KV-694-309

WITHDRAWN FROM STOCK

Department for Work & Pensions
Legal Information Centre

WITHDRAWN FROM STOCK

600134

Date: 18/1/07

Classmark: EQUL UND

343.D64 UND

current ed. ✓
2/10 PS

8th ed expected
Dec 2010

STOCK

Law Relating to Trusts and Trustees

Publishing History

First edition (1878) – Arthur Underhill
Second edition (1884) – Arthur Underhill
Third edition (1889) – Arthur Underhill
Fourth edition (1894) – Arthur Underhill
Fifth edition (1901) – Arthur Underhill
Sixth edition (1904) – Arthur Underhill
Seventh edition (1912) – Arthur Underhill
Eighth edition (1926) – Arthur Underhill
Ninth edition (1939) – Sir Arthur Underhill and Edward Bagshaw
Tenth edition (1950) – C Montgomery White QC and MM Wells
Eleventh edition (1959) – C Montgomery White QC and MM Wells
Twelfth edition (1970) – RT Oerton
Thirteenth edition (1979) – DJ Hayton
Fourteenth edition (1987) – DJ Hayton
Fifteenth edition (1995) – DJ Hayton
Sixteenth edition (2003) – DJ Hayton
Seventeenth edition (2006) – DJ Hayton, PB Matthews and CCJ Mitchell

Underhill and Hayton

Law Relating to Trusts and Trustees

Seventeenth Edition

General Editor

David Hayton
LLB, LLD (Newcastle), MA, LLD (Cantab)
Justice of the Caribbean Court of Justice, Additional Bencher of Lincoln's Inn and Fellow of King's College, London

with

Paul Matthews
BCL (Oxon), LLB, LLD (London)
Professor of Law, King's College, London, Solicitor of Withers London, and HM Coroner City of London

Charles Mitchell
BA (Oxon), LLM, PhD (London)
Professor of Law, King's College, London

LexisNexis®
Butterworths

Members of the LexisNexis Group worldwide

United Kingdom	LexisNexis Butterworths, a Division of Reed Elsevier (UK) Ltd, Halsbury House, 35 Chancery Lane, London, WC2A 1EL, and RSH, 1–3 Baxter's Place, Leith Walk Edinburgh EH1 3AF
Argentina	LexisNexis Argentina, Buenos Aires
Australia	LexisNexis Butterworths, Chatswood, New South Wales
Austria	LexisNexis Verlag ARD Orac GmbH & Co KG, Vienna
Benelux	LexisNexis Benelux, Amsterdam
Canada	LexisNexis Canada, Markham, Ontario
Chile	LexisNexis Chile Ltda, Santiago
China	LexisNexis China, Beijing and Shanghai
France	LexisNexis SA, Paris
Germany	LexisNexis Deutschland GmbH, Munster
Hong Kong	LexisNexis Hong Kong, Hong Kong
India	LexisNexis India, New Delhi
Italy	Giuffrè Editore, Milan
Japan	LexisNexis Japan, Tokyo
Malaysia	Malayan Law Journal Sdn Bhd, Kuala Lumpur
Mexico	LexisNexis Mexico, Mexico
New Zealand	LexisNexis NZ Ltd, Wellington
Poland	Wydawnictwo Prawnicze LexisNexis Sp, Warsaw
Singapore	LexisNexis Singapore, Singapore
South Africa	LexisNexis Butterworths, Durban
USA	LexisNexis, Dayton, Ohio

First published in 1878

© Reed Elsevier (UK) Ltd 2007

© David J. Hayton 2007

Published by LexisNexis Butterworths

All rights reserved. No part of this publication may be reproduced in any material form (including photocopying or storing it in any medium by electronic means and whether or not transiently or incidentally to some other use of this publication) without the written permission of the copyright owner except in accordance with the provisions of the Copyright, Designs and Patents Act 1988 or under the terms of a licence issued by the Copyright Licensing Agency Ltd, 90 Tottenham Court Road, London, England W1T 4LP. Applications for the copyright owner's written permission to reproduce any part of this publication should be addressed to the publisher.

Warning: The doing of an unauthorised act in relation to a copyright work may result in both a civil claim for damages and criminal prosecution.

Crown copyright material is reproduced with the permission of the Controller of HMSO and the Queen's Printer for Scotland. Parliamentary copyright material is reproduced with the permission of the Controller of Her Majesty's Stationery Office on behalf of Parliament. Any European material in this work which has been reproduced from EUR-lex, the official European Communities legislation website, is European Communities copyright.

A CIP Catalogue record for this book is available from the British Library.

ISBN 10: 1405708638

ISBN 13: 9781405708630

Typeset by Letterpart Limited, Reigate, Surrey

Printed and bound in Great Britain by CPI Bath Press, Bath

Visit LexisNexis Butterworths at www.lexisnexis.co.uk

Preface

Having produced a new edition every eight years (commencing with the 13th edition in 1979), but faced with the need for more frequent editions in the light of increasingly rapid developments in the trust world, I was delighted to have persuaded Paul Matthews and Charles Mitchell to join me in producing this 17th edition. Under my general editorship, Paul Matthews has been responsible for preparing the hefty Division Four ('The Administration of a Trust'), while Charles Mitchell has been responsible for preparing Division Three ('Trusts Imposed by Law') and Division Five ('The Consequences of a Breach of Trust').

As in previous editions, the principles of the law of private (as opposed to charitable) trusts are extracted and formulated along the lines of Articles of a Code. This is a salutary exercise in itself to help clarify matters, but has the practical function of enabling the busy practitioner to see at a glance the general principles governing a particular topic. To resolve a particular problem, the practitioner can then turn to the appropriate sub-heading in the subsequent commentary which, in its detailed discussion of cases and any relevant legislation, illustrates and explains the application of the relevant principles.

This approach, revealing the structure of relevant principles and their relationships, should also help to provide a good overall picture of trust law. As a developing and primarily judge-made picture, the picture will always be unfinished, but an attempt is made to indicate how parts of the picture are likely to be developed at the extremities and how even some of the inner parts may be touched up. After all, as Sir George Jessel MR pointed out in *Re Hallett's Estate* (1880) 13 Ch D 696 at 710, 'It is perfectly well-known that [the rules of Courts of Equity] have been established from time to time – altered, improved and refined from time to time. The doctrines are progressive, refined and improved'. The guidelines provided by the Articles reflect the modern tendency in equity to put less emphasis on detailed rules that have emerged from the cases and more weight on the underlying principles that engendered those rules, treating the rules less as rules requiring complete compliance and more as guidelines to assist the court in applying the principles, as Sir Robert Megarry V-C remarked in *Re Montagu's Settlements* [1987] Ch 264 at 278. Sadly, he died on 11th October 2006 aged 96, after a very distinguished career as academic, author, QC and judge, while a staunch Bencher of Lincoln's Inn.

In this edition there has been some significant re-writing of Articles, taking account of over a hundred new cases and many newly published articles or books, and taking advantage of the knowledge and experience of my new co-editors.

Paul Matthews has added significant new material to Article 43 ('The effect of the trustee's bankruptcy'), Article 47 ('Duty of trustee to obey the directions of the settlement'), Article 60 ('Duty of trustee to be ready with his accounts'), Article 61 ('General principles applicable to trustees' powers' eg the *Hastings-Bass* principle and the fraud on a power doctrine) and Article 69 ('Power of a sole beneficiary or of the beneficiaries collectively to extinguish the trust').

Charles Mitchell has substantially re-written Article 28 ('Analysis of trusts of property imposed by law') and the first part of Articles 89 ('Measure of the trustee's liability for breach of trust'), while adding significant new material to Article 29 ('Resulting trusts where express trusts do not exhaust the beneficial interest') and to the first part of Article 33 ('Constructive trusts of unauthorised fiduciary gains or their traceable proceeds').

For my part, I have substantially re-written the first part of Article 1 dealing with the nature of the trust concept, dealt with the Mental Capacity Act 2005 and introduced a new Article 27 to deal with the termination of a trust. All of us have interwoven new case law from England, Australia, New Zealand, Jersey, Guernsey and the Cayman Islands into the text so as to help clarify the state of the law as at October 1st 2006.

What are the principal reflections that arise from reviewing the new material? *Schmidt v Rosewood Trust Limited* will probably come to be seen as the most significant new case. It affirms the trust as a trustee-beneficiary centred property concept, with core obligations owed by the trustee to beneficiaries extending to objects of a fiduciary power of appointment that have some realistic possibility of receiving trust assets, Equity looking to the substance of the matter and not to the form. It seems (correctly in my view) that the trend is to empower such 'beneficiaries' and make it harder for settlors and trustees to keep them in the dark. The challenge for some practitioners will be how to use settlor-autonomy and the flexibility of trust instruments to try to outflank the Schmidt approach (though an open frank relationship between trustee and beneficiaries should be the normal one because secrecy is a breeding ground for suspicion and antagonistic action).

The ramifications of the *Hastings-Bass* principle are clearly too extensive under the current case law: as a matter of policy, can a settlor really be allowed to create a situation where his beneficiaries can insist that the trustee must always exercise its powers as a paragon of legal virtue or, otherwise, the exercise is void, so that a trustee's mistakes can always be undone and put right? A case on the principle needs to proceed through the appellate process or Her Majesty's Revenue and Customs need to seek to have some limiting legislative provision in a Finance Bill.

Hitherto, Equity lawyers have been very pragmatic about resulting trusts and constructive trusts, the life of the law being experience rather than logic, with such trusts imposed in traditionally recognised special circumstances. The late Professor Birks, however, emphasised the need for ascertaining the event to which legal rights – including rights arising under a trust – respond eg an agreement or some wrongdoing or some unjust enrichment, and we have sought to analyse constructive and resulting trusts in these terms.

The constructive trust imposed on a trustee of an express trust in respect of property rightfully or wrongfully representing traceable trust property, and in respect of profits arising from a conflict between the trustee's personal interest and his duty as trustee, should be regarded as a response to the trustee's agreement to take on the office of trustee. On T becoming trustee, T agrees not to act in his own interest but to act exclusively in the best interests of his beneficiaries, and to hold the original trust assets, added trust assets, and assets in his hands that have rightly or wrongly been substituted for such assets on express trust for the beneficiaries. When the beneficiaries claim that a particular asset or a particular profit in the hands of the trustee belongs to them because he agreed not to act in his own interest but in their best interests, he cannot deny that he holds such asset or profit as part of the assets held on express trust for them.

If it so happens that a loss flows from a conflict of interest and duty, then the beneficiaries should also be able to claim substitutive performance of the trustee's obligation not to act in his own interest but only in their best interests: they should not be relegated to a claim for reparation of a loss that was caused by the trustee's breach of duty. He is not authorised to act in his own interest where there is a conflict of interest and duty, so that an investment in breach of such duty should be treated like an unauthorised investment Thus, if £10 million of trust money was invested in a land development project in breach of the trustee's duty to act in the beneficiaries' best interests, not his own, and the loss would only have been £1 million but for a crash in the market increasing the loss to £3 million, the beneficiaries should be able to claim the full £3 million. The reason is that they are entitled to say that the trustee must have used his own £10 million, so that he still has their £10 million to restore with interest.

Principles of equitable liability are thus justifiably different from those of common law liability in tort or for breach of contract. However, equitable compensation for reparation of loss flowing from a trustee negligently or improperly doing what he is authorised to do should be ascertained in the same way as at common law for negligence, though this remains to be authoritatively resolved.

But enough of reflections upon modern developments, because it is time to express my deep gratitude not just to Paul Matthews and Charles Mitchell for keeping to schedule in preparing their Divisions but also to Jonathan Harris, Professor of International Commercial Law, Birmingham University, for updating Article 102 on Conflict of Laws and The Hague Trusts Convention, the Convention codifying many principles. Having headed the UK delegation to the XVth Session of The Hague Conference that was responsible for the Convention (and having been on the drafting committee), I had written the Article for the 14th and 15th editions, but for the 16th edition Jonathan substantially developed the Article when Hart Publishing had just published his book, *The Hague Trusts Convention*, and I was very pressed for time. Despite being pressed for time himself for this edition, within the schedule he kindly updated the Article (taking account, of course, of *Charalambous v Charalambous*), subject to some fine-tuning of mine. As with previous editions, I am most grateful to the publishers for preparing the index and the tables of cases and statutes.

While it is hoped that the law is accurately stated as at 1st November 2006, please note that the views herein are for the purpose of further consideration only, and are not be acted upon without professional advice. No responsibility can be accepted for any loss occasioned to any person, no matter howsoever caused or arising as a result of, or in consequence of, action taken or refrained from in reliance on the contents hereof.

The Honourable Mr. Justice David Hayton
Caribbean Court of Justice
Port of Spain, Trinidad and Tobago
All Saint's Day 2006

Contents

Division One Preliminary terminology

Chapter 1 Preliminary terminology

Division Two Express trusts

Chapter 2 Introduction

Chapter 3 Matters essential to the prima facie validity of an express trust

Chapter 4 Validity of express trusts in relation to latent matters

Contents

Division Four The Administration of a Trust

Chapter 10 Disclaimer and acceptance of trusts

Chapter 11 The estate of the trustee and its incidents

Chapter 12 Trusts of land

Chapter 13 The trustee's duties

Contents

Chapter 19 Administration of new trusts created under limited powers in the original settlement

Chapter 20 The rights of the trustee

Chapter 21 The right of trustees and beneficiaries to seek the assistance of the Public Trustee or the court in auditing or in administering the trust

Division Five The Consequences of a Breach of Trust

Chapter 22 The liability of the trustees

Chapter 23 Protection accorded to trustees in case of breach of trust

Contents

Chapter 24 Liability of third parties and beneficiaries

Division Six The Hague Trusts Convention

Chapter 25 Conflict of Laws and The Hague Trusts Convention

Table of Statutes

Paragraph references printed in **bold** type indicate where the Statute is set out in part or in full.

Table of Statutes

Table of Statutes

Table of Statutes

Table of Statutory Instruments

Paragraph references printed in **bold** type indicate where the Statutory Instrument is set out in part or in full.

Table of European Legislation

Paragraph references printed in **bold** type indicate where the Legislation is set out in part or in full.

SECONDARY LEGISLATION
DIRECTIVES

REGULATIONS

Table of Cases

A

PARA

Table of Cases

Table of Cases

C

Table of Cases

G

PARA

I

PARA

PARA

J

M

Table of Cases

Table of Cases

PARA

PARA

Table of Cases

Table of Cases

S

Table of Cases

PARA

Table of Cases

T

Table of Cases

PARA

Table of Cases

Division One

PRELIMINARY TERMINOLOGY

Article

Chapter 1
PRELIMINARY TERMINOLOGY

ARTICLE 1
TERMINOLOGY OF TRUST, TRUSTEE, TRUST FUND, TRUST
PROPERTY, BREACH OF TRUST, BENEFICIARY, SETTLOR,
EQUITABLE INTEREST AND BENEFICIAL INTEREST

1.1

(1) A trust is an equitable obligation, binding a person (called a trustee) to deal with property (called trust property) owned by him as a separate fund, distinct from his own private property, for the benefit of persons (called beneficiaries or, in old cases, *cestuis que trust*), of whom he may himself be one[1], and any one of whom may enforce the obligation[2].

(2) Trust property within the separate fund is immune from claims of the trustee's private creditors because the beneficiaries have equitable proprietary interests in such property. The trust fund comprises not just the trust property originally owned by the trustee as trustee and all the fruits from time to time thereof (eg interest payments, rents, dividends from shares or bonus issues of shares), but also *authorised* substituted property subsequently acquired by the trustee on behalf of the trust. Indeed, if the beneficiaries so require, the trust fund comprises *unauthorised* substituted property purportedly acquired by the trustee on behalf of the trust, and any property purportedly acquired by the trustee *for himself* from his sale or exchange of trust property or from his misuse of his position as trustee (eg secret commissions or bribes)[3].

(3) It is the trustee who sues third parties or is sued by third parties in relation to the trust property, the trust, unlike a company, having no legal personality. Any act or neglect on the part of a trustee which is not authorised or excused by the terms of the trust instrument, or by law, is called a breach of trust[4]. The

beneficiaries can then sue the trustee for such breach. Exceptionally instead, if in breach of trust the trust has refused to sue a third party, the beneficiaries may directly sue the third party but joining the trustee as co-defendant, so that all interested parties are bound by the court's judgment[5]. Here a beneficiary sues not in his own right but 'in right of the trust and in the room of the trustee'[6], the trustee, before the Judicature Acts 1873–75, being compelled by the Court of Chancery to let the beneficiary use the trustee's name to sue the third party in the common law court[7].

(4)   The trustee's functions, whether management functions in managing or administering the trust property or distributive functions in distributing income or capital to beneficiaries, may, under the terms of a trust, be subject to fiduciary powers or personal powers vested in another person[8], such as a person designated as protector or a beneficiary currently entitled to income or, even, the settlor or his widow. Any act or neglect of such a person in respect of a fiduciary power, which is not authorised or excused by the terms of the trust instrument or by law, may be called a breach of fiduciary duty.

(5)   The settlor of property is the person who creates a trust of that particular property[9], whether, as normal, by transferring – or doing everything necessary to be done by him[10] to transfer – title to that property to the trustee and declaring trusts thereof or, exceptionally, by retaining certain designated property over which he declares trusts of which he is to be trustee.

(6)   The settlor, by creating a trust, imposes obligations on the trustee owed only to, and enforceable only by, the beneficiaries and not the settlor[11], unless he is one of the beneficiaries or unless he reserved rights to himself within the trust instrument, eg as the donee of a power of appointment over capital or as a protector with specific powers for the protection of beneficiaries that are as yet unborn or unascertained.

(7)   The core primary obligation[12] created by the settlor is the personal obligation of the trustee of the trust fund to produce accounts of the trusteeship available to be falsified (for unauthorised conduct) or surcharged (for authorised but negligent conduct) by the beneficiaries. This is crucial so that the beneficiaries can monitor or 'police' the trustee's fundamental duty to keep within the terms of the trust instrument and in doing so (subject to any dilution in the settlor's trust instrument) always to act exclusively in the best interests of the beneficiaries – and so act with undivided loyalty in their best interests – and also the duty to act with appropriate care except so far as ousted in the trust instrument. Breach of the fundamental duty leads to a substitutive performance of such duty, where the trustee cannot deny the

beneficiaries' claim that he must be taken to have performed his duty in the way that most furthers their interests.

(8) The settlor also confers on a beneficiary an equitable proprietary interest in the trust property and its fruits, which enables the beneficiary to trace the product thereof[13] into the hands of the apparent owner and claim all or a proportionate part thereof as part of the trust fund that must be restored to the trust fund (or himself if an absolutely entitled beneficiary). If the product has depreciated in value the beneficiary will claim instead an equitable lien thereon as security for the amount due to be restored to the trust fund under the accounting process. A beneficiary's proprietary interest arises as soon as the settlor has transferred – or has done everything necessary to be done by him to transfer – title to the trust property to a trustee, but the personal obligations of trusteeship do not arise until the trustee has knowledge of the trust[14], yet does not disclaim the trusteeship[15]. A beneficiary's equitable proprietary interest in the trust property binds a third party to whom trust property is wrongfully transferred unless the latter proves that he has a defence such as bona fide purchaser of the legal title to such property without notice of the beneficiary's interest or protection under a statutory provision (eg conferring good title on a purchaser of land if he pays the purchase money to two trustees or a trust corporation)[16]. The third party does not take on the obligations of the trustee for the beneficiaries but must return the trust property to the trustee as soon as practicable after learning of the wrongful transfer and must account for what has happened to the property in his hands, eg receipt of income therefrom or selling the property to purchase another asset (requiring to be restored to the trust).

(9) The owner of the beneficial interest in property is the person personally entitled to the full economic benefit of the property. A beneficiary with an equitable interest in property will normally have a beneficial interest, but can be a trustee of the equitable interest for others. The absolutely entitled legal owner of property is also the beneficial owner, but has no equitable interest[17] until there is separation of the legal interest from the equitable interest, so that one person owes a duty to another, there can be no equitable interest.

(10) History is responsible for the terminology of a trustee owning a legal interest in property and beneficiaries owning equitable interests. The courts of the common law treated the trustee as full owner, but the Court of Chancery, presided over by the Lord Chancellor (originally the King's right-hand man) and acting on equitable principles so as to become known as the court of equity, compelled the trustee to manage the legal interest in the best interests of the beneficiaries, regarded as having

equitable interests in the property owned at law by the trustee. Equity prevailed over the common law if any conflict arose, the court of equity, the Court of Chancery, being able to grant an injunction to restrain a defendant from suing in the common law courts or from enforcing a common law judgment[18]. If the trustee in breach of trust refused to take proceedings in the common law courts against an outsider liable only in the common law courts (eg for breach of contract or a tort), the beneficiaries could be authorised by the Court of Chancery to take legal proceedings in the trustee's name as plaintiff. Since 1875 the rules of equity and of common law have been concurrently applied and administered in all courts[19]; nowadays, in such a case the beneficiaries will simply bring an action as claimant but join the wrongdoing trustee as a co-defendant, so ensuring that all necessary parties will be bound by the court's decision[20].

1   Unless he takes on the face of a will as trustee of a half-secret trust when evidence not complying with the Wills Act 1837 is inadmissible to contradict the apparently exclusive status of trustee: *Re Rees Will Trusts* [1950] Ch 204 [1949] 2 All ER 1003, CA.
2   Charitable purpose trusts enforceable by the Attorney General or the Charity Commission (representing the Crown as *parens patriae*) are outside the scope of this work, though the trust property is also a separate fund, distinct from the trustee's private property alone available to satisfy his private creditors. The anomalous valid testamentary 'trusts' for erection and maintenance of sepulchral monuments, for maintenance of pet animals of the deceased and for saying of masses in private for the soul of the deceased (see paras 8.173–8.184) are essentially powers to perform those activities, since no-one has positive rights to compel performance of such activities. It is possible that the courts may develop the obligation characteristic of the trust so that a trust validly arises where a trustee owns property not just for the benefit of charitable purposes (enforceable by the Attorney-General or the Charity Commission) but also for the benefit of non-charitable purposes where the settlor has appointed an enforcer so that positive enforcement of the purposes is possible: see paras 8.157–8.167.
3   *A-G of Hong Kong v Reid* [1994] 1 AC 324 at 331 and see para 3.7 and Article 33 below. If the acquired property has appreciated in value the beneficiaries adopt it as authorised property. If it has depreciated, the trustee cannot deny that he was a good man who acted in the best interests of the beneficiaries, so he cannot deny he personally borrowed the money to acquire the assets for himself but secured the loan by an equitable lien or charge against the acquired assets which the beneficiaries can sell in part satisfaction of their claim against the trustee.
4   This sentence was expressly approved by Romer LJ in *Green v Russell* [1959] 2 QB 226 at 241.
5   *Hayim v Citibank* [1987] AC 730 at 748; *Parker-Tweedale v Dunbar Bank plc* [1991] Ch 12 at 19, 23 and 25; but not where T has the benefit of a non-assignable contract with X and, T having declared a trust of the contract for B, B tries to sue X as if B were an assignee of T which is the very thing forbidden by the contract: *Barbados Trust Co Ltd v Bank of Zambia* [2006] EWHC 212 (Comm), [2006] All ER (D) 37 (Jan) *Don King Productions Inc v Warren* [2000] Ch 291.
6   *Parker-Tweedale v Dunbar Bank plc* [1991] Ch 12 at 19 per Nourse LJ.
7   See paragraph (10) below.
8   See paras 1.76–1.92 below.
9   Sometimes a dummy settlor is used to create a trust of £100 before the real settlor transfers property of significant value to the trustee: *Re TR Technology Investment Trust plc* [1988] BCLC 256, 263–264; *West v Lazard* [1993] Jersey LR 165, 201–204. When X adds property to an existing trust fund such property is new trust property of which X is the

settlor: *CIR v Dick* (2001) 4 ITELR 317 at para 40. Also see *Air Jamaica Ltd v Charlton* [1999] 1 WLR 1399 at 1409 for an employee's separate settlement within a pension trust fund.

10 See para 9.32 below.
11 *Re Astor's Settlement Trusts, Astor v Scholfield* [1952] Ch 534 at 542; *Bradshaw v University College of Wales* [1987] 3 All ER 200 at 203; *Re Murphy's Settlements* [1999] 1 WLR 282 at 295.
12 *Foreman v Kingstone* [2004] 1 NZLR 84 [2005] WTLR 823 at paras 85 to 88, *Armitage v Nurse* [1998] Ch 241 at 253.
13 See Arts 92 and 101 below and *Foskett v McKeown* [2001] 1 AC 102, HL.
14 *Westdeutsch Landesbank Girozentrale v Islington London Borough Council* [1996] AC 669 at 689, 705, 707 and 709; *Re Montagu's Settlement Trusts, Duke of Manchester v National Westminster Bank Ltd* [1987] 1 Ch 264 at 271–273, 278, and 285. See also *Naas v Westminster Bank* [1940] AC 366. It is possible for a settlor, without the trustee's knowledge, to transfer land or shares to the trustee as new registered proprietor or to covenant with the trustee that the settlor's executor will transfer £1million to the trustee within one year of the settlor's death to the intent that the trustee holds the benefit of the covenant forthwith for specified beneficiaries. A testator's will may also create trusts without the knowledge of the intended trustee.
15 Equity will not allow a trust to fail for want of a trustee: see para 8.8 and Article 38 below. If the trustee disclaims then the settlor (or his personal representative) holds the property as trustee: it is thus the unilateral act of the settlor that creates this trust as if he had declared himself trustee in the first place.
16 Further see Article 101 below.
17 *Westdeutsch Landesbank Girozentrale v Islington London Borough Council* [1996] AC 669 at 706; *Re DKLR Holding Co (No 2) Pty Limited v Commissioner of Stamp Duties* (1982) 149 CLR 431; *Duggan v Governor of Sutton Prison* [2004] EWCA Civ 78, [2004] 1 WLR 1010, para 28.
18 *Earl of Oxford's Case* (1615) Ch Cas 1.
19 Supreme Court of Judicature Act 1873; currently Supreme Court Act 1981 s 49, rules of equity still prevailing in the case of any conflict or variance.
20 *Parker-Tweedale v Dunbar Bank* [1991] Ch 12 at 19; *Hayim v Citibank* [1987] AC 730 at 747–748.

Ownership-management of a fund

1.2 Until the sixteenth edition, the first sentence of this Article defined a trust as 'an equitable obligation, binding a person (who is called a trustee) to deal with property *over which he has control* (which is called the trust property) for the benefit of persons ... [continuing as in the above first sentence],' such sentence being expressly approved by Romer LJ in *Green v Russell*[1] and by Cohen J in *Re Marshall's Will Trusts*[2]. However, James LJ in *Smith v Anderson*[3] stated, 'A trustee is a man who is the *owner of the property* and deals with it as principal as owner and as master, subject only to an equitable obligation to account to some persons to whom he stands in the relation of trustee and who are his *cestuis que trust*', and Mason P stated[4] 'it is of the essence of a trust that property is vested in the trustee'. Indeed, as Lord Diplock stated in a speech[5] with which all the other Law Lords concurred, 'the full ownership in the trust property was split into two constituent elements which became vested in different persons: the "legal ownership" in the trustee, the "beneficial ownership" in the *cestui que trust*'.

1 [1959] 2 QB 226 at 241.
2 [1945] Ch 217 at 219.
3 (1880) 15 Ch D 247 at 275.

4   *Chief Commissioner of Stamp Duties v ISPT Pty Ltd* (1999) 2 ITELR 1 at 15 (New South Wales CA).
5   *Ayerst v C & K (Construction) Ltd* [1976] AC 167 at 177.

1.3 Trusteeship is ownership-management, not agency-management or bailee-management. A person who deals with property owned by another but over which he has control as agent or as bailee or as attorney under a power of attorney for the benefit of another person, is not a trustee of property, although in relation to particular property he may in certain circumstances, like a director of a company, be under fiduciary duties similar to those of a trustee. One can understand that, where a trustee is interested in 10,000 shares out of 5 million shares of XYZ plc owned by a custodian, a layman may regard the trustee as having control over 10,000 of those shares but a lawyer regards the trustee as owning a one five-hundredth equitable interest in the pool of 5 million shares as equitable tenant in common with all others interested in such pool of securities owned by the custodian. Thus, Article I(I) of *Principles of European Trust Law*[1] states, 'In a trust, a person called the trustee owns assets segregated from his private patrimony and must deal with those assets (the "trust fund") for the benefit of another person called "the beneficiary" or for the furtherance of a purpose.'

1   Published by Kluwer Law International and edited by D Hayton, S Kortmann and H Verhagen. The Principles, prepared by an international working group, are intended to guide non-trust jurisdictions desirous of implementing The Hague Trusts Convention.

1.4 Whether or not spelled out in the definition section of a trust instrument, the concept of a trust fund extends beyond the original settled assets (often of a small value, eg £100) and the fruits thereof and further assets subsequently transferred by the settlor or another settlor to the trustees. It extends to assets subsequently from time to time successively substituted for such assets. The ring-fenced fund extends beyond assets that the trustee is *authorised* to acquire on behalf of the trust using the proceeds of sale of trust assets. If the beneficiaries so claim, it extends also to *unauthorised* assets that the trustee wrongfully acquired on behalf of the trust[1] and, most significantly, extends to assets that the trustee wrongfully tried to acquire for himself as part of his private estate or patrimony[2], eg by using proceeds of sale of trust property as if his own money so as to buy a house for himself (or for himself and his spouse or for his spouse alone[3]). The ring-fenced protected nature of trust property would be wholly illusory if the protection could simply be removed by the trustee-guardian of the fence taking trust money or other property 'over the fence' out of the trust and claiming it to be his own private property, so that it and property exchanged for it or purchased with the proceeds of sale thereof is his own private property available to satisfy his creditors' claims. Equity does not allow him to deny a claim of the beneficiaries that he holds such property on trust for his beneficiaries.

1   The beneficiaries can adopt the transaction if the unauthorised assets are worth more than the authorised assets sold to acquire them; if worth less, then the beneficiaries will have an equitable lien over the assets as security for their claim, thereby entitling them to the assets in part satisfaction of their claim, the trustee not being able to deny their claim that he was an honest good man and so must have borrowed the money to enable him to buy the unauthorised assets for himself and secured the loan on those assets.

²   *Att-Gen of Hong Kong v Reid* [1994] 1 AC 324 (where a house acquired using bribes was part of the trust fund).
³   On proprietary interests acquired via the tracing process see Arts 92 and 101 below.

1.5 Believing that the term 'breach of trust' had not been defined in any case or textbook Megarry V-C in *Tito v Waddell (No 2)*¹ concerned himself with two American formulations: (a) 'every omission or violation by a trustee of a duty which equity lays on him is a breach of trust'; (b) 'a trustee commits a breach of trust if he violates any duty which he owes as trustee to the beneficiaries'. The first formulation is the wider since it would make a breach by a trustee of some duty imposed on him otherwise than under the law of trusts into a breach of trust. In any event defining a breach of trust in terms of a breach of duty raises the further question of what is meant by a breach of duty. Megarry V-C took the view that a trustee owed no 'duty' not to purchase the trust property or not to purchase a beneficiary's interest in the trust property without making proper disclosure, but was under a disability in respect of such matters, such disability being not a specific part of the law of trusts but part of a general rule of equity that certain persons (eg agents, solicitors, directors, trustees, personal representatives, liquidators) are subject to fiduciary obligations creating certain consequences if they carry through certain transactions without, where appropriate, complying with certain requirements. It thus followed that the six year limitation period in Limitation Act 1939, s 19(2) (now Limitation Act 1980, s 21(3)), for 'an action by a beneficiary in respect of any breach of trust' did not apply to a trustee's purchase of the trust property or of a beneficiary's interest without proper disclosure.

¹   [1977] 3 All ER 129 at 246–248.

1.6 This approach, however, has been rejected by the Court of Appeal¹, which refused to accept that the liability to account for profits on breach of the self-dealing rule or the fair-dealing rule is the consequence of an equitable disability rather than a breach of duty. Such liability arises from the fiduciary's breach of his primary duty to act loyally in the beneficiaries' best interests and not his own, and so the six year period in Limitation Act 1980, s 21(3) applies.

¹   *Gwembe Valley Development Co Ltd v Koshy* [2003] EWCA Civ 1048, [2004] WTLR 97.

1.7 Other definitions¹ have been formulated to summarise the effect of all the various rules that are responsible for the concept of the trust which, unlike a corporation, is not a legal person, but it is not considered worthwhile to examine such definitions since it is the rules from which the definitions result that are of much greater practical concern. However, the distinctive features of a trust are well illuminated by Article 2 of The Hague Convention on the Law Applicable to Trusts and on their Recognition as follows.

> 'For the purposes of this Convention, the term "trust" refers to the legal relationships created—inter vivos or on death—by a person, the settlor, when assets have been placed under the control of a trustee for the benefit of a beneficiary or for a specified purpose.

A trust has the following characteristics—

a   the assets constitute a separate fund and are not a part of the trustee's own estate;

b   title to the trust assets stands in the name of the trustee or in the name of another person on behalf of the trustee;

c   the trustee has the power and the duty, in respect of which he is accountable, to manage, employ or dispose of the assets in accordance with the terms of the trust and the special duties imposed upon him by law.

The reservation by the settlor of certain rights and powers, and the fact that the trustee may himself have rights as a beneficiary, are not necessarily inconsistent with the existence of a trust.'

¹   Keeton and Sheridan, *Law of Trusts* (13th edn) p 3; Lewin, *The Law of Trusts* (18th edn) paras 1–01 to 1–08; Pettit, *Equity and the Law of Trusts* (9th edn) pp 24–25; Scott, *Law of Trusts* (4th edn) para 2.

1.8   This last sentence reflects the impossibility of A holding on trust for A alone¹, whilst recognising the possibility of A vesting property in A and B on trust for A for life, remainder to B and C equally, with express power for A as settlor to revoke the trust or to delete or add persons as beneficiaries and with express power in A's lifetime for whoever happen to be trustees from time to time to appoint trust capital to or settle it upon spouses or children of beneficiaries. Such a flexible trust is valid though it may be unsatisfactory from a tax point of view and may be liable to be set aside on A's bankruptcy.

¹   *Re Cook* [1948] Ch 212, [1948] 1 All ER 231; *Re Lord Grimthorpe* [1908] 2 Ch 675, CA; cf *Rye v Rye* [1962] AC 496, [1962] 1 All ER 146, HL.

1.9   Unfortunately Article 2, in its references to assets 'under the control of a trustee' and 'title to assets ... in the name of another person on behalf of a trustee', reflects the layman's viewpoint where a custodian owns a million shares in XYZ plc and the trustee is interested in 10,000 of them so that the layman believes the trust assets to be 10,000 shares in XYZ plc rather than a one hundredth equitable interest in the million shares. At first sight, the width of Article 2 allows agency-management of assets owned by another to qualify as a trust, but if 'title to assets' managed by an agent is 'in the name of' the owner this surely is not 'on behalf of' the agent but on the owner's own behalf. Moreover, if agency-management were intended to qualify as a trust, then the Trusts Convention would have a provision dealing with its relationship to the earlier Agency Convention and it has no such provision. Furthermore, as Article 11 indicates, at the core of the Convention is an owner of property, but that part of his property which is trust property constitutes a separate fund immune from claims of the owner-trustee's creditors, heirs and spouse. Thus the Trusts Convention should not be construed as extending to agency and bailment arrangements: if it did there would be no scope for Article 13 to enable states that do not have the 'trust' to refuse to recognise trusts that are local except for the choice of a foreign governing law and a foreign trustee, because all states have 'agency'.

1.10   Article 1 of *Principles of European Trust Law*¹, designed to help countries efficiently implement The Hague Trust Convention (whether or not

1.10 *Preliminary terminology*

they want to restrict the trust concept to a special personal obligation, simply making the separate trust fund immune from the claims of the trustee's private creditors, rather than having the effect of creating proprietary rights against third parties) is based upon the trust as 'ownership management'. Under Article 1(1) 'In a trust, a person called "the trustee" owns assets segregated from his private patrimony and must deal with those assets ("the trust fund") for the benefit of another person for the furtherance of a purpose.'

1 See *Principles of European Trust Law* (Edited by D Hayton, S Kortmann and H Verhagen) Kluwer Law International, 1999.

1.11 The nature of an English trust is probably best appreciated by contrasting other ways in which English law may provide for someone to deal with property for the benefit of others.

Trust and governmental or public obligation

1.12 The Crown will often be administering property for others in the exercise of the Crown's governmental functions. Such a relationship is not an equitable relationship enforceable in the courts[1]. The Crown will have the whole legal and beneficial interest in the property and will be subject to no equitable obligations in administering the property. Similarly, the Law Society acting in a public capacity under s 37 of the Solicitors Act 1974 so as to obtain insurance cover for practising solicitors was not acting in any fiduciary capacity and so was entitled to retain the commission it received in arranging the 'master policy' for solicitors[2]. Furthermore, in exercising its powers under s 35 and para 6 of Pt II of Sch 1 of the 1974 Act, when intervening in the affairs of improperly run solicitors' practices and holding money found as a result of such intervention 'on trust to exercise' its statutory powers 'and subject thereto upon trust for the persons beneficially entitled to them', the Law Society was not under the duties of a private law trustee[3]. Its statutory powers had to be exercised in accordance with public law principles, though these would require taking account of private trust law principles in relation to money provided to solicitors by clients on trust for the clients.

1 *Kinloch v Secretary of State of India* (1880) 15 Ch D 1, (1882) 7 App Cas 619; *Tito v Waddell (No 2)* [1977] 3 All ER 129 at 216–228. Cf *Mabo v State of Queensland (No 2)*(1993) 175 CLR 1 (Aust HC); *Phillip Brothers Ltd v Sierra Leone* [1995] 3 CL 316.
2 *Swain v Law Society* [1983] 1 AC 598, [1982] 2 All ER 827, HL.
3 *Re Ahmed & Co* [2006] EWHC 480 (Ch), [2006] NLJR 512.

Trust and agency

1.13 Agency is a common law relationship arising where a person, known as the agent, has express or implied authority to act on behalf of another, known as the principal, and consents so to act. An agent, like a trustee, is thus acting to promote the interests of another but the agency relationship is based on agreement between principal and agent: this is not so in the case of trustee and beneficiary (unless the settlor is the sole beneficiary). During his agency the agent can act on behalf of the principal as a means whereby the principal and

10

third parties are placed in contractual relations: a trustee cannot involve his beneficiaries in such relations but must act so as to be personally liable (though with a right of indemnity from the trust property for properly incurred expenses). An agent need never have any control over his principal's property and even where he is employed to deal with his principal's property he will not have title to it: a trustee always has the title to the trust property (except for settled land under the Settled Land Act 1925 – but no more such settled land can be created after the Trusts of Land and Appointment of Trustees Act 1996).

1.14 Agency is normally terminated on death of either principal or agent. A trust will not terminate merely because the trustees have died and a beneficiary's death will only terminate his particular interest. The settlor's death is immaterial after his gift has created the trust. Once a trust has been created the settlor cannot intervene at all, even with the agreement of the trustees, unless the trust deed reserved a power for him to intervene for a specified purpose: the contract of agency can be modified at any time by agreement between the principal and agent. If the beneficiaries are all ascertained adults of full capacity they can terminate the trust at will: a principal cannot terminate the agency at will unless he reserves such a specific right in the contract of agency.

1.15 The common law governing the agency relationship has been supplemented by intervention by the equitable jurisdiction, which is prepared to treat the relationship as a fiduciary relationship for the purpose of imposing a liability to account upon an agent who makes a personal profit out of his privileged position without his principal's informed consent. To this extent agents are under similar obligations as trustees but with the disadvantage that the protection of the Trustee Act 1925, ss 57 and 61, is unavailable to them.

1.16 The common law relationship between principal and agent is that of creditor and debtor giving rise to a personal claim: thus if the debtor is insolvent the personal claim will abate with the claims of the other creditors. The equitable relationship of trustee and beneficiary, whereunder the nominal ownership is vested in the trustee so that the beneficiary has an equitable proprietary interest, is such that if the trustee is insolvent the trust property is unavailable for the trustee's creditors. The trust property is claimed as their own by the trust beneficiaries if it is identifiable and, for this purpose, the beneficiaries have an equitable right to trace the trust property into other property into which it has been converted after the trust property has been mixed with the trustee's own funds and claim a proprietary interest in the traced property.

1.17 In certain circumstances equity intervenes to treat an agent as a constructive trustee or under fiduciary duties similar to those of a trustee. Thus, if the principal instructs his agent to purchase Blackacre for the principal and the agent purports to purchase Blackacre for himself the agent will be held constructive trustee thereof for the principal[1]. If an agent has property given to him by his principal for sale, investment or safe custody the agent will be under fiduciary duties similar to those of a trustee[2]. The position is the same when an agent receives property on behalf of his principal, eg by way of collection of rents or debts, so long as he is required contractually or otherwise to keep such moneys separately identifiable from his own property: otherwise he is liable to account as debtor only[3]. Where the agent is a fiduciary in respect of property, not liable as debtor only, then the equitable right to trace will be available so as to establish a proprietary claim. On the agent's insolvency the principal's original or traced property will be claimed by the principal and not be available for the agent's creditors. This will also be the case where property is received by an agent on his own behalf as a bribe or by way of secret profit so that he ought to account for it to his principal and 'Equity considers done that which ought to be done'[4].

1   *Longfield Parish Council v Robson* (1913) 29 TLR 357.
2   *Re Hallett's Estate* (1880) 13 Ch D 696; *De Bussche v Alt* (1878) 8 Ch D 286; *Burdick v Garrick* (1870) 5 Ch App 233.
3   *Kennedy v Lyell* (1889) 14 App Cas 437; *Foley v Hill* (1848) 2 HL Cas 28; *Aluminium Industrie Vaassen BV v Romalpa Aluminium Ltd* [1976] 2 All ER 552, [1976] 1 WLR 676; *Clough Mill Ltd v Martin* [1984] 3 All ER 982, [1985] 1 WLR 111, CA.
4   *A-G for Hong Kong v Reid* [1994] 1 AC 324, [1994] 1 All ER, PC.

Trust and contract

1.18 A contract is a creature of the common law and creates a personal right against the other party to the contract. At common law, only the parties to the contract can sue on it, but under the Contracts (Rights of Third Parties) Act 1999 it is now possible for third parties to enforce contracts for their benefit where intended by the contracting parties. A contract is essentially a bargain: it is based upon agreement and it requires for its validity some valuable consideration or to be incorporated in a deed, the formalities for a deed importing the consideration.

1.19 A trust is an equitable obligation which creates a proprietary interest in the beneficiaries capable of binding third parties. No consideration[1] is required for its validity: it is, perhaps, best regarded as the equitable equivalent of a common law gift and so leaves no right in the creator of the trust, known as the settlor, to enforce, vary or revoke the terms of the trust, unless such rights be expressly reserved at the time of the creation of the trust. Thus, if S vests property in B on trust to pay the income to C for life and after C's death to divide the capital among X, Y and Z, then C, X, Y and Z being of full capacity can together (if unanimous) insist on B dividing the property between them at once, notwithstanding the protests of S[2]. It is the beneficiaries alone who can enforce the trust (or terminate the trust if unanimous and of full capacity).

1   Consideration may be present, eg where a trust is created in consideration of the primary beneficiary's marriage or where in consideration of a £20,000 loan by F to G in 1997 G agrees to settle and does settle £60,000 on X, Y and Z in 2007.
2   *Saunders v Vautier* (1841) 4 Beav 115; *Stephenson v Barclays Bank Trust Co Ltd* [1975] 1 All ER 625.

1.20 A person may enter into a contract to create a trust and if the contract is enforceable, whether specifically or in damages, this will ensure that property ultimately becomes vested in trustees upon trust for the beneficiaries[1]. However, if the promise to create a trust is merely in a deed unsupported by valuable consideration it will be unenforceable by an equitable decree for specific performance since 'equity will not assist a volunteer'[2], although equity will not prevent a covenantee who is also a beneficiary from suing at common law for damages on his own account[3].

[1] A contract to create a trust over an unascertained part of a larger fund of money or gold ingots confers no equitable proprietary interest until allocation of the relevant amount, and if the obligee is insolvent a damages claim is of no assistance: *MacJordan Construction Ltd v Brookmount Erostin Ltd* (1991) 56 BLR 1, [1992] BCLC 350, CA, endorsed in *Re Goldcorp Exchange Ltd* [1994] 2 All ER 806 at 823, PC. If the contract relates to specific property that becomes vested in the obligee then the trust will affect such property: *Pullan v Koe* [1913] 1 Ch 9; *Re Gillott's Settlement* [1934] Ch 97.

[2] *Re Pryce* [1917] 1 Ch 234; *Re Kay's Settlement* [1939] Ch 329; *Re Cook's Settlement Trusts* [1965] Ch 902, [1964] 3 All ER 898. Further see paras 9.104–9.112 below.

[3] *Cannon v Hartley* [1949] Ch 213, [1949] 1 All ER 50.

1.21 Contractual rights, like other choses in action, may be the subject matter of a trust[1]. Thus, if S is entitled to be repaid a loan of £10,000 at 10% pa he may assign this to trustees to hold on trust for certain beneficiaries. He may similarly assign to trustees rights to royalties or competition prize rights entitling him or his assignees to £500 per week for ten years. Indeed, contractual rights not assignable at law, because involving the benefit of agreements for personal services or because of an express contractual restriction, may be the subject matter of a declaration of trust by the person having the benefit of the contract[2]. Such person as trustee must then hold the fruits of the benefit of the contract for his beneficiary, but such beneficiary cannot directly sue the other party to the contract as he would then be in the same position as an assignee of the benefit of the contract which is not permitted[3]. This is an exception to the rule that if T holds rights against X as trustee for B then if, in breach of trust, T refuses to enforce those rights then B can directly sue X but joining T as co-defendant so that all relevant parties are bound by the court's judgment[4].

[1] *Lloyd's v Harper* (1880) 16 Ch D 290; *Harmer v Armstrong* [1934] Ch 65; *Re Patrick* [1891] 1 Ch 82.

[2] *Don King Productions Inc v Warren* [2000] Ch 291, [1999] 2 All ER 218, CA.

[3] *Don King Productions Inc v Warren* [2000] Ch 291, [1999] 2 All ER 218, CA; *Barbados Trust Co Ltd v Bank of Zambia* [2006] EWHC 222 (Comm).

[4] *Don King Productions Inc v Warren* [2000] Ch 291, [1999] 2 All ER 218, CA; *Parker-Tweedale v Dunbar Bank plc* [1990] 2 All ER 577 at 582–583, 587.

1.22 Since contractual rights may be trust property it is possible for X to obtain the benefit of a contract made between A and B for the benefit of X, although X is not a party to the contract, if X can show that A contracted expressly or impliedly as trustee of the benefit of the contract for X so that A is at once both settlor and trustee: as a beneficiary, X can enforce his interest in the trust property against B[1]. Everything hinges upon whether or not A intended to create a trust of the benefit of the contract. The courts have become increasingly reluctant to find such an intention if only because this renders the contract between A and B incapable of being varied by them without X's consent, a result often not contemplated by A[2]. Usually, the courts rightly adjudge the claim to a trust relationship to be a transparent device to evade the privity of contract doctrine[3]. Nowadays, X can seek to have A and B confer enforceable contractual rights upon him under the Contracts (Rights of Third Parties) Act 1999.

[1] A can recover substantial damages from B to be held on trust for X where A holds the benefit of the contract on trust for X: *Lloyd's v Harper* (1880) 16 Ch D 290. If no such trust can be imported then the general rule is that A can only claim for his own actual loss and so usually recover only nominal damages: *West v Houghton* (1879) 4 CPD 197; *Albacruz (Cargo Owners) v Albazero (Owners),The Albazero* [1977] AC 774, [1976] 3 All ER 129. *Jackson v Horizon Holidays* [1975] 3 All ER 92, [1975] 1 WLR 1468 appears out of line in applying a dictum in *Lloyd's v Harper* (1880) 16 Ch D 290 at 321 out of context as pointed out by the House of Lords in *Woodar Investment Development Ltd v Wimpey Construction UK Ltd* [1980] 1 All ER 571 at 576; cf *Coulls v Bagot's Executor and Trustee Co Ltd* (1967) 119 CLR 460 at 501–502. In an appropriate case where A's damages will be inadequate he may be able to satisfy the requirements for a decree of specific performance: *Beswick v Beswick* [1968] AC 58, [1967] 2 All ER 1197. Further see para 9.87 below.

[2] *Vandepitte v Preferred Accident Insurance Corpn of New York* [1933] AC 70, PC; *Re Sinclair's Life Policy* [1938] Ch 799, [1938] 3 All ER 124; *Re Schebsman ex p Official Receiver, Trustee v Cargo Superintendants (London) Ltd and Schebsman* [1944] Ch 83; *Green v Russell* [1959] 2 QB 226, [1959] 2 All ER 525; *Beswick v Beswick* [1968] AC 58, [1967] 2 All ER 1197; *Trident General Insurance Co Ltd v McNiece Bros* (1988) 165 CLR 107; *DG Finance Ltd v Scott & Eagle Star Insurance Ltd* (unreported), CA, discussed by NJ Price in (1996) 59 MLR 738–741.

[3] The intent to create a trust must be affirmatively proved: *West v Houghton* (1879) 4 CPD 197 at 203; *Vandepitte v Preferred Accident Insurance Corpn* [1933] AC 70 at 79–80.

1.23 However, it is still very important to realise that there are many key differences between a contract and a trust (which are mutually exclusive concepts). They are as follows:

(a)   A trust cannot exist without there being property owned by someone subject to obligations as trustee of the trust, while a contract may or may not concern property.

(b)   A settlor can be sole trustee of designated property of his own[1] for others or for charity, so as to give rise to an obligation enforceable by others, but a person cannot contract with himself[2] (just as X cannot be trustee of property for X alone[3]).

(c)   A settlor can unilaterally create a trust conferring rights forthwith on the beneficiaries without telling the trustee[4] as in cases where A can transfer ownership of property to T without T knowing (eg by registering property in T's name or executing a deed or making T his executor and trustee by a testamentary document) but a contract creating rights cannot arise until there is an agreement between the contracting parties; however, T cannot be subject to any trusteeship obligations without his knowledge and consent[5] which is deemed present if he does not disclaim the trusteeship as soon as reasonably practicable after discovering that title to trust property has been vested in him.

(d)   Once a settlor has created his trust by vesting his property in the trustee, T, he drops out of the picture, having no rights or liabilities[6] (so his later death or mental incapacity is immaterial) except to the extent created by him within his trust structure[7] (eg a right to appoint himself to be discretionary portfolio manager with liabilities as such or a right to replace T or to appoint capital or income to beneficiaries or to veto specified proposed actions by T); a contracting party has extensive rights and liabilities as such: he must be joined in any action relating to the contract and his later death or mental incapacity is critical in terminating the contract.

(e) Automatically attached to the office of trustee are rights to take expenses and remuneration out of the trust fund[8], *proscriptive* fiduciary duties[9] preventing him from preferring his own interests to those of his beneficiaries and making him strictly liable to account for any unauthorised gains he makes for himself, his family and associates (irrespective of no loss being suffered by the beneficiaries or of the gain not being capable of being obtained for the trust)[10], and *prescriptive* duties to act in authorised fashion, fairly and in good faith[11] and to exercise management powers (expressly or automatically conferred on him[12] with due care and skill[13] – except to the extent protected from liability by express clauses in the trust instrument[14]. There is little like this for parties to a contract except for a developing obligation of good faith[15] and protective consumer contracts legislation against unfair contract terms[16].

(f) A trustee as the holder of an office can be removed and replaced by the court for good cause[17] or by a person given a power in the trust instrument if acting within the terms of such power[18], while a trustee can resign and appoint a replacement trustee; a party to a contract remains always a party to the contract.

(g) A trust is not terminated before its specified duration[19] (not exceeding the perpetuity period permitted by law[20]) by the death or mental incapacity of the trustee[21], while neither the settlor nor a beneficiary can terminate the trust for a major breach of trust; a contract can be terminated by one party for a major breach of contract by the other party and by the death or mental incapacity of a party.

(h) A beneficiary need suffer no loss before requiring the trustee to restore to the trust fund value lost due to any breaches of trust[22], such liability of the trustee being a strict liability where his accounts are falsified by reason of his conduct being beyond his powers and so unauthorised, causation being relevant where the accounts are surcharged due to the trustee doing negligently or improperly what is within his powers[23]; a person suing in respect of a breach of contract can sue only in respect of personally suffered loss (as is the position of a beneficiary absolutely entitled to lost income or capital, though such beneficiary, unlike a contracting party, also has a right to any gain made by the trustee even if suffering no loss[24]).

(i) During the life of a trust the court has an extensive supportive or paternalistic role to play under its inherent jurisdiction supplemented by some statutory powers (eg conferring extra powers on trustees where expedient in the interests of the beneficiaries[25] certifying that defending or pursuing specific legal proceedings is reasonable so that the trustees can be sure that all legal costs can be taken out of the trust fund[26], declaring that a proposed course of action that is controversial is safely within the discretionary leeway afforded to the trustee in exercising a particular power so the action will be valid[27]) as well as an extensive range of remedies[28]; this is not the case for a contract.

(j)   Crucially, the trust confers proprietary interests, first, on the trustee in the form of a trustee's lien[29] as security for payment of remuneration and expenses (with creditors of the trustee duly acting in his capacity as fund-owner-manager being subrogated to such lien[30]), and, second, on the beneficiaries in the form of equitable interests vested in the beneficiaries, whether under fixed or discretionary trusts[31]. Such proprietary interests are attached to the trust fund. This comprises authorised assets rightfully representing the original trust assets, and, if so claimed by the beneficiaries, unauthorised assets acquired by the trustee on behalf of the trust or on behalf of himself, together with assets added by the settlor or others to the assets of the trust, and the fruits of any trust assets[32]. The creation of these proprietary interests under trust law confers priority over the trustee's private creditors for creditors dealing with the trustee as trustee and also for the beneficiaries: it also makes it possible for the trustee to be guilty of theft of the beneficiaries' property[33]. The law of contract cannot create proprietary interests (except, in common law countries, for contracts relating to land or other unique property which are specifically enforceable, leading 'Equity to look on as done that which ought to be done' so as to regard the claimant as having an equitable proprietary interest in the relevant property[34]).

(k)   Because all the beneficiaries, if ascertained and of full capacity, are between them the absolutely entitled collective owner of the trust property, they can terminate the trust and require the trustee to transfer the trust property to themselves or as they otherwise unanimously direct, after satisfying any trustee's lien – even though the settlor and the trustee oppose this[35]. A contract cannot be terminated without the agreement of all the parties.

(l)   With the traditional emphasis on the proprietary nature of the trust, a trust must be for beneficiaries (so they have enforceable equitable proprietary interests even if only interested under a discretionary trust[36]) or, exceptionally for a charitable purpose (so that in the public interest on the Crown's behalf, the Attorney General or a statutory body, the Charity Commission, can ensure the trustees duly use the trust property for the charitable purpose). Thus, a trust cannot be used for the furthering of non-charitable purposes[37] (eg political purposes or the purposes of a self-interested group like solicitors, accountants or bankers) unless the courts are prepared to place a modern emphasis on the obligational nature of the trust to validate a non-charitable purpose trust if the trust instrument expressly provides for an enforcer to enforce the obligations of the trustee[38]. A contract, of course, can be utilised for carrying on non-charitable purposes.

---

[1]   Eg *Paul v Constance* [1977] 1 WLR 527.
[2]   *Rye v Rye* [1962] AC 496; *Ingram v IRC* [2000] 1 AC 293.
[3]   *Re Cook, Beck v Grant* [1948] Ch 212.
[4]   *Fletcher v Fletcher* (1844) 4 Hare 67, *Mallott v Wilson* [1903] 2 Ch 494.
[5]   *Westdeutsche Landesbank Girozentrale v Islington London Borough Council* [1996] AC 669.

6   *Re Astor's Settlement Trusts* [1952] Ch 534 at 542; *Re Murphy's Settlements, Murphy v Murphy* [1999] 1 WLR 232 at 295.

7   Exceptionally, he may separately oblige himself by contract or a covenant in a deed to transfer to T a sum of money or other property in certain future events: indeed such obligation could be expressly undertaken in the trust instrument creating the bi-partite trustee-beneficiaries relationship.

8   See below, Articles 58 and 83 and Trustee Act 2000, ss 28, 29, 31 and 32. These are not contractual rights against beneficiaries or the settlor: *Re Duke of Norfolk's Settlement Trusts, Earl of Perth v Fitzalan-Howard* [1982] Ch 61, 77–78; *Galmerrow Securities Ltd v National Westminster Bank* [2002] WTLR 125, 155–156.

9   *Bristol & West Building Society v Mothew* [1998] Ch 1.

10 *Boardman v Phipps* [1967] 2 AC 46.

11 *Edge v Pensions Ombudsman* [2000] Ch 602.

12 Trustee Act 2000, ss 3, 4, 5, 8, 11, 16, 17.

13 Trustee Act 2000, ss 2, 23, Sch 1.

14 *Armitage v Nurse* [1998] Ch 241.

15 See O Lando & H Beale, *Principles of European Contract Law Part I* (Martinus Nijhoff, 1999) Article 1.106, 'Good Faith and Fair Dealing' and notes thereon; R Brownsword, N Hird & G Howells (eds), *Good Faith in Contract* (Aldershot 1999); J Smits, *The Making of European Private Law* (Intersentia 2002) pp 193–195.

16 Unfair Contract Terms Act 1977, EC Directive 93/13/EEC on Unfair Contract Terms.

17 Trustee Act 1925, s 41.

18 *Virani v Guernsey International Trustees Ltd* [2004] WTLR 1007, CA.

19 Unless no property remains subject to the terms of the trust because distributed to beneficiaries by the trustees.

20 In England a period of years not exceeding 80 may be prescribed or a period of 21 years from the death of the last survivor of then-living descendants of a specified person, such as Queen Elizabeth II.

21 Trustee Act 1925, ss 36 and 41.

22 *Target Holdings Ltd v Redferns* [1996] AC 421, 434. Accountability, via production of the trusteeship accounts and detailed examination of them, is at the core of the trust concept.

23 See Lord Millett when Millett LJ in 'Equity's Place in the Law of Commerce' (1998) 114 LQR 214, 226–227, and D J Hayton, 'Unique Rules for a Unique Institution, The Trust' in S Degeling and J Edelman (eds), *Equity in Commercial Law* (Thomson, 2005).

24 *Boardman v Phipps* [1967] 2 AC 46. In very exceptional circumstances a claimant may recover a gain made by the defendant in breach of contract: *Att-Gen v Blake* [2001] 1 AC 268.

25 Trustee Act 1925, s.57.

26 *Re Beddoe, Downes v Cottam* [1893] 1 Ch 547; *Alsop Wilkinson v Neary* [1996] 1 WLR 1220.

27 *Public Trustee v Cooper* [2001] WTLR 901.

28 Orders for the trustee to pay compensation for loss to the trust fund or to a beneficiary suffering the loss, or to pay the fund or absolutely entitled beneficiaries the amount of profit made out of wrongful use of the trust property or the office of trustee; orders removing the trustee and replacing him with another person; declarations that property owned by the trustee or a third party is to be held wholly or partly on trust for the beneficiaries under a particular trust or subject to a lien or charge for money due from the trustee or a third party; orders for a third party unconscionably involved in a breach of trust to compensate the trust fund or absolutely entitled beneficiaries suffering loss from such breach; orders for accounts to be taken, for the defendant to disclose the whereabouts of trust assets and for such assets owned by the defendant to be frozen until trial of the claim to them.

29 *X v A* [2000] 1 All ER 490; *Octavo Investments Pty Ltd v Knight* (1979) 144 CLR 260; *Dimos v Dikeakos Nominees Ltd* (1997) 149 ALR 113.

30 *Re Ballman ex p Garland* (1804) 10 Ves 110; *Re British Power Traction and Lighting Co Ltd, Halifax Joint Stock Banking Co Ltd v British Power Traction and Lighting Co Ltd* [1910] 2 Ch 470.

31 'If the beneficiaries have no rights enforceable against the trustees, there are no trusts' [except in the case of charitable trusts]: *Armitage v Nurse* [1998] Ch 241, 253.

32 *A-G of Hong Kong v Reid* [1994] 1 AC 324; *Foskett v McKeown* [2001] 1 AC 102, R Nolan, 'Property in a Fund' (2004) 120 LQR 108.

33 Theft Act 1968, ss 1, 3(1), 4(1), 5(1).

1.23 *Preliminary terminology*

34 *Lysaght v Edwards* (1876) 2 Ch D 499.
35 *Saunders v Vautier* (1841) 4 Beav 115; *Stephenson v Barclays Bank Trust Co Ltd* [1975]
    1 WLR 882; *Goulding v James* [1997] 2 All ER 239.
36 *Schmidt v Rosewood Trust Co* [2003] UKPC 26,[2003] 2 AC 709. Trusts may be for
    beneficiaries not yet in existence but alive on expiry of an accumulation of income period,
    though the person entitled in default of such beneficiaries will be a beneficiary with
    enforceable rights.
37 *Re Denley's Trust Deed, Holman v HH Marlyn & Co Ltd* [1969] 1 Ch 373; *Re Grant's
    Will Trusts, Harris v Anderson* [1980] 1 WLR 360.
38 See D Hayton, 'Developing the Obligation Characteristic of the Trust' (2001) 117 LQR 97
    and paras 8.157–8.167 below.

Trust and loans

1.24 Loans require special examination. First, a loan must be distinguished
from the resulting trust that arises where A provides B with £50,000 towards
the purchase of Blackacre (or other property) in B's name, when B will hold
the property upon trust for A and himself in proportion to their contributions,
so that A will have a beneficial interest in the property which will appreciate
(or depreciate) with the value of the property[1]. In the event of B's bankruptcy
A's interest will not be available for B's creditors. If A had merely lent B
£50,000 at 10% pa repayable over 20 years then, when B had purchased
Blackacre, A would merely have had a personal contractual claim against B
for the principal and interest irrespective of how much the property might
appreciate with inflation over the years[2]. If A had had the £50,000 debt and
interest thereon secured on Blackacre by means of a mortgage A would still
only have been entitled to the principal and interest, but he would have the
right to sell the security, Blackacre, in order to ensure that he received his
principal and interest (and legal costs) but no more. A would be a secured
creditor in the event of B's bankruptcy if his £50,000 loan had been secured by
means of a mortgage: if no such mortgage had been created then A would
rank as an ordinary unsecured creditor with priority subsequent to secured
creditors.

1   *Dyer v Dyer* (1788) 2 Cox Eq Cas 92; *The Venture* [1908] P 218, CA; *Shephard v
    Cartwright* [1955] AC 431, [1954] 3 All ER 649. In *Hussey v Palmer* [1972] 3 All ER 744,
    [1972] 1 WLR 1286, the dissenting judgment of Cairns LJ is to be preferred: (1973) 89
    LQR 2; (1973) 37 Conv 65; *Re Sharpe (a bankrupt)* [1980] 1 All ER 198, [1980] 1 WLR
    219, *Trustee of the Bankrupt v Sharpe.*
2   *Aveling v Knipe* (1815) 19 Ves 441; *Guardian Ocean Cargoes Ltd v Banco de Brasil (Nos
    1 & 3)* [1994] 2 Lloyds Rep 152 (a trust requires money not to be usable as the recipient's
    own free money, as also emphasised in *Paragon Finance Ltd v Thakerar & Co* [1999]
    1 All ER 400 at 416 per Millett LJ) and in *Twinsectra Ltd v Yardley* [2002] UKHL 12 at
    para [74] per Lord Millett, [2002] 2 AC 164.

QUISTCLOSE TRUSTS

1.25 A loan arrangement may commence as a trust of the money loaned to
enable the borrower only to carry out a particular purpose resulting, if the
purpose is performed, in a pure debtor-creditor relationship excluding any
trust, but in the event of non-performance of the purpose the lender can rely
on the loaned money being held on trust for the lender. This was the situation
in *Barclay's Bank Ltd v Quistclose Investments Ltd*[1].

1   [1970] AC 567, [1968] 3 All ER 651, analysed in detail in W Swadling (ed), *Quistclose Trust* (Hart Publishing, 2004).

1.26 Rolls Razor Ltd (with a large overdraft with Barclays Bank) had declared a dividend on its shares which it could not pay except under an arrangement with Quistclose whereby a loan of £209,719 8s 6d was made by Quistclose to Rolls Razor 'for the purpose of paying the final dividend on 24 July next'. The money was paid into a separate account at Barclays Bank with whom it was agreed by confirming letter of 15 July that the account would 'only be used to meet the dividend due on 24 July'. On 17 July Rolls Razor went into liquidation.

1.27 The Bank claimed that the money was owned beneficially by Rolls Razor subject to a personal debtor-creditor relationship to repay an equivalent sum of money to Quistclose: thus the Bank could set off the money against Rolls Razor's overdraft.

1.28 Quistclose claimed that the money had been given to Rolls Razor impressed with a primary trust to pay out the segregated money to the shareholders of Rolls Razor as a dividend (so long as such payment would still have been lawful if made out of the company's own money)[1] and a secondary trust to repay it to Quistclose if the primary trust failed: only if payment had been made to the shareholders in accordance with the primary trust would Rolls Razor's status have been converted from that of trustee into that of a contractual debtor.

1   This qualification seems required by necessary implication for otherwise the shareholder beneficiaries of the primary trust would have acquired an indefeasible interest at the time of payment of Quistclose's money to Rolls Razor. They were not even joined as parties. Further see F Oditah (1992) 108 LQR 459.

1.29 The House of Lords unanimously accepted Quistclose's claim to the money. As Peter Gibson J subsequently explained it:

> 'The principle is that equity fastens on the conscience of the person who receives from another property transferred for a specific purpose only and not therefore for the recipient's own purposes, so that such person will not be permitted to treat the property as his own or to use it for other than the stated purpose ... if the common intention is that property is transferred for a specific purpose ... the transferee cannot keep the property if for any reason that purpose cannot be fulfilled.'[1]

1   *Carreras Rothmans Ltd v Freeman Mathews Treasure Ltd* [1985] Ch 207 at 222, [1985] 1 All ER 155 at 165. Thus the receipt by a solicitor of loan funds from a third party under a solicitor's undertaking to apply them for a particular purpose renders the solicitor a trustee of such funds: *Barclays Bank plc v Weeks Legg & Dean* [1999] QB 309 at 324, CA, and *Twinsectra Ltd v Yardley* [2002] UKHL 12 at paras [13], [99] and [100], [2002] 2 AC 164.

1.30 In *Quistclose* the Bank, a purchaser, had notice of the arrangement of Rolls Razor with Quistclose and so had notice that it would be a breach of trust for it to take the money for itself. Subsequently in *R v Common*

1.30 *Preliminary terminology*

Professional Examination Board, ex p Mealing-McCleod[1] Lloyd's Bank lent M £6,000 to be used as a 'Deposit to Court Funds' to cover the £6,000 payment into court required as security for M's appeal against a decision in favour of the CPE Board so as to cover the Board's costs. The Loan Agreement stated 'You will hold the loan on trust for us until you have used it for that purpose'. As it happened, M won her appeal and so did not have to pay the Board's costs, but the Board sought to have the £6,000 paid to it to cover costs owed to it in earlier proceedings against it that M had lost.

[1]   [2000] EWCA Civ 138, (2000) Times, 2 May.

1.31 The Court of Appeal rejected the Board's claim, the two-man court considering that the trust continued after the payment into court and 'as trustee of the money the appellant was under an obligation to take steps to see that the money was returned to the bank', while the court, a volunteer not having given consideration for receipt of the money, once it had notice of the trust in favour of the bank, had to give effect to it.

1.32 This is a dubious decision. Clearly, there was a trust of the money until M paid it into court pursuant to the power to transfer the legal beneficial ownership to the court to enable such to be delivered to the CPE Board if the appeal failed. No doubt by necessary implication M's right to the money (subject to costs rules involving the same parties) if the appeal succeeded was held on trust for the bank. The court knew nothing of the Loan Agreement and had every reason to believe it received full legal beneficial ownership of the money and was not a trustee under a duty to keep the money segregated as trust money. Its receipt of the money was not in breach of any trust. On receiving notice that M's right to the money (subject to costs rules concerning other proceedings involving the same parties) was held on trust for the bank, the court as a volunteer had to respect such trust but, of course, could exercise its overriding powers as to costs so as to defeat the banker's interest under the trust.

1.33 In *Twinsectra Ltd v Yardley*[1] the House of Lords considered *Quistclose* trusts. Twinsectra had loaned £1 million on the terms that a solicitor gave an undertaking that the money would 'be utilised solely for the acquisition of property' on behalf of the solicitor's client 'and for no other purpose', and would be 'retained until such time as applied in the acquisition of property on behalf of the client'. Their Lordships unanimously concluded the money was held on trust.

[1]   [2002] UKHL 12, [2002] 2 AC 164, applied in *Re Margaretta Ltd, Freeman v Customs & Excise Commissioners* [2005] EWHC 582 (Ch), [2005] STC 610.

1.34 Lord Hoffman[1] *(with whom Lord Slynn*[2] *agreed)* seemed simply to consider the trust to be an express trust of the money subject to a power to apply it by way of loan to the solicitor's client in the acquisition of property. Lord Millett[3] analysed the *Quistclose* trust:

'to be an entirely orthodox example of the kind of default trust known as a resulting trust. The lender pays the money to the borrower by way of a loan, but he does not part with the entire beneficial interest in the money, and insofar as he does not, it is held on a resulting trust for the lender from the outset ... it is the borrower who has a very limited use of the money, being obliged to apply for it for the stated purpose or to return it. He has no beneficial interest in the money, which remains throughout in the lender subject only to the borrower's power or duty to apply the money in accordance with the lender's instructions. When the purpose fails, the money is returnable to the lender, not under some new trust in his favour which only comes into being on the failure of the purpose, but because the resulting trust in his favour is no longer subject to any power on the part of the borrower to make use of the money. Whether the borrower is obliged to apply the money for the stated purpose or is merely at liberty to do so and whether the lender can countermand the borrower's mandate while it is still capable of being carried out, must depend on the circumstances of the particular case ... .Provided the power is stated with sufficient clarity for the court to be able to determine whether it is still capable of being carried out or whether the money has been misapplied, it is sufficiently certain to be enforced. If it is uncertain, then the borrower has no authority to make any use of the money at all and must return it to the lender under a resulting trust.'

1   *Twinsectra Ltd v Yardley* [2002] UKHL 12, [2002] 2 AC 164, para 13.
2   *Twinsectra Ltd v Yardley* [2002] UKHL 12, [2002] 2 AC 164, para 2.
3   *Twinsectra Ltd v Yardley* [2002] UKHL 12, [2002] 2 AC 164 at paras [100] and [101].

1.35 Lord Hutton[1] agreed with the reaons of Lords Hoffmann and Millett for the solicitor's undertaking creating a trust, while Lord Steyn[2] agreed with Lords Hoffman and Hutton. Lord Millet's analysis may appear to pose problems in the case where the borrower does not merely have a power but 'is obliged to apply the money for the stated purpose', especially where the lender cannot countermand the borrower's obligation, because the third party benefiting from the application of the money for the stated purpose then has an equitable interest. However, so long as there is a possiblility that the occasion for such application may not arise, the lender will have an equitable interest under a resulting trust.

1   *Twinsectra Ltd v Yardley* [2002] UKHL 12, [2002] 2 AC 164, para 25.
2   *Twinsectra Ltd v Yardley* [2002] UKHL 12, [2002] 2 AC 164, para 7.

RESERVATION OF TITLE, CHARGES OR TRUSTS

1.36 Company liquidations create many situations where it is claimed that a company's obligations have been transformed from contract to property, from debt to trust, so that the claimant may claim property as his own in priority to mere creditors. The form of words used can be decisive in establishing whether the requisite intent to create a trust was present. The words may be part of a contract.

1.37 A customer may send money to a company for goods under a contract for the company to supply him with the goods. If the goods are not supplied (eg because of the liquidation of the company) the customer will merely be a general unsecured creditor of the company for the amount of the money he sent unless a trust has been created. He may create a trust of his money until he receives title to the goods by using appropriate words when he sends the money, or the company may similarly create a trust covering customers' moneys when received by the company[1]. The customer's equitable interest in the money or its traceable product will protect him until he is supplied with the goods unless the company wrongfully uses the money to pay off debts of creditors having no notice of the misapplication so that the equitable right to a proprietary remedy against substituted assets ascertained via the tracing process (explained in Articles 92 and 101) is of no avail. In such a way he may retain the beneficial ownership of his money until supplied with the goods.

1   *Re Kayford Ltd* [1975] 1 All ER 604, [1975] 1 WLR 279 cogently criticised by Goodhart and Jones (1980) 43 MLR 489, 496–498 for not holding that the company's unilateral declaration of trust was a voidable preference of the customers under Companies Act 1948, s 320 (now Companies Act 1985, s 615), though it has been applied by the Court of Appeal in *Re Chelsea Cloisters* (1980) 41 P & CR 98 to tenants' damage deposits paid into a separate account after a company was having financial problems that subsequently led to its liquidation.

1.38 If a vendor supplies goods to a company under a contract of sale, he may provide, by appropriate words in the contract, for title to such goods unsold by the company to remain in himself until he has received payment in full for the supplied goods[1] or until he has received payment in respect of all debts due to him from the company, including debts concerning other supplied goods[2]. In such a case he will be no mere debtor if the company goes into liquidation but will be fully entitled to his own property in the company's possession.

1   *Clough Mill Ltd v Martin* [1984] 3 All ER 982, [1985] 1 WLR 111, CA. Indeed, in *Re Highway Foods International Ltd* [1995] 1 BCLC 209 it was held that if goods were sold subject to a retention of title clause and the buyer then sold the goods on to a sub-purchaser, that sale also being subject to a retention of title clause, and delivered the goods to the sub-purchaser, unless and until the sub-purchaser paid the buyer the price of the goods, the original seller could claim title to the goods in the hands of the sub-purchaser, irrespective of ss 2(1) and 9 of the Factors Act 1889.
2   *Armour v Thyssen Edelstahlwerke A-G* [1991] 2 AC 339, [1990] 3 All ER 481, HL though there were no outstanding debts for other goods: if the vendor recovers goods for which he has been paid then, to prevent unjust enrichment, it seems he should refund their price for total failure of consideration: *Rowland v Divall* [1923] 2 KB 500 CA; *Clough Mill Ltd v Martin* [1984] 3 All ER 982, example of Goff LJ at 987–988.

1.39 However, if the legal and beneficial title passes to the company or if legal title alone purports to pass to the company and the vendor is entitled to repossess the goods if the company does not make full payment for them, then the company will be treated as having created a charge[1] over the goods which will be void against a liquidator or administrator or a purchaser of the property subject to the charge if not registered under Companies Act 1985, s 395[2]. Equity looks to the substance and reality of the transaction which is the provision of security for a debt[3], the company having the right to the property once it has repaid the relevant debt.

1   *Re Bond Worth Ltd* [1980] Ch 228, [1979] 3 All ER 919. Where the vendor is legal beneficial owner he cannot acquire a separate equitable interest until he has passed full ownership to the purchaser: *Westdeutsche Landesbank v Islington London Borough Council* [1996] AC 669, 706, 714; *DKLR Holding Co (No 2) Pty Ltd v Commissioner of Stamp Duties* (1982) 149 CLR 431.

2   See Companies Act 1985, s 399 substituted by Companies Act 1989, s 95 and *Stroud Architectural Systems Ltd v John Laing Construction Ltd* [1994] BCC 18.

3   A similar problem arises as to whether a transaction is a sale or a secured loan, i e a charge: see *Welsh Development Agency v Export Finance Co* [1992] BCLC 148, CA; *Lloyds and Scottish Finance Ltd v Cyril Lord Carpets Sales Ltd* [1992] BCLC 609, HL.

1.40 Where the vendor supplies to the company material to use to manufacture new goods, the vendor's contract with the company may provide for the vendor to have legal and beneficial title to such goods or for the company to hold such goods on trust for the vendor until payment in full for the material or until the company sells the goods to its customers. Here the company will be treated as having created a charge over the goods which will be void against a liquidator or administrator or a purchaser of the property subject to the charge if not registered under Companies Act 1985, s 395[1].

1   *Clough Mill Ltd v Martin* [1984] 3 All ER 982, [1985] 1 WLR 111, CA; *Re Peachdart Ltd* [1984] Ch 131, [1983] 3 All ER 204; *Modelboard Ltd v Outer Box Ltd* [1992] BCC 945.

1.41 If the vendor seeks to protect himself further by providing that the proceeds of sale of his materials or of new goods manufactured using his materials are to be paid into a separate bank account to be held by the company on trust for him until he receives payment, it seems that a fund is being set aside by the company as security for payment of a debt so that there is a charge which will be void if not registered under Companies Act 1985, s 395[1]. After all, the vendor is surely supposed only to be entitled to a sum equal to the undischarged balance due from the company and not to obtain as a windfall the remainder of the moneys in the account representing the company's profit.

1   *Pfeiffer (E) Weinkellerei-Weineinkauf GmbH & Co v Arbuthnot Factors Ltd* [1988] 1 WLR 150; *Re Weldtech Equipment Ltd* [1991] BCC 16; *Compaq Computer Ltd v Abercorn Group* [1991] BCC 484; *Ian Chisholm Textiles Ltd v Griffiths* [1994] 2 BCLC 291. It seems that the Court of Appeal in *Aluminium Industrie Vaasen BV v Romalpa Aluminium Ltd* [1976] 2 All ER 552, [1976] 1 WLR 676, CA overlooked the underlying charge nature of the contract so that the decision has been distinguished to death.

1.42 However, there will be no charge within s 395 if the company purchaser expressly contracted that it will be trustee of a specified percentage or fractional part of re-sale proceeds received by it or such a percentage or fractional part[1] of such proceeds as is equivalent to the amount owing to the vendor by the purchaser at the time of receipt of such proceeds. On receipt of the proceeds Equity treats as done that which ought to be done[2] and because of this, 'even if the proceeds were paid into a general bank account there could be a tracing remedy where the recipient was obliged to hold a particular portion of the proceeds on trust'[3]. To reinforce the vendor's position the recipient purchaser should be expressly placed under an obligation to transfer the relevant amount of money into the vendor's own account within a short period of five to ten working days and under an obligation in that period not to permit the amount credited in its general account to fall below the relevant amount held on trust for the vendor[4].

1   Assuming £50,000 is owed by P to V in respect of goods made with V's materials and sold for £100,000, P will hold the £100,000 on the agreed trust for itself and V equally. Assuming P's bank account was not overdrawn by more than £50,000, an equitable lien or

charge arises by operation of law to enable V to trace an amount of £50,000 into and out of such an account (see Article 92 below). If the agreement related not to a trust of a specific portion of the £100,000 proceeds but only to a trust of an amount corresponding to the amount of the debt (of £50,000) then owed by P to V, a problem arises as to the certainty of subject-matter because there is no £50,000 fund segregated from the remaining money (unless reliance can be placed on the unsatisfactory *Hunter v Moss* [1994] 3 All ER 215, CA, discussed at paras 8.12–8.22 below), so that no more than a contractual charge can arise requiring registration under s 395.

2   Consideration having been fully given for acquisition of the after-acquired asset: *Pullan v Koe* [1913] 1 Ch 9; *Re Lind, Industrials Finance Syndicate Ltd v Lind* [1915] 2 Ch 345; *Barclays Bank plc v Willowbrook International Ltd* [1987] BCLC 717n, CA; *Associated Alloys Pty Ltd v ACN 001 452 106 Pty Ltd* (2000) 202 CLR 588.

3   Per Gaudron, McHugh, Gummow and Hayne JJ in *Associated Alloys Pty Ltd v ACN 001 452 106 Pty Ltd* (2001) 74 ALJR 862. Also see *Stephens Travel Service International Pty Ltd v Quantas Airways Ltd* (1988) 13 NSW LR 331, CA applied in *Re ILG Travel Ltd* [1995] 2 BCLC 128 and *Air Canada v M&L Travel Ltd* [1993] 3 SCR 787 at 804–805.

4   *Royal Trust Bank v National Westminster Bank* [1996] 2 BCLC 682, CA; *Re Lewis' of Leicester* [1995] 1 BCLC 428.

1.43 Of course, the arrangement must not be a sham (disguising a debtor-creditor relationship) in form[1] or substance where from the outset the company purchaser, to take advantage of the cash flow, is permitted by the vendor to use all the general account money as if beneficially owned by the company purchaser. Even if there be a real trust arrangement one must be aware that the vendor's equitable right, to trace assets and impose a lien over them or claim proportionate ownership of them, will be worthless if the purchaser in breach of trust uses all the general account money to pay off creditors without notice of the vendor's rights.

1   *Customs & Excise Commissioners v Richmond Theatre Management Ltd* [1995] STC 257.

Trust and bailment

1.44 Bailment is a common law institution which only applies to personal chattels, being a deposit (a transfer of possession) of personal chattels for redelivery to the bailor or according to his direction after the purpose of the bailment (eg safe custody, cleaning, repair, hire etc) has been carried out. Trusts are equitable only and any property may be held on trust. It is the bailor who can enforce or vary the bailment whilst the settlor cannot enforce or vary the trust (unless he specially reserves such power). The general property or general ownership remains in the bailor, whilst the bailee is said to have only a special property or special ownership in the chattels bailed: thus an unauthorised sale by a bailee normally[1] does not pass title to the chattels. A transfer (eg of shares in a company) which simultaneously confers both possession and ownership upon the transferee cannot create a bailment because an owner of assets cannot constitute himself their bailee at common law. A trustee has full legal title (not merely possession) so an unauthorised sale by him will vest a good title in a bona fide purchaser of a legal interest for value without notice of the trust. In the event of the bankruptcy of the bailee or of the trustee the bailor and beneficiaries remain respectively entitled to the bailed chattels or the trust property. A bailee is in a similar position to a trustee in that both are subject to fiduciary obligations concerning the property in their control: in the case of unauthorised sales by either of them, the proceeds are subject to an equitable proprietary remedy against substituted assets ascertained via the tracing process[2]. In the special case where a vendor retains legal and beneficial title to goods supplied to a purchaser who has authority to sell the goods but is bailee of them until sale one has to examine the facts carefully to discover whether or not the relationship of bailor and bailee is fiduciary[3]. One must ask whether the bailee was selling on his own account with an obligation merely to account as a debtor for the purchase price due to the vendor-bailor or whether the bailee had to pay proceeds of sale into a separate account for the vendor-bailor subject to some remuneration being paid for the bailee's services.

[1] Exceptions exist under the Factors Act 1889, Sale of Goods Act 1979, estoppel. On bailment generally see N E Palmer, in his chapter 13 on Bailment in PBH Birks (ed), *English Private Law* (Oxford, 2000).

[2] *Re Hallett's Estate* (1880) 13 Ch D 696 at 710; *Aluminium Industrie Vaassen BV v Romalpa Aluminium Ltd* [1976] 2 All ER 552, [1976] 1 WLR 676.

[3] *Re Andrabell Ltd (in liquidation) Airborne Accessories Ltd v Goodman* [1984] 3 All ER 407; *Hendy Lennox (Industrial Engines) Ltd v Grahame Puttick Ltd* [1984] 2 All ER 152, [1984] 1 WLR 485; approved by the Court of Appeal in *Clough Mill Ltd v Martin* [1984] 3 All ER 982, [1985] 1 WLR 111, CA. The presumption is that the purchaser is selling on his own account and is not a fiduciary bailee: *Pfeiffer v Arbuthnot Factors* [1988] 1 WLR 150; and see *Compaq Computers Ltd v Abercorn Group* [1991] BCC 484.

Trusts and the administration of a deceased's estate

1.45 Personal representatives, like trustees, are subject to fiduciary obligations preventing them from profiting from their administration of a deceased's estate[1]. However, the duty of personal representatives is owed to the estate as a whole and thus, unlike trustees, the personal representatives do not have to hold the balance evenly between those interested in income and those interested in capital[2]. Furthermore, if assets are wrongfully abstracted from the estate a pecuniary or residuary legatee (or a creditor) may follow and recover the assets on behalf of the estate for use in due course of administration: this remedy 'asserts the estate's right of property, not the property right of creditor or legatee'[3]. A trust beneficiary follows and recovers assets on his own behalf by virtue of his equitable proprietary right although exercise of his right may also require restitution to the trust of assets for the benefit of other beneficiaries as well. An unpaid or underpaid legatee (or creditor) also has a well-established special personal claim against even innocent persons benefiting under a wrongful administration of a deceased's estate[4]. The claim is limited to the amount which cannot be recovered from the personal representatives and will not lie against a bona fide purchaser without notice or a person who can make out the defence of change of position. The orthodox view is that trust beneficiaries have no such personal claim against third parties and are restricted to tracing trust assets, if traceable, or seeking to make personally liable to account as constructive trustees persons involved in trustees' wrongful conduct[5]. However, it now seems likely that to prevent the unjust enrichment of the recipient of trust property a personal claim will lie against such recipient subject to the defence of bona fide purchaser without notice and of change of position[6].

[1] *Stamp Duties Comr v Livingston* [1965] AC 694, [1964] 3 All ER 692; *Re Thomson, Thomson v Allen* [1930] 1 Ch 203; *Vyse v Foster* (1874) LR 7 HL 318.

2   *Re Charteris, Charteris v Biddulph* [1917] 2 Ch 379; *Re Hayes' Will Trusts* [1971]
    2 All ER 341, [1971] 1 WLR 758.
3   *Stamp Duties Comr v Livingston* [1965] AC 694 at 713–714.
4   *Ministry of Health v Simpson* [1951] AC 251, [1950] 2 All ER 1137, HL.
5   See Articles 33, 92 100 and 101.
6   See Article 100(4).

1.46 Whilst the task of a trustee generally is the continuous administration of trust property for the beneficiaries, the task of a personal representative is to collect the assets of the deceased, discharge taxes, debts and expenses and distribute the remaining assets amongst the persons entitled under the deceased's will or intestacy. For this purpose 'whatever property comes to the executor virtute officii comes to him in full ownership without distinction between legal and equitable interests: the whole property is his'[1] subject to the fiduciary obligation to wind up the estate in the proper manner. Thus 'no legatee, devisee or next-of-kin has any beneficial interest in the assets being administered'[2]. During the period of administration those interested under a will or intestacy only have an equitable right or chose in action to have the deceased's estate properly administered, though this chose may be disposed of by will or inter vivos, whether expressly or by operation of law upon the bankruptcy of the residuary legatee[3]. Thus, while a devisee of land comprised in an unadministered estate cannot convey the land *in specie* until completion of the administration, he can validly contract to sell land before such completion[4]. By way of contrast beneficiaries under a trust (not being a charitable trust or a discretionary trust[5] where the beneficiaries are not all ascertained and sui juris) have the equitable beneficial ownership, whilst the trustee only has the nominal ownership. It should be mentioned that though it is clear that a residuary devise or bequest does not confer a vested defeasible equitable interest in the subject matter thereof as from the testator's death, subject to the personal representatives' right to have resort thereto for payment of debts and expenses, some cases indicate that a *specific* devise or bequest does confer a vested defeasible equitable interest in the subject matter thereof from the testator's death, subject to the personal representatives' right of resort[6]: this appears very doubtful in view of the general statement of principles discussed above[7].

1   *Stamp Duties Comr v Livingston* [1965] AC 694 at 701. See also *Pagels v MacDonald*
    (1936) 54 CLR 519 at 526; *Passant v Jackson* [1986] STC 164, CA.
2   *Re Hayes' Will Trusts* [1971] 1 WLR 758 at 764; *Cochrane v IRC* [1974] STC 335.
3   *Re Leigh's Will Trusts* [1970] Ch 277, [1969] 3 All ER 432; *Official Receiver in
    Bankruptcy v Schultz* (1990) 170 CLR 306; *Crowden v Aldridge* [1993] 3 All ER 603,
    [1993] 1 WLR 433; *Marshall v Kerr* [1995] 1 AC 148, 157–158, HL.
4   *Wu Koon Tai v Wu Yau Loi* [1997] AC 179, PC.
5   See Article 5.
6   *IRC v Hawley* [1928] 1 KB 578 at 583; *Re Neeld* [1962] Ch 643 at 687–688; *Williams v
    Holland* [1965] 1 WLR 739 at 743–744; *Re K* [1986] Ch 180 at 188.
7   *Stamp Duties Comr v Livingston* [1965] AC 694 at 713–714; *Re Hayes' Will Trusts*
    [1971] 1 WLR 758 at 764; *Kavanagh v Best* [1971] NI 89 at 93–94; *Re K* [1986] Ch 180
    at 197; Law Com No 188 (1989) para 2.16.

1.47 Whilst 'trustee' in the Trustee Act 1925 includes a personal representative where the context admits[1] many distinctions exist. The authority of trustees to deal with all types of property is joint only[2]. The general rule is that personal representatives have joint *and several* authority so that the act of any one of them in exercise of their power is binding on the others and the deceased's estate[3]. Exceptionally, a conveyance of freehold or leasehold land and contracts relating thereto made after 30 June 1995[4] must be made by all the personal representatives or under a court order[5], though one of several personal representatives could previously enter into a valid contract of sale of land binding the others and the estate, so long as he did not purport to act for the others without their authority[6]. The other exception is that all the personal representatives who are registered shareholders of a company must execute any transfer of the shares if it is to be valid[7].

1   Trustee Act 1925, ss 68(1), (17), 69(1).
2   *Attenborough v Solomon* [1913] AC 76.
3   *Attenborough v Solomon* [1913] AC 76; *Re Houghton* [1904] 1 Ch 622 (executor compromising claim by co-executor against estate); *Warner v Sampson* [1958] 1 QB 404, [1958] 1 All ER 44, CA (denial of claimant landlord's title by one executor binds co-executors in forfeiture proceedings).
4   Law of Property (Miscellaneous Provisions) Act 1994, s 16.
5   Administration of Estates Act 1925, ss 2(2), 3(1).
6   *Fountain Forestry Ltd v Edwards* [1975] Ch 1, [1974] 2 All ER 280, where since one personal representative had purported to contract for himself and the other representative (when the other had no knowledge of this and refused to ratify the contract) there was no contract to be enforced, the first personal representative being open to action for breach of warranty of authority; cf *Colyton Investments Pty Ltd v McSorley* (1962) 107 CLR 177.
7   *Barton v North Staffordshire Rly Co* (1888) 38 Ch D 458; *Barton v London and North Western Rly Co* (1889) 24 QBD 77; Companies Act 1985, ss 182, 183, Table A, Part I, arts 29–31.

1.48 A sole personal representative acting as such (unlike a sole trustee other than a trust corporation) can give a valid receipt for capital money arising on a trust for sale of land[1]. A personal representative (unlike a trustee) has the statutory power of appropriation under Administration of Estates Act 1925, s 41. A twelve year limitation period applies to claims to the estate of a deceased person[2] whilst a six year period applies to breach of trust actions[3], though no limit exists in the case of fraudulent trustees or property retained by a personal representative or trustee or converted to his own use[4]. Whilst a trustee is permitted to retire[5] a personal representative holds his office for life unless the grant of probate or letters of administration was for a limited period or he is released by the court appointing a substitute[6]. If the personal representative dies without having completed administration of the deceased's estate the court will appoint an *administrator de bonis non administratis* to continue the administration unless the personal representative is an executor who appoints an executor when such executor upon taking out a grant of probate becomes executor by representation of the estate being administered as well as the estate of the deceased executor[7]. The statutory power of appointing new trustees is available to trustees[8] or the personal representative of a last surviving trustee[9] but is not available to a personal representative qua personal representative[10].

1   Law of Property Act 1925, s 27(2).
2   Limitation Act 1980, s 22.
3   Limitation Act 1980, s 21(3).Once an executor and trustee completes administration of the estate he continues in office only as a trustee: *Davies v Sharples* [2006] WTLR 839, paras 43–47.
4   Limitation Act 1980, s 21(1).

5   Trustee Act 1925, ss 36, 39.
6   *Harvell v Foster* [1954] 2 QB 367, [1954] 2 All ER 736; Administration of Justice Act 1985, s 50.
7   Administration of Estates Act 1925, s 7.
8   Trustee Act 1925, s 36.
9   Trustee Act 1925, ss 36(1)(b), 18(2). An executor who has not obtained a grant of probate may appoint under s 36(1)(b) but his title to appoint can only be proved by production of a grant of probate or letters of administration with the will annexed: *Re Crowhurst Park* [1974] 1 WLR 583 at 593–594.
10 *Re Ponder* [1921] 2 Ch 59.

1.49 Since the offices of personal representative and trustee are not mutually exclusive[1] it is often the case that the same persons are appointed executors and trustees or a personal representative becomes also a trustee of the deceased's property owing to the maxim that equity will not let a trust fail for want of a trustee. It is well established that once a personal representative has discharged all the debts and liabilities of the estate he becomes a trustee for the purposes of having the trustee's statutory power of appointing new trustees[2], though qua personal representative he remains liable as such until the estate has been properly distributed to the appropriate beneficiaries[3]. The statutory appointment of trustees by a personal representative who has discharged all the debts and liabilities is effective to confer on the newly appointed trustees the powers and discretions contained in the will[4]. However, they cannot deal with the legal estate in land until a written assent is executed in their favour owing to the much criticised decision of Pennycuick J in *Re King's Will Trusts*[5] where there was overlooked the line of cases concerned with establishing that a personal representative on completing administration of the estate becomes a trustee thereof[6]. Counsel accepted the correctness of *Re King's Will Trusts* in *Re Edwards' Will Trusts*[7] where the Court of Appeal held that an assent to the vesting of a beneficial interest in land may be inferred from conduct of the personal representative in circumstances where he is also the person beneficially entitled to the land under the deceased's will or intestacy.

1   *Harvell v Foster* [1954] 2 QB 367, [1954] 2 All 736.
2   *Eaton v Daines* [1894] WN 32; *Re Ponder* [1921] 2 Ch 59; *Re Pitt* (1928) 44 TLR 371; *Re Yerburgh* [1928] WN 208; *Re Cockburn's Will Trusts* [1957] Ch 438, [1957] 2 All ER 522.
3   *Harvell v Foster* [1954] 2 QB 367, [1954] 2 All ER 736.
4   *Re Cockburn's Will Trusts* [1957] Ch 438, [1957] 2 All ER 522.
5   [1964] Ch 542, [1964] 1 All ER 833.
6   See 1.23, note 21, above, and E C Ryder (1976) Current Legal Problems 60; R R A Walker (1964) 80 LQR 328; but contrast C Stebbings [1984] Conv 423.
7   [1982] Ch 30 at 40, CA. Note that in *Mohan v Roche* [1991] 1 IR 560 Keane J held that because E as executor has the legal and beneficial interest nothing needs to be executed to pass such interest to E if also sole devisee.

Trust and fiduciary relationship

1.50 The archetypal fiduciary relationship is that of trustee and beneficiaries, the trustee with undivided loyalty to the beneficiaries having to further their interests and not his own (except to the extent authorised in the trust instrument). Apart from this relationship set up by the settlor, a fiduciary relationship exists as Ford and Lee indicated[1] where:

(a)   one person, the fiduciary, has undertaken to act in the interests of another person, the principal, or in the interest of the fiduciary and another person;

(b)   as part of the arrangement between the fiduciary and the principal the fiduciary has a power or discretion capable of being used to affect the interests of the principal in a legal or practical sense;

(c)   the principal is vulnerable to abuse by the fiduciary of his or her position; and

(d)   the principal has not agreed as a person of full capacity who is fully informed, to allow the fiduciary to use the power or discretion solely in his or her own interests.

---

[1]   *Principles of the Law of Trusts* (2nd edn), p 1002. Also see J C Shepherd in 'Towards a Unified Concept of Fiduciary Relationships' (1981) 97 LQR 51; Goff and Jones, *Law of Restitution*, Chapter 33; P D Finn, 'The Fiduciary Principle', being Chapter 1 in T G Youdan (ed), *Equity, Fiduciaries and Trusts* (1989, Carswell, Canada) concluding at p 54: 'A person will be a fiduciary in his relationship with another when and insofar as that other is entitled to expect that he will act in that other's or in their joint interest to the exclusion of his own several interest'; P D Finn, 'Fiduciary Law and the Modern Commercial World', being Chapter 1 in E McKendrick (ed), *Commercial Aspects of Trusts & Fiduciary Obligations* (1992, Clarendon Press). *Hospital Products Ltd v United States Surgical Corpn* (1985) 156 CLR 41, 55 ALR 417; *LAC Minerals Ltd v International Cocoa Resources Ltd* (1989) 61 DLR (4th) 14; *Hodgkinson v Simms* [1994] 3 SCR 377; *Re Goldcorp Exchange Ltd* [1995] 1 AC 74 at 98, [1994] 2 All ER 806 at 821, Lord Mustill emphasising that if a fiduciary relationship is alleged to exist where there is a contractual relationship, 'the essence of a fiduciary relationship is that it creates obligations of a different character from those deriving from the contract itself.' The extent of a fiduciary relationship may, of course, be restricted by a contract: *Kelly v Cooper* [1993] AC 205, PC. A fiduciary in breach of his obligations cannot rely on an exclusion clause: *Baskerville v Thurgood* (1992) 100 Sask LR 214, CA; *Rutanen v Ballard* (1997) Mass 723 at 733.

1.51   The key is that the fiduciary's conduct has reasonably led the principal to expect that the fiduciary will subordinate his own private interest to the interest of the principal[1]. Thus, a fiduciary relationship can exist not just where there has been an express or an implied undertaking by the fiduciary to the principal but also where the fiduciary's relationship with the principal is one in which subordination of the former's interest to the latter's interest is reasonably expected by the latter – fiduciary relationships with fiduciary duties are imposed by equity not by agreement of the parties.

---

[1]   See chapters by L Hoyano, J Glover and D Hayton in PBH Birks (ed), *Privacy and Loyalty* (Oxford, 1997). The court is quite prepared to lift the corporate veil to find on the facts that a solicitor acting in conveyancing matters for a company owed fiduciary duties to the controller of the company who placed trust in and reliance upon the solicitor, so the solicitor could not bid against the controller for the purchase of a property near property being acquired by the company: *Ratiu v Conway* [2005] EWCA Civ 1302, [2006] 1 All ER 571n.

1.52   The categories of cases in which fiduciary duties and obligations arise spring from factual circumstances so the types of relationship of the parties are no more closed than the categories of negligence at common law. Where a fiduciary qua fiduciary does have vested in him – or under his control – property, such property has the essential characteristic of trust property in that it cannot be used or disposed of by the fiduciary for his own benefit but must be used or disposed of for the benefit of other persons[1].

[1] *Tito v Waddell (No 2)* [1977] 3 All ER 129 at 230–231; *Ayerst v C & K (Construction) Ltd* [1976] AC 167 at 180; *Wates Construction (London) Ltd v Franthom Property Ltd* (1991) 53 BLR 23, CA.

1.53 Equity is seen at its flexible pragmatic best (or worst) in dealing with fiduciaries since even the extent and content of the duties of a fiduciary varies according to the particular category of fiduciary in the context under consideration. As Lord Mustill has emphasised[1], to describe someone as a fiduciary without more, is meaningless for, as Frankfurter J said in *SEC v Chenery Corp*[2]:

> 'to say that a man is a fiduciary only begins an analysis; it gives direction to further inquiry. To whom is he a fiduciary? What obligation does he owe as a fiduciary? In what respect has he failed to discharge these obligations? And what are the consequences of his deviation from duty?'

[1] *Re Goldcorp Exchange Ltd* [1995] 1 AC 74 at 98, [1994] 2 All ER 806 at 821.
[2] 318 US 80, 85–86 (1943). Further see *Chirnside v Fay* [2006] NZSC 68.

1.54 Moreover, 'a person may be in a fiduciary position quoad a part of his activities and not quoad other parts'[1]. In respect of particular activities in various contexts the following have been held to be fiduciaries: a protector having powers under a trust deed[2], personal representatives[3], agents[4], a prospective purchaser of land purporting to act as the vendor's agent in making a planning application[5], bailees[6], directors[7], solicitors and other professional advisers (eg accountants, stock-brokers)[8], company promoters[9], partners[10], receivers[11], liquidators[12], members of a committee of inspection in bankruptcy[13], borough treasurers[14], guardians[15], employees[16], tenants for life[17]. If certain fiduciaries, eg trustees, personal representatives, agents, tenants for life, renew a lease subject to the fiduciary relationship it must always be held automatically on a constructive trust for the beneficiaries[18]. Other fiduciaries may retain the lease for themselves if they show they have not in fact abused their position[19].

[1] *New Zealand Netherlands Society Oranje Inc v Kuys* [1973] 2 All ER 1222 at 1225. Thus a director qua director owes a fiduciary duty to his company (though not its shareholders or creditors) whilst qua shareholder he does not owe any fiduciary duty in respect of his voting power as shareholder except that it cannot be used to perpetrate a fraud on the minority shareholders: *Regal (Hastings) Ltd v Gulliver* [1967] 2 AC 134n, [1942] 1 All ER 378; *Re AM Wood's Ships Woodite Protection Ltd* (1890) 62 LT 760; *Percival v Wright* [1902] 2 Ch 421; *North-West Transportation Co v Beatty* (1887) 12 App Cas 589; cf *Coleman v Myers* [1977] 2 NZLR 225; revsd [1977] 2 NZLR 225, (NZCA); see also (1977) 40 MLR 471 and (1978) 41 MLR 585. Exceptionally in *Platt v Platt* [1999] 2 BCLC 745 the active director-shareholder was held to owe fiduciary duties to his passive brother director-shareholders when he misrepresented the company's position to enable him to buy them out cheaply. *Waxman v Waxman* (2004) 186 Ont AC 201 is a similar exceptional case.
[2] *Steel v Paz Ltd* [1993–1995] Manx LR 426; *Re Osiris Trustees* (2000) 2 ITELR 404.
[3] *Stamp Duties Comr v Livingston* [1965] AC 694, [1964] 3 All ER 692; *Re Diplock* [1948] Ch 465, [1948] 2 All ER 318; *Vyse v Foster* (1874) LR 7 HL 318.
[4] *Kirkham v Peel* (1880) 43 LT 171 at 172; *New Zealand Netherlands Society Oranje Inc v Kuys* [1973] 2 All ER 1222 at 1225.
[5] *English v Dedham Vale Properties Ltd* [1978] 1 All ER 382, [1978] 1 WLR 93.

6   *Aluminium Industrie Vaassen BV v Romalpa Aluminium Ltd* [1976] 2 All ER 552, [1976] 1 WLR 676; *Clough Mill Ltd v Martin* [1984] 3 All ER 982, [1985] 1 WLR 111, CA.
7   *Sinclair v Brougham* [1914] AC 398; *Regal (Hastings) Ltd v Gulliver* [1967] 2 AC 134n, [1942] 1 All ER 378.
8   *Re Hallett's Estate* (1880) 13 Ch D 696; *Conway v Ratiu* [2005] EWCA Civ 1302, [2006] 1 All ER 571n; *Brown v IRC* [1965] AC 244 at 265; *Nocton v Lord Ashburton* [1914] AC 932, HL; *Glennie v McDougall & Cowans Holdings Ltd* [1935] SCR 257; *Clark Boyce v Mouat* [1994] 1 AC 428, [1993] 4 All ER 268, PC; *Farrington v Rowe McBride & Partners* [1985] 1 NZLR 83; *Hodgkinson v Simms* (1994) 117 DLR (4th) 161.
9   *Gluckstein v Barnes* [1900] AC 240; *Jubilee Cotton Mills Ltd (official receiver and liquidator) v Lewis* [1924] AC 958; (1970) 86 LQR 493 (J H Gross).
10 *Clegg v Edmondson* (1857) 8 De GM & G 787; *Thompson's Trustee v Heaton* [1974] 1 All ER 1239, [1974] 1 WLR 605.
11 *Nugent v Nugent* [1908] 1 Ch 546.
12 *Tito v Waddell (No 2)* [1977] 3 All ER 129 at 229–230.
13 *Re Bulmer* [1937] Ch 499, [1937] 1 All ER 323.
14 *A-G v De Winston* [1906] 2 Ch 106. In *Appleby v Cowley* (1982) Times, 14 April a head of barristers' chambers was held to be a fiduciary.
15 *Hatch v Hatch* (1804) 9 Ves 292.
16 *Reading v A-G* [1951] AC 507, [1951] 1 All ER 617; *A-G v Goddard* (1929) 98 LJKB 743 at 745.
17 *Rowe v Chichester* (1773) Amb 715; *Re Biss* [1903] 2 Ch 40 at 56, 61.
18 *Keech v Sandford* (1726) Sel Cas Ch 61; *Re Morgan* (1881) 18 Ch D 93; *Re Biss* [1903] 2 Ch 40.
19 *Re Biss* [1903] 2 Ch 40; *Thompson's Trustee in Bankruptcy v Heaton* [1974] 1 All ER 1239 at 1250.

1.55 One must distinguish the proscriptive[1] fiduciary duties inherent in a fiduciary relationship from prescriptive duties (eg to use proper care and skill) arising at common law out of a contract or in equity out of a fiduciary relationship. As Millett LJ stated[2]:

> 'The expression "fiduciary duty" is properly confined to those duties which are peculiar to fiduciaries and the breach of which attracts legal consequences differing from those consequent upon the breach of other duties. Unless the expression is so limited it is lacking in practical utility. In this sense it is obvious that not every breach of duty by a fiduciary is a breach of fiduciary duty … . It is similarly inappropriate to apply the expression to the obligation of a trustee or other fiduciary to use proper skill and care in the discharge of his duties … . The distinguishing obligation of a fiduciary is the obligation of loyalty. The principal is entitled to the single-minded loyalty of his fiduciary … . Breach of fiduciary obligation connotes disloyalty or infidelity. Mere incompetence is not enough'.

1   The 'no profit' and 'no conflict of interest' rules summarised by Millett LJ in *Bristol & West BS v Mothew* [1996] 4 All ER 698 at 711–712, [1998] Ch 1 at 18 endorsed by Hobhouse LJ in *Swindle v Harrison* [1997] 4 All ER 705 at 720.
2   *Bristol & West BS v Mothew* [1998] Ch 1 at 18. Lord Walker accepted this distinction between breach of the proscriptive duty of loyalty and breach of the prescriptive duty of care: *Hilton v Barker Booth & Eastwood* [2005] UKHL 8, [2005] 1 WLR 567 at para 29.

1.56 All fiduciaries are subject to the rule 'that no person standing in a fiduciary position, when a demand is made upon him by the person to whom he stands in the fiduciary relationship to account for profits acquired by him by reason of the opportunity and the knowledge, or either, resulting from it, is entitled to defeat the claim upon any ground save that he made the profits with the knowledge and assent of the other person'[1]. It matters not that the fiduciary acted in good faith and that the profit made by the fiduciary could not have been made by the person to whom he stands in the fiduciary relationship[2]. The extent to which a fiduciary can ever use for his own benefit (or for strangers to the fiduciary relationship under consideration) information received by him in his fiduciary capacity is uncertain[3]. It seems that partners may take advantage of information received as a partner (unless received on terms that it will be kept confidential)[4] so long as the use made of the information is outside the scope of the partnership business[5].

[1]   *Boardman v Phipps* [1967] 2 AC 46 at 105; *Chan v Zachariah* (1983) 154 CCR 178; *Swain v Law Society* [1982] 1 WLR 17 at 37 endorsed [1983] 1 AC 598, 619, though reversing the Court of Appeal; *Warman International Ltd v Dwyer* (1995) 69 ALJR 362; *Murad v Al-Saraj* [2005] EWCA Civ 959, [2005] 32 LS Gaz R 31.
[2]   *Boardman v Phipps* [1967] 2 AC 46, [1966] 3 All ER 721; *Regal (Hastings) Ltd v Gulliver* [1967] 2 AC 134n, [1942] 1 All ER 378; *Industrial Development Consultants Ltd v Cooley* [1972] 2 All ER 162, [1972] 1 WLR 443; *Warman International Ltd v Dwyer* (1995) 69 ALJR 362.
[3]   *Boardman v Phipps* [1967] 2 AC 46 at 102–103, 126. See Article 33 below.
[4]   *North and South Trust Co Ltd v Berkeley* [1971] 1 All ER 980, [1971] 1 WLR 470.
[5]   *Aas v Benham* [1891] 2 Ch 244. Also see *Framlington Group v Anderson* [1995] 1 BCLC 475.

1.57 A fiduciary cannot purchase property affected by the fiduciary relationship unless he can show that, in fact, he did not abuse his position, ie he gave the best price after making full disclosure of all material facts[1]. In the case of a trustee purchasing trust property the purchase is automatically voidable *ex debito justitae* except in very limited special circumstances[2]. A fiduciary cannot purchase any beneficial interest of his beneficiary in property affected by the fiduciary relationship unless he can show that, in fact, he did not abuse his position, ie he gave the best price after making full disclosure of all material facts[3]. Unlike cases where undue influence is presumed there is nothing to stop the fiduciary purchasing from his beneficiary property not affected by the fiduciary relationship.

[1]   *Dunne v English* (1874) LR 18 Eq 524 at 533.
[2]   *Holder v Holder* [1968] Ch 353, [1968] 1 All ER 665; *Tito v Waddell (No 2)* [1977] 3 All ER 129 at 241; see Article 59 below.
[3]   *Coles v Trecothick* (1804) 9 Ves 234 at 247; *Wright v Carter* [1903] 1 Ch 27; *Tito v Waddell (No 2)* [1977] 3 All ER 129 at 241; see Article 59 below. In making a loan to his principal the fiduciary must prove the transaction was fair and that he had disclosed all material facts: *Swindle v Harrison* [1997] 4 All ER 705, CA.

1.58 Any sale of a fiduciary's property to his beneficiary is voidable unless full and proper disclosure of his interest is made[1]. If the right to rescind is lost (eg owing to a disposition of the property by the beneficiary) or if the beneficiary does not wish to rescind but to recover the fiduciary's profits can such profits be recovered? They clearly can if the fiduciary sold to the beneficiary property acquired after he became a fiduciary because such property and therefore the profits therefrom are regarded as held on behalf of the beneficiary[2]. If the fiduciary, however, had acquired the property before he became a beneficiary the old orthodox view[3] is that the beneficiary cannot recover the profit because to allow him to do so would be to make a fresh bargain between the parties. Today[4] there is much to be said for the strict prophylactic view that in both cases[5] the crucial vitiating factor is the failure to disclose the self-dealing, so making the fiduciary in the latter of the two cases also personally liable to account for the profit (even in the absence of deceit, misrepresentation or undue influence).

1   *Imperial Mercantile Credit Association v Coleman* (1873) LR 6 HL 189; *Armstrong v Jackson* [1917] 2 KB 822.
2   *Cooke v Deeks* [1916] 1 AC 554 at 563; *Bentley v Craven* (1853) 18 Beau 75; *Regier v Campbell-Stuart* [1939] Ch 766, [1939] 3 All ER 235; *Re Cape Breton Co* (1885) 29 Ch D 795 at 803–804; *Longfield Parish Council v Robson* (1913) 29 TLR 347; *Gluckstein v Barnes* [1900] AC 240; *Gray v New Augarita Porcupine Mines* [1952] 3 DLR 1 at 12–14; *Robinson v Randfontein Estates* [1921] App D 168 (SA SC App Div).
3   *Re Cape Breton Co* (1885) 29 Ch D 795; *Tracy v Mandalay Pty Ltd* (1952) 88 CLR 215 at 241; *Burland v Earle* [1902] AC 83.
4   Goff & Jones, *Law of Restitution* (6th edn) para 33–011: at the very least the fiduciary must be liable to the extent that he sold his property above market value: *Cavendish Bentinck v Fenn* (1887) 12 App Cas 652 at 659.
5   In *Re Sharpe* [1909] 2 Ch 241 at 249 no distinction was made between goods supplied before or after the trusteeship arose.

1.59 It should be noted that if a fiduciary in a position of conflict between his self interest and his fiduciary duty provides advice tainted by such conflict (or if a solicitor with a conflict between a duty owed to one client, A, and a duty owed to another client, B, fails to make a disclosure required by his duty to A)[1] then he may be personally liable to replace any loss caused thereby, with interest thereon[2]. Indeed, if a claimant shows that he suffered loss from any breach of the defendant's fiduciary duty (including such a duty arising from the defendant's undue influence over the claimant[3]) the court can order the defendant to compensate the claimant for that loss[4].

1   *Hilton v Barker Booth & Eastwood* [2005] UKHL 8, [2005] 1 WLR 567.
2   *Nocton v Lord Ashburton* [1914] AC 932, HL; *Farrington v Row McBride & Partners* [1985] 1 NZLR 83, CA; *Swindle v Harrison* [1997] 4 ALL ER 705, CA.
3   *Mahoney v Purnell* [1996] 3 All ER 61.
4   *Swindle v Harrison* [1997] 4 All ER 705, CA; *Platt v Platt* [1999] 2 BCLC 745.

1.60 In most circumstances a fiduciary will not be allowed to carry on a business which competes with that carried on behalf of his beneficiary[1]. Oddly enough, an 1891 case[2] indicates that a director may escape this rule, at least if he is a non-service director[3], though this has been trenchantly criticised[4].

1   *Re Thomson* [1930] 1 Ch 203; cf *Moore v McGlynn* [1894] 1 IR 74; Partnership Act 1890, s 30.
2   *London and Mashonaland Exploration Co Ltd v New Mashonaland Exploration Co Ltd* [1891] WN 165; *Bell v Lever Bros Ltd* [1932] AC 161 at 145.
3   *Scottish Co-operative Wholesale Society v Meyer* [1959] AC 324 at 366–367.
4   By Sedley LJ in *In Plus Group Limited v Pyke* [2002] EWCA Civ 370, [2002] 2 BCLC 201 at paras 79–90.

1.61 In certain circumstances equity intervenes further by treating a fiduciary as a constructive trustee of particular property. Thus, a fiduciary instructed to acquire Blackacre or to acquire the benefit of certain contracts will be a constructive trustee thereof despite any claim that he intended his acquisition was for his personal benefit[1]. A fiduciary, who exploits property or confidential information the subject of a fiduciary relationship, is constructive trustee of any profits made out of such exploitation[2]. A fiduciary who exploits his fiduciary position so as to obtain a secret commission or a bribe is also a constructive trustee thereof (if it or its traceable product is still retained by the fiduciary)[3]. Where a fiduciary is a constructive trustee of property the equitable right to trace will be available and on the fiduciary's insolvency the beneficiary's property or its traceable product will be claimed by the beneficiary and will not be available for the fiduciary's general creditors.

[1]   *Cook v Deeks* [1916] 1 AC 554 at 563; *Re Edwards Will Trusts* [1982] Ch 30 at 41, CA.
[2]   *Boardman v Phipps* [1967] 2 AC 46, [1966] 3 All ER 721; *Nanus Asia Co Inc v Standard Chartered Bank* [1990] Hong Kong LR 396 (dishonest 'tippee' liable); *Satnam Investments Ltd v Dunlop Heywood & Co Ltd* [1999] 3 All ER 652, CA (no liability of a stranger who took advantage of opportunity first discovered through breach of a fiduciary's duty to his principal).
[3]   *A-G for Hong Kong v Reid* [1994] 1 AC 324, [1994] 1 All ER 1, PC (holding *Lister & Co v Stubbs* (1890) 45 Ch D 1, CA and *Metropolitan Bank v Heiron* (1880) 5 ExD 319, CA to be wrong).

Fiduciary relationship and debt

1.62 Beneficiaries' proprietary rights to property held on constructive trust for them must not be confused with their personal rights as mere creditors in equity or at law.

1.63 Thus, where a bank trustee lawfully deposits money with itself as banker pursuant to express authority in the trust instrument so that the beneficiaries' moneys, like other customers' moneys, belong absolutely and beneficially to the bank, there can only be an unsecured personal claim for a sum corresponding to the amount paid into the deposit account with interest thereon[1]. The new trustee appointed in place of the insolvent bank trustee can only rank in the liquidation of the bank as an unsecured creditor on behalf of the trust in respect of the chose in action that was acquired in place of the trust moneys, which ceased to be impressed with the trust on payment into the bank account.

[1]   *Space Investments Ltd v Canadian Imperial Bank of Commerce Trust Co (Bahamas) Ltd* [1986] 3 All ER 75, [1986] 1 WLR 1072, PC.

1.64 Similarly, if an employee of a stockbroking firm advises D to leave his money on deposit with the firm until appropriate investments can be made when the market picture becomes clearer, when the firm has not told the employee or D that the firm's parlous financial situation makes such deposit precarious, the firm will be in breach of its duty of disclosure as a fiduciary. However, upon the insolvency of the firm D will only have a personal claim for the debt owed him[1]. If D had rescinded the transaction in time so as to revest the equitable title to the money in himself this may have enabled him to make an equitable proprietary claim against any traceable product of such money[2].

[1]   *Daly v Sydney Stock Exchange* (1986) 160 CLR 371, 65 ALR 193 (Aust HC) where a claim against the Stock Exchange Compensation Fund failed because the firm had not received the money for or on behalf of D or as trustee and so there had been no defalcation of trust funds. D had an equitable right to avoid the voidable contract of loan but he had not elected to exercise this right before the firm failed: he could not at the same time treat

the contract as on foot and yet deny the borrower's title to the money which the contract conferred. For other instances of debtor-creditor relationships see *Chief Constable of Leicestershire v M* [1988] 3 All ER 1015; *Customs and Excis Comrs v Richmond Theatre* [1995] STC 257; and *Re Goldcorp Exchange Ltd* [1995] 1 AC 74; [1994] 2 All ER 806, PC. Cf *Re Fleet Disposal Services Ltd* [1995] 1 BCLC 345.

2 *El Ajou v Dollar Land Holdings plc* [1993] 3 All ER 717 at 734; *Daly v Sydney Stock Exchange* (1986) 160 CLR 371, 371 at 388–390; and *Twinsectra Ltd v Yardley* [2000] WTLR 527 at 568, CA; but see *Re Goldcorp Exchange Ltd* [1994] 2 All ER 806 at 825–826. Further see Article 35(2)(f) below.

Trusts and powers

1.65 A power is the authority to deal with or dispose of property which one does not own and which may or may not be vested in one. Some powers are legal such as the power of attorney[1] which enables the holder of the power to perform various functions like the conveyance of a legal estate in land, and the mortgagee's power of sale under Law of Property Act 1925, ss 88, 101 and 104. Trustees have statutory powers of investment[2], sale[3], leasing[4], maintenance[5], advancement[6], and a power of appointing new trustees[7].

1 Powers of Attorney Act 1971, Enduring Powers of Attorney Act 1985 until replaced by Mental Capacity Act 2005 creating lasting powers of attorney extending beyond a person's property and affairs to his personal welfare.
2 Trustee Investments Act 1961 until replaced by the Trustee Act 2000, ss 3–7.
3 Trusts of Land and Appointment of Trustees Act 1996, s 6.
4 Trusts of Land and Appointment of Trustees Act 1996, s 6.
5 Trustee Act 1925, s 31.
6 Trustee Act 1925, s 32.
7 Trustee Act 1925, s 36.

1.66 A particularly significant distributive (as opposed to administrative) power is the power of appointment which enables the donee of the power (whether a trustee or a relative of the settlor or whoever) to determine who are to be the beneficial recipients of property whether of an income or capital nature. Such category of power is always equitable[1]. Essentially, a power will be *general* if the power-holder (known as the donee of the power) may appoint to anyone including himself, otherwise it will be a special power[2]. Where a special power is exercisable in favour of everyone but a small excepted class (eg the settlor, his spouse, and past and present trustees) it is often referred to as a hybrid or an intermediate power[3]. These powers are usually to be found in instruments creating trusts (eg in wills or deeds) and are often held by the person(s) holding office as trustee so as to be fiduciary powers, but they may be held by an individual (eg the settlor or the testator's widow or eldest son) so as to be personal powers[4].

1 Law of Property Act 1925, s 1(7).
2 *Re Penrose* [1933] Ch 793; Perpetuities and Accumulations Act 1964, s 7.
3 *Re Hay's Settlement Trusts* [1981] 3 All ER 786, [1982] 1 WLR 202; *Re Beatty's Will Trusts* [1990] 3 All ER 844; *Schmidt v Rosewood Trust Ltd* [2003] UKPC 26,[2003] 2 AC 709 at para 35.
4 See paras 1.76–1.77 below for the distinctions between fiduciary powers and personal powers.

1.67 The essential difference between a trust and a power is succinctly expressed in the statement 'A trust is imperative, a power discretionary'. A trustee *must* act in accordance with the terms of the trust: the donee of a power, even if a trustee, *may* act or not as he chooses in his discretion. Thus, if T holds on trust for A for life, then for B absolutely but has power to appoint income or capital to, or for the benefit of, X's descendants, T *must* distribute income to A during A's lifetime and capital to B after A's death, but T *may* or *may not choose* to exercise his discretionary power to benefit X's descendants: they only have a hope (often called in Latin, a *spes*) that T may choose to exercise his discretion.

1.68 If T held income on trust to distribute it as T sees fit to, or for the benefit of, X's descendants, this is a discretionary trust, which is a combination of a trust duty and a discretionary power. T *must* distribute all the income to one or more beneficiaries but T may decide whether a particular beneficiary receives a lot or a little or nothing. A beneficiary thus only has a hope of benefiting, although it is a higher hope than the hope of an object of a power of appointment. After all, if in this discretionary trust a power had also been conferred on T to appoint income, instead, to any of the descendants of O, then T would be under no duty to appoint any income whatsoever to any of the descendants of O, such persons only having a hope of benefiting after T had first considered if the interests and needs of X's descendants required use of all the income.

1.69 If a discretionary trust is not being carried out, the court can replace the obstructive trustees or authorise representative persons of classes of beneficiaries to prepare a scheme of distribution or, if a proper basis for distribution appears, itself direct a distribution, such distribution not having to be an equal distribution at all[1]. Indeed, the court has been prepared to exercise a trustee's power to augment pensions under pension fund trusts (where the beneficiaries had purchased their rights and expectations)[2] and to order an advance of capital to a beneficiary under a power of advancement[3]. The Privy Council[4] has indicated that the objects of a power of appointment have rights to invoke the court's intervention on the same lines as for beneficiaries of discretionary trusts, though one would expect that replacing obstructive trustees with new trustees will normally be the limit of the court's intervention: the key mechanism for the exercise of optional powers of appointment is surely the trustee[5].

[1] *McPhail v Doulton* [1971] AC 424 at 457.
[2] *Mettoy Pension Trustees Ltd v Evans* [1991] 2 All ER 513, [1990] 1 WLR 1587, *Thrells v Lomas* [1993] 2 ALL ER 546.
[3] *Klug v Klug* [1918] 2 Ch 67.
[4] *Schmidt v Rosewood Trust Ltd* [2003] UKPC 26, [2003] 2 AC 709.
[5] Further see D Hayton, 'Beneficiaries' and Objects' Rights to Information' [2003] 10 JITCP 139.

1.70 An instrument by its terms may confer powers on a particular individual as an individual or it may confer powers on a trustee as a trustee.

1.71 So far as concerns an individual, there are the following possibilities:

(a)   P may be donee of an absolute gift subject only to a moral obligation, so that he has power if he wishes to implement such obligation, but he need not, eg if T leaves the contents of his house 'to P trusting that P will see to it that my friends receive some decent bottles of wine from my cellar.'

(b)   P may be a donee of a personal power of appointment under a trust in circumstances where no obligations whatever are owed to anyone in respect of the power[1], eg if T settles property by will on his executors and trustees on trust for P for life, remainder to P's children equally unless P by will or deed chooses to appoint the trust property as P sees fit amongst P's children and grandchildren.

(c)   P may be a donee of a power of appointment under a trust in rare special circumstances where P is under a duty to exercise the power, so that the court will intervene to exercise the power in the obligatory fashion intended by the donor of the power, eg where T settles property by will on his executors and trustees on trust for P for life and then for such of P's children as P shall appoint. Depending upon the size of the class of objects of the power, the court may treat the power either as in the nature of a discretionary trust or as a simple power of appointment where, exceptionally, in default of the exercise thereof a necessarily implied trust arises in favour of the objects equally[2].

So far as concerns a trustee, there are the following possibilities

(d)   As with case (c) for individuals, in rare special circumstances (usually of a testamentary nature) the power of appointment vested in a trustee, T, may be construed either as in the nature of a discretionary trust or as a simple power of appointment where, exceptionally, in default of the exercise thereof a necessarily implied trust arises in favour of the objects equally.

(e)   Normally, a trust instrument will make it clear that T has a fiduciary power of appointment in favour of a class of objects by expressly providing that in default of exercise of such power the trust property passes elsewhere, though T is under a duty[3] from time to time to consider whether or not it is appropriate to exercise the power, though, of course, he can choose not to exercise the power.

(f)   Where the trust instrument indicates that T is not just under a duty from time to time to consider whether or not to exercise the power to benefit those within its ambit, but must actually exercise the power, although having discretion as to who benefits and to what extent, then this is a discretionary trust. It is sometimes referred to as a 'trust power' or 'power in the nature of a trust' owing to the discretionary power of selection the trustees are *obliged* to exercise but it is submitted that it is conceptually clearer to refer to it as a discretionary trust[4].

---

[1]   Other than under the fraud on a power doctrine: *Re Wright* [1920] 1 Ch 108. Thus, so long as he does not try to benefit someone outside the scope of the power, he can exercise the power capriciously or spitefully or he can simply ignore it.

[2]   For example, *Burrough v Philcox* (1840) 5 My & Cr 72; Article 8(2)(a). Where, after a special power, the court implies a trust in default of appointment in favour equally of the objects of the special power the terms 'trust power' or 'power in the nature of the trust' have sometimes been used to describe such a situation. Such a shorthand description is dangerously misleading especially since the same description has sometimes confusingly

been used for situation (f), more properly regarded as a discretionary trust, and the test for certainty of objects for a fixed trust for a class of persons equally is stricter than the test for certainty of objects of a discretionary trust for a class of persons: Article 8(1)(c), post.

3   *Re Hay's Settlement Trusts* [1981] 3 ALL ER 786 at 793.
4   For example, per Stamp LJ in *Re Baden's Deed Trusts (No 2)* [1973] Ch 9 at 26; Megarry V-C in *Re Hay's Settlement Trusts* [1981] 3 All ER 786 at 793 Warner J in *Mettoy Pension Trustees Ltd v Evans* [1991] 2 All ER 513 at 546 and Lord Walker in *Schmidt v Rosewood Trust Ltd [2003] UKPC 26*, [2003] 2 AC 709 at paras 37, 40. A discretionary trust is said to be 'exhaustive' if all its income has to be distributed among beneficiaries and 'non-exhaustive' if some of its income may be accumulated: *Sainsbury v IRC* [1970] Ch 712, [1969] 3 All ER 919.

1.72 It is a question of construction[1] to determine which of the six situations in 1.71 was intended to be created by the words used by the person executing the instrument in question. Apart from the differences apparent in the above specification of the six situations, in (f) (where there is a discretionary trust) if all possible beneficiaries are adults under no disability and entitled between them to the whole beneficial interest, they can terminate the trust and divide the trust property between them or they can jointly assign their interest so that their assignee becomes absolutely entitled under a bare trust. In contrast[2] all the beneficial objects of a *power* are helpless except to the extent they may individually compel the donee of the power to consider exercising the power; however, after such consideration, he may lawfully refuse to exercise the power. A trustee as the holder of a fiduciary power must consider periodically whether to exercise it, consider the range of objects, and the appropriateness of individual appointments[3]. The test for certainty of beneficiaries is the same for the discretionary trust in situation (f) as for the powers in situations (e), (d) and (c)[4], though a stricter test applies in situations (d) and (c) to the trust in default of appointment if it is for equal division amongst a fixed class[5]. The trustees' duty of inquiry and ascertainment of possible beneficiaries is higher where trustees have to carry out discretionary trusts than where they merely have to consider whether or not to exercise a power: a wider more systematic survey is required in the case of a discretionary trust[6].

1   See approach of Buckley J in *Re Leek* [1967] Ch 1061 and of HL in *McPhail v Doulton* [1971] AC 424.
2   *Schmidt v Rosewood Trust Ltd [2003] UKPC 26*, [2003] 2 AC 709 at para 40; *Re Smith* [1928] Ch 915; *Saunders v Vautier* (1841) Cr & Ph 240. Often beneficiaries will be unborn or minors. If the discretionary class is very wide or a fluctuating class there is the further practical difficulty that it will be impossible to ascertain every class member so making it impossible to take advantage of the *Re Smith* principle.
3   *Re Hay's Settlement Trusts* [1981] 3 All ER 786 at 793.
4   It may be that the test for certainty of objects of a personal power in 1.71, situation (b) above is less strict than the test for objects of a fiduciary power: see paras 8.67–8.70 below.
5   *McPhail v Doulton* [1971] AC 424, [1970] 2 All ER 228 and para 8.42 below.
6   *McPhail v Doulton* [1971] AC 424, [1970] 2 All ER 228; *Re Baden's Deed Trust (No 2)* [1973] Ch 9, [1972] 2 All ER 1304; *Re Manisty's Settlement* [1974] Ch 17, [1973] 2 All ER 1203; *Re Hay's Settlement Trusts* [1982] 1 WLR 202.

1.73 For there to be the necessary accountability of the trustees to the beneficiaries that is at the core of the trust obligation requiring correlative rights and duties regarding beneficiaries and trustees[1], beneficiaries of full capacity[2] need to be informed so far as practicable that they are beneficiaries so that they have a meaningful efficacious right upon which to found the trust obligation[3]. The fundamental right of any beneficiary[4] is the right to see the trust documents, especially the trust accounts (with supporting documentation and explanations) with a view to falsifying or surcharging them, so that the trustees are under an enforceable meaningful obligation. However, in exceptional circumstances (eg to prevent disclosure of sensitive commercial or personal details) some matters need not be disclosed by trustees[5]. The settlor is normally taken to intend to confer a similar *locus standi* on the objects of powers of appointment[6], but it would seem that the settlor can expressly exclude this if desired, on the basis that it is only the trustee-beneficiary obligation that is the foundation of the trust concept[7].

[1] *Armitage v Nurse* [1998] Ch 241 at 253 referring to 'an irreducible core of obligations owed by the trustees to the beneficiaries and enforceable by them which is fundamental to the concept of a trust. If the beneficiaries have no rights enforceable against the trustees there are no trusts.' Also, *Foreman v Kingstone* [2004] 1 NZLR 841, [2005] WTLR 823 at paras 85 to 88. See Article 60.

[2] *Hawkesley v May* [1956] 1 QB 304.

[3] *Re Murphy's Settlement* [1998] 3 All ER 1; and see *Scally v Southern Health & Social Services Board* [1992] 1 AC 294 at 306–307.

[4] *Foreman v Kingstone* [2004] 1 NZLR 841, [2005] WTLR 823 at paras 85 to 88; *Re Murphy's Settlement* [1998] 3 All ER 1; *Armitage v Nurse* [1998] Ch 241 at 261, but a particular beneficiary may temporarily have no rights (eg where the settlor-beneficiary is the Chancellor of the Exchequer) or may have a significant conflicting interest adverse to the trust that excludes his right (*Rouse v 100F Australia Trustees Ltd* [2000] WTLR 111; *Re Rabaiotti's 1989 Settlement* [2000] WTLR 953) or disclosure of sensitive commercial or personal details may be excluded (*Schmidt v Rosewood Trust Ltd* [2003] 2 AC 709).

[5] *Schmidt v Rosewood Trust Ltd* [2003] AC 709.

[6] *Schmidt v Rosewood Trust Ltd* [2003] AC 709; *Spellson v George* (1987) 11 NSWLR 300.

[7] D J Hayton, 'Beneficiaries' and Objects' Rights to Information' (2003) 10 JITCP 139: the obligation of a trustee as a power-holder could be restricted to that of a holder of a personal power: see paras 1.67–1.68 and Article 60 below.

1.74 Where it is hoped that certain purposes (other than charitable purposes) may be carried out, a power for these purposes has the advantage that its validity does not depend upon the existence of someone positively interested in supervising its exercise[1]: the lack of someone to enforce a trust is fatal to its validity save in special anomalous cases that are not to be extended[2]. If a trust were intended to be created it cannot be saved by being treated as a power: a finding of an intention to create an imperative obligation to act is inconsistent with a finding of an intention to confer only an opportunity to act[3].

[1] *Re Douglas* (1887) 35 Ch D 472; *Re Shaw* [1957] 1 All ER 745, [1957] 1 WLR 729.

[2] *Re Endacott* [1960] Ch 232, [1959] 3 All ER 562.

[3] *Re Shaw* [1957] 1 WLR 729 at 746; *Re Endacott* [1960] Ch 232 at 246.

1.75 In the absence of express authorisation to the contrary in the instrument creating powers or trusts, neither powers nor trusts can be released by the donees or trustees respectively except where the donee is a personal donee as opposed to a fiduciary donee[1]. Potential beneficiaries under powers or discretionary trusts may validly release the donees or trustees from their duties so that the potential beneficiaries cease to be such[2]. If trustees' discretionary *powers* over income are not exercised within a reasonable time the discretion is extinguished[3] whereas discretionary *trusts* over income remain exercisable despite the passing of time, though only in favour of such persons as would have been objects of the discretion had it been exercised within a reasonable time[4].

¹ *Re Wills' Trust Deeds* [1964] Ch 219, [1963] 1 All ER 390; *Mettoy Pension Trustees Ltd v Evans* [1991] 2 All ER 513 at 545. Powers or trusts may, of course, be deleted on an application under the Variation of Trusts Act 1958.
² *Re Gulbenkian's Settlement Trusts (No 2)* [1970] Ch 408, [1969] 2 All ER 1173.
³ *Re Allen-Meyrick's Will Trusts* [1966] 1 All ER 740, [1966] 1 WLR 499; *Re Gulbenkian's Settlement Trusts (No 2)* [1970] Ch 408, [1969] 2 All ER 1173.
⁴ *Re Locker's Settlement Trusts* [1978] 1 All ER 216, [1977] 1 WLR 1323.

Fiduciary powers, personal powers and protectors

PERSONAL AND FIDUCIARY POWERS

1.76 A personal power may be one of three types. In a rare case a settlor may confer a beneficial personal power on a donee with intent to confer full dominion over the relevant property on the donee or full power to withhold consent to particular courses of action[1] so as to enable the donee to protect his own interests, so that the donee can act as selfishly as he wishes purely to benefit himself, eg in discharging his legal or moral obligations to persons whom he would otherwise seek to benefit from his own resources[2]. More commonly, a settlor will confer a non-beneficial personal power on a donee (eg his widow) with intent that the donee is to be wholly unaccountable in the courts in respect of the power's exercise or non-exercise, so long as upon any exercise of the power only objects of the power are to benefit[3], it being a fraud upon the power (actionable by the beneficiaries entitled in default of a proper exercise of the power) if the donee exercises it to benefit persons (like herself) who are not objects of the power[4]. Otherwise, the donee of the power is under no duty to consider exercising it and 'is entitled to prefer one object to another from any motive he pleases, and however capriciously he exercises the power the court will uphold it'[5]. In a third scenario, the holder of the power will be under a fiduciary duty from time to time to consider whether or not it is appropriate to exercise a power (eg a trustee with power to add anyone in the world other than a member of an excepted class to the class of beneficiaries or of objects of powers of appointment or to delete anyone from such a class), but the actual decision to exercise or not to exercise the power is to be an unchallengeable personal function[6] unless amounting to a fraud on the power.

¹ *Rawson v Perlman* 1 BOCM 135 (Bahamas Supreme Court Eq No 194 of 1984); *Re Z Trust* [1997] CILR 248.
² *Re Wills' Trust Deeds* [1964] Ch 219 at 228.
³ *Re Gulbenkian's Settlement* [1970] AC 508 at 518; *Re Hay's Settlement Trusts* [1982] 1 WLR 202; *Re Wills' Trust Deed* [1964] Ch 219; *Re Somes* [1896] 1 Ch 250; *Steele v Paz Ltd* [1993–95] Manx LR 426.
⁴ *Vatcher v Paull* [1915] AC 372; *Re Dick* [1953] Ch 343; *Palmer v Locke* (1880) 15 Ch D 294; *Mettoy Pension Trustees Ltd v Evans* [1991] 2 All ER 513 at 545.
⁵ Per Lawrence J in *Re Wright* [1920] 1 Ch 108 at 118.
⁶ See para 8.88 below.

1.77 In contrast, a fiduciary power is one conferred upon someone (usually holding an office like that of trustee or protector) for the benefit of the beneficiaries, so that he must independently consciously consider from time to time whether or not to exercise it and he must exercise it responsibly according to the purpose for which it was conferred on him and not perversely to any sensible expectation of the settlor, e g by exercising it capriciously or arbitrarily or in bad faith; moreover, a fiduciary power cannot be released unless the trust instrument specifically authorises it[1].

1   *Re Hay's Settlement Trusts* [1981] 3 All ER 786, [1982] 1 WLR 202; *Re Manisty's Settlement* [1974] Ch 17, [1973] 2 All ER 1203; *Re Skeats Settlement* (1889) 42 Ch D 522. Further see D J Hayton in (1999) 32 Vanderbilt J Transnat Law 555 at 579–589.

ROLE OF A PROTECTOR

1.78 A trust instrument sometimes provides for a 'protector' in its definition clause and goes on to confer some powers and rights on such protector to enable the protector to play a role in the life of the trust. The protector can then be regarded as holding an office, just as a trustee holds an office. The same office can be fulfilled by a 'committee' or 'board' or 'company', which could be independent of, or be controlled by, the settlor. The rights and powers of the protector that create the nature of his role will depend upon the terms of the trust instrument. The protector may have negative powers, as where his consent is requisite before the trustees carry out certain transactions, or have positive overriding powers enabling him to direct the trustees in certain matters or to appoint or remove trustees. Because the protector merely has powers vested in him and not trust property he is not a trustee. Exceptionally, if the trusteeship is a sham[1] so that the trustees are wholly nominees for the protector bound to do his bidding for the benefit of the beneficiaries (or, perhaps, of himself) then the protector will be regarded as a trustee[2] for the beneficiaries (or, in an extreme case, as where the settlor is the protector, as sole beneficial owner).

1   *Rahman v Chase Bank (CI) Trust Co Ltd* [1991] JLR 103; *Midland Bank plc v Wyatt* [1995] 1 FLR 697; see paras 4.6–4.14 below.
2   Perhaps managing trustee: *Re Arnott* [1899] Ir R 201.

1.79 The particular powers conferred upon a protector normally are fiduciary powers intended to enable him to play a fiduciary role[1] (unless expressly or necessarily implied otherwise in the trust instrument or from the circumstances, as where the settlor or a beneficiary is a protector with power to protect his own selfish interests). The fiduciary powers are to enable the protector to safeguard the trust from various hazards, whether relating to the trustee (e g exorbitant charges, inadequate investment performance, unsatisfactory exercise of distributive functions vis-á-vis discretionary beneficiaries) or to beneficiaries (e g disputing what the trustees might do on their own) or to the trust arrangements (e g tax or other problems relating to the trust jurisdiction or to a corporate trustee's change of residence or ownership or opening of offices in a jurisdiction where pressure could be exerted). Examples of powers expressly given to a protector are powers to:

(a)   monitor and agree the trustees' fees;
(b)   require an accounting or audit, with power to nominate the auditors;

(c)   conduct periodic reviews of the administration of the trust;

(d)   approve self-dealing by the trustees;

(e)   remove and appoint trustees;

(f)   initiate the migration of the trust or to be the judge of facts concerning whether the trust has automatically migrated upon the occurrence of certain events;

(g)   be consulted or have veto powers before the trustees make any discretionary payments to beneficiaries or objects of a power;

(h)   be consulted or have veto powers over sales of particular shareholdings or other trust property;

(i)   withhold consent where requisite before any beneficiary can institute legal proceedings against the trustee (for its conduct during the settlor's lifetime)[2];

(j)   withhold consent to trustees' proposed exercise of a power to amend the administrative or managerial terms of the trust;

(k)   direct generally or only in specific areas the exercise of trustees' investment or other managerial discretions;

(l)   veto the settlor's exercise of a reserved power if believing him to be under duress in his home jurisdiction or to be suffering from a mental disorder;

(m)   make or approve additions to, or deletions from, the class of beneficiaries or objects of powers; and

(n)   amend any clause in the trust instrument, other than one setting out beneficiaries or objects of the settlor's bounty, in any fashion that the protector subjectively considers will better further the purposes of the settlor.

[1]   *Steele v Paz* [1993–95] Manx LR 426; *Re Osiris Trustees* (2000) 2 ITELR 404; *IRC v Schroder* [1983] STC 480; *Sociedad Financiera Sofimeca v Kleinwort Benson (Jersey) Trustees Ltd* (13 July 1993, unreported, Jersey Royal Court) discussed in Matthews & Sowden, *Jersey Law of Trusts* (Third edn, Keyhaven) p 130; *Von Knierem v Bermuda Trust Co Ltd and Grosvenor Trust Co Ltd* (13 July 1994, Supreme Court of Bermuda 1 BOCM 116) *Scott on Trusts* (Fourth edn) vol IIA, para 185. Statutory recognition of a protector is found in the Cook Islands, The Bahamas, Belize and British Virgin Islands. Further, see R Ham, E Campbell and M Tennet, 'Protectors' in J Glasson (ed), *The International Trust* (Jordans, 2006), D W M Waters, 'The Protector: New Wine in Old Bottles' in A J Oakley (ed), *Trends in Contemporary Trust Law* (Clarendon Oxford, 1996) and A Duckworth, *Protectors-Fish or Fowl* (1995) 4 JTCP 131 and (1996) 5 JTCP 18.

[2]   This can, however, negate the trust obligation if the protector is the settlor or the settlor's dummy, so that in the settlor's lifetime capital and income in substance are held to the order of the settlor, no beneficiary having any right to complain of this, because the power is a personal one.

RIGHTS AND DUTIES OF A PROTECTOR

1.80 Of course, the existence of some of these express powers will give rise to some necessarily implied rights, eg to see trust accounts and to an indemnity out of the trust fund for properly incurred expenses, but an express power to charge fees will be needed[1]. Indeed, the courts[2] have assumed that protectors, who are office holders, have the right to appear before the court in matters involving their powers because recognition of their office and their powers requires this.

1   *Re Representation Blampied* Jersey Royal Court, 28 January 1994 (a fiduciary cannot profit from his position without authorisation).
2   *Re Representation Blampied* Jersey Royal Court, 28 January 1994; *Von Knierem v Bermuda Trust Co* Vol 1 BOCM pp 116–125; *Re Omar Family Trust* [2000] WTLR 713, 714; *Re Hare Trust* (2001) 4 ITELR 288. In England see the width of Civil Procedure Rules 1998, Part 64 and Practice Directions thereto: see Article 87 below.

1.81 In determining the scope of duties affecting particular powers of a protector a court will need to consider the settlor's purposes[1] in conferring particular powers on the protector so that, ideally, the purposes should be properly documented, eg in a general letter of wishes or a specific protectors' memorandum. The court also needs to consider the terms of any exemption or other clause in the trust instrument that in any way relates to the protector's position. Indeed, a court may well take the view that if the protector is an unpaid friend or relative of the settlor then there may be no duties in relation to some protector's powers (eg of appointment or of consenting or not to a trustee's proposed appointment), but that in relation to other powers, eg to remove the trustee and appoint a new trustee, the extent of the fiduciary duty is to act in good faith in the best interests of the beneficiaries, while if the protector is a paid professional then he is subject to the full fiduciary responsibilities applicable to trustees[2], but, like trustees, he can be expressly exempted from liability for breach of fiduciary duty if a clause so provides, so long as the breach does not involve recklessness or dishonesty[3].

1   *Re Hay's Settlement Trusts* [1981] 3 All ER 786 at 792. Exceptionally, the protector may be intended by the settlor to protect the settlor's interests rather than the beneficiaries' interests, which seems the real justification for the court's decision in the *Von Knierem* case (see para 1.81, footnote 2).
2   Except to the extent that the circumstances of his appointment by the settlor may necessarily impliedly relieve him from a need to avoid a conflict of interest and duty as in *Re Z Trust* [1997] Cayman ILR 248.
3   *Armitage v Nurse* [1998] Ch 241, CA.

1.82 Exceptionally, where the first protector office-holder is the settlor with a selfish interest to promote in respect of a particular trust asset it will be possible to hold that some of his powers are personal, as also is likely where the first protector is a beneficiary with selfish interests that the settlor must have taken into account[1]. Alternatively, if it be fiduciary, the court may hold that there is a necessarily implied authorisation of a conflict of interest which allows the beneficiary, after due consideration of other beneficiaries' interests, to exercise the power despite personal benefit accruing therefrom[2].

1   *Rawson Trust v Perlman* (Bahamas Sup. Ct Eq No 194 of 1984) BOCM Vol 1 pp 35–54.
2   *Re Z Trust* [1997] CILR 248 where the judge held the beneficiary-protector's power was probably personal, but if it was fiduciary there was a necessarily implied authority to exercise the power and thereby benefit the beneficiary-protector, so upholding the consent of a protector committee to an amendment of the beneficial provisions of the trust fund so as to benefit beneficiary members of the protector committee at the expense of other beneficiaries.

1.83 However, normally where the settlor or a beneficiary is a protector the powers of such protector that affect the investment and managerial role of the trustee will be presumed fiduciary so far as concerns the exercise of a power of removal and appointment of trustees and the exercise of a power to direct investments to be made by the trustees, because those powers will be presumed to be exercisable to promote the interests of the beneficiaries as a whole[1]. In respect of the trustees' role as discretionary distributors of income or capital to beneficiaries it seems that there is good scope for argument that the protector's power to withhold consent to proposed distributions or to direct distributions is a personal power, especially in the case of a settlor who is the protector[2].

[1]   *Vestey's Executors v IRC* [1949] 1 All ER 1108; *Re Rogers* (1928) 63 Ontario LR 180; *IRC v Schroder* [1983] STC 480; *Re Burton* (1994) 126 Australia LR 557; *Re Osiris Trustees* (2000) 2 ITELR 404. It is unlikely that the settlor or beneficiary will be under a duty to monitor the trustee with a view to discovering when, if at all, the trustee needs to be removed.

[2]   Cf *Re Triffit's Settlement* [1958] Ch 852; *Re Penrose* [1933] Ch 793; *Palmer v Locke* (1880) 15 Ch D 294.

1.84 Rather than rely on default law, a settlor should consider (with the benefit of professional advice) what mechanism should be employed for succession to the protectorship (even though it appears[1] that the court has inherent jurisdiction to appoint someone to be protector, where it is clear that such an office is crucial to the operation of the trust, and, equally, has inherent jurisdiction to remove[2] a protector in breach of protectorship duties or mentally incapacitated) and what particular powers, duties, rights and exemptions he wishes to confer on his protector. It is up to the settlor alone to decide how to deal with the settlor's property by transferring it to trustees for the benefit of beneficiaries, who will not look a gift-horse in the mouth and so must take the benefit with associated burdens arising from the existence of fiduciary or personal powers – unless they choose to disclaim their interest.

[1]   *Steele v Paz Ltd* [1993–95] Manx LR 426.
[2]   *Re Papadimitriou* [2004] WTLR 1141, para 71.

1.85 Where it is the settlor who has reserved to himself personal powers as protector which will enable him to act capriciously and irresponsibly without being accountable before any court, no doubt, he will not expect that he could ever be accused of acting capriciously, irresponsibly or recklessly; but to guard against such an irritating ungrateful accusation he can block any court action by expressly ensuring that his powers are exclusively merely personal. However, if he has an expressly personal power from time to time to replace the current trustee with a new one, there is a grave danger that the trustee will be regarded as in his thrall, so that the trust is in substance a bare trust for the settlor or, perhaps a true trust for several beneficiaries, including himself, but one where there is virtually no likelihood that the trustees will fail to comply with the settlor's request for trust funds to be distributed to him (so such funds can be regarded as available assets where claims of divorcing spouses[1] – but not other creditors[2] – are concerned).

[1]   *Browne v Browne* [1989] 1 FLR 291; *Thomas v Thomas* [1995] 2 FLR 668 and Australian cases; *Re Marriage of Goodwin* (1990)14 Fam LR 801; *Re Marriage of Davidson* (1990) 14 Fam LR 817.
[2]   *Re Esteem Settlement* [2004] WTLR 1; *Shalson v Russo* [2003] WTLR 1165 rejecting the approach in *Private Trust Corpn v Grupo Torras SA* (1997/98) 1 OFLR 443.

1.86 If the settlor can expressly confer personal powers on himself as concerns particular aspects of his trust, the question arises whether he can expressly authorise others as protector to have exclusively personal powers so as to block any court challenges to the exercise of the protector's discretion unless amounting to a fraud on the power, eg in adding or deleting persons as beneficiaries or objects of powers or removing Trustee A and appointing Trustee B, whether or not also exporting the trust through Trustee B being in a different jurisdiction, the law of which is chosen by the protector to govern the trust. Such challenges can obviously be detrimental to the smooth running of the trust and provoke lengthy and costly litigation[1]. The answer to the question hinges on whether or not there is an irreducible core minimum content of protectorship in the same way that there is for trusteeship and whether or not there should be less concern over protectors than over trustees.

[1] For example, *Von Knierem v Bermuda Trust Co* (Bermuda Equity nos 154 and 162 of 1994 of 1994 Butts OCM Vol 1 pp 116–125). The problem can be avoided by employing a custodian trustee to hold the trust assets. A managing trustee sacked by the protector will not need to be informed of the identity of the new trustee and will have no cause to complain if the trust instrument provides that a replaced trustee cannot be liable for anything happening as a result of the appointment of the replacement trustee.

1.87 In *Armitage v Nurse* Millett LJ stated[1]:

'There is an irreducible core of obligations owed by the trustees to the beneficiaries and enforceable by then which is fundamental to the concept of a trust. If the beneficiaries have no rights enforceable against the trustees there are no trusts. But I do not accept that these core obligations include the duties of care and skill, prudence and diligence. The duty of the trustees to perform the trusts honestly and in good faith for the benefit of the beneficiaries is the minimum necessary to give substance to the trusts.'

[1] [1998] Ch 241, 253.

1.88 He then held that exemption clauses cannot exempt trustees from liability for dishonest or reckless breaches of trust but can exempt them from liability for negligence, whether gross or ordinary negligence. This has since been glossed by the Court of Appeal[1] holding that if a professional trustee (like a solicitor) deliberately commits a breach of duty subjectively honestly believing this to be in the best interests of the beneficiaries, he cannot rely on the protection of a clause exempting him from liability unless dishonest if no honest reasonable professional trustee could have held such belief.

[1] *Walker v Stones* [2001] QB 902. A professional person who has knowingly accepted a trusteeship should not be treated as leniently as such a person who did not know he was a trustee as in *Twinsectra Ltd v Yardley* [2002] UKHL 12, [2002] 2 AC 164 as explained in *Barlow Clowes International Ltd v Eurotrust International Ltd* [2005] UKPC 37 [2006] 1 All ER 333.

1.89 One can therefore argue that particular powers of a protector (or of any designated person) expressly or by necessary implication in all the circumstances require the protector (or other person) to consider whether or not to exercise them from time to time, as appropriate in all the circumstances, and, if relating to investment or managerial matters, must be exercised with the standard of care applicable to trustees, while particular powers may only be required to be exercised honestly and in good faith for the benefit of the beneficiaries as a whole. Otherwise, however, if the settlor understands what he is doing and clearly intends that the powers of a protector, even a professional independent protector, are to be exclusively personal, so that their exercise is to be beyond challenge in the courts unless they are proved to have committed a fraud upon their powers, then the court should respect the settlor's intentions, as they should any exemptions from liability for behaviour that is neither dishonest nor reckless.

1.90 Where a trustee cannot act without the protector's consent and the giving or withholding of such consent is a fiduciary power the trustee should not simply acquiesce in the refusal of consent if he reasonably believes such refusal is perverse. He should apply to the court under ss 14 and 15 of the Trusts of Land and Appointment of Trustees Act 1996 if English land be involved or s 57 of the Trustee Act 1925[1] if the administrative disposition of trust property is involved or otherwise ask the court for directions, as also ought to be done if the protector positively directs the trustee to take certain steps which the trustee reasonably believes would amount to a breach of fiduciary duty (as perverse to any sensible expectations of the settlor) or would otherwise involve the trustee in a breach of its equitable standards of care[2]. However, it should be open to the settlor to deal with the interrelationship of trustees and protector by expressly providing that if the protector withholds his consent or gives a positive direction then the trustees are under no liability whatsoever if they simply acquiesce in what the protector has decided, being always irrebuttably regarded as having no reasonable grounds for questioning the decisions of the protector unless they actually believe the protector to be acting dishonestly. Any beneficiary's remedy for improper breach of fiduciary duty should then only lie against the protector if he were under such a duty.

[1]   *Re Beale's Settlement Trusts* [1932] 2 Ch 15 which also indicates that it may be that the withholding of consent under a personal power can be overridden under the Trusts of Land and Appointment of Trustees Act 1996, ss 14 and 15 replacing Law of Property Act 1925, s 30 or Trustee Act 1925, s 57 where such withholding is clearly disproportionately detrimental to the interests of the beneficiaries as a whole in the proper administration of the trust property.
[2]   *Re Arnott* [1899] Ir R 209; *Commonwealth of Australia v Colonial Weaving Co* (1922) 31 CLR 421 at 470; *Scott on Trusts* (Fourth edn) Vol IIA, para 185, and c f express exclusion in s 36 of the Fines and Recoveries Act 1833 of court's power to control or interfere with exercise by the protector of a settlement of his power of consent.

1.91 After all, the settlor may be the protector with a personal power to direct the trustees' in their asset management functions (so long as such directions do not personally benefit himself or his spouse). He may have successfully built up a £40 million portfolio of investments which he transferred to trustees on discretionary trusts for his descendants, their spouses and cohabitees under which he requires the trustees to speculate with the trust fund as if they were absolute beneficial owners thereof who could afford to lose the whole fund without it in any way whatsoever affecting their standard of living, and the trustees are not to be liable for any investment or speculation losses if they acted honestly. Indeed, to avoid delay in implementing his directions, it will be better if the settlor's trust instrument requires delegation of the trustees' asset management duties to the settlor or his dummy company (obliged not to exercise their powers for personally benefiting the settlor or his spouse or *alter ego*) with the trustees having no power in the settlor's lifetime to revoke such delegation unless they have actual knowledge of the settlor's mental incapacity or unless at the end of a relevant accounting year they discover the trust fund is worth one tenth of its value the preceding year: title to trust assets should be in the name of the trustee[1] or a custodian, with the trustee having to maintain proper accounts and take action if discovering the settlor had moved from a managerial role to a distributive role for his own benefit.

[1]   So the settlor cannot be a trustee: *Re Carapiet's Trusts* [2002] WTLR 989.

1.92   Ultimately, one must be aware that the intentions of the settlor govern the position and that all settlors are different. It is up to the draftsperson (or, in default, the court) to make clear what was authorised by the power so long as giving effect to the purposes for which the settlor conferred the powers; what was the extent of the duties, if any, intended to apply to the exercise of, or the consideration of exercising or not, particular powers of the power-holder; what rights were intended to be conferred on the power-holder to enable him to perform his duties; and what were the obligations of the trustee in respect of exercises of powers by the power-holder.

Trusts and charges, personal obligations and conditional or absolute gifts

1.93   If T makes a testamentary or inter vivos gift to B and requires B to make some payment to C or perform some obligation in C's favour there are five possible legal consequences[1]:

(a)   T's words may be treated as creating B a trustee for C[2].

(b)   T's words may be treated as creating an equitable charge in C's favour on the property given to B. The charge attaches to the property (whether taken by B or someone else upon B's disclaimer) so as to give C an equitable security interest though it imposes no personal fiduciary obligations upon B[3]. Thus, on the charge being satisfied B will hold the property beneficially[4] unlike a trustee who, on the termination of express trusts, holds the property on a resulting trust for the settlor[5]. During the subsistence of the charge B will not be accountable for rents and profits arising from the charged property[6]: a trustee is so accountable in respect of the trust property. B is in a similar position to a trustee only in that neither he nor a trustee is ordinarily personally responsible for any insufficiency of the property to produce the sum charged or the expected beneficial interest[7]. C is in a similar position to the beneficiary of a trust in that his rights are equitable and so may only be overridden if the property affected by those rights is purchased by a bona fide purchaser of a legal interest for value without notice[8] or, in the case of land, by a purchaser protected under the Land Charges Acts 1925 or 1972 or the Land Registration Act 1925 owing to absence of an entry protecting the equitable charge[9]. C is in a different position from a beneficiary under a trust in that C's remedy, if his charge is not met, is to apply for sale of the charged property and payment out of the proceeds thereof.

(c)   T's words may be construed as making a gift to B if B undertakes a personal equitable obligation in C's favour signified by B's acceptance of the gift. C will then obtain a personal right against B but no right against the gifted property. Then B has the choice of taking the property and performing the obligation in C's favour *or* of declining both in which case C will receive nothing. If a trust had been created C would have been secure for a trust does not fail for want of a trustee, eg if the trustee predeceases the testator or disclaims[10]. On the other hand, B's obligation if he accepts the gift may be greater than those of a trustee for he is personally required to perform the obligation even if it costs him more than the value of the property received[11]. In an exceptional case the court may find that an equitable charge and a personal obligation were intended by the testator to co-exist[12].

(d)   T's words may be construed as giving property to B subject to a condition subsequent so that if B, after receiving the property, goes on to infringe the condition he will forfeit his interest in the property. So long as B does not infringe the condition the property is B's absolutely beneficially[13]. If B breaks the condition (eg where freehold land has been devised to him subject to a condition subsequent) then T's specific devisee or residuary devisee or next of kin, as the case may be, having the right of entry for breach of condition, may enter and determine B's estate. The disadvantage of this is that C, who on the face of it takes the property upon forfeiture of B's interest, thereby loses all hope of obtaining his interest from B and so suffers unless he happens to have the right of entry[14]. For this reason the courts are more likely to protect C if they find this accords with T's intention by construing T's words as creating a trust or charge or personal obligation[15].

(e)   Finally, T's words may be treated merely as indicating his motive for leaving property to B so that B takes an absolute beneficial interest, eg 'to my wife, B, that she may support herself and the children according to their needs' or 'for the Hull Judeans (Maccabi) Association in memory of my late wife to be used solely in the work of constructing new buildings for the Association'[16]. If a gift in absolute terms is accompanied by a desire, wish, recommendation, hope or expression of confidence that the donee will use it in a certain way for benefiting others, no trust to that effect will attach to it unless, on the will as a whole the court concludes that a trust was intended[17]. Indeed, s 22 of the Administration of Justice Act 1982 provides 'Except where a contrary intention is shown, it shall be presumed that if a testator devises or bequeaths property to his spouse in terms which themselves would give an absolute interest to the spouse, but by the same instrument purports to give his issue an interest in the same property, the gift to the spouse is absolute notwithstanding the purported gift to the issue.'

---

[1]   See (1952) 11 Camb LJ 240 (Thomas). See also *Countess of Bective v Federal Commissioner of Taxation* (1932) 47 CLR 417 and *Muschinski v Dodds* (1985) 106 CLR 583 at 605–607.

[2]   See Article 8(1)(a) and 8(2)(c) below.

3   *Cunningham v Foot* (1878) 3 App Cas 974 at 992–993.
4   *Re Oliver* (1890) 62 LT 533.
5   *Re West* [1900] 1 Ch 84.
6   *Re Oliver* (1890) 62 LT 533.
7   *Re Cowley* (1885) 53 LT 494.
8   *Parker v Judkin* [1931] 1 Ch 475.
9   Settled Land Act 1925, s 1(1)(v), will apply if the charge is voluntary in which case no protection is possible under the Land Charges Act for the overreachable charge.
10   *Re Armitage* [1972] Ch 438, [1972] 1 All ER 708; *Mallott v Wilson* [1903] 2 Ch 494.
11   *Re Hodge* [1940] Ch 260; *Re North* [1952] Ch 397, [1952] 1 All ER 609. The cases on conditional gifts concern testamentary gifts but inter vivos gifts should be subject to the same principles: *Countess of Bective v Federal Comr of Taxation* (1932) 47 CLR 417 at 418; *Muschinski v Dodds* (1985) 160 CLR 583 (Aust HC) per Brennan and Dawson JJ.
12   *Re Lester* [1942] Ch 324, [1942] 1 All ER 646. It will be important to distinguish between a charge and a condition where property is devised, say, to a son and two daughters in unequal shares subject to payment by the son and daughters of an annuity to their widowed mother for her life: as a charge the annuity will be borne rateably but as a personal obligation the annuity will be payable equally by the joint obligors: *Pearce v Wright* (1926) 39 CLR 16.
13   *A-G v Cordwainers' Co* (1883) 3 My & K 534, as will also be the case if the condition is void for uncertainty. In *Ellis v Chief Adjudication Officer* [1998] 1 FLR 184, CA, a mother's gift of her flat to her daughter on condition she cared for her mother in the flat was upheld, so that on evicting the mother and selling the flat, part of the proceeds had to be paid to the mother, after allowing for mortgage payments by the daughter.
14   See (1952) 11 Camb LJ 240 at 242–245 (Thomas); Megarry and Wade, *The Law of Real Property* (Sixth edn) pp 65–71; *Re Gardiner* [1971] 2 NSWLR 494.
15   *Lambe v Eames* (1871) 6 Ch App 597; *Re Brace* [1954] 2 All ER 354, [1954] 1 WLR 955; Article 8(2)(b) and (c) below.
16   *Re Lipinski's Will Trust* [1976] Ch 235.
17   See the position on 'precatory' trusts at paras 8.214–8.232 below.

Summary analysis of a trust

1.94 From the foregoing comparisons with other legal relationships it will be seen it is convenient to regard a trust as 'an obligation', that is to say, 'a tie of equity (*vinculum juris*), whereby one person is bound to perform or forbear some act for another'[1]. The obligation is an equitable one, and until the amalgamation of the courts of common law and equity, was enforceable only in courts of equity; and although, by the Judicature Act 1873, all courts take cognisance of trusts, yet they are treated as equitable rights giving rise to defences applicable only to equitable rights, and remediable only by equitable remedies. It is also an obligation relating exclusively to property. An obligation to do or forbear from doing some act not relating to property is not a trust, whatever else it may be. A trust is 'of property': the trustee is under obligations owed to beneficiaries in respect of specific property owned by the trustee, such that the beneficiaries have an equitable interest in such property.

1   The words quoted are an adaptation of the description of 'obligation', referring to the Roman *Obligatio*, in the Article on 'Obligation' in vol 16 of the *Encyclopaedia Britannica* (15th edn 1955), under the editorship in respect of law of Abraham Wolf.

1.95 An English trust has the following characteristics:

(a)   Title to the trust property is vested in the trustee[1], who alone can sue[2] or be sued, a trust not being a legal person. Thus, a purported transfer to 'The Smith Family Trust' should strictly rank as a nullity as a transfer to no-one: it should be to the legal persons (eg X and Y) who are to own the property as trustees subject to the obligations set out in the instrument creating The Smith Family Trust. However, since it is easy to see what was intended, the courts[3] are prepared to construe the transfer as to the trustees of The Smith Family Trust.

(b)   The trust property is not part of the trustee's own estate but must be kept for the benefit of beneficiaries or for charitable or other permitted purposes as a separate protected fund immune from any claims of the trustee's creditors, heirs or spouse[4]: this fund extends beyond the original trust assets to accruals thereto (of a capital or income nature), to assets representing the rightful product of trust assets and, if so claimed by the beneficiaries, the wrongful product of trust assets[5], eg unauthorised assets purchased by a trustee as new investments with the proceeds of sale of authorised investments and also assets wrongfully acquired by a trustee purportedly for himself as his private property with such proceeds of sale.

(c)   The trustee holds an office for the duration of the trust, such office being subject to onerous fiduciary proscriptive duties[6] and to equitable prescriptive duties in default of contrary provision in the terms of the trust. Enforceability of these duties by the beneficiaries (not the settlor) is at the core of the trust concept[7], although in the case of charitable purpose trusts the trustees' duties are enforceable in the public interest by the Attorney-General or the Charity Commission (as the representatives of the Crown as *parens patriae*).

(d)   Many trusts are in operation for a lengthy period (which can be as long as 125 years[8]) so that many unforeseeable matters may arise in vastly changing social and economic circumstances during the life of the trust. Thus court has a supportive, supervisory jurisdiction[9] (in addition to its punitive enforcement role) that the trustees or the beneficiaries can invoke to help further the settlor's purposes in creating the trust, eg the court can advise the trustees whether they have power to act in particular circumstances and, if they do not, then the court can authorise them to act in an expedient manner; and where the trustees fear that they might be held to have acted improperly in bringing or defending proceedings, so that they would not be able to recover their costs from the trust fund, the trustees can obtain the court's authority for them to act, so ensuring that they can so recover their costs even if losing the legal proceedings.

(e)   The beneficiaries (or the Attorney-General or the Charity Commission in the case of charitable purpose trusts) not only have personal rights against a trustee to have the value of the trust fund restored to what it should have been but for a breach of trust (which rights may extend to a third party[10] who dishonestly interferes with the obligations owed to the beneficiaries) but have equitable proprietary rights[11] in the trust fund (as defined in (b) above). These rights bind not just the trustees but also third parties unless such are bona fide purchasers of the legal title without notice of the equitable rights or are protected by statutory overreaching provisions (eg when purchasing land from two trustees or a trust corporation). Third parties owning property bound by the trust do not take over the duties of the trustees but must return the property (or assets that have replaced such property by virtue of a sale or exchange of the original trust property) to the current trustees (or the absolutely entitled beneficiaries if the beneficiaries are absolutely entitled to the trust property). The settlor has no right to enforce his trust unless he happens to be a beneficiary or takes exceptional steps to reserve such a right in his trust instrument[12].

(f)   Where the settlor has effectively transferred legal title to trustees but has failed effectively to divest himself of all his beneficial interest in favour of beneficiaries or of charitable purposes, then the trustees hold the trust fund under a resulting trust for the settlor to the extent he failed so to divest himself[13] (unless in the case of charitable trusts the settlor had a paramount general charitable intention, in which event the trust fund is applied cy-près to a closely allied purpose[14]).

---

[1]   *Smith v Anderson* (1880) 15 Ch D 247 at 275; *CCSD v ISPT Pty Ltd* (1999) 2 ITELR 1 at 15; *Ayerst v C & K Construction* [1976] AC 167 at 177. At law the trustee appears to be the owner, having absolute rights in respect of the property and the benefit thereof, but in equity the benefit is vested in the beneficiaries to whom the trustee is accountable for the exercise of his legal rights.

[2]   Exceptionally, if T holds a right to sue X on trust for beneficiaries, but in breach of trust T refuses to sue X, a beneficiary can directly sue X, joining T as co-defendant so that all interested parties are bound by the court's judgment: *Hayim v Citibank* [1987] AC 730 at 748; *Parker-Tweedale v Dunbar Bank plc* [1991] Ch 12 at 19 emphasising that the beneficiary sues on behalf of the trust and in place of the trustee.

[3]   *Choithram International SA v Pagarani* [2001] 1 WLR 1.

[4]   *Henry v Hammond* [1913] 2 KB 515 at 521 endorsed by *R v Clowes (No 2)* [1994] 2 All ER 316 at 325, CA.

[5]   'That which is the fruit of the trust property or the trusteeship is itself trust property', per Oliver LJ in *Swain v Law Society* [1982] 1 WLR 17 at 36; *A-G of Hong Kong v Reid* [1994] 1 AC 324 at 338; *Re Hallett's Estate* (1880) 13 Ch D 696 at 709.

[6]   For the distinction between proscriptive fiduciary duties (the 'no profit' and 'no conflict of interest and duty' rules) and prescriptive equitable duties see *Bristol & West Building Society v Mothew* [1998] Ch 1, CA.

[7]   *Armitage v Nurse* [1998] Ch 241 at 253 where Millett LJ refers to 'an irreducible core of obligations owed by the trustees to the beneficiaries and enforceable by them which is fundamental to the concept of a trust. If the beneficiaries have no rights enforceable against the trustees there are no trusts.' However, it is possible that the court will come to uphold trusts for furthering non-charitable purpose trusts within a valid perpetuity period so long as expressly made enforceable by a person designated by the trust instrument and positively interested in enforcing the purposes: see paras 8.157–8.167 below.

[8]   For example, where a perpetuity period is chosen of royal lives plus 21 years, so that the Law Commission in its Report *The Rules against Perpetuities and Excessive Accumulations* (Law Com no 251) recommends a fixed period of 125 years as the maximum perpetuity period.

[9]   For example, *Re New* [1901] 2 Ch 534; *Rafidian Bank v Saipem* (2 March 1994, unreported, CA); Trustee Act 1925, s 57; *Re Beddoe* [1893] 1 Ch 547; *Public Trustee v Cooper* [2001] WTLR 901.

[10]   *Twinsectra Ltd v Yardley* [2002] UKHL 12, [2002] UKHL 12, [2002] 2 AC 164; *Ultraframe (UK) Ltd v Fielding* [2005] EWHC 1638 (Ch) [2005] All ER (D) 397 (Jul).

[11]   *Re Diplock* [1948] Ch 465; *Foskett v McKeown* [2001] 1 AC 102.

[12]   Once the settlor has unilaterally transferred his entire interest in particular property to the trustee this amounts to complete fulfilment of his purposes, so that he drops out of the picture: *Re Astor's Settlement Trusts* [1952] Ch 534 at 542; *Bradshaw v University College of Wales* [1987] 3 All ER 200 at 203. Exceptionally, he could enter into a contract with the trustee whereby the trustee agrees to produce accounts to the settlor in his lifetime and to restore to the trust fund any amount due on the taking of accounts, to be enforceable under *Beswick v Beswick* [1968] AC 58 principles; or, under trust law, the settlor could perhaps expressly reserve to himself *locus standi* as enforcer of the trustee's obligations in addition to the beneficiaries: see paras 8.157–8.167 below.

13   See Article 29 below.
14   For example, *Re Lysaght* [1966] Ch 191.

1.96 It has already been noted[1] how far these and other characteristics distinguish a trust from a contract.

1   See para 1.23 above.

The attractive commercial qualities of the trust[1]

1.97 It has been seen that a trust is, essentially, a fiduciary relationship with respect to property, subjecting the trustee who holds or controls the property to duties to deal with the property for the benefit of persons (including himself if so designated). Any one of these persons, known as beneficiaries, can enforce the obligations of the trustee, which arise as the result of a manifestation of an intention to create a trust by a person known as the settlor. The trustee is the legal person who acts on behalf of the trust because it has no legal personality of its own, unlike a company. However, the assets of the trust constitute a separate fund available only for the beneficiaries and not for the trustee's creditors if the trustee becomes insolvent[2]. The beneficiaries are regarded as having equitable ownership of the assets in the legal ownership of the trustee. If the trustee in breach of trust wrongfully transfers the legal ownership in particular assets to a third party, then the beneficiaries can still assert their equitable ownership against those assets and so trace such assets (or, even, the product of such assets) into the hands of anyone who is neither a bona fide purchaser of the assets without notice of the breach of trust, nor protected by statutory overreaching provisions[3], as where the purchase price of land is paid to two trustees or a trust corporation, though the proceeds of sale may then be traced and claimed.

1   Generally see chapters of D Hayton, J Langbein and D Waters in D Hayton (ed), *Modern International Developments in Trust Law* (Kluwer Law International 1999); chapters of D Hayton and S Worthington in D Hayton (ed), *Extending the Boundaries of Trusts and Similar Ring-Fenced Funds in the Twenty-First Century* (Kluwer Law International 2002); D Hayton, *The Association of Corporate Trustees: English Trusts and Their Commercial Counterparts in Continental Europe: A Report* (2002); M Grazladei, V Mattei and L Smith (eds), *Commercial Trust in European Private Law*, CUP, 2005.
2   Insolvency Act 1986, s 283(3); *Re Solicitor* (1951 M 234) [1952] Ch 328.
3   Law of Property Act 1925, ss 2, 27(2).

1.98 It can therefore be seen that strong security is provided for beneficiaries by virtue of their equitable ownership of trust assets. Furthermore, the settlor has freedom to lay down all the terms of the trust creating whatever rights and duties he wishes in the trustee, so long as they are not uncertain, illegal or contrary to public policy, and he does not have to comply with the formal rules for the incorporation and regulation of a company.

1.99 The trust is, therefore, a very flexible, useful device: its uses are as unlimited as the imagination of lawyers in taking account of the wishes of bankers, financiers and businessmen in the commercial context.

Trusts as a commercial security device

1.100 The trust is particularly useful as a means of holding security over the same assets of the debtor (eg land and stocks and shares) for a large number of creditors. It is most convenient for the security to be vested in an independent trustee or one of the creditors to be held on trust for all the creditors. Administration and realisation of the security are made much easier when there is one security holder rather than many. The major advantage, however, is that it is very easy to replace one creditor with another without the need to assign interests in security and to comply with the relevant formalities to reflect the new ownership of the interest in security. The security remains vested in the trustee: there is simply a change in the identities of the beneficiaries for whom the trustee holds the security; and the new beneficiary's interest is the old equitable interest of the old beneficiary so that rights of priority are unaffected without the need for the co-operation of the other creditors, or of the debtor as required for the novation of debts at common law.

1.101 The holding of security on trust also facilitates security structures where the same security is to benefit successive groups of creditors whose claims will come into existence at different times, eg where, in project financing, security is granted over the project assets to a trustee for the benefit not only of the bank participating in the initial grant of finance but also for banks who may at some future time provide additional finance. If the trust were not used, the banks participating in each successive grant of finance would have to take separate security over the same assets with the priority problems this would raise for them. Indeed, pari passu ranking in respect of the security would require complex contracts between all the creditors. However, the trust instrument will set out how the proceeds of realisation are to be applied and the order of application may be pari passu or howsoever set out.

1.102 Incidentally, it does not matter that the trustee is an independent trustee not in its personal capacity a creditor of the debtor or is a bank in a syndicate holding the security as trustee for all and so personally a creditor of the debtor for an amount less than the total amount secured. The full amount due and the security for such amount are respectively due to and held by the trustee qua trustee who can claim for the benefit of the beneficiaries the full amount due and enforce the security for such amount.

1.103 If less than the full amount is recovered the trustee will distribute proportionately reduced amounts to the beneficiaries. While reserving certain exclusive powers to the trustee[1] (eg on agreeing amendments to the trust instrument or on waiving defaults) it is, however, possible for the debtor to give parallel payment undertakings to the trustee and to the beneficiary bondholders as in the typical Eurobond issue: payment under one undertaking (normally to the bondholders) will pro tanto discharge liability under the other, but the trustee alone can bring proceedings if the issuer defaults.

[1]   For a saga involving the rights and duties of a trustee of a bond issue see *Concord Trust v Law Debenture Trust Corporation p/c* [2005] UKHL 27, [2005] 1 All ER (Comm) 699 and *Law Debenture Trust Corporation plc v Elektrim* [2005] EWHC 1999 (Ch).

1.104 In the case of the trust for debenture holders where a company charges property to a trustee and confers rights on it as security to be held on trust for the debenture holders, who lend money to the company in return for debenture stock, the trustee also exclusively has the right to sue on the covenant to repay and to enforce the security. The debenture stock trustee will normally be given power to appoint administrative receivers or managers to carry on the business of the company, though the trust deed will normally confer some powers upon the majority of the debenture stock holders in general meeting, eg the power to assent to modifications of the rights of the holders as a class. The Companies Act 1985, s 192 negatives any clause purporting to exclude a debenture trustee from liability for negligent breaches of trust, but allows the debenture holders at a meeting to give a subsequent release to a trustee relating to specific acts or omissions. Moreover, the London Stock Exchange imposes requirements on debenture trusts, eg as to who can be a trustee and the need to have at least one trustee independent of the company.

1.105 The trust is also crucial to efficiency in national and international financial markets by the successful exploitation of other intermediate securities where an underlying security is issued (or agreed to be issued) in paper form to an intermediate depositary or custodian or nominee, who holds the paper security (or the issuer's obligation to issue it) for the investors. To avoid problems over the need for specific allocation of certain identified assets to be held on trust for the specific investors, the intermediary will hold its proprietary interest or its personal chose in action on trust for the investors as equitable tenants in common in fractional shares appropriate to the value of the relevant investments by the respective investors, of whom there may well be thousands rather than hundreds. The investors may be financial institutions[1] which then constitute themselves trustees of a sub-trust of their rights for sub-investors as equitable tenants in common.

[1]   In Europe bond issues are dominated by the commercial custodians, Clearswift and Euroclear based in Belgium and Luxembourg, with whom financial institutions have accounts for dematerialised numbers of bonds, and individual or corporate investors will themselves have accounts with such institutions. Further see J Benjamin, *The Law of Global Custody* (Butterworth, Second edn, 2002)

1.106 The trust is also used as a security device where a buyer raises finance on the security of imported goods (so that he can pay for, obtain and sell the goods so that he can then repay the loan) by pledging the bill of lading and other shipping documents to the lender. This requires delivery of the bill and the other documents to the lender, either indorsed to the lender or left blank. The problem is that the buyer needs these very documents to obtain the goods from the shipping company but if the lender parts with possession unconditionally the pledge will be extinguished since it requires the pledgee to have possession. The solution is to have the buyer provide the lender with a 'trust letter' or 'trust receipt' in which he undertakes that, in consideration of the release of the documents to him, he will hold them on trust for the lender and will hold the goods and the proceeds of sale on trust for the lender. This enables the lender to be deemed to continue in constructive possession so that the pledge remains valid.

1.107 There are limits to the use of the trust as a security device because it is not always possible to make something a trust simply by having documents that use the terminology of trusts nor is it possible to have a trust until assets have been specifically transferred or appropriated (ie set apart) to be held upon trust. A supplier of materials to a company can safeguard the supplier's interests, in the event of the company's insolvency without having paid for the materials, if it has reserved legal beneficial ownership of the materials until paid for them and such unpaid for materials remain unsold in the company's possession[1]. The supplier can repossess them. However, if legal title to the materials has passed to the company but the company is supposed, by virtue of the supplier's terms of contract, to hold the materials on trust for the supplier until payment, this is regarded not as a true trust but as an equitable charge over the materials to secure moneys due[2]. Such charge will be void against the company's creditors on liquidation of the company unless registered under the Companies Act 1985 which would then make it impractical to have frequent expeditious dealings with the company's property.

[1]   *Clough Mill v Martin* [1984] 3 All ER 982, [1985] 1 WLR 11, CA; *Armour v Thyssen Edelstahlwerke AG* [1991] 2 AC 339.
[2]   *Clough Mill v Martin* [1984] 3 All ER 982, [1985] 1 WLR 111, CA; *Re Weldtech Equipment Ltd* [1991] BCC 16.

1.108 The position is the same if the so-called 'trust' for the supplier until payment purports to extend to goods manufactured using the supplier's materials and to the proceeds of sale of such goods, such proceeds being required to be paid into a separate 'trust account' to be held as security for payment of moneys due[1]. The position is different, however, and there is a true trust if the manufacturing company holds the legal title to the proceeds on trust for itself and the supplier as equitable tenants in common in ascertainable shares. This will be the case if the company contracts that it will be trustee of a specified fraction of re-sale proceeds received by it or of such fractional part of such proceeds as is equivalent to the amount owing to the supplier at the time of receipt of such proceeds[2].

[1]   *Compaq Computer Ltd v Abercorn Group Ltd* [1991] BCC 484.
[2]   *Associated Alloys Pty Ltd v CAN 001 452 806 Pty Ltd* (2000) 202 CLR 588; *Air Canada v M & L Travel Ltd* (1994) 108 DLR (4th) 592; *Palette Shoes Pty Ltd v Krohn* (1937) 58 CLR 1. Further see para 1.42 above.

1.109 Where a settlor declares itself trustee of only some of its property other than a specific fraction or percentage of a specific asset (eg £5,000 or 500 XYZ Limited shares), then, it should actually set apart the relevant property (eg £5,000 or 500 XYZ Limited shares), as emphasised in a Court of Appeal decision concerned with the retention money trust fund in building construction contracts[1]. Take a contract between an employer and a building contractor containing a clause entitling the employer to retain, say, 5% of money certified by the architect as due to the contractor: half becomes payable when the architect provides the certificate of practical completion and the other half becomes payable when the architect provides the certificate of making good defects. The clause requires the 5% to be paid into a separate retention trust fund to be held by the employer without any obligation to invest it but with a right to any interest produced by the money and a right to use the money to remedy defects in the construction of the contracted for building. If it so happens that the employer does not actually pay the relevant amount of money into a separate account but leaves the money in its own account for its general purposes and then becomes insolvent, the contractor is simply an ordinary unsecured creditor even if, say, £200,000 is due to the contractor under the retention trust clause and there happens to be £250,000 in the employer's own account.

1. *Mac-Jordan Construction Ltd v Brookmount Erostin Ltd* [1992] BCLC 350, approved in *Re Goldcorp Exchange Ltd* [1994] 2 All ER 806, 823, PC; but see paras 8.12–8.21 below.

1.110 By way of contrast, if the employer had contracted or covenanted that it would hold upon trust for the contractor any money received from a specific third party (like the company funding the project releasing an amount equivalent to the retention moneys due) and did so receive, say, £200,000 then, on receipt, that specific £200,000 would become impressed with the trust for the contractor[1]. Equity looks on that as done which ought to be done. The contractor will be able to trace this £200,000 into the company's own account, assuming that there had never been less than £200,000 in such account[2]. If £200,000 had, instead, been spent on acquiring an asset now worth £220,000 then the contractor would instead be able to claim equitable ownership of this traceable product of the £200,000[3].

1. *Pullan v Koe* [1913] 1 Ch 9; *Re Irving ex p Brett* (1877) 7 Ch D 419; *Re Lind* [1915] 2 Ch 345, CA.
2. *Roscoe v Winder* [1915] 1 Ch 62.
3. *El Ajou v Dollar Land Holdings plc* [1993] 3 All ER 717, 735–736; *Foskett v McKeown* [2001] 1 AC 102, 132.

1.111 Similarly, if a solicitor or accountant or architect had received money from a client not paid into the office account, as fees belonging beneficially to the professional person, but paid into the client trust account as money paid on account for fees yet to be incurred and disbursements yet to be made to other, the client could trace payments wrongly paid out of the client account.

1.112 Subordination trusts well exemplify the use of trusts as another means of segregating a person's assets for the benefit of other persons so as to make their position more secure. Subordination is a transaction whereby one creditor, the 'subordinated' or 'junior' creditor, agrees not to be paid by a borrower or other debtor until another creditor, the 'senior' creditor, of the common debtor has been paid. Like the taking of security, subordination is relevant only if the debtor is insolvent because until then both junior and senior creditor can be paid in full. The fundamental object of a subordination is that it should be successful on the debtor's insolvency but, for full efficiency, it needs also to be successful if the junior creditor becomes insolvent. For these purposes, under a 'turnover' agreement the junior creditor can agree to hold whatever he might recover in respect of the junior debt up to the amount of the senior debt upon trust for the senior creditor.

1.113 However, to avoid practical problems (over the registrability of such agreements under the Companies Act 1985, s 395) raised by any doubts as to whether such agreement might constitute a security interest (as in substance a charge over the proceeds of the junior debt to secure the senior debt), it is common to use a trust deed[1]. Under this the junior debt is payable by the debtor to a trustee, who holds what is recovered in respect of the debt on trust first for the benefit of the senior creditor by paying it the amount of the senior debt and, then, anything remaining is held for the benefit of the junior creditors. The debtor's covenant in favour of the trustee can be a covenant parallel to the obligation of the debtor to pay the junior creditors (eg by virtue of their holding of subordinated bonds) and the debtor can be authorised to pay the bondholders direct until an event of default occurs whereupon the debtor must pay the trustee. In these circumstances, there is no charge because the trustee has no property of its own which it can charge, while the junior creditors are simply taking a limited interest under a trust. Payments in respect of the junior debt after the junior creditor's insolvency will not fall into the junior creditor's insolvent estate. The subordination trust will bite on the proceeds as soon as they come into existence even if this is after the insolvency.

1   A trust deed will always be used if there is a large class of junior creditors. Neither subordination trusts nor contractual subordination contravene the application of the fundamental pari passu rule for treatment of creditors in insolvency: *Re British and Commonwealth Holdings plc (No 3)* [1992] 1 WLR 672; *Re Maxwell Communications Corpn plc* (No 2) [1994] 1 All ER 737, [1993] 1 WLR 1402. Also see *Squires v AIG Europe (UK) Ltd* [2006] EWCA Civ 7, [2006] 2 WLR 1369.

1.114 Subordination trusts fulfil many purposes. A senior creditor, like a bank, may wish to subordinate insiders of the debtor, such as a parent company or a major shareholder, eg in the case of project financing. Alternatively, insiders or major suppliers may be persuaded to subordinate their claims to induce bank creditors not to enforce their loans in the hope that the borrower will survive and prosper. A debtor may wish to increase its capital base and have subordinated debt ranking as new primary capital for the purpose of supervision of capital adequacy of banks or insurance companies. Where loans are to finance a take-over or a management buyout on highly leveraged terms, lenders may be prepared to lend on a subordinated basis, encouraging senior lenders to lend more because of the cushion of the junior debt. Because this type of financing is located midway between debt and equity it is referred to as mezzanine debt by professionals, though, because such financing is risky newspapers refer to such bond issues as junk bonds.

1.115 Trusts of corporate special purpose vehicles (SPVs) have a vital role to play in debt securitisation transactions where X Limited with valuable rights to income (eg royalties from intellectual property rights or receivables arising from mortgage or credit card debts or instalments of a debt due to it) wants to sell those rights for an immediate capital sum – and not to have to make any provision in its accounts for possible non-payment of such future income. X Limited can incorporate an SPV the shares in which are held by trustees of a charitable purpose trust or a valid foreign non-charitable purpose trust (and not by X Limited because, if so, the accounts of the SPV would have to appear in the group accounts of X Limited)[1].

[1]   The purpose of securitisation transactions is often to take the creditor's contract claims off the balance sheet of the creditor company, so it is important for the SPV not to be a subsidiary of the company so as to avoid consolidation of the accounts of the SPV and the company. This will be achieved by the company holding the SPV shares on charitable trusts (though expecting little value to be ultimately available for the charitable purposes). Getting assets off the creditor company's balance sheet makes its gearing look better, whilst its financial covenants will not be breached if the SPV gets into difficulties; and in the case of banks it makes it easier to comply with capital ratio requirements.

1.116 On the basis of the income stream flowing to the SPV, it is able to raise the necessary capital by issuing debt securities (eg under a debenture trust deed) with the income stream as security for the capital lent by investors. The SPV is not a commercial company out to make a profit and, ultimately, little is left for the charitable or non-charitable purpose.

1.117 It is also common to use SPVs in ring-fenced project finance. Z Limited may want to acquire an aeroplane or a ship but, because of uncertainties over its financial situation or potential difficulties litigating against it or in respect of the plane or ship as security, Bank B plc will not lend the necessary money to Z Limited. Thus, Z Limited sets up a purpose trust with a reputable trust company, which incorporates an SPV, which buys the plane or ship, using money lent by Bank B plc to the trustee and passed on to the SPV. The Bank's security is the shares in the SPV which will lease the plane or ship to Z Limited for sub-leasing to its customers. The income passing to the SPV is passed up to the trustee and on to the Bank to repay the loan with interest. The Bank is in a strong position with the trustee as the liable borrower and the shares in the SPV as security. If Z Limited does not pay the hire or becomes insolvent the plane or ship can be leased out afresh.

1.118 *Quistclose*[1] trusts are useful temporary security devices. On the basis of the House of Lords' decision in that case, Q Ltd can lend £1 million to R Ltd on trust for a specified purpose (like paying a dividend in 14 days' time or purchasing certain property) but until the specified purpose is carried out, the money is held on trust by R Ltd for Q Ltd, though if the purpose is achieved then R Ltd is simply to be a debtor of Q Ltd in respect of the loan. Thus, if R Ltd went into liquidation within the 14 day period so that it could not pay out the dividend or before purchasing the requisite property, Q Ltd would be treated as equitable owner of the money, which would therefore be unavailable for R Ltd's creditors.

[1]   *Barclays Bank Ltd v Quistclose Investments Ltd* [1970] AC 567, [1968] 3 All ER 651, HL, explained by Lord Millett in *Twinsectra v Yardley* [2002] UKHL 12, paras [68]–[103], [2002] 2 AC 164 on which see para 1.34 above.

1.119 Sinking fund trusts usefully provide security for a lengthy period. Money is regularly paid to trustees so that an adequate amount of money will be available in due course to carry out a particular purpose benefiting persons, eg major repairs or renewals for blocks of flats or for old heritage property, or replacement of oil drilling rigs or land reclamation after working-out of a mine[1].

[1] See 'The Role of the Trust in Environmental Law' by D W M Waters (ed), *Equity, Fiduciaries and Trusts* (1993, Carswell, Canada).

Trading trusts

1.120 Instead of forming a limited company, a trading trust can be created to enable the trustees to carry on a trade for the benefit of beneficiaries under the trust. It is possible for the trust to be simply for A for life, remainder to B, or a discretionary trust for A, B, C and D, their spouses and their descendants and their spouses but, as a business proposition, a trading trust will normally be for the benefit of such persons as may or may become the holders of transferable certificates evidencing beneficial fractional interests or units in the trust fund. In America it seems such persons, under special legislation (eg in Delaware and Massachusetts), can have the same limitation of liability as is extended to shareholders of private companies but in England this is not the case, so that an indemnity can be claimed from such persons by creditors if the trustee, which is usually a limited liability company, does not satisfy their claims.

1.121 Except for tax considerations, there are very few cases where it is sensible to use a trust rather than a company for the conduct of a business because of the risks to creditors that makes them wary of dealing with a trustee[1], eg if the trustee is not wealthy enough to pay the debt or if the trustee acted beyond its or his or her powers or exercised its or his or her powers improperly or if there may be special circumstances preventing any indemnity being obtained from beneficiaries. In England tax considerations rarely favour the creation of a trading trust.

[1] See D J Hayton in J Glasson, *International Trust Laws* (Jordan Publishing, Second edn), Chapter 8 'Trading Trusts, Trustees' Liability & Creditors' Rights'. Further see Trust Law Consultation Paper and the Report *Rights of Creditors Against Trustees and Trust Funds* (www.kcl.ac.uk/depsta/law/tlc).

Unit trusts (or collective investment schemes)

1.122 A unit trust[1] is an investment trust, as opposed to a trading trust[2], and is known in the UK as a collective investment scheme or in the USA as a mutual fund. In the UK one must distinguish between 'unit trust' and 'investment trust' because the latter expression is used as shorthand for an investment trust *company*, a *company* quoted on the London Stock Exchange with the sole activity of making investments, generally in the shares of other companies. A shareholder in an investment trust company has no legal or equitable interest in the investments owned by the company, and the share price will stand at a discount to the net asset value because the current value of the shareholder's shares will depend not just on the underlying current value of the company's investments but also on the dividend policy of the company's board of directors, who generally are subject to fewer controls than the manager of a unit trust. In contrast[3], any unitholder has the right to sell his units to the manager at a price directly corresponding to the underlying current value of the investments in the unit trust, while the manager can issue new units all the time (a unit trust being open-ended with a variable capital, unlike an investment trust company). However, open-ended investment companies[4] (OEICs) as open-ended as unit trusts can now be created with share prices directly reflecting the value of underlying assets, the shareholders having the right to sell their shares to the company for the company to purchase at a price reflecting the value of the underlying assets.

1 Generally, see K F Sin *The Legal Nature of the Unit Trust* (Oxford University Press, 1997) especially pp 284–292.

2 Exceptionally, it is possible, however, to insert in a private trust deed that the trustees are to carry on trading activities and to divide the income and capital profits into, say, 100 units then allocated amongst specified beneficiaries, who could then dispose of such units, e g by sale or by declaring discretionary sub-trusts of such units.

3 Another contrast is that shareholders have a right to attend an Annual General Meeting and vote on various matters so as to bind the company, whilst beneficiaries have no right to such a meeting where they can exercise voting rights to bind the trustees unless the trust instrument expressly confers such a right upon them, e g debenture trusts. Unit trust holders are not members of any company or partnership: *Smith v Anderson* (1880) 15 Ch D 247, CA.

4 See Financial Services and Markets Act 2000, s 236, and Regulations thereunder in the Financial Services Authority's Collective Investment Scheme Sourcebook. Both OEICs and authorised unit trusts rank as Undertakings for Collective Investment in Transferable Securities within the EU UCITS Directive [1985] OJ L375/3 as amended inter alia by Directive 2001/108 in [2002] OJ L041.

1.123 It is the manager who sets up the arrangement embodied in the trust deed with the independent corporate trustee and then finds investors to provide the money to be forwarded by the manager to the trustee, who then issues unit certificates to the investors. The trustee acts as a type of custodian trustee to hold the investors' money and investments purchased with the money on the terms of the trust deed subject to the provisions of the Financial Services and Markets Act 2000. It must follow all instructions properly given by the manager who manages the portfolio of investments but, where the unit trust is an authorised unit trust open to public subscription, it must take reasonable care to ensure that the manager acts within its powers, keeps adequate records and manages the scheme in accordance with the Regulations for Collective Investment Schemes. Section 253 of the Financial Services and Markets Act 2000 prevents the trustee or manager being exempted from liability for 'any failure to exercise due care and diligence in the discharge of' their functions, while s 243(4) and (5) require the manager and the trustee to be companies incorporated in the UK or another European Economic Area state and to be independent of each other.

1.124 Unit trusts not authorised by the Financial Services Authority under the Financial Services and Markets Act 2000, ss 242–248 cannot be sold to the public and have such tax disadvantages that, in practice, unit holders are confined to bodies exempt from charge to tax on capital gains, eg pension funds and charities. In recent years the types of investments that can be held by a unit trust if it is to be an authorised unit trust have been much extended so that there can be futures and options funds, geared futures and options funds, property funds and warrant funds.

1.125 The persons who participate in a unit trust by subscribing for units are not beneficiaries with equitable proprietary interests as equitable co-owners of the property held by the custodian trustee until the time comes for termination of the trust pursuant to the terms of the trust deed as set up by the manager of the trust[1]. Before such termination they have no *Saunders v Vautier*[2] collective right to divide the assets held by the trustee between themselves, the terms of their contract of subscription as reflected in the trust deed ousting such right. They only have individual contractual rights to a sum of money representing a proportion of the net value calculated and realisable as provided in the trust deed, though, as in the case of a pension trust[3], the trust property is available as security for their personal claim as is the traceable product of the trust property (such product itself being part of the trust fund) while the existence of the trust automatically imposes fiduciary obligations upon the trustee and the manager, except to the extent of any contrary provision in the trust deed, so far as permitted by the Financial Services and Markets Act 2000.

[1] The manager will only be settlor of the nominal sum initially transferred to the trustee so as to create a completely constituted trust of such sum before (as in the case of pension trusts: *Air Jamaica Ltd v Charlton* [1999] 1 WLR 1399, paras 32–33) each participant contributes money as a settlor of a separate settlement with contractual rights and ultimately equitable tenancy in common proprietary rights if still a unit-holder when the trust terminates.
[2] (1841) 10 LJ Ch 354, Article 69 below.
[3] *Air Jamaica Ltd v Charlton* [1999] 1 WLR 1399, para 33.

1.126 Thus, while it is true that s 237(1) of the Financial Services and Markets Act 2000 states 'Unit Trust Scheme' means 'a collective investment scheme under which the property is held on trust for the participants', one needs to appreciate that during the continuance of the unit trust the participants are to be regarded as passive investors[1] owning choses in action to produce a cash return from a ring-fenced fund which is security for such claims. This is because they have contractually agreed to this.

[1] See Financial Services and Markets Act 2000, s 235(2).

Pension fund trusts

1.127 Occupational pension schemes are the main form of private pension arrangement in the UK, their main purpose being to provide income after retirement from work but they usually also provide a lump sum on retirement or death during employment and make provision for early retirement on grounds of ill-health or disability. Over 11 million employees are members of occupational pension schemes while 6 million receive occupational pensions. Outside statutory schemes for public sector employees occupational pension schemes are set up as irrevocable trusts so that they are approved by the Revenue[1] and so receive favourable tax treatment.

[1]   Income and Corporation Taxes Act 1988, ss 590–591: see Revenue Practice Notes on the Approval of Occupational Pension Schemes.

1.128 In the case of defined benefit (or final salary) schemes both employer and employee pay contributions to trustees for them to build up a large trust fund that is security[1] for payment to scheme members of their pensions (eg one sixtieth or one eightieth of the final pensionable salary for each year of employment with the employer or a group of employers). The scheme will often also provide death-in-service benefits or disability benefits, a lump sum benefit on retirement (eg of the amount of one year's salary) and benefits for a widow or dependants. The employee's contributions are fixed so it is the employer which bears the risk of ensuring it covers the cost of providing the benefits. It also meets the costs of running the scheme which is much more complex than running a defined contribution (or money purchase) scheme.

[1]   *Air Jamaica Ltd v Charlton* [1999] 1 WLR 1399, 1408; *Wrightson Ltd v Fletcher Challenge Nominees Ltd* [2001] UKPC 23, para 28.

1.129 In such a scheme the employee and usually the employer, but to a lesser extent than the employee, pay contributions to trustees, to invest with a life assurance company[1] on behalf of each contributing employee. The benefits obtained by the employee depend on the returns achieved by the assurance company when investing the contributions so as to achieve an aggregate amount that the employee uses to purchase an annuity depending upon annuity rates at the relevant time. The employer is thus free from the risk and extra cost inherent in defined benefit schemes, while its balance sheet does not have to provide for any prospective deficit that needs to be made good.

[1]   Life assurance companies are strictly regulated so as to make their insolvency most unlikely.

1.130 Employees receive less than under defined benefit schemes but mobile employees benefit by carrying their rights with them from one employment to another: in defined benefit schemes such employees have to leave their benefits in their old scheme as deferred benefits to be taken at retirement or have their new employment scheme receive from the trustees of the defined benefit scheme a transfer value as determined by such trustees[1].

[1]   If the employee left employment within two years he is only entitled to a return of his actual contributions.

1.131 Due to the government removing from pension trusts the tax-free perquisite for share dividends (worth £5 billion pa), a poor three year performance of the stock markets, and a tightening up of accounting rules for deficits in defined benefit schemes, many employers have closed their defined benefit schemes and replaced them with defined contribution schemes. Indeed, some employers have gone into liquidation and wound up their pension schemes in deficit, leading to the government in the Pensions Act 2004 establishing a Pension Protection Fund and conferring strong regulatory powers upon a Pensions Regulator assisted by a Determinations Tribunal.

1.132 The Pensions Act 2004 has also built upon the protection accorded scheme-members by the Pensions Act 1995 and the Pension Schemes Act 1993, the latter creating a Pensions Ombudsman with wide powers to intervene to remedy injustice in consequence of maladministration or breaches of trust.

1.133 Because scheme-members are settlor-beneficiaries, each being settlor of a separate settlement[1], who have earned their rights as deferred remuneration and so are not volunteers like beneficiaries in family trusts, they have more extensive rights against the trustees than volunteer beneficiaries have when trustees' discretion is involved[2].

1   *Air Jamaica Ltd v Charlton* [1999] 1 WLR 1399.
2   See D J Hayton, 'Pension Trusts and Traditional Trusts: Drastically Differing Species of Trusts' [2005] Conv 229; *Sieff v Fox* [2005] WTLR 891, para 77.

Employee trusts

1.134 It is in the public interest to encourage employees of a company to work hard so as to improve the profitability of the company and thereby increase the value of shares in the company. Accordingly, favourable tax exemptions exist to enable shares in the company to be transferred to trustees to set them aside for particular employees, who will then only be liable to income tax on dividends and who, on sale of their shares after five years, will only be liable to capital gains tax[1]. An employee share ownership plan involves two trusts. First, a general employee trust which buys shares in the company, using company funds or borrowed money guaranteed by the company, and, second, a profit sharing trust which buys from the general trust company shares with moneys provided by the company and appropriates shares to particular employees. This structure has tax advantages, while the employee trust provides a ready market for the sale of shares in a private company and provides a possible defence mechanism against a hostile take-over bid.

1   See Income and Corporation Taxes Act 1988, ss 186–187 and Schs 9 and 10; Finance Act 1989, ss 67–73 and Sch 5; Taxation of Chargeable Gains Act 1992, ss 227–229 as amended.

Miscellaneous commercial uses of trusts

1.135 Businessmen can use trusts for any purpose benefiting persons if such purpose be a sensible business purpose and the use of the trust involves no practical or tax disadvantages. Some miscellaneous examples are as follows:

(a)   To deal with the death of a partner there may be a partnership buy-sell agreement funded by insurance held by a trustee for the partners. The insurance money will provide funds to enable the surviving partners to buy the interest of the deceased partner, thereby avoiding sale of the partnership assets which might jeopardise the business.

(b)   To reduce or eliminate tax relating to intellectual property royalties the owner may assign the right to receive royalties to a trust situated in a low tax or no-tax jurisdiction (or to a company so situated). It is important that the jurisdiction is party to various international conventions enabling the mutual recognition of each other's intellectual property rights so that rights to royalties can be enforced.

(c)   To further the best interests of a family in a family company, the elderly founder of the company may rely much on his second son, B, who is managing director and who has a 26% shareholding. By his will the founder might leave his 54% shareholding to B on trust for the founder's three other children, A, C and D, if alive at B's death or his earlier attainment of the age of 65 years (with a substitutionary clause for the issue of A, C and D if A, C or D die before the contingency[1] is satisfied). This allows the business-minded B to control matters in the best interests of the family.

[1]   If the interests are not contingent but absolute then the beneficiaries will be able to call for the trust property to be transferred to themselves and so frustrate the settlor's purposes: see Article 69 below.

1.136 At B's death aged 64 it may be that his children, E and F, have a 13% shareholding each, while the deceased A's only child has an 18% shareholding, the deceased C's two children each have a 9% shareholding, while D has an 18% shareholding. They can contract with each other for their shares to be held by a trustee to vote the rights on the shares as the parties direct in respect of the shares to which they are respectively entitled but, in the event of an offer being made to acquire all or any part of the shares, if a specified majority of the parties wish to dispose of their shares then the trustee is to take such action as in his opinion is likely to result in all the trust shares being disposed of to the best advantage. There can be further provisions preventing any party from disposing of his equitable interest in his shares under the trust unless first offering it to the other parties at a fair value to be fixed by an independent valuer if not agreed[1].

[1]   See, eg *Booth v Ellard* [1980] 3 All ER 569, [1980] 1 WLR 1443, CA.

1.137 Another example of a voting trust is to cater for a joint venture of A and B carried on via a company the shares in which are mainly owned by A but B is to enjoy a higher percentage of voting rights than his minority shareholding warrants. A could contractually bind himself to vote certain of his shares as B directs but if A broke the agreement and voted against B's instructions the votes would be validly cast and bind the company. To avoid this the shares and voting rights can be vested in an independent trustee to hold dividends, etc for A but to vote as directed by B who will know that the trustee will vote as directed.

Conclusion

1.138 The lack of rigid formal requirements for the creation and operation of trusts, unlike companies, and the tremendous flexibility allowed in inserting clauses in trust instruments make the trust a very useful device for achieving any commercial purpose if there are no tax disadvantages in its use and no practical disadvantages flowing from its lack of legal personality. Maitland, a great legal historian and trusts lawyer, has written[1]:

> 'If we were asked what is the greatest and most distinctive achievement performed by Englishmen in the field of jurisprudence I cannot think that we should have any better answer to give than this, namely the development from century to century of the trust idea.'

[1] *Selected Essays* (1936) p 129.

ARTICLE 2
LEGAL AND EQUITABLE ESTATES AND INTERESTS

2.1

The interest of a beneficiary in trust property is called an equitable interest because it was originally only recognised in courts of equity. A legal estate or interest, on the other hand, is that proprietary interest which has been acquired with all the formalities which are required by the common or statute law for conferring a complete title to such interest, though it may have subsequently devolved automatically upon the death of one or more title-holders. A trustee usually, but not necessarily or always, has the legal title to trust property: it is, however, possible for a trustee to hold an equitable interest upon trust for beneficiaries.

Estates and interests

2.2 As a preliminary matter, since 1925 the only legal estates in land[1] are an estate in fee simple absolute in possession (a freehold estate) and a term of years absolute (a leasehold estate), while all other estates in land (eg an estate for life) take effect only as equitable interests[2]. Technically, the Crown owns all land in England and Wales, so that persons can only own an estate or interest in land (or a charge or right over land[3]). In the case of chattels and choses in action, a person can be absolute beneficial owner thereof or can be owner thereof as trustee for persons with equitable interests under fixed or discretionary trusts.

[1] Law of Property Act 1925, s 1(1).
[2] Law of Property Act 1925, s 1(3). The fee tail estate or entailed interest (enduring so long as the grantee had issue, whether restricted to makes or unrestricted) can no longer be created: Trusts of Land and Appointment of Trustees Act 1996, Sch 1, para 5.
[3] For legal charges and legal rights over land see Law of Property Act 1925, s 1(2).

Distinction between legal and equitable interests still important

2.3 The fundamental and ineradicable distinctions which existed between legal and equitable estates or interests remain despite the so-called 'fusion' of law and equity[1]. As Lord Selborne said, in introducing the Judicature Act 1873 into the House of Lords:

2.3 Preliminary terminology

'if trusts are to continue, there must be a distinction between what we call a legal and equitable estate. The legal estate is in the person who holds the property for another; the equitable estate is in the person beneficially interested. The distinction between law and equity is, within certain limits, real and natural, and it would be a mistake to suppose that what is real and natural ought to be disregarded.'[2]

1   For exposure of the fusion fallacy see Jill Martin [1994] Conv 13, Meagher, Gummow and Lehane, *Equity: Doctrines and Remedies* (Fourth edn) paras2–100 to 2–320; *Schalit v Joseph Nadler Ltd* [1933] 2 KB 79; *Chan v Cresdon Pty Ltd* (1989) 168 CLR 242 at 252–256; *Parker-Tweedale v Dunbar Bank plc* [1991] Ch 12, [1990] 2 All ER 577, CA; *Downsview Nominees Ltd v First City Corpn Ltd* [1993] AC 295, [1993] 3 All ER 626, PC; *Silven Properties v Royal Bank of Scotland* [2003] EWCA Civ 1409, [2004] 1 WLR 997, CA; *MCC Proceeds Inc v Lehman Bros International (Europe) Ltd* [1998] 4 All ER 675 at 691. The Act was intended only to be procedural as recognised by Jessel MR in *Salt v Cooper* (1880) 16 Ch D 544 at 549, though 'there is no reason why the courts in shaping principles, whether their origins lie in the common law or in Equity, should not have regard to both common law and equitable concept and doctrines, borrowing from either as may be appropriate' as Sir Anthony Mason stated in Waters (ed), *Equity, Fiduciaries and Trusts* (1993, Carswell) pp 7–8. Further, see S Degeling and J Edelman (eds), *Equity in Commercial Law*, Chapter 11 'Unique Rules for the Unique Institution, the Trust' (D J Hayton).
2   Hansard (NS), Vol 214, p 333, and see Lord Cairns' views in *Pugh v Heath* (1882) 7 App Cas 235 at 237.

2.4 Legal estates and interests still subsist; and although equitable interests are now recognised by all branches of the Supreme Court, and may therefore in a sense be called legal, it has been found more convenient to retain the old nomenclature, 'legal' and 'equitable', signifying, as it does, a real and substantial difference, which would still exist, even although the terms had themselves been abolished. In the case of land this is recognised by the Law of Property Act 1925[1].

1   See Settled Land Act 1925, s 1(1), (3), s 4 and s 205(1) which defines 'legal estates' and 'equitable interests'.

Title of trustees not necessarily legal

2.5 It must not, however, be assumed that the title or interest of a trustee is always legal. The beneficial interest of the beneficiary is always equitable, so long as the trust subsists; but so also may be the interest of the trustee. For instance, the trust property may consist of the equitable interest of a tenant in common or an equitable life interest under another settlement. Exceptionally, under the Settled Land Act 1925, the trustees of settled land, unless they are statutory owners, have no interest or estate therein at all. Instead, the beneficiary who is the life tenant holds the legal estate on trust for himself and the other beneficiaries. This enables him to manage the trust, though capital moneys (eg arising upon a sale) must be paid to the Settled Land Act trustees, who then need to invest or apply the monies in their discretion after consulting the tenant for life, so as to give effect to his wishes so far as consistent with the general interest of the settlement[1].

1   Settled Land Act 1925, s 75 as substituted by Trustee Act 2000, Sch 2, para 10.

Importance of difference between legal and equitable interests

2.6 The difference between legal and equitable interests is not merely of theoretical interest. A legal title prevails against the whole world unless statute-barred[1] whilst an equitable title does not prevail against a bona fide purchaser of a legal interest for value without notice of the equitable interest affecting it[2] or against a purchaser of a legal estate who, by paying capital money to two trustees or a trust corporation, complies with the overreaching provisions of the Law of Property Act 1925 or the Settled Land Act 1925 or the Land Registration Act 1925 or 2002. Where a question of priority arises between two claimants with equitable interests then the equitable interest that arose first in time will prevail over the second unless the first claimant was fraudulent or grossly negligent or is otherwise estopped from claiming priority[3]. Thus a purchaser of an equitable interest without notice will not normally take free of prior equitable interests even if, in the case of registered land, he protects his interest, being a minor interest, by an entry (eg of a notice) on the register[4].

1   *Wyld v Silver* [1963] Ch 243, [1962] 3 All ER 309; *Benn v Hardinge* (1992) 66 P & CR 246, CA.
2   *Pilcher v Rawlins* (1872) 7 Ch App 259; *Wilkes v Spooner* [1911] 2 KB 473; *MCC Proceeds Inc v Lehman Brothers International (Europe) Ltd* [1998] 4 All ER 675 where it was crucial whether the claimant had a legal interest as bailee or only an equitable interest as beneficiary under a trust.
3   *Freeguard v Royal Bank of Scotland plc* (1998) 79 P & CR 81, CA; *Rice v Rice* (1854) 2 Drew 73; *Capell v Winter* [1907] 2 Ch 376. If the second claimant was a purchaser of his equitable interest without notice he could obtain priority over the prior equitable interest if he subsequently acquired the legal estate without being a party to a breach of trust: *Bailey v Barnes* [1894] 1 Ch 25 at 36; *McCarthy & Stone Ltd v J S Hodge & Co Ltd* [1971] 1 WLR 1547 at 1556.
4   Land Registration Act 2002, s 28.

Distinction between equitable interests and mere equities

2.7 An equity which is ancillary to or dependent upon an interest in land[1] (eg a right to recover property by having a conveyance or lease set aside for fraud or undue influence or rectified)[2] must be distinguished from an equitable interest, though some old cases refer indiscriminately to equitable interests as equities. A purchaser of an equitable (or legal) interest without notice of the equity will take free of the equity[3] and the nature of a mere equity means that a purchaser is quite likely to have no notice of it[4]. It follows that a purchaser of an equitable interest without notice should also be immune from any equitable proprietary remedy against any substituted assets ascertained via the tracing process, where the claim relates to a mere equity, eg to rescind for undue influence.

1   *National Provincial Bank Ltd v Ainsworth* [1965] AC 1175 at 1238, HL per Lord Upjohn.
2   *Ernest v Vivian* (1863) 33 LJ Ch 513; *Latec Investments Ltd v Hotel Terrigal Pty Ltd* (1965) 113 CLR 265; *Bainbrigge v Browne* (1881) 18 Ch D 188; *Garrard v Frankel* (1862) 30 Beav 445; *Smith v Jones* [1954] 2 All ER 823, [1954] 1 WLR 1089.
3   *Philips v Philips* (1861) 4 De GF & J 208 at 218; *Allied Irish Banks Ltd v Glynn* [1973] IR 188; Lord Millett in (1998) 114 LQR 399 at 416.
4   *Smith v Jones* [1954] 1 WLR 1089.

2.8 Preliminary terminology

Registered land: overriding and minor interests

2.8 If a person in actual occupation of land happens to have either an equitable interest[1] or a mere equity[2], that is not protected by entry on the register, this ranks as an overriding interest[3], unless inquiry was made of him and he failed to disclose his interest. An overriding interest binds the whole world irrespective of notice[4]. Exceptionally, equitable interests under Settled Land Act settlements cannot be overriding interests and so, as minor interests, will be void against subsequent purchasers unless protected by entry of a restriction on the register of title[5].

1   *Hodgson v Marks* [1971] Ch 892, [1971] 2 All ER 684, CA; *Williams & Glyn's Bank v Boland* [1981] AC 487, [1980] 2 All ER 408, HL.
2   *Blacklocks v J B Developments (Godalming) Ltd* [1982] Ch 183, [1981] 3 All ER 392, Land Registration Act 2002, s 116.
3   Land Registration Act 1925, ss 70(1)(g), 3(xvi) replaced by Land Registration Act 2002, ss 29–30 and Sch 3, para 2. However, if the inherent nature of the interest (eg a co-ownership interest) is overreachable then it will be overreached on payment of capital moneys to two trustees or a trust corporation: *City of London Building Society v Flegg* [1988] AC 54, [1987] 3 All ER 435, HL; *Birmingham Midshires Mortgage Services Ltd v Sabherwal* (1999) 80 P & CR 256, CA. In an exceptional case, irrespective of the position according to principles of property law, equity may act in personam against the conscience of the purchaser or mortgagee to prevent him getting away with unconscionable behaviour: *Ashburn Anstalt v Arnold* [1989] Ch 1, [1988] 2 All ER 147, CA.
4   *Williams & Glyn's Bank v Boland* [1981] AC 487, [1980] 2 All ER 408, HL; Land Registration Act 2002, ss 29–30.
5   Land Registration Act 2002, ss 33(a), 40 and Sch 3, para 2(a).

Rights in rem and in personam

2.9 There has been some controversy over the nature of an equitable interest under a trust[1]. To what extent is the beneficiary's interest a right in rem and to what extent a right in personam?

1   (1899) 15 LQR 294 (Hart); (1917) 17 Col LR 269 (A W Scott); (1917) 17 Col LR 467 (H Stone); (1954) 32 Can BR 510 (V Latham); (1967) 45 Can BR 219 (D Waters).

2.10 It has often been said that legal interests are rights in rem whilst equitable interests are rights in personam. Since rights are given only against persons not things, what is meant is that legal rights prevail against persons generally whilst equitable rights prevail against a limited group of persons[1]. This limited group originally comprised persons who were not bona fide purchasers of a legal estate for value without notice and now includes persons who are not able to take advantage of special protective provisions in the 1925 property legislation, eg the overreaching provisions of the Law of Property Act 1925, the registration provisions of the Land Charges Acts 1925 and 1972 and of the Land Registration Act 1925 or 2002.

1   Exceptionally, if the equitable interest is owned by an actual occupier of registered land it can rank as an overriding interest so as to bind persons generally: Land Registration Act 2002, Sch 3, para 2.

2.11 It is also said that equitable rights under trusts are rights *in personam* because each trust beneficiary has a personal right against the trustees to ensure due performance of the trusts and to ensure that the trustees properly discharge their duties. This well reflects the practical working of the trust. Thus where D holds a French immovable on trust for C but refuses to transfer it to C when C demands this, C's legal proceedings in England are not 'proceedings which have as their object rights *in rem* in immovable property'[1], when the court of the French *lex situs* would have had exclusive jurisdiction. C's action is only *in personam*, seeking only to assert rights against D. The immovable nature of the property and its location are irrelevant to the issues (whether D held the property on trust for C under a resulting trust and so could be compelled to transfer it to C), which would have been the same if the dispute had concerned a London flat or a yacht.

[1] *Webb v Webb* [1994] QB 696. Also see *Ashurst v Pollard* [2001] 2 All ER 75. However, if a foreign court is first seised of divorce proceedings, an English resident spouse will have any Trusts of Land and Appointment of Trustees Act 1996 application concerning a share in English immovables stayed under Article 28 of Regulation 44 of 2001 so that the foreign court can deal with all property owned by the spouses in resolving the financial side of the divorce: *Prazic v Prazic* [2006] EWCA Civ 497 [2006] All ER (D) 246 (May).

2.12 On the other hand, a beneficiary does have a right in rem in the sense of a 'real' or 'proprietary' right because he can exercise equitable proprietary remedies against strangers in possession of the trust property or its traceable product, taking advantage of the tracing process to ascertain such product[1]. If, however, the trustee sold the trust property to a bona fide purchaser and then dissipated the proceeds of sale, the beneficiary is left merely with his equitable chose in action against the trustee which will be worthless if the trustee is bankrupt.

[1] In *Re Diplock* [1948] Ch 465 at 475–476 the Court of Appeal thus used 'in rem' to cover the equitable proprietary remedy against substituted assets ascertained via the tracing process.

2.13 A beneficiary may similarly be regarded as interested in the res, the subject of the trust, where he is a sane adult absolutely indefeasibly entitled as against the trustees to the trust property within the *Saunders v Vautier* principle[1]. Where a beneficiary (eg an adult life tenant) is currently entitled to income produced by the trust property he is taxable on his income from the stocks, shares etc comprising the trust property as soon as it is received by the trustees[2] rather than when it is received by him from the trustees pursuant to their personal duty to account to him for it[3]. He is regarded as having part of the equitable ownership of the assets themselves[4] so if they are foreign he is treated as interested in foreign assets. Thus, if property is held in trust for A for life, remainder to B absolutely, A is regarded as having an equitable life interest in the actual property and B an absolute equitable interest in remainder in such property: after all, between them, A and B, if they agree, can call for the property to be vested in them or otherwise dealt with as they direct.

[1] See Article 69 below.
[2] *Baker v Archer-Shee* [1927] AC 844; *IRC v Hamilton-Russell's Executors* (1943) 25 TC 200 at 207–208; *Spens v IRC* [1970] 3 All ER 295 at 299; *IRC v Berrill* [1982] 1 All ER 867 at 880; *New Zealand Insurance Co Ltd v Probate Duties Commissioner (Victoria)* [1973] VR 619.

3   Some foreign jurisdictions take this view or used to take this view: *Archer-Shee v Garland*
     [1931] AC 212, HL, also making it clear that English law will recognise the nature of
     rights under a foreign settlement as governed by the foreign proper law; see also *Re
     Fitzgerald* [1904] 1 Ch 573.
4   *New Zealand Insurance Co Ltd v Probate Duties Comr* [1973] VR 659; *Cholmondeley v
     IRC* [1986] STC 384; *Perpetual Trustee Co Ltd v Commissioner of Stamp Duties* [1977]
     2 NSWLR 472.

2.14 A beneficiary under a discretionary trust (eg to trustees on trust to distribute the income in their absolute discretion between such of B, C and D, their spouses and issue as they see fit) is in a specially weak position. His hope of receiving income is not a full equitable proprietary interest capable of assignment by way of gift, though he can release his equitable right to be considered for receipt of income[1]. It seems that the discretionary trustees (somewhat like personal representatives of an unadministered estate[2] and a company subject to a winding up order)[3] have ownership subject to onerous fiduciary duties in circumstances where the beneficiaries have no full equitable proprietary interest but only a hope that the trustees in performing their duty to distribute income in their discretion will actually exercise their discretion in favour of the hopeful beneficiary. However, discretionary beneficiaries, as well as having personal rights to make their trustees account for the trusteeship[4], may exercise proprietary remedies to restore property or its traceable product to the trust, taking advantage of the tracing process to ascertain such product. They can be in no less a position than that of beneficiaries of an unadministered estate, who, on behalf of such estate, are entitled to have the estate's property or the traceable product thereof restored to the estate if the personal representative wrongly takes no action[5].

1   *Re Gulbenkian's Settlement (No 2)* [1970] Ch 408, [1969] 2 All ER 1173.
2   *Stamp Duties Comr (Queensland) v Livingston* [1965] AC 694, [1964] 3 All ER 692;
     Marshall v Kerr [1995] 1 AC 148.
3   *Commissioner of Taxation v Linter Textiles Australia Ltd (in liquidation)* [2005] High Ct
     of Australia 20.
4   *Schmidt v Rosewood Trust Ltd* [2003] UKPC 26, [2003] 2 AC 709.
5   *Re Atkinson* [1971] VR 613.

2.15 Because a beneficiary under a fixed or a discretionary trust has proprietary remedies against third parties owning substituted trust assets ascertained via the tracing process, it is proper to regard beneficiaries under either type of trust as having proprietary *in rem* rights. However, a discretionary beneficiary only has the right to have the recovered traced property added back to the trust fund in the hope that some thereof may, perhaps, be distributed to him pursuant to an exercise of the trustee's discretion. In contrast, L, a life tenant, is himself absolutely entitled to obtain traceable income, while the lost traceable capital has to be restored to the trust fund, to which R will become absolutely entitled on L's death where the trust was for L for life, remainder to R. Thus, in concerning oneself with external aspects of the trust in trying to trace and recover trust property and its traceable product, beneficiaries have *in rem* rights, but so far as concerns the internal operation of a trust the beneficiaries have *in personam* rights against the trustees for the proper performance of the trusts. The *situs* of a discretionary beneficiary's equitable chose in action has to be where the trustee resides and administers the trust (in the absence of contrary statutory provision), although in the case of a beneficiary absolutely entitled to income or to both capital and income, the Revenue can justifiably claim that such beneficiary has an *in rem* interest located where the trust assets are located.

ARTICLE 3
EXPRESS, STATUTORY, RESULTING AND CONSTRUCTIVE TRUSTS

3.1

(1) Trusts:
   (a) are duly[1] created intentionally by an express or inferred declaration of trust of the settlor, in which case they are called express trusts; or
   (b) are imposed by a statute[2] expressly or by necessary implication, in which case they are called statutory trusts; or
   (c) are imposed by a court applying principles of equity so that, while the legal title to property is in one person, the equitable right to the beneficial enjoyment thereof is in another, the legal title then being subject to a resulting trust or a constructive trust.

(2) A resulting trust[3] of property is imposed in a transferor's favour where (i) a transferor gratuitously transfers or causes a transfer of property he owns or purchases to a transferee (other than the transferor's spouse or child) or where there is an enforceable[4] express or inferred declaration of trust affecting property transferred to the trustee but the transferor fails to divest himself wholly of his beneficial interest so that an undisposed-of interest is in the trustee's hands, and in either case (ii) there is no evidence that the transferor intended to make a gift or loan or to abandon all interest in the property.

(3) A constructive trust[5] of property is imposed on proof of recognised categories of special circumstances where a court considers it unconscionable for the owner of the property to hold it for his own benefit to the entire exclusion of the claimant.

(4) The term 'implied trust' has been used by parliamentary counsel and the courts as a generic term connoting resulting and constructive trusts, but confusingly they have also used the term in several other ways. To avoid such confusion the term is best avoided altogether.

[1] Duly complying with requisite formalities, eg Law of Property Act 1925, s 53(1)(b).
[2] For example, the trusts declared by ss 313 and 314 of the Companies Act 1985 of certain sums improperly received by directors as compensation for loss of office; the trusts arising in respect of legal estates conveyed to minors or co-owned under Law of Property Act 1925, ss 19, 34–36 (as amended by Trusts of Land and Appointment of Trustees Act 1996); the trusts arising on intestacy under Administration of Estates Act 1925, s 33.
[3] See Articles 28 and 29–32.

3.1 *Preliminary terminology*

⁴   See Law of Property Act 1925, s 53(1)(b).
⁵   See Articles 28 and 33–36.

Express trusts distinguished from resulting and constructive trusts

3.2 The distinction between (1) express trusts and (2) resulting or constructive trusts is vital as far as the formalities for the creation of trusts are
concerned[1]. Furthermore, a person incapable of being an express trustee may
be a trustee of a resulting or constructive trust[2]. A trust is an express trust
whether expressed in certain unambiguous language or inferred from relatively uncertain ambiguous words and conduct of the settlor, eg where a
testator uses some precatory words of entreaty, prayer or expectation intending them exceptionally to be imperative and binding in a special context[3]. In
the event that a person intending to declare an express trust fails to comply
with the requisite statutory formalities, his intention may still be perfected in
some cases by the imposition of a resulting trust or a constructive trust or a
proprietary estoppel interest.

1   Law of Property Act 1925, s 53(1), (2).
2   *Re Vinogradoff* [1935] WN 68.
3   *Comiskey v Bowring-Hanbury* [1905] AC 84; *Paul v Constance* [1977] 1 WLR 527.

Resulting trusts

3.3 Resulting trusts are trusts imposed by law on property in the hands of a
gratuitous transferee (ie a transferee who has provided no valuable consideration for the transfer) and which carry the beneficial interest back to the
transferor. The transferor is either the owner of the transferred property or in
the case of property purchased by him and caused to be transferred to such
transferee is the purchaser rather than the actual transferor-vendor. In many
cases where property is gratuitously transferred, there is evidence that the
transferor intended to make a gift or loan or, in a very rare case, to abandon
his interest in the property, in which cases the law will give effect to that
intention, and no question will arise of a resulting trust being imposed[1].
Likewise, if the evidence reveals that the transferor made an enforceable
express or inferred declaration of trust of property gratuitously transferred
into the name of, or bought by the transferor in the name of, the transferee,
then the law will give effect to that express trust, assuming compliance with
the requisite formalities[2]. Thus resulting trusts are imposed only in cases
where property is gratuitously transferred and there is insufficient evidence to
ascertain the transferor's intention. In these circumstances the law will raise a
presumption in the transferor's favour that the transferor 'does not intend to
part with the beneficial interest in the property'[3].

1   *Air Jamaica Ltd v Charlton* [1999] 1 WLR 1399 at 1412 per Lord Millett; *Twinsectra Ltd
     v Yardley* [2000] WTLR 527 at 562 per Potter LJ; *Lavelle v Lavelle* [2004] EWCA Civ
     223, [2004] 2 FCR 418 at [14] per Lord Phillips MR.
2   In *Hodgson v Marks* [1971] Ch 892, where A transferred her house to B on oral trust for
     A (unenforceable for failing to satisfy Law of Property Act 1925, s 53(1)(b)) the CA held
     that B held the house on trust for A nonetheless. On one view this was an express trust
     imposed to prevent statute being used as an instrument of fraud (*Rochefoucauld v
     Boustead* [1897] 1 Ch 196, CA, applying: W J Swadling, 'A Hard Look at *Hodgson v*

Marks' in P Birks and F Rose (eds), *Restitution and Equity Vol 1: Resulting Trusts and Equitable Compensation* (2000) at p 61). Alternatively, it was a resulting trust responding to A's lack of intent to benefit B: R Chambers, *Resulting Trusts* (1997) at p 25.

3   Per Lord Phillips MR in *Lavelle v Lavelle* [2004] EWCA Civ 223, [2004] 2 FCR 418 at [14].

3.4 Failure to rebut this presumption by the transferee will then lead to the imposition of a resulting trust, but it should always be borne in mind that, as Lord Upjohn once observed[1], 'In reality, the so-called presumption of a resulting trust is no more than a long-stop to provide the answer when the relevant facts and circumstances fail to yield a solution.'. Exceptionally, even where there is no evidence of the transferor's intention, a presumption will not be raised if the property in question is land because s 60(3) of the Law of Property Act 1925 ousts the presumption where a person gratuitously transfers land to another[2]. Note also that a presumption will not be raised if the transferor is the transferee's spouse or parent because in those circumstances the law raises a presumption of advancement, presuming that the transferor intended to make a gift to the transferee[3].

1   *Vandervell v IRC* [1967] 2 AC 291 at 313. See too *Stockholm Finance Ltd v Garden Holdings Inc* (26 October 1995, unreported) Ch D per Robert Walker J and *Ali v Khan* (2002) 5 ITELR 232 at [30] per Morritt V-C.
2   See paras 31.62–31.63.
3   See paras 31.36–31.42.

3.5 Resulting trusts were formerly understood to fall into two separate categories: 'automatic' and 'presumed' resulting trusts. In *Re Vandervell's Trusts (No 2)*[1] Megarry J held that the former arise 'automatically' when some or all of the beneficial interest in property held on an express trust has not been disposed of by the settlor, whereas the latter arise following a gratuitous transferee's failure to rebut the presumption that the transferor intended to retain the beneficial interest in the property. However, in *Westdeutsche Landesbank Girozentrale v Islington London Borough Council*[2], Lord Browne-Wilkinson rightly observed that there is no real difference between these two classes of case. In the first case, as in the second, a resulting trust will not arise if the evidence clearly shows that the settlor intended some other outcome, eg to abandon his undisposed-of beneficial interest, or to give it to the trustees not as trustees but as absolute beneficial owners. In the first case, as in the second, property is transferred by a transferor who receives nothing in return for it. In the first case, as in the second, the imposition of a resulting trust leads to the creation of a new equitable property right for the transferor[3], and, as a new right as Professor Chambers has written, 'It cannot be explained as the inertia of a pre-existing beneficial interest'[4]. Thus there are not two types of resulting trust, but only one, imposed by law when property is transferred gratuitously and there is no evidence that the transferor meant to make a gift or loan or to abandon his beneficial interest.

1   [1974] Ch 269 at 288, glossing *Vandervell v IRC* [1967] 2 AC 291 at 312 per Lord Upjohn.
2   [1996] AC 669 at 708.
3   [1996] AC 669 at 706 and see *DKLR Holding Co v Stamp Duties Commissioner* (1982) 149 CLR 431.
4   R Chambers, 'Resulting Trusts in Canada' (2000) 38 Alberta LR 379 at p 389.

3.6 Preliminary terminology

Constructive trusts

3.6 A constructive trust of property is a trust imposed by equity in respect of property on proof of a variety of special circumstances (discussed in Articles 34 to 36) where equity considers it unconscionable for the owner of particular property to hold it purely for his own benefit. It confers a *proprietary* right on the claimant and so must be distinguished from the *personal* right afforded by Equity to a claimant against a defendant who no longer has, or who never had, any trust property in his hands, but whose conscience is affected by his dishonest involvement in a breach of trust (or other fiduciary duty), so that Equity historically made him personally liable to account as if he had been an express trustee acting in breach of trust: this is the meaning of the expression that a defendant is 'personally liable to account as a constructive trustee'[1].

[1]   See Article 100 below.

3.7 To impose a constructive trust in respect of specific property it is necessary to prove facts which fit the accepted special circumstances directly or by analogy, for the court cannot impose a constructive trust whenever justice and good conscience require it and thereby indulge idiosyncratic notions of fairness and justice[1]. Often the constructive trust is imposed to vindicate equitable proprietary rights under an express or resulting trust and to give effect to the settlor's intentions (binding the trustee as an incident of his office) that the original trust property and subsequent additions to it and the fruits thereof and property subsequently replacing such property (in the rightful or even wrongful operation of the trust) are to be held as the trust fund for the beneficiaries[2]. Sometimes, the special circumstances require parties' actual, apparent or presumed intentions to be taken into account, where it has become unconscionable for the defendant to repudiate such intentions which would be possible but for the intervention of equity[3].

[1]   Lord Denning's attempts to do this (condemned in 13th and 14th editions hereof) have been rejected in England and in Australia: *Grant v Edwards* [1986] Ch 638, [1986] 2 All ER 426, CA; *Burns v Burns* [1984] Ch 317; *Muschinski v Dodds* (1986) 62 ALR 429; *Lloyds Bank v Rosset* [1991] 1 AC 107, [1990] 1 All ER 1111, HL; *Ivin v Blake* (1993) 67 P & CR 263, CA see Article 35(2)(a).
[2]   *Re EVTR* [1987] BCLC 646 at 651, CA; *Swain v Law Society* [1981] 3 All ER 797 at 813, CA; *A-G of Hong Kong v Reid* [1994] 1 AC 324.
[3]   For example, mutual wills, secret trusts, common intention constructive trusts and see *Allen v Snyder* [1977] 2 NSWLR 685 at 699 per Samuel JA; *Re Rose* [1952] Ch 499; and *Re Japan Leasing (Europe) plc* [2000] WTLR 301.

3.8 Express, resulting and constructive trusts tend to be mentioned in one breath as if they are similar substantive institutions, so enhancing the legitimacy of constructive trusts of property which play a vital role in supporting express and resulting trusts of property and which developed as a vital adjunct of such trusts[1]. In the case of express and resulting trusts the court compels the trustees to give effect to the beneficiaries' rights because they are express or resulting trustees. It is now apparent that a constructive trust is a vindicatory institution which equity imposes to preclude the retention or assertion of beneficial ownership of property (by persons who are express or resulting trustees or who, for special reasons, are to be treated as if they were express trustees) to the extent that such retention or assertion would be contrary to some principle of equity[2]. It is because some principle of equity compels the defendant to hold the whole or part of particular property in equity for the claimant that the defendant is constructive trustee thereof: it is not because the defendant is a constructive trustee that he is compelled to hold his property in equity for the claimant[3]. Such defendant is not under the same extensive duties as an express trustee, his obligation being to restore the trust property to express trustees for the beneficiaries – or to the beneficiaries if absolutely beneficially entitled thereto – and to account for what happened while he owned the trust property or its traceable product.

[1] For example, transferees of trust property hold it as constructive trustees for the trust beneficiaries unless bona fide purchasers for value without notice, while trustees hold a lease renewed to themselves or profits made from their trust on constructive trust for the trust beneficiaries.

[2] See per Deane J in High Court of Australia in *Muschinski v Dodds* (1986) 62 ALR 429 at 451–453 and per Lord Browne-Wilkinson in *Westdeutsche Landesbank Girozentrale v Islington London Borough Council* [1996] AC 669 at 714.

[3] Cf *Scott on Trusts* (Fourth edn) para 462.

3.9 Under English law, constructive trusts arise as a result of Equity's rules which state that they arise in particular circumstances at the time of those circumstances[1], even though this may not be appreciated until a court subsequently clarifies matters. These rules do not give the courts any discretion to impose constructive trusts, or to refuse to do so, according to their assessment of the equities of a case: the courts' role is purely declaratory. In contrast, some Commonwealth jurisdictions, eg Canada[2] and Australia[3], distinguish 'substantive' or 'Institutional' constructive trusts from 'remedial' constructive trusts. Different courts use these terms in different fashions, but most use them to distinguish constructive trusts which arise through the inflexible operation of rules of Equity from constructive trusts which arise following the exercise of a judicial discretion, either retrospectively or prospectively from the date of the court order[4]. These latter 'remedial' constructive trusts are not currently recognised by English courts[5]. It remains to be seen if this may change, given the current drift towards assimilating common intention constructive trusts with the flexible doctrine of proprietary estoppel in family homes cases[6].

[1] *Westdeutsche Landesbank Girozentrale v Islington London Borough Council* [1996] AC 669 at 714.

[2] *Sorochan v Sorochan* [1986] 2 SCR 38; *LAC Minerals Ltd v International Corona Resources Ltd* [1989] 2 SCR 574; *Soulos v Korkontzilas* [1997] 2 SCR 217.

[3] *Muschinski v Dodds* (1986) 160 CLR 583; *Re Stevenson Nominees Pty Ltd* (1987) 76 ALR 485; *Giumelli v Giumelli* (1999) 196 CLR 101.

[4] Eg *Fortex Group Ltd v Macintosh* [1998] NZLR 171 at 172–173 per Tipping J.

[5] *Re Goldcorp Exchange Ltd* [1995] 1 AC 74 at 104 per Lord Mustill; *Westdeutsche Landesbank Girozentrale v Islington London Borough Council* [1996] AC 669 at 714–716 per Lord Browne-Wilkinson; *Re Polly Peck International Ltd (No 2)* [1998] 3 All ER 812 at 827 per Mummery LJ and at 831 per Nourse LJ.

[6] See paras 35.9–35.48 below.

3.10 Constructive and resulting trusts have often been insufficiently distinguished by judges[1] dealing with family homes since both are exempt from written formalities. There is a danger that confusion of the requirements for the two types of trust may follow from a confusion of the two[2]. A significant practical distinction where the legal owner is insolvent is that a purchaser's resulting trust share proportionate to her contribution is safe from being upset under s 339 of the Insolvency Act 1986 unlike the gift element under a constructive trust[3].

[1]   For example, Lord Denning in *Hussey v Palmer* [1972] 1 WLR 1286 at 1289, CA: 'This [question of resulting or constructive trust] is more a matter of words than anything else. The two run together.'
[2]   For example, *Heseltine v Heseltine* [1971] 1 All ER 952, [1971] 1 WLR 342, CA.
[3]   *Re Densham (a bankrupt)* [1975] 3 All ER 726, [1975] 1 WLR 1519 dealing with its predecessor, Bankruptcy Act 1914, s 42.

'Implied' trusts

3.11 Acting from an abundance of caution, parliamentary draftsmen have used the compendious expression 'implied resulting or constructive trusts' on several occasions to describe trusts imposed by law other than statutory trusts[1]. However, the inclusion of 'implied' trust in the series is redundant and potentially misleading because there are no trusts imposed by law other than statutory, resulting and constructive trusts. The courts have also used the expression 'implied trust' as a synonym for 'resulting or constructive trust'[2], but confusingly neither they nor parliamentary counsel have been particularly consistent in this usage. They have also used the term as a synonym for 'resulting trust'[3], as a synonym for 'constructive trust'[4], and as a synonym for an express trust which has been intentionally created by a settlor whose intention had to be inferred from his ambiguous words and conduct[5]. This makes it difficult to be sure what meaning is attached to the term from one case to the next, and ideally the term should cease to be used.

[1]   Law of Property Act 1925, s 53(2); Law of Property (Miscellaneous Provisions) Act 1989 s 2(5); Trusts of Land and Appointment of Trustees Act 1996, ss 1(2), 17(4).
[2]   *Cowcher v Cowcher* [1972] 1 All ER 943 at 949; *McKenzie v McKenzie* [2003] EWHC 601 (Ch) at [89]; *TL v ML [2005] EWHC 2860 (Fam)*, [2006] 1 FCR 465 at [42].
[3]   Trustee Act 1925, s 68(17). See too *Re Vandervell's Trusts (No 2)* [1974] Ch 269 at 285; *Tinsley v Milligan* [1994] 1 AC 340 at 371.
[4]   *Midland Bank v Cooke* [1995] 2 FLR 915 at 927.
[5]   *Westdeutsche Landesbank Girozentrale v Islington London Borough Council* [1996] AC 669 at 705; *Bristol & West Building Society v Mothew* [1998] Ch 1 at 26; *Abbey National plc v Frost* [1999] 1 WLR 1080 at 1082.

ARTICLE 4
SIMPLE AND SPECIAL TRUSTS OR BARE AND ACTIVE TRUSTS

4.1

Trusts are divided into simple and special trusts according to the nature of the duty imposed on the trustee.

(1)   A simple trust is a trust in which the trustee is a mere repository of the trust property, with no active management duties to perform: such a trustee is called a passive or, more frequently, a

bare trustee, though the expressions 'bare trustee' and 'bare trust' when used in a statute derive their meaning from the statutory context.

(2) A special trust is a trust in which a trustee is appointed to carry out some scheme particularly pointed out by the settlor, and is called upon to exert himself actively in the execution of the settlor's intention: the trustee of a special trust is called an active trustee.

Example of a simple trust

4.2 A devised property to B in trust for C, a person who is of full age and capacity. Here the trust is a simple trust, as the only duty which B has to perform is to convey the legal estate to C, or C's nominee if so requested; and B is a passive or bare trustee[1]. His function is to hold the property to convey it to C or to whom C might direct. B has no active management duties, though under a basic duty to preserve the trust property so long as the trusteeship subsists[2]. If X, a transferee of such property from B knows (or suspects but deliberately abstains from inquiry lest the truth be discovered) that B is a bare trustee he will not acquire a good title unless C authorised the transfer[3]. B is not independent of C but neither is he a mere cypher[4] so that B cannot be compelled by C to grant a lease or create other obligations binding B. Indeed, in the case of a trust of any property, B has power to convey the property to C (if of full age and capacity) even if C had not required this[5], although C can prevent this by directing B to convey the property to X for C.

[1] *Christie v Ovington* (1875) 1 Ch D 279; *Re Cunningham and Frayling* [1891] 2 Ch 567. Cf *Morgan v Swansea Urban Sanitary Authority* (1878) 9 Ch D 582; *Re Blandy Jenkins Estate* [1917] 1 Ch 46.
[2] *Herdegen v Federal Commissioners of Taxation* (1988) 84 ALR 271 at 281. Also see *Hulbert v Avens* [2003] WTLR 387 at paras 24, 54, 62.
[3] *MacMillan Inc v Bishopsgate Investment Trust* (10 December 1993, unreported) decision of Millett J delivered in redacted form; also see *Kronheim v Johnson* (1877) 7 Ch D 60.
[4] *Ingram v IRC* [1997] 4 All ER 395 at 424, approved by the House of Lords in [2000] 1 AC 293, 305, 310.
[5] Trusts of Land and Appointment of Trustees Act 1996, s 6(2).

4.3 Where the term 'bare trust' is used in a statutory context its meaning will depend on such context and any statutory definition, so that it may cover all cases where all the beneficiaries together (taking account not just of concurrent interests but also successive interests) are of full age and capacity[1]. A custodian trustee is not a bare trustee[2].

[1] Trustee Act 1925, s 19(3) as substituted by Trustee Act 2000, s 34. In a similar situation where all the beneficiaries have *Saunders v Vautier* rights (see Article 69) the Trusts of Land and Appointment of Trustees Act 1996, s 19 enables them to direct the trustees to retire and convey the trust fund to a new trustee or trustees as if only a bare trust existed. For a classic bare trust see Land Registration Act 2002, s 7.
[2] *IRC v Silverts* [1951] Ch 521, CA.

4.4 Preliminary terminology

Example of a special trust

4.4 However, if the trust had been during C's life to collect the rents and profits, and to pay thereout the cost of repairs and insurance, and to pay the residue of such rents and profits to C during his life, and after C's death to hold the property in trust for D, the trust would have been a special trust during the life of C, and B would have been an active trustee, since during that period he would have had active duties to perform. Upon C's death, however, the trust would have become a simple trust, and B a bare trustee, inasmuch as the active duties originally attached to the trustee's office would have lapsed on the death of C, and the only duty remaining (apart from the basic duty of preservation) would have been to convey the legal estate to D or at his direction and to account to D for B's stewardship of the property.

4.5 Where a trustee holds property for a beneficiary or beneficiaries absolutely entitled to call for the property to be transferred to them or at their direction under the rule in *Saunders v Vautier*[1], but until such call the trustee has powers and discretions to exercise[2], then he will be an active trustee[3] and not an agent or nominee or bare trustee. However, usage of the term 'bare trustee' may extend in context to trusts where beneficiaries are absolutely entitled under the rule in *Saunders v Vautier*[4], so the property is held to their order.

[1]   (1841) 4 Beav 115.
[2]   *Re Brockbank* [1948] Ch 206, [1948] 1 All ER 287. A power of sale during a minority or a life tenancy will suffice: *Re Lashmar* [1891] 1 Ch 258 at 267 and 269. Further see *ISPT Nominees Pty Ltd v Chief Commissioner for State Revenue* [2003] NSWSC 697 at paras 267 to 282.
[3]   *Booth v Ellard* [1980] 3 All ER 569, [1980] 1 WLR 1443, CA. A, B and C will be regarded as 'absolutely entitled against the trustees' for Capital Gains Tax purposes if they are concurrently entitled but not if they are together successively entitled with *Saunders v Vautier* rights.
[4]   Further see *Herdegen v Federal Comr of Taxation* (1988) 84 ALR 271 at 282; *Blue Resources Ltd v Law Society of Upper Canada* (1995) 120 DLR (4th) 751 and Trustee Act 1925, s 19(3).

Sham trusts

4.6 One must note that a trust which appears on its face to be an active trust with sundry beneficiaries may be held to be a sham[1], so that, despite the appearance of creating equitable rights in others, the equitable beneficial ownership is intended to remain with the settlor. The agreed[2] real duty of the trustee is only to distribute the property as the settlor directs, while managing investments as directed by the settlor or as the trustee considers best in the absence of directions from the settlor. The subsequent conduct of the parties is admissible evidence that they were parties to the sham[3].

[1]   *Rahman v Chase Bank (CI) Trust Co Ltd* [1991] JLR 103; *Midland Bank plc v Watt* [1994] EGCS 113; *R v Dimsey* [2000] QB 744, 772–773, [1999] STC 846, 870–871, CA; *Shalson v Russo* [2003] WTLR 1165; *Re Esteem Settlement* [2004] WTLR 1; *R v Kumar* [2005] EWCA Crim 1979 [2006] Crim LR 271; *Minwalla v Minwalla* [2004] EWHC 2823 (Fam), [2005] 1 FLR 771, (2004) 7 ITELR 457; *Hill v Spread Trustee Co Ltd* [2005] BPIR 842. On sham documents generally see *Hitch v Stone* [2001] EWCA Civ 63, [2001] STC

214, CA. For a Zurich court holding a Guernsey trust to be a sham see *O-D Bank v Bankrupt Estate of WKR* (1999) ZR 98 No 52 pp 225 ff discussed [2000] JTCP 141–158.

2   Where the settlor declares himself trustee his intention is crucial, but trustees who knowingly become trustees receiving trust assets from the settlor need to agree to receiving trust assets and acting as trustee of a true trust or a sham trust. However, if a settlor's poor English led him to believe that in executing the trustee's discretionary trust instrument the trust fund was held to his order like a glorified bank account, in circumstances where he had been misled (perhaps confused over the proper meaning of 'We are legally obliged to take all decisions but our moral obligations to observe your wishes are of crucial significance, so you have nothing to worry about over our independent control of the trust fund') because the trustee intended to operate a proper trust for beneficiaries, then the settlor's intention should be honoured, although if regarded as creating a proper trust by mistake he could, anyhow, set it aside for mistake: *Gibbon v Mitchell* [1990] 3 All ER 338. The onus should be on the knowledgeable trustee to ensure it knows the real intention of the ignorant settlor which it can then accept, reject or change.

3   *AG Securities v Vaughan* [1990] 1 AC 417; *Midland Bank plc v Wyatt* [1995] 1 FLR 697 (declaration of trust of their house by H and W in favour of W and their children held a sham, W being a party to the sham when she 'merely went along with the "shammer" neither knowing or caring about what she was signing'); *Hitch v Stone* [2001] EWCA Civ 63, [2001] STC 214.

4.7 The key to the sham is that the settlor and the trustees intend to give a false impression from the outset[1], not intending the persons appearing to be beneficiaries on the face of the trust instrument to have any rights enforceable against the trustees[2] even though they appear to have such rights. The substance of the matter is that, despite appearances, the settlor has retained all the rights. Indeed, it may be that, to keep a nervous settlor happy and to protect nervous trustees where beneficiaries appear to have been given significant interests, there is inserted a term in the trust instrument which is inconsistent with the specified beneficiaries having any rights (eg a clause stating that in respect of events occurring in the settlor's[3] lifetime, the trustees in no circumstances are under any duty to account to the 'beneficiaries' and are always to be exempt from any liabilities howsoever arising to such 'beneficiaries'). The intentional insertion of such a specific clause should lead the court to give effect to the clause by holding that the whole equitable interest remains in the settlor, although in exceptional circumstances, it would be open to the court to disregard such a clause as a pretence repugnant to, or inconsistent with, a true trust intended by the settlor[4]. The law recognises that the concept of a sham or pretence can relate either to the whole of a document or to provisions thereof[5].

1   *Hitch v Stone* [2001] EWCA Civ 63, [2001] STC 214;*Shalson v Russo* [2003] WTLR 1165; *Hill v Spread Trustee Co Ltd* [2005] BPIR 842; *MacKinnon v Regent Trust Co Ltd* [2005] WTLR 1367, para 19: 'What is required in a case based on sham is a common intention to give a false impression'.

2   As Millett LJ stated in *Armitage v Nurse* [1998] Ch 241 at 253, 'If the beneficiaries have no rights enforceable against the trustees' there are no trusts.

3   If the beneficiaries are only intended to have rights arising on the settlor's death then the disposition on death of such rights is testamentary, requiring compliance with the Wills Act formalities: cf *Re Pfrimmer's Estate* [1936] 2 DLR 400; *Kauter v Hilton* (1953) 90 CLR 86 at 100; *Anderson v Patton* [1948] 2 DLR 202; *Baird v Baird* [1990] 2 AC 548, PC; *Tampson v Browne* (1835) My & K 32 at 35–36.

4   Indeed, such term could be void as an attempt to oust the jurisdiction of the courts: *Jones v Shipping Federation of Canada* (1963) 37 DLR (2d) 273.

5   *National Westminster Bank v Jones* [2001] 1 BCLC 98, paras 42, 45, 59; *AG Securities Ltd v Vaughan* [1990] 1 AC 417; *Hill v Spread Trustee Co Ltd* [2005] BPIR 842.

4.8 Close attention must be paid to the terms of a trust. Thus, where S transfers property to trustees on trust in S's lifetime to pay the income *or capital* to him or at his direction and, after his death, to hold the capital equally for his children or for such persons in such shares as S may designate in signed writing, the trustees will be holding the property to S's order, the full equitable interest remaining in him, with the purported disposition after his death being testamentary[1] and void if not complying with the Wills Act 1837, while if complying with the Wills Act it might be accidentally revoked by a subsequent will. By way of contrast, S would have formally divested himself of his equitable ownership if he had settled his property on trusts for others but had reserved a general power of appointment or a power of revocation[2]: the trustees would not hold such property to the order of S *until* he ordered it in the exercise of his reserved powers. The presence of such powers, however, will normally have very adverse tax consequences and may expose the trust assets to claims of a deceased settlor's dependants or forced heirs.

1 *Baird v Baird* [1990] 2 AC 548 at 566. Under the American Uniform Trust Code, ss 603, 604 and 608 such a trust, if revocable, is characterised as a lifetime, not a testamentary disposition, as is the case under the Bahamian Trustee Act 1998, s 3(2)(c) even if the trust is irrevocable, but the English forum will use its own characterisation rules to treat such trusts as testamentary, so as to create a resulting trust of English assets as part of the settlor's estate at death which will need to have been disposed of in a formally valid will.
2 *Young v Sealey* [1949] Ch 278 at 284, 294; *Kauter v Hilton* (1953) 90 CLR 86, 98–99, 100–101; *T Choithram International SA v Pagarani* [2001] 2 All ER 492 at 500; *Scott on Trusts* (Fourth edn) Vol 1A pp 125–129, 141–142. In form this is a proper trust but in substance it might be run as a sham: one indicator may be nominal fees paid to the trustee of a very valuable trust fund; another indicator might be if the trustee were removable at the whim of someone holding a personal power to replace the trustee, particularly if that someone were the settlor, but there may be good reason for an independent protector to have such a personal power in order to avoid the problems that a disgruntled removed trustee could raise if the power were fiduciary as in *Von Knierem v Bermuda Trust Co* (1994) 1 Butts OCM 116. Delivering two contradictory letters of wishes to the trustee, naming different beneficiaries in the event of the settlor's death, can also indicate a lack of intention to create a true trust: *Minwalla v Minwalla* [2004] EWHC 2823 (Fam), [2005] 1 FLR 771, [2006] WTLR 311.

4.9 Furthermore, the critical distinction[1] between a trustee holding to the order of the settlor and a trustee holding to the order of the settlor *only* if the settlor orders it is a fine one which a trustee can easily overlook by treating itself as bound to do what the settlor directs, even though he has not exercised his power of appointment or revocation to recover full equitable ownership of the settled property. Where the settlor does wish to exercise much significant influence over the conduct of the trustee, an informal arrangement with the trustee may leave the trust wide open to allegations of being a sham. It is better for the settlor to reserve specific powers of direction or veto so that the trustee can explain its actions by reference to these powers in a true trust.

1 Accepted by the Revenue in interpreting Taxation of Chargeable Gains Act 1992, ss 60(2), 70.

4.10 The courts are not restricted to examining the four corners of a document which appears to be a true trust. It can examine contemporary correspondence and e-mails and circumstantial evidence, such as the subsequent conduct of the settlor and the trustees[1]. In case trusts that are true trusts in form are subsequently attacked as sham trusts in substance, it will be necessary to have plenty of written evidence documenting either the exercise by the settlor or a protector of specific powers reserved in the trust instrument or independent conscious discretions exercised by the trustee: unless such written evidence of the trustee's discretion is established by oral cross-examination to be a sham (perhaps amounting to conspiracy to defraud the Revenue) the trust will then be proved a true trust. It is purely a question of fact whether or not a trust is in substance a sham.

¹   *Stone v Hitch* [2001] EWCA Civ 63, [2001] STC 214, para 65.

4.11   Once a true trust always a true trust, so that if, after running a true trust for a while, the trustee in breach of trust does as directed by the settlor as if the trust at the outset had been a sham, this does not enable the court to ignore the terms of the trust and permit the beneficiaries' property be transferred to the settlor¹. The court must enforce the duties owed by the trustee to the beneficiaries.

¹   *Shalson v Russo* [2003] WTLR 1165; *Hill v Spread Trustee Co Ltd* [2005] BPIR 842.

4.12   Exceptionally, a few years after creating a true named trust, a settlor may add property to this trust, but under an arrangement with the trustee that really such added property is to be regarded as the settlor's, regardless of the terms of the named trust: the added property is then treated as the subject of a separate sham trust¹.

¹   *Re Esteem Settlement* [2004] WTLR 1, para 60; *Hill v Spread Trustee Co Ltd* [2005] BPIR 842 citing D J Hayton (2004) 8 Jersey LR 8. On separate trusts of added property see *Air Jamaica Ltd v Charlton* [1999] 1 WLR 1399.

4.13   A conclusion that a trust instrument or a provision therein is a sham or pretence means that the settlor and trustees will not be able to rely on it as representing the true position as to the rights and obligations they have created so the court can ignore it, though as against an innocent third party it cannot lie in the mouths of the pretenders to assert to the disadvantage of that innocent third party that the trust was a sham or pretence¹.

¹   *National Westminister Bank plc v Jones* [2001] 1 BCLC 98, para 60; *Hill v Spread Trustee Co Ltd* [2005] BPIR 842.

4.14   The sham doctrine is a general one capable of applying to all transactions¹. It may apply not just to the creation of a trust but to an appointment under a special power sub-settling trust assets (as where property is settled on accumulation trusts for 21 years for the settlor's five children equally if alive at the end of the 21 years but with power to appoint income or capital revocably or irrevocably to the settlor's children or grandchildren and after 20 years 363 days the trust assets are revocably re-settled in five stirpital shares on the settlor's grandchildren, but with power to appoint all or part of the one fifth shares to a relevant child, in circumstances where a child alleges the substance was that the trustees were to hold to the order of the children, so that he is entitled to one fifth of the trust assets when the trustees break the alleged agreement to let him have his fifth share whenever he wants it).

4.14 *Preliminary terminology*

[1]   *Chase Manhattan Equities Ltd v Goodman* [1991] BCLC 897; *Snook v London and West Riding Investments Ltd* [1967] 2 QB 786, [1967] 1 All ER 518, CA; *Antoniades v Villiers* [1990] 1 AC 417, [1988] 3 All ER 1058, HL; *Atlas Maritime Co SA v Avalon Maritime Ltd* [1991] 4 All ER 769 at 779, CA.

LETTERS OF WISHES: THEIR SIGNIFICANCE

4.15 Where the settlor has provided a letter of wishes or let the trustees make a memorandum of his wishes (a factual distinction which should make no legal difference when both are utilised to indicate the settlor's intention), the trustees must be careful to provide documentation revealing that they consciously exercised an independent discretion when making decisions, naturally taking serious account of the settlor's wishes but appreciating that the ultimate decision was theirs. For the trustees to give effect exactly to the settlor's wishes is very dangerous because it lays them wide open to the charge that either the trust deed on its own is a sham, because the real trust terms incorporate the legally *binding* letter of wishes, or the trustees have committed a breach of trust in automatically following the settlor's *legally significant* (but not legally binding) wishes without consciously exercising an independent discretion.

4.16 To prevent them from being legally binding, letters of wishes should be written at a distinctly different date from that of creation of the trust or a transfer of substantial assets to the trustees, should be expressed to have no legally binding force and the wishes should not be expressed in too precise or forceful a manner. If the letter is expressed to be confidential and not to be revealed to the beneficiaries then, on current authority[1], a beneficiary has no absolute right to see the letter, though there is much to be said[2] for the view that just as purporting to make a trust deed confidential between the settlor and the trustees is ineffective, so should be making a letter of wishes confidential where without the letter the trustees would not be able properly to know how to exercise their very broad discretionary powers, so that the letter is a key document. However, if somehow (eg by discovering a copy of a draft letter of wishes in the deceased settlor's safe and comparing its terms with what the trustees have done) the beneficiary establishes a prima facie case either that the trust terms should include the letter as incorporated into the trust instrument[3] or that the trustees have not exercised a dispositive power 'in a responsible manner according to its purpose'[4] but have acted 'for reasons which are irrational perverse or irrelevant to any sensible expectation of the settlor'[5], then he may bring a legal action against the trustees and thereby take advantage of Civil Procedure Rule 31 to obtain disclosure of the letter of wishes. However, so long as the trustees do take into account the legally significant letter of wishes the decision is theirs, so that they can properly decide to act contrary to the settlor's wishes taking account of all the relevant circumstances[6] or they can properly decide to act in accordance with the settlor's wishes without such compliance sufficing to indicate that the trust is a sham[7].

[1]   *Hartigan Nominees Pty Ltd v Rydge* (1992) 29 NSWLR 405, CA; *Re Rabbaiotti's Settlement* [2000] WTLR 953.
[2]   See paras 60.52–60.56 below.

3   It may be that pleading the letter of wishes is a legally binding part of the settlor's trust instrument will suffice on its own, a beneficiary being entitled to see the trust instrument (even if expressed to be confidential): see *Chase Manhattan Equities Ltd v Goodman* [1991] BCLC 897 at 923.

4   *Re Hay's Settlement Trust* [1981] 3 All ER 786 at 792.

5   *Re Manisty's Settlements* [1973] 2 All ER 1203 at 1210.

6   *Bank of Nova Scotia Trust (Bahamas) Ltd v Borletta* (11 March 1985, Bahamas Supreme Court unreported) discussed [1994] 1 JIP 35–38.

7   *Re Esteem Settlement* [2004] WTLR 1, para 122; *Charman v Charman* [2005] EWCA Civ 1606, para 12 [2006] 1 WLR 1053.

4.17 Of course, if the trustees act contrary to a legally significant letter of wishes it will place them on the defensive if they are attacked by a beneficiary who has a copy of the letter. As a result, it seems, in principle, that a settlor should be able to create a letter of wishes intended only to be of *moral* significance and not legal significance. Thus, the following letter should be taken at its face value (unless the court is prepared to find that it should be treated as a mere pretence[1]):

'This letter is not to be regarded as indicating in a legally significant way the purposes for which the powers in my trust deed have been conferred on my trustees because I do not want them to have any extra legal obligations placed upon them by this letter so as to have to go out of their way to defend their conduct. I believe the imposition of such extra legal obligations would cause more difficulties than benefits to accrue, creating greater cost burdens and proving likely to upset relationships between my beneficiaries. Thus, my trustees are only to be under a moral obligation to take into account the following wishes of mine and shall not be accountable before the courts in relation to taking into account or failing to take into account such wishes. Indeed, they are not legally obliged to pass this letter on to successor trustees although I would hope they would consider themselves morally bound to do so.'

1   *Aslan v Murphy (No 2)* [1989] 3 All ER 130, 133; *Fitzwilliam v IRC* [1990] STC 65, 118; *Bankway Properties v Dunsford* [2001] EWCA Civ 528, [2001] 1 WLR 1369; *Hitch v Stone* [2001] EWCA Civ 63, [2001] STC 214.

4.18 While a morally binding letter of wishes can always be replaced, a legally binding letter of wishes can never be replaced or varied because it and the trust deed together amount to the documents creating an irrevocable trust (assuming no power of revocation is present). A legally significant letter of wishes should be capable of being replaced or varied as a letter indicating from time to time in the light of changing circumstances how very broad discretionary powers should hopefully be exercised in relatively specific fashion. This will certainly be the case where the first letter of wishes expressly makes clear that it merely indicates the settlor's current hopes in the light of current circumstances and that further letters of wishes are likely to be provided to give more up-to-date hopes as to how the trustee's broad discretionary powers might well be exercised.

AVAILABLE RESOURCE OF SETTLOR SCENARIO

4.19 Where there is not a trust for the settlor absolutely as a matter of form or substance, but the settlor is the primary beneficiary to whom trust funds can be distributed, perhaps with the trustee being expressly authorised to do this without the need to consider the interests of other beneficiaries, so that in practice there is no real likelihood of the independent trustee turning down a request for funds from the settlor, then the trust funds (like trust funds subject to a settlor having a power of revocation or a power to appoint to himself) can be regarded as an available resource of the settlor where claims of divorcing spouses are concerned. Thus, a spouse may have a substantial financial order made against her in the belief the trustees will put her in funds to relieve her of financial embarrassment[1]. The approach of the court is that trust capital (or income) will be a resource of the spouse within s 25(2)(a) of the Matrimonial Causes Act 1973 if the trustee would be likely to transfer the whole of the capital (or income) to the spouse if the spouse requested it[2].

[1]   *Browne v Browne* [1989] 1 FLR 291; and also see *Thomas v Thomas* [1995] 2 FLR 668 and a pair of Australian cases *Re Marriage of Goodwin* (1990) 14 Fam LR 801; *Re Marriage of Davidson* (1990) 14 Fam LR 817.
[2]   *Charman v Charman* [2005] EWCA Civ 1606, para 12, [2006] 1 WLR 1053.

4.20 However, such trust funds are not assets of the settlor for the purpose of satisfying claims of his creditors[1] and so no freezing injunction can be granted over such assets in aid of court proceedings against him by claimant creditors.

[1]   *Re Esteem Settlement* [2004] WTLR 1; *Shalson v Russo* [2003] WTLR 1165. There is no half-way house between a sham trust and a true trust.

4.21 Of course, the borderline is a narrow one between the case where an independent trustee in the exercise of its discretion will almost invariably exercise it in favour of the settlor-beneficiary when requested by him and the case where a nominee trustee will always exercise its discretion as directed by the settlor-beneficiary. If the court considers that there is good reason to suppose that a trust created by the defendant falls on the sham side of the borderline then it may grant a freezing injunction over the trust fund in aid of the claimant[1]. The court is likely to find such good reason where it appears that the defendant is seeking to hide or dissipate his assets via trusts and companies and Anstalts controlled by him[2].

[1]   *Dadourian Group International Inc v Azuri Ltd* [2005] EWHC 1768 (Ch), [2006] WTLR 239.
[2]   Piercing the veil of controlled companies is possible (eg *International Credit and Investment Co (Overseas) Ltd v Adham* [1998] BCC 134, and *Trustor AB v Smallbone (No 2)* [2001] 1 WLR 1177) but trusts are either full legally controlled so as to be sham trusts or they are true trusts: see antepenultimate footnote.

ARTICLE 5
FIXED AND DISCRETIONARY TRUSTS

5.1

Beneficiaries have rights either under fixed trusts or discretionary trusts.

(1)   A fixed trust is a trust in which a beneficiary has a current fixed entitlement to an ascertainable part of the net income, if any, of

the trust fund after deduction of sums paid by the trustees in the exercise of their *administrative* powers of management: the beneficiary has an interest in possession under the trust.

(2) A discretionary trust is a trust in which a beneficiary has no such absolute current right to direct the trustees to pay him an ascertainable part of the net income. Typically, this is the case where a beneficiary will receive income only if the trustees positively decide to carry out their duty to distribute income by favouring him rather than another member of the class of potential beneficiaries. There is also the atypical case where a beneficiary must receive the income unless the trustees exercise *dispositive* (or *distributive*) powers to divert the income elsewhere (eg under a power to appoint income within six months of receiving it to charity) or to withhold it (eg a power to accumulate income by adding it to the capital where there is no certainty that accumulations will ultimately pass to the beneficiary or his personal representatives): the discretion-conferring dispositive (or distributive) powers prevent an interest in possession arising (eg where B is a life tenant subject to dispositive powers)[1]. A discretionary trust will be exhaustive where all income *must* be distributed in the trustees' discretion amongst the class of beneficiaries: it will be non-exhaustive where all income must be distributed in the trustees' discretion amongst the class of beneficiaries *except* to the extent that income may be otherwise dealt with pursuant to a power in that behalf, eg a power of accumulation or a power to pay income to charity[2].

[1] *Gartside v IRC* [1968] AC 553, [1968] 1 All ER 121; *Pearson v IRC* [1981] AC 753, [1980] 2 All ER 479, HL; *Re Trafford's Settlement* [1985] Ch 32, [1984] 1 All ER 1108 (present sole object of class of beneficiaries that was open and not closed has no interest in possession since another class member might come into existence before a reasonable time for the distribution of accrued income had elapsed); *Miller v IRC* [1987] STC 108.

[2] *Sainsbury v IRC* [1970] Ch 712, [1969] 3 All ER 919.

Significance

5.2 The inheritance tax treatment of discretionary trusts is radically different from the treatment of fixed trusts[1]. Significant capital gains tax[2] and income tax[3] differences also exist. The test for certainty of beneficiaries for the validity of a trust differs according to whether the trust is a fixed trust or an 'atypical' discretionary trust on the one hand or a 'typical' discretionary trust on the other hand[4].

[1] Inheritance Tax Act 1984, ss 49–84.

[2] Taxation of Chargeable Gains Act 1992, ss 71, 72; where a life interest in possession is a narrower concept than an interest in possession.

[3] Finance Act 1973, ss 16, 17 replaced by Income and Corporation Taxes Act 1988, ss 686, 687 as amended; *Corbett v IRC* [1938] 1 KB 567 at 577; *Baker v Archer-Shee* [1927] AC 844; *IRC v Miller* [1930] AC 222; *Hamilton Russell's Executors v IRC* (1943) 25 TC 200; *IRC v Berrill* [1982] 1 All ER 867, [1981] 1 WLR 1449.

[4] *McPhail v Doulton* [1971] AC 424.

5.3 Preliminary terminology

Illustrations of fixed and discretionary trusts

5.3 A trust is a fixed trust where property (whether or not income-producing) has been settled on an adult, A, for life or for an entailed interest or on A until he attains the age of 50. It matters not that the trust is revocable or the trustees have power to appoint capital elsewhere so that thenceforth A's interest in possession will have ceased wholly or partly. However, a discretion or a power which can be exercised after income arises so as to withhold it from A, prevents A having an interest in possession at all. A power to accumulate income is treated as a power to withhold income unless any accumulations must be held for the otherwise entitled beneficiary or his personal representatives[1].

1 Revenue Press Notice [1976] BTR 418.

5.4 A trust is a discretionary trust in the obvious case where property is given to trustees to distribute the income therefrom amongst such of A's children, grandchildren, nephews, nieces, great-nephews and great-nieces as the trustees see fit. Less obviously there is a discretionary trust where property is settled on a minor, M, for life or on M for an entailed interest where Trustee Act 1925, s 31, is not ousted: the effect of s 31 is to convert M's apparently vested interest into a contingent interest for it imposes a trust to accumulate income during M's minority, but with power to apply income for M's maintenance, education or benefit, and it provides that if M does not attain 18 years or marry thereunder the accumulations are not to pass to M's personal representatives but, instead, are to pass as an accretion to the capital to the person entitled to capital[1].

1 Trustee Act 1925, s 31(2)(ii); *Stanley v IRC* [1944] KB 255, [1944] 1 All ER 230; *Cornwell v Barry* (1955) 36 TC 268. Exceptionally, s 31(4) provides that in the case of a vested annuity accumulations made during the annuitant's minority are, in any event, to be held upon trust for the annuitant or his personal representatives absolutely. Freehold land settled on a minor absolutely is treated as conferring a life interest if the minor dies childless without attaining 18 years or marrying thereunder: Administration of Estates Act 1925, s 51(3) as amended by Trusts of Land and Appointment of Trustees Act 1996, Sch 3, para 6.

Administrative powers and dispositive (or distributive) powers

5.5 An administrative power is, but a dispositive (or distributive) power is not, compatible with a beneficiary having an interest in possession under a fixed trust. 'The line between [them] may be difficult to draw but that does not mean that there is not a valid distinction ... A life tenant has an interest in possession but his interest only extends to the net income of the property after deduction from the gross income of expenses etc properly incurred in the management of the trust by the trustees in the exercise of their powers. A dispositive power is a power to dispose of the net income'[1]. There is a distinction 'properly to be drawn between powers directed to the preservation of the trust estate for the benefit of life tenant and remaindermen alike, and a discretionary power the exercise of which is intended to have an effect on the actual benefits which the beneficiaries as such become entitled to receive'[2].

1   *Pearson v IRC* [1981] AC 753 at 774–775 per Viscount Dilhorne, HL.
2   *Pearson v IRC* [1981] AC 753 at 785 per Lord Keith. In *Miller v IRC* [1987] STC 108 the
     Court of Session held that a power to make a payment out of income in order to meet the
     depreciation of capital value was an administrative power.

5.6 A power which might affect the destination of net income after it has arisen (eg a power to accumulate income or to divert it for the benefit of other beneficiaries) is a dispositive (or distributive) power. What then is the status of the common power enabling the trustees 'to apply any income of the Trust Fund in or towards the payment or discharge of any duties, taxes, costs, charges, fees or other outgoings which but for the provisions of this clause would be payable out of or charged upon the capital of the Trust Fund'? It amounts to authorising 'taking income away from the income beneficiaries and bestowing it on the capital beneficiaries, so that capital is augmented'[1], so that prima facie it seems a dispositive (or distributive) power, though in obiter dicta Viscount Dilhorne has asserted that it was an administrative power in context[2]. This may be justified on the basis that the clause is merely an ancillary power intended to emphasise the flexibility of trustees' powers to utilise income or capital (especially if mixed in one bank account) as is most convenient for dealing with pressing liabilities from time to time without affecting the trustees' duty overall to maintain a fair balance between life tenant and remaindermen in apportioning or allocating expenditure.

1   *Carver v Duncan (Inspector of Taxes)* [1985] AC 1082 at 1122, [1985] 2 All ER 645 at
     654, HL, per Lord Templeman.
2   *Pearson v IRC* [1981] AC 753 at 775. See also *IRC v Lloyd's Private Banking* [1998] STC
     559. Further see J Kessler *Drafting Trusts and Will Trusts* (Seventh edn), Chapter 16.

ARTICLE 6
EXECUTED AND EXECUTORY TRUSTS

6.1

Express trusts when created are either executed or executory.
(1)   An executed trust is one where the trust property is vested in trustees or personal representatives and the particular interests taken by the beneficiaries are exactly delimited[1]. The settlor has done everything within his inter vivos or testamentary powers to give effect to specific trusts.
(2)   An executory trust is one where the trust property is vested in trustees or personal representatives but the interests to be taken by the beneficiaries remain to be delimited in some subsequent instrument pursuant to the settlor's clear general intention or where the property intended to be subjected to trusts is the subject of an enforceable agreement to create a trust whether for delimited beneficiaries or beneficiaries that remain to be delimited[2].

1   *Stanley v Lennard* (1758) 1 Eden 87; *Egerton v Earl Brownlow* (1853) 4 HL Cas 1 at 210.

6.1 Preliminary terminology

²   Sackville-West v Viscount Holmesdale (1870) LR 4 HL 543; Papillon v Voice (1728) 2 P
    Wms 471. This definition was applied in Davis v Richards & Wallington Industries Ltd
    [1991] 2 All ER 563 at 588.

Significance

6.2 The language of executed trusts is interpreted in a strict technical fashion whilst the language of executory trusts is interpreted in a liberal untechnical fashion[1]. A trust will be executed where the settlor has been his own conveyancer or draftsman and executory where he has contemplated, expressly or by necessary implication, the execution of some further instrument providing detailed clauses to implement his general intentions[2]. However, even an executory trust will fail if its language is insufficiently clear to indicate generally the trusts intended by the settlor, eg where a testator left a share of residue to trustees 'for the formation of a superannuation bonus fund for the employees' of a named company[3].

¹   Re Bostock's Settlement [1921] 2 Ch 469 but cf Re Arden [1935] Ch 326; Lord Glenorchy
    v Bosville (1733) Cas temp Talb 3.
²   Egerton v Earl Brownlow (1853) 4 HL Cas 1.
³   Re Flavel's Will Trusts [1969] 2 All ER 232, [1969] 1 WLR 444; Magrath v Morehead
    (1871) LR 12 Eq 491.

6.3 The abolition or simplification of technicalities involving words of limitation has made the difference between executed and executory trusts much less significant since the Law of Property Act 1925, ss 60, 130, 131 and since the abolition of entails in 1996[1].

¹   Trusts of Land and Appointment of Trustees Act 1996, Sch 1, para 5.

6.4 The ramifications of tax law are now such that executory trusts are rare for it is normally better to specify executed trusts at the outset, having then fully considered all the tax implications.

Marriage articles, wills and interim pension trusts

6.5 Executory trusts are always found in marriage articles[1]. They are sometimes found in wills (usually home-made), though it is possible to find them in inter vivos dispositions other than marriage articles[2], such as in company's interim pension deeds[3], or in trustees transferring assets to non-resident trustees to declare trusts thereof to substantially the same effect as the original trusts. Most trusts created in professionally drafted wills are executed trusts where the beneficial interests are exactly specified, though the personal representatives of the testator may subsequently have to vest the trust property in themselves qua trustees or in other trustees. However, will trusts are executory, for example, where a testator directs that on B's marriage a strict settlement of Blackacre shall be made in B's favour as counsel shall advise[4] (so taking effect after 1996 as a trust of land[5]) or where a testator in his home-made will gives 'All my property in trust for my wife and children' when it is up to the court to decide whether the wife was meant to have a life interest or an absolute interest, whether as joint tenant or tenant in common. However under s 22 of the Administration of Justice Act 1982, 'Except where a contrary intention is shown it shall be presumed that if a testator devises or bequeaths property to his spouse in terms which in themselves would give an absolute interest to the spouse but by the same instrument purports to give his issue an interest in the same property, the gift to the spouse is absolute notwithstanding the purported gift to the issue.'

1   There is a strong presumption to favour children and so restrict a wife's interest to a life interest if a remainder is given for the 'wife and children': *Rossiter v Rossiter* (1863) 14 I Ch R 247.
2   *Mayn v Mayn* (1867) LR 5 Eq 150. A settlor's executory trusts may be contained in correspondence with a trustee in an off-shore trust jurisdiction which is to execute a trust deed on the face of which it appears as settlor.
3   *Davis v Richards & Wallington Industries Ltd* [1991] 2 All ER 563, [1990] 1 WLR 1511.
4   Cf *Re Spicer* (1901) 84 LT 195; *Re Potter's Will Trusts* [1944] Ch 70, [1943] 2 All ER 805; *Shelley v Shelley* (1868) LR 6 Eq 540 at 549.
5   Trusts of Land and Appointment of Trustees Act 1996, s 2.

Relationship to completely and incompletely constituted trusts

6.6 An express trust is said to be completely constituted[1] when the trust property has been effectively transferred to trustees by the settlor and subjected by him to enforceable trusts, whether the beneficiaries' interests are exactly delimited or remain to be delimited. Thus, in such circumstances both executed and executory trusts are completely constituted trusts, though something remains to be done to perfect an executory trust.

1   See Article 9 below.

6.7 However, if the settlor gratuitously declares himself a trustee of 1,000 specific shares in a private company, part of a larger shareholding held by him, in which he is to retain the remaining beneficial interest, or of £10,000 in a building society account containing a larger sum, in which he is also to retain the remaining beneficial interest, then no completely constituted trust, capable of being an executed trust, should exist until the relevant property intended to be subject to trusts has been separated from the settlor's property and so set aside on the relevant trusts[1]. In contrast, testamentary trusts to similar effect will be completely constituted trusts, the deceased by his death having automatically vested his legal beneficial ownership in his personal representative subject to the equitable duty[2] to transfer the specific number of shares or amount of money to the designated legatee with the remaining shares or money passing to the residuary legatee (or, if none, to the next of kin).

1   *Re Goldcorp Exchange Ltd* [1994] 2 All ER 806; at para 8.16 below indicating that *Hunter v Moss* [1994] 3 All ER 215, [1994] 1 WLR 452, CA was incorrectly decided. There would be no uncertainty of subject matter if it was a proportion of the shareholding or chose in action: *Associated Alloys Pty Ltd v ACN 001 452 106 Pty Ltd* (2000) 202 CLR 588.
2   See *Stamp Duties Comr (Queensland) v Livingston* [1965] AC 694, [1964] 3 All ER 692; *Marshall v Kerr* [1995] 1 AC 148, [1994] 3 All ER 106, HL; Inheritance Tax Act 1984, ss 83, 91.

6.8 *Preliminary terminology*

6.8 An executory inter vivos trust requires property to be vested in trustees but with the beneficiaries' interests ascertainable though not precisely delimited or the property in question (though not yet vested in trustees) to be the subject of an enforceable agreement.

Division Two

EXPRESS TRUSTS

Chapter 2

INTRODUCTION

ARTICLE 7
ANALYSIS OF AN EXPRESS TRUST

7.1

(1) In order for a settlor to create an express trust of property vested in a trustee the following conditions are essential.

    (a) The settlor must have used language from which the court finds, as a fact, an intention to create a trust of ascertainable property in favour of ascertainable persons whose ability to enforce the trust underpins the binding obligation inherent in the trust concept[1]. The test for ascertaining such persons is stricter for fixed trusts than for discretionary trusts[2]. If either the property or the beneficiaries cannot be ascertained with certainty, there can be no trust for the beneficiaries, the settlor remaining beneficial owner of the property[3]. If the trust is for abstract, impersonal purposes rather than for persons, whether individual or corporate, it will be void[4] unless the purposes are exclusively charitable[5], except for certain anomalous testamentary cases relating to the maintenance of animals, tombs and the performance of private religious rituals[6], though there is some scope to develop the law so as to accept as valid non-charitable purpose trusts enforceable by an enforcer expressly designated as such in the trust instrument[7]. However, any trust other than a charitable trust[8] must be administratively workable[9].

    (b) For an inter vivos (or lifetime) trust of property to be created gratuitously (*viz* without the provision of any valuable consideration for the settlor), in which case it is known as a voluntary trust (or a trust in favour of volunteers):

> (i)   the settlor's interest in the property must have been effectively transferred to the trustee(s) or
>
> (ii) the settlor must have done everything necessary for him to do to enable the property (eg registered land or shares) to be transferred to the trustee(s) even if he subsequently changes his mind or
>
> (iii) the settlor must have declared himself to become trustee of identified segregated property retained by him[10]

(c)   For a testamentary trust of property to be created, the testator must declare the trusts in his will or codicil. On his death, legal beneficial ownership of all his property automatically vests in his personal representatives, who must duly gather in all his assets and pay debts taxes and funeral expenses before wholly – or to the extent possible after paying such debts etc – transferring the relevant property to the trustees of the testamentary trusts[11]. If the personal representatives are also the trustees, then they need to segregate from their other property the trust property that they are now holding as trustees, having completed administration of the testator's estate.

(d)   For a trust to be created by a contract (for valuable consideration covering money, money's worth, marriage or a civil partnership for same-sex couples), the settlor must have entered into a valid contract that in a specified eventuality (eg marriage or, after receiving the relevant consideration, the receipt in the future of a specified type of property, like income to be received from an identified source) he himself will hold specified existing property or future property when it materialises on trust for specified beneficiaries or on trust to transfer it to specified trustees for such beneficiaries. The court acts on the maxim that Equity considers done that which ought to be done, so the trust automatically arises at the time of the specified eventuality[12].

(e)   The trust property must be of such a nature as to be capable of being settled[13].

(f)   The object of the trust must be lawful[14] so that the trust must satisfy the rules against remoteness, accumulations and inalienability as well as not be illegal, immoral etc.

(g)   The settlor must comply with any requisite formalities for declaring trusts, creating contracts or assigning equitable interests where a purported declaration of trust amounts to an assignment of an equitable interest[15].

These essentials for prima facie validity are examined at length in Chapter 2.

(2)   But a trust, prima facie valid, may yet be impeachable:

(a) by the settlor or his successors in title, by reason of his incapacity[16]; or the failure to co-operate of someone whose cooperation is vital to carrying out the trusts[17]; or by reason of some mistake made by, or fraud practised on, the settlor, at its creation[18]; or

(b) by the settlor's creditors, by reason of it having been made with an intention to put assets beyond their reach[19]; or because it infringes ss 339 and 340 of the Insolvency Act 1986[20]; or

(c) by future purchasers of the property from the settlor without notice of the trust, where the trust property is land, and the trust was intended by the settlor to defeat the claims of future purchasers[21];

(d) by a settlor's dependants if the trust were designed to defeat their claims under the Matrimonial Causes Act 1973 or the Inheritance (Provision for Family and Dependants) Act 1975[22];

(e) under specific ad hoc legislation preventing criminals from profiting from their crimes[23].

These latent flaws are considered in Chapter 3.

(3) Lastly, where the trust is executory[24] a very liberal construction is given to the language, so as to give effect to the manifest intentions of the settlor[25].

These questions of construction are dealt with in Chapter 4.

1   Article 8 below.
2   See paras 8.42–8.76 below.
3   See paras 8.34–8.36 below.
4   See paras 8.144–8.156 below.
5   See para 8.34 below.
6   See paras 8.173–8.184 below.
7   See paras 8.157–8.167 below.
8   Where there is evidence of a clear general charitable intention, the court under its cy-près jurisdiction can make the charitable trust administratively workable so that the general purpose can be carried out: Charities Act 1993, s 13.
9   See paras 8.71–8.88 below.
10 Article 9 below.
11 See para 1.49 above.
12 See paras 1.42 and 10.8–10.10 below.
13 Article 10 below.
14 Article 11 below.
15 Article 12 post.
16 Article 13 below.
17 See para 8.9 below.
18 Article 15 below.
19 Article 16 below.
20 Article 17 below.
21 Article 18 below.
22 Article 19 below.
23 Article 19 below.
24 See Article 6 above.
25 Articles 20–26 below.

Chapter 3

MATTERS ESSENTIAL TO THE PRIMA FACIE VALIDITY OF AN EXPRESS TRUST

Article

ARTICLE 8
LANGUAGE SUFFICIENT TO CREATE A TRUST FOR PERSONS

8.1

(1) No technical expressions are necessary for the creation of an express trust, which may be created without the settlor being aware of this[1], so long as he intends to create a state of affairs that can only be accomplished if he creates a trust[2]. It is sufficient if the settlor evinces with reasonable certainty:
  (a) an intent to create a trust, involving the trust property being intended to be kept separate from other property of the trustee[3];
  (b) the trust property[4];
  (c) the persons (individual or corporate) intended to be beneficiaries[5]; and
  (d) the purpose of the trust so that the trust is administratively workable and not capricious[6];
  providing always that for there to be a valid, and therefore enforceable, trust the trust must be intended to be directly or indirectly for the benefit of persons (individual or corporate) so that some person has locus standi to enforce the trust[7] unless the trust is for charitable purposes, when enforceable by the Attorney General or the Charity Commission, or for a limited anomalous number of non-charitable purposes relating to the maintenance of animals, tombs and the performance of private religious rituals[8], although there is scope[9] for

the courts to uphold non-charitable purpose trusts if the settlor's trust instrument provides for a person with locus standi to enforce the purpose trust, assuming it to be workable and restricted to a valid perpetuity period.

(2)   Whether an intention to create a trust is sufficiently evinced is in each case a question of interpretation. There is a well-established rule of construction that where an instrument is capable of two interpretations, one of which would give effect to the purpose of the person who drew it up, and the other of which would frustrate such purpose, one should prefer the former interpretation to the latter[10]. Whether or not[11] there is an intention to create a trust may be inferred from the context.

In particular:

(a)   an apparent power of appointment among such of a class as the donee of the power may select, unaccompanied by a gift over in default of appointment[12], may raise an inference that a fixed trust was intended in favour of the class in default of appointment if there appears to be a general intention to benefit the objects of the power[13], alternatively, the apparent power may be treated as in the nature of a discretionary trust for the class members[14];

(b)   a gift by will to a person, followed by precatory words expressive of the testator's request, recommendation, desire, hope or confidence, that the property will be applied in favour of others, may exceptionally create a trust, if, on the will as a whole, it appears that the testator intended the words to be imperative[15], but the court will not presume the imposition of a precatory trust merely from the presence of particular precatory words[16];

(c)   a devise or bequest 'upon condition' or 'to the intent' that a benefit may be conferred on a third party, may create a trust for the third party if, on construing the whole will, the court comes to the conclusion that a trust, and not a charge merely, or a personal obligation, or a condition entailing forfeiture, was intended[17];

(d)   a contract to create a trust of which specific performance would be ordered is considered to be an executory trust, conferring on parties who could sue for specific performance the same rights and imposing the same liabilities as if the contract had been actually performed[18].

(3)   On the other hand, persons to whom payments are directed to be made by trustees are not necessarily beneficiaries, and cannot enforce such directions if the object of the payments, as gathered from the whole instrument, was not to confer benefits on the payees, but to facilitate the administration of an estate or to relieve the owner of trouble or inconvenience. In many cases the so-called trustee is regarded as an agent[19].

1 *Paul v Constance* [1977] 1 WLR 527, CA; *Rowe v Prance* [2000] WTLR 249; *Dipple v Corles* (1853) 11 Hare 183; *Page v Cox* (1852) 10 Hare 163; *Moore v Darton* (1851) 4 De G & Sm 517.
2 He is presumed to intend the legal consequences of his acts: *Swiss Bank Corpn v Lloyds Bank Ltd* [1982] AC 584 at 595–596.
3 *Paragon Finance plc v Thakerar* [1999] 1 All ER 400 at 416; *Commissioners of Customs & Excise v Richmond Threatre Management* [1995] STC 257.
4 *Boyce v Boyce* (1849) 16 Sim 476; *Knight v Knight* (1840) 3 Beav 148; affd sub nom *Knight v Boughton* (1844) 11 Cl & Fin 513 at 548, HL; and explained by CA in *Re Oldfield* [1904] 1 Ch 549, CA.
5 *McPhail v Doulton* [1971] AC 424; *Re Wright's Will Trusts* [1981] LS Gaz R 841.
6 *R v District Auditor, ex p West Yorks CC* [2001] WTLR 795.
7 *Re Denley's Trust Deed* [1969] 1 Ch 373.
8 See paras 8.173–8.184 below.
9 See paras 8.157–8.167 below.
10 *Universe Tankships Inc of Monrovia v International Transport Workers' Federation* [1983] 1 AC 366 at 406, [1982] 2 All ER 67 at 93; *IRC v McMullen* [1981] AC 1 at 14, [1980] 1 All ER 884 at 890, CA; *Charles v Barzey* [2002] UKPC 68, para 12 [2003] 1 WLR 437.
11 *Re B (A Child: Property Transfer)* [1999] EWCA Civ 1313, (1999) Times, 10 May, (divorce consent order transferring house to mother as to 70% 'for the benefit of the child, J', and 30% for the father, held by the Court of Appeal not to create a trust for J, so the mother could retain such percentage of proceeds of sale); *Duggan v Governor of Sutton Prison* [2004] EWCA Civ 78, [2004] 1 WLR 1010 (Governor did not hold prisoners' money on trust); *Re Chelsea Cloisters Ltd* (1981) 41 P & CR 98 (tenants' damage deposit moneys held on trust by landlord).
12 *Burrough v Philcox* (1840) 5 My & Cr 72; *Grieveson v Kirsopp* (1838) 2 Keen 653; *Brown v Higgs* (1799) 4 Ves 708.
13 *Re Weekes' Settlement* [1897] 1 Ch 289; *Re Llewellyn's Settlement* [1921] 2 Ch 281.
14 *McPhail v Doulton* [1971] AC 424.
15 *Shelley v Shelley* (1868) LR 6 Eq 540; *Re Steele's Will Trusts* [1948] Ch 603, [1948] 2 All ER 193.
16 *Re Adams and Kensington Vestry* (1884) 27 Ch D 394; *Re Diggles* (1888) 39 Ch D 253; *Re Hamilton* [1895] 1 Ch 373; on appeal [1895] 2 Ch 370, and cases there cited; *Re Steele's Will Trusts* [1948] Ch 603, [1948] 2 All ER 193; and *Mussoorie Bank v Raynor* (1882) 7 App Cas 321.
17 See paras 8.233–8.242 below.
18 *Pullan v Koe* [1913] 1 Ch 9; *Collyer v Isaacs* (1881) 19 Ch D 342 at 351.
19 See paras 8.252–8.255 below.

Paragraph (1)

Reasons for the rule that technical language is unnecessary

8.2 The latitude of expression allowed to the creator of a trust is an instance of the maxim that 'Equity regards the intention rather than the form'. Wherever the intent to create a trust is apparent, it will (other matters being in order) be carried into effect, however crudely or elliptically it may have been expressed.

Express direction or declaration

8.3 Of course, the words 'in trust for', or 'upon trust to', are the most proper for expressing a fiduciary purpose; but wherever a person vests property in another and shows an intention that it is to be applied for the benefit of third parties who are sufficiently pointed out, an express trust will be created, whatever form of words may have been used. Thus where S devised or granted freehold lands unto and to the use of B, and 'directed' him to sell it and pay the proceeds to C, or directed him to apply the property for the benefit of C a trust was created in favour of C[1], although the word 'trust' was not used.

1   *White v Briggs* (1848) 2 Ph 583. See also *Re Endacott* [1960] Ch 232, [1959] 3 All ER 562, CA, where a testator gave his residuary estate to a parish council 'for the purpose of providing some useful memorial to myself'. The Court of Appeal held that the words quoted were not merely expository but intended to impose an obligation in the nature of a trust which was void as a pure purpose trust.

8.4 Similarly, if a person states that particular property he owns is to be regarded as as much his cohabitee's as his own, this will reveal an intention to create a trust for both of them, a person being able to create a trust without knowing it, just as he may speak prose without knowing it. Thus, as in *Paul v Constance*[1] a man might open a bank deposit account in his name alone, having ensured that his female co-habitant could be authorised to draw on the account using a note with his signature, and pay in a capital sum. Bingo winnings treated as their winnings might subsequently be paid in and £150 might be withdrawn for their Christmas presents and their Christmas food. At various times the man might say to the female, 'The money is as much yours as mine'. These words will be interpreted in context as amounting to an express declaration of trust of the bank account moneys in equal shares, the court 'dealing with simple people, unaware of the subtleties of equity, but understanding very well indeed their own situation'[2].

1   [1977] 1 All ER 195, [1977] 1 WLR 527. Also see *Dhingra v Dhingra* (1999) 2 ITELR 262.
2   [1977] 1 All ER 195 at 197, [1977] 1 WLR 527 at 530. Also see the benevolent decision in *Re Vandervell's Trusts (No 2)* [1974] Ch 269, [1974] 3 All ER 205, CA.

8.5 However the use of 'our house', 'our flat' or 'our home' in ordinary social contexts will not be regarded as indicative of ownership, only of joint occupation or residence[1], but the use of 'our boat' in a serious discussion between the owner and his cohabitee may indicate shared beneficial owner-ship under a trust[2].

1   *Lloyds Bank v Rosset* [1991] 1 AC 107 at 130 and *Otway v Gibbs* [2001] WTLR 467 at 472. Declarations of trusts of land are unenforceable in any event unless evidenced in signed writing within Law of Property Act 1925, s 53(1)(b) or there is a resulting trust or detrimental reliance sufficient to create a constructive trust or an equitable proprietary estoppel.
2   *Rowe v Prance* [2000] WTLR 249, [1999] 2 FLR 787.

Trust property to be separate from other property

8.6 An intent to create a trust of specific property will involve an intent that such property be kept separate from other trust or private property of the trustee, so that a property relationship is intended and not a personal debtor-creditor relationship[1]. Thus if a recipient of money:

'is not bound to keep the money separate, but is entitled to mix it with his own money and deal with it as he pleases, and when called upon to hand over an equivalent sum of money, then he is not a trustee of the money but merely a debtor.'[2]

¹ See para 1.24 above and *Paragon Finance plc v Thakerar* [1999] 1 All ER 400 at 416, per Millett J; *Hinckley Singapore Trading Pte Ltd v Sogo Department Stores Pte Ltd* (2001) 4 ITELR 301 (Singapore CA); *Re English & American Insurance Co Ltd* [1994] 1 BCLC 649; *Re Fleet Disposal Services Ltd* [1995] 1 BCLC 345; *Guardian Ocean Cargoes Ltd v Banco da Brasil* [1994] 2 Lloyd's Rep 152, CA.

² *Henry v Hammond* [1913] 2 KB 515 at 521, endorsed by CA in *R v Clowes (No 2)* [1994] 2 All ER 316 at 325 and applied in *Commissioners of Customs and Excise v Richmond Theatre Management* [1995] STC 257.

8.7 A requirement to keep moneys separate is an indicator that they are impressed with a trust: the absence of such a requirement, if there are no other indicators of a trust, normally negatives it. The fact that a transaction contemplates the mingling of funds is, therefore, not necessarily fatal to a trust, eg where investors' moneys are to be pooled for the purposes of buying a particular type of investment to be held on trust for them as equitable tenants in common[1]. Similarly, a valid trust exists where B contracts with C that after receiving full consideration from C, if he receives proceeds of sale materialising from some specified future property he will hold it (or a specified percentage or fractional part thereof[2]) on trust for C, though he can hold such money briefly in his own bank account before transmitting it on to C: such money belongs in Equity to C from the moment received by B so that C has the benefit of the tracing rules[3]. The contract should spell out that the relevant amount of money is to be transferred into C's account or a trust account for C within a short period of receipt (eg five working days) and that B should not let the amount credited in its general account receiving the proceeds of sale fall below the relevant amount to be held on trust for C[4].

¹ *Re Goldcorp Exchange Ltd* [1995] 1 AC 74, [1994] 2 All ER 806, PC; *R v Clowes (No 2)* [1994] 2 All ER 316, CA.

² See *Associated Alloys Pty Ltd v ACN 001 452 106 Pty Ltd* (2001) 74 ALJR 862, para 1.42 above.

³ *Associated Alloys Pty Ltd v ACN 001 452 106 Pty Ltd* (2001) 74 ALJR 862 and *Re Irving* (1877) 7 Ch D 419; *Pullan v Koe* [1913] 1 Ch 9; *Re Gillott's Settlements* [1934] Ch 97; *Palette Shoes Pty Ltd v Krohn* (1937) 58 CLR 1, at 27.

⁴ *Royal Trust Bank v National Westminster Bank* [1996] 2 BCLC 682, CA; *Re Lewis' of Leicester* [1995] 1 BCLC 428. If, despite such terms, C ignores B's breach of them and, in practice allows B to use the money as B's own, then the trust will have been replaced with a debtor-creditor relationship.

Trusts do not fail for want of a trustee

8.8 In the case of a will trust it matters not that the testator fails to appoint trustees[1] or that the appointed trustees predecease the testator[2] or disclaim the trust[3] or are not capable of taking the trust property[4]. The personal representatives will hold the property with power to appoint trustees who can then exercise all the powers vested in the trustees[5]. In the case of inter vivos trusts the settlor must do all that he can to vest the trust property in specific existing persons of full capacity[6] but disclaimer by them[7] or refusal of registration of them as shareholders by the board of directors in the case of shares[8] will not invalidate the trust since the settlor will hold the property subject to the trusts.

1   *Ellison v Ellison* (1802) 6 Ves 656; *Dodkin v Brunt* (1868) LR 6 Eq 580; *Pollock v Ennis* [1921] 1 IR 181.
2   *A-G v Stephens* (1834) 3 My & K 347; *Moggridge v Thackwell* (1792) 3 Bro CC 517; *A-G v Lady Downing* (1766) Amb 550; *Tempest v Lord Camoys* (1866) 35 Beav 201; *Re Smirthwaite's Trusts* (1871) LR 11 Eq 251.
3   *Robson v Flight* (1865) 4 De GJ & Sm 608; *Re Wilson-Barksworth* (1933) 50 TLR 82.
4   *Sonley v Clock-makers Co* (1780) 1 Bro CC 81.
5   See cases in footnote 2.
6   If property is vested in a trustee of unsound mind his co-trustees or the court can appoint another trustee to replace him: Trustee Act 1925, ss 36, 41 as amended.
7   *Mallott v Wilson* [1903] 2 Ch 494 criticised by P Matthews [1981] Conv 141, but accepted as good law by the Court of Appeal in *Harris v Sharp* (21 March 1989, unreported).
8   *Tett v Phoenix Property and Investment Co Ltd* [1984] BCLC 599; *Mascall v Mascall* (1984) 50 P & CR 119, CA.

Trusts will fail if key figure uncooperative

8.9 As Buckley J has stated[1], 'if it is of the essence of a trust that the trustees selected by the settlor and no-one else shall act as the trustees of it and those trustees cannot or will not undertake the office, the trust must fail. This is because the co-operation of the trustees is the key to carrying out the trusts'[2]. The position would be the same if co-operative trustees were under a duty to distribute the trust fund only to persons nominated by X, but X was unco-operative so nothing could be distributed as required, X having a personal power of nomination but not being obliged to exercise it. A resulting trust in favour of the settlor then arises[3].

1   *Re Lysaght* [1966] Ch 191 at 207, [1965] 2 All ER 888 at 896.
2   As pointed out in J E Penner, *The Law of Trusts* (Fourth edn, 2004) para 13. 44.
3   *Boyce v Boyce* (1849) 16 Sim 476.

Trusts intended may amount to charges

8.10 As already explained at para 1.41, if contracting parties enter into a transaction using the terminology of 'trust', but the legal effect of the transaction is to give rise to an equitable charge because the intended 'trust' fund is simply to provide security for an obligation then no trust arises, the parties being taken to intend the legal consequences of their acts[1].

1   *Clough Mill Ltd v Martin* [1985] 1 WLR 111, CA; *Swiss Bank Corpn v Lloyds Bank* [1980] 2 All ER 419 at 426.

Trusts intended may yet be void for uncertainty

8.11 However, intention to create a trust is not of itself sufficient (even where the most direct and imperative words are used)[1], if either the property, or the persons to be benefited, or the way in which they are to be benefited be not indicated with reasonable certainty.

1   See *Mussoorie Bank v Raynor* (1882) 7 App Cas 321 at 331.

Illustrations of uncertainty where settlor declares self trustee of part of own property

8.12 If a settlor intends to create a trust by transferring property to trustees then, of necessity, he must effectively transfer specific property to those trustees and declare trusts relating to such specific property. One would logically expect that if he is to declare himself trustee of some of his own property for particular beneficiaries, his declaration must relate to specific property identified as trust property separate from his private property that remains subject to claims of his private creditors, divorcing spouse and persons with claims on his death under the Inheritance (Provision for Family and Dependants) Act 1975.

FRACTIONS OR PERCENTAGES OF SETTLOR'S PROPERTY

8.13 If the settlor intends to hold all of the £50,000 in his building society account or all his 200 shares in Smith Co Ltd, a private company, or all his 20 cases of Chateau Lafite 1961 or all his flock of sheep on trust for himself and another as equitable tenants in common as to four fifths and one fifth respectively, there is certainty as to the money, the shares, the wine and the sheep and as to the factional shares in such certain property. Thus, the other equitable tenant in common via the tracing process can claim a proprietary interest in one fifth of the traceable product of such property.

ENUMERATED AMOUNTS OF SETTLOR'S PROPERTY

8.14 A fundamental problem arises, however, if, instead, the settlor intends to create a trust of 4 of his 20 cases of wine or 20 out of his flock of 100 sheep for B. As Oliver J has stated, in *Re London Wine Company (Shippers) Ltd*[1].

'Of course, he could by appropriate words, declare himself to be a trustee of a specified proportion of his whole flock and thus create an equitable tenancy in common between himself and the named beneficiary, so that a proprietary interest would arise in the beneficiary in an undivided share of all the flock and its produce. But the mere declaration that a given number of animals would be held upon trust could not, without very clear works pointing to such an intention, result in the creation of an interest in common in proportion which that number bears to the whole at the time of the declaration'.

[1] [1986] PCC 121 at 137; though in *Hunter v Moss* [1994] 1 WLR 452 the Court of Appeal erroneously treated it as only concerned with the passing of legal title, while the Court of Appeal was concerned with a declaration of trust of property whose legal title was retained by the declarer. Also see *Re Wait* [1927] 1 Ch 606.

8.15 An intention to create a trust of a specific quantity of assets cannot be construed as being the different intention to create an equitable tenancy in common in a larger quantity of assets. In the former case a small quantity of assets is trust property, tying the settlor's hands; in the latter case a large quantity of assets is trust property, so tying the settlor's hand to a greater extent.

8.16 Where a settlor, S, has the former intention he cannot create a trust for B of 4 cases of wine or 20 sheep, when owning a larger number, until he has identified them by clearly segregating them from his other cases or sheep[1]. B can acquire no equitable title (and so no right to vindicate an equitable proprietary interest via the tracing process) until such identification has occurred. The position is the same if S intends to transfer legal title to B. As Lord Mustill stated in *Re Goldcorp Exchange Ltd*[2]: 'It makes no difference what the parties intended if what they intend is impossible as is the case with an immediate transfer of title[3] to goods whose identity is not yet known ... It is impossible to have title to goods when nobody knows to which goods the title relates'.

1   *Re London Wine Co Shippers Ltd* [1986] PCC 121; *Re Goldcorp Exchange Ltd* [1995] 1 AC 74.
2   [1995] 1 AC 74 at 90 and 92.
3   In *Re Goldcorp Exchange Ltd* [1995] 1 AC 74 at 90, Lord Mustill makes it clear that there is no distinction between creating a new legal or equitable title: 'the same conclusion applies, and for the same reason, to any argument that a title in equity was created by the sale'.

8.17 Here, Lord Mustill was reinforcing the point made by Oliver J but ignored by the Court of Appeal in *Hunter v Moss*[1], such case and *Re Goldcorp Exchange Ltd* being decided without reference to each other owing to their timing.

1   [1994] 3 All ER 215, [1994] 1 WLR 452, criticised in detail by D J Hayton (1994) 110 LQR 335, but applied in two cases not to be cited in court by *Practice Note* [2001] 2 All ER 510 (*Re Harvard Securities* [1997] 2 BCLC 369, an undefended case, and *Re CA Pacific Finance* [2000] 1 BCLC 494, a Hong Kong case).

8.18 In *Hunter v Moss*[1], Moss owned 950 of 1,000 shares in a private company, MEL, the other 50 being owned by the managing director. Moss wanted the finance director, Hunter, to have 5% of the MEL shares like the managing director and so said: 'that he would henceforth hold 5 per cent of the MEL shares either for, or in trust for, the plaintiff'. At first instance the deputy judge found[2]: 'that the defendant had declared himself a trustee for the plaintiff of 50 shares in MEL, being 5 per cent of the share capital of that company,' and held the trust valid.

1   [1994] 1 WLR 452 at 457.
2   [1994] 1 WLR 452 at 455.

8.19 The Court of Appeal upheld the defendant's gratuitous declaration of trust of 50 of his 950 shares for Hunter[1]. Ignoring the significance of *Re London Wine Company (Shippers)*[2] (as later reinforced by *Re Goldcorp Exchange*) it held[3]: 'just as a person can give by will a specified number of his shares in a certain company, so equally he can declare himself a trustee of 50 of his shares in MEL and that is effective to give a beneficial proprietary interest to the beneficiary under the trust.' This is a false analogy because it overlooks the crucial difference between inter vivos and testamentary dispositions. On death a testator is totally divested of all his legal and beneficial title in all his assets in favour of his executor[4] who becomes subject to equitable obligations to effect the testator's wishes so far as practicable after payment of debts, expenses and taxes. In his lifetime a settlor is only divested of his beneficial entitlement to his assets where one knows to which assets such divestment relates.

1   The appellate committee of the House of Lords refused leave to appeal but this does not mean it approved the judgment of the Court of Appeal: *Re Wilson* [1985] AC 750 at 756. It just means it did not consider the House of Lords should hear any appeal, eg because the House was too busy for hearing a case not regarded as significant or because other reasoning might well justify the actual decision (perhaps an intent to create a trust of one twentieth of the 1000 shares should be treated as an intent to create a trust of one nineteenth of Moss's 950 shares).

2   [1986] PCC 121.

3   [1994] 3 All ER 215 at 222, [1994] 1 WLR 452 at 459.

4   Thus the true lifetime analogy is with the situation where S declares he holds 50 of his 950 shares for B and 900 for C, so that B and C between them have full beneficial ownership entitling them under the *Saunders v Vautier* principle to demand the shares from S.

8.20 It is surely impossible to confer equitable title to an enumerated number of shares in a larger shareholding when nobody knows to which shares the title relates until the registered shareholder has sent to the company his share certificate for the whole shareholding (950 shares) in order to receive back two share certificates, for one shareholding (900 shares) to be retained for himself and one shareholding (50 shares) to be held on trust. Equitable duties only then arise in respect of the latter shareholding with the tracing process available only in respect of gifts or sales of such shareholding. The fact that it is more difficult to perfect a gift of assets, like a private company, that require registration than a gift of assets transferable by delivery or by a formal deed does not justify by-passing fundamental rules. Imperfectly gifted property on trust cannot be traced because no trust can arise till the relevant intention has been duly implemented and an intention to create a trust of a specific number out of a larger number of shares in a private company is not an intention to create a trust of a specific proportion of the large shareholding. Only a statute can treat the former intention as the latter intention as witness the Sale of Goods (Amendment) Act 1995.

8.21 In view of the erroneous analogy in *Hunter v Moss* and of the ringing endorsement of *Re London Wine (Shippers) Ltd* by the Privy Council in *Re Goldcorp Exchange Ltd*[1] (argued before the Court of Appeal decision in *Hunter v Moss*) it is respectfully submitted that *Hunter v Moss* should not be followed where a registered shareholder declares himself trustee of a specific number of his shares rather than a specific fraction or percentage of his whole shareholding: there is no sound reason for distinguishing trusts of goods from trusts of intangibles[2].

1   [1995] 1 AC 74, [1994] 2 All ER 806, PC. Also see *MacJordan Construction Ltd v Brookmount Erostin Ltd* (1991) 56 BLR 1, [1992] BCLC 350, CA; a specifically enforceable contractual right of a contractor to have his employer set aside a retention fund trust of money for the contract does not relate to specific money happening to be in the contractor's general bank account, so the contractor has no equitable proprietary interest till the retention fund is actually set up; similarly see *McKee v Paradise* 575 Sup Ct 124, 299 US 122 (1936).

2   The Court of Appeal in *Hunter v Moss* [1995] 1 AC 74, [1994] 2 All ER 806, PC did not focus on this (mass-produced tangibles being as identical as intangible fungibles), though this had been done at first instance: [1993] 1 WLR 934 at 946; and this distinction was used in *Re Harvard Securities* [1997] 2 BCLC 369 to try to reconcile *Hunter v Moss* with

Re Goldcorp Exchange Ltd. Where A is owed £5,000 by B, A can declare himself trustee of his chose in action for C, but, despite *Hunter v Moss*, surely B, whether having 10,000 in cash or in a bank account, cannot be trustee of £5,000 for C till he segregates it: *McFadden v Jenkyns* (1841) 1 Ph 153, cf *Re Innes* [1910] 1 Ch 188 at 193 and Australian High Court in *Herdegen v Federal Commissioner of Taxation* (1988) 84 ALR 271. Further see Sir Roy Goode in 'Are Intangible Assets Fungibles?' [2003] LMCLQ 309, disputed by G Morton in S Worthington (ed), *Commercial Law and Commercial Practice* (Hart Publishing, 2003) pp 296–302 and Hayton & Marshall, *Commentary & Cases on Trusts* (12th edn by D Hayton & Mitchell) para 3–85.

8.22 However, where the intangibles are shares in a public company whose shares are held by a nominee under the CREST system with, say, 1 million shares recorded as held, say, for Cazenove & Co, whose records state that 20,000 shares are held for S, S does not actually own 20,000 shares: he owns a one fiftieth equitable interest in Cazenove's pool of 1 million shares which may amount to a one fifth equitable interest in the public company's shares held by the nominee. Thus, if S declares himself trustee of his 20,000 shares in the company, the court will need to construe this otherwise nonsensical, impossible declaration as a declaration of trust of his one fiftieth interest in Cazenove's interest. It would seem to follow that if S happened to declare himself trustee of 10,000 of his 20,000 shares then, because he does not own any shares, his declaration should be construed as a trust of half of the one fiftieth interest he does own in Cazenove's interest. Thus certainty of subject matter of the trust is present[1].

[1]   Due to reg 38(5) of the Uncertified Securities Regulations 2001 no problem arises over the possible application of Law of Property Act, s 53(1)(c) where S declares himself trustee of his equitable interest for B absolutely or B and C absolutely where they are of full age and capacity: see paras 12.15–12.36 below.

Uncertainty as to testamentary trusts

8.23 A testator may validly settle his residuary estate (after payment of debts, expenses, taxes and legacies) on trusts because whatever is left after specified payments is ascertainable. Similarly, if property is left on trust for W for life, with W also having a general power of appointment over capital, and whatever remains on W's death is to be held on trust for her children equally, the latter trust is valid[1]. It has been said that a testator's gift of the bulk of his property to X (as donee or as trustee for others) will be void since it is impossible to determine what is the trust property[2]. However, if the rest is given to Y so that the testator has divested himself of all his property in favour of X and Y, there seems no reason why X and Y should not take advantage of the *Saunders v Vautier* principle to claim all the property and divide it between them in such way as they agree.

[1]   *Re Richards* [1902] 1 Ch 76.
[2]   *Palmer v Simmonds* (1854) 2 Drew 221; cf *Bromley v Tyron* [1952] AC 265, [1951] 2 All ER 1058, HL. (Bulk means anything over one half, so shifting clause conditioned on Stoke Hall Estate 'or the bulk thereof' vesting in X was upheld).

8.24 Where a testator gives property to, or in trust for, his wife, and directs that *such part of it as may not be required by her* shall, after her death, be held in trust for his children, the latter trust is void for uncertainty, for no one can say how much the wife may or may not require[1]. Thus the wife takes the property absolutely. The Administration of Justice Act 1982, s 22 now states, 'Except where a contrary intention is shown it shall be presumed that if a testator devises or bequeaths property to his spouse in terms which in themselves would give an absolute interest to the spouse but by the same instrument purports to give his issue an interest in the same property the gift to the spouse is absolute notwithstanding the purported gift to the issue.'

[1] Per Sir A Hobhouse in *Mussoorie Bank v Raynor* (1882) 7 App Cas 321 at 331; and see *Pope v Pope* (1839) 10 Sim 1; and *Re Minchell's Will Trust* [1964] 2 All ER 47 (wife taking absolutely where estate bequeathed to her 'for her life', with precatory words for disposing of whatever was left at her death). See also *Re Dunstan* [1918] 2 Ch 304; but cf *Re Wilson* (1916) 142 LT Jo 41 and *Re Last* [1958] P 137, [1958] 1 All ER 316 where on the construction of the wills it was held that the first taker was limited to a life interest only.

8.25 On similar uncertainty grounds, directions to a legatee 'to remember' certain persons[1], or 'to give what should remain at her death'[2], or 'to reward very old servants and tenants according to their deserts'[3], or (after an absolute gift to a wife) a direction that at her death 'such parts of my estate as she shall not have sold or disposed of' should be held in trust for certain other persons[4], have all been held void for uncertainty as to the property. The trust property has to be certain when the trust is created not just when the trust terms are to begin to operate. Thus in Canada an inter vivos trust set up on the separation of the settlor from his wife to take effect upon the settlor's death when the trustee was to hold three fifths of the settlor's net estate for the wife for life or until re-marriage, remainder for their two children, was held void for uncertainty as to the property[5].

[1] *Bardswell v Bardswell* (1838) 9 Sim 319.
[2] *Parnall v Parnall* (1878) 9 Ch D 96; *Sprange v Barnard* (1789) 2 Bro CC 585; *Tibbits v Tibbits* (1816) 19 Ves 657; *Pope v Pope* (1839) 10 Sim 1.
[3] *Knight v Knight* (1840) 3 Beav 148; affd sub nom *Knight v Boughton* (1844) 11 Cl & Fin 513, HL; and see *Stead v Mellor* (1877) 5 Ch D 225.
[4] *Re Jones* [1898] 1 Ch 438; distinguished in *Re Sanford* [1901] 1 Ch 939. For other examples of trusts void for uncertainty as to the property, see *Sale v Moore* (1827) 1 Sim 534; *Hoy v Master* (1934) 6 Sim 568; *Curtis v Rippon* (1820) 5 Madd 434; *Cowman v Harrison* (1852) 10 Hare 234; and *Green v Marsden* (1853) 1 Drew 646. See also *Re Booth* (1917) 86 LJ Ch 270; and *Re Howell* [1915] 1 Ch 241.
[5] *Re Beardmore* [1952] 1 DLR 41 (the inter vivos equivalent of *Sprange v Barnard* (1789) 2 Bro CC 585).

8.26 On the other hand, a trust to pay a 'reasonable income' to a beneficiary has been held to refer to an objective standard, which could if necessary be quantified by the court, and therefore not to fail for uncertainty[1]. Similarly, a trust will be valid if it is to purchase an annuity of £10,000 pa for X for life or to purchase a school fees annuity policy to enable X to attend public school for five years by providing no less than is considered sufficient to cover the fees of a boarder at the Leys School, Cambridge. It suffices that there is a formula or method for identifying the subject matter of a trust, eg where a testator wishes to ensure that he takes advantage[2] of the whole of the nil per cent band for inheritance tax applicable on his death so as to leave on trust or otherwise a cash legacy (or a legacy of such number of shares in a private company as shall ultimately be agreed with the Revenue to be of the value) of such an amount as may be bequeathed before inheritance tax becomes payable thereon at a rate above 0%.

1   *Re Golay* [1965] 2 All ER 660, [1965] 1 WLR 969; *Ellis v Chief Adjudication Officer* [1998] 1 FLR 184, CA (valid condition requiring donee-daughter to allow donor-mother to live in donated flat so long as was reasonably practicable and to provide the donor with an acceptable standard of living); cf 'reasonable price' or 'reasonable rent' in *Talbot v Talbot* [1968] Ch 1, [1967] 2 All ER 920, CA; *Smith v Morgan* [1971] 2 All ER 1500, [1971] 1 WLR 803; *Brown v Gould* [1972] Ch 53, [1971] 2 All ER 1505; *King's Motors (Oxford) Ltd v Lax* [1969] 3 All ER 665, [1970] 1 WLR 426; *Ponsford v HMS Aerosols Ltd* [1979] AC 63, [1978] 2 All ER 837, HL; *Sudbrook Trading Estate Ltd v Eggleton* [1983] 1 AC 444, [1982] 3 All ER 1, HL; *Re Malpass* [1985] Ch 42, [1984] 2 All ER 313 (testamentary option to purchase at value 'as agreed with the District Valuer' upheld and inquiry directed as to price where the valuer refused to value since there was no official need to value).
2   If a testator's will is not tax-efficient the legatees within two years of his death may re-write the will with effect from death for capital gains tax and inheritance tax purposes: Inheritance Act 1984, s 142, and Taxation of Chargeable Gains Act 1992, s 62(6).

8.27 However a bequest of 'such minimal part of my estate as [my wife] might be entitled to under English law for maintenance purposes' was held void for uncertainty in the absence of adequate criteria for ascertaining the wife's entitlement[1], so the wife's course of action was to apply for reasonable financial provision under the Inheritance (Provision for Family and Dependants) Act 1975.

1   *Anthony v Donges* [1998] 2 FLR 775.

8.28 A curious example of uncertainty in regard to the beneficial shares in property is afforded by the case of *Boyce v Boyce*[1]. Here a testator devised his four houses in Southwold to trustees in trust for his wife for life, and after her death in trust to convey one of them, whichever she might choose, to his daughter Maria in fee, and to convey the others to his daughter Charlotte in fee. Maria died in the testator's lifetime and therefore could not choose any particular house, and it was held that in consequence the trust in favour of Charlotte was void for uncertainty, so that on the widow's death the four houses were held on resulting trust. If the trustees had been given a discretion to determine the quantum of the beneficiaries' interest, then there would have been a valid discretionary trust, but any failure to exercise the discretion would enable the court to intervene and appoint new trustees or, if a basis for distribution appears, order distribution, whether on an equal or unequal basis[2].

1   (1849) 16 Sim 476. Nowadays, a court might be more ready to construe the trust as of four houses for Charlotte subject to the right of Maria to choose one of them for herself.
2   *McPhail v Doulton* [1971] AC 424 at 457, HL. *Salusbury v Denton* (1857) 3 K & J 529; *Re Coxen* [1948] Ch 747, [1948] 2 All ER 492.

Defendant unconscionably relying on uncertainty

8.29 Where a court is imposing a constructive trust over the defendant's property in order to prevent his unconscionable behaviour in trying, to the detriment of the claimant, to take advantage of uncertainty created by the defendant, the court will circumvent the uncertainty[1]. Thus, a common intention constructive trust of a 'fair share' of a home will not be void for uncertainty but will be converted into a trust of a specific share that the court considers fair in the circumstances[2].

1   For commercial joint venture cases where no valid contract existed to protect the claimant see *Banner Homes Group plc v Luff Development Ltd* [2000] Ch 372.
2   *Gissing v Gissing* [1971] AC 886 at 909; *Passee v Passee* [1988] 1 FLR 263 at 271; *Oxley v Hislock* [2004] EWCA Civ 546, [2004] 3 All ER 703.

Floating (or suspended) trusts

8.30 It used to be thought that if property were bequeathed essentially to X to pass on whatever was left at his death to Y, then this would normally be treated as an absolute gift to X[1] but, in an exceptional case, the court in context might be able to find that the property had to be held on trust for X for life, remainder to Y absolutely[2].

1   *Sprange v Barnard* (1789) 2 Bro CC 585.
2   *Re Last* [1958] P 137, [1958] 1 All ER 316.

8.31 There is now a third possibility where the testator and X have reached an express or implied agreement, since Brightman J in *Ottaway v Norman* stated[1]:

'I am content to assume for present purposes, but without so deciding, that if property is given to [X] on the understanding that [X] will dispose by his will of such assets, if any, as he may have at his command at his death in favour of [Y], a valid trust is created in favour of [Y] which is in suspense during the lifetime of [X] but attaches to the estate of [X] at the moment of [X's] death.'

1   [1972] Ch 698 at 713.

8.32 Further elucidation is present in an earlier Australian case, *Birmingham v Renfrew*[1], where Dixon J (as he then was) stated[1]:

'The purpose must often be to enable the survivor during his life to deal as absolute owner with the property passing under the will of the party first dying. The object is to put the survivor in a position to enjoy for his own benefit the full ownership so that he may convert it and expend the proceeds if he choose. But when he dies he is to bequeath what is left in the manner agreed upon. It is only by the special doctrines of equity that such a floating obligation, suspended, so to speak, during the lifetime of the survivor can descend upon the assets at his death and crystallise into a trust. No doubt, gifts and settlements inter vivos, if calculated to defeat the intention of the compact, could not be made by the survivor and his right of disposition inter vivos is therefore not unqualified.'

1   (1937) 57 CLR 666.
2   (1937) 57 CLR 666 at 689, endorsed by Nourse J in *Re Cleaver* [1981] 2 All ER 1018, [1981] 1 WLR 939. The survivor must not give away considerable portions of the capital or do anything else with it that would be inconsistent with the spirit and the obvious intention and purpose of the agreement: *Edell v Sitzer* (2001) 4 ITELR 149 at 169–170.

8.33 Where this third possibility arises it thus seems that X has an absolute interest subject to an equitable fiduciary obligation during his lifetime neither to transfer the property nor to contract to transfer the property with destructive intent to prevent the property passing to Y[1]. The obligation is rather nebulous so that a well-advised testator would leave the property to trustees for X for life, remainder to Y but give X and the trustees a joint power to appoint capital to X.

1   It would seem that Y should have a proprietary base to justify a proprietary remedy via the tracing process. Quaere whether Y should have a right to ensure that X kept a separate account of the property received by him subject to the fiduciary obligation? Presumably, if Y predeceased X then X's fiduciary obligation would cease. Further see *Palmer v Bank of New South Wales* (1975) 113 CLR 150.

Uncertainty as to the beneficiaries or as to the way in which the property is to be applied

8.34 Where the uncertainty arises in relation either to the persons intended to be benefited[1], or to the way in which[2], or the period for which, the property is to be applied, then unless the trust is for charitable purposes, in which event if a general charitable intention is present the court[3] or the Charity Commission[4] can always settle a scheme, the trust is void[5].

1   See *Re Astor's Settlement Trusts* [1952] Ch 534, [1952] 1 All ER 1067; see also *Re Shaw* [1957] 1 All ER 745, [1957] 1 WLR 729; compromised on appeal [1958] 1 All ER 245n, CA (trusts for alphabet reform). The whole trust for a class of beneficiaries fails if although part of the class is certain, part is uncertain: *Re Wright's Will Trusts* (21 July 1982, unreported) CA, (1999) 13 Trust L I 48.
2   See *Briggs v Hartley* (1850) 19 LJ Ch 416; *Re Endacott* [1960] Ch 232, [1959] 3 All ER 562, CA (for 'providing some useful memorial to myself'); *Re Atkinson's Will Trusts* [1978] 1 All ER 1275, [1978] 1 WLR 586 ('worthy causes'); *R v District Auditor No 3 Audit District of West Yorkshire Metropolitan County Council, ex p West Yorkshire Metropolitan County Council* [1986] RVR 24, [2001] WTLR 785.
3   *Re Gott* [1944] Ch 193, [1944] 1 All ER 293; *Re Shaw* [1957] 1 All ER 745, [1957] 1 WLR 729; compromised on appeal [1958] 1 All ER 245n, CA. Note, however, that the court's powers to order a scheme arises only when the gift concerned is made by way of trust: when it is a direct gift (eg a testamentary gift to a non- existent beneficiary, from which a general charitable intention can be deduced) the court cannot order a scheme and the subject matter of the gift must be administered as directed by Her Majesty the Queen: *Re Bennett* [1960] Ch 18, [1959] 3 All ER 295.
4   See the Charities Act 1993, ss 13, 14, 16 and Charities Act 2006.
5   See *Thomason v Moses* (1842) 5 Beav 77; *Re Porter* [1925] Ch 746; *Re Endacott* [1960] Ch 232, [1959] 3 All ER 562, CA; *Re Flavel's Will Trusts* [1969] 2 All ER 232, [1969] 1 WLR 444.

8.35 There is, however, an important difference to be noted between trusts void for uncertainty as to the property, and those void for uncertainty as to beneficiaries, or as to the way in which the property is intended to be applied. Where it is held that there is uncertainty as to the property intended to be settled, it is obvious that no further question can arise; for if there is no property capable of identification there is nothing to litigate about. But where the property is described with sufficient certainty, and the words actually used, or the surrounding circumstances, make it clear that, although the donor has not sufficiently specified the objects of his bounty or the way in which the property was intended to be dealt with, yet he never meant the trustee to take the entire beneficial interest, it is different; and in such cases (which are treated of in Division Three, below) the law imposes a resulting trust in favour of the donor or persons claiming under him.

8.36 Where a trust for beneficiaries is intended to benefit them absolutely but in specified ways which are uncertain or exhaustively carried out then the specified purposes are regarded as the motive of the trust which is thus valid for the beneficiaries[1].

1   *Re Andrew's Trust* [1905] 2 Ch 48; *Re Osoba* [1979] 2 All ER 393, [1979] 1 WLR 247, CA; *Hancock v Watson* [1902] AC 14, HL. Further see paras 8.154–8.155.

8.37 Where it is the way in which a valid trust fund is to be invested that is void for uncertainty (eg a direction to trustees to invest in shares in the 'blue chip' category) then one falls back on the statutory powers of investment applicable in the absence of express powers of investment[1].

1   *Re Kolb's Will Trusts* [1962] Ch 531.

8.38 Uncertainty may sometimes be avoided if it arises from a provision which does not properly express the settlor's intention and which the court can construe so as to express this intention correctly and thus to eliminate the uncertainty[1].

1   As, eg in *Re Wootton's Will Trusts* [1968] 2 All ER 618 and *Re Gulbenkian's Settlement Trusts* [1970] AC 508, [1968] 3 All ER 785, HL. By Administration of Justice Act 1982, s 21, discussed by R Kerridge and J Rivers in 'The Construction of Wills' (2000) 116 LQR 311, extrinsic evidence, including evidence of the testator's intention, may be admitted to assist in the interpretation of a will in so far as it is meaningless or the language used is ambiguous on the face of it or in so far as evidence, other than evidence of the testator's intention, shows that the language used is ambiguous in the light of the surrounding circumstances. Evidence of counsel's opinion given at or prior to the execution of an inter vivos trust deed is not admissible to explain the meaning of the deed since this will be a breach of the parol evidence rule: *Rabin v Gerson Berger Association Ltd* [1986] 1 All ER 374, [1986] 1 WLR 526, CA. See also *Re Tepper's Will Trusts* [1987] 1 All ER 970; *Re Benham's Will Trusts* [1995] STC 210.

Uncertainty as to period of duration of trust

8.39 Trusts of income limited to a period which is impossible of ascertainment are void for uncertainty.

8.40 Thus, where a testatrix bequeathed £500 to trustees to be applied in keeping up a tomb until the expiration of the period of 21 years from the death of the last survivor of all persons living at her death, it was held that, quite apart from any question whether the rule against perpetuities was infringed, the trust was void for uncertainty, as it would be impossible to ascertain when the last life would be extinguished[1].

1   *Re Moore* [1901] 1 Ch 936. This case was considered and distinguished in *Muir v IRC* [1966] 3 All ER 38, [1966] 1 WLR 1269, CA, where it was said that if there was no present uncertainty, the mere possibility of uncertainty arising in the future did not invalidate the trust.

8.41 On the other hand, a trust limited in the 1930s by reference to the life of the survivor of a large class, eg the descendants of Queen Victoria, is not void: it is merely difficult and expensive, but not actually impossible, to discover when such survivor dies[1]. For a royal lives perpetuity clause it is nowadays safer to use the descendants of King George VI.

1   *Re Villar* [1929] 1 Ch 243, CA; and see *Re Leverhulme (No 2)* [1943] 2 All ER 274.

Uncertainty as to beneficiaries under fixed trusts

8.42 A fixed trust is void unless at the outset it can be seen clearly that *all* the beneficiaries thereunder are then ascertainable or will be ascertainable when the time comes under the trust to distribute capital or income[1]. Just as a trust for A for life remainder to B absolutely is valid, so is a trust for A (a bachelor) for life remainder to his children equally and a trust to divide a fund equally between such persons as shall on X's death be his statutory next of kin or his dependants. However, a trust to divide a fund equally between next of kin and dependants of persons currently or formerly employed by ICI plc or by any company on the board of which an ICI plc director currently sits will be void unless a comprehensive list of such beneficiaries can be drawn up so as to enable an equal division to be made[2]. Except where the potential number of beneficiaries is very high and the value of the trust fund relatively low[3] it will usually be possible to draw up a comprehensive list of the persons ranking as beneficiaries at the time for distribution of the trust fund. However, a small class may be void for conceptual uncertainty, eg a trust for 'my old friends' or 'my business associates' where no criteria can be ascertained from the trust instrument or other admissible evidence for determining exactly who can be old friends or business associates[4]. Thus a trust for equal division among 'my friends' will be void[5].

1   *Re Gulbenkian's Settlement Trusts* [1970] AC 508 at 524, [1968] 3 All ER 785 at 793B; *Kinsels v Caldwell* (1975) Austr LR 337; *Re Ahmed & Co* [2006] EWHC 480 (Ch) para 116, [2006] NLJR 512.
2   *IRC v Broadway Cottages Trusts* [1955] Ch 20, [1954] 3 All ER 120; *McPhail v Doulton* [1971] AC 424 at 450, [1970] 2 All ER 228 at 244f; *Re Sayer* [1957] Ch 423, [1956] 3 All ER 600.
3   *Re Gulbenkian's Settlement Trusts* [1970] AC 508 at 519, [1968] 3 All ER 785 at 788, HL. The court requires substantial probability that all the beneficiaries can be ascertained even if much difficulty and much expense is likely: *Re Saxone Shoe Co Ltd's Trusts Deed* [1962] 2 All ER 904, [1962] 1 WLR 943 not following *Re Eden* [1957] 2 All ER 430, [1957] 1 WLR 788.
4   *Re Baden's Deed Trusts (No 2)* [1973] Ch 9, [1972] 2 All ER 1304; *Brown v Gould* [1972] Ch 53, [1971] 2 All ER 1505; *Re Connor Estate* (1970) 10 DLR (3d) 5; *Re Bethel* (1971) 17 DLR (3d) 652; affd sub nom *Jones v Executive Officers of the T Eaton Co Ltd* (1973) 35 DLR (3d) 97; *Re Tuck's Settlement Trusts* [1978] Ch 49, [1978] 1 All ER 1047; *Re Tepper's Will Trusts* [1987] 1 All ER 970.
5   *Brown v Gould* [1972] Ch 53 at 57 and *Re Barlow's Will Trusts* [1979] 1 All ER 296 at 299, [1979] 1 WLR 278 at 281, 282. A fixed or discretionary trust for 'customers' would also seem void for uncertainty due to difficulties of distinguishing 'ex-customers': *Spafax (1965) Ltd v Dommett* (1972) 116 Sol Jo 711, (1972) Times, 14 July, CA.

Uncertainty as to beneficiaries under discretionary trusts

THE OLD TEST

8.43 Until the House of Lords' three to two majority decision in *McPhail v Doulton*[1] it was taken for granted that a trust, whether fixed or discretionary, was void for uncertainty if a comprehensive list of beneficiaries could not be drawn up[2]. After all, trusts are imperative: they must be carried out by trustees, though, in default, it must be possible for the court to enforce and carry out the trusts. If trustees failed to carry out discretionary trusts then, since it would be invidious and injudicious for the court to discriminate between the possible discretionary beneficiaries, the court would have to act on the maxim 'Equality is equity' and so distribute the trust fund equally between the beneficiaries. This is impossible unless a comprehensive list is capable of being drawn up so as to know into what number of shares to divide the fund equally.

[1]   [1971] AC 424, [1970] 2 All ER 228; (1971) 87 LQR 31 (J W Harris); [1971] CLJ 68 (J A Hopkins); (1974) 37 MLR 643 (Y Grbich).
[2]   *Re Gulbenkian's Settlement Trusts* [1970] AC 508, [1968] 3 All ER 785.

THE NEW TEST: AS FOR OBJECTS OF FIDUCIARY POWERS OF APPOINTMENT

8.44 However, in *McPhail v Doulton* the House of Lords assimilated the test for uncertainty of beneficiaries under discretionary trusts to the test for certainty of objects under a mere power. Earlier in *Re Gulbenkian's Settlement Trusts*[1] the House of Lords had laid down that a mere power is valid, even though a comprehensive list of its objects cannot be drawn up, so long as it is possible to say with certainty of any given postulant that he definitely is an object of the power or that he definitely is not an object of the power.

[1]   [1970] AC 508, [1968] 3 All ER 785.

8.45 Indeed, a mere power will be void if, although one or a few persons can definitely be said to be within the power, there are persons of whom it cannot be said 'with certainty who is within and who is without the power'[1]. The underlying reasoning was that trustees with a mere power do not *have* to exercise it, so that the court cannot compel the trustees to exercise it: the objects of the power have a mere spes or hope of benefiting, and the persons entitled in default of exercise of the power have full equitable interests which entitle them to restrain the trustees from exercising the power in favour of persons outside the power. Thus, 'the trustees or the court must be able to say with certainty who is within and who is without the power'[2]. In obiter dicta the House of Lords (Lord Reid reserving his position) clearly affirmed the comprehensive list test of certainty for beneficiaries under discretionary trusts, since such trusts have to be executed by the court in the event of default by the trustees, execution being impossible unless there can be equal division.

[1]   [1970] AC 508 at 524, [1968] 3 All ER 785 at 794A per Lord Upjohn, with whom Lords Hodson and Guest concurred. It seems the possibility of the power being exercised to confer equal interests on all the objects is ignored in ascertaining the validity of the power. Any such exercise would presumably be void for capriciousness.

2   [1970] AC 508 at 525. The authority of *Re Allen* Ch 810, [1953] 2 All ER 898, for the
view that conceptual uncertainty does not vitiate conditions precedent is most doubtful in
view of the favoured 'is or is not' approach of the House of Lords in *Gulbenkian* and in
McPhail despite the views of Browne-Wilkinson J in *Re Barlow's Will Trusts* [1979]
1 All ER 296, paras 8.92–8.94 below.

8.46 In *McPhail v Doulton* Lords Hodson and Guest reaffirmed their view in
Re Gulbenkian's Settlement Trusts but Lord Wilberforce (with whom
Lord Reid and Viscount Dilhorne concurred) held that the test for certainty of
beneficiaries under discretionary trusts should be assimilated to the 'is or is
not' test for certainty of objects under a mere power: after all, in practical
substance there is very little difference between the position of objects of a
discretionary power and beneficiaries under a discretionary trust: they only
have a hope of benefiting, though the hopes of beneficiaries will nomally be
higher than the hopes of objects of powers of appointment (unless favoured in
a letter of wishes)[1]. Lord Wilberforce relied on certain 18th century cases for
the proposition that execution by the court does not require equal division,
especially where equal division is surely the last thing the settlor ever
intended[2]. Referring to the discretionary trust in question as a 'trust power'
(as opposed to a mere power) he laid down[3]:

'In the case of a trust power, if the trustees do not exercise it, the court will do
so in the manner best calculated to give effect to the settlor's or testator's
intentions. It may do so by appointing new trustees, or by authorising or
directing representative persons of the classes of beneficiaries to prepare a
scheme for distribution, or even, should the proper basis for distribution
appear, by itself directing the trustees so to distribute.'

1   Further see *Schmidt v Rosewood Trust Ltd* [2003] UKPC 26, [2003] 2 AC 709,
paras 40–42.
2   The comprehensive list test will only apply at the end of the trust period if the discretionary
trust instrument reveals that the settlor requires equal division at the end of the trust
period.
3   [1971] AC 424 at 457, [1970] 2 All ER 228 at 247b; *Re Locker's Settlement Trusts* [1978]
1 All ER 216 at 219. Lord Wilberforce [1971] AC 424 at 449 accepted that it was 'legally
correct' 'to say that there is no obligation to exercise a mere power and that no court will
intervene to compel it, whereas a trust is mandatory and its execution may be compelled'.
This passage was endorsed by Lord Walker in *Schmidt v Rosewood Trust Ltd* [2003]
UKPC 26, [2003] 2 AC 709, para 39, but see paras 42 and 51.

8.47 Having stated the law, Lord Wilberforce then remitted the case to the
High Court[1], whence an appeal was made to the Court of Appeal[2], for a
determination whether the discretionary trust in question was valid or void for
uncertainty. Certain problems then emerged as to the proper scope of what, at
first sight, seems a simple clear test.

1   *Re Baden's Deed Trusts (No 2)* [1972] Ch 607, [1971] 3 All ER 985.
2   [1973] Ch 9, [1972] 2 All ER 1304.

SCOPE OF THE NEW TEST

8.48 The discretionary trust in question was for the trustees to make 'at their
absolute discretion grants to or for the benefit of any of the officers and
employees or ex-officers or ex-employees of the Company or to any relatives

or dependants of any such persons in such amounts at such times and on such conditions (if any) as they think fit'. When the trust was created the company had about 1,300 officers and employees, the company having been incorporated 14 years previously in 1927. It became clear that the trustees could not trace numbers of short-term ex-employees (who had moved on since 1927) or, therefore, their relatives and dependants[1].

1   [1972] Ch 607. Where the discretionary trust is for future as well as existing persons it must be restricted to the perpetuity period or reliance must be placed on Perpetuities and Accumulations Act 1964: see paras 11.17–11.18 below.

8.49 In the Court of Appeal, Stamp LJ took the view that the 'is or is not' test, for certainty of beneficiaries under discretionary trusts and of objects under powers, required that the court must be able to say of any given postulant that he definitely *is* a member of the class of beneficiaries or he definitely is *not* such a member, ie the name of any given person must be capable of being put either in a 'Yes' box or a 'No' box. Thus, a discretionary trust would be void if it was impossible to say of a given postulant either that he was or that he was not a member of the beneficial class, ie if his name had to be put into a 'Don't know' box. Accordingly, if 'relative' meant descendant of a common ancestor, so that A was a relative of B if at some time over hundreds or thousands of years they both traced their descent from a common ancestor, the discretionary trust would be void. Whilst many persons definitely would be relatives within the 'Yes' box there would be an infinitely greater number of persons, neither known to be relatives nor known to be non-relatives, needing to be placed within the 'Don't know' box. The apparently clear concept thus turned out, in effect, to be an uncertain 'grey' concept. However, Stamp LJ was prepared to treat relatives as meaning statutory next of kin in which case any given postulant would be bound to fall within the 'Yes' box or the 'No' box. 'Dependants' created no problems of conceptual certainty, only of evidential certainty, which of itself does not invalidate a trust since the court can always resolve the matter on the evidence presented to it on an application for directions.

8.50 Sachs and Megaw LJJ disagreed with Stamp LJ on the issue of 'relatives'. Sachs LJ took the robust practical view that the expression 'relatives' in its broadest sense would not cause the slightest difficulty in practice since the trustees would not distribute to a person who failed to prove he was a relative: if a person is not proved to be within the class of relatives then he is not in it.

8.51 Megaw LJ endorsed this. He also pointed out, first, that, since *McPhail v Doulton*, a discretionary trust does not fail simply because it is impossible to ascertain every member of the class of beneficiaries and to draw up a comprehensive list thereof. Second, the view of Stamp LJ that the 'is or is not' test means that a discretionary trust will fail if it cannot be shown of any individual that he definitely is *or definitely is not* a member of the class, is to contend 'in substance and reality that it does fail simply because it is impossible to ascertain every member of the class'[1]. With respect, this second point seems fallacious since in ascertaining whether *any* (as opposed to every) individual is or is not a member of the class it is not necessary to ascertain *every* member of the class and draw up a comprehensive list, e g if there are roughly 5,000 potential class members the trustees need only survey each of say 2,000 individuals placing each of them definitely inside or definitely outside the discretionary class according to clear conceptual criteria.

¹   [1973] Ch 9 at 23, [1972] 2 All ER 1305 at 1313.

8.52 Be that as it may, Megaw LJ went on to say¹:

'In my judgment, much too great emphasis is placed on the words "or is not". To my mind, the test is satisfied if, as regards at least a substantial number of objects, it can be said with certainty that they fall within the trust, even though as regards a substantial number of other persons, if that ever for some fanciful reason fell to be considered, the answer would have to be, not "they are outside the trust", but "it is not proven whether they are in or out". What is a "substantial number" may well be a question of common sense and of some degree in relation to the particular trust; particularly where, as here, it would be fantasy, to use a mild word, to suggest that any practical difficulty would arise in the fair, proper and sensible administration of this trust in respect of relatives and dependants.'

¹   [1973] Ch 9 at 24, [1972] 2 All ER 1305 at 1313.

8.53 Two comments may be made on the above remarks. First, is it wrong to emphasise the need to ascertain those who are not class members when a person alleging a breach of trust will need to show that the trustees distributed to an individual who was not a class member? Second, the rule that a discretionary trust is valid if a 'substantial' number of persons can be placed in the 'Yes' box of clear beneficiaries, even though a substantial number have to be placed in the 'Don't know' box of persons of whom it cannot be said they *are* beneficiaries or they are *not* beneficiaries, introduces uncertainty into the test of certainty of beneficiaries. Apart from the obvious uncertainty in the word 'substantial' does the rule operate to validate a discretionary trust as in *McPhail v Doulton* but to which there was added a conceptually uncertain clause such as 'any other person to whom I may be under a moral obligation and any of my old friends'¹? Moreover, it is not so far removed from the view rejected by the House of Lords in *Re Gulbenkian's Settlement Trusts*² in relation to powers (and so in relation to discretionary trusts by *McPhail v Doulton*)³ namely the view⁴ that a power (or discretionary trust) is valid if the trustees can say with certainty of any one person or any few persons⁵ that he or they are within the scope of the power (or discretionary trust), though uncertainty exists as to whether other persons are within or without the power (or discretionary trust).

¹   Alternatively, may the court have power to strike out the offending concept and sever it from the valid concepts within the class or classes of beneficiaries? Cf *Re Leek* [1969] 1 Ch 563 at 586; *Re Gulbenkian's Settlement Trusts* [1968] Ch 126 at 138. The orthodox view is that there is no authority in the trustees or the court to make any distribution among a smaller class than that pointed out by the donor: *Whishaw v Stephens* [1970] AC 508 at 524, sub nom *Re Gulbenkian's Settlement Trusts* [1968] 3 All ER 785 at 792, HL, per Lord Upjohn, with whom Lords Hodson and Guest concurred; *McPhail v Doulton* [1971] AC 424 at 456, [1970] 2 All ER 228 at 246, HL per Lord Wilberforce. Consider also the implications of the views of Megaw LJ for cases like *Re Astor's Settlement Trusts* [1952] Ch 534, [1952] 1 All ER 1067, where a substantial number of persons came within

clause 7(b) for the relief or benefit of persons, or families or dependants thereof, actually or formerly engaged in journalism or in the newspaper business or any branch thereof, applied by the Court of Appeal in *Re Wright's Will Trusts* (21 July 1982) reported in (1999) 13 Trust L I 48.

2   [1970] AC 508 at 524, [1968] 3 All ER 785 at 794.
3   [1971] AC 424, [1970] 2 All ER 228.
4   *Re Gulbenkian's Settlement Trusts* [1968] Ch 126, [1967] 3 All ER 15, CA.
5   Megaw LJ in *Re Baden's Deed Trusts (No 2)* [1973] Ch 9 at 24, [1972] 2 All ER 1304 at 1313, treats the rejected view as concerning one single person being within the power or the trust but Lord Upjohn in *Re Gulbenkian's Settlement Trusts* [1970] AC 508 at 524, [1968] 3 All ER 785 at 792, in his example of two or three individuals being clearly 'old friends' treats the rejected view as concerning one or a few persons clearly within a power or trust.

8.54 Ultimately, everything must hinge upon how the court will deal with B's allegation that the trustees wrongfully paid income to X, whom B alleges is not a relative of S, where there is no evidence capable of proving whether or not X is a relative. If the evidential burden of proof rests on B as well as the legal burden of proof[1] so that the trustees are free to pay income to X or, indeed, to any Tom, Dick or Harry since it is impossible to prove that they are not relatives of S through some possible ancient common ancestor, then the 'trust' should be void for uncertainty and administrative unworkability. However, if the evidential burden of proof rests on the trustees once B has provided prima facie evidence that X is not a relative, then the trust will be valid, since the trustees will be under an enforceable duty to pay only those who can produce the relevant birth and marriage certificates. This justifies the majority view of Sachs and Megaw LJJ who endorsed the views of Brightman J at first instance when he had pointed out[2]. 'A supposed relative to whom a grant is contemplated would, in strictness, be bound to produce the relevant birth and marriage certificates or other sufficient evidence to prove his or her relationship. If the relationship is sufficiently proved the trustees will be entitled to make the grant. If no sufficient evidence can be produced the trustees would have no option but to decline to make a grant.'

1   On legal and evidential burdens see *Cross on Evidence* (Ninth edn) Ch 4.
2   [1972] Ch 607 at 626, [1971] 3 All ER 985 at 995.

8.55 The ease with which common ancestry can be traced back many thousands of years by DNA testing makes it necessary for a settlor or testator not to create a discretionary trust or power for his relatives generally, which could extend to an unworkable[1].100 million Europeans, but to restrict them in some way to descendants of a designated ancestor alive 100 years ago or so. Old trusts, for relatives, like those in *McPhail v Doulton*, should remain valid[2].

1   Two and a half million members of a class made a discretionary trust for such class void for administrative unworkability in *R v District Auditor, ex p West Yorkshire MCC* [1986] RVR 24, [2001] WTLR 785. In *Re Baden's Deed Trusts (No 2)* [1973] Ch 9 at 20 it appears counsel disclaimed any reliance on the class being so large as to be unworkable. If advertising under s 27 of the Trustee Act 1925 or as directed by the court led to a workable group of relatives being known to the trustees then, perhaps, the discretionary trust could be upheld.
2   See para 8.91.

RESOLUTION OF UNCERTAINTY

8.56 Questions of evidential uncertainty will be resolved by the court if need be, though it is possible[1] to make express provision for the trustees or the Chief Rabbi or the testator's widow conclusively to resolve any evidential uncertainty, so obviating any need to apply to the court.

1   *Re Tuck's Settlement Trusts* [1978] Ch 49, [1978] 1 All ER 1047, CA; *Dundee General Hospitals Board of Management v Walker* [1952] 1 All ER 896, HL (where a hospital was to benefit if in the opinion of the trustees a particular event had not occurred).

8.57 Since conceptual uncertainty cannot be resolved by the court it would seem that a fortiori it cannot be resolved by a provision purporting to make the opinion of the trustees conclusive in cases of such uncertainty. If ex hypothesi the court cannot decide who are persons with whom B 'has had a social or other relationship', or persons who 'have moral claims' on a testator, or persons who are 'old friends' of the testator, it is difficult to see how the trustees can[1]. In exercising their fiduciary power or defending it against a challenge in the courts there are surely no clear conceptual criteria to guide them or justify their actions so that the matter is not justiciable, not capable of resolution.

1   *Re Coxen* [1948] Ch 747, [1948] 2 All ER 492; *Re Jones* [1953] Ch 125; *Re Burton's Settlement* [1955] Ch 82 at 95; *Re Wright's Will Trusts* [1981] LS Gaz R 841.

8.58 As Jenkins J said in *Re Coxen*[1]:

'If the testato r had insufficiently defined the state of affairs on which the trustees were to form their opinion he would not have saved the condition from invalidity on the ground of uncertainty merely by making their opinion the criterion, although the declaration by the trustees of this or that opinion would be an event about which in itself there could be no uncertainty.'

1   [1948] Ch 747 at 761–762.

8.59 This view was followed in two other cases where a beneficiary's interest would be forfeited on the happening of a condition subsequent[1], *Re Jones*[2] and *Re Burton's Settlement*[3]. It was also followed in a case where persons were to benefit if satisfying certain conditions, *Re Wright's Will Trusts*[4], where a bequest to trustees 'to use the same at their absolute discretion for such people and institutions as they think have helped me or my late husband' failed for conceptual uncertainty. Any apparent objective-subjective distinction between (i) a trust for 'such persons as have helped me or otherwise have moral claims upon me' with a subsequent clause empowering the opinion of the trustees to be decisive in cases of doubt and (ii) a trust for 'such persons as my trustees consider to have helped me or otherwise to have moral claims upon me' was considered a 'distinction without a difference' as Sir George Jessel MR would have said[5].

1   In the case of a condition subsequent a beneficiary loses what he had actually enjoyed for some time and needs to know precisely what conduct will induce forfeiture, but in the case of a person qualifying as a beneficiary if he satisfies certain conditions (so that the default beneficiary will not begin to have any actual enjoyment) the settlor intends such person to be a primary beneficiary if possible: see para 8.96 below.

²   [1953] Ch 125, [1953] 1 All ER 357.
³   [1955] Ch 82 at 95.
⁴   [1981] LS Gaz R 841 (and on appeal reported in (1999) 13 Trust L I 48) despite the dicta
    of Lord Denning in *Re Tuck's Settlement Trusts* [1978] Ch 49 at 60 and 62, [1978]
    1 All ER 1047 at 1052–1054, CA favouring allowing the Chief Rabbi to resolve any
    conceptual uncertainty. It may well be that resolution by the Chief Rabbi can be justified in
    Re Tuck's Settlement Trusts either because it related to a particular baronet satisfying a
    condition precedent where a 'core meaning' will suffice according to *Re Allen* [1953]
    Ch 810 cited by Lord Denning, or because the matter of Jewish faith can be resolved as an
    evidential matter (c f *Re Tepper's Will Trusts* [1987] Ch 358, para 8.105 below), or because
    the Chief Rabbi can be regarded as an expert acting as such, rather than an arbitrator, so as
    to be able to resolve related questions of law and fact: *Brown v Glo Insurance Ltd* [1998]
    Lloyd's Rep IR 201; *Nikko Hotels (UK) Ltd v MEPC* [1991] 2 EGLR 103 at 108.
⁵   See also Eveleigh LJ in *Re Tuck's ST* [1978] Ch 49 at 66.

8.60 However, in *Re Leek*¹ Harman and Russell LJJ had no difficulty accepting the certainty of a trust for such other persons as the trustees may consider to have a moral claim upon the late Colonel Leek. 'I do not see why they should not be able to make up their minds and arrive at a decision'². This seems based upon the trustees' decisions being unchallengeable so long as not made capriciously or otherwise not in good faith, so that the trustees' duties are not fully fiduciary and so capable of justiciable challenge on the wide-ranging grounds³ available to a beneficiary disgruntled by the trustees' exercise of a fiduciary power of appointment or of a trust power within a discretionary trust for beneficiaries. Thus, so long as the trustees do not stray beyond the 'black core' or the 'grey penumbra' of what they can consider to be a moral claim into the 'white area' where no reasonable possibility of such a claim can exist, their decisions will stand unless amounting to a fraud on a power⁴.

¹   [1969] Ch 563 concerned with a trust of life assurance monies to provide benefits on
    Colonel Leek's death for his widow, issue and such other persons as the trustee might
    consider to have a moral claim upon him. Cross J took the same approach in *Re Kolb's
    Will Trusts* [1962] Ch 531 at 537, 539 and in *Re Saxone Shoe Company Ltd's Trust Deed*
    [1962] 1 WLR 943 at 953.
²   Per Harman LJ [1969] Ch 563 at 579 and see Russell LJ at 582.
³   See Article 61.
⁴   Under the fraud on a power doctrine, a trustee within the 'white' area will not be able to
    distribute trust money to someone within the 'black' or 'grey area under an arrangement
    with that person for the personal benefit of the trustee.

8.61 By way of contrast, if the discretionary trust is objectively for persons who have a moral claim upon the late X or who were friends of X, and the trustees are separately given power conclusively to determine whether or not a person had a moral claim or was a friend of X in instances of doubt, this legalistic structure can justifiably be held to be one where the trustees' power is a fully fiduciary power, the draftsperson not having proceeded in legalistic fashion expressly to add a proviso to the effect that in making such determinations the decisions of the trustees are to be final unless it is proved that they were made capriciously or otherwise not in good faith¹. Thus, the trust is void because too uncertain to be capable of justiciable challenge on the wide-ranging grounds available to challenge the exercise of a fully fiduciary power.

1   The jurisdiction of the court over fully or partly fiduciary powers cannot be ousted: trustees cannot delimit the scope of their own obligations: *Re Raven* [1915] 1 Ch 673; *Re Wynn's Will Trusts* [1952] Ch 271. However, the extent to which the court can intervene can be limited by limiting the content of fiduciary powers.

8.62 The moral is always to spell out any intended dilution of trustees' fiduciary duties.

8.63 If the arbiter was not the trustees but the testator's widow the position is very likely different. An individual, like a widow, having a personal power, as opposed to a trustee having a fiduciary power, is unhampered by fiduciary duties and cannot have the power taken away from her[1]. She can release the power[2], or decide never to bother to consider exercising it, or exercise the power initially by an appointment to trustees of a discretionary trust who then can exercise the discretion that formerly she had despite the *Delegatus non potest delegare* principle[3], or exercise it capriciously without bothering to consider the range of objects[4], though she cannot go outside the range of objects or commit a fraud on the power (eg by exercising the power in B's favour subject to obtaining a pre-arranged benefit from B).

1   *Re Park* [1932] 1 Ch 580 at 582.
2   *Re Wills' Trust Deeds* [1964] Ch 219 at 237.
3   *Re Triffitt's Settlement* [1958] Ch 852 at 864.
4   *Re Hay's Settlement Trusts* [1981] 3 All ER 786 at 792, [1982] 1 WLR 202 at 209.

8.64 In *Re Coates*[1] a testator provided, 'If my wife feels that I have forgotten any friend I direct my executors to pay to such friend or friends as are nominated by my wife a sum not exceeding £25 per friend with a maximum aggregate payment of £250 so that such friends may buy a small memento of our friendship' and this was upheld[2]. Similarly, in *Re Gibbard*[3] a life tenant's power to appoint to 'old friends' was upheld. Nowadays, these cases could be followed but on the ground that the testator-settlor intended the exercise of the power to be unchallengeable unless in favour of someone beyond the 'black' core or the 'grey' penumbra of persons who could qualify as friends and into the 'white' area, where there is no reasonable possibility of persons qualifying as friends, or unless amounting to a fraud on a power[4]. After all, it is clear from *Re Hay's Settlement Trusts*[5] that one can validly confer on the widow power, for example, to add to the class of beneficiaries anyone else (other than herself or the trustees) or power to appoint to anyone (except herself or the trustees) so that one may certainly qualify that by adding 'particularly anyone she considers a friend of the testator'.

1   [1955] Ch 495, [1955] 1 All ER 26.
2   Roxburgh J seemed to regard the concept in context as certain enough but the decision pre-dated *Re Gulbenkian's Settlement Trusts* [1970] AC 508, [1968] 3 All ER 785, HL and *McPhail v Doulton* [1971] AC 424, [1970] 2 All ER 228, HL. On 'friends' see *Re Barlow's Will Trusts* [1979] 1 All ER 296 and *Brown v Gould* [1972] Ch 53, [1971] 2 All ER 1505.
3   [1967] 1 WLR 42, [1966] 1 All ER 273.
4   See Art 61(1)(h).
5   [1981] 3 All ER 786, [1982] 1 WLR 202.

8.65 Apparent conceptual uncertainty may be saved from actual uncertainty by benignant construction. As Lord Hailsham has emphasised[1]:

'Where it is claimed that there is an ambiguity, a benignant construction should be given if possible. This was the maxim of the civil law: *semper in dubiis benigniora praeferenda sunt.* There is a similar maxim in English law: *ut res magis valeat quam pereat.* It applies where a gift is capable of two constructions one of which would make it void and the other effectual.'

[1] *IRC v McMullen* [1981] AC 1 at 11, [1980] 1 All ER 884 at 890, HL. Also see *Re Lloyd's Trust Instrument* cited in *Brown v Gould* [1972] Ch 53, [1971] 2 All ER 1505 and *Universe Tankships Inc of Monrovia v International Transport Worker's Federation* [1983] 1 AC 366 at 406, [1982] 2 All ER 67 at 93, HL. See the benevolent *Re Lipinski's Will Trusts* [1976] Ch 235.

8.66 Thus, a residuary bequest 'to those beneficiaries who have only received small amounts' may be validated in context by being restricted to those who had received legacies of £25, £50 and £100 where other legatees had received £200 or £250[1]. Similarly, a private discretionary trust for 'Cambridge students' might be validated by restricting it to students from time to time studying as junior members of the University of Cambridge, so excluding foreigners studying English at Cambridge language schools, students at Cambridge Sixth Form Colleges and students whose homes are in Cambridge but who are studying elsewhere.

[1] *Re Steel* [1978] 2 All ER 1026 at 1032. See also *O'Rourke v Binks* [1992] STC 703, CA for 'small' in s 72(4), Capital Gains Tax Act 1979.

Uncertainty as to objects of personal powers

8.67 While the 'is or is not' test of conceptual certainty applies to certainty of beneficiaries under a trust and objects of trustees' fiduciary powers of appointment, a good arguable case may be made to apply a lesser test of certainty to objects of personal powers of appointment, eg vested in a deceased's widow or sibling. After all, as seen in para 8.63 above, the donee of a personal power is not under the extensive duties of the donee of a fiduciary power. The only duty is not to exercise the power so as to favour someone outside the scope of the power, while there is no possibility of the court exercise the power or appointing someone else to exercise the power, so that there is no need for positive administrative workability of the power[1].

[1] On which see paras 8.71–8.88 below.

8.68 In the light of cases[1] dealing with personal powers of appointment it is open to the courts to accept the validity of such powers so long as the donee can appoint in favour of one or more persons who, on any view, are within the core meaning of the concept (eg 'old friend') even though there are other persons (in a grey area) of whom it cannot be said with certainty whether they qualify as objects of the power.

[1] *Re Coates* [1955] Ch 495; *Re Gibbard* [1966] 1 All ER 273; and in a pre *Re Gulbenkian's Settlement Trusts* [1970] AC 508 case, *Re Leek* [1967] Ch 1061 at 1076 where Buckley J upheld a fiduciary power where one or more persons could well fall clearly within the core meaning of a concept so uncertain that it would be impossible to say of many persons whether or not they qualified as objects of the power. Further see C T Emery (1982) 98 LQR 177 at 582.

8.69 This, however, affords very little leeway to the donee before those entitled in default of appointment can claim the exercise of the power to be ultra vires and void because in favour of someone not within the 'black' core meaning of the concept.

8.70 Surely, the donor of the power, often a testator, would expect his personal donee to have more leeway than that. By necessary implication, should the donee not be allowed to appoint to anyone within the 'black' core or the 'grey' penumbra of the meaning of 'old friends', so that an appointment will be ultra vires and void only if in favour of someone in the 'white' area for persons with no reasonable possibility of falling within the grey penumbra? 'The problem being one of interpretation every case must depend upon its own circumstances'[1], so that there is leeway for a liberal approach when appropriate.

1   As Buckley J stated in *Re Leek* [1967] Ch 1061 at 1074.

A trust must be administratively workable

8.71 As long ago as 1805 Lord Eldon stated[1]:

'As it is a maxim that the execution of a trust shall be under the control of the court it must be of such a nature that it can be under that control; so that the administration of it can be reviewed by the court, or the court itself can execute the trust: a trust, therefore, which in case of maladministration could be reformed and a due administration directed.'

1   *Morice v Bishop of Durham* (1805) 10 Ves 522 at 539–540.

8.72 Thus he held void a purported trust for 'objects of benevolence and liberality' since no clear criteria existed to enable the court to control or execute the trust. Here the administrative unworkability arises, as it always must, in the case of conceptual uncertainty. However, a discretionary trust may be conceptually certain but, nevertheless, may be administratively unworkable. Thus, a trust of funds to be applied in such manner as the trustee sees fit (otherwise than for his own benefit) or for such persons (other than himself) as the trustee sees fit will be void since no clear criteria exist to enable the court to control or execute the trust[1], though it is clear that anything can be done otherwise than for the trustee's benefit and that everyone in the world is a beneficiary except the trustee. How would the trustee begin to try to decide what to do? As Clauson J stated in *Re Park*[2]:

'It is clearly settled that if a testator creates a trust he must mark out the metes and bounds which are to fetter the trustee, or as has been said, the trust must not be too vague for the court to enforce, and that is why a gift to trustees for such purposes as they in their discretion think fit is an invalid trust: there are no metes and bounds within which the trust can be defined, and unless the trust can be defined the court cannot enforce it.'

1   *Re Pugh's Will Trusts* [1967] 3 All ER 337, [1967] 1 WLR 1262; *Re Carville* [1937] 4 All ER 464; *Re Chapman* [1922] 1 Ch 287; *Blausten v IRC* [1972] Ch 256 at 266, 271, 272, 273, per Buckley LJ; *Re Hay's Settlement Trusts* [1981] 3 All ER 786, [1982] 1 WLR 202 where Megarry V-C, if necessary, would have been prepared to hold a discretionary

trust for everyone, but the settlor her spouse and the trustees, void for administrative unworkability, but upheld a fiduciary power of appointment for such huge class.
2   *Re Park, Public Trustee v Armstrong* [1932] 1 Ch 580 at 583, approved in *Blausten v IRC* [1972] Ch 256 at 271.

8.73 Essentially, the terms of the trust must be justiciable: a court must act judicially according to some clear criteria expressly or impliedly provided by the trust instrument or by extrinsic admissible evidence. If such criteria do not exist then, obviously, the court is not in a position to have the information required to carry out or control the trust. It is in 'a judicial no man's land'[1] where it cannot resort to pure guesswork for this is to fulfil a non-justiciable function.

1   Per Lord Wilberforce in *Buttes Gas and Oil Company v Hammer (No 3)* [1982] AC 888 at 938.

8.74 In the case of discretionary trusts, as Lord Wilberforce made clear in *McPhail v Doulton*[1], the court may execute the trust by appointing appropriate persons to be new trustees to carry out the trusts, or if it is appropriate to distribute the trust fund, by directing representative persons of different classes of beneficiaries to prepare a scheme of distribution for distributing the funds amongst the different classes, or, even, should the proper basis for distribution appear, by itself directing distribution of the trust fund. However, as Lord Wilberforce went on to say[2], the trust will be void 'where the meaning of the words used is clear but the definition of beneficiaries is so hopelessly wide as not to form anything like a class so that the trust is administratively unworkable or in Lord Eldon's words one that cannot be executed. I hesitate to give examples for they may prejudice future cases, but perhaps 'all the residents of Greater London' will serve. I do not think that a discretionary trust for 'relatives' even of a living person falls within this category'[3].

1   [1971] AC 424 at 457, [1970] 2 All ER 228 at 247.
2   [1971] AC 424, [1970] 2 All ER 228. In *Re Gulbenkian's Settlement Trusts* [1970] AC 508, [1968] 3 All ER 785 at 788, Lord Reid had stated, 'There may be a class of case where, although the description of a class of beneficiaries is clear enough, any attempt to apply it to the facts would lead to such administrative difficulties that it would for that reason be held to be invalid'.
3   Note the problems that DNA evidence provides nowadays: see para 8.55 above. However, if advertising under s 27 of the Trustee Act 1925 or as directed by the court led to the trustees knowing of a workable group of relatives then the discretionary trust would be upheld.

8.75 Lord Wilberforce's example of a discretionary trust for all the residents of Greater London being void is perhaps borderline[1] since it can be envisaged that a former Chairman of the Greater London Council[2] could create such a trust to provide benefits for Greater London residents, though, in practice, it is likely that for such a huge class there would be further words indicative of a charitable purpose[3]. However, in the absence of admissible evidence of any intent of the settlor it seems the trustees (and the court) could not begin to ascertain criteria for determining which residents are to benefit and in what degree: thus resort would be needed to guesswork and this is a non-justiciable function. It seems necessary for there to be criteria expressly or impliedly provided by the trust instrument or by extrinsic admissible evidence sufficient to enable the court to 'police' matters after deciding upon persons appropriate to be appointed trustees in place of recalcitrant trustees or after appointing representatives of appropriate classes of beneficiaries to draw up a scheme of distribution for approval by the court.

1   (1974) 38 Conv 269 (L McKay); (1974) 37 MLR 643.
2   An example suggested by Megarry V-C in *Re Hay's Settlement Trusts* [1981] 3 All ER 786 at 795, [1982] 1 WLR 202 at 212.
3   If the trust were exclusively charitable it could be valid, a cy prés scheme making the trust administratively workable if a paramount charitable intention existed.

8.76 In practice it seems from *McPhail v Doulton*[1], *Re Denley*[2] and *Re Gestetner*[3] that the court will be loath to inhibit the flexibility of widely drafted discretionary trusts by holding them void for administrative unworkability. However, in *R v District Auditor No 3 Audit District of West Yorkshire Metropolitan County Council, ex p West Yorkshire Metropolitan County Council*[4] the Divisional Court held that a discretionary trust for the purpose of benefiting as many as two and a half million inhabitants of West Yorkshire would be administratively unworkable, even assuming the presence of conceptual certainty. The inhabitants had to be benefited within eleven months in any of four specified ways: (1) to assist economic development in the county in order to relieve unemployment and poverty, (2) to assist bodies concerned with youth and community problems, (3) to assist and encourage ethnic and other minority groups and (4) to inform all interested and influential persons of the consequences of the proposed abolition of the Council (and other metropolitan county councils) and of other proposals concerning local government in the county. The trust was thus also void as a pure purpose trust since administrative unworkability prevented anyone having locus standi to enforce the trust. To be on the safe side, it will be as well for draftsmen of discretionary trusts for the 'benefit' of large classes of persons to provide guiding criteria for the trustees to consider in exercising their discretion.

1   [1971] AC 424, [1970] 2 All ER 228; *Re Baden's Deed Trusts (No 2)* [1973] Ch 9, [1972] 2 All ER 1304, where the trust was valid for the trustees to make 'at their absolute discretion grants to or for the benefit of any of the officers and employees or ex-officers or ex-employees of the Company or to any relatives or dependants of any such persons in such amounts at such times and on such conditions (if any) as they think fit'.
2   [1969] 1 Ch 373, [1968] 3 All ER 65.
3   [1953] Ch 672, [1953] 1 All ER 1150, where a special power was valid though exercisable in favour of four named individuals, any descendant (or spouse thereof) of the settlor's father and uncle, five named charities, any former employee of the settlor or his wife, any director or employee (or spouse thereof) or ex-director or ex-employee (or spouse thereof) of Gestetner Ltd or of any company of which the directors for the time being included any director of Gestetner Ltd. If a Gestetner director became a director of Woolworth or ICI or Unilever the expansion in numbers would be dramatic. *McPhail v Doulton* [1971] AC 424, [1970] 2 All ER 228, and *Re Gulbenkian's Settlement Trusts* [1970] AC 508, [1968] 3 All ER 785, HL seem to treat *Re Gestetner* as a good decision though the administrative unworkability point seems never to have been raised in respect of the decision. This has encouraged Templeman J and Megarry V-C to treat special powers as not subject to the test of administrative workability: *Re Manisty's Settlement* [1974] Ch 17, [1973] 2 All ER 1203; *Re Hay's Settlement Trusts* [1981] 3 All ER 786, [1982] 1 WLR 202: see paras 8.80–8.86 below.
4   [1986] RVR 24, [2001] WTLR 785.

Must powers be administratively workable ?

8.77 *Re Gestetner*, in fact, concerned a special power of very wide ambit[1] rather than a discretionary trust, and the question arises whether a power needs to be administratively workable at all or to the same degree as a discretionary trust. It seems that a power vested in someone not as trustee but as a private individual need not be administratively workable since the private individual as donee of a personal or non-fiduciary power is under no fiduciary obligation subject to the control of the court[2] (though an appointment cannot be made if it is ultra vires or otherwise a fraud on the power, ie for a purpose beyond the scope of the power)[3]. Thus, a personal power conferred on a widow to appoint amongst a conceptually uncertain class such as the testator's old friends should be validly exercised if confined to those within the 'core' meaning of the concept and might even be effective unless in favour of some person clearly outside the uncertain grey 'penumbra' of meaning[4].

1 See para 8.76, footnote 4.
2 *Re Park* [1932] 1 Ch 580; *Re Jones* [1945] Ch 105; *Re Gulbenkian's Settlement Trusts* [1970] AC 508 at 518, [1968] 3 All ER 785 at 787; *Re Hay's Settlement Trusts* [1981] 3 All ER 786 at 792, [1982] 1 WLR 202 at 209, so justifying *Re Coates* [1955] Ch 495 and *Re Gibbard* [1967] 1 WLR 42 if needing a post-*Re Gulbenkian* [1970] AC 508 justification.
3 *Vatcher v Paull* [1915] AC 372; *Re Somes* [1896] 1 Ch 250 at 256.
4 See para 8.70 above.

8.78 Trustees with special powers are under a fiduciary obligation to consider from time to time whether, and if so, in what way they shall exercise their powers and they must not exceed their powers[1], whether by going outside the class of objects or using their powers mala fide or for reasons that are irrational, perverse or irrelevant to any sensible expectation of the settlor or for a purpose other than one for which the powers were given to them. Indeed, in an extreme case an improper refusal to consider exercising a power may lead the court to intervene positively to correct the situation by replacing the intransigent trustee or even by directing an exercise of the power[2]. Admittedly, except in pension fund cases, where a power to augment benefits exists for the benefit of beneficiaries who have earned their rights and is very different from a power of appointment in favour of objects of a gratuitous trust, it is exceptionally difficult to find instances where the court has exercised positive control, but the negative control exercised by the court on justiciable grounds is significant, for those entitled in default of a valid exercise of the power must clearly be entitled to restrain the trustees from exercising it save among those within the power[3] and taking into account factors within the scope or purpose of the power[4].

1 *Re Gulbenkian's Settlement Trusts* [1970] AC 508 at 518, [1968] 3 All ER 785 at 787; *McPhail v Doulton* [1971] AC 424 at 449, 456, [1970] 2 All ER 228 at 240, 247; *Re Hay's Settlement Trusts* [1981] 3 All ER 786, [1982] 1 WLR 202; *Edge v Pensions Ombudsman* [2000] Ch 602.
2 *Klug v Klug* [1918] 2 Ch 67; *White v Grane* (1854) 18 Beav 571; *Re Lofthouse* (1885) 29 Ch D 921; *Mettoy Pension Trustees Ltd v Evans* [1991] 2 All ER 513, [1990] 1 WLR 1587; *Thrells Ltd v Lomas* [1993] 2 All ER 546, [1993] 1 WLR 456; *Schmidt v Rosewood Trust Ltd* [2003] UKPC 26, [2003] 2 AC 709 paras 42, 51.
3 This is the rationale for the 'is or is not' test in *Re Gulbenkian's Settlement Trusts* [1970] AC 508, [1968] 3 All ER 785.

⁴ *Re Hastings-Bass* [1975] Ch 25 at 41, [1974] 2 All ER 193 at 203; *Sieff v Fox* [2005] WTLR 891.

8.79 Accordingly, Buckley LJ (with whom Orr and Salmon LJJ agreed) in *Blausten v IRC*¹ took the view that a power would be void if 'of so wide an extent that it would be impossible for the court to say whether or not the trustees were properly exercising it and so wide that it would be impossible for the trustees to consider in any sensible manner how they should exercise it, if at all, from time to time'. He went on to hold valid a power for trustees during the settlor's lifetime to add to a specified class of beneficiaries anyone in the world (other than the settlor or the trustees) *if approved in writing by the settlor*: this meant the settlor had set metes and bounds to the beneficial interests which he intended to permit to be created under the settlement. Buckley LJ clearly would have regarded such power void but for the requirement of the settlor's written approval². One might consider that a power to add anyone in the world to the class of beneficiaries (other than the settlor or the trustees) is so wide that, in the absence of admissible evidence of restrictive criteria, it would be impossible for the court to invalidate an appointment of everyone in the world (except the settlor and the trustees) to the class of beneficiaries, made to simplify matters by obviating the need for innumerable ad hoc appointments of particular individuals from time to time in order to benefit them³. A trust for everyone in the world (except the settlor and the trustees) has long been treated as void for administrative unworkability⁴.

¹ [1972] Ch 256 at 273, [1972] 1 All ER 41 at 50. However, see *Re Edwards* [1947] 2 All ER 521, where a testamentary power for trustees to appoint to such persons and for such purposes as they might see fit was held void for uncertainty by Jenkins J though the validity of such a power in an inter vivos trust seems to have been assumed. In [1948] Ch 440 the Court of Appeal made the same assumption though reversing Jenkins J on another ground.
² [1972] Ch 256 at 271, 272, [1972] 1 All ER 41 at 49, 50.
³ Despite this, there is plenty of scope for the court to strike down such a broad exercise of the power as capricious as appears from *Re Manisty's Settlement* [1974] Ch 17 and *Re Hay's Settlement Trusts* [1981] 3 All ER 786.
⁴ *Re Pugh's Will Trusts* [1967] 3 All ER 337, [1967] 1 WLR 1262; *Neo v Neo* (1875) LR 6 PC 382; *Re Hay's Settlement Trusts* [1981] 3 All ER 786 at 796. If the trustees exercised the power by adding a conceptually uncertain or administratively unworkable class of beneficiaries this should not invalidate the whole trust but should be an invalid exercise of the power.

8.80 However, in *Re Manisty's Settlement*¹ Templeman J held valid a power to add anyone in the world (other than members of a defined small 'Excepted Class') to the class of beneficiaries under a discretionary trust. After all, there were instances like *Re Gestetner*² where special powers had been upheld despite being in favour of a very wide class of objects of potentially 'immeasurable width'; so why draw a line between such powers and powers to add anyone (except a tiny excepted class) to the class of beneficiaries, the latter advantageously arming the trustees against all developments and contingencies. A response to this argument is that in the case of discretionary trusts the administrative workability test determines as a matter of degree when a wide class of beneficiaries has become too wide to be acceptable for the trustees to perform their role in justiciable fashion, and this test should apply to powers, the House of Lords having indicated that, except for the mandatory duty to distribute funds of a discretionary trust, discretionary trusts and discretionary powers should be assimilated (as endorsed by the Privy Council in 2003 in *Schmidt v Rosewood Trust Ltd*).

¹ [1974] Ch 17, [1973] 2 All ER 1203. A similar power in *Schmidt v Rosewood Trust Ltd* [2003] UKPC 26, [2003] 2 AC 709 was not questioned by counsel or the Privy Council.
² [1953] Ch 672.

8.81 Nevertheless, Templeman J boldly treated the obiter dicta of Buckley LJ as having been made without the benefit of counsel having fully explored the implications of *Re Gestetner*¹, *Re Gulbenkian's Settlement Trusts*², *McPhail v Doulton*³ and *Re Baden's Deed Trusts (No 2)*⁴. He treated the test of administrative workability as formulated in *McPhail v Doulton* as applying only to trusts which may positively have to be executed and administered by the court and not to powers where the court has a more limited function⁵: thus 'a power cannot be uncertain merely because it is wide in ambit'⁶. However, he accepted the court could intervene if the trustees exercised a power 'capriciously, that is to say, act for reasons which could be said to be irrational, perverse or irrelevant to any sensible expectation of the settlor'⁷. He continued⁸:

'The objection to the capricious exercise of a power may well extend to the creation of a capricious power. A power to benefit residents of Greater London is capricious because the terms of the power negative any sensible intention on the part of the settlor. If the settlor intended and expected the trustees would have regard to persons with some claims on his bounty or some interest in an institution favoured by the settlor, or if the settlor had any other sensible intention or expectation, he would not have required the trustees to consider only an accidental conglomeration of persons who have no discernible link⁹ with the settlor or with any institution. A capricious power negatives a sensible consideration by the trustees of the exercise of the power. But a wide power, be it special or intermediate, does not negative or prohibit a sensible approach by the trustees to the consideration and exercise of their powers.'

¹ [1953] Ch 672.
² [1953] Ch 672, [1953] 1 All ER 1150.
³ [1970] AC 508, [1968] 3 All ER 785.
⁴ [1971] AC 424, [1970] 2 All ER 228.
⁵ [1972] Ch 607, [1971] 3 All ER 985; affd [1973] Ch 9, [1972] 2 All ER 1304. He might also have mentioned *Re Denley's Trust Deed* [1969] 1 Ch 373, [1968] 3 All ER 65, where Goff J held valid a power to allow a sports ground to be used for the benefit of such other persons in the world as the trustees might see fit.
⁶ *Re Manisty's Settlement, Manisty v Manisty* [1974] Ch 17 at 29, [1973] 2 All ER 1203 at 1213. He played down the court's function in respect of powers: see *Klug v Klug* [1918] 2 Ch 67; *Re Hastings-Bass* [1975] Ch 25, [1974] 2 All ER 193, CA and RSC Ord 85, r 2(3)(e), now CPR Part 64.
⁷ [1974] Ch 17 at 24, [1973] 2 All ER 1203 at 1213.
⁸ [1974] Ch 17 at 26, [1973] 2 All ER 1203 at 1208.
⁹ Would it make a difference if the settlor were a proud retired Mayor of London?

8.82 However, it seems a wide power must be capable of being exercised sensibly and the court must be able to intervene if it is exercised for reasons which are irrational, perverse or irrelevant to any sensible expectation of the settlor. Thus, the settlor's expectations must somehow be discerned and so some degree of administrative workability is required for trustees' fiduciary powers. It is noteworthy that Templeman J remarked[1]:

> 'In *Gestetner* it was impossible to derive any assistance from the terms of the power, save that the trustees, it could be assumed, were expected to have regard to the considerations which might move the settlor to confer bounty on the beneficiaries. A similar expectation may be implied from an intermediate power, and in the present case *if the settlement is read as a whole the expectations of the settlor are not difficult to discern.*'

1   [1974] Ch 17 at 24–25, [1973] 2 All ER 1203 at 1209.

8.83 In *Re Hay's Settlement Trusts*, however, Megarry V-C endorsed the views of Templeman J on a power to add any persons (except X, Y, and Z) to the existing beneficiaries (when one may, perhaps, discern that such persons ought to relate in some way to such beneficiaries) and upheld a *power to appoint to anyone in the world* (except X, Y and Z), considering that 'dispositions ought, if possible, to be upheld and the court ought not to be astute to find grounds on which a power can be invalidated'[1]. He rejected the submission 'that the power is so wide that it would be impossible for the trustees to consider in any sensible manner how to exercise it and also impossible for the court to say whether or not they were properly exercising it', stating, 'If I have correctly stated the extent of the duties of trustees in whom a mere power is vested, I do not see what there is to prevent the trustees from performing these duties'[2].

1   [1981] 3 All ER 786 at 795, [1982] 1 WLR 202 at 213.
2   [1981] 3 All ER 786 at 794, [1982] 1 WLR 202 at 212.

8.84 Earlier he had stated[1]:

> 'A trustee to whom, as such, a power is given is bound by the duties of his office in exercising that power to do so in a responsible manner according to its purpose. It is not enough for him to refrain from acting capriciously; he must do more. He must make such a survey of the range of objects ... as will enable him to carry out his fiduciary duty ...
>
> Apart from the obvious duty of obeying the trust instrument, and in particular of making no appointment that is not authorised by it, the trustee must, first, consider periodically whether or not he should exercise the power; second, consider the range of objects of the power; and third, consider the appropriateness of individual appointments.'

1   [1981] 3 All ER 786 at 793, [1982] 1 WLR 202 at 210 and 211.

8.85 On the basis of the view of Megarry V-C, a settlor can thus make provision for his conceptually uncertain friends or business associates by conferring on his trustee (s) power 'to appoint to anyone in the world (except X, Y and Z) in the hope that my old friends and business associates may be benefited' or, even, just a power 'to appoint to anyone in the world except X, Y and Z' without any guidance at all in the document creating the trust, though having a statement of his hopes in a letter of wishes.

8.86 Currently, first instance decisions[1] establish that administrative workability is essential for discretionary trusts because they are positively justiciable, a beneficiary having the right to obtain the intervention of the court positively to ensure the trusts are carried out, while administrative workability is not essential for discretionary powers because they are only negatively justiciable, an object of the power having only the right to obtain the intervention of the court negatively to restrain or invalidate wrongful actions by the trustees, (though does the court not have power positively to replace a trustee in breach of duty in relation to his discretionary powers of appointment?) Logically, one would have thought that the need for justiciability, whether positive or negative, underlies the requirement of administrative workability. Furthermore, as *Mettoy Pension Trustees Ltd v Evans*[2] emphasises, and as seemingly accepted by the Privy Council in *Schmidt v Rosewood Trust Ltd*[3], there are some extreme cases where discretionary powers are positively carried out by the courts: thus, it is not correct to distinguish discretionary trusts from discretionary powers by saying that the former are positively and negatively justiciable while the latter are only negatively justiciable.

[1] *Re Manisty's Settlement* [1974] Ch 17, [1973] 2 All ER 1203 and *Re Hay's Settlement Trusts* [1981] 3 All ER 786, [1982] 1 WLR 202 were followed in *IRC v Schroder* [1983] STC 480 and in *Re Beatty's Will Trusts* [1990] 3 All ER 844, [1990] 1 WLR 1503 where counsel conceded that a power in an inter vivos deed for trustees to appoint to anyone in the world would be valid, and Hoffmann J held that such a power in a will was valid because there was no so-called rule against the delegation of a testator's will-making function to invalidate it.

[2] [1991] 2 All ER 513, [1990] 1 WLR 1587 and *Thrells Ltd v Lomas* [1993] 2 All ER 546, [1993] 1 WLR 456, both being pension fund cases where the beneficiaries had earned their rights and where the company employer and sole trustee had become insolvent so its liquidator could not exercise powers relating to the surplus that could favour either creditors or beneficiaries because of an irreconcilable conflict of interest. Pensions Act 1995, s 25(2) now makes provision for there to be an independent person as trustee to exercise the power. Also see *Klug v Klug* [1918] 2 Ch 67 (court will intervene to direct positive exercise of power if a trustee's attitude is that he is not going to bother considering using his powers to benefit B because B is not worthy of consideration and a situation arises where no trustee could refuse to exercise the power in favour of B unless acting capriciously, i e for reasons irrational, perverse or irrelevant to any sensible expectation of the settlor).

[3] *Schmidt v Rosewood Trust Ltd* [2003] 2 Ch 709.

8.87 Therefore, on the safety first principle a power of appointment should be restricted to a sensible class of persons and then there should be a power for trustees to add persons to the specified class which should provide some express guidance for the trustees (eg to add persons proposed in writing by existing class members taking account of the proposer's written reasons why such addition would have been likely to meet with the settlor's approval) unless a letter of wishes provides such guidance or more detailed guidance to set workable parameters for the exercise of the trustees' discretion.

8.88 Indeed, the best course to take in order to provide the greatest flexibility will be expressly to provide that the trustee's power to appoint to anyone in the world (other than, say, the trustee and its employees, their spouses, descendants and dependants, and the settlor and his spouse) is a *fiduciary* one only in the limited sense that the trustee must periodically consider whether or not to exercise it, but that, otherwise, it may be exercised in favour of any object without considering the merits of other objects, while any exercise or non-exercise of the power is to be a *personal* decision unchallengeable in the courts unless ultra vires or apparently intra vires but a fraud on the power[1]. One sympathises with the view of Megarry V-C that[2] 'dispositions ought, if possible to be upheld and the court ought not to be astute to find grounds on which a power can be invalidated', but, to uphold this view, it is neither necessary nor logical to draw a distinction between fiduciary discretionary trusts and fiduciary discretionary powers. For future courts to produce the result he reached they should hold that, in context, by necessary implication the exercise of the power to appoint to anyone in the world is a personal and not a fiduciary function (except for the need periodically to consider the exercise of the power), such benignant construction saving the settlor's intentions from being ineffective.

1   For detailed discussion of the distinction between fiduciary powers and personal powers see paras 1.76–1.77 above.
2   *Re Hay's Settlement Trust* [1981] 3 All ER 786 at 795, [1982] 1 WLR 202 at 213.

8.89 In the case of testamentary trusts there is no so-called rule against the delegation of a testator's will-making function to invalidate the broadest powers of appointment[1].

1   *Re Beatty's Will Trusts* [1990] 3 All ER 844, [1990] 1 WLR 1503.

Initial and supervening administrative unworkability

8.90 The question of administrative workability or not has to be determined (like the issue of conceptual certainty) as of the date property is effectively subjected to trusts[1]. Are the trusts then valid thereafter or are they inherently voidable in that they may subsequently become void for administrative unworkability, eg where there are initially 1,000 members of a discretionary trust class consisting of (1) issue of X and of X's spouse and (2) employees or ex-employees or directors or ex-directors of X Ltd or of any company of which the directors for the time being included any director of X Ltd and (3) issue of persons within class (2), and after 70 years (when the trust fund with many X Ltd shares is worth £2 billion) the class consists of about 80 million members with X Ltd's directors being on the boards of various multi-national companies as well as of taken-over companies? Harman J and Goff J in *Gestetner*[2] and *Re Denley*[3] seem to have assumed that a trust must be certain or administratively workable at any given time. On this basis subsequent supervening unworkability could invalidate a trust, the ever-present possibility of a resulting trust in the settlor's favour causing him tax problems in respect of any undistributed income[4]. However, in *Muir v IRC*[5] the Court of Appeal endorsed the view of Pennycuick J that the possibility of future uncertainty did not make a presently certain trust invalid so the settlor was not liable for tax on undistributed income.

1   *Re Baden's Deed Trusts (No 2)* [1972] Ch 607 at 619.
2   [1953] Ch 672 at 684, 685.
3   [1969] 1 Ch 373 at 386, [1968] 3 All ER 65 at 71; *IRC v Broadway Cottages Trust* [1955] Ch 20 at 29.

4 Income and Corporation Taxes Act 1988, s 673.
5 [1966] 3 All ER 38 at 44, 45 per Harman LJ.

8.91 One may expect that the courts will be reluctant to be driven to find a trust administratively unworkable when, on its creation, it was possible to find it workable owing to the settlor's clear express or implied criteria for the carrying out of the trusts and when DNA testing was unavailable to reveal the millions of relatives a person has. Perhaps the solution lies in the trustees advertising for beneficiaries under s 27 of the Trustee Act 1925 or under directions from the court so as to identify a workable number of beneficiaries known to the trustees for the trustees to keep computerised records of them and their issue. Alternatively, assuming a valid workable discretionary trust initially, when the class becomes larger the trustees could take it upon themselves to make a valid sub-settlement or re-settlement on a smaller certain workable class of beneficiaries pursuant to a power in that behalf. Another solution could lie in Lord Wilberforce's dicta in *McPhail v Doulton*[1] laying down that the court, if called on to execute a discretionary trust, will do so in the manner best calculated to give effect to the settlor's intentions as by authorising or directing representative persons of the classes of beneficiaries to prepare a scheme of distribution or, should the proper basis for distribution appear, by itself directing the trustees so to distribute. This heralds a jurisdiction similar to the cy près jurisdiction for charitable trusts despite the denials of such jurisdiction by the High Court in *Re Astor*[2] and *Re Denley*[3]. So far as concerns persons originally within a certain administratively workable settlement, *Re Hain*[4] indicates that the settlement cannot subsequently be invalidated because some of the class of beneficiaries may have disappeared or become impossible to find or it has been forgotten who they were.

1 [1971] AC 424 at 457, [1970] 2 All ER 228 at 247.
2 [1952] Ch 534, [1952] 1 All ER 1067.
3 [1969] 1 Ch 373 at 388, [1968] 3 All ER 65 at 72.
4 [1961] 1 All ER 848, [1961] 1 WLR 440.

Uncertain conditions for benefiting: conditions precedent

8.92 In the case of a fixed trust for division equally between my tall friends the trust will fail since a comprehensive list of beneficiaries cannot be drawn up. If there is a discretionary trust or a fiduciary power for the benefit of such of my tall friends as my trustees may see fit, then the trust will also fail due to the lack of conceptually clear criteria for determining whether any given postulant is or is not a member of the class of possible beneficiaries[1].

1 *McPhail v Doulton* [1971] AC 424, [1970] 2 All ER 228, HL paras 8.44–8.47 above.

8.93 If, however, there is a testamentary gift of £1,000 or of a painting to each of my tall friends, this should be valid according to Browne-Wilkinson J in *Re Barlow's Will Trusts*[1]. By applying *Re Allen*[2], without distinguishing it[3] or considering it inconsistent with *McPhail v Doulton*[4], Browne-Wilkinson J held such testamentary gifts to be valid if it is possible to say of one or more persons that he or they undoubtedly qualify, even though it may be impossible to say of others whether or not they qualify[5]. Query whether his benevolent

Matters essential to the prima facie validity of an express trust

decision should be restricted to testamentary trusts like the decisions in the anomalous purpose trust cases that are regarded as concessions to human sentiment[6].

1   [1979] 1 All ER 296, [1979] 1 WLR 278 applying *Re Allen* [1953] Ch 810 decided before the new post-1970 approach.
2   [1953] Ch 810.
3   Should one distinguish '£x to A if he marries a woman of Jewish parentage and of Jewish faith' from '£x to each of F's friends if marrying a woman' so qualified? See C T Emery (1982) 98 LQR 551 at 564–565.
4   [1971] AC 424.
5   The testatrix by will directed her executor 'to allow any member of my family and any friends of mine who may wish to do so to purchase' various of her paintings at a low 1970 valuation. If one painting was the best bargain by far, how could the offeree be found except by putting all names of potential offerees into a hat and drawing out one name? How could all such names be ascertained? Can they really be restricted just to persons within the 'core' meaning of family and friends?
6   See paras 8.173–8.184 below.

8.94 In any event, it seems anomalous and illogical to have a less strict approach for trusts to make gifts to individuals than for class gifts under a discretionary trust or fiduciary power. An executor or trustee directed to make payments or transfer paintings to qualifying beneficiaries owes an enforceable obligation to such beneficiaries, who are in a stronger position than objects of discretionary trusts or powers. The default beneficiary, entitled to the balance after proper payments or transfers, has a right to sue the executor or trustee if benefiting persons who are not qualifying beneficiaries. To protect himself where the default beneficiary is claiming particular persons are not qualifying beneficiaries, the executor or trustee must have a right to obtain the court's directions as to precisely whom he may or may not benefit, so that a comprehensive list needs to be capable of being drawn up. The uncertain penumbra of meaning attached to 'tall friends' makes the concept uncertain so that in many instances the court will find it impossible to decide whether or not a person is a tall friend. If the court, like Browne-Wilkinson J, allows just persons within the restricted 'core' meaning of friends to qualify in the case of a trust to make individual gifts to qualifying persons, then, consistently, discretionary trusts and powers for members of a qualifying class ought to be valid and be capable of being exercised in favour of persons within the 'core' meaning of the class description. However House of Lords authority[1] is to the contrary, so that Brown-Wilkinson J accepted[2] that a discretionary trust or power for 'my friends' would be void for uncertainty.

1   *Re Gulbenkian's Settlement Trusts, Whishaw v Stephens* [1970] AC 508, [1968] 3 All ER 785; *McPhail v Doulton* [1971] AC 424, [1970] 2 All ER 228, HL.
2   *Re Barlow's Will Trusts* [1979] 1 WLR 278 at 281.

8.95 Where the individual gifts are not to each person who comes within a qualifying class description (eg £5,000 to each of my friends' children who marry persons of the Jewish faith and of Jewish parentage) but to specific ascertained individuals if they satisfy the qualifying conditions (eg Shalom House to my elder son, Abraham, if he marries a woman of Jewish faith and of Jewish parentage, but if he does not, then for my younger son, Gideon, if he marries such a woman) there seems more scope, as a concession to human sentiment, to accept the individual's entitlement if he satisfies the 'core' meaning of the requisite concept. Thus, a gift to the eldest son of A if he is a member of the Church of England and an adherent to the doctrine of that Church is valid[1].

[1]   *Re Allen* [1953] Ch 810 at 817; L Mackay [1980] Conv 263 at 277; C T Emery (1982) 98 LQR 551 at 564.

Uncertain conditions for forfeiture: conditions subsequent

8.96 Uncertainty frequently arises in the case of conditions for forfeiture and particularly in conditions for forfeiture on non-residence, engaging in professional or public activities, marrying outside a particular religion or race or failing to comply with a name and arms clause. Such conditions subsequent where a vested interest is subsequently, upon a certain condition, to be divested must be distinguished from conditions precedent where an interest is only to be taken in the first place if the qualifying condition is satisfied[1]. The former type of condition is negative and destructive: it operates to take away someone's actual enjoyment of an existing interest. The latter type is positive and constructive: it operates to give actual enjoyment of an interest to someone who is a primary object of the settlor's bounty, the settlor only intending the default beneficiary to take if there is no primary beneficiary. This is the justification for the test of certainty for a condition subsequent being strict and that for a condition precedent being liberal as seen above. Whether a condition is precedent or subsequent can be a very nice point[2]. Matters are straightforward where the position under testamentary trusts is resolved forthwith in favour of a beneficiary satisfying the condition precedent, but are more complex where someone satisfying a condition precedent at a late stage leads to another person losing enjoyment of an interest in the trust fund, so the distinction between the two sorts of condition is difficult to justify, though only the House of Lords can now abolish the distinction[3].

[1]   *Re Allen* [1953] Ch 810, [1953] 2 All ER 898; *Blathwayt v Baron Cawley* [1976] AC 397, [1975] 3 All ER 625; *Re Tuck's Settlement Trusts* [1978] Ch 49, [1978] 1 All ER 1047, CA; *Re Abrahams' Will Trusts* [1969] 1 Ch 463, [1967] 2 All ER 1175.
[2]   *Re Tuck's ST* [1978] Ch 49.
[3]   *Re Tuck's Settlements Trusts* [1978] Ch 49 at 60 and 65, *Blathwayt v Baron Cawley* [1976] AC 397 at 424–425.

8.97 In order that a condition subsequent may be valid it must at all times be possible to predicate with absolute certainty what event will cause forfeiture. The rule was expressed by Lord Cranworth in *Clavering v Ellison*[1] as follows:

> 'Where a vested estate is to be divested by a condition on a contingency that is to happen afterwards that contingency must be such that the court can see from the beginning precisely and distinctly upon the happening of what event it was that the preceding estate was to determine.'

[1]   (1859) 7 HL Cas 707 at 725; but see *Re Coxen* [1948] Ch 747, [1948] 2 All ER 492.

8.98 This language must, however, be closely analysed[1], for there is a distinction between uncertainty in expression and uncertainty in operation, and a provision will not be void for uncertainty merely because it is difficult to construe[2]. Where the language employed embodies a concept of sufficient certainty a condition will not be void although there may be difficulty in ascertaining whether the conceived event has occurred[3], but it is otherwise where the concept is itself uncertain[4]. A condition can thus be void for conceptual uncertainty but if the condition is conceptually certain it will not be vitiated by any evidential uncertainty.

1   See *Re Lanyon* [1927] 2 Ch 264.
2   *Re Wilson's Will Trusts* [1950] 2 All ER 955 at 963, CA, per Sir Raymond Evershed MR; affd sub nom *Bromley v Tyron* [1952] AC 265, [1951] 2 All ER 1058, HL; *Re Denley* [1969] 1 Ch 373.
3   *Blathwayt v Baron Cawley* [1976] AC 397, [1975] 3 All ER 625, HL ('be or become a Roman Catholic'); *Re Gape* [1952] Ch 743, [1952] 2 All ER 579, ('permanent residence') CA; *Re Burton's Settlements* [1955] Ch 82, [1954] 3 All ER 193; and see *Re Hatch* [1948] Ch 592, [1948] 2 All ER 288. See also *Re Baden's Deed Trusts (No 2)* [1973] Ch 9, [1972] 2 All ER 1034; *Re Tepper's Will Trusts* [1987] 1 All ER 970.
4   See *Sifton v Sifton* [1938] AC 656, [1938] 3 All ER 435, PC; *Re Brace* [1954] 2 All ER 354, [1954] 1 WLR 955 ('provide a home' held to be uncertain).

8.99 A condition subsequent, otherwise void for *conceptual* uncertainty, will not be saved by the fact that the opinion of the trustees or some third party is the deciding factor. The concept on which the trustees or third party are to found their opinion must, itself, be certain[1]. Exceptionally, it would seem that a condition subsequent would be valid, though turning on the view of a trustee, if worded along the following fashion: 'provided that if B marries a "disqualified person" being a person considered by my trustee to be an enemy of mine or a member of the family of such an enemy, so long as my trustee at B's request shall give a decision before any contemplated marriage on the position of the proposed spouse and so long as such decision is not one that no reasonable person could possibly make, then on marriage to such a disqualified person ...'

1   *Re Coxen* [1948] Ch 747, [1948] 2 All ER 492; *Re Jones* [1953] Ch 125, [1953] 1 All ER 35. Further see paras 8.57–8.64 above.

8.100 There is no doubt that the opinion of the trustees or third party may, be used to resolve matters where there would otherwise be *evidential* uncertainty.

Conditions as to residence

8.101 When a testator directed that certain payments should be made to his daughter 'only so long as she shall continue to reside in Canada', it was held by the Privy Council that, inasmuch as a categorical answer could not be given to the question upon what event the daughter's interest would determine so that she would know at all times if she was committing a breach of the condition, that condition as a condition subsequent was void for uncertainty[1].

1   *Sifton v Sifton* [1938] AC 656, [1938] 3 All ER 435. However in *Ellis v Chief Adjudication Officer* [1998] 1 FLR 184 the Court of Appeal upheld a deed of gift of a flat by a mother to her daughter, D, on condition D repaid the mortgage and allowed her mother to reside in the flat under D's care, so on eviction the mother was entitled to part of the proceeds of sale.

8.102 This decision appears to have met with the approval of the House of Lords[1], but in subsequent cases the court has been able to escape its results by finding sufficient distinctions in the language to be construed. Thus a condition for forfeiture if in the opinion of trustees a beneficiary should have ceased 'permanently to reside' in a certain house has been upheld on the grounds that in the context of the particular will 'residence' meant personal residence, that permanent cesser of personal residence connoted removal with no animus revertendi and that it would not be impossible to decide whether this event had or had not happened[2]. Likewise a condition for forfeiture on failing to 'take up permanent residence in England' has been upheld as embodying a concept of sufficient certainty known to English law in ascertaining the issue of domicile. Here again 'permanent' was regarded as the decisive word[3].

1   See *Clayton v Ramsden* [1943] AC 320, [1943] 1 All ER 16, HL.
2   *Re Coxen* [1948] Ch 747, [1948] 2 All ER 492.
3   *Re Gape* [1952] Ch 418, [1952] 1 All ER 827; affd [1952] Ch 743, [1952] 2 All ER 579, CA.

8.103 On the other hand, a condition that a beneficiary should occupy certain freehold property has been held to be void for uncertainty since it was impossible to ascertain the degree of occupation necessary to fulfil it[1].

1   *Re Field's Will Trusts* [1950] Ch 520, [1950] 2 All ER 188.

Conditions as to professions or offices

8.104 Where a testator gave life interests to two ladies and provided that they should forfeit such interests if they should 'willingly adopt and carry on any profession or professional calling, whether for gain or otherwise', the condition was held void for uncertainty[1], and where a testator stipulated that his sons should not 'become candidates for or enter Parliament or undertake any other public office', the court, though not expressing any view as to whether or not the condition was void for uncertainty, thought there were good grounds for suggesting that it might be[2].

1   *Re Reich* (1924) 40 TLR 398.
2   *Re Edgar* [1939] 1 All ER 635, actually decided on grounds of public policy.

Conditions as to religion and parentage

8.105 A strict approach was heralded by the House of Lords in *Clayton v Ramsden*[1] which concerned a condition subsequent providing for forfeiture on marriage with a person 'not of Jewish parentage and of the Jewish faith'[2]. It was unanimously held that the first limb (and therefore the whole condition) was void for uncertainty and in obiter dicta a four to one majority concluded that the second limb was also void. A more liberal approach subsequently prevailed in the House of Lords in *Blathwayt v Baron Cawley*[3] where a condition for forfeiture upon someone being or becoming a Roman Catholic was upheld as a less vague conception than someone being or not being of the Jewish faith. However, even Jewish faith may validly be the subject matter of a

135

condition precedent qualifying an ascertained person to take a particular interest[4] for the test of certainty for a condition precedent is less than that for a condition subsequent[5]. The Court of Appeal has continued the liberal approach in dealing with a condition precedent concerned with marriage to an 'approved wife' being 'a wife of Jewish blood by one or both of her parents and who has been brought up in and has never departed from and at the date of her marriage continues to worship according to the Jewish faith'[6]. It was held that this meant that the wife should have some Jewish blood so that there were not the problems met in a case[7] where it was required simply that X should be 'of Jewish blood' or 'of Jewish parentage' and it was uncertain whether 100 or 75 or 50% blood or parentage would suffice. Subsequently[8], a condition subsequent providing for forfeiture on marriage outside the Jewish faith was not automatically struck down. Scott J rather benevolently gave leave for evidence to be adduced as to the settlor's concept of Jewish faith on the basis that if this was sufficiently certain the clause would be upheld.

1   [1943] AC 320, [1943] 1 All ER 16.
2   See also *Re Gott* [1944] Ch 193, [1944] 1 All ER 293; *Re Evans* [1940] Ch 629; *Re Krawitz's Will Trusts* [1959] 3 All ER 793, [1959] 1 WLR 1192; *Re Blaiberg* [1940] Ch 385, [1940] 1 All ER 632; *Re Donn* [1944] Ch 8, [1943] 2 All ER 564; *Re Moss' Trusts* [1945] 1 All ER 207.
3   [1976] AC 397, [1975] 3 All ER 625.
4   *Re Abrahams' Will Trusts* [1969] 1 Ch 463, [1967] 2 All ER 1175; *Re Selby's Will Trusts* [1965] 3 All ER 386, [1966] 1 WLR 43; *Re Tuck's Settlement Trusts* [1978] Ch 49, [1978] 1 All ER 1047, CA; *Re Tepper's Will Trusts* [1987] Ch 358, [1987] 1 All ER 970.
5   *Re Allen* [1953] Ch 810, [1953] 2 All ER 898; *Blathwayt v Baron Cawley* [1976] AC 397, [1975] 3 All ER 625; *Re Tuck's Settlement Trusts* [1978] Ch 49, [1978] 1 All ER 1047.
6   *Re Tuck's Settlement Trusts* [1978] Ch 49, [1978] 1 All ER 1047.
7   *Re Tarnpolsk* [1958] 3 All ER 479, [1958] 1 WLR 1157.
8   *Re Tepper's Will Trusts* [1987] Ch 358, [1987] 1 All ER 970.

8.106 Draftsmen, of course, should err as much as possible on the side of particularising forfeiting events (eg by referring to particular religious rites upon marriage or conversion under the religion in question) or, if more flexibility is required, should provide for the settlor's concept of someone being of the Jewish faith or the Roman Catholic faith to be the concept of a particular Chief Rabbi or Bishop for the time being when the matter arises for resolution, the decision of such Chief Rabbi or Bishop to be conclusive as the opinion of an expert, not merely that of an arbitrator[1].

1   *Re Tuck's Settlement Trusts* [1978] Ch 49, [1978] 1 All ER 1047 explained at para 8.59, footnote 4 above.

8.107 The High Court of Australia[1] has accepted resolution of a condition subsequent concerning 'professing the Protestant faith' by the opinion of the trustees. However, the majority struck down the condition as void for public policy. The divesting of the testator's Protestant sons' vested interests in remainder after their mother's life interest, if on her death being married to a person not professing the Protestant faith, was calculated to make them divorce their Catholic wives so that on their mother's death they were not married to a person not professing the Protestant faith.

1   *Church Property Trustees of Newcastle Diosese v Ebbeck* (1960) 104 CLR 394.

Names and arms clauses

8.108 The former tendency of the courts to hold that provisions for forfeiture in the traditional form of name and arms clauses are void for uncertainty has been reversed by the decision of the Court of Appeal in *Re Neeld*[1]. The clause in that case required each of several beneficiaries within the space of one year to

'... take upon himself and use upon all occasions the surname of "Neeld" only and quarter the arms of "Neeld" with his or her own family arms ...'

and it extended to the husband of a female beneficiary. The clause went on to provide that if a beneficiary

'... shall refuse or neglect or discontinue to take or use such surname and arms ... then after the expiration of the said space of one year ...'

his interest should cease. The court, in upholding the clause, held that in general a name and arms clause following the language of established precedent is not void for uncertainty merely because it imposes an obligation to 'take and use' or to 'assume' or to 'use on all occasions' a surname, or because it provides for defeasance if the beneficiary in question 'disuses' or 'ceases to use' the surname, for these expressions are not so uncertain as to make the provision invalid and they satisfy the test laid down in *Clavering v Ellison*[2] as restated in *Sifton v Sifton*[3] – that is to say, can the court and the parties concerned see from the beginning precisely and distinctly upon the happening of what events it is that the previous vested estate is to determine? Earlier cases in a contrary sense[4] were disapproved.

1   [1962] Ch 643, [1962] 2 All ER 335, CA.
2   (1859) 7 HL Cas 707.
3   [1938] AC 656, [1938] 3 All ER 435, PC.
4   On the question of uncertainty, the following cases were expressly disapproved: *Re Lewis' Will Trusts* [1951] WN 591; *Re Bouverie* [1952] Ch 400, [1952] 1 All ER 408; *Re Wood's Will Trusts* [1952] Ch 406, [1952] 1 All ER 740; and *Re Kersey* [1952] WN 541. The case of *Re Murray* [1955] Ch 69, [1954] 3 All ER 129 was not disapproved because the decision in that case rested upon the use of particular language in the provision in question.

8.109 Questions may clearly arise as to what acts or events amount to a disuse of, or to a discontinuance of use of, or to ceasing to use, a surname. In *Re Howard's Will Trusts*[1], Wilberforce J held that one single instance of failure to use a surname on an occasion when a surname could appropriately be used would be sufficient of itself to bring about a forfeiture. But this dictum was disapproved in *Re Neeld*[2] by Upjohn and Diplock LJJ, who took the view that the inadvertent use by a beneficiary of his former surname on one or more occasions after he had assumed the new one should be treated as de minimis and would not therefore result in defeasance.

1   [1961] Ch 507, [1961] 2 All ER 413.
2   [1962] Ch 643, [1962] 2 All ER 335, CA.

8.110 The Court of Appeal also held in *Re Neeld*[1] that a clause such as that with which they were concerned is not void as being contrary to public policy merely because it imposes an obligation of change of name on a man to whom a female beneficiary is married or whom she may subsequently marry[2].

1   [1962] Ch 643, [1962] 2 All ER 335, CA.
2   On this question of public policy, the following cases were expressly disapproved: *Re Fry* [1945] Ch 348, [1945] 2 All ER 205; and *Re Kersey* (see 8.109, footnote 1, above). It may also be assumed that the case of *Re Howard's Will Trusts* [1961] Ch 507, [1961] 2 All ER 413 has been overruled on this question.

8.111 As has already been noted, the clause with which this case was concerned required each beneficiary not only to change his surname but also to 'quarter the arms of 'Neeld' with his or her own family arms'. The case has a sequel in *Re Neeld (No 3)*[1], in which Megarry J considered the practical effect of this requirement. During the time which had elapsed since the decision of the Court of Appeal in the first case the plaintiff beneficiary had (as appears from the title of the second case) changed his surname, but he had not quartered the arms of Neeld with his family arms, because he had no family arms with which to quarter them. Megarry J held, however, that the effect of the clause was to require the plaintiff to obtain some family arms for himself and then to quarter the arms of Neeld with those arms (and that he must do both these things within the time limit specified by the clause).

1   [1969] 2 All ER 1025, [1969] 1 WLR 988.

Conditions for forfeiture if challenging will or trust

8.112 Sometimes a will may contain a condition preventing a legatee or devisee from obtaining the relevant legacy or devise if taking any legal proceedings to contest the will or to undermine the effectiveness of any gifts to trustees or individuals made by the testator before death, but capable of being taken into account to assess the amount of any forced heirship share that the legatee or devisee could claim[1].

1   In many European countries a person with three children must leave them three quarters of his estate, notionally regarded as including property given away within thirty years (or in some States, ten years) of his death. A personal action for compensation to make up the full amount of the forced heirs' claims can be brought by them against donees (whether trustees or individuals), suing more recent ones before later ones.

8.113 Such a deprivation of the benefits given by will is valid so long as the condition is not purely *in terrorem* but expressly provides for the benefits to pass to someone else on breach of the condition[1], so long as worded clearly enough for the beneficiary and any other affected person[2] to know distinctly what behaviour will amount to breach of the condition[3].

1   *Cooke v Turner* (1846) 15 M & W 727; *Evanturel v Evanturel* (1874) LR 6 PC 1.
2   To bring extra pressure to bear on a beneficiary, B, it can be provided that if B triggers the condition then gifts to others will be forfeited to a person or organisation detested by B: *Nathan v Leonard* [2003] 1 WLR 827, [2002] WTLR 1061.
3   *Nathan v Leonard* [2003] 1 WLR 827.

8.114 The English equivalent of the mandatory protection for forced heirs under a foreign law of succession is the Inheritance (Provision for Family & Dependants) Act 1975. Proceedings under such Act will amount to contesting or challenging the testator's will[1]. However, the loss of the benefit under the will due to application of the forfeiture clause will be taken into account in assessing the measure of reasonable provision to be made under the 1975 Act[2].

1   *Nathan v Leonard* [2003] 1 WLR 827.
2   *Nathan v Leonard* [2003] 1 WLR 827.

8.115 Where contesting the will leads to the will being wholly ineffective eg due to lack of capacity or formalities, then the will and the condition therein are ignored[1]. Similarly, if it proved possible to strike down the condition for lack of the requisite knowledge and approval of the testator, the condition will be ignored. Otherwise, the condition will be fully operative.

1   *Nathan v Leonard* [2003] 1 WLR 827, para 25; *Evanturel v Evanturel* (1874) LR 6 PC 1 at 26.

8.116 However, the terms of some conditions (eg not to intermeddle with or interfere in the administration of the testator's estate[1], or if bringing an action for administration then the claimant's share under the will must meet the costs of all parties[2]) may be construed as not intended to apply where the claimant beneficiary's proceedings were successful in preventing unjustified interference with his rights under the will.

1   See *Adams v Adams* [1892] 1 Ch 369 (testator could not have intended to discourage a beneficiary's justifiable interference to enforce his rights).
2   *Williams v Williams* [1912] 1 Ch 399 (construed not to apply where the beneficiary sued for executor's wilful default, though if had so applied it would have been struck down as repugnant to the absolute beneficial ownership conferred on the beneficiary).

Discretionary trusts for benevolent purposes

8.117–8.127 Cases in which the question of uncertainty has arisen have frequently come before the courts in relation, first, to attempts on the part of testators to create discretionary trusts in favour of vague objects of benevolence not falling within the legal definition of charity and, second, to trusts where the objects are so described that the property could be used exclusively for charitable purposes but could, nevertheless, be devoted in whole or in part to non-charitable purposes. Only if every purpose to which trust property can lawfully be devoted is charitable are trusts charitable in law[1] and thus exempt from failure through uncertainty (unless they were in existence before 16 December 1952, and were validated by the Charitable Trusts (Validation) Act 1954)[2]. Vague purpose trusts may be void not just because they are too uncertain but because there is no-one with locus standi to enforce them, or because they infringe the rule against inalienability which prevents income being tied up to be used in a particular way for longer than the perpetuity period. It seems that they cannot be attacked for contravening the so-called principle against delegation of the will-making power[3].

1   *Chichester Diocesan Fund and Board of Finance Inc v Simpson* [1944] AC 341, [1944] 2 All ER 60, HL; *A-G of the Bahamas v Royal Trust Co* [1986] 3 All ER 423, [1986] 1 WLR 1001, PC.
2   See paras 8.131–8.143 below.
3   *Re Beatty's Will Trusts* [1990] 3 All ER 844, [1990] 1 WLR 1503.

8.128 An example of the first class is afforded by *Grimond v Grimond*[1]: where the testator had directed his trustees to divide a part of his residuary estate among 'such charitable or religious institutions and societies as they think fit'. If, however, the trust had been for charitable or religious *purposes*, instead of for charitable or religious *institutions* it would have been good[2], but being partly for charitable objects and partly for objects not charitable (since the purposes of a religious institution may lack the element of public benefit, and thus, not be charitable)[3], the beneficiaries were not pointed out with sufficient certainty.

1   [1905] AC 124 overlooked in *Attorney General of Cayman Island v Wahr-Hansen* [2001] 1 AC 75, para 10 where Privy Council assumed 'for any one or more religious institutions' was a valid charitable trust but it failed as also alternatively 'for any institutions operating for the public good.' See also *Blair v Duncan* [1902] AC 37 ('charitable or public'); *Ellis v Selby* (1836) 1 My & Cr 286 ('charitable or other'); *Re Jarman's Estate* (1878) 8 Ch D 584; and *Re Macduff* [1896] 2 Ch 451 ('charitable or benevolent'); see also *Houston v Burns* [1918] AC 337; *Re Gardom* [1914] 1 Ch 662; revsd sub nom *Le Page v Gardom* [1915] WN 216 HL.
2   *Re White* [1893] 2 Ch 41, CA; *Re Ward* [1941] Ch 308, [1941] 2 All ER 125, CA; a trust simply 'for religious purposes' or 'for educational purposes' is valid in the absence of a context subverting it e g restriction to a contemplative order of nuns or to employees of a particular company.
3   *Gilmour v Coats* [1949] AC 426, [1949] 1 All ER 848, HL.

8.129 Trusts for purposes vaguely described as 'benevolent'[1], 'charitable *or* benevolent'[2], 'philanthropic'[3], 'hospitable'[4], 'patriotic'[5], or for 'religious, social and physical well-being'[6], or 'for parochial purposes' or 'for parish work'[7] (not necessarily equivalent to 'church purposes' by which are meant purposes connected with the services of the church)[8] or 'generally useful'[9] or 'worthy causes'[10] are void for uncertainty because these purposes might be satisfied without applying any part of the fund for charity, and the court will not intervene to direct the fund into charitable channels[11]. Thus the Attorney General cannot interfere on behalf of charity, and no other person can interfere because no one can predicate of himself that he is a beneficiary[12]. But a bequest to 'my country England' or to a defined area is a good charitable bequest and enforceable by the Attorney General[13], possibly on the ground that, where no purpose is defined, a charitable purpose is implicit in the context[14]. Again, trusts for purposes 'charitable *and* pious'[15], 'charitable *and* deserving'[16], 'religious *and* charitable'[17] have been upheld, for in such cases the purposes are not alternatively charitable *or* not charitable as the trustee may decide, but are confined to charities of a particular class.

1   *Morice v Bishop of Durham* (1804) 9 Ves 399; *James v Allen* (1817) 3 Mer 17; *Re Freeman* [1908] 1 Ch 720; *Houston v Burns* [1918] AC 337; and see *Re Simson* [1946] Ch 299, [1946] 2 All ER 220, where a gift to an individual for his 'benevolent work' was held to fail.
2   *Chichester Diocesan Fund and Board of Finance Inc v Simpson* [1944] AC 341, [1944] 2 All ER 60, HL, and see *Re Bawden's Settlement* [1953] 2 All ER 1235 ('objects or purposes of charity or benevolence or amelioration of human suffering'). See also *Re Wootton's Will Trusts* [1968] 2 All ER 618, [1968] 1 WLR 681 where the objects of a trust included any 'organisation or body not being registered as a charity but in the opinion of my trustees as having charitable objects', and it was held by Pennycuick J that this definition was not limited to objects which were charitable in law, and *A-G of Bahamas v Royal Trust Co* [1986] 3 All ER 423, [1986] 1 WLR 1001, PC.
3   *Re Macduff* [1896] 2 Ch 451.
4   *Re Hewitt's Estate* (1883) 53 LJ Ch 132.

5 *Re Tetley* [1923] 1 Ch 258; affd sub nom *A-G v National Provincial and Union Bank of England* [1924] AC 262, HL.

6 *IRC v Baddeley* [1955] AC 572, [1955] 1 All ER 525, HL (distinguished in *Re Banfield* [1968] 2 All ER 276, [1968] 1 WLR 846), but see now the Recreational Charities Act 1958.

7 *Farley v Westminster Bank* [1939] AC 430, [1939] 3 All ER 491, HL; *Re Bain* [1930] 1 Ch 224; *Re Stratton* [1931] 1 Ch 197, CA; *Dunne v Byrne* [1912] AC 407, but a gift to the holder of an office of a charitable character virtute officii, which is prima facie a gift on charitable trusts, will not be avoided by the addition of words confining the use of the fund to the area in which the office is exercised, see *Re Rumball* [1956] Ch 105, [1955] 3 All ER 71, CA (gift to bishop for time being of named diocese to be used as he thinks fit in his diocese upheld—but this case was distinguished in *Re Endacott* [1960] Ch 232, [1959] 3 All ER 562, CA, where it was held the mere fact that a gift was made to a parish council did not render it charitable), and see *Re Simson* [1946] Ch 299, [1946] 2 All ER 220 (gift to a vicar for his work in the parish upheld), and *Re Eastes* [1948] Ch 257, [1948] 1 All ER 536, distinguishing *Re Davies* (1932) 49 TLR 5, CA. In *Re Rumball* [1956] Ch 105, [1955] 3 All ER 71, the Court of Appeal expressly reserved the question whether *Re Beddy* (1953) unreported (gift to bishop for such purposes in his diocese as he might choose held void for uncertainty) was rightly decided.

8 *Re Gare* [1952] Ch 80, [1951] 2 All ER 863.

9 *Kendall v Granger* (1842) 5 Beav 300; *Re Woodgate* (1886) 2 TLR 674; and see *Re Endacott* [1960] Ch 232, [1959] 3 All ER 562, CA.

10 See *Re Gillingham Bus Disaster Fund* [1959] Ch 62, [1958] 2 All ER 749, CA.

11 *Re Strakosch* [1948] Ch 37, [1947] 2 All ER 607; affd [1949] Ch 529, [1949] 2 All ER 6.

12 See *Hunter v A-G* [1899] AC 309; *Re Davis* [1923] 1 Ch 225; *Re Chapman* [1922] 2 Ch 479, where the words were 'to be retained by my executor for such objects and such purposes as he may at his discretion select and to be at his own disposal'; and *Re Carville* [1937] 4 All ER 464.

13 *Re Smith* [1932] 1 Ch 153, CA; *Re Baynes* [1944] 2 All ER 597; *Re Norton's Will Trusts* [1948] 2 All ER 842 upholding a gift for the benefit of a parish as distinct from a gift 'for parish work', as to which, see *Farley v Westminster Bank* [1939] AC 430.

14 *Williams' Trustees v IRC* [1947] AC 447, [1947] 1 All ER 513, HL; *Re Strakosch* [1949] Ch 529, [1949] 2 All ER 6.

15 *A-G v Herrick* (1772) Amb 712. But cf *Re Eades* [1920] 2 Ch 353, where 'and' was read 'or'.

16 *Re Sutton* (1885) 28 Ch D 464.

17 *Baker v Sutton* (1836) 1 Keen 224; *Re Scowcroft* [1898] 2 Ch 638. See also *Re Hood* [1931] 1 Ch 240, where the dominant provision was religious.

8.130 In this connection the case of *Re Clarke*[1] is instructive as showing that where there is a trust to divide a residue among four objects, three of which are charitable and the fourth is not and is too uncertain, the property will be divided into fourths, three of which will go to the charities and the fourth to the next of kin of the testator as on a partial intestacy.

1 [1923] 2 Ch 407. Followed in *Re King* [1931] WN 232.

Statutory validation of certain trusts

8.131 Certain trusts which would otherwise have failed for the reasons just discussed may be validated by the Charitable Trusts (Validation) Act 1954. This Act validates what it calls 'imperfect trust provisions' contained in instruments taking effect *before* 16 December 1952 eg where a testator died before then, leaving his estate to his widow for life, remainder on imperfect trust provisions. An imperfect trust provision means

'... any provision declaring the objects for which property is to be held or applied, and so describing those objects that, consistently with the terms of the

141

provision, the property could be used exclusively for charitable purposes, but could nevertheless be used for purposes which are not charitable.'[1]

1   See s 1(1) of the Act.

8.132 It should be noted that a trust provision falls within this definition only if it enables the property to be used 'exclusively for charitable purposes'. Thus a trust primarily for the benefit of non-charitable purposes will not be an imperfect trust provision within the Act merely because the trustees have power to administer it so that charitable objects can benefit in addition to, but not to the exclusion of, the non-charitable objects[1].

1   *Vernon v IRC* [1956] 3 All ER 14, [1956] 1 WLR 1169; *Buxton v Public Trustee* (1962) 41 TC 235; *Sir Howell Jones Williams Trust* Annual Report of the Charity Commissioners 1977, paras 71–80, applying the 1954 Act to the London Welsh trust held non-charitable in *Williams Trustees v IRC* [1947] AC 447, the social and recreational element being excluded.

8.133 Again, if a trust provision is to fall within the terms of the Act, it must (1) declare the objects of the trust and (2) describe them in such a way that the property could be used exclusively for charitable purposes but could nevertheless be used for non-charitable *purposes*[1]. This condition is not fulfilled by a provision which simply requires property to be transferred to one or more institutions, since this does not amount to a declaration of the objects of the trust, still less are those objects described so as to indicate the purposes for which the property can be used[2]. The condition is similarly not fulfilled where trust property can be paid or applied for the direct benefit of individuals with no purposes prevailing[3].

1   Thus in *Buxton v Public Trustee* (1962) 41 TC 235 Plowman J held the Act did not apply to trusts 'to promote and aid the improvement of international relations and intercourse' since such trusts did not allow the property to be used exclusively for charitable purposes.
2   *Re Harpur's Will Trusts* [1962] Ch 78, [1961] 3 All ER 588 criticised by Picarda's *Law Relating to Charities* (1st edn) pp 161–162. The trust in this case was to divide a fund 'between such institutions and associations having for their main object the assistance and care of soldiers, sailors, airmen, and other members of H M Forces who have been wounded or incapacitated during recent world wars' in such manner and proportions as the trustees thought fit. It was conceded that these words were not apt to confine the institutions to those devoted exclusively to charitable objects. The trust was held not to be a trust to apply property for certain purposes but to distribute it among certain institutions.
3   *Re Saxone Shoe Co Ltd's Trust Deed* [1962] 2 All ER 904, [1962] 1 WLR 943 (essentially a private discretionary trust). Contrast the more liberal approach in Australia and New Zealand where legislation goes further: *Re Thureau* [1948] ALR 487; *Re Ingram* [1951] VLR 424; *Leahy v A-G for New South Wales* [1959] AC 457, [1959] 2 All ER 300.

8.134 Another question arising out of s 1(1) is whether the Act applies to all trust provisions which would in fact allow property to be used exclusively for charitable purposes but would nonetheless allow it to be used for non-charitable purposes, or whether the trust provision must itself differentiate in some way between these two purposes and include both an express reference to a charitable purpose and an express reference to a non-charitable purpose. In other words, would the Act apply to a trust simply 'for public purposes', which could include both charitable and non-charitable objects, or is its operation confined to trusts which provide for the property to be used 'for charitable or benevolent purposes' or adopt some wording of that kind? In *Re Gillingham Bus Disaster Fund*[1], Harman J at first instance adopted the latter (narrower) interpretation, but his comments were obiter[2]. When this case went to appeal, his decision was affirmed by the majority of the Court of Appeal who expressed some sympathy with his view on this point, but did not decide it or express an opinion of their own. On the other hand, Ormerod LJ, who dissented and to whose decision alone the point was relevant, decided in favour of the former (wider) interpretation, and considered the subsection unambiguous. In these circumstances, Buckley LJ felt free to adopt the wider interpretation in a later case, that of *Re Wykes*[3], where he was concerned with a trust of property to be used ' ... as a benevolent or welfare fund or for welfare purposes for the sole benefit of the past, present and future employees ... ' of a company.

[1]   [1958] Ch 300, [1958] 1 All ER 37; affd [1959] Ch 62, [1958] 2 All ER 749.
[2]   It would appear, however, from his remarks in *Re Harpur's Will Trusts* [1962] Ch 78, [1961] 3 All ER 588, that Harman LJ may have intended these comments to amount to an alternative ground for his decision.
[3]   [1961] Ch 229, [1961] 1 All ER 470.

8.135 This decision was subsequently considered in two cases which came before Cross J. In the first[1] he impliedly supported it, while in the second case[2], he assumed that it was correct and added:

'In such a phrase as "welfare purposes" there is at least some flavour of charity which may justify ... saying that the testator was seeking to benefit the public through the relief of a limited class.'

[1]   *Re Mead's Trust Deed* [1961] 2 All ER 836, [1961] 1 WLR 1244 at 1212. In this case Cross J held that a trust to provide a convalescent home for members of a trade union and a home for aged members no longer able to support themselves and for the wives of such members was validated by the Act and restricted to those members of the union only who were poor persons and, in the case of the home for the aged, retired members and their wives.
[2]   *Re Saxone Shoe Co Ltd's Trust Deed* [1962] 2 All ER 904, [1962] 1 WLR 943. As to this case, see the text, below. The broader approach was conceded to be correct in *Re Chitty's Will Trust* [1970] Ch 254, [1969] 3 All ER 1492.

8.136 Recently, in *Ulrich v Treasury Solicitor*[1] Hart J upheld the wider interpretation, so that the Act is not confined to cases where a charitable purpose has been expressed. Where a trust provision permits both charitable and non-charitable applications of the trust fund and if, upon examining the objects of the trust in context, no one could have a legitimate complaint if the whole fund had been devoted to the relief of poverty of the small class of beneficiaries, the trust is validated by the Act.

[1]   [2006] 1 WLR 33.

8.137 He was concerned with a 1927 trust of a small fund for the benefit of employees of a company, their widows and children, where employee was defined to exclude anyone in a managerial role and one clause purported to exclude any beneficiary from having a right to insist that he benefit. The trustees had used the income as a hardship fund.

8.138   This leads naturally to another point. The Act does not operate to validate what are essentially private trusts. It is true that it may validate a trust for the benefit of a particular group of people who do not amount to a section of the community for the purposes of the law relating to charitable trusts[1], but this will be so only if the trust is to promote purposes rather than to benefit these people as individuals, and, of course the trust will be confined to those charitable purposes. Thus it was held that the words used in the trust provision with which Buckley J was concerned in *Re Wykes* (quoted above) did create a trust for purposes and that the provision was therefore validated by the Act. The effect of the Act, in that case, was to confine the purposes of the trust to the sole, charitable purpose for which, having regard to the class of its beneficiaries, it could be used—that is, the relief of poverty.

1   See *Dingle v Turner* [1972] AC 601, [1972] 1 All ER 878, HL (on public benefit for a section of the community with relief of poverty the purpose of the trust).

8.139   But in *Re Saxone Shoe Co Ltd's Trust Deed*[1] Cross J distinguished this type of provision from the one then before him, which he held to amount essentially to a trust for the application of capital and income for the benefit of a class of persons in any way the trustees might think fit and was more in the nature of a private discretionary trust than of a trust for purposes. Hart J in *Ulrich*[2] distinguished *Saxone* because there the beneficiaries would have had a legitimate complaint if the whole fund had been applied to relieve poverty while, in context in *Ulrich* no beneficiary could have had such a complaint if the whole fund had been so applied.

1   [1962] 2 All ER 904, [1962] 1 WLR 943. Compare *Re Flavel's Will Trusts* [1969] 2 All ER 232, [1969] 1 WLR 444.
2   [2006] 1 WLR 33 at paras 33–34.

8.140   The Act goes on to provide that if the trust in question does amount to an imperfect trust provision contained in an instrument taking effect before 16 December 1952[1], then it is to be treated:

(a)   as respects the period before the commencement of the Act (30 July 1954) as if the whole of its declared objects were charitable; and

(b)   as respects the period after the commencement of the Act as if it had required the property in question to be held or applied for its declared objects in so far, and only in so far, as they authorised use for charitable purposes[2].

1   A document inviting gifts of property for objects declared by the document is to be treated as an instrument taking effect when it is first issued; s 1(3) of the 1954 Act.
2   Section 1(2).

8.141   The Act applies to dispositions of all kinds, and to covenants to make dispositions, which would otherwise be invalid but which would have been valid if their objects had been exclusively charitable[1], except to the extent that the capital or income of the property to which they relate has, before 16 December 1952, been paid or conveyed to or for the benefit of the persons who were entitled on the footing that the trust was invalid[2]. For the purposes of the Act a disposition which creates more than one interest in the same property, whether by way of settlement or otherwise, is to be treated as a separate disposition in relation to each interest created[3]. This provision was considered in *Re Gillingham Bus Disaster Fund*[4] where an appeal had been made for funds for three purposes, two of which were not charitable and the third (worthy causes) included both charitable and non-charitable objects. Section 1(1) could not apply to the fund as a whole since it could not be used in its entirety for charitable purposes and it was held (Ormerod LJ dissenting) that there was no separate disposition for the third purpose.

1   Section 2(1).
2   Section 2(2).
3   Section 2(3); *Re Chitty's Will Trust* [1970] Ch 254, [1969] 3 All ER 1492.
4   [1958] Ch 300, [1958] 1 All ER 37; affd [1959] Ch 62, [1958] 2 All ER 749.

8.142   The Act provides for limitation periods and contains limited savings for the rights of persons who had become entitled, on the footing that the trust in question was invalid, to property comprised in it[1].

1   Section 3. As to this section, see *Re Harpur's Will Trusts* [1962] Ch 78, [1961] 3 All ER 588.

8.143   The Act does not apply to trusts contained in instruments which take effect on or after 16 December 1952. In respect of these the law stated in the immediately preceding section of this book remains unaffected.

The beneficiary principle

8.144   There are plenty of judicial statements that for there to be a valid trust there must be a beneficiary or cestui que trust (corporate or human) in whose favour performance of the trust may be decreed[1] unless the trust falls within a group of exceptional anomalous cases relating to the maintenance of animals, tombs etc, when it is valid but unenforceable so that it is regarded as a power that the trustees may exercise if they wish[2]. However charitable trusts for purposes are valid since they are enforceable by the Attorney General[3]. Mere powers for abstract, impersonal but certain, workable purposes are valid[4] but they merely enable trustees to exercise them and, of course, do not compel the trustees. It has been suggested that all pure purpose 'trusts' should be treated as not being in the nature of trusts since unenforceable but in the nature of powers so as to be valid, but this approach seems only to be open to the House of Lords[5].

1   *Morice v Bishop of Durham* (1804) 9 Ves 399 at 404–405; *Re Chardon* [1928] Ch 464; *Re Astor's Settlement Trusts* [1952] Ch 534, [1952] 1 All ER 1067; *Leahy v A-G for New South Wales* [1959] AC 457 at 478, PC; *Re Denley's Trust Deed* [1969] 1 Ch 373, [1968] 3 All ER 65.
2   *Re Endacott* [1960] Ch 232, [1959] 3 All ER 562; paras 8.173–8.184 below.
3   *Leahy v A-G for New South Wales* [1959] AC 457 at 479. On charitable trusts see generally *Tudor on Charities* and Picarda's *Law Relating to Charities*. Nowadays, enforcement is also possible by the Charity Commission or an 'interested person' within Charities Act 1993, s 33.
4   *Re Wooton's Will Trusts* [1968] 2 All ER 618 at 623.

5   *IRC v Broadway Cottages Trust* [1955] Ch 20 at 36, CA; *Re Shaw* [1957] 1 WLR 729 at 731; *Re Endacott* [1960] Ch 232 at 246, CA. Further see Morris & Leach *Rule against Perpetuities* (Second edn) pp 319 ff; (1945) 58 Harvard LR 548 (Scott). If it is unclear whether a trust or power was intended then the court should find in favour of a power on the basis, 'Verba ita sunt intelligenda ut res magis valeat quam pereat': *IRC v McMullen* [1981] AC 1 at 11, HL; *Universe Tankships Inc of Monrovia v International Transport Workers Federation* [1983] 1 AC 366 at 406, HL.

8.145 The beneficiary principle first became apparent in *Morice v Bishop of Durham* where Sir William Grant MR stated[303]:

> 'There can be no trust over the exercise of which this court will not assume control; for an uncontrollable power of disposition would be ownership and not trust. If there be a clear trust but for uncertain objects the property, that is the subject of the trust, is undisposed of ... But this doctrine does not hold good with regard to trusts for charity. *Every other trust must have a definite object. There must be somebody in whose favour the court can decree performance.*'

1   *Morice v Bishop of Durham* (1804) 9 Ves 399 at 404–405.

8.146 This quotation usefully reveals how inter-related are the three principles that a trust will be void if (1) administratively unworkable so as not to be capable of being controlled or executed by the court or (2) if uncertain as to its objects or (3) if there is no beneficiary able to enforce the trust in his favour in the courts. A fourth principle is also interrelated, namely the *Saunders v Vautier*[1] principle whereby the beneficiaries, if unanimous, can terminate their trust and obtain the trust property for themselves if they are all ascertained and between themselves absolutely entitled to the trust property, each being of full age and capacity. If the beneficiaries between them can obtain the trust property then clearly the beneficiary principle is satisfied.

1   See Article 69 below.

8.147 This century the beneficiary principle has come into prominence as a ground on its own for invalidating purported trusts. In *Re Wood*[1] Harman J held, 'A gift on trust must have a cestui que trust and there being here no cestui que trust the gift must fail.' In *Re Astor*[2] Roxburgh J held trusts void on the ground that they were not trusts for individuals but for purposes. In *Re Endacott*[3] the Court of Appeal endorsed this, treating the anomalous cases of valid pure purpose trusts as concessions to human sentiment that were not to be extended. In *Leahy v A-G for New South Wales*[4] a gift upon trust for a contemplative, and therefore non-charitable, Order of Nuns was held by the Privy Council to be void for perpetuity as a gift intended to be by way of endowment for the religious purposes of the Order for the benefit of future nuns as much as (if not more than) existing nuns. However, Viscount Simonds, dealing with an extra ground for invalidating the gift as a purpose trust, said[5]:

> 'A gift can be made to persons (including a corporation) but it cannot be made to a purpose or to an object: so also a trust may be created for the benefit of persons as cestuis que trust but not for a purpose or object unless the purpose or object be charitable. For a purpose or object cannot sue, but, if it be charitable, the Attorney General can sue and enforce it.'

1   [1949] Ch 498 at 501.

2   [1952] Ch 534, [1952] 1 All ER 1067. Also *Re Grant's Will Trusts* [1979] 3 All ER 359, [1980] 1 WLR 360.
3   [1960] Ch 232, [1959] 3 All ER 562.
4   [1959] AC 457, [1959] 2 All ER 300.
5   [1959] AC 457 at 478, [1959] 2 All ER 300 at 307.

The beneficiary principle and purpose trusts for beneficiaries with standing to sue

8.148 Since then the position in respect of purpose trusts has been developed by Goff J in *Re Denley* who, after quoting Viscount Simonds' words, above, stated[1]:

> 'Where, then, the trust though expressed as a purpose is directly or indirectly for the benefit of an individual or individuals, it seems to me that it is in general outside the mischief of the beneficiary principle.'

1   [1969] 1 Ch 373 at 383–384, [1968] 3 All ER 65 at 69.

8.149 Earlier he had said[1]:

> 'I think there may be a purpose or object trust, the carrying out of which would benefit an individual or individuals, where that benefit is so indirect or intangible or which is otherwise framed so as not to give those persons any locus standi to apply to the court to enforce the trust, in which case the beneficiary principle would apply to invalidate the trust, quite apart from any question of uncertainty or perpetuity. Such cases can be considered if and when they arise. The present is not of that character and it will be seen that clause 2(d) of the trust deed expressly states that, subject to any rules and regulations made by the trustees, the employees of the company shall be entitled to the use and enjoyment of the land. Apart from this possible exception the beneficiary principle is confined to purpose or object trusts which are abstract or impersonal. The objection is not that the trust is for a purpose or object per se, but that there is no beneficiary or cestui que trust.'

1   [1969] 1 Ch 373 at 382–383, [1968] 3 All ER 65 at 69.

8.150 In *Re Lipinski's Will Trusts*[1] Oliver J (as he then was) expressly adopted these remarks in upholding a residuary bequest upon trust 'as to one half thereof for the Hull Judeans (Maccabi) Association to be used solely in the work of constructing the new buildings for the Association and/or improvements to the said buildings' since the prescribed purpose was clearly intended for the benefit of the members of the Association. In *Re Denley's Trust Deed* Goff J had upheld inter vivos trusts for a specified perpetuity period of land to be maintained and used for the purpose of a recreation or sports ground for the benefit of the employees of Martyn & Co Ltd. In both cases the Association members[2] and the employees respectively had a right to have the court enforce the trusts in their favour.

1   [1976] Ch 235, [1977] 1 All ER 33. In *Re Northern Development (Holdings)* (6 October 1978, unreported) Megarry V-C accepted purpose trusts 'of the type recognised in *Re Denley*' (see (1985) 101 LQR 280) as did the Divisional Court in *R v District Auditor No 3 Audit District of West Yorkshire Metropolitan County Council, ex p West Yorkshire Metropolitan County Council* [1986] RVR 24 discussed at para 8.76 above.

2   Oliver J regarded the members as beneficially entitled with the expressed purpose only being morally binding: see para 8.192 below.

8.151 The employees in *Re Denley* had locus standi as beneficiaries intended to obtain personal enjoyment out of the recreation ground and who could indeed be regarded as licensees under clause 2(d) of the Settlement Deed (analogous to irrevocable contractual licensees). The court could execute the trust positively by ordering the trustees to allow the employees to use the land for recreational purposes and negatively by restraining any improper use or disposition of the land[1]. In view of the later *McPhail v Doulton*[2] presumably the court could, as in the case of discretionary trusts, appoint new trustees to carry out the trusts in place of defaulting trustees or even, perhaps, authorise or direct representative persons to prepare a scheme, eg of regulations respecting use of the land. It would seem also from *McPhail v Doulton* that the beneficiaries, not being intended to take equal fixed interests, need not be capable of ascertainment in a comprehensive list so long as any given postulant can be ascertained as being a beneficiary or not being a beneficiary. Thus a trust as in *Re Saxone Shoe Co Ltd's Trust Deed*[3] for 'the provision of pensions for and donations to present and past employees and the education and benefit of their dependants' might now be held valid as a purpose trust directly or indirectly for the benefit of beneficiaries, if limited to the perpetuity period or, otherwise, saved by s 3(3) of the Perpetuities and Accumulations Act 1964. Indeed, in *Wicks v Firth*[4] it was assumed that a trust to provide educational scholarships for the settlor employer's employees' children and restricted to a specified perpetuity period was valid.

1   [1969] 1 Ch 373 at 388, [1968] 3 All ER 65 at 72.
2   [1971] AC 424, [1970] 2 All ER 228; para 8.44 above.
3   [1962] 2 All ER 904, [1962] 1 WLR 943.
4   [1983] 2 AC 214, [1983] 1 All ER 151, HL.

8.152 The beneficiary principle requires a beneficiary with locus standi to have the trust positively enforced. It will not be satisfied merely by the presence of a person who will be benefited by the carrying out of the trust, eg the owner of a school where a trust provides for the education of the settlor's son at that school[1] or a settlor who would feel benefited and fulfilled if his desires were carried out[2]. A person cannot enforce a trust merely because he may incidentally benefit from the performance of the trust just as a person who incidentally may benefit by the performance of a contract cannot enforce that contract (assuming after the Contracts (Rights of Third Parties) Act 1999, the parties did not intend the benefiting term to be enforceable by him).

1   *Shaw v Lawless* (1838) 5 Cl & Fin 129 at 155; *Gandy v Gandy* (1885) 30 Ch D 57; para 8.257 below.
2   *Re Astor's Settlement Trusts* [1952] Ch 534 at 542.

8.153 The beneficiary principle will not be satisfied by the fact that there is some person in the background (eg a residuary legatee of the testator-settlor or his next of kin under a resulting trust) with an interest in applying to the court if the primary purpose trust is not effectively carried out, for there will virtually always be such a person[1] so validating virtually all purpose trusts, which is not the position[2]. Such a person, after all, is not interested in having the purpose trust enforced in his favour: his interest is only in the failure, or the declaring to be invalid, of the purpose trust.

1   In a rare case (as in *Re Sayer* [1975] Ch 423) he might not currently be ascertainable (eg be unborn or the person who is Warden of All Souls College at the expiry of the perpetuity period).
2   *Re Davidson* [1909] 1 Ch 567 at 571. *Re Shaw* [1957] 1 All ER 745, [1957] 1 WLR 729; *Re Endacott* [1960] Ch 232, [1959] 3 All ER 562; *Leahy v A-G for New South Wales* [1959] AC 457, [1959] 2 All ER 300.

8.154 The question arises whether purpose trusts of the valid *Re Denley* type should be categorised as an intermediate category between trusts for individuals and trusts for pure abstract purposes rather than as trusts for individuals. It seems better to regard them as trusts for individuals[1]. After all under the rule in *Saunders v Vautier* if S creates a trust to spend £10,000 on planting trees on land held for A for life remainder to B, A and B can claim the £10,000[2]. If S creates a trust for the maintenance and care of B for B's life it is a question of construction whether B has absolute entitlement to the income for whatever purpose he wants[3] or whether B is only entitled to claim what is necessary for the specified purpose[4]. As trusts for individuals the trusts will benefit from the application of the 'wait and see' and other provisions of the Perpetuities and Accumulations Act 1964[5].

1   *Re Grant's Will Trusts* [1979] 3 All ER 359 at 368, [1980] 1 WLR 360; P J Millett (later Lord Millett) (1985) 101 LQR 268 at 281–282.
2   *Re Bowes* [1896] 1 Ch 507 from which Goff J in *Re Denley's Trust Deed* claimed assistance; also *Re Skinner's Trusts* (1860) 1 John & H 102 (bequest of £1,000 to provide for publishing testator's manuscript books to the best advantage of the testator's grandson, G, to provide a fund for his university education, was construed as being for G's benefit so he could claim the £1,000 when publication was not a paying proposition).
3   *Re Andrew's Trust* [1905] 2 Ch 48; *Re Osoba* [1979] 2 All ER 393, [1979] 1 WLR 247, CA.
4   *Re Sanderson's Trusts* (1857) 3 K & J 497; *Re Abbott Fund Trust* [1900] 2 Ch 326; *Re Gillingham Bus Disaster Fund* [1958] Ch 300, [1958] 1 All ER 37.
5   See paras 11.17–11.18 below. Purpose trusts for people validated by *Re Denley* should not be regarded as purpose trusts, subject at the outset to the rule against inalienability, but as people trusts, subject to the benevolent provisions of the Perpetuities and Accumulations Act 1964, despite the apparent view of Megarry V-C to the contrary based on *Re Denley* trusts being an intermediate category of purpose trust: *Re Northern Development (Holdings) Ltd* (6 October 1978, unreported) discussed by C E F Rickett (1991) 107 LQR 608 at 611 fn 13. A trust created today in the terms of the *Re Denley* trusts should be saved by s 3(3) of the 1964 Act covering discretionary trusts, though a resulting trust should arise at the end of the statutory perpetuity period: a *Re Denley* endowment trust for present and future members of a club should on expiry of the statutory period (without any earlier dissolution of the club) be saved by s 4(4): see para 8.190 below.

8.155 In the case of apparent purpose trusts it is submitted that it is a question of construction in every case whether the trust is primarily for the benefit of a class of individuals, with the specified way in which they are to enjoy the benefit being secondary, or whether the specified purpose in which they will be involved to a greater or lesser extent is of the essence of the gift, with the indirect benefit to individuals being secondary. In the former category there will be scope for application of the rule in *Saunders v Vautier* so long as a fluctuating class is not involved[1], while in the latter category there will be no such scope and the purpose trust will be void for infringing the beneficiary principle unless it is a charitable trust. Within the former category will be trusts providing a maintenance fund for historic buildings and gardens owned by trustees for the benefit of beneficiaries[2] or providing a sinking fund for repairs to a block of flats for the benefit of the lessees[3] or providing for the education of employees' children[4]. Within the latter category will be trusts for furthering the overriding purposes of a political party[5] or of a non-charitable religious order[6] or of an unincorporated society[7].

1   *Re Levy* [1960] Ch 346 at 363, CA; *Re Westphal* [1972] NZLR 792 at 794–795.
2   *Re Aberconway's Settlement Trusts* [1953] Ch 647, [1953] 2 All ER 350, CA; *Raikes v Lygon* [1988] 1 All ER 884, [1988] 1 WLR 281; Inheritance Tax Act 1984, Sch 4.
3   Landlord and Tenant Act 1987, s 42.
4   *Wicks v Firth* [1983] 2 AC 214, [1983] 1 All ER 151, HL.
5   *Re Grant's Will Trusts* [1979] 3 All ER 359, [1980] 1 WLR 360; *Bacon v Pianta* (1966) 114 CLR 634 (Aust HC).
6   *Leahy v A-G for New South Wales* [1959] AC 457, [1959] 2 All ER 300, PC.
7   *Carne v Long* (1860) 2 De GF & J 75; *Re Macaulay's Estate* [1943] Ch 435n, HL.

8.156 Incidentally, if property is transferred inter vivos on void pure purpose trusts it seems that the transferee trustee will hold the property on resulting trust for the transferor but will be regarded as authorised by the transferor to have power to apply the property for the stated purpose until the transferor decides otherwise[1] (eg by demanding a re-transfer of the property to himself) or the transferor dies: in the case of similar void testamentary trusts there can be no such deemed authority on the part of the deceased testator or the residuary legatee or next of kin entitled on failure of such trusts.

1   See *Re Sayer* [1957] Ch 423 at 437 where the trust for an uncertain class of beneficiaries of whatever surplus remained after the exercise of certain powers (to make grants to, or buy annuities for the benefit of, company employees, ex-employees, their widows and dependent relatives) was void for uncertainty, but the powers were valid till the end of the trust period when the resulting trust of capital in favour of the settlor would operate and *Vandervell v IRC* [1967] 2 AC 291 at 317 per Lord Upjohn.

Scope to develop the enforcer principle

8.157 Where lack of a beneficiary to enforce a trust has been a ground for holding a non-charitable purpose trust to be void, there have also been other grounds such as the absence of an express valid perpetuity period rendering the trust void for infringing the rule against inalienability[1] or the absence of workable certain purposes[2]. Moreover, in none of the cases rejecting non-charitable purpose trusts did the settlor in his trust instrument expressly arrange for there to be an enforcer positively interested in performance of the purposes.

1   *Re Nottage* [1895] 2 Ch 649; *Leahy v A-G for New South Wales* [1959] AC 457.
2   *Re Astor's Settlement Trusts* [1952] Ch 534; *Re Endacott* [1960] Ch 232; *Re Shaw* [1957] 1 WLR 729.

8.158 Nowadays, many trusts governed by foreign trust laws, such as the laws of Jersey, Isle of Man, Bermuda, Cayman Islands or s 409 of the American Uniform Trust code, have an enforcer expressly appointed as such in the trust instrument that creates valid non-charitable purpose trusts according to the relevant governing law. Under the Recognition of Trusts Act 1987, incorporating The Hague Trusts Convention, those trusts[1] need to be recognised as such[2], unless the English court is prepared to apply Article 18 so as to disregard the Convention if its application would be manifestly incompatible with public policy. Is it really manifestly incompatible with English public policy to permit a non-charitable purpose trust to be enforceable where an expressly appointed enforcer has locus standi positively to apply to the court for enforcement of the trust against the trustees, just as a charitable purpose trust is enforceable against the trustees by the Attorney-General or the Charity Commission or 'an interested person'[3], and a trust for beneficiaries is enforceable against the trustees by the beneficiaries or by new trustees?[4]

1 Article 2.
2 Article 11.
3 With the consent of the Commission or the court: Charities Act 1993, s 33.
4 *Young v Murphy* [1996] 1 VR 279.

8.159 This non-charitable purpose trust is hardly different from the case where, at the end of a valid perpetuity and accumulation[1] period, capital is to pass to R, but until then[2] the trustees have a valid power to accumulate the income subject to a valid power to use income or capital to further a non-charitable purpose specified in certain and workable fashion[3] eg to further the purposes of the Conservative Party as clarified if need be by the Leader of the Party[4], who has power to replace the trustees from time to time, the exercise of such power not to be challengeable in the courts except by proof beyond reasonable doubt that the Leader acted dishonestly, while the settlor's expressed intention in establishing the trust is for the trustees to use their powers to exhaust virtually all the income and capital within the trust period so that no more than £10,000 passes to R.

1 The English government has accepted the Law Commission's recommendation that the current 21-year period should be increased to match the perpetuity period as in other common law jurisdictions, and that this period should be raised to 125 years. The Legislative and Regulatory Reform Bill when enacted is intended to enable these reforms to be implemented swiftly. Recognition of foreign trusts with perpetuity periods in a range up to one hundred and fifty years should not be manifestly incompatible with English public policy, while foreign trusts for ever should be valid at least till expiry of the English default statutory period,
2 Eg *Re Sayer* [1957] Ch 423 at 437.
3 *Re Shaw* [1957] 1 All ER 745 at 759 endorsed in *Re Wooton's WT* [1968] 2 All ER 618 at 624.
4 So ensuring workable certainty: *Re Tuck's ST* [1978] Ch 49; *Church Property Trustees of Newcastle Diocese v Ebbeck* (1960) 104 CLR 394.

8.160 If the English Court of Appeal[1] over 100 years ago could accept the inalienability of a life interest under a trust governed by Scot's law, though English life interests cannot be inalienable, surely the English courts today can accept a non-charitable purpose trust where there is an expressly appointed enforcer (eg a trust to further the purposes of the Conservative Party to be enforceable by the Leader of that Party from time to time), such enforcer being in substantially the same position as the Leader of the Conservative Party in the example in the last paragraph.

1 *Re Fitzgerald* [1904] 1 Ch 573.

8.161 Indeed, why should the English courts not recognise that enforceable obligations to account to an interested person are at the core of the trust concept (as evident from *Schmidt v Rosewood Trust Ltd*[1]), whether such person is a beneficiary under a trust or an object of a power of appointment or a new trustee or, in the case of a charitable trust, the Attorney-General or the Charity Commission or 'an interested person', or in the case of a non-charitable purpose trust, the expressly appointed enforcer?

[1] [2003] 2 AC 709 where Privy Council held that rights to disclosure of documents and supporting information are not based on beneficiaries' proprietary interests but on the court's inherent jurisdiction to supervise matters and make trustees account for their trusteeship at the behest of sufficiently interested persons, including objects of powers.

8.162 Just as a car needs an engine so a trust needs an enforcer. If this be correct[1], then non-charitable purposes of a trust governed not just by a relevant foreign law but also by English law should be valid if the trust instrument has expressly provided for an enforcer and the purposes are certain and workable[2] and limited to a valid perpetuity period[3]. Thus, trusts (restricted to a royal lives plus twenty-one years perpetuity period) to further the purposes of the Labour Party to be enforceable by the Leader of such Party from time to time or to further the purposes of a particular self-interested group (the profession of barrister, solicitor or doctor or accountant) to be enforceable by the head of such group from time to time, should be valid.

[1] For favourable and unfavourable views respectively, see D J Hayton, *Overview and Comment* and *Developing the Obligation Characteristic of the Trust*, reprinted from (2001) 117 LQR 97, and P B Matthews *From Obligation to Property and Back Again?* in D J Hayton (ed) *Extending the Boundaries of Trusts and Similar Ring-Fenced Funds* (Kluwer Law International, 2002).
[2] No cy-près jurisdiction exists for non-charitable, as opposed to charitable, trusts unless created by statute, as in the case of most foreign non-charitable trusts.
[3] No 'wait and see' is possible since the Perpetuities and Accumulations Act 1964 does not apply to non-charitable purpose trusts which, by the rule against inalienability, are void from the outset if not restricted to a valid common law perpetuity period.

8.163 By expressly using language imposing a duty owed to the enforcer upon the trustee to use the trust fund exclusively for the non-charitable purposes (and hence not for the benefit of the settlor), the settlor by necessary implication has abandoned any beneficial interest in the fund so as to oust any resulting trust[1]. The trustee has legal beneficial ownership of the fund (as in the case of charitable trusts) but subject to fiduciary and equitable duties owed to the enforcer.

[1] 'If the settlor has expressly, or by necessary implication, abandoned any beneficial interst in the trust property, there is in my view no resulting trust': Lord Browne-Wilkinson in *Westdeutsche Landesbank v Islington London Borough Council* [1996] AC 669 at 708.

8.164 However, it would seem that if, instead of the trust fund having to be used up for a purpose like those in the penultimate paragraph, the purpose was merely holding and maintaining particular assets (eg an art collection as an undivided private collection) or developing the value of the trust fund, then the alleged purpose would be regarded as an investment power, with the settlor not having disposed of his underlying beneficial interest in the assets transferred to trustees[1].

1   This characterisation of the matter by English courts should lead to non-recognition of a non-charitable holding purpose trust even though stated a fully valid trust under the foreign governing law: the ring-fenced fund will be held on resulting trust for the settlor.

8.165 Furthermore, it is fundamental to an English trust for beneficiaries that the beneficiaries have rights to enforce the trust[1]. Thus, if a settlor used the most extreme type of Cayman Special Trusts Alternative Regime (STAR) trust to create a discretionary trust for the purpose of benefiting his descendants, none of whom had any right under STAR to enforce the trust, such right of enforcement being expressly vested in another person, then it seems that the English court should characterise the descendants as only objects of a personal power of appointment under a resulting trust for the settlor, but the power would be exercisable until the end of the specified trust period[2], assuming it to be a valid perpetuity period under conflicts of law principles and the Recognition of Trusts Act 1987.

1   Per Millett LJ in *Armitage v Nurse* [1998] Ch 241 at 253; and see para 60.21 below.
2   *Re Sayer* [1957] Ch 423.

8.166 A final issue is whether a settlor or a protector can have locus standi conferred on him by the trust instrument so as to become an enforcer where the trust is a trust for beneficiaries. Here, there is in England the core *Saunders v Vautier* principle whereby, if unanimous and all of full age and capacity and between them absolutely entitled to the whole beneficial interest, the beneficiaries can terminate the trust, regardless of the settlor's intentions, and obtain the property for themselves, so frustrating any other purposes of the settlor[1]. Clearly, any rights of enforcement of an English trust that would encroach upon such principle must be ineffective so as not to encroach upon the core of the English trust concept, although the English court would surely accept as fully valid trusts governed by foreign trust laws (such as those of all but one States in the USA) which have no *Saunders v Vautier* principle and insist on the carrying out of material purposes of the settlor regardless of all the beneficiaries' wishes.

1   See Article 69.

8.167 However, in principle, there seems no reason why a person other than the beneficiaries should not be capable of having locus standi conferred upon him by the settlor's trust instrument (eg to safeguard the interests of a beneficiary as yet unborn or unascertained) so long as he does not interfere with beneficiaries' *Saunders v Vautier* rights. Objects of a power of appointment can have locus standi to make the trustee account for its conduct even though the trust fund belongs beneficially to the beneficiaries entitled in default of appointment[1]. Why should the court not facilitate the wish of the settlor in his trust deed that he or a protector[2] should have the right to make the trustee account so long as there is a beneficiary unborn, unascertained or not of full age and capacity? Indeed, nowadays the settlor can take advantage of the Contracts (Rights of Third Parties) Act 1999 to contract with the trustee for the trustee to produce to him annual accounts and provide any requested information or documents and to add to the trust fund for the benefit of the beneficiaries any amount found due on the taking of accounts, to the intent that minor beneficiaries and beneficiaries not yet in existence shall have rights to have the trustee make up any deficiency in the trust fund and the settlor shall be trustee of those rights for them.

1   *Schmidt v Rosewood Trust Ltd* [2003] 2 AC 709.
2   In the foreign cases, *Re Hare Trust* (2001) 4 ITELR 288; *Von Knierem v Bermuda Trust* (1994) 1 Butts O.C.M. 116 and *Re Omar Family Trust (No 565 of 1997)* [2000] WTLR 713 at 714 the protector had locus standi. CPR Part 64 is drafted broadly enough to cover protectors.

Loan purpose trusts

8.168 The beneficiary principle has been considered in connection with the *Barclays Bank Ltd v Quistclose Investments Ltd*[1] type of trust where A lends money to B under a primary temporary trust to use the money only for the purpose of paying B's creditors, resulting if the purpose is performed in a pure loan relationship between A and B (excluding any trust relationship), but with a trust arising in A's favour if the purpose is not performed. Where is the beneficial interest in the money pending its application by B? Must it remain in A or may it be in B's creditor, C, or may it be in suspense, with C merely having a right to compel B to apply the property in accordance with A's directions, analogous to the right of a residuary legatee under a will[2] to compel the executor to administer the estate according to the testator's directions? In special circumstances Megarry V-C[3] took the last view which Peter Gibson J regarded as a general rule in *Carreras Rothmans Ltd v Freeman Matthews Treasure Ltd*[4].

1   [1970] AC 567, paras 1.25–1.35 above; applied in *Re EVTR Ltd* [1987] BCLC 646 CA; *Rowan v Dann* (1991) 64 P & CR 202, CA; *Guardian Ocean Cargoes Ltd v Banco de Brasil* [1991] 2 Lloyd's Rep 68, 87 but rejected by CA in [1994] CLC 243; *Tropical Capital Investment Ltd v Stanlake Holdings Ltd* (unreported, CA, noted [1992] LMCLQ 3).
2   *Stamp Duties Comr (Queensland) v Livington* [1965] AC 694, [1964] 3 All ER 692, para 1.46 above.
3   *Re Northern Developments (Holdings) Ltd* (6 October 1978, unreported) cited in *Carreras Rothmans Ltd v Freeman Matthews Treasure Ltd* [1985] 1 All ER 155 at 166. In *Twinsectra Ltd v Yardley* [2002] UKHL 12 Lord Millett at para [87] considered there was a powerful argument for the result of the arrangements in *Northern Developments* being to vest a beneficial interest in the company's subsidiary from the start, so that there was no *Quistclose* trust.
4   [1985] Ch 207, [1985] 1 All ER 155.

8.169 However, Peter Millett QC has emphasised[1] that the matter turns on A's intention and that no new enforceable purpose trust arises enforceable by the settlor qua settlor or where the beneficial interest is in suspense. He considered guidelines for ascertaining A's intentions to be as follows[2]:

'1.   If A's intention was to benefit C, or his object would be frustrated if he were to retain a power of revocation, the transaction will create an irrevocable trust in favour of C, enforceable by C but not by A. The beneficial interest in the trust property will be in C.

2.   If A's intention was to benefit B (though without vesting a beneficial interest in him), or to benefit himself by furthering some private or commercial interest of his own, and not (except incidentally) to benefit C, then the transaction will create a trust in favour of A alone and B will

hold the trust property in trust to comply with A's directions. The trust will be enforceable by A but not by C. The beneficial interest will remain in A.

3. Where A's object was to save B from bankruptcy by enabling him to pay his creditors, the prima facie inference is that set out in paragraph 2 above. Wherever that is the correct inference:

   (i)   Where A has an interest of his own, separate and distinct from any interest of B, in seeing that the money is applied for the stated purpose, B will be under a positive obligation, enforceable by A, to apply it for that purpose. Where A has no such interest, B will be regarded as having a power, but no duty, to apply it for the stated purpose, and A's remedy will be confined to preventing the misapplication of the money.

   (ii) Prima facie, A's directions will be regarded as revocable by him; but he may contract with B not to revoke them without B's consent.

   (iii) Communication to C of the arrangements prior to A's revocation will effect an assignment of A's equitable interest to C, and convert A's revocable mandate into an irrevocable trust for C.'

1   (1985) 101 LQR 269.
2   (1985) 101 LQR 290. For valuable discussion on the nature of *Quistclose* trusts see W Swadling (ed), *The Quistclose Trust (Hart Publishing, 2004).*

8.170 Since then, as Lord Millett in *Twinsectra Limited v Yardley*[1], he has rejected any question of the beneficial ownership being in suspense, holding that where the loaned monies are not freely at the disposal of the borrower but must be kept separate to be used only for a particular purpose, whether benefiting people or for an abstract purpose, then there is a resulting trust for the lender with the transferee having a power (or a duty) to apply the money for the stated purpose. Whether the borrower is obliged to apply the money for the stated purpose or is merely at liberty to do so, and whether the lender can countermand the borrower's mandate while it is still capable of being carried out, must depend on the circumstances of the particular case, taking account of the above guidelines in his LQR article. So long as the power is stated with sufficient clarity for the court to be able to determine whether it is still capable of being carried out or whether the money has been misapplied, it is sufficiently certain to be enforced. Otherwise, the borrower cannot make any use of the money and must return it to the lender under the resulting trust.

1   [2002] UKHL 12, [2002] 2 AC 164, at paras [77]–[102], especially [100], and Lord Hoffmann at para [13].

Points for draftsperson

8.171 Of course, a draftsman should ensure that no problems arise. If a settlor or testator wishes pure purposes to be carried out powers in that behalf may be created if trustees can be relied upon to exercise the powers[1] within an expressly restricted perpetuity period (eg royal lives plus twenty one years) and the purposes are certain and workable[2] with, perhaps an internal cy-près mechanism. Otherwise, a company can be created with the pure purposes (eg anti-vivisection) as its objects and the requisite funds can be given outright to the company. Alternatively, it seems that funds may be given as an accretion to the funds of an unincorporated association subject to the contractual rights and liabilities of the members inter se but subject to no trusts[3]. Otherwise, funds can be given to trustees to pay the income therefrom to the A Charity Co for such company to dispose of as it wishes for so long as the following purposes ... shall happen to be carried out but as soon as such purposes shall not be carried out then to pay such income to the B Charity Co for such company to dispose of as it wishes for so long as the said purpose shall happen to be carried out and so on to the Z Charity Co if need be, ensuring that the balance of income is sufficient to interest a charity[4]. It will be advisable to have the trustees or some other person as expert to decide whether or not the determining event has occurred[5].

[1] Of course, a trustee could be given a substantial beneficial interest liable to forfeiture if he failed to spend £x a year in exercising his power to carry out pure abstract purposes.
[2] *Re Shaw* [1951] 1 ALL ER 745 at 759, endorsed in *Re Wooton's WT* [1968] 2 ALL ER 618 at 624.
[3] *Re Recher's Will Trusts* [1972] Ch 526, [1971] 3 All ER 401; *Re Lipinski's Will Trusts* [1976] Ch 235, [1977] 1 All ER 33; *Universe Tankships Inc of Monrovia v International Transport Workers Federation* [1983] 1 AC 366, [1982] 2 All ER 67, HL; *Re Bucks Constabulary Widows' and Orphans' Fund Friendly Society (No 2)* [1979] 1 All ER 623, [1979] 1 WLR 936; *Conservative and Unionist Central Office v Burrell (Inspector of Taxes)* [1982] 2 All ER 1 at 7, CA.
[4] *Re Chardon* [1928] Ch 464; *Christ's Hospital v Grainger* (1849) 1 Mac & G 460, ousting the Perpetuities and Accumulations Act 1964, s 12. The income must be freely alienable and so not subject to trusts preventing this: *Re Dalziel* [1943] Ch 277, [1943] 2 All ER 656; *Re Wightwick's Will Trusts* [1950] Ch 260, [1950] 1 All ER 689.
[5] *Re Tuck's ST* [1978] Ch 49; *Church Property Trustees of Newcastle Diocese v Ebbeck* (1960) 104 CLR 394.

8.172 In the earlier cases of *Re Bowes*[1] and *Re Aberconway's Settlement Trusts*[2] it had been assumed that trusts were valid respectively for planting trees on the estate and for the upkeep and development of gardens within an estate since indirectly for the benefit of the individuals interested in the estate. Nowadays, when the beneficiary principle is more prominent it will be as well if draftsmen specifically express in the trust instrument the persons intended to be benefited making it clear that they are to have the right to have the trusts positively enforced[3], eg when drafting trusts of maintenance funds for historic buildings to obtain advantageous inheritance tax and capital gains tax treatment or when drafting sinking fund trusts for the upkeep of blocks of flats.

[1] [1896] 1 Ch 507.
[2] [1953] Ch 647, [1953] 2 All ER 350.
[3] Under *Re Denley's Trusts Deed* [1969] 1 Ch 373, [1968] 3 All ER 65, principles endorsed in *Re Lipinski's Will Trusts* [1976] Ch 235, [1977] 1 All ER 33. Also see *Raikes v Lygon* [1988] 1 All ER 884, [1988] 1 WLR 281.

The exceptional cases

8.173 In what follows, consideration is given to the exceptional, or anomalous, group of cases in which a testamentary trust, though it is not charitable nor for the benefit of any beneficiary, is still valid (if unenforceable, so operating as if a power). They were reviewed by the Court of Appeal in the

case of *Re Endacott*[1]. The court accepted the classification put forward by
Dr Morris and Professor Barton Leach in the following passage from their
book, *The Rule against Perpetuities*:

> 'We proceed to examine these "anomalous" exceptions. It will be found that
> they fall into the following groups: (1) trusts for the erection or maintenance of
> monuments or graves; (2) trusts for the saying of masses, in jurisdictions where
> such trusts are not regarded as charitable; (3) trusts for the maintenance of
> particular animals; (4) trusts for the benefit of unincorporated associations
> (though this group is more doubtful); (5) miscellaneous cases'.

[1]   [1960] Ch 232, [1959] 3 All ER 562, CA.

8.174 Of the miscellaneous cases in group (5), only one was specifically
referred to in *Re Endacott*, above, and that was *Re Catherall*[1], where a gift to
a vicar and churchwardens for a suitable memorial to the testator's parents
and sisters was upheld by Roxburgh J, who said: 'Such a trust as this is valid
whether charitable or not'; but the Court of Appeal held that in any event the
decision could be justified on the ground 'that in its context the purposes were
limited to religious (ie charitable) purposes'. A number of the other miscellaneous cases had been reviewed in *Re Astor's Settlement Trusts*[2], where
Roxburgh J had shown that in many instances they must have been decided
per incuriam and held that they did not justify the conclusion that a Court of
Equity will recognise a direction to apply funds for non-charitable purposes in
a manner which no court could control or enforce. In *Re Endacott*, above, this
view was impliedly affirmed by Lord Evershed, MR while Harman LJ said[3]:

> 'I applaud the orthodox sentiments expressed by Roxburgh J in *Re Astor's
> Settlement Trusts*, and I think, as I think he did, that though one knows that
> there have been decisions at times which are not satisfactorily classified, but are
> perhaps merely occasions when Homer had nodded, at any rate these cases
> stand by themselves and ought not to be increased in number, nor indeed
> followed, except where the one is exactly like another. Whether it would be
> better that some authority should now say that those cases were wrongly
> decided, this perhaps is not the moment to consider. At any rate, I cannot think
> that a case of [the present] kind, the case of providing outside a church an
> unspecified and unidentified memorial is the kind of instance which should be
> allowed to add to those troublesome, anomalous and aberrant cases.'

[1]   (3 June 1959, unreported).
[2]   [1952] Ch 534, [1952] 1 All ER 1067.
[3]   [1960] Ch 232 at 250–251.

8.175 On a strict view it would be possible for these exceptional testamentary
trusts to be confined to those so drafted that trust property not applied for the
prescribed purpose should fall into residue[1]. The traditional form of order can
then be made, the trustees undertaking to apply the trust property for the
prescribed purpose but the residuary beneficiary being given liberty to apply
to the court on the trustees failing to do so[2]. However, it would seem the
principle must extend to a will trust of residue for prescribed purposes, the
next of kin being given liberty to apply[3].

[1]   *Re Thompson* [1934] Ch 342 at 344; *Re Astor's Settlement Trusts* [1952] Ch 534 at 546.
[2]   *Pettingall v Pettingall* (1842) 11 LJ Ch 176.
[3]   *Re Endacott* [1960] Ch 232 at 240.

THE RULE AGAINST INALIENABILITY

8.176 The rule against inalienability applies to non-charitable purpose trusts where the capital is to be kept intact for a period so that only the income is to be spent in that period. If the trust fund can be spent without distinction between capital and income then the rule has no application[1]. It is the inalienability of the income that must be used for the designated purpose that leads to the rule being known as the rule against inalienability[2], while the trust capital fund itself (as opposed to the actual assets from time to time comprising the trust fund) is also inalienable.

1   *Trimmer v Danby* (1856) 26 LJ Ch 424; *Musset v Bingle* [1876] WN 170.
2   Eg *Re Chardon* [1928] Ch 464.

8.177 Non-charitable purpose trusts of capital to be kept intact for a period are void from the outset unless it is then certain that persons will become absolutely entitled to the property by the end of the common law perpetuity period[1] expiring 21 years from the death of the last survivor of causally relevant lives-in-being, if any. Thus the trust must be restricted directly or indirectly[2] to such period. Restricting a bequest expressly 'so far as the law allows' will be construed as restricting to 21 years[3] but the court will not imply such a clause[4].

1   The Perpetuities and Accumulations Act 1964 only deals with the rule against remoteness of interests vesting in *people*, though in that Act the draftsman uses 'the rule against perpetuities' in s 1 when referring to the rule against remoteness, and 'rule against remoteness' in s 15(4) when excluding the rule against inalienability.
2   *Pedilla v Nasti* (1990) 20 NSWLR 720.
3   *Re Hooper* [1932] Ch 38.
4   *Re Compton* [1946] 1 All ER.

TRUSTS TO RAISE AND KEEP IN REPAIR GRAVES AND SEPULCHRAL MONUMENTS

8.178 Although it would seem that the court could not *enforce* a testamentary trust for applying money in the erection of a tomb or monument or the repair of a grave or tomb not forming part of the fabric of a church[1] (insomuch as there would be no beneficiary interested in applying to the court to enforce the trust)[2] it was said in *Re Dean* that such trusts are not *void*, but merely duties of imperfect obligation, and that the trustees may safely spend the moneys on the prescribed object if they please[3]. North J added that he knew of nothing to prevent a gift of a sum of money to trustees upon trust to apply it for the repair of such a monument, if the donor took care to limit the time for which the trust was to last, so as to provide for its cesser within the perpetuity period applicable under the rule against inalienability[4]. If the time is not so limited the trust will fail at the outset.

1   It would be a valid charitable trust if the tomb could be regarded as part of the fabric of the church or if the trust were for the maintenance of the churchyard generally: *Re King* [1923] 1 Ch 243; *Re Vaughan* (1886) 33 Ch D 187; *Re Eighmie* [1935] Ch 524.
2   See *Re Astor's Settlement Trusts* [1952] Ch 534, [1952] 1 All ER 1067; *Re Shaw* [1957] 1 All ER 745 at 758, per Harman J.
3   (1889) 41 Ch D 552 at 557, per North J.

4   Cf *Pirbright v Salwey* [1896] WN 86; *Re Hooper* [1932] 1 Ch 38, cases where the trust
was for upkeep so long as the law allows, and see *Re Astor's Settlements Trusts* [1952]
Ch 534, [1952] 1 All ER 1067. See paras 11.38–11.43 below.

8.179 In *Re Chardon*[1], Romer J, in a considered judgment, held that a legacy
in trust to pay the income therefrom to a cemetery company, so long as the
company kept a grave in order, was a good trust, as the rule against
remoteness was directed against interests which vested outside the perpetuity
period, not against interests which, having vested, continued beyond it; and
the interests both of the company and of the residuary legatees were vested
interests, subject to no trusts, and they could combine to dispose of the whole
legacy. The rule against inalienability could not be infringed since the
company's determinable interest in income could be freely disposed of since no
trusts were imposed on the use of the income. In *Re Chardon* the learned
judge did not decide what would happen in the case of a gift over in the event
of a condition being broken. It appears, however, that at common law a gift
over to commence on the breach of the condition would be bad and that on
such breach the property would fall into residue[2]. A simple direction that on
breach of the condition the fund should fall into residue would, it seemed, be
unobjectionable[3]. However, where the disposition taking advantage of *Re
Chardon* is made after 15 July 1964 the position is altered by the Perpetuities
and Accumulations Act 1964. After creating the trust to pay income to the
cemetery company so long as the grave is kept in good order[4], the disposition
might continue in any one of three basic ways.

(1)   It could go on to make an express gift over to designated beneficiaries
       upon the grave not being kept in good order. The gift over may be void
       for remoteness but the 'wait and see' provisions of the Act (see
       11.17–11.18 below) mean that the voidness of the gift over cannot be
       taken for granted until it is known that the corporation had not in fact
       broken the condition within the perpetuity period. Once the remoteness
       has rendered the gift over invalid, the only consequence of the happen-
       ing of the determining event would be a resulting trust, and this would
       seem to attract the application of s 12(1) of the Act. The end result
       would seem to be that once the perpetuity period is past (ie the
       perpetuity period notionally supplied by s 3(4) and (5) of the Act)
       without the happening of the determining event, so that the gift over
       must fail, the corporation's interest becomes an absolute interest under
       s 12(1).
(2)   Alternatively, the disposition might not go on at all—that is, it might
       stop after making the initial gift. In this event a resulting trust would
       arise as soon as the determining event occurred, and so the disposition
       would fall squarely and from the outset within the terms of s 12(1). The
       resulting trust would be subject to the rule against perpetuities and if
       the perpetuity period passed without the happening of the determining
       event, so that the resulting trust became void for remoteness, the
       corporation would again acquire an absolute interest.
(3)   Or again, the disposition might go on (as the disposition in *Re Chardon*
       itself actually did) in a way which fell in a sense between the two
       possibilities already mentioned, by spelling out the resulting trust which
       would have arisen in any case—that is, by stating specifically the trusts

which would have arisen automatically if nothing had been stated. For example, if the disposition was contained in a will it might simply say that on the happening of the determining event the gift was to fall into residue. Whether this would also attract the operation of s 12(1) is not quite so clear, but it certainly seems illogical that a disposition of this kind should escape. On this basis, the position would be as in (2) above, rather than the residuary gift taking effect as before 1964.

1   [1928] Ch 464. The case has been criticised mainly in relation to the gift over not to the determinable interest (see e g *Tudor on Charities* (5th edn) p 701, and articles by W O Hart in 53 LQR 24, and M J Albery in 54 LQR 258), but, counsel having admitted it to be indistinguishable, it was followed in *Re Chambers' Will Trusts* [1950] Ch 267, though distinguished in *Re Wightwick's Will Trusts* [1950] Ch 260, [1950] 1 All ER 689, where income was subjected to trusts so as not to be freely alienable: c f *Re Dalziel* [1943] Ch 277, [1943] 2 All ER 656.
2   *Re Chambers' Will Trusts* [1950] Ch 267; *Re Gage* [1898] 1 Ch 498; *Re Hooper* [1932] 1 Ch 38; *Re Vaughan* (1886) 33 Ch D 187. See also *Re Moore* [1901] 1 Ch 936, where an unsuccessful attempt was made to extend the period to twenty-one years after the death of the survivor of all persons living at the testator's death, which made it void for uncertainty. A bequest to a club of a portrait in trust to hang it up and retain it in a conspicuous part of the Hall of a City company was upheld; but a further gift, conditional upon the acceptance of the gift aforesaid, of £4,000 upon trust out of the income to keep the picture in repair and to apply the surplus income to persons of a particular description without reference to age or poverty was held not charitable and therefore void on grounds of perpetuity: *Re Gassiot* (1901) 70 LJ Ch 242.
3   *Re Randell* (1888) 38 Ch D 213, and see *Re Wightwick's Will Trusts* [1950] Ch 260, [1950] 1 All ER 689.
4   Although it has nothing to do with trusts, note the Parish Councils and Burial Authorities (Miscellaneous Provisions) Act 1970, which provides one solution to the problem posed by the desire to have a grave or tomb maintained. Section 1 of the Act permits local authorities or burial authorities to make an agreement to maintain (inter alia) certain graves, vaults, tombstones or other memorials for a period not exceeding 99 years.

8.180   A testator may make a gift to a charity conditionally upon his tomb being kept in repair, with a gift over to another charity in the event of the tomb being allowed to fall into disrepair[1]. In *Re Dalziel*[2], Cohen J pointed out that such a gift will only be upheld where there is no more than an inducement to the first charity to repair the tomb and the testator has not imposed any legal obligation to apply part of the income for that purpose. The American courts have held that a trust to keep in repair for ever the tombs *of a class* (eg the testator's family) is a charitable trust and valid, although a similar trust to keep up the tomb of an individual is not; but the distinction seems somewhat unreal[3], and it is believed that it would not be made in English law.

1   *Re Tyler* [1891] 3 Ch 252; *Chamberlayne v Brockett* (1872) 8 Ch App 206 at 211; *Re Davies* [1915] 1 Ch 543. But dist. *Re Porter* [1925] Ch 746.
2   [1943] Ch 277, [1943] 2 All ER 656.
3   *Swasey v American Bible Society* 57 Me 527 (1869); *Piper v Moulton* 72 Me 155 (1881). Contrast *Neo v Neo* (1875) LR 6 PC 382.

TRUSTS FOR THE BENEFIT OF DOGS, HORSES, ETC

8.181   On similar principles, a testamentary trust, limited in point of time within the rule against perpetuities, to apply money for keeping specified pet animals in comfort during their lives, is perfectly legal, although no person could enforce it[1]. Testamentary expressions like 'so far as the law allows' will validly restrict the period to 21 years but the court will not treat such an expression as implicit in order to save the gift[2]. Moreover, a trust of undefined continuance for the benefit of animals will be upheld as a valid charitable trust if, in its execution there is 'necessarily involved benefit to the public'[3], as in the case of a gift for 'the welfare of cats and kittens needing care and attention' which has been held to develop the finer side of human nature of which care for old and sick animals is a manifestation[4]. Applying this test the House of Lords has held that an anti-vivisection society is not a charity[5] since the material benefits of vivisection to man outweigh the moral benefit alleged to flow from the success of the society's project and since the need to change the law in order to prohibit vivisection gave the trust a disqualifying political complexion.

1   *Pettingall v Pettingall* (1842) 11 LJ Ch 176; *Re Dean* (1889) 41 Ch D 552 though wrong in suggesting lives other than human lives may be used in ascertaining the perpetuity period: *Re Haines* (1952) Times, 7 November and *Mitford v Reynolds* (1848) 16 Sim 105; and see *Re Kelly* [1932] IR 255. These cases must be regarded as anomalous and exceptional and in no way destructive of the principle laid down in *Morice v Bishop of Durham* (1805) 10 Ves 522, that there must be someone in whose favour the court could decree specific performance (*Re Astor's Settlement Trusts* [1952] Ch 534, [1952] 1 All ER 1067, and see *Re Shaw* [1957] 1 All ER 745, [1957] 1 WLR 729, compromised on appeal [1958] 1 All ER 245n).
2   *Re Compton* [1946] 1 All ER 117; *Re Kelly* [1932] IR 255.
3   *Re Grove-Grady* [1929] 1 Ch 557 at 882, CA, per Romer LJ; on appeal sub nom *A-G v Plowden* [1931] WN 89, HL.
4   *Re Moss* [1949] 1 All ER 495.
5   *National Anti-Vivisection Society v IRC* [1948] AC 31, [1947] 2 All ER 217, overruling *Re Foveaux* [1895] 2 Ch 501. Trustees who had acted on the basis that the latter case was good law were relieved against breach of trust in *Re Wightwick's Will Trusts* [1950] Ch 260, [1950] 1 All ER 689.

8.182 A trust to promote fox-hunting has been upheld[1], though fox-hunting may be promoted otherwise than by maintaining and exercising horses and hounds, the judge, being over-influenced by the fact that the executors and trustees could hold the property subject to an undertaking to apply it to the named object, with the residuary beneficiary being given leave to apply to the court upon the trustees failing in their duty[2]. It may well be that the residuary beneficiary, Trinity Hall, Cambridge only objected pro forma in respect of this gift from an alumnus. This anomalous case should not be extended to other sports (like angling) and if any of these anomalous cases is to be overruled this seems a prime candidate. Indeed, by virtue of the Hunting Act 2004, outlawing the hunting of wild animals by dogs unless no more than two dogs are used and only for the purpose of stalking and flushing out the animals so that they can be shot, fox-hunting trusts are illegal.

1   *Re Thompson* [1934] Ch 342.
2   This 'negative' enforceability by persons not positively wanting the purposes to be enforced does not suffice on its own or all purpose trusts would be valid: *Re Davidson* [1909] 1 Ch 567 at 571.

GIFTS FOR MASSES

8.183 In *Re Caus*[1] it was held that a gift for the saying of masses is charitable, on the grounds that it enables a ritual act, recognised by a large proportion of Christians as the central act of their religion, to be performed and assists in the endowment of priests to perform that act, and accordingly the rule against perpetuities does not apply to it. *Re Hetherington*[2] has accepted *Re Caus* as good law in respect of the saying of masses in public though not in private.

1   [1934] Ch 162, but some doubt was cast on this decision in *Gilmour v Coats* [1949] AC 426 at 451–452, 454, [1949] 1 All ER 848 at 858, 859, HL.
2   [1990] Ch 1, [1989] 2 All ER 129 (*sed quaere* when the justification of assisting in the endowment of the priesthood applies equally to masses said in public or in private).

8.184 However even if a gift for the saying of private masses be non-charitable it seems it could still be valid if restricted to the perpetuity period[1].

1   *Bourne v Keane* [1919] AC 815 at 874–75, per Lord Buckmaster; in Malaysia and Singapore trusts for ancestor worship (Sin Chew or Chin Shong ceremonies) have been held valid anomalous non-charitable purpose trusts if restricted to the perpetuity period: *Re Khoo* (1933) 2 MLJ 119; *Phan v Phan* (1940) 9 MLJ 44; *Tan v Tan* (1946) 12 MLJ 159; *Hong Kong Bank Trustee Co v Farrer Tan* [1988] 1 MLJ 485.

CAPRICIOUS TRUSTS RELATING TO THE MANAGEMENT OF INANIMATE OBJECTS

8.185 Where directions are given to trustees to manage property in a manner absolutely capricious, and without either human interest or benefit to any living being, it would seem that the trust is absolutely void, and that the person entitled to the property by law can claim it at once as if the trust had never been declared. Thus, where a house was devised to trustees in trust to block up windows and doors for twenty years, and at the end of that period to convey it to A in fee, it was held that the first trust was void, and that the heir-at-law took the house during the twenty years[1]. So in America it has been held that a trust to keep a favourite clock of the testator in repair was void[2]. It is, however, difficult in principle to distinguish these cases from those relating to the keeping up of tombs, unless the latter are allowed as a concession to human weakness or sentiment[3]. The whole of the cases relating to this question require to be reviewed by the House of Lords before any intelligible principle can be extracted from them.

1   *Brown v Burdett* (1882) 21 Ch D 667. But cf *Re Cassel* [1926] Ch 358, where a trust to keep in repair and pay rent, rates, and taxes of a dwelling house was held good until it vested absolutely in possession.
2   *Kelly v Nichols* (1891) 17 RI 306, but now see Uniform Trust Code 2000, ss 404 and 409 for valid purpose trusts for twenty-one years. For antagonistic Scots cases see, eg *McCaig v University of Glasgow* 1907 SC 231; *McCaig's Trustees v Kirk Session of United Free Church of Lismore* 1915 SC 426.
3   As explained in *Re Astor's Settlement Trusts* [1952] Ch 534, [1952] 1 All ER 1067 and *Re Endacott* [1960] Ch 232, CA.

Unincorporated associations

8.186 An unincorporated association has the following features[1]: (1) it is composed of two or more persons bound together for a common purpose; (2) those persons have mutual rights and duties arising from a contract between them; (3) the association has rules to determine (a) who controls the association and its funds and (b) the terms on which such control is exercisable; (4) the association can be joined or left at will. This fourth feature was not at issue in *Conservative and Unionist Central Office v Burrell (Inspector of Taxes)* and it seems too restrictive since there may well be rules restricting new membership or the freedom to leave at will and why should such rules negative the existence of an unincorporated association?

1   *Conservative and Unionist Central Office v Burrell (Inspector of Taxes)* [1982] 2 All ER 1, [1982] 1 WLR 522, CA.

8.187 Gifts to or in trust for unincorporated associations raise technical problems that will amaze or confound laymen wishing to benefit such an association. The technical problems flow from the fact that an unincorporated association is not a legal person capable of owning property and of being the subject of legal rights and duties. Association property thus has to be vested in a few leading members as trustees for all the members of the association, though moneys will be dealt with by a treasurer operating an association bank account separate from his personal account. The trust will be a straightforward trust for the members (except to the extent that some specific statute might prevent members of certain societies from winding up the society and dividing up its property between themselves). The trustees or other organ under the club's constitution (eg the chairman or the executive committee) may enter into contracts or, exceptionally may be authorised to create trusts binding the club's property. To the extent such valid trusts have not been created the club's property belongs beneficially to the members subject to their contract inter se under the club's constitution (whether an inward-looking or outward-looking constitution) and subject to creditors' claims resulting from contracts made by the trustees or other organ[1].

1   See *Re Bucks Constabulary Widows' and Orphans' Fund Friendly Society (No 2)* [1979] 3 All ER 623, [1979] 1 WLR 936. However, exceptionally, the beneficiaries of the bare trust are not liable to indemnify the trustees in respect of any liabilities incurred beyond the extent of the assets of the club unless, as often is the case, the club rules provide otherwise: *Wise v Perpetual Trustee Co* [1903] AC 139.

8.188 The technical problems in the way of gifts to or in trust for such clubs relate to the need for trusts to satisfy the beneficiary principle[1], the test for certainty of objects[2], the rule against remoteness of vesting ensuring that beneficiaries' interests must vest in interest within the perpetuity period[3], and the rule against inalienability ensuring that income, subject to non-charitable trusts or powers is not rendered inalienable for longer than the perpetuity period[4]. Whether or not such principles, tests or rules are satisfied hinges upon the construction placed upon the settlor's or testator's intentions[5], taking into account the terms of his gift, the rules and nature[6] of the association to which he is giving (he being presumed to know such)[7] and the nature of the gifted property[8].

1   *Re Denley's Trust Deed* [1969] 1 Ch 373, [1968] 3 All ER 65; *Re Lipinski's Will Trusts* [1976] Ch 235, [1977] 1 All ER 33; *Leahy v A-G for New South Wales* [1959] AC 457, [1959] 2 All ER 300.
2   See para 8.43 ff.
3   See para 11.55 ff.
4   See para 11.38 ff.

5   *Leahy v A-G for New South Wales* [1959] AC 457, [1959] 2 All ER 300.
6   *Re Recher's Will Trusts* [1972] Ch 526, [1971] 3 All ER 401; cf *Re Lipinski's Will Trusts*
     [1977] 1 All ER 33 at 43.
7   *Carne v Long* (1860) 2 De GF & J 75 at 79.
8   *Leahy v A-G for New South Wales* [1959] AC 457, [1959] 2 All ER 300.

8.189 The first question is whether or not the donor intended to create a straightforward trust of his property in the hands of the treasurer or other officer so that it can be freely spent on everyday expenses (without the need to distinguish capital from income and to spend only the income) or an endowment trust requiring the capital to be set apart from the club's general assets and only the income to be used in the specified manner. Until the Perpetuities and Accumulation Act 1964 endowment trusts were void unless restricted to the perpetuity period: after that Act they are valid for the statutory perpetuity period if not restricted to the common law perpetuity period, unless they are pure abstract purpose trusts that are non-charitable, in which event they will be void for infringing the rule against inalienability (unaffected by the 1964 Act) as well as void for infringing the beneficiary principle. The critical question in the case of an endowment trust is, therefore, whether it satisfies the beneficiary principle as clarified by *Re Denley's Trust Deed*[1] or contravenes it as a non-charitable purpose trust (assuming that the law does not develop so as to allow such a trust to be valid if enforceable by an expressly designated enforcer having locus standi to sue).

1   See para 8.148 ff.

8.190 The following constructions are possible, though the modern trend is to validate gifts by adopting the fourth construction (post) in the absence of a clear intention on the part of the donor or testator to create an endowment trust of his property. Thus, a gift or legacy to an unincorporated society will be valid under the fourth construction as accruing to society funds generally under a straightforward trust, in the absence of a clear intention that the property is to be held as an endowment trust, as would be the case if one million pounds were bequeathed to the English Dart – Playing Association on trust to use the income for furthering the dart playing standards of English people of all ages, such trust being void for infringing the beneficiary principle and the rule against inalienability, whether the Association be an unincorporated body or a company limited by guarantee. Where the trust is an endowment trust for present and future members of the unincorporated body, it would now seem to be valid under the third construction (post).

(1)   No trust exists for the gift is a valid absolute out-and-out gift to the present[1] aggregate of persons described by the group name under which they associate[2], eg the X Club, the Y Society, the Z Association. Any member of the association may claim his aliquot share under a joint tenancy or tenancy in common. This construction is possible even if the gift is to the association with the motive of being used for its general purposes[3] though nowadays the recently developed fourth construction, below, will be more likely since the settlor/testator would probably not intend that the individual members could forthwith divide up his gift among themselves[4]. However, the old approach was benevolent in

preventing the gift being for the future members and so necessarily upon an endowment trust and so void under the common law rule against remoteness before the 1964 Perpetuities and Accumulations Act.

(2)   A trust exists for the present members (ie those at the date of the gift) of the association jointly or equally[5]. Where there is a clear trust this has the merit of validating the gift, though since a straightforward trust for present members with *Saunders v Vautier* rights is equivalent in effect to an absolute out-and-out gift it is perhaps a little unusual to create a trust if only present members are intended to be benefited rather than future members as well.

(3)   A trust exists for present and future members of the association, including instances where the trust is for purposes primarily for the personal benefit of present and future members thereby satisfying the beneficiary principle[6], so the gift is in the nature of an endowment, the capital having to be set aside and kept intact so that the income may be used for the benefit of the members of the club from time to time. Such trust would have been void under the old common law rule against remoteness since persons could become members and obtain a beneficial interest outside the perpetuity period[7]. To be valid the trust would have needed to be restricted to members from time to time until 21 years after the death of the last survivor of all the descendants of, eg King George VI, living at the date of creation of the trust or the earlier dissolution of the club. Without such restriction the trust would now seem to be valid if created after the 1964 Perpetuities and Accumulations Act. Under s 3(1) of the Act the trust is treated as valid until it becomes established that a vesting of beneficial interests must occur (if at all) after the statutory period of 21 years from the death of the last survivor of the statutory lives in being. Thus, one waits and sees if the club is dissolved before expiry of this period, because in such event the then members will take absolute vested interests in the trust property to the exclusion of all others. If it becomes apparent at the expiry of the statutory period that, since the club has not been dissolved, persons can still become members and obtain a beneficial interest outside the statutory period, then it seems that s 4(4) of the 1964 Act may apply to exclude such future persons from the class of beneficiaries, so the then class members take absolute vested interests in the trust property to the exclusion of all others[8].

(4)   No endowment trust exists because the gift is a valid absolute out-and-out gift to the present members of the association beneficially as an accretion to the body's property to be dealt with according to the rules of the body by which the members are contractually bound[9]. Moneys will thus be paid over to the treasurer to go into the account he maintains separately from his own personal account, whilst other property will be vested in trustees under a straightforward trust for the members in accordance with the body's rules[10].

---

[1]   If the organisation or trustees were intended to be legally bound to benefit future members, so that the property would still be held for them when they materialised, a trust would necessarily arise.

2 *Cocks v Manners* (1871) LR 12 Eq 574 (share of residue 'to the Dominican Convent at Carisbrooke payable to the superior for the time being'); *Re Smith* [1914] 1 Ch 937 (bequest to 'the society or institution known as the Franciscan Friars of Clevedon in the County of Somerset'); *Re Ogden* [1933] Ch 678; *Leahy v A-G for New South Wales* [1959] AC 457, [1959] 2 All ER 300, PC.

3 *Re Ogden* [1933] Ch 678 at 681; *Re Clarke* [1901] 2 Ch 110 (bequest to the committee for the time being of the Corps of Commissionaries in London to aid in the purchase of their barracks or in any other way beneficial to the Corps).

4 *Re Recher's Will Trusts* [1972] Ch 526, [1971] 3 All ER 401; *Re Lipinski's Will Trusts* [1976] Ch 235, [1977] 1 All ER 33; *Re Goodson* [1971] VR 801.

5 *Re Drummond* [1914] 2 Ch 90, though the Privy Council in *Leahy v A-G for New South Wales* [1959] AC 457, [1959] 2 All ER 300, PC had reservations as to whether it would have come to the same conclusion on the facts since an intention to benefit future members seemed present. The same objection applies to *Re Prevost* [1930] 2 Ch 383 and *Re Turkington* [1937] 4 All ER 501. Nowadays, it seems these cases would be validated under the fourth construction, below. The cases decided before Brightman J first fully explained in *Re Recher's Will Trusts* [1972] Ch 526 at 538–539 how unincorporated bodies held their property are most unsatisfactory, since they failed to recognise that the imagined problems arising in respect of legacies to unincorporated bodies arose equally in respect of property already held by such bodies and yet such bodies could validly hold and use such property for the benefit of purposes and of future members.

6 See para 8.144 above. Where the members have joined together for a social and recreational purpose or to secure some personal advantage the beneficiary principle will be satisfied: where they combined in pursuit of some altruistic non-charitable purpose the beneficiary principle should still be satisfied if the members under the constitution can wind up the association and divide the property between themselves and the settlor's trust terms are not construed as overriding the members' rights under the constitution and creating an enduring non-charitable purpose trust within the fifth construction below.

7 The gift cannot be saved by the principle that a gift of income indefinitely for A and his successors in title is a gift of the capital to A for such principle cannot be applied where the beneficiary is a fluctuating group of successive generations of members: *Re Levy* [1960] Ch 346 at 363, CA; *Re Westphal* [1972] NZLR 792 at 794–795.

8 Exceptionally, if the trust were construed as a discretionary endowment trust for the members until dissolution of the club, then on such dissolution or the later expiry of the statutory perpetuity period there should be a resulting trust to the settlor or his estate under s 3(3) of the 1964 Act. Trusts for persons (as opposed to trusts for purposes) are not invalidated by the rule against inalienability: see paras 11.2–11.4 and 11.38–11.43 below. On the 1964 Act see paras 11.14–11.36 below.

9 *Re Lipinski's Will Trusts* [1976] Ch 235, [1977] 1 All ER 33; *Re Recher's Will Trusts* [1972] Ch 526; *Re Bucks Constabulary Widows' and Orphans' Fund Friendly Society (No 2)* [1979] 1 All ER 623; *Universe Tankship Inc of Monrovia v International Transport Workers Federation* [1983] 1 AC 366, [1982] 2 All ER 67, HL, [1980] 2 Lloyd's Rep 523, CA; *Conservative and Unionist Central Office v Burrell (Inspector of Taxes)* [1982] 2 All ER 1 at 7; *Re Goodson* [1971] VR 801; *Boddington v Lawton* [1994] ICR 478; *Hunt v McLaren* [2006] EWHC 2386 (Ch).

10 *Re Bucks Constabulary Widows' and Orphans' Fund Friendly Society (No 2)* [1979] 1 All ER 623, [1979] 1 WLR 936; Friendly Societies Act 1974, s 53.

8.191 Usually, the members will be able by a contractually specified majority (or, otherwise, unanimously)[1] to divide the subject-matter of the gift between themselves so that there is a valid trust for themselves. In the very rare case where beneficiaries cannot obtain beneficial interests by dividing the property up between themselves because statute prohibits this[2] or because on dissolution the assets must pass on to another body to carry on the purposes of the dissolved club[3], then the trust cannot be a bare trust for members: it would seem to be a purpose trust with the gifted assets often being regarded as an endowment, so that one will need to consider the fifth and subsequent constructions that follow. However, a legacy not by way of endowment but intended to augment the general funds of a body available for discharging any liabilities, should be valid as directly or indirectly benefiting the members with locus standi to ensure their body's funds are properly spent.

1   *Re Grant's Will Trusts* [1979] 2 All ER 359 at 366; *Re Recher's Will Trusts* [1972] Ch 526 at 539; *Re William Denby & Sons Ltd Sick and Benevolent Fund* [1971] 1 WLR 973 at 978–979 but of *McKenny v Barnsley Corpn* (1894) 10 TLR 533, CA; *Abbatt v Treasury Solicitor* [1969] 1 WLR 1575 at 1583.
2   For example, Literary and Scientific Institutions Act 1854, s 30, *Re Bristol Athenaeum* (1889) 43 Ch D 236.
3   *Re Grant's Will Trusts* [1979] 3 All ER 359 at 366 discussed below.

8.192 In *Re Lipinski's Will Trusts*[1] Oliver J upheld a residuary bequest 'upon trust as to one half thereof for the Hull Judeans (Maccabi) Association in memory of my late wife to be used solely in the work of constructing the new buildings for the Association and/or improvements to the said buildings'. Benevolently, he treated the reference to the wife as a tribute, a motive, throwing no light on the question whether or not a permanent endowment was intended, and he treated the 'used solely' reference as a superadded direction of no legal force, though a strong moral intimation of which of the Association's purposes the testator would most like carried out. He held that the testator's moneys could be spent on capital or income expenses or could even be divided between the members if they took the necessary measures under the Association's constitution. The testator's moneys accrued to the general funds of the Association held for the benefit of the members.

1   [1976] Ch 235, [1977] 1 All ER 33.

8.193 In *Re Grant's Will Trusts*[1] Vinelott J did not uphold the gift of a testator's estate 'to the Labour Party Property Committee for the benefit of [which he construed as "in trust for"] the Chertsey HQ of the Chertsey & Walton Constituency Labour Party' ('CLP'), providing that if the headquarters ceased to be in the Chertsey UDC Area (1972) his estate should pass to the National Labour Party ('NLP'). He held the estate was intended to be kept intact to provide a permanent endowment to pass to the NLP if the prescribed event occurred, so that the gift was void for perpetuity (whether under the rule against remoteness if construed as a gift for present and future members of the CLP, or the rule against inalienability if construed as a purpose trust, quite apart from infringing the beneficiary principle if construed as an abstract political purpose trust).

1   [1979] 3 All ER 359, [1980] 1 WLR 360 where the impact of Perpetuities and Accumulations Act 1964, ss 3 and 4 was not considered.

8.194 He could not accept that the bequest should be construed as a gift to the CLP members at the testator's death with the superadded direction of no legal force that they would use it for HQ purposes, though accruing to the general funds of the CLP. He said[1], 'The fact that it is a gift to trustees and not in terms to an unincorporated association militates against construing it as a gift to the members at the date the gift takes effect and against construing the words indicating the purposes for which the property is to be used as expressing the testator's motive and not as imposing any trust'. Furthermore, the CLP members were not under the CLP rules entitled to divide the CLP

167

funds amongst themselves but were subordinated to the NLP who could demand the funds, and the CLP rules were unalterable except with the NLP's consent. He might have added that any finding of a gift to the CLP members, whether directly or as an accrual to the CLP general funds, was already precluded by his prior holding that the bequest was meant as a permanent endowment, the Committee having to keep the capital intact to use the income for ever for HQ purposes, unless the HQ political ceased to be in Chertsey when the capital was to be handed over to the NLP for its political purposes.

1   [1979] 3 All ER 359, [1980] 1 WLR 360 at 372.

8.195 The real reason for the judge emphasising the point that the CLP members could not divide the trust fund between themselves could well be that, if an outward looking purpose of a non-charitable character could be made effective for a perpetuity period by a gift for such purpose being made to an unincorporated association, this would wholly undermine the orthodox principle[1] that a trust must be for persons or for charitable purposes if it is to be valid.

1   See paras 8.144–8.156 above.

8.196 In *Neville Estates Ltd v Madden*[1] Cross J appears to treat this fourth construction as creating a new limited form of proprietary interest, while in *Artistic Upholstery Limited v Art Forma (Furniture) Ltd*[2] Lawrence Collins J held that members of an unincorporated association can collectively own goodwill subject to the express or implied terms of the contract into which they enter with one another upon becoming members, following the view of Cross J who stated that a gift to an unincorporated association is construed as 'a gift to the existing members not as joint tenants but subject to their respective contractual rights and liabilities towards one another as members. In such a case a member cannot sever his share. It will accrue to the other members on his death or resignation, even though such members include persons who became members after the gift took effect. It will not be open to objection on the score of perpetuity or uncertainty unless there is something in its terms or circumstances or in the rules of the association which preclude the members at any given time from dividing the subject of the gift between them.' These views have not yet been subject to thorough judicial scrutiny, though often cited.

1   [1962] Ch 832 at 849.
2   [1999] 4 All ER 277.

8.197 Perhaps, the proper analysis is that the ordinary form of equitable co-proprietary interest subsists in each member but that each member has contracted not to sever his joint interest and not to exercise his right to claim an aliquot share on resignation or death or, even, whilst a member unless under the appropriate rules the members between them decide to divide up the assets. As a matter of contract or of estoppel when a member resigns (or dies) he (or his executor) cannot claim his aliquot share or claim that his equitable interest could not have passed on resignation (or death) to the other members without signed writing as required by Law of Property Act 1925, s 53 (or the

Wills Act 1837)[1]. Alternatively, the equitable interest automatically determines on resignation or death, being a limited and not an absolute, equitable interest.

[1] See also Ford *Unincorporated Non-Profit Associations*, pp 5–7, 21–23; Morris and Leach, *The Rule against Perpetuities* (2nd edn) pp 313 ff, *Re Vandervell's Trusts (No 2)* [1974] Ch 269, [1974] 1 All ER 47, B. Green (1980) 43 MLR 628.

8.198 The final sentence of Cross J requires qualification. If the fourth construction is ousted by the terms or circumstances of the gift or the rules of the association, an endowment trust for present and future members within the third construction will not be open to objection on the score of uncertainty or perpetuity after the Perpetuities and Accumulations Act 1964: an endowment trust for non-charitable purposes will, however, be open to objection on the score of uncertainty or perpetuity (ie the rule against inalienability) or of infringing the beneficiary principle (unless some expressly appointed enforcer exists and the courts are prepared to develop the beneficiary principle into the enforcer principle, as discussed[1].)

(5)   An endowment trust exists for abstract or impersonal non-charitable purposes. Here the trust will be void for infringing the beneficiary principle, unless it falls within the anomalous group of exceptional cases earlier discussed[2], though even then the rule against inalienability will need to be satisfied by restriction to the common law perpetuity period if the trust is to be valid[3]. Thus, a trust to provide a Jewish community centre in Hull would be void[4], just as an endowment trust for a contemplative order of nuns[5] or for the Communist Party[6] or for the Socialist Party[7] is void unless the courts are prepared to develop an enforcer principle validating such trusts if the settlor's trust instrument expressly arranges for there to be an enforcer[8] (eg, the leader from time to time of the Socialist Party to be enforcer of a trust to further the purposes of the Socialist Party).

(6)   A trust exists for charitable purposes, so there is no need to satisfy the beneficiary principle or the rule against inalienability or, indeed, the certainty principle as long as the charitable intent is sufficiently certain[9].

[1] See paras 8.157–8.167 above.
[2] See paras 8.173–8.184 above.
[3] *Re Hooper* [1932] 1 Ch 38; *Re Astor's Settlement Trusts* [1952] Ch 534, [1952] 1 All ER 1067.
[4] *Re Lipinski's Will Trusts* [1976] Ch 235 at 248, [1977] 1 All ER 33 at 44.
[5] *Leahy v A-G for New South Wales* [1959] AC 457, [1959] 2 All ER 300, PC.
[6] *Bacon v Pianta* (1966) 114 CLR 634.
[7] Cf *Re Grant's Will Trusts* [1979] 3 All ER 359, [1980] 1 WLR 360.
[8] See paras 8.157–8.167 above.
[9] *Re Banfield* [1968] 2 All ER 276, [1968] 1 WLR 846; *Re Finger's Will Trusts* [1972] Ch 286, [1971] 3 All ER 1050; *Chamberlayne v Brockett* (1872) 8 Ch App 206.

Associations neither corporate nor unincorporated

8.199 Where there is an *inter vivos* gift to an association of people, like a campaign group, that is not a corporate body nor an unincorporated association as defined in *Conservative and Unionist Central Office v Burrell*[1], the donor is regarded as giving the treasurer a mandate to deal with the gifted property of which the treasurer becomes the full legal beneficial owner. Under the mandate the treasurer is liable to be sued to apply the property for the designated purpose and can be restrained from misapplying the property. No such agency can be set up at the moment of death between a testator and his chosen agent[1]. Perhaps, a testator's legacy to a campaign group or its treasurer could be regarded as a conditional gift, with the property falling back into the testator's estate for the residuary legatee (or the next of kin if the legacy was of the residuary estate) to the extent not applied in the manner required by the condition.

1   [1982] 2 All ER 1, [1982] 1 WLR 522.
2   [1982] 2 All ER 1, [1982] 1 WLR 522.

Paragraph 2(a)

Powers in the nature of trusts

8.200 When faced with an apparent special power of appointment amongst a defined class where there is no gift over in default of appointment the court may treat the apparent power as being in the nature of a discretionary trust for the class members[1] or as a mere power followed by an implied fixed trust in default of appointment in favour of the class members equally[2]. In reading the cases care must be taken in ascertaining which of these alternatives prevailed in the light of the ambiguous language often used by the courts to describe either alternative, eg 'trust power', 'power in the nature of a trust'. For large classes the former alternative is likely and for small classes the latter alternative: the test for certainty of objects of a trust is less strict for discretionary trusts than for fixed trusts[3].

1   *Re Parker's Will* [1966] IR 309; *McPhail v Doulton* [1971] AC 424, [1970] 2 All ER 228; *Re Leek* [1967] Ch 1061, [1967] 2 All ER 1160; affd [1969] 1 Ch 563, [1968] 1 All ER 793, CA.
2   *Wilson v Duguid* (1883) 24 Ch D 244; *Walsh v Wallinger* 91830) 2 Russ & M 78; *Re Kieran* [1916] 1 IR 289.
3   See paras 8.42–8.55 above.

8.201 If the power is just a power and no trust can be implied in default of appointment then there will be a resulting trust in favour of the settlor/testator if the power is not exercised[1]. The crucial question is whether the court can ascertain a general intention to benefit the objects of the power. The leading authority is *Burrough v Philcox*[2]. There, a testator directed that certain property should be held in trust for his two children for life, with remainder to their issue. He declared that if they should both die without issue, the survivor of them should have power to dispose of the property by will amongst such of the testator's nephews and nieces or their children as such survivor should select. No appointment was made. It was held that the class members took the property equally. Lord Cottenham said:

'Where there appears *a general intention in favour of a class*, and a particular intention in favour of individuals of a class to be selected by another person,

170

and the particular intention fails, from that selection not being made, the court will carry into effect the general intention in favour of the class.'

1   *Re Sayer* [1957] Ch 423, [1956] 3 All ER 600; *Re Perowne* [1951] Ch 785, [1951] 2 All ER 201.
2   (1840) 5 My & Cr 72; *Wilson v Duguid* (1883) 24 Ch D 244.

8.202 So, where a testator gave personalty to his widow for life, and to be at her disposal by her will, 'therewith to apply part for charity, the remainder to be at her disposal among my relations, in such proportions as she may be pleased to direct', and the widow died without appointing the property, it was held that half was to be held in trust for charitable purposes, and the residue for the testator's relatives determined according to the Statutes of Distribution laying down those entitled to an intestate's personal estate[1].

1   *Salusbury v Denton* (1857) 3 K & J 529; *Re Caplin* (1865) 2 Drew & Sm 527; *Little v Neil* (1862) 10 WR 592; *Gough v Bult* (1847) 16 Sim 45; affd (1848) 17 LJ Ch 401; and see also *Re Susanni* (1877) 47 LJ Ch 65; *Butler v Gray* (1869) 5 Ch App 26; *Croft v Adam* (1842) 12 Sim 639; and *Re Cammell* [1925] WN 36.

Gift over in default of appointment destroys implied trust

8.203 The fact of there being a gift over in default of selection of any member of the class is, of course, fatal to any such trust for such class, even although the gift is void[1]. But a residuary gift is not 'a gift over' for this purpose[2].

1   *Re Sprague* (1880) 43 LT 236.
2   *Re Brierley* (1894) 43 WR 36.

No implied trust unless general intention to benefit apparent

8.204 On the other hand, the question is always one of construction of the particular instrument, the lack of a gift over being no more than an argument as to what the settlor's intention really was; for a resulting trust may be implied[1].

1   *Re Sayer* [1957] Ch 423 at 437, [1956] 3 All ER 600 at 607.

8.205 The tendency of the court has for many years been against inferring trusts from powers unless there are some other expressions indicating a general intention to benefit the class. Thus, in *Re Weekes' Settlement*[1] there was a gift to the testatrix's husband for life, with power by deed or will to dispose of the property amongst their children.

1   [1897] 1 Ch 289; and see also *Carberry v M'Carthy* (1881) 7 LR Ir 328.

8.206 Romer J, after elaborately examining all the decisions, pointed out that there was no *gift to such of the class* as the husband might appoint, but merely a bare power to appoint among a class, and that the mere giving of a power did not itself show that general intention to benefit the class which was apparent in cases where the selection only was confided to the donee of the power.

8.207 Similarly in *Re Combe*[1], Tomlin J refused to infer a trust in default of appointment in favour of the testator's 'relations of the whole blood', a vague phrase which of itself raised no inference of any intention to benefit them.

1   [1925] Ch 210. It is conceived that the decision of Malins V-C, in *Tweedale v Tweedale* (1878) 7 Ch D 633, cannot be supported.

8.208 In *Re Perowne*[1] Harman J refused to imply a gift over in favour of the objects of the power where the power of appointment was in favour of persons described by the testatrix as her 'family', saying:

'Where, in a marriage settlement, there is a gift to such of the children as A shall appoint, or in trust for such class as he shall be writing indicate, it is very easy to assume a gift over in default, because that is the natural thing to suppose; but where the class is large and indefinite it seems to me much more difficult to imply a gift over.

1   [1951] Ch 785, [1951] 2 All ER 201.

8.209 The case visualised by Harman J, at the beginning of the passage quoted had occurred in *Re Llewellyn's Settlement*[1], where Russell J inferred the existence of an implied trust in a marriage settlement containing a trust to convey to such children as the wife should appoint with no gift over in default of appointment. An additional ground for making the necessary inference was in that case afforded by the fact that there was an *express trust to convey* to such of the children as the wife should appoint.

1   [1921] 2 Ch 281.

8.210 More recently the cases have concerned broader classes of beneficiaries where the question was not whether there could be implied a trust in default of exercise of the power of appointment but whether the power was not itself really a discretionary trust.

8.211 *Re Leek*[1] is most helpful, though every case must depend on its own circumstances, the question being whether there is a fiduciary duty to distribute amongst members of a specified class of objects, the only discretion given to the donee of the power being to decide which particular objects shall benefit and when and how[2], or whether there is no duty to distribute so that whether any object at all is to benefit is left entirely to the discretion of the donee[3].

1   [1967] Ch 1061, [1967] 2 All ER 1160 (discretionary power); result affd [1969] 1 Ch 563, [1968] 1 All ER 793 (although discretionary trust not power).
2   *Re Ogden* [1933] Ch 678; *Re Saxone Shoe Co Ltd's Trust Deed* [1962] 2 All ER 904, [1962] 1 WLR 943; *Re Hain's Settlement Trust* [1961] 1 All ER 848, [1961] 1 WLR 440; *McPhail v Doulton* [1971] AC 424, [1970] 2 All ER 228; reversing sub nom *Re Baden's Deed Trust* [1969] 2 Ch 388, [1969] 1 All ER 1016.
3   *Re Sayer* [1957] Ch 423, [1956] 3 All ER 600.

Distinction between express and implied gifts in default

8.212 Where there is an express gift in default of appointment the takers in default take a vested defeasible interest from the date the trust took effect[1]. However, where there is an implied gift in default of appointment the court implies an intention either to give the property in default of appointment equally or as the donee of the power sees fit to those only to whom the donee might have given it. Thus, if the power be exercisable only by will the takers in default can only be those objects living at the death of the holder of the power[2].

1   *Re Brooks' Settlement Trusts* [1939] Ch 993, [1939] 3 All ER 920.
2   *Lambert v Thwaites* (1866) LR 2 Eq 151; *Perpetual Trustee Co Ltd v Tindal* (1940) 63 CLR 232 at 247.

The release of powers

8.213 For various reasons (eg tax) it may be advisable for powers to be released and a well drafted trust instrument will normally contain an express authorisation enabling the donees of powers to release them, in which case there is no problem in releasing a power[1]. Otherwise, the position seems to be as follows[2]:

(a)   If a 'power' of appointment is one in the nature of a trust, it can never be released.
(b)   If a power is not in the nature of a trust, then:
   (i)   it cannot be released if it was conferred upon the trustees of the property to which it relates in virtue of their office;
   (ii)   it cannot be released if it was conferred upon persons who were in fact the trustees of the property to which it relates and, although it was conferred upon them by name and not by reference to their office, they were selected as donees of the power because they were the trustees;
   (iii)   if it was not conferred upon the trustees of the property to which it relates, but upon other office-holders such as the trustees of some other trust, a release binds those executing the release but cannot exclude their successors in office from being capable of exercising the power[3];
   (iv)   otherwise the power can be released (eg a personal power of a widow).
(c)   Whether the 'power' is a power or really a trust, an arrangement under the Variation of Trusts Act 1958 may effectively release or extinguish the 'power' expressly or impliedly[4].

1   A power may similarly cease to be capable of exercise if a power is completely exercised, so exhausting it (as where all the trust property is appointed out of the trust), or if the property is so dealt with that the power is implicitly extinguished: *Re Christie-Miller's Settlement* [1961] 1 All ER 855n, [1961] 1 WLR 462; *Re Courtauld's Settlement* [1965] 2 All ER 544n, [1965] 1 WLR 1385; *Muir v IRC* [1966] 3 All ER 38, [1966] 1 WLR 1269; *Blausten v IRC* [1972] Ch 256, [1972] 1 All ER 41.
2   *Re Will's Trust Deeds* [1964] Ch 219, [1963] 1 All ER 390; (1968) 84 LQR 77 (A.J. Hawkins); *Muir v IRC* [1966] 3 All ER 38, [1966] 1 WLR 1269. The actual decision in *Re Wills' Trust Deeds* probably cannot stand with the CA decision in *Muir v IRC*: see *Mettoy*

Pension Trustees Ltd v Evans [1991] 2 All ER 513 at 546, [1990] 1 WLR 1587 at 1614.
Re Will's Trust Deeds [1964] Ch 219, [1963] 1 All ER 390.

3   Buckley J suggested that where in default of exercise of the power of appointment there is
a trust express or implied in favour of the objects of the power then the power cannot be
released, but this seems erroneous in view of *Smith v Houblon*(1859) 26 Beav 482; *Re
Radcliffe* [1892] 1 Ch 227, CA; *Re Evered* [1910] 2 Ch 147.

4   Re Courtauld's Settlement [1965] 2 All ER 544n, [1965] 1 WLR 1385.

Paragraph 2(b)

Precatory trusts depend wholly on interpretation

8.214 The subject of precatory trusts, ie transfers or bequests of property to
another, coupled with words of prayer, entreaty, recommendation, expectation, or the like (which according to ordinary usage would not bear an
imperative connotation), is not free from difficulty, owing to the conflict
between the modern decisions and those of an earlier age. If, however, it be
borne in mind that this question is not one of *law*, but merely one of the true
interpretation of the document which contains the precatory words, much
confusion will be avoided. Regarded in that light, and applying the dictum of
Lord Lindley[1], that

> 'when I see an intention clearly expressed in a will, and find no rule of law
> opposed to giving effect to it, I disregard previous cases',

the conflict of authorities to a large extent becomes immaterial.

1   [1897] 2 Ch 12 at 27.

8.215 The expression 'precatory trusts' is a little misleading in that where
precatory words are construed as creating a trust then such trust is a perfectly
ordinary trust with no unusual characteristics as pointed out by Rigby LJ in
Re Williams[1].

1   [1897] 2 Ch 12 at 27. Also see Goff LJ in *Re Osoba* [1979] 2 All ER 393 at 396, CA.

The modern rule as to precatory words stated and contrasted with the former rule

8.216 The modern way of judging whether precatory expressions are
intended to impose enforceable trusts might be stated thus:

> 'If a gift in terms absolute is accompanied by a desire, wish, recommendation,
> hope, or expression of confidence that the donee will use it in a certain way, no
> trust to that effect will attach to it, unless, on the will as a whole, the court
> comes to the conclusion that a trust was intended'[1].

1   See *Comiskey v Bowring-Hanbury* [1905] AC 84; *Hill v Hill* [1897] 1 QB 483 at 487; *Re
Hamilton* [1895] 2 Ch 370; *Re Williams* [1897] 2 Ch 12; *Lambe v Eames* (1871) 6 Ch
App 597; *Re Adams and the Kensington Vestry* (1884) 27 Ch D 394; *Re Diggles* (1888)
39 Ch D 253; *Mussoorie Bank v Raynor* (1882) 7 App Cas 321; *Re Conolly* [1910]
1 Ch 219; *Re Williams* [1933] Ch 244; *Re Green* [1935] WN 151. Extrinsic evidence may
be allowed: Administration of Justice Act 1982, s 21.

8.217 In other words, it is a question of construction of the particular instrument, and not a question of any supposed rule of courts of equity[1].

1   *Re Steele's Will Trusts* [1948] Ch 603, [1948] 2 All ER 193.

8.218 This is almost the precise opposite of the rule laid down in the older cases which might have been stated as follows:

> 'If a gift in terms absolute is accompanied by a desire, wish, recommendation, hope, or expression of confidence that the donee will use it in a certain way, a trust to that effect will attach to it'[1].

1   *Malim v Keighley* (1795) 2 Ves 333 at 529; *Knight v Knight* (1840) 3 Beav 148; affd sub nom *Knight v Boughton* (1844) 11 Cl & Fin 513 ('I trust to the liberality of my successors ... '); *Palmer v Simmonds* (1854) 2 Drew 221 ('having full confidence'); *Curnick v Tucker* (1874) LR 17 Eq 320; *Le Marchant v Le Marchant* (1874) LR 18 Eq 414 ('in full confidence'); *Hart v Tribe* (1854) 18 Beav 215 ('being convinced'); *Gully v Cregoe* (1857) 24 Beav 185 ('feeling assured and having every confidence'). See also *Wace v Mallard* (1851) 21 LJ Ch 355; *Shovelton v Shovelton* (1863) 32 Beav 143.

8.219 But even when the older rule stood unimpeached there was a clear consensus of judicial opinion that precatory expressions were only prima facie imperative and that the inference was capable of being rebutted by the context[1], while, even now that the modern rule has become firmly established, the court will not hesitate to infer the existence of a trust where the testator has made apparently conscious use of a formula held in a case decided before the emergence of the modern rule, but never since questioned, to create a trust[2].

1   See for example *McCormick v Grogan* (1869) LR 4 HL 82.
2   *Re Steele's Will Trusts* [1948] Ch 603, [1948] 2 All ER 193; see para 8.223 below.

Authorities for modern rule

8.220 As Lindley LJ observed in *Re Hamilton*[1]:

> 'We are bound to see that the beneficiaries are not made trustees unless intended to be made so by their testator ... You must take the will which you have to construe and see what it means, and if you come to the conclusion that no trust was intended, you say so, although previous judges have said the contrary on some wills more or less similar to the one which you have to construe'.

1   [1895] 2 Ch 370 at 373, approved in *Re Oldfield* [1904] 1 Ch 549, CA.

8.221 The same view was expressed later by Romer J in *Re Williams*[1]:

> 'The rule you have to observe is simply this. In considering whether a precatory trust is attached to any legacy, the court will be guided by the intention of the testator apparent in the will, and not by any particular words in which the wishes of the testator are expressed'.

1   [1897] 2 Ch 12 at 14; and see also *Re Burley* [1910] 1 Ch 215.

8.222 And in *Comiskey v Bowring-Hanbury*[1] Lord Davey said:

'The words "in full confidence", are, in my opinion, neutral. I think it would be impossible to regard them as technical words in any sense. They are words which may or may not create a trust, and whether they do so or not must be determined by the context'.

1   [1905] AC 84 at 89.

8.223 While in *Re Steele's Will Trusts*[1] Wynn-Parry J summarised the matter thus:

'The manner in which the modern view has evolved is, I think, simply that the courts have indicated that there is established in the older authorities no binding or overriding rule of construction which would disentitle one to look at each will and to extract from that will what was the true intention of the particular testator or testatrix.'

1   [1948] Ch 603, [1948] 2 All ER 193.

Illustrations of the application of the modern rule

8.224 It may be useful to look at the relevant words in certain wills which the court has construed in accordance with the modern rule. The case which, perhaps, marks the turn of the tide is *Lambe v Eames*[1], where a testator had given his estate to his widow 'to be at her disposal in any way she may think best *for the benefit of herself and family*'. It was held that the latter words imposed no trust on the widow in favour of the family, and Lord Justice James commented severely on former decisions which had imposed trusts where none were intended.

1   (1871) 6 Ch App 597, followed in *Re Hutchinson and Tenant* (1878) 8 Ch D 540.

8.225 A similar decision was given in *Re Adams and the Kensington Vestry*[1], where a testator gave all his estate unto and to the absolute use of his wife, her heirs, executors, administrators and assigns, in full confidence that she would do what was right as to the disposal thereof between his children, either in her lifetime or by will after her decease. It was held that, under these words, the widow took an absolute interest in the property, unfettered by any trust in favour of the children.

1   (1884) 27 Ch D 394. This case appears to overrule *Curnick v Tucker* (1874) LR 17 Eq 320; *Le Marchant v Le Marchant* (1874) LR 18 Eq 414, where the precatory words were practically identical, since any argument to the contrary based on difference in meaning between 'absolute use' and 'sole use and benefit' seems too refined to be acceptable.

8.226 On the other hand, in *Comiskey v Bowring-Hanbury*[1], the House of Lords held that the words 'in full confidence' were, on the construction of the whole will, intended to create a trust. There the testator gave all his property to his wife 'absolutely, in full confidence that she will make such use of it as I should have made myself, and that at her death she will devise it to such one or more of my nieces as she may think fit. *And in default of any disposition by* *her thereof by her will or testament, I here direct* that all my estate and property acquired by her under this my will shall at her death be divided among the surviving said nieces.'

1   [1905] AC 84.

8.227 Besides being of the highest authority this case forms an excellent example of the application of the present rule that intention must be gathered from the will as a whole. Although the testator's language was ambiguous it is difficult to resist the inference, collected from the whole of the passage quoted, that his intention was to restrict his widow to a life estate with a power of appointment among the nieces[1]. This interpretation appears to ignore the word 'absolutely', but to place too unbending and strict an interpretation on any single word in a will irrespective of other expressions of an inconsistent character therein would in many cases lead to the disappointment of the testator's intentions.

1   See *Re Jones* [1898] 1 Ch 438 and *Re Parsons* [1927] 2 DLR 1001; but cf *Re Sanford* [1901] 1 Ch 939.

8.228 In *Re Steele's Will Trusts*[1], it was again held that a binding precatory trust had been created. There the testatrix had, in a will prepared with professional aid, used with regard to certain jewellery, the identical formula which, in a case[2] which had stood for eighty years without any doubt being cast on the correctness of the decision, had been held to create a valid trust and it was held that the testatrix here intended the jewellery to devolve in the same manner as the jewellery in the earlier case was directed to devolve by the order made therein.

1   [1948] Ch 603, [1948] 2 All ER 193; (1968) 32 Conv (NS) 361 (P. St. J. Langan).
2   *Shelley v Shelley* (1868) LR 6 Eq 540.

Gift in will and precatory words in codicil

8.229 If the gift is contained in a will and the precatory expressions in a codicil, there is more chance of an inference in favour of a trust than where the gift and the precatory words are contained in the same instrument. Thus where a testatrix by her will gave a legacy of £2,300 to R and by a first codicil said 'I wish R to use £1,000 part of the legacy for the endowment in his own name of a cot' at a named hospital, and by a second codicil said 'I wish R after endowing the cot to use the balance of the legacy for charitable purposes', it was held that R was merely a trustee[1].

1   *Re Burley* [1910] 1 Ch 215.

Spouse or civil partner and testator's issue under wills

8.230 By the Administration of Justice Act 1982, s 22, 'Except where a contrary intent is shown[1], it shall be presumed that if a testator devises or bequeaths property to his spouse in terms which in themselves would give an absolute interest to the spouse but by the same instrument purports to give his issue an interest in the same property, the gift to the spouse is absolute notwithstanding the purported gift to the issue.' This has been extended by paragraph 5 of Schedule 4 to the Civil Partnership Act 2004 to cover a testamentary gift to a testator's civil partner.

1   See *Harrison v Gibson* [2006] WTLR 289. To resolve matters quickly and relatively
    cheaply advantage may be taken of s 48 of the Administration of Justice Act 1985.

8.231 This is a narrow provision, restricted to testamentary legacies or devises between spouses or civil partners where only the testator's descendants are the other persons interested in such legacies or devices and receive such interest under the same testamentary instrument as the spouse or civil partner –and not, for example, under a separate codicil.

Interpretation of wills

8.232 Extensive evidence, including evidence of the testator's intention, may be admitted to assist in the interpretation of a will (a) insofar as any part of it is meaningless, or (b) insofar as the language used in any part of it is ambiguous on the face of it, or (c) insofar as evidence, other than evidence of the testator's intention, shows that the language used in any part of it is ambiguous in the light of the surrounding circumstances[1].

1   Administration of Justice Act 1982, s 21, discussed by R Kerridge and J Rivers (2000) 116
    LQR 287 at 311–316.

Paragraph 2(c)

How far apparent testamentary[1] conditions are construed as charges, trusts or personal obligations

8.233 Whether a devise or bequest to A in terms *upon condition* or *to the intent* that some benefit may be conferred on B creates a trust or merely a charge or a personal liability on A if he accepts the devise or bequest is often a most difficult question. As in the case of precatory words, however, it is entirely a question of interpretation of the will[2]. If the true interpretation is that the property was beneficially given to A subject to a definite sum being paid to B, then the gift to A will not be construed as a conditional gift; for failure to perform such a condition, whether due to A's refusal to perform it or to his death in the lifetime of the testator, would result not merely in forfeiting A's interest, but also in depriving B of the benefits which were intended to be conferred on him[3]. Nor will the gift be construed as a trust, if a charge or equitable lien for the sum payable to B would meet the case[4], though such a charge may be coupled with a personal obligation[5]. If on the other hand the true interpretation is that the testator intended that A should hold the property for the benefit of himself and B or a fortiori if he did not intend A to take beneficially at all, a trust and not a mere charge will be created[6]. It should be added that words which on their face appear to impose a condition may be construed as merely precatory and explanatory of the testator's motive in making the gift[7].

1   For inter vivos contractual conditions creating trusts or charges in the context of commercial contracts for the supply of goods and for the protection of the vendor see paras 1.36–1.43 and 1.107–1.110 above, and for an inter vivos gift of a flat subject to a valid condition requiring the donee to allow the donor to live in the flat as long as was reasonably practicable and to provide the donor with a reasonable standard of living, see *Ellis v Chief Adjudication Officer* [1998] 1 FLR 184, CA.
2   *Re Lester* [1942] Ch 324, [1942] 1 All ER 646. Further see paras 8.224–8.232 above.
3   *Re Oliver* (1890) 62 LT 533, where the principles of the court are very lucidly stated by Chitty J.
4   *Cunningham v Foot* (1878) 3 App Cas 974, per Lord Cairns; *Hughes v Kelly* (1843) 3 Dr & War 482, ii; *Wood v Cox* (1837) 2 My & Cr 684; *Re Foord* [1922] 2 Ch 519.
5   See *Re Lester* [1942] Ch 324, [1942] 1 All ER 646.
6   *Cunningham v Foot* (1878) 3 App Cas 974; *Merchant Taylors' Co v A-G* (1871) 6 Ch App 512; *A-G v Wax Chandlers' Co* (1873) LR 6 HL 1; *Bird v Harris* (1870) LR 9 Eq 204; *Re Cowley* (1885) 53 LT 494; *Re Oliver* (1890) 62 LT 533; *Re G* [1899] 1 Ch 719; *Re Booth* [1894] 2 Ch 282; *Re Rees' Will Trusts* [1950] Ch 204, CA.
7   *Re Brace* [1954] 2 All ER 354, [1954] 1 WLR 955 (condition that A 'will always provide a home for B' precatory only); *Re Lipinski's Will Trusts* [1976] Ch 235, para 8.192 above; but binding inter vivos condition in *Ellis v Chief Adjudication Officer* [1998] 1 FLR 184, CA for donor-mother to be cared for in donated flat by donee-daughter.

Illustrations

8.234 As is always the case in questions depending on the interpretation of particular documents and not on rules of positive law the authorities are unsatisfactory, but the following illustrations will, at least, serve to show the effect attributed by the courts to different forms of words which have been variously construed as imposing trusts, charges or personal obligations.

8.235 In *Cunningham v Foot*[1] property was devised to A on condition of his well and truly paying legacies.

1   (1878) 3 App Cas 974.

8.236 Lord Cairns LC said[1]:

'Well and truly pay must mean simply on condition of well and truly paying; and therefore, it being established in law that a devise to A "paying" a sum of money to B is not a trust, but is a charge, it must also be the law that a devise to A "to well and truly pay" to B is not a trust but is a charge; and a devise to A, "on the condition of well and truly paying", must be a charge and not a trust.'

1   (1878) 3 App Cas 974 at 990; and see also *Re Oliver* (1890) 62 LT 533.

8.237 On the other hand, in *Merchant Taylors' Co v A-G*[1] a testator had devised houses to the company 'to this intent and upon this condition', viz, to provide garments for twenty-four poor persons each year and to 'gather the whole residue of the rents into a stock and therewith repair and if need be rebuild the houses', with a gift over to another City company for the same purposes if the Merchant Taylors failed to carry out his behests. The income in course of time greatly exceeded what was required for the purposes expressed in the will, and the question then arose whether the will created a charitable trust (in which case the balance would have to be applied for charity cy près), or whether it was a beneficial devise to the company merely charged with the charitable dole.

1   (1871) 6 Ch App 512.

8.238 It was ultimately held that it was a trust and not a mere charge on the ground, apparently, that there was no indication that any beneficial interest whatever was intended to be given to the company, the testator having expressly provided what was to be done with the whole of the rents and having merely not foreseen that there would in course of time be more than was needed for the purposes expressed.

8.239 In *Re Frame*[1] property was bequeathed to A on condition that she adopted one of the testator's daughters and made certain payments to two other daughters.

1   [1939] Ch 700.

8.240 Simonds J said[1]:

'A devise or bequest, on condition that the devisee or legatee makes certain payments does not import a condition in the strict sense of the word, but imports a trust, so that though the devisee or legatee dies before the testator, and the gift does not take effect, yet the payments must be made for it is a trust, and no trust fails for want of trustees ... Much argument has been directed as to what is involved in the condition that she adopts my daughter. It seems clear that ... what is intended is not any single formal act but a series of acts to establish the relationship of parent and child ... So far as adoption involves the giving of care, advice and affection, this court cannot compel that such things be given. However, seeing that it involves the duty of maintenance that is a trust which the court can enforce ... It will not allow the whole to fail because a part cannot be enforced.'

1   [1939] Ch 700 at 703–704.

8.241 In *Re Lester*[1], where a testator had bequeathed certain shares to his son 'subject ... to the payment by him' of an annuity to another son and, after the latter's death, of certain deferred annuities, it was held that a personal obligation was imposed on the legatee but that the words used were not apt to create a charge on the shares.

1   [1942] Ch 324, [1942] 1 All ER 646.

Words of expectation or explanatory of motive

8.242 It is well settled that mere words of expectation, or words explanatory of the donor's motive, never impose trusts on the donee. Thus, if a legacy be given to a father 'the better to enable him to bring up his children', no trust is thereby created; for such words are only explanatory of the donor's motive[1]. But where, on the other hand, there was a bequest of income to A, *'that he may use it* for the benefit of himself, and the maintenance and education of his children', it was held that a trust was intended to be imposed upon A to maintain and educate his children[2].

[1] *Brown v Casamajor* (1799) 4 Ves 498; *Benson v Whittam* (1831) 5 Sim 22; and cf *Re Brace* [1954] 2 All ER 354, [1954] 1 WLR 955.

[2] *Woods v Woods* (1836) 1 My & Cr 401; *Crockett v Crockett* (1848) 2 Ph 553; and *Talbot v O'Sullivan* (1880) LR 6 Ir 302; and see *Bird v Maybury* (1864) 33 Beav 351; *Hora v Hora* (1863) 33 Beav 88; *Castle v Castle* (1857) 1 De G & J 352. On motive also see *Re Lipinski's Will Trusts* [1976] Ch 235, [1977] 1 All ER 33, p 106.

Paragraph 2(d)

Agreement to create trusts

8.243 The rule that a valid agreement to create a trust in futuro, is sufficient to create a trust in praesenti, so as to bind the property in the hands of the parties, or those having notice of the agreement, depends on the maxim that 'Equity regards that as done which ought to be done.' As Lindley LJ stated[1], 'Where the obligation to do what ought to be done is not an absolute duty, but only an obligation arising from contract, that which ought to be done is only treated as done in favour of some person entitled to enforce the contract or against the person liable to perform it.'

[1] *Re Anstis* (1886) 31 Ch D 596 at 605, CA.

8.244 It follows, therefore, that where a trust is alleged to have been created by an *agreement* to do something, its validity depends on the question whether the agreement is one of which courts of equity would decree specific performance[1]. If it was merely a voluntary promise (or even a covenant under seal, not supported by valuable consideration), no trust will be created; for equity gives no assistance to volunteers, and consequently there is nothing which can, under the foregoing maxim, be regarded by the court as done. This distinction between trusts depending on contracts, and trusts actually declared, will be emphasised in Article 9, below.

[1] See *Westminster Bank v Wilson* [1938] 3 All ER 652; *Macjordan Construction Ltd v Brookmount Erostin Ltd* [1992] BCLC 350, CA; *Pullan v Koe* [1913] 1 Ch 9 (after-acquired property within marriage settlement covenant automatically subject to settlement trusts).

8.245 It is worth noting that one can declare a trust of property one presently owns, including choses in action like existing book debts, but there is also a doctrine of Equity that when a person contracts to hold on trust for X or to assign to X property of a certain description which is either not then in existence (like future book debts) or is not then owned by the contractor, who has received the consideration for the contract, then when property satisfying the contractual description is acquired by the contractor he is regarded as trustee of the property for X whose claims therefore prevail over his creditors[1].

1   *Re Lind* [1915] 2 Ch 345 at 360; *Palette Shoes Pty Ltd v Krohn* (1937) 58 CLR 1 at 26–27; *Associated Alloys Pty Ltd v ACN 001452106 Pty Ltd* (2002) 74 ALJR 862, 202 CLR 588.

Marriage articles

8.246 An instance of trusts arising out of contract is afforded by marriage articles though these are very much less common than they used to be. Where it is desired to settle property on a marriage which is arranged to take place upon such short notice that there is no time to draw up a formal settlement, articles of agreement are signed, by which, in consideration of the marriage, the parties agree to execute a formal settlement, vesting certain property upon trusts indicated more or less roughly. Thereupon equity, regarding that as done which ought to be done, fastens a trust on the property, and treats any dealings with it inconsistent with the agreement, not only as a breach of contract, but also as a breach of trust.

8.247 So, also, where a father, in contemplation of his daughter's marriage, *contracts* to leave her a specified sum, or an aliquot part of his estate, and dies without fulfilling his promise, his estate will be bound to make good the contract[1]. There must, however, have been a binding contract; a mere representation of intention will not suffice, even although the marriage took place on the faith of it[2].

1   *Luders v Anstey* (1799) 4 Ves 501; (1800) 5 Ves 213; *Hammersley v de Biel* (1845) 12 Cl & Fin 45 at 61n; *Coverdale v Eastwood* (1872) LR 15 Eq 121; *Synge v Synge* [1894] 1 QB 466. See also *Parker v Clark* [1960] 1 All ER 93, [1960] 1 WLR 286, especially at 100; *Palmer v Bank of New South Wales* (1975) ALJR 320, and *Schaefer v Schuhmann* [1972] AC 572, [1972] 1 All ER 621, PC for the problems relating to testamentary contracts generally.
2   *Hammersley v de Biel* (1845) 12 Cl & Fin 45 at 61n; *Jorden v Money* (1854) 5 HL Cas 185; *Maddison v Alderson* (1883) 8 App Cas 467 at 473; *Re Fickus* [1900] 1 Ch 331. It would be difficult to use marriage as a detriment for the purposes of establishing a proprietary estoppel claim in relation to land promised to be given: cf. *Coombes v Smith* [1986] 1 WLR 808. Further see paras 12.56–12.57 below.

Mutual wills and joint wills

8.248 Mutual wills and joint wills were dealt with under this head in previous editions.

8.249 Where two persons (usually, but not necessarily, husband and wife) make an arrangement as to the disposal of their property after their respective deaths and agree not to alter such arrangement and make mutual wills in pursuance of that arrangement, then if one dies, and the survivor subsequently revokes[1] or alters his own will, then although probate will be granted of the last-mentioned will the survivor's personal representatives will hold his estate on trust to give effect to the provisions of his mutual will[2].

1   This includes revocation on subsequent marriage; see *Re Green* [1951] Ch 148, [1950] 2 All ER 913.
2   *Stone v Hoskins* [1905] P 194.

8.250 As Lord Camden LJ said in *Dufour v Pereira*[1]:

'The parties by the mutual will do each of them devise, upon the engagement of the other, that he will likewise devise in manner therein mentioned. The instrument is the evidence of agreement; and he that dies first, does by his death carry the agreement on his part into execution. If the other then refuses, he is guilty of fraud, can never unbind himself and becomes a trustee of course.'

1   (1769) 1 Dick 419; and see *Stone v Hoskins* [1905] P 194.

8.251 However, the agreement at the date of making the wills to create a trust in futuro does not then create a trust in praesenti. Not only is mutual revocation possible during their joint lives but individual revocation is possible provided notice is given to the other, such notice even being supplied by the death of the first to die with a revoked or altered will[1]. The trust is only operative at the death of the first to die and is really in the nature of a constructive trust[2] so it is dealt with at paras 35.53–35.72 below.

1   *Dufour v Pereira* (1796) 1 Dick 419; *Stone v Hoskins* [1905] P 194; *Lewis v* Cotton [2001] WTLR 1117 at 1129, [2000] NZCA 399 para 44. *Pratt v Johnson* (1959) 16 DLR (2d) 385.
2   *Kasperbauer v Griffith* [2000] WTLR 333 at 342; *Gillett v Holt* [2001] Ch 210 at 228, [2002] 2 All ER 289 at 305.

Paragraph 3

Illusory trusts

8.252 Sometimes a disposition which at first sight appears to be a trust in favour of another or others may prove to be illusory, if the document or the surrounding circumstances lead to the conclusion that no trust for the benefit of such person or persons was intended[518].

1   Where A lends money to B for the specific purpose of enabling B to pay creditors or particular creditors see paras 8.168–8.173. For sham trusts see para 4.6, above.

8.253 Thus, where a man who is in debt makes provision for payment of his debts generally, by vesting property in trustees upon trust to pay them, but does so without the knowledge of his creditors, the trustees do not necessarily become trustees *for the creditors*.

'The motive of the party executing the deed may have been either to benefit his creditors or to promote his own convenience; and the court there has to examine into the circumstances, for the purpose of ascertaining what was the true purpose of the deed; and this examination does not stop with the deed itself, but must be carried on to what has subsequently occurred, because the party who has created the trust may, by his own conduct, or by the obligations which he has permitted his trustee to contract, have created an equity against himself.'[1]

---

[1]   Per Turner V-C in *Smith v Hurst* (1852) 10 Hare 30.

Inferences arising with regard to creditors' deeds[1]

8.254 Prima facie a trust deed for payment of the settlor's creditors *generally*, is deemed to have been made for the debtor's convenience. The transaction is regarded as being the same as if he had put a sum of money into the hands of an agent with directions to apply it in paying certain debts, and such a trust is revocable, the debtor being, in fact, the sole beneficiary[2]. On the other hand, where the creditors are parties to the arrangement, the inference then is that the deed was intended to create a trust in *their* favour, which they are entitled to call on the trustee to execute[3]. However, even though they are not made parties, yet if the debtor has given them notice of the existence of the deed, and has expressly or impliedly told them that they may look to the trust property for payment, they may become beneficiaries[4]:

(1)   if they have been thereby induced to exercise forbearance in respect of their claims[5], or

(2)   if they have assented to the deed and actively (and not merely passively) acquiesced in it, or

(3)   if they have acted under its provisions and complied with its terms, and the other side has expressed no dissatisfaction;

but not otherwise[6].

---

[1]   The general law as to such deeds is outside the scope of this work. Under the Deeds of Arrangement Act 1914, s 2 a deed of arrangement for the benefit of creditors generally, or if the debtor was insolvent at the date of execution thereof, for the benefit of any three or more of them is void if not registered within seven days of its execution. If it is for the benefit of creditors generally it will be void unless it has received the written assent of a majority in number and value of the creditors within twenty-one days of registration: s 3 of the 1914 Act. If the deed affects unregistered land it should be registered under Land Charges Act 1972, s 7 whilst if it affects registered land it should be protected by a caution against dealing: Land Registration Act 1925, s 59(1) and (6). Use of deeds of arrangement can be frustrated by a dissenting creditor petitioning for bankruptcy. To avoid this the Insolvency Act 1986 (as amended by the Insolvency Act 2000) introduced 'voluntary arrangements,' which provide a moratorium on other insolvency proceedings. A qualified insolvency petitioner must be the 'nominee' to act in relation to the voluntary arrangement either as trustee or otherwise for the purpose of supervising its implementation: Insolvency Act 1986, s 253. There is a public register of voluntary arrangements, the Deeds of Arrangement Act 1914 not applying to such arrangements. The trusts created by a voluntary arrangement take effect according to the terms of the arrangement, and in default of such terms providing for what is to happen on liquidation or bankruptcy, the trusts continue thereafter: *Re N T Gallagher & Son Limited* [2002] EWCA Civ 404 [2002] 1 WLR 2380.

[2]   *Walwyn v Coutts* (1815) 3 Sim 14; *Garrard v Lauderdale* (1830) 3 Sim 1; affd (1831) 2 Russ & M 451; *Acton v Woodgate* (1833) 2 My & K 492; *Bill v Cureton* (1835) 2 My & K 503 at 511; *Gibbs v Glamis* (1841) 11 Sim 584; *Henriques v Bensusan* (1872) 20 WR 350; *Johns v James* (1878) 8 Ch D 744; *Henderson v Rothschild* (1886) 33 Ch D 459. But see *Re Fitzgerald's Settlement* (1877) 37 Ch D 18; and *Priestley v Ellis* [1897] 1 Ch 489, deciding otherwise as to trusts for creditors after settlor's death.

[3]   *Mackinnon v Stewart* (1850) 1 Sim NS 76; *La Touche v Earl of Lucan* (1840) 7 Cl & Fin 772; *Montefiore v Browne* (1858) 7 HL Cas 241; and see *Smith v Cooke* [1891] AC 297.

4   Lord Cranworth in *Synnot v Simpson* (1854) 5 HL Cas 121; *Biron v Mount* (1857) 24 Beav 642.
5   Per Sir John Leach in *Acton v Woodgate* (1833) 2 My & K 492.
6   Per Lord St Leonards in *Field v Donoughmore* (1841) 1 Dr & War 227; see also *Nicholson v Tutin* (1855) 2 K & J 18; *Kirwan v Daniel* (1847) 5 Hare 493; *Griffith v Ricketts* (1849) 7 Hare 299; *Cornthwaite v Frith* (1851) 4 De G & Sm 552; *Siggers v Evans* (1855) 5 E & B 367; *Gould v Robertson* (1851) 4 De G & Sm 509; *Re Ashby, ex p Wretford* [1892] 1 QB 872. In essence, it seems the debtor needs to be estopped in all the circumstances from alleging he had no intention to create the trust.

8.255 Moreover, where the trust is for particular named creditors (at all events where the facts show that the object of the settlor was to give them a preference over the general body of his creditors)[1], the inference is that they were intended to be benefited; and a similar inference arises where the deed provides for payment of the settlor's debts *at his death* with remainders over[2]. And where it provides for such payment *either* in the settlor's lifetime *or* after his death, it can (it would seem) be enforced by the creditors unless he revokes it in his lifetime[3].

1   *New, Prance and Garrard's Trustee v Hunting* [1897] 2 QB 19.
2   See per Lord Cranworth in *Synnot v Simpson* (1854) 5 HL Cas 121; *Re Fitzgerald's Settlement* (1887) 37 Ch D 18.
3   *Priestley v Ellis* [1897] 1 Ch 489.

Direction to trustees to pay costs, etc

8.256 Where the trustees are, by the settlement, directed to pay all costs, charges, and expenses of the deed, and other incidental charges and expenses of the trust, and to reimburse themselves, and then to pay over the residue to third parties, the solicitor who prepared the deed, and acted as solicitor to the trustees, is not a beneficiary. The trust might, of course, be enforced, but not by him[1].

1   *Worrall v Harford* (1802) 8 Ves 4; *Foster v Elsley* (1881) 19 Ch D 518. See also *Strickland v Symons* (1884) 26 Ch D 245; and *Staniar v Evans* (1886) 34 Ch D 470, negating the right of a creditor of trustees to proceed against the *estate*.

Direction to employ and pay a named person

8.257 Even a positive direction to the trustees of a will to employ a particular person and to allow him a salary, does not create a trust in his favour[1]. Thus, a direction in a will appointing a particular person solicitor to the trust estate, imposes no trust or duty on the trustees of the will to employ and pay him[2]. Whilst there is a very strong presumption against construing such directions as constituting trusts, in principle, it would appear that a sufficiently strong expression by a settlor/testator of his intention to create a trust could be effective as held in Australia[3].

1   *Shaw v Lawless* (1838) 5 Cl & Fin 129.
2   *Foster v Elsley* (1881) 19 Ch D 518; *Finden v Stephens* (1846) 2 Ph 142.
3   *Taylor v Lewis* (1891) 12 LR NSW Eq 258; *Re Larkin* (1913) 13 SRNSW 691.

Funds confined to state officials for distribution

8.258 The funds voted by Parliament for the public service are not trust funds in the hands of the Secretaries of State (who receive them from the Treasury) in favour of private persons[1]. And on similar grounds, where Queen Victoria, by royal warrant, granted booty of war to the Secretary of State to India, *in trust* to distribute amongst the persons found entitled to share in it by the Court of Admiralty, it was held that the warrant did not operate as a declaration of trust in favour of such persons, but merely made the Secretary of State the *agent of the Sovereign* for the purpose of distributing the fund[2]. Similarly in *Tito v Waddell (No 2)*[3] the Crown was held to be merely under a governmental obligation to the Banabans in respect of the phosphate-rich Ocean Island so that no fiduciary obligations existed. The position is exhaustively analysed by Megarry V-C[4].

1 *Grenville-Murray v Earl of Clarendon* (1869) LR 9 Eq 11.
2 *Kinloch v Secretary of State for India* (1880) 15 Ch D 1; on appeal (1882) 7 App Cas 619, HL, reaffirmed by the House of Lords in *Town Investments Ltd v Department of the Environment* [1978] AC 359.
3 [1977] Ch 106, [1977] 3 All ER 129.
4 [1977] Ch 106 at 219–230, [1977] Ch 106 at 219–230, [1977] 3 All ER 129 at 219–228; cf *Phillip Brothers v Sierra Leone* [1995] 3 CL 316 and Australian cases, *Aboriginal Development Corpn v Treka Aboriginal Arts & Crafts Pty Ltd* [1984] 3 NSWLR 502, CA and *Registrar of the Accident Compensation Tribunal v Commissioner of Taxation* (1993) 178 CLR 145, HC.

Injured claimant's claims for voluntary carers' services

8.259 The law with respect to the services of a third party who provides voluntary care for a tortiously injured claimant and who has no cause of action of his or her own against the tortfeasor is that the claimant may recover the value of the services, past and anticipated, so that he may recompense the voluntary carer, eg his spouse or daughter. The House of Lords has held[1] that the claimant recovers such damages on trust for the carer. This will lead to a bare trust of the amount due to the carer for past services, but what is the position concerning the sum received in respect of future services, especially if the claimant dies prematurely or recovers more speedily than anticipated so that a surplus is available? Surely, it will not be held on resulting trust for the tortfeasor but will be retained by the claimant or his estate. Moreover, the current carer is surely not intended to have any right to insist on being the 'beneficiary-carer', eg if the claimant prefers to replace his wife by his daughter or by some paid third party. Thus, it seems that the amount representing cover for future services is held by the claimant on discretionary trust for paying for such care as he wants but otherwise for himself absolutely: this is an illusory trust because in reality he is in the position of absolute beneficial owner of such money.

1 *Hunt v Severs* [1994] 2 AC 350, [1994] 2 All ER 385, HL well criticised by P. Matthews [1994] CJQ 302.

ARTICLE 9
THE CONSTITUTION OF TRUSTS

9.1

(1) A trust is completely constituted by the settlor (or the donee of a power[1]) either:

(a) declaring that certain property vested in him (or otherwise subject to the donee's power) is to be held henceforth by him (or the holder of the property affected by the exercise of the power) on certain trusts; or

(b) effectively transferring certain property to trustees and declaring the trusts upon which the trustees are to hold such property.

Thus, if the settlor voluntarily intends to constitute a trust by the second method (or to make a gift directly to a person) but fails because the property has not been effectively transferred to the intended trustees (or to the person) then the settlor cannot be treated as retaining the property qua trustee thereof for the intended beneficiaries (or the person) except if statute so provides specifically or if he has done everything necessary to be done by him in order to make it possible for another to transfer the property (eg in the case of shares or land not yet transferred by entry on the appropriate register). Exceptionally, a settlor may be estopped from denying that he holds certain property on trust. It may be that (under an extension of the *Strong v Bird*[2] principle) the appointment by the settlor of one or more of his trustees to the executorship of his will could on his death completely constitute a trust of specific property not effectively transferred to trustees in his lifetime, so long as his intention to create a trust still existed at his death.

(2) A completely constituted trust is binding upon the settlor (and his personal representatives), though voluntary, just as a gift is binding upon the donor (and his personal representatives): it is irrevocable unless an express power of revocation was reserved at the time of constituting the trust.

(3) An incompletely constituted trust is unenforceable by a volunteer, since equity will not assist a volunteer, but is enforceable (even if volunteers are thereby benefited) by someone who gave consideration for the settlor's promise or covenant or, where the settlement was made in consideration of marriage, by someone (eg children) within the marriage consideration. Equity will not frustrate a volunteer suing at common law (unless special circumstances involving fraud, undue influence, etc are present) so a volunteer who is a covenanting party to the deed can sue the settlor as the other party the covenant at common law and obtain full damages. Just as the benefit of a contract may be the subject matter of a completely constituted trust if this is intended by the settlor, so may the benefit of a voluntary covenant (whether relating to existing property or future property) be the subject matter of a completely constituted trust if this is intended

187

by the settlor, in which case the trustees and the volunteer beneficiaries can enforce the trusts in the usual way. If the settlor intended not to create a trust of the benefit of the covenant itself, but only to create a trust of the property within the covenant when or if he transferred it to the trustees, the covenant is unenforceable by volunteers. If the trustees seek the court's directions whether or not they should sue the settlor for common law damages for breach of covenant they will be directed not to sue: it will not be a breach of trust if, in view of this, they decide not to sue without first seeking the court's directions. Indeed, since ex hypothesi the trustees are not holding the benefit of the covenant itself on trust for the beneficiaries they must hold it on a resulting trust for the settlor, so that the action on the covenant against the settlor is groundless.

[1] Trustees often have a special power of appointment in favour of a class of objects which enables them to appoint or declare new sub-trusts for the benefit of some of the objects or to transfer trust property to trustees of a new separate trust for the benefit of some of the objects so that new trusts are completely constituted: *Commissioner of State Revenue v Lam & Kym Pty Limited* [2004] VSCA 204.

[2] (1874) LR 18 Eq 315, paras 9.46–9.68 below.

Paragraph 1

Declaration of self as trustee

9.2 Here the property is already vested in the settlor/trustee so the problems can only relate to whether the settlor intended not merely to benefit someone, but to make himself a trustee for that person, and to which of his property the settlor intended his trusteeship obligation to relate. The court has to ascertain that the settlor manifested an intention[1] to become a trustee of certain of his property set aside[2] for certain beneficiaries, though there is no need for such intention to be communicated to the beneficiaries[3]. However, if no communication of an informal declaration is made to any beneficiary it will be strongly, but rebuttably, presumed that no final unequivocal intention had been formed to create a binding declaration of trust[4]. Even a formal declaration of trust will be open to the allegation of a sham trust if put in the settlor's safe and not communicated to any beneficiary[5].

[1] The intention must be manifested in writing if the trust property is land but may be oral or even inferred from conduct otherwise; though where a beneficiary directs his trustees to hold the trust property for A this amounts to a disposition of the beneficiary's equitable interest to A and so must be in writing within the Law of Property Act 1925, s 53(1)(c), and it seems that a beneficiary, B, declaring that he holds his interest on trust absolutely for X will, as a bare trustee, drop out of the picture if X is of full capacity, so that the trustees hold for X instead of for B, so that B has essentially assigned his interest, which again requires writing within s 53(1)(c): *Grey v IRC* [1960] AC 1, [1959] 3 All ER 603; *Re Lashmar* [1891] 1 Ch 258; para 12.15 below.

[2] *Re Goldcorp Exchange Ltd* [1995] 1 AC 74, [1994] 2 All ER 806, PC.

[3] *Middleton v Pollock, ex p Elliott* (1876) 2 Ch D 104; *Standing v Bowring* (1885) 31 Ch D 282; *Rose v Rose* (1986) 7 NSWLR 679 at 686; *Fletcher v Fletcher* (1844) 4 Hare 67.

[4] *Re Cozens* [1913] 2 Ch 478.

[5] *Midland Bank plc v Wyatt* [1995] 1 FLR 697.

9.3 Informal expressions of intent to declare himself a trustee will suffice, (eg 'This property is as much your's as mine'[1]). However, the layman will have to select his informal words carefully for the courts insist on the nice distinction between the expression 'I give and make over this property to you' and 'I undertake to hold this property for you'[2]. The first is a purported out-and-out transfer whilst the second is a declaration of trust of retained property, though in both cases a layman might well broadly think of himself as making a gift.

1 *Paul v Constance* [1977] 1 All ER 195.
2 *Richards v Delbridge* (1874) LR 18 Eq 11.

9.4 However, if the layman attempted to transfer property to another out-and-out, but failed to effect it in accordance with legal requirements as far as he could[1], then equity will not assist the volunteer donee by construing the attempted transfer as a declaration of trust; otherwise, all attempted and imperfect transfers would take effect as declarations of trust when, after all, the attempted out-and out *transfer* is the clearest evidence that the donor did not intend to *retain* the property and create a trust thereof with himself as trustee[2]. Where the donor's intentions are unclear then the court, in order to give effect to the general intention of the donor to benefit the donee, may be prepared to apply the maxim 'Verba ita sunt intelligenda ut res magis valeat quam pereat'[3] particularly where the court is 'dealing with simple people unaware of the subtleties of equity but understanding well their own domestic situation' as remarked by Scarman LJ in *Paul v Constance*[4].

1 See the *Re Rose* [1952] Ch 499 Principle, paras 9.32–9.43 below.
2 *Milroy v Lord* (1862) 4 De GF & J 264; *Richards v Delbridge* (1874) LR 18 Eq 11.
3 *Re Gulbenkian's Settlement Trusts* [1968] Ch 126, [1967] 3 All ER 15; *Re Leek* [1969] 1 Ch 563, [1968] 1 All ER 793; *Re Baden's Deed Trusts* [1969] 2 Ch 388, [1969] 1 All ER 1016; *IRC v McMullen* [1981] AC 1 at 11, [1980] 1 All ER 884 at 890, HL per Lord Hailsham.
4 [1977] 1 All ER 195 at 197. Contrast the lack of an immediate donative intent in *Otway v Gibbs* [2002] WTLR 467, PC.

9.5 This case concerned an effective oral express declaration of trust in informal terms.

9.6 C and P lived together as man and wife. C received £950 damages for personal injuries. C and P saw a bank manager to open a deposit account telling him they were not married. They accepted his suggestion that the account should be in C's name, though P could draw on it with C's signed authority. On many occasions C told P, 'The money is as much yours as mine'. Some joint bingo winnings were paid into the account and there was one withdrawal only of money from the account which was for the shared purposes of C and P. It was held that in context C's words were equivalent to C declaring himself a trustee of the moneys in the account for P and himself equally, so P was entitled on his death to half the moneys.

9.7 Scarman LJ usefully summarised the two leading cases on the subject of declarations of trust as follows[1]:

'The first of the two cases is *Jones v Lock*[2]. In that case Mr Jones, returning home from a business trip to Birmingham, was scolded for not having brought back anything for his baby son. He went upstairs and came down with a cheque made out in his own name for £900 and said, in the presence of his wife and nurse: "Look you here, I give this to baby", and he then placed the cheque in the baby's hand. It was obvious that he was intending to make a gift of the cheque to his baby son but it was clear, as Lord Cranworth LC held, that there was no effective gift then and there made of the cheque; it was in his name and had not been endorsed over to the baby. Other evidence showed that he had in mind to go and see his solicitor, Mr Lock, to make proper provision for the baby boy, but unfortunately he died before he could do so. *Jones v Lock* was a classic case where the intention to make a gift failed because the gift was imperfect. So an attempt was made to say: "Well, since the gift was imperfect, nevertheless, one can infer the existence of a trust." But Lord Cranworth LC would have none of it.

In the other case *Richards v Delbridge*[3] the facts were that a Mr Richards, who employed a member of his family in his business, was minded to give the business to the young man. He evidenced his intention to make this gift by endorsing on the lease of the business premises a short memorandum to the effect that:

> "This deed [ie the deed of leasehold] and all thereto belonging I give to *Edward* ... [ie the boy] from this time forth with all the stock in trade"

Jessel MR, who decided the case, said that there was in that case the intention to make a gift, but the gift failed because it was imperfect; and he refused from the circumstances of the imperfect gift to draw the inference of the existence of a declaration of trust or the intention to create one. The ratio decidendi appears clearly from the report[4]. It is a short passage, and because of its importance I quote it:

> "In *Milroy v Lord*[5] Lord Justice Turner, after referring to the two modes of making a voluntary settlement valid and effectual, adds these words: 'The cases, I think, go further, to this extent, that if the settlement is intended to be effectuated by one of the modes to which I have referred, the court will not give effect to it by applying another of those modes. If it is intended to take effect by transfer, the court will not hold the intended transfer to operate as a declaration of trust, for then every imperfect instrument would be made effectual by being converted into a perfect trust.' It appears to me that that sentence contains the whole law on the subject".'

1   [1977] 1 All ER 195 at 198.
2   (1865) 1 Ch App 25.
3   (1874) LR 18 Eq 11.
4   (1874) LR 18 Eq 11.
5   (1862) 4 De GF & J 264 at 274–275.

9.8 In exceptional cases it may be possible for a court to find that though there has been no actual express declaration of trust it is possible to infer a declaration of trust from acts showing that a person has constituted himself a trustee, ie from conduct evincing an intent to deal with his property so that somebody else to his own exclusion acquires the beneficial interest (or part thereof) in his property[1]. Thus G, an executor and residuary legatee, directed by the testator to pay 8% interest on £2,000 to W for life might, if satisfied that the testator really meant the sum to be £3,000, actually so tell W and himself till his death pay interest on £3,000 to W. This will make G trustee of the additional £1,000 for W's life[2]. Similarly, where a residuary legatee, R, purchases £2,000 of X stock in his own name to give effect to the testator's wishes, expressed but not effected before death to add such stock to trusts of which R was trustee and R gives the beneficiary a power of attorney to receive the dividends from the stock, there will be held to be a trust of the £2,000 X stock[3].

1   *Paul v Constance* [1977] 1 All ER 195 at 198; *Richards v Delbridge* (1874) LR 18 Eq 11 at 14; *Heartley v Nicholson* (1875) LR 19 Eq 233 at 242; *Re Fleet Disposal Services Ltd* [1995] 1 BCLC 345 (agency account under agency agreement held in surrounding circumstances to be trust account).
2   *Gee v Liddell* (1866) 35 Beav 621; *New, Prance and Garrard's Trustee v Hunting* [1897] 2 QB 19.
3   *Gray v Gray* (1852) 2 Sim NS 273; *Robertson v Morrice* (1845) 9 Jur 122; *Wheatley v Purr* (1837) 1 Keen 551.

9.9 An exceptional case, and so requiring detailed consideration, is *T Choithram International SA v Pagarani*[1] where, a month before he died of cancer, P organised an elaborate ceremony one afternoon at his London bedside in the house of his son, Lekhraj, to establish a philanthropic Foundation in the form of a Jersey trust of which he was settlor and one of the Trustees. The trust deed recited that the settlor had transferred £1,000 to the trustees and that further property might be paid, transferred or otherwise placed under the control of the trustees. The settlor, P, executed the trust deed in the presence of three other Trustees and his accountant and the First Secretary of the Indian High Commission. Their evidence was that he uttered works to the effect 'I give to the Foundation all my wealth, shareholdings and credit balances with my BVI companies.' Indeed, the minutes of those companies' meetings held in the evening of that day recorded that the directors (including P, who signed the minutes) acknowledged P's gift of such wealth to the Foundation and that the Trustees of the Foundation were henceforth the holders of the shares and credit balances with the companies. Before P died the gifted shares and balances were not legally transferred to the other Trustees, so it was alleged that the gift to the Foundation was imperfect.

1   [2001] 2 All ER 492.

9.10 Lord Browne-Wilkinson for the Privy Council held, in context, that[1]:

'The words "I give to the Foundation"[a non-existent legal entity] can only mean "I give to the Trustees of the Foundation trust deed to be held by them on the trusts of the Foundation trust deed". Although the words are apparently words of outright gift they are essentially words of gift on trust.'

1   [2001] 2 All ER 492, para 31.

9.11 Had P intended to make a gift to trustees of his legal interest in the shares and credit balances, so that his oral gift was imperfect, or had he intended to make a perfect gift of his beneficial interest by way of holding his legal interest subject to the trusts of the Foundation deed? Was he to be regarded as having, in substance, said, 'Because I am sole legal beneficial owner of the shares and credit balances and also trustee of the Foundation trusts, I am giving my beneficial interest to be held on such trusts and so as trustee I am now holding my legal title to such assets on such trusts'.

9.12 Lord Browne-Wilkinson believed so. The reason was that Lekhraj, P's son and one of the trustees, was the liaison between P and third parties, such as P's lawyers and accountant and the intended trustees. Documents sent by P's lawyers to Lekhraj, to discuss with P five days before the ceremony establishing the Foundation, revealed that it was intended for P to sign these documents acknowledging and declaring that particular assets were to be held on trust for the trustees of the Foundation[1]. However, P never signed these when asked to do so a few days after the ceremony, because he believed 'he had done his bit' at the ceremony and nothing further needed to be done by him[2]. 'The machinery actually adopted was the same as that proposed by Messrs Macfarlanes [the solicitors] save that the written declaration of trust was replaced by an immediate oral gift'[3] as held by Lord Browne-Wilkinson.

[1]   [2001] 2 All ER 492, para 14.
[2]   [2001] 2 All ER 492, para 15.
[3]   [2001] 2 All ER 492, para 23; also see para 26.

9.13 Did it matter that P had not transferred the shares and credit balances to all the Trustees? As Lord Browne-Wilkinson stated[1]:

'What then is the position where the trust property is vested in one of the body of Trustees viz TCP? TCP has, in the most solemn circumstances, declared that he is giving (and later that he has given) property to a trust which he himself has established and of which he has appointed himself to be a Trustee. All this occurs in one composite transaction taking place on February 17. There can be no distinction between the case where the donor declares himself to be sole Trustee for a donee or a purpose and the case where he declares himself to be one of the Trustees ... in the absence of special factors[2], where one out of a larger body of trustees has the trust property vested in him he is bound by the trust and must give effect to it by transferring the trust property into the name of all the Trustees.'

[1]   [2001] 2 All ER 492, para 33.
[2]   A special factor would exist if no trust was intended to arise till the intended trust property had been vested in all the intended trustees.

9.14 No problems arise as to certainty of subject matter of a declaration of trust where the settlor's declaration relates to specific property, eg 'my one and only Picasso painting, all my shares in ICI plc, all my money currently in my Woolwich Building Society account'. However, if it relates to part of his unascertained property in which he retains an interest[1] and he has not declared himself trustee for himself and another as equitable co-owners with specified fractions or percentages, no trust can arise till there has been a segregation or appropriation of specific property out of the larger mass of property where tangible assets are concerned, eg where it is intended to create a trust for B of 20 cases out of 80 cases of Chateau Latour 1982 in the settlor's cellar[2]. However, where intangible assets are concerned eg 500 of my 1,000 shares in Private Company Limited or £10,000 out of £50,000 in my

Woolwich Building Society account[3], the Court of Appeal[4] surprisingly has upheld trusts of such assets as if involving equitable co-owners of fractional interests.

1   If he divests himself of all his equitable interest, eg I hold 20 of my 80 cases of Chateaux Lafite 1961 for X and 60 for Y, this should be effective in favour of X and Y as to one quarter and three quarters of the whole 80 cases due to their *Saunders v Vautier* rights to the 80.
2   *London Wine Co (Shippers) Ltd* [1986] PCC 121 endorsed in *Re Goldcorp Exchange Ltd* [1995] 1 AC 74, [1994] 2 All ER 806, PC.
3   A person for value, may create an immediate charge for say £1,000 on property but a company chargor will need to register the charge under Companies Act 1985, s 395 and an individual chargor will need to comply with the Bills of Sale Acts 1878 in respect of movable property. Further see paras 1.40–1.43 above.
4   *Hunter v Moss* [1994] 1 WLR 452 [1994] 3 All ER 215: see detailed discussion at paras 8.16–8.21 above.

A present irrevocable declaration of trust

9.15 Superficially, there appear to be some dicta of Romilly MR[1] and Neville J[2] indicating that a declaration of trust to be valid needs not only to be a present declaration but also to be 'irrevocable'. Of course, a declaration of trust must be 'present' in the sense that 'I declare I hold my ICI Ltd shareholding in trust for myself for life, remainder to X for life, remainder to Y absolutely' is a valid trust[3] whilst 'I declare that on my death I will declare a trust of my ICI shareholding for X for life, remainder to Y absolutely' is a mere promise to constitute a testamentary trust in the future[4]. However, there is no reason in principle why S should not declare 'I hold my shareholding in ICI Ltd on trust for A for life, remainder to B absolutely, providing that I reserve a power to revoke the settlement without prejudice to any prior distribution of income or capital'[5]. The use of the word 'irrevocable' in the dicta is surely meant to indicate merely that the settlor must have made a final binding unequivocal decision to take upon himself forthwith the role of trustee, rather than that the incorporation of a power of revocation prevents the constitution of any valid trust. A transfer or declaration of trust of property will be presumed irrevocable[6]. The reservation to the settlor of power to revoke an inter vivos trust does not make the trust testamentary[7]. In exercising its powers to settle the property of a mental patient the court will normally make the settlement revocable just in case the patient recovers his capacity[8].

1   *Grant v Grant* (1865) 34 Beav 623 at 625.
2   *Re Cozens* [1913] 2 Ch 478 at 486 'Where a declaration of trust is relied on the court must be satisfied that a present irrevocable declaration of trust has been made'.
3   Cf *Kelly v Walsh* (1878) 1 LR Ir 275; *Re Smith* (1890) 64 LT 13.
4   *Bayley v Boulcott* (1828) 4 Russ 345.
5   *Beecher v Major* (1865) 2 Drew & Sm 431 at 437; *Smith v Deshaw* 116 V 441 (1951) (Supreme Court of Vermont); *Copp v Wood* [1962] 2 DLR (2d) 224; *T Choithram International SA v Pagarani* [2001] 1 WLR 1 [2001] 2 All 492 at para 27.
6   *Newton v Askew* (1848) 11 Beav 145; *Miller v Harrison* (1871) IR 5 Eq 324; *Dhingra v Dhingra* [1999] EWCA Civ 1899, (1999) 2 ITELR 262; *Re Beesty's Will Trusts* [1966] Ch 223 at 233 pointing out that while the exercise of powers of appointment construed in a deed or will and exercisable by deed is irrevocable unless the contrary is stated, there is flexibility for powers that are exercisable informally to be regarded as exercised revocably in context.

7   *Young v Sealey* [1949] Ch 278 at 284 and 294; *Kauter v Hilton* (1953) 90 CLR 86 at
     98–101; *T Choithram International SA v Pagarani*, [2001] 2 All ER 492, at para 27.
8   *Re TB* [1967] Ch 247, [1966] 3 All ER 509.

The effective transfer of the trust property to trustees

9.16 Gifts to trustees for the benefit of beneficiaries have to satisfy the same
rules as gifts directly to donees[1]: otherwise the transfer is incomplete and the
intended beneficiary cannot sue to enforce completion of the transfer since he
is a volunteer[2] nor can he claim that the donor should be treated as having
declared a trust of the property for him, since the donor's attempted
incomplete transfer of the property is absolutely inconsistent with an intention
to retain the property on trust for him[3]. In an exceptional case, however,
where the donor has done all in his power that it is necessary for him to do,
but some further act is necessary to perfect the gift (eg registration of a share
transfer or of a transfer of registered land) the court will artificially treat the
donor as himself trustee of the property until the gift is perfected by the
requisite further act[4]. Furthermore, if a trustee, T, declares that henceforth
particular property of his is to be held on the trusts of which he is a trustee or
is to be held on trust for a named Trust or Foundation, construed as on trust
for the trustees of such Trust or Foundation, then he is bound to transfer such
property into the names of all the trustees[5].

1   Quaere whether a trustee/donee is free to accept cash offered as a gift not as a gift but as a
     loan, eg in the case of family trusts holding shares in the family company where the
     'donor' may perhaps need the money later to support the company; cf *Dewar v Dewar*
     [1975] 2 All ER 728, [1975] 1 WLR 1532, decided in ignorance of *Hill v Wilson* (1873)
     8 Ch App 888 where Mellish J at 896 stated, 'In order to make out a gift it must be shown
     not only that the cheque was sent as a gift. It requires the assent of both minds to make the
     gift as it does to make a contract.'
2   'Equity will not assist a volunteer', para 9.74 below.
3   *Milroy v Lord* (1862) 4 De GF & J 264; *Richards v Delbridge* (1874) LR 18 Eq 11.
4   *Re Rose* [1949] Ch 78, [1948] 2 All ER 971; para 9.32 below.
5   *T Choithram International SA v Pagarani* [2001] 2 All ER 492.

9.17 The gift may be inter vivos or by way of a donatio mortis causa or by
will. Assuming the will satisfies the requisite formalities and the debts,
expenses and liabilities do not exhaust the intended subject matter of the gift,
then the personal representatives must in the appropriate manner vest the
subject matter in the trustees for the beneficiaries[1].

1   Until then the beneficiaries have a chose in action and not an equitable interest under a
     trust: see para 1.46 above.

9.18 The donatio mortis causa requires the donor's intention in contemplation of death to make a gift immediately, but conditional on death, so as to be
subject to a right of revocation until the donor's death[1]. There must be
delivery of the subject matter of the gift or of something representing it which
provides the donee with some effective means of obtaining it[2]. It is most
unusual for a gift to a trustee to be by means of a donatio mortis causa and a

nice distinction has to be drawn between a donatio mortis causa and an attempt to make a testamentary gift which must satisfy the Wills Act formalities[3].

1   *Wilkes v Allington* [1931] 2 Ch 104; *Re Lillingston* [1952] 2 All ER 184.
2   *Re Wasserberg* [1915] 1 Ch 195; *Birch v Treasury Solicitor* [1951] Ch 298, [1950] 2 All ER 1198; *Sen v Headley* [1991] Ch 425, [1991] 2 All ER 636, CA (delivery of title deeds to land suffices); *Woodard v Woodard* [1991] Fam Law 470, [1995] 3 All ER 980, CA (car keys).
3   See Wills Act 1837 s9 as amended by Wills Act 1968.

9.19 Inter vivos gifts have to be completed according to the nature of the property involved.

9.20 A legal estate in unregistered land requires delivery[1] of a duly executed[2] deed to the intended trustee (except for grants of leases not exceeding three years)[3]. If he disclaims the donor takes over as trustee of the trusts[4].

1   While physical delivery is common, technical delivery is simply the intention that the deed is to be binding forthwith so that the grantor may be bound before his deed comes into the custody of the grantee or even before the grantee knows of it, although the grantee can disclaim once he knows of it: *Macedo v Stroud* [1922] 2 AC 330 at 337, PC.
2   A signature needs to be made in the presence of a witness attesting the signature, but a signatory is estopped from claiming the witnesses' attestation was made in the signatory's absence where the other party had been led to rely on the deed being valid: *Shah v Shah* [2001] EWCA Civ 527, [2002] QB 75.
3   If required to be registered within two months with the Land Registry but this is not done then the legal title reverts to the transferor to hold on a bare trust for the transferee: Land Registration Act 2002 s 7.
4   *Mallot v Wilson* [1903] 2 Ch 494.

9.21 Registered land requires the transferee to be registered on the Land Register as proprietor of the land before he becomes the legal owner[1].

1   Further see Land Registration Act 2002, ss 91–93 for electronic transfer provisions.

9.22 Traditionally company shares (other than bearer securities transferable merely by delivery) require delivery of a duly executed form of transfer to the intended trustee, coupled with delivery of the share certificates relating thereto, and finally registration of the intended trustee as registered owner of the shares[1]. If this final step has not yet taken place the donor will be treated exceptionally as himself holding the shares on a trust enforceable at the suit of the beneficiaries[2], assuming he has done everything else required of him, eg obtaining Exchange Control consent[3]. However shares in public limited companies within the CREST system for transfer of shares are transferred electronically with electronic recording of the names of transferees, who receive no share certificates and who have no legal title to the relevant shares because they are equitable tenants in common with proportionate equitable interests in the pool of relevant shares. Assignments of such equitable interests in the CREST system do not need to comply with s 53(1)(c) of the Law of Property Act 1925[4].

1   Companies Act 1985, s 183; Stock Transfer Act 1963, s 1. Inessential irregularities, eg the transferee's signature or the addresses of the transferor and transferee or even the failure to state the amount of consideration may be ignored: *Re Paradise Motor Co Ltd* [1968] 2 All ER 625, [1968] 1 WLR 1125, CA; *Nisbet v Shepherd* [1994] 1 BCLC 300, CA.
2   *Re Rose* [1949] Ch 78, [1949] 2 All ER 971; *Tett v Phoenix Property and Investment Co Ltd* [1984] BCLC 599 at 619.
3   *Re Fry* [1946] Ch 312, [1946] 2 All ER 106.
4   Regulation 38(5) of the Uncertificated Securities Regulations 2001, SI 2001/3755.

9.23 Chattels require the donor to deliver them actually or constructively[1] with the intention to give or to deliver a duly executed deed of gift.

1   *Cochrane v Moore* (1890) 25 QBD 57; *Re Cole* [1964] Ch 175, [1963] 3 All ER 433; *Thomas v Times Book Co Ltd* [1966] 2 All ER 241, [1966] 1 WLR 911.

9.24 Negotiable instruments are transferable by delivery. However, a gift of money by cheque drawn on the donor is not complete until the cheque is cleared, for until then the cheque is merely a revocable authority or mandate[1]. Where the donor endorses and hands over to trustees a cheque drawn by a third party for full consideration it seems this should effectively constitute the trust. Similarly, an irrevocable banker's draft given to trustees should constitute the trust[2].

1   *Re Swinburne* [1926] Ch 38; *Re Owen* [1949] 1 All ER 901, though see *Blackett v Darcy* [2005] NSWSC 65, paras 24–31. A cheque cleared by a bank before having notice of the drawer's death amounts to an effective payment.
2   *Carter v Sharon* [1936] 1 All ER 720.

9.25 Where the donor only has an equitable interest, whether an interest under a trust or an interest in land, like an equitable lease[1] or an estate contract or an equitable chose in action, it must be disposed of in writing signed by the person disposing of the same or by his agent lawfully authorised in writing[2]. The assignment will take effect immediately if so intended even if the assignee is unaware of it, although the assignee can disclaim once aware of it[3].

1   *Gilbert v Overton* (1864) 2 Hem & M 110; *Kekewich v Manning* (1851) 1 De GM & G 176.
2   Law of Property Act 1925, s 53(1)(c). This principle of gifts of equitable choses being complete in equity without any valuable consideration is not affected by the Law of Property Act, s 136, which enables such gifts to be made in a further manner; *Re Pain* [1919] 1 Ch 38 at 44–45; *William Brandt's Sons & Co v Dunlop Rubber Co Ltd* [1905] AC 454 at 461, 'The statute does not forbid or destroy equitable assignments or impair their efficacy in the slightest degree'; *Norman v Federal Comr of Taxation* (1962) 109 CLR 9 at 30; *Timpson's Executors v Yerbury* [1936] 1 KB 645, [1963] 1 All ER 186. The dictum of Parker J in *Glegg v Bromley* [1912] 3 KB 474 at 491, 'If there be no consideration there can be no equitable assignment' must be confined to the assignment of a *future* debt taking effect as an agreement to assign it when it is an existing debt; see per Lush J in *German v Yates* (1915) 32 TLR 52.
3   *Re Way's Trust* (1864) 2 De G J & S 365.

9.26 Certain legal choses in action, like patents, copyrights, life assurance policies, bills of lading and shares, require to be transferred according to the appropriate statutory formalities or require the donor to have done everything required of him to enable the transfer to become effective. Otherwise (eg for debts) the Judicature Act 1873, s 25(6), replaced by the Law of Property Act 1925, s 136, created a statutory form of assignment enabling legal[1] choses in action to be assigned at law as a new possibility[2] where previously only an equitable assignment had been possible. Nowadays, a donor seeking to make a gift of a legal chose in action, like a debt, should ideally satisfy Law of Property Act 1925, s 136, which requires and authorises an absolute assignment (not purporting to be by way of charge only) (1) to be in writing signed by the assignor and (2) to be notified in writing by the assignor or assignee or whoever to the debtor before proceedings are commenced. However, by satisfying requirement (1) the donor has done all that is necessary by *him* to be done in order to make the gift at law so the gift will be complete in equity[3]. If the absolute assignment were made orally then requirement (1) would not be satisfied and so the gift would be incomplete, taking effect merely as a promise to make a complete gift which would be unenforceable unless valuable consideration had been provided, as held by the High Court of Australia[4]. However, the vexed question[5] remains in England whether under equitable assignment rules existing independently of s 136[6] there can be an effective oral or unsigned equitable assignment of a legal chose in action for no consideration. There is authority that where s 136 is unavailable, as where part of a debt is assigned[7], so it is necessary to rely on equitable assignment rules, then the gift of part of the debt will be complete in equity if the donor orally or in writing revealed an intention to assign which he communicated to the trustee/donee[8].

[1] This is read as if 'lawfully assignable chose in action' so as to extend to equitable choses in action: *Re Pain* [1919] 1 Ch 38 at 44, *Federal Commissioner of Taxation v Everett* (1980) 143 CLR 440 at 447.

[2] *William Brandt's Sons & Company Limited v Dunlop Rubber Company Limited* [1905] AC 454 at 461.

[3] *Holt v Heatherfield Trust Ltd* [1942] 2 KB 1, [1942] 1 All ER 404: the absence of consideration is immaterial since the gift is treated as a completed gift: *Re McArdle* [1951] Ch 669 at 676.

[4] *Olsson v Dyson* (1969) 120 CLR 365.

[5] See G J Tolhurst (2002) 118 LQR 98 at 101, *Lewin on Trusts* (17 edn), para 3–31, Meagher Gummow and Lehane, *Equity: Doctrine and Remedies* (4th edition) paras 6–075 to 6–155.

[6] However, because s 136 makes legal choses in action assignable at law if the requirements therein are met, for the assignor to do everything necessary by him to be done to perfect a gift before equity will treat the gift as effective, surely he must use signed writing: otherwise equity should not assist a volunteer: *Re Westerton* [1919] 2 Ch 104 at 111; *Holt v Heatherfield Trust Limited* [1942] 2 KB 1 at 5; *Olsson v Dyson* (1969) 120 CLR 365.

[7] *Re Steel Wing Co Ltd* [1921] 1 Ch 349; *Walter & Sullivan Ltd v J Murphy & Sons Ltd* [1955] 2 QB 584, [1955] 1 All ER 843, CA.

[8] *Shepherd v Federal Taxation Comr* (1965) 113 CLR 385 (Aust HC) applying view of Windeyer J in *Norman v Federal Taxation Comr* (1963) 109 CLR 9.

9.27 Only existing property, and not future property, is capable of being assigned, so that a purported assignment of future property can only take effect if it is for valuable consideration and so regarded as a contract[1]. A trust may be validly created of an existing debt (eg due from a bank to the settlor) even, it seems, if the debtor (eg the bank) is the trustee of the trust , in which event the debtor has an equitable obligation to the beneficiaries on the same terms as the debt to make payment into the trust fund[2].

1   *Tailby v Official Receiver* (1888) 13 App Cas 523 at 543; *Re Ellenborough* [1903] 1 Ch 697; *Shepherd v Federal Taxation Comr* (1965) 113 CLR 385. Expectancies under wills or under the exercise of a power of appointment are classic future property, but a chose in action relating to future property is no less an existing chose in action because it is not immediately recoverable by action: *Re Landau* [1997] 3 All ER 322 at 328.
2   *Re Bank of Credit and Commerce International SA (No 8)* [1998] AC 214 at 226–228 on analagous charge of bank over customer's deposit account. The value of the trust of the debt or contractual promise will depend on the solvency of the debtor-promisor.

9.28 The settlor must be responsible for the trust property becoming vested in the trustees, whether he or his duly authorised agent is directly responsible. If Trust 'A' property settled by A is appointed by the trustees in favour of S then S can actually receive the property and subsequently settle it under the 'S' trust, an existing trust already created by him, or under a fresh trust. Alternatively, S may authorise or mandate the 'S' trustees to receive the property and so inform the 'A' trustees: on receipt by the 'S' trustees, without having received any revocation of their authority or mandate, the property will be fully subject to the 'S' trust[1]. If S wishes he can create a trust and make as its trustees the Trust 'A' trustees, directing them in the trust deed to hold any property held by them qua Trust 'A' trustees, but which is subsequently appointed to him absolutely to be held by them qua his trustees[2] though, in principle, this direction, if voluntary[3] and therefore unenforceable, should be capable of being effectively revoked before any such appointment is made[4].

1   *Re Bowden* [1936] Ch 71.
2   *Re Burton's Settlements* [1955] Ch 82, [1954] 3 All ER 193.
3   Or not otherwise binding as being to give effect to a condition contained in a will as in *Re Burton's Settlements* [1955] Ch 82, [1954] 3 All ER 193, or being an irrevocable power of attorney.
4   *Re Bowden* [1936] Ch 71, though cf *Re Burton's Settlements* [1955] Ch 82 at 104.

9.29 If S voluntarily covenants to transfer to the 'S' trustees any property appointed to S under a special power in that behalf, contained in the 'A' trust set up by A, and property is appointed to S absolutely at a time when a third party has fortuitously appointed the 'S' trustees to be trustees of the 'A' trust (not so unlikely if the 'S' trustees are a major trust corporation) then S is entitled to obtain the appointed property for himself free from any trusts since his voluntary obligation is unenforceable and he is in no way responsible for vesting title to the appointed property in the trustees[1]. However, if S authorises the trustees holding the appointed property qua trustees of the 'A' trust to hold the property qua S's trustees then the 'S' trust of the property will be completely constituted.

1   *Re Brooks' Settlement Trusts* [1939] Ch 993, [1939] 3 All ER 920.

9.30 As will be seen later in dealing with the rule in *Strong v Bird*[1], it seems that a settlor who has not effectively transferred property to trustees in his lifetime may regularise the position if he appoints one or more of the trustees to be his executors, thereby obtaining the property on his death, so long as the intention to transfer the property for the benefit of the trust beneficiaries continued unchanged till the settlor's death.

1   See para 9.46 below.

9.31 If the settlor dies without having effectively transferred property to his trustees in his lifetime and his executor, mistakenly believing himself legally bound to effect the transfer, then effects the transfer to trustees, Astbury J[1] has opined that this would be effective as against those interested under the deceased's will. Even then it would seem that the personal representative should be personally liable to the will beneficiaries, and can the executor really be allowed to perfect the transfer so as to prevent the will beneficiaries claiming the property from the transferees, since the executor does not have as much freedom as the deceased settlor had to perfect the transfer, for the executor holds the property subject to fiduciary obligations owed to the will beneficiaries and not as absolute owner like the settlor?[2]

1   *Carter v Hungerford* [1917] 1 Ch 260 at 273.
2   Cf *Re Diplock* [1948] Ch 465, [1948] 2 All ER 318; *Stamp Duties Comr (Queensland) v Livingston* [1965] AC 694, [1964] 3 All ER 692, PC.

Exceptional cases

SETTLOR DOES EVERYTHING NECESSARY FOR HIM, AS OPPOSED TO OTHERS, TO DO TO TRANSFER THE PROPERTY TO TRUSTEES

9.32 *Milroy v Lord*[1] laid down that the transferor/settlor must 'have done everything which according to the nature of the property was necessary to be done in order to transfer the property'[2]. The question then arose whether for the transfer to be perfect or complete in equity the transferor (1) must ensure that all necessary acts are done to transfer title irrespective of the fact that the participation of a third party is necessary (eg in transferring shares, in a private company), (2) must do all acts which he *can* do even though it may be equally possible for the transferee to do them[3] (eg forwarding the appropriate documents to a company) (3) must do only those acts which it is obligatory *upon him* to do[4] (eg giving the transfer form to the transferee who can himself forward them to the appropriate registering authority).

1   (1862) 4 De GF & J 264.
2   *Milroy v Lord* (1862) 4 De GF & J 264 at 274.
3   *Anning v Anning* (1907) 4 CLR 1049 at 1079–1082, per Higgins J.
4   *Anning v Anning* (1907) 4 CLR 1049 at 1079–1082, per Griffith CJ.

9.33 The third approach has prevailed[1]. In *Re Rose*[2] the donor on 30 March 1943 had executed valid transfers of certain shares in a private company and handed them to the donee together with the relevant certificates by 5 April 1943. The donee forwarded the documents to the company which registered the transfer on 30 June 1943. The Court of Appeal held that the gift was perfected by 5 April, it being crucial to the estate duty position on the donor's death in 1947 that the gift was perfected by 10 April 1943. In respect of the interregnum period the donor held the legal title to the shares upon trust for the donee so that any dividends in that period would be held for the donee. If the company directors had exercised their right under the company's articles to refuse to register the transfer the indications are that the court would still have treated the gift as perfect by 5 April and the legal interest thereafter vested in the donor as trustee[3]. An analogy may be drawn with the position after disclaimer by a trustee[4].

1   *Pennington v Waine* [2002] EWCA Civ 227, [2002] 1 WLR 2075, para 56. The position is the same in Australia: *Corin v Patton* (1990) 169 CLR 540.
2   [1952] Ch 499, [1952] 1 All ER 1217, followed in *Tett v Phoenix Property and Investment Co Ltd* [1984] BCLC 599. See also *Vanderell v IRC* [1967] 2 AC 291 at 330; (1967) 30 MLR 461 (N. Strauss).
3   [1952] Ch 499 at 510. The trust would determine when, the directors having chosen not to object to a proposed transferee, the legal interest passed on registration of the transferee as owner. Meanwhile, voting rights and dividends would be held to the transferee's order. The trust seems constructive rather than express since the transferor did not intend to hold upon trust but to have the transferee hold the property beneficially or on trust for others;see paras 35.75–35.77 below.
4   *Mallott v Wilson* [1903] 2 Ch 494, Article 38.

9.34 The Court of Appeal distinguished the earlier decision of Romer J in *Re Fry*[1] whilst accepting it as correct, on the basis that there the American donor had not done everything required of him since his transfer of shares in an English company could not be registered without Treasury consent. The donor completed the necessary forms and submitted them to the Treasury but died before consent was obtained. Romer J held the gift was not perfected by the time of the donor's death so that the donor's executors could not go on to complete the gift. If the gift in *Re Fry* was imperfect because Treasury consent, necessary for the share transfer to proceed, had not been obtained by the relevant time, why was the gift in *Re Rose* not imperfect because the directors' consent necessary for the share transfer to proceed had not been obtained by the relevant time?[2] The Court of Appeal did not face up to this but its views may be supported on the basis that the directors' consent is the ultimate consent and is a negative requirement, rather than a positive requirement, in that the transfer must automatically be registered within two months unless the directors' discretion to refuse to register is exercised within the two months[3].

1   [1946] Ch 312, [1946] 2 All ER 106.
2   (1976) 40 Conv (NS) 139 (L. McKay); (1955) 33 Canadian BR 284 (L.A. Sheridan).
3   Companies Act 1948, s 78 (now Companies Act 1985, s 183); *Re Swaledale Cleaners Ltd* [1968] 3 All ER 619, [1968] 1 WLR 1710; *Tett v Phoenix Property and Investment Co Ltd* [1984] BCLC 599.

9.35 For types of property other than shares where third party acts are required for legal title to pass (eg registered land before instantaneous electronic conveyancing became the norm) a similar principle applies, namely, that the transferor must do all according to the nature of the property that it is obligatory upon him alone to do (eg deliver an executed transfer and the land certificate in pre-electronic conveyancing times)[1].

1   See Australian and New Zealand cases on Torrens title land: *Re Ward* [1968] WAR 33, 42 ALJ 227; *Norman v Federal Taxation Comr* (1962) 109 CLR 9 at 24–34 (Aust HC) per Windeyer J; *Brunker v Perpetual Trustee Co* (1937) 57 CLR 555; *Scoones v Galvin and the Public Trustee* [1934] NZLR 1004. Also *Mascall v Mascall* (1984) 50 P & CR 119; *Corin v Patton* (1990) 169 CLR 540.

9.36 It would seem that if the transferee lost the transfer form or it was destroyed in a fire then the equitable interest he had acquired should justify the court requiring the transferor to execute a fresh transfer[1].

[1]   *Mascall v Mascall* (1984) 50 P & CR 119; *Corin v Patton* (1990) 169 CLR 540 at 559–560; Trustee Act 1925, s 51.

9.37 In *Re Rose*[1] sufficient emphasis was put on the early April delivery of the share certificates together with the transfer forms executed on 30 March for the probable *ratio* to be that equitable title did not pass on 30 March but only passed once the share certificates were delivered together with the transfer forms. Minds did not focus clearly on this issue since it sufficed if equitable title passed by 10 April and delivery had occurred before then.

[1]   [1952] Ch 499.

9.38 However, in *Pennington v Waine*[1] Clarke LJ (but not Arden or Schiemann LJJ) held that execution of a stock transfer form forthwith took effect as an equitable assignment in favour of the transferee without the necessity of delivering the form and the relevant certificate either to the transferee or the relevant company – unless the transferor intended the assignment not to have effect until a later date. He regarded this as following from basic principle and some unguarded dicta of Evershed MR and Jenkins LJ in *Re Rose* which indicated 30 March as the date from which legal title was held on trust for the transferee (despite earlier emphasis on the importance of delivery of certificates and forms).

[1]   [2002] EWCA Civ 227, [2002] 1 WLR 2075.

9.39 It follows from this view of Clarke LJ that there is no difference between O, the owner, of 1,000 shares in XY Co Ltd writing a letter to D stating 'I hold my 1,000 shares in XY Co Ltd on trust for you', or 'I hereby assign my beneficial interest in my 1,000 shares in XY Co Ltd to you', or executing a stock transfer form 'I hereby transfer 1,000 shares in XY Co Ltd out of my name to D of such and such an address. I request that such entry is made in the register as is necessary to give effect to this transfer.' However, in the last case, unlike the first two, O is not intending to create an equitable interest in favour of D. He is intending to transfer to D legal title which, when transferred, will carry with it the beneficial interest. His intention to transfer ownership is premised upon an effective transfer of the legal title.

9.40 Thus, when O has put it out of O's power to prevent D becoming registered with legal title, then O cannot deny D's equitable entitlement, but not before then. So long as O or O's agent has the transfer form or the relevant certificate without which D cannot become registered, O retains beneficial ownership[1] unless there are special circumstances which make it unconscionable for O to deny D equitable entitlement, as held by Arden and Schiemann LJJ in *Pennington v Waine* (and also by Clarke LJ as an alternative *ratio*).

[1]   Hence the emphasis in *Mascall v Mascall* (1984) 50 P & CR 119, CA and *Trustee of the Property of Pehrsson v Greyerz* (16 June 1999, unreported) PC, on the necessity for the donee to have under his control everything necessary to constitute his title completely, so the donor has no power to prevent this.

9.41 Here, Ada owned 1,500 shares in a private family company with 2,000 issued shares, and her share certificate was in the company's custody. She told her nephew Harold she was giving him 400 shares and wanted him to become a director. She instructed a partner in the company's firm of auditors to prepare a transfer form, which she executed and returned to the partner, who happened to put it in the company's file (not Ada's file) in his office, told Harold of Ada's gift saying Harold (who was company secretary) need take no action, and asked Harold to sign a prescribed form of consent to act as a director, which Harold did and which Ada countersigned. Shortly afterwards, Ada made a will leaving Harold 620 shares so that with the 400 shares he would have a 51% shareholding. Within a month Ada was dead, the above events occurring in the preceding three months.

9.42 Despite delivery of the transfer form to the partner as Ada's agent, and not the agent of Harold or the company, so that Ada had it within her power to change her mind and destroy the transfer form so as to prevent Harold becoming registered share-holder, Arden and Schiemann LJJ held it had become unconscionable for Ada to change her mind and refuse to hand over the transfer form once Harold signed the consent to act as director and so subjected himself to potential liabilities as a director. It followed it also was unconscionable for her executors to refuse to hand over the share transfer form to Harold[1].

[1] See *Pennington v Waine* [2002] EWCA Civ 227, [2002] 1 WLR 2075 Arden LJ at paras 4, 64 and 66.

9.43 Alternatively, when Ada's agent, the partner, had informed Harold of Ada's gift of 400 shares to him and assured Harold that this required no action on his part, this should be construed as meaning that Ada and the partner became agents for Harold for the purpose of submitting the share transfer form to the company, and Harold 'must be taken to have proceeded on the basis that [this assurance] would be honoured'[1]. The implication is that no revocation of such agency could occur because Harold had altered his position to his detriment by acting as director despite the apparent absence of qualification shares for a directorship which would have led to vacation of the directorship before Ada's death[2] if equity did not treat him as owner of the requisite shares.

[1] See *Pennington v Waine* [2002] EWCA Civ 227, [2002] 1 WLR 2075 Arden LJ at para 68.
[2] [2002] EWCA Civ 227, [2002] 1 WLR 2075, para 7.

CONVEYANCE TO A MINOR

9.44 A minor cannot hold a legal estate in land[1] so a conveyance attempting to vest a legal estate in a minor operates as a declaration that the land is held in trust for the minor, the grantor being the trustee; although if the legal estate is purportedly conveyed to persons of full age as well, then those persons hold in trust for the minor.

[1] Law of Property Act 1925, s 1(6).

EQUITABLE PROPRIETARY ESTOPPEL

9.45 If a settlor tells his son that the son can take possession of a plot of land, Blackacre, which is to be held for the son for life, remainder to his widow, remainder to his children equally, and the son to the settlor's knowledge builds a house thereon, then the son can compel the settlor or the settlor's personal representatives to perfect the gift on principles of equitable proprietary estoppel epitomised in cases such as *Dillwyn v Llewelyn*[1]; *Ramsden v Dyson*[2]; *Inwards v Baker*[3]; and *Pascoe v Turner*[4], discussed at paras 12.47–12.61 below. Similarly, if A tells B that his house is now hers absolutely so that she acts to her detriment in reliance thereon the court may find that A holds the house on a bare trust for B so that he can be compelled to vest the legal title in B beneficially[5]. If he had told her that the house was half hers so that she acted to her detriment in reliance thereon the court can find that he held the house on trust for himself and her in equal shares[6].

[1] (1862) 4 De GF & J 517.
[2] (1866) LR 1 HL 129.
[3] [1965] 2 QB 29, [1965] 1 All ER 446.
[4] [1979] 2 All ER 945, [1979] 1 WLR 431.
[5] *Pascoe v Turner* [1979] 2 All ER 945, [1979] 1 WLR 431, CA.
[6] *Lloyd's Bank v Rosset* [1991] 1 AC 107; *Grant v Edwards* [1986] 2 All ER 426 at 439, CA.

THE RULE IN STRONG V BIRD

9.46 To appreciate *Strong v Bird*[1] it is necessary to consider the position at law and in equity where a deceased creditor had appointed his debtor as his executor. As pointed out by Mason J in *Bone v Stamp Duties Comr*[2] the common law treated the appointment as extinguishing or releasing the debt (but not as against creditors where the executor was treated as having in his hands the amount of the debt). The basis for such extinction or release was:

'that a debt was no more than the right to sue for the money owing by the debtor and that a personal action was discharged when it was suspended by the voluntary act of the person entitled to bring it. An executor could not maintain an action against himself; the action to recover the debt was suspended by his appointment which came about by the voluntary act on the part of the testator ... [the true basis of the common law rule] lay in the significance attributed to a voluntary act on the part of the testator, the person entitled to bring the action. Once this is recognised, the true character of the rule is perceived. It reflected the presumed intention of the party having the right to bring the action and was not absolute in its operation.'

[1] (1874) LR 18 Eq 315.
[2] (1974) 132 CLR 38 at 53, appeal allowed on other grounds by Privy Council in *Stamp Duties Comr v Bone* [1977] AC 511, [1976] 2 All ER 354, PC.

9.47 Since the administrators are not selected by the voluntary act of the testator the common law did not treat the appointment by the court of the administrator as the release of any debt due to the deceased from the administrator[1]. The procedural obstacle prevented the administrator from suing himself in his life-time but after his death an action could be brought against his estate for the debt if still outstanding.

1   *Wankford v Wankford* (1704) 1 Salk 299; *Seagram v Knight* (1867) 2 Ch App 628, CA; *Re Gonin* [1977] 2 All ER 720 at 734. Presumably there would be no release if the debtor as executor of the deceased creditor's executor became executor by representation of the deceased creditor. Now Administration of Estates Act 1925, s 21A, added by Limitation Amendment Act 1980, s 10, extinguishes a debt due to the deceased from his administrator or executor by representation though such person remains accountable for the debt where he would be so accountable if he had been appointed an executor by the deceased's will.

9.48 In equity the debtor (whether the creditor's executor or administrator) was treated as having paid the debt to the estate and hence having assets in his hands which were distributable amongst creditors and persons beneficially interested in the estate[1].

1   *Berry v Usher* (1805) 11 Ves 87; *Jenkins v Jenkins* [1928] 2 KB 501.

9.49 *Strong v Bird* decided that equity should allow the common law position to prevail and thus not require the executor to account for the debt if the testator had manifested an intention to forgive the debt in his lifetime and this intention had continued till his death.

9.50 The common law position thus takes on special significance and so should be elaborated further. The cases[1] seem to establish the debt was released if the debtor appointed executor took out a grant of probate or if he intermeddled but died before taking out a grant of probate or, it seems, if he died before intermeddling or taking out a grant since the executor's title to sue commences as from the testator's death[2]. The release operated to extinguish the debt against beneficiaries but not against creditors. However, there was no release if the debtor renounced probate (or upon being cited to take out probate did not appear to the citation) since he was then treated as if he had never been appointed executor. The Administration of Estates Act 1925, s 5 (replacing the provisions in the Court of Probate Acts 1857 and 1858) now provides that where a person appointed executor survives the testator but dies without having taken out probate the representation to the testator and the administration of his estate are to devolve and be committed as if such person had not been appointed executor. However, it seems unlikely that this has affected the common law release of such person's debt[3] since such person's death cannot be said to be a wilful voluntary act (eg renunciation) rejecting the testator's intention to release the debt manifested in the appointment of the debtor as executor.

1   *Wankford v Wankford* (1704) 1 Salk 299; *Re Bourne* [1906] 1 Ch 697; *Jenkins v Jenkins* [1928] 2 KB 501; *Bone v Stamp Duties Comr* (1974) 132 CLR 38; *Re Applebee* [1891] 3 Ch 422.
2   Where the debtor was jointly or jointly and severally liable with others there was a release if he was appointed executor, and, where as sole debtor he was appointed one of several executors there was also a release even, it seems, if only the others took out probate so long as he did not renounce or refuse to appear to a citation.
3   *Re Applebee* [1891] 3 Ch 422.

9.51 In *Strong v Bird* B borrowed £1,100 from his stepmother living with him and paying £212.10s each quarter for her board. The loan was to be repaid by £100 deductions from the stepmother's next eleven quarterly payments. She did this for two quarters but then she expressly forgave B the debt and insisted on paying the full £212.10s each quarter. She continued to make these full quarterly payments till her death. She had appointed B executor in her will and he proved the will. The residuary legatees sought to make B account to them for the debt due to the estate since the oral release of the debt was ineffective.

9.52 Jessel MR held, however, that the debt had been released at common law by B's appointment as executor and although in equity B would be liable to account for the amount of the debt this had been displaced in equity by B proving that his stepmother up to her death had an unchanged intention to forgive him the outstanding £900. This intention was perfected at law by B becoming his stepmother's executor and there was 'no equity against him to take the property away from him'[1]. In his judgment Jessel MR vacillates between treating the appointment of B as executor as releasing the debt at law and treating the grant of probate in B's favour as releasing the debt at law. On balance it would seem he treated the grant of probate as perfecting the gift of the £900 by causing 'a change of the property at law'[2] to take place. Strictly speaking, though immaterial to the facts of *Strong v Bird*, it would seem at law that it is the intention of the testator manifested in appointing his debtor as his executor and leaving this part of his will unchanged till his death that is itself the making of a gift of the debt so causing a change of the property at law[3].

1 (1874) LR 18 Eq 315 at 318.
2 (1874) LR 18 Eq 315 at 318.
3 *Wankford v Wankford* (1704) 1 Salk 299; *Bone v Stamp Duties Comr* (1974) 132 CLR 38; *Brazier v Hudson* (1836) 8 Sim 67.

EXTENSION FROM FORGIVENESS OF DEBTS TO PERFECTING GIFTS

9.53 Where a donor intends to make a gift of specific property but fails to comply with the legal formalities for transferring the legal title to the intended donee and goes on to appoint the donee his executor and then dies, the appointment itself is no perfect gift at law of the specific property unlike the case of a debt due from a previously imperfectly released debtor. Nevertheless, in *Re Stewart*[1] Neville J extended the principle of *Strong v Bird* to an imperfect gift of specific bonds made by the testator in his lifetime to his wife, by handing to her his brokers' letter that they had purchased specified bonds for him, after she had proved his will alongside his other appointed executors. He said[2]:

> 'Where a testator has expressed the intention of making a gift of personal estate belonging to him to one who upon his death becomes his executor, the intention continuing unchanged, the executor is entitled to hold the property for his own benefit. The reasoning by which the conclusion is reached is of a double character—first, that the vesting of the property in the executor at the testator's death completes the imperfect gift made in the lifetime and secondly, that the

intention of the testator to give the beneficial interest to the executor is sufficient to countervail the equity of beneficiaries under the will, the testator having vested the legal estate in the executor. The whole of the property in the eye of the law vesting in each executor, it seems to me immaterial whether the donee is the only executor or one of them; nor do I think the rule is confined to cases of the release of a debt owing by the donee.'

1   [1908] 2 Ch 251.
2   [1908] 2 Ch 251 at 254.

9.54 Whilst *Strong v Bird* negatively left the situation as it was at law *Re Stewart* went a bold step further by positively treating a gift as effective even though the law did not. However, it has been followed at first instance[1] and treated as good law in the Court of Appeal[2].

1   *Re Comberbach* (1929) 73 Sol Jo 403; *Re James* [1935] Ch 449; *Re Nelson* [1947] 91 Sol Jo 533; see also *Re Ralli's Will Trusts* [1964] Ch 288, [1963] 3 All ER 940; *Re Gonin* [1979] Ch 16, [1977] 2 All ER 720.
2   *Re Freeland* [1952] Ch 110, [1952] 1 All ER 16, counsel unreservedly accepting *Re Stewart* as correct. In *Corin v Patton* (1990) 169 CLR 540 at 557 Mason CJ and Mc Hugh J described the rule as clearly established.

9.55 A problematic question is what suffices as an imperfect gift. Must there be delivery of some indicia of title? Take X with £50,000 in a building society deposit account where 90 days' notice of withdrawal is required. He signs the withdrawal form but, on being informed of the interest penalty if 90 days' notice is not given, he then gives the requisite notice and takes away the withdrawal form. He tells Y that his intention is to open an account in the joint names of X and Y and pay the £50,000 into this. Upon expiry of the 90 days X feels unwell and in the evening hands the withdrawal form to Y, together with a note authorising the building society to pay Y if opening a new account in the names of X and Y. The following morning X dies and the building society therefore correctly refuses to pay the £50,000 out when Y presents the document in the afternoon, stating that X is dead so that he should have the whole £50,000. Y then takes out a grant of probate as X's executor. By virtue of *Re Stewart* Y should be entitled to the £50,000 but would this be the case if X had not delivered the signed withdrawal form to Y? Presumably, there could be no requisite[1] intention to make an immediate gift before expiry of the 90 days period and, once such period expired, would an intent to make an immediate gift require handing over the withdrawal form with accompanying authorisation or writing a cheque out for £50,000 and handing it to Y to open a joint account with it? Indeed should the perfection of imperfect gifts under *Re Stewart* principles require the same sort of delivery of indicia as is required for donationes mortis causa?

1   See 9.57, footnote 1 and text to which it relates.

9.56 *Strong v Bird* itself was based not on delivery of anything but simply on evidence of an express intention to forgive the debt, supported by full quarterly payments. This would justify mere evidence of intention without delivery of any indicia as sufficient for the *Re Stewart* extension to imperfect gifts, but it is arguable that in extending the negative release of debts principle of *Strong v Bird* to the perfection of positive gifts, positive delivery of some indicia should be required. However, in most cases of imperfect gifts if there is no delivery of some indicia relating to the subject of the purported immediate gift it is unlikely that there will be found an intent to make an immediate gift as opposed to an intent to make a gift in the future.

9.57 This adds significance to the requirement[1] for an intent to make a present gift. However, once the pass has been sold by Equity assisting a volunteer and perfecting an imperfect immediate gift, it is, arguably, illogical for Equity to refrain from assisting a volunteer under an imperfect gift of specific property to be made at a future time (other than the donor's death when testamentary requirements must be satisfied) once that time has arrived, assuming that the donor has not changed his intention by then.

[1]   *Re Innes* [1910] 1 Ch 188; *Re Freeland* [1952] Ch 110, [1952] 1 All ER 16; *Cope v Keene* (1968) 118 CLR 1, and a fortiori when the donor's death is the future occasion so the gift is testamentary in nature; *Re Hyslop* [1894] 3 Ch 522; *Re Pink* [1912] 2 Ch 528 at 536 and 538–539. It follows that *Re Goff* (1914) 111 LT 34 is of doubtful authority (donor intended to forgive debt only if donor predeceased donee yet Sargant J applied *Strong v Bird*).

ERRONEOUS EXTENSION TO ADMINISTRATORS

9.58 In *Re James*[1] Farwell J further extended *Re Stewart* to perfect an imperfect gift of real property made by a donor by merely handing the title deeds to his housekeeper who, on the donor's intestacy, had herself appointed by the court one of two *administratrices* of the donor's estate, thereby obtaining the legal estate to the house. This is difficult to justify and it has been doubted by Walton J in *Re Gonin*[2] and rejected by the British Virgin Islands' Court of Appeal[3]. After all, it is the voluntary act of the testator in appointing his debtor as his executor that at law released or extinguished the debt while the appointment of an administrator is an act of the law and, even then, it is often pure chance that determines which of many persons entitled to a grant of letters of administration finally takes them out. For this reason at law the appointment by the court of an administrator, who happened to be a debtor of the deceased, did not release the debt so that *Strong v Bird* itself would have been differently decided if the defendant had been an administrator and not an executor.

[1]   [1935] Ch 449.
[2]   [1977] 2 All ER 720 at 734.
[3]   *Re Pagarani* (1998/99) 2 OFLR 1, not dealt with on appeal in *T Choithram International SA v Pagarani* [2001] 1 WLR 1.

THE NEED FOR INTENT TO MAKE AN IMMEDIATE GIFT

9.59 The rule in *Strong v Bird* has so developed that an imperfect *immediate* gift of *specific*[1] existing[2] real[3] or personal property will be perfected if the intended donee is appointed the donor's executor alone or with others[4] (whether or not he proves the will or intermeddles)[5] or becomes one of the donor's administrators[6] or executors by representation, so long as the intention to make an immediate gift continues unchanged till the donor's death[7].

9.59 *Matters essential to the prima facie validity of an express trust*

Whether the donee's title derived from the donor can then be relied on against creditors (as opposed to the beneficiaries' under the will or a partial intestacy) is doubtful: in principle it should not avail against creditors since a common law release of a debt by appointment of the debtor as executor did not avail against creditors[8].

1   The subject matter of the intended gift must be specific so that a sum of money must be 'sufficiently identified to enable it to be separated from the rest of the estate of the testator': *Re Innes* [1910] 1 Ch 188 at 193.

2   *Morton v Brighouse* [1927] 1 DLR 1009; a present intention to make an immediate gift of after-acquired property does not suffice to attract the *Strong v Bird* principle. Arguably, once the pass is sold and equity assists a volunteer and perfects an imperfect gift as in *Re Stewart* [1908] 2 Ch 251, is it not inconsistent for equity to draw back and refrain from assisting a volunteer who is not a volunteer under an immediate gift of existing property but a volunteer under an imperfect gift of specific property to be made at a future time once that time has arrived (not being the time of the donor's death so that testamentary formalities must be satisfied)? In *Re Ralli's WT* [1964] Ch 288 Buckley J assumed a covenant to transfer property as soon as circumstances would admit could come within the rule; also see *Re Goff* (1914) 111 LT 34. However, such imperfect gift amounts merely to a promise to make a gift.

3   *Re James* [1935] Ch 449.

4   *Re Stewart* [1908] 2 Ch 251. Each joint tenant is treated as having the whole property.

5   *Re Applebee* [1891] 3 Ch 422; *Re Harvey* (1932) 41 OWN 420 (donor a minor appointed as a joint executor though only permitted by the will to take out probate on attaining his majority); *Wankford v Wankford* (1704) 1 Salk 299.

6   *Re James* [1935] Ch 449.

7   In *Re Stoneham* [1919] 1 Ch 149 at 158, P.O. Lawrence J indicates that if the imperfect gift is confirmed by the will this suffices to satisfy the requirement of continuing intention up to death even if there were contrary expressions of the testator between the date of his will and his death: also see *Cope v Keene* (1968) 118 CLR 1 at 8. A contrary intention ousting *Strong v Bird* will be present if the testator lends to X a car which she had previously intended to give to B, or if a testator later takes security for a debt which she had previously forgiven, or if a testatrix forgets that investments had been settled by her ineffectually and for the rest of her life treats them as still her own or, it seems, if a testator specifically devises or bequeaths property to a third party or otherwise demonstrates that he has forgotten or is overriding his original intent to give the property to B: *Re Freeland* [1952] Ch 110, [1952] 1 All ER 16; *Re Eiser's Will Trusts* [1937] 1 All ER 244; *Re Wale* [1956] 3 All ER 280, [1956] 1 WLR 1346; *Morton v Brighouse* [1927] 1 DLR 1009.

8   *Bone v Stamp Duties Comr* (1974) 132 CLR 38; *Stamp Duties Comr v Bone* [1976] 2 All ER 354 at 359, 360, PC.

9.60 Where the intended donee of the title to the subject matter of the intended gift is a trustee or one of several trustees it seems that the rule in *Strong v Bird* can apply to perfect the trust, for the equity of the beneficiaries under the intended trust of the property should be sufficient to countervail the equity of the testamentary beneficiaries[1]. Thus, if S makes an imperfect immediate gift of specific existing property to the trustees of his settlement then if one (or more) of the trustees is appointed S's executor or one of his executors this should completely constitute the trusts relating to the property so long as S's intention to make the gift continues unchanged till his death[2].

1   This adopts the reasoning of Neville J in *Re Stewart* [1908] 2 Ch 251 at 254 cited at para 9.53 above.

2   See *Re Ralli's Will Trusts* [1964] Ch 288, [1963] 3 All ER 940, where counsel submitted that the rule in *Strong v Bird* could only apply 'where the plaintiff was claiming on his own behalf and not on behalf of volunteers' at 294 but Buckley J rejected this at 301: 'In my judgment the circumstance that the plaintiff holds the fund because he was appointed a trustee of the will is irrelevant. He is at law the owner of the fund and the means by which

he became so have no effect upon the quality of his legal ownership. The question is: For whom if anyone does he hold the fund in equity?' Also see *Re Wale* [1956] 3 All ER 280, [1956] 1 WLR 1346 where the executors would have taken as trustees and *Carter v Hungerford* [1917] 1 Ch 260 at 273 where the imperfect gift to trustees was treated as perfect (though wrongly so, because the legal title was passed by the donor's executor). For a contrary restrictive view see *Blackett v Darcy* [2005] NSWSC 65, para 35, *Re Halley* (1959) 43 MPR 79.

9.61 If S voluntarily covenants to pay £20,000 to his trustees or to transfer stocks and shares or lands to the value of £80,000 to his trustees then *Strong v Bird* cannot apply if a trustee becomes S's executor because separate specific identifiable property is not concerned[675].

1   *Re Innes* [1910] 1 Ch 188 at 193. If S had intended forthwith to create a binding trust of the covenant then the beneficiaries would have an interest under the trust: *Fletcher v Fletcher* (1844) 4 Hare 97.

9.62 There is a further problem with voluntary covenants in that the very fact that the subject matter thereof is not immediately transferred to trustees[1] indicates that the settlor, S, did not have 'a present intention to make an immediate gift'[2] of the subject matter if, indeed, the covenant does not expressly state that the property is to be transferred upon some future date or future event, eg the falling into possession of a reversionary interest owned by S. The covenant is thus 'an announcement of what a man intends to do in the future and is not intended by him as a gift in the present'[3] so as to fall outside the *Strong v Bird* requirement of a present intention to make an immediate gift as laid down in *Re Freeland*[4] and in *Re Innes*[5].

1   And the settlor does not expressly declare that the *covenant* itself is to be held on trust: see para 9.84 below.
2   *Re Freeland* [1952] Ch 110 at 118, per Jenkins LJ.
3   *Re Innes* [1910] 1 Ch 188 at 193, per Parker J.
4   [1952] Ch 110.
5   [1910] 1 Ch 188.

9.63 It may be argued that once the pass has been sold and equity assists a volunteer and perfects an imperfect gift as in *Re Stewart*[1] it is inconsistent for equity to draw back and refrain from assisting a volunteer under an imperfect gift of specific property to be made at a future time (other than the donor's death when testamentary formalities must be observed) once that time has arrived, when the donor's intention continued till death and the donee became his executor. In *Re Innes*[2] Parker J considered it would be 'exceedingly dangerous' if this were the case but his underlying reasoning is that a promise to give in the future is unenforceable, unless given for value, and equity will not assist a volunteer: however, an imperfect immediate gift is unenforceable unless made for value and equity will not assist a volunteer *except* where the donor's intention continued till death and the donee became his executor[3]. Logically the *Strong v Bird* exception should exist in both cases, though in *Re Freeland*[4] the Court of Appeal assumed that the views of Parker J in *Re Innes* represented the law since counsel apparently accepted this. In principle, a voluntary covenant to transfer specific property in the future to trustees should thus fall within *Strong v Bird* (as dramatically extended by *Re Stewart*) if a trustee is appointed an executor of the settlor[5]. However, this should probably be regarded' as extending the extension to the original *Strong v Bird* principle too far.

1   [1908] 2 Ch 251.
2   [1910] 1 Ch 188.
3   *Re Stewart* [1908] 2 Ch 251.
4   [1952] Ch 110.
5   Alternative grounds for supporting this view would be to treat the covenant as manifesting an ever-continuing intent so that when the future time arrived there could then be said to be an intent to make an immediate gift.

DOUBTFUL EXTENSION TO LIFETIME ACQUISITION OF LEGAL TITLE BY TRUSTEE WITHOUT IMPROPRIETY PERFECTING GIFTS

9.64 Indeed, in *Re Ralli's Will Trusts*[1], taking his cue from the extension of *Strong v Bird* principles to acquisition of legal title to imperfectly gifted property by an administrator-donee, Buckley J upheld the fortuitous vesting in T, the sole surviving *trustee of S's voluntary settlement*, of property that was the subject of S's covenant to transfer certain existing and after-acquired property and that was owned by T in his capacity as sole surviving *trustee*[2] *of S's father's will trusts* for S's mother for life, remainder to S and her sister equally. T had been appointed trustee of the latter trusts by a third party some years after his appointment as trustee of S's voluntary settlement.

1   [1964] Ch 288, with clause 7 fully set out in [1963] 3 All ER 940.
2   If there had been another trustee, Y, of the will trusts, Y might need to obtain the directions of the court, trustees holding property jointly and having to act unanimously. Because Y is not a trustee-covenantee of S's voluntary settlement does he not hold the will trust fund on trust for S and her personal representatives, so that he will be liable for breach of trust if he co-operates with T to transfer the assets to T to be held as part of the voluntary settlement? If Y will not co-operate with T, then T cannot be liable to the voluntary settlement beneficiaries. Indeed, if T does not co-operate as co-trustee with Y of the will trusts to transfer the assets to S or her personal representatives will T not be acting in breach of trust?

9.65 Buckley J first held that, pending transfer to the trustees of S's voluntary settlement of property within clause 7 thereof, the effect of clause 8 was that S's existing equitable interest in remainder should in the hands of S (or her personal representatives on her death) be held on the trusts of S's settlement. That was decisive in entitling the beneficiaries there under to equitable interests in half of the actual assets happening to comprise the will trust fund on S's mother's death.

9.66 However, as an alternative ratio, under clause 7 S had covenanted to transfer to the trustees all existing and after-acquired property she owned or would come to own (with specified exceptions) and, because T, her covenantee, had legal title to the actual assets within that covenant which comprised half the trust fund held by T fortuitously as sole surviving trustee of S's father's will trusts, such property automatically became held on the trusts of S's voluntary settlement at her mother's death. Thus, if S were still alive (rather than dying before her mother died in 1961) it was 'indisputable'[1] that she could not claim that T was disentitled from insisting he held on the trusts of her settlement half the assets in the father's fund at the death of her mother because S had 'solemnly covenanted under seal to assign [half] the fund to'[2] T, and her personal representatives could be no better off than she.

1   [1964] Ch 288 at 301.
2   [1964] Ch 288 at 301.

9.67 With respect, *Re Brooks' Settlement Trusts*[1] not cited to Buckley J, makes it clear that S could have claimed that the assets became hers on her mother's death despite her solemn but voluntary covenant. Only the settlor or her duly authorised agent can completely constitute a trust, just as at common law only the donor or his duly authorised agent can make a gift. Thus, in *Re Brooks' Settlement Trusts*, S solemnly covenanted with T in his 1929 voluntary settlement that he would transfer to T anything appointed to him under his father's will trusts. T then fortuitously happened to be trustee of the will trusts when S's mother in 1939 exercised her power of appointment thereunder to appoint £3,517 to S. Although T owned this money as trustee of the will trusts, and so claimed the money would now be held by it as trustee of S's voluntary settlement, Farwell J rejected this, so that S was personally entitled to the £3,517.

1   [1939] Ch 993.

9.68 It follows that the alternative ratio in *Re Ralli's Will Trusts* is based on an erroneous premise, although the decision is fully justifiable on the basis of its first ratio, that clause 8 was an effective valid declaration of S's existing property, which included her half interest in remainder under her father's will trusts. Only if S had expressly or by necessary implication authorised T, holding assets *qua* trustee of another trust for S, to hold those assets qua trustee of S's trust should there be a completely constituted trust of such assets as part of S's trust[1].

1   As in *Re Bowden* [1936] Ch 71 (where the settlor, before becoming a nun, covenanted to settle on trustees what she might inherit under her father's will or intestacy and in her deed expressly authorised the trustees as her agents to receive such inheritance to hold on the trusts, but over 30 years after such receipt sought unsuccessfully to claim the property) and *Re Adlard* [1954] Ch 29 (where the sister-settlors had entered into voluntary covenants to settle after-acquired property and after authorising the trustees of such actual property to transfer it to themselves as trustees of the sister-settlors' trusts, later sought unsuccessfully to claim such property for the themselves).

MISTAKEN PERFECTION OF GIFTS BY EXECUTORS

9.69 If S makes an imperfect gift of property to trustees of his settlement and dies, his intention to make the gift continuing unchanged till his death, and his executor, mistakenly believing himself legally bound to perfect the gift, perfects the gift, Astbury J opined[1] that this would be effective against the beneficiaries entitled under S's will. This seems an extremely doubtful extension of *Strong v Bird*[2] which itself would surely have been decided differently if the debtor had not been appointed executor but had had his debt released by the executor. After all, an executor does not have as much freedom as the deceased had to release debts and perfect gifts since the executor holds the property under fiduciary obligations owed to the beneficiaries under the deceased's will and not as absolute owner like the deceased[3]. Thus, the position is different from that where the donor makes an incomplete gift of property and afterwards *himself,* unintentionally, includes it in a conveyance to the donee when the later conveyance is held to perfect the gift.

1   *Carter v Hungerford* [1917] 1 Ch 260 at 273. Also see *McCathie v McCathie* [1971] NZLR 58 at 63.
2   (1874) LR 18 Eq 315.
3   *Stamp Duties Comr (Queensland) v Livingston* [1965] AC 694, [1964] 3 All ER 692; *Re Diplock* [1948] Ch 465, [1948] 2 All ER 318.

Paragraph 2

9.70 Many cases establish the elementary proposition that just as a gift is binding upon a donor and his personal representatives so a completely constituted trust is binding upon a settlor and his personal representatives, unless at the time of the gift or of constituting the trust a power of revocation was expressly reserved to the donor/settlor.

9.71 Thus in *Re Wale*[1] a settlor executed a voluntary settlement containing a recital that the settlor had transferred certain investments into the names of the trustees (the settlor's two sons) to be held on the trusts thereof. In fact, none of the investments were so transferred but at the date of the settlement some of them, the 'A' investments, were registered in the settlor's name, whilst the 'B' investments were registered in the names of the settlor and the two sons, though held for the settlor absolutely beneficially. The settlement was clearly ineffective as regards the 'A' investments since the settlor had neither declared herself trustee of them nor transferred them to the trustees. However, it was effective as regards the 'B' investments since the settlement amounted to an effective assignment of the settlor's equitable interest in the 'B' investments. Thus, whilst the 'A' investments formed part of the settlor's estate on her death, the 'B' investments could not be claimed by her personal representatives but were fully subject to the trusts of her voluntary settlement.

1   [1956] 3 All ER 280, [1956] 1 WLR 1346; *Jefferys v Jefferys* (1841) Cr & Ph 138.

9.72 Similarly, if a settlor voluntarily covenants with trustees to settle any property to which she might become entitled on her father's death and then knowingly allows this property after her father's death to be transferred to the trustees she will not be able to reclaim this property nor to obtain rectification of the deed so as to contain a power of revocation[1].

1   *Re Bowden* [1936] Ch 71; *Re Adlard* [1954] Ch 29, [1955] 2 All ER 1437; *Paul v Paul* (1882) 20 Ch D 742. Rectification would only be possible if there were clear evidence that a power of revocation had originally been intended to be inserted in the voluntary settlement: *Re Butlin's Settlements Trusts* [1976] Ch 251, [1976] 2 All ER 483. Further see *Racal Group Services Ltd v Ashmore* [1994] STC 416 at 425 and [1995] STC 1151, CA; *Tankel v Tankel* [2002] EWCA Civ 227.

9.73 Once a trust has been completely constituted it matters not that the beneficiaries are volunteers[1] (ie persons not providing consideration in money or money's worth or within marriage consideration). However, where equity's assistance is necessary to constitute a trust as yet incompletely constituted then it is crucial whether or not beneficiaries are volunteers in view of the general maxim, 'Equity will not assist volunteers'[2].

1   *Paul v Paul* (1882) 20 Ch D 742.
2   Contrast *Pullan v Koe* [1913] 1 Ch 9 (consideration) with *Re Plumptre's Marriage Settlement* [1910] 1 Ch 609 (volunteers).

Paragraph 3

Equity will not assist a volunteer

9.74 As Lord Browne-Wilkinson stated in *T Choithram International SA v Pagarani*[1]: 'Although equity will not aid a volunteer, it will not strive officiously to defeat a gift'. A court of equity will not assist a volunteer by requiring a would-be donor to perfect an inchoate intention to confer a bounty. For this reason the maxim is often referred to as 'Equity will not perfect an imperfect gift'[2]. Thus the would-be donor must make a perfect gift to the intended beneficiary (whether inter vivos or by testamentary disposition) or create a completely constituted trust by making a perfect gift to the intended trustees for the intended beneficiaries or by declaring himself trustee of property appropriated for the intended beneficiaries[3].

1   [2001] 2 All ER 492 at 501 applied in *Pennington v Waine* [2002] EWCA Civ 227, [2002] 1 WLR 2075.
2   Certain exceptions exist as seen at paras 9.32–9.68 above.
3   *Milroy v Lord* (1862) 4 De GF & J 264 at 274–275.

9.75 However, the would-be donor/settlor can be specifically compelled to perfect his gift if the intended beneficiary provided valuable consideration[1] (whether in money or money's worth or by marriage) or comes within the scope of marriage consideration: the fact that the promise to make the gift is contained in a deed and so a covenant avails the intended beneficiary nought so far as equity is concerned[2].

1   P. Birks (ed) English Private Law: Vol. II paras 8.29–8.46. In *Milroy v Lord* a settlement was considered as not for value where expressed to be in consideration of one dollar though in *Mountford v Scott* [1975] Ch 258, [1975] 1 All ER 198, the Court of Appeal treated £1 as value to enable specific performance to be ordered. It is insufficient to show 'good consideration' viz natural affection for family or friends or moral obligation. Inadequacy of consideration is no ground for resisting specific performance unless it is 'so gross as of itself to prove fraud or imposition on the part of the purchaser': *Borell v Dann* (1843) 2 Hare 440 at 450.
2   *Re Plumptre's Marriage Settlement* [1910] 1 Ch 609; *Re Brooks' Settlement Trusts* [1939] Ch 993. In circumstances where the settlor intended a trust of the benefit of the covenant (a chose in action) a volunteer may enforce the trust of that property like trusts of other types of property: see para 9.84 below.

9.76 A settlement is in consideration of marriage if made before and in consideration of marriage or if agreed to be made before and in consideration of marriage and actually executed after the marriage[1]. Within the scope of marriage consideration are the parties, their children, and more remote issue[2]. Early cases allowing children of a former marriage or a possible later marriage or illegitimate children to be within the scope of marriage consideration can now, it seems, only be supported on the basis that such children's interests were so closely interwoven with the interests of the children of the marriage that the latter could benefit only on terms allowing the former to benefit[3].

¹ *Re Holland* [1902] 2 Ch 360; *Hill v Gomme* (1839) 5 My & Cr 250 at 254; *De Mestre v West* [1891] AC 264.
² *A-G v Jacobs-Smith* [1895] 2 QB 341; *Re Cook's Settlement Trusts* [1965] Ch 902, [1964] 3 All ER 898.
³ *Mackie v Herbertson* (1884) 9 App Cas 303 at 337; *De Mestre v West* [1891] AC 264 at 270; *A-G v Jacobs-Smith* [1895] 2 QB 341; *Rennell v IRC* [1962] Ch 329 at 341; affd sub nom *IRC v Rennell* [1964] AC 173, [1963] 1 All ER 803; *Re Cook's Settlement Trusts* [1965] Ch 902 at 914. If of full capacity, such children should be made parties and covenantees so as to be able to enforce their rights at common law on *Cannon v Hartley* principles [1949] Ch 213, [1949] 1 All ER 50, para 9.83 below.

9.77 Where an intended beneficiary who has provided consideration or is within a marriage consideration does enforce a contract or covenant to create a trust of certain property this may enure for the benefit of volunteers. Thus, if someone within a marriage consideration and having a life interest sues to have covenanted property brought into the settlement, the court will order this and will not exclude volunteers taking under the settlement when the life interest determines[1]. But for this the volunteers would have been unable to claim any of the covenanted property as *Re Plumptre's Marriage Settlement* shows[2], because 'that which ought to be done is only treated as done in favour of some person entitled to enforce the contract as against the person liable to perform it'.

¹ *Davenport v Bishopp* (1843) 2 Y & C Ch Cas 451; affd (1846) 1 Ph 698; *Re D'Angibau* (1880) 15 Ch D 228 at 242, CA.
² [1910] 1 Ch 609 at 619; *Re Cook's Settlement Trusts* [1965] Ch 902, [1964] 3 All ER 898.

9.78 Here, a settlement in consideration of marriage contained the usual covenant by husband and wife with the trustees for the settlement of after-acquired property of the wife. The husband subsequently gave some stocks to the wife and, after her death without issue, the question arose whether the next of kin of the wife (who took the settled fund in default of issue) could call upon the trustees to enforce the covenant against the wife's personal representative, who happened to be the husband. Eve J held that since the next of kin were volunteers and since there was neither a completely constituted trust of the stocks that were the subject matter of the covenant, nor of the benefit of the covenant itself the next of kin's claim failed.

9.79 By way of contrast, in a similar situation, but where a wife did not settle £285 pursuant to an after-acquired property covenant in her marriage settlement but died leaving nine children, Swinfen-Eady J held[1] that, since the children were within the marriage consideration, the moment the wife received the £285 it was specifically bound by the covenant enforceable in the children's favour[2]. Thus, part of the £285 paid by the wife to the husband and invested by him in bearer bonds deposited with his bank could be traced and had to be transferred to the settlement trustees, whose claim at law for damages for breach of the covenant had long since been statute-barred, more than 30 years having elapsed since the breach of covenant.

1   *Pullan v Koe* [1913] 1 Ch 9.
2   Where a covenant is specifically enforceable in B's favour then at B's behest (but not volunteers of an incompletely constituted trust) 'equity looks on as done that which ought to be done': *Re Anstis* (1886) 31 Ch D 596 at 605, per Lindley LJ, though if B does have the trust completely constituted then volunteers will benefit: *Davenport v Bishopp* (1843) 2 Y & C Ch Cas 451.

9.80 It should be noted that a covenant merely to pay a capital sum of money not specifically earmarked (such as in a safety deposit box or a bank deposit account or received under someone's will) does not attract the equitable remedy of specific performance for equity to look on that as done which ought to be done and treat the money as subject to trusts. Thus in *Stone v Stone*[1] the beneficiaries, though purchasers and not volunteers, were without remedy when the action at law on a covenant to settle £1,000 had become barred under the Statute of Limitations. Similarly, in *MacJordan Construction Ltd v Brookmount Erostin Ltd*[2] the beneficiary-contractor under a contract requiring the employer to set up a retention trust fund was without a proprietary remedy when the employer became insolvent without having set aside out of money in its bank account the requisite amount required for the retention trust fund. The contractor would, however, have had an equitable proprietary interest if the employer's obligation had related to specified funds payable and paid to it by a third party financier[3].

1   (1869) 5 Ch App 74; cf *Beswick v Beswick* [1968] AC 58, [1967] 2 All ER 1197.
2   [1992] BCLC 350, CA endorsed by PC in *Re Goldcorp Exchange Ltd* [1995] 1 AC 74, [1994] 2 All ER 806.
3   *Pullan v Koe* [1913] 1 Ch 9; *Re Lind* [1915] 2 Ch 345, CA; *Palette Shoes Pty Ltd v Krohn* (1937) 58 CLR 1 at 26–27; *Associated Alloys Pty Ltd v ACN 001 452 106 Pty Ltd* (2000) 202 CLR 588.

Possible impact of Contracts (Rights of Third Parties) Act 1999 on post 10 May 2000 contracts or covenants to settle property

9.81 Section 1 of the Act which 'does not affect any right or remedy of a third party that exists apart from this Act' provides that 'a person who is not a party to a contract ("a third party") may in his own right enforce a term of the contract if (a) the contract expressly provides that he may or (b) the term purports to confer a benefit on him' unless 'on a proper construction of the contract it appears that the parties did not intend the term to be enforceable by the third party.' Section 7 (3) assumes that section 1 covers not just actions relating to a simple contract but actions relating to a specialty, a term covering agreements in deeds, whether gratuitous or for value.By s 1(5) 'there shall be available to the third party any remedy that would have been available to him in an action for breach of contract if he had been a party to the contract (and the rules relating to damages, injunctions, specific performance and other relief shall apply accordingly).' It follows that, since a volunteer-beneficiary who is actually a party to a deed can only recover damages for his own loss[1]

215

and not obtain specific performance for the benefit of the trust fund, a volunteer-beneficiary-third-party cannot obtain specific performance; but if the parties to the deed were not volunteers, as in the case of settlements in consideration of marriage, so that they could obtain specific performance, then the third parties will similarly be able to obtain specific performance, unless on a proper construction it appears that the parties did not intend the relevant term to be enforceable by the third parties.

[1]   *Cannon v Hartley* [1949] Ch 213.

9.82 It seems likely that the courts will hold that, in properly construing marriage settlements, the traditional intention of the parties is for the covenant to settle after-acquired property of the spouses to be enforceable by the spouses and their issue, but not by the next-of-kin beneficiaries entitled in default of issue and who are intended only to benefit to the extent of property actually transferred to the trustees. Thus the 1999 Act is probably of no assistance to such default beneficiaries but, in drafting modern settlements, it should be made clear that such beneficiaries are not to have enforcement rights if this position is desired.

Equity will not frustrate a volunteer suing at law

9.83 Assuming that fraud, mistake, undue influence or oppressive uncon-scionable conduct[1] is not involved, equity will not intervene to injunct a volunteer from suing at common law for damages for breach of covenant. Thus in *Cannon v Hartley*[2] a volunteer, who was a party to a settlement deed and covenantee thereunder, was held entitled to recover full damages at common law for her loss from breach of the covenant with her, Romer J stating[3]:

> 'The plaintiff, although a volunteer, is not only a party to the deed but is also a direct covenantee under the very covenant upon which she is suing. She does not require the assistance of the court to enforce the covenant for she has a legal right to enforce it. She is not asking for equitable relief but for damages at common law for breach of covenant.'

[1]   See Meagher, Gummow and Lehane *Equity: Doctrines and Remedies*, (4th edn) Part IV.
[2]   [1949] Ch 213, [1949] 1 All ER 50. See also *Milroy v Lord* (1862) 4 De GF & J 264 at 278, per Turner LJ and *Davenport v Bishopp* (1843) 2 Y & C Ch Cas 451 at 460, per Knight-Bruce VC.
[3]   [1949] Ch 213 at 223.

9.84 To succeed at common law and obtain damages for his own loss, the volunteer, if not being a covenantee under a deed poll, had to be a party to the inter partes deed[1] as well as a covenantee since Law of Property Act 1925, s 56, allowing non-parties to sue if covenantees, had been treated as covering only land or other real property[2]. It follows that B cannot sue at common law where S in a deed with T promised T that S would transfer to T personal property to be held on trust for B. However, for deeds after 10 May 2000, B, under the Contracts (Rights of Thirds Parties) Act 1999, will have the same remedies as if he had been a party to the deed unless, on a proper construction, it appears that the parties did not intend the relevant term (eg relating to the settlor's after-acquired property from specified sources) to be enforceable by B[3]. Traditionally, in creating a voluntary settlement with an after-acquired property covenant in favour of the trustee, the settlor did not intend any beneficiary to be able to enforce the covenant[4], and it seems likely that the courts will follow such traditional approach and not assist beneficiaries. Clearly, nowadays the draftsman should expressly state that the beneficiaries are not to have enforcement rights if this is the desired position.

1   *Lord Southampton v Brown* (1827) 6 B & C 718; *Gardner v Lachlan* (1836) 8 Sim 123.
2   *Beswick v Beswick* [1968] AC 58, at 76, 81, 87, 94, and 105. HL a 3 to 2 majority view.
3   See Contracts (Rights of Third Parties) Act 1999 outlined at paras 9.81 and 9.121.
4   See *Re Pryce* [1917] 1 Ch 234; *Re Kay's Settlement Trusts* [1939] Ch 329; *Re Cook's Settlement Trusts* [1965] Ch 902; and para 9.104 below.

Completely constituted trusts of the benefit of contracts or covenants

9.85   Just as money, shares or land may be the subject matter of a trust so may choses in action like a debt or the benefit of a contract or covenant to transfer specific shares or land[1] or of a contract or covenant to transfer property, if any, materialising under a will or under the exercise of a power of appointment[2].

1   *Gregory v Williams* (1817) 3 Mer 582; *Les Affréteurs Réunis SA v Leopold Walford (London) Ltd* [1919] AC 801; *Re D'Angibau* (1880) 15 Ch D 228; *Re Empress Engineering Co* (1880) 16 Ch D 125; *Lloyd's v Harper* (1880) 16 Ch D 290; *Re Flavell* (1883) 25 Ch D 89; *Gandy v Gandy* (1885) 30 Ch D 57; *Re Schebsman* [1944] Ch 83.
2   'A chose in action is no less a chose in action because it is not immediately recoverable by action', per Lord Oliver in *Kwok Chi Leung Karl v Commissioner of Estate Duty* [1988] 1 WLR 1035 at 1040, applied in *Re Landau* [1997] 3 All ER 322 at 328. Thus, a covenant by C to transfer to T whatever C inherits from D or whatever is appointed to C by D can be held by T on trust for B, so that after D's death or an appointment by D, T will be entitled to hold the inherited or appointed property for B, and B can enforce this.

CONTRACTS

9.86   The common law position before the Contracts (Rights of Third Parties) Act 1999 was that where contracts are concerned if A promises B for value that A will pay money or transfer property to C there is a perfectly valid contract between A and B but C cannot sue on the contract since he is not a party to the contract and has not provided the consideration therefor[1]. However, if B at the time of making the contract was acting as trustee for C or intended to hold the benefit of the contract as trustee for C, or later declares himself trustee thereof for C, then from the time of the contract or the subsequent declaration of trust, C, with equity's assistance (though a volunteer) because he is a beneficiary[2], will be able to enforce the contract, joining B as co-defendant, if B is not prepared to be plaintiff, and C will obtain specific performance or full damages as appropriate to the subject matter of the contract[3]. If a trust exists then C as a beneficiary is much better off than under the common law contractual position.

1   *Tweddle v Atkinson* (1861) 1 B & S 393; *Dunlop Pneumatic Tyre Co Ltd v Selfridge & Co Ltd* [1915] AC 847; *Scruttons Ltd v Midland Silicones Ltd* [1962] AC 446, [1962] 1 All ER 1, HL.

2   Since there is a completely constituted trust it is immaterial that he is a volunteer.
3   *Affréteurs Réunis SA v Leopold Walford (London) Ltd* [1919] AC 801; *Lloyd's v Harper*
     (1880) 16 Ch D 290; *Vandepitte v Preferred Accident Insurance Corpn of New York*
     [1933] AC 70 at 79, PC.

9.87 At common law where the contract between A and B was expressed to
be for C's benefit C has no rights and if B sues for damages for breach the
general rule[1] is that B can only secure nominal damages, for a plaintiff can
only receive substantial damages (as in tort) to the extent that he suffers
damage[2]. However, in an appropriate case B may be able to obtain a decree of
specific performance, so obtaining full benefits for C as in *Beswick v
Beswick*[3], all the more so where damages would be inadequate. Of course, if A
carries out the contract and benefits C then B cannot complain and C is
absolutely entitled to do as he wishes with the money or property transferred
to him by A so long as not intended to be a nominee for B[4].

1   Certain statutory exceptions exist (eg Married Women's Property Act 1882, s 11; Road
     Traffic Act 1972, s 148(4); Solicitors Act 1974, s 37) and there is a general common law
     exception: 'In a commercial contract concerning goods where it is in the contemplation of
     the parties that the proprietary interests in the goods may be transferred from one owner to
     another after the contract has been entered into and before the breach which causes loss or
     damage to the goods, an original party to the contract, if such be the intention of the
     parties, is to be treated in law as having entered into the contract for the benefit of all
     persons who have or may acquire an interest in the goods before they are lost or damaged
     and is entitled to recover by way of damages for breach of contract the actual loss
     sustained by those for whose benefit the contract is entered into': *The Albazero* [1976]
     3 All ER 129 at 137, per Lord Diplock. For an extension of this to building contracts see
     Linden Gardens Trust Ltd v Lenesta Sludge Disposals Ltd [1994] 1 AC 85 at 114–
     115, HL and *Darlington Borough Council v Wiltshier Northern Ltd* [1995] 1 WLR
     68, CA. There may also be an exception where B may claim full damages where A
     contracted with B to discharge a debt owed to C by B and, perhaps, where B has actually
     performed in C's favour that (or part of that) which A failed to perform *Coulls v Bagot's
     Executor Co Ltd* (1967) 119 CLR 460 at 501–502, per Windeyer J; (1948) 21 Aust LJ 424
     (Dr J.G. Starke); *Beswick v Beswick* [1968] AC 58 at 88, per Lord Pearce.
2   *West v Houghton* (1879) 4 CPD 197; *Beswick v Beswick* [1968] AC 58, [1967] 2 All ER
     1197; *The Albazero* [1977] AC 774, [1976] 3 All ER 129, HL; *Woodar Investment
     Developments Ltd v Wimpey Construction UK Ltd* [1980] 1 All ER 571, [1980] 1 WLR
     277, HL disapproving the reasoning of Lord Denning MR in *Jackson v Horizon
     Holidays Ltd* [1975] 3 All ER 92, [1975] 1 WLR 1468, CA; where Lord Denning MR
     based himself on a dictum of Lush LJ in *Lloyd's v Harper* ignoring the fact that Lush LJ (as
     pointed out by Dillon LJ in *Darlington Borough Council v Wiltshier Northern Ltd* [1995]
     1 WLR 68 at 73) was concerned with a completely constituted trust of a contract held by
     A on trust for B when he said, 'I consider it to be an established rule of law that where a
     contract is made with A for the benefit of B, A can sue on the contract for the benefit of B
     and recover all that B could have recovered if the contract had been made with B himself'.
3   [1968] AC 58, [1967] 2 All ER 1197.
4   *Re Schebsman* [1943] Ch 366, [1943] 2 All ER 387; affd [1944] Ch 83, [1943] 2 All ER
     768; *Re Stapleton-Bretherton* [1941] Ch 482; *Re Miller's Agreement* [1947] Ch 615,
     [1947] 2 All ER 78; *Beswick v Beswick* [1968] AC 58 at 71, per Lord Reid.

9.88 To circumvent the circumscribed common law contractual position
many attempts have been made on C's behalf to claim that B holds the benefit
of the contract on trust for C. Originally, the courts were quite sympathetic to
such claims, sometimes being prepared to find that an intention to benefit C
sufficed to show an intention to create a trust, just as originally the courts
were quite willing to find that precatory words sufficed to show an intention
to create a trust.

9.89 The position then developed that C has a heavy onus to discharge in proving that B intended to make himself a trustee of the benefit of the contract for C for it is became crystal clear that 'An intention to provide benefits for someone else and to pay for them does not in itself give rise to a trusteeship'[1]. As du Parcq LJ said in *Re Schebsman*[2], 'It is true that by the use possibly of unguarded language a person may create a trust ... but unless an intention to create a trust is clearly to be collected from the language used and the circumstances of the case I think the court ought not to be astute to discover indications of such an intention.' In *Re Webb Farwell* J said[3], 'It is for a person to make clear by the language used that he is constituting himself a trustee and the absence of any clear words to that effect makes it difficult to establish a trust.' 'The intention to constitute the trust must be affirmatively proved.'[4]

1   *Green v Russell* [1959] 2 QB 226 at 231, per Romer LJ.
2   [1944] Ch 83 at 104; (1944) 7 MLR 123 (G.L. Williams).
3   [1941] Ch 225, [1941] 1 All ER 321.
4   *West v Houghton* (1879) 4 CPD 197 at 203; *Vandepitte v Preferred Accident Insurance Corpn of New York* [1933] AC 70 at 79–80, PC per Lord Wright.

9.90 The crux of the matter is that one must not 'disregard the dividing line between the case of a trust and the simple case of a contract made between two persons for the benefit of a third party'[1]. If an express or implied intention on B's behalf to constitute himself a trustee cannot be found then the court cannot impose a constructive trusteeship in order to do 'justice' and benefit C: a constructive trust[2] cannot be used as a means of conferring rights on C where B has merely failed to declare a trust for C in proper fashion, otherwise all imperfect express trusts would take effect as constructive trusts!

1   *Re Schebsman* [1944] Ch 83 at 84, per Lord Greene MR.
2   See Article 35 below. A constructive test would only be imposed to prevent a person taking an advantage for himself where to do so would be inequitable or unconscionable.

9.91 Most of the cases concern policies of assurance[1] or other arrangements taking effect on death, eg under partnership deeds or company schemes[2]. In respect of policies two points emerge as stated by Plowman J[3]: 'First that the mere fact that [B] takes out a policy which is expressed to be for the benefit of [C] or on behalf of [C] does not constitute a trust for [C]; second that the mere fact that the policy provides that policy moneys are to be payable to [C] does not create a trust in favour of [C]'. As Farwell J stated in *Re Webb*[4]:

> 'The whole matter rests entirely upon the true construction of the policy in question. I think that one must take it that unless there is in the policy something which does establish reasonably clearly that the assured was in fact constituting, and intending to constitute, himself a trustee for the third party of the assurance moneys, the third party is not and the personal representatives of the assured are, entitled to the money payable'.

1   *Re Webb* [1941] Ch 225, [1941] 1 All ER 321 (reviewing earlier cases); *Re Foster's Policy* [1966] 1 All ER 432, [166] 1 WLR 222.
2   *Re Flavell* (1883) 25 Ch D 89; *Re Schebsman* [1944] Ch 83, [1943] 2 All ER 768; *Re Miller's Agreement* [1947] Ch 615, [1947] 2 All ER 78.
3   *Re Foster's Policy* [1966] 1 All ER 432 at 436.

4   [1941] Ch 225 at 234. However, for varying reasons the majority of the Australian High
     Court in *Trident General Insurance Co Ltd v McNeice Bros Pty Ltd* (1988) 165 CLR 107,
     80 ALR 574 (Aust HC) held that third party beneficiaries under contracts of insurance
     could, even apart from special statutory provision, sue the promisor directly. Further see
     Re Australian Elizabethan Theatre Trust (1991) FCR 491 at 503.

9.92 The fact that rights under the policy can be varied without the consent
of the third party does not mean that no trust can exist[1]: after all, a
beneficiary can have an interest that is defeasible upon revocation of the trust
or upon the exercise of a power of appointment in someone else's favour.
Indeed the subject-matter of a trust may be a contract inherently variable by B
if in his absolute unfettered discretion a variation is in the best interests of C.
A trust can still exist where powers of surrender or agreeing to modification
are vested in the alleged trustee so as to be exercisable only in the third party's
best interests[2]. However, if surrender moneys can be held by the alleged
trustee for his own benefit[3] and not for the third party this will negative any
trust, at least until a time arises when the alleged trustee ceases to be entitled
to hold surrender moneys or other benefits for himself alone[4].

1   Cf *Re Flavell* (1883) 25 Ch D 89; *Re Webb* [1941] Ch 225, [1941] 1 All ER 321.
2   *Re Webb* [1941] Ch 225, [1941] 1 All ER 321.
3   *Re Sinclair's Life Policy* [1938] Ch 799, [1938] 3 All ER 124; *Re Schebsman* [1944] Ch 83,
     [1943] 2 All ER 768, CA.
4   *Re Foster's Policy* [1966] 1 All ER 432, [1966] 1 WLR 222; *Re Webb* [1941] Ch 225,
     [1941] 1 All ER 321.

9.93 Where B is deceased and no trust of the benefit of his contract with A
exists his personal representative (who may happen to be the third party, C, in
question) may be able to obtain an order qua B's representative against A
compelling A to perform the obligation in favour of C as happened in *Beswick
v Beswick*[1], so a finding of no trust need not necessarily be fatal to C.

1   [1968] AC 58, [1967] 2 All ER 1197.

VOLUNTARY COVENANTS

9.94 If A voluntarily covenants (ie promises in a deed) with B to pay money
or transfer property to B for the benefit of C then C cannot have any rights[1]
(other than any conferred by the Contracts (Rights of Third Parties)
Act 1999[2]) unless he can show that A intended B to hold property on trust for
C and that this property is vested in B on trust for C. Assuming there is shown
to be an intent to create a trust for C, there is no problem when the subject
matter of the covenant is actually transferred to B[3]. If it has not yet been
transferred, and if as existing property it is not subject to an express
declaration of trust until it or its subject matter is actually transferred[4], then C
has no rights (other than any conferred by the above 1999 Act) unless the
covenant itself is the subject matter of the trust, so the question arises whether
A intended to create a trust *of the covenant* for C or intended only to create a
trust *of the subject matter of the covenant* if or when transferred to B.

1   He is neither a party nor a convenantee nor has he provided any consideration.
2   See para 9.81 above.

220

3   A may do this voluntarily or someone within a marriage consideration may enforce it, so
    indirectly benefiting the volunteer.
4   *Re Ralli's Will Trusts* [1964] Ch 288, [1963] 3 All ER 940. If the subject matter is a spes it
    may not be the subject matter of an effective declaration of trust (or assignment): *Re
    Ellenborough* [1903] 1 Ch 697; *Williams v IRC* [1965] NZLR 395; see para 9.102 below.

9.95   The crux of the matter for C's claims is thus *intention to create a trust* of
the benefit of the voluntary covenant just as in the cases of alleged trusts of the
benefit of contracts. Originally, the courts were quite sympathetic to such
claims[1] just as originally they were quite ready to find an intention to create a
trust in precatory words or situations[2]. Alternatively, the courts were prepared
to assume that, even if no completely constituted trusts of the covenant
existed, B could be left to pursue his common law remedy for damages for
breach of covenant[3] without considering whether such damages should be,
nominal or otherwise, held for C or for A under a resulting trust[4]. Indeed, in
Milroy v Lord[5] the Court of Appeal, if B were not willing to pursue his
common law remedy, was prepared to insert in its decree a direction that C be
at liberty to use B's name in the common law action overlooking that this
would be equity assisting a volunteer where the court had already held that no
completely constituted trust existed. The possibility of B obtaining common
law damages and thus *himself* constituting A's trusts will be examined after the
question of completely constituted trusts of the benefit of covenants has been
investigated.

1   *Williamson v Codrington* (1750) 1 Ves Sen 511. *Cox v Barnard* (1850) 8 Hare 310;
    Watson v Parker (1843) 6 Beav 283; *Fletcher v Fletcher* (1844) 4 Hare 67.
2   See para 8.214 above.
3   *Davenport v Bishopp* (1843) 2 Y & C Ch Cas 451 at 460, per Knight-Bruce V-C; *Milroy v
    Lord* (1862) 4 De GF & J 264 at 278, per Turner LJ: *Re Flavell* (1883) 25 Ch D 89 at 99,
    per North J; *Re Plumptre's Marriage Settlement* [1910] 1 Ch 609, where, though holding
    that no completely constituted trust existed to assist volunteer next of kin, Eve J
    investigated without demur the trustees' claim for common law damages, though finding it
    statute-barred.
4   See para 9.114 below.
5   (1862) 4 De GF & J 264.

9.96   If A merely covenants with X that he will transfer £20,000 to B on trust
for C it is clear that A does not intend X to be trustee of the covenant so that
A is liable at law only to X or X's personal representative if he fails to transfer
the money[1].

1   *Colyear v Countess of Mulgrave* (1836) 2 Keen 81.

9.97   In *Fletcher v Fletcher*[1] essentially, A covenanted in a voluntary deed with
B that if his illegitimate sons C1 and C2 or either of them should survive him
his personal representatives should within 12 months of his death pay
£60,000 to B upon trust for C1 and C2 or such of them as should attain 21. A
retained possession of the deed and the first B heard of the deed was after A's
death. B then refused to act as trustee or sue A's executors or hold any money
on trust for C1, the survivor of C1 and C2. Wigram VC held the voluntary
deed was effective and that the executors should pay the £60,000 to C1[2] on
the footing that A intended to create a completely constituted trust of the
covenant, a debt being a perfect chose in action capable of being the subject

matter of a trust. In the circumstances involving secrecy and the fact that the whole deed would be futile unless it was really intended to confer equitable rights on the only possible beneficiaries C1 and C2, it is quite understandable that Wigram VC treated the deed as if it had had expressly inserted therein some clause such as 'to the intent that the benefit of this covenant shall be held by B upon trust'.

1   (1844) 4 Hare 67.
2   This avoided circuity of actions.

9.98   Wigram VC stated[1]:

'I cannot, I admit, do anything to perfect the liability of the author of the trust if it is not already perfect. The covenant, however, is already perfect. The covenantor is liable at law, and the court is not called upon to do any action to perfect it. One question made in argument has been whether there can be a trust of a covenant the benefit of which shall belong to a third party but I cannot think there is any difficulty in that ... [citing *Clough v Lambert*[2]]. Where the transaction is of such a nature that there is no doubt of the intention of A, while dealing with his own property to constitute B a trustee for C and B has accepted the trust may not C be in a position to compel B to enforce the legal right which the trust deed confers upon him? If the trustees have in this case accepted the trust I think the decision in *Clough v Lambert*[3] applies [allowing C to succeed]; and if they have not accepted the trust I scarcely think that fact can make a difference. It is an extraordinary proposition that nothing being wanted to perfect the liability of the estate to pay the debt, the plaintiff has no right in equity to obtain the benefit of the trust ... The testator has bound himself absolutely. There is a debt created and existing. I give no assistance against the testator. I only deal with him as he has dealt by himself and, if in such a case the trustee will not sue without the sanction of the court I think it is right to allow the cestui que trust to sue for himself, in the name of the trustee, either at law, or in this court, as the case may require. The rights of the parties cannot depend on mere accident or caprice.'

1   *Fletcher v Fletcher* (1844) 4 Hare 67 at 74.
2   (1839) 10 Sim 174.
3   (1839) 10 Sim 174.

9.99   The case may be invoked as authority for the broad proposition that a covenant to create a money debt of a sum certain, even though payable on a future uncertain date, will always be the subject of a completely constituted trust or with the narrow proviso that this is only if the settlor/covenantor intended to create a trust of the covenant rather than a trust of the moneys if or when transferred. This narrower proposition is clearly to be preferred in principle with its emphasis on intention rather than the nature of the subject matter of the covenant.

9.101   Indeed, covenants to transfer other property such as specific shares or land create choses in action similar to debts (though requiring straightforward quantification) and, whilst some cases concerning such covenants have been held to be instances of completely constituted trusts of the covenant[1], other cases concerning such covenants have been held not to be instances of completely constituted trusts of the covenant[2]. Even a covenant for further assurance has been held to create a debt so that there was a completely constituted trust of such covenant[3]. However, it has been suggested[4] that a covenant to settle after-acquired property is not a chose in action capable of being the subject matter of a trust just as future property or a spes cannot be the subject of a trust or of an assignment.

1   *Williamson v Codrington* (1750) 1 Ves Sen 511; *Cox v Barnard* (1850) 8 Hare 310.
2   *Green v Paterson* (1886) 32 Ch D 95; *Re D'Angibau* (1880) 15 Ch D 228.
3   *Cox v Barnard* (1850) 8 Hare 310 at 312, per Knight-Bruce VC.
4   W.A. Lee (1969) 85 LQR 213 based on *Re Cook's Settlement Trusts* [1965] Ch 902, [1964] 3 All ER 898.

9.102 At law, an assignment of future property (ie an expectancy or hope of receiving property in the future[1] such as under someone's will or intestacy or future book-debts to arise in a business or future royalties or future income from a particular source) is void since a man cannot assign what he does not have and he only has existing property[2]. Equity, however, where the assignment was for value will treat the assignment as a contract to assign the property when received, if received, and will compel the assignor to transfer the property received[3]: if no value was given the assignment is wholly inoperative[4]. A trust must be of existing property and not future property, so, just as an assignment of future property to trustees is void at law and inoperative in equity unless for value, a declaration of trust by A that he holds future property on trust for C is inoperative unless for value[5]. If A *contracts* for value to assign future property when received, if received, equity will enforce such obligation and common law damages can be claimed for breach of contract[6]. If A *covenants* to assign future property when received, if received, then equity will not enforce such obligation in favour of volunteers, but only in favour of someone who provided value or is within marriage consideration provided for the marriage settlement containing such covenant to transfer after-acquired property[7]. However, a volunteer who is a covenantee can obtain full damages at common law under a deed poll or, if also a party, under a deed inter partes, so if A covenants to assign to a volunteer, B, any property A may acquire on A's father's death under the will or intestacy of such father, B may obtain full damages if the covenant is broken[8].

1   Distinguish a present existing property right, eg a contingent equitable interest in remainder under a trust.
2   *Robinson v Macdonnell* (1816) 5 M & S 228 at 236; *Holroyd v Marshall* (1862) 10 HL Cas 191 at 220; *Re Tilt* (1896) 74 LT 163.
3   The assignee's equitable interest under a specifically enforceable contract attaches to the property on the assignor acquiring it: *Holroyd v Marshall* (1862) 10 HL Cas 191.
4   *Re Tilt* (1896) 74 LT 163; *Re Ellenborough* [1903] 1 Ch 697.
5   *Williams v IRC* [1965] NZLR 395.
6   *Re Parkin* [1892] 3 Ch 510; *Re Burton's Settlements* [1955] Ch 82, [1954] 3 All ER 193; *Re Ellenborough* [1903] 1 Ch 697; *Re Lind* [1915] 2 Ch 345.
7   *Re Brooks' Settlement Trusts* [1939] Ch 993; *Re Ellenborough* [1903] 1 Ch 697.
8   *Cannon v Hartley* [1949] Ch 213, [1949] 1 All ER 50.

9.103 Since there is a presently existing covenant in favour of B, vesting rights in B, it seems B may himself subsequently declare a trust of the after-acquired property covenant in favour of C. Thus, there seems no reason in principle why A, when entering into the after-acquired property covenant with B, cannot intentionally create a completely constituted trust of the benefit of the covenant with B in favour of C, eg 'I, A, hereby covenant to assign to B any property that I may subsequently acquire under the will or intestacy of my father, F, now aged 70 years, to the intent that B shall immediately hold the benefit of this present covenant on trust for C absolutely'. It will then be immaterial that C is a volunteer since the trust is completely constituted. Indeed, in *Davenport v Bishopp*[1] Knight-Bruce VC indicated there could be a completely constituted trust of a covenant to settle after-acquired property. Moreover, in *Lloyd's v Harper*[2] the Court of Appeal held there was a trust of the benefit of a promise to pay an uncertain amount on an uncertain future date, which is hardly different from a promise to assign an expectancy, and in *Royal Exchange Assurance v Hope*[3] Tomlin J recognised a trust of a promise to pay a sum of money arising only on a person's death before a certain date which might or might not occur. Thus, it would seem that a covenant to settle after-acquired property or an analogous covenant can itself be the subject matter of a completely constituted trust[4]. After all, 'a chose in action is no less a chose in action because it is not immediately recoverable by action'[5]. In the case of such covenants concerning future property it seems sensible to presume rebuttably that the settlor intended not to create a trust of the covenant but only a trust of the property after it had materialised and had been transferred to the trustees.

[1]   (1843) 2 Y & C Ch Cas 451 at 460.
[2]   (1880) 16 Ch D 290.
[3]   [1928] Ch 179, CA.
[4]   Further see (1976) 92 LQR 427 (Meagher and Lehane) though not dealing with the resulting trust difficulty where the covenantee sues the settlor; (1975) 91 LQR 236 (Barton).
[5]   Per Lord Oliver in *Kwok Chi Leung Kaul v Commissioner of Estate Duty* [1988] 1 WLR 1035 at 1040 applied in *Re Landau* [1997] 3 All ER 322 at 328.

9.104 In *Re Plumptre's Marriage Settlement*[1], *Re Pryce*[2], *Re Kay's Settlement*[3] and *Re Cook's Settlement Trusts*[4] particular covenants to settle after-acquired property or analogous covenants were treated as not themselves the subject matter of a completely constituted trust, so that volunteers had no rights to enforce the covenants against the settlors once the settlors had acquired the property, the subject matter of the covenants.

[1]   [1910] 1 Ch 609.
[2]   [1917] 1 Ch 234.
[3]   [1939] Ch 329, [1939] 1 All ER 245.
[4]   [1965] Ch 902, [1964] 3 All ER 898.

9.105 The first two cases concerned marriage settlements where there were no issue so that in default the next of kin, who were volunteers, were entitled to the settled property, and where the settlor had not carried out his obligations under the usual after-acquired property covenant to settle such property on the trusts of the settlement. In both cases[1] Eve J treated the volunteer next of kin as interested only in a voluntary executory contract to create a trust as distinct from being interested under a complete voluntary trust of a covenant such as existed in *Fletcher v Fletcher*[2]. It would seem this was because the settlor did not intend to create a trust of the covenant so as to confer immediate rights on the next of kin (as well as the issue) but only intended to create a trust of the property, the subject matter of the covenant, if or when, having acquired it, he actually transferred it to the trustees. Thus, only at that future time would the next of kin have equitable rights, though in the interval the issue, if any, would be able to enforce the covenant as being within the marriage consideration, but not the next of kin since they were mere volunteers.

1   Particularly see *Re Plumptre's Marriage Settlement* [1910] 1 Ch 609 at 618 and [1917] 1 Ch 234 at 241.
2   (1844) 4 Hare 67.

9.106 In *Re Kay's Settlement*[1] a voluntary settlement executed by a spinster contained a covenant in the usual form to settle after-acquired property. Six years later she married: she then had three children. Having become entitled to property within the scope of the covenant she refused to settle it. The trustees applied to the court for directions. Counsel for the volunteer children began by submitting that the children were not interested only in a voluntary executory agreement to settle the after-acquired property but under a completely constituted trust. However, he then conceded despite this[2] that the trustees could not obtain an order in equity for specific performance of the covenant and so concentrated on submitting that they could be left to their remedy of damages at common law for breach of the after-acquired property covenant and the settlor's implied covenant for further assurance. Not surprisingly, Simonds J treated the volunteer children as interested only in a voluntary executory agreement to settle the after-acquired property: the settlor's obligation lay in an unenforceable voluntary covenant and not under any trust[3].

1   [1939] Ch 329, [1939] 1 All ER 245.
2   [1939] Ch 329 and 339. An intent to confer immediate equitable rights when they are born on children, who are volunteers and have no other rights, is more likely than an intent to confer immediate equitable rights on next of kin, who are volunteers as in *Re Pryce* when the issue, if any, had rights as being within the marriage consideration.
3   [1939] Ch 329 at 342. In context it would seem the settlor did not intend her children to have enforceable rights to after-acquired property.

9.107 Finally, in *Re Cook's Settlement Trusts*[1] Sir Herbert, as life tenant, and his son Sir Francis, as remainderman, for value agreed that certain settled property (including a Rembrandt) should become Sir Francis' absolutely subject to Sir Francis resettling some of the property (not the Rembrandt) and covenanting with the trustees of the resettlement that, in case any of certain pictures (including the Rembrandt) should be sold in Sir Francis' lifetime, the net proceeds of sale should be paid over to the resettlement trustees on the resettlement trusts in favour of Sir Francis' children, who were volunteers. The resettlement was executed. Later Sir Francis gave the Rembrandt to his third wife who desired to sell it. The trustees took out a summons to determine their obligations upon any such sale.

1   [1965] Ch 902, [1964] 3 All ER 898.

9.108 In a somewhat elliptical judgment Buckley J stated[1]:

'Counsel [for Sir Francis] submits that the covenant was a voluntary and executory contract to make a settlement in a future event ... Counsel for the second and third defendants have contended that on the true view of the facts there was an immediate settlement of the obligations created by the covenant and not merely a covenant to settle something in the future. It was said that by the agreement Sir Herbert bought the rights arising under the covenant for the benefit of the cestuis que trust under the settlement and that, the covenant being made in favour of the trustees, these rights became assets of the trust. He relied on *Fletcher v Fletcher, Williamson v Codrington* and *Re Cavendish Browne's Settlement Trusts*. I am not able to accept this argument. The covenant with which I am concerned did not, in my opinion, create a debt enforceable at law, that is to say, a property right, which although to bear fruit only in the future and on a contingency was capable of being the subject of an immediate trust, as was held to be the case in *Fletcher v Fletcher*[2]. Nor is this covenant associated with property which was the subject of an immediate trust as in *Williamson v Codrington*[3]. Nor did the covenant relate to property which then belonged to the covenantor as in *Re Cavendish Browne's Settlement Trusts*[4]. In contrast to all these cases, this covenant on its true construction is, in my opinion, an executory contract to settle a particular fund or particular funds of money which at the date of the covenant did not exist and which might never come into existence. It is analogous to a covenant to settle an expectation or to settle after-acquired property. The case, in my judgment, involves the law of contract not the law of trusts.'

[1]   *Re Cook's Settlement Trusts* [1965] Ch 902 at 913.
[2]   (1844) 4 Hare 67; see para 9.97 above.
[3]   (1750) 1 Ves Sen 511 (an American plantation including slaves!).
[4]   [1916] WN 341 (realty and personalty to which covenantor was already entitled under the wills of persons already deceased).

9.109 In any event, Buckley J went on to hold that the covenant operated only upon a sale by Sir Francis and not by his wife-donee. However, it is submitted that Buckley J's approach is erroneous if it is concerned merely with the type of property that happens to be the subject of the covenant in question for, as already seen, it seems that any covenant is an existing chose in action that may be the subject of a trust, regardless of the type of property that happens to be within the scope of the covenant. Surely it is the intention of the settlor/covenantor that is the crucial factor. It is very difficult to believe that Buckley J would have held that no trust of the covenant could exist if the settlor/covenantor had ended his covenant with the clause, 'to the intent that the benefit of this covenant shall immediately be held by my Trustees upon the Trusts hereof'. In the circumstances Buckley J's judgment is best interpreted as finding that there was no intention to create a trust of property in the form of the covenant so as to be immediately enforceable by the children volunteers, but only an intention to create a trust of the subject matter of the covenant if or when it materialised and was transferred to the trustees for the children, so that only at that future time would the children have equitable rights, though in the interval Sir Herbert (or, it seems, his executors)[1] would be able to enforce the covenant, having provided consideration therefor.

[1]   *Beswick v Beswick* [1968] AC 58, [1967] 2 All ER 1197, HL. Such action by Sir Herbert or his personal representatives would completely constitute the trust for the children, but the trustees could not compel Sir Herbert or his personal representatives to take such action nor could they join them as co-defendants in an attempt to take advantage of their contractual rights. Sir Herbert and his personal representatives owe no duty to the children or the trustees to exercise their contractual rights and so they cannot be forced to become parties to an action concerning such rights.

9.110 It is thus considered that nothing displaces the fundamental require-ment of intention in the law of trusts so that if the settlor/covenantor intended to create immediate equitable rights in the beneficiaries to enforce the covenant (whether relating to existing or future property) there will be a completely constituted trust of the covenant. On the other hand, if he only intended the beneficiaries to have equitable rights in the property within the scope of the covenant if or when he actually transferred such property to the trustees, then there will be no completed constituted trust of the covenant. This will normally be the intention in respect of next of kin under marriage settlements, issue within the marriage consideration having their interests safeguarded by their contractual rights and the equitable maxim 'Equity looks on as done that which ought to be done'. Whilst this test of intention is a clear one, like the test of intention to create a trust of the benefit of a contract[1], there is plenty of scope for controversy over the application of the test in particular circumstances.

[1] See paras 9.86–9.92 above.

9.111 It would seem that if the deed containing the voluntary covenant also contains a covenant for further assurance then the court will be more likely to find that there was an intention to create a completely constituted trust of either or both covenants[1] and should so find if, otherwise, there is no real scope for the operation of the covenant for further assurance. It would further seem that if the deed does not contain an express covenant to assign future or after-acquired property but contains a purported assignment of future prop-erty (taking effect in equity, if consideration is provided, as a covenant to assign it when acquired) the court should not find that there was any intention to create a trust of the covenant but only of the property when acquired and transferred to trustees[2]. Indeed, where the covenant relates to future property there should be a rebuttable presumption that the settlor/covenantor intended not to create a trust of the covenant but only a trust of the property when acquired and transferred to trustees[3]. Finally, in the straightforward case of A, in a deed only consisting of one covenant, covenanting with B on trust wholly for C it seems there should, perhaps, be a presumption that A intended to create immediate equitable rights in C's favour by creating a trust of the covenant where the whole transaction would be futile except on the basis that this is the case[4]. However, for post 10 May 2000 convenants it would seem such covenant would be enforceable under the Contracts (Rights of Third Parties) Act 1999 without the need to find a trust of the covenant.

[1] *Cox v Barnard* (1850) 8 Hare 310 at 312 and 313; *Milroy v Lord* (1862) 4 De GF & J 264 at 278; *Re Cavendish-Browne's Settlement Trust* [1916] WN 341.
[2] As in *Re Kay's Settlement* [1939] Ch 329, [1939] 1 All ER 245, in respect of property appointed under a special power. Cf *Cox v Barnard* (1850) 8 Hare 310.
[3] See *Re Plumptre's Marriage Settlement* [1910] 1 Ch 609.
[4] *Fletcher v Fletcher* (1844) 4 Hare 67.

9.112 For the draftsman the moral is to insert a clause expressly stating the intention of the settlor/covenantor, whether to create a trust of a covenant or to confer enforcement rights on a third party beneficiary under the 1999 Act.

Trustees' common law action for damages for breach of voluntary covenant

9.113 If there is a completely constituted trust of the benefit of the voluntary covenant then not only can the volunteer beneficiaries enforce it specifically but the trustees themselves as the covenantees can obtain full damages for breach of covenant and they will, of course, hold such damages (as the fruit or product of the covenant) on trust for the volunteer beneficiaries[1].

[1]   *Cox v Barnard* (1850) 8 Hare 310; *Ward v Audland* (1845) 8 Beav 201; (1847) 16 M & W 862; *Re Cavendish-Browne's Settlement Trust* [1916] WN 341. If no trust of the covenant exists but consideration has been provided therefor (eg by issue under a marriage settlement) then damages may also be claimed: *Re Parkin* [1892] 3 Ch 510.

9.114 If there is no completely constituted trust of the benefit of the voluntary covenant the trustees as covenantees can prima facie still claim full damages[1] for breach of the voluntary covenant. However, ex hypothesi they are not holding the covenant itself on a completely constituted trust for the volunteer beneficiaries and since ex hypothesi they hold the covenant qua trustees they surely must, therefore, hold the covenant on a resulting trust for the covenantor/settlor[2]. If the covenant, with the right to damages for breach of covenant, is held on resulting trust for the covenantor/settlor then surely so must any damages obtained for breach of covenant. It follows that since the settlor is, under the resulting trust, an absolutely entitled beneficiary of full capacity he must under the *Saunders v Vautier*[3] principle be able to terminate such trust and prevent the trustees from launching upon such a pointless exercise as a suit against himself for damages. It should thus be an end of the matter as soon as the settlor (or his personal representative) makes it clear to the trustees that he does not want to be sued[4].

[1]   At common law if property valued at £x was not transferred to the covenantee then clearly the covenantee's loss was £x, the position in equity of the beneficiaries being immaterial to the common law position before the Judicature Acts. Thus, full damages and not nominal damages will be awarded: cf *Re Cavendish-Browne's Settlement Trust* [1916] WN 341 and D. W. Elliott (1980) 76 LQR 100 at 112; J. L. Barton (1975) 91 LQR 236 at 238.

[2]   The prospective beneficiaries only have a spes that the subject matter of the covenant will be transferred to the trustees by the settlor. See also (1969) 85 LQR 213 (W. A. Lee).

[3]   (1841) 4 Beav 115; see Article 72, below.

[4]   See *IRC v Ingram* [1997] 4 All ER 395 at 424 where Millett J also endorses *Hirachand Punamchand v Temple* [1911] 2 KB 330, where plaintiff money-lenders accepted a lesser sum from the defendant's father in satisfaction, of a debt and then sued the defendant for the balance. It is noteworthy that Vaughan-Williams J held that any money recovered would be held in trust for the defendant's father and 'there might have been a defence in a court of law on the ground that any money recoverable by the plaintiffs was recoverable by them merely as trustees for the father and that, under the circumstances disclosed by the correspondence the relations between father and son were such that it was impossible to suppose that the father wished to insist on payment by the son' (p 337), and Fletcher-Moulton LJ said, 'If there be any difficulty in formulating a defence at common law I have no hesitation in saying that a court of equity would have regarded the plaintiffs as disentitled to sue except as trustees for the father and would have restrained them from suing' (p 342). Also see *Hunt v Severs* [1994] 2 All ER 385 at 394, HL where it was held that a plaintiff claiming damages for personal injury can recover damages in respect of the care voluntarily provided by X and will hold them on trust for X (see para 8.259 above) except where X is also the defendant tortfeasor because it would he pointless and circular if the plaintiff were to recover £y from X which was then to be held on trust for X.

9.115 After all, whilst prospective volunteer beneficiaries with a spes that the settlor will carry out his voluntary promise to transfer property to trustees for them are dependent upon the whim of the settlor, it is surely wrong that they should be dependent upon the whim of the trustees suing or not suing[1]. Indeed, if the settlor has chosen not to constitute a trust of certain property surely the trustees cannot themselves have a right to constitute the trust[2]. The essence of the matter seems that since the settlor has not created a completely constituted trust of the voluntary covenant he must ex hypothesi have reserved to himself the right if he chooses to constitute a trust of the property, the subject of the covenant, at a later date, having lined up the trustees as his agents to receive the trust property[3] but, meanwhile, they are to hold the covenant on a resulting trust for him.

[1] The acts, neglects or default of trustees cannot be allowed to affect the rights of their beneficiaries: *Fletcher v Fletcher* (1844) 4 Hare 67 at 78; *Re Richerson* [1892] 1 Ch 379.
[2] Only the settlor (or his agent) can constitute his trust: see para 9.67 above and *Re Brook's Settlement Trusts* [1939] Ch 993 where the trustees obtaining title to the intended trust property without the settlor's consent did not completely constitute the trust.
[3] Cf *Milroy v Lord* (1862) 4 De GF & J 264 at 277 where Turner LJ in discussing the fact that the settlor's imperfect gift of shares to the intended trustee could have been carried out under a power of attorney held by the trustee stated, 'A court of Equity could not I think, decree the agent of the settlor to make the transfer, unless it could decree the settlor himself to do so and it is plain that no such decree could have been made against the settlor.'

9.116 In practice, if trustees are considering taking action on behalf of the trust they will need to obtain the leave of the court for otherwise they will be at personal risk as to the costs unless they can establish the costs were properly incurred[1]. If their position is doubtful they may also, at the cost of the trust fund, obtain directions from the court as to the position[2]. It is clear that if the court is involved it will direct the trustees that they ought not to sue for common law damages for breach of covenant where the settlor did not create a completely constituted trust of the benefit of the covenant[3]. Since this is well established there is no need for the trustees to bother the court and the trustees have a complete defence if any beneficiary seeks to make them liable for breach of trust for not suing the covenantor for damages[4].

[1] *Re Beddoe* [1893] 1 Ch 547; *Re Yorke* [1911] 1 Ch 370.
[2] CPR Part 64.2.
[3] *Re Pryce* [1917] 1 Ch 234; *Re Kay's Settlement* [1939] Ch 329, [1939] 1 All ER 245; *Re Cook's Settlement Trusts* [1965] Ch 902, [1964] 3 All ER 898.
[4] *Re Ralli's Will Trusts* [1964] Ch 288 at 301–302. For consideration of the Contracts (Rights of Third Parties) Act 1999 where the beneficiary might have tried to sue under the Act but failed or have been advised that he would fail see para 9.121 below.

9.117 Three cases of first instance establish that the trustees will be directed not to sue for damages for breach of a voluntary covenant where the settlor/covenantor did not create a completely constituted trust of the covenant. *Re Pryce*[1] established the proposition in 1917 and it has simply been followed in *Re Kay's Settlement*[2] and, despite academic criticism[3], by *Re Cook's Settlement Trusts*[4].

[1] [1917] 1 Ch 234.
[2] [1939] Ch 329, [1939] 1 All ER 245.
[3] (1960) 76 LQR 100 (D. W. Elliot); (1962) 78 LQR 228 (J. A. Hornby).
[4] [1965] Ch 902, [1964] 3 All ER 898; [1965] CLJ 46 (G. H. Jones).

9.118 In *Re Pryce* trustees took out a summons asking whether they needed to take proceedings in respect of a breach of the wife's covenant in her marriage settlement to transfer after-acquired property to trustees. Eve J in a reserved judgment held there was no completely constituted trust of the covenant and directed the trustees that they ought not to take proceedings, stating[1]:

> '[Her next of kin] are volunteers and although the court would probably compel fulfilment of the contract to settle at the instance of any persons within the marriage consideration[2] and in their favour will treat the outstanding property as subjected to an enforceable trust[3] "volunteers have no right whatever to obtain specific performance of a mere covenant which has remained as a covenant and has not been performed": see per James LJ in *Re D'Angibau*. Nor could damages be awarded either in this court, or, I apprehend, at law where since the Judicature Act 1873, the same defences would be available to the defendant as would be raised in an action brought in this court for specific performance or damages. In these circumstances, seeing that the next of kin could neither maintain an action to enforce the covenant nor for damages for breach of it, and that the settlement is not a declaration of trust constituting the relationship of trustee and cestui que trust between the defendant and the next of kin, in which case effect could be given to the trusts even in favour of volunteers, but is a mere voluntary contract to create a trust, ought the court now for the sole benefit of volunteers to direct the trustees to take proceedings to enforce the defendant's covenant? I think it ought not; to do so would be to give the next of kin by indirect means relief they cannot obtain by any direct procedure and would in effect be enforcing the settlement.'

1   [1917] 1 Ch 234 at 241.
2   *Re D'Angibau* (1880) 15 Ch D 228 at 242, 246.
3   *Pullan v Koe* [1913] 1 Ch 9.

9.119 Whilst the result in *Re Pryce* is correct Eve J's reasoning is insupportable. It is a fallacy that the Judicature Act 'fusion' made defences available to a defendant in Chancery also available to a defendant at law so that the Chancery defence of 'volunteer' is available to a defendant at law[1]. Moreover, except in specially limited cases of fraud, undue influence etc equity never actively intervened to prevent a volunteer pursuing his rights at law, equity's maxim being 'equity will not assist a volunteer' and not 'equity will frustrate a volunteer in equity and at law'[2].

1   After all, hardship maybe a defence to an action in equity for specific performance but not to a common law action for damages. Moreover, the Judicature Acts did not alter the substantive law by making promises under seal unenforceable at common law without valuable consideration: *Cannon v Hartley* [1949] Ch 213, [1949] 1 All ER 50; (1960) 76 LQR 100,109,111 (D.W. Elliot); Meagher, Gummow and Lehane, *Equity Doctrine and Remedies*, (4th ed) para 2–170.
2   *Davenport v Bishopp* (1843) 2 Y & C Ch Cas 451 at 260; *Ward v Audland* (1845) 8 Beav 201 at 211; *Milroy v Lord* (1862) 4 De GF & J 264 at 273 and 278; *Cannon v Hartley* [1949] Ch 213, [1949] 1 All ER 50.

9.120 Since the result in *Re Pryce* has been followed in *Re Kay's Settlement*[1] (or, indeed, extended from 'the trustees ought not to sue' to 'the trustee must not sue') and *Re Cook's Settlement Trusts* and since it also accords with the resulting trust reasoning already propounded, it is submitted that it is now beyond doubt that where there is no completely constituted trust of a voluntary covenant the trustees will be directed not to sue the covenantor for common law damages. If a bold trustee did sue (eg because also a beneficiary or married to a beneficiary or indemnified fully as to costs by a beneficiary) it is submitted that it is likely that such action would fail on the basis that the covenant, the right to damages for breach of the covenant and any actual damages, must in principle be held on a resulting trust for the settlor/ covenantor, making the action groundless.

[1]   Where Simonds J emphasised [1939] Ch 329 at 339, 'The question before me is not whether if she [the settlor] were sued such an action would succeed (as to which she might have a defence, I know not what) but whether in the circumstances the trustees ought to be directed to take proceedings against her'.

9.121   This is reinforced if one considers that the beneficiaries have no rights to damages under the Contracts (Rights of Third Parties) Act 1999 because in the absence of creating a completely constituted trust of the benefit of the covenant the settlor did not intend the covenant to be enforceable by the beneficiaries already benefiting sufficiently in the trust property already vested in the trustee for them. Nowadays, a well-drafted settlement should make clear that beneficiaries are not to have enforcement rights in respect of the settlor's covenants with his trustee if this be the desired position as often will be the case.

ARTICLE 10
WHAT PROPERTY IS CAPABLE OF BEING MADE THE SUBJECT OF A TRUST

10.1

All assets real or personal[1], legal or equitable, at home or abroad and whether in possession or action, remainder or reversion, and whether vested or contingent, may be made the subject of a trust, unless:
(1)   the policy of the law or some statutory enactment has made it inalienable; or
(2)   where the property is land abroad, the trusts sought to be created are inconsistent with the lex loci situs[2].

[1]   Even a herd of deer may be the subject of a trust: (*White v Paine* (1914) 83 LJKB 895) or a milk quota (*Swift v Dairywise Farms Ltd* [2000] 1 All ER 320).
[2]   *Earl Nelson v Lord Bridport* (1846) 8 Beav 547.

Equitable interests

10.2   A person, holding an agreement for a lease, assigned all his interest under it to trustees upon certain trusts. Here, although the legal term was not in the settlor, it was held to be a good settlement, because he had conveyed his equitable interest in the property[1]. In *Re Ralli's Will Trusts*[2] there was held to be an effective declaration of trust by the settlor under which she held her equitable remainder interest on trust for certain beneficiaries until she transferred to the trustees the actual property that would become hers absolutely upon her remainder falling into possession. The interest of a beneficiary in default of appointment is an existing equitable interest but the interest or, rather, spes or hope of the object of a power is a mere expectancy[3], as is the interest of one of a number of beneficiaries under a discretionary trust. However, if all the discretionary beneficiaries (as opposed to mere objects of a power of appointment) who between them are absolutely beneficially entitled to the whole equitable interest in income or capital or both, are of full capacity and of one mind, then they can dispose of the equitable interest as they see fit[4].

[1] *Gilbert v Overton* (1864) 2 Hem & M 110; and see also *Re Way's Trust* (1864) 2 De GJ & Sm and *Knight v Bowyer* (1857) 23 Beav 609; affd (1858) 2 De G & J 421.
[2] [1964] Ch 288, [1963] 3 All ER 940. Also see *Fitzwilliam v IRC* [1993] 1 WLR 1189, HL.
[3] *Re Brooks' Settlement Trusts* [1939] Ch 993, [1939] 3 All ER 920.
[4] *Re Smith* [1928] Ch 915; *Schmidt v Rosewood Trust Ltd* [2003] UKPC 26, [2003] 2 AC 709, para 40.

Choses in action

10.3 A owes £1,000 to B. B assigns this debt to trustees upon certain trusts. This transaction is perfectly good. Equity, almost always, enforced contracts for the sale of choses in action though, subject to certain exceptions the common law did not; but the common law rule is abrogated as regards absolute assignments of debts or other legal choses in action by s 136(1) of the Law of Property Act 1925. By s 4(2) of the same Act, replacing part of s 6 of the Real Property Act 1845, contingent and future interests and possibilities, *coupled with an interest in real estate,* may be granted or assigned at law. But it is otherwise in the case of possibilities in personal estate which still remain assignable only in equity if for value[1].

[1] See *Joseph v Lyons* (1884) 15 QBD 280; *Collyer v Isaacs* (1881) 19 Ch D 342; and *Re Ellenborough* [1903] 1 Ch 697.

10.4 Lord Shaw has emphasised[1], 'The scope of the trusts recognised in equity is unlimited. There can be a trust of a chattel or of a chose in action or of a right or obligation under an ordinary legal contract; just as much as a trust of land.' Thus, it has been held[2] that a plaintiff can assign his interest in litigation to trustees on protective trusts for himself and his son or can assign to trustees exclusive contractual burial rights in a plot for family members[3]. Moreover, even though a contract is not assignable at law, a trust may be declared of it unless the terms of the contract prohibit this[4], though only the trustee – and not the beneficiary – has rights to enforce the contract[5].

[1] *Lord Strathcona SS Co Ltd v Dominion Coal Co Ltd* [1926] AC 108 at 124, PC.
[2] *Harrison v Tew* (1988) Times, 30 November.
[3] Re West Norwood Cemetery [2005] 1 WLR 2176.
[4] *Don King Productions Inc v Warren* [2000] Ch 291 at 321, affd at 335–336, CA.
[5] Barbados Trust Company Limited v Bank of Zambia [2006] EWHC 222 (Comm), [2006] 1 Lloyd's Rep 723.

Reversionary interests

10.5 A reversion, whether vested or contingent, is assignable both at law and in equity, and may therefore be made the subject of a trust[1].

1   *Shafto v Adams* (1864) 4 Giff 492; *Fitzwilliam v IRC* [1993] 3 All ER 184, [1993] 1 WLR 1189, HL.

Expectancies or future property

10.6 At law, assignments of property to be acquired in the future pass nothing. Thus, a gratuitous assignment of all X's 'right title and interest in and to all the dividends' which might be declared in respect of certain shares is an ineffective transfer of a mere expectancy[1]. However, a gratuitous assignment of all X's 'right title and interest in and to an amount equal to 90% of the income which may accrue during a period of three years from the date hereof under a' specified licence agreement providing for royalties to be paid by the licensee to the assignor was held an effective transfer of presently existing property, namely 90% of that portion of the assignor's existing contractual rights entitling him to royalties at a fixed rate during the period (rather than the mere expectancy of 90% of such payments, as might accrue due to the assignor during the period)[2].

1   *Norman v Federal Comr of Taxation* (1963) 109 CLR 9 (Aust HC). An assignment of property to which one might become entitled on the death of a specified living person is clearly ineffective: *Re Ellenborough* [1903] 1 Ch 697.
2   *Shepherd v Federal Comr of Taxation* (1965) 113 CLR 385 (Aust HC). Further see Meagher, Gummow & Lehane (4th edn) paras 6–215 to 6–235 on these fine distinctions.

10.7 Equity, however, may be able to regard assignments of expectancies, *if for value*, as contracts to assign the property when it comes into existence[1]; and although they are uncertain in their inception (inasmuch as the property is incapable of ascertainment at the date of the assignment) the property is nevertheless capable of identification when the subject has come into existence and the assignment becomes enforceable[2]. Such assignments, which do not require any particular form of words so long as the intention to assign is reasonably clear[3], are therefore not void for uncertainty. Thus, an assignment for value (to cover advanced money) of all moneys to which the assignor was or might become entitled under any settlement, will, or other document, was held to be good in equity as to money inherited under a will[4], and a similar conclusion was arrived at by the House of Lords where the property assigned was all book debts due and owing or which during a named period *might become due* and owing to the assignor[5]. In the early case of *Lewis v Madocks*[6], specific performance was ordered of a covenant by the husband in a marriage settlement that he would:

> 'by deed or will convey give devise and assure all and singular his ready money goods chattels and personal estate and effects to and for the use and behoof of the spouses and the survivor of them'

upon certain trusts. An assignment of the copyright of an unwritten book has also been held to be good[7]. Another example is the covenant to settle after-acquired property of the wife commonly found in marriage settlements. As, however, such assignments are really only regarded as contracts, it follows that equity will not enforce them unless the conscience of the assignor is bound by valuable consideration having been given[8] or for some other reason[9].

1   *Wethered v Wethered* (1828) 2 Sim 183, and see also *Beckley v Newland* (1723) 2 P Wms 182; *Harwood v Tooke* (1812) 2 Sim 192; *Higgins v Hill* (1887) 56 LT 426; *Collyer v Isaacs* (1881) 19 Ch D 342; *Re Clarke* (1887) 36 Ch D 348; *Tailby v Official Receiver* (1888) 13 App Cas 523, HL; *Hardy v Fothergill* (1888) 13 App Cas 351; *Thomas v Kelly* (1888) 13 App Cas 506, HL; *Re Ellenborough* [1903] 1 Ch 697 at 700.
2   See per Lord Herschell in *Tailby v Official Receiver* (1888) 13 App Cas 523 at 530, HL; and *Holyroyd v Marshall* (1862) 10 HL Cas 191 at 210, per Lord Westbury.
3   *Fyfe v Garden* [1946] 1 All ER 366 at 372, HL, per Viscount Maugham.
4   *Re Clarke* (1887) 36 Ch D 348.
5   *Tailby v Official Receiver* (1888) 13 App Cas 523. See *Re Lind* [1915] 2 Ch 345, CA; *Palette Shoes Pty Ltd v Krohn* (1937) 58 CLR 1, at 27–28; and *Re Green* [1979] 1 All ER 832 at 843.
6   (1810) 17 Ves 48, stated to be good law in *Re Reis* [1904] 2 KB 769 at 783, per Stirling LJ.
7   *Ward, Lock & Co v Long* [1906] 2 Ch 550.
8   *Re Ellenborough* [1903] 1 Ch 697; *Re Brooks' Settlement Trusts* [1939] Ch 993, [1939] 3 All ER 920. And see Article 9, above.
9   *Re Burton's Settlement Trusts* [1955] Ch 82, [1954] 3 All ER 193, where the assignor's conscience was bound because the assignment was made in compliance with a condition in a will and to enable her to take benefits thereunder. On possible impact of Contracts (Rights of Third Parties) Act 1999, see paras 9.81–9.84 above.

Effect of bankruptcy on assignments of future or after-acquired property or covenants relating thereto

10.8 *Tailby v Official Receiver*[1] establishes that where X for consideration agrees to assign, or purports presently to assign an expectancy to Y, and the consideration has been paid or executed, then any property acquired by X within his obligation forthwith automatically vests the equitable interest therein in Y, because Equity regards as done that which ought to be done. As Dixon J said in *Palette Shoes Pty Ltd v Krohn*[2]:

'because value has been given on the one side, the conscience of the other party is bound when the subject matter comes into existence. Because his conscience is bound, equity fastens upon the property itself and makes him a trustee of the legal rights of ownership for the assignee ... [the assignee's right] may survive the assignor's bankruptcy because it attaches without more eo instanti when the property arises and gives the assignee an equitable interest therein.'

1   (1888) 13 App Cas 523, HL.
2   (1937) 58 CLR 1 at 26–27. Also see *Re Andromo Pty Limited* [1987] 2 Qd R 134 at 152–154 and *Raiffeisen Zentralbank Osterrecch AG v Five Star General Trading LLC* [2001] QB 825 at 858.

10.9 He endorsed *Re Lind*[1] to similar effect where L had assigned his expectancy (in what he hoped to inherit on the death of his mother, who was alive but not of sound mind) as security for loans by A and then B. L then became bankrupt but, later, after being discharged, assigned his expectancy to C. The Court of Appeal held that A and B had priority over C.

1   [1915] 2 Ch 345.

10.10 Commercial advantage of the principle enshrined in the above remarks of Dixon J can be taken in reservation of title clauses where a supplier of raw materials has a manufacturer contract that it will be trustee of proceeds of sale of manufactured goods (incorporating the raw materials) as to one fifth for the supplier and four fifths for itself or holding on trust for the supplier such fractional part of such proceeds then received as is equivalent to the amount then owing by it to the supplier and the rest on trust for itself[1]. In cases where there are covenants in marriage settlements relating to after-acquired property, it seems that there should be no automatic arising of an equitable interest in favour of volunteers as well as those providing (or being within) the marriage consideration[2]. The equitable interest ought only to attach to the property if there is then some beneficiary who gave value with an interest to enforce the covenant: there may be no such beneficiary by reason of the previous death of that beneficiary or from the property in question having become vested in him or her so that the property is 'at home'[3]. Thus, if in consideration of marriage, property was settled on A for life then B for life with remainder to their children, but in default of children for their statutory next of kin and A and B entered into the usual after- acquired property covenants, then if B inherited property within the scope of such covenant after A had died childless, no equitable interest in favour of the volunteer next of kin would arise.

1   *Associated Alloys Pty Ltd v ACN 001 452 106 Pty Ltd* (2000) 202 CLR 588 (High Court of Australia); para 1.42 above.
2   *Re Reis ex p Clough*[1904] 2 KB 769, CA: the availability of specific performance is crucial, unlike the position in commercial cases mentioned in the three preceding footnotes.
3   *Re Anstis* (1886) 31 Ch D 596, CA; *Re Plumptre's Marriage Settlement* [1910] 1 Ch 609.

Paragraph (a)

Property inalienable by reason of public policy

10.11 Salaries or pensions are inalienable only if given to enable persons to perform duties connected with the public service, or so that they may be in a fit state of preparation to perform those duties. In *Grenfell v Dean and Canons of Windsor*[1] a canon of Windsor had assigned the canonry and the profits to the plaintiff to secure a sum of money. There was no cure of souls, and the only duties were residence within the castle and attendance in the chapel for twenty-one days a year.

1   (1840) 2 Beav 544.

10.12 In giving judgment for the plaintiff and upholding the assignment the Master of the Rolls said:

'If he (the canon) had made out that the duty to be performed by him was a public duty, or in any way connected with the public service, I should have thought it right to attend very seriously to that argument, because there are various cases in which public duties are concerned, in which it may be against public policy, that the income arising from the performance of those duties should be assigned; and for this simple reason, because the public is interested, not only in the performance from time to time of the duties, but also in the fit state of preparation of the party having to perform them. Such is the reason in the cases of half-pay where there is a sort of retainer, and where the payments which are made to officers, from time to time, are the means by which they, being liable to be called into public service, are enabled to keep themselves in a state of preparation for performing their duties.'

10.13 So, in *Davis v Duke of Marlborough*[1], the Lord Chancellor said:

'A pension for past services may be aliened, but a pension for supporting the grantee in the performance of future duties is inalienable.'

1   (1818) 1 Swan 74.

10.14 Alimony or maintenance granted to a spouse by the Family Division or the magistrates is similarly not assignable.

Property inalienable by statute

10.15 Some classes of property are expressly made inalienable by statute. Thus, in *Davis v Duke of Marlborough*[1], it was held that a pension granted by statute to the first duke and his successors in the title 'for the more honourable support of the dignities' was not alienable, since it was held that, the object of Parliament in granting it was that 'it should be kept in mind that it was for a memento and a perpetual memorial of national gratitude for public services'.

1   (1818) 1 Swan 74. However, the land granted to the Duke is subject to the court's powers under Settled Land Act 1925, s. 64: *Hambro v Duke of Marlborough* [1994] Ch 158, [1994] 3 All ER 332.

10.16 Deferred pay or military reward payable to any officer, soldier or airman of the Army, Air Force or Royal Marines, or any pension, allowance or relief payable to any such officer, soldier or airman, or to his wife, or to his widow, child or other dependant, or to any person in respect of military or air force service, are also made unassignable by statute[1]. It has been held[2] that, while such legislation inhibits the court from making any order which would prevent the receipt by the pensioner in due course of any pension or gratuity, etc to which he is entitled in the future, it does not inhibit the court in making any other kind of order (like a lump sum order on divorce) once the pensioner has safely received the sum of money to which he is due. While statute[3] makes unassignable naval pensions payable to an officer, seaman or a marine, or to an officer's widow, allowances from the compassionate fund, marine half pay, and payments, rewards etc, in respect of services in the navy and marines to a subordinate officer, marine or seaman, the Court of Appeal has held[4] that such statute does not restrict the court's powers to make orders eg under the Matrimonial Causes Act 1973. In general, salaries or pensions, not given in respect of public services, are freely assignable[5].

1   Army Act 1955, ss 141, 190, 203; *Walker v Walker* [1983] Fam 68, [1983] 2 All ER 909, CA; *Roberts v Roberts* [1986] 2 All ER 483, [1986] 1 WLR 437, Air Force Act 1955, ss 141, 190; *Ranson v Ranson* [1988] 1 WLR 183, CA.
2   *Happé v Happé* [1991] 4 All ER 527, [1990] 1 WLR 1282, CA.
3   Naval and Marine Pay and Pensions Act 1865, ss 4, 5.

10.17 By s 5(1) of the Superannuation Act 1972 any assignment or agreement to assign any benefit payable under a scheme made under s 1 of the Act is void.

10.18 To qualify for favoured tax treatment as approved pension arrangements, the benefits of such arrangements have to be made non-assignable expressly in their terms, but this did not prevent them falling into the ownership of the pensioner's trustee on bankruptcy[1] until so provided by the Welfare Reforms and Pensions Act 1999[2]. This Act[3] also contains overriding provisions for the sharing of rights under pensions arrangements upon divorce.

¹ *Rowe v Sanders* [2002] EWCA Civ 242, [2002] 2 All ER 800; *Krasner v Dennison* [2001] Ch 76, CA.
² Welfare Reforms and Pensions Act 1999, s 11.
³ Welfare Reforms and Pensions Act 1999, Pt IV.
³ *Freke v Lord Carbery* (1873) LR 16 Eq 461 (leaseholds); *Re Berchtold* [1923] 1 Ch 192 (trust for sale).

Paragraph (b)

Trusts of foreign immovables

10.19 The distinction between immovables and movables is not the same as that between real and personal property. Leasehold land ranks as personalty but is an immovable, while a trust for sale of land, until s 3 of the Trusts of Land and Appointment of Trustees Act 1996 came into force, was personalty, but also an immovable[1]. Naturally and practically the lex situs has crucial significance for immovables, especially where it has particular policy interests, e g prohibiting unbarrable entails altogether[2], or future interests which might vest at too remote a time[3], or testamentary gifts for charitable purposes made within one year of death[4], or testamentary dispositions contrary to forced indefeasible shares in favour of the widow and children[5]. The lex situs may even lead to a restrictive interpretation of an after-acquired property covenant, e g so that it did not extend to after-acquired Jersey land when Jersey law prohibited married women from conveying such land except for adequate pecuniary compensation[6].

¹ *Freke v Lord Carbery* (1873) LR 16 Eq 461 (leaseholds); *Re Berchtold* [1923] 1 Ch 192 (trust for sale).
² *Earl Nelson v Bridport* (1846) 8 Beav 547. Nowadays entails can no longer be created: Trusts of Land and Appointment of Trustees Act 1996, Sch 1, para 5.
³ *Freke v Lord Carbery* (1873) LR 16 Eq 461. Nowadays, one can wait and see so that trusts are not void from the outset: Perpetuities and Accumulations Act 1964, s 3.
⁴ *Curtis v Hutton* (1808) 14 Ves 537; *Duncan v Lawson* (1889) 41 Ch D 394: since then the Mortmain and Charitable Uses Acts 1736 and 1888 have been repealed.
⁵ *Re Ross* [1930] 1 Ch 377 (legitima portio). A foreign state concerned only with its own nationals may let an English national domiciled in England devise land in the foreign state free from any legitima or legitim: cf *Re Duke of Wellington* [1948] Ch 118, [1947]

237

2 All ER 854, CA, and the current position in Spain, Netherlands, Greece, Finland and Denmark: see D J Hayton (ed) *European Succession Laws* (2 edn 2002, Jordans).
6   *Re Pearse's Settlement* [1909] 1 Ch 304.

10.20 If the lex situs does not sanction trusts of land a settlor's creation of inter vivos 'trusts', of specific land transferred to 'trustees' subject to an express choice[1] of English law will be ineffective to create equitable or other proprietary interests under the lex situs in favour of the beneficiaries[2]; though the rights or powers of the trustees may be recognised to some extent. If the matter be litigated in the courts of the lex situs it seems the transfer will either be void so that the land still is the settlor's or the 'trustees' will hold the land as nominee of or agent for the settlor (though the trustees may be treated as having power to deal with the land effectively without the settlor's consent). This leaves it open to the settlor to sell the land and settle the proceeds or to take advantage of some analogous institution of the lex situs to enable the land to be held for the benefit of others. However, if exceptionally, the English courts have jurisdiction[3] to determine an equitable in personam matter between A and B resident in England concerning foreign land, then the court may find that B holds the foreign land on trust for A and order B to execute such documents as the foreign law requires to vest ownership in the land in A[4] or order B to sell the land and remit the proceeds to a in England[5].

1   On choice of law see Article 107 below.
2   See Rule 117 of Dicey & Morris, *Conflict of Laws* (13th edn).
3   See Rule 116 of Dicey & Morris, *Conflict of Laws* (13th edn).
4   *Webb v Webb* [1991] 1 WLR 1410 accepted by *European Court* [1994] QB 696, [1994] 3 All ER 911; *Cook Industries Inc v Galliher* [1979] Ch 439, [1978] 3 All ER 945.
5   *Ashurst v Pollard* [2001] 2 All ER 75, CA.

10.21 In the case of English testamentary trusts, where necessarily the English settlor-testator is dead, it seems that a trust of foreign land comprised within the testator's residuary estate held on the usual trusts for sale will be given effect, as will a specific devise of foreign land on trust for sale[1] except to the extent that the foreign lex situs gives effect to heirs' indefeasible shares[2]. The English trustees will be under valid in personam obligations enforceable by the beneficiaries in the English courts to sell the land and hold the proceeds on trust for the beneficiaries. In the exceptionally rare case where the draftsman does not employ a trust for sale it seems the intended trust will fail where the trust concept is unknown to the lex situs, except to the extent that The Hague Convention on the Recognition of Trusts[3] may have been implemented so as to enable some effect to be given to the intended trust, so that a resulting trust does not arise.

1   *Re Piercy* [1895] 1 Ch 83.
2   Most European countries (except, eg Italy, Spain, Netherlands, Finland and Denmark) accept the English renvoi to the lex situs as being the lex successionis: see Hayton (ed), *European Succession Laws* (2 edn 2002, Jordans).
3   See Article 107 below.

10.22 English inter vivos or testamentary trusts of foreign movables will be valid except to the extent they conflict with any mandatory rules (relating to matter like insolvency, transfer of title to property, heirs' indefeasible rights[1]) of the law applicable under the choice of law rules of the forum or any strong principle of public policy of the lex situs[2]. The English trustees will often owe beneficiaries valid in personam obligations enforceable in the English courts[3] even if in the lex situs the concept of the trust is unknown, but it is possible that there may be a resulting trust for the settlor in some circumstances.

[1] Testamentary trusts will be subject to forced heirs' rights under a foreign lex successionis, but *inter vivos* gifts to trusts or persons fall outside the deceased's estate at death which is subject to the lex successionis.

[2] Hague Convention on the Law Applicable to Trusts and on their Recognition Articles 11, 15, 16, 18, paras 102.189–102.210 below.

[3] *Chellaram v Chellaram* [1985] Ch 409, [1985] 1 All ER 1043; *Webb v Webb* [1994] QB 696; *Ashurst v Pollard* [2001] 2 All ER 75, CA.

ARTICLE 11
THE LEGALITY OF THE EXPRESSED OBJECT OF THE TRUST[1]

11.1

(1) A trust created for a purpose illegal by English law is void[2]. Private trusts of this character mostly fall under one of the following classes:

    (a) trusts for the tying-up of property for an unlawful period[3] whether the tying-up is achieved by the trusts creating contingent interests for persons which might not vest till too remote a time or ensuring the immediate application of income for purposes which will continue for too long a period during which the trust income will be inalienable;

    (b) trusts for accumulation of income beyond the period allowed by law;

    (c) trusts by which it is sought to alter the devolution of property as prescribed by law, eg in the event of intestacy[4], bankruptcy or seizure of property in execution of a judgment[5];

    (d) trusts restricting the power of alienation of the beneficiaries' interest[6];

    (e) trusts ousting the jurisdiction of the courts[7] or operating in terrorem to induce the beneficiary not to apply to the courts[8];

    (f) trusts promoting or encouraging immorality[9], the separation of spouses, fraud, dishonesty, or other matters contrary to public policy;

    (g) trusts tending to the general restraint of marriage[10] (unless of a second marriage)[11], or encouraging breach of the sanctity of marriage[12] or interfering drastically with parental duties or otherwise infringing the Human Rights Act 1998;

    (h) trusts made illegal by statute[13].

(2)   An illegal or impossible trust will not normally vitiate other provisions in the settlement unconnected with the illegal purpose[14].

(3)   Testamentary trusts of English movables (but not English immovables[15]) created by a testator domiciled abroad are only valid to the extent that the testator's *lex domicilii* as his *lex successionis* according to the English forum allows such to be disposed of free from mandatory rules protecting the interests of the testator's children or other relatives or dependants[16]; inter vivos trusts of English movables and immovables transferred validly under the *lex situs* to trustees of an English (or other trust jurisdiction) trust by a settlor of foreign domicile, habitual residence or nationality are valid and unimpeachable except, perhaps, to the extent that the settlor reserves a general power of appointment or revocation and his *lex successionis* has mandatory rules protecting the interests after his death of his children or other relatives or dependants[17].

---

1   In addition to trusts that are void for illegality, trusts may become void for breach of conditions so long as those conditions are lawful. Such conditions may be either precedent (so that the trust never comes into force at all unless and until the condition is performed), or subsequent so as to cause a forfeiture after the trust has arisen. If a condition is subsequent and is impossible, uncertain, contrary to public policy or illegal the condition is void and the interest becomes absolute: *Re Beard* [1908] 1 Ch 383. If a condition is precedent and attached to realty then failure to perform the condition defeats the gift. In respect of personalty 'where a condition precedent is originally impossible or is made so by the act or default of the testator or is illegal as involving malum prohibitum, the bequest is absolute just as if the condition had been subsequent. But where the performance of the condition is the sole motive of the bequest or its impossibility was unknown to the testator or the condition which was possible in its creation has since become impossible by act of God or where it is illegal as involving malum in se ... both gift and condition are void': per Harman J in *Re Elliott* [1952] Ch 217 at 221; *Re Wolffe* [1953] 1 WLR 1211 at 1216; *Re Piper* [1946] 2 All ER 503.
2   *A-G v Sands* (1668) Hard 488; *Pawlett v A-G* (1667) Hard 465; *Burgess v Wheate* (1759) 1 Eden 177; *Duke of Norfolk's Case* (1678) 3 Ch Cas 1. As to trusts void for attempting to alter the law of devolution of an absolute equitable gift, see *Re Dixon* [1903] 2 Ch 458.
3   *Cadell v Palmer* (1833) 1 Cl & Fin 372; Tud Lead Cas Conv (ed 4) 578; *Griffiths v Vere* (1803) 9 Ves 127; Tud Lead Cas Conv (ed 4) 618; *Re Dalziel* [1943] Ch 277, [1943] 2 All ER 656; *Re Wightwick's Will Trusts* [1950] Ch 260, [1950] 1 All ER 689.
4   *Re Walker* [1908] 2 Ch 705; *Re Dixon* [1903] 2 Ch 458.
5   *Graves v Dolphin* (1826) 1 Sim 66; *Snowdon v Dales* (1834) 6 Sim 524; *Brandon v Robinson* (1811) 18 Ves 429; *Re Machu* (1882) 21 Ch D 838; *Re Dugdale* (1888) 38 Ch D 176 at 182; *Rowe v Sanders* [2002] EWCA Civ 242, [2002] All ER 800; *Krasner v Dennison* [2001] Ch 76, CA.
6   *Floyer v Bankes* (1869) LR 8 Eq 115; *Sykes v Sykes* (1871) LR 13 Eq 56.
7   *Re Wynn* [1952] Ch 271.
8   *Re Hanlon* [1933] Ch 254.
9   *Blodwell v Edwards* (1596) Cro Eliz 509.
10   See per Wilmot LCJ in *Low v Peers* (1770) Wilm 375; *Morley v Rennoldson* (1843) 2 Hare 570; *Lloyd v Lloyd* (1852) 2 Sim NS 255.
11   *Marples v Bainbridge* (1816) 1 Madd 590; *Lloyd v Lloyd* (1852) 2 Sim NS 255; *Craven v Brady* (1869) 4 Ch App 296; and as to second marriage of a man, *Allen v Jackson* (1875) 1 Ch D 399.
12   *Re Caborne* [1943] Ch 224, [1943] 2 All ER 7. This was a decision upon a condition; but it is thought that the same principles would be applied in the case of a trust.

13 For example, by the Exchange Control Act 1947, s 29 (settlement of property, otherwise than by will, so as to confer an interest on a person resident outside 'the scheduled territories'). These controls terminated on 23 October 1979. See further para 11.103 below.

14 *H v W* (1857) 3 K & J 382; *Cartwright v Cartwright* (1853) 3 De GM & G 982; *Merryweather v Jones* (1864) 4 Giff 509; *Cocksedge v Cocksedge* (1844) 14 Sim 244; *Evers v Challis* (1859) 7 HL Cas 531; *Watson v Young* (1885) 28 Ch D 436; *Re Harvey* (1888) 39 Ch D 289; and *Re Bence* [1891] 3 Ch 242.

15 Succession to English immovables is governed by English Law.

16 *Re Annesley* [1926] Ch 692.

17 See para 11.132 below.

Paragraph 1 (a)

Distinguish rule against remoteness from rule against inalienability

11.2 Where trust property cannot be applied for people or purposes without distinguishing between capital and income, so that the capital has to be kept intact as endowment capital for the income therefrom to be applied for people or purposes for some time, two mutually exclusive rules prevent the endowment trust from lasting too long a time. The two rules appeared relatively similar before the Perpetuities and Accumulations Act 1964 so that in the case law trusts are often said to be void for perpetuity without it being made clear whether the perpetuity arises from the prospect of a contingent interest not becoming vested in *persons* till too remote a time or from the prospect of income having to be used forthwith for particular *purposes* for too long a period. In the former case it is clearer to refer to the rule against remoteness of vesting as making the trusts void. In the latter case it is proposed to refer to the rule against inalienability as making the trusts void though it can also be referred to as the rule against purpose trusts of excessive duration. After the 1964 Act came into operation it has become crucial to distinguish between a trust for people (or other legal persons) and a trust for purposes: it will be seen that there is a 'wait and see' validity for people trusts while purpose trusts (if non-charitable) remain void from the outset if not restricted to a valid perpetuity period.

11.3 The rule against remoteness applies to trusts where some persons are intended to obtain beneficial interests and ensures that some person or persons will ultimately become absolutely entitled to the trust property on or before expiry of the perpetuity period (it sufficing that at the end of the period the property is held for Y for life, remainder to Z, Y having a vested interest in possession and Z a vested interest in remainder). It thus covers trusts where persons have contingent equitable interests and even discretionary trusts for a huge unlistable class of beneficiaries where at the end of the perpetuity period the trust property will have to be distributed by the trustees between the beneficiaries on a discretionary *McPhail v Doulton*[1] basis.

1 [1971] AC 424, HL; para 8.46 above.

11.4 The above rule has no scope where persons are not intended to obtain beneficial interests ie where from the outset the trust capital has to be held on abstract purpose trusts of a non-charitable nature, which will normally fall foul of the beneficiary principle unless within the small anomalous class of testamentary purpose trusts that are concessions to human sentiment[1] or unless such purpose trusts come to be enforceable if an enforcer has been expressly appointed so as to create workable obligations upon the trustee(s)[2]. Here, it is the rule against inalienability which fulfils the function of ensuring that some person or persons will become absolutely entitled to the trust property on or before expiry of the perpetuity period.

¹ See para 8.173 above.
² See para 8.157 above.

The rule against remoteness

11.5 A detailed examination of this rule is beyond the scope of this work but may be found in Morris and Leach, *The Rule against Perpetuities*, or Megarry and Wade, *The Law of Real Property*. The rule developed in the seventeenth century, though trusts void under the common law rule may now be saved by the Perpetuities and Accumulations Act 1964 if created in an instrument taking effect after 15 July 1964 (not being an appointment under a special power in a trust created before then). Since the 1925 property legislation and the Trustee Investments Act 1961 enable trust capital to be freely transposed, the modern rationale of the rule is probably to prevent the dead from ruling the actions of the living for too long (by imposing requirements for entitlement to benefits) and to strike a balance between trust capital (which is safe capital, except where very broad powers of investment are conferred on trustees who are given full protection in exercising these powers) and 'risk' capital by converting trust capital into risk capital at the end of the perpetuity period. Indeed, economic and fiscal circumstances are such that trusts normally do not run for the full perpetuity period: instead, the trustees terminate the trust period at an earlier time pursuant to express powers in that behalf or exercise powers to distribute capital such that no trust property remains before expiry of the trust period.

11.6 The rule against remoteness is that a future interest in real or personal property is void unless at the outset it can be seen that the future interest is absolutely certain to vest in interest (as opposed to vest in possession[1]) if at all, not later than twenty-one years after the death of the last surviving causally relevant life in being at the creation of the interest[2]. The most fantastic outlandish possibilities of interests vesting outside the perpetuity period can thus destroy those interests.

¹ For an interest to vest in interest the person(s) entitled must be ascertained (eg by having been born) and the interest must be ready to take effect in possession forthwith upon cesser of prior interests (eg by the beneficiary having satisfied the contingency such as attaining 25 years) while if the gift is a gift to a class the size of the benefit must also be known (so the exact number within the class must be known).
² *Cadell v Palmer* (1833) 1 Cl & Fin 372; Tud Lead Cas Conv (ed 4) 578; *London and South Western Rly Co v Gomm* (1882) 20 Ch D 562, CA; *Edwards v Edwards* [1909] AC 275; *Pearks v Moseley* (1880) 5 App Cas 714. A period of gestation may be added to the 21 years where it exists.

11.7 Under the Perpetuities and Accumulations Act 1964, effective as of 16 July 1964 for instruments taking effect on or after that date (not being the exercise of a special power contained in a pre-16 July 1964 trust), it is possible to wait and see what actually happens until it becomes absolutely clear that a future interest is certain to vest outside the perpetuity period and only then is the interest void[1] unless it can be saved by application of the statutory class-closing rules in s 4 of the Act or by s 5 dealing with the unborn widow problem[2]. The Act also replaces causally relevant lives by a list of statutory lives in being[3] and allows a specific number of years not exceeding eighty to be chosen as the perpetuity period so long as expressly specified in that behalf[4]. However, an instrument exercising a special power of appointment can only use a specific period of years if the trust deed creating the power used a specific period of years[5].

1   Perpetuities and Accumulations Act 1964, s 3.
2   *Re Frost* (1889) 43 Ch D 246, and paras 11.19–11.21 below.
3   Perpetuities and Accumulations Act 1964, s 3(5).
4   Perpetuities and Accumulations Act 1964, s 1(1) on which see *Re Green's Will Trusts* [1985] 3 All ER 455.
5   Perpetuities and Accumulations Act 1964, s 1(2).

11.8 Only where a future interest is void under the common law rule against remoteness is there to be applied the 'wait and see' provisions and the statutory lives provisions of the 1964 Act. Thus, reliance is still often to be placed upon validity at common law with a royal lives perpetuity clause ensuring that all vesting in interest takes place 'within 21 years of the death of the last survivor of all the descendants of King George VI now living'.

11.9 The rule against remoteness cannot be evaded by imposing a condition that the person who receives the capital absolutely at the end of the perpetuity period must resettle the property upon certain trusts for his issue or forfeit the capital: such a condition is void as being repugnant to the absolute nature of the interest in capital[1]. However out of a sense of responsibility, the person ultimately receiving the capital (perhaps under the exercise of a power of appointment by the trustees) may well re-settle it on family discretionary trusts to preserve the wealth and influence of his family.

1   *Re Wenger's Settlement* (1963) 107 Sol Jo 981; *Re Brown* [1954] Ch 39, [1953] 2 All ER 1342.

Whether a trust is void for remoteness depends on possible, not actual, events

11.10 In considering whether limitations or trusts offend against the rule against remoteness *possible* events are to be considered[1]. If the trust contingency *might* in some event be too remote, it will be void, notwithstanding that in the events which have actually happened it would have occurred so that someone obtained an interest that vested within the prescribed period. To be good the limitation must be one of which, at its creation, it could be predicated that it *must* necessarily vest within the prescribed period[2]. For this purpose, physical impossibility was ignored so that female octogenarians were assumed capable of child bearing[3]. However, it had to be assumed that trustees would observe legal proprieties and not commit a breach of trust[4] and that legitimate children would not be born to persons under the age of marriage. Thus, a gift by will to such of G's grandchildren living at the testatrix's death or born within five years therefrom and attaining twenty-one was upheld[5], since it would be impossible for a child of G born after the death of the testatrix to have a child within the five year period. On the other hand, with regard to marriage settlements coming into operation before 1926, a trust for such of the children of the marriage as should attain the age of twenty-two years, or any greater age, was necessarily void for remoteness because both husband and wife *might* die leaving the child under one year of age who could not attain a vested interest within twenty-one years. For class gifts to vest in interest not only must (1) the person or persons entitled be ascertained and (2) the interest be ready to take effect in possession forthwith, subject only to prior interests, but (3) the size of the benefit must be known[6]. Thus, if a single member of the class might possibly not satisfy requirements (1) and (2) till after expiry of the perpetuity period the whole gift failed since the other class members could not satisfy requirement (3) till after expiry of the perpetuity period.

1   For a restatement of this principle see *Re Wills' Will Trusts* [1959] Ch 1, [1958] 2 All ER 472, where a power of advancement was possibly too remote in relation to some trusts but was held not to be too remote in relation to others under the same will.
2   *Re Atkins' Will Trusts* [1974] 2 All ER 1, [1974] 1 WLR 761; *Re Wood* [1894] 3 Ch 381; *Lord Dungannon v Smith* (1845) 12 Cl & Fin 546; *Smith v Smith* (1870) 5 Ch App 342; *Re Handcock's Trusts* (1889) 23 LR Ir 34; *Re Johnson* (1914) 111 LT 130; *Re Nash's Settlement* (1882) 51 LJ Ch 511; *Re Connell's Settlement, Re Benett's Trust* [1915] 1 Ch 867; *Re Engels* [1943] 1 All ER 506; and *Re Fry* [1945] Ch 348, [1945] 2 All ER 205. As to trusts to take effect in remainder upon the failure of such trusts, see para 11.110.
3   *Jee v Audley* (1787) 1 Cox Eq Cas 324; *Re Deloitte* [1926] Ch 56.
4   *Re Atkins' Will Trusts* [1974] 2 All ER 1, [1974] 1 WLR 761.
5   *Re Gaite's Will Trusts* [1949] 1 All ER 459.
6   *Leake v Robinson* (1817) 2 Mer 363; *Pearks v Moseley* (1880) 5 App Cas 714 at 723.

11.11 Fortuitously, in some cases the rule in *Andrews v Partington*[1] might apply to close the class when the first member became entitled to claim his share in possession[2]. This closing of the class against those born later will fix the maximum number of shares and so may often save the gift[3]. The primary purpose of the *Andrews v Partington* rule is to enable beneficiaries within the class to know their shares so that the property can be distributed to them by executors or trustees as soon as possible but the rule is only a rule of presumptive construction so that it can be ousted expressly or impliedly[4].

1   (1791) 3 Bro CC 401; *Re Bleckley* [1951] Ch 740, [1951] 1 All ER 1064; *Re Chapman's Settlement Trusts* [1978] 1 All ER 1122, [1977] 1 WLR 1163; (1954) 70 LQR 61 (J.H.C. Morris).
2   If, however, the beneficiaries qualify simply by being born then if no child has been born when the will or deed takes effect the first child born does not scoop the pool, the class remaining open for all after-born children to be included: *Re Ransome* [1957] Ch 348 at 359.
3   It will not assist if it could not be invoked at the time of the disposition creating the class gift (certainty being required at the outset) or if it closed a class of beneficiaries taking at 25 years of age since the closed class might comprise a person under four years of age who would not attain 25 within 21 years of the death of the last life in being.

⁴ *Re Drummond's Settlement* [1988] 1 All ER 449; [1988] 1 WLR 234, CA; *Re Tom's Settlement* [1987] 1 All ER 1081, [1987] 1 WLR 1021.

11.12 For trusts in instruments coming into operation after 1925 but before the application of the 1964 Act, s 163 of the Law of Property Act 1925 ensured that where a gift would be void for remoteness by reason of its being expressed to vest at an age exceeding twenty-one years, the latter age is to be substituted for the age stated if it would then make the gift valid. This provision, however, was without prejudice to any provision whereby absolute vesting is made dependent on marriage or any other event before the age stated in the instrument creating the trust.

11.13 The rule against remoteness will not be transgressed when, although the specified event might not happen within the perpetuity period the gift is only to take effect if it does happen within the period[1], but it will be transgressed by a provision for defeasance on the notification to trustees of the happening of an event which, if it happens at all, *must* happen within the perpetuity period if the notification may not be received by the trustees until after the end of the period[2].

[1] *Re Grotrian* [1955] Ch 501, [1955] 1 All ER 788.
[2] *Re Spitzel's Will Trusts* [1939] 2 All ER 266.

The 1964 Act improvements to the common law rule where otherwise the rule would make dispositions void

11.14 In relation to instruments to which it[1] applies the Act of 1964 makes substantial changes in the previous law stated above so as to save a gift that would be void at common law.

[1] See paras 11.7 and 11.31.

11.15 New provisions are made with regard to the possibility of parenthood[1]:

(a) Where in any proceedings a question arising on the rule against perpetuities turns on the ability of a person to have a child, it is to be presumed that a male can have a child at the age of fourteen or over but not under that age, and that a female can have a child at the age of twelve or over, but not under that age[2]. A female is to be presumed incapable of childbearing over the age of fifty-five, but there is no corresponding presumption as to males[3]. These presumptions apply also to the possibility that a person may have a child by adoption, legitimation 'or other means'[4]. In the case of a living person the presumptions may be rebutted by evidence showing that he or she will or will not be able to have a child at the time in question[5], but this provision for rebuttal does not apply to the possibility of having children by adoption, legitimation or other means[6].

(b) If such a question is decided by treating a person as unable to have a child at a particular time, and he or she does in fact have a child at that time, the court may make such order as it thinks fit for placing the persons interested in the property, so far as may be just, in the position in which they would have been if the question had not been decided in that way[7].

(c)   Subject to the point just mentioned, where such a question is decided by making a presumption that a person is able or unable to have a child at a particular time, the same presumption shall be made if any question arises on the rule against perpetuities in any subsequent proceedings in connection with the same disposition[8].

[1]   Perpetuities and Accumulations Act 1964, s 2.
[2]   Perpetuities and Accumulations Act 1964, s 2(1)(a).
[3]   Perpetuities and Accumulations Act 1964, s 2(1)(a).
[4]   Perpetuities and Accumulations Act 1964, s 2(4).
[5]   Perpetuities and Accumulations Act 1964, s 2(1)(b). Thus evidence of incurable incapacity may be given or that a woman over 55 recently had a child by the insertion of an embryo or could have a child in such fashion, she being the mother and her husband the father under the Human Fertilisation and Embryology Act 1990, ss 27 and 28.
[6]   Perpetuities and Accumulations Act 1964, s 2(4).
[7]   Perpetuities and Accumulations Act 1964, s 2(2).
[8]   Perpetuities and Accumulations Act 1964, s 2(3).

11.16   The Act also enables a draftsman, instead of using common law lives in being for ascertaining the perpetuity period, to use a fixed period of years not exceeding eighty specified in that behalf[1].

[1]   Perpetuities and Accumulations Act 1964, s 1. In *Re Green's Will Trusts* [1985] 3 All ER 455 Nourse J held it was unnecessary to specify a number of years and upheld a period specified as follows in a codicil: 'The period from the date of my death to 1 January 2020 is hereby specified as the Perpetuity Period for the trusts of the residue of my estate contained in my will'.

THE 1964 ACT 'WAIT AND SEE' PRINCIPLE SAVING TRUSTS OTHERWISE VOID

11.17   The Act introduces the principle of 'wait and see' by providing that where, *apart from* this newly introduced principle[1] and the provisions of ss 4 and 5 (considered at paras 11.19–11.21 below):

(a)   a disposition would otherwise be void on the ground that the interest disposed of might not become vested until too remote a time, the disposition is to be treated (unless and until it becomes established that the vesting must in fact occur too late) as if it was not subject to the rule against remoteness at all; and its becoming so established is not to affect the validity of anything previously done by way of advancement, application of intermediate income or otherwise[2];

(b)   a disposition which consists of the conferring of a general power of appointment would be void on the ground that the power might not become exercisable until too remote a time, the disposition is to be treated (unless and until it becomes established that the power will not in fact be exercisable within the perpetuity period) as if the disposition were not subject to the rule against remoteness[3];

(c)   a disposition (eg in the case of discretionary trusts) which consists of the conferring of any power, option or other right would be void on the ground that the right might be exercised at too remote a time, the disposition is to be treated as regards any exercise of the right which is in fact made within the perpetuity period as if it were not subject to the rule against remoteness, and is to be treated as void for remoteness only if, and so far as, the right is not fully exercised within that period[4].

1 The 'wait and see' principle in s 3 always applies in priority to ss 4 and 5.
2 Perpetuities and Accumulations Act 1964, s 3(1).
3 Perpetuities and Accumulations Act 1964, s 3(2).
4 Perpetuities and Accumulations Act 1964, s 3(3). As to the *administrative* powers of trustees, see also s 8, summarised at para 11.34 below.

11.18 In cases where the 'wait and see' principle comes into play, it is of course necessary to wait and see whether the event concerned does take place within the perpetuity period. The question then arises as to how the perpetuity period is to be determined for this purpose. Here, the Act contains special provisions[1] to the effect that where any one or more of certain persons listed and described in the Act[2] are individuals in being and ascertainable at the start of the perpetuity period, the duration of the period is in general to be the time during which they (or any of them) remain alive and twenty-one years thereafter. In other cases, the period is to be simply twenty-one years.

1 Perpetuities and Accumulations Act 1964, s 3(4) and (5). As to the desirability of this, see 80 LQR 486, 81 LQR 106, 86 LQR 357, 97 LQR 593 and (1986) 102 LQR 250.
2 See Perpetuities and Accumulations Act 1964, s 3(5).

11.19 Section 163 of the Law of Property Act 1925, which deals with the reduction of a beneficiary's age to twenty-one to avoid the failure of his gift for remoteness and is summarised above, is repealed by the Act of 1964 and replaced by new provisions[1].

(a) The first of these applies where a disposition is limited by reference to the attainment by any person or persons of a specified age greater than twenty-one, and it is apparent when the disposition is made (or it becomes apparent later) that the disposition would (but for the Act) fail for remoteness, but that it would be saved if the specified age were to be reduced to the age of twenty-one. In such a case, the disposition is to be treated for all purposes as if the age specified had been the nearest age to twenty-one which would have saved it[2].

(b) Where different ages exceeding twenty-one are specified in a disposition in regard to different persons, the provisions summarised in paragraph (a) above are to apply as if the reference to the disposition being saved if the specified age were to be reduced to the age of twenty-one were read as a reference to it being saved by the similar reduction of all the specified ages. Each one of the several ages specified is then to be notionally reduced so far as is necessary to save the disposition from failure through remoteness[3].

1 Perpetuities and Accumulations Act 1964, s 4. It is provided by sub-s (5) that where this section has effect in relation to a disposition to which s 3 (summarised above) applies, the operation of s 4 is not to affect the validity of anything previously done in relation to the interest disposed of by way of advancement, application of intermediate income or otherwise. The defect arising from the fact that the repeal of s 163 was contained in s 4(6)

will probably be held to have been remedied by the Children Act 1975. Sch 3, para 43, treating s 4(6) as a separate section despite the fact that para 43 does this as s 4(7) of the 1964 Act.

2   Perpetuities and Accumulations Act 1964, s 4(1). Where there are several beneficiaries it is unclear whether there must be a once-for-all reduction to an age which will save all beneficiaries for certain or whether age reduction can be by stages as one waits and sees what happens: [1969] CLJ 286 (M.J. Prichard). The former is more probable.

3   Perpetuities and Accumulations Act 1964, s 4(2).

11.20 In the case of class gifts, if not valid at common law or under the effect of the class-closing rule in *Andrews v Partington*[1] or under the statutory 'wait and see' principle, s 4(4) of the 1964 Act operates to exclude from the class any potential members whose inclusion would cause the disposition to fail for remoteness. Section 4(3) makes special provision for combining this class reduction with the age reduction provisions already discussed where needed to save a disposition.

1   See para 11.11 above.

11.21 It may also be noted here that the Act[1] contains provisions designed to deal with a draftsman's trap sometimes called the trap of the 'unborn widow'. These apply where a disposition is limited by reference to the time of death of the survivor of two people, one of them a person in being at the start of the perpetuity period and the other any spouse of that person. If that time has not arrived when the perpetuity period ends, then the disposition is to be treated for all purposes (if this would save it from being void for remoteness) as being limited by reference to the time immediately before the end of the period so that a beneficiary's interest vests in interest at that time.

1   Perpetuities and Accumulations Act 1964, s 5.

Property need not vest in possession within the prescribed period so long as it vests in interest

11.22 The rule against perpetuities does not require that the trust property shall vest absolutely *in possession* within the prescribed period. It suffices that it must necessarily vest absolutely *in interest*[1] in some person or persons, so that one can say with certainty at some time within that period that A as life tenant and B as absolute owner in remainder can collectively deal with the property. Thus, a trust for A for life, with remainder for any woman who may become his widow for life, with remainder for his children who shall attain twenty-one, is good as a whole[2]. For although it is possible that the woman who may become A's widow has not been born at the date when the settlement comes into operation, yet at the end of twenty-one years after the death of A it will be possible to say that his widow (if any) and his children who have attained twenty-one are together the absolute owners of the property.

1   This is the prima facie meaning of 'vested,' see *Re Wills' Will Trusts* [1959] Ch 1, [1958] 2 All ER 472, per Upjohn J. Also see para 11.6 above.

2   *Re Hargreaves* (1889) 43 Ch D 401 at 405; *Re Roberts* (1881) 19 Ch D 520; *Evans v Walker* (1876) 3 Ch D 211; *Re Lodwig* [1916] 2 Ch 26.

How far related trusts are invalidated

11.23 The question how far a trust which is void for remoteness invalidates other trusts connected with it is discussed at para 11.108.

Validity of powers

11.24 At common law a general power was void if it might be acquired outside the perpetuity period[1], though the 1964 Act allows a 'wait and see' period so that the power only becomes void if it becomes established that it cannot be acquired, and so become exercisable, within the perpetuity period[2]. A general power exercisable only by will ranks as a special power for determining its validity for perpetuity purposes[3]. At common law a special power was void if it might be exercised outside the perpetuity period[4], though the 1964 Act allows a 'wait and see' period so that the power only becomes void in so far as it is not exercised within the perpetuity period[5]. This applies to the powers of selection between the beneficiaries under a discretionary trust.

[1] *Bray v Hammersley* (1830) 3 Sim 513.
[2] Perpetuities and Accumulations Act 1964, s 3(2).
[3] *Wollaston v King* (1869) LR 8 Eq 165; *Morgan v Gronow* (1873) LR 16 Eq 1.
[4] *Re Abbott* [1893] 1 Ch 54.
[5] Perpetuities and Accumulations Act 1964, s 3(3).

Validity of trusts created under exercise of powers of appointment

THE LAW APART FROM THE 1964 ACT

11.25 Where a person has a *general* power to appoint a trust fund to such persons as he may think fit, the rule against perpetuities applies to an appointment made thereunder in the same way as it would to a disposition by an absolute owner, the reason being that the property is treated as vesting in the donee of the power[1]. But where, under a settlement or will, a person has a limited or *special* power (such as the power to appoint among issue commonly found in marriage settlements) or a power to appoint with the consent of another[2] or a joint power[3] a person taking under the power is deemed to take directly under the instrument creating it, so the perpetuity period runs from the date of the settlement creating the power[4]. However, for the purposes of the rule, under the 'second – look' doctrine, the effect of the appointment at the date when it comes into operation, and not what the possibilities might have been if the actual wording of the appointment had been in force from the outset of the trust are considered[5]. If, judged on the facts at the date the appointment took effect, it would have been void for remoteness as an original trust, it will equally be void for remoteness as an appointment[6]. An example is afforded by the case of *Re Thompson*[7] which emphasises the fact that it is the factual situation at the date of the power's exercise that is crucial in ascertaining whether or not the perpetuity period, running from the date of the creation of the power, can be exceeded. There the original will gave a life interest to the testator's widow, with remainder upon such trusts for the

249

11.25 *Matters essential to the prima facie validity of an express trust*

testator's brother CT and his issue as the widow should appoint. The widow by her will appointed in favour of CT for life with remainder to his children who being born in her lifetime should attain twenty-five, or being born after her death should attain twenty-one. At her death (when the appointment first came into operation) all of CT's then existing children were twenty-five.

¹ Per Roxburgh J in *Re Churston Settled Estates* [1954] Ch 334 at 346. In the report in [1954] 1 All ER 725 at 733, the more picturesque phrase 'being at home' in the donee of the power is used.
² *Re Watts* [1931] 2 Ch 302; *Re Churston's Settled Estates* [1954] Ch 334, [1954] 1 All ER 725.
³ *Re Churston's Settled Estates* [1954] Ch 334, [1954] 1 All ER 725. This decision ran counter to the practice of many conveyancers (see Mr F.E. Farrer's note in Key and Elphinstone, *Precedents in Conveyancing*, (14th edn) Vol 2, at p 1049), but stands as an authority, especially since it has been applied in *Re Earl of Coventry's Indentures* [1974] Ch 77, [1973] 3 All ER 1.
⁴ *Re Brown and Sibly's Contract* (1876) 3 Ch D 156; *Re Pratt's Settlement Trusts* [1943] Ch 356, [1943] 2 All ER 458.
⁵ *Re Thompson* [1906] 2 Ch 199; *Re Paul* [1921] 2 Ch 1.
⁶ Law of Property Act 1925, s 163 (2) applied to appointments where the *appointment* (not necessarily the power) came into operation after 1925.
⁷ [1906] 2 Ch 199.

11.26 It was contended that if the *words of appointment* had been written into the husband's will the trusts in favour of the children of CT who should attain twenty-five would have been void for remoteness. But Joyce J said¹:

'When it is stated that the test by which the validity of such a gift must be tried is to read it as inserted in the deed or will creating the power in the place of the power, it is not meant that the precise language of the instrument exercising the power is to be read into the instrument creating it ... Inasmuch, therefore, as the will of the widow was so made that the persons who, according to the true construction of such will, were to take under it, and the shares they were to take would necessarily be ascertained and their interests vest not later than the expiration of twenty-one years from the death of CT, who was alive at the death of the testator, the appointment was perfectly valid.'

¹ *Re Thompson, Thompson v Thompson* [1906] 2 Ch 199 at 205.

11.27 On the other hand, in *Re Legh's Settlement Trusts*¹, where in exercise of a special power in a settlement the donee of the power appointed to two objects of the power for their joint lives, with remainder to the survivor for life, it was held that the appointment to the survivor for life was void as it was a contingent interest and neither of the appointees was a life in existence at the date of the settlement creating the power.

¹ [1938] Ch 39, [1937] 3 All ER 823, following *Whitby v Von Leudecke* [1906] 1 Ch 783; and see *Re Johnson's Settlement Trusts* [1943] Ch 341, [1943] 2 All ER 499.

11.28 Where the appointor has both a general and a special power of appointment over the same fund and makes a single testamentary appointment it may be material to know which power was in fact exercised. In general a special power will not be held to have been exercised in the absence of some expression of intention to exercise it¹.

250

1   *Re Holford's Settlement* [1945] Ch 21, [1944] 2 All ER 462, reviewing many of the earlier cases.

11.29 Powers of advancement are subject to the rule against remoteness in the same way as special powers of appointment[1].

1   *Pilkington v IRC* [1964] AC 612, [1962] 3 All ER 622; cf *Hart (Inspector of Taxes) v Briscoe* [1979] Ch 1, [1978] 1 All ER 791.

CHANGES MADE BY THE 1964 ACT

11.30 In relation to instruments taking effect after its commencement, the Act of 1964 contains provisions of two different kinds.

11.31 First, the 'wait and see' provisions of the Act are applied by a special provision to powers of appointment, including powers of selecting between beneficiaries under a discretionary trust[1]. However, the Act only applies when both the creation and the exercise of the special power were under instruments taking effect after 15 July 1964[2].

1   See the Perpetuities and Accumulations Act 1964, s 3(2), (3).
2   Perpetuities and Accumulations Act 1964, s 15(5).

11.32 Second, the Act contains a statement of rules, designed to clarify rather than to change the law, for ascertaining whether, for the purposes of the rule against perpetuities, a power of appointment is to be treated as a general or a special one[1]. If the power was expressed in the instrument creating it to be exercisable by one person only and is such that, at all times during its currency when that person is of full age and capacity, he could exercise it so as immediately to transfer to himself the whole of the interest governed by the power (and could do so without the consent of anyone else and without having to comply with any other condition except a purely formal one relating only to the mode of exercising the power), then the power is to be treated as a general one. Otherwise it is to be treated as special. But a power which is exercisable by will only is to be treated as a general power where it would be treated in that way if exercisable by deed.

1   See the Perpetuities and Accumulations Act 1964, s 7.

Power of or trust for sale not limited in duration

11.33 Prior to the commencement of the Act of 1964, a trust of real estate forbidding a sale until the happening of an event (eg when the settlor's gravel pits were worked out) which might not happen within the allowed period was void[1]. A power of or trust for sale not expressly limited in point of duration was not, however, necessarily void; for there was a presumption that it was intended to be exercisable only before all beneficial interest should have vested absolutely in persons of full capacity, or, possibly, within a reasonable time after such interests were ascertained[2]. Even where it could be gathered that the settlor intended it to be exercised after that for purposes of division, it could still be exercised within the period allowed by the rule[3]. But where no successive interests were given and the property vested absolutely in persons of full capacity directly the settlement took effect, and no intention could be gathered that a power of a sale was merely given for facility of division, it was void for remoteness[4]. However, although the trust for, or power of, sale might be void, it was looked upon as mere machinery and would not avoid the trusts in favour of the beneficiaries if they took vested interests within the prescribed period[5].

[1] *Re Wood* [1894] 3 Ch 381; *Goodier v Edmunds* [1893] 3 Ch 455; *Re Daveron* [1893] 3 Ch 421.
[2] *Re W and R Holmes and Cosmopolitan Press Ltd's Contract* [1944] Ch 53, [1943] 2 All ER 716. In some of the cases reference has been made to vesting *in possession* (eg *Re Lord Sudeley and Baines & Co* [1894] 1 Ch 334; but vesting in possession might occur after the expiry of the perpetuity period; see *Re Allott* [1924] 2 Ch 498, CA (power of leasing held invalid), and cf *Re Wills' Will Trusts* [1959] Ch 1, [1958] 2 All ER 472 (power of advancement).
[3] *Re Lord Sudeley and Baines & Co* [1894] 1 Ch 334.
[4] *Re Dyson and Fowke* [1896] 2 Ch 720; *Re Jump* [1903] 1 Ch 129; and see *Re Kaye and Hoyle's Contract* (1909) 53 Sol Jo 520; and *Kennedy v Kennedy* [1914] AC 215, distinguished, however, in *Re Cassel* [1926] Ch 358 which was followed in *Beachway Management Ltd v Wisewell* [1971] Ch 610, [1971] 1 All ER 1.
[5] *Re Appleby* [1903] 1 Ch 565; *Goodier v Edmunds* [1893] 3 Ch 455; *Re Daveron* [1893] 3 Ch 421.

11.34 The law has however been changed by s 8 of the Perpetuities and Accumulations Act 1964, which is almost unique among the provisions of the Act in applying to instruments taking effect before, as well as after, its commencement[1]. This section provides that the rule against perpetuities is not to apply at all to a power conferred upon trustees or other persons to sell, lease, exchange or otherwise dispose for full consideration, or to do any other act in the administration (as opposed to the distribution) of any property. Nor is the rule to prevent the payment to trustees or other persons of reasonable remuneration for their services. It is to be noted that the administrative powers which fall within this provision are strictly defined: they would not, for instance, include a power to dispose of property for less than full consideration, though they may well include a power to mortgage or charge. It is clear, however, that although administrative powers which did not fall within this definition would still be subject to the rule against perpetuities, they would have the benefit of the 'wait and see' provisions of the Act which have already been discussed[2].

[1] This is so at least 'for the purpose of enabling a power to be exercised at any time after the commencement of [the] Act notwithstanding that the power is conferred by an instrument which took effect before that commencement'; Perpetuities and Accumulations Act 1964, s 8(2).
[2] See para 11.17 ff.

Exceptions from rule against remoteness

11.35 The rule does not apply to trusts following estates tail since they can be barred[1], nor to a joint tenant's right of survivorship[2], nor to a contingent gift over from one charity to another[3]. However, if a gift to a private person is followed by a gift over to charity the gift over is subject to the rule[4] as is any trust for charity conditional upon a future uncertain event[5]. Pension trusts (otherwise subject to the rule[6]) will normally be exempt due to statutory exemption[7].

1   *Heasman v Pearse* (1871) 7 Ch App 275; *Re Haygarth* [1912] 1 Ch 510.
2   *Re Roberts* (1881) 19 Ch D 520; *Re Smith* [1914] 1 Ch 937 at 948; *Re Goode* [1960] VR 117 at 124; but for a gift to a survivor of two persons see *Re Legh's Settlement Trusts* [1938] Ch 39.
3   *Christ's Hospital v Grainger* (1849) 1 Mac & G 460; *Re Tyler* [1891] 3 Ch 252; *Re Hanbey's Will Trusts* [1956] Ch 264, [1955] 3 All ER 874. There is a similar statutory exception for gifts over to charitable trusts from gifts for the' endowment of a historic building or garden: Historic Buildings and Ancient Monuments Act 1953, ss 8(5), 8A(5), 8B(5) as amended by National Heritage Act 1983, s 33, Sch 4, para 10.
4   *Re Johnson's Trusts* (1866) LR 2 Eq 716.
5   *Chamberlayne v Brockett* (1872) 8 Ch App 206 at 211; *Re Lord Stratheden and Campbell* [1894] 3 Ch 265.
6   *Air Jamaica Ltd v Charlton* [1999] 1 WLR 1399, PC.
7   Superannuation and Other Funds (Validation) Act 1927 followed by Social Security Act 1973, s 69 as amended by Social Security Pensions Act 1975, s 65(1), Sch 4 and Social Security Act 1986, s 86(1), Sch 10, Pt I; Personal and Occupational Pension Schemes (Perpetuities) Regs 1990; Pension Schemes Act 1993, s 163.

11.36 Furthermore, to put doubts at rest s 162 of the Law of Property Act 1925 is as follows:

'162.—(1) For removing doubts, it is hereby declared that the rule of law relating to perpetuities does not apply and shall be deemed never to have applied—

(a)   To any power to distrain on or to take possession of land or the income thereof given by way of indemnity against a rent, whether charged upon or payable in respect of any part of that land or not; or

(b)   To any rentcharge created only as an indemnity against another rentcharge, although the indemnity rentcharge may only arise or become payable on breach of a condition of stipulation; or

(c)   To any power, whether exercisable on breach of a condition or stipulation or not, to retain or withhold payment of any instalment of a rentcharge as an indemnity against another rentcharge; or

(d)   To any grant, exception, or reservation of any right of entry on, or user of, the surface of land or of any easements, rights, or privileges over or under land for the purpose of—

     (i)   winning, working, inspecting, measuring, converting, manufacturing, carrying away, and disposing of mines and minerals;

     (ii)   inspecting, grubbing up, felling and carrying away timber and other trees, and the tops and lops thereof;

     (iii)   executing repairs, alterations, or additions to any adjoining land, or the buildings and erections thereon;

     (iv)   constructing, laying down, altering, repairing, renewing, cleansing, and maintaining sewers, watercourses, cesspools, gutters, drains, water-pipes, gas-pipes, electric wires or cables or other like works.

(2)This section applies to instruments coming into operation before or after the commencement of this Act.'

Further reform of rule against remoteness

11.37 The Law Commission in a Report[1] (with a draft bill annexed) accepted by the Government has recommended a fixed period of 125 years within which an equitable interest must vest in instruments made after the reform is enacted (including appointments under a special power of appointment created beforehand).

1   Report on the Rules against Perpetuities and Excessive Accumulations (Law Com No. 251, 1998).

The rule against inalienability or purpose trusts of excessive duration

11.38 This rule, makes void endowment[1] trusts for purposes of a non-charitable nature where one cannot be sure by the end of the perpetuity period the trust fund will be available to be spent freely on non-trust purposes because beneficially owned by persons who can spend the capital on themselves. The fact that the income has to be spent on trust purposes means that the income is inalienable and this has the effect of rendering the trust fund inalienable in that the trust fund must always be retained in one form or another to give effect to the income trusts[2].

1   If the trust fund can be freely disposed of without distinction between capital and income there are no perpetuity problems, eg *Re Lipinski's Will Trusts* [1976] Ch 235, [1977] 1 All ER 33.
2   It is immaterial that the investments within the capital fund can be freely transposed into other investments.

11.39 The following are examples of trusts void for inalienability: a devise of 'Elmslea' to trustees upon trust for the purposes of a contemplative (and therefore non-charitable) order of nuns[1]; a bequest to trustees for the provision of an annual cup for the most successful yacht in a sailing club[2]; a bequest to trustees for the maintenance of a tomb that is not part of the fabric of a church[3].

1   *Leahy v A-G for New South Wales* [1959] AC 457, [1959] 2 All ER 300.
2   *Re Nottage* [1895] 2 Ch 649; *Re Gwyon* [1930] 1 Ch 255.
3   *Re Rickard* (1862) 31 Beav 244; *Re Dean* (1889) 41 Ch D 552 at 557; *Re Elliott* [1952] 1 All ER 145; *Re Dalziel* [1943] Ch 277, [1943] 2 All ER 656.

11.40 As already discussed at paras 8.189–8.190, gifts for unincorporated associations raise special problems in connection with the rule against inalienability and the rule against remoteness.

11.41 The rule against inalienability may be avoided by creating alienable determinable interests in income[1]. Thus a fund can be left to T1 and T2 upon trust to pay the income therefrom to the A Charity Co for such company to dispose of as it wishes for so long as the following purpose ... shall be carried out but as soon as such purpose shall not be carried out then on trust to pay the income to the B Charity Co for such company to dispose of as it wishes for so long as the purpose aforesaid shall be carried out [and so on to the Z Charity Co][2].

1   *Re Chardon* [1928] Ch 464; *Re Chambers' Will Trusts* [1950] Ch 267; contrast *Re Wightwick's Will Trusts* [1950] Ch 260, [1950] 1 All ER 689.

2   The gifts over from one charity to another are exempt from the rule against remoteness and unaffected by Perpetuities and Accumulations Act 1964, s 12. Maintenance of private graves is possible for 99 years under the Parish Council and Burial Authorities (Miscellaneous Provisions) Act 1970, s 1.

11.42 The perpetuity period beyond which an interest may not be inalienable is the same as for the common law rule against remoteness[1], ie causally relevant lives (if applicable) and 21 years because the operation of the rule against inalienability (or perpetual purpose trusts) is expressly excluded from the 1964 Act. The curiously worded s 15(4) of the Perpetuities and Accumulations Act 1964 expressly provides that nothing in the Act is to affect the operation of the rule rendering void[2] certain dispositions under which property is limited to be applied for purposes other than the benefit of any person or class of persons where the property may be so applied after the end of the perpetuity period applicable to the relevant disposition under such rule. Thus the perpetuity period, so far as the rule against inalienability is concerned, cannot be a period of years not exceeding 80 as allowed by s 1 of the Act for the rule against remoteness.

1   *Thellusson v Woodford* (1805) 11 Ves 112 at 135, 146; *Re Dean* (1889) 41 Ch D 552 at 557 (though wrong in allowing animal lives to count as lives in being); *Re Moore* [1901] 1 Ch 936; *Re Astor's Settlement Trusts* [1952] Ch 534, [1952] 1 All ER 1067; *Re Khoo Cheng Teow* [1932] Straits Settlement Reports 226.
2   The draftsman actually states 'void for remoteness', considering the rule against inalienability or perpetual purpose trusts to make trusts for purposes void if they can continue till too remote a time, while using in s 1 'the rule against perpetuities' when referring to what we have earlier referred to, strictly, as the rule against remoteness concerned with trusts for people as opposed to trust for purposes.

11.43 The rule against inalienability does not apply to charitable trusts[1].

1   *Chamberlayne v Brockett* (1872) 8 Ch App 206 at 211. Thus a 1585 charitable trust was upheld in *A-G v Webster* (1875) LR 20 Eq 483.

Paragraph 1 (b)

Excessive Accumulations of income

No accumulation beyond one of six periods

11.44 At common law, the period for which money could be tied up so as to accumulate at compound interest was co-extensive with the period for which property might be tied up under the rule against remoteness, and the Law Commission in a Report[1] accepted by the Government has recommended that the accumulation period should be co-extensive with the recommended 125 year period for the rule against remoteness. However, when a testator directed his property to be accumulated during the lives of all his descendants living at his death[2], the common law power was seen to be unreasonably wide, especially by Members of Parliament who were sons of wealthy men and did not want themselves or their descendants kept out of income for too long. Accordingly, by the statute 39 & 40 Geo 3, c 98 (commonly known as the Thellusson Act after the testator of that name whose will provoked the Act)[3], now repealed and re-enacted by ss 164 and 165 of the Law of Property Act 1925, the period allowed for accumulations was restricted to one (and one only) of the following:

(a)   the life of the grantor or settlor[4];
(b)   21 years from the death of the grantor, settlor, devisor or testator;
(c)   the duration of the minorities of any persons who should be living, or en ventre sa mère, at the death of the grantor, settlor, devisor or testator; or
(d)   the duration of the minority or respective minorities of any persons who, under the instrument directing the accumulation, would for the time being, if of full age, be entitled to the income directed to be accumulated. This period is not restricted to the minority of persons in existence at the time when the settlement came into force[5], although the statute does not permit the accumulations in that case to be made during the period before their birth[6].

1   Report on the Rules against Perpetuities and Excessive Accumulations (Law Com No 251, 1998).
2   *Thellusson v Woodford* (1805) 11 Ves 112.
3   See *Bassil v Lister* (1851) 9 Hare 177.
4   *Stewart's Trustees v Stewart* 1927 SC 350.
5   *Re Cattell* [1907] 1 Ch 567; affd by the CA [1914] 1 Ch 177, dissenting from *Haley v Bannister* (1819) 4 Madd 275; *Jagger v Jagger* (1883) 25 Ch D 729, and *Re Watts' Will Trusts* [1936] 2 All ER 1555.
6   *Ellis v Maxwell* (1841) 3 Beav 587 at 596.

11.45 In respect of instruments which take effect after the commencement, on 16 July 1964, of the Perpetuities and Accumulations Act 1964, however, it is provided[1] that the periods for which accumulation is permitted by s 164 of the Law of Property Act 1925 shall include two other periods, namely:

(e)   a term of 21 years from the date of the making of the disposition (a disposition contained in a will being deemed to be made at the testator's death)[2]; or
(f)   the duration of the minority or respective minorities of any person or persons in being at that date.

1   See the Perpetuities and Accumulations Act 1964, s 13(1).
2   Perpetuities and Accumulations Act 1964, s 15(2).

11.46 The Act also contains a declaration[1] that the restrictions imposed by s 164 apply in relation to a power to accumulate income whether or not there is a duty to exercise it, and whether or not it extends to income produced by the investment of income previously accumulated (viz whether compound or simple interest is involved). Companies, however, that are settlors are wholly exempt[2] though if S transfers property to a company which declares that it, as settler, is settling the property on particular trusts, S, as the provider of the property settled as he directed, will be treated as the real settlor[3]. If S adds perperty to a trust genuinely created by a company settler, S will be regarded as settlor of the added property[4].

1 Perpetuities and Accumulations Act 1964, s 13(2). This confirms the view in *Re Robb's Will Trusts* [1953] Ch 459, [1953]1 All ER 920 (overruled on another point in *Re Berkley* [1968] Ch 744) endorsed by HL in *Baird v Lord Advocate* [1979] AC 666, [1979] 2 All ER 28, HL.
2 *Re Dodwell & Co Ltd's Trust Deed* [1979] Ch 301, [1978] 3 All ER 738.
3 *Re TR Technology Investment Trust p/c* [1988] BCLC 256 at 263–264.
4 *CIR v Dick* (2001) 4 ITELR 315, para 40.

11.47 The statutory provisions set out above must be construed in the light of the Family Law Reform Act 1969, the relevant parts of which came into force on 1 January 1970. By virtue of s 1(1) of the Act, a person attains full age at eighteen, instead of twenty-one and by virtue of the general provision in s 1(2) the references in the Acts of 1925 and 1964 to 'minority' or 'minorities' are to be construed accordingly. This does not, of course, affect the specific references in those Acts to periods of twenty-one years, which are not affected by the 1969 Act. Furthermore, it is provided by s 1(4) and Sch 3, para 7, that these changes are not to invalidate any direction for accumulation in a settlement or other disposition made by a deed, will or other instrument which was made before 1 January 1970 (and a will or codicil executed before that date is not to be treated for this purpose as having been made on or after that date merely because it has been confirmed by a codicil executed on or after that date: s 1(7)).

RIGHT TO TERMINATE ACCUMULATIONS

11.48 The principle sometimes known as the rule in *Saunders v Vautier*[1] permits a beneficiary who is of full capacity to put an end to an accumulation which is entirely for his benefit. Thus a beneficiary (or beneficiaries acting together) may sometimes be able to prevent accumulation from continuing by bringing it to an end. In determining whether an existing beneficiary (or existing beneficiaries) were entitled to exercise this right, however, the law as it stood before the Act of 1964 did not permit a woman's incapacity to bear children to be taken into account[2]. But with respect to instruments taking effect after its commencement, the 1964 Act provides[3] that the new provisions relating to the possibility of future parenthood[4], which are contained in the Act and have already been mentioned[5], are to apply where any question arises as to the right of beneficiaries to put an end to accumulations of income, in the same way as they apply to questions arising on the rule against perpetuities.

1 (1841) 4 Beav 115; *Wharton v Masterman* [1895] AC 186. See also Article 72, below.
2 *Re Deloitte* [1926] Ch 56. This case was doubted by the House of Lords in *Berry v Green* [1938] AC 575, [1938] 2 All ER 362, but in *IRC v Bernstein* [1960] Ch 444, [1960] 1 All ER 697, Danckwerts J said that despite the doubts cast upon it the former case was plainly binding on him as regards the principle which it laid down. It would now be saved by the operation of ss 14 and 2 of the 1964 Act.
3 Perpetuities and Accumulations Act 1964, s 14.
4 See the Perpetuities and Accumulations Act 1964, s 2.
5 See para 11.15 above.

EXCLUSIONS FROM ACCUMULATION RULES

11.49 The statutory restriction of accumulations does not extend to any provision for payment of debts, or for raising portions for the legitimate children of the settlor, grantor, or devisor, or of any person taking any interest under the instrument directing such accumulations; nor to any direction as to the produce of timber upon any lands; nor to a trust or direction for keeping property in repair[1]; nor to the accumulation of surplus income under any statutory power or under the general law (powers of maintenance of infants etc) made during a minority[2], nor to a direction to apply income for keeping up an insurance policy to mature on expiry of a lease, so preserving capital value[3].

[1] *Vine v Raleigh* [1891] 2 Ch 13, CA; *Re Mason* [1891] 3 Ch 467. Maintaining property at its present value is not a true accumulation since the capital of the property is not augmented.
[2] Law of Property Act 1925, s 165. An express trust for accumulation for any other permitted period is not invalidated by reason of accumulations also having been made under such statutory power or the general law. See *Re Maber* [1928] Ch 88. As to 'minority', see the provisions of the Family Law Reform Act 1969, discussed above.
[3] *Re Gardiner* [1901] 1 Ch 697; and see *Miller v IRC* [1987] STC 108. Income applied for life policy premiums to increase capital may be an accumulation, *Carver v Duncan* [1985] AC 1082 at 1099–1100 querying *Bassil v Lister* (1851) 9 Hare 177. Lord Templeman at 1122–1124 seems to suggest that the test to be applied is whether the income is directed to be applied on a capital, as opposed to an income, expense; if so, there is an accumulation. The modern approach is to consider payment of premiums as a purchase of a commercial investment that falls outside the Acts: see Law Commission Consultation Paper No 133, paras 3–34 to 3–36 and Law Commission Report No 251, paras 9.33 to 9.35 and 11.57.

11.50 The case of *Re Rochford's Settlement Trusts*[1] bears on the principles just stated. In that case the settlor had provided that estate duty payable in certain events should in effect be borne by the income of a trust fund. Some time after the settlement was made, events occurred which gave rise to estate duty liability, and if this liability was to be discharged out of the income of the fund the income would have to be accumulated for this purpose for a number of years.

[1] [1965] Ch 111, [1964] 2 All ER 177.

11.51 Cross J held that these provisions fell within the terms of s 164 of the Law of Property Act 1925 and, since they made use of none of the accumulation periods permitted by that section, they were void with the consequence that the estate duty liability should be met out of capital. The provisions were not within the exception to s 164 whereby that section does not apply to accumulations for the payment of debts, because for this purpose the debt in question must be in existence as a legal liability (if only a contingent one) when the instrument providing for the accumulation takes effect. Had the settlement in this case been made after the commencement of the Perpetuities and Accumulations Act 1964, the provision would no doubt have been valid to the extent that it fell within the first of the two new accumulation periods permitted by that Act and mentioned above (ie accumulation for a term of twenty-one years from the date of the making of the disposition).

258

11.52 The exception for provisions for raising portions[1] was considered by the Court of Appeal in *Re Bourne's Settlement Trusts*[2]:

> 'The phrase "raising portions" is a technical phrase of conveyancing. A more accurate way to express the intention of the legislature might possibly have been to use the phrase "for creating portions"... It has been settled quite clearly that the phrase "raising portions" does not cover the case where all that is done is to treat the accumulations as, and deal with them as, an addition to capital. Indeed, if that were what the phrase meant, any accumulation for the benefit of children would have fallen within the exception. The authorities come to this: that accumulations do not fall within this language unless they are themselves, as separate items, used for the purpose of portions. This must not be merely by way of addition to a capital gift ... Where the settlement ... merely gives a power to deal with the accumulations so that the result could be described as a portion, it does not, in my opinion, satisfy the section. You cannot predicate of the provision in the settlement that it is a provision for "raising portions" when whether it is so used depends entirely on the discretion of some third person, who may use it that way, or who may not.'

[1] As to the meaning of 'portions', see *Re Elliott* [1918] 2 Ch 150; *Watt v Wood* (1862) 2 Drew & Sm 56 at 60.
[2] [1946] 1 All ER 411. See also *Wildes v Davies* (1853) 1 Sm & G 475; *Bourne v Buckton* (1851) 2 Sim NS 91.

11.53 There is little doubt that the statutory restrictions on accumulation apply to an implied trust to accumulate as well as to an express one, but it is sometimes difficult in such cases to determine whether there really is an implied trust to accumulate or not. Thus two cases[1] previously relied upon in support of the proposition just stated were disapproved by the Court of Appeal in *Re Berkeley*[2], not because the proposition was held to be wrong but because the court considered that those two cases (in common with the case they were themselves considering) did not involve any trust to accumulate, implied or otherwise, within the ambit of s 164. The facts were that the surplus income of a trust fund had been accumulated by trustees of a will in fulfilment of their obligation to protect an annuitant by securing the payment of an annuity which, under the will, was a continuing charge on the income of the trust fund. The court held that this retention of income to meet a possible future income need did not amount to an '[accumulation] for [a] ... period' within s 164. The court's reasons for reaching this conclusion may shed some light on the meaning of accumulation itself. Harman LJ said:

> 'Is this an accumulation? I think not. Accumulation to my mind involves the addition of income to capital, thus increasing the estate in favour of those entitled to capital and against the interests of those entitled to income.'

[1] *Re Robb's Will Trusts* [1953] Ch 459, [1953] 1 All ER 920; *Re Nash* [1965] 1 All ER 51.
[2] [1968] Ch 744, [1968] 3 All ER 364, CA.

11.54 This seems a narrow definition of accumulation which would render its meaning more restricted than has hitherto been supplied[1]. Widgery LJ, at least, preferred a wider definition. He said:

> 'I doubt if the word "accumulation" signifies more than a simple aggregation of instalments of income to create a single fund ... '

¹   It seems, for instance, that the 'accumulation' involved in *Re Rochford's Settlement Trusts* [1965] Ch 111, [1964] 2 All ER 177, might not fall within this definition.

11.55 But he added, referring to the words used in s 164:

'... but the reference to accumulation for a *period* clearly implies in my judgment, a mounting fund which reaches a climax at the end of the period.'

11.56 Russell LJ did not venture a definition of accumulation, but rested his judgment on the ground that the case involved only a de facto accumulation made necessary by the trustees' uncertainty as to the availability of assets of the estate, and this at any rate was not an accumulation for a period within the meaning of s 164.

11.57 The statutory restrictions have no application to provisions for the accumulation of sums available for distribution, but not in fact distributed, under a deed constituting a unit trust¹, whether because all the unit holders could end the trust (or even ask in any year for all the income to be distributed and not added to capital) or because the legislation did not have any application to commercial situations. This latter reason followed the reasoning in *Bassil v Lister*² where a testator's direction to his trustees to pay the premiums on a policy of life assurance he had taken out on the life of his son out of the income of his residuary estate was held not to be an accumulation. Statute provides that no person (which has been held to mean individuals and not corporations) may 'settle or dispose' of property in breach of the restrictions against accumulations and there are many commercial transactions or commercial investments which are not properly within those terms, eg partnership agreements involving accumulation of profits for long periods, life insurance policies on the lives of debtors, a settlement of insurance policies with shares transferred to pay the premiums out of the dividends, unit trusts that capitalise part of their income, investment trusts split into capital and income shares. Such transactions and provisions for making payments in respect of them should therefore fall outside the rule³. This should also be the case for pension scheme trusts⁴ though normally they will be created by a company settlor so as to fall outside the legislation anyway⁵.

¹   *Re AEG Unit Trust (Manager) Ltd's Deed* [1957] Ch 415, [1957] 2 All ER 506.
²   (1851) 9 Hare 177 followed in *Re Vaughan* [1883] WN 89; *Re AEG Unit Trust (Managers) Ltd's Deed* [1957] Ch 415, [1957] 2 All ER 506, though cf comments in *Carver v Duncan* [1985] AC 1082 at 1100, 1122–1124.
³   Megarry & Wade, *Law of Real Property* (6th edn) para 7–177, Law Com Consultation Paper No 133 para 3.35. Similarly on expiry of the accumulation period the trustees, if authorised by the trust deed, could transfer investments to a company wholly owned by them which could retain the income from such investments and effectively accumulate it.
⁴   Hansard (HC) 1 July 1964 vol 697, cols, 1503–1504.
⁵   *Re Dodwell & Co Ltd's Trust* [1979] Ch 301, [1978] 3 All ER 738, assuming the company is not acting merely as nominee for an individual.

Accumulations for the purpose of purchasing land

11.58 By an Act passed in 1892, and now repealed, and re-enacted in altered form in s 166 of the Law of Property Act 1925¹, the period allowed by the

Thellusson Act is further restricted, where the accumulation is to be made either wholly or partially for the purchase of land only, to the minority or respective minorities[2] of any person or persons who, under the instrument directing the accumulations, 'would for the time being (if of full age) be entitled to receive the rents, issues, profits, or income so directed to be accumulated'.

[1]   But not where the accumulations are directed for the purchase of land and other purposes (*Re Knapp* [1929] 1 Ch 341).
[2]   As to 'minority', see the provisions of the Family Law Reform Act 1969, discussed at para 11.47 above.

Excessive accumulation

11.59 If an express or implied trust for accumulation infringes the perpetuity period allowed under the rule against remoteness it is wholly void[1]. If within the perpetuity period but exceeding the authorised accumulation periods, the trust is restricted to the nearest period of the six authorised periods and only the excess is void[2]. The income for the excess period goes to the person or persons who would have been entitled to such income if accumulation had not been directed[3] eg the settlor of a lifetime trust or the person entitled to residue or undisposed of property in the case of a testamentary trust[4].

[1]   *Curtis v Lukin* (1842) 5 Beav 147; *Martin v Maugham* (1844) 14 Sim 230. The Perpetuities and Accumulations Act 1964 does not seem to provide for the wait and see rules to apply, which seems unsatisfactory, unless one can strain the language of s 3(3) to treat 'any power option or other right' as extending to powers and duties to accumulate: see Megarry and Wade, *Law of Real Property* (6th edn) para 7–162 and Law Com Consultation Paper No 133 para 3.23 and Law Com Report No 251, para 9.24.
[2]   *Re Watt's Will Trusts* [1936] 2 All ER 1555 at 1562; *Re Ransome* [1957] Ch 348 at 361.
[3]   Law of Property Act 1925, s 164(1). However, where there is a general charitable intention expressed with regard to the income it will be devoted to charity cy-près: *Re Bradwell* [1952] Ch 575, [1952] 2 All ER 286.
[4]   If the residue is held on trust for A for life, remainder to B it seems the excess income should be paid to A: *Re Hawkins* [1916] 2 Ch 570; *Re Garside* [1919] 1 Ch 132.

Paragraph 1 (c)

Attempts to alter the rules of devolution prescribed by law

11.60 If there is a trust of real or personal property for A absolutely, but if he dies intestate then for B, the divesting gift over to B is void as an attempt to alter the ordinary law of devolution[1]. In short, any trust creating an *absolute* equitable interest in A, but attempting to negative the statutory devolution on intestacy or the power of testamentary disposition, or the right of committing waste, or of alienating or charging the estate (even where there is a condition subsequently purporting to create a forfeiture) is, qua such attempt, void[2].

[1]   *Gulliver v Vaux* (1746) 8 De GM & G 167n; *Holmes v Godson* (1856) 8 De GM & G 152; *Barton v Barton* (1857) 3 K & J 512; *Re Wilcock's Settlement* (1875) 1 Ch D 229; *Re Dixon* [1903] 2 Ch 458; *Krasner v Dennison* [2001] Ch 76, CA. See also *Re Ashton* [1920] 2 Ch 481 (gift over if donee should die non compos held void).

² Co Litt 222 b; *Portington's Case* (1613) 10 Co Rep 35 b, 39 a: *Shaw v Ford* (1877) 7 Ch D 669; *Re Dugdale* (1888) 38 Ch D 176; *Braithwaite v A-G* [1909] 1 Ch 510; and see also *Carr v Living* (1860) 28 Beav 644; *Re Brown* [1954] Ch 39 and *Re Dixon* [1903] 2 Ch 458.

Settlements against the policy of bankruptcy law

11.61 A trust, with a condition or proviso that the interest of the beneficiary shall not be liable to the claims of creditors, is void so far as the condition or proviso is concerned[1]. The beneficiary's conditional interest (whether absolute or for life) will vest in his trustee in bankruptcy for the benefit of his creditors regardless of the condition. Similarly a man cannot make a settlement of his own property[2] upon *himself* until bankruptcy, and then over[3], and this is so even in the case of an ante-nuptial settlement, where it might fairly be urged to be part of *the wife's* terms of the marriage bargain[4]. However, a man might on marriage settle his own property on an immediate discretionary trust for himself, etc, during his life, as there would then be no alteration of the trust to take effect on bankruptcy.

¹ For example, see *Younghusband v Gisborne* (1844) 1 Coll 400; affd (1846) 15 LJ Ch 355; *Green v Spicer* (1830) 1 Russ & M 395; *Graves v Dolphin* (1826) 1 Sim 66; *Piercy v Roberts* (1832) 1 My & K 4; *Snowdon v Dales* (1834) 6 Sim 524; *Re Sanderson's Trust* (1857) 3 K & J 497.
² See *Re Holland* [1902] 2 Ch 360, overruling *Re Pearson* (1876) 3 Ch D 807; *Re Ashby* [1892] 1 QB 872.
³ *Knight v Browne* (1861) 7 Jur NS 894; *Brooke v Pearson* (1859) 27 Beav 181; *Re Burroughs-Fowler* [1916] 2 Ch 251; *Re Wombwell* (1921) 125 LT 437.
⁴ *Higinbotham v Holme* (1812) 19 Ves 88; *Ex p Hodgson* (1812) 19 Ves 206; *Re Pearson* (1876) 3 Ch D 807; but consider *Re Detmold* (1889) 40 Ch D 585, and *Re Johnson* [1904] 1 KB 134.

11.62 On the other hand, a trust created by a third party, to pay the income to A until he dies or becomes bankrupt or alienates or charges his life interest, and then over to B, is perfectly good[1], and may even take effect in respect of bankruptcy or alienation preceding the settlement[2]. The distinction between this valid determinable interest and the void conditional interest is that the determinable limitation is allowed since the limitation merely sets a natural limit to the interest whilst a condition or proviso cuts down the interest before it reaches its natural limit[3].

¹ See *Billson v Crofts* (1873) LR 15 Eq 314; *Re Aylwin's Trusts* (1873) LR 16 Eq 585, and cases there cited; and as to income accrued before forfeiture but not paid over, see *Re Jenkins* [1915] 1 Ch 46. Such a clause will be strictly construed; see *Re Longman* [1955] 1 All ER 455, [1955] 1 WLR 197 (gift over on an act whereby income vested in another; authority to pay dividends to creditors held not to cause a forfeiture because no dividend declared).
² *West v Williams* [1898] 1 Ch 488; *Re Walker* [1939] Ch 974, [1939] 3 All ER 902.
³ *Brandon v Robinson* (1811) 18 Ves 429; *Rochford v Hackman* (1852) 9 Hare 475; Megarry and Wade, *Law of Real Property* (6th edn) pp 64–70.

11.63 A trust creating a determinable life interest determining naturally upon bankruptcy or alienation (giving what is known as 'a protected life interest') is equally good where the trustee is, upon bankruptcy of or alienation by the beneficiary, given a discretion to apply the income for the benefit or maintenance of the bankrupt or his wife or issue[1], or any other indicated persons, *or any of them*. Such trusts were so common (though discretionary trusts with a letter of wishes are normally now utilised) that the Trustee Act 1925, in s 33, contains the following provisions intended to shorten wills and settlements by substituting a reference to 'protective trusts' for the rather lengthy clause formerly employed[2].

'(1)Where any income, including an annuity or other periodical income payment, is directed to be held on protective trusts for the benefit of any person[3] (in this section called 'the principal beneficiary') for the period of his life or for any less period, then, during that period[4] (in this section called the 'trust period') the said income shall, without prejudice to any prior interest, be held on the following trusts, namely:

   (i)   Upon trust for the principal beneficiary during the trust period or until he, whether before or after the termination of any prior interest, does or attempts to do[5] or suffers any act or thing, or until any event happens, other than an advance under any statutory or express powers[6], whereby, if the said income were payable during the trust period to the principal beneficiary absolutely during that period, he would be deprived of the right to receive the same or any part thereof, in any of which cases, as well as on the termination of the trust period, whichever first happens, this trust of the said income shall fail or determine[7],

   (ii)   If the trust aforesaid fails or determines during the subsistence of the trust period, then, during the residue of that period, the said income shall be held upon trust for the application[8] thereof for the maintenance or support, or otherwise for the benefit, of all or any one or more exclusively[9] of the other or others of the following persons (that is to say)

      (a)   the principal beneficiary and his or her wife or husband, if any, and his or her children or more remote issue[10], if any; or

      (b)   if there is no wife or husband or issue of the principal beneficiary[11] in existence, the principal beneficiary and the persons who would, if he were actually dead, be entitled to the trust property or the income thereof or to the annuity fund, if any, or arrears of the annuity, as the case may be[12], as the trustees in their absolute discretion, without being liable to account for the exercise of such direction, think fit.

(2)This section does not apply to trusts coming into operation before the commencement of this Act, and has effect subject to any variation of the implied trusts aforesaid contained in the instrument creating the trust.

(3)Nothing in this section operates to validate any trust which would, if contained in the instrument creating the trust, be liable to be set aside.'

1   Note that by virtue of s 15 of the Family Law Reform Act, references in disposition made on or after 1 January 1970, to the child or children of any person, or to a person or persons related in some other manner to any person, are in certain circumstances to be construed as including references to illegitimate children and persons related through illegitimacy.

2   The effect is to engraft trusts on the life interest so that if the life interest is extinguished (eg by order of the divorce court) the engrafted trusts are extinguished also (*Re Allsopp's Marriage Settlement Trusts* [1959] Ch 81, [1958] 2 All ER 393). In *General Accident Fire and Life Assurance Corpn Ltd v IRC* [1963] 3 All ER 259, the Court of Appeal held that an order of the court under s 192 of the Supreme Court of Judicature (Consolidation) Act 1925 (now s 24 of the Matrimonial Causes Act 1973) to pay an annual sum of money during the wife's life did not bring about a forfeiture of the husband's protected life interest

under s 33 of the Trustee Act 1925, and accordingly the discretionary trusts under s 33(1) did not arise. This was because the court order overrode the settlement trusts, was an event to which both life tenant and trustee had to bow, and was not such an event as was contemplated by s 33(1), this being intended as a protection to spendthrift or improvident or weak-minded life tenants.

3   Natural persons, not companies: *IRC v Brandenbury* [1982] STC 555.

4   See *Cholmondeley v IRC* [1986] STC 384.

5   He need have no responsibility for this event unlike the position on a proper construction of some express trusts: *Re Hall* [1944] Ch 46, [1943] 2 All ER 753; *Re Pozot's Settlement Trust* [1952] Ch 427, [1952] 1 All ER 1107.

6   Cf *Re Hodgson* [1913] 1 Ch 34; *Re Rees* [1954] Ch 202, [1954] 1 All ER 7. A court order that the principal beneficiary shall charge his interest will create an equitable charge, and thus work a forfeiture, even though no deed of charge is executed (*Re Richardson's Will Trusts* [1958] Ch 504, [1958] 1 All ER 538). See also *Edmonds v Edmonds* [1965] 1 All ER 379n (attachment of earnings order to secure former wife's maintenance held to cause forfeiture).

7   Where the corpus becomes vested in the same person who has a protected life estate there is no merger: *Re Chance's Settlement Trusts* [1918] WN 34. Whether on the true construction of this sub-clause the principal beneficiary would on bankruptcy forfeit his interest absolutely so as to bring the discretionary trust into force, or whether if the bankruptcy was annulled or suspended under a compromise his interest would be restored does not seem very clear (see *Re Clark* [1926] Ch 833, and *Re Forder* [1927] 2 Ch 291). It is settled, however, that an order to discharge has no effect on the previous forfeiture: *Re Walker* [1939] Ch 974, [1939] 3 All ER 902.

8   The trustees must apply all income for the benefit of the persons mentioned under (a) and (b): *Re Gourju's Will Trusts* [1943] Ch 24, [1942] 2 All ER 605. If any income remains in the trustees' hands at the death of the first beneficiary it must be so applied thereafter: *Re Forster's Settlement* [1942] Ch 199, [1942] 1 All ER 180. All sums paid out of income in exercise of the trustees' discretion form part of the total income of the recipient for tax purposes (*Lindus and Hortin v IRC* (1933) 17 TC 442).

9   The donee of a power of appointment may sometimes wish to exercise it by giving a protected life interest to a beneficiary, but, with the possibility of a discretionary trust arising thereunder, this will only be effective if the power is construed as wide enough to permit the creation of new dispositive discretionary powers. Nineteenth century powers of appointment in their context were construed narrowly but in more modern contexts the courts have too unquestioningly followed old case law (like *Re Joicey* [1915] 2 Ch 115): see *Re Boulton's Settlement Trust* [1928] Ch 703; *Re Morris' Settlement Trusts* [1951] 2 All ER 528, CA. The latter case was followed, but reluctantly, in *Re Hunter's Will Trusts* [1963] Ch 372, [1962] 3 All ER 1050. Further see paras 67.7 and 82.17–82.18.

10   The Family Law Reform Act 1969, s 15(3), provides that in relation to any disposition made after the coming into force of the section (on 1 January 1970) this reference to 'children or more remote issue' is to be construed as including a reference to any illegitimate child of the principal beneficiary and to anyone who would rank as such issue if he, or some other person through whom he is descended from the principal beneficiary, had been born legitimate.

11   See preceding note.

12   This sub-clause is not very lucid as it might very well happen that it would be impossible to determine who would be entitled at the death of the principal beneficiary. It has, therefore, been suggested that in using the statutory words 'on protective trusts' it might be wise to add the following words, viz: 'In the event of its being impossible to ascertain with certainty who would be entitled to the trust property or the income thereof or to the annuity fund, if any, or arrears of the annuity as the case may be, the income shall be held in trust for any relations of the principal beneficiary who would be entitled to his personal estate if he were then dead intestate under the provisions of the Administration of Estates Act 1925.' See 'relations' thus defined in *Re Bridgen* [1938] Ch 205, [1937] 4 All ER 342. But note that in regard to deaths intestate on or after 1 January 1970, the Administration of Estates Act 1925 is amended so as to confer certain rights upon illegitimate persons: Family Law Reform Act 1969, s 14. See also s 15.

11.64 A danger signal, however, appears in sub-s (3), from which it will be perceived that the pre-existing law is preserved as to the invalidity of such trusts; so that *where the settlor himself* is to take the income until some of the events mentioned in sub-s (1)(i) happen, then if the event which actually happens is bankruptcy, the income during the rest of his life will go to his creditors.

11.65 So far as the authorities go, however, such trusts are not invalid where the event which works a forfeiture is alienation or charge, whether it be voluntary by assignment, either legal or equitable[1], or mortgage of the settlor's defeasible life interest, or involuntary as by reason of a judicial charge created by a judgment or an order for the appointment of a receiver by way of equitable execution[2]. And, moreover, in such cases the *subsequent* bankruptcy of the settlor will not invalidate the gift over which has already happened.

---

1   *Re Gillott's Settlement* [1934] Ch 97; *Re Haynes Will Trusts* [1949] Ch 5, [1948] 2 All ER 423.
2   *Re Detmold* (1889) 40 Ch D 585; *Re Johnson* [1904] 1 KB 134; *Re Perkin's Settlement Trusts* [1912] WN 99; and *Re Balfour's Settlement* [1938] Ch 928, [1938] 3 All ER 259. As to what constitutes a forfeiture under such trusts, see *Re Potts* [1893] 1 QB 648 at 661; *Re Beaumont* (1910) 79 LJ Ch 744; *Re Mair* [1909] 2 Ch 280 (no forfeiture where under the Trustee Act 1925, s 57, the court authorised capital moneys to be raised to enable the principal beneficiary to pay certain pressing liabilities since all settlements are subject to the overriding s 57); *General Accident Fire and Life Assurance Corpn Ltd v IRC* [1963] 3 All ER 259, [1963] 1 WLR 1207 (no forfeiture where under, what is now, the Matrimonial Causes Act 1973, s 24, the court orders income to be diverted from the husband to the wife, all settlements being subject to such overriding powers); *Re Swannell* (1909) 101 LT 76; *Re Williams* [1912] 1 Ch 399; and *Re Smith* [1916] 1 Ch 369, distinguished in *Re Forder* [1927] 2 Ch 291; *Re Baring's Settlement Trusts* [1940] Ch 737, [1940] 3 All ER 20; *Re Dennis's Settlement Trusts* [1942] Ch 283, [1942] 1 All ER 520; *Re Haynes Will Trusts* [1949] Ch 5, [1948] 2 All ER 423; *Re Richardson's Will Trusts* [1958] Ch 504, [1958] 1 All ER 538.A forfeiture has also been held to take place if the principal beneficiary becomes an enemy for the purposes of the Trading with the Enemy Act 1939 (*Re Gourju's Will Trusts* [1943] Ch 24, [1942] 2 All ER 605; *Re Wittke* [1944] Ch 166; [1944] 1 All ER 383); but contrast *Re Hall* [1944] Ch 46, [1943] 2 All ER 753, and *Re Harris* [1945] Ch 316, [1945] 1 All ER 702, where the protective trusts were not in the statutory form, and it was held that no forfeiture was incurred by becoming an alien enemy; and *Re Pozot's Settlement Trusts* [1952] Ch 427, [1952] 1 All ER 1107, where, again the trusts were not in the statutory form and it was held that there was no forfeiture because although the income was payable to the Custodian of Enemy Property the beneficiary's proprietary right to a life interest had not vested in the Custodian.The appointment of a receiver in lunacy is not, of itself, sufficient to bring discretionary trusts into operation (*Re Marshall* [1920] 1 Ch 284; nor does charge of a lunacy percentage under the Lunacy Act 1890, s 148(3)). (NB The Lunacy Act 1890 has been repealed. Currently the Mental Health Act 1983, is applicable.) In any event such a charge is not such an incumbrance as is contemplated by the normal forfeiture clause (*Re Westby's Settlement* [1950] Ch 296, [1950] 1 All ER 479, overruling *Re Custance's Settlements* [1946] Ch 42, [1945] 2 All ER 441). The fees payable to the percentage account are, analogous to the remuneration payable to an agent (*Re Westby's Settlements*, above) an arrangement for payment whereof will not lead to a forfeiture (*Re Tancred's Settlement, Re Selby* [1903] 1 Ch 715). Where trustees were directed to pay income to the principal beneficiary 'so long as he shall be able to give a personal discharge therefore' it was held that the appointment of a receiver in lunacy did not work a forfeiture, since the beneficiary could give a personal discharge through the receiver who was his statutory agent (*Re Oppenheim's Will Trust* [1950] Ch 633, [1950] 2 All ER 86).

11.66 Another point that not infrequently arises is whether, under a discretionary trust (such as the statutory trust above set forth) *where the settlor is a third party*, and the defeasible life interest has been forfeited either by bankruptcy or alienation (voluntary or involuntary), the trustees can, *under the discretion* vested in them, continue to pay the income to the person whose life interest has determined. Obviously the object of such trusts is to enable this to be done if it can be. The authorities are, however, against the right of the trustees to do this[1], on the ground apparently that the life tenant, being bound to hand over to his creditor or assignee whatever his interest in the income may be, is none the less bound with regard to such part of the income as may be paid to him by the trustees in the exercise of their discretion; and that they, having notice of this equity, are equally bound not to pay him. This may seem to be a reductio and absurdum, since the trustees could not under any circumstances pay any part of the income to the creditor or assignee[2], so that it is difficult to see how the latter could suffer by the payment being made to the life tenant himself, or what claim he could have upon the trustees. Nevertheless, trustees under such circumstances have been made liable to the creditor or assignee[3], although, curiously enough, it is well settled that they are at liberty to *expend* the income for his benefit[4]. In one case it was held that the trustees might apply such part as they thought fit of the income for the benefit of the person whose life interest had determined without reference to any debt which such person might owe to the trust estate[5]. This case is distinct from that which has been more frequently before the courts where the contest is between the tenant of a protected life interest and his own assignee. The law is, therefore, in an anomalous and unsatisfactory state; and it is not considered that it has been in any way altered by the introduction by s 33 of the Trustee Act 1925 of the statutory 'protective trusts'. However, it seems that trustees can properly pay directly to a bankrupt discretionary beneficiary the basic amount necessary for supporting himself, his wife and his family[6]. Indeed, if he has a wife she can be paid money as a discretionary beneficiary and she is free to use it for benefiting her husband and family, while expenses (eg of schooling children) can be paid directly to the creditor.

1   *Re Coleman* (1888) 39 Ch D 443; *Re Neil* (1890) 62 LT 649, explained by Stirling LJ in *Re Fitzgerald* [1904] 1 Ch 573 at 593.
2   *Re Bullock* (1891) 64 LT 736; *Train v Clapperton* [1908] AC 342; *Re Laye* [1913] 1 Ch 298; *Re Hamilton* (1921) 124 LT 737. But cf *Lord v Bunn* (1843) 2 Y & C Ch Cas 98; which seems contra at first sight, but really turned on a question of construction.
3   *Re Coleman* (1888) 39 Ch D 443; *Re Neil* (1890) 62 LT 649, explained by Stirling LJ in *Re Fitzgerald* [1904] 1 Ch 573 at 593.
4   *Re Bullock* (1891) 64 LT 736; and cf *Re Coleman* (1888) 39 Ch D 443; and *Re Neil* (1890) 62 LT 649. But see *Re Ashby* [1892] 1 QB 872, where Vaughan Williams J thought that the bankrupt might be liable to account for sums paid to him, though, perhaps, just for the surplus above that needed for his mere support. See also *Re Allen-Meyrick's Will Trusts* [1966] 1 All ER 740 at 743.
5   *Re Eiser's Will Trusts* [1937] 1 All ER 244.
6   See Insolvency Act s 310 and *Re Ashby* [1892] 1 QB 872.

11.67 It need scarcely be said that, until they have notice of an act amounting to forfeiture, the trustees are justified in paying the income to the principal beneficiary[1]. Indeed, where forfeiture occurs on bankruptcy, now that the bankrupt's property does not vest retrospectively in the trustee in bankruptcy on the first available act of bankruptcy, it seems the trustees can pay the principal beneficiary until the bankruptcy order is made[2].

1   *Re Long* [1901] WN 166.
2   See Insolvency Act 1986, s 306.

11.68 Upon forfeiture no apportionment of income occurs under the Apportionment Act 1870[1].

> 1   *Re Gourju's Will Trust* [1943] Ch 24, [1942] 2 All ER 605.

11.69 If a protected life tenant overlooks the forfeiture of his interest when surrendering his life interest in favour of the remaindermen, so that he believes that he has thereby vested the entire beneficial interest in both capital and income in the remaindermen to the exclusion of everyone else, he may have the court set aside the surrender by reason of his mistake[1].

> 1   *Gibbon v Mitchell* [1990] 3 All ER 338, [1990] 1 WLR 1304.

Express and implied protective trusts

11.70 Protective trusts in the statutory form may be created by any words evincing a clear enough intention, eg 'upon protective trusts for the benefit of my sister'[1] or to B 'for a protective life interest'[2]. However, s 33 applies only where there is a human being and not a company as the principal beneficiary[3].

> 1   *Re Wittke* [1944] Ch 166, [1944] 1 All ER 383.
> 2   *Re Platt* (1969) unreported Current Law consolidation 10917.
> 3   *IRC v Brandenburg* [1982] STC 555 at 565, 569.

11.71 The statutory form may be expressly varied. The trustees may be given power to waive and determine the protective trust so that the beneficiary takes a full life interest[1]. Express provision may be made to enable the protected life tenant if he obtains the written approval of the trustees to enter into arrangements with the other settlement beneficiaries for dividing up the trust funds or otherwise re-arranging the beneficial interests as if he had an absolute life interest[2]. In the case of youthful indiscretions it may be advantageous to have a settlement contain a series of protective trusts, eg one set till B is 25, another from 25 to 35, another from 35 to 50 and another for the rest of B's life[3].

> 1   *Re Gordon's Will Trusts* [1977] Ch 27, [1976] 2 All ER 577.
> 2   This can avoid the need for an application under Variation of Trusts Act 1958.
> 3   (1958) 74 LQR 184 (R. E. Megarry).

Paragraph 1 (d)

Restraint on alienation

11.72 Trusts designed to prevent the barring of entails, or imposing restrictions on the alienation of property *which has once been given absolutely* to the beneficiary are contrary to the policy of the law, and are therefore void[1], and the former exception to this rule in the case of trusts limiting the power of married women to alienate their separate property *during coverture* has been abolished by statute[2]. It has, however, been held by the Court of Appeal that a restraint on alienation may be good even in the case of a man, if under the proper law of the trust such restraints are allowed[3]. And, of course, a trust creating a determinable interest for a person *until* he attempts to alienate, and then a gift over in favour of someone else, is good[4]. Even in the case of conditional interests, however, some partial restraint on alienation is possible[5].

1 *Floyer v Bankes* (1869) LR 8 Eq 115; *Sykes v Sykes* (1871) LR 13 Eq 56; and as to alienation *Snowdon v Dales* (1834) 6 Sim 524; *Green v Spicer* (1830) 1 Russ & M 395; *Graves v Dolphin* (1826) 1 Sim 66; *Brandon v Robinson* (1811) 18 Ves 429; *Ware v Cann* (1830) 10 B & C 433; *Hood v Oglander* (1865) 34 Beav 513; *Re Dugdale* (1888) 38 Ch D 176; *Re Cockerill* [1929] 2 Ch 131; *Re Elliot* [1896] 2 Ch 353; *Re Brown* [1954] Ch 39, [1953] 2 All ER 1342. A contract or covenant against alienation is valid since breach gives rise to a claim for damages and not to forfeiture of the property interest: *Caldy Manor Estate Ltd v Farrell* [1974] 3 All ER 753, [1974] 1 WLR 1303. Since an absolute equitable interest cannot be inalienable, the Finance Act 1978, s 54, concerned with trustees holding company shares on trust absolutely for company employees, had to resort to the contract device to give effect to the government's scheme to benefit employees.

2 Married Women (Restraint upon Anticipation) Act 1949, whereby every restraint upon anticipation, whenever imposed, has ceased to have effect. Previously by the Law Reform (Married Women and Tortfeasors) Act 1935 restraints upon anticipation imposed by a statute or instrument passed or executed on or after 1 January 1936, had been declared void. On the construction of the 1935 Act, see *Re Heath's Will Trusts* [1949] Ch 170, [1949] 1 All ER 199.

3 *Re Fitzgerald* [1904] 1 Ch 573 (Scots law); *Trustees Executors and Agency Co Ltd v Margottini* [1960] VR 417. If the trust consists of immovables the lex situs will govern the matter.

4 *Re Detmold* (1889) 40 Ch D 585.

5 *Re Macleay* (1875) LR 20 Eq 186, distinguished in *Re Brown* [1954] Ch 39, [1953] 2 All ER 1342.

Paragraph 1 (e)

Trust terms ousting the jurisdiction of the courts

11.73 Except as provided by statute (eg under the Arbitration Act 1996) no-one can exclude the jurisdiction of the courts upon questions of law as opposed to questions of fact. It is contrary to public policy to attempt to oust the court's jurisdiction to construe and control the construction and administration of a trust or a deceased's estate, while it is also repugnant to the actual rights conferred by a deed or a will (as would be determined by the court) to permit some third party to determine that the rights are such different rights as he or she considers them to be[1].

1 *Re Wynn's Will Trusts* [1952] Ch 271 (trustees cannot conclusively determine what moneys are to be capital and what are to be income, although they can have power to pay moneys to X whether the moneys happen to be income or capital); *Re Raven* [1915] 1 Ch 673; *Jones v Shipping Federation of British Columbia* (1963) 37 DLR (2d) 273.

11.74 Trustees may be allowed to be the final arbiter on questions of fact, but the court has a residual part to play if the decision on fact is open to challenge on the ground of fraud or of being a perverse decision that no reasonable trustees would have reached unless ignoring a relevant factor or taking account of an irrelevant factor[1]. However, if the factual circumstances involve conceptual uncertainty that the court itself cannot resolve (eg the meaning of 'friend' or 'persons who have helped me' or 'persons who have a moral claim to share in my estate'), then the trustees cannot be allowed to exercise their fiduciary function to resolve the issue under a special arbitral clause, because if such resolution is challenged the court has no justiciable criteria to enable it to adjudicate upon the matter[2].

1   *Dundee General Hospitals Board v Bell's Trustees* [1952] 1 All ER 896, HL (valid legacy to an Infirmary if my trustees [one of whom was Treasurer of the Infirmary] shall be satisfied that the Infirmary has not been taken over or otherwise placed under the control of the State); *West of England Shipowners Mutual Insurance Association (Luxembourg) v Cristal Ltd, The Glacier Bay* [1996] 1 Lloyds Rep 370, CA; *Brown v GIO Insurance Ltd* [1998] Lloyds Rep IR 201, CA; *Re Hastings – Bass* [1975] Ch 25 at 41; *Sieff v Fox* [2005] WTLR 891.
2   *Re Wright's Will Trusts* [1981] LS Gaz R 841; *Re Coxen* [1948] Ch 747; *Re Jones* [1953] Ch 125, discussed at para 8.56 above.

11.75 Exceptionally, it seems, some third party, like the settlor-testator's widow or eldest child, may be given a personal, as opposed to a fiduciary, power to determine whether or not any particular individual was a 'friend' of the testator, such determination to be unchallengeable unless such individual could not possibly fall within the black core meaning of 'friend' nor the grey surrounding penumbra of meaning[1]. It would seem to follow that if a widow can resolve such issues by virtue of a personal power, then it should be open to a settlor-testator expressly to make this particular aspect of the functions of a trustee or executor subject only to a personal, as opposed to a fiduciary, obligation, so that a valid adjudication can be made. Indeed, on the basis of *Re Leek*[2] a trust 'for such persons as my trustees consider to have helped me or otherwise to have moral claims upon me' could be upheld not as a personal power but as a diluted fiduciary power intended to be unchallengeable so long as not exercised capriciously or otherwise not in good faith, as by straying beyond the black or grey penumbra of meaning.

1   *Re Coates* [1955] Ch 495; *Re Gibbard* [1966] 1 All ER 273; and paras 8.64 and 8.70.There should be no difference between a trust 'for my friends, providing that my widow's opinion as to who is such a friend shall be final and conclusive' and a trust 'for such persons as my widow considers to be my friends'.
2   [1969] 1 Ch 563 at 579 and 582, discussed at para 8.60 above.

11.76 Furthermore, if the trust instrument refers to the final and conclusive judgment of an independent expert an issue of fact which necessarily involves a solution of a question of construction, the expert's decision will be final and conclusive, so long as he did not address himself to the wrong question[1]. This explains why the Chief Rabbi can validly determine whether or not beneficiaries are of the Jewish faith[2].

1   *West of England Shipowners Mutual Insurance Association (Luxembourg) v Cristal Ltd, The Glacier Bay* [1996] 1 Lloyds Rep 370 at 377–378.
2   *Re Tuck's Settlement Trusts* [1978] Ch 49.

11.77 If a settlement simply contains a clause that no breaches of trust actions are to be taken against the trustees without first resorting to arbitration under the Arbitration Act 1996, there is the problem that this does not amount to an arbitration agreement or contract within the Arbitration Act 1996[1]. A trust is not a contract but a unilateral transfer of assets to a person prepared to accept the office of trustee with the benefits and burdens attached to such office, one benefit being that the trustee can debit the trust fund with the expenses and costs of properly acting as trustee: it is not a contract between the settlor and the trustee that enables the trustee (or a successor-trustee) to debit the trust for the cost of trusteeship services.

1   Although see L Cohen & M Sieff in [1999] JTCP 203, 217–220. In *Schoneberger v Oelze* 96 P. 3d 1078 (Arizona App. 2004) the court held that a settlor's clause cannot unilaterally strip beneficiaries of their right to access the courts.

11.78 However, it would seem that if a settlor, on behalf of himself and the beneficiaries deriving their interests through him, expressly contracts in the trust instrument with the trustee, on behalf of itself and its successors in title, that in consideration of undertaking the office of trustee (for the benefit of the settlor, the beneficiaries and itself) any breach of trust claim against the trustees shall be referred to arbitration by an arbitrator appointed by the Chair of the Chancery Bar Association or, failing such, by the Chair of the Bar Council, then this should amount to an arbitration agreement or contract. By taking the benefit of the trust deed the beneficiaries and trustee all become parties to the arbitration agreement and bound by it[1].

1   Arbitration Act 1996, s 82(2).

11.79 If a settlement contained a clause that the beneficiaries have no rights to see the trust accounts or to make the trustees account for their administration of the trust fund, this would be ineffective if the settlor intended to create a trust for beneficiaries[1], rather than a sham trust under which the trustee holds the fund to the order of the settlor. As Millett LJ stated[2], 'If the beneficiaries have no rights enforceable against the trustees there are no trusts'. If a settlement contained a clause that the accounts would be conclusive as to their accuracy if signed by all adult income beneficiaries this would not exclude the rights of capital beneficiaries whose interests conflict with the income beneficiaries' interests[3]. If the accounts were to be conclusive if signed by all adult beneficiaries and there were such beneficiaries interested in capital and in income then it may well be that the courts would uphold this. However, it would seem that beneficiaries would still be permitted to surcharge and falsify the accounts if the trustees were guilty of fraud, a flexible concept in equity[4], extending to recklessness, as where a trustee continued to pay income to a widow with a life interest determinable on remarriage without asking her before regular payments whether she had remarried[5]. After all, the principle is well-settled that if a person makes a representation of a fact, as of his own knowledge, in relation to a matter susceptible of knowledge and such representation is not true, then if the party to whom it is made relies and acts upon it as true, and sustains damage by it, it is fraud for which the representor is responsible[6].

1   *Briggs v Crowley* 224 NE 2d 417 (Mass 1967) : cannot so deprive court of jurisdiction and beneficiary of standing to require trustees to show performed their duties.
2   *Armitage v Nurse* [1998] Ch 241 at 253, *Foreman v Kingstone* [2004] 1 NZLR 841, [2005] WTLR 823, para 85; *Raak v Raak* 428 NW 2d 778 at 780 (Michigan CA, 1998).
3   *Re Crane* 34 NYS 2d 9, affd 41 NYS 2d 940 (1943).
4   See Meagher, Gummow & Lehane, *Equity: Doctrines & Remedies* (4h ed) Chapter 12.
5   *National Academy of Sciences v Cambridge Trust Company* (1976) 370 Mass 303, 346 NE 2d 879.

[6] *National Academy of Sciences v Cambridge Trust Company* (1976) 370 Mass 303, 346 NE 2d 879.

Trust terms operating to prevent beneficiaries applying to the courts

11.80 An *in terrorem* condition in a will or a trust to induce a legatee or beneficiary not to contest the will or trust on pain of receiving nothing or some token gift will be ineffective, but a similar no-contest condition which expressly provides for the interest to pass or accrue to another person if the will or trust is contested is valid where the contest is unsuccessful and the will or trust is upheld[1]. An essential attribute of property is the right to go to court to vindicate and protect such property so that such right cannot be ousted directly or indirectly[2]. A gift on trust for B until he brings court proceedings concerning the trust other than for the bona fide vindication and protection of his rights under the trust, and then over to others, should clearly be valid by analogy with determinable interests under protective trusts. Thus, where it is feared that a settlor's children may dispute his settlement once he dies, so that they can claim more under forced heirship rules or his will, their interests as discretionary beneficiaries can be made to determine, so as to improve the position of the remaining beneficiaries, if they bring any court proceedings in respect of the trust other than bona fide to assert their rights as beneficiaries thereunder to have the trust fund duly administered and distributed. If a disputant beneficiary subsequently repents before his case is heard or there is a subsequent family reconciliation, it will be helpful if the trust instrument confers a power on the trustees or another person (eg a protector) to add such automatically excluded person back into the class of beneficiaries.

[1]   *Nathan v Leonard* [2002] EWHC 1701 (Ch), [2003] 1 WLR 827 (accepted in a Cayman inter vivos trust case discussed in 'To sue or not to sue' by S Collins in STEP Journal Sept 2006 p 27); *Evanturel v Evanturel* (1874) LR 6 PC 1, 29, PC, endorsing *Cooke v Turner* (1846) 15 M & W 727; and for related conditions against marriage see *Leong v Lim Beng Chye* [1955] AC 648, PC; *Re Whiting's Settlement* [1905] 1 Ch 96.
[2]   *Adams v Adams* [1892] 1 Ch 369, CA (properties left on trust to pay annuities thereout but if annuitant intermeddled or interfered with the trustees' management of the properties the annuity was to cease, so that a groundless frivolous action for appointing receiver in place of trustees caused loss of annuity, although seeking the protection of the court to vindicate and enforce rights would not cause such loss).

11.81 It is, of course, possible for the trustee or a third party to have power to delete beneficiaries from the class of beneficiaries, so that such exclusion is not automatic upon certain events occurring but left to the discretion of the holder of the exclusionary power. However, a court may take the view that if trustees exercise this power against a beneficiary who has instituted legal proceedings, then this power has been exercised in breach of fiduciary duty so as to benefit and protect the trustees or the exercise amounts to a contempt of court as punishing the beneficiary for applying to the court[1]. On the other hand, if the settlor's letter of wishes clearly indicates that upon a son seeking to prefer his own interest via a forced heirship or other claim in preference to the settlor's broader family interests for successive generations, the settlor wants the trustees to exclude such son from being a beneficiary under the trustees' power in that behalf, then an experienced Chancery judge should uphold the trustees' actions and not consider them as any possible contempt of court, the son's defeasible interest only continuing until being properly defeated at the time anticipated and intended by the settlor.

¹ As in the *Lemos v Coutts & Co (Cayman) Ltd* litigation, some reported [1992–93] CILR 460.

Paragraph 1 (f)

Trusts for future illegitimate children

11.82 Since the Family Law Reform Act 1969 came into force on 1 January 1970 not only are dispositions in favour of existing 'en ventre sa mere' illegitimate children valid but also dispositions in favour of future illegitimate children. Section 15(7) in fact provides that as respects such dispositions¹ 'any rule of law that a disposition in favour of illegitimate children not in being when the disposition takes effect is void as contrary to public policy' is abolished. Not only is the rule abolished but, broadly, whenever there is a reference in such dispositions to beneficiaries who are described by their relationship to another person, the reference (in the absence of contrary intention) is deemed to include a reference to beneficiaries who are so related through illegitimacy². Section 15(7) has now been repealed and replaced by s 19 of the Family Law Reform Act 1987 which replaces the concept of the illegitimate child with that of the child of unmarried parents.

¹ A disposition made by will is made on the date of execution of the will even though it cannot, of course, take effect till death: see s 15(8) of the 1969 Act.
² Also see Family Law Reform Act 1987, s 1.

Trusts on separation or divorce of spouses

11.83 A trust to take effect upon the future separation or divorce of a husband and wife is void, as being contrary to public morals¹; but a trust in reference to an immediate separation, *already agreed upon*, is good and enforceable². If, however, the separation does not in fact take place, the trust becomes wholly void³.

¹ *Westmeath v Westmeath* (1831) 1 Dow & Cl 519; *Re Moore* (1888) 39 Ch D 116. The High Court of Australia in *Newcastle Diocese v Ebbeck* (1960) 104 CLR 394 held void a testamentary trust clause forfeiting a son's interest if not married to a Protestant on the death of his mother, so being pressurised to divorce his Catholic wife unless she changed her religion.
² *Wilson v Wilson* (1848) 1 HL Cas 538; (1854) 5 HL Cas 40; *Vansittart v Vansittart* (1858) 2 De G & J 249; *Jodrell v Jodrell* (1845) 9 Beav 45; and see *Jodrell v Jodrell* (1851) 14 Beav 397, and *Egerton v Egerton* [1949] 2 All ER 238 at 242.
³ *Bindley v Mulloney* (1869) LR 7 Eq 343.

11.84 On the other hand, a trust in favour of a wife so long only as she shall cohabit with her husband, and on the cesser of such cohabitation a gift over to the husband, has been held valid¹. Similarly a trust in favour of a deserted wife so long only as she shall be separated from her husband is good². It has been pointed out[3] that 'only in a case where there is still a generally accepted moral code can the court refuse to enforce rights in such a way as to offend that generally accepted code'.

1   *Re Hope-Johnstone* [1904] 1 Ch 470, where the earlier cases are elaborately reviewed.
2   *Re Charleton* [1911] WN 54; *Re Lovell* [1920] 1 Ch 122 (will leaving annuity to deceased testator's mistress, W, living apart from H, 'so long as she shall not return to live with H or remarry' upheld).
3   *Stephens v Avery* [1988] 2 All ER 477 at 481 per Browne-Wilkinson V-C.

Miscellaneous trusts contrary to public policy

11.85   Case law indicates that the following trusts are void as against public policy (quite apart from problems concerning the beneficiary principle): trusts to provide for payment of fines of convicted poachers[1], to procure a peerage[2], to block up a house for 20 years[3], to provide a school for pickpockets or prostitutes[4], to place money to the credit of a company to create a false picture in case of enquiries of the bankers by persons about to do business with the company[5], to provide B with property only if he becomes destitute, so encouraging irresponsibility with money[6].

1   *Thrupp v Collett* (1858) 26 Beav 125.
2   *Earl of Kingston v Lady Elizabeth Pierepont* (1681) 1 Vern 5.
3   *Brown v Burdett* (1882) 21 Ch D 667.
4   *Re Pinion* [1965] Ch 85, [1964] 1 All ER 890, CA.
5   *Re Great Berlin Steamboat Co* (1884) 26 Ch D 616, CA.
6   *Re Hepplewhite's Will Trusts* (1977) Times, 21 January.

11.86   However, if a trust term is designed to induce a separation of husband and wife it will be void, eg if providing a large amount of income for W upon separation, divorce or H's death but only a tiny amount whilst W lives with H[1]. The effect of finding the term void will depend upon whether the term is treated as a condition precedent or condition subsequent[2].

1   *Re Johnson's Will Trusts* [1967] Ch 387, [1967] 1 All ER 553; *Re Caborne* [1943] Ch 224, [1943] 2 All ER 7; *Wilkinson v Wilkinson* (1871) LR 12 Eq 604.
2   See para 11.126 below.

Paragraph 1 (g)

Human Rights Act 1998

11.87   By virtue of Article 8 of the Convention for the Protection of Human Rights and Fundamental Freedoms:

'1.   Everyone has the right to respect for his private life and family life, his home and his correspondence.

2.   There shall be no interference by a public authority with the exercise of this right except such as is in accordance with the law and is necessary in a democratic society in the interests of national security, public safety or the economic well-being of the country, for the prevention of disorder or crime, for the protection of health or morals, or for the protection of the rights and freedoms of others.'

11.88 By Article 9:

'1.   Everyone has the right to freedom of thought, conscience and religion; this right includes freedom to change his religion or belief and freedom ... to manifest his religion or belief in worship, teaching, practice and observance.

2.   Freedom to manifest one's religion or beliefs shall be subject only to such limitations as are prescribed by law and are necessary in a democratic society in the interests of public safety, for the protection of public order, health or morals, or for the protection of the rights and freedoms of others.'

11.89 Article 14, then incidentally provides:

'The enjoyment of the rights [as in Article 8] and freedoms as set forth in this Convention shall be secured without discrimination on any ground such as sex, race, colour, language, religion, political or other opinion, national or social origin, association with a national minority, property, birth or other status.'

11.90 Article 1 of Protocol No 1 (20 March 1952) provides:

'Every natural or legal person is entitled to the peaceful enjoyment of his possessions. No one shall be deprived of his possessions except in the public interest and subject to the conditions provided for by law and the general principles of international law.'

11.91 The Human Rights Act 1998 came into force on 22 October 2000 making it[1] 'unlawful for a public authority to act in a way which is incompatible with a Convention right', but trustees of private trusts[2] (including the Public Trustee) are not public authorities, although a court is a public authority[3] so that in dealing with trusts it will favour an approach that does not interfere with rights and freedoms protected in the Convention. It seems, however, that the impact upon lawful or unlawful conditions is likely to be limited.

[1]   Human Rights Act 1998, s 6(1).
[2]   Trustees of charitable trusts are also not to be regarded as public authorities unless carrying out public duties delegated to them by a public authority: *R (on the application of Heather) v Leonard Cheshire Foundation* [2002] EWCA Civ 366, [2002] 2 All ER 936.
[3]   Human Rights Act 1998, s 6(3)(a). For narrow approach of the courts see *R (on the application of Begum) v Dendigh High School* [2006] UKHL 15.

Trusts in restraint of marriage

11.92 Where property is settled in trust for a woman *for life*, with an executory gift over if she marry a man with an income from freeholds in 1795 of less than £500 a year, or if she marry any person of a particular nationality or religion, or if she marry a blood relation[1], (but not apparently if she cease to bear a particular surname)[2], the divesting gift over is prima facie bad, where its object, as gathered from its probable result[3], is to restrain marriage altogether. If, however, the trust over is to take effect only upon the first beneficiary marrying a particular person, it will be good, as not being in *general* restraint of marriage[4]. Partial restraints, if sufficiently certain in their terms[5], are prima facie valid except that where personality is concerned a partial restraint will be void if intended merely in terrorem as where there is no clear gift over or no clear revocation of the gift upon the restraint being infringed[6].

1   *Re Lanyon* [1927] 2 Ch 264; *Keily v Monck* (1795) 3 Ridg Parl Rep 205.
2   *Re Fry* [1945] Ch 348, [1945] 2 All ER 205, which suggested that a divesting gift over was bad in these circumstances, was disproved in *Re Neeld* [1962] Ch 643, [1962] 2 All ER 335, CA.
3   *Lloyd v Lloyd* (1852) 2 Sim NS 255; and see also *Re Bathe* [1925] Ch 377; and *Re Hanlon* [1933] Ch 254.
4   *Re Hanlon* [1933] Ch 254.
5   *Perrin v Lyon* (1807) 9 East 170; *Jenner v Turner* (1880) 16 Ch D 188. See cases on religious conditions such as persons 'not of Jewish parentage and of the Jewish faith': *Clayton v Ramsden* [1943] AC 320, [1943] 1 All ER 16; *Blathwayt v Baron Cawley* [1976] AC 397, [1975] 3 All ER 625; *Re Tepper's Will Trust*, [1987] 1 All ER 970, discussed at para 8.105, above.
6   *Re Whiting's Settlement* [1905] 1 Ch 96, CA; *Leong v Lim Beng Chye* [1955] AC 648 at 660; *Re Hanlon* [1933] Ch 254.

Exception in case of other motive

11.93 Where it appears that the intention of the testator or settlor was not to restrain the beneficiary from marrying but to achieve some other object a gift over on marriage may be upheld. Thus in *Re Hewett*[1], a testator gave an annuity of £1,200 to a woman with whom he was living and declared that if she should marry it should be reduced to £800 and that an annuity of £400 should then be applied to the benefit of his son by her. It was held that the testator's intention was not to restrain the woman from marrying but to provide for the son if she did, and that the declaration was valid.

1   [1918] 1 Ch 458; see also *Re Fenton* [1950] 2 All ER 1073 and *Jones v Jones* (1876) 1 QBD 279. Cf *Re Michelham's Will Trusts* [1964] Ch 550, [1963] 2 All ER 188.

Exception in cases of second marriage

11.94 The rule does not apply to second marriages. Thus Mellish LJ in *Allen v Jackson*[1] in delivering this judgment, after stating the general rule, said:

> 'It has never been decided that it (the rule) applies to second marriages ... It appears to me very obvious that if it is regarded as a matter of policy, there may be very essential distinctions between a first and second marriage. At any rate, there is this, that in the case of a second marriage, whether of a man or a woman, the person who makes the gift to the man or the woman may have been influenced by their friendship towards the wife in the one case, and towards the husband in the other.'

1   (1875) 1 Ch D 399.

Gifts until marriage are good

11.95 But although conditional or executory gifts over *divesting* an estate on marriage are void if the probable effect would be to discourage marriage altogether, yet it is well established that a trust in favour of a person *until* marriage and then over is unobjectionable.

11.96 As was said by Wigram V-C in *Morley v Rennoldson*[1]:

'Until I heard the argument of this case, I had certainly understood that, without doubt, where property was limited to a person *until* she married, and when she married then over, the limitation was good. It is difficult to understand how this could be otherwise, for in such a case there is nothing to give an interest beyond the marriage. If you suppose the case of a gift of a certain interest, and that interest *sought to be abridged by a condition*, you may strike out the condition, and leave the original gift in operation; but if the gift is *until* marriage and no longer, there is nothing to carry the gift beyond the marriage.'

[1]   (1843) 2 Hare 570. See also *Re Lovell* [1920] 1 Ch 122.

11.97 This distinction between executory gifts over on marriage and gifts *until* marriage is a fine one. But the distinction between a trust temporary in character and one unlimited but liable to be forfeited on the happening of an event is well established[1]. The law leans strongly against forfeiture, and there-fore refuses to enforce it where it would tend to discourage acts which public policy regards as desirable. But it is quite a different matter to forbid temporary trusts which are to end on the happening of the same desirable event.

[1]   Formerly there was some tendency to construe gifts over on marriage as gifts until marriage; see *Allen v Jackson* (1875) 1 Ch D 399 at 404, per James LJ; *Jones v Jones* (1876) 1 QBD 279. But it is thought unlikely that such a construction would be adopted now.

CONDITION REQUIRING CONSENT TO MARRIAGE

11.98 Although a provision for *forfeiture* on marriage is prima facie invalid, the same invalidity, according to *Re Whiting's Settlement*[1], does not attach to a condition subsequent requiring some person's consent to a marriage. The reasons for this are obscure and not very satisfactory[2]. Article 8 of the Human Rights Convention is likely nowadays to prevent such interference with a person's private life and family life. A consent once given cannot be revoked[3].

[1]   [1905] 1 Ch 96, CA.
[2]   Per Vaughan Williams LJ in *Re Whiting's Settlement* [1905] 1 Ch 96.
[3]   *Re Brown* [1904] 1 Ch 120.

Trusts tending to separate parent and child

11.99 Analogous to trusts in restraint of marriage are those tending to separate parent from child which are also void as being contrary to public policy. Thus, a condition was held void where it provided for the forfeiture of two grandchildren's interests if one or both of them should 'live with or be or

276

continue under the custody, guardianship or control of their father'[1]. It is immaterial that the parent from whom the trust seeks to separate the child has been divorced by the other[2].

[1]   *Re Boulter* [1922] 1 Ch 75; *Re Sandbrook* [1912] 2 Ch 471.
[2]   *Re Piper* [1946] 2 All ER 503.

Trusts interfering with parental duty

11.100 Similarly, in *Re Borwick*[1], a condition subsequent providing that an interest which would otherwise vest at twenty-one should be forfeited if, before attaining that age, the beneficiary should 'be or become a Roman Catholic or not be openly or avowedly Protestant', was held void on the ground that it interfered with a parent in the exercise of his parental duty, which ought to be discharged solely with a view to the moral and spiritual welfare of the child and without being influenced by mercenary considerations affecting the child's worldly welfare. This was followed in *Re Tegg*[2] where a condition requiring that 'at no time may any child of hers go to or be sent to any Roman Catholic school for education' was held void as a fetter on the parent doing what she might think best for the welfare and education of her children.

[1]   [1933] Ch 657.
[2]   [1936] 2 All ER 878.

11.101 However, these two decisions must now be treated as of doubtful authority in view of *Blathwayt v Baron Cawley*[1] where the House of Lords upheld a forfeiture clause concerned with any tenant for life who 'shall be or become a Roman Catholic'. Such a clause may obviously influence the decision of an infant's parents as to what, if any, religious education he is to receive. However, where an infant is involved, the time for choice as to compliance or non-compliance with a condition must be postponed until majority and a reasonable time thereafter[2] when the beneficiary should be regarded as free from parental influence and able to choose a religion for *himself*. Thus, on one view such conditions do not interfere with parental duty[3]. On another—and preferable—view[4] such conditions may influence or interfere with parental duty since the religious teaching provided for the child by the parents must have a strong influence on the child's choice when adult, but such conditions ought not to be outlawed on ground of public policy. As Lord Fraser said[5];

'If a parent has strong convictions he may well regard the religious upbringing of his child as of overriding importance not to be set against purely material considerations; if, on the other hand, his religious convictions are weak or non-existent, he can weigh a testamentary benefit with a religious condition attached as one among the many factors affecting the welfare of his child. In neither case does the existence of the religious condition offend against public policy merely because it might affect the parent's action. One must remember also the public policy that a testator should be free ... to dispose of his property as he pleases. It would surely be going too far to say that a bequest for the benefit of a child to help with paying his school fees, payable on condition of his going to a particular school, would be contrary to public policy. Conversely, a condition of his not going to a particular type of school—say a fee- paying public school—ought not to be contrary to public policy either. In my opinion the same rules should apply to conditions about the religious upbringing of a child.'

1   [1976] AC 397, [1975] 3 All ER 625.
2   *Re May* [1917] 2 Ch 126; *Re May* [1932] 1 Ch 99, CA.
3   *McCausland v Young* [1949] NI 49; *Blaythwayt v Baron Cawley* [1976] AC 397 at 426, per Lord Wilberforce, and at 427 per Lord Simon.
4   [1976] AC 397 at 435, per Lord Cross, and at 442 per Lord Fraser.
5   [1976] AC 397 at 442.

11.102 Taking these views into account, while 'everyone has the right to freedom of though, conscience and religion' subject to such limitations as are 'for the protection of the rights and freedom of others'[1], it seems likely that the potential for interference with a person's religious views will not infringe the Human Rights Act 1998.

1   Under Article 9 of the Human Rights Convention.

Paragraph 1 (g)

Trusts made illegal by statute

11.103 Exchange Control restrictions were abolished in their entirety as from 23 October 1979. In case a future Government reintroduces them (but restricted to non-EU countries) it seems worth noting that by s 29 of the Exchange Control Act 1947[1], a resident in the United Kingdom had to obtain Treasury consent to any settlement inter vivos (including the exercise of a power of appointment) which conferred an interest in trust property on a person who was resident outside the scheduled territories (ie the UK, including the Isle of Man and the Channel Islands, Gibraltar and the Republic of Ireland), but the settlement was only invalid so far as it purported to confer an interest on such person.

1   A transaction which was invalid under this section might be validated by Treasury certificate given subsequently, see sub-s (3) and s 18(2). The Treasury had delegated to the Bank of England the power to grant permission and certificates. Validation by certificate was unlikely if the trustees were, or had become, resident outside the jurisdiction.

11.104 The Race Relations Act 1968 may also have a limited application in this context. Taking effect on 25 November 1968, the Act is directed against certain acts of racial discrimination. For the purposes of the Act a person discriminates against another if on the ground of colour, race or ethnic[1] or national origins he treats that other, in any situation to which the Act applies, less favourably than he treats or would treat other persons (and it is expressly declared that if a person is segregated from other persons he is treated less favourably than they are treated)[2]. The situations in which the Act operates to forbid acts of discrimination are those relating to the provisions of goods, facilities and services[3], to employment[4], to trade unions, and employers' and trade organisations[5], and to the provisions of housing accommodation, and business and other premises⁶. There are also provisions relating to advertisements and notices⁷. The Act refers expressly to charities and to acts which are done for charitable purposes⁸. As regards charitable trusts in existence when the Act took effect, the Act does not render unlawful any act done to comply with their provisions; but as regards charitable trusts created after this date the Act merely states that it is not to be construed as affecting any provision which confers benefits on persons of a particular race, particular descent or particular ethnic or national origins, or as rendering unlawful any acts done to comply with such a provision. Although it is not entirely clear, the intention apparently is to draw a distinction between discriminating in favour of persons for whom one feels particular sympathy, particular goodwill, or a particular affinity, and discriminating *against* persons for whom one has negative feelings. In relation to charities, discrimination of the former kind is not attacked by the Act, so that, for instance, it would not be unlawful for trustees to carry out a trust for the benefit of poor persons of a particular race. But discrimination of the latter kind is attacked; so that, for instance, it would seem to be unlawful for trustees to carry out a trust in favour of poor persons *except* those of a particular race—at least in so far as, in doing so, they committed acts of discrimination in any of the situations with which the Act is concerned (see above). As already mentioned, however, this applies only to trusts established after the coming into effect of the Act.

¹ Jews were held to be an ethnic group in *King-Ansell v Police* [1979] 2 NZLR 531 approved by HL in *Mandla v Dowell Lee* [1983] 2 AC 548, [1983] 1 All ER 1062, HL where Sikhs were held to be a racial group.
² Race Relations Act 1968, s 1.
³ Race Relations Act 1968, s 2.
⁴ Race Relations Act 1968, s 3
⁵ Race Relations Act 1968, s 4.
⁶ Race Relations Act 1968, s 5.
⁷ Race Relations Act 1968, s 6.
⁸ Race Relations Act 1968, s 9.

11.105 So far as private trusts are concerned, the Act contains no provisions which affect them expressly, but it does of course affect the actions of both trustees and beneficiaries in the same way as it affects those of other people. Thus trustees must not practice racial discrimination in their capacity as employers or in disposing of trust property; and the Race Relations Act 1965, s 5 is directed against landlords and others (whether trustees or not) who refuse consent to the assignment of a tenancy because of the colour, race or ethnic or national origins of the proposed assignee. But none of these matters is peculiar to trusts. It is just possible that the courts will become more ready to hold that provisions in private trusts which savour of racial discrimination (for example, one designed to discourage the marriage of a beneficiary to any person of a particular race or colour) are void as contrary to public policy, but the act contains no express provisions in this respect and the House of Lords in *Blathwayt v Baron Cawley*¹ exhibited no enthusiasm for moving in this direction to reduce the fundamental freedom of testamentary disposition.

¹ [1976] AC 397, [1975] 3 All ER 625.

11.106 The Sex Discrimination Act 1975, like the Race Relations Act, does not invalidate provisions in private trusts.

11.107 In the context of the Human Rights Act 1998[1] it remains to be seen how extensive will be the impact of a court ranking as a public authority in deciding cases where no public authority is involved as claimant or as defendant when it is unlawful only for a public authority to act in a way which is incompatible with a Convention right. Why should a settlor not have freedom to choose to confer beneficial interests upon descendants who satisfy clauses related to religion, race or colour and arrange for terminated or forfeited interests to accrue to qualifying descendants or to pass to a charity concerned with persons of a particular religion, race or colour[2]? The descendants will still have a right to pursue whatever religion they wish and to marry whomsoever they choose.

[1]   See para 11.87 above.
[2]   As Lord Wilberforce stated in *Blathwayt v Lord Cawley* [1976] AC 397 at 426, 'Discrimination is not the same thing as choice; it operates over a larger and less personal area and neither by express provision nor by implication has private selection yet become a matter of public policy.'

Paragraph 2

Illegal trusts do not necessarily avoid other trusts in same settlement

11.108 Assuming that a trust is void for illegality, it is sometimes difficult to determine whether, and, if so, to what extent, the illegality affects other trusts in the same instrument. Where the illegality is the consideration for the trust, then, of course, the whole instrument is tainted, as used to be the case in trusts in favour of a mistress and her future illegitimate children which were wholly void as tending to promote continued immorality[1]. Where an ascertainable part of the property is to be denoted to lawful trusts then those trusts of that part may be carried out[2]. If some conditions are valid and some void as contrary to public policy the valid conditions are severable and effective[3].

[1]   But see now the Family Law Reform Act 1969, para 11.82 above and *Tanner v Tanner* [1975] 1 WLR 1346.
[2]   *Mitford v Reynolds* (1842) 1 Ph 185; and cf *Fisk v A-G* (1867) LR 4 Eq 521.
[3]   *Re Hepplewhite's Will Trusts* (1977) Times, 21 January.

Cases arising under rule against perpetuities and accumulations

11.109 Cases, in which it is not so easy to follow the reasoning of the court, occur with regard to the rules against remoteness and accumulations. The underlying principle is, however, that a trust is illegal so far as it tends to infringe the object of the rule which forbids it, but no farther.

Trusts in remainder after trusts void under rule against perpetuities

THE LAW APART FROM THE 1964 ACT

11.110 The objects of the rule against remoteness (more fully explained at para 11.2 ff) are to prevent the dead from ruling the living from the grave and to prevent a trust fund (as opposed to the investments comprised therein) from being made entrepeneurially unavailable (as not in the hands of an absolute beneficial owner) for too long a period through having to be kept intact to await the outcome of contingencies. Consequently, not only trusts which may take effect beyond the prescribed limit but also trusts in remainder to take effect upon their failure—even though they be trusts in favour of living persons—are void in some circumstances[1].

1   *Cambridge v Rous* (1802) 8 Ves 12; *Re Thatcher's Trusts* (1859) 26 Beav 365; *Hale v Hale* (1876) 3 Ch D 643; and see *Watson v Young* (1885) 28 Ch D 436; and *Re Frost* (1889) 43 Ch D 246; *Re Abbott* [1893] 1 Ch 54.

11.111 Such trusts in remainder are, however, void only if they are dependent upon the previous void trust, that is to say, if upon the terms of the trust instrument, construed without regard to the rule against remoteness, it cannot from the beginning be affirmed that the ulterior trust must best indefeasibly, if it ever vests at all, before the expiration of the perpetuity period[1]. If at the expiration of that period the ulterior trust may still be accelerated or postponed or defeated by some event operating under the offending previous trust, the ulterior trust is dependent upon the previous void trust, and is itself void[2].

1   An independent limitation is one intended to take effect whether or not the prior gift takes effect.
2   To be valid the ulterior trust must 'dovetail in and accord with previous limitations which are valid'; per Lord St Leonards LC in *Monypenny v Dering* (1852) 2 De GM & G 145 at 182; and see *Re Mill's Declaration of Trust* [1950] 1 All ER 789; affd [1950] 2 All ER 292, CA.

11.112 In *Re Abbott*[1], Stirling J said:

'It is settled that any limitation depending or expectant upon a prior limitation which is void for remoteness is invalid. The reason appears to be that the persons entitled under the subsequent limitation are not intended to take *unless and until the prior limitation is exhausted*; and as the prior limitation which is void for remoteness can never come into operation, much less be exhausted, it is impossible to give effect to the intentions of the settlor in favour of the beneficiaries under the subsequent limitation.'

1   [1893] 1 Ch 54 at 57. It is odd that the courts do not apply the presumption in favour of early vesting illustrated by *Phipps v Ackers* (1842) 9 Cl & Fin 583; *Re Mallinson's Consolidated Trusts* [1974] 2 All ER 530, [1974] 1 WLR 1120.

11.113 This passage was cited with approval by Farwell J in *Re Canning's Will Trusts*[1], and again by Clauson J in *Re Coleman*[2], where the learned judge said:

'Where, as in the present case, ... the limitation which it is sought to impeach creates a future interest which becomes vested in interest (though not in possession) within the limits of the rule against perpetuities and cannot in any event be subsequently divested by the operation of the earlier trust, it would be entirely inconsistent with the principle on which the decision in *Re Canning's Will Trusts* proceeds to hold such a future interest to be adversely affected by the invalidity of the trusts which it follows, but of which it is wholly independent.'

¹   [1936] Ch 309.
²   [1936] Ch 528 at 535, [1936] 2 All ER 225 at 230; followed in *Re Allan's Will Trusts*
    [1958] 1 All ER 401, [1958] 1 WLR 220; *Re Backhouse* [1921] 2 Ch 51 is of doubtful
    authority; see Megarry and Wade, *Law of Real Property* (5th edn) p 272 and Buckley J in
    Re Hubbard's Will Trusts [1963] Ch 275, [1962] 2 All ER 917.

11.114 Difficulties of interpretation may arise where the settlor had expressly
provided (perhaps by way of an accruer clause or a substitutional gift) for
what is to happen to the trust property in the event of the 'failure' or the
'failure or determination' of the previous trust¹.

¹   See 16th edition hereof pp 226–227.

CHANGES MADE BY THE 1964 ACT

11.115 The Perpetuities and Accumulations Act 1964, s 6 states:

'A disposition shall not be treated as void for remoteness by reason only that
the interest disposed of is ulterior to and dependent upon an interest under a
disposition which is so void, and the vesting of an interest shall not be
prevented from being accelerated¹ on the failure of the prior interest by reason
only that the failure arises because of remoteness.'

¹   As to acceleration, see para 29.7 below.

11.116 The effect of this section is, in relation to instruments taking effect on
or after 16 July 1964, to reverse the rule which formerly applied. Thus in
those (now rarer) cases where a prior limitation is void for remoteness, a
subsequent limitation will not be tainted with this fault and will remain
effective even if it is dependent on the prior one. Each limitation must stand or
fall by itself.

Trusts in favour of a class, some of which infringe rule against perpetuities

11.117 Under the law as it existed before the Perpetuities and Accumulations
Act 1964 (and as it still applies to instruments which took effect before the
commencement of the Act), in the case of a trust for A for life, and after her
death for her children who may attain twenty-one and the issue *who shall
attain twenty-one* of such of them as shall die under that age, per stirpes, the
whole of the limitations after the life estate of A were void. For although the
children must attain twenty-one within the prescribed period, the issue of
deceased children may not; and the gift being to a class as a whole, the one
could not be separated from the other¹.

¹   *Pearks v Moseley* (1880) 5 App Cas 714; *Re Lord's Settlement* [1947] 2 All ER 685; *Re
    Hooper's Settlement Trusts* [1948] Ch 586, [1948] 2 All ER 261.

11.118 In regard to instruments to which it applies, the Act of 1964 has made
extensive changes in the position. It will be remembered that s 4 of the Act
introduced new provisions to validate a disposition which would otherwise
fail for remoteness because it was limited by reference to the attainment of an

age greater than twenty-one, and that further provision was made for a case where different ages were specified for different persons. These provisions have already been discussed[1]. So far as the subject matter of the present part of the text is concerned, the same section of the Act goes on to make two further provisions. The first[2] excludes from the class of beneficiaries all those persons whose inclusion (as potential members of it, or as unborn persons who would at birth become actual or potential members of it) prevents the foregoing provisions of the section from saving the disposition. Such persons having been thus excluded from the class, the foregoing provisions of the section are then to operate to save the disposition. The second of the two provisions[3] applies to class dispositions to which the first does not apply (ie to those where the exclusion of class members would not allow the age reduction provisions to save the disposition). It excludes from the class of beneficiaries all those persons whose inclusion (as potential members of it, or as unborn persons who would at birth become actual or potential members of it) makes it apparent (at the time when the disposition is made or at some later time) that the disposition would be void for remoteness. This exclusion is not to be made, however, if it would exhaust the class altogether. It is also provided[4] that the operation of these provisions is not to affect the validity of anything previously done in relation to the interest disposed of by way of advancement, application of intermediate income or otherwise.

1   See para 11.19 above.
2   Perpetuities and Accumulations Act 1964, s 4(3).
3   Perpetuities and Accumulations Act 1964, s 4(4).
4   Perpetuities and Accumulations Act 1964, s 4(5).

Alternative trusts, one legal and the other illegal

11.119 But when there are alternative trusts (A and B), A being illegal and B legal, then if the contingency happens on which B was to take effect, it will not be affected by the illegality of A[1]. For by giving effect to trust B the courts would in no way aid the illegality intended by Trust A, nor (the contingency having happened on which B was to come into force) would the intentions of the settlor be disregarded. If, however, the contingency on which B was to come into operation should never occur, then, of course, the whole instrument would be void, because the contingency contemplated by the settlor had not happened.

1   *Evers v Challis* (1859) 7 HL Cas 531; *Watson v Young* (1885) 28 Ch D 436; *Re Harvey* (1888) 39 Ch D 289; *Re Bence* [1891] 3 Ch 242; and see also *Re Abbott* [1893] 1 Ch 54. See *Re Bullock's Will Trusts* [1915] 1 Ch 493; and *Re Davey* [1915] 1 Ch 837; *Curryer's Will Trusts* [1938] Ch 952, [1938] 3 All ER 574; *Re Hay* [1932] NI 215; *Re Canning's Will Trusts* [1936] Ch 309; *Re Coleman* [1936] Ch 528, [1936] 2 All ER 225. As to the effect of adding *surplus* income (under a discretionary trust) to corpus after the expiration of twenty-one years, see *Re Hawkins* [1916] 2 Ch 570, and cases there cited; following *Re Garside* [1919] 1 Ch 132; dissenting from *Re Pope* [1901] 1 Ch 64.

11.120 So again, where a trust for sale is void for remoteness but the beneficial interests in the proceeds are vested absolutely within the period limited by the rule, the latter will be good although the former may be bad[1].

1   *Re Appleby* [1903] 1 Ch 565.

11.121 *Matters essential to the prima facie validity of an express trust*

Appointment of absolute interest with provision for defeasance which infringes the rule

11.121 Where under a special power of appointment an absolute interest is appointed subject to a provision for defeasance on the happening of a stated event, and the gift over fails for remoteness, the absolute appointment is unimpaired and remains in full force and effect[1].

1   *Re Pratt's Settlement Trusts* [1943] Ch 356, [1943] 2 All ER 458, following *Re Brown and Sibly's Contract* (1876) 3 Ch D 156.

11.122 In regard to instruments taking effect on or after 16 July 1964, the Perpetuities and Accumulations Act 1964[1] provides that in the case of a possibility of reverter on the determination of a determinable fee simple, or a possibility of a resulting trust on the determination of any other determinable interest in property, the rule against perpetuities shall apply to the provision which makes the interest determinable in the same way as it would apply if that provision were a condition subsequent giving rise on its breach to a right of re-entry (or to an equivalent right in the case of property other than land). Where the provision falls to be treated as void for remoteness, the determinable interest is to become an absolute one. However, if a determining event occurs or a condition is broken and the right of entry exercised during the valid wait and see period then the interest fails. The Act also provides[2] that where a disposition is subject to any such provision, or to any such condition subsequent, or to any exception or reservation, the disposition is to be treated for the purposes of the Act as including a separate disposition of any rights which arise by virtue of the provision, condition subsequent, exception or reservation.

1   Perpetuities and Accumulations Act 1964, s 12(1).
2   Perpetuities and Accumulations Act 1964, s 12(2).

Trusts infringing the law restricting accumulations

11.123 It might perhaps be thought that, by analogy to the action of the courts with regard to trusts which transgress the rule against remoteness, a trust which endeavoured to go beyond the period allowed for accumulations (see para 11.44) would be wholly void; but this is not so. The statute merely prohibits accumulations going beyond the period prescribed by it, and, being in derogation of a common law right it is construed strictly. Consequently, since accumulations which exceed the most appropriate statutory period of accumulation, but are within the perpetuity period prescribed under the rule against remoteness, are not contrary to public policy as defined by common law, a trust for accumulation is good pro tanto, unless, of course, it exceeds the perpetuity in which case it is void in toto[1].

1   See *Griffiths v Vere* (1803) 9 Ves 127; see para 11.59 above.

Trusts in remainder after illegal trust to accumulate

11.124 On similar principles, remainders to take effect after the period prescribed by the settlement for the accumulation of income are not rendered void on the ground that the prescribed period exceeds the statutory period. All that the statute does is to prohibit *accumulations* beyond a certain period. When that period comes to an end the accumulations stop, and the fact of the subsequent remainder being allowed in no way tends to a breach of the statutory rule. On the other hand, such remainders are not accelerated (for that would be contrary to the settlor's intentions); but there is a resulting trust in favour of the persons who, if no accumulation had been directed, would have been entitled to the income during the time which elapses between the expiration of the statutory period and the period prescribed by the settlement[1]. In the case of an illegal trust to accumulate declared by will, however, a resulting trust for the testator's next-of-kin may be excluded by the evidence of a general charitable intention and the court will carry this intention into effect by means of a scheme[2].

1   Law of Property Act 1925, s 164(1).
2   *Martin v Maugham* (1844) 14 Sim 230; *Re Bradwell* [1952] Ch 575, [1952] 2 All ER 286.

Trusts subject to impossible or illegal condition

11.125 If a term of a trust is a condition subsequent and is impossible, uncertain, contrary to public policy or illegal then the term is void and the interest becomes absolute[1].

1   *Re Beard* [1908] 1 Ch 383; *Re Caborne* [1943] Ch 224.

11.126 If the term is a condition precedent and attached to realty then failure to perform the condition for whatever reason defeats the gift. In respect of personalty.

> 'where a condition precedent is originally impossible or is made so by the act or default of the testator or is illegal as involving malum prohibitum, the bequest is absolute just as if the condition had been subsequent. But where the performance of the condition is the sole motive of the bequest or its impossibility was unknown to the testator or the condition which was possible in its creation has since become impossible by Act of God or where it is illegal as involving malum in se ... both gift and condition are void'[1].

1   *Re Elliott* [1952] Ch 217 at 221; *Re Wolffe* [1953] 1 WLR 1211 at 1216; *Re Piper* [1946] 2 All ER 503; cf *Re Thomas' Will Trusts* [1930] 2 Ch 67. In *Re McBride* (1980) 107 DLR (3d) 233 testamentary condition precedent designed to promote the divorce of the testator's son was held not to be malum in se but only malum prohibitum so the gift was good, passing to the son free from the condition.

11.127 It is high time these archaic, illogical[1] and anomalous rules were reformed.

1   *Leong v Lim Beng Chye* [1955] AC 648 at 662; *Exham v Beamish* [1939] IR 336; *Re Blake* [1955] IR 89. See Law Commission Consultation Paper No 154 (1999).

Paragraph 3

Testamentary trusts unknown to the law of settlor's domicile

11.128 English law distinguishes between immovables and movables for succession purposes, so that the *lex situs* governs immovables while the *lex domicilii* of the deceased at his death is his *lex successionis* for movables[1]. Thus English law governs succession to English immovables[2], and so gives effect to trusts thereof, though a deceased's foreign *lex successionis* applicable to his other property may allow countervailing compensation to be payable thereout in the foreign forum in satisfaction of the claims of forced heirs entitled indefeasibly to a fraction of the deceased's estate (including the value of his immovables). Succession to English movables of a foreign domiciliary is governed by the foreign *lex domicilii* so that forced heirship rights to English movables owned at his death by the foreign deceased will be recognised and implemented[3], and so pro tanto diminish the subject matter of trusts thereof.

[1]   See generally Hayton (ed), *European Succession Laws* (Jordans), Dicey & Morris, *Conflict of Laws* (14th edn) chap 27.
[2]   Dicey & Morris, *Conflict of Laws* (14th edn) rules 135 and 140; *Re Collens* [1986] Ch 505; *Re Hernando* (1884) 27 Ch D 284.
[3]   Dicey & Morris, *Conflict of Laws* (14th edn) rules 134 and 139; *Re Annesley* [1926] Ch 692.

11.129 At birth a person ahs a domicile of origin, being that of the father, if a marital child, or that of the mother, if a non-marital child. There is then a domicile of dependency, dependent on the father or mother's domicile, respectively. At sixteen an independent domicile of choice can be acquired by residence in a jurisdiction with intent permanently or indefinitely to reside there. It a domicile of choice is abandoned without acquiring a new domicile of choice then the domicile of origin ranks as the domicile. Before 1974 a woman took, on marriage, the domicile of her husband and her domicile was dependent upon his, changing with his whilst the marriage lasted. On 1 January 1974, s 1 of the Domicile and Matrimonial Proceedings Act 1973 has the domicile of a wife ascertained by reference to the same factors as in the case of any other individual capable of having an independent domicile. However, where immediately before 1 January 1974 she was married, so having her husband's domicile by dependence, she is to be treated as retaining that domicile (as a domicile of choice if it is not also her domicile of origin) unless and until it is changed by acquisition or revival of another domicile either on or after that date.

Inter vivos trusts unknown to law of settlor's domicile

11.130 It is clear that questions of capacity, form and essential validity affecting English land are governed by the English *lex situs* irrespective of the settlor's domicile, habitual residence or nationality[1]. Thus, a foreign settlor can create valid inter vivos trusts of English land if complying with English domestic requirements, especially if he reinforces the significance of English law by express (or implied) choice of English law to govern his trust. The position seems to be the same for gratuitous transfers to trustees by foreign settlors of English movables as discussed below at paras 102.193–102.197.

1   Dicey & Morris, *Conflict of Laws* (14th edn) rule 117.

11.131 Thus, if a foreign domiciliary has validly transferred by the *lex situs* English assets to English trustees of a trust governed by English law, such assets will not form part of the deceased settlor's estate governed by his foreign *lex successionis*, just as any inter vivos joint tenancy of English assets would require such assets to vest in the survivor and not to pass as part of the deceased's estate. Care should be taken, however, to ensure that no part of the trust fund is invested in the jurisdiction of the foreign heirs or a sympathetic jurisdiction or it could be appropriated in satisfaction of the heirs' claims.

Danger of general power of appointment or revocation

11.132 Reservation to the settlor of a general power of appointment or revocation is likely to lead to problems if claims are subsequently brought by the foreign settlor's forced heirs, because property settled inter vivos in respect of which such powers are reserved is automatically treated as part of the deceased's 'net estate' for claims under the Inheritance (Provision for Family and Dependants) Act 1975[1] if the deceased died domiciled in England. Because such property is automatically available for satisfying the provisions of the English *lex successionis* mandatory rules for the protection of heirs, why should it not be automatically available for satisfying forced heirship claims under the mandatory rules of the foreign *lex successionis*? What of the position if the settlement were made within six years of death with the intention of defeating a claim under the 1975 Act, so that there is a judicial discretion to set aside the settlement to the extent necessary to make reasonable provision for the applicant, taking account of various discretionary factors, if the deceased died domiciled in England? It is considered unlikely that the English court would be prepared to take on such a hypothetical discretionary exercise if the deceased died domiciled abroad, so as to ascertain an amount available for satisfying forced heirship claims. It may well be that the matter will not arise for decision because most foreign settlors who set up English trusts will make reasonable provision for their forced heirs (though not such extravagant provision as is provided by the law on forced heirship in the case of wealthy testators).

1   See Inheritance (Provision for Family and Dependants) Act 1975, s 25(1).

ARTICLE 12
NECESSITY OR OTHERWISE OF WRITING AND SIGNATURE

12.1

(1)(a) A contract for the sale or other disposition of an interest in land
       (so covering a contract to create a trust of an interest in land or
       to dispose of a subsisting equitable interest in land) is void unless

made in writing incorporating all the terms which the parties have expressly agreed in one document or, where contracts are exchanged, in each[1]. The document incorporating the terms (whether set out in itself or by reference to some other document) or, where contracts are exchanged, one of the documents incorporating the terms (but not necessarily the same one) must also be signed by or on behalf of each party to the contract[2];

(b) An express trust of any interest in land is unenforceable unless evidenced by writing signed by the person able to declare such trust or by his will[3];

(c) An oral declaration is sufficient to create a trust of pure personalty by a person both legally and beneficially entitled[4], or by a person authorised by a trust instrument orally to declare or appoint new trusts unless his declaration or appointment amounts to a disposition by him of his own subsisting equitable interest[5]. A disposition inter vivos of a subsisting equitable interest must be in writing signed by the disposor or his agent lawfully authorised in writing[6], and for this purpose a direction given by a person entitled in equity to trustees directing them to hold the trust property on trust for donees is a disposition of his equitable interest[7] as, it seems, is a declaration by such person that he holds his equitable interest on a simple bare trust for another person of full capacity[8];

(d) An express trust of any kind of property, if intended to be testamentary, must be created by a duly executed and attested will or codicil[9]. Even where property is devised or bequeathed to a person *as trustee* the trust cannot be declared by a subsequent instrument other than a codicil[10]. Failure to comply with the testamentary formalities leads to a resulting trust in favour of the testator's residuary legatee or devisee or, if there is no residuary legatee or devisee, or if residue were the subject of the intended trust, in favour of the persons entitled on his intestacy.

(2) Absence of the requisite formalities will not matter if a person otherwise prejudiced by such absence can invoke the principle that equity will not allow a statute to be used as an instrument of fraud[11] or the principle of equitable proprietary estoppel[12] or the doctrine of part performance[13] (available for unenforceable trusts but not void contractual arrangements) or can rely on the operation of resulting or constructive trusts[14]. The principle that equity will not allow a statute to be used as an instrument of fraud has taken on special refinements, in the case of secret or half secret testamentary trusts: see paras 12.77–12.112 below.

---

[1] Law of Property (Miscellaneous Provisions) Act 1989, s 2(1).
[2] Law of Property (Miscellaneous Provisions) Act 1989, s 2(2),(3).

3   Law of Property Act 1925, ss 53(1)(b), 40; *Kronheim v Johnson* (1877) 7 Ch D 60; *Tierney v Wood* (1854) 19 Beav 330; *Rudkin v Dolman* (1876) 35 LT 791.

4   *M'Fadden v Jenkyns* (1842) 1 Ph 153; *Milroy v Lord* (1862) 4 De GF & J 264; *Grey v IRC* [1960] AC 1, [1959] 3 All ER 603, HL: *Paul v Constance* [1977] 1 All ER 195, [1977] 1 WLR 527, CA.

5   *Re Vandervell's Trusts (No 2)* [1974] Ch 269, [1974] 3 All ER 205, CA, *Grey v IRC* [1960] AC 1.

6   Law of Property Act 1925, s 53(1)(c). But see *Vandervell v IRC* [1967] 2 AC 291, [1967] 1 All ER 1, HL, para 12.31 below (if T holds on trust for B and, at B's request, transfers the property to X, this is effective to dispose of B's interest without writing signed by B).

7   *Grey v IRC* [1960] AC 1, [1959] 3 All ER 603, HL.

8   *Grey v IRC* [1958] Ch 375 at 382; on appeal [1958] Ch 690 at 715, CA, para 12.17 below.

9   Wills Acts 1837, s 9. In regard to attestation, the Wills Act 1837 is slightly amended by the Wills Act 1968. A disposition of a subsisting equitable interest or trust may be made by will: Law of Property Act 1925, s 53(1)(c).

10   *Adlington v Cann* (1744) 3 Atk 141; *Briggs v Penny* (1851) 3 Mac & G 546; *Re Boyes* (1884) 26 Ch D 531; *Habergham v Vincent* (1793) 2 Ves 204.

11   *Rochefoucauld v Boustead* [1897] 1 Ch 196; *McCormick v Grogan* (1869) LR 4 HL 82.

12   *Inwards v Baker* [1965] 1 All ER 446; *Dillwyn v Llewelyn* (1862) 4 De GF & J 517; *Re Basham* [1987] 1 All ER 405; *Gillett v Holt* [2001] Ch 210, CA.

13   *Re Gonin* [1979] Ch 16, [1977] 2 All ER 720; *Steadman v Steadman* [1976] AC 536, [1974] 2 All ER 977, HL; Law of Property Act 1925, s 55(d).

14   Law of Property Act 1925, s 53(2); *Hodgson v Mark* [1971] Ch 892, [1971] 2 All ER 684.

Contracts to create trusts

12.2 By the Law of Property (Miscellaneous Provisions) Act 1989, s 2:

> '(1) A contract for the sale or other disposition of an interest in land can only be made in writing and only by incorporating all the terms which the parties have expressly agreed in one document or, where contracts are exchanged in each.
>
> (2) The terms may be incorporated in a document either by being set out in it or by reference to some other document.
>
> (3) The document incorporating the terms or, where contracts are exchanged, one of the documents incorporating them (but not necessarily the same one) must be signed by or on behalf of each party to the contract.'

12.3 It follows that if, after 26 September 1989, the above requirements are not satisfied when S purports to contract to create a trust of an interest in land (which expressly extends to interests in the proceeds of sale of land, eg co-ownership interests behind a trust for sale) there is no contract at all. Thus, there is no scope[1] for the doctrine of part performance[2], available for unenforceable but otherwise valid arrangements, though nothing in s 2 affects the creation or operation of resulting or constructive trusts[3], which may arise independently or as a result of equitable proprietary estoppel principles[4]. The requisite writing may comprise several documents read together if they refer to the relevant transaction commencing with the document bearing the signature of the defendant or his agent and working back from there[5]. If the writing be defective because of the omission of a term expressly agreed by the parties in circumstances enabling the court to rectify the document, then the rectified document can satisfy the requirements of s 2[6]. A liberal purposive interpretation has been given to the section by the courts in holding that it does not apply to the exercise of an option to purchase land[7], a collateral contract[8] (contained in a side letter signed only by one party) and an agreement supplemental to a contract which was no longer executory, having been duly carried out[9]. It does, however, apply to the subsequent variation of a contract within s 2[10], eg if the completion date is postponed.

1   *Yaxley v Gotts* [2000] Ch 162 at 172, CA.
2   *Steadman v Steadman* [1976] AC 536, [1974] 2 All ER 977, as narrowly interpreted in *Re Gonin* [1979] Ch 16, [1977] 2 All ER 720 and commented upon in *Actionstrength Limited v International Glass Engineering SPA* [2003] UKHL 17, [2003] 2 AC 541, paras 23 and 47.; Jones & Goodhart, *Specific Performance*, pp 96–106.
3   Law of Property (Miscellaneous Provisions) Act 1989, s 2(5); *Kinane v Mackie – Conteh* [2005] EWCA Civ 45, [2005] WTLR 345.
4   *Yaxley v Gotts* [2000] Ch 162, CA; *Re Basham* [1986] 1 WLR 1498 at 1504, [1987] 1 All ER 405 at 410; *Lim Teng Huan v Ang Swee Chuan* [1992] 1 WLR 113.
5   *Timmins v Moreland Street Property Co Ltd* [1958] Ch 110, [1957] 3 All ER 265; *Elias v George Sahely & Co (Barbados) Ltd* [1983] 1 AC 646, [1982] 3 All ER 801. These cases concerned with Law of Property Act 1925, s 40, replaced by the 1989 Act, are still relevant here. Note that mutual wills expressed to be irrevocable amount to contracts so that, to the extent they devise land they need to satisfy s 2(1) but a constructive trust is exempted by s 2(5) from s 2(1): *Healey v Brown* [2000] WTLR 780 (where the constructive trust ought to have extended beyond half the flat to the whole).
6   *Wright v Robert Leonard (Developments) Ltd* [1994] EGCS 69; s 2(4), 1989 Act.
7   *Spiro v Glencrown Properties Ltd* [1991] Ch 537.
8   *Record v Bell* [1991] 1 WLR 853; *Pitt v PHH Asset Management Ltd* [1994] 1 WLR 327, [1993] 4 All ER 961.
9   *Tootal Clothing v Guinea Properties Management Ltd* (1992) 64 P & CR 452.
10 *McCausland v Duncan Lawrie Ltd* [1997] 1 WLR 38, CA.

12.4 A contract to create a trust of property other than land or an interest in land need satisfy no special formalities.

Contracts to dispose of existing equitable interests

12.5 If A has an equitable interest in pure personalty held by T prima facie no formalities need to be observed if he contracts to sell his interest. However, it can be argued that the constructive trusteeship imposed upon A when he enters into a specifically enforceable contract[1] to sell his equitable interest to B means that T holds on trust for A who holds on trust for B so that if A is a simple bare trustee with no active duties to perform he disappears from the picture leaving T holding on trust for B[2]. Since T formerly held on trust for A it can be said that A by his contract with B has made a disposition in B's favour of his equitable interest which must actually be in writing signed by A (or A's agent authorised in writing) or be void: Law of Property Act 1925, s 53(1)(c)[3]. To this it may be riposted that s 53(2) itself states that s 53(1) is not to affect the creation or operation of resulting or constructive trusts so that without the need for any s 53(1)(c) writing B becomes equitable owner due to the constructive trust in his favour: this view has been taken by Upjohn J[4], Lord Radcliffe[5], Megarry J[6] and by Goff and Shaw LJJ[7] and has been held to be correct by the Court of Appeal in *Neville v Wilson*[8]. Furthermore, once the purchase price had been paid by B to A, A would not in any case be able to put forward successfully any claim to the equitable interest as Lord Cohen has indicated[9]. Indeed, the best riposte may be that where A contracts to sell his equitable interest to B the nature of his 'interested' constructive trustee-ship, vitally dependent upon the contractual obligations being carried out (particularly payment of the purchase price) means that A is not at the outset a simple bare trustee, so there is a true sub-trust and not a full assignment of A's equitable interest to B so that s 53(1)(c) is inapplicable. The position is analogous to the case where A declares a sub-trust of his equitable interest in property other than land for X for one year, remainder to Y absolutely (outside s 53) and after a year X's interest automatically ceases and Y becomes full beneficial owner (outside s 53).

¹   See Article 36.
²   Per Upjohn J in *Grey v IRC* [1958] Ch 375 at 382 and per Evershed MR [1958] Ch 690 at 715, CA; *Grainge v Wilberforce* (1889) 5 TLR 436; *Re Lashmar* [1891] 1 Ch 258.
³   Lord Denning in *Oughtred v IRC* [1960] AC 206 at 233.
⁴   *Oughtred v IRC* [1958] Ch 383, [1958] 1 All ER 252.
⁵   *Oughtred v IRC* [1960] AC 206 at 227–228.
⁶   *Re Holt's Settlement* [1969] 1 Ch 100, [1968] 1 All ER 470.
⁷   *DHN Food Distributors Ltd v London Borough of Tower Hamlets* [1976] 3 All ER 462 at 472, 473, [1976] 1 WLR 852 at 865, 867.
⁸   [1997] Ch 144.
⁹   *Oughtred v IRC* [1960] AC 206 at 230. The case concerned a remainderman, R, who orally agreed to transfer his interest under the settlement in certain shares to the life tenant, L, in return for other shares owned absolutely by L. After L had transferred her shares to R the trustees transferred the trust shares to L. The House of Lords majority held, whatever the effect of s 53 on the oral agreement, the transfer by the trustees was stampable ad valorem as a transfer on sale giving full effect to the agreement.

12.6 In *Chinn v Collins*¹ the House of Lords held that no formalities were required for contractual dealings related to an equitable interest in shares in an English public company: 'As soon as there was an agreement for their sale accompanied or followed by payment of the price, the equitable title passed at once to the purchaser and all that was needed to perfect his title was notice to the trustee'. Since the contract related to shares in a public company specific performance was not available as a remedy, so that no constructive trust could arise: thus the availability or otherwise of specific performance and the creation of a constructive trust is immaterial. A contract to make a disposition of an equitable interest is thus not in itself a disposition within s 53(1)(c).

¹   [1981] AC 533 at 548, Lord Wilberforce mentioning that the assignee should give notice to the trustee because if the trustee were to pay dividends to the vendor and did not have notice of the purchaser's interest he would be discharged from any liability to the purchaser who would have to trace against the vendor holding the dividends as constructive trustee. Moreover, a further reason for giving notice to the trustee is that if the assignor were to make several assignments for value of his one equitable interest priority under the rule in *Dearle v Hall* (1828) 3 Russ 1, as affected by Law of Property Act 1925, s 137 depends not on the order of making the assignments but on the order in which assignees gave notice to the trustee: further see J De Lacy, *The Priority Rule of Dearle v Hall Restated* [1999] Conv 311.

Declarations (or creations) of trusts of land and other property

12.7 Assuming that the appropriate formalities have been observed for property becoming vested in S or in S vesting property in his trustees for his beneficiaries, problems may arise as to the formalities to be observed in S declaring the trusts upon which he himself is to hold specific property henceforth or upon which his trustees are to hold specific property henceforth.

12.8 By the Law of Property Act 1925, s 53(1)(b),

'A declaration of trust respecting any land or any interest therein must be manifested and proved by some writing signed by some person who is able to declare such trust or by his will.'

12.9 As for s 40 of the 1925 Act before replaced by the 1989 Act, the trust is not required to be created by signed writing but only evidenced, so that the writing may come into existence at any time after the declaration of the trusts[1]. Absence of the written evidence makes the trust unenforceable but not void[2] so that the doctrine of part-performance[3] may enable the trust to be enforced. The writing need not be in any special form[4] but it must comprehensively set out the terms of the trust and recognise that there was a clear intention to create a trust[5]. The written evidence may comprise several linked documents read together, working back from the document bearing the appropriate signature[6].

1   *Forster v Hale* (1798) 3 Ves 696; *Gardner v Rowe* (1828) 5 Russ 258; *Rochefoucauld v Boustead* [1897] 1 Ch 196 at 206; *Re Holland* [1902] 2 Ch 360. The failure to comply with s 53(1)(b) must be expressly pleaded.
2   See the cases in preceding note. It seems that s 53(1)(b) requires s 53(1)(a) to be construed as not extending to a declaration of trust, so as to leave scope for s 53(1)(b) under the maxim 'generalia specialibus non derogant': *Secretary, Department of Social Security v James* (1990) 95 ALR 615.
3   Preserved by LPA 1925, s 55(d).
4   For example, in correspondence *Forster v Hale* (1798) 3 Ves 696; *Childers v Childers* (1857) 1 De G & J 482; in a telegram *McBlain v Cross* (1871) 25 LT 804; a recital *Re Hoyle* [1893] 1 Ch 84; an affidavit *Barkworth v Young* (1856) 26 LJ Ch 153; an answer to interrogatories *Wilson v Dent* (1830) 3 Sim 385.
5   *Smith v Matthews* (1861) 3 De GF & J 139 at 151; *Morton v Tewart* (1842) Y & C Ch Cas 67 at 80.
6   *Forster v Hale* (1798) 3 Ves 696; *Oliver v Hunting* (1890) 44 Ch D 205.

12.10 The requisite signature is of 'some person who is able to declare such trust'. It has been assumed that the absence of an express reference to an agent found in ss 40(1), 53(1)(a) and 53(1)(c) precludes a settlor's agent lawfully authorised in writing from providing the requisite written evidence to satisfy s 53(1)(b), but it may yet prove to be the case that such authorised agent will be regarded as 'some person who is able to declare' a trust on the settlor's behalf. The necessary signatory will be A where A declares himself trustee of Blackacre for B and will then be B if B subsequently declares himself trustee of his equitable interest therein for C for life, remainder to D absolutely[1]. If B had declared himself to be a simple bare trustee for E absolutely this really means that A holds for E instead of B because E can directly sue A, so that B's disposition of his subsisting equitable interest seems to need to satisfy s 53(1)(c)[2].

1   *Tierney v Wood* (1854) 19 Beav 330; *Kronheim v Johnson* (1877) 7 Ch D 60.
2   *Grey v IRC* [1958] Ch 375 at 382; revsd [1958] Ch 690 at 715, *Re Lashmar* [1891] 1 Ch 258, *ISPT Nomiminees Pty Limited v Chief Commissioner* of State Revenue [2003] NSWSC 697; see para 12.15 below.

12.11 Where A has conveyed land to B for C without signing a contemporaneous declaration of trust for C then it seems to be B as the apparent landowner who can declare the trust with subsequent signed writing in C's favour[1]. It seems to be assumed that A cannot supply the written evidence subsequently to the conveyance to B, but because there is a valid but unenforceable trust why cannot A later supply the written evidence to make such trust enforceable, while also allowing B as A's authorised agent (until A revokes his mandate) to supply the written evidence? After all, until such written evidence is provided B must hold on a resulting trust for A[2], who ordinarily would then need to satisfy the tougher s 53(1)(c) to dispose of his equitable interest but who, exceptionally, because of the earlier transfer of the legal title to B on an unenforceable valid oral trust for C, ought retrospectively to be able to make such trust enforceable by providing the written evidence. If A had conveyed land (or other property) to B to hold to A's order and subsequently A told B to hold on trust for C this would amount to A disposing of his subsisting equitable interest and so would need to satisfy s 53(1)(c)[3].

1   *Gardner v Rowe* (1828) 5 Russ 258; *Smith v Matthews* (1861) 3 De G F & J 139; *Mountain v Styak* [1922] NZLR 131; T. G. Youdan [1984] Camb LJ 306 at 316–320.
2   Because A did not intend B to be legal beneficial owner.
3   *Grey v IRC* [1960] AC 1, [1959] 3 All ER 603, HL.

12.12 Where land has been conveyed by A to B on oral trusts for C or for A the interests of C or A are, in the absence of writing signed by B, fully protected against B by the maxim that Equity will not allow a statute to be used as an instrument of fraud[1]. However, in a competition between A and C the better view[2] is that C cannot prove his claim due to the absence of writing satisfying s 53(1)(b), so that B holds on a resulting trust for A (assuming that C has not acted to his detriment in reliance upon having the equitable interest so as to obtain an equitable proprietary interest) for, otherwise, the impact of s 53(1)(b) would be restricted to cases where the settlor declares himself trustee of his own land[3].

1   See para 12.67 below.
2   See paras 12.73–12.74 below.
3   *Wratten v Hunter* [1978] 2 NSWLR 367; *Morris v Whiting* (1913) 15 DLR 254.

12.13 A declaration of trusts of property other than interests in land need satisfy no special formalities: thus unsigned writing, word of mouth or conduct will suffice[1].

1   *Re Vandervell's Trusts (No 2)* [1974] Ch 269, [1974] 3 All ER 205; *Paul v Constance* [1977] 1 All ER 195, [1977] 1 WLR 527; *Rowe v Prance* [2000] WTLR 249.

Dealings with equitable interests

12.14 Dealings by a person, S, in respect of his equitable interest under a trust create problems requiring special care to be taken. It may be that S purports to declare that he himself is henceforth to hold the equitable interest on trust for a person or persons or S may direct the trustees that they are henceforth to hold the trust property not for himself but for certain other persons. It is crucial to determine whether S is declaring or creating trusts within s 53(1)(b) or whether, in reality, he is disposing of his equitable interest when s 53(1)(c) will apply, laying down that 'a disposition of an equitable interest [in realty or personalty] subsisting at the time of the disposition must be in writing signed by the person disposing of the same, or by his agent lawfully authorised in writing or by will'.

SUB-TRUST OR ASSIGNMENT?

12.15 Take the situation where T holds property on trust for S, when S declares that he is henceforth holding his equitable interest on trust for B absolutely. Here, if B is of full capacity, S is a simple or bare trustee so it seems he disappears from the picture leaving T holding on trust for B[1] whereas before T held on trust for S. Thus S had divested himself of his equitable interest which he has passed to B. This means that S's declaration is treated as a disposition of his equitable interest which must actually itself be in writing or be void owing to the Law of Property Act 1925, s 53(1)(c). However, if S's declaration had left him with active duties to perform[2] so as not be a bare simple trustee then it would be a true declaration creating a sub-trust with S as sub-trustee holding the equitable interest for his beneficiaries with their subsidiary equitable interests[3], eg if S declared himself trustee for B for life with remainder to C, or discretionary trustee of discretionary trusts for D, E and F and their wives and children. In this latter case no formalities would need to be satisfied unless S's interest was in land and even then the s 53(1)(b) formalities would only be evidential and not prerequisite to the very validity of the trusts declared by S.

[1]   *Grey v IRC* [1958] Ch 375 at 382, per Upjohn J; revsd [1958] Ch 690 at 715 per Evershed MR, CA; *Grainge v Wilberforce* (1889) 5 TLR 436; *Re Lashmar* [1891] 1 Ch 258; *ISPT Nominees Pty Limited v Chief Commissioner of State Revenue* [2003] NSWC 697, paras 246, 250 and 270; *Corin v Patton* (1990) 169 CLR 540 at 579. Under the principle in *Saunders v Vautier* (1841) 4 Beav 115, B should then be able to bring an action directly against T so as to ensure that T vests the property in B. However, where T holds on trust for S, who declares he holds his interest on trust for B, one can argue that until B directs T to hold on trust for B instead of S, S holds his old equitable chose in action against T on a true trust for B who has a new equitable close in action against S who has thereby made a part disposal for capital gains tax purposes of his old equitable interest: see B. Green (1984) 47 MLR 385 at 397–398.

[2]   Including reserving to himself a power of sale, like the trustee's power of sale in *Re Lashmar* [1891] 1 Ch 258, the trustee being under an active duty to consider from time to time whether or not to exercise it.

[3]   *Onslow v Wallis* (1849) 1 Mac & G 506; *Re Lashmar* [1891] 1 Ch 258.

BENEFICIARY DIRECTING T TO HOLD FOR ANOTHER

12.16 The other way in which S may purportedly declare trusts of his equitable interest arises where T1 and T2 are trustees of property for S and S directs them to hold the property on trust for B instead of S. The essence of this direction is that S divests himself of his equitable interest and vests it in B. Thus S's direction is treated as a disposition of his equitable interest which must actually itself be in writing or be void owing to the Law of Property Act 1925, s 53(1)(c).

12.17 The leading case is *Grey v IRC*[1] where S had already created six settlements (each with the same persons as trustees) and wished to transfer 18,000 shares to those trustees in such a way as only to pay nominal stamp duty, a tax levied on *documents* effecting transactions. Thus, on 1 February he transferred the 18,000 shares to the trustees as nominees holding the shares to his order, so that since he had not divested himself of his equitable interest the trustees held the shares on trust for him[2]. On 18 February he orally directed the trustees to divide the shares into six blocks of 3,000 each to be appropriated to each of the six pre-existing settlements. On 25 March the trustees executed documents confirming that as from 18 February they held the blocks of the shares on the trusts of the relevant settlements and S also executed these documents, though not expressed to be a party thereto.

[1] *Grey v IRC* [1960] AC 1, [1959] 3 All ER 603. Like so many cases on formalities the problems arose from trying to avoid ad valorem stamp duty payable on documents. Conveyances or transfers by way of gift are no longer subject to ad valorem duty: Since Finance Act 1985, s 82.

[2] The trust was probably express, though it may have been resulting, but no court treated the matter as of any significance.

12.18 No stamp duty was payable if the oral direction of 18 February created the trust as it would if it truly amounted to a declaration of trust of personalty. However, if the direction really amounted to an assignment or disposition of S's equitable interest then this was void until effected in writing on 25 March, in which case stamp duty would be payable on the instruments of 25 March[1].

[1] The 25 March documents were regarded not as ineffective subsequent written evidence but as a 'belt and braces' device capable of making a disposition as of that date insofar as necessary if the 18 February disposition were void: *Grey v IRC* [1958] Ch 690 at 706–707, CA and B. Green (1984) 47 MLR 385 at 391–392.

12.19 The House of Lords unanimously held that S's oral direction was a disposition of S's equitable interest since S intended thereby to divest himself of his equitable interest and vest it in the beneficiaries under his six pre-existing settlements. As such, the oral direction was void, so that it was the documents of 25 March signed by S that validly disposed of S's equitable interest and thus ad valorem stamp duty was payable.

EXERCISE OF T'S OVERRIDING POWERS

12.20 By way of contrast, if property is held by trustees upon such trusts as trustees shall from time to time appoint or declare[1], and the trustees appoint or declare trusts, thereby divesting the existing beneficiaries of their equitable interests and vesting equitable interests in the new beneficiaries, this is not a disposition of subsisting equitable interests within s 53(1)(c): it is the creation of new equitable interests automatically extinguishing the old equitable interests. If, however, the absolutely entitled beneficiary under an express or resulting trust, takes advantage of such absolute beneficial ownership to direct the trustees to hold the trust fund wholly for others, then he is divesting himself of his equitable interest in favour of the newly declared beneficiaries, so this should be a disposition within s 53(1)(c)[2]; indeed, Viscount Simonds in

12.20 *Matters essential to the prima facie validity of an express trust*

Grey v IRC[3] stated, 'If the word disposition is given its natural meaning it cannot be denied that a direction given by [the settlor-beneficiary] whereby the beneficial interest theretofore vested in him became vested in another is a disposition.' It should not matter whether the direction is made under the powers inherent in an absolute beneficial owner or under a 'spelled-out' express personal power of appointment vested in the express personal power of appointment vested in the absolute beneficial owner, Equity looking to the substance and not the form.

1   On the excessively broad scope of such powers see paras 8.77–8.88 above.
2   There are unsound dicta of Lord Denning to the contrary in *Re Vandervell's Trusts (No 2)* [1974] Ch 269, [1974] 3 All ER 205, which cannot be supported even if restricted to a resulting trust in the settlor's favour—distinguishing between a resulting and an express trust in this context appears to fly in the face of *Grey v IRC* [1960] AC 1, [1959] 3 All ER 603 and of Lord Denning in *Oughtred v IRC* [1960] AC 206 at 233, HL where he considered that dispositions of equitable interests under a constructive trust need to satisfy s 53(1)(c).
3   [1960] AC 1 at 12.

12.21 *Re Vandervell's Trusts (No 2)*[1] is the case in point, though somewhat enigmatic. V wished to endow a Chair of Pharmacology at the Royal College of Surgeons by providing it with about £150,000. To this end, in 1958 he had 100,000 'A' shares in his private company transferred to the College, so that he might declare dividends on the shares amounting to £145,000[2] in the next few years, and he had the College grant an option to the trustee company of V's children's settlement enabling the 100,000 shares to be acquired for £5,000. Nothing was stated as to the trusts on which the trustee company was to hold the option. Thus, the House of Lords in the earlier *Vandervell v IRC*[3] held that the option was held by the trustee company on a resulting trust for V so that V, not having divested himself absolutely of all interest in the shares, was personally liable for surtax on all the dividends paid to the College in the period from 1958 until 1961, when the option was exercised, the appropriate amount of dividends having then been paid to endow the Chair.

1   [1974] Ch 269 on which see [1979] Conv 17 (G. Battersby) and (1975) 38 MLR 557 (J.W. Harris).
2   The dividends were paid net of tax but the Royal College of Surgeons as a charity could recover the tax to make up the £145,000: see *Vanderwell v IRC* [1967] 2 AC 291 at 321.
3   [1967] 2 AC 291, [1967] 1 All ER 1.

12.22 The trustee company used £5,000 of the children's settlement moneys to exercise the option and acquire the 100,000 shares. The trustee company and V then believed, and acted on the footing, that the shares were held on the trusts of the children's settlement (erroneously believing that the option had been so held) so that V's private company declared £770,000 dividends on the shares and the dividends were added to the funds of the children's settlement in the period 1961 onwards.

12.23 However, doubts arose as to whether or not V had effectively divested himself absolutely of all interest in the shares so the Revenue claimed that V was still personally liable for surtax on dividends paid to the children's settlement from 1961. In 1965 V made sure he had divested himself of all interest by executing a deed transferring all his interest to the trustee company on the trusts of the children's settlement.

12.24 In 1967 probably worn out by his Revenue problems, V died, leaving his personal representatives allegedly responsible for £628,000 tax due on the dividends paid to the children's settlement 1961–1965.

12.25 The personal representatives were thus forced to claim these dividends back from the trustee company on the basis that the option, and then the shares (after the exercise of the option), were held on a resulting trust for V until V executed the 1965 deed since (1) there was insufficient evidence of any intention to have the option and then the shares held on trust for the children's settlement, or (2) even if there were sufficient evidence, V could divest himself of his equitable interest in favour of the children only by signed writing within s 53(1)(c) and no such document came into existence until 1965.

12.26 The Revenue claim against the personal representatives for the £628,000 tax was stood over pending the outcome of the personal representatives' claim against the trustee company. After all, if the personal representatives' claim against the trustee company failed this would be on the basis that V had effectively divested himself of his equitable interest in the shares in 1961 so that no tax assessment should lie against the personal representatives in respect of the dividends on the shares paid to the trustee company. However, if the Revenue felt that the personal representatives had not pressed their claim against the trustee company hard enough then the Revenue, not being a party to that action[1], would not be bound by its findings and so could still pursue its claim. As things turned out, the personal representatives' claim against the trustee company succeeded before Megarry J but, on a new ground, failed according to all three judges in the Court of Appeal, and the Revenue accepted this failure, so there was no need for the personal representatives to take the case to the House of Lords to impress the Revenue with their good faith. The net result of the *Re Vandervell (No 2)* litigation was that the Revenue lost and the Vandervell family won, though the Revenue had won in respect of the 1958–61 period in *Vandervell v IRC*.

[1]   In *White v Vandervell Trustees* [1971] AC 912, the trustee company had successfully resisted the personal representatives' claim to join the Revenue as a party so that the Revenue would be bound by the findings of the facts. The Rules of the Supreme Court were then changed to allow the Revenue to be joined in future cases if they consent.

12.27 In *Re Vandervell (No 2)* the Court of Appeal held that the additional evidence available since *Vandervell v IRC* did not change the inference drawn by Lord Upjohn[1] (with whom Lord Pearce agreed) that the option and, after its exercise, the shares, were to be held by the trustee company on such trusts as V *or the trustee company* should from time to time declare (V presumably having such power as an incident of the option being held on resulting trust for him as absolute beneficial owner thereof, and the trustee company having such power under the oral trusts created by V[2]). Further, there was sufficient evidence that the trustee company had declared new trusts at the time of exercising the option in October 1961 since it had paid the £5,000 from the children's settlement, its solicitors in November had written to the Revenue so informing them stating, 'Consequently such shares will henceforth be held by the company upon the trusts of the settlement', and the trustee company thenceforward paid all dividends received into the children's settlement. Of course, the company's exercise of its power to appoint or declare trusts (which was probably restricted by necessary implication to exercising such power only in favour of beneficiaries under trusts of which the private trust company was trustee, as believed by the directors of the trust company according to paragraph 9(3) of the facts found by the Special Commissioners), since it concerned personalty, did not need to be in any special written form but could be manifested orally or by conduct[3].

1   [1967] 2 AC 291 at 315, 317.
2   A power to appoint or declare new trusts may be unrestricted in its terms, particularly where the donee of the power knows enough of the settlor's intentions to make it administratively workable: see paras 8.77–8.88 above.
3   However, there are 'difficulties in the way of a limited company declaring a trust by way of parol or conduct and without a resolution of the board of directors' per Stephenson LJ [1974] Ch 269 at 323. Furthermore since the trustee company thought they were already trustees of the option for the children (rather than V) and thus automatically became trustees for the children of the shares acquired upon exercising the option, it is difficult to find an intention to create a new trust in favour of the children to displace the old trust in favour of V.

12.28   The trustee company's declaration of valid trusts in favour of the children extinguished V's equitable interest under the resulting trust in his favour. Thus s 53(1)(c) was inapplicable since it required only that 'a disposition of an equitable interest subsisting at the time of the disposition must be in writing signed by the person disposing of the same'. After all, V did not dispose of his existing equitable interest: the trustee company did not dispose of an existing equitable interest, but created a new equitable interest thereby automatically extinguishing V's old equitable interest. As Stephenson LJ stated[1], 'Lord Denning MR and Lawton LJ are able to hold that no disposition is needed because (1) the option was held on such trusts as might thereafter be declared by the trustee company or by Mr. Vandervell himself and (2) the trustee company has declared that it holds the shares in the children's settlement.'

1   [1974] Ch 269 at 323.

12.29   Unfortunately some of Lord Denning's remarks in the case are couched in misleading broad terms sufficient to lead the unwary to believe that s 53(1)(c) is inapplicable, and so no formalities are required, where property is held on a resulting trust for the settlor and the *settlor* terminates the resulting trust by directing the trustees to hold on new trusts for new beneficiaries. In such a case s 53(1)(c) is surely applicable as apparent from *Grey v IRC* where trustees held shares for the settlor and were then orally told by him to hold the shares for certain beneficiaries, and the House of Lords held that this amounted to a disposition by the settlor of the settlor's equitable interest to the new beneficiaries which was void for lack of the writing required by s 53(1)(c).

12.30 Lord Denning and Lawton LJ[1] were also quite ready to hold that V during his lifetime (so binding his personal representatives) had by his conduct estopped himself from denying the existence of his children's beneficial interest in the shares acquired upon exercise of the option. However, they made no attempt to meet the difficulties over this, as fully set out in the judgment of Megarry J. Essentially, how could V be shown to have acted unconscionably or inequitably in letting the option be exercised for the benefit of the children's settlement and letting them receive the dividends on the shares acquired by exercising the option, when at the relevant time he believed he had no right to the option or dividends entitling him to object? Since Megarry J made this point it has become established that (whilst this point may still be valid where V has merely negatively acquiesced in what has occurred) where someone like V has positively encouraged particular conduct it is not necessary for him to know that he has a legal right to prohibit such conduct[2]. However, even if V's encouragement of the trustees spending £5,000 of the moneys of the trust for V's children upon purchasing the shares is capable of founding an estoppel one would have thought that the requisite minimum equity to do justice to the children's settlement was to order repayment of the £5,000 with interest rather than allowing the children's settlement to retain the £770,000 still in the settlement trustee's hands[3].

[1] Lawton LJ was also prepared to base his judgment on an unrealistic distinction between the option held on a resulting trust and the shares acquired upon exercising the option: after the option had been exercised it had been extinguished, so the resulting trust had been extinguished so no old equitable interest existed to be capable of assignment, so that only new equitable interests could be created. However, the option is surely not distinct from the shares but merely a limited right created out of the larger bundle of rights inherent in the ownership of the shares; for this very reason the House of Lords in *Vandervell v IRC* held that V, as beneficial owner of the *option*, had failed to divest himself absolutely of the shares which it controlled. Moreover, if the right to the shares under the option was held by the trustee company not for itself, but for V, then surely the actual shares acquired by exercising the right were held for V.
[2] *Taylor Fashions Ltd v Liverpool Victoria Trustees Co Ltd* [1982] QB 133n, [1981] 1 All ER 897, approved in *Habib Bank Ltd v Habib Bank AG Zurich* [1981] 2 All ER 650 at 666; *Amalgamated Investment and Property Co v Texas Commerce International Bank Ltd* [1982] QB 84 at 104; *Lim Teng Huan v Ang Swee Chuan* [1992] 1 WLR 113 at 117.
[3] B. Green (1984) 47 MLR 385 at 418, and the need for a proportionate response emphasized in *Jennings v Rice* [2003] EWCA Civ 159 [2002] WTLR 367.

BENEFICIARY DIRECTING T TO TRANSFER TO X ABSOLUTELY

12.31 Further problems concerning s 53(1)(c) arise where T holds property on trust for A absolutely and A directs T to transfer the property to X to the intent that X shall have the full legal and beneficial interest therein. Whilst there is something to be said for the view that since A formerly had a separate equitable interest, which he no longer has, he must have disposed of his equitable interest to X, *Vandervell v IRC*[1] provides clear House of Lords' authority that where the legal title to the property is transferred at the direction of the absolutely entitled beneficiary intending to part with his beneficial interest (or the beneficiaries together entitled to the entire beneficial interest) no separate assignment within s 53(1)(c) is required of the beneficial interest co-extensive with the legal title.

[1] [1967] 2 AC 291.

12.32   The reasoning in the speeches of Lord Upjohn[1] and Lord Donovan[2] is based on likening A's position as absolutely entitled equitable owner to the position of an absolute legal beneficial owner, O, who transfers property, when there is clearly no need for O to sign a separate written assignment of the beneficial[3] interest. This accords with the object of s 53(1)(c) which 'is to prevent hidden oral transactions in equitable interests ... and making it difficult, if not impossible, for the trustee to ascertain who are in truth his beneficiaries'[4]. However, the reasoning is not very convincing because in the case of transfer by the legal beneficial owner the beneficial interest is subsumed or merged in the legal interest, whereas where T holds the legal title on trust for A the legal and equitable interests are obviously separated and the issue is whether they can be joined without a separate assignment or surrender by A, so that the legal and equitable interest may become at home in T and so be transferred by T to X. Perhaps, the position might be better justified on the ground that where T does transfer the legal title to X at the instigation of, or with the concurrence of, A then A's interest is overreached[5] and he cannot claim there has been a breach of trust and assert his interest against the new legal owner, X. By operation of law outside s 53(1)(c) A's equitable interest is extinguished[6] just as much as it would have been extinguished if A in signed writing had expressly surrendered his equitable interest to T, so that T might then pass the legal (and thus automatically the co-extensive equitable) interest to X[7].

1   [1967] 2 AC 291 at 311.
2   [1967] 2 AC 291 at 317.
3   O is not regarded as having separate legal and equitable interests, his beneficial interest being subsumed in the legal interest: *Westdeutsche Landesbank v Islington London Borough Council* [1996] AC 669 at 706; *DKLR Holding Co v Commissioner for Stamp Duties* (NSW) (1982) 149 CLR 431.
4   [1967] 2 AC 291 at 311.
5   See R C Nolan [2002] Camb LJ 169.
6   (1967) 31 Conv 175 (S. M. Spencer); [1979] Conv 17 (G. Battersby). The position of X will be even stronger if he provided consideration in reliance upon acquiring title.
7   Where T holds on trust for A it seems possible for A orally to direct T that he is to hold on trust for A until A or T declares new trusts so if it is T who declares new trusts, then T's declaration need not satisfy s 53(1)(c): conferring such a power does not confer an interest in property: see *Townshend v Harrowby* (1858) 27 LJ Ch 553.

12.33   On either basis it would seem to follow that it is the transfer by T to X that is crucial and not the earlier direction by A to T to make the transfer, so that A does not cease to be equitable owner upon giving his gratuitous oral direction to T. What if A dies before T carries out his direction or revokes his direction where the transaction is voluntary?[1] In the case of shares, where the legal title is transferred only upon the company registering the transferee on the register of members of the company, there must be considered the *Re Rose* principle[2] which treats gifts as complete when the donor has done all that is necessary, according to the nature of the property, that is required to be done by him. What if X has received the share certificates in question and the duly executed share transfer form but at the time of A's death or revocation of his voluntary direction X has not sent the document to the company or the company has not yet registered X as the new member? Strictly, it would seem that since T originally has the legal interest and since A originally has the equitable interest (until assigned under s 53(1)(c) or extinguished upon a transfer to a third party with A's concurrence) A has not done everything possible within his power to transfer his equitable interest for he has not taken advantage of s 53(1)(c). Thus, in the case of voluntary transactions A's death or revocation of his direction before the legal interest is effectively transferred from T to X should ensure that the equitable interest does not pass to X. However, it seems likely that a more liberal view will be taken, treating A as if he were the legal as well as the equitable owner so that X will obtain the equitable interest on *Re Rose* principles[3].

[1]   See para 9.74 above.
[2]   See para 9.32 above.
[3]   Per Lord Wilberforce in *Vandervell v IRC* [1967] 2 AC 291 at 330; (1967) 30 MLR 461 (N. Strauss) but see B. Green (1984) 47 MLR 385 at 410.

BENEFICIARY DIRECTING T TO TRANSFER TO TT FOR ANOTHER

12.34 Finally, there must be considered the position where T holds property on trust for A absolutely and A directs T to transfer the property to X who is to hold on trust for B[1]. Nothing was said of this position in *Vandervell v IRC*[2] where A directed T to transfer shares to X and where X, the Royal College of Surgeons, as a corporate charity received legal and beneficial ownership. However, if, as there, the position of the absolutely entitled A is likened to the position of an absolute legal beneficial owner, O, who transfers property to X on trust for B, it is clear that O would not need to execute a separate written assignment of O's beneficial interest to B: O's transfer of the legal title to X would have to satisfy the requisite formalities for the nature of the transferred property but the trusts declared by O at the time of the transfer could be oral, though if land were involved subsequent written evidence thereof would be required under s 53(1)(b).

[1]   The trust for B must commence with X's title to the property, otherwise X will hold on a resulting trust for A so that if X is subsequently to hold for B A will be making a disposition within s 53(1)(c); *Grey v IRC* [1960] AC 1, [1959] 3 All ER 603, HL.
[2]   [1967] 2 AC 291, [1967] 1 All ER 1. The statement of Harman LJ in [1966] Ch at 296, 's 53(1)(c) in dealing with dispositions of an equitable interest only applies where the disposer is not also the controller of the legal interest' is misleadingly succinct since it contradicts *Grey v IRC* [1960] AC 1, [1959] 3 All ER 603, HL.

12.35 Here the analogy between A and O is obviously less convincing than in *Vandervell v IRC* especially when such an argument would undermine the decision in *Grey v IRC*[1], based on the need for trustees and their successors in title to have a paper trail where a separate equitable interest subsists, so as to know where they stand without any problems of oral evidence, so avoiding the mischief against which s 53(1)(c) is directed. In *Vandervell v IRC* the effect of the disposition was that the legal and beneficial interest was at home in X, while in *Grey v IRC* and the present case, where the transferee X is to hold on trust for B, there is a clear separation of the legal interest from the equitable interest which has passed from its owner, A, to B by virtue of A's direction, thereby falling within s 53(1)(c). Indeed, in *Grey v IRC*, while the factual position was that T1 and T2 held shares on trust for A and were directed by A to hold them instead, in their existing capacities as trustees, for B, the legal position was that A directed his trustees to transfer shares to trustees of a trust for B, nowadays being a capital gains tax disposal from one set of trustees to a new set absolutely entitled against the other set, it being immaterial that the same individuals happen to comprise both sets of trustees[2].

1 [1960] AC 1.
2 *Hoare Trustees v Gardner* [1978] 1 All ER 791; Taxation of Capital Gains Act 1992, s 71.

REGISTERS OR DATABASES OF EQUITABLE INTERESTS

12.36 What is the position where there is an unincorporated society which keeps a register of members with absolute co-ownership interests under a trust of the society's assets (subject to the contractual position under the society's constitution) or where a nominee holder of securities maintains a register or database of the persons for whom it holds the securities from time to time? Does s 53(1)(c) as interpreted in *Grey v IRC* create insuperable problems if a club member resigns or dies, or if a beneficial owner of an interest in securities (like shares in a company) orally declares he holds them on trust absolutely for X (a person of full capacity)[1] or orally sells them to X? At first sight it does, but the practical inconvenience thereof indicates that the courts are likely to circumvent s 53(1)(c) if they can find, as a matter of contract law, that certain interests are automatically defeasible[2] or that agreed acts of the member or beneficiary amount to authority to the society's trustees or the nominee to recognise that he no longer has any equitable interest and that some other person or persons now have enlarged equitable interests or new equitable interests, so that he is prevented from asserting any claim[3].

1 Probably a disposition within LPA 1925 s 53 (1) (c): *Re Lashmar* [1891] 1 Ch 258, *ISPT Nominees Pty Limited v Chief Commissioner of State Revenue* [2003] NSWSC 697, paras 246, 250 and 270.
2 Compare the defeasibility of interests subject to an overriding power of appointment.See para 12.20 above.
3 *Ashby v Blackwell and the Million Bank Co* (1765) Amb 503; K F Sin *The Legal Nature of the Unit Trust* (Oxford University Press, 1997); *Clarke v Dunraven* [1897] AC 59, HL; Contracts (Rights of Third Parties) Act 1999. To put matters beyond doubt, disposition of equitable interests in shares within the CREST system and dealings in gilt-edged securities settled through the Central Gilts Office are exempted from compliance with s 53(1)(c) by the Uncertified Securities Regulations 2001, SI 2001/3755, reg 38(5) and Stock Transfer Act 1982, s 1(2).

'DISPOSITIONS' WITHIN SECTION 53(1)(C)

12.37 'Disposition' within s 53(1)(c) includes a conveyance which is defined[1] to include a mortgage, charge, lease, assent, vesting declaration, vesting instrument, disclaimer, release and every other assurance of property unless the context otherwise requires. However, the Court of Appeal in *Re Paradise Motor Co Ltd*[2] briefly held that s 53(1)(c) is inapplicable to a disclaimer since 'a disclaimer operates by way of avoidance and not by way of disposition'[3]. The case concerned A making a gift of shares to B, B's name being registered in the company's register of members. Within a reasonable time of learning of this B orally disclaimed any interest. His subsequent claim that this disclaimer was ineffective for failure to satisfy s 53(1)(c) failed on the short ground given above by the court. No fuller explanation was given by the court.

1   Law of Property Act 1925, s 205(1)(ii).
2   [1968] 2 All ER 625, [1968] 1 WLR 1125, CA; and see *Dewar v Dewar* [1975] 1 WLR 1532; *Re Smith* [2001] 3 All ER 552; *Sembalink v Sembalink* (1984) 15 DLR 4th 303 at 309–310. Note also that disclaimer of a unilateral transfer of land may be oral: *Re Birchall* (1889) 40 Ch D 436.
3   [1968] 2 All ER 625 at 632, [1968] 1 WLR 1125, at 1143.

12.38 It would seem that the court must have assumed that only the legal title to the shares had passed to B and that the beneficial interest would only pass to B when, having become aware of the gift, he failed to disclaim it within a reasonable time: his disclaimer within a reasonable time prevented the beneficial interest passing to him and since he avoided having the beneficial interest he could not be treated as having disposed of it[1]. Thus the essence of disclaimer is that it is a refusal to accept an intended gift, not a disposal of property.

1   Cf *Re Stratton's Disclaimer* [1958] Ch 42 at 54.

12.39 Since that decision Lord Browne-Wilkinson has explained[1]

'A person solely entitled to the full beneficial ownership of property, both at law and in equity, does not enjoy an equitable interest in that property. The legal title carries with it all rights. Unless and until there is a separation of the legal and equitable estates there is no separate equitable title. Therefore to talk about the bank [the full beneficial owner at law and in equity] retaining its equitable interest is meaningless'.

1   *Westdeutsche Landesbank Girozentrale v Islington London Borough Council* [1996] AC 669 at 706.

12.40 It could not have an equitable interst in its own property. Thus, the High Court of Australia[1] has held that if A transfers property to B to hold on trust for A, A's full beneficial ownership at law and in equity passes to B and is subject to stamp duty before a new equitable interest arises in favour of A. A cannot transfer only the bare legal estate because A cannot hold such estate on trust for A: he cannot have rights against himself and cannot owe duties to himself.

1   *DKLR Holding Company (No 2) Pty Ltd v Commissioner of Stamp Duties* (1982) 149 CLR 431.

12.41 On this basis a modern justification of *Re Paradise Motor Company Ltd* is that when B disclaimed any interest in the shares transferred to him by A (registering B as the new shareholder) s 53 (1) (c) concerned with any disposition 'of an equitable interest subsisting at the time of the disposition' could not apply because B did not have a subsisting equitable interest separate from the legal title which absorbed the beneficial interest.

12.42 Where a release or surrender of a subsisting equitable interest is concerned it may be argued that it takes effect by way of extinguishing the existing equitable interest and that extinction is not disposition[1] just as avoidance (in the case of disclaimer) is not disposition. Indeed, some support may be obtained from *Vandervell v IRC*[2] where T held on trust for A absolutely and A directed T to transfer the whole legal and beneficial interest to B and there was held to be no disposition within s 53(1)(c) on the part of A, though the result was that the whole interest was in B so that A's interest had somehow been released, surrendered or otherwise extinguished. However, *Vandervell v IRC* is likely to be restricted to the situation where an absolutely entitled beneficiary, A, directs a disposition of the legal estate and the beneficial interest therewith. Take the case where T holds on trust for A for life, remainder to B, and A releases or surrenders his equitable interest, so accelerating B's interest in remainder. A has divested himself of his subsisting equitable intest so that B benefits to the extent of such interest. Surely A's dealing with his interest is a disposition of it[3]. Thus writing should be required under s 53(1)(c). This is supported by the view of the House of Lords[4] that the surrender of a lease merging in the freehold reversion would be a disposition within s 37 of the Matrimonial Causes Act 1973.

¹   [1960] BTR 20 (J.G. Monroe); *Re Tancred's Settlement* [1903] 1 Ch 715 at 725; *Re Earl Leven* [1954] 3 All ER 81, [1954] 1 WLR 1228.
²   [1967] 2 AC 291, [1967] 1 All ER 1, HL.
³   As observed by Viscount Simonds in *Grey v IRC* [1960] AC 1 at 12, 'If the word disposition is given its natural meaning it cannot be denied that a direction given by [the beneficiary] whereby the beneficial interest in the shares theretofore vested in him became vested in another is a disposition.' See also *IRC v Buchanan* [1958] Ch 289, [1957] 2 All ER 470.
⁴   *Newlon Housing Trust v Alsulaimen* [1999] 1 AC 313 at 317.

12.43 Variations of trusts by the court under the Variation of Trusts Act 1958 do not have to satisfy s 53(1)(c)[1], nor, apparently, nominations made under a staff pension fund allowing a beneficiary to nominate a beneficiary to take on his death what would otherwise vest in his personal representatives[2]. Similarly, if a person takes out a policy on his own life where rights to a money payment only crystallise on death, there is no disposition of a subsisting equitable interest if he orally nominates X to receive the money to which he is contractually entitled and hold it on trust for B and C[3].

¹   *Re Holt's Settlement* [1969] 1 Ch 100, [1968] 1 All ER 470.
²   *Re Danish Bacon Co Staff Pension Fund Trusts* [1971] 1 WLR 248 approved in *Baird v Baird* [1990] 2 AC 548 at 561.
³   *Gold v Hill* (1998–99) 1 ITELR 27, [1999] 1 FLR 54, while as pointed out in *Kasperbauer v Griffiths* [2000] WTLR 333 at 347, the doctrine of secret trusts has no application to nominations of beneficiaries under life policies.

12.44 Where s 53(1)(c) does apply to an assignment in writing of an equitable interest and the assignee is to take as trustee the assignment is valid without the need to disclose particulars of the trust[1]. Furthermore, the requirement for signed writing can be satisfied as for ss 40 and 53(1)(b) by two or more sufficiently interconnected documents[2].

¹   *Re Tyler Funds Trusts* [1967] 3 All ER 389, [1967] 1 WLR 1269.
²   *Re Danish Bacon Co Staff Pension Fund* [1971] 1 All ER 486, [1971] 1 WLR 248.

Testamentary trusts

12.45 Clearly, when a testator is intending in his will or codicil to create trusts of property to take effect on his death such trusts will only take effect if the Wills Act 1837 formalities are satisfied as respects the trust property and the intended beneficiaries by virtue of the testator's signature being attested by two witnesses present together. An apparent inter vivos trust will only be regarded as testamentary in nature if it has no immediate effect on the settlor's full beneficial ownership and purports to dispose of such equitable interest only on his death, eg a transfer to trustees of property to be held on trust in S's lifetime as to income *and capital* for S or such persons as he directs and on his death for X or such other person signified to the trustees by S in signed writing in his lifetime or by will[1]. If such trust happened to comply with testamentary formalities it would only take effect (other than as a bare trust for S) on S's death – if not revoked by some later will – when its subject matter, being whatever is left at S's death after S has done whatever he wanted with it, will be certain.

1   See *Anderson v Patton* [1948] 2 DLR 202 where three judges in the Alberta Court of Appeal upheld the trial judge's construction of a trust as a gift of $5000 to a trustee upon trust for the settlor for life, then for X and Y, with a power of revocation in the settlor, so there was a valid trust, while two judges held the trust to be of capital and income for the settlor absolutely but if he did not demand the money in his lifetime then it was to pass to X and Y, so there was a void testamentary disposition. As Dixon and Evatt JJ stated in *Russell v Scott* (1936) 55 CLR 440 at 454, 'What can be accomplished only by will is the voluntary transmission on death of an interest which up to the moment of death belongs absolutely [and indefeasibly] to the deceased.' The bracketed words are correct if referring to an interest defeasible by the death of the deceased but not by some subsequent event. Also see *Governors of Foundling Hospital v Crane* [1911] 2 KB 367 at 379–380.

12.46 In contrast, there will be an effective inter vivos trust where S transfers property in his lifetime to trustees on trust for S for life, remainder to B or such other persons signified to the trustees by S in signed writing in his lifetime or by will, even if the trustees or S have power to revoke the trust or to appoint the property to anyone other than the trustees[1]. B has a defeasible vested interest in remainder capable of passing to his trustee in bankruptcy if he becomes bankrupt or of being disposed of by B inter vivos or by will, while S has a defeasible vested life interest entitling him to the income until exercise of the power of revocation or appointment.

1   *Kauter v Hilton* (1953) 90 CLR 86 at 98–99 and 100–101; *Young v Sealey* [1949] Ch 278 at 284 and 294; *T Choithram International SA v Pagarani* [2001] 2 All ER 492 at 500; Scott on Trusts (4th edn) para 57.1, but if the settlor retains such control that the trust is a sham in his lifetime the dispositions after his death will be testamentary: *Scott on Trusts* (4th edn) para 57.2. Where S in his lifetime sets up a joint account of cash or investments for S and B jointly then, in the absence of any resulting trust, B will become automatically entitled to the cash or investments on S's death but by virtue of the lifetime gift and not any testamentary disposition: *Aroso v Coutts & Co* [2001] WTLR 797; *Re Figgis* [1969] 1 Ch 123 at 149; *Lynch v Burke* [1995] 2 IR 159.

Equitable proprietary estoppel

12.47 Equity is seen as its flexible best or worst in its doctrine that if a defendant encourages, or acquiesces in, the claimant acting to his detriment, in the belief that the defendant's property is the claimant's property or that the defendant has given or will give the claimant the property or an interest therein, then equity will estop the defendant (and his personal representatives) from asserting his full legal and beneficial ownership and from claiming that non-compliance with statutory formalities under the Law of Property Act 1925 or the Wills Act 1837 bars the claimant's claim. Such estoppel gives the claimant an equitable right which may be for a sum of money[1] perhaps supported by an equitable lien on the defendant's property for the claimant's expenditure[2] or the value of his improvements[3], or lost expected occupancy rights[4] or a decree perfecting the defendant's imperfect gift by ordering the defendant to convey[5] or lease[6] land to the claimant, or grant the claimant an easement[7] or a licence to use the premises as long as the claimant permanently resides there[8] or until the claimant receives compensation from the defendant[9].

[1] *Jennings v Rice* [2002] EWCA Civ 159, [2002] WTLR 367.
[2] *Unity Joint Stock Mutual Banking Association v King* (1858) 25 Beav 72; *Morris v Morris* [1982] 1 NSWLR 61; *Lee-Parker v Izzet (No 2)* [1972] 2 All ER 800 at 804–805; *Burrows v Sharp* (1989) 23 HLR 82; *Baker v Baker* (1993) 25 HLR 408.
[3] *Raffaele v Raffaele* [1962] WAR 29; (1963) 79 LQR 228 (D. E. Allen); (*Cbbe v Yeomans Row Management Limited* [2005] WTLR 625 (lien for amount equal to half the increase in value of the property as a result of grant of planning permission obtained by claimant's efforts and money).
[4] *Campbell v Griffin* [2001] EWCA Civ 990, [2001] WTLR 981.
[5] *Pascoe v Turner* [1979] 2 All ER 945, [1979] 1 WLR 431, CA; *Dillwyn v Llewelyn* (1862) 4 De G F & J 517; *Thomas v Thomas* [1956] NZLR 785; *Re Basham* [1987] 1 All ER 405; *Voyce v Voyce* (1991) 62 P & CR 290; *Lim Teng Huan v Ang Swee Chuan* [1992] 1 WLR 113 (where the transfer to the claimant was conditional upon payment of suitable compensation).
[6] *Taylor Fashions Ltd v Liverpool Victoria Trustees Co Ltd* [1982] QB 133n, [1981] 1 All ER 897; *Siew Soon Wah v Yong Tong Hong* [1973] AC 836, [1973] 2 WLR 713, PC; *Griffiths v Williams* (1977) 248 Estates Gazette 947, CA.
[7] *Ward v Kirkland* [1967] Ch 194, [1966] 1 All ER 609; *Ives Investments Ltd v High* [1967] 2 QB 379, [1967] 1 All ER 504, CA; *Crabb v Arun District Council* [1976] Ch 179, [1975] 3 All ER 865, CA.
[8] *Inwards v Baker* [1965] 2 QB 29, [1965] 1 All ER 446, CA; *Greasley v Cooke* [1980] 3 All ER 710, [1980] 1 WLR 1306, CA; *Williams v Staite* [1979] Ch 291, [1978] 2 All ER 928, CA; *Makaraj v Chand* [1986] AC 898, [1986] 3 All ER 107, PC; *Matharu v Matharu* [1994] 2 FLR 597, CA. If the court finds the plaintiff to have a life interest, as opposed to a licence then the plaintiff becomes a Settled Land Act tenant for life: *Ungurian v Leshoff* [1990] Ch 206.
[9] *Re Sharpe (a bankrupt)* [1980] 1 All ER 198, [1980] 1 WLR 219; *Hussey v Palmer* [1972] 3 All ER 744, [1972] 1 WLR 1286, CA; *Dodsworth v Dodsworth* (1973) 228 Estates Gazette 1115; *Taylor v Taylor* [1956] NZLR 99; *Stratulatos v Stratulatos* [1988] 2 NZLR 424.

12.48 The question arises whether, in the event of detrimental reliance, the court should order a remedy which fulfils the expectations of the claimant so as to perfect imperfect gifts (just like a contract is fully enforced irrespective of the consideration therefor being relatively slight) or a remedy which merely reverses the claimant's detriment. It seems that the aim is 'the minimum equity to do justice to'[1] the claimant so that the Australian courts' approach[2] is to reverse detriment or prevent unjust enrichment, because it would normally be inequitable to assist a volunteer by providing a remedy which is disproportionate to the detriment. However there may be exceptional reasons for going further in some cases, as in *Pascoe v Turner*, where according to the Court of Appeal[3], 'The court must decide what is the minimum equity to do justice to [the claimant, Mrs Turner] having regard to the way in which she changed her position for the worse by reason of the acquiescence and encouragement of the legal owner.' This was a Mr Pascoe who had told Mrs Turner, 'The home is yours', when he left her to move in with another woman. Believing the house was now hers Mrs Turner spent £230 on improvements to it over three years, such expenditure representing a significant part of her small capital. Mr Pascoe's 'ruthless disregard of the obligations binding on his conscience' led him to try to recover the house but the court ordered him to convey the fee simple to Mrs Turner. Otherwise, she might be at risk of him selling to a bona fide purchaser of the legal estate for value without notice (when she was away, ill or on holiday) and would not have a mortgageable interest as security for loans for repairs and improvements.

1   *Crabb v Arran District Council* [1976] Ch 179; *Pascoe v Turner* [1979] 1 WLR 431; *Baker v Baker* (1993) 25 HLR 408; *Stedmore v Dalby* (1996) 72 P & CR 196; *Gillett v Holt* [2001] Ch 210.
2   *Waltons Stores (Interstate) Ltd v Maher* (1988) 164 CLR 387; *Commonwealth of Australia v Verwayen* (1990) 170 CLR 394.
3   *Pascoe v Turner* [1979] 2 All ER 945 at 950, CA, endorsing the approach of Scarman LJ in *Crabb v Arun District Council* [1976] Ch 179, [1975] 3 All ER 865, CA.

12.49 From *Jennings v Rice*[1] the Court of Appeal approach now appears to be to look at the claimant's expectation as indicating the maximum extent of the equity but the court's award is a proportionate one taking account of the combination of expectations, detrimental reliance and the unconscionability of allowing the benefactor-defendant (or the deceased benefactor's estate) to go back on his assurances. In *Grundy v Ottey* the Court of Appeal stated[2], 'the purpose of proprietary estoppel is not to enforce an abligation that does not amount to a contract nor yet to reverse the detriment which the claimant has suffered, but to grant an appropriate remedy in respect of the unconscionable conduct'. The court also takes account of any misconduct of the claimant[3], any particularly oppressive conduct of the defendant[4] and the difficulties in compelling people to live under one roof so that there may be a need for a clean break[5]. Indeed, a claim will fail if the claimant fails to come to Equity with 'cleans hands'[6].

1   [2002] EWCA Civ 159, [2002] WTLR 367, applied in *Grundy v Ottey* [2003] EWCA Civ 1176, [2003] WTLR 1253.
2   [2003] WTLR 1253, para 61.
3   *J Willis & Son v Willis* [1986] 1 EGLR 62; *Williams v Staite* [1979] Ch 291.
4   *Pascoe v Turner* [1979] 1 WLR 431; *Crabb v Arun District Council* [1976] Ch 179.
5   *Campbell v Griffin* [2001] EWCA Civ 990, [2001] WTLR 981; *Burrows and Burrows v Sharpe* (1991) 23 HLR 82; *Baker v Baker* [1993] 2 FLR 247.
6   *Gonthier v Orange Contract Scaffolding Ltd* [2003] EWCA Civ 873, [2003] All ER (D) 332 (Jun).

12.50 Where the assurances and the claimant's reliance have a consensual character, like that involved in common intention constructive trusts, relating to specific property the court will normally vindicate the claimant's expectations[1]. However, where the expectations are uncertain or extravagant or out of all proportion to the detriment which the claimant has suffered the court will satisfy the equity in another more limited way[3].

12.50 *Matters essential to the prima facie validity of an express trust*

1   *Yaxley v Gotts* [2000] Ch 162 at 176 and *Oxley v Hiscock* [2004] EWCA Civ 546, [2004] 3 All ER 703, para 66, (proprietary estoppel and common intention constructive trusts often co-existing). A typical case will involve sexual cohabitants or an elderly benefactor and a carer residing with him under a common understanding the latter will inherit the benefactor's house or will have a home for life: *Jennings v Rice* [2002] EWCA Civ 159, para [45], [2003] 1 P & CR 100.
2   *Jennings v Rice* [2002] EWCA Civ 159, [2002] WTLR 367 para [50]; *Campbell v Griffin* [2001] EWCA Civ 900, [2001] WTLR 981; *Gillett v Holt* [2001] Ch 210.

DEVELOPMENT OF BROAD APPROACH

12.51 The starting point for proprietary estoppel claims used to be the five *probanda* of Fry J in *Willmott v Barber*[1]:

> 'In the first place the plaintiff must have made a mistake as to his legal rights. Secondly, the plaintiff must have expended some money or must have done some act (not necessarily upon the defendant's land) on the faith of his mistaken belief. Thirdly, the defendant, the possessor of the legal right, must know of the existence of his own right which is inconsistent with the right claimed by the plaintiff. If he does not know of it he is in the same position as the plaintiff, and the doctrine of acquiescence is founded upon conduct with a knowledge of your legal rights. Fourthly, the defendant, the possessor of the legal right, must know of the plaintiff's mistaken belief of his rights. If he does not, there is nothing which calls upon him to assert his own rights. Lastly, the defendant must have encouraged the plaintiff in his expenditure of money or in the other acts which he has done, either directly or by abstaining from asserting his legal right ... Nothing short of this will do.'

1   (1880) 15 Ch D 96 at 105–106.

12.52 The courts originally considered matters from the viewpoint of the defendant, the possessor of the legal right, so that he had to be at fault in some way before the claimant could claim an equity. Thus, if the defendant did not know the true position and so did not know of his right to object when he either acquiesced in or encouraged the claimant's belief then he was not estopped from subsequently asserting his rights against the claimant[1]. This may still be the case where he has merely acquiesced whilst his rights were being infringed at a time when he did not realise he had such rights[2].

1   *Willmott v Barber* (1880) 15 Ch D 96; *Falcke v Scottish Imperial Insurance Co* (1886) 34 Ch D 234 at 243, 253, CA; *Re Vandervell's Trusts (No 2)* [1974] Ch 269 at 300–301.
2   *Taylor Fashions Ltd v Liverpool Victoria Trustees Co Ltd* [1982] QB 133n at 147; *Amalgamated Investment and Property Co Ltd v Texas Commerce International Bank Ltd* [1982] QB 84 at 204, CA.

12.53 In cases of encouragement the court now seems to regard matters from the claimant's viewpoint. It is not fault on the defendant's part that is significant: attention is directed at how unconscionable it would be if the claimant were to suffer from the defendant asserting his strict legal rights. The court adopts a broad approach[1] 'directed at ascertaining whether in particular circumstances it would be unconscionable for a party to be permitted to deny that which, knowingly or unknowingly, he has allowed or encouraged another to assume to his detriment.' The defendant's ignorance is merely one of the relevant factors in the overall inquiry. The court's inquiry focuses upon unconscionability at the date it deals with the case so events occurring well after particular encouragement are taken into account[2].

1   *Taylor Fashions Ltd v Liverpool Victoria Trustees Co Ltd* [1982] QB 133n at 151, approved in *Habib Bank Ltd v Habib Bank Ag Zurich* [1981] 2 All ER 650 at 666, CA; *A-G of Hong Kong v Humphreys Estate Ltd* [1987] 2 All ER 387 at 392, PC; *Lim Teng Huan v Ang Swee Chuan* [1992] 1 WLR 113 at 117, PC; *Jones v Stones* [1999] 1 WLR 1739; and Blue Haven Enterprises Limited v Tully [2006] UKPC I7, para 23, [2006] All ER (D) 428 (Mar). Cf the broad approach to consents to breach of trust in *Re Pauling's Settlement Trusts* [1962] 1 WLR 86 at 208 endorsed by the Court of Appeal in *Re Freeston's Charity* [1979] 1 All ER 51, [1978] 1 WLR 741, CA.
2   *Uglow v Uglow* [2004] WTLR 1183.

DETRIMENTAL RELIANCE

12.54 It is necessary to prove that the plaintiff acted to her detriment in the belief that she had or would have an interest in the defendant's property[1]. The detrimental acts do not need to be expenditure of money or be inherently referable to the property[2]. Once the claimant shows that the defendant assured the claimant she was to have an interest in the property and that the claimant suffered detriment it will be presumed that the claimant acted to her detriment in reliance on the assurance: the onus of rebutting this presumption of reliance will then be on the defendant[3].

1   *Greasley v Cooke* [1980] 1 WLR 1306 at 1313–1314, CA; *Watts and Reading v Storey* (1983) 134 NLJ 631, CA cited in Maudsley & Burn's *Land Law: Cases & Materials* (6th edn) p 575; *Grant v Edwards* [1986] 2 All ER 426 at 439; *Brinnand v Ewens* (1987) 19 HLR 415. *Midland Bank v Dobson* [1986] 1 FLR 171.
2   *Grant v Edwards* [1986] Ch 638 at 657 [1986] 2 All ER 426 at 439, CA; *Jones v Jones* [1977] 2 All ER 231; *Greasley v Cooke* [1980] 1 WLR 1306; *Re Basham* [1987] 1 All ER 405, [1986] 1 WLR 1498.
3   *Greasley v Cooke* [1980] 1 WLR 1306; *Coombes v Smith* [1986] 1 WLR 808 at 821; *Evans v HSBC Trust Company (UK) Limited* [2005] WTLR 1289, para 71.

12.55 In *Grant v Edwards*[1] Browne-Wilkinson V-C stated obiter:

'In many cases it is impossible to say whether or not the claimant would have done the act relied on as a detriment even if she thought she had no interest in the house. Setting up house together, having a baby and making payments to general housekeeping expenses (not strictly necessary to enable the mortgage to be paid) may all be referable to the mutual love and affection of the parties and not specifically referable to the claimant's belief that she has an interest in the house. Once it has been shown that there was a common intention that the claimant should have an interest in the house, any act done by her to her detriment relating to the joint lives of the parties is sufficient detriment to qualify. The acts do not have to be inherently referable to the house. The holding out to the claimant that she had a beneficial interest in the house is an act of such a nature as to be part of the inducement to her to do the acts relied on. Accordingly, in the absence of evidence to the contrary, the right inference is that the claimant acted in reliance on such holding out and the burden lies on the legal owner to show that she did not do so.'

1   [1986] Ch 638 at 657, [1986] 2 All ER 426 at 439, CA.

12.56 Earlier a tough approach had been taken in *Coombes v Smith*[1] where the claimant's belief, encouraged by the defendant house-owner whilst she was his mistress, that he would always provide her with a roof over her head was held to be something quite different from a belief that she had an interest in the house. Even if she had had such a belief the judge was of the view that the claimant had failed to prove that her following acts constituted detriment in the context of proprietary estoppel:

(1)   leaving her husband and moving to a house owned but not occupied by the defendant[2] (who lived elsewhere with his wife and children, though indicating for ten years he would shortly be leaving them to live with the plaintiff);

(2)   allowing herself to become pregnant and giving birth to their child Clare[3];

(3)   looking after and redecorating the house, looking after Clare and being ready for the defendant's visits[4];

(4)   taking no other steps like looking for a paid job (or, presumably, a rich husband) to provide for herself and Clare, when the defendant was happy to pay all the bills and pay an allowance to her and Clare[5].

1   [1986] 1 WLR 808. *Contrast Lalani v Crump Holdings Limited* (18 June 2004, unreported), para 47.
2   She preferred to have a relationship with, and a child by, the defendant rather than continue living with her husband.
3   She wished to bear his child.
4   She was the occupier of the house, Clare's mother and his mistress.
5   The deputy judge, Jonathan Parker QC, considered her omission to look for a job, once Clare was born, as 'more readily arguable' as beneficial then detrimental since this meant the defendant provided her with the money she needed: sed quaere [1986] Camb LJ 394 (D.J. Hayton).

12.57 Nowadays, a more sympathetic approach is taken to the question of detrimental reliance. As Robert Walker LJ states in *Gillett v Holt*[1]:

'Detriment is required. But the authorities show that it is not a narrow or technical concept. The detriment need not consist of the expenditure of money or other quantifiable financial detriment, so long as it is something substantial. The requirement must be approached as part of a broad inquiry as to whether repudiation of an assurance is or is not unconscionable in all the circumstances ... There must be sufficient causal link between the assurance relied on and the detriment asserted. The issue of detriment must be judged at the moment when the person who has given the assurance seeks to go back on it. Whether the detriment is sufficiently substantial is to be tested by whether it would be unjust or inequitable to allow the assurance to be disregarded – that is, again, the essential test of unconscionability. The detriment alleged must be pleaded and proved.'

1   [2001] Ch 210 at 232, applied in *Evans HSBC Trust Company (UK) Limited* [2005] WTLR 1289.

12.58 Once it is proved that the assurance was made and that there has been conduct by the claimant of such a nature that inducement may be inferred, then the burden of proof switches to the defendant to establish that the claimant did not rely on the assurance[1].

1   *Wayling v Jones* (1993) 69 P & CR 170; *Grundy v Ottey* [2003] EWCA Civ 1176, [2003] WTLR 1253.

12.59 In *Wayling v Jones*[1] the claimant chef was promised by his homosexual cohabitee that the latter's hotel (where the chef worked for inadequate wages) would be devised to him. It was, but a new hotel was bought without the will being altered to take account of this, so the old devise was adeemed. The new hotel was sold on the owner's death but the claimant successfully obtained the proceeds of sale to satisfy his equity, despite having answered 'Yes' in cross-examination to the question, 'If he had not made the promise to you would you have stayed.' This indicated that he stayed for low wages because he loved the hotel owner, not because he had been promised the hotel on the owner's death. However, the Court of Appeal held that since the owner had made the promise to his chef-lover who, in evidence, had said that if the owner had reneged on his promise he, the chef, would have left to find a job elsewhere, this was sufficient to prevent the owner's executors from showing that the chef had not relied upon the promise[2].

[1] (1993) 69 P & CR 170.
[2] The court could just as easily have held that such leaving of the defendant was in reliance upon the ending of the loving relationship between the parties.

12.60 In the testamentary context where the benefactor assures the claimant that the benefactor will leave all his estate or a particular house to the claimant-carer or will see to it in his will that the claimant will be all right, the Court of Appeal[1] has rejected the view[2] that a claimant relies on testamentary promises at his own risk (because wills are always ambulatory and revocable) unless the benefactor has created or encouraged the claimant to believe he would not revoke his promise. After all, because estoppel claims concern promises unsupported by contractual consideration they must always be initially revocable: it is the claimant's detrimental reliance that thereafter makes the promises binding and irrevocable.

[1] *Gillett v Holt* [2001] Ch 210.
[2] *Taylor v Dickens* [1998] 1 FLR 806.

12.61 Thus in *Gillett v Holt*[1] the defendant landowner of substantial means had repeatedly made assurances to the claimant that he would inherit the defendant's farming business. On this basis the claimant as friend and then farm manager worked for the defendant from the age of sixteen and deprived himself of the opportunity to better himself. After nearly forty years the defendant unjustifiably sacked the claimant, made gifts to a new favourite and altered his will (under which the residuary estate went to the claimant) so as to make no provision for the claimant. The Court of Appeal awarded the claimant one of the defendant's three farms (a farmhouse and 42 hectares of land) and £100,000 to compensate him for exclusion from the rest of the defendant's farming business.

[1] [2001] Ch 210.

Status of estoppel from purchasers' viewpoint

12.62 When the court's order creates a recognised property interest the position is clear thereafter, but beforehand there will be uncertainty over how the court will tailor the remedy to fit the circumstances under its flexible jurisdiction which, increasingly, seems concerned not simply with upholding already existing rights but with a complex exercise of discretion which may confer not just a property right but a licence or just a right to compensation. If the court ultimately confers a property interest or a licence it matters not to the parties involved (as representor and representee) what the position was before the court order. Clearly, the representee had no rights before the relevant act of detrimental reliance occurred. Thereafter, can one say that the estoppel interest is too uncertain and unstable to qualify at all as a property interest[1] before the court decree (particularly when factors up to the date of the court hearing are taken into account in searching for whether conduct was ultimately unconscionable[2]), or can it rank as a mere equity, ancillary to and dependant upon an interest in land, so as to be capable of binding a purchaser of any legal or equitable interest with notice[3], or can it retrospectively be treated as having the characteristics of a full equitable interest once the court order crystallises such a property interest?[4]

[1] *National Provincial Bank Ltd v Ainsworth* [1965] AC 1175, D.J. Hayton [1990] Conv 370 at 380–384, P. Ferguson (1993) 109 LQR 114; N Glover and P Todd (1996) 16 LS 325 at 342.
[2] *Uglow v Uglow* [2004] WTLR 1183.
[3] J Warburton (1991) 5 Trust Law Int 9. It is more uncertain than a mere equity to set aside a deed or rectify a deed where the ultimate court decision is predestined if the case is established.
[4] G Battersby [1991] Conv 36.

12.63 So far, the courts have not had to address these issues though, inevitably, there are various obiter dicta[1] assuming that donees and purchasers with notice will be bound by inchoate estoppel interests. When the point comes to be fully argued it is possible that the court decree should only have prospective effect unless the court in its in personam jurisdiction to restrain unconscionable conduct decrees that a third party should be subject to the property interest or even licence decreed to exist between the representor and representee[2]. For the third party's conscience to be affected, so as to bring down upon him the in personam jurisdiction, it should suffice that he has actual knowledge of the estoppel claim or would have had such knowledge but for turning a Nelsonian blind eye or but for deliberately or recklessly failing to make the inquiries an honest reasonable man would have made in all the circumstances[3].

[1] *Lloyd's Bank v Carrick* [1996] 4 All ER 630 at 642; *Voyce v Voyce* (1991) 62 P & CR 290 at 294; *Sen v Headley* [1991] Ch 425 at 440; *Re Sharpe* [1980] 1 WLR 219 at 224; *Campbell v Griffin* [2001] WTLR 981 at 994. *Ives Investments Ltd v High* [1967] 2 QB 379.
[2] *Ashburn Anstalt v Arnold* [1989] Ch 1; *United Bank of Kuwait plc v Sahib* [1997] Ch 107 at 142. This can explain cases like *Duke of Beaufort v Patrick* (1853) 17 Beav 60 and *Ives Investments Ltd v High* (supra).
[3] Cf actual 'Nelsonian' and 'naughty' knowledge sufficing for the want of probity needed to make a defendant personally liable to account for knowingly assisting in a dishonest breach of trust or other fiduciary duty: see paras 100.31–100.39 and 100.72–100.73.

12.64 Take the sole legal beneficial owner of a house, M, who represented to F, who became his cohabitee, that she would have a half share or a life interest in the house, so leading her to act to her detriment in reliance thereon. If she is warned about M obtaining a mortgage from X having priority over her, she can have M expressly grant her a prior property interest before creating the mortgage or, if M refuses, she can issue a writ (protected as a *lis pendens*) claiming a proprietary estoppel interest against M and an injunction restraining him from proceeding with the mortgage. If X deliberately or recklessly failed to take the elementary conveyancing precaution of asking F as occupier whether she claimed any interest in the house and thereby divested her of the opportunity she would otherwise have had to take the only sensible precaution of taking the legal proceedings mentioned, is it not clearly unconscionable if X can then take advantage of his own wrong to have priority for his interest over whatever interest the court subsequently confers on F?

12.65 However, it seems nowadays that the courts are prepared to treat proprietary estoppel interests arising between parties involved in land acquisition enterprises as if essentially the same as common intention constructive trusts[1], where it is assumed an equitable proprietary interest arises once detrimental reliance has occurred, thereby protecting F in the above example. However, if the interest is of a family overreachable type then it may be overreached by a disposition to two trustees or a trust corporation[2].

[1] *Yaxley v Gotts* [2000] Ch 162 at 176; *Banner Homes Holdings Ltd v Luff Developments Ltd* [2000] Ch 372 at 384; *Birmingham Midshires BS v Sabherwal* (1999) 80 P & CR 256 at 263; *Oxley v Hiscock* [2004] EWCA Civ 546, [2005] Fam 211, para 66.
[2] *Birmingham Midshires BS v Sabherwal* (1999) 80 P & CR 256.

12.66 Section 116 of the Land Registration Act 2002 is intended to clarify matters in the case of registered land so that an equity by estoppel will have effect as a proprietary interest 'from the time the equity arises as an interest capable of binding successors in title (subject to the rules about the effect of dispositions on priority)', such time presumably being the time of the detrimental reliance[1]. The bracketed clause relates to the new priority rule that mere equities are to be treated like full equitable interests, with both being incapable of being defeated by a purchaser of a later equitable interest in registered land[2].

[1] See Law Com no 271, *Land Registration for the 21st Century*, paras 5.30–5.31 and B Macfarlane, 'Proprietary Estoppel and Third Parties after the Land Registration Act 2002' (2003) 62 Camb LJ 661.
[2] Law Com no 271, Land Registration for the 21st Century, para 5.36.

Statute may not be used as an instrument of fraud

12.67 As Lord Westbury stated in *McCormick v Grogan*[1]:

'the court has, from a very early period, decided that even an Act of Parliament shall not be used as an instrument of fraud; and that equity will fasten on the individual who gets a title under that Act, and impose upon him a personal obligation, because he applies the Act as an instrument for accomplishing a fraud. In this way a court of equity has dealt with the Statute of Frauds, and in this manner, also, it deals with the Statute of Wills.'

[1] (1869) LR 4 HL 82 at 97.

12.68   *Matters essential to the prima facie validity of an express trust*

INTER VIVOS TRUSTS

12.68   Where written evidence is required under Law of Property Act 1925, s 53(1)(b) of declarations of trust respecting land and A unilaterally transfers land to B to hold on trust for A, there is a perfect express trust if the trust for A is in signed writing, even if B knows nothing of the transfer, so that he can disclaim the trust if he wishes as soon as he discovers it[1].

[1]   See Article 38.

12.69   However, if B had orally agreed to hold the land on trust for A he cannot disclaim the trust nor can he claim to be beneficial owner of the land. According to Lindley LJ in *Rochefoucauld v Boustead*[1], the equitable principle preventing statute being used as an instrument of fraud prevents B from exploiting the statute, so that it is an express trust (within s 25(2) of the Judicature Act 1873 and so not statute-barred as a constructive trust under the Statute of Limitations) that is enforced. However, Millett LJ in *Paragon Finance plc v Thakerar & Co*[2] in a detailed historical examination of Limitation Statutes pointed out[3] that 'before 1890 constructive trusts of the first kind were treated in the same way as express trusts and were often confusingly described as such', having categorised as constructive trusts of the first kind cases where the defendant received property not in his own right but by a transaction by which both parties intended to create a trust from the outset, so that the defendant's ownership is coloured from the first by the trust and confidence by means of which he obtained it[4].

[1]   [1897] 1 Ch 196.
[2]   [1999] 1 All ER 400.
[3]   [1999] 1 All ER 400 at 409.
[4]   [1999] 1 All ER 400 at 409, where Millett LJ stated, 'Well-known examples of such a constructive trust are *McCormick v Grogan* (1869) LR 4 HL 82 (a case of a secret trust); *Rochefoucauld v Boustead* [1897] 1 Ch 196 (where the defendant agreed to buy property for the plaintiff but the trust was imperfectly recorded) and *Pallant v Morgan* [1953] Ch 43 (where the defendant sought to keep for himself property which the plaintiff trusted him to buy for both parties).'

12.70   Section 53(2) of the Law of Property Act 1925 expressly exempts constructive and resulting trusts from the formalities prescribed in s 53(1), and the case where A transfers land to B on oral trusts for A can also be regarded as a resulting trust[1] in the absence of A's intent to part with the beneficial interest.

[1]   *Hodgson v Marks* [1971] Ch 892, CA.

12.71   The equitable principle preventing statutes being used as instruments of fraud and leading to the imposition of a constructive trust is not confined to cases in which the conveyance was itself fraudulently obtained. 'The fraud which brings the principle into play arises as soon as the absolute character of the conveyance is set up for the purpose of defeating the beneficial interest'[1]. Thus, if A sells her two adjoining cottages to B for below market value on the basis that they agreed orally that she is to be allowed to live in a particular cottage rent-free for the rest of her life, B will be compelled to hold that cottage on trust for her if later he attempts to defeat her interest by relying on s 53(1)(b).

¹   *Bannister v Bannister* [1948] 2 All ER 133 at 136.

12.72 It can be argued that the equitable principle extends to the case where A's oral understanding with B is that B will hold the land on trust not for A but for C[1]. After all, if B were to append his signature to an appropriate document this would make enforceable[2] what had hitherto been an unenforceable but valid trust and B's act or omission should not determine whether B holds on trust for A or for C. Also, if A had conveyed the land to B as a beneficial gift A would have effectively divested himself of all interest and it should make no difference that the beneficial gift was to C with the interposition of B's trusteeship[3].

¹   *Lyus v Prowsa Developments Ltd* [1982] 2 All ER 953 at 962, though this involved not a gift but a sale of land by A to B so that A lost all his interest and it would have been fraudulent for B to claim that C's rights (subject to which A had sold the land) were unenforceable against him: see *Ashburn Anstalt v Arnold* [1989] Ch 1.
²   *Gardner v Rowe* (1828) 5 Russ 258; *Smith v Mathews* (1861) 3 De GF & J 139; *Mountain v Styak* [1922] NZLR 131.See para 12.11 above.
³   T.G. Youdan [1984] Camb LJ 306 at 335–336.

12.73 Against this it can be argued that if A had orally declared himself a trustee of the land for C he would not have divested himself of his beneficial interest because s 53(1)(b) precludes C relying on oral evidence: it should make no difference that A transferred the land to B and declared oral trusts for C or there would hardly be any scope for the application of s 53(1)(b). Moreover, B's authority to sign the requisite writing can be revoked at will by A or by A's death[1] because A's failure to satisfy s 53(1)(b) means that his beneficial entitlement remains with him, C being incapable of proving the contrary and so not being unjustly deprived of something that he can prove is his. No constructive trust in favour of C can be imposed because it is not unconscionable for A to assert his own beneficial interest in the property.

¹   *Rudkin v Dolman* (1876) 35 LT 791; *Scheurman v Scheurman* (1916) 52 SCR 625 at 636; *Vandervell v IRC* [1967] 2 AC 291 at 317.

12.74 C may invoke as analogous the case where X by will devises land to Y on the oral understanding with Y that Y will hold the land on trust for Z when X's fully secret trust in favour of Z will be enforced against Y. However, here X has died happy in the belief that he has done all he can to benefit Z while A is alive and kicking against C being benefited. The better view is thus that B holds on trust for A where s 53(1)(b) is not complied with[1], the doctrine of secret trusts not applying to inter vivos trusts.

¹   Ford & Lee, *Principles of Law of Trusts* (2nd edn) pp 209–211.

12.75 The equitable principle against fraudulent use of statutes has been applied not just to the transferee-trustee but to volunteers claiming under him[1]. Indeed, it has been applied[2] to a purchaser for value without notice at the time of his purchase when subsequently he attempted to set up the absolute nature of the title of his vendor to defeat the equitable interest of the vendor's beneficiary. However, surely the equitable interest which is allowed to be proved despite s 53(1)(b) will in any case be void against a bona fide purchaser for value without notice, just as trusts satisfying s 53(1)(b) will be void against a purchaser without notice.

1   *Re Duke of Marlborough* [1894] 2 Ch 133.
2   By Ungoed-Thomas J in *Hodgson v Marks* [1971] Ch 892 at 909, [1970] 3 All ER 513 at 522, but see inconsistency with *Dodds v Hill* (1865) 2 Hem & M 424, endorsed in *Macmillan v Bishopsgate Investment Trust (No 3)* [1995] 3 All ER 747 at 773; also see *Russell v Jackson* (1852) 10 Hare 204 at 212.

12.76 Where certain interests are required to be registered or protected by entry on a register such as under the Land Charges Act 1972[1] or the Land Registration Act 1925[2] or 2002 or the Companies Act 1985[3] on pain of a purchaser[4] taking free from such interests, it is not fraud for the purchaser to take advantage of his strict statutory rights by relying on the absence of the registration or protection stipulated for in the statute.

1   *Hollington Bros Ltd v Rhodes* [1951] 2 TLR 691; *Miles v Bull (No 2)* [1969] 3 All ER 1585; *Kitney v MEPC Ltd* [1978] 1 All ER 595, [1977] 1 WLR 981; *Midland Bank Trust Co Ltd v Green* [1981] AC 513, [1981] 1 All ER 153, HL.
2   *De Lusignan v Johnson* (1973) 230 Estates Gazette 499; *Freer v Unwins Ltd* [1976] Ch 288, [1976] 1 All ER 634; *Williams and Glyn's Bank v Boland* [1981] AC 487, [1980] 2 All ER 408, HL.
3   *Re Monolithic Building Co* [1915] 1 Ch 643.
4   A genuine purchaser, not just the alter ego of a vendor, for example, trying to escape an estate contract entered into by him with X, but unprotected on the register, by selling to the vendor's controlled company; *Jones v Lipman* [1962] 1 All ER 442, [1962] 1 WLR 832.

TESTAMENTARY TRUSTS

12.77 The equitable principle of not allowing statutes to be used as an instrument of fraud applies not just to inter vivos transactions but also to testamentary gifts. Indeed, originally the Statute of Frauds provided formalities for inter vivos and testamentary gifts, though testamentary gifts are now covered by the Wills Act 1837 and inter vivos transactions by the Law of Property Act 1925.

12.78 Just as there is some old authority[1] that it is an express trust that the court enforces when it applies the equitable principle to prevent the intended inter vivos trustee setting up the Statute of Frauds or the Law of Property Act as a defence, so there is some old authority that it is an express trust that the court enforces when it applies the equitable principle to prevent the intended testamentary trustee setting up the Statute of Frauds or the Wills Act as a defence[2]. However the better modern approach is to treat secret trusts as based on enforcing a gratuitous promise because it would be fraudulent or unconscionable to allow the person who had agreed to carry out the obligation in another's favour to refuse to do so. After all, there is not just a fraud on the testator in betraying his confidence but there is a fraud on the secret beneficiary who would be deprived of the benefit which, but for the trustee agreeing to carry out the testator's wishes, the testator would surely have secured for him by other means[3]. Indeed, the requirement for the intended trustee's consent distinguishes secret trusts (and mutual wills) from express trusts, so the better view is that the court is imposing a constructive trust in favour of the secret beneficiaries. As Robert Walker LJ stated[4], 'There must be an agreement between A and B conferring benefit upon C because it is the agreement which would make it unconscionable for B [the secret trustee] to resile from his agreement'. Exceptionally, in some circumstances there may be an automatic resulting trust in favour of the deceased settlor's estate, eg where a devisee or legatee takes absolutely beneficially on the face of a will, though having orally agreed to hold on trusts to be communicated to him by the testator, yet no communication of any trusts was made to him in the testator's lifetime[5].

1   *Rochefoucauld v Boustead* [1897] 1 Ch 196, see para 12.69 above.
2   See *Jones v Badley* (1868) 3 Ch App 362 at 364; *McCormick v Grogan* (1869) LR 4 HL 82 at 88–89; *Walgrave v Tebbs* (1855) 2 K & J 313 at 321–322; *Re Baillie* (1886) 2 TLR 660 at 661 though the express oral half-secret trust of land should have been saved under the principle that equity does not allow a statute to be used as an instrument of fraud: *Rochefoucauld v Boustead* [1897] 1 Ch 196; *Lyus v Prowsa Developments Ltd* [1982] 2 All ER 953 at 962.
3   See D.R. Hodge [1980] Conv 341.
4   *Gillett v Holt* [2001] Ch 210 at 228.
5   *Re Boyes* (1884) 26 Ch D 531.

12.79 Whilst the existence of the two approaches concerned with an express trust on the one hand and a constructive or resulting trust on the other hand is recognised by Lord Cairns, the Lord Chancellor, in *Jones v Badley*[1] in connection with testamentary trusts and by the Court of Appeal[2] in connection with inter vivos trusts the distinction between the two approaches has been lost sight of in many cases concerned with testamentary trusts. The distinction is no longer significant for limitation period purposes, while because a constructive trust is exempt from formalities by s 53(2) of the Law of Property Act 1925, judicial utilisation of it avoids the embarrassment of Equity refusing to implement a statute. Secret trusts should be categorised as constructive trusts[3] even though being treated here within the Division dealing with 'express trusts' because of the close affinity with express trusts that many secret trusts have.

1   (1868) 3 Ch App 362 at 364.
2   *Rochefoucauld v Boustead* [1897] 1 Ch 196; *Hodgson v Marks* [1971] Ch 892, [1971] 2 All ER 684.
3   *Paragon Finance plc v Thakerar & Co* [1999] 1 All ER 400 at 409 per Millett LJ; *Kasperbauer v Griffith* [2000] WTLR 333 at 343, per Peter Gibson LJ; *Gillett v Holt* [2001] Ch 210 at 228.

DISTINCTION BETWEEN FULLY AND HALF-SECRET TRUSTS

12.80 A testamentary trust is fully secret where a testator leaves property by will to X, who takes the property beneficially on the face of the will, or where a person dies intestate so that by operation of the intestacy rules X takes property beneficially, but where the deceased intended X to hold the property on trusts, communicated this intention in his lifetime to X, who agreed so to hold the property.

12.81 A testamentary trust is half-secret where a testator leaves property by will to X in such manner that X appears to take as trustee on the face of the will, though the terms of the trust are not apparent from the will itself or any document incorporated as part of the will under the probate doctrine of incorporation by reference. This doctrine admits to probate with the will a document referred to in the will as being already in existence if it is sufficiently described in the will to enable it to be identified from the will itself, eg 'to hold according to the directions contained in my letter to him dated 5 May 2005[1]. Confusion of half-secret trusts with the doctrine of incorporation by reference[2] has probably led to the requirements that communication of the trust terms to the intended trustee must comply strictly with any terms regarding such communication expressed in the will and must occur prior to, or contemporaneously with, the execution of the will.

[1]   *Re Smart* [1902] P 238; *Re Garnett* [1894] P 90; *Re Schintz' Will Trusts* [1951] Ch 870, [1951] 1 All ER 1095.
[2]   For the differences see Hayton and Marshall, *Commentary and Cases on the Law of Trusts* (12th edn), paras 2–117 to 2–119.

12.82 In *Re Keen's Estate*[1] £10,000 was left to the testator's executors and trustees, H and E, 'to be held upon trust and disposed of by them among such person, persons or charities as may be notified by me to them or either of them during my lifetime'. Some time before making the will the testator had given a sealed envelope to E directing that it be not opened till his death. It was then found to contain the name of a lady. However, the Court of Appeal held that the £10,000 had to be held for the residuary beneficiaries.

[1]   [1937] Ch 236, [1937] 1 All ER 452.

12.83 Lord Wright, giving the judgment of the Court of Appeal, held that communication of the trust had occurred when the sealed envelope had been delivered to E prior to execution of the will and such communication was inconsistent with the express terms of the will which contemplated future communication only, so that evidence of the earlier communicated trust was inadmissible. Even if the terms of the will could have been construed as contemplating past and future communications this would not have helped to establish a valid half-secret trust for 'the trusts referred to, but undefined in the will, must be described in the will as established prior to, or at least contemporaneously with, its execution'[1].

[1]   [1937] Ch 236 at 247; *Re Bateman's Will Trusts* [1970] 3 All ER 817, [1970] 1 WLR 1463; *Johnson v Ball* (1851) 5 De G & Sm 85.

12.84 The objection to allowing communication to be made to the half-secret trustee after execution of the will is that this would enable the testator to 'give the go-by' to the provisions of the Wills Act by reserving to himself a power of making future testamentary dispositions orally or by unattested writing[1].

However, in the case of fully secret trusts the testator is allowed to reserve to himself such a power to 'give the go-by' to the Wills Act[2]. The principle that equity will not allow a statute to be used as an instrument of fraud is the very basis for giving the 'go-by' to statutes[3].

1 *Blackwell v Blackwell* [1929] AC 318 at 339; *Re Keen's Estate* [1937] Ch 236 at 246.
2 *McCormick v Grogan* (1869) LR 4 HL 82.
3 *Re Pitt-Rivers* [1902] 1 Ch 403 at 407.

12.85 Furthermore, should strict compliance with the terms of the will really be necessary? If T leaves property on a half- secret trust to A, B, C and D 'to be dealt with in accordance with my wishes which I have made known to them' why should the trust for the secret beneficiaries fail[1] if it turns out that by an oversight T had only informed three of his four trustees of his wishes? Secret trusts seem to rest on the assumption that the will must first operate so as to vest the secret trust property in the fully or half-secret trustee but then the secret trusts themselves arise dehors the will for equity 'makes him do what the will in itself has nothing to do with; it lets him take what the will gives him and then makes him apply it as the court of conscience directs, and it does so in order to give effect to the wishes of the testator which would not otherwise be effectual'[2]. It is thus illogical[3] for the court to concern itself so strictly with the wording of the will and also to claim, in the case of half-secret trusts, that oral evidence of communication and acceptance made after execution of the will but in the testator's lifetime should be inadmissible as allowing the Wills Act to be avoided.

1 *Re Spence* [1949] WN 237.
2 *Blackwell v Blackwell* [1929] AC 318 at 335; *Cullen v A-G for Ireland* (1866) LR 1 HL 190 at 198. Dispositions taking effect outside the confines of the will are still testamentary: P Critchley (1999) 115 LQR 631 at 639–641.
3 (1951) 67 LQR 413 (L.A. Sheridan); (1937) 53 LQR 501 (Holdsworth); *Re Browne* [1944] IR 90; *Restatement of Trusts*, para 55(c)(h); *Ledgerwood v Perpetual Trustee Co Ltd* (1997) 41 NSWLR 532, *Re Prendiville* noted by John Mee [1992] Conv 202.

PAROL OR EXTRINSIC EVIDENCE MAY NOT BE ADDUCED TO VARY OR
CONTRADICT A WILL

12.86 The rule that is intended to prevent the 'go-by' from being given to the Wills Act is the rule that parol or extrinsic evidence may not be adduced to vary or contradict a will.

12.87 However, this rule has no application in the case of fully secret trusts where the will gives property to X apparently absolutely beneficially[1]. The standard of proof on the person seeking to establish the trust is the ordinary civil standard of proof on a balance of probabilities unless fraud is involved when a higher standard is required[2]. Where the will uses precatory words insufficient to make X a trustee of a half-secret trust the claimant will have to prove why the communication of the testator's wishes should not be treated as merely fulfilling a precatory intention rather than a trust intention[3]. If, indeed, the will leaves property to X and Y 'relying, but not by way of trust, on their applying' it as informed by the testator, it will be even harder for a claimant to prove that a fully secret trust existed dehors the will, but not impossible as held by the Court of Appeal in *Re Spencer's Will*[4].

1   *Blackwell v Blackwell* [1929] AC 318.
2   *Re Snowden* [1979] 2 All ER 172 at 179 where Megarry V-C rejected the view of Brightman J in *Ottaway v Norman* [1972] Ch 698, [1971] 3 All ER 1325 that the standard was that required for rectification of written documents. One might have thought it logical for the standard of proof of intention to create a trust to depend always on a balance of probabilities, regardless of other circumstances: C. Rickett [1979] Camb LJ 260, *Re Cleaver* [1981] 2 All ER 1018 at 1024. Generally on the single civil standard see *R (on the application of N) v Mental Health Review Tribunal* [2005] EWCA Civ 1605, [2006] QB 468.
3   *Hayman v Nicoll* [1944] 3 DLR 551.
4   (1887) 57 LT 519, CA. Cf *Re Falkiner* [1924] 1 Ch 88; *Re Stirling* [1954] 2 All ER 113, [1954] 1 WLR 763.

12.88 In the case of a half-secret trust where the trust property is left expressly to X on trust for purposes communicated to him, then parol evidence is inadmissible to allow the trustee to prove that he was intended to have some part of the property for himself beneficially[1]. It is said not to be in the public interest to admit an exception to the parol evidence rule so that a trustee's personal interest might conflict with his duty qua trustee[2]. However in some circumstances the court may be able to find that X was intended not to take as trustee but was intended to take a beneficial interest himself subject to satisfying some condition or equitable charge[3].

1   *Re Rees Will Trusts* [1950] Ch 204, [1949] 2 All ER 1003; *Re Pugh's Will Trusts* [1967] 3 All ER 337, [1967] 1 WLR 1262.
2   However, a settlor may expressly and validly create a trust under which T is a trustee and also a beneficiary. One will naturally be suspicious if a half secret trustee claims some beneficial interest but why should he not have a beneficial interest if the evidence is clear enough eg a non-testamentary document in the testator's signed handwriting or an oral statement in the presence of an independent witness? Cf *Re Tyler's Fund Trusts* [1967] 3 All ER 389, [1967] 1 WLR 1269.
3   *Irvine v Sullivan* (1869) LR 8 Eq 673; *Re Foord* [1922] 2 Ch 519.

FULLY SECRET TRUSTS

12.89 The three necessary requirements are an *intention* on the part of the deceased to create a trust (despite the property passing apparently beneficially to the recipient under the will or the intestacy rules), *communication* thereof to the intended recipient of the property and *acceptance* thereof by the intended recipient, provided these requirements are satisfied in the deceased's lifetime[1]. Acceptance by the recipient is readily inferred once communication occurs unless he protests[2].

1   *Ottaway v Norman* [1972] Ch 698, [1971] 3 All ER 1325; *Moss v Cooper* (1861) 1 John & H 352; *Re Boyes* (1884) 26 Ch D 531.
2   *Moss v Cooper* (1861) 1 John & H 352; *Tee v Ferris* (1856) 2 K & J 357.

12.90 Where intention is present but not the other requirements, as where after the testator's death an unattested set of instructions is found addressed to the person taking apparently beneficially on the face of the will, then that person does so take since no trust is established[1].

1   *Wallgrave v Tebbs* (1855) 2 K & J 313.

12.91 Where communication of the fact that the property is to be held upon trust is made and agreed to, but the terms of the trust are not communicated at all or are not communicated until after the deceased's death (eg when found in a letter in the deceased's bureau) then the property is held on a resulting trust for the deceased's estate, so benefiting the residuary beneficiaries or, if the property was itself the residuary property, the statutory next of kin[1]. If the intended trustee happens to be the residuary beneficiary or next of kin, as the case may be, there is the obvious possibility that he might be tempted to make self-serving statements, where other evidence prevents him from going so far as to claim that he was not even informed of the fact that he was intended to hold on some sort of trust. However, in the case of fully secret trusts the testator obviously runs risks with his trustee (unless having the trustee sign a witnessed document delivered into the hands of the intended beneficiaries) and his donee-volunteers claiming under him should perhaps run the same risks. It seems the court should allow all possible evidence to clarify the situation rather than impose an arbitrary salutary rule removing all temptation by prohibiting an intended fully secret trustee from ever being able to benefit from failure of the trust qua residuary legatee or qua next of kin. If, however, the intended trustee appeared to be lying and it was otherwise impossible to ascertain the terms of the intended trust then public policy must prevent the intended trustee from obtaining any advantage from his own wrong[2].

1   *Re Boyes* (1884) 26 Ch D 531.
2   *Re Sigsworth* [1935] Ch 89.

12.92 Communication of the terms of the intended trust need not be made so that the intended trustee actually knows all the terms in the deceased's lifetime, so long as the terms are expressed in the deceased's lifetime and the intended trustee has the means of discovering them once the deceased dies, having been informed in the deceased's lifetime that he is to take as trustee. Thus, delivery to the intended trustee of a sealed envelope containing the terms of the trust will suffice if done in the deceased's lifetime though the envelope is directed not to be opened till the deceased's death[1]. The same principle will apply if a key to a locked box containing a letter with the terms of the trust is delivered by the deceased to the intended trustee[2].

1   *Re Keen's Estate* [1937] Ch 236; *Re Boyes* (1884) 26 Ch D 531.
2   Cf *McDonald v Moran* (1938) 12 MPR 424 (Prince Edward Island).

12.93 Communication to the legatee/devisee must make it clear how much property is to vest in the legatee/devisee. Thus if £5,000 is bequeathed to X and Y absolutely and they agree to hold it on certain secret trusts communicated to them by the testator and, later, the testator in terms increases the legacy to £10,000, X and Y will only hold £5,000 qua secret trustees, the other £5,000 being taken by them beneficially[1]. Presumably, if the testator in terms reduces the legacy to £2,500 there will be a valid secret trust of the

£2,500, the greater including the lesser figure. It would also seem that if the intended trustees agreed with the testator to hold whatever they obtain under the testator's will, then changes in the nature or value of the property resulting from codicils or fresh wills should not affect the validity of the secret trust arising on the testator's death.

1   *Re Cooper* [1939] Ch 811, [1939] 3 All ER 586.

HALF-SECRET TRUSTS

12.94 The same requirements have to be satisfied as in the case of fully secret trusts (discussed above) except there are two further requirements in that the communication must conform strictly to the language of the will and must be made prior to, or contemporaneously with, the execution of the will[1]. As already seen the justification for these two refinements is not convincing but the refinements must be taken as established law unless the House of Lords overrules *Re Keen's Estate*, a most unlikely event when the latter decision is over seventy years old. Presumably, revocation by a testator of a half secret trust (agreed to before or at the time of the will) after making his will should be effective because it will not then be fraudulent or unconscionable for the legatee-trustee to disregard his earlier undertaking[2]. However, if it is not a simple revocation but revocation by virtue of replacing one secret beneficiary with another, it seems that effect should not be given to such revocation if conditional on the replacement trust being effective[3], which it is not.

1   *Re Keen's Estate* [1937] Ch 236, [1937] 1 All ER 452; *Re Spence* [1949] WN 237; *Re Bateman's Will Trusts* [1970] 3 All ER 817, [1970] 1 WLR 1463.
2   See *Guest v Webb* [1965] VR 427 at 432.
3   Cf conditional revocation of wills, eg *Re Finnemore* [1992] 1 All ER 800.

12.95 In the case of half-secret trusts ex hypothesi a trust must exist. If the specific terms of the trust are not communicated in accordance with the language used in the will[1] or are not communicated prior to or contemporaneously with the execution of the will, then the trust will be a resulting trust for the testator's estate and not an express trust for the intended beneficiaries[2]. If the half-secret trustee himself is a beneficiary under the resulting trust qua residuary legatee or next of kin there is an obvious temptation for him to allege there was either no communication to him at all or there was communication but it was after the date of the will or did not comply with the terms of the will, eg because oral and not written. Some dicta of Lord Buck-master[3] suggest that the trustee should be excluded from benefiting under the resulting trust. However, this seems difficult to justify except where the court takes the view that there probably was a proper communication of full details of the trusts before the execution of the will despite the trustee's evidence to the contrary, in which case where the trust details cannot be ascertained public policy should prevent the trustee benefiting from his own wrongful conduct[4].

1   *Re Spence* [1949] WN 237.
2   *Johnson v Ball* (1851) 5 De G & Sm 85; *Re Keen's Estate* [1937] Ch 236, [1937] 1 All ER 452.
3   *Blackwell v Blackwell* [1929] AC 318 at 341.
4   Cf *Re Sigsworth* [1935] Ch 89.

12.96 In *Re Baillie*[1] the view was taken that a half secret trust of land needs to satisfy s 53(1)(b) of the Law of Property Act, whereas it was assumed without argument in *Ottoway v Norman*[2] that a fully secret trust of land need not satisfy s 53(1)(b), presumably because fully secret trusts are clearly constructive trusts imposed to prevent the legatee-trustee taking beneficially. However, fully secret trusts, like half-secret trusts, go further in requiring the legatee-trustee not to hold on a resulting trust for the deceased's estate but to hold for the intended beneficiaries, so that both give effect to gratuitous promises that it would be fraudulent or unconscionable for the promisor to dishonour[3]. Both types of secret trust should therefore be treated as constructive trusts exempted from formal requirements by s 53(2), as already explained at para 12.78.

1   (1886) 2 TLR 660.
2   [1972] Ch 698.
3   Fraud can be perpetuated without gain to the perpetrator: *Re Dale* [1994] Ch 31; *Twinsectra Ltd v Yardley* [2002] UKHL 12, [2002] 2 All ER 377 at paras [41] and [137].

GIFTS TO SEVERAL INTENDED TRUSTEES WITHOUT COMMUNICATION TO ALL

12.97 Farwell J laid down the position as follows where fully secret trusts are concerned[1]:

> 'If A induced B either to make, or leave unrevoked, a will leaving property to A and C as *tenants in common*, by expressly promising or tacitly consenting, that he and C will carry out the testator's wishes and C knows nothing of the matter until after the testator's death, A is bound but C is not bound: *Tee v Ferris*[2]; the reason stated being, that to hold otherwise would be to enable one beneficiary to deprive the rest of their benefits by setting up a secret trust. If however the gift were to A and C as *joint tenants*, the authorities have established a distinction between those cases in which the will is made on the faith of an antecedent promise by A and those in which the will is left unrevoked on the faith of a subsequent promise. In the former case the trust binds both A and C: *Russell v Jackson*[3], *Jones v Badley*[4], the reason stated being that no person can claim an interest under a fraud committed by another; in the latter case A and not C is bound: *Burney v Macdonald*[5] and *Moss v Cooper*[6], the reason stated being that the gift is not tainted with any fraud in procuring the execution of the will. Personally, I am unable to see any difference between a gift made on the faith of an antecedent promise and a gift left unrevoked on the faith of a subsequent promise to carry out the testator's wishes.'

1   *Re Stead* [1900] 1 Ch 237 at 241.
2   (1856) 2 K & J 357.
3   (1852) 10 Hare 204.
4   (1868) 3 Ch App 362.
5   (1845) 15 Sim 6.
6   (1861) 1 John & H 352.

12.98 However, a good case can be made out that the only question to be asked is: was the gift to C induced by A's promise? If yes, C is bound, if no he is not bound. It can be said that whether A and C are tenants in common or joint tenants[1] 'C is not bound if his gift was not induced by the promise of A because to hold otherwise would be to enable A to deprive C of his benefit by setting up a secret trust; but C is bound if his gift was induced by the promise of A because he cannot profit by the fraud of another; and if the trust was communicated to A after the will was made, then C takes free if [as will almost certainly be the case] his gift was not induced by the promise of A because if there is no inducement there is no fraud affecting C.'

1   (1972) 88 LQR 225 (B. Perrins).

12.99   In the case of half-secret trusts communication must comply strictly with the terms of the will but if the will permits communication to be made to one only of several trustees a communication made to one trustee before or at the time of the execution of the will binds all of them, the trust being a joint office[1]. A subsequent communication is ineffective[2].

1   *Blackwell v Blackwell* [1929] AC 318; *Re Spence* [1949] WN 237; *Ward and Pemberton v Duncombe* [1893] AC 369.
2   *Re Keen* [1937] Ch 236.

SECRET BENEFICIARY PREDECEASING TESTATOR

12.100   If D by will leaves property to T on trust expressly for B, and B predeceases D, the gift to B lapses[1]. One would expect the position to be the same if D, having obtained T's agreement to hold the property on trust for B, leaves property 'to T absolutely' or 'to T upon trusts which I have communicated to him.' However, in *Re Gardner*[2] Romer J held that B's interest did not lapse since B obtained an interest as soon as D communicated the terms of the trust to T and T accepted the trust.

1   However, if B is D's child and leaves issue of his own surviving D the gift takes effect in favour of B's issue: Wills Act 1837, s 33 as amended by Administration of Justice Act 1982, s 19.
2   [1923] 2 Ch 230.

12.101   D communicated the trust terms to T in 1909 and D died in 1919, B having died in the interval. It is difficult to understand Romer J's reasoning since no completely constituted trust of D's property could arise till D died without having revoked or altered the will and without having become insolvent, so that B would only have a mere spes till D died. However, if B had an absolute vested interest in a 1909 settlement and funds accruing under a will taking effect in 1919 were treated as an accretion to the 1909 settlement (rather than comprising a separate 1919 referential settlement) then if B died before 1919 the funds would accrue to his estate[1]. Romer J did state[2]:

'The rights of the parties appear to me to be exactly the same as though the husband (T), after the memorandum had been communicated to him by the testatrix (D), in 1909 had executed a declaration of trust binding himself to hold any property that should come to him under his wife's (D's) partial intestacy upon trust as specified in the memorandum.'

1   *Re Playfair* [1951] Ch 4, [1950] 2 All ER 285.
2   [1923] 2 Ch 230 at 233.

12.102   Such a declaration, however, does not create a completely constituted trust since the subject is future property, a spes[1]. Thus, the beneficiaries could have had no rights in 1909 particularly since they were volunteers. Further-more, even if T could be treated as declaring trusts in favour of the secret beneficiaries as soon as D died in 1919 this could not assist a predeceasing beneficiary[2] (assuming the trusts declared were not for the beneficiaries or their estates). The authority of *Re Gardner*, is thus exceptionally doubtful.

1   *Re Ellenborough* [1903] 1 Ch 697; *Re Northcliffe* [1925] Ch 651; *Williams v IRC* [1965] NZLR 395; *Brennan v Morphett* (1908) 6 CLR 22. Further see para 9.102 above.
2   If B is dead when an interest is purported to be created in his favour under an inter vivos disposition the interest fails: *Re Corbishley's Trusts* (1880) 14 Ch D 846; *Re Tilt* (1896) 74 LT 163.

THE EXTENT TO WHICH SECRET TRUSTS OPERATE INDEPENDENTLY OF SETTLOR'S WILL

12.103   In *Re Gardner*[1] Romer J treated the predeceasing beneficiary's interest as arising independently of the will so as not to lapse. In *Re Young*[2] Danckwerts J held that the beneficiary under a half-secret trust may take the interest intended for him even though he acted as a witness to the will so as prima facie to fall foul of Wills Act 1837, s 15, which makes void beneficial gifts to attesting witnesses of wills. He stated[3]:

'The whole theory of the formation of a secret trust is that the Wills Act has nothing to do with the matter because the forms required by the Wills Act are entirely disregarded, since the persons do not take by virtue of the gift in the will, but by virtue of the secret trusts imposed upon the beneficiary who does in fact take under the will.'

Secret trusts thus give the 'go-by' to s 15[4].

1   [1923] 2 Ch 230.
2   [1951] Ch 344.
3   [1951] Ch 344 at 346.
4   Danckwerts J treated fully and half-secret trusts on the same footing, refusing to follow *Re Fleetwood* (1880) 15 Ch D 594 where Hall V-C held that a half-secret trust in favour of a secret beneficiary failed by reason of the beneficiary being an attesting witness.

12.104   If this view is taken to its logical conclusion issue will not need to bring their secret trust beneficial interests into hotchpot under Administration of Estates Act 1925, s 49(1)(a), and the issue of a testator's child taking as secret beneficiary but who predeceases the testator leaving issue alive at the testator's death will not benefit under the exception to the doctrine of lapse in Wills Act 1837, s 33[1407].

1   Assuming *Re Gardner* [1923] 2 Ch 230 is erroneous in itself creating an equitable exception to the doctrine of lapse so that recourse to s 33 is necessary.

12.105   On the other hand in *Re Maddock*[1] residuary personalty was left to T absolutely but T undertook to hold a specified portion thereof for certain secret beneficiaries. In paying the testator's debts the Court of Appeal held that debts should not be paid out of the residuary personalty as a whole, but that they should be paid primarily out of that part of residuary personalty intended for T beneficially, and, if that were exhausted, then resort could be had to the secret trust portion of residue as if there had been a specific legacy of the amount of that portion set out in the will, though this should be resorted to for payment of debts before any specific legacies actually expressed in the will.

¹   [1902] 2 Ch 220.

12.106   In principle, there is much to be said for the view that all secret trusts are testamentary in character[1] since they are dispositions of property (albeit operating outside the confines of the will) to take effect on death, such property forming part of the testator's estate available to satisfy any claims under the Inheritance (Provision for Family and Dependants) Act 1975. As Viscount Sumner states[2], 'the doctrine must, in principle, rest on the assumption that the will has first operated according to its terms'.

¹   P Critchley (1999) 115 LQR 631 at 639–641.
²   [1929] AC 318 at 334. Also Romer J in *Re Gardner* [1923] 2 Ch 230 at 232, 'The obligation can be enforced *if the donee becomes entitled'*. In *Re Snowden* [1979] 2 All ER 172 at 177 Megarry V-C said, 'The whole basis of secret trusts is that they operate outside the will, changing nothing that is written in it and allowing it to operate according to its tenor, but then fastening a trust on the property in the hands of the recipient.'

12.107   Thus, secret trusts must fail if the testator revokes the relevant clause in his will or if the testator dies insolvent or the relevant property is not available due to ademption or abatement.

12.108   If a fully secret trustee dies, alone knowing of the secret trust then the trust must fail. Even if some other person, like the secret beneficiary, knows of the secret trust and may even have documentary evidence of it signed by the testator or the fully secret trustee, it would seem that the secret trusts should fail[1] on the basis that the will cannot operate according to its terms due to the predecease of an apparently absolutely entitled beneficiary who therefore receives nothing that can be held on secret trusts. Whether secret trusts should fail if the will fails due to technicalities over the attestation procedures yet the intended trustee obtains the intended secret trust property qua statutory next of kin will depend upon whether his equitable obligations strictly relate only to what he received under the will or extend to property whether received under the will or under the intestacy rules. Presumably, if the fully secret trustee happened to attest the will the secret trust should fail since a beneficial interest is given *by the will* to the fully secret trustee though dehors the will, trusts are intended to operate.

¹   'If the legatee dies in the lifetime of the testator the persons claiming under the memorandum [ie the secret trusts] can take nothing' per Cozens-Hardy LJ in *Re Maddock* [1902] 2 Ch 220 at 231. However, the contrary was held to be the case in *Lord Inchiquin v French* (1745) 1 Cox Eq Cas 1.

12.109   In the case of half-secret trusts the death of the trustee before the will takes effect cannot affect the position (unless his personality was vital to the trusteeship or unless all knowledge of the trusts died with him) for equity will not allow a trust to fail for want of a trustee. Any attestation of the will by the half-secret trustee would fall outside Wills Act 1837, s 15. Any disclaimer by the half-secret trustee would normally be immaterial owing to Equity not allowing a trust to fail for want of a trustee.

12.110 Disclaimer by a fully secret trustee was treated by Cozens-Hardy LJ obiter[1] as causing the fully secret trusts to fail though preferable obiter dicta[2] of Lords Buckmaster and Warrington treat disclaimer as not invalidating the secret trusts which are assumed to take effect on the testator's death[3] making it a fraud or breach of trust for the secret trustee to renounce the legacy. Disclaimer would, it seems, be fully effective if the testator's communication to his legatee were construed not as imposing trusts but as conferring a gift subject to a condition[4].

1   *Re Maddock* [1902] 2 Ch 220 at 231.
2   [1929] AC 318 at 328 and 341 respectively.
3   Cf mutual wills being effective on death: *Re Dale* [1994] Ch 31.
4   See para 8.233 above.

12.111 Revocation of his acceptance of the trust by the intended secret trustee raises further problems. If revocation occurs when the testator has plenty of time to alter his will but he fails to do so then the fully secret trustee should be allowed to take beneficially. In the case of a half-secret trustee it would seem that he should not be allowed to make the trusts fail by retracting his acceptance of the intended trusts, so that the maxim, equity will not allow a trust to fail for want of a trustee, should come into play if on the testator's death he claims to have earlier renounced his acceptance of the trust. If the testator has not reasonable time to alter his will, taking into account any physical or mental illness, then the trusts should be enforced whether fully or half-secret.

SECRET 'FLOATING' TRUSTS

12.112 The obligation on the intended secret trustee is usually to hold specific property for a secret beneficiary absolutely, resulting normally in the trustee making an inter vivos transfer to the beneficiary. However, the obligation may be that the secret trustee is to make a will in favour of the secret beneficiary transferring to him property formerly belonging to the settlor/testator but left to the secret trustee absolutely. In *Ottaway v Norman*[1] Brightman J was prepared to assume, but without so deciding,

> 'that if property is given to the [trustee] on the understanding that the [trustee] will dispose by his will of such assets, if any, as he may have at his command at his death in favour of the [secret beneficiary], a valid trust is created in favour of the [secret beneficiary] which is in suspense during the lifetime of the [trustee] but attaches to the estate of the [trustee] at the moment of the latter's death.'

1   [1972] Ch 698 at 713.

12.113 In such a case it would appear that the trustee takes an absolute interest in the property subject to an equitable fiduciary obligation of good faith during his lifetime neither to transfer the property nor to contract to transfer the property with destructive intent to prevent the property passing to the secret beneficiary[1], but otherwise he can resort to capital for his own purposes. In *Healey v Brown*[2] in separate mutual wills H and W left all to the survivor of them absolutely, with a specific flat (or the subsequent matrimonial home) to be devised to N by the survivor. H became sole owner of the flat as surviving joint tenant but transferred it into the names of himself and his son, S, as joint tenants, so S owned the flat on H's death. N claimed that S held the flat on constructive trust for her. While H had not revoked or amended his will in contravention of his agreement, the judge held that his gift of the flat was calculated to defeat the intention of the mutual contract between H and W that gave rise to a constructive trust. One would have expected that the constructive trust would affect the whole flat to prevent the fraudulent frustration of W's dying belief, encouraged by H's contract with her. Oddly, the judge held that the constructive trust only extended to W's half share as if there had been a secret trust accepted by H which would only cover W's property and not property owned by H, as Morritt LJ had pointed out in *Re Goodchild*[3] where no contractual agreement not to revoke the will had been found. However, here there was such a contractual agreement that extended to H's property so the constructive trust should have extended to the whole flat.

[1]   Further see paras 8.30–8.33 above and *Birmingham v Renfrew* (1937) 57 CLR 666 at 689 approvingly cited in *Re Cleaver* [1981] 2 All ER 1018 at 1023–1024. Cf Inheritance (Provision for Family and Dependants) Act 1975, s 10. Also see *Edell v Sitzer* (2001) 4 ITELR 149 at 169–170.
[2]   [2002] WTLR 789.
[3]   [1997] 1 WLR 1216 at 1231.

Chapter 4

VALIDITY OF DECLARED TRUSTS IN RELATION TO LATENT MATTERS

ARTICLE 13
WHO MAY BE A SETTLOR OR TRUSTEE

13.1

Every person, male or female, married or unmarried, human or corporate, who has power to hold and dispose of any legal or equitable[1] estate or interest in assets can create a trust in respect thereof, and can be a trustee thereof.

[1]   *Gilbert v Overton* (1864) 2 Hem & M 110; *Kekewich v Manning* (1851) 1 De GM & G 176; *Donaldson v Donaldson* (1854) Kay 711; *Re Ralli's Will Trust* [1964] Ch 288, [1963] 3 All ER 940.

Minors

13.2   An infant, or minor in the modern parlance, attains full age on attaining eighteen instead of twenty-one which was the case until 1 January 1970[1].

[1]   Family Law Reform Act 1969, ss 1, 12.

13.3 Since 1925 a minor cannot hold a legal estate in land and so cannot settle it[1]. Otherwise, capacity to settle is treated in the same way as capacity to contract. Thus settlements that are obviously prejudicial will be wholly void[2] whilst the minor may plead non est factum if too young to understand the nature of the arrangement he purported to make[3]. An inter vivos settlement made by an infant which, if made by an adult, would bind the property itself, is voidable but not void; and, unless the infant repudiates it on or shortly after attaining his majority, it will be binding[4], and this is so whether the property settled is reversionary or not[5]. But where by the law of the infant's domicile or the proper law of the settlement ratification is not allowed, the settlement will not be binding, even though not expressly repudiated[6].

1   Law of Property Act 1925, ss 1 (6), 19. He may settle his equitable interest.
2   *IRC v Mills* [1975] AC 38, [1974] 1 All ER 722; *De Francesco v Barnum* (1890) 45 Ch D 430.
3   *IRC v Mills* [1975] AC 38, [1974] 1 All ER 722. The House of Lords unanimously reversed the view of the Court of Appeal [1973] Ch 225 at 240 and 247 that a contract or settlement was void if made by a person below the age of discretion (14 years for boys and 16 years for girls) when he is presumed by law not to have sufficient understanding to know what it involved or, at any rate, not a sufficient discretion to exercise a sound judgment on it.
4   *Duncan v Dixon* (1890) 44 Ch D 211; *Edwards v Carter* [1893] AC 360; *Chaplin v Leslie Frewin (Publishers) Ltd* [1966] Ch 71 at 89 per Lord Denning MR.
5   *Carnell v Harrison* [1916] 1 Ch 328, overruling *Re Jones* [1893] 2 Ch 461; and see *Hamilton v Hamilton* [1892] 1 Ch 396. The Infants Relief Act 1874, s 2, has no application as it only prohibits action on a ratification: cf *Edwards v Carter* [1893] AC 360; *Re Hodson* [1894] 2 Ch 421; and see *Harle v Jarman* [1895] 2 Ch 419 at 428.
6   *Viditz v O'Hagan* [1900] 2 Ch 87, CA.

13.4 A minor cannot make a settlement by will unless a privileged testator, ie a soldier or airman in actual military service or a mariner or seaman at sea: Wills Act 1837 as amended by Wills (Soldiers and Sailors) Act 1918.

13.5 By s 20 of the Law of Property Act 1925 the appointment of an infant to be a trustee in relation to any settlement or trust is void.

Persons who lack capacity

13.6 A person who lacks capacity to exercise the functions of a trustee cannot act as a trustee[1] and is liable to be replaced as a trustee under section 36 (1) of the Trustee Act 1925[2], while a person cannot create a testamentary trust or an *inter vivos* trust unless having capacity to make such a decision.

1   *Re East* (1873) 8 Ch App 735; *Re Blake* [1887] WN 173.
2   See para 73.16 below and note s. 36 (9) where, if the trustee has a beneficial interest, the consent of the Court of Protection is needed.

13.7 Under s 2(1) of the Mental Capacity Act 2005 'a person lacks capacity in relation to a matter if at the material time he is unable to make a decision for himself in relation to the matter because of an impairment of, or a disturbance in the functioning of, the mind or brain.' It matters not whether the impairment or disturbance is temporary or permanent[1].

'A person is unable to make a decision for himself if he is unable
(a)   to understand the information relevant to the decision,
(b)   to retain that information,
(c)   to use or weigh that information as part of the process of making the decision, or
(d)   to communicate his decision (whether by talking, using sign language or any other means)'[2].

1   Mental Capacity Act 2005, s 2(2).
2   Mental Capacity Act 2005, s 3(1). Under the previous law a 'patient' was a person who by reason of mental disorder was incapable of managing and administering his property and affairs: Mental Health Act 1983, S. 94(2); 'mental disorder' meant mental illness, arrested or incomplete development of mind, psychopathic disorder and any other disorder or disability of the mind: s 1 (2) on which see *Masterman-Lister v Jewell* [2002] EWCA Civ 1889, [2003] 3 All ER 162. The new law is intended to come into effect in April 2007.

13.8 However, 'a person is not to be regarded as unable to understand the information relevant to a decision if he is able to understand an explanation of it given to him in a way that is appropriate to his circumstances (using simple language, visual aids or any other means')[1], while 'the fact that a person is able to retain the information relevant to a decision for a short period only does not prevent him from being regarded as able to make the decision'[2]. The information relevant to a decision includes information about the reasonably foreseeable consequences of (a) deciding one way or another or (b) failing to make the decision[3].

1   Mental Capacity Act 2005, s 3(2).
2   Mental Capacity Act 2005, s 3(3).
3   Mental Capacity Act 2005, s 3(4).

13.9 Section 1 of the 2005 Act establishes the following principles:

(a)   a person must be assumed to have capacity unless it is established (on the balance of probabilities[1]) that he lacks capacity;
(b)   a person is not to be treated as unable to make a decision unless all practicable steps to help him to do so have been taken without success;
(c)   a person is not to be treated as unable to make a decision merely because he makes an unwise decision.

1   Mental Capacity Act 2005, s 2(4).

13.10 Section 2 (3) emphasises that the above tests of capacity are decision-specific in that a lack of capacity cannot be established merely by reference to a person's age or appearance or a condition of his or an aspect of his behaviour which might lead others to make unjustified assumptions about his capacity.

13.11 The greater the complexity of the decision the greater degree of understanding required of the decision maker. As stated in *Re Beaney*[1]:

'The degree or extent of understanding required is relative to the particular transaction ... In the case of a will the degree required is always high. In the case of a contract, a deed made for consideration or a gift inter vivos the degree required varies with the circumstances of the transaction. Thus, at one extreme, if the subject matter and value of a gift are trivial in relation to the donor's assets a low degree of understanding will suffice. But, at the other, if its effect is to dispose of the donor's only asset of value and thus for practical purposes to pre-empt the devolution of his estate under his will or on his intestacy, then the degree of understanding required is as high as that required for a will and the donor must understand the claims of all potential donees and the extent of the property to be disposed of.'

1   [1978] 2 All ER 595 at 601, [1978] 1 WLR 770 at 774 applied in *Re Morris* [2001] WTLR 1137 and endorsed in *Masterman – Lister v Jewell* [2002] EWCA Civ 1889, [2003] 3 All ER 162.

13.12 However, where a person who is of unsound mind in fact, but is not known to be so to persons privy to valuable consideration, enters into a settlement or other contract, it would seem that it would not be set aside, either at law or in equity[1]. A voidable marriage[2] entered into by a person of unsound mind is probably valuable consideration for a marriage settlement.

1   See *Molton v Camroux* (1848) 2 Exch 487 at 503; affd (1849) 4 Exch 17; and *Hart v O'Connor* [1985] AC 1000, [1985] 2 All ER 880, PC; *Masterman – Lister v Jewell* [2002] EWCA Civ 1889 [2003] 3 All ER 162, para 57.
2   Nullity of Marriage Act 1971, ss 11, 12.

13.13 The Mental Capacity Act 2005[1] also allows a person to execute a lasting power of attorney to enable an attorney to act on his behalf if he should lose capacity in the future. Such a power goes further than an enduring power of appointment[2] because it can extend to health and welfare matters and not just cover property and financial matters. The power has to comply with the requirements of section 10 and be in the prescribed form and registered in accordance with Schedule 1 with the Public Guardian. The attorney cannot make gifts[3] except on customary occasions to persons (including himself) who are related to or connected with the donor of the power or to any charity to whom the donor made or might have been expected to make gifts, and then only if the value of each gift is not unreasonable having reqard to all the circumstances and, in particular, the size of the donor's estate.

1   Mental Capacity Act 2005, s 9.
2   Enduring Powers of Attorney Act 1985.
3   Mental Capacity Act 2005, s 12.

13.14 The Court of Protection has extensive powers[1] to settle the property of the incapable person or to make a will for him, whether or not involving testamentary trusts. While the Court will itself make the major decisions (eg as to settlements and wills) on behalf of such person it can appoint deputies to take decisions, but their powers are to be as limited in scope and duration as it reasonably practicable in the circumstances[2].

1   Mental Capacity Act 2005, ss 16–18.
2   Mental Capacity Act 2005, s 16(4) and restrictions on deputies' powers in s 20.

13.15 The Public Guardian is responsible for establishing and maintaining a register of lasting powers of attorney and a register of orders appointing deputies, and has supervisory duties in relation to how attorneys and deputies are operating[1].

¹ Mental Capacity Act 2005, s 58.

Foreigners

13.16 Testamentary trusts of English movables (but not English immovables) created by a testator domiciled abroad are only valid to the extent that the testator's *lex domicilii* (as his *lex successionis* according to the English forum) allows such to be disposed of free from mandatory rules protecting the interests of the testator's children or other relatives or dependants[1]. Inter vivos trusts of English movables and immovables transferred validly under the *lex situs* to trustees of an English or other trust by a settlor of foreign domicile, habitual residence or nationality are valid and uninpeachable[2] except, perhaps, to the extent that the settlor reserved a general power of appointment or revocation and his *lex successionis* at his death has mandatory rules protecting the interests after his death of his children or other relatives or dependants[3].

¹ *Re Annesley* [1926] Ch 692.
² *Re Megret* [1901] 1 Ch 547; *Pouey v Hordern* [1900] 1 Ch 492: see paras 102.193–102.197.
³ See para 11.132 above.

Corporations

13.17 A corporation is an artificial person having no capacity beyond its express objects and powers[1] set out in its memorandum of association and those implied objects and powers that are reasonably incidental to the carrying on of the corporation's business[2]. The creation of trusts especially for the benefit of employees of the company[3] and perhaps even for endowing a professorship[4] may be intra vires the company where conducive to the continued progress of the company's business.

¹ *Bell Houses Ltd v City Wall Properties Ltd* [1966] 2 QB 656, [1966] 2 All ER 674.
² *Charterbridge Corpn v Lloyds Bank Ltd* [1970] Ch 62, [1969] 2 All ER 1185; *Re Lee Behrens & Co Ltd* [1932] 2 Ch 46; *Rolled Steel Products (Holdings) Ltd v British Steel Corpn* [1982] Ch 478, [1982] 3 All ER 1057; reversed in part on appeal [1986] Ch 246, [1985] 3 All ER 52, CA.
³ See Inheritance Tax Act 1984, ss 72, 75; Taxation of Chargeable Gains Act 1992, ss 227–231 for some tax advantages.
⁴ *Evans v Brunner Mond & Co* [1921] 1 Ch 359.

13.18 By s 35 of the Companies Act 1985 substituted by s 108 of the Companies Act 1989:

> '(1)The validity of an act done by a company shall not be called into question on the ground of lack of capacity by reason of anything in the company's memorandum.

13.19 *Validity of declared trusts in relation to latent matters*

(2)A member of a company may bring proceedings to restrain the doing of an act which but for sub-s (1) would be beyond the company's capacity; but no such proceedings shall lie in respect of an act to be done in fulfilment of a legal obligation arising from a previous act of the company.'

13.19 By s 35A:

'(1)In favour of a person dealing with a company in good faith, the power of the board to bind the company, or authorise others to do so, shall be deemed to be free of any limitation under the company's constitution.

(2)For this purpose
(a)   a person deals with a company if he is a party to any transaction or other act to which the company is a party;
(b)   a person shall not be regarded as acting in bad faith by reason only of knowing that an act is beyond the powers of the directors under the company's constitution; and
(c)   a person shall be presumed to have acted in good faith unless the contrary is proved.'

13.20 By s 35(B):

'A party to a transaction is not bound to enquire as to whether it is permitted by the company's memorandum or as to any limitation on the powers of the board of directors to bind the company or authorise others to do so.'

13.21 Shareholders may thus still restrain a proposed ultra vires matter and directors may still be liable for breach of duty. The section does not affect the possibility of personal liability to account as a constructive trustee if the facts otherwise give rise to such liability[1].

[1]   *International Sales and Agencies Ltd v Marcus* [1982] 3 All ER 551.

Regulation under Financial Services and Markets Act 2000

13.22 While trust corporations (other than those established to act only as trustee of trusts established by one family or one settlor) are required to be registered and licensed in some off-shore trust jurisdictions (eg Bermuda, Turks and Caicos Islands, Jersey, Guernsey, Isle of Man, Cayman Islands) if resident there or carrying on business there, no such requirement exists in England. However, if a trustee deals in investments or arranges deals in investments or manages investments or safeguards and administers assets belonging to another[1] it will need to be authorised under the Financial Services and Markets Act 2000 and to comply with rules laid down by the Financial Services Authority eg the Conduct of Business Rules.

[1]   Financial Services and Markets Act 2000, ss 19, 22 and Sch 2.

13.23 If the trustee restricts itself to managing investments it will fall outside the 1986 Act if (a) it does not hold itself out as offering investment management services, or (b) is not remunerated for providing such services 'in addition to any remuneration' received for discharging its duties as a trustee, and 'for these purposes a person is not to be regarded as receiving additional remuneration merely because his remuneration is calculated in reference to time spent'[1]. It might be argued that (a) seems capable of catching all trustees who hold themselves out as professional trustees (ie carrying on business as trustee) since investment management is one of the two major inherent functions of trusteeship, the other function being the trustee's distributive function which can only operate in respect of the results of the investment function. However, this would afford such little scope to the exemption that a purposive interpretation should lead the court to restrict (a) to those professional trustees who advertise their investment management expertise, though this will catch most trustees who try to attract business by marketing themselves.

[1] Financial Services and Markets Act 2000 (Regulated Activities) Order 2001, SI 2001/544, article 66.

13.24 For (b) to exempt a trustee, investment management services must not be remunerated in addition to remuneration for trusteeship duties. Thus, it seems that a trustee who charges not on a time basis but by way of a fixed percentage of the trust fund's value will be outside the Financial Services Act 1986.

13.25 Where a trustee is regulated under the Financial Services and Markets Act 2000 the ordinary Conduct of Business Rules will not apply to the trustee if delegating investment management to a Permitted Third Party which has to comply with such Rules[1].

[1] Conduct of Business Rules, Chapter 11, particularly section 11.6.

13.26 A Permitted Third Party is an authorised or an exempt person under the 2000 Act or lawfully carrying on a regulated activity in another European Economic Area State.

ARTICLE 14
WHO MAY BE BENEFICIARIES

14.1

Every person who would be capable of owning property if of full age and sound mind may be a beneficiary under a trust even if not of full age and sound mind.

Aliens

14.2 Aliens[1] generally have the same capacity as British subjects to own, and therefore may be beneficiaries under trusts of, real and personal property of every kind. However, ships and aircraft cannot be registered in the UK and so operate in the UK or elsewhere if an unqualified person has the legal or equitable interest therein. In essence, qualified persons are British or Commonwealth citizens or bodies and also nationals or bodies of a European Economic Area State[2]. Trustees for aliens in wartime must also bear in mind the provisions of the Trading with the Enemy Act 1939.

1   The definition of 'alien' in the British Nationality Act 1981, s 50, is a 'person who is neither a Commonwealth citizen nor a British protected person nor a citizen of the Republic of Ireland'.
2   S 9 Merchant Shipping Act 1995, Merchant Shipping (Registration of Ships) Regulations 1993 SI 3138 (as amended by 1998 SI 2976) Regs 7, 8 and 9; and Air Navigation Order 2005 SI 1970 article 4.

Minors and persons of unsound mind

14.3   Although a minor is incapable of holding a legal estate in land[1] he can be a beneficiary under a trust of property of any kind, as can a person, who lacks capacity under the Mental Capacity Act 2005, though incapable of acting as a trustee.

1   See paras 13.2–13.3 above, where the reduction in the age of majority from 21 to 18 by the Family Law Reform Act 1969 is also noted.

Settlors and trustees

14.4   A settlor may be the beneficiary or one of the beneficiaries under the trust he creates. A trustee may also be a beneficiary, but a sole trustee cannot hold on trust for himself as sole beneficiary since it is impossible to have rights and duties at home in one person[1]. No trust can exist where the entire property, legal and equitable, is vested in one person[2]. Indeed, no separate equitable interest exists where O is absolute legal beneficial owner[3], and O does not need to comply with s 53(1)(c) of the Law of Property Act 1925 (which is concerned with a person disposing of his subsisting equitable interest) when he fully disposes of his property[4] or creates a trust of it in favour of others, thereby creating a fresh equitable obligation.

1   *Rye v Rye* [1962] AC 496, [1962] 1 All ER 146, HL (B cannot grant a lease to B).
2   *Re Cook* [1948] Ch 212, [1948] 1 All ER 231; *Re Heberley* [1971] NZLR 325; *DKLR Holding Co (No2) Pty Ltd v CSD (NSLU)* (1982) 40 ALR 1 at 26.
3   *Westdeutsche Landesbank Girozentrale v Islington London Borough Council* [1996] AC 669 at 706.
4   *Vandervell v IRC* [1967] 2 AC 291, [1967] 1 All ER 1, HL.

ARTICLE 15
WHEN A TRUST IS VOIDABLE OR RECTIFIABLE FOR MISTAKE OR FRAUD OR UNDUE INFLUENCE

15.1

At the suit of the settlor or his representatives[1], the court will set aside or rectify (as the case may require) a settlement executed under duress or in ignorance or mistake[2], or procured by fraud, misrepresentation[3], or undue influence[4], provided that the settlor has not acquiesced in the settlement after the influence has ceased, or after he has become aware of its legal effect[5], and that the parties can be restored substantially to their original positions[6].

1   *Anderson v Elsworth* (1861) 3 Giff 154; *Tayars v Alsop* (1889) 37 WR 339, CA; *Morley v Loughman* [1893] 1 Ch 736; *Frey v Royal Bank of Scotland (Nassau) Limited* (2001) 3 ITELR 775.
2   *Phillips v Mullings* (1871) 7 Ch App 244; *Forshaw v Welsby* (1860) 30 Beav 243; c f *North Ocean Shipping Co Ltd v Hyundai Construction Co Ltd, The Atlantic Baron* [1979] QB 705, [1978] 3 All ER 1170; *Re Daniel's Settlement* (1875) 1 Ch D 375; *Clark v Girdwood* (1877) 7 Ch D 9; *Re Hargreaves' Trusts* [1937] 2 All ER 545; *Lady Hood of Anderson v Mackinnon* [1909] 1 Ch 476; *Gibbon v Mitchell* [1990] 3 All ER 338.
3   *Re Glubb* [1900] 1 Ch 354.
4   *Huguenin v Baseley* (1807) 14 Ves 273; *Morley v Loughnan [1893] 1 Ch 736; Hoghton v Hoghton* (1852) 15 Beav 278; *Cooke v Lamotte* (1851) 15 Beav 234; *Bullock v Lloyds Bank Ltd* [1955] Ch 317, [1954] 3 All ER 726.
5   *Davies v Davies* (1870) LR 9 Eq 468, *Allcard v Skinner* (1887) 36 Ch D 145; *Bullock v Lloyds Bank Ltd* [1955] Ch 317, [1954] 1 All ER 726.
6   *Johnston v Johnston* (1884) 52 LT 76; *O'Sullivan v Management Agency and Music Limited* [1985] QB 428, CA.

Distinguish resulting trusts resulting from failure of purposes

15.2 In *Essery v Cowlard*[1] by a settlement in consideration of a then intended marriage, executed in 1877, it was declared that a sum of stock, which had been transferred by the intended wife to trustees, should be held by them on trusts for her benefit and that of the intended husband and the issue of the intended marriage. The marriage was not solemnised, but the parties cohabited without marriage, and three children were born. In 1883 an action was brought by the father and mother of these children. It was held that, the contract to marry having been absolutely put an end to, the trusts declared by the settlement to take effect after the solemnisation of the then intended marriage had become inoperative[2]. Delivery up of the deed to the settlor for cancellation and destruction is a short-cut for there being held to be a resulting trust for the settlor, entitling the settlor to require the trustees formally to transfer the legal title to the property to the settlor, but if title is registered in the trustees' names then a formal transfer will be needed. Similar decisions were arrived at in *Bond v Walford*[3], where an intended marriage had been simply broken off, and *Re Garnett*[4], where a decree of nullity of marriage had been made. However, a decree of nullity no longer has retrospective effect, so that such decree, like a decree of divorce, should not bring about a failure of the trust in respect of which the courts have a broad jurisdiction to make orders under the Matrimonial Causes Act 1973[5].

1   (1884) 26 Ch D 191; and see *Chapman v Bradley* (1863) 4 De GJ & Sm 71.
2   Thus treated as a resulting trust case by Lord Denning in *Burgess v Rawnsley* [1975] Ch 429 at 437.
3   (1886) 32 Ch D 238.
4   (1905) 93 LT 117; *Re Wombwell's Settlement* [1922] 2 Ch 298; *Re Ames' Settlement* [1946] Ch 217, [1946] 1 All ER 689, discussed as a resulting trust case by Lord Browne-Wilkinson in *Westdeutsche Landesbank Girozentrale v Islington London Borough Council* [1996] 2 AC 669 at 715.
5   Part II, as amended by the Family Law Act 1996.

15.3 Validity of declared trusts in relation to latent matters

15.3 The above cases all concern failure of marriages but the principle is, of course, capable of wider application[1] as recognised by Browne LJ in *Burgess v Rawnsley* as follows[2]:

> 'It is clear that where a person creates a trust for a particular purpose or in contemplation of a particular event and that purpose fails or that event does not happen, there is a resulting trust for the settlor.
>
> The same would also apply where two people join in creating a trust both having the same purpose or contemplating the same event. The resulting trust in such a case is for each settlor in proportion to the amount he or she put into trust.'

[1] See Article 29.
[2] [1975] Ch 429 at 441, [1975] 3 All ER 142 at 149. Also see *Westdeutsche Landesbank Girozentrale v Islington London Borough Council* [1996] AC 669 at 683.

15.4 The case concerned H, a 63 year-old tenant of the lower flat of a house divided into two flats and his friend Mrs R, a 60 year-old widow. They purchased the house paying half each and took the conveyance jointly upon trust for sale for themselves as joint tenants. H's purpose was marriage to her, though he had not mentioned this to her. In Lord Denning's opinion Mrs R's purpose was to have the upper flat to live in but H refused to let her move in when, after the purchase, she refused to marry him. If a common purpose had failed a resulting trust for each in half shares would have arisen and the fact that each had a different purpose which failed should make no difference, so that on H's death Mrs R was not entitled to the whole property.

15.5 Browne LJ and Sir John Pennycuick disagreed: a common purpose which fails must be established; or, at any rate, a failure of purpose of one settlor, not communicated to the other, cannot destroy a trust; and, in any event, Mrs R's purpose had not failed since it was not just to obtain the upper flat to live in but to take an interest in the whole house as beneficial joint tenant, as expressed in the conveyance, incidentally sharing the house in a particular manner. However, further facts showed H and Mrs R had effectively orally severed the joint tenancy, so that Mrs R was only entitled to half the house.

15.6 Another situation where a resulting trust arises from a failure of purposes is where a testator devises four properties to trustees to transfer the house which X chooses to X and then to transfer the remaining properties to Y, but X died shortly before the testator and so cannot make the requisite choice[1].

[1] *Boyce v Boyce* (1849) 16 Sim 476. Also see *Muschinski v Dodds* (1985) 160 CLR 583.

Onus of proof to set aside a deed

15.7 Setting aside on the ground of ignorance, mistake, fraud, or undue influence is more frequently sought in the case of voluntary settlements than those made for consideration. The remedy is not, however, confined to voluntary settlements, although the court will more readily set aside a settlement for which no consideration was given than one based on value.

15.8 It is now settled that where the settlor invokes the aid of the court to set aside a voluntary settlement the *onus* of showing mistake, fraud, or undue influence is upon him[1], except that the evidential burden shifts:

(1)   where the provisions of the settlement are so absurd and improvident as to raise a presumption that no reasonable person would have agreed to them knowingly so that the settlor did not understand what he was doing[2], or

(2)   where the beneficiary occupied at the date of the settlement a fiduciary position towards the settlor, of a character recognised as creating a strong prima facie presumption of undue influence[3].

1   *Henry v Armstrong* (1881) 18 Ch D 668.
2   *Dutton v Thompson* (1883) 23 Ch D 278. A sale at an undervalue or settlement may be set aside if of an improvident unconscionable character made by a poorly educated person acting without independent advice: *Fry v Lane* (1888) 40 Ch D 312. This principle has had a new lease of life where a wife in circumstances of emotional strain transfers her interest in the matrimonial home: *Backhouse v Backhouse* [1978] 1 All ER 1158, [1978] 1 WLR 243; *Cresswell v Potter* [1978] 1 WLR 255n; *Butlin-Sanders v Butlin* [1985] FLR 204, [1985] Fam Law 126. In *Watkin v Watson-Smith* (1986) Times, 3 July, Michael Wheeler QC as deputy judge opined that a vendor's desire for a quick sale and his old age with accompanying diminution of capacity and judgment would suffice in place of poverty and ignorance for *Fry v Lane* principles. Further see *Simpson v Simpson* [1992] 1 FLR 601; *Credit Lyonnais v Birch* [1997] 1 All ER 144 at 151, per Nourse LJ and *Portman Building Society v Dusangh* [2001] WTLR 117, CA. The unconscionable bargains doctrine does not apply to gifts so that undue influence or mistake will need to be relied upon to upset gifts: *Langton v Langton* [1995] 2 FLR 890.
3   *Huguenin v Baseley* (1807) 14 Ves 273; *Tate v Williamson* (1866) 2 Ch App 55; *Allcard v Skinner* (1887) 36 Ch D 145; *Morley v Loughnan* [1893] 1 Ch 736; *Royal Bank of Scotland plc v Etridge (No. 2)* [2001] UKHL 44 [2002] AC 773. For such special relationships see para 15.38 below.

15.9 The absence of a power of revocation will not operate to transfer the onus of proof from the settlor to the beneficiary[1].

1   *Hall v Hall* (1873) 8 Ch App 430.

15.10 As Lindley LJ stated[1]:

'Gifts cannot be revoked nor can deeds of gift be set aside simply because the donors wish they had not made them. Where there is no fraud, no undue influence, no fiduciary relation between donor and donee, no mistake induced by those who derive any benefit by it, a gift, whether by mere delivery or by deed, is binding on the donor ... In the absence of all such circumstances of suspicion, a donor can only obtain back property which he has given away by showing that he was under some mistake of so serious a character as to render it unjust on the part of the donee to retain the property.'

1   *Ogilvie v Littleboy* (1897) 13 TLR 399, affd as *Ogilvie v Allen* (1889) 15 TLR 294, HL.

15.11 In the case of a gift to trustees by way of a settlement there is the further possibility of seeking to rectify the settlement, whether by deleting or adding provisions.

Mistake justifying rectification

15.12 Although a settlor cannot obtain the setting aside or variation of a voluntary trust for the mere asking, yet some relief will be given to him where he can show that he misunderstood, or did not understand, the effect thereof. In the case of *James v Couchman*[1] it appeared that the plaintiff had, by a voluntary settlement (made with the object of protecting himself against extravagant habits), assigned property to trustees, upon trust for himself for life, remainder to his wife (if any) for life, remainder to his issue, and in default of issue to his *paternal* next of kin. North J, while refusing to set aside the settlement, thought that the ultimate limitation was unusual, and that it was odd that there was the omission of a usual power, namely, a general power of appointment vested in the plaintiff, antecedent to the default clause in favour of paternal next of kin. His Lordship stated,[2]

> 'I think that he did not understand that the effect of what he was doing was to deprive himself of a power which might have been given to him after every purpose of protecting himself, his wife and children had been answered.'

[1] (1885) 29 Ch D 212; (and see *Cavendish v Strutt* (1903) 19 TLR 483).
[2] (1885) 29 Ch D 212 at 215.

15.13 Accordingly, his Lordship ordered the settlement to be rectified so as to give the settlor a power of appointment in default or failure of issue. His Lordship, however, was careful to add:

> 'The fact that a usual power was omitted here would not weigh with me in the least if I were satisfied that the omission of such power had been brought to the attention of the settlor, as he would then have been competent to judge for himself. But it seems to me that in the present case his attention was not called to the omission'.[1]

[1] (1885) 29 Ch D 212 at 215.

15.14 Where a person, apparently at the point of death, executed a voluntary settlement, of which he recollected nothing, which was never read to him, and in which a power of revocation was purposely omitted by the solicitor on the ground that he knew the variable character of the settlor, and there was also evidence that the settlor thought that he was executing the settlement in place of a will, it was held that the settlement was revocable[1].

[1] *Forshaw v Welsby* (1860) 30 Beav 243; *Re Blake* (1889) 37 WR 441. See also *Constantinidi v Ralli* [1935] Ch 427, where it was sought, without success, to compromise an action for rectification of a settlement brought upon the ground that the settlor, a foreigner, did not understand the true effect of the settlement, it being held on the evidence that she took part in the negotiations for the settlement and that it was her deed. In the same case it was held that rectification will not be made on affidavit evidence, but in s clear-cut case rectification can be ordered on affidavit evidence as in *Frey v Royal Bank of Scotland (Nassau) Ltd* (2001) 3 ITELR 775 (settlement of Marc Bolan rectified 24 years after his death to extend to illegitimate children of the rock star or his wife); *Hanley v Pearson* (1879) 13 Ch D 545.

15.15 If a settlement involves bargaining between the parties then rectification may be obtained where it is clearly proved by convincing evidence[1] that owing to a mistake of the draftsman the settlement does not express the real intention of the parties: the mistake must thus be mutual[2]. Exceptionally where the bargaining parties had a common intention and it is shown (i) that the claimant erroneously believed that the instrument gave effect to that intention, (ii) that the defendant knew that it did not because by reason of the claimant's mistake the instrument contained or omitted something, (iii) that the defendant failed to bring the mistake to the claimant's notice and (iv) that the mistake would benefit the defendant or, perhaps, merely be detrimental to the claimant, then rectification will be ordered to give effect to the common intention, despite the fact that the mistake was merely a unilateral mistake[3].

1   *AMP (UK) plc v Barker* [2001] WTLR 1232 at 1256.
2   *Re Butlin's Settlement Trusts* [1976] Ch 251, [1976] 2 All ER 483; *Joscelyne v Nissen* [1970] 2 QB 86, [1970] 1 All ER 1213.
3   *Thomas Bates & Son Ltd v Wyndham's (Lingerie) Ltd* [1981] 1 All ER 1077, [1981] 1 WLR 505, CA; *Commission for New Towns v Cooper (GB) Ltd* [1995] 2 All ER 929; *Littman v Aspen Oil* [2005] EWCA Civ 1579, [2006] 2 P & CR 35.

15.16 In the case of a unilateral transaction it is necessary only to prove that the settlement fails to express the real intention of the settlor. In *Re Butlin's Settlement Trust* Brightman J summarised the law as follows[1]:

> 'In the absence of an actual bargain between a settlor and trustees: (i) a settlor may seek rectification by proving that the settlement does not express his true intention, or the true intention of himself and any party with whom he has bargained, such as a spouse in the case of an antenuptial settlement; (ii) it is not essential for him to prove that the settlement fails to express the true intention of the trustees if they have not bargained; but (iii) the court may in its discretion decline to rectify a settlement against a protesting trustee who objects to rectification.'

1   [1976] Ch 251 at 262, [1976] 2 All ER 483 at 489. See also *Behrens v Heilbut* (1956) 222 L Jo 290; *Re Walton's Settlement* [1922] 2 Ch 509, CA.

15.17 The settlor had intended his voluntary discretionary settlement to contain a power for a majority of trustees to bind a minority in more situations than allowed for by the settlement as finally executed. Brightman J held that rectification (which has retrospective effect) was 'available not only in a case where particular words have been added, omitted or wrongly written as the result of careless copying or the like' but 'also where the words of the document were purposely used but it was mistakenly considered that they bore a different meaning from their correct meaning as a matter of construction'[1]. Applying his summary of the law (above) he ordered rectification despite the trustees' absence of intention and despite the opposition of one trustee, though not swearing any affidavit to disclose the reasons for her opposition.

1   [1976] Ch 251 at 260, [1976] 2 All ER 483 at 487. Whilst a mistake as to the interpretation of words used can be rectified, so that 'children' in a Bahamian trust can be rectified to include illegitimate children (*Frey v Royal Bank of Scotland (Nassau) Ltd* (2001) 3 ITELR 775), a mistake as to material facts which led to the words used cannot be rectified: *Frederick Rose Ltd v William Pim Junior & Co Ltd* [1953] 2 QB 450, [1953] 2 All ER 739, CA ('horsebeans' used in contract under mistaken belief it meant the same as 'feveroles').

15.18 It is not enough that it would have been better if the settlor had executed a deed which was from the outset in the form to which the settler seeks it to be changed or that, if asked at the time of preparation of the deed it she would prefer the form now sought, she would have said that she would[1].

¹ Thus there was a refusal to rectify a settlement in *Tankel v Tankel* [1999] 1 FLR 676 where appointments had been made in favour of the settlor's daughters, who were beneficiaries who had become two of the trustees in whose favour no distributions of income or capital could be made due to a prohibitory clause of which rectification was sought, so as retrospectively to validate the appointments.

15.19 Where rectification is sought which will attract tax benefits the case law[1] has been summarised by Vinelott J as follows[2]: 'the court will make an order for the rectification of a document if satisfied that it does not give effect to the true agreement or arrangement between the parties, or to the true intention of a grantor or covenantor, and if satisfied that there is an issue, capable of being contested, between the parties or between a covenantor or grantor and the person he intended to benefit, it being irrelevant first that rectification is sought or consented to by them all and second that rectification is desired because it has beneficial fiscal consequences. On the other hand, the court will not order rectification of a document as between the parties or as between a grantor or covenantor and an intended beneficiary, if their rights will be unaffected and if the only effect of the order will be to secure a fiscal benefit.' The court needs to be convinced that the clause to be rectified was intended to be in some precisely different form from that that appearing in the deed[3].

¹ *Whiteside v Whiteside* [1950] Ch 65; *Re Slocock's Will Trust* [1979] 1 All ER 358; *Sherdley v Sherdley* [1986] 1 WLR 732, *Lake v Lake* [1989] STC 865; *Re Smouha Family Trust* [2000] WTLR 133.
² *Racal Group Services Ltd v Ashmore* [1995] STC 1151, CA.
³ *Racal Group Services Ltd v Ashmore* [1995] STC 1151, CA. Also, see *Martin v Nicholson* [2005] WTLR 175; *Farmer v Sloan* [2005] WTLR 521.

15.20 For rectification, as with rescission, of a deed the mistake of law or fact needs to be a mistake as to the legal or factual effect of the transaction and not merely as to its fiscal or other consequences or as to the advantages to be gained by entering into it[1].

¹ *Whiteside v Whiteside* [1950] Ch 65 at 74; *AMP (UK) plc v Barker* [2001] 1 WTLR 1237 at 1260; *Commissioner of Stamp Duties (NSW) v Carlenka Pty Limited* (1995) 41 NSWLR 329; *Eroc Pty Limited v Amalgamated Resources NL* [2003] QSC 74 at para 38: and see paras 15.28–15.33.

15.21 Rectification is a last resort and it may be possible where words have been omitted from a deed by inadvertence so to construe a deed as to give effect to the clear intentions of the parties where it is clear what correction was required to carry out the intentions of parties[1]. Thus is *Schnieder v Mills*[2] a clause was construed with the implication therein of the words 'which has arisen prior to the date hereof' after the word 'income' so as to reflect the fact that deeds of variation of wills executed within two years of a testator's death are retrospective for the purposes of inheritance tax[3] and capital gains tax[4] but not income tax.

1   *Re Whitrick* [1957] 1 WLR 884; *Re Bacharach's Will Trust* [1959] Ch 245; *Littman v Aspen Oil [2005] EWCA Civ 1579, [2006] 2 P & CR 35.*
2   [1993] STC 430.
3   Inheritance Taxes Act 1984, s 142.
4   Taxation of Chargeable Gains Act 1992, s 62(6).

Rectification of marriage settlements or pension trusts

15.22 Even a marriage settlement or pension trust where valuable consideration has been provided will be rectified on clear evidence of mistake.

15.23 Thus in *Banks v Ripley*[1], Morton J ordered the rectification of a marriage settlement by the insertion of words of limitation even though the only evidence that they had been omitted by mistake was afforded by the document itself. There was also rectification of a marriage settlement in *Re Alexander's Settlement*[2] where by mistake a gift over was directed in the event of a son becoming tenant in tail male under the will of a deceased person, it appearing that under that will a son could only become tenant in tail general.

1   [1940] Ch 719, [1940] 3 All ER 49.
2   [1910] 2 Ch 225.

15.24 In *AMP(UK) Ltd v Barker*[1] trustees of a pension trust, with the requisite consent of the employer ,exercised their power to amend the trust in terminology intended to increase benefits of members retiring early through incapacity but mistakenly extending to all early leavers. Convincing evidence of the separate intentions of the trustees and of the employer to affect only incapacity benefits justified retrospective rectification without the need to show that there was some outward expression of any agreement or accord between the trustees and the employer (although it was possible on the facts to find that 'there was in effect such an accord'[2]). Early leavers for reasons unrelated to their incapacity could not resist rectification as bona fide purchasers, not having given any additional consideration for the rights mistakenly conferred on them, so that it was wholly unrealistic to treat them as purchasers of anything other than such rights as were properly granted under the pension trusts.

1   [2001] WTLR 1237.
2   [2001] WTLR 1237 at 1259.

Rectification of wills

15.25 By s 20 of the Administration of Justice Act 1982 it is now possible for a court to rectify a will if it is satisfied that the will fails to carry out the testator's intentions in consequence of a clerical error or a failure to understand his instructions[1]. The words 'clerical error' are wide enough to include a solicitor's omission to record or include a clause from a previous will[2]. The application for rectification cannot be made, except with the court's leave, more than six months after the date on which the grant of representation to the estate was taken out. If after the six months the personal representatives distribute the estate they will not be liable for failing to take into account the possibility of the court allowing an application for rectification out of time: the estate will be recoverable from its recipients, so long as they are not bona fide purchasers[3].

1 If the testator has misunderstood the effect of the wording he has used then s 20 is not available so decisions like *Collins v Elstone* [1893] P 1, may still occur. In *Walker v Medlicott* [1999] 1 All ER 685 a solicitor's failure to implement the testatrix's intention to devise her house to the claimant was regarded as based on a failure to understand the testatrix's intention. In *Goodman v Goodman* [2006] EWHC 1757 (Ch) rectification led to omission of a clause.
2 *Wordingham v Royal Exchange Trust Co* [1992] Ch 412, [1992] 3 All ER 204; *Re Segelman* [1996] Ch 171.
3 Whether on tracing principles (Article 101) or under the in personam action vindicated by *Ministry of Health v Simpson* [1951] AC 251, [1950] 2 All ER 1137, HL (para 100.80).

15.26 Apart from this statutory power a court may rectify a will in the case of fraud[1]. It is also possible that a court as a matter of construction may be able to correct an obvious mistake or error appearing on the face of the will[2], especially now that by s 21 of the 1982 Act extrinsic evidence, including evidence of the testator's intention, may be admitted to assist in the interpretation of a will in so far as it is meaningless or the language used is ambiguous on the face of it or in so far as evidence, other than evidence of the testator's intention, shows that the language used is ambiguous in the light of the surrounding circumstances.

1 *Collins v Elstone* [1893] P 1.
2 *Re Bacharach's Will Trusts* [1959] Ch 245, [1958] 3 All ER 618; *Re Doland's Will Trust* [1970] Ch 267, [1969] 3 All ER 713; *Re Reynette-James* [1975] 3 All ER 1037, [1976] 1 WLR 161; *Re Chambers* [2001] WTLR 1375.

Potential negligence liability of legal advisers

15.27 While a solicitor may be liable for negligent breach of contract for any loss caused to the person instructing him to prepare a deed or a will, he may also be liable for the tort of negligence to third party beneficiaries suffering a loss through the solicitor's failure to achieve what he was instructed to achieve, eg negligently failing to advise a testator that a beneficiary's spouse should not attest the will[1] or negligently failing to prepare an ill elderly testator's will timeously[2] or negligently failing to use the appropriate wording or to have the will validly executed[3], or, it would seem[4], negligently failing to create an effective inter vivos trust for X after the death of the settlor, when, instead, a bare trust for the settlor containing an unattested testamentary disposition for X was actually created. While claimants have a duty to mitigate losses, there is no rule that rectification must be sought before suing the solicitor for negligence[5].

1 *Ross v Caunters* [1980] Ch 297.
2 *White v Jones* [1995] 2 AC 207, HL.
3 *Corbett v Bond Pearce* [2001] WTLR 419, CA.
4 *White v Jones* [1993] 3 All ER 481 at 492–493, *Hemmens v Wilson Browne* [1993] 4 All ER 826.
5 *Horsfall v Haywards* [1999] 1 FLR 1182, CA. Contrast *Walker v Medlicott* [1999] 1 All ER 685 where rectification should have been sought.

Setting aside for mistake

15.28 Millett J (as he then was) summarised the case law as showing[1]:

'that, wherever there is a voluntary transaction by which one party intends to confer a bounty upon another, the deed will be set aside if the court is satisfied that the disposer did not intend the transaction to have the effect which it did. It will be set aside whether the mistake is of law or of fact, so long as the mistake is as to the effect of the transaction itself and not merely as to its consequences or the advantages to be gained by entering into it.'

[1]   [1990] 3 All ER 338 at 343, [1990] 1 WLR 1304 at 1309.

15.29 Thus, he set aside a voluntary deed whereby G purported to surrender his protected life interest, believing this would be effective to accelerate his children's interest in remainder into an immediate absolute interest. However, the purported surrender actually forfeited his life interest and caused discretionary trusts to spring up in favour of himself and his children. There was a clear mistake as to the effect of the transaction.

15.30 Similarly, in *Lady Hood of Avalon v Mackinnon*[1], Lady Hood, on the marriage of her younger daughter, exercised her personal power of appointment in favour of such daughter and then exercised it again in favour of her elder daughter so as to maintain equality between them, believing that no earlier appointment had been made in favour of the elder daughter, though, in fact such an appointment had been made six years previously. There was a clear factual mistake as to the effect of the appointment which mistakenly gave the elder daughter very much more than the younger daughter had received, instead of the same amount.

[1]   [1909] 1 Ch 476.

15.31 In *Ellis v Ellis*[1] the donor husband made a clear mistake as to the effect of an outright gift to his wife when he did not realise it was automatically caught up on the trusts of a settlement due to falling within an after-acquired property covenant of his wife. In *Anker-Petersen v Christenson*[2] the claimant beneficiaries made a clear mistake as to the effect of assigning their equitable interests so that they could be held on new trusts which they believed to be similar to old trusts, when, this was not the case. Davis J there[3] accepted that rescission would not be possible if the mistake had, instead, been as to the fiscal consequences or advantages to be gained by entering into a transaction as to the effect of which as a transaction there was no mistake.

[1]   (1909) 26 TLR 166.
[2]   [2002] WTLR 313.
[3]   [2002] WTLR 313 at 330–331. Further see *Baird v BCE Holdings Pty Limited* (1996) 40 NSWLR 374.

15.32 In *Sieff v Fox*[1] Lloyd LJ, giving a reserved judgment in a case heard by him when Lloyd J, provisionally accepted this[2] where there was a mistake as to the fiscal consequences on the part of an *individual* dealing with his own property. However, in examining the *Re Hastings-Bass* principle[3] available to *trustees* who would not have acted as they did but for mistakenly failing to take into account a relevant consideration, he held that fiscal consequences could bea relevant consideration[4]. He was influenced by the special position of trustees[5] and by dicta of Lindley LJ[6] that a donor could recover property given away 'by showing that he was under some mistake of so serious a character as to render it unjust on the part of the donee to retain the property.' He indicated[7] that this could justify allowing fiscal consequences to be taken into account if they were sufficiently serious.

1   [2005] EWHC 1312 (Ch), [2005] 3 All ER 693.
2   [2005] EWHC 1312 (Ch), [2005] 3 All ER 693, paras 106, 108.
3   See Article 61(1)(e).
4   [2005] EWHC 1312 (Ch), [2005] 3 All ER 693, paras 108, 114.
5   [2005] EWHC 1312 (Ch), [2005] 3 All ER 693, paras 85, 108.
6   *Ogilvie v Littleboy* (1897) 13 TLR 399 at 400, endorsed by Lord Halsbury on appeal in *Ogilvie v Allen* (1899) 15 TLR 294.
7   [2005] EWHC 1312 (Ch), [2005] 3 All ER 693, paras 106, 108.

15.33 However, first instance decisions concerned with setting aside transactions of individuals for a fundamental mistake on their part have taken a narrower approach seeking to restrict the right to rescind within reasonable bounds, so as not to undermine the certainty of transactions and so as not to allow persons to reverse the effect of a transaction merely because they were mistaken about the fiscal or commercial consequences of the transaction[1] as opposed to the direct or indirect effect of the transaction in creating legal or beneficial proprietary interests.

1   See *AMP (UK) plc v Barker* [2001] WTLR 1237 at 1260 per Lawrence Collins J.

15.34 The above principles in these decisions extend beyond the exercise of a non-fiduciary power of appointment[1] to the exercise of a non-fiduciary power of consent to the exercise of fiduciary power and apply whether the settlement was voluntary or for consideration[2] – though, of course, in the latter case the principles cannot affect bona fide purchasers[3]. While these principles many also apply to the exercise of fiduciary powers by *trustees*, in practice it is easier to satisfy the less strict requirements of the *Re Hastings-Bass* principle as interpreted by first instance decisions culminating in *Sieff v Fox*[4].

1   As in *Lady Hood of Avalon v Mackinnon* [1909] 1 Ch 476.
2   *AMP (UK) plc v Barker* [2001] WTLR 1237.
3   See para 15.54 below.
4   [2005] EWHC 1312 (Ch), [2005] 3 All ER 693.

Fraud

15.35 If ignorance or mistake suffices to invalidate a settlement, a fortiori it will be cancelled where the settlor has been induced to make it by fraud; as, for instance, where a wife by falsely denying her previous adultery induces her husband to execute a deed of separation containing a stipulation not to take proceedings in respect of previous offences[1].

¹   *Brown v Brown* (1868) LR 7 Eq 185; and see *Evans v Carrington* (1860) 2 De G F & J 481; *Evans v Edmonds* (1853) 13 CB 777; *Gordon v Gordon* (1816) 3 Swan 400. Restitutio in integrum must be possible: *Johnston v Johnston* (1884) 52 LT 76 (marriage settlement could not be set aside).

Undue influence

15.36 A gift or settlement may be set aside on the ground of undue influence not on the principle that it is right and expedient to save persons from the consequences of their own folly but on the principle that it is right and expedient to save them from being victimised by other people by ensuring that the influence of the ascendant person over the claimant is not abused so as to prevent the claimant's conduct from being an expression of his free will¹.

¹   *Allcard v Skinner* (1887) 36 Ch D 145 at 182–183 endorsed by Lord Scarman in *National Westminster Bank plc v Morgan* [1985] AC 686 at 705, [1985] 1 All ER 821 at 828, HL; and see *Royal Bank of Scotland plc v Etridge (No. 2)*[2001] UKHL 44, [2002] 2 AC 773, paras 6, 7.

15.37 As a result of the House of Lords' scrutiny¹ of two of their earlier decisions², one can state that there are two categories of undue influence. The first category is that of actual undue influence where the claimant proves affirmatively that the wrongdoer exerted undue influence on the claimant ('twisted the mind' of the claimant³) to have the claimant enter into the particular impugned transaction; such influence may arise from conduct including duress or misrepresentations⁴.

¹   *Royal Bank of Scotland plc v Etridge (No 2)* [2001] UKHL 44, [2002] 2 AC 773, [2001] 4 All ER 449.
²   *Barclays Bank plc v O'Brien* [1994] 1 AC 180; *National Westminster Bank v Morgan* [1985] AC 686.
³   See *Daniel v Drew* [2005] EWCA Civ 507, [2005] WTLR 807 at para 31.
⁴   *Royal Bank of Scotland plc v Etridge (No 2)* [2001] UKHL 44, [2002] 2 AC 773, [2001] 4 All ER 449 at para 103.

15.38 The second category arises where undue influence is inferred or presumed on a *res ipsa loquitur* basis¹ (where the circumstances speak loudly for themselves) which switches the evidential burden from the claimant to the defendant, so that the defendant needs to show that actually there was no undue influence² eg because of independent legal advice given to the claimant. For such switch of the evidential burden it is necessary first to show that the relationship between the parties to the transaction was (A) one where the law *de iure* irrebuttably presumes there to have been a relationship of trust and confidence³ (eg always between parent and child who has not, or who has only recently, achieved maturity⁴, guardian and ward⁵, solicitor and client⁶, trustee and beneficiary⁷, doctor and patient⁸, spiritual mentor and disciple⁹) or (B) one where the claimant proves *de facto* there was a relationship of trust and confidence¹⁰ (eg often between husband and wife¹¹ or sometimes between siblings or banker and customer¹² or employer and employee¹³). Second, to produce the equitable equivalent of the common law *res ipsa loquitur*, the impugned transaction must be shown to be one that clearly calls for an

15.38 *Validity of declared trusts in relation to latent matters*

explanation[14] eg as so bountiful to the recipient or so detrimental to the donor as to seem explicable only on the basis that undue influence had been exercised to procure it.

1   *Royal Bank of Scotland plc v Etridge (No 2)* [2001] UKHL 44, [2002] 2 AC 773, [2001] 4 All ER 449 at paras 16, 107 and 161.
2   'It is more a case of what has not been done': *Daniel v Drew* Supra para 31.
3   *Royal Bank of Scotland plc v Etridge (No 2)* [2002] AC 773, [2001] 4 All ER 449 at paras 18, 105, 157 and 161 for Class 2A cases within the *Barclays Bank plc v O'Brien* [1994] 1 AC 180 classification.
4   *Lancashire Loans Ltd v Black* [1934] I KB 380; *Powell v Powell* [1900] 1 Ch 243; *Bainbrigge v Browne [2001] UKHL 44,* (1881) 18 Ch D 188.
5   *Hatch v Hatch* (1804) 9 Ves 292.
6   *Wright v Carter* [1903] 1 Ch 27; *Wintle v Nye* [1959] 1 WLR 284.
7   *Liles v Terry* [1895] 2 QB 679 at 686; *Re Brocklehurst* [1978] 1 All ER 767 at 785.
8   *Re CMG* [1970] Ch 574.
9   *Allcard v Skinner* (1887) 36 Ch D 145.
10   *Royal Bank of Scotland plc v Etridge (No 2)* [2002] 2 AC 773, [2001] 4 All ER 449 at paras 14,16, 18, 106–107, 153, 156 and 161.
11   *Barclays Bank plc v O'Brien* [1994] 1 AC 180 or between engaged couples as in *Zamet v Hyman* [1961] 1 WLR 1442, CA, there being no irrebuttable presumption of undue influence in such case, though overlooked in *Stevens v Leeder* [2005] EWCA Civ 50, [2005] All ER (D) 40 (Jun).
12   *Lloyds Bank Ltd v Bundy* [1975] QB 326.
13   *Goldsworthy v Brickell* [1987] Ch 378; *Credit Lyonnais Bank v Burch* [1997] 1 All ER 144; *Re Craig* [1971] Ch 95.
14   *Royal Bank of Scotland plc v Etridge (No 2)* [2001] UKHL 44 [2002] 2 AC 773, [2001] 4 All ER 449 at paras 24, 25, 29, 104, 106, 107, and 161; *Turkey v Awadh* [2005] EWCA Civ 382 [2005] 2 P & CR 29 para 11; *Macklin v Dowsett* [2004] EWCA Civ 904 [2005] WTLR 1561, para 10.

15.39 Once it is proved that there is a disadvantage to the settlor-donor that is sufficiently grave to raise the inference that undue influence has probably been exerted whether knowingly or unknowingly[1], the onus is thrown on the donee-beneficiary to prove affirmatively that there was no undue influence exerted. This will normally require proof that the settlor had independent advice[2] or was strongly urged to obtain such advice and that the settlement contains all usual and proper powers and provisions; and, if there are any unusual provisions, that they were brought to the notice of, and understood by, the settlor[3]. Exculpatory clauses benefiting the trustee should clearly be brought to the attention of the settlor, the trustee prior to creation of the trust being in a fiduciary position where there is a conflict of interest preventing him from taking advantage of his position[4].

1   Public policy will not allow the transaction to stand even if the ascendant fiduciary was innocent in preventing the claimant from exercising his free will: *Pesticcio v Huet* [2004] EWCA Civ 372, [2004] WTLR 699.
2   Whether it will be proper to infer that such advice had an emancipating effect, so that the transaction was not brought about by the exercise of undue influence, is a question of fact to be decided having regard to all the evidence: *Royal Bank of Scotland plc v Etridge (No 2)* [2001] UKHL 44, [2002] 2 AC 773, [2001] 4 All ER 449 at paras 20 and 1531. In *Pesticcio v Huet* [2004] EWCA Civ 372 [2004] WTLR 699 such advice did not suffice.
3   *Everitt v Everitt* (1870) LR 10 Eq 405; *Bester v Perpetual Trustee Co Ltd* [1970] 3 NSWLR 30; *Huguenin v Baseley* (1807) 14 Ves 273; *Re Lloyds Bank Ltd* [1931] 1 Ch 289; *Bullock v Lloyds Bank Ltd* [1955] Ch 317, [1954] 3 All ER 726.
4   *Bogg v Raper* (1998) 1 ITELR 267, CA; *Scott on Trusts* (4th edn) para 222.4; also see *Baskerville v Thurgood* (1992) 100 Sask LR 214, CA where a fiduciary in breach of his obligations could not rely on an exclusion clause.

Undue influence in relation to wills

15.40 It must be understood that the onus of proof stated above only applies in the case of settlements and gifts inter vivos. With regard to dispositions by will when once it has been proved that a will has been executed with due solemnities by a person of competent understanding, and apparently a free agent, the burden of proving that it was executed under undue influence rests on the person who so alleges[1]. Thus in *Parfitt v Lawless*[2] no presumption of undue influence arose where T left her residuary estate to a Catholic priest who resided with her as her domestic chaplain and confessor. Actual coercion must be proved rather than mere persuasion[3].

1   *Craig v Lamoureux* [1920] AC 349; (1970) 86 LQR 447.
2   (1872) LR 2 P & D 462.
3   *Hall v Hall* (1868) LR 1 P & D 481; *Craig v Lamoureux* [1920] AC 349; *Killick v Pountney* [2000] WTLR 41 at 66–69.

Undue influence by solicitor

15.41 A gift made by a client to a solicitor, while the relation of solicitor and client exists, if of such amount as not to be a small gift but one large enough to seem explicable only on the basis of the exertion of undue influence[1] is presumed voidable. Although such gift may be ratified after the relation has ceased to exist, yet, in order to establish ratification, it must be proved to the satisfaction of the court that the donor, at the time when he was a free agent, and knew of his right to recall the gift, intentionally determined to forgo that right. In the absence of such evidence, the gift may be avoided, not only by the donor, but by his personal representatives[2]. As Cotton LJ said[3]:

> 'We must find something equivalent to a present gift when the influence arising from the existence of the relationship had ceased to exist: in the words of Turner LJ in *Wright v Vanderplank*[4], there must be "a fixed, deliberate, and unbiased determination that the transaction should not be impeached". In the case of a gift to a solicitor, the court looks most carefully to see if there has been a fixed, deliberate, and unbiased determination on the part of the donor that the transaction should not be impeached.'

1   See *Royal Bank of Scotland plc v Etridge (No 2)* [2001] UKHL 44, [2001] 4 All ER 449 at paras 24, 92, 104 and 156.
2   *Tyars v Alsop* (1889) 37 WR 339, CA.
3   *Tyars v Alsop* (1889) 37 WR 339 at 340, CA; and see also *Nanney v Williams* (1856) 22 Beav 452; and *Wright v Carter* [1903] 1 Ch 27.
4   (1856) 8 De GM & G 133; and see also *Mitchell v Homfray* (1881) 8 QBD 587, CA.

15.42 Indeed, the Court of Appeal has laid it down that, in the absence of competent independent advice, the presumption that the settlor was unduly influenced is absolute and irrebuttable[1]; and has also extended the doctrine not only to gifts to the solicitor himself, but also to his wife[2], or his son[3]. The same principle applies to an option to purchase given by a client to his solicitor[4].

1   *Liles v Terry* [1895] 2 QB 679; *Barron v Willis* [1900] 2 Ch 121; *Wright v Carter* [1903] 1 Ch 27 at 57. In the last case the settlement was set aside only as to the one tenth of capital passing to the solicitor, so that nine twentieths remained held for each of the settlor's two children.

2   *Liles v Terry* [1895] 2 QB 679; *Wright v Carter* [1903] 1 Ch 27.
3   *Barron v Willis* [1900] 2 Ch 121; affd sub nom *Willis v Barron* [1902] AC 271; *Wright v Carter* [1903] 1 Ch 27; but contra in Scotland, *Burrell v Burrell's Trustees* 1915 52 SLR 312.
4   *Demerara Bauxite Co Ltd v Hubbard* [1923] AC 673.

Undue parental influence

15.43 The expression 'undue influence' is not confined to cases in which the influence is exerted to secure a benefit for the person exerting it, but extends also to cases in which a person of imperfect judgment is placed, or places himself, under the direction of one possessing not only greater experience but also such force as that which is inherent in such a relationship as that between a father and his own child[1]; and the influence may be exerted not directly by the parent but through his solicitor[2]. A fortiori undue influence will be presumed where the deed confers a benefit on the parent. Thus it seems that where a deed conferring a benefit on the settlor's father is executed by a child who is not yet emancipated[3] from his father's control, and the deed is subsequently impeached by the child, the onus is on the father to prove that the gift was the result of the free exercise of independent will, and this may most readily be done by showing that the child had independent advice[4], and that he executed the deed with full knowledge of its contents, and with the full intention of giving the father the benefit conferred by it[5].

1   *Bullock v Lloyds Bank Ltd* [1955] Ch 317, [1954] 3 All ER 726; and see *Lancashire Loans Ltd v Black* [1934] 1 KB 380, CA.
2   *Bullock v Lloyds Bank Ltd* [1955] Ch 317, [1954] 3 All ER 726.
3   Marriage of a daughter even when she has gone to live with a husband is not conclusive proof of emancipation *Lancashire Loans Ltd v Black* [1934] 1 KB 380, CA. The presumption of undue influence of a parent over his child endures for a 'short time' (its precise length being in each case a question of fact) after the child has attained majority: *Re Pauling's Settlement Trusts* [1964] Ch 303, [1963] 3 All ER 1, CA.
4   In *Powell v Powell* [1900] 1 Ch 243 (approved in *Wright v Carter* [1903] 1 Ch 27), independent legal advice was regarded as essential. The common law judges have been inclined to rely more on individual proof than on general presumption, and to consider the nature of the relationship and presence of independent advice as important but not essential matters to be considered on the question whether the transaction can be supported, cf *Inche Noriah v Shaik Allie Bin Omar* [1929] AC 127, PC; see *Lancashire Loans Ltd v Black* [1934] 1 KB 380 at 404, [1933] All ER Rep 201 at 208, per Scrutton LJ. It seems that there are some circumstances in which independent legal advice is essential; see *Bullock v Lloyds Bank Ltd* [1955] Ch 317, [1954] 3 All ER 726.
5   *Bainbrigge v Browne* (1881) 18 Ch D 188; and see *Tate v Williamson* (1866) 2 Ch App 55; *Kempson v Ashbee* (1874) 10 Ch App 15, and cases cited; and *Tucker v Bennett* (1887) 38 Ch D 1, CA.

15.44 Where the settlor has been advised 'carefully, deliberately, separately and independently'[1], the fact that he has not taken the advice he has been given is not fatal to the deed.

1   *Bullock v Lloyds Bank Ltd* [1955] Ch 317 at 326, [1954] 3 All ER 726 at 730, per Vaisey J.

15.45 The above rules as to rebutting the presumption of undue influence were formulated in the Privy Council case of *Inche Noriah v Shaik Allie Bin Omar*[1]. Lord Hailsham, delivering the judgment of the Board said:

'their Lordships are not prepared to accept the view that independent legal advice is the only way in which the presumption [of undue influence] can be rebutted; nor are they prepared to affirm that independent legal advice, when given, does not rebut the presumption, unless it be shown that the advice was taken. It is necessary for the donee to prove that the gift was the result of the free exercise of independent will. The most obvious way to prove this is by establishing that the gift was made after the nature and effect of the transaction had been fully explained to the donee by some independent qualified person so completely as to satisfy the court that the donor was acting independently of any influence from the donee and with the full appreciation of what he was doing and in cases where there are no other circumstances this may be the only means by which the donee can rebut the presumption. But ... if evidence is given of circumstances sufficient to establish this fact (ie that the gift was the result of a free exercise of the donor's will) their lordships see no reason for disregarding them merely because they do not include independent advice from a lawyer.'

1   [1929] AC 127 at 135, approved in *Lancashire Loans Ltd v Black* [1934] 1 KB 380 at 413, [1933] All ER Rep 201 at 213, CA, per Lawrence LJ. See also *Bruty v Edmundson* (1915) 85 LJ Ch 568; *Re Coomber* [1911] 1 Ch 723 and *Kali Bakhsh Singh v Ram Gopal Singh* (1913) 30 TLR 138, PC. Further see *Royal Bank of Scotland plc v Etridge (No 2)* [2001] 4 All ER 449 at paras 20 and 153 per Lords Nicholls and Scott.

Trustees need beware undue parental (or other) influence

15.46 In *Re Pauling's Settlement Trusts*[1] the Court of Appeal put forward the view (but without expressing a final opinion) that a trustee who is carrying out a transaction in breach of trust will not escape liability by obtaining the consent of the beneficiary concerned if the trustee knew, or should have known, that the consent was, or might be presumed to be, induced by undue influence; but that the trustee would escape liability if it could not be shown that he knew or should have known this.

1   [1964] Ch 303, [1963] 3 All ER 1, CA.

Independent advice to youthful settlors

15.47 The duty of the person tendering independent advice to a young intending settlor was laid down by Vaisey J in *Bullock v Lloyds Bank Ltd* as follows[1]:

'Such a settlement as this can, in my judgment, only be justified after prolonged consideration, being made, as it was, by a young girl only just of age, and can only stand if executed under the advice of a competent adviser capable of surveying the whole field with an absolutely independent outlook, and who explains to the intending settlor, first, that she could do exactly as she pleased, and, secondly that the scheme put before her was not one to be accepted or rejected out of hand, but to be discussed, point by point, with a full understanding of the various alternative possibilities.'

1   [1955] Ch 317 at 326, [1954] 3 All ER 726 at 730. See also *Re Pauling's Settlement Trusts* [1964] Ch 303, [1963] 3 All ER 1, CA; *Re Coomber* [1911] 1 Ch 723; *Bester v Perpetual Trustee Co Ltd* [1970] 3 NSWLR 30. A solicitor acting for both parties cannot give independent advice: *Powell v Powell* [1900] 1 Ch 243.

15.48 *Validity of declared trusts in relation to latent matters*

Acquiescence by settlor

15.48 The settlor will get no relief if he has knowingly acquiesced in the settlement. Thus where a father induced a young son, who was still under his roof, and subject to his influence, to make a settlement in favour of his stepbrothers and sisters, it was held that, if the son had applied promptly, the court would have set it aside. But as he had remained quiescent for some years, and had made no objection to the course which he had been persuaded to follow, he was not entitled to relief. For by so doing he had in his more mature years practically adopted and confirmed that which he had done in his early youth[1]. Nor will the court interfere where the settlor subsequently acts under the deed, or does something which shows that he recognises its validity; unless, indeed, he was ignorant of the effect of the settlement at the date of such recognition[2].

1 *Turner v Collins* (1871) 7 Ch App 329.
2 *Jarratt v Aldam* (1870) LR 9 Eq 463; *Motz v Moreau* (1860) 13 Moo PCC 376; *Davies v Davies* (1870) LR 9 Eq 468. As to ignorance, see *Lister v Hodgson* (1867) LR 4 Eq 30. Ignorance of the *right* to rescind is no bar to the defence of acquiescence: *Goldsworthy v Brickell* [1987] 1 All ER 853 at 873, CA.

15.49 So where a lady entered a religious sisterhood, and, under circumstances which amounted to undue influence, made a voluntary settlement in its favour, but omitted, for more than six years after severing her connection with it, to seek to have the settlement set aside, it was held that her acquiescence barred her claim for relief. As Lindley LJ said[158]:

> 'In this particular case the plaintiff considered when she left the sisterhood what course she should take, and she determined to do nothing, but to leave matters as they were. She insisted on having back her will, but she never asked for her money until the end of five years or so after she had left the sisterhood. In this state of things I can only come to the conclusion that she deliberately chose not to attempt to avoid her gifts but to acquiesce in them ... I regard this as a question of fact, and upon the evidence I can come to no other conclusion than that which I have mentioned.'

1 *Allcard v Skinner* (1887) 36 Ch D 145. See also *Mitchell v Homfray* (1881) 8 QBD 587, CA.

15.50 On the other hand, in *Bullock v Lloyds Bank Ltd*[1], relief was granted to a settlor who had been aware of objections to the validity of her settlement for four years before the issue of the writ, but during those four years had been endeavouring to recover her property by obtaining the trustee's consent to the exercise by her of a power of revocation which was only exercisable with the consent of the trustee. Moreover, in *Bester v Perpetual Trustee Co Ltd*[2] a woman had a settlement made 20 years earlier when she was 21 set aside, the defence of laches being rejected because no persons other than the two trustees had altered their position on the faith of the validity of the settlement.

1 [1955] Ch 317, [1954] 3 All ER 726. See also *Re Pauling's Settlement Trusts* [1964] Ch 303, [1963] 3 All ER 1, CA.
2 [1970] 3 NSWLR 30 where under her voluntary settlement she was merely a protected life tenant with no access to capital, no right of revocation being reserved.

Change of status: restitutio in integrum

15.51 Even a settlement induced by most serious misrepresentations will not be set aside and cancelled unless the parties can be replaced in their original position. In one case[1], a settlor had married a lady who represented to him that she had divorced her first husband for adultery and cruelty, whereas, in point of fact, she herself had been divorced for adultery at his suit. The settlor, on discovering this, commenced an action to have the settlement set aside. Pearson J dismissed it as being frivolous and vexatious; and the Court of Appeal confirmed his decision, on the ground that the plaintiff could not set aside the settlement and yet keep the only consideration which was given for it, namely, the marriage; one essential condition of cancellation being (as Fry LJ observed) restitutio in integrum, which was there impossible.

[1]   *Johnston v Johnston* (1884) 52 LT 76.

15.52 However, nowadays where no change of status is involved rescission will be ordered if 'the situation is such that by the exercise of its power including the power to take account of profits and to direct inquiries as to allowances for deterioration [the court] can do what is practically just between the parties and restore them substantially to the status quo.'[1] In special circumstances where rescission is impossible equitable compensation may become payable[2].

[1]   *Alati v Kruger* (1955) 94 CLR 216 at 223–224 applied in *O'Sullivan v Management Agency & Music Ltd* [1985] QB 428; *Goode & Durrant Administration v Biddulph* [1994] 2 FLR 551.
[2]   *Mahoney v Purnell* [1996] 3 All ER 61.

Absolute right of claimant or only on making counter-restitution?

15.53 In *TSB v Camfield*[1] the Court of Appeal has taken the strict view that if a claimant establishes a right to set aside a transaction for undue influence or misrepresentation, then it must be set aside entirely, even where she would have agreed to the mortgage on the matrimonial home for £x rather than the actual £2x. The Australian High Court[2] has rejected this so that in such a case the mortgage for £2x would be set aside only on terms that the wife joins in a valid mortgage for £x. it seems likely that the English House of Lords will follow the view of their Australian counterparts. Indeed, Millett J (as he then was) has already indicated[3] the need for counter-restitution to the extent it is proved that the wife actually benefited from the loan that is set aside.

[1]   [1995] 1 All ER 951.
[2]   *Vadasz v Pioneer Concrete SA Pty Ltd* (1995) 184 CLR 102; also see *Maguire v Makaronis* (1998) 188 CLR 449.
[3]   *Dunbar Bank v Nadeem* [1998] 3 All ER 876.

Third parties

15.54 On general principles of property law[1] a court will make no order that would prejudice a person who proves that he or she is a purchaser of a legal or equitable interest in the property for value without notice of the claim to avoid the trust affecting the property or a purchaser protected by statutory overreaching or registration provisions.

1 Subject to Land Registration Act 2002, s 116 which, when in force, will make earlier mere equities to set aside dispositions of registered land bind later purchasers of equitable interests: Law Com no 271, *Land Registration for the 21st Century*, paras 5.32–5.36.

15.55 Where co-owners of a home charge their home to a bank as security for a loan to one co-owner or the company which he operates as a business[1], the issue arises whether or not the other co-owner is to be bound by her apparent consent to the grant of security to the bank if such consent has been vitiated by her co-owner's conduct. The House of Lords[2] has held that this is not a question of priority of competing proprietary interests but one of suretyship contracts, where the burden is on the innocent co-owner to prove that it is unconscionable for the bank-chargee to be able to enforce its charge against her because it had failed to take reasonable steps to satisfy itself that there was no vitiating factor like undue influence or misrepresentation of the other co-owner.

1 No problem arises if the loan appears to be for the benefit of both co-owners; *CIBC Mortgages plc v Pitt* [1994] 1 AC 200.
2 *Royal Bank of Scotland plc v Etridge (No 2)* [2002] 2 AC 773, [2001] UKHL 44, [2001] 4 All ER 449 at paras 40–43, 101, 144–146. Their Lordships detailed the reasonable steps required but they fall outside the scope of a trusts book.

ARTICLE 16
EFFECT OF THE BANKRUPTCY OF THE SETTLOR ON THE
VALIDITY OF A SETTLEMENT

16.1

(1) Where
  (a) an individual[1], 'the settlor', has subjected property to a trust gratuitously or in consideration of marriage or for a consideration the value of which, in money or money's worth, is significantly less than the value, in money or money's worth, of the settlor's consideration[2]; and
  (b) he is adjudged bankrupt either (i) having made such disposition within the period of two years ending with the day of the presentation of the bankruptcy petition[3] or (ii) having made such disposition no less than two years nor more than five years from the day of the presentation of the bankruptcy petition[4] and it is shown that he was insolvent[5] at the time of the disposition or became insolvent in consequence of the disposition, such being rebuttably presumed to be the case where the disposition was in favour of his associates[6],then, on the application of the trustee of the bankrupt's estate, the court must make such

order as it thinks fit for restoring the position to what it would have been if the settlor had not made the disposition[7].

(2) Where

(a) the settlor creates a settlement which desiredly[8] has the effect of putting one of his creditors or a surety or guarantor for any of his debts or liabilities into a position which, in the event of the settlor's bankruptcy, will be better than the position he would have been in if the settlement had not been created; and[9]

(b) the settlor is adjudged bankrupt either (i) having given such preferential treatment to an associate of his within two years of the day of the presentation of the bankruptcy petition[10] or (ii) having given such preferential treatment in any other case within six months of the day of the presentation of the bankruptcy petition[11]; and

(c) the settlor at the time of the preferential treatment was insolvent or became insolvent in consequence of such preference[12], then on the application of the trustee of the bankrupt's estate the court must make such order as it thinks fit for restoring the position to what it would have been if the settlor had not given such preferential treatment[13].

(3) A court order cannot prejudice any interest in property which was acquired from a person other than the settlor and was acquired in good faith for value and without notice of the relevant circumstances, nor prejudice any interest deriving from such an interest, nor require a person who received a benefit from the disposition in good faith for value and without notice of the relevant circumstances to pay a sum to the trustee of the bankrupt's estate except where he was a party to the disposition[14].

1   For corporate settlors see Insolvency Act 1986, ss 238 and 239.
2   Insolvency Act 1986, s 339(3). The court must determine the actual value of the transferred property against which the consideration therefor must be measured: *Jones v National Westminster Bank plc* [2001] EWCA Civ 1541, [2002] BPIR 361.
3   Insolvency Act 1986, ss 339(1), 341(1)(2). Where the settlor has been made criminally bankrupt under s 264(1)(d) it is only necessary that the disposition was made on or after the date specified for the purposes of s 341(4) in the criminal bankruptcy order.
4   Insolvency Act 1986, ss 339(1), 341(1)(2).
5   Insolvency Act 1986, s 341(3).
6   Insolvency Act 1986, s 435.
7   Insolvency Act 1986, s 339(2).
8   Insolvency Act 1986, s 340(4); *Re M C Bacon Ltd* [1991] Ch 127. Preferences in favour of an associate are rebuttably presumed to be desired to improve his position. The section has extra-territorial effect as concerns persons preferred: *Re Paramount Airways Ltd* [1993] Ch 223: s 340(5).
9   Insolvency Act 1986, s 340(3).
10 Insolvency Act 1986, s 341(1)(b).
11 Insolvency Act 1986, s 341(1)(c).
12 Insolvency Act 1986, s 341(2).

The Insolvency Act 1986

16.2 Sections 339, 341 and 342 of the Insolvency Act 1986 have replaced provisions, formerly in s 42 of the Bankruptcy Act 1914, which enabled dispositions to be set aside pro tanto where the dispositions were made within two years of the bankruptcy or after two but within ten years where the bankrupt was not solvent at the date of the disposition without the aid of the property comprised in it. The old case law on what amounts to a gratuitous disposition still remains good so that the new provisions will catch a house purchased by H in the name of W[1] or an agreement that a house purchased by H in H's name will be owned by them jointly so leading W to act to her detriment, though not having provided half the purchase moneys for the half share she is intended to have[2]. Similarly, in estimating solvency where the settlor reserves for himself a life interest out of the disposition it seems that the life interest should still be taken into account[3]. Where H lets out his farmhouse and land to W at a full market rent as a protected tenancy the court will still look to the transaction as a whole (eg the safeguarding of the family home and the farming business and the 'ransom' surrender value to permit H's mortgagee to take vacant possession and enforce the security) and so set aside the transaction[4].

1 *Re A Debtor* [1965] 3 All ER 453, [1965] 1 WLR 1498.
2 *Re Densham (a bankrupt)* [1975] 3 All ER 726, [1975] 1 WLR 1519.
3 *Re Lowndes* (1887) 18 QBD 677.
4 *Agricultural Mortgage Corpn v Woodward* [1996] 1 FLR 226, CA.

16.3 The Court of Appeal decision in *Clarkson v Clarkson*[1] is illuminating on the ambit of s 339. A, B and C were directors and equal shareholders in ABC Ltd which they valued at £1.5 million. To cater for the death of any of them and provide the cash to buy out the deceased they each took out in 1989 an insurance policy for £0.5 million. C's policy was held on trust by A, B and C with power to appoint to C's spouse and issue or A and B, and in default of appointment for A and B equally. The premiums in respect of the policy that C took out were deducted from his remuneration by the company, and afterwards paid for directly by C and after his bankruptcy by his family. ABC Ltd had become insolvent in 1991 and had gone into administrative receivership. The guarantees of A, B and C for the company's indebtedness were invoked in October 1991. In November 1992 A, B and C as trustees appointed the proceeds of the policy to Mrs C. In February 1993 A, B and C were adjudicated bankrupt.

1 (26 April 1994, unreported).

16.4 It was argued against Mrs C that she had benefited from a transaction at an undervalue within two years of the bankruptcy of A, B and C within s 339. After all, A, B and C could have appointed everything to A and B, or by refusing to co-operate in any proposed appointment by C, A and B could have engineered matters so that they took in default of appointment.

16.5 The Court of Appeal held that the creation of the trust in 1989 by C was a gift by C, and the appointment in 1992:

> 'was merely the exercise of a fiduciary power to select the person to whom the gift should go. It has been for centuries a principle that an appointment under a special power takes effect as if it had been written into the instrument creating the power. The appointee takes the property of the settlor and not that of the donee of the power. So, if the settlement had been made less than two years before the bankruptcy petition was presented it would have been open to attack under section 339. But since it was made earlier and at a time when Mr Clarkson was solvent it cannot be set aside ... This is a very simple case. Mr Clarkson made a gift into settlement which has vested in his wife. That gift is unaffected by his subsequent bankruptcy more than two years later, and the fact that the trustees who jointly exercised the power in favour of the wife became bankrupt less than two years afterwards is irrelevant.'

16.6 The new provisions have much more flexibility than the old provisions. To restore the position to what it would have been if the settlor had not made the gift, the court can require any property transferred as part of the transaction to be vested in the trustee of the bankrupt's estate as well as any property representing in any person's hands the application either of the proceeds of sale of property so transferred or of money so transferred[1]. The court can also require any person to pay in respect of benefits received by him (eg as beneficiary under the settlor's settlement) such sums to the trustee of the bankrupt settlor's estate as the court may direct[2]. The court may provide for a person against whom it makes an order to be able to prove in the settlor's bankruptcy, eg for debts incurred for less than full consideration[3].

[1]   Insolvency Act 1986, s 342(1)(a) and (b).
[2]   Insolvency Act 1986, s 342(1)(d).
[3]   Insolvency Act 1986, s 342(1)(g).

Dispositions in the two to five year period

16.7 An individual is treated as insolvent if (a) he is unable to pay his debts as they fall due or (b) the value of his assets is less than the amount of his liabilities, taking into account his contingent and prospective liabilities[1]. For the presumption of insolvency, where the transaction at an undervalue is with an associate of the settlor, there is a broad and lengthy statutory definition[2] of an associate, but a person who is an associate by reason only of being the settlor's employee is deemed not to be an associate[3]. For present purposes it suffices that an associate of the settlor includes his spouse, his relatives and their spouses, her relatives and their spouses, his partners and their spouses and relatives. A person in his capacity as trustee of a trust is an associate of X if the trust beneficiaries include, or the trust terms confer, a power that may be exercised for the benefit of X or an associate of X[4].

[1]   Insolvency Act 1986, s 341(2). Such liabilities would not seem to extend to future uncertain liabilities.
[2]   Insolvency Act 1986, s 435.
[3]   Insolvency Act 1986, s 341(2).

⁴ Insolvency Act 1986, s 435(5). But there is an exception where the body of trustees manages a pension trust or an employee share scheme: *Re Thirty-Eight Building Ltd* [1999] 1 BCLC 416.

Unfair preferences

16.8 The principles just discussed deal with transactions at an undervalue and not with the case where full consideration has been provided. Where an individual[1] has many creditors for value it is clearly unfair for him to give preferential treatment to some creditors (eg by creating a settlement on a creditor, his spouse and issue in satisfaction of the debt) at a time when he is insolvent so that the remaining creditors will be prejudiced in the event of his bankruptcy. Thus the Insolvency Act 1986 in ss 340, 341 and 342 extends to cover unfair preferences as well as transactions at an undervalue[2]. A preference will only be unfair if there was a subjective positive desire to improve the creditor's position[3].

¹ For companies see s 239.
² On 'undervalue' see *Re Kumar* [1993] 2 All ER 700.
³ *Re M C Bacon Ltd* [1991] Ch 127.

No prejudice to persons without notice of relevant circumstances

16.9 A problem arises from the fact that a purchaser from a donee of unregistered land will inevitably have notice of relevant circumstances so freezing the land in his hands for two or perhaps, five years. Thus the Insolvency (No 2) Act 1994 amends s 342 so that a purchaser will only be vulnerable if he was either an associate of the person initiating the undervalue transaction or preference or of the person benefiting under it, or if he can be shown to have had knowledge of the bankruptcy or pending bankruptcy.

Criminal offences

16.10 By virtue of ss 357 and 352 of the Insolvency Act 1986 a bankrupt is guilty of an offence if in the five years before his bankruptcy commenced he made or caused to be made any gift or transfer of or any charge on his property unless he proves that at the time of such conduct he had no intent to defraud or to conceal the state of his affairs. Conduct defrauding creditors covers transactions entered into for the purpose of putting assets beyond the reach of a person who is making, or may at some time make, a claim against him or of otherwise prejudicing the interests of such a person in relation to the claim which he is making or may make as appears from s 423(3) discussed below in Article 17. Assisting a person to commit such a crime will be an offence under the general aiding and abetting offence in the Accessories and Abettors Act 1861, s 8 as amended by the Criminal Law Act 1977; those involved in asset protection trusts must beware.

ARTICLE 17
EFFECT OF SETTLEMENTS INTENDED TO PREJUDICE CREDITORS
WHETHER OR NOT SETTLOR BECOMES BANKRUPT

17.1

(1)   Where
  (a)   a person, 'the settlor', has subjected property to a trust gratuitously or in consideration of marriage or for a consideration the value of which, in money or money's worth, is significantly less than the value, in money or money's worth, of the settlor's consideration[1], and;
  (b)   the court is satisfied that the settlement was entered into for the purpose[2] of putting assets beyond the reach of a person[3] who is making or may at some time make a claim against the settlor, or of otherwise prejudicing the interests of such claimant or potential claimant[4], then the court may make such order as it thinks fit for restoring the position to what it would have been if the settlement had not been entered into and for protecting the interests of prejudiced persons[5].

(2)   A court order cannot prejudice any interest in property which was acquired from a person other than the settlor and was acquired in good faith for value and without notice of the relevant circumstances, nor prejudice any interest deriving from such an interest, nor require a person who received a benefit from the settlement in good faith for value and without notice of the relevant circumstances to pay any sum unless he was a party to the settlement[6].

---

[1]   Insolvency Act 1986, s 423(1). The court must assess from the transferor-settlor's viewpoint whether any consideration provided was significantly less than the ascertained value received: *Jones v National Westminster Bank plc* [2001] EWCA Civ 1541, [2002] BPIR 361. Valuation can take account of subsequent events: *Re Thoars Reid v Ramlort Limited [2002] EWHC 2416 (Ch)* [2003] 1 BCLC 499 (assignment of life policy one week after assignor learned of assured's imminent death which followed two months later).
[2]   As to need for a 'substantial' purpose see *IRC v Hashmi* [2002] WTLR 19 at 28–29.
[3]   Any person anywhere: *Re Paramount Airways Ltd* [1993] Ch 223, CA. Leave to serve outside the jurisdiction needs to be sought, e g under CPR 6.20(10) if the claim relates to property located within the jurisdiction: *Banca Carige v Banco Nacional de Cuba* [2001] 3 All ER 923.
[4]   Insolvency Act 1986, s 423(3).
[5]   Insolvency Act 1986, s 423(2).
[6]   Insolvency Act 1986, s 425(2).

Insolvency cases

17.2   In a case where the settlor has been adjudged bankrupt or is a company which is being wound up or in relation to which an administration order is in force, the application for an order under s 423 of the Insolvency Act 1986 must be by the Official Receiver, by the trustee of the bankrupt's estate or the liquidator or administrator of the company or, with the leave of the court, by a person who is, or is capable of being, prejudiced by the settlement[1].

1   Insolvency Act 1986, s 424(1)(a).

17.3 In a case where a person who is, or is capable of being, prejudiced by the settlement is bound by a voluntary arrangement under Pts I or VIII of the Insolvency Act 1986, the application must be by the supervisor of the voluntary arrangement or by any person who (whether or not so bound) is, or is capable of being, so prejudiced[1].

1   Insolvency Act 1986, s 424(1)(b).

17.4 Any application is treated as made on behalf of every victim of the relevant transaction(s)[1].

1   Insolvency Act 1986, s. 424 (2).

Other cases

17.5 In any other case any person who is or is capable of being prejudiced by the settlement may apply to the court but whenever an application is made in relation to a settlement it is treated as made on behalf of every person who is, or is capable of being, prejudiced by the settlement[1]. A trustee against whom hostile litigation has been brought challenging the validity of the settlement does not have a duty to defend the trust but is obliged to remain neutral and offer to submit to the court's directions where there are rival claimants to the beneficial interest able to fight their own battles, though he will be entitled to an indemnity and a lien for his costs necessarily and properly incurred in serving a defence, agreeing to submit to the court's direction and in making discovery[2].

1   Insolvency Act 1986, s 424(1)(c), (2).
2   *Alsop Wilkinson v Neary* [1995] 1 All ER 431; see paras 87.36–87.38.

Onus of proof

17.6 The onus of proof is on the applicant[1] to show that the settlement was a transaction entered into for the purpose of putting assets beyond the reach of a person who is making or may make a claim against the settlor or of otherwise prejudicing the interests of such claimant or potential claimant. However, once the applicant has established his case[2], then it seems that a person seeking escape from having an order made against him must discharge the onus of showing that he falls within the protection afforded by s 425(2), eg proving good faith, value and lack of notice of the relevant circumstances, which will include the debtor's substantial purpose to prejudice creditors[3].

1   *Law Society v Southall* [2001] WTLR 719 at 729–730, per Hart J.
2   On requisite evidence see *Law Society v Southall* [2001] EWCA Civ 2001, [2002] WTLR 1151reversing Hart J's refusal to strike out the claim.

3   Cf *Lloyds Bank Ltd v Marcan* [1973] 3 All ER 754, [1973] 1 WLR 1387 on Law of Property Act 1925, s 172 (now repealed due to the broader effect of s 423 of the 1986 Act). Notice will include constructive notice, cf *Lloyds Bank Ltd v Marcan* [1973] 2 All ER 359 at 369 per Pennycuick V-C.

Flexible orders

17.7 Inter alia court orders may provide for any property transferred as part of the settlement to be vested in any person either absolutely or for the benefit of all the persons on whose behalf the application is treated as made[1], or for any property to be so vested if it represents in any person's hands the application either of the proceeds of sale of property so transferred or of money so transferred[2]. The order may also require any person to pay to any other person in respect of benefits received from the settlor such sums as the court may direct[3].

1   Insolvency Act 1986, s 425(1)(a). See *Law Society v Southall* [2001] WTLR 719 at 726–727 and *Chohan v Saggar (No 2)* [1992] BCC 750.
2   Insolvency Act 1986, s 425(1)(b).
3   Insolvency Act 1986, s 425(1)(d).

Liberal time limit for claims

17.8 There is a twelve year time limit for an action on a specialty which is a covenant under seal or an obligation, like that in the Insolvency Act, imposed by statute[1] (except that if the action is to recover a sum of money recoverable by statute, a six year period applies[2]). However, time does not begin to run when the relevant transaction was entered into for the purpose of putting assets beyond the reach of actual or potential victims. If an action is brought by a trustee in bankruptcy, time does not begin to run till the date of the bankruptcy order – and the action is for the collective benefit of all victims[3]. If the action is brought by a victim it seems likely that he cannot be a victim until his debtor becomes insolvent[4] and time does not begin to run till then.

1   *Hill v Spread Trustee Co Ltd* [2006] EWCA Civ 542 para 116, (2006) Times, 10 July, Limitation Act 1980 s. 8.
2   Limitation Act 1980 s. 9.
3   *Hill v Spread Trustee Co Ltd* [2006] EWCA Civ 542, paras 145,151,152 (2006) Times, 10 July, Insolvency Act 1986 s. 424 (2).
4   *Hill v Spread Trustee Co Ltd* [2006] EWCA Civ 542, para 125 (2006) Times, 10 July.

Settlements impeachable even if unascertainable future creditors

17.9 The new statutory section avoids the difficulties of interpretation that surrounded s 172 of the Law of Property Act 1925[1]. It probably encapsulates the effect of the old case law[2] so that an attempt to prejudice future creditors, even though there may be no existing creditors, will suffice to make a transaction impeachable, eg where H transfers his house to trustees on trust for his wife, remainder to his children or purchases a house in the name of his wife alone or puts his house into the joint names of himself and his wife on trust for each other equally. As Jessel MR stated[3],

17.9   Validity of declared trusts in relation to latent matters

'a man is not entitled to go into a hazardous business, and immediately before doing so, settle all his property voluntarily, the object being this: "If I succeed in business, I make a fortune for myself. If I fail, I leave my creditors unpaid. They will bear the loss." That is the very thing the Statute of Elizabeth[4] was meant to prevent.'

1   See 13th Edition hereof pp 211–219.
2   *Mackay v Douglas* (1872) LR 14 Eq 106; *Re Butterworth* (1882) 19 Ch D 588, CA; *Cadogan v Cadogan* [1977] 1 All ER 200, [1977] 1 WLR 1041.
3   *Re Butterworth* (1882) 19 Ch D 588 at 598; *Midland Bank v Wyatt* [1995] 1 FLR 697.
4   The predecessor of Law of Property Act 1925, s 172.

17.10   Thus, if a professional man about to become a partner is worried that the amount of professional indemnity assurance cover may prove insufficient for possible future claims so that he had better preserve his house as his major asset, and so vests it in his wife as sole absolute beneficial owner or on trust for his wife for life, remainder to their children, then it seems that the transaction will be impeachable, irrespective of the man being adjudged bankrupt and so quite apart from investigating any possibilities under the Insolvency Act 1986 ss 339, 341 and 342. If the conscience of an existing partner is pricked by fear that certain events that have already occurred may lead to a negligence claim then he will clearly fall within s 423 if he then off-loads significant assets on to trustees for his family. After all, there is a clear actual fraudulent intent aimed at the particular subsequent creditor rather than a predominant anxiety that any person may somehow someday make a claim. It seems harsh that the latter suffices to make settlements impeachable for a lengthy period according to *Re Butterworth*. If circumstances arise to highlight such harshness, it may be that *Re Butterworth* might be able to be circumvented if the court is prepared to find that the reference in s 423(3) to purposely putting assets beyond the reach of 'a person' [not 'any person'] requires the purpose of prejudicing a particular subsequent creditor whose debt was in contemplation at the time of the prejudicial transaction[1]. This point was not argued in *Midland Bank plc v Wyatt* where s 423 was held to cover the voluntary disposition of assets to avoid future but unknown creditors and whether or not the transferor was about to enter into a hazardous business or whether his business was as sole practitioner or as partner or as participant in a limited liability company where personal guarantees are normally required.

1   *Law Society v Southall* [2001] WTLR 719 at 730.

PURPOSE: PREDOMINANT, SUBSTANTIAL OR SIGNIFICANT

17.11   The claimant must prove 'that the transaction was entered into for the purpose of putting assets beyond the reach of[1] an existing or potential creditor or 'of otherwise prejudicing the interests of such a person'. Purpose seems to have the same meaning as 'object', 'end' or 'with a view to' and stops short at what was in a man's mind[2] so that it does not include the necessary effect of an act[3]. Thus, identical transactions carried out by different settlors may have different results[4]. Putting assets beyond the reach of creditors, or otherwise prejudicing them may be a necessary effect of a transaction without it being a purpose of the transaction. If the settlor had more than one purpose (eg where another purpose is to minimise liability to inheritance tax) the settlement will be impeachable if the predominant[5] or substantial[6] purpose was prejudicing creditors, substantial purpose extending to a purpose of equal power with another purpose[7], and it is possible that it would be impeachable if prejudicing creditors was a significant purpose but of less power than another purpose[8]. Some hallmarks of such purpose may include the following[9]: virtually all the settlor's assets may have been settled, the settlement may have been carried out secretly or in great haste, false statements may be found in the recitals, the settlor may continue to remain in possession of the settled property or retain some advantage under the terms of the settlement. In *Agricultural Mortgage Corpn v Woodward*[10] the Court of Appeal held that where a farmer granted a protected agricultural tenancy of his farm to his wife at full market value in order to prevent his major creditor from obtaining vacant possession of the farm with a view to enforcement of the debt the transaction could be set aside under s 423. The wife achieved benefits greater than those conferred by the value of the consideration provided by her, namely the safeguarding of the family home, the carrying on of the family farming business and a 'ransom' surrender value against the creditor: the substantial detriment incurred by the creditor was largely matched by the substantial benefit conferred on the wife beyond the rights conferred by the tenancy agreement for which she provided full market value.

[1]   Cf the language used by Russell LJ in *Lloyds Bank Ltd v Marcan* [1973] 3 All ER 754 at 759.
[2]   This is a question of fact.
[3]   In a tax context see *IRC v Brebner* (1966) 43 TC 705 at 713 per Lord Clyde and Lord Pearce [1967] 2 AC 18 at 27–28, HL 'that which has to be ascertained was the object (not the effect) of each interrelated transaction in its actual context', and *Mallalieu v Drummond (Inspector of Taxes)* [1983] 2 AC 861 at 870, HL 'The object of the taxpayer in making the expenditure must be distinguished from the effect of the expenditure.' Intention goes beyond purpose in including necessary effects and so is objective: *Re M C Bacon Ltd* [1991] Ch 127.
[4]   Cf *Philippi v IRC* [1971] 3 All ER 61, [1971] 1 WLR 1272, CA.
[5]   *Chohan v Saggar* [1992] BCC 306 at 323; *Midland Bank plc v Wyatt* [1995] 1 FLR 697.
[6]   *Royscott Spa Leasing Ltd v Loverr* [1995] BCC 502, CA; *Hill v Spread Trustee Company Limited* [2006] EWCA Civ 542 para 131, (2006) Times, 10 July..
[7]   It would be odd if a claim failed because although the statutory purpose exists another purpose exists of equal power: *IRC v Hashmi* [2002] WTLR 19 at 29 endorsing *Pinewood Joinery v Starelm Properties Ltd* [1994] 2 BCLC 412 at 418.
[8]   *IRC v Hashmi* [2002] WTLR 19 at 28–29.
[9]   *Twyne's Case* (1602) 3 Co Rep 80b; *Re Sinclair* (1884) 26 Ch D 319, CA; *Lloyds Bank Ltd v Marcan* [1973] 3 All ER 754, [1973] 1 WLR 1387.
[10] [1995] 1 BCLC 1.

17.12 Lawyer-client privilege from disclosure of documents cannot be claimed by the client where there is a strong prima facie case that the purpose of the transaction involving the use of the solicitor was to prejudice a creditor[1].

[1]   *Barclays Bank plc v Eustice* [1995] 1 WLR 1238, CA; also see *Kuwait Airways Corpn v Iraqi Airways Company (No 6)* [2005] EWCA Civ 286, [2005] 1 WLR 2734.

ARTICLE 18
WHEN A TRUST DESIGNED TO DEFEAT DEPENDANTS MAY BE SET
ASIDE PRO TANTO UNDER A COURT ORDER

18.1

(1) Under the Matrimonial Causes Act 1973, s 37, a reviewable disposition of property may be set aside by the court if made with the intention of defeating a person's claim for financial relief under ss 22, 23, 24, 27, 31 (except sub-s 6) and 35 of the said Act. Any disposition of property, eg to trustees, is a reviewable disposition[1] unless made for valuable consideration (other than marriage) to a person who, at the time of the disposition, acted in relation to it in good faith and without notice of any intent to defeat a claim for financial relief;

(2) Under the Inheritance (Provision for Family and Dependants) Act 1975, s 10, a disposition of property, eg to trustees, may be set aside by the court if (i) made less than six years before his death by the deceased with the intention of defeating an application for financial provision under the said Act and (ii) if full valuable consideration[2] for the disposition was not given by the person to whom or for the benefit of whom the disposition was made ('the donee') and (iii) if the exercise of the court's power to set aside the disposition pro tanto by ordering a sum of money or other property to be provided will facilitate the making of financial provision for the applicant under the said Act. Similarly a contract to leave property by will cannot defeat an application for financial provision under the said Act unless made for full valuable consideration[3].

[1] Matrimonial Causes Act 1973, s 37(4).
[2] On the meaning of this see *Re Wilkinson* [1978] Fam 22, [1978] 1 All ER 221. Marriage is not valuable consideration: s 25(1).
[3] Inheritance (Provision for Family and Dependants) Act 1975, ss 11 and 12(2).

Paragraph 1

18.2 An intent to defeat a person's claim for financial relief is an intent to prevent financial relief from being granted to that person or to that person for the benefit of a child of the family or to reduce the amount of any financial relief that might be so granted or to frustrate or impede the enforcement of any court order which might be or has been made[1].

[1] Matrimonial Causes Act 1973, s 37(1).

18.3 Where the application to the court is made within three years of the disposition it is to be presumed, unless the contrary is shown[1], that the disposition was made with intent to defeat the applicant's claim for financial relief[2]. The intent does not need to be the respondent's sole intent[3]. The court may give consequential directions[4] for giving effect to its order which may cover property abroad[5] though, it seems, not the proceeds of sale of property previously disposed of by a purchaser with notice of a husband's intent to defeat his wife's claim by selling property to the purchaser[6]. For a purchaser to lack good faith requires 'something akin to fraud: at the very least it connotes a lack of honesty'[7]. Notice covers constructive notice[8] as well as actual notice.

1   As in *Shipman v Shipman* [1991] 1 FLR 250.
2   Matrimonial Causes Act 1973, s 37(5); *Whittingham v Whittingham* [1979] Fam 9, [1978] 3 All ER 805.
3   Cf *Re Kennedy* [1980] CLY 2820; *Kemmis v Kemmis* [1988] 1 WLR 1307, CA.
4   *Green v Green (Barclays Bank, Third Party)* [1981] 1 All ER 97, [1981] 1 WLR 391 holding these are incidental ancillary powers.
5   *Hamlin v Hamlin* [1986] Fam 11, [1985] 2 All ER 1037, CA.
6   *Sherry v Sherry* [1991] 1 FLR 307, CA; J. Fortis [1991] Conv 370.
7   *Whittingham v Whittingham* [1979] Fam 9 at 12, [1978] 3 All ER 805 at 808.
8   *Kemmis v Kemmis* [1988] 1 WLR 1307, CA; *Sherry v Sherry* [1991] 1 FLR 307.

18.4 'Disposition' does not include any provision in a will or codicil but otherwise includes any conveyance, assurance or gift of property of any description whether made by an instrument or otherwise[1].

1   Matrimonial Causes Act 1973, s 37(6). The section does not apply to the case where H and W are leasehold joint tenants and H serves a notice to quit on the landlord (which could be a body of trustees): *Newlon Housing Trust v Al-Sulaimen* [1999] 1 AC 313; but the court can grant an injunction to restrain serving such a notice or require an undertaking to be given to it: *Baker v Greenwich London Borough Council* [1999] 4 All ER 944.

Paragraph 2

18.5 An arbitrary six year time limit applies here[1]. The requisite intent will be present if the court is of opinion that on a balance of probabilities the intention of the deceased (though not necessarily his sole intention)[2] in making the disposition or contract was to prevent an order for financial provision being made or to reduce the amount of the financial provision that might otherwise be made[3]. A disposition does not include an appointment under a special power of appointment so the appointee will be safe so long as the settlement was made more than six years before the death of the deceased settlor[4].

1   Inheritance (Provision for Family and Dependants) Act 1975, s 10(2)(a).
2   *Re Dawkins, Dawkins v Judd* [1986] 2 FLR 360, [1986] Fam Law 295; *Hanbury v Hanbury* [1999] 2 FLR 255.
3   Inheritance (Provision for Family and Dependants) Act 1975, s 12(1).
4   Inheritance (Provision for Family and Dependants) Act 1975, s 10(7).

18.6 Where an application is made under s 10 of the 1975 Act in respect of a disposition made by the deceased to trustees or, under s 11, in respect of any payment made or property transferred, in accordance with a contract made by the deceased, to trustees then the court's powers are expressly limited[1]. The amount of money or the value of any property that the court can order to be provided *cannot*

(i)   in the case of a disposition or contract consisting of the payment of money, exceed the aggregate of so much of that money as is at the date of the court order in the hands of the trustees and the value at that date of any property which represents that money or is derived therefrom and is at that date in the hands of the trustees;

(ii)   in the case of a disposition or contract consisting of the transfer of property (other than money), exceed the aggregate of the value at the date of the court order of so much of that property as is at that date in the hands of the trustee and the value at that date of any property which represents the first-mentioned property or is derived therefrom and is at that date in the hands of the trustees.

[1]   Inheritance (Provision for Family and Dependants) Act 1975, s 13(1).

18.7 Furthermore, the trustees are not to be liable for having distributed any money or other property on the ground they ought to have taken into account the possibility that an application might be made under ss 10 or 11 of the 1975 Act[1]. Of course, beneficiaries receiving such money or other property may be subject to a court order[2].

[1]   Inheritance (Provision for Family and Dependants) Act 1975, s 13(2).
[2]   Inheritance (Provision for Family and Dependants) Act 1975, ss 10(2)(b), 11(2)(c).

ARTICLE 19
MISCELLANEOUS INSTANCES WHERE A TRUST MAY BE SET ASIDE TO THWART CRIMINALS

19.1

There are miscellaneous legislative instances where the court can confiscate what are, or are regarded as, the proceeds of crime in a trust fund created by a criminal.

19.2 Outside the scope of this work are wide-ranging tracing and confiscation provisions in statutes concerned with the proceeds of drug-trafficking, terrorism and other serious crimes, whether in the hands of the criminal or of trustees of trusts created by the criminal or of beneficiaries of such trusts[1]. Even 'clean' money can be attacked so as to deal with the criminal who lives off his 'black' criminal money, so that he can afford to put his 'white' money, earned or inherited by him, into the trust. Various assumptions against the criminal are made where he had a criminal lifestyle[2].

[1]   Part IV Criminal Justice Act 1988 as amended by Pt III Criminal Justice Act 1993, and Proceeds of Crime Acts 1995 and 2002; Anti-terrorism, Crime and Security Act 2001 (enabling gains of trustees to be traced and recovered rather than only the original value of the benefit received as under the CJA 1988 as amended); Serious Organised Crime and Police Act 2005.
[2]   Proceeds of Crime Act 2002, s 11.

Chapter 5

THE INTERPRETATION OF EXECUTORY TRUSTS

ARTICLE 20
EXECUTORY TRUSTS NOT CONSTRUED AS STRICTLY AS
EXECUTED TRUSTS

20.1

(1)   In the construction of executed trusts of legal or equitable interests in property, technical terms are construed in their legal and technical sense[1].

(2)   In the construction of executory trusts (as defined in Article 6), the court is not confined to the language used. Where, therefore, such language is improper or informal[2], or would create a wholly or partly void trust[3], or one which is impossible to execute[4], or would otherwise defeat the settlor's intentions, as gathered from the motives which led to the settlement, and from its general object and purpose, or from other instruments to which it refers, or from any circumstances which may have influenced the settlor's mind[5], the court will direct a settlement to be executed in such form as will best answer the intent of the parties[6], unless the executory trust instrument required the consent of some third party who refused consent in circumstances where the court

367

could not find that such refusal was in breach of a fiduciary obligation or a contractual obligation not unreasonably to withhold consent[7].

1   *Wright v Pearson* (1758) 1 Eden 119; *Austen v Taylor* (1759) 1 Eden 361; *Brydges v Brydges* (1796) 3 Ves 120; *Jervoise v Duke of Northumberland* (1820) 1 Jac & W 559; *Re Whiston's Settlement* [1894] 1 Ch 661.
2   See *Earl Stamford v Hobart* (1710) 3 Bro Parl Cas 31.
3   *Humberston v Humberston* (1716) 1 P Wms 332.
4   *Re Shelton's Settled Estates* [1945] Ch 158, [1945] 1 All ER 283.
5   See per Lord Chelmsford in *Sackville-West v Viscount Holmesdale* (1870) LR 4 HL 543.
6   *Earl Stamford v Hobart* (1710) 3 Bro Parl Cas 31; *Surtees v Surtees* (1871) LR 12 Eq 400; and see *Cogan v Duffield* (1876) 2 Ch D 44. As to the construction to be placed on an executory trust of heirlooms, see *Re Beresford-Hope* [1917] 1 Ch 287, where the form of settlement is indicated, and *Re Steele's Will Trusts* [1948] Ch 603, [1948] 2 All ER 193.
7   *Davis v Richards & Wallington Industries Ltd* [1991] 2 All ER 563 at 589 where a definitive pension trust deed required the consent of the trustees as fiduciaries and the consent of the employer-company's subsidiary companies not as fiduciaries but as a contractual obligation.

Paragraph 1

20.2 The general rule with regard to executed trusts is as stated above, and the omission of apt words of limitation from equitable estates in land created by deed before 1926 was held by the Court of Appeal in *Re Bostock's Settlement*[1] to reduce the estate so given to a life estate only, even though a clear intention to pass the fee simple could be found.

1   [1921] 2 Ch 469, applying the principle in *Re Whiston's Settlement* [1894] 1 Ch 661, and overruling *Re Tringham's Trusts* [1904] 2 Ch 487.

20.3 The point is not now of great practical importance since the necessity for words of limitation was abolished in deeds executed after 1925 except for executed trusts creating entails[1], but since 1996 no new entails may be created[2]. Moreover, the court will in appropriate cases rectify a settlement by the insertion of words of limitation where it is satisfied on the evidence afforded by the document that they were omitted by mistake, and without them the document would not give effect to the intention of the parties[3]. However, if a testator by will gave his 'personal property' to his executor and trustee on trust for beneficiaries real property would not be part of the trust[4].

1   See ss 60, 130, 131 Law of Property Act 1925.
2   Trusts of Land and Appointment of Trustees Act 1996, s 2 and Sch 1, para 5.
3   *Banks v Ripley* [1940] Ch 719, [1940] 3 All ER 49.
4   *Re Cook* [1948] Ch 212.

Paragraph 2

Distinction between executed and executory trusts well settled

20.4 This rule has been acted on for over 300 years, and was stated by Lord Cowper[1] in 1710 in the following words:

'In matters executory, as in the case of articles or a will directing a conveyance, where the words of the articles or will are improper or informal, this court will not direct a conveyance according to such improper or informal expressions in the articles or will, but will order the conveyance or settlement to be made out in a proper and legal manner, so it may best answer the intent of the parties.'

[1] *Earl Stamford v Hobart* (1710) 3 Bro Parl Cas 31. Also see *Papillon v Voice* (1728) 2 P Wms 471; *Trevor v Trevor* (1847) 1 HL Cas 239; *Parker v Bolton* (1835) 5 LJ Ch 98; and *Thompson v Fisher* (1870) LR 10 Eq 207.

20.5 More recently, the Court of Appeal[1] in dealing with an executory charitable trust accepted that 'although the objects of a trust must be certain, it is not essential that the instrument creating the trust should mark out precisely the interests which the objects are to take in the trust property; that may be left to be done by formal settlement to be prepared afterwards.' The case concerned a trust to provide a Fellowship in Paediatric Surgery at a specified hospital, to be set up and its scope determined by a named paediatrician or the head of the Department of Paediatric Surgery.

[1] *Harris v Sharp* [2003] WTLR 1541.

20.6 Executory trusts nowadays most commonly arise in the creation of pension trusts[1]. There are very many old cases on executory trusts in contracts for settlements on marriage, commonly known as marriage articles. Such articles, however fell out of use a long time ago in preference for executed trusts leaving no room for the implication of provisions[2].

[1] Eg *Davis v Richards and Wallington Industries Limited* [1991] 2 All ER 563.
[2] For such provisions see *Cogan v Duffield* (1876) 2 Ch D 44 at 49.

Where strict construction would make execution impossible or the trust void

20.7 Equity will not permit a referential trust to fail and the intentions of the settlor to be frustrated for want of the necessary ingenuity of adaptation and will direct it to be executed cy-près where execution modo et forma is impossible[1]; but this power of adaptation will not be resorted to merely to suit altered circumstances where execution of the original trusts remains possible[2].

[1] *Re Shelton's Settled Estates* [1945] Ch 158, [1945] 1 All ER 283.
[2] *Re Benett-Stanford Settlement Trusts* [1947] 1 All ER 888.

20.8 Similarly, the words of an executory trust will be departed from where a strict construction would render the trust void. Thus, in an early case[1] a testator devised lands to a corporation, in trust to convey to A for life, and afterwards, upon the death of A, to his first son for life, and then to the first son of that first son for life, with remainder (in default of issue male of A) to B for life, and to his sons and their sons in like manner. That was, of course, an attempt to create a perpetuity, yet Lord Cowper held that the device ought to be complied with, so far as was consistent with the rules of law, and he directed that all the sons already born at the testator's death should take estates for life, with limitations to their unborn sons in tail. It must, however, be remembered that where the words of an instrument are plain they are construed as they stand, and without regard to the consequences of the rule against perpetuities when applied thereto. It is only where the meaning of the words used is not plain and unambiguous that the court will in construing the instrument have regard to such consequences[2].

1   *Humberston v Humberston* (1716) 1 P Wms 332; *Williams v Teale* (1847) 6 Hare 239. See also *Re Mountgarret* [1919] 2 Ch 294.
2   *Re Flavel's Will Trusts* [1969] 2 All ER 232, [1969] 1 WLR 444.

20.9 Since the Perpetuities and Accumulations Act 1964 if a trust would be void at common law one waits for the period of statutory lives plus twenty-one years to see if someone might acquire a vested interest outside such period, in which eventuality a resulting trust arises[1], except for a class gift eg for my great-grandchildren. In the latter case the class is closed to include only great-grandchildren alive at the expiry of the statutory period[2]. In other cases it may be possible to construe executory trusts so as to oust any resulting trust.

1   Perpetuities and Accumulations Act 1964, s 3(1), (2), (3).
2   Perpetuities and Accumulations Act 1964, s 4(3), (4).

ARTICLE 21
HOW FAR THE WIFE IS BOUND BY COVENANTS TO
SETTLE PROPERTY

21.1

(1)   A wife is bound by a covenant contained in a marriage settle-ment, to which she is a party, to settle her other, or her after-acquired property not just where she is a covenantor but also if the words used consist of an agreement or declaration, or even a covenant by the husband alone, that the wife's property 'shall be settled' or that he, *and his wife*, or that he and all necessary parties, will settle the property;

(2)   If the covenant would be binding on the wife but for her minority[1], it will be voidable only and not void; and if she wishes to repudiate it, she must do so promptly;

(3)   Breach of such covenants may give rise to an ordinary claim for damages. by those within the marriage consideration but not by or on behalf of volunteers[2].

1   Family Law Reform Act 1969 lowered the age of majority from 21 to 18.
2   *Re Cavendish Browne's Settlement Trusts* [1916] WN 341; and see *Cannon v Hartley* [1949] Ch 213, [1949] 1 All ER 50. See discussion at paras 9.113–9.121.

Paragraph 1

21.2 The position under the old case law was complicated by the rule that the wife's property, unless held for separate use, automatically belonged to the husband, the wife and husband being one and that one being the husband.

Old principles still applicable are the principle that a declaration binds all parties to the deed[1] and that if a wife is an assenting party to a covenant she cannot afterwards obstruct its performance[2].

1   *Townshend v Harrowby* (1858) 27 LJ CH 553.
2   *Butcher v Butcher* (1851) 14 Beav 222; *Re De Ros' Trust* (1885) 31 Ch D 81; *Re Haden* [1898] 2 Ch 220; *Lee v Lee* (1876) 4 Ch D 175.

21.3   On the other hand, a covenant by the husband as to acts to be done by him will not bind the wife[1].

1   *Dawes v Tredwell* (1881) 18 Ch D 354; and see *Re Smith* [1900] WN 75 (covenant by husband that he and all other necessary parties would settle; held to include only persons that the husband had a right to call on to join, and not to include the wife).

Paragraph 2

21.4   Assuming that a woman, who is a minor[1], purports to covenant to settle her after-acquired property, and subsequently becomes entitled to property is she bound? The answer is yes, unless she has, after attaining her majority, and becoming aware of her right to repudiate, promptly disaffirmed her liability[2].

1   Eighteen years is the age of majority under the Family Law Reform Act 1969.
2   See *Wilder v Pigott* (1882) 22 Ch D 263; *Greenhill v North British and Mercantile Insurance* Co [1893] 3 Ch 474; and *Re Hodson* [1894] 2 Ch 421; and see Article 13, above.

ARTICLE 22
PROPERTY WHICH IS PRIMA FACIE EXCLUDED FROM A
COVENANT TO SETTLE OTHER OR AFTER-ACQUIRED PROPERTY

22.1

Prima facie, covenants to settle other or after-acquired property (not definitely described) do not comprise:
(1)   income, or (semble) capitalisations of income;
(2)   immovable property which cannot by the lex situs be vested in trustees;
(3)   property over which the covenantor has merely a general power of appointment, or which she has a statutory power of making her own, unless she exercises such powers in her own favour;
(4)   [probably] gifts made by her husband;
(5)   [probably] property substituted for that which she possessed at the date of the marriage[1];
(6)   property expressly excepted by the terms of the covenant[2];
(7)   any interest of the wife in the settled property which is excluded from the settlement[3];
(8)   property which is already in the settlement and on which the settlement has operated[4];
(9)   property which the covenantor would forfeit if the covenant applied to it[5].

1   *Re Biscoe* [1914] WN 302.

2   See *Re Thorne* [1917] 1 Ch 360; *Vanneck v Benham* [1917] 1 Ch 60 (any property which
    the donor expresses a wish should not be brought into settlement).
3   See *Re Wyatt* (1889) 60 LT 920.
4   *Re Roger's Settlement* [1951] Ch 450, [1951] 1 All ER 236.
5   *Re Smith* [1928] Ch 10.

Paragraph 1

Ordinary covenant binds corpus only, and not income

22.2 A settlement was made by a husband of all his personal estate to which
he was then or might thereafter become entitled, in trust for himself for life
with remainders over: it was held not to comprise his interest in a fund
bequeathed to him for life[1].

1   *St Aubyn v Humphreys* (1856) 22 Beav 175; *Townshend v Harrowby* (1858) 27 LJ
    Ch 553; *Lewis v Madocks* (1810) 17 Ves 48; *Re Dowding* [1904] 1 Ch 441.

22.3 The same principle applies to an annuity bequeathed to a wife[1]. But, of
course, such limited interests may be caught by the covenant where it is plainly
intended that they should be[2].

1   *Re Dowding* [1904] 1 Ch 441.
2   *Scholfield v Spooner* (1884) 26 Ch D 94, explained in *Re Dowding* [1904] 1 Ch 441;
    Beatty v Vance [1916] 1 IR 66.

Whether covenant binds property purchased out of savings of income

22.4 Where a woman covenants to settle after-acquired property she contemplates merely the settlement of property which may come to her by gift or
bequest, and not property which she may acquire out of the savings of her
income, so the covenant should not extend to such savings[1]. She should not be
penalised for saving her income instead of spending it as she received it.

1   So held in *Finlay v Darling* [1897] 1 Ch 719 and *Re Clutterbuck's Settlement* [1905]
    1 Ch 200.

Paragraph 2

Immovable property incapable of being vested in trustees by the lex situs

22.5 In *Re Pearse's Settlement*[1] it was held that since land in Jersey could not
be conveyed by a married woman to someone except for adequate pecuniary
compensation her after-acquired property covenant should be construed as
not intended to include within its scope after-acquired Jersey land.

1   [1909] 1 Ch 304. Jersey law now recognises trusts of movables but not of Jersey
    immovables. A covenant will thus be construed as not intended to include Jersey
    immovables unless expressly extending to foreign immovables, in which case it may well be
    that the equitable in personam jurisdiction might force the covenantor to transfer the land
    to the trustees as apparent beneficial co-owners or to sell the land and vest the proceeds in
    the trustees as trustees.

Paragraph 3

Covenant to settle after-acquired property does not oblige donee of general power to appoint the property to herself

22.6 In *Townshend v Harrowby*[1] the wife had joined in a covenant to settle after-acquired property. She subsequently became the donee of a general power of appointment over some property; but it was held that the covenant did not apply to it so as to oblige her to exercise the power in favour of herself or the trustees of the settlement.

[1] (1858) 27 LJ Ch 553; and see also *Ewart v Ewart* (1853) 11 Hare 276; *Bower v Smith* (1871) 19 WR 399.

22.7 Kindersley V-C said:

'It was very important to uphold the broad distinction between property and power, and he (the Vice-Chancellor) had always endeavoured to do so. It was true that power might result in property, and the exercise of it, if general, might affect property in an indirect manner; but so long as it was unexercised it was distinct from property. In one sense it was interest in property, because if there was a power it could not be said that there was not some interest. Technically, however, in the eye of a court of law or equity, a power was not an interest, and an interest was not a power. This covenant[1] was clearly not intended to apply to a mere power.'

[1] The definition clause in a settlement could give an extended meaning to property so as to include 'rights and interests of any description' as in Inheritance Tax Act 1984, s 272 which was held to cover a general power of appointment in *Melville v IRC* [2001] EWCA Civ 1247, [2002] 1 WLR 407.

22.8 But where property was given for such purposes as A should appoint, and in default of appointment to her absolutely, it was held that she could not defeat a covenant in her marriage settlement to settle after-acquired property exceeding £200 by making a succession of appointments to herself of £199 each[1]. It would indeed seem that wherever there is *a gift to the lady herself in default of appointment* the fund is caught by the covenant since she has a vested interest capable of being divested only by her own act[2].

[1] *Re O'Connell* [1903] 2 Ch 574; but see *Bower v Smith* (1871) 19 WR 399, explained in *Steward v Poppleton* [1877] WN 29; and *Re Lord Gerard* (1888) 58 LT 800, observed upon in *Re O'Connell*, above; and see also Article 25, below.
[2] For example, *Re Brook's Settlement Trusts* [1939] Ch 993 at 996–997.

22.9 On the other hand, a wife was not bound to disentail an estate tail in order to convey the fee simple to the trustees of her settlement[1].

[1] *Hilbers v Parkinson* (1883) 25 Ch D 200; *Re Dunsany's Settlement* [1906] 1 Ch 578.

Paragraph 4

Whether covenants to settle after-acquired property extend to gifts made by husband himself

22.10 Whether such covenants prima facie exclude gifts made by the husband to the wife is at present doubtful. In *Coles v Coles*[1], Joyce J held that such gifts were excluded. On the other hand, in *Re Ellis' Settlement*[2], Swinfen Eady J held the contrary view, and said that he did not think that Joyce J meant to lay down any general rule; and in *Re Plumptre's Marriage Settlement*[3] Eve J (while admitting that it seemed somewhat anomalous), followed the view of Swinfen Eady J. Sir Arthur Underhill took the view that Joyce J did lay down a general rule of prima facie interpretation, and that he was right in that view. These covenants are (as decided by Eve J in *Re Plumptre's Marriage Settlement*) purely executory, and should therefore, like marriage articles, be construed so as to answer the presumed intentions of the parties. But if so, it is difficult to believe that any man and woman, about to marry, ever intended by such covenants to preclude the husband making a present to his wife. A covenant so construed might embrace every chattel (such as a diamond necklace, a motor car, a ring, or even a dog) which the husband might wish to give to his wife for her personal use and enjoyment, and every cheque which he might give her to take a trip on the Continent, which is, it is submitted, a reductio ad absurdum. Moreover, the original object of these covenants, as stated by James LJ in *Re Edwards*[4] was to protect the wife against the old common law doctrine which handed her chattels to her husband absolutely and her lands to him for his life. Swinfen Eady J seems to have dissented from this last view, and said that such covenants were also intended for the benefit of the issue. No doubt the issue are within the valuable consideration which supports them, for otherwise the issue could not enforce them; but the view that these covenants are intended for the benefit of the issue seems to be inconsistent with the cases in which it has been held that they apply only to property falling to the wife during the coverture although they extend to property falling to the husband jure mariti after the coverture has been determined by death or divorce (see Article 24, below), the ratio decidendi of which is that these covenants are intended for the wife's protection. However, since the wife now needs no protection, being treated as a full separate independent person, it seems the covenants are better regarded as for the benefit of the issue.

[1] [1901] 1 Ch 711, following Malins V-C in *Dickinson v Dillwyn* (1869) LR 8 Eq 546 at 551, and followed by the Irish court in *Kingan v Matier* [1905] 1 IR 272.
[2] [1909] 1 Ch 618.
[3] [1910] 1 Ch 609, followed in *Leigh-White v Ruttledge* [1914] 1 IR 135.
[4] (1873) 9 Ch App 97 at 100.

22.11 If it be argued that these covenants may exclude personal chattels, but not gifts of money or securities, it is answered that such exclusion can only be justified by implied intention and that it is a safer and more logical rule to apply the intention to all gifts made by a husband than to some only. It must also not be forgotten that, before the Married Women's Property Acts a husband was incapable of making a common law gift to his wife; so that, as a matter of law, such apparent gifts remained his property, and could not be caught by such covenants; and it would be a strange effect of the Act to bring within such covenants common law gifts which the law previously excluded from them.

22.12 The question is one which can only be settled by the Court of Appeal, but it seems unlikely to arise nowadays: all well-drafted covenants contain an exception for gifts from the husband[1].

1   Cf 40 Encyclopaedia of Forms & Precedents (5th edn) form 13.

Paragraph 8

Property already in the settlement

22.13 Where successive life interests were given to husband and wife and, in the events which happened, the reversion expectant on the death of the survivor was irrevocably appointed to the son of the marriage who died an infant, it was held that the moiety of the son's reversionary interest to which the wife became entitled on his death was not caught by her covenant to settle after-acquired property.

22.14 In that case[1] Harman J said:

'It would be ridiculous that property already in the settlement should come into the settlement again and go on the limitations of the settlement and so on, in an everlasting succession. I cannot think that that is what the after-acquired property clause was intended to do. Although the wife acquired this property after the date of the settlement on her son's death ... , this was the very property in which, under the settlement itself, she had a life interest already, and it is ridiculous to suppose that she would have to re-settle in order to give herself another life interest in the same property.'

1   *Re Rogers' Settlement* [1951] Ch 450 at 455, [1951] 1 All ER 236 at 238.

ARTICLE 23
WHAT PROPERTY IS COMPRISED IN A GENERAL COVENANT TO
SETTLE PROPERTY TO WHICH THE WIFE IS PRESENTLY ENTITLED

23.1

Where the covenant is to settle property to which the wife 'is now entitled', or words to that effect, all property to which she then has any title, whether it be in possession, reversion, or contingency, is bound.

23.2 In *Re Jackson's Will*[1] the covenant was, 'that if at the time of the solemnisation of the said intended marriage, the wife shall be, or if at any time thereafter, and during the joint lives of the husband and wife she or her husband in her right shall become beneficially entitled ... to any real or personal property, estate, or effects ... for any estate or interest whatsoever ... then and in every such case' it should be settled.

1   (1879) 13 Ch D 189.

23.3 It was held that a reversionary interest in personalty which was vested in the wife at the date of the marriage, but was liable to be divested by the exercise of a power of appointment, was included in the covenant, although it did not fall into possession until after the husband's death[1].

[1] See also *Re Mackenzie's Settlement* (1867) 2 Ch App 345; *Agar v George* (1876) 2 Ch D 706; *Cornmell v Keith* (1876) 3 Ch D 767; and *Sweetapple v Horlock* (1879) 11 Ch D 745.

ARTICLE 24
WHAT IS COMPRISED IN A COVENANT TO SETTLE
AFTER-ACQUIRED PROPERTY OF THE WIFE

24.1

(1) A covenant to settle after-acquired property of the wife is limited, prima facie, to property acquired during the marriage;

(2) A covenant to settle property to which the wife *shall* become entitled is equivalent to a covenant to settle property to which she becomes entitled in possession or reversion[1], and binds:

   (a) property to which she is then only contingently entitled, provided that she attains a vested interest during the period covered by the covenant; and

   (b) property to which she has no title at the date of the marriage, but in which she acquires a reversionary or contingent interest during the period covered by the covenant, even although it may not fall into possession during that period.

   But it does not bind property in which she has a vested (or a vested but defeasible)[2] interest in reversion at the date of the marriage.

[1] *Blythe v Granville* (1842) 13 Sim 190; *Re Maltby Marriage Settlement* [1953] 2 All ER 220, [1953] 1 WLR 765. See also *Re Peel's Settlement Trusts* [1964] 3 All ER 567, [1964] 1 WLR 1232.
[2] *Re Peel's Settlement Trusts* [1964] 3 All ER 567, [1964] 1 WLR 1232.

Paragraph 1

Wife's covenant limited to property acquired during marriage

24.2 In *Re Edwards*[1], James LJ said:

'The primary object of a covenant to settle the future property of a wife is to prevent its falling under the sole control of the husband, and it therefore prima facie is to be supposed not to be intended to apply to property the wife's title to which does not accrue until after the husband's death. We have consulted the Lord Chancellor [Selbourne] on the case, and he agrees with us in the opinion that, in the absence of any expression showing that a covenant of this nature was intended to have a more extended operation, it is to be construed as if the usual words, "during the said intended coverture", had been inserted.'

[1] (1873) 9 Ch App 97 at 100.

24.3 The rule was subsequently carried to its logical conclusion, the court holding that it applies where the coverture has been determined either by divorce or judicial separation[1].

[1]   *Davenport v Marshall* [1902] 1 Ch 82; *Re Simpson* [1904] 1 Ch 1. But not where there has merely been a decree nisi; *Sinclair v Fell* [1913] 1 Ch 155.

But where the husband survives, it binds him to settle property acquired jure mariti after the wife's death

24.4 The rule, as above stated, was however, expressed somewhat too broadly by James LJ; for a general covenant by a husband and wife (or a husband alone) to settle a wife's property will not be restricted to property falling in during the coverture if the *husband* survives, though it will be so restricted when the wife survives. In *Fisher v Shirley*[1] the wife was entitled to a vested reversionary interest in personal estate, which fell into possession after her death, and was claimed by her husband jure mariti.

[1]   (1889) 43 Ch D 290.

24.5 Stirling J, however, held that it was bound by the husband's covenant to settle the wife's after-acquired property. The learned judge, commenting upon Lord Justice James' judgment in *Re Edwards*, above, said:

> 'No doubt the concluding words of the Lord Justice in that judgment at first sight support the contention on behalf of the husband. But when the literal construction of a covenant is departed from one ought to look at the reason for so doing, and the reason assigned is that the object of the covenant is to protect the property,the subject of the covenant, from the husband's marital right, and preserve it for the benefit of the wife and children. There is no need to protect property against the husband's marital right where the wife does not become entitled until after the husband's death: but there is need of such protection where the husband is the survivor, and the property falls in after the wife's death. If effect were given to the husband's claim his marital right would be enforced instead of the wife's property being protected against it, and the very object of the covenant would be defeated. The words of the covenant in the present case are quite general, and the reason assigned for limiting them does not appear to apply, and, in my opinion, they cannot in the present case be limited as suggested.'

A fresh approach?

24.6 It is clear, then, that the basis for the view that covenants of this kind operate (at least in the case of the wife) only during coverture is that their purpose is to protect the wife's property from falling into the hands of the husband. In *Re Peel's Settlement Trusts*[1], Buckley J commented:

> 'There is authority for the view that in the absence of an express contrary intention a covenant of this kind will operate only during coverture, although it does not say so expressly (*Re Edwards* (1873) 9 Ch App 97); but it seems to me at least arguable that the basis for this view has disappeared with the enactment

of the Married Women's Property Act 1882. This point has not been fully argued before me and I do not propose to express any concluded view on it.'

1   [1964] 3 All ER 567, [1964] 1 WLR 1232.

24.7 Nowadays, a court may very well consider that a particular covenant in context was intended to protect the issue of the marriage and so extend beyond coverture. The draftsman should expressly specify the duration of the covenant.

Paragraph 2

If the covenant only relates to future property, the question arises what future property is bound

24.8 Assuming that the covenant is restricted to *future* property of the wife, the question then arises, what constitutes *future* property. The cases are not easy to reconcile, but paragraph (2) is believed to state the modern view.

24.9 A covenant to settle future-acquired property (without more) is sufficiently wide to embrace:

(1)   that which may be thereafter acquired in both title and possession; and
(2)   that which may be acquired in title only, although possession may never be obtained during the coverture[1]; but it does not embrace that to which a *title* has already been acquired, whether or not that title is followed during the coverture by the actual right to possession.

1   *Hughes v Young* (1862) 32 LJ Ch 137; *Dickinson v Dillwyn* (1869) LR 8 Eq 546; *Cowper-Smith v Anstey* [1877] WN 28; *Cannon v Hartley* [1949] Ch 213, [1949] 1 All ER 50.

A reversion vested at the marriage apparently not bound

24.10 The authorities are clear that where a vested reversion, to which the wife is entitled at the date of the settlement, does *not* fall in during the marriage or the life of the husband (if he be survivor), it will not be bound by the covenant to settle future-acquired property[1]. On the question whether a reversion which is vested at the date of the settlement and falls into possession during the marriage (or, where the period for which the covenant is to be operative is not named, during the life of the husband)[2] is bound, the better view appears to be that *property which was vested in interest at the date of the settlement is not caught* irrespective of the date when it falls in[3]. The same is true of property which was vested in interest, but defeasibly, at the date of the settlement[4].

1   See *Re Jones* (1876) 2 Ch D 362; *Re Pedder's Settlement Trusts* (1870) LR 10 Eq 585; *Re Clinton's Trust* (1871) LR 13 Eq 295.
2   *Fisher v Shirley* (1889) 43 Ch D 290.

3   *Re Maltby Marriage Settlement* [1953] 2 All ER 220, [1953] 1 WLR 765; following *Re
     Bland's Settlement* [1905] 1 Ch 4, and not following *Re Clinton's Trust* (1871) LR 13 Eq
     295; *Re Crook's Settlement* [1923] 2 Ch 339. *Re Maltby Marriage Settlement*, above, was
     followed in *Re Peel's Settlement Trusts* [1964] 3 All ER 567, [1964] 1 WLR 1232, where
     the covenant was not expressly limited within the period of the continuance of the
     marriage.
4   *Re Peel's Settlement* [1964] 3 All ER 567, [1964] 1 WLR 1232.

Contingent interests

24.11 Where the wife has a contingent interest at the date of the marriage
which both becomes vested and falls into possession during the marriage, it is
bound by the covenant[1]. It seems, however, that a contingent interest which,
though it becomes vested during the marriage, does not fall into possession
until afterwards is not bound[2].

1   *Archer v Kelly* (1860) 1 Drew & Sm 300; *Brooks v Keith* (1861) 1 Drew & Sm 462; *Re
     Williams' Settlement* [1911] 1 Ch 441; and see *Re Maltby Marriage Settlement* [1953]
     2 All ER 220, [1953] 1 WLR 765 and *Re Peel's Settlement Trusts* [1964] 3 All ER 567,
     [1964] 1 WLR 1232.
2   *Re Michell's Trusts* (1878) 9 Ch D 5, CA concerned with the clause 'come to or devolve
     upon the wife'. Also see *Re Peel's Settlement Trusts* [1964] 3 All ER 567 at 576.

Transformed interests

24.12 Even if a particular interest does not (for example, because it is vested
at the time when the covenant was made) fall within the ambit of a covenant
to settle future property, it seems that it may do so if it is later transformed
into something new. Thus in a case[1] where the trusts of a settled fund in which
a wife was interested were terminated with the court's approval by family
arrangements and the fund divided among the beneficiaries, Buckley J said
that what the wife received under the arrangements:

> '... was not the fruition of any rights which she had under the relevant trusts,
> but something new, to which she became entitled for the first time under and in
> consequence of the arrangements, that is, after the date of her marriage. It is
> consequently clear, in my opinion, that what she so received was caught by the
> covenant ...'

1   *Re Peel's Settlement Trusts* [1964] 3 All ER 567 at 574.

ARTICLE 25
COVENANTS TO SETTLE A DEFINITE INTEREST IN PROPERTY

25.1

Where the covenant is to settle a definite estate or interest in property
which subsequently becomes enlarged, the covenant does not bind the
enlarged interest; and, conversely, if the definite interest fails, but the
covenantor acquires the property under another title, it will not be
bound.

25.2 *The interpretation of executory trusts*

25.2 In *Sweetapple v Horlock*[1] (corrected in *Re Jackson's Will*[2]) the intended wife, being entitled to a reversionary interest under her parents' settlement, liable to be defeated by the exercise by her father of a power of appointment, covenanted to settle all property which she was '*then* seised of or interested in or entitled to'. The father subsequently exercised his power, and appointed to her exactly the same proportion of the property which she would have taken in default of appointment.

[1]   (1879) 11 Ch D 745.
[2]   (1879) 13 Ch D 189.

25.3 On these facts, Jessel MR held that the wife's covenant did not comprise the appointed share, although it would have done so if the share had come to her in default of appointment, saying:

> 'A conveyance by a person by an innocent assurance of an interest expressed as being subject to be defeated by the exercise of a power, does not convey an interest which that person might take under the power. This is not like a settlement of all property which might come to the wife in any event, but only of that which was then vested in or belonging to her.'

25.4 So, in *Smith v Osborne*[1], it was laid down that where a man, in his marriage settlement, describes himself as entitled to an expectant estate in remainder in two pieces of land, and covenants that when 'such remainder' shall become vested in possession he will convey it to the uses of his settlement, the covenant will not bind him if he becomes possessed of either of these pieces of land by a title different from that described in the covenant. As Lord Wensleydale put it, the point resolved itself into this:

> 'Is this a covenant to convey the townlands of Stonehouse to the trustees absolutely, whenever the covenantor was entitled to them in possession? Or is it a bargain only with respect to the contingent interest, or spes successionis, or more correctly, a bargain to convey the estates conditionally, if they should vest in possession in Mr Boyse Osborne, the covenantor, under the will of the grandfather Thomas Carr?'

[1]   (1857) 6 HL Cas 375.

25.5 His lordship then pointed out that, in the words of the covenant, it was only to take effect if the estates became vested in the covenantor under the will of his grandfather, and that, as a matter of fact, they became vested in him in defiance of that will, by gift from a tenant in tail under that will, who had disentailed. He further remarked (in reference to an argument of the trustee's counsel that there was an obvious intention to settle the estates themselves) that that was:

> 'to apply a wrong rule of construction. It is to interpret the covenant, not according to the meaning of the words used, but according to what the parties may be reasonably supposed (judging from the circumstances in which they were placed) to have been likely to intend to do when they entered into the contract ... The only safe rule of construction is to ascertain the meaning of the words used, and in this case I think it is too clear to admit of any doubt.'

ARTICLE 26
COVENANTS TO SETTLE PROPERTY EXCEEDING A
CERTAIN VALUE

26.1

Where the covenant is to settle property exceeding a certain value:
(1)   that value is normally the actual value of the property itself after
      deducting estate duty or capital transfer tax or inheritance tax[1],
      and not the actuarial value of the covenantor's interest in it; and
(2)   that value is, prima facie, construed to mean the value of funds
      derived from the same source: two legacies under the will of the
      same testator are so derived[2];
(3)   where part of an estate falls under the covenant it must be
      valued, and where the covenant excludes specified chattels, yet
      they will be included if they merely form part of a residuary
      estate[3].

---

1   *Re Pares* [1901] 1 Ch 708. But cf *Re Harcourt's Trusts* [1911] WN 214, where Swinfen
    Eady J held that an endowment policy effected by the husband in favour of the wife was
    not caught, because it was not worth the limit at the date when she first became entitled to
    the policy, and the marriage had necessarily determined when the money (beyond the limit)
    became payable.
2   *Re Pares* [1901] 1 Ch 708.
3   *Vanneck v Benham* [1917] 1 Ch 60. For a case where chattels were excluded and £1,000
    was bequeathed to the wife to purchase a necklace, see *Re Thorne* [1917] 1 Ch 360.

Where the covenant is to settle property which is worth more than a
minimum sum, it is a matter of construction whether the property itself or
the value of the covenantor's interest in it governs the question

26.2 In *Re Mackenzie's Settlement*[1] a marriage settlement contained a covenant that, if the wife then was, or should at any time during the coverture
become, entitled to any real or personal estate of the value of £400, for any
estate or interest, it should be settled. At the date of the settlement she was
entitled (under a prior settlement) in remainder, expectant on her mother's
death, to (a) a share of a sum of stock in her own right, and (b) a further share
of the same stock as one of the next of kin of a deceased brother. The value of
the two shares taken together was above £400, but the actuarial value of the
wife's reversionary interest in them, at the date of the settlement, was
considerably less than £400. It was held that both shares were included in the
settlement, the true interpretation of the covenant being that it referred to the
value of the property itself, and not to the value of the wife's reversionary
interest in it.

---

1   (1867) 2 Ch App 345.

26.3 But in such a case, the value is the value when it falls into possession, so
that if there is a depreciation of a reversionary interest so as to bring it below
the stipulated minimum at the date when it falls into possession it will be
excluded from the covenant[1].

---

1   *Re Hughes Settlement* [1924] 2 Ch 356.

26.4 In *Cannon v Hartley*[1], a separation deed contained a covenant to settle 'any money or property exceeding in net amount or value £1,000'. After the date of the deed the covenantor became entitled to a reversionary interest in certain property and it was conceded that both the property itself and the reversionary interest were worth more than £1,000. Romer J, however, who was careful to point out that his judgment proceeded entirely on the actual language used, appears to have assumed that the 'net amount or value' on which the liability to settle depended was the amount or value of the reversionary interest itself.

1   [1949] Ch 213, [1949] 1 All ER 50.

Implied term that the prescribed value refers to property derived from the same source

26.5 It will be seen that, in *Re Mackenzie's Settlement* (above), the aggregate of the two funds was held to be bound, although singly they were of insufficient amount. But although they accrued to the lady under two titles, they were derived from the same source, namely, the original settlement. Care must, however, be taken to distinguish between covenants where nothing is said upon this point, and those in which the question is distinctly dealt with. For instance, in *Re Mackenzie's Settlement* it appeared that there were two distinct funds, neither of which taken alone would have fallen under the covenant, but which, taken together, exceeded the value mentioned in the covenant, and although they came to the lady under different titles, they were held to be bound by the covenant. Nevertheless, it seems to be well settled that in such cases the fund will not be bound unless all its parts are derived from *the same source*[1]. The same source, however, does not necessarily mean under the same title. In *Re Mackenzie* both funds were derived from the same source (namely, the prior settlement) although part was derived by the lady directly and part as the next of kin of her brother. And in the same way two legacies derived from the same testator are derived from the same source[2].

1   *Re Hooper* (1865) 13 WR 710; *Hood v Franklin* (1873) LR 16 Eq 496; *Re Hughes' Settlement* [1924] 2 Ch 356.
2   *Re Pares* [1901] 1 Ch 708.

Cases where the covenant limits the fund to be settled to funds acquired 'at one time'

26.6 Care must also be taken to distinguish between covenants where nothing is said upon the point[1], and those in which the fund to be settled is expressly declared to be a minimum sum derived from one and the same source and 'at one and the same time'. For instance, in *Bower v Smith*[2]:

> 'the covenant was to settle property exceeding £500 in value which the wife should acquire 'at any one time'. She afterwards became the donee of a general power of appointment over a fund of £5,499 19s 1d. This power she exercised by eleven successive appointments in favour of herself for sums under £500 each.'

1   Eg *Re Hooper* (1865) 13 WR 710 and *Hood v Franklin* (1873) LR 16 Eq 496.

2   (1871) 19 WR 399 (the report in LR 11 Eq 279 is misleading and incorrect: see *Steward v Poppleton* [1877] WN 29).

26.7 On these facts it was held that the appointed funds were not bound, for although they were all derived from the same source, they were not acquired at the same time, ie at the same moment.

Sums already advanced out of the fund

26.8 Where the fund originally exceeds the minimum named in the covenant, but, by reason of advances made to the lady while it was still reversionary, the fund has been reduced below that minimum, the amount so advanced must be included for the purpose of determining whether the fund is large enough to be brought into settlement[1].

1   *Hood v Franklin* (1873) LR 16 Eq 496.

Conclusion

26.9 The whole subject of covenants to settle future property is in an unsatisfactory state, although skilled drafting can avoid the pitfalls emerging in this Chapter. In the light of the Married Women's Property Acts, and the Law Reform (Married Women and Tortfeasors) Act 1935 (which collectively have taken away the jus mariti of husbands in respect of their wives' capital except under their intestacies), such covenants ought not to be inserted in marriage settlements except after due consideration[1], taking into account the utility of preserving the family 'nest egg' for three or four generations and the ability to vary such trusts under the Matrimonial Causes Act 1973, s 24[2].

1   *Re Maddy* [1901] 2 Ch 820 (such covenants not being usual covenants even in 1901).
2   *Brooks v Brooks* [1996] AC 375.

Chapter 6

THE TERMINATION OF TRUSTS OF PROPERTY

ARTICLE 27
HOW TRUSTS TERMINATE

27.1

(1)   A trust terminates once all the assets of the trust fund have been distributed in accordance with the provisions of the trust, whether found in a trust instrument or an oral declaration of trust.

(2)   Where the application of such provisions does not exhaust the trust fund, the assets remaining within the fund will be held on a resulting trust for the settlor or, if dead, his estate[1] (so as to be distributed to the settlor or those entitled to his estate), unless the settlor had expressly or by necessary implication abandoned any beneficial interest in the trust fund, in which exceptionally rare eventuality the assets will vest in the Crown as *bona vacantia*[2].

(3)   A trust terminated by distribution of all its assets in accordance with its provisions cannot be revived. However, if someone transfers assets to the trustees of a terminated or 'dead' trust to be held on terms incorporating by reference the provisions of the 'dead' trust, such person is settlor of a new trust of such assets, as also is the case if the trustees of such new trust are persons different from the trustees of the 'dead' trust.

[1]   See Article 29.
[2]   *Westdeutsche Landesbank v Islington London Borough Council* [1996] AC 669 at 708.

Paragraph 1

No trust if no property

27.2 Because a trust of property cannot exist unless there is property held on trust[1], once a trust has been duly emptied of all of its assets, there is no trust. Thus, in a simple case of a fixed trust for A for life, remainder to B, once A dies the trustees hold the assets on a bare trust[2] for B; and such trust terminates once all the trusts assets are transferred to B or to others as directed by B. In the case of a discretionary trust to distribute capital amongst a class of beneficiaries alive at the end of the trust period, the trust terminates once all the trust assets have been transferred by the trustees to such of the beneficiaries as they have selected in their discretion, a temporary bare trust arising of identified property that the trustees have decided to transfer to a particular beneficiary but have not yet transferred to him.

[1]   See Article 9.
[2]   See Article 4.

27.3   A trust can terminate before the end of the original trust period (or any shorter trust period designated pursuant to a power in that behalf) if a power is exercised to decant all the trust assets out of the trust eg into another trust[1] or to individuals as absolute legal beneficial owners.

[1]   Even if this trust has the same persons as are trustees of the old trust as in *Hart v Briscoe* [1979] Ch 1, but note the distinction between a re-settlement on separate independent trusts as in *Hart v Briscoe* and a sub-settlement grafting new trusts onto the old trusts as in *Swires v Renton* [1991] STC 490. Generally see Article 82.

Paragraph 2

Resulting trust of trust property

27.4   Where for some reason, such as the impact of a rule of the law of trusts or the settlor's failure to provide comprehensively for what is to happen to the income and capital of his trust fund, the provisions of a particular trust fail to exhaust the income and capital of a trust fund, the unexhausted income and capital are almost invariably held on a resulting trust for the settlor or his estate[1]. Thus, if the settlor is dead the relevant property passes as part of his residuary estate under his will or intestacy.

[1]   See Article 29.

27.5   In an exceptionally rare case, it may be that at the time of creating the trust the settlor had expressly or by necessary implication abandoned any beneficial interest in the trust fund[1]. It then follows that any unexhausted trust assets can only vest in the Crown as *bona vacantia*.

[1]   *Westdeutsche Landesbank v Islington London Borough Council* [1996] AC 669 at 708.

Paragraph 3

A terminated trust cannot be revived, but a new trust with provisions identical to the terminated or 'dead' trust can be created

27.6   A trust is not like a company or a box which continues to exist even if the company owns no property or the box is empty. However, the settlor of the terminated or 'dead' trust or, indeed, anyone knowing the provisions of such trust, can create a new separate trust on terms identical to the provisions of the 'dead' trust, whether in the same lengthy fashion or simply by an incorporating reference to such provisions but perhaps with a longer trust (or perpetuity) period. It is immaterial whether this new settlement involves transferring new assets to new trustees or to the same persons who were trustees of the terminated dead trust.

Division Three

TRUSTS IMPOSED BY LAW

Chapter 7

INTRODUCTION

ARTICLE 28
ANALYSIS OF TRUSTS OF PROPERTY IMPOSED BY LAW

28.1

(1) Trusts of property are imposed by law where property is held by T, the person having title to the property, either:
- (a) by statute, expressly or by necessary implication, in which case they are called statutory trusts; or
- (b) on resulting trust for B, where B transfers or causes a transfer of property he owns or purchases to T, without receipt of any consideration, such trust arising at the time of the transfer to T, and being founded on the presumption that B does not intend to part with the beneficial interest; or
- (c) on constructive trust for X, where it would be unconscionable for T to retain the property for his own benefit to the exclusion of X, either because the parties intended that X should receive the beneficial interest and this intention would be thwarted by T's subsequent change of mind or failure to comply with applicable formalities, or because the property consists of the profits of wrongdoing against X, or possibly because the property consists of an enrichment unjustly gained at X's expense.

(2) Resulting trusts of property are imposed:
- (a) when property is transferred to a trustee, upon trusts which do not wholly effectively dispose of the beneficial interest[1], or when property is gratuitously transferred or caused to be transferred by the owner or purchaser to a transferee (not being the transferor's spouse or child)[2], and
- (b) there is no evidence that the transferor intended to make a gift or loan or to abandon his beneficial interest in the property, so that as a backstop measure to determine the

390

whereabouts of the beneficial interest, the law raises a presumption in the transferor's favour that he did not intend to part with this interest, failure to rebut which presumption by the transferee will lead to the imposition of a resulting trust.

(3)   Constructive trusts of property are imposed:

    (a)   when a trustee or other fiduciary makes an unauthorised profit from his office, for example by receiving unauthorised remuneration, or by taking a bribe to act against his principal's best interests, or by misappropriating a profit-making opportunity which comes to him in his fiduciary capacity, or by acquiring a new asset for himself with misapplied trust or other fiduciary property[3],

    (b)   when a stranger receives misdirected trust or other fiduciary property, and the stranger is not a bona fide purchaser of the legal interest for value without notice, nor is he protected by statutory overreaching provisions or exceptions to the rule *nemo dat quod non habet* or the defence of change of position[4],

    (c)   when a property-owner fraudulently or unconscionably attempts to take advantage of statutory provisions or other fundamental legal principles to deny the beneficial interest therein of another[5], and

    (d)   when a vendor of property has entered into a specifically enforceable contract[6].

(4)   This Chapter is concerned only with trusts *of property* and beneficiaries' *proprietary* interests and not with the personal accountability of strangers to a trust who, in some circumstances (eg if they dishonestly assist in a breach of trust) can be made *personally* liable to account to the beneficiaries as if they were trustees although they are not actually trustees of property, such liability being referred to traditionally as 'personal accountability as a constructive trustee'[7].

[1]   Articles 29 and 30, below.
[2]   Article 31, below.
[3]   Article 33, below.
[4]   Article 34, below.
[5]   Article 35, below.
[6]   Article 36, below.
[7]   The personal liability of strangers implicated in a breach of trust is covered in Article 100, below.

Statutory trusts

28.2   Trusts are either express trusts or trusts imposed by law. There are three categories of trusts imposed by law: statutory trusts, resulting trusts and constructive trusts[1]. Statutory trusts arise under various statutes which stipulate that property shall be held on trust in different circumstances. Examples are the trusts arising in respect of legal estates co-owned under the Law of Property Act 1925, ss 34 and 36[2], the trusts arising on intestacy under the Administration of Estates Act 1925, s 33; the trusts arising under the Companies Act 1985, ss 313–5, of certain sums improperly received by directors as compensation for loss of office; and the trust arising under the Postal Services Act 2000, s 92, of certain sums recovered by another party on behalf of the sender or addressee of a packet lost or damaged in the post.

[1]   There is no separate category of 'implied trust': see Article 3.
[2]   As amended by the Trusts of Land and Appointment of Trustees Act 1996.

Resulting and constructive trusts

28.3 The word 'resulting' derives from the Latin word *resalire*: 'to jump back'. Hence a resulting trust is literally a trust which returns beneficial ownership of the trust property to a person who owned the property before it reached the trustee's hands: in equity, the beneficial interest 'jumps back' to its previous owner. Using the term 'resulting trust' in a literal sense, it could therefore meaningfully be said that an 'express resulting trust' would be created if B transferred £500 to T with the express instruction that T should hold the money on trust for B. However, English trust lawyers very rarely use the term 'resulting trust' to describe an *express* trust or *bare* trust which carries the beneficial interest back to its previous owner[1]. They almost always use the term to describe a trust which conforms to this pattern, *and which is imposed by law*[2].

[1]   But see eg *Latimer v IRC [2004] UKPC 13* [2004] 1 WLR 1466 at [41] per Lord Millett.
[2]   As in eg *Lane v Dighton* (1762) Amb 409 at 411 per Sir Thomas Clarke MR; *Barton v Muir* (1874) LR 6 PC 134 at 145 per Sir John Stuart; *Churcher v Martin* (1889) 42 Ch D 312 at 319 per Kekewich J; *Re English & American Insurance Co Ltd* [1994] 1 BCLC 649 at 651 per Harman J; *Air Jamaica Ltd v Charlton* [1999] 1 WLR 1399 at 1412 per Lord Millett.

28.4 The verb 'to construe' means 'to interpret'. Hence the word 'constructive' is used to denote the fact that the law interprets – or, effectively, deems – a party's actions or words to have had some effect in law, even though they may not actually have had this effect in fact[1]. For example, a person with 'constructive notice' is deemed to know the answers to questions that a reasonable person in his position would have asked[2], even if he does not actually know the answers because he has not actually asked the questions. In the case of a 'constructive trust', the law deems a defendant to have conferred the same proprietary rights on the claimant as he would have acquired, had the defendant validly declared an express trust in his favour, even though no such valid declaration has actually been made. However, the defendant does not normally take on the duties of an express trustee nor have the powers of an express trustee: his obligation is just to transfer the relevant property to the express trustees for the claimant or to the claimant himself if of full capacity and absolutely entitled to the property. Exceptionally, if the constructive trust was imposed on the defendant as a result of his conduct as an express trustee (or other fiduciary) he must treat the property as if it had always been held by him as express trustee (or other fiduciary), and so he will owe the same duties in relation to his stewardship of this property as he owes in relation to the rest of the property which he holds in a fiduciary capacity. Note, too, that if he is replaced as a trustee (whether by an appointment made by him under section 36 of the Trustee Act 1925 or by the court or by a person having an express power of replacement) he must transfer the relevant property to the new trustees.

1 Sir R Megarry 'Historical Development' in *Special Lectures of the Law Society of Upper Canada 1990 – Fiduciary Duties* (1991) 1 at p.5: '"Constructive" seems to mean "It isn't, but has to be treated as if it were".'
2 Eg Law of Property Act 1925 s 199(1)(ii).

28.5 It seems to follow from the foregoing account that the classifications 'resulting trust' and 'constructive trust' cut across one another. If a constructive trust is a trust imposed by law in circumstances where no express trust has been declared, and a resulting trust is a trust which returns beneficial ownership of the trust property to a previous owner, then it seems to follow that some trusts can be both resulting trusts and constructive trusts. Different judges have drawn different conclusions from this. On one view, all trusts imposed by law are constructive trusts, and resulting trusts are a sub-set of constructive trusts which conform to a particular fact-pattern[1], so that the two are effectively interchangeable whenever these facts are encountered[2]. On another view, resulting trusts and constructive trusts are distinct categories of trust, imposed by the courts for different underlying reasons[3]. It cannot be known which of these views is correct unless the underlying reasons for the imposition of constructive and resulting trusts are identified. These are considered at the end of the chapter.

1 *Re Llanover Settled Estates* [1926] Ch 626 at 637 per Astbury J, approving the statement to this effect in A Underhill *The Law Relating to Trusts and Trustees* (8th edn, 1926) at p.9.
2 Eg Law of Property Act 1925 s 199(1)(ii).
3 Article 33, below.

Personal and proprietary rights arising under resulting and constructive trusts

28.6 There is a significant difference between a beneficiary's proprietary rights under a resulting or constructive trust, and his personal rights against the trustee. In *Westdeutsche Landesbank Girozentrale v Islington London Borough Council*[1], Lord Browne-Wilkinson thought that it would be inappropriate to fix a resulting or constructive trustee with personal liability to account to the beneficiaries for the trust property, unless his conscience was affected by knowledge of the circumstances which led to the creation of the beneficiary's equitable proprietary interest. Situations can certainly be imagined in which it would be harsh to hold a resulting or constructive trustee liable to make good losses out of the trust funds when he does not know that the beneficiary has an equitable interest in the property: where the trustee is an infant, for example[2]. However, it need not follow from this, as Lord Browne-Wilkinson also held, that a resulting or constructive trust should not arise at all unless and until the trustee's conscience is affected by knowledge of the relevant circumstances[3].

28.6   *Introduction*

1   [1996] AC 669 at 705–6.
2   As in eg *Re Vinogradoff* [1935] WN 68.
3   [1996] AC 669 at 706–7, recognising that an equitable proprietary interest, whether a restrictive covenant affecting land or an equitable charge or an interest under a trust, can burden a defendant's legal estate before his conscience is affected, but refusing to use the term 'trust' to describe the case where an interest under a trust binds the legal estate.

28.7 Less drastic strategies than denying the existence of the trust altogether are open to a court that wishes to avoid fixing an innocent resulting or constructive trustee with personal liability for spending the trust assets: for example, placing the trustee under no greater duty than 'an obligation to restore the property on demand, if still in possession of it' at the time when the trustee becomes aware of the trust's existence[1]. Various authorities contradict the view that trusts cannot be imposed by law unless and until the trustee's conscience is affected[2], and in Professor Chambers' words[3]:

> 'delaying the creation of the trust until the trustees have sufficient notice to affect their consciences may have a drastic effect on a number of important matters which depend on the timing of the creation of the resulting [or constructive] trust, such as entitlement to income, liability for taxation, risk and insurance, commencement of limitation periods, transfer and transmission of property interests, and priority of competing claims.'

1   J Hackney *Understanding Equity & Trusts* (1987) at p.167. Other possible strategies are explored in R Chambers *Resulting Trusts* (1997) at pp.209–212.
2   *Birch v Blagrave* (1755) Amb 264; *Childers v Childers* (1857) 1 De G & J 482; *Re Vinogradoff* [1935] WN 68; *Re Diplock* [1948] Ch 465; *Re Muller* [1953] NZLR 879.
3   R Chambers *Resulting Trusts* (1997) at p.206.

28.8 In principle, therefore, the best view is that a resulting or constructive trust can arise whatever the state of the trustee's conscience, and that when it does so the beneficiary immediately acquires an equitable proprietary interest in the trust assets[1], along with a concomitant right to see an account of the trustee's dealings with the property from the moment of receipt. However, this need not mean that the trustee will be personally liable for disposing of the trust assets before his conscience is affected by knowledge of the circumstances which led to the imposition of the trust[2]. Moreover, once the trustee becomes aware of the existence of the trust, he may disclaim his trusteeship, but in that case he must obviously transfer the trust property to the beneficiary (where the beneficiary is absolutely entitled to the equitable interest) or to other trustees for the beneficiaries (where the property forms part of an ongoing settlement)[3]. Where necessary he may also be obliged to get in the trust estate from third parties for payment over to the beneficiary[4]. However, that is the limit of his personal obligations, and he does not also owe the beneficiaries a fiduciary duty of loyalty which attaches to express trusteeship[5],since this must be undertaken voluntarily[6]. Nor need he undertake the administrative and managerial duties with which express trustees are commonly charged, although it seems that if he does incur legitimate costs in the course of managing the trust affairs, he will enjoy the same right of indemnity as an express trustee[7].

1   Cf *Hardoon v Belilios* [1901] AC 118 at 123 per Lord Lindley: a trust exists when 'the legal title [is] in the plaintiff and the equitable title in the defendant.'

2   *R v Chester and North Wales Legal Aid Area Office, ex parte Floods of Queensferry Ltd* [1998] 1 WLR 1496 at 1500 per Millett LJ; *Allan v Rea Brothers Trustees Ltd* [2002] PLR 169 at [55] per Robert Walker LJ; *Waxman v Waxman* (2004) 7 ITELR 162 at [583] (Ontario CA); *Clark v Cutland [2003] EWCA Civ 810,* [2004] 1 WLR 783 (D can hold property on constructive trust although C concedes that D not personally liable to account). See too R Chambers *Resulting Trusts* (1997) at pp.200–209; Lord Millett 'Restitution and Constructive Trusts' (1998) 114 LQR 399, at pp.403–6.

3   *Allied Carpets Group plc v Nethercott (28 January 2000, unreported)* QBD, Colman J; *Re Holmes* [2005] 1 All ER 490 at [22] per Burnton J. Hence the beneficiary can obtain an order against the trustee to the orders for conveyance made in *Dillwyn v Llewelyn* (1862) 4 De G F & J 517 at 523 per Lord Westbury LC, and more recently in *Riches v Hogben* [1985] 2 Qd R 292 at 302 per McPherson J.

4   *Evans v European Bank Ltd* (2004) 7 ITELR 19 at [116] per Spigelman CJ; *Bracken Partners Ltd v Gutteridge* [2004] 1 BCLC 377.

5   *Lonrho plc v Fayed (No 2)* [1992] 1 WLR 1 at 12 per Millett J; Lord Millett 'Restitution and Constructive Trusts' (1998) 114 LQR 399 at pp.404–5.

6   A Scott 'The Fiduciary Principle' (1949) 37 Cal LR 539 at p.540; *Hospital Products Ltd v United States Surgical Corp* (1984) 156 CLR 41 at 96–7.

7   Cf *James v Williams* [2000] Ch 1 at 10–11; *Nolan v Collie* (2003) 7 VR 287 at [32]–[34]. For an express trustee's indemnity right see Article 83.

Personal accountability of intermeddlers in trust affairs

28.9 The personal liability owed by the trustee of a constructive trust of property should not be confused with the personal liability of a stranger to a trust who intermeddles with the beneficiaries' equitable property rights, such as a dishonest assistant in a breach of trust. The two are easily confused because equity has traditionally described liability under the latter head as 'personal liability to account as a constructive trustee'. Since this liability can arise whether or not the intermeddler has received property which might be impressed with a trust[1], it would describe the liability more accurately to say that the intermeddler is 'constructively liable to account as a trustee' or simply 'accountable in equity', as this would make it clearer that 'he is not in fact a trustee at all, even if he may be liable to account as if he were'[2]. The personal liability of strangers implicated in a breach of trust is covered in Article 100 below.

1   *Royal Brunei Airlines Sdn Bhd v Tan* [1995] 2 AC 378 at 382 per Lord Nicholls; *Houghton v Fayers* [2000] Lloyd's Rep Bank 145 at 149 per Nourse LJ.

2   *Paragon Finance plc v D B Thakerar & Co* [1999] 1 All ER 400 at 409 per Millett LJ. Compare Lord Millett's later statement in *Dubai Aluminium Co Ltd v Salaam [2002] UKHL 48,*[2003] 2 AC 366 at [142] that 'we should now discard the words "accountable as constructive trustee" in this context and substitute the words "accountable in equity".'

Resulting trusts

28.10 Resulting trusts only arise either in respect of express trusts of property, where there has been a failure effectively to dispose wholly of the settlor's interest, or in respect of purchases or gifts of property where the apparent new owner has given no consideration (or only a fraction of the consideration) for the property and was not really intended to have the beneficial interest (or the whole beneficial interest). In both cases the beneficial interest forthwith results (or 'jumps back') to the person who provided the value transferred, whether by directly providing the property transferred or by providing the resources as purchaser to enable another to vest the property in the transferee's name.

28.11 In many cases where property is gratuitously transferred, there is evidence that the transferor intended to make a gift, to make a loan, or (much less likely) to abandon his interest in the property. In all such cases, the law will give effect to that intention, and no question will arise of a resulting trust being imposed[1]. Likewise, if the evidence reveals that the transferor made an enforceable declaration of trust of property gratuitously transferred into the transferee's name, then again the law will give effect to that express trust in the normal way, assuming compliance with applicable formalities[2]. Thus resulting trusts are imposed only in cases where property is gratuitously transferred and there is insufficient evidence to determine the transferor's intention. In these circumstances the law will raise a presumption in the transferor's favour as a 'long-stop' measure to locate the beneficial interest in the absence of any evidence decisively establishing its whereabouts[3]. Failure to rebut this presumption by the transferee will lead to the imposition of a resulting trust.

[1] *Air Jamaica Ltd v Charlton* [1999] 1 WLR 1399 at 1412 per Lord Millett; *Twinsectra Ltd v Yardley* [2000] WTLR 527 at 562 per Potter LJ; *Lavelle v Lavelle* [2004] EWCA Civ 223, [2004] 2 FCR 418 at [13] per Lord Phillips MR.
[2] In *Hodgson v Marks* [1971] Ch 892, where A transferred her house to B on oral trust (not satisfying Law of Property Act 1925, s 53(1)(b)) for A, the CA held that B held the house on trust for A nonetheless. On one view this trust was an express trust, the court applying the doctrine in *Rochefoucauld v Boustead* [1897] 1 Ch 196, CA, to prevent statute being used as an instrument of fraud: see W J Swadling 'A Hard Look at *Hodgson v Marks*' in P Birks & F Rose (eds) *Restitution and Equity Vol 1: Resulting Trusts and Equitable Compensation* (2000) 61. On another view, it was a resulting trust responding to A's lack of intention to benefit B: R Chambers *Resulting Trusts* (1997) at p.25.
[3] *Vandervell v IRC* [1967] 2 AC 291 at 313 per Lord Upjohn; *Stockholm Finance Ltd v Garden Holdings Inc (26 October 1995, unreported)* Ch D 26 October 1995, per Robert Walker J; *Ali v Khan* (2002) 5 ITELR 232 at [30] per Morritt V-C.

28.12 In *Westdeutsche Landesbank Girozentrale v Islington London Borough Council*[1], Lord Browne-Wilkinson described the presumption raised in the transferor's favour as a 'presumption that [the transferor] did not intend to make a gift to [the transferee]', but in the same passage of his speech, he also described it as a 'presumption of resulting trust', ie a presumption that the transferor intends that the transferee should hold the property on trust for the transferor. In some cases, the same result will follow whichever way the presumption is characterised, since a transferor who does not intend to benefit the transferee may also intend that the beneficial interest should come back to him. However, as Lord Millett pointed out in *Air Jamaica Ltd v Charlton*[2], resulting trusts have been imposed in cases where it was clear on the facts that the transferor did not wish the transferor to be his trustee. For example, in *Vandervell v IRC*[3], the transferor thought that he had disposed of his property completely, and did not wish the remainder of the property to result to him, as this rendered him liable to tax that he had sought to avoid; in *Re Vinogradoff*[4], the transferor could not have intended the transferee to be trustee for her because the transferee was her seven year-old grand-daughter; and in *El Ajou* *v Dollar Land Holdings*[5], the transferor had no such intention because it was unaware of the fact that the property had been taken from it in the first place. These cases all suggest that the first of Lord Browne-Wilkinson's formulations is to be preferred, because (unlike the second) it dovetails with all the cases in which resulting trusts have been imposed, including those mentioned above: it is clear, for example, that although Vandervell did not wish the share option to result to him, he did not wish to make an outright gift of it to the trustee company, either. Thus as Lord Phillips MR recently held in *Lavelle v Lavelle*[6], the best view of the law is that where property is gratuitously transferred and there is no evidence conclusively determining the transferor's intention,' there will be a presumption that [he] does not intend to part with the beneficial interest in the property.'

1   [1996] AC 669 at 708.
2   [1999] 1 WLR 1399 at 1412. See too *Twinsectra Ltd v Yardley* [2000] WTLR 527 at 562 per Potter LJ; [2002] 2 AC 164 at [91] per Lord Millett.
3   [1967] 2 AC 291.
4   [1935] WN 68.
5   [1993] 3 All ER 717.
6   [2004] EWCA Civ 223, [2004] 2 FCR 418 at [13]–[14].

'Automatic' and 'presumed' resulting trusts

28.13 Resulting trusts were formerly understood to fall into two separate categories: 'automatic resulting trusts' and 'presumed resulting trusts'. Thus, for example, Megarry J held in *Re Vandervell's Trusts (No 2)*[1] that a resulting trust arises 'automatically' when some or all of the beneficial interest in property held on an express trust has not been disposed of by the settlor, whereas a resulting trust is imposed where property is gratuitously transferred, there is no evidence determining the transferor's intentions, and the transferee fails to rebut a presumption raised in the transferor's favour that the property should be held on trust for him. Laying to one side the proper characterisation of the presumption raised in the transferor's favour in the latter class of case, which has already been discussed, his Lordship's statement of the law is also problematic for another reason – namely, that there is no real difference between the two classes of case which he identifies. Lord Browne-Wilkinson made this point in *Westdeutsche*[2], observing that in the first class of case, as in the second, a resulting trust will not arise if the evidence clearly shows that the settlor intended some other outcome, eg to abandon the remaining beneficial interest. In the first class of case, as in the second, property is transferred by a transferor who receives nothing in return for it. In the first, as in the second, the imposition of a resulting trust leads to the creation of a new equitable property right for the transferor[3], and as Professor Chambers has written, a new right 'cannot be explained as the inertia of a pre-existing beneficial interest'[4]. This all suggests that there are not two types of resulting trust, but only one, imposed by law when property is transferred gratuitously and there is no evidence that the transferor meant to make a gift or loan or to abandon his beneficial interest. For the purposes of exposition, and when examining the duties of a resulting trustee, it remains useful to distinguish between cases where express trusts are declared which fail to dispose completely of the beneficial interest, and other cases where property is gratuitously transferred or bought in the name of the transferee[5]. However, these two classes of cases are analytically identical, in the sense that the underlying reasons for imposing a resulting trust in both types of case are the same.

1 [1974] Ch 269 at 288 ff, glossing *Vandervell v IRC* [1967] 2 AC 291 at 312 ff per Lord Upjohn.
2 [1996] AC 669 at 708.
3 See Lord Browne-Wilkinson's comments in the *Westdeutsche* case at 706; also *DKLR Holding Co (No 2) Pty Ltd v Commissioner for Stamp Duties* (1982) 149 CLR 431.
4 R Chambers 'Resulting Trusts in Canada' (2000) 38 Alberta LR 379 at p.389.
5 Writing extra-judicially, Lord Millett described these two classes of case as 'failing trusts' and 'apparent gifts': Lord Millett 'Pension Schemes and the Law of Trusts' (2000) 14 Tru LI 66 at p.73.

Constructive trusts

28.14 Constructive trusts of property originated in respect of express trusts: they were imposed on the traceable proceeds of misdirected assets belonging to the beneficiaries of express trusts as a means of vindicating the beneficiaries' pre-existing equitable interest. They have been extended so as to arise in respect of other fiduciary relationships concerning property and to prevent unconscionable conduct in relation thereto. They may retain or return value whether for the benefit of the person providing the value in the fiduciary property or for the benefit of persons he intended to benefit, but, unlike resulting trusts, they cannot be ousted by evidence of the real intention of the relevant party, although real intentions can be taken into account in preventing unconscionable behaviour.

'Institutional' and 'remedial' constructive trusts

28.15 Under English law, constructive trusts arise as a result of legal rules which state that they arise in particular circumstances. These rules do not give the courts a discretion to impose constructive trusts, or to refuse to do so, according to their assessment of the equities of a case: the courts' role is purely declaratory. In contrast, some other Commonwealth jurisdictions, eg Canada[1], Australia[2], and New Zealand[3], distinguish 'substantive' or 'institutional' constructive trusts from 'remedial' constructive trusts. Different courts use these terms to mean different things[4], but most use them to distinguish constructive trusts which arise through the inflexible operation of legal rules from constructive trusts which arise following the exercise of a judicial discretion, either retrospectively or prospectively from the date of the court order[5]. It is controversial whether the courts should have a discretion to vary property rights in this way[6] but whatever the rights and wrongs of this question in principle, it is clear as a matter of authority that English law does not currently recognise 'remedial' constructive trusts of this kind[7].

1 *Sorochan v Sorochan* [1986] 2 SCR 38; *LAC Minerals Ltd v International Corona Resources Ltd* [1989] 2 SCR 574; *Soulos v Korkontzilas* [1997] 2 SCR 217; *Hartman Estate v Hartfam Holdings Ltd* (2006) 205 OAC 369.
2 *Muschinski v Dodds* (1986) 62 ALR 429; *Re Stevenson Nominees Pty Ltd* (1987) 76 ALR 485; *Bathurst CC v PWC Properties Pty Ltd* (1998) 195 CLR 566; *Giumelli v Giumelli* (1999) 196 CLR 101; *Robins v Incentive Dynamics Pty Ltd (in liquidation)* (2003) 45 ACSR 244.

3   *Gillies v Keogh* [1989] 2 NZLR 327; *Powell v Thompson* [1991] 1 NZLR 597; *Phillips v Phillips* [1993] 3 NZLR 159; *Fortex Group Ltd v Macintosh* [1998] 3 NZLR 171; *Commonwealth Reserves v Chodar* [2001] 2 NZLR 374.

4   G Elias *Explaining Constructive Trusts* (1990) at pp. 159–163; C Rotherham *Proprietary Remedies in Context* (2002) at pp. 7–32. Some English judges have used the term 'remedial constructive trust' to refer to the *personal* liability of strangers who dishonestly participate in a breach of trust, eg *Clarke v Marlborough Fine Art (London) Ltd* [2002] 1 WLR 1731 at [66] per Patten J; *Kilcarne Holdings Ltd v Targetfollow (Birmingham) Ltd* [2004] EWHC 2547 (Ch), [2005] 2 P & CR 105 at [261], *per* Lewison J. This usage seems to have been prompted by *Paragon Finance plc v D B Thakerar & Co (a firm)* [1999] 1 All ER 400 at 408–9, where Millett LJ distinguished constructive trusts of property from the personal liability of dishonest participants in a breach of trust, but it is best avoided, lest this personal liability become confused with the 'discretionary proprietary remedy' to which Millett LJ also refers at 414.

5   eg *Fortex Group Ltd v Macintosh* [1998] 3 NZLR 171 at 172–3 per Tipping J.

6   P Loughlan 'No Right to the Remedy? An Analysis of Judicial Discretion in the Imposition of Equitable Remedies' (1989) 17 Melbourne LR 132; P D Finn 'Equitable Doctrine and Discretion in Remedies' in W Cornish et al (eds) *Restitution: Past, Present and Future* (1998) 251; D Wright *The Remedial Constructive Trust* (1998), reviewed by P Birks (1999) 115 LQR 681; P Birks 'Rights, Wrongs, and Remedies' (2000) 20 OJLS 1; S Evans 'Defending Discretionary Remedialism" (2001) 23 Sydney LR 463; DWM Waters 'Liability and Remedy: An Adjustable Relationship' (2001) 64 Sask LR 426; DM Jensen 'The Rights and Wrongs of Discretionary Remedialism' [2003] SJLS 178; S Gardner *Introduction to the Law of Trusts* 2nd edn (2003) at pp.124–6.

7   *Re Goldcorp Exchange Ltd* [1995] 1 AC 74 at 104 per Lord Mustill; *Westdeutsche Landesbank Girozentrale v Islington London Borough Council* [1996] AC 669 at 714–6 per Lord Browne-Wilkinson; *Re Polly Peck International Ltd (No 2)* [1998] 3 All ER 812 at 827 per Mummery LJ, and at 831 per Nourse LJ; *Shalson v Russo* [2003] EWHC 1637 (Ch), [2005] Ch 281 at [118] per Rimer J; *Sinclair Investment Holdings SA v Versailles Trade Finance Ltd* [2005] EWCA Civ 722, [2006] 1 BCLC 60 at [37] and [42] per Arden LJ.

28.16 Instead, English law imposes constructive trusts in defined circumstances in accordance with settled principles of Equity, as a way of protecting or vindicating a pre-existing equitable interest in property[1], eg where property is settled on B for life remainder to C, and the trustee, T, purports to keep for himself dividends and bonus shares arising in respect of trust property or a bribe paid to him, or a company claims from a director (a fiduciary) a bribe paid to him; or X, to whom T wrongly gave trust property, purports to keep it or its product for himself; or Y, to whom S bequeathed property on Y's agreement to hold it for A for life, remainder to B absolutely, purports on S's death to keep it for himself or on resulting trust for the residuary beneficiary in S's estate; or where H and W each made wills, agreeing not to revoke them, in favour of the survivor for life, remainder to Z and then, after H's death, W revokes her will and purports to leave everything not to Z but to her new husband; or where L, as registered owner of shares in a private company having done everything he needs to do to transfer legal title to M (by handing M or M's agent the share certificate together with the signed transfer form) so that Equity regards the equitable title as having passed, purports as legal owner to keep the dividends for himself, having changed his mind and the company having refused (as it can) to register M as shareholder. In all these cases, inevitably, the result of the court's intervention will be the retrospective assertion or vindication of pre-existing equitable rights.

1   Scott & Fratcher: *The Law of Trusts* (4th edn) Vol 5 (Boston 1989) para 462.4; *US v Fontana* 528 F Supp 137 (1981); *Rawluk v Rawluk* (1990) 65 DLR (4th) 161; *Re Sharpe* [1980] 1 All ER 198 at 203, [1980] 1 WLR 219 at 225; *Chase Manhattan Bank v Israel-British Bank (London)* [1981] Ch 105; *Re Jonton Pty Ltd* [1992] 1 Qd R 105.

28.17 *Introduction*

28.17 A traditional doctrine which might have been thought to lead to the award of a 'remedial' constructive trust is equitable proprietary estoppel. Successful proprietary estoppel claims lead to the discretionary award of some type of proprietary interest in land to satisfy the claimant's equity, and one could argue that in such cases the court tailors the remedy to fit all the circumstances right up to the date of the hearing rather than declaring the existence of (previously inchoate) rights of a proprietary nature[1]. Moreover the courts have increasingly tended to favour the view that the doctrines of proprietary estoppel and common intention constructive trusts are under-pinned by a common set of principles[2], suggesting that such a trust should be viewed as one of several remedies which could be awarded by the court in a proprietary estoppel case, depending on its assessment of the equities. Against this line of argument, however, must be set the fact that common intention constructive trusts have been assumed by the courts to take effect from the date of the claimant's detriment, binding subsequent mortgagees of the property[3], while s 116 of the Land Registration Act 2002 similarly appears to have been designed to treat equitable proprietary estoppel interests affecting registered land as arising not at the date of the court order but at the date of the claimant's detriment[4].

[1]   See *Stokes v Anderson* [1991] 1 FLR 391 at 399 per Nourse LJ; *Gillett v Holt* [2001] Ch 210 at 235 ff per Robert Walker LJ; *Jennings v Rice* [2002] EWCA Civ 159,[2003] 1 FCR 501 at [42] ff per Robert Walker LJ. See too P Ferguson (1993) 109 LQR 114; D J Hayton (1993) 109 LQR 485; E Cooke (1997) 17 LS 258; S Gardner (1999) 115 LQR 438 and (2006) 122 LQR 492.
[2]   See eg *Grant v Edwards* [1986] Ch 638 at 656 per Browne-Wilkinson V-C; *Birmingham Midshires Mortgage Services Ltd v Sabherwal* (1999) 80 P & CR 256 at 263 per Robert Walker LJ; *Yaxley v Gotts* [2000] Ch 162 at 176 per Robert Walker LJ; *Banner Homes Group plc v Luff Developments Ltd* [2000] Ch 372 at 397 per Chadwick LJ; *Chan Pui Chun v Leung Kam Ho* [2003] BPIR 29 at [91] per Jonathan Parker LJ; *Oxley v Hiscock* [2004] EWCA Civ 546 [2005] Fam 211 at [66] per Chadwick LJ; *Kinane v Mackie-Conteh* [2005] WTLR 345 at [25] per Arden LJ. But for the view that the two concepts are not yet one, see *Hyett v Stanley* [2003] EWCA Civ 942, [2004] 1 FLR 394 at [27] per Sir Martin Nourse.
[3]   As in eg *Midland Bank plc v Cooke* [1995] 4 All ER 562, CA; *Lloyds Bank v Rosset* [1989] Ch 350 (but no proprietary interest on appeal).
[4]   Further see paras 12.66 and 35.49–35.51.

Purchaser's undertaking to respect a contractual licence

28.18 A contractual licence to occupy a house or flat is not an interest in land, and binds the contracting parties alone[1]. However, a purchaser P may undertake to a vendor V that he will take the property positively subject to the rights of a contractual licensee C. After completion of the purchase, C might be able to take advantage of a term for his benefit in V and P's contract under the Contracts (Rights of Third Parties) Act 1999. But if he cannot, then P might try to evict C by claiming that C only has contractual personal rights against V. In *Ashburn Anstalt v Arnold*[2], the Court of Appeal held that Equity would prevent this by imposing a constructive trust on the property, compel-ling P to recognise C's rights under the contractual licence. However, as this case also reveals, if V conveys or contracts to convey Blackacre defensively subject to whatever rights C may happen to have, so as to satisfy V's obligation to disclose all possible incumbrances and to protect him against any possible claim by P, then P is not bound by C's rights which are merely personal and not proprietary. In other words, it is essential that P must have agreed to confer a new right on C. He must have[3]:

> 'undertaken a new obligation, not otherwise existing, to give effect to the relevant incumbrance or prior interest. If, but only if, he has undertaken such a new obligation will a constructive trust be imposed.'

1   *Ashburn Anstalt v Arnold* [1989] Ch 1 at 15–22.
2   [1989] Ch 1.
3   *Lloyd v Dugdale* [2001] EWCA Civ 1754, [2002] 2 P & CR 167 at [52] per Sir Christopher Slade.

28.19 This new right may give C the same rights against P as he would have enjoyed against V, had V never sold the land[1]. But it may also protect C even if C had no right against V, e g because he failed to register his interest[2], and equally if C's valid right against V was destroyed by the transfer to P[3]. However the 'constructive trust' used by the courts to protect C's interests in cases of this sort is probably not a trust at all. The courts find P's conscience to be personally affected by an obligation to give effect to C's interest, and therefore treat him constructively as though he were a trustee, to the limited extent that is necessary to place him under a personal obligation to C. This does not mean that C acquires an equitable interest in the land, for otherwise his contractual licence would be a valid equitable interest binding the land, as would an unregistered void estate contract.

1   *Clowes Developments (UK) Ltd v Walters* [2006] 1 P&CR 1 at [44].
2   *Lyus v Prowsa Developments Ltd* [1982] 1 WLR 1044; *Bahr v Nicolay (No 2)* (1988) 62 ALJR 268 at 288–9, per Brennan J; *IDC Group Ltd v Clark* [1992] 1 EGLR 187 at 190.
3   *Melbury Road Properties 1995 Ltd v Kreidi* [1999] 3 EGLR 10; *Lloyd v Dugdale* [2002] 2 P & CR 167.

Why are resulting and constructive trusts imposed?

28.20 Recently some legal scholars have sought to explain the underlying reasons for the imposition of resulting and constructive trusts by analysing them as 'responses' to legally significant 'causative events', methodology which was first propounded by the late Professor Birks[1]. On this approach, legal rights are understood to respond to various causative events, e g consent, wrongs, and unjust enrichment. In some cases these rights include not only personal rights, but also proprietary rights arising under trusts of property imposed by law. On this view, the key to understanding resulting and constructive trusts is therefore to identify the source of the rights which they afford to the beneficiaries: ie the 'causative events' to which these rights respond. The writers who have taken this approach have differed in their conclusions, but their work confirms that Professor Birks' methodology is a powerful analytical tool which can facilitate a clearer understanding of the ways in which the law of trusts might align with the law of obligations, and the ways in which resulting and constructive trusts might differ from one another.

1   eg P Birks 'Equity in the Modern Law: An Exercise in Taxonomy' (1996) 26 UWALR 1; P Birks 'Equity, Conscience, and Unjust Enrichment' (1999) 23 Univ of Melbourne LR 1.

28.21 So far as resulting trusts are concerned, there is the traditional view that resulting trusts are imposed in order to give effect to the transferor's intention to create a trust for himself[1], while there is the contrasting restitutionary view that they are imposed in order to reverse the transferee's unjust enrichment at the transferor's expense[2]. In *Westdeutsche Landesbank Girozentrale v Islington London Borough Council* [3], Lord Browne-Wilkinson rejected the argument that resulting trusts respond to unjust enrichment, and favoured the view that they respond to the transferor's intention to create a trust. In *Air Jamaica Ltd v Charlton*[4], however, Lord Millett preferred the view that resulting trusts respond to the absence of an intention on the part of the transferor to pass the entire beneficial interest, and in *Twinsectra Ltd v Yardley*[5], he considered that the 'surer ground' for the decision in *Westdeutsche* was another reason given by Lord Browne-Wilkinson for rejecting a resulting trust, namely that the claimant's 'money was paid and received with the intention that it should become the absolute property of the recipient.' Following upon the support for Lord Millett's view given by Lord Phillips MR in *Lavelle v Lavelle*[6], the best view is that resulting trusts are imposed to locate the beneficial interest in property where B gratuitously has transferred property or caused it to be transferred to T but there is no evidence that he intended to part with the beneficial interest. After all, the main objection to the theory that resulting trusts respond to the transferor's intention to create a trust for himself is that it cannot explain cases where resulting trusts have been imposed in the teeth of evidence that the transferor never formed any intention with regard to the disposal of the beneficial interest, or else formed a clear intention that he did not wish to acquire a new equitable beneficial interest in the property, as in *Vandervell v IRC*[7].

[1]   CEF Rickett 'The Classification of Trusts' (1999) 18 NZ Law Rev 305; CEF Rickett and R Grantham 'Resulting Trusts: A Rather Limited Doctrine' in P Birks and FD Rose (eds) *Restitution and Equity* (2000) 39. Cf WJ Swadling 'A New Role for Resulting Trusts?' (1996) 16 LS 110 and WJ Swadling 'A Hard Look at *Hodgson v Marks*" in Birks and Rose, supra, 61, distinguishing 'presumed resulting trusts' which he takes to respond to the transferor's intention, from 'automatic resulting trusts', which he regards as *sui generis*.

[2]   P Birks 'Restitution and Resulting Trusts' in S Goldstein (ed) *Equity and Contemporary Legal Developments* (1992) 361; R Chambers *Resulting Trusts* (1997); R Chambers 'Resulting Trusts in Canada' (2000) 38 Alberta LR 378, reprinted (2002) 16 Tru LI 104 and 138.

[3]   [1996] AC 669 at 708–9. Also see Lords Goff, Slynn, Woolf and Lloyd at 689–690, 718, 720 and 738 respectively.

[4]   [1999] 1 WLR 1399 at 1412.

[5]   [2002] UKHL 12, [2002] 2 AC 164 at 189–190.

[6]   [2004] EWCA Civ 223, [2004] 2 FCR 418 at [13]–[14].

[7]   [1967] 2 AC 291.

28.22 Meanwhile, the main objection to the theory that resulting trusts respond to unjust enrichment is that it seems to prove too much. Pushed to its logical limits, it suggests that a resulting trust should arise whenever a claimant transfers property to a defendant, and his intention to benefit the defendant is vitiated by mistake or undue influence, or is conditional on the happening of a future event which subsequently fails to materialise. Yet in principle it seems very doubtful that claimants in these various situations should all be given proprietary rights and thus priority over the defendant's unsecured creditors, rather than a personal restitutionary remedy or a right to rescind the transfer[1]. It certainly might seem most surprising that a claimant who pays money to a defendant under a standard unsecured loan agreement should be given a proprietary remedy when the defendant defaults, although Professor Chambers would argue that even here a distinction should be drawn between cases where the basis for the claimant's payment fails at some time after receipt of the benefit, and cases where it fails immediately, so that there is no moment at which the defendant has held the relevant asset free of any claim[2]. If that were right, then it would suggest that *Sinclair v Brougham*[3], overruled by the House of Lords in *Westdeutsche*[4], was rightly decided after all, depending on whether the ultra vires depositors' claim to recover their money on the ground of failure of consideration was founded on the assertion that the building society had failed to repay their money, or on the assertion that their contracts with the building society had been void from the outset[5].

1   Lord Millett 'Restitution and Constructive Trusts' (1998) 114 LQR 399 at p.416; Lord Millett 'The Law of Restitution: Taking Stock' (1999) 14 *Amicus Curiae* 1 at pp.7–8.
2   R Chambers *Resulting Trusts* (1997) at pp. 110 and 155–170. See too P Birks 'Retrieving Tied Money' in W Swadling (ed) *The Quistclose Trust: Critical Essays* (2004) 121, at pp.130–138; P Birks, *Unjust Enrichment* 2nd edn (2003) at pp. 180–198.
3   [1914] AC 398.
4   [1996] AC 669 at 709–714.
5   Another example of immediate failure of basis is arguably provided by *Nesté Oy v Lloyds Bank plc* [1983] 2 Lloyd's Rep 658, where to the knowledge of the payee no performance at all could have taken place under the contract for which the payment formed the consideration. See too *Re Ames' Settlement* [1946] Ch 217; *Criterion Properties plc v Stratford* [2004] UKHL 28, [2004] 1 WLR 1846 at [4] per Lord Nicholls.

28.23 Turning to constructive trusts, there is little consensus with regard to the underlying reasons for their imposition, perhaps inevitably in light of the fact that the courts of different Commonwealth jurisdictions have varied quite widely in the approaches which they have taken to this question. It has often been said that constructive trusts do not give effect to the parties' intentions, but are imposed 'against the intentions of the trustee'[1]. Nevertheless, there are good reasons for thinking that some constructive trusts are imposed on property in response to the parties' intention that beneficial ownership of the property should pass from one to the other[2]. Obviously constructive trusts are not needed in such situations unless the parties' intentions have been thwarted in some way: by failure to comply with applicable formality rules, for example, or by the property-owner's change of heart. In cases of the latter sort it could be said that the constructive trust is imposed against the *current* wishes of the property-owner, and that it responds to his 'wrongdoing' in denying the claimant's beneficial interest[3]. However, if attention is focussed on his *original* intention, then it can be said that in these cases, just as in the cases where an intended transfer has failed for non-compliance with a formality, the function of the constructive trust is 'perfectionary': it perfects the parties' original intention that beneficial ownership should be transferred[4].

1   *Westdeutsche Landesbank Girozentrale v Islington London Borough Council* [1996] AC 669 at 708 per Lord Browne-Wilkinson. See too *Rathwell v Rathwell* [1978] 2 SCR 436 at 454 per Dickson J; *Air Jamaica Ltd v Charlton* [1999] 1 WLR 1399 at 1412 per Lord Millett.
2   R Chambers 'Constructive Trusts in Canada' (1999) 37 Alberta LR 173, reprinted in (2001) 15 Tru LI 214 and (2002) 16 Tru LI 2; S Gardner *Introduction to the Law of Trusts* 2nd edn (2003) at pp. 159 ff; D Hayton and C Mitchell (eds) *Hayton & Marshall's Commentary & Cases on The Law of Trusts & Equitable Remedies* 12th edn (2005) Chapter 6.

28.23 *Introduction*

3   *Lonrho plc v Fayed (No 2)* [1992] 1 WLR 1 at 10 per Millett J.
4   G Elias *Explaining Constructive Trusts* (1990) p. 157.

28.24 Authorities supporting this analysis include the statement by the High Court of Australia in *Bathurst CC v PWC Properties Pty Ltd* that[1]:

> 'One species of constructive trust is concerned with cases where the intent of a settlor or testator in transferring or devising property otherwise would fail for want of compliance with the formalities for creation of express trusts inter vivos or by will. The necessary elements on which the question turns in many cases are "intention, communication, and acquiescence".'[2]

1   (1998) 195 CLR 566 at [39]. See too *Allen v Snyder* [1977] 2 NSWLR 685 at 693 per Glass JA; *Re Australian Elizabethan Theatre Trust* (1991) 30 FCR 491 at 510 per Gummow J, considering *Le Compte v Public Trustee* [1983] 2 NSWLR 109.
2   Citing *Vosges v Monaghan* (1954) 94 CLR 231 at 233, 235, and 237; *Blackwell v. Blackwell* [1929] AC 318 at 334.

28.25 Millett LJ also held in *Paragon Finance plc v D B Thakerar & Co* that some constructive trusts arise where the trustee receives the trust property[1]:

> 'by a transaction *which both parties intend to create a trust from the outset* and which is not impugned by the plaintiff. [The defendant's] possession of the property is coloured from the first by the trust and confidence by means of which he obtained it, and his subsequent appropriation to his own use is a breach of that trust. Well known examples of such a constructive trust are *McCormick v Grogan*[2] (a case of secret trust) and *Rochefoucauld v Boustead*[3] (where the defendant agreed to buy property for the plaintiff but the trust was improperly recorded). *Pallant v Morgan*[4] (where the defendant sought to keep for himself property which the plaintiff trusted him to buy for both parties) is another. In these cases the plaintiff does not impugn the transaction by which the defendant obtained control of the property. He alleges that the circumstances in which the defendant obtained control make it unconscionable for him thereafter to assert a beneficial interest in the property.'

1   [1999] 1 All ER 400 at 408–9.
2   (1869) 4 App Cas 82.
3   [1897] 1 Ch 196.
4   [1953] Ch 43.

28.26 In line with these authorities, many constructive trusts can be seen as responding to the parties' original intention that beneficial ownership of the trust property should be vested in the beneficiary. Further examples besides those enumerated by Millett LJ are: constructive trusts imposed on unauthorised fiduciary gains which cannot be denied to have been obtained by acting to further the best interests of the beneficiaries, rather than the selfish interests of the fiduciary[1]; constructive trusts of property which forms the subject matter of a specifically enforceable contract of sale; constructive trusts of property which has been assigned for value before it comes into the assignor's hands; constructive trusts arising under the rule in *Re Rose*[2]; and common intention constructive trusts of family homes. Assuming that it is correct to characterise these constructive trusts as perfectionary, however, there are still some outstanding questions to be answered[3]. It is currently uncertain what significance should be attached to the parties' failure to comply with a statutory formality, as the courts have sometimes thought it undesirable to impose a constructive trust where this would undermine the integrity of statutory formalities, but at other times have imposed a constructive trust nonetheless[4]. Again, the role of detriment in attracting Equity's attention is not yet fully understood. One might have thought that detriment suffered by the claimant would always be a necessary pre-requisite for the imposition of the constructive trust, as the element which makes it unconscionable for the defendant to act in a manner contrary to the parties' original intentions. However, while this is true of some cases (eg the family homes cases), it is not true of others, such as cases arising under the rule in *Pallant v Morgan* and cases concerned with unauthorised gains by fiduciaries, where the defendant has expressly undertaken to act always to further the best interests of the beneficiaries (or of himself and his co-beneficiary)[5].

[1] Cf Lord Millett 'Book Review' (2002) 2 OUCLJ 291, at p.295; Lord Millett 'Proprietary Restitution' in S Degeling and J Edelman (eds) *Equity in Commercial Law* (2005) 309 at p.324.
[2] [1952] Ch 499.
[3] For discussion of these and other problems see: T Youdan 'Formalities for Trusts of Land and the Doctrine in *Rochefoucauld v Boustead*' (1984) 43 CLJ 306; N Hopkins 'Acquiring Property Rights from Uncompleted Sales of Land' (1998) 61 MLR 486; P Critchley 'Instruments of Fraud, Testamentary Dispositions, and the Doctrine of Secret Trusts' (1999) 115 LQR 631; N Hopkins 'The *Pallant v Morgan* "Equity"?' [2002] Con. 35; S Gardner *Introduction to the Law of Trusts* 2nd edn (2003) at pp.86–93 and 159–162; J Cartwright 'Formality and Informality in Property and Contract' in J Getzler (ed) *Rationalizing Property, Equity and Trusts* (2003) 36; B Macfarlane 'Constructive Trusts Arising on a Receipt of Property *Sub Conditione*' (2004) 120 LQR 667.
[4] See *Yaxley v Gotts* [2000] Ch 162.
[5] Fiduciaries must account for unauthorised profits whether or not their actions have caused their principals a loss, and even though there is no actual conflict between their personal interests and their principals' interests: see paras 33.2–33.6 below.

28.27 Other constructive trusts cannot be explained by reference to intention. For example, a court order to convey a specific asset can lead to the imposition of a constructive trust on the property even though the order itself is not couched in these terms, and in this case it seems that the order itself is the event to which the trust responds[1]. Again, constructive trusts are sometimes imposed as a response to wrongdoing, most obviously where they capture the proceeds of crime[2], but also where they are imposed on property in the hands of those who wrongfully intermeddle with the equitable property rights of trust beneficiaries[3]. It has also been said that some constructive trusts respond to unjust enrichment. Under Canadian law it was formerly held that all constructive trusts do this[4], although it has now been recognised that some do not[5]. In contrast, the English and Australian courts have never subscribed to the view that *all* constructive trusts respond to unjust enrichment, but they have held that some do. Perhaps the best known English case is *Chase Manhattan Bank v Israel-British Bank (London) Ltd*[6] in which Goulding J held that money paid by mistake should be held on constructive trust for the payor by the recipient[7]. In various jurisdictions, constructive trusts have also been imposed on property stolen from a claimant or obtained from him by fraud[8], and on property transferred by a claimant who has been unduly influenced by the recipient[9], or whose ability to make decisions has otherwise been compromised by his relationship with the recipient[10].

[1] *Mountney v Treharne* [2002] EWCA Civ 1174, [2003] Ch 135, affirming *Re Flint (a bankrupt)* [1993] Ch 319.

28.27 *Introduction*

2   *Beresford v Royal Insurance Co Ltd* [1938] AC 586 at 600; *Rasmanis v Jurewitsch* [1970] NSWLR 650; *Re K* [1985] 1 All ER 403.
3   *Blyth v Fladgate* [1891] 1 Ch 337; *Nonus Asia Co Inc v Standard Chartered Bank* [1990] 1 HKLR 396 at 417–9.
4   *Deglman v Guaranty Trust Co* [1954] SCR 725; *Pettkus v Becker* [1980] 2 SCR 834; *Sorochan v Sorochan* [1986] 2 SCR 38; *Peter v Beblow* [1993] 1 SCR 980.
5   *Korkontzilas v Soulos* [1997] 2 SCR 217.
6   [1981] Ch 105.
7   *Chase Manhattan* remains good law in England, and was recently followed in e g *Commerzbank Aktiengesellschaft v IMB Morgan plc* [2005] 1 Lloyd's Rep 298 at [36]. However its status was diminished by Lord Browne-Wilkinson's gloss on the case in *Westdeutsche Landesbank Girozentrale v Islington London Borough Council* [1996] AC 669 at 714–5, and by judicial reactions to this gloss in *Box v Barclays Bank plc* [1998] Lloyd's Rep Bank 185 at 200–201; *Papamichael v. National Westminster Bank plc* [2003] 1 Lloyd's Rep 341 at [232]–[242]; and *Shalson v Russo* [2003] EWHC 1637 (Ch) [2005] Ch 281at [108]–[127], *per* Rimer J.
8   *Westdeutsche Landesbank Girozentrale v Islington London Borough Council* [1996] AC 669 at 715–6 per Lord Browne-Wilkinson, followed in *Niru Battery Manufacturing Co v Milestone Trading Ltd (No 1)* [2002] EWHC 1425 (Comm), [2002] 2 All ER (Comm) 705 at [55]–[56] per Moore-Bick J. See too *Black v S Freedman & Co* (1910) 12 CLR 105 at 109; *Creak v James Moore & Sons Pty Ltd* (1912) 15 CLR 426 at 432; *Australian Postal Corpn v Lutak* (1991) 12 NSWLR 584 at 589; *Zobory v Commissioner of Taxation* (1995) 64 FCR 86 at 90–93; *Evans v European Bank Ltd* (2004) 7 ITELR 19 at [111].
9   *Janz v McIntosh* (1999) 182 Sask R 197.
10 *Louth v Diprose* (1992) 175 CLR 621; *McCulloch v Fern* [2001] NSWSC 406; *Smith v Smith* [2004] NSWSC 663. On the Australian law governing unconscionable transactions and the law of unjust enrichment, see M Bryan 'Unjust Enrichment and Unconscionability in Australia: A False Dichotomy?' in JW Neyers et al (eds) *Understanding Unjust Enrichment* (2004) 47.

28.28 These authorities are difficult for a number of reasons. Many of the Canadian cases concern shared homes, and in their wish to do justice between the parties, the courts have made awards designed to fulfil the claimant's expectations rather than to reverse a transfer of value to the defendant, riding roughshod over the requirement that a claimant in unjust enrichment must prove that the defendant's enrichment has been acquired at her expense[1]. More generally, some hard questions arise, once it is accepted that at least some claimants in unjust enrichment are entitled to a proprietary rather than a personal restitutionary remedy.

1   J Mee *The Property Rights of Cohabitees* (1999) at pp.213–4; J D McCamus 'Restitution on Dissolution of Marital and Other Intimate Relationships: Constructive Trust or *Quantum Meruit?*' in J D Neyers et al (eds) *Understanding Unjust Enrichment* (2004) 359. Also, note Cory J's comment in *Peter v Beblow* [1993] 1 SCR 980 at 1012 that 'if there is enrichment ... it [will] almost invariably follow that there is a corresponding deprivation suffered by the person who provided the enrichment'.

28.29 First, should *all* claimants in unjust enrichment be entitled to a proprietary remedy, and if not, then how should the law distinguish those who are from those who are not? Different writers offer different answers to this question, many of them focussing on the question whether the claimant has taken the risk of the defendant's insolvency[1], others focussing on the question whether the basis of the claimant's transfer to the defendant has immediately failed at the moment of receipt[2]. In *Westdeutsche*[3], Lord Browne-Wilkinson took another approach, suggesting that a claimant in unjust enrichment should be entitled to a proprietary remedy against a defendant only if his conscience is affected by knowledge of the circumstances making his enrichment unjust, at a time when the property he has received from the claimant is still identifiable in his hands. However, it is hard to see why the claimant's position relative to the defendant's other creditors should be improved by a change in the defendant's state of mind at some time between the date of receipt and the date of his insolvency[4].

1   eg C Rotherham *Proprietary Interests in Context* (2002) chaps. 4, 6, 9, 11 and 12; A Burrows *The Law of Restitution* 2nd edn. (2002) pp. 69–73.
2   eg P Birks, *Unjust Enrichment* 2nd edn (2003) at pp. 180–198.
3   [1996] AC 669 at 707 and 709.
4   Cf Lord Millett 'Restitution and Constructive Trusts' (1998) 114 LQR 399 at p. 413: 'By itself notice of the existence of a ground of restitution is obviously insufficient to found a proprietary remedy; it is merely notice of a personal right to an account and payment.'

28.30 Second, if a trust is to be imposed on assets in a defendant's hands in order to reverse his enrichment at a claimant's expense, then why should this trust be regarded as a constructive trust rather than a resulting trust? Given that resulting trusts are always restitutionary in pattern and constructive trusts are not, then it might make more sense to say that trusts imposed to reverse unjust enrichment are always resulting trusts[1]. Developing the law in this way would make it easier to understand why trusts are imposed by law, and how resulting and constructive trusts differ from one another. It would enable us to say that resulting trusts align with unjust enrichment and that constructive trusts align with intention, wrongdoing, and other causative events. As already explained, aligning resulting trusts with unjust enrichment would make it difficult to restrain their imposition within reasonable bounds so as not to prejudice the defendant's creditors, which is why Lord Browne-Wilkinson rejected this line of thinking in *Westdeutsche*[2]. Of course, the same objection can also be raised to aligning *constructive* trusts with unjust enrichment as they are currently understood to operate under English law – which is why his Lordship went on to suggest that the solution might be to introduce the remedial constructive trust into English law, a form of constructive trust which 'can be tailored to the circumstances of the particular case' to avoid prejudice to 'innocent third parties'[3].

1   As mooted in *El Ajou v Dollar Land Holdings plc* [1993] 3 All ER 717 at 734 per Millett J; *Evans v European Bank Ltd* (2004) 7 ITELR 19 at [112] per Spigelman CJ. See too PJ Millett 'Tracing the Proceeds of Fraud' (1991) 107 LQR 71 at p. 81.
2   [1996] AC 669 at 703–5.
3   [1996] AC 669 at 716.

28.31 Third, should the law distinguish between consensual and non-consensual transfers? In *Twinsectra Ltd v Yardley*, Potter LJ gave a positive answer to this question, holding that in cases where a defendant has acquired a claimant's money by fraudulent means[1]:

'the distinction of importance ... is that between non-consensual transfers and transfers pursuant to contracts which are voidable for misrepresentation. In the latter case, the transferor may elect whether to avoid or affirm the transaction and, until he elects to avoid it, there is no constructive (resulting) trust[2]; in the former case the constructive trust arises from the moment of transfer. The result, so far as third parties are concerned, is that, before rescission, the owner has no proprietary interest in the original property; all he has is the "mere equity" of his right to set aside the voidable contract.'

1   [1999] Lloyd's Rep Bank 438 at [99], considered in *Halley v Law Society* (2003) 6 ITELR 40 at [46]–[48].
2   It is uncertain what his Lordship meant by 'constructive (resulting) trust'.

28.32 Thus, where a claimant, C, concludes a contract with a defendant, D, under which he transfers legal and beneficial[1] ownership in particular assets to D, and his intention to benefit D is vitiated by a factor such as undue influence or induced mistake, C can rescind the transaction and ask the court to exercise its discretion to restore the assets[2]. Once C elects to rescind[3], the court can treat equitable title as retrospectively vesting in C for the purpose of allowing C to trace what happened to his assets in D's hands[4]. Since D, his trustee in bankruptcy, and his personal representatives are all bound to retransfer the original assets to C from the time when he elects to rescind and demands the return of the assets, it can be said that C enjoys a proprietary interest in the assets from that time[5]. This interest can be devised[6] or assigned[7], but it is a mere equity rather than an equitable interest: ie it will bind a third party who is a volunteer or a purchaser with notice, but it will not bind a bona fide purchaser without notice of a legal *or equitable* interest in the assets[8].

1   A case of undue influence 'assumes a transfer of the beneficial interest but in circumstances which entitle the transferor to recall it': *Hodgson v Marks* [1971] Ch 892 at 929 per Russell LJ. So does a case of fraudulent misrepresentation: *Shalson v Russo* [2003] EWHC 1637 (Ch), [2005] Ch 281 at [119] per Rimer J.
2   *Lonrho plc v Fayed (No 2)* [1992] 1 WLR 1 at 9 per Millett J; *Re Goldcorp Exchange Ltd* [1995] 1 AC 74 at 103 per Lord Mustill; *Cheese v Thomas* [1994] 1 All ER 35 at 42.
3   A claimant's action in issuing proceedings can amount to an implied election to rescind in itself: *Shalson v Russo* [2003] EWHC 1637 (Ch), [2005] Ch 281 at [120] per Rimer J, relying on *Banque Belge pour l'Etranger v Hambrouck* [1921] 1 KB 321 at 332 per Atkin LJ.
4   *O'Sullivan v Management Agency & Music Ltd* [1985] QB 428 at 475; *El Ajou v Dollar Land Holdings plc* [1993] 3 All ER 717 at 734 per Millett J; *Bristol & West BS v Mothew* [1996] 4 All ER 698 at 716 per Millett LJ.
5   *Load v Green* (1846) 15 M & W 216; *Re Eastgate* [1905] 1 KB 465; *Tilley v Bowman* [1910] 1 KB 745 at 750; *Banque Belge pour l'Etranger v Hambrouck* [1921] 1 KB 321 at 332 per Atkin LJ; *Shalson v Russo* [2003] EWHC 1637 (Ch), [2005] Ch 281 at [122]–[126] per Rimer J. See generally S Worthington 'The Proprietary Consequences of Rescission' [2002] RLR 28.
6   *Stump v Gaby* (1852) 2 De G M & G 623.
7   *Dickinson v Burrell* (1866) LR 1 Eq 337; *Bruty v Edmundson* (1915) 85 LJ Ch 568.
8   *Phillips v Phillips* (1861) 4 De G F & J 208 at 218 and 221–3; *Lancashire Loans Ltd v Black* [1934] 1 KB 380; *Latec Investments Pty Ltd v Terrigal Pty Ltd* (1965) 113 CLR 265; *Blacklocks v J B Developments Ltd* [1981] 3 All ER 392 at 400. See too Lord Millett 'Restitution and Constructive Trusts' (1998) 114 LQR 399 at p.416.

Chapter 8

RESULTING TRUSTS

ARTICLE 29
RESULTING TRUSTS WHERE PROPERTY TRANSFERRED ON
EXPRESS TRUST WHICH DOES NOT EXHAUST THE
BENEFICIAL INTEREST

29.1

(1)   When property is transferred gratuitously and it appears to have
       been the transferor's intention that the transferee should not take
       beneficially[1], but as an express trustee, and there is no evidence
       that the transferor expressly or by necessary implication aban-
       doned any beneficial interest in the trust property[2], a resulting
       trust will be imposed in favour of the transferor or his repre-
       sentatives where the trust declared does not exhaust the whole
       beneficial interest[3] as exemplified by the following cases, namely:
       (a)   if the transferor fails to declare comprehensive trusts upon
              which the property is to be held; or
       (b)   if the transferor directs that the property shall be applied
              for a particular purpose (as distinguished from merely
              being subjected to a charge for such purpose)[4] which turns
              out to be insufficient to exhaust the property; or
       (c)   if an express trust cannot wholly be carried into effect[5]
              (though if this is because of illegality special considerations
              arise[6]).

(2)   If money is lent to a borrower for a specific purpose, it was formerly thought that the money might be held on a 'primary' purpose trust, the failure of which would trigger the imposition of a 'secondary' resulting trust in the lender's favour[7], but the better view is now that the law achieves this effect by imposing a resulting trust of the money for the lender from the outset, which is defeasible by the exercise of a power vested in the borrower to apply the money to the purpose, until the purpose cannot be carried out or a specified period elapses or the lender countermands the mandate, depending on the terms of their contract[8].

(3)   Where the non-beneficial character of the transfer appears on the face of the instrument, no evidence to the contrary is admissible[9]. But where it is merely presumed from the general scope of the instrument, parol evidence is admissible both in aid and in contradiction of the presumption made in the transferor's favour[10].

(4)   A resulting trust is a trust which the court can execute even though all that is required is the transfer of the property back to the settlor[11].

[1]   Lord Reid in *Vandervell v IRC* [1967] 2 AC 291 at 307 citing the 11th edition hereof; also *Hill v Bishop of London* (1738) 1 Atk 618; *Walton v Walton* (1807) 14 Ves 318; *King v Denison* (1813) 1 Ves & B 260.

[2]   See Lord Browne-Wilkinson in *Westdeutsche Landesbank v Islington London Borough Council* [1996] AC 669 at 708.

[3]   See *Westdeutsche Landesbank v Islington London Borough Council* [1996] AC 669 at 708; *Vandervell v IRC* [1967] 2 AC 291 at 313, 329.

[4]   *Watson v Hayes* (1839) 5 My & Cr 125; *Wood v Cox* (1837) 2 My & Cr 684; *Cunningham v Foot* (1878) 3 App Cas 974; *Re West* [1900] 1 Ch 84.

[5]   *Stubbs v Sargon* (1838) 3 My & Cr 507; *Ackroyd v Smithson* (1780) 1 Bro CC 503.

[6]   See Article 30.

[7]   *Barclays Bank Ltd v Quistclose Investments Ltd* [1970] AC 567, HL.

[8]   *Twinsectra Ltd v Yardley* [2002] UKHL 12, [2002] 2 AC 164, HL.

[9]   See *Langham v Sanford* (1811) 17 Ves 435 at 442; *Irvine v Sullivan* (1869) LR 8 Eq 673; *Re Rees' Will Trusts* [1949] Ch 541, [1949] 1 All ER 609; affd [1950] Ch 204, [1949] 2 All ER 1003; *Vandervell v IRC* [1967] 2 AC 291 at 312.

[10]   Statute of Frauds 1677, s 8; Law of Property Act 1925, s 53 (2); *Gascoigne v Thwing* (1685) 1 Vern 366; *Willis v Willis* (1740) 2 Atk 71; *Cook v Hutchinson* (1836) 1 Keen 42. As to parol evidence explanatory of a *testator's* intention, see *Docksey v Docksey* (1708) 2 Eq Cas Abr 506; *North v Crompton* (1671) 1 Cas in Ch 196; *Walton v Walton* (1807) 14 Ves 318; *Langham v Sanford* (1811) 17 Ves 435; *Lynn v Beaver* (1823) Turn & R 63; *Biddulph v Williams* (1875) 1 Ch D 203; *Vandervell v IRC* [1967] 2 AC 291 at 312 and Administration of Justice Act 1982, s 21.

[11]   *Re Sayer* [1957] Ch 423, [1956] 3 All ER 600.

Paragraph 1

'Automatic' resulting trusts

29.2 In *Re Vandervell's Trusts (No 2)*[1], Megarry J distinguished between 'presumed' resulting trusts, imposed when property is gratuitously transferred and there is no evidence determining the transferor's intentions, and 'automatic' resulting trusts, imposed when some or all of the beneficial interest in property held on an express trust has not been disposed of by the settlor. However, this terminology is misleading to the extent that it suggests that these two types of trust are underpinned by different principles. As Lord Browne-Wilkinson observed in *Westdeutsche Landesbank Girozentrale v Islington London Borough Council*[2], a resulting trust will not be imposed in either type of case if the evidence shows that the settlor intended some other outcome, eg to abandon the remaining beneficial interest, or give it to the transferee. In both classes of case, property is transferred by a transferor who receives nothing in return for it; and in both, the imposition of a resulting trust leads to the creation of a new equitable property right for the transferor[3].

[1]   [1974] Ch 269 at 294.
[2]   [1996] AC 669 at 708.
[3]   See Lord Browne-Wilkinson's comments in the *Westdeutsche* case at 706; also *DKLR Holding Co (No 2) Pty Ltd v Commissioner for Stamp Duties* (1982) 149 CLR 431.

Disposition to trustees

29.3 If a settlor declares himself trustee of a trust which fails, then he will then become the absolute beneficial owner of the property once more. No resulting trust is needed to produce this result, and in fact it would be an impossibility, because a person cannot be a trustee solely for his own benefit[1]. However, if property is transferred to others as trustees, or left by will to trustees, but no defined trusts are delimited then there can be a resulting trust for the settlor or his estate (when the residuary beneficiary or the next of kin will respectively benefit according to whether the property was the subject of a specific gift or of a residuary gift[2]).

[1]   *Westdeutsche Landesbank Girozentrale v Islington London Borough Council* [1996] AC 669 at 703.
[2]   *Rudkin v Dolman* (1876) 35 LT 791; *Re Boyes* (1884) 26 Ch D 531; *Re Chapman* [1922] 1 Ch 287; *Re Pugh's Will Trusts* [1967] 3 All ER 337, [1967] 1 WLR 1262.

29.4 In *Vandervell v IRC*[1], a settlor transferred certain shares to an institution so that the institution would receive the dividends. By arrangement with him, the institution granted to the trustees of the settlor's family settlement an option to buy back the shares for £5,000, but the trusts on which the trustees were to hold the option were not declared. The Inland Revenue claimed that the settlor had not divested himself absolutely of all interest in the shares within s 415 (1)(d) and (2) of the Income Tax Act 1952. It was held that the settlor should be treated as having settled the option on the settlement trustees and that these trustees held the option on a resulting trust for the settlor, and that he had therefore not divested himself of all interest in the shares.

[1]   [1967] 2 AC 291, [1967] 1 All ER 1; *Re Vandervell's Trusts (No 2)* [1974] Ch 269, [1974] 3 All ER 205; and see paras 12.20–12.33.

Uncertainty or failure of express trust

29.5 If a declared trust is too uncertain or vague to be executed[1] or cannot be carried out by reason of lapse[2] or of complete failure of beneficiaries[3] or becomes in the event void for remoteness[4] then, since it appears from the face of the instrument that the trustee was not intended to take beneficially, there will be a resulting trust. Similarly if the declared trust fails to satisfy the requisite formalities[5].

1   *Morice v Bishop of Durham* (1804) 9 Ves 399; on appeal (1805) 10 Ves 522; *Re Osmund* [1944] Ch 66, [1944] 1 All ER 12; *Re Pugh's Will Trusts* [1967] 3 All ER 337, [1967] 1 WLR 1262; *Re Atkinson's Will Trusts* [1978] 1 All ER 1275, [1978] 1 WLR 586.
2   *Ackroyd v Smithson* (1780) 1 Bro CC 503.
3   *Hedderwick's Trustees v Hedderwick's Executors* 1910 SC 333.
4   *Tregonwell v Sydenham* (1815) 3 Dow 194 at 210; *Re Drummond's Settlement* [1986] 3 All ER 45, [1986] 1 WLR 1096; *Air Jamaica Ltd v Charlton* [1999] 1 WLR 1399, PC.
5   *Hodgson v Marks* [1971] Ch 892, [1971] 2 All ER 684, CA.

29.6 If a settlement is executed in contemplation of a marriage and the contract to marry is definitely and absolutely put an end to, so that there is a total failure of the consideration for, or purpose of, the settlement, the trustees hold on a resulting trust for the settlor[1].

1   *Essery v Cowlard* (1884) 26 Ch D 191; also see *Burgess v Rawnsley* [1975] Ch 429, [1975] 3 All ER 142, CA.

Failure of life interest

29.7 A resulting trust will be imposed on failure of a life interest in cases where the interest in remainder does not take effect forthwith under the doctrine of acceleration. To bring this doctrine into effect there must be something equivalent to the gift of a vested remainder[1] to a person expressed to take effect on the death of the first taker[2] so that the postponement of the subsequent interest is merely in order that the life interest may be enjoyed. The principle was first established in regard to remainders in real estate[3], but has been extended to personalty and to partial as well as residuary interests[4], and it applies to settlements inter vivos as well as to wills[5]. There will, however, be no acceleration where the character of the disposition made by the settlement shows that the settlor's intention was that the person interested in remainder should take no benefit until the actual death of the person entitled to the life interest[6], or where the interests in remainder are still contingent at the determination of the life interest[7]. However when the contingent interest becomes vested acceleration will occur[8].

1   *Re Flower's Settlement Trusts* [1957] 1 All ER 462, CA.
2   Even though liable to be divested, see *Re Taylor* [1957] 3 All ER 56, [1957] 1 WLR 1043.
3   A distinction was made between legal remainders which could not be accelerated (*Re Scott* [1911] 2 Ch 374), and equitable remainders which could (*Re Conyngham* [1921] 1 Ch 491) but even if this distinction was valid, as to which there is some doubt, the legislation of 1925 has swept away distinctions of this kind between legal and equitable limitations (*Re Hatfeild's Will Trusts* [1958] Ch 469, [1957] 2 All ER 261).
4   *Re Hodge* [1943] Ch 300, [1943] 2 All ER 304.
5   *Re Flower's Settlement Trusts* [1957] 1 All ER 462, [1957] 1 WLR 401, CA, but it may be more difficult to collect between settlement the intention necessary to bring the principle of acceleration into play in the case of a settlement than a will (*Re Flower's Settlement Trusts*, above). See also *Re Harker's Will Trusts* [1969] 3 All ER 1, [1969] 1 WLR 1124 showing that acceleration probably does not close class gifts despite *Re Davies* [1957] 3 All ER 52, [1957] 1 WLR 922; [1973] CLJ 246 (A.M. Prichard).
6   *Re Flower's Settlement Trusts* [1957] 1 All ER 462, [1957] 1 WLR 401, CA.

7   *Re Townsend's Estate* (1886) 34 Ch D 357; *Re Taylor* [1957] 3 All ER 56, [1957] 1 WLR 1043; *Re Scott* [1975] 2 All ER 1033, [1975] 1 WLR 1260.
8   *Re Townsend's Estate* (1886) 34 Ch D 357.

29.8 In regard to instruments taking effect after 16 July 1964, it is expressly provided by s 6 of the Perpetuities and Accumulations Act 1964 that the vesting of an interest shall not be prevented from being accelerated on the failure of a prior interest merely because the prior interest failed for remoteness. It is doubtful whether this provision makes any change in the law[1].

1   See *Re Coleman* [1936] Ch 528, [1936] 2 All ER 225; *Re Allan's Will Trusts* [1958] 1 All ER 401, [1958] 1 WLR 220; and *Re Hubbard's Will Trusts* [1963] Ch 275, [1962] 2 All ER 917.

Residue after satisfaction of express trust

29.9 Where there is a devise to A upon trust to pay debts, or to answer an annuity, there is a resulting trust of what remains after payment of the debts or satisfaction of the annuity[1]. And, on similar principles where income under a settlement was payable to the wife so long as she lived with her husband and on her death, or the prior determination of the trust in her favour, to the husband during his life with a gift over on the death of the survivor, it was held that, the wife having ceased to live with the husband during the subsistence of the marriage but having survived him, there was a resulting trust of income during the rest of her life since the court could not see clearly what words ought to be written into the settlement to provide for the eventuality for which the settlement made no provision[2]. Where, however, the court can see from the document itself what words should be supplied it will fill the gap and thus prevent a resulting trust from arising[3].

1   *King v Denison* (1813) 1 Ves & B 260; *Watson v Hayes* (1839) 5 My & Cr 125; but see contra *Croome v Croome* (1889) 61 LT 814.
2   *Re Cochrane* [1955] Ch 309, [1955] 1 All ER 222; see also *Re Wyatt* (1889) 60 LT 920; though the assumption in that case that the gift over only took effect on death seems to have been wrong on the authorities and as a matter of interpretation, see *Upton v Brown* (1879) 12 Ch D 872; and *Underhill v Roden* (1876) 2 Ch D 494, and cases there cited; and *Re Akeroyd's Settlement* [1893] 3 Ch 363.
3   *Re Akeroyd's Settlement* [1893] 3 Ch 363; *Re Cochrane* [1955] Ch 309, [1955] 1 All ER 222; and cf *Re Cory* [1955] 2 All ER 630, [1955] 1 WLR 725; distinguished *Re Follett* [1955] 2 All ER 22, [1955] 1 WLR 429, CA.

29.10 Even though it may appear, at the time of execution, that a settlement effectively disposes of the whole of the settlor's interest in the property comprised in it, later events may nonetheless give rise to a resulting trust. This may be so if the beneficial interests fail for want of beneficiaries. Equally, it may be so if a beneficiary, though qualified to take his interest, chooses instead to surrender or release it without declaring trusts in respect of it and in such circumstances that the subsequent interests (if any) under the settlement are not accelerated. Thus in *Re Guinness's Settlement*[1], a tenant for life executed a deed which released her life interest to the settlement trustees but did not declare trusts in respect of it. Goff J held that the income must be held

413

on a resulting trust for the settlor: it was very unlikely that the life tenant had intended this, but then ' ... it is rarely, if ever, that anyone intends to create a resulting trust'.

¹   [1966] 2 All ER 497, [1966] 1 WLR 1355. Also *Re Scott* [1975] 2 All ER 1033, [1975] 1 WLR 1260.

No resulting trust where it appears that donee was to take beneficially

29.11 On the other hand, there will be no resulting trust where an intention to exclude the settlor appears from the evidence. Thus, where debtors assigned their property to trustees in trust to sell, and *divide the proceeds* amongst their creditors in rateable proportions according to the amounts of their respective debts, it was held by the House of Lords that there was no resulting trust in favour of the debtors, in the event of there being more than sufficient to pay twenty shillings in the pound¹. This decision, was, however, founded entirely on the construction of the particular deed, and turned apparently to some extent upon the fact that all the best precedents contained an *express* trust of any surplus in favour of the debtors. It must, therefore, not be rashly assumed that the same decision would be arrived at if, on the language of another creditor's deed, it should appear that the object was to *pay debts* (or a dividend on debts), and not to assign the property for better or for worse by way of accord and satisfaction. It may be observed that where, under a similar assignment to that mentioned in the last illustration, there is not enough to pay all the creditors in full, any unclaimed dividends must be applied in augmentation of the dividends of those creditors who have claimed².

¹   *Smith v Cooke* [1891] AC 297. It is difficult, if not impossible, to reconcile this case with *Green v Wynn* (1869) 4 Ch App 204, which does not seem to have been quoted to their lordships. Lord Halsbury spoke, in his judgment, of it being the 'ordinary and familiar method in such cases to *express a resulting* trust on the fact of the instrument'. This, at first sight, seems to be inconsistent with the idea of a resulting trust; but doubtless his lordship used the phrase 'resulting trust', not in the narrow technical sense of an implied resulting trust, but in the wider original etymological sense, of a trust (whether express or implied) springing back, or resulting, to its creator.
²   *Wild v Banning* (1866) LR 2 Eq 577.

29.12 Where there is a devise to A, *charged* with the payment of debts and legacies¹, or charged with the payment of a contingent legacy² which does not take effect, there will be no resulting trust; but the whole property will go to the devisee beneficially, subject only to the charge. And the same result will follow even where property is devised to A 'upon trust' to pay specific legacies, if on the whole will it appears that the testator merely meant to charge the legacies on the property³. In all such cases the inference is that the donee was to take everything not required to satisfy the *charge*. Thus in *Re Foord*⁴ where a testator left his estate to his sister absolutely on trust to pay his widow an annuity and the estate income exceeded the annuity the sister was held beneficially entitled to the balance.

¹   *King v Denison* (1813) 1 Ves & B 260; *Wood v Cox* (1837) 2 My & Cr 684.
²   *Tregonwell v Sydenham* (1815) 3 Dow 194.
³   *Croome v Croome* (1889) 61 LT 814; *Re West* [1900] 1 Ch 84.
⁴   [1922] 2 Ch 519; contrast the resulting trust in *Re West* [1900] 1 Ch 84.

29.13 In *Re Osoba*[1] the Court of Appeal held that a testator's bequest to his widow upon trust 'for her maintenance and for the training of my daughter Abiola up to university grade and for the maintenance of my aged mother' was a trust for the three females absolutely as joint tenants. There was no resulting trust when, after the deaths of the testator's widow and mother, Abiola finished her education, so that Abiola was absolutely entitled to the property.The specified purposes were regarded merely as the testator's motives for making an absolute gift.

[1]   [1979] 2 All ER 393, [1979] 1 WLR 247, CA.

29.14 In *Bath and North East Somerset Council v A-G*[1], land was conveyed to a city corporation on condition that it would be held on trust for the purposes of public recreation. Hart J held that this was a valid charitable trust, but went on to consider whether the land would have resulted to the transferor if the trust had not been valid. He held it to be relevant that the corporation had probably paid the market price for the land, so that even if the trust had been void, the corporation would still have been entitled to insist on specific performance of the contract, to acquire the full beneficial interest in the land. Hence no resulting trust would have been imposed in favour of the transferor.

[1]   (2002) 5 ITELR 274. Cf *Fraser v Canterbury Diocesan Board of Finance (No 2)* [2005] UKHL 65, [2006] 1 AC 377, considering the School Sites Act 1841, s 2, and the Reverter of Sites Act 1987, s 1.

Resulting trusts of voluntary contributions for assisting distressed individuals

29.15 It is sometimes a difficult question whether or not the balance of a fund formed by means of voluntary contributions for the relief of particular individuals (and therefore not falling within the legal conception of a charitable trust, in which latter case the presence of general charitable intention will exclude a resulting trust)[1], results pro rata to the contributors. In *Re Abbott's Trust*[2], a fund had been subscribed for the maintenance of two distressed ladies, and on the death of the survivor, Stirling J held that the balance resulted to the subscribers. On the other hand, in *Re Andrew's Trust*[3], where a fund had been subscribed solely for the education of the children of a distressed clergyman and 'not for equal division among them', Kekewich J held that when their education was completed there was no resulting trust of the balance, and that it was divisible equally among the children, on the ground that education was merely the special purpose assigned for the gift—the motive—and that the subscribers parted with all interest in the money when they gave it. This seems to be common sense, but the distinction between the two cases is somewhat fine and seems to consist only in the fact that the first fund was subscribed for the personal support of living ladies and not for the benefit of their next of kin, whereas in the second case the money was given for the benefit of living children generally with special reference to their education.

[1]   See para 29.33 below.

[2] [1900] 2 Ch 326 and *Re Sanderson's Trust* (1857) 3 K & J 497. Also see *Re British Red Cross Balkan Fund* [1914] 2 Ch 419, where in the absence of the Attorney-General a resulting trust was erroneously admitted: *Re Welsh Hospital (Netley)* [1921] 1 Ch 655 at 622; and *Re Customs and Excise Officers' Mutual Guarantee Fund* [1917] 2 Ch 18, in both of which a resulting trust was found. Where the balance of a mutual benevolent fund is returned to the subscribers those who have received benefits out of the fund must bring them into hotchpot (*Re Hobourn Aero Components Ltd's Air Raid Distress Fund* [1946] Ch 86, [1945] 2 All ER 711; affd [1946] Ch 194, [1946] 1 All ER 501, where this point was not raised). Society rules, nowadays, often provide for equal division amongst those who are members at the date of dissolution, irrespective of benefits earlier received: *Re Sick and Funeral Society of St John's Sunday School, Golcar* [1973] Ch 51, [1972] 2 All ER 439.

[3] [1905] 2 Ch 48 at 52–53 applied in *Re Osoba* [1979] 2 All ER 393, [1979] 1 WLR 247, CA.

29.16 The fact that the fund was contributed by a large number of anonymous small donors does not prevent a resulting trust from arising in their favour or entitle the Treasury Solicitor to come in and claim the balance as bona vacantia. The trustees must in such a case pay the balance into court like any other trustee who cannot find his beneficiary[1].

[1] *Re Gillingham Bus Disaster Fund* [1958] Ch 300, [1958] 1 All ER 37; affd [1959] Ch 62, [1958] 2 All ER 749, CA, where this point was not under consideration.

Bona vacantia

29.17 Where a donor has parted with his money out and out in pursuance of some contract this normally suffices to prevent any resulting trust arising so that the money will either be owned according to the terms of the contract (eg the constitution of a members' club) or be bona vacantia. Thus, no resulting trust will arise where the donors part absolutely with their moneys for tickets contractually entitling them to participate in raffles, sweepstakes, beetle drives, whist drives, discotheques or to watch films or live entertainment, and the purposes for which the profits from such moneys have been used fail to exhaust the profits[1].

[1] *Re West Sussex Constabulary's Widows, Children and Benevolent (1930) Fund Trusts* [1971] Ch 1, [1970] 1 All ER 544. The funds came from (1) contributions of past and present members, (2) entertainments, raffles, sweepstakes, collecting boxes, (3) outside donations and legacies and Goff J held that (1) and (2) were bona vacantia though (3) were held on resulting trusts for the donors but it appears from *Re Bucks Constabulary Widows' and Orphans' Fund Friendly Society (No 2)* [1979] 1 All ER 623, [1979] 1 WLR 936 that all three sources of funds belonged to the society and so to the members of the society equally: see para 29.29 below.

29.18 If the contractual element is absent and the money has been given for certain purposes, then it can be difficult to show that the donors had a general intention to part with their money absolutely beyond all recall, rather than a qualified intention to part with their money solely to the extent that the money is required to carry out the relevant purposes. However, the modern trend where street collections are concerned with thousands of anonymous small donors is for the court to be increasingly ready to find a general intention to part with money absolutely beyond all recall so as to exclude any resulting trust[1]. In such a case if the purpose does not exhaust the money then the money will pass to the Crown as bona vacantia except where the purpose was charitable, so the property is applied cy-près (see para 29.33 below) or the money was paid to an unincorporated association which is not moribund (see para 29.31 below) 'when it will pass to the members according to the association's constitution'.

1   *Re West Sussex Constabulary's Widows, Children and Benevolent (1930) Fund Trusts* [1971] Ch 1, [1970] 1 All ER 544. The funds came from (1) contributions of past and present members, (2) entertainments, raffles, sweepstakes, collecting boxes, (3) outside donations and legacies and Goff J held that (1) and (2) were bona vacantia though (3) were held on resulting trusts for the donors but it appears from *Re Bucks Constabulary Widows' and Orphans' Fund Friendly Society (No 2)* [1979] 1 All ER 623, [1979] 1 WLR 936 that all three sources of funds belonged to the society and so to the members of the society equally: see para 29.29 below.

29.19   In *Davis v Richards & Wallington Industries Ltd*[1] Scott J held that the contractual origin of rights under a pension trust was not necessarily conclusive against a resulting trust in favour of the providers of the trust fund. The trust deed may expressly exclude a resulting trust or such might be implied in suitable circumstances. Thus, surplus funds where the employer's obligation was to top up employee's contractually fixed contribution if the trust fund was not adequate to provide benefits in full, were held on a resulting trust for the employer to the extent they represented its contributions. However, so far as the surplus reflected employee's contributions, Scott J surprisingly found that the employees impliedly intended to exclude any resulting trust in their favour so that their share of the surplus passed as bona vacantia to the Crown – or would have done, but for the learned judge's prior holding that a defective deed executed after the pension trust scheme had been terminated was effective with its power to use surplus funds to augment members' benefits.

1   [1991] 2 All ER 563.

29.20   Scott J found[1] an implied intention to exclude a resulting trust because an intent to have a resulting trust would be unworkable (the value of individual's benefits being so various and involving complex calculations) and would give the employees more than the maximum intended by Parliament in the statutory requirements for benefits under exempt approved schemes. Would these thoughts have entered the employees' minds? Would not they expect to be able to have worked out for them what each was entitled to, and why should Parliament's intention provide evidence of the employees' intention?

1   [1991] 2 All ER 563 at 595.

29.21   A further criticism is that he accepted *Re West Sussex Constabulary's Widows Children and Benevolent Fund Trusts*[1] as authority for surplus moneys either passing as bona vacantia or on resulting trust without considering the third alternative preferred in *Re Bucks Constabulary Widows' and Orphans Fund Friendly Society*[2], namely, that the surplus should be divided between the members of an unincorporated society or by analogy between the employee contributors.

1   [1971] Ch 1.
2   [1979] 1 All ER 623.

29.22 Lord Millett in *Air Jamaica Ltd v Charlton*[1] was critical of Scott J's opinion in *Davis v Richards & Wallington Industries Ltd* because he believed that tax considerations should not distort legal principle and it seemed more likely that the employees lacked intentions (rather than being capable of having rather artificial intentions being inferred), lack of intention provoking the response of a resulting trust. For tax-relief reasons the trust deed stated, 'No moneys which at any time have been contributed by the Company under the terms hereof shall in any circumstances be repayable to the Company'. Despite this, Lord Millett, giving the Privy Council's reasons, held that this clause was not intended to cover what happened outside, rather, than within, the terms of the pension scheme. The surplus moneys upon the trust being void for perpetuity were 'held on resulting trust for those who provided it ... contributions were payable by the Members with matching contributions by the Company .. the surplus must be treated as provided as to one half by the Company and as to one half by the Members'[2].

1   [1999] 1 WLR 1399.
2   [1999] 1 WLR 1399 at 1411.

29.23 Lord Millett rejected the Jamaica Government's claim to the Members' half share as *bona vacantia*. The Members had not received what they had contracted for when the provisions as to surplus funds on discontinuance of the pension scheme were void for perpetuity. Their $200 million half share should not be *bona vacantia* but should be divided proportionately among the Members and the estates of deceased Members in proportion to the contributions made by each Member, without regard to the benefits received by each of them and irrespective of the dates on which contributions were made.

Dissolution of clubs or societies

29.24 Where a members' club (viz a club existing for the members' own personal benefit) is dissolved it is now clear that resulting trust principles are of no application.

> 'Membership of a club or association is primarily a matter of contract. The members make their payments and in return they become entitled to the benefits of membership in accordance with the rules. The sums they pay cease to be their individual property and so cease to be subject to any concept of resulting trust. Instead, they become the property, through the trustees of the club or association, of all the members for the time being, including themselves. A member who, by death or otherwise ceases to be a member thereby ceases to be part owner of any of the club's property: those who remain continue owners. If, then, dissolution ensues there must be a division of the property of the club or association among those alone who are owners of that property to the exclusion of former members'[1].

1   *Re Sick and Funeral Society of St John's Sunday School, Golcar* [1973] Ch 51 at 59–60. Cf *Re Recher's Will Trusts* [1972] Ch 526 at 538–539.

29.25 Division will be to existing members equally per capita or, in the case of societies with rules contemplating advantages related to contributions, rateably per contributions, assuming no society rule (contractually binding all members) provides for surplus assets on a dissolution to be distributed in some other way[1].

> [1] *Re Sick and Funeral Society of St John's Sunday School, Golcar* [1973] Ch 51, [1972] 2 All ER 439; *Re St Andrews Allotment Association Trusts* [1969] 1 All ER 147, [1969] 1 WLR 229; *Re William Denby & Sons Ltd Sick and Benevolent Fund* [1971] 2 All ER 1196, [1971] 1 WLR 973; *Re GKN Bolts and Nuts Ltd Sports and Social Club* [1982] 2 All ER 855, [1982] 1 WLR 774; *Hunt v McLaren* [2006] EWHC 2386 (Ch).

29.26 Where a club is formed to benefit non-members (eg widows and orphans of members) the destination of surplus assets on a dissolution or when the substratum or purpose of the club no longer subsists is very probably the same as in the case of members' clubs since gifts to clubs, unless expressly on an endowment trust for the club[1], are construed as gifts to the current members by way of accrual to the property already held on a bare administrative trust for them according to the contractually binding rules of the club[2].

> [1] An endowment trust for the benefit of club members from time to time within a specified valid perpetuity period will need to be held by club officers separate from general assets of the club and will be held on resulting trust for the donor if the club is dissolved.
> [2] See para 8.190; *Re Recher's Will Trusts* [1972] Ch 526, [1971] 3 All ER 401; *Re Lipinski's Will Trusts* [1976] Ch 235, [1977] 1 All ER 33; *Universe Tankships Inc of Monrovia v International Transport Workers Federation* [1983] 1 AC 366, [1982] 2 All ER 67, HL; *Re Bucks Constabulary Widows' and Orphans' Fund Friendly Society (No 2)* [1979] 1 All ER 623, [1979] 1 WLR 936.

29.27 One must first deal with *Cunnack v Edwards*[1] where a society, formed to provide annuities for widows of deceased members, had surplus assets after the death of the last member and the last widow, and the assets were held to pass to the Crown as bona vacantia. Lord Halsbury and A L Smith LJ held there could be no resulting trust for members' personal representatives since the members in paying their subscriptions intended to part with their moneys out-and-out subject only to their collective power (unexercised) to change the society's rules for their own benefit subject to then existing contractual rights. Rigby LJ concerned himself with the Friendly Societies Act 1829 under which the society had been registered and which in his judgment required the society's rules expressly to provide for the surplus assets to pass to members if such was to happen, so that in default thereof the surplus had to pass as bona vacantia.

> [1] [1896] 2 Ch 679.

29.28 In *Re West Sussex Constabulary's Widows, Children and Benevolent (1930) Fund Trusts*[1] Goff J followed *Cunnack v Edwards* in holding that surplus funds (in the form of past and present members' subscriptions and the proceeds of entertainments, sweepstakes, raffles and collecting boxes) of a police fund for their widows and orphans passed to the Crown as bona vacantia subject to any existing contractual claims on the funds. He rejected the proprietary claim to the surplus funds of the members existing at the date of dissolution since the society was not a members' club.

¹   [1971] Ch 1, [1970] 1 All ER 544.

29.29 In *Re Bucks Constabulary Widows and Orphans' Fund Friendly Society (No 2)*¹ Walton J distinguished the *West Sussex Constabulary* case but otherwise he would have refused to follow it.

¹   [1979] 1 All ER 623, [1979] 1 WLR 936. In *Re Bucks Constabulary Widows' and Orphans' Fund Friendly Society* [1978] 2 All ER 571, [1978] 1 WLR 641, Megarry V-C had already held that Friendly Societies Act 1896, s 79 (4), conferred no power to distribute surplus assets among those not entitled under the general law.

29.30 He distinguished the case on the footing that he was concerned with a friendly society registered under the Friendly Societies Act 1896. Section 49 (1) in his judgment ensured that, in the absence of any provision to the contrary in the society's rules, any assets belonged to the existing members subject only to any contractual rights created against the assets or to any trusts expressly declared of the assets.¹

¹   See also *Elvridge v Coulson* [2003] EWHC 2089 (Ch) at [8] per Peter Smith J: 'In the absence of any express contract and provision, the principle is that there should ordinarily be equality of distribution per capita as between those members who were alive and members at the time of the dissolution.'

29.31 Otherwise, he considered that *Cunnack v Edwards* hinged on the Friendly Societies Act 1829 or the fact that no surviving members existed when the society became defunct, whilst the *West Sussex Constabulary* case made an invalid distinction between members' club cases and other cases. After all, all cases of persons forming societies (whether members' clubs for social or sporting purposes, or societies establishing a widows and orphans fund or formed to obtain a separate Cornish Parliament or to further the advance of alchemy) involve a contract between the members whereunder the only persons interested in the society's property are the current members to the extent that no trusts thereof are expressly declared and no contractual rights therein are given to third parties. The members, subject to any such trusts or contractual rights, are in complete control of the society's property and can alter the society's rules and appropriate the property for themselves if they see fit¹. Thus members in existence at the date of dissolution take the society's assets to the total exclusion of any bona vacantia claim by the Crown. Only if the society has become moribund with no existing members or only one member can the Crown claim the assets. This approach of Walton J seems more consistent with principle than the approach of Goff J in the *West Sussex Constabulary* case. It has the advantage of refusing to recognise any distinction between inward-looking and outward-looking clubs and of avoiding problems of distinguishing between members' club cases and friendly society and other cases: the uncertain questions of degree involved in ascertaining when a club or society is moribund are inevitable in all club cases.

¹   See also *Re Sick and Funeral Society of St John's Sunday School, Golcar* [1973] Ch 51 at 59–60; *Re Recher's Will Trusts* [1972] Ch 526 at 538–539; *Re Grant's Will Trusts* [1979] 3 All ER 359 at 365.

Effect of liquidation or bankruptcy of debtor after creation of a Voluntary Arrangement for benefit of creditors

29.32 If the voluntary arrangement of a company's or individual's assets for the benefit of creditors does provide for what is to happen on liquidation or bankruptcy then effect must be given to such provision, but otherwise, the trust will continue notwithstanding the liquidation or bankruptcy and must take effect according to its terms[1] (subject to the exercise of *Saunders v Vautier* termination rights by all the beneficiaries acting unanimously). The creditor-beneficiaries can prove in the liquidation or bankruptcy for so much of their debt as remains after payment of what is recovered under the trust.

[1]   *Re Gallagher & Son Ltd, Shierson v Tomlinson* [2002] EWCA Civ 404, [2002] 3 All ER 474.

Resulting trusts of contributions to charitable funds

29.33 Once property has been given to a charitable institution or to trustees of charitable purpose trusts which are carried into effect (as opposed to failing in limine due to insufficiency of funds, unavailability of an appropriate site or whatever) then the property is forever dedicated to charity, so that the property will be applied cy-près if the institution is subsequently dissolved or surplus funds are available after particular purposes have been effected. As Jenkins LJ remarked[1], 'once the charity for which the fund was raised had been effectively brought into action the fund was to be regarded as permanently devoted to charity to the exclusion of any resulting trust.'

[1]   *Re Ulverston and District New Hospital Building Trusts* [1956] Ch 622 at 637, CA endorsing *Re Wokingham Fire Brigade Trusts* [1951] Ch 373, [1951] 1 All ER 454; and see also *Re Cooper's Conveyance* [1956] 3 All ER 28, [1956] 1 WLR 1096. It is thus unnecessary for courts to exclude a resulting trust by finding (as they did in *Re Welsh Hospital (Netley) Fund* [1921] 1 Ch 655; *Re North Devon and West Somerset Relief Fund Trusts* [1953] 2 All ER 1032, [1953] 1 WLR 1260; *Re British School of Egyptian Archaeology* [1954] 1 All ER 887, [1954] 1 WLR 546) that the subscribers intended to give their money outright under a general charitable intention, so that the property may be applied cy-près.

29.34 Where the source of funds for charitable trusts that have failed at the outset has been the profits from some lottery, competition, entertainment, sale, or similar money-raising activity, then special considerations arise. Profits from such activities cannot be held on resulting trust for the subscribers who will have received their contractual consideration[1]. Hence such profits will be bona vacantia, in which case the Crown will usually waive its rights so that the money can be applied cy-près.

[1]   *Re West Sussex Constabulary's Widows, Children and Benevolent (1930) Fund Trusts* [1971] Ch 1, [1970] 1 All ER 544.

29.35 In contrast, where the source of the funds has been a gift there will be a resulting trust for the donor unless a general charitable intention was present at the time of the gift, in which case the property will be applicable cy-près[1]. The question arises, however, what should happen where street collections have been held and money has been given by numerous anonymous donors who cannot subsequently be identified? An attempt was made to resolve this problem by enacting what is now the Charities Act 1993, s 14, which deems a general charitable intention to have been present 'where any difficulty in applying property to charitable purposes makes that property or the part not applicable cy-près available to be returned to the donors', presumably by virtue of a resulting trust[2]. However, there seems to be hardly any scope for s 14 to apply, since it applies only where the property is held on a resulting trust under the general law. It does not apply where the property passes to the Crown as bona vacantia, as an out and out gift without any general charitable intention,[3] in which case the Crown will allow the property to be applied cy-près. Nor does it apply where the property is in any event applicable cy-près as an out and out gift with a general charitable intention[4]. It is very unlikely, nowadays, that the cash will be treated as given only for a specific purpose so that on failure of such purpose it will be held on resulting trust for the donor[5] (who, of course, almost invariably will be anonymous). Moreover, since 2006 cy-près applications of donations have been permitted by statute, irrespective of the donors' general intentions, provided that they are told at the time when their gifts are solicited that these will be applied cy-près if the purposes for which the money is solicited fail, and they raise no objection to this[6].

[1] *Re University of London Medical Sciences Institute Fund* [1909] 2 Ch 1, CA.
[2] Section 14(5) of the 1960 Act and s 14(7) of the 1993 Act; see D Wilson [1983] Conv 40.
[3] *Re Ulverston and District New Hospital Building Trusts* [1956] Ch 622, [1956] 3 All ER 164, CA.
[4] *Re Hillier* [1954] 2 All ER 59, [1954] 1 WLR 700, CA.
[5] *Re West Sussex Constabulary's Widows, Children and Benevolent (1930) Fund Trusts* [1971] Ch 1, [1970] 1 All ER 544.
[6] Charities Act 1993 s 14A, inserted by the Charities Act 2006 s 17.

Paragraph 2

Quistclose trusts

29.36 Where L lends money to B for a specific purpose in sufficiently certain terms for a court to adjudge whether or not that purpose can be, or has been, carried out, and where B is bound in equity not to treat the money as beneficially owned by B but to be kept apart to be used only for the specific purpose, then on the money being applied for that purpose L only has a personal remedy in debt. Otherwise, the money from the outset is held on a resulting trust for the lender. It will depend on the terms of the contract whether B has a power or, in some circumstances a duty to apply the money for the specific purpose, and whether the power or duty ceases when the purpose becomes incapable of achievement or when a specified period has elapsed or when L countermands his mandate.

29.37 The source of these rules is *Twinsectra Ltd v Yardley*[1], where Lord Millett reinterpreted the House of Lords' previous decision in *Barclays Bank Ltd v Quistclose Investments Ltd*[2]. In *Quistclose*, a company lent money to another company in the same corporate group for the purpose of paying a dividend to the shareholders of the second company, and the second company became insolvent before the dividend was paid. The House of Lords held that the money was held for the first company on a resulting trust which arose on the failure of a primary express trust to pay the dividend. However, this was difficult to reconcile with various trust law principles, eg the beneficiary principle which suggests that if the primary trust was a trust for a private purpose then it should have been void[3]. Building on his extra-judicial criticisms of the reasoning in *Quistclose*[4], Lord Millett therefore held in *Twinsectra* that where L lends money to B on the basis that it does not become part of B's general assets, but must be applied to a specific purpose, a trust of the money immediately arises in L's favour, but this trust is defeasible by the exercise of a power vested in B to apply the money to the specified purpose[5]. It seems from his extra-judicial writings that Lord Millett formerly thought that the trust for L would always be an express trust, but his speech in *Twinsectra* suggests that he was persuaded by Professor Chambers' general work on resulting trusts to modify this opinion[6], and to hold that in cases where the transferor does not declare an express trust for himself when he lends the money to the transferee, a resulting trust arises in his favour[7].

1   [2002] UKHL 12, [2002] AC 162.
2   [1970] AC 567. See too *Re ETVR* [1987] BCLC 646.
3   R Chambers *Resulting Trusts* (1997) at pp 68–89; W J Swadling 'Orthodoxy' in W J Swadling (ed) *The Quistclose Trust: Critical Essays* (2004) 9.
4   PJ Millett QC 'The *Quistclose* Trust: Who Can Enforce It?' (1985) 101 LQR 269.
5   The nature of which is discussed in L Smith 'Understanding the Power' in Swadling (above n 77) 67.
6   Although not his analysis of *Quistclose*, which his Lordship thought vulnerable to the criticisms made in L Ho and P St J Smart 'Reinterpreting the *Quistclose* Trust: A Critique of Chambers' Analysis' (2001) 21 OJLS 267. Professor Chambers answers these criticisms, and restates his position on *Quistclose*, in 'Restrictions on the Use of Money' in Swadling (above n 77) 77; see too J Glister 'The Nature of *Quistclose* Trusts: Classification and Reconciliation' [2004] CLJ 632.
7   As noted in J Penner 'Lord Millett's Analysis' in Swadling (above n 77) 41, at pp 50–56. See also Lord Millett's own comments in the foreword to this book, at p ix, and compare his analysis of the trust in *Latimer v CIR* [2004] UKPC 13, [2004] 1 WLR 1466 (PC) at [41]. See too *Salvo v New Tel Ltd* [2005] NSWCA 281, where the members of the court could not agree whether the trust arising in the lender's favour should be characterised as express or resulting.

29.38 To bring a case within the scope of the (reinterpreted) *Quistclose* principle it seems the parties need not have expressly agreed that the money should be applied for a 'sole purpose' or 'exclusive purpose', provided that this is the substance of their arrangement[1]. Nor does it matter if the relevant purpose is couched in broad terms (eg 'purchase of suitable property' or 'purchase of Korean investments'[2]) or described more precisely (eg 'payments to specified creditors'[3]), provided that it is expressed sufficiently clearly for a court to be able to say of any application of the money that it does or does not fall within the terms of the power given to the borrower[4].

1   *Templeton Insurance Ltd v Penningtons Solicitors LLP* [2006] EWHC 685 (Ch) at [11]–[15], [2006] All ER (D) 191 (Feb). But for cases falling on the wrong side of the line, cf *Shalson v Russo* [2003] EWHC 1637 (Ch), [2005] Ch 281 at [128]–[130] and *Abou-Rahmah v Abacha* [2005] EWHC 2662 (QB), [2006] 1 All ER (Comm) 247 at [78]–[80].
2   As in *R v Prestney* [2003] 1 NZLR 21 (NZCA).

³   *Industrial & General Insurance Co Ltd v A O N Group Ltd* [2003] EWHC 240 (Comm) at [51], [2003] All ER (D) 460 (Mar).
⁴   *Twinsectra v Yardley Ltd* [2002] UKHL 12, [2002] 2 AC 164 at [16] per Lord Hoffmann, invoking *McPhail v Doulton* [1971] AC 424, although *Re Gulbenkian's Settlements* [1970] AC 508 would have been more exactly in point as it concerned a power of appointment rather than a discretionary trust.

29.39 Since *Quistclose* trusts most commonly arise in practice in situations where L lends money to B for the purpose of paying B's creditor, C, the question arises, whether C, rather than L, can ever acquire a beneficial interest in the fund in cases of this kind? This question was considered in *Re Margaretta Ltd*¹ where the judge considered that this might happen in two types of case:

'Where the obvious intention of the transaction would be frustrated if the donor were to retain a power of revocation of the trust² ... [and where] the existence of the trust arrangements is communicated to the intended payee and the latter gains a beneficial interest in the money either because of the creation of an estoppel in his favour or because communication perfects an assignment of the donor's equitable interest to him³.'

¹   [2005] STC 610 at [24] (Michael Crystal QC), drawing on Lord Millett's 1985 LQR article cited in n 78.
²   Citing *New, Prance and Garrads Trustee v Hunting* [1897] 2 QB 19.
³   Citing *Acton v Woodgate* (1833) 2 My & K 492, 495; *Ellis v Cross* [1915] 2 KB 654, 659; *Browne v Cavendish* (1844) 1 Jo & Lat 606, 635–6; *Morrell v Wootten* (1852) 16 Beav 197, 202–3; *Re Hamilton* (1921) 124 LT 737.

29.40 The judge went on to hold that the facts of the case placed it within the second of these situations, and that the creditor therefore had a beneficial interest in the money paid over to the borrower, and subsequently to the fruits of the borrower's action against its agent who dishonestly dealt with the property and thereby incurred a personal liability to reconstitute the trust fund¹

¹   For discussion of the personal liability incurred by those who dishonestly deal with trust property, see Article 100.

Paragraph 3

Evidence not admissible where donee is trustee and not a beneficiary on face of settlement

29.41 In *Re Rees' Will Trusts*¹ the testator bequeathed his residuary estate to his 'trustees absolutely, they well knowing my wishes concerning the same.' Before signing his will the testator had orally communicated to the trustees certain wishes which he desired them to implement, but which were not sufficient to exhaust the residuary estate and told them that any surplus was to be retained by them for their own benefit. It was held that, the gift having been made to the trustees, the evidence that they were intended to take some part beneficially must be disregarded and the surplus, after implementing the testator's other wishes, must be held on trust for the testator's statutory next of kin.

¹ [1950] Ch 204, [1949] 2 All ER 1003; followed in *Re Pugh's Will Trusts* [1967] 3 All ER 337, [1967] 1 WLR 1262, distinguished in *Re Tyler's Fund Trusts* [1967] 3 All ER 389, [1967] 1 WLR 1269.

29.42 The Court of Appeal distinguished *Irvine v Sullivan*¹. There the testator appointed A, B and C as trustees and gave them his property on trust for sale. Then he gave the residue to D the lady to whom he was betrothed 'trusting she will carry out my wishes with regard to the same with which she is fully acquainted', and it was held that D was beneficially entitled to the surplus remaining after satisfying the purposes communicated to her by the testator. After all trustees, of whom D was not one, were appointed to carry out the trusts, and D who was engaged to be married to the testator was the sort of person for whom one would assume he would wish to provide so that D did not take as trustee on the face of the will.

¹ (1869) LR 8 Eq 673.

Evidence admissible in other cases

29.43 Where a person purchased sums of stock in the names of herself and the son of her daughter-in-law, parol evidence was admitted to ascertain her intentions because there was nothing to show on the face of the instrument that she intended the son of her daughter-in-law to hold the stock as her trustee, or to take some part beneficially for himself. James LJ said:

> 'Where the Court of Chancery is asked, *on an equitable assumption of presumption*, to take away from a man that which by the common law of the land he is entitled to, he surely has a right to say: "Listen to my story as to how I came to have it, and judge that story with reference to all the surrounding facts and circumstances".'¹

¹ *Fowkes v Pascoe* (1875) 10 Ch App 343 at 349.

29.44 So evidence is admissible to rebut the legal presumption as to part only—for instance, to prove that the donee was intended to take a *life interest*, although there is a resulting trust as to the remainder; and vice versa¹.

¹ *Lane v Dighton* (1762) Amb 409; *Rider v Kidder* (1805) 10 Ves 360; *Benbow v Townsend* (1833) 1 My & K 506; *London and County Banking Co v London and River Plate Bank* (1888) 21 QBD 535 at 542, CA; *Re Blake* (1889) 60 LT 663.

ARTICLE 30
RESULTING TRUSTS ARISING WHERE TRUSTS DECLARED ILLEGAL

30.1

When a person has intentionally created an executed trust¹ for an illegal consideration or purpose which therefore fails, then a resulting trust will only be imposed in favour of the settlor if:

(a)   he voluntarily withdrew from the illegal purpose before it was wholly or partly carried into execution[2]; or

(b)   he does not have to disclose the illegal purpose in order to rebut the presumption of advancement, but can simply rely on the fact that he transferred or purchased the property without receiving any consideration from the transferee or person in whose name the property was purchased[3], it being irrelevant whether or not the illegal purpose had been wholly or partly carried into effect[4]; or

(c)   the effect of allowing the trustee to retain the property might be to effectuate an unlawful object, to defeat a legal prohibition, or to protect a fraud[5].

[1]   Where an illegal trust (or contract) is executory it simply cannot be enforced: *Tinsley v Milligan* [1993] 3 All ER 65, [1994] 1 AC 340, HL.
[2]   *Tribe v Tribe* [1996] Ch 107 at 135, no genuine repentance being required; *Symes v Hughes* (1870) LR 9 Eq 475; *Childers v Childers* (1857) 1 De G & J 482; *Davies v Otty (No 2)* (1865) 35 Beav 208; *Birch v Blagrave* (1755) Amb 264; *Platamone v Staple* (1815) Coop G 250.
[3]   *Tinsley v Milligan* [1993] 3 All ER 65, [1994] 1 AC 340, HL, applied in *Silverwood v Silverwood* (1997) 74 P & CR 453, CA; *Macdonald v Myerson* [2001] EWCA Civ 66, [2001] NPC 20; and *Lowson v Coombes* [1999] Ch 373, CA.
[4]   *Gorog v Kiss* (1977) 78 DLR (3d) 690 endorsed by *Tinsley v Milligan* [1994] 1 AC 340 at 376; and *Tribe v Tribe* [1996] Ch 107 at 111 per Nourse LJ.
[5]   See per Lord Selborne in *Ayerst v Jenkins* (1873) LR 16 Eq 275 at 283; and see per Knight-Bruce LJ in *Reynell v Sprye* (1852) 1 De Gm & G 660, where he said: 'Where the parties are not *in pari delicto*, and where public policy is considered as advanced by allowing either party, or at least the more excusable of the two, to sue for relief, relief is given to him'. And see also, to same effect, *Law v Law* (1735) 3 P Wms 391, and *Lord St John v Lady St John* (1803) 11 Ves 526. Confiscation of the proceeds of crime is now a possibility under the Criminal Justice Act 1988 as amended by the Criminal Justice Act 1993.

Conveyance to qualify for game licence

30.2 Thus where a father granted land to his son, in order to give him a colourable qualification to shoot game under the old game laws, and without any intention of conferring any beneficial interest upon him, the court would not enforce any resulting trust in favour of the father, for he and the son were in pari delicto, and there was no detriment to the public in allowing the son to retain the estate[1]. Of course, if there had been no illegality (if, for instance, a bare legal estate had been a sufficient qualification), there would have been a resulting trust[2].

[1]   *Brackenbury v Brackenbury* (1820) 2 Jac & W 391. See also *Chettiar v Chettiar* [1962] AC 294, [1962] 1 All ER 494, PC, where a Malayan father conveyed 40 acres of his 139 acres of rubber land to his son in order to evade certain regulations which applied to those who owned more than 100 acres. In order to rebut the presumption of advancement the father had to disclose his illegal purpose, and the court refused to declare a resulting trust.
[2]   *Childers v Childers* (1857) 1 De G & J 482.

Settlement for illegal consideration

30.3 In *Ayerst v Jenkins*[1] a widower, two days before going through the ceremony of marriage with his deceased wife's sister (which ceremony was invalid under the law then in force and was known so to be by both parties), had executed a settlement reciting that he was desirous of making a provision for the lady, and had transferred certain shares into the names of trustees, upon the trusts thereinafter declared, being the separate and inalienable use of the lady during her life, and after her death as she should by deed or will appoint. They afterwards lived together as man and wife until the widower's death. Some time afterwards, his personal representatives instituted a suit to set aside the settlement, on the ground that it was founded on an immoral consideration, being to secure her future cohabitation with him.

[1]   (1873) LR 16 Eq 275.

30.4 Lord Selborne, however, said:

> 'Relief is sought by the representative, not merely of a *particeps criminis*, but of a voluntary and sole donor, on the naked ground of the illegality of his own intention and purpose; and that, not against a bond or covenant or other obligation resting *in fieri*, but against a completed transfer of specific chattels, by which the legal estate in those chattels was absolutely vested in trustees ... for the sole benefit of the defendant. I know of no doctrine of public policy which requires, or authorises, a court of equity to give assistance to such a plaintiff under such circumstances. When the immediate and direct effect of an estoppel in equity against relief to a particular plaintiff might be *to effectuate an unlawful object, or to defeat a legal prohibition, or to protect a fraud*, such an estoppel may well be regarded as against public policy. But the voluntary gift of part of his own property by one particeps criminis to another, is in itself neither fraudulent nor prohibited by law; and the present is not the case of a man repenting of an immoral purpose before it is too late, and seeking to recall, while the object is yet unaccomplished[1], a gift intended as a bribe to iniquity. If public policy is opposed (as it is) to vice and immorality, it is no less true, as was said by Lord Truro in *Benyon v Nettlefold*[2], that the law, in sanctioning the defence of *"particeps criminis"*, does so *"*on the grounds of public policy, namely, that those who violate the law must not apply to the law for protection"*.'

[1]   As in *Symes v Hughes* (1870) LR 9 Eq 475.
[2]   (1850) 3 Mac & G 94 at 102.

30.5 In *Phillips v Probyn*[1], North J distinguished *Ayerst v Jenkins* on the ground that in the case before him the settlement was made *in consideration* of a contemplated and then invalid *marriage* with a deceased wife's sister, and that there was a total failure of consideration. It is, however, humbly submitted that the settlement in *Ayerst v Jenkins* was also made in contemplation of, and as part of, the arrangements consequent on such a marriage, and that there is really no valid distinction between the two cases. In the very changed social climate today courts will be very averse to find a transaction tainted with illegality because in consideration of future immoral cohabitation: at the least a court is likely to find a valid consideration severable from the immoral consideration[2].

[1]   [1899] 1 Ch 811.
[2]   See *Chitty on Contracts* (25th edn) para 1085 and *Tanner v Tanner* [1975] 3 All ER 776, [1975] 1 WLR 1346, CA.

30.6 Resulting trusts

30.6 Moreover in *Tinsley v Milligan*[1] it seems that a trust set up for an illegal consideration is valid and enforceable by any beneficiary unless the beneficiary needs to lead evidence of the illegality to establish his claim. It seems he will only need to lead evidence of the declaration of trusts and of the acquisition of trust property by the trustee and so will always be able to enforce the trust.

> [1] *Chettiar v Chettiar* [1962] AC 294 at 302, PC; *Perpetual Executors and Trustees Association of Australia Ltd v Wright* (1917) 23 CLR 185 (Aust HC); *Martin v Martin* (1959) 110 CLR 297 (Aust HC; *Tinsley v Milligan* [1993] 3 All ER 65, [1994] 1 AC 340, HL.

Fraudulent conveyance

30.7 But where an illegal purpose is only contemplated, there is a locus poenitentiae[1]. Thus, in *Symes v Hughes*[2] the plaintiff, being in pecuniary difficulties, assigned certain leasehold property to a trustee with a view to defeating his creditors. Two and a half years afterwards he was adjudicated bankrupt, but obtained the sanction of his creditors to an arrangement by which his estate was revested in him, he covenanting to prosecute a suit for the recovery of the assigned property, and to pay a composition to two-and-sixpence in the pound to his creditors, in case his suit should prove successful.

> [1] *Chettiar v Chettiar* [1962] AC 294 at 302, PC; *Perpetual Executors and Trustees Association of Australia Ltd v Wright* (1917) 23 CLR 185 (Aust HC); *Martin v Martin* (1959) 110 CLR 297 (Aust HC; *Tinsley v Milligan* [1993] 3 All ER 65, [1994] 1 AC 340, HL.
>
> [2] (1870) LR 9 Eq 475. Contrast *Chettiar v Chettiar* [1962] AC 294, [1962] 1 All ER 494, PC.

30.8 Lord Romilly MR in delivering judgment, said:

> 'Where the purpose for which the assignment was given is not carried into execution, and nothing is done under it, the mere intention to effect an illegal object when the assignment was executed does not deprive the assignor of his right to recover the property from the assignee who has given no consideration for it.'

30.9 So, again in *Davies v Otty*[1] the plaintiff, being apprehensive of an indictment for bigamy (conviction for which then involved forfeiture of property), conveyed his real estate to the defendant, on a parol agreement to re-transfer when the difficulty should have passed over. It subsequently transpired that the plaintiff was not liable to be indicted, and thereupon he filed a bill praying for a re-transfer of his property.

> [1] *Davies v Otty (No 2)* (1865) 35 Beav 208. See also *Sekhon v Alissa* [1989] 2 FLR 94, [1989] Fam Law 355 (where a mother recovered a share in her house conveyed into her daughter's name where her alleged purpose of capital gains tax evasion had not been carried out because the house had not been sold) and *Rowan v Dann* (1991) 64 P & CR 202, CA (where R, who had granted a lease to D with a view to a joint venture with D and to prejudicing R's creditors, recovered the property by way of resulting trust when the joint venture failed to materialise and no creditors had been prejudiced).

30.10 It was held, that although there was no enforceable express trust (inasmuch as there was no written proof of it), yet there was a resulting trust to which the statute did not apply; and as there was no illegality in fact, but only in intention, the court ordered the transfer prayed for.

30.11 Similarly in *Tribe v Tribe*[1] the claimant father transferred his major shareholding in a company to his son to deceive his creditors and protect his assets. In the event he did not have to carry out repairs as tenant of property used by his company and the need to deceive his creditors did not arise. He claimed to recover the shares from his son who refused to return them. The Court of Appeal held he could lead evidence of his illegal purpose to rebut the presumption of advancement. No genuine repentance was needed, it being sufficient to withdraw voluntarily from the illegal transaction when it had ceased to be needed.

[1] [1996] Ch 107. See too *Collier v Collier* (2002) 6 ITELR 270 at [107]–[112] per Mance LJ.

Spouses' fraudulent designs

30.12 In *Gascoigne v Gascoigne*[1] a husband transferred land into his wife's name solely in order to protect the land from his existing and future creditors and tax was paid on the basis the land belonged to his wife, but it was held he could not succeed in his claim that she held the land not for herself but on trust for him. He could not be allowed to rebut the presumption that he had made an advancement or gift in his wife's favour by producing evidence of his fraudulent design even though his wife was a party to it. Similarly in *Re Emery's Investment Trust*[2] where a husband had registered some American securities in his wife's name, though it was intended that she should hold them in trust for herself and him in equal shares, evidence to this effect so as to rebut the presumption of advancement was not allowed when the rationale and effect of the transaction was to evade American withholding tax in respect of the husband's half share.

[1] [1918] 1 KB 223; *Elford v Elford* (1922) 69 DLR 284.
[2] [1959] Ch 410, [1959] 1 All ER 577.

30.13 These cases were approved in *Tinker v Tinker*[1] where a husband on purchasing the matrimonial home had it conveyed into his wife's name to protect it from creditors if his new garage business failed.

> 'As against his wife he wants to say that it belongs to him. As against his creditors that it belongs to her. That simply will not do. The presumption is that it was conveyed to her for her own use, and he does not rebut the presumption by saying that he only did it to defeat his creditors.'[2]

[1] [1970] P 136, [1970] 1 All ER 540 applied to man and mistress in *Cantor v Cox* (1976) 239 Estates Gazette 121.
[2] *Tinker v Tinker* [1970] P 136 at 141, [1970] 1 All ER 540 at 542, per Lord Denning MR.

30.14 Where property is purchased in the wife's name to avoid tax or defeat creditors the husband has to face the argument that since the design could not honestly be achieved unless the equitable beneficial ownership was conferred with the legal title on the wife the presumption is strengthened that it was so conferred.

30.15 Perhaps, mention should be made of *Heseltine v Heseltine*[1] where a husband persuaded his wealthy wife to transfer £20,000 to him in order to enable him to become a 'name' at Lloyd's and to transfer £40,000 to him to save estate duty if she predeceased him.

> 'The wife here has done no wrong. She only did what her husband asked her. That should not be taken against her. The court can and should impute a trust by him for her.'[2]

[1] [1971] 1 All ER 952, [1971] 1 WLR 342. See (1973) Current Legal Problems 17 (A J Oakley); (1971) 115 Sol Jo 614 (S Cretney).
[2] [1971] 1 All ER 952 at 955. Such broad approach has now been overridden by a stricter approach; *Grant v Edwards* [1986] Ch 638; *Lloyds Bank plc v Rosset* [1991] 1 AC 107.

30.16 However, in imposing this trust the Court of Appeal seem to have been imposing a constructive trust on the ground that it would be inequitable to allow the husband to deny the wife the equitable interest in the sums. This would certainly have been the case if the husband had exercised undue influence but otherwise it is difficult to justify a constructive trust in favour of the wife so permitting her to trace the moneys and preferring her over the general creditors of the husband. A resulting trust would seem to be out of the question since the spouses knew that the husband could only become a 'name' at Lloyd's if the beneficial interest passed to him and estate duty could only be saved if the beneficial interest passed to him.

30.17 In *Lowson v Coombes*[1] the claimant and his mistress together bought a house in the mistress' name to defeat claims of the claimant's wife if divorcing him, under s 37 of the Matrimonial Causes Act 1973. There was no room for any presumption of advancement as in *Tinker v Tinker*, so the claimant could rely on a resulting trust, the defendant holding the house on resulting trust for herself and the claimant in equal shares.

[1] [1999] Ch 373, CA.

Crucial significance of presumption of advancement

30.18 In *Tinsley v Milligan*[1] two females, T and M, jointly purchased a house which they registered only in T's name to enable M, with the knowledge and assent of T, to make false social security benefit claims for the benefit of both of them cohabiting as lovers. On M claiming half the house, their Lordships held 3:2 in M's favour on the basis that an equitable interest under a resulting trust was presumed to arise in favour of M without the need for M to rely in any way on the underlying illegality. Lord Browne-Wilkinson for the majority emphasised, however, that if a presumption of advancement arises where A has transferred property to B (eg A being the husband or father of B) then A will need to rebut the presumption by leading evidence of the true purpose of the transfer and if such purpose be illegal then he cannot plead it, so that the property will remain with B and A's claim will fail:

> 'A party to an illegality can recover by virtue of a legal or equitable property interest if, but only if, he can establish his title without relying on his own illegality. In cases where the presumption of advancement applies, the plaintiff is faced with the presumption of gift and therefore cannot claim under a resulting trust unless and until he has rebutted that presumption of gift: for those purposes the plaintiff does have to rely on the underlying illegality and therefore fail.'[2]

1 [1993] 3 All ER 65, [1994] 1 AC 340. M had made her peace with the Department of Social Security, having told it what she had done; T had been prosecuted, convicted and fined and had had to make some repayments to the Department.
2 [1993] 3 All ER 65 at 90 and 148; see further N. Enonchong (1995) 111 LQR 135 at 148–155.

Reliance on resulting trust after carrying out illegal purpose

30.19 As Nourse LJ has pointed out[1], 'It is inherent in [*Tinsley v Milligan*] that it makes no difference whether or not the illegal purpose has been carried into effect, as it clearly had been in that case'. Thus, once the coast is clear and the transferor has defrauded his creditors etc., he can recover his property simply by relying on a resulting trust if there is no applicable presumption of advancement. The unattractiveness of this iniquitous result led Millett LJ to suggest that if X transfers property to his nephew N to conceal it from creditors and, then, settles with his creditors on the basis he owns no interest in the property, then 'the transferor's own conduct would be inconsistent with the retention of any beneficial interest in the property', so there should be no resulting trust for him. However, this suggestion seems inconsistent with *Tinsley v Milligan* where Miss Milligan had dealt with the DHSS on the basis she had no ownership of the house owned by Miss Tinsley and where *Gorog v Kiss*[2] was endorsed.

1 *Tribe v Tribe* [1996] Ch 107 at 111.
2 (1977) 78 DLR (3d) 690, Ontario CA.

Reform

30.20 As pointed out by the High Court of Australia[1], the English Court of Appeal[2], and the English Law Commission[3], it is unsatisfactory for the law to make a transferor's ability to recover property transferred for an illegal purpose turn on the essentially irrelevant question of whether or not he and the transferee are in a special relationship giving rise to a presumption of advancement. Thus, the minority of the House of Lords in *Tinsley v Milligan* preferred the harsh but certain approach that 'a court of equity will not assist a claimant who does not come to equity with clean hands', producing the result that the transferred property is left in the hands of the defendant.[4] However, all their Lordships rejected the flexible rule relied upon by the Court of Appeal,[5] which made the transferor's ability to recover the property turn upon the extent to which the public conscience would be affronted by recognising rights arising out of illegal transactions[6].

30.20 *Resulting trusts*

1   *Nelson v Nelson* (1995) 184 CLR 538.
2   *Tribe v Tribe* [1996] Ch 107 at 118 per Nourse LJ; *Silverwood v Silverwood* (1997) 74 P & CR 453 at 458–9 per Nourse LJ; *Lowson v Coombes* [1999] Ch 373 at 385 per Robert Walker LJ; *Collier v Collier* (2002) 6 ITELR 270 at [105]–[106] per Mance LJ.
3   Law Commission Illegal Transactions: The Effect of Illegality on Contracts and Trusts (Law Com No 154, 1999) at paras 3.19–3.24.
4   'Let the estate lie where it falls': *Muckleton v Brown* (1801) 6 Ves 52 at 69.
5   [1992] Ch 310.
6   Quaere whether this firm line has been compromised by Lord Walker's disposal of the illegality point which arose in *Bakewell Management Ltd v Brandwood* [2004] UKHL 14, [2004] 2 AC 519? See especially his comment at [60] that 'the maxim *ex turpi causa* must be applied as an instrument of public policy, and not in circumstances where it does not serve any public interest'.

30.21 In principle, however, matters would be greatly improved if the law were amended in line with the Law Commission's view[1] that there should be a structured statutory discretion to decide the effects of illegality. Factors to be taken into account would be (a) the seriousness of the illegality; (b) the knowledge and intent of the illegal trust beneficiary; (c) whether invalidity would tend to deter the illegality; (d) whether invalidity would further the purpose of the rule which renders the trust 'illegal'; and (e) whether invalidity would be a proportionate response to the claimant's participation in the illegality.

1   Law Commission *Illegal Transactions: The Effect of Illegality on Contracts and Trusts* (Law Com No 154, 1999) at para 8.63; on which see N Enonchong 'Illegal Transactions: The Future' [2000] RLR 82 at pp 99–104.

Claimants through transferor or settlor

30.22 If the transferor or settlor cannot recover then his personal representative should be in no better position[1] even though not personally *in delicto*. His trustee in bankruptcy should be in no better position unless public policy considerations dictate otherwise[2], despite the availability of statutory provisions in the Insolvency Act 1986.

1   *Ayerst v Jenkins* (1873) LR 16 Eq 275 at 281 per Lord Selborne LC: the contrary view of Lord Eldon in *Muckleston v Brown* (1801) 6 Ves 52 at 68 seems unsound in principle.
2   Cf *Trautwein v Richardson* [1946] ALR 129 at 134 per Dixon J; *Ayerst v Jenkins* (1873) LR 16 Eq 275 at 283.

Attempt to evade rule against perpetuities or accumulations

30.23 There will also be a resulting trust where otherwise the illegal object might be attained. Thus, where a settlor attempts to settle property so as to infringe the law against perpetuities, the offending trusts will not only not be carried into effect, but the person nominated to carry them out will be held to be a mere trustee for the settlor or his representatives. This is because the attempt must have been made either through ignorance or carelessness, or else with a direct intention to contravene the law. In the former case, as there would be no *delictum*, the usual maxim would not apply. In the latter, equity would not allow the trustee to retain the property, and so put it in his power to carry out the illegal intention of the testator, and to defeat the policy of the law[1]. So where the settlor directs accumulations beyond the statutory period, there is a resulting trust between the end of the twenty-one years and the period for which the accumulations were directed[2].

[1] *Carrick v Errington* (1726) 2 P Wms 361; *Tregonwell v Sydenham* (1815) 3 Dow 194; *Gibbs v Rumsey* (1813) 2 Ves & B 294.
[2] *Re Travis* [1900] 2 Ch 541, CA.

ARTICLE 31
RESULTING TRUSTS WHERE PURCHASE MADE IN ANOTHER'S NAME OR PROPERTY VOLUNTARILY TRANSFERRED TO ANOTHER

31.1

(1) When real or personal property[1] is conveyed to a purchaser jointly with others, or to one or more persons other than the purchaser, it will be presumed that he does not intend the others to take beneficially, provided that he is proved (by parol[2] or other evidence) to have paid the purchase-money[3] in the character of purchaser (as opposed to that of donor or lender)[4]; and failure to rebut this presumption will lead to the imposition of a resulting trust.

(2) This presumption may be rebutted:
    (a) by parol[5] or other evidence that the purchaser intended to benefit the others; or
    (b) by the fact that the person in whom the property was vested was the lawful[6] wife[7] or fiancée[8] or child of the purchaser[9] or was some person towards whom he stood in loco parentis[10], or, it seems nowadays[11], was the lawful husband or fiancé or child or some other person to whom a female purchaser stood in loco parentis, or the registered civil partner in a same sex relationship – or was trustee of a settlement by which he previously settled property[12]. In any of these cases a prima facie (but rebuttable)[13] presumption will arise that the purchaser intended the ostensible grantee or grantees to take beneficially, or, in the last mentioned case, upon the trusts of the settlement in question.

(3) Similar principles apply to voluntary transfers of property except to the extent that section 60 (3) of the Law of Property Act 1925 alters the position concerning land[14].

[1] *Dyer v Dyer* (1788) 2 Cox Eq Cas 92; *Ebrand v Dancer* (1680) 2 Cas in Ch 26; *Wheeler v Smith* (1860) 1 Giff 300.
[2] *Ryall v Ryall* (1739) 1 Atk 59; *Lench v Lench* (1805) 10 Ves 511; *Rochefoucauld v Boustead* [1897] 1 Ch 196.
[3] *Dyer v Dyer* (1788) 2 Cox Eq Cas 92; *Wray v Steele* (1814) 2 Ves & B 388.
[4] *Rochefoucauld v Boustead* [1897] 1 Ch 196.
[5] *Rider v Kidder* (1805) 10 Ves 360; *Standing v Bowring* (1885) 31 Ch D 282. The onus is on the grantee to prove the purchase-money-provider intended to be a donor if alleging this: *Seldon v Davidson* [1968] 2 All ER 755, CA.

31.1 Resulting trusts

6   See *Re Scottish Equitable Life Assurance Society (Policy No 6402)* [1902] 1 Ch 282.
7   *Re Eykyn* (1877) 6 Ch D 115; *Drew v Martin* (1864) 2 Hem & M 130; *Calverley v Green* (1984) 56 ALR 483 (Aust HC); *Re Condrin* [1914] 1 IR 89.
8   *Mossop v Mossop* [1989] Fam 77, [1988] 2 All ER 202, Law Reform (Miscellaneous Provisions) Act 1970, s 2(1).
9   *Soar v Foster* (1858) 4 K & J 152; *Beckford v Beckford* (1774) Lofft 490; *Webb v Webb* [1992] 1 All ER 17 at 27.
10 *Beckford v Beckford* (1774) Lofft 490; *Current v Jago* (1844) 1 Coll 261; *Tucker v Burrow* (1865) 2 Hem & M 515; *Forrest v Forrest* (1865) 13 WR 380; *Re Paradise Motor Co Ltd* [1968] 1 WLR 1125.
11 *Brown v Brown* (1993) 31 NSWLR 582 at 591 CA (mother and child); *Nelson v Nelson* (1995) 184 CLR 538 (mother and child); *Calverley v Green* (1984) 155 CLR 242, 268–269; *Dullow v Dullow* [1985] 1 NSWLR 531 at 536 and European Union law requiring equality of treatment of the sexes e g in the pensions context.
12 *Re Curteis* (1872) LR 14 Eq 217; *Muggeridge v Stanton* (1859) 1 De G F & J 107.
13 *Tumbridge v Care* (1871) 19 WR 1047; *Williams v Williams* (1863) 32 Beav 370; *Westdeutsche Landesbank v Islington London Borough Council* [1996] AC 669 at 708. On the other hand, if there is actual evidence of a gift, this solves the issue before any recourse needs to be made to the long-stop of a resulting trust, as emphasised by E Simpson in P Birks and F Rose (eds) *Restitution and Equity Vol 1, Resulting Trusts and Equitable Compensation* (2000).
14 As to personal estate see *Vandervell v IRC* [1967] 2 AC 291, [1967] 1 All ER 1, and per Cotton LJ in *Standing v Bowring* (1885) 31 Ch D 282; and per Jessel MR in *Fowkes v Pascoe* (1875) 10 Ch App 345n.

Paragraph 1

Where purchase-money contributed by two persons

31.2 Where the purchase-money is contributed, partly by the person in whose name the property is taken, and partly by another, then, if they contribute it in equal shares, they will (in the absence of evidence or circumstances showing a contrary intention[1]) take as joint tenants, because the advance being equal the interest is equal; but if in unequal shares, then a trust results to each of them of an undivided share in proportion to his advance[2] where this can be calculated with reasonable certainty[3]. Since undivided shares in land can now only take effect behind a trust[4] persons contributing to the purchase of land conveyed to one of them are equitable tenants in common, so that each is entitled concurrently with the other to possession of the land and use and enjoyment of it in a proper manner[5].

1   See *Robinson v Preston* (1858) 4 K & J 505; *Edwards v Fashion* (1712) Prec Ch 332; *Lake v Gibson* (1729) 1 Eq Cas Abr 290; *Bone v Pollard* (1857) 24 Beav 283; Megarry and Wade: *Law of Real Property* (6th edn) para 9–022; *Delehunt v Carmody* (1986) 161 CLR 464.
2   *Lake v Gibson* (1729) 1 Eq Cas Abr 290; *Rigden v Vallier* (1751) 3 Atk 731; *Crisp v Mullings* (1975) 239 Estates Gazette 119, CA; *Re Densham (a bankrupt)* [1975] 3 All ER 726, [1975] 1 WLR 1519; *Pettit v Pettit* [1970] AC 777 at 814.
3   *Diwell v Farnes* [1959] 2 All ER 379, [1959] 1 WLR 624, CA and *Finch v Finch* (1975) 119 Sol Jo 793, CA indicating that where precise quantification is impossible it seems that the principle is that 'Equity delighteth in equality' though reliance on this should be a last resort: *Gissing v Gissing* [1971] AC 886 at 897 and 903, HL.
4   Law of Property Act 1925, s 34(1); Settled Land Act 1925, s 36(4), as amended by the Trusts of Land and Appointment of Trustees Act 1996, Schs 2 and 3.
5   *Bull v Bull* [1955] 1 QB 234, [1955] 1 All ER 253, CA; *Jones v Jones* [1977] 2 All ER 231, [1977] 1 WLR 438, CA; *Williams & Glyn's Bank v Boland* [1981] AC 487, subject to the Trusts of Land and Appointment of Trustees Act 1996, ss 12 and 13.

31.3 Payments of an income (as opposed to capital) nature for the use of property, eg rent and bills for everyday living expenses do not give the payer any interest in the property. Thus in *Savage v Dunningham*[1], where a tenancy agreement was in the name of the defendant, who had the plaintiffs living with him sharing the rent and other day-to-day expenses, it was held that no resulting trust arose in favour of the plaintiffs so as to enable them to have an interest in the freehold reversion which the defendant subsequently purchased.

[1]   [1974] Ch 181, [1973] 3 All ER 429.

TITLE TAKEN IN ONE NAME

31.4 When property is bought[1] by A and B in the name of A, and there is no evidence that B intended a gift, and no express written declaration of trust[2], and no presumption of advancement between the parties[3], it is presumed that B does not intend A to take the whole property beneficially for himself. Failure to rebut this presumption by A will lead to the imposition of a resulting trust in B's favour, to the extent of his contribution. Thus, if the property cost £100,000 and A paid £60,000 and B paid £40,000 the property will be held by A on resulting trust for A and B in the proportions 3:2[4]. The position will be the same if the property is worth £100,000 but a discount worth £60,000 is allowed to A as sitting tenant so that A only needs to pay the £40,000 provided by B[5]. The position is the same if A, as legal owner, mortgages the legal title in order to provide his £60,000 contribution[6].

[1]   *The Venture* [1908] P 218 at 230; *Gissing v Gissing* [1971] AC 886 at 897, 900, 905; *Bernard v Joseph's* [1982] Ch 391 at 404; and the approach of the Court of Appeal in *Huntingford v Hobbs* [1993] 1 FLR 736, (1992) 24 HLR 65; *Springette v Defoe* (1992) 65 P & CR 1, (1992) 24 HLR 552; *Sekhon v Alissa* [1989] 2 FLR 94.

[2]   *Goodman v Gallant* [1986] Fam 106, CA, [1986] 1 All ER 311; *Turton v Turton* [1988] Ch 542, CA, [1987] 2 All ER 641.

[3]   See paras 31.36–31.58 below.

[4]   It is unclear whether capital acquisition costs like legal fees, survey fees and stamp duties should be treated as part of the cost of purchase when making this calculation. Yes: *Huntingford v Hobbs* [1993] 1 FLR 736; *Currie v Hamilton* [1984] 1 NSWLR 687 at 691. No: *Curley v Parkes* [2004] EWCA Civ 1515 at [22], [2004] All ER (D) 344.

[5]   *Abbey National BS v Cann* (1989) 57 P & CR 381, CA; *Springette v Defoe* (1992) 65 P & CR 1, (1992) 24 HLR 552 (CA); *Mckenzie v Mckenzie* [2003] EWHC 601 (Ch) at [81]; *R (on the application of Kelly) v Hammersmith & Fulham London Borough Council* [2004] EWHC 435 (Admin) at [19], [2004] All ER (D) 388 (May); *Day v Day* [2005] EWHC 1455 (Ch), [2005] All ER (D) 268 (Jun). Cf *Ashe v Mumford* (2001) 33 HLR 756 at 769 (para 50), a declaration of trust by A of holding on trust for herself for life, remainder to B's son, C and a surrender of A's life interest being disregarded by the Court of Appeal as shams, A fronting B's transactions (paras 19 and 54).

[6]   *Huntingford v Hobbs* [1993] 1 FLR 736, (1992) 24 HLR 65, CA.

31.5 A's and B's equitable interests under resulting trusts are fixed at the time they purchased the property by paying the purchase price[1]. They get the shares they paid for when they provided the purchase price, whether by way of their own cash (whether saved, inherited, or borrowed on mortgage) or a discount arising from their status. Exceptionally, it seems that if at the time of purchase A and B agreed that B would undertake responsibility for the mortgage payments, then A will hold on resulting trust for B as to the proportion of the price provided by the mortgage, equity regarding as done that which has to be

31.5 *Resulting trusts*

done by B[2]. This holds true even if B subsequently fails to make the mortgage payments as agreed, and these are made instead by A, although on sale of the property, equitable accounting principles may require deductions to be made against B's share of the sale proceeds[3].

[1] Lord Browne-Wilkinson 'Constructive Trusts and Unjust Enrichment' (1996) 10 Tru LI 98 at 100: 'Under a resulting trust the existence of the trust is established once and for all at the date on which the property is acquired'. See too *Pettitt v Pettitt* [1970] AC 777 at 800 per Lord Morris, and at 816 per Lord Upjohn; *Gissing v Gissing* [1971] AC 886 at 900 per Viscount Dilhorne; *Calverley v Green* (1984) 155 CLR 242 at 257 per Mason CJ and Brennan J; *Crisp v Mullings* (1975) 239 Estates Gazette 119, CA; *Huntingford v Hobbs* [1993] 1 FLR 736, (1992) 24 HLR 65, CA; *Harwood v Harwood* [1991] 2 FLR 274 at 292; *Curley v Parkes* [2004] EWCA Civ 1515 at [14] per Peter Gibson LJ, [2004] All ER (D) 344 (Oct). The mortgage instalments are not part of the price already paid to the vendor but are sums paid for discharging the mortgagor's personal obligations and ultimately the incumbrance on the property: *Carlton v Goodman [2002] EWCA 545, [2002] 2 FLR 259* at [22] per Mummery LJ. For common intention constructive trusts or proprietary estoppel, payments of mortgage instalments, most of which will represent interest in the early years of the mortgage, or of interest and premiums on endowment policies to pay off the mortgage on maturity will be taken into account: *Gissing v Gissing* [1971] AC 886 at 906; *Grant v Edwards* [1986] Ch 638, CA; *Stokes v Anderson* [1991] 1 FLR 391, CA; *Lloyds Bank v Rosset* [1991] 1 AC 107.
[2] *Kronheim v Johnson* (1877) 7 Ch D 60 (title in A); *Ivin v Blake* (1994) 67 P & CR 263, CA, where the resulting trust in B's favour was not ousted by a common intention trust in favour of A, the title holder; *Huntingford v Hobbs* [1993] 1 FLR 736; *Springette v Defoe* (1992) 65 P & CR 1 (title in A and B).
[3] *Huntingford v Hobbs* [1993] 1 FLR 736. See too *Bernard v Jacobs* [1982] Ch 391; *Re Gorman* [1990] 1 WLR 616; *Re Pavlou* [1993] 1 WLR 1046; *Ryan v Dries* (2002) 4 ITELR 829; *Re Byford* [2003] EWHC 1267 (Ch), [2004] 1 FLR 56; and para 31.16.

31.6 If B did not contribute to the cost of purchase when the property was bought on mortgage by A, but subsequently provides £10,000 whether towards discharging A's mortgage liability for capital moneys or in paying for a capital improvement like a conservatory, this is regarded as a gift and will not confer on B a one-tenth or other proportionate share in the property[1] unless an agreement with A or a representation by A enables B to claim an equitable interest under a common intention constructive trust or proprietary estoppel principles. The position is *a fortiori* if B's £10,000 happens to represent periodic contributions to interest due under the mortgage or to premiums on the endowment policy that on maturity will ensure that the capital moneys due under the mortgage will be repaid. Lax use of language and confusion between resulting and constructive trusts has, however, led some judges to treat subsequent mortgage payments as giving rise to resulting trusts rather than constructive trusts or proprietary estoppel interests.

[1] *Winkworth v Edward Baron Developments Ltd* [1986] 1 WLR 1512 at 1515, [1987] 1 All ER 114 at 117, HL: payment not referable to acquisition of house 'which had already been bought and paid for in full'; *Pettit v Pettit* [1970] AC 777 at 818; *Davis v Vale* [1971] 1 WLR 1022 at 1025; *Harwood v Harwood* [1991] 2 FLR 274 at 294; *Falcke v Scottish Imperial Insurance Co* (1886) 34 Ch D 234. However, if A and B were married or engaged to be married and contributed money or money's worth to the improvement of the property B could claim a beneficial interest under s 37 of the Matrimonial Proceedings and Property Act 1970, but this section is not available if A and B are beneficial joint tenants: *Barclays Bank Ltd v Abbas* (7 May 1985, unreported), Nicholls J.

31.7 Where A purchases property in the name of a company or trust controlled by him the normal natural (but rebuttable) inference is that beneficial ownership was intended to pass to the company or trustee[1],but if A transfers property from his name into that of a company or trust controlled by him, the court is ready to infer that in the circumstances the transferee was to be a nominee for A[2].

1   *Nightingale Mayfair Ltd v Mehta* [2000] WTLR 901 at 925–926, per Blackburne J.
2   *United Overseas Bank Ltd v Iwuanyanwu* Ch D 5 March 2001, affirmed [2001] EWCA Civ 616.

TITLE TAKEN IN BOTH NAMES

31.8 When property is bought by A and B in their joint names, it is presumed in the absence of clear evidence as to their intentions that neither intends to make a gift or loan of his own contribution to the others. Unless this presumption is rebutted, the property will then be held on resulting trust for the pair of them, the amount of their respective equitable interests corresponding to the contributions which they made to the purchase[1]. Because A and B have legal title any mortgage moneys will be a joint and several liability, so giving A and B joint or equal shares in the proportion of the property purchased with the mortgage moneys unless A and B have agreed that one of them undertakes all mortgage liability or, say 75% of liability under the mortgage, when the 'undertaker' will acquire an equitable interest under a resulting trust in the proportion that the amount of his liability bears to the acquisition cost of the property[2]. If any subsequent improvements to the property paid for by one party or any subsequent payments greater than his share are alleged to give the payer a greater interest in the property, then again[3], this can only be on the basis of some agreement or representation generating a common intention constructive trust or a proprietary estoppel interest.

1   *Pettitt v Pettitt* [1970] AC 777 at 814.
2   *Huntingford v Hobbs* [1993] 1 FLR 736; *Springette v Defoe* (1992) 65 P & CR 1; *Mckenzie v Mckenzie* [2003] EWHC 601 (Ch) at [80]–[81]; *Trowbridge v Trowbridge* [2002] EWHC 3114 (Ch), [2003] 2 FLR 231. Cf *Carlton v Goodman [2002] EWCA Civ 545*, [2002] 2 FLR 259, where no resulting trust arose in B's favour over a house bought in the names of A and B by virtue of a joint mortgage by them where the purchase from A's landlady was only for A's occupation where A alone could not obtain the relevant mortgage and B's function was as a facilitator, likely to 'come off' the mortgage within a year or so, and whose contribution to such arrangement was regarded as a gift and her payments of mortgage instalments after A's death payments as trustee for which she was entitled to be indemnified.
3   See para 31.5 above.

Where purchase money provided by one person

31.9 Of course, if A buys property in B's name A will be beneficially entitled thereto unless intending to make a gift to B. Thus, where a married couple, A and B, each subscribed for a one fifteenth share in a National Lottery syndicate but, on separating, A continued to pay B's share as well as her own, so that B's name was ticked off the list each week, Lindsay J held[1] that a resulting trust arose for A in respect of B's fifteenth share of the lottery winnings. There was acceptable evidence that B had rudely refused to continue paying his share and that A intended herself to benefit as to both one fifteenth shares for which she was paying.

1   *Abrahams v Abrahams* [2000] WTLR 593.

Resulting and constructive trusts contrasted

31.10 A purchaser under a resulting trust acquires at the outset an equitable interest representing the share he or she provided for the vendor at the time the property was bought. Thus, if a claimant seeks a larger share than originally paid for, especially where subsequent direct or indirect financial contributions to mortgage payments have been made or a representation has been made to the claimant that she is to have a half share and in reliance thereon she acts significantly to her detriment, she will have to rely on a common intention constructive trust or an equitable proprietary estoppel interest.

31.11 A person with an equitable interest under a purchase money resulting trust is fully a purchaser so as to be protected in the event of the bankruptcy of the other co-owner, while a person with an equitable interest under a constructive trust or a proprietary estoppel will be regarded as a donee or a purchaser at an undervalue[1].

1   *Re Densham* [1975] 3 All ER 726, [1975] 1 WLR 1519. One-ninth share under a resulting trust valid against husband's trustee in bankruptcy but the one-half share under a constructive trust was voidable as a voluntary settlement; see now Insolvency Act 1986, ss 339, 340.

31.12 The interest that a non-owning cohabitee expects to have under a constructive trust may be specified at the outset or it may be specified at a later date or it may be what will represent a fair share at the date the parties separate or the property is sold, taking account of the parties' direct and indirect financial contributions[1]. Detrimental reliance is crucial to both common intention constructive trusts and proprietary estoppel and in both instances there can be much uncertainty as to what interest arises, when it arises and how it is quantified because, essentially, the court appears to be tailoring a remedy to fit the circumstances.

1   *Austin v Keele* (1981) 61 ALJR 605, PC; *Stokes v Anderson* [1991] 1 FLR 391, CA.

31.13 One needs to be aware that the courts are apt to use the terminology of resulting and constructive trusts as if the terms were interchangeable. This should not matter for the purposes of formalities, since both types of trust fall within the scope of s 53(2) of the Law of Property Act 1925. However, this loose usage can sometimes lead the courts into error. One example is the view expressed by Lord Browne-Wilkinson that 'a resulting trust arises in order to give effect to the intention of the parties'[1]. This is not borne out by cases where resulting trusts have been imposed on property held by transferees who had no intention of becoming trustees, eg because they were legally incapable of forming any intention at all[2], and the better view is that the only person whose intentions are relevant is the transferor[3]. Another example is the tendency displayed by some judges to treat subsequent payments of mortgage instalments which are potentially relevant for constructive trusts as being relevant for resulting trusts. This ignores the essence of resulting trusts which can be summarised as the claimant having a share in the property proportionate to the share of the purchase price that she paid or undertook to pay at the time the purchase price was paid over: she gets what she then paid for or undertook to pay for. If a resulting trust claim is therefore unavailable or would result in nothing more than a small share, then she can try to rely upon a common intention constructive trust or an equitable estoppel claim to seek what she was led to believe she would acquire.

[1] 'Constructive Trusts and Unjust Enrichment' (1996) 10 Tru LI 98 at 99, echoed in *Tinsley v Milligan* [1994] 1 AC 340 at 371, and *Westdeutsche Landesbank Girozentrale v Islington London Borough Council* [1996] AC 669 at 708. It seems likely that his Lordship was misled by Lord Diplock's unfortunately expressed speech in *Gissing v Gissing* [1971] AC 886 at 904–5 and 922. Certainly a misreading of this speech led the Canadian courts to use unorthodox 'common intention resulting trusts' to resolve shared homes cases (see e g *Rathwell v Rathwell* [1978] 2 SCR 436), an approach which has now given way to the application of statutes and constructive trust reasoning: *Oosterhoff on Trusts* 6th edn (2004) 554–560.

[2] e g *Lench v Lench* (1805) 10 Ves 511; *Childers v Childers* (1857) 1 De G & J 482; *Re Vinogradoff* [1935] WN 68.

[3] R Chambers *Resulting Trusts* (1997) 35–37; J Mee *The Property Rights of Cohabitees* (1999) 39–43. This is not to deny that a transferee's intentions can be relevant as circumstantial evidence of the transferor's intentions, as in e g *Ali v Khan* (2002) 5 ITELR 232 at [28] per Morritt V-C.

Express declaration of trust advisable

31.14 To avoid problems appertaining to resulting and constructive trusts and concomitant court proceedings, the Court of Appeal has emphasised many times how advisable it is for there to be an express declaration of trust setting out the precise equitable interests conclusively in the absence of fraud or mistake[1], although those who were not parties to the declaration of trust cannot be prejudiced by such a declaration if they have contributed to the purchase price[2].

[1] *Goodman v Gallant* [1986] Fam 106 (CA); *Turton v Turton* [1988] Ch 542, CA; *Carlton v Goodman* [2002] EWCA Civ 545 at para 44. An express declaration of trust of a fair share will be void for uncertainty, though many parties would like to do this, not being prepared at the outset to bind themselves to precise shares.

[2] *City of London BS v Flegg* [1988] AC 54, HL.

31.15 Declarations of trust of land require to be evidenced in signed writing but where a transfer of registered land stated, 'It is hereby agreed and declared that the transferees are entitled to the land for their own benefit and that the survivor of them can give a valid receipt for capital money arising on a disposition of land' and was not signed by the transferees, it was still held to be conclusive evidence of the parties' intention to be beneficial joint tenants[1]. However, if the printed form contains the statement, 'The transferees declare that the survivor of them can/cannot give a valid receipt for capital money

31.15 *Resulting trusts*

arising on a disposition of the land' and cannot is deleted such statement is not treated as a declaration of trust of a beneficial joint tenancy[2].

1   *Re Gorman* [1990] 1 All ER 717, [1990] 1 WLR 616 (Div Ct).
2   *Huntingford v Hobbs* [1993] 1 FLR 736, CA; *Harwood v Harwood* [1991] 2 FLR 274; *Stack v Dowden* [2005] EWCA Civ 857, [2006] 1 P & CR 244.

Equitable accounting

31.16 Whether the co-ownership interests arise under an express or resulting or constructive trust, equitable accounting principles will apply where the parties have split up and one has then made all the mortgage payments and spent money improving the property although enjoying rent-free occupation of the property[1]. Some cases will illustrate how these accounting principles operate: they apply to joint tenants as well as to tenants in common[2].

1   For example, *Re Pavlou* [1993] 3 All ER 955; *Re Gorman* [1990] 1 All ER 717; *Bernard v Josephs* [1982] Ch 391; *Ryan v Dries* (2002) 4 ITELR 829; *Byford v Butler* [2003] EWHC 1267 (Ch), [2004] 1 FLR 56. Further see E Cooke 'Equitable Accounting' [1995] Conv 391.
2   *Re Pavlou* [1993] 3 All ER 955.

31.17 In *Bernard v Josephs*[1] in October 1974 an unmarried couple, M and W, bought a house in their joint names for £11,750 and took a 100% mortgage jointly in order to purchase the house. M contributed £650 and W £200 to the costs incidental to the conveyance, the mortgage and the moving in. Their intention was to pay the mortgage by taking in tenants, and M spent £2,000 on decorations and repairs to enable part of the house to be let. The resulting rents were used towards the mortgage payments which were made by M throughout, though they treated their resources primarily as pooled, W working all the time and using her money for joint household expenses, M for a time being unemployed. As a result of M's violence W left him in July 1976. M continued to live in the house, taking rents and paying the mortgage.

1   [1982] Ch 391, [1982] 3 All ER 162, CA.

31.18 The Court of Appeal held that there was a common intention constructive trust in equal shares, M and W being regarded as having contributed to the mortgage, and thus the purchase price, in substantially equal shares, with a common intention that they should receive credits for their initial contributions and sums spent on improvements. The balance of the equity value of the house after deduction of the outstanding mortgage was about £15,000 so W was prima facie entitled to half this. However, M had to be given credit for £2,450 (being the £650 at acquisition plus £2,000 on improvements less W's £200 at acquisition). He was entitled to a further credit because, since W left, M had paid £4,743 on mortgage instalments though receiving £2,080 rent, leaving a balance of £2,663. M was credited with half this, ie £1,331.50 (in effect, paying an occupation rent for ousting his co-owner)[1]. M's total credit of £3,781.50 was rounded up to £3,800 so that deducting this from the £15,000 left £11,200, of which W's half share amounted to £5,600, which the court rounded up to £6,000 in view of the growth of property values since the proceedings began. If M did not pay W this sum within four months then the house was to be sold[2] so that W could realise her share.

1   A co-owner if in sole occupation does not have to pay rent to the other co-owner unless he has ousted her *Dennis v McDonald* [1982] Fam 63, [1982] 1 All ER 590, CA or as a matter of equitable accounting ancillary to an order or suspended order for sale under Law of Property Act 1925, s 30 or Trusts of Land and Appointment of Trustees Act 1996 s 14, 43.45–43.55. In *Re Pavlou* [1993] 3 All ER 955 at 959 Millett J stated, 'A court of equity will order an inquiry and payment of an occupation rent, not only in the case where the co-owner in occupation has ousted the other, but in any other case in which it is necessary in order to do equity between the parties that an occupation rent should be paid.' This was endorsed in *Byford v Butler* [2003] EWHC 1267 (Ch), [2004] 1 FLR 56.
2   W had sought a declaration that she had a half share and that the house ought to be sold under Law of Property Act 1925, s 30, 43.45 and 43.58.

31.19 Here the court did not distinguish between the capital and interest parts of the instalments of the repayment mortgage, though the usual practice as appears from *Suttill v Graham*[1] is just to set off the interest element against a notional occupational rent so that they cancel each other out and to credit the occupying payer of the mortgage with the capital element. This is a rule of convenience because much will depend upon the amount of the mortgage debt and the value of the property providing the basis for the notional occupation rent: in *Re Gorman*[2] Vinelott J was thus prepared to set off against half the notional rent half the actual mortgage instalments paid. More recently, in *Re Pavlou*[3] Millett J was prepared to order inquiries to ascertain the notional rent and then to set off against it actual mortgage payments if the trustee in bankruptcy was not agreeable to the interest element of mortgage instalments being taken to match the notional rent, or if it could not be seen in advance that the taking of the two accounts would be a waste of time because the amounts would be likely to be so similar. He also held that the bankrupt's wife, an express joint tenant, was entitled to credit for one-half of any repairs or improvements paid for by her since her husband had left her or if it were lesser one-half of the increase in value of the property realised by such repairs or improvements.

1   [1977] 3 All ER 1117, [1977] 1 WLR 819.
2   [1990] 1 All ER 717, [1990] 1 WLR 616.
3   [1993] 3 All ER 955, [1993] 1 WLR 1046.

Loans

31.20 Where the purchase money is provided by a third party at the request of and by way of loan to the person to whom the property is conveyed there is no resulting trust in favour of the third party, for the lender did not advance the purchase-money as purchaser[1], but merely as lender.

1   *Aveling v Knipe* (1815) 19 Ves 441.

31.21 In *Hussey v Palmer*[1] this last sentence was accepted as a correct statement of the law by Cairns LJ though in a dissenting judgment. The case is a very unsatisfactory one, partly due to the course events took in the county court before the registrar and then the judge. The plaintiff, the defendant's mother-in-law, having sold her condemned house, was invited by the defendant to live with the defendant and his wife. The house was rather small so an extra bedroom was built on for £607 which the plaintiff paid directly to the builder, having agreed with the defendant that this was to be treated as a loan to him.

1   [1972] 3 All ER 744, [1972] 1 WLR 1286 criticised (1973) 89 LQR 2, (1973) 37 Conv 65; and see *Re Sharpe (a bankrupt)* [1980] 1 All ER 198 at 201; *Spence v Browne* [1988] 1 Fam Law 291.

31.22 Differences arose so the plaintiff left the house and later claimed repayment of the loan. She submitted to a non suit before the registrar when he intimated he thought she should not be claiming for money lent. A fresh plaint claimed the £607 on resulting trust principles but the judge rejected this since he found the money had been lent. Unfortunately, he rejected the plaintiff's application to amend the particulars to a claim for money lent. The plaintiff appealed against the rejection of the resulting trust and the refusal of the amendment.

31.23 Cairns LJ held[1] 'as it was a loan it is quite inconsistent with that to say that it could create a resulting trust at the same time' so that she could only claim for money lent for which amendment of her particulars should be allowed.

1   *Hussey v Palmer* [1972] 3 All ER 744 at 749.

31.24 Surprisingly, Phillimore LJ[1] held that the loan would not be 'inconsistent with the transaction also being or involving a resulting trust' so that the plaintiff had an interest in the house proportionate to the £607 she had paid. However, a transaction of paying money over qua lender is quite different from a transaction of paying money over qua purchaser: a lender can recover just the money lent[2] whilst a purchaser acquires a proportionate interest in the property usually being an appreciating interest. The two transactions are thus mutually exclusive.

1   [1972] 3 All ER 744 at 748.
2   As emphasised by *Westdeutsche Landesbank v Islington London Borough Council* [1996] AC 669, HL.

31.25 Lord Denning in a robust judgment flying in the face of the plaintiff's evidence of a loan arrangement held that there was no loan but that a constructive trust existed proportionate to the plaintiff's contribution because 'justice and good conscience required it'[1]. With respect, this is far too broad an approach[2] to the use of constructive trusts and is now discredited[2]. A further justification put forward by Lord Denning was the equitable proprietary estoppel principle illustrated by cases such as *Chalmers v Pardoe*[3] and *Inwards v Baker*[4] , though he overlooked the requirement that there must be words or conduct on the part of the defendant from which the plaintiff can reasonably assume that he is to have an interest proportionate to his contribution to the defendant's property. No such words or conduct were proved by the plaintiff as inducing the required expectation on her part and in the absence of such as Lord Upjohn has said[5] 'It has been well settled that if A expends money on the property of B prima facie A has no claim on such property'. Indeed in *Davis v Vale*[6] Lord Denning himself assumed this was the law.

1. [1972] 3 All ER 744 at 747.
2. See para 35.11 below.
3. [1963] 3 All ER 552, [1963] 1 WLR 677. On this principle see paras 12.47–12.66.
4. [1965] 2 QB 29, [1965] 1 All ER 446.
5. [1970] AC 777 at 818.
6. [1971] 1 WLR 1022 at 1025.

31.26 *Risch v McFee*[1], however was an exceptional case where a female not seeking repayment of her loan (and therefore making a gift) to a male house owner with whom she cohabited was found to be thereby acting to her detriment in reliance on a common intention that she should acquire a beneficial interest in the house: she thus had a pro tanto share in the house under a constructive trust.

1. (1991) 61 P & CR 42, CA.

31.27 In *Assured Quality Construction Ltd v Thompson*[1], the parties agreed that the defendant would contribute to the purchase price and development costs of two properties, and that when the properties were sold the defendant's money would be repaid with interest, and that he would additionally receive a share of the profits. The parties fell out, and in the proceedings which followed the defendant sought a declaration that he had an equitable interest in the properties under a resulting trust. Lewison J declined to make such a declaration, holding that the parties' contractual arrangement was for a loan and profit share only.

1. (2006) Times, 21 April.

Paragraph 2

Evidence of intention to benefit

31.28 In *Standing v Bowring*[1] the plaintiff, a widow, in the year 1880 transferred £6,000 consols into the joint names of herself and her godson, the defendant. This she did *with the express intention* that the defendant, in the event of his surviving her, should have the consols, but that she herself should retain the dividends during her life. She had been previously warned that her act was irrevocable.

1. (1885) 31 Ch D 282; and see also *Wheeler v Smith* (1860) 1 Giff 300; and *Fowkes v Pascoe* (1875) 10 Ch App 343.

31.29 In delivering judgment, Cotton LJ said:

'The rule is well settled that where there is a transfer by a person into his own name jointly with that of a person who is not his child, or his adopted child, then there is prima facie a resulting trust for the transferor. But that is a presumption capable of being rebutted by showing that at the time the transferor intended a benefit to the transferee, and in the present case there is ample evidence that at the time of the transfer, and for some time previously, the plaintiff intended to confer a benefit by this transfer on her late husband's godson.'

31.30 Thus the resulting trust was rebutted for the period after the plaintiff's death as was the case in *Fowkes v Pascoe*[1] where the circumstances of a wealthy widow, with plenty of consols already in her own name, putting £250 of consols into the names of herself and her lady companion and of herself and the young son of her daughter-in-law were held after her death to be explicable only on the basis of an intent to make a gift. Unfortunately, this case was not drawn to the attention of Farwell J in *Re Vinogradoff*[2] where Mrs Vinogradoff had transferred £800 of war loan stock into the joint names of herself and her four year old granddaughter but Farwell J held there was resulting trust for Mrs Vinogradoff's estate when one would have thought that the transaction could only be explicable on the basis that a gift was intended.

1 (1875) 10 Ch App 343.
2 [1935] WN 68.

Banking or portfolio accounts in joint names

31.31 Where a bank balance has been transferred into joint names similar principles have been applied even though the transferor has retained dominion and control over the account during his life so that all the donee could take by survivorship was the balance standing to the credit of the account at the donor's death[1]. The point that, where the donor retains not only the right to income but the right to use, during his life, the substance of the gift itself, the gift is of a testamentary character not made in conformity with the Wills Act 1837, does not appear to have been raised in any reported English case before *Young v Sealey*[2]. There, after reviewing certain cases in the Supreme Court of the Irish Free State[3] and the Canadian Courts[4], where it had been held that the transfer into joint names was in substance and in fact a testamentary disposition and, as such, ineffectual, Romer J said that their reasoning appealed to him. But he declined to apply such reasoning on the grounds that:

> ' ... the cases which have come before the courts of this country in which a depositor has put funds in the joint names of himself and another, intending to retain control over the funds, and to withdraw them if he thought proper, but with the further intention that the other party (if surviving) should take beneficially whatever might be left of the funds at the death of the depositor have all, so far as I am aware, resulted in the surviving beneficiary taking free from any trust, and it is impossible to say that the point was not raised in any of those cases although it is not mentioned in any report.
>
> Further, the Appellate Division of the Supreme Court of Ontario had the point before it[5] but did not accept it.'

1 See *Marshal v Crutwell* (1875) LR 20 Eq 328 at 330, per Jessel MR; *Re Harrison* (1920) 90 LJ Ch 186. The first of these two cases was distinguished, and the second followed, in *Re Figgis* [1969] 1 Ch 123, [1968] 1 All ER 999.

2   [1949] Ch 278, [1949] 1 All ER 92. This case was considered in *Re Figgis* [1969] 1 Ch 123, [1968] 1 All ER 999.
3   *Owens v Green* [1932] IR 225 overruled by *Lynch v Burke* [1995] 2 IR 159 so as no longer to amount to testamentary dispositions.
4   *Hill v Hill* (1904) 5 OWR 2; *Shortill v Grannen* (1920) 47 NBR 463; *McKnight v Titus* (1933) 6 MPR 282. See also *Russell v Scott* (1921) 55 CLR 440.
5   *Re Reid* (1921) 64 DLR 598.

31.32 He went on to say that, in these circumstances, and having regard to the disturbing effect which an acceptance of the arguments might have on existing titles, any change in the current of English authority must be made, if at all, by the Court of Appeal, and there the matter now stands, *Re Figgis*[1] having endorsed the *Young v Sealey* approach, finding that there is 'an immediate gift [at the opening of the account] of a fluctuating asset consisting of the chose in action for the time being constituting the balance in the bank account'. While this analysis is appropriate for cash deposits there are difficulties in applying it to a changing portfolio of investments but there has been held[2] to be no conceptual difficulty in a gift via a joint portfolio investment account extending to assets actually acquired by the bank and placed to the credit of the joint account-holders. In such a case the surviving donee needs to do nothing more to constitute his title and can give instructions to the bank in accordance with the mandate.

1   [1969] 1 Ch 123 at 149, per Megarry LJ.
2   *Aroso v Coutts & Co* [2001] WTLR 797 (account in name of donor and his cousin's son).

Joint banking account of husband and wife

31.33 Where husband and wife have a joint bank account, the beneficial ownership of money in it, and of assets acquired from it, will depend upon their intention. When their intention is that the account is to be a pool of their joint resources, the money in it will be treated as belonging to them jointly, and no attempt will be made to divide it between them according to their respective contributions to it. This was established by *Jones v Maynard*[1], in which Vaisey J also held that since the spouses had agreed that investments thereout were to be 'our savings', then if investments were purchased out of such an account in the name of the husband, he would hold one half of them as trustee for the wife. But he went on to suggest, obiter, that if investments were purchased in the sole name of the wife they would belong to her absolutely because the presumption of advancement would apply.

1   [1951] Ch 572, [1951] 1 All ER 802 (approved in *Rimmer v Rimmer* [1953] 1 QB 63, [1952] 2 All ER 863, CA). But in *Re Cohen* [1953] Ch 88, [1953] 1 All ER 378, a cache of notes found secreted in the matrimonial home after the deaths of both spouses (who died within a few months of each other) was, in the absence of evidence of ownership, held to be the property of the wife to whom the residence belonged.

31.34 In *Re Bishop*[1], Stamp J questioned this last point and suggested that if money in an account was intended to belong to the spouses equally, and that investments purchased out of that money should also belong to them equally, it would not be possible to presume a trust of investments purchased in the husband's name for both spouses without presuming a similar trust in respect of those purchased in the name of the wife. This latter case also made it clear that in so far as the decision in *Jones v Maynard* related to investments, it was based upon its own facts particularly the common intention that investments were to be treated as 'our savings'. In general, where spouses open a joint account on terms that cheques may be drawn by either, then (unless the account is kept for some specific or limited purpose) each spouse can draw on it for his or her own benefit and any investment purchased out of the account belongs to the spouse in whose name the purchase was made. If an investment is purchased by one spouse in the joint names, there is no equity to displace the joint legal ownership and they do not hold it 'as trustees [for themselves] in equal or some other shares'[2]. On the husband's death, money standing to the credit of the account will belong to the wife[3].

[1]   [1965] Ch 450, [1965] 1 All ER 249.
[2]   See also *Re Young* (1885) 28 Ch D 705, and *Gage v King* [1961] 1 QB 188, [1960] 3 All ER 62.
[3]   *Re Bishop* [1965] Ch 450, [1965] 1 All ER 249.

31.35 When a joint account is opened by a husband in the names of his wife and himself, and the only money paid into the account is that of the husband, the question whether the presumption of advancement applies in favour of the wife may be difficult to answer. If the joint account was opened merely for convenience, the wife will not have the benefit of this presumption and will not be entitled to the money standing to the credit of the account on the husband's death[1]. But if it was opened with the intention of making provision for the wife (an intention which will be more readily inferred if the only person to operate the account was the husband), then the wife will be so entitled[2].

[1]   *Marshal v Crutwell* (1875) LR 20 Eq 328; *Thompson v Thompson* (1970) 114 Sol Jo 455, CA; *Hoddinott v Hoddinott* [1949] 2 KB 406; *Heseltine v Heseltine* [1971] 1 All ER 952, [1971] 1 WLR 342, where H purchased 4 houses in his own name, paying for them out of a joint account the money in which had been wholly provided by W, and the CA held the joint account had been opened purely for convenience and not with the intention that W should make a gift to H, so H held the houses on trust for W.
[2]   *Re Figgis* [1969] 1 Ch 123, [1968] 1 All ER 999. Further see (1969) 85 LQR 530 (M. C. Cullity).

Presumption of advancement

31.36 The rule was stated thus by Viscount Simonds in *Shephard v Cartwright*[1]:

'The law is clear that, on the one hand, where a man purchases shares and they are registered in the name of a stranger, there is a resulting trust in favour of the purchaser; on the other hand, if they are registered in the name of a child or one to whom the purchaser then stood in loco parentis there is no such resulting trust, but a presumption of advancement. Equally it is clear that the presumption may be rebutted but should not give way to slight circumstances.'

[1]   [1955] AC 431 at 445, [1954] 3 All ER 649 at 652, HL; *Pettitt v Pettitt* [1970] AC 777 at 815.

31.37 The presumption is particularly strong for property bought in the name of a child who is a minor[1] and it seems it should make no difference whether the child is legitimate, legitimated or adopted[2].

[1]   *Shephard v Cartwright* [1955] AC 431 at 452.
[2]   Legitimacy Act 1976, ss 2, 8; Adoption Act 1976, s 39; *Seldon v Davidson* [1968] 2 All ER 755 at 758.

31.38 Where the presumption has arisen and not been rebutted it will not be destroyed by anything (such as change of mind on the part of the donor) that happens subsequently.

31.39 Thus in *Crabb v Crabb*[1] a father transferred a sum of stock from his own name into the joint names of his son and of a broker, and told the latter to carry the dividends to the son's account. The father, by a codicil to his will, executed subsequently, bequeathed the stock to another; but it was held that the son took absolutely. Lord Brougham LC said:

> 'If the transfer is not ambiguous, but a clear and unequivocal act, as I must take it to be on the authorities, for explanation there is plainly no place ... The transfer being held an advancement, nothing contained in the codicil, nor any other matter ex post facto, can ever be allowed to alter what has been already done.'

[1]   (1834) 1 My & K 511; and see also *Birch v Blagrave* (1755) Amb 264; and *Batstone v Salter* (1875) 10 Ch App 431, where a mother transferred stock into the joint names of herself, her daughter, and her son-in-law.

31.40 Similarly, it has been held that even in the days when a nullity decree had retrospective effect a subsequent decree of nullity of marriage did not destroy the presumption of advancement which existed where the husband had transferred property into the name of the wife[1].

[1]   *Dunbar v Dunbar* [1909] 2 Ch 639.

31.41 The presumption arises where a man transfers property to his wife or his fiancée whom he subsequently marries[1], or after 1970 even if he does not[2], but not where he transfers property to his mistress or a woman with whom he cohabits as if they were man and wife[3]. It also applies where a man transfers property to his child or a person to whom he stands in loco parentis[4] or to trustees of a settlement by him on his children[5], but it must be the man's own property not just property belonging to a company controlled by the man[6].

[1]   *Moate v Moate* [1948] 2 All ER 486; *Ulrich v Ulrich and Felton* [1968] 1 All ER 67, [1968] 1 WLR 180. Nowadays the presumption is a very weak one as a judicial instrument of last resort if there is not even circumstantial evidence to clarify the transferor's intentions: *McGrath v Wallis* [1995] 2 FLR 114, CA.
[2]   Section 2 of Law Reform (Miscellaneous Provisions) Act 1970; *Mossop v Mossop* [1989] Fam 77 [1988] 2 All ER 202, CA.
[3]   *Rider v Kidder* (1805) 10 Ves 360; *Crisp v Mullings* (1974) 233 Estates Gazette 511; *Calverley v Green* (1984) 56 ALR 483 (Aust HC).
[4]   *Shephard v Cartwright* [1955] AC 431 at 445, HL. For a woman and her child see para 31.51.
[5]   *Re Curteis* (1872) LR 14 Eq 217.

⁶ *Re Vandervell's Trusts (No 2)* [1974] Ch 269 at 302–303, [1974] 1 All ER 47 at 75–76 per Megarry J.

31.42 In these days of sexual economic equality it is surely time that the presumption of advancement also operated for transfers by a wife to her husband or by a mother to her child[1].

¹ See paras 31.51–31.57 below; *Nelson v Nelson* (1995) 184 CLR 538 (presumption of advancement by mother to her child); *Brown v Brown* (1993) 31 NSWLR 582 at 591, CA; *Calverley v Green* (1984) 155 CLR 242 at 268–269.

Rebutting presumption of advancement

31.43 A declaration made by the father, *at or before* the date of the purchase, is admissible to rebut the presumption, although it might not be enforceable as a declaration of trust, on account of its not being reduced into writing in the case of land. The reason for this is that, as the trust would result to the father were it not rebutted by the relation of father and son as a circumstance of evidence, the father may counteract that circumstance of evidence by his parol declaration[1]. The transferor cannot, however, rebut the presumption of advancement by evidence showing that he intended to retain the beneficial interest in the property and made the transfer to effect a fraudulent or illegal purpose[2], unless he repented before such purpose had been partially achieved.

¹ *Williams v Williams* (1863) 32 Beav 370; *Warren v Gurney* [1944] 2 All ER 472, CA.
² See paras 30.18–30.19 above and *Tinsley v Milligan* [1994] 1 AC 340, [1993] 3 All ER 65, HL.

Surrounding circumstances

31.44 Surrounding circumstances may also tend to rebut the presumption. Thus a father, upon his son's marriage, gave him a considerable advancement, though there were several younger children who had no provision. He subsequently sold an estate, but £500 only of the purchase-money being paid, he took a security for the residue in the joint names of himself and his said son. He himself, however, received the interest and a great part of the principal without any opposition from the son, as did his executrix after his death, the son writing receipts for the interest.

31.45 In these circumstances it was held that the son took nothing, the Lord Chancellor (Lord Hardwicke) saying:

'Where a father takes an estate in the name of his son, it is to be considered as an advancement; but that is liable to be rebutted by subsequent acts. So if the estate be taken jointly, so that the son may be entitled by survivorship, that is weaker than the former case, and still depends on circumstances. The son knew here that his name was used in the mortgage, and must have known whether it was for his own interest or only as a trustee for the father; and instead of making any claim, his acts are very strong evidence of the latter; nor is there any colour why the father should make him any further advancement when he had so many children unprovided for.'[1]

¹   *Pole v Pole* (1748) 1 Ves Sen 76; *Stock v McAvoy* (1872) LR 15 Eq 55; *Marshal v Crutwell* (1875) LR 20 Eq 328; *McGrath v Wallis* [1995] 2 FLR 114, CA, emphasising that the presumption is a 'judicial instrument of last resort'. Further see *Damberg v Damberg* (2001) 4 ITELR 65 (NSWCA).

31.46 The 'subsequent acts' referred to in this dictum are not subsequent acts *of the father*, which were only admissible against, and not for, him¹, but subsequent acts of the son and these are only admissible when there is nothing to show that the father did actually intend to advance the son². Evidence of acts which, though not part of the same transaction, indicate a course of dealings is not admissible. In determining whether subsequent events can be regarded as forming part of the original transaction so as to be admissible evidence of intention there is no universal criterion by which a link can be established between one transaction and another. Evidence of subsequent conduct of a child amounting to an admission of his parent's original intention may be admitted in a proper case, but should be regarded jealously, and it is an indispensable condition of such conduct being admissible that it was performed with knowledge of the material facts³.

¹   *Redington v Redington* (1794) 3 Ridg Parl Rep 106 at 177; *Shephard v Cartwright* [1955] AC 431, [1954] 3 All ER 649, HL. Also see note 235 below.
²   *Sidmouth v Sidmouth* (1840) 2 Beav 447; *Hepworth v Hepworth* (1870) LR 11 Eq 10.
³   *Shephard v Cartwright* [1955] AC 431, [1954] 3 All ER 649, HL.

31.47 The fact that the father had previously made provision for the son, would not of *itself* be sufficient to rebut the usual presumption, although, taken together with other circumstances, it may be a strong link in the chain¹. Similarly, the retention by the father of the title deeds (the 'sinews of the land') of property purchased in the name of a child is not of itself conclusive to rebut the presumption of advancement but is of great significance when coupled with *contemporaneous* declarations by the father². Traditionally, 'The acts and declarations of the parties before or at the time of the purchase, or so immediately after it as to constitute a part of the transaction are admissible in evidence either for or against the party who did the act or made the declaration; subsequent acts and declarations are only admissible as evidence against the party who made them and not in his favour'³. However, the Court of Appeal⁴ has recently indicated that a less rigid approach to the rules of evidence should now be taken in searching for the subjective intention of the apparent donor.

¹   See per Lord Loughborough, *Redington v Redington* (1794) 3 Ridge Parl Rep 106 at 190; *Hepworth v Hepworth* (1870) LR 11 Eq 10.
²   *Warren v Gurney* [1944] 2 All ER 472, CA.
³   *Abrahams v Abrahams* [2000] WTLR 593 at 607.
⁴   *Lavelle v Lavelle* [2004] EWCA Civ 223, [2004] 2 FCR 418 at [19], cited at para 31.65.

31.48 The fact that a son permits his father to receive income (eg rents, dividends) from the property has been said to be insufficient to rebut the presumption of advancement for it is an 'act of reverence and good manners'¹ though it will be most significant if the father retains the share certificates or title deeds² and significant if the son returns the share certificates or deed to

31.48 *Resulting trusts*

his father[3]. In present irreverent times a court may well be prepared to treat it as significant in the father's favour if the adult son does allow his father to receive all income from the property.

1   *Grey v Grey* (1677) 2 Swan 594; *Stamp Duties Comrs v Byrnes* [1911] AC 386, PC.
2   *Warren v Gurney* [1944] 2 All ER 472, CA.
3   *Re Gooch* (1890) 62 LT 384; *Stock v McAvoy* (1872) LR 15 Eq 55.

31.49 The relationship of solicitor and client between the son and the parent has been considered a circumstance that will rebut the presumption of advancement[1] unless there is clear evidence of intention to make a gift.

1   *Garrett v Wilkinson* (1848) 2 De G & Sm 244.

Augmentation of settled property

31.50 In one case[1] a sum of consols was vested in the trustees of a marriage settlement upon the usual trusts. The husband directed the bankers who received the dividends (and paid them to him as tenant for life under a power of attorney from the trustees) to invest an additional sum of £2,000 consols in the names of the same trustees, so that they might receive the dividends as before. This was done, and the husband received the income of the whole during his life. No notice of the new investment was ever given to the trustees. It was held that there was no resulting trust of the £2,000 to the husband, but that it became subject to the trusts of the settlement as an augmentation of the trust fund.

1   *Re Curteis* (1872) LR 14 Eq 217.

Presumption of advancement: mother and child

31.51 In *Re De Visme*[1] it was laid down that, where a married woman had, out of her separate estate, made a purchase in the name of her children, no presumption of advancement arose, inasmuch as a *married* woman was under no obligation to *maintain* her children. This case was followed by Sir George Jessel MR in *Bennet v Bennet*[2], where a mother was entitled to property under the Married Women's Property Act 1870 by which married women were made as liable *as widows* for the maintenance of their children. The Master of the Rolls, however, gave it as his opinion that the presumption of intention to advance depended, not on the *liability to maintain*, but on the moral obligation on the part of a father to provide a provision or fortune for a child; and that there was no such obligation recognised on the part of a mother. If that be so, the law still remains the same, notwithstanding that the *statutory* liability for the maintenance of children has for some time been the same in the case of both spouses[3]. However, it is conceived that the point is still an open one, as Sir George Jessel's judgment is admittedly in direct conflict with that of Vice-Chancellor Stuart in *Sayre v Hughes*[4], where the presumption of intention to benefit was based by the Vice-Chancellor rather on motive than on duty. His lordship said:

450

'Maternal affection, *as a motive* of bounty, is, perhaps, the strongest of all, although *the duty* is not so strong as in the case of a father, inasmuch as it is the duty of a father to advance his child. That, however, is a moral obligation, and not a legal one.'

[1]   (1863) 2 De GJ & Sm 17.
[2]   (1879) 10 Ch D 474.
[3]   See Supplementary Benefits Act 1976, s 17 and Children Act 1989, s 2, each having parental responsibility for their child.
[4]   (1868) LR 5 Eq 376. This was the case of a *widowed* mother, but the principle appears to be the same. See also *Re Orme* (1883) 50 LT 51 and *Gore-Grimes v Grimes* [1937] IR 470.

31.52 On the whole, it is with much diffidence conceived that if the authorities should ever come to be reviewed, the views of Vice-Chancellor Stuart would be found to have as much to be said in their favour as those of Sir George Jessel. Neither judge bases the presumption on legal obligation. Both admit that the presumption is found on a moral presumption of intention. But, if so, surely there is as much moral presumption of an intention by a mother to benefit her offspring as there is in the case of a father. And if neither law nor equity imposes any obligation on a father to advance his child, it is difficult to see on what principle an equity judge should invent an imperfect obligation of this kind as a foundation for a presumption of intention to benefit, while at the same time rejecting a similar moral obligation on the part of a wealthy mother. In reason and in custom there is assuredly as much obligation on the part of a mother who has the command of money to benefit her children with it as there is in the case of a father. It must in any case be borne in mind (even if the view of Jessel MR, be the correct one) that if it be proved by other evidence, as will often be the case, that the mother did in fact intend to benefit her offspring, there will be no resulting trust, so that the presumption of advancement ought to apply to the mother-child relationship whether in a stable marital relationship or in a single unmarried mother's relationship with her child where she is in loco parentis[1].

[1]   *Brown v Brown* (1993) 31 NSWLR 582 at 591. See also *Nelson v Nelson* (1994) 184 CLR 538 (presumption of advancement from mother to child).

31.53 Indeed in *Gross v French*[1] the Court of Appeal held that even if the presumption of advancement operates against a mother in favour of her child there was sufficient evidence to rebut any such presumption. It will be a rare case indeed where there is no evidence available to affirm or negative any presumption, especially where the property in question is valuable.

[1]   (1975) 238 Estates Gazette 39, CA; in *Sekhon v Alissa* [1989] 2 FLR 94 there was sufficient evidence to clarify the matter between mother and daughter though a resulting trust appeared to be presumed.

No presumption of advancement where wife's money is invested in husband's name

31.54 Although, where a man purchases property in the name of his wife or intended wife[1], there is a prima facie presumption of an intention to advance the wife[2], the converse does not hold good according to traditional case law which must be assumed to be applicable[3] until a bold court takes a sensible modern view requiring equality of treatment for spouses. Therefore, if property is purchased in the name of the husband wholly or partly out of money belonging to his wife, there is a presumption that the wife does not intend her husband to take the whole property beneficially for himself. This presumption is, of course, capable of being rebutted by parol or other evidence showing that it was intended to be a gift or, where the purchase-money has been contributed by the spouses, that it was intended that they should be entitled to the proceeds of sale in the proportions in which they found the purchase price[4] or, where it is not possible to quantify their interests, in equal shares[5].

1   *Moate v Moate* [1948] 2 All ER 486. For fiancées see *Mossop v Mossop* [1989] Fam 77 at 82 and Law Reform (Miscellaneous Provisions) Act 1970, s 2(1).
2   *Silver v Silver* [1958] 1 All ER 523, [1958] 1 WLR 259, CA.
3   As in *Abrahams v Abrahams* [2000] WTLR 593.
4   *Re Rogers' Question* [1948] 1 All ER 328, CA.
5   *Rimmer v Rimmer* [1953] 1 QB 63, [1952] 2 All ER 863, CA; *Fribance v Fribance* [1957] 1 All ER 357, [1957] 1 WLR 384, CA; *Macdonald v Macdonald* [1957] 2 All ER 690; *Finch v Finch* (1975) 119 Sol Jo 793, CA.

31.55 It was formerly thought that a presumption would only be made in the wife's favour where the property was purchased with the wife's capital, and not where it was purchased with her income. But in *Mercier v Mercier*[1], the Court of Appeal laid it down that there is no such inherent distinction between capital and income except in degree. Romer LJ said:

> 'No doubt in certain cases, in considering whether a gift was intended, the fact of the money having been income received by him with her consent may be material in respect of the weight of evidence; but there is no other distinction, so far as I am aware, between capital and income.'

1   [1903] 2 Ch 98, CA.

31.56 In short, it would seem that where there is no evidence one way or the other, it will be presumed that the wife did not intend to benefit her husband, whether the property was paid for out of capital or income; but that where there is some evidence of intention to benefit the husband, then the fact that the payment was made out of income will, to some extent, support that evidence.

31.57 In *Pettitt v Pettitt*[1] three of the Law Lords took the view that the changing conditions of society had much diminished the usefulness of the law's presumptions at least in property disputes between husband and wife. This suggests that the presumptions will be applied only as a last resort and greater efforts will be made to ascertain from direct or even circumstantial evidence what the parties really intended[2]. However, the Law Lords in *Tinsley v Milligan*[2] subsequently invested the question whether a presumption of advancement arises with a new significance, since this will affect the claim where a transferor had an illegal purpose: his claim to recover the property will fail if the application of the presumption of advancement forces him to plead his illegal purpose, while he will succeed if this is unnecessary because no presumption of advancement is made.

1   [1970] AC 777 at 793, 811 and 824, but c f Lord Upjohn at 813.
2   For example *Falconer v Falconer* [1970] 3 All ER 449, [1970] 1 WLR 1333.
3   [1993] 3 All ER 65, [1994] 1 AC 340 discussed at paras 30.18–30.20 above.

Advancement by persons in loco parentis

31.58 The presumption of advancement in favour of persons to whom the purchaser stands in loco parentis, has been held to arise in the case of an illegitimate child[1], a grandchild *whose father was dead*[2], the nephew of a wife who had been practically adopted by the husband as his child[3], and a stepson who had not come to live with the person alleged to have been in loco parentis until he was sixteen years old[4]. But it would seem that the person alleged to have been in loco parentis must have intended to put himself in the situation of the person described as the natural father of the child with reference to those parental offices and duties which consist in *making provision for a child*. The mere fact that a grandfather took care of his daughter's illegitimate child and sent the child to school, has been held to be insufficient to raise the presumption, Page-Wood V-C saying:

> 'I cannot put the doctrine so high as to hold that if a person educate a child to whom he is under no obligation either morally or legally the child is therefore to be provided for at his expense'.[5]

1   *Beckford v Beckford* (1774) Lofft 490; *Kilpin v Kilpin* (1834) 1 My & K 520 at 542, *sed quaere Soar v Foster* (1858) 4 K & J 152.
2   *Ebrand v Dancer* (1680) 2 Cas in Ch 26.
3   *Currant v Jago* (1844) 1 Coll 261; and see *Re Howes* (1905) 21 TLR 501, the case of a niece.
4   *Re Paradise Motor Co Ltd* [1968] 2 All ER 625, [1968] 1 WLR 1125, CA. In this case the Court of Appeal gave express approval to the statement of the law which is contained in this section of the text.
5   *Tucker v Burrow* (1865) 2 Hem & M 515; and see per Jessel MR in *Bennet v Bennet* (1879) 10 Ch D 474 at 477. In *Kirpalani v Hathiramani* (1992) 46 Estates & Trusts R (Ontario) it was held that a person is not relevantly in loco parentis towards another unless he provides regular and systematic assistance and undertakes a moral obligation to ensure the welfare of that other.

Paragraph 3

Gratuitous transfers

31.59 Gratuitous transfers of property by a person in loco parentis to a child or by a man to his wife or children (and, if new case law will reflect the current sexual socio-economic equality of women, by a wife to her husband or children) are subject to the presumption of advancement and so are treated as outright gifts. Otherwise it will be presumed in the absence of evidence to the contrary that the transferor does not intend to make a gift, and if the transferee cannot rebut this presumption, then a resulting trust will be imposed. Note, however, that these rules apply only to transfers of personal property, and do not apply to transfers of land.

31.60 The presumption will be raised whenever the property gratuitously transferred is personal property. So in *Re Vinogradoff*[1], where a testatrix had transferred £800 War Loan into the joint names of herself and her four year old granddaughter but continued to receive the dividends until her death, Farwell J held that after the testatrix's death the granddaughter held the War Loan on a resulting trust for the testatrix's estate (although the judge did not have the benefit of having cited to him cases[2] indicating that a strong inference from the circumstance of the transferee only being a minor is that a gift was intended). The presumption will also be raised where there is a gratuitous transfer of personalty into the name of another alone[3]. Much will depend on the nature of the property in question, eg personal jewellery or clothing on the one hand, or property like stocks and shares where legal title and beneficial ownership are often divorced. If it is alleged by the recipient that moneys were provided by way of gift in respect of a house bought by the recipient and not by way of loan or purchase then the onus is on him to prove this[4]. However, in the simpler case of payment of money (by cash, cheque or bank transfer) to another this, it seems, is presumed to be to satisfy a debt or some other obligation[5].

[1] [1935] WN 68. See also *Re Howes* (1905) 21 TLR 501; *Re Muller* [1953] NZLR 879; and *Young v Sealey* [1949] Ch 278, [1949] 1 All ER 92.
[2] *Fowkes v Pascoe* (1875) 10 Ch App 343; also see *Shephard v Cartwright* [1955] AC 431 at 452.
[3] *Vandervell v IRC* [1967] 2 AC 291 at 312–3; *Re Vandervell's Trusts (No 2)* [1974] Ch 269, [1974] 3 All ER 205, *Fowkes v Pascoe* (1875) 10 Ch App 343 at 348; *Hepworth v Hepworth* (1870) LR 11 Eq 10; *Crane v Davis* (1981) Times, 13 May.
[4] *Seldon v Davidson* [1968] 2 All ER 755, [1968] 1 WLR 1083, CA; *Dewar v Dewar* [1975] 2 All ER 728, [1975] 1 WLR 1532.
[5] *Re Cooper* [1882] WN 96, CA.

31.61 Where land is concerned the position is somewhat controversial. Before 1925 a voluntary conveyance of freehold land 'unto the grantee and his heirs' raised a resulting use to the grantor which the Statute of Uses executed so that the legal estate forthwith reverted to the grantor. If the gift of land were 'unto and to the use of the grantee and his heirs' this prevented there being a resulting use to be executed so as to place the legal estate in the grantor and, instead, the legal estate was effectively vested in the grantee. Whether this grantee then held the legal estate on trust for himself or on resulting trust for the grantor was never decided[1].

[1] Against a resulting trust are dicta in *Fowkes v Pascoe* (1875) 10 Ch App 343 at 348; *Young v Peachy* (1741) 2 Atk 254 at 257 whilst in favour are *Maitland's Equity* (2nd edn) p 77; White and Tudor, *Leading Cases in Equity* (9th edn) Vol 2, p 762 and *Neazor v Hoyle* (1962) 32 DLR (2d) 131.

31.62 The Law of Property Act 1925 repealed the Statute of Uses so that it is no longer necessary to transfer the fee simple 'unto and to the use of' the grantee to prevent a resulting use or trust in favour of the grantor. Then section 60(3) oracularly provides that:

> 'In a voluntary conveyance a resulting trust for the grantor shall not be implied merely *by reason that* the property[1] is not expressed to be conveyed for the use or benefit of the grantee.'

[1] In context this seems to mean land only. See Law of Property Act 1925, s 205(1)(ii).

31.63 The meaning of this sub-section has troubled the courts[1], but recent authority holds that it should be taken at face value: if A gratuitously conveys freehold or leasehold land to B or, probably, to A and B, then no presumption will be made in A's favour, that he does not intend B to take beneficially[2] It follows that s 60(3) creates inconsistencies between the rules for real and personal property, and also between the rules for purchase of property in another's name and transferring property into another's name. Arguably, however, these inconsistencies are justified[3]. There are many reasons why X might buy property in Y's name without intending to make a gift to Y that do not obtain in the case of a transfer of property from X to Y: eg overlooking the need to protect X's position in the course of a complex transaction involving vendors and mortgagees[4]. Moreover, formality rules apply to conveyances of land which do not apply to transfers of personal property, increasing the likelihood that a transferor has thought carefully about whether he really wants to hand his property over to another person, and so reducing the need for a backstop rule that he should be presumed not to have intended this.

1   See eg *Hodgson v Marks* [1971] Ch 892 at 933 per Russell LJ; *Tinsley v Milligan* [1994] 1 AC 340 at 371 per Lord Browne-Wilkinson.
2   *Lohia v Lohia* [2001] WTLR 101, affirmed on a different point [2001] EWCA Civ 1691, and cited with approval in *Ali v Khan* (2002) 5 ITELR 232 at [24] per Morritt V-C.
3   R Chambers (2001) 15 Tru LI 26 at 29.
4   Cf *Brown v Brown* (1993) 31 NSWLR 582.

Rebutting the presumption

31.64 In some cases, the presumption that a transferor does not intend a gift can be rebutted by comparatively slight evidence,[1] but speaking generally, the strength of the evidence required to rebut the presumption will vary with the strength of the presumption, which in turn will depend on the facts and circumstances giving rise to it[2]. To give some examples: 'if a young woman in her first job, not very well paid, were to raise as much as she could on mortgage in order to buy a flat, what would we make of the fact that her well-to-do uncle, a man on affable terms with her, provided a minor part of the purchase price? The most obvious explanation is not that he wanted a part of the speculation. It is more credible that it was meant to be a loan or, perhaps, a gift[3].' Again, if land is purchased in the name of a company which is formed for the purpose and controlled by the provider of the funds, then it would be 'perverse' to think that he does not wish the company to take the property beneficially for itself, since his likely intention is to use the company to deal with the property[4]'

1   *Pettitt v Pettitt* [1970] AC 777 at 813 and 824; *Falconer v Falconer* [1970] 1 WLR 1333; *McGrath v Wallis* [1995] 2 FLR 114.
2   *Vajpeyi v Yusaf* [2004] WTLR 989 at [71] per Peter Prescott QC (sitting as a deputy High Court judge), following *Fowkes v Pascoe* (1875) 10 Ch 343 at 352–3, per Mellish LJ.
3   *Vajpeyi v Yusaf* [2004] WTLR 989 at [77].
4   *Arab Monetary Fund v Hashim* (15 June 1994, unreported) Ch D 15 June 1994 per Chadwick J, followed in *Trade Credit Finance (No 1) Ltd v Dinc Bilgin* [2004] EWHC 2732 (Comm), 2004] All ER (D) 47 (Nov). Cf *United Overseas Bank Ltd v Iwuanyanwu* Ch D 5 March 2001, affirmed [2001] EWCA Civ 616.

31.65 In *Shephard v Cartwright*[1] Viscount Simonds held that evidence of acts subsequent to the transfer, though not admissible in favour of the party doing the acts, is admissible against him. However, this rule was abandoned in *Lavelle v Lavelle*[2], in favour of the 'less rigid' approach taken in *Pettitt v Pettitt*[3]. According to Lord Phillips MR:[4]

> 'Equity searches for the subjective intention of the transferor. It … is not satisfactory to apply rigid rules of law to the evidence that is admissible to rebut the presumption of advancement. Plainly, self-serving statements or conduct of a transferor, who may long after the transaction be regretting earlier generosity, carry little or no weight. But words or conduct more proximate to the transaction itself should be given the significance that they naturally bear as part of the overall picture. Where the transferee is an adult, the words or conduct of the transferor will carry more weight if the transferee is aware of them and makes no protest or challenge to them.'

1 [1955] AC 431.
2 [2004] EWCA Civ 223, [2004] 2 FCR 418.
3 [1970] AC 777.
4 [2004] EWCA Civ 223, [2004] 2 FCR 418 at [19].

ARTICLE 32
TO WHOM PROPERTY RESULTS

32.1

(1)   Where a resulting trust arises under an instrument inter vivos, the beneficial interest results to the settlor himself[1]. Where the instrument is a will, the property results to the testator's estate, passing as part of his residuary estate if the failed gift was a specific or general gift or passing as undisposed of property (to his statutory next of kin under the intestacy rules) if the failed gift was of the whole or part of the residuary estate. No distinction has been made since 1925 between the devolution of real estate and personal estate upon intestacy, but if the testator devised residuary real estate to R separately from his bequest of personal estate to P, then a failed gift of real estate will result to R, while a failed gift of personal estate will result to P[2], whether or not the will directed a conversion of the subject matter of the failed gift as by subjecting it to a trust for sale[3];

(2)   provided that where, on the true interpretation of the instrument, property is first given to A absolutely, and then trusts are engrafted or imposed on that absolute interest which fail, the property (whether it be real[4] or personal estate) results to A absolutely to the exclusion of the donor or the persons entitled under his will or on his intestacy[5];

(3)   provided also that where after waiting and seeing for the appropriate perpetuity period the event has not occurred that would make the property result to the settlor or his estate, then

the interest in the property becomes absolute to the exclusion of the donor or the persons entitled to his estate under his will or intestacy[6];

(4) where a resulting trust has once arisen under an instrument which directs a conversion, and the person to whom it results dies before getting it in, then as between persons entitled to his real and personal estate it devolves (whether actually converted at the date of his death or not) as if it were actually converted, where money was directed to be laid out in the purchase of realty, unless the trust for conversion has wholly failed[7]; except that in other cases of conversion where realty is held on trust for sale or personal property is subject to a trust for sale in order that the trustees may acquire realty, no conversion takes place after 1996[8];

(5) where there is no other person to whom the trust property can result, it is held in trust for the Crown[9].

[1] *Symes v Hughes* (1870) LR 9 Eq 475; *Davies v Otty (No 2)* (1865) 35 Beav 208; *Rowan v Dann* (1991) 64 P & CR 202, CA.

[2] *Ackroyd v Smithson* (1780) 1 Bro CC 503; 1 Wh & Tud LC (8th edn) 394, and cases there cited.

[3] *Curteis v Wormald* (1878) 10 Ch D 172; *Ackroyd v Smithson* (1780) 1 Bro CC 503.

[4] *Moryoseph v Moryoseph* [1920] 2 Ch 33.

[5] *Lassence v Tierney* (1849) 1 Mac & G 551; *Hancock v Watson* [1902] AC 14; *Re Cohen* [1915] WN 361; *O'Connor v Tanner* [1917] AC 25; *Re Marshall* [1928] Ch 661; *A-G v Lloyds Bank Ltd* [1935] AC 382; *Re Hatch* [1948] Ch 592, [1948] 2 All ER 288; *Watson v Holland (Inspector of Taxes)* [1985] 1 All ER 290, [1984] STC 372.

[6] Perpetuities and Accumulations Act 1964, s 12 where the settlor's disposition was after 15 July 1964.

[7] *Re Richerson* [1892] 1 Ch 379; *Curteis v Wormald* (1878) 10 Ch D 172; *Cogan v Stephens* (1835) 5 LJ Ch 17; *Clarke v Franklin* (1858) 4 K & J 257; *Re Lord Grimthorpe* [1908] 2 Ch 675; *Re Ffennell's Settlement* [1918] 1 Ch 91; *Re Lyne's Settlement Trusts* [1919] 1 Ch 80.

[8] Trusts of Land and Appointment of Trustees Act 1996, s 3.

[9] *Re West Sussex Constabulary's Widows Children and Benevolent Fund Trusts* [1971] Ch 1; *Davies v Richards & Wallington Industries Ltd* [1990] 1 WLR 1511 overlooking the possibility of members' ownership apparent from *Re Bucks Constabulary's Widows' & Orphans' Fund Friendly Society (No 2)* [1979] 1 WLR 936 and so considering only the options of either a resulting trust or bona vacantia. See, as to both real and personal estate, Administration of Estates Act 1925 ss 45 ff and as to estates vested in a company at the date of dissolution and not subject to any trust, see Companies Act 1985, s 654.

Historical background

32.2 Under the Administration of Estates Act 1925, both real and personal estate devolve on intestacy in the same way instead of realty passing to the heir and personalty passing to the next of kin. In the case of deaths after 1925, therefore, no questions arise as between heirs and next of kin. Nevertheless, questions may arise where a testator has devised his residuary real estate to A and his residuary personal estate to B. For this reason the old cases are retained in this edition (even where they dealt with the rival claims of heirs and next of kin) as illuminating cases where the rival claimants are devisees of real estate and legatees of personal estate.

32.3 Resulting trusts

Paragraph 1

Examples

RESULTING TRUST OF SURPLUS MONEYS

32.3 Where expressed trusts do not exhaust the trust property there is a resulting trust in favour of those subscribing the moneys rateably in proportion to the amounts subscribed by them. Thus in *Re British Red Cross Balkan Fund*[1] an unexpected surplus at the close of the Balkan War was held to belong to the subscribers in proportion to their subscriptions: the 'first in first out' rule in *Clayton's Case*[2] was not applied although the subscriptions had been paid at various times and the moneys had been spent while the subscriptions were coming in.

1 [1914] 2 Ch 419 where in the absence of the Attorney-General a resulting trust was erroneously admitted; *Re Welsh Hospital (Netley) Fund* [1921] 1 Ch 655 at 662.
2 See para 92.26 below.

32.4 However, there can be no resulting trust where the original purpose that was carried into effect was charitable because the surplus moneys will then be applied cy-près[1].

1 See para 29.33 above.

Resulting trust under marriage settlement

32.5 By a marriage settlement, real estate of the husband, and personal estate of the wife, are vested in trustees, in trust for the husband for life, with remainder in trust for the wife for life, with remainder upon the usual trusts in favour of the issue of the marriage, without any gift over in default of issue. Upon the death of the wife without issue, the real estate will result to the husband; and similarly, on the death of the husband without issue, the personal estate will result to the wife.

Resulting trust under will where no conversion directed

32.6 A testator by his will gives real and personal estate to trustees, upon trust for certain persons for life, with an ultimate remainder in trust for the testator's two nephews B and C as tenants in common in equal shares, and devises his residuary real estate to X and bequeaths his residuary personal estate to Y. B dies in the testator's lifetime. His share of the real estate results to X as residuary devisee, and his share of the personalty to Y as residuary legatee.

Resulting trust where conversion directed

32.7 The preceding examples speak for themselves, and require no comment. But the following case at first sight presents more difficulty. A testator specifically devises real estate to trustees, *upon trust to sell* and divides the proceeds between his nephews B and C. If B should die in the testator's lifetime, his share of the proceeds of the sale will lapse, and before 1926 would have resulted to the testator's heir or residuary devisee, and not to his next of kin or residuary legatees, although the trust for sale was still effective and had turned the land into pure personalty. After 1925, it will go to the residuary devisee, or, where the testator leaves no residuary devisee, to the persons entitled to any estate as to which he dies intestate.

32.8 The principle from which this proceeds (settled by the leading case of *Ackroyd v Smithson*[1]) is that conversion directed by a will is presumed to be intended only for the purposes therein expressed; and, so far as these purposes fail, equity presumed that the testator did not intend to rob his heir or residuary devisee of property which, but for those objects, would have been his, and to give such property to his next of kin or residuary legatees, whose only possible ground of claim arises from the fact that the testator's expressed intentions have been disappointed. Moreover, so far as the heir at law was concerned, this presumption was not rebutted even by a declaration that the proceeds of the sale of realty were to be personalty *for all purposes*[2], the latter words being construed as meaning all purposes *of the will*. But whether this would be so where the question in dispute is between residuary devisees and residuary legatees may be open to question.

[1] (1780) 1 Bro CC 503, 1 Wh & Tud LC (8th edn) 394.
[2] *Shallcross v Wright* (1850) 12 Beav 505; *Taylor v Taylor* (1853) 3 De GM & G 190; and see also *Fitch v Weber* (1848) 6 Hare 145.

32.9 The question was explained by Sir George Jessel MR in *Curteis v Wormald*[1]. Where personal estate had been bequeathed upon trust to purchase real estate which was to be held on trusts some of which eventually failed. It was held that land, purchased before the failure, resulted in favour of the testator's next of kin, and not his heir[2]. The Master of the Rolls, in giving judgment, after stating the facts, said:

> 'The limitations took effect to a certain extent, and then, by reason of failure of issue of the tenants for life, the ultimate limitations failed, and there became a [resulting] trust for somebody. Now, for whom? According to the doctrine of the court of equity ... this kind of conversion is a conversion for the purposes of the will, and does not affect the rights of the persons who take by law *independent of the will*. If, therefore, there is a trust to sell real estate for the purposes of the will, and the trust takes effect, and there is an ultimate beneficial interest undisposed of, that undisposed-of interest goes to the heir. If, on the other hand, it is a conversion of personal estate into real estate, and there is an ultimate limitation which fails of taking effect, the interest which fails results for the benefit of the persons entitled to the personal estate, that is, the persons who take under the Statute of Distribution as next of kin[3]. Their right to the residue of the personal estate is a statutory right independent of the will.'

[1] (1878) 10 Ch D 172. As to settled land ordered to be sold by the court, see *Pole v Pole* [1924] 1 Ch 156, CA.
[2] This case can, of course, never occur where the testator dies after 1925, as the same persons are now heirs and next of kin.
[3] *Cogan v Stephens* (1835) 5 LJ Ch 17; *Bective v Hodgson* (1864) 10 HL Cas 656.

32.10 However, for testators who died after 1996 having in their wills created trusts to sell land or trusts to buy land, s 3(1) of the Trusts of Land and Appointment of Trustees Act 1996 states, 'where land is held by trustees subject to a trust for sale, the land is not to be regarded as personal property; and where personal property is subject to a trust for sale in order that the trustees may acquire land, the personal property is not to be regarded as land'. This section is poorly drafted[1] not being apt to cover a testamentary trust of money, say £500,000, to be laid out in the purchase of land, while there is an overlap between 'land' and 'personal property' since leaseholds fall into both categories; and it would have been better not to focus on the trustees' interest but on the beneficiary's interest, so that the interest of a beneficiary under a trust for sale of realty should have been treated for the future as an interest in realty until sale – and an interest of a beneficiary under a trust of personalty to be used for the purchase of realty should have been treated for the future as an interest in personalty until sale. However, on a purposive construction, the section should be held to abolish the doctrine of conversion[2] where freehold land (realty) is held on trust for sale or where pure personalty is held on trust to sell it to acquire freehold land (realty) but not, it seems, where money is held on trust to be laid out in the purchase of realty[3]. However, as seen in the preceding paragraph, any conversion directed by the will is ignored in any event where the will trust fails eg for lack of a surviving beneficiary.

[1] See P Matthews (1996/97) 5 PTPR 87 and also P H Pettit (1997) 113 LQR 207.
[2] As indicated by the head-note to s 3 which has no legislative force but may be taken into account: *Stephens v Cuckfield RDC* [1960] 2 QB 373 at 383 per Upjohn LJ.
[3] Query the position where T did not leave enough cash in a deposit account, so that his executor and trustee is obliged to sell personalty to provide enough cash to buy a house so there is an implied trust for sale, when it would be odd to have the original cash part dealt with differently from the part of the purchase price provided by selling personalty.

Paragraph 2

Rule in Lassence v Tierney

32.11 This principle usually known as the Rule in *Lassence v Tierney*[1], but more accurately as the Rule in *Hancock v Watson*[2] is well exemplified by the latter case where a testator directed his estate to be divided into five portions and then said 'to SD I give two of such portions'. He then directed that the two portions given to SD should remain in trust for her for life, and after her decease for her children upon attaining twenty-five if sons, or upon attaining twenty-one or marrying in the case of daughters, 'but in default of any such issue' there was a gift over to the children of C. It was held that the limitation after the life estate to SD being void for remoteness, the original gift to her remained intact and passed to her representatives and did not go to the testator's next of kind under a partial intestacy. Lord Davey said:

'In my opinion, it is settled law that if you find an absolute gift to a legatee in the first instance, and trusts are engrafted or imposed on that absolute interest which fail, either from lapse or invalidity or any other reason, then the absolute gift takes effect so far as the trusts have failed to the exclusion of the residuary legatee or next of kin as the case may be. Of course, as Lord Cottenham has pointed out in *Lassence v Tierney*[3], if the terms of the gift are ambiguous, you may seek assistance in constructing it – in saying whether it is expressed as an absolute gift or not – from the other parts of the will, including the language of the engrafted trusts. But when the court has once determined that the first gift is in terms absolute, then if it is a share of residue (as in the present case) the next of kin are excluded in any event. In the present case I cannot feel any doubt that the original gift of two-fifths of the residuary estate to SD was in terms an absolute gift to her ... In other words, as between herself and the estate there is a complete severance and disposition of her share so as to exclude an intestacy, though as between her and the parties taking under the engrafted trusts she takes for life only.'[4]

1   (1849) 1 Mac & G 551.
2   [1902] AC 14. See also *Re Bernard's Settlement* [1916] 1 Ch 552, where there was a good appointment to a daughter by will, and an attempt to settle it on her and her issue by codicil which was void for remoteness. The doctrine is equally applicable whether the fund is bequeathed to a trustee for the legatee and then settled, or it is bequeathed directly to the legatee and trusts declared of it (*Re Harrison* [1918] 2 Ch 59).
3   (1849) 1 Mac & G 551.
4   See also *Kellett v Kellett* (1868) LR 3 HL 160; *Re Marshall* [1928] Ch 661; *Re Gatti's Voluntary Settlement Trusts* [1936] 2 All ER 1489; *Re Hatch* [1948] Ch 592, [1948] 2 All ER 288. But contrast *Re Goold's Will Trusts* [1967] 3 All ER 652.

32.12 Subsequently, the rule was considered by the House of Lords in the Scottish case of *Fyfe v Irwin*[1]. There Lord Romer said:

'the court endeavours to reconcile the two inconsistent dispositions made by the trust on the one hand and the absolute gift on the other hand, and it does so by imputing to the testator the intention to modify the absolute gift only so far as is necessary to give effect to the trusts, whatever those trusts may be ... The fact that the engrafted trusts are more than usually inconsistent with the idea that an absolute interest has been given to the legatee is not a reason for denying that such an interest has been conferred.'

1   [1939] 2 All ER 271.

32.13 So where there is a gift to A for life with remainder to his children, with a proviso that if any child dies in A's lifetime then the property shall go to the issue of that child, the original gift to a child of A remains absolute if he dies in A's lifetime *without issue*[1]. Similarly where there is a devise to A in fee simple, with an executory limitation over to B *for life* if A dies without issue, the fee simple remains in A, subject to letting in B's life estate[2].

1   *Smither v Willock* (1804) 9 Ves 233; *Hodgson v Smithson* (1856) 8 De GM & G 604.
2   *Gatenby v Morgan* (1876) 1 QBD 685.

32.14 In every case before it applies the rule the court must find something that is in form an absolute initial gift. A direction to divide a fund into parts and appropriate one of such parts to each of the beneficiaries may amount to such a gift so that the rule will be applied on failure of the trusts declared of an appropriated part[1].

1   *Re Burton's Settlement Trusts* [1955] Ch 348, [1955] 1 All ER 433, CA; but cf *Re Payne* [1927] 2 Ch 1, where on similar words Astbury J found that there was no absolute gift and also *Re Cohen's Will Trusts* [1936] 1 All ER 103.

461

32.15 Peter Gibson J has summarised the guidance to be obtained from the cases as follow[1]:

'(1)   in each case the court must ascertain from the language of the instrument as a whole whether there has been an initial absolute beneficial gift onto which inconsistent trusts have been engrafted[2];

(2)   if the instrument discloses no separate initial gift but merely a gift coupled with a series of limitations over so as to form one system of trusts, then the rule will not apply[3];

(3)   in most of the cases where the rule has been held to apply, the engrafted inconsistent trusts have been separated from the absolute gift either by being placed in a separate clause or sentence or by being introduced by words implying a contrast, such as a proviso or words such as ''but so that''[4] But this is not an essential requirement, and in an appropriate context the engrafted trusts may be introduced by the word ''and'' or the words ''and so that'' ... [5];

(4)   references in parts of the instrument, other than the initial gift claimed to be absolute, to the share of the donee are usually[6] treated as indicative that the share is owned by the donee ... ;[7]

(5)   if a donor, by the trusts which follow the initial gift, has sought to provide for every eventuality by creating what prima facie are exhaustive trusts, it is the more difficult to construe the initial gift as an absolute gift.'[8]

---

[1]   *Watson v Holland (Inspector of Taxes)* [1985] 1 All ER 290 at 300.
[2]   For example *Lassence v Tierney* (1849) 1 Mac & G 551 at 562; *Re Burton's Settlement Trusts* [1955] Ch 348 at 360, CA.
[3]   For example *Rucker v Scholefield* (1862) 1 Hem & M 36.
[4]   For example *Hancock v Watson* [1902] AC 14, HL; *A-G v Lloyds Bank Ltd* [1935] AC 382, HL.
[5]   For example *Re Johnson's Settlement Trusts* [1943] Ch 341, [1943] 2 All ER 499; *Re Norton, Wyatt v Bain* [1949] WN 23.
[6]   In *Re Goold's Will Trusts* [1967] 3 All ER 652, Buckley J held that an express provision that the share was not to be held in trust for a beneficiary was decisive.
[7]   For example *A-G v Lloyds Bank Ltd* [1935] AC 382 at 345, HL; *Fyfe v Irwin* [1939] 2 All ER 271 at 282–283; *Re Burton's Settlement Trusts* [1955] Ch 348 at 356, 361, CA.
[8]   *Lassence v Tierney* (1849) 1 Mac & G 551 at 567; *A-G v Lloyds Bank Ltd* [1935] AC 382 at 395, HL.

Gift to a class or such of them as shall survive A goes to all if none survives A

32.16 A bequest to several, or to a class, 'or to such of them as shall be living at' the period of distribution or any other specified time, is a vested gift to all, subject to being divested for the benefit of those living at the time indicated. Consequently, if *none* survives, the original vested gift will remain intact, and all will be held to have taken as tenants in common[1]. The rule equally applies where there is an absolute gift by will which is afterwards settled by a codicil[2].

---

[1]   *Browne v Lord Kenyon* (1818) 3 Madd 410; *Sturgess v Pearson* (1819) 4 Madd 411; *Belk v Slack* (1836) 1 Keen 238; *Re Sanders' Trusts* (1866) LR 1 Eq 675; *Marriott v Abell* (1869) LR 7 Eq 478; *Monck v Croker* [1900] 1 IR 56.
[2]   *Re Wilcock* [1898] 1 Ch 95.

Rule equally applicable to settlements inter vivos

32.17 The rule is not confined to wills[1]. Thus, where on the marriage of his daughter a father settled £800 on her and her children, it being held that on the true construction of the settlement he gave her the £800 on condition of its being settled, it followed that on her death without issue the £800 resulted to her estate and not to the father[2].

1 See, for example, *Re Burton's Settlement Trusts* [1955] Ch 348, [1955] 1 All ER 433, CA.
2 *Doyle v Crean* [1905] 1 IR 252; but cf *Re Connell's Settlement* [1915] 1 Ch 867, where Sargant J held that a sum of £1,670 Consols settled by a father on his daughter's marriage resulted to him, but that a share of his residuary estate bequeathed to the trustees of that settlement resulted to her, the distinction being that there was no antecedent gift of the Consols to the daughter, but that the share of residue was referred to in the will as the daughter's share.

Applications of rule to accrued shares

32.18 In *Re Litt's Will Trusts*[1] it was held that the rule applied to shares passing under an accruer clause in the same way as to original shares; Lord Greene saying:

'I can see no logical reason whatsoever why a trust engrafted upon an absolute interest should not, among the trusts which are so engrafted, include a further absolute interest, which is in its turn subject to settlement.'

1 [1946] Ch 154, [1946] 1 All ER 314, CA.

32.19 In that case the accruer clause directed that the share of a child dying without issue who attained a vested interest and any additional share or shares which might accrue or be added thereto should 'go and accrue to such of my children as shall be living at the death of such child of mine ... and so that the share which shall accrue to any child of mine ... shall be held upon the trusts' of his or her original share. But where there was no absolute gift in the accruer clause, but a mere direction that the share should accrue *to the share* of another child and be held upon the trusts of that share, and the trusts of both shares failed, Upjohn J[1] held that the accruer clause was itself part of the engrafted trusts which failed, and that the original absolute interest prevailed on the principle of *Lassence v Tierney*[2].

1 *Re Atkinson's Will Trust* [1957] Ch 117, [1956] 3 All ER 738. In *Re Burton's Settlement Trusts* [1955] Ch 60, [1954] 3 All ER 231; reversed on appeal [1955] Ch 348, [1955] 1 All ER 433; Roxburgh J inclined to the same view of the accruer clause in the settlement before him, but the Court of Appeal did not find it necessary to decide the point.
2 (1849) 1 Mac & G 551.

Initial difficulty in all cases is to determine whether the gift over is a divesting gift or a gift in remainder

32.20 In all cases, however, the initial difficulty must be borne in mind of determining whether, on the true interpretation of the instrument, there really was an absolute gift afterwards partially divested, or whether all that the beneficiary was intended to take was the restricted interest[1]. Of course, where the gift is by will, and the partial divesting is by a codicil, there is no difficulty[2], nor where, as in *Hancock v Watson*[3], there are clear words of gift and allotment. But there are numerous cases on the border line which nothing but verbal criticism of the particular instrument will solve; and, as was said in *Lassence v Tierney*[4], in the case of a will containing such a disposition, the intention of the testator:

'is to be collected from the whole of the will, and not from there being words which, standing alone, would constitute an absolute gift.'

1   As in *Re Goold's Will Trusts* [1967] 3 All ER 652.
2   *Norman v Kynaston* (1861) 3 De GF & J 29.
3   See para 32.11 above.
4   (1849) 1 Mac & G 551.

32.21 In doubtful cases, the subsequent disposition of the subject-matter of the gift in every possible event which can arise, forms an important considera-tion in putting a construction on the instrument; such a disposition being apparently inconsistent with the intention of giving an absolute interest in the first instance[1].

1   Examples will be found in *Rucker v Scholefield* (1862) 1 Hem & M 36; *Gompertz v Gompertz* (1846) 2 Ph 107; *Re Richards* (1883) 50 LT 22; *Waters v Waters* (1857) 26 LJ Ch 624; *Harris v Newton* (1877) 46 LJ Ch 268; *Re Payne* [1927] 2 Ch 1; and *Re Cohen's Will Trusts* [1936] 1 All ER 103; and see *Re Bickerton's Settlement* [1942] Ch 84, [1942] 1 All ER 217; where the existence of an ultimate trust for the settlor excluded the application to the rule.

Paragraph 3

No resulting trust where gift becomes void for remoteness

32.22 Possibilities of reverter or of resulting trust under dispositions taking effect before 16 July 1964 could validly take effect in favour of the settlor's estate after an interest terminated, even where an express gift over after that interest would be void for perpetuity[1]. For dispositions after 15 July 1964 one waits and sees[2] if the interest terminates within the statutory perpetuity period for, if it does so, then there will be a valid reverter or resulting trust in favour of the settlor or his estate[3]. If the interest does not so terminate then the interest becomes absolute to the exclusion of the settlor and his estate[4].

1   *Re Cooper's Conveyance Trusts* [1956] 3 All ER 28, [1956] 1 WLR 1096.
2   Of course, one only needs to wait and see under the 1964 Perpetuities and Accumulations Act if the trust is not expressly restricted to a valid common law perpetuity period: see para 11.17 above.
3   Perpetuities and Accumulations Act 1964, ss 3, 12.
4   Perpetuities and Accumulations Act 1964, ss 3, 12.

Paragraph 4

How the person to whom converted property results holds it

32.23 Where the person, taking under a resulting trust property which is subject to conversion, dies before he has received the property, having made a will giving his real estate to A and his personal estate to B, or, as sometimes happens, having effectively disposed of his personal estate only so that there is intestacy as to his real estate, a question may still arise as to whether it results to him as realty or personality. In *Curteis v Wormald*[1] Sir George Jessel MR said:

> 'Then the next question which arises is, how does the heir-at-law [or A above] in the first case, or the next of kin [or B above] in the second, take the undisposed-of interest? The answer is, *he takes it as he finds it*. If the heir-at-law becomes entitled to it in the shape of personal estate, and dies, there is no equitable reconversion as between his real and personal representatives, and consequently his executor takes it as part of his personal estate. On the other hand, if the next of kin, having become entitled to a freehold estate [under a resulting trust of converted personalty], dies, there is no equity to change the freehold estate into anything else on his death.'

[1] (1878) 10 Ch D 172.

32.24 The broad statement quoted above that the party to whom property results 'takes it as he finds it', is apt to mislead the unwary. It would be more accurate to say that he takes it as he *ought* to find it. That is to say, if the trust for conversion *wholly* fails, he takes it as unconverted[1], but if it only partially fails, then, as the conversion dates from the death of the testator (even though it is directed to be made at a future date)[2], he takes it as converted, and it devolves accordingly, notwithstanding that in point of fact the conversion is not, as it ought to be, carried out in accordance with the trust[3].

[1] *Re Lord Grimthorpe* [1908] 2 Ch 675; cf *Re Newbould* (1913) 110 LT 6, CA; *Re Hopkinson* [1922] 1 Ch 65.
[2] *Clarke v Franklin* (1858) 4 K & J 257.
[3] *Re Richerson* [1892] 1 Ch 379, and cases there cited; distinguished in *Re Hopkinson* [1922] 1 Ch 65.

32.25 However the effect of s 3 of the Trusts of Land and Appointment of Trustees Act 1996 is that for testators dying after 1996 no conversion takes place for land held on trust for sale or personal property held on trust for sale in order that the trustees may acquire land, but it seems it can still take place for money directed to be used to acquire realty[1] if such trusts only fail partially.

[1] See para 32.10 above.

Same rules applicable to instruments inter vivos

32.26 Precisely the same rule applies where property results on failure of trusts, whenever created by instruments inter vivos. As has been pointed out above, such property results to the settlor in the first instance; but the character in which he retains it is determined by the same principles as have been indicated in the last illustration, so that, nowadays, the settlor will take the property resulting to him in its actual state except for the case of moneys directed to be used to purchase realty where the trusts only fail partially.

32.27 *Resulting trusts*

Paragraph 5

Rights of the Crown

32.27 By the Administration of Estates Act 1925, s 45, all existing modes, rules and canons of descent and devolution and escheat for want of heirs were abolished, and by s 46(1)(vi) of that Act, as set out in the First Schedule to the Intestates' Estates Act 1952, it is provided that in default of any person taking an absolute interest under the foregoing provisions of that section as to distribution of real and personal estate[1] on intestacy the residuary estate of an intestate shall belong to the Crown or to the Duchy of Lancaster or to the Duke of Cornwall for the time being, as the case may be, as bona vacantia and in lieu of any right to escheat.

[1] See the definition of 'the residuary estate of intestate' in Administration of Estates Act 1925, s 33(4). The persons who can take an interest are extended by the Family Law Reform Act of 1969 and of 1987 to include persons related to the intestate through illegitimacy.

32.28 It follows that if when a resulting trust arises the settlor has died intestate leaving no persons entitled to his estate under s 46(1)(i)–(v) of the Administration of Estates Act 1925, as set out in the First Schedule to the Act of 1952, the beneficial interest results to the Crown.

32.29 The Crown will also receive property as bona vacantia where a donor has parted with his money (or other property) out and out in circumstances excluding any resulting trust and where the trusts for use of the money fail in circumstances where the money does not belong to the members of an incorporated association and no general charitable intention exists to found the cy-près jurisdiction[1].

[1] See para 29.33 above.

Chapter 9

CONSTRUCTIVE TRUSTS

ARTICLE 33
CONSTRUCTIVE TRUSTS IMPOSED ON UNAUTHORISED FIDUCIARY
GAINS OR THEIR TRACEABLE PROCEEDS

33.1

(1) Where a person has the management of property, as express trustee or trustee de son tort or partner or director or other person clothed with a disinterested fiduciary character, he may not make any personal gain from such property; nor may a fiduciary make a personal gain by exploiting his position in any other way; and a fiduciary who makes any such gain must account for it to his principal, in whose favour a constructive trust will be imposed on the gain or its traceable proceeds[1].

(2) No constructive trust will be imposed on gains in a fiduciary's hands if they derive from activities which fall outside the scope of his fiduciary engagement[2], nor will a trust be imposed on gains in a fiduciary's hands even though they are the traceable proceeds of trust property or the unauthorised profits of his fiduciary office, if they have been duly authorised or made with the informed consent of all the beneficiaries[3].

467

33.1 Constructive trusts

1 *Williams v Barton* [1927] 2 Ch 9 at 11; *Re Edwards* [1981] 2 All ER 941 at 950, CA; *A-G v Guardian Newspapers (No 2)* [1990] 1 AC 109, 161, 211, 262–263, 288: *A-G for Hong Kong v Reid* [1994] 1 AC 324, PC (where bribes were traced into land in New Zealand); *Don King Productions Inc v Warren* [2000] Ch 291 at 322, 341–342, CA (boxing contracts renewed after dissolution of partnership held by partner on constructive trust for partnership); *Foskett v McKeown* [2001] 1 AC 102 at 127. For tracing see Article 92 below.
2 *Murad v Al-Saraj* [2005] WTLR 1573 at [62], CA.
3 *Boardman v Phipps* [1967] 2 AC 46.

Paragraph 1

Unauthorised fiduciary gains

33.2 Trustees and other fiduciaries must account to their principals for unauthorised gains which they make in the course of their engagement. This rule takes in the situation where a trustee makes unauthorised gains through the misuse of trust property, whether by using trust funds to acquire a new asset[1], or by other means[2]. It also takes in many other situations where a fiduciary makes unauthorised gains by reason of his office: for example, where he is paid unauthorised remuneration for his services[3], takes a bribe to act against his principal's best interests[4], or misappropriates a profit-making opportunity which comes to him in his fiduciary capacity[5]. The rule is strictly applied. It makes no difference that the fiduciary has acted in good faith, that his actions have caused the principal no loss, nor even that they have left him better off[6].

1 *Foskett v McKeown* [2001] 1 AC 102 at 127 per Lord Millett.
2 eg *Aberdeen Town Council v Aberdeen University* (1877) 2 App Cas 544 (Crown grant of salmon fishings made to trustees as owners of trust land); *Brown v IRC* [1965] AC 244 (interest earned on money in solicitors' client account); *Wells v Wells* (1967) 204 EG 687 (trust property let to trustee for less than market rent).
3 Fiduciaries must act gratuitously unless payment is authorised: *Robinson v Pett* (1734) 3 P Wms 249; *Barrett v Hartley* (1866) LR 2 Eq 789.
4 *A-G for Hong Kong v Reid* [1994] 1 AC 324.
5 *Boardman v Phipps* [1967] 2 AC 46; *Bhullar v Bhullar* [2003] EWCA Civ 424, [2003] 2 BCLC 241.
6 *Regal (Hastings) Ltd v Gulliver* [1967] 2 AC 134n at 144–5; *Warman International Ltd v Dwyer* (1995) 182 CLR 544 at 558.

33.3 Where a trustee uses trust property to acquire new property, the beneficiaries can trace the value inherent in the trust property into the value inherent in the new property[1], and assert a proprietary interest in the new property. Likewise, where a trustee or other fiduciary makes an unauthorised gain by some other means, Equity will consider as done that which ought to have been done, and treat the fiduciary as holding this gain for his principal from the moment of receipt, and if the fiduciary uses the gain to acquire a new asset then his principal can trace into the new asset, and will have an equitable lien or charge over such traceable product to the extent of his claim or, if a profit has been made, then the traceable product will be held on constructive trust for the principal[2]. Temptation is thus put beyond the reach of the fiduciary by the absolute automatic appropriation to his beneficiaries of his unauthorised gains and the traceable proceeds thereof. The imposition of the constructive trust thus fulfils a crucial role in underpinning express trusts and other fiduciary relationships.

1   For discussion of tracing see Articles 92 and 101, below.
2   *A-G for Hong Kong v Reid* [1994] 1 AC 324.

33.4 According to Dillon LJ[1], 'It is a long-established principle of Equity that if a person who is a trustee receives money or property because of, or in respect of, trust property, he will hold what he receives as constructive trustee on the trusts of the original trust property'. However, there is no need for the law to impose a constructive trust on assets which have been wrongfully acquired by an express trustee with misappropriated trust assets. The reason is that the substitute asset becomes part of the express trust fund from the moment when it is acquired, the trustee being unable to deny the beneficiaries' claim that he acted on their behalf when he bought the new asset[2], so that unauthorised sales and purchases are treated as authorised overreaching dispositions. Thus, as Lord Templeman stated[3]:

'Property acquired by a trustee innocently but in breach of trust and the property from time to time representing the same belong in equity to the *cestui que trust* and not to the trustee personally, whether he is solvent or insolvent. Property acquired by a trustee as a result of a criminal breach of trust and the property from time to time representing the same must also belong in equity to his *cestui que trust* and not to the trustee, whether he is solvent or insolvent'.

1   *Re EVTR* [1987] BCLC 646 at 651.
2   *A-G for Hong Kong v Reid* [1994] 1 AC 324 at 337 endorsing Sir Peter Millett, 'Bribes and Secret Commissions' [1993] Restitution LR 7 at 20.
3   *A-G for Hong Kong v Reid* [1994] 1 AC 324 at 331.

33.5 In essence, the trust property comprises the original trust property, property subsequently added to the trust and the property from time to time representing the original or added property. This is necessarily implicit if not made explicit in the definition of the 'Trust Fund' in the trust instrument, as often is the case[1]. Hence, as Lord Millett has written[2],

'It is often said that wrongfully substituted assets are held on a constructive trust. I do not think they are. I think that they continue to be held on the same trusts throughout. If the claimant was the beneficiary under an express trust, the substituted assets are held on the same express trusts.'

1   See 1.1(2).
2   'Proprietary Restitution' in S Degeling and J Edelman (eds) *Equity in Commercial Law*, Thomson, Sydney, 2005, 309 at 315–316. See too *Foskett v McKeown* [2001] 1 AC 102 at 130 per Lord Millett.

33.6 Obviously, this reasoning does not apply to situations where unauthorised gains have been made by a fiduciary who does not hold property on an express trust, such as a company director or partner, for example. Nor does it apply to situations where the traceable proceeds of trust assets have come into the hands of third parties who have never agreed to act as express trustees[1].

33.6   Constructive trusts

Subject to the proviso that a constructive trust is not needed to capture the proceeds of misapplied trust assets in the trustee's hands, the situation can therefore be summarised as follows[2]:

> 'The principle of Equity is that a person who is under a fiduciary obligation must account to the person to whom the obligation is owed for any benefit or gain (1) which has been obtained or received in circumstances where a conflict or significant possibility of conflict existed between his fiduciary duty and his personal interest in the pursuit or possible receipt of such a benefit or gain or (2) which was obtained or received by use or by reason of his fiduciary position or of opportunity or knowledge resulting from it. Any such benefit or gain is held by the fiduciary as constructive trustee'.

[1]   Discussed in Articles 34 and 101.
[2]   *Chan v Zachariah* (1984) 154 CLR 178 at 198 per Deane J. This summary has been endorsed and applied in various English cases, eg *Don King Productions Inc v Warren* [2000] Ch 291 at 341per Morritt LJ; *Gencor ACP Ltd v Dalby* [2000] 2 BCLC 734 at [16] per Rimer J; *John Taylors (a firm) v Masons (a firm)* [2005] WTLR 1519 at [24] per Arden LJ.

Distinct proprietary and personal liability

33.7 The fiduciary is personally accountable to his beneficiaries for the amount of his unauthorised gains, and these gains are also impressed with a trust in their favour. If the fiduciary is sufficiently solvent then the beneficiaries will normally be happy to elect for payment to them of the appropriate amount, thereby leaving the fiduciary, as purchaser, entitled to the particular assets that represent his unauthorised gain. However, if the fiduciary is insolvent then the beneficiaries should insist on their proprietary rights because their personal remedy will be worth very little.

The nature of the fiduciary's duty to account

33.8 Nowadays the courts often speak of a fiduciary's duty to account for unauthorised gains as though this were a wrong-based liability[1]. The liability is said to be triggered by the wrong committed by the fiduciary when he breaches his duty[2]:

> 'not to promote his personal interest by making or pursuing a gain in circumstances in which there is a conflict or a real or substantial possibility of a conflict between his personal interests and those of the persons whom he is bound to protect'.

[1]   See eg *New Zealand Netherlands Society 'Oranje' Inc v Kuys* [1973] 1 WLR 1126 at 1129; *Chan v Zacharia* (1984) 154 CLR 178 at 189; *International Corona Resources Ltd v LAC Minerals Ltd* (1987) 25 DLR (4th) 504 at 647, affirmed [1989] 2 SCR 574; *Henderson v Merrett Syndicates Ltd* [1995] 2 AC 145 at 206; *Maguire v Makaronis* (1997) 188 CLR 449 at 468; *United Pan-Europe Communications NV v Deutsche Bank AG* [2000] 2 BCLC 461 at [44]; *Walsh v Deloitte & Touche Inc* [2001] UKPC 58 at [13], [2002] 4 LRC 454; *Lindsley v Woodfull* [2004] 2 BCLC 131 at [28]–[30].
[2]   *Hospital Products Ltd v United States Surgical Corpn* (1984) 156 CLR 41 at 103 per Mason J.

33.9 This way of thinking about fiduciary liability for unauthorised gains emerged during the course of the twentieth century, but it entails a departure from the courts' traditional conception of the relationship between trustee and beneficiary. Formerly, the Chancery courts held this relationship to be governed by a set of proscriptive rules disabling the trustee from acting in particular ways, rather than a set of prescriptive rules requiring the trustee to perform positive duties[1], and consistently with this, they understood the source of a fiduciary's liability to account for unauthorised gains to be a rule which disables the fiduciary from keeping such gains for himself, rather than a rule which prohibits him from accumulating them in the first place. On this understanding of the fiduciary's liability, it arises out of his agreement to act in his principal's best interest by turning over all the gains of his office to the principal – ie it is a consent-based rather than a wrong-based liability.

---

1   See eg *York Buildings Co v Mackenzie* (1795) 8 Bro Parl Cas 42, 64 and 66. And cf T Lewin *A Practical Treatise on the Law of Trusts and Trustees* (1837) at p. 376; J Hill *A Practical Treatise on the Law Relating to Trustees* (1845) at pp 554–61.

33.10 Important twentieth century authorities have kept this conception of the fiduciary's liability alive[1], and it has recently been championed in the extra-judicial writings of Lord Millett. Thus, His Lordship has written that a court order directing a fiduciary to pay over the amount of an unauthorised gain:[2]

> 'is not a monetary award for wrongdoing. It is simply that she must be taken to have received the money for and on behalf of her principal and accordingly must account to him for it.'

---

1   *Jacobus Marler Estates Ltd v Marler* [1916–17] All ER Rep 291 at 291; *Furs Ltd v Tomkies* (1936) 54 CLR 583 at 592; *Scott v Scott* (1963) 109 CLR 649; *Regal (Hastings) Ltd v Gulliver* [1967] 2 AC 134n at 144; *Tito v Waddell (No 2)* [1977] Ch 106 at 246–50; *Soulos v Korkontzilas* [1997] 2 SCR 217 at [45]. See too L S Sealy 'Some Principles of Fiduciary Obligation' [1963] CLJ 119 at pp. 128–9.
2   Lord Millett 'Book Review' (2002) 2 OUCLJ 291 at p. 295.

33.11 Elsewhere, he has also written that *A-G for Hong Kong v Reid*[1], where bribe monies received by a fiduciary were declared to be held on constructive trust[2]:

> 'does not belong in the law of wrongs at all.... You cannot say ... that the bribe belonged to the claimant because it was wrong for the defendant to receive it. The claimant did not complain of the receipt, without which his claim must have failed! He complained of the defendant's failure to pay it over.'

---

1   [1994] 1 AC 324.
2   Lord Millett 'Proprietary Restitution' in S Degeling and J Edelman (eds) *Equity in Commercial Law* (Sydney, 2005) 309 at p. 324.

33.12 Does this orthodox disability-based understanding of the fiduciary's liability still represent the law, or has it been superseded by a wrong-based analysis? Does it make a practical difference if a claim is pleaded in line with one approach or the other? These questions were addressed by Rimer J in *Gwembe Valley Development Co Ltd (in rec) v Koshy (No 3)*[1]. He held that a principal can now plead his claim either way, and that disability-based claims and duty-based claims are governed by different limitation rules. On appeal, however, while the Court of Appeal agreed that a claim can be pleaded either way, the court also held that the same limitation rule will apply whichever way the claim is pleaded[2]. Subsequently, in *Murad v Al-Saraj*, Arden LJ also held that same causation rules apply to both types of claim[3]. As matters currently stand, therefore, no practical advantage can be gained from pleading a claim in one way or the other. However, it would be eminently desirable for the courts to commit themselves to one idea of the fiduciary's liability or the other, preferably following Lord Millett's view. To persist in treating them as equally valid is conceptually incoherent and renders the law unnecessarily complex.

1   [2002] 1 BCLC 478.
2   [2003] EWCA Civ 1048, [2004] 1 BCLC 131. See para 96.25 below.
3   [2005] WTLR 1573 at [49], CA. See para 33.74 below.

Trustees de son tort

33.13 As A L Smith LJ stated in *Mara v Browne*[1],

> 'If one, not being a trustee and not having authority from a trustee, takes upon himself to intermeddle with trust matters or to do acts characteristic of the office of trustee he may thereby make himself what is called in law a trustee of his own wrong, ie a trustee de son tort, or as it is also termed, a constructive trustee.'

1   [1896] 1 Ch 199 at 209.

33.14 Distinguishing features of a trustee de son tort are that he does not claim to act in his own right but for the beneficiaries and his assumption to act as trustee is not of itself a ground of liability (save in the sense of liability to account and for any failure in the duty so assumed) so that his status as trustee precedes the occurrence which may be the subject of a claim against him[1]. It matters not that the intermeddler was honest and well intentioned, a busy-body of excessive probity[2]. From the outset he will be constructive trustee of trust property received by him and thereafter he may be liable for any breach of his duty to account to the beneficiaries for his stewardship of the trust property. His conduct is equated to a declaration of himself as a trustee[3], and he is treated 'in every respect as if [he] had been duly appointed', with the result that he is 'fully subject to fiduciary obligations'[4]. Thus in *Kennedy v Lyell*[5] it took twenty-two years to discover the identity of a deceased landowner's heir. In this period the defendant, who had managed the land for its owner, continued to collect the rents and place them in a separate bank account. The House of Lords held that these moneys as the product of the trust property were held on constructive trust for the heir[6].

1   See per Ungoed-Thomas J in *Selangor United Rubber Estates Ltd v Cradock (No 3)* [1968] 1 WLR 1555 at 1579.
2   *Kennedy v Lyell* (1889) 14 App Cas 437 at 459; *Life Association of Scotland v Siddal* (1861) 3 De G F & J 58.
3   *Life Association of Scotland v Siddal* (1861) 3 De GF & J 27 at 72 per Turner LJ.
4   *Dubai Aluminium Co Ltd v Salaam* [2002] UKHL 48, [2003] 2 AC 366 at [138]–[139] per Lord Millett, following *Taylor v Davies* [1920] AC 636 at 651 per Viscount Cave.

5   (1889) 14 App Cas 437.
6   Similarly a solicitor or other agent investing trust funds while there are no trustees will be constructive trustee of the investments: *cf Blyth v Fladgate* [1891] 1 Ch 337.

33.15 One should be alert to the fact that some authors and judges have formerly used the expression 'trustee de son tort' to cover someone who has dishonestly assisted the trustees in a breach of trust and who has therefore been treated as a constructive trustee for the purpose of being made personally liable to account, though having no specific trust property of which he could be said to be constructive trustee[1].

1   See paras 100.2–100.6 below.

Executors de son tort

33.16 An executor de son tort is a person who[1], 'to the defrauding of creditors or without full valuable consideration, obtains, receives or holds any real or personal estate of a deceased person or effects the release of any debt or liability close to the estate of the deceased'. Where he appears to be acting for the benefit of the beneficiaries then, like a trustee de son tort[2], he is regarded as a constructive trustee and cannot plead that an action against him is barred by a fixed limitation period[3]. However, if he appears to be solely acting in his own interest then he may plead such a limitation period[4]. Thus, in *Martin v Myers*[5], the unmarried partner of the deceased remained in occupation of their shared home following his death intestate. She took no steps to have the property vested in her, something to which she would not have been entitled as she had no standing to apply for a grant of administration, but there was no evidence that she knew this, and the judge was satisfied that she did not act unconscionably. It followed that she had never held the property on constructive trust, and had acquired possessory title to the property, by the time of her own death.

1   Administration of Estates Act 1925, s 28.
2   *Paragon Finance Ltd v Thakerar* [1999] 1 All ER 400 at 408, CA; *Soar v Ashwell* [1893] 2 QB 390 at 396, 402 and 405.
3   *James v Williams* [2000] Ch 1, CA.
4   *Paragon Finance Ltd v Thakerar* [1999] 1 All ER 400 at 408, such distinction being ignored in *James v Williams* [2000] Ch 1, as well as *Pollard v Jackson* (1993) 67 P & CR 327: just because a person knows another person is entitled to the property does not mean he should be presumed to be acting on that person's behalf.
5   [2004] EWHC 1947 (Ch), [2004] All ER (D) 396 (Jul).

Trustee taking renewal of lease to himself

33.17 In the leading case of *Keech v Sandford*[1] a lessee of the profits of a market had devised the lease to a trustee for an infant. On the expiration of the lease, the trustee applied for a renewal; but the lessor would not renew, on the ground that the infant could not enter into the usual covenants. Upon this, the trustee took a lease to himself for his own benefit. It was, however, decreed by Lord King that he must hold it in trust for the infant; his Lordship saying:

33.17 Constructive trusts

'If a trustee, on the refusal to renew, might have a lease to himself, few trust estates would be renewed to cestuis que trust.'

1   (1726) Sel Cas Ch 61. See too *Fitzgibbon v Scanlan* (1813) 1 Dow 261; *Re Morgan* (1881) 18 Ch D 93; *Re Lulham* (1885) 53 LT 9; and *Re Biss* [1903] 2 Ch 40, where the whole subject is elaborately discussed. The history of *Keech v Sandford* and subsequent authorities is interestingly discussed in J Getzler 'Rumford Market and the Genesis of Fiduciary Obligations' in A Burrows and A Rodger (eds) *Mapping the Law: Essays in Honour of Peter Birks* (2006) 577.

33.18   The same principle is equally applicable to renewals by the husband or wife of a trustee[1]. It seems executors will be treated the same as trustees[2].

1   *Ex p Grace* (1799) 1 Bos & P 376; explained in *Re Biss* [1903] 2 Ch 40 at 58.
2   *Re Morgan* (1881) 18 Ch D 93; *James v Dean* (1808) 15 Ves 236.

33.19   The same beneficial trusts as apply to the original equity of the original lease apply to the extension of that entity obtained by renewal, whether the original lease itself contains a right to call for a renewal, or the trustee obtains a renewal merely by virtue of his position as a sitting tenant[1]. Where the demised property consists of business premises the trustee will be accountable for the whole profits of the business carried on by him though the form of inquiry will vary according to the circumstances. Thus, in *Re Jarvis*[2] one executrix obtained a new lease to herself of premises, where the testator had carried on business until they suffered war damage, and resurrected the testator's business there. Upjohn J held that but for the laches, acquiescence and delay of the other beneficiary, she would have been accountable as constructive trustee of the business, subject to all just allowances for her own time, energy and skill, for certain assets which she had contributed, and for certain payments she had made to an annuitant.

1   *Re Knowles' Will Trusts* [1948] 1 All ER 866.
2   [1958] 2 All ER 336, [1958] 1 WLR 815.

Tenant for life of leaseholds renewing to himself

33.20   A tenant for life of leaseholds (even though they be held under a mere yearly tenancy[1]), who claims under a settlement, cannot renew them for his own sole benefit. For he is not permitted to avail himself of his position, as the person in possession under the settlement, to get a more durable term, and so to defeat the probable intentions of the settlor that the lease should be renewed for the benefit of *all* persons claiming under the settlement[2].

1   *James v Dean* (1808) 15 Ves 236.
2   *Eyre v Dolphin* (1813) 2 Ball & B 290; *Mill v Hill* (1852) 3 HL Cas 828; *Yem v Edwards* (1857) 1 De G & J 598; *James v Dean* (1808) 15 Ves 236; *Lloyd-Jones v Clark-Lloyd* [1919] 1 Ch 424. See too *Re Payne's Settlement* (1886) 54 LT 840; and Article 34, below. But cf *Blake v Blake* (1786) 1 Cox Eq Cas 266.

33.21   In *Longton v Wilsby*[1], Stirling J is reported to have said that the above cases must be restricted to leases where there was a *right* of renewal either by custom or contract; but Warrington J pointed out[2] that this is an obvious mistake, and that the learned judge was only referring to the purchase of *reversions on*, and not to the *renewal* of, leases.

1 (1897) 76 LT 770, strangely omitted from the authorised reports. See also *Holmes v Williams* [1895] WN 116.
2 *Bevan v Webb* [1905] 1 Ch 620. For other cases of renewals of leases by fiduciary persons, see *Smyth v Byrne* [1914] 1 IR 53; *Hahesy v Guiry* [1917] 1 IR 371; affd [1918] 1 IR 135; *Re Smith* (1918) 52 ILT 113; *Kiernan v M'Cann* [1920] 1 IR 99; and *Brady v Brady* [1920] 1 IR 170.

Fiduciary lessee purchasing the reversion expectant on the lease

33.22 Whether a trustee or other fiduciary person is equally precluded from purchasing for his own benefit the reversion expectant on a lease of which he is trustee, is not quite so clear. Until *Protheroe v Protheroe*[1], the authorities suggested that he was not[2], unless the lease was one which was renewable by contract or, short of that, was one in respect of which a long-standing custom of granting renewals made it possible to infer that a renewal would be highly probable[3]. This view of the law found support in a dictum of Wilberforce J at first instance in the case of *Phipps v Boardman*[4], when he said:

> 'By contrast with the familiar case of a renewal of the lease, typified by *Keech v Sandford*, which, if made by a person in a fiduciary position, becomes the property of the trust, the purchase of a reversion does not have this effect, unless the lease is renewable by contract or by custom ... '

1 [1968] 1 All ER 1111, [1968] 1 WLR 519, CA.
2 *Randall v Russell* (1817) 3 Mer 190; *Hardman v Johnson* (1815) 3 Mer 347; *Longton v Wilsby* (1897) 76 LT 770; *Bevan v Webb* [1905] 1 Ch 620. But cf *Re Lord Ranelagh's Will* (1884) 26 Ch D 590.
3 *Phillips v Phillips* (1885) 29 Ch D 673; *Bevan v Webb* [1905] 1 Ch 620.
4 [1964] 2 All ER 187 at 201–202. In the case of a renewal the trustee is in effect buying a part of the trust property; in the case of a reversion this is not so: it is a separate item altogether.

33.23 But in *Protheroe v Protheroe* the Court of Appeal based its decision on the view that no trustee of a lease could in any circumstances purchase the freehold for his own benefit. Lord Denning MR, who delivered the only judgment, said simply[1]:

> 'There is a long established rule of equity from *Keech v Sandford* downwards that if a trustee who owns the leasehold, gets in the freehold, that freehold belongs to the trust and he cannot take the property for himself.'

1 [1968] 1 All ER 1111 at 1112.

33.24 In this case, a husband and wife had purchased a leasehold house as their matrimonial home and, although the assignment was taken in the husband's name alone, it was admitted that he held on trust for himself and his wife in equal shares. The parties had separated, the wife had petitioned for divorce, and the husband had then bought the freehold reversion for a sum raised by a mortgage. It was held that, because of the Rule in *Keech v Sandford*, the wife was entitled equally with the husband to the proceeds of sale of the freehold property, but that the husband was entitled to be repaid the cost of the reversion and his expenses in acquiring it. Although this does not appear with certainty, it seems that the lease was not renewable, either by contract or by custom: certainly the court's decision did not rest on the ground that it was. No cases at all were cited in argument, and the only case mentioned in the judgment, *Keech v Sandford* itself, was of course concerned with the renewal of a lease, not with the purchase of a reversion. Moreover, the fact that *Protheroe v Protheroe* was a case concerning husband and wife may perhaps have given rise not only to the neglect, by counsel and the court, of the earlier cases (concerned, as they were, with the rights of beneficiaries and trustees who were at arms' length), but also to a desire on the part of the court to do justice as between the spouses rather than to seek and apply the principles of law which were strictly applicable as between trustee and beneficiary.

33.25 It would seem, however, that the case can be justified by the need to prevent the conflict of interest arising where otherwise the trustee would personally be the landlord of the trust tenancy and so have to deal with himself[1]. In *Thompson's Trustees in bankruptcy v Heaton*[2] Pennycuick V-C merely followed *Protheroe v Protheroe*. The Court of Appeal[3] has since applied *Thompson's Trustees* so that in *Don King Productions Inc v Warren*[4] Morritt LJ rejected counsel's suggestion that it was still an open question whether the rule in *Keech v Sandford* applied to the purchase of the reversion.

[1]   See the concern with this in *Re Thompson's Settlement* [1986] Ch 99, [1985] 2 All ER 720.
[2]   [1974] 1 WLR 605.
[3]   *Popat v Shonchhatra* [1997] 1 WLR 1367.
[4]   [2000] Ch 291 at 340. See too *John Taylors (a firm) v Masons (a firm)* [2005] WTLR 1519 at [39]–[40] per Arden LJ; *Fairclough v Salmon* [2006] EWCA Civ 320 at [28] per Mummery LJ . In *Ward v Brunt* [2000] WTLR 731 the reversion would have been held on constructive trust by a partner but for having been acquired by her pursuant to an option under the will of the freeholder, her grandfather, rather than *qua* partner.

Renewal of leases by partial owners other than tenants for life

33.26 In the case of renewals of leases by trustees or tenants for life, the presumption against the validity of the renewal for the sole benefit of the party renewing, is absolute and irrebuttable[1]. But when we come to consider renewals by mortgagees[2] mortgagors[3], equitable co-owners not holding the legal estate as trustees for sale[4] and perhaps partners[5], the proposition requires modification. In such cases there is no irrebuttable presumption of law against the validity of the transaction, but at most a rebuttable presumption of fact that it lies on the party renewing to show that he acted bona fide, and took no undue advantage of the other parties interested[6]. If, therefore, on the evidence, the court considers that there was no bad faith and no undue advantage taken, the renewer will be allowed to retain the benefit of the renewed lease. For instance, where a lease formed part of the personal estate of an intestate, and the lessor refused to renew to the administratrix, a subsequent renewal obtained by one of the next of kin was held to be unimpeachable[7].

[1]   *Re Biss* [1903] 2 Ch 40.
[2]   *Rushworth's Case* (1676) Freem Ch 13.
[3]   *Leigh v Burnett* (1885) 29 Ch D 231.

4   *Palmer v Young* (1684) 1 Vern 276; *Holmes v Williams* [1895] WN 116; *Hunter v Allen*
     [1907] 1 IR 212; *Kennedy v De Trafford* [1897] AC 180; *Re Biss* [1903] 2 Ch 40; *Re
     Jarvis* [1958] 2 All ER 336, [1958] 1 WLR 815. The Law of Property Act 1925, ss 34–36,
     makes express trustees of persons taking legal title to land as co-owners.
5   *Featherstonhaugh v Fenwick* (1810) 17 Ves 298; *Clegg v Fishwick* (1849) 1 Mac & G 294;
     Re Biss [1903] 2 Ch 40; *Clegg v Edmondson* (1857) 8 De G M & G 787 at 807; *Bell v
     Barnett* (1872) 21 WR 119; *Dean v MacDowell* (1878) 8 Ch D 345; *Piddocke v Burt*
     [1894] 1 Ch 343; *Bevan v Webb* [1905] 1 Ch 620 at 625; *Gordon v Gonda* [1955]
     2 All ER 762, CA; *Thompson's Trustees in Bankruptcy v Heaton* [1974] 1 All ER 1239,
     [1974] 1 WLR 605.
6   *Re Biss* [1903] 2 Ch 40.
7   *Re Biss* [1903] 2 Ch 40.

Tenant for life of mortgaged property purchasing interest of mortgagee

33.27 The principle precluding a tenant for life from renewing a lease for his
own benefit, equally precluded a tenant for life of an equity of redemption
under the old law from purchasing the fee simple from the mortgagee. It is
thought that a tenant for life of mortgaged property taking an assignment of
the mortgage would hold it upon the trusts of the settlement subject, of
course, to a charge for what he had paid[1].

1   It is submitted that the principle is the same as where the tenant for life of an equity of
     redemption purchased the fee simple from the mortgagee as to which see *Griffith v Owen*
     [1907] 1 Ch 195.

Additions to trust property

33.28 It need scarcely be said that any property acquired by trustees by
reason of their legal ownership of the trust property (for instance, a Crown
grant of salmon fishings opposite the trust property[1]), must be held by them as
trustees only. As Oliver LJ said in *Swain v Law Society*[2] 'that which is the fruit
of trust property or of the trusteeship is itself trust property'. Similarly, where
trust moneys were lent on a mortgage and the mortgagor, an eccentric, in
devising properties to persons unknown to him, devised the equity of
redemption to 'the mortgagee' it was held that, although the mortgagor did
not know the mortgagee was a trustee, the mortgagor's intention was to
increase the interest which the mortgagee already had in the property so that
the equity of redemption belonged to the trust and not to the trustee
beneficially[3]. If the devise had been intended personally for the trustee it seems
he could have retained it beneficially since it would have come to him without
his volition[4].

1   *Aberdeen Town Council v Aberdeen University* (1877) 2 App Cas 544.
2   [1981] 3 All ER 797 at 813.
3   *Re Payne's Settlement* (1886) 54 LT 840; cf *Re Bagnall's Trusts* [1901] 1 IR 255.
4   *Re Northcote's Will Trusts* [1949] 1 All ER 442.

Tenant for life receiving money in relation to settled land

33.29 Upon similar grounds, if a tenant for life accepts money in consideration of his allowing something to be done which is prejudicial to the trust

property (as, for instance, where for a consideration he refrains from opposing a private Bill prejudicial to the trust estate), he will be a trustee of such money for all the persons interested under the settlement[1], but it seems that it would be otherwise where moneys come to him without his volition[2]. Where a tenant for life has refunded to him out of capital moneys the cost of improvements effected by him, he is nevertheless entitled to retain for his own benefit reliefs or allowances for income tax purposes obtained by him in respect of such improvements, since he is entitled to the whole income of the settled property[3].

1   *Re Thorpe* [1891] 2 Ch 360; see also *Fawcett v Whitehouse* (1829) 1 Russ & M 132 and *Owen v Williams* (1733) Amb 734 where trustee benefited self instead of acting in the best interests of his beneficiaries.
2   *Re Northcote's Will Trusts* [1949] 1 All ER 442.
3   *Re Pelly* [1957] Ch 1, [1956] 2 All ER 326, CA.

Profits made by trustee or fiduciary from property or position

33.30 As Lord Reid stated in *Brown v IRC*[1], 'If the person in a fiduciary position does gain or receive any financial benefit arising out of the use of the property of the beneficiary he cannot keep it unless he can show authority', eg by the trust deed or by contract or by the assent of all the beneficiaries. There the House of Lords held that interest earned on a solicitor's clients' moneys put in a deposit account earmarked for clients generally belonged to the clients and never belonged to the solicitor: the moneys and the interest thereon were held on an express and constructive trust respectively. Similarly, in *Patel v Brent LBC (No 2)*[2] a trustee failed to deposit trust funds in an interest-bearing account as required by the trust deed, and put the money to uses which generated nearly twice as much profit as would have been made in the form of interest, had the trustee done what it was meant to do. The Vice-Chancellor held[3] that even after the trustee had paid over a sum equivalent to the amount of interest that would have been made, if the money had been placed in the bank account, it remained liable to account for the balance.

1   [1965] AC 244, [1964] 3 All ER 119; see also *Reid-Newfoundland Co v Anglo-American Telegraph Co Ltd* [1912] AC 555 and *A-G v Guardian Newspapers (No 2)* [1990] 1 AC 109.
2   [2004] WTLR 577.
3   [2004] WTLR 577 at [35].

33.31 Of course, if A holds no money of B but is merely under an obligation to account to B for a certain amount of money then A can retain profits made from the use of what is his own money subject to his obligation to account for the principal sum to B and for such interest, if any, as may have been agreed with B[1]. Similarly, if A by fraudulent misrepresentations borrows £x from B secured by a mortgage over the house purchased with the £x, A cannot be liable to B beyond his liability to repay £x with interest even if the house has doubled in value[2].

1   *Kirkham v Peel* (1881) 44 LT 195; *York and North Midland Rly Co v Hudson* (1853) 16 Beav 485.
2   *Halifax Building Society v Thomas* [1996] Ch 217, CA.

33.32 A fiduciary[1], as part of the wider rule that a fiduciary must not place himself in a position where his fiduciary duty and his private interest may conflict[2], is very strictly prohibited from obtaining any profit from his fiduciary relationship unless duly authorised[3]. This is to deliver him from any temptation to misuse his fiduciary position[4] and to ensure that he positively fulfils his duty to act in the best interests of his beneficiaries or principal. He is liable to account (so long as not holding the property subject to the relationship as debtor only) to his principal for such profit. It is immaterial that the principal could not otherwise have obtained the profit, that the fiduciary acted honestly and in his principal's best interest, that the principal benefited from the fiduciary's actions, and that the profit was obtained through use of the fiduciary's own assets and resulted from the fiduciary's personal skills[5]. Indeed, the fiduciary will be constructive trustee of the profit even if arising from misuse of his position (as opposed to the fiduciary property) as where he takes advantage of information obtained by him qua fiduciary[6] or where he takes a bribe or secret commission[7] or uses the opportunity and facilities arising by virtue of his fiduciary position to make profits for himself instead of for his principal[8].

[1]   For who is a fiduciary see para 1.50.
[2]   *Boardman v Phipps* [1967] 2 AC 46 at 123, per Lord Upjohn; *Re Thompson's Settlement* [1985] 2 All ER 720 at 730. If there be a conflict then he must subordinate his private interest to his fiduciary duty: *Swain v Law Society* [1981] 3 All ER 797 at 813; *Bristol & West Building Society v Mothew* [1998] Ch 1 at 19, CA.
[3]   See para 33.89 below.
[4]   *Swain v Law Society* [1981] 3 All ER 797 at 809.
[5]   *Boardman v Phipps* [1967] 2 AC 46, [1966] 3 All ER 721, though in exceptional circumstances (as there) the fiduciary may be awarded an allowance for his expertise: see paras 58.25–58.30 below.
[6]   *Boardman v Phipps* [1967] 2 AC 46, [1966] 3 All ER 721 as interpreted in *A-G for Hong Kong v Reid* [1994] 1 AC 324, PC.
[7]   *A-G for Hong Kong v Reid* [1994] 1 AC 324, PC, rejecting *Lister v Stubbs* (1890) 45 Ch D 1, CA. In *Daraydan Holdings Ltd v Solland International Ltd* [2005] Ch 119 at [75]–[85], Lawrence Collins J considered that the rules of precedent allowed him to follow *Reid* in preference to *Lister* (although see further *National Westminster Bank plc v Spectrum Plus Ltd* [2005] UKHL 41, [2005] 2 AC 680 at [93], [155] and [163]), but it was unnecessary for him to depart from *Lister* which was distinguishable on the facts. A principal can recover the bribe from his agent whether he affirms or repudiates the contract between the agent and the briber, and is not obliged to return the bribe to the briber if he repudiates the contract: *Logicrose Ltd v Southend United FC* [1988] 1 WLR 1256.
[8]   *A-G for Hong Kong v Reid* [1994] AC 324 implicitly rejecting *A-G's Reference (No 1 of 1985)* [1986] QB 491, CA: see J.C. Smith (1994) 110 LQR 180.

33.33 If the profit, in the form of specific property or cash, held on constructive trust is used to acquire new property then the beneficiaries can trace into the new property and assert a proprietary claim to that. However, if the fiduciary is good for the money it will be necessary only to make him personally liable to account as was the case in *Swain v Law Society*[1], where Oliver LJ stated

> 'What one has to do is to ascertain first of all whether there was a fiduciary relationship and, if there was, from what it arose and what, if there was any, was the trust property; and then to inquire whether that of which an account is claimed either arose, directly or indirectly, from the trust property itself or was acquired not only in the course of, but by reason of, the fiduciary relationship.'

[1]   [1981] 3 All ER 797 at 813–814, [1982] 1 WLR 17 at 37.

33.34 On appeal Lord Brightman (with whom the others agreed) endorsed[1] this approach but held that no fiduciary relationship existed since the Law Society was performing a public duty under s 37 of the Solicitors Act 1974 when it received large commission in respect of premiums paid by solicitors under the Solicitors' Indemnity Assurance Scheme.

[1]   [1983] 1 AC 598 at 619, [1982] 2 All ER 827 at 838, HL.

Profits made by trustee's parent company

33.35 If a corporate trustee places business with its parent company, eg invests trust moneys in a fund managed for a fee by the parent company will this amount to a breach of trust making the trustee or its parent company liable? In *Jones v AMP Perpetual Trustee Co NZ Ltd*[1], where the trustee was a trustee company but not a fund manager, Thomas J held that the trustee was not liable (from which it would seem to follow that its parent could not be liable). He regarded the rule preventing a trustee from profiting as arising from the more general principle that no one who has a duty to perform shall place himself in such a position that his interest will conflict with his duty and that, if interest and duty do conflict, interest must give way. As a matter of fact and degree he held that no real sensible possibility of conflict arose which could impair the trustee's ability to serve the best interests of the beneficiaries: the parent company was a pre-eminent company with an attractive investment record, while the equivalent fee would be payable to any similar company selected to be investment manager. An alternative approach in line with *Swain v Law Society*[2] is to regard the trustee as providing its parent with the opportunity to profit in the course of its management of the trust property but not by reason of that management relationship. One needs to bear in mind the warning uttered by Lord Selborne in *Barnes v Addy*[3] that 'there is no better mode of undermining the sound doctrines of equity than to make unreasonable and inequitable applications of them.'

[1]   [1994] 1 NZLR 690.
[2]   [1981] 3 All ER 797 at 813–814 per Oliver LJ endorsed by Lord Brightman, [1983] 1 AC 598 at 619, discussed at para 33.33 above.
[3]   (1874) 9 Ch App 244 at 251.

Trustee obtaining directorship fees by use of trust shareholding

33.36 As Cohen J said in *Re Macadam*[1]:

'The root of the matter really is: Did the trustee acquire the position in respect of which he drew the remuneration by virtue of his position as trustee?'

[1]   [1946] Ch 73 at 82.

33.37 Harman J (as he then was) reviewed the case law thoroughly in *Re Gee*[1] concluding:

'A trustee who either uses a power vested in him as such to obtain a benefit as in *Re Macadam*[2] or who (as in *Williams v Barton's* case)[3] procures his co-trustees to give him, or those associated with him, remunerative employment must account for the benefit obtained. Further, a trustee who has the power by the use of trust votes to control his own appointment to a remunerative position and refrains from using them, with the result that he is elected to a position of profit, would also be accountable. On the other hand, it appears not to be the law that every man who becomes a trustee, holding, as such, shares in a limited company is made ipso facto accountable for remuneration received from the company independently of any use by him of the trust holding, whether by voting or refraining from so doing. For instance, A, who holds the majority of shares in a limited company becomes the trustee of the estate of B, a holder of a minority interest. This cannot, I think, disentitle A to use his own shares to procure his appointment as an officer of the company nor compel him to disgorge the remuneration he so receives, for he cannot be disentitled to the use of his own voting powers nor could the use of the trust votes in a contrary sense prevent the majority prevailing. Many other instances could be given of a similar kind. Of these *Re Dover Coalfield Extension Ltd*[4] is really one. There the trustees did not earn their fees by virtue of the trust shares[5] though, no doubt, the continued holding of those shares was a qualification necessary for the continued earning of the fees.'

[1]   [1948] Ch 284 at 295.
[2]   [1946] Ch 73, [1945] 2 All ER 664.
[3]   [1927] 2 Ch 9.
[4]   [1908] 1 Ch 65.
[5]   They became directors before they held any trust shares.

33.38 Thus, a trustee will not be a constructive trustee of director's fees if using his own shares in his own favour but using the trust shares against himself he happens to be appointed to the directorship. Otherwise, he will be constructive trustee of the fees and liable to account unless, of course, authorised by the trust instrument to become director and expressly or implicitly made not liable to account for director's fees[1].

[1]   *Re Llewellin's Will Trusts* [1949] Ch 225.

Trustee obtaining commission

33.39 As Fox LJ stated in *Swain v Law Society*[1]:

'I do not think that the fact that a trustee receives a benefit otherwise than from some direct dealing with the trust property or from the exercise of a trust power is conclusive of the question whether he has to account to the beneficiaries for the benefit he has received. If, for example, a trustee propounds a tax saving scheme to beneficiaries under which they are required to effect at their own expense policies on their own lives, I apprehend that if the trustee took commission from the insurers in respect of such policies he would be liable to account for the commission, even though he received the commission without any exercise of his powers as trustee and even though the commission did not derive from a dealing with the trust fund itself.'

[1]   [1981] 3 All ER 797 at 823–824.

33.40 Earlier[1] he had made it clear that the fact that the contract under which a fiduciary received a benefit by virtue of his trust was a contract which antedated the trust would not affect his obligation to account. If a man enters

33.40 *Constructive trusts*

into an agreement under which he is entitled to a commission in certain circumstances and subsequently accepts a trusteeship under which he enters into such transactions and obtains a commission he is still obliged to account to the trust.

¹   [1981] 3 All ER 797 at 823.

Director obtaining profits from his directorship

33.41 Directors are subject to the strict rule preventing them from profiting from their fiduciary relationship with their company. Thus, in *Cook v Deeks*¹, where the directors diverted to themselves contracts which they should have taken up on behalf of their company, the Privy Council held that the contracts belonged to the company in equity so that the directors held the benefit of the contracts on constructive trust for the company. The company resolution in general meeting ratifying the directors' actions and secured by the directors' majority shareholding was ineffective: the directors could not make a present to themselves of company property and defraud the minority shareholders.

¹   [1916] 1 AC 554.

33.42 In *Industrial Development Consultants v Cooley*¹ the managing director of the plaintiff company was found to be a constructive trustee of the benefit of a contract with the Eastern Gas Board and was made liable to account for the profits thereof. The Gas Board had privately told the managing director that he would not obtain a contract from them for the benefit of his company, but that he would have a good chance of privately obtaining the contract for himself if he severed his connection with the company. Pretending poor health and concealing his true reason he secured his release from employment by the company. He then obtained for himself the contract with the Gas Board that he had unsuccessfully tried to obtain for the plaintiff company. He was held liable to account for all the profit, even though the chance of his persuading the Gas Board to change their stance and contract with the plaintiff company was no greater than 10%.

¹   [1972] 2 All ER 162, [1972] 1 WLR 443. Also see *Pre-Cam Exploration and Development Ltd v McTavish* (1966) 57 DLR (2d) 557; *Canadian Aero Service Ltd v O'Malley* (1973) 40 DLR (3d) 371 and *Abbey Glen Property Corpn v Stumborg* (1976) 65 DLR (3d) 235.

33.43 *Regal (Hastings) Ltd v Gulliver*¹ is a particularly salutary case where the fiduciaries acted honestly in the best interests of the company, which received a totally unmerited windfall. The company formed a subsidiary company to take up leases of some cinemas. The landlord required the directors personally to guarantee the rents unless the subsidiary had a paid up capital of £5,000. The directors did not wish to give guarantees since they intended that the company and the subsidiary company should sell their properties in the near future. The company could only afford to subscribe for £2,000 paid up capital of the subsidiary. Acting honestly and in the best interests of the company, the directors ensured that the remaining £3,000 capital was subscribed for by themselves, by the chairman as nominee for someone else and by the company's solicitor. It does not seem that they considered themselves lending (or guaranteeing a loan of) the £3,000 to the company to enable it to subscribe for the shares, nor did they approach the other fifteen shareholders to let them in on the probable future profits. A proposed sale of the property of the company and the subsidiary company fell through, but a later sale was arranged involving the purchaser buying all the shares in the two companies and thereby obtaining the companies' property. Since the 5,000 £1 shares in the subsidiary company were sold at £3 16s 1d each, the directors, the chairman's beneficiary, and the solicitor made quite a profit on the 3,000 shares they had subscribed for at £1 each.

1   [1942] 1 All ER 378 later reported in [1967] 2 AC 134n.

33.44 The purchaser, as controller of the company, had the audacity to bring an action in the company's name to make the former directors, chairman and solicitor liable to account for the profit which had been made by them taking advantage of their position: a rather sharp way of recovering part of the purchase price!

33.45 The action failed against the solicitor since he subscribed for the shares from which the profit arose not only with the knowledge and consent of the plaintiff company (as represented by its directors) but at its request. The action also failed against the chairman since, as nominee, the shares and the profits never belonged to him (and no proprietary claim via the tracing process was made against the persons for whom he was nominee[1]). However, it succeeded against the directors[2] since 'the directors, standing in a fiduciary relationship to (the plaintiff company) in regard to the exercise of their powers as directors, and having obtained these shares by reason and only by reason of the fact that they were directors and in the course of the execution of that office, are accountable for the profits which they have made out of them'.

1   As donees they could be in no better position than the chairman, if, as fiduciary, he had retained the profit for himself in breach of the fiduciary duty – cf the innocent donees in *Foskett v McKeown* [2001] 1 AC 102.
2   The chairman and the solicitor, the prime movers, thus escaped. For further details of their involvement see *Luxor (Eastbourne) Ltd v Cooper* [1941] AC 108, [1941] 1 All ER 33, HL; especially [1939] 4 All ER 411 at 416, CA.

33.46 As Lord Russell said[1]:

'The rule of equity which insists on those who by use of a fiduciary position make a profit, being liable to account for that profit in no way depends on fraud or absence of bona fides; or upon such questions or considerations as whether the profit would or should otherwise have gone to the plaintiff, or whether the profiteer was under a duty to obtain the source of the profit for the plaintiff, or whether he took a risk, or acted as he did for the benefit of the plaintiff, or whether the plaintiff has in fact been damaged or benefited by his action. The liability arises from the mere fact of a profit having in the stated circumstances been made. The profiteer, however honest and well intentioned, cannot escape the risk of being called upon to account.'

1   [1967] 2 AC 134n at 144–145 endorsed by *Warman International v Dwyer* (1995) 69 ALJR 362.

33.47 In *Queensland Mines Ltd v Hudson*[1] the Privy Council took a liberal view in stark contrast to the strict approach of the House of Lords in earlier cases. Queensland was formed to exploit the anticipated award of mining licences. Hudson was its managing director. At the last minute Queensland's financial backing collapsed so Hudson in 1961 took the licences in his own name and resigned as managing director, though remaining a director for 10 more years. At a 1962 board meeting Hudson honestly admitted he held the licences for Queensland but candidly warned of the risks attendant upon attempting to exploit the licences. The board then resolved not to pursue the matter further, so leaving Hudson free to go it alone. It was held that Hudson was not liable for his profits in successfully exploiting the licences either because the board had given a fully informed consent or because the board had placed the licences venture outside the scope of Hudson's fiduciary relationship. However, the consent of the board members (especially if they were Hudson's cronies) is surely not enough, especially when the consent of all the directors of Regal (Hastings) Ltd was not sufficient to protect them. However, because Queensland Mines Ltd had only two (corporate) shareholders, both of whom were represented on the board of directors, and Hudson was a representative of the shareholder with a 49% holding, the board's decision may be treated as a decision of the shareholders where the majority was not controlled by the defendant[2].

1   (1978) 18 ALR 1, PC cogently criticised by G.R. Sullivan (1979) 42 MLR 711. See also *Peso-Silver Mines Ltd v Cropper* (1966) 58 DLR (2d) 1 criticised (1967) 30 MLR 450 (D Prentice), (1971) 49 Can BR 80 (S M Beck).
2   This satisfies the test suggested by Vinelott J in *Prudential Assurance Co v Newman Industries (No 2)* [1980] 3 WLR 543 at 568.

33.48 As for the second reason, to allow fiduciary managers to define the scope of their own fiduciary obligations, and so immunise themselves from liability, is startling when there is obviously such a conflict of interest if the directors can acquire for themselves what they have rejected on behalf of the company, though, in exceptional circumstances, it may be that such a resolution could be passed bona fide in the interests of the company[1]. Nowadays, approval for otherwise objectionable benefits to be conferred on directors can be given by the company in general meeting under ss 320 and 322A of the Companies Act 1985.

1   See *Rolled Steel (Holdings) Ltd v British Steel Corpn* [1986] Ch 246.

33.49 In *Guinness plc v Saunders*[1] the House of Lords reaffirmed the impossibility of a director profiting from his fiduciary position unless duly authorised[2], so that unauthorised remuneration of £5.2 million was received by the defendant as constructive trustee thereof so that he was personally accountable therefor. The principle has since been applied in many further cases, including *Bhullar v Bhullar*[3]. The defendants there were directors of a family company which operated a chain of supermarkets, and ran a property development business as a side line. Following a breakdown in relations between the shareholders, the board of directors resolved that the company should acquire no further properties for development purposes. The defendants then learnt that a property adjoining one of the company's properties was up for sale, and bought it in the name of a second company under their control without disclosing their actions to the board. The Court of Appeal held that they were liable to account for their profits, and that the property was held on constructive trust for the family company. The court rejected the defendants' arguments that directors owe no duty to offer their company business opportunities which come to them privately, and that they need only account for gains made by taking 'maturing business opportunities' which have come to them in the course of managing the company's affairs. The relevant test is instead whether the director has entered a transaction in which he 'has, or can have, a personal interest conflicting, or which may possibly conflict, with the interests of those whom he is bound to protect'[4]. This rule leaves directors with very little room for arguing that opportunities have come to them in a personal rather than a fiduciary capacity.

1   [1990] 2 AC 663.
2   Such authorisation is not precluded by Companies Act 1985, s 310: *Movitex Ltd v Bulfield* [1988] BCLC 104.
3   [2003] EWCA Civ 424, [2003] 2 BCLC 241. See too *Gencor ACP Ltd v Dalby* [2000] 2 BCLC 734; *CMS Dolphin Ltd v Simonet* [2001] 2 BCLC 704; *Coleman Taymar Ltd v Oakes* [2001] 2 BCLC 749; *Item Software (UK) Ltd v Fassihi* [2002] EWHC 3116 (Ch), [2003] 2 BCLC 1; *Tesco Stores Ltd v Pook [2003] EWHC 823 (Ch)*, [2004] IRLR 618; *Crown Dilmun v Sutton [2004] EWHC 52 (Ch)*, [2004] 1 BCLC 468; *Quarter Master UK Ltd (in liq) v Pyke* [2005] 1 BCLC 145; *Shepherds Investments Ltd v Walters* [2006] EWHC 836 (Ch), [2006] All ER (D) 213 (Apr).
4   [2003] 2 BCLC 241.at [27] per Jonathan Parker LJ, quoting *Aberdeen Railway Co v Blaikie Bros* (1854) 1 Macq 461 at 471 per Lord Cranworth LC.

Profits made by agents

33.50 As James LJ stated in *Parker v McKenna*[1]:

'No agent in the course of his agency, in the matter of his agency, can be allowed to make any profit without the knowledge and consent of his principal; that rule is an inflexible rule, and must be applied inexorably by this Court which is not entitled, in my judgment, to receive evidence, or suggestion, or argument as to whether the principal did or did not suffer any injury in fact by reason of the dealing of the agent; for the safety of mankind requires that no agent shall be able to put his principal to the danger of such an inquiry as that.'

1   (1874) 10 Ch App 96 at 124–125.

33.51 Except to the extent the agent-principal relationship is a debtor-creditor relationship the agent is a fiduciary for the purpose of imposing constructive trusteeship, liability to account and of allowing the proprietary remedies via the tracing process[1].

1   *New Zealand Netherlands Society Oranje Inc v Kays* [1973] 2 All ER 1222, [1973] 1 WLR 1126; *Boardman v Phipps* [1967] 2 AC 46, [1966] 3 All ER 721, HL; *Re Hallett's Estate* (1880) 13 Ch D 696; *Sinclair v Brougham* [1914] AC 398 at 420; *Burdick v Garrick* (1870) 5 Ch App 233; *Metropolitan Bank v Heiron* (1880) 5 Ex D 319, CA; *Lister & Co v Stubbs* (1890) 45 Ch D 1; *Makepeace v Rogers* (1865) 4 De GJ & Sm 649, CA.

33.52 The leading case is *Boardman v Phipps*[1]. Assets were held upon trust to provide an annuity for the testator's widow and subject thereto for the testator's children. The trustees were an accountant, Fox, the deceased's daughter and the deceased's widow. The active trustee, Fox, was unhappy with the trust's sizeable minority shareholding in a private textile company. The solicitor to the trustees, Boardman, and a beneficiary knowledgeable in the textile business, Tom Phipps, as agents of the trust tried unsuccessfully at a general meeting to pave the ground for improvement. Boardman and Tom Phipps reckoned that a purchase of a majority holding in the company would be advisable and necessary if things were to improve, assuming a detailed investigation of the situation did not prove unsatisfactory. They so informed Fox but he made it clear that it was entirely out of the question for the trust to attempt to obtain a majority shareholding. Fox and the daughter-trustee both agreed that Boardman and Tom Phipps could go ahead and themselves personally attempt to acquire a majority shareholding. The widow-trustee was virtually senile and so was left out of the picture.

[1]   [1967] 2 AC 46, [1966] 3 All ER 721.

33.53 Purporting to act on behalf of the trust with its sizeable minority holding, Boardman and Tom Phipps had detailed negotiations with the company directors which provided them with information they would not otherwise have obtained. They then realised what worthwhile advantages might well flow from acquiring control of the company, reorganising its structure and realising its assets. They then put the trust beneficiaries in the picture, the widow having died so the beneficiaries were absolutely entitled under a bare trust, but not sufficiently enough for a fully informed consent to be given as the court subsequently held[1]. With much time, trouble and skill Boardman and Tom Phipps succeeded in their design so that the trust made roughly £47,000 profit from its shareholding and they made roughly £75,000 profit from their personal shareholdings.

[1]   Wilberforce J so held and no appeal from this was made.

33.54 The plaintiff beneficiary, Tom's brother John, entitled to a five-eighteenths share of the trust assets, then had the audacity to claim that Boardman and Tom Phipps held the shares, which they had acquired by virtue of exploiting an opportunity arising by virtue of their fiduciary position, as constructive trustees as to five-eighteenths of them for the plaintiff and that they were liable to account for profits made from the shares. He sought an order that the defendants should transfer to him the shares held by them as constructive trustee for him (subject to satisfying their lien for the money they had paid for the shares) and should pay him five-eighteenths of the profit found on the taking of the account.

33.55 The plaintiff succeeded in his claim but an inquiry was directed to allow the defendants on a liberal scale a sum in respect of their work and skill in obtaining the shares and making a profit therefrom.

33.56 All Law Lords agreed that Boardman was a fiduciary as solicitor to the trustees and as purporting to act as agent for the trust in the negotiations which provided the extra information for going on with the takeover. His opportunities thus arose by virtue of his fiduciary position. Tom Phipps did not seek to be treated any differently from Boardman. All agreed that the defendants would not have been able to obtain the information on which they based their successful takeover but for their ability to represent that they were acting for the trust with a sizeable minority shareholding.

33.57 Lords Hodson and Guest therefore held that the information was trust property and since the defendants had made a profit out of using this property they were clearly liable to account for the profit. Lord Cohen, however, stated[1]:

> 'Information is not property in the strict sense of that word and it does not necessarily follow that because an agent acquired information and opportunity while acting in a fiduciary capacity he is accountable to his principals for any profit that comes his way as the result of the use he makes of that information and opportunity. His liability to account must depend on the facts of the case. In the present case much of the information came the [defendants'] way when Mr Boardman was acting on behalf of the trustees on the instructions of Mr Fox, and the opportunity for bidding for the shares came because he purported for all purposes except for making the bid to be acting on behalf of the owners of the 8,000 shares in the company. In these circumstances the principle of *Regal (Hastings) Ltd v Gulliver* applies.'

[1]   [1967] 2 AC 46 at 102–103, [1966] 3 All ER 721 at 743.

33.58 Lords Cohen, Hodson and Guest further applied the broad principle (of which the rule that a fiduciary may not make a profit out of his trust is a part[1]) that[2] 'an agent is liable to account for profits which he makes out of the trust property if there is a possibility of conflict between his interest and his duty to his principal'. After all, the trustees might have sought Boardman's advice on an application to the court to acquire power to purchase the outstanding shares in the company; they would need not just legal advice but practical advice as to the likelihood of the assured success of the proposed takeover and reorganisation of the company. Boardman would not have been able to give unprejudiced advice if, when his plans were well advanced ('at the third phase'), he had been consulted by the trustees as to whether they should then try to take advantage of what he had done so as to obtain profits otherwise passing to him, thereby dashing the cup of profit from his lips.

[1]   [1967] 2 AC 46 at 123, [1966] 3 All ER 721 at 756, per Lord Upjohn.
[2]   [1967] 2 AC 46 at 103, [1966] 3 All ER 721 at 743, per Lord Upjohn.

33.59 Viscount Dilhorne and Lord Upjohn dissented. They took the view that the information obtained by the defendants purporting to be agents of the trust was not trust property. Viscount Dilhorne treated information as not being trust property unless use of the information was of value to the trust and was a use in which the trust was interested: the trust had no power (except upon applying to court) to purchase further shares in the company and Fox had made it clear that the trustees did not want any involvement in purchasing shares, waging a takeover bid and reorganising the company. Lord Upjohn[1] made the good point that information 'is not property in any normal sense but equity will restrain its transmission to another if in breach of some confidential relationship' which was not the case before him.

> 'The real rule is that knowledge learnt by a trustee in the course of his duties as such is not in the least property of the trust and in general may be used by him for his own benefit or for the benefit of other trusts unless it is confidential information which is given to him (i) in circumstances which, regardless of his position as a trustee, would make it a breach of confidence for him to communicate to anyone, for it has been given to him expressly or impliedly as confidential; or (ii) in a fiduciary capacity and its use would place him in a position where his duty and his interest might possibly conflict'[2].

1   [1967] 2 AC 46 at 128, [1966] 3 All ER 721 at 759. Further on confidential information see *De Maudsley v Palumbo* [1996] EMLR 460; *Fraser v Thames Television Ltd* [1984] QB 44, [1983] 2 All ER 101; *Faccenda Chicken Ltd v Fowler* [1987] Ch 117, [1986] 1 All ER 617. In *Satnam Investments Ltd v Dunlop Heywood Ltd* [1999] 3 All ER 652 at 669–671, CA, confidential information was regarded as property.
2   [1967] 2 AC 46 at 128–129, [1966] 3 All ER 721 at 759.

33.60 Viscount Dilhorne and Lord Upjohn concurred also in the view that there was no conflict between the defendants' private interest and their fiduciary duty to the trust. Lord Upjohn considered that a conflict requires[1]:

> 'that the reasonable man looking at the relevant facts and circumstances of the particular case would think that there was a real sensible possibility of conflict not that you could imagine some situation arising which might in some conceivable possibility in events not contemplated as real sensible possibilities by any reasonable person, result in a conflict.'

1   [1967] 2 AC 46 at 124, [1966] 3 All ER 721 at 756.

33.61 At the outset, Fox had refused to consider purchasing shares to obtain a majority shareholding and the trustees had no power to purchase further shares and the whole venture would have been too speculative. At the later stage when the defendants had discovered the information that made them consider it worthwhile taking over the company and reorganising its business, though they did not approach Fox, which they ought to have done, the venture was still rather speculative, so no court would have sanctioned the trust purchasing the shares to take over the company, unless Tom Phipps was willing to enter into a contract to run the company. Fox was an experienced accountant with as much knowledge of the company's situation as Boardman and in evidence had stated that he would not consider the trustees buying the shares in any circumstances. There was thus no reasonable sensible possibility of conflict of interest: indeed, Fox thought it would be to the advantage of the trust if the defendants themselves purchased the shares and took over the company.

33.62 Both the majority and the minority agreed that it could not be said that all information received by a fiduciary in his fiduciary capacity was trust property so that it could never be used by the fiduciary for his own benefit—that would place a trustee of more than one trust in an impossible position. The essential difference between the majority and the minority was that the majority favoured the traditional strict deterrent approach, so that (*non-de-minimis*) possibility of a conflict between private interest and fiduciary duty arising out of use of information received in a fiduciary capacity should give rise to constructive trusteeship of the shares purchased as a result of such information, whilst the minority favoured a liberal reasonable approach[1] that only a real sensible possibility of a conflict should give rise to a constructive trusteeship of the shares and there was not such a real sensible possibility (though the majority decision can, perhaps, be justified on the basis that it was possible to take the view that there was such a real sensible possibility on the facts[2]).

1   Favoured in *Manufacturers Trust Co v Becker* 338 US 304, 70 Sup Ct 127 (1949); *Peso-Silver Mines Ltd v Cropper* (1966) 58 DLR (2d) 1; (1967) 30 MLR 450 (D.D. Prentice) and in *Consul Development Pty Ltd v DPC Pty Ltd* (1975) 49 ALR 74. See also *Pine Pass Oil and Gas Ltd v Pac Petroleum Ltd* (1968) 70 DLR (2d) 196 and (1968) 84 LQR 472.
2   On the other hand, in the remote possibility of the trustees seeking the solicitor-defendant's advice at the time of the crucial third phase he could have openly declared his interest and declined to advise them other than to seek the advice of another solicitor.

33.63 It would seem that the question of possibility of conflict or not must be judged at the time when the fiduciary carried out the acts leading to the making of the profit (the third phase in *Boardman v Phipps*) so that the fiduciary can then judge whether he needs to seek the sanction of the trustees or beneficiaries or the court. As Lindley LJ said in *Re Hurst*[1], 'The conduct of trustees ought to be regarded with reference to the facts and circumstances existing at the time when they had to act and which were known or ought to have been known by them at that time.'

1   (1892) 67 LT 96 at 99; also *Nestle v National Westminster Bank plc* [1993] 1 WLR 1260, CA.

33.64 It is submitted that the strict deterrent approach of the majority in *Boardman v Phipps* is to be supported with its clear practical advantage that should save much litigation. It protects the beneficiaries who will usually be at a substantial informational disadvantage vis-à-vis the trustees or other fiduciary, who could have avoided the problem whether by obtaining an informed consent or court approval before commencing the activity leading to the making of the profit or otherwise by refraining from such activity and any risk of loss to the trust fund resulting therefrom.

33.65 In *A-G for Hong Kong v Reid*[1] the Privy Council endorsed *Boardman v Phipps* 'which demonstrates the strictness with which equity regards the conduct of a fiduciary and the extent to which equity is willing to impose a constructive trust on property obtained by a fiduciary by virtue of his office' before holding that 'if a fiduciary acting honestly and in good faith and making a profit which his principal could not make for himself becomes a trustee of that profit, then a fiduciary acting dishonestly who accepts a bribe must also be a constructive trustee [thereof].'

1   [1994] 1 AC 324 at 338.

33.66 An agent who has been employed by his principal to purchase land cannot purchase it for himself, so if he does so he will be constructive trustee thereof for his principal[1]. Where he contracts to purchase land for himself which he should have bought for his principal and then assigns the benefit of the contract to a purchaser, then the equitable interest of the principal will have priority over the later equitable interest of the assignee-purchaser as Jessel MR held in *Cave v Mackenzie*[2].

1 *Longfield Parish Council v Robson* (1913) 29 TLR 357. Similarly, if an agent is employed to find another person as purchaser of a house, but by fraudulent misrepresentations has the owner transfer the house into the name of an alias of the agent, such house will be held on constructive trust for the owner: *Collings v Lee* [2001] 2 All ER 332.
2 (1877) 46 LJ Ch 564.

33.67 In *English v Dedham Vale Properties Ltd*[1] self-appointed agents were held liable to account for profits. The plaintiff had sold her bungalow and four acres to the defendant for £7,750. However, seven days before contracts had been exchanged the defendant had applied for planning permission for one acre, making the application in the plaintiff's name and signed by the defendant as agent for the plaintiff. Under the Planning Acts the plaintiff did not then need to be notified of the application or informed of its outcome. Planning permission was granted after exchange of contracts but before completion. It was only after completion that the plaintiff learnt about the application. She thereupon brought an action claiming inter alia an account of profits for breach of fiduciary relationship.

1 [1978] 1 All ER 382, [1978] 1 WLR 93.

33.68 Slade J held[1]:

'(1)Where, during the course of negotiations for a contract for the sale and purchase of property, the proposed purchaser in the name of and purportedly as an agent on behalf of the vendor, but without the consent or authority of the vendor, takes some action in regard to the property (whether it be the making of a planning application, a contract for the sale of the property or anything else) which, if disclosed to the vendor, might reasonably be supposed to be likely to influence him in deciding whether or not to conclude the contract, a fiduciary relationship arises between the two parties. (2) Such fiduciary relationship gives rise to the consequences that there is a duty on the proposed purchaser to disclose to the vendor before the conclusion of the contract what he has done as the vendor's purported agent, and correspondingly, in the event of non-disclosure, there is a duty on him to account to him for any profit made in the course of the purported agency, unless the vendor consents to his retaining it. In such circumstances, the person who, for his private purpose, uses the vendor's name and purports to act as his agent cannot reasonably complain if the law subjects him to the same consequences vis-à-vis his alleged principal as if he actually had the authority which he purported to have.'

1 [1978] 1 All ER 382 at 399.

33.69 Since the plaintiff's name was used in respect of the plaintiff's property, the defendant was clearly liable to account for his profit ultimately received as a result of the making of the application for planning permission. If it had been material it seems likely that the defendant could have been held to be constructive trustee of the benefit of the planning permission so that upon a sale of the acre plot with a dwelling house thereon, if the proceeds (including the profit resulting from the planning permission) had been mixed with other moneys of the defendant an equitable tracing claim would have been available if the defendant had become bankrupt, so giving the plaintiff a prior interest in the defendant's assets. Indeed, Slade J stated[1]:

> 'If the plaintiffs had learned of the application which had been made in their names and in respect of their property before contracts had been exchanged they would have been entitled to say to the defendants: "We ratify and adopt this application, which has been made in our names as our own application, and neither of you are to have anything more to do with it". Furthermore, this is, I think, effectively the course which the plaintiffs would actually have adopted unless a more favourable form of contract had been offered to them. This being so, I do not think that a court of equity should, or will, allow the defendants to be in a better position than that in which they would have found themselves if, before exchange of contracts, the defendants had told the plaintiffs of the application which had been made in their names as I think they should have told them.'

[1]   [1978] 1 All ER 382 at 398.

33.70 This seemingly treats the benefit of the planning application as belonging in equity to the plaintiffs[1].

[1]   Like the benefit of the contracts in *Cook v Deeks* [1916] 1 AC 554.

33.71 Indeed, though Slade J assumed that ratification was impossible after contracts had been exchanged there seems no reason why ratification could not have occurred. The plaintiffs were full legal and equitable owners at the time of submission of the planning application in their name, and the rule that a principal loses his right to ratify the act done on his behalf if, since the act, property rights have become vested only relates to the vesting of rights in third parties, so that the self-appointed agent cannot plead the vesting of rights in himself as a bar to ratification. Thus, on ordinary agency principles the plaintiffs should have been entitled to the benefit of the planning application and the profits flowing therefrom.

Profits by partners or prospective partners

33.72 A partner, though a fiduciary, may profit personally from information received by him qua partner so long as the use made by him of the information is outside the scope of the partnership business[1]. Where the use is for a purpose within the scope of the partnership business then the profits belong to the partnership. Profits made out of partnership property must also be held on constructive trust for the partnership[2], and the concept of partnership 'property' is sufficiently flexible to include goodwill built up by the firm, so that agreements entered by a former partner on the back of such goodwill will be held on constructive trust for the firm[3]. Note, too, that a prospective partner or joint venturer who is given confidential information not to be exploited other than pursuant to the prospective partnership or joint venture will be constructive trustee of that which he obtains through using such confidential information after negotiations between the parties have failed to lead to a partnership or joint venture agreement[4].

¹   *Aas v Benham* [1891] 2 Ch 244 approved in *Boardman v Phipps* [1967] 2 AC 46, [1966] 3 All ER 721.
²   *Don King Productions Inc v Warren* [2000] Ch 291 at 341–342, CA; *Gordon v Gonda* [1955] 2 All ER 762 at 766, where 'not' in line 33 in the clause 'would not be held' on trust for the firm seems to have been inserted by mistake in a long convoluted sentence.
³   *Pathirana v Pathirana* [1967] 1 AC 233, followed in *John Taylors (a firm) v Masons (a firm)* [2005] WTLR 1519, CA. See too *Lindsley v Woodfull* [2004] EWCA Civ 165, [2004] 2 BCLC 131, CA.
⁴   *Lac Minerals Ltd v International Corona Resources Ltd* (1989) 61 DLR (4th) 14.

33.73 In *Sandhu v Gill*[1], the Court of Appeal was asked to construe the Partnership Act 1890 s 42(1), which provides that after the departure of an outgoing partner, if there has been no final settlement of accounts 'the outgoing partner ... is entitled ... to such share of the profits made since the dissolution as the Court may find to be attributable to the use of his share of the partnership assets.' The question before the court was whether the words 'share of the partnership assets' referred to the partner's share in the *gross* assets on a notional dissolution or his share of the *net* assets. The outgoing partner argued for the former construction because his debt to the partnership exceeded any capital payment that would have been made to him. Hence he would have had no entitlement to profits on the latter approach. However, the court held that although each partner has a proprietary interest or share in all the assets of the partnership, the relevant words refer not to this proprietary interest but to the outgoing partner's entitlement to the net assets on a notional dissolution. The reason is that the continuation of the partnership business, using assets in which the outgoing partner has a proprietary interest, is a breach of fiduciary duty, and the profits attributable to the breach are those which relate to the net financial interest of the outgoing partner.

¹   [2005] EWCA Civ 1297, [2006] Ch 456.

33.74 In *Murad v Al-Saraj*[1] the parties entered a joint venture to buy a hotel under an agreement which provided that the claimants would put up £1 million in cash and that the capital profits realised when the hotel was resold would be split between the claimants and the defendant on a 50:50 basis. After the hotel had been resold, the claimants discovered that the defendant had misrepresented the nature of his own contribution to the purchase of the property. The Court of Appeal upheld their claim that the defendant's misrepresentation constituted a breach of fiduciary duty, and ordered him to account for the whole of his profit, subject to a deduction for the contribution which he had actually made to the purchase. However this was an unsatisfactory way of resolving the case[2], because it overlooked the significance of two Privy Council decisions, *Burland v Earle*[3] and *Cook v Deeks*[4], both of which establish that where a fiduciary fails to disclose all relevant facts when entering a contract with his principal, the principal can rescind or affirm the contract, but he cannot affirm the contract and then effectively change its terms by taking the fiduciary's profit. In Lord Buckmaster LC's words[5], 'this would be for the court to make a new contract between the parties'. This suggests that in *Murad* the proper response would have been for the court to give the claimants the option of rescinding the contract; if they exercised this option, there would then have been no agreed basis for splitting the profits on the sale of the hotel, which should therefore have been held for the parties on resulting trust in proportion to their contributions to the purchase price.

1 [2005] WTLR 1573, CA.
2 As noted by R Chambers (2005) 16 KCLJ 186, at pp 192–3.
3 [1902] AC 83.
4 [1916] 1 AC 554.
5 [1916] 1 AC 554 at 564.

Profits by tippees

33.75 Where information acquired by a fiduciary is confidential (so that its disclosure could be prevented by a court injunction) and is passed on to another (the 'tippee') who exploits it, then just as the profit if directly made by the fiduciary would be held on constructive trust, so should the profit made by the tippee[1]. Indeed, use by a tippee of knowledge of an opportunity of a non-confidential but special nature, like that in *Boardman v Phipps* (whose strictness has been endorsed twice by the Privy Council[2]) may well give rise to accountability and to a constructive trust[3].

1 *Nanus Asia Inc v Standard Chartered Bank* [1990] HKLR 396; *A-G v Guardian Newspapers (No 2)* [1990] 1 AC 109, 161, 211, 262–263, 278, 288. However, if the information shortly becomes readily available in the public domain so the tippee could have made the profit by relying on that, then there will be no liability: *Satnam Investments Ltd v Dunlop Heywood & Co Ltd* [1999] 3 All ER 652 at 672, CA.
2 *New Zealand Netherlands Society Oranje Inc v Kays* [1973] 1 WLR 1126; *A-G for Hong Kong v Reid* [1994] 1 AC 324.
3 An alternative explanation for *Nanus Asia Inc v Standard Chartered Bank* [1990] HKLR 396; but courts are reluctant to find a third party liable unless dishonest or becoming a fiduciary: *Satnam Investments Ltd v Dunlop Heywood & Co Ltd* [1999] 3 All ER 652 at 672, CA. In *Fyffes Group Ltd v Templeman* [2000] 2 Lloyd's Rep 643 at 672 it was held that the briber of an agent may be required to account to the principal for benefits obtained from the corruption of the agent.

Commercial transactions

33.76 The courts should be very wary of extending the ambit of fiduciary obligations (with the concomitant liability to account for, and constructive trusts of, profits). Such obligations should only arise in a relationship involving some inequality of footing or opportunity between the parties arising out of a particular relationship or special circumstances surrounding such relationship. If experienced businessmen with access to legal advice contract at arms' length then their relationship should not be held to be a fiduciary one, even if a continuing business relationship is contemplated and one party as a result of the business generated by the contract knows that he will receive, unknown to the other, valuable commissions and discounts from third parties[1]. The contractual position should exclusively be the position, while 'the essence of a fiduciary obligation is that it creates obligations of a different character from those deriving from the contract itself'[2]. However, property acquired in breach of confidence by a prospective partner or co-venturer will be held on constructive trust[3].

33.76 *Constructive trusts*

1   See eg *Jirna Ltd v Mister Dount of Canada Ltd* (1971) 22 DLR (3d) 639 (Ont CA), affd (1973) 40 DLR (3d) 303 (Can SC); *Hanson v Lorenz and Jones* [1986] NLJ Rep 1088, [1987] 1 FTLR 23 where a solicitor was held by CA not to be liable to account for his profit from a joint venture (concerning purchase renovation and sale of a house) between himself and a business client where the client fully understood a fair agreement; *Frame v. Smith* [1987] 2 SCR 99 at 137–8 (Can SC); *Indata Equipment Supplies Ltd (t/a Autofleet) v ACL Ltd* [1998] 1 BCLC 412, CA; *Cadbury Schweppes Inc v FBI Foods Ltd* (1999) 167 D.L.R. (4th) 577 at 592 (Can SC); *Paper Reclaim Ltd v Arotearoa International Ltd* [2006] 3 NZLR 188.
2   *Re Goldcorp Exchange Ltd* [1994] 2 All ER 806 at 821, PC; also *Clark Boyce v Mouat* [1993] 4 All ER 268 at 275, PC; and *Kelly v Cooper* [1993] AC 205, para 33.97.
3   *Lac Minerals Ltd v International Corona Resources Ltd* (1989) 61 DLR (4th) 14.

33.77 Businessmen should be regarded as voluntarily taking the risk of sharp practice of other businessmen: they are free to take extensive legal advice on their responsibilities during negotiations for contracts and can enter into a pre-contract bargaining agreement defining their duties and liabilities in respect of information acquired in the course of negotiations[1]. The courts should not allow the device of fiduciary obligations in a relationship to be extended to create a degree of uncertainty and vagueness that will jeopardise the operation of commercial transactions and inhibit the parties' ability to determine their legal relations quickly and cheaply. These practical problems are well brought out in a passage from the judgment of Robert Goff LJ (as he then was) in *Scandinavian Trading Tanker Co AB v Flota Petrolera Ecuatoriana*[2] which Lord Diplock (with whom the others concurred) cited[3] in extenso on appeal:

> 'The courts should so far as possible desist from placing obstacles in the way of either party ascertaining his legal position, if necessary with the aid of advice from a qualified lawyer, because it may be commercially desirable for action to be taken without delay, action which may be irrevocable and which may have far-reaching consequences. It is for this reason that the English courts have time and again asserted the need for certainty in commercial transactions, for the simple reason that the parties are entitled to know where they stand and to act accordingly. [It is no answer that the] problem may in a particular case prove to be capable of solution by entering into a without prejudice agreement with the [other party]. This is not always possible ... Nor is it an answer that the parties can immediately apply to arbitrators or to a court for a decision. For, quite apart from the fact that some delay inherent in the legal process, if the question to be decided is whether the tribunal is to grant equitable relief, investigation of the relevant circumstances and the collection of evidence for that purpose cannot ordinarily be carried out in a very short period of time.'

1   *Hospital Products Ltd v United States Surgical Corpn* (1985) 55 ALR 417 (Aust HC) (liability for breach of contract, no liability to account for profits).
2   [1983] QB 529 at 540–541, [1983] 1 All ER 301 at 308–309.
3   [1983] 2 AC 694 at 713–714, [1983] 2 All ER 763 at 768–769.

33.78 Significantly in *Satnam Investments Ltd v Dunlop Heywood & Co Ltd*[1] the Court of Appeal reversed the trial judge's holding that a development company, which bought a site through taking advantage of disclosures made to it by a surveyor in breach of fiduciary duty to the surveyor's principal, held the site on trust for the principal (subject to paying the purchase price of the site). There had been no finding that the company had come under any fiduciary obligation as a result of receiving the disclosed confidential information, nor that it had encouraged or participated in the agent's breach of duty. Thus, the Court of Appeal considered it would be contrary to commercial sense that the company should disgorge property which it had acquired merely through an opportunity provided by a breach of fiduciary duty of another in which it itself was not implicated.

[1]   [1999] 3 All ER 652 criticised by Goff and Jones *Law of Restitution* (6th edn) paras 33–019 to 33–020.

Identifying the relevant gain

33.79 When a court comes to identify the gain for which a fiduciary must account, the question can arise whether the court should allow a deduction for the fiduciary's costs and expenses – ie whether the fiduciary should account for his net profits or his gross receipts? The courts usually take the former to be the relevant gain, and order fiduciaries to account for their net profits only[1].

[1]   eg *Strata Consolidated (Australia) Pty Ltd v Bradshaw* [1999] NSWSC 22; *Medcalf v Mardell* unreported Ch D 31 March 1999; *Nottingham University v Fishel* [2000] ICR 1462 at1498–9; *J J Harrison (Properties) Ltd v Harrison* [2002] 1 BCLC 162 at [50]; *Stocking v Montila* [2005] EWHC 2210 (Ch) at [43], [2005] All ER (D) 191 (Oct).

33.80 The question can also sometimes arise, whether the relevant gain should be valued at the date of receipt, the date of judgment, or some other date. In cases where the fiduciary improperly receives property which fluctuates in value, he will be liable to account to his principal for the highest market value of the property between the date of receipt and the date of judgment[1]. The justification for this rule is that the fiduciary owes a continuing duty throughout this period to realise the assets for the principal at the most opportune moment.

[1]   *Nant-y-Glo and Blaina Ironworks Co v Grave* (1878) 12 Ch D 738, accepted in *Target Holdings Ltd v Redferns* [1996] AC 421 at 440.

33.81 In *Crown Dilmun v Sutton*[1] the defendant misappropriated an opportunity to develop property, in a deal that would still take time, effort, and cash to bring to fruition by the time when the case came to trial. The success or failure of the deal would turn on the hypothetical future actions of various parties, including the resolution of a planning application, and possibly also the provision of cash by the defendant's company. Peter Smith J held that the claimants could elect to postpone the taking of an account of profits until it became clearer whether the deal would go through, rejecting the defendant's argument that this would effectively enable the claimants to force him to act for their benefit in the future. In the judge's view, the claimants could have achieved this result in any case, by waiting to bring their claim after the deal have been brought to fruition; he also thought that a charge for the defendant's skill, labour and expenses might conceivably be appropriate when the account of profits was eventually taken.

[1]   [2004] EWHC 52 (Ch), [2004] 1 BCLC 468 esp at [205]–[214].

Paragraph 2

No liability for gains made in a personal capacity

33.82 Obviously a fiduciary is not liable to account for *every* gain accruing in his hands: he is only liable for gains which have been made in his fiduciary capacity[1]. Hence a court must determine the exact nature and extent of the fiduciary's obligations, and satisfy itself that a gain fell within the scope of his fiduciary engagement, before it will order him to account for the gain and/or declare that it is held on constructive trust for the principal. This can be a straightforward matter where the fiduciary's obligations derive from his special status as trustee, partner, etc, but it can also present the court with difficulties in a case where the fiduciary's obligations derive instead from the fact-specific context of his dealings with the principal[2].

1   *Murad v Al-Saraj* [2005] WTLR 1573 at [62], CA; *3464920 Canada Inc v Strother* (2005) 7 ITELR 748 at [47], British Columbia CA.
2   For further discussion see the Hon Mr Justice J B Kearney 'Accounting for a Fiduciary's Gains in Commercial Contexts' in P D Finn (ed) *Equity and Commercial Relationships* (1987) 186.

33.83 One case where a fiduciary escaped liability because his gain was made in a personal capacity, rather than a fiduciary capacity, was *Appleby v Cowley*[1]. There Megarry V-C held that the head of a barristers' set of chambers was in a fiduciary position to the members thereof, but that he did not hold the building he had purchased for chambers on constructive trust for the members since he purchased the building on his own account and not as agent or delegate of the members. The building was purchased in the course of the fiduciary relationship but not by reason of that relationship. Another example is *Hanson v Lorenz and Jones*[2] where the Court of Appeal held that a solicitor was under no duty to account to a client for his profit from a joint venture (purchase, renovation and sale of a house through the medium of companies controlled by him and by his client) in circumstances where the business or financial prudence of the deal was outside the scope of the solicitor-client relationship, and the client understood the terms of the venture agreement, which were fair in any event. A third example is *Ward v Brunt*[3], *where* the freehold reversion to a lease to a partnership was purchased by a partner, not in her capacity as partner owing fiduciary duties to her fellow partners, but in her capacity as devisee of an option to purchase the freehold under the will of her grandfather, who had owned the freehold.

1   (1982) Times, 14 April.
2   [1986] NLJ Rep 1088, [1987] 1 FTLR 23.
3   [2000] WTLR 731.

Causation

33.84 Cases can arise in which gains accrue in a fiduciary's hands as a result of activities, some of which he is bound to pursue on his principal's behalf, but some of which he can legitimately pursue in his own interest. In cases of this kind, there is a need for the courts 'to specify criteria for a sufficient connection (or "causation") between breach of duty and the profit derived' in order to distinguish the gains for which the fiduciary must account to his principal from the gains which he is entitled to keep for himself[1]. The test which they use is a simple one. The breach must have been one cause of the gain. It need not have been the only cause, nor need it have been the predominant cause, for 'in this sort of case the court "does not allow an examination into the relative importance of contributory causes" '[2]. Nor can the fiduciary escape liability by proving that he would have made the gain even if he had not breached his duty: 'the question whether or not the benefit would have been obtained but for the breach of trust has always been treated as irrelevant'[3]. Furthermore, 'the court lays the burden on the defaulting fiduciary to show that the profit is not one for which he should account'[4]. In effect, therefore, he must prove that his breach of duty had no causative effect whatsoever, by showing that the gain came into his hands exclusively as a result of activities legitimately undertaken in his own interest.

[1] *Maguire v Makaronis* (1997) 188 CLR 449 at 468. See too *Swain v Law Society* [1982] 1 WLR 17 at 37; *Estate Realties Ltd v Wignall* [1992] 2 NZLR 615 at 631; *Kao Lee & Yip v Koo Hoi Yan* [2003] HKLRD 296 at [142]; *Loizou v Derrimut Enterprise Pty Ltd* [2004] VSC 176 at [116]; *Say-Dee Pty Ltd v Farah Constructions Pty Ltd* [2005] NSWCA 309 at [196]; *Button v Phelps* [2006] EWHC 53 (Ch) at [66], [2006] All ER (D) 33 (Feb).

[2] *Fexuto Pty Ltd v Bosnjak Holdings Pty Ltd (No 2)* (1998) 29 ACSR 290 at 297 per Young J, quoting *Barton v Armstrong* [1976] AC 104 at 118.

[3] *Industrial Development Consultants Ltd v Cooley* [1972] 1 WLR 443 at 453 per Roskill J. See too *Beach Petroleum NL v Kennedy* (1999) 48 NSWLR 1 at [440], followed and applied in *Say-Dee Pty Ltd v Farah Constructions Pty Ltd* [2005] NSWCA 309 at [191]–[193]; *Gwembe Valley Development Co Ltd (in rec) v Koshy (No 3)* [2003] EWCA Civ 1048, [2004] 1 BCLC 131 at [145]–[146].

[4] *Murad v Al-Saraj* [2005] WTLR 1573 at [77] per Arden LJ.

33.85 Thus in *Manley v Santori*[1] the surviving members of a partnership continued to carry on the firm's business following the death of a partner until a winding up order was made. Pursuant to the Partnership Act 1890, s 42, Romer J ordered the surviving partners to account to the personal representatives of the deceased partner for the profits made between his death and the winding-up order. The section provided that the surviving members were accountable for those profits which were attributable to their use of the deceased's share of the partnership assets. Romer J held that they would have to pay a proportionate share of *all* the profits made by the firm during the relevant period unless they could prove that they had been earned by some means other than by use of the partnership assets.

[1] [1927] 1 Ch 157.

33.86 In *Gray v New Augarita Porcupine Mines Ltd*[1] a company director bought shares in the company at a discount and sold them on at higher prices. He failed to disclose these dealings to the board of directors. Hence he owed the company a duty to account for his profits. Subsequently the board agreed to settle the company's claim for these profits at a meeting where he failed again to disclose all the relevant details of his transactions. When the truth came out, the company argued that the settlement agreement had left him with gains for which he should account, because his failure to make full disclosure of his prior wrongdoing itself constituted a further breach of fiduciary duty. He replied that it would have made no difference if he had revealed everything to the board because they had already decided on the terms of the settlement, calculating that they could get no more out of him, and wishing to recover some cash to keep the company running. Lord Radcliffe made the following comments[2]:

> 'There may be an element of truth in all this, but in fact it constitutes an irrelevant speculation. If a trustee has placed himself in a position in which his interest conflicts with his duty and has not discharged himself from responsibility to account for the profits that his interest has secured for him, it is neither here nor there to speculate whether, if he had done his duty, he would not have been left in possession of the same amount of profit.'

1   [1952] 3 DLR 1, PC.
2   [1952] 3 DLR 1, PC at 15.

33.87 Hence the director was liable for the difference between the amount which he had owed to the company at the time of the agreement and the amount for which the board had released the company's claims.

33.88 The same rule was applied in *Murad v Al-Saraj*[1]. The claimants were induced to enter a property development joint venture with the defendant by his misrepresentations relating to the nature of his contributions to the purchase of the property. The claimants conceded that if they had known the truth they would still have entered the venture, but would have done so on a different profit-splitting basis. The defendant argued that he should therefore be obliged to account for no larger sum than the difference between the profits he had actually made and the profits he would have made, had he told the truth. However the majority of the Court of Appeal rejected this, holding that the causation test used to identify the profits for which the defendant was liable to account was not a 'but-for' test, but a simple 'cause of the gain' test.

1   [2005] WTLR 1573.

Due authorisation

33.89 No constructive trusteeship of profits will arise if the conduct generating the profit is authorised by the trust instrument or by the contract of agency, or by the deed of partnership or by the original articles of a company providing the contractual basis upon which persons become members of the company[1].

1   *Boardman v Phipps* [1967] 2 AC 46, [1966] 3 All ER 721; *Brown v IRC* [1965] AC 244, [1964] 3 All ER 119; *New Zealand Netherlands Society Oranje Inc v Kays* [1973] 2 All ER 1222, [1973] 1 WLR 1126; *Phillips v Manufacturers Securities Ltd* (1917) 116 LT 290. See also *Re Drexel Burnham Lambert* [1995] 1 WLR 32.

33.90 A further defence is for a trustee or fiduciary to show he had the informed consent of all the beneficiaries being each of full age and capacity and between them absolutely entitled to the trust property[1] or that he had the sanction of the court[2]. The court may authorise a trustee to sell his property to the trust and retain his profit, while it may also allow a trustee remuneration for his skill and labour in making a profit for which he is accountable to the trust[3]. A partner will need the informed consent of the other partners. A director will need the informed consent of all the members of the company[4] or of a majority acting bona fide in the interests of the company[5] except where advantage is taken of ss 320 and 322A of the Companies Act 1985[6].

1   *Boardman v Phipps* [1967] 2 AC 46, [1966] 3 All ER 721; *Borland's Trustees v Steel Bros & Co Ltd* [1901] 1 Ch 279; *Boulting v Association of Cinematograph, Television and Allied Technicians* [1963] 2 QB 606 at 636.
2   *Farmer v Dean* (1863) 32 Beav 327; *Boardman v Phipps* [1967] 2 AC 46, [1966] 3 All ER 721; Trustee Act 1925, s 42.
3   *Phipps v Boardman* [1967] 2 AC 46 at 104, 112; *Guinness v Saunders* [1990] 2 AC 663 at 694, 701; *Re Badfinger* [2001] WTLR 1 at 13–17.
4   *Cook v Deeks* [1916] 1 AC 554; *Borland's Trustees v Steel Bros & Co Ltd* [1901] 1 Ch 279.
5   *Rolled Steel Products Ltd v British Steel Corpn* [1986] Ch 246, CA.
6   Gower, *Principles of Modern Company Law* (6th edn) p 202–206.

33.91 It would seem that someone employed by trustees in a fiduciary position (eg a solicitor, discretionary portfolio manager, surveyor, land agent, or accountant) or a beneficiary acquiring special information whilst purportedly representing the trust so as to be treated as a fiduciary, may be able to escape liability as constructive trustee by obtaining the informed consent of independent trustees[1] as an alternative to obtaining the informed consent of all the beneficiaries. Indeed, where the business reality is such that profits could never have been earned at all as between fully independent persons except on a profit-sharing basis then a fiduciary may be allowed a share of the profits[2].

1   *Regal (Hastings) Ltd v Gulliver* (1942) [1967] 2 AC 134n, [1942] 1 All ER 378, HL; *Boardman v Phipps* [1967] 2 AC 46 at 93, 117, and implicit in Lord Upjohn's speech at 130–133. See also *Anson v Potter* (1879) 13 Ch D 141. The trustees should be independent just as company directors must be if disclosure to them is to protect a promoter; *Gluckstein v Barnes* [1900] AC 240. In *Boardman v Phipps* [1967] 2 AC 46 at 104 Lord Cohen indicates that where a fund is to the fiduciaries' knowledge distributable, because the beneficiaries are each of full capacity and between them absolutely entitled to call for the capital, then the informed consent of the beneficiaries is required.
2   *O'Sullivan v Management Agency and Music Ltd* [1985] 3 All ER 351 at 373, CA; *Re Badfinger* [2001] WTLR 1; c f *Warman International Ltd v Dwyer* (1995) 128 ALR 201 at 211 and see paras 58.25–58.30 below.

33.92 It will always be a defence to a claim by a particular plaintiff that that particular plaintiff himself gave his fully informed consent to the conduct in question of the defendant[1].

1   See Article 98 below.

Mere use of knowledge or opportunity acquired qua fiduciary: problems of trustees of two or more trusts

33.93 There must be more than *mere* use of any knowledge or opportunity which comes to the fiduciary in the course of his fiduciary relationship[1].

1   *Boardman v Phipps* [1967] 2 AC 46 at 88, 89–90, 100, 102–103, 107, 126, 128–129.
    Directors are treated leniently so long as not acting in breach of contract or confidence: see
    London and Mashonaland Exploration Co Ltd v New Mashonaland Exploration Co Ltd
    [1891] WN 165; *Bell v Lever Bros Ltd* [1932] AC 161 (on which see Sedley LJ in *In Plus
    Group Ltd v Pyke* [2002] EWCA Civ 370, [2002] 2 BCLC 201at [79] onwards);
    cf *Hivac Ltd v Park Royal Scientific Instruments Ltd* [1946] Ch 169, [1946] 1 All ER 350;
    Marshall (Thomas) Exports Ltd v Guinle [1979] Ch 227, [1978] 3 All ER 193. As
    emphasised by Oliver LJ in the passage covered by note 88 above, the profits have to have
    been acquired not only in the course of, but *by reason of*, the fiduciary relationship.

33.94 Lord Upjohn in *Boardman v Phipps* stated[1]:

'There is no general rule that information learnt by a trustee during the course
of his duties is property of the trust and cannot be used by him. If this was to be
the rule it would put the Public Trustee and other corporate trustees out of
business and make it difficult for private trustees to be trustees of more than
one trust. This would be the greatest possible pity for corporate trustees and
others may have much information which they may initially acquire in
connection with some particular trust but, without prejudice to that trust, can
make it readily available to other trusts to the great advantage of those other
trusts.

The real rule is that knowledge learnt by the trustee in the course of his duties
as such is not in the least property of the trust and in general may be used by
him for his own benefit or for the benefit of other trusts unless it is confidential
information which is given to him (i) in circumstances which, regardless of his
position as a trustee would make it a breach of confidence for him to
communicate it to anyone, for it has been given to him expressly or impliedly as
confidential; or (ii) in a fiduciary capacity, and its use would place him in a
position where his duty and his interest might possibly conflict. Let me give
examples. A, as trustee of two settlements X and Y holding shares in the same
small company, learns facts as trustee of X about the company which are
encouraging. In the absence of special circumstances (such, for example, that X
wants to buy more shares) I can see nothing whatever which would make it
improper for him to tell his co-trustees of Y who feel inclined to sell that he has
information that this would be a bad thing to do. Another example: A as
trustee of X learns facts that make him and his co-trustees want to sell. Clearly
he could not communicate this knowledge to his co-trustees of Y until at all
events the holdings of X have been sold for there would be a plain conflict,
reflected in the prices that might or might possibly be obtained.'

1   [1967] 2 AC 46 at 128–129.

33.95 An equitable obligation of confidence arises from the receipt of
confidential information in the knowledge that it is to be kept confidential[1].
Indeed 'if the circumstances are such that any reasonable man standing in the
shoes of the recipient of the information would have realised that upon
reasonable grounds the information was being given to him in confidence then
this should suffice to impose upon him the equitable obligation of confidence'[2]. Thus, if a trustee of two settlements, X and Y, obtains as trustee of Y
information subject to the equitable obligation of confidence then he cannot
use it for the benefit of X and, it seems, even if he was trustee of X before he
became trustee of Y, he cannot be sued by the X beneficiaries for breach of
trust for failing to take advantage of the confidential information obtained
qua trustee of Y[3]. After all, where clients of auditors consent to them acting

for competing clients the auditors 'must of course keep confidential the information obtained from their respective clients'[4].

1 *Seager v Copydex* [1967] 2 All ER 415, [1967] 1 WLR 923, CA; *De Maudsley v Palumbo* [1996] EMLR 460; *Fraser v Evans* [1969] 1 QB 349, [1969] 1 All ER 8; *A-G v Jonathan Cape Ltd* [1976] QB 752, [1975] 3 All ER 484; *Dunford and Elliot Ltd v Johnson and Firth Brown Ltd* [1977] 1 Lloyd's Rep 505. Generally see F. Gurry, *Breach of Confidence* on this topic which falls outside the scope of this work.
2 *Coco v A N Clark (Engineers) Ltd* [1969] RPC 41 at 48, per Megarry J.
3 Cf *North and South Trust Co v Berkeley* [1971] 1 All ER 980, [1971] 1 WLR 470; [1978] Conv 114 (B. Rider).
4 *Bolkiah v KPMG* [1999] 1 All ER 517 at 526–527, per Lord Millett.

33.96 Partners are not at such a disadvantage as many other fiduciarie for a partner may make a profit from information obtained in the course of the partnership business where he does so in another firm with business outside the scope of the partnership business[1]. As Lord Hodson stated in *Boardman v Phipps*[2]:

'The case of partnership is special in the sense that a partner is the principal as well as the agent of the other partners and works in a defined area of business so that it can normally be determined whether the particular transaction is within or without the scope of the partnership. It is otherwise in the case of a general trusteeship or fiduciary position such as was occupied by Mr Boardman, the limits of which are not readily defined.'

1 *Aas v Benham* [1891] 2 Ch 244.
2 [1967] 2 AC 46 at 108.

Contractual ouster of fiduciary obligations

33.97 *Kelly v Cooper*[1] provides further assistance for professional trustees who act as trustee of many trusts. The case concerned an estate agent, employed to sell two adjoining properties, who, having obtained X to purchase one property, did not so inform the vendor of the other property when communicating to him X's offer of purchase, so depriving such vendor of the opportunity to obtain a higher price. The Privy Council held that there must be an implied term of the contract with the agent (known to act often for competing principals where properties are of similar description) that he is entitled to act for other principals selling competing properties and to keep confidential the information obtained from each of his principals. Moreover[2], 'the scope of the fiduciary duties owed by the defendants to the plaintiff (and in particular the alleged duty not to put themselves in a position where their duty and their interest conflict) are to be defined by the terms of the contract of agency.' The Privy Council endorsed the following dicta of Mason J[3]:

'That contractual and fiduciary relationships may co-exist between the same parties has never been doubted ... In these situations it is the contractual foundation which is all important because it is the contract that regulates the basic rights and liabilities of the parties. The fiduciary relationship, if it is to exist at all, must accommodate itself to the terms of the contract so that it is consistent with, and conforms to, them. The fiduciary relationship cannot be superimposed upon the contract in such a way as to alter the operation which the contract was intended to have upon its true construction.'

¹ [1993] AC 205.
² [1993] AC 205 at 215.
³ *Hospital Products Ltd v United States Surgical Corpn* (1984) 156 CLR 41 at 97.

33.98 Thus in *Clark Boyce v Mouat*¹ the Privy Council held that a fiduciary duty cannot be prayed in aid to enlarge the scope of contractual duties so that, there being no contractual duty on the solicitor to advise the plaintiff on the wisdom of entering into the relevant transaction, the plaintiff could not claim that he nevertheless owed her a fiduciary duty to give advice.

¹ [1993] 4 All ER 268 at 275.

33.99 However, there are limits to this principle, as the House of Lords held in *Hilton v Barker, Booth and Eastwood*¹. Here a firm of solicitors acted for both the vendor and purchaser in a conveyancing transaction. The firm failed to disclose to the vendor that the purchaser had recently been released from prison after convictions for criminal fraud (the firm having previously acted in his defence), and also that the firm had itself provided the money paid by the purchaser as a deposit. When the property deal subsequently fell through the vendor sought to recover his losses from the firm, which sought to avoid liability on the ground that the vendor had impliedly agreed not to require the firm to disclose the purchaser's confidences in the course of the parties' dealings. However Lord Walker held that the vendor's ignorance of the purchaser's criminal past meant that he could not have agreed to waive the firm's disclosure duty in relation to this information, and in the absence of the vendor's agreement to waive his right to disclosure of relevant information, the firm was liable for losses flowing from its failure to disclose.

¹ [2005] UKHL 8, [2005] 1 All ER 651, [2005] 1 WLR 567.

Fiduciary cannot use the equitable principle as a shield

33.100 Upjohn LJ made it clear in *Boulting v Association of Cinematograph, Television and Allied Technicians*¹ that the principle that a trustee or other person with fiduciary duties to perform should not place himself in a position where his private interest might conflict with his fiduciary duties is a principle for the protection of the person to whom the fiduciary duties are owed, not for the benefit of the trustee or fiduciary. The person to whom the duties are owed may relax them if he sees fit but the trustee or fiduciary cannot invoke the principle for some ulterior purpose of his own.

¹ [1963] 2 QB 606 at 636–637.

Can the strict rule be flexibly diluted?

33.101 As can be seen from the foregoing discussion the rule requiring fiduciaries to account for unauthorised gains is very strictly applied, so ensuring that the fiduciary is regarded as fulfilling his duty to act in the best interests of his beneficiaries or principal. The courts have traditionally given two reasons for this firm approach: first, that fiduciaries must be given 'an incentive ... to resist the temptation to misconduct themselves'[1]; and secondly, that a principal would often face insuperable evidential difficulties, were he required to prove that his fiduciary acted in bad faith and failed to do everything he could have done[2]. The latter justification dates back to a time when shortcomings in the fact-finding processes of the Chancery courts set a premium on rules that avoided fact-finding, and it seems less convincing now that the fusion of the Chancery and common law courts, and successive reforms of civil procedure, have left the courts far better equipped in this respect; at the same time, as Professor Langbein has observed[3]:

> 'improvements in the standards, practices and technology of trust recordkeeping, as well as enhanced duties of disclosure ... have largely defused the old concern that a trustee operating under a potential conflict could easily conceal wrongdoing.'

[1]   *Murad v Al-Saraj* [2005] WTLR 1573 at [74] per Arden LJ. The reports contain many similar dicta, eg *Keech v Sandford* (1726) Sel Cas Ch 61 at 62; *Killick v Flexney* (1792) 4 Bro CC 161 at 163n; *Docker v Somes* (1834) 2 My & K 655 at 665; *Bray v Ford* [1896] AC 44 at 51; *Swain v Law Society* [1982] 1 WLR 17 at 29; *Guinness plc v Saunders* [1990] 2 AC 663 at 701; *Lindsley v Woodfull* [2004] EWCA Civ 165, [2004] 2 BCLC 131 at [30].

[2]   This was a frequent refrain of Lord Eldon's: see eg *ex parte Lacey* (1802) 6 Ves 625 at 627; *ex parte James* (1803) 8 Ves Jun 337 at 345. Lord Wright expressed similar concerns in *Regal (Hastings) Ltd v Gulliver* [1967] 2 AC 134n at 154.

[3]   J H Langbein 'Questioning the Trust Law Duty of Loyalty: Sole Interest or Best Interest?' (2005) 114 Yale LJ 929 at p. 932.

33.102 The need to deter fiduciaries from misconducting themselves remains prominent in the courts' thinking, but they are also alive to the fact that strict application of the rules can produce harsh results, and they have developed a number of strategies to moderate the law's severity.

33.103 First, some flexibility is inherent in the leeway afforded to the court to find that the alleged possibility of conflict was fanciful or insignificant in all the particular circumstances[1], because this will oust any liability. Secondly, there is also flexibility in defining the scope of a fiduciary relationship which may make a person a fiduciary for part of his activities but not for other parts and in ascertaining whether the profit was actually acquired by reason of the fiduciary relationship[2]. Thirdly, there is scope to mitigate the harsh effects of the rule by making an equitable allowance in favour of the defendant constructive trustee[3]-although the English courts have become less willing to make such an award following Lord Goff's statement in *Guinness plc v Saunders*, that the exercise of the courts' jurisdiction should be restricted to cases where an award would not have the effect of encouraging fiduciaries to put themselves in a position of conflict[4]. Fourthly, flexible relief may be available under s 61 of the Trustee Act 1925. Fifthly, in Canada[5], Australia[6], and New Zealand[7] there are suggestions that equity in its discretion in particular circumstances should not automatically impose a constructive trust but a lesser remedy such as a lien or a personal liability to account; the policy underlying liability should help determine what remedies will best further that policy and the honesty and solvency of the defendant should be important factors.

1   See *Industrial Development Consultants Ltd v Cooley* [1972] 2 All ER 162; *Jones v AMP Perpetual Trustee Co* [1994] 1 NZLR 690.
2   *Queensland Mines v Hudson* (1978) 52 ALJR 399; *New Zealand Netherlands Society Oranje Inc v Kuys* [1973] 1 WLR 1126; *Arklow Investments Ltd v Maclean* [2000] 1 WLR 594.
3   *Boardman v Phipps* [1967] 2 AC 46; *O'Sullivan v Management Agency & Music Ltd* [1985] QB 428; *Re Badfinger* [2001] WTLR 1 at 13–17; *Chirnside v Fay* [2006] NZSC 68; see paras 58.25–58.30.
4   [1990] 2 AC 663 at 701, followed in eg *Quarter Master UK Ltd (in liq) v Pyke* [2004] EWHC 1815 (Ch), [2005] 1 BCLC 245 at [76]–[77], though cf *Nottingham University v Fishel* [2000] ICR 1462 at 1499–1500. The Australian courts have been more generous: see eg *Llewellyn v Derrick* (1999) 33 ACSR 213; *Say-Dee Pty Ltd v Farah Constructions Pty Ltd* [2005] NSWCA 309 at [252].
5   *Lac Minerals Ltd v International Corona Resources Ltd* (1989) 61 DLR (4th) 14; *Canson Enterprises Ltd v Boughton* (1991) 85 DLR (4th) 129.
6   *Chan v Zacariah* (1984) 154 CLR 178 at 204–205.
7   *Official Assignee of Collier v Creighton* [1993] 2 NZLR 534, CA.

33.104 Finally, the suggestion has also been made that in some circumstances the courts should apply a remoteness rule to cap the gains for which a fiduciary should account. This may be the best explanation of the High Court of Australia's decision in *Warman International Ltd v Dwyer*[1]. Warman was the distribution agent for an Italian company that manufactured gearboxes. In breach of fiduciary duty, Warman's employee, Dwyer, formed a joint venture with the Italian manufacturer in competition with his employer, and made substantial profits. The question arose whether Dwyer and his associated companies should account for all of these profits, and the court held not, ordering them instead to account only for the profits made in the first two years of business.

1   (1995) 182 CLR 544.

33.105 In his dissenting judgment in *Murad v Al-Saraj* Clarke LJ interpreted *Warman* to mean that a 'but-for' causation test can sometimes be used to determine the scope of a fiduciary's liability to account. His Lordship considered that proof of this lay in the attention paid by the court to the trial judge's finding that Warman's business relationship with the Italian manufacturer would have continued for about another year if Dwyer had not breached his duty[1]. However, a different view of the case is possible – namely, that the court effectively held that the profits made by Dwyer and his companies after the first two years were too remote a consequence of his breach of duty to justify ordering them to account for these subsequent profits. On this view, the significance of the trial judge's finding about the counterfactual was that it provided the court with one means of assessing the point in time at which the defendant's gains could fairly be attributed to his own efforts rather than his breach of duty[2].

1   [2005] WTLR 1537 at [154].
2   Cf *3464920 Canada Inc v Strother* (2005) 7 ITELR 748 at [60], British Columbia CA. There Newbury JA considered that the time-limited order made in *Warman* reflected 'the dilution of the causal link' between the defendant's breach and the gains accruing in his hands. However, this presupposes a sliding scale of causative potency which is hard to conceptualise, and which is difficult to reconcile with the all-or-nothing nature of the standard causation test, discussed above at para 33.84.

33.106 This interpretation of *Warman* was adopted in a recent Hong Kong case, *Kao Lee & Yip v Koo Hoi Yan*[1]. The defendant was a partner in the claimant solicitors' firm. One of the firm's major clients was the Bank of China. The defendant advised the bank to set up a law centre which would provide the bank and its customers with legal services. However, the bank opted to use the services of a 'friendly outside law firm'. The defendant left the claimant firm and set up a new firm of his own, with the help of the bank which took its custom to the defendant's new firm. Ma J held that this diversion of the bank business to the new firm constituted a breach of the defendant's fiduciary duty to his former partners. However, he declined to order the defendant to account for all the profits of the bank business. He held that 'the duty to account is not completely open-ended'[2], and he cited *Warman* for the proposition that:[3]

> 'in some cases there comes a point when the profits of the relevant business are so remote from the breach of the fiduciary duty that it would simply be unfair to force the fiduciary to continue to account.'

1   [2003] 2 HKC 113.
2   [2003] 2 HKC 113 at [139].
3   [2003] 2 HKC 113 at [143]. *Watson v Holyoake* (1986) 15 CPC (2d) 262 at [353] is to the same effect.

33.107 Ma J concluded on the facts that it would only be appropriate to award an account for one year, on the basis that thereafter profits would be too far away from the wrongful diversion of the bank business[1]. One reason for reaching this conclusion was that the bank would only have given its business to the claimant for a year even if the defendant had not breached his fiduciary duty, but the judge was at pains to stress that this was 'not relevant as far as deciding whether an account of profits should be ordered' but was merely an 'aid' in deciding how long the account should extend for'[2].

1   [2003] 2 HKC 113 at [157].
2   [2003] 2 HKC 113 at [158].

'Chinese Walls' or information barriers

33.108 To avoid conflicts of interests and liabilities arising therefrom large companies or firms may well erect physical or geographical barriers between particular departments to try to deal with the general rule that the knowledge of a company or firm depends on the knowledge of all its employees with authority to acquire or receive such knowledge[1], although one cannot put the knowledge of one employee in one department together with the knowledge of another employee in a separate department where each acts honestly so as to conclude that the company acted dishonestly because, had the two employees pooled their information, they would have discovered an act was dishonest[2].

1   *Lloyds Bank Ltd v Savory & Co* [1933] AC 201; *Harrods Ltd v Lemon* [1931] 2 KB 157; *El Ajou v Dollar Land Holdings plc* [1994] 2 All ER 238, CA.
2   *Galmerrow Securities Ltd v National Westminster Bank* [2002] WTLR 125.

33.109 In the case of solicitors and of accountants providing litigation support services they owe a continuing professional duty to a former client following termination of the client relationship to preserve the confidentiality of information imparted during the relationship. Such former client can obtain an injunction preventing the professional firm from acting for someone with an adverse interest to him, assuming it is shown that the firm is in possession of confidential information, unless the firm can prove effective measures had been taken to ensure no disclosure would occur and there was no risk of the information coming into the possession of those acting for the other client. The risk must be a real one, and not merely fanciful or theoretical, but it need not be substantial. There is a presumption that unless special measures are taken information moves within a firm. The court should restrain the firm from acting for the other client unless there is clear and convincing evidence that effective measures have been taken to ensure the other client receives no confidential information[1]. An effective Chinese wall needs to be an established part of the organisational structure of the firm, not artificially created ad hoc and dependent on the acceptance of evidence sworn for the purpose by persons engaged in the relevant work[2]. However, no Chinese wall can affect the situation as between existing clients due to the inescapable conflict of interest inherent in such situation, which is also the case where a trustee will be contravening the fundamental rule against self-dealing[3] (in purchasing trust property for himself or selling his own property to the trust). If it is only the fair-dealing rule[4] that applies (as where a trustee purchases the beneficial interest of a beneficiary) then a Chinese wall can help to show that no advantage was taken of the trustee's position and the transaction was proper and reasonable.

1   *Bolkiah v KPMG* [1999] 2 AC 222, HL
2   *Re Firm of Solicitors* [2000] 1 Lloyd's Rep 31 (effective Chinese wall); also see *Halewood International v Addleshaw Booth* [2000] Lloyd's Rep PN 298. Further see C Hollander & S Salzedo *Conflicts of Interest and Chinese Walls* (2000, Sweet & Maxwell) and review thereof by Waller LJ in (2001) 117 LQR 335–340; *Laker Airways v FLS Aerospace Ltd* [2000] 1 WLR 113; *Koch Shipping Inc v Richards Butler* [2002] Lloyd's Rep PN 201; *Marks and Spencer plc v Freshfields Bruckhaus Deringer* [2004] EWHC 1337 (Ch), [2004] 3 All ER 773; *GUS Consulting GmbH v Leboeuf Lamb Greene & Macrae* [2006] PNLR 32.
3   See para 59.4.
4   See para 59.44.

ARTICLE 34
CONSTRUCTIVE TRUSTS IMPOSED ON TRUST ASSETS OR THEIR
TRACEABLE PROCEEDS RECEIVED BY STRANGERS TO THE TRUST

34.1

Equity imposes a constructive trust upon trust or other property subject to a fiduciary relationship or upon its traceable product where such property has wrongfully been transferred by the fiduciary to a stranger, so long as the stranger is not protected by statutory over-reaching provisions[1] or exceptions to the rule *nemo dat quod non habet*[2] or the defence of change of position[3] or is not a bona fide purchaser of a legal interest for value without notice or a registered proprietor of land protected under the Land Registration Act 1925 or 2002[4]. However, the stranger only becomes subject to personal duties and liabilities from the time he knows of the claimant's proprietary interest or would have known but for turning a blind eye to what would otherwise be obvious or from the time when his suspicions were aroused that the transfer to him might well have been improper but he deliberately or recklessly failed to make the inquiries an honest and reasonable person would make in the circumstances[5].

1   Law of Property Act 1925, ss 2, 27.
2   Eg Factors Act 1889, Sale of Goods Act 1979, Hire Purchase Act 1964.
3   See paras 100.82–100.86.
4   LRA 1925, ss 5, 9, 20(1), 23(1), 59(6) or LRA 2002, ss 11, 12, 28, 29 and 30.
5   *Re Montagu's Settlement* [1987] Ch 264; *Westdeutsche Landesbank v Islington London Borough Council* [1996] AC 669 at 705–707; *Re Diplock* [1948] Ch 465 at 478, CA.

34.2 The foundation for the fundamental principle enshrined in the above Article is based on the property law rules for the priorities of competing interests supplemented by the equitable tracing rules discussed in Article 103. If T holds property on trust for A for life, remainder to B absolutely, but wrongfully makes a gift of it to G, who subsequently sells it and purchases with the proceeds a valuable painting, then the court will treat the gifted property as held on constructive trust by G from the moment of receipt[1] so that any income arising therefrom will similarly be held on constructive trust, as will the proceeds of sale and, then, the painting[2]. Thus G, when the facts are discovered, must account to A and B for everything that has happened in respect of the property since he received it, thereby assisting them in their proprietary claim via the tracing process. However, as Millett J has observed[3]:

> 'It is a mistake to suppose that in every situation in which a constructive trust arises the legal owner is necessarily subject to all the fiduciary obligations and disabilities of an express trustee.'

1   See *Re Sharpe* [1980] 1 All ER 198 at 203h; *A-G for Hong Kong v Reid* [1994] 1 AC 324 at 331; *Guinness v Saunders* [1990] 2 AC 663 at 696 and 701; Lord Millett in (1998) 114 LQR 399 at 402, 404–406.
2   See Article 103.
3   *Lonhro plc v Al Fayed (No 2)* [1992] 1 WLR 1 at 12. Further see his remarks in (1998) 114 LQR 399 at 404–406.

34.3 Lord Browne-Wilkinson has also made it clear[1] that no personal liability to account ('as a constructive trustee' in the old misleading terminology) can arise until the defendant's conscience is affected by actual 'Nelsonian' or 'naughty'[2] knowledge of the claimant's interest[3]. Thus, so long as G remains an innocent volunteer without cognisance of the trust, he will owe no duties to safeguard or sensibly invest the property[4] and he will have the defence of change of position available to him[5].

1   *Westdeutsche Landesbank v Islington London Borough Council* [1996] AC 669 at 705–707. Indeed he would prefer the recipient subject to the claimant's equitable interest from the time of receipt not to be termed a constructive trustee until the time he becomes personally liable but to be treated just like a transferee of land subject to an equitable charge or easement or restrictive covenant. However, since he is subject to equitable interests of beneficiaries under a trust it seems reasonably preferable to regard him as a constructive trustee for such beneficiaries from the outset. See para 29.8 above.

2   This arises, where, despite being suspicious, the defendant deliberately or recklessly fails to make the inquiries an honest reasonable person would make: see paras 100.72–100.74 below.
3   As in eg *Campden Hill Ltd v Chakrani* [2005] EWHC 911 (Ch), [2005] All ER (D) 238 (May).
4   *Re Diplock* [1948] Ch 465 at 477–479, *Re Montagu's Settlement* [1987] 2 WLR 1192 at 1211.
5   See paras 100.82–100.86 below.

34.4 If G were a purchaser and not a donee then he could take advantage of any statutory protection accorded to purchasers or the defence of bona fide purchaser of a legal interest without notice, if such defence be not ousted by statute as in the case of registered land. In the commercial context, not involving the conveyancing aspects of the purchase of land the courts are very reluctant to inhibit commercial dealings, so that a purchaser will only be treated as having constructive notice if he turned a Nelsonian blind eye to what would otherwise be obvious or if he deliberately or recklessly failed to make the inquiries that an honest, reasonable man would have made, though considering that there was something suspicious about the honesty of the circumstances but not wanting to probe matters for fear of what he might then discover[1]. In the case of the purchase of unregistered land there are well-established standard procedures that justify treating a purchaser as having constructive notice of those matters he would have discovered if he had followed such procedures rather than negligently failed to do so[2]. In the case of registered land[3] the new registered proprietor for value of the land or a charge over the land will not take subject to interests of beneficiaries unless they are protected by entry on the register or by being overriding interests or by the application of the principle that equity will not allow a statute to be used as an instrument of fraud[4].

1   *Polly Peck International plc v Nadir (No 2)* [1992] 4 All ER 769, at 778–779.
2   Law of Property Act 1925, s 199.
3   Land Registration Act 1925, ss 5, 9, 20, 23, 70; LRA 2002, ss 11, 12, 28, 29, 30, Schs 1 and 3.
4   *Lyus v Prowsa Developments Ltd* [1982] 1 WLR 1044.

ARTICLE 35
CONSTRUCTIVE TRUSTS IMPOSED ON PROPERTY TO PREVENT
FRAUDULENT OR UNCONSCIONABLE CONDUCT

35.1

(1)   Equity imposes a constructive trust upon property which a person might attempt to obtain or retain for himself exclusively (or might prevent the equitable interest therein passing to persons for whom he had agreed to hold the property[1]) by fraudulently or unconscionably taking advantage of statutory provisions[2] or other fundamental legal principles, eg the *ius accrescendi* in a joint tenancy and the need for certainty of subject-matter of trusts. The constructive trust will be in favour of those to whose disadvantage the invocation of the provisions or principles would otherwise operate.

(2) In particular, but without prejudice to the generality of the foregoing, equity imposes a constructive trust on property:

(a) where it was the common but otherwise unenforceable intention (due to non-compliance with formalities requirements) or understanding, express or inferred (but not imputed) of the proprietor and the claimant that the claimant was to have some beneficial interest in the property and the claimant acted to his detriment in reliance thereon;

(b) where two persons, concerned with disposing of their estates on their death, enter into a contractual arrangement to subject property to a legally binding arrangement and make mutual wills pursuant to the arrangement, which is intended irrevocably to take effect on the first death, and that death occurs without the survivor having repudiated the arrangement to the deceased's knowledge (it would seem in sufficient time to enable the deceased to alter his will);

(c) where, on D's death, T becomes entitled to property, arranged by D to pass to T under D's will or intestacy, on the understanding that T is to hold on trust for a beneficiary or beneficiaries where otherwise the trust would fail for lack of compliance with formalities requirements;

(d) where a donor having legal title to property does everything he needs to do to transfer that title to a donee and that donee has not become registered with that legal title or where the donor has made an effective *donatio mortis cansa* without having effectively vested legal title in the donee;

(e) where such property would otherwise belong to a person involved in an unlawful killing as a result of his crime (eg benefiting under his victim's will or intestacy or assurance policy or a joint tenancy with the victim);

(f) where a transferor's legal and beneficial title to his property has passed to the transferee according to basic principles of property law but in circumstances (eg involving fraud, misrepresentation, mistake, undue influence) where the transferor has an equitable right (ie a mere equity) to recover the property by having the transfer set aside, and the court declares that the property must be transferred *in specie* to the transferor;

(g) where money has been received by an agent and it would be unconscionable for the agent to claim beneficial title against the principal having regard to the insolvency problems of the agent when there is no express, or *Quistclose* resulting trust for the principal;

(h) where property not owned by the seller when he contracted to assign it to the purchaser is received by the seller, having already received the consideration from the purchaser.

1   For example, secret trusts and mutual wills.
2   For example, Wills Act 1837; Law of Property Act 1925, s 53; Administration of Estates Act 1925, s 46.

Paragraph 1

Fraudulent or unconscionable abuse of statutory provisions

35.2 Where statute has prescribed formalities for wills and for dispositions of land the courts have long applied the maxim, 'Equity will not allow a statute to be used as an instrument of fraud'. Thus, as has been seen in dealing with secret trusts[1], an apparently absolutely entitled beneficiary on the face of a will can be compelled to hold his legacy on a trust communicated to him and accepted by him before the testator's death: it would be fraudulent for him to retain the property for himself. A person taking as trustee on the face of a will, disclosing no beneficiaries for whom the trustee is to hold the willed property, can be compelled to hold for beneficiaries disclosed to him outside the will before or at the time the testator made the will: as a trustee he cannot retain the property for himself, but it would be unconscionable to deny the secret beneficiaries their benefits which, but for the trustee agreeing to carry out the testator's wishes, would have been secured to them by other means. Indeed, in *Bulkley v Wilford*[2] a solicitor had his client enter into a transaction (levying a fine) that revoked the client's will but failed to advise the client to make a new will. The solicitor then happened to benefit upon the intestacy of his client. The House of Lords held it would be unconscionable if the solicitor were to do anything other than hold his interest in his client's estate for the beneficiaries under the revoked will.

1   See para 12.80 above.
2   (1834) 2 CL & Fin 102.

35.3 In an inter vivos disposition case, *Bannister v Bannister*[1], a constructive trust was imposed by the Court of Appeal upon the defendant cottage owner to hold the cottage for the plaintiff for life: the defendant failed in his claim that the absence of a written declaration of trust enabled him to take free of the life interest he had orally agreed the plaintiff was to have when she sold him the cottage and an adjoining property at a lower price than would have otherwise been the case.

1   [1948] 2 All ER 133. The plaintiff was held to be a Settled Land Act tenant for life and the Court of Appeal by a majority followed this in *Binions v Evans* [1972] Ch 359, [1972] 2 All ER 70. See also *Ungurian v Lesnoff* [1990] Ch 206.

35.4 However, it appears from *Hodgson v Marks*[1] that a plaintiff can plead as alternatives the application of the equitable principle that equity will not allow a statute to be used as an instrument of fraud and the imposition of a constructive trust.

1   [1971] Ch 892, [1971] 2 All ER 684.

35.5 Neither alternative plea will succeed where the statute (eg the Land Charges Act 1972, the Land Registration Act 1925, the Companies Act 1985) expressly requires certain interests to be registered or protected by entry on a register upon pain of a purchaser taking property free from such interests. It is not fraudulent or unconscionable for a purchaser[1] to take advantage of his strict statutory rights by relying on the absence of the registration or protection stipulated for in the statute[2] unless he misled the plaintiff so as to make it unconscionable to allow him to insist on the position being different from what he led the plaintiff to believe[3].

[1] There must be a genuine purchaser and not someone agreeing to take property as trustee for the unprotected person or someone who is the alter ego of the vendor endeavouring to evade the grasp of the unprotected person: *Peffer v Rigg* [1978] 3 All ER 745, [1977] 1 WLR 285 though probably erroneous on another point which cannot now stand with *Williams & Glyn's Bank Ltd v Boland* [1981] AC 487, [1980] 2 All ER 408, HL and see [1977] Camb LJ 227 and [1978] LQR 239; *Jones v Lipman* [1962] 1 All ER 442, [1962] 1 WLR 832.

[2] *Hollington Bros Ltd v Rhodes* [1951] 2 TLR 691; *Miles v Bull (No 2)* [1969] 3 All ER 1585; *Kitney v MEPC Ltd* [1978] 1 All ER 595, [1977] 1 WLR 981; *De Lusignan v Johnson* (1973) 230 Estates Gazette 499; *Re Monolithic Building Co* [1915] 1 Ch 643; *Midland Bank Trust Co Ltd v Green* [1981] AC 513, [1981] 1 All ER 153, HL; *Lloyds Bank plc v Carrick* [1996] 4 All ER 630, CA.

[3] *Lyus v Prowsa Developments Ltd* [1982] 1 WLR 1044; *Taylor Fashions Ltd v Liverpool Victoria Trustees Co Ltd* [1982] QB 133n.

Fraudulent or unconscionable use of property principles

35.6 Just as A cannot take advantage of the *ius accrescendi* of a joint tenant by killing B, where A and B hold land on trust for themselves as joint tenants, so as to claim the land exclusively for himself[1], so A cannot evict B where B merely has a contractual licence over land purchased by A from X if A had positively undertaken with X to take such land subject to B's contractual licence, thereby paying X a lower price and saving X from being sued by B for breach of contract[2]. Although, as a matter of property law, a contractual licence is not an interest in property capable of binding third parties like A, equity will regard B as having a right personally binding A's conscience so that A will be compelled to recognise B's personal rights under the contractual licence[3]. This would also seem to be the case if A's undertaking had been with B and caused B to act to his detriment[4].

[1] *Rasmanis v Jurewitsch* [1968] 2 NSWLR 166; *Re Stone* [1989] 1 QHR 351.
[2] *Ashburn Anstalt v Arnold* [1989] Ch 1, [1988] 2 All ER 147, CA. Further see Contracts (Rights of Third Parties) Act 1999.
[3] *Ashburn Anstalt v Arnold* [1989] Ch 1, [1988] 2 All ER 147, CA.
[4] Equitable estoppel principles come into play here: see para 12.47 ff.

35.7 However, if V sells property to P and in defensive fashion makes the sale subject to such property rights, if any, that B may happen to have, so as to satisfy V's obligations to disclose all possible incumbrances and so protect V against possible claims from P, then P is not bound by B's rights as a contractual licensee which are merely personal and not proprietary. In other words it is essential that P must have agreed to confer a new right on C: he must have 'undertaken a new obligation, not otherwise existing, to give effect to the relevant incumbrance or prior interest. If, but only if, he has undertaken such a new obligation will a constructive trust be imposed[1].' This new right may give C the same rights against P as he would have enjoyed against V, had V never sold the land. But it may also protect C even if C had no right against V eg because he failed to register his interest[2], and equally if C's valid right against V was destroyed by the transfer to P[3].

1   *Lloyd v Dugdale* [2001] EWCA Civ 1754, [2002] 2 P & CR 167 at [52] per Sir Christopher Slade.
2   *Lyus v Prowsa Developments Ltd* [1982] 1 WLR 1044; *Bahr v Nicolay (No 2)* (1988) 62 ALJR 268 at 288–9 per Brennan J; *IDC Group Ltd v Clark* [1992] 1 EGLR 187 at 190.
3   *Melbury Road Properties 1995 Ltd v Kreidi* [1999] 3 EGLR 10; *Lloyd v Dugdale* [2001] EWCA Civ 1754, [2002] 2 P & CR 167.

35.8 Where a defendant unconscionably tries to take advantage of uncertainty of subject matter of a trust (eg a trust of a 'fair share' of a house) the court will not allow him such advantage but find some means to prevent it (eg somehow ascertain a fair share in all the circumstances[1]). Similarly, the court will intervene to prevent a defendant claiming to be absolute beneficial owner of a property acquired by him in furtherance of a pre-acquisition unenforceable[2] arrangement with the claimant for the claimant to acquire some interest in the property: the advantage to the defendant or the detriment of the claimant makes it unconscionable to allow the defendant to retain the property for himself inconsistently with the arrangement which enabled him to acquire it[3]. If the defendant cannot agree with the claimant what precise part of the property should be held on trust for the claimant or be transferred to the claimant, then the court will order a sale of the property and, usually, an equal division of the proceeds[4].

1   *Passee v Passee* [1988] 1 FLR 263 at 271; *Stokes v Anderson* [1991] 1 FLR 391, CA.
2   Whether because not contractual or too uncertain.
3   *Banner Homes Group plc v Luff Developments Ltd* [2000] Ch 372, CA; *Cox v Jones* [2004] EWHC 1486 (Ch), [2004] 2 FLR 1010; *Kinane v Mackie-Conteh* [2005] WTLR 345; *Kilcarne Holdings Ltd v Targetfollow (Birmingham) Ltd* [2005] EWCA Civ 1355, [2006] 1 P & CR D55; *Yeomans Row Management Ltd v Cobbe* [2006] EWCA Civ 1139. No trust will be imposed if the parties have expressly agreed not to be bound unless and until formal contracts have been exchanged, because where they have expressly negatived an intention to create legal intentions, equity should follow the law in declining to place them under legally enforceable obligations: *London & Regional Investments Ltd v TBI plc* [2002] EWCA Civ 355, [2002] All ER (D) 360.
4   *Pallant v Morgan* [1952] 2 All ER 951, [1953] Ch 43; *Banner Homes Group plc v Luff Developments Ltd* [2000] Ch 372 at 388, 391, 393 and 396,CA.

Paragraph 2(a)

Common intention constructive trusts

35.9 A constructive trust may be imposed on specific property, such as a house in M's name, in order to give effect to an express or inferred common intention of M and W (whether at the time of the purchase or subsequently[1]) that W is to have a beneficial interest therein, so leading W to act to her detriment in reliance on that intention, so making it unconscionable to allow M to deny W any interest by pleading the lack of the necessary written formalities for a valid declaration of trust[2] or contract[3]. In such circumstances, the positive common intention can oust any prima facie resulting trust treating M and W as acquiring the shares they paid for at the time they completed the purchase with their saved, inherited or borrowed money, so that if M bought the house in his name with a mortgage (in his name, of course) having paid the deposit with his money, he will be sole legal beneficial owner, though if W provided the deposit and at the outset undertook with M to provide all the mortgage payment M will hold on resulting trust for her[4].

1 *Austin v Keele* (1987) 61 ALJR 605, PC; *Lloyds Bank plc v Rosset* [1991] 1 AC 107 at 132.
2 *Yaxley v Gotts* [2000] Ch 162.
3 *Lloyds Bank plc v Rosset* [1991] 1 AC 107, [1990] 1 All ER 1111, HL; *Gissing v Gissing* [1971] AC 886, [1970] 2 All ER 780, HL; *Burns v Burns* [1984] Ch 317, [1984] 1 All ER 244, CA; *Grant v Edwards* [1986] Ch 638, [1986] 2 All ER 426 approved by PC in *Maharaj v Chand* [1986] 3 WLR 440 at 446, PC.
4 *Ivin v Blake* (1994) 67 P & CR 263, CA and see para 31.5.

35.10 If the common intention was that W was to have a specific interest, eg a half or a quarter, or a share to be quantified on sale of the house or earlier separation of the parties as a fair share[1], taking account of W's financial contributions or their real and substantial equivalent to the acquisition of the house (without penalising her or him when prevented from making their usual contributions eg because of childbirth or illness), there will be a constructive trust of the specified share or of a fair share. Case law based on Lord Diplock's leading speech in *Gissing v Gissing* tends to stress the element of common intention and detrimental reliance thereon so as to impose a constructive trust, rather than a resulting trust, since the flexibility of constructive trust principles affords more scope for achieving a just result.

1 *Gissing v Gissing* [1971] AC 886 at 909, [1970] 2 All ER 780, HL; *Burns v Burns* [1984] Ch 317 at 327, [1984] 1 All ER 244 at 251, CA; *Grant v Edwards* [1986] Ch 638, [1986] 2 All ER 426; *Stokes v Anderson* [1991] 1 FLR 391, CA

35.11 Indeed, Lord Denning developed what he called 'a constructive trust of a new model'[1] by imposing a constructive trust 'whenever justice and good conscience required it'[2]: 'the shares may be half and half or any such other proportion as in the circumstances of the case appears to be fair and just'[3]. He was able to do this by imputing or ascribing to the parties a common intention they ought to have formed as reasonable persons if they had thought about the matter. This ignored what the House of Lords, and Lord Diplock in particular, had laid down in *Gissing v Gissing*[4]. The Court of Appeal in *Burns v Burns*[5] and *Grant v Edwards*[6] and the House of Lords in *Lloyds Bank plc v Rosset*[7] have now rejected Lord Denning's views and made it very clear that if there is no express or inferred common intention then the court cannot impute or ascribe a common intention to the parties in an attempt to produce a fair and just result. However, the principles underlying proprietary estoppel may provide some flexibility in the light of Lord Oliver's view[8] that, 'in essence, the common intention doctrine is an application of proprietary estoppel,' Lord Browne-Wilkinson's preference[9] for the use of proprietary estoppel and Lord Bridge's three references[10] to 'constructive trust or proprietary estoppel,' as if they both arise wherever there is a common intention followed by detrimental reliance, in his speech in *Lloyds Bank plc v Rosset* (with which the other Lords simply concurred). He there laid down[11]:

> 'Neither a common intention that a house is to be renovated as a joint venture nor a common intention that the house is to be shared by parents and children as the family home throws any light on their intentions with respect to the beneficial ownership of the property ...
>
> The first and fundamental question which must always be resolved is whether, independently of any inference to be drawn from the conduct of the parties, there has at any time prior to acquisition, or exceptionally at some later date, been any agreement, arrangement or understanding reached between them that the property is to be shared beneficially. The finding of an agreement or arrangement to share in this sense can only be based on evidence of express discussions between the partners, however imperfectly remembered and however imprecise their terms may have been. Once a finding to this effect is made it will only be necessary for the partner asserting a claim to a beneficial interest against the partner entitled to the legal estate to show that he or she has acted to his or her detriment or significantly altered his or her position in reliance on the agreement in order to give rise to a constructive trust or proprietary estoppel.
>
> In sharp contrast with this situation is the very different one where there is no evidence to support a finding of an agreement or arrangement to share however reasonable it might have been for the parties to reach such an agreement if they had applied their minds to the question, and where the court must rely entirely on the conduct of the parties both as the basis from which to infer a common intention to share the property beneficially and as the conduct relied on to give rise to a constructive trust. In this situation direct contributions to the purchase price by the partner who is not the legal owner, whether initially or by payment of mortgage instalments, will readily justify the inference necessary to the creation of a constructive trust. But, as I read the authorities, it is at least extremely doubtful whether anything less will do.'

1   *Eves v Eves* [1975] 3 All ER 768 at 771.
2   *Hussey v Palmer* [1972] 3 All ER 744 at 747, CA. Also see *Hardwick v Johnson* [1978] 2 All ER 935 at 938, CA.
3   *Bernard v Josephs* [1982] Ch 391 at 399, [1982] 3 All ER 162 at 167, CA, where he erroneously treated *Hine v Hine* [1962] 3 All ER 345, [1962] 1 WLR 1124, CA discredited by *Pettitt v Pettitt* [1970] AC 777, [1969] 2 All ER 385, HL as still being good law.
4   [1971] AC 886 at 898, 900, 904, [1970] 2 All ER 780 at 784, 786, 789.
5   [1984] Ch 317, [1984] 1 All ER 244, CA.
6   [1986] Ch 638, [1986] 2 All ER 426 accepted by PC in *Maharaj v Chand* [1986] AC 898, at 907, PC.
7   [1991] 1 AC 107, [1990] 1 All ER 1111.
8   *Austin v Keele* (1987) 61 ALJR 605 at 609, PC.
9   *Grant v Edwards* [1986] Ch 638, (1991) Birmingham University Holdsworth Lecture, 'Constructive trusts and unjust enrichment', published in (1996) 10 Trust LI 98. Also see Nicholls LJ in *Lloyds Bank v Rosset* [1989] Ch 350 at 387.
10 [1991] 1 AC 107 at 129, 132 and 133; [1990] 1 All ER 1111 at 1116 and 1119. Further on equation of constructive trusts and proprietary estoppel see *Yaxley v Gotts* [2000] Ch 162 at 176, CA and *Birmingham Midshires Mortgage Services v Sabherwal* (1999) 80 P & CR 256 at 263 and for a flexible approach to detrimental reliance see *Gillett v Holt* [2001] Ch 210, CA.
11 [1991] 1 AC 107 at 130 and 132–133. It matters not that the man does not have legal title himself but has it vested in a company he controls: *Re Schuppan* [1997] 1 BCLC 256 at 268.

Express common intention

35.12 Lord Bridge placed primary emphasis on searching for express agreement arising out of express discussions, so that in *Hammond v Mitchell*[1] Waite J emphasised that as much particularity as possible of such discussion should be pleaded, although this 'means that the tenderest exchanges of courtship may assume an unforeseen significance many years later when they are brought under equity's microscope and subjected to an analysis under which many thousands of pounds of value may be liable to turn on fine questions as to whether the words were spoken in earnest or in dalliance and with or without representational effect.'

1 [1991] 1 WLR 1127 at 1139.

35.13 As Lord Diplock emphasised in *Gissing v Gissing*[1]:

'The relevant intention of each party is the intention which was reasonably understood by the other party to be manifested by that party's words or conduct, notwithstanding that he did not consciously formulate that intention in his own mind or even acted with some different intention which he did not communicate to the other party. On the other hand, he is not bound by any inference which the other party draws as to his intention unless that inference is one that can reasonably be drawn from his words or conduct.'

1 [1971] AC 886 at 906, [1970] 2 All ER 780 at 790, HL; *Burns v Burns* [1984] Ch 317 at 336, [1984] 1 All ER 244 at 258, CA.

35.14 There will thus be sufficient direct evidence of an express common intention not just where the parties treated the house as 'our house' and had 'a principle of sharing everything'[1], but also where the man put up an excuse for not putting the house in joint names which he says he would otherwise have done[2]: if there was no apparent common intention that the woman was to have a proprietary interest then the man would not have needed to put up an excuse[3]. The court will consider the parties' common intention when the property was initially purchased but a subsequent common intention will suffice if followed by detrimental reliance[4]. When ascertaining the parties' common intention the court will view their discussions in the round and will not focus on one aspect of their arrangements to the exclusion of others[5]. Note, though, that it does not suffice that each party happened separately to form the same intention because a common intention means one that is communicated between them[6].

1 *Midland Bank plc v Dobson and Dobson* [1986] 1 FLR 171, [1986] Fam Law 55, 75, CA.
2 *Eves v Eves* [1975] 3 All ER 768, [1975] 1 WLR 1338, CA (alleged 20 year old girl needed to be 21 to have house in joint names); *Grant v Edwards* [1986] Ch 638, [1986] 2 All ER 426 (alleged her matrimonial proceedings be prejudiced if house put in joint names); *Hammond v Mitchell* [1991] 1 WLR 1127 (in his sole name for tax reasons, though he also said, 'Don't worry about the future because when we are married it will be half yours anyway').
3 However, note the criticisms made of this reasoning in Gardner (1993) 109 LQR 263, which Lawrence Collins J thought were well taken in *Van Laethem v Brooker* [2005] EWHC 1478 (Ch), [2006] 1 FCR 697 at [64]–[67].
4 *Bernard v Josephs* [1982] Ch 391 at 404, [1982] 3 All ER 162 at 171; *Burns v Burns* [1984] Ch 317, [1984] 1 All ER 244 at 251, CA. *Austin v Keele* (1987) 61 ALJR 605, PC. The legal owner must implicitly agree that the contributor of finance is to be a purchaser

and not a donor for 'It has been well settled that if A expends money on the property of B prima facie he has no claim on such property': *Pettitt v Pettitt* [1970] AC 777 at 818, HL, per Lord Diplock and *Davis v Vale* [1971] 1 WLR 1022 at 1025, CA, per Lord Denning.

5   *Vinaver v Milton Ashbery Ltd* [2006] EWCA Civ 363, where D's stated intention that C should have an option to purchase had to be read against his further statements, and her concurring statements, that she should have a beneficial interest.

6   *Springette v Defoe* (1992) 24 HLR 552, CA. Also *Mollo v Mollo* [2001] WTLR 227 at 241–242; *Lightfoot v Lightfoot-Brown* [2005] EWCA Civ 201, [2005] WTLR 1031, CA.

Inferred common intention

35.15 In inferring a common intention from the conduct of the parties the court must look at the true state of affairs and cannot impute to the parties an intention they never actually possessed[1]. However, in the case of a couple who are married or engaged, s 37 of the Matrimonial Proceedings and Property Act 1970 is available to enable the contributor in money or money's worth to acquire a share or an enlarged share in the property, depending on the extent to which it seems just to the court, eg the share represented by the value added by the contribution[2].

1   *Grant v Edwards* [1986] Ch 638, [1986] 2 All ER 426, *Lloyds Bank plc v Rosset* [1991] 1 AC 107.
2   See para 31.6 above.

35.16 Much significance has to be given to the obiter dicta of Lord Bridge (with whose speech the other Lords simply concurred) in *Lloyds Bank v Rosset*[1]. Here H and W decided to buy as their family home a derelict farmhouse for £57,000 using money provided by trustees of a family trust for H (inter alia) and who insisted that the property be bought in H's name alone. Without W's knowledge H mortgaged the property to Lloyds Bank to secure a £15,000 loan with interest. W spent some time supervising builders doing renovation work, did some preparatory cleaning work herself and some painting and decorating. It was held that there was no express common intention that W was to have an interest but even if there had been, the value of her work in relation to a farmhouse costing £72,000 was so trifling (as to be almost de minimis) that there was 'considerable doubt'[2] whether such work would amount to detrimental reliance linked to acquisition of the property so as to support a constructive trust[3]:

> 'In these circumstances [of trying to have the home ready for occupation by Christmas] it would seem the most natural thing in the world for any wife, in the absence of her husband [a courier] abroad, to spend all the time she could spare and to employ any skills she might have in doing all she could to accelerate progress of the work, quite irrespective of any expectation she might have of enjoying a beneficial interest in the property. The judge's view that some of this work was work "on which she could not reasonably have been expected to embark unless she was to have an interest in the house" seems to me quite untenable.'

1   [1991] 1 AC 107, [1990] 1 All ER 1111.
2   [1991] 1 AC 107 at 131 and 1118.
3   [1991] 1 AC 107 at 131, [1990] 1 All ER 1111 at 1118.

35.17 Thus, there could be no inferred common intention. In the situation where the court must rely entirely on the conduct of the parties both as the basis from which to infer a common intention to share the property beneficially and as the detrimental conduct relied upon to give rise to a constructive trust[1]:

> 'direct contributions to the purchase price by the partner who is not the legal owner, whether initially or by payment of mortgage instalments, will readily justify the inference necessary to the creation of a constructive trust. But, as I read the authorities, it is at least extremely doubtful whether anything less will do'.

[1]   [1991] 1 AC 107 at 133 and 1119.

35.18 Of course, initial payments will give rise to a resulting trust anyhow[1], while some consider that subsequent mortgage payments can create or enlarge a share under a resulting trust by being regarded as deferred payment of the price (rather than repayment of the moneys paid as the purchase price to the purchaser on completion of the purchase), though the better view is that for subsequent mortgage payments to displace the resulting trust shares arising at the time of purchase there must be a common intention to such effect[2].

[1]   See para 31.2 above.
[2]   See paras 31.5–31.6 above; *Bernard v Josephs* [1982] Ch 391 at 404; *Ivin v Blake* (1993) 67 P & CR 263; *Curley v Parkes* [2004] EWCA Civ 1515 at [14].

35.19 Lord Bridge then examined *Eves v Eves*[1] and *Grant v Edwards*[2] as 'outstanding examples'[3] where the 'indirect contributions to the acquisition or enhancement of the value of the houses made by the female partners' were 'sufficient to give rise to a constructive trust or proprietary estoppel' because of direct evidence of a common intention that the female was to have some share in the house but 'fell far short of such conduct as would by itself have supported the claim in the absence of an express representation by the male partner that she was to have an interest.'

[1]   [1975] 3 All ER 768, [1975] 1 WLR 1338.
[2]   [1986] Ch 638, [1986] 2 All ER 426.
[3]   [1991] 1 AC 107 at 133.

35.20 In *Eves v Eves*[1] Stuart led Janet to believe that she was to have a fair share in the dilapidated house purchased in his name, taking account of her renovatory work. She cleaned the house and did extensive decorative work, painted the brickwork at the front of the house, wielded a 14lb sledgehammer to demolish the concrete front garden, disposed of the rubble and prepared the front garden for turfing, and helped renovate the back garden demolishing an old shed and replacing it with a new shed. The Court of Appeal held that Stuart held the house on constructive trust for himself and Janet in the proportions 3:1, the equity of redemption being worth about £10,000. Thus, in view of Lord Bridge's remarks, odd-job work even if cumulatively quite significant does not, of itself, enable any inference to be drawn of a common intention that such conduct is to be sufficient for acquiring an interest in the property: it is regarded as the 'most natural thing in the world'[2] for Janet to spend her time to have a nicer place to live in for the benefit of her relationship.

1   [1975] 3 All ER 768.
2   [1991] 1 AC 107 at 131 and [1990] 1 All ER 1111 at 1118.

35.21 In *Grant v Edwards*[1] the man led the woman to believe that she would have a beneficial interest in the house purchased in his name, saying it would have been taken in their joint names but for a particular excuse. For most of the time, except for three years when she had two young babies to look after, she went out to work and earned roughly the same as he did. He paid all the mortgage instalments but he would not have been able to do so and maintain the family standard of living but for her substantial contributions to household expenses, so that she could indirectly be regarded as having paid roughly half the mortgage instalments. Moreover, the £1,037 balance of a fire insurance claim paid in respect of the house was paid into a joint account. The Court of Appeal held that the man held the house on constructive trust for himself and the woman equally.

1   [1986] Ch 638.

35.22 Lord Bridge's remarks indicate a strong belief that the woman's conduct would not nowadays justify an inferred common intention that she was to have an interest in the house so that substantial indirect contributions to mortgage payments, via payments of household expenses freeing up the man's moneys for paying the mortgage instalments, only count where an express common intention is found that they are to be treated as contributions to the purchase price or can be inferred from a direct initial contribution to the purchase indicating a common intention that some beneficial interest is to be acquired. However, his Lordship did not refer to Lord Diplock's previous statement in *Gissing v Gissing* that a court might draw the necessary inference where[1]:

'the wife's efforts or her earnings made it possible for the husband to raise the initial loan or the mortgage or [where] the relieving of the husband from the expense of buying clothing for [the wife] and for their son was undertaken in order to enable him the better to meet the mortgage instalments of to repay the loan.'

1   [1971] AC 886 at 910–911.

35.23 Likewise Fox and May LJJ indicated in *Burns v Burns*[1] that the courts will infer a common intention from a claimant's substantial financial contributions to household expenses, which are necessary to enable her partner alone to keep up the mortgage payments without affecting their standard of living. Reviewing these authorities in *Le Foe v Le Foe* the judge therefore concluded that it was open to him to hold that[2]:

by virtue of her indirect contributions to the mortgage I am entitled to infer that the parties commonly intended that [the claimant wife] should have a beneficial interest in the former matrimonial home.'

¹ [1984] Ch 317 at 328–9 per Fox LJ and at 344 per May LJ.
² [2001] 2 FLR 970 at [50] per Nicholas Mostyn QC (sitting as a deputy High Court judge).

35.24 In *McHardy v Warren*¹ the Court of Appeal was happy to infer that the man held on constructive trust for himself and his wife equally where the man's parents were regarded as giving him and his wife £650 in paying the £650 deposit on a house bought in the man's name when his wife was a minor. Subsequent replacement houses were bought in the man's name, but a £5,000 personal loan was made to both jointly, while the mortgage instalments and the £5,000 loan were always paid or repaid out of a joint account. Thus, the wife did not obtain just a proportionate 8.97% share on resulting trust principles².

¹ [1994] 2 FLR 338 endorsed in *Halifax Building Society v Brown* [1996] 1 FLR 103, CA and applied in *Drake v Whipp* [1996] 1 FLR 826, CA.
² Contrast *Springette v Defoe* (1992) 65 P & CR 1, CA, (no more than resulting trust percentage).

35.25 The position was developed in *Midland Bank plc v Cooke*¹ where the husband's parents contributed £1,000 to the purchase of the house in his name where the money was again held to be a gift to husband and wife equally. This direct contribution of 6.47% under resulting trust principles was held by the Court of Appeal to indicate a common intention that the wife was to have some beneficial interest and the court was 'free to attribute to the parties an intention to share the beneficial interest in some different proportions'², *despite* the fact that both parties had in their evidence expressly stated on oath that they had neither made, nor intended, any agreement. Adopting a holistic approach of looking at the parties' global dealings over the span of their ownership of the property, 'one could hardly have a clearer example of a couple who had agreed to share everything equally ... the conclusion becomes inescapable that their presumed intention was to share the property in equal shares'³.

¹ [1995] 4 All ER 562, CA.
² [1995] 4 All ER 562 at 574.
³ [1995] 4 All ER 562 at 576.

35.26 In essence, from the springboard of a resulting trust (arising from the wife's lack of intention to make a gift of her share of the money to her husband), the Court of Appeal imposed on the parties a common intention that the wife was to have some beneficial interest in the house which was to be a fair interest in all the circumstances during their ownership thereof, which amounted to a half interest held on constructive trust for her. It is difficult to reconcile this approach with Lord Morris' previous insistence in *Pettitt v Pettitt* that¹:

> 'In reaching a decision the court does not, and, indeed, cannot find that there was some thought in the mind of a person which was never there at all. The court must find out exactly what was done or what said and must then reach a conclusion as to what was the legal result. The court does not devise or invent a legal result.'

35.26 *Constructive trusts*

1 [1970] AC 777 at 804. See too Lord Hodson's comments at 810 and Lord Upjohn's comments at 816. The same point was also made in *Gissing v Gissing* [1971] AC 886 at 898 per Lord Morris, at 900 per Viscount Dilhorne, and at 904, per Lord Diplock.

35.27 Nevertheless, in *Oxley v Hiscock*[1] the Court of Appeal accepted that a common intention can be attributed to the parties where they give evidence that they had no intention at the outset but that even so the claimant contributed to the purchase price. In such cases, the court will treat the fact of the claimant's contribution as evidence of a common intention that she is to have a share of the property, but not a share which is limited to the proportion represented by her contribution; rather the parties' deemed intention is said to be that she should have a fair share in the property as subsequently determined in the light of their life together.

1 [2004] EWCA Civ 546, [2005] Fam 211, reaffirmed in *Stack v Dowden* [2006] WTLR 511. See too *Crossley v Crossley* [2006] WTLR 225.

35.28 In the absence of a deposit or other payment to found a resulting trust and of direct or indirect payments of mortgage instalments to found an inferred common intention trust, the court will not assist a woman who acted as the man's unpaid assistant, supported him in his speculative ventures and looked after the home and their children[1] nor a daughter who worked full time in her mother's public house for pocket money only, thereby assisting her mother make profits facilitating the purchase of a house[2]. This can produce harsh results, for which reason the Law Commission has issued a Consultation Paper recommending statutory reforms[3].

1 *Hammond v Mitchell* [1992] 2 All ER 109 for Spanish house.
2 *Ivin v Blake* (1994) 67 P & CR 263 at 276, CA, endorsing *McFarlane v McFarlane* [1972] NI 59 (already endorsed by *Lloyds Bank plc v Rosset* [1991] 1 AC 107 at 133), but see deputy judge in *Haywood v Haywood*, (13 July 2000, unreported).
3 Law Commission Cohabitation: The Financial Consequences of Relationship Breakdown (LCCP No 179, 2006).

Detrimental reliance

35.29 Where there has been direct evidence of an express common intention that W is to have a specific share or a fair share in return for an explicit or implicit undertaking[1] to act in a particular way, W's conduct only needs to be that undertaken. It is immaterial whether it takes the form of a contribution to the costs of acquiring the property or is of quite a different character[2]. Whatever the court decides the *quid pro quo* to have been, it will suffice if the claimant has furnished it[3]. Expenditure or other detrimental acts insufficiently referable to acquisition of the house and insufficient to support an inferred common intention may thus be sufficient detriment to enable a claimant to succeed upon proving an express common intention that such expenditure or other acts were to entitle her to an interest[4].

1 *Grant v Edwards* [1986] Ch 638 at 652.
2 *Grant v Edwards* [1986] 2 All ER 426 at 435–436.
3 *Grant v Edwards* [1986] 2 All ER 426 at 435–436.
4 *Grant v Edwards* [1986] 2 All ER 426 at 432, 435, 437; *Ogilvie v Ryan* [1976] 2 NSWLR 504.

35.30 In order to show that W acted to her detriment in reliance upon the common intention there has to be some 'link' or 'referability' between the common intention and the conduct claimed to have been based upon that intention: Where the express common intention was that W was to acquire over the years a fair share based on her financial contributions to the costs of acquisition or improvement of the house (without penalising her or M when prevented from making their usual contribution, eg because of childbirth or illness[1]) then W obviously needs to prove she made such contributions. Where W was supposed to provide a clear *quid pro quo* for the intended share of the house then the provision of this will suffice in itself even if, apart from the clear agreement, it would not of itself be an act inherently referable to acquisition of a house[2].

[1]   This may help instead to establish an inferred intention for a half share: *Gissing v Gissing* [1971] AC 886 at 908–909, [1970] 2 All ER 780 at 793, HL.
[2]   *Grant v Edwards [1986] Ch 638*, [1986] 2 All ER 426.

35.31 It further seems that if in the case of a *quid pro quo* common intention W does not provide the *quid pro quo* but does act to her detriment, believing she will be acquiring an interest in the home through subsequently doing what was envisaged, then the courts will be ready to grant W an interest in the home. After all, the court will grant W an interest where there is no *quid pro quo* common intention (ie no bargain) but only M's unilateral declaration of intention to create a trust which is made known to W, so that M and W have an understanding or agreement that W has a share in the home[1]. As Lord Bridge stated[2]:

'Once a finding to this effect is made it will only be necessary for the partner asserting a claim to a beneficial interest to show that he or she has acted to his or her detriment or significantly altered his or her position in reliance on the agreement in order to give rise to a constructive trust or a proprietary estoppel.'

[1]   *Lloyds Bank plc v Rosset* [1989] Ch 350 at 381.
[2]   *Lloyds Bank plc v Rosset* [1991] 1 AC 107 at 133.

35.32 Further in *Grant v Edwards*[1], in a passage endorsed by Nicholls LJ in *Lloyds Bank plc v Rosset*[2] and by the Privy Council in *Maharaj v Chand*[3], Sir Nicholas Browne-Wilkinson V-C stated[4]:

'Once it has been shown that there was a common intention that the claimant should have an interest in the house, any act done by her to her detriment relating to the joint lives of the parties is sufficient detriment to qualify. The acts do not have to be inherently referable to the house. The holding out to the claimant that she had a beneficial interest in the house is an act of such a nature as to be part of the inducement to her to do the acts relied on. Accordingly, in the absence of evidence to the contrary, the right inference is that the claimant acted in reliance on such holding out and the burden lies on the legal owner to show that she did not do so: *Greasley v Cooke*.'

[1]   [1986] Ch 638.
[2]   [1989] Ch 350 at 381, (Mustill LJ agreed at 388).
[3]   [1986] AC 898 at 907.
[4]   [1986] Ch 638 at 657.

35.33 However, subsequently in *Lloyds Bank plc v Rosset*[1] the Law Lords opined that even if Mr and Mrs Rosset had an express common intention that she was to have some interest in the house they had 'considerable doubt' whether Mrs Rosset's assistance with renovating work would amount to detriment or a significant alteration of position when 'it would seem the most natural thing in the world for any wife' to assist with such work. Their Lordships, none the less, had no doubt that the woman's conduct *in Eves v Eves*[2] and the woman's substantial contributions to household expenses in *Grant v Edwards*[3] clearly amounted to sufficient detrimental reliance to justify the imposition of a constructive trust where there was evidence of an express common intention, although in both such cases the behaviour of the woman[4] 'fell far short of such conduct as would by itself have supported the claim' by enabling an inferred common intention to be discovered.

[1] [1991] 1 AC 107 at 131.
[2] [1975] 3 All ER 768.
[3] [1986] Ch 638.
[4] [1991] 1 AC 107 at 133. Lord Bridge echoes Lord Diplock's views in *Gissing v Gissing* [1971] AC 886 at 909, [1970] 2 All ER 780 at 793.

35.34 In *Hyett v Stanley*[1], Sir Martin Nourse reaffirmed his own finding in *Grant v Edwards*[2] that W's conduct 'must have been conduct on which [she] could not reasonably have been expected to embark unless she was to have an interest in the house.' However, this is difficult to reconcile with Browne-Wilkinson V-C's finding in the latter case that examples of detrimental reliance might include 'setting up house together' and 'having a baby'[3], and with his further finding that by analogy with the rules governing proprietary estoppel claims, the burden of proof should lie on M to show that W's conduct was attributable to mutual love and affection rather than reliance on the parties' common intention[4].

[1] [2003] EWCA Civ 942, [2004] 1 FLR 394 at [19]. On the facts, W had acted to her detriment by rendering herself jointly and severally liable for M's debts, the repayment of which was secured by way of mortgage on their shared home.
[2] [1986] 1 Ch 638 at 648.
[3] [1986] 1 Ch 638 at 657.
[4] [1986] 1 Ch 638 at 657.

Where legal title is in both names instead of one

35.35 Where the legal title is taken in both names, but there is no express declaration of beneficial interests, the beneficial interest will prima facie be shared[1]. Where the house is bought outright without the assistance of any mortgage then the extent of the respective shares will depend on the proportion of the purchase price respectively contributed[2].

[1] *Pettitt v Pettitt* [1970] AC 777 at 813–814; *Bernard v Josephs* [1982] Ch 391; *Burns v Burns* [1984] Ch 317; *Springette v Defoe* (1992) 65 P & CR 1; *Mortgage Corpn Ltd v Shaire* [2001] Ch 743 at 751 and 754, also pointing out that an express declaration of the extent of the beneficial interest is conclusive (in the absence of fraud or undue influence: *Goodman v Gallant* [1986] Fam 106); for the latter point, see too *Fairclough v Salmon* [2006] EWCA Civ 320 at [18]–[19]. A land registry form that the survivor of the joint registered proprietors can give a valid receipt for capital moneys is not equivalent to a declaration of a beneficial joint tenancy (*Mortgage Corpn Ltd v Shaire* [2001] Ch 743;

Stack v Dowden [2006] WTLR 511,CA): in addition, one needs a statement that the transferees are entitled 'for their own benefit' (*Re Gorman* [1990] 1 All ER 717).
²   *Burns v Burns* [1984] Ch 317 at 344–345, [1984] 1 All ER 244 at 264.

35.36 Where, as is much more usual, the house is bought with the assistance of a mortgage then the parties will have a joint and several liability for the mortgage money that became their money and was paid over as part of the purchase price due to the vendor upon completion of the purchase. Such money, together with the money paid by way of deposit and for stamp duty and legal costs, should be taken into account for establishing a beneficial interest under a resulting trust[1].

¹   *Huntingford v Hobbs* [1993] 1 FLR 736; *Springette v Defoe* (1992) 65 P & CR 1; *Stack v Dowden* [2006] WTLR 511; see paras 31.5–31.6 above.

35.37 Exceptionally, if M and W agreed at the outset that M was to pay all or 75% of the mortgage payments then M will be treated as providing all or 75% of the borrowed money for the purposes of establishing a proportionate interest under a resulting trust[1] (or it may be possible to find a common intention that irrespective of deposit payments etc M was to be 100 or 75% equitable owner)[2]. The fact that subsequently W actually paid 30% of the mortgage payments should not alter the beneficial interests established originally[3] under the resulting (or constructive) trust, unless paid pursuant to a common intention that W was to have a beneficial interest or an increased beneficial interest, though an equitable accounting between the parties may be required in respect of the proceeds of sale when the house is sold[4].

¹   *Huntingford v Hobbs* [1993] 1 FLR 736; *Springette v Defoe* (1992) 65 P & CR 1; *Stack v Dowden* [2006] WTLR 511; see also *Ivin v Blake* (1993) 67 P & CR 263.
²   *Bernard v Josephs* [1982] Ch 391 at 403, [1982] 3 All ER 162 at 170. See too *Abbey National plc v Stringer* [2006] EWCA Civ 338, where a mother and son were jointly liable on the purchase mortgage but there was no real prospect that the son would pay any of the mortgage instalments, and the court concluded that the entire beneficial interest belonged to the mother. *Wilson v Wilson* [1969] 1 WLR 1470 is to similar effect.
³   *Re Gorman* [1990] 1 All ER 717 at 724; *Currie v Hamilton* [1984] 1 NSWLR 687 at 691.
⁴   *Re Gorman* [1990] 1 All ER 717; *Currie v Hamilton* [1984] 1 NSWLR 687, and see para 31.16 above.

35.38 Of course, it is also possible that M and W equally provided for the deposit and legal costs and undertook liability under the mortgage, but agreed that each was to have a fair share taking account of who directly or indirectly contributed to payments of the mortgage. Here the court has to assess each of the parties' contributions in a broad sense but 'nevertheless the court is only entitled to look at the financial contributions or their real and substantial equivalent'[1]. Payments of mortgage instalments out of pooled earnings or a joint account clearly will support a claim for a half share[2], as will the repayment of the whole capital sum by a third party with the intention of making a gift to M and W jointly[3].

¹   *Burns v Burns* [1984] Ch 317 at 344, [1984] 1 All ER 244 at 264.
²   *Burns v Burns* [1984] Ch 317; *McHardy v Warren* [1994] 2 FLR 338.
³   *Hurst v Supperstone* [2005] EWHC 1309 (Ch), [2006] 1 FLR 1245.

35.39 *Constructive trusts*

Size of share

35.39 It is necessary to distinguish between cases involving reliance on an express common intention and cases involving reliance on an inferred common intention[1]. In dealing with express common intention cases it further seems necessary to distinguish between cases where the claimant is relying on having performed the *quid pro quo* of a *quid pro quo* common intention and cases where the quid pro quo has not been performed or there was no *quid pro quo* required[2]. Finally, it is important whether the claimant, W, was led to believe she would acquire a specific (eg half or quarter) share or a vague fair share[3].

1   *Lloyds Bank plc v Rosset* [1991] 1 AC 107.
2   *Grant v Edwards* [1986] Ch 638.
3   *Gissing v Gissing* [1971] AC 886; *Passee v Passee* [1988] 1 FLR 263; *Stokes v Anderson* [1991] 1 FLR 391.

35.40 W's position will be strongest where there was an express agreement that she was to have a specific share, say a half share, if she acted in a certain way, eg gave birth to M's child (the agreement, even if a contract not being in signed writing as required by s 2 of the Law of Property (Miscellaneous Provisions) Act 1989). Here, once W has acted as promised, so that M should be holding the house on trust for them equally, but has provided no signed writing to satisfy s 53(1) (b) of the Law of Property Act 1925, it seems that almost as of course equity will impose a constructive trust upon M[1] so as to provide[2] 'the remedy by which [W] seeks to vindicate an express trust founded upon a common intention which [M] later repudiates.' Indeed, it would seem to be open to a court to hold that the doctrine of part performance preserved by the Law of Property Act 1925, s 55(d) enables the express trust to be enforced despite the lack of signed writing[3]. Thus W will obtain a half share.

1   *Gissing v Gissing* [1971] AC 886 at 908.
2   *Allen v Snyder* [1977] 2 NSWLR 685 at 699.
3   W's conduct would need to be unequivocally referable to some such agreement as alleged: *Steadman v Steadman* [1976] AC 536; *Wakeham v Mackenzie* [1968] 1 WLR 1175.

35.41 Where there has been an express oral agreement it is open to the court to depart from the agreement only if there is a very good reason for doing so[1]. What, therefore, if W only had done one-half of what she was supposed to do, eg where she had agreed to contribute whatever she could to help with mortgage payments and household expenses (taking account of the exigencies of child-bearing and child-rearing) and she had held back for her secret nest-egg some money she had inherited so as only to have contributed half of what she could have contributed? There would seem to be flexibility to award her only a quarter share. Indeed, if, due to becoming unemployed shortly after acquisition of the home, the childless W had contributed very little and a year later ran off with X there would seem to be sufficient flexibility to award her little, if anything. When detrimental acts may be placed on a scale from 1 to 99 should a tiny scale 5 detriment really entitle W to the full half interest? Surely not.

1   *Clough v Killey* (1996) 72 P & CR D 22 at 24, CA; *Mortgage Corpn Ltd v Shaire* [2001] Ch 743 at 750; *Crossley v Crossley* [2006] WTLR 225 at [32].

35.42 This scale of detriment will be taken into account where the parties have agreed that W is to have a fair share or some share when equity will give effect to this and not allow M to claim that W's interest is void for uncertainty, because this would be unconscionable[1]. As Lord Diplock has stated[2]:

> 'There is nothing inherently improbable in their acting on the understanding that the wife should be entitled to a share which was not to be quantified immediately on the acquisition of the home but should be left to be determined when the mortgage was repaid or the property disposed of, on the basis of what would be fair having regard to the total contributions, direct or indirect, which each spouse had made by that date ... it would be for the court to give effect to the common intention of the parties by determining what in all the circumstances was a fair share.'

1   *Gissing v Gissing* [1971] AC 886 at 908; *Pallant v Morgan* [1953] Ch 43; *Chattlock v Muller* (1878) 8 Ch D 177 at 181.
2   *Gissing v Gissing* [1971] AC 886 at 908.

35.43 After citing these dicta of Lord Diplock, Nourse LJ has stated[1]:

> 'Those observations ... support a more general proposition that all payments made and acts done by the claimant are to be treated as illuminating the common intention to the extent of the beneficial interest ... . The court must supply the common intention by reference to that which all the material circumstances have shown to be fair. ... . I think that both *Eves v Eves*[2], where no financial contribution was made by the claimant, and *Grant v Edwards*[3], where the claimant had made substantial indirect contributions to the mortgage repayments and the balance of the fire insurance moneys had been equally divided, are explicable on this basis, albeit that neither was clearly expressed to be so decided.'

1   *Stokes v Anderson* [1991] 1 FLR 391 at 400.
2   [1975] 3 All ER 768.
3   [1986] Ch 638.

35.44 Significantly, after Lord Bridge commented on these last two cases he recognised that[1] 'in no sense could these shares have been regarded as proportionate to what the judge in the instant case described as a "qualifying contribution" in terms of the indirect contributions to the acquisition or enhancement of the value of the houses made by the female partners.' In *Eves v Eves* W's odd-job work produced for her a quarter interest in an equity of redemption worth £10,000 in 1975 though she had borne two children for M, while in *Grant v Edwards* indirect contributions of less than half, due to W having M's babies in the first three years at the house, produced a half interest for W.

1   *Lloyds Bank plc v Rosset* [1991] 1 AC 107 at 133.

35.45 Thus, where the courts find that there was an express agreement or understanding they are prepared when awarding a precise share on a rough and ready broad basis[1] to take account of 'all payments made and acts done by the claimant'[2]. Strictly speaking, it seems a 'fair' share requires the taking into account only of direct and indirect financial contributions[3] or their real and substantial equivalent[4], but the court has leeway, in investigating all the circumstances where there was an express intention that W was to have some share, to find that the intention was really to have a half or quarter share[5].

1 'There is, of course, an air of unreality about the whole exercise': per Griffith LJ in *Bernard v Josephs* [1982] Ch 391 at 404, [1982] 3 All ER 162 at 170. See also *Cox v Jones* [2004] EWHC 1486 (Ch) [2004] 2 FLR 1010.(25% share).
2 *Stokes v Anderson* [1991] 1 FLR 391 at 400. No distinction is made between capital and interest elements of mortgage payments: *Passee v Passee* [1988] 1 FLR 263.
3 *Gissing v Gissing* [1971] AC 886 at 909; *Grant v Edwards* [1986] Ch 638 at 657, [1986] 2 All ER 426 at 439.
4 *Burns v Burns* [1984] Ch 317 at 344.
5 This seems reasonable in *Grant v Edwards* [1986] Ch 638 but artificial in *Eves v Eves* [1975] 3 All ER 768, which, perhaps, would be better justified as an intention for joint legal and equitable ownership (but not fair equitable ownership), but where equity did not perfect the imperfect gift because the minimum equity to do justice and undo the defendant's unconscionable conduct only required a quarter share.

35.46 Where W's claim is based on an inferred common intention in ascertaining the size of her share, one first focuses upon her direct financial contributions, whether to the initial purchase (eg deposit, stamp duty and legal costs) or to subsequent mortgage payments[1]. However, once an inferred common intention that she should have some share in the home has arisen by virtue of her contribution to the initial purchase, then other expenditure by W can also be taken into account when ascertaining the size of her share, including indirect contributions to mortgage payments (arising from her payment of household expenses without which M could not have afforded to pay the mortgage and keep the household going), council tax, utility bills, insurance, housekeeping, repairs, refurbishments, and/or participation in joint business activities[2].

1 *Lloyds Bank plc v Rosset* [1991] 1 AC 107.
2 *Gissing v Gissing* [1971] AC 886 at 908; *Burns v Burns* [1984] Ch 317 at 345; *Lloyd v Pickering* [2004] EWHC 1513 (Ch), [2004] NLJR 1014; *Cox v Jones* [2004] EWHC 1486 (Ch), [2004] 2 FLR 1010.

35.47 Further according to the Court of Appeal in *Midland Bank plc v Cooke[1]* one can go beyond the direct or indirect financial contributions, where the parties have been honest enough to admit that they never gave ownership a thought or reached any agreement about it and formulate 'a fair presumed basis'[2] for the sharing of the beneficial title upon surveying the parties' whole course of dealings relating to the property, including non-financial conduct. 'That scrutiny will not confine itself to the limited range of acts of direct contribution that are needed to found a beneficial interest in the first place. It will take into consideration all conduct which throws light on the question what shares were intended. Only if that search proves inconclusive does the court fall back on the maxim "equality is equity" '[3].

1 [1995] 4 All ER 562.
2 [1995] 4 All ER 562 at 575.
3 [1995] 4 All ER 562 at 574 and 576. Applied in *Le Foe v Le Foe* [2001] 2 FLR 970; *Mollo v Mollo* [2000] WTLR 227; *Oxley v Hiscock* [2004] EWCA Civ 546, [2005] Fam 211; *Holman v Howes* [2005] EWHC 2824 (Ch), [2006] Fam Law 176.

Date of valuation of interest

35.48 Once it has been established that W is entitled to a specific share (eg a half) it follows that the value[1] 'must be determined at the date when the property is sold, but that may have to give way to circumstances, eg one of the parties may buy out the other, in which case the value of the party's interest may have to be determined at a different date.' Valuation is not to be made as at the date when W and M separate (unless, unusually, M and W had so agreed) though separation will often bring the purpose of the trust to an end[2], but not the trust itself. Events after separation may be taken into account for the purpose of equitable accounting in respect of the proceeds of sale, eg H may be credited with mortgage instalments paid while staying in possession but debited with a notional occupation rent for using the ousted W's share of the house[3].

1   *Marsh v Von Sternberg* [1986] 1 FLR 526; *Gordon v Douce* [1983] 2 All ER 228 at 230; *Turton v Turton* [1988] Ch 542, CA disapproving authority favouring date of separation.
2   Enabling a sale to be sought under Trusts of Land and Appointment of Trustees Act 1996, ss 14 and 15; see para 45.45 above.
3   See *Re Gorman* [1990] 1 All ER 717; *Re Pavlou* [1993] 3 All ER 955; *Clarke v Harlowe* [2005] WTLR 1473; see para 31.16 above.

Constructive trusts and equitable estoppel

35.49 The above flexibility in determining the size of the interest to be awarded to W leads one to consider whether the doctrine of the common intention constructive trust should be regarded as subsumed within the broader head of equitable estoppel or proprietary estoppel[1], which is concerned with the discretionary prevention of unconscionable conduct arising out of a defendant, M, having induced the claimant, W, to act to her detriment in respect of specific property, eg by making an informal unenforceable gift of part of his property to W[2]. After all, in any case where the elements necessary to found a common intention constructive trust are present so are the elements necessary to found a proprietary estoppel, namely, that M, by virtue of his bilateral agreement with W or of his unilateral representation to W, has created an expectation or belief that W has or will have an interest in the house and on the basis of that expectation or belief W has acted to her detriment with M's encouragement or acquiescence. Thus in *Yaxley v Gotts*[3], Robert Walker LJ has stated, 'In the area of a joint enterprise for the acquisition of land the two concepts coincide'.

1   'In essence the doctrine is an application of proprietary estoppel' per Lord Oliver in *Austin v Keele* (1987) 61 ALJR 605 at 609. Further support is provided by Browne-Wilkinson V-C in *Grant v Edwards* [1986] Ch 638 and in his 1991 Holdsworth Lecture 'Constructive trusts and Unjust Enrichment', reprinted in (1996) 10 TLI 98, Nicholls LJ in *Lloyds Bank plc v Rosset* [1989] Ch 350, Nourse LJ in *Stokes v Anderson* [1991] 1 FLR 391, and in his Hong Kong *Law Lectures for Practitioners* 1991 Lecture 'Unconscionability and the Unmarried Couple' discussed by Cooke P in *Phillips v Phillips* [1993] 1 NZLR 159 at 168, while Lord Bridge in *Lloyds Bank plc v Rosset* [1991] 1 AC 107 in three places (pp 129, 132 and 133) refers to 'constructive trusts or proprietary estoppels' but avoids dealing with the reported arguments thereon of M. Crystal QC.
2   See para 12.47 above.

3   [2000] Ch 162 at 176–177 (citing *Gissing v Gissing* [1971] AC 886 at 905; *Lloyds Bank plc v Rosset* [1991] 1 AC 107 at 132; *Grant v Edwards* [1986] Ch 638 at 656), endorsed by Chadwick LJ in *Banner Homes Group plc v Luff Developments* [2000] Ch 372 at 384. See too *Oxley v Hiscock* [2004] EWCA Civ 546 [2005] Fam 211 at [66]. Overreaching applies to co-owned interests whether established under resulting or constructive trusts or equitable estoppel principles: *Birmingham Midshires Mortgage Services Ltd v Saberhwal* (1999) 80 P & CR 256, CA.

35.50 The estoppel approach has many advantages. It avoids the search for an express or inferred common intention, which is often a difficult and somewhat artificial exercise when cohabitees often do not give detailed consideration to the matter, if, indeed, any consideration is really given. Instead, if to M's knowledge, because of M's behaviour W thinks that the house is partly hers, then good conscience requires that M should not stand by allowing W to act to her detriment or significantly alter her position on a mistaken basis or, if he does, then equity may intervene in some appropriate fashion to counteract his unconscionable behaviour. Moreover, not just financial detriment should be taken into account but any act done by her to her detriment relating to the joint life of the parties based on their home[1]. Furthermore, the flexibility of equity revealed in proprietary estoppel cases will afford the court leeway to deny a claimant the agreed interest and confer a smaller interest if award of the agreed interest would be inequitable and disproportionate in all the circumstances[2].

1   See *Midland Bank plc v Cooke* [1995] 4 All ER 562, discussed at para 35.47 above.
2   See paras 12.48–12.49 above.

35.51 Just as an interest under a common intention constructive trust arises when the claimant first acts to his detriment[1], so an equitable proprietary estoppel interest will be treated as arising when the claimant first acted to his detriment[2], even though the precise size of such interest will not be ascertained until the court decides the issue. This has the advantage of protecting co-owning occupiers with only an equitable interest from subsequent mortgagees, though, in any event, even if such an occupier had no proprietary interest until the date of the court hearing the court could have held the subsequent mortgagee's conscience to be bound by the co-owner's rights as ultimately laid down by the court.

1   *Turton v Turton* [1988] Ch 542 at 55; *Lloyds Bank plc v Rosset* [1989] Ch 350 at 386, 393 and 402, per Nicholls , Mustill and Purchas LJJ respectively.
2   *Voyce v Voyce* (1991) 62 P & CR 290 at 294, 296; *Lloyds Bank plc v Carrick* [1996] 4 All ER 630 at 642 (but cf *United Bank of Kuwait plc v Sahib* [1997] Ch 107 at 142. For registered land, the Land Registration Act 2002, s 116 seems to make an equitable interest arise from the date of detrimental conduct of the claimant.

Availability of Matrimonial Causes Act 1973 for spouses

35.52 The uncertainties and, at times, artificiality of applying principles of resulting trusts and constructive trusts and proprietary estoppel principles to ascertain the precise property rights of the parties should not concern spouses unless facing a claim by a creditor. This is because until the applicant remarries or the respondent dies matters should be resolved in the Family

Division[1] under the jurisdiction conferred by s 24 of the Matrimonial Causes Act 1973, whereby there is a broad discretion to make orders as to property (taking into account the wife's contribution to looking after the children and the home) without the need first to ascertain precisely the beneficial shares in the property[2].

[1] *Williams v Williams* [1976] Ch 278, [1977] 1 All ER 28, CA; *Fielding v Fielding* [1978] 1 All ER 267, [1977] 1 WLR 1146n, CA.
[2] Eg *P v P* [1978] 3 All ER 70, [1978] 1 WLR 483, CA.

Paragraph 2(b)

Mutual wills

35.53 To prevent the fraudulent or unconscionable revocation of a will in certain circumstances Equity has developed the doctrine of mutual wills which relies upon the imposition of a constructive trust upon the death of the first testator to die[1].

[1] *Dufour v Pereira* (1769) 1 Dick 419; *Birmingham v Renfrew* (1937) 57 CLR 666; *Re Cleaver* [1981] 2 All ER 1018, [1981] 1 WLR 939; *Re Dale* [1994] Ch 31.

35.54 Where two persons (eg husband and wife or brother and sister) make a contractually binding arrangement as to the disposal of their property and make mutual wills pursuant to that arrangement, which they agree are to be unalterable, then, if one person dies but the survivor subsequently alters his testamentary dispositions in breach of the arrangement, the survivor's personal representatives will be granted probate (or letters of administration) in the ordinary way. However, they will hold the relevant part of his estate on constructive trust to give effect to the arrangement effected by the mutual wills[1]. If instead of executing separate mutual wills the parties make a joint will agreeing that the arrangement embodied therein shall be unalterable then the arrangement will also be binding on the survivor under a constructive trust[2]. It would seem that the principles underlying mutual wills should extend to cases where there are more than two parties (eg to wills of 70-year-old triplets), to where the agreement is subsequent to the making of the wills[3] (eg if it could be proved that A expressly agreed with B that he would not revoke his will if she agreed not to revoke her will and she agreed), to where the agreement is not the same mutatis mutandis (eg I will leave my property to you for life, remainder to X if you leave your property to me for life, remainder to Z), and where there is an agreement between joint tenants of property not to sever their interest on condition the survivor disposes of the property in an agreed manner[4].

[1] *Re Oldham* [1925] Ch 75; *Gray v Perpetual Trustee Co* [1928] AC 391; *Birmingham v Renfrew* (1937) 57 CLR 666. See also (1951) 14 MLR 140 (J.D.B. Mitchell); (1970) 34 Conv 230 (R. Burgess); A.J. Oakley *Constructive Trusts*, pp 131–140.
[2] *Re Hagger* [1930] 2 Ch 190. However the practical and legal problems are such that joint wills are to be deprecated and practitioners should do their utmost to ensure that separate wills are drafted.
[3] *Re Fox* [1951] OR 378, [1951] 3 DLR 337 (agreement to alter their wills).
[4] *Healey v Brown* [2002] WTLR 849; *University of Manitoba v Sanderson Estate* (1998) 15 DLR (4th) 40.

35.55 While the cases concentrate on whether or not the parties agreed not to revoke or amend their agreed wills, the crux of the obligation is not dealing with the relevant property contrary to the agreement[1], so that the survivor should still be bound by the agreement if the first to die revoked or altered the will but the relevant property continued to be dealt with in accordance with their agreement – unless the will is restrictively worded, eg 'I shall not amend nor revoke my will after the death of my spouse if the will [dated — day of —] of my spouse has not been amended nor revoked before death'. Such wording is fine where a spouse's *whole* estate is left absolutely to the surviving spouse but for the latter to bequeath or devise what remains of specific property to X, but if *part* only of the spouse's estate is to be subject to the agreed obligation then the survivor should be placed under a binding obligation in respect only of that part 'if the will of my spouse has not been amended nor revoked before death so as to deal with [specified property] inconsistently with [clause 3 of her will dated — day of —].'

1   *Lewis v Cotton* [2001] WTLR 1117 at 1129, NZCA.

Binding agreement for survivor to carry out agreed arrangement

35.56 It is vital to show on a balance of probabilities that each person agreed that if he was the survivor then he would be legally bound to carry out the agreed arrangement[1]. The agreement is a contractual one made in consideration of the mutual promises of the parties[2], though for the benefit to some extent of persons who are neither parties to the contract nor suppliers of consideration, eg where the testator's will leaves a life interest to the other mutual testator with remainders over or a limited type of 'absolute' ownership to the other with remainders over[3]. It depends on the construction of the contract whether a breach arises (i) if one party openly tells the other that he no longer is going to give effect to the arrangement because he is to change his will, or (ii) if the party's will is revoked automatically by remarriage and a new will is not made to give effect to the arrangement, or (iii) if the party revokes his will without informing the other but predeceases the other so that his secret becomes public. Usually, the contract will be presumed revocable upon notice to the other party or upon the will becoming revoked by operation of law so as not to be broken if such circumstances materialise[4]. Even where a breach arises during the lifetime or on the death of one party the uncertain variables make it difficult to see what the survivor's measure of damages would be[5], especially since he would then be free to rearrange his own will as he wished[6].

1   *Re Cleaver* [1981] 2 All ER 1018, [1981] 1 WLR 939.
2   This is a factor which distinguishes mutual wills from secret trusts which involve voluntary undertakings. Further see *Re Goodchild* [1997] 3 All ER 63, CA and *Re Dale* [1994] Ch 31, [1993] 4 All ER 129 holding that it is not a necessary condition for the imposition of a constructive trust that the testators should confer benefits on each other.
3   See para 35.68 below, for such 'absolute ownership'.
4   *Dufour v Pereira* (1769) 1 Dick 419 at 420; *Stone v Hoskins* [1905] P 194 at 197; *Re Marsland* [1939] Ch 820, CA; *Birmingham v Renfrew* (1937) 57 CLR 666 at 682–683. Further see *Re Newey* [1994] 2 NZLR 590 at 593 and *Bigg v Queensland Trustees Ltd* [1990] 2 Qd R 11, critically noted by CEF Rickett (1991) 54 MLR 581, emphasising that the constructive trust remedy only becomes available after the death of the first party having performed the agreement. If such party dies failing to perform the agreement the

survivor's action against the deceased's executor can only be a breach of contract action for an equitable estoppel claim if the survivor had earlier acted to his detriment in reliance on the other's promises.

5   *Lewis v Cotton* [2001] WTLR 1117 at 1129, NZCA.
6   See *Re Hobley* (1997) Times, 16 June (codicil revoking devise of property within the agreement held to leave survivor free to dispose of all property as she wished).

35.57 It is necessary to prove that the arrangement was intended to affect legal relations and was intended to bind the surviving party after the death of the other party so that the survivor could not revoke his will unless he made a new will continuing to give effect to the arrangement[1]. Thus, the arrangement must be more than an agreement to make wills in almost identical terms[2]. A recital or declaration in the wills that no alteration or revocation is to be made except by mutual consent will be sufficient[3] as will similar proof obtained outside the four corners of the will, eg in family conversations[4].

1   *Re Oldham* [1925] Ch 75; *Gray v Perpetual Trustee Co* [1928] AC 391 where the mere fact that husband and wife simultaneously had made wills mutatis mutandis in identical form was not of itself sufficient evidence to raise a constructive trust binding the survivor; see too *Osenton v Osenton* [2004] EWHC 1055 at [33]. With joint mutual wills the court is more ready to find sufficient evidence: *Re Gillespie* (1969) 3 DLR (3d) 317.
2   *Lewis v Cotton* [2001] WTLR 1117, NZCA.
3   *Re Green* [1951] Ch 148, [1950] 2 All ER 913.
4   *Re Heys* [1914] P 192 at 194; *Re Cleaver* [1981] 1 WLR 939; *Re Newey* [1994] 2 NZLR 590.

35.58 An agreement not to revoke a testamentary disposition of land is the same in effect as a promise to make such a disposition, so that it falls within the Law of Property (Miscellaneous Provisions) Act 1989, s 2(1) so that a problem arises where there is not a joint will signed by them both but separate mutual wills not containing identical terms and not signed by both parties. As a result, in *Healey v Brown*[1] the Deputy Judge held that land owned by the survivor was not subject to a valid contract, and so could not be held on any constructive trust under the mutual wills doctrine because such doctrine was founded on there being an enforceable contract. He did, however, hold that land owned by the first to die was held on constructive trust under secret trust principles which are not dependent on any contract but on a voluntary undertaking. The land in question was their matrimonial home when the first died and was a flat beneficially owned by them as joint tenants so as to pass automatically on death to the survivor.

1   [2002] WTLR 849.

35.59 Shortly after Mrs Brown's death Mr Brown had vested the flat in himself and his son as beneficial joint tenants so that two years later, on Mr Brown's death, his son acquired the flat as surviving joint tenant. As the judge said[1] '[This] could scarcely run more directly and fully counter to the intention of the mutual will compact that the flat should pass to his deceased wife's niece on his own death'. 'It would in my judgment be entirely inequitable now to frustrate Mrs Brown's expectation and it was unconscionable for Mr Brown to do so after her death in seeking to pass the flat to the First Defendant'[2] his son. Yet the failure to comply with the 1989 Act formalities led the judge to hold that the niece only acquired a half interest in the flat, despite the fact that Equity does not allow statutes to be used as an instrument of fraud and will impose a constructive trust over particular property to prevent the owner retaining exclusive beneficial ownership where this would be unconscionable – and s 2(5) of the 1989 Act provides an exception for constructive trusts.

¹   [2002] WTLR 849 at [14].
²   [2002] WTLR 849 at [26].

35.60 In *Dufour v Pereira*¹ Lord Camden stated the basis for imposing a constructive trust:

'The instrument itself is the evidence of the agreement; and he that dies first, does by his death carry the agreement on his part into execution. If the other then refuses he is guilty of a fraud, can never unbind himself, and becomes a trustee of course. For no man shall deceive another to his prejudice. By engaging to do something that is in his power, he is made a trustee for the performance, and transmits that trust to those that claim under him ...there is not an instance to be found since the jurisdiction was established where one man has ever been released from his engagement after the other has performed his part' [until *Healey v Brown*].

¹   (1769) 2 Hargrave's Judicial Arguments 304 at 310.

35.61 Thus, Mr Brown and, then, his son should have been found to hold the flat on constructive trust for Mrs Brown's niece absolutely. Mrs Brown had died, reasonably believing that Mr Brown was subject to a legally binding agreement to give effect to what they had both believed to be a legally binding obligation. It should have been immaterial that unknown to them the agreement happened not to satisfy the formalities required by s 2(1) of the 1989 Act: its certain existence should have led to a legally binding obligation under a constructive trust.

Trust giving effect to arrangement

35.62 Assuming the terms of the mutual arrangement were not unusual in expressly providing that the survivor was only bound to give effect to the arrangement *if* he accepted property passing under the will of the deceased party, the survivor is bound as from the death of the deceased, irrespective of taking any property under the will¹. After all, in the usual case the benefit that the ultimately surviving party contracted for was to have the ultimately predeceasing party make testamentary dispositions in the agreed form and die without altering them. Once this party dies with testamentary dispositions in the agreed form, thus having deprived himself of the chance to make alternative testamentary dispositions, then the surviving party obtains the contracted for benefit so that it would be a fraud if thereafter the survivor made testamentary dispositions inconsistent with those previously mutually agreed².

¹   Especially if disclaimer under the will enables the disclaiming party to take under the intestacy rules: cf secret trusts, para 12.110 above.
²   *Re Dale* [1994] Ch 31, [1993] 4 All ER 129.

35.63 Thus, while Equity does not interfere with the fundamental principle that all wills are revocable till death[1] it does, if the survivor revokes his will without making a new one giving effect to the mutual arrangement, impose a constructive trust on the property subject to the arrangement that passes to the survivor's personal representatives under his new will or intestacy. The constructive trust is in favour of the mutually agreed beneficiaries. In such manner Equity is able to prevent the survivor fraudulently frustrating the arrangement with the deceased and to benefit the third party beneficiaries of the arrangement, who themselves can enforce the constructive trusts[2].

[1] *Stone v Hoskins* [1905] P 194.
[2] They may also have rights under the Contracts (Rights of Third Parties) Act 1999 which leave unaffected, rights under constructive trusts: see s 10 of the 1999 Act.

35.64 It follows that if a third party beneficiary of the mutual arrangement survives one party, but predeceases the surviving party, then the third party's interest does not lapse since it arose under the constructive trust imposed at the date of death of the first party to die. Thus in *Re Hagger*[1] H and W executed a joint mutual will leaving their moiety of their property at Wandsworth to the survivor for life, with remainder to various beneficiaries including a certain EP. It happened that W died in 1904, EP died in 1923, and H died in 1928, having made a will inconsistent with the mutually agreed arrangement. Clauson J held that EP had a vested interest in remainder in the Wandsworth property (both W's moiety passing under W's will *and H's own moiety*) as from 1904.

[1] [1930] 2 Ch 190. The interest could be protected by an entry on the land register: *Fisher v Mansfield* [1997] 2 NZLR 230.

The property subject to the trust

35.65 In *Re Hagger* it was clear that the Wandsworth property was the subject matter of the trust and that H was, after W's death, to take a life interest in W's moiety and his own moiety. Where the mutual agreement is clear as to the property intended to be subject to the agreement and the interest to be taken therein then obviously there are no problems. The agreement may provide only for certain property of the first to die to be affected or it may also provide for the survivor's property to be affected[1].

[1] See *Re Green* [1951] Ch 148, [1950] 2 All ER 913; *Re Goodchild* [1997] 3 All ER 63 at 75; *Healey v Brown* [2002] WTLR 849.

35.66 In the former case there is no problem where a life interest is expressly conferred on the survivor. Problems, however, arise as to the scope of the survivor's obligation where an apparently 'absolute' interest in the deceased's property is conferred on the survivor who is then intended to be subject to some equitable obligation to pass the interest on to third parties after his death.

35.67 In the latter case there is no problem if the survivor takes a life interest in some part of his own property, though practical problems arise if he takes a life interest in all his property unless he has power to resort to capital and wide powers of investment. Furthermore, it must be ascertained whether all his property at the date of the deceased party's death is intended or all his property including after-acquired property. These problems become more acute where the survivor is apparently intended to retain an 'absolute' interest in his own property but subject to some equitable obligation to pass the interest on to third parties after his death.

35.68 In the case of 'absolute' interests if the courts are not to hold that a mere moral obligation exists it will be necessary for them to find an implied life interest with implied power to resort to capital and implied wide powers of investment as absolute owner or to introduce some new concept such as a floating trust as envisaged by Dixon J in *Birmingham v Renfrew*[1] in stating:

> 'The purpose of an arrangement for corresponding wills must often be to enable the survivor during his life to deal as absolute owner with the property passing under the will of the party first dying. That is to say the object of the transaction is to put the survivor in a position to enjoy for his own benefit the full ownership so that, for instance, he may convert it and expend the proceeds if he choose. But when he dies he is to bequeath what is left in the manner agreed upon. It is only by the special doctrines of equity that such a floating obligation, suspended, so to speak, during the lifetime of the survivor can descend upon the assets at his death and crystallize into a trust. No doubt gifts and settlements inter vivos, if calculated to defeat the intention of the compact, could not be made by the survivor and his right of disposition, inter vivos, is therefore not unqualified. But, substantially, the purpose of the arrangement will often be to allow full enjoyment for the survivor's own benefit and advantage upon condition that at his death the residue shall pass as arranged.'

[1] (1937) 57 CLR 666 at 689 endorsed by Nourse J in *Re Cleaver* [1981] 2 All ER 1018, [1981] 1 WLR 939 who also pointed out, 'No objection could normally be taken to ordinary gifts of small value.' Further see endorsement and discussion in *Edell v Sitzer* (2001) 4 ITELR 149 at 169–170.

35.69 Does the third party beneficiary then have a 'quasi' defeasible vested equitable interest in remainder under a quasi certain trust and, if such beneficiary, having survived the 'settlor', predeceases the 'trustee', is the trustee then entitled to make larger inroads into the capital for whatever purposes he wishes, or, indeed, is the beneficiary's interest really contingent upon being alive at the survivor's death? Many matters remain to be resolved unless great care is taken in drafting mutual wills in those relatively rare circumstances where they may be justified.

35.70 In the sole English case[1] the position was clear-cut. H and W left all their property to each other absolutely, except the survivor was to leave their matrimonial home and the proceeds thereof to W's niece, N: they agreed not to amend or revoke these wills. Their home was owned as beneficial joint tenants, so on W's death H became sole beneficial owner. Shortly thereafter he transferred the home into the name of himself and his son, S, as beneficial joint tenants, so that two years later, on H's death, S became sole beneficial owner to the apparent exclusion of N. This could scarcely run more directly and fully counter to the intention of the mutual will compact so S could not rely on being beneficial sole owner as seen at paras 35.58–35.61 above.

[1]   *Healey v Brown* [2002] WTLR 849.

Affinity with secret trusts

35.71 There is much affinity between mutual wills and secret trusts except that the arrangement giving rise to the trust is in the former case contractual[1] and in the latter case voluntary.

[1]   Despite *Healey v Brown* [2002] WTLR 849 it ought to be immaterial that the contract turns out to be void for lack of complying with the requisite formalities under s 2(1) of the Law of Property (Miscellaneous Provisions) Act 1989: see paras 35.58–35.61 above and also M Cope, *Constructive Trusts* (Law Book Co, Australia 1992) Chap 12.

35.72 As Nourse J has stated[1]:

'These cases of mutual wills are only one example of a wider category of cases, for example, secret trusts, in which a court of equity will intervene to impose a constructive trust ... . The principle of all these cases is that a court of equity will not permit a person to whom property is transferred by way of gift, but on the faith of an agreement or clear understanding that it is to be dealt with in a particular way for the benefit of a third person, to deal with that property inconsistently with that agreement or understanding.'

[1]   *Re Cleaver* [1981] 2 All ER 1018 at 1024.

Paragraph 2(c)

Secret trusts

35.73 Secret trusts arising on a deceased's testacy or intestacy have already been fully dealt with and the fraud noted (which justifies the imposition of a constructive trust) where the deceased's wishes would be frustrated and the secret beneficiary be deprived of the benefit which, but for the trustee's agreement, would have been secured to him by the deceased by other means[1].

[1]   See para 12.96 and *Re Dale* [1994] Ch 31 at 48–49, [1993] 4 All ER 129 at 142.

35.74 In the case of an inter vivos trust where A transferred land to B on the oral understanding that B is to hold it for C it seems that it should not be regarded as fraudulent for A to plead Law of Property Act 1925, s 53(1)(b) and retain his interest, not having made a perfect gift and not having died happy in the belief that he had made such a gift[1].

[1]   See paras 12.73–12.74 above.

Paragraph 2(d)

Donor doing all he is obliged to do to transfer legal title or make a donatio mortis causa

35.75 In the case of shares and registered land legal title only passes when the transferee becomes registered as shareholder or proprietor of the land, the latter being deemed to occur when all the relevant documents have been delivered to the appropriate Land Registry office, although it will occur electronically in due course. Company directors of private companies may refuse to register a transferee. The acquisition of the equitable title may be important for the three to seven year survival period required for potentially exempt transfers under inheritance tax or for the transferee to be entitled to require further assistance from the transferor if the transfer form should happen to be lost or destroyed after the transferee had received it.

35.76 As already discussed a constructive trust arises as soon as the transferor has done all which it is obligatory for him to do to make the transfer effective[1], eg signed and handed over the transfer form together with the share certificate or the land certificate to the transferee or the transferee's agent, so that the transferor no longer has power to prevent delivery of the requisite documents for registration of the transferor as legal owner. Once this has happened it becomes unconscionable for the transferor to insist in being regarded as still beneficial owner so the transferee then obtains equitable title entitling him to dividends, rents and, presumably, a freshly executed transfer form if the earlier one were lost or burnt, the transferor being his nominee under *Saunders v Vautier*[2].

1   See para 9.33.
2   (1841) 4 Beav 115.

35.77 To make an effective donatio mortis causa there must be delivery of the subject matter of the gift or the essential indicia of title in circumstances amounting to a parting with dominion and not mere physical possession over the subject matter of the gift. Where legal title remains in the donor and passes to his personal representatives they will hold it on constructive trust for the donee of the effective donatio mortis causa[1]. It makes no difference that in the case of shares the company directors may refuse to register the transferee as shareholder.

1   *Sen v Headley* [1991] Ch 425 at 439–440, [1991] 2 All ER 636 at 646–647, CA.

Paragraph 2(e)

No criminal may benefit from his crime

35.78 As Fry LJ stated in *Cleaver v Mutual Reserve Fund Life Association*[1]

'No system of jurisprudence can with reason include among the rights which it enforces rights directly resulting to the person asserting them from the crime of that person.'

1   [1892] 1 QB 147 at 156 but in special circumstances bigamists may have rights to ancillary statutory relief: *Rampal v Rampal (No 2)* [2001] EWCA Civ 989, [2002] Fam 85.

35.79 Thus, when Crippen was hanged for murdering his wife it was held that the property passing on his wife's intestacy did not pass to him and through his will to his mistress, Miss Le Neve, but, instead passed to his wife's blood relatives[1]. Here, as in other English instances[2], the property was intercepted before passing to the criminal. However, it seems, as established in American and Commonwealth jurisdictions, that if the property did vest in the criminal then he would hold the property on constructive trust for those really entitled to the property[3] who would thus have priority in the event of the criminal's bankruptcy and also the right to trace the property if transferred to others. A transferee would be safe if a bona fide purchaser of the legal interest for value or protected by the change of position defence[4].

1   *Re Crippen* [1911] P 108; *Re Sigsworth* [1935] Ch 89. Cf *Re DWS (deceased)* [2001] Ch 568 where X murdered his parents who died intestate leaving no other children, the Court of Appeal rejected the claim of X's only child, Y, under s 47 of the Administration of Estates Act 1925, refusing to treat the situation as if X had predeceased his parents: the property devolved on class of next of kin ranking after issue of the intestate. Kerridge (2001) 117 LQR 371 argued that this result could have been avoided if the court had allowed the parents' property to pass to X, subject to a constructive trust in Y's favour. However this solution did not commend itself to the Law Commission, which prefers the certainty of statutory reform to undo the decision: Law Commission *The Forfeiture Rule and the Law of Succession* (Law Com No 295, 1995) esp paras 3.21–3.23.
2   For example, *Davitt v Titcumb* [1990] Ch 110, [1989] 3 All ER 417 (proceeds of life assurance policy payable on death of murderer's co-owner).
3   *Schobelt v Barber* (1966) 60 DLR (2d) 519; *Rasmanis v Jurewitsch* [1970] 1 NSWR 650; *Re Pechar* [1969] NZLR 574.
4   Cf *Bradley v Fox* Ill App 2d 106, 129 NE 2d 699 (1955); *Beresford v Royal Insurance Co Ltd* [1938] AC 586 at 600.

35.80 Where one joint tenant murders another it seems the criminal should hold the property as constructive trustee for himself and his victim in equal shares[1]. If the remainderman murders the life tenant it seems that the victim should be deemed to have lived as long as predicted by actuarial mortality tables (except for death-bed killings, e g 'mercy' killings) so that for this notional period the victim's interest should be held on a constructive trust for the victim's estate and, thereafter, the remaining interests should devolve normally[2].

1   *Rasmanis v Jurewitsch* [1970] 1 NSWR 650; *Re K* [1985] Ch 85 (affd [1986] Ch 180 without considering this point); (1973) 89 LQR 235 (T.G. Youdan); (1974) 37 MLR 481 (Earnshaw and Pace); *Re Dreger* (1976) 69 DLR (3d) 47. If X, Y and Z are joint tenants and X kills Y then X should become tenant in common of one-third and Z of two-thirds. Generally see M Cope *Constructive Trusts* (Law Book Co, Australia 1992) Chap 13.
2   (1973) 89 LQR 235 at 250–251 (T.G. Youdan).

35.81 It is not only murder that invokes the principle but also manslaughter[1] including manslaughter by reason of diminished responsibility[2]. However, the principle does not apply to insane killers[3].

1   *Re Estate of Hall* [1914] P 1, CA; *Re Giles* [1972] Ch 544, [1971] 3 All ER 1141.

35.81 *Constructive trusts*

²   *Re Giles* [1972] Ch 544, [1971] 3 All ER 1141 and *Dunbar v Plant* [1998] Ch 412 at 436 and 437, [1997] 4 All ER 289 at 310 and 311, per Phillips LJ; *Permanent Trustee Co Ltd v Gillett* (2004) 6 ITELR 1063 at [36] ff, NSW Sup Ct (Eq Div). See further (1973) LQR 235 at 237–248 (T.G. Youdan); (1974) 37 MLR 481 at 492–496 (Earnshaw and Pace).
³   *Re Houghton* [1915] 2 Ch 173; *Re Pitts* [1931] 1 Ch 546; Criminal Procedure (Insanity) Act 1964, s 1 (verdict now not guilty by reason of insanity).

POSSIBLE RELIEF UNDER FORFEITURE ACT 1982

35.82 Where the court is satisfied that in all the circumstances the justice of the case requires it[1], the court can modify the effect of the forfeiture rule as it applies to the 'offender' ie the unlawful killer or the person who has unlawfully aided, abetted, counselled or procured the victim's death[2], but not someone who has been convicted of murder[3]. The offender must bring proceedings within three months of conviction[4]. The Act applies to killings even before it came into operation on 13 October 1982 unless, in consequence of the forfeiture rule, the property had before then been acquired by someone else[5]. 'Acquired' denotes property which has actually been transferred to a person or to which a person has acquired an indefeasible right to have it transferred to him[6]. The Act applies to benefits under the deceased's will, nomination, intestacy, or donatio mortis causa, and to property held on trust before the death which would devolve on the offender as a result of the death[7].

¹   Forfeiture Act 1982, s 2(1). See *Dunbar v Plant* [1998] Ch 412, CA. Contrast *Re H* [1990] 1 FLR 441 with *Jones v Roberts* [1985] 2 FLR 422, High Court, discussed by R A Buckley (1995) 111 LQR 196. See too *Dalton v Latham* [2003] EWHC 796 (Ch), [2003] WTLR 687.
²   Forfeiture Act 1982, s 1(2). *Re Paterson, Petitioner* 1986 SLT 121.
³   Forfeiture Act 1982, s 5.
⁴   Forfeiture Act 1982, s 2(3).
⁵   Forfeiture Act 1982, s 2(7).
⁶   *Re K* [1986] Ch 180, [1985] 2 All ER 833, CA.
⁷   Forfeiture Act 1982, s 2(4).

Paragraph 2(f)

Rescission of voidable property transfers

35.83 Where C deliberately transfers legal and beneficial ownership in particular property to D under a legally binding agreement, but C's intention was vitiated by some factor such as fraud, undue influence, mistake or misrepresentation, C can elect to rescind the transaction[1]. In fixing upon the appropriate remedy the court may then order D or a donee from D to transfer the property or its traceable product to C, so that D or his donee is regarded as holding the property on trust for C[2]. Alternatively, payment of compensation may be a more appropriate (or indeed the only possible) remedy. For example, if the vitiated transaction was an unsecured contract of loan, C cannot be placed in a better position than if the loan had been valid and so can only be a personal creditor for the amount lent[3].

1. The situation is different where C transfers legal ownership of property to D for some reason other than the fact that he is contractually bound to do so, as here, a trust is imposed on the property at the moment of receipt by the fraudster D: *Twinsectra v Yardley* [1999] Lloyd's Rep Bank 438 at [99] per Potter LJ; *Collings v Lee* [2001] 2 All ER 332 at 337 per Nourse LJ; *Halley v Law Society* [2003] WTLR 845 at [46]–[48] per Carnwath LJ. The situation is also different where D steals property from C and legal title does not pass to D, as D cannot be declared trustee of property which he does not own: *Shalson v Russo* [2003] EWHC 1637 (Ch), [2005] Ch 281 at [110] per Rimer J; *Sinclair Investment Holdings SA v Versailles Trade Finance Ltd* [2005] EWCA Civ 722, [2006] 1 BCLC 60 at [43] per Arden LJ. For this reason Lord Browne Wilkinson's comments to the contrary in *Westdeutsche Landesbank Girozentrale v Islington London Borough Council* [1996] AC 669 at 715–716 must be doubted.

2. As in eg *Robins v Incentive Dynamics Pty Ltd (in liquidation)* (2003) 45 ACSR 244, NSWCA. According to some authorities, the trust imposed in C's favour may be a resulting trust rather than a constructive trust: see eg *Halley v Law Society* [2003] WTLR 845 at [99] per Mummery LJ; *Cripps v Lakeview Farm Fresh Ltd (in rec)* [2006] 1 NZLR 238 at [75], NZ High Ct. For discussion see paras 28.31–28.32.

3. *Halifax Building Society v Thomas* [1996] Ch 217; *Daly v Sydney Stock Exchange* (1986) 160 CLR 271.

35.84 However, if D's fraudulent misrepresentation or undue influence resulted in C transferring a house or a painting to D[1] then, clearly, C should be able to obtain an order for the reconveyance to C of the house or painting and such order should also be made against a donee from D. Indeed, if D had sold the house or painting and used the proceeds to buy another asset, then such traceable asset should be conveyed to C by D or by a donee thereof from D[2]. Once C's rescission has been made known to D or a donee from him[3], then clearly D and the donee should be regarded retrospectively from that date as constructive trustees when the court makes its order for the property to be transferred to C[4]. Indeed, because D's conscience is affected from the time when C transferred the property, he should be constructive trustee from that time and personally accountable for any profits made out of the transferred property[5].

1. Where D is a fiduciary apparently authorised by C so as to fall outside the constructive trust automatically arising under Article 33 it seems he should be estopped from taking advantage of his own wrongdoing by relying on such consent, which he knew was not a true consent.

2. Where no constructive trust automatically arises against a fiduciary under the preceding footnote, it seems C only has a mere equity (*Phillips v Phillips* (1862) 4 De GF & J 208 at 218 and 222 endorsed by Lord Millett in (1998) 114 LQR 399 at 416 but see *Eyre v Burmester* (1862) 10 HL Cas 90 and *Gresley v Mousley* (1859) 4 De G & J 78 at 86) so it binds all but a bona fide purchaser of a legal or equitable interest for value without notice.

3. A claimant's action in issuing proceedings can amount to an implied election to rescind in itself: *Shalson v Russo* [2005] Ch 281 at [120] per Rimer J, relying on *Banque Belge pour l'Etranger v Hambrouck* [1921] 1 KB 321 at 332 per Atkin LJ.

4. *El Ajou v Dollar Land Holdings plc* [1993] 3 All ER 717 at 734; *Bristol and West Building Society v Mothew* [1998] Ch 1 at 23 [1996] 4 All ER 678 at 716, CA; *O'Sullivan v Management Agency & Music Ltd* [1985] QB 428 at 457, CA; *Twinsectra Ltd v Yardley* [1999] Lloyd's Rep Bank 438 at [99] per Potter LJ. See too Lord Millett (1998) 114 LQR 399 at 416.

5. *Westdeutsche Landesbank v Islington London Borough Council* [1996] AC 669 at 705–706, 707, 709.

35.85 *Constructive trusts*

Paragraph 2(g)

Unconscionable money receipts by agents with insolvency problems where principal cannot be benefited

35.85 In *Neste Oy v Lloyds Bank plc[1]* claimant ship owners made regular payments to the general bank account of PSL, their agents, to discharge present and future liabilities relating to services provided for their ships. '[The last] payment was credited to PSL at a time when Peckston Group Ltd had already resolved that it and its group companies should cease trading immediately (one of the directors supporting the resolution being a director of PSL) at a time when PSL had not paid for the services for which the funds had been remitted and at a time when, in all the circumstances, there was no chance that PSL could pay for the services'[2]. It thus appears that the directors of PSL would have been liable for wrongful trading if they had continued PSL's business. Bingham J held[3], 'Given the situation of PSL when the last payment was received, any honest and reasonable directors (or the actual directors had they known of it) would, I feel sure, have arranged for the repayment of that sum to the plaintiffs without hesitation or delay ... and, accordingly, a constructive trust is to be inferred'. Therefore, the defendant Bank could not set-off the plaintiffs' payment to PSL against money due from PSL to the Bank, which had notice of the trust.

[1] [1983] 2 Lloyd's Rep 658.
[2] [1983] 2 Lloyd's Rep 658 at 666.
[3] [1983] 2 Lloyd's Rep 658 at 665.

35.86 In *Re Japan Leasing (Europe) plc[1]*, a purchaser paid an instalment payment for purchase of an aeroplane to A Ltd, the head vendor, to divide the instalment between itself and three other companies, co-vendors with A Ltd. The intended beneficial payment to A Ltd discharged the purchaser of its liability to the four co-vendors under contractual arrangements which also expressly excluded any trust relationship arising between A Ltd and the other three co-vendors in respect of instalments received by A Ltd: it was only under a personal contractual obligation as agent to account to each of the three co-vendors in respect of such instalments. However, the judge held that the exclusion clause did not help A Ltd for the instalment received after its financial problems had led to it going into administration. Such clause excluded an express trust but not the constructive trust that the judge held to arise by operation of law against A because[2] 'it would be unconscionable for the Company [A Ltd], as agent, to receive money as agent knowing that it could not account for it to its principal [the other three co-vendors]'. The instalment was held on constructive trust for the four co-vendors.

[1] [2000] WTLR 301.
[2] [2000] WTLR 301 at 316.

Paragraph 2(h)

Assignments for value of future property

35.87 As Swinfen–Eady LJ stated in *Re Lind[1]*:

'an assignment for value of future property actually binds the property itself directly it is acquired—automatically on the happening of the event, and without any further act on the part of the assignor—and does not merely rest in, and amount to, a right in contract, giving rise to an action. The assignor having the consideration, becomes in equity, on the happening of the event, trustee for the assignee of the property devolving upon or acquired by him, and which he had previously sold and been paid for.'

[1]   [1915] 2 Ch 345 at 360; also see *Re Gillott's Settlement* [1934] Ch 97 at 108–109 and *Pullan v Koe* [1913] 1 Ch 9.

35.88   The constructive trust arises as a result of the maxim 'Equity regards as done that which ought to be done'[1], the assignor being bound to hold the materialised former future property on trust for the assignee by virtue of his earlier receipt of consideration from the assignee. As Dixon J stated in *Palette Shoes Pty Ltd v Krohn*[2]:

'Because value has been given on the one side, the conscience of the other party is bound when the subject matter comes into existence, that is, when, as is generally the case, the legal property vests in him. Because his conscience is bound in respect of a subject of property, equity fastens upon the property itself and makes him a trustee of the legal right or ownership for the assignee. But although the matter rests primarily in contract, the prospective right in property which the assignee obtains is a higher right than to have specific performance of a contract and it may survive the assignor's bankruptcy because it attaches without more *eo instanti* when the property arises and gives the assignee an equitable interest therein.'

[1]   'The principle that is applied is not a principle depending upon the possibility of a court of equity decreeing specific performance. The relevant principle is that equity considers as done that which ought to be done': Latham CJ in *Palette Shoes Pty Ltd v Krohn* (1937) 58 CLR 1 at 16; Meagher Gummow & Lehane *Equity: Doctrines & Remedies* (4th edn) paras 6–275 to 6–330.
[2]   (1937) 58 CLR 1 at 27. Also see *Associated Alloys Pty Ltd v ACN 001 452 106 Pty Ltd* [2001] HCA 25, (2000) 74 ALJR 862.

ARTICLE 36
CONSTRUCTIVE TRUSTS IMPOSED ON PROPERTY SUBJECT TO A SPECIFICALLY ENFORCEABLE CONTRACT OF SALE

36.1

When a vendor enters into a specifically enforceable contract for the sale of property he becomes a constructive trustee thereof for the purchaser until the contract is completed by transfer of the property to the purchaser or to the order of the purchaser[1]. Once the purchaser has wholly fulfilled his side of the contract (eg by paying over the purchase price) but the vendor still has title to the property then the vendor holds the property on a bare trust for the absolutely entitled purchaser[2]. Until then the vendor's trusteeship is a highly self-interested modified form of trusteeship.

[1]   *Wall v Bright* (1820) 1 Jac & W 494 at 503; *Shaw v Foster* (1872) LR 5 HL 321; A-J Oakley *Constructive Trusts* (3rd edn) Chap 6, M. Cope *Constructive Trusts* (Law Book Co of Australia, 1992) Chap 25.

36.1 *Constructive trusts*

2   *Shaw v Foster* (1872) LR 5 HL 321 at 349 and 356; *Bridges v Mees* [1957] Ch 475, [1957] 2 All ER 577; *Williams on Title* (4th edn) p 713.

The effect of the doctrine of conversion

36.2 Where the contract for sale is specifically enforceable the equitable doctrine of conversion looks on that as done which ought to be done. Thus equity looks on the purchaser as owner of the property the subject of the contract (eg specific real property) and the vendor as the owner of the purchase money (ie personal property)[1]. However, the vendor retains the legal title to the property (or the primary equitable title if he is selling an equitable interest) until full performance of the contract. By operation of law the vendor then holds the property on constructive trust for the purchaser[2]. Owing to absence of the necessary certainty of subject matter the purchaser does not hold the purchase money on a corresponding constructive trust for the vendor; instead, the vendor has a lien or charge on the property for the unpaid purchase money[3]. Only if the contract had been one of exchange of properties (eg if V sold Blackacre to P in exchange for P selling Whiteacre to V) would reciprocal constructive trusts have arisen.

1   For example *Re Birmingham* [1959] Ch 523, [1958] 2 All ER 397.
2   Whether the vendor's property is a legal or equitable interest: *Oughtred v IRC* [1958] Ch 383, [1958] 1 All ER 252; affd [1960] AC 206, [1959] 3 All ER 623, HL (Viscount Radcliffe and Lord Cohen); *Re Holt's Settlement* [1969] 1 Ch 100, [1968] 1 All ER 470; *DHN Food Distributors Ltd v London Borough of Tower Hamlets* [1976] 3 All ER 462, [1976] 1 WLR 852. Where there is a vendor and a purchaser and a sub-purchaser (as distinct from an assignee of the purchaser's contract) Stamp LJ has taken the view that the vendor is not a trustee for the sub-purchaser and the sub-purchaser cannot sue the vendor for specific performance. However, Goff LJ thought the sub-purchaser had acquired an equitable interest which the vendor was bound to recognise and the vendor and purchaser could not with notice of the sub-purchaser's claim agree to rescind or vary the head contract leaving the sub-purchaser with no more than a remedy against the purchaser. See *Berkley v Poulett* (1976) 242 Estates Gazette 39, CA. The absence of mutuality, because the vendor is not entitled to sue the sub-purchaser directly even if the sub-purchaser could sue such vendor, should prevent there being a specifically enforceable obligation between then so that the view of Stamp LJ seems preferable.
3   *Nives v Nives* (1880) 15 Ch D 649; *London and Cheshire Insurance Co Ltd v Laplagrene Property Co Ltd* [1971] Ch 499, [1971] 1 All ER 766.

36.3 Once the equitable doctrine of conversion has operated the vendor is subject to certain trusteelike obligations in respect of the property, whilst the purchaser becomes liable for risks inherent in the nature of ownership of the property, eg if destroyed by fire. If freehold land is the subject of the contract under the doctrine of conversion the vendor's interest is treated as one in pure personalty (the purchase proceeds) whilst the purchaser's interest is treated as one in land[1]. This can be crucial where a testator leaves his realty and personalty (or land and pure personalty) to different persons[2].

1   *Re Birmingham* [1959] Ch 523, [1958] 2 All ER 397.
2   Before 1926 the doctrine of conversion was more crucial since on intestacy realty passed to the heir and personalty to the next of kin. Section 3 of the Trusts of Land and Appointment of Trustees Act 1996 only abolishes conversion for trusts for sale of land: see para 32.10 above.

When doctrine of conversion operates

36.4 The doctrine of conversion operates from the time a contract is specifically enforceable. Few contracts for the sale of goods will be specifically enforceable since the equitable remedy of specific performance will only be granted if the breach of contract is incapable of being adequately compensated by an award of damages, eg in the case of a contract to sell a rare antique. From the moment of entering such a contract the remedy of specific performance will be available so that a constructive trust immediately arises.

36.5 Every piece of land is regarded as unique so as to make damages inadequate as compensation for the loss of an interest in land so that specific performance is prima facie available as a remedy. However, a contract for sale of land is only enforceable if either the vendor is in a position to make title in accordance with the contract or the purchaser agrees to accept the title notwithstanding that it is not in accordance with the contract[1]. Only after the contract has been concluded does the purchaser investigate the title so that the contract will only become enforceable some period thereafter. The question arises whether conversion only occurs when the contract has become enforceable (upon the vendor being able to make title in accordance with the contract or the purchaser otherwise accepting the title the vendor has).

[1]   *Lysaght v Edwards* (1876) 2 Ch D 499 at 506–507.

36.6 The authorities[1] establish that no conversion will occur if the vendor cannot make title in accordance with the contract and the purchaser does not agree to accept such other title as the vendor has. If the vendor can make title in accordance with the contract or if the purchaser otherwise accepts the title the vendor has, then conversion occurs with retrospective effect from the conclusion of the binding contract[2]. In fact, where the purchaser accepts the title the vendor has (the vendor not having been able to make title in accordance with the contract) there is no authority deciding that conversion is retrospective so that it has been suggested that conversion should only be retrospective when the vendor is able to make title in accordance with the contract and not where the purchaser agrees to accept some other title[3]. It is submitted that there should be retrospectivity in both cases. The date of concluding a binding contract (usually the date of exchange of contracts) will usually occasion no difficulty, whilst the ascertainment of the day when the purchaser agrees to accept what title the vendor has may well occasion difficulty. Moreover, if retrospectivity did not occur then the vendor would be under no trusteeship obligation in respect of the property till the purchaser accepted the vendor's actual title, so that before accepting such title, the purchaser ought to carry out a further inspection of the property to ensure that it had not deteriorated since conclusion of the contract. Since this would afford scope to the purchaser to withdraw from the contract if deterioration had occurred, the vendor *de facto* would need to preserve the property from deterioration, so there seems no reason why this situation shall not be regularised *de iure* by making the vendor under a trusteeship obligation from the date of the contract if the purchaser accepts title from the vendor otherwise than in accordance with the contract.

36.6 *Constructive trusts*

1   *Re Thomas* (1886) 34 Ch D 166; *Broome v Monck* (1805) 10 Ves 597; *Plews v Samuel* [1904] 1 Ch 464.
2   *Lysaght v Edwards* (1876) 2 Ch D 499 at 506–507, 510, 518.
3   P H Pettit (1960) 24 Conv (NS) 47, D W M Waters *The Constructive Trust*, pp 76–87.

36.7 Conversion should thus occur from the conclusion of a binding contract of sale of land once the vendor has been able to make title in accordance with the contract or the purchaser has otherwise accepted the vendor's title. Exceptionally and anomalously, owing to *Lawes v Bennett*[1], conversion is retrospective not just to the conclusion of a binding contract but to the date of grant of an option to purchase an interest in land where such an option has been granted and then exercised[2]. The exception has been restricted so as not to apply as between those interested in the estate of the grantee of the option[3] nor between the grantor and the grantee of the option so as to make the grantor liable as trustee between the grant and exercise of the option[4] nor where the property in question is the subject matter of a specific devise after the grant of the option so that the testator can be taken to have intended to pass to the devisee the entire interest therein, no matter what its nature[5]. Although many regard the rule in *Lawes v Bennett* as anomalous in redeeming specific devises in wills made before the grant of an option relating to the devised property Nicholls J[6] accepted it as well-established and extended it to a conditional contract entered into after the date of the testator's will where the condition was only fulfilled after the testator's death.

1   (1785) 1 Cox Eq Cas 167 applied in *Townley v Bedwell* (1808) 14 Ves 591; *Weeding v Weeding* (1861) 1 John & H 424; *Re Blake* [1917] 1 Ch 18; *Re Carrington* [1932] 1 Ch 1.
2   Even if the purchase does not subsequently go through: *Re Blake* [1917] 1 Ch 18.
3   *Re Adams and Kensington Vestry* (1884) 27 Ch D 394.
4   *Edwards v West* (1878) 7 Ch D 858.
5   *Weeding v Weeding* (1861) 1 John & H 424; *Emuss v Smith* (1848) 2 De G & Sm 722 (codicil after option republishing the will); *Re Pyle* [1895] 1 Ch 724 (will and option grant on same day).
6   *Re Sweeting* [1988] 1 All ER 1016.

The nature of the vendor's trusteeship

36.8 The vendor's trusteeship is of an unusual nature. As Lord Cairns remarked in *Shaw v Foster*[1]:

> 'There cannot be the slightest doubt of the relation subsisting in the eye of a court of equity between the vendor and the purchaser. The vendor was a trustee of the property for the purchaser; the purchaser was the real beneficial owner in the eye of a court of equity of the property, subject only to this observation, that the vendor, whom I have called a trustee, was not a mere dormant trustee, he was a trustee having a personal and substantial interest in the property, a right to protect that interest, and an active right to assert that interest if anything should be done in derogation of it. The relation, therefore, of trustee and cestui que trust subsisted, but subsisted subject to the paramount right of the vendor and trustee to protect his own interest as vendor of the property.'

1   (1872) LR 5 HL 321 at 338.

36.9 Similarly, in *Jerome v Kelly* Lord Walker observed that[1]:

36.10 'It would ... be wrong to treat an uncompleted contract for the sale of land as equivalent to an immediate, irrevocable declaration of trust (or assignment of beneficial interest) in the land. Neither the seller nor the buyer has unqualified beneficial ownership. Beneficial ownership of the land is in a sense split between the seller and buyer on the provisional assumptions that specific performance is available and that the contract will in due course be completed, if necessary by the court ordering specific performance. In the meantime, the seller is entitled to enjoyment of the land or its rental income. The provisional assumptions may be falsified by events, such as rescission of the contract (either under a contractual term or on breach). If the contract proceeds to completion the equitable interest can be viewed as passing to the buyer in stages, as title is made and accepted and the purchase price is paid in full.'

1   [2004] UKHL 25, [2004] 1 WLR 1409 at [32].

36.11 The vendor, unless the contract otherwise provides, has the following rights. He has a right to remain in possession of the property until completion and he has an equitable lien on the property for payment of the purchase money[1]. He has a right to rents and profits due before the contractual completion date[2], but is under a corresponding duty to discharge outgoings (eg rates) payable in respect of the property[3]. Once the vendor has received the purchase price he will become a bare trustee pending transfer of his legal title and will have to pass on all benefits to the purchaser.

1   *Phillips v Silvester* (1872) 8 Ch App 173; *Re Birmingham* [1959] Ch 523, [1958] 2 All ER 397.
2   *Cuddon v Tite* (1858) 1 Giff 395.
3   *Barsht v Tagg* [1900] 1 Ch 231; *Re Highett and Bird's Contract* [1902] 2 Ch 214.

36.12 The vendor is under a duty to 'use reasonable care to preserve the property in a reasonable state of preservation, and, so far as may be, as it was when the contract was made' or 'to take reasonable care that the property is not deteriorated in the interval before completion'[1]. He must keep the property in repair[2] and must not himself damage the property[3] or let others damage the property through lack of reasonable precautions on his part[4]. He must not withdraw any application for planning permission[5] and it seems that if the purchaser is not buying for his own occupation but for speculation, then the vendor may well be under a duty to pass on to the purchaser higher offers for the property received by the vendor[6]. However it also seems that the vendor's duty does not encompass an obligation as lessor to impose covenants on purchasers of adjoining properties unless this obligation is imposed by the contract of sale of the property in question[7].

1   *Clarke v Ramuz* [1891] 2 QB 456 at 460, 468.
2   *Royal Bristol Permanent Building Society v Bomash* (1887) 35 Ch D 390.
3   *Phillips v Lamdin* [1949] 2 KB 33, [1949] 1 All ER 770.
4   *Clarke v Ramuz* [1891] 2 QB 456; *Davron Estates Ltd v Turnshire Ltd* (1982) 133 NLJ 937, CA; *Cedar Transport Group Ltd v First Wyvers Property Trustee Co Ltd* (1980) 258 Estates Gazette 1077 (damage by vandals); *Lucie-Smith v Gorman* [1981] CLY 2866 (burst pipe).
5   *Sinclair-Hill v Sothcott* (1973) 26 P & CR 490, but note Lawrence Collins J's doubts about this application of the principle in *Englewood Properties Ltd v Patel* [2005] EWHC 188 (Ch), [2005] 1 WLR 1961 at [56]–[57].

36.12 *Constructive trusts*

6   *Lake v Bayliss* [1974] 2 All ER 1114 at 1118.
7   *Englewood Properties Ltd v Patel* [2005] EWHC 188 (Ch), [2005] 1 WLR 1961.

36.13 Where land is sold subject to tenancies which come to an end before the contract is completed the vendor has a duty to inform the purchaser, so that a vendor who re-lets the property without informing the purchaser will be liable for any loss thereby suffered[1]. If the purchaser directs the vendor not to re-let and undertakes to compensate the vendor for any loss thereby suffered then the vendor should not re-let. If the purchaser does not respond to notification that the property (or part thereof) has fallen vacant and that the vendor is considering re-letting then the vendor should re-let[2] unless it is in his best interests to retain the property with vacant possession the better to assist a re-sale at a good price if the sale falls through. Whether the whole or only a small part of the premises falls vacant will often be crucial. If the whole becomes vacant then it will very often be in the interest of both vendor and purchaser not to re-let before completion. Where the premises comprise several lettings and have been purchased for their rental income then re-letting of the vacated part will often be best, though the purchaser may be happy to do this himself after completion, in which case he should offer to compensate the vendor for what the vendor may lose through not re-letting before completion.

1   *Earl Egmont v Smith* (1877) 6 Ch D 469.
2   *Abdulla v Shah* [1959] AC 124, [1959] 2 WLR 12, PC.

36.14 The vendor's duties should be performed as much in his interest as in the purchaser's interest since the sale may fall through and, as a result, the vendor is not entitled to be reimbursed for any expenses thereby incurred[1].

1   *Re Watford Corpn and Ware's Contract* [1943] Ch 82, [1943] 1 All ER 54.

The purchaser's position

36.15 Unless the purchaser has expressly waived his rights he can sue the vendor for breach of the vendor's trusteeship duties even after completion of the contract: the duties do not merge in the conveyance and completion does not amount to waiver of any breach of the vendor's trusteeship duties[1].

1   *Clarke v Ramuz* [1891] 2 QB 456 at 561; *Cumberland Consolidated Holdings Ltd v Ireland* [1946] KB 264 at 269.

36.16 Since the purchaser is regarded under the doctrine of conversion as the owner of the property, the subject of the contract, he takes the benefit and burden of gains and losses of a capital nature accruing to the property itself.

36.17 Except in unforeseen extreme circumstances, a contract for the sale of land cannot be frustrated[1]. Thus (in the absence of a contrary contractual provision like that in Standard Conditions of Sale Condition 5.1) a purchaser bears the risk, for example, of total destruction of the buildings by fire as long as not caused by breach of the vendor's trusteeship duties[2]. If a purchaser has been foolish enough not to have insured the property he cannot, if the vendor has insured the property, recover insurance moneys from the vendor[3]. He will have to pay the purchase money to the vendor's insurance company who, having satisfied the vendor's claim, will be subrogated to the vendor's right to the purchase price[4].

1   *Wong Lai-Ying v Chinachen Investments Co Ltd* [1978] HKLR 1, PC; *Cricklewood Property and Investment Trust Ltd v Leighton's Trust Ltd* [1945] AC 221, [1945] 1 All ER 252; *Total Oil Great Britain Ltd v Thompson Garages (Biggin Hill) Ltd* [1972] 1 QB 318, [1971] 3 All ER 1226, CA; *Hillingdon Estate Co v Stonefield Estates Ltd* [1952] Ch 627 at 631; *National Carriers Ltd v Panalpina (Northern) Ltd* [1981] AC 675, [1981] 1 All ER 161, HL; *Amalgamated Investments & Property Co v John Walker & Sons* [1977] 1 WLR 164, CA.
2   *Rayner v Preston* (1881) 18 Ch D 1, CA; *Paine v Meller* (1801) 6 Ves 349.
3   *Rayner v Preston* (1881) 18 Ch D 1, CA.
4   *Castellain v Preston* (1883) 11 QBD 380, approved by House of Lords in *Lord Napier and Ettrick v RF Kershaw Ltd* [1993] AC 713.

36.18 Section 83 of the Fires Prevention (Metropolis) Act 1774, where buildings have been destroyed or damaged by fire, enables any person interested to require the insurance company to lay out the insurance money towards rebuilding or reinstating the building in question so long as the money has not already been paid to the assured. However it seems that this obligation only arises where the assured was under an obligation to the person interested to reinstate the premises (eg where a landlord has so covenanted with a tenant)[1]: this is unlikely as between vendor and purchaser.

1   *Lonsdale & Thompson Ltd v Black Arrow Group plc* [1993] Ch 361.

36.19 Section 47 of the Law of Property Act 1925 was enacted with a view to assisting purchasers, but did not achieve its object, as it obliges the vendor to pay over money which 'becomes payable' by the vendor's insurer following an insured loss: the problem with this wording is that nothing 'becomes payable' by the insurer where the vendor can recover the full purchase price from the purchaser as in this case the vendor suffers no loss. For this reason the Law Commission thought that legislation might be desirable to change the law by ruling that the risk of loss does not pass to the purchaser until completion of the contract. However, it made no recommendation for statutory intervention because the same effect has been achieved by the Law Society's *Standard Conditions of Sale*[1]. Condition 5.1.1 enables a purchaser on or after completion to recover from the vendor any insurance money paid 'in respect of any damage to or destruction of property included in the contract' (whether caused by fire or not). However, this is subject to any contrary stipulation in the contract, any requisite consent of the insurance company, and the payment by the purchaser of the proportionate part of the premium from the date of the contract.

1   Law Commission Transfer of Land: Passing of Risk from Vendor to Purchaser (Law Com WP No 109, 1988) Part II; Law Commission Transfer of Land: Risk of Damage After Contract of Sale (Law Com No 191, 1990) Parts II and III.

36.20 The purchaser is entitled to all gains or benefits of a capital nature *accruing to the property itself*, eg improvements financed by the vendor[1]. He is not entitled to benefits accruing to the vendor qua vendor unless expressly provided for by the contract for sale. Thus the vendor, in the absence of statutory intervention or a contrary contractual term, can retain insurance money payable to him[2]. He can retain sums due in respect of dilapidations arising between contract and conveyance payable under a lease expiring in that period[3]. In *Re Hamilton-Snowball's Conveyance*[4] H-S, occupying a requisitioned house, contracted to buy it from its owner, the conveyance to him going to have the effect of derequisitioning the house. Later the same day H-S contracted to re-sell the house to the purchaser at a much higher price, not mentioning the requisitioning since the subsequent conveyance to H-S would derequisition the house. The house was conveyed to H-S, derequisitioned, and then conveyed by H-S to the purchaser. As houseowner at the time of derequisitioning H-S received a substantial sum under the Compensation (Defence) Act 1939. The purchaser's claim that H-S held this sum as constructive trustee for the purchaser failed since the sum was not paid as an accrual to the property that was the subject matter of the purchaser's contract.

1   *Monro v Taylor* (1848) 8 Hare 51 at 60.
2   *Rayner v Preston* (1881) 18 Ch D 1, CA.
3   *Re Lyne-Stephens and Scott-Miller's Contract* [1920] 1 Ch 472. If the sale had been subject to, but with the benefit of, an existing lease the position would have differed.
4   [1959] Ch 308, [1958] 2 All ER 319.

36.21 Since the vendor holds the property as constructive trustee for the purchaser it follows that, if the vendor in breach of trust sells the property to a third party, the purchaser may trace the property into the proceeds of sale received by the vendor from the third party[1]. This will be useful where the purchaser has no claim against the third party for want of protecting his estate contract on the appropriate register and where the contractual claim against the vendor for damages is not worthwhile, eg because the vendor is bankrupt or because more financial benefit can be obtained from the tracing claim than from the damages claim.

1   *Lake v Bayliss* [1974] 2 All ER 1114, [1974] 1 WLR 1073.

Division Four

THE ADMINISTRATION OF
A TRUST

Chapter 10

DISCLAIMER AND ACCEPTANCE OF TRUSTS

Article

ARTICLE 37
THE NUMBER OF TRUSTEES PERMISSIBLE

37.1

As a general rule the number of trustees is not prescribed by law, one being sufficient, and any greater number permissible. But, in the case of trusts of land and trustees for the purposes of the Settled Land Act, the maximum number is four and the minimum for giving a good receipt for purchase-money two, unless the sole trustee is a trust corporation.

37.2 Section 34 of the Trustee Act 1925 provides that:

(1) Where, at the commencement of this Act, there are more than four trustees of a settlement of land, or more than four trustees holding land on trust for sale, no new trustees shall (except where as a result of the appointment the number is reduced to four or less) be capable of being appointed until the number is reduced to less than four, and thereafter the number shall not be increased beyond four.

(2) In the case of settlements[1] and dispositions creating trusts[2] of land made or coming into operation after the commencement of this Act—
   (a) the number of trustees thereof shall not in any case exceed four, and where more than four persons are named as such trustees, the four first named (who are able and willing to act) shall alone be the trustees, and the other persons named shall not be trustees unless appointed on the occurrence of a vacancy;
   (b) the number of the trustees shall not be increased beyond four.

(3) This section applies to settlements and dispositions of land, and the restrictions imposed on the number of trustees do not apply—

(a)   in the case of land vested in trustees for charitable, ecclesiastical, or public purposes; or

(b)   where the net proceeds of the sale of the land are held for like purposes; or

(c)   to the trustees of a term of years absolute limited by a settlement on trusts for raising money, or of a like term created under the statutory remedies relating to annual sums charged on land.

1   Under the Settled Land Act 1925: Trusts of Land and Appointment of Trustees Act 1996, s 23(1), Law of Property Act 1925, s 205(1)(xxvi), Settled Land Act 1925, s 117(1)(xxiv), Trustee Act 1925, s 68(1), (15). No new SLA settlements can be created after 1996: see s 2 of the 1996 Act.

2   See Sch 3, para 3(9) of the Trusts of Land and Appointment of Trustees Act 1996 substituting 'creating trusts of land' for 'on trust for sale of land', the former expression covering any trust of land (including trusts for sale) other than SLA settled land: s 1(1)(a) of the 1996 Act.

37.3 The requirement for a minimum of two trustees[1] to *give a good receipt for the purchase-money of English and Welsh land* applies whether the sale be by trustees or by a tenant for life or statutory owner selling under the powers of the Settled Land Act[2]. This is further referred to in Article 64, below. But it does not apply to a sole personal representative acting as such[3.] Nor does it apply where the sole trustee is a 'trust corporation', as defined.[4]

1   This applies to Settled Land Act trustees: Settled Land Act 1925, s 18. Exceptionally, a sole personal representative acting as such may give valid receipts for capital moneys:

2   As to trustees by s 27(2) of the Law of Property Act 1925, and as to Settled Land Act trustees by s 94 of the Settled Land Act 1925.

3   Law of Property Act 1925, s 27(2).

4   A 'trust corporation' is defined in the statutes as 'the Public Trustee or a corporation either appointed by the Court [or the Charity Commissioners] in any particular case to be a trustee or entitled by rules made under subsection (3) of section 4 of the Public Trustee Act 1906 to act as custodian trustee' (Law of Property Act 1925, s 205(1)(xxviii); Settled Land Act 1925, s 117(1)(xxx); Trustee Act 1925, s 68(18) and by the Law of Property (Amendment) Act 1926, s 3 and Charities Act 1993, s 35, the definition was extended to include the Treasury Solicitor, the Official Solicitor, and certain other official persons and trustees of charitable, ecclesiastical and public trusts. See also the Public Trustee Rules 1912, r 30 as substituted by the Public Trustee (Custodian Trustee) Rules 1975 under SI 1975/1189 as amended by SI 1987/1891 and SI 1994/2519, which require the company to be a company constituted under the law of a European Union Member State and to have an issued share capital of £250,000 (or its foreign currency equivalent) of which not less than £100,000 (or its equivalent) paid up and to have a place of business in the UK (and, of course, be empowered under its constitution to undertake trust business-):see paras 79.5–79.6 below. It must also be authorised under the Financial Services and Markets Act 2000.

37.4 There is no restriction on the number of tenants for life in whom settled land may be vested as joint tenants.

37.5 Where a trust with more than four trustees is not a trust of land initially, but English or Welsh land is later acquired by the trustees, a problem will arise. Such land should not be vested in more than four persons as trustees, so if sufficient trustees do not retire[1] to reduce their number to four the first four named will become trustees to the exclusion of the others[2].

1   See Trustee Act 1925, s 39, para 72.11 below.

2   Trustee Act 1925, s 34(2)(a). An alternative would be to acquire the land through a holding company owned by all the trustees.

37.6 When a trust ceases to be a trust of land, either because the land has been distributed to one or more beneficiaries or it has been sold, so that the trustees are holding money on deposit and investments other than land, then the restriction on the number of trustees will cease[1].

1   See ss 17(3) and 1(1) of the 1996 Act.

ARTICLE 38
DISCLAIMER OF A TRUST

38.1

No one is bound to accept the office of trustee[1]. Both the office and the estate may be disclaimed before acceptance (but not afterwards[2]) by deed or by conduct tantamount to a disclaimer[3]. It is not possible to accept the estate whilst disclaiming the office[4].The disclaimer should be made within a reasonable period of acquiring knowledge, having regard to the circumstances of the particular case[5]. Part of a trust cannot be disclaimed if other parts be accepted[6], though If appointed trustee of two separate trusts a person may accept one and reject the other unless this would be contrary to the settlor's intention. The onus of proving disclaimer is on those who assert it[7].

1   *Robinson v Pett* (1734) 3 P Wms 249, 2 White & Tud LC 605.
2   *Re Lister* [1926] Ch 149; *Re Sharman's Will Trusts* [1942] Ch 311, [1942] 2 All ER 74, where this Article was cited with approval by Bennett J.
3   *Stacey v Elph* (1833) 1 My & K 195; *Townson v Tickell* (1819) 3 B & Ald 31; *Begbie v Crook* (1835) 2 Bing NC 70; *Bingham v Lord Clanmorris* (1828) 2 Mol 253; and *Re Birchall* (1889) 40 Ch D 436.
4   *Re Birchall* (1889) 40 Ch D 436, CA (trustee by conduct disclaimed office; must of necessity have also disclaimed estate); and see *Lancashire v Lancashire* (1848) 2 Ph 657; and *Re Clout and Frewer's Contract* [1924] 2 Ch 230.
5   See *Doed Chidgey v Harris* (1847) 16 M & W 517 at 522; *Paddon v Richardson* (1855) 7 De GM & G 563; *James v Frearson* (1842) 1 Y & C Ch C as 370.
6   *Re Lord and Fullerton's Contract* [1896] 1 Ch 228. Cf *Wellesley v Withers* (1855) 4 E & B 750.
7   See *Re Arbib and Class's Contract* [1891] 1 Ch 601, CA: also paras 39.6–39.7 below.

Consent to undertake future trust not binding

38.2 Even though a person may have agreed in the lifetime of a testator to be his executor, he is still at liberty to resile from his promise at any time before proving the will[1]. However, a person can be made a constructive or resulting trustee against his will, eg under the doctrines of secret trusts[2] and mutual wills[3].

1   *Doyle v Blake* (1804) 2 Sch & Lef 231.
2   See para 12.80 above.
3   See para 35.53 above.

38.3 Disclaimer and acceptance of trusts

Methods of disclaiming

38.3 A prudent person will, of course, always disclaim by deed[1], in order that there may be no question of the fact; but a disclaimer by counsel at the bar[2], or even by conduct inconsistent with acceptance, is sufficient[3]. It seems mere inaction over a long period may be evidence of disclaimer[4].

1   Married women are in the same position as men: Statute Law (Repeals) Act 1969, Sch, P III, repealing Law of Property Act 1925, ss 167–170.
2   *Norway v Norway* (1834) 2 My & K 278; *Bray v West* (1838) 9 Sim 429.
3   *Foster v Dawber* (1860) 8 WR 646; *Stacey v Elph* (1833) 1 My & K 195; *Re Gordon* (1877) 6 Ch D 531.
4   *Re Clout and Frewer's Contract* [1924] 2 Ch 230.

38.4 Where a deed is executed with the intention that it shall operate as a disclaimer, it will have that effect, notwithstanding that the disclaiming trustee purports to convey or release his estate to the accepting trustees, an action which logically raises the inference that he has accepted the estate[1]. However it is best to execute a deed poll expressed as a disclaimer[2].

1   *Nicolson v Wordsworth* (1818) 2 Swan 365 at 370–371, 372.
2   *Re Schar* [1951] Ch 280 at 284, [1950] 2 All ER 1069 at 1071).

Costs of disclaimer

38.5 A person nominated to be a trustee who refuses to accept the office ought not to be put to expense. He is therefore entitled, as a condition of executing a deed of disclaimer, to be paid out of the trust estate all his costs of and incident thereto, including the costs of taking counsel's opinion[1]. If (not having previously disclaimed) he is made a defendant to an action concerning the trust, he should, generally speaking, disclaim at once and offer to execute all necessary documents on his costs being paid. He will then be entitled to have the action against him dismissed, with costs[2]. What would happen in the case of a person nominated as trustee who unreasonably refuses either to accept or disclaim seems never to have been decided in any reported case. It is apprehended, however, that he would get no costs of any proceedings rendered necessary by his ill-conditioned conduct, though it is difficult to see how he could be ordered to pay costs. Indeed, in one case (before the present wide judicial discretion as to costs) where the executrix of a deceased trustee refused to act in the trust (she could not disclaim) she was allowed her costs of a suit for the appointment of new trustees and a transfer of the trust property[3].

1   *Re Tryon* (1844) 7 Beav 496.
2   See *Benbow v Davies* (1848) 11 Beav 369; *Norway v Norway* (1834) 2 My & K 278; *Bray v West* (1838) 9 Sim 429. As to where he is a defendant in a foreclosure action by a mortgagee of the trustee estate, see *Ford v Lord Chesterfield* (1853) 16 Beav 516. Costs would probably be only on the standard basis which has replaced party and party costs.
3   *Legg v Mackrell* (1860) 2 De GF & J 551.

Effect of disclaimer

38.6 The effect of disclaimer is to avoid the devise, bequest, or grant *ab initio*, so that where there are two trustees and one disclaims, the title of the other who accepts is complete *ab initio*, and devolves on his death as such[1]. This equally applies to powers annexed to the office[2], but not to personal powers[3].If a person appointed sole trustee disclaims (unless his personality was regarded by the settlor as critical to the running of the trust[4]), the trust does not fail: the property is held by the settlor or, if he is dead, his personal representatives upon the trusts specified in the settlement or will[5].

[1]   *Peppercorn v Wayman* (1852) 5 De G & Sm 230; *JW Broomhead (Vcc) Pty Ltd v JW Brownhead Pty Ltd* [1985] VR 891; *Re Paradise Motor Co Ltd* [1968] 2 All ER 625, [1968] 1 WLR 1125, CA
[2]   *Browell v Reed* (1842) 1 Hare 434; *Adams v Taunton* (1820) 5 Madd 435.
[3]   *Wetherell v Langston* (1847) 1 Exch 634; *Crawford v Forshaw* (1890) 43 Ch D 643.
[4]   *Re Lysaght* [1966] Ch 191.
[5]   *Mallott v Wilson* [1903] 2 Ch 494, criticised by P Matthews [1981] Conv. 141, but applied in *Harris v Sharp* (1989) [2004] WTLR 1541, CA. Further on the unilateral and bilateral nature of gifts see J Hill (2001) 117 LQR 127.

38.7 The effect of a disclaimer of a legal estate in land by a person who has been entered on the land register as proprietor of that estate is less clear. The legislation[1] does not deal explicitly with this situation. Probably, however, the disclaimer does not take effect immediately, and he remains the proprietor[2], unless and until steps are taken to alter the register.[3]

[1]   Ie Land Registration Act 2002, Land Registration Rules 2003.
[2]   Land Registration Act 2002, s 58 (conclusiveness of entry on register).
[3]   Under Land Registration Act 2002, s 65 and Sch 4.

ARTICLE 39
ACCEPTANCE OF A TRUST

39.1

A person may accept the office of trustee expressly, or he may do so constructively by doing such acts as are only referable to the character of trustee or executor, or he may do so by long acquiescence. In the absence of evidence to the contrary, acceptance will be presumed[1].

[1]   *In Re Sharman's Will Trusts* [1942] Ch 311, [1942] 2 All ER 74, Bennett J cited this Article, for which authority is to be found in *Townson v Tickell* (1819) 3 B & Ald 31; *Standing v Bowring* (1885) 31 Ch D 282; *Re Arbib and Class's Contract* [1891] 1 Ch 601.

Express acceptance

39.2 A trustee expressly accepts the office by executing the settlement[1], or by making an express declaration of his assent[2].

[1]   *Buckeridge v Glasse* (1841) Cr & Ph 126; *Jones v Higgins* (1866) LR 2 Eq 538.
[2]   *Doe d Chidgey v Harris* (1847) 16 M & W 517.

39.3 Disclaimer and acceptance of trusts

Acceptance by acquiescence

39.3 Permitting an action concerning the trust property to be brought in his name[1], or otherwise allowing the trust property to be dealt with in his name[2], is such an acquiescence as will be construed to be an acceptance of the office.

[1]   *Lord Montford v Lord Cadogan* (1810) 17 Ves 485.
[2]   *James v Frearson* (1842) 1 Y & C Ch C as 370.

Acceptance by acts of ownership

39.4 Exercising any act of ownership, such as advertising the property for sale, giving notice to the tenants to pay the rents to himself or an agent, or requesting the steward of a manor to enrol a deed in relation to the trust property, and a fortiori active interference in the affairs of the trust[1], is sufficient to constitute acceptance of a trust[2], as normally will be opening a trust bank account, signing cheques, endorsing insurance policies and instructing solicitors[3].

[1]   *Doyle v Blake* (1804) 2 Sch & Lef 231; *Harrison v Graham* (unreported, but cited in I P Wms (6th edn) 241n; *Urch v Walker* (1838) 3 My & Cr 702.
[2]   *Bence v Gilpin* (1868) LR 3 Exch 76. As to acceptance of executorship by intermeddling, and its effect on subsequent devastavit by administrator, see *Doyle v Blake* (1804) 2 Sch & Lef 231.
[3]   *Holder v Holder* [1968] Ch 353, [1968] 1 All ER 665, where it was conceded by counsel that this was an acceptance of the executorship (eg *Cummins v Cummins* (1845) 3 Jo & Lat 64, not cited to CA) but the concession was doubted by the court.

Acceptance by taking out probate

39.5 Where the office of executor is clothed with certain trusts, or where the executor is also nominated the trustee of real estate under a will, he is treated as having accepted the office of trustee if he takes out probate to the will[1].

[1]   *Mucklow v Fuller* (1821) Jac 198; *Ward v Butler* (1824) 2 Mol 533; *Booth v Booth* (1838) 1 Beav 125; *Styles v Guy* (1849) 1 Mac & G 422; *Re Sharman's Will Trusts* [1942] Ch 311, [1942] 2 All ER 74.

Acceptance by conduct

39.6 Where a person appointed as trustee of a will receives trust rents from the lessee to whom he is also agent, he cannot be heard to say that he is not also acting as trustee[1]. However an interference with trust property which is plainly (not ambiguously) referable to some other ground will not operate as an acceptance[2]. It was said in an old case that merely taking charge of a trust until a new trustee can be found does not constitute, of itself, a constructive acceptance[3]. However, it is considered that this view would be rejected nowadays especially where such acts would make even a stranger a trustee or executor de son tort[4].

[1]   *Conyngham v Conyngham* (1750) I Ves Sen 522; and see *Re Sharman's Will Trusts* [1942] Ch 311, [1942] 2 All ER 74.

2   *Stacey v Elph* (1833) I My & K 195; *Dove v Everard* (1830) I Russ & M 231; *Lowry v Fulton* (1838) 9 Sim 104.
3   *Evans v John* (1841) 4 Beav 35.
4   See para 100.2.

39.7 In another dubious case, the joining in the legacy duty receipt for the trust fund, unaccompanied by the actual receipt of the money, was held to be of itself insufficient to fix a trustee, who desired to disclaim, with acceptance of the trusteeship, though he need not have signed if he were not a trustee[1].

1   *Jago v Jago* (1893) 68 LT 654.

Acceptance by long silence

39.8 There is a prima facie presumption of acceptance; so that where a trustee, with notice of the trust, has indulged in a passive acquiescence for some years, he will be presumed to have accepted it, in the absence of any satisfactory explanation[1]. And where a testator nominated A, who was living in Australia, to be one of his trustees if he should return to England, and some years after the testator's death he did return for a temporary visit, and there was no evidence of disclaimer, it was held that the prima facie presumption of acceptance had not been rebutted, and that a title could not be made by the other trustees[2]. But a long period of silence and inaction can rebut the presumption of acceptance[3]. After all, to presume that inaction amounts to acceptance is to presume an intention to neglect a duty to act: is it not better to presume from long inaction an intention never to be under any duty?

1   *Wise v Wise* (1845) 2 Jo & Lat 403; *Re Uniacke* (1844) 1 Jo & Lat 1; *Re Needham* (1844) 1 Jo & Lat 34; *Doed Chidgey v Harris* (1847) 16 M & W 517.
2   *Re Arbib and Class's Contract* [1891] 1 Ch 601. There was, however, some evidence that whilst in Australia A intended to become a trustee.
3   *Re Clout and Frewer's Contract* [1924] 2 Ch 230, casting doubt on *Re Uniacke* (1844) 1 Jo & Lat 1 and *Re Needham* (1844) 1 Jo & Lat 34 and preferring views expressed in *Re Gordon* (1877) 6 Ch D 531 and *Re Birchall* (1889) 40 Ch D 436. See also *JW Broomhead (Vic) Pty Ltd v JW Broomhead Pty Ltd* [1985] VR 891 at 931–932.

Acceptance of part and attempted disclaimer of other part

39.9 Acceptance of part of a trust is acceptance of the whole, notwithstanding any attempted disclaimer of part[1]. Thus, where a testator, having property here and abroad, gave the whole to trustees upon the same trusts, it was held that one of the trustees could not disclaim the English property while accepting the trusts of the foreign property. Consequently he was a necessary party to a sale of the former[2]. However it would seem that a person appointed by the same settlor to be trustee of two separate trusts could accept one and disclaim the other, unless this would be against the intention of the settlor.

1   It is different in, eg, Jersey and Guernsey law.
2   *Re Lord and Fullerton's Contract* [1896] 1 Ch 228; *Re Lister* [1926] Ch 149 at 166.

39.10 Lastly, when once a trust has been effectually disclaimed, interference by the disclaiming trustee will not cancel the disclaimer or raise an inference of acceptance of the trust—as, for example, where he acts as agent for the trustees or adviser to the family[1].

1   *Dove v Everard* (1830) 1 Russ & M 231; *Lowry v Fulton* (1838) 9 Sim 104; *Stacey v Elph* (1833) 1 My & K 195.

39.11 The position of a trustee de son tort (ie a person not nominated as trustee who gets possession of trust property with notice of the trust) is dealt with elsewhere[1].

1   See Article 100(1).

Chapter 11

THE ESTATE OF THE TRUSTEE AND ITS INCIDENTS

ARTICLE 40
ESTATE TAKEN BY THE TRUSTEE

40.1

The trustee takes such legal or equitable estate in the trust property as the settlor (or testator) has power to dispose of and as may be expressed to be vested in him by conveyance, assignment or other form of transfer inter vivos appropriate to property of the nature of the trust property[1], assent, vesting declaration[2], vesting order[3] or vesting deed[4] or as may be already vested in him.

[1] Eg the usual form of share transfer.
[2] See para 75.3 below.
[3] See para 75.14 below.
[4] This will only be appropriate where settled land is vested in the Settled Land Act trustees as statutory owners, see Settled Land Act 1925, s 9(2).

Legal or equitable estate

40.2 The only estates in land capable of subsisting or of being conveyed *at law* are an estate in fee simple absolute in possession and a term of years absolute. An attempt to create any other estate in land operates only to create equitable interests[1].

[1] Law of Property Act 1925, ss 1, 4.

Assent

40.3 An assent is the act by which a personal representative releases an asset from the administration of the estate and perfects the title of the person entitled to it as a result of the death. A personal representative may assent to the vesting in any person who (whether by devise, bequest, devolution, appropriation or otherwise) may be entitled thereto as trustee of any estate or interest in freehold or leasehold property which devolved upon the personal representative[1]. In order to pass a legal estate the assent must be in writing signed by the personal representative, and name the person in whose favour it is made[2]. An equitable interest in land may be assented without the need for writing[3].

1   Administration of Estates Act 1925, ss 36(1), 55(1)(xix).
2   Administration of Estates Act 1925, s 36(4).
3   *Re Edwards' Will Trust* [1982] Ch 30, CA.

40.4 A personal representative who has cleared the estate becomes a trustee for those entitled. The court may appoint a new trustee to act jointly with him[1] , or he may himself exercise the statutory power to appoint new or additional trustees[2]. However, if a personal representative wishes to pass a legal estate in land to a new co-trustee he cannot do so by the deed of appointment coupled with the statutory automatic vesting in a new trustee[3], unless he has first assented in writing to the vesting of the legal estate in himself[4], for only then is the land vested in him in the capacity of trustee[5].

1   *Re Ponder* [1921] 2 Ch 59; *Re Yerburgh* [1928] WN 208.
2   *Re Cockburn's Will Trust* [1957] Ch 438, [1957] 2 All ER 522; and CVIII Law Journal 36 ff.; *Re Pitt* (1928) 44 TLR 371.
3   Trustee Act 1925, s 40; see para 75.3.
4   And, in the case of registered land, registered himself as proprietor.
5   *Re King's Will Trusts* [1964] Ch 542, [1964] 1 All ER 833, *not challenged in Re Edwards' WT* [1982] Ch 30, [1981] 2 All ER 941, CA, discussed [1981] Conv 450 and [1982] Conv 4; *Jemma Trust Co v Kippax Beaumont Lewis* [2005] EWCA Civ 248, [2005] WTLR 683, at para 119; and see also paras 1.49 and 75.8, and JT Farrand 1964 Sol Jo 698 and 719; RR Walker (1964) 80 LQR 328; JF Garner (1964) 28 Conv 298; EC Ryder (1976) 29 Current Legal Problems 60 and *Williams on Title* (4th edn) pp 354–361. *Re King's Will Trusts* has not been followed in Ireland: *Mohan v Roche* [1991] 1 IR 560.

40.5 Since April 1998 any disposition of unregistered land effected by an assent has triggered the requirement of compulsory registration of the land[1]. If the title to the land was registered before the owner's death, the personal representatives should become registered themselves, whether as trustees or personal representatives, or a sole executor-beneficiary should become registered as sole proprietor[2].

1   Land Registration Act 1997, s 1; Land Registration Act 2002, s 4(1)(a).
2   Land Registration Act 1925, s 41; Land Registration Act 2002, ss 24, 27(5)(a).

ARTICLE 41
THE INCIDENTS OF THE TRUSTEE'S ESTATE

41.1
At law the estate of the trustee is subject to the same incidents, whether privileges or burdens, as if he were also beneficial owner, except where such incidents are modified by case law or statute.

Power to commence actions

41.2 Thus, he is the proper person to bring actions arising out of wrongs formerly cognisable by common law courts, and which necessitated the possession of the legal estate in those bringing them[1]. However, there are exceptional circumstances in which the beneficiary may bring an action against a third party 'in the room of the trustee'[2].

1   *May v Taylor* (1843) 6 Man & G 261; *Schalit v Joseph Nadler Ltd* [1933] 2 KB 79.
2   *Parker-Tweedale v Dunbar Bank plc (No 2)* [1991] Ch 26, CA; see para 1.1(3) above.

Trustee's right to prove in bankruptcies

41.3 Where a debtor to the trust estate becomes bankrupt, the trustee is the proper person to prove without the concurrence of the beneficiaries[1], except in the case of a simple trust. Where, however, it is probable that the debtor has paid the beneficiaries direct, it lies in the discretion of the judge to require their concurrence in the proof[2].

1   *Ex p Green* (1832) 2 Deac & Ch 113.
2   *Ex p Dubois* (1787) 1 Cox Eq Cas 310; *Ex p Gray* (1835) 4 Deac & Ch 778.

Trustee liable for rates and taxes

41.4 The trustee of a private trust is, as legal owner of land, liable to pay rates or council tax in respect of the trust property[1]. A trustee may also be liable in certain circumstances for income tax, capital gains tax, inheritance tax and value added tax. These matters are, however, beyond the scope of this work. But a trustee of a head trust, considering creating separate sub-trusts with separate non-resident trustees, should be wary, since he may remain liable for capital gains made by the separate trustees, the body of trustees comprising the head trustees together with the sub-trusts trustees[2]. A prospective new trustee of the head trust needs to be aware of his potential liability if capital gains are subsequently made. Care must also be taken in case the retirement or appointment of a trustee converts a non-resident trust into a resident trust[3], or the addition of further funds 'taints' an existing trust with tax disadvantages[4].

1   *R v Sterry* (1840) 12 Ad & El 84; *R v Stapleton* (1863) 4 B & S 629.
2   *Roome v Edwards (Inspector of Taxes)* [1982] AC 279, [1981] 1 All ER 736, HL.
3   *Green v Cobham* [2000] WTLR 1100, though the judge was persuaded that the relevant appointment should be treated as void on applying the *Re Hastings-Bass* [1975] Ch 25 principle (see para 61.6 below).
4   See eg *Federal Trust Co Ltd v Macdonald-Smith* (2001) 4 ITELR 211, R Ct Guernsey.

Trustee of a business liable to creditors

41.5 If the trustee, in pursuance of the trust, carries on a business for the benefit of the beneficiaries, he will nonetheless be personally liable to the

41.5 *The estate of the trustee and its incidents*

creditors of the business[1], or to others to whom tortious rights may accrue[2], and may be made bankrupt in respect of such liabilities[3]. But of course he has a right of indemnity[4].

1   *Farhall v Farhall* (1871) 7 Ch App 123; *Owen v Delamere* (1872) LR 15 Eq 134.
2   Eg *Benett v Wyndham* (1862) 4 De G F & J 259; *Re Raybould* [1900] 1 Ch 199.
3   *Wightman v Townroe* (1813) 1 M & S 412; *Ex p Garland* (1804) 10 Ves 110; *Farhall v Farhall* (1871) 7 Ch App 123. See Article 86, below.
4   As to which see Article 83, below.

Trustee entitled to custody of deeds

41.6 A trustee in whom the legal estate is vested is entitled to the custody of the deeds[1]; but the beneficiaries are entitled, at all reasonable times, to inspect them[2].

1   *Evans v Bicknell* (1801) 6 Ves 174.
2   *Wynne v Humberston* (1858) 27 Beav 421.

Rights under Land Compensation Act 1961

41.7 Where the right to claim compensation under s 23 of the Land Compensation Act 1961 (which deals with the effect of planning decisions increasing the value of land already compulsorily acquired) becomes exercisable by reference to an interest in land which is, at the time when the right is exercisable, subject to a settlement, then (a) the right to make the claim is exercisable by the trustees; and (b) where a claim has been made by reference to such an interest as aforesaid and compensation falls to be paid, the principal amount of the compensation is payable to the trustees, and to the extent that it ought (as between the beneficiaries) to be treated as capital it is applicable as capital money under the Settled Land Act 1925, or as proceeds of sale arising under a trust of land, as the case may be[1].

1   Land Compensation Act 1961, Sch 3 para 7, inserted by the Planning and Compensation Act 1991, s 66 and Sch 14 para 2.

Individual rights of tenants of houses to freehold or extended lease and of tenants of flats to a new 90 year lease[1]

41.8 The Leasehold Reform Act 1967, as amended by the Housing Act 1996 and the Commonhold and Leasehold Reform Act 2002 (the 'CLRA'), makes it possible for trustees of land to purchase the freehold or an extended lease if the long lease of the house has been held subject to the trust for two years. The Leasehold Reform Housing and Urban Development Act 1993 ('the LRHUDA'), as amended by the CLRA, makes it possible for trustees holding the tenancy of a flat to purchase a new 90 year lease from the expiry date of the existing long lease if it has been held subject to the trust for two years.

1   See Hill & Redman's *Law of Landlord & Tenant* on the immense technical detail; and the broad powers of trustees of land in Trusts of Land and Appointment of Trustees Act 1996, s 6.

Collective enfranchisement rights of tenants of flats[1]

41.9 The tenants of a block of flats have a right to have the freehold thereof acquired on their behalf by a company known as a 'RTE company' at a price determined in accordance with a statutory formula, so long as notice to the freeholder is given by the RTE company – having amongst its participating members those having tenancies of no less than half of the total number of flats in the premises. The LRHUDA[2], as amended by the CLRA, makes it possible for trustee-tenants to be involved in such purchase at the expense of the trust fund.

[1]   Further see *Hill & Redman's Law of Landlord & Tenant.*
[2]   Section 93A, CLRA, Sch 8, para 33.

Right to manage block of flats[1]

41.10 The CLRA gives leaseholders under long leases of flats the right to manage their block of flats via a company known as a 'RTM company' without having to prove shortcomings on the landlord's part and without having to pay him compensation. Trustee-tenants are enabled to be involved in such enterprise[2]. The right to manage does not extend to premises which have a resident landlord and do not contain more than four flat units, the residence of a person having an interest under the trust ranking as that of the landlord where the actual landlord is a body of trustees[3].

[1]   Further see Hill & Redman (above).
[2]   CLRA, s 109.
[3]   CLRA, Sch 6 para 3(7).

Commonhold ownership[1]

41.11 The CLRA provides for the ownership of the freehold of interdependent properties, 'units', and the corporate ownership and management of the associated common parts by the unit owners as a commonhold association. Each unit-holder owns the freehold in his own unit, while the commonhold association owns the freehold in the common parts. A commonhold community statement governs the use and maintenance of the units and common parts. Where there are joint unit-holders, only one (nominated by one of themselves) can be registered as a member of the commonhold association, but in default, the person whose name first appears on the proprietorship register will be the registered owner[2].

[1]   On this topic see e g T Aldridge, *Commonhold* or D Clarke, *Commonhold.*
[2]   CLRA, Sch 3 para 8.

ARTICLE 42
THE EFFECT OF THE LIMITATION ACT 1980 ON THE
TRUSTEE'S ESTATE

42.1

(1)   A trustee of land is divested of the legal estate by the exclusive possession of a beneficiary solely and absolutely entitled to the

land or the proceeds of sale thereof for the statutory period. But where land is in the possession of a beneficiary not solely and absolutely entitled to the land or the proceeds thereof time does not run either against the trustee or against any other person having a beneficial interest in the land or the proceeds of sale thereof[1];

(2) A trustee, like a beneficial owner, may be barred by the adverse possession of a stranger; and if he be so barred, his beneficiaries will be barred also. But the legal estate of trustees will not be extinguished until every right of action of the persons beneficially interested (who for this purpose are deemed to be entitled to the same right of action to recover the land as if their estates were legal and not equitable) is barred.

(3) An action to recover land held on trust may be brought by the trustees on behalf of any person entitled to a beneficial interest in possession in the land or proceeds of sale whose right is not barred notwithstanding that the trustees' right of action would otherwise be barred.

(4) The registered title to land cannot be lost by adverse possession alone, while a person is not to be regarded as being in adverse possession of registered land subject to a trust unless the interest of each of the beneficiaries is an interest in possession.

[1] Limitation Act 1980, Sch 1, para 9.

Paragraph 1

Exclusive possession of a beneficiary

42.2–42.5 Time runs against a bare trustee, which includes a fully paid vendor still holding the legal title[1]. However, a beneficiary under a trust of land or settled land, not being a person solely or absolutely entitled, cannot adversely possess and so cannot acquire statutory title against his fellow beneficiaries or the trustees[2]. But the rule only applies to a trust of land (including land held on trust for sale) and to settled land, and so it is apprehended that any trustee, including a constructive trustee (as, for example, a vendor under an uncompleted contract), is liable to be divested of the legal estate by possession of a person entitled in equity in exactly the same way as if the latter were a stranger[3]. But where a purchaser acknowledges that he is in possession under an uncompleted contract time will not run against the unpaid vendor since the purchaser's possession is not adverse[4].

[1] *Bridges v Mees* [1957] Ch 475, [1957] 2 All ER 577.
[2] Paragraph 9 of Sch 1 to the Limitation Act 1980 (replacing s 7(5) of the 1939 Act).
[3] This statement was expressly approved in *Bridges v Mees* [1957] Ch 475, [1957] 2 All ER 577, by Harman J, in dealing with s 7(5).

⁴   *Hyde v Pearce* [1982] 1 All ER 1029, [1982] 1 WLR 560, CA. It may be the purchaser is
a licensee. *Bridges v Mees* (supra) was not cited.

Paragraph 2

Adverse possession of a stranger

42.6 This paragraph is believed to state the effect of s 18 of the Limitation
Act 1980. It had long ago been held by the courts that:

> 'the rule that the Statute of Limitations does not bar a trust estate, holds only as
> between cestui que trust and trustee, and between the cestuis que trust inter se,
> and not between cestui que trust and trustee on the one side and strangers on
> the other ... and therefore, where a cestui que trust and his trustee are both out
> of possession for the time limited, the party in possession has a good bar
> against them both'[1].

1   Per Lord Hardwicke in *Lewellin v Mackworth* (1740) 2 Eq Cas Abr 579; and to same
effect per Lord Redesdale in *Hovenden v Annesley* (1806) 2 Sch & Lef 607; and per
Lord Manners in *Pentland v Stokes* (1812) 2 Ball & B 68 at 75. As to whether a purchaser
of the equitable interest of a beneficiary gets the legal estate by 12 years' possession, see *Re
Cussons Ltd* (1904) 73 LJ Ch 296, and *Bolling v Hobday* (1882) 31 WR 9.

42.7 The 1980 Act makes it clear that though the trustee's right of action may
be barred by the adverse possession of a stranger[1], his estate is not to be
divested until the right of action of every beneficiary has been barred, and that
even after his right of action would otherwise be barred he may sue to recover
the land on behalf of a person beneficially interested in possession. Time
begins to run against a beneficiary when his right of action first accrues: in the
case of a future interest, the right of action first accrues when the interest falls
into possession[2]. If land (not being settled land) is held on trust for sale for A
for life remainder to B, 12 years' adverse possession of the land by S will bar
A's equitable interest but time will not begin to run against B until A's death.
After expiry of the twelve years the trustees will hold the legal estate on trust
for B as from A's death. On A's death B (if of full age and sound mind) or the
trustees will be able to recover the land.

1   On the meaning of adverse possession in the light of the Human Rights Act and Article 1
of the First Protocol see *Beaulane Properties Ltd v Palmer* [2005] EWHC 1071 (Ch),
[2005] 4 All ER 461 endorsed by the ECHR in *J A Pye (Oxford) Ltd v United Kingdom
(Application 44302/02)* when considering breach of the applicant's rights in *J A Pye
(Oxford) Ltd v Graham* [2002] UKHL 30 [2003] 1 AC 419.
2   Limitation Act 1980, s 15. As an alternative to the 12 year period there is a period of six
years from the falling into possession of a remainderman's interest: s 15(2).

42.8 In the case of registered land, there is a new regime for the registration
of an adverse possessor of an estate in such land who may apply to the
registrar to be registered as proprietor if he has been in adverse possession for
a period of ten years ending on the date of the application[1]. The registrar will
send notices of this to the registered proprietor and mortgagees. An objection
from one of them will prevent registration of the adverse possessor unless this
would be unconscionable (eg on proprietary estoppel principles) or he
occupied the land under a reasonable mistake about the boundary or he has

some other entitlement to be registered, eg as unpaid vendor or devisee under a will[2]. The registered proprietor has two years from the date of objection to take possession proceedings; otherwise the adverse possessor can apply a second time and be registered as proprietor pursuant to that application[3]. It will, however, no longer be possible for there to be any adverse possession[4] of land subject to a trust unless the interest of each of the beneficiaries is an interest in possession[5]. Thus, it is now impossible to use adverse possession to resolve boundary disputes if the land is held in trust for successive interests.

[1] Land Registration Act 2002, Sch 6, para 1.
[2] Land Registration Act 2002, Sch 6, paras 2, 3 and 5.
[3] Land Registration Act 2002, Sch 6, paras 6 and 7.
[4] Land Registration Act 2002, Sch 6, para 11.
[5] Land Registration Act 2002, Sch 6, para 12.

ARTICLE 43
THE EFFECT ON THE TRUSTEE'S ESTATE OF CREDITORS' CLAIMS
(INCLUDING THE TRUSTEE'S BANKRUPTCY OR LIQUIDATION)

43.1

(1) Where judgment has been obtained against a trustee, execution may be obtained by the judgment creditor on one or more of various classes of assets, including (i) those owned beneficially by the trustee, (ii) those held by the trustee of the trust in respect of which the liability was incurred, (iii) those held by the trustee as trustee of another trust, and (iv) those held by the trustee jointly with another person, depending on the method of execution employed.

(2) The property of a bankrupt divisible among his creditors does not include property held by him on trust for any other person[1], notwithstanding that it is property in his order and disposition at the commencement of the bankruptcy[2]; property held on trust by a company at the commencement of winding-up is similarly not divisible among the company's creditors[3];

(3) If the trustee has converted trust property into money or other property which would be subject to the trust in the hands of the trustee, it will remain so subject notwithstanding the trustee's bankruptcy or liquidation[4].

[1] Insolvency Act 1986, s 283(3).
[2] *Re Fox, ex p Barry* (1873) LR 17 Eq 113;*Ex p Marsh* (1744) 1 Atk 158. As to constructive trustees, see *Re Boldero, ex p Pease* (1812) 19 Ves 25 at 46, and *Whitfield v Brand* (1847) 16 M & W 282.
[3] For example, *Barclays Bank Ltd v Quistclose Investments Ltd* [1970] AC 567, HL; *Re Kayford Ltd* [1975] 1 WLR 279.
[4] *Frith v Cartland* (1865) 2 Hem & M 417; *Re Hallett's Estate* (1880) 13 Ch D 696 at 719.

Paragraph 1

43.2 There are various methods of execution of judgments in English law, which are considered individually hereafter. In considering these methods being used against a trustee, it is necessary to bear in mind that assets belonging to the trustee may fall into a number of different categories:

1 assets belonging to the trustee beneficially;
2 assets belonging to the trustee and held subject to the trust in respect of which the liability was incurred;
3 assets belonging to the trustee but held in some other fiduciary capacity;
4 assets belonging to the trustee and another person or persons jointly.

43.3

FIERI FACIAS[1]

Fieri facias (often simply called 'fi fa') is the primary form of execution. Goods are seized and sold to meet the judgment debt. Assets in category 1 can be taken in execution of the judgment, although they have nothing to do with the trust. The trustee will have to recoup himself out of the trust assets, if he can. Those in category 3 cannot be taken by *fieri facias*[2]. This is not because of some special protection for trusts, but because it was and is legally wrong for the sheriff to execute on chattels in the hands of the judgment debtor knowing that they belong to another *or are held on trust for another*[3] .The creditor receiving the proceeds of sale would be accountable as a trustee[4]. It is moreover the duty of a trustee whose trust assets are being subjected to execution to object and to protect the trust interests in any interpleader proceedings[5]. As to assets in category 2, in theory the answer is the same as for category 3[6]. However, the trustee has a right of indemnity against the trust assets[7]. Normally this means that the judgment creditor can be subrogated to that right, and by that means can reach the trust assets[8]. However, in some cases there will be no subrogation[9]. Jointly owned assets, *ie* those in category 4, can in principle be taken by *fieri facias*[10]. If there were an interpleader, the court would order the sheriff to divide the proceeds with the co-owner claimant[11] .But this regime does not now apply in the case of partnership property, which by statute cannot be taken by *fieri facias*[12]. Instead, a charging order can be obtained on the partner's interest,[13] and, if the assets are seized, the partners can interplead[14]. Nor will it apply if the jointly owned assets are held on trust for others, making them fall into category 2 or category 3.

[1] See RSC Ords 46 and 47, CCR Ord 26.
[2] *Re Morgan* (1881) 18 Ch D 93; *Jennings v Mather* [1901] 1 KB 108; affd [1902] 1 KB 1, CA.
[3] *Farr v Newman* (1792) 4 Term Rep 621, 645; *Cailland v Eastwick* (1794) 2 Anst 381.
[4] *Foley v Burnell* (1783) 1 Bro CC 274, 278.
[5] *Wright v Redgrave* (1879) 11 Ch D 24, CA.
[6] *Re Morgan* (1881) 18 Ch D 93, 99, 104; *Jennings v Mather* [1901] 1 KB 108; affd [1902] 1 KB 1, CA.
[7] *Jennings v Mather* [1901] 1 KB 108; affd [1902] 1 KB 1, CA; Trustee Act 2000, s 31; see para 83.2 below.
[8] *Re Pumphrey* (1882) 22 Ch D 255; *Re Frith* [1902] 1 Ch 342. See para 83.47 below.
[9] See para 83.47 below.
[10] *Farrar v Beswick* (1836) 1 M & W 682, 685; *Mayhew v Herrick* (1849) 7 CB 229, 240, 248, 250.
[11] Cf *The James W Elwell* [1921] P 351.

12   Partnership Act 1890, s 23(1).
13   Partnership Act 1890, s 23(2).
14   *Peake v Carter* [1916] 1 KB 652, 655–66, CA.

43.4

CHARGING ORDERS[1]

A charge may be imposed by charging order on any interest held by a judgment debtor beneficially (i) in land, UK government stocks and company shares (connected with England and Wales), unit trusts, and funds in court, or (ii) under a trust[2]. It may also be imposed on any such interest held by a person as trustee of a trust (*ie* not beneficially), where *either* the judgment or order in respect of which the charging order is to be imposed was made against him as trustee of the trust, *or* the trust is for the sole unencumbered benefit of the judgment debtor (or judgment debtors, if there is more than one)[3]. So a charging order can be made in respect of any appropriate assets in categories 1 and 2, and in respect of similar assets in category 3 and category 4 where the judgment debtor is (or two or more judgment debtors together are) absolutely beneficially entitled under the trust, but (in relation to assets in categories 3 and 4) not in other cases.

1   CPR Part 73; formerly RSC Ord 50.
2   Charging Orders Act 1979, s 2(1)(a).
3   Charging Orders Act 1979, s 2(1)(b).

43.5

THIRD PARTY DEBT ORDERS[1]

Third party debt orders (formerly 'garnishee orders') are orders against a person in the jurisdiction[2] to pay to the judgment creditor the amount of any debt due or accruing due to the judgment debtor from the third party, or so much of it as will satisfy the judgment debt and costs of the application[3]. A trustee may of course be the third party in such a case, and if he owes money to a judgment debtor be ordered to pay the judgment creditor, with the result that he is to that extent discharged from the debt to the judgment debtor[4]. If the trustee is the judgment debtor, debts owed to the trustee can be diverted in this way to the judgment creditor. Such debts may be in category 1, *ie* owed to the trustee in his personal capacity (*eg* his private bank account) or in category 2, as trustee of the trust in respect of which the liability was incurred (*eg* the 'trust's' bank account). There is no authority (as there is for seizure of chattels) for limiting third party debt orders to debts in category 1. But the court will not make a final third party debt order against a trustee if the debt is owed to him as trustee of a different trust (*ie* an asset falling within category 3 above)[5] .If the trustee does not make the objection, as he should[6], the beneficiary can intervene to do so[7]. Where the debt is owed to the debtor trustee and another person or persons jointly (*ie* category 4 above), it is not possible to attach the debt, as the debtor cannot sue for it by himself[8].

1   CPR Part 72; formerly RSC Ord 49.
2   CPR rule 72.1(1); *SCF Finance Co Ltd v Masri (No 3)* [1987] QB 1028.
3   CPR rule 72.2.
4   CPR rule 72.9.
5   *Roberts v Death* (1881) 8 QBD 319.
6   *Wright v Redgrave* (1879) 11 Ch D 24, CA.
7   CPR rule 72.8; see *eg Philipp Bros Ltd v Republic of Sierra Leone* [1995] 1 Lloyd's Rep 289, CA (allegation of trust failed on facts).
8   *Macdonald v Tacquah Gold Mines* (1884) 13 QBD 535, 539; *Beasley v Roney* [1891] 1 QB 509, 512; *Hirschorn v Evans* [1938] 2 KB 801, CA.

43.6

APPOINTMENT OF RECEIVER[1]

Historically, the appointment of a receiver by way of equitable execution was not so much a means of execution of a judgment as a kind of equitable relief employed by the Court of Chancery when common law methods of execution were inapplicable to the form in which the debtor's property was found[2].Nowadays, the court may appoint a receiver in all cases where it appears just and convenient to do so[3]. It is not now confined to those cases where the Court of Chancery would have done so before the Judicature Acts[4]. The power of the court to appoint a receiver of land or interests in land is now statutory, and extends to all legal estates and interests in land[5]. In most land cases, however, a charging order is a more suitable remedy. In non-land cases, a receiver is still convenient in cases of execution against a life interest under a trust[6], or a reversionary interest under a will[7], because a charging order requires a debt that is due or accruing due. In such a case, appointment of a receiver does not interfere with the possession of the trustees or others in whom the property is vested[8].

1   See CPR Part 69; formerly RSC Ords 30, 51.
2   See *eg Anglo-Italian Bank v Davies* (1878) 9 Ch D 275, 283; *Salt v Cooper* (1880) 16 Ch D 544, 552, CA; *Re Shephard* (1890) 43 Ch D 131.
3   Supreme Court Act 1981, s 37(1); County Courts Act 1981, s 38.
4   *Soinco SACI v Novokuznetsk Aluminium Plant* [1998] QB 406, not following earlier authority.
5   Supreme Court Act 1981, s 37(4); County Courts Act 1981, s 107.
6   *Webb v Stenton* (1883) 11 QBD 518, 530.
7   *Fuggle v Bland* (1883) 11 QBD 711; *Tyrell v Painton* [1895] 1 QB 202, CA; *Ideal Bedding Co v Holland* [1907] 2 Ch 157.
8   *Re Peace and Waller* (1883) 24 Ch D 405, 407, CA.

43.7 There do not appear to be any cases governing the appointment of a receiver in cases where the assets of a trustee are those of the trust in question (category 2) or of another trust entirely (category 3). It is nevertheless considered that the court would not appoint a receiver in the case of category 3 assets, but would do so in the case of those in category 2, not being hampered by the common law rules on the execution of writs of *fieri facias*. Indeed, category 2 may be just the case where the court should appoint a receiver, as the common law did not allow execution in such a case. In the case of assets owned by the trustee and another person or persons jointly (*ie* category 4 above), there is a dearth of authority[1]. This may be explained by the fact that it is possible to execute judgment by writ of *fieri facias* on co-owned chattels[2], and charging orders cover nearly all interests in land[3]. On principle it should be possible to obtain the appointment of a receiver by way of equitable execution in respect of a joint interest in property at least in the (relatively) few cases where no other form of execution is available.

1   *Cf Wild v Southwood* [1897] 1 QB 317 (partnership property).
2   *Farrar v Beswick* (1836) 1 M & W 682, 685; *Mayhew v Herrick* (1849) 7 CB 229, 240, 248, 250.
3   See s 2 Charging Orders Act 1979.

43.8

VESTING ORDERS

The court has wide statutory powers to make orders in litigation vesting trust assets in other persons, whether successor trustees, persons beneficially entitled, or indeed others[1]. The existence of these vesting powers means that, in litigation against a trustee or trustees where what is sought (either principally or consequentially upon some other order) is a conveyance of property to a person entitled, it may be unnecessary to seek to execute the order against the trustee concerned. The vesting is, so to speak, self-executing.

1   See para 75.14 below.

43.9

COMMITTAL

Although imprisonment for debt was largely abolished in 1869[1], a number of exceptional cases remain. One of these is where there is 'default by a trustee or person acting in a fiduciary capacity and ordered to pay by [the High Court of Justice] any sum in his possession or under his control ...'[2] This applies to trustees expressly so called[3], and to those becoming trustees by virtue of the order itself[4], as well as to certain others. However, the exception only applies where the trustee has been ordered to pay sums actually in his possession or under his control[5] ,including control jointly with another[6] .Hence if he cannot be proved ever to have had the monies in question[7], even if he failed to get them in[8] ,he cannot be committed for failure to pay what is ordered. But if the sums were in his possession or control, the fact that he was not personally at fault in losing them, or is not guilty of fraud[9], does not take the case out of the exception[10]. The court now has a discretion in cases falling within the exception as to whether a committal will be ordered[11]. Conflicting views have been expressed as to whether the provision is punitive, and whether the discretion should be exercised in favour of a defaulting trustee[12] .Where there is no fraud or other moral fault, the court is more likely so to exercise its discretion[13]. If committal is ordered, the order must state under which exception the case falls[14]. No imprisonment under this power may last longer than one year[15].

1   Debtors Act 1869, s 4.
2   Debtors Act 1869, s 4, exception 3.
3   *Re Lord Berwick* (1900) 81 LT 797.
4   *Preston v Etherington* (1887) 37 Ch D 104.
5   *Re Fewster* [1901] 1 Ch 447; *Re Wilkins* [1901] WN 202.
6   *Evans v Bear* (1875) 10 Ch App 76.
7   *Re Hincks, ex p Cuddeford* (1878) 45 LJ Bcy 127; *Middleton v Chichester* (1871) 6 Ch App 152; *Re Hickey* (1866) 35 WR 53; *Re Fewster* [1901] 1 Ch 447.
8   *Ferguson v Ferguson* (1875) 10 Ch App 661.
9   *Preston v Etherington* (1887) 37 Ch D 104, 110.
10 *Middleton v Chichester* (1871) 6 Ch App 152; *Evans v Bear* (1875) 10 Ch App 76.
11 Debtors Act 1878. Before the 1878 Act there was no discretion: *Evans v Bear* (1875) 10 Ch App 76.
12 *Barrett v Hammond* (1879) 10 Ch D 285; *Marris v Ingram* (1880) 13 Ch D 338; *Re Knowles* (1883) 52 LJ Ch 685; *Re Freston* (1883) 11 QBD 545; *Re Dudley* (1883) 12 QBD 44; *Re Gent* (1889) 40 Ch D 190; *Re Edgcome* [1902] 2 KB 403; *Church's Trustee v Hibbard* [1902] 2 Ch 784, CA.
13 *Earl Aylesford v Earl Poulett* [1892] 2 Ch 60; *Re Bourne* [1906] 1 Ch 697, CA.
14 *Re Wilde* [1910] WN 128, CA.
15 Debtors Act 1869, s 4, proviso.

Paragraph 2

43.10 If some person other than the trustee has a beneficial interest in property held by the trustee, the property will not vest in the trustee in bankruptcy. Thus in one case, involving a solicitor's client account, Roxburgh J said:

> 'It is to be noted that the only property which vests in the trustee [in bankruptcy] is property divisible amongst his [the bankrupt's] creditors, because section 38 [of the Bankruptcy Act 1914] points out what is meant in this Act by "the property of the bankrupt"; accordingly this client account is not vested, and will not vest, in the trustee if it is property held by the bankrupt on trust for any other person. The words "on trust for any other person," in my judgment, are of very wide import ... If it can be said of any asset that though the title is in the bankrupt, a beneficial interest therein resides in some person other than the bankrupt, even though the bankrupt himself may also have a beneficial interest therein, the asset does not vest in the trustee [in bankruptcy], though the beneficial interest, if any, which the bankrupt himself has would vest in the trustee.[1]'

1   *Re A Solicitor* [1952] Ch 328, [1952] 1 All ER 133. Distinguish *St Thomas's Hospital Governors v Richardson* [1910] 1 KB 271, CA, where the legal estate in property held on an onerous lease by a husband, who had contracted to sell it to his wife for a price which she had paid, was held to have vested in the husband's trustee in bankruptcy, apparently on the ground that the husband's right of indemnity against the rent and covenants would have entitled him in the particular circumstances of that case to retain all the rents as an indemnity fund; see per Farwell LJ at 283–284.

43.11 A power given to a bankrupt is only 'property' for this purpose if it can be exercised for the benefit of the bankrupt[1]. Thus a fiduciary power to appoint or remove trustees[2] or to appoint property among a class[3] will not vest in the appointor's trustee in bankruptcy.

1   Insolvency Act 1986, s 283(4).
2   *Re Burton* (1994) 126 ALJ 557, FCA.
3   *Clarkson v Clarkson* [1994] BCC 921, CA.

43.12 Where a sole trustee holds property on trust for a *purpose* (charitable or non-charitable[1]) it will not fall within the definition of 'property' vesting in the trustee in bankruptcy and according to English law will not be available for the creditors. But where there are two or more trustees, holding as joint tenants, and only one becomes bankrupt, the trustee in bankruptcy cannot take the property free of the interests of the other trustees.

[1]   As to non-charitable purpose trusts in English law, see para 8.148 ff. But there are many other jurisdictions where such trusts are permitted.

43.13 In the case of a corporate trustee in liquidation the trust property does not automatically vest in the liquidator, but remains vested in the company until disposed of the course of winding-up or the company is dissolved.

43.14 An insolvent trustee, unless the trust instrument otherwise provides, remains a trustee until retirement or replacement (or dissolution if a corporation). A bankrupt trustee may be 'unfit to act' within s 36 of the Trustee Act 1925 but this need not be the case[1]: if doubts exist and the trustee is happy to retire then it is best to replace him on the grounds of retirement. Unlike the trustee in bankruptcy of a bankrupt individual trustee[2], the liquidator[3] of a corporate trustee in liquidation or the administrator[4] of a corporate trustee in administration has power to conduct a trusteeship vested in the company, and the power of the company to appoint new trustees is exercisable by the liquidator or administrator[5]. The costs and expenses of winding-up (including the liquidator's remuneration) are payable out of the company's own assets and not out of assets held on trust[6], though the latter assets are available for fees and expenses incurred in sorting out what is trust property and continuing to manage the trust as opposed to winding-up the corporate trustee. In a special case[7] where the company's liabilities have all been incurred in discharging the duties imposed by a trust then the costs of winding-up may be regarded as incurred in discharging such duties, e g if the company had been specially formed to administer a particular trust.

[1]   For example, *Re Barker's Trusts* (1875) 1 Ch D 43; *Re Betts* (1897) 41 Sol Jo 209.
[2]   See above.
[3]   *Re Cyest Realty* [1977] 1 NSWLR 664; *Re Berkely Applegate (Investment Consultants) Ltd* [1989] Ch 32; *Re William Makin & Son Ltd* [1993] BCC 453.
[4]   *Polly Peck International plc v Henry* [1999] 1 BCLC 407.
[5]   *Simpson Curtis Pension Trustees Ltd v Readson Ltd* (1994) 8 Tru LI 86, Ch D; *Denny v Yeldon* [1995] 3 All ER 624. For pension trusts there is a need for an independent trustee: Pensions Act 1995, ss 22–25.
[6]   *Re Berkely Applegate (Investment Consultants) Ltd* [1989] Ch 32 at 40–41;*Re Eastern Capital Futures (in liquidation)* [1989] BCLC 371 at 375;*Re French Caledonia Travel* [2003] NSWSC 1008; *Re Matheson* (1994) 121 ALR 605 at 615.
[7]   See *Re Suco Gold Pty Ltd* (1983) 33 SASR 99.

Paragraph 3

43.15 The doctrine of tracing trust property into other property into which it has been converted is fully dealt with in Articles 92 and 101, below.

43.16 If a trustee holding money in one capacity on trust for B is authorised to, and does, invest the money by lending it to itself in another capacity, then the invested money no longer represents property held on trust for B who will only be an unsecured creditor[1].

1   *Space Investments Ltd v Canadian Imperial Bank Commerce Trust Co (Bahamas) Ltd* [1986] 3 All ER 75, [1986] 1 WLR 1072, PC; *Customs and Excise Comrs v Richmond Theatre Management Ltd* [1995] STC 257 (see P Matthews [1995] BTR 332).

Chapter 12

TRUSTS OF LAND

ARTICLE 44
PRE-1997 'OLD' SETTLED LAND ACT SETTLEMENTS

44.1

(1)   Before 1997, where a legal estate in land was intended to be enjoyed by persons in succession or by a minor when adult or to be subject to family (as opposed to commercial) charges, then, unless the legal estate was vested in trustees on trust for sale[1], a settlement arose under the Settled Land Act 1925 ('SLA 1925')[2]. The trust instrument was required to be supported by a second document, a 'vesting' deed or assent vesting the legal estate[3] in the tenant for life[4] (or, exceptionally, the statutory owner[5]), who had unfettered[6] statutory powers of disposition[7]. However, when capital money arose, it had to be paid[8] to two Settled Land Act trustees (or a trust corporation acting as SLA trustee), although the investment or other application of the money had to be made according to the direction of the tenant for life (or statutory owner)[9].

(2)(i)   After 1996, old SLA settlements continue but no new SLA settlements can be created[10], except under powers contained in an old SLA settlement[11] if no express election be made that the exercise of such powers is not to create a SLA settlement[12]. Moreover, in any event, no new entailed interests can be created after 1996[13]. Since 1 February 2001 section 75(2) of the Settled Land Act 1925 has been amended so that the investment or other application of capital money is to be made according to the discretion of the SLA trustees[14], and investments (but not land occupied by the tenant for life) must be in the names or under the control of the trustees[15]. However, the trustees' actions are subject to any consent required by the settlement[16] and they must, so far as practicable, consult the tenant for life and, so far as consistent with the general interest of the settlement, give effect to his wishes[17].

(ii)   An old SLA settlement will cease to be one if there is a deed of discharge executed by the trustees[18] or if a conveyance or assent of the land does not state who are the SLA trustees[19] or, after 1996, if there is no relevant land or heirlooms subject to the settlement[20] (eg where the whole of the settled land and heirlooms, if any, have been sold).

(3)   Charitable, ecclesiastical and public trusts of land, whether deemed before 1997 to be SLA settlements[21] or created after 1996, now rank as trusts of land[22], although exempted from some of the trusts of land regime[23], and subject to sections 37 to 39 of the Charities Act 1993.

(4)   From 1 January 1997 a new 'trust of land'[24] regime has been introduced by the Trusts of Land and Appointment of Trustees Act 1996 ('TLATA 1996') whereby land is vested in trustees, whether for charitable, ecclesiastical or public purposes or for a person or persons absolutely or successively, and whether under a trust for sale[25] or a complex trust or a bare trust[26] (as will be dealt with in Article 45 following this Article). This trust of land regime applies to any trust of property which consists of or includes land, whenever it was created[27], so long as it was not a pre-1997 old Settled Land Act 1925 settlement.

---

1   Settled Land Act 1925 ('SLA 1925'), s 1(7); thus the two methods for settling land were mutually exclusive.
2   SLA 1925, s 1(1).
3   SLA 1925, ss 4–10.
4   SLA 1925, ss 19–21.
5   SLA 1925, ss 23, 24 and 117(xxvi), as where the tenant for life was a minor.
6   SLA 1925, ss 104, 106 and 108.
7   For example, sale: SLA 1925, ss 38, 39; limited leasing powers: SLA 1925, ss 41–48.
8   SLA 1925, s 18(1)(c).
9   SLA 1925, s 75(2).
10   Trusts of Land and Appointment of Trustees Act 1996 ('TLATA 1996'), s 2(1).
11   TLATA 1996, s 2(2).
12   TLATA 1996, s 2(3).
13   TLATA 1996, Sch 1, para 5.
14   Trustee Act 2000, Sch 1, para 10(1)(a).
15   Trustee Act 2000, Sch 1, para 10(1)(b).
16   Trustee Act 2000, Sch 1, para 10(1)(a).
17   Trustee Act 2000, Sch 1, para 10(2).
18   SLA 1925, s 17.
19   SLA 1925, s 110(5).
20   TLATA 1996, s 2(4).
21   SLA 1925, s 29.
22   TLATA 1996, s 2(5).
23   For example, TLATA 1996, ss 8(3), 11 and 16(6).

²⁴ TLATA 1996, s 1.
²⁵ Land held on trust for sale is no longer personalty due to no conversion now taking place: TLATA 1996, s 3 and para 32.10 above.
²⁶ TLATA 1996, s 1(2)(a).
²⁷ TLATA 1996, s 1(2)(b).

44.2 Old Settled Land Act 1925 settlements are of a 'special and complicated statutory character'¹ that all previous editions omitted to deal with in detail, on the basis that this real property and conveyancing topic 'would unreasonably encumber this work if treated in any detail'². Now there will be increasingly fewer of these relatively rare³ settlements. Such settlements are sometimes loosely referred to as 'strict' settlements, though there is no single meaning to be ascribed to that phrase.⁴

¹ See 15th edition hereof at p 451.
² See 15th edition hereof at p 451.
³ See *Transfer of Land: Trusts of Land* (Law Com No 181, June 1989), para 4.3 note 72 on result of consultation with practitioners.
⁴ *D'Abo v Paget (No 1)*, (2000) Times, 10 August, Lawrence Collins QC.

44.3 Reference for details should therefore be made to the latest editions of Megarry & Wade, *Law of Real Property* ; *Emmett on Title* (looseleaf); and Ruoff & Roper, *Law and Practice of Registered Conveyancing* (looseleaf).

44.4 Most practitioners were happy to see the demise of the complexities of the Settled Land Act settlement where the tenant for life owned the freehold or leasehold land and was 'king of the castle'¹, though capital moneys had to be paid to the SLA trustees. Some, however, regret the reduction in freedom of choice given to the settlor, who may have wished to create a trust of the land having just these effects (perhaps with himself as tenant for life). It was particularly popular with large landed estates of country families. A decade after the Settled Land Act was closed to new business, a considerable number still remain in existence. But they will die out over the next decades.

¹ See SLA 1925, ss 104, 106 and 108, while the courts were remarkably liberal in the leeway afforded to the tenant for life, despite his fiduciary position under s 107, eg *Re Thornhill's Settlement* [1941] Ch 24; *England v Public Trustee* (1968) 112 So Jo 70; *Re Lord Boston's Will Trusts* [1956] Ch 395 at 405.

44.5 Under the trusts of land regime the trustees (being two or a trust corporation) have in relation to the land all the powers of an absolute owner¹. However, if, for example, a spouse on divorce obtains a life interest in the former matrimonial home and wants to have absolute control over sale and purchase of her home, then it may well be that Equity would enforce a right of direction conferred upon her against the trustees², just as in a trust of personalty a settlor may confer upon himself or a designated protector the right to direct the trustees in respect of certain prescribed functions of the trustees. In any event, it is clear that the spouse's consent to any disposition of the trustees can be a binding precondition³. Similarly, the trustees can be required to consult her on exercise of their powers and the use of the capital money on a sale and to give effect to her wishes⁴, especially where the terms of the trust make clear the purpose of providing accommodation for her wherever she desires in her lifetime. Indeed, in such circumstances it would seem that the trust instrument could expressly require the trustees to exercise their power to delegate by power of attorney[5] their power of sale to the spouse, though proceeds of sale would still need to be paid to the trustees[6], whose function in respect of the proceeds is not capable of delegation under TLATA 1996[7].

1   TLATA 1996, s 6(1).
2   TLATA 1996, s 6(6).
3   TLATA 1996, ss 6(8), 8(2), 10(1).
4   TLATA 1996, s 11(1).
5   TLATA 1996, s 9(1).
6   TLATA 1996, s 9(7).
7   Section 9(1) only permits delegation of 'functions as trustees which relate to the land'.

ARTICLE 45
POST-1996 TRUSTS OF LAND

45.1

(1)   A trust of land is any trust[1] of property which consists of or includes land other than land which is land[2] to which the Universities and College Estates Act 1925 or the Settled Land Act 1925 applies, as explained in Article 44.

(2)   Such a trust may be created inter vivos or by will. In the former case it is the practice, though not essential, to use two deeds, one vesting the title to the land in the trustees and the other declaring the detailed trusts, thus keeping the trusts off the title.

(3)   Where a trust of land is land subject to an immediate trust for sale there is implied, despite any contrary provision, a power for the trustees to postpone sale of the land[3]; and the trustees are not liable in any way for postponing sale of the land, in the conscious exercise of their discretion, for an indefinite period[4].

(4)   The doctrine of conversion no longer applies to regard land held on trust for sale as personal property or to regard as realty personal property directed to be sold in order that realty be acquired[5].

(5)   Trustees of land, for the purpose of exercising their functions as trustees, have in relation to the land subject to the trust all the powers of an absolute owner[6], which need to be exercised in accordance with the duty of care under section 1 of the Trustee Act 2000[7].

(6)   Trustees of land have power to acquire 'freehold or leasehold land' in the UK as an investment or for occupation by a beneficiary or for any other reason[8], as explained in Article 53(5), and subject to the duty of care in section 1 of the Trustee Act 2000.

(7)   Trustees of land have power to partition land subject to the trust and provide (by way of mortgage or otherwise) for the payment

of any equality money, but only where beneficiaries of full age are absolutely entitled in undivided shares to the land and give their consent[9].

(8)   Trustees of land have power compulsorily to transfer land subject to the trust to the beneficiaries interested in the land where they are each of full age and capacity and between them absolutely entitled to the land[10].

(9)   The above powers of trustees of land cannot be exercised in contravention of any enactment or subordinate legislation or any rule of law or equity[11], but they can be restricted or excluded[12] or be made subject to a requirement of consent[13].

(10)   Trustees of land may, by power of attorney, delegate to any beneficiary or beneficiaries of full age and beneficially entitled to an interest in possession in land subject to the trust any of their functions as trustees which relate to the land[14] (as opposed to the proceeds of sale and receipts therefor), with the duty of care under section 1 of the Trustee Act 2000 applying to the trustees in deciding whether to delegate, in keeping the delegation under review and in intervening if need be[15] (this is explained in more detail in Article 55(1)(e) and (2), below).

(11)   Where the consent of more than two persons is required under the trust to the exercise by the trustees of any function relating to the land, the consent of any two is sufficient for the protection of a purchaser[16]. If a person whose consent is required is not of full age a purchaser can ignore the need for such consent, though the trustees should obtain the consent of a parent having parental responsibility for him or of a guardian[17].

(12)   In the exercise of any function relating to land subject to the trust, the trustees of land must, so far as practicable, consult the beneficiaries of full age and beneficially entitled to an interest in possession in the land and, so far as consistent with the general interest of the trust, give effect to the wishes of those beneficiaries, or (in case of dispute) of the majority (according to the value of their combined interests)[18]. This obligation applies to all trusts of land created after 1996 except where the disposition provides to the contrary or the trust arises under a will made before 1997[19]. For trusts created before 1997 no duty to consult exists unless provision that it should is made by a deed executed by the settlor or settlors if still alive and of full capacity[20].

(13)   A beneficiary who is beneficially entitled to an interest in possession in land subject to a trust of land is entitled by reason of his interest to occupy the land at any time if at that time either (a) the purposes of the trust include making the land available for his occupation (or for the occupation of beneficiaries of a class of which he is a member or of beneficiaries in general) or (b) the land is held by the trustees so as to be so available[21]; but a

beneficiary has no such right to occupy land if it is either unavailable or unsuitable for occupation by him[22].

(14) Where two or more beneficiaries would be entitled to occupy the land, the trustees may exclude or restrict the entitlement of any one or more (but not all) of them[23], but the trustees must act reasonably[24] and they may impose reasonable conditions[25], having taken account of the settlor's intentions, the purposes for which the land is held and the circumstances and wishes of each of the beneficiaries seeking to occupy the land[26].

(15) Any person who is a trustee of land or has an interest in property subject to a trust of land may apply to the court for an order relating to the exercise by the trustees of any of their functions (including an order relieving them of any obligation to obtain the consent of, or to consult, any person concerning exercise of any of their functions) or an order declaring the nature or extent of a person's interest in the trust property[27], but this provision does not enable the court to make any order as to the appointment or removal of trustees[28]. Except on an application made by the trustee of a bankrupt's estate for an order for the sale of the land, the court must have regard to[29] (a) the intentions of the settlor, (b) the purposes for which the property subject to the trust is held, (c) the welfare of any minor who occupies, or might reasonably be expected to occupy, any trust land as his home, (d) the interests of any secured creditor of the beneficiary and[30] (e) the circumstances and wishes of any beneficiaries of full age entitled to an interest in possession in trust property or (in case of dispute) of the majority according to the value of their combined interest. However, if the application is made by a trustee of a bankrupt's estate for an order *for the sale of the land*,[31] the court makes such order as it thinks just and reasonable having regard to (a) the interests of the bankrupt's creditors and (b) where the application relates to the home of the bankrupt or his spouse or civil partner or former spouse or former civil partner, to (i) the conduct of the spouse or civil partner or former spouse or former civil partner, so far as contributing to the bankruptcy, (ii) the needs and financial resources of the spouse or civil partner or former spouse or former civil partner and (iii) the needs of any children, and (c) all the circumstances of the case other than the needs of the bankrupt[32]. Where the application is made one year after the first vesting of the bankrupt's estate in a trustee, the court must assume, unless the circumstances of the case are exceptional, that the interests of the bankrupt's creditors outweigh all other considerations[33].

(16) Purchasers of land from trustees of land are not concerned to see whether or not any duty to consult beneficiaries has been complied with[34], and so long as capital monies are paid to two

trustees or a trust corporation or a sole personal representative acting as such, interests under the trust of land will be over-reached[35] unless, in the case of unregistered land, the purchaser or his agent had actual notice that the trustees were exceeding their powers (by ignoring any exclusion or restriction placed upon them)[36] or, in the case of registered land, there was an entry in the register limiting the trustees' powers[37].

[1] Whether express, resulting or constructive and including a trust for sale and a bare trust: TLATA 1996, s 1(2)(a).
[2] TLATA 1996, s 1(3).
[3] TLATA 1996, s 4(1).
[4] TLATA 1996, s 4(1). This does not affect any liability incurred before 1997: s 4(3).
[5] TLATA 1996, s 3; see P Matthews, *Nice Try, Shame about Conversion*, (1997) 5 PTPR 87.
[6] TLATA 1996, s 6(1).
[7] TLATA 1996, s 6(9).
[8] TLATA 1996, s 6(3) as substituted by Trustee Act 2000, Sch 2, para 45(1).
[9] TLATA 1996, s 7.
[10] TLATA 1996, s 6(2).
[11] TLATA 1996, s 6(6).
[12] TLATA 1996, s 8(1), but not applicable to charitable, ecclesiastical or public trusts.
[13] TLATA 1996, s 8(2).
[14] TLATA 1996, s 9.
[15] TLATA 1996, s 9A inserted by Trustee Act 2000, Sch 2, para 47.
[16] TLATA 1996, s 10(1).
[17] TLATA 1996, s 10(3).
[18] TLATA 1996, s 11(1).
[19] TLATA 1996, s 11(2).
[20] TLATA 1996, s 11(3).
[21] TLATA 1996, s 12(1).
[22] TLATA 1996, s 12(2).
[23] TLATA 1996, s 13(1).
[24] TLATA 1996, s 13(2).
[25] TLATA 1996, s 13(3).
[26] TLATA 1996, s 13(4).
[27] TLATA 1996, s 14(1) and (2).
[28] TLATA 1996, s 14(3).
[29] TLATA 1996, s 15(1).
[30] TLATA 1996, s 15(4).
[31] But not for any other order (eg lease, mortgage etc).
[32] TLATA 1996, s 15(4); Insolvency Act 1986, s 335A.
[33] Insolvency Act 1986, s 335A(3).
[34] TLATA 1996, s 16(1).
[35] Law of Property Act 1925, ss 2 and 27 as amended by TLATA 1996, Sch 3, para 4.
[36] TLATA 1996, s 16(2) and (3).
[37] Land Registration Act 2002, s 26, resolving the problem identified by Ferris & Battersby in [1998] Conv 168.

Paragraph 1

Trusts of Land

45.2 Settled Land Act settlements created before 1997 continue, and powers exercised thereunder may create Settled Land Act settlements if no election is made that such are not to be Settled Land Act settlements. Otherwise, if land is not subject to the Universities and College Estates Act 1925 it will be a 'trust of land' covered by the Trusts of Land and Appointment of Trustees Act 1996 ('TLATA 1996'). Personal property, however, may well be within a 'trust of land', since this is defined to cover 'any trust of property which consists of *or includes* land'[1], while the reference to 'trust' is to any description of trust (whether express, implied, resulting or constructive) including a trust for sale and a bare trust[2].

1 TLATA 1996, s 1(1)(a).
2 TLATA 1996, s 1(2)(a).

45.3 Implied trusts of land arise by virtue of statute where a person dies intestate leaving land[1] or where two or more persons are entitled to land as joint tenants or tenants in common but no express trust for them has been created[2]. Prior to 1997 all co-owned land was subject either to an express or to a statutorily implied trust[3] for sale with a power to postpone sale (unless ousted expressly or by necessary implication)[4]. Thus, there was a duty to sell unless the trustees unanimously exercised their power to postpone sale. So, in the absence of unanimity, the courts would enforce the letter of the trust for sale unless so to do would defeat the spirit or purpose of the trust[5].

1 Administration of Estates Act 1925, s 33 as amended by TLATA 1996, Sch 2, para 5.
2 Law of Property Act 1925, ss 34 and 36 as amended by TLATA 1996, Sch 2, paras 3 and 4.
3 See Administration of Estates Act 1925, s 33 and Law of Property Act 1925, ss 34 and 36 before amendment by TLATA.
4 Law of Property Act 1925, s 25(1).
5 *Jones v Challenger* [1961] 1 QB 176; *Re Buchanan-Wollaston's Conveyance* [1939] Ch 738.

45.4 After 1996 a settlor can still deliberately create an express trust for sale, although he can no longer oust the trustees' power to postpone sale[1].

1 TLALTA 1996, s 4(1).

Paragraph 2

Desirability of two deeds for lifetime trusts of land

45.5 A major object of the 1925 property legislation was to simplify conveyancing and to facilitate sales by keeping trusts off the title or behind a curtain past which a purchaser could not peep. The Settled Land Act system required the use of two deeds, a simple one for purchasers to see who was the legal title-owner, and a complex one detailing the trusts. Although it was not compulsory to do so, conveyancing practice for land held on trusts for sale made it desirable to use two deeds, with only the conveyance to the trustees on unspecified trusts for sale needing to be abstracted and produced on the sale taking place.

45.6 This desirable practice has continued and is recognised in s 35 of the Trustee Act 1925, as amended by TLATA 1996:

'Appointments of new trustees of land and of new trustees of any trust of the proceeds of sale shall, subject to any order of the court, be effected by separate instruments, but in such manner that the same persons become trustees of land and trustees of the proceeds of sale'.

45.7 Thus, as also recognised in s 24 of the Law of Property Act 1925, the same persons will be appointed in one deed to be trustees of the conveyance of the legal title and in another deed to be trustees of the detailed trusts of land and any proceeds thereof.

45.8 Where there is a testamentary trust, so that the legal estate is vested in the personal representatives, they should, on completing the administration of the estate, assent to the legal estate simply vesting in themselves as trustees[1], if the two offices are united, or in other persons as trustees, thereby keeping the testamentary trusts off the title[2].

[1] *Re King's Will Trusts* [1964] Ch 542; Administration of Estates Act 1925, s 36(4); see further para 1.49 above.
[2] The assent should be registered with the Land Registry within two months: Land Registration Act 2002, s 4 replacing Land Registration Act 1997, s 1.

45.9 If a purchaser or his agent sees the trust instrument and it contains exclusions or restrictions upon the trustees' powers, then a purchaser will not take a good title if he ignores those limits on the trustees' powers[1].

[1] If title is registered then a purchaser is protected if no entry of any exclusions or restrictions appears on the register: Land Registration Act 2002, s 26 resolving the difficulty identified by Ferris & Battersby in [1998] Conv 168.

Paragraph 3

Trusts for sale of land

45.10 Where a disposition expressly creates a trust for sale of land, then, if it does not expressly create a power to postpone sale, there is implied a power for the trustees to postpone sale of the land[1]. This implied power cannot be ousted by any provision to the contrary in the disposition, whether before or after TLATA came into force[2]. Disposition[3] should be regarded as broad enough to cover trusts for sale whether created by a transfer to trustees or by the settlor declaring himself trustee of his own designated property and whether created in writing or orally but subsequently evidenced in writing: there is no reason at all to treat any of those trusts differently from any other of them.

[1] TLATA 1996, s 4(1).
[2] TLATA 1996, s 4(2) but by s 4(3) his does not affect any liability incurred by trustees before 1997.
[3] TLATA 1996, s 23(2); Law of Property Act 1925, s 205(1)(ii).

45.11 Trust for sale means an immediate trust for sale, whether or not exercisable at the request or with the consent of any person[1]. Until a trust for sale becomes an immediate one there is no need for any power to postpone sale, but such a power will arise as soon as the trust becomes immediate eg upon the happening of some specified future event.

1 Law of Property Act 1925, s 205(1)(xxi) as amended by TLATA 1996, Sch 4 and incorporated by TLATA 1996, s 23(2).

45.12 The Act provides[1] that 'the trustees are not liable in any way for postponing sale of the land, in the exercise of their discretion, for an indefinite period'. The potential opposition to postponing for a lengthy *definite* period is curious. But on a purposive interpretation it seems the intention should be to exempt trustees from liability if, from time to time as they review matters[2], they consciously exercise their discretion to postpone sale of the land for a definite or indefinite period, so that sale is postponed indefinitely until the time comes when they ultimately decide to sell. 'The exercise of their discretion' clearly means a conscious exercise[3], but it cannot be implicitly restricted to 'the *proper* exercise of their discretion' since they could not then be liable anyhow.

1 TLATA 1996, s 4(1).
2 Breach of their duty to review whether to exercise their powers to sell or retain trust assets can give rise to liability.
3 For example, *Rowlls v Bebb* [1900] 2 Ch 107; *Re Guinness's Settlement* [1966] 2 All ER 497.

45.13 One view would be implicitly to restrict the clause to 'the bona fide exercise of their discretion'. Thus, for example, if within 12 months of B's death the house has not been sold by private treaty or by auction as directed by the settlor within that period, the trustees can be made liable if their postponement of the sale is not bona fide. Another view would be that the phrase was included simply to contrast with the previous law (which merely conferred a power to postpone which was, however, subject to contrary intention). On that view, there is no wider significance in the reference to an indefinite period. In any event, if one trustee refuses to postpone, the power to postpone cannot be validly exercised since this requires unanimity, while applications can be made to the court for an order for sale under s 14, taking account of the settlor's directions.

Paragraph 4

No conversion under trusts for sale of land or of personalty

45.14 Except where a trust was created by the will of a testator who died before 1997[1], land held on trust for sale of land is not to be regarded as personal property (the notional proceeds of sale), nor is personalty subject to a trust to sell in order to acquire realty to be regarded as land (the notionally acquired realty)[2]. Thus the effects of the equitable doctrine of conversion have to that extent been negatived. Strangely, the provision does not catch the case of money paid to trustees to acquire realty[3].In such a case the doctrine still applies. The interests of the beneficiaries are in realty from the outset.[4]

1   TLATA 1996, s 3(2).
2   TLATA 1996, s 3(1) and (3).
3   See P Matthews, *Nice Try, Shame about Conversion*, (1997) 5 PTPR 87.
4   *Re Scarth* (1879) 10 Ch D 499.

Paragraphs 5, 6 and 9

Trustees of land have all the powers of an absolute owner

45.15   For the purposes of exercising their functions as trustees, the trustees of land have in relation to the land subject to the trust all the powers of an 'absolute owner'[1]. They also have power to acquire UK land under s 8 of the Trustee Act 2000 as an investment or for occupation by a beneficiary or for any other reason[2] and have all the powers of an absolute owner in relation to this land[3]. Such powers must not be exercised in contravention of any legislation or any rule of law or equity or any order of the court or of the Charity Commissioners[4]. Moreover, they can be excluded or restricted by the terms of the disposition creating the trust of land[5].

1   TLATA 1996, s 6(1). Presumably the draftsman meant 'absolute *beneficial* owner', as the trustees being owners of the legal estate already have all the powers of an absolute owner.
2   TLATA 1996, s 6(3) as amended by Trustee Act 2000, Sch 2, para 45(1).
3   Trustee Act 2000, s 8 (3). Further see para 53.35 ff.
4   TLATA 1996, s 6(6).
5   TLATA 1996, s 8(1) but inapplicable to charitable, ecclesiastical or public trusts.

45.16   Thus, trustees cannot make gifts of trust land to persons who are not beneficiaries or objects of powers of appointment in the trust instrument. Similarly, if investing in land they must comply with the duty to take advice, taking account of the standard investment criteria[1]. In exercising any function relating to land they must consult the beneficiaries so far as practicable and give effect to their wishes so far as consistent with the general interest of the trust[2], unless the trust instrument precludes this, or the trust is a pre-1997 trust[3].

1   Trustee Act 2000, ss 4 and 5.
2   TLATA 1996, s 11(1). See para 45.29 below.
3   TLATA 1996, s 11(2). Law of Property Act 1925, s 26(3) requiring statutory trustees for sale to consult beneficiaries was repealed by TLATA. See para 45.29 below.

45.17   The trust instrument can also exclude or restrict the trustees' powers eg by (a) requiring consents of a specific person or persons before any particular function is exercised[1] or by (b) requiring particular trust land to be inalienable for the duration of the trust or some lesser period or, it would seem, by (c) stipulating that the trustees must sell the trust land or any part thereof when directed by the life tenant and not before then, and must use the proceeds as directed by the life tenant in the acquisition of land or other property[2]. In an extreme situation where such exclusion or restriction was particularly disadvantageous and more prejudicial than probably contemplated by the settlor, it is likely that the court could either override any restrictions[3] or confer a requisite power[4].

1   See TLATA 1996, s 10. See para 45.26 below.

2 See TLATA 1996, s 6(6) preserving rules of equity coupled with s 8(1) and the possibility of the settlor or his designated protector expressly having the right to direct the trustees in respect of particular prescribed functions.
3 TLATA 1996, s 14(1); *Re Beale's Settlement Trusts* [1932] 2 Ch 15.
4 Trustee Act 1925, s 57; cf *Re Cockerell's Settlement Trusts* [1956] Ch 372.

45.18 When exercising their powers the trustees are subject to the duty of care[1].

1 TLATA 1996, s 6(9) inserted by Trustee Act 2000, Sch 2, para 45(3). See para 52.2 below.

Paragraphs 7 and 9

Partition by trustees

45.19 Where beneficiaries of full age[1] are absolutely entitled in undivided shares to land subject to the trust, the trustees may partition the land, or any part of it, and provide for the payment of any equality money by way of mortgage or otherwise[2], but only if each of the beneficiaries consents[3]. In case of disagreements application may be made to the court which may make such order as it thinks fit[4], eg an order for sale or to partition the land. On partition, accounts may need to be taken as if there had been a sale eg taking account of who paid for improvements[5].

1 If a beneficiary is a minor, however, the trustees can act on his behalf to carry out a partition as if he had been a consenting adult: TLATA 1996, s 7(5).
2 TLATA 1996, s 7(1), but an interest in part only of a commonhold unit cannot be created: Commonhold and Leasehold Reform Act 2002, Sch 5, para 8.
3 TLATA 1996, s 7(3).
4 TLATA 1996, s 14; *Rodway v Landy* [2001] Ch 703, CA.
5 For example, *Re Pavlou* [1993] 3 All ER 955, [1993] 1 WLR 1046.

45.20 Effect is given to the partition by conveying relevant parts of the land to the person entitled thereto, whether absolutely or as a trustee[1]. Where a share is vested in a beneficiary who is a minor the trustees can act in his behalf and retain land or other property representing his share upon trust for him[2].

1 TLATA 1996, s 7(2).
2 TLATA 1996, s 7(5).

Paragraphs 8 and 9

Compulsory transfer to absolutely entitled beneficiaries

45.21 Without the need to consult the beneficiaries[1], let alone obtain their consent, the trustees (unless precluded by the terms of the trust instrument[2]) can off-load their trusteeship of the land (under s 6(2) of TLATA 1996) where 'each of the beneficiaries interested in the land is a person of full age and capacity who is absolutely entitled to the land'. Thus, where land is held on trust for A for life, remainder to B, C and D (whether equally or jointly), it is not until A dies that the trustees can convey the land to B, C and D on trust for themselves as joint tenants or as tenants in common in equal shares, as appropriate. The beneficiaries must do whatever is necessary to secure that the land vests in them (eg execute the conveyance, entering into covenants therein) and, if they fail to do so, the court may make an order requiring them to do so[3].

1   TLATA 1996, s 11(2)(c).
2   TLATA 1996, s 8(1).
3   TLATA 1996, s 6(2).

45.22 It is noteworthy, however, that under s 19 of TLATA 1996 where 'the beneficiaries under the trust are of full age and capacity and (taken together) are absolutely entitled to the property subject to the trust' they can compel the trustees to retire in favour of new trustees specified by the beneficiaries (if the power of appointing new trustees is not vested in a person, eg the settlor, designated in the trust instrument). Thus, the beneficiaries can pro-actively intervene to prevent themselves becoming the new trustees, while once they are trustees they will normally have the statutory[1] power to appoint new trustees in their place.

1   Trustee Act 1925, s 36.

45.23 It will be noted that there is a subtle difference in wording between (a) s 19 covering beneficiaries with *Saunders v Vautier* rights to terminate a trust[1]and (b) s 6(2) which is not intended to apply where one of the beneficiaries has a limited interest as opposed to an absolute interest. The latter is intended to apply where all beneficiaries are of full age and capacity and each has an absolute interest in the land. In such a case, as between themselves they are absolutely entitled to the land whether such absolute interests are beneficially owned or held on trust[2] for others. Unfortunately, s 6(2) is not drafted as unambiguously as ought to be the case but, looking at the parliamentary debates[3] the Lord Chancellor made it clear[4] that the section is concerned with concurrent interests as joint tenants or tenants in common.

1   See Article 70, below.
2   TLATA 1996, s 22(1).
3   Under *Pepper v Hart* [1993] AC 593, HL.
4   571 HL Official Report (5th Series) col 957, April 22, 1996.

45.24 While the plural can include the singular under the Interpretation Act, it seems in context that the statutory power is confined to the situation where there are two or more beneficiaries under a continuing trust of land[1]. Where trustees convey to a sole beneficiary absolutely entitled to the land that trust terminates and it does not seem that any statutory authority is needed for the trustees to execute such a conveyance.

1   See Megarry & Wade *Law of Real Property* (6th edn). by C Harpum (Law Commissioner responsible for TLATA), para 8–138.

Paragraph 10

Delegation to interest in possession beneficiaries

45.25 This topic is fully dealt with in Article 55 1(e) and 2, below.

Paragraph 11

Requisite consents for trustees or purchasers

45.26 Trustees commit a breach of trust if the terms of the disposition creating the trust of land require the consent of a person to the exercise of a particular function relating to the land but the trustees proceed to exercise such function without such requisite consent[1]. Because this can make it difficult to market the land s 10(1) of TLATA 1996 protects purchasers in whose favour trustees of land exercise their functions by providing that it is sufficient if the consent of any two requisite persons is obtained[2] (except in the case of charitable, ecclesiastical or public trusts[3]). Moreover, if the person whose consent is requisite is a minor, his consent is not, in favour of a purchaser, required for the exercise of the trustees' function[4]. However, the trustees will be liable for breach of trust unless they obtain the consent of the minor's parent who has parental responsibility for him (within the meaning of the Children Act 1989) or of a guardian of his[5].

1   In the case of the powers conferred by the 1996 Act, see also s 8(2).
2   However, it seems that a non-consenting requisite person could seek an injunction to restrain a disposition proceeding in breach of trust.
3   TLATA 1996, s 10(2): see also Sch 1 para 4.
4   TLATA 1996, s 10(3)(a). 'Purchaser' means a person who acquires an interest in, or charge on, property for money or money's worth: s 23(1).
5   TLATA 1996, s 10(3)(b). Presumably a parental consent, like that of a receiver or attorney for a mental patient, could count towards the two requisite consents under s 10(1).

45.27 Where the person whose consent is requisite has no power to consent because of a mental disorder then the position is more complex. There are three possible ways forward without resorting to the court. One is that there are two others whose consent is requisite and they give their consent. A second possibility is that a receiver of the mental patient's property[1] gives a duly authorised consent[2]. A third possibility is that consent is given by an attorney under an enduring power of attorney entered into by the mentally disordered person at a time when he was not suffering from the disorder.

1   Under s 99 of the Mental Health Act 1983.
2   Mental Health Act 1983, s 96(1)(k).

45.28 If problems arise over a requisite consent not being forthcoming, then application can be made to the court by a trustee of land or any person with an interest in property subject to a trust of land for an order relating to the exercise by the trustees of any of their functions including an order relieving them of their obligation to obtain the consent of a particular person in connection with the exercise of any of their functions[1]. Often, however, the settlor will have intended the beneficiary (eg if a life tenant occupying the house) to be entitled to veto a sale pursuant to selfish personal interests, so that no court order will be made unless such beneficiary is unreasonably acting to the prejudice of all beneficiaries including himself and so exercising his power to withhold consent beyond the parameters contemplated by the settlor[2].

¹   *Re Beale's Settlement Trusts* [1932] 2 Ch 15, decided under LPA 1925, s 30, but now dealt with by s 14 of the 1996 Act; see para 45.45 below.
²   In some cases this may even amount to a fraud on the power; see para 61.9 below.

Paragraph 12

Due consultation with interest in possession beneficiaries

45.29 Except when compulsorily transferring land to the beneficiaries absolutely entitled thereto¹, trustees of land in the exercise of any function relating to the land² subject to the trust must, so far as is practicable, consult the beneficiaries of full age and 'beneficially entitled to an interest in possession in the land'³ and, so far is consistent with the general interest of the trust, give effect to the wishes of those beneficiaries or of the majority according to the value of their combined interests⁴. In a deliberate change from the old law, annuitants are excluded from the scope of this duty.⁵

¹   TLATA 1996, s 11(2)(c).
²   But not any personalty comprised within the trust of land.
³   This meaning is examined in Article 55(1)(e) and does not extend to interests under discretionary trusts or the tax-favoured accumulation and maintenance settlements or under pension trusts, on which see *Wrightson Ltd v Fletcher Challenge Nominees* [2001] UKPC 23 [2001] OPLR 249 at para 28.
⁴   TLATA 1996, s 11(1), widening provisions formerly applying to implied statutory trusts for sale by Law of Property Act 1925, s 26(3) which TLATA 1996 repealed. Query whether three otherwise equally entitled life tenants' interests should be treated as of the same value or whether the greater actuarial value of younger life tenants should be taken into account.
⁵   TLATA 1996, s 22(3).

45.30 This duty applies to all post-1996 trusts of land except those existing under a pre-1997 will, unless the terms of the disposition on trusts of land provide to the contrary¹, as is customary practice. For pre-1997 trusts (and property added thereto) no duty to consult exists unless provision for such duty is made by a deed executed by the settlor or settlors if still alive and of full capacity², when such deed is irrevocable³. The duty is to listen to the views of those adult beneficiaries with interests in possession whom it has proved practicable to contact, but the views of the majority according to the value of their beneficial interests in possession can be rejected if the trustees consider them not to be consistent with the general interest of the trust⁴, taking account of the interests of beneficiaries who are not consulted because minors or unborn or interested in remainder.

¹   TLATA 1996, s 11(2).
²   TLATA 1996, s 11(3). The real economic creator of the trust needs to execute the deed, so that if it were the trustee which declared the trust as apparent 'dummy' creator it should not be the trustee which has to execute the necessary deed.
³   TLATA 1996, s 11(4).
⁴   *Smith v Smith* (1975) 120 Sol Jo 100.

45.31 The duty only applies to the exercise of any function relating to trust land. The giving of notice by one joint tenant, A, terminating a joint periodic leasehold tenancy held by A and B on trust for A and B is not any such function: 'it is no more than the exercise by the joint tenant of his or her right to withhold his or her consent to the continuation of the tenancy into a further period'[1]. The court considered it most unlikely that Parliament would have intended the time, trouble and cost of proceedings under s 14 of TLATA 1996 to be capable of invocation[2].

[1] *Notting Hill Housing Trust v Brackley* [2001] EWCA Civ 601, [2002] HLR 10 at para 23. B has a sufficient interest in the home to be protected by Article 8(1) of the Human Rights Convention (*Harrow London Borough Council v Qazi* [2001] EWCA Civ 1834, [2002] HLR 276) but it seems interference with it by local authority landlords will almost always be justifiable under Article. 8(2):*Kay v Lambeth LBC* [2006] 2 WLR 570, HL.
[2] *Notting Hill Housing Trust v Brackley* [2001] EWCA Civ 601, [2002] HLR 10 at para 26.

45.32 The decision can be justified on the basis that the duty to consult only applies to joint functions of trustees qua trustees[1] and not to the case where one of the trustees has a right to act in his or her own interest and to the prejudice of other beneficiaries[2], as is taken to be necessarily authorised by the settlor-trustee-beneficiaries in accepting the grant of a periodic residential tenancy on trust for themselves as cohabitees.

[1] For example, *Harris v Black* (1983) 46 P & CR 366, CA: joint business tenants holding partnership assets must join in giving notices exercising statutory rights of continuation.
[2] Contrast *Sykes v Land* (1984) 271 Estates Gazette 1264 at 1266 per Fox LJ, 'In general, it must be the duty of trustees to preserve trust property for the benefit of the ultimate beneficiaries and not let it be destroyed ... if Mr Sykes required Ms Land to consent to the service of a counter-notice it would be her duty to comply, and that if necessary the court in the exercise of its general jurisdiction over trustees would order her to do so.'

Paragraphs 13 and 14

Right to occupy of beneficiary with interest in possession

45.33 By s 12(1) a beneficiary who is beneficially entitled to an interest in possession in land subject to the trust is entitled by reason of his interest to occupy the land at any time if at that time (a) the purposes of the trust include making the land available for his occupation (or for the occupation of beneficiaries of a class including him or of beneficiaries in general) or (b) the land is held by trustees so as to be so available. There can be no right of occupation if the land is either unavailable or unsuitable for occupation by him[1]. The right is subject to the trustees' powers under s 13(1) to exclude or restrict the entitlement where two or more beneficiaries would qualify under s 12, and to the trustees' powers under s 13(3) to impose reasonable conditions on any beneficiary.

[1] TLATA 1996, s 12(2).

45.34 The meaning of 'beneficially entitled to an interest in possession in land subject to the trust' is considered in Article 55(1)(e)[1]. In the present context an important question is whether or not a beneficiary with a beneficial interest in possession in an undivided share in land[2] under a sub-trust has an interest in the trust of land. This is the case eg where A and B are co-owners of land with undivided equal shares and A dies leaving his share on trust for his children equally or for his son X for life remainder to Y absolutely. A purposive, rather than a narrow, interpretation would enable B not to be the only person with a right of occupation. Indeed, as pointed out in *Lewin on Trusts*[3] it would be particularly odd if A, by settling his half share on himself for life, remainder to Y, would thereby lose his former right of occupation.

[1] See para 55.23 below.
[2] An undivided share in land qualifies as land, the exclusion of undivided shares from the Law of Property Act 1925 definition of land being repealed by TLATA 1996, Sch 4.
[3] (17th edn), para 37–55.

45.35 The settlor's purposes within s 12(1)(a) in creating the trust are ascertained from the trust instrument itself, and from the circumstances in which it was made eg to purchase land adjoining the properties of four home-owners to preserve it as open space[1], to purchase land for the joint occupation of the male and female purchasers and, perhaps, any family they may have[2], to have the testator's bungalow sold and the proceeds divided between his five children, one of whom happens to be living with him in the bungalow[3], transferring the family home, where the testator and his wife resided and which by survivorship vested in the widow, from the widow into the names of herself and her daughter jointly, but to enable the widow to stay residing there on her own for as long as she wished[4].

[1] *Re Buchanan-Wollaston's Conveyance* [1939] Ch 738.
[2] *Jones v Challenger* [1961] 1 QB 176, CA; *Rawlings v Rawlings* [1964] P 398, CA.
[3] *Barclay v Barclay* [1970] 2 QB 677, CA
[4] *Abbey National plc v Moss* (1993) 26 HLR 249, CA.

45.36 If the purposes of the trust do not include making the land available for occupation of some beneficiary or beneficiaries, then, to have a right to occupy, a beneficiary with an interest in possession will need to show that the land is held by the trustees so as to be available for occupation by some beneficiary or beneficiaries[1]. It will not be so available if the trustees are marketing it for sale with vacant possession so as to have proceeds of sale to divide between the beneficiaries as directed by the testator-settlor[2]. However, if to obtain the best price the trustees or personal representatives seek in November not to market the house till May, then it is available for them to permit a beneficiary to reside there. But this will probably be on condition[3] that he pays an appropriate percentage of a fair occupation rent so as not to have preferential treatment over his co-beneficiaries. Again, if leased commercial and residential premises are held on trust for a testator's widow for life but, after a few years she finds her own country house to be too large and inconvenient at a time when a nice city flat belonging to the trustees has just become vacant, then it seems that, if the house were sold, the flat would be held by the trustees so as to be available for her occupation[4].

[1] TLATA 1996, s 12(1)(b). Note the present tense 'is held' as emphasised in *Rodway v Landy* [2001] Ch 703, CA.
[2] Cf *Barclay v Barclay* [1970] 2 QB 677, CA.
[3] TLATA 1996, s 13(3) and (6).
[4] See *Lewin on Trusts* (17th edn) para 32–56.

45.37 Of course, the beneficiary will have no right to occupy the land if it is unavailable (eg because leased out to a tenant) or if it is unsuitable for him[1](eg because of personal physical disabilities or it is farmland and he has no farming experience whatever). 'Suitability' involves consideration not only of the property but also of the personal characteristics, circumstances and requirements of the particular beneficiary[2]. A property suitable for two to occupy together may still be suitable for one if the other leaves[3].

1 TLATA 1996, s 12(2).
2 *Chan v Leung* [2002] EWCA Civ 1075, [2003] 1 FCR 520, at para 101.
3 *Chan v Leung* [2002] EWCA Civ 1075, [2003] 1 FCR 520, at para 102. Probably the house needs to continue to be suitable which may not be the case if the widow becomes permanently infirm.

45.38 Where two or more beneficiaries qualify under s 12(1) the trustees may exclude or restrict their rights of occupation so long as this is not unreasonable and so long as the restriction is not to an unreasonable extent. Moreover, they may impose reasonable conditions on any of the beneficiaries[1]. These may include conditions requiring a beneficiary allowed into occupation to pay any outgoings or expenses in respect of the land or to assume any other obligations in relation to the activity which is or is proposed to be conducted there[2]. Thus, a house can be divided into two self-contained flats with the beneficiaries sharing the burden of the conversion costs and taking over payment of outgoings and expenses in relation to their respective flats[3].

1 TLATA 1996, s 13(2).
2 TLATA 1996, s 13(5).
3 *Rodway v Landy* [2001] EWCA Civ 471, [2001] Ch 703.

45.39 Moreover, where the entitlement of any beneficiary to occupy has been excluded or restricted, then the occupying beneficiary can be required to make payments by way of compensation to the excluded or restricted beneficiary or to forgo any payment or other benefit to which he would otherwise be entitled under the trust so as to benefit that beneficiary[1].

1 TLATA 1996, s 13(6).

45.40 If only one beneficiary has the statutory right to occupy the trust land, the right cannot be excluded or restricted, though reasonable conditions can be imposed. Thus, if the beneficiary had only an interest in possession in 5% of the land[1], the rest being held on discretionary trusts or accumulation and maintenance trusts, he may qualify under s 12(1) and occupy the whole, thus benefiting as if life tenant of 100%. In such a case, under their duty to act fairly between the beneficiaries the trustees should normally require payment of a 95% fair occupation rent. But it might be different if, say, that beneficiary's minor children resident with him happened to be the beneficiaries under the accumulation and maintenance trusts.

1 Cf *IRC v Eversden* [2002] EWHC 1360 (Ch), [2002] STC 1109.

45.41 In exercising all the above powers the trustees must have regard to the intentions of the settlor, the purposes for which the land is held, and the circumstances and wishes of each of the beneficiaries who is, or would otherwise be, entitled to occupy trust land under s 12[1]. Thus the settlor's intentions alone are not the decisive factor: the circumstances of a beneficiary may be more crucial, as in the case of the testator's widow discussed above[2].

1   TLATA 1996, s 13(4).
2   See para 45.36 above.

45.42 Finally, protection is conferred upon any beneficiary already in occupation of land and anyone occupying the land with him, such as a spouse or elderly parent. The trustees' powers under s 13 cannot be exercised to prevent such a person from occupying the land or result in cesser of such occupation unless the occupant consents or the court has given approval[1]. However, if the trustees' exercise of a power of appointment causes cesser of the beneficial interest by virtue of which the occupant occupies the land with his family members, then the land will have to be vacated, as also if the beneficiary's determinable interest in possession determines on the happening of the prescribed event.

1   TLATA 1996, s 13(7), taking account of the settlor's intentions, the purposes for which the land is held and the circumstances of the beneficiaries qualifying within s 12(1): ss 13(8) and 15(2). See *Rodway v Landy [2001] EWCA Civ 471,*[2001] Ch 703.

Paragraph 15

Court assistance for trustees and persons interested in trust property

THE OLD LAW

45.43 Before TLATA 1996, land held on trust, not being settled land within the Settled Land Act 1925 or held on a bare trust, was held on trust for sale with a power to postpone sale (unless ousted expressly or by necessary implication). Of course, powers of trustees must be exercised unanimously[1] (unless otherwise authorised by statute or by the trust instrument). Then, under s 30 of the Law of Property Act 1925, 'If the trustees for sale refuse to sell or to exercise any of the powers conferred [by ss 28 and 29], or any requisite consent cannot be obtained, any person interested may apply to the court for a vesting or other order for giving effect to the proposed transaction or for an order directing the trustees for sale to give effect thereto, and the court may make such order as it thinks fit.'

1   *Re Mayo* [1943] Ch 302.

45.44 Because there was a trust or duty to sell, the court concentrated upon the need to sell the land unless this would defeat the spirit or purpose of the trust[1]. Of course, if the trustees did not unanimously exercise the power to postpone sale, the duty to sell must take effect, as where M and F held on trust for sale for themselves but terminated their cohabitation.

1   *Jones v Challenger* [1961] 1 QB 176 CA; *Re Buchanan-Wollaston's Conveyance* [1939] Ch 738.

THE NEW STATUTORY POWERS

45.45 Section 14 of TLATA 1996 is much broader than the old s 30,[1], and s 15 gives more guidance for the exercise of the court's discretion. They provide:

'14(1) Any person who is a trustee of land or has an interest in property subject to a trust of land may make an application to the court for an order under this section.

(2) On an application for an order the court may make any such order–
  (a) relating to the exercise by the trustees of any of their functions (including an order relieving them of any obligation to obtain the consent of, or to consult, any person in connection with the exercise of any of their functions), or
  (b) declaring the nature or extent of a person's interest in property subject to the trust,as the court may think fit.

(3) The court may not under this section make any order as to the appointment or removal of trustees.

15(1) the matters to which the court is to have regard in determining an application for an order under section 14 include–
  (a) the intentions of the person or persons (if any) who created the trust,
  (b) the purposes for which the property subject to the trust is held,
  (c) the welfare of any minor who occupies or might reasonably be expected to occupy any land subject to the trust as his home, and
  (d) the interests of any secured creditor of any beneficiary

(3) the matters to which the court is to have regard also include[2] the circumstances and wishes of any beneficiaries of full age and entitled to an interest in possession in property subject to the trust or (in case of dispute) of the majority (according to the value of their combined interests).

(4) This section does not apply to an application if section 335A of the Insolvency Act 1986[3] applies to it.'

[1] Except in only applying to trustees and not to personal representatives: TLATA 1996, s 18(1).
[2] *Mortgage Corpn v Shaire* [2001] Ch 743.
[3] This is dealt with below, in paras 45.53–45.55.

45.46 Under s 17(2), s 14 applies in relation to a trust of proceeds of sale of land and trustees of such a trust as in relation to a trust of land and trustees of land. A trust of proceeds of sale of land[1] is any trust of property (other than a trust of land) which consists of, or includes, any proceeds of a disposition of land held in trust (including settled land unless the proceeds remain subject to the Settled Land Act 1925) or any property representing any such proceeds. An application under s 14 is not an action falling within the *in rem* exclusive jurisdiction provision in reg 22 of the Council Regulation (EC) 44/2001.[2]

[1] TLATA 1996, s 17(3) and (5).
[2] *Prazic v Prazic* [2006] EWCA Civ 497.

LOCUS STANDI TO APPLY TO COURT

45.47 Those who are entitled to apply to the court are the trustees (but not personal representatives)[1], and any person who 'has an interest in property' (which could be personal property[2]) subject to the trust of land or of its proceeds or property representing such proceeds. This could be a claimant alleging a resulting or constructive trust in his favour[3]. But only an *interest* is required, not an interest *in possession* nor an interest *as a beneficiary*. Thus, those who can apply include a beneficiary under a discretionary trust[4], an annuitant[5], a creditor with a charge or a charging order over a beneficiary's interest[6], a spouse or civil partner with a Class F charge or registered notice under the Family Law Act 1996[7], and the trustee in bankruptcy of a beneficiary[8], though probably not a receiver by way of equitable execution[9]. A creditor who thinks he is taking a legal charge from a person claiming to be sole legal owner, but who is in fact only a co-owner of land, will generally obtain a charge (necessarily equitable) over that co-owner's beneficial interest[10], and will thus have standing to apply to the court.

1 TLATA 1996, s 18(1).
2 TLATA 1996, s 1(1)(a).
3 Eg *Oxley v Hiscock* [2004] EWCA Civ 546, [2005] Fam 211.
4 As indicated in Megarry & Wade *Law of Real Property* (6th edn) by C Harpum (Law Commissioner responsible for TLATA 1996), para 8–142; *Gartside v IRC* [1968] AC 553, HL.
5 Like a chargee and only excluded from having an interest in possession by TLATA 1996, s 22(3).
6 *Bank of Ireland Home Mortgages Ltd v Bell* [2001] 2 FLR 809 (equitable charge) as for Law of Property Act 1925, s 30 in *Midland Bank plc v Pike* [1988] 2 All ER 434; *Lloyds Bank v Byrne* [1993] 1 FLR 369, CA; and see TLATA 1996, s 15(1)(d).
7 Application under the FLA 1996 may be preferable due to the considerations to be taken into account under s 33(6) thereof.
8 *Re Solomon* [1967] Ch 573; *Re Ng* [1997] BCC 507.
9 *Stevens v Hutchinson* [1953] Ch 299 (held not to be a 'person interested' for the purposes of s 30 of the Law of Property Act 1925).
10 *First National Securities Ltd v Hegerty* [1985] QB 850; *Ahmed v Kendrick* [1988] 2 FLR 22; *Bowers v Bowers*, [2004] 1 FCR 18, 3 February 1997 unreported, Hoffmann J; *First National Bank v Achampong* [2003] EWCA Civ 487 [2004] 1 FCR 18; *Edwards v Lloyds TSB Bank plc* [2004] EWHC 1745 (Ch), [2005] 1 FCR 139.

DETERMINATION OF APPLICATIONS (OTHER THAN FOR AN ORDER FOR SALE UNDER INSOLVENCY ACT 1986, S 335A)

45.48 The court may make such orders as it thinks fit so as to declare, but not vary[1], the nature or extent of a person's interest in trust property[2] or affect the exercise of any of the functions of the trustees. This may include orders relieving them of any obligation to obtain the consent of, or to consult, any person, even (as under the old LPA s 30) where that person has expressly told the trustees not to do what they propose.

1 See Law Commission Discussion Paper 'Sharing Homes' (July 2002) para 2.26. No varying power existed under Law of Property Act 1925, s 30: *Stott v Ratcliffe* (1982) 126 Sol Jo 310; *Ahmed v Kendrick* (1987) 56 P & CR 120 at 127.
2 Proprietary estoppel principles may make a person's interest uncertain so as to need to be determined and declared.

45.49 The terms of the statute are very wide, and it seems that they even extend to overcoming any exclusions by the settlor of the powers conferred upon trustees by TLATA 1996 in those exceptional cases where such exclusions wholly undermine the trustees' fundamental functions to act in the best interests of the beneficiaries as a whole and to further the purposes of the trust, acting fairly between income and capital beneficiaries (except to the extent clearly ousted by the trust instrument)[1].

1   As indicated in Megarry & Wade *Law of Real Property* (6th edn) by C Harpum, the Law Commissioner responsible for TLATA 1996, para 8–142.

45.50 It is in the sphere of co-owned land that most applications to the court are made. Case law under s 30 of the Law of Property Act 1925 established that, where the power to postpone sale was not unanimously exercised by the cohabiting, co-owning trustees, the courts favoured enforcement of the trust for sale.However, the courts did look at the intentions of the settlor-trustees when becoming co-owners of the house or flat and the purposes for which they held such property, to see whether enforcing the letter of the trust for sale would defeat the purpose of the trust[1].

1   *Jones v Challenger* [1961] 1 QB 176, CA.

45.51 Some judges[1] found that the purpose was to provide a matrimonial or quasi-matrimonial home for the two settlor-trustee-beneficiaries so that the purpose did not continue once they separated, even if the home housed one parent and their children, so the welfare of the children was only an incidental factor affecting postponement of a sale only for a short period. Other judges[2], however, were prepared to find that the purpose was to provide a family home so that such purpose persisted when one parent had left the home occupied by the other parent and the children.

1   *Burke v Burke* [1974] 1 WLR 1063, CA; *Re Halliday* [1981] Ch 405, CA.
2   *Williams v Williams* [1976] Ch 278, CA; *Re Evers' Trust* [1980] 1 WLR 1327, CA.

45.52 In any event, the voice of a secured creditor or of the trustee in bankruptcy would prevail unless the circumstances were most exceptional[1].

1   *Re Citro* [1991] Ch 142, CA; *Lloyds Bank plc v Byrne* [1993] 1 FLR 369, CA.

45.53 Section 15 has changed the pre-1996 law, requiring the court to consider whether any matters mentioned in the section are present, and in giving it greater discretion as to the weight to be given to such matters in deciding what order to make[1]. (But it should be noted that, where the trustee in bankruptcy of a bankrupt beneficiary applies for an order for sale, different criteria are provided[2].) The authorities on LPA s 30 have now to be treated with caution and in many cases they are unlikely to be of great assistance[3]. Where trusts for sale were created before 1997 as a matter of standard conveyancing practice, there is now no presumption of sale. No doubt, if an express trust for sale were deliberately imposed after 1996, this would indicate the settlor's intention that there should be a sale, and the purpose of the trust at the time of its creation, so in that case there may well be a presumption in favour of sale. Even so, the other matters mentioned in s 15 must also be considered, noting that it is the purposes for which the property *is* held at the time of the application which are relevant[4].

1   *Mortgage Corpn v Shaire* [2001] Ch 743 at 757; *Bank of Ireland Home Mortgages Ltd v Bell* [2001] 2 FLR 809 at 816 per Peter Gibson LJ. *Edwards v Lloyds TSB Bank plc* [2004] EWHC 1745 (Ch) [2005] 1 FCR 139, at paras 28–30.
2   See para 45.56 below.
3   *Mortgage Corpn v Shaire* [2001] Ch 743 at 761.
4   *Rodway v Landy [2001] EWCA Civ 471*,[2001] Ch 703 at 711 per Peter Gibson LJ. Where there are two co-owners it is their common intention at the time of creation of the trust that counts, while their common purpose at the outset is what counts unless both agree to a change of purpose: *White v White* [2003] EWCA Civ 924, [2004] 2 FLR 321 at [21] to [23].

45.54 While the interests of secured creditors are not almost invariably conclusive as under s 30[1], a powerful consideration swaying the court is the unfairness of keeping such a creditor out of his money if he is not receiving proper recompense for this[2].

1   See *Williams v Williams* [1976] Ch 278: *Re Evers Trust* [1980] 1 WLR 1327.
2   *Williams v Williams* [1976] Ch 278, CA; *Bank of Ireland Home Mortgages Ltd v Bell* [2001] 2 FLR 809; *Edwards v Lloyds TSB Bank plc* [2004] EWHC 1745 (Ch), [2005] 1 FCR 139; *Pritchard Englefield v Steinberg* [2004] EWHC 1908 (Ch).

45.55 The welfare of any minor who occupies or might reasonably be expected to occupy land as his home is a factor always to be taken into consideration, so that there is scope to give more prominence to this than before when considering the interests of any secured creditor[1]. However, as before, where there are children of a marriage matters should still be dealt with so far as possible under the flexibility of the matrimonial homes legislation rather than under the more general trusts of land legislation[2]. Similarly, if there is an application under Schedule 1 to the Children Act 1989 relating to children of an unmarried couple as well as a TLATA application, the flexibility under the 1989 Act is to be preferred[3].

1   *Mortgage Corpn v Shaire* [2001] Ch 743 at 760; *Edwards v Lloyds TSB Bank plc* [2004] EWHC 1745 (Ch), [2005] 1 FCR 139 at para 29.
2   *Williams v Williams* [1976] Ch 278, CA; *Tee v Tee* [1999] 2 FLR 613, CA.
3   *White v White* [2003] EWCA Civ 924, [2004] 2 FLR 321.

Trustee in bankruptcy's application for order for sale under Insolvency Act 1986, s 335A[1]

45.56 An application by the trustee of a bankrupt's estate for an order for sale of the land under s 14 must be made to the bankruptcy court having jurisdiction in the bankruptcy (which may not be the court which would otherwise have jurisdiction under s 14). On such an application, the court must make such order as it thinks just and reasonable, having regard to–

(a)   the interests of the bankrupt's creditors;
(b)   where the application concerns the home of the bankrupt or the bankrupt's spouse or civil partner or former spouse or former civil partner–

   (i) the conduct of the spouse or civil partner or former spouse or former civil partner, so far as contributing to the bankruptcy;

   (ii) the needs and financial resources of the spouse or civil partner or former spouse or former civil partner, and

   (iii) the needs of any children; and

(c) all the circumstances of the case other than the needs of the bankrupt.

¹ Inserted by TLATA 1996, Sch 3, para 23.

45.57 Crucially, where the application is made after one year has elapsed since the bankrupt's estate first vested in a trustee, the court must assume, unless the circumstances of the case are exceptional, that the interests of the bankrupt's creditors outweigh all other considerations¹. In *Harrington v Bennett*², the judge explained 'exceptional circumstances' as follows:

'The essence of this appeal is whether there are exceptional circumstances which would justify a departure from the assumption that the interests of creditors are paramount in this type of application. The principles to be derived from the authorities which were cited to me can be summarised as follows:

(a) The presence of exceptional circumstances is a necessary condition to displace the *assumption* that the interests of the creditors outweigh all other considerations, but the presence of the exceptional circumstances does not debar the court from making an order for sale: *Re D R Raval* [1998] BPIR 389;

(b) Typically, the exceptional circumstances in the modern cases relate to the personal circumstances of one of the joint owners, such as a medical or mental condition: see *Judd v Brown* [1977] BPIR 470; *Re DR Raval* [1998] BPIR 389; *Claughton v Charalamabous* [1998] BPIR 558.

(c) But the categories of exceptional circumstances are not to be categorised or defined. The court makes a value judgment after looking at all the circumstances: *Claughton v Charalamabous* [1998] BPIR 558, 562.

(d) But the circumstances must be "exceptional", and this expression was intended to apply the same test as the pre-Insolvency Act 1986 decisions on bankruptcy: *Re Citro* [1991] Ch 142, 159, 160 referring to the identical wording in section 336(5), i.e. exceptional or special circumstances which are outside the usual "melancholy consequences of debt and improvidence", at 157, *per* Nourse LJ; or "compelling reasons, not found in the ordinary run of cases", at 161, *per* Bingham LJ.

For the purposes of weighing the interests of the creditors, the creditors have an interest in the order for sale being made even if the whole of the net proceeds will go towards the expenses of the bankruptcy; and the fact that they will be swallowed up in paying those expenses is not an exceptional circumstance justifying the displacement of the assumption that the interests of the creditors outweigh all other considerations: *Trustee of the Estate of Bowe v Bowe* [1997] BPIR 747.'

¹ Insolvency Act 1986, s 335A(3).
² [2000] BPIR 630, [2000] EGCS 41.

45.58 Article 8 (respect for the home) and Article 1 of Protocol 1 (the right to peaceful enjoyment of possessions) of the European Convention on Human Rights are not automatically breached when the court makes an order for the sale of the family home.¹

¹ *Nicholls v Lan*, [2006] EWHC 1255 (Ch), (2006) Times, 4 August.

EQUITABLE ACCOUNTING AFTER SALE

45.59 As already seen[1], accounts may need to be settled between co-owners after sale of their property. These will take into account any co-owner bearing a disproportionate part of the mortgage payments, or being entitled to an occupation rent having been forced out of the property well before the sale, or being entitled to an allowance for improvements to the property, or not being paid for a business being carried on in the premises by the other co-owner[2].

[1]   See para 31.16 ff.
[2]   *Abbott v Price* [2003] EWHC 2760 (Ch).

Paragraph 16

Protection of Purchasers

45.60 A purchaser (meaning a person who acquires an interest in land or a charge on property for money or money's worth) need not be concerned to see that the trustees have complied with their duty under s 6(5) to have regard to the rights of the beneficiaries and to consult them under s 11(1) (if not ousted) nor to see that they had obtained the consent of each beneficiary to any earlier partition of the land[1].

[1]   TLATA 1996, s 16(1).

45.61 So long as capital money is paid to two trustees or a trust corporation or a sole personal representative acting as such[1], interests under the trust of land will be overreached unless, in the case of unregistered land, the purchaser or his agent had actual notice that the trustees were exceeding their powers (by ignoring any limitations on them in s 6(6) and (8)[2]) or, in the case of registered land, there was an entry in the register limiting the trustees' powers[3].

[1]   Law of Property Act 1925, ss 2 and 27 as amended by TLATA 1996, Sch 3, para 4.
[2]   TLATA 1996, s 16(2) and (3).
[3]   Land Registration Act 2002, s 26, resolving the problem identified by Ferris & Battersby in [1998] Conv 168.

45.62 To avoid the need to investigate the underlying equitable interests, where the trustees have conveyed their land to the persons believed by them to be beneficiaries of full age and capacity and have executed a deed of discharge declaring themselves discharged from the trust in relation to that land, then a purchaser is entitled to assume that the land has been free from that trust since the date of the deed of discharge[1] – unless he has actual notice that the trustees were mistaken in their belief[2].

[1]   Cf Settled Land Act 1925, s 17.
[2]   TLATA 1996, s 16(5).

Chapter 13

THE TRUSTEE'S DUTIES

ARTICLE 46
DUTY OF TRUSTEE CONCERNING ACCEPTANCE OF TRUST OR
ADDITIONAL TRUST PROPERTY

46.1

(1)   Before accepting a trust or additional trust property, the potential
or actual trustee ought to discover:

  (i)   if he might be about to put himself in a position where
there would be a sensible possibility of a conflict between
his personal self-interest and his fiduciary duty, because in
such event he should refuse the trusteeship unless such
conflict is authorised by the trust instrument (or by all the
beneficiaries of full age and capacity who between them
are absolutely beneficially entitled to the trust property);

  (ii)   how onerous the task is likely to be, taking account of the
value and nature of the trust property, the range of the
beneficiaries and of the trustees' powers, the provisions for
remuneration and for exculpation from liability, and the
possibilities for dissension and animosity among beneficiaries or classes of beneficiaries;

  (iii)   whether there is a sensible possibility that the validity of
the transfer of the trust or a transfer of property to the
trustees could be attacked;

  (iv)   whether there is a sensible possibility that he could find
himself criminally liable under extensive anti-money laundering legislation.

(2)   Having accepted the trust, it is the duty of the trustee to acquaint
himself, as soon as possible, with the nature and circumstances of
the trust property, the terms of the trust, and the contents of the
documents handed over to him relating to the trust. Where
necessary, he should obtain a transfer of the trust property to
himself, and (subject to the provisions of the settlement) get in
debts and trust money invested on insufficient or hazardous
security[1].

[1]   Eg in trade: *Kirkman v Booth* (1848) 11 Beav 273; *Re Strahan* (1856) 8 De GM & G 291.

Paragraph 1(i)

Avoidance of conflict between fiduciary duty and self-interest

46.2–46.3   If a prospective original trustee is related by blood or marriage to a
beneficiary or owed a significant sum by a beneficiary[1] or may want to
purchase for himself trust property at some stage (eg the large house from
which he and the testator-settlor have conducted a dental or medical practice),
then the trusteeship of the lifetime or testamentary trust should be refused
unless the trust instrument confers express authority for such conflicts of

interest or self-dealing[2], eg so long as there are co-trustees who concur in the payment to a related beneficiary or the self-dealing. Where the relevant facts were known to the settlor, who still went ahead with appointing the interested person as an original trustee, the courts are easily persuaded to find a necessarily implied authority for conflicts of interest[3], except where such conflict is at its greatest in the case of self-dealing[4], but it is always better to avoid possible problems with an express authority in the trust instrument.

[1] *Peyton v Robinson* (1823) 1 LJOS Ch 191. A bargain between a trustee and a beneficiary that payment of trust money will only be made if the trustee then receives thereout payment of his debt will be a fraud on the power of payment (so the payment will be void) unless the power expressly authorises payment on such terms so indirectly allowing the trustee to be a beneficiary to the extent of debts due from a beneficiary to him: see, generally, see paras 61.31–61.41.
[2] See para 59.30 below.
[3] As where the settlor and spouse are trustees for their children and grandchildren or the settlor makes X and Y trustees for their children and grandchildren. For other instances see *Sargeant v National Westminster Bank* (1991) 61 P & CR 518, CA; *Edge v Pensions Ombudsman* [2000] Ch 602 at 621–622, 632–633.
[4] See paras 33.89 and 59.30.

46.4 Where a person is asked to become new trustee of an established trust, then, unless there is some broad general authority in the trust instrument that can be relied upon, the only foolproof protection in the event of a conflict of interest is if all the beneficiaries of full age and capacity, who between them are absolutely beneficially entitled to the trust property, agree to the impeachable transaction[1]. Such a situation is, in practice, very rare because the lengthy duration of most trusts means that all the beneficiaries will not have been ascertained at the relevant time, so that a subsequently born or ascertained beneficiary may subsequently bring legal proceedings.

[1] *Saunders v Vautier* (1841) 4 Beav 115, Article 70 below.

Paragraph 1(ii)

Avoiding onerous responsibilities that are not worthwhile

46.5 As a matter of commonsense, a prospective trustee should consider the value and nature of the actual or potential trust assets and the terms of the trust instrument to ascertain how complex and difficult his task will be and how extensive his potential liability may be. Particular regard should be paid to clauses concerned with remuneration and with exculpation from liability, and he may well wish to be able to retire without the consent of his co-trustees[1], although if his co-trustees can also do this, then this is double-edged, involving a possibility of benefit or of burden. Caution is also needed if there is, or there is to be, a protector, in considering the relationship between the trustee and the protector and the impact of any powers of supervision or removal vested in the protector. Difficulties can also arise if there is only one trust for the issue of three or four marriages of the settlor or only one trust for the benefit of a settlor's family as well as for employees and ex-employees of the settlor's company and their families.

[1] Trustee Act 1925 ('TA 1925'), s 39.

Paragraph 1(iii)

Vitiated transfers to trustees or vitiated trusts

46.6 The settlor's transfer of property to trustees will be vitiated if the settlor was not the beneficial owner thereof[1] or made the transfer to prejudice his creditors[2] or under undue influence[3] or when he had no capacity[4]. Where there was a valid transfer of property to trustees the trust may be void for uncertainty[5] or administrative unworkability[6] or as a non-charitable purpose trust[7], or it may be that the trust was a sham trust for the designated beneficiaries, really being a trust of property for the settlor[8], with any dispositive provisions taking effect on the settlor's death being testamentary ones requiring compliance with the Will Act 1837. Certain trusts subject to an exotic foreign governing law may stretch the elasticity of the trust concept beyond that permitted by English public policy or that required for the irreducible core content of a trust, so that the trust is a 'limping trust', valid under its governing law but a resulting trust of assets situated in England or other traditional trust jurisdictions[9].

1   The real owner may follow or trace the property so as to recover it.
2   See Article 17.
3   See Article 15.
4   See Article 13.
5   See Article 8(1).
6   See para 8.71 above.
7   See para 8.144 above.
8   See para 4.6 above.
9   See para 102.209 below.

46.7 If a prospective trustee believes that there is a sensible possibility that he will become involved in the time, trouble and expense of litigation, then it is only common sense to refuse the trusteeship. In addition, he could be personally liable if he had actual, Nelsonian or naughty knowledge that the settlor's transfer to him was a breach of the settlor's fiduciary duty[1], while there may be problems over recourse to the trust fund for liabilities incurred in performance of the trusts or in defending the trust fund against third parties, particularly where those parties' claims succeed[2].

1   See paras 100.72–100.74 below.
2   See para 87.48 ff.

Paragraph 1(iv)

Criminal liabilities under anti-money-laundering legislation

46.8 Money laundering[1] is an act which:

(a)   constitutes an offence under ss 327, 328 or 329 of the Proceeds of Crime Act 2002;

(b)   constitutes an attempt, conspiracy or incitement to commit an offence within (a);

(c)   constitutes aiding, abetting, counselling or procuring the commission of an offence within (a); or

(d)   would constitute an offence within (a), (b) or (c) if done in the UK.

¹   Proceeds of Crime Act 2002 ('PCA 2002'), s 340(11). 14 years is the maximum sentence for ss 327, 328 and 329 offences: see s 334.

46.9 Under s 327 a person commits an offence if he conceals, disguises, converts or transfers criminal property or removes criminal property from England and Wales or from Scotland or from Northern Ireland. 'Concealing or disguising' criminal property includes concealing or disguising its nature, source, location, disposition, movement or ownership or any rights with respect to it¹. The act of accepting property to hold on trust could amount to such concealing or disguising. Similarly, a bank or other entity which received money from trustees could also commit the offence². (Payment out to beneficiaries of the trust, of course, would amount to 'transferring'.) Property is 'criminal property' if³ (a) it constitutes a person's benefit from 'criminal conduct' or it represents such a benefit (in whole or part and whether directly or indirectly eg via the tracing process), and (b) the alleged offender knows or suspects that it constitutes or represents such a benefit. 'Criminal conduct' is conduct⁴ which (a) constitutes an offence in any part of the UK or (b) would constitute an offence in any part of the UK if it occurred there. The prosecution must prove that the property is indeed criminal property, not merely that the defendant so believed⁵.

¹   PCA 2002, s 327(3).
²   Hence the need for 'know your customer' guidance in relation to trusts: UK Joint Money Laundering Steering Group's Guidance Notes for the Financial Sector, Jan 2006, Part 1, paras 5.4.100–5.4.123.
³   PCA 2002, s 340(3).
⁴   PCA 2002, s 340(2).
⁵   *R v Montilla* [2004] UKHL 50, [2004] 1 WLR 3141, paras 21–22.

46.10 Under s 328 a person commits an offence if he enters into or becomes concerned in an arrangement which he knows or suspects facilitates (by whatever means) the acquisition, retention, use or control of criminal property by or on behalf of another person. Again, accepting property to hold on trust could amount to such an arrangement. (So could the preparation of the trust documents by a professional, such as a lawyer, accountant or banker.) On the other hand, the ordinary conduct of litigation by legal professionals¹ or consensual settlement by them of such litigation² does not fall within this provision.

¹   *Bowman v Fels* [2005] EWCA Civ 226, [2005] 4 All ER 609, paras 83–84. Even if it did, the section would not override legal professional privilege (paras 85–87) or the implied obligation of confidence in relation to information obtained by compulsory disclosure in litigation (paras 88–89).
²   *Bowman v Fels* [2005] EWCA Civ 226, [2005] 4 All ER 609, paras 99–102.

46.11 Under s 329 a person commits an offence if he acquires, uses or has possession of criminal property, unless he be a purchaser for adequate consideration¹, but the provision by a person of goods or services which he knows or suspects may help another to carry out criminal conduct is not consideration for this purpose[2]. A trustee holding criminal property on trust or acquiring it so to hold may commit this offence.

1   PCA 2002, s 329(2).
2   PCA 2002, s 329(3).

46.12 It is a defence to charges under ss 327, 328 and 329 that (i) the alleged offender knew or believed on reasonable grounds that the relevant criminal conduct occurred in a place outside the UK, (ii) that conduct was not then unlawful under the criminal law applying in that place, and (iii) it is not of a description prescribed by the Secretary of State[1]. (There is also a further defence available in most cases to deposit-takers accepting small sums of money[2], but this will rarely apply to trustees).

1   PCA 2002, ss 327(2A), 328(3), 329(2A).
2   PCA 2002, ss 327(2C), 328(5), 329(2C).

46.13 It is also a defence[1] to charges under ss 327, 328 and 329 that the alleged offender on his own initiative as soon as practicable had made an authorised disclosure under s 338 (eg to someone authorised by the Serious Organised Crime Agency[2], or a person nominated by his employer under an established procedure[3]) or he had intended to make such a disclosure but had a reasonable excuse for not doing so, or the act he did was done in carrying out a function he has relating to the enforcement of any provision of the 2002 Act or of any other Act relating to criminal conduct.

1   PCA 2002, ss 327(2), 328(2), 329(2) and (3).
2   Replacing the former National Criminal Intelligence Service.
3   There is a separate procedure for disclosure (and possible offence of non-disclosure to be committed) by this nominated officer: POCA 2002, ss 331–32.

46.14 Where the potential defendant made the authorised disclosure before performing the act constituting an offence under ss 327, 328 or 329 and obtained an appropriate consent then no offence has been committed[1]. The appropriate consent is the consent of the officer nominated by the employer or of someone authorised by the SOCA to do a prohibited act after receiving an authorised disclosure[2]. In the case of a person authorised by the SOCA, the consent will be deemed to have been given if either notice refusing consent is not received within seven working days of disclosure to such person (starting with the first working day after disclosure) or such notice was received but thirty-one days have elapsed since receipt of such notice[3]. In the case of a nominated officer, he must not give the appropriate consent unless either he does not believe his act is prohibited or he is authorised by some person authorised by the SOCA or unless notice refusing consent is not received from such person within seven working days of disclosure to him or unless such notice of refusal was received but thirty-one days have elapsed since receipt of such notice[4].

1   PCA 2002, ss 327(2)(a), 328(2)(a), 329(2)(a).
2   PCA 2002, s 335(1). See UK Joint Money Laundering Steering Group's Guidance Notes for the Financial Sector, Jan 2006, Part 1, paras 7.45–7.53.
3   PCA 2002, s 335(2)–(6).
4   PCA 2002, s 336.

46.15 An offence of failure to make an authorised disclosure occurs[1] if all the following four conditions are satisfied:

(i)   the defendant knows[2] or suspects[3] or has *reasonable grounds for* knowing or *suspecting* that another person is engaged in money-laundering; and

(ii) the information or other matter on which his knowledge or suspicion is based or which gives reasonable grounds for such knowledge or suspicion came to him in the course of a business in the regulated sector[4]; and

(iii) he can identify either the other person in (i) above or the whereabouts of any of the laundered property, or he believes (or it is reasonable to expect him to believe) that the information in (ii) above will or may assist in identifying that person or those whereabouts; and

(iv) he fails to make the authorised disclosure as soon as practicable without a reasonable excuse.

1   PCA 2002, s 330: 5 years is the maximum sentence: s 334.
2   It suffices that the defendant deliberately refrained from inquiry because he suspected the truth but did not want to have his suspicion confirmed: *Westminster City Council v Croyalgrange Ltd* [1986] 2 All ER 353 at 359, HL, per Lord Bridge.
3   Suspicion requires some foundation, as opposed to speculation, but not prima facie proof and can take account of matters that could not be put in evidence: *Hussein v Chong Fook Kam* [1970] AC 942, PC, *Welsh v Loughman* [1992] 2 VR 351.
4   PCA 2002, Sch 6, Pt I defines the regulated sector essentially to cover persons regulated under the Financial Services and Markets Act 2000, but also lawyers and trustees.

46.16 It is however a defence to a charge of this offence that (i) the defendant knew or believed on reasonable grounds that the relevant criminal conduct occurred in a place outside the UK, (ii) that conduct was not then unlawful under the criminal law applying in that place, and (iii) it is not of a description prescribed by the Secretary of State[1].

1   PCA 2002, s 330(7A).

46.17 It is also a defence that the defendant was a professional legal adviser and the information or other matter came to him in privileged circumstances (and so was not communicated or given with the intention of furthering a criminal purpose)[1]. In determining whether a person knows or suspects or has reasonable ground for knowing or suspecting money-laundering, the court must consider whether the defendant had followed any relevant guidance issued by a supervisory or other appropriate body and published in a manner in its opinion appropriate to bring the guidance to the attention of persons likely to be affected by it[2]. Indeed, the defendant will be safe if he does not know or suspect another person is engaged in money-laundering if he had not been provided by his employer with such training as is specified by the Secretary of State for the purposes of s 330[3].

1   PCA 2002, s 330(6), (10) and (11).
2   PCA 2002, s 330(8).
3   PCA 2002, s 330(7). On the other hand the employer would have committed an offence in not supplying the training.

46.18 Tipping off the alleged money-launderer is a further offence[1] once the defendant knows or suspects that a disclosure has been made *by anyone* to the relevant person (eg to the SOCA or the person designated by the employer)[2]. But this does not apply[3] if he did not know or suspect that his tipping-off conduct was likely to be prejudicial to investigation of the alleged money launderer, or if such conduct occurred in carrying out a function relating to enforcement of the 2002 Act or any other Act relating to criminal conduct. Nor does it apply if he was a professional legal adviser advising the alleged criminal but not with the intention of furthering a criminal purpose[4]. A trustee who knows of or suspects that a disclosure has been made to the relevant person must therefore be very careful what information he passes to others, including his beneficiaries, who under the general law might otherwise be entitled to such information[5].

1   PCA 2002, s 333(1): 5 years is the maximum sentence under s 334.
2   UK Joint Money Laundering Steering Group's Guidance Notes for the Financial Sector, Jan 2006, Part 1, paras 7.55–7.62. For resolution of practical difficulties see *Bank of Scotland v A Ltd [2001] EWCA Civ 52*, [2001] 3 All ER 58; *Amalgamated Metal Trading Ltd v City of London Financial Investigation Unit* [2003] EWHC 703 (Comm), [2003] 4 All ER 1225, [2003] 1 WLR 2711; see also *Ani v Barclays Private Bank & Trust Ltd* [2004] JRC 069, R Ct Jersey.
3   PCA 2002, s 333(3) and (4).
4   PCA 2002, s 333(3) and (4).
5   As to provision of information to beneficiaries generally, see Article 60.

46.19 Property that is not criminal property within the Proceeds of Crime Act 2002 but which is 'terrorist property'[1] is governed by the Terrorism Act 2000. The term 'terrorist property' extends to property not acquired by criminal conduct but likely to be used for the purposes of terrorism (including any resources of a proscribed organisation). A person commits an offence if he enters into or becomes concerned in an arrangement which facilitates the retention or control by or on behalf of another person of terrorist property by concealment, by removal from the jurisdiction, by transfer to nominees or in any other way, unless he can prove he did not know and had no reasonable cause to suspect that the arrangement related to terrorist property[2]. The Act was amended in 2001[3] by introducing a further offence[4] of failure to disclose that he knows or suspects or has reasonable grounds for knowing or suspecting that another person has committed an offence under ss 15 to 18 of the 2000 Act[5]. Similar defences exist as under the Proceeds of Crime Act 2002[6]. But unlike in the 2002 Act, there is no provision in the Terrorism Act for consent to be given for a proposed transaction within a specified period, and such transaction must not proceed until authorised[7].

1   Terrorism Act 2000, s 14.
2   Terrorism Act 2000, s 18.
3   By the Anti Terrorism, Crime and Security Act 2001.
4   Terrorism Act 2000, s 21A.
5   These concern fund-raising, use and possession of property for purposes of terrorism, being concerned in arrangements to make property available to another for purposes of terrorism as well as money-laundering, so long as there is reasonable cause for suspicion.
6   Terrorism Act 2000, ss 19, 20, 21 and 21A.
7   UK Joint Money Laundering Steering Group's Guidance Notes for the Financial Sector, Jan 2006, Part 1, para 7.54.

Suspicious transaction reports: professional trustees and advisers

46.20 Professional trustees and their advisers need to be aware of the extensive width of the Proceeds of Crime Act 2002 and the Terrorism Act 2000 (as amended) so as to consider whether they need to make a suspicious transaction report to the SOCA[1]. After all, they need only to have reasonable grounds for suspecting[2] that a person is involved in money-laundering 'criminal property' or 'terrorist property'. Moreover, criminal property is so broadly defined[3] as to cover not just false accounting or forgery or obtaining benefits by fraud[4] but also the benefits obtained from pure tax evasion (like non-declaration of taxable income or capital), while conduct occurring anywhere is 'criminal conduct' (potentially giving rise to 'criminal property') if it 'would constitute an offence in any part of the UK if it occurred there' (though subject to defences in some cases for conduct not criminal where it was believed to have occurred). Relying on analogous extradition provisions[5], prosecution authorities are prepared to argue that the courts will transpose conduct amounting to cheating the Taxopian revenue (eg by non-disclosure), whether occurring in Taxopia or in England, into conduct amounting to cheating the national revenue, which would constitute an offence if occurring in England, but there is much to be said for respecting human rights by treating conduct cheating the Taxopian revenue as not constituting an offence in England if occurring in England or Taxopia. However, breach of another jurisdiction's exchange controls cannot of itself amount to 'criminal conduct'[6].

[1]   See generally UK Joint Money Laundering Steering Group's Guidance Notes for the Financial Sector, Jan 2006, Part 1, Chap 7.
[2]   Terrorism Act 2000, s 21A; PCA 2002, s 330(2); UK Joint Money Laundering Steering Group's Guidance Notes for the Financial Sector, Jan 2006, Part 1, paras 7.13–7.15.
[3]   PCA 2002, s 340.
[4]   Though not *attempted* fraud: UK Joint Money Laundering Steering Group's Guidance Notes for the Financial Sector, Jan 2006, Part 1, paras 7.40–7.42.
[5]   *R v Chief Metropolitan Stipendiary Magistrate, ex p Secretary of State for Home Department* [1988] 1 WLR 1204.
[6]   Though of course there may be other offences involved in the activity concerned, e g false accounting, which can amount to 'criminal conduct'.

46.21 Finally, in the regulated sector the due diligence requirements[1] to help prevent money-laundering may well lead to information being available that provides reasonable grounds for money-laundering suspicions so that a suspicious transaction report should be made to the SOCA. However, financial institutions with proper systems in place can reasonably assume their clients will meet their tax liabilities unless there is some reason to suspect otherwise, and are not required actively to investigate clients' affairs to ascertain whether any criminal conduct has occurred[2].

[1]   UK Joint Money Laundering Steering Group's Guidance Notes for the Financial Sector, Jan 2006, Part 1, Chap 5.
[2]   See generally UK Joint Money Laundering Steering Group's Guidance Notes for the Financial Sector, Jan 2006.

Paragraph 2

Inquiries as to the property and the trusts and the trust documents

46.22 A person who undertakes to act as a trustee takes upon himself serious and onerous duties; and when, as too often happens, he adopts a 'policy of masterly inactivity', he entirely misapprehends the nature of the office to which he has been appointed. As Kekewich J said in *Hallows v Lloyd*[1]:

> 'What are the duties of persons becoming new trustees of a settlement? Their duties are quite onerous enough, and I am not prepared to increase them. I think that when persons are asked to become new trustees, they are bound to inquire of what the property consists that is proposed to be handed over to them, and what are the trusts. They ought also to look into the trust documents and papers to ascertain what notices appear among them of incumbrances and other matters affecting the trust.'

[1]   (1888) 39 Ch D 686 at 691. Precisely the same duties are binding on persons appointed as *original* trustees.

46.23 So that the new trustees may carry out these duties, they are entitled to require the old trustees to produce all trust documents, papers, and memoranda relating to the administration of the trust (including any letter of wishes necessary to be considered before exercising any flexible discretionary functions), and where there was previously a corporate trustee, the documents to be produced may include internal correspondence and memoranda. But what should be so produced, and whether it should be only produced or actually handed over depends upon the circumstances of each case and the nature and contents of the document[1]. Everything relating to the management and administration of the trust property should be produced, at the least, but so far as concerns documents relating to discretionary distributive functions it would seem that only those of them that should be take into account when considering fuure exercise of such functions need to be produced. It would seem that a former trustee should be obliged to supply information to the new trustee on matters not clear from the trust papers[2], just as he would be so obliged to a beneficiary of full age and capacity[3], the new trustee being no worse off than the beneficiaries to whom he owes a duty to collect in and safeguard all the property for which the former trustee should account.

[1]   *Tiger v Barclays Bank Ltd* [1952] 1 All ER 85, CA. See also Article 60, below.
[2]   *Mond v Hyde* [1999] QB 1097 at 1104 per Beldam J.
[3]   See Article 60, below.

46.24 If there are any doubts as to the scope of the trustees' powers, eg of investment then steps must be taken to obtain legal advice[1].

[1]   *Nestle v National Westminster Bank plc* [1993] 1 WLR 1260 at 1265.

Inquiries as to acts of predecessors

46.25 New trustees should further ascertain that the trust fund is properly invested and review the trust investments[1], to see that the trust portfolio comprises not just authorised investments but is sensibly balanced as far as capital and income growth is concerned taking account of the terms, purposes and distribution requirements of the trust. They do not need to incur time, trouble and expense to hunt for breaches of trust committed by former trustees[2], since they can assume their predecessors acted properly in the absence of circumstances indicating a breach of trust or possible breach[3]. If, through not inquiring into suspicious circumstances, the trust estate should suffer, a new trustee may be liable, although he himself took no part, and could have taken no part, in committing the original breaches of trust[4]. There is, however, no obligation upon a new trustee to make a new investigation of the title to, or value of, existing securities of a nature authorised by the trust[5].

[1] *Nestle v National Westminster Bank plc* [1993] 1 WLR 1260: there is a duty to make periodic reviews of the investments.
[2] *Re Forest of Dean Coal Mining Co* (1878) 10 Ch D 450 at 453–454, per Jessel MR.
[3] *Re Strahan, ex p Geaves* (1856) 8 De G M & G 291 at 309.
[4] *Harvey v Olliver* (1887) 57 LT 239; and see *Millar's Trustees v Polson* (1897) 34 SLR 798; *Re Strahan* (1856) 8 De GM & G 291.
[5] *Rawsthorne v Rowley* (1907) 24 TLR 51, [1909] 1 Ch 409n.

Duty of new trustees to inquire as to losses

46.26 Where part of the trust estate has been lost, it is the duty of new trustees to inquire as to the circumstances, and as to whether there is a probability of recovering the loss or any part of it by appropriate proceedings[1]. Nor can new trustees escape this duty by purporting to be appointed trustees of what remains of the estate only[2], for the effect of doing so might be to discharge parties who were liable for breach of trust from their liability, or at least to interpose difficulties in the way of the beneficiaries recovering the loss. The proper course in such cases is to appoint the new trustees to be trustees of the whole, and for them then to take out a summons for directions as to whether any and, if so, what steps ought to be taken at the cost of the estate for the recovery of the loss[3].

[1] *Bennett v Burgis* (1846) 5 Hare 295.
[2] See *Bennett v Burgis* (1846) 5 Hare 295.
[3] *Bennett v Burgis* (1846) 5 Hare 295. Further on *Beddoes* applications see Article 88, below.

Effect of not searching for notices of incumbrances

46.27 A new trustee is liable to make good moneys which he may have honestly paid to a beneficiary, if the papers relating to the trust contain a notice of an incumbrance created by that beneficiary; for if the trustee had acquainted himself, as he was bound to do, with the trust documents and papers, he would have found what was the true state of the case[1]. Where, however, no amount of search would have disclosed the notice, the trustee would, of course, not be liable, as his liability entirely depends upon his failure to perform the duty of search which the law casts upon him[2].

[1] See *Hallows v Lloyd* (1888) 39 Ch D 686.
[2] *Hallows v Lloyd* (1888) 39 Ch D 686.

46.28 *The trustee's duties*

46.28 This is because trustees are not insurers, and their conduct ought to be judged with reference to the facts and circumstances existing at the time when they have to act, and which either are known *or ought to be known* by them at that time[1]. Moreover, a new trustee is not bound to inquire of the old trustees whether they have received notice of any incumbrances[2]. Old case law establishes that he is not even liable if he honestly, but erroneously (eg from forgetfulness), informs an intended incumbrancer that he has no knowledge of any prior incumbrancer[3].

1   *Re Hurst* (1892) 67 LT 96; *Youde v Cloud* (1874) LR 18 Eq 634.
2   *Phipps v Lovegrove* (1873) LR 16 Eq 80.
3   *Low v Bouverie* [1891] 3 Ch 82; *Porter v Moore* [1904] 2 Ch 367.

46.29 However, under Law of Property Act 1925, s 137(3) and (8) written notices are required to be given to trustees in respect of any dealings with an equitable interest in real or personal property if it is to affect priorities of competing claims; the trustees from time to time are entitled to custody of such notices and, subject to the payment of costs, any person interested in the equitable interest may require production of the notice(s). An intending assignee or incumbrancer may very well be a person interested, which will certainly cover a person contractually bound to acquire the intended interest subject to there being no notices other than those of which he was aware at the date of the contract, while *Hedley Byrne v Heller*[1] has extended liability in negligence for honest mis-statements where reliance is placed on a person in a specially knowledgeable position. Thus, nowadays a trustee who honestly but negligently fails to inform an intending incumbrancer of a written notice is likely to find himself liable for loss thereby suffered.

1   [1964] AC 465, HL; *MLC v Evatt* [1971] AC 793 PC; *Pirelli General Cable Works Ltd v Oscar Faber & Partners* [1983] 2 AC 1, HL.

Obtaining control of trust property and properly investing it

46.30 A trustee who leaves the trust fund in the sole name, or under the sole control, of his co-trustee will be liable if it be lost[1]. Thus trust property must be brought under the joint control of the trustees, with trust property being placed in the joint names of the trustees unless they take advantage of express or statutory powers to employ and remunerate nominees or custodians. Trustees should, of course, ensure that trust funds are properly invested in authorised investments[2].

1   *Lewis v Nobbs* (1878) 8 Ch D 591, *Underwood v Stevens* (1816) 1 Mer 712.
2   See Article 53, below.

46.31 A trustee who keeps money for an unreasonable length of time without investing it is liable if it be lost, however pure his motives may have been[1].

1   *Moyle v Moyle* (1831) 2 Russ & M 710.

ARTICLE 47
DUTY OF TRUSTEE TO OBEY THE DIRECTIONS OF THE
SETTLEMENT UNLESS DEVIATION SANCTIONED BY
APPROPRIATE AUTHORITY

47.1

(1)   A trustee must obey the lawful directions of the settlement if
practicable, except so far as these directions are modified by (i)
the consent of all the beneficiaries collectively (if they can all be
ascertained and are of full age and capacity), or (ii) in the case of
a pension fund, the trustees for authorised purposes within
section 68 of the Pensions Act 1995 (in some cases with the
consent of the employer), or the Pensions Regulator[1] for authorised purposes within section 69 of that Act, or (iii) the exercise of
a power of amendment conferred by the trust instrument, or (iv)
the court pursuant to statute. In relation to the first category
mentioned above, consent to a scheme of variation put forward
by an adult beneficiary may be given by the court on behalf of
beneficiaries who are not of full age and capacity, or potential
beneficiaries who are incapable of ascertainment, or are unborn[2].
In relation to the last category, the court has power in divorce or
analogous proceedings to vary for the benefit of the parties to the
marriage and of the children of the family or either or any of
them any ante-nuptial or post-nuptial settlement made on the
parties to the marriage, except (in most cases) one in the form of
a pension arrangement[3].

(2)   Subject to the foregoing, the court has no power to authorise the
application of the income or capital of the trust fund for the
benefit of persons outside the trusts or powers contained in the
settlement[4].

(3)(i)   Where in the management or administration of any property vested in trustees, any disposition, or any transaction,
is, in the opinion of the court, expedient, but cannot be
effected by reason of the absence of any power for that
purpose vested in the trustees by the trust instrument, if
any, or by law, the court may by order confer upon the
trustees, either generally or in any particular instance, the
necessary power for the purpose, on such terms, and
subject to such provisions and conditions, if any, as the
court may think fit and may direct in what manner any
money authorised to be expended, and the costs of any
transaction, are to be paid or borne as between capital and
income[5];

(ii)   the jurisdiction of the court to sanction the above dispositions or transactions includes power in certain circumstances to make an order authorising any expense of action

taken or proposed in or for the management of land held on trust for sale to be treated as a capital outgoing, notwithstanding that in other circumstances that expense could not properly have been so treated[6];

(4)   A trustee who ventures (without the sanction of the court) to deviate from the letter of his trust, does so at the peril of afterwards having to satisfy the court that the deviation was necessary and beneficial or amounted to honest conduct covered by an exemption clause in the trust instrument[7].

[1]   Originally the Occupational Pensions Regulatory Authority, but see the Pensions Act 2004, s 7, transferring the Authority's functions to the Pensions Regulator set up by that Act.
[2]   Variation of Trusts Act 1958, s 1.
[3]   Matrimonial Causes Act 1973, s 24(1)(c), as amended; Matrimonial and Family Proceedings Act 1984, s 17.
[4]   *Polly Peck International plc (in liquidation)(No 2)*, [2005] Ch 397 [1998] 3 All ER 812; and see also *A–G v Trustees of the British Museum* [2005] EWHC 1089 (Ch), [2005] Ch 397. Cf *FM v ASL Trustee Co Ltd* [2006] JRC 20A, R Ct Jersey.
[5]   The power referred to in para (2)(i), above, is conferred by the TA 1925, s 57(1), which specifically refers to 'any sale, lease, mortgage, surrender, release or other disposition, or any purchase, investment, acquisition, expenditure or other transaction'. For Settled Land Act settlements see ampler powers conferred by the Settled Land Act 1925 ('SLA 1925'), s 64.
[6]   Settled Land and Trustee Acts (Courts' General Powers) Act 1943, s 1, as permanently continued and amended by Emergency Laws (Miscellaneous Provisions) Act 1953, s 9.
[7]   *Harrison v Randall* (1851) 9 Hare 397; *Armitage v Nurse* [1998] Ch 241; *Walker v Stones* [2001] QB 902. See also TA 1925, s 61.

Paragraph 1

Duty to obey directions of settlement

47.2 This is the most important of all the rules relating to the duties of trustees. Although trustees have full power as individuals or as companies to transfer their legal title to others[1], they must not act beyond the limits of the powers conferred upon them by law or the terms of the trust instrument, so that they are strictly obliged to comply with such terms, although it may be that an exemption clause in the trust instrument may excuse them from liability[2], while the court has a discretion to relieve them from liability if they acted honestly and reasonably and ought fairly to be excused for the breach and for omitting to obtain the directions of the court in the matter in question[3]. Thus, if trustees act beyond the capacity conferred upon them by law or the trust instrument and a loss be sustained then such trustees or executors 'will be liable to make it good, however unexpected the result, however little likely to arise from the course adopted and however free such conduct may have been from any improper motive'[4].

[1]   *Rolled Steel Products (Holdings) Ltd v British Steel Corpn* [1986] Ch 246 at 303, per Browne-Wilkinson LJ.
[2]   *Armitage v Nurse* [1998] Ch 241, CA.
[3]   TA 1925, s 61; see Article 95.
[4]   *Clough v Bond* (1838) 3 My & Cr 490 at 496–497; *Target Holdings Ltd v Redferns* [1996] AC 421 at 434, HL. Technically, the trustee's accounts are falsified, with new accounts being drawn up to reflect the position if the trustees had not acted beyond their

powers; if they act within such powers but act negligently, then the accounts will be surcharged to reflect what would have been the position but for such negligence: see para 89.30 below.

47.3 The rule is, as we have seen[1], not binding upon a trustee where the directions of the settlement are illegal. Other exceptions necessarily arise where the directions of the settlement are impracticable (eg if it directs an immediate sale, and no purchaser can be found) or are varied or rendered impossible of fulfilment by statute[2], or are uncertain so that no valid trust is created[3].

1   Articles 11 and 30, above.
2   Eg under the National Health Service Act 1946, s 7(2) or where the cases are collected; or where the trusts of premises used for the purposes of a voluntary school were modified by the Minister of Education under the powers conferred by the Education (Miscellaneous Provisions) Act 1953, s 14.
3   See Article 8(1).

Duty to act in accordance with actuary's advice

47.4 Where pension fund trusts provide for the trustees to act only in accordance with the advice or determination of the duly appointed actuary then they must so act. As Buckley J said in *Re George Newnes Group Pension Fund*[1], 'where a discretion of this kind is reposed in an expert, the burden rests on any party who criticises the decision of the expert to show that the expert has acted fraudulently or with some improper motive or that he has been guilty of some mistake of a substantial character or has materially misdirected himself ... The court should be very slow to criticise or seek to control the exercise of any discretion or judgment reposed in or required of an expert of this kind.' As Walton J emphasised in *Re Imperial Food Ltd's Pension Scheme*[2], 'The function of an actuary in any situation which is not governed precisely by the provisions of the trust deed is to achieve the greatest possible degree of fairness between the various persons interested under the scheme.' He then upheld an actuary's valuation of the portion of a group fund to pass to purchasers of subsidiaries in the group, where the valuation was based on the 'past service reserve method' which gave rise to a lower figure than an alternative possible valuation based on the 'share of fund method' which would have taken account of a share of the group fund's surplus over the amount required to cover actuarial liabilities. It seems that either view could be held by a competent actuary so that was the end of the case. However, he did indicate *obiter* that if the choice of method had been for him to make (as it was not) he had no doubt that the 'past service reserve method' was the method to adopt. It still seems[3] that it is open to a competent actuary who has read Walton J's judgment to disagree with it when reviewing all the circumstances and to make a binding valuation on the 'share of fund method'.

1   [1986] 2 All ER 802; (1969) 98 J Inst of Actuaries 251; and see *Dean v Prince* [1954] Ch 409, [1954] 1 All ER 749, CA.
2   [1986] 2 All ER 802, [1986] 1 WLR 717.
3   See on trustees' discretion *Wrightson Ltd v Fletcher Challenge Nominees Ltd* [2001] UKPC 23, [2001] OPLR 249, PC at para 29.

47.5 Where trustees are to transfer part of the trust fund as certified by the actuary into another pension scheme, but a significant delay occurs during which there is a significant change in the value of the trust fund, with resulting implications for the alternative actuarial valuation principles, then the trustees will need to have the position reviewed by the actuary if the transferred amount is to be properly determined[1].

[1] *Stannard v Fisons Pension Trust Ltd* [1992] IRLR 27, CA.

Failure to purchase or sell where directed to do so

47.6 If trustees are, by the settlement, directed to call in trust moneys, and to lay them out on a purchase, and they fail to do so, and the fund is lost, they are liable for the loss[1]. Similarly if a trustee for sale omits to sell property as soon as convenient and an event occurring after the convenient period causes loss, although without any default on his part, he is liable for the loss, which would not have happened had he not failed in performing the prescribed duty[2]. Again if a trustee fails to sell real property within a directed 21 year period, so that it is producing mining rents for the life tenant that are higher than a reasonable percentage yield, the life tenant will be entitled only to a reasonable yield from expiry of the 21 year period[3].

[1] *Craven v Craddock* [1868] WN 229 (actual decision reversed by CA (1869) 20 LT 638, on the interpretation of a will).
[2] *Fry v Fry* (1859) 27 Beav 144.
[3] *Wentworth v Wentworth* [1900] AC 163, PC.

Payment to beneficiaries

47.7 Trustees must pay income and capital to the persons entitled without any demand[1]. If there is a permissive power to distribute income amongst a discretionary class with trusts to take effect in default of exercise of the power then failure to exercise the power within a reasonable time of receiving the income extinguishes the power in respect of such income which thereupon is held upon the default trusts[2]. Where there is a compulsory duty to distribute amongst a discretionary class the failure to execute this trust duty leaves the unfulfilled duty still in existence[3].

[1] *Hawksley v May* [1956] 1 QB 304, [1955] 3 All ER 353.
[2] *Re Allen-Meyrick's Will Trusts* [1966] 1 All ER 740, [1966] 1 WLR 499; *Re Gulbenkian's Settlement Trusts* (No 2) [1970] Ch 408, [1969] 2 All ER 1173.
[3] *Re Locker's Settlement Trusts* [1978] 1 All ER 216, [1977] 1 WLR 1323.

Direction to invest on particular securities

47.8 Where the settlement orders trust funds to be invested on particular securities, but does not clearly restrict the trustee's powers of investment *only* to such securities, the trustees are bound to invest in such securities *or* in those prescribed by statute[1].

[1] Trustee Act 2000 ('TA 2000'), ss 6(1), 7 and 9.

Trustees must observe conditions imposed on their discretionary powers

47.9 Where there are any conditions attached to the exercise of any of their functions, trustees must strictly perform those conditions. For instance, where they are authorised to lend to a husband with the consent of his wife, they cannot make the advance without first obtaining the required consent, even though they subsequently get it[1].

> 1   *Bateman v Davis* (1818) 3 Madd 98; but see *Stevens v Robertson* (1868) 37 LJ Ch 499, where it was held that a consent as to the mode of investing the trust fund might be given, ex post facto. It would seem that where there is a trust for sale *at such time* as A shall approve, the trustees may sell after the death of A, see *Re Powell (No 2)* (1918) 144 LT Jo 459, following *Pearce v Gardner* (1852) 10 Hare 287, 292; and also *Re Ffennell's Settlement* [1918] 1 Ch 91.

47.10 In one case trustees were empowered to vary investments with the consent of the tenant for life. They sold consols, and first made an investment with such consent upon a contributory mortgage (which was not an authorised security), and subsequently called the money in, and *without* such consent reinvested it upon a mortgage which was an authorised one. It was held that, although there was no loss of capital, they were nevertheless bound to *replace the consols* which had since risen in price. For they sold the consols for the purpose of investing in an unauthorised security, which was contrary to the directions of the settlement; and then, when they realised that investment, they reinvested the proceeds without the consent of the tenant for life, which was again contrary to the directions of the settlement. In both transactions, therefore, they disobeyed the rule now under consideration, and consequently committed breaches of trust, and were bound to place the beneficiaries in the same position as they would have occupied if no such breach had been committed[1].

> 1   *Re Massingberd's Settlement* (1890) 63 LT 296; and see also *Re Bennison* (1889) 60 LT 859; and *Stokes v Prance* [1898] 1 Ch 212.

Trustees duty to consult with expert

47.11 To help ensure that trustees exercise due care, trustees are required not to invest or disinvest without obtaining and considering expert advice[1] if not themselves expert enough. However, they need not follow that advice if in their honest judgment there appear to be reasonable grounds for such. It seems likely that failure to obtain such advice before selling a particular investment to purchase a new investment within the range of authorised investments will not make the new investment unauthorised and so make the trustees strictly liable to replace the sold investment (unless, fortuitously, the new investment is of better value[2]). The position is surely different from that where the acquisition of a particular type of asset is only authorised if X consents.The trustees' power of investment over a wide authorised range of investments has arisen under the Trustee act 2000 or the trust deed, though not to be exercisable till proper advice has been obtained and considered – and perhaps even rejected on reasonable grounds. Failure to comply with the advice requirements of section 5 of the Trustee Act 2000 should amount to a

47.11 *The trustee's duties*

negligent failure to take proper care, so that liability could be escaped if the relevant loss would have occurred even if proper advice had been obtained[3].

1 TA 2000, s 5.
2 *Re Massingberd's Settlement* (1890) 63 LT 296 and *Re Bell's Indenture* [1980] 3 All ER 425 at 437–439 (in both of which clearly unauthorized conduct had taken place.
3 Further see paras 53.22–53.23 on 'Status of Investments'.

Modification by beneficiaries

47.12 As will be seen in Article 69, the rule that trustees must obey the directions of the settlement is subject to modification if all parties beneficially interested are of full age and capacity[1], and concur in putting an end to or amending the trust. For the beneficiaries collectively, being the only parties beneficially interested, are entitled, at any moment, provided that they are of age and not under any disability, to depose the trustee, and distribute the trust property between themselves as they may think fit, though (except for exercising their right[2] to replace the trustees with nominated new trustees) they cannot control the exercise by the trustees of their fiduciary powers without putting an end to the trusts altogether[3]. The trustees are nevertheless entitled, if they think fit, to accept the collective directions of the beneficiaries and to act upon them without requiring the trusts to be brought to an end, and a new trust to be constituted. In the case of a modification which involves the distribution of trust property, the trustees should, for their own protection, ensure that any capital gains tax or inheritance tax payable is properly provided for.

1 This phrase must now be understood in the light of s 1 of the Family Law Reform Act 1969, which came into force on 1 January 1970, providing that as from that date a person attains full age (so ceasing to be an infant) on attaining the age of 18. If on that date a person had attained 18 but not 21, he attained full age on that date.
2 Trusts of Land and Appointment of Trustees Act 1996 ('TLATA 1996'), s 19.
3 *Re Brockbank* [1948] Ch 206, [1948] 1 All ER 287.

47.13 If the trust instrument (eg a debenture trust deed or a unit trust deed) expressly provides for its terms to be varied upon a majority vote of voting beneficiaries then, of course, a variation so obtained will be effective[1].

1 *Graham Australia Pty Ltd v Perpetual Trustees Ltd* [1992] PLR 193.

Power of amendment in trust instrument

47.14 Powers of revocation, general powers of appointment, special powers of appointment (enabling re-settlements or only sub-settlements)[1] and powers of advancement[2] have been well-known features of trusts. In the last few decades powers of amendment have become features of many trusts, especially pension trusts (which can last indefinitely and where many significant changes can occur in the circumstances of the employer and the number of beneficiaries) and broad discretionary trusts (where circumstances can change dramatically in the course of a trust period of 80 years or more).

618

¹   See Article 82.
²   See Article 67.

47.15 An occupational pension scheme will usually contain a very wide power of amendment (eg 'The Trustees may at any time by deed with the consent of the Principal Company amend, extend, modify, revoke or replace all or any of the trusts powers and provisions of this Deed or of the Rules with effect from such date as is specified in that deed to the effect that any such amendment, extension, modification, revocation or replacement may be retrospective or retroactive in effect'), although the Pensions Act 1995 (as amended) provides some protection against the power being exercised to prejudice members of the pension scheme.

47.16 A discretionary trust will often contain a power for the settlor, and the trustees after his death, to add persons to the class of persons who are beneficiaries under a discretionary trust or objects of a discretionary power of appointment as well as a power to exclude persons from such a class. The discretionary trustees will often be given power to vary or revoke any of the administrative powers and provisions of the settlement or to add any further administrative powers and provisions as the trustees may consider expedient (including provisions as to the incidence of costs and expenses between income and capital)¹.

¹   Cf TA 1925, s 57.

47.17 Often there will be restrictions on the exercise of such powers to ensure that there are no adverse tax consequences for the settlor¹ or the beneficiaries², while such powers may well be fiduciary powers³ preventing those powers from being exercised to benefit the exerciser (except as authorised expressly or by necessary implication) or a personal power vested in an employer subject to the obligation not to exercise it in a way that could damage the relationship of confidence between employer and employee⁴. The power may be exercisable only with the consent of X, whose power to withhold consent can be a fiduciary power or merely a personal power⁵ or a personal power subject to the employer-employee relationship of confidence.

¹   For example, Income and Corporation Taxes Act 1988, ss 672, 675; Taxation of Chargeable Gains Act 1992, s 86.
²   Inheritance Act 1984, s 71 as affected by Finance Act 2006. In the favoured accumulation and maintenance trusts it is common to provide power to vary the shares of the trust fund to which the beneficiaries will become entitled on or before attaining the relevant age: see J Kessler *Drafting Trusts & Will Trusts* (7th edn) para 14–16 ff.
³   See para 1.76 ff.
⁴   *Imperial Group Pensions Trust Ltd v Imperial Tobacco Ltd* [1991] 1 WLR 589; *British Coal Corporation v British Coal Staff Superannuation Scheme Trustees Ltd* [1995] 1 All ER 912 (overruled in part by *National Grid Co plc v Mayes* [2001] UKHL 20, [2001] 2 All ER 417).
⁵   See para 1.76 ff.

47.18 The scope of the relevant power and the obligations attaching to its exercise are a matter of construction of the wording of the clause in question in accordance with the surrounding context and in the light of admissible

47.18 *The trustee's duties*

extrinsic evidence[1]. The matrix of facts relating to pension schemes leads to a particularly practical and purposive approach to construction.

> [1]   *Re Courage Group's Pension Schemes* [1987] 1 WLR 495 at 505–506; *Mettoy Pension Trustees Ltd v Evans* [1990] 1 WLR 522; *Investors Compensation Scheme Ltd v West Bromwich Building Society* [1998] 1 All ER 98 at 114–115 per Lord Hoffmann; *Cameron v M & W Mack (ESOP) Trustee Ltd* [2002] WTLR 647 at 663–667; *National Grid Co plc v Mayes* [2001] UKHL 20, [2001] 2 All ER 417 paras 16–63 per Lord Hoffmann.

47.19 There seems[1] a rebuttable presumption that a power of amendment cannot be used to extend its own scope or amend its own terms, particularly where there are express restrictions or limitations on the exercise of such power eg the requisite consent of a third party. On whether exercise of such a power can be retrospective the courts seem to be open-minded in construing the clause in its practical context where a likely need for retrospective amendment may well incline the court to permit this[2].

> [1]   *Aitken v Christy Hunt plc* [1991] PLR 1; *British Coal Corpn v British Coal Staff Superannuation Scheme Trustees Ltd* [1995] 1 All ER 912. It seems a power to alter any provision or to amend any provision will permit the addition of new beneficiaries: *Kearns v Hill* (1990) 21 NSWLR 107, CA, cited with apparent approval in *Napier and Ettrick v R F Kershaw Ltd (No 2)* [1999] 1 WLR 756, HL.
> [2]   For example, in the context of pension trusts and, now, Pensions Act 1995, s 71; also unit trusts in *Graham Australia Pty Ltd v Perpetual Trustees Ltd* [1992] PLR 193.

Deviation sanctioned by the court

47.20 It frequently happens that it is not possible to obtain the concurrence of all the beneficiaries, either because some of them are not of age or are otherwise under disability, or because potential beneficiaries include unascertained or unborn persons. Pressure of economic circumstances and the burden of heavy taxation, particularly since the Second World War, have, moreover, diminished the attractions of rigid settlements and much ingenuity has been devoted to the production of schemes by which trust funds might be divided up, or trusts rearranged, to the mutual advantage of those interested in income and capital respectively, often at the expense of the Revenue. Many such schemes were, it is believed, sanctioned by judges of the Chancery Division in chambers, and a belief that the jurisdiction to do so was unlimited was growing[1], when a sharp rebuff was administered by the House of Lords in *Chapman v Chapman*[2], affirming the decision of the Court of Appeal[3] but further narrowing the jurisdiction therein recognised.

> [1]   See, eg the arguments of counsel for the trustees, and the dissenting judgment of Denning LJ in *Re Chapman's Settlement Trusts* [1953] Ch 218 at 226, 227 [1953] 1 All ER 103 at 129, CA; and the argument of counsel for the appellant trustees in *Chapman v Chapman* [1954] AC 429 at 433 ff, [1954] 1 All ER 798; *Re Duke of Leeds and the Coal Acts 1938 to 1943* [1947] Ch 525 at 557, [1947] 2 All ER 200 at 216.
> [2]   [1954] AC 429, [1954] 1 All ER 798.
> [3]   *Re Chapman's Settlement Trusts* [1953] Ch 218, [1953] 1 All ER 103.

47.21 It may now be taken to be settled that, apart from statute, the court's jurisdiction to sanction a deviation from the terms of the trust is limited to three cases which may conveniently be grouped under the following heads:

(1)   cases in which the court has allowed the trustees to enter into some business transaction, or to make some investment, which was not authorised by the settlement[1];

(2)   cases in which the court has allowed maintenance out of income, which the settlor or testator directed to be accumulated[2];

(3)   cases in which the court has approved a compromise on behalf of minors and possible after-born beneficiaries.

[1]   This jurisdiction has been almost entirely superseded by the statutory jurisdiction to vary trusts under the Variation of Trusts Act 1958, below, and by that under the TA 1925, s 57, and the SLA 1925, s 64, and is further considered in the notes to paragraph (2) of this Article; at 47.101 ff. Trustees' powers of investment have been greatly widened by the TA 2000: see para 53.9 ff.

[2]   As to this jurisdiction, and the powers of trustees apart from it, see further *Re Collins* (1886) 32 Ch D 229, *Re Alford* (1886) 32 Ch D 383 and Article 66.

47.22 The first two groups of cases are dealt with subsequently, but there remains the power of the court to sanction a compromise. It was decided by the majority of the House of Lords in *Chapman v Chapman*[1] that the court's jurisdiction in this regard is limited to cases where the beneficial interests are in dispute, and have not yet been ascertained: it is not a jurisdiction to alter ascertained interests. It was said by Lord Morton of Henryton[2] that—

'If ... there is no doubt as to the beneficial interests, the court is ... exceeding its jurisdiction if it sanctions a scheme for their alteration, whether the scheme is called a "compromise in the wider sense" or an "arrangement" or is given any other name ... I think that Farwell J ... was right when in 1901 he used the words ... "I decline to accept any suggestion that the court has an inherent jurisdiction to alter a man's will because it thinks it beneficial. It seems to me that is quite impossible" '[3].

[1]   [1954] AC 429, [1954] 1 All ER 798.
[2]   [1954] AC 429 at 461, [1954] 1 All ER 798 at 814.
[3]   *Re Walker* [1901] 1 Ch 879 at 885.

47.23 It was accordingly held that orders sanctioning compromises in a number of cases[1] where the beneficial interests were undisputed and were ascertained, had been made without jurisdiction.

[1]   For example, *Re Duke of Leeds and Re the Coal Acts 1938 to 1943* [1947] Ch 525, [1947] 2 All ER 200. The decisions in *Re Downshire Settled Estates*, and *Re Blackwell's Settlement Trusts* [1953] Ch 218, [1953] 1 All ER 103 (which were heard by the Court of Appeal at the same time as *Re Chapman's Settlement Trusts*), though overruled so far as they rested on the inherent jurisdiction to sanction compromises, may, perhaps, be supported as an exercise of the statutory jurisdiction to sanction a 'transaction' under s 64 of the SLA 1925; see para 47.115 below.

47.24 A bona fide compromise of a genuine dispute, however, does not involve a departure from the basic principle that trust interests cannot be varied by the court without statutory authority. This is because the compromise is an estoppel preventing the parties from asserting that the position is otherwise than as agreed[1]. Accordingly, the court is enforcing the trusts as they are agreed to be, and (assuming all necessary and property parties have joined in or are otherwise bound[2]) no-one has standing to assert otherwise.

1   *Binder v Alachouzos* [1972] 2 QB 151; *A–G v Trustees of the British Museum* [2005] EWHC 1089 (Ch),[2005] Ch 397, para 39.
2   Eg through the operation of CPR Part 19 Part II.

47.25 The inconvenience and anomalies resulting from this decision[1] led to the enactment of the Variation of Trusts Act 1958.

1   Cf *Re Harrison's Share under a Settlement, Re Williams' Will Trusts, Re Ropner's Settlement* [1955] Ch 260, [1954] 2 All ER 453, where Roxburgh J recalled certain orders made but not drawn up before the House of Lords decision.

Variation of Trusts Act 1958

47.26 This Act (which does not extend to Scotland or Northern Ireland[1]) applies whenever any property, real or personal, is held on trusts arising under any will, settlement or other disposition, other than trusts affecting property settled by Act of Parliament[2]. It applies to the case of a bare trust for a minor[3] (who accordingly cannot terminate the trust and give a good receipt for the trust assets). It authorises the court[4] order to approve on behalf of a person who comes within any one of four specified categories of persons any arrangement (by whomsoever it is proposed, and whether or not there is any other person beneficially interested who is capable of assenting to it) varying or revoking all or any of the trusts or enlarging the powers of the trustees of managing or administering any of the property subject to the trusts.

1   But which has been copied in many Commonwealth trust jurisdictions.
2   Variation of Trusts Act 1958, s 1(1), (5).
3   *D (a child) v O* [2004] EWHC 1036 (Ch), [2004] 3 All ER 780 (trust of life assurance polices)
4   See paras 47.84–47.87 below.

Persons on whose behalf approval may be given

47.27 The categories of persons are thus specified in the Act[1]:

'(1)(a) any person having, directly or indirectly, an interest, whether vested or contingent, under the trusts who by reason of infancy or other incapacity is incapable of assenting, or

(b)   any person (whether ascertained or not) who may become entitled, directly or indirectly, to an interest under the trusts as being at a future date or on the happening of a future event a person of any specified description or a member of any specified class of persons, so however that this paragraph shall not include any person who would be of that description, or a member of that class, as the case may be, if the said date had fallen or the said event had happened at the date of the application to the court, or

(c)   any person unborn, or

(d)   any person in respect of any discretionary interest of his under protective trusts where the interest of the principal beneficiary has not failed or determined'[2].

1   Variation of Trusts Act 1958, s 1(1).

2   'Protective trusts' means the trusts specified in s 33(1)(i) and (ii) of the TA 1925 or any like trusts, and 'the principal beneficiary' has the same meaning as in that section; 'discretionary interest' means an interest arising under s 33(1)(ii) of the TA 1925, or any like trust: Variation of Trusts Act 1958, s 1(2). As to protective trusts, see para 11.63 above. Of 'like trusts' Megarry J in *Re Wallace's Settlement* [1968] 1 WLR 711 at 716, said, 'The word "like" requires not identity but similarity; and similarity in substance suffices, without the need for similarity in form or detail or wording'. In *Re Bristol's Settled Estates* [1965] 1 WLR 469, where discretionary trusts were to arise for six months on the life tenant's death whether or not there had been a forfeiture, the trusts were held to be outside paragraph (d).

47.28 Broadly the effect of the Act is to enable the court to give approval on behalf of persons who are unable to give approval for themselves (eg because minors or unborn or not yet ascertained) so long as for the benefit of such persons, unless those persons are only potentially interested as beneficiaries of the discretionary trust that springs up on failure of the principal beneficiary's interest, but which has not sprung up.

47.29 As Mummery LJ states[1], 'The court is merely contributing on behalf of infants and unborn and unascertained persons the binding assents to the arrangements which they, unlike an adult beneficiary, cannot give. The 1958 Act has thus been viewed by the courts as a statutory extension of the consent principle embodied in the rule in *Saunders v Vautier*[2]. The principle recognises the rights of beneficiaries who are *sui juris* and together absolutely entitled to the trust property, to exercise their proprietary rights to overbear and defeat the intentions of a testator or settlor'. Lord Maugham LC has also emphasised[3] that, 'The rule has no application unless all the persons who have any present[4] or contingent interest in the property are *sui juris* and consent.'

1   *Goulding v James* [1997] 2 All ER 239 at 247.
2   On which see Article 70 below.
3   *Berry v Geen* [1938] AC 575 at 582.
4   Presumably by this Lord Maugham meant 'vested', in opposition to 'contingent'.

47.30 A distinction needs to be drawn between a contingent interest, which is property capable of being assigned or subjected to trusts, and a mere expectancy or *spes* incapable of being so assigned or subjected[1], although it can be the subject of a contract for value[2].

1   *Re Brooks' Settlement Trusts* [1939] Ch 993; *Lovett v Lovett* [1898] 1 Ch 82.
2   *Holroyd v Marshall* (1862) 10 HLCas 191; *Re Ellenborough* [1903] 1 Ch 697 at 200; *Williams v IRC* [1965] NZLR 395, CA.

47.31 A trust in favour of A, if on the death of B he shall be the heir of B, (so becoming the holder of any peerage or baronetcy of B), or one of the next of kin of B or the spouse of B or a member of the Athenaeum club, confers on A a present contingent interest, which becomes vested if on B's death A has the required characteristic. In contrast, a trust in favour of whomsoever shall at the death of B be the spouse or heir of B or one of his next of kin or a member of the Athenaeum, confers no interest contingent or otherwise on anyone until the death of B, whereupon a proprietary interest is acquired by any person with the required characteristic[1]. Until then such person has no more than an expectancy or hope of qualifying as a person with the relevant characteristic, but if he does so qualify then he obtains a proprietary interest to which the trustees must give effect.

1   *Re Earl of Midleton's Will Trusts* [1969] 1 Ch 600 at 607.

47.32 Such a presumptive person is thus not in the same position as someone who is merely an object of a power of appointment and who hopes it will be exercised in his favour some day[1]. The difference is that a person who is an object of a power is already a person of the specified description or a member of the specified class and is ready to benefit as soon as the trustees wish to exercise the power in his favour, but they are under no obligation to exercise such power. A presumptive person has to wait and see if on the specified future date or event he will become entitled to an interest under the trust as then a person of the specified description or a member of the specified class, when the trustees *must* benefit him as required under the trust. Thus, the consent of the presumptive person is required before the trust property can be dealt with in any way prejudicial to the proprietary rights such person is bound to acquire if qualifying as a person of the specified description or class. It will be seen that paragraph (b) enables the court to consent on behalf of presumptive persons, except where persons of full age and capacity have been ascertained who would be qualifying persons if the future date or future event had occurred at the date of the application to the court, so that they can decide for themselves whether or not to consent.

1   *Re Brooks' Settlement Trusts* [1939] Ch 993.

PARAGRAPH (A)

47.33 The effect of paragraph (a) is to enable the court to give approval on behalf of a minor or a mental patient[1] who has, 'directly or indirectly[2]', an interest, whether vested[3] or contingent, under the trusts', but not on behalf of a person of full age and capacity with such 'an interest'. 'An interest' and 'a discretionary interest of his under protective trusts' are used in paragraphs (b) and (d), so that an interest should clearly cover not just vested or contingent fixed interests but also interests of a beneficiary under a discretionary trust[4], especially when a discretionary trust can be terminated if all the discretionary beneficiaries between them entitled to the equitable proprietary interest in the trust property so agree, being of full age and capacity[5].

1   Under s 1(3) of the VTA 1958 the Court of Protection needs to determine the question of benefit eg *Re CL* [1969] 1 Ch 587.
2   For example, under a sub-settlement.
3   This includes a bare trust for a minor: *D (a child) v O* [2004] EWHC 1036 (Ch), [2004] WTLR 751 (trust of life assurance polices).
4   As assumed in *Re Clitheroe's Settlement Trusts* [1959] 1 WLR 1159; *Re Bristol's Settled Estates* [1965] 1 WLR 469; *Re Steed's Will Trusts* [1960] Ch 407 at 420 per Lord Evershed MR. Contrast the meaning of 'interest, whether vested or contingent' in TA 1925, s 32(1)(c): *Re Beckett's Settlement* [1940] Ch 279.
5   *Re Smith* [1928] Ch 915; *Re Beckett's Settlement* [1940] Ch 279 at 285.

47.34 It has been held that the word 'interest' in the Act has a technical legal meaning that excludes a mere hope of inheriting from a person (a '*spes* *successionis*')[1]. So the court has no power to approve an arrangement on behalf of persons who may take under the terms of a trust merely because they are or would be the heirs or next of kin of a particular person still living. This is on the basis that no-one can be the heir (or next of kin) of a person who is still alive: *nemo est haeres viventis*[2].

1 *Knocker v Youle* [1986] 2 All ER 914 at 916–917; *Gartside v IRC* [1968] AC 553 at 606 and 617–618. Section 22 of the TLATA 1996 defines 'beneficiary' for the purpose of a *Saunders v Vautier* removal of trustees under s 19 as 'any person who under the trust has an *interest* in property subject to the trust': see para 72.23.
2 *Re Parsons* (1890) 45 Ch D 51; *Re Ellenborough* [1903] 1 Ch 697; *Re Midleton's Will Trusts* [1969] 1 Ch 600; *Re Smith* [2001] 3 All ER 552.

47.35 However, this does not deal with the question whether *an object of a special power of appointment*, also sometimes referred to as having an 'expectancy', has an interest within the meaning of the Act. The matter is not covered by any express authority on the point. There is no doubt that the object of such a power, unless and until released[1], has rights, justiciable before the court, against the trustee in respect of his position[2].

1 Personal powers may be released to avoid problems as in *Re Christie-Miller's Settlement Trusts* [1961] 1 All ER 855n; *Re Courtauld's Settlement* [1965] 2 All ER 544n, and *Re Ball's Settlement Trusts* [1968] 2 All ER 438, but fiduciary powers cannot be released without authority in the trust instrument: *Re Wills Trust Deeds* [1964] Ch 219.
2 See para 60.4 ff.

47.36 Such authority as there is arises in other contexts. There is one decision at first instance holding that an assignment by such an object for no consideration[1] does not transfer his rights to the assignee[2]. There is another at first instance holding that beneficiaries of a trust fund subject only to a special power of appointment are not (even together) 'absolutely entitled' within s 31(2)(i)(b) of the Trustee Act 1925[3]. There is a dictum in the House of Lords to the effect that, where a trustee holds property on trust for the settlor subject to a power[4] of appointment, the settlor could at any time revoke the power and demand the reconveyance of the property[5]. And there is a dictum in the Privy Council to the effect that such a *Saunders v Vautier* requirement of the trustee to convey as the beneficiaries direct cannot be validly made without every such object joining in[6].

1 Certainly, if for valuable consideration, it is clear that the object's rights can be and are transmitted: *Re Coleman* (1888) 39 Ch D 443, CA. It is also clear that the object's right are transmitted, without consideration, where the object becomes bankrupt: *Re Ashby, ex p Wreford* [1892] 1 QB 872.
2 *Re Brooks' Settlement Trusts* [1939] Ch 993.
3 *Re Sharp's Settlement Trusts* [1973] Ch 331.
4 Not, however, stated to be a special power, and, in context, likely to be a general power.
5 *Vandervell v IRC* [1967] 2 AC 291 at 317, per Lord Upjohn. An explanation for the right to revoke the power could be that the settlor had not made a completed perfect gift of the whole bundle of his legal and beneficial proprietary rights in the property, but had only made it possible for someone to receive a future gift by authorising the trustee to make such a gift. This gratuitous authority could be revoked at will by the settlor: the conferment of a special power to make a gift is not itself a gift of any property: *Melville v IRC* [2001] EWCA Civ 1247 [2002] 1 WLR 407; *Re Armstrong* (1886) 17 QBD 521, CA.
6 *Schmidt v Rosewood Trust Ltd* [2003] UKPC 26, [2003] 2 AC 709.

47.37 These expressions of judicial opinion pull in different directions. But none of them was made in the context of the 1958 Act, although, given the *Saunders v Vautier* conceptual underpinning of the 1958 Act[1], the Privy Council dictum may be considered particularly significant. In principle, the bundle of rights accruing to an object of a special power in respect of the trust property ought to amount to an interest within the Act. Like other bundles of rights accepted to amount to interests in property[2], those rights affect specific property, and are binding on third party acquirers of the property (not being bona fide purchasers for value of a legal estate without notice). Moreover, they arise from *the existing trust instrument*, a property conveyance, even though they do not at present give rise to a right to actual enjoyment, and (just like a conventional contingent future interest) may never do so. This is all very different from the expectation that a person has of succeeding to the property of another who is still alive. No conveyance has yet been made, and no death has occurred, to confer any rights (however contingent) upon anyone.

[1]   See para 47.29 above.
[2]   Eg a restrictive covenant.

47.38 If this analysis is right, then the court can give consent for an infant under paragraph (a) when the infant is merely the object of a special power of appointment.

PARAGRAPH (B)

47.39 As already discussed, the effect of paragraph (b) is that the court can consent to an arrangement if for the benefit of persons who will presumptively become entitled, directly or indirectly, to an interest under a trust (but not a *spes*) as being on a future date or event a person of any specified description (eg the heir or widow of a living person) or a member of any specified class of persons (eg the next of kin of a living person or a member of the Athenaeum club). However, as the section itself makes clear, no consent can be given in respect of such a presumptive person if already ascertained on the basis that the future date or event had occurred at the date of the application to the court.

47.40 If an object of a power of appointment has an interest for the purposes of the Act (as submitted above in relation to paragraph (a)), then the court cannot give consent for such an object under paragraph (b) in respect of *that* interest, for ex hypothesi he already has it, and so cannot become entitled to it at a future date, though of course the court could do so in respect of any *other* interest which he might later acquire.

47.41 A case which illustrates paragraph (b) is *Re Suffert's Settlement*[1]. There a trust fund was held on protective trusts for the applicant during her life and after her death on trust for any children of hers who should attain twenty-one. If no child attained a vested interest, the applicant had a general testamentary power of appointment and, subject to that, the fund was to be held after her death on trust for her statutory next of kin. The applicant was a spinster aged

61 and sought the court's approval to an arrangement. Of the three people who would have been her statutory next of kin at the time of the case, all were of full age and capacity but only one had consented. Buckley J held that he had no power to give approval on behalf of, and thus to bind, the other two people because they fell within the ambit of the concluding words of paragraph (b).

¹   [1961] Ch 1, [1960] 3 All ER 561 (where it was assumed without any discussion that consent could be given on behalf of unascertained objects of power).

47.42 A similar case is *Re Moncrieff's Settlement Trust¹*. There a trust fund was held on trust for the settlor for life, with remainder to such persons or purposes as the settlor should by will or codicil appoint and in default of appointment for her statutory next of kin if she had died an intestate widow. The settlor applied for an order approving apportionment of the fund between those contingently entitled and herself. She had one adopted son who would become entitled as statutory next of kin under the default clause if he survived her. Buckley J held he had no power to give approval on behalf of the adopted son since the son fell within the ambit of the concluding words of para-graph (b), but he could give approval on behalf of all other possible next of kin who could only become entitled if the adopted son predeceased the settlor since they fell outside the ambit of the concluding words of paragraph (b): the only possible next of kin on the hypothesis that the settlor had died at the date of the application was the adopted son.

¹   [1962] 3 All ER 838n, [1962] 1 WLR 1344.

47.43 These two cases were followed by Warner J in *Knocker v Youle¹* where ultimately the issue of the settlor's four sisters were to take the trust fund in certain remote contingencies defeasible by A or B exercising a testamentary power of appointment. At the date the originating summons was issued A and B (still alive) had made wills fully exercising their powers of appointment. It was held that since such issue *now* had contingent defeasible interests they could not fall within (b) as persons 'who *may become* entitled to an interest', so (b) only covers persons who have an interest in the eyes of the law. Even if they had prima facie fallen within (b), they would have been excluded by the proviso, since there were 17 cousins who would have satisfied the class description at the date of the application to the court if all prerequisities had been satisfied at that date. It did not matter not that A and B had made wills exercising their powers of appointment, since the proviso was merely designed to identify the presumptive members of the class and did not advert to the question whether they would or would not have become entitled at the date of the application.

¹   [1986] 2 All ER 914, [1986] 1 WLR 934.

47.44 The provisions outlined above give rise to several difficulties. It has been assumed¹ that 'at the date of the application to the court' in para-graph (b) means the date on which the originating summons or, nowadays, the claim form was issued, so that the relevant parties can then be ascertained. However, take the case where there is a trust for A for life, remainder if she dies without having been made bankrupt during her lifetime to A absolutely and, subject thereto, to her statutory next of kin living at her death in equal shares, otherwise for the Red Cross absolutely. A's spouse is deceased, like her parents, and she has a daughter, D, and a 45 years old sister, S, 12 years younger than herself. Under paragraph (b) the court can approve on S's behalf but not D's behalf since D is alive at the date of the issue of the claim form. But what if D dies of a terminal disease just before the court hears the VTA application? Can the court ignore S or, upon hearing S refuses to consent, override her refusal? Under s 3(1) of the Human Rights Act 1998 ambiguous legislation must be interpreted, so far as possible, compatibly with the Human Rights Convention (and Article 1 of the First Protocol protecting persons from being deprived of their possessions) so that the court could well construe 'at the date of application to the court' as covering the date of the court hearing.

1   *Re Suffert's Settlement* [1961] Ch 1 at 5; *Knocker v Youle* [1986] 1 WLR 934 at 938.

47.45 Another difficulty lies in the relationship of paragraph (a) to paragraph (b). On the face of it, they appear to be mutually exclusive, the first applying where a person has an interest under the trusts, the second where he has no actual interest but some kind of presumptive *spes successionis*. But this leads to strange consequences. Suppose an infant with a *spes successionis* within the terms of paragraph (b) fell within the ambit of the concluding words of that paragraph, so that the court had no power under paragraph (b) to give approval on his behalf. Would the court then have power to give it under paragraph (a)? Buckley J in *Re Suffert's Settlement*[1] expressed the opinion *obiter* that it would: he said that the persons on whose behalf the court was precluded by the concluding words of paragraph (b) from giving approval under that paragraph did not include 'infants, because they come under a different heading in the Act'. Yet it is not clear from the wording of the Act that this is so. Counsel had argued that it was not (at the same time raising other points of difficulty) and the learned judge did not deal with his arguments. The view of Buckley J is certainly a commonsense one, since it would be extraordinary if the court could bind an infant with an actual interest but could not bind one with a mere presumptive *spes successionis*.

1   [1961] Ch 1 at 5.

47.46 On the face of it, doubts might also arise as to whether the Act authorised the court to give approval to an arrangement on behalf of unascertained future spouses under paragraph (b). Any unmarried woman over sixteen years of age is a person who would be the wife of a propositus if the event of the marriage had happened at the date of the application to the court so that such a person would prima facie appear to be excluded by the closing words of paragraph (b) from the jurisdiction of the court. However, the courts have tacitly assumed they have power to approve arrangements on behalf of unascertained future spouses[1]. This can be supported by construing 'any person' as meaning 'any ascertained person' in view of the fact that 'any person' is not as in the opening words of paragraph (b) qualified by the words (whether ascertained or not).

[1]   *Re Clitheroe's Settlement Trusts* [1959] 3 All ER 789, [1959] 1 WLR 1159; *Re Roberts'*
      Settlement Trusts (1959) Times, 8 April; *Re Steed's Will Trusts* [1960] Ch 407 at 420; *Re*
      Lister's Will Trusts [1962] 3 All ER 737, [1962] 1 WLR 1441. Further see JW Harris,
      Variation of Trusts (1975) pp 36–40.

PARAGRAPH (C)

47.47 Consent can be given by the court in respect of any person unborn
without any restrictions as to prospective interests or expectancies so the
problems canvassed in relation to paragraphs (a) and (b) do not arise.

PARAGRAPHS (A), (B) AND (C) GENERALLY

47.48 Since the paragraphs (a), (b), (c) and (d) are listed in the alternative if
beneficiaries fall within paragraph (d), as well as earlier paragraphs, approval
may be given under paragraph (d) so as to dispense with the need to prove
benefit in respect of the beneficiaries' interests under the protective trusts[1].

[1]   *Re Turner's Will Trusts* [1960] Ch 122 at 127.

47.49 The jurisdiction of the court under the Act is, it is thought, limited to
authorising an arrangement which the beneficiaries themselves could have
authorised if they had all been ascertained and of full age and capacity.
Certainly, the court has no power to override the objections (however
unreasonable), or to dispense with the consent, of persons on whose behalf the
Act does not expressly authorise it to give approval, even when such persons
are very numerous and difficult to ascertain[1]. If a beneficiary has disappeared
in circumstances where his death is very probable but not certain it may be
that a court might make more use of a Benjamin order[2], permitting a variation
affecting the beneficiary's interest and so freeing the trustees from potential
personal liability but preserving for the beneficiary the right to trace assets and
enforce a proprietary claim.

[1]   As, for instance, the class of beneficiaries in *Re Eden* [1957] 2 All ER 430, [1957] 1 WLR
      788 and *Knocker v Youle* [1986] 2 All ER 914, [1986] 1 WLR 934.
[2]   *Re Benjamin* [1902] 1 Ch 723; *Re Green's Will Trusts* [1985] 3 All ER 455.

47.50 The court has power to approve an arrangement which the trustees do
not consider desirable, though the views of the trustees are entitled to respect
and will be considered[1]. Nor need the court be satisfied that the arrangement
is for the benefit of the person who proposes it[2] or for that of other
beneficiaries who are of full age and capacity and consent on their own
behalf[3]. Except for applications involving protective trusts, the views of the
settlor have little, if any, relevance or weight[4].

[1]   *Re Steed's Will Trusts* [1960] Ch 407, [1960] 1 All ER 487, CA.
[2]   *Re Steed's Will Trusts* [1960] Ch 407, [1960] 1 All ER 487, CA.
[3]   *Re Berry's Settlement* [1966] 3 All ER 431n, [1966] 1 WLR 1515.
[4]   *Goulding v James* [1997] 2 All ER 239 at 251, per Mummery LJ.

BENEFICIAL ARRANGEMENTS FOR WHICH APPROVAL MAY BE GIVEN

47.51 The power of the court is to approve 'if it thinks fit'

> 'any arrangement ... varying or revoking all or any of the trusts, or enlarging
> the powers of the trustees of managing or administering any of the property
> subject to the trusts: Provided that except by virtue of paragraph (d) ... the
> court shall not approve an arrangement on behalf of any person unless the
> carrying out thereof would be for the benefit of that person.'

47.52 'ARRANGEMENT'. First, then, what is an arrangement? Apparently
the meaning of this word is not confined to an arrangement which two or
more people have worked out. Lord Evershed MR said in *Re Steed's Will
Trusts*[1]:

> 'I think that the word ... is deliberately used in the widest possible sense so as to
> cover any proposal which any person may put forward for varying or revoking
> the trusts [or, presumably for varying or enlarging the powers of the trustees].'

[1]   [1960] Ch 407, [1960] 1 All ER 487, CA.

47.53 'VARYING OR REVOKING'. So far as the trusts are concerned, the
arrangement must be one which either varies or revokes[1] them. It seems that it
cannot be one which replaces the trusts with quite different ones, because this
would amount neither to a variation nor to a simple revocation. But the line
dividing variation from replacement is sometimes indistinct. Thus in one case[2],
although the proposed arrangement would revoke all the prior trusts and
establish new ones, it was held to amount only to a variation because the new
trusts would in many respects be similar to the old. Megarry J said that

> '... the old trusts may fairly be said to be varied by the arrangement whether the
> variation is effected directly by leaving some of the old words standing and
> altering others, or indirectly, by revoking all the old words and then setting up
> new trusts partly, though not wholly, in the likeness of the old.'

[1]   For a case involving revocation, see *Re Seale's Marriage Settlement* [1961] Ch 574, [1961]
      3 All ER 136.
[2]   *Re Holt's Settlement* [1969] 1 Ch 100, [1968] 1 All ER 470. Contrast *Re Purves* (1984) 14
      DLR 4th 738.

47.54 In a later case[1] the same judge went still further, saying:

> 'If an arrangement changes the whole substratum of a trust, then it may well be
> that it cannot be regarded merely as varying that trust. But if an arrangement,
> while leaving the substratum, effectuates the purpose of the original trust by
> other means, it may still be possible to regard that arrangement as merely
> varying the original trusts, even though the means employed are wholly
> different and even though the form is completely changed.'

[1]   *Re Ball's Settlement* [1968] 2 All ER 438, [1968] 1 WLR 899.

47.55 In this latter case, Megarry J expressly distinguished the case of *Re T's
Settlement Trusts*[1]. In that case Wilberforce J had declined to approve a
proposed arrangement on the ground that it amounted to a completely new
re-settlement, not to a variation, and that there was therefore no jurisdiction

under the Act to approve it. But this was only one of the grounds on which he rested his decision, the other being that even if the court did have such jurisdiction it should nonetheless refuse approval in the particular circumstances of the case.

¹   [1964] Ch 158, [1963] 3 All ER 759.

47.56 ENLARGEMENT OF POWERS. In cases in which the arrangement has proposed to enlarge the powers of the trustees, the most frequent desire appears to have been to enlarge their powers of investment¹. However the Trustee Act 2000 now confers extensive powers of investment so the need for extra powers is very limited, eg to permit purchase of land outside the UK² or the acquisition of an asset that is not the 'making of an investment' but the 'application' of trust funds³.

¹   *Trustees of the British Museum v A-G* [1984] 1 WLR 418; *Steel v Wellcome Custodian Trustees* [1988] 1 WLR 167; *Anker-Petersen v Anker-Petersen* [2000] WTLR 581.
²   TA 2000, s 8(1).
³   TA 2000, s 3(1).

47.57 Cases in which the court will approve an arrangement enlarging the powers of the trustees are not, of course, confined to those involving investment. Thus in one case¹ approval was given to the retention of remuneration by director-trustees; and in another², involving the trusts of a will where the testator had died before 1926, approval was given to an arrangement which gave the trustees the power of advancement contained in s 32 of the Trustee Act 1925³.

¹   *Re Cooper's Settlement* [1962] Ch 826, [1961] 3 All ER 636.
²   *Re Lister's Will Trusts* [1962] 3 All ER 737, [1962] 1 WLR 1441.
³   See Article 67.

47.58 Nowadays, where no alteration of beneficial interests is sought so that it is only wider administrative powers that are sought, it is more convenient to use s 57 of the Trustee Act 1925 as emphasised in *Anker-Petersen v Anker-Petersen*¹. The advantages of s 57 are that the trustees are normally the applicants (unlike the position under the 1958 Act²), it is not essential to obtain the consent of every beneficiary of full age and capacity, the court is not required to given consent on behalf of every category of beneficiary separately but considers their interests collectively in income on the one hand and in capital on the other, so that s 57 applications are cheaper and more straight-forward, especially because they are taken in chambers while 1958 Act applications are taken in open court.

¹   [2000] WTLR 581.
²   *Re Druce's Settlement Trusts* [1962] 1 WLR 363.

47.59 'BENEFIT': STATEMENT OF GENERAL RULE AND EXCEPTION. Having noted the extent of the court's power under the Act, it is appropriate to consider its exercise. The power is of course discretionary and the only guidance which the Act gives on its exercise is that the courts shall not approve an arrangement on behalf of any person unless the carrying out of that arrangement would be for his benefit. To this, however, there is one exception: where the arrangement is approved by virtue of paragraph (d) of s 1(1)–that is, on behalf of a person who has a discretionary interest under protective trusts where the interest of the principal beneficiary has not failed or determined—no benefit need be shown to accrue to the person on whose behalf approval is given.

47.60 'BENEFIT': THE EXCEPTION DISCUSSED. This exception means that the provision of a 'compensation fund' for persons who fall within its terms, as was customary in some schemes presented to the court before the passing of the Act, is not an essential pre-requisite to the court's approval. But this does not imply that the interests of such persons can be ignored entirely; and the court must consider not only their interests but also the reason why they figure in the trust at all—in other words, the settlor's intention in providing the principal beneficiary with a protected rather than a full life interest[1]. The exception does not, therefore, lessen the extent of the court's discretion[2]. Thus even where, in the case of a spinster with a protected life interest, the only persons interested under the prospective discretionary trust are issue (whose advent is made very unlikely by the age of the life tenant) and a future husband (whose existence is made unlikely by the life tenant's lack of desire to marry) the court will still refuse to give approval on behalf of the 'spectral' discretionary beneficiaries to an arrangement which would frustrate the settlor's intention to protect the life tenant against her own possible improvidence[3]. And where a compensation fund *is* provided for the prospective discretionary beneficiaries, provisions affecting it must be fair: thus, the court may refuse to approve an arrangement which benefits only those beneficiaries who are already born and ignores entirely the possibility of unborn beneficiaries[4]. Where property is held on protective trusts and the protected life tenant applies to the court to vary them evidence, including evidence of the financial position of the applicant and the applicant's spouse, must be put before the court to show to what extent the protective trusts continue to serve any useful purpose[5].

[1]   *Re Steed's Will Trusts* [1960] Ch 407, [1960] 1 All ER 487, CA; *Re Burney's Settlement Trusts* [1961] 1 All ER 856, [1961] 1 WLR 545; *Gibbon v Mitchell* [1990] 3 All ER 338 at 343; *Goulding v James* [1997] 2 All ER 239, CA.
[2]   *Re Steed's Will Trusts* [1960] Ch 407, [1960] 1 All ER 487, CA; *Re Burney's Settlement Trusts* [1961] 1 All ER 856, [1961] 1 WLR 545; *Gibbon v Mitchell* [1990] 3 All ER 338 at 343; *Goulding v James* [1997] 2 All ER 239, CA.
[3]   *Re Steed's Will Trusts* [1960] Ch 407, [1960] 1 All ER 487, CA.
[4]   *Re Poole's Settlement's Trusts* [1959] 2 All ER 340, [1959] 1 WLR 651.
[5]   *Re Baker's Settlement Trusts* [1964] 1 All ER 482n, [1964] 1 WLR 336n.

47.61 It should be noted that the exception applies only to discretionary trusts which will arise on the forfeiture of a protected life interest. It does not apply to discretionary trusts which, though still future ones, are not framed to arise in this way, or are not framed to arise *only* in this way[1]. Still less does it apply to immediate discretionary trusts[2]. In cases where it does not apply, the arrangement proposed must therefore be shown to be for the benefit of the discretionary beneficiaries[3]. But where the discretionary trust does fall within the terms of paragraph (d), the court has power to approve it under that paragraph on behalf of potential beneficiaries who are unborn as well as those who are already in existence[4]. It should also be noted that the protective trusts must be either those specified in s 33(1)(i)–(ii) of the Trustee Act 1925 'or any like trusts'[5]. As to the last four words, see the discussion in *Re Wallace's Settlements*[6], where Megarry J said:

> 'The word "like" requires not identity but similarity; and similarity in substance suffices, without the need of similarity in form or detail or wording.'

1   *Re Bristol's Settled Estates* [1964] 3 All ER 939, [1965] 1 WLR 469.
2   *Re Clitheroe's Settlement Trusts* [1959] 3 All ER 789, [1959] 1 WLR 1159.
3   *Re Bristol's Settled Estates* [1964] 3 All ER 939, [1965] 1 WLR 469.
4   *Re Turner's Will Trusts* [1968] 1 All ER 321, [1968] 1 WLR 227. Strictly, the views expressed on this point by Danckwerts J in this case were obiter, but later cases have been decided on the implicit assumption that the position is as stated in the text, and there would certainly seem to be no sensible reason why benefits should have to be proved in the case of unborn beneficiaries but not in the case of those already in existence.
5   1958 Act, s 1(2).
6   [1968] 2 All ER 209, [1968] 1 WLR 711 and see *Thomas v IRC* [1981] STC 382 at 390.

47.62 'BENEFIT': THE GENERAL RULE DISCUSSED. Having considered the exception, it is necessary to return to the general rule: that the court cannot approve an arrangement on behalf of any person unless it is for his benefit.

47.63 In deciding whether a scheme is for a person's benefit the court will consider it as a whole. Typically a scheme will enhance a protected life interest into an ordinary life interest, eliminate the interests of unborn children unlikely to come into existence, insert a new perpetuity or accumulation period into the new trust arising by virtue of the 1958 Act, postpone the vesting of capital or, even income in a young person, or avoid or mitigate taxation by modifying or deleting discretionary powers or by partitioning the trust fund between income and capital beneficiaries. In the latter event the emphasis is on tax savings and not just the actuarial value of the interests of the various capital beneficiaries but also the sudden death values, the scheme being disadvantageous to them to the extent that the risk materialises of an income beneficiary failing to survive for his normal life expectancy, so that provision for any shortfall is normally required to be made via insurance or a personal covenant. However, the word 'benefit' is not to be narrowly interpreted or restricted to matters of finance. Thus:

(a)   If a person derives no financial benefit from a proposed arrangement the court may still approve it on his behalf. In one case[1] a settlement provided that a beneficiary should be entitled absolutely to certain capital at the age of 21. The beneficiary had shown herself to be immature and irresponsible as regards money and the court was asked, just before she attained 21, to approve on her behalf an arrangement which would deprive her of her right to capital entirely and give her a mere protected life interest instead. Wilberforce J refused approval to this, but he did approve on her behalf a less drastic scheme which had the effect of postponing her right to the capital for a period and giving her a protected life interest during that period. It could no doubt be argued that, although the immediate effect of this arrangement was one of financial deprivation, it was however for the beneficiary's financial benefit in the long term and thus that the decision does not conclusively support the proposition just advanced. The point has, however, been considered in two other reported cases: *Re Tinker's Settlement*[2] and *Re C L*[3].

1   *Re T's Settlement Trusts* [1964] Ch 158, [1963] 3 All ER 759, followed in *Re Holt's Settlement* [1969] 1 Ch 100 at 121 Megarry J stating, 'The word "benefit" is plainly not confined to financial benefit but may extend to moral or social benefit'. See also *Re Estate Trust* [2001] WTLR 571.
2   [1960] 3 All ER 85n, [1960] 1 WLR 1011.
3   [1969] 1 Ch 587, [1968] 1 All ER 1104.

47.64 In the first of these a male beneficiary was to receive his share of settled capital absolutely on attaining 30. If he died under that age, his share was to accrue to his sister's share, which was settled on her for life with remainder to her children. Apparently through a drafting error, a provision that if the male beneficiary died under 30 leaving children his share should go to those children rather than accrue to the share of the sister had been omitted. The court was asked to approve, on behalf of the sister's unborn children, an arrangement whereby this provision would be inserted on the ground that, although this could not be for their financial benefit and might be to their financial detriment, it was 'reasonable and fair'. Russell J refused approval, saying that he could not bring himself to think that he would be benefiting the children if he gave away property which might accrue to them. But in *Re C L* a patient who was of advanced age and mentally ill[1] owned substantial property and had a large income. A small part of this income was derived from property in which she had a protected life interest under a settlement made by her late husband. Her adopted daughters applied to the court for approval on her behalf to an arrangement whereby she would give up her protected life interest and all other interest under the settlement in order to benefit them. Cross J gave approval, saying that although the arrangement would involve the patient in financial loss this was comparatively small and it was for her benefit to do what she herself would have done had she been of full capacity. He distinguished *Re Tinker's Settlement* above (though agreeing with it) on the basis that there one could not say that the relevant beneficiaries, if of full capacity, would in all probability have consented to the proposed variation of the settlement[2]. He added:

'If and so far, however, as the judge was saying that there must always be some element of financial advantage to the infant or otherwise incapable person in question before an arrangement can be said to be for his benefit, I think he went too far.'

1   As to the special provisions applicable to certain patients who are mentally ill, see para 47.89.
2   See also *Re Mr & Mrs N's 1989 Settlement* (1998/99) 1 ITELR 803.

47.65 In *Re Remnant's Settlement Trusts*[1] the children of two sisters, Dawn and Merrial, had contingent interests under a testamentary trust which contained a forfeiture provision in respect of any child who practised Roman Catholicism or was married to a Roman Catholic at the time of vesting, with an accruer provision in favour of the children of the other sister. Dawn's children were Protestant whilst Merrial's children were Catholic. In the interests of family harmony an application was made inter alia for deletion of the forfeiture provision.

¹   [1970] Ch 560, [1970] 2 All ER 554. See also *Re Zekelman* (1971) 19 DLR (3d) 652.

47.66   Pennycuick J acceded to the application, though defeating the testator's clear intentions and though financially disadvantageous to Dawn's children who otherwise had a good chance of gaining under the accruer clause. Pennycuick J was much influenced by the fact that the forfeiture clause operated as a deterrent in the selection of a spouse and was the source of possible family dissension. He emphasised that 'benefit' included educational and social benefit in a broad sense:

> 'I think I am entitled to take a broad view of what is meant by "benefit", and so taking it, I think this arrangement can be fairly said to be for [the children's] benefit ... I think the court is entitled and bound to consider not merely financial benefit but benefit of any other kind'¹.

¹   [1970] Ch 560 at 566. *In theory* either side of the family might benefit.

47.67   Unfortunately, *Re Tinker's Settlement¹* was not cited to Pennycuick J and no counsel seems to have presented submissions against the proposed arrangement where the judge took on a paterfamilial role in sublimating the individual interests to broader family interests without considering, as Cross J had suggested², whether the Protestant children, when adult, would in all probability be happy to forgo a larger share in the trust funds resulting from their cousins' Roman Catholicism.

(b)   Conversely, the mere fact that a person does derive financial benefit from a scheme does not necessarily mean that the court will sanction it on his behalf. For one thing, the financial benefit, though present, may be unfairly small, so that the scheme is not—in the wider sense— beneficial to the person concerned. Thus Ungoed-Thomas J pointed out in one case³ that if a proposed arrangement would give infants and unborn persons an entitlement which is actuarially greater than their entitlement under the existing trusts, but which is still not as great as their bargaining strength should have enabled them to obtain, the court should not approve it. In the event, the judge did approve the arrangement in question because he held, with some hesitation, that the benefit was sufficient. It is apprehended that there may be difficulties here, unless the court can be sure that the refusal of its approval will result in the proposal being made more beneficial to the persons concerned; for otherwise the refusal may merely deprive them of the benefit, however small, which they would have obtained. For another thing, the financial benefit to a person may be outweighed by disadvantages of a different kind. Thus in *Re Weston's Settlements⁴*, approval was sought on behalf of infant and unborn persons to the insertion in certain English settlements of a power for the trustees to discharge the trust property from the settlements and to subject it to the trusts of new Jersey settlements containing substantially the same beneficial trusts. The purpose behind the proposed arrangement was to establish the settlements in Jersey (where the adult beneficiaries claimed already to have taken up permanent residence and acquired a domicile[5]) and so save capital gains tax and estate duty. Although the arrangement would thus have brought financial benefit to the persons on whose behalf its approval was sought, the court refused approval; and Lord Denning MR, with whom Danckwerts LJ agreed, based this refusal on the view that:

'... the court should not consider merely the financial benefit to the infants or unborn children but also their educational and social benefit. There are many things in life more worth-while than money. One of these things is to be brought up in this our England, which is still "the envy of less happier lands". I do not believe it is for the benefit of children to be uprooted from England and transported to another country simply to avoid tax.'

[1] [1960] 3 All ER 85n, [1960] 1 WLR 1011.
[2] *Re CL* [1969] 1 Ch 587 at 599. One might try to reconcile *Re Remnant's Will Trusts* with *Re Tinker's Settlement* on the basis that in the former both sides of the family could benefit in theory while in the latter only one side could benefit.
[3] *Re Van Gruisen's Will Trusts* [1964] 1 All ER 843n, [1964] 1 WLR 449.
[4] [1969] 1 Ch 223, [1968] 3 All ER 338, CA. Further see tax avoidance discussion at para 47.72 below.
[5] In fact, the family *did* settle permanently in Jersey.

47.68 This case also brings out the fact that the court may often be able to refuse its approval on either one of two grounds: it may either decide, as did Lord Denning here, that the arrangement is not for the benefit of the persons concerned, perhaps interpreting the word 'benefit' widely for this purpose; or it may by-pass the question of benefit, as Harman LJ seems to have done in the same case, and simply decide that (whether there is a benefit or not) the arrangement is not one which the court 'thinks fit' to approve.

47.69 The general requirement that an arrangement must be for a person's benefit if it is to be approved on his behalf by the court does not mean, of course, that all its provisions must be beneficial to him: it is enough if the provisions, taken as a whole and (if necessary) balanced one against another, are beneficial to him[1]. Benefit may sometimes be found on the principle that a bird in the hand is worth two in the bush: thus an arrangement under which a beneficiary would receive £100 a year certain instead of remaining a member of a class of discretionary beneficiaries has been held to be beneficial[2].

[1] *Re Lister's Will Trusts* [1962] 3 All ER 737, [1962] 1 WLR 1441.
[2] *Re Clitheroe's Settlement Trusts* [1959] 3 All ER 789, [1959] 1 WLR 1159.

47.70 The court must consider individually each person on whose behalf it is asked to give approval. Thus it is not sufficient that the proposed arrangement is for the benefit of a class of persons, considered together, if some members of the class—ie those born after a certain date—would not participate in that benefit; and this is so even if the arrangement is likely to result in more persons being born in time to qualify, or in greater benefits for those who do qualify[1].

[1] *Re Cohen's Settlement Trusts* [1965] 3 All ER 139, [1965] 1 WLR 1229.

47.71 Although arrangements must generally be for the benefit of those on whose behalf the court approves them, it is not essential that this benefit should be the inevitable result of the arrangement provided that it is an overwhelmingly likely one: the court will be prepared to take, on behalf of those for whom its approval is sought, the kind of risk which an adult beneficiary of full capacity would take on his own behalf[1]. The court may take a broad, reasonable view but not a galloping, gambling view as Templeman J pointed out in *Re Robinson's Settlement Trusts*[2]. Insurance can usually take care of most risks.

1   *Re Cohen's Will Trusts* [1959] 3 All ER 523, [1959] 1 WLR 865.
2   [1976] 3 All ER 61, [1976] 1 WLR 806.

47.72 TAX AVOIDANCE. It is clear that there is in principle no objection to schemes designed to avoid taxation by lawful means. In *Chapman v Chapman*[1], decided before the Act of 1958, Lord Morton of Henryton deprecated the alteration by the court of settlements for the purpose of avoiding tax, saying that if the court had power to approve, and did approve, schemes for that purpose 'the way would be open for a most undignified game of chess between the Chancery Division and the legislature'. But substantially the same scheme was later approved by the court under the 1958 Act[2], and having regard to the fact that (subject to the exception already mentioned) any arrangement must be for the benefit of all the beneficiaries (either, in the case of those on whose behalf the court's approval is given, because the Act so provides or, in the case of the others, because they would not otherwise be likely to agree to it) it is perhaps inevitable that some of this benefit must often be gained at the expense of the revenue. Indeed in *Re Weston's Settlements*, Harman LJ above went so far as to say that[3]:

> '... it is well known that much and perhaps the main use which has been made of the Variation of Trusts Act 1958 has been to produce schemes which will have the effect of reducing the liabilities either on capital[4] of the trusts or the income[5] of the beneficiaries.'

1   [1954] AC 429 at 468, [1954] 1 All ER 798 at 818, HL.
2   *Re Chapman's Settlement Trusts (No 2)* [1959] 2 All ER 47n, [1959] 1 WLR 372.
3   See also the remarks of Lord Denning MR [1969] 1 Ch at 245, [1968] 3 All ER 338 at 342.
4   As in *Re Drewe's Settlement* [1966] 2 All ER 844n, [1966] 1 WLR 1518, and *Re Lloyd's Settlement* [1967] 2 All ER 314n, [1967] 2 WLR 1078.
5   As in *Clitheroe's Settlement Trusts* [1959] 3 All ER 789, [1959] 1 WLR 1159 (income tax and surtax), and *Re Sainsbury's Settlement* [1967] 1 All ER 878, [1967] 1 WLR 476 (capital gains tax).

47.73 And when the court does approve a scheme the benefit of which depends on estate duty (or, now, inheritance tax) being avoided, it will seek to ensure that its avoidance is not jeopardised by future acts: thus in a case[1] where the incautious exercise of a power of appointment might result in a liability to estate duty which the arrangement was designed to avoid, the court required the documents to provide that the power:

> '... shall not be exercisable without the consent of the trustees which consent the trustees shall not withhold if advised by counsel of not less than ten years standing [at the Bar] that any proposed appointment will not under the law in

force for the time being give rise to any claim for estate duty on the reversioners' fund or any part thereof on the death of [the appointor].'

1   *Re Drewe's Settlement* [1966] 2 All ER 844n, [1966] 1 WLR 1518.

47.74 But the case of *Re Weston's Settlements*, above, indicates that a line may have to be drawn somewhere. The main facts of this case have already been mentioned. At first instance[1], Stamp J refused his approval and rested this refusal at least partly on the ground that the scheme was an artificial one designed solely to save tax, saying:

> 'I am not persuaded that this application represents more than a cheap exercise in tax avoidance which I ought not to sanction, as distinct from a legitimate avoidance of liability to taxation.'

1   [1969] 1 Ch 223, [1968] 1 All ER 720.

47.75 With respect, however, the distinction between these two activities is difficult to define and seems to consist only in the differently coloured language in which they are described. The Court of Appeal[1] affirmed the decision at first instance, but it is not easy to decide how much weight it placed, in dismissing the appeal, upon the tax avoiding nature of the arrangement. Certainly this played a large part in the judgments of Lord Denning MR and Harman LJ with both of which Danckwerts LJ agreed, as did the fact that the beneficiaries' move to Jersey had apparently been prompted solely by the hope of obtaining the tax advantage in question. In this latter respect, the case was contrasted with that of *Re Seale's Marriage Settlement*[2] where, although the scheme sanctioned did involve the transfer of a settlement to another country and the consequent avoidance of tax, the beneficiaries had emigrated to the other country some time before and for reasons quite unconnected with the scheme. And indeed in *Re Windeatt's Will Trusts*[3], a case decided since the *Weston* case, Pennycuick J applied *Seale* and distinguished *Weston* in order to approve an arrangement which was similar to that proposed in *Weston* but which concerned beneficiaries who had already been resident in Jersey for 19 years and seemed clearly to have acquired a domicile there. Equally certainly, however, the *Weston* case does not mean that schemes which have tax avoidance as their sole purpose will no longer be approved by the courts. All that can be said, perhaps, is that the courts prefer such schemes to be presented with decorum. Where this is the only purpose of a proposed arrangement, and the arrangement itself is particularly artificial or reveals its purpose in too blatant a way, the court may be ready to refuse its approval, if not on the express ground that the scheme is simply an exercise in tax avoidance, then on the ground that it is not truly for the benefit of the beneficiaries on whose behalf approval is sought or on the ground that the court does not 'think fit' to approve it.

1   [1969] 1 Ch 223, [1968] 3 All ER 338, CA.
2   [1961] Ch 574, [1961] 3 All ER 136.
3   [1969] 2 All ER 324, [1969] 1 WLR 692 where Lord Denning MR stated, 'Nearly every variation that has come before the court has tax avoidance for its principal object and no-one has ever suggested that this is undesirable or contrary to public policy'.

47.76 In *Re Chamberlain*[1] Walton J approved an arrangement transferring assets of a trust, the proper law of which was English, to trustees of a Guernsey trust where the primary beneficiaries were domiciled and resident in France and the remaindermen were domiciled and resident in Indonesia. Unlike *Re Seale's Marriage Settlement* and *Re Windeatt's Will Trusts* the beneficiaries under the settlement had no connection with the country to which the settled funds were to be exported so as to become subject to an alien proper law. The settlement had been created many years previously by an English domiciled settlor so as to remain liable to UK capital transfer tax. Foreign trustees had been appointed in place of UK trustees and the trust assets had been switched into exempt gilts so that no capital transfer tax arose on determining the settlement and once the assets had been received into the Guernsey settlement no capital transfer tax would subsequently arise: no exchange control problems arose since Guernsey is in the sterling area. Trust exporting for the purpose of avoiding tax is thus still possible despite *Re Weston* which must be restricted to its special facts.

[1]   (1976) 126 NLJ 104 reported in an article by JB Morcom, barrister.

47.77 In *Richards v Mackay*[1] Millett J contrasted cases where the court is asked to exercise an original discretion of its own (as under the 1958 Act) with those where the proposed export of a trust or other arrangement is to be carried out by the trustees in exercise of their own discretion. In the former case the applicants have to make out a positive case for the exercise of a judicial discretion and 'the court is unlikely to assist them where the scheme is nothing more than a device to avoid tax and has no other advantages of any kind'. In the latter case the court only needs to be satisfied that the proposed appointment of foreign trustees or other arrangement is not so inappropriate that no reasonable trustee could entertain it. It is also significant that since *Re Weston* was decided Parliament has intervened with substantial provisions for preventing capital gains tax being avoided by means of exporting trusts[2], so that naked tax avoidance will rarely be involved where trusts are exported.

[1]   [1990] 1 OTPR 1, (R. Bramwell QC) and (1997) 11 Trust LI 123, applied by Vinelott J in *Re Beatty's Will Trusts (No 2)* (28 February 1991, unreported, except in 11 Trust LI 77).
[2]   [1966] Ch 257, [1966] 1 All ER 913. Taxation of Chargeable Gains Act 1992, ss 80–84, 87.

47.78 WOMEN PAST CHILDBEARING. The Act has no special effect in cases where a woman, although in theory capable of having children who would or might become beneficiaries under a trust, is thought to be, or is in fact, past the age of childbearing. Of course, the court's power to approve an arrangement on behalf of unborn persons allows it to approve an arrangement on behalf of children who may be born to a middle-aged mother just as much as those who may be born to a younger one. But when the woman concerned is clearly past the age of childbearing it is inappropriate to apply under the Act for approval on behalf of her potential children of an arrangement whereby the trust property can be dealt with on the assumption that they will not in fact be born. This was made clear by Pennycuick J in *Re Pettifor's Will Trusts*[1], where it was proposed to take out an insurance policy against the possibility of future children in such a way that the insurance money would benefit such children if they were born and thus make up their loss. He said that where the woman in question is clearly past the age of childbearing, eg 70 years old, the trustees will normally be prepared to act, without any insurance cover, on the assumption that no children will in fact be born; but if the intervention of the court is to be sought at all, an application should be made to it in its administrative jurisdiction for leave to carry out the existing trusts on the basis that no children will be born. He added that:

> '... it is well established that in administration the court will allow funds to be distributed on the footing that at a certain age, normally in the late or middle fifties, a woman has become incapable of childbearing.'

[1]   [1966] Ch 257, [1966] 1 All ER 913; also see *Re Westminster Bank's Declaration of Trust* [1963] 1 WLR 820 (VTA order for woman aged 50).

47.79 A distinction must of course be drawn between cases like that described above, where the court is asked to approve on behalf of the unborn children of a woman past the age of childbearing an arrangement which allows the trustees to proceed on the assumption that they will not be born, and cases in which an arrangement has been drawn up for some larger purpose but has as one of its elements the assumption that children will not be born to a woman past the age of childbearing. In one such case[1] it was not proposed to give any benefit to such children, so that the court could not in any case approve the proposed arrangement on their behalf, but the court was asked to approve it on behalf of the other beneficiaries. The court did so, and authorised the trustees to deal with the trust fund on the basis that the woman in question was past the age of childbearing, but without extinguishing any rights that her potential children might have.

[1]   *Abbott v Service* (1963) 107 Sol Jo 681.

47.80 PUBLIC POLICY. The court will not approve an arrangement which is contrary to public policy, eg which amounts to a general restraint of mariage[1].

[1]   *Re Michelham's Will Trusts* [1964] Ch 550, [1963] 2 All ER 188.

47.81 FRAUD ON A POWER OF APPOINTMENT[1]. Powers of appointment may be either exercised or released in order to prepare the ground for an arrangement to be submitted to the court. When the power has been released (so that the default beneficiaries take) no question of fraud on a power can, of course, arise. But when it has been exercised this question may be pertinent. If the appointment has been made in order (or partly in order) to benefit the appointor, either directly, or indirectly by creating a situation in which the court might be expected to approve an arrangement which is for his benefit and which it would not otherwise have approved, or to approve an arrangement more favourable to him than it would otherwise have approved, then the appointment will be invalid and an arrangement based upon it will not be approved[2]. But the mere fact that the appointment does benefit the appointor in any of these ways is not enough of itself to make it fraudulent, and if the court does not find, or infer, an intention to exercise it *for that purpose* the appointment will be valid and can form the basis of an arrangement which the court will approve[3].

1   See generally para 61.31 ff.
2   *Re Brook's Settlement* [1968] 3 All ER 416, [1968] 1 WLR 1661.
3   *Re Robertson's Will Trusts* [1960] 3 All ER 146n, [1960] 1 WLR 1050.

47.82 Although it is clear that a power of appointment may be released without any question of fraudulent intention being raised, the courts have none the less been confronted in several cases under the Act with the question of how this release can be effected. If the power of appointment has not been released, expressly and by deed, before the application under the Act comes to court, but the arrangement proposed is inconsistent with the continued existence of the power, does the application itself, or the court's approval of the arrangement, amount to a release of the power? It is clear that, although an express release must be by deed[1], the donee of a power makes an effective implied release if he deals with the property in a way which is inconsistent with its exercise. It has been suggested that the donee of a power may therefore, by applying for the court's approval of an arrangement inconsistent with its continued existence, or even by merely concurring in such a scheme, release the power. In *Re Christie-Miller's Settlement Trusts*[2] Wilberforce J left this question open and accepted an oral release by the donee's counsel. In *Re Courtauld's Settlement*[3] Plowman J pointed out that an oral release of this kind could be of only evidential value and approved an arrangement on the basis that the mere fact that the donee had propounded it was enough to release the power. He said, however, that he could not decide this point in such a way as to bind persons who were not parties to the proceedings. Finally, in *Re Wallace's Settlement*[4], Megarry J was asked to approve an arrangement which revoked certain clauses in a settlement, including one conferring a power of appointment which had not been expressly released. He held that the revocation could not amount to an express release of the power. He added, referring to *Re Courtauld's Settlement*, above, that there might well be an implied release but said: 'The difficulty in such cases may be, however, that an implied release will not, as in *Re Courtauld's Settlement*, necessarily bind all persons'. These words may give rise to some confusion. It seems clear enough that if an implied release is in fact made it will bind all persons in just the same way as an express one would do. What Plowman J said in *Re Courtauld's Settlement* was merely that his *decision* that the implied release *was* made would not bind anyone who was not a party to the proceedings. At all events, Megarry J said that it was preferable that the power should be expressly released by deed, so that this is the proper course to take, Megarry J in *Re Ball's Settlement Trusts*[5] requiring an express release of the power.

1   Law of Property Act 1925 ('LPA 1925'), s 155.
2   [1961] 1 All ER 855n, [1961] 1 WLR 462.
3   [1965] 2 All ER 544n, [1965] 1 WLR 1385.
4   [1968] 2 All ER 209, [1968] 1 WLR 711.
5   [1968] 2 All ER 438.

47.83 In *IRC v Cookson*[1] Stamp LJ laid down the general law on implied release of powers as follows:

'In the absence of words which actually have that effect an instrument or the transaction which it effects will only operate to release a power if it operates in such a way that the power cannot thereafter be exercised without interfering with the operation of the earlier instrument or transaction. However probable it may be that the author of the instrument intended to destroy a power you must, in order to destroy it, find words which have that effect or something which shows by necessary implication an intention so to do.'

1   [1977] 2 All ER 331 at 335.

THE EFFECT OF THE COURT'S APPROVAL

47.84 On the precise effect of the court's approval, and of the order by which this is expressed, there has been a conflict of judicial opinion. The following propositions can, it is submitted, be deduced from the cases, some more tentatively than others:

(a)   whatever the precise way in which the result is achieved (and this is discussed below) the arrangement, to which those beneficiaries who act on their own behalf have assented, coupled with the order by which the court approves it on behalf of the other beneficiaries, has the immediate effect of varying or revoking the trusts (or enlarging the powers of the trustees, as the case may be). It is therefore not necessary or appropriate for the court to add to its order a direction that the arrangement shall be carried into effect, for it becomes effective automatically. The action of Vaisey J, in making such an addition to the order in the case of *Re Joseph's Will Trusts[1]* must, in the light of the cases mentioned below, be considered mistaken;

(b)   but some doubt remains as to the exact way in which the variation (or revocation or enlargement) is made. In *Re Viscount Hambleden's Will Trusts[2]*, Wynn-Parry J said that it was made by the court's order of approval: 'If I approve an arrangement, I vary the trusts'. But this view was rejected by Megarry J in *Re Holt's Settlement[3]* where he held (and his view is supported by dicta of the House of Lords in *Re Holmden's Settlement Trusts[4]*) that it was the arrangement, made binding on certain beneficiaries by the court's order, which varied the trusts and not the order itself. This must therefore be considered the better view;

(c)   it would be wrong to conclude, however, that the sole effect of the Act is to allow the court to make good the lack of assent to an arrangement of beneficiaries who are unborn or lacking in capacity. The arrangement, after all, is not a written document signed by the beneficiaries and if the Act merely allowed the court, as it were, notionally to supply the signatures of some of the beneficiaries, it would still lack those of the others. In particular it would in many cases fail to meet the requirements of s 53(1)(c) of the Law of Property Act 1925 which provides that:

'a disposition of an equitable interest or trust subsisting at the time of the disposition, must be in writing signed by the person disposing of the same, or by his agent thereunto lawfully authorised in writing or by will.'

1   [1959] 3 All ER 474n, [1959] 1 WLR 1019.
2   [1960] 1 All ER 353n, [1960] 1 WLR 82.
3   [1969] 1 Ch 100, [1968] 1 All ER 470. See also *Spens v IRC* [1970] 1 WLR 1173 at 1183–1184.

⁴ [1968] AC 685 at 701, 710–711, 713. See also *Thorn v IRC* [1976] 2 All ER 622 at 631, per Walton J.

47.85 In *Re Holt's Settlement*, above, Megarry J acceded to the argument of counsel that by enacting the Variation of Trusts Act the legislature had provided an implied exception to these requirements where the order of the court re-worded the consent of the parties by their counsel to the arrangement. The Act contemplated that the court's order should conclude all the steps necessary to make the variation effective and 'one should construe the Act ... as authorising an order which is efficacious to achieve its avowed object'. In his judgment, Megarry J gave assent also to an alternative means of escape under s 53(2)¹ from the provisions of s 53(1)(c) of the 1925 Act, namely:

> 'Where ... the arrangement consists of an agreement made for valuable consideration, and that agreement is specifically enforceable, then the beneficial interests pass to the respective purchasers on the making of the agreement ... by virtue of the species of constructive trust made familiar by contracts for the sale of land, whereunder the vendor becomes a constructive trustee for the purchaser as soon as the contract is made ... '

¹ This is a little difficult to reconcile with the majority view in *Oughtred v IRC* [1960] AC 206, [1959] 3 All ER 623 (see J W Harris, *Variation of Trusts*, pp 107–109) but it has subsequent support from *DHN Food Distributors Ltd v Tower Hamlets* [1976] 1 WLR 852 and *Neville v Wilson* [1997] Ch 144, CA, though contracts for sale of interests in land are now void unless all their terms are in writing signed by both parties due to the Law of Property (Miscellaneous Provisions) Act 1989, s 2, so the remarks of Megarry J now have to be confined to personalty unless one can impose a constructive trust within s 2(5) of the 1989 Act to prevent unconscionable behaviour on proprietary estoppel grounds, as in *Yaxley v Gotts* [2000] Ch 162.

47.86 Another point decided by Megarry J in the same case is that the arrangement coupled with the court's order constitutes an 'instrument' for the purposes of s 15(5) of the Perpetuities and Accumulations Act 1964¹, so that provisions which derive their validity from that Act may be included in the arrangement, the perpetuity and accumulation period starting afresh.

¹ See also Article 11, para 1(a), above and *Re Lansdowne's Will Trusts* [1967] Ch 603.

47.87 It is normally desirable that the court's order should give approval on behalf of, and thus bind all the beneficiaries who are not able to assent on their own behalf. Indeed Stamp J has doubted¹, *obiter*, whether it would be right to approve an arrangement which would not bind all the beneficiaries, since such approval might also fail to bind the Inland Revenue.

¹ *Re Brook's Settlement* [1968] 3 All ER 416, [1968] 1 WLR 1661. But see eg *Re Clarke's Will Trusts* [1961] 3 All ER 1133, [1961] 1 WLR 1471. No doubt this may depend upon the kind of variation proposed.

Jurisdiction and practice

47.88 The jurisdiction conferred by the Act is exercisable by the High Court, except that the question whether the carrying out of any arrangement would

47.88 *The trustee's duties*

be for the benefit of a person falling within s 1(1)(a) is to be determined by order of the authority having jurisdiction under Pt VII of the Mental Health Act 1983 if that person is a patient within the meaning of that Part of that Act. But the county court has all the jurisdiction of the High Court to hear and determine proceedings under s 1 of the Variation of Trusts Act where the estate or fund subject to the trust does not exceed £30,000 in amount or value, and in these proceedings the country court judge has, in addition to any other powers and authorities which he possesses, all the powers and authorities of a judge of the Chancery Division of the High Court[1].

[1] County Courts Act 1984, s 23. The £30,000 limit on the county court jurisdiction cannot be exceeded even if all the parties agree: County Courts Act 1984, s 24 (3).

47.89 In regard to the exception which applies to a beneficiary who is a patient within Pt VII of the Mental Health Act 1983, it should be noted that the procedure required is for the Court of Protection to approve the arrangement on behalf of the patient as being for his benefit: it is not appropriate for the Court of Protection to direct the patient's receiver to consent to the arrangement on the patient's behalf[1]. But if the arrangement subsequently comes before the Chancery Division for approval on behalf of other beneficiaries, an order may be made that the costs in the Court of Protection shall be paid out of the trust estate[2].

[1] *Re CL* [1969] 1 Ch 587, [1968] 1 All ER 1104.
[2] *Re Sanderson's Settlement Trusts* [1961] 1 All ER 25n, [1961] 1 WLR 36.

47.90 The court's jurisdiction to vary trusts is not confined to those to which English law applies. Thus it extends to a Northern Ireland settlement[1], and indeed to a settlement governed by any law. But careful consideration is given to the question of whether it is proper to exercise this jurisdiction 'where there are substantial foreign elements in the case'[2]. In particular the court pays attention to the effectiveness of any order which it may make[3], eg whether the trustees and the trust property are situate in England and whether there is any possibility of 'limping' trust provisions valid under the English Act but void under some applicable law governing validity.

[1] *Re Ker's Settlement Trusts* [1963] Ch 553, [1963] 1 All ER 801.
[2] Per Cross J in *Re Paget's Settlement* [1965] 1 All ER 58, [1965] 1 WLR 1046 (New York Trust).
[3] *Re Paget's Settlement* [1965] 1 All ER 58, [1965] 1 WLR 1046; cf *C v C* [2004] EWCA Civ 1030,[2005] Fam 250 under the matrimonial variation jurisdiction (para 47.95), where only one of the three judges mentioned this aspect, and then only as something for the claimant to think about after successfully obtaining the order: see para 54.

47.91 The Recognition of Trusts Act 1987, implementing Article 8 of The Hague Convention on Trusts, allows trusts to be varied by the English court under its VTA jurisdiction but only if variation by a court is permitted to be effective by the law governing validity of the trust if alteration of beneficial interests is involved, or the law governing administration if alteration or deletion or enlargement of administrative powers is involved[1]. Obviously, it will normally be best and most appropriate to vary the trust in the jurisdiction of the applicable law for validity and/or administration. If however in the case of a foreign trust the variation is made by the English court, whether applying the foreign variation law or Englsh law , and the trustees are not subject to the jurisdiction, it will generally be necessary to take proceedings in the foreign court to the jurisdiction of which the trustees are subject, before the variation can be made effective[2].

1   See para 102.159 below.
2   *Compass Trustees Ltd v MacBarnett* [2002] JLR 321, R Ct Jersey; *Re the Bald Eagle Trust* [2003] JLR N[16], R Ct Jersey; *C v C* [2004] EWCA Civ 1030, [2005] Fam 250, para 54; *FM v ASL Trustee Co Ltd* [2006] JRC 020A, R Ct Jersey (where, however, it is not clear which jurisdiction the Jersey court was employing in varying the trust). Futher see para 102.177 below.

47.92 Section 1(1) of the Act gives the court power to approve any arrangement 'by whomsoever proposed'. But in applications to vary beneficial interests the beneficiaries, and not the trustees, should generally be the applicants unless the trustees are satisfied that the proposed arrangement is beneficial to the beneficiaries and that no beneficiary is willing to make the application. This was said by Russell J in *Re Druce's Settlement Trusts*[1], and he added:

'In particular it would not be right if it became the general practice for such applications to be made by the trustees on the supposition that should the application fail it will be more probable ... that the costs of all parties will be directed to be paid out of the trust funds.'

1   [1962] 1 All ER 563, [1962] 1 WLR 363.

47.93 It is not proposed to deal here in any more detail with matters which relate purely to practice under the Variation of Trusts Act. The relevant rules and practice directions[1] are fully summarised and discussed in the established works on practice[2].

1   For example, RSC Ord 85 and RSC PD 85; Civil Procedure Rules 1998, rr 19.7, 21.2 and 24.0.
2   Atkin's *Encyclopaedia of Court Forms* Vol 41; *Chancery Practice and Procedure* (Jordans, 2001); *Lewin on Trusts* (17th edn) paras 45–79 to 45–96; E Campbell *Changing the Terms of Trusts* (Butterworths 2002), Ch 4, paras 4.94 to 4.129.

OTHER POWERS ARE NOT LIMITED BY THE ACT

47.94 It is expressly provided[1] that the Act is not to limit 'the powers conferred by s 64 of the Settled Land Act 1925, s 57 of the Trustee Act 1925[2] or the powers of the authority having jurisdiction under Pt VII of the Mental Health Act 1983'[3]. Since these powers do not require unanimity on the part of all beneficiaries who are ascertainable and of full age and capacity they will doubtless still be resorted to in many cases to which they are appropriate[4]. But the jurisdiction under the Act of 1958 has the advantage that under it the powers of the trustees of management and administration may be enlarged at the same time as dealing with the alteration of beneficial interests. If no such alteration is required then it is cheaper, more convenient and more straightforward to have particular transactions or an enlargement of management and administrative powers authorised in Chambers under the Trustee Act 1925 or the Settled Land Act 1925[5].

47.94 *The trustee's duties*

1   Section 1(6) of the 1958 Act, as amended by Mental Health Act 1959, s 149(1), Sch 7, Pt I
     and Mental Health Act 1983, s 148, Sch 4, para 14.
2   As to this, see also the notes to Paragraphs 2 and 3 of the present Article.
3   Sections 95 and 96, especially s 96(3) replacing s 103(4) of the Mental Health Act 1959 on
     which see *Re CWHT* [1978] Ch 67, [1978] 1 All ER 210.
4   Eg *Mason v Farbrother* [1983] 2 All ER 1078.
5   *Anker-Petersen v Anker-Petersen* [2000] WTLR 581 discussed at para 47.56 and 47.114.

Variation in connection with matrimonial proceedings

47.95 Since 1857 the courts have had power to order the property of a wife
divorced or judicially separated for adultery to be settled for the benefit of the
other spouse and the children[1], and since 1859 they have had power to vary
ante-nuptial and post-nuptial settlements made on the parties to a marriage
the subject of a divorce or nullity decree[2]. In each case the legislation has been
widened, and s 24 of the Matrimonial Causes Act 1973 now provides:

1   Matrimonial Causes Act 1857, s 45.
2   Matrimonial Causes Act 1859, s 5.

47.96

'(1) On granting a decree of divorce, a decree of nullity of marriage or a decree
of judicial separation or at any time thereafter (whether, in the case of a decree
of divorce or of nullity of marriage, before or after the decree is made absolute),
the court may make any one or more of the following orders, that is to say (a)
an order that a party to the marriage shall transfer to the other party, to any
child of the family or to such person as may be specified in the order for the
benefit of such a child such property as may be so specified, being property to
which the first-mentioned party is entitled, either in possession or reversion;
(b) an order that a settlement of such property as may be so specified, being
property to which a party to the marriage is so entitled, be made to the
satisfaction of the court for the benefit of the other party to the marriage and of
the children of the family or either or any of them;
(c) an order varying for the benefit of the parties to the marriage and of the
children of the family or either or any of them any ante-nuptial or post-nuptial
settlement (including such a settlement made by will or codicil) made on the
parties to the marriage [, other than one in the form of a pension arrangement
(within the meaning of section 25D below)]1;
(d) an order extinguishing or reducing the interest of either of the parties to the
marriage under any such settlement[, other than one in the form of a pension
arrangement (within the meaning of section 25D below)]2;
subject, however, in the case of an order under paragraph (a) above, to the
restrictions imposed by section 29(1) and (3) below on the making of orders for
a transfer of property in favour of children who have attained the age of
eighteen.
(2) The court may make an order under subsection (1)(c) above notwithstanding that there are no children of the family.
(3) Without prejudice to the power to give a direction under section 30 below
for the settlement of an instrument by conveyancing counsel, where an order is
made under this section on or after granting a decree of divorce or nullity of
marriage, neither the order nor any settlement made in pursuance of the order
shall take effect unless the decree has been made absolute'.

1   Words inserted by Welfare Reform and Pensions Act (1999 c.30), Sch 3 Para 3.
2   Words inserted by Welfare Reform and Pensions Act (1999 c.30), Sch 3 Para 3.

47.97 Although s 24 requires that the (English) court should first have granted a decree of divorce, nullity or judicial separation before becoming able to make any order under the section, the court may make similar orders in relation to foreign decrees[1], provided that it otherwise has jurisdiction over the parties[2].

1   Matrimonial and Family Proceedings Act 1984, s 17.
2   But see Matrimonial and Family Proceedings Act 1984, s 20, for a limitation where jurisdiction arises only because the matrimonial home was in England and Wales.

47.98 This power of variation is really a matter for specialist family law texts, but some important features of the jurisdiction can be noted here. The critical provision is s 24(1)(c), referring to 'any ante-nuptial or post-nuptial settlement ... made on the parties to the marriage'. This has been interpreted widely[1], and includes a trust conferring discretion on the trustees[2], the acquisition by the parties of a matrimonial home in joint names,[3] a deed of separation[4], a deed of covenant[5], some annuities[6], and even (until the law was subsequently amended[7]) some pension arrangements[8]. Moreover the settlement does not have to have been made *by* the parties, only *on* them[9] (even by will[10]), 'made on the parties to the marriage' means 'made on the parties to the marriage *or either of them*'[11], and 'made' refers back to the moment of creation of the 'settlement'[12]. Nor does the settlement need to have been made under English law[13]. Jurisdiction to vary does not depend on there having been children of the marriage[14]. And a settlement which once fell with the scope of the provision may still be varied even if the spouses have been removed as beneficiaries by the date of the hearing[15].

1   See *Prinsep v Prinsep* [1929] P 225; *Brooks v Brooks* [1996] AC 375, [1995] 3 All ER 257, HL.
2   *Marsh v Marsh* (1877) 47 LJP 34; *Vallance v Vallance* (1907) 77 LJP 33.
3   *Brown v Brown* [1959] P 86, [1959] 2 All ER 266, CA; *Dinch v Dinch* [1987] 1 All ER 818, [1987] 1 WLR 252, HL.
4   Rayden & Jackson on Divorce and Family Matters, 18th ed, para 16.172.
5   *Prinsep v Prinsep* [1929] P 225, at 232.
6   *Jump v Jump* (1883) 8 PD 159; *Nepean v Nepean* [1925] P 97; *Bosworthick v Bosworthick* [1927] P 64; cf *Brown v Brown* [1937] P 7, [1936] 2 All ER 1616, CA.
7   By the Welfare Reform and Pensions Act 1999, with effect from 1 December 2000. But there is now provision for so called 'pension-splitting' orders under ss 25B-D, and for 'pension-sharing' orders under ss 21A, 24B, 24C and 24D.
8   *Brooks v Brooks* [1996] AC 375, [1995] 3 All ER 257, HL.
9   *Paul v Paul* (1870) LR 2 P & D 93; *E v E (financial provision)* [1990] 2 FLR 233.
10 S 24(1)(c).
11 *Melvill v Melvill* [1930] P 99.
12 *C v C* [2004] EWCA Civ 1030, [2005] Fam 250 at para 53.
13 *Goff v Goff* [1934] P 107.
14 S 24(2).
15 *Compton v Compton* [1960] P 201, [1960] 2 All ER 70; *C v C [2004] EWCA Civ 1030*, [2005] Fam 250.

47.99 But there are limits. An absolute transfer or assignment is not a settlement for this purpose[1]. Nor is a trust conferring a protective life interest on the wife in the will of her father[2], or a pre-marital settlement by either party reserving power to the settlor to appoint an interest to a future spouse[3], unless (in either case) it was made in contemplation of marriage. The court's power does not extend to property which is not part of the settled property. Thus in one case it did not extend to a pension surplus which belonged to the employer company[4].

1   *Prescott v Fellowes* [1958] P 260, [1958] 3 All ER 55, CA.
2   *Loraine v Loraine* [1912] P 222, CA.
3   *Hargreaves v Hargreaves* [1926] P 42; cf *Lort-Williams v Lort-Williams* [1951] P 395, [1951] 2 All ER 241 (settlement in contemplation of marriage conferring interest on spouse by subsequent marriage).
4   *Brooks v Brooks* [1996] AC 375, [1995] 3 All ER 257, HL.

47.100 In practice all suits for divorce or nullity are commenced in the county court, and most claims for ancillary relief are dealt with there. But in big or difficult cases the whole suit, or perhaps the ancillary relief claims after the decree of divorce or nullity is granted, are transferred to the High Court. In that court, applications under s 24 to vary settlements are assigned to the Family Division rather than to the Chancery Division[1]. Once the court has jurisdiction, it may vary, not only the interest of the spouses, but also those of others taking under the settlement[2]. It may also reduce or extinguish the interest under the settlement of either spouse[3]. Where a proposed variation may affect minor children they should be separately represented[4]. The trustees may intervene or be joined to the proceedings[5]. The court may also remove the trustees from office[6]. The costs of the variation are sometimes ordered to be paid out of the settled assets[7].

1   Supreme Court Act 1981, Sch 1, para 3(a).
2   *Marsh v Marsh* (1878) 47 LJP 34; *Blood v Blood* [1902] P 78.
3   1973 Act, s 24(1)(d).
4   Family Proceedings Rules 1991, r 2,57(1); *Meldrum v Meldrum* [1970] 3 All ER 1084, [1971] 1 WLR 5.
5   *T v T* (joinder of third parties) [1996] 2 FLR 357.
6   *E v E* (financial provision) [1990] 2 FLR 233.
7   *E v E* (financial provision) [1990] 2 FLR 233.

Paragraph 2

Jurisdiction before 1926

47.101 Before 1926 the power of the court to authorise trustees to carry out transactions not expressly authorised by the settlement was derived from the inherent administrative jurisdiction of the court, and until 1901 the extent of such jurisdiction was a matter of considerable doubt.

47.102 In *Re Morrison*[1] Buckley J held that he had no jurisdiction to sanction an agreement by which trustees concurred in the conversion into a limited company of a business in which the testator was a partner, on the terms of the testator's share in the business being exchanged for shares and debentures in the new company, which were not investments authorised by the will. On the other hand, in *West of England and South Wales District Bank v Murch*[2] Fry J found it possible to sanction such an agreement.

1   [1901] 1 Ch 701; and see, to same effect, *Re Crawshay* (1888) 60 LT 357.
2   (1883) 23 Ch D 138.

Decision of the Court of Appeal in Re New

47.103 In July 1901, however, the leading case of *Re New*[1] came before the Court of Appeal, which, in the exercise of its general jurisdiction, authorised the trustees of three separate trust instruments to concur in a shareholders' scheme for the reconstruction of a limited company, under which shares settled in specie were to be exchanged for shares in a new company which the trustees were not, by their settlements, authorised to hold; the court imposed on them an undertaking to apply for leave to retain the new shares and debentures if they desired to do so beyond one year.

1   [1901] 2 Ch 534, approved by the House of Lords in *Chapman v Chapman* [1954] AC 429, [1954] 1 All ER 798.

47.104 Although the jurisdiction invoked in that case is now largely super-seded by the statutory jurisdiction discussed below (and by the rather different jurisdiction under the Variation of Trusts Act 1958, discussed in the preceding pages), the inherent jurisdiction still remains, and the principles enunciated in the judgment of the court delivered by Romer LJ still command respect, and may still afford some guidance in the exercise of the statutory jurisdiction. The following passage from the judgment was cited at length and with approval by Lord Morton of Henryton in *Chapman v Chapman*:

'As a rule, the court has no jurisdiction to give, and will not give, its sanction to the performance by trustees of acts with reference to the trust estate which are not, onthe face of the instrument creating the trust, authorised by its terms ... But in themanagement of a trust estate, and especially where that estate consists of a business or shares in a mercantile company, it not infrequently happens that some peculiar state of circumstances arises for which provision is not expressly made by the trust instrument, and which renders it most desirable, and it may be even essential, for the benefit of the estate and in the interest of all the cestuis que trust, that certain acts should be done by the trustees which in ordinary circumstances they would have no power to do. In a case of this kind, *which may reasonably be supposed to be one not foreseen or anticipated by the author of the trust*, where the trustees are embarrassed by the emergency that has arisen and the duty cast upon them to do what is best for the estate, and the consent of all the beneficiaries cannot be obtained by reason of some of them not being sui juris or in existence, then it may be right for the court, *and the court in a proper case would have jurisdiction*, to sanction on behalf of all concerned such acts on behalf of the trustees as we have above referred to. By way merely of illustration, we may take the case where a testator has declared that some property of his shall be sold at a particular time after his death, and then, owing to unforeseen change of circumstances since the testator's death, when the time for sale arrives it is found that to sell at that precise time would be ruinous to the estate, and that it is necessary or right to postpone the sale for a short time in order to effect a proper sale: in such a case the court would have jurisdiction to authorise, and would authorise, the trustees to postpone the sale for a reasonable time. It is a matter of common knowledge that the jurisdiction we have been referring to, which is only part of the general administrative jurisdiction of the court, has been constantly exercised, chiefly at chambers. Of course, the jurisdiction is one to be exercised with great caution, and the court will take care not to strain its powers. It is impossible, and no attempt ought to be made, to state or define all the circumstances under which, or the extent to which, the court will exercise the jurisdiction; but it need scarcely be said that the court will not be justified in sanctioning every act desired by trustees and beneficiaries *merely because it may appear beneficial to the estate*; and certainly the court will not be disposed to sanction transactions of a speculative or risky character. But each case brought before the court must be considered and dealt with according to its special circumstances. As a rule, these circumstances are better investigated and dealt with in chambers. Very often they involve matters of a delicate and private nature, the publication of which is not requisite on any good ground and might cause great injury to the trust estate.'

47.105 From this statement it clearly appears that even the limited and exceptional jurisdiction to sanction transactions in the nature of 'salvage' of the trust property must be exercised with the greatest caution, and does not extend to any alteration of the beneficial interests[1].

1   Cf *Re Forster's Settlement* [1954] 3 All ER 714, [1954] 1 WLR 1450, and the majority judgment in *Re Downshire Settled Estates, Re Chapman's Settlement Trusts, Re Black-well's Settlement Trusts* [1953] Ch 218 at 236, [1953] 1 All ER 103 at 112, CA; approved in *Chapman v Chapman* [1954] AC 429 at 465, [1954] 1 All ER 798 at 816, HL.

47.106 Applying the principle laid down in *Re New*[1], orders were made before 1926 to authorise or approve making advances out of capital for the benefit of an infant[2]; carrying on a business which was not presently saleable until it could be sold as a going concern; selling a business to a company in exchange for shares therein, and holding such shares for a limited period; holding, for a period, land which had been mortgaged to the trustees, and which mortgage they had foreclosed; the raising of money by mortgage of the trust property, where the estate would be ruined if money were not expended on it, or a settled policy would lapse if premiums were not paid[3]; a sale of a trust policy where it had become impossible to pay the premiums[4]; a compromise or scheme of family arrangement on behalf of infants interested under the trust[5] and making to an infant a larger allowance for maintenance than the settlor had named where the result would otherwise have been to injure the infant's prospects or to cause real property belonging to him to fall into ruin[6]. In the last-mentioned case the court even went to the extent of allowing subscriptions to charities, on the ground that the testator must have intended that the infant should be brought up and the property maintained in the mode usual amongst gentlemen holding the position to which he was born, so as to keep up the reputation of the family and estate which incidentally involved the payment of subscriptions to local charities[7].

1   [1901] 2 Ch 534.
2   Per Kekewich J in *Re Tollemache* [1903] 1 Ch 457; affd [1903] 1 Ch 955.
3   *Neill v Neill* [1904] 1 IR 513, and *Moore v Ulster Bank* (1909) 43 ILTR 136.
4   *Hill v Trenery* (1856) 23 Beav 16; *Beresford v Beresford* (1857) 23 Beav 292; *Re Wells* [1903] 1 Ch 848.
5   *Re Wells* [1903] 1 Ch 848.
6   *Re Walker* [1901] 1 Ch 879; and see also *Griggs v Gibson* (1866) 14 WR 538; *Havelock v Havelock* (1881) 17 Ch D 807; *Re Collins* (1886) 32 Ch D 229; *Bennett v Wyndham* (1857) 23 Beav 521; *Revel v Watkinson* (1748) 1 Ves Sen 93; *Greenwell v Greenwell* (1800) 5 Ves 194; and *Barnes v Ross* [1896] AC 625.
7   See *Re Walker* [1901] 1 Ch 879.

Modern inherent and statutory powers to sanction deviation

47.107 The Court of Appeal[1] recently utilised the inherent salvage juris-diction to provide the key to release of retention trust money in a building construction contract where an impasse had been reached (the unobtainability of a necessary certificate frustrating the purpose of the trust) which could not be resolved under the terms of the contract. Most of the inherent jurisdiction is now to be found in s 57 of the Trustee Act 1925, the substance of which is stated in paragraph (2), above, and with regard to settled land in s 64 of the Settled Land Act 1925, the substance of which is also stated in paragraph (2), above.

1   *Rafidain Bank v Saipem* (2 March 1994, unreported), CA.

Jurisdiction under Trustee Act 1925, s 57

47.108 With regard to s 57 of the Trustee Act 1925, it was held by the majority of the Court of Appeal in *Re Downshire's Settled Estates, Re Chapman's Settlement Trusts* and *Re Blackwell's Settlement Trusts*[1], that it must be presumed to have been the intention of Parliament in enacting the section to confer new powers on the court rather than to codify or define existing powers, though it may well be that the jurisdiction thereunder does in some degree overlap the pre-existing inherent jurisdiction. The section envis-ages (1) an act unauthorised by the trust instrument, (2) to be effected by the trustees, (3) in the management or administration of the trust property, (4) which the court will empower them to perform, (5) if in its opinion the act is expedient. The key words here are 'management' and 'administration', and though it is possible that each is capable of some shade of meaning which could not properly be attributed to the other, the subject matter of both is trust property which is vested in trustees, and this cannot, by any legitimate use of language, include the equitable interests which the settlor has created in that property. The object of s 57 is to secure that trust property should be managed as advantageously as possible in the interests of the beneficiaries and, with that object in view, to authorise specific dealings or types of dealings with the property which the court might have felt itself unable to sanction under the inherent jurisdiction, either because no actual 'emergency' had arisen, or because of inability to show that the position which called for intervention was one which the creator of the trust could not reasonably have foreseen, but it was no part of the legislative aim to disturb the rule that the court will not re-write a trust or to add to such exceptions to that rule as had already found their way into the inherent jurisdiction.

1   *Re Chapman's Settlement Trusts* [1953] Ch 218, [1953] 2 All ER 103; affd sub nom
    Chapman v Chapman [1954] AC 429, [1954] 1 All ER 798, HL; counsel stated that they
    could not contend that s 57 of the TA 1925, had any application. None of their Lordships
    either affirmed or disapproved the part of the judgment of the majority of the Court of
    Appeal, summarised above, and, accordingly, this must be taken to be good law.

47.109 The jurisdiction under s 57 co-exists side by side with that under the Variation of Trusts Act 1958[1] and, as has been seen[2], where proposals involve only the management and administration of the settled property (as opposed to the attention of beneficial interests therein) application to the court to sanction departure from the terms of a trust may be made more conveniently under s 57 than under the Act of 1958[3].

1   See para 47.26 above.
2   See para 47.56 above.
3   See eg *Re Shipwrecked Fishermen and Mariners' Royal Benevolent Society Charity* [1959] Ch 220, [1958] 3 All ER 465 (extension of a charity's investment powers) applied in *Mason v Farbrother* [1983] 2 All ER 1078; and *Anker-Petersen v Anker-Petersen* [2000] WTLR 581.

47.110 Application to the court under s 57 may be made by the trustees or a beneficiary[1] and the court may from time to time vary or rescind any order made under s 57 or may make a new or further order[2].

1   TA 1925, s 57(3).
2   TA 1925, s 57(2).

Transactions sanctioned under Trustees Act 1925, s 57

47.111 In order that it may be sanctioned by the court under s 57 of the Trustee Act 1925, the proposed transaction must be for the benefit of the whole trust and not of one beneficiary only[1] and must not be one which could be effected without praying in aid the jurisdiction of the court under the section[2].

1   *Re Craven's Estate* [1937] Ch 431, [1937] 3 All ER 33.
2   *Re Basden's Settlement Trusts* [1943] 2 All ER 11; *Re Pratt's Will Trusts* [1943] Ch 326, [1943] 2 All ER 375.

47.112 Apart from using its jurisdiction under the section to sanction a partition or sale to which the necessary consent could not be obtained[1] the court has made orders thereunder enabling the trustees of the wills of two testatrices, who had made identical residuary bequests for the foundation of a poor person's home, to blend the residuary estates into a single fund[2]; authorising a transaction involving the expenditure of capital in the purchase at a low price of the life tenant's interest thus making it possible to pay off certain mortgages of the reversionary interests, which had been sanctioned by the court, and a sum owing for estate duty on the death of a former life tenant and to preserve something for distribution among the reversioners[3]; authorising the sale by trustees of a reversionary interest, which they had no power under the settlement to sell until it fell into possession[4]; and conferring on the trustees power to invest in certain shares which were not included amongst the investments authorised by the settlement[5].

1   *Re Hope's Will Trusts* [1929] 2 Ch 136; *Re Thomas* [1930] 1 Ch 194; *Re Beale's Settlement Trusts* [1932] 2 Ch 15.
2   *Re Harvey* [1941] 3 All ER 284. In each case the testatrix had directed that the home should have the same name.
3   *Re Forster's Settlement* [1954] 3 All ER 714, [1954] 1 WLR 1450.
4   *Re Cockerell's Settlement Trusts* [1956] Ch 372, [1956] 2 All ER 172, distinguishing *Re Heyworth's Contingent Reversionary Interest* [1956] Ch 364, [1956] 2 All ER 21; but a transaction similar to that which Upjohn J was unable to sanction in the latter case for want of jurisdiction could now be approved under the Variation of Trusts Act 1958, para 47.26 ff.

5   *Re Brassey's Settlement* [1955] 1 All ER 577, [1955] 1 WLR 192. Also see *X v A* [2000] 1 All ER 490 at 495.

47.113 In considering what extended powers of investment should be conferred the court should consider the object of the trust (eg if capital appreciation were sought to enable capital purchases), the size of the trust fund (more latitude for larger funds), the width and efficacy of provisions for advice and control, while the wider the proposed powers the more should consideration be given to restricting them to a specific fraction of the fund.

47.114 In *Anker-Petersen v Anker-Petersen*[1] involving a trust fund of over £4 million the court authorised under s 57 many transactions, so enabling the trustees to take full advantage of the services of a discretionary portfolio manager authorised under the Financial Services Act 1986. First, the trustees were given power to invest in assets of any kind anywhere as if they were beneficial owners, subject to obtaining advice from an Investment Adviser, being from any person reasonably believed by the trustees to be qualified by his ability in and practical experience of financial matters to advise them on investment matters, and having regard to the need for diversification, the suitability of investments, the desirability of diminishing the risk of loss and need to strike a balance between income yield and capital appreciation. Second, the trustees were given power to hold investments in the name of nominees. Third, the trustees were given a general power to borrow money. Fourth, the trustees were empowered to employ an Investment Adviser to act as discretionary portfolio manager (thereby delegating their crucial investment role), subject to an annual review of this delegation, subject to laying down policy guidelines for the manager and using reasonable endeavours to ensure that the guidelines were observed and subject to the trustees being liable for any failure to take reasonable care in selecting a manager, fixing or enforcing the terms on which he was employed, or remedying any breaches of those terms or otherwise in supervising the manager, but not otherwise being liable for the acts or defaults of the manager. Little scope for resort to s 57 now remains after the Trustee Act 2000 conferred on trustees the powers of investment and delegation to agents, custodians or nominees.

1   [2000] WTLR 581. It must be remembered that even if trustees have power to do something they must still exercise the appropriate degree of care in deciding whether or not to do what they have power to do.

Jurisdiction under the Settled Land Act 1925, s 64

47.115 It was held by the majority of the Court of Appeal in *Re Downshire's Settled Estates*[1] that the jurisdiction under s 64 of the Settled Land Act 1925 was ampler than that under s 57 of the Trustee Act 1925. In order that a transaction may be sanctioned under the former section, it is only necessary that it should (a) be one to be effected by the tenant for life, (b) be for the benefit of the settled land or some part thereof or of the persons interested under the settlement[2] but not necessarily of both, and (c) affect or concern the settled land or other land, in England or abroad, and whether settled or not. The last requirement could, in the view of the majority of the Court of Appeal, be satisfied by transactions only indirectly operating on the settled land providing that such operation was real and substantial by ordinary common-sense standards.

1   [1953] Ch 218, [1953] 1 All ER 103, CA. There was no appeal from the Court of Appeal's decision in this case, and the SLA 1925, s 64, was not referred to by the House of Lords in *Chapman v Chapman* [1954] AC 429, [1954] 1 All ER 798. 'Trusts of land' cannot benefit from s 64 although trustees for sale of land could, until the 1996 repeal of LPA 1925, s 28 which had been held to enable reliance on s 64: *Re Simmons* [1956] Ch 125.
2   See *Re White-Popham Settled Estates* [1936] Ch 725, [1936] 2 All ER 1486, CA; *Re Earl Mount Edgcumbe* [1950] Ch 615, [1950] 2 All ER 242.

47.116 Section 64 has also been held[1] wide enough to enable trustees to transfer part of their trust property to another settlement in order to help maintain other settled property vested in the trustees, notwithstanding that such transaction might benefit some persons who were not beneficiaries under the trust. It has also been used to deal with the Duke of Marlborough's parliamentary estate at Blenheim when the Eleventh Duke and the trustees concluded that the Eleventh Duke's son as likely successor as tenant in tail would not be capable of managing the Blenheim estate. To provide for the proper future management of the estate it was held that the court could approve the Eleventh Duke conveying the estate to trustees of a new settlement on trust for sale for himself for life, then upon protective trusts for his son for life, thereafter upon the trusts of the parliamentary settlement[2].

1   *Raikes v Lygon* [1988] 1 All ER 884, 1988 1 WLR 28.
2   *Hambro v Duke of Marlborough* [1994] Ch 158, [1994] Conv 492.

Extension of powers under Trustee Act 1925 and Settled Land Act 1925

47.117 The powers conferred by s 57 of the Trustee Act 1925 and s 64 of the Settled Land Act 1925 have been extended by the Settled Land and Trustee Acts (Courts' General Powers) Act 1943[1] as stated in this paragraph.

1   Made permanent by the Emergency Laws (Miscellaneous Provisions) Act 1953, s 9.

47.118 Section 1 of this Act, as subsequently amended by s 9 of the Emergency Laws (Miscellaneous Provisions) Act 1953, provides that those powers shall include power, in the circumstances specified in subs (2), to make an order authorising any expense of action taken or proposed in or for the management of settled land or of land held on trust for sale to be treated as a capital outgoing notwithstanding that in other circumstances it could not properly have been so treated. The Act then goes on:

> (2)   The said circumstances are that the court is satisfied
>   (a)   that the action taken or proposed was or would be for the benefit of the persons entitled under the settlement, or under the trust for sale, as the case may be, generally; and either
>   (b)   that the available income from all sources of a person who, as being beneficially entitled to possession or receipt of rents and profits of the land or to reside in a house comprised therein, might otherwise have been expected to bear the expense of the action taken or proposed has been so reduced by reason of

circumstances as to render him unable to bear the expense thereof, or unable to bear it without undue hardship; or

(c)   in case in which there is no such person as aforesaid, that the income available for meeting that expense has become insufficient.

(3)   In determining whether to make such an order as aforesaid the court shall have regard to all the circumstances of the case, including the extent of the obligations, whether legally enforceable or not and whether or not relating to the land, of the person referred to in paragraph (b) of the last preceding subsection, the extent to which other persons entitled under the settlement or trust for sale are likely to benefit from the action taken or proposed or from the relief which would accrue to that person from the making of the order, and the extent to which the making of the order would be likely to involve a loss to any other person so entitled without his receiving any corresponding benefit.

(4)   Such an order as aforesaid may be made notwithstanding that the action in question was taken, or the expense thereof discharged, before the passing of this Act or before the application for the order, and the court may direct such adjustments of accounts and such repayments to be made as may appear to the court to be requisite for giving full effect to the purposes of any such order.

(5)   In this section the expression 'management' includes all the acts referred to in subsection (2) of section one hundred and two of the Settled Land Act, 1925, and references in this section to expense of management include references to the expense of the employment of a solicitor, accountant, surveyor, or other person in an advisory or supervisory capacity.

47.119 The object of this extension of powers is to enable the court to authorise the use of capital for meeting expenses which would otherwise be income expenses. Since the intention is not merely to relieve the person entitled to income but to maintain the estate for the general benefit of all persons interested under the trust, the power of the court is carefully hedged about by the provisions of subsections (2) and (3).

47.120 In *Re Scarisbrick Re-settlement Estates*[1] it was argued that the effect of the section was to restrict and not to extend the powers of the court under s 64 of the Settled Land Act 1925 since all that is authorised is the application of capital moneys in 'management' as defined by subsection (5), and that any other application of capital moneys which was formerly authorised by the 1925 Act must be treated as excluded by the 1943 Act. This contention was, however, rejected and the extent of the jurisdiction formerly exercised under section 64 of the Settled Land Act 1925 was confirmed.

[1]   [1944] Ch 229, [1944] 1 All ER 404.

Paragraph 3

47.121 As Sir GJ Turner stated in *Harrison v Randall*[1]:

'A trustee is not, in all cases, to be made liable upon the mere ground of his having deviated from the strict letter of his trust. The deviation may be necessary, or may be beneficial to the interests of the cestuis que trust, but when a trustee ventures to deviate from the letter of his trust, he does so under the obligation and at the peril of afterwards satisfying the court that the deviation was necessary or beneficial.'

¹ (1851) 9 Hare 397. Also see *Re New* [1901] 2 Ch 534, para 47.103 above.

47.122 It may be that the trust instrument contains a clause exempting a trustee from liability for any breach of trust unless dishonest or reckless¹. Such a clause will protect a trustee from liability for a deliberate breach of trust honestly believed to be in the best interests of the beneficiaries unless such belief is so unreasonable that no honest reasonable person in the shoes of the particular trustee could have held such belief².

¹ Such clauses are valid: *Armitage v Nurse* [1998] Ch 241, CA.
² *Walker v Stones* [2001] QB 902, CA.

ARTICLE 48
DUTY OF TRUSTEE TO ACT IMPARTIALLY IN THE SENSE OF
FAIRLY AND DISINTERESTEDLY, BETWEEN THE BENEFICIARIES

48.1

(1) A trustee must act fairly and disinterestedly in the execution of his trust, and not exercise his powers so as to confer an advantage on one beneficiary or class of beneficiary at the expense of another unless this apparent partiality results from the exercise of the power in question for the purpose of which it was given, affording proper consideration to the matters which are relevant and excluding from consideration matters which are irrelevant¹; he must act fairly in making investment decisions which may have differing consequences for differing classes of beneficiaries²;

(2) where the capital of the trust property is in any way augmented, the augmentation accrues for the benefit of all the beneficiaries, and is accordingly to be treated as capital and not as income³;

(3) a trustee may pay over a share to a beneficiary to whom it is presently payable without liability for any subsequent inequality which may occur by reason of the depreciation of the invest- ments of one share, or the appreciation of the investments of another, although in the absence of an express or statutory power of appropriation it seems a trustee should not appropriate a share of income of the trust property to beneficiaries without seeking the guidance of the court;

(4) where advances have to be brought into hotchpot, then, in the absence of a direction to the contrary, the necessary valuation must be made as at the date of actual distribution⁴ and, between the date for notional distribution and the actual payment or appropriation of the property to or among the persons entitled,

interest at 4% per annum must for the purposes of computation be charged against the advances and added to the income of the whole estate which is then divisible, each advanced person taking his share of the income less the 4% on his advance[5].

1   *Edge v Pensions Ombudsman* [2000] Ch 602 at 618 and 627. Also see *Lloyds Bank plc v Duker* [1987] 1 WLR 1324 where the duty of the trustee was to reject the claim of D, entitled to forty-six eightieths of the trust fund including 999 shares in a private company with share capital of 1000 shares, to have 574 of the 999 shares transferred to him, the trustees having to sell the 999 shares and then transfer forty-six eightieths of the proceeds of sale to D, so that D could not acquire a greater amount by acquiring the majority shareholding and selling it.
2   Per Hoffmann J in *Nestle v National Westminster Bank plc* [2000] WTLR 795 at 803.
3   *Re Barton's Trust* (1868) LR 5 Eq 238; *Bouch v Sproule* (1887) 12 App Cas 385. As to apportionment of income on death of life tenant, see *Re Jowitt* [1922] 2 Ch 442. It cannot be left to trustees to resolve problems by determining whether an augmentation is to capital or to income, so ousting the jurisdiction of the court: *Re Raven* [1915] 1 Ch 673 at 677; *Re Bronson* (1958) 14 DLR (2d) 51. However, the settlor can confer power on his trustees to allocate augmentations, whether objectively capital or income augmentations, to the income or capital accounts, so leaving the trustees unhampered in their efforts to act impartially or fairly between income and capital beneficiaries.
4   *Re Hillas-Drake* [1944] Ch 235, [1944] 1 All ER 375, and *Re Slee* [1962] 1 All ER 542, [1962] 1 WLR 496, not following *Re Gunther's Will Trusts* [1939] Ch 985, [1939] 3 All ER 291; *Re Oram* [1940] Ch 1001, [1940] 4 All ER 161.
5   *Re Forster-Brown* [1914] 2 Ch 584; and *Re Cooke* [1916] 1 Ch 480, and cases there cited.

Paragraph 1

Discretionary distributive powers

48.2 Where trustees are trustees for a class of discretionary beneficiaries with wide-ranging powers of appointment or are trustees of a pension scheme with flexible powers capable of benefiting the employer or current employees or pensioners or particular classes thereof, it is envisaged that the trustees will benefit some persons or classes of persons more than others where the trustees consider it appropriate. As Chadwick LJ has stated[1]:

'Properly understood, the so-called duty to act impartially is no more than the ordinary duty which the law imposes on a person who is entrusted with the exercise of a discretionary power: that he exercises the power for the purpose for which it is given, giving proper consideration to the matters which are relevant and excluding from consideration matters which are irrelevant. If trustees do that, they cannot be criticised if they reach a decision which appears to prefer the claims of one interest over others. The preference will be the result of a proper exercise of the discretionary power.'

1   *Edge v Pensions Ombudsman* [2000] Ch 602 at 627.

48.3 Scott V-C has pointed out[1]:

'The judge may disagree with the manner in which the trustees have exercised their discretion but, unless they can be seen to have taken into account irrelevant, improper or irrational factors, or unless their decision can be said to be one that no reasonable body of trustees properly directing themselves could have reached, the judge cannot interfere. In particular, he cannot interfere simply on the ground that the partiality showed to the preferred beneficiaries was, in his opinion, undue.'

[1]   [2000] Ch 602 at 618. Further see Article 61 below.

Choice of investments

48.4 Again, where trustees have a choice of investments, they must not exercise that choice for the *sole* benefit of the tenant for life, by investing upon a highly productive but insecure property[1]. 'The obligation of a trustee is to administer the trust fund impartially or fairly, having regard to the different interests of beneficiaries'[1]. He can take into account the income needs of a life tenant and the fact that the life tenant was close to the settlor (eg his widow) and a primary object of the trust, whilst the remainderman is a remoter relative or wealthy stranger, so as to tilt the balance in favour of the penurious life tenant even if this could lead to the real value of the capital being eroded[2].

[1]   *Raby v Ridehalgh* (1855) 7 De GM & G 104; and *Stuart v Stuart* (1841) 3 Beav 430; cf *Beauclerk v Ashburnham* (1845) 8 Beav 322. The first of these cases was applied in *Re Pauling's Settlement, Younghusband v Coutts & Co (No 2)* [1963] Ch 576, [1963] 1 All ER 857. There, Wilberforce J made it clear that the trustee's duty in matters of investment to hold an equitable balance between capital and income is paramount. A trustee who has committed a breach of trust and claims that this was instigated by the life tenant and that he has therefore a right to recoup his liability out of the trust income, has no right to regulate investment policy for the purpose of ensuring that the income is substantial enough to cover this liability; still less to oppose the appointment by the court of other trustees to replace him on the ground that it would prevent him from exercising such a right. A trustee's right of recoupment does not end with his trusteeship.

[2]   *Nestle v National Westminster Bank* [1994] 1 All ER 118 at 136 per Staughton LJ. This may require sale of a shareholding settled by S on his mother for life, remainder to himself where income is low though capital appreciation is high: *Re Smith* (1971) 16 DLR (3d) 130 upheld 18 DLR (3d) 405.

[3]   *Nestle v National Westminster Bank* [1994] 1 All ER 118 at 137 and by Hoffmann J at first instance (29 June 1988, unreported) where he emphasised that the trustees must not be judged on individual investments but on the whole portfolio of investments.

48.5 However, if, to benefit the testator's widow as life tenant of a testamentary trust, the trustees sell the main asset, a farm, and invest the proceeds solely in fixed interest securities to produce a high income, without diversifying into stocks and shares for capital growth purposes, the trustees will be liable for breach of trust[1].

[1]   *Re Mulligan* [1998] 1 NZLR 481.

48.6 A trustee can even take its own position into account where it has an equitable lien over the trust fund covering its liabilities as trustee to third parties, but it must act in a fair even-handed fashion as between the beneficiaries and itself[1].

[1]   *X v A* [2000] 1 All ER 490 at 495.

Discretionary distribution of capital growth as if income

48.7 In trust law capital is to income as land is to the harvest therefrom and as a tree is to the fruit thereof, while economists and investors consider income to be the maximum amount a person can spend in a year and still expect to be as well off at the end of the year as at the beginning. This is the concept of total return consisting of income yield plus capital growth[1]. Thus, if £1 million of trust assets appreciate to be worth £1,100,000 at the end of the year and yield income of £40,000, then the total return of £140,000 (less an amount for inflation) can be distributed as if it were income, and not just the actual £40,000 income, if the terms of the trust permit payment of capital (at least to the extent of £100,000) to income beneficiaries. While the trustee is obliged to pay out the actual £40,000 income to income beneficiaries, it has a discretion as to what extent, if any, it exercises any discretionary power to distribute capital to income beneficiaries. It must bear in mind that if, in its discretion pursuant to a power in that behalf, it distributes the whole of the total return each year, then the value of the trust fund will not grow so as to protect the capital beneficiaries from inflation.

[1] *Cowan v Scargill* [1985] Ch 270 at 287; Lord Nicholls in 'Trustees and their Broader Community' (1995) 9 Trust LI 71 at 75; *JW v Morgan Trust Company of the Bahamas Ltd* (2002) 4 ITELR 541.

48.8 It may be that the trustee forms an investment company to hold the portfolio of investments or that such a company with an extensive portfolio of investments is transferred to the trustee to create the trust property. If the company accounts are properly drawn up on the basis that profits and gains on investments are income of the company, this does not mean that such profits and gains are to be regarded as income of a life tenant under the trust that owns the company. However, dividends declared by such company out of the company's available income (including profits and gains) would rank as income of the trust to be distributed to the life tenant, but the trustee controlling the company under a duty as trustee to act fairly is not obliged to distribute by way of dividend all profits and gains on investments, although it should so distribute for the benefit of the life tenant the actual income yield from the investments owned by the company[1] as income to which the life tenant is entitled on trust accountancy principles.

[1] *JW v Morgan Trust Company of the Bahamas Ltd* (2002) 4 ITELR 541; and *see Lloyds Bank plc v Duker* [1987] 1 WLR 1324. If there was a power in the trust instrument for the trustees not to exercise their controlling rights to ensure the company declares a dividend (often a standard power), then the trustees would not be obliged to declare a dividend of the actual income yield unless they considered this appropriate in all the circumstances.

Trustee must not exert influence against the interest of a beneficiary

48.9 On the principle enunciated in the article now under consideration, trustees must not threaten to exert their influence with third parties to the prejudice of one of their beneficiaries, in order to coerce him into consenting to a disposition of the trust property more favourable to another of the beneficiaries than would be the case if the settlement were strictly performed[1].

1   *Ellis v Barker* (1871) 7 Ch App 104.

Annuities

48.10 On the principle that one beneficiary should not be preferred at the expense of another, where an annuity is payable out of income, the trustees will often have no power to accumulate surplus income for the purpose of better securing the annuity[1]. But the question is one of intention, and the position will usually be different if the annuity constitutes a continuing charge on income: thus Russell LJ said in *Re Berkeley*[2]:

> 'It is well settled that in the ordinary case where a testamentary annuity is charged on both income and capital of the estate, the annuitant is entitled to require the executors not to part with any income or capital of residue lest it should turn out later that the estate is in fact otherwise insufficient to meet the annuity: see *Re Coller's Deed Trusts*[3]. This right is not, however, absolute, and distribution is not held up where it could not prejudice the annuitant: see *Re Coller*.'

1   *Re Platt* [1916] 2 Ch 563. See also *Re Chance's Will Trusts* [1962] Ch 593, [1962] 1 All ER 942.
2   [1968] Ch 744, [1968] 3 All ER 364, CA.
3   [1939] Ch 277, [1937] 3 All ER 292.

48.11 Where resort may be had to capital for the payment of an annuity if the income of a fund is insufficient to discharge it, and the trustees have had such resort, the capital beneficiaries are not entitled to be recouped from surplus income of subsequent years the amounts of capital applied in this way[1].

1   *Re Croxon* [1915] 2 Ch 290, followed in *Re Berkeley* [1968] Ch 744, [1968] 3 All ER 364, CA.

48.12 Where the payment of an annuity falls into arrears because there is insufficient income to pay it, and the income of the trust fund later increases, the arrears must be discharged but the annuitant cannot claim interest on them[1].

1   *Torre v Browne* (1855) 5 HL Cas 555, followed in *Re Berkeley* [1968] Ch 744, [1968] 3 All ER 364, CA.

48.13 An annuitant is not entitled to require the capitalised value of his annuity to be paid to him[1]. But if T by will directs that an annuity be purchased for A for life A is entitled to take the purchase money instead of the annuity[2]. If, instead, T had conferred a power on his executors and trustee to purchase an annuity for A, the executor and trustee has power to pay the purchase money to A instead of purchasing an annuity[3].

1   *Wright v Callender* (1852) 2 De GM & G 652. Only if those entitled to capital consented could the annuitant obtain the capitalised value of his annuity.

2   *Stokes v Cheek* (1860) 28 Bear 620; *Re Robbins* [1907] 2 Ch 8.
3   *Messeena v Carn* (1870) LR 9 Eq 260; *Re Mabbett* [1891] 1 Ch 707.

Tax-free annuities: rule in Re Pettit

48.14 An annuitant under a trust is in the same position with regard to income tax as any other annuitant. The annuity is a separate source of taxable income[1] from which, whether or not it is paid out of taxed income, tax at the basic rate is deductible on payment by the trustees to the annuitant[2].

1   Schedule D, Case III (Income and Corporation Taxes Act 1988, s 18(3)).
2   Income and Corporation Taxes Act 1988, s 348.

48.15 An agreement for the payment of an annuity without deduction of tax is void[1], but this rule applies only to agreements to pay in full without allowing for the deduction of tax[2], and does not apply when the true agreement is merely that the payer, and not the payee, is to bear the tax. Provisions for the payment of an annuity 'free of tax' have been construed in this way and held valid[3], and the House of Lords has confirmed this construction and indicated that it should be applied to all such provisions[4]. An annuity incorporating a provision of this kind is therefore considered as an annuity of a gross sum from which tax at the basic rate has been deducted on payment[5]. The beneficiary's circumstances (with personal allowances and reliefs) may, however, be such as not to render him liable to suffer tax at the basic rate on the whole annuity, and in that event he is accountable to the trustees for so much of the repayment received as is attributable to the annuity in accordance with the rule in *Re Pettit*[6]. This rule applies only where the annuity is free of tax at the annuitant's effective rate (ie a rate dependent on the annuitant's personal circumstances); where the annuity is free of tax at the basic rate irrespective of the annuitant's personal circumstances, no refund of tax recovered falls to be made by the annuitant to the trustees[7]. This distinction must be drawn upon a proper interpretation of the wording of the will or settlement[8]. The question whether the annuity is or is not free of higher rate tax requires to be settled similarly.

1   Taxes Management Act 1970, s 106(2).
2   *Ferguson v IRC* [1970] AC 442, [1969] 1 All ER 1025, HL.
3   *Festing v Taylor* (1862) 3 B & S 235; *Burroughes v Abbott* [1922] 1 Ch 86; *Re Goodson's Settlement* [1943] Ch 101, [1943] 1 All ER 201.
4   *Ferguson v IRC* [1970] AC 442, [1969] 1 All ER 1025, HL.
5   See per Lord Sands in *Hunter's Trustees v Mitchell* 1930 SC 978, approved in *IRC v Cook* [1946] AC 1, [1945] 2 All ER 377, HL.
6   [1922] 2 Ch 765.
7   *Re Jones* [1933] Ch 842.
8   In *Re Pettit* [1922] 2 Ch 765, an annuity 'free of tax' was held to mean free of tax at the annuitant's effective rate. Decisions to the same effect were reached in *Re Maclennan* [1939] Ch 750, [1939] 3 All ER 81, CA, on the words 'clear of all deductions for income tax'; in *Re Jubb* (1941) 20 ATC 297, on the words 'free of death duties and all other taxes'; and in *Re Tatham* [1945] Ch 34, [1945] 1 All ER 29, where the annuitant was held accountable, inter alia, for postwar credits. In *Re Jones* [1933] Ch 842, the words 'such annuity as after deducting income tax at the current rate for the time being would amount to a clear yearly sum of ... ' was held to mean free of tax at the standard rate; cf *Re Eves* [1939] Ch 969, where an annuity free of income tax at the current rate for the time being deductible at source was considered to be free of tax at the annuitant's effective rate. For

cases where the tax-free element was restricted to a certain rate by the instrument itself, see *Re Bates' Wills Trust* [1946] Ch 83, [1945] 2 All ER 688; *Re Arno* [1947] Ch 198, [1947] 1 All ER 64, CA.

48.16 Where the rule applies the annuitant is obliged[1] to claim the allowances and reliefs[2] due to him and to pay to the trustees the whole or part of any refund of tax so received, the proportion being calculated in accordance with the method laid down in *IRC v Cook*[3]. The annuitant's refund to the trustees is calculated from the value of his personal allowances and reliefs which is apportioned between the gross annuity and the annuitant's total income; the part apportioned to the annuity is refunded to the trustees. The refund so received by the trustees may be regarded as net income of the trust in the year in which it is received by the trustees. It may be distributed to beneficiaries as a net sum which has borne tax, and, in appropriate cases, will reduce any liability under s 3 of the Income and Corporation Taxes Act 1988 if the gross amount of the annuity exceeds the taxed income of the trust. If the annuitant is liable to higher rate tax (or the investment income surcharge if reintroduced) he is entitled to claim a proportion of his excess liability (that is, the liability in excess of tax at the basic rate) from the trustees, calculated in the ratio which the gross annuity bears to his total income.

1 *Re Kingcome* [1936] Ch 566, [1936] 1 All ER 173.
2 As to the allowances and reliefs which come within the rule, see Simon's Taxes, E 2.1123 ff.
3 [1946] AC 1, [1945] 2 All ER 377, HL. The calculation of the refund is explained in detail in Simon's Taxes E 2.1125 ff from which the following comment is quoted: 'It is apparent from a study of the speeches of the majority (Viscount Maugham, Lord Thankerton and Lord Porter) and of the dissenting speeches (Lord Russell of Killowen and Lord Simonds) in *IRC v Cook* [1946] AC 1, [1945] 2 All ER 377 and from the formula employed before that decision, that the whole method of calculation is fraught with difficulty. It would appear that no method suggested in argument or in speeches completely carries out the intention of the testator and is at the same time completely in accordance with the provisions of the Income Tax Acts. But the present method of calculating the gross annuity, whatever the results and complications in applying it, is in itself simple and definite.'

Depreciation reserves

48.17 Where trustees are lawfully managing a business the trustees are justified in setting aside part of the profits for depreciation before determining net profits[1], though where trustees own a company carrying on a business it is the dividends declared in respect of shares in the company that are the income of the trust[2]. There seems scope for developing the trustees' duty of fairness or impartiality so as to justify taking a depreciation reserve where assets in the trust fund are in fact depreciating to the point where the remainderman is suffering an actual disadvantage in relation to the income beneficiary[3], particularly if the trustees have power in the trust instrument to allocate receipts or expenditure to income or capital as they deem appropriate.

1 *Re Crabtree* [1912] WN 24, 106 LT 49, CA; *McBride v Hudson* (1962) 107 CLR 604 at 623; *Re Hunter* [1958] 77 NZLR 654 at 660; *Re Katz* (1980) 112 DLR (3d) 529.
2 *Comr of Taxes v Pratt Estate Co Ltd* [1934] NZLR 347.
3 *Re Zive* (1977) 77 DLR (3d) 669 at 680 where the trust fund consisted almost entirely of 19 investment properties leased to tenants.

Paragraph 2

Augmentation of capital[1]

48.18 Where a company, out of a reserve fund, pays up unissued capital, and allots it credited as fully paid among old shareholders, any shares so allotted to trustees will be held by them as capital and as an accretion to the shares originally held by them, and will not belong to the person entitled to the trust income[2].This is only logical when it is remembered that the true effect of the new issue is not to increase the holding because the persons to whom the new shares are issued will continue to hold the same proportion of the capital[3].

---

[1]   The notes to this paragraph deal with the question of when an accretion to the trust fund is to be treated as capital, and when as income.
[2]   *Bouch v Sproule* (1887) 12 App Cas 385; *Re Northage* (1891) 60 LJ Ch 488; *Re Joel* [1936] 2 All ER 962; *Re Wright's Settlement Trusts* [1945] Ch 211, [1945] 1 All ER 587.
[3]   *Re Whitfield* [1920] WN 256.

Bonuses

48.19 So where bonuses are paid *as part of capital*, they will be retained as capital by the trustee; but where bonuses are mere expressions for extra dividend income, this will not be the case. As Fry LJ said in *Re Bouch*[1] in a passage quoted with approval by Lord Herschell in giving judgment on the same case in the House of Lords (where the House of Lords rejected the Court of Appeal's inference of fact that the company intended the bonuses to be income rather than capital)[2]:

> 'When a testator or settlor directs or permits the subject of his disposition to remain as shares or stock in a company which has the power either of distributing its profits as dividend, or of converting them into capital, and the company validly exercises this power, such exercise of its power is binding on all persons interested under him, the testator or settlor, in the shares, and consequently what is paid by the company as dividend goes to the tenant for life, and what is paid by the company to the shareholder as capital, or appropriated as an increase of the capital stock in the concern, enures to the benefit of all who are interested in the capital'[3].

---

[1]   (1885) 29 Ch D 635 at 653; For capital intentions see *Re Evans* [1913] 1 Ch 23; *Re Ogilvie* (1919) 35 TLR 218; *IRC v Blott* [1921] 2 AC 171; *Re Taylor* [1926] 1 Ch 923; *IRC v Wright* [1927] 1 KB 333.
[2]   (1887) 12 App Cas 385 at 397.
[3]   For income intentions see *Re Northage* (1891) 60 LJ Ch 488; *Re Tindal* (1892) 9 TLR 24; *Re Malam* [1894] 3 Ch 578; *Re Despard* (1901) 17 TLR 478 and *Re Hume Nisbet's Settlement* (1911) 27 TLR 461, where Eve J admitted that but for *Re Northage* (supra) (which may, in any event, be distinguished as a more complex scheme where the option to take bonus shares was not available to all shareholders receiving the dividend) he would have had difficulty in distinguishing his case from *Bouch v Sproule* (supra) where a capital intention was found: perhaps the income cases other than *Re Northage* were wrongly decided. As to the principles on which profits ought to be ascertained by companies, see *Lubbock v British Bank of South America* [1892] 2 Ch 198; and *Re Taylor* [1926] Ch 923. In *Re Outen's Will Trusts* [1963] Ch 291, [1962] 3 All ER 478, Plowman J held, following *Bouch v Sproule*, above, that a company's decision to capitalise reserves of profits by issuing loan stock to ordinary shareholders effected a capitalisation of the profits which was binding on the shareholders so as to make the loan stock capital in the hands of trustees.

48.20 To understand problems in ascertaining, in the light of case law, what a company's intentions were, it is necessary to appreciate that by virtue of s 25 of the Companies Act 1867 the procedure adopted in *Bouch v Sproule* (and cases after the Companies Act 1900 where old habits died hard) in issuing new shares involved the company: (a) declaring a dividend and issuing a dividend warrant to its shareholders; (b) allotting the new shares to those shareholders; and (c) giving the shareholders the option either to cash the dividend warrant or have the dividend applied in paying up the allotted shares.

48.21 An illuminating explanation of *Bouch v Sproule* was given in the Privy Council case of *Hill v Permanent Trustee Co of New South Wales*[1], where Lord Russell of Killowen laid down the following principles:

'(1)   A limited company when it parts with moneys available for distribution among its shareholders is not concerned with the fate of those moneys in the hands of any shareholder. The company does not know and does not care whether a shareholder is a trustee of his share or not. It is of no concern to a company which is parting with moneys to a shareholder whether that shareholder (if he be a trustee) will hold them as trustee for A absolutely or as trustee for A for life only.

(2)   A limited company not in liquidation can make no payment by way of return of capital to its shareholders except in an authorised reduction of capital. Any other payment made by it by means of which it parts with moneys to its shareholders must and can only be by way of dividing profits. Whether the payment is called "dividend" or "bonus", or any other name, it must still remain a payment on division of profits.

(3)   Moneys so paid to a shareholder will (if he be a trustee) prima facie belong to the person beneficially entitled to the income of the trust estate. If such moneys or any part thereof are to be treated as part of the corpus of the trust estate there must be some provision in the trust deed which brings about that result.

(4)   Other considerations arise when a limited company with power to increase its capital and possessing a fund of undivided profits, so deals with it that no part leaves the possession of the company, but the whole is applied in paying up new shares which are issued and allotted proportionately to the shareholders, who would have been entitled to receive the fund had it been, in fact, divided and paid away as dividend.

(5)   The result of such a dealing is obviously wholly different from the result of paying away the profits to the shareholders. In the latter case the amount of cash distributed disappears on both sides of the company's balance sheet ... the cash necessary to provide the dividend is raised and paid away, the company's assets being reduced by that amount. In the former case the assets of the company remain undiminished ... '

[1]   [1930] AC 720 at 730–732; following *Re Bates* [1928] Ch 682. *Re Ward's Will Trusts* [1936] Ch 704, [1936] 2 All ER 773, appears not to be good law; see *Re Doughty* [1947] Ch 263, [1947] 1 All ER 207; *Hill v Permanent Trustee Co of New South Wales*, above, was distinguished in *Re Outen's Will Trusts* (see para 48.19 above).

48.22 Moneys received by trustees on the distribution amongst shareholders of a share premium account through the medium of a reduction petition are capital assets in their hands. Section 130 of the Companies Act 1985, which requires all premiums on the issue of shares to be placed to the credit of a share premium account which can only be applied in specified ways, takes the moneys in the account out of the category of divisible profit and prevents them from being distributed by way of dividend. The only way in which they can be distributed among the shareholders is by a transaction to which the provisions relating to reduction of capital apply or in the guise of the premium payable on the redemption of redeemable preference shares. In the former case there is a reduction in the value of every share and thus a reduction of capital though not of share capital[1].

¹   *Re Duff's Settlement Trusts* [1951] Ch 923, [1951] 2 All ER 534, CA.

48.23 Where shares are transferred under a scheme of arrangement or debentures are issued in lieu of arrears of dividend or interest they must be treated as income even although an additional bonus of 1% is added as a solatium[1], and the same course is adopted on the distribution of a reserve fund which has never been capitalised[2]. In another case, a scheme was sanctioned by the court under what is now s 425 of the Companies Act 1985, and cash and debentures of another company were issued to trustees in satisfaction of amounts due to them from a company under debentures in respect of both capital and arrears of interest (and in respect of interest agreed to be paid on these arrears). It was held that a fraction of the assets thus received by the trustees should be treated as income, the fraction bearing the same proportion to the whole of the assets received as the arrears of interest (and the interest thereon) bore to the total amount of principal and arrears of interest (and interest thereon) secured by the original debentures when the scheme was approved[3].

¹   *Re Pennington* [1915] WN 333; *Re Sandbach* [1933] Ch 505; *Re Smith's Will Trusts* [1936] 2 All ER 1210.
²   *Re Thomas* [1916] 2 Ch 331, CA.
³   *Re Morris' Will Trusts* [1960] 3 All ER 548, [1960] 1 WLR 1210, following *Re Atkinson* [1904] 2 Ch 160, and *Smith v Law Guarantee and Trust Society Ltd* [1904] 2 Ch 569, and explaining and distinguishing *Re Pennington* [1914] 1 Ch 203.

48.24 As Lord Reid stated in *Rae v Lazard Investments Co Ltd*[1] the current position is that 'there is no doubt that every distribution of money or money's worth by an English company must be treated as income in the hands of the shareholders unless it is either a distribution in a liquidation, a repayment in respect of reduction of capital (or a payment out of a special premium account) or an issue of bonus shares (or it may be bonus debentures)'. To these exceptions must be added, by analogy with reductions of share capital, the proceeds of a purchase by a company of its own shares; also the declaration of a dividend immediately used to satisfy a contemporaneous call of unpaid share capital[2] and the type of indirect merger dealt with in *Sinclair v Lee*[3], which can be understood after considering the 'capital profits dividends' cases arising out of the nationalisation of Thomas Tilling & Co Ltd.

¹   [1963] 1 WLR 555 at 565.
²   *Re Hatton* [1917] 1 Ch 357.
³   [1993] Ch 497.

48.25 *The trustee's duties*

'Capital profits dividends'

48.25 In *Re Doughty*[1] a company had declared an 'additional dividend or distribution' out of capital profits, ie profits resulting from the realisation of capital assets, and it was held that they fell under the word 'income' in the will in question, although not subject to income tax in the hands of the recipient.

1   [1947] Ch 263, [1947] 1 All ER 207.

48.26 The distribution of a sum of British Transport Stock by way of 'capital profits dividend' upon the nationalisation of a part of the undertaking of Thomas Tilling & Co Ltd led to a number of applications to the court[1].

1   See CII Law Journal 270.

48.27 In *Re Sechiari*[1] and *Re Kleinwort's Settlements*[2], in neither of which cases any special circumstances existed, it was held that the British Transport Stock was received by trustee shareholders as income and not as capital and, accordingly, it belonged to the tenant for life, but Romer J in the one case, and Vaisey J in the other, indicated that jurisdiction to apportion existed and would be exercised in a proper case.

1   [1950] 1 All ER 417.
2   [1951] Ch 860, [1951] 2 All ER 328.

48.28 In *Re Rudd's Will Trusts*[1] it was held that the failure of the trustees to sell the whole or part of the Tilling Stock before it went ex-dividend and thus realise a large profit for capital was not a breach of trust such as would bring the jurisdiction to apportion into play, and that no part of the British Transport Stock ought to be apportioned to capital.

1   [1952] 1 All ER 254.

48.29 In *Re Winder's Will Trusts*[1] the application was made by trustees of the will of a testator who had died before the distribution of British Transport Stock, but after the right to it crystallised so that it formed an asset of his estate before his death. It was held by Romer J that in the circumstances the stock when received ought to be treated as capital for the purposes of the trusts of the will.

1   [1951] Ch 916, [1951] 2 All ER 362.

48.30 In *Re Maclaren's Settlement Trusts*[1] the tenant for life assented to the purchase as a capital investment of stock of Thomas Tilling & Co Ltd at a time when it was known that that company proposed to distribute the British Transport Stock it received amongst its stockholders. He subsequently requested the sale of both the Tilling Stock and British Transport Stock and its re-investment in the purchase of a freehold house as a residence for himself. It was held that in the circumstances the Transport Stock and the proceeds of its sale had 'assumed the guise of capital'.

1   [1951] 2 All ER 414.

Demergers

48.31 A demerger involves a company hiving off part of its business to a new company and arranging for its shareholders to receive the shares in the new company. Thus one capital asset, the shares in the distributing company, is converted into two capital assets, the shares in the distributing company plus the shares in the new demerged company. A direct demerger involves the distributing company hiving off a part of its business to a subsidiary and then distributing shares in the subsidiary or a holding company thereof by way of an in specie dividend to its shareholders. In such a case the receipt by trustees of shares in the demerged company will continue to be an income receipt following *Re Sechiari*[1], *Re Kleinworts Settlements*[2] and *Briggs v IRC*[3] unless the House of Lords on appeal can be persuaded to take a more realistic course.

1   [1950] 1 All ER 417.
2   [1951] Ch 860.
3   (1932) 17 TC 11 and *Re Doughty* [1947] Ch 263.

48.32 In the case of indirect demergers Nicholls V-C[1] was able to distinguish the above cases to take the realistic course of holding the shares in the new indirectly demerged company to be capital, it being crucial in such an indirect demerger that the distributing company does not own the shares in the demerged company which are transferred to its shareholders.

1   *Sinclair v Lee* [1993] Ch 497.

Enhanced scrip dividends

48.33 With conventional scrip dividends a company declares a dividend but gives each shareholder the option to take the dividend either as cash or as bonus shares. The receipt is income in nature, even if the shareholder elects to take the bonus shares because the company's intention was to pay a dividend and not to capitalise its profits: the number of bonus shares is calculated by dividing the amount of the dividend receivable by the ex-dividend market value of the shares. Enhanced scrip dividends differ because the bonus shares are issued at a price below their current market value, so that if a shareholder elects to receive shares he will get assets of greater value than the cash dividend. Indeed, the company often arranges for a third party to be ready to purchase the bonus shares at market value so that the shareholders can quickly realise the cash value of the shares. In ascertaining the company's intention as required by *Bouch v Sproule* it seems that for various reasons (like avoiding Advance Corporation Tax, before its abolition, while maintaining a regular distribution policy) the company intends shareholders to take scrip, because it is deliberately made worth much more than the cash dividend, so that the bonus shares, and the proceeds of sale thereof, are capital[1].

1   *Hawkins v Hawkins* (1920) SR (NSW) 550.

48.34 To obtain most for the trust the trustees should take the bonus shares but to reimburse the life tenant for lost income they could exercise, if it exists, a power to pay out of capital a sum corresponding to the amount of cash dividend. Alternatively, because the Revenue have accepted[1] that *Re Malam*[2] can be applied to capital profits, the trustees can elect to allow the life tenant a lien over the bonus shares to the amount of the cash dividend, and satisfy the lien out of capital cash.

[1] SP4/94.
[2] [1894] 3 Ch 578.

48.35 It is, however, possible for trustees to take the factual view that the company with its enhanced scrip dividend policy was not, as in the *Bouch v Sproule* capitalisation cases, concerned to find a way of capitalising profits and issuing new shares, but had a policy developed from the conventional scrip dividend scheme where the intention is to pay dividend income but with the difference that the bonus shares are issued well below market value, such being part of a regular distribution policy so as not to be a 'special' or 'bonus' dividend.

48.36 The Revenue will accept the capital approach, the *Malam* approach or the income approach if supportable, as will often be the case on the particular facts involved, so that the tax consequences will much influence the approach to be adopted.

Profit on realisation of investments

48.37 It need scarcely be pointed out that where, on a change of investment, trust securities realise more than was given for them originally, the profit accrues to capital, and is not considered as income payable to the tenant for life. In the same way, where trustees of a mortgage debt foreclose, and subsequently sell the property for more than the debt and arrears of interest and costs, the balance is to be held by them as an augmentation to the capital of the trust fund. For as any diminution of the trust property would have to be borne by all the beneficiaries, and would not fall on the tenant for life only, so it is only fair that any casual augmentation should belong to all, and not merely to the life tenant.

Stocks purchased or sold by trustees 'cum dividend'

48.38 When trustees invest capital in the purchase of stocks or shares, on which, at the date of purchase, dividends have been earned and declared, but not paid, such dividends must be carried to capital and not paid as income[1]. The fairness of this is obvious. But it is also settled (with less obvious fairness) that, in the absence of special circumstances, no apportionment of income will be made where stocks are sold between two dividend days[2]. This appears to

be founded merely on convenience, for Kindersley V-C in *Scholefield v
Redfern*[3], while admitting that much might be said in favour of apportionment in such cases, said:

> 'When we consider a little further, it is obvious, that if the tenant for life is to
> have something out of the sale money, as representing income, then when the
> trustees invest the money, unless they invest it on the very day on which the
> dividend has just accrued due, the same equity ought to be administered the
> other way, and we ought to take from the tenant for life something of his next
> dividend ... and add that to the capital, in order to make things equal as
> between him and the remainderman. It is clear that if there is an equity one
> way, there is an equity the other way. It is obvious that the reason why such
> equity on either side has never been administered habitually by this court is,
> that by attempting it, a grievous burden would be imposed upon the estates of
> testators, by reason of the complex investigations which it would lead to.'

[1]   *Re Sir Robert Peel's Settled Estates* [1910] 1 Ch 389.
[2]   *Bulkeley v Stephens* [1896] 2 Ch 241; *Scholefield v Redfern* (1863) 2 Drew & Sm 173;
      Freman v Whitbread (1865) LR 1 Eq 266; *Re Henderson* [1940] Ch 368, [1940] 1 All ER
      623.
[3]   (1863) 2 Drew & Sm 173 at 182.

48.39 Again, in *Re Henderson*[1] Morton J pointed out the difficulty of
ascertaining by what sum the purchase price was increased by reason of the
fact that a dividend was accruing, and said:

> 'Let me assume that the dividend was paid half-yearly, that the tenant for life
> dies when three months of the half-year has expired, and that the investment is
> sold two months later. Can it ever be ascertained with accuracy what portion of
> the purchase-price represents five-sixths of the half-yearly dividend which is
> accruing?'

[1]   [1940] Ch 368, [1940] 1 All ER 623.

48.40 But the practice does not hold where the dividend is declared, but not
paid at the date of the sale[1].

[1]   *Re Sir Robert Peel's Settled Estates* [1910] 1 Ch 389.

48.41 In *Re Winterstoke's Will Trusts*[1] Clauson J with a view to preserving
the rights between tenant for life and remainderman, declared that the trustees
ought to apportion the purchase price of shares in a certain way between
capital and income. His decision was shortly afterwards criticised in *Re Firth*[2]
by Farwell J who said that only very special circumstances would justify the
process applied by Clauson J and found no such circumstances in the case
before him.

[1]   [1938] Ch 158, [1937] 4 All ER 63.
[2]   [1938] Ch 517, [1938] 2 All ER 217; explained, *Re Henderson* [1940] Ch 368, [1940]
      1 All ER 623.

48.42 These two cases were considered in *Re MacLaren's Settlement Trusts*
by Harman J who said[1]:

'The court can, then, in special circumstances apportion between capital and income on sale or purchases of stock cum dividend or ex dividend, although it is not the practice to do so in the ordinary way because the various persons interested under settlements ought to take the rough with the smooth, and in order to ease the burden falling on trustees. The jurisdiction, however, exercised in special circumstances seems to be only the exercise of a right to make a more exact distinction of income from capital. As a matter of convenience, the practice is in the ordinary case that no apportionments are made, with the result that capital sometimes gets what, on a more exact scrutiny, would prove to be income or vice versa. Where this produces a glaring injustice, the court will cause a more exact calculation to be made, but it does not treat as income that which is capital, or as capital that which is income.'

1   [1951] 2 All ER 414 at 420; para 48.30 above.

48.43 In *Re Ellerman*[1] Nourse J therefore considered *Re Winterstoke's WT* to be wrong so that it ought not to be followed.

1   [1984] LS Gaz R 430, more fully reported sub nom *Hitch v Ruegg* [1986] TL & P 62.

48.44 Where stocks were directed to be transferred in specie to a class on the death of a life tenant, but for convenience of division were sold and the proceeds divided, then, as his personal representatives would, under the Apportionment Act, have been entitled to an apportionment of the income up to his death if the trust had been strictly carried out, the court directed that a similar apportionment should be made in respect of the proceeds of the sale[1]. On the other hand, where there has been no dividend paid during the tenancy for life on cumulative preferred shares, it has been held that the life tenant's executors have no claim to any part of the dividends paid after his death[2].

1   *Bulkeley v Stephens* [1896] 2 Ch 241; *Re Muirhead* [1916] 2 Ch 181; *Re Oppenheimer* [1907] 1 Ch 399; and see *Re Henderson* [1940] Ch 368, [1940] 1 All ER 623.
2   *Re Sale* [1913] 2 Ch 697; and *Re Grundy* (1917) 117 LT 470; following *Re Taylor's Trusts* [1905] 1 Ch 734; and distinguishing *Re Griffith* (1879) 12 Ch D 655; *Re Wakley* [1920] 2 Ch 205, CA.

48.45 Where executors sell stocks to a beneficiary pursuant to a direction in the will no question of apportionment of accruing dividends arises, for the beneficiary, like any other purchaser, 'has bought the tree, and with it the fruits that are ripening on the tree'[1].

1   *Re Wimbush* [1940] Ch 92, [1940] 1 All ER 229.

Profit on reconstruction of company

48.46 In *Re Armitage*[1] a testator gave his estate upon the usual trusts for conversion, with power to postpone, and directed that, pending conversion, the income actually produced should be treated as income. Part of the residue consisted of shares in a company with £8 per share paid up. The company was reconstructed, and the new company paid £9 5s for each of the old shares. The £1 5s was the proceeds partly of the regular reserve fund, and partly of profits which the directors had retained to meet contingencies. It was held that the right of a tenant for life of shares is only to receive dividends and *bonuses in the shape of dividends*, and that, although £1 5s was profits, it was under the circumstances not payable as income.

¹   [1893] 3 Ch 337.

Director's fee

48.47   If trustees are accountable for their fees as directors, having unauthorisedly obtained the directorships by using shares owned as trustee, then the fees are capital of the trust¹.

¹   *Re Macadam* [1946] Ch 73 at 76–77.

Unit trusts

48.48   In *Re Whitehead's Will Trusts¹* it was held that trustees who own units in a unit trust need to inquire whether the source of any alleged capital distribution by the managers of the unit trust requires such distribution to be treated as of income or capital, just as if the trustees directly owned the shares in the portfolio of the unit trust, applying the rules earlier explained in relation to distributions by companies where the intentions of the directors of the companies need to be ascertained. This is a difficult task and one that is often overlooked.

¹   [1959] Ch 579.

Paragraph 3

Whether trustees can safely pay the share of one beneficiary before paying the others

48.49   The question sometimes arises whether trustees can safely pay the share of one beneficiary who has attained a vested interest in possession, before paying the other beneficiaries who may not have attained a vested interest or whose shares (by reason of incapacity or otherwise) are not presently payable¹. If they do so, it may happen that, by reason of subsequent depreciation of securities, the balance retained by the trustee may be insufficient to pay the other beneficiaries in full, in which case the first beneficiary will have more than the others. It appears, however, to be well settled that if, when the first payment was made, the trustees have, and retain in their hands, assets which, fairly valued, are then sufficient to meet shares which are not presently payable, but have to be held in trust, they are justified in paying other shares payable pari passu but payable at once, and are not liable if the assets so retained should, in the event, prove insufficient to pay the unpaid beneficiaries in full². This is because the sui juris beneficiary has a right to call for his appropriate share³ and the conduct of trustees is regarded with reference to the facts and circumstances existing at the time when they have to act; and therefore, if they make the variation impartially at that time, they are

671

48.49 *The trustee's duties*

not liable for an unforeseen loss[4]. Trustees should employ a duly qualified valuer, taking advantage of ss 11(2)(a) and 23(1) of the Trustee Act 2000 or s 22(3) of the Trustee Act 1925.

[1] Where the trustees do this and the beneficiary takes the distribution in the form of investments rather than cash the beneficiary will be treated as having received the cash value of these investments (*Re Gollins Declaration of Trust* [1969] 3 All ER 1591, [1969] 1 WLR 1858) unless the investments were specifically appropriated as having a value equivalent to a specific proportion of the whole trust fund: *Re Leigh's Settlement Trusts* [1981] CLY 2453.
[2] Per Lindley LJ in *Re Hurst* (1892) 67 LT 96 at 99; *Re Swan* (1864) 2 Hem & M 34 at 37; *Re Winslow* (1890) 45 Ch D 249; *Fenwick v Clarke* (1862) 4 De GF & J 240; *Re Lepine* [1892] 1 Ch 210; and see also *Re Hall* [1903] 2 Ch 226; *Re Gardiner* [1942] NZLR 199; *Re Chirnside* [1974] VR 160.
[3] See Article 69.
[4] Cf Administration of Estates Act 1925, s 41 which authorises appropriation by personal representatives, subject to certain conditions, of part of the estate of the deceased to answer legacies, including annuities and other shares and interests in the estate: see para 48.55 below.

Appropriation to answer particular shares

48.50 Another question which sometimes arises is whether trustees of a settlement or will can treat their trust as several trusts, appropriating specific securities to each; or whether they must treat the trust property as one undivided fund until it becomes necessary, on the death of a life tenant, to pay and distribute his share among his children. For instance, where a settlor settles money either in a specific sum or as a share of residue upon each of his daughters for life, with remainder for her children, ought the trustees to treat the daughters' fortunes as one trust, or as several? If a severance and appropriation of securities be lawful, it may sometimes be convenient; but on the other hand the result may obviously be that (by reason of the appreciation of one appropriated set of securities, or the depreciation of another, or from both such causes) one family may get less, and the other more, than their due proportion of the entire fund. Where the trust is a trust of specific sums (eg £50,000 to be held upon trust for a settlor's daughter A for life, with remainder for her children equally, and £50,000 to be held upon a similar trust for his daughter B and her children), an appropriation is not only undoubtedly legitimate, but ought to be made[1].

[1] *Fraser v Murdoch* (1881) 6 App Cas 855; *Re Walker* (1890) 62 LT 449; and see also *Re Lepine* [1892] 1 Ch 210; *Barclay v Owen* (1889) 60 LT 220; *Re Nicholson's Will Trusts* [1936] 3 All ER 832. Unlike the position under the statutory power of appropriation conferred by the Administration of Estates Act 1925, s 41, an appropriation of securities is only valid if the appropriated securities were both authorised and sufficient at the date of the appropriation; see *Re Waters* [1889] WN 39. See also *Re Forster-Brown* [1914] 2 Ch 584. It is not, however, necessary that where a trustee appropriates securities to one beneficiary he should appropriate contemporaneously to all (*Re Richardson* [1896] 1 Ch 512; *Re Nickels* [1898] 1 Ch 630) though he should consider whether equality is not best achieved by contemporaneous appropriations.

48.51 Where property is left on trust for sale or there is a trust of land within s 1 of the Trusts of Land and Appointment of Trustees Act 1996, and there is nothing in the trust instrument indicating that no appropriation between the

672

beneficiaries is to be made until some specified event (eg the death of a life tenant interested in one quarter of a fund) then it seems an appropriation can be made[1]. After all, the property could be sold to the beneficiary so he can have the property appropriated to him, being credited with its value at the time[2]. However, it seems that infant beneficiaries incapable of consenting to the appropriation could be bound to an appropriation in their favour if done fairly upon a proper valuation[3].

[1]   *Re Nickels* [1898] 1 Ch 630; *Re Brooks* (1897) 76 LT 771. Of course an appropriation must be made if directed by the trust instrument, eg *Pexton (Inspector of Taxes) v Bell* [1976] 2 All ER 914 at 949.
[2]   *Re Beverly* [1901] 1 Ch 681, *followed Re Craven* [1914] 1 Ch 358. Trustees of UK land have all the powers of an absolute owner in relation to the land and so have a power of partition: see TA 2000, s 8(3).
[3]   *Re Ruddock* (1910) 102 LT 89, CA. TA 1925, s 22(3).

48.52 Doubts now exist in the case of income interests since it has been held that 'an interest in half the income of an undivided fund is quite different from the whole income of a divided half of that fund'[1] so that an appropriation varies the beneficial interests necessitating an application under the Variation of Trusts Act[2] if the statutory power conferred on personal representatives by s 41 of the Administration of Estates Act 1925 is not available and there is no express power of appropriation contained in the trust instrument. A properly drawn trust instrument should contain express powers of appropriation unless the settlor specifically desires no appropriation to take place until the time for distribution to absolutely entitled beneficiaries.

[1]   *Re Freeston's Charity* [1978] 1 WLR 741 at 751, per Goff LJ stating the effect of *Macculloch v Anderson* [1904] AC 55.
[2]   See *Re Freeston's Charity* [1978] 1 WLR 741 at 752, per Goff LJ.

48.53 When the appropriation is made the beneficiary absolutely entitled can call for a transfer of the appropriated securities[1]. On similar principles it has been held that the court has jurisdiction to distribute in specie real estate directed to be sold even where there are settled shares if the trustees have power to invest in the purchase of land[2].

[1]   *Re Marshall* [1914] 1 Ch 192. As to stamp duty, see *Jopling v IRC* [1940] 2 KB 282, [1940] 3 All ER 279.
[2]   *Re Wragg* [1919] 2 Ch 58; and see also *Re Cooke's Settlement, Tarry v Cooke* [1913] 2 Ch 661. For the statutory power now to acquire land in the UK, see TA 2000, s 8.

Appropriation at cash value or as proportion of trust fund

48.54 The general principle is that an appropriation of assets to satisfy the interest of a beneficiary is treated as payment of the cash equivalent to the beneficiary[1]. This may prove unsatisfactory and frustrate the settlor's real intentions if this cash sum is brought into account on final division of the trust fund many years later[2]. It will often be better for the trustees to treat the appropriated assets as having a value equivalent to a specified proportion of the trust fund and to obtain the beneficiary's consent to this or the leave of the court[3]. If such consent or leave had not been obtained then on final division it may be possible with leave of the court to bring actual or notional cash sums into account at final division at their value at the time of the beneficiary's receipt multiplied by the increase in the retail price index[4].

1   *Re Gollins Declaration of Trust* [1969] 3 All ER 1591, [1969] 1 WLR 1858.
2   Law Reform Committee (23rd Report) Cmnd 8733, para 4.43.
3   *Re Leigh's Settlement Trusts* [1981] CLY 2453.
4   Cmnd 8733, para 4.47.

Statutory power of appropriation

48.55 By s 41 of the Administration of Estates Act 1925 a *personal representative* (which expression does not comprise a trustee)[1] may appropriate any part of the real or personal estate of the deceased in the actual condition or state of investment thereof at the time of appropriation[2] in or towards satisfaction of any legacy bequeathed by the deceased or of any other interest or share in his property, *whether settled or not*, as to the personal representative may seem just and reasonable according to the respective rights of the persons interested in the property of the deceased, but an appropriation may not be made so as to affect prejudicially any specific devise or bequest. When an appropriation is made in respect of any settled legacy share or interest, the consent must be obtained either of the trustee thereof, if any (not being also the personal representative himself), or of the person who may for the time being be entitled to the income, or (if the latter is an infant or is incapable, by reason of mental disorder within the meaning of the Mental Health Act 1983, of managing and administering his property and affairs) of his guardian or receiver (if any), or of the court. No consent (save that of that trustee, if any) is required of any person coming into existence after the appropriation, and no consent of any such guardian or receiver is required if the appropriated property is an investment authorised by law or by the trust. Any property so appropriated (though until then not an investment authorised by law or the will) is thereafter to be treated as an authorised investment and may be retained.

1   But an express power of appropriation is often conferred upon *trustees* of wills by reference to this section: otherwise personal representatives should consider exercising the power before fully administering the estate and becoming trustees, e g by assenting in favour of themselves as trustees.
2   The deceased's property being appropriated must be revalued at the date of appropriation: *Re Charteris* [1917] 2 Ch 379 at 386; *Re Collins* [1975] 1 WLR 309; *Re Gollins Declaration of Trust* [1969] 3 All ER 1591, [1969] 1 WLR 1858.

48.56 The personal representative may ascertain and fix the value of the respective parts of the real and personal estate and the liabilities of the deceased as he may think fit, employing a duly qualified valuer where necessary, and may make any conveyance (including an assent) which may be required for giving effect to the appropriation. The appropriation will bind all parties interested, but in making it the personal representative is to have due regard to the rights of persons who may subsequently come into existence. This statutory power of appropriation is not to prejudice any other power of appropriation conferred by law, or by the will of the deceased, and the property appropriated is to be subject to all trusts for sale and powers of leasing, disposition and management in varying investments which would have been applicable if no appropriation had been made. Any appropriation *purporting to have been made under this statutory power* is, in favour of a purchaser, to be deemed to have been made in accordance with the requirements of the section. For the purposes of the section 'settled legacy, share or interest' includes any legacy share or interest to which a person is not absolutely entitled in possession at the date of the appropriation. It will be observed that the statute does not expressly authorise the trustee of the settled property to consent to the appropriation. However, it is considered that is implied, that it is left to his discretion whether he will consent or not, and that he runs no risk in giving consent so long as it is reasonable to do so.

Paragraph 4

Application of hotchpot provisions

48.57 Cases in which children have to bring sums, whether advances or loans[1], into hotchpot sometimes present great difficulty. An express hotchpot clause should be drawn up in clear terms resolving potential difficulties. Beneficiaries may also have to bring property into hotchpot as a result of the application of the equitable presumption against double portions[2], but since January 1996 spouses and issue of a person dying wholly or partly intestate no longer are subject to the hotchpot provisions in s 47(1)(iii) or s 49(1)(a) of the Administration of Estates Act 1925 which were repealed by the Law Reform Succession Act 1995.

[1] *Re Horn* [1946] Ch 254, [1946] 2 All ER 118, CA, affords a good example of a hotchpot clause adapted to meet the case of outstanding loans. Generally see (1961) 25 Conv 468 (JT Farrand); *Theobald on Wills* (15th edn) pp 757 ff.
[2] A legacy or share of residue is presumed adeemed if the testator made an earlier gift by way of portion when *in loco parentis*: generally see *Re Cameron* [1999] Ch 386 applied to a half share in realty in *Race v Race* [2002] EWHC 1868 (Ch), [2002] WTLR 1193 (5 July 2002, unreported).

48.58 The actual amount brought into hotchpot is normally the value of the portion or advancement as at the date received by the beneficiary[1].

[1] *Watson v Watson* (1864) 33 Beav 574; *Re Innes* (1908) 125 LTJo 60; *Re Crocker* [1916] 1 Ch 25.

48.59 It seems the impact of inheritance tax should be dealt with by bringing into account the net value of the benefit to the beneficiary against the net estate of the deceased where it is the deceased's estate that is distributable[1]. Where a trust fund is distributable on some event occurring (such as a life tenant's death) it seems likely that the gross amount (subject to inheritance tax) advanced to the beneficiary should be brought into account against the gross amount available on eventual distribution[2]. In a hotchpot calculation it is crucial whether the value of the distributable assets is to be reckoned as of the date of actual distribution or of the date of notional distribution. The date of notional distribution will usually be the date of a testator's death or of a life tenant's death or of a beneficiary satisfying some contingency. The date of actual distribution is the subsequent date when the distributable assets are actually distributed. In the absence of some indication in the will or trust deed that the distributable assets are to be valued at the date for notional distribution[3] valuation is taken as of the date of actual distribution[4]. So far as hotchpot on intestacy is concerned it would seem that since the advancement is to be valued at the intestate's death this is an indication that the distributable assets are also to be valued at death[5].

[1]   *Re Beddington* [1900] 1 Ch 771; *Re Crocker* [1916] 1 Ch 25; *Re Turner's Will Trusts* [1968] 1 All ER 321, [1968] 1 WLR 227; (1961) 25 Conv 468 at 487 (JT Farrand).
[2]   *Re Tollemache* [1930] WN 138; *Re Slee* [1962] 1 All ER 542, [1962] 1 WLR 496.
[3]   *Re Hargreaves* (1903) 88 LT 100; *Re Mansel* [1930] 1 Ch 352; *Re Gunther's Will Trusts* [1939] Ch 985; *Re Oram* [1940] Ch 1001, [1940] 4 All ER 161.
[4]   *Re Poyser* [1908] 1 Ch 828; *Re Forster-Brown* [1914] 2 Ch 584; *Re Cooke* [1916] 1 Ch 480; *Re Tod* [1916] 1 Ch 567; *Re Wills* [1939] Ch 705, [1939] 2 All ER 775; *Re Hillas-Drake* [1944] Ch 235, [1944] 1 All ER 375; *Re Slee* [1962] 1 All ER 542, [1962] 1 WLR 496.
[5]   *Re Slee* [1962] 1 All ER 542, [1962] 1 WLR 496; (1961) 25 Conv 468 (JT Farrand).

48.60 So far, only the capital side of hotchpot calculations has been considered but there will be income accruing from the capital between the notional time for distribution and the actual time of distribution. The date of the valuation of the distributable capital assets controls not only the division of the capital but also the mode of controlling the intermediate income.

48.61 If the valuation of the capital is reckoned at the date of notional distribution the advancement is brought into account to reduce the gross share of capital otherwise passing to the advanced beneficiary so that, for example, as from the date of notional distribution the beneficiary is treated as entitled to a net one-third share of the capital and not a gross one-half share. He is thus entitled to one-third of the income for the period between the notional and actual distribution[1].

[1]   See para 48.59 note 3, above.

48.62 If valuation of the capital is not reckoned till the date of actual distribution then interest at 4% on the sums brought into hotchpot is added to the income for the period between notional and actual distribution: the total is then divided between the beneficiaries according to their gross shares of capital but the shares of the advanced beneficiaries are then debited with the 4% interest notionally payable in respect of the advanced sums[1].

[1]   See para 48.59 note 4, above.

48.63 The computation should be made on the basis of the gross amount of the income actually produced by the distributable capital and the gross notional 4% payable in respect of the sums brought into hotchpot as laid down in *Re Foster*[1]. However, without argument, the computation has been made on the basis of net amounts after tax[2].

[1]   [1920] 1 Ch 391.
[2]   *Re Wills* [1939] Ch 705, [1939] 2 All ER 775; *Re Hillas-Drake* [1944] Ch 235, [1944] 1 All ER 375.

48.64 Funds appointed by the deceased under a special power of appointment do not have to be brought into statutory hotchpot under s 47(1)(iii) of the Administration of Estates Act 1925[1] though they do have to be brought into equitable hotchpot arising from the application of the presumptions against double portions[2].

[1]   *Re Reeve* [1935] Ch 110.
[2]   *Re Peel's Settlement* [1911] 2 Ch 165.

48.65 Whether a person brings into hotchpot benefits received by him or also benefits received by his issue depends on the wording of the hotchpot clause. If he only has to bring into hotchpot a life interest (and not a remainder passing to his issue) then the life interest will be valued on actuarial principles[1]. Under s 49(1)(a) beneficial interests acquired by issue had to be taken into account[2], but the equitable presumption against double portions only requires benefits received by the donee of the portion to be brought into hotchpot.

[1]   *Re Gordon* [1942] Ch 131, [1942] 1 All ER 59; *Re West* [1921] 1 Ch 533.
[2]   *Re Grover's Will Trusts* [1971] Ch 168, [1970] 1 All ER 1185; *Re Young* [1951] Ch 185, [1950] 2 All ER 1040.

ARTICLE 49
DUTY OF TRUSTEE TO SELL IMPROPER PROPERTY

49.1

Where *residuary personal estate* is settled by will for the benefit of persons in succession, all such parts of it as consist of improper securities must be converted into proper authorised securities being property of a sensible and prudent character satisfying the trustee's obligations under the Trustee Act 2000, unless the will reveals a contrary intention, eg

(a)   the will contains a direction or implication that the life tenant is to enjoy the income from the property in its actual state of investment (*'in specie'*); or

(b)   the will confers on the trustee a discretion to postpone such conversion, not merely as an ancillary power for the more convenient realisation of the estate but as an independent power for the benefit of the life tenant, and the trustee bona fide and impartially exercises the discretion.

Rule in Howe v Lord Dartmouth

49.2 The above rule, known as the rule in *Howe v Earl of Dartmouth*[1], is really a corollary of the principle stated in Article 48, namely, that the trustee must act impartially between the beneficiaries, for if unauthorised or improper [2] investments producing a high rate of interest but with little capital security were to be retained, the tenant for life would profit at the expense of the remaindermen, and if unauthorised or improper investments producing no income, only capital appreciation, were not converted the remaindermen would profit at the expense of the tenant for life. It must, however, be borne in mind that the rule is based upon an implied or presumed intention of the testator that the legatees shall successively enjoy the same fund, with neither life tenant nor remainderman benefiting at the expense of the other. Courts of equity have, consequently, always declined to apply the rule in cases where the settlor has indicated an intention that the property should be enjoyed *in specie* ('in its actual state'), though he may not have said so in express words. The real question, therefore, in all such cases, is whether the settlor has, with sufficient distinctness, indicated his intention that the property should be enjoyed *in specie*[3], for the burden of showing this lies upon the party who desires that the rule in *Howe v Earl of Dartmouth* should not be applied[4].

1   (1802) 7 Ves 137, 1 White Tud LC 68; and see also *Hinves v Hinves* (1844) 3 Hare 609; and *Pickering v Pickering* (1839) 4 My & Cr 289.
2   The huge width of unauthorised investments (in the absence of broad express powers of investment) was reduced by the TA 1925, significantly reduced by the Trustee Investment Act 1961, and almost abolished by the TA 2000 (in the absence of express restriction in the trust instrument); however many investments within the range of authorised investments will be improper ones as breaching the trustees' duties under the TA 2000 if retained or purchased by them for the trust.
3   Per Baggallay LJ in *Macdonald v Irvine* (1878) 8 Ch D 101 at 112, CA.
4   Per James LJ in *Macdonald v Irvine* (1878) 8 Ch D 101 at 112; *Re Wareham* [1912] 2 Ch 312 at 315, CA.

49.3 The rule in *Howe v Earl of Dartmouth*, as well as requiring conversion, has certain financial apportionment consequences as between life tenant and remainderman (see Article 50,below) and reference to the rule is often made in order to allude both to the duty to convert and to these financial consequences. Understood in this sense, therefore, the rule applies to cases where the testator has expressly directed conversion (because although there is no room for any implied duty to convert the financial consequences of the rule still normally apply). Although the rule can be excluded by the use of appropriate words, it is not excluded merely by the addition of an express power for the trustees to postpone conversion for the more convenient realisation of the estate[1].

1   *Re Berry* [1962] Ch 97, [1961] 1 All ER 529. In this case Pennycuick J said that in so far as *Re Fisher* [1943] Ch 377, [1943] 2 All ER 615, had decided that a mere power to postpone was enough to exclude the rule it was 'contrary to the whole current of authority'.

Impact of Trustee Act 2000 vast extension of authorised investments

49.4 Under the Trustee Act 2000[1] a trustee or personal representative[2] is authorised to make any kind of investment that he could make if he were absolutely entitled to the assets of the trust, except that he cannot invest in land (other than in loans secured on land) except for freehold or leasehold land in the UK which, under s 8(1), can be acquired as an investment or for occupation by a beneficiary or for any other reason.

49.5 The philosophy is for trustees to have vast powers of investment, but subject to significant safeguards requiring exercise of such powers to be subject to equitable and statutory duties. Moreover, trustees, like wealthy individual investors, are entitled to be judged by the standards of modern portfolio theory which emphasises the risk level of the entire portfolio. Each particular investment is not taken in isolation but in the context of the overall portfolio[1]. Traditional warnings against the need for trustees to avoid speculative or hazardous investments are not to be read as inhibiting trustees from maintaining a portfolio which contains a sensible and prudent mixture of low risk and higher risk securities and of high-yielding investments with capital growth investments with no or little yield[2].

1   *Nestle v National Westminster Bank* [2000] WTLR 795 at 802.
2   See Lord Nicholls (1995) 9 Trust LI 71 at 73, and see para 53.9 ff.

49.6 If it so happens that in exercising its powers within the vast range of possible investments the trustee breaks its duty of care[1] or to obtain and consider investment advice[2] or to act fairly and disinterestedly[3], then the trustee is personally liable to make reparation for the losses he caused[4], whether to all the beneficiaries or just to the life tenant or just to the remainderman.

1   TA 2000, ss 1 and 2, Sch 1.
2   TA 2000 s 5.
3   *Edge v Pensions Ombudsman* [2000] Ch 602, CA; *Nestle v National Westminster Bank* [2000] WTLR 795.
4   See Article 89.

49.7 The question arises whether the rule in *Howe v Dartmouth* should not apply where the testator's personal representative or trustee has power (whether express or statutory) to invest in any kind of investment (other than in land outside the UK) on the basis that this indicates that the testator is prepared for his executor or trustee to retain such testator's investments until he considers it expedient to replace them[1]. Thus, the testator should not be regarded as requiring them to be sold forthwith under an implied trust for sale only in order for the same kind of investments possibly to be purchased as authorised investments.

1   See *Brown v Gellatly* (1867) 2 Ch App 751 at 758; *Re Pitcairn* [1896] 2 Ch 199 at 209; *Re Nicholson* [1909] 2 Ch 111; J Kessler *Drafting Trusts and Will Trusts* (5th edn) para 18.33.

49.8 However, an investment within the range of statutory or, even, expressly authorised investments only becomes a proper one once the executor or trustee has obtained and considered advice[1] (unless he reasonably concludes that in all the circumstances it is unnecessary or inappropriate to do so[2]). Thus, the key issue is whether the testator can be taken to have intended the life tenant to receive all income actually produced by the residuary investments before the executor's or trustee's conscious investment decisions were duly taken. In the absence of some special wording in the testator's will which might permit the court to reach such a convenient construction, it seems likely that the testator's intention will be for the life tenant to receive the income from those residuary investments that the executor or trustee duly decides to retain as proper investments[3], but not the other investments that are duly sold. Therefore, it will be advisable for a testator's will to spell out an intention to permit enjoyment *in specie* of income from existing residuary investments from his death if so intending.

[1] TA 2000, ss 4, 5 and 35; and see para 53.22 below. Until the executor or trustee does this and decides to retain an investment within the authorised range such investment is an improper one and so (in the absence of contrary intent) subject to *Howe v Dartmouth* (see *Re Rowlls* [1900] 2 Ch 107 and *Re Guinness' Settlement* [1966] 1 WLR 1355 and R Mitchell [1999] Conv 84 at 99–103).
[2] TA 2000, s 5(3).
[3] *Re Sheldon* (1888) 39 Ch D 50.

Small scope for implied trust for sale under Howe v Dartmouth

49.9 From the above it seems likely that only in respect of residuary personalty that the trustee decides not to retain or only if the testator expressly or by necessary implication restricts the range of investments otherwise permitted by the Trustee Act 2000 to a restricted class, but dies owning assets outside the restricted class, will there be room for an implied trust for sale. Even then, the old case law reveals that no such trust for sale arose if the property[1] were real property or the subject of a specific (as opposed to a residuary) bequest[2], the court in such cases presuming the testator's intention to be that the property be enjoyed *in specie*[3].

[1] *Re Woodhouse* [1941] Ch 332.
[2] *Macdonald v Irvine* (1878) 8 Ch D 101, CA; *Re Van Straubenzee* [1901] 2 Ch 779.
[3] Lifetime settlements inevitably deal specifically with particular property and so an *in specie* intention is present: *Re Van Straubenzee* [1901] 2 Ch 779.

Paragraph (a), (b)

Rule in Howe v Lord Dartmouth not applicable where contrary intention expressed

49.10 As already stated, the rule in *Howe v Earl of Dartmouth* will yield to any contrary intention which may be expressed or implied in the settlement. Moreover, it is immaterial whether the contrary intention is imperatively expressed, or whether a discretion to convert or not is expressly given to the trustees; for the court will not interfere with a discretion so long as trustees exercise it in good faith[1].

[1] *Gisborne v Gisborne* (1877) 2 App Cas 300; *Tabor v Brooks* (1878) 10 Ch D 273; *Re Rogers* [1915] 2 Ch 437; and *Re Slater* (1915) 113 LT 691.

49.11 Thus, in one case a testator gave his residuary estate, which included several leasehold houses (held upon short terms), to trustees, upon trust to pay the income to his wife for life, with remainder to his grandchildren, and gave his trustees *power to retain any portion of his property in the same state in which it should be at his decease,* or to sell and convert the same as they should think fit. It was held that the special power to retain existing investments took the case out of the general rule as to conversion of perishable property, and that the trustees were at liberty to retain the short leaseholds, and any other investments held by the testator, for such period as they should think fit[1]. A similar decision was arrived at where a testator authorised his trustees to postpone the sale of his business[2].

1   *Gray v Siggers* (1880) 15 Ch D 74; *Re Fisher* [1943] Ch 377, [1943] 2 All ER 615.
2   *Re Crowther* [1895] 2 Ch 56; followed in *Re Elford* [1910] 1 Ch 814; but see *Re Smith* [1896] 1 Ch 171.

49.12 So, again, where the testator devised wasting property to trustees, upon trust to sell 'when in their discretion they should deem it advisable', it was held that the trustees were not bound to sell until they thought fit[1].

1   *Miller v Miller* (1872) LR 13 Eq 263; *Thursby v Thursby* (1875) LR 19 Eq 395; and see also *Re Chancellor* (1884) 26 Ch D 42; and *Re Crowther* [1895] 2 Ch 56, in both of which cases the property consisted of a business.

Rule not applicable where impliedly negatived

49.13 The above cases are instances of an express intention that the trustees should have a discretion; but the same result will follow where that intention, though not expressed in so many words, can be implied. Thus, a testator, after a special bequest, gave all his residuary estate, both real and personal, to trustees, upon trust, to *sell as much and such part thereof as they might think necessary for paying all his mortgage and other debts and funeral and testamentary expenses,* and to invest the balance of the proceeds, and to stand possessed of such investments, *and all other his residuary estate,* upon trust for several persons successively for their respective lives, with remainders over. Part of the testator's estate consisted of leaseholds, which were retained unsold. On this state of facts it was held that, on the construction of the will, the trustees had a discretion as to what part of the testator's estate should be converted, and that the court could not interfere with the exercise of such discretion[1].

1   *Re Sewell's Estate* (1870) LR 11 Eq 80; and see also *Simpson v Earles* (1847) 11 Jur 921.

49.14 So it has been held that an express direction for sale at a particular period indicates an intention that there should be no previous sale[1] and even a *power* to sell all or any part of the estate in the absolute discretion of the trustees, has been held to negative the prima facie duty of selling wasting or reversionary property forthwith[2]. A similar view has been taken of a discretion to *divide* property after the death of the life tenant[3], though it has subsequently been held that a mere provision that residue is to be divided between certain persons after the life tenant's death does not exclude the rule where the division may be of the residue as converted under the rule[4]. So, in some cases, it has been decided that a trust to pay *rents* to the tenant for life, *where the testator has only leaseholds*[5], or a direction that the trustees should

49.14 *The trustee's duties*

give a power of attorney to the life tenant to receive the income[6], is a sufficient indication of a contrary intention to take the case out of the general rule.

1   *Alcock v Sloper* (1833) 2 My & K 699; *Daniel v Warren* (1843) 2 Y & C Ch Cas 290; *Re North* [1909] 1 Ch 625.
2   *Re Pitcairn* [1896] 2 Ch 199.
3   *Collins v Collins* (1833) 2 My & K 703.
4   *Re Evans' Will Trusts* [1921] 2 Ch 309.
5   *Goodenough v Tremamondo* (1840) 2 Beav 512; *Cafe v Bent* (1845) 5 Hare 24; *Vachell v Roberts* (1863) 32 Beav 140; *Re Wareham* [1912] 2 Ch 312, CA.
6   *Neville v Fortescue* (1848) 16 Sim 333.

ARTICLE 50
DUTY OF TRUSTEE, AS BETWEEN TENANT FOR LIFE AND
REMAINDERMAN, IN RELATION TO PROPERTY
PENDING CONVERSION

50.1

(1)   Where property ought to be converted, and the proceeds invested, whether under an implied *Howe v Dartmouth* trust for sale or an express trust for sale, the tenant for life is entitled, pending actual conversion, to the whole net income of income-bearing property, if a direction to that effect is expressed in or can be implied from the trust[1] or if the trust is of land[2];

(2)   but in the absence of any such direction or implication, he is entitled to receive or be credited with income in accordance with the following rules, namely:

  (a)   where the property is personal estate (other than lease-holds), he is only entitled to a fair equivalent for the income which he would have received if the property had been sold and invested in proper authorised investments[3];

  (b)   where the property is of a reversionary nature, he is entitled, when it falls in, to a proportionate part of the capital, representing compound interest (with yearly rests[4]) on the true actuarial value of the property at the testator's death, calculated on the assumption that the actual date when the property fell into possession could have been then predicted with certainty[5];

(3)   upon complete realisation of an insufficient investment, where interest is in arrears, the money realised must be divided between tenant for life and remainderman in proportion to the amount due for arrears of interest and the amount of capital remaining due[6]; but this does not apply to settled shares or stock of such a nature that dividend is payable only if earned[7];

(4)   this article has no application to investments made by trustees in breach of trust where no loss results; but is confined to cases where unavoidable delay takes place in converting property in

due course of administration[8], and to cases where a security (whether authorised or not) has turned out to be insufficient.

1   See *Re Sheldon* (1888) 39 Ch D 50; *Re Thomas* [1891] 3 Ch 482. Where the property is of a non-wasting nature, the court will accept very slight evidence of implied intention.
2   *Re Oliver* [1908] 2 Ch 74; *Re Earl of Darnley* [1907] 1 Ch 159; *Re Berton* [1939] Ch 200; before LPA 1925, s 28 repealed for position to be governed by TLATA 1996, s 4 and TA 2000, s 8.
3   *Brown v Gellatly* (1867) 2 Ch App 751; See para 50.15 below; *Meyer v Simonsen* (1852) 5 De G & Sm 723; *Wentworth v Wentworth* [1900] AC 163.
4   See *Re Goodenough* [1895] 2 Ch 537; *Re Morley* [1895] 2 Ch 738; *Re Hobson* (1885) 53 LT 627; and *Re Duke of Cleveland's Estate* [1895] 2 Ch 542; *Rowlls v Bebb* [1900] 2 Ch 107, CA. As to the rate of interest, see para 50.22 below.
5   *Re Earl of Chesterfield's Trusts* (1883) 24 Ch D 643; followed, with variations as to rate of interest, in *Re Goodenough* [1895] 2 Ch 537; *Re Morley* [1895] 2 Ch 738; *Re Hobson* (1885) 53 LT 627; and *Re Duke of Cleveland's Estate* [1895] 2 Ch 542.
6   *Re Atkinson* [1904] 2 Ch 160; over-ruling *Re Foster* (1890) 45 Ch D 629; and *Re Phillimore* [1903] 1 Ch 942; and see *Re Walker's Settlement Trusts* [1936] Ch 280; *Re Atkinson*, above, was applied in *Re Morris' Will Trusts* [1960] 3 All ER 548, [1960] 1 WLR 1210 (see para 48.23 above).
7   See *Re Taylor's Trust* [1905] 1 Ch 734. Cf *Re Sale* [1913] 2 Ch 697; *Re Grundy* (1917) 117 LT 470; *Re Wakley* [1920] 2 Ch 205, CA; and *Re Marjoribanks* [1923] 2 Ch 307.
8   See per Byrne J in *Re Appleby* [1903] 1 Ch 565 at 566; and *Stroud v Gwyer* (1860) 28 Beav 130; but cf *Re Hill* (1881) 50 LJ Ch 551; *Slade v Chaine* [1908] 1 Ch 522; *Re Hoyles* [1912] 1 Ch 67.

Not confined to settled residue

50.2 This article is a further corollary of Article 48, and its main principle forms the second part of the rule in *Howe v Earl of Dartmouth*, namely, that, pending a conversion which ought to be made, the tenant for life is, prima facie, entitled only to the income which would have been produced by the proceeds of the conversion if it had in fact been made.

50.3 It is not (like the main rule) confined to settled residuary personal estate under a will, but is equally applicable to all settled personal property which is subject to a direction for sale exercisable forthwith. However, it does not apply where the sale is only to take place at a future date, for in that case the intention must have been that until that date arrived the tenant for life should enjoy the property in specie, though a mere power to postpone conversion, without more, is normally not enough to indicate such an intention[1].

1   *Re Berry* [1962] Ch 97, [1961] 1 All ER 529.

A question of interpretation of the trust instrument

50.4 Where it is possible that the rule applies, the first question that arises is one of fact, namely, whether on the true interpretation of the trust instrument the tenant for life is either expressly or impliedly intended to take the actual income pending the sale. If that question is answered in the affirmative, that is an end of the matter. But if no such intention is expressed or can reasonably be inferred, the question becomes one of law, to be answered in accordance with the rules in paragraph (2).

50.5 The trustee's duties

Paragraph 1

Rules have no application where a future sale is directed

50.5 The rules in paragraph (2) have no application where only a *future* sale is directed. In *Re North*[1] a testator, part of whose property consisted of land with brick earth upon it which was being worked under a lease granted by him at a royalty, gave his real estate to trustees upon trust 'to pay the rents issues and profits' to certain persons for life, with remainder *after the death of the last surviving life tenant* upon trust for sale. It was held that the trustees had power, after the expiration of the lease, to let the brick earth from year to year at a royalty, and that the life tenants were entitled to the whole of such royalty. No one seems to have suggested (nor indeed could have suggested) that the rules in paragraph (2) applied, the argument being mainly directed to the power of the trustees to let the brick earth at all, and the fact that if the tenants for life had let it under the powers of the Settled Land Acts, a proportion of the royalties would have had to be carried to capital account. The judge holding, on the interpretation of the will, that the trustees had power to continue the letting of the brick earth, it followed that the tenants for life were entitled to the royalties, there being no immediate trust for conversion.

[1]   [1909] 1 Ch 625. For a case where a direction for a future sale was implied, see *Re Barratt* [1925] Ch 550.

50.6 Similarly, where a testator devised and bequeathed 'a life rent in all my property' to his wife, and gave his trustees a mere power to sell and invest the proceeds, it was held that the wife was entitled to the whole of the income[1].

[1]   *Re Bentham* (1906) 94 LT 307; see also *Gray v Siggers* (1880) 15 Ch D 74.

Exclusion of rules in the case of intestacy

50.7 By the Administration of Estates Act 1925, s 33(5), it is provided that the income of so much of the real and personal estate of the deceased as may not be disposed of by will, or may not be required for administration purposes, may, however the estate is invested, be treated and applied as income as from the death of the deceased[1].

[1]   See and cf *Re Trollope's Will Trusts* [1927] 1 Ch 596; and *Re Sullivan* [1930] 1 Ch 84.

Rules may be expressly or impliedly negatived

50.8 Even where mineral property is subject to a trust for immediate sale, yet, if the trust expressly or impliedly gives the whole of the royalties pending sale to the tenant for life, he will be entitled to them. Thus where a testator devised his brickfield to trustees upon trust to sell when in their discretion it might seem advisable, and directed that the rents and profits should until sale be *applicable and applied in the same manner as the dividends or interest to arise from the investments of the sale moneys*, it was held that the tenant for life was entitled to the whole of the royalties paid by tenants of the brickfield, although the trustees did not sell the property for ten years[1]. If, however, the italicised words had not been inserted in the will, it seems plain that the power to postpone conversion would not of itself have authorised the payment of the whole of the royalties to the tenant for life. For, in that case, the inference would have been that the power to postpone conversion was for the purpose of efficiently selling the estate, and not for the benefit of the tenant for life[2]. And the words used must be clear: thus a declaration in a will against apportionment of 'dividends rents interests of moneys of the nature of income' has been held *not* to exclude the rule in relation to the profits of a business carried on by the testator[3].

1   *Miller v Miller* (1872) LR 13 Eq 263; and see also *Thursby v Thursby* (1875) LR 19 Eq 395; where the whole of colliery royalties were held to be payable to the tenant for life, and *Re Crowther* [1895] 2 Ch 56.
2   *Re Woods* [1904] 2 Ch 4. See *Re Carter* (1892) 41 WR 140; *Brown v Gellatly* (1867) 2 Ch App 751; *Re Owen* [1912] 1 Ch 519; and *Re Aste* (1918) 87 LJ Ch 660. See also *Re Berry* [1962] Ch 97, [1961] 1 All ER 529.
3   *Re Berry* [1962] Ch 97, [1961] 1 All ER 529.

Sale of business directed as soon as practicable

50.9 A case illustrating this part of the rule is *Re Elford[1]* where a testator directed the sale of his business as soon as practicable, but in a subsequent clause declared that pending conversion 'all the income arising from my estate' shall be applied as if it were income arising from the proceeds of the conversion. It was held, that the tenant for life was entitled to the whole of the profits of the business. It is conceived, however, that even in such a case the trustees ought to set aside a reasonable sum of profits for depreciation[2].

1   [1910] 1 Ch 814; following *Re Chancellor* (1884) 26 Ch D 42; and *Re Crowther* [1895] 2 Ch 56. A direction that pending sale the whole income is to be paid to a tenant for life does not negative the Apportionment Act 1870 (*Re Edwards* [1918] 1 Ch 142); *Re Elford*, above, was distinguished in *Re Berry* [1962] Ch 97, [1961] 1 All ER 529.
2   See *Re Crabtree* [1912] WN 24.

Purchase of land directed with all convenient speed

50.10 On the other hand, where a testator directs that a fund shall be invested in the purchase of land 'with all convenient speed', and that in the meantime the income shall be accumulated, the rule of the court is that a year is a reasonable time, and that if the purchase is not made within such year the accumulations stop, and the income is payable to the tenant for life of the land[1].

1   *Parry v Warrington* (1820) 6 Madd 155; followed by Jessel MR in *Wing v Wing* (1876) 34 LT 941; and see *Sitwell v Bernard* (1801) 6 Ves 520.

50.11 The question is really one of construction, namely, whether the testator intended that the power to postpone should be exercised for the benefit of the tenant for life, or merely for the more convenient realisation of the estate; and, if the former intention is found, no distinction is made by the court between unauthorised securities of a wasting and those of a permanent nature[1].

¹   *Re Nicholson* [1909] 2 Ch 111. This statement of the law was approved and adopted by Neville J in *Re Inman* [1915] 1 Ch 187.

Settlement implying that income is to be enjoyed in specie

50.12   In one case[1] a testator empowered his trustees, at their discretion, *to continue* all or any part of his personal estate in the state of investment in or upon which the same should be at his death; or to convert it, and invest the proceeds in the names of the trustees in certain specified securities. Part of the personal estate consisted of securities not specially authorised, which were retained. It was held that the tenants for life were entitled to receive the actual income of those securities which were retained. It will be perceived that the testator authorised the *continuance* of securities and not merely the temporary postponement of their conversion; otherwise the decision would have been different, as was the case in *Re Chaytor*[1], where the testator only authorised the *continuance pending a favourable opportunity for selling*. The real point in such cases is whether the power to continue or retain is to be construed as a power to continue or retain permanently, or only until the trustees can sell advantageously. In the first case, the inference is that the power was for the benefit of the tenant for life; in the latter, the inference is that it was merely for the convenient administration of the estate.

¹   *Re Sheldon* (1888) 39 Ch D 50; *Gray v Siggers* (1880) 15 Ch D 74; *Re Bates* [1907] 1 Ch 22; (power 'to retain'); and *Re Wilson* [1907] 1 Ch 394; and *Re Nicholson* [1909] 2 Ch 111, to same effect. See also *Re Rogers* [1915] 2 Ch 437; *Re Slater* (1915) 113 LT 691; and *Re Fisher* [1943] Ch 377, [1943] 2 All ER 615; But cf *Re Wareham* [1912] 2 Ch 312, CA.
²   [1905] 1 Ch 233; and see cases under paragraph 2 (b), below. Cf *Re Johnson* [1915] 1 Ch 435. But see *Re White's Settlement* [1930] 1 Ch 179.

50.13   Another example of an implied intention that income should be enjoyed in specie pending conversion is afforded by the case of *Re Thomas*[1]. A testator gave his residuary estate to trustees upon trust for conversion and investment of the proceeds in specified securities; with power to the trustees in their absolute discretion to retain any securities or property belonging to him at his death unconverted, for such period as they should think fit. He then declared that they should stand possessed of 'the stocks, funds, shares, and securities for the time being *constituting* or representing the residuary personal estate and effects therein before bequeathed *and of the income thereof*', upon trust to pay the income to certain persons for life with remainders over. The estate comprised certain American bonds, which were not included among the securities authorised by the will as investments, but were retained by the trustees in exercise of the discretion given to them. It was held that, on the true construction of the will, the tenants for life were entitled to the whole income of the bonds in specie. In giving judgment, Kekewich J said:

'I am not prepared to hold that where there is a direction for conversion of personal estate, followed by a power of retention of existing securities in the absolute discretion of the trustees, and then there are trusts for tenants for life, and afterwards for remainderman, the power of retention *necessarily* gives the tenants for life the enjoyment in specie of the securities retained by the trustees in the exercise of their discretion ... But I have no doubt that one looks out with an expectant eye for a direction to the trustees to retain securities, or any indication of the testator's intention that they shall retain indefinitely for so long as they may think fit.'

¹   [1891] 3 Ch 482; followed by Warrington J in *Re Godfree* [1914] 2 Ch 110.

Discretionary power to retain

50.14 Even when the power to retain investments is such that it does imply the exclusion of the rule, the rule will not be excluded in fact unless and until the trustees consciously determine to exercise the power. Thus in *Re Guinness's Settlement*¹ the trustees, who had a general power to retain assets, had not exercised it in relation to one particular asset because they did not know that it applied to this asset although they had in fact retained the asset, and it was held that until they actually decided to retain the asset in exercise of their discretion, its income fell within the ambit of the rules discussed in this Article.

¹   [1966] 2 All ER 497, [1966] 1 WLR 1355.

Paragraph 2(a)

Tenant for life not entitled to whole income of wasting property or unauthorised investments if settlement silent

50.15 In the leading case of *Brown v Gellatly*¹ the testator, who was a shipowner, directed his trustees to convert his personal estate into money, when and in such manner as they should see fit, and *gave them power to sail his ships until they could be disposed of satisfactorily*. The proceeds of his personal estate were then settled upon tenants for life, with remainders over. The will contained a wide power of investment in specified securities. On his death, the testator possessed: (1) numerous ships; (2) securities falling within those authorised by the will; and (3) shares and investments not so authorised. The ships could not be immediately sold, nor could the unauthorised securities. Both, pending sale, produced a high rate of income; and the question arose whether the tenants for life were entitled to the whole of that income, or only to some, and, if so, what, proportion thereof.

¹   (1867) 2 Ch App 751; and see also *Hume v Richardson* (1862) 4 De GF & J 29; *Re Lynch Blosse* [1899] WN 27; and *Mousley v Carr* (1841) 4 Beav 49. Followed in *Re Hazeldine* [1918] 1 Ch 433; *Re Trollope's Will Trusts* [1927] 1 Ch 596.

50.16 In giving judgment, Lord Cairns said:

'We find no indication whatever of an intention that the ships were to remain unconverted for any specific time. The testator, who had been engaged in the shipping business, knew perfectly well, and shows that he knew, that some time would necessarily be taken in converting the ships, and therefore he very wisely provided that until they were sold the executors should have power which otherwise they would not have possessed, namely, the power to sail the ships for the purpose of making profit, but in giving that power, he does not *give it as a power to be exercised for the benefit of the tenant for life as against the parties in remainder*, or for the benefit of the parties in remainder as against the interest of the tenant for life, but says that it is to be exercised for the benefit of the estate, meaning as I apprehend, for the benefit of the estate generally, without disarranging the equities between the successive takers ... In that state of things, it seems to me that the case falls exactly within the third division pointed out by Sir James Parker in the case of *Meyer v Simonsen*[1], and that a value must be set upon the ships as at the death of the testator, and the tenant for life must have 4% on such value, and the residue of the profits must of course beinvested, and become part of the estate. Then, secondly, as to the authorisedsecurities ... The tenant for life is, in my opinion, entitled to the specific income of the securities, just as if they had been £3 per cent consols. I understand the words of the will as amounting to the constitution by the testator of a larger class of authorised securities than this court itself would have approved of, and the court has merely to follow his directions, and treat the income accordingly, as being the income of authorised securities. Then comes the third question in the case, the securities not ranging themselves under any of those mentioned in the last clause of the will ... As they do not come within the class of authorised securities it was the duty of the trustees to convert them at the earliest moment at which they properly could be converted. I do not mean to say that the trustees were by any means open to censure for not having converted them within the year [after testator's death], but I think that the rights of the parties must be regulated as if they had been so converted. I think the proper order to make is that which was made in *Dimes v Scott*[2], followed by Wigram V-C in the case of *Taylor v Clark*[3], namely, to treat the tenant for life as entitled, during the year after the testator's death, to the dividends upon so much 3% stock as would have been produced by the conversion and investment of the property at the end of the year.'

[1] (1852) 5 De G & Sm 723.
[2] (1828) 4 Russ 195.
[3] (1841) 1 Hare 161.

50.17 The first branch of this decision, that relating to the ships where the trust for sale *was subject to a power to postpone sale*, was considered in *Re Parry*[1], where Romer J said:

'And, finally, not only was the order regarding the ships not inconsistent with previous authority, but it seems to me that it was plainly right. Notional conversion is very understandable when the executors are under a duty, express or implied, to sell; such a duty readily lets in the doctrine that equity regards that as done which ought to be done and the notional conversion arising from the doctrine (subject to a year's grace) acted as a convenient medium for preserving the balance between life tenant and remainderman. If no duty exists, however, the medium is not available, and another has to be found in its place. If there is no duty upon the executor to sell at once, or within a year, or at any other time, I can see no reason for assuming a notional conversion at once, or within a year, or at any other time. The essential equity, however—the balance between the successive interests—remains equally compelling even where there is no immediate obligation to convert and property is retained for the benefit of the estate as a whole; it is accordingly rational, and indeed obvious, to substitute a valuation of the testator's assets in the place of a hypothetical sale, and, if so, it is difficult to think of a better date for the valuation than *the day when the testator died* and the assets passed to his executors.'

[1] [1947] Ch 23, [1946] 2 All ER 412.

50.18 Thus, where residuary personalty is subject to a power to postpone sale, one has to wait until the residuary estate is ascertained (after collecting in all assets and paying debts, taxes and expenses) and then make a retrospective valuation at the testator's death. It might have been better to restrict *Brown v Gellatly* to a power to postpone the sale of specific assets comprised within residuary personalty and conveniently have the end of the executor's year as the date of valuation of the residuary state which should have been ascertained by them.

50.19 This is the basic rule laid down in *Re Fawcett¹* where Farwell J laid down the following rules as to the respective rights of persons entitled to the capital and income of a residuary estate comprising unauthorised investments *where there is no express power to postpone conversion*:

(1)   In the case of investments retained more than one year after the death of the testator the tenant for life is entitled to interest at 4% from the death till realisation on their value one year after the death. [As to the rate of interest see para 50.22 below]

(2)   In the case of investments sold within one year from the death the tenant for life is entitled to the interest on the net proceeds of sale from the date of the death till completion of the sale.

(3)   The unauthorised investments for the time being unsold must be treated en bloc as one aggregate for the purpose of the rule in *Howe v Lord Dartmouth²*.

(4)   In applying that rule the Apportionment Act 1870 ought not to be applied to income accounts with reference to unauthorised investments.

(5)   Any excess income from unauthorised investments over that payable to the tenant for life ought to be invested in authorised investments and the subsequent income thereof paid to the tenant for life.

(6)   If actual income from unauthorised investments is less than 4% payable to the tenant for life then the tenant for life is entitled to have his income made up at 4% simple interest (less tax) out of excess income subsequently arising from unauthorised investments or from the proceeds of subsequent sale of unauthorised investments. The deficit cannot be made up out of past excess income from unauthorised investments since such excess income will have become authorised capital.

¹   [1940] Ch 402.
²   (1802) 7 Ves 137.

Annuities of varying amount or uncertain duration

50.20 Where the property consists of an annuity of varying amount or uncertain duration (so that no reasonably accurate valuation can be made) then each instalment must be treated as a reversion falling in, as in *Re Earl of Chesterfield's Trusts¹* and *Re Busfield²*.

¹   (1883) 24 Ch D 643.
²   (20 February 1919, unreported) per Sargant J; *Michael v Callil* (1945) 72 CLR 509.

50.21 *The trustee's duties*

*Income derived from property of which testator was mortgagee
in possession*

50.21 On the same principle, where part of a testator's residuary estate consisted of a colliery of which he was mortgagee in possession, the question arose as to how accumulations of the income, derived from working the colliery since the testator's death, were to be apportioned between tenant for life and remaindermen. It was held that the proper principle was that so much as would, if invested at the testator's death at 4% with yearly rests, have amounted to the sum in the hands of the trustees, should be treated as capital, and the rest as income[1].

1   *Re Godden* [1893] 1 Ch 292.

Rate of interest allowed to tenant for life

50.22 It will be perceived that in all the above cases the rate of interest on the capital value allowed to the life tenant was 4%. About the turn of the century, owing to the drop in the current rate of interest, 3% was substituted for four[1], but 4% was reverted to in 1920[2], and this was the rate allowed as late as 1946 in relation to a death occurring in 1936[3]. But in *Wentworth v Wentworth*[4] the Privy Council stated that they did not think it expedient to hamper the court by laying down any fixed rule as to the rate of interest to be allowed to tenants for life on the estimated value of the capital of the property and directed an inquiry as to what annual sum would, under all the circumstances of the case, be fair. On the other hand, Eve J in *Re Beech*[5] pointed out that:

> 'a departure from a salutary rule in matters of this kind introducing as it does an element of uncertainty in practice and administration can only be justified if the changed conditions on which it is founded continue at least as constant as those upon which the rule was itself framed.'

1   *Re Goodenough* [1895] 2 Ch 537; and *Re Duke of Cleveland's Estate* [1895] 2 Ch 542. But cf *Re Owen* [1912] 1 Ch 519.
2   *Re Beech* [1920] 1 Ch 40; *Re Baker* [1924] 2 Ch 271.
3   *Re Parry* [1947] Ch 23 at 46, [1946] 2 All ER 412 at 423.
4   [1900] AC 163; also see *Re Laner and Stekl* (1974) 47 DLR (3d) 286, (1975) 54 DLR (3d) 159.
5   [1920] 1 Ch 40 at 44; and cf *Re Parry* [1947] Ch 23 at 47, [1946] 2 All ER 412 at 422; and *Re Ellis* [1935] Ch 193 at p 200.

50.23 The period of low interest rates which followed the Second World War proved to lack that constancy, and no instance has been reported in which the court adopted a rate of interest lower than 4%. This time-honoured 4% rate was confirmed in 1961[1]. Since then there have been periods when 4% may have been regarded as the 'real' rate of interest when higher actual rates of interest have reflected compensation for loss of capital value due to high rates of inflation[2]: indeed, in one case[3] actual interest at the court's special account rate in respect of lost capital was divided equally between life tenant and remainderman. It is now clear that the courts are well aware of the impact of inflation and so will be much concerned with 'real' interest rates as opposed to high actual interest rates[4].

1   *Re Berry* [1962] Ch 97, [1961] 1 All ER 529.
2   *Bartlett v Barclays Bank Trust Co* [1980] Ch 515 at 547.
3   *Jaffray v Marshall* [1994] 1 All ER 143 at 154.
4   *Jaffray v Marshall* [1994] 1 All ER 143; *Wright v British Railways Board* [1983] 2 AC 773. Further see para 89.46 ff.

Paragraph 2(b)

Tenant for life entitled to part of corpus of non-income-bearing property when realised

50.24 In the above cases the income actually received by the trustees exceeded that which they were authorised to pay to the tenant for life. But the same principle applies in favour of the tenant for life where personal[1] property is not presently saleable or realisable except at an unreasonable loss, and, pending realisation, produces no income; for instance, where part of the estate consists of a policy of assurance on another's life which does not fall in for some years after the testator's death, or a reversion in the strict sense of that word[2]. This is true even though, when the asset in question does fall in, a sum is received in respect of interest in addition to the cash or other property representing its capital value[3]. In such cases, unless the settlor contemplated that it should not be sold[4], it would be unfair to the tenant for life that he should lose intervening income. Therefore, when it does fall in, the money must be apportioned, as between capital and income, by ascertaining the sum which, put out at 4% per annum[5] on the day of the testator's death, and accumulated at compound interest with yearly rests, and deducting income tax, would, with the accumulations, have produced the amount actually received. The sum so ascertained must be treated as capital, and retained by the trustees. The residue is income, and must be paid to the tenant for life[6]. The same principle applies where a debt due to the estate is recovered by the trustees without interest[7]. It has no application to trust property consisting of an absolute interest in possession subject to a charge on income[8].

1   See *Re Woodhouse* [1941] Ch 332, [1941] 2 All ER 265.
2   *Re Hobson* (1885) 53 LT 627; *Rowlls v Bebb* [1900] 2 Ch 107, CA.
3   *Re Chance's Will Trusts* [1962] Ch 593, [1962] 1 All ER 942, where Wilberforce J considered this part of the text of the 11th edition of this book.
4   *Re Pitcairn* [1896] 2 Ch 199; but cf *Re Hubbuck* [1896] 1 Ch 754.
5   As to the rate of interest, see para 50.22 above.
6   *Re Earl of Chesterfield's Trusts* (1883) 24 Ch D 643; and see also *Massy v Gahan* (1889) 23 LR Ir 518; *Re Morley* [1895] 2 Ch 738; and *Wilkinson v Duncan* (1857) 23 Beav 469.
7   *Re Duke of Cleveland's Estate* [1895] 2 Ch 542. It also applies to instalments of purchase-money payable over a series of years.
8   *Re Holliday* [1947] Ch 402, [1947] 1 All ER 695.

50.25 Where a testator's estate includes national savings certificates the tenant for life is not entitled to any part of the sum received on encashment which represents interest earned before the death, since there is an agreement between the purchaser of the certificates and the government that, unless they are encashed, a sum shall be added to the principal month by month with the result that at the end of each completed month the addition is capitalised[1].

1   *Re Holder* [1953] Ch 468, [1953] 2 All ER 1.

Rule may be negatived expressly or by inference

50.26 This branch of the rule, like all the others, is subject to any express or implied direction to the contrary in the trust instrument; and it is now common to find in wills a clause expressly providing that, pending sale, calling in, and conversion of property, the whole of the income shall be applied as income, and on the other hand that no part of the proceeds of the sale, calling in, or conversion of reversionary property or policies of assurance shall be paid or applied as income[1]. A usual form of the clause[2] is:

> 'The income of my estate, however invested, and whether received in respect of a period wholly or only partly prior to my death but actually received after my death shall form part of and be applied as if the same were income of authorised investments thereof[3] and a reversionary or other future interest forming part of my residuary estate shall not be sold before falling into possession unless my trustees shall see special reason for such earlier sale.'

1   Cf Administration of Estates Act 1925, s 33(5), which relates to intestacy.
2   See 42 *Encyclopaedia of Forms and Precedents* (5th edn) Forms 341–343. See also Form 8 of Statutory Will Forms 1925.
3   These words will not exclude also the rule in *Allhusen v Whittell* (1867) LR 4 Eq 295; as to which see para 51.5 below (*Re Ullswater* [1952] Ch 105, [1951] 2 All ER 989).

50.27 Sometimes the latter part of such a clause is so worded that:

> 'no property not actually producing income shall be treated as producing income or as entitling any tenant for life to the receipt of income.'

50.28 This form is not, however, desirable, as it may raise awkward questions as to whether it extends beyond the case of reversionary property, eg to interest in arrear or to interest which is only payable at a future date. Thus, in one case, where the testator used the above form of words, the question arose whether they applied to a mortgage made in the testator's favour, where the principal, together with simple interest, was only to be paid on the mortgagor's death. It was held that they did not, however, on the ground that such clauses only apply to property which is not *producing* income, and not to property which is *producing* income, payment of which is merely postponed[1].

1   *Re Lewis* [1907] 2 Ch 296.

50.29 In cases where the testator does not exclude the rule entirely but gives the trustees a discretionary power to retain assets which do not produce income the rule will be excluded in respect of any particular asset when, but not until, the trustees consciously determine to exercise this power of retention in respect of that asset[1].

1   *Re Guinness's Settlement* [1966] 2 All ER 497, [1966] 1 WLR 1355.

Paragraph 3

Proceeds of insufficient security are divided between capital and income if latter in arrear

50.30 Where a trust security turns out to be insufficient, and interest is in arrear, the sum ultimately realised by the depreciated security is divisible between capital and overdue income—even where the settlor has directed that the actual income of his estate pending conversion shall be treated as income, but that no property not actually producing income shall be treated as producing any[1]. The principles on which such division ought to be made were settled by the Court of Appeal in *Re Atkinson*[2] where it was held that the sum realised ought to be apportioned between tenant for life and remainderman in the proportion which the amount due for arrears bears to the amount due in respect of the capital debt.

1   *Re Hubbuck* [1896] 1 Ch 754; and *Re Lewis* [1907] 2 Ch 296.
2   [1904] 2 Ch 160; and see *Re Walker's Settlement Trusts* [1936] Ch 280. See also *Re Morris' Will Trusts* [1960] 3 All ER 548, [1960] 1 WLR 1210.

Prior to realisation of insufficient security tenant for life entitled to whole of income actually received

50.31 The rule only applies where the insufficient security has been realised. Until then, the tenant for life is entitled to keep all the interest actually paid, or which is in hand ready to be paid[1]. Thus, where the trustees were mortgagees in possession of property, and interest was in arrear at their testator's death, it was held that they must first apply each instalment of rent in satisfaction of the arrears of interest due to the testator, and then distribute the balance as income up to but not exceeding the interest accrued since the testator's death on the mortgage, and apply any excess as capital[2].

1   *Re Broadwood's Settlement* [1908] 1 Ch 115.
2   *Re Coaks* [1911] 1 Ch 171. Ought it not to be net rental income after payment of management expenses?

50.32 The rule has no application where an investment is of such a nature (eg preference shares specifically settled) that a dividend is only payable if earned; and this is so even in the case of cumulative preference shares where the dividend which is unpaid in one year has to be made good out of the profits earned in a subsequent year. In all such cases the actual dividends declared belong to the tenant for life at the time when the dividend is declared, and the representatives of a deceased tenant for life have no claim to have arrears made good out of the dividend[1].

1   *Re Taylor's Trusts* [1905] 1 Ch 734; *Re Sale* [1913] 2 Ch 697; *Re Wakley* [1920] 2 Ch 205, CA; *Re Marjoribanks* [1923] 2 Ch 307. For a case where under a scheme by the court ordinary shareholders had surrendered some of their shares to preference shareholders whose dividends were in arrear, see *Re MacIver's Settlement* [1936] Ch 198.

Paragraph 4

How far rule applies to unauthorised investments made by trustee

50.33 The rule as to the tenant for life being only entitled to 4% on investments made by the settlor which ought to be converted, does not apply to investments made by the trustee in breach of trust. In these circumstances, if no loss of capital is sustained, the remainderman is not entitled to have the capital increased by adding to it the difference between the income actually paid to the tenant for life and 4%, or such other rate as is for the time being allowed[1]; the reason being that in such cases (herein differing from speculative or wasting property settled by the settlement) the amount of the trust fund is definitely ascertained, and if it has not in fact been depreciated by the breach of trust the remainderman has no equity to have it appreciated at the expense of the life tenant. This principle holds good where no loss has been sustained, even although the tenant for life was also one of the trustees[2].

[1] Per Byrne J in *Re Appleby* [1903] 1 Ch 565 at 566; *Stroud v Gwyer* (1860) 28 Beav 130; but cf *Re Hill* (1881) 50 LJ Ch 551; which was distinguished in *Slade v Chaine* [1908] 1 Ch 522.
[2] *Re Hoyles* [1912] 1 Ch 67.

50.34 Where, however, by reason of a breach of trust, the capital has become depreciated, then when it is realised, although the tenant for life, who was no party to the breach, cannot be ordered to refund income, yet he will not get any part of the amount realised to make up arrears (if any), without bringing into hotchpot all the income he has received from the security during its entire continuance. For that is the only way of placing the beneficiaries in the approximate positions in which they would have been if no breach had been committed[1].

[1] *Re Bird* [1901] 1 Ch 916; and comments thereon of Warrington KC arguendo in *Re Alston* [1901] 2 Ch 584 at 587.

ARTICLE 51
DUTY OF TRUSTEE IN RELATION TO THE PAYMENT OF
OUTGOINGS OUT OF CORPUS AND INCOME RESPECTIVELY

51.1

Subject to particular statutes[1] a trustee has a general discretion to allocate outgoings out of income or capital as he sees fit, but using his powers to effectuate the settlor's purposes and in accordance with his duty to keep a fair balance between the interests of income beneficiaries and capital beneficiaries, and so taking account of the following traditional principles governing the incidence of outgoings (after the trustees have taken advantage of their initial right to resort to capital or income as they find easiest to discharge outgoings):

(a) the corpus bears capital charges incurred for the benefit of the whole trust estate, and the income bears the interest on them[2], while if the current income is insufficient, arrears of interest on capital charges must be paid out of subsequent income[3];

(b) the income usually bears current expenses[4], including the entire cost of keeping leaseholds in repair[5];

(c) where repairs to trust freeholds are necessary to save them from destruction[6], or fines become payable for the renewal of leases[7], or for putting in repair leasehold property which was out of repair at the date of the creation of the trust[8], the court may empower the trustees to raise the necessary amount in such a way as will be equitable between income and corpus;

(d)   all costs incident to the administration and protection of the trust property, including legal proceedings, are borne by corpus[9], unless they relate exclusively to the tenant for life[10], the corpus bearing all costs, charges and expenses incurred for the benefit of the whole estate.

[1]   Eg the War Damage Act 1943.
[2]   *Marshall v Crowther* (1874) 2 Ch D 199; *Whitbread v Smith* (1854) 3 De GM & G 727; and see and consider *Norton v Johnstone* (1885) 30 Ch D 649.
[3]   *Honywood v Honywood* [1902] 1 Ch 347; *Frewen v Law Life Assurance Society* [1896] 2 Ch 511.
[4]   *Fountaine v Pellet* (1791) 1 Ves 337 at 342 (rates and taxes); *Shore v Shore* (1859) 4 Drew 501 (receiver's commission and expenses of passing account); *Carver v Duncan (Inspector of Taxes)* [1985] AC 1082 at 1120 per Lord Templeman.
[5]   See *Re Gjers* [1899] 2 Ch 54; and *Re Betty* [1899] 1 Ch 821; but cf *Re Baring* [1893] 1 Ch 61; and *Re Owen* [1912] 1 Ch 519; distinguished in *Re Shee* [1934] Ch 345.
[6]   *Re Courtier* (1886) 34 Ch D 136; per Cotton and Lindley LJJ in *Re Hotchkys* (1886) 32 Ch D 408.
[7]   *White v White* (1804) 9 Ves 554; *Nightingale v Lawson* (1785) 1 Bro CC 440.
[8]   *Re Copland's Settlement* [1900] 1 Ch 326.
[9]   *Lord Brougham v Lord Poulett* (1855) 19 Beav 119 at 135; *Sanders v Miller* (1858) 25 Beav 154; *Re Earl De La Warr's Estates* (1881) 16 Ch D 587; *Stott v Milne* (1884) 25 Ch D 710; explained in *Re Weall* (1889) 42 Ch D 674.
[10]   See *Re Marner's Trusts* (1866) LR 3 Eq 432; *Re Evans' Trusts* (1872) 7 Ch App 609; *Re Smith's Trusts* (1870) LR 9 Eq 374.

Section 31(1) Trustee Act 2000 general discretion

51.2 By s 31(1) 'a trustee (a) is entitled to be reimbursed from the trust funds or (b) may pay out of the trust funds expenses properly incurred by him when acting on behalf of the trust', while 'trust funds' is defined in s 39 for the purposes of the Trustee Act 2000 as 'income or capital funds of the trust'. This right of reimbursement or exoneration has always operated as a first charge on the capital and income within the trust, so that the trustees can use whatever is to hand and then make later adjustments to the accounts so as to throw the ultimate incidence of the expense on income or capital as appropriate[1] in accordance with well-established equitable principles developed on a case-by-case basis or in accordance with statute (eg the old s 19 of the Trustee Act 1925 before the new one substituted by s 34 of the Trustee Act 2000).

[1]   *Stott v Milne* (1884) 25 Ch D 710 at 715 per Lord Selborne LC; *Carver v Duncan* [1985] AC 1082 at 1120 per Lord Templeman.

51.3 The old s 19 only permitted premiums to be paid out of income, but the substituted s 19(5) states that 'trust funds' means 'any income or capital funds of the trust' and the Law Commission[1] clearly intended the trustees to have a discretion as to the ultimate incidence of those premiums. The Law Commission[2] also clearly intended that the cost of employing a nominee or custodian or other agent should ultimately be allocated as the trustees decided in their discretion and believed that the s 39 definition of 'trust funds' as 'income or capital funds of the trust' achieved this.

¹   Law Com No 260 'Trustees' Powers and Duties' at paras 6.6, 8.39, and at p119 note on cl 34 draft Bill.
²   Law Com No 260 at paras 5.13, 8.33, and p 117 note on clauses 31 and 32 of draft Bill.

51.4 There seems no reason to restrict the operation of 'income or capital funds of the trust' to the initial payment of outgoings so as not to cover the ultimate incidence of outgoings. The words should be taken at their face¹ value in accordance with the modern philosophy (eg with broad powers of investment) to confer very flexible discretionary powers on trustees, but subject to the safeguards of the duties imposed on trustees when coming to exercise those powers eg the duty to act fairly between life tenant and remainderman, enabling the remainderman to challenge apportioning the cost of collecting rental income onto capital and the life tenant to challenge any attempt to apportion the cost of selling a capital asset onto income.

¹   As indicated in J Kessler *Drafting Trusts and Will Trusts* (7th edn), para 20.28, although the contrary view has been taken by *Lewin on Trusts* (17th edn) para 25–26B. The power in TA 2000, s 31(1) and in TA 1925, s 19 is merely an administrative power, like that in TA 1925, s 22(4), and so will not prevent a life tenant having an interest in possession for tax purposes.

Paragraph (a)

Charges and incumbrances

51.5 Where a capital sum is secured on property, it is payable out of corpus; but the interest on it is payable out of income¹ arising not only from the incumbered property, but from all other property subject to the same trust. If the current income is insufficient to keep down the interest, the arrears are payable out of subsequent income², and this is so, even where the charge in respect of which the arrears have arisen has been paid off by means of a sale of part of the property³.

¹   *Marshall v Crowther* (1874) 2 Ch D 199; *Whitbread v Smith* (1854) 3 De GM & G 727; and see *Allhusen v Whittell* (1867) LR 4 Eq 295. *Allhusen v Whittell* deals with the situation where a testator leaves his residuary estate to A for life, remainder to B absolutely and in accordance with the general law debts, expenses and legacies have to be paid out of the residue. The payments are treated as coming partly from income and partly from capital. That sum has to be ascertained which together with interest for the year succeeding death would amount to the total expended on debts, expenses and legacies: the sum so ascertained is borne by B entitled to capital and the excess of the total expenditure over the sum is borne by A entitled to income. The rate of interest to be used depends on the ratio subsisting between the actual net income after tax for the year succeeding death and the value of the residuary estate: *Re Oldham* [1927] WN 113. The calculation should be modified if payment of debts, etc is significantly before or after the end of the executor's year: rough and ready calculations will suffice: *Re Wills* [1915] 1 Ch 769. For words inappropriate to exclude the rule in *Allhusen v Whittell*, see *Re Ullswater* [1952] Ch 105, [1951] 1 All ER 989. Also see *Re Hogg* [1983] LS Gaz R 2838.
²   *Honywood v Honywood* [1902] 1 Ch 347; *Frewen v Law Life Assurance Society* [1896] 2 Ch 511; *Re Hotchkys* (1886) 32 Ch D 408.

³ *Honywood v Honywood* [1902] 1 Ch 347; *Frewen v Law Life Assurance Society* [1896] 2 Ch 511; *Re Hotchkys* (1886) 32 Ch D 408. Capital must be reimbursed if used to discharge an income expense when insufficient income was available.

51.6 The rule as to capital charges being borne by corpus prevails even where a debt is secured by, or is payable as, an *annuity* or by instalments. In such a case the tenant for life will have to contribute an amount equal to interest on the capital value¹.

¹ *Bulwer v Astley* (1844) 1 Ph 422; *Playfair v Cooper* (1853) 17 Beav 187; *Ley v Ley* (1868) LR 6 Eq 174; *Re Muffett* (1888) 39 Ch D 534 (purchase-money consisting of a life annuity). But this does not apply to the case of a jointure, or other charge, where there is no covenant and therefore no debt: *Re Popham* [1914] WN 257; *Re Darby* [1939] Ch 905, [1939] 3 All ER 6.

How the respective liabilities of corpus and income are computed

51.7 There has, however, been a curious conflict of judicial authority as to how the respective contributions of capital and income ought to be computed in such cases. In *Re Bacon¹* and *Re Henry²*, Kekewich J laid it down that the proper way was to raise the required amount out of corpus as required, in which way the tenant for life would lose a corresponding amount of income. This view was, however, dissented from by Swinfen Eady J in *Re Dawson³*, where his Lordship held that the successive instalments of the annuities must be borne by income and capital in proportion to the actuarial values of the life estate and reversion at the testator's death. But in the subsequent case of *Re Perkins⁴* where it was pointed out that this actuarial method would act unfairly, the same judge directed that each instalment of the annuity should be met by calculating what sum with 3% simple interest from the commencement of the life tenancy to the day of payment would have met the instalment, the sum so ascertained to come out of capital and the balance out of income. This case was subsequently followed by Joyce J in *Re Thompson⁵*, by Parker J in *Re Poyser⁶* and by the Court of Appeal in *Re Berkeley⁷* and may now be taken as establishing the recognised rule⁸.

¹ (1893) 62 LJ Ch 445.
² [1907] 1 Ch 30.
³ [1906] 2 Ch 211.
⁴ [1907] 2 Ch 596.
⁵ [1908] WN 195.
⁶ [1910] 2 Ch 444; and *Re Craven* [1914] 1 Ch 358; and *Re Tod* [1916] 1 Ch 567.
⁷ [1968] Ch 744, [1968] 3 All ER 364.
⁸ But as to the rate of interest, see para 50.22 above.

Purchase of annuities

51.8 If, for example, a testator settles his residuary estate but directs that an annuity be purchased for A for life, then A is entitled to take the amount of money required to produce such annuity¹. A has a vested legacy as from the testator's death and is entitled to interest thereon from such date². In the absence of a gift over, a direction that A shall not receive the capital value of the annuity or shall not alienate the annuity is void as a naked in terrorem prohibition and probably also as repugnant to A's absolute interest in the capital value[3]. If the annuity is charged on the whole income or the whole income and corpus A is not entitled to anything except the annuity and having sufficient assets set aside to cover the annuity[4]. If there is a further provision empowering the trustees on sale of corpus to purchase annuities for annuitants and the trustees decide to exercise this power then on completion of the sale when the trustees receive the capital moneys A will have a vested right to the amount of capital required to produce the annuity[5].

1   *Stokes v Cheek* (1860) 28 Beav 620.
2   *Re Robbins* [1907] 2 Ch 8, CA; *Re Brunning* [1909] 1 Ch 276.
3   *Woodmeston v Walker* (1831) 2 Russ & M 197; *Re Mabbett* [1891] 1 Ch 707.
4   *Harbin v Masterman* [1896] 1 Ch 351, CA; *Re Coller's Deed Trusts* [1939] Ch 277, CA.
5   *Re Mabbett* [1891] 1 Ch 707 (where A received nothing when dying before completion of the contract for sale).

Local government charges

51.9 Expenses incurred by a local authority in sewering, paving and flagging a new street, and charged by statute on the adjacent land, are a charge on corpus and not income, even although they, with interest, are repayable to the local authority by instalments[1], and by s 213 of the Highways Act 1980 any person who could sell such lands under the Compulsory Purchase Act 1965 may mortgage them for raising the charge.

1   *Re Legh's Settled Estate* [1902] 2 Ch 274; but cf Highways Act 1980, ss 212, 213.

Arrears of interest accrued during the settlor's life

51.10 Arrears of interest on incumbrances accrued in the lifetime of the settlor before the tenant for life became such, are a charge on corpus, the tenant for life merely paying interest on them[1].

1   *Revel v Watkinson* (1748) 1 Ves Sen 93; *Playfair v Cooper* (1853) 17 Beav 187.

51.11 The strong inclination of the court to saddle capital charges on corpus was well exemplified by *Norton v Johnstone*[1] where a testator had directed that the income of certain estates should be accumulated until the amount of the accumulations should be sufficient to pay off existing mortgages; and that, subject thereto, the property should be held to the use of the plaintiff for life, with remainders over. Before the accumulations were sufficient to discharge the mortgages, the mortgagees sold a part of the property; and with the moneys so produced, and part of the moneys already accumulated, the mortgages were paid off. The tenant for life then claimed to be let into possession, and also to have the balance of the accumulations paid to him. On the other hand, the remainderman urged that, inasmuch as the mortgage debt had been paid off by means of a sale of the corpus (which was not what was contemplated by the testator), the accumulation of rents ought to continue, until such a sum was obtained as would be equal to the amount raised by the sale; and that the sum thus obtained ought to be employed in recouping the inheritance, the tenant for life receiving only the interest of it.

[1] (1885) 30 Ch D 649; and see also *Re Harrison* (1889) 43 Ch D 55; and *Re Brandon* (1932) 49 TLR 48.

51.12 Pearson J, however, decided in favour of the tenant for life, on the ground that the mortgage debts had been paid in a way different from that which the testator intended, that he had not provided for that event, and that, consequently, the ordinary rule as to the incidence of capital charges must govern the case.

51.13 Where, however, on the expiration of a lease granted by the settlor, the tenant for life is obliged to pay compensation for improvements to the outgoing lessee *under a covenant in the lease*, he has no claim to saddle the compensation on corpus. For, as Jessel MR said,

> 'If he lives long enough he will let the land again and get the outlay from the incoming tenant, and so if he recovered it now ... he would be repaid it twice over'[1].

[1] *Mansel v Norton* (1883) 22 Ch D 769.

51.14 But this seems to assume that the life tenant is empowered to require (and keep for his own use) a premium from the new lease. However, this rule does not apply to compensation payable under the Agricultural Holdings Act 1986, as such compensation is expressly provided for by ss 86 and 87 of that Act. Under s 86(1) a landlord can obtain from the Minister of Agriculture an order charging the holding with repayment of compensation and the trustees can redeem this charge out of capital moneys pursuant to s 73(1)(ii) of the Settled Land Act 1925[1].

[1] *Re Duke of Wellington's Parliamentary Estates* [1972] Ch 374, [1971] 2 All ER 1140.

Calls on shares

51.15 Calls on shares which form part of a trust estate are outgoings attributable to capital and not to income, and are accordingly payable out of corpus[1].

[1] *Todd v Moorhouse* (1874) LR 19 Eq 69; and now TA 1925, s 11(2).

Paragraph (b)

Current annual charges

51.16 All charges of an annual character, except annual charges to secure capital sums, are payable out of income, for otherwise the corpus would inevitably decrease year by year, and would ultimately be swallowed up. As Lord Templeman said in *Carver v Duncan* (Inspector of Taxes)[1], 'The general rule is that income must bear all ordinary outgoings of a recurrent nature, such as rates and taxes, and interest on charges and incumbrances'. It has been held that the income must bear rates and taxes[2]; the commission of house

699

agents for obtaining tenants[3]; the rent payable for, and the expenses incident
to the observance and performance of the covenants and conditions in relation
to, leasehold hereditaments[4]. But a tenant for life is not liable to have his
income taken for breaches of covenant not occurring in his time[5]. It would
seem that even the cost of complying with a sanitary notice under the Public
Health (London) Act 1936[6], or a dangerous structure notice under the
London Building Act 1930, are, as a rule, payable by the tenant for life; but
not, apparently, the cost of a thorough reconstruction of the sewers of a
house[7], or other permanent improvements insisted on by the local authority[8].
Of course, annuities charged on income[9], the commission or poundage
payable to a receiver, and the expenses incident to the preparation and passing
of his accounts must be borne by income[10].

1   [1985] AC 1082 at 1120, HL.
2   *Fountaine v Pellet* (1791) 1 Ves 337, 342; including income tax even where there is a
    direction to pay income not exceeding £x per annum to A (*Re Cain's Settlement*) [1919]
    2 Ch 364.
3   *Re Leveson-Gower's Settled Estate* [1905] 2 Ch 95. But see *Re Watson* [1928] WN 309.
4   *Re Gjers* [1899] 2 Ch 54; *Re Betty* [1899] 1 Ch 821; cf *Re Tomlinson* [1898] 1 Ch 232.
5   *Re Betty* [1899] 1 Ch 821.
6   See *Re Copland's Settlement* [1900] 1 Ch 326; and *Re Lever* [1897] 1 Ch 32. See now
    London Government Act 1963, s 40.
7   *Re Thomas* [1900] 1 Ch 319; and see *Re McClure's Trusts* [1906] WN 200.
8   See *Re Farnham's Trusts* [1904] 2 Ch 561. The cost of private street works is specially
    provided for by the Highways Act 1980, ss 212, 213.
9   *Playfair v Cooper* (1853) 17 Beav 187 at 193; *Miller v Huddleston* (1851) 3 Mac & G
    513.
10 *Shore v Shore* (1859) 4 Drew 501. Where leaseholds have to be let at a loss, the loss falls
    on income (*Re Owen* [1912] 1 Ch 519).

Insurance premiums

51.17 Where a life policy is maintained for the benefit of capital, the
premiums are (in the absence of express direction) payable out of capital
raised from time to time by a charge on the policy[1]. In practice such premiums
are usually paid in the first instance out of income, and are then repayable to
the tenant for life when the policy falls in with interest at 4%[2]. Of course,
where a policy is specifically settled, express directions are almost invariably
given for payment of the premiums; and where they are directed to be paid out
of income, and for some reason the policy lapses without breach of trust, the
amounts which would have been paid for keeping it up must thenceforth be
paid to capital account[3].

1   *Carver v Duncan (Inspector of Taxes)* [1985] AC 1082 at 1180, HL; *Macdonald v Irvine*
    (1878) 8 Ch D 101, CA. Expenditure for the benefit of the whole estate is a capital expense
    so premiums in respect of inheritance tax protection and endowment policies are capital
    expenses.
2   *Re Morley* [1895] 2 Ch 738.
3   *Re Fitzgerald* (1904) 90 LT 266 at 274, CA.

51.18 As a result of s 34 of the Trustee Act 2000, s 19 of the Trustee
Act 1925 now confers on trustees of all trusts (including bare trusts[1]) power to
insure any trust property against risks of loss or damage due to any event and
to pay the premiums out of the 'trust funds' defined[2] to mean 'any income or

capital funds of the trust'. A trustee of land in the UK, who has all the powers of an absolute owner in relation to the land[3], will thereby incidentally have a further power to insure the land against any risks.

1   When the *Saunders v Vautier* beneficiaries can collectively direct the trustees as to the exercise or not of the statutory power: a trustee with an equitable lien ranks as a beneficiary (see para 83.27 below) so that the other beneficiaries will need his consent to their proposals.
2   TA 2000, s 19(5).
3   TA 2000, s 8(3).

51.19 Trustees exercising these statutory administrative powers may initially pay premiums out of either capital or income, as is most administratively convenient, before allocating the burden of the premiums taking account of the general principle that the insurance is for the benefit of the whole estate capital and so should normally be borne by capital in the absence of express provision as to the incidence of premiums[1]. However, where there are not different beneficiaries or classes of beneficiaries interested in income and capital but, for example, co-owners of income-yielding land, then premiums should be paid out of income and not out of capital necessitating sale or mortgage of the land.

1   *Re Betty* [1899] 1 Ch 821 at 829; *Re McEacharn* (1911) 103 LT 900 at 902; *Carver v Duncan* [1985] AC 1082, HL. As seen at para 51.2 above, the substituted TA 1925, s 19(5) confers upon trustees much discretion on the ultimate incidence of premiums, subject to their duty to act fairly.

51.20 When exercising a statutory or an express power to insure, the statutory duty of care applies[1] (unless excluded by the trust instrument[2]) but it does not seem that it applies to the decision whether or not to exercise the power[3].

1   TA 2000, Sch 1, para 4.
2   TA 2000, Sch 1, para 5.
3   'Trustees' Powers and Duties' Law Com No 260 (1999) para 6.9 and see terminology 'in deciding' in TLATA 1996, s 9A inserted by TA 2000, Sch 2, para 47.

51.21 It seems that, nowadays, a trustee, having extensive powers of insurance, is under an equitable duty to insure property to the extent that an ordinary prudent business person would have insured his or her own property in the circumstances[1], taking account of the value and liquidity of the trust capital and the cost of premiums. The trustee should be afforded reasonable leeway in balancing the risk of substantial loss against the burden of very expensive insurance, so that it may be proper to take out an insurance policy with a high excess to be borne first by the trust and only to cover some basic risks rather than all risks or even not to insure, although it would then be wise to obtain the written consents thereto of existing beneficiaries of full age and capacity[2].

1   *Re Betty* [1899] 1 Ch 821 at 829; *Kingham v Kingham* [1897] 1 IR 170 at 174; 'Trustees' Powers and Duties' Law Com No 260 (1999) p 163; *Lewin on Trusts* (17th edn) para 34–37; P Reed & R Wilson *The Trustee Act 2000: A Practical Guide* (Jordans 2001) paras 7.11–7.14.

² Then they cannot sue for the breach of the trust and they are liable to indemnify the trustee.

51.22 Trustees have to exercise their powers unanimously (unless otherwise authorised by the trust instrument or by statute) so that one trustee can prevent his co-trustees from exercising the power of insurance to any greater extent than he wishes. His co-trustees cannot then be liable for any breach of trust unless his view was outside the reasonable limits for the exercise of the trustees' discretion such that they should have applied to the court for directions pursuant to their paramount duty to act in the best interests of present and future beneficiaries[1].

¹ *Cowan v Scargill* [1985] Ch 270 at 286–287.

Money paid for redemption of rentcharge

51.23 Where a rentcharge is redeemed by the tenant for life, he is only entitled to be recouped, out of corpus, the amount paid, less the value of the redemption of his life estate[1].

¹ *Re Duke of Leinster* (1889) 23 LR Ir 152.

Losses on trust business

51.24 Where a business is vested in trustees in trust for successive tenants for life and a remainderman, the net losses on one year's trading must generally be made good out of the profits of subsequent years, and not out of capital[1]. This is because the outgoings of a business are part of the regular current expenses, and there can be no profits until all losses are paid, whether such losses are incurred in a year in which gross profits exceed the losses, or were incurred in prior years. This rule, however, will not apply where a business is not carried on under a direction in the settlement, but all interested parties do not want a sale at a loss to occur so that the business is merely carried on temporarily until it can be sold profitably and the remaindermen concede that a *Re Earl of Chesterfield* appointment[2] is appropriate. In such cases the annual loss or profit (if any) ought to be apportioned between capital and income as follows. Calculate the sum which, put out at interest at 4% per annum on the day when the business ought to have been sold (if it could have been) and accumulated at compound interest at the like rate, with yearly rests, would, together with such interest and accumulations, after deducting income tax, be equivalent at the end of each year to the amount of the loss or profit sustained or made during that year. The sum so ascertained will be charged against, or credited to, capital, and the rest of the loss will be charged against, or the rest of the profit will be credited to, income[3].

¹ *Upton v Brown* (1884) 26 Ch D 588.
² See para 50.24 above.
³ *Re Hengler* [1893] 1 Ch 586. Cf *Re Owen* [1912] 1 Ch 519.

Where intention can be implied that losses shall be borne by capital

51.25 However, where, on the facts, it appears to have been the settlor's intention that losses in a trust business should be borne by capital, effect will be given to that intention. For instance, where *it has been the custom of a partnership* to write off the losses of unprosperous years from each partner's share of capital, that custom will be continued, even as between a tenant for life and remainderman after the death of a partner who has bequeathed his share to persons in succession[1].

1   *Gow v Foster* (1884) 26 Ch D 672.

51.26 So, where the settlement empowers trustees to make improvements out of capital or income, they must exercise a fair discretion, and not throw the cost wholly on income[1].

1   *Re Earl of Stamford and Warrington* [1916] 1 Ch 404.

Paragraph (c)

Repairs

51.27 Well-drawn settlements of house property on trust usually provide that the trustees shall keep it in repair, and insured against loss or damage by fire, out of the rents and profits.

51.28 Before 1997, s 28(2) of the Law of Property Act 1925 otherwise provided that:

(2)   Subject to any direction to the contrary in the disposition on trust for sale or in the settlement of the proceeds of sale, the net rents and profits of the land until sale, after keeping down costs of repairs and insurance and other outgoings shall be paid or applied, except so far as any part thereof may be liable to be set aside as capital money under the Settled Land Act 1925 in like manner as the income of investments representing the purchase-money would be payable or applicable if a sale had been made and the proceeds had been duly invested[1].

1   See also the SLA 1925, s 102, applicable to the trusts for sale by LPA 1925, s 28(1) until 1997.

51.29 Maugham J in *Re Smith*[1] held that the subsection did not take away the discretion of the court to decide in a proper case[2] that the cost of certain repairs ought to be borne by capital. Section 1 of the Settled Land and Trustee Acts (Courts' General Powers) Act 1943[3] then extended the courts' jurisdiction under s 57 of the Trustee Act 1925 and s 64 of the Settled Land Act 1925 (which applied to land held on trust for sale as a result of s 28(1) of the Law of Property Act 1925[4]) so as to enable it to order that the cost of any repairs shall be treated as a capital outgoing when they are for the benefit of all persons beneficially interested and the income out of which their cost would ordinarily have been payable has become inadequate for the purpose.

703

1   [1930] 1 Ch 88.
2   See *Re Hotchkys* (1886) 32 Ch D 408; *Re Farnham's Trusts* [1904] 2 Ch 561.
3   Set out at para 47.117 above, as amended and made permanent by the Emergency Laws (Miscellaneous Provisions) Act 1953.
4   *Re Simmons* [1956] Ch 125.

51.30   After 1996 and, now as a result of s 8(3) of the Trustee Act 2000[1], trustees of land[2] have all the powers of an absolute owner in relation to the land and so can carry out repairs and improvements. Whether such expenditure should be borne by capital or income now depends on equitable principles.

1   Replacing s 6(1) of the TLATA 1996.
2   The SLA 1925 as amended by the TA 2000, Sch 2, paras 7–17 governs the position of tenant for life and the SLA trustees. Many repairs to freehold land amount to improvements which can be thrown onto capital under SLA 1925 as amended by the Agricultural Holdings Act 1986: see para 51.33 below.

51.31   It has been held that trustees may, without any order, do such repairs to leasehold property as are necessary to prevent a forfeiture of the lease, and repay themselves out of the income[1], but without prejudice to the rights of tenant for life and remainderman between themselves[2], on the ground that trustees may expend money by way of salvage, and have a lien both on income and corpus for expenses properly incurred by them, as will be seen later on[3].

1   *Re Fowler* (1881) 16 Ch D 723.
2   *Re Hotchkys* (1886) 32 Ch D 408.
3   Article 86, below.

51.32   The following propositions founded on the practice prior to 1926 are submitted as offering some guidance as to the principles on which the court might be expected to act in the exercise of its jurisdiction to throw the cost of repairs on to capital and upon which the trustees should base the proper exercise of their discretion[1].

(1)   Where the property was in disrepair when the tenant for life came into possession, then, whatever its tenure may be, the court would probably not throw the cost exclusively on him, but would sanction a mortgage, equitably apportioning the ultimate cost between corpus and income[2]. There is, however, no reported case showing how this equitable apportionment will be carried out; but in one case in which Sir Arthur Underhill appeared before Romer J in chambers, that learned judge approved a scheme under which the trustees were to pay for a new roof in a tropical climate (which was estimated to last for twenty years only) by a sinking fund extending over that period. And where trustees, under a power, invested money in the purchase of real estate out of repair, the cost of putting it in repair was thrown exclusively on capital[3]. On the other hand, cases have been known where the judge made a rough and ready apportionment, such as an arbitrator might make. There is in fact no technical rule—the judge directs what he considers to be fair and reasonable.

(2)   Where the property was not in disrepair when the tenant for life came into possession, the question is governed by the maxim qui sensit

commodum debet sentire et onus, unless it becomes a clear case of salvage; and as regards leaseholds the person entitled to enjoy the income of the property must perform the conditions of the lease as to repairs[4].

(3)   The fact that the trustees are expressly authorised to pay for repairs out of income or capital will not justify them in throwing on to capital the cost of repairs which ought to be borne by income for the purpose of relieving the person entitled to that income, such powers being prima facie intended for the benefit of the estate and to be used so as to adjust the burden equitably[5].

[1]   For further examples see *Re Jackson* (1882) 21 Ch D 786; *Re Hawker's Settled Estates* (1897) 66 LJ Ch 341; *Re Lord Sherborne's Settled Estate* [1929] 1 Ch 345; *Re Smith* [1930] 1 Ch 88; *Re Whitaker* [1929] 1 Ch 662; *Re Conquest* [1929] 2 Ch 353; *Re Jacques Settled Estates* [1930] 2 Ch 418; and *Re Borough Court Estate* [1932] 2 Ch 39. For a case involving special circumstances, see *Re Earl Berkeley* [1968] Ch 744, [1968] 3 All ER 364, CA.

[2]   *Re Courtier* (1886) 34 Ch D 136; as explained in *Re Redding* [1897] 1 Ch 876; *Re Betty* [1899] 1 Ch 821; and *Re Kingham* [1897] 1 IR 170; acquiesced in by Kekewich J in *Re Gjers* [1899] 2 Ch 54; contrary to his previous decision in *Re Tomlinson* [1898] 1 Ch 232.

[3]   *Re Freman* [1898] 1 Ch 28; but cf *Re Lord De Tabley* (1896) 75 LT 328; *Re Freman*, above, was distinguished by Eve J in *Re Jervis* (1919) 146 LT Jo 215.

[4]   *Re Kingham* [1897] 1 IR 170; *Re Redding* [1897] 1 Ch 876; *Re Betty* [1899] 1 Ch 821; *Re Gjers* [1899] 2 Ch 54; and see *Re Partington* [1902] 1 Ch 711, as to re-drainage of a leasehold house being borne by income.

[5]   *Re Lord De Tabley* (1896) 75 LT 328; *Re Earl of Stamford and Warrington* [1916] 1 Ch 404; *Re Lord Boston's Will Trusts* [1956] Ch 395.

Alterations in the nature of repairs under the Settled Land Act

51.33 By the Third Schedule to the Settled Land Act 1925 improvements on which capital moneys are authorised by that Act to be expended[1] are to include structural or other[2] *additions to* or *alterations in* buildings reasonably necessary or proper to enable the same to be let, and also the rebuilding of the principal mansion house. But, in the latter case, the sum to be applied out of capital money is not to exceed one-half of the annual rent of the settled land. Under a similar provision in the Settled Land Act 1890 it was held, that although mere repairs and improvements will not amount to a 'rebuilding' of the principal mansion house[3]; yet reconstruction, alteration, and enlargement of a considerable part of the house may[4]. For instance, the Act was held to apply where the house had become infested with dry rot, and portions had to be rebuilt in order to save the whole[5]. It has likewise been held that the substitution of a block floor over concrete for ordinary floor boards in order to keep dry rot out of the basement of a large house let in separate offices was an alteration reasonably necessary or proper to enable the same to be let[6]. By virtue of the Agricultural Holdings Act 1986, s 89(1), and Seventh Schedule, the improvements authorised by the Settled Land Act 1925, s 83 and Third Schedule[7], include repairs to fixed equipment reasonably necessary for the proper farming of agricultural land.

[1]   SLA 1925, ss 73 (1) (iii), 83 and Sch 3. See also *Re Duke of Wellington's Parliamentary Estates* [1972] Ch 374, [1971] 2 All ER 1140.

[2]   *Re Lindsay's Settlement (No 2)* [1941] Ch 119, [1941] 1 All ER 143.

3   *Re De Teissier's Settled Estates* [1893] 1 Ch 153; *Re Lord De Tabley* (1896) 75 LT 328; *Re Wright's Settled Estates* (1900) 83 LT 159.
4   *Re Walker's Settled Estate* [1894] 1 Ch 189; and see *Re Leveson-Gower's Settled Estate* [1905] 2 Ch 95.
5   *Re Legh's Settled Estate* [1902] 2 Ch 274.
6   *Stanford v Roberts* [1901] 1 Ch 440; and see also *Re Clarke's Settlement* [1902] 2 Ch 327; *Re Gaskell's Settled Estates* [1894] 1 Ch 485; both approved by Court of Appeal in *Re Blagrave's Settled Estates* [1903] 1 Ch 560; *Standing v Gray* [1903] 1 IR 49; *Re Battle Abbey Settled Estate* [1933] WN 215; and *Re Swanwick House, Prestbury* [1939] 3 All ER 531; where the cost of conversion into flats was held to be proper expenditure to enable the property to be let to the greatest advantage.
7   See *Re Duke of Northumberland* [1951] Ch 202, [1950] 2 All ER 1181; *Re Sutherland Settlement Trusts* [1953] Ch 792, [1953] 2 All ER 27; *Re Lord Brougham and Vaux's Settled Estates* [1954] Ch 24, [1953] 2 All ER 655.

Fencing of unfenced land

51.34 Where the question arises as to the incidence of the cost, not of mere repairs, but of putting property into a better condition than it was in originally, it would seem that no part of the cost falls on income. Thus, the expense of fencing waste lands granted to a trustee for the benefit of the estate must be paid out of corpus exclusively[1].

1   *Earl of Cowley v Wellesley* (1866) LR 1 Eq 656; and see SLA 1925, s 83, and judgment of Kekewich J in *Re Verney's Settled Estates* [1898] 1 Ch 508.

Paragraph (d)

General costs incident to administration

51.35 Legal expenses or investment advice incident to the administration of a trust almost exclusively fall on capital, unless the settlor has expressly provided for them, for they are for the benefit of all persons interested. Thus:

the costs of the appointment of new trustees[1],

the costs incident to the investment or change of investment of trust funds[2],

the costs of obtaining investment advice, since such affects the future value of corpus and the future level of income[3],

the costs of obtaining legal advice[4], and of taking the direction of the court[5],

the costs of an administration action[6],

the costs of paying money into court under the Trustee Act[7],

the costs of bringing or defending actions against third parties for the protection of the estate[8] (eg lessees for breach of their covenants to repair[9]), and the like,

have all been held to be payable out of corpus.

1   *Re Fellows' Settlement* (1856) 2 Jur NS 62; *Re Fulham* (1850) 15 Jur 69; *Ex p Davies* (1852) 16 Jur 882.
2   But not of petition to vary investment of funds in court, see Equitable *Reversionary Interest Society v Fuller* (1861) 1 John & H 379.
3   *Carver v Duncan (Inspector of Taxes)* [1985] 2 All ER 645 at 653, HL.

4   *Poole v Pass* (1839) 1 Beav 600.
5   *Re Elmore's Will Trusts* (1860) 9 WR 66; *Re Leslie's Settlement Trusts* (1876) 2 Ch D 185.
6   *Re Turnley* (1866) 1 Ch App 152.
7   *Re Whitton's Trusts* (1869) LR 8 Eq 352.
8   See *Stott v Milne* (1884) 25 Ch D 710; *Hamilton v Tighe* [1898] 1 IR 123; and see also *Re Earl De La Warr's Estates* (1881) 16 Ch D 587, and *Re Earl of Berkeley's Will* (1874) 10 Ch App 56. And as to defending foreclosure actions and obtaining transfers of the mortgage, see *More v More* (1889) 37 WR 414.
9   *Re McClure's Trusts* (1906) 76 LJ Ch 52. Here corpus did not exclusively bear the burden of £200 incurred in survey fees and legal fees for serving notices of disrepair: Kekewich J said, 'The burden is to be cast not wholly upon the tenant for life nor upon the remainderman but is to be borne by each in fair proportion. That can be done by raising the amount required by mortgage of the property, the tenant for life bearing the burden of the interest payments.'

51.36 Even where the costs of management are directed by the settlement to be paid out of income, the court may, in exceptional cases, order them to be paid out of corpus[1]. On the other hand, where money is paid into court under the Trustee Act, the costs of all necessary parties to a petition for obtaining an order for the payment of the *income* to the tenant for life have been held to be payable out of income[2].

1   See *Re Tubbs* [1915] 2 Ch 137, CA; and *Re Hicklin* [1917] 2 Ch 278.
2   *Re Marner's Trusts* (1866) LR 3 Eq 432; *Re Evans' Trusts* (1872) 7 Ch App 609; *Re Whitton's Trusts* (1869) LR 8 Eq 352; *Re Smith's Trusts* (1870) LR 9 Eq 374; *Scrivener v Smith* (1869) LR 8 Eq 310; *Longuet v Hockley* (1870) 22 LT 198; but see *Eady v Watson* (1864) 12 WR 682.

Trust accounts and audit

51.37 If trust accounts are audited no more than once in every three years, the trustees have a discretion under s 22(4) of the Trustee Act 1925 as to the incidence of the cost between capital and income, but in default of exercise of such discretion costs attributable to capital shall be borne by capital and those attributable to income by income, so that the auditor should be asked to advise on such attribution. If accounts are audited more than once in every three years because the nature of the trust or any special dealings with the trust property make a more frequent exercise of the right reasonable, s 22(4) continues to apply. On principle, the cost should fall on capital because the audit is for the benefit of the estate as a whole to ensure that after falsification and surcharge of the accounts, if necessary, the due amount of capital is present, but this provides the basis for checking that the due amount of income was, and should be, provided, so that it would be difficult for an income beneficiary to complain if there was an apportionment according to the default provision in s 22(4).

51.38 With professionally prepared annual trust accounts, it is common to pay for them out of the income available for the income beneficiaries (especially if there are liquidity problems with capital assets) without complaint from such beneficiaries. However, where, as should be the case, the accounts include balance sheets and capital accounts for the benefit of the estate as a whole and the capital beneficiaries in particular, it is wholly justifiable[1] to charge the costs thereof to the capital beneficiaries and the costs of the income accounts to the income beneficiaries in accordance with the default provision in s 22(4) for the analogous costs of independent audits.

[1] *Shore v Shore* (1859) 4 Drew 501 and *Earl of Cowley v Wellesley* (1866) LR 1 Eq 656 are not authority to the contrary because the costs there related respectively to the costs of a receiver of rents to which the income beneficiary was entitled and to the costs of accounts for succession duty payable by the life tenant.

ARTICLE 52
DUTY OF TRUSTEE TO EXERCISE REASONABLE CARE AND SKILL

52.1

(1) Trustees are not insurers[1], and, except where courts of equity have imposed distinct and stringent duties upon them (which duties are mentioned in the succeeding Articles of this Chapter) not to breach their obligation of undivided disinterested loyalty nor to act beyond the powers conferred upon them by the trust instrument or by law[2], a trustee must exercise such care and skill as is reasonable in the circumstances, having regard in particular (a) to any special knowledge or experience that he has or holds himself out as having and (b), if he acts as trustee in the course of a business or profession, to any special knowledge or experience that it is reasonable to expect of a person acting in the course of that kind of business or profession[3].

(2) the conduct of trustees is to be judged with reference to the facts and circumstances existing at the time when they had to act and which were known or ought to have been known to them at the time[4];

(3) though it cannot oust the jurisdiction of the court to determine matters of law, the trust instrument may to a greater or lesser extent qualify or exclude the duties otherwise imposed by equity upon the trustees, so long as there remains a sufficient inner core of duties owed to the beneficiaries to enable a trust to subsist (as opposed to an agency or nomineeship arrangement on behalf of the settlor), while exemption may expressly be granted to trustees against liability for a breach of duty which is not dishonest, unless the trustee's belief is so unreasonable that no honest reasonable person with the objective attributes of the trustee in question (eg a solicitor paid to act as trustee) could have held such belief.

[1] *Re Hurst* (1892) 67 LT 96; *Re Chapman* [1896] 2 Ch 763 at 775, per Lindley LJ; *Bartlett v Barclays Bank Trust Co Ltd* [1980] Ch 515, [1980] 1 All ER 139.
[2] For strict liability on falsification of account for acting ultra vires see Article 89(1).
[3] TA 2000, ss 1, 2, Sch 1.
[4] *Re Hurst* (1892) 67 LT 96 at 99 per Lindley LJ, CA; *Nestle v National Westminster Bank* [1994] 1 All ER 118 at 134 per Staughton LJ: 'the trustees performance must not be judged with hindsight'.

Paragraph 1

The duty of care under Trustee Act 2000

52.2 The Trustee Act 2000 in enacting[1] 'the duty of care', which applies[2] to the extensive range of powers derived from the 2000 Act and ss 15, 19 and 22 of the Trustee Act 1925 as well as to equivalent types of powers derived from the trust instrument and to the investment and reviewing duties imposed by ss 4, 5 and 22 of the 2000 Act, seems to codify the general equitable duty of care[3], breach of which enables the trust accounts to be surcharged[4] with the amount of income or capital that would have been trust income or capital but for the trustee's breach of the equitable duty of care in acting within the powers conferred by law or the trust instrument. It applies to trusts in existence when it came into force on 1 February 2001, but out of an abundance of caution it does not apply to acts or omissions before then.

[1] TA 2000, s 1.
[2] TA 2000, Sch 1, extending to powers of investment, acquisition of land, appointment of agents, nominees and custodians, compounding liabilities, insurance, and valuing interests.
[3] As intended by Law Com Report No 260 (1999) 'Trustees' Powers and Duties', para 2.35.
[4] See Article 89(2).

52.3 The general equitable duty of care was a developing one which had not been laid down with precision. The general duty was to take the care of an ordinary prudent businessman in managing his own affairs[1], except that in selecting investments he had to consider that he was making an investment for the benefit of other people for whom he felt morally obliged to provide[2], so that there could be no question of making a speculative investment that an ordinary prudent businessman might occasionally make for himself: 'safety first' was the cardinal principle[3]. A paid trustee was expected to exercise a higher standard of diligence and knowledge than an unpaid trustee[4], while a professional corporate trustee was expected to use the special care and skill which it professed itself to have in its advertising literature and its dealings with the settlor[5].

[1] *Brice v Stokes* (1805) 11 Ves 319; *Massey v Banner* (1820) 1 Jac & W 241; *Bullock v Bullock* (1886) 56 LJ Ch 221; *Speight v Gaunt* (1883) 22 Ch D 727 at 736 and 754 and (1883) 9 App Cas 1, at 19 per Lord Blackburn.
[2] *Re Whiteley* (1886) 33 Ch D 347 at 355 and 358; *Cowan v Scargill* [1985] Ch 270 at 288; *Nestle v National Westminster Bank* [1994] 1 All ER 118 at 126 and 140, CA; Lord Nicholls in (1995) 9 Trust LI 71 at 73.
[3] See *Nestle v National Westminster Bank* [1994] 1 All ER 118 at 142 per Leggatt LJ.
[4] *Re Waterman's Will Trusts* [1952] 2 All ER 1054 at 1055; *National Trustees Co of Australian v General Finance Co* [1905] AC 373 at 381.
[5] *Bartlett v Barclays Bank Trust Co Ltd* [1980] Ch 515 at 534.

52.4 The statutory duty of care is to 'exercise such care and skill as is reasonable in the circumstances', which will include the fact that in his investment function a trustee is investing not for his own benefit but for the benefit of others and also the fact that he is acting gratuitously or being paid for his services. In particular, regard must be had under s 1(1)(a) to any special knowledge or experience that the trustee subjectively has or holds himself out as having and under s 1(1)(b), if he 'acts as a trustee in the course of a business or profession' (and so is a paid trustee), to any special knowledge or experience that it is objectively reasonable to expect of a person acting in the course of that kind of business or profession.

52.5 Section 1 (1)(b) of the 2000 Act imposes an objective minimum standard on a solicitor or accountant or fund-manager acting as a paid trustee, but s 1(1)(a) raises that standard if such trustee has or holds himself out as having special knowledge or experience.

Trustees of pension schemes, common investment schemes for charities and authorised unit trusts; bare trustees and constructive trustees.

52.6 The statutory duty of care does not apply to many functions of pension scheme trustees already covered by the Pensions Act 1995[1], while many of the powers conferred by the 2000 Act or their corresponding express powers are inappropriate for trustees of authorised unit trusts[2] or of common investment schemes for charities[3] or are regulated by other laws.

[1]   TA 2000, s 36.
[2]   TA 2000, s 37.
[3]   TA 2000, s 38.

52.7 Otherwise, any trustee having statutory or express powers of investment or of acquisition of land or of appointing agents, nominees and custodians or of compounding liabilities or of insuring or of valuing assets, is subject to the statutory duty of care[1] (except to the extent excluded by the trust instrument[2]) when exercising any of those powers. 'Trustee' is not defined anywhere in the 2000 Act, although its substitution of a new s 19 power to insure into the 1925 Act is in terminology apt to cover a bare trustee in that context because the substituted s 19(2) creates a special exception from s 19(1) for property held on a bare trust. On the other hand, s 16 of the 2000 Act, in permitting trustees to appoint a nominee unless there is already a custodian trustee, indicates that a nominee is not to be regarded as being a trustee with the powers of a trustee under the 2000 Act subject to the duty of care in their exercise. Where T has agreed to be nominee or bare trustee for B, T should have no power to do anything other than as directed by B[3], but if B, subject to revocation by B, confers powers on T then T becomes subject to the statutory duty of care[4]. It should be noted that if T has a prior beneficial lien to cover T's liabilities, then the other beneficiaries cannot terminate the trust: T is entitled to continue managing so much of the trust property as he retains with the same powers as were conferred in the trust instrument[5].

[1]   TA 2000, Sch 1, paras 1–6.
[2]   TA 2000, Sch 1, para 7.
[3]   See para 4.2 above.
[4]   TA 2000, Sch 1.
[5]   *X v A* [2000] 1 All ER 490.

52.8 Where a person is a constructive trustee of property as trustee *de son tort*, having undertaken to act as if trustee though not validly appointed as such, then the statutory duty of care will apply. Otherwise, it is only from the time that the conscience of the constructive trustee of property was affected (viz such person had actual, Nelsonian or 'naughty' knowledge of the trust) that there can be personal liability for breach of any duty of care[1]. If express trustees are extant or all the beneficiaries collectively entitled are present and demanding the property, then the constructive trustee's duty is to transfer the property as soon as practicable to the trustees or the beneficiaries as the case may be, the trustee merely being a nominee. If there are no trustees and the beneficiaries include minor or unborn persons, then it seems the constructive trustee will have to fulfil the role of a trustee until the property can be vested in new trustees, and the duty of care will apply.

[1] *Westdeutsche Landesbank v Islington London Borough Council* [1996] AC 669 at 705 and 707.

Realisation of debts

52.9 It is the duty of a trustee to realise debts owing to the trust estate with all convenient speed[1]. He should not only press for payment, but, if they are not paid within a reasonable time, should enforce payment by means of legal proceedings[2]. However, one trustee ought not to commence proceedings without consulting his co-trustees; and if he does so and is condemned in costs to a third party he will have to bear them himself[3]. Under the Trustee Act 1925, s 15 until 1 February 2001, trustees who had failed to take proceedings to get in a debt were not liable for failure so to do where they had acted in good faith. 'Good faith,' however, involves the exercise of 'active discretion' on the part of the trustees, so they would be liable for loss arising from supineness or recklessness[4]. Since 1 February 2001[5] trustees in compounding, compromising or abandoning claims under the Trustee Act 1925, s 15 are not to be liable for any loss thereby occasioned if they had discharged their statutory duty of care.

[1] *Buxton v Buxton* (1835) 1 My & Cr 80.
[2] *Re Brogden* (1888) 38 Ch D 546; and *Millar's Trustees v Polson* (1897) 34 SLR 798; *Fenwick v Greenwell* (1847) 10 Beav 412; *Grove v Price* (1858) 26 Beav 103.
[3] *Re England's Settlement Trusts* [1918] 1 Ch 24.
[4] *Re Greenwood* (1911) 105 LT 509 (where a debt was uncollected and no action brought for seven years although the debtor was possessed of considerable means). Overdue payments under a covenant are income of the trust for the year in which the payments were due, so a claim for repayment of tax made later than 6 years after a covenanted payment fell due will be out of time. Trustees must bear in mind that delay in enforcing a covenant may result in loss of a claim for repayment of tax: *IRC v Crawley* [1987] STC 147.
[5] TA 2000, Sch 2, para 20.

52.10 In one very old case where a beneficiary would have been ruined by the immediate realisation of a debt due from him to the trust estate, and other beneficiaries (his children) would have been seriously prejudiced, the House of Lords held that the trustee exercised a reasonable discretion in refraining from suing the debtor and in allowing him time, and that the trustee was consequently discharged from liability for any consequent losses[1]. Where a trustee needs reassurance that it will be a proper unimpeachable exercise of its s 15 powers to compromise a debt, it should obtain the directions of the court that this will be the case. This will require the court to be satisfied[2] that the trustee has in fact formed the opinion in good faith, that the special circumstances render it desirable and proper to take the particular course of action, the opinion is one at which a reasonable trustee, properly instructed, could have arrived and the opinion is not vitiated by any actual or potential conflict of interest. This would be appropriate where the debt was owed to trustees by the deceased settlor's family company in which the trustees held a significant shareholding upon trust for the settlor's issue, some of whom were in the employ of the company, and where postponement of calling in the debt might either see the company through a difficult situation or lose the debt upon the company's subsequent liquidation, though suing for the debt, whilst occasioning a short-term benefit, might precipitate events leading to liquidation of the company. Indeed, such steps were recently taken[3] where trustees of a pension scheme sought to use s 15 to compromise a claim against the employer to fund the scheme up to the statutory minimum funding requirements.

[1]   *Ward v Ward* (1843) 2 HL Cas 777n at 784; *Clack v Holland* (1854) 19 Beav 262; and see *Re Hurst* (1892) 67 LT 96.
[2]   See *Public Trustee v Cooper* [2001] WTLR 901 at 925 applied in *Representation of I* (2001) 4 ITELR 446.
[3]   *Bradstock Group Pension Scheme Trustees Ltd v Bradstock Group plc* [2002] EWHC 1461 (Ch), [2002] ICR 1427. The beneficiaries need to be informed of the Part 8 application and the proposed compromise: *Re Owens Corning Fiberglass (UK) Pension Plan Ltd* (2002) Times, 8 July.

Trustees bound to realise an investment which has ceased to be authorised

52.11 Section 4 of the Trustee Act 1925 provided that:

> 'A trustee shall not be liable for breach of trust by reason *only* of his continuing to hold an investment which has ceased to be an investment authorised by the trust instrument or by the general law.'

52.12 However there was a duty to conduct regular reviews of investments[1], so that once such review indicated an investment had become unauthorised, then it needed to be sold as soon as reasonable practicable, not necessarily immediately[2]. The Trustee Act 2000 repealed s 4 as from 1 February 2001, taking account of the immensely wide powers of investment generally and of acquisition of land in particular, so that (unless restricted by the trust instrument) investments in any assets other than non-UK land, will be authorised if the trustees obtain and consider proper advice having regard to the standard investment criteria of s 4 of the Trustee Act 2000 and the need to review investments regularly under s 4(2).

[1]   *Nestle v National Westminster Bank plc* [1994] 1 All ER 118, CA.
[2]   See *Wright v Ginn* [1994] OPLR 83; *Re Medland* (1889) 41 Ch D 476.

Allowing rents to fall in arrears

52.13 Where trustees allowed rents to get in arrears, it was held that they were liable to make good the arrears, though without interest[1].

1   *Tebbs v Carpenter* (1816) 1 Madd 290; and see as to interest, *Lowson v Copeland* (1787) 2 Bro CC 156; *Wiles v Gresham* (1854) 2 Drew 258; *Rowley v Adams* (1849) 2 HL Cas 725.

Bankrupt trustee indebted to trust

52.14 Where a trustee, indebted to the trust, becomes bankrupt, it is his duty to prove the debt; and if he neglects to do so he will be liable for the loss[1]. If he absconds, the beneficiaries may prove[2]; and if a co-trustee has paid part, the beneficiaries may nevertheless prove for the whole[3].

1   *Orrett v Corser* (1855) 21 Beav 52.
2   *Re Bradley* (1910) 54 Sol Jo 377.
3   *Edwards v Hood-Barrs* [1905] 1 Ch 20.

Life policies

52.15 Where part of the trust property was a life policy, and default was made in payment of the premium for keeping it alive, the trustees were held liable for not surrendering the policy and obtaining the surrender value[1].

1   *Re Godwin's Settlement* (1918) 87 LJ Ch 645.

Neglect to register when necessary

52.16 Again, it has been held that a trustee will be liable if he fails to register the trust instrument (where it requires to be registered), and the settlor is thereby enabled to effect a mortgage on the property[1].

1   *Macnamara v Carey* (1867) 1 IR Eq 9; and as to neglect to give notice to an assurance company of an assignment to the trustees of a policy, see *Kingdon v Castleman* (1877) 25 WR 345. But *query* whether these neglects of a skilled agent would now be held to fall on the trustee. Further see TA 1925, s 61, Article 95, below.

Joining in sale of contiguous properties

52.17 Trustees must use their best endeavours to sell to the best advantage[1]. They should, therefore (in general), abstain from joining with the owners of contiguous property in a sale of the whole together, unless such a course would be clearly beneficial to their beneficiaries. For, by doing so, they expose the trust property to deterioration on account of the flaws, or possible flaws, in the title to the other property. But:

> 'suppose there were a house belonging to trustees, and a garden and forecourt belonging to somebody else; it must be obvious that those two properties would fetch more if sold together than if sold separately. You might have a divided

portion of a house belonging to trustees and another divided portion belonging to somebody else. It would be equally obvious, if these two portions were sold together, that a more beneficial result would thereby take place ... But in those cases where it is not *manifest on a mere inspection* of the properties that it is more beneficial to sell them together, then you ought to have reasonable evidence ... that it is a prudent and right thing to do, and that evidence, as we know by experience, is obtained from surveyors and other persons who are competent judges'[2].

[1] See *Buttle v Saunders* [1950] 2 All ER 193, (1950) 14 Conv (NS) 228 (EH Bodkin); (1975) 39 Conv (NS) 177 (A Samuels).
[2] Per Jessel MR in *Re Cooper and Allen's Contract for Sale to Harlech* (1876) 4 Ch D 802 at 816, 817. See also *Rede v Oakes* (1864) 4 De GJ & Sm 505; *Re Parker and Beech's Contract* [1887] WN 27.

52.18 The trustees must, of course, ensure that their apportioned part of the purchase price is duly paid to them alone.

52.19 Where trustees are reversioners, it is obvious that they may in general join in a sale; for everybody knows that as a general rule (of course there are exceptions to every rule) the entirety of freehold estate fetches more than the sum total of the separate value of the particular estate and reversion[1]. This view has since received the express sanction of the legislature[2]. Likewise, trustees of an undivided share in the proceeds of land directed to be sold, or in any other property are empowered by statute to concur in a sale jointly with the persons entitled to or having power in that behalf over the other share or shares[3].

[1] Per Jessel MR in *Re Cooper and Allen's Contract for Sale to Harlech* (1876) 4 Ch D 802 at 816, 817. See also *Rede v Oakes* (1864) 4 De GJ & Sm 505; *Re Parker and Beech's Contract* [1887] WN 27.
[2] TA 1925, s 12. Also see TA 2000, s 8(3).
[3] TA 1925, s 24. Also see TA 2000, s 8(3).

Depreciatory conditions of sale

52.20 Trustees ought not to do any act which will depreciate the property. No sale made by a trustee can be impeached on the ground that any of the conditions was unnecessarily depreciatory unless the beneficiaries prove that the consideration was thereby rendered inadequate; and, after the execution of the conveyance, no such sale can be impeached at all as against the purchaser, unless the beneficiaries also prove that such purchaser was acting in collusion with the trustee at the time when the contract for sale was made[1].

[1] TA 1925, s 13.

Improvident sale

52.21 If trustees for sale fail in reasonable diligence in inviting competition, or if they contract to sell under circumstances of great improvidence or waste, they will be personally responsible[1], and the onus of proving that they acted reasonably is upon them[2]. It is, therefore, the duty of trustees for sale to inform themselves of the real value of the property and to fix a reserve price, and for that purpose to employ, if necessary, some independent experienced person to value it[3]. Planning permission or planning potential should be emphasised in the sale particulars[4]. But if they perform this duty, they will not be responsible if the beneficiaries seek to impeach the sale as improvident[5].

1 *Ord v Noel* (1820) 5 Madd 438; and *Anon* (1821) 6 Madd 10; *Pechel v Fowler* (1795) 2 Anst 549; cf *Cuckmere Brick Co Ltd v Mutual Finance Ltd* [1971] Ch 949, [1971] 2 All ER 633; *Downsview Nominees v First City Corpn* [1993] AC 295, [1993] 3 All ER 626, PC.
2 *Norris v Wright* (1851) 14 Beav 291.
3 *Oliver v Court* (1820) 8 Price 127; *Campbell v Walker* (1800) 5 Ves 678; and see per Jessel MR in *Re Cooper and Allen's Contract for Sale to Harlech* (1876) 4 Ch D 802 at 816.
4 *Cuckmere Brick Co Ltd v Mutual Finance Ltd* [1971] Ch 949, [1971] 2 All ER 633.
5 *Grove v Search* (1906) 22 TLR 290; and cf *Reliance Permanent Building Society v Harwood-Stamper* [1944] Ch 362 at 369 ff, [1944] 2 All ER 75 at 79, per Vaisey J.

Non-renewal of fixed or periodic tenancies

52.22 While it is the duty of trustees to preserve the trust assets, they need not necessarily renew a fixed term business tenancy or allow a periodic tenancy to continue. Thus, if A and B Ltd hold a tenancy on trust for themselves, but they are partners in a firm which they have dissolved and are at loggerheads with each other, one cannot obtain an interlocutory order to force the other to join in serving a counter-notice under the Landlord and Tenant Act 1954 to enable the business tenancy to be renewed: the court considered it unlikely that at the trial of the action it would be held to be a breach of trust to fail to join in the application for a new tenancy[1].

1 *Harris v Black* (1983) 46 P & CR 366, CA.

52.23 Indeed, where A and B were cohabitees and their relationship had broken down, the Court of Appeal[1] has held it not to be a breach of trust for A[2] (who has no need to consult B[3] under s 11 of the Trusts of Land and Appointment of Trustees Act 1996) to serve a notice to quit in respect of their joint periodic tenancy (held on a statutory trust for sale) so as to bring the tenancy to an end for both of them. Thus, the landlord local authority could evict B, such conduct not amounting to dishonest assistance in a breach of trust or knowing inconsistent dealing with trust property[4]. Although B has sufficient interest in the family home where he lives to fall within the Human Rights Act 1998, Sch 1, Pt I, para 8(1), interference with such right in these circumstances is almost always going to be justified under Article 8(2)[5].

1 *Crawley Borough Council v Ure* [1996] QB 13, [1995] 1 FLR 806.
2 *Hammersmith and Fulham London Borough Council v Monk* [1992] 1 AC 478, [1992] 1 All ER 1, HL (notice by only one joint tenant suffices to terminate periodic tenancy).
3 *Notting Hill Housing Trust v Brackley* [2001] EWCA Civ 601, [2002] HLR 10, CA.
4 See Article 100.
5 *Harrow London Borough Council v Qazi* [2003] UKHL 43 [2003] 4 All ER 461; *Kay v Lambeth London Borough Council* [2006] UKHL 10, [2006] 2 WLR 570, HL.

52.24 The landlord's position is not affected if B had obtained against A a standard non-molestation and non-exclusion court order prohibiting A from molesting B or excluding B from the premises, the court order applying only so long as A has a proprietary interest in the premises entitling A to take action to exclude B, as the House of Lords held in *Harrow London Borough Council v Johnstone*[1]. Since the non-exclusion order had there been made in divorce proceedings between A and B it is submitted that to prevent the landlord being able to evict B, B should have claimed a transfer of the tenancy to B alone and until such claim was resolved A should have been restrained from serving a notice to quit on the landlord. Once notice to quit has been served, A has no property of which to dispose so that it cannot amount to a reviewable disposition of property that B can attack under s 37 of the Matrimonial Causes Act 1973[2].

[1]   [1997] 1 All ER 929, HL.
[2]   *Newlon Housing Trust v Alsulaimen* [1999] 1 AC 313, HL.

Dishonourable duty to 'gazump'

52.25   Where trustees who have entered into negotiations for the sale of the trust property receive a subsequent higher offer from another party they should at least probe the subsequent offer irrespective of any questions of commercial morality which might have led a vendor who was not a trustee to close the deal with the original purchaser. Nevertheless the trustees retain such a discretion as will allow them to act with proper prudence, and may pray in aid the commonsense rule underlying the old proverb 'A bird in the hand is worth two in the bush'; so that there may be cases in which they could properly refuse a higher offer and proceed with a lower one[1].

[1]   *Buttle v Saunders* [1950] 2 All ER 193; *Cowan v Scargill* [1984] 2 All ER 750 at 761, 193; *Selby v Bowie* (1863) 8 LT 372; *R v Commissioner for New Towns, ex p Tomkins* [1988] RVR 106 affd, (1988) 58 P & CR 57.

Improvident leasing or letting

52.26   Precisely the same principles apply to the leasing or letting of trust property; and if the trustees do not take proper steps, by consulting a practical valuer, to ascertain the proper rent, or, a fortiori, knowing the proper rent accept a lower rent, they will be liable to make good the difference[1]. Nowadays, indeed, trustees should very seriously consider whether it is in the best interests of a trust to let or re-let property (rather than sell with vacant possession) balancing the capital growth potential and the actual realisable income, taking into account repairing obligations and the statutory protection as to tenure of, and rents payable by, tenants.

[1]   *Ferraby v Hobson* (1847) 2 Ph 255.

Grant of leases and options as if absolute owner

52.27   Having, for the purpose of exercising his functions as a trustee, all the powers of an absolute owner in relation to trust land, a trustee of land can grant leases or options on such terms (eg rent review clauses, break clauses, option to purchase at market value as ascertained by a properly qualified third party, a price other than money) as satisfy the statutory duty of care, without being restricted by the wording of sections of earlier statutes. Proper advice, however, must be taken and considered.

Improvident purchase

52.28 The same principles hold good in the case of trustees of a trust for the purchase of land or of trustees exercising their statutory or other powers to acquire land, who ought clearly to satisfy themselves of the value of the property, and for that purpose to employ a valuer of their own, and not trust to the valuer of the vendor. For a man may bona fide form his opinion, but he looks at the case in a totally different way when he knows on whose behalf he is acting; and if the trustees rely upon the vendor's valuer, and he, however bona fide, values the property at more than its true value, they will be liable[1].

1 *Ingle v Partridge* (1865) 34 Beav 411; and see also *Fry v Tapson* (1884) 28 Ch D 268; *Waring v Waring* (1852) 3 I Ch R 331.

52.29 Trustees for purchase should also take reasonable care that they get a good marketable title, and that they do not, by conditions of sale, bind themselves not to require one[1]; and they should never purchase without getting the legal estate unless they are expressly authorised[2] to acquire an equitable interest, when all precautions should be taken to protect the vulnerability of such interest if the land be sold to a bona fide purchaser or to a new registered proprietor.

1 *Eastern Counties Rly Co v Hawkes* (1855) 5 HL Cas 331.
2 The TA 2000 only extends to acquisition of legal estates (s 8(2) thereof) and not even legal rentcharges.

Purchasing with the assistance of a mortgage

52.30 It seems that when trustees are acquiring land under s 8(1) of the Trustee Act 2000 they have power to purchase it with the assistance of a mortgage over it[1], the acquisition of the legal estate and the legal charge thereon being one indivisible transaction[2] by the trustees with all the powers of an absolute owner in relation to the land they are acquiring.

1 See Law Com Report No 260, 'Trustees' Powers and Duties' para 2.44; *Lewin on Trusts* (17th edn) para 35–194L.
2 *Abbey National Building Society v Cann* [1991] 1 AC 56, HL.

52.31 Indeed, for the purpose of exercising their functions as trustees they have all the powers of an absolute owner in relation to the land that they acquire. Because an absolute owner can mortgage his subsisting legal estates in land in order to help purchase new investments can trustees mortgage trust land in order to help purchase new investments in exercising their investment functions? This creation of a new liability imposed on subsisting trust land to create a new fund of money to be invested in the purchase of new investments seems one step removed from a power to invest as if an absolute owner, which seems implicitly restricted to making investments out of subsisting cash or investments currently available for the purchase or exchange of investments[1]. Thus, it would seem that 'gearing up' is not possible under the 2000 Act unless there is an express power in that behalf.

[1] *Re Suenson-Taylor's Settlement* [1974] 3 All ER 397.

Error of judgment

52.32 Even apart from s 61 of the Trustee Act 1925 which gives the court power to excuse a trustee who has acted reasonably and honestly and ought fairly to be excused for the breach and for omitting to obtain the directions of the court in the matter[1], a trustee is not responsible for a mere error of judgment, if he has exercised a reasonable discretion and acted with diligence and good faith. Thus, where an executor omitted to sell some foreign bonds for a year after the testator's death, although there was a direction in the will to convert with all reasonable speed, he was held not to be responsible for a loss caused by the bonds falling in price, for although the conclusion he came to was unfortunate, yet having exercised a bona fide discretion, the mere fact of the loss was not sufficient to charge him[2]. A fortiori will this be so where there is power to postpone a sale[3]. As to what constitutes a reasonable delay, this depends on the particular circumstances affecting each case. Prima facie, a trustee ought not to delay realisation beyond a year, even where he has apparently unlimited discretion[4]; and, if he procrastinates beyond that period, the onus will be cast upon him of proving that the delay was reasonable and proper[5]. If he considers further delay very desirable he should apply to the court[6].

[1] See Article 95.
[2] *Buxton v Buxton* (1835) 1 My & Cr 80; and see *Paddon v Richardson* (1855) 7 De GM & G 563.
[3] *Re Schneider* (1906) 22 TLR 223.
[4] *Sculthorpe v Tipper* (1871) LR 13 Eq 232; and as to the propriety of an executor allowing the testator's money invested on mortgage to remain so until wanted, see *Orr v Newton* (1791) 23 Cox Eq Cas 274, PC; *Robinson v Robinson* (1851) 1 De GM & G 247.
[5] See per Wood LJ in *Grayburn v Clarkson* (1868) 3 Ch App 605 at 606; and *Hughes v Empson* (1856) 22 Beav 181.
[6] See *Morris v Morris* (1858) 4 Jur NS 802.

52.33 In *Re Chapman*[1] Lopes LJ said:

'A trustee who is honest and reasonably competent is not to be held responsible for a mere error in judgment when the question which he has to consider is whether a security for a class authorised, but depreciated in value, should be retained or realised, provided he acts with reasonable care, prudence and circumspection'.

[1] [1896] 2 Ch 763 at 778.

52.34 Brightman J in *Bartlett v Barclays Bank Trust Co Ltd*[1] endorsed this, saying,

'Nor must the court be astute to fix liability on a trustee who has committed no more than an error of judgment, from which no business man, however prudent, can expect to be immune'.

¹   [1980] 1 All ER 139 at 150.

52.35 In *Re Lucking's Will Trusts¹* Mr Lucking as active trustee and main beneficiary under a trust which had a controlling shareholding in the Lucking family company and as director of that company brought in D to manage the business. From D's appointment in 1954 to his dismissal in 1961 he was allowed to remain living in Stirling in Scotland though the company business was in Chester: he was thus allowed hotel expenses in Chester and travelling expenses to and from Chester in addition to his salary. Of this Cross J said, 'It may very well have been an unnecessary concession and an error of judgment, but not, in my judgment, a breach of trust'. The learned judge went on to hold that signing blank cheques on the No 2 account was also not a breach of trust so long as Mr Lucking had no reason to think that D was abusing the confidence reposed in him, ie until the summer of 1957 when Mr Lucking realised that D was overdrawing at a rate of £1,400 pa on top of his salary and his expenses and his travel allowance.

¹   [1967] 3 All ER 726, [1968] 1 WLR 866.

Theft of trust property

52.36 A trustee will not be liable if the trust property be stolen, provided he has taken reasonable care of it[1], even although the thief be his own servant, if, on the facts proved, it appears that the trustee was justified in entrusting the custody of the property to such servant as for example in the managing of a trust business[2]. On the other hand, it has been held that a trustee is liable if he is induced by fraud or forgery to hand it over to the wrong person[3] because he is then acting beyond his powers as as to be strictly liable upon falsification of the accounts unless protected by an exemption clause in the trust instrument or afforded relief by the court under s 61 of the Trustee Act 1925[4]. As has been shown in this article, a trustee is in the position of a bailee; he must take reasonable care of the trust property, and if it is lost or stolen he is discharged from responsibility provided that he was not guilty of negligence, which would lead to surcharging of the accounts.

¹   *Jones v Lewis* (1751) 2 Ves Sen 240; *Job v Job* (1877) 6 Ch D 562.
²   *Jobson v Palmer* [1893] 1 Ch 71; and see also *Weir v Bell* (1878) 3 ExD 238, CA. Compare *Re Lucking's Will Trusts* [1967] 3 All ER 726.
³   See Article 54 and Illustrations thereto, below.
⁴   See Article 96, below; *Re Smith* (1902) 71 LJ Ch 411.

Neglect in keeping trust securities

52.37 Where a trustee of a policy of insurance neglected to indorse on it a memorandum of the trust, or to give notice to the office, and by his subsequent carelessness allowed it to get into the hands of the settlor, who mortgaged it to a third party, the trustee was held liable[1]. Again, where part of the trust property was a policy of assurance on the settlor's life which he failed to keep on foot, and the trustees neglected to get the surrender value, they were held liable[2], but a trustee was held not to be liable where he kept up the policy, but forgot the receipt, and the company wrongly refused to pay in consequence[3].

1   *Kingdon v Castleman* (1877) 25 WR 345; and see *Barnes v Addy* (1874) 9 Ch App 244; and *Hobday v Peters (No 3)* (1860) 28 Beav 603.
2   *Re Godwin's Settlement* (1918) 87 LJ Ch 645.
3   *Re McGaw* [1919] WN 288.

52.38 Where trustees hold securities payable to bearer, they appoint a person to act as custodian of the securities unless otherwise authorised in the trust instrument[1].

1   TA 2000, s 18 but this does not apply if the trust has a custodian trustee or securities are vested in the official custodian for charities.

Inventory of chattels

52.39 A trustee of chattels should make and keep an inventory of them, so that, if lost by the neglect or fraud of others, proper evidence of the nature and value of the chattels may be preserved[1].

1   *Temple v Thring* (1887) 56 LJ Ch 767.

Neglect to invest trust fund

52.40 A trustee ought to invest moneys in his hands subject to the trust within a reasonable time; and if he omits to do so, he will be charged interest[1]; and if the fund be lost, he will be liable to make it good[2]. A fortiori will he be liable where he has left the trust fund in the sole custody of his co-trustee[3]. And, on similar grounds, trustees ought to accumulate the income of infants' property (in so far as it is not applied for maintenance, etc) by way of compound interest[4].

1   See *Gilroy v Stephens* (1882) 30 WR 745; *Stafford v Fiddon* (1857) 23 Beav 386; and *Re Jones* (1883) 49 LT 91. In *Cann v Cann* (1884) 51 LT 770, Kay J considered that six months was the maximum period. Cf also *Re Waterman's Will Trusts* [1952] 2 All ER 1054; where, however, no beneficiary desired to attack the trustee on the basis of breach of trust in failing to invest. Nowadays, there seems little excuse for not investing money forthwith in a deposit account unless a particular investment is to be made within days, requiring money to be available in a current account.
2   *Moyle v Moyle* (1831) 2 Russ & M 710; *Cann v Cann* (1884) 33 WR 40; *Astbury v Beasley* (1868) 17 WR 638.
3   *Lewis v Nobbs* (1878) 8 Ch D 591; or left it with his law agent for five months: *Wyman v Paterson* [1900] AC 271.
4   TA 1925, s 31(2); and see Article 69 where the provision itself is more fully discussed.

Controlling interest in private company

52.41 The duties of trustees whose investment holdings give them a controlling interest in a private company were considered in *Re Lucking's Will*

Trusts[1]. In that case a sole trustee had, by virtue of such an interest, appointed a manager of the company business who also became a director. Losses occurred through the misconduct of the manager and the trustee was held liable because he had failed adequately to supervise the manager's drawings from the company after the summer of 1957 when it had become apparent that some check ought to be imposed on such drawings. But a second trustee, who had been appointed in the meantime and had relied on what the first trustee told him, was held in the circumstances not to have failed to exercise ordinary prudence. Cross J stated:

> 'I do not look on him as a passive trustee who has allowed his co-trustee to decide for him matters on which they ought to have exercised a joint discretion. He was entitled to rely on what Mr Lucking told him about the company's affairs as being accurate and adequate unless he had some positive reason to think the contrary which he had not.'

[1]   [1967] 3 All ER 726, [1968] 1 WLR 866.

52.42 Earlier Cross J had considered the general position:

> 'What steps, if any, does a reasonably prudent man who finds himself a majority shareholder in a private company take with regard to the management of the company's affairs? He does not content himself with such information as to the management of the company's affairs as he is entitled to as shareholder, but ensures that he is represented on the board. He may be prepared to run the business himself as managing director or, at least, to become a non-executive director while having the business managed by someone else. Alternatively, he may find someone who will act as his nominee on the board and report to him from time to time as to the company's affairs. In the same way trustees holding a controlling interest ought to ensure so far as they can that they have such information as to the progress of the company's affairs as directors would have. If they sit back and allow the company to be run by the minority shareholder and receive no more information than shareholders are entitled to, they do so at their risk if things go wrong.
>
> In this case the trust was represented on the board by Mr Lucking. One ought not to regard him as performing a duty to the trust which it was incumbent on the trustees to perform personally, so that [the second trustee] became automatically responsible for any deficiences of Mr Lucking as does a passive trustee who allows his co-trustee to exercise alone discretions which it is their duty to exercise jointly. If these trustees had decided, as they might have done, to be represented on the board by a nominee they would have been entitled to rely on the information given them by the nominee even though such information was inaccurate or inadequate, unless they had reason to suspect that it was inaccurate or inadequate. [The second trustee] cannot have been in a worse position because his co-trustee was the trust's representative on the board than he would have been if the trust's representative had not been a trustee at all.'

52.43 In *Re Miller's Deed Trusts*[1] Oliver J did not read Cross J's judgment as imposing on trustees having a controlling interest in a private company a necessary requirement that one of them or a nominee must be on the board of directors where one trustee was an accountant whose firm acted as auditors to the company and who, or a member of his staff, was normally in regular monthly attendance at the company's premises dealing with accounts.

1   [1978] LS Gaz R 454.

52.44 In *Bartlett v Barclays Bank Trust Co Ltd¹* Brightman J endorsed this saying:

> '[Cross J] was merely outlining convenient methods by which a prudent man of business (as also a trustee) with a controlling interest in a private company can place himself in a position to make an informed decision whether any action is appropriate to be taken for the protection of his asset ... Alternatives which spring to mind are the receipt of copies of the agenda and minutes of board meetings, the receipt of monthly management accounts in the case of a trading concern or quarterly reports. Every case will depend on its own facts ... *The purpose to be achieved* is not that of monitoring every move of the directors, but of *making it reasonably probable ... that the trustees or one of them will receive an adequate flow of information in time to enable the trustees to make use of their controlling shareholding should this be necessary for the protection of their trust asset, namely the shareholding²...* It was not proper for the bank to confine itself to the receipt of the annual balance sheet and profit and loss account, detailed annual financial statements and the chairman's report and statement, and to attendance at the annual general meetings and the luncheons that followed, which were the limits of the bank's regular sources of information. Had the bank been in receipt of more frequent information it would have been able to step in and stop, and ought to have stopped the board embarking on the Old Bailey project.'

1   [1980] Ch 515 at 533–534.
2   Editor's italics.

Bound to insure against risks in many circumstances

52.45 As already discussed¹, nowadays trustees should exercise their powers (as absolute owner of land under s 8(3) of the Trustee Act 2000 or their substituted², s 19 of the Trustee Act 1925 powers) to insure any trust property against risks of loss or damage due to any event, when exercising the care and skill of an ordinary prudent businessman in furthering the financial interests of present and future beneficiaries. The extent of such cover will take account of the value and liquidity of the trust capital and the cost of premiums in balancing the risk of substantial loss against the expense of the premiums.

1   At para 51.21 above.
2   See TA 2000, s 34.

Application of insurance money where policy kept up under any trust, power or obligation

52.46 And by s 20 it is provided that:

> (1)   Money receivable by trustees or any beneficiary under a policy of insurance against the loss or damage of any property subject to a trust or to a settlement within the meaning of the Settled Land Act, 1925,

shall, where the policy has been kept up under any trust in that behalf or under any power statutory or otherwise, or in performance of any covenant or of any obligation statutory or otherwise, or by a tenant for life impeachable for waste, be capital money for the purposes of the trust or settlement, as the case may be.

(2)   If any such money is receivable by any person, other than the trustees of the trust or settlement, that person shall use his best endeavours to recover and receive the money, and shall pay the net residue thereof, after discharging any costs of recovering and receiving it, to the trustees of the trust or settlement, or, if there are no trustees capable of giving a discharge therefore, into court.

(3)   Any such money—

(a)   if it was receivable in respect of settled land within the meaning of the Settled Land Act 1925 or any building or works thereon, shall be deemed to be capital money arising under that Act, from the settled land, and shall be invested or applied by the trustees, or, if in court, under the direction of the court, accordingly;

(b)   if it was receivable in respect of personal chattels settled as heirlooms within the meaning of the Settled Land Act 1925 shall be deemed to be capital money arising under that Act, and shall be applicable by the trustees, or, if in court, under the direction of the court, in like manner as provided by that Act with respect to money arising by a sale of chattels settled as heirlooms as aforesaid;

(c)   if it was receivable in respect of property held upon trust for sale, shall be held upon the trusts and subject to the powers and provisions applicable to money arising by a sale under such trust;

(d)   in any other case, shall be held upon trusts corresponding as nearly as may be with the trusts affecting the property in respect of which it was payable.

(4)   Such money, or any part thereof, may also be applied by the trustees, or, if in court, under the direction of the court, in rebuilding, reinstating, replacing, or repairing the property lost or damaged, but any such application by the trustees shall be subject to the consent of any person whose consent is required by the instrument, if any, creating the trust to the investment of money subject to the trust, and, in the case of money which is deemed to be capital money arising under the Settled Land Act, 1925, be subject to the provisions of that Act with respect to the application of capital money by the trustees of the settlement.

(5)   Nothing contained in this section prejudices or affects the right of any person to require any such money or any part thereof to be applied in rebuilding, reinstating, or repairing the property lost or damaged, or the rights of any mortgagee, lessor, or lessee, whether under any statute or otherwise.

(6)   This section applies to policies effected either before or after the commencement of this Act, but only to money received after such commencement.

52.47 These sections do not, however, apply to property held by bare trustees on trust for beneficiaries absolutely entitled.

52.48 If trustees do not insure, and a beneficiary does so out of his own moneys, he may keep whatever is paid under the policy for himself[1]; but not where the premiums are paid out of the trust income[2].

1   *Gaussen v Whatman* (1905) 93 LT 101.
2   Section 20(1); *Re Quicke's Trusts* [1908] 1 Ch 887.

Liability for repairs

52.49 Trustees are generally bound to see that trust premises do not fall into decay[1]. But, as we have seen, the cost of repairs is not necessarily thrown exclusively on income[2], and trustees should apply to the court for directions as to raising the necessary money[3]. It has, however, been decided that when *leasehold* houses are held in trust to receive the rents and pay them to A for life, and after his death in trust for B, the trustees, in order to avoid forfeiture, are entitled to apply the rents in keeping the houses in a proper state[4]. But this is without prejudice to the ultimate incidence of the cost[5].

1   Per Cotton LJ in *Re Hotchkys* (1886) 32 Ch D 408.
2   Article 51, above.
3   *Re Fowler* (1881) 16 Ch D 723. But see *Re Courtier* (1886) 34 Ch D 136; and also Article 51, above.
4   *Re Fowler* (1881) 16 Ch D 723. But see *Re Courtier* (1886) 34 Ch D 136; and also Article 51, above.
5   *Re Courtier* (1886) 34 Ch D 136 and *Re Hotchkys* (1886) 32 Ch D 480; and see para 51.30 ff.

Liability of retired trustee

52.50 A retired trustee, while remaining liable for breaches of trust committed during his trusteeship, will not be liable for breaches of trust after his retirement except that where a trustee retires from the trust in order, as he thinks, to relieve himself from the responsibility of a wrongful act which his co-trustee has in mind, he will be held as fully responsible as if he had been *particeps criminis*[1]. To make him responsible however it must be proved that the very breach of trust which was in fact committed was not merely the outcome of, or rendered easy by, the retirement, but was contemplated by the trustee who retired, so he was an accessory before the fact[2].

1   *Norton v Pritchard* (1845) 5 LTOS 2; *Webster v Le Hunt* (1861) 9 WR 918; *Palairet v Carew* (1863) 32 Beav 564; *Clark v Hoskins* (1868) 37 LJ Ch 561.
2   *Head v Gould* [1898] 2 Ch 250 at 273–274.

Liability of trustee where loss results from act or default of agents nominees or custodians

52.51 Trustees will often employ agents nominees or custodians under the Trustee Act 2000[1] or express powers in the trust instrument. When trustees act within such powers they are not automatically responsible for any act or default of such persons: they are only liable for any personal failure to comply with their duty of care when entering into the arrangements under which another person acts as agent, nominee or custodian and when keeping those arrangements under review[2] (needing to consider if they need to intervene by giving directions to or dismissing such a person and so acting if there is such a need[3]). Any right of action against the agent, nominee or custodian will be an asset of the trust which the trustees should seek to realise, if appropriate[4], on pain of personal liability if not complying with their own duty of care and skill.

1   See paras 53.77–53.83 below.
2   TA 2000, s 23(1).
3   TA 2000, s 22.
4   Taking account of the wealth of the defendant and the strength of the trustee's claim and the possibility of compromising the matter under s 15 of the TA 1925: a *Beddoe* application will usually be appropriate (see para 87.48 below).

Paragraph 2

Relevant time for judging trustees' conduct

52.52 As Lindley LJ stated in *Re Hurst*[1]:

'The conduct of trustees ought to be regarded with reference to the facts and circumstances existing at the time when they had to act and which were known or ought to have been known by them at the time.'

1   (1892) 67 LT 96 at 99, CA; *Re Chapman* [1896] 2 Ch 763 at 777–778, CA; *Nestle v National Westminster Bank (No 2)* [1993] 1 WLR 1260, CA.

52.53 In *Nestle v National Westminster Bank* Hoffmann J emphasised[1] that, 'in reviewing the conduct of trustees over a period of more than 60 years one must be careful not to endow the prudent trustee with prophetic vision or expect him to have ignored the received wisdom of his time'.

1   [2000] WTLR 795 at 802.

Paragraph 3

No ousting the jurisdiction of the court

52.54 On matters of law, the jurisdiction of the court cannot be ousted by provisions in the trust instrument[1] eg a specific power to decide whether a receipt is an income or capital receipt or a general power to determine all questions arising in the execution of the trust provisions. However, trustees may be authorised to distribute receipts whether of a capital or income nature as they see fit in their discretion, irrespective of whether the recipient is otherwise only interested in capital or only in income.

1   *Re Wynn* [1952] Ch 271; *Re Raven* [1915] 1 Ch 673; *Re Bronson* (1958) 14 DLR (2d) 51; *Boe v Alexander* (1987) 41 DLR (4th) 520.

52.55 If a clause is designed to oust any possibility of contesting the validity of a trust or will or the decisions of the trustee it will be void for trying to oust the jurisdiction of the court. An essential attribute of an equitable interest is the ability to obtain its full benefit by recourse to the courts if need be.Thus justifiable contesting of trusts or wills or decisions of trustees cannot be ousted and a clause providing for a beneficiary's interest to pass to others if an action is unjustifiably brought will be upheld[1].

[1]   *Nathan v Leonard [2002] EWHC 1701 (Ch)*, [2002] WTLR 1061, discussed at para 11.80 above. See also 'To sue or not to sue' by S Collins in STEP Journal Sept 2006 p 27 on a Cayman trust case.

Excluding duties in respect of particular property

52.56 If a very wealthy testator wants to be kind to his brother and sister living in one of his houses and wants to avoid any death duties payable on their deaths he may provide in his will trust, 'My trustees shall have no responsibility or duty with respect to such house' until both are dead, though subject thereto the testator's estate is left on trust for sale (with power to postpone sale) for the testator's children with remainders over. At the testator's death his brother and sister were 92 and 87 and the property market was falling. The Privy Council in *Hayim v Citibank*[1] upheld the testator's clause, so rejecting the children's claim for breach of trust when the house was sold after the death of the last surviving sibling for much less than would have been obtained if a speedy sale had occurred. The provision was:

> 'in the circumstances designed to enable Albert and Marie to remain in the house so long as [the trustee] saw fit ... If clause 10 were exploited for any other purpose the beneficiaries could complain and the court could find that [the trustee] had not properly exercised the discretion conferred on it to postpone sale either in the interests of the beneficiaries or of Albert and Marie.'

[1]   [1987] AC 730, not cited in *IRC v Lloyds Private Banking Ltd* [1998] STC 559, [1999] 1 FLR 147.

52.57 Here the house was only a small part of the testator's estate and some residual duties (eg not to use the house for the trustee's own purposes) remained even in respect of the house.

52.58 However there are implications for the case where the trust property consists almost wholly of a company transferred by the settlor to the trustees, whether the settlor's trading company or investment company, where the settlor or the settlor's nominee is intended to continue running the company. Most of the trustees' duties, under *Bartlett v Barclays Bank Trust Co*[1], *Cowan v Scargill*[2] and the Trustee Act 2000[3] will be capable of exclusion.

[1]   [1980] Ch 515.
[2]   [1985] Ch 270.
[3]   Sections 6(1), 21(3), 26 and Sch 1, para 7.

52.59 The settlor's trust instrument can provide, for example, that the controlling shareholding in the settlor's company that is to be the trust's only significant asset is to be retained and not sold until its value falls a specified percentage below its value when transferred to the trustee or until a specified person consents, but whose power to withhold consent is not to be a fiduciary power, only a personal one incapable of challenge unless amounting to a fraud on the power. Thus, the duty to consider diversification is negated.

52.60 The settlor could also exclude the trustee's duty to take such steps as make it reasonably probable that the trustee will receive an adequate flow of information in time to enable it to use its controlling interest to protect the beneficiaries' interests if necessary. Indeed, he could go on to exclude the trustee's duty to interfere in the affairs of the company in any way whatsoever unless it has actual knowledge that one or more of the directors is acting dishonestly in the running of the company.

52.61 However, the trustee does have *power* to obtain information and interfere (by virtue of its controlling shareholding) so far as necessary to protect beneficiaries' interests, while it seems that the trustee has an overriding duty to exercise its powers so as to safeguard and further the beneficiaries' interests as a whole[1] and that this duty at the core of the trust cannot be ousted[2]. Thus, the trustee would need to exercise its power to obtain information, so as to be able to interfere before obtaining actual knowledge of dishonesty on the part of directors, because by that time it will almost always be too late to protect the beneficiaries' interests, dishonest persons often dissipating their assets so as to have nothing left to satisfy creditors.

[1] *Cowan v Scargill* [1985] Ch 270; *Beauclerk v Ashburnham* (1845) 8 Beav 322.
[2] This is surely part of 'the duty of the trustees to perform the trusts honestly and in good faith for the benefit of the beneficiaries' (*Armitage v Nurse* [1998] Ch 241 at 253) so they should not ignore a significant drop in profits from a preceding year. If they then relied on the presence of an exemption clause exempting them from liability for a breach of trust unless dishonest to justify refusing to inquire about such a fall crying out for an explanation, they should lose its protection because in so refusing they acted recklessly which equates to dishonesty: *Armitage v Nurse* [1998] Ch 241 at 254.

52.62 To exclude the trustee's power to intervene and replace the directors of the company, the settlor would need to arrange for the company to be created under a foreign law[1] under which the managing director (being the settlor's nominee or the settlor himself) cannot be removed until certified mentally incompetent by two qualified medical practitioners in the foreign jurisdiction, so staying on until resigning or dying, with directors being removable only by the managing director. This will mean that the settlor has transferred a flawed asset (a pig in a poke) to the trustee for the beneficiaries, who will not be able to complain that all they have is a flawed asset as intended by the settlor, the trustees having run the trust to the extent income materialised from company dividends but the settlor or his nominee having run the company owned by the trustee. However, if significant income has not been made available to give the trustee something to do, the company having power to make gifts or loans to the settlor's family, relatives and friends, then the trust is likely to be regarded as a sham.

[1] For example, British Virgin Islands.

52.63 Where the settlor wants himself or his nominee to perform the role of discretionary portfolio manager he may (like a billionaire who has just won £5 million lottery money) provide, 'The Trustee shall speculate with the Trust Fund (but have power to invest[1] it while awaiting speculative opportunities) as if he were an absolutely entitled beneficial owner speculating on his own behalf in circumstances where he could afford to lose the whole Fund in acquiring any assets of whatsoever nature anywhere without it affecting his standard of living one iota; and the Trustee shall be under no duty to exercise care and skill mindful that he is acting for the benefit of others but shall only be liable for losses caused by his own dishonesty'[2]. To protect the Trustee and to further the settlor's interests, the trust instrument may also provide, 'The Trustee must employ the settlor as discretionary manager of the Fund (without payment of any fee and without authority to self-deal directly or indirectly so as to benefit himself or his spouse in any way) until the settlor resigns such post or dies or is certified as a mental patient, so that in all the circumstances it is unnecessary and inappropriate for the Trustee to review the investments and other assets comprising the fund'[3].

[1]   This would be a power of investment within TA 2000, s 4(1) but it is very doubtful whether the duty to speculate could be so regarded, although, in any event, the power to make an authorised investment after proper advice having regard to the standard investment criteria can be subject to any restriction or exclusion imposed by the trust instrument: TA 2000, s 6(1)(b).
[2]   *Armitage v Nurse* [1998] Ch 241; TA 2000, Sch 1, para 7.
[3]   Because employment is required by the trust instrument delegation is not under TA 2000, Pt IV but even if it were the duty to review can be ousted: TA 2000, s 21(3).

Non-excludable duties: irreducible core content of a trust

52.64 As Millett LJ has stated[1], 'There is an irreducible core of obligations owed by the trustees to the beneficiaries and enforceable by them which is fundamental to the concept of a trust. If the beneficiaries have no rights enforceable against the trustees there are no trusts'. The Court of Appeal[2] has held that these core obligations do not include the duties of care and skill, prudence and diligence, and so has upheld a clause exempting a trustee from liability for loss or damage unless caused by the trustee's own actual fraud, but they do include the duty to perform the trusts honestly and in good faith for the benefit of the beneficiaries[3]. To enforce this duty the beneficiaries – and objects of a fiduciary power of appointment with a realistic possibility of benefiting under an appointment – have a right to see the trust accounts[4] so that they are then able to falsify or surcharge those accounts.

[1]   *Armitage v Nurse* [1998] Ch 241; also D J Hayton 'The Irreducible Core Content of Trusteeship', Chapter 3 in AJ Oakley (ed) *Trends in Contemporary Trust Law* (Oxford, 1996).
[2]   *Armitage v Nurse* [1998] Ch 241.
[3]   *Armitage v Nurse* [1998] Ch 241 at 253; *Green v Wilden Pty Ltd* [2005] WASC 83, Sup Ct WA, paras 482–502.
[4]   See Article 60 and *Schmidt v Rosewood Trust Ltd* [2003] UKPC 26, [2003] 2 AC 709.

52.65 Thus, if a clause stated that the trustees are not to account to the beneficiaries or objects[1] for anything happening in the lifetime of the settlor or that the beneficiaries and objects are to have no right to sue the trustees for any alleged breach of trust occurring in the settlor's lifetime, there is no trust for the benefit of beneficiaries and objects while the settlor is alive, the substance of the matter simply being that the trust fund is held to his order[2]; on his death a trust of whatever remains may be intended to arise, but this will be a testamentary trust that will be void if not complying with the formalities required for a valid will[3].

1   A clause intended to prevent any meaningful right to account from arising (eg 'The Trustee shall keep this Trust Deed secret and confidential to itself alone and shall not inform any beneficiary that he or she be a beneficiary and shall always ensure that benefits provided to any beneficiary are provided in untraceable fashion so far as possible') would also be repugnant to the trust concept: *Cf Scally v Southern Health Services Board* [1992] 1 AC 294 at 306–307 and *Re Murphy's Settlement* [1998] 3 All ER 1.

2   Since the settlor did not intend the beneficiaries to have any rights in his lifetime nor did he intend the trustees to be beneficial owners, there is a resulting trust in his favour with a power, which he can revoke (*Vandervell v IRC* [1967] 2 AC 291 at 317) to benefit the so-called beneficiaries.

3   *Re Pfrimmer Estate* [1936] 2 DLR 123; *Baird v Baird* [1990] 2 AC 548, PC.

Exemption from liability for breach of duty unless dishonest

52.66 The benefit of an exemption clause conferred by the settlor on the trustee is construed so as to cover no more than its wording is apt to cover[1] but not so as restrictively to cover less than would appear on a fair reading of the wording. Thus, a clause exempting from loss or damage not caused by the trustee's own fraud will not extend to a beneficiary claiming to recover trust property purchased by the trustee in breach of the 'no self-dealing' rule[2]. However, a clause exempting trustees for liability for 'omissions made in good faith' is taken at its face value to cover both non-negligent and negligent omissions[3], rather than restricted under a *contra proferentem* construction[4] to cover non-negligent omissions only where strict liability arises on falsification of the accounts[5].

1   For example, *Wight v Olswang (No 1)* (1988) 1 ITELR 783; *Bogg v Raper* (1998) 1 ITELR 267; *Walker v Stones* [2001] QB 902 at 935.

2   *Armitage v Nurse* [1998] Ch 241 at 253.

3   *Bogg v Raper* (1998) 1 ITELR 267, CA, and *Walker v Stones* [2001] QB 902 at 941, CA. It should follow that a clause exempting a trustee from liability 'for any negligent breach of trust' should cover gross and ordinary negligence.

4   As to which see *Green v Wilden Pty Ltd* [2005] WASC 83, Sup Ct WA, at paras 498, 858.

5   As held under a restrictive approach by the Minnesota CA in *Re Williams Trust* (2000) 2 ITELR 313. In *Bonham v Blake Lapthorn Linell* [2006] EWHC 2513 (Ch) 'loss' was held to cover not just amounts payable for reparation of a loss on surcharging principles but also amounts payable by way of substitutive performance on falsification principles.

52.67 The Court of Appeal[1] has accepted that an aptly worded exemption clause can protect a trustee from liability for any breach of trust other than a dishonest (including reckless[2]) breach of trust, it not being repugnant to the core concept of a trust nor contrary to public policy to exempt a trustee from liability for negligence extending to gross negligence. Such view may still be challenged[3] because the court did not have cited to it English cases[4] that distinguish gross negligence from ordinary negligence, so the court, believing that 'English lawyers have always had a healthy disrespect for the distinction'[5], regarding gross negligence as 'ordinary negligence with a vituperative epithet'[6], assumed that such distinction could not be made. Exemption from negligence of all degrees therefore had to be accepted or rejected, and, in modern times, when exemption from negligence is commonplace in the contractual context and the trust context, one could hardly justify outlawing exempting liability for negligence[7].

1   *Armitage v Nurse* [1998] Ch 241 at 253.

2 *Armitage v Nurse* [1998] Ch 241 at 251,'dishonesty' covering a trustee pursuing a course of action recklessly indifferent whether or not it is contrary to the beneficiaries' interests. A trustee relying on a clause exempting him from liability for breach to justify what he is about to do is acting recklessly ie dishonestly: *Armitage v Nurse* [1998] Ch 241 at 254.

3 As in the appeal to the Privy Council from the Jersey CA in *Midland Bank Trustee (Jersey) Ltd v Federated Pension Services* [1996] PLR 179 which settled on the morning it was to be opened in the PC.

4 Bailment cases where gratuitous bailees can only be liable if guilty of gross negligence (*Gibbon v McMullen* (1868) LR 2 PC 317; *Beal v South Devon Rly Co* (1864) 3 H & C 337) and mortgage cases postponing a legal mortgagee's priority if guilty of gross negligence (eg *Colyer v Finch* (1856) 5 HL Cas 905, 928–929). The court also believed Scots law permitted exemption from liability for gross negligence but it does not: *Lutea Trustees Ltd v Orbis Trustees Guernsey Ltd* 1997 SCLR 735, 1998 SLT 471.

5 *Armitage v Nurse* [1998] Ch 241 at 254.

6 *Armitage v Nurse* [1998] Ch 241.

7 *Armitage v Nurse* [1998] Ch 241.

52.68 The Law Commission issued a Consultation Paper No 171 leading to a Report on Trustee Exemption Clauses (Law Com No 301) to see whether the liability of paid trustees for negligence should be outlawed, the Trustee Act 2000[1] having deliberately permitted ouster of trustees' duty of care until the Law Commission investigated the matter further. The Report recommends adoption of a rule of practice in the trust industry, with the Society of Trusts and Estates Practitioners setting the lead. As part of the STEP Code of Practice any paid trustee who causes a settlor to include in his trust instrument a clause which has the effect of excluding or limiting liability for negligence, must before creation of the trust use his reasonable endeavours to ensure that the settlor is notified of the clause and gives his full and informed acceptance to the clause.

1 TA 2000, Sch 1, para 7.

Exemption from liability for deliberate breaches

52.69 Lord Nicholls[1] considered that it was dishonest for a trustee knowingly to act beyond his powers and so take a risk to the prejudice of another's rights, which risk is known to be one which there is no right to take. If the risk materialises and causes loss then the trustee who knowingly took the risk will be accountable accordingly. However, Millett LJ[2] considered that if trustees deliberately commit a breach of trust but in good faith in the honest belief that they are acting in the best interests of the beneficiaries their conduct is not dishonest.

1 *Royal Brunei Airlines v Tan* [1995] 2 AC 378 at 390, PC.

2 *Armitage v Nurse* [1998] Ch 241 at 252, and subsequently as Lord Millett in *Three Rivers District Council v Governor of Bank of England (No 3)* [2000] 2 WLR 1220 at 1274.

52.70 In *Walker v Stones*[1] Rattee J followed the view of Millett LJ so as to allow a trustee to rely on an exemption clause exempting him from liability unless dishonest. On appeal[2], the Court of Appeal considered 'it most unlikely that [Millett LJ] would have intended his dicta to apply to a case where [as here] a solicitor-trustee's perception of the interests of the beneficiaries was so unreasonable that no reasonable solicitor-trustee could have held such belief.

Indeed, in my opinion, such a construction of the clause could well render it inconsistent with the very existence of an effective trust.' After all, a settlor intends the trustee only to have the powers conferred upon him by law and the settlor, and not also to have power to do anything else that the trustee subjectively honestly believes to be in the interests of the beneficiaries even if no reasonable trustee could possibly have held such belief.

¹   [2000] WTLR 79 striking out the beneficiaries' claim.
²   [2001] QB 902 at 941; leave to appeal given by HL, but the appeal was compromised just before it was due to be heard.

52.71 Thus, a clause exempting a trustee from liability for breaches of trust, other than dishonest breaches, does not extend to a deliberate breach committed in the genuine belief that the course taken was in the interests of the beneficiaries if such belief was so unreasonable that no reasonable trustee of the actual trustee's type could have held that belief¹.

¹   Compare the rejection by the PC in *Barlow Clowes International Ltd (in liquidation) v Eurotrust International Ltd* [2005] UKPC 37, [2006] 1 All ER 333 of the apparently subjective view in *Twinsectra Ltd v Yardley [2002] UKHL 12, [2002] 2 AC 164* which was interpreted as really supporting an objective approach in dishonest assistance cases.

Ouster of duty better for trustees than exemption from liability for breach of duty

52.72 Ouster of a duty is preferable for a trustee than exemption from liability for a breach of trust. A trustee can be removed for a breach of trust even if exempted from liability therefor. More importantly, a trustee who deliberately relies on an exemption clause so as to proceed to commit a breach of trust is acting recklessly which amounts to acting dishonestly, against which no exemption clause can be effective. However, if a provision expressly provides that the trustee is not placed under a duty otherwise applicable under trust law then a trustee relying on the absence of such a duty cannot be made liable for such conduct.

Statutory prohibitions on exemption clauses in trust instruments

52.73 Where there is a trust deed for securing an issue of debentures any provision therein is void¹, 'in so far as it would have the effect of exempting a trustee from, or indemnifying him against, liability for breach of trust where he fails to show the degree of care and diligence required of him as trustee, having regard to the provisions of the trust deed conferring any powers, authorities or discretions'; but a three-quarters majority of debenture holders may release him from liability².

¹   Companies Act 1985, s 192(1).
²   Companies Act 1985, s 192(2).

52.74 For authorised unit trusts any provision is void¹ so far as it would have the effect of exempting the trustee or the manager from liability for any failure to exercise due care and diligence in discharge of his functions.

52.74 *The trustee's duties*

1   Financial Services and Markets Act 2000, s 253 re-enacting Financial Services Act 1986, s 84.

52.75 In the case of pension trust schemes liability for breach of any obligation to take care or exercise skills in the performance of any investment functions cannot be excluded or restricted by an instrument or agreement[1] where the function is exercisable by a trustee or by a person to whom any investment function has been delegated under s 34 of the Pensions Act 1995 (permitting discretionary investment functions to be delegated eg to a portfolio fund manager).

1   Pensions Act 1995, s 33.

52.76 Trusts are not contracts, trustees as an incident of their office being entitled to charge remuneration provided for in the trust instrument or by law; so trusts are unaffected by the Unfair Contracts Terms Act 1977[1] and so far, have not been affected by regulations made under the European Directive[2].

1   Sir William Goodhart 'Trust Law for the 21st Century' in AJ Oakley (ed) *Trends in Contemporary Trust Law* (Oxford 1996) p 270. A *contra proferentem* approach applies to exemption clauses in contracts but not in trusts: see para 52.66 above.
2   Council Directive 93/13 EEC; Law Commission Consultation Paper, 'Trustee Exemption Clauses', Oct 2002.

The effect of undue influence or breach of fiduciary duty

52.77 Fiduciary duties can exist before formal creation of the trust relationship[1] and it will be wise to minimise the chances of the settlor or a beneficiary alleging that an exemption clause had been included in the trust instrument as a result of a breach of fiduciary duty or by means of undue influence such that the trustee cannot be allowed to rely on the terms of such clause[2]. The settlor's attention must be drawn to the clause and its effect, and until *Bogg v Raper*[3] it would have been thought wise to take the precaution of advising the settlor to consult an independent lawyer[4]: a document signed by the settlor acknowledging such matters would provide helpful evidence. In the light of *Bogg v Raper* it is only necessary to show that the settlor-testator knew and approved the clause, the Court of Appeal considering[5] that an exemption clause, unlike a remuneration clause did not confer a benefit on the solicitor preparing his client's will trust of which the solicitor was to be an executor and trustee, However, there is much to be said for the view that the solicitor was unjustly enriched at the expense of the beneficiaries in saving himself from paying the requisite insurance premiums to cover possible liability and saving himself from the claimant's claim for £8 million[6].

1   *Swain v Law Society* [1981] 3 All ER 797 at 805–806, [1982] 1 WLR 17 at 26, per Stephenson LJ; *Galmerrow Securities Ltd v National Westminster Bank* [2002] WTLR 125 at 148; *Bogg v Raper* (1998) 1 ITELR 267, CA.
2   To this effect see *Rutanen v Ballard* 424 Mass 723 (1997) at 733; *Baskerville v Thurgood* (1992) 100 Sask LR 214, CA; *Jothann v Irving Trust Co* 270 NYS 721, 277 NYS 955 (1934) and *Scott on Trusts* Vol III para 222.4.
3   (1998) 1 ITELR 267.
4   Eg precautions suggested by *Barclays Bank plc v O'Brien* [1994] 1 AC 180 and *Royal Bank of Scotland v Etridge (No 2)* [2001] UKHL 44, [2002] 2 AC 773.

⁵ (1998) 1 ITELR 267 at 285.
⁶ The saving of expense is a benefit or enrichment: *Peel v Canada* (1992) 98 DLR (4th) 140; *Peter v Beblow* (1993) 101 DLR 621 at 645; A Burrows *Law of Restitution* (3rd edn) p 8; Goff & Jones *Law of Restitution* (6th edn) para 1–017.

52.78 It would seem that successor trustees as donees of the legal title with an equitable interest under exemption and remuneration clauses will only acquire the benefit of such clauses as already vitiated by the circumstances surrounding their creation[1].

¹ Successor trustees should not be regarded as purchasers: remuneration clauses are regarded as gifts subject to a condition (*Re Pooley* (1880) 40 Ch D 1; *Re White* [1898] 2 Ch 217; *Re Brown* [1918] WN 118; *Re Duke of Norfolk's Settlement Trusts* [1982] Ch 61) while exemption clauses may be regarded as conferring a bounty upon the trustees at least to the cost of insuring against the liabilities relieved. The first equity prevails against the later equity: *Cave v Cave* (1880) 15 Ch D 639.

ARTICLE 53
POWERS AND DUTIES OF TRUSTEE IN RELATION TO THE INVESTMENT OF TRUST FUNDS

53.1

(1) Trustees cannot lawfully invest trust funds upon any securities other than those authorised by the settlement or by statute (or, in rarer cases, by the court).

(2) Statutory powers of investment are now contained almost entirely in the Trustee Act 2000 except[1] for trustees of occupational pension schemes[2], authorised unit trusts and charitable common investment schemes. Whether any provision relating to the powers of trustees which is contained in the settlement or other relevant instrument can limit the powers of investment conferred by the Act will depend upon the date and nature of the instrument. Unless the instrument is an enactment or instrument made under an enactment, in which case it may limit those powers whatever its date, it can limit them only if it is made after the passing of the Trustee Investments Act on 3 August 1961[3].

(3) Under section 3 of the Trustee Act 2000 a 'general power of investment' is conferred upon a trustee so that he 'may make any kind of investment that he could make if he were absolutely entitled to the assets of the trust', but[4] this power does not permit him to make investments in land, other than in loans secured on land, because powers to acquire legal estates in land in the UK are conferred by section 8.

(4) Before exercising any power of investment, whether the general power of investment or an express power of investment, a trustee must obtain and consider 'proper advice' about the way in which, having regard to the 'standard investment criteria', the power should be exercised[5] unless he reasonably concludes that,

in all the circumstances, it is unnecessary or inappropriate to do so[6]; this is also the case[7] when a trustee is performing his duty[8] from time to time to review the investments of the trust.

(a)   'Proper advice' is the advice of a person who is reasonably believed by the trustee to be qualified to give it by his ability in and practical experience of financial and other matters relating to the proposed investment[9].

(b)   The 'standard investment criteria' are[10]:

(i)   the suitability to the trust of investments of the same kind as any particular investment proposed to be made or retained and of that particular investment as an investment of that kind, and

(ii)   the need for diversification of investments of the trust, in so far as is appropriate to the circumstances of the trust.

(5)   Under section 8(1) of the Trustee Act 2000, except for trusts governed by the Settled Land Act 1925 or the Universities and College Estates Act 1925, a trustee may acquire 'freehold or leasehold land' in the UK whether as an investment or for occupation by a beneficiary or for any other reason; 'freehold or leasehold land' covers a legal estate or interest in English or Welsh land[11], and, in relation to Scotland, (i) the estate or interest of the proprietor of the *dominium utile* or, in the case of land not held on feudal tenure, the estate or interest of the owner or (ii) a tenancy, and, in relation to Northern Ireland, a legal estate in land, including land held under a fee farm grant.

(6)   A trustee of land initially settled upon him or a trustee of land or of pure personalty acquiring land under section 8(1) has, for the purpose of exercising his functions as a trustee, all the powers of an absolute owner in relation to the land[12]; but in the case of pre 1997 Settled Land Act settlements[13] the inter-related position of the tenant for life and the Settled Land Act trustees is governed by the Settled Land Act 1925 as amended by the Trustee Act 2000 Schedule 2 paras 7–17.

(7)   Wide express powers of investment are very common so as to confer wider powers than those conferred by the Trustee Act 2000, and the courts[14] are not astute to limit the scope of these express powers if the natural and proper meaning of the words used allows for wide powers of investment or other application of trust property by trustees in the exercise of their managerial and administrative functions.

(8)   Trustees act beyond their powers if investing in unauthorised investments so that their accounts can be strictly falsified[15], but even if they invest in authorised investments their accounts can be surcharged[16] if the value of the trust fund would have been higher but for their breach of any equitable or statutory duty in exercising their powers of investment[17].

(9)   Trustees will often transfer trust investments[18] to a nominee[19] or a custodian[20] or purchase investments in the name of a nominee or custodian, either under express powers in that behalf or under powers in the Trustee Act 2000[21], while bearer securities must be deposited with a qualifying custodian[22] unless there is a sole trustee which is a trust corporation[23] or the trust instrument otherwise provides[24].

(10) Trustees will often delegate their asset management functions to a discretionary portfolio manager or a land manager, either under express powers in that behalf or under the powers contained in the Trustee Act 2000[25].

1   TA 2000, ss 36, 37 and 38.
2   Pensions Act 1995, ss 34 and 35.
3   TA 2000, ss 6(2) and 7. See also para 53.2 below. In the case of a will, the date on which it is made will be the date of its execution, not that of the testator's death; but it seems that a will confirmed by a codicil is for this purpose 'made' at the date of execution of the codicil (see the Wills Act 1837, s 34 though this section applies only 'for the purposes of the Act'; and see *Berkeley v Berkeley* [1946] AC 555, [1946] 2 All ER 154, HL). Support is lent to this view by the fact that the draftsman of the Family Law Reform Act 1969 felt it necessary expressly to negative this construction: see s 1(7) of the Act.
4   TA 2000, s 3(3).
5   TA 2000, s 5(1).
6   TA 2000, s 5(3).
7   TA 2000, s 5(2).
8   TA 2000, s 4(2).
9   TA 2000, s 5(4).
10 TA 2000, s 4(3).
11 TA 2000, s 8(2)(a) and presumably LPA 1925, s 1(4) as for TLATA 1996, s 6(3) by s 23(2) thereof: see para 53.37 below.
12 TA 2000, s 8(3).
13 See Article 44 above.
14 For example, *Re Harari's Settlement Trusts* [1949] 1 All ER 430; *Re Peczenik's Settlement* [1964] 2 All ER 339; *R v Barlow Clowes (No 2)* [1994] 2 All ER 316, CA.
15 See Article 89(1).
16 See Article 89(2).
17 *Nestle v National Westminster Bank* [1994] 1 All ER 118, CA; *Re Mulligan* [1998] 1 NZLR 481.
18 A transferee may have custody of tangibles but title to intangibles must be transferred, title and custody being inseparable for intangibles ie choses in action.
19 TA 2000, s 16.
20 TA 2000, s 17.
21 TA 2000, ss 16–23.
22 TA 2000, ss 18 and 19.
23 TA 2000, s 25(2).
24 TA 2000, s 18(2).
25 TA 2000, ss 11–15.

Paragraphs 2,3 and 4

Availability of the general power of investment

53.2 The general power of investment is conferred on trustees (except for trustees of pension schemes, authorised unit trusts and charitable common investment schemes[1] and, probably, bare trustees[2]) in addition to powers conferred on trustees otherwise than by the Trustees Act 2000, but subject to any restriction or exclusion imposed by the trust instrument[3] if made after 2 August 1961 or by any enactment or subordinate legislation[4]. However, a power to invest only in authorised investments or in investments authorised under the Trustee Investments Act 1961 is treated as conferring the general power of investment on the trustee[5]. A post-1961 power to invest in any UK securities will not work as a restriction or exclusion imposed by the trust instrument despite the necessary implication that it is forbidden to invest in non-UK securities[6]. However, the express addition of the words 'but not in any non-UK securities' would appear to amount to an exclusion or restriction of the general power[7]. It is then most likely that an application to the court under s 57 could successfully be made for conferment of the general power, a settlor conferring the power in 1962 in substance conferring as an addition, to the power to invest in investments authorised under the 1961 Act, the power to invest in any UK securities not so authorised – so not having any excluding or restrictive intent in respect of investments then ranking as authorised investments.

1 TA 2000, ss 36, 37 and 38.
2 See para 4.2 above.
3 TA 2000, s 6(1). In the absence of a definition of 'trust instrument' such instrument is capable of extending to an instrument exercising a special power of appointment in the original trust deed: *Lewin on Trusts* (17th edn) para 35–01D.
4 TA 2000, s 7(2).
5 TA 2000, s 7(3).
6 Cf *Re Burke* [1908] 2 Ch 248.
7 Cf *Ovey v Ovey* [1900] 2 Ch 524.

Trustees of occupational pension schemes

53.3 Section 34(1) of the Pensions Act 1995 ensures that trustees of a pension trust scheme[1] 'have, subject to any restrictions imposed by the scheme, the same power to make an investment of any kind as if they were absolutely entitled to the assets of the scheme'. The Trustee Act 2000[2] followed this model in conferring on a trustee power to 'make any kind of investment that he could make if he were absolutely entitled to the assets of the trust'.

1 Defined in Pension Act 1995, s 124(1).
2 TA 2000, s 3(1).

53.4 It is noteworthy that subjective, and not objective, powers of an absolute beneficial owner are conferred, so that the statutory powers of a corporate trustee may be limited if it is limited in what it can do with its own beneficially owned assets. Furthermore, no clarification of the meaning of investment[1] is given so as to make clear that non-income-yielding assets may be purchased in accordance with modern portfolio theory.

1 See para 53.9 below.

53.5 Trustees of a pensions trust scheme can delegate discretionary portfolio management to a fund manager[1] authorised under s 192(1)(a)–(c) of the Financial Services Act 1986 or, now, article 4 of the Financial Services and

Markets Act 2000 (Carrying on of Regulated Activities by Way of Business) Order 2001 and, subject to taking certain limited precautions in the appointment and supervision of such manager, are protected from liability for the manager's acts or defaults[2]. They can also delegate to a manager not so authorised or to two of themselves the exercise of investment discretions but they then remain liable for the acts or defaults of such persons as if their own[3].

[1]   Pensions Act 1995, s 34(2).
[2]   Pensions Act 1995, s 34(3).
[3]   Pensions Act 1995, s 34(5).

53.6 Unless exempted[1], the trustees must ensure that there is prepared, maintained and from time to time revised a written statement of the principles governing investment decisions[2] setting out the kinds of investments to be held, the balance between risk, expected return, realisation of investments and such other matters as may be prescribed[3]. Such statement must also cover the trustees' policy for securing compliance with s 36 and the minimum funding requirements of s 56[4].

[1]   Pensions Act 1995, s 35(7).
[2]   Pensions Act 1995, s 35(1). Proper advice needs to be obtained and the employer must be consulted: s 35(5).
[3]   Pensions Act 1995, s 35(3). For example, the extent to which social environmental or ethical considerations are taken into account and the trustees' policy as to the exercise of voting rights attached to investments: SI 1999/1849.
[4]   Pensions Act 1995, s 35(2).

53.7 Section 36 is concerned to ensure the trustees or fund manager consider the need for diversification and the suitability of the kind of investment proposed and the particular one of that kind[1]. The trustees, before investing in any manner, must obtain and consider proper advice taking account of the above criteria and the above written statement[2], while in retaining investments they must determine at what intervals to obtain proper advice and then obtain and consider it accordingly[3].

[1]   Pensions Act 1995, s 36(1).
[2]   Pensions Act 1995, s 36(3).
[3]   Pensions Act 1995, s 36(4).

53.8 The trustees' power of investment cannot be restricted by reference to the consent of the employer[1], and tight restrictions are imposed[2] on the proportion of the trust fund that may be invested in 'employer-related investments'.

[1]   Pensions Act 1995, s 35(4).
[2]   Pensions Act 1995, s 40; SI 1996/3127.

Ambit of the general power of investment

53.9 Section 3 empowers a trustee (subject to ss 4, 5, 6 and 7) to 'make any kind of investment that he could make it he were absolutely entitled to the assets of the trust', except for 'investments in land [dealt with in s 8] other than in loans secured on land'. Many years ago an investment was considered to be an asset acquired for the sake of the income it would yield[1], but nowadays with the emphasis placed on 'total return', taking account of income yield and capital appreciation[2] in accordance with modern portfolio theory[3], an investment is considered to cover any asset acquired for a portfolio for the sake of its income yield or anticipated capital profit or both. Thus, the purchase by trustees of depreciating chattels for a villa that is trust property or the purchase of a depreciating car for use by a beneficiary would not amount to an investment.

1   *Re Somerset* [1894] 1 Ch 231 at 247; *Re Wragg* [1919] 2 Ch 58 at 65.
2   *Harries v Church Comrs* [1992] 1 WLR 1241 at 1246, 'the purposes of the trust will be best served by the trustees seeking the maximum return, whether by way of income or capital growth, which is consistent with commercial prudence'; Lord Nicholls (1995) 9 Trust LI 71 at 73; *Cowan v Scargill* [1985] Ch 270 at 287.
3   See J Langbein (1996) 81 Iowa LR 641; I N Legair (2000) 14 Trust LI 75.

53.10 However, because investing in investments covers the 'laying out of money in anticipation of a profitable capital or income return'[1] the purchase of a valuable painting or a rare stamp or antique desk that the trustees believe to have a good chance of capital appreciation will be an investment[2].

1   *Cook v Medway Housing Society* [1997] STC 90 at 98; also *Marson v Morton* [1986] 1 WLR 1343 at 1350.
2   Law Com No 260 'Trustees' Powers and Duties' page 22 note 56 and Explanatory Notes to TA 2000, paras 22 and 23.

53.11 It may be argued that if a trustee can 'make any kind of investment that he could make if he were absolutely entitled to the assets of the trust', then he can not only use money donated by the settlor and the proceeds of the sale of investments to purchase new investments, but he can exchange an old investment to substitute a new investment therefor, and even mortgage an old investment so as to raise new money to make a new investment. After all, an absolute owner of assets can sell those assets or exchange those assets or mortage those assets in order to make a new investment.

53.12 On the other hand, it can be argued that the making of any kind of investment implicitly needs to be made out of subsisting cash or investments that currently are trust assets available for the purchase or exchange of investments, so that the creation of a mortgage liability imposed on old trust assets to create a new fund of money to be used in the purchase of a new investment is one step removed from the power conferred by s 3 of the Trustee Act 2000. This argument seems the better one in the light of *Re Suenson-Taylor's Settlement*[1] although, in any event, such gearing-up would not be authorised unless proper advice had been obtained and considered[2] in the light of the statutory duty of care[3], to the extent not excluded in the trust instrument[4]. In many circumstances it would be unlikely that gearing-up would be advised in the light of the duty of care.

1   [1974] 3 All ER 397, [1974] 1 WLR 1280.
2   TA 2000, ss 4 and 5.
3   TA 2000, ss 1 and 2.
4   TA 2000, Sch 1, para 7.

Duty to obtain proper advice before exercise of the general power of investment or of express powers

53.13 By s 5(1) of the Trustee Act 2000 'before exercising any power of investment, whether arising under this Part or otherwise, a trustee must (unless the exception applies) obtain and consider proper advice about the way in which, having regard to the standard investment criteria, the power should be exercised.' The exception[1] is that 'a trustee need not obtain such advice if he reasonably concludes that in all the circumstances it is unnecessary or inappropriate to do so.' The trustee's conclusion needs to be objectively reasonable[2], taking account of all the circumstances eg the financial experience of the trustee, the amount of cash or the value of investments involved, the nature of the investment being considered. The trustee, to protect himself, should provide contemporaneous written evidence of the reason(s) for considering the exception applied.

1   TA 2000, s 5(3).
2   See next but one footnote.

53.14 Obtaining and considering proper advice is needed if there are doubts over the applicability of the exception. 'Proper advice'[1] is 'the advice of a person who is reasonably believed by the trustee to be qualified to give it by his ability in, and practical experience of, financial and other matters relating to the proposed investment'. The advisor must be subjectively believed by the trustee to be qualified on objective reasonable grounds so that the choice of advisor was one which a reasonable trustee could have made in all the circumstances even if the court might have taken a different view[2]. The advice need not be given or confirmed in writing but it will be wise for the trustees to require such in case problems arise later. There are no provisions similar to those in s 6(4) and (6) of the Trustee Investments Act 1961 concerning a trustee being advised by a co-trustee or an officer or servant of a corporate trustee, but it would seem that the advice of a co-trustee reasonably believed to be duly qualified could be 'proper advice'. It is less clear whether the advice of a senior employee of a corporate sole or co-trustee is capable of being proper advice. It should probably suffice when an individual sole trustee who is duly qualified can act without[3] taking proper advice. The advice obtained has to be considered, not followed, so it need not be followed, but it is wise to provide contemporaneous written evidence as to why the advice was not followed in case of subsequent complaints from beneficiaries.

1   TA 2000, s 5(4).
2   *Edge v Pensions Ombudsman* [2000] Ch 602 at 618–619, 627 and 630.
3   TA 2000, s 5(3).

53.15 A trustee must from time to time review the investments of the trust[1] and then (unless the s 5(3) exception applies) obtain and consider proper advice about whether, having regard to the standard investment criteria, the investments should be varied[2].

1   TA 2000, s 4(2).
2   TA 2000, s 5(2).

53.16 The standard investment criteria to which a trustee must have regard are[1]:

'(a)   the suitability to the trust of investments of the same kind as any particular investment proposed to be made or retained and of that particular investment as an investment of that kind, and

(b)   the need for diversification of investments of the trust, in so far as is appropriate to the circumstances of the trust'.

[1]   TA 2000, s 4(3).

53.17 Thus, trustees need to consider the different types of investment open to them (eg land, quoted stocks and shares, unit trusts, investment trusts, mortgages, bonds, building society deposits, tax reserve certificates) and to consider that the more diversified the portfolio of investments the lower the overall level of risk for the portfolio, the trustees being entitled to be judged according to modern portfolio theory[1]. However, the circumstances of the case must be taken into account eg restrictions on sale (whether by articles of a private company or by a consent required in the trust instrument), the settlor's purposes as, for example, indicated in his letter of wishes, especially where beneficiaries may have interests as employees in the family company controlled by the trustees[2].

[1]   *Nestle v National Westminster Bank* [2000] WTLR 795 at 802; *JW v Morgan Trust Company of the Bahamas Ltd* (2002) 4 ITELR 541, Lord Nicholls, 'Trustees and their Broader Community' (1995) 9 Trust LI 71 at 75.
[2]   For example, *Public Trustee v Cooper* [2001] WTLR 901.

53.18 The statutory duty of care applies to a trustee[1] 'when exercising the general power of investment or any other power of investment, however conferred' and 'when carrying out a duty to which he is subject under ss 4 or 5 (Duties relating to the exercise of a power of investment or to the review of investments'.

[1]   TA 2000, Sch 1, para 1.

Exclusions or restrictions relating to investment powers

53.19 The 'general power of investment' is in addition to powers conferred on trustees otherwise then by the trustee Act 2000 but is subject[1] to any restriction or exclusion imposed by the trust instrument after 2 August 1961[2] or by any enactment or subordinate legislation, while the statutory duty of care does not apply in so far as it appears from the trust instrument that the duty is not meant to apply[3].

[1]   TA 2000, s 6(1).
[2]   TA 2000, s 7(2).
[3]   TA 2000, Sch 1, para 7.

53.20 The 'general power of investment' is[1] the power of a trustee to make any kind of investment that he could make if he were absolutely entitled to the assets of the trust 'subject to the provisions of this Part' viz ss 4, 5, 6 and 7.

Thus, the general power of investment is the power so to invest only if the trustee has obtained and considered proper advice, having regard to the standard investment criteria, and it is this that is subject to exclusion or restriction expressly or by necessary implication, as where an express power of investment in a wider range of assets than those permitted by the general power of investment is subject to an exclusion or restriction which should apply *a fortiori* to the narrower general power of investment.

¹   TA 2000, s 3(1) and (2).

53.21 It follows that a settlor can exclude any duty to consider the need for diversification eg for so long as the trustees retain the controlling shareholding in a particular company, or can exclude any duty to take proper advice, eg for so long as the trustees consult the settlor before making any investment decision.

Investments purchased without requisite proper advice are authorised but improper

53.22 A key issue is whether investments within the range permitted by the general power of investment or an express power of investment, but which are purchased without obtaining and considering the requisite 'proper advice', amount to unauthorised investments, the trustees having acted beyond their powers, or amount to merely improper investments, the trustees having acted improperly in breach of trust but within their powers. In the case of unauthorised investments the trustees are strictly liable upon a falsification of the trust accounts¹, while in the case of improper investments the accounts will be surcharged in the amount of any loss which would not have been incurred but for the improper conduct of the trustees².

¹   See Article 89(1). Good title will pass to a purchaser because the individual trustees (or a corporation with a broad objects clause) have power or capacity as such to transfer title: *De Vigier v IRC* [1964] 2 All ER 907 at 914, HL; *Hammersmith and Fulham London Borough Council v Monk* [1992] 1 AC 478 at 493; *Rolled Steel Products (Holdings) Ltd v British Steel Corpn* [1986] Ch 246 at 303, [1985] 3 All ER 52 at 91,CA.
²   See Article 89(2).

53.23 It seems that a general power of investment or an express power of investment can be likened to a mortgagee's statutory power of sale which first *arises* and on further requirements being satisfied becomes *exercisable*, though a valid sale can be made once the power has arisen¹. The power of investment arises under s 3 of the Trustee Act 2000 or the trust instrument, but does not become exercisable until the requisite proper advice has been obtained and considered under ss 4 and 5 of the 2000 Act. It is significant that ss 4(1) and 5(1) use the terminology of '*exercising* any power of investment, whether *arising* under this Part of otherwise'. It also makes sense that strict liability by way of falsification of accounts should only be imposed in clearly defined, easily ascertainable circumstances and not in circumstances, like those involved in ss 4 and 5, where the opposite may well be the case.

[1]   LPA 1925, ss 104(2) and 101 and 103. See Gray & Gray , *Elements of Land Law*(4th ed) paras 15.176 to 177.

Investment in loans secured on land

53.24 Trustees can invest in a loan secured on land if they have rights under any contract under which they provide another with credit and the obligation of the borrower to repay is secured on land[1]. Such an investment falls within the trustee's power[2] to 'make any kind of investment that he could make if he were absolutely entitled to the assets of the trust'.

[1]   TA 2000, s 3(3) and (4). For 'land' see under paras (5) and (6) below.
[2]   TA 2000, s 3(1).

53.25 Such powers to invest in a loan secured on land are broad enough to enable trustees to be sole or co-lenders and sole or co-mortgagees or co-chargees[1] and to invest not just in legal mortgages or charges over freehold or leasehold land or in legal sub-mortgages, but also equitable mortgages or charges or sub-mortgages and, even, in second or subsequent mortgages or charges or sub-mortgages as opposed to first mortgages or charges or sub-mortgages.

[1]   See Law Com Report No 260 'Trustees' Powers and Duties' para 2.28.

53.26 Traditionally[1], trustees could not invest in contributory mortgages, second mortgages or equitable charges of freeholds or leaseholds nor on first legal mortgages of leaseholds with fewer than 60 years to run. The potential inadequacy or vulnerability of such types of mortgage meant they had to be avoided at all costs. Nowadays, there may well be circumstances where some such types of mortgage can be invested in in accordance with the duties imposed on trustees to safeguard their beneficiaries' interests.

[1]   See 15th edn hereof pp 603–605.

53.27 Sections 8, 9 and 10 of the Trustee Act 1925, until repealed by the Trustee Act 2000, provided assistance for trustees lending on mortgage by permitting dispensing with production of the lessor's title where the lessee was mortgaging the leasehold interest to the trustees[1], permitting loaned money not to be called in for a period not exceeding seven years[2], permitting up to two thirds of the sale price of trust land to be secured by a legal mortgage[3], and protecting trustees from liability for loss arising by reason only of the loan exceeding two thirds of the value of the property if certain precautions had been taken[4] or making trustees only liable to the extent the amount advanced was larger than the proper amount that should have been lent on mortgage[5]. The repeal of ss 8 and 9 does not affect their operation[6] in relation to loans made before 1 February 2001[7].

[1]   TA 1925, s 8(2) in light of LPA 1925, s 44(2), but registration of the superior title under the Land Registration Acts 1925, s 44(2), but registration of the superior title under the Land Registration Acts 1925 and 2002 increasingly simplifies matters by enabling the inferior title to be title absolute, not just good leasehold title.
[2]   TA 1925, s 10(1).

3   TA 1925, s 10(2).
4   TA 1925, s 8(1).
5   TA 1925, s 9.
6   On these sections see 15th edn hereof pp 587–589 and 605–608.
7   TA 2000, s 40(2), Sch 3, paras 2 and 3.

Particular duties when investing in mortgages or charges

53.28 Trustees need to focus upon the title of the borrower (so that it is readily saleable if need be) and upon the value of the property and its sufficiency for the amount of the loan once they have made the preliminary decision that an investment by way of mortgage, as opposed to any other kind of investment, is appropriate for the portfolio of trust assets. Thus, unless themselves having particular expertise, they will need to take the advice of a financial consultant on the balance of the portfolio and, then, of a surveyor-valuer and a solicitor.

53.29 Case law and s 8 of the Trustee Act 1925 indicate that compliance with the duty of care will require the trustees to give written instructions to the valuer (preferably a local one or, otherwise, with the assistance of the trustees he will need to take extra time to familiarise himself with all material circumstances affecting the locality[1]). They should select as valuer someone they adjudge on reasonable grounds to be an able practical valuer and who is independent of the mortgagor and whose fee is not dependent on the mortgage transaction being completed[2]. The valuer should be instructed that his valuation is for the trustees for the purpose of considering the advisability of investing trust funds on the security of the property (so any matters tending to decrease the present or future value of the property should be stated) and that he must advise the trustees in the light of his valuation as to what amount could safely be lent upon the security of the property[2]. Section 8 used to provide protection for advances up to two thirds of the value of the property if so advised, but there is now no hard and fast rule. Thus trustees, therefore, ought to be regarded as complying with their duty of care if their valuer recommends that any amount of three quarters of his valuation can safely be advanced on the security of the well-located residential property which he has conservatively valued.

1   *Fry v Tapson* (1884) 28 Ch D 268.
2   *Re Walker* (1890) 59 LJ Ch 386; *Re Somerset* [1894] 1 Ch 231; *Re Dive* [1909] 1 Ch 328.
3   *Re Solomon* [1912] 1 Ch 261 compromised [1913] 1 Ch 200, CA; *Shaw v Cates* [1909] 1 Ch 389.

Possible problems in replacing Trustee Act 1925, Pt I with general power of investment

53.30 As just seen, s 10 of the Trustee Act 1925 has been repealed. Under s 10(3) trustees holding securities in a company had power to 'concur in any scheme or arrangement.

(a)   for the reconstruction of the company;

(b)   for the sale of all or any part of the property and undertaking of the company to another company;

(bb) for the acquisition of the securities of the company, or of control thereof, by another company;

(c) for the amalgamation of the company with another company;

(d) for the release, modification or variation of any rights, privileges or liabilities attached to the securities or any of them

in like manner as if they were entitled to such securities beneficially[1], with power to accept any securities of any denomination or description of the reconstructed or purchasing or new company in lieu of or in exchange for all or any of the first mentioned securities'.

[1]   But consent was required of anyone whose consent would be required to a change of investments: TA 1925, s 10(5).

53.31 The general power of a trustee to 'make any kind of investment that he could make if he were absolutely entitled to the assets of the trust' appears to cover (a), (bb) and (c), but not (b) and (d). In (b) where it is the company selling its assets or undertaking and it cannot do this without the concurrence of its shareholders (as in the case of a reconstruction under s 110 of the Insolvency Act 1986) it seems the trustees will not by their concurrence be making an investment. However, in dissenting from the reconstruction they can require their shares to be purchased, having of course power to sell those investments in order to make a new investment. In (d) it does not seem that releasing modifying or varying rights for no consideration can amount to the making of an investment.

53.32 Thus trust deeds should expressly confer on trustees the powers of an absolute beneficial owner to exercise any rights attached to trust investments or expressly confer powers in the terms of s 10(3).

53.33 Section 11 has also been repealed. Sub-section (1) conferred power pending the making of an investment to pay any trust money into a bank to a deposit or other account (with the interest thereon being applied as income) separate from the trustee's personal account, of course. This seems to have been declaratory of the general law[1] and such temporary income-yielding investment before making a longer term investment would seem, in any event, to fall within the ambit of the general power of investment.

[1]   *Ex p Belchier* (1754) Amb 218; *Massey v Banner* (1820) 1 Jac & W 241 at 248; *Ex p Kingston* (1871) 6 Ch App 632.

53.34 Section 11(2) permitted trustees to 'apply capital money subject to a trust in payment of the calls on any shares subject to the same trust'. The general power to make any kind of investment a trustee could make if he were absolutely entitled to the assets of the trust clearly extends to him purchasing shares issued partly paid, but subject to the obligation to pay the amount unpaid when called upon, where the trustees were the original subscribers to whom the shares were first issued, and there seems no reason why it should make any difference that the trustees purchased the partly-paid shares from the original subscriber or a successor in title thereto: in each case the purchase is in exchange for some money to be paid forthwith and for incurring the obligation to pay the remainder when duly called for.

Paragraphs 5 and 6

Specific power of trustees to acquire 'freehold or leasehold land' in UK in respect of which the trustees have all the powers of an absolute owner

53.35 Trustees may, under s 8(1) of the Trustee Act 2000, 'acquire freehold or leasehold land in the UK (a) as an investment (b) for occupation by a beneficiary or (c) for any other reason'. Such English or Welsh land must be a legal estate, as for Northern Irish land, but this includes land held under a fee farm grant. Scots land must be the estate or interest of the proprietor of the *dominium utile* or of the owner of land not held on feudal tenure or must be a tenancy. For trustees who acquire land other than under s 8(1), eg because they already have land settled on them initially by the settlor[1], the amended s 6(3) of the Trustees of Land and Appointment of Trustees Act 1996 provides, 'The trustees of land have power to acquire land under the power conferred by section 8 of the Trustee Act 2000'. Under s 8(3), 'For the purpose of exercising his functions as a trustee, a trustee who acquires land under this section has all the powers of an absolute owner in relation to the land'. To cover land initially settled on the trustees and not subsequently acquired by them, s 6(1) of the 1996 Act provides, 'For the purpose of exercising their functions as trustees, the trustees of land have in relation to the land subject to the trust all the powers of an absolute owner.' Such powers necessarily enable trustees to be co-purchasers if otherwise complying with their duties of care.

[1]   Not being settled land under the SLA 1925; see Article 44 above.

53.36 In exercising their powers as an absolute owner the trustees of land or just of movables can purchase land (together with appurtement easements profits and restrictive covenants) by way of mortgage *over that land* acquiring the benefit of the legal estate in land at the same time as incurring the burden of the mortgage without which the legal estate could not have been acquired[1], but they cannot create a liability by mortgaging *other trust property* in order to generate money to be used in the acquisition of further investments, whether purchased outright or with the assistance of a mortgage over them[2].

[1]   *Abbey National Building Society v Cann* [1991] 1 AC 56, HL.
[2]   See para 53.12 above.

53.37 'Land' is not defined in the Trustee Act 2000[1], but by the Interpretation Act 1978[2], unless the contrary intention appears, '"land" includes buildings and other structures, land covered with water, and any estate, *interest, easement, servitude* or right in or over land.' 'Legal estate' is not defined in either the 2000 or the 1978 Act but, presumably, should have the meaning set out in s 1(4) of the Law of Property Act 1925[3] so as to include not just legal estates but also interests and charges like legal profits relating to game-shooting or legal rentcharges, as was the case for trustees of land under s 6(3) of the Trust of Land and Appointment of Trustees Act 1996 having powers to purchase a 'legal estate in any land', with the LPA 1925 definitions applying to such terminology, until such powers were replaced by the powers in s 8 of the 2000 Act. It would, indeed, be most strange if trustees investing under the 1996 Act in perpetual rentcharges[4] or in shooting rights over estates in the nature of a legal profit or in acquiring a useful legal easement from the new owner of neighbouring land could no longer do so after January 2001 and would need to sell such existing assets[5].

1   Which refers to Scots and Northern Ireland land as well as English and Welsh land.
2   Sch 1.
3   s 205(1)(x).
4   Perpetual rentcharges were even authorised under Trustee Investments Act 1961, Sch 1, Pt II, para 14 as well as s 6(3) of the TLATA 1996.
5   Section 8 of the TA 2000 was intended in similar terms to replace s 6(3) of the 1996 Act without changing matters: Law Com Report No 260 'Trustees' Powers and Duties' page 101 Explanatory Note. It would seem that the draftsperson of Sch 3, para 7(1) of the 2000 Act, worried about the repeal of the Trustee Investments Act 1961, put in a provision for continuing to hold rentcharges without appreciating that this was unnecessary because, as legal interests, they fell within the definition of legal estates: if it had been necessary, then all other legal interests should have been similarly protected.

53.38 'Freehold or leasehold land' means 'a legal estate in land', but, in the light of the above, this should extend beyond a freehold or leasehold estate to a legal rentcharge or a legal easement or profit, because it seems likely that legal estate does not have the narrow meaning in s 1(1) of the Law of Property Act 1925 restricting legal estate to freeholds and leaseholds[1] but the broad meaning in s 1(4) thereof.

1   Although *Lewin on Trusts* (17th edn) para 35–194F takes this narrow view, but cf para 35–194 M on acquiring a profit.

Acquisition as investment or for occupation or other reasons

53.39 When land is acquired by way of 'investment' as earlier discussed[1], then the duties to take advice, having regard to the standard investment criteria, and the equitable duty to act fairly between the beneficiaries will need to be complied with. While leaseholds of any duration may be acquired, the acquisition of leaseholds of short duration that are wasting assets will normally be out of the question having regard to such duties.

1   See para 53.9 above.

53.40 Originally, land purchased for occupation by a beneficiary was not regarded as an investment because it was not intended to produce income[1], although if purchased also with a view to capital growth as part of a balanced portfolio in accord with modern portfolio theory it might nowadays be regarded as an investment. Acquisition 'for occupation by a beneficiary' is now expressly permitted, but since it may well be regarded as also an investment the trustees should take advice as with any other investment and fairly consider the potential impact on all beneficiaries.

1   *Re Power's Will Trusts* [1947] Ch 572.

53.41 Clearly, occupation by a beneficiary cannot extend to a beneficiary with an interest in remainder after an interest in possession. Only the beneficiary with an interest in possession could occupy the land because to oust his interest in favour of the interest of the remainderman would be for the trustees to alter the beneficial interests laid down by the settlor. Purchasing for occupation by a beneficiary is merely an administrative power, not a distributive one permitting the trustees to distribute to the remainderman a benefit intended only for the life tenant. However, trustees should be able to purchase land for occupation by beneficiaries interested in income under a discretionary trust[1]. Thus, trustees could purchase a house for occupation of a discretionary income beneficiary and his family and permit him a licence to live there revocable at the whim of the trustees, although if there is a power to appoint income in a sufficient amount of capital to such a beneficiary so as to confer upon him an interest in possession therein, then he may have an interest in possession in the house[2]. Indeed, the trustees may acquire a house in the Lake District or Cornwall to be used as a holiday home from time to time by discretionary beneficiaries and their families.

[1] By TA 2000, s 35(2)(c) the reference to a beneficiary in s 8(1)(b) is to be read as referring to a person who, under the will of the deceased or under the law of intestacy, is beneficially interested in the estate, not merely interested in the due administration of the estate. Thus, one waits till the executors have completed their administration and themselves become trustees or transfer property to trustees whether on fixed or discretionary trusts.

[2] For inheritance tax danger if an interest in possession is created see Inheritance Tax Act 1975, s 65.

53.42 In the case of mere object of a power of appointment it would seem that a house cannot be acquired for occupation for such a person until, pursuant to the power, an income interest is appointed in the capital used to acquire the house for the benefit of such person or until the power has been exercised (if it can be) to appoint him a discretionary beneficiary in trust income[1].

[1] Objects only have a spes or hope or expectancy and have no interest in the trust property (*Re Brooks' Settlement Trusts* [1939] Ch 993), but a beneficiary under a discretionary trust does have a proprietary interest of sorts: *Knocker v Youle* [1986] 2 All ER 914; *Re Smith* [1928] 1 Ch 915.

53.43 In the case of the favoured accumulation and maintenance trusts[1], where income is to be accumulated to the extent not used for maintenance of a beneficiary who is to take a beneficial interest in possession or absolute interest on or before attaining 25 years of age, it should also be permissible for trustees to buy land for occupation by such beneficiary eg buying a land for the beneficiary-student to occupy while studying for a degree in that locality.

[1] Inheritance Act 1984, s 71.

53.44 With the powers of an absolute owner, the trustees can impose reasonable conditions related to the occupation of the trust land. One naturally assumes that purchase 'for occupation by a beneficiary' relates to physical residence by that beneficiary and, if appropriate, his family, but it could extend to occupation for a business purpose of the beneficiary, though the trustees would need to ensure they act fairly between income and capital beneficiaries[1] in going ahead with such a proposed purchase.

¹   *Nestle v National Westminster Bank* [1994] 1 All ER 118, CA; *Edge v Pensions Ombudsman* [2000] Ch 602; *Beauclerk v Ashburnham* (1845) 8 Beav 322.

53.45 In any event such a purchase for occupation for a business purpose of a beneficiary comes with s 8(1)(c) as an acquisition 'for any other reason'. This is primarily concerned with the functional purposes of charitable trusts but can otherwise authorise the trustees to acquire land not as an investment and not for residential occupation by a beneficiary currently interested in income of the trust, but for some other reason connected with furthering the interests of the beneficiaries as a whole and not the furthering of the trustees' interests at all (except to the extent otherwise authorised expressly or by necessary implication in the trust instrument). Thus, if the trustees have power under the trust instrument to carry on a business for the benefit of the beneficiaries then the trustees may acquire land for the purpose of carrying on and developing that business. In the absence of such a power, however, they cannot go off on frolic of the own so as to acquire land to commence a business role as trustee in addition to their fundamental investment role.

Settled Land Act 1925 trustees and tenant for life

53.46 Pre-1997 settlements under the Settled Land Act 1925 and new settlements made by virtue of powers thereunder unless designated not to be SLA settlements[1] are subject to the Settled Land Act 1925 regime as amended by the Trustee Act 2000[2]. While the tenant for life (or the statutory owner e g if there be no tenant for life of full age and capacity) decides whether to sell, lease, or otherwise dispose of the settled land, any capital money arising thereby which needs to be invested is invested in investments within s 73 of the Settled Land Act 1925[3] by the trustees (who must be paid the capital money), although they must so far as practicable consult the tenant for life and give effect to his wishes so far as is consistent with the general interest of the settlement[4]. Such investments are held in the names of or under the control of the SLA trustees[5]. However, freehold or leasehold land with at least 60 years unexpired acquired at the request of the tenant for life for occupation by the tenant for life is vested in the tenant for life[6].

¹   TLATA 1996, s 2(3).
²   TA 2000, Sch 2, paras 7–17.
³   These extend to investments authorised under the general power of investment within s 3 of TA 2000 as well as expressly authorised investments.
⁴   SLA 1925, s 75(2) and (4) as substituted by TA 2000, Sch 2, para 10(1) and (2).
⁵   SLA 1925, s 75(2) as substituted above.
⁶   SLA 1925, ss 10, 73(1)(xi) for moneys to be invested 'or otherwise applied' e g for occupation; substituted s 73(2).

Paragraph 7

Expressly and necessarily impliedly authorised investments

53.47 It is well-established that wills impliedly authorise the retention of investments that are specifically referred to in a specific bequest[1] or are intended to be capable of being retained for the benefit of the income beneficiary even if the subject of a residuary bequest[2]. However, where there is a power to retain specific shares this does not authorise the purchase of more of the same shares[3].

1   *Re Pugh* [1887] WN 143; *Re Whitfield* (1920) 125 LT 61.
2   *Re Pitcairn* [1896] 2 Ch 199; *Brown v Gellatley* (1867) 2 Ch App 751.
3   Hence the need in *Phipps v Boardman* [1967] 2 AC 46 for the trustees to obtain court
     permission under TA 1925, s 57 if they were to purchase more shares in Lester &
     Harris Ltd.

53.48 Where, under s 41 of the Administration of Estates Act 1925, there is an appropriation by personal representatives of a deceased's property towards satisfying a settled legacy, with the consent of the trustee or the income beneficiary, such appropriated property becomes an authorised investment so far as concerns its retention[1].

1   Administration of Estates Act 1925, s 41(2).

53.49 Investment clauses are now construed fairly and straightforwardly rather than in a restrictive fashion, but the court must first consider whether the relevant clause is truly an investment clause or not. Thus, in *Re Barlow Clowes (No 2)*[1] the Court of Appeal construed a clause which authorised the trustee to buy and sell British Government stock 'and to place any uninvested funds with any bank, local authority or other body on such terms and conditions as you see fit whether bearing interest or not' as authorising him to *invest* in British Government stock and merely *place* uninvested moneys temporarily pending investment in British Government stock. The words used were not intended to enable the trustee to invest in any corporate or other body he saw fit apart from investing in British Government stock.

1   [1994] 2 All ER 316 at 327–330, CA.

53.50 However in *Nestle v National Westminster Bank*[1] a lengthy clause 13 declaring 'all moneys liable to be invested may be invested upon any stocks or securities of or guaranteed by the UK Government or any British Colony or Dependency or any Foreign State or the stocks, shares, bonds, debentures or securities of any Railway or other Company established in the UK' was held to extend to investment in the purchase of ordinary shares in companies incorporated in the UK.

1   [1994] 1 All ER 118, CA.

53.51 If the trustee be given power to invest in such securities as he sees fit, it will be construed as power to invest in such investments as he sees fit (whether or not authorised by the general law), so that any investment honestly thought to be in the interests of the beneficiaries will be authorised[1], except, according to an old case of doubtful authority nowadays[2] a loan of money at interest on a mere personal contract to repay it with interest. If the power is to invest in investments in his absolute discretion in all respects as if he were the absolute beneficial owner of the Trust Fund this does not exempt him from the need to satisfy the duty of care[3].

53.51 *The trustee's duties*

1   *Re Douglas' Will Trusts* [1959] 2 All ER 620; *Re Harari's Settlement Trusts* [1949]
    1 All ER 430; *Re McEachern's Settlement Trusts* [1939] Ch 858; *Re Peczenik's Settlement*
    Trusts [1964] 2 All ER 339.
2   *Khoo Tek Keong v Ch'ng Joo Tuan Neoh* [1934] AC 529, PC. If a secured loan is an
    investment it is difficult to see why an unsecured loan is not also an investment that could
    form part of a well-balanced portfolio if balanced by little or no risk investments;
    especially where the loan was an urgent one made in the subsequently unfulfilled
    expectation that security would be provided.
3   *Bartlett v Barclays Bank Trust Co Ltd* [1980] Ch 515 at 536.

53.52 If, to avoid doubt, express power to lend money at interest is to be conferred on trustees its terms should make clear whether a bond or promissory note from the borrower will suffice or whether the loan should only be made on the security of real or personal property[1]. Where there is an express power to lend, with or without security for such loan, the trustee must not make it merely to accommodate the borrower but must consider whether such loan is in the best financial interests of the beneficiaries as a whole, especially if the borrower is a beneficiary[2]. If the loan can only be made to a specified partnership then upon a change in the membership of the partnership the loan becomes unauthorised unless the terminology of the power can be construed as permitting the loan to be made to the firm known as 'X and partners' irrespective of who are the partners from time to time[3].

1   *Re Laing's Settlement* [1899] 1 Ch 593.
2   *Re Laing's Settlement* [1899] 1 Ch 593. Joint trustees cannot lend to one of themselves in
    breach of their undivided duty of loyalty unless authorised by the trust deed.
3   *Re Tucker* [1894] 1 Ch 724; affd [1874] 3 Ch 429; *Smith v Patrick* [1901] AC 282, HL.

53.53 For over forty years it has been common to use very wide express investment powers and such continue to be used due to the limits of the statutory default powers in the Trustee Act 2000. Thus, to avoid uncertainties in construing the 2000 Act and to extend the powers upon trustees for the next eighty or more years and relying on the safeguards provided by the trustees' equitable and statutory duties[1], many trust instruments contain a broad power along the following lines: 'In performing their managerial or administrative functions the Trustees may apply or invest the Trust Fund as if they were the absolute beneficial owners thereof in the purchase or acquisition or protection of assets or investments of whatsoever nature and wherever situated, and whether or not yielding income, [or of a speculative or hazardous nature] [and including the acquisition of derivatives but only for the purpose of limiting risks and not for the purpose of speculation]'.

1   Many of these duties, however, may be expressly ousted: see para 52.56 ff.

53.54 Without the optional clauses in brackets such express power solves any problems caused by the repeal of s 10(3) of the Trustee Act 1925 and the ambit of the restrictions concerning acquisition of interests in land in s 8 of the Trustee Act 2000, and should extend to permitting unsecured loans and to mortgaging some of the trust property in order to acquire money to enable further trust property to be purchased. However, many draftspersons play safe by expressly including specific powers for the avoidance of any doubt.

Paragraph 8

Trustees not necessarily protected by investing in authorised securities

53.55 A trustee is not necessarily safeguarded merely because the investments he makes are authorised by the settlement or by statute. To invest in any other way would, of itself, be a breach of trust leading to a strict falsification of the trust accounts. However, a breach of trust will arise if he fails to obtain and consider proper advice, having regard to the standard investment criteria, or fails from time to time to review the investments with a view to vary them[1] or fails to exercise the duties of care[2] and fairness[3] when exercising his powers of investment or carrying out his duties to obtain and consider proper advice and to review the trust investments from time to time. If, but for such a breach, no loss would have resulted, then the trusteeship accounts will be surcharged with the amount of the loss[4].

1   TA 2000, ss 4 and 5.
2   TA 2000, ss 1, 2, Sch 1, paras 1 and 2.
3   *Nestle v National Westminster Bank* [1994] 1 All ER 118, CA.
4   Loss can cover loss of profit if proved: *Nestle v National Westminster Bank* [1994] 1 All ER 118, CA, applied in *Re Mulligan* [1998] 1 NZLR 481.

53.56 Where, however, the trustees are required by the settlement to comply with the directions as to investment of one of the beneficiaries, then if this power of direction be a personal power as opposed to a fiduciary power[1], and the beneficiary is not acting in wholly unreasonable fashion[2] beyond that contemplated by the settlor, their only responsibility is to see that they are not paying a higher price than is reasonable and proper[3]. Nevertheless, if the trust is a trust of land, then if the trustees believe the direction to be one that no reasonable beneficiary should give or if his consent to their action is requisite and no reasonable beneficiary should withhold his consent, the trustees may apply to the court for such order as the court thinks fit under ss 14 and 15 of the Trusts of Land and Appointment of Trustees Act 1996[4]. If the trustees believe a fiduciary power is being exercised in breach of fiduciary duty and fear liability as accessory to such breach, they can obtain directions from the court[5].

1   Nowadays, it seems clear wording would be needed to justify a power of a beneficiary, or a third party to be merely a personal power when concerned with investment of the trust property at the heart of the trust: *Vestey's Executors v IRC* [1949] 1 All ER 1108 at 1115, HL; *Comr of Stamp Duties v Way* [1942] 1 All ER 198, PC.
2   A fraud on the power. Indeed, *Beauclerk v Ashburnham* (1845) 8 Beav 322 at 328 indicates that the trustees should seek directions from the court if directed to lay out the trust moneys in a low, bad and deteriorating situation, e g purchasing land in Ireland in 1886 as required by the trust instrument but excused by the court in *Re Maberly* (1886) 33 Ch D 455.
3   *Re Hart's Will Trust* [1943] 2 All ER 557.
4   *Re Beale's Settlement Trust* [1932] 2 Ch 15.
5   *Finers v Miro* [1991] 1 All ER 182; *Re Arnott* [1899] 1 IR 201; the complaining power exerciser can also issue a claim seeking directions: *Re Sutherland's Settlement Trust* [1953] Ch 792.

Trustees' duties and standard of care

53.57 In *Cowan v Scargill*[1], where trustees had very wide powers of investment, Megarry V-C made the following points.

1   'It is the duty of trustees to exercise their powers in the best interests of
       the present and future beneficiaries of the trust, holding the scales
       impartially between the different classes of beneficiaries ... When the
       purpose of the trust is to provide financial benefits for the beneficiaries,
       as is usually the case, the best interests of the beneficiaries are normally
       their best financial interests. The power must be exercised so as to yield
       the best return for the beneficiaries, judged in relation to the risks of the
       investments in question; and the prospects for the yield of income and
       capital appreciation both have to be considered in judging the return
       from the investment'[2]. Only if investments are of equal financial merits
       can moral considerations influence the choice of investment. Otherwise,
       trustees must put on one side their own social or political views. Where
       trusts are set up to provide financial benefits then financial considera-
       tions are paramount except for the very rare case eg where all the
       beneficiaries are adult, teetotal, non-smoking, peace campaigners with
       the same moral attitude to investment in alcohol, tobacco or arma-
       ments.

2   The trustees must 'take such care as an ordinary prudent man would
       take if he were minded to make an investment for the benefit of other
       people for whom he felt morally bound to provide. This duty includes
       the duty to seek advice on matters which the trustee does not under-
       stand, such as the making of investments, and, on receiving that advice,
       to act with the same degree of prudence. Although a trustee who takes
       advice on investments is not bound to accept and act on that advice, he
       is not entitled to reject it merely because he sincerely disagrees with it,
       unless in addition he is acting as an ordinary prudent man would act'[3].

3   The trustees must consider the need for diversification of investments
       and the suitability of the investments proposed as laid down by s 6 of
       the Trustee Investments Act 1961, now s 4 of the Trustee Act 2000.

4   If trustees are deadlocked on investment policy because five favour one
       policy and five another and no casting vote is available, then the court
       has jurisdiction to intervene and determine which policy is appropriate.

[1]   [1985] Ch 270, [1984] 2 All ER 750. This has been applied in *Martin v City of Edinburgh
       District Council* 1988 SLT 329, (1989) 1 Pensions LR 9; *Harries v Church Comrs* [1992]
       1 WLR 1241 (though accepting that in charitable trusts there is more scope for taking
       account of ethical considerations) and *Jones v AMP Perpetual Trust to NZ Ltd* [1994] 1
       NZLR 690.
[2]   [1985] Ch 270 at 286–287. In selling land where no written contract yet subsists trustees
       must negotiate with a serious bidder making a higher offer, even as honourable men they
       would prefer to stick with their original bargain: *Buttle v Saunders* [1950] 2 All ER 193.
[3]   [1985] Ch 270 at 289, also saying 'Honesty and sincerity are not the same as prudence and
       reasonableness'.

53.58 On the facts Megarry V-C held the five defendant trustees to be in
breach of their fiduciary duties in their attempt to restrict the investment
policy of the trustees of the mineworkers' pension fund in such fashion as to
ensure the general prosperity of the coal industry eg prohibiting investment in
competing industries and reducing overseas investment. If such restrictions are
desired then they should be inserted in the original trust deed.

53.59 It is considered that the Trustee Act 2000 has not changed the position
as set forth by Megarry V-C. It leaves unaffected the duty to maximise

financial returns holding the scales fairly[1] or impartially between different classes of beneficiaries. It spells out[2] the duty[3] from time to time to review the investment portfolio with a view to varying it and the duty to obtain and consider proper advice[4] having regard to the standard investment criteria[5] (diversification of investments and suitability to the trust of proposed investments).

[1] As emphasised by the Court of Appeal in *Nestle v National Westminster Bank* [1994] 1 All ER 118 and *Edge v Pensions Ombudsman* [2000] Ch 602.
[2] TA 2000, s 4(2).
[3] *Nestle v National Westminster Bank* [1994] 1 All ER 118, CA, where there was a blatant breach of this duty.
[4] TA 2000, s 5.
[5] TA 2000, s 4(3).

53.60 The Trustee Act 2000[1] does lay down the duty of care of trustees, so far as not excluded by the trust instrument, so that a trustee 'must exercise such care and skill as is reasonable in the circumstances, having regard in particular (a) to any special knowledge or experience that he has or holds himself out as having, and (b) if he acts as trustee in the course of a business or profession, to any special knowledge or experience that it is reasonable to expect of a person acting in the course of that kind of business or profession'.

[1] TA 2000, s 1 and Sch 1.

53.61 Because this statutory duty of care is deliberately worded flexibly in imposing a duty to 'exercise such care and skill as is reasonable in all the circumstances' it permits taking account of whether or not the trustee is a paid professional, whether or not he has held himself out as having higher abilities than other trustees, and the circumstance that he is selecting investments for sale or purchase not for himself but for other persons, who may be much worse off than himself and very dependent on the trust for their support. Thus, it is not considered that a trustee's duty of care in selecting appropriate investments has been reduced by the Trustee Act 2000 to a duty only to take as much care as if he were investing on his own behalf. It remains at the level indicated by Megarry V-C[1].

[1] *Cowan v Scargill* [1985] Ch 270 at 289, endorsed by Lord Nicholls in 'Trustees and their Broader Community', (1995) 9 Trust LI 71 at 73.

53.62 Exercising such care and skill as is reasonable in all the circumstances should involve the trustees taking account of considerations like the following spelled out in the American Uniform Prudent Investor Act:

(1) general economic conditions;
(2) the possible impact of inflation or deflation;
(3) the expected tax consequences of investment decisions or strategies;
(4) the role that each investment or course of action plays within the overall portfolio;
(5) the expected total return from income and the appreciation of capital;
(6) other resources of the beneficiaries;
(7) needs for liquidity, regularity of income, and preservation or appreciation of capital; and

(8)   an asset's special relationship or special value, if any, to the purposes of the trust or to one or more of the beneficiaries.

53.63 Of course, the trustees should make reasonable efforts to verify facts relevant to the investment and management of the trust assets[1] eg wealth of beneficiaries, domicile if relevant to tax treatment of assets on beneficiary's death, residence if cared for in residential accommodation (especially if the trust income would all be used to defray expenses under the National Assistance (Assessment of Resources) Regulations, so it would be better to invest only for capital appreciation).

[1]   *Nestle v National Westminster Bank* [1994] 1 All ER 118, CA.

53.64 Where confrontation is not sought between the trustees and the beneficiaries (unlike the *Cowan v Scargill* situation) there is still much scope for trustees quietly to take into account the moral, social and political views of beneficiaries and of themselves[1], since it will in practice be difficult to prove that at the time a particular investment was made it was not as equally financially meritorious as certain other possible investments. The inevitable uncertainty in the stock market makes it difficult to assess which particular investment or type of investment would be the best in terms of capital growth, income and risk: a reasonable amount of leeway must be afforded to trustees.

[1]   Indeed, pension trustees should regard to their beneficiaries on the extent to which they have taken account of ethical and environmental considerations. Charitable trustees should not invest in companies whose products (eg armaments or alcohol) are incompatible with the purposes of the charity (eg Society of Friends, Alcoholics Anonymous) or where shareholdings in particular companies might well hamper a charity's work by making potential recipients of aid unwilling to be helped, or by alienating those who support the charity financially or by voluntary work: *Harries v Church Comrs* [1993] 2 All ER 300.

53.65 Indeed, the difficulty that faces a beneficiary who wishes to complain that the selection of a particular type of investment was, in terms of capital growth, infelicitous was illustrated in *Nestle v National Westminster Bank plc*[1] where the trustee, having wider powers of investment than it had appreciated, failed to seek advice on the true extent of its powers under the trust instrument and accordingly restricted its actual investments to those of a type which, in the event, resulted not merely in a failure to achieve the kind of capital growth that more adventurous investment in equities rather than gilts would have achieved but also a depreciation in real terms of the capital value of the fund. It also failed to conduct regular reviews of the investment portfolio between 1922 and 1959. Whilst finding that the bank had acted in breach of trust the Court of Appeal held that it could not fix the trustee with liability for default. Staughton LJ held that failure to to diversify up to 1960 was not a breach of trust because he could not accept that at that time failure to diversify 'was a course which no prudent trustee would have followed'[2]. Leggatt LJ stated:

> 'The appellant ... had to prove that a prudent trustee, knowing of the scope of the bank's investment powers and conducting regular reviews, would so have invested the trust funds as to make it worth more than it was worth when the plaintiff inherited it'[3].

1   [1994] 1 All ER 118, CA.
2   [1994] 1 All ER 118 at 138. Nowadays, it would appear to be reckless if a trustee failed to consider diversification for a decade and it ought to be the case that such recklessness, a type of dishonesty (according to *Armitage v Nurse* [1998] Ch 241, CA) should lead to a presumption that loss flowed from such recklessness unless disproved by the trustee, everything being presumed against a dishonest trustee (see para 92.23 below).
3   [1994] 1 All ER 118 at 141.

53.66 She failed to produce enough evidence to prove any 'loss' incurred by making a gain less than would have been made by trustees acting as prudent businessmen investing for persons for whom they felt morally obliged to provide. Because there was no loss there was no cause of action.

53.67 At first instance, Hoffmann J had taken the opportunity to restate what he took to be the duty of a trustee in balancing the interests of life tenant and remainderman as regards selection of the type of investment. He had said:

> 'Modern trustees acting within their investment powers are entitled to be judged by the standards of current portfolio theory, which emphasises the risk level of the entire portfolio rather than the risk attaching to each investment taken in isolation ... A trustee must act fairly in making investment decisions which may have different consequences for differing classes of beneficiaries ... The trustees have a wide discretion. They are, for example, entitled to take into account the income needs of the tenant for life or the fact that the tenant for life was a person known to the settlor and a primary object of the trust whereas the remainderman is a remoter relative or a stranger. Of course, these cannot be allowed to become the overriding considerations but the concept of fairness between classes of beneficiaries does not require them to be excluded. It would be an inhuman rule which required trustees to adhere to some mechanical rule for preserving the real value of capital when the tenant for life was the testator's widow who had fallen upon hard times and the remainderman was young and well off'[1].

1   [2000] WTLR 795 at 802–803.

53.68 The Court of Appeal, not finding it necessary to comment on his reformulation of the test laid down by Megarry V-C (in terms of 'holding the scales impartially')[1] to permit the trustee to aim at 'fairness' between the classes of beneficiaries, none the less agreed in substance that the personal circumstances of the life tenant might be taken into account in, for example, deciding to choose a high-income yield investment, inevitably at the expense of the remainderman to the extent that a high growth investment might, instead, have been chosen[2].

1   *Cowan v Scargill* [1985] Ch 270 at 286.
2   *Nestle v National Westminster Bank plc* [1993] 1 WLR 1260 at 1270–1272, 1279. See also *Karger v Paul* [1984] VR 161 and *Re Saunders and Halom* (1986) 32 DLR (4th) 503.

53.69 In dealing with the investment of proceeds of sale of the family home the Court of Appeal rejected the appellant's prima facie strong claim by applying the view of Megarry V-C[1]:

> 'If trustees make a decision on wholly wrong grounds, and yet it subsequently appears, from matters which they did not express or refer to, that there are in

fact good and sufficient reasons for supporting their decisions, then I do not think that they would incur any liability for having decided the matter on erroneous grounds, for the decision itself was right.'

¹ [1985] Ch 270 at 294.

53.70 The appellant, having a difficult and costly onus of proof to discharge in *Nestle v National Westminster Bank* despite having the advantage of deficient behaviour by the trustee, may have been entitled to feel aggrieved, but not the claimants in *Galmerrow Securities Ltd v National Westminster Bank¹* where in the context of a clause absolving the trustee of a unit trust for liability for loss that might arise from 'the exercise or non-exercise' of its powers, except in the cases of fraud or negligence, the question arose whether it was negligent not to have removed the property fund manager, whose investment strategy had, because of the London property market crash of 1974, been unsuccessful. As, on the facts, the unit holders needed to vary the trust deed to provide better remuneration terms, the trustee would have been unable to replace the manager sufficiently quickly, so it had not been negligent:

'The venture was a speculation and like all speculations carried with it the risk of failure. It would not be right to visit the consequences of that misjudgment of the market upon NatWest which is not shown to have had any power open to it which would remedy or mitigate the consequence ... it is not negligent to fail to act where no alternative course of conduct to the continuance of the present arrangement is proved to have been available to the person who has a power to act'².

¹ [2002] WTLR 125.
² [2002] WTLR 125 at 155.

53.71 Essentially¹, to succeed in a claim that negligent or unfair investment of the trustees caused loss, a claimant beneficiary has to prove that no trustee, acting with the requisite minimum care and skill and suffering from the bad luck² that can affect investors, could possibly have ended up with a trust fund of the complained-of value. Thus in *Re Mulligan³*, to favour the life tenant-widow of the testator-settlor, the trustees did not diversify at all by investing in equities, but invested the proceeds of the testator's farm in high-yielding investments allowing depreciation of the value of capital. The New Zealand High Court held that the trustees should in 1972 have diversified to the extent of investing 40% of the capital in equities which would have appreciated not at 100% of an appropriate index of equities but only at 75% thereof, taking account of dealing costs and the fact that the fund was not large enough for the trustees to be able to rival the index.

¹ *Wight v Olswang* [2001] WTLR 291, CA, following the lead in the court below [2000] WTLR 783, taking account of *Bristol and West Building Society v Mothew* [1998] Ch 1.
² See Staughton LJ in *Nestle v National Westminster Bank* [1994] 1 All ER 118 at 133.
³ [1998] 1 NZLR 481.

53.72 In *Re Smith¹* only Imperial Oil Company Stock was held on trust for S's mother for life, remainder to S. From the outset there was only an average dividend of two and a half per cent for the mother, when returns of up to 8 to

10 per cent were available in respect of good quality bonds and mortgages. The trustee ignored the mother's requests for diversification and a better income when S preferred retention of the stock. The Ontario Court of Appeal held there had been a breach of trust and replaced the trustee.

1   (1971) 16 DLR (3d) 130; on appeal (1971) 18 DLR (3d) 405.

53.73 In *Bartlett v Barclays Bank Trust Co Ltd*[1] trustees with power to invest in investments that an absolute beneficial owner might invest in were held liable for hazarding money in a development project concerning a site near the Old Bailey. This project 'was a gamble because it involved buying into the site at prices in excess of the investment values of the properties, with no certainty or probability, with no more than a chance, that planning permission might be obtained for a financially viable redevelopment, that the numerous proprietors would agree to sell out or join in the scheme, that finance would be available on acceptable terms, and that the development would be completed, or at least become a marketable asset, before the time came to start winding up the trust'. In fact it was a company which was controlled by the trustees with a 99.8% shareholding that actually carried out the hazardous speculation leading the company to lose over half a million pounds but this did not alter the liability of the trustees. The trustee had failed to use their controlling shareholding to ensure that they received an adequate flow of information concerning the intentions and activities of the company, and, if they had received such information, they would have been under a duty to use their controlling shareholding to stop the speculative project. No prudent business-man, mindful he was trustee for the benefit of others, would have failed to stop the speculative project[2].

1   [1980] Ch 515, [1980] 1 All ER 139. For a further case of hazardous investment via a controlled company so as to cause loss to the beneficiaries under the trust, see *Walker v Stones* [2001] QB 902, CA.
2   For clauses to protect trustees in such a situation see para 52.56 ff.

Paragraph 9

Holding investments in name of nominee or custodian

53.74 Originally, when investment was relatively simple and leisurely, all investments had to be held in the names of all the trustees[1], unless otherwise expressly authorised in the trust instrument. However, changes in trust law had to follow upon changing investment practices. Speed in making and acting upon investment decisions became crucial, while the time for settlement of transactions on the London Stock Exchange has gradually been reduced to three working days. Indeed, to cut costs and speed up transactions, the holding of many securities has been dematerialised via an electronic database, so that securities are held in certificated form and settlement of dealings takes place electronically[2]. This is a system called CREST governing dealings in most public companies' shares.

1   *Lewis v Nobbs* (1878) 8 Ch D 591; *Re Flower and Metropolitan Board of Works* (1884) 27 Ch D 592.

2   Companies Act 1989, s 207; Uncertificated Securities Regulations 1995, SI 1995/3272.
     Dispositions of equitable interests in such securities are exempted by reg 32(5) thereof from
     the need for signed writing within LPA 1925, s 53(1)(c) but overreaching authorised sales
     or gifts by trustees take effect without such need, anyhow: RC Nolan [2002] Camb LJ 169.

53.75 Trustees may become system-members of CREST having direct access
to the system or sponsored members, who act by instructing system-members
to act as their agent in implementing their instructions and debiting their bank
account. The dematerialised securities will be held in the name of the trustees[1].
However, if the trustees act via a sponsored member they may require their
shares to be certificated[2], although extra cost and time will be taken up for
subsequent sales of the shares needing to be in dematerialised form.

1   Authorised directly and indirectly by reg 33(1)(c).
2   Uncertificated Securities Regulations 1995, Sch 1, para 13.

53.76 Often it is easier for trustees to hold interests in securities via a
nominee or custodian which is a member of CREST or to hire a discretionary
portfolio manager[1] which holds all its interests in securities via such a
nominee or custodian. It would appear that authorisation of the trustees to
invest in foreign securities will necessarily authorise the acquisition of dematerialised securities in the names of the trustees where a dematerialised system
is in operation or in the name of a nominee if so required by the foreign
system. However, use of a nominee or custodian under ss 16 to 20 of the
Trustee Act 2000 will normally be desirable in any event.

1   See para 53.87 below.

Statutory powers to appoint nominees and custodians

53.77 By s 16 trustees (other than of pension schemes, authorised unit trusts
or charitable common investment schemes[1]) may appoint a person to act as
their nominee in relation to such of the trust assets as they determine (other
than settled land within the Settled Land Act 1925) and then take such steps
as are necessary to secure that those assets are vested in the nominee. The
appointment must be in or evidenced in writing but cannot be made if the
trust has a custodian *trustee*[2] or the assets are vested in the official custodian
for charities.

1   See TA 2000, ss 36, 37, 38.
2   See Article 79.

53.78 Custodians undertake the safe custody of assets or of any documents
or records concerning the assets and normally fulfil many administrative tasks
e.g. keeping track of dividend payments, bonus issues, and of any tax
repayment claims. Trustees[1] (other than of pension schemes, authorised unit
trusts or charitable common investment schemes) may appoint a person to act
as custodian in relation to such of the trust assets as they determine[2] and,
unless otherwise authorised, must appoint a custodian of any bearer securities

of the trust[3]. The appointment must be in or evidenced in writing but cannot be made if the trust has a custodian trustee or the assets are vested in the official custodian for charities.

[1] TA 2000, s 17. The powers in ss 16 and 17 are additional to any express powers: s 26(a).
[2] Settled Land Act trustees' investments (other than land vested in the tenant for life) can thus be vested in a custodian.
[3] TA 2000, s 18. Under s 25 (2) there is no such duty on a sole trustee if it be a trust corporation. Where there are two trustees, one of which is a trust corporation, they can appoint the trust corporation to be custodian of bearer securities: s 19(5).

53.79 To be eligible for appointment as a nominee or custodian[1] or as nominee and custodian and agent[2] if so desired, a person must either (a) carry on a business which consists of or includes acting as a nominee or custodian or (b) be a body corporate controlled by the trustees or (c) a body corporate recognised under s 9 of the Adminstration of Justice Act 1985 (by the Council of the Law Society for the provision of such professional services), although trustees of a charity (other than an exempt charity) must act in accordance with any guidance given by the Charity Commissioners[3]. Trustees may appoint one of themselves if a trust corporation, or two or more of themselves acting jointly[4].

[1] TA 2000, s 19(1) and (2).
[2] TA 2000, s 19(6) and (7).
[3] TA 2000, s 19(4).
[4] TA 2000, s 19(5).

53.80 The terms of appointment are such terms as to remuneration and other matters as the trustees may determine[1]. However, unless it is objectively reasonably necessary for them to do so, they must not include terms permitting the nominee or custodian to appoint a substitute, or restricting the liability of the nominee or custodian or his substitute to the trustees or to any beneficiary, or permitting the nominee or custodian to act in circumstances capable of giving rise to a conflict of interest[2].

[1] TA 2000, s 20(1).
[2] TA 2000, s 20(2).

53.81 It will be wise to have written evidence recording why the trustees considered it reasonably necessary to include any of the proscribed terms in case there arises the question of fact as to whether or not such terms were at that time reasonably necessary. The trustees are only allowed to remunerate the nominee or custodian out of trust funds if there is a term for payment of remuneration and the amount does not exceed such remuneration as is objectively reasonable in the circumstances for the provision of the relevant services[1]. The trustees may reimburse the nominee or custodian out of trust funds for any expenses properly incurred by him acting as such[2].

[1] TA 2000, s 32(2). The excess amount will have to be paid by the trustees out of their own pockets.
[2] TA 2000, s 32(3).

53.82 If the trustees fail to act within the limits of the above statutory powers in appointing a nominee or custodian this does not invalidate the appointment[1], so protecting persons dealing with the appointee, but the trustees remain liable to the beneficiaries for acting beyond their powers.

[1]   TA 2000, s 24.

Duty of care

53.83 The statutory duty of care applies[1] (subject to contrary intention in the trust instrument[2]) to a trustee when 'entering into arrangements' under which a person is appointed as agent, nominee or custodian under the Trustee Act 2000 powers or any other powers (eg in the trust instrument) and when carrying out the duty to review the arrangements and how they are being put into effect. 'Entering into arrangements' includes selecting the person who is to act and determining the terms on which he is to act[3].

[1]   TA 2000, Sch 1, para 3(1).
[2]   TA 2000, Sch 1, para 7.
[3]   TA 2000, Sch 1, para 3(2).

53.84 In reviewing matters, if circumstances make it appropriate to do so, the trustees must consider whether there is a need to intervene by giving directions or even by revoking the arrangements and if there is such a need, they must so intervene[1].

[1]   TA 2000, s 22(1), (4), unless ousted by inconsistent terms in the trust instrument: s 21(3).

53.85 A trustee is not liable for any act or default of the agent nominee or custodian unless he personally failed to comply with the above duty of care[1].

[1]   TA 2000, s 23, unless ousted as above.

Restriction or exclusion of statutory provisions

53.86 Not only the statutory duty of care can be ousted[1] (up to the point of excluding liability for all breaches of trust except dishonest or reckless breaches[2]) but the power-conferring provisions concerning nominees, custodians and agents are subject to any restriction or exclusion imposed by the trust instrument[3], while the reviewing duties and liabilities in ss 22 and 23 are capable of being ousted by inconsistent terms in the trust instrument or subordinate legislation[4].

[1]   TA 2000, Sch 1, para 7.
[2]   *Armitage v Nurse* [1998] Ch 241.
[3]   TA 2000, s 26(b). Also by s 26(a) the statutory powers only need to relied upon if no express power is available eg to employ nominees, custodians and agents on whatever terms the trustees honestly believe to be appropriate to help them fulfil their investment functions.
[4]   TA 2000, s 21(3).

Paragraph 10

Delegation of asset management functions

53.87 Where trustees are not themselves skilled portfolio managers they may very well prefer to delegate discretionary portfolio management, rather than making their own discretionary decisions after having obtained and considered proper advice[1], leaving them leeway necessitating the exercise of some discretion[2]. A discretionary portfolio manager can then make and implement decisions instantaneously at a particular market price, without needing to consult the trustees, by which time the market could well have moved against them.

[1]   TA 2000, s 5.
[2]   If the adviser came up with 'take it or leave it' advice which the trustees always took, they would be very vulnerable to the allegation that they had wrongfully delegated investment management to the adviser and had not consciously exercised their own discretion.

53.88 Before the Trustee Act 2000 came into force on 1 February 2001 there was no power to employ a discretionary portfolio manager unless there was an express power in the trust instrument[1] or unless s 25 of the Trustee Act 1925[2] was exploited to permit delegation of discretions by power of attorney for up to twelve months at a time (though there was then automatic liability for the acts or defaults of the delegate)[3].

[1]   Hence the need for applications to the court under TA 1925, s 57 to obtain the requisite powers e g *Anker-Petersen v Anker-Petersen* [2000] WTLR 581.
[2]   As substituted by Powers of Attorney Act 1971, s 9(2).
[3]   TA 2000, s 25(5).

53.89 The Trustee Act 2000, taking inspiration from the Pensions Act 1995[1], now authorises delegation of the 'asset management functions' of trustees[2] consisting of 'the investment of assets subject to the trust, the acquisition of property which is to be subject to the trust, and managing property which is subject to the trust and disposing of, or creating or disposing of an interest in, such property'. However, before authorising a delegate to exercise any such functions, they must have prepared a 'policy statement' and the agreement in, or evidenced in, writing must include a term requiring compliance with such statement or any revised statement after a regular review.

[1]   Pensions Act 1995, ss 34–36.
[2]   TA 2000, ss 11 and 15.

53.90 This power, therefore, does not arise unless and until the policy statement has been prepared and there is some writing containing a term for securing compliance with such statement. However, a failure by the trustees to act within the limits of the powers capable of being conferred[1] by the Trustee Act 2000 in authorising a person to exercise any function of theirs as an agent does not invalidate the authorisation[2].

[1]   If they were actually conferred there would be no ultra vires problem.

2   TA 2000, s 24. The delegate may however be liable for dishonestly assisting in a breach of trust if having actual, Nelsonian or naughty knowledge (see paras 100.72–100.74 below) of failure to comply with the statutory requirements.

53.91 An express power to delegate asset management functions that is broader than the statutory power, not containing the restrictions attached to the statutory power, may be relied upon by the trustees, the statutory power being in addition to express powers[1]. Alternatively, it seems that the trust instrument may impose a restriction or exclusion on the statutory power to delegate[2].

1   TA 2000, s 26(a).
2   TA 2000, s 26(b).

53.92 In deciding whether or not to exercise their powers of delegation the trustees can suit themselves and do not need to prove it was reasonably necessary or in the best interests of the beneficiaries. However, once they have decided to delegate they come under extensive duties of care in selecting and supervising such delegates as dealt with below in Article 55.

ARTICLE 54
DUTY OF TRUSTEE TO SEE THAT HE TRANSFERS TRUST PROPERTY ONLY TO BENEFICIARIES OR OBJECTS OF A POWER OF APPOINTMENT OR ONLY TO PERSONS AUTHORISED UNDER THE TRUST INSTRUMENT OR THE GENERAL LAW TO RECEIVE SUCH PROPERTY (EG AS CUSTODIAN OR PORTFOLIO MANAGER)

54.1

(1)   The responsibility of handing the trust property to the persons entitled lies upon the trustee, so that if he acts beyond his powers his accounts are falsified and he is strictly liable for a substitutive performance of his obligations. However, if he acts within his powers (eg in transferring trust property to a nominee, custodian or discretionary portfolio manager) his accounts can only be surcharged to the extent that but for his failure to observe some equitable or statutory duty caused the trust fund to have suffered the particular loss in question. Formerly neither mistake[1] nor fraud[2] afforded any excuse against the strict liability arising upon falsification of conduct that was beyond the trustee's powers, but now the court has power to excuse such a mistake made honestly and reasonably[3], and by section 27 of the Trustee Act 1925 a trustee is granted further protection by giving notice by advertisement. Nevertheless, in cases of doubt the trustee should apply to the court for its direction[4]. To deal with problems otherwise arising in the case of legitimated or adopted persons some statutory protection is granted to trustees and personal representatives[5];

(2) if, however, the person who is really entitled to trust property is not the beneficiary who appears on the face of the settlement (but someone who claims through him), and the trustees have neither express nor constructive notice of such derivative title, they cannot be made to pay over again[6];

(3) on the other hand, if they have notice of the derivative title, they cannot refuse to pay to the person entitled under it on the ground that such title has been improperly obtained and is liable to be set aside[7], unless it is on the face of it prima facie voidable, or is an appointment under a power in the trust instrument which they suspect is a fraud on the power.

[1] *Re Hulkes* (1886) 33 Ch D 552. As to fraud, see *Re Bennison* (1889) 60 LT 859. See comments, para 52.36 above.

[2] *Eaves v Hickson* (1861) 30 Beav 136.

[3] If the court also feels he ought fairly to be excused for omitting to obtain the directions of the court. TA 1925, s 61; as to which see Article 98, below.

[4] *Talbot v Earl of Radnor* (1834) 3 My & K 252; *Merlin v Blagrave* (1858) 25 Beav 125; *Ashby v Blackwell* (1765) 2 Eden 299; *Eaves v Hickson* (1861) 30 Beav 136; *Sporle v Barnaby* (1864) 10 Jur NS 1142.

[5] Adoption Act 1976, s 45; Legitimacy Act 1976, s 7.

[6] *Cothay v Sydenham* (1788) 2 Bro CC 391; *Leslie v Baillie* (1843) 2 Y & C Ch Cas 91; *Re Lord Southampton's Estate* (1880) 16 Ch D 178.

[7] *Devey v Thornton* (1851) 9 Hare 222 at 231.

Paragraph 1

Duty to inform beneficiaries of their interests

54.2 Trustees are under a fundamental primary duty to distribute the trust property only to a beneficiary or object of a power of appointment, and to the right beneficiary or object and only to transfer trust property to another person if they have power under the trust instrument or the general law to do so (eg so as to avail themselves of the services of a discretionary portfolio manager or a custodian). For such duty to be an enforceable meaningful obligation[1], a beneficiary of full age and capacity has a right to be told by the trustees that he is a beneficiary[2] and, indeed, a right to be told by the settlor the name and address of the trustees to whom demands for accounts and requests for discretionary distributions can be sent[3]. Every beneficiary is entitled to see the trust accounts, with a view to falsification of such accounts if trust property has been transferred to a person who is not a beneficiary or an object of a power of appointment or who is not an authorised managerial or administrative recipient, such as a portfolio manager or a custodian. It matters not that the beneficiary's interest is vested or contingent, or in possession or not, or that of a beneficiary under a discretionary trust[4].

[1] Cf *Scally v Southern Health and Social Services Board* [1992] 1 AC 294, 304–306.

[2] *Hawkesley v May* [1956] 1 QB 304, 332. Further see Article 60, below.

[3] *Re Murphy's Settlement* [1998] 3 All ER 1.

[4] *Armitage v Nurse* [1998] Ch 241 at 253 and 261; *Re Tillott* [1892] 1 Ch 86; *A-G of Ontario v Stavro* (1995) 119 DLR (4th) 750; *Re Murphy's Settlement* [1998] 3 All ER 1.

54.3 However, the Privy Council has recently made it clear that the court has an inherent jurisdiction to supervise and, if need be, intervene in the affairs of a trust, so that any discretionary beneficiary or object of a fiduciary power of appointment can seek to invoke this jurisdiction – though if the applicant has no more than a theoretical possibility of benefiting he will receive no assistance[1].

1   *Schmidt v Rosewood Trust Ltd* 60, below.[2003] UKPC 26, [2003] 2 AC 709, also see *Foreman v Kingstone* [2004] 1 NZLR 841, [2005] WTLR 823.

54.4 Trustees are not, however, required to give the beneficiaries legal advice or to inform them of rights such as a right to sever a joint tenancy[1]. Executors have been held to be under no duty to inform will beneficiaries of their interests since wills are open to public inspection[2] but there is much to be said for the view that once the executors competed their administration so as to become trustees[3], and certainly once they have assented to property vesting in themselves or others as trustees, then the trustees should be in the same position as trustees of inter vivos trusts.

1   *Hawksley v May* [1956] 1 QB 304, [1955] 3 All ER 353 on which see (1970) 34 Conv 29 (A. Samuels).
2   *Re Mackay* [1906] 1 Ch 25.
3   *Re Cockburn* [1957] Ch 438.

Payment under a forged document

54.5 Where a trustee made a payment to one who produced a forged authority from the beneficiary, it was held that the trustee and not the beneficiary had to bear the loss, for, as was said by Lord Northington[1]:

'A trustee, whether he be a private person or a body corporate, must see to the reality of the authority empowering him to dispose of the trust money; for if the transfer is made without the authority of the owner, the act is a nullity.'

1   *Ashby v Blackwell* (1765) 2 Eden 299; but see *Re Smith* (1902) 71 LJ Ch 411.

54.6 So, again, trustees who paid over the trust fund to wrong persons, upon the faith of a forged marriage certificate, were made responsible for so much of the trust fund as could not be recovered from those who had wrongfully received it[1], or from the father responsible for altering the marriage certificate so as to make his children appear to be legitimate and thus be beneficiaries.

1   *Eaves v Hickson* (1861) 30 Beav 136; and see also *Bostock v Floyer* (1865) LR 1 Eq 26; and *Sutton v Wilders* (1871) LR 12 Eq 373.

54.7 The question whether an honest and reasonable mistake as to the nature of a forged document, or as to the construction of an obscure one, would now be excused under s 61 of the Trustee Act 1925, is discussed in Article 96, below.

Non-delegable nature of distributive functions of trustees

54.8 Section 11(2)(a) of the Trustee Act 2000 does not authorise trustees to delegate any functions relating to whether, or in what way, any assets of the trust should be distributed to beneficiaries or to objects of powers of appointment. Thus it is solely the responsibility of the trustees to distribute trust assets correctly subject to any protection from an exemption clause or relief from the court under the Trustee Act 1925, s 61.

Transfer to unauthorised person

54.9 If trustees or executors with no authority to entrust trust funds to the management of a third party do so entrust the funds and a loss is sustained then such trustees or executors 'will be forced to make it good, however unexpected the result, however little likely to arise from the course adopted and however free such conduct may have been from any improper motive'[1]. Mitigation of such strict liability may be possible under s 61 of the Trustee Act 1925 or by a clause in the trust instrument s trustees from liability for negligence if the conduct be negligent rather than reckless or deliberate.

[1]   *Clough v Bond* (1838) 3 My & Cr 490 at 496–497.

Duty to pay at right time on satisfaction of a condition

54.10 Where a solicitor holding a lender's money on trust to pay it over on the completion of a purchase by the borrower and in return for receiving documentary security, deliberately in breach of trust paid the money over to the borrower ten days early, he became strictly liable to replace such money. However, falsification of accounts ceased to be available when three weeks later completion of the purchase took place and the solicitor obtained the required documentary security for the lender and so performed his duty. To surcharge the accounts it was necessary to show that but for the early payment the alleged loss would not have occurred: a trial would be necessary to establish this so the application for summary judgment was rejected by the House of Lords[1].

[1]   *Target Holdings Ltd v Redferns* [1996] AC 421 as explained by Lord Millett in (1998) 114 LQR 214 at 225–227. The plaintiff simply had claimed the £1,500,000 loan less the £500,000 received on selling the property despite it having been fraudulently valued at £2 million. See para 89.18 below.

Statutory protection for illegitimate, legitimated and adopted persons

54.11 Where illegitimate persons or their relatives are entitled to property by reason of ss 14 to 16 of the Family Law Reform Act 1969 protection was afforded under s 17 thereof to trustees and personal representatives who, without notice of a claim, distributed the property without having ascertained that no person was entitled under ss 14 to 16. However, s 17 has been repealed in the belief that protection by advertisement under s 27 of the Trustee Act 1925 should be sufficient[1].

1   Family Law Reform Act 1987, s 20 commented upon by G. Miller [1988] Conv 410 at 417–419.

54.12 However, a trustee or personal representative is not under a duty to inquire before distributing any property whether any adoption had been effected or revoked or whether any person is illegitimate or has been adopted by one of his natural parents or could be legitimated (or, if deceased, treated as legitimated) if that fact could affect entitlement to the property[1]. The fiduciary is not to be liable for any distribution of property made without regard to any such fact if he has not received notice thereof before such distribution[2].

1   Adoption Act 1976, s 45; Legitimacy Act 1976, s 7.
2   Adoption Act 1976, s 45; Legitimacy Act 1976, s 7.

54.13 None of the above statutory protection afforded to trustees and personal representatives is to prejudice the right of any person to follow the property, or any property representing it, into the hands of another person, other than a purchaser, who has received it[1].

1   Adoption Act 1976, s 45(3); Legitimacy Act 1976, s 7(3).

Mistake as to construction of settlement

54.14 A trustee who, by mistake, pays the capital to the tenant for life, instead of investing it and paying him the income only, will in general have to make good the loss to the estate, although he will, as will be seen hereafter, be entitled to be recouped out of the life estate[1]. Similarly, trustees who had distributed a trust fund upon what turned out to be an erroneous, although bona fide, construction of the trust instrument were formerly always held liable to refund the property distributed, together with interest thereon at 4%[2], and this notwithstanding that they have acted under the advice of counsel[3]. But now the court has power[4], which it will exercise in a proper case, of excusing a trustee who has acted on legal advice in such a case[5].

1   *Barratt v Wyatt* (1862) 30 Beav 442; *Davies v Hodgson* (1858) 25 Beav 177; *Griffiths v Porter* (1858) 25 Beav 236.
2   *Hilliard v Fulford* (1876) 4 Ch D 389; and see also *Re Ward* (1878) 47 LJ Ch 781; and *Re Hulkes* (1886) 33 Ch D 552.
3   See *National Trustees Co of Australasia v General Finance Co of Australasia* [1905] AC 373.
4   Under s 61 of the TA 1925. See Article 98, below.
5   *Re Allsop* [1914] 1 Ch 1, CA.

Reliance on counsel's opinion and court authorisation

54.15 Where a question of construction has arisen out of the terms of a will or a trust and an opinion in writing of a barrister of at least ten years' standing has been obtained thereon by the personal representatives or trustees, then such persons can safely proceed to take such steps in reliance on the opinion as the High Court specifies without hearing argument[1]. The High Court will not make an order under this summary procedure if it appears that a dispute exists which would make it inappropriate for the court to make the order without hearing argument[2].

[1] Administration of Justice Act 1985, s 48(1). See Practice Direction – Pt 8, section A, paras A.1(1) and A.2(1) and CDPD 12, section A.
[2] Administration of Justice Act 1985, s 48(2).

Protection by means of advertisements

54.16 Trustees and personal representatives may protect themselves against their strict liability by advertising for 'interested' persons (viz beneficiaries[1] and creditors of the estate) whose claims they are not aware of, although, oddly, the statutory protection does not extend to trusts of property not comprising land[2] and not subject to a trust for sale. By s 27 of the Trustee Act 1925, as amended by the Law of Property (Amendment) Act 1926, s 7 and Schedule and the Trusts of land an Appointment of Trustees Act 1996 Schedule 3 para 3(7), it is enacted as follows:

(1)   With a view to the conveyance to or distribution among the persons entitled to any real or personal property, the trustees of a settlement, trustees of land, trustees for sale of personal property or personal representatives, may give notice by advertisement[3] in the Gazette, and [in a newspaper circulating in the district in which the land is situated], and such other like notices, including notices elsewhere than in England and Wales, as would, in any special case, have been directed by a court of competent jurisdiction in an action for administration, of their intention to make such conveyance or distribution as aforesaid, and requiring any person interested to send to the trustees or personal representatives within the time, not being less than two months, fixed in the notice or, where more than one notice is given, in the last of the notices, particulars of his claim in respect of the property or any part thereof to which the notice relates.

(2)   At the expiration of the time fixed by the notice the trustees or personal representatives may convey or distribute the property or any part thereof to which the notice relates, to or among the persons entitled thereto, having regard only to the claims, whether formal or not, of which the trustees and personal representatives then had notice and shall not, as respects the property so conveyed or distributed, be liable to any person of whose claim the trustees or personal representatives have not had notice at the time of conveyance or distribution; but nothing in this section—

  (a)   prejudices the right of any person to follow the property, or any property representing the same, into the hands of any person, other than a purchaser, who may have received it; or

  (b)   frees the trustees or personal representatives from any obligation to make searches or obtain official certificates of search similar to those which an intending purchaser would be advised to make or obtain.

(3)   This section applies notwithstanding anything to the contrary in the will or other instrument, if any, creating the trust.

[1] *Re Aldhous* [1955] 2 All ER 80, [1955] 1 WLR 459.

² Trustees are 'trustees of land' if any part of the trust property is land: TLATA 1996, s 1(1)(b).

³ The advertisement should follow accurately the wording of the statute and should indicate that it is not only the claims of creditors but also those of beneficiaries which are required to be sent in (*Re Aldhous* [1955] 2 All ER 80, [1955] 1 WLR 459). For a form to use, see *Law Society's Gazette*, for July 1955, p 307; 42 *Encycl Forms & Precedents* (5th edn) Form 537.

54.17 Application may be made to the court in the administration of the estate of a deceased person for an inquiry what notices or advertisements should be issued in a special case¹; a like application may, it is thought, properly be made by trustees seeking to avail themselves of the protection of s 27, above, in a case where the circumstances are special.

¹ *Re Letherbrow* [1935] WN 34; *Re Holden* [1935] WN 52. Where it is impracticable to advertise in a foreign country where the deceased resided the court may authorise distribution without advertisements there: *Re Gess* [1942] Ch 37.

Payment under a power of attorney

54.18 Section 29 of the Trustee Act 1925 used specifically to provide protection for trustees making a distribution to an agent of a beneficiary. Now the section has been repealed and the position is governed generally by s 5 of the Powers of Attorney Act 1971 which is as follows:

5(1) A donee of a power of attorney who acts in pursuance of the power at a time when it has been revoked shall not, by reason of the revocation, incur any liability (either to the donor or to any other person) if at that time he did not know that the power had been revoked.

(2) Where a power of attorney has been revoked and a person [eg a trustee or executor], without knowledge of the revocation, deals with the donee of the power, the transaction between them shall, in favour of that person, be as valid as if the power had then been in existence.

(3) Where the power is expressed in the instrument creating it to be irrevocable and to be given by way of security then, unless the person dealing with the donee knows that it was not in fact given by way of security, he shall be entitled to assume that the power is incapable of revocation except by the donor acting with the consent of the donee and shall accordingly be treated for the purposes of subsection (2) of this section as having knowledge of the recovation only if he knows that it has been revoked in that manner.

(4) Where the interest of a purchaser depends on whether a transaction between the donee of a power of attorney and another person was valid by virtue of subsection (2) of this section, it shall be conclusively presumed in favour of the purchaser that that person did not at the material time know of the revocation of the power if—

(a) the transaction between that person and the donee was completed within twelve months of the date on which the power came into operation; or

(b) that person makes a statutory declaration, before or within three months after the completion of the purchase, that he did not at the material time know of the revocation of the power.

(5) Without prejudice to subsection (3) of this section, for the purposes of this section knowledge of the revocation of a power of attorney includes

knowledge of the occurrence of any event (such as the death of the donor) which has the effect of revoking the power.

Paragraph 2

Trustees not bound to know of derivative title

54.19 In *Leslie v Baillie*[1] a testator who died, and whose will was proved in England, bequeathed a legacy to a married woman whose domicile, as well as that of her husband, was in Scotland. The husband died a few months after the testator. After his decease, the executors of the testator paid the legacy to the widow. It was proved that, according to Scots law, the payment should have been made to the husband's personal representatives. It was, however, held that, in the absence of proof that the executors of the settlor knew the Scots law on the subject, the payment to the widow was a good payment.

1   (1843) 2 Y & C Ch Cas 91; and see also *Re Cull's Trusts* (1875) LR 20 Eq 561.

54.20 Where B is a person entitled in default of an appointment by the life tenant who has died, then the trustees can safely pay the trust fund to B if the life tenant's solicitor swears that to his knowledge no appointment was ever made[1]. If a power of appointment has been exercised, apparently properly, in favour of Y so that the trustees, having made reasonable inquiries, pay the trust funds to Y, then the trustees will not be liable to pay the money again to Z if it turns out there was a prior appointment in Z's favour[2].

1   *Re Cull's Trusts* (1875) LR 20 Eq 561.
2   *Cothay v Sydenham* (1788) 2 Bro CC 391: cf *Re Lord Southampton's Estate* (1880) 16 Ch D 178. It could be submitted that this situation falls within paragraph 1 for it is difficult to distinguish between a payment made on the faith of a void forged marriage certificate and a payment made on the faith of a void appointment in favour of Y. In any event a trustee in such a case should have the protection of TA 1925, s 61 if not protected by an exemption clause.

Disputes between beneficial claimants

54.21 Trustees are not bound to hand over the trust fund to the mortgagee of their beneficiary, where accounts are pending between the mortgagee and mortgagor[1].

1   *Hockey v Western* [1898] 1 Ch 350.

Effect of not searching for notices of incumbrances

54.22 On the other hand, a new trustee is liable to make good moneys paid by him bona fide to a beneficiary, if the papers relating to the trust include a notice of an incumbrance created by that beneficiary depriving him of the right to receive the money[1], and so is a trustee who dispenses with an investigation of the title of an alleged assign whose title is in fact bad[2]. Kekewich J held that this is none the less so if the alleged assign is the trustee's own solicitor[3], on the ground that if the trustee had acquainted himself, as he was bound to do with the trust documents and papers, he would have found what the true state of the case was. But the Court of Appeal has since held[4] that at all events it would be good ground for excusing the trustee from the consequences of such a technical breach under the statutory provisions aforesaid, as to which see Article 96, below. Where no amount of search would have disclosed the notice, the trustee would, of course, not be liable.

1   *Hallows v Lloyd* (1888) 39 Ch D 686. This is so even where the trustees have a discretion to pay the income to or for the benefit of the assignor, 'his wife or children', if they do in fact pay it to the assignor: *Re Neil* (1890) 62 LT 649; *Lord v Bunn* (1843) 2 Y & C Ch Cas 98. See also *Burrowes v Lock* (1805) 10 Ves 470; and *Re Coleman* (1888) 39 Ch D 443.
2   *Davis v Hutchings* [1907] 1 Ch 356.
3   *Davis v Hutchings* [1907] 1 Ch 356.
4   *Re Allsop* [1914] 1 Ch 1.

Trustee not entitled to the deed of assignment

54.23 Where a person claims as the assign of a beneficiary, it might be thought that the trustee would, on payment, be entitled to the custody of the deed of assignment as evidence of authority for paying the assign. But this is not so[1], although it would seem that he is entitled to the statutory acknowledgment for production and undertaking for safe custody, and he would be wise also to take an attested copy. As Swinfen Eady J said in *Re Palmer*[2]:

'Where money is paid by a trustee to a person who receives it under a power of attorney, the trustee cannot claim that the power of attorney should be given up to him. It was said that the trustee would be in a very unfortunate position if an action were brought against him for the fund and he had not the deeds; but it might equally be said that the company [the assigns] would be in a very unfortunate position if they handed over the deeds and the assignor disputed the assignment and brought an action against the company to set it aside.'

1   *Re Palmer* [1907] 1 Ch 486.
2   [1907] 1 Ch 486 at 488.

Paragraph 3

Whether a trustee is to investigate where he merely suspects mala fides by assignee of beneficiary

54.24 The question of how far a trustee can refuse to pay an assign where he suspects unfair dealing, is by no means easy.

54.25 It appears to be well settled, that, where his beneficiary is dead, he cannot refuse to pay his personal representative on the ground that he obtained probate or administration unfairly[1]. It is for other persons interested to take action in such a case, and not the trustee.

1   *Devey v Thornton* (1851) 9 Hare 222 at 226.

54.26 The same principle also seems to apply to an assignment inter vivos. It is not for the trustee to question its validity if the assignor does not do so. If the deed is not a forgery it stands good until it is cancelled by the court, and it cannot be cancelled by the court at the instance of the trustee[1]. This class of cases would, it seems, cover assignments and mortgages by reversioners where the trustees may suspect unfair dealing or oppression.

[1]   *Devey v Thornton* (1851) 9 Hare 222 at 226.

54.27 But the problem becomes much more difficult when we approach transactions which are either:

(1)   prima facie invalid, or
(2)   appointments in the exercise of powers contained in the trust instrument.

54.28 Generally where a reasonable doubt arises as to the claimant's title the prudent course is to apply to the court for directions. If the trustee is forced to defend a claim he could well be at risk of being ordered personally to pay the costs of both sides[1] or of being deprived of a right to reimburse his own costs from the trust fund[2].

[1]   *Re Knox's Trusts* [1895] 2 Ch 483; *Moss v Integro Trust (BVI) Ltd* (1998) 1 OFLR 427.
[2]   *Griffin v Brady* (1869) 39 LJ Ch 136.

Trustee bound to investigate where instrument is prima facie invalid

54.29 (1) With regard to instruments prima facie invalid, one may take, as typical, an assignment, whether voluntary or for value, by a beneficiary to one of the trustees. It is apprehended that in such a case the other trustees would not only be justified, but bound, to refuse payment to their co-trustee without an order of the court; for the facts speak loudly for themselves and the deed, on the face of it, cannot be supported without some outside evidence that the parties were at arms' length, and that no unfair advantage was taken by the assign. Anyhow, it is scarcely open to doubt that, in such a case, the co-trustee would be justified in issuing an originating summons for the direction of the court.

Trustee suspecting a fraud on a power

54.30 (2) Where the trustee has reasonable ground for suspicion that an appointment made by a predecessor or a third party is a fraud on a power[1] in the trust instrument, he certainly ought not to pay without the direction of the court. For, as pointed out by Farwell LJ in *Cloutte v Storey*[2], an appointee can only claim an equitable right if the appointment is valid. If it is not valid it passes nothing, and the property remains the property of the person who takes in default of appointment. It is, therefore, the duty of a trustee to satisfy himself that an alleged appointment is valid before acting on it; and if he has reasonable doubts, he is not only justified in acting but bound to act under the direction of the court[3].

1   See generally para 61.31. Essentially an appointment is a fraud on a power if made for a corrupt or foreign purpose outside the intended scope of the power: further see *Re Crawshay* [1948] Ch 123 at 133 ff, [1948] 1 All ER 107 at 113 ff, CA; *Re Simpson* [1952] Ch 412, [1952] 1 All ER 963; but see *Re Burton's Settlement* [1955] Ch 82, [1954] 3 All ER 193. The doctrine of frauds on powers does not apply to an exercise of a power of revocation contained in a revocable appointment: *Re Greaves' Will Trusts* [1954] Ch 434, [1954] 1 All ER 771. As to frauds on a power in relation to the Variation of Trusts Act 1958, see para 47.81 above.
2   [1911] 1 Ch 18 at 32 and 33; and see *Duke of Portland v Topham* (1864) 11 HL Cas 32; and see order thereon, Seton on Judgments (7th edn) p 1672; and see also *Hopkins v Myall* (1830) 2 Russ & M 86; *Cocker v Quayle* (1830) 1 Russ & M 535; *Reid v Thompson and M'Namara* (1851) 2 I Ch R 26; *Cochrane v Cochrane* [1922] 2 Ch 230.
3   See *Hannah v Hodgson* (1861) 30 Beav 19; *King v King* (1857) 1 De G & J 663.

54.31 One may perhaps ask: if a fraudulent appointment is futile and void ab initio, is not a trustee who acts upon it, although without knowledge of the fraud, paying to the wrong beneficiary, and if so, are his accounts not falsified so that he is strictly liable? It is apprehended that this would be so but for the possibility of relief under s 61 of the Trustee Act 1925, as it is difficult to distinguish between a payment made on the faith of a fraudulent certificate of marriage, and one made on the faith of an appointment which turns out to be fraudulent. There can, however, be no reasonable doubt that under s 61, a trustee who innocently, and reasonably, assumed the bona fides of an appointment would be excused[1] if not already protected by a broad exemption clause.

1   See *Re Smith* (1902) 71 LJ Ch 411; *Re Allsop* [1914] 1 Ch 1; and Article 96, below.

ARTICLE 55
DUTY OF TRUSTEES NOT TO DELEGATE THEIR DUTIES OR
POWERS UNLESS AUTHORISED

55.1

(1)   Trustees must not collectively delegate their duties or powers either to a stranger or to a beneficiary or to a co-trustee[1], unless authorised by the settlement[2], except in the following cases, namely:

(a)   they may engage and pay reasonable remuneration[3] to a person to act as nominee or custodian under sections 16 to 20 of the Trustee Act 2000, as already discussed within Article 53;

(b)   subject to (c), (d) and (e), they may engage and pay reasonable remuneration to any person (including a co-trustee[4] but not a beneficiary[5]) as agent to exercise any or all of their 'delegable functions' which in the case of a trust other than a charitable trust, consist of any function other than[6]

(i)   any functions relating to whether or in what way any assets of the trust should be distributed,

(ii)   any power to decide whether any fees or other payment due to be made out of the trust funds should be made out of income or capital,

(iii) any power to appoint a person to be a trustee of the trust, or

(iv)   any power conferred by any other enactment or the trust instrument which permits the trustee to delegate any of their functions or to appoint a person to act as a nominee or custodian,

but in the case of a charitable trust consist of[7]

(i)   any function consisting of carrying out a decision the trustees have taken,

(ii)   any function relating to the investment of assets subject to the trust,

(iii) any function relating to the raising of funds for the trust otherwise than by means of profits of a trade which is an integral part of carrying out the trusts charitable purposes, and

(iv)   any other function prescribed by an order made by the Secretary of State;

(c)   they may not authorise a person to act as agent on terms permitting the agent to appoint a substitute or to act in circumstances capable of giving rise to a conflict of interest or restricting the liability of the agent or his substitute to the trustees or any beneficiary, unless it is reasonably necessary for them to do so[8];

(d)   in the case of asset management functions, they may not delegate except by an agreement which is in, or evidenced in, writing[9] and unless[10]

(i)   they have prepared a policy statement, in, or evidenced in writing, giving guidance as to how the functions should be exercised, and

(ii)   there is a term in the agreement that the agent will secure compliance with the policy statement and any revised or replacement policy statement;

(e)   in the case of trusts of land, they may, by power of attorney, delegate to any beneficiary or beneficiaries of full age and beneficially entitled to an interest in possession in land subject to the trust, any of their functions as trustees which relate to the land, the beneficiary or beneficiaries then being in the same position as the trustees as to duties and liabilities except for the purpose of any enactment permitting the delegation of functions by trustees or imposing requirements relating to receipts for capital money[11].

2(a)   Except in respect of delegation under (e) above, trustees owe no duty of care in deciding whether or not to exercise their statutory or express powers of delegation, but they do owe a duty of care (unless ousted in the trust instrument[12]) when entering into arrangements[13] for delegating to agents, nominees or custodians under statutory or express powers and when carrying out[14] their duty[15] to review the arrangements under which such delegates act (including the policy statement for asset management) with a view to intervening if need be; they will not be personally liable for any act or default of the agent, nominee or custodian unless they failed to comply with their duty of care[16].

(b)   In respect of trustees of land delegating by power of attorney to currently entitled beneficiaries, the trustees are under a duty of care in deciding whether to delegate any of their functions on particular terms[17] and, if they delegate, they are under a duty to keep the delegation under review[18] with a view to intervening if need be, a duty of care applying[19] to such reviewing duty; they will not be personally liable for any act or default of the beneficiary unless they failed to comply with their duty of care[20].

(3)   Each trustee individually may by power of attorney[21] delegate for a period not exceeding twelve months the execution or exercise of all or any of the trusts, powers and discretions vested in him as trustee[22]: he is, however, liable for the acts or defaults of the donee of the power of attorney as if they were his own acts or defaults[23].

---

1   *Adams v Clifton* (1826) 1 Russ 297; *Chambers v Minchin* (1802) 7 Ves 186; *Wood v Weightman* (1872) LR 13 Eq 434; *Re Bellamy and Metropolitan Board of Works* (1883) 24 Ch D 387; *Langford v Gascoyne* (1805) 11 Ves 333; *Clough v Bond* (1838) 3 My & Cr 490; *Cowell v Gatcombe* (1859) 27 Beav 568; *Eaves v Hickson* (1861) 30 Beav 136; *Re Flower and Metropolitan Board of Works* (1884) 27 Ch D 592.
2   *Kilbee v Sneyd* (1828) 2 Mol 186; *Doyle v Blake* (1804) 2 Sch & Lef 231; *Re Airey* [1897] 1 Ch 164 at 170. For delegation via the exercise of a special power of appointment se Article 83 below.
3   TA 2000, s 32.
4   TA 2000, s 12(1).
5   TA 2000, s 12(3).
6   TA 2000, s 11(2).
7   TA 2000, s 11(3).
8   TA 2000, s 14(2).
9   TA 2000, s 15(1).
10   TA 2000, s 15(2).
11   TLATA 1996, s 9.
12   TA 2000, Sch 1, para 7.
13   TA 2000, Sch 1, para 3(1)(a)–(d).
14   TA 2000, Sch 1, para 3(1)(e).
15   TA 2000, s 22, unless ousted by trust instrument: TA 2000, s 21(3).
16   TA 2000, s 23(1).
17   TA 2000, Sch 2, para 47 inserting s 9A into the TLATA 1996.
18   TLATA 1996, s 9A(3).
19   TLATA 1996, s 9A(5).
20   TLATA 1996, s 9A(6).

21 The Trustee Delegation Act 1999, ss 1, 2 and 3 makes special provision for co-owners of land so that a trustee with a beneficial co-ownership interest in trust land can simply grant an ordinary power of attorney under the Powers of Attorney Act 1971 to his co-owner to enable a valid overreaching sale of the land to be made by such co-owner on his own.
22 TA 1925, s 25 as substituted by the Trustee Delegation Act 1999, s 5.
23 TA 1925, s 25(7).

The original position

55.2 Originally the rule was strictly observed that an agent could only be properly employed where such employment was expressly authorised by the settlement, or where out of necessity in the particular transaction it was impossible for the trustee satisfactorily to do the act himself[1], or where the act was merely ministerial and employment of an agent was not the delegation of a function but the performance of a function though an agent, normally necessary or in the ordinary course of affairs from the point of view of a prudent man of business[2]. The care of a prudent businessman had to be exercised in the choice of agent (who had to be employed within the scope of his expertise[3]) and in the supervision of the agent[4]. An express or statutory provision authorising wider use of agents and exempting a trustee from liability for loss caused by the acts or defaults of an agent unless the loss occurred by reason of the trustee's 'wilful default' did not relieve the trustee of his duty to exercise the care of the prudent man of business in the appointment and in the supervision of agents: a beneficiary's action would still succeed if he could prove 'wilful default which includes want of ordinary prudence on the part of the trustees' as where trustees negligently appointed an unsuitable agent or negligently supervised an agent[5].

1 For example, trusts of property in the far-flung British Empire where a local manager could run huge plantations and make maintenance payments for beneficiaries out there who were children: recognised in TA 1925, s 23(2).
2 *Speight v Gaunt* (1883) 9 App Cas 1; *Re Parsons, ex p Belchier* (1754) Amb 218.
3 *Fry v Tapson* (1884) 28 Ch D 268.
4 *Re Weall* (1889) 42 Ch D 674; *Mathew v Brise* (1845) 15 LJ Ch 39.
5 *Underwood v Stevens* (1816) 1 Mer 712; *Rehden v Wesley* (1861) 29 Beav 213; Law of Property Amendment Act 1859, s 31; Trustee Act 1893, s 24; *Re Chapman* [1896] 2 Ch 763 at 776; *Re Brier* (1884) 26 Ch D 238 at 243; *Speight v Gaunt* (1883) 9 App Cas 1 at 13–15 and 22–23.

The effect of the Trustee Act 1925

55.3 The Trustee Act 1925 radically enlarged trustees' collective powers to delegate implementation of their decisions[1], but not their own discretionary decision-making powers to agents. Section 23 enabled them to delegate, whether or not there was any reasonable need for this, so lazy trustees could even delegate matters they could have seen to personally. It was clear that, as before, trustees who in good faith employed an agent whom they had power to employ under the general law or s 23, would not be automatically liable for the acts or defaults of such agent. It was, however, uncertain whether trustees still owed a duty to select and supervise such agents with the care of a prudent businessman[2].

55.3 *The trustee's duties*

1   See 15th edn hereof, pp 620–624 on TA 1925, ss 23 and 30.
2   See 15th edn hereof, pp 620–624 on TA 1925, ss 23 and 30.

55.4 Traditionalists considered that this duty continued after 1925, so that trustees would still be personally liable if themselves personally guilty of wilful default in the traditional equitable sense which covered deliberate, reckless and negligent conduct.

55.5 Modernists, believing in a literal, rather than an historical interpretation of ss 23(1) and 30(1) of the Trustee Act 1925 considered trustees would only be personally liable in respect of acts or defaults of agents if themselves guilty of wilful default in the common law sense of deliberate or reckless conduct, but not negligent conduct. In *Armitage v Nurse*[1] the Court of Appeal, in *obiter dicta* without full argument, accepted the modernist interpretation that permits trustees to get away with negligent conduct in the selection and supervision of agents. This helped to provide momentum for the Trustee Act 2000 which imposes a duty of care on the trustees in the arrangements for employing and supervising agents, whether employed under statutory or express powers[2].

1   [1998] Ch 241 at 252.
2   TA 2000, Sch 1, para 3.

55.6 The Trustee Act 2000 has repealed ss 23 and 30 of the Trustee Act 1925. Section 23(2) automatically permitted discretions to be exercised by delegates authorised by the trustees in respect of non-UK trust property. whether or not it was otherwise impossible for the trustees satisfactorily to run the trust or reasonably necessary for the operation of the trust. In the light of the repeal of s 23(2) and the modern ease of communication by e-mail, phone and fax there now seems no scope for this exceptional position provided for under general law when communications took many months[1].

1   *Stuart v Norton* (1860) 14 Moo PCC 17. Now also consider TA 2000, s 11(2)(a); and Law Com Report No 260, 'Trustees Powers and Duties', para 4.13.

Paragraph 1(b)

Delegable functions of trustees

55.7 The power to employ agents under s 11 of the Trustee Act 2000 is not available to trustees of authorised unit trusts[1] or of charitable common investment schemes[2], while trustees of pension schemes[3] cannot use it in relation to any investment functions nor to authorise a person to act as their agent if being the employer in relation to the scheme or if connected with, or an associate of, such employer.

1   TA 2000, s 37.
2   TA 2000, s 38.
3   TA 2000, s 37(4).

55.8 Otherwise, trustees of a non-charitable trust[1] whenever they wish can delegate functions:

'other than
(a)   any function relating to whether or in what way any assets of the trust should be distributed,
(b)   any power to decide whether any fees or other payment due to be made out of the trust funds should be made out of income or capital,
(c)   any power to appoint a person to be trustee of the trust, or
(d)   any power conferred by any other enactment or the trust instrument which permits the trustees to delegate any of their functions or to appoint a person to act as nominee or custodian'.

[1]   TA 2000, s 11(2).

55.9 The clear intention behind (a) is to ensure that distributive discretions[1] concerning payment of capital to beneficiaries or to objects of powers of payment or accumulation of income are not to be delegated: only administrative or managerial functions concerning the trustees' running of the trust in the best interests of the beneficiaries are to be delegable. For the same reason, if trustees have a discretion as to paying outgoings of an income nature out of capital and vice versa, so as to have adverse distributive effect on an income or capital beneficiary, they must exercise it themselves.

[1]   These should extend to the exercise of powers of appropriation to individual beneficiaries or to trust funds for beneficiaries as steps on the way to a distribution.

55.10 As for (d) the reference to any power conferred by any *other* enactment indicates that a power conferred by the Trustee Act 2000 itself to appoint an agent[1] enables the trustees to appoint an agent whose function can include the appointment of another agent[2].

[1]   Note that terms permitting an agent to appoint a *substitute* and restricting the liability of such substitute are not authorised unless reasonably necessary: TA 2000, s 14(2) and (3).
[2]   A discretionary portfolio manager may well be given power to appoint a nominee or custodian.

55.11 In the case of charitable trusts, delegable functions are[1]:

(a)   any function consisting of carrying out trustees' decisions,
(b)   any function relating to investment of trust assets (including managing any trust land and creating or disposing of an interest in such land),
(c)   any fund-raising function otherwise than by trading which is an integral part[2] of carrying out the trust's charitable purposes, and
(d)   any function prescribed by an order[3] made by the Secretary of State.

[1]   TA 2000, s 11(3).
[2]   A trade is an integral part of carrying out a trust's charitable purpose if, whether carried on in the UK or elsewhere, the profits are applied solely for trust purposes and either the trade is exercised in the course of the actual carrying out of a primary purpose of the trust or the work in connection with the trade is mainly carried out by beneficiaries of the trust: TA 2000, s 11(4).
[3]   Exercisable by a statutory instrument subject to annulment by resolution of either House of Parliament: TA 2000, s 11(5).

55.12 The trustee's duties

Eligibility as a delegate

55.12 Trustees can appoint anyone under s 11 including one of themselves[1] to exercise any of their delegable functions, but they can never under s 11 so authorise any beneficiary (even if also a co-trustee)[2]. The appointee may also act as the trustees' nominee or custodian if qualifying under statutory or other powers[3]. If trustees appoint two or more persons to exercise the same function they can only do this on the basis that such persons are to exercise the function jointly[4].

[1] TA 2000, s 12(1).
[2] TA 2000, s 12(3).
[3] TA 2000, s 12(4).
[4] TA 2000, s 12(2).

Burdens attached to trustees' specific functions attach to the delegate

55.13 A delegate exercising any particular function delegated to him by the trustees under s 11 is, of course, subject to any specific duties or restrictions attached to that function[1]. Thus, a discretionary portfolio manager must have regard to the standard investment criteria, although he will not be subject to the requirement to obtain advice if he is the kind of person from whom it would have been proper for the trustees to obtain advice[2]. However, it is not considered that such portfolio manager is subject to the general duty to act fairly imposed upon trustees as such and who should comply with this duty in preparing their policy statement[3] for the manager to comply with and in monitoring such statement and the conduct of the manager[4].

[1] TA 2000, s 13(1).
[2] TA 2000, s 13(2).
[3] TA 2000, s 15(2), (3).
[4] TA 2000, s 22.

55.14 Where trustees of land are subject under s 11(1) of the Trusts of Land and Appointment of Trustees Act 1996 to the duty to consult with the beneficiaries it is they who must perform this duty: they cannot delegate it, and, indeed, any delegate cannot be subjected to s 11 of the 1996 Act[1]. The position is similar[2] where Settled Land Act trustees own investments and must so far as practicable consult the tenant for life and give effect to his wishes so far as consistent with the general interest of the settlement. If a discretionary portfolio manager is to operate speedily and effectively the tenant for life's consent to the policy statement guidelines, after consultation, should suffice to oust the need for consultation by the trustees before every sale or purchase by the manager.

[1] TA 2000, s 13(4) and (5).
[2] TA 2000, Sch 2, para 10 inserting into SLA 1925, s 75(4), (4B) and (4C).

Paragraph 1(c)

Terms of delegation

55.15 Subject to complying with the duty of care[1], trustees have a very broad discretion as to the terms upon which they engage a delegate under s 11[2], so long as remuneration does not exceed such amount as is objectively reason-able in all the circumstances for the provision of the relevant services[3]. However, unless it is objectively reasonably necessary[4], the contractual terms must not include terms permitting the agent to appoint a substitute or to act in circumstances capable of giving rise to a conflict of interest or 'restricting the liability of' the agent or his substitute to the trustees or any beneficiary[5]. It would accord with the philosophy of such proscription if terms 'restricting' the liability of an agent or his substitute extended to terms 'ousting' liability by ousting duties[6] (so there can be no breach thereof to give rise to any liability) but, in any event, compliance with the duty of care could well prevent agreeing to any terms ousting liability altogether in particular circum-stances.

[1] TA 2000, Sch 1, para 3.
[2] TA 2000, s 14(1).
[3] TA 2000, s 32(2). These restrictions are inapplicable if an express power in the trust instrument is being used (TA 2000, s 26(a)) or if the trust instrument expressly restricts or excludes s 14(2) and (3) (TA 2000, s 26(b)).
[4] TA 2000, s 14(2).
[5] TA 2000, s 14(3).
[6] If Parliament intended to proscribe terms 'restricting' liability then, *a fortiori*, terms going beyond that by 'ousting' liability should be proscribed.

55.16 To avoid any future problems, trustees will be wise to preserve contemporaneous written evidence of the factors that led them to think it was objectively reasonably necessary in the best interests of the beneficiaries as a whole to agree to the proscribed terms. Usually, there will be presentations by, say, three prospective discretionary portfolio managers, so that the trustees should probe the need for such terms if they are to obtain the services of the manager likely to perform best for the trust and, perhaps, attach some conditions, eg as to notification to them by the agent when it has acted in circumstances capable of giving rise to a conflict of interest.

Paragraph 1(d)

Asset management delegation

55.17 Special restrictions apply if trustees exercise their s 11 power[1] to delegate any of their asset management functions defined[2] as functions relating to:

'(a)   the investment of assets subject to the trust,
(b)   the acquisition of property which is to be subject to the trust, and
(c)   managing property which is subject to the trust and disposing of, or creating or disposing of an interest in, such property.'

[1] The s 11 power to employ an agent for asset management only if certain conditions are satisfied is in addition to powers expressly conferred by the trust instrument (per s 26(a)) and is also subject to any restriction or exclusion in the trust instrument (per s 26(b)).
[2] TA 2000, s 15(5).

55.18 This clearly covers a discretionary portfolio manager dealing with stocks and shares and bonds and gilts or of a land agent dealing with rented-out residential and commercial property. However, the definition is broad enough to extend to an estate agent or an auctioneer selling a trust house or painting for the best price reasonably obtainable.

55.19 No authority is conferred on an agent to exercise any asset management function until the trustees have (1) prepared a policy statement giving guidance as to how the function should be exercised[1] and being in writing or evidenced in writing[2], and (2) entered into an agreement, which is in writing or evidenced in writing[3], containing a term[4] that the agent will secure compliance with the policy statement, except that failure to comply with these conditions does not invalidate the authorisation of the agent[5], thereby protecting third parties and the agent. As to be expected, the guidance given in the policy statement has to be formulated with a view to ensuring that the asset management functions will be exercised in the best interest of the trust beneficiaries[6].

[1] TA 2000, s 15(2)(a).
[2] TA 2000, s 15(4).
[3] TA 2000, s 15(1).
[4] TA 2000, s 15(2)(b).
[5] TA 2000, s 24.
[6] TA 2000, s 15(3).

55.20 The above statutory power is in addition to any express power conferred by the trust instrument[1], so trustees may prefer to act pursuant to the express power rather than be subject to the statutory restrictions, although to achieve the same end as a self-sufficient express power it is possible[2] for the trust instrument to restrict or exclude the conditions attached to the statutory power.

[1] TA 2000, s 26(a).
[2] TA 2000, s 26(b).

Paragraph 1(e)

Delegation by trustees of land functions to a beneficiary

55.21 'Trustees of land may, by power of attorney, delegate to any beneficiary or beneficiaries of full age and beneficially entitled to an interest in possession in land subject to the trust any of their functions as trustees which relate to the land'[1]. It seems implicit that these functions are only administrative or managerial functions and not distributive functions involving the exercise of powers of appointment or discretionary trusts so as to favour certain persons over others. Moreover, it is only functions relating to the land that can be delegated, not functions relating to the proceeds of sale of land or investments thereof or of originally settled assets that are not land. There seems no reason why delegation may not relate to separate parts of the land so that one beneficiary then manages one part and another beneficiary another part.

[1] TLATA 1996, s 9(1). This cannot be an enduring power within Enduring Powers of Attorney Act 1985: see s 9(6).

55.22 Delegation may only occur where there is some beneficiary[1] entitled to an interest in possession in the relevant land. Beneficial entitlement is required so that entitlement as personal representative or as trustee, eg of a sub-trust, is not sufficient[2].

[1] TLATA 1996, s 22(1) for definition of a beneficiary as a person who has an interest in property subject to the trust.
[2] TLATA 1996, s 22(2). Cf *Olsanecki v Hillocks* [2002] EWHC 1997 (Ch). Annuitants are not beneficiaries interested in possession: s 22(3).

55.23 A beneficiary has an interest in possession if entitled to occupy the land or to receive the rents and profits[1] therefrom, having an immediate right to present enjoyment of the land or the rents and profits. Where a beneficiary currently has a life interest but it is subject to a power of accumulation of income vested in the trustees, the beneficiary does not have an immediate right of present enjoyment for inheritance tax purposes[2], although his interest is not in remainder or in reversion and so can be regarded as in possession. The onus will be on those alleging that interest in possession has the simple latter meaning to prove that this was intended[3] rather than the stricter inheritance tax meaning. Because the position is ambiguous there should be an express power permitting delegation to a beneficiary currently interested in income but subject to a power of accumulation if the settlor desires such flexibility.

[1] TLATA 1996, s 23(2) incorporating LPA 1925, s 205(1)(xx).
[2] *Pearson v IRC* [1981] AC 753, HL where, by a majority, the House of Lords held that a life tenant subject to a power of accumulation did *not* have an 'interest in possession' for the purposes of capital transfer tax (now inheritance tax); all the Chancery judges involved in the various stages of the appeal considered the the taxing statute was referring to the established Chancery meaning of the phrase, and that accordingly there *was* an interest in possession, because it was not in remainder or in reversion.
[3] See SLA 1925, s 20(1) and *Pearson v IRC* [1980] Ch 1 at 9, but cf *Re Earl of Stamford and Warrington* [1925] Ch 162 at 171, not challenged on appeal [1925] Ch 589 at 591.

55.24 Where a beneficiary under an accumulation and maintenance trust will become entitled to income or capital upon some future event (eg on attaining 25 years of age) but, until then, the trustees are under a duty to accumulate income, so far as not applied for the maintenance of the beneficiary, it is clear that he does not have an interest in possession. Moreover, any beneficiary interested under a discretionary trust of income does not seem someone entitled to an interest in possession for the purposes of the 1996 Act[1] unless and until the trustees exercise any discretionary power that they may have to appoint an interest in possession to such person.

[1] In context see 'entitled' in s 12 of the 1996 Act and consider the unascertainable value of a discretionary interest for purposes of s 11(1)(b).

55.25 Finally, delegation can only be to someone beneficially entitled to an interest in possession in *land*, while a trust of an undivided share in land is itself a trust of land[1] so the trustee thereof can delegate to a beneficiary with an interest in possession under the sub-trust. More significant is whether the head trustees can delegate to such a beneficiary under the sub-trust. It seems clear that they can if the sub-trust was created by the settlor of the head trust as a subsidiary part thereof or if they themselves, pursuant to powers in this behalf, created the sub-trusts within the umbrella of the head trust. However, where the beneficial co-owner of the undivided share under S's settlement created an independent settlement of his undivided share, eg on B for life, delegation to B by the trustees of S's settlement will only be permissible if a broad non-technical construction is taken of s 9, which would seem to be in keeping with the purpose of the section.

1   TLATA 1996, s 23(2) incorporating LPA 1925, s 205(1)(ix) as amended by the 1996 Act s 25 (2) and Sch 4. See *Olsanecki v Hillocks* [2002] EWHC 1997 (Ch) (A, surviving joint tenant at law, held legal estate on trust as to one half for self and as to one half for estate of deceased joint tenant B, joint tenancy having previously been severed in equity, B's share being held by will on trust to permit A to reside for life and subject thereto for B's children absolutely: B's half share was subject to a trust of land).

Duration of delegation

55.26 The power of attorney may be for a defined period or it may be indefinite[1], but it must be given by all the trustees jointly and then be revocable by any one or more of them (unless expressed to be irrevocable and to be given by way of security). The power is automatically revoked by the appointment of a new trustee, but not by a current trustee dying or otherwise ceasing to be a trustee[2].

1   TLATA 1996, s 9(5).
2   TLATA 1996, s 9(3).

55.27 When the attorney ceases to be a person beneficially entitled to an interest in possession in land the power is automatically revoked if given to him alone[1]. If given to him and two or more other beneficiaries to be exercised jointly (not separately) the power is revoked if each of the other beneficiaries ceases to be so entitled, but otherwise it remains in force for the remaining beneficiaries. If the power were given to beneficiaries to be exercised by them separately, or either separately or jointly, the power is revoked only as concerns the beneficiary ceasing to be a person beneficially entitled to an interest in possession[2].

1   TLATA 1996, s 9(4).
2   TLATA 1996, s 9(4).

Delegates as trustees of their functions relating to land

55.28 Beneficiaries to whom functions have been delegated by power of attorney under s 9 of the 1996 Act are, in relation to the exercise of their functions, in the same position as trustees with the same duties and liabilities, but are not regarded as trustees for any other purposes, particularly the purposes of any enactment permitting the delegation of functions by trustees or imposing requirements relating to the payment of capital money[1]. Thus, a beneficiary-attorney cannot sub-delegate the functions delegated to him by the trustees. It also seems clear that a sole life tenant or joint life tenants cannot give a valid receipt for capital money arising from the exercise of a delegated function, eg a power to sell the land or grant an easement over it. The delegated functions must relate to the land, while giving a valid overreaching receipt relates to the proceeds of sale of land. Thus, the trustees themselves must provide the receipt to satisfy s 27 of the Law of Property Act 1925 or exercise their power under s 11 of the Trustee Act 2000 to appoint an agent, eg a solicitor, to provide a receipt on their behalf.

1   TLATA 1996, s.9(7).

Paragraph 2

Duties of care where trustees of land delegate to a beneficiary

55.29 Trustees of land in deciding whether to delegate any of their functions relating to land to a currently entitled beneficiary under s 9 of the Trusts of Land and Appointment of Trustees Act 1996 must comply with the statutory duty of care[1] except to the extent ousted by the trust instrument[2]. Once they have decided to make and have made a delegation on particular terms that is not an irrevocable one by way of security, they must keep the delegation under review with a view to intervening and if they consider they should intervene (eg by revoking the delegation or giving directions to the delegate) they must do so[3]. The duty of care (unless ousted by the trust instrument) applies to 'trustees in carrying out any duty under subs (3)' to keep the delegation under review and to intervene if appropriate[4].

1   TLATA 1996, s 9A inserted by TA 2000, Sch 2, para 47.
2   TA 2000, Sch 1, para 7.
3   TLATA 1996, s 9A(3).
4   TLATA 1996, s 9A(5).

55.30 'Unless the trustee fails to comply with the duty of care in deciding to delegate any of the trustee's functions under section 9 or in carrying out any duty under subsection (3)' he is not liable for any act or default of the delegate[1]. It seems clear that 'in deciding to delegate' must cover the terms of delegation as an integral part of the decision to delegate, which must depend on the terms of the delegation and the attributes of the delegate-beneficiary. It also seems that 'in carrying out any duty' under subs (3) to review and, then, to intervene, if appropriate, should cover the whole nil to one hundred per cent band of the duty, thereby preventing the trustee from arguing unmeritoriously that his total failure to review the conduct of the delegate means that he cannot be liable for any act or default of the delegate. Alternatively, such argument could be trumped by holding that breach of his duty to review and then intervene, if appropriate, is a personal default of the trustee for which he is personally liable.

1   TLATA 1996, s 9A(6).

Duties of care where trustees delegate under s 11 of the Trustee Act 2000

55.31 The same arguments as those canvassed in the preceding paragraph arise where s 23(1) of the Trustee Act 2000 provides 'unless he has failed to comply with the duty of care applicable to him under paragraph 3 of Schedule 1 ... when carrying out his duties under section 22' to keep under review the arrangements under which an agent, nominee or custodian continues to act for the trustees, 'a trustee is not liable for any act or default of the agent, nominee or custodian'. To prevent the trustee from escaping all liability when he totally failed to keep the agency arrangements under review, 'carrying out his duties' must extend to the whole nil to one hundred per cent band of the duties or, otherwise, such a total breach of his duties is a personal default for which he is personally liable, unaffected by s 23(1).

55.32 Unless inconsistent with the trust instrument[1], once trustees, pursuant to their powers under the Trustee Act 2000, have entered into arrangements for someone to act as agent (or nominee or custodian) they must keep the arrangements under review, checking how those arrangements are being implemented, considering whether they need to exercise their powers to intervene (by giving directions or revoking the arrangements) and they must exercise them if there be a need[2]. In the case of an agent exercising asset management functions, the reviewing duty extends to considering whether there is any need for a revised or replacement policy statement and, if there is such a need, then to producing such a revised or replacement policy, and to assessing whether the current policy statement is being complied with[3]. The duty of care applies to these reviewing and intervention duties[4] except to the extent ousted by the trust instrument[5].

[1] TA 2000, s 21(3).
[2] TA 2000, s 22(1).
[3] TA 2000, s 22(2).
[4] TA 2000, Sch 1, para 3(1)(e).
[5] TA 2000, Sch 1, para 7.

55.33 The duty of care (except to the extent ousted by the trust instrument) also applies to a trustee when 'entering into arrangements' for the appointment of an agent (nominee or custodian) under the Trustee Act 2000 or under express powers in the trust instrument[1]. 'Entering into arrangements' covers selecting the person who is to act, determining any terms on which he is to act, and, if the person is being authorised to exercise asset management functions, the preparation of a policy statement[2].

[1] TA 2000, Sch 1, para 3(1).
[2] TA 2000, Sch 1, para 3(2).

Paragraph 3

Temporary delegation by a trustee of all or any of his discretions

55.34 Totally distinct from the collective power of the body of the trustees to delegate pursuant to the Trustee Act 2000 or express powers in the trust instrument is the power (under the substituted[1] s 25 of the Trustee Act 1925) of each trustee personally, by power of attorney, to 'delegate the execution or exercise of all or any of the trusts, powers and discretions vested in him as trustee either alone or jointly with any other person or persons'. This extends beyond administrative or managerial functions to every function including distributive functions. The delegate becomes the *alter ego* of the trustee in respect of the delegate functions, so the delegating trustee is automatically liable for the acts or defaults of the delegate as if they were the acts or defaults of the delegating trustee[2].

1   By Trustee Delegation Act 1999, s 5.
2   TA 1925, s 25(7).

55.35 Because a trustee can delegate every function so that the delegate can essentially become a substitute trustee, the delegation can continue only for a period of 12 months or any shorter period stipulated in the power of attorney, the period commencing with the date of execution of the power of attorney by the trustee or as expressly provided in such power of attorney[1]. Furthermore, to give those with the power to appoint a replacement trustee the opportunity to exercise such power, the delegating trustee, before or within seven days after giving the power of attorney, must give written notice of it to each person (other than himself), if any, who has express power under the trust instrument to appoint a new trustee, and to each of the other trustees (who have statutory default powers[2] to appoint a replacement trustee)[3]. The written notice must specify the date on which the power comes into operation and its duration, the donee of the power, the reason why the power is given, and, where some only are delegated, the particular trusts, powers and discretions delegated[4]. Failure to comply with this notice requirement, however, does not, in favour of a person dealing with the donee of the power, invalidate any act done or instrument executed by the donee[5].

1   TA 1925, s 25(2).
2   TA 1925, s 36(1).
3   TA 1925, s 25(4). In the case of delegation by a personal representative notice must be given to each of the other personal representatives, if any, except an executor who has renounced probate.
4   TA 1925, s 25(4).
5   TA 1925, s 25(4).

55.36 For the purpose of performing the delegated functions the donee may exercise any of the powers conferred on the trustee-donor by statute (eg in s 11 of the Trustee Act 2000) or the trust instrument, including power, for the purpose of transferring any inscribed stock, himself to delegate to an attorney power to transfer, but not including the power of delegation under the substituted s 25 of the Trustee Act 1925[1].

1   TA 1925, s 25(8).

55.37 A statutory 'General Trustee Power of Attorney' is provided by s 25(6): a separate power of attorney is required for each trust to which the delegation is to apply. Otherwise, a power in a form to like effect but expressed to be made under s 25(5) can be used: it would then seem that a trustee of say, five trusts, could use that power of attorney to delegate his trusteeship functions in relation to the five singly specified trusts to a colleague of his while on a six month sabbatical from work, but it will be safer to use a separate power of attorney for each separate trust.

55.38 The persons who may be donees of the power of attorney include a trust corporation[1] or a co-trustee, but the requirement for capital money to be paid to a trust corporation or two persons continues to apply[2], eg if one of two trustees, A, delegated his functions to his co-trustee, B, who is not a trust corporation, then B cannot give a valid receipt for capital money on sale of property nor execute an overreaching deed.

1   TA 1925, s 25(3).
2   Trustee Delegation Act 1999, s 7.

55.39 The donee may recover expenses incurred in performing his duties just as his donor could have recovered such expenses if incurring them[1]. Section 25 does not make any reference to payment of reasonable remuneration to the donee, but it would be strange if the remuneration to which the donor was entitled as trustee could not be diverted to the donee performing the functions that the donor would otherwise have to perform. Indeed, if the donor-trustee is entitled to be indemnified out of trust funds for the costs of the power of attorney as properly incurred by him acting as trustee on behalf of the trust[2], should he not also be entitled to the costs of employing the donee-attorney?

1   TA 1925, s 25(8).
2   TA 2000, s 31.

Enduring or Lasting Powers of Attorney and Co-owners of Land

55.40 It is possible[1] for the temporary delegation of trusteeship functions under the substituted s 25 of the Trustee Act 1925 to be by way of an enduring power of attorney under the Enduring Powers of Attorney Act 1985 or by way of a lasting power of attorney with the Mental Capacity Act 2005[2] replacing the 1985 Act, so as to survive the loss of mental capacity of the donor. However, with a maximum twelve months duration, this is not very significant.

1   Trustee Delegation Act 1999, s 6.
2   See s 18(1)(j).

55.41 Much more significant is that where M and W hold land on trust for M and W each can confer a power of attorney on the other under s 1 of the Trustee Delegation Act 1999[1] which can be by way of an enduring power of attorney or its replacement, the lasting power of attorney, enabling the other to exercise any trustee function of the donor, eg to sell the land. The key feature is that the donor-trustee had a beneficial interest in the land, its proceeds or income at the time of the donee's act[2]. In favour of a purchaser an 'appropriate statement' is conclusive evidence, being a signed statement of the donee when doing the act in question or within three months thereof that the donor has or had a beneficial interest in the property at the time of the donee doing the act[3].

1   Not under TA 1925 or an express power in the trust instrument: Trustee Delegation Act 1999, s 1(8).
2   Trustee Delegation Act 1999, s 1(1).
3   Trustee Delegation Act 1999, s 2(2), (3).

55.42 A sole individual donee cannot give a valid receipt for capital money or execute an overreaching deed[1], but if the enduring or lasting power of attorney is registered such sole donee can appoint an additional trustee[2].

1   Trustee Delegation Act 1999, s 7.
2   Trustee Delegation Act 1999, s 8.

ARTICLE 56
DUTY OF TRUSTEES TO ACT JOINTLY WHERE MORE THAN ONE

56.1

In the case of a non-charitable[1] trust which is not a pension trust scheme[2] where there are more trustees than one, all must join in the execution of the trust[3], save only:
(a)   where the settlement[4] or a competent court otherwise directs;
(b)   as to the receipt of income[5];
(c)   as to such matters as can be lawfully delegated under Article 55.

1   *Re Whiteley* [1910] 1 Ch 600 (majority decisions are valid). If decision by a majority is allowed it is not enough that a majority sign a paper recording the decision (unless this be authorised by the trust instrument); the trustees must meet so the matter can be considered by them: *A-G v Scott* (1750) 1 Ves Sen 413.
2   Pensions Act 1995, s 32 (majority decisions are not valid).
3   *Luke v South Kensington Hotel Co* (1879) 11 Ch D 121; *Re Dixon* (1826) 2 GI & J 114; *Re Flower and Metropolitan Board of Works* (1884) 27 Ch D 592; but retrospective assent to the decision of the other trustees by a non-consulted trustee will validate such decision: *Messeena v Carr* (1870) LR 9 Eq 260; *Libby v Kennedy* (1998) OPLR 213.
4   *Re Butlin's Settlement Trust* [1976] Ch 251.
5   As to shares and stocks, see Companies Act 1985, s 360; but consider *Binney v Ince Hall Coal and Cannel Co* (1866) 35 LJ Ch 363. As to rents, see *Townley v Sherborne* (1633) J Bridg 35, 2 Wh & Tu Lead Cas (8th edn) 627; *Gouldsworth v Knights* (1843) 11 M & W 337; and *Gough v Smith* [1872] WN 18.

56.2 This article is a corollary of Article 55 for, if trustees cannot delegate their duties, it follows that they must all personally perform those duties, and not appoint one of themselves to manage the business of the trust. It is not unusual to find one of several trustees spoken of as the 'acting trustee', meaning the trustee who actively interests himself in the trust affairs, and whose decisions are merely indorsed by his co-trustees. The court, however, does not recognise any such distinction; for the settlor has trusted *all* his trustees, and it behoves each and every one of them to exercise his individual judgment and discretion on every matter, and not blindly to leave any questions to his co-trustees or co-trustee[1].

1   *Munch v Cockerell* (1840) 5 My & Cr 178; *Re Lucking's Will Trusts* [1967] 3 All ER 726.

56.3 Exceptionally, as where the settlor would prefer to have X alone as trustee managing the affairs of the trust, but a second trustee, Y, is needed (because the trust assets include land, so two trustees are needed to give a good receipt and overreach the beneficiaries' interests) the trust instrument may expressly stipulate that Y, or any successor trustee, while X is a trustee, must always act as directed by X unless aware that X is thereby committing a breach of trust[1]. Similarly there is no reason why a trust instrument should not effectively provide for X to have a casting vote if X and Y (or Y's successor) cannot agree on a matter concerning the trust[2], although if aware that X is seeking to commit a breach of trust, Y must not join X in carrying out such breach, and indeed, should seek an injunction to restrain X if X is in a position on his own, without Y's assistance, to commit a breach of trust[3].

[1]   *Re Arnott* [1899]1 IR 201. Y will be personally liable if dishonestly facilitating a breach of trust.
[2]   After all, the settlor can provide for majority decisions and for the chairman of the trustees to have a casting vote where the trustees are evenly divided.
[3]   *Booth v Booth* (1838) 1 Beav 125; *Gough v Smith* [1872] WN 18.

Majority of trustees cannot bind the rest

56.4 Thus, the act of a majority of private (as opposed to charitable or pension scheme) trustees cannot bind either a dissenting minority, or the trust estate. In order to bind the trust estate the act must be the act of all unless the trust instrument expressly authorises the trustees to act according to the majority view where they are not unanimous[1]. Where there is a trust for sale of real estate with a discretionary power to postpone the sale, the property must be sold within a reasonable time, unless the trustees are unanimously in favour of a postponement[2], and the same rule applies to a trust for sale with power to retain existing investments[3]. At the same time, in such cases a trustee, if acting bona fide, may defer to what he considers to be the better judgment of his co-trustee, although he does so with reluctance[4]. On the same ground, if one of several trustees incurs costs without consultation with his co-trustees, he cannot recover them from the estate where his efforts have resulted in loss[5].

[1]   *Luke v South Kensington Hotel Co* (1879) 11 Ch D 121; *Swale v Swale* (1856) 22 Beav 584; *Re Butlins Settlement Trust* [1976] Ch 251, [1976] 2 All ER 483. It may be otherwise, however, with regard to charitable trustees; (see Charities Act 1960, ss 28 and 34) and pension trustees (Pensions Act 1995, s 32).
[2]   *Re Roth* (1896) 74 LT 50; *Jones v Challenger* [1961] 1 QB 176, CA.
[3]   *Re Hilton* [1909] 2 Ch 548.
[4]   *Re Schneider* (1906) 22 TLR 223.
[5]   *Re England's Settlement Trusts* [1918] 1 Ch 24.

Revocable or periodic obligations terminable by notice

56.5 Exceptionally, if T1 and T2 contract with C on terms which are revocable or are to continue in operation for one year in the first place and thereafter from year to year unless determined by notice at the end of the first or any subsequent year, the contract will only continue or only persist beyond the initial period so long as both T1 and T2 are willing that it should do so[1]. Thus, either T1 or T2 can alone give notice unless restrained by an injunction, as where the giving of such a notice would in the circumstances amount to a breach of trust, eg the loss of a valuable leasehold (as opposed to an unsatisfactory contract with a discretionary portfolio manager who is a friend of T2).

¹   *Hammersmith and Fulham London Borough Council v Monk* [1992] 1 AC 478, [1992] 1 All ER 1, HL, also indicating that all trustees must join in the operation of a break clause in a lease, a surrender of the lease, an application for relief against forfeiture and the exercise of an option to renew the lease.

All trustees must join in receipt

56.6   Likewise, all the trustees must join in the receipt of money, unless, of course, the settlement authorises one of them to give good receipts and discharges, assuming capital moneys on the sale of land in England and Wales are not involved when receipt must be by two trustees or a trust corporation¹. As Kay J said in *Re Flower and Metropolitan Board of Works*²:

> 'The theory of every trust is that the trustees shall not allow the trust moneys to get into the hands of any one of them, but that all shall exercise control over them. They must take care that they are in the hands of all, or invested in their names, or placed in a proper bank in their joint names ... The reason why more than one trustee is appointed, is that they shall take care that the moneys shall not get into the hands of one of them alone ... and they have no right, as between themselves and the cestuis que trust, unless the circumstances are such as to make it imperatively necessary to do so, to authorise one of themselves to receive the moneys'³.

¹   LPA 1925, s 27.
²   (1884) 27 Ch D 592.
³   *See also Lee v Sankey* (1872) LR 15 Eq 204; *Clough v Bond* (1838) 3 My & Cr 490; and *Walker v Symonds* (1818) 3 Swan 1 at 61.

56.7   In practice, trustees receiving capital money on sale of land will, under s 11 of the Trustee Act 2000¹, authorise their solicitor to receive such money on their behalf.

¹   Replacing TA 1925, s 23(1) and (3).

Investments should be in joint names

56.8   Unless advantage is taken of the Trustee Act 2000 to appoint nominees or custodians, all investments of trust moneys should be made in the joint names of the trustees, for otherwise one trustee would be able to realise and appropriate the money¹. But this must of course yield to necessity; as, for instance, where shares are specifically bequeathed to trustees upon certain trusts (so that retention of such shares is authorised), and it is found that by the regulations of the company the shares can only be registered in the name of one person²; or where investments that the trustees are authorised to purchase can only be held in the name of a nominee for the purchasers.

¹   *Lewis v Nobbs* (1878) 8 Ch D 591; *Swale v Swale* (1856) 22 Beav 584.
²   *Consterdine v Consterdine* (1862) 31 Beav 330.

Income

56.9   As a general rule, however, although trustees must join in the receipt of capital, it is permissible for them to allow one of their number to receive the income. Thus, in the case of rents, the trustees may delegate the collection to one of their number or to a rent collector, for it would be impossible for them all to collect the rents[1]. If, however, there is any fear of misappropriation by the collecting trustee, the others should notify the tenants not to pay him again[2]. A similar rule applies to the receipt of dividends on stocks or shares, from the necessity of the case, where the Articles of Association of limited companies provide that trusts shall not be recognised and that payment shall be made to the first of several joint holders[3].

1   *Townley v Sherborne* (1633) J Bridg 35, 2 White & Tud LC 627.
2   *Gough v Smith* [1872] WN 18.
3   Companies Act 1985, s 360; Companies (Tables A to F) Regulations 1985, SI 1985/805, Table A, arts 5 and 106.

Trustee joining in receipt for conformity

56.10 In cases where a trustee permits his co-trustee to receive moneys owing to the estate (eg where he permits him to collect rents), then, even though he join in the receipt for such moneys, and thereby acknowledge that he has received them, he will not be liable *if he can prove[1]* that he did not in fact receive them, and that he only joined in the receipt for the sake of conformity[2].

1   *Brice v Stokes* (1805) 11 Ves 319, 2 White & Tud LC 631; *Townley v Sherborne* (1633) J Bridg 35, 2 White & Tud LC 627; *Re Fryer* (1857) 3 K & J 317.
2   *Fellows v Mitchell* (1705) 1 P Wms 81; *Re Fryer* (1857) 3 K & J 317. There is less need for this nowadays in the light of TA 2000, ss 11 and 12(1).

Trustee must not permit co-trustee to retain money

56.11 Even where a trustee may safely permit his co-trustee to receive trust moneys, he will, nevertheless, be liable for breaching his duty of care if he permit him to retain them for a longer period than the circumstances of the case require[1].

1   *Brice v Stokes* (1805) 11 Ves 319, 2 White & Tud LC 631. *Thompson v Finch* (1856) 8 De GM & G 560; *Walker v Symonds* (1818) 3 Swan 1; *Hanbury v Kirkland* (1829) 3 Sim 265; distinguished in *Re Munton* [1927] 1 Ch 262; *Styles v Guy* (1849) 1 Mac & G 422; *Wiglesworth v Wiglesworth* (1852) 16 Beav 269; *Egbert v Butter* (1856) 21 Beav 560; *Rodbard v Cooke* (1877) 25 WR 555; *Lewis v Nobbs* (1878) 8 Ch D 591; *Consterdine v Consterdine* (1862) 31 Beav 330; and *Carruthers v Carruthers* [1896] AC 659.

Trustee must not permit co-trustee alone to sign cheques

56.12 For like reasons, trustees in whose names trust moneys are banked should not authorise the bankers to pay cheques signed by one only of their number, for that would be equivalent to giving the sole control of the trust funds to one trustee; whereas the beneficiaries are entitled to the safeguard of the control of all[1]. A trustee may, however, entrust his co-trustee with a crossed cheque, signed by both of them, for delivery to the beneficiary[2]. He may well be at risk if he entrusts his co-trustee with a blank cheque signed by him and the co-trustee takes advantage of this for his own purposes: there will certainly be liability if he knew or ought to have known that his co-trustee had earlier obtained a similar advantage[3].

1   *Clough v Bond* (1838) 3 My & Cr 490; *Trutch v Lamprell* (1855) 20 Beav 116. Note that delegable functions under TA 2000, s 11 do not extend to distribution of assets.
2   *Lake Bathurst Australasian Gold Mining Co, Re Barnard v Bagshaw* (1862) 3 De GJ & Sm 355.
3   Cf *Re Lucking's Will Trusts* [1967] 3 All ER 726, [1968] 1 WLR 866.

56.13 If one trustee forges the signature of the other to a cheque, and obtains payment from the bank to which the trustees had given a mandate to honour drawings signed by them both, the bank does not obtain a good discharge; but it was surprisingly held by McNair J in *Brewer v Westminster Bank Ltd*[1], that the innocent trustee cannot obtain a declaration of the bank's liability since the obligation of the bank is owed to both trustees jointly, and the delinquent trustee must be a party to the action and the forgery by him is an essential link in the claim.

1   [1952] 2 All ER 650 (a case as to executors' joint banking account). It is understood that an appeal in this case was compromised.

56.14 That case was justifiably not followed in *Welch v Bank of England*, by Harman J who said:

> 'I confess that I do not follow that decision. None of the cases in equity were cited to the judge. It may be however that this would be a good defence at law. It is certainly, I think, no defence in equity'[1].

1   [1955] Ch 508 at 532, [1955] 1 All ER 811 at 821 (a case as to forged transfers of stocks).

ARTICLE 57
DUTY OF TRUSTEE NOT TO SET UP JUS TERTII

57.1

A trustee, who has acknowledged himself as such, must not set up, or aid, the adverse title of a third party against his beneficiary[1]. But he has a right to have the direction of the court as to whether he should resist an adverse claim which has been made[2] or as to what he should do in respect of or an adverse claim which he has reasonable grounds to believe could make him personally liable to the claimant if the claimant knew what he was doing[3]; if, with notice of the adverse claim, he continues to pay his beneficiaries and himself he will do so at his own peril[4].

1   *Newsome v Flowers* (1861) 30 Beav 461; *Devey v Thornton* (1851) 9 Hare 222. Exceptionally, a trustee will be allowed to substantiate a claim that property allegedly devolving upon testamentary trusts is really his property: *Re Tucker* [1918] VLR 460, *Allen v Roughly* (1955) 94 CLR 98.
2   *Neale v Davies* (1854) 5 De GM & G 258, per Wood V-C and Turner LJ (Knight-Bruce LJ dissenting surprisingly). See also *Alsop Wilkinson v Neary* [1995] 1 All ER 431, para 87.37 below.

Trustees must not contest the title of their beneficiaries

57.2 In *Newsome v Flowers*[1] a chapel was vested in trustees, in trust for
Particular Baptists. Subsequently part of the congregation seceded, and went
to another chapel. Still later, the surviving trustees were induced (not knowing
the real object) to appoint new trustees, and vest the property in them.
Immediately afterwards the new trustees—who were in fact attached to the
seceding congregation—brought an action to obtain possession of the chapel.
Their appointment was, however, set aside, and it was held that they could not
plead the adverse claims of the seceders as a defence against the congregation
of the chapel, who were their beneficiaries.

1   (1861) 30 Beav 461.

57.3 Nor, however honestly trustees may believe that the trust property
belongs of right to a third party, are they justified in refusing to perform the
trust they have once undertaken, or in communicating with such other person
on the subject; but they must assume the validity of the title of their
beneficiaries until it be negatived[1].

1   *Beddoes v Pugh* (1859) 26 Beav 407.

Obtaining the directions of the court

57.4 The above cases show that trustees are not justified in taking an actively
hostile attitude towards the validity of their trust. Where they have received
notice of a paramount claim, and of the intention of the claimant to hold them
responsible if they deal with the fund in a manner contrary to such claim, the
trustees can hardly be expected at their own personal risk to go on steadily
executing the trust which they have undertaken, but must be able to apply to
the court for directions and relief. Thus, in *Neale v Davies*[1], Vice-Chancellor
Wood and in the Court of Appeal Turner LJ held that the trustees were
entitled to refuse to execute the trust under such circumstances, and had a
right to come to the court for its direction. Surprisingly, Knight-Bruce LJ,
however, dissented.

1   (1854) 5 De GM & G 258.

57.5 Nowadays, it is clear that a trustee is always entitled to act under the
direction of the court when he is placed in a position of difficulty or danger
whether under the inherent jurisdiction or Part 64 of the Civil Procedure
Rules[1]. Thus, in *Finers v Miro*[2] there were reasonable grounds for believing
that the defendant had defrauded X Ltd of millions of dollars indirectly held
by the plaintiff solicitor through an intricate network of overseas companies,
trusts and foundations held by the plaintiff on trust for the defendant
absolutely. Because the plaintiff was potentially personally liable to account to
X Ltd for knowing assistance in a dishonest breach of fiduciary duty, the

Court of Appeal held, despite the solicitor-client relationship between plaintiff and defendant, the plaintiff was entitled to obtain the court's directions. The plaintiff was authorised to inform X Ltd sufficiently to enable it to decide whether or not to make a claim against the defendant's assets held by the plaintiff and frozen except for releasing 100,000 dollars to the defendant for his legal expenses.

1   See para 87.1 below.
2   [1991] 1 All ER 182, [1991] 1 WLR 35, CA.

57.6 However, in *United Mizrahi Bank v Doherty*[1] the court was not prepared to assist a firm of solicitors seeking a direction that they would have an unimpeachable title to moneys paid to them out of their client's bank account which was frozen except for payment thereout of legal expenses, the claimant alleging that the account contained money belonging to the claimant having been misappropriated from it by the defendant. The court was not prepared to close off the possibility that knowledge of someone in the firm might mean that the firm could not qualify as a bona fide purchaser without notice once all the facts emerged after the defendant's trial[2], so that the claimant might be able to recover the payments made for legal expenses.

1   [1998] 2 All ER 230, [1998] 1 WLR 435.
2   Doherty, the Bank's Chief Lending Officer, subsequently pleaded guilty and was jailed for five years: the court's ruling meant that solicitors faced the risk of having to repay fees received out of the defendant's account, so working for nothing.

Notice of adverse claim

57.7 In *Carl-Zeiss-Stiftung v Herbert Smith & Co (a firm) (No 2)*[1] the Court of Appeal held that knowledge of a claim being made against a solicitor's client by the other party to the action (in which the solicitor represented the client) was not sufficient to amount to notice of a trust (the East German plaintiff company claiming that the assets of the West German defendant company were held on trust for it) and of misapplication of trust moneys by the client so as to make the solicitor constructive trustee of the moneys for the other party. The solicitor was a bona fide purchaser without notice. Significantly, the claim was a strongly disputed one involving unsolved questions of fact and difficult questions of German and of English law so that it was impossible for the solicitor to know whether or not the claim was well-founded.

1   [1969] 2 Ch 276, [1969] 2 All ER 367, CA but cf *Guardian Trust and Executors Co of New Zealand Ltd v Public Trustee of New Zealand* [1942] AC 115 at 125, per Lord Romer (executor with notice from next-of-kin that they intended to challenge the will was held personally liable for the amount of legacies paid thereafter when the challenge succeeded).

57.8 In the commercial context (other than the purchase of land) it seems[1] that a purchaser of property will not have notice that it is trust property unless he has actual knowledge or deliberately turned a blind eye so as to avoid actual knowledge or deliberately or recklessly failed to make the inquiries an honest reasonable man would have made due to the circumstances appearing suspicious to him, such latter types of knowledge being regarded in shorthand as 'Nelsonian' and 'naughty' knowledge respectively. A person who with actual, Nelsonian or naughty knowledge thereby dishonestly assists in a breach of fiduciary duty is personally liable to account to those suffering loss thereby[2].

1 *Polly Peck International plc v Nadir (No 2)* [1992] 4 All ER 769.
2 See Article 100.

ARTICLE 58
DUTY OF TRUSTEE TO ACT GRATUITOUSLY UNLESS OTHERWISE AUTHORISED, AS IS USUAL NOWADAYS

58.1

A trustee, other than the Public Trustee[1] or a custodian trustee[2], or an independent trustee of a pension scheme[3] or a trust corporation[4], A has no right to charge for his time and trouble[5] except:

(a)   where the settlement so provides[6];

(b)   where he acts in a professional capacity and each other trustee has agreed in writing that he may be remunerated[7];

(c)   where he has entered into a legally binding agreement with the beneficiaries being of full age and capacity who have freely and without unfair pressure entered into the agreement[8];

(d)   where the trustee is a solicitor authorised under the exceptional rule in *Cradock v Piper*[9];

(e)   where the court has authorised payment of remuneration under its inherent jurisdiction;

(f)   where the trust property is abroad, and it is the custom of the local courts to allow remuneration[10].

1   By s 7 of the Public Trustee Act 1906, the Public Trustee is authorised to charge fees to be fixed by the Treasury with the sanction of the Lord Chancellor.
2   A body appointed to be a custodian trustee may charge fees not exceeding those charged by the Public Trustee; see paras 58.32, 77.8 and 79.2 below.
3   On insolvency of the employer company, an independent trustee of the pension scheme has to be appointed: he is entitled to payment out of the Scheme's resources for his reasonable fees and expenses in priority to all other claimants: Pensions Act 1995, s 20.
4   TA 2000, s 29(1) where no express provision in the trust instrument.
5   *Robinson v Pett* (1734) 3 P Wms 249, 2 White & Tud LC 605; *Barrett v Hartley* (1866) LR 2 Eq 789.
6   *Robinson v Pett* (1734) 3 P Wms 249; *Webb v Earl of Shaftesbury* (1802) 7 Ves 480; *Willis v Kibble* (1839) 1 Beav 559. Section 23 of TA 1925, although allowing trustees to employ and pay agents probably did not authorise the employment and payment of one of themselves, but section 12(1) of TA 2000 now does.
7   TA 2000, s 29(2).
8   TA 2000, s 29(2).
9   *Re Sherwood* (1840) 3 Beav 338: only those beneficiaries who are party to the contract have to provide the remuneration.
10 *Chambers v Goldwin* (1804) 9 Ves 254; cf *Re Northcote's Will Trusts* [1949] 1 All ER 442.

Basis of the rule

58.2 While a trustee has always been entitled to be indemnified against costs and expenses properly incurred by him as trustee, he has had to perform his office gratuitously for, otherwise 'the trust estate might be loaded and made of little value'[1], his self interest in doing as much remunerated work as possible prevailing over his fiduciary duty with undivided loyalty to further the interests of the beneficiaries, unless the trust instrument authorised such conflict and provided openly for payment of remuneration as an incident[2] of the office.

1   *Robinson v Pett* (1734) 3 P Wms 249 at 251.
2   *Galmerrow Securities Ltd v National Westminster Bank plc* [2002] WTLR 125 at 156.

Charging may be authorised by the settlement

58.3 If, however, the settlement provides that the trustee *may* charge, he will be allowed to do so; but charging clauses were strictly construed[1] before the Trustee Act 2000. Thus, if a solicitor-trustee was authorised to make 'professional charges'[2] (even where the words 'for his time and trouble' are added[3]), he was not allowed to charge for time and trouble expended otherwise than in his position as solicitor. On the other hand, where a will authorised any trustee thereof who may be a solicitor to make:

'the usual professional, *or other proper and reasonable charges*, for all business done and time expended in relation to the trusts of the will, *whether such business is usually within the business of a solicitor or not*',

the taxing master had power to allow to a solicitor-trustee the proper charges for business not strictly of a professional nature transacted by him in relation to the trust estate[4], although not for work altogether outside his professional vocations[5]. Thus, a well-drafted clause needed to authorise a professional trustee to charge for services which a layman could do personally.

1   *Re Gee* [1948] Ch 284, [1948] 1 All ER 498; *Mackie v BCB Trust Co Ltd* [2005] WTLR 1253, Sup Ct Bermuda.
2   *Harbin v Darby* (1860) 28 Beav 325; *Re Chapple* (1884) 27 Ch D 584.
3   *Re Chalinder and Herington* [1907] 1 Ch 58.
4   *Re Ames* (1883) 25 Ch D 72. Where the trust was created by will, the solicitor's charges in such cases were considered to be general legacies for purposes of legacy duty (*Re Thorley* [1891] 2 Ch 613), and for purposes of abatement (*Re Brown* [1918] WN 118), and for him losing the legacy if he or his spouse attested the will (*Re Pooley* (1888) 40 Ch D 1) (though a solicitor who attested the will might take advantage of a charging clause if he was not appointed a trustee until after the testator's death: *Re Royce's Will Trusts* [1959] Ch 626, [1959] 3 All ER 278, CA). He could not charge at all if the estate was insolvent (*Re White* [1898] 2 Ch 217, CA) or if the estate had been exhausted by specific legacy. However, the charges were taxable as income: *Dale v IRC* [1954] AC 11, HL.
5   *Clarkson v Robinson* [1900] 2 Ch 722. If a clause were to allow a trustee to charge for services which a layman can do personally then this had to be explained to the settlor or testator: *Re Orwell's Will Trusts* [1982] 3 All ER 177 at 179.

58.4 It has been held in Guernsey that a trustee with the benefit of a trustee remuneration clause could not charge remuneration for the period between the date on which it was removed from office by the protector and (there

58.4 *The trustee's duties*

being a dispute about the validity of the removal) the date more than two years later on which it finally handed over the trust assets to its successor[1].

[1]   *Virani v Guernsey International Trustees Ltd* [2004] WTLR 1035, R Ct Guernsey (Patrick Talbot QC, Lieutenant Bailiff).

58.5 Now, by s 28 of the Trustee Act 2000, if there is a provision in the trust instrument entitling a trustee who is 'acting in a professional capacity' or is a trust corporation to receive payment out of trust funds in respect of services provided to, or on behalf of, the trust, such provision extends to services even if they are services capable of being provided by a 'lay trustee'[1]. However, this only applies to a trustee of a charitable trust[2], if a trust corporation or an individual trustee who is not a sole trustee and who has the agreement of a majority of the other trustees. Significantly, payment for such trustee services is now not regarded as a gift[3] but as remuneration for the purposes of the Wills Act 1837 and the Administration of Estates Act 1925[4].

[1]   Unless the trust instrument makes inconsistent provision, eg my trustees shall only charge for professional services that a layman could not provide: TA 2000, s 28(1).
[2]   TA 2000, s 28(3).
[3]   See note 1241 above.
[4]   TA 2000, s 28(4).

58.6 A 'lay trustee' is someone who is neither a trust corporation nor a person acting in a professional capacity[1]. A trustee 'acts in a professional capacity' if he acts in the course of a profession or business which consists of, or includes, the provision of services in connecction with (a) the management or administration of trusts generally or a particular kind of trust or (b) any particular aspect of the management or administration of trusts generally or a particular kind of trust and if the services he provides fall within that description[2]. It seems that a Schedule D Case I or II taxable trade or profession is required but that a corporation, not being a trust corporation could qualify as a professional trust services provider[3], though it is likely that an express clause entitling any corporation to charge its scale fees from time to time[4] will be regarded as inconsistent with s 28 if in some special circumstance it sought to charge additional fees under s 28.

[1]   TA 2000, s 28(6).
[2]   TA 2000, s 28(5).
[3]   TA 2000, s 29(2) and 'person' in Interpretation Act 1978, Sch 1.
[4]   Express provision had to be made for standard scale fees as opposed to fees from time to time relating to specific services: *Re Cooper* (1939) 160 LT 453.

Cradock v Piper exception where solicitor acts for himself and another

58.7 There is a curious exception to the old rule that a solicitor-trustee cannot, in the absence of an enabling clause, charge profit costs. This exception (known as the rule in *Cradock v Piper*[1]) has been enunciated in the following terms:

> 'Where there is work done *in a suit*, not on behalf of the trustee, who is a solicitor alone, but on behalf of himself and a co-trustee, the rule will not prevent the solicitor or his firm from receiving the usual costs, if the costs of

appearing for and acting for the two have not increased the expense; that is to say, if the trustee himself has not added to the expense which would have been incurred if he or his firm had appeared only for his co-trustee'[2].

1   (1850) 1 Mac & G 664.
2   Per Cotton LJ in *Re Corsellis* (1887) 34 Ch D 675; and see to same effect *Re Barber* (1886) 34 Ch D 77.

58.8 This exception is, however, limited to the costs incurred in respect of business done in an *action or matter*, and does not apply to business done out of court[1].

1   *Stocken v Dawson* (1843) 6 Beav 371; *Burden v Burden* (1813) 1 Ves & B 170.

Trustee Act 2000, s 29 authorisation

58.9 In the absence of any provision about remuneration in legislation or in the trust instrument (which should cover a charging clause for persons other than the settlor or his spouse), not only is as trust corporation (not being trustee of a charitable trust) entitled to receive remuneration out of trust funds for trust services[1], but also any trustee who acts in a professional capacity, but is not a trust corporation, a trustee of a charitable trust or a sole trustee, if each other trustee has agreed in writing to his being remunerated for his trust services[2]. It matters not that the trust services are capable of being provided by a lay trustee[3].

1   TA 2000, s 29(1).
2   TA 2000, s 29(2). For 'in a professional capacity' see s 28(5) discussed in the preceding paragraph.
3   TA 2000, s 29(4).

58.10 Reasonable remuneration[1] is such remuneration as is reasonable in the circumstances for provision of the trust services, and in relation to the services of a trust corporation that is an authorised institution under the Banking Act 1987 providing trust services in that capacity, the institution's reasonable charges for such services.

1   TA 2000, s 29(3).

58.11 Those in the invidious position of having to agree to their co-trustee being remunerated and then hoping such co-trustee will agree to themselves being remunerated have been placed in that position by the Trustee Act. Thus merely entering into the agreement is not in itself impeachable at one extreme[1] while, at the other extreme, the agreements would be impeachable if entered into under a reciprocal arrangement whereby each agrees to the other's remuneration only on the basis that they will agree to his remuneration[2]. However, if they consider what is in the best interests of the beneficiaries, taking account of the cost of employing delegates to act on behalf of the trustees if they are unpaid and so desire to minimise their own involvement, and the possibility of the trustees resigning and replacing themselves with a trust corporation with its scale fees and difficulties in establishing close ties with the beneficiaries for some time, then there should be no problems. And this should be so even if there are only two trustees who are partners in the same firm of solicitors, where there is a home made will trust appointing them trustees or appointing lay trustees who have appointed the two partners as trustees to replace themselves. Indeed, in the latter case it seems acceptable for the professional trustees to make it plain that they will not accept appointment unless remuneration is agreed at the time of appointment, so they know where they stand. Thus the appointing lay trustees continue as trustees to appoint one professional trustee agreeing in the deed of appointment to remuneration, and, then, the three trustees appoint the other professional trustee as an additional trustee agreeing in the deed of appointment to remuneration before the two lay trustees retire.

1   *Edge v Pensions Ombudsman* [2000] Ch 602, CA.
2   A fraud on the power.

58.12 Once remuneration has been authorised under s 29(2), as a result of each of the other trustees having agreed in writing to a trustee, T, being remunerated for his services, that should be T's position for the duration of his trusteeship, irrespective of one or more of the trustees being replaced by other persons as trustees. On this basis T, having once been duly authorised to receive remuneration, one might think he should continue to be so authorised even if subsequently becoming a sole trustee. However, it may be[1] that it is only so long as T is not a sole trustee that T can continue to charge remuneration. In that case T will need to execute a deed of appointment appointing X to act in a professional capacity and to be remunerated therefor. No doubt, taking account of the trust's history, X will shortly agree in writing that T may be remunerated for trust services[2]. If the latter strict construction be correct, then statute has placed T in an invidious position having taken office believing thereafter he would be entitled to remuneration, so as probably implicitly authorising him to take account of his self-interest when looking to appoint a new trustee. To avoid such problems T should ensure that once the number of trustees falls to two then a third trustee is appointed, although the downside will be the extra costs remunerating three trustees and obtaining unanimity for decisions. Taking account of these considerations, it is hoped the courts will construe s 29(2) so that 'once duly authorised thereafter duly authorised'. After all, a beneficiary is entitled to challenge the charges made by a professional trustee[3].

1   TA 2000, s 29(2)(b) applying throughout, not just at the time of the remuneration agreement.
2   This should be capable of authorising remuneration retrospectively for the period when T was sole trustee: *Messeena v Carr* (1870) LR 9 Eq 260; *Libby v Kennedy* (1998) OPLR 213.
3   *Re Fish* [1893] 2 Ch 413, CA; *Re Wells* [1962] 2 All ER 826, 1 WLR 397, [1962]; the trustee must account for the amount overcharged.

The court's inherent jurisdiction

58.13 Although much less likely to be needed after the Trustee Act 2000, the court has inherent jurisdiction to authorise prospectively or retrospectively remuneration or extra remuneration for an express or constructive trustee but the jurisdiction 'should be exercised only sparingly and in exceptional cases'[1], eg where the execution of the trust is more than ordinarily burdensome and especially beneficial for the trust beneficiaries[2] or where inflation has had disastrous consequences on fixed remuneration[3].

1   Per Upjohn J in *Re Worthington* [1954] 1 All ER 677, [1954] 1 WLR 526. Further, see *Re Duke of Norfolk's Settlement Trusts* [1982] Ch 61, [1981] 3 All ER 220, CA; *Marshall v Holloway* (1820) 2 Swan 432; *Re Freeman* (1887) 37 Ch D 148; *Re Masters* [1953] 1 All ER 19, [1953] 1 WLR 81.
2   *Boardman v Phipps* [1967] 2 AC 46, [1966] 3 All ER 721; *Re Duke of Norfolk's Settlement Trusts* [1982] Ch 61, [1981] 3 All ER 220, CA; *John v James* [1986] STC 352 at 358.
3   *Re Barbour's Settlement* [1974] 1 All ER 1188 at 1192.

58.14 Where the jurisdiction is invoked it should be plainly sought by direct application: there should certainly not be inserted in the terms of a compromise a remuneration provision which has nothing to do with the matter in dispute and which is directly for the trustee's benefit[1].

1   *Re Barbour's Settlement* [1974] 1 All ER 1188; *Re Codd* [1975] 2 All ER 1051n, [1975] 1 WLR 1139.

58.15 In *Re Duke of Norfolk's Settlement Trusts*[1] the Court of Appeal in reserved judgments reversed Walton J[2] in part and clarified the law. There was no appeal against the extra remuneration which Walton J had authorised for exceptionally burdensome work in connection with the development of Arundel Court in The Strand and which was entirely outside anything which could reasonably have been foreseen when the trustees accepted office.

1   [1982] Ch 61, [1981] 3 All ER 220, CA. Applied in *Re Drexel Burnham Lambert's Pension Plan* [1995] 1 WLR 32.
2   [1979] Ch 37, [1978] 3 All ER 907.

58.16 However, Walton J had held that the court had no general inherent jurisdiction to authorise for the future any general increase in the trustee company's remuneration, eg to increase the management fee to 40p from 10p per £100 on the aggregate amount of the market values of the trust property. The Court of Appeal[1] held that:

> 'the court has an inherent jurisdiction to authorise the payment of trustees and that jurisdiction extends to increasing the remuneration authorised by the trust instrument. In exercising that jurisdiction the court has to balance two influences which are to some extent in conflict. The first is that the office of trustee is, as such, gratuitious; the court will accordingly be careful to protect the interests of the beneficiaries against claims by the trustees. The second is that it is of great importance to the beneficiaries that the trust should be well administered. If, therefore, the court concludes, having regard to the nature of the trust, to the experience and skill of a trustee and to the amounts which he seeks to charge when compared with what other trustees might require to be paid for their services and to all the other circumstances of the case, that it would be in the best interests of the beneficiaries to increase the remuneration, then the court may properly do so.'

1   [1982] Ch 61 at 79, [1981] 3 All ER 220 at 230, CA. The consent of beneficiaries is not required as under the Variation of Trusts Act 1958, but their objections will be considered, eg *Polly Peck International plc v Henry* [1999] 1 BCLC 407.

58.17 The case was then remitted to the Chancery Division for consideration to be given to the exercise of the jurisdiction.

58.18 Unfortunately, the Court of Appeal did not mention *Re Keeler's Settlement Trusts*[1], where Goulding J had followed Walton J in *Re Duke of Norfolk's Settlement Trusts,* but *Re Keeler's Settlement Trusts* can no longer be authoritative so far as regards future remuneration of trustees.

[1]   [1981] Ch 156, [1981] 1 All ER 888.

58.19 Goulding J was also asked to allow the trustees to retain past remuneration earned in directorships to which they had been elected by virtue of trust shareholdings. He held that they could only retain the fees if 'it is plainly expedient in the interests of the trust for the directorship in question to be held by a trustee' as was the case, but that a director-trustee can only 'be allowed to retain reasonable remuneration for effort and skill applied by him in performing the duties of the directorship *over and above* the effort and skill ordinarily required for a director appointed to represent the interests of a substantial shareholder. The latter is something that a prudent man of business would in general undertake in the management of his own investments, and so is in general an exertion reasonably expected of a trustee'[1]. Since there was no evidence of the scale or intensity of the director-trustees' activities their claim was rejected, but an inquiry was directed to ascertain what effort and skill had been applied over and above the effort and skill ordinarily required.

[1]   [1981] Ch 156 at 162, [1981] 1 All ER 888 at 893.

58.20 The companies were the settlor's family companies and, as he swore in an affidavit, he had envisaged that his two sons would become trustees and directors after acquiring the necessary experience in the family business. Clause 4 of the Settlement, indeed, authorised the transfer of shares into the name of a trustee to enable him to have sufficient qualifying shares to be eligible for a directorship 'if at the request of the Trustees appointed or to be appointed as director of any Company in which the Trustees have an interest'.

58.21 On the authority of *Re Llewellin's Will Trust*[1] (not cited in *Re Keeler's Settlement Trusts*) it is unfortunate that the above clause was not treated as authorising the appointment of a trustee to a remunerated office and thus retention of such remuneration. In *Re Llewellin's Will Trusts* a will authorised the trustees 'to make arrangements with the … company … for the appointment of my said trustees or either of them or any other person as director or managing director of the said company'. Jenkins J, observing that the company articles provided for remunerating directors, remarked that 'the testator has expressly empowered his trustees to make arrangements for the appointment of themselves to offices which can fairly be described as remunerated' and so held that the trustees could retain their directors' fees even though 'the trustees are in the invidious position of fixing their own remuneration, being completely in control of the company … but that is the result which must inevitably ensue'[2].

1 [1949] Ch 225, [1949] 1 All ER 487.
2 [1949] Ch 225 at 229, [1949] 1 All ER 487 at 489. Further see liberal tendencies in
Sargeant v National Westminister Bank (1990) 61 P & CR 518 at 523 and *Re Drexel
Burnham Lambert's Pension Plan* [1995] 1 WLR 32.

58.22 In *Foster v Spencer*[1] the judge awarded remuneration for past services
to trustees of a decaying cricket ground ultimately sold by them with planning
permission for over £900,000. The services they rendered were wholly outside
their contemplation when appointed as unpaid trustees and refusal of remuneration would lead to unjust enrichment of the beneficiaries at their expense.
The court was happy with the retrospective application because the true
extent of the trustees' tasks and services could not be known until it was
possible to market and sell the land well, while no money was available for
paying remuneration for a long time. Indeed, interest was awarded at 8%
from the time that funds were available to pay remuneration[2].

1 [1996] 2 All ER 672.
2 No interest, however, was allowed in respect of expenses properly incurred by the trustees.

58.23 In offshore trust jurisdictions the courts are well-used to entertaining
applications for trustee remuneration. In Jersey, for example, the Royal Court
has several times in recent years authorised a professional trustee to charge
remuneration where no or no sufficient provision is made for this in the terms
of the trust, on the basis that

> 'It would be unreasonable and unrealistic to expect a professional trustee to
> undertake the responsibilities of administering a trust without any remunera-
> tion. It is in the interests of the beneficiaries that the trust should be managed
> professionally by those with the appropriate skills ...'[1]

1 *Rathbone Trust Co (Jersey) Ltd v Kane* [2004] JRC 041, at para 28; see also *Re RF
Norman Settlement,*(14 March 2002, unreported), R Ct Jersey; *HSBC Trustees (CI) Ltd v
Rearden* [2005] JRC 130, R Ct Jersey.

58.24 Similar examples can be found in Guernsey[1].

1 Eg *Re H Sossen 1969 Settlement,* (28 May 2004, unreported) , R Ct Guernsey (extending
to remuneration for past services).

Remuneration where breach of fiduciary duty

58.25 In *Boardman v Phipps*[1] the House of Lords upheld the trial judge's
allowance of generous remuneration to the solicitor to the trustees who had
been guilty of an innocent breach of trust and whose exceptional abilities had
proved to be of exceptional benefit to the trust for whom the solicitor held his
profits on constructive trust. In *O'Sullivan v Management Agency and
Music Ltd*[2] Fox LJ stated:

> 'A hard and fast rule that the beneficiary can demand the whole profit without
> an allowance for the work without which it could not have been created is
> unduly severe. Nor do I think that the principle is only applicable in cases
> where the personal conduct of the fiduciary cannot be criticised. The justice of
> the individual case must be considered on the facts of that case. Accordingly,

where there has been dishonesty or surreptitious dealing or other improper conduct then it might be appropriate to refuse relief; but that will depend on the circumstances.'

1   [1967] 2 AC 46.
2   [1985] QB 428 at 468 endorsed in *Cheese v Thomas* [1994] 1 All ER 35 at 43, CA; see also *Warman International Ltd v Dwyer* (1995) 182 CLR 544.

58.26 Thus, the Court of Appeal held that a fiduciary agent whose contract with his performer was set aside for undue influence was entitled to remuneration and a reasonable sum by way of profit because of a significant contribution to the performer's success[1]. In *Re Berkeley Applegate Ltd*[2] it was stated:

'The authorities establish a general principle that where a person seeks to enforce a claim to an equitable interest in property, the court has a discretion to require as a condition of giving effect to that equitable interest that an allowance be made for costs incurred and for skill and labour expended in connection with the administration of the property. It is a discretion which will be sparingly exercised; but factors which will operate in favour ... include the fact that if the work had not been done ... it would have had to be done either by the person entitled to the equitable interest or by a receiver appointed by the court whose fees would have been borne by the trust property, and the fact that the work has been of substantial benefit to the trust property ... '

1   See also *John v James* [1986] STC 352 at 358.
2   [1988] 3 All ER 71 at 83.

58.27 Thus, where a company went into liquidation and held mortgage loans and funds on trust for investors (who had advanced funds to be invested in mortgages) and it was likely that the costs incurred and skill and labour expended by the liquidator in administering the trust property would greatly exceed the company's free assets, the court declared that the liquidator would be entitled to be paid his costs and remuneration out of the trust property to the extent that the company's free assets, were insufficient.

58.28 In *Guinness plc v Saunders*[1] Lord Goff made the general point that the exercise of the jurisdiction should be 'restricted to those cases where it cannot have the effect of encouraging trustees in any way to put themselves in a position where their interests conflict with their duties as trustees.' However, these dicta seem too sweeping in the light of the authorities. In *Guinness* a director's claim to reasonable equitable remuneration for work done without an intra vires authorisation from the committee of directors failed, the court not being entitled to usurp the functions conferred on the directors by the company's articles, especially when it still remained open to the company to award the director appropriate remuneration.

1   [1990] 2 AC 663 at 701, [1990] 1 All ER 652 at 667, HL.

58.29 In *Badfinger Music v Evans*[1] the court considered that Lord Goff's dicta were too strict, the existence or absence of a conflict of interest being an important consideration but not the only factor to be taken into account. Indeed, reasonable remuneration could be calculated by reference to a percentage of profits in a case where a flat fee of similar amount (or even larger amount) could have been recoverable.

¹ [2001] WTLR 1: where the claimant's conduct was open to serious criticism though not dishonest, he was entitled to a flat fee, though a fiduciary, and his sound-engineer was entitled to a percentage of the profits.

58.30 In *Chirnside v Fay*¹ Elias CJ took the traditonal English approach to an allowance claimed by a joint venturer who had dishonestly diverted from his co-venturer a profitable venture, so the allowance was denied. However, the rest of the New Zealand Supreme court took a liberal approach in view of the fact that the defendant was not a trustee but a commercial joint venturer, a lesser fiduciary relationship,and if things had duly gone ahead the claimant would have permitted the defendant an allowance.

¹ [2006] NZSC 68.

The court's statutory jurisdiction

58.31 Where the court appoints a corporation, other than the Public Trustee, to be a trustee it is empowered by s 42 of the Trustee Act, 1925, to authorise such remuneration for its services as the court thinks fit¹. The court may also authorise remuneration for a person whom it appoints as a judicial trustee under the Judicial Trustees Act 1896, s 1(5).

¹ *Re Young* (1934) 103 LJP 75; *Re Masters* [1953] 1 All ER 19, [1953] 1 WLR 81 (both cases where remuneration of an administrator was authorised); and see *Hearn v Morgan* [1945] 2 All ER 480 at 481, where the relevant terms of the orders of the court are set out in the case stated; the decision is reported on a question of liability to income tax.

The Public Trustee and custodian trustees

58.32 The Public Trustee is allowed to charge such fees as may be fixed by the Treasury¹. A custodian trustee is allowed to charge such fees as the Public Trustee could charge for acting as custodian trustee². A trust corporation could not be appointed custodian trustee and managing trustee so as to enable it to charge fees³, but it can now charge under s 29(1) of the Trustee Act 2000 if not trustee of a charitable trust and there is no charging clause in the trust instrument.

¹ Public Trustee Act 1906, s 9, as amended by the Administration of Justice Act 1965, s 2; Public Trustee (Fees) Act 1957 and orders made thereunder.
² Public Trustee Act 1906, s 4.
³ *Arning v James* [1936] Ch 158; *Forster v Williams Deacon's Bank Ltd* [1935] Ch 359.

Agreement with beneficiaries

58.33 A trustee is entitled to remuneration if the beneficiaries are all of full age and capacity and between them absolutely entitled to the settled property and so agree¹, so long as undue influence was not exercised by him². If one beneficiary (eg the life tenant) agrees that the trustee may be paid out of his interest then that beneficiary will be bound and will not be able to sue for breach of trust for past payments and, if contractually bound, will be unable to revoke his agreement.

1   It seems that the agreement (unless in a deed) needs to be concluded before the trustee accepts office (as indicated by *Re Sherwood* (1840) 3 Beav 338 and *Douglas v Archbutt* (1858) 2 De G & J 148) since once the trustee has accepted office he is already under a duty to the beneficiaries to act gratuitously so that no consideration exists for a contractually binding agreement. However, the acquiescence of a beneficiary prevents a beneficiary from suing for breach of trust for past payments of remuneration.
2   *Ayliffe v Murray* (1740) 2 Atk 58.

Challenging trustee's fees

58.34 Remuneration chargeable under s 29 of the Trustee Act 2000 is such remuneration as is reasonable in the circumstances[1], so that the beneficiaries may make the trustee account for the amount by which his remuneration exceeds that which is reasonable in all the circumstances. Where there is an express clause in the trust instrument authorising the trustee to charge for his services as trustee, the beneficiaries can also seek to make the trustee account for the amount by which his remuneration exceeds what is reasonable for him to charge in all the circumstances[2].

1   TA 2000, s 29(2).
2   *Re Fish* [1893] 2 Ch 413, although Lindley LJ contemplated that the beneficiaries' accounting rights could be ousted by a provision in the trust instrument authorising a co-trustee's bona fide approval of his co-trustee's account to bind the beneficiaries: *Re Wells* [1962] 2 All ER 826, [1962] 1 WLR 874.

ARTICLE 59
DUTY OF TRUSTEE NOT TO TRAFFIC WITH OR OTHERWISE PROFIT BY TRUST PROPERTY NOR TO CAUSE LOSS FROM A CONFLICT BETWEEN HIS FIDUCIARY DUTY AND HIS SELF-INTEREST

59.1

(1)   A trustee must not use or deal with trust property or exploit his position for his own private advantage for he will be strictly liable to account for his profits of which he will be constructive trustee[1] and he will also be personally accountable for losses arising where there is a real sensible possibility of a conflict between his fiduciary duty and his self-interest[2].

(2)   A disposition of trust property to a trustee is automatically voidable by a beneficiary 'ex debito justitiae', however fair the transaction may be (the 'self-dealing' rule) unless:

   (a)   under an express or necessarily implied[3] power in the settlement; or
   (b)   by leave of a competent court; or
   (c)   under a contract or option made before the fiduciary relationship arose[4]; or

(d)   carried out under section 68 of the Settled Land Act 1925 or section 39 of the Pensions Act 1995; or

(e)   the beneficiary acquiesced in the transaction; or

(f)   exceptional circumstances exist and it is proved by the party seeking to uphold the transaction that it was a fair and reasonable one not vitiated by any conflicting interest or duty[5].

(3)   A trustee may purchase, or accept a mortgage of, the equitable interest of a beneficiary in the trust property[6], but, if the transaction be impeached, it is incumbent on the trustee to prove[7] affirmatively and conclusively (the 'fair-dealing' rule):

(a)   that he and the beneficiary were at arm's length and that no confidence was reposed in him;

(b)   that the transaction was for the advantage of the beneficiary; and

(c)   that full information was given to the beneficiary of the value of the property, of the nature of his interest therein and of the circumstances of the transaction[8].

(4)   A trustee cannot qualify himself to become a purchaser by retiring from the trusteeship with that view[9].

[1] *A-G for Hong Kong v Reid* [1994] 1 AC 324, PC; *Webb v Earl of Shaftesbury* (1802) 7 Ves 480; *Ex p Lacey* (1802) 6 Ves 625; and see *Re Imperial Land Co of Marseilles* (1877) 4 Ch D 566; *Aberdeen Town Council v Aberdeen University* (1877) 2 App Cas 544; and *Rochefoucauld v Boustead* [1898] 1 Ch 550. Cf also *Brown v IRC* [1965] AC 244, [1964] 3 All ER 119, HL (but see, now, Solicitors' Accounts Rules 1991). This has been dealt with in Article 33, above.

[2] *Clark Boyce v Mouat* [1994] 1 AC 428; *Nocton v Lord Ashburton* [1914] AC 932; *Canson Enterprises Ltd v Boughton & Co* (1991) 85 DLR (4th) 129; *Glennie v McDongall & Lowans Holdings Ltd* [1935] 2 DLR 561 at 579; *Swindle v Harrison* [1997] 4 All ER 705, CA; *Bristol and West Building Society v Mothew* [1998] Ch 1; *Hodgkinson v Simms* [1994] 3 SCR 377, (1994) 117 DLR (4th) 161.

[3] *Sargeant v National Westminister Bank plc* (1991) 61 P & CR 518, CA; *Edge v Pensions Ombudsman* [2000] Ch 602, CA.

[4] *Re Mulholland's Will Trust* [1949] 1 All ER 460.

[5] *Holder v Holder* [1968] Ch 353.

[6] *Gibson v Jeyes* (1801) 6 Ves 266; *Phipps v Lovegrove* (1873) LR 16 Eq 80; *Newman v Newman* (1885) 28 Ch D 674.

[7] See penultimate note and also *Randall v Errington* (1805) 10 Ves 423; *Coles v Trecothick* (1804) 9 Ves 234.

[8] See *Chillingworth v Chambers* [1896] 1 Ch 685.

[9] *Ex p James* (1803) 8 Ves 337; *Spring v Pride* (1864) 4 De GJ & Sm 395. But cf *Re Boles and British Land Co's Contract* [1902] 1 Ch 244.

Paragraph 1

59.2 These matters have already been fully dealt with in Article 33 (concerned with constructive trusts of profits) to which reference should be made. If losses arise instead of profits then, assuming that no defence is available that would have been available if a profit had been made, the trustee or fiduciary is personally accountable for such loss. It is noteworthy that if non-disclosure of material facts is at the heart of the breach of fiduciary duty the defendant 'cannot be heard to maintain that disclosure would not have altered the decision to proceed with the transaction, because the [claimant's] action would be surely determined by some other factor ... Once the court has determined that the non-disclosed facts were material, speculation as to what course the [claimant], on disclosure, would have taken is not relevant'[1]. However, these remarks have been restricted[2] to a claim to rescind the transaction, although it may well be that if the defendant fiduciary is being sued for an account or equitable compensation, then misrepresentation or non-disclosure by him in breach of his duty of undivided loyalty should place the onus of proof upon him to prove that the losses would have occurred even if there had been no such breach[3], particularly if the fiduciary's breach was fraudulent[4].

[1] *Brickenden v London Loan & Savings Co* [1934] 3 DLR 465 at 469, PC; *Farrington v Rowe McBride & Partners* [1985] 1 NZLR 83 at 99. Misrepresentations are *a fortiori* non-disclosures.

[2] *Swindle v Harrison* [1997] 4 All ER 705 at 726, per Hobhouse LJ.

[3] *Bank of New Zealand v New Zealand Guardian Trust Co* [1999] 1 NZLR 664 at 687, CA.

[4] *Swindle v Harrison* [1997] 4 All ER 705 at 716–717, per Evans LJ, but rejected by Tuckey LJ in *Collins v Brebner* [2000] Lloyd's Rep PN 587, CA, where the defendant's ultimate obtaining of a 50% shareholding in the specified company with the claimant's £524,000 held on trust for the claimant was held to prevent the defrauded claimant from recovering for further losses, unless proved to result from the defendant's fraud, following *Target Holdings v Redferns* [1996] AC 421. It may be that where a commercial bare trust arises incidentally in the course of a contractual relationship with a fiduciary element as in the solicitor-client relationship, contractual principles should prevail, (implicitly ousting equitable principles).

59.3 However, in the case of a trustee, as opposed to a lesser fiduciary relationship, who acts where there is a conflict of interest, there is much to be said for the trustee to be strictly liable to a substitutive performance claim on the basis he acted in wholly unauthorised fashion in his own personal interest, not acting (as agreed) in the exclusive furtherance of his beneficiaries' best interests. Thus, he is liable for consequential losses not caused by his act eg a market crash[1].

[1] As was the defendant portfolio manager in *Hodgkinson v Simms* (1994) 117 DLR (4th) 161.

Paragraph 2

The self-dealing rule

59.4 As Megarry V-C said in a reserved judgment in *Tito v Waddell (No 2)*[1]:

'The self-dealing rule is (to put it very shortly) that if a trustee sells the trust property to himself the sale is voidable by any beneficiary ex debito justitiae, however fair the transaction'.

[1] *Tito v Waddell (No 2)* [1977] 3 All ER 129 at 241, per Megarry V-C.

59.5 Vinelott J has stated[1]:

'It is clear that the self-dealing rule is an application of the wider principle that a man must not put himself in a position where duty and interest conflict or where his duty to one conflicts with his duty to another.'

¹ *Re Thompson's Settlement* [1985] 2 All ER 720 at 730 and *Movitex Ltd v Bulfield* [1988] BCLC 104 at 117.

59.6 Until *Holder v Holder*[1] the rule was considered to stand much more upon general principle than upon the circumstances of any individual case. It rested upon this: that 'the purchase is not permitted in any case, however honest the circumstances, the general interest of justice requiring it to be destroyed in every instance; because no court is equal to the examination and ascertainment of the truth'[2]. Consequently, under no circumstances could an active trustee, nor, indeed, a passive trustee *who had been* (at all events within a recent period) *an active one*, nor even a person who had been erroneously treated by all parties as a trustee[3] (ie a trustee de son tort), purchase trust property from himself or his colleagues, either directly, or through the intervention of a third party[4]. It mattered not that an independent third party fixed the purchase price.

[1] [1968] Ch 353, [1968] 1 All ER 665.
[2] Per Lord Eldon in *Ex p James* (1803) 8 Ves 337 at 345; and see *Beningfield v Baxter* (1886) 12 App Cas 167.
[3] *Plowright v Lambert* (1885) 52 LT 646. As to executor, see *Hall v Hallett* (1784) 1 Cox Eq Cas 134.
[4] *Campbell v Walker* (1800) 5 Ves 678; *Knight v Marjoribanks* (1849) 2 Mac & G 10; and see *Re Walters* [1954] Ch 653, [1954] 1 All ER 893. But in one case it was held that a trustee who had retired for upwards of twelve years was not precluded from purchasing part of the trust property (*Re Boles and British Land Co's Contract* [1902] 1 Ch 244).

59.7 Thus in *Wright v Morgan*[1] a testator left land on trust for sale with power to postpone sale for seven years and provided that it should be offered at a price to be fixed by valuers to one of his sons, A, who was one of the trustees. A assigned his right (which was treated as an option and not a right of pre-emption) to his brother, B, who was also one of the trustees but who, unlike A, was not authorised to purchase by the terms of the will. B arranged for the sale to himself, retired from the trusteeship and purchased at a price fixed by the valuers. The Privy Council set the purchase aside: after all, B was one of those responsible for determining when the land was to be sold and prices could fluctuate over the years.

[1] [1926] AC 788.

Exceptional circumstances

59.8 In *Holder v Holder*[1] the Court of Appeal refused to treat the rule as inflexible, not being impressed by Lord Eldon's view that no court is equal to the examination and ascertainment of the knowledge and intention of a trustee since the Court of Appeal considered that courts were daily engaged in ascertaining parties' knowledge and intentions. In the case a testator had appointed his widow, daughter and son to be his executors and trustees. The son took a very few minor incidental steps at the outset in connection with the administration of the estate but then took no further part. He executed a deed of renunciation of the executorship so only the widow and the daughter took out probate. The deed was ineffective owing to his technical intermeddling with the estate. The son had a tenancy of a farm comprised in his father's estate. The farm was offered for sale at auction subject to the son's tenancy and the son purchased the freehold reversion in the farm at well above the reserve price. The Court of Appeal refused to set aside the purchase on the application of a beneficiary under the will.

¹   [1968] Ch 353.

59.9 The purchase was not voidable due to the following special circumstances: the son had played no real part in the administration of the estate; there was, in fact, no conflict of duty and self-interest for the beneficiaries knew the son was a prospective purchaser and did not look to him to protect their interests; the son had taken no part in instructing the valuers or in the preparations for the auction sale and was not in the position of being both vendor and purchaser; any special knowledge which the son had was acquired by him as tenant of the farm and not as executor.

59.10 Subsequently, in *Hillsdown plc v Pensions Ombudsman*¹ Knox J refused to treat the self-dealing rule as inflexible where directors of limited companies dealing with each other are concerned, but held that the fact that negotiations have been conducted by persons one or more of whom had a conflict of duties places upon those seeking to uphold the transaction the onus of proving that it was, indeed, reasonable and proper on a full investigation of the facts.

¹   [1997] 1 All ER 862 at 895–896 two persons were directors of the relevant three companies, being the trustee of pension scheme A, the trustee of pension scheme B (to whom the pension funds of A were being transferred) and the employer.

59.11 A flexible approach was also taken in *Public Trustee v Cooper*¹ where an unconnected outsider had made a take-over offer for shares in a private company where a key share-holding was held on trust for company employees (largely opposed to the take-over) and one trustee had a substantial minority shareholding that he himself owned beneficially, while also being a trustee of a charitable trust with a minority shareholding (the charity being keen to accept the offer). Hart J held the self-dealing rule did not apply in respect of the trust for employees but the trustees thereof, if they wanted to be able to exercise their discretion without surrendering it to the court, had to discharge the onus of proving that the conflicting interest or duty had not operated in a vitiating way: the onus had been discharged.

¹   [2001] WTLR 901, especially at 933.

59.12 He stated¹:

'The beneficiary is entitled to the decision of all his trustees, but, at the same time, he is entitled to require that the decision is made independently of any private interest or competing duty of any of the trustees. Where a trustee has such a private interest or competing duty there are three possible ways in which the conflict can successfully be managed. One is for the trustee concerned to resign. This will not always provide a practical or sensible solution. The trustee concerned may represent an important source of information or advice to his co-trustees or have a significant relationship to some or all of the beneficiaries such that his departure as a trustee will be potentially harmful to the interests of the trust estate or its beneficiaries.

Secondly, the nature of the conflict may be so pervasive throughout the trustee body, that they, as a body, have no alternative but to surrender their discretion to the court.

Thirdly, the trustees may honestly and reasonably believe that, notwithstanding a conflict affecting one or more of their number, they are nevertheless able fairly and reasonably to take the decision. In this third case, it will usually be prudent, if time allows, for the trustees to allow their proposed exercise of discretion to be scrutinised in advance by the court in proceedings in which any opposing beneficial interests are properly represented, and for them not to proceed unless and until the court has authorised them to do so. If they do not do so, they run the risk of having to justify the exercise of their discretion in subsequent hostile litigation and then satisfy the court that their decision was not only one which any reasonable body of trustees might have taken but was also one that had not in fact been influenced by the conflict.'

¹ [2001] WTLR 901 at 933–934.

No need for self-dealing rule if only one party or transaction not genuine

59.13 T cannot contract with himself and so cannot purchase from himself or sell to himself¹, nor can he make a gift of a chattel to himself or grant a lease to himself², nor could he convey land to himself until statute permitted this³ (eg for an executor⁴ to transfer land to himself beneficially or as trustee). Thus, the purported transaction is of no effect.

¹ *Williams v Scott* [1900] AC 499; *Ellis v Kerr* [1910] 1 Ch 529; LPA 1925, s 82.
² *Rye v Rye* [1962] AC 496.
³ LPA 1925, s 72(4).
⁴ Administration of Estates Act 1925, s 36(4). Also see Law of Property Act 1925 s 72.

59.14 However, a trust instrument may authorise a bank trustee to deposit money with itself by way of unsecured loan, so that the beneficiaries' equitable proprietary interest in the deposited money becomes only a proprietary interest in the chose in action against the bank, which will be of little value if the bank becomes heavily insolvent¹. Similarly, if a trustee of four sub-trusts for four branches of the settlor's family has an express power to switch assets from one sub-trust to another for a compensating transfer of cash or other assets², and the trustee does so, this should be effective to move the equitable interests in assets 'xyz' of the beneficiaries of sub-trust 'X' to the beneficiaries in sub-trust 'Y', whose equitable interests in assets 'abc' pass to the 'X' beneficiaries. The 'X' and 'Y' beneficiaries now have different rights against the trustee. At law the legal title remains in the trustee, but in equity different beneficiaries have become interested in different assets. The position is analogous to that where a trustee exercises a power of appointment in favour of Z for life remainder to his children in relation to specific trust assets,

59.14 *The trustee's duties*

so that the default beneficiaries' rights in those assets pass to Z and his children, though the legal title remains with the trustee.

¹ *Space Investments Ltd v Canadian Imperial Bank of Commerce Trust Co (Bahamas) Ltd* [1986] 3 All ER 75, PC.
² Provision should be made either for an independent valuation or for the trustee's decision in good faith on the value to be treated as made by an expert and so be unchallengeable in the absence of dishonesty.

59.15 A sale or lease to a nominee does not breach the requirement for two parties to a transaction capable of overreaching the beneficiaries' interests[1].

¹ It is an unauthorised transaction, unless in a special case authorised, eg where T holds land for A absolutely and is authorised to grant a lease to A: *Ingram v IRC* [2000] 1 AC 293 at 305 and 310, HL, approving Millett LJ, below in the Court of Appeal, [1997] 4 All ER 395 at 426–427.

Sale to the wife of trustee

59.16 A sale to a trustee's wife is not automatically voidable but the circumstances will be closely examined[1]. After all,

'there are wives and wives. In one case the trustee may have sold privately to his wife with whom he was living in perfect amity; in another the property may have been knocked down at auction to the trustee's wife from whom he has been living separate and in enmity for a dozen years'[2].

¹ *Burrell v Burrell's Trustees* 1915 SC 333; *Re King's Will Trust* (1959) 173 Estates Gazette 627. Cf *Re McNally* [1967] NZLR 521.
² *Tito v Waddell (No 2)* [1977] 2 All ER 129 at 241.

59.17 One must look at realities to see if she should be treated as the trustee's alter ego.

Sale to company in which trustee holds shares

59.18 The rule vitiating purchases by trustees does not prevent a trustee from selling to a limited company (other than a 'one man company'[1]) in which he is a mere shareholder; for a sale by a person to a corporation of whom he is a member is not, either in form or in substance, a sale by him to himself and others. Nevertheless, in such a case, there is such a conflict of interest and duty that, if the sale be impeached by the beneficiaries, the onus will lie on the company to show affirmatively that the trustee had taken all reasonable pains to secure a purchaser at the best price, and that the price given by the company was not inadequate at the time, although a better price might have been obtained by waiting[2].

¹ *Silkstone and Haigh Moor Coal Co v Edey* [1900] 1 Ch 167 or presumably a company of which he is managing director and (with his and his wife's shares) majority shareholder: *Re Thompson's Settlement* [1985] 2 All ER 720 at 729 where Vinelott J at pp 730–731 also indicated that sale by a trustee to a partnership of which he was a member would be automatically voidable.
² *Farrar v Farrars Ltd* (1888) 40 Ch D 395; *Tse Kwong Lam v Wong Chit Sen* [1983] 3 All ER 54, [1983] 1 WLR 1349, PC.

Employment of parent company by subsidiary company

59.19 What happens if a company-trustee places business with its holding company, eg invests trust moneys in a fund managed by its holding company for a fee? It seems that the onus will lie on the trustee to show that the placement of its business with its holding company did not create a real sensible possibility of conflict which could impair the trustee's ability to serve the best interests of the beneficiaries, as where the holding company is a pre-eminent company with an attractive investment record and where the equivalent fee would be payable to any similar company selected to be investment manager[1].

[1] *Jones v AMP Perpetual Trustee Company NZ Ltd* [1994] 1 NZLR 690 at 710–711 where Thomas J would also have excused the trustee, if necessary, from liability under the New Zealand equivalent of TA 1925, s 61, the loss of value of the investments being caused by the October 1987 stockmarket crash.

Subsequent repurchase by trustee without collusion

59.20 The fact that a trustee has sold trust property in the hope, subsequently realised, of being able to repurchase it for himself at a future time, is not of itself a sufficient ground for setting aside the sale, where the price was not inadequate at the time, and there was no agreement or understanding existing at the time of the first sale that the purchaser should sell or reconvey the property to the trustee. The fact that the trustee many years afterwards made a handsome profit by repurchasing and selling the property makes no difference[1]. However, in the case just cited, more than twenty years had elapsed without the sale being impeached, and many of the parties were dead; and, as the court said, the presumption of law that a transaction was legal and honest is a presumption that is strengthened by lapse of time. It is, however, clear that where trustees have rightly sold to A, so long as that sale is not completed and remains executory, one of the vendor trustees cannot repurchase the property from A for himself[2].

[1] *Re Postlethwaite* (1888) 37 WR 200, CA; and see also *Dover v Buck* (1865) 5 Giff 57; and *Baker v Peck* (1861) 9 WR 472; but cf *A-G v Lord Dudley* (1815) Coop G 146.
[2] *Williams v Scott* [1900] AC 499; *Delves v Gray* [1902] 2 Ch 606; *Parker v McKenna* (1874) 10 Ch App 96 at 125.

Application of the rule to other fiduciary persons

59.21 The general self-dealing rule that a purchase by a trustee can be set aside applies to all persons in a fiduciary position, who are involved in disposing of fiduciary property to themselves or their nominee. Thus it has been held that an agent employed for the sale of an estate cannot purchase it for himself or another[1].

[1] *Ex p Bennett* (1805) 10 Ves 381; *Re Bloye's Trust* (1849) 1 Mac & G 488; affd sub nom *Lewis v Hillman* (1852) 3 HL Cas 607; *De Bussche v Alt* (1878) 8 Ch D 286.

59.22 On the other hand where there are genuinely two parties to the transaction as where a client was very desirous of selling property, and, after vainly endeavouring to do so, finally sold it to his solicitor (who was, of course, a fiduciary) and it was proved that the transaction was fair and the price adequate, and indeed more than could have been obtained elsewhere at the time, and that the client quite understood his position, it was held that such a sale was good and binding, although it lay upon the solicitor to prove that it was unimpeachable[1]. A solicitor purchasing from his client should, however, to avoid allegations of undue influence always make him employ a separate solicitor[2]; and this is so even where the solicitor purchases, not directly from the client, but from the latter's trustee in bankruptcy[3].

[1] *Spencer v Topham* (1856) 22 Beav 573, 2 Jur NS 865; *Gibson v Jeyes* (1801) 6 Ves 266; *Johnson v Fesemeyer* (1858) 3 De G & J 13; *Edwards v Meyrick* (1842) 2 Hare 60.
[2] *Cockburn v Edwards* (1881) 18 Ch D 449.
[3] *Luddy's Trustee v Peard* (1886) 33 Ch D 500; and see also *Barron v Willis* [1900] 2 Ch 121; affd sub nom *Willis v Barron* [1902] AC 271.

59.23 The rule applies even where the party from whom advice is sought is not a professional adviser; for the fact that he accepts the position of adviser places him under a fiduciary obligation towards the party seeking advice[1].

[1] *Tate v Williamson* (1866) 2 Ch App 55.

Trustee cannot lease to himself or sell or lease own property to trust

59.24 Trustees cannot lease the trust estate to one of themselves, and if they do so the lessee will have to account for the profits[1]. Just as agents cannot sell or lease their own property to their principal except with his knowledge and approval[2], so a trustee cannot sell or lease his own property to himself and his co-trustees, although there is no English case directly in point[3].

[1] *Re Dumbell ex p Hughes* (1802) 6 Ves 617; *Re John's Assignment Trusts* [1970] 1 WLR 955 at 960.
[2] *Bentley v Craven* (1853) 18 Beav 75; *Re Cape Breton Co* (1885) 29 Ch D 795, CA; Goff & Jones *Law of Restitution* (5th edn) Ch 33(B) 3.
[3] *Bentley v Craven* (1853) 18 Beav 75 at 76; *Re Cape Breton Co* (1885) 29 Ch D 795 at 803, CA; *Scott on Trusts* (4th edn) Vol IIA para 170.12 to 170.13; *National Trust Co Ltd v Osadchuk* [1943] SCR 89.

Sine qua non concurrence of trustee

59.25 In *Re Thompsons' Settlement*[1] it was held that the self-dealing rule extends to cases where a trustee concurs in a transaction (eg the grant or assignment of a lease) which cannot be effected without his concurrence and where he also has an interest in, or holds a fiduciary duty to another in relation to, the same transaction.

[1] [1986] Ch 99, [1985] 2 All ER 720.

Mortgages

59.26 In one case concerning the property of a charity, the trustees of which could act by a majority, it was held that one of several trustees might himself become a mortgagee of the trust property and exercise over it all the rights of a mortgagee[1]. It does not appear whether the mortgagee-trustee concurred with his co-trustees in exercising their discretion.

> [1] *A-G v Hardy* (1851) 1 Sim NS 338 accepted by Stirling J in *Re Mason's Orphanage* [1896] 1 Ch 54 at 59.

59.27 Where trustees must act unanimously, as in the case of private trusts unless the trust instrument otherwise provides, it is clear that a conflict of duty and self-interest may arise in the case of a mortgagee-trustee so that prima facie the mortgage will be voidable in the absence of special circumstances entirely satisfying the court as to the complete propriety of the mortgage.

Personal representative's appropriation of deceased's assets for himself

59.28 In satisfaction of a pecuniary legacy or the statutory pecuniary legacy on intestacy or a debt due to him, the personal representative can appropriate[1] to himself, cash or the equivalent of cash (like quoted government securities and quoted shares with a clear market value) but not shares in an unquoted company[2]. The rationale is that the open market value of securities equivalent to cash could have been obtained by a sale and the proceeds then remitted to the personal representative as his own property[3]. Thus, a trustee should also be able similarly to appropriate to himself to satisfy a fixed sum due to him as beneficiary or by way of indemnity.

> [1] Administration of Estates Act 1925, s 41.
> [2] *Kane v Radley-Kane* [1999] Ch 274.
> [3] *Kane v Radley-Kane* [1999] Ch 274.

59.29 In satisfaction of a share in the deceased's residuary estate the cases seem to establish that an appropriation of assets can be made by the personal representative to himself if it is fairly made without an eye to obtaining for himself those assets that are more likely to appreciate than others[1].

> [1] *Barclay v Owen* (1889) 60 LT 220; *Re Richardson* [1896] 1 Ch 512; *Kane v Radley-Kane* [1999] Ch 274. For the need to act fairly see *Lloyds Bank v Duker* [1987] 3 All ER 193 and *Edge v Pensions Ombudsman* [2000] Ch 602.

Express or necessarily implied authorisation

59.30 A trust instrument may expressly authorise trustees to act in ways benefiting themselves where they are also beneficiaries under the trust or objects of powers therein, eg a clause entitling a trustee to act and exercise discretionary powers notwithstanding any direct personal interest therein[1]. The onus is then on those attacking the exercise of the function by the trustees to impeach it (eg as ignoring a relevant factor or taking account of an irrelevant factor or perverse to any sensible expectation of the settlor)[2] whether the authorisation is express or necessarily implied from the circumstances[3] (eg the settlor appointed A and B to be trustees but also beneficiaries under his discretionary trust)[4].

1   *Re Beatty's Will Trust* [1990] 3 All ER 844 at 846, [1990] 1 WLR 1503 at 1506; *Blair v
    Vallely & Blair* [2000] WTLR 615 at 639.
2   See Article 61 below.
3   *Edge v Pensions Ombudsman* [2000] Ch 602 at 622 and 631–633, CA.
4   *Edge v Pensions Ombudsman* [2000] Ch 602 at 622 and 631–633, CA; *Re Drexel
    Burnham Lambert UK Pension Plan* [1995] 1 WLR 32; *Sargeant v National Westminster
    Bank* (1990) 61 P & CR 518, CA.

Purchase by trustee by leave of the court

59.31 Where there are infant beneficiaries or unborn beneficiaries the court
will, on the application of the trustee, allow him to purchase, if it can see that,
in the circumstances, it is clearly for the benefit of the beneficiaries, but not
otherwise[1]. The best course of procedure in such an application is to issue a
Part 8 claim form invoking CPR Part 64. The master will make an order
approving the sale in clear cases and in cases of greater difficulty the summons
will be adjourned to the judge (usually as a Monday morning chambers
summons). The usual practice is for costs to be paid by the purchasing trustee.
An alternative method would be an application under s 57 of the Trustee
Act 1925[2]. It is apprehended that no such application could succeed in the
face of opposition by any beneficiary, unless the court considered such
opposition to be merely capricious and unreasonable.

1   *Farmer v Dean* (1863) 32 Beav 327; *Campbell v Walker* (1800) 5 Ves 678.
2   See para 47.108 above.

Pensions Act 1995, s 39

59.32 Doubts (subsequently assuaged by the courts[1]) as to the extent that
members of pension trust schemes who were also trustees could exercise
discretions so as to benefit themselves led to s 39 of the Pensions Act 1995,
stating:

> 'No rule of law that a trustee may not exercise the powers vested in him so as to
> give rise to a conflict between his personal interest and his duties to the
> beneficiaries shall apply to a trustee of a trust scheme, who is also a member of
> the scheme, exercising the powers vested in him in any manner, merely because
> their exercise in that manner benefits, or may benefit, him as a member of the
> scheme'.

1   *Edge v Pensions Ombudsman* [2000] Ch 602, CA; *Re Drexel Burnham Lambert UK
    Pension Plan* [1995] 1 WLR 32.

59.33 The trustee-member problem ceased to be one so far as concerns
pension schemes of insolvent employer-trustees when the Pension Schemes
Act 1993, ss 119 and 121 required independent trustees to be appointed for
the exercise of discretions.

Purchase under contract made before the fiduciary relationship arose

59.34 Where the contract for purchase was made before the fiduciary
relationship came into existence the creation of that relationship will not

prevent the trustee from asserting his rights under the contract[1]. Thus, where a lessor had granted an option to purchase the demised premises at a fixed price it was held that the lessee was not prevented from exercising the option after the lessor's death by having become his executor[2].

1   *Vyse v Foster* (1874) LR 7 HL 318.
2   *Re Mulholland's Will Trusts* [1949] 1 All ER 460.

Purchase by bare trustees

59.35 The rule as to selling to himself only applies where the express or constructive trustee is substantially an active trustee having the opportunity of thereby acquiring information concerning the trust property. He may purchase where he is the mere depositary of the legal estate without any duties, and without ever having had any[1], or is a person nominated trustee who has disclaimed[2]. However, a trustee who was originally an executive trustee, and has become a mere bare trustee by performance of the trusts, would, it is apprehended, be disqualified; for he would have had an opportunity of becoming acquainted with the property and its value[3].

1   Eg a trustee to preserve contingent remainders, see *Sutton v Jones* (1809) 15 Ves 584. Also see *Pooley v Quilter* (1858) 4 Drew 184; *Denton v Donner* (1856) 23 Beav 285.
2   *Stacey v Elph* (1833) 1 My & K 195.
3   *Ex p Bennett* (1805) 10 Ves 381. But cf *Re Boles and British Land Co's Contract* [1902] 1 Ch 244.

Purchase from person to whom trustee's functions delegated

59.36 Where a collective delegation has been made to a person or persons beneficially interested in possession under a trust of land[1] and a trustee seeks to purchase the land, he faces the difficulties that he may well have acquired useful information about the land while trustee and that his interest in purchasing conflicts with his duty to consider revoking the delegation which would interfere with his purchase. Thus, it is likely that his purchase will be impeachable unless with the consent of the court or of all the beneficiaries if ascertained and of full age and capacity[2].

1   TLATA 1996, s 9.
2   If the delegation were made with a view to facilitating the purchase, such would be clearly impeachable.

59.37 In the case of an individual delegation by a trustee by a power of attorney it seems that the acts of the delegate are treated as acts of the trustee[1], so that any purchase by the latter will be impeachable.

1   TA 1925, s 25(5) as substituted by the Trustee Delegation Act 1999, s 5.

Purchase by trustees of subsidiary settlement

59.38 A question sometimes arises in practice whether, on a sale by trustees, the property can be purchased beneficially by a person who is a trustee of a subsidiary settlement by which a share in the proceeds of the sale is settled. Curiously enough, this point seems never to have been decided; but it is submitted that such a purchase might be impeached, for it is the duty of the trustee of the subsidiary settlement to watch over the interests of *his* beneficiaries. It is obviously to their interest that the sale shall realise a high price, whereas it is to the interest of a purchaser that it shall be sold cheaply. By himself becoming a purchaser, therefore, the subsidiary trustee is acting in a character wholly inconsistent with his fiduciary duty; and little doubt is entertained that, if the sale were impeached by his beneficiaries, the onus would be on him under the fair-dealing rule of proving that he acted bona fide and gave an adequate price.

Acquiescence or concurrence by knowledgeable beneficiaries of full age and capacity

59.39   In *Holder v Holder*[1] an additional ground upon which a beneficiary failed to have a purchase set aside was that he had acquiesced in the purchase. It would be inequitable to allow him to assert any equity to set the auction sale aside (if he had such equity) because he had full knowledge of the sale and stood by making no attempt to stop completion, and *restitutio in integrum* was impossible.

[1]   [1968] Ch 353, [1968] 1 All ER 655.

59.40   In principle, a trustee should be able to purchase trust property if this is agreed by all the beneficiaries, being of full age and capacity and between them absolutely entitled to the settled property, and so long as the beneficiaries were given full information and freely gave their agreement. The onus is on the trustee to prove this and in the case of land he will normally find the property unmarketable, purchasers with constructive notice of the equity to set aside being bound by the equity[1] and not being able to be sure that fully informed free consent was given by the beneficiaries.

[1]   *Cookson v Lee* (1853) 23 LJ Ch 473; *Aberdeen Town Council v Aberdeen University* (1877) 2 App Cas 544.

The beneficiaries' remedies

59.41   If the trustee has resold the property at a profit the beneficiaries can adopt the sale and recover the profit[1].

[1]   *Baker v Carter* (1835) 1 Y & C Ex 250. If the purchaser had notice of the beneficiary's equity the beneficiary may recover the property from the purchaser. If sale were to a purchaser without notice for less than the true value the beneficiaries can claim from the trustee the difference between the price paid and the true value with interest at 4%; *Lord Hardwicke v Vernon* (1799) 4 Ves 411.

59.42   If the trustee has not re-sold the beneficiaries may, if they all agree, insist that the property be reconveyed by the purchasing trustee to the vendor trustees; otherwise the property will be re-sold under the direction of the court on the footing that if it realises more than the reserve price fixed by the court the surplus belongs to the trust whereas if it realises less, then the purchasing trustee is held to his bargain[1]. All beneficiaries should be notified of the course proposed by the court on the application of a particular beneficiary so that all may have the opportunity of being heard and all will be bound. The reserve price must be calculated as the sum of the price paid by the purchasing trustee and, at least where he acted in good faith, a figure appropriate for any improvements made to the property which, it seems, should be based on the difference between the improved and the unimproved value of the property[2]. Any balance on income account should, as the case may be, be added to or deducted from the reserve. The purchasing trustee will be credited with interest at 5%[3] on the purchase price and the improvements figure and debited with a proper rent. Any excess of interest over rent will be added to the reserve whilst any deficiency will be subtracted from the reserve. If the property fetches more than the reserve and the costs of re-sale then it seems the costs are borne by the trust. If the reserve is not reached or only exceeded by an amount not covering the costs of re-sale then there is something to be said for the plaintiff beneficiary seeking re-sale to pay the costs in some circumstances.

1   *Holder v Holder* [1966] 2 All ER 116 at 128–131, Harman LJ in [1968] 1 All ER 665 at 669 approving the form of order obiter whilst allowing the appeal. See also *Price Waterhouse v MacCulloch* (1986) 25 DLR (4th) 126 where an executor was liable.
2   *Holder v Holder* [1966] 2 All ER 116 at 169. In principle, to prevent the trustee profiting he should only recover for improvements the lesser of (a) the actual cost of improvements or (b) the difference between the improved and unimproved value of the property.
3   *Holder v Holder* [1966] 2 All ER 116 at 130, Cross J considering that the traditional 4% would be 'unfair in present day conditions'.

59.43 Upon ordering re-sale the court has discretion to allow the purchasing trustee to bid at the auction but it will not normally exercise this discretion if any adult beneficiary objects though, in principle, there is much to be said, if the beneficiaries disagree as to this, for the view that the matter ought to be decided by the court in the interests of the trust as a whole[1].

1   *Tennant v Trenchard* (1869) 4 Ch App 537; *Holder v Holder* [1966] 2 All ER 116 at 130.

Paragraph 3

Purchase by trustee of beneficiary's equitable interest

59.44 But although a trustee is incapable of purchasing from himself or his colleagues, there is no fixed and arbitrary rule that he cannot, in any circumstances, purchase the interests of his beneficiaries from the beneficiaries themselves. Thus a purchase by a trustee for sale of the interest of a beneficiary in the proceeds of sale is unobjectionable[1]. Yet the court regards such transactions with great jealousy; and, if impeached, they cannot stand unless the trustee can affirmatively and clearly show that the parties were completely at arm's length in making the bargain, that the bargain was a beneficial one to the beneficiaries, and that the trustee candidly disclosed all facts known to him which could in any way influence the vendors[2].

59.44 *The trustee's duties*

1   *Coles v Trecothick* (1804) 9 Ves 234; and *Clarke v Swaile* (1762) 2 Eden 134.
2   See per Lord Cairns in *Thomson v Eastwood* (1877) 2 App Cas 215 at 236, HL; *Williams v Scott* [1900] AC 499; *Dougan v Macpherson* [1902] AC 197, where the trustee had had a valuation made for himself which he did not communicate to the beneficiary.

59.45 In *Tito v Waddell (No 2)*[1] Megarry V-C called the rule the 'fair-dealing' rule summarising it as:

'that if a trustee purchases the beneficial interest of any of his beneficiaries, the transaction is not voidable *ex debito justitiae*, but can be set aside unless the trustee can show that he has taken no advantage of his position and has made full disclosure to the beneficiary, and that the transaction is fair and honest'.

1   [1977] 3 All ER 129 at 241.

59.46 Thus, in *Hill v Langley*[1] where an executor and trustee had taken an assignment of his sister's half interest in their father's residuary estate without disclosing information relevant to the value of that interest, the assignment was set aside so that the traceable assets within the half interest could be recovered.

1   (1988) Times, 28 January.

59.47 The rule can apply where the transaction with the beneficiary is effected not by the trustee but by some person or body which is merely the trustee's alter ego. Short of the alter ego case where they must disclose the true position, trustees are not under any duty to proffer information to their beneficiary, or to see that he has proper advice merely because they are trustees for him and know that he is entering into a transaction with his beneficial interest with some person or body connected in some way with, but independent of, the trustees such as a company in which the trustees own some shares beneficially[1].

1   *Tito v Waddell (No 2)* [1977] 3 All ER 129 at 242–243.

Mortgage of equitable interest of trustee

59.48 A trustee may take a fair mortgage from his beneficiary; and, in an appropriate case, may obtain priority over prior equitable mortgagees of whose claims he had no notice when he made the advance[1].

1   *Newman v Newman* (1885) 28 Ch D 674.

ARTICLE 60
DUTY OF TRUSTEE TO BE READY WITH HIS ACCOUNTS

60.1

(1)   A trustee:
       (a)   must keep clear and accurate accounts of the trust property[1]; and

(b)   may be ordered by a court, at the request of a beneficiary, to give him full and accurate information as to the amount and state of the trust property[2], and to permit him or his solicitor[3] or accountant to inspect[4] the accounts and vouchers[5], and other documents (including legal advice[6]) relating to the trust[7], so long as such documents do not reveal the reasons or the reasoning process for the exercise of the trustees discretions[8] and so long as supplying the documents in an exceptional case would not prejudice the interests of the beneficiaries as a whole and the ability of the trustee to discharge its obligations under the trust, particularly management of a business[9]. Where a notice in writing of a dealing with an equitable interest in real or personal property has been served on a trustee under section 137 of the Law of Property Act 1925 any person interested in the equitable interest may require production of the notice subject to paying any costs, otherwise a trustee is under no duty to volunteer such information[10].

(2)   A trustee is, nevertheless, not bound to supply copies of accounts or trust documents[11], or to supply information which necessitates expenditure[12], except at the cost of the beneficiary requiring them.

(3)   A trustee must comply with the general law relating to disclosure of information, including (so far as applicable) the Data Protection Act 1998 and the Freedom of Information Act 2000.

---

1   *Springett v Dashwood* (1860) 2 Giff 521; *Burrows v Walls* (1855) 5 De GM & G 233; *Newton v Askew* (1848) 11 Beav 145 at 152; *Pearse v Green* (1819) 1 Jac & W 135.

2   *Re Tillott* [1892] 1 Ch 86; *Re Page* [1893] 1 Ch 304 at 309; *Re Dartnall* [1895] 1 Ch 474; *Talbot v Marshfield* (1868) 3 Ch App 622 (explained and distinguished in *Re Londonderry's Settlement* [1965] Ch 918, [1964] 3 All ER 855, CA); *Ryder v Bickerton* (1743) 3 Swan 80n. Particularly detailed disclosure of informationis required for beneficiaries under occupational pension schemes by virtue of subordinate legislation. See also *Wilson v Law Debenture Trust Corpn* [1995] 2 All ER 337.

3   *Kemp v Burn* (1863) 4 Giff 348.

4   *Marigold Pty Ltd v Belswan (Mandurah) Pty Ltd* [2001] WASC 274.

5   *Pearse v Green* (1819) 1 Jac & W 135; *West v Lazard Bros & Co (Jersey) Ltd* 1987–88 JLR 414.

6   *Wynne v Humberston* (1858) 27 Beav 421; *O'Rourke v Darbishire* [1920] AC 581, HL; *Hawkesley v May* [1956] 1 QB 304, [1955] 3 All ER 353; *Re Londonderry's Settlement* [1965] Ch 918, [1964] 3 All ER 855, CA; *A–G for Ontario v Stavro* (1994) 119 DLR (4th) 750.

7   *Re Cowin* (1886) 33 Ch D 179; *Ottley v Gilby* (1845) 8 Beav 602; see also *Re Londonderry's Settlement* [1965] Ch 918, [1964] 3 All ER 855, CA: paras 60.5, 60.23 and 60.30.

8   *Re Londonderry's Settlement* [1965] Ch 918, CA.

9   *Re Rabaiotti Settlement* [2000] WTLR 953; *Rouse v 100F Australian Trustees Ltd* [2000] WTLR 111.

10   *Low v Bouverie* [1891] 3 Ch 82 at 99.

11   *Ottley v Gilby* (1845) 8 Beav 602; *Marigold Pty Ltd v Belswan (Mandurah) Pty Ltd* [2001] WASC 274.

12   *Re Bosworth* (1889) 58 LJ Ch 432.

60.2 The trustee's duties

Paragraph 1

Irreducible core of accountability to beneficiaries

60.2 As Millett LJ (as he then was) stated in *Armitage v Nurse¹*, when dealing with a private trust as opposed to a charitable trust, 'there is an irreducible core of obligations owed by the trustees to the beneficiaries and enforceable by them which is fundamental to the concept of a trust. If the beneficiaries have no rights enforceable against the trustees there are no trusts'². The rights of a beneficiary to monitor and protect his interest by obtaining accounts from the trustee so that they can then be falsified or surcharged is at the very core of the trust concept.

¹ [1998] Ch 241 at 253 and see DJ Hayton 'The Irreducible Core Content of Trusteeship', Ch 3 in AJ Oakley (ed) *Trends in Contemporary Trust Law* (Oxford 1996).
² While there will be no trusts for beneficiaries , there will be a resulting trust for the settlor.

60.3 As Millett LJ also stated¹, 'Every beneficiary is entitled to see the trust accounts, whether his interest is in possession or not', so that he has the means to discover whether there has been a breach of trust which can be remedied. Thus, beneficiaries with a life interest or an interest in remainder, whether in income or in capital and whether vested or contingent², have accounting rights, as do beneficiaries under discretionary trusts³ and also (in principle) objects of a fiduciary power of appointment⁴.

¹ *Armitage v Nurse* [1998] Ch 241 at 261.
² *Re Tillott* [1892] 1 Ch 86; *A-G of Ontario v Stavro* (1995) 119 DLR (4th) 750.
³ *Chaine Nickson v Bank of Ireland* [1976] IR 393; *Spellson v George* (1987) 11 NSWLR 300; *Re Murphy's Settlement* [1998] 3 All ER 1.
⁴ *Re Murphy's Settlement* [1998] 3 All ER 1 at 9 treating the claimant like an object of a power of appointment as in *Re Manisty's Settlement* [1974] Ch 17; *Schmidt v Rosewood Trust Ltd* [2003] UKPC 26, [2003] 2 AC 709.

60.4 Until the decision of the Privy Council in *Schmidt v Rosewood Trust Ltd¹* it could be argued that a distinction was to be drawn between fixed and discretionary beneficiaries on the one hand, and objects of a power of apointment on the other. In the former case the beneficiaries had to have accounting rights (unless, perhaps, some of them could be excluded e g while their father was a beneficiary). In the case of objects of a fiduciary power they could be argued to have no accounting rights unless specifically conferred. The reason was that the presence of objects of powers of appointment with hopes that they might receive assets was an optional extra in a trust, while the presence of beneficiaries was a core characteristic of a trust, there being no trust if the beneficiaries had no rights to make the trustee account for stewardship of the trust property. Thus, the settlor could well have intended the objects of a power to have no accounting or enforcement rights, but only a right to retain whatever assets might be appointed to them, unless he had expressly or by necessary implication given the objects such rights².

¹ [2003] UKPC 26, [2003] 2 AC 709.
² *Re Manisty's Settlement* [1974] Ch 17 at 25; *Spellson v George* (1987) 11 NSWLR 300.

60.5 Since *Schmidt v Rosewood Trust Ltd*[1], however, the landscape has changed. It is now clear that in terms of accounting rights there is no brightline division between objects of a discretionary *trust* and objects of a fiduciary *power*[2] :after all, both only have a hope of having assets appointed to them, though a discretionary trust power must be exercised. The right to seek disclosure was held simply to be an aspect of the inherent jurisdiction of the court to supervise and, if need be, intervene in the administration of the trust[3], and the object of a power is, in principle, as much entitled to invoke that jurisdiction as is the fixed or discretionary beneficiary. That does not of course mean that the court will necessarily order disclosure to an object. The nub of the matter, it seems, is whether the settlor intended the claimant to have a realistic possibility of receiving bounty from the trust fund, not having a remote or peripheral or theoretical likelihood of benefiting. As Lord Walker said in *Schmidt v Rosewood Trust Ltd,*

1   [2003] UKPC 26, [2003] 2 AC 709, examined in detail by D Hayton in (2003) 10 JTCP 139.
2   For the focus on fiduciary, as opposed to personal, powers, see paras 37 and 66.
3   *Schmidt v Rosewood Trust Ltd [2003] UKPC 26, [2003] 2 AC 709.*

60.6

'Evaluation of the claims of a beneficiary (and especially of a discretionary object) may be an important part of the balancing exercise which the court has to perform on the materials placed before it. In many cases the court may have no difficulty in concluding that an applicant with no more than a theoretical possibility of benefit ought not to be granted any relief'[1].

1   [2003] UKPC 26, [2003] 2 AC 709, at para 67.

60.7 Earlier he had stated[1]

'There are three such areas in which the court may have to form a discretionary judgment: whether a discretionary object (or some other beneficiary with only a remote or wholly defeasible interest) should be granted relief at all; what classes of documents should be disclosed, either completely or in redacted form; and what safeguards should be imposed (whether by undertakings to the court, arrangements for professional inspection, or otherwise) to limit the use which may be made of documents or information disclosed under the order of the court'

1   At para 54.

60.8 But, discretion aside, there are nevertheless limits. It is clear that a former beneficiary may seek to invoke the jurisdiction in relation to matters occurring up to the point at which he or she ceased to be a beneficiary[1], but no further, unless successfully challenging the removal as beneficiary by the trustee. Similarly, a person who is within the scope of a power in the trust instrument to add to a class of beneficiaries is not able to invoke this jurisdiction until he or she has been so added[2], unless, most exceptionally, there is clear evidence (eg in a letter of wishes) that the primary beneficiary was meant to be added pursuant to such power[3]. And it does not follow that an admitted beneficiary can see everything. Thus, an income beneficiary cannot invoke the jurisdiction in relation to matters *solely* relating to capital[4].

Nor can one beneficiary invoke it in order to find out what another beneficiary may have done with his or her interest[5]. Finally, a person who claims to be a beneficiary or an object under a trust must first establish his or her status as such before being allowed to invoke this jurisdiction[6]. Otherwise, 'any stranger might come and claim the estate and see all the opinions and cases and a very serious injury might be caused to the persons really entitled to the property'[7]. Nevertheless, there may be exceptional cases where it is necessary to direct the provision of information to persons before they have established their status as beneficiaries[8].

1   *Budgen v Tylee* (1856) 21 Beav 544; *Millar v Hornsby*, (28 June 2000, unreported) , Sup Ct Vic; *Bathurst v Kleinwort Benson (CI) Trustees Ltd*, (4 August 2004, unreported) R Ct Guernsey.
2   *West v Lazard Bros & Co (Jersey) Ltd* 1987–88 JLR N-22, R Ct Jersey; *West v Lazard Bros & Co (Jersey) Ltd* [1993] JLR 165, R Ct Jersey.
3   Like the claimant under the Everest Trust in *Schmidt v Rosewood Trust Ltd* [2003] UKPC 26, [2003] 2 AC 309 para 68 point 4.
4   *Nestle v National Westminster Bank plc* (1988) 10 Tru LI 112 at 124, affd [1993] 1 WLR 1260, CA. But capital distributions, however, do concern income beneficiaries as reducing the fund producing their income, and so reducing their income.
5   *Re Tillott* [1892] 1 Ch 86.
6   *Wynne v Humberston* (1858) 27 Beav 421; *O'Rourke v Darbishire* [1920] AC 581; *Re CA Settlement* [2002] JLR 312, R Ct Jersey.
7   *Wynne v Humberston* (1858) 27 Beav 421.
8   *Re Internine Trust and the Intertraders Trust* (2004) 7 ITELR 308, R Ct Jersey (weak allegation that B had disclaimed beneficial interest); see also *Re Murphy's Settlement* [1998] 3 All ER 1.

Concomitant duty to notify beneficiaries

60.9 To give meaningful substance[1] to the duty of trustees to account to their beneficiaries, the trustees are under a duty to take reasonable practicable steps to inform their beneficiaries of the trusts favouring the beneficiaries, although problems over sanctions undermine this duty of notification[2]. If a beneficiary does not know he is a beneficiary how can he enforce the trustees' duty to account? Indeed, if he does not know who are the trustees how can he exercise his rights against them? Thus, in *Re Murphy's Settlement*[3] the settlor's son, as beneficiary under a discretionary trust, obtained a court order for the settlor to give him the names and addresses of the trustees of a foreign trust (that the settlor admittedly knew) so that he could apply to them for a discretionary distribution, having fallen out with his father and being poor enough to be in receipt of legal aid for his application to the court.

1   See *Scally v Southern Health & Social Services Board* [1992] 1 AC 294 at 306–307, HL.
2   Removal of the trustee could be sought; otherwise, since there would normally be no loss to the trust fund to account for, the claimant beneficiary would need to seek equitable compensation eg for personal loss incurred a month before the trustees paid him £1 million on a contingency being satisfied (eg attaining 30 years of age) of which he knew nothing until the payment arrived and the loss would have been avoided if he had known.
3   [1998] 3 All ER 1.

60.10 Whether beneficiaries' interests are under fixed[1] or discretionary trusts[2], whether in income or capital, and whether vested or contingent, trustees are necessarily under a duty to take reasonable practicable steps to inform beneficiaries of full age and capacity of their beneficial interests. Those currently interested in income cannot be expected to look after the capital beneficiaries' interested in capital growth and, due to their personal wealth or their relationships with a trustee, might not bother monitoring what is happening to the trust fund. The sooner a capital beneficiary has any lost capital restored to the trust fund the better, the trustee's ability to restore it usually diminishing as time goes by. Moreover, a capital beneficiary may need to make out the case for a power of advancement or appointment to be exercised in his favour. Beneficiaries under discretionary trusts of income or capital also need to be able to make out a case for discretions to be exercised in their favour.

1   *Hawkesley v May* [1956] 1 QB 304; *Brittlebank v Goodwin* (1868) LR 5 Eq 545. Trustees must do everything possible to ascertain a life tenant to whom to pay income. In the case of discretionary trusts and powers they need only take reasonable practicable steps, enabling them to size up their task and invoke and deal with any applications to them: *Re Hay's Settlement Trust* [1981] 3 All ER 786.
2   *Re Murphy's Settlement* [1998] 3 All ER 1.

60.11 What then of the position of persons who only are objects of a fiduciary power of appointment vested in the trustees and hope discretions will be exercised in their favour? In principle they have the right to make the trustees account[1], with the trustees being under a duty to consider from time to time whether to exercise the power and, if they so decide, in what manner to exercise the power, so, of course, they must consider cases made to them by objects for the power of appointment to be exercised[2]. Thus, the trustees must take all reasonable practiable steps to notify objects they are objects. Formerly, where the class of objects of a power comprised two sub-classes, like descendants of the settlor and employees and ex-employees of the settlor's company, then, while there would ordinarily be a duty to notify descendants within the primary class, there would not normally be a duty to notify the more remote class[3]. The position is now less clear. How far the settlor is able in the trust instrument to modify the position under the general law is the subject of the next section.

1   *Schmidt v Rosewood Trust Ltd [2003] UKPC 26*, [2003] 2 AC 709.
2   *Re Hay's Settlement Trust* [1981] 3 All ER 786.
3   *Re Manisty's Settlement* [1974] Ch 17 at 25.

60.12 However, the general law position of the objects of a personal (as opposed to a fiduciary) power of appointment remains to be considered because this was ignored in *Schmidt v Rosewood Trust Ltd*[1]. The exercise of a personal power is unchallengeable in the courts unless the appointment is outside the scope of the power viz to persons who are not objects of the power; thus the donee of the power can refuse to consider exercising the power or can exercise it spitefully or maliciously[2]. Where an individual, as opposed to the trustee, has the power of appointment, there seems no reason why the courts should not give effect to an express provision that objects of the personal power are to have no rights at all other than the right to retain any assets appointed to them. After all, the beneficiaries (and also any objects of a fiduciary power) will be able to check that appointments are not made to persons who are not objects of the personal power – and they have a very strong interest in so checking. Thus, the integrity of the trust concept is not under threat.

1   [2003] UKPC 26, [2003] 2 AC 709, the focus only being on fiduciary powers: see paras 37 and 66.
2   See para 1.76 above.

60.13 If such a weak interest can be created by making persons objects of a personal power vested in individuals, with a clause stating that such persons are to have no rights at all other than the right to retain any assets appointed to them, why cannot such weak interests also be created if the power is vested in trustees, with plenty of fiduciary duties under the trust, but who are expressly stated to owe no duties whatsoever as regards the power of appointment in favour of class 'X', whose only rights are to retain whatever assets might happen to be appointed to them? Why should the courts frustrate the reasonable wishes of the settlor, which do not undermine the trust concept but advance it by extending its flexibility?

Modification of trustees' duties and beneficiaries' correlative rights

60.14 There cannot be any obligation, and hence there cannot be any trust, if the trustee does not owe a duty to account to any beneficiary[1]. For this purpose even objects of fiduciary powers are treated like beneficiaries if there is a realistic prospect of receiving bounty under the trust[2]. On the other hand, it is irrelevant that there is currently no ascertained beneficiary to enforce the trustee's duty to account[3], so long as there is such a beneficiary ascertained by the end of the trust period who will retrospectively have the right to make the trustee account for the operation of the trust throughout the trust period. Thus, a settlor can create a 'blackhole trust'[4] under a foreign governing law that permits accumulations for the whole perpetuity period and which is not retrospectively enforceable by a beneficiary till near the end of a lengthy trust period when the discretionary beneficiaries are to be charitable companies formed in a specific jurisdiction in the last five years of the trust period and such persons (other than the settlor and spouse thereof and the trustee or employees thereof) as are added to such class by the trustees. It would appear[5] that if, throughout the trust period, there was also a fiduciary power to appoint income or capital to any member of class 'X', and the settlor's expectation was that there would be significant use made of this power before expiry of the trust period, then the objects of this fiduciary power could not have their rights to make the trustee account excluded by any provision in the trust instrument.

1   *Armitage v Nurse* [1998] Ch 241 at 253.
2   *Schmidt v Rosewood Trust Ltd [2003] UKPC 26,* [2003] 2 AC 709, PC.
3   For example, there may be a duty to accumulate income (with powers of appointment over income and capital) for a prescribed period, at the end of which the beneficiaries can be ascertained but not till then.
4   On 'blackhole trusts' see D J Hayton, *Modern International Developments in Trust Law* (Kluwer, 2000) Chapter 13, and P Matthews, The Black Hole Trust : Uses, Abuses and Possible Reforms [2002] PCB 42, 110. note that *Schmidt v Rosewood Trust Ltd*[2003] 2 AC 709 has vitiated some of the views there expressed.
5   From *Schmidt v Rosewood Trust Ltd [2003] UKPC 26,* [2003] 2 AC 709.

60.15 However, a settlor can create a 'blind trust' for himself (or himself and his family) under which he prevents himself (or himself and his family) from having any rights as a beneficiary to see the accounts (with supporting information) for a prescribed limited period, eg while he holds a senior political or other sensitive public position.

60.16 If a trust instrument did not directly try to oust the duty of the trustees to account, but stipulated that the trust instrument was not to be disclosed to any beneficiary and any distributions to beneficiaries were to be achieved so far as practicable in untraceable fashion, (to ensure that no beneficiary could discover the existence of the trust and the whereabouts of the trustees), then this indirect ouster of the duty to account would negate the existence of any trust for the 'beneficiaries'. There would either be a resulting trust for the settlor, or the offending clause would be struck out[1].

1   Cf *Re Wynn's Will Trusts* [1952] Ch 271 (clause seeking to exclude recourse to court struck out); *Jones v Shipping Federation of British Columbia* (1963) 37 DLR (2d) 273 at 274–75 (clause in pension trust restricting right to seek accounting to employers held ineffective).

60.17 More difficult is the case where the settlor wishes, for understandable reasons, to restrict accounting rights to some only of the beneficiaries or objects at a given time. Suppose a settlor created a discretionary trust for a class consisting of his four children, his grandchildren and great-grandchildren, with the trustees having a power of appointment in favour of persons being spouses or cohabitants of beneficiaries. Suppose, further, that there were a provision that no person capable of benefiting under the trust was to be informed of the trust except for the four children and the persons who after their respective deaths became the eldest of the next generation in each of the four branches of the family, to the intent that such four children and the eldest member of each successor generation in each family branch were alone to have the right to see trust accounts and other documents, and to bring the trustees to account for any breaches of trust. If then child B died, survived by three children, X, Y and Z, born in that order, could Y and Z, having fortuitously learned of the trust, succeed in a claim to see the trust accounts so that they could then sue in respect of any breaches of trust that might then be discovered?

60.18 Before the decision of the Privy Council in *Schmidt v Rosewood Trust Ltd*[1], it could perhaps have been argued that their claims should fail because X alone of X, Y and Z ranked as a beneficiary with the inherent rights necessary for the status of beneficiary. In essence Y and Z without such rights would have been re-characterised as merely objects of a fiduciary power of appointment[2]. But, whatever the merits of that argument in the past[3], after *Schmidt* at least it is clear that it will not work. Objects of powers with a realistic possibility of receiving bounty have the same ability as fixed or discretionary beneficiaries to invoke the court's jurisdiction to order disclosure of information.

1   [2003] UKPC 26, [2003] 2 AC 709.Resort would need to be made to make members of class 'X' objects of a personal power expressed to have no rights at all other than a right to retain any assets appointed to them, as discussed under the preceding heading.

² See Millett LJ in *Armitage v Nurse* [1998] Ch 241 at 253.
³ It could not have worked, for example, where Y or Z had a *fixed* interest.

60.19 A clause in the trust instrument restricting accounting rights to some only of the beneficiaries or objects has been held void on public policy grounds in Canada¹, and in New Zealand it has been held, following *Schmidt*, that the trustees must be accountable to 'all beneficiaries'¹². Similarly, in England clauses more generally restricting access to the court to decide entitlements have been struck down³. Whilst there is little doubt that the court in deciding whether to order disclosure to beneficiaries or objects could properly take into account the settlor's wishes in the matter, as expressed in the trust instrument, or (perhaps) in a letter of wishes⁴, it does not seem open to the settlor definitively to exclude the ability of a beneficiary or an object to invoke the jurisdiction of the court.

¹ *Jones v Shipping Federation of British Columbia* (1963) 37 DLR (2d) 273 at 274–75.
² *Foreman v Kingstone* [2005] WTLR 823, [2004] 1 NZLR 841, para 93.
³ Eg *Re Wynn's Will Trusts* [1952] Ch 271.
⁴ See the discussion in *Foreman v Kingstone* [2004] WTLR 823, at 844–45, paras 85 to 98.

60.20 Perhaps the best method to try achieve a similar effect is to make persons objects of a power vested in the trustee but expressed to be a personal power in respect of which the trustee owes no duties and the objects have no rights at all other than to retain any assets appointed to them¹. Otherwise, one could create a trust for a limited class, with power to add further persons to such class. Until so added, persons outside the class will have no right to seek disclosure². However, a provision in a pension trust that the trustees should 'observe strict secrecy with regard to the affairs, accounts and transactions' of the trust, but not 'so as to prevent the publication of ... information' to beneficiaries generally when thought fit by the trustees, was regarded as valid and influential in persuading an Australian court not to order disclosure to an individual beneficiary of an actuary's report³.

¹ See under the preceding heading.
² *West v Lazard Bros & Co (Jersey) Ltd* 1987–88 JLR N-22, R Ct Jersey; *West v Lazard Bros & Co (Jersey) Ltd* [1993] JLR 165, R Ct Jersey, but see the very exceptional case of the claimant under the Everest Trust in *Schmidt v Rosewood Trust Ltd* [2003] UKPC 26, [2003] 2 AC 709, para 68 point 4.
³ *Tierney v King* [1983] 2 Qd R 580, Sup Ct Qld.

60.21 A settlor needs to be aware that when he creates a trust for persons (whether beneficiaries or objects of fiduciary powers of appointment) then those persons must have full rights to see the trust accounts and bring the trustees to account. Suppose for instance that the settlor stipulated that 'The Protector [or 'Enforcer'] alone shall have rights to see trust accounts and documents and to bring an action against the trustees'. The court, rather than strike down the clause, or even hold that this caused the whole trust to fail and meant the property was held on resulting trust for the settlor, would more likely hold that the Protector held these rights as a fiduciary for the benefit of the beneficiaries¹ as part of the Protector's irreducible core function², but that these rights of the Protector were in addition to the beneficiaries' rights³. However, suppose that a Cayman 'special trust'⁴ for beneficiaries were involved, where none of the beneficiaries had been appointed an enforcer. Because the Cayman statute[5] , surprisingly, expressly prescribes such beneficiaries have no interest whatsoever in the trust property and have no right to sue the trustee or the enforcer in any way whatsoever, then the English court should hold there to be a resulting trust for the settlor[6]. The absence of enforceable rights for the beneficiaries is of the essence of this novel Cayman legal structure, and there is no particular clause that can be struck down to leave an otherwise conventional trust standing.

[1] The beneficiaries will then be entitled to see the accounts and obtain the information acquired by the Protector, will have a right to ensure he acquires such material for their benefit and that he sues the trustees if necessary: if he did not, then they themselves could sue the trustee joining the Protector as co-defendant: cf *Parker-Tweedale v Dunbar Bank plc* [1990] 2 All ER 577 at 582–583 and 587.
[2] A fiduciary is bound to account to those for whom he is a fiduciary: *A-G v Cocke* [1988] 2 All ER 391 at 395. It would seem to be repugnant to, or inconsistent with, the core content of protectorship not to hold as a fiduciary the core right to make the trustee account.
[3] Beneficiaries' fundamental proprietary *Saunders v Vautier* rights to terminate a trust and claim property from the trustee cannot be affected by any rights of a protector (or enforcer) where there is a valid trust governed by English law. Under a foreign law beneficiaries may have no *Saunders v Vautier* rights as in virtually all States in USA. See generally Article 69.
[4] See the Special (Trusts (Alternative Regime) Law 1997 (now in Trusts Law (2001) Revision Part VIII), discussed by P Matthews, *Shooting STAR* (1997) 11 Tru LI 67, A Duckworth, *STAR WARS: The Colony Strikes Back* (1998) 12 Tru LI 16, P Matthews, *STAR: Big Bang or Red Dwarf* (1998) 12 Tru LI 98, and Duckworth, *STAR WARS: Smiting the Bull* (1999) 13 Tru LI 158.
[5] Trusts Law (2001) Revision s 100(1).
[6] As Millett LJ stated in *Armitage v Nurse* [1998] Ch 241 at 253, 'If the beneficiaries have no rights enforceable against the trustees there are no trusts.'

Accounting duties of trustees

60.22 Trustees must keep clear and distinct accounts of property administered as trustee[1] with supporting vouchers and other documentation[2]. They must always be ready to give full information as to the investment of trust funds, producing mortgage deeds or other appropriate documentation to support their claims[3].

[1] *Pearse v Green* (1819) 1 Jac & W 135.
[2] *Clarke v Earl of Ormonde* (1821) Jac 108 at 120.
[3] *Re Tillott* [1892] 1 Ch 86 at 88.

Nature of beneficiaries' rights to inspect trust documents

60.23 In less complex times where trusts conferred fixed interests eg on A for life remainder to B, it was easy to consider that the right of A and B to inspect the trust documents was based on A and B having equitable proprietary rights in all trust assets which extended to trust documents[1]. Nowadays, where beneficiaries interested under complex discretionary trusts and powers of appointment have rights to inspect trust documents, such rights can be seen to be based not so much on equitable proprietary rights in such documents but on the core right to make trustees account for their trusteeship of the trust property[2].

1   *O'Rourke v Darbishire* [1920] AC 581, HL, followed in *Re Londonderry's Settlement* [1965] Ch 918.
2   *Re Rabaiotti 's Settlement Trust* [2000] WTLR 953 at 963–964; *Hartigan Nominees Pty Ltd v Rydge* (1992) 29 NSWLR 405; *Morris v Morris* (1993) 9 WAR 150; *Schmidt v Rosewood Trust Ltd* [2003] UKPC 26, [2003] 2 AC 709.

60.24 It follows that, instead, of concentrating upon whether particular documents should be appropriately termed 'trust documents' the real question should be whether or not particular documents need to be capable of being inspected by a beneficiary if he is to be able properly to bring the trustees to account. This would be the case for example if the trustees did not exercise their functions for the purposes for which those functions were conferred upon them by the settlor but acted irrationally or negligently or for reasons perverse to any sensible expectation of the settlor.

Costs on failure to keep or furnish accounts

60.25 Failure by trustees to keep accounts and vouchers may lead to them having to bear their own costs even where an administration action is dismissed[1]. If, however, the action succeeds the trustee will normally[2] have to pay the claimant's costs as well[3] up to the hearing[4]. But, as the reason of this is that such costs are caused by the trustee's neglect to keep and furnish accounts, the claimant will not in general be entitled to costs against the trustee beyond the time when the account is actually rendered, or ordered by the court to be rendered. From this time, if the accounts are substantially accurate, the trustee will be entitled to his costs out of the estate[5], or, if the claimant sues alone, out of his share in the estate[6].

1   *Payne v Evens* (1874) LR 18 Eq 356; and see to same effect, *Re Page* [1893] 1 Ch 304.
2   If the claimant has been over hasty in seeking the assistance of the court he, or even his solicitor, may be ordered to pay the costs: *Re Dartnall* [1895] 1 Ch 474.
3   *Eglin v Sanderson* (1862) 3 Giff 434; *Newton v Askew* (1848) 11 Beav 145.
4   *Springett v Dashwood* (1860) 2 Giff 521; *Re Linsley* [1904] 2 Ch 785. Trustees who deliberately try to keep the beneficiaries in the dark will be liable to have costs awarded against them on the indemnity basis: *Re Den Haag Trust* (1998) 1 OFLR 495.
5   *Ottley v Gilby* (1845) 8 Beav 602.
6   *Thompson v Clive* (1848) 11 Beav 475.

60.26 It has been held that where a trustee by his gross and indefensible neglect to furnish accounts renders a claim necessary, he may be ordered to pay all the costs, including the costs of taking and vouching the account[1]. It is no defence that the trustees are illiterate and incapable of keeping accounts; for in that case they would be justified in employing, and be bound in point of law to employ, a competent agent to keep the accounts for them[2].

1   *Re Skinner* [1904] 1 Ch 289; explained in *Re Holton's Settlement Trusts* [1918] WN 78. See also *West v Lazard Brothers & Co (CI) Ltd* 1987–88 JLR 414; *Bhander v Barclays Private Bank and Trust Co Ltd* (1997) 1 OFLR 497; *Re Den Haag Trust* (1997) 1 OFLR 495; *James v Newington* [2004] WTLR 863, R Ct Jersey; *Longworth v Allen* [2005] SASC 469, Sup Ct S Aus.

2 *Wroe v Seed* (1863) 4 Giff 425 at 429. Any trustee may employ an agent to keep their accounts: TA 2000, s 11.

Inaccurate accounts

60.27 The importance of keeping accounts is shown by the fact that, although the court will generally saddle with costs a trustee whose only fault is that he has failed to do so, yet where a trustee has kept and furnished accounts, which, by an honest mistake, turn out to be inaccurate, he will be allowed his costs[1].

1 *Smith v Cremer* (1875) 24 WR 51.

Information as to investment of trust funds

60.28 'A trustee is bound to give his cestui que trust proper information as to the investment of the trust estate, and where the trust estate is invested on mortgage, it is not sufficient for the trustee merely to say, "I have invested the trust money on a mortgage", but he must produce the mortgage deeds, so that the cestui que trust may thereby ascertain that the trustee's statement is correct, and that the trust estate is so invested ... Where a portion of the trust estate is invested in consols, it is not sufficient for the trustee merely to say that it is so invested, but his cestui que trust is entitled to an authority from the trustee to enable him to make proper application to the bank, ... in order that he may verify the trustee's own statement; there may be stock standing in the name of a person who admits he is a trustee of it, which at the same time is incumbered, some other person having a paramount title may have obtained a charging order on the stock or placed a distringas upon it'[1].

1 Per Chitty J in *Re Tillott* [1892] 1 Ch 86 at 88; see also *Re Dartnall* [1895] 1 Ch 474; *Gough v Ottley* (1852) 5 De G M & Sm 653 (property deeds).

Other documents relating to the trust

60.29 Apart from the trust accounts and their supporting vouchers[1], the trustees may be required by the court to disclose other forms of information. These include trust deeds (original, supplemental, deeds of appointment or advancement to beneficiaries[2], deeds of appointment and retirement of trustees), agendas for and minutes of trustees' meetings[3] (except to the extent that they reveal trustees' confidential deliberations as to the exercise of discretion[4]), legal advice[5], and, in relation to pension trusts at least, financial information relevant to such trusts[6]. In Jersey, in particular, the class of disclosable documents is very wide indeed[7].

1 *Pearse v Green* (1819) 1 Jac & W 135; *West v Lazard Bros & Co (Jersey) Ltd* 1987–88 JLR 414; *Armitage v Nurse* [1998] Ch 241, CA.
2 *Lemos v Coutts & Co* [1992] CILR 460, Grand Ct Cayman Is.
3 *Wilson v Law Debenture Trust Corp plc* [1995] 2 All ER 337.
4 *Re Londonderry's Settlement* [1965] Ch 918, [1964] 3 All ER 855, CA; see para 60.30.

5   *Wynne v Humberston* (1858) 27 Beav 421; *O'Rourke v Darbishire* [1920] AC 581, HL; *Hawkesley v May* [1956] 1 QB 304; *Re Londonderry's Settlement* [1965] Ch 918, [1964] 3 All ER 855, CA; *A-G of Ontario v Stavro* (1995) 119 DLR (4th) 750.
6   *Crowe v Stevedoring Employers Retirement Fund Pty Ltd* [2003] VSC 316, Sup Ct Vic; cf *Allen v TKM Group Pension Trust Ltd* [2002] PLR 333.
7   *West v Lazard Brothers & Co (CI) Ltd* 1987–88 JLR 414; *Re Representation Herminia Umberti, Re Lombardo Settlement*, (5 December 1990; unreported), *Re a Settlement* [1994] JLR 149, R Ct Jersey; *Bhander v Barclays Private Bank and Trust Co Ltd* (1997) 1 OFLR 497; *Re Den Haag Trust* (1997) 1 OFLR 495; *Re Rabaiotti's Settlement* [2000] WTLR 953; *James v Newington* [2004] WTLR 863.

60.30 More generally, the extent of the trustee's duty to disclose other documents relating to the trust was considered by the Court of Appeal in *Re Londonderry's Settlement*[1] which concerned the confidentiality of documents emanating from the trustees and which disclosed their reasons for exercising distributive discretions or contained material on which their reasons might well have been based. In this case a beneficiary under a discretionary trust of income, who was also the object of a power of appointment over capital, dissatisfied with the amount of capital proposed to be distributed to her, sought to obtain information to enable her to launch an attack on the trustees' allocation of trust capital. The right of beneficiaries to inspect counsel's opinions taken by the trustees at the expense of the trust fund to guide them on their obligations as trustees was confirmed. Apart from that, the court laid down certain general propositions, making it clear, however, that they were not intended to be all-embracing and that they might not be applied inflexibly and in all circumstances. These propositions are:

(a)   the principle that where the trustees have, in good faith, reached certain decisions as to the exercise of their discretionary powers over trust property they are under no duty to disclose their reasons holds good even when those reasons have been committed to paper. So they are not bound to disclose to a beneficiary the agenda of their meetings, nor any documents (including minutes of meetings) relating to the deliberations in which they engaged before taking their decisions, or disclosing their reasons for taking them or the material on which those reasons were or might have been based. The court considered that such documents were not, in fact, trust documents, adding that, even if they were, it was in the interests of all concerned that they should be confidential and the court would not order their disclosure;

(b)   where trustees have power, subject to the consent of certain appointors, to appoint shares of capital to beneficiaries, no beneficiary has the right to inspect communications between individual trustees and appointors, or between any of the trustees or appointors and an individual beneficiary because, it seems, they are not trust documents;

(c)   but if a solicitor advising the trustees commits to paper an aide-memoire summarising the state of the fund, or of the family concerned, and reminding the trustees of past distributions and future possibilities, it seems that this is a document which beneficiaries have a right to inspect.

1   [1965] Ch 918, [1964] 3 All ER 855, CA; see also *Lemos v Coutts & Co* [1992–93] CILR 460 (CA Cayman).

Duty to keep trust information confidential

60.31 As a general proposition, trustees must keep the affairs of the trust confidential[1], as well as personal information relating to the beneficiaries, as part of the law relating to breach of confidence[2]. Of course this is subject to compliance with obligations of disclosure imposed by the general law, such as to relevant tax authorities, anti-money laundering authorities[3], the rules of civil[4] and criminal procedure in court, and so on. (On the other hand trustees may be able to resist such general disclosure by reference to other principles of general application, such as the privilege against self-incrimination, which remains available even to trustees[5]).

1   Eg *Heerema v Heerema* 1985–86 JLR 293, R Ct Jersey.
2   *Argyll v Argyll* [1967] Ch 302; *Faccenda Chicken Ltd v Fowler* [1987] Ch 117, CA; *X v Y* [1988] 2 All ER 648; *A v B* [2002] EWCA Civ 337, [2003] QB 195, [2002] 2 All ER 345, CA; *Campbell v Mirror Group Newspapers Ltd [2004] UKHL 22, [2004] 2 AC 457.*
3   See paras 46.8–46.19.
4   See below.
5   *Bishopsgate Investment Management Ltd v Maxwell* [1993] Ch 1, CA; see para 60.63 below.

60.32 If a trustee is a trustee of several trusts, he will have information relating to all of them and their beneficiaries. Certainly information acquired in acting as trustee of trust A should not (in the absence of fraud) *prejudice* trust B, in the sense of causing the trustee to have notice of some fact affecting the assets of trust B, merely because he acquired that notice while acting as trustee of trust A[1]. But how far may/must he disclose (or use) this information for the benefit of the beneficiaries of trust B? The problem is that the trustee by accepting the second trusteeship has put himself into a position where he owes – or at least, may owe – two inconsistent duties. On the one hand, he owes a duty to keep confidential trust A's information. On the other, he owes a duty to do the best he can for trust B and its beneficiaries, which may involve disclosing to the beneficiaries, or simply using for their benefit, information available to him that may or will be useful to them. Now it is clear that – from the point of view of the first trust in which he acts – a trustee cannot use his position as trustee, or information acquired as trustee, for his *personal* benefit[2]. It should be no different if, instead, he subsequently undertakes the duty of trustee for others as beneficiaries. Those others should be in no better position than he would be himself had he not so undertaken.

1   Trustee Act 1925, s 28.
2   Eg *Boardman v Phipps* [1967] 2 AC 46, HL; see para 33.52.

60.33 In cases involving fiduciary agents who have accepted agency relationships with several principals leading to inconsistent duties of this kind, it has been held that prima facie the agent owes his duties to *all* such principals. This means that, whatever he does, he will breach at least one duty, and it is no answer to an action for such breach that he was obliged to do this because of his duty to another principal[1]. But of course it is open to the agent in accepting the second and subsequent agencies to stipulate for a modification of his duty to such second or subsequent principals to exclude the need to disclose information in respect of which he owes a duty of confidentiality to an earlier principal[2]. In some kinds of contract, such as that made by an estate agent with his client to try to sell the client's property, it may even be possible to imply a term to this effect generally into the contract[3].

1   *Moody v Cox* [1917] 2 Ch 71, CA.

²   *Moody v Cox* [1917] 2 Ch 71, at 81, per Lord Cozens-Hardy MR.
³   *Kelly v Cooper* [1993] AC 205, PC. See para 33.97 [under Article 33].

60.34 So far as trusts are concerned, there seems no justification for applying a general rule of a lower standard than is applied to fiduciary agents. Thus the fact that the trustee owes a duty of confidence in respect of information held to the beneficiaries of trust A does not of itself prevent him from being in breach of his duty to the beneficiaries of trust B if he fails to use such information for the benefit of the latter. Plainly, provision may be made by the settlor in the trust instrument for trust B to modify the duty that the trustee would otherwise owe to the beneficiaries of trust B. However, unlike the case of estate agents, there is no authority suggesting that such a provision can be routinely implied into trust instruments. It is a wise counsel therefore for a trustee accepting multiple trusteeships to ensure, if there is any risk of conflict between the various trusteeships he holds or may hold, that appropriate provision is made in the trust instrument before accepting any trusteeship after the first.

60.35 In one Jersey case[1] where a trust company was trustee of several trusts for related persons, the beneficiaries of trust A complained about action taken by the trustee as trustee of that trust, and sought disclosure of information from the trustee under the normal beneficiary rules[2]. This included information which also related to trust B, most of the beneficiaries of which were not beneficiaries of trust A. The trustee sought consent for disclosure from the protector of trust B (who apparently had power to authorise such disclosure under the terms of the trust), but consent was refused on grounds of confidentiality. The trustee therefore sought the directions of the court as to whether it should disclose the requested information (ie relating to *both* trusts) to the beneficiaries of trust A. Unfortunately the Jersey Court of Appeal preferred to analyse the situation as one of *discovery in civil proceedings* (and third party pre-action discovery at that), rather than in terms of beneficiaries' rights, and determined that the trustee should be permitted to disclose the information concerned.

¹   *Re Representation of JP Morgan Trust Co (Jersey) Ltd, Re the Internine Trust and the Azali Trust* [2006] JCA 093.
²   Ie not on discovery in civil proceedings.

Right to disclosure in civil litigation

60.36 It should be noted that the court order in *Re Londonderry's Settlement*[1] was made 'without prejudice to any right of the defendant to discovery in separate proceedings against the plaintiffs'. Thus if a beneficiary bona fide instituted hostile litigation against trustees alleging improper exercise of their discretions then he could obtain discovery of documents relevant to exercise of these discretions[2]. At that time a litigant in ordinary civil proceedings was entitled to discovery from his opponent of any document in the latter's possession, custody or power 'which may fairly lead him to a train of inquiry' that may 'either directly or indirectly enable the party either to advance his own case or to damage the case of his adversary'[3].

¹   [1965] Ch 918, [1964] 3 All ER 855, CA.
²   Eg *Talbot v Marshfield* (1865) 2 Drew & Sm 549.
³   *Compagnie Financiere du Pacifique v Peruvian Guano Co* (1882) 11 QBD 55 at 63. See (1965) 81 LQR 196 (R.E.Megarry).

60.37 'Discovery' under the Rules of the Supreme Court 1965 has now been replaced by 'disclosure' under the Civil Procedure Rules 1998¹. The main principles of disclosure are similar to those of discovery. If a claimant can make out a properly particularised claim (so that it cannot be struck out as a mere 'fishing expedition' to see if material can be obtained on disclosure to support the claim) this triggers 'standard disclosure' of documents that can advance or hinder either party's case². Subsequent applications can then be made in relation to *specific* disclosure of documents. It is also possible to obtain pre-action disclosure of documents if this is desirable to assist fair expedient resolution of the dispute³.

¹   CPR Pt 31 and Practice Direction thereof.
²   However, 'standard' disclosure under the CPR 1998 is less extensive than ordinary discovery under the RSC 1965.
³   Under CPR, r 34.6: see *Bermuda International Securities Ltd v KPMG* [2001] EWCA Civ 269, [2001] CP Rep 73, *Black v Sumitomo Corpn [2001] EWCA Civ 1819,* [2003] 3 All ER 643, CA: *BSW Ltd v Balltec Ltd* [2006] EWHC 822 (Ch).

60.38 However, despite the change in the procedural rules, the broad distinction between on the one hand disclosure to a trust beneficiary as such beneficiary and on the other disclosure to a litigant in civil proceedings remains the same. Disclosure is a process only coming into play once civil proceedings have been commenced, and only in relation to matters in issue in those proceedings. But trust beneficiaries or objects have the right to seek to hold their trustees to account irrespective of litigation, and covering the whole range of their interests in the trust, not restricted to any matters which might be in dispute. But it should be noted that the scope of disclosure in civil procedure is more pervasive than the right to hold trustees to account, and covers, for example, documents withheld under the latter right because they might reveal the trustees' private deliberations¹.

¹   See para 60.43 below.

60.39 Where the English court otherwise has power to make a disclosure order against foreign trustees who allege that such disclosure would put them in breach of their local law, the court may be persuaded not to make that order, or to restrict it in some way. But the court will first need to be satisfied that there is a real risk of prosecution in their home jurisdiction, and not just a theoretical possibility¹. Thus at a minimum the trustees will need to show that the local law contains no applicable exceptions (eg for legal proceedings), and that it is regularly enforced².

¹   *Canada Trust Co v Stolzenberg* (1997) 1 OFLR 606; *Morris v Banque Arabe et Internationale d'Investissement SA* (1999) 2 ITELR 492.
²   *Partenreederei M/S 'Heidberg' v Grosvenor Grain and Feed Co Ltd* [1993] 2 Lloyd's Rep 324 at 332.

60.40 At the international level, it is usually possible, by means of letters of request, to obtain *evidence* for use in civil proceedings. But it is not permitted to use such procedures to obtain general *disclosure*. The law as laid down by the House of Lords[1] is that, in order to obtain evidence under an incoming letter of request, the documents sought must be *specified*, and it must also be shown both that they are likely to exist and that they will be adduced in evidence in the foreign proceedings. These principles have been held to apply to outgoing as to incoming letters of request[2].

1   *Re Asbestos Insurance Coverage Cases* [1985] 1 WLR 331, HL; *Rio Tinto Zinc Corpn v Westinghouse Electric Corpn* [1978] AC 547, HL.
2   *Panayiotou v Sony Music Entertainment* (U.K.) Ltd [1994] Ch 142.

60.41 But recently the Court of Appeal has departed from this approach and has held that, in the context of matrimonial proceedings in England where the wife seeks information from trustees offshore, as a preliminary to the hearing of an application for relief ancillary to a divorce[1], it is not necessary to specify the documents sought or to show that they probably exist[2]. In other words, in matrimonial cases only, 'fishing' is permitted. Whether this exceptionalist view will prevail if the matter is ever taken to the House of Lords must be regarded as doubtful. In any event, however, this does not mean that the receiving (foreign) court will necessarily take the same view. When the letter of request the subject of the Court of Appeal's order reached its destination, Bermuda, the court there held it should follow the House of Lords authorities rather than the Court of Appeal, and refused to implement the English letter of request, on the basis that it was in the nature of a fishing expedition[3].

1   See para 47.95 ff.
2   *Charman v Charman* [2005] EWCA Civ 1606, [2006] 1 WLR 1053.
3   *Charman v Charman*, (22 December 2005, unreported), Sup Ct Bermuda (Bell J).

60.42 US courts may adopt an even more brazen approach, not bothering with letters of request, but simply making discovery orders against foreign trustees who (i) are not parties to the proceedings, (ii) are outside the jurisdiction and (iii) have not submitted to it. In one Jersey case the trustee recipient of such an order sought the directions of the court, and was directed to take no part in the US proceedings and not to comply with the US discovery order[1].

1   *Re M Trust, Re L Trust* [2003] JLR N[6], [2003] WTLR 491, R Ct Jersey.

Confidentiality of trustees' deliberations

60.43 It is well established[1] that trustees are not obliged to give reasons for their exercise of distributive discretions so that they are not obliged to disclose their reasons or their reasoning processes but are entitled to keep them confidential: otherwise embitterment and embarrassment could well arise and persons could well be deterred from acting as trustees. This applies not just to private family trusts but to pension trusts where the members of the pension scheme have purchased their interests under the trusts[2]. If reasons are not given then the trustees have plenty of leeway because their exercise of a discretion can only be challenged[3] if (which is often difficult) prima facie evidence can be found by a claimant to justify alleging the discretion was exercised mala fide, capriciously, spitefully, perversely to any sensible expectation of the settlor, or without any real and genuine consideration, or the trustees would not have done what was done if irrelevant considerations had not been taken into account or if relevant considerations, which were not taken into account, had been taken into account. Disclosure of documents in such litigation can then lead to the trustees' reasons becoming apparent.

[1]   *Re Londonderry's Settlement* [1965] Ch 918, CA.
[2]   *Wilson v Law Debenture Trust Corpn plc* [1995] 2 All ER 337. However, *Schmidt v Rosewood Trust Ltd [2003] UKPC 26,* [2003] 2 AC 709 has undermined this: see D Hayton 'Pension Trusts and Traditional Trusts' [2005] Conv 229 at 236–237.
[3]   *Gisborne v Gisborne* (1877) 2 App Cas 300; *Re Hay's Settlement Trust* [1982] 1 WLR 202; *Turner v Turner* [1984] Ch 100; *Mettoy Pension Trustees Ltd v Evans* [1990] 1 WLR 1587; *Edge v Pensions Ombudsman* [2000] Ch 602, CA.

60.44 Whether the trustees volunteered reasons at the outset or only later at the stage of disclosure or of cross-examination[1], the exercise of their distributive discretion should stand unless the claimant makes out any of the above allegations, in which event the trustees or new trustees, replacing the old trustees, should be free to exercise their discretion afresh but on a proper basis.

[1]   As Robert Walker J pointed out in *Scott v National Trust* [1998] 2 All ER 705 at 719, 'If a decision taken by trustees is directly attacked in legal proceedings, the trustees may be compelled either legally (through discovery or subpoena) or practically (in order to avoid adverse inferences being drawn) to disclose the substance of the reasons for their decision'. However, before then, if the trustees themselves are not prepared to give up the confidentiality of their reasons and reasoning processes then nothing can be done.

Letters of Wishes[1]

60.45 Separate from a trust instrument, there is increasingly found in the case of very flexible discretionary trusts a letter of wishes signed by the settlor or a memorandum of wishes drawn up by the trustee after discussion with the settlor to indicate the latter's wishes. The settlor is normally not very interested in the technical trust instrument that confers immense discretions, but he does spend much time and thought as to what should guide the trustees in the exercise of those discretions, and he puts these thoughts into his letter of wishes. It is the letter of wishes that fleshes out the skeletal trust provisions.

[1]   See generally P Matthews, Letters of Wishes, (1995) 5 OTPR 181.

60.46 Some professional advisers recommend the use of a memorandum of wishes rather than a letter of wishes, apparently on the grounds that the settlor does not sign the former, and therefore the risk of its being held to impose trusts forming part of the trust instrument is removed. But the fact is that it serves the same purpose, ie to inform of the settlor's intentions, and, since it is these intentions that determine what exactly are the trusts on which the assets are held, it is of the same significance as a letter signed by the settlor. Hence there is no reduction in risk achieved by using a memorandum of wishes. Accordingly, they are treated here together, and references hereafter to 'letter of wishes' include references to 'memorandum of wishes'.

LEGALLY BINDING LETTERS

60.47 In an exceptional case, the letter of wishes may be intended by the settlor and accepted by the trustees as a *legally binding* document, overriding the terms of the trust instrument to the extent inconsistent therewith. Factors that may persuade the court that this was so intended include not only the use of mandatory language, but also the length and complexity of the trust instrument compared to the shortness and simplicity of the letter of wishes, the fact that the settlor did not speak or read the language of the trust instrument, whereas the letter of wishes is in his own language, and the degree of precision (sometimes mathematical) with which the letter of which is couched.

60.48 Just as the beneficiaries have a right to see the formal trust instrument, so they have a right to see the informal letter of wishes where the legally binding terms of the trust are found by incorporating both documents[1]. Moreover, any term that the trust instrument or the legally binding letter of wishes is not to be disclosed to any beneficiary but to be kept secret and confidential would, of course, be rejected as repugnant to, or inconsistent with, the trust concept, such obligation requiring beneficiaries to have a meaningful right to make the trustees account for their trusteeship[2].

1   *Chase Manhattan Equities Ltd v Goodman* [1991] BCLC 897 at 923, the trust instrument being a sham or pretence in those parts overridden by the legally binding letter. It is thus advantageous to allege this in bringing legal proceedings.
2   *Armitage v Nurse* [1998] Ch 241 at 253; voidness of clause 15 purporting to oust accountability to beneficiaries in *Re Levy* [1960] Ch 346 at 366; *Scally v Southern Health & Social Services Board* [1992] 1 AC 294 at 306–307; and paras 60.2 and 60.19 above.

LEGALLY SIGNIFICANT LETTERS

60.49 Normally, the key letter of wishes is intended to have legal significance only. An example might be: 'This letter is not intended to be legally binding upon the trustees in any way. It is intended only to provide some guidance for the trustees in exercising their functions, but, having considered whatever guidance may appear to be provided herein, they are, of course, free to exercise their independent judgment in ever-changing circumstances'.

60.50 This *legally significant* letter has to be considered by the trustees and passed on to replacement trustees, because it normally is the key document to guide the trustees in exercising very broad flexible discretions in a fairly standard-form trust deed. It will make clear to the trustees what are the purposes and expectations of the settlor in conferring such immense discretions upon the trustees.

60.51 Since disclosure of information to beneficiaries is now based on the core accountability of trustees to them[1], this letter is a key document that needs to be available for inspection by beneficiaries if they are going to be in a position where it becomes possible for them to bring the trustees properly to account. If the beneficiaries cannot ascertain the purposes and expectations of the settlor they cannot possibly allege that the trustees did not responsibly exercise their discretion for furthering the purposes and expectations of the settlor, but exercised their discretion arbitrarily or contrary to the settlor's purposes and expectations or irrationally, failing to take account of relevant factors or taking account of irrelevant factors. Thus for the beneficiaries to have a meaningful right to make the trustees account for the exercise of their discretions, they will need to see the key letter of wishes as well as the trust instrument. However, it may well be that this is subject to deletion from the letter of any embarrassing personal information regarded as confidential to the settlor, his trustees and the person named in the letter.

[1]   *Schmidt v Rosewood Trust Ltd [2003] UKPC 26*, [2003] 2 AC 709.

CONFIDENTIALITY OF LEGALLY SIGNIFICANT LETTERS

60.52 The question then arises whether the settlor can expressly or impliedly provide that the legally significant letter of wishes is not to be disclosed to any beneficiary but to be kept secret and confidential. One argument is that the inherent nature of a letter of wishes independent of the trust instrument makes it inherently confidential and unavailable to the beneficiaries if requesting to inspect it. Opinions of foreign judges are divided on this issue[1].

[1]   *Hartigan Nominees Pty Ltd v Rydge* (1992) 29 NSWLR 405; *Re Rabaiotti's Settlement* [2000] WTLR 953; *Bathurst v Kleinwort Benson (Channel Islands) Trustees Ltd*, (4 August 2004, unreported), R Ct Guernsey.

60.53 In principle, the key letter of wishes, separate from a broad, bland but skeletal trust instrument, is normally intended by the settlor to be for the benefit of the settlor (dispensing vicarious benevolence via the trustees), and the beneficiaries and the trustees, so they all know the sort of music that the trustees are supposed to be playing with their immense orchestra of powers and discretions. There is thus no implied necessity to make the key letter of wishes confidential to the trustees and not available to beneficiaries to inspect[1].

[1]   The fact that the letter, like the trust instrument, is given to the trustees and not to the beneficiaries should be a neutral indicator, though not so considered in *Re Rabbaiotti's Settlement* [2000] WTLR 953. It may be that, in any event, beneficiaries have a right of access to letters of wishes affecting them under the Data Protection Act 1998: see M Shillingford 'The Data Protection Act 1998' in the TACT Review, Issue No 11, April 2000, pp 3–8. On the Act, see further para 60.72.

60.54 However, if the settlor chooses expressly to stipulate that his legally significant letter of wishes is not to be made available to beneficiaries but to be kept secret and confidential, will the law accept this? After all, it will not accept a similar stipulation in respect of the trust instrument because any stipulation preventing any obligation of accountability to beneficiaries arising is repugnant to, or inconsistent with, the concept of the trust[1]. A similar argument can be made in relation to the confidentiality of a legally significant letter of wishes, that is crucial to the operation of a bland, flexible discretionary trust. Without sight of the letter of wishes making clear the purposes and expectations of the settlor as to the parameters within which he expects his trustees to exercise their immense discretions, a beneficiary can hardly raise a particularised claim that the trustees exercised their discretions contrary to the purposes for which the settlor conferred the discretions and took account of irrelevant factors or ignored relevant factors. Thus, on this view, in order to place trustees under a meaningful obligation, a legally significant letter of wishes should be made available to a beneficiary upon request (though subject to deletion of any information given by a person in confidence to the settlor to be shared only with the trustees).

[1]   EG *Armitage v Nurse* [1998] Ch 241 at 253 *Foreman v Kingstone* [2005] WTLR 823, para 93.

60.55 On the other hand, some accountability remains in respect of trustees' functions even if the letter of wishes is not disclosed. If in a blatant case a particularised claim can be made out that the trustees in exercising distributive functions had not acted in good faith, disclosure of the letter of wishes will then be possible under the Civil Procedure Rules[1]. And in respect of trustees' investment and managerial functions a particularised claim involving breach of statutory and equitable duties will be possible if appropriate after inspecting trust accounts and supporting documents (other than any letter of wishes). There is thus substance in accountability for the investment and managerial side of trustees' functions. It is true that, on the distributive side of a flexible discretionary trust, accountability is very limited because it is difficult to make out a particularised claim of lack of good faith unless one has a very extreme case where the facts cry out for an explanation by the trustees, eg only male beneficiaries benefited or only those of a particular religion, or an appointee of £250,000 capital had a sexual relationship with a trustee just before the appointment.

[1]   CPR, Part 31. See para 60.37.

60.56 This need to particularise lack of good faith in order to make out a claim takes on more significance when one considers that often an exemption clause will oust liability of trustees for everything unless they did not act honestly and in good faith, so that Millett LJ could state[1], 'The duty of the trustees to perform the trusts honestly and in good faith for the benefit of the beneficiaries is the minimum necessary to give substance to the trusts'. Thus, the only way to circumvent such common exemption clause is to allege the trustees did not act in good faith. If a clause in a letter of wishes stating that it is an expressly confidential letter of wishes that is not to be disclosed to the beneficiaries (except pursuant to disclosure under Civil Procedure Rules if litigation can be instituted without being struck down as a 'fishing expedition') is upheld so that evidence for alleging lack of good faith cannot be found, then the rights of beneficiaries have been very much minimised and marginalised. There is thus much to be said for the courts refusing to uphold such confidentiality clauses, though being prepared to delete from a disclosed letter of wishes information given by a person in confidence to the settlor to be shared only with the trustees or information of an embarrassing personal nature that need not be more widely known.

[1] *Armitage v Nurse* [1998] Ch 241 at 253–254.

MORALLY BINDING LETTERS

60.57 However, a settlor determined upon secrecy could make his letter of wishes merely morally binding and of no legal signficance, so that, perhaps, no disclosure even needs to be made of it if by some chance legal proceedings are duly instituted against the trustees. He could state, 'This letter is not to be regarded as a legally significant letter indicating the purposes for which the discretions in my trust deed have been conferred on my trustees because I do not want my trustees to have legal obligations placed upon them by this letter so as to be forced to go out of their way to justify the exercise of their discretions. I believe the imposition of any legal obligations by this letter would cause more difficulties than benefits to accrue, creating greater cost burdens and proving likely to upset relationships between my beneficiaries. Thus, my trustees are only under a moral obligation to take account of the following wishes of mine and shall not be accountable before the courts in relation to taking into account or failing to take into account such wishes. It is on this basis only that they have been prepared to take on the invidious task of exercising discretions under my Trust Deed. I trust the courts will respect my views and my trustees' expectations'

Trustees' discretion in exceptional case to withhold documents in interests of beneficiaries as a whole

60.58 Even where a beneficiary may invoke the court's jurisdiction to seek an order to see trust documents, the trustees may decline in an appropriate case to provide documents and other information to a particular beneficiary[1]. This is where they reasonably consider that providing the relevant documents and information to that beneficiary will not be in the best interests of the beneficiaries as a whole, but will be prejudicial to the ability of the trustees to discharge their obligations under the trust[2].

[1] *Re Cowin* (1886) 33 Ch D 179; *Schmidt v Rosewood Trust Ltd* [2003] UKPC 26, [2003] 2 AC 709 paras 54 & 67.
[2] *Rouse v 100F Australian Trustees Ltd* (1999) 2 ITELR 289, [2000] WTLR 111 at 128–129; *Re Rabbaiotti's Settlement* [2000] WTLR 953 at 962; *Re Lemos Trust* (1992) CILR 26; *Bathurst v Kleinwort Benson (CI) Trustees Ltd* (4 August 2004, unreported), R Ct Guernsey (disclosure only to claimant's lawyer).

60.59 Examples might be a trust involving the conduct of a business where that beneficiary runs a competing business and seeks the information to provide him with a competitive advantage, or is an employee of a competing business seeking to advance his interests with his employer by providing his employer with the information in return for promotion and a pay-rise, or where the beneficiary is seeking the information to support a claim in another jurisdiction that the trust is a sham[1]. And a provision in a pension trust that the trustees should 'observe strict secrecy with regard to the affairs, accounts and transactions' of the trust, but not so as to prevent the disclosure of information to beneficiaries as a whole when thought fit by the trustees, was regarded as justifying an Australian court in not ordering disclosure to an individual beneficiary of an actuary's report[2].

[1]   *Re M Trust, Re L Trust [2003]* JLR N[6], [2003] WTLR 1491, R Ct Jersey.
[2]   *Tierney v King* [1983] 2 Qd R 580, Sup Ct Qld.

60.60 If a beneficiary is dissatisfied with the trustees' refusal to make documents and information available, he may seek the directions of the court so that the court can decide whether the presumption in favour of disclosure should be overridden in the best interests of the beneficiaries as a whole.

60.61 While an assignee of a beneficiary's interest and the personal representative of a deceased beneficiary will have the same rights as the beneficiary[1], it may be that while the beneficiary would have had the usual full rights to trust documents and supporting documentation the assignee or personal representative will not be allowed such full rights because endeavouring to use them for their personal ends which conflict with the interests of the beneficiaries as a whole[2].

[1]   For example, to ensure a life tenant received the income he should have received when alive.
[2]   Cf *Global Custodians Ltd v Mesh* (2000) 2 ITELR 327.

60.62 In some cases it may be possible for confidential or sensitive information to be disclosed subject to an undertaking not to use for other than specified purposes or to publish more widely[1].

[1]   *Lemos v Coutts & Co* 1992–93 CILR 460, Cayman CA; *Morris v Morris* (1993) 9 WAR 150, Sup Ct WA; *Re AG Manchester Ltd [2005]* JLR N[13], R Ct Jersey.

Use of privilege against self-incrimination

60.63 It might be thought that the privilege against self-incrimination could not extend to a trustee or other fiduciary sued for breach of his duty so as to protect a criminally fraudulent trustee (but not a negligent trustee). However, it has been held[1] that it does so extend, unless, it seems, the trustee or other fiduciary expressly covenanted or contracted to waive any claim he might have to the privilege in respect of matters arising from his trusteeship or fiduciary relationship[2].

[1]   *Bishopsgate Investment Management Ltd v Maxwell* [1993] Ch 1, [1992] 2 All ER 886, CA.
[2]   [1992] 2 All ER 886 at 881 and 991; *East India Co v Atkyns* (1720) 1 Com 346. This assumes that the settlor's fair insistence upon this to protect the vulnerable beneficiaries from exploitation of the trustee's office does not amount to an Article 17 abuse of the trustee's Article 6 right to a fair trial under the Convention on Human Rights as incorporated by the Human Rights Act 1998.

*Trustee bound upon demand to give information as to notices
of incumbrances*

60.64 Subject to payment of any costs any person interested in the equitable
interest is entitled to see any notices of dealings with the equitable interest[1].
An intending assignee is probably a person interested in the equitable interest[2].
A trustee should take care in answering enquiries for he may be liable for
honest but negligent misrepresentation[3].

[1] LPA 1925, s 137(8).
[2] See Wolstenholme and Cherry, *Conveyancing Statutes* (13th edn) vol 1, discussion of
s 137(8), but cf (1935) 20 Conv 137 (Gower). A person would certainly be interested if
contractually bound to acquire the interest subject to being relieved of his obligation if any
notices materialised other than those of which he was aware at the time of the contract.
[3] Misrepresentation Act 1967, s 2(1); *Hedley Byrne & Co Ltd v Heller* [1964] AC 465,
[1963] 2 All ER 575, HL.

*Information as to private company where substantially all shares held
by trustees*

60.65 In *Butt v Kelson*[1] substantially all the shares of a private company were
held upon trust and the trustees were directors of the company. It was held
that the beneficiaries were subject to the restrictions imposed by the Articles,
which provided that no member, not being a director, should have any right to
inspect any account, book or document of the company except as conferred
by statute or authorised by the directors or by the company in general
meeting. Romer LJ, delivering the leading judgment in the Court of Appeal,
said that if a beneficiary:

> 'firstly, specifies the documents of the company that he wants to see, secondly,
> makes out a proper case for seeing them, and, thirdly, is not met by any valid
> objection by the other beneficiaries or by the directors from the point of view of
> the company, then the directors should give inspection, not because they, as
> directors, can be compelled to do so, but as a short-circuit, if one may so
> describe it, to an order compelling them to use their voting powers so as to
> bring about what the plaintiff desires to achieve.'

[1] [1952] Ch 197, sub nom *Re Butt* [1952] 1 All ER 167, CA, followed in *Walker v Cherry*,
(15 July 1994, unreported), Ch D.

60.66 However, it is difficult to reconcile this with the principle that, whilst
all beneficiaries being of full age and capacity and between them absolutely
entitled to the settled property can terminate the trust, they cannot whilst the
trust continues control the trustees in the exercise of their powers and
discretions under the trust[1].

[1] See *Re Whichelow* [1953] 2 All ER 1558, [1954] 1 WLR 5, and *Re Brockbank* [1948]
Ch 206, [1948] 1 All ER 287. This aspect is considered at paras 69.25–69.26 below.

60.67 So far as concerns documents relating to the day-to-day running of
underlying companies, normally the balance sheet and profit and loss accounts
should suffice[1]. But, where trustees are allowed to retain fees as directors,

beneficiaries must be allowed to check documents indicating the actual amount of the fees to see if such fees are reasonable and proper.

1   *Chaine-Nickson v Bank of Ireland* [1976] IR 393; *Re Ojjeh Trust* (1992–93) CILR 348.

60.68 Yet there are cases in other jurisdictions holding that trustees should make available to trust beneficiaries accounting and other documents relating to underlying companies[1].

1   *Re Representation Herminia Uberti, re Lombardo Settlement*, (5 December 1990, unreported) R Ct Jersey; *Alhamrani v Russa Management Ltd* [2004] JRC 076A, R Ct Jersey.

Information where trustee a partner

60.69 In *Morris v Morris*[1] a distinction was drawn from *Butt v Kelsen*, namely that between (i) the information and obligations of a trustee acting as a partner with other partners, in making day-by-day discretionary decisions in relation to the running of the business, and (ii) the obligations of a trustee to the beneficiaries of the trust to provide them with information. The beneficiaries should not be able to interfere with the workings of the partnership business: thus, they were not entitled to see the books of account of the partnership business and documents relating to such business other than the balance sheets and profit and loss accounts.

1   (1993) 9 WAR 150.

Paragraph 2

Expensive information

60.70 As above stated, a beneficiary is entitled, either personally or by his solicitor or accountant, to *inspect* the trust accounts and documents. If, however, he requires a copy of an account or document, he must either take copies himself at the trustee's office using his own portable copier or, for a reasonable fee, using an office copier, or pay the necessary expense himself. It is not fair that it should be saddled on the trust estate, nor, of course, can the trustee be expected to incur the expense personally[1]. On the same ground, where a beneficiary demands information as to his rights under the settlement which cannot be furnished by the trustee without the assistance of a solicitor, the trustee is not bound to incur that expense (or if he be himself a solicitor, with power to charge, he is not bound to incur the loss of time), unless the beneficiary is willing to pay the reasonable costs of complying with his requisition[2].

1   *Ottley v Gilby* (1845) 8 Beav 602; *Kemp v Burn* (1863) 4 Giff 348; *Re Watson* (1904) 49 Sol Jo 54.
2   *Re Bosworth* (1889) 58 LJ Ch 432. See also *Gray v Guardian Trust Australia* [2003] NSWSC 704.

Paragraph 3

General law of disclosure

60.71 In recent years legislation has been enacted to give members of the public the right to access information held by others, particularly but not exclusively about them. This legislation includes the Access to Personal Files Act 1987[1], the Access to Medical Reports Act 1988, the Access to Health Records Act 1990 and the Data Protection Act 1998[2]. Most of this legislation is unlikely to apply to trustees as such, but it should not be entirely ignored. In particular, the significance of the Data Protection Act 1998 should not be under-estimated[3]. Detailed comment is beyond the scope of this work, but the following general points can be made.

[1] Repealed by the 1998 Act.
[2] Replacing an earlier Act of 1984.
[3] See M Shillingford 'The Data Protection Act 1998' in the TACT Review, Issue No 11, April 2000, pp 3–8.

60.72 Information about a living person, which can identify him, and which is either processed by automated systems (such as a computer) or recorded in certain kinds of manual filing system, is known as 'personal data'. The person who controls the information is known as the 'data controller' and the living person the subject of the information is known as the 'data subject'[1]. Some of the data may even be 'sensitive personal data'[2], in respect of which special rules apply. A data controller is only subject to the Act if he is established in the UK or processes the data there[3]. In the trust context, personal data will include information about the living beneficiaries and their families, their resources and needs, and so on. The trustees will be the data controllers. No processing of personal data may take place unless the data controller concerned has registered with the Information Commissioner under the Act[4].

[1] Data Protection Act 1998, s 1.
[2] Data Protection Act 1998, s 2.
[3] Data Protection Act 1998, s 5.
[4] Data Protection Act 1998, s 17. There are some exemptions, notably for 'non-automated processing, 'personal, family or household affairs' and 'accounts and records': see the Data Protection (Notification and Notification Fees) Regulations 2000, SI 2000/188.

60.73 An individual has the right in writing and on payment of a fee, and subject to certain exceptions, to require to be informed by a data controller whether he is processing any of that individual's data, and if so to make that data and its source available to him[1]. This may enable a beneficiary to ask a trustee to disclose to him information about that beneficiary, including, say, whether he is a beneficiary, what his entitlement is, whether he is mentioned in a letter of wishes, and in what terms, and so on.

[1] Data Protection Act 1998, s 7.

60.74 The Freedom of Information Act 2000 is very different. This requires 'public authorities' (as defined[1]) to disclose information held by them (not necessarily about the enquirer) on request[2]. In the nature of things it is unlikely that trustees of a private trust would be such public authorities, but the list of such authorities is long[3], and sometimes public bodies act as trustees even of private trusts, such as employee pension trusts.

1   Freedom of Information Act 2000, s 3, 4 and Sch 1.
2   Freedom of Information Act 2000, s 1.
3   Freedom of Information Act 2000, Sch 1.

Chapter 14

THE POWERS OF THE TRUSTEE[1]

ARTICLE 61
GENERAL PRINCIPLES APPLICABLE TO POWERS OF TRUSTEES

61.1

(1)   Unless and until his powers are suspended by an administration action[2], a trustee
    (a)   must consider from time to time the exercise of his distributive and managerial discretions;
    (b)   must not fetter the future exercise of his discretions;
    (c)   must consciously exercise his own discretion in good faith and not passively fall in with suggestions of the settlor or his co-trustees;
    (d)   must exercise his discretions only within the scope of the terms of the relevant power and, then, only for the purposes for which the discretions were conferred on him by the settlor and not perverse to any sensible expectation of the settlor, thereby keeping an even hand among all the beneficiaries except in so far as he may properly discriminate between them[3];
    (e)   must exercise his distributive discretions responsibly in properly informed fashion, taking account of relevant matters and ignoring irrelevant matters;

845

(f)   must exercise his managerial discretions in accordance with the duty of care, so far as not ousted in the trust instrument;

(g)   must not exercise any discretions directly or indirectly for his own benefit unless authorised by the trust instrument or by statute;

(h)   must not commit a fraud on the powers conferred on him.

(2)   If he complies with the above duties the exercise of his discretions will be unchallengeable even if the court itself would consider it reasonable and better to have exercised the discretion in different fashion.

1   The powers of managing infants' estates or settled property conferred by the Settled Land Act 1925 on trustees for purposes of that Act, are outside the scope of this work.
2   See Article 68, below. Also, no discretionary powers can be exercised in the very rare case where the trustees have paid the trust fund into court: *Re Murphy's Trusts* [1900] 1 IR 145; *Re Nettlefold's Trusts* (1888) 59 LT 315.
3   As where the settlor intends discretionary trusts and powers to benefit some more than others and some not at all, or intends his life-tenant-widow to be the main object of his bounty and not a remote wealthy remainderman.

Paragraph 1(a)

Duty to keep discretions under review

61.2   In the case of a discretionary trust, the income or capital subject thereto must be distributed. The trustees have a discretion as to which of the beneficiaries will take what amount, which they must exercise within a reasonable time of the income or capital becoming distributable[1]. In the case of a discretionary power of appointment, the trustees are not bound to exercise it and distribute the income or capital. However, they must consider from time to time whether or not to exercise the power, taking account of the range of objects of the power and then considering the appropriateness of individual appointments[2].

1   *Re Locker's Settlement Trust* [1978] 1 All ER 216.
2   *Re Hay's Settlement Trust* [1981] 3 All ER 786. Without undermining the integrity of the trustee-beneficiary obligation, it seems it would be possible for the trust instrument to provide that the actual exercise of a power of appointment or a power to add or delete beneficiaries shall be unchallengeable like the exercise of a personal power (see paras 1.76, 8.63–8.64, 8.88) unless a fraud on the power (see para 61.31) or, even, that the trustee is to be under no obligation to consider from time to time the exercise of a particular power so that the particular power is to be regarded as a personal power. Note that a fiduciary power can be expressly authorised in the trust instrument to be released.

61.3   Where the trustees have managerial discretions, particularly in investing the trust fund, then they must keep the position under review, taking advice and taking account of the standard investment criteria where investments are concerned[1]. If losses to the trust fund would not have occurred but for breach of the duty to review managerial discretions or breach of specific duties in the investment function, then the trustees will have to account for them.

¹ *Nestle v National Westminster Bank* [1994] 1 All ER 118, CA; Trustee Act 2000 ('TA 2000'), ss 3, 4 and 5.

61.4 Failure to execute discretionary *trusts* of income or capital within a reasonable time leaves such capital or income available for distribution amongst those who were possible recipient beneficiaries within such period¹. Innocent trustees (eg awaiting resolution by the courts of the validity of the trusts) may subsequently exercise their discretions². Wrongdoing trustees may be replaced by new trustees to exercise the discretions or, where distribution of funds is required, the court may direct preparation of a scheme by representative members of the beneficial class or in a simple case fix the basis of distribution itself³.

¹ *Re Locker's Settlement Trust* [1978] 1 All ER 216.
² *Re Locker's Settlement Trust* [1978] 1 All ER 216.
³ *McPhail v Doulton* [1971] AC 424 at 457.

61.5 Failure to exercise a discretionary *power* of appointment over income or capital within a reasonable time or any stipulated time leaves the income or capital belonging to the default beneficiaries¹. Nothing can then be done by a disgruntled object except, it seems, that equitable compensation in the appointed amount will be available where the trustees actually prepared the deed of appointment but negligently executed it a day too late². The court cannot intervene except to remove a trustee (as where the trustee told the object he hated him and would never make an appointment in his favour) where the power of appointment was not exercised in favour of a complaining object of such power, because the court does not positively exercise such power: it only intervenes negatively to restrain the improper exercise of such a power³.

¹ *Re Allen-Meyrick's Will Trust* [1966] 1 All ER 740; *Re Gulbenkian's Settlement Trust* [1970] Ch 408; or capital if the power relating thereto must be exercised before a particular date: *Breadner v Granville-Grossman* [2001] Ch 523.
² *Breadner v Granville-Grossman* [2001] Ch 523 implications discussed by D J Hayton in PBH Birks & A Pretto *Breach of Trust* (Hart Publishing, 2002), Chapter 13 'Overview' p 388.
³ *Re Manisty's Settlement* [1974] Ch 17 at 25–26 and 27–28; *Re Hay's Settlement Trusts* [1981] 3 All ER 786 at 792; *Re Gulbenkian's Settlement Trust* [1970] AC 508 at 525 per Lord Upjohn.

61.6 Exceptionally, if the object of some power like a power of advancement or a power to augment benefits under a pension scheme is also a beneficiary, then the court will intervene to direct exercise of the power in a special case. One example is where a trustee refused to consider exercising her discretion to advance capital to a beneficiary, her daughter, who had married against her wishes, though her co-trustee, the Public Trustee considered it to be a plain case for the advancement to be made¹. Another is where the employer-trustee of its pension trust for employees was in liquidation and the liquidator was in the impossible position of looking after creditors interested in the non-exercise of a power to benefit scheme members and looking after scheme-members interested in that power being exercised in their favour².

61.6 *The powers of the trustee*

1   *Klug v Klug* [1918] 2 Ch 67; also see *White v Gane* (1854) 18 Beav 571 and *Re Lofthouse* (1885) 29 Ch D 921.
2   *Mettoy Pension Trustees Ltd v Evans* [1991] 2 All ER 513 where the remarks of Warner J at p 549 on the extensive powers of the court to carry out discretionary trusts (in ways indicated in *McPhail v Doulton* [1971] AC 424 at 457) need to be restricted to the context of powers to increase the benefits of beneficiaries who also had earned their expectations as deferred pay; and *Thrells v Lomas* [1993] 2 All ER 546. Now under Pensions Act 1995, s 25(2) an independent person should become trustee to exercise such power.

Paragraph 1(b)

Duty not to fetter exercise of discretions

61.7 Just as powers vested in trustees ex officio cannot be released by the trustees (unless expressly authorised)[1], it is trite law that trustees cannot fetter the future exercise of powers vested in trustees ex officio[2]. Any fetter is of no effect. Trustees need to be properly informed of all relevant matters at the time they come to exercise a relevant power. However, the settlor can by conferring appropriate powers, effectively authorise the fettering by the trustees of their discretion. In this way the current exercise of a particular power that has irrevocable impact on part of the trust fund is unimpeachable. The power may be a power of appointment, eg if part of the settled property is settled revocably or irrevocably on B contingent upon attaining 25 years, thereby providing intermediate income for the education of B, or it may be an administrative power, such as a power of investment or management, as where money is invested in a bond that cannot be redeemed for five years, or an option is granted over part of the property[3].

1   *Re Wills' Trust Deeds* [1964] Ch 219.
2   *Swales v IRC* [1984] 3 All ER 16 at 24; *Re Gibson's Settlement Trust* [1981] Ch 179 at 182–183.
3   Trustees now have much wider powers conferred on them than previously, when grants of options were impermissible as fettering trustees' functions: *Oceanic Steam Navigation Co v Sutherberry* (1880) 16 Ch D 236, CA.

Paragraph 1(c)

Duty consciously to act in good faith

61.8 A discretion is not properly exercised by a trustee unless he consciously directs his mind to the fact that he only has to exercise his discretion if he considers this appropriate in all the circumstances. Thus, where a trustee automatically signs a deed of appointment placed before him by the settlor the deed will be void[1]. Again, if trustees automatically pay all the income of the trust fund to the infant beneficiary's father without appreciating they have a discretion to pay only the amount needed for the infant's maintenance, the infant's father will have to repay all the money[2]. Similarly, a power to retain assets and not sell them had to be consciously exercised to oust a *Howe v Dartmouth* apportionment between life tenant and remainderman[3].

Any decision actuated by caprice[4] or spite,[5] or by a bribe[6] will be a nullity[7].

1   *Turner v Turner* [1984] Ch 100, like an equitable *non est factum.*
2   *Wilson v Turner* (1883) 22 Ch D 521, CA.
3   *Re Guinness' Settlement* [1966] 2 All ER 497.
4   *Re Manisty's Settlement* [1973] 2 All ER 1203 at 121; *Re Pauling's Settlement Trust* [1964] Ch 303 at 333.
5   *Klug v Klug* [1918] 2 Ch 67.
6   This will also fall foul of the principle that a fiduciary power cannot be exercised in the power-holder's own favour unless authorised: *Re Skeats Settlement* (1889) 42 Ch D 522 at 526.
7   See also under Paragraph 1(e), para 61.22.

Paragraph 1(d)

Duty to exercise discretions only for purposes intended by settlor so as fairly to benefit the beneficiaries

61.9 First, trustees must not exercise any discretionary power ultra vires its terms, so they must keep within the specified class of beneficiaries or objects[1] and otherwise act in accordance with the terminology of the trust instrument[2] or of statutory default powers. Any requisite consents to the exercise of powers must be obtained[3], unless the court can dispense with them in the case of land held on trust[4] or circumvent the matter by granting managerial powers[5] or by the replacement of a person, such as a protector, refusing consent in breach of his fiduciary obligation[6].

1   *Re Gulbenkian's Settlement Trust* [1970] AC 508 at 518.
2   *Harris v Lord Shuttleworth* [1994] ICR 991 at 999, [1995] OPLR 79 at 86–87 per Glidewell LJ; *Wrightson Ltd v Fletcher Challenge Nominees Ltd* [2001] UKPC 23, [2001] OPLR 249 at para 11. Decisions must be implemented in any requisite form: *Kain v Hutton* [2004] 1 NZLR 318.
3   Eg the consent of the life tenant to a power of advancement: *Re Forster's Settlement* [1942] Ch 199.
4   Trusts of Land and Appointment of Trustees Act 1996, s 14; see para 45.45 above.
5   Under Trustee Act 1925, s 57; see para 47.108.
6   There being such inherent power (*Re Papadimitriou* [2004] WTLR 1141, para 71) if there is inherent power to appoint a protector as established in *Steele v Paz Ltd* [1993–95] Manx LR 102, and on appeal at 426; as to protectors, see para 1.78 above.

61.10 Second, trustees must not exercise their powers other than for the purposes for which the settlor conferred those powers so that the trustees fulfil the settlor's expectations[1]. This is of particular significance where the settlor has provided his trustees with exceptionally broad flexible powers, though expecting them to be used for relatively narrow purposes: it may be said that he provides the trustee as conductor with a large orchestra of powers in the trust instrument but he expects the trustee to play only music of the type indicated by him eg in a letter of wishes or in oral discussions with the trustees.

1   *McPhail v Doulton* [1971] AC 424 at 449, HL; *Re Hay's Settlement Trust* [1981] 3 All ER 786 at 792; *Hayim v Citibank* [1987] AC 730 at 746, PC; *Re Beatty's Will Trust* [1990] 3 All ER 844 at 846; *Edge v Pensions Ombudsman* [1998] Ch 512 at 535 per Scott V-C and on appeal [2000] Ch 602 at 627 per Chadwick LJ.

61.11 Where a range of beneficiaries is intended to be benefited throughout the duration of the trust, the settlor expects the trustees to act fairly in

61.11 *The powers of the trustee*

exercising their powers by holding an even hand between all the beneficiaries except where he intends different discriminatory treatment to be accorded to the beneficiaries[1]. Examples of this are where he has created extensive discretionary trusts or powers of appointment in a family trust or where trustees of a pension trust have extensive discretionary powers capable of discriminating between different classes of beneficiaries[2] or where he intends his life-tenant-widow to be well looked-after as the main object of his bounty rather than a remote wealthy remainderman, like a charity or a cousin who is next of kin[3].

1   Or in favour of persons who technically are not beneficiaries like the two elderly occupants of the Hong Kong house as to which the trustee-executors had no duties (other than not to benefit themselves) in *Hayim v Citibank* [1987] AC 730, PC.
2   *Edge v Pensions Ombudsman* [2000] Ch 602.
3   *Nestle v National Westminster Bank* [1994] 1 All ER 118, CA affirming Hoffmann J, reported [2000] WTLR 795. Breach gives rise to personal accountability here (eg *Re Mulligan* [1998] 1 NZLR 481) though exercise of a power could contravene the fraud on a power doctrine: see para 61.31 below.

61.12 It is perverse to any sensible expectation of the settlor for trustees to exercise their powers for purposes they know were not intended by the settlor so that they commit a fraud on the power[1]. However, in the area of pension trusts where beneficiaries have earned their rights and so have higher expectations than beneficiaries under family trusts, there has developed the idea[2] that trustees 'must not arrive at a perverse decision ie a decision to which no reasonable body of trustees could arrive'.

1   See Paragraph 1(h), para 61.31.
2   Enunciated by Glidewell LJ in *Harris v Shuttleworth* [1994] ICR 991 at 999, [1995] OPLR 79 at 86–87, CA.

61.13 This resembles the public law, judicial review *Wednesbury* principle[1], that the decision of a public body (such as a domestic tribunal) would be void if it was so unreasonable that no reasonable body could have arrived at it. Where the decision of a body of pension trustees relates to whether someone should receive a pension early, on grounds like incapacity or disablement that is likely to be irremediable, or should receive a lump sum as the deceased's cohabitee, the body is acting rather like a domestic tribunal[2]. Hence it was natural for an experienced judicial review judge[3] expressly to adopt judicial review principles as laid down in an earlier public law case[4].

1   Named after *Associated Provincial Picture Houses Ltd v Wednesbury Corporation* [1948] 1 KB 223, CA.
2   And see Pensions Act 1995, s 50 on procedural arrangements needing to be in place for resolution of disputes.
3   As in *Harris v Lord Shuttleworth* [1994] ICR 991 at 999, [1995] OPLR 79 at 86–87, CA; see also *Wild v Pensions Ombudsman* [1996] 2 FLR 680 at 688 and 691.
4   *Lee v Showmen's Guild of Great Britain* [1952] 2 QB 329, CA.

61.14 In *Edge v Pensions Ombudsman*[1], where a pension scheme's rules were amended by the trustees to take account of an actuarial surplus, but did not benefit one class of beneficiaries, Scott V-C accepted this judicial review approach stating[2]:

'The judge may disagree with the manner in which the trustees have exercised their discretion, but, unless they can be seen to have taken into account irrelevant, improper or irrational factors, or unless their decision can be said to be one that no reasonable body of trustees properly directing themselves would have reached, the judge cannot interfere.'

1   [1998] Ch 512.
2   [1998] Ch 512 at 534.

61.15 On appeal, the Court of Appeal[1] thought it 'no coincidence that courts considering the exercise of discretionary powers by those to whom such powers have been entrusted (albeit in different contexts), should reach similar and consistent conclusions and should express these conclusions in the same language'. However, it considered[2] it 'unnecessary to consider, in the present case, how far an analogy between the principles applicable in public law cases can or should be pressed in the different context of a private pension scheme'.

1   [2000] Ch 602 at 628.
2   [2000] Ch 602 at 630.

61.16 In a pension scheme trust, an employee enters into a contract of employment and as a condition thereof pays his first contribution to the trustees, thereupon making him a settlor-beneficiary[1]. It may well be that, in that context, it is proper to regard that employee as having a reasonable and legitimate expectation[2] that the trustees will not be permitted to make a decision adversely affecting his interests that is a decision that no reasonable body of trustees could have made[3]. Nonetheless, it is still a matter of property law, and not public law.

1   *Air Jamaica Ltd v Charlton* [1999] 1 WLR 1399, PC.
2   See D Hayton, *Pension trusts and traditional trusts: drastically different species of trusts*, [2005] Conv 229, and cf implied terms giving effect to the reasonable expectations of the mortgagor and mortgagee in *Paragon Finance plc v Staunton* [2001] EWCA Civ 1466, [2002] 2 All ER 248 at paras 36–42: mortgagee not to exercise interest-rate-changing discretion dishonestly, for an improper purpose, capriciously or arbitrarily nor in a way that no reasonable mortgagee would do.
3   Cf *Scott v National Trust* [1998] 2 All ER 705 (not a pension case).

61.17 However, certainly in the context of a private family trust where the beneficiaries are neither settlors nor parties to the transaction, there is no need to invoke *Wednesbury* public law principles. The beneficiaries have well-established private law rights, relating to the doctrine of fraud on a power, that are focused upon the purposes and expectations of the settlor[1]. Once one public law principle is held to apply there is a danger that judges not steeped in trust law will begin to apply other public law principles, for example, concerned with natural justice and due process, as to the way in which decisions are arrived at. As has been stated[2], 'The difference between the public law and the trust approach is that the former focuses on the individual's opportunity to be heard before a decision, whereas the trust concept focuses on the information available to the person making the decision'. The latter aspect will now be examined.

1   See para 61.31 below.
2   *R v Charity Commissioners, ex p Baldwin* [2001] WTLR 137 at 148–149.

Paragraph 1(e)

*Duty in exercising distributive discretions to make a properly
informed decision*

61.18 For trustees to act responsibly they must inform themselves, before
making a decision, of matters which are relevant to the decision[1]. Their
decision must then take account of such relevant matters and ignore irrelevant
matters[2]. However, the rules of natural justice do not apply to the exercise of
a discretion by trustees (unless imported by the terms of a trust), so that
trustees, minded to benefit X, do not have to inform Y (for whom less will be
available) so as to afford Y the opportunity to make representations against
such a course of action[3].

Examination is thus focused upon the matters known to, and considered by,
the trustees in their decision-making process[4]. The principle is known as the
Hastings-Bass principle, from the decision in *Re Hastings-Bass*[5] of the Court
of Appeal. This stated:

> 'Where a trustee is given a discretion as to some matter under which he acts in
> good faith, the court should not interfere with his action, notwithstanding that
> it does not have the full effect which he intended unless
> (1)   what he has achieved is unauthorised by the power conferred on him, or
> (2)   it is clear that he would not have acted as he did (a) had he not taken
>   into account considerations which he should not have taken into
>   account or (b) had he not failed to take into account considerations
>   which he ought to have taken into account'.

The decision in *Re Hastings-Bass* was based on the earlier decision in *Re
Abrahams' WT*[6], though these were not the first cases to raise the same
problem[7]. Both *Hastings-Bass* and *Abrahams* concerned trusts which were
ultimately held to be partly void for perpetuity. Ignorant of the partial
invalidity, the trustees in each case had purported to exercise powers of
advancement 'for the benefit of' particular beneficiaries. In the earlier case, the
effect of the invalidity was that the exercise of the power was not 'for the
benefit of' the intended beneficiary, and was thus *ultra vires* and void. But in
the later case the invalidity was less serious, and the exercise of the power
could still be said to be 'for the benefit of' the beneficiary, the trustees' actions
saving a large amount of estate duty. Hence it was intra vires, and valid.
However, in *Mettoy Pension Trustees Ltd v Evans*[8] Warner J held that the
principle was wider than mere ultra vires, and involved a failure to take
account of relevant considerations, which might be of law or fact. But he
stated the proposition in positive rather than negative terms:

> 'Where a trustee acts under a discretion given to him by the terms of the trust,
> the court will interfere with his action if it is clear that he would not have acted
> as he did had he not failed to take into account considerations which he ought
> to have taken into account.'[9]

Of course, a statement that the court will not intervene *unless* certain
conditions are fulfilled is not logically equivalent to a (positive) statement that
the court *will* intervene if the same conditions are fulfilled[10].However that

may be, a fuller, more modern restatement of the rule, taking into account subsequent case law developments, is this:

> 'Where trustees act under a discretion given to them by the terms of the trust, in circumstances in which they are free to decide whether or not to exercise that discretion, but the effect of the exercise is different from that which they intended, the court will interfere with their action if it is clear that they would not have acted as they did had they not failed to take into account considerations which they ought to have taken into account, or taken into account considerations which they ought not to have taken into account.'[11]

The rule has been applied in some offshore jurisdictions, such as Jersey[12] and the Cayman Islands[13].

It is thus clear that if, say, trustees mistakenly believe that material considerations, eg the wishes of the settlor[14], or the funding implications of their proposed action[15], are different from what they in fact are, and act on that basis, when they would not have done so otherwise, the exercise of discretion falls within the scope of the rule. Similarly, if they act in the belief and on the basis that the trusts provide a particular route to take, but in fact they do not so provide[16], or they fail to appreciate the impact of the rules against perpetuities on those trusts[17] .But the driving force in recent cases has been tax. It has been held that where trustees are advised that acting in a certain way will achieve particular tax objectives, and they act upon that basis, but the advice given is wrong and the tax objectives are not achieved, their action will fall within this principle, and the position be reversed[18]. The same appears to apply if the trustees never think about the tax consequences of their action at all, which then turn out to be unacceptable[19], or if they are correctly advised but mistakenly ignore the advice and act in a way which causes unwanted tax consequences[20].

Although the principle is usually invoked against trustees by disgruntled objects of a power, or by others adversely affected, such as the employer in a pension scheme trust[21], it can equally be used by the trustees against their own decisions, so as to protect themselves from claims by beneficiaries in respect of disastrous tax consequences of their negligent exercise of powers of appointment[22]. And, if (as is discussed below) the consequences of the application of the principle are that the decision is void rather than voidable, third parties such as the Revenue authorities could invoke it too[23].

1   *Stannard v Fisons Pension Trust* [1992] IRLR 27, CA; *Scott v National Trust for places of Historic and Natural Beauty* [1998] 2 All ER 705 at 717; *R v Charity Commissioners, ex p Baldwin* [2001] WTLR 137 at 148.
2   *Re Hastings-Bass* [1975] Ch 25 at 41.
3   *Karger v Paul* [1984] VR 161 at 166 endorsed in *R v Charity Commissioners, ex p Baldwin* [2001] WTLR 137 at 148; *Scott v National Trust for places of Historic and Natural Beauty* [1998] 2 All ER 705 at 717; *Re B* [1987] 2 All ER 475 at 478.
4   See *Stannard v IRC* 1991 Pensions LR 225 at para 65 per Staughton LJ, applied in *Hearn v Younger* [2002] EWHC 963 (Ch) at para 91, [2002] WTLR 1317. However, until Civil Procedure Rules on disclosure can be invoked, it is difficult to obtain sufficient evidence as to the reasoning of the trustees to enable litigation to be instituted: see para 60.37 above.
5   [1975] Ch 25 at 41.
6   [1969] 1 Ch 463.
7   Eg *Re Vestey's Settlement* [1951] Ch 209; *Re Pilkington's Will Trusts* [1961] Ch 466, CA (in HL [1964] AC 612).

8   [1991] 2 All ER 513.
9   [1991] 2 All ER 513 at 552.
10   Edward Nugee QC, 'Re Hastings-Bass Again – Void Or Voidable? And Further Reflections' [2003] PCB 173 at 184; Tax Bulletin 83, June 2006, 1292 at 1293.
11   *Sieff v Fox* [2005] EWHC 1312 (Ch), [2005] WTLR 891, 8 ITELR 93, per Lloyd LJ, followed by Lightman J in *Betafence Ltd v Veys* [2006] EWHC 999 (Ch), [2006] WTLR 941, [2006] Pens LR 137, and by Smellie CJ in *A v Rothschild Trust Cayman Ltd* [2006] WTLR 1129 (Cayman Grand Court).
12   *Re Green GLG Trust* (2002) 5 ITELR 590; *Re Representation Dubham and La Ville Trustees Ltd* [2005] JRC 142.
13   *Barclays Private Bank & Trust (Cayman) Ltd v Chamberlain* (5 May 2005, unreported); *A v Rothschild Trust Cayman Ltd* [2006] WTLR 1129.
14   *Abacus Trust Co (IOM) v Barr* [2003] Ch 409.
15   *Hearn v Younger* [2002] WTLR 1317.
16   *AMP (UK) plc v Barker* [2001] PLR 77, [2001] WTLR 1265, 3 ITELR 414.
17   *Re Hastings-Bass* [1975] Ch 25, CA.
18   *Burrell v Burrell* [2005] EWHC 245 (Ch), [2005] WTLR 313, [2005] STC 569; *Sieff v Fox* [2005] EWHC 1312 (Ch), [2005] WTLR 891, 8 ITELR 93; *A v Rothschild Trust Cayman Ltd* [2006] WTLR 1129 (Cayman Grand Court). HM Revenue and Customs consider that the principle should not apply at all in this case: *Tax Bulletin 83*, 1291 at 1294.
19   *Green v Cobham* [2002] STC 820, [2000] WTLR 1101;
20   *Abacus Trust Co (IOM) Ltd v NSPCC* [2001] STC 1344, [2001] WTLR 953. HM Revenue and Customs consider that the principle should not apply at all in this case: *Tax Bulletin 83*, 1291 at 1294.
21   *AMP (UK) plc v Barker* [2001] PLR 77, [2001] WTLR 1265, 3 ITELR 414.
22   *Green v Cobham* [2002] STC 820, [2000] WTLR 1101; *Abacus Trust Co (IOM) Ltd v NSPCC* [2001] STC 1344, [2001] WTLR 953; *Abacus Trust Co (IOM) v Barr* [2003] EWHC 114 (Ch), [2003] Ch 409; *Burrell v Burrell* [2005] EWHC 245 (Ch), [2005] STC 569. But see Brian Green QC, *The law relating to trustees' mistakes – where are we now?* (2003) 17 Tru LI 114, at 122–23.
23   See *Sieff v Fox* [2005] EWHC 1312 (Ch), [2005] WTLR 891, 8 ITELR 93, para 78. In the past the UK Revenue have generally declined to become involved (though they were actually defendants in both *Re Abrahams' WT* and *Re Hastings-Bass*). But in June 2006 they announced their intention to give active consideration to intervening in appropriate cases to argue against the application of the principle: *Tax Bulletin 83*, 1291 at 1293.

WHAT ARE MATERIAL CONSIDERATIONS?

61.19 If the principle involves failing to take into account considerations which trustees ought to have taken into account, or taking into account considerations which they ought not to have taken into account, the obvious question is, which considerations are material for this purpose? There seems no doubt that the settlor's wishes are[1]. That apart, the cases give no very clear answer. For example, in one case the judge distinguished between tax considerations which were material for trustees of one family trust but not trustees of another, yet were material for another family member whose consent to a transaction was requisite[2] .It seems to be largely a matter of impression and common sense.

1   *Abacus Trust Co (IOM) v Barr* [2003] EWHC 114 (Ch), [2003] Ch 409, at paras 23, 25; *Re Esteem Settlement* [2003] JRC 092, [2004] WTLR 1, at para 122; Hayton, Pension trusts and traditional trusts: drastically different species of trusts, [2005] Conv 229.
2   *Sieff v Fox* [2005] EWHC 1312 (Ch), [2005] WTLR 891, 8 ITELR 93, para 92. HM Revenue and Customs agree: *Tax Bulletin 83*, 1291 at 1294.

THE ANALOGY WITH PUBLIC LAW

61.20 The possible analogy between attacking the exercise of trustees' discretion and attacking that of public bodies in public law has already been discussed and rejected[1]. For the reasons given it is submitted that the analogy is no more compelling in the context of the *Hastings-Bass* principle[2]. This concerns interests in private property, not the control of powers given to public bodies in the public interest.

1   See paras 61.13–61.17.
2   See eg S Taube QC, The principle in Hastings-Bass and *Sieff v Fox*: Analogies with administrative law, [2006] PCB 155.

WOULD OR MIGHT?

61.21 One problem which has arisen in the cases is the degree of likelihood that the trustees, not having made the mistake which in fact they made, would have made a different decision. In some cases, including *Hastings-Bass* itself, it has been said that the court must be satisfied that the trustees *would* have decided differently. In others, it has been said that it is enough if the trustees *might* have done so[1]. Sometimes it has made no difference on the facts[2]. In *Sieff v Fox* the matter was fully argued and Lloyd LJ (as a judge of first instance) concluded that

> 'for the purposes of a case where the trustees are not under a duty to act, the relevant test is still that stated in *Re Hastings-Bass*, namely whether, if they had not misunderstood the effect that their actual exercise of the discretionary power would have, they *would* have acted differently. In my judgment that is correct both on authority, starting with *Re Hastings-Bass* itself, and on principle. Only in a case where the beneficiary is entitled to require the trustees to act, such as *Kerr* or *Stannard*, should it suffice to vitiate the trustees' decision to show that they *might* have acted differently.'[3]

The distinction between powers that *may* be exercised and powers that *must* be exercised is a convenient one for some purposes, but it is one which is less and less relevant in other areas of trust law, such as certainty of objects[4], the non-assignability of an object's interest, the right of an object to have his claim considered, the need for all objects to join in an application to the trustee to terminate the trust[5], and the right to information about the trust[6]. It does not seem an altogether satisfactory distinction in the present context. Although the trustee is obliged to exercise a trust power, the actual exercise of it, as an act, is not different in quality or degree from the exercise of a mere power. It is therefore difficult to see why, in this context, there should be a different test for upsetting that exercise, rather than complaining about its non-exercise (where it would make a difference).

A different argument is that a better more functional distinction lies between cases involving voluntary family settlements by patriarchs providing the 'icing on the cake' for family members and cases involving pension trusts where the beneficiaries have earned significant benefits crucial to a decent retirement for themselves or their cohabitees. 'Would' is the appropriate test for the former, whereas 'might' is appropriate for the latter. This fits most of the cases, but is inconsistent with Lloyd LJ's view[7]. The thinking is that the hurdle for those who have paid for such crucial rights to have the trustees think again about not accepting a claim (eg to an early disability retirement if sufficiently disabled or a pension if the deceased's 'cohabitee') should be lower than for those who have not[8]. Some may consider this to be a significant difference in considering the constitution and construction of trusts in the first place[9], but find it difficult to see why it should govern once the trusts have been fully established, considering the matter then to be a matter of property, not contract. However, where beneficiaries of pension trusts are also settlors contributing to the trust fund, the trustees have to exercise their powers in accordance with the settlor's expectations which are justifiably high as to how the trustees should fulfil their functions concerning the trust property. Pensions trusts are a special case. It remains to be seen how the law might develop with regard to other kinds of trusts created for consideration. It is noteworthy that a special regime already exists for disputes concerning the co-ownership of land[10].

[1] *Kerr v British Leyland (Staff) Trustees Ltd* (1986) [2001] WTLR 1071, CA; *Stannard v Fisons Pensions Trust Ltd* [1992] IRLR 27, CA; *AMP (UK) plc v Barker* [2001] PLR 77, [2001] WTLR 1265, 3 ITELR 414; *Hearn v Younger* [2002] WTLR 1317.

[2] *AMP (UK) plc v Barker* [2001] PLR 77, [2001] WTLR 1265, 3 ITELR 414; *Re Green GLG Trust* (2002) 5 ITELR 590, at para 29; *Gallaher Ltd v Gallaher Pensions Ltd* [2005] EWHC 42 (Ch), [2005] All ER (D) 177 (Jan).

[3] [2005] EWHC 1312 (Ch), [2005] 3 All ER 693, para 77, [2005] WTLR 891, dutifully followed by Lightman J in *Betafence Ltd v Veys* [2006] EWHC 999 (Ch), para 72 [2006] All ER (D) 91 (May) despite sympathy for the apt distinction being between trusts where beneficiaries had earned their rights and trusts where they were mere volunteers.

[4] *McPhail v Doulton* [1971] AC 424, HL.

[5] Under *Saunders v Vautier* (1841) 4 Beav 115, Cr. & Ph. 240; see *Rosewood Trust Ltd v Schmidt* [2003] 2 AC 709, para 41.

[6] *Rosewood Trust Ltd v Schmidt* [2003] UKPC 26, [2003] 2 AC 709, PC.

[7] *Sieff v Fox* [2005] EWHC 1312 (Ch), [2005] WTLR 891 [2005] 3 All ER 693, at paras 76, 77.

[8] See D Hayton, Pension trusts and traditional trusts: drastically different species of trusts, [2005] Conv 229.

[9] See *Re National Grid Group* [1997] Pensions LR 167 (on appeal [1999] EWCA Civ 961, and [2001] UKHL 20, [2001] 1 WLR 864.

[10] See Article 45.

VOID OR VOIDABLE?

61.22 Another problem relates to the result of the principle applying to a decision by trustees: is the decision *void*, or merely *voidable*? If the former, third parties may take the point, and the court has no discretion to set aside on terms. If the latter, only the beneficiaries and other objects of the power can complain, but the court has more flexibility in dealing with the consequences of its decision.

In some of the cases, the decision was held to be void[1]. In others, the principle was held not to apply[2], or, if it did, it made no difference whether the decision was void or voidable[3], and so (in either case) the court did not need to reach a conclusion. In one case, where the point was argued but rectification of the trust instrument was granted, so rendering the point academic, the judge observed *obiter* 'that the language of the cases strongly suggests that the application of the principle leads to the act being void rather than voidable'[4] .But in *Abacus Trust Co (IOM) v Barr*, again after argument, Lightman J decided that

> 'A successful challenge made to a decision under the Rule should in principle result in the decision being held voidable and not void. This accords with the ordinary principles of Equity that (leaving aside the separate and distinct self-dealing rule) a decision challenged on grounds of breach of fiduciary duty is voidable and not void.'[5]

This view had powerful extra-curial support[6]. It reasoned that, if the common law doctrine of 'non est factum', rendering a transaction *void*, only applied where the transaction was essentially different in substance or in kind from the transaction intended, so in a case where the trustees had indeed made a decision, albeit flawed, this was not essentially different, and hence it should be voidable rather than void[7] .Moreover, gifts or appointments made by individuals due to a mistake as to the effect of the voluntary transaction (and not merely as to the consequences or the advantages to be gained by it) are only voidable. Thus, the court should be able to side-step at least some of the potentially disruptive and unfair consequences of holding a trustee's decision void. Yet in *Sieff v Fox* the matter was argued again, and Lloyd LJ expressed the view that Lightman J's decision, though attractive, was open to doubt in light of the earlier authority[8]. However, he himself had no need to reach a conclusion on the point, and his remarks were therefore *obiter*.

The main problem with Lightman J's solution is that it seems erroneously based upon the effect of flawed consent upon a transaction such as a gift. In such a context one may talk of a transaction completely different from that intended being void, but others which are flawed merely voidable. Instead, however, the transaction concerned here is the exercise of a fiduciary power of appointment under a trust. The appointor does not give away his own beneficial property[9]. On the contrary, his requisite conduct constitutes the event stipulated for by the *settlor* upon the happening of which the equitable interest concerned passes to the appointee as a due gift from the settlor. It satisfies the relevant contingency, and works out the trusts[10]. It is no different in principle from the case of a trust for A for life but if A attempts to alienate then for B for life. The interest of B is contingent on A's conduct.

The correct analogy therefore ought to be, not with gifts, but with other purported exercises of powers. And it is well established that both an attempt to appoint outside the class of objects[11] ,and an attempt to subvert the power by committing a fraud on it[12],are *void* rather than voidable. The power has simply not been exercised. It is notable that in *Hastings-Bass* itself the Court of Appeal commented on the earlier case of *Abrahams* by saying:

> 'Cross J might well have been justified in that case in considering that the intended sub-settlement in its attenuated form could not reasonably be regarded as beneficial to the daughter intended to be advanced and so could not be treated as an exercise of discretion falling within the terms of section 32. If so, we think he reached the right conclusion.'[13]

The interesting question in a *Hastings-Bass* case therefore is, what exactly is the conduct required if a beneficial interest is to pass? Is it the execution of the stipulated formality with all the accompanying mental attributes and non-attributes *required in the case of a gift*? Or will something less do, and if so what? This must be a question of the settlor's intention in every case[14], as established by the words used in the factual matrix concerned. For the sake of convenience, however, the cases could establish a default position as to the settlor's intention, and to assume *that* intention unless it is made clear in the trust instrument that it is not so. This is a familiar technique in other contexts. Unfortunately, there are no cases dealing explicitly with this question in the context of the *Hastings-Bass* rule. But there are cases dealing with the exercise of powers of appointment more generally.

Thus, for example, where a power of appointment has been conferred upon a person who, at the time when he comes to exercise the power, has no capacity to dispose of property at all (eg a minor), such a power may nonetheless be validly exercised by inter vivos instrument by that person[15]. The reason is that 'the authority to dispose proceeds from the donor of the power and not from the donee'[16]. The sole question is, has the stipulated event occurred?[17] Similarly it is no objection that the appointment is contained in a will made by a foreigner who has no testamentary capacity to alienate property to the same extent[18].

Hence, in the *Hastings-Bass* context, *if* the conduct stipulated for by the settlor is a decision with due formality, the trustee-appointor being required to have taken into account all and only relevant considerations, and the trustee has not done so, the conduct has not occurred and so the power has not been exercised. On the other hand, if the stipulated conduct is a simple decision with due formality, *whether the trustee has taken such considerations into account or not*, then a failure to do so is simply irrelevant. The stipulated conduct or event – the decision – has occurred, and the power has been exercised. There is simply no room for an 'equitable' halfway house leading to voidability.

The matter can be simply tested by supposing a trust instrument conferring a power of appointment which expressly required a decision 'taking into account all and only relevant considerations'. Plainly a failure to observe this requirement would be fatal, and the power would not have been exercised. However, in the converse case (of a power exercisable regardless of what considerations are or are not taken into account) not so, and the power would have been properly exercised. All that therefore is in issue is, what is the default position? On this view, then, the case-law before *Barr* had implicitly concluded that the default position was that part of the stipulated conduct required for a trustee's power of appointment or advancement to be effectively exercised was a requirement that all and only relevant considerations be taken into account. That seems a reasonable position to adopt, given (i) that trustees exercising a discretion have a duty to take relevant considerations into account[19], and (ii) that the alternative construction, ie that the settlor intended the powers he conferred on trustees to be properly exercised even where the trustee-appointor took into account irrelevant considerations, or failed to take into account relevant ones, would lead to absurdity. Thus, for example, in another case where trustees had made appointments but had failed to consider whether they had a discretion at all, the judge, relying on the *Hastings-Bass* line of authority, said:

'If appointors fail altogether to exercise the duties of consideration referred to by Sir Robert Megarry V.-C.[20]then *there is no exercise of the power and the purported appointment is a nullity.*'[21]

Barr has thus subverted the *Hastings-Bass* default position, though could be supported by cases holding individual's mistaken appointments to be voidable. However, *Sieff v Fox*[22] brought up the distinction between mistakes made by individual donors or appointors and mistakes made by trustees of fiduciary powers. Where an appointor with a personal power executes a deed drafted by his lawyer intended to exercise the power in a limited way, but the deed in fact goes further than the appointor's intentions or the draftsman's instructions, it is *voidable* at the instance of the appointor[23]. Similarly, where such an appointor exercised the power forgetting that she had already provided for the appointee earlier, and the result was the opposite of what she intended[24] But these cases dealt with appointors owing no fiduciary duty to the objects, and not with trustees[25], and in any event in none of them was there any argument as to voidness or voidability. For an individual to make a mistake of this kind is not in principle the same as a trustee failing to take into account all and only relevant considerations: an individual is not obliged to take account of all relevant considerations and is free to take account of irrelevant considerations. Thus, a condition for the effective exercise of a personal power of appointment is not taking account of all and only relevant considerations. However, it is submitted that such conduct is requisite for the exercise of a fiduciary power of appointment or advancement, and if not present the exercise will be void in the absence of a contrary intent in the trust instrument.

1   *Re Abrahams' Will Trusts* [1969] 1 Ch 463; *Green v Cobham* [2002] STC 820, [2000] WTLR 1101; *Abacus Trust Co (IOM) Ltd v NSPCC* [2001] STC 1344, [2001] WTLR 953; *Hearn v Younger* [2002] WTLR 1317, at paras 86, 91; *Re Green GLG Trust* (2002) 5 ITELR 590, at para 31; cf *A v Rothschild Trust Cayman Ltd* [2006] WTLR 1129, at paras 28, 38 (void on facts, but not deciding that that is only response available).
2   *Re Hastings-Bass* [1975] Ch 25, CA; *Mettoy Pension Trustees Ltd v Evans* [1991] 2 All ER 513.
3   *Burrell v Burrell* [2005] EWHC 245 (Ch), [2005] STC 569; *Sieff v Fox* [2005] EWHC 1312 (Ch), [2005] WTLR 891, 8 ITELR 93.
4   *AMP (UK) plc v Barker* [2001] PLR 77, [2001] WTLR 1265, 3 ITELR 414, at para 90.
5   [2003] Ch 409, at para 33; followed in *Gallaher Ltd v Gallaher Pensions Ltd* [2005] EWHC 42 (Ch), paras 169–70, [2005] All ER (D) 177 (Jan). HM Revenue and Customs agree: *Tax Bulletin 83*, 1291 at 1293.
6   Sir Robert Walker, *The Limits of the Rule in Re Hastings-Bass* [2002] PCB 226, 13 KCLJ 173; see also the 16th edition of this work, at 698–99. A similar view has since been taken in the context of company law: *Hunter v Senate Support Services Ltd* [2004] EWHC 1085 (Ch), para 179, [2005] 1 BCLC 175. Contrast Edward Nugee QC, 'Re Hastings-Bass Again – Void Or Voidable? And Further Reflections' [2003] PCB 173.
7   See [2003] EWHC 114 (Ch), [2003] Ch 409, at para 32.
8   [2005] EWHC 1312 (Ch), [2005] WTLR 891, 8 ITELR 93, at paras 79, 81, 119.
9   As pointed out by Lloyd LJ in *Sieff v Fox* [2005] EWHC 1312 (Ch), [2005] WTLR 891, 8 ITELR 93, at para 85.
10   See *Muir v Muir [1943]* AC 468, *Pilkington v IRC [1964]* AC 612.
11   See para 61.9.
12   *Cloutte v Storey* [1911] 1 Ch 18, CA; see para 61.31.
13   [1975] Ch 25 at 41.
14   *Von Brockdorff v Malcolm* (1885) 30 Ch D 172 at 179.

[15] *Re D'Angibeau* (1880) 15 Ch D 228.
[16] *Pouey v Horden* [1900] 1 Ch 492 at 495.
[17] Hence there would be a problem if the appointor became incapable of selecting, e g through mental disorder: *Pouey v Horden* [1900] 1 Ch 492 at 494.
[18] *Re Price* [1900] 1 Ch 442; *Pouey v Horden* [1900] 1 Ch 492; *Re Megret* [1901] 1 Ch 547; *Re Waite's Settlement Trusts* [1958] Ch 100; cf Morris (1957) 73 LQR 459.
[19] *Scott v National Trust for places of Historic Interest and Natural Beauty* [1998] 2 All ER 705 at 717.
[20] In *Re Hay's Settlement Trusts* [1982] 1 WLR 202 at 209–10.
[21] *Turner v Turner* [1984] Ch 100 at 111 (emphasis supplied).
[22] [2005] EWHC 1312 (Ch), [2005] 3 All ER 693, [2005] WTLR 891 at para 108.
[23] *Walker v Armstrong* (1856) 8 De G M & G 531; *Re Walton's Settlement* [1922] 2 Ch 509; followed in *Gibbon v Mitchell* [1990] 1 WLR 1304 (mistake in releasing a protective life interest; not in exercising a power); see also *Re Ellis's Settlement, Ellis v Ellis* (1909) 26 TLR 166, *Anker-Petersen v Christensen* [2002] WTLR 313 and *Wolff v Wolff* [2004] WTLR 1349.
[24] *Lady Hood of Avalon v Mackinnon* [1909] 1 Ch 476 (the authority of this decision is somewhat reduced by the surprising endorsement in the judgment of Eve J of counsel's proposition that 'whether it is rescission or whether it is rectification is only a question of degree' (at 481)).
[25] A point adverted to by Davis J in *Anker-Petersen v Christensen* [2002] WTLR 313, at para 38; and cf *Sieff v Fox* [2005] EWHC 1312 (Ch), [2005] WTLR 891, 8 ITELR 93, at para 85.

BONA FIDE PURCHASER

61.23 Resolution of the void/voidable question may well resolve the next issue, which is whether a bona fide purchaser of the affected assets for value without notice obtains a clear title[1]. On principle, if an appointment is void, there is no title for a bona fide purchaser from the 'appointee' ever to obtain. However, while the appointment may be void in equity, the trustees having legal title have it within their power to transfer the legal title[2] subject to the equitable interests of those entitled on the basis that the appointment in equity was void[3].If an appointment is voidable, a purchaser may obtain that flawed title from the appointee, and then (as a bona fide purchaser for value) successfully oppose any claim to set aside the appointment[4]. In a family trust, the beneficiaries are volunteers (except for any who are within marriage consideration)[5]. On the other hand, in a pension scheme trust, scheme members give consideration for their rights, and so may be bona fide purchasers for value[6].However they are not purchasers from any appointee. Thus, if a mistakenly enhanced appointment in their favour is voidable rather than void, it may still be set aside, since they gave no additional consideration for their enhanced rights[7]. Whether the Revenue authorities could be regarded as a third party entitled to retain a tax payment has been said to be 'open to debate'[8].

[1] Cf Brian Green QC, *The law relating to trustees' mistakes – where are we now?* (2003) 17 Tru LI 114, at 122 and 123 n 63.
[2] *De Vigier v IRC* [1964] 2 All ER 907 at 914, *Hammersmith and Fulham London Borough Council v Monk* [1992] 1 AC 478 at 493, *Rolled Steel Products (Holdings) Ltd v British Steel Corporation* [1986] Ch 246 at 303.
[3] *Cloutte v Storey* [1911] 1 Ch 18 at 31; and see s 157 Law of Property Act 1925, para 61.38 below.
[4] *Oakes v Turquand* (1867) LR 2 HL 325, HL; *Re Eastgate ex p Ward* [1905] 1 KB 465.
[5] As to which, see para 9.76 above.

6   *Kerr v British Leyland (Staff) Trustees Ltd* (1986) [2001] WTLR 1071, CA; *Stannard v Fisons Pensions Trust Ltd* [1992] IRLR 27, CA; *Imperial Group Pension Trust Ltd v Imperial Tobacco Ltd* [1991] 1 WLR 589 at 597; *McDonald v Horn* [1995] 1 All ER 961 at 972–73; *AMP (UK) plc v Barker* [2001] PLR 77, [2001] WTLR 1265, 3 ITELR 414, at para 76.
7   *AMP (UK) plc v Barker* [2001] PLR 77, [2001] WTLR 1265, 3 ITELR 414, at para 77; *Gallaher Ltd v Gallaher Pensions Ltd* [2005] EWHC 42 (Ch), para 180, [2005] All ER (D) 177 (Jan).
8   Sir Robert Walker, *The Limits of the Rule in Re Hastings-Bass* [2002] PCB 226 at [ ], 13 KCLJ 173 at 184, referring to *Re Slocock's Will Trusts* [1979] 1 All ER 358 at 363.

THE LIMITS OF THE RULE

61.24 One's instinctive reaction is that the *Hastings-Bass* principle is too wide – too good to be true – and that trustees, unlike others, can use it whenever it suits them to wriggle out of their reckless or negligent decisions which turn out to have unfortunate consequences[1]. In one case the judge said:

'It cannot be right that whenever trustees do something which they later regret and think that they ought not to have done, they can say that they never did it in the first place.'[2]

Thus, it is argued, there must be some means of limiting its scope and effect. The *Barr* decision[3], that the principle renders the appointment voidable rather than void, was one response to this concern. And in the same case the view was also expressed[4] that the *Hastings-Bass* principle only applied where the trustees' failure to take all and only relevant considerations into account amounts to a breach of duty on their part, so that if the mistake had been made by the settlor or the settlor's agent as opposed to the trustees or the trustees' agent, the principle would not have applied. However, in *Sieff v Fox* Lloyd LJ disagreed with this view[5]. Since there are two inconsistent decisions of co-ordinate jurisdiction, the second having considered the first after full argument, the High Court should in future follow the latter[6], until a higher court pronounces conclusively.

The response of Lloyd LJ to this concern has been that:

'the main ways at present open to the court to control the application of the principle are: (a) to insist on a stringent application of the tests as they have been laid down, (b) to take a reasonable and not over-exigent view of what it is that the trustees ought to have taken into account, and (c) to adopt a critical approach to contentions that the trustees would have acted differently if they had realised the true position, perhaps especially so in cases (unlike the present) where it is in the interests of all who are before the court that the appointment should be set aside.'[7]

The answer to the rhetorical question why trustees should be in a different position than ordinary individuals who make a mistake is of course that they are not disposing of their beneficial property[8] .On the contrary, the settlor has given them power (subject to fiduciary duties) to make gifts on his behalf, and stipulated certain conditions before such gifts can be made. The question is whether those conditions have been satisfied. On one view of the conditions, part of the inquiry is into the considerations taken into account by the trustees. None of this is the case with an ordinary individual.

Logically, one can be driven to accept that, whether expressly or under the current law, a settlor can ensure that the trustees perform their job perfectly in the best interests of the beneficiaries and the worst interests of HM Revenue and Customs by the trustees having to take account of all relevant considerations (including fiscal considerations) and only those if particular actions are to be valid. If the trustees, being imperfect, do not get everything right then their decisions will be reversed, so they can start over again – and this time make sure that they get things right. Oh brave new world where all assets should be held by trustees. Countervailing legislation inspired by the Revenue can be expected.

The cases at present establish, however, two outer limits. First, the principle does not apply to every kind of trustee decision. In particular it does not apply to the trustees' exercise of a power to appoint new trustees[9]. Secondly, the principle invalidates decisions to *do* something, rather than turning a decision not to do something into a *positive* decision. Thus a failure by trustees acting under a misapprehension to execute a deed of appointment (which they had in principle resolved to do) until one day after the period within which it was exercisable could not be turned into an appointment within the period and so valid[10].

[1] Hayton, *Some major developments in trust law*, [2001] PCB 361 at 368–89; Mitchell, *Reining in the rule in Hastings-Bass* (2006) 122 LQR 35 at41; HM Revenue and Customs, *Tax Bulletin 83*, June 2006, 1292 at 1293.
[2] *Breadner v Granville-Grossman* [2001] Ch 523 at para 61; cf *Re Green GLG Trust* (2002) 5 ITELR 590, at para 18, where Birt DB said: 'After all, it is not the law that whenever trustees do something which they later regret and think that they ought not to have done, they can say that they never did them in the first place.'
[3] *Abacus Trust Co (IOM) v Barr* [2003] EWHC 114 (Ch), [2003] Ch 409.
[4] *Abacus Trust Co (IOM) v Barr* [2003] EWHC 114 (Ch), [2003] Ch 409, per Lightman J; this view was criticised by counsel and noted (but not ruled on) by the judges in *Gallaher Ltd v Gallaher Pensions Ltd* [2005] EWHC 42 (Ch), para 165, [2005] All ER (D) 177 (Jan) and *Burrell v Burrell* [2005] EWHC 245 (Ch), para 22, [2005] STC 569, see also Brian Green QC, *The law relating to trustees' mistakes – where are we now?* (2003) 17 Tru LI 114, at 119–22.
[5] [2005] EWHC 1312 (Ch), [2005] WTLR 891, 8 ITELR 93, paras 80–81, 119. HM Revenue and Customs agree with Lloyd LJ: *Tax Bulletin 83*, 1291 at 1294.
[6] *Colchester Estates (Cardiff) v Carlton Industries plc* [1986] Ch 80; *Salvidge v Hussein* [2000] BCC 36, [1999] BPIR 410; *IRC v Trustees of Sema Group Pension Scheme* [2002] EWHC 94 (Ch), [2002] STC 276, paras 44–47 (revsd [2003] STC 95).
[7] *Sieff v Fox* [2005] EWHC 1312 (Ch), [2005] WTLR 891, 8 ITELR 93 at para 82.
[8] *Sieff v Fox* [2005] EWHC 1312 (Ch), [2005] WTLR 891, 8 ITELR 93 at para 85.
[9] *Re Duxbury's Settlement Trusts* [1995] 3 All ER 145, CA.
[10] *Breadner v Granville-Grossman* [2001] Ch 523.

Paragraph 1(f)

Duty to exercise managerial discretions with due care

61.25 Distributive discretions involve decisions about the distribution of income or capital to or for the benefit of beneficiaries under discretionary trusts or objects of powers of appointment or to or for the benefit of beneficiaries via exercise of powers of maintenance and advancement or powers of accumulation. In exercising these, trustees are exercising only internal functions relating to the trustee-beneficiary or trustee-object relationship. The recipients of the settlor's vicarious bounty are almost always volunteers and so can have no protection as bona fide purchasers for value without notice. However, they may be protected if they change their position as a result of receiving such bounty. They are also 'insiders' with rights to see the trust instrument and trust accounts. This means that they are in a position when receiving benefits to know whether or not the trustees are acting within the limits of the powers conferred on them by the settlor or by law and not for purposes perverse to any sensible expectation of the settlor. They are also in a position to make the trustees fully informed of facts which may justify an exercise of a distributive discretion in their favour. By contrast, in exercising managerial or administrative discretions, the trustees will be dealing with third parties. These are not 'insiders', but may well be bona fide purchasers for value without notice or be protected by statutory overreaching provisions (as where the proceeds of sale of land are paid to two trustees or to a trust corporation), or by equitable overreaching under authorisations in the trust instrument (as where jewels or shares in X Co Ltd are authorised to be sold and the proceeds are used to buy Y Co Ltd shares as authorised investments).

61.26 One also has to remember that the persons who are trustees will have full legal ownership of the trust assets and will not be acting beyond their own powers and capacity when transferring legal title to a third party, so that legal title will validly pass[1]. If the trustees are acting beyond the limits imposed upon them by the trust instrument or the general law of trusts, then they will be acting in breach of trust, but the third party now owning the legal title will often be a bona fide purchaser thereof for value without notice of any trusts or be protected by statutory or equitable overreaching provisions despite any notice of the trusts.

[1] *Rolled Steel Products (Holdings) Ltd v British Steel Corpn* [1986] Ch 246 at 303 per Browne-Wilkinson LJ, *De Vigier v IRC* [1964] 2 All ER 907 at 914 per Lord Upjohn.

61.27 Because the beneficiaries then have no remedy against the third party, the focus turns upon the internal obligations owed by the trustees to their beneficiaries. The trustees may be liable for breach of specific duties, eg not having taken proper advice when making investments[1], not having taken account of the statutory standard investment criteria[2], not having provided a proper-policy statement for their asset manager[3], not having made regular reviews of investments or of delegations to others[4]. More often, the trustees will be liable for failure to observe the statutory duty of care[5] (if not ousted in the terms of the trust instrument[6]) eg in selecting investments or in selecting and supervising any delegates they employ to carry out or help carry out their managerial functions.

[1] TA 2000, s 5.
[2] TA 2000, s 4(3).
[3] TA 2000, s 15.
[4] TA 2000, ss 4(2) and 22.

5   TA 2000, s 1 and Sch 1.
6   See Article 52, above.

61.28 Breaches of specific duties when acting within their powers and breaches of the duty of care will lead to the trustees' accounts being surcharged with an amount to make up the extra value the trust fund would have had but for their breaches of duty.

Paragraph 1(g)

Duty of undivided loyalty

61.29 More fundamental than the prescriptive duties laid down by trust law and the trust instrument is the proscriptive fiduciary obligation of undivided loyalty owed to the beneficiaries[1]. This fiduciary obligation is the obligation to put the interests of the particular beneficiaries above all other interests (unless otherwise authorised). Thus for example no profit can be made from the trust property or the office of trustee (unless authorised), and (unless authorised) the trustee must not place himself in a position where his own interest conflicts with the interests of his beneficiaries or his duty in one capacity conflicts with his duty in another capacity or in a position where there is a sensible possibility of such conflict arising. If however there is a conflict or possibility of conflict the trustee must prefer his duty to his interest, except as permitted by the trust instrument, the beneficiaries or the court to consider his interest.

1   See Articles 33, 58 and 59, above.

61.30 Breach of fiduciary obligation connotes disloyalty or infidelity: mere incompetence is not enough[1]. To uphold the fundamental fiduciary obligation owed to vulnerable beneficiaries the trustee is strictly liable for profits[2] made in breach of the obligation and, indeed, a constructive trust is automatically imposed on the profits and the traceable product thereof[3]. It seems that the logic of strict personal liability for losses is not followed, but that the onus of proof lies on the trustees to show that the losses were not caused by the trustee's breach because they would have occurred even if there had been no such breach[4].

1   *Bristol & West BS v Mothew* [1998] Ch 1 at 18, CA.
2   See Article 59, above.
3   See Article 33, above.
4   *Bank of New Zealand v New Zealand Guardian Trust Co* [1999] 1 NZLR 664 at 687, CA; *Swindle v Harrison* [1997] 4 All ER 705 at 716–717.

Paragraph 1(h)

Duty not to commit a fraud on the power

61.31 The doctrine of fraud on a power occupies a central position in the range of regulatory rules imposed by equity on powers and their exercise. It is squarely concerned with an attempt by the appointor deliberately to subvert the original power conferred upon him, and is closely related therefore to the case where the appointor seeks directly to exercise the power outside the class otherwise specified. The origins of this doctrine lie in the middle of the eighteenth century[1], though cases in equity dealing with other aspects of powers go back a century or more before that. In the mid-nineteenth century the doctrine was confirmed by the House of Lords[2] .

1   *Lane v Page* (1755) Amb 233.
2   Eg *The Duke of Portland v Topham* (1864) 11 HLC 32.

61.32 However, the phrase *'fraud on a power'* is misleading. The word *'fraud'* does not actually refer to fraudulent conduct in the ordinary sense of the word:

'The term fraud in connection with frauds on a power does not necessarily denote any conduct on the part of the appointor amounting to fraud in the common law meaning of the term or any conduct which could be properly termed dishonest or immoral. It merely means that the power has been exercised for a purpose, or with an intention, beyond the scope of or not justified by the instrument creating the power. [...] It is enough that the appointor's purpose and intention is to secure a benefit for himself, or some other person not an object of the power.'[1]

1   *Vatcher v Paull* [1915] AC 372, 378.

61.33 The doctrine was built up in cases relating to the exercise of special powers of appointment, ie powers for the appointor to select, within a limited class of objects, the person or persons who should benefit from the property. The classic case is where property is appointed to A on the basis of a prior agreement that A should give all or part to B, not an object of the power[1]. In normal circumstances the doctrine cannot apply to a general power of appointment (where anyone in the world can be appointed) or to a hybrid power, unless the hybrid power is misused in order to get property to a person who is actually excluded from the scope of that power (eg a trustee). The special powers of appointment that are covered by the doctrine include powers of advancement, powers to jointure and powers to create portions for younger children. The doctrine has also been applied to the power of amendment conferred upon a management committee or an employer company in relation to a pension trust[2]. But the matter goes further. Although it is not often referred to as an application of the doctrine of a fraud on the power, there can be little doubt that other powers such as powers of investment of trustees, must also be exercised for the proper purpose[3] .As it was put in a recent New Zealand case,

'The notion of a fraud on a power itself rests on the fundamental juristic principle that any form of authority may only be exercised for the purposes conferred, and in accordance with its terms. This principle is one of general application.'[4]

1   Eg *Wong v Burt* [2005] WTLR 291, at para 27, NZ CA; *Kain v Hutton* [2005] WTLR 977, NZ HCt.

2   *Re Courage Group's Pension Schemes* [1987] 1 WLR 495; *Hillsdown Holdings plc v Pensions Ombudsman* [1997] 1 All ER 862; *Bank of New Zealand v Board of Management of the Officers' Provident Association* [2003] UKPC 58, [2003] OPLR 281, (2003) 6 ITELR 142, at paras 19–20.
3   *Cowan v Scargill* [1985] Ch 270.
4   *Wong v Burt* [2005] WTLR 291, at para 27, NZ CA.

61.34 However, the doctrine normally does not apply to the exercise of a power (where one is reserved) to *revoke* an appointment that has been made[1]. This is because the remaindermen cannot be prejudiced by the revocation of an appointment that would otherwise take the property away from them, and the person to whom the property was appointed cannot complain, because the appointment was a flawed appointment in the sense that it always contained the possibility of revocation. Again, the *release* of a power cannot be complained of as a fraud on the power, because there is no duty to make an appointment[2]. Similarly, an agreement not to appoint, and to let the property go in default of appointment, cannot be a fraud on the power[3].

1   *Re Greaves* [1954] Ch 434.
2   *Re Somes* [1896] 1 Ch 250, at 255.
3   *Vatcher v Paull* [1915] AC 372.

61.35 It has always been clear that the effect of a fraud being committed in relation to an equitable power is that the exercise of the power is *void* rather than merely voidable[1]. Any asset transferred must be restored, or equitable compensation paid[2]. This also shows the close alliance between this doctrine and the doctrine of simply attempting to appoint outside the class of objects. The power does not extend that far, and therefore an attempt to appoint to a non-object is of no effect at all. Similarly, the attempt to appoint for the benefit of someone who is not within the class (even though through the pretence of attempting to appoint to someone who is) is equally without effect. It is simply that the events stipulated by the settlor for the particular person to benefit have not come to pass and are therefore as nothing in equity.

1   *Re Cohen* [1911] 1 Ch 37; *Vatcher v Paull* [1915] AC 372, 378.
2   *Kain v Hutton* [2005] WTLR 977, at para 239.

61.36 It is irrelevant that the appointee is not aware of the appointor's intentions. Moreover, if an appointment is a *joint* appointment (because the power has been conferred upon two or more persons to act jointly in the matter) and only one of the persons concerned had the relevant 'fraudulent' intention, then the appointment is still void. This is because the appointment was only to be valid if made jointly by all and in relation to one of them it cannot be said that the appointment has properly been made. Hence, again, the event upon which the property in equity was to belong to the appointee has not occurred.

61.37 Unlike the position with common law powers, a ratification of the position by all concerned after the power has been fraudulently exercised is not possible. This is because the equitable interest has simply not been transferred to the beneficiary. In order for that to happen the power must be properly exercised and that has not occurred.

61.38 The purchaser of an asset in relation to which there has been a fraud on the power exercised may set up the defence that he is the bona fide purchaser for value of a legal estate without notice, actual or constructive. In addition, there is some protection conferred by section 157 of the Law of Property Act 1925. This reads as follows:

'(1) an instrument purporting to exercise a power of appointment over property which, in default of and subject to any appointment, is held in trust for a class or number of persons of whom the appointee is one, shall not (save as hereinafter provided) be void on the ground of fraud on the power as against a purchaser in good faith: provided that, if the interest appointed exceeds, in amount or value, the interest in such property to which immediately before the execution of the instrument the appointee was presumptively entitled under the trust in default of appointment, having regard to any advances made in his favour and to any hotchpot provision, the protection afforded by this section to a purchaser shall not extend to such excess;

(2) in this section 'a purchaser in good faith' means a person dealing with an appointee of the age of not less than 25 years for valuable consideration in money or money's worth, and without notice of fraud, or of any circumstances from which, if reasonable enquiries had been made, the fraud might have been discovered;

(3) persons deriving title under any purchaser entitled to the benefit of this section shall be entitled to the like benefit.'

61.39 This protection is of course limited. It only applies at all where the appointee whose title is being impeached is one of the persons entitled in default of appointment. This is obviously not the case with every power. Moreover, only 'a purchaser in good faith', as defined, is protected. This requires that the appointee should be at least 25 years old.

61.40 Generally an appointment cannot be severed, discarding only the bad and leaving the good untouched[1]. However, in rare cases this can be done, especially where consideration has been given which cannot be restored, or where the good and the bad intentions of the appointors can be distinguished[2].

[1] *Daubeny v Cockburn* (1816) 1 Mer 626; *Rowley v Rowley* (1854) Kay 242; *Re Chadwick's Trusts* [1939] 1 All ER 850.
[2] *Rowley v Rowley* (1854) Kay 242; *Vatcher v Paull* [1915] AC 372, 378.

61.41 From the point of view of trustees, the doctrine is relevant in two ways. First, they may be the appointors, and the purported exercise of their powers may be attacked. Second, they may not be the appointors in relation to the power, and may have only received notice from an appointee that the appointor has actually made the appointment. The trustees must then be satisfied that the power has indeed been effectively and validly exercised, not just in the formal sense (if any special formalities are prescribed) but also in the substantive sense, that there should not be any suspicion that there had

61.41 *The powers of the trustee*

been any kind of fraud on the power. The risk for the trustees is that, if having any suspicion about the validity of the appointment they pay away the asset concerned to the appointee and subsequently it is established that there was a fraud on the power, the trustees will be liable to replace the property if it is lost[1]. But if they are misled and innocently transfer the assets under what appeared to be a valid appointment, they will not be liable[2]. This means that in practice trustees would be well advised to check the circumstances of the appointment with some care, and indeed will not only want to see the relevant documents but in some case also have witness statements or statutory declarations made.

1   See e g *Mackechnie v Marjoribanks* (1870) 39 LJ Ch 604.
2   *Re Deane* (1888) 42 Ch D 9.

61.42 In the textbooks and in the literature the cases of fraud on a power are often collected into three distinct groups of cases: (i) cases where there is an antecedent agreement or a bargain to benefit a non-object; (ii) where there is a corrupt purpose involved; (iii) where the power is exercised for a purpose foreign to the power[1]. However, this classification is purely for convenience, and has no legal significance. A bargain is certainly not necessary[2]. Indeed, some cases will fall under more than one of these heads, and it is entirely conceivable that cases will arise which do not fall under any of them. As has been said,

'These distinctions are useful for analytic and descriptive purposes, but it is necessary to recall that the *sine qua non* which makes the exercise of a discretion or power "improper" is the improper intention of the person exercising it. The central principle is that if the power is exercised with the intention of benefiting some non-object of the discretionary power, whether that person is the person exercising it, or anybody else for that matter, the exercise is void. If, on the other hand, there is no such improper intention, even although the exercise does in fact benefit a non-object, it is valid.'[3]

1   See e g *Halsbury's Laws of England*, 4ᵗʰ ed Reissue, vol 36(2), paras 365–67; *Snell's Equity*, 31ˢᵗ ed, paras 9–13 – 9–15; *Hanbury & Martin's Equity*, 17ᵗʰ ed, paras 6–019–6–021; Thomas, *Powers*, 1998, paras 9–21–9–48.
2   *Vatcher v Paull* [1915] AC 372, 378.
3   *Wong v Burt* [2005] WTLR 291, at para 30, NZ CA; see also *Kain v Hutton* [2005] WTLR 977, NZ HCt.

Paragraph 2

Much discretionary leeway afforded to trustees

61.43 As the Court of Appeal pointed out in *Edge v Pensions Ombudsman*[1], if trustees exercise their discretionary power for the purpose for which it is given, giving proper consideration to the matters which are relevant and excluding from consideration matters which are irrelevant, they cannot be criticised if they reach a decision which appears to prefer the claims of one interest over others: the preference will be the result of a proper exercise of the discretionary power.

1   [2000] Ch 602 at 627.

61.44 The Court of Appeal endorsed the approach of Scott V-C[1] who had emphasised that it was not for a judge to exercise the discretion of trustees unless they had surrendered it to the court in a particular situation[2]. The judge may disagree with the trustees' exercise of their discretion because he would have exercised it differently if in their shoes, but, nevertheless, he cannot interfere where the trustees had complied with the applicable duties in coming to their decision.

1   [2000] Ch 602 at 618 and 630.
2   See Article 87.

61.45 It is thus a 'well-established rule that where a discretion is entrusted to a trustee, the trustee is not required to give reasons for the exercise of that discretion and that, in the absence of evidence that the trustee has acted improperly, whether from an improper motive or by taking account of factors which the trustee should not have taken into account or not taking into account factors which the trustee should have taken into account, the court will not interfere with the exercise of the trustee's discretion'[1]. However, 'If a decision taken by trustees is directly attacked in legal proceedings, the trustees may be compelled either legally (through discovery or subpoena) or practically (in order to avoid adverse inferences being drawn) to disclose the substance of the reasons for their decision'[2]. Normally, if the exercise of distributive discretions is in issue it is difficult to acquire sufficient evidence at the outset to support a claim and so prevent its being struck out as a mere 'fishing expedition'.

1   *Wilson v Law Debenture Trust Corp plc* [1995] 2 All ER 337 at 343 per Rattee J based on *Re Beloved Wilkes Charity* (1851) 3 Mac & G 440 and *Re Londonderry's Settlement* [1965] Ch 918, CA; see further para 60.43.
2   *Scott v National Trust* [1998] 2 All ER 705 at 719, per *Robert Walker J and Taylor v Midland Bank Trust Co* (2000) 2 ITELR 439 at 459–461 per Buxton LJ.

61.46 Often trustees are given a power to distribute income or capital between members of a class as they see fit in their absolute discretion or to invest the trust fund as they see fit in their absolute discretion, but this is subject to the implicit restriction that their discretion should be exercised properly within the limits of the general law[1]. It makes no difference if the words used are 'in their uncontrollable discretion'[2]. To take such words at face value would prevent the beneficiaries having any enforceable rights, so that there would be no trust[3]. In carrying out their fundamental investment role and their fundamental distributive role in favour of beneficiaries, trustees must exercise their discretions within the limits of the general law.

1   *Gisborne v Gisborne* (1877) 2 App Cas 300, HL; *Re Gulbenkian's Settlement Trust* [1970] AC 508 at 518, HL; *Tempest v Lord Camoys* (1882) 21 Ch D 571, CA; *Bishop v Bonham* [1988] 1 WLR 742 at 751–752, CA.
2   *Gisborne v Gisborne* (1877) 2 App Cas 300, HL; *Re Gulbenkian's Settlement Trusts* [1970] AC 508 at 518.
3   *Armitage v Nurse* [1998] Ch 241 at 253, CA; D J Hayton, 'The Irreducible Core Content of Trusteeship', Chap 3 in A J Oakley (ed) *Trends in Contemporary Trust Law* (Oxford, 1996).

61.47 It is a question how far a settlor may expressly or by necessary implication prevent beneficiaries or objects of a power of appointment from having the rights as to accountability of the trustees[1]. It would be impermissible to exclude *all* accountability[2]. But can the settlor exclude accountability towards, say, minor beneficiaries, or objects of powers, and leave only adult beneficiaries, or objects of discretionary trusts, or even only some representative examples of these, with the right to hold the trustees to account? There are obvious problems with this course, especially where the only persons able to hold the trustees accountable are connected to them, whilst those unconnected with the trustees have no such rights. And it is always difficult to know where to draw the line. The question is discussed in more detail in relation to information disclosure to beneficiaries[3].

[1]   *Schmidt v RosewoodTrust Ltd* [2003] UKPC 26, [2003] 2 AC 709, [2003] 3 All ER 76, PC; see para 60.5.
[2]   *Jones v Shipping Federation of British Columbia* (1963) 37 DLR (2d) 273, 274–5; *Armitage v Nurse* [1998] Ch 241 at 253, CA.
[3]   See paras 60.30, 60.37, 60.43 and 60.58.

ARTICLE 62
MANAGERIAL POWERS OF TRUSTEES WITH PARTICULAR
REFERENCE TO SALES

62.1

Subject to modification in the trust instrument or by ad hoc legislation,
(1)   trustees of land have power to manage their land as if absolute owners[1] and to employ agents in this behalf[2]; they may delegate their functions relating to the land to a beneficiary or beneficiaries of full age beneficially entitled to an interest in possession[3];
(2)   trustees of property other than land have power to sell it to make any kind of investment they could make if absolutely entitled to it; however, except for investing in loans secured on land[4], the only land which they may acquire is 'freehold or leasehold land' in the UK[5]. If they do acquire land under this power, they have all the powers of an absolute owner in relation to it[6].

[1]   TLATA 1996, s 6 and Article 45 above.
[2]   TA 2000, ss 11–27, and Article 55 above.
[3]   TLATA 1996, s 9 and Article 55(1)(e) above.
[4]   TA 2000, s 3(8).
[5]   TA 2000, s 8(1).
[6]   TA 2000, s 8(3).

Paragraphs 1 and 2

Very extensive general powers of trustees

62.2 In simpler, more static times, the rule had been that trustees were supposed to preserve the settled property in specie for the beneficiaries interested in it[1]. They could not dispose of it unless directed or empowered to do so by the trust instrument or by the court or by some statutory authority[2]. Moreover, the settlor was relying on the trustees personally to do this, so that they could not employ agents, even for the implementation of their decisions, unless this was reasonably necessary or in the ordinary course of affairs[3].

Nowadays, in view of the protective panoply of equitable and statutory duties imposed upon trustees in the exercise of their powers[4], trust instruments and trust legislation (in default of express powers in the relevant trust instrument) confer very extensive powers to manage the trust property[5] and purchase or acquire new trust property[6]. For this purpose they may use the services of nominees and custodians and agents[7], who may have discretionary, and not merely ministerial, functions delegated to them eg discretionary portfolio management[8]. These matters have all been considered in earlier Articles (as footnoted) dealing with the duties of trustees.

[1]   Nowadays the emphasis is on preserving the capital value of the trust property, taking account of inflation, unless the settlor clearly intended the life tenant (eg his widow) to be the primary object of his bounty rather than the remainderman (eg a cousin as next of kin or some charity): *National Westminster Bank v Nestle* [1994] 1 All ER 118 at 133, 137 and 140, CA; *Karger v Paul* [1984] VR 161; *Re Saunders & Halom* (1986) 32 DLR (4th) 503.
[2]   See 15th edn hereof, Article 64.
[3]   See Article 55 above.
[4]   See Articles 48, 52, 53 and 55 above.
[5]   See Article 45 above.
[6]   See Article 53 above.
[7]   See Article 55 above
[8]   See Article 55 above, TA 2000, s 15.

Power to raise capital money

62.3   Trustees (other than trustees of charities or Settled Land Act trustees who are not also statutory owners) who are authorised under the trust instrument or by law[1] to pay or apply capital money subject to the trust for any purpose or in any manner have power to raise the money required by sale, conversion, calling in, or mortgage of all or any part of the trust property for the time being in possession[2]. This statutory power cannot be ousted by the trust instrument[3]. Where the property is land a similar power is within the general powers of trustees of land as if they were absolute owners of it[4].

It has been held that the specific statutory power does not authorise trustees to raise money to purchase further investments by mortgaging existing investments[5]. As already seen[6], the new general absolute powers do not appear apt to empower such 'gearing up' the value of the trust fund.

[1]   Eg s 32 of the Trustee Act 1925.
[2]   TA 1925, s 16(1).
[3]   TA 1925, s 16(2).
[4]   TA 2000s 8(3).
[5]   *Re Suenson-Taylor's Settlement* [1974] 3 All ER 397.
[6]   See para 53.12 above.

Conduct of sales

62.4   Where a trustee has a duty or power to sell real or personal property then, unless there is a contrary intention expressed in the trust instrument[1], he may sell or concur with any person in selling all or any part of the property, either subject to prior charges or not, and either together or in lots, by public auction or by private contract, subject to any such conditions respecting title or evidence of title or other matter as the trustee thinks fit, with power to vary any contract for sale, and to buy in at any auction, or to rescind any contract for sale and to re-sell, without being answerable for any loss[2].

Specific statutory power[3] is also conferred on trustees of land to dispose of surface and mines and minerals separately. This too is now covered by the absolute owner powers conferred by law[4]. They also empower trustees of leases to sell via underleases at apportioned rents[5] and to sell for a price other than money.

Purchase money must be apportioned before completion where trustees make a sale jointly with another and the purchaser must pay the apportioned trust money only to the trustees[6].

Where trustees hold an undivided share in property on trust they can execute any trust or power vested in them in relation to such share in conjunction with persons owning the other share or shares, and notwithstanding that one or more of the trustees may be entitled to an undivided share in his own right or as trustee for others[7]. The last proviso goes beyond the absolute owner powers given by statute[8].

Specific performance will not be granted of a contract made by the trustees in breach of trust[9], while it is possible that some of the conditions of a contract of sale of land may be depreciatory conditions that may or may not amount to a breach of trust. Accordingly, it is provided that no sale shall be impeached by a beneficiary (or objected to by the purchaser) on the basis that any condition thereof was unnecessarily depreciatory unless thereby making the sale price inadequate. Similarly, after conveyance, no sale can be impeached as against the purchaser on the ground that any condition was unnecessarily depreciatory unless the purchaser was acting in collusion with the trustees when the contract was made[10].

1   TA 1925, s 69(2).
2   TA 1925, s 12(1).
3   TA 1925, s 12(2).
4   TLATA 1996, s 6.
5   Also see *Re Judd and Poland's Contract* [1906] 1 Ch 684, CA.
6   *Re Cooper and Allen's Contract* (1876) 4 Ch D 802.
7   TA 1925, s 24.
8   Ie under TLATA 1996, s 6.
9   *Dunn v Flood* (1885) 28 Ch D 586, CA.
10 TA 1925, s 13.

ARTICLE 63
POWER OF TRUSTEES TO GIVE RECEIPTS

63.1

(1)   The receipt in writing of a trustee for any money, securities, investments or other personal property or effects payable, trans-ferable, or deliverable to him under any trust or power is a

sufficient discharge to the person paying, transferring, or delivering the same and effectually exonerates him from seeing to the application or being answerable for any loss or misapplication thereof[1].

(2) Except where the trustee is a trust corporation constituted under the law of a Member State of the European Union[2], a sole trustee cannot give a valid receipt for the proceeds of sale or other capital money arising under a trust of land[3] or for capital money arising under the Settled Land Act 1925.

(3) Paragraphs 1 and 2 of this Article apply notwithstanding anything to the contrary in the instrument, if any, creating the trust[4].

1   TA 1925, s 14(1), as amended by TA 2000, Sch 2, para 19.
2   See the Law of Property Act 1925, s 205(1)(xxviii); see note 4 of 37.3 and 79.5–79.6.
3   TA 1925, s 14(2), as amended by TLATA 1996, Sch 3, para 3(3).
4   TA 1925, s 14(3).

63.2 The above Article states the effect of s 14 of the Trustee Act 1925, as amended. Sub-section (2) is complementary to s 27(2) of the Law of Property Act 1925, which provides that notwithstanding anything to the contrary in the instrument (if any) creating a trust for sale of land or in the settlement of the net proceeds, the proceeds of sale are not to be paid to or applied by the direction of fewer than two trustees except where the trustee is a trust corporation. However, a bona fide purchaser of a legal estate in unregistered land for value without notice of an equitable interest may obtain a good title from a sole legal owner[1]. In the case of registered land a purchaser from a sole registered proprietor will obtain a good title, free from any equitable interest whose priority is not protected, whether as an 'overriding' interest, or by entry on the register[2], at all events so long as the purchaser is not using the statutory provision as an instrument of fraud[3].

1   *Kingsnorth Trust Ltd v Tizard* [1986] 2 All ER 54; *Williams and Glyn's Bank v Boland* [1979] Ch 312 at 330, 341, [1979] 2 All ER 697 at 704, 713, CA.
2   Land Registration Act 1925, ss 20, 23; Land Registration Act 2002, ss 26, 29 and 30.
3   *Jones v Lipman* [1962] 1 All ER 442, [1962] 1 WLR 832; see also *Lyus v Prowsa Developments Ltd* [1982] 2 All ER 953.

63.3 Until 1997, while the proceeds of sale of land in England and Wales could be properly paid to two *persons* (whether individuals or companies or one individual and one company)[1], a trustee was not validly discharged from his trust unless there would be either a trust corporation constituted in a State within the European Union or at least two *individuals* to perform the trust[2](though this latter requirement could be ousted by the terms of the trust instrument[3]). The law was then changed from 'individuals' into 'persons'[4], thus mirroring the position for payment of sale monies, and so closing the trap[5].

1   LPA 1925, s 27(2).
2   TA 1925, s 37(1)(c).
3   *London Regional Transport Pension Fund Trust Co Ltd v Hatt* [1993] Pens LR 227 at 260–262.
4   TLATA 1996, Sch 3, para 4(8)(b).
5   See further para 72.3 ff.

ARTICLE 64
POWERS WITH REGARD TO REVERSIONARY INTERESTS

64.1

(1)   Where trust property includes any share or interest in property
not vested in the trustees, or the proceeds of the sale of any such
property, or any other thing in action, the trustees on the same
falling into possession, or becoming payable or transferable may:
>   (a)   agree or ascertain the amount or value thereof[1] or any part
>   thereof in such manner as they may think fit;
>   (b)   accept in or towards satisfaction thereof, at the market or
>   current value, or upon any valuation or estimate of value
>   which they may think fit, any authorised investments;
>   (c)   allow any deductions for duties, costs, charges and
>   expenses which they may think proper or reasonable;
>   (d)   execute any release in respect of the premises so as effectu-
>   ally to discharge all accountable parties from all liability in
>   respect of any matters coming within the scope of such
>   release;

without being responsible in any such case for any loss occasioned by
any act or thing so done by them if they have discharged the duty of
care set out in section 1 of the Trustee Act 2000.

(2)   The trustees are not under any obligation and are not chargeable
with any breach of trust by reason of any omission:
>   (a)   to place any distringas notice[2] or apply for any stop or
>   other like order upon any securities or other property out
>   of or on which such share or interest or other thing in
>   action as aforesaid is derived, payable or charged; or,
>   (b)   to take any proceedings on account of any act, default, or
>   neglect on the part of the persons in whom such securities
>   or other property or any of them or any part thereof are
>   for the time being, or had at any time been, vested; unless
>   and until required in writing so to do by some person, or
>   the guardian of some person, beneficially interested under
>   the trust, and unless also due provision is made to their
>   satisfaction for payment of the costs of any proceedings
>   required to be taken.

(3)   Nevertheless nothing in paragraphs (1) and (2) of this article
relieves the trustees of the obligation to get in and obtain
payment or transfer of such share or interest or other thing in
action on the same falling into possession.

[1]   See also TA 1925, s 22(3), as to valuations.
[2]   Now a stop notice: RSC Ord 50, rr 11–14.

64.2 The above Article reproduces s 22(1) and (2) of the Trustee Act 1925 as
amended by the Trustee Act 2000, Sch 2, para 22(a), substituting for 'good

faith' the need to comply with the statutory duty of care. It will be noticed that it is restricted to interests in property not vested in the trustees and to choses in action.

ARTICLE 65
GENERAL ADMINISTRATIVE POWERS OF TRUSTEES

65.1

(1)   A personal representative, or two or more trustees acting together, or, subject to the restrictions imposed in regard to receipts by a sole trustee not being a trust corporation, constituted under the law of a State within the European Union[1], a sole acting trustee where by the instrument, if any, creating the trust, or by statute, a sole trustee is authorised to execute the trusts and powers reposed in him, may, if and as he or they think fit:

    (a)   accept any property, real or personal, before the time at which it is made transferable or payable; or

    (b)   sever and apportion any blended trust funds or property; or

    (c)   pay or allow any debt or claim on any evidence that he or they may think sufficient; or

    (d)   accept any composition or any security, real or personal, for any debt or for any property, real or personal, claimed; or

    (e)   allow any time of payment of any debt; or

    (f)   compromise, compound, abandon, submit to arbitration, or otherwise settle any debt, account, claim, or thing whatever relating to the testator's or intestate's estate or to the trust;

and for any of those purposes may enter into, give, execute, and do such agreements, instruments of composition or arrangement, releases, and other things as to him or them seem expedient, without being responsible for any loss occasioned by any act or thing so done by him or them if he has or they have discharged the duty of care set out in section 1 of the Trustee Act 2000.

[1]   See paras 37.3, 79.5–79.6.

65.2 This Article reproduces s 15 of the Trustee Act 1925, as amended by the Trustee Act 2000[1] so as to require not merely good faith but compliance with the statutory duty of care in exercising the extensive powers conferred by s 15.

[1]   TA 2000, Sch 2, para 20.

65.3 In *Re Ezekiel's Settlement Trusts*[1] where the trustees had surrendered to the court their discretion as to whether they should accept a compromise that had been offered, the Court of Appeal directed the trustees to proceed with a compromise for £7,750 of a claim for £15,000, and Lord Greene MR pointed out that 'the court, just the same as any trustee, has to act on the balance of possibilities and the balance of apparent advantages'.

1   [1942] Ch 230, [1942] 2 All ER 224, CA.

65.4 In order to justify a payment by way of compromise there must have been a claim, but it is not necessary to establish that the claim would have succeeded, for the effect of that would be to reduce the power to compromise to a nullity[1]. It seems the section only applies where the trustee has actively exercised some discretion so that loss has not arisen from passive inactivity[2].

1   *Re Ridsdel* [1947] Ch 597, [1947] 2 All ER 312. See also *Re Shenton* [1935] Ch 651.
2   *Re Greenwood* (1911) 105 LT 509; *Partridge v Equity Trustees Executors and Agency Co Ltd* (1947) 75 CLR 149, Aus HC.

65.5 Whilst the nature of executorship enables an executor in a proper case to compromise a claim by his co-executor against the estate[1], it seems that trustees should not compromise a claim by one of themselves against the trust property unless there is a special authority for a majority to bind the minority[2] or the court sanctions such compromise.

1   *Re Houghton* [1904] 1 Ch 622. Administration of Estates Act 1971, s 10(2), provides some additional protection for a personal representative who pays a debt to a creditor.
2   *Luke v South Kensington Hotel Co* (1879) 11 Ch D 121.

65.6 The power to compromise is very broad indeed. Any disparity between the beneficiaries arising upon exercise of the power is to be judged by ascertaining whether the compromise is desirable and fair as regards all the beneficiaries. Thus, where the consideration for the compromise of a claim against a party extraneous to the trust, who owned a beneficial interest in the trust, included the surrender of that interest and the consequential alteration of the beneficial interests, the compromise lay within the power to compromise[1], although the power does not enable trustees to effect a variation of the trusts.

1   *Re Earl of Strafford* [1978] 3 All ER 18, [1978] 3 WLR 233; affd [1980] Ch 28, [1979] 1 All ER 513, CA.

65.7 The need to act not merely in good faith, but also to comply with the duty of care in the Trustee Act 2000, means that trustees will often be advised to apply to the court to confirm that they will be acting properly if they decide to compromise a valuable or difficult claim as proposed to the court, and the costs of such application should be ordered to be paid out of the trust fund[1].

1   *Re Owens Corning Fiberglas (UK) Pension Plan Ltd* [2002] Pens LR 323, (2002) Times, 8 July; *Bradstock Pension Scheme Trustees Ltd v Bradstock Group plc* [2002] Pens LR 327, (2002) Times, 10 July.

ARTICLE 66
POWER TO ALLOW MAINTENANCE TO INFANTS

66.1

(1)   Where any property is held by trustees in trust for any person for any interest whatsoever, whether vested or contingent, then, subject to any prior interests[1] or charges affecting that property, the trustees *may*, during the period when that beneficiary is under the age of 18, if his interest so long continues, make an all(1) Where any property is held by trustees in trust for any person for any owance of the whole or part of the income of that property for or towards his maintenance, education, or benefit[2].

(2)   This power is discretionary, but is exercisable notwithstanding that there is another fund applicable to the same purpose, or some person bound by law to provide for such maintenance or education[3].

(3)   In deciding whether the whole or any part of the income of the property is, during the period when a beneficiary is under 18, to be paid or applied for the purposes aforesaid, the trustees must have regard to his age and his requirements and generally to the circumstances of the case[4], and in particular to what other income, if any, is applicable for the same purposes. Where trustees have notice that the income of more than one fund is applicable for those purposes, then, as far as practicable, unless the entire income of the funds is paid or applied as aforesaid or the court otherwise directs, a proportionate part only of the income of each fund ought to be so paid or applied[5].

(4)   The trustees may pay the allowance to the parent or guardian of the beneficiary under 18, instead of expending it directly themselves[6].

(5)   The balance of the income not applied for the maintenance, education, or benefit of the beneficiary under 18 *must* during the period when he remains under 18 (if his interest so long continues) be accumulated at compound interest, but the trustees may, at any time during the period when he is under 18 (if his interest so long continues) apply the accumulations or any part thereof as if they were income of the current year[7].

(6)   Even if the beneficiary on attaining the age of 18 years has not a vested interest in the income, the trustees must thenceforth pay the *income* of the property and of any accumulations thereto, made under paragraph 5 of this Article, to the beneficiary until he either attains a vested interest or dies, or until failure of his interest[8].

(7)(i)   If the beneficiary:

(a)   attains the age of 18 years, or marries under that age and his interest in such income while he is under 18 or until his marriage is a vested interest; or

(b)   on attaining the age of 18 years or on marriage under that age becomes entitled to the property from which such income arose in fee simple, absolute or determinable, or absolutely, or for an entailed interest;

the trustees must hold the accumulations in trust for such person absolutely[9], and the receipt of such person after marriage, and though still under 18, is a good discharge[10]. This provision operates without prejudice to any provision with respect to such accumulations contained in any settlement by him made under any statutory powers during his infancy.

(ii)   In any other case the trustees must, notwithstanding that such person had a vested interest in such income[11], hold the accumulations as an accretion to the capital of the property from which they arose[12]. If such property is settled land within the Settled Land Act 1925, the accumulations should be treated as if they were capital moneys.

(8)   The above provisions apply to a contingent interest only if the limitation or trust carries the intermediate income of the property[13], but they apply to a future or contingent legacy by the parent of, or a person standing in loco parentis to, the legatee, if and for such period as, under the general law, the legacy carries interest for the maintenance of the legatee[14].

(9)   These provisions apply to a vested annuity in like manner as if the annuity were the income of property held by trustees in trust to pay the income thereof to the annuitant for the same period for which the annuity is payable, save that in any case accumulations made whilst the annuitant is under 18 must be held in trust for the annuitant or his personal representatives absolutely[15].

(10)   These provisions do not apply where the instrument, if any, under which the interest arises came into operation before 1 January 1926[16]. Where the instrument under which the interest arises came into operation before 1 January 1970, when the age of majority became 18[17], they do apply, but with 21 years replacing 18 years; and they may be negatived or modified by the instrument creating the trust[18], but any period of accumulation must be one permitted by statute.

[1]   The question has been raised as to whether, and in what circumstances, the mere fact that remaindermen will or may become entitled to the capital of the trust fund, and thus to any accumulations of income which may augment it (so that they have an interest in ensuring that income is accumulated rather than spent), gives them a 'prior interest' within the meaning of this provision (TA 1925, s 31(1)). The point was deliberately left undecided by Clauson J in *Re Spencer* [1935] Ch 533, and by the Court of Appeal in *Re Turner's Will Trusts* [1937] Ch 15, [1936] 2 All ER 1435, CA. See also *IRC v Bernstein*, where the point

was considered in relation to the power of advancement (TA 1925, s 32) at first instance [1960] Ch 444, [1960] 1 All ER 697; and on appeal [1961] Ch 399, [1961] 1 All ER 320, CA; see note 2 of para 67.2 below.

2   In *Re Heyworth's Contingent Reversionary Interest* [1956] Ch 364 at 370, [1956] 2 All ER 21 at 23, Upjohn J said that these were words of the widest import. Also see *Allen v Coster* (1839) Beav 202.

3   Section 31(1)(i).

4   Section 31(1). As to the former law see *Wilson v Turner* (1883) 22 Ch D 521, CA.

5   See, as to the former law, *Smith v Cock* [1911] AC 317. Paragraph 3 here sets out the proviso to s 31(1) which trust instruments commonly exclude.

6   In pre-1970 trusts the trustees *may* pay the beneficiary at 18.

7   Section 31(2).

8   Section 31(1)(ii). The beneficiary's entitlement to income confers an interest in possession upon him so as to attract inheritance tax if he dies or assigns the interest: Inheritance Tax Act 1984, ss 51, 52; *Swales v IRC* [1984] 3 All ER 16 at 24; *Re Jones' Will Trusts* [1947] Ch 48, [1946] 2 All ER 281.

9   *Re Fulford* [1930] 1 Ch 71.

10   Section 31(2)(i).

11   The words 'notwithstanding that such person had a vested interest in such income' refer to the nature of the interest conferred by the settlement on the infant and are not an affirmation that the infant's interest in the surplus income remains a vested interest despite the alteration of his rights into a contingent interest by the subsection: *Stanley v IRC* [1944] KB 255 at 261.

12   Section 31(2)(ii).

13   Section 31(3).

14   In any such case the rate of interest (if the income available is sufficient, and *subject to any rules of court to the contrary*) is to be five pounds per cent per annum. However, it may be that RSCO 44, r 10, applicable under CPR, Pt 50, r 50.1 now makes 6% the rate payable when accounting for legacies if the income available is sufficient.

15   Section 31(4).

16   Section 31(5).

17   Family Law Reform Act 1969.

18   Section 69(2); *Re Turner's Will Trusts* [1937] Ch 15, [1936] 2 All ER 1435; where a power of appointment is exercised 'the document' exercising the power is the instrument under which the appointed interest arises: *Re Dickinson's Settlement* [1939] Ch 27; *Begg-McBrearty v Stilwell* [1996] 4 All ER 205. The age of 21 years is relevant for testamentary trusts of a testator who died after 1969 but made his will before 1970: Family Law Reform Act 1969, s 1(7).

Application of Trustee Act 1925, s 31

66.2 The section can only apply if the trust limitations in favour of the beneficiary in question carry the intermediate income[1] and if no express or implied contrary intention appears in the trust instrument[2].

Where the section does apply the trustees must apply their discretion rather than merely pay the income automatically to the beneficiary's parent[3]. The circumstances of the beneficiary and his parents should be reviewed regularly. A special point should be made to review the position a month or so before the beneficiary attains 18 since the statutory power to apply income and accumulations thereof expires on his 18th birthday and, before then, such could be allocated to him absolutely or contingent upon attaining his majority, such being applications of money for his benefit[4].

It is apprehended that, in spite of the wide words of the section, trustees should ask the parent or guardian for some reasonable explanation as to how he intends to apply the sum allowed by them, although they are not bound to see to its application. It does not matter that parents of the infant being maintained are incidentally benefited though, of course, a trustee should not maintain an infant with the purpose of benefiting the parents[5].

The power being discretionary, the court will not interfere with the trustees' discretion so long as they exercise it bona fide and rationally[6].

Sums paid by trustees in the exercise of their discretion form part of the total income of the infant for tax purposes as soon as the trustees exercise their discretion[7]. Income applied for an infant unmarried child of the settlor is treated as the settlor's income. Any sum paid out of trust funds to the settlor's child is treated as income to the extent that accumulated income is available[8].

1   Section 31(3); see below.
2   Section 69(2).
3   *Wilson v Turner* (1883) 22 Ch D 521.
4   *Re Vestey's Settlement* [1951] Ch 209, CA; *Pilkington v IRC* [1964] AC 612, HL on benefit via settlements.
5   *Re Lofthouse* (1885) 29 Ch D 921.
6   *Re Bryant* [1894] 1 Ch 324; *Re Senior* [1936] 3 All ER 196.
7   *Drummond v Collins* [1915] AC 1011, HL.
8   See the Income and Corporation Taxes Act 1988, s 660B, as substituted by Finance Act 1995, s, 68, Sch 17.

Statutory power not always applicable

66.3 Section 31 applies in two cases only. The first is where, in the case of a future or contingent legacy by the parent of, or of a person in loco parentis to, the legatee, under the general law[1] the legacy carries interest for the maintenance of the legatee. The second is *where the gift carries the intermediate income.* Thus if, on the true construction of the settlement, that income is payable to someone else during the infancy, or if there is an express direction to the trustees to accumulate the income during the minority of the contingent life tenant and to add that income to the corpus[2], the infant will not (with one exception referred to later in the case of portions charged on land) be entitled to be maintained.

Consequently, except in the first case set out above, the preliminary question which the practitioner has to resolve in all cases of maintenance, is whether or not the income of the fund will go along with the capital if and when the latter vests. If it *will,* then, unless there is an express direction to accumulate all the income until the corpus vests, maintenance may be safely allowed. If it will not, then maintenance must be refused. So must it also be where there is an express direction for accumulation.

Where trustees hold property on discretionary trusts before holding it for persons with vested or contingent interests and, pursuant to their discretions, the trustees allocate income absolutely to a discretionary beneficiary, this income does not fall within s 31. On the other hand, income arising from such income will do so[3]. An infant discretionary beneficiary in such a case is thus absolutely entitled to the allocated income and does not have his interest converted into a contingent interest by the application of s 31[4].

1   See para 66.5 below.
2   *Re Stapleton* [1946] 1 All ER 323.
3   *Re Vestey's Settlement* [1951] Ch 209, [1950] 2 All ER 891.
4   For such conversion, see para 66.9 below.

What gifts carry actual intermediate income

66.4 An inter vivos settlement must be of specific property, and, even if a beneficiary's interest is contingent, it will carry the intermediate income (unless a contrary intent is present as where the income is disposed of in favour of someone else or directed to be accumulated to the capital). A testamentary contingent bequest of residuary personalty will carry intermediate income[1] unless a contrary intent is present e g where it is expressly deferred to some future date[2].

With regard to specific devises and bequests and residuary devises contained in wills coming into operation after 1925, s 175 of the Law of Property Act 1925 provides as follows:

(1)   A contingent or future specific devise[3] or bequest of property, whether real or personal, and a contingent residuary devise of freehold land, and a specific or residuary devise of freehold land to trustees upon trust for persons whose interests are contingent or executory shall, subject to the statutory provisions relating to accumulations, carry the intermediate income of that property from the death of the testator, except so far as such income, or any part thereof, may be otherwise expressly disposed of.

In considering s 175 a distinction has to be drawn between gifts which are merely contingent (or vested subject to defeasance) and those which are expressly deferred to a future date. Prima facie, a gift of residue which is deferred to a future date does not carry the intermediate income whether it is vested, or vested subject to defeasance, or contingent, unless the will contains words indicating an intention that the income is to go with the capital[4].

1   *Re Adams* [1893] 1 Ch 329 at 334. The intermediate income is carried for as long as the law allows it thereby to be accumulated for the beneficiary: *Re McGeorge* [1963] Ch 544, [1963] 1 All ER 519.
2   *Re Oliver* [1947] 2 All ER 162 at 166; *Re Gillett's Will Trusts* [1950] Ch 102, [1949] 2 All ER 893; *Re Geering* [1964] Ch 136, [1962] 3 All ER 1043: such express deferral may even prevent a vested residuary bequest from carrying intermediate income.
3   In *Re McGeorge* [1963] Ch 544, [1963] 1 All ER 519, the testator had devised land to his daughter and declared that 'the ... devise ... shall not take effect until after the death of my ... wife should she survive me', going on to make substitutionary provision for the land if his daughter should die before the survivor of the testator and his wife. Cross J held that the land was the subject of a 'future specific devise' within s 175 and therefore carried the income but that, since it was liable to defeasance during the lifetime of the testator's widow, the income should be accumulated and the daughter could not claim that it be paid to her under s 31(1)(ii) because (a) her interest was vested and not contingent and (b) since the gift was a future gift, the will showed a contrary intention within s 69(2).
4   *Re Geering* [1964] Ch 136, [1962] 3 All ER 1043. In this case, Cross J held that this prima facie rule was in fact rebutted by the wording of the will. But in *Re Nash* [1965] 1 All ER 51, [1965] 1 WLR 221, Ungoed-Thomas J held that no such rebuttal was to be found in

the will and that the normal rule should be applied: the intermediate income was therefore ordered to be accumulated for 21 years or until the ultimate gift vested in possession (whichever period was the shorter), and if the gift failed to vest within 21 years the intermediate income which accrued after the end of that period would pass on intestacy.

General or pecuniary legacies that merely carry interest

66.5 Section 175 does not refer to contingent or future general legacies (eg 'I bequeath 1,000 ordinary shares in ICI Ltd') or pecuniary legacies (eg 'I bequeath £5,000'). The basic principle is that a general or pecuniary legacy carries interest (at 5% if the income available is sufficient[1] and there is no rule of court to the contrary[2]) from the time at which it is payable[3]. If not specified by the testator, this will, in the case of an immediate legacy, be one year after the testator's death[4] (ie at the end of the executor's year) and in the case of a contingent or deferred legacy will be the time the contingency is satisfied or the deferred event occurs[5].

In four exceptional cases, interest runs from the testator's death. First, if a vested legacy is given in satisfaction of a debt[6]; second, if a vested legacy is charged on realty alone[7]; third, if a legacy is given to a minor and the will shows an intention to provide for the minor's maintenance or education[8] even if the legacy is contingent upon an event having no reference to the legatee's minority, eg the attainment of twenty-five years of age[9]; fourth, if a testator gives a legacy to his minor child or to a minor to whom he stands in loco parentis[10], so long as the testator makes no other provision for maintenance of the minor[11], so long as the legacy is given directly to the minor and not to trustees for the minor[12] and so long as any specified contingency has some reference to the child's minority (eg attaining an age no greater than 18 years)[13].

There is one special case where a contingent general or pecuniary legacy carries actual intermediate income: where a legacy is directed to be set apart from the rest of the testator's estate for the purpose of benefiting the minor legatee (and not merely for convenience of administration) this will carry the actual intermediate income produced by such separate fund as from the end of the executor's year[14] (or from such earlier date as the separate fund is established if that is the testator's intention[15]). If, in the third or fourth exceptional case mentioned in the preceding paragraph, a fund to provide the legacy is set aside for the sake of convenience, then any excess of income over the applicable interest rate will fall to be distributed as part of the residuary bequest. By oversight it seems that s 31(3) only applies to the fourth exceptional case, and not to the third, so that in the latter case the contingent legatee will not be affected by s 31.

1   TA 1925, s 31(3).
2   SI 1983/1181; CPR, Practice Direction to Part 40, para 15 (formerly RSC, Ord 44, r 10) may perhaps rank as such a rule.
3   *Re Hall* [1951] 1 All ER 1073; *Re Raine* [1929] 1 Ch 716.
4   *Re Hall* [1951] 1 All ER 1073.
5   *Re Raine* [1929] 1 Ch 716.
6   *Re Rattenberry* [1906] 1 Ch 667.
7   *Shirt v Westby* (1808) 16 Ves 393.

8   *Re Churchill* [1909] 2 Ch 431; *Re Selby-Walker* [1949] 2 All ER 178; *Re Stokes* [1928]
     Ch 716; *Re West* [1913] 2 Ch 345.
9   *Re Jones* [1932] 1 Ch 642 (the headnote is wrong).
10   *Re Bowlby* [1904] 2 Ch 685.
11   *Re George* (1877) 5 Ch D 837.
12   *Re Pollock* [1943] Ch 338.
13   *Re Abrahams* [1911] 1 Ch 108.
14   *Re Medlock* (1886) 55 LJ Ch 738; *Re Woodin* [1895] 2 Ch 309, CA; *Re Couturier* [1907]
     1 Ch 470.
15   Until establishment of the separate fund the applicable interest rate thereon may be payable
     from the date of the testator's death if the exceptional circumstances referred to in the
     preceding paragraph are present.

Portions charged on land

66.6 There is, however, an exception to the general rule with regard to
contingent portions charged on land. Although such gifts do not vest until
they are wanted, namely, in case of sons at full age, or in case of daughters at
full age or marriage, and do not carry intermediate income, yet an infant
contingent portioner is entitled to such a rate of interest or allowance in
respect of his or her portion as the court may deem necessary for maintenance[1].

1   Per Farwell J *Re Greaves' Settled Estates* [1900] 2 Ch 683.

Residuary gift to infant

66.7 A gift of residue to an infant *makes the executor a trustee*, and enables
him to allow maintenance under this Article[1].

Personal representatives have power[2] to appoint new trustees of an infant's
absolute[3] share of residue, and thereby to obtain a discharge themselves. This
power may be exercised even where the personal representatives are attorneys,
and trustees appointed by such attorneys have the powers of trustees constituted by English law, and so may allow maintenance[4].

1   *Re Smith* (1889) 42 Ch D 302. The same rule applies to an administration, see *Re Adams*
     (1906) 51 Sol Jo 113.
2   Under s 42 of the Administration of Estates Act 1925.
3   Upon an English intestacy after 1925 the statutory trusts mean that a minor beneficiary has
     only a contingent interest unless married: Administration of Estates Act 1925, s 47(1)(i).
4   Under the Trustee Act 1925, s 31: *Re Kehr* [1952] Ch 26, [1951] 2 All ER 812.

Contrary intention

66.8 All the provisions of s 31 of the Trustee Act 1925, whether expressed as
permissive or as imperative, are 'powers conferred by this Act' within the
meaning of s 69(2) of that Act, and therefore apply if and so far only as a
contrary intention is not expressed in the instrument creating the trust, and
have effect subject to the terms of that instrument[1]. An express direction (as
opposed to a power) to accumulate income during infancy will almost
invariably amount to a contrary intention sufficient to negative the statutory

power[2]. But, in any event, it may cause the gift not to carry the intermediate income, as has been seen above[3]. The statutory duty under s 31(1)(ii) to pay income to adult contingent beneficiaries has been held to be negatived by an express power for the trustees to make payments to certain of the persons who claimed its benefit 'on account of their respective expectant shares of the trust fund and the income thereof', this express power being held inconsistent with the existence of the statutory duty[4], and by a provision expressly deferring the enjoyment of a gift[5].

Where an express direction to accumulate does amount to an expression of contrary intention the fact that it is partially invalidated by s 164 of the Law of Property Act 1925 does not render s 31 applicable as from the date of the express direction becoming invalid: the income will be treated as undisposed of[6] unless carried to beneficiaries with vested interests by Law of Property Act 1925, s 164[7].

Section 31 will be excluded if its application would be inconsistent with the purport of the instrument in question. Thus the statutory duty in s 31(2)(ii) to hold accumulations as an accretion to capital will be excluded where an appointment of income to six minors 'in equal shares *absolutely*' reveals in context an intention that each is to take an indefeasible share even if dying before attaining 18 years of age[8].

[1] *Re Turner's Will Trusts* [1937] Ch 15, [1936] 2 All ER 1435, CA (overruling *Re Spencer* [1935] Ch 533, and *Re Ricarde-Seaver's Will Trusts* [1936] 1 All ER 580). And see also *Re Watt's Will Trusts* [1936] 2 All ER 1555; *Re Rees* [1954] Ch 202, [1954] 1 All ER 7. See also para 67.9.
[2] *Re Turner's Will Trusts* [1937] Ch 15, [1936] 2 All ER 1435; *IRC v Bernstein* [1961] Ch 399, [1961] 1 All ER 320; *Re Erskine's Settlement Trusts* [1971] 1 All ER 572, [1971] 1 WLR 162; cf *Re Thatcher's Trusts* (1884) 26 Ch D 426; *Re Cooper* [1913] 1 Ch 350.
[3] See para 66.4 above.
[4] *Re Geering* [1964] Ch 136, [1962] 3 All ER 1043.
[5] *Re McGeorge* [1963] Ch 544, [1963] 1 All ER 519: see note 3 at para 66.4 above.
[6] *Re Ransome* [1957] Ch 348, [1957] 1 All ER 690; *Re Erskine's Settlement Trusts* [1971] 1 All ER 572, [1971] 1 WLR 162. In *Brotherton v IRC* [1978] 2 All ER 267 at 272 Stamp LJ giving the judgment of the Court of Appeal spoke of *Re Ransome* as follows, 'I would not wish to throw any doubt on that decision but it is right to say that it has not been considered'.
[7] *Brotherton v IRC* [1978] 2 All ER 267, [1978] 1 WLR 610.
[8] *Re Delamere's Settlement Trusts* [1984] 1 All ER 584, [1984] 1 WLR 813, CA.

Vested interests converted into contingent interests

66.9 Section 31(2)(ii) is significant, because accumulations of income will not pass to a beneficiary with a vested interest in income under the terms of a settlement unless he satisfies a contingency within s 31(2)(i) or unless he is also entitled to the capital to which the accumulations automatically accrue. This has important tax consequences, since if a beneficiary (or his personal representative if he died immediately after the income arose) is not entitled to the income then the disadvantageous income tax treatment accorded to accumulation and discretionary trusts under the Income and Corporation Taxes Act 1988, ss 686–687, applies, while absence of an interest in possession is very significant for inheritance tax purposes.

A beneficiary becomes entitled to accumulations only if (a) he attains 18 or marries under that age and his interest beforehand was vested under the terms of the settlement, eg to B for life, or (b) on attaining 18 or marrying under that age he becomes entitled to the capital from which the income arose in fee simple absolute or determinable[1] in relation to realty, or absolutely and indefeasibly[2] in relation to personalty, or for an entailed interest in relation to realty and personalty.

In other cases the accumulations pass with the capital to the persons interested in capital so that the beneficiary (or his personal representative) only obtains the accumulations if he is entitled to the capital.

It follows that where B is an unmarried minor he only has a contingent interest in income as it arises under a 1996 settlement conferring an interest on B for life or for B in tail[3]. If personalty is settled on B absolutely then B's entitlement to capital ensures that he receives all accumulations of income not otherwise applied for his maintenance etc. However, if freehold land was settled on B absolutely then the effect of the Administration of Estates Act 1925, s 51(3), is to make B's interest contingent, for if he dies unmarried before attaining majority the land and the accumulations pass as if B had merely had an entail. For inheritance tax purposes a settlement will be taxed as one where no interest in possession subsists where B is a minor and is not entitled to capital (so that he is not entitled to accumulations of income not applied for his maintenance etc)[4]. Exceptionally, B as a minor will have an interest in possession where he has a vested annuity since the Trustee Act 1925, s 31(4), entitles B or his personal representatives to accumulations.

1   It seems this means a determinable fee in the strict sense distinct from a fee simple on condition: *Re Sharp's Settlement Trusts* [1973] Ch 331, [1972] 3 All ER 151, but cf the Settled Land Act 1925, s 117(1)(iv), treating 'determinable fee' as meaning a fee determinable whether by limitation or condition.
2   The interest will not be absolute if defeasible by an overriding power or upon the fulfilment of a condition: *Re Sharp's Settlement Trusts* [1973] Ch 331, [1972] 3 All ER 151.
3   *Stanley v IRC* [1944] KB 255, [1944] 1 All ER 230; *Re Delamere's Settlement Trusts* [1984] 1 All ER 584, [1984] 1 WLR 813, CA. Entailed interests cannot be created after 1996: TLATA 1996, s 2(6).
4   See B McCutcheon, *Inheritance Tax* (3rd ed) para 17–05 paras 16–72 to 16–80.

Class gifts

66.10 The Apportionment Act 1870 requiring apportionment of income on trust assets on a day-to-day basis applies to trusts within s 31 of the Trustee Act[1]. It will apply when a beneficiary attains 18, though producing an anomalous result where income is received after such date. To the extent that income is apportioned in respect of the period before such date such income 'cannot be applied for maintenance etc. because the trustees cannot exercise their discretion in advance so as to affect the income when it is received, and they cannot apply it in arrears because the infancy will have ceased'[2]. It also applies when a class member dies or is born.

Suppose a 1985 settlement on X's grandchildren, now alive or born within 21 years, if they attain twenty-six, where five grandchildren now exist aged twenty-five, nineteen, twelve, seven and two. A fifth share of income must be paid to the two eldest and a fifth share of income may be used for the maintenance etc of each of the others and to the extent not so used must be accumulated. The allocations to the three minor beneficiaries must each be kept separate[3]. If a sixth grandchild is born then sixth shares are allocable. If a grandchild then dies before attaining twenty-six the relevant shares of income will be fifths once more. Income provisionally accumulated and allocated to such deceased grandchildren is treated as an accretion to the capital of the whole fund, divisible amongst all beneficiaries ultimately becoming entitled to the capital even if not alive during the period when such accumulated income arose[4]. Otherwise, a beneficiary can only be maintained etc out of income attributable to the period when he was alive and allocated to him as his proportionate share of income.

1   *Re Joel's Will Trust* [1967] Ch 14, [1966] 2 All ER 482.
2   *Re Joel's Will Trust* [1967] Ch 14 at 29.
3   *Re Joel's Will Trust* [1967] Ch 14, [1966] 2 All ER 482; *Re Sharp's Settlement Trusts* [1973] Ch 331, [1972] 3 All ER 151. Allocated accumulations will pass to the beneficiaries when they obtain vested interests.
4   *Re Joel's Will Trust* [1967] Ch 14, [1966] 2 All ER 482. The Law Reform Committee 23rd Report 1982 (Cmnd 8733) para 3.41 recommends abrogation of the *Re Joel's Will Trust* time apportionment: the income from the trust should be apportioned between the class of beneficiaries as constituted on the day the income is received by the trustees. A draftsman may expressly provide for this in the settlement.

ARTICLE 67
POWER OF ADVANCEMENT

67.1

(1)   Trustees may at any time or times pay or apply any capital money subject to a trust, for the advancement or benefit, in such manner as they may, in their absolute discretion, think fit, of any person entitled to the capital of the trust property or of any share thereof, whether absolutely or contingently on his attaining any specified age or on the occurrence of any other event, or subject to a gift over on his death under any specified age or on the occurrence of any other event[1], and whether in possession or in remainder or reversion, and such payment or application may be made notwithstanding that the interest of such person is liable to be defeated by the exercise of a power of appointment or revocation, or to be diminished by the increase of the class to which he belongs[2].

(2)   The money so paid or applied for the advancement or benefit of any person must not exceed altogether in amount one-half of the presumptive or vested share or interest of that person in the trust property. It seems that the power ceases to be exercisable in respect of a particular beneficiary once it has been exercised in respect of such beneficiary's presumptive half share, so that a

subsequent appreciation of the assets remaining in the settlement will not enable any further advancement to be made to such beneficiary.

(3)   If that person is or becomes absolutely and indefeasibly entitled to a share in the trust property the money so paid or applied must be brought into account as part of such share.

(4)   No such payment or application may be made so as to prejudice any person entitled to any prior life or other interest, whether vested or contingent, in the money paid or applied unless such person is in existence and of full age and consents in writing to such payment or application.

(5)   This power does not apply to money applicable as capital money for the purposes of the Settled Land Act 1925.

(6)   This power does not apply to trusts constituted or created before 1 January, 1926 and may be negatived or modified by the instrument creating the trust, eg so that if the power is extended to the whole of a prospective share the consent of the life tenant remains requisite[3].

1   See *Re Garrett, Croft v Ruck* [1934] Ch 477.
2   The power of revocation in Mental Health Act 1983, s 96(3) does not prevent an advancement of capital: *Re CWHT* [1978] Ch 67, [1978] 1 All ER 210 on the corresponding s 103(4) of the 1959 Act.
3   TA 1925, s 69(2); *Henley v Wardell* (1988) Times, 29 January.

Application of statutory power

67.2   The above statutory power of advancement conferred by s 32 of the Trustee Act 1925 is to the same effect as the usual advancement clause formerly contained in most well-drafted wills and settlements[1]. Its operation may be excluded or modified by the expression of a contrary intention in the will or settlement,[2] and it only relates to trusts constituted or created after 1925.

For this purpose a trust in a will is not 'constituted or created' until the death of the testator[3]. Trusts created by a deed of appointment executed pursuant to a special power of appointment conferred by will are constituted by the will, that is, from the death of the testator since an appointment under a special power must be read into the instrument creating it[4]. It is otherwise in the case of trusts created by a deed exercising a general power of appointment given by will which derive their force from and originate in the appointment only. The result is that s 32 applies to the trusts arising on the exercise after 1925 of a general power whenever created[5].

1   *Re Stimpson's Trusts* [1931] 2 Ch 77. The express power is still required in Settled Land Act settlements created under powers in pre-1997 settlements (TA 1925, s 32(2), the effect whereof is stated in para 5 of this Article).
2   TA 1925, s 69(2). See *IRC v Bernstein* [1961] Ch 399, [1961] 1 All ER 320, CA, where the statutory power of advancement was held to be impliedly excluded by the manifest intention of the settlor that there should be no distribution during his lifetime (compare *Re Henderson's Trusts* [1969] 3 All ER 769, [1969] 1 WLR 651). See also *Re Evans' Settlement* [1967] 3 All ER 343, [1967] 1 WLR 1294 where Stamp J held that although an

express power of advancement did not necessarily exclude the statutory power, the express power in this case, being limited to a stated sum, did do so. For a case in which the statutory power was restricted, but not in such a way as to affect its operation in the circumstances which had arisen, see *Re Collard's Will Trusts* [1961] Ch 293, [1961] 1 All ER 821 (a provision that the power should not be exercised 'for any purposes connected with business' did not prevent its exercise for the purpose of saving estate duty).

3   *Re Darby* (1943) 59 TLR 418.
4   *Re Batty* [1952] Ch 280, [1952] 1 All ER 425; as explained in *Re Bransbury's Will Trusts* [1954] 1 All ER 605, [1954] 1 WLR 496.
5   *Re Bransbury's Will Trusts* [1954] 1 All ER 605, [1954] 1 WLR 496.

Cash or property may be advanced subject to being brought into account

67.3 The power of advancement is primarily a power to make payments of cash and can be exercised informally, though the trustees should record what they have done. The court will not insist on circuity of action: thus, instead of advancing cash to a beneficiary to enable him to purchase land forming part of the trust property, the trustees may simply transfer the land in question to him[1]. Money paid or applied by way of advancement must, of course, be brought into account when the beneficiary's share of capital becomes distributable to him, as should the money-equivalent of any assets directly advanced to the beneficiary irrespective of any depreciation or appreciation of such assets or the traceable product thereof[2].

1   *Re Collard's Will Trusts* [1961] Ch 293, [1961] 1 All ER 821, where Buckley J also said: 'There is no doubt that the statutory power of advancement is constantly exercised by trustees transferring to beneficiaries Stock Exchange investments by way of advancement'. See also *Pilkington v IRC* [1964] AC 612, [1962] 3 All ER 622, HL.
2   Money or assets advanced are from the date of such advancement no longer part of the trust property: *Re Fox* [1904] 1 Ch 480; *Re Pilkington's Will Trusts* [1959] Ch 699 at 705. Their value at that date is thus the relevant value: see *Re Gollins Declaration of Trust* [1969] 3 All ER 1591 and contrast advancements caught by Administration of Estates Act 1925, s 47(1)(iii) where it is the date of the intestate's death that is the valuation date.

Exhausting the exercise of the power

67.4 In *Re Marquess of Abergavenny's Estate Act Trusts*[1] the trustees had express power from time to time to advance to the life tenant any part or parts not exceeding in all one half in value of the settled fund. Goulding J held that an advance of half the value of the fund exhausted the exercise of the power, so that it ceased to be exercisable in the life tenant's favour, even though the retained settled assets had subsequently much increased in value. It is difficult to distinguish the statutory power from such express power, so that to retain flexibility the trustees should, therefore, never quite exercise the statutory power of advancement to the full value of half the settled assets at the date of exercise of the power.

If a settlor would wish half of any subsequent increase in value of the settled assets retained by the trustees to be available for further advancement then the statutory power should be expressly varied by the trust instrument[2]. Where a fund is held for a minor absolutely, and the one half in value limit on advancement has been reached, the court may vary the trust so as to remove the limit[3].

1   [1981] 2 All ER 643, [1981] 1 WLR 843.
2   Consideration might also be given to how advanced or appropriated property should be brought into account on final distribution: see para 48.54 above.
3   *CD (a minor) v O* [2004] EWHC 1036 (Ch).

Purpose of the advance

67.5 The word 'benefit' is the widest possible word which could be employed and includes a payment direct to the beneficiary. That, however, does not absolve the trustees from making up their minds whether the payment in the particular manner which they contemplate is for the benefit of the beneficiary[1]. Clearly a payment direct to the beneficiary which will effect a substantial saving of tax on the death of the tenant for life will be for the benefit of the beneficiary[2], as may be a payment to enable him to discharge his debts[3]. Payment of capital under a scheme to provide for prospective public school fees will also be for the benefit of an infant beneficiary.

Where the statutory power did not apply an express clause authorising the application of moneys for the 'advancement' of the beneficiary but *not* containing the wider word 'benefit'[4] has been held to authorise payments for

purchasing a commission in the army[5];
putting out as an apprentice[6];
emigrating[7];
purchasing an outfit[8];
furnishing a house[9];
payment of legacy duty[10];
establishing in business[11] (but not making a deposit with the Trustees of Lloyd's for the purpose of becoming an underwriter[12]) or even establishing a husband in business[13];
and a power to raise money for starting the testator's son in business has been held to authorise the trustees to apply money towards the purchase of a house, with or without a surgery, for him to live in while practising medicine[14].

It is plain, therefore, that if the power of advancement is exercised for the benefit of the beneficiary, its exercise will not be made improper by the fact that other people benefit incidentally as a result[15]. It has indeed been held[16] that trustees may exercise a power of advancement in the normal form to pay a sum to a charity at the request of a wealthy beneficiary: the discharge of the beneficiary's moral obligation to make charitable donations was held to be for his benefit but, said Pennycuick J it is essential:

'that the beneficiary himself should recognise the moral obligation. It is not open to trustees to pay away the beneficiary's prospective capital over his head or against his will in discharge of what they consider to be his moral obligation.'

In line with this, under an express power to apply capital for the benefit of a beneficiary it has been held proper to re-settle it on the beneficiary's children, with a view to avoiding tax, in a case where the beneficiary was already well provided for[17].

67.5 *The powers of the trustee*

The word 'advancement' does not imply that the interest of the beneficiary need be in any sense accelerated: thus the power of advancement may be properly exercised by the trustees settling the property advanced upon trusts which in fact defer the beneficiary's physical possession of the property longer than the original settlement would have done[18]. (The question of the trustees making an advancement by way of settlement is dealt with below).

In no case, however, must a power of advancement be exercised so as to procure a benefit to the trustees[19].

Although the trustees must decide, before exercising the power that there is some good reason for doing so and must, in the words of Willmer LJ[20], 'weigh on the one side the benefit to the proposed advancee, and on the other hand the rights of those who are or may ... become interested under the trusts', there is no need for the advance to be 'personal' to the beneficiary in the way suggested by the Court of Appeal in *Re Pilkington's Will Trusts*[21]. In that case, Lord Evershed MR said that the statutory power of advancement could not be exercised unless the benefit to be conferred was 'personal to the person concerned in the sense of being related to his or her own real or personal needs' and the exercise was 'an exercise done to meet the circumstances as they present themselves in regard to a person within the scope of the section whose circumstances call for that to be done which the trustees think fit to be done'. But the House of Lords in reversing (sub nom *Pilkington v IRC*[22])the decision of the Court of Appeal, found it impossible to import a restriction of this kind into the statutory power. Lord Radcliffe said that it seemed to him 'uncontrollably vague as a guide to a general administration'.

1   *Re Moxon's Will Trusts* [1958] 1 All ER 386, [1958] 1 WLR 165; *Re Pauling's Settlement Trust* [1964] Ch 303, [1963] 3 All ER 1, CA.
2   *Re Moxon's Will Trusts* [1958] 1 All ER 386, [1958] 1 WLR 165. See also *Pilkington v IRC* [1964] AC 612, [1962] 3 All ER 622, HL, per Viscount Radcliffe.
3   Cf *Lowther v Bentinck* (1874) LR 19 Eq 166.
4   A discussion of these two words is to be found in *Pilkington v IRC* [1964] AC 612, [1962] 3 All ER 622, HL. See also *X v A* [2006] EWHC 2706 (Ch), [2006] WTLR 171; *Kleinwort Benson (Jersey) Trustees Ltd* [2004] JRC 047.
5   *Lawrie v Bankes* (1857) 4 K & J 142.
6   *Swinnock v Crisp* (1681) Freem Ch 78; *Simpson v Brown* (1865) 13 WR 312.
7   *Re England* (1830) 1 Russ & M 488; *Re Salters Trusts* (1866) 17 ICh R 176.
8   *Re Welch* (1854) 23 LJ Ch 344.
9   *Perry v Perry* (1870) 18 WR 482.
10 *Klug v Klug* [1918] 2 Ch 67.
11 *Re Mead* (1918) 88 LJ Ch 86, CA; also see *Hardy v Shaw* [1975] 2 All ER 1052.
12 *Re Craven's Estate* [1937] Ch 431, [1937] 3 All ER 33.
13 *Re Kershaw's Trusts* (1868) LR 6 Eq 322.
14 *Re Williams' Will Trusts* [1953] Ch 138, [1953] 1 All ER 536.
15 This was confirmed by the House of Lords in *Pilkington v IRC* [1964] AC 612, [1962] 3 All ER 622, HL. Also see *Re Hampden Settlement Trusts* [1977] TR 177 and [2001] WTLR 195 (where in the case of a wealthy beneficiary with plenty to support himself it was held for his benefit to appoint trust property on trust for his family though they were not beneficiaries) and *Re Lesser* [1947] VLR 366 (purchase of house for infant beneficiaries to live in with their parents).
16 *Re Clore's Settlement Trusts* [1966] 2 All ER 272, [1966] 1 WLR 955; contrast *X v A* [2006] EWHC 2706 (Ch), [2006] WTLR 171.
17 *Re Earl of Buckinghamshire's Settlement Trusts* (1977) Times, 29 March.
18 *Pilkington v IRC* [1964] AC 612, [1962] 3 All ER 622, HL; and see 'benefit' under the Variation of Trusts Act jurisdiction: *Re Estate Trust* [2001] WTLR 571.

19 *Molyneux v Fletcher* [1898] 1 QB 648 (advance to daughter to enable her to pay father's debt to one of the trustees a fraud on the power).
20 In *Re Pauling's Settlement Trust* [1964] Ch 303, [1963] 3 All ER 1, CA.
21 [1961] Ch 466, [1961] 2 All ER 330, CA.
22 [1964] AC 612, [1962] 3 All ER 622, HL.

Ensuring purpose effected

67.6 If trustees do make an advance for a particular purpose, which they state, the question arises as to whether and how far they must ensure that it is used for that purpose. In *Re Pauling's Settlement*[1] the Court of Appeal held that in such a case the trustees can properly pay the advance to the person for whose benefit it is made if they reasonably believe that he can be trusted to carry out the purpose prescribed; but if the person concerned had, to the trustees' knowledge, applied any previous advance in some way other than the one prescribed, the trustees would not be justified in paying another advance to him for a specific purpose and should themselves apply it for the purpose for which they wished it to be used. Alternatively, the person to whom an advance is made for a stated purpose can expressly be placed under a *Quistclose* trust obligation[2] to carry out that purpose, and the trustees should not relieve him of that obligation or pay the advance to him in such a way as to leave him free to carry it out or to disregard it without any responsibility on their part to enquire as to its application.

Re Pauling's Settlement further indicates that requests from and consents of young adult beneficiaries in respect of advancements must be carefully considered, since until such beneficiaries are 'emancipated' from their parents questions of undue influence arise. A beneficiary's consent to an advancement in breach of trust (as for the benefit of the beneficiary's parent and not for the benefit of the beneficiary) will be no defence if obtained from the beneficiary by undue influence[3].

1 [1961] Ch 466.
2 Explained at para 8.169 above.
3 *Re Pauling's ST* [1964] Ch 303, at 335–36, CA.

Advancement by way of settlement

67.7 Trustees exercising a power of advancement may make settlements on objects of the power if the particular circumstances of the case warrant that course as being for the benefit of the object of the power[1]. However, trustees should be cautious about re-settling the property so as to postpone the beneficiary's entitlement (though there may be justifiable tax or special personal reasons)[2]. To strengthen 'benefit' for the beneficiary for whose benefit there is to be a re-settlement it is common to confer powers of appointment on such beneficiary. The consent of the beneficiary to the re-settlement is not needed[3].

In at least one case[4] the court has even refused to sanction an advancement unless the beneficiary settled the sum advanced.

The provisions that may be included in a settlement were considered by Upjohn J in *Re Wills' Trusts*[5], where he opined:

> 'What the authorities typified by *Re May's Settlement*[6] and *Re Mewburn's Settlement*[7] establish to my mind is that any settlement made by way of advancement on an object of the power by trustees must not conflict with the principle delegatus non potest delegare. Thus, unless upon its proper construction the power of advancement permits delegation of powers and discretions, a settlement created in exercise of the power of advancement cannot in general delegate any powers or discretions, at any rate in relation to beneficial interests, to any trustees or other persons, and in so far as the settlement purports to do so it is pro tanto invalid. I say that without prejudice to the propriety of including ordinary powers of advancement in such settlement; see *Re Morris' Settlement Trusts*'[8].

In *Pilkington v IRC*, however, the House of Lords held that trustees could properly exercise their statutory power of advancement by adding the property advanced to another settlement, which was already in existence and of which they themselves happened to be the trustees. Viscount Radcliffe dealt with several arguments which had been raised by the Revenue against the propriety of such an exercise, including one based on the maxim delegatus non potest delegare, mentioned above. In this connection he said[9]:

> 'I am unconvinced by the argument that the trustees would be improperly delegating their trust by allowing the money raised to pass over to new trustees under a settlement conferring new powers on the latter. In fact I think the whole issue of delegation is here beside the mark. The law is not that trustees cannot delegate: it is that trustees cannot delegate unless they have authority to do so. If the power of advancement which they possess is so read as to allow them to raise money for the purpose of having it settled [as the House of Lords considered that it was] then they do have the necessary authority to let the money pass out of the old settlement into the new trusts. No question of delegation of their powers or trusts arises. If, on the other hand, their power of advancement is read so as to exclude settled advances, cadit quaestio.'

The House of Lords considered that the statutory power of advancement in substance gave the trustees power to free money from the trust and subject it to another trust, whether indirectly by advancing it to the beneficiary for the binding purpose of being settled by the beneficiary on new trusts or directly by transferring it themselves to new trustees of new trusts. The new trustees then are to exercise original discretions of their own, there being no question of them exercising delegated functions of the old trustees. However, in light of the dicta of Upjohn J cited above and some cases[10] narrowly construing the scope of special powers of appointment so as not to authorise the creation of independent new trusts conferring extensive new discretions upon the new trustees, the conservative practice arose of expressly extending the statutory power of advancement to permit advancements to trustees of new trusts upon discretionary trusts or upon protective trusts, and whether or not containing flexible powers of appointment. There is no harm in this practice but there is no need for it either[11].

The statutory power of advancement does not contain any express reference to 'raising' money or part of the trust funds for the purpose of an advancement, although s 16 of the Trustee Act 1925 seems available for this purpose.

Where such words do occur in an express power, the requirement is sufficiently met by taking specified investments out of the general trust fund and holding them upon new trusts for the benefit of the beneficiary advanced[12]. The power to 'pay or apply' is sufficiently exercised by a resolution of the trustees allocating money (or property) to a beneficiary[13] or by the trustees appropriating it to the trusts of another settlement of which they are themselves the trustees[14].

1   *Re Halsted's WT* [1937] 2 All ER 570; *Re Ropner's ST* [1956] 3 All ER 332n, [1956] 1 WLR 902; *Re Meux* [1958] Ch 154, [1957] 2 All ER 630; *Re Wills' Will Trusts* [1959] Ch 1, [1958] 2 All ER 472; *Pilkington v IRC* [1964] AC 612, [1962] 3 All ER 622, HL; cf *Kleinwort Benson (Jsy) Tees Ltd v Pinto* [2004] JRC 047.
2   *Pilkington v IRC* [1964] AC 612, [1962] 3 All ER 622, HL; for tax reasons see *Re Estate Trust* [2001] WTLR 571.
3   *Re Cameron* [1999] 2 All ER 924 at 948–949.
4   *Roper-Curzon v Roper-Curzon* (1871) LR 11 Eq 452, where the beneficiary who was already married was studying for the law.
5   [1959] Ch 1, [1958] 2 All ER 472 but the re-settlement did not contain discretionary powers.
6   [1926] Ch 135.
7   [1934] Ch 112.
8   [1951] 2 All ER 528, CA.
9   [1964] AC 612 at 639.
10 *Re Morris' Settlement Trusts* [1951] 2 All ER 528, CA; *Re Hunter's Will Trusts* [1963] Ch 372, [1962] 3 All ER 1050; *Re Hay's Settlement Trusts* [1981] 3 All ER 786, [1982] 1 WLR 202.
11 See *Lewin on Trusts* (17th edn), para 32–18; J Kessler *Drafting Trusts and Will Trusts* (6th edn), paras 10.5 and 10.11; A J Oakley (ed) Parker & Mellows *The Modern Law of Trusts* (7th edn), pp 626–627.
12 *Re Wills' Will Trusts* [1959] Ch 1, [1958] 2 All ER 472.
13 *Re Baron Vestey's Settlement* [1951] Ch 209, [1950] 2 All ER 891, CA.
14 *Pilkington v IRC* [1964] AC 612, [1962] 3 All ER 622, HL.

The rule against perpetuities

67.8 For the purpose of the rule against perpetuities, there is an effective analogy between powers of advancement and special powers of appointment, so that if the trustees exercise their power of advancement by imposing new trusts upon the property advanced the validity of those new trusts from the point of view of perpetuity is to be judged in the same way as the trusts declared by the exercise of a special power of appointment[1] because 'the new settlement is only effected by the operation of a fiduciary power which itself "belongs" to the old settlement'[2]. The Perpetuities and Accumulations Act 1964 will not apply to the advancement unless the original settlement was created after 15 July 1964 as a result of s 15(5) of the 1964 Act applying by analogy.

If part of the exercise of a power of advancement is void for perpetuity and this alters the resultant effect of the advancement so drastically that it cannot reasonably be regarded as beneficial to the beneficiary intended to be advanced, or that the trustees cannot reasonably be supposed to have addressed their minds to the questions relevant to the true effect of the advancement, then the whole advancement is void[3]. Otherwise the part of the advancement not void for perpetuity (eg a life interest in B's favour) stands even if no effective trusts of the capital interest have been created: the fact that trustees now hold the capital for B for life is an application of capital within s 32[4].

1   See para 11.25 ff.
2   *Pilkington v IRC* [1964] AC 612, [1962] 3 All ER 622, HL.
3   *Re Hastings-Bass* [1975] Ch 25, [1974] 2 All ER 193 (restrictively interpreting *Re Abraham's Will Trusts* [1969] 1 Ch 463, [1967] 2 All ER 1175) discussed and clarified in *Mettoy Pension Trustees Ltd v Evans* [1991] 2 All ER 513 at 552–555: see para 61.18 above. For adverse tax consequences that may flow from a void advancement see *Spens v IRC* [1970] 3 All ER 295, [1970] 1 WLR 1173.
4   *Re Hastings-Bass* [1975] Ch 25, [1974] 2 All ER 193.

Consent of persons having prior interests

67.9 Beneficiaries under a discretionary trust are not persons 'entitled to any prior life or other interest etc', and therefore their consent to the exercise of the power is unnecessary[1]. Likewise the consent of persons who would be interested should the discretionary trusts arise out of statutory protective trusts need not be obtained[2] ,though the principal beneficiary with the protected life interest must give his consent. If such a person gives his or her consent to an advance under the above power, he or she will not forfeit his or her beneficial interest in the trust fund whether the advancement is made under an express advancement clause[3] or under the statutory power[4] except where the statutory power applies in the case of a will made before, but coming into operation after 1925[5].

The court has no power to dispense with any consent to the exercise of an express power of advancement required by the settlement[6] and, presumably, it has no power to dispense with any requisite consent to the exercise of the statutory power. This could create a difficulty if the person having the prior interest were a minor or unborn.

In *IRC v Bernstein*[7] clause 2 of the settlement directed that the income of the trust fund should be accumulated during the settlor's lifetime 'in augmentation of the capital of the trust fund and for the benefit of the person or persons who shall eventually become entitled thereto'. Subsequent clauses provided that on the settlor's death the relevant portion of the fund (in fact two-thirds) should be held on trust for his wife absolutely or, if she were then dead, for the children of the marriage then living, with a further gift over. At the date of the case, no children had been born.

The main point of the case was whether the statutory power of advancement was in fact applicable to the settlement at all, and it was held at first instance and on appeal that it was not. While a duty to accumulate is necessarily inconsistent with the statutory power of maintenance, it is not necessarily inconsistent with the power of advancement, though in context it was, since the main object of the trust was to build up an intact capital fund. The question was also raised as to whether, if the power had applied, the unborn children would have had a 'prior ... interest' necessitating their consent to its exercise in the wife's favour. The argument that they did have a prior interest seems to have been based on the contention that clause 2 made a separate disposition of the accumulations of income which went to augment the capital (as distinct from the original capital itself) and that this disposition gave the wife and children an interest, in ensuring that all income was applied in augmentation of capital, which was prior to the remaining dispositions. At first instance, Danckwerts J held that they did not have prior interests, saying simply that 'the first interest seems to me to be that of the wife' and that he therefore could not see how 'the interest of possible children ... can be regarded as a prior interest at all', adding that they had 'only a contingent interest which is subject to her first interest ... '

The approach of the Court of Appeal was less robust in two respects: first, because the Court did not consider it necessary to decide this point and deliberately refrained from doing so; and secondly, because it gave more recognition to the subtlety of the argument. Thus since the 'prior interest' was alleged to exist in the accumulations of income rather than in the original capital, the Court of Appeal treated the point involved as being the same as that which was raised, but not decided, in connection with s 31 of the Act in *Re Spencer, Lloyds Bank Ltd v Spencer*[8] and *Re Turner's Will Trusts*[9]. Evershed MR, like the judges involved in those two cases, shrank from finding that the children had prior interests when they had no present right to call for income, though Harman LJ had a slight preference for the Special Commissioners' view that the children did have prior interests.

[1] *Re Beckett's Settlement, Re Beckett* [1940] Ch 279.
[2] *Re Harris' Settlement* (1940) 162 LT 358.
[3] *Re Shaw's Settlement* [1951] Ch 833, [1951] 1 All ER 656; following *Re Hodgson* [1913] 1 Ch 34, and distinguishing *Re Stimpson's Trusts* [1931] 2 Ch 77.
[4] *Re Rees* [1954] Ch 202, [1954] 1 All ER 7.
[5] *Re Stimpson's Trust* [1931] 2 Ch 77, as explained in *Re Rees' Will Trusts* [1954] Ch 202, [1954] 1 All ER 7.
[6] *Re Forster's Settlement* [1942] Ch 199, [1942] 1 All ER 180. Presumably, in a case appropriate for the application of equitable proprietary estoppel principles a person with a prior interest who had orally consented would not be permitted to prevent the advancement.
[7] At first instance [1960] Ch 444, [1960] 1 All ER 697; and on appeal [1961] Ch 399, [1961] 1 All ER 320, CA.
[8] [1935] Ch 533.
[9] [1937] Ch 15, [1936] 2 All ER 1435, CA. See para 66.8 above.

Capital Gains Tax considerations

67.10 A line can be drawn between 'resettlement' cases where an advancement is made so that new trusts, powers and provisions supersede the original trusts, powers and provisions (even if the same persons happen to be trustees of the new trusts and the original trusts) and 'sub-settlement' cases where an advancement by way of allocation of part of the capital otherwise leaves the trusts, powers and provisions of the original settlement applicable thereto[1]. In the former situation a capital gains tax charge will arise since the trustees of the separate new trust become absolutely entitled against the trustees of the original trusts within Taxation of Chargeable Gains Act 1992, s 71.

1   *Hoare Trustees v Gardner* [1979] Ch 10, [1978] 1 All ER 791; *Roome v Edwards
    (Inspector of Taxes)* [1982] AC 279, [1981] 1 All ER 736, HL; *Bond v Pickford* [1983]
    STC 517, CA; *Swives v Renton* [1991] STC 490. See para 82.10 ff.

ARTICLE 68
SUSPENSION OF THE TRUSTEE'S POWERS BY
ADMINISTRATION ACTION

68.1

(1)   Where a judgment has been given for the execution of the trust
       by the court, or (before judgment) an injunction has been
       granted, or a receiver appointed, the trustee can only exercise his
       powers with the sanction of the court[1].

(2)   But, although its sanction must be obtained, the court will not
       interfere with a discretion reposed in a trustee and expressed to
       be absolute and uncontrollable, so long as it is exercised in good
       faith[2].

(3)   A decree for administration does not absolve a trustee or
       personal representative from the performance of his duties[3], but
       he should obtain the sanction of the court to each transaction or
       type of transaction[4].

1   *Mitchelson v Piper* (1836) 8 Sim 64; *Shewen v Vanderhorst* (1830) 2 Russ & M 75; *Minors
    v Battison* (1876) 1 App Cas 428; *Re Gadd* (1883) 23 Ch D 134. The mere issue of a claim
    for administration does not affect the trustee's powers (*Berry v Gibbons* (1873) 8 Ch App
    747), nor does the issue of a claim under RSC Ord 85, r 3 (preserved in CPR, Pt 50, Sch 1),
    except so far as interference with or control of any power or discretion is necessarily
    involved in the particular relief sought.
2   *Gisborne v Gisborne* (1877) 2 App Cas 300; *Tempest v Lord Camoys* (1882) 21 Ch D
    571; and see Article 65, above.
3   *Garner v Moore* (1855) 3 Drew 277, and *Bernhardt v Galsworthy* [1929] 1 Ch 549.
4   *Re Viscount Furness* [1943] Ch 415, [1944] 1 All ER 66.

After judgment

68.2 Thus, a trustee or personal representative cannot, after an order for
execution of the trust or for general administration (even though only one
account is to be proceeded with forthwith[1]) prosecute or defend legal
proceedings[2], or execute a power of sale[3], or appoint trustees[4] or do repairs[5],
or invest[6], or exercise any other power, or deal in any way with the assets,
even in due course of administration[7], without applying to the court to
sanction his doing so. It remains his duty to bring before the court questions
upon which the direction of the court is required, and if he acts, or omits to
act, without the direction of the court he does so at his peril[8]. However it
seems a good title can be conferred on innocent purchasers[9].

It has been suggested[10] that the restrictions imposed by an administration
order apply only to powers of management (eg the appointment of trustees,
the transposing of investments, the sale of assets) and not to the exercise of an
absolute discretionary power over beneficial distribution of the trust funds. To

be on the safe side[11] it will be advisable to seek the court's confirmation of this or the court's leave, if the court should take the view that leave is necessary.

1   *Re Viscount Furness* [1943] Ch 415, [1944] 1 All ER 66.
2   *Jones v Powell* (1841) 4 Beav 96.
3   *Walker v Smalwood* (1768) Amb 676. But the trustee can give a good title to a specific chattel to a purchaser who has no notice of the order (*Berry v Gibbons* (1873) 8 Ch App 747, as explained in *Re Viscount Furness* [1943] Ch 415, [1944] 1 All ER 66).
4   *Webb v Earl of Shaftesbury* (1802) 7 Ves 480.
5   *Mitchelson v Piper* (1836) 8 Sim 64.
6   *Bethell v Abraham* (1873) LR 17 Eq 24.
7   *Re Viscount Furness* [1943] Ch 415, [1944] 1 All ER 66.
8   *Garner v Moore* (1855) 3 Drew 277.
9   *Berry v Gibbons* (1873) 8 Ch App 747.
10 AJ Hawkins (1968) 84 LQR 64 at 68–73; *Bethell v Abraham* (1873) LR 17 Eq 24 at 26 per Jessel MR.
11 In view of obiter dicta of Morton J in *Re Viscount Furness* [1943] Ch 415, [1944] 1 All ER 66, envisaging the court's sanction as requisite to any distribution of assets.

Before judgment

68.3 But where an executor or administrator, after the commencement of a creditor's administration action, and before judgment, has voluntarily paid any creditor in full, he will be held to have made a good payment, and will be allowed it in passing his accounts, even though he may have had notice of the action before payment; and, it is apprehended, the same principle would be equally applicable to trustees. To prevent such payments being made in any such case, the claimant should, immediately upon issuing his writ, apply for and obtain a receiver[1].

In *Cafe v Bent*[2] Wigram V-C stated:

'There is no reason why the mere institution of a suit which may never be prosecuted should have the effect of preventing trustees from exercising their discretion ... the mere filing of a bill cannot have the effect of preventing trustees from doing acts which are necessary to the due execution of the trust which is imposed upon them.'

Powers of appointment[3] and powers of advancement[4] survive as well as powers of management.

1   *Re Radcliffe* (1878) 7 Ch D 733, and see also *Re Barrett* (1889) 43 Ch D 70.
2   (1843) 3 Hare 245.
3   *A-G v Clack* (1839) 1 Beav 467; *Thomas v Williams* (1883) 24 Ch D 558.
4   *Sillibourne v Newport* (1855) 1 K & J 602; *Talbot v Marshfield* (1867) LR 4 Eq 661; *Brophy v Bellamy* (1873) 8 Ch App 798.

Loss of powers by trustees who have paid money into court

68.4 It may be conveniently mentioned here that, where trustees have paid the trust fund into court under s 63 of the Trustee Act 1925, they can no longer exercise any of their powers, discretionary or otherwise. This is because the payment into court is, in effect, a retirement by the trustees from their office, and a relinquishment of the judgment and discretion confided to them by the settlor[1]. New trustees may be appointed or in a special case the court may even exercise discretions or powers[2].

1   *Re Nettlefold's Trusts* (1888) 59 LT 315.
2   *Re Ashburnham's Trust* (1885) 54 LT 84; *Klug v Klug* [1918] 2 Ch 67; *McPhail v Doulton* [1971] AC 424, [1970] 2 All ER 228; *Mettoy Pension Trustees Ltd v Evans* [1991] 2 All ER 513; see paras 8.46 and 8.86 above.

Chapter 15

POWERS OF THE BENEFICIARIES

Article

69 Power of a sole beneficiary or of the beneficiaries collectively to extinguish the trust 69.1
70 Power of one of several beneficiaries partially interested in a special trust 70.1

ARTICLE 69
POWER OF A SOLE BENEFICIARY OR OF THE BENEFICIARIES
COLLECTIVELY TO EXTINGUISH THE TRUST

69.1

Where
(a)   the person who is solely absolutely entitled under a trust, not being under disability[1], so decides, or, if there is no such person,
(b)   the persons who are all those who may possibly benefit under a trust, whether concurrently or successively, and whether under fixed trusts, discretionary trusts, or powers of appointment, none being under any disability[2], unanimously so decide,
the specific performance of the trust may be arrested, and the trust extinguished by that person or persons collectively without reference to the wishes of the settlor or the trustees[3]. The equitable owners of the trust property are entitled to claim it for themselves even if the settlor wants the trustees to manage it for them for particular purposes of his own[4]. They cannot, however, compel the trustees to continue to run the trust in a form modified by themselves, but their authority to the trustees so to run the trust, if the trustees wish, will provide the trustees with a defence to any claim that the trustees thereby committed a breach of trust. Exceptionally, section 19 of the Trusts of Land and Appointment of Trustees Act 1996 permits the beneficiaries under the trust of full age and capacity and, taken together, absolutely entitled to the trust property, to rid themselves of unwanted trustees without the

need to terminate the trust, because they can compel those trustees to retire and appoint as new trustees the persons specified by all those beneficiaries collectively, so long as the power of appointing new trustees is not reserved to others under the trust instrument.

1   Ie minors and persons of unsound mind. As to the power of the court under the Variation of Trusts Act 1958 to give consent on behalf of beneficiaries under disability or not ascertainable, see para 47.28 ff.
2   See note 1, above.
3   Cf *Goulding v James* [1997] 2 All ER 239, CA.
4   Contrast the position in the USA under the so-called Claflin doctrine: *Claflin v Claflin*, 149 Mass. 19, 20 N.E. 454 (1889); see generally P Matthews, 'The Comparative Importance of the Rule in *Saunders v Vautier*' (2006) 122 LQR 266.

Illustration in case of a simple trust

69.2 Thus, if property is devised to the trustees in fee simple, upon trust for sale and to invest the proceeds of sale and to pay the income thereof to the testator's widow for life, and after her death to hold such investments upon trust for B absolutely, B, on the death of the widow, is entitled to call upon the trustees to vest the property if still unsold in him absolutely, or may by writing declare new trusts thereof[1], for in equity B is the sole and absolute owner, and the court will not permit a person solely and absolutely entitled, to be subjected to the tutelage or interference of a trustee. The court, in fact, regards a trustee as a kind of intermediary or stakeholder, whose office is to hold the scales evenly, and to see that the rights of several persons are mutually respected. Where there is only one person interested, however, and that person is of full age and capacity, the trustee's raison d'être ceases to exist; and consequently he himself becomes merely a person in the legal possession of another person's estate[2], and if the beneficiary refuses to accept a transfer of trust funds the trustee can pay them into court just as the beneficiary can insist on a transfer to himself against the trustee's wishes[3].

1   *Grey v IRC* [1960] AC 1, [1959] 3 All ER 603, HL.
2   *Smith v Wheeler* (1669) 1 Mod Rep 16; *Brown v How* (1740) Barn Ch 354; *A-G v Gore* (1740) Barn Ch 145; *Kaye v Powel* (1791) 1 Ves 408; and *Re Cotton's Trustees and London School Board* (1882) 19 Ch D 624 at 627.
3   *IRC v Hamilton-Russell Executors* [1943] 1 All ER 474, CA.

Illustration in case of a special trust where parties interested elect to stop it

69.3 The same result follows even where the settlor has contemplated and intended that the trustee shall have the control of the property, if the sole person beneficially interested is of full age and capacity and in favour of 'breaking the trust', or if all the persons collectively beneficially interested (if there are several of them) are all of full age and capacity and are unanimously in favour of doing so. For a trust is the equitable equivalent of a common law gift, and, when once declared, the settlor, like the donor of a gift, has no further rights over the property unless he be also one of the beneficiaries or has reserved to himself a power of revocation or appointment[1].

1   *Re Bowden* [1936] Ch 71.

69.4 Thus, in one case[1] a testator gave his residuary personal estate to an infant, and directed his executors to place it out at interest to accumulate, and to pay the principal and accumulations to the infant on his attaining twenty-*four*, and in the meantime to allow £60 a year for his maintenance. In the event of the infant's dying under 21 the testator gave the estate to third persons. The court held that, on the true construction of the will, the infant took an absolute vested and transmissible interest on attaining 21; and that, consequently, being the only person beneficially interested, he could put an end to the trust, and was entitled to have the residue and accumulations at once transferred to him. For, as Page Wood V-C said, in the case of *Gosling v Gosling* (when 21 years represented the age of majority)[2]:

> 'The principle of this court has always been to recognise the right of all persons who attain the age of 21 to enter upon the absolute use and enjoyment of the property given to them by will, notwithstanding any directions by the testator to the effect that they are not to enjoy it until a later age—unless, during the interval, the property is given for the benefit of another. If the property is once theirs, it is useless for the testator to attempt to impose any fetter upon their enjoyment of it in full so soon as they attain 21.'

[1] *Josselyn v Josselyn* (1837) 9 Sim 63; *Saunders v Vautier* (1841) Cr & Ph 240; *Wharton v Masterman* [1895] AC 186; *Re Johnston* [1894] 3 Ch 204; *Re Smith* [1928] Ch 915; *Re Nelson* [1928] Ch 920n; *Thorn v IRC* [1976] 2 All ER 622 at 631; and distinguish *Re Lord Nunburnholme* [1911] 2 Ch 510; reversed on appeal [1912] 1 Ch 489, CA, on the construction of the will; *Re Travis* [1900] 2 Ch 541, CA; *Berry v Geen* [1938] AC 575, [1938] 2 All ER 362; and *IRC v Hamilton-Russell Executors* [1943] 1 All ER 474, CA. *Talbot v Jevers* (1875) LR 20 Eq 255, appears to be inconsistent with the other cases.
[2] (1859) John 265 endorsed by Lord Herschell *in Wharton v Masterman* [1895] AC 186 at 192.

69.5 Section 14 of the Perpetuities and Accumulations Act 1964 applies s 2 of the Act as to presumptions of future parenthood in determining whether all beneficiaries are ascertained so as to have a right to stop accumulations.

69.6 However, the *Saunders v Vautier* principle has developed well beyond utilisation for stopping accumulations. Now, 'the principle recognises the rights of beneficiaries who are *sui juris* and together absolutely entitled to the trust property to exercise their proprietary rights to overbear and defeat the intentions of a testator or settlor'[1]. This is in stark contrast to the position in most of the USA where, if a material purpose of the settlor remains to be carried out, those beneficially entitled cannot bring the trust to an end even if unanimous[2].

[1] *Goulding v James* [1997] 2 All ER 239 at 247, per Mummery LJ.
[2] *Claflin v Claflin*, 149 Mass. 19, 20 N.E. 454 (1889); see generally P Matthews, 'The Comparative Importance of the Rule in *Saunders v Vautier*' (2006) 122 LQR 266.

Absolute gift with superadded direction

69.7 If a trust settles property in a way which will benefit another, but stipulates *how* that person should benefit, such as requiring money to be spent on his education[1], support and maintenance[2], advancement in life[3], improvement to his other property[4], or laid out in the purchase of particular property[5] or an annuity[6], it is a matter of construction whether the provision is intended to create a non-charitable purpose trust, or a beneficial interest for that person[7]. If the former, the gift is in English law generally void[8], though a gift framed as one equal in value to money spent by a beneficiary on certain purposes is a gift to a person[9]. If the gift is construed as a purpose trust for the benefit of a beneficiary, then, on the principle that you cannot give a property right to a person and then prevent him from having all the incidents of a property owner[10], the gift is good, but he is not fettered by the direction as to the mode of application, and can claim the interest under the rule in *Saunders v. Vautier*, if the other conditions are satisfied.

1   *Barlow v Grant* (1684) 1 Vern. 255; *Webb v Kelly* (1839) 9 Sim. 469; *Lewes v Lewes* (1848) 16 Sim. 266; *Re Skinner's Trusts* (1860) 1 John & H 102; *Presant v Goodwin* (1860) 1 Sw & Tr 544; *Re Andrew's Trust* [1905] 2 Ch 48; *Re Osoba* [1979] 1 WLR. 247.
2   *Younghusband v Gisborne* (1848) 1 Coll. 400; *Re Sanderson's Trust* (1857) 3 K.& J. 497; *Re Abbott Fund* [1900] 2 Ch. 326 (life interest only).
3   *Cope v Wilmot* (1772) Amb 704; *Re Johnston* [1894] 3 Ch. 204.
4   *Re Bowes* [1896] 1 Ch. 507; *Re Lipinski's Will Trusts* [1976] Ch. 235.
5   *Pearson v Lane* (1809) 17 Ves 101; cf. *Gott v Nairne* (1876) 3 Ch. D 278.
6   *Re Browne's Will* (1859) 27 Beav. 324.
7   See *e.g. Re Osoba* [1979] 1 WLR. 247, 253C; P J Millett (1985) 101 LQR 269 at 282.
8   *Re Endacott* [1960] Ch. 232. See para 8.148 ff.
9   *Re Sanderson's Trust* (1857) 3 K & J 497.
10 *Re Machu* (1882) 21 Ch D 838; *Re Brown* [1954] Ch 39.

Need for collective absolute beneficial entitlement

69.8   If property is settled on B contingent upon attaining 30 years of age B cannot claim entitlement to the property till attaining 30[1]. However, if property were settled upon B for life if attaining 30 and subject thereto for C absolutely, then B and C between them as the only persons beneficially interested in the property could compel the trustees to divide it between themselves as they directed[2].

1   *Re Lord Nunburnholme* [1912] 1 Ch 489.
2   *Berry v Geen* [1938] AC 575 at 582 per Lord Maugham.

69.9   If property were settled on discretionary trusts for D, E, F and G such that income and capital had to be distributed between them before the death of the last survivor, then D, E, F and G could terminate the trust and acquire the property in such shares as they agreed[1]. However if there is a fluctuating class, like D, E, F and G and their spouses and issue for 80 years or members of a club for 80 years so there is a fluctuating class of trust beneficiaries, then all the beneficiaries between them absolutely entitled to the property cannot be ascertained until the end of the period, so that the trust cannot be terminated before expiry of the 80 years[2].

1   *Re Smith* [1928] Ch 915.
2   *Re Jeffries* [1936] 2 All ER 626; *Re Levy* [1960] Ch 346 at 363; *Re Westphal* [1972] NZLR 792 at 794–795.

69.10   Thus, where property is settled on B for life, remainder to B's statutory next of kin, then no termination can be achieved while B is still alive, because until his death one cannot ascertain for sure who will be his next of kin[1]. His current presumptive next of kin could die, so that his actual next of kin turn out to be different persons.

1   *Re Earl of Midleton's Will Trust* [1969] 1 Ch 600 at 607 discussed at para 47.31.

69.11 It is clear that the *Saunders v Vautier* principle 'recognises the rights of beneficiaries who are *sui juris* and together absolutely entitled to the trust property to exercise their proprietary rights to overbear and defeat the intentions of a testator or settlor'[1] by terminating the trust and dividing the property up as they unanimously agree. This poses a problem where beneficiaries have rights which are defeasible by the rights of others that are current (eg any right of revocation reserved by the settlor) or can arise upon the happening of a future event (eg satisfaction of a condition or the exercise of a power of appointment). In particular, is it insufficient to have the consent of only the default beneficiaries, and is it not also necessary to have the consent of all those who will benefit if they do not?

1   *Goulding v James* [1997] 2 All ER 239 at 247 per Mummery LJ. Note that while a trust may be declared a non-assignable contract, the beneficiaries cannot call for assignment of the contract: *Don King Productions Inc v Warren* [2000] Ch 291 at 321, CA.

69.12 Suppose eg that the collective proprietary right of the beneficiaries is defeasible because the trust contains a power of appointment in favour of a class of objects which might from time to time be exercised in favour of one or more of the objects. It is commonly said that an object has no proprietary interest until an appointment is made in his favour: before then he only has a hope that he might acquire a proprietary interest. The settlor has made a completed gift of an equitable proprietary interest to the beneficiaries collectively entitled in default of any exercise of the power but has merely provided a gratuitous mandate[1] to the trustees so as to enable them, if they wish, to confer a proprietary interest on one or more objects at some future time[2].

1   This could justify the remarks of Lord Upjohn in *Vandervell v IRC* [1967] 2 AC 291 at 317 that if trustees held property on trust for the settlor but with the trustees having a power of appointment the settlor could at any time revoke that power.
2   Conferment of a power is not a gift of property: *Re Armstrong* (1886) 17 QBD 521; *Melville v IRC* [2001] EWCA Civ 1247, [2002] 1 WLR 407, CA.

69.13 However, in *Re Sharp's Settlement Trust*[1] Pennycuick V-C held that beneficiaries had not become 'absolutely' entitled to trust property when the property remained subject to a special power of appointment vested in trustees because the beneficiaries' interests were defeasible. Taking the matter a step further, in *Schmidt v Rosewood Trust Ltd*[2], Lord Walker considered obiter that the object of a mere power of appointment had the negative ability to block a *Saunders v Vautier* application (unless the trustees had power to release their power of appointment)[3].

1   [1973] Ch 331 at 338 in particular.
2   [2003] 2 AC 709, PC.
3   [2003] 2 AC 709, at paras 40–41.

69.14 Under s 19 of the Trusts of Land and Appointment of Trustees Act 1996,[1] the persons who can force the trustees to retire by replacing themselves as directed are 'the beneficiaries under the trust of full age and capacity and (taken together) absolutely entitled to the property subject to the trust' where 'beneficiary' means[2] 'any person who under the trust has an interest in property subject to the trust'. It may be that the object of a mere power, with the negative blocking ability explained by Lord Walker as conferred by *Saunders v Vautier*, has such an interest[3].

[1]   See para 72.27.
[2]   Trusts of Land and Appointment of Trustees Act 1996 ('TLATA 1996'), s 22(1).
[3]   See also *Gartside v IRC* [1968] AC 553: an interest under a discretionary trust was capable of being an interest in property in some circumstances, but not the estate duty context in question, but it was accepted (at p 607) that an object of a power of maintenance (where there was a trust to accumulate under Trustee Act 1925, s 31) could not be regarded as having an interest; *IRC v Eversden* [2002] EWHC 1360 (Ch), [2002] STC 1109.

69.15 A recent development in this area of the law is the appreciation that the trustee himself may have a beneficial interest in the trust assets, such as his right to remuneration[1] and indemnity[2], the latter of which has certainly been held to prevent the rule in *Saunders v Vautier* being applied without his consent[3]. This was perhaps not taken into account in earlier English cases[4], although there are analogous cases holding for example that beneficiaries cannot terminate the trust as of right where there are legacies contingently charged on the trust fund[5]. It is true that a trust beneficiary does not cease to be entitled to an interest in possession in trust assets merely because some or all of the income or capital *may* be consumed in trust expenses[6], but that does not make him absolutely entitled. And it is also true that, in practice, as long as the trustee is protected (eg confining the right to an appropriate part of the trust assets, or replacing it with some other security, real or personal) the court is likely to sanction a distribution of the balance to the beneficiaries otherwise entitled[7]. But this is not a matter of *right*. It is similar to the jurisdiction of the court to sanction a distribution on the footing that a beneficiary is already dead[8], or will never come into existence[9]. On the other hand, the right to remuneration is a right which subsists only so long as the trust does; at least in the absence of contrary provision the trustee could hardly rely on his continuing right to remuneration as the sole reason for preventing all the beneficiaries putting an end to the trust.

[1]   *Re Duke of Norfolk's Settlement Trusts* [1982] Ch 61, CA; *Galmerrow Securities Ltd v National Westminster Bank plc* (1993) 8 Tru LI 21 at 25. A trustee has a beneficial equitable lien. See Article 83.
[2]   *X v A* [2000] 1 All ER 490; *CPT Custodian Property Co v Commissioner of State Trading* [2005] HCA 5, at paras 49–51.
[3]   See in particular *X v A* [2000] 1 All ER 490; *CPT Custodian Property Co v Commissioner of State Trading* [2005] HCA 5, at para 49.
[4]   *CPT Custodian Property Co v Commissioner of State Trading* [2005] HCA 5, at para 50.
[5]   *Weatherall v Thorborough* (1878) 8 Ch D 261, CA.
[6]   *Pearson v IRC* [1981] AC 753, HL.
[7]   *Weatherall v Thorborough* (1878) 8 Ch D 261, CA; *Harbin v Masterman* [1896] 1 Ch 351, CA (protection of annuitant).
[8]   *Re Benjamin* [1902] 1 Ch 723; *Re Green's Will Trusts* [1985] 3 All ER 455.
[9]   *Re Westminster Bank Ltd's Declaration of Trust* [1963] 1 WLR 820.

69.16 A related problem is that where an apparently absolutely entitled beneficiary requires the trustee to convey the trust fund to his order, and the trustee suspects that the trust fund was in fact the product of, say, embezzlement of a third party, or some other criminal activity. In such circumstances the trustee cannot justify a refusal to convey as the beneficiary requires by reference to mere suspicion[1], and should apply to the court for directions[2] .The matter is complicated by the fact that, if the trustee's suspicions are correct, compliance with the beneficiary's direction may involve, not only civil liability to the third party[3], but also criminal liability under anti-money laundering legislation[4].

1   *Moss v Integro Trust (BVI) Ltd* (1997) 1 OFLR 427, HCt BVI.
2   *Finers v Miro* [1991] 1 WLR 35.
3   As to which see para 46.7.
4   As to which see para 46.8 ff.

Special cases

69.17 Some trusts however present special problems in the possible application of the rule in *Saunders v Vautier*. For example, in defined benefit pension scheme trusts[1], the interest of the beneficiaries is to receive the particular money payments in the particular circumstances stipulated for in the scheme rules, rather than to share more generally in the scheme assets. The risk that the fund does not grow to match the employer's liabilities is that of the employer. Thus it has been stated that, in such trusts, 'the trust fund is only a security for the payment of benefits'[2]. What this apparently means is that, just as a debtor can charge his own asset to secure the debt he owes his creditor, the employer (and usually, the employee) pursuant to contract pay sums at regular intervals to a trustee to build up a fund, which is then charged to secure the employer's (or perhaps the trustee's) obligations to pay the pension benefits in due course, but, subject to that security interest, the trust assets belong in equity to the debtor-employer rather than the creditor-employees. The employees therefore cannot terminate the trust under *Saunders v Vautier*. The employer can, but only subject to the rules and/or with the consent of the secured employees.

1   Usually based on final salary (or an average over the last few years) and length of service.
2   *Air Jamaica Ltd v Charlton* [1999] 1 WLR 1399 at 1409 per Lord Millett; *Wrightson Ltd v Fletcher Challenge Nominees Ltd* [2001] UKPC 23 at para 28, [2001] OPLR 249, per Lord Millett.

69.18 But the position may well be different in the case of a defined *contribution* pension scheme trust[1], where the (contractual) contributions of employer and (usually) employee make up a sub-fund in the hands of the trustee, and the level of benefits to be obtained by the individual employee depends on the investment value achieved by his subfund at the time of retirement and taking benefits. In this case the risk of poor growth falls on the employee, not the employer. Hence in the absence of clear intention to the contrary the employees have a beneficial interest in the trust assets, and are not merely secured creditors. But it does not follow that the employer has no interest. That must depend on the terms of the scheme and the trusts themselves. If, as is commonly the case, the employer does, then the employees cannot terminate such a trust under *Saunders v Vautier* without its consent. It will be rare to find a pension scheme trust where the employees are able to use the rule in *Saunders v Vautier* to terminate the trust without the consent of the employer or some other third party[2].

1   Often called a 'money purchase scheme', as the subfund is commonly used to purchase an annuity to fund retirement.
2   See eg *Bushau v Rogers Communications Inc* [2006] SCC 28.

69.19   The position of an investor of a unit trust may well be similar. It has been argued that unit holders have merely a contractual right to money payments secured on the assets held by the custodian trustee[1]. This would make the position analogous to the defined *benefit* pension scheme trusts first mentioned. But that was not the analysis in the only English case (now rather old) to consider the matter so far[2]. Much, perhaps everything, will turn of course on the precise terms of the contract between investor and manager and trustee, and of the trust instrument itself[3]. Do they make the investor just a secured creditor, or a real beneficiary under the trust?[4] In any event, even if he is the latter, the consent of others with rights in the trust fund (including, perhaps, the trustee's remuneration and indemnity)[5] may be needed before *Saunders v Vautier* can apply. Whatever the position, it seems that there is no *Saunders v Vautier* difference between a single investor who holds all the units and a group of investors between them holding all of them[6]. Depending on the terms of the trust, either the rule can be applied by the investor(s) without the consent of others in both cases, or it can be so applied in neither.

1   K F Sin, *The Legal Nature of the Unit Trust*, (Oxford, 1997), pp 114–120.
2   *Re AEG Unit Trust (Managers) Ltd's Deed* [1957] Ch 415 at 422.
3   *CPT Custodian Property Co v Commissioner of State Trading* [2005] HCA 5, at paras 30–36. Changes in standard unit trust documentation since 1957 may explain the different stance taken by Sin from the views expressed in the *AEG* case: see Sin, at pp 284–92.
4   As stated in *Read v Commonwealth* (1988) 167 CLR 57 at 61.
5   See notes 2 and 3 at para 69.14.
6   *CPT Custodian Property Co v Commissioner of State Trading* [2005] HCA 5, at paras 41–46, reversing the Victorian Court of Appeal (2003) 8 VR 502.

Position summarised in Stephenson v Barclays Bank Trust Co Ltd

69.20   Walton J stated as elementary principles[1]:

'(1) In a case where the persons who between them hold the entirety of the beneficial interests in any particular trust fund are all sui juris and acting together ("the beneficial interest holders"), they are entitled to direct the trustees how the trust fund may be dealt with. (2) This does not mean, however, that they can at one and the same time override the pre-existing trusts and keep them in existence. Thus, in *Re Brockbank*[2] itself the beneficial interest holders were entitled to override the pre-existing trusts by, for example, directing the trustees to transfer the trust fund to X and Y, whether X and Y were the trustees of some other trust or not, but they were not entitled to direct the existing trustees to appoint their own nominee as a new trustee of the existing trust. By so doing they would be pursuing inconsistent rights. (3) Nor, I think, are the beneficial interest holders entitled to direct the trustees as to the particular investment they should make of the trust fund. I think this follows for the same reasons as the above. Moreover, it appears to me that once the beneficial interest holders have determined to end the trust they are not entitled, unless by agreement, to the further services of the trustees. Those trustees can of course be compelled to hand over the entire trust assets to any person or persons selected by the beneficiaries against a proper discharge, but they cannot be compelled, unless they are in fact willing to comply with the directions, to do anything else with the trust fund which they are not in fact willing to do. (4) Of course, the rights of the beneficial interest holders are always subject to the right of the trustee to be fully protected against such matters as duty, taxes, costs or other outgoings; for example, the rent under a lease which the trustees have properly accepted as part of the trust property.

So much for the rights of the beneficial interest holders collectively. When the situation is that a single person who is sui juris has an absolutely vested beneficial interest in a share of the trust fund, his rights are not, I think, quite as extensive as those of the beneficial interest holders as a body. In general, he is entitled to have transferred to him (subject, of course, always to the same rights of the trustees as I have already mentioned above) an aliquot share of each and every asset of the trust fund which presents no difficulty so far as division is concerned. This will apply to such items as cash, money at the bank or an unsecured loan, stock exchange securities and the like. However, as regards land, certainly, in all cases[3], as regards shares in a private company in very special circumstances (see *Re Weiner's Will Trusts*[4]) and possibly (although the logic of the addition in fact escapes me[5]) mortgage debts (see *Re Marshall*[6] per Cozens-Hardy MR) the situation is not so simple, and even a person with a vested interest in possession in an aliquot share of the trust fund may have to wait until the land is sold, and so forth, before being able to call on the trustees as of right to account to him for his share of the proceeds.'

1   [1975] 1 All ER 625 at 637. See also *Booth v Ellard* [1978] 1 WLR 927, CA applied in *Jenkins v Brown* [1989] STC 577 no capital gains tax charge if 6 people vest their farms in a trust for themselves and one later obtains back what he put into the trust or its equivalent value.
2   [1948] Ch 206, [1948] 1 All ER 287.
3   *Re Horsnaill* [1909] 1 Ch 631; *Re Kipping* [1914] 1 Ch 62.
4   [1956] 2 All ER 482, [1956] 1 WLR 579.
5   In *Crowe v Appleby* [1975] 3 All ER 529 at 537, Goff J endorsed the views of Walton J, but pointed out that 'the logic of the addition of mortgages is that they include not only the debt but the estate and powers of the mortgagee'.
6   [1914] 1 Ch 192 at 199.

Possible future beneficiaries

69.21 Where it is not absolutely certain that no more beneficiaries can come into existence so as to enable the existing beneficiaries to take advantage of the *Saunders v Vautier* principle, the court may give leave to the trustees to distribute the trust property according to the directions of the existing beneficiaries (so long as the contingent rights of living persons are not prejudiced without their consent)[1]. The classic case is where the ultimate beneficiaries are the children of a living person when adopted children and children born as a result of medical advances may possibly feature.

1   *Re White* [1901] 1 Ch 570; *Davidson v Kimpton* (1881) 18 Ch D 213; *Re Widdow's Trust* (1871) LR 11 Eq 408; *Re Millner's Estate* (1872) LR 14 Eq 245; *Re Benjamin* [1902] 1 Ch 723; *Re Jordan's Trust* [1903] 1 IR 119; *Re Cazenove* (1919) 122 LT 181; *Re Smith* [1928] Ch 915; *Re Whichelow* [1954] 1 WLR 5 at 8; *Re Pettifor's Will Trusts* [1966] Ch 257; but cf *Croxton v May* (1878) 9 Ch D 388.

69.22 If appropriate evidence is obtained, eg as to the physical impossibility of a parent creating future children[1] and the strong possibility that there will be no adoption[2] nor exploitation of medical advances, then the court may authorise distribution in the exercise of its administrative jurisdiction[3], without prejudice to the rights of any child subsequently coming into existence. Alternatively, application can be made under the Variation of Trusts Act 1958 to approve an arrangement eliminating the interests of unborn persons, but some provision against the eventuality of birth or adoption of such persons will need to be made, eg via insurance[4].

1   *Bullas v Public Trustee* [1981] 1 NSWLR 641 (hysterectomy); *Re Pettifor's Will Trust* [1966] Ch 257 (women over 70 years).
2   It is presumed a woman over 54 years will not adopt a child: Adoption Act 1976, s 42(5). In Australian context see *Re Cassidy* [1979] VR 369 at 372; *National Trustees Executors & Agency Co v Tuck* [1967] VR 847; *Bullas v Public Trustee* [1981] NSWLR 641.
3   In *Figg v Clarke* [1997] 1 WLR 603 the court held that children did not become absolutely entitled to trust property for capital gains tax purposes the moment their father had an accident making him incapable of having further children but only on his death. If leave to distribute had been sought after the accident it seems likely it would have been granted.
4   Care will have to be taken to avoid committing a fraud on the power: see para 61.31.

Modification of trusts so as to control trustees

69.23 Although the beneficiaries acting collectively can require the trustees to transfer the trust property to themselves absolutely or to other persons upon trusts identical with, or corresponding to, or even completely different from the trusts of the settlement, it is conceived that they cannot force upon the trustees against their will modifications of the trusts which would impose upon the trustees new duties involving an exercise of discretion nor can they, without the consent of the trustees, abrogate discretions or powers conferred upon the trustees by the instrument creating the trust, or seek to control the exercise of such discretions or powers.

69.24 Thus, it was held[1] that the beneficiaries cannot compel the retirement of a trustee or control the exercise of the statutory power of appointing new trustees conferred on a continuing trustee. Since that decision, power has now been conferred on the beneficiaries, acting unanimously, to compel a trustee to retire under s 19 of the Trusts of Land and Appointment of Trustees Act 1996 if the power of appointing new trustees is not conferred on someone else by the trust instrument[2]. However, they can collectively consent or acquiesce in the trustees doing something beyond their powers, whereupon they will not be able to sue for breach of trust in respect of the act concerned.

1   *Re Brockbank* [1948] Ch 206, [1948] 1 All ER 287 endorsed in *Stephenson v Barclays Bank Trust Co* [1975] 1 All ER 625 at 637, p 714, above and in *Holding & Management Ltd v Property Holding plc* [1990] 1 All ER 938 at 948 CA. Also see *Napier v Light* (1974) 236 Estates Gazette 273, CA where the two absolutely entitled sui juris beneficiaries of a trust for sale of land could not commit their trustees to tenancies purportedly created by the beneficiaries to whom no power had been delegated by the trustees under Law of Property Act 1925, s 29.
2   See para 72.27.

69.25 Where the trust estate included shares in a limited company of which the trustees were directors it was held by the Court of Appeal in *Butt v Kelson*[1] that the beneficiaries were not entitled to call on these directors to use their powers as directors as if they held those powers on trust for them, but that they could compel them to use their votes as shareholders as the beneficiaries should think proper even to the extent of altering the articles of association if the trust shares carried sufficient votes. This is difficult to reconcile with the line of cases (not cited to the Court of Appeal) establishing the principle that beneficiaries cannot compel the trustees to do as the beneficiaries wish (and so control the trustees' discretions) except so as to transfer the trust assets to persons nominated by the beneficiaries of full age and capacity and between them absolutely entitled to the entire beneficial interest[2].

[1] [1952] Ch 197, [1952] 1 All ER 167.
[2] *Re Whichelow* [1953] 2 All ER 1558, [1954] 1 WLR 5, citing *Re Brockbank* [1948] Ch 206, [1948] 1 All ER 287; *Re Higginbottom* [1892] 3 Ch 132; and *Tempest v Lord Camoys* (1882) 21 Ch D 571.

69.26 Perhaps *Butt v Kelson* might be justified on the basis that, to prevent any possibility of the trustees as directors being liable to the company for breach of duty, it was necessary for the court not merely to point out that the trustees qua shareholders could exercise their votes as they saw fit (so long as not perpetrating a fraud on minority shareholders) and so against what the directors might consider in the best interests of the company, but to direct the trustees qua shareholders to vote as desired by the beneficiaries as in their best interests since the trustees being directors were not in a position to exercise their discretion impartially and properly. *Butt v Kelson* should thus be restricted to trustee shareholders who are also directors. Alternatively, it has been suggested[1] that the circumstances could have been regarded as exceptional, so that the trustees had come under a duty to exercise their discretionary power as indicated so that a duty was being enforced.

[1] *Lewin on Trusts* (17th edn) paras 23–09 and 24–08.

ARTICLE 70
POWER OF ONE OF SEVERAL BENEFICIARIES PARTIALLY
INTERESTED IN A SPECIAL TRUST

70.1

(1)   The authority of one of several beneficiaries interested in a special trust in general depends upon the terms of the trust as construed by the court, coupled with the powers conferred on persons entitled to equitable interests by the Settled Land Act 1925 and the Trusts of Land and Appointment of Trustees Act 1996; but a beneficiary who is of full age and capacity cannot be prohibited from assigning his or her interest, while such a beneficiary with an absolutely vested beneficial interest in a share of a trust fund will be entitled to an aliquot share of each

and every asset of the trust fund which presents no difficulty so far as division is concerned, there being difficulties with land, mortgage debts and, in very special circumstances, shares in a private company[1].

(2)(a) In the case of a trust of land, a sole beneficiary beneficially entitled to an interest in possession in the land is entitled by reason of his interest to occupy the land at any time, if then the purposes of the trust include making the land available for his occupation or the land is held by the trustees so as to be so available, unless it is unsuitable for occupation by him[2], though the trustees may impose reasonable conditions upon him[3]; where there is more than one such beneficiary they are in a weaker position[4] because the trustees may exclude or restrict the entitlement of any one or more (but not all) of them[5] so long as this is not unreasonable[6].

(b) In this behalf, trustees of land have a power revocably to delegate any of their functions as trustees which relate to the land (but not to proceeds of sale thereof)[7]; the beneficiaries can apply to the court for an order relating to the exercise by the trustees of any of their functions[8].

(c) A tenant for life under the Settled Land Act 1925 has the legal estate in the settled land vested in him[9] and so is thereby entitled to possession.

[1] *Stephenson (Inspector of Taxes) v Barclays Bank Trust Co Ltd* [1975] 1 All ER 625 at 637, cited, para 69.20.
[2] TLATA 1996, s 12(1) and (2).
[3] TLATA 1996, s 13(3).
[4] Also a weaker position than before the Act: *IRC v Eversden* [2002] EWHC 1360 (Ch), [2002] STC 1109 at paras 21 and 24; *Bull v Bull* [1955] 1 QB 234; *City of London Building Society v Flegg* [1988] AC 54 at 78 and 79.
[5] TLATA 1996, s 13(1).
[6] TLATA 1996, s 13(2).
[7] TLATA 1996, s 9.
[8] TLATA 1996, s 13(7), 14(1).
[9] Settled Land Act 1925, ss 4 and 6.

Paragraph 1

Equitable interest of beneficiary cannot generally be made inalienable

70.2 Under English[1] law, the interest of a beneficiary cannot be made inalienable[2]. Thus a trust to apply income for another's maintenance entitles him to have the income paid to him or to his alienee, even although he be restrained from alienation; for no one in remainder is injured by it and he alone was absolutely entitled to the income being applied for his benefit as he saw it[3]. If an absolute interest in capital or income is given to a person, then it is repugnant to, or inconsistent with, the nature of that absolute interest to prevent it being dealt with as an absolute interest: thus it passes to the owner's trustee in bankruptcy if he becomes bankrupt[4].

1   It is not contrary to public policy to recognise in England inalienable alimentary life
     interests created under a Scottish trust: *Re Fitzgerald* [1904] 1 Ch 573.
2   *Snowdon v Dales* (1834) 6 Sim 524; *Green v Spicer* (1830) 1 Russ & M 395; *Brandon v
     Robinson* (1811) 18 Ves 429; *Hood v Oglander* (1865) 34 Beav 513; *Re Dugdale* (1888)
     38 Ch D 176 at 182.
3   *Younghusband v Gisborne* (1844) 1 Coll 400; affd (1846) 15 LJ Ch 355; *Snowdon v Dales*
     (1834) 6 Sim 524.
4   *Re Machu* (1882) 21 Ch D 838.

Protective trusts

70.3 But if a *determinable* interest only be given, there is no repugnancy, even if then followed by a discretionary trust for a class including the principal beneficiary[1]. Where, however, there is a trust to pay income to A *until* he shall alienate it or become bankrupt etc; and, upon the happening of any of those events, a further trust to pay to him, or apply for his benefit during the remainder of his life, the whole *or so much only* of such income as the trustees may in their discretion think fit, and, subject thereto, the residue of such income (if any) is to be *paid to other persons*; then, as the trustees have an absolute discretion as to what part of the income they will apply for the benefit of the tenant for life, his alienees or creditors cannot force the trustees to pay them any part of the income[2].

1   Trustee Act 1925, s 33; see para 11.63.
2   *Re Bullock* (1891) 64 LT 736; *Train v Clapperton* [1908] AC 342; and cf *Lord v Bunn*
     (1843) 2 Y & C Ch Cas 98; which seems contra at first sight, but really turned on a
     question of construction; see also *Re Laye* [1913] 1 Ch 298; and *Re Hamilton* (1921) 124
     LT 737; and as to such trusts generally, see para 11.64 ff.

Partial restraint on alienation

70.4 A provision that a beneficiary may only alienate his interest in favour of one of a small class of named persons which inevitably diminish in course of time is tantamount to a general restraint on alienation and, therefore, void[1]. Where, however, the class of permitted alienees is a large and indeterminate one (such as the beneficiary's 'family') which may increase as time goes on a restriction against alienating outside that class may be good[2].

1   *Attwater v Attwater* (1853) 18 Beav 330; *Re Brown* [1954] Ch 39, [1953] 2 All ER 1342.
2   *Re Macleay* (1875) LR 20 Eq 186 (criticised by Pearson J in *Re Rosher* (1884) 26 Ch D
     801).

Right to aliquot share

70.5 A beneficiary of full age and capacity with an absolute vested beneficial interest in a share of a trust fund will be entitled to an aliquot share of each and every asset of the fund which presents no difficulty so far as division is concerned[1] eg cash, bank deposits, shares in quoted companies. He is not entitled to an aliquot share if it is in land[2] or mortgage debts[3]. Shares in a

70.5 *Powers of the beneficiaries*

private company are in a special position. A beneficiary cannot be refused an aliquot share of such shares merely because this would break up a controlling interest, and so reduce the value of the whole[4]. But it was refused, a sale of the whole ordered, with distribution of a share of the proceeds to follow, in one case where the beneficiary would thereby be entitled to a controlling interest in the company, so giving him more by value per share than any other beneficiary[5].

Stephenson v Barclays Bank Trust Co Ltd [1975] 1 All ER 625 at 637–638, cited at para 69.20.
2 *Re Kipping* [1914] 1 Ch 62; *Crowe v Appleby* [1975] 3 All ER 529.
3 *Re Marshall* [1914] 1 Ch 192 at 199; *Crowe v Appleby* [1975] 3 All ER 529 at 537.
4 *Re Sanderson's Will Trusts* [1937] 1 All ER 368; *Re Weiner's Will Trusts* [1956] 2 All ER 482.
5 *Lloyds Bank plc v Duker* [1987] 3 All ER 193, [1987] 1 WLR 1324.

Paragraph 2

How far beneficiary with interest in possession may claim actual possession of land

70.6 The position of a beneficiary currently entitled to an interest in possession of land is summarised in paragraph 2 itself and discussed in detail in Article 45.

Chapter 16

THE DEATH, RETIREMENT, OR REMOVAL OF TRUSTEES AND THE APPOINTMENT OF NEW TRUSTEES

ARTICLE 71
DEVOLUTION OF THE OFFICE AND ESTATE ON DEATH
OF TRUSTEES

71.1

(1)   Upon the death of one of two or more trustees the office, as well as the estate, survives to the surviving trustees or trustee[1], who can carry out the trust and exercise all such powers as were given to the original trustees as such[2].

(2)   Upon the death of a sole or last surviving trustee, the trust property devolves on his legal personal representative[3].

(3)   Until the appointment of new trustees, the personal representatives or representative for the time being of a sole trustee, or, where there were two or more trustees, of the last surviving or continuing trustee, can exercise or perform any power or trust which was given to, or capable of being exercised by, the sole or last surviving or continuing trustee, or other the trustees or trustee for the time being of the trust[4].

(4)   This article must be read subject to the restrictions imposed in regard to receipts by a sole trustee, not being a trust corporation[5].

(5)   The person upon whom the estate devolves cannot be compelled to act in the trusts[6]; nor, on the other hand, can he insist upon doing so against the wishes of a donee of a power of appointing new trustees in substitution for deceased ones[7].

(6)   In this article 'personal representative' does not include an executor who has renounced probate or has not proved[8].

1   *Warburton v Sandys* (1845) 14 Sim 622; *Eyre v Countess of Shaftesbury* (1725) 2 P Wms 103; and now Trustee Act 1925 ('TA 1925'), s 18(1); *Re Harding* [1923] 1 Ch 182.
2   TA 1925, s 18(1), re-enacting 1893 Act, s 22; and *Lane v Debenham* (1853) 11 Hare 188; *Re Cookes' Contract* (1877) 4 Ch D 454; and *Re Harding* [1923] 1 Ch 182. As to whether the court will pay out trust money in court to a sole surviving trustee, see *Leigh v Pantin* [1914] 2 Ch 701.
3   See Administration of Estates Act 1925, ss 1, 3.
4   TA 1925, s 18(2).
5   These restrictions are in TA 1925, ss 14 and 18; Law of Property Act 1925 ('LPA 1925'), s 27; and Settled Land Act 1925, s 94.
6   *Re Benett* [1906] 1 Ch 216 at 225; *Re Ridley* [1904] 2 Ch 774; and cases there cited.
7   *Re Routledge* [1909] 1 Ch 280.
8   TA 1925, s 18(4).

Paragraph 1

Death of co-trustee

71.2 The law as to survival stated in this paragraph has always applied with regard to trusts as distinguished from bare powers[1], and since 1881 has been statute law. The law as to powers incident to the office of trustee is now set forth in s 18(1) of the Trustee Act 1925[2] in the following words:

'Where a power or trust is given to or imposed on two or more trustees jointly, the same may be exercised or performed by the survivors or survivor of them for the time being.'

1   *Warburton v Sandys* (1845) 14 Sim 622; *Eyre v Countess of Shaftesbury* (1725) 2 P Wms 102; *Lane v Debenham* (1853) 11 Hare 188. *Re Cookes' Contract* (1877) 4 Ch D 454; *Doe d Read v Godwin* (1822) 1 Dow & Ry KB 259; *Re Bacon* [1907] 1 Ch 475.
2   Re-enacting s 22 of the Trustee Act 1893, which in turn re-enacted s 38 of the Conveyancing Act 1881. The words 'unless the contrary is expressed in the instrument, if any, creating the trust' which were present in the former enactments are omitted in reliance on s 69(2) of the 1925 Act.

71.3 It would seem however, that the statute applies only to powers which are fiduciary, ie incident to the office of trustee; and that it is in all cases a question of interpretation whether a discretionary power was intended to be incident to the office, or was a mere naked personal power given to the individuals who were also nominated as trustees[1]. However,

'every power given to trustees which enables them to deal with or affect the trust property is prima facie given them ex officio as an incident of their office, and passes with the office to the holders or holder thereof for the time being'[2].

1   *Crawford v Forshaw* [1891] 2 Ch 261, CA; and see also *Re Perrott and King's Contract* (1904) 90 LT 156. See *Re Eades* [1920] 2 Ch 353; and *Re Willis* [1920] 2 Ch 358 per Astbury J but reversed by CA [1921] 1 Ch 44. See para 1.76 ff.
2   Per Farwell J in *Re Smith* [1904] 1 Ch 139 at 144; cf *Re De Sommery* [1912] 2 Ch 622; and see *Re Symm's Will Trusts* [1936] 3 All ER 236 and *Re Will's Trust Deeds* [1964] Ch 219.

71.4 The mere fact that the power is one requiring the exercise of a very wide personal discretion is not enough to exclude this prime facie presumption, and little regard is now paid to such minute differences as those between such expressions as 'my trustees', 'my trustees, A & B', and 'A & B, my trustees'. In short, the testator's reliance on the individuals to the exclusion of the holders of the office for the time being must be expressed in clear and apt language[1].

1 Per Farwell J in *Re Smith* [1904] 1 Ch 139 at 144; cf *Re De Sommery* [1912] 2 Ch 622; and see *Re Symm's Will Trusts* [1936] 3 All ER 236 and *Re Will's Trust Deeds* [1964] Ch 219.

Paragraph 2

Devolution on death of sole or last surviving trustee

71.5 Since 1925 all trust estates devolve on the general personal representatives of the sole or last surviving trustee, in whom the estate was vested, and it is conceived that a sole or last surviving trustee cannot appoint 'special executors' for the purpose of executing the trust[1]. This view receives some support from the case of *Re Cohen's Executors and LCC*[2], where the general executors were held to be alone the personal representatives within the meaning of the Land Transfer Act 1897.

1 See *Re Parker's Trusts* [1894] 1 Ch 707; *Rose v Bartlett* (1633) Cro Car 292; *Clough v Dixon* (1841) 10 Sim 5 64. The devolution of settled land under the Settled Land Act 1925 is outside the scope of this work: see Megarry and Wade, *Real Property* (6th edn) paras 8–031 ff.
2 [1902] 1 Ch 187.

71.6 Where powers and trusts have devolved upon the personal representative of a trustee the question arises whether upon the death of such personal representative (having failed to appoint further trustees) the powers and trusts can devolve further upon his own personal representative or whether such powers and trusts revert to the trustee's estate so as to be exercisable by an administrator de bonis non administratis. If the executor of the deceased personal representative is executor by representation of the trustee then he has the capacity to perform powers and trusts under the Trustee Act 1925, s 18(2)[1]. It would also seem that if the deceased personal representative had accepted the trust then he should be treated as a trustee within s 18(2) for his powers to devolve thereunder to his own personal representative[2], though the position is not free from doubt[3].

1 Administration of Estates Act 1925, s 7; TA 1925, s 68(9).
2 *Williams on Title* (4th edn) p 490, Pettit *Equity and the Law of Trusts* (7th edn) p 341; (1977) 41 Conv 423 (P.W. Smith); *Re Timmis* [1902] 1 Ch 176.
3 Wolstenholme and Cherry, *Conveyancing Statutes* (13th edn) p 21.

Paragraph 3

Execution of trusts by personal representatives of sole or last surviving trustee

71.7 This paragraph reproduces s 18(2) of the Trustee Act 1925 which in turn re-enacts s 8 of the Conveyancing Act 1911 with the difference that it is not restricted to trusts which have come into operation since 1881[1]. Where a deceased trustee's powers have devolved upon his personal representative, who then dies before having appointed new trustees but having accepted the role of trustee, it seems[2] that he should be treated as trustee for his powers to devolve under s 18(2) to his own personal representative. If he was executor of the deceased trustee and himself appointed an executor, who obtained probate, then his executor would be executor by representation[3] of the trustee and so have the s 18(2) powers in any event.

[1] The application of s 18(2) of the TA 1925 to trusts whenever created depends on s 69(1) of that Act.
[2] See PW Smith (1977) 41 Conv 423, *Williams on Title* (4th edn) p 490.
[3] Administration of Estates Act 1925, s 7.

ARTICLE 72
RETIREMENT OR REMOVAL OF A TRUSTEE

72.1

(1)   A trustee can only retire:
    (a)   under an express or a necessarily implied[1] power;
    (b)   under the statutory power conferred by the Trustee Act 1925, either on the appointment of a new trustee in his place, or without such appointment if at least two trustees will continue in office or if the continuing trustee is a trust corporation;
    (c)   by the consent of *all* the beneficiaries, which can only be obtained where all are of full age and capacity[2]; or
    (d)   by order of the court[3].
(2) A trustee may be removed from his office:
    (a)   under an express power;
    (b)   by the direction of all the beneficiaries who, take together, are absolutely entitled to the trust property and all of full age and capacity if the trust instrument has not conferred power to appoint new trustees on someone else or otherwise ousted the right of the beneficiaries[4];
    (c)   under the statutory power of appointing new trustees contained in sections 36 and 37 of the Trustee Act 1925 in cases where he remains out of the kingdom for more than twelve months consecutively[5], refuses or is unfit to act, or is incapable of acting; or
    (d)   by the court[6] appointing a new trustee in his place (or, exceptionally, under its inherent jurisdiction[7] by simply removing the trustee without replacing him if sufficient trustees remain), at the instance of any trustee or beneficiary, where he has behaved improperly[8], or is incapable of acting properly[9], or from faults of temper or want of tact is in a permanent condition of hostility with his co-trustees

and beneficiaries[10], or has been convicted of an offence involving dishonesty or is a recent bankrupt[11], or is residing permanently, or for a long or indefinite period, abroad[12], or cannot be heard of[13], or where any other good reason exists[14];

(e) if he is a trustee of a pension trust scheme by the Pensions Regulator if the Regulator is satisfied that he is in serious or persistent breach of any of his duties under the Pensions Act 1995 or the Pension Schemes Act 1993, sections 6, 113, 175, or Chapter IV of Part IV and may be suspended for a period not exceeding twelve months pending consideration being given to his removal[15], while he will cease to be a trustee[16] if he becomes disqualified under section 29 of the Pensions Act 1995.

[1] *Davis v Richards and Wallington Industries Ltd* [1991] 2 All ER 563 at 581.
[2] *Wilkinson v Parry* (1828) 4 Russ 272; and see Art 69, above.
[3] *Re Gregson's Trusts* (1886) 34 Ch D 209; *Re Chetwynd's Settlement* [1902] 1 Ch 692.
[4] Trusts of Land and Appointment of Trustees Act 1996 ('TLATA 1996'), ss 19 and 21.
[5] See para 73.20 below.
[6] Under s 41 of the TA 1925 or under its inherent jurisdiction.
[7] *Re Harrison's Settlement Trusts* [1965] 3 All ER 795 at 799; *Clarke v Heathfield (No 2)* [1985] ICR 606; *Re Chetwynd's Settlement* [1902] 1 Ch 692.
[8] *Millard v Eyre* (1793) 2 Ves 94; *Palairet v Carew* (1863) 32 Beav 564.
[9] *Buchanan v Hamilton* (1801) 5 Ves 722; and *Re Lemann's Trusts* (1883) 22 Ch D 633; and *Re Phelp's Settlement Trusts* (1885) 31 Ch D 351, where trustees were incapable from old age and infirmity.
[10] *Letterstedt v Broers* (1884) 9 App Cas 371 at 386; see *Earl of Portsmouth v Fellows* (1820) 5 Madd 450.
[11] *Re Adams Trust* (1879) 12 Ch D 634; *Re Barker's Trusts* (1875) 1 Ch D 43.
[12] *Buchanan v Hamilton* (1801) 5 Ves 722; *Re Bignold's Settlement Trusts* (1872) 7 Ch App 223; and *Re Moravian Society* (1858) 26 Beav 101.
[13] *Re Harrison's Trusts* (1852) 22 LJ Ch 69.
[14] See *Assets Realisation Co v Trustees etc Corpn* (1895) 65 LJ Ch 74; *Re Henderson* [1940] Ch 764, [1940] 3 All ER 295.
[15] Pensions Act 1995, ss 3 and 4. The Pensions Regulator took over the powers of the abolished Occupational Pensions Regulatory Authority: Pensions Act 2004 s 7.
[16] Pensions Act 1995, s 30.

Paragraph 1

Retirement under powers of appointing new trustees

72.2 The most usual way in which a trustee retires is under a power enabling some person or persons to appoint a new trustee in his place in the event (inter alia) of his desiring to retire. This mode of retiring necessitates the appointment of a new trustee in the place of the one retiring[1]. No question, however, can ever arise as to the costs of such an appointment, inasmuch as ex hypothesi the power provides for the retirement of the trustee *if he so desires*. The costs, therefore, in such cases always fall on the estate and not on the retiring trustee. Such a power may be expressly given by the settlement, but, unless a contrary intention is expressed in the settlement, will also be implied into it by statute irrespective of the date at which the settlement came into operation. This statutory power will be discussed in the next article.

¹   *Adam and Company International Trustees Ltd v Theodore Goddard* [2000] WTLR 349 at 355.

Danger of trustees not being discharged

72.3 It must be noted that by s 37(1)(c) of the Trustee Act 1925 (as amended by the Trusts of Land and Appointment of Trustees Act 1996¹ substituting 'persons' for 'individuals') even though a new trustee is appointed in place of the old trustee such old trustee will not be discharged from his trust unless there will then be either a trust corporation (which has a special definition²) or at least two persons to act as trustees (except where only one trustee was originally appointed and a sole trustee is able to give valid receipts for capital money)³.

¹   TLATA 1996, Sch 3, para 3(12).
²   See paras 79.5–79.6.
³   Ie the trust is of pure personalty and not of English or Welsh land: LPA 1925, s 27(2); TA 1925, s 14(2).

72.4 The question arises whether s 37(1)(c) is an inflexible mandatory rule or can be ousted by a contrary provision in the trust instrument¹. Originally, under s 10(2)(c) of the Trustee Act 1893 trustees were not discharged unless there were 'at least two trustees to perform the trust', though by s 10(5) 'This section applies only if and so far as a contrary intention is not expressed in the instrument, if any, creating the trust and shall have effect subject to the terms of that instrument'. In 1893 a limited company could not be a joint tenant of property, and hence plural trustees were invariably individuals. The Law of Property Act 1922, s 110(9) substituted for the quoted words in s 10(2)(c) 'either a trust corporation or at least two individuals to perform the trust' but, of course, still subject to s 10(5).

¹   *Mettoy Pension Fund Trustees Ltd v Evans* [1991] 2 All ER 513 at 534.

72.5 The Law of Property (Amendment) Act 1924 made no direct amendment to s 10, but added in Pt II, Sch 5, para 5(4), 'Nothing in the Trustee Acts shall authorise the appointment of a sole trustee not being a trust corporation where the trustee when appointed will not be able to give valid receipts for all capital money arising under the trust'. This reflected the policy of the new legislation that a sole trustee, not being a trust corporation, should not be able to give a valid receipt for capital money arising in respect of English or Welsh land held on trust for sale or subject to a Settled Land Act settlement.

72.6 Thus, the position immediately before the Trustee Act 1925 was that, if no English or Welsh land be comprised in the trust, a trust instrument could *expressly* provide for trustees to be validly discharged when the settlor or trustees, as the case may be, appointed as new sole trustee an individual or a body corporate.

918

72.7 The Trustee Act 1925 was stated in terms to be 'An Act consolidating certain enactments relating to trustees in England and Wales' (eg Trustee Act 1893, Law of Property Act 1922, Law of Property Amendment Act 1924), so as to simplify the Parliamentary procedure. The position under the Trustee Act 1925 ought therefore to be as stated in the preceding paragraph, because Parliament's intention was not to change the law.

72.8 However, the draftsman in his consolidation exercise boldly inserted a *general* contrary intention provision at the end of the 1925 Act in s 69(2):

'The powers conferred by this Act on trustees are in addition to the powers conferred by the instrument, if any, creating the trust, but those powers, unless otherwise stated, apply if and so far only as a contrary intention is not expressed in the instrument, if any, creating the trust, and have effect subject to the terms of that instrument ... '

72.9 Since s 36 is headed 'Powers of appointing new or additional trustees' and s 37 headed 'Supplemental provisions as to appointment of trustees', it might have been thought that those provisions were amongst 'the powers conferred by this Act on trustees'. The consequence would be that, if so authorised by the terms of the trust instrument, trustees should be able validly to retire from the trust when they exercise their s 36 power to appoint a *sole* trustee as successor, unless the trust includes any land in England or Wales[1]. Yet it has been held that only the powers in Part II of the Act are within the scope of this phrase[2]. Sections 36 and 37 are, however, within Part III, not Part II. On the other hand, if it is the *settlor* (or anyone other than the trustees) who has power to appoint, and does appoint, a sole trustee in place of the existing trustees, the 1925 Act should have no impact, because it does not deal with such powers conferred on the settlor (or other third party). The appointment and retirement should be as valid as they would have been before 1926.

[1] Section 37(2) is mandatory: 'Nothing in this Act shall authorise the appointment of a sole trustee not being a "trust corporation" where the trustees when appointed would not be able to give valid receipts for all capital money arising under the trust'; but this only applies to provisions *in the Act* and not to an express power, which can thus be used to authorise the appointment, as pointed out in *London Regional Transport Pension Fund Trust Company Ltd v Hatt* [1993] Pens LR 227 at 261.
[2] *Re Turners's Will Trusts* [1937] Ch 15, CA.

72.10 In *London Regional Transport Pension Fund Trust Co Ltd v Hatt*[1], *however,* it was held, despite earlier doubts[2], that s 37(1)(c) was subject to a contrary intention expressed in the trust instrument, and that this should also follow for s 39. The judge recognised that the 1925 Act was a consolidating Act, but nonetheless looked at the previous law[3], which persuaded him that the earlier law should govern the construction of the present. Another approach (not discussed in *Hatt*) would have been simpler. Section 37 only relates to the position 'on the appointment of a trustee'. So if an express (not statutory) power is exercised to *remove* a trustee, and so to reduce the number of remaining trustees to one, there is no problem[4].

72.10   *The death, retirement, or removal of trustees*

1   [1993] Pens LR 227 at 260–262, discussed by D. Way [1993] 2 J Int P 100 and accepted in *Adam and Company International Trustees Ltd v Theodore Goddard* [2000] WTLR 349.
2   *Mettoy Pension Trustees Ltd v Evans* [1991] 2 All ER 513 at 534.
3   Despite eg *R v West Yorkshire Coroner, ex p Smith* [1983] QB 335, CA.
4   *Chamberlain v IRC* [1945] 2 All ER 351, at 355D, CA.

Retirement under statutory power without appointment of successor

72.11 Section 39 of the Trustee Act 1925 provides that:

(1)   Where a trustee is desirous of being discharged from the trust, and after his discharge there will be either a trust corporation[1] or at least two persons[2] to act as trustees to perform the trust, then, if such trustee as aforesaid by deed declares that he is desirous of being discharged from the trust, and if his co-trustees and such other person, if any, as is empowered to appoint trustees, by deed consent to the discharge of the trustee, and to the vesting in the co-trustees alone of the trust property, the trustee desirous of being discharged shall be deemed to have retired from the trust, and shall, by the deed, be discharged therefrom under this Act, without any new trustee being appointed in his place.

(2)   Any assurance or thing requisite for vesting the trust property in the continuing trustees alone shall be executed or done.

1   See definition, paras 79.5–79.6. Companies incorporated outside the European Union cannot be 'trust corporations' however well capitalised.
2   See TLATA 1996, Sch 3, para 3(13).

72.12 The position on reducing the number of trustees to one should be the same mutatis mutandis under this section as for s 37 of the Trustee Act 1925. The Law of Property Act 1922, s 110(10) substituted corresponding words in s 11(1) of the Trustee Act 1893, leaving scope for contrary intention under s 11(3). And, as pointed out above, s 37 has no effect in relation to an express power to remove a trustee[1].

1   *Chamberlain v IRC* [1945] 2 All ER 351, at 355D, CA.

72.13 It would seem that the power to obtain his discharge without appointment of a successor is one of the powers conferred on trustees which under s 69(2) thereof[1] yield to the express terms of the settlement, as should the need for there to be a trust corporation incorporated in a state within the European Union or at least two individuals. A deed is required if advantage is to be taken of s 40(2) of the Trustee Act to vest relevant property in the continuing trustees alone[2].

1   See *Re Warren* [1939] Ch 684, [1939] 2 All ER 599 and *Adam and Company International Trustees Ltd v Theodore Goddard* [2000] WTLR 349 at 355. When English or Welsh land comes to be sold, however, no valid capital receipt can be given to protect a purchaser unless there are two trustees or a trust corporation: LPA 1925, s 27(2).
2   See para 75.3 below.

Retirement by consent of all the beneficiaries

72.14 The method of retirement by consent of all the beneficiaries is merely a corollary of Article 69. The beneficiaries collectively being the sole owners of the property, and able to put an end to the trust, can a fortiori permit the trustee to retire, even though the result may be to leave a single individual to act as trustee. But for this to happen, all the beneficiaries or objects must join in, and thus if even one is a minor or unborn it cannot in practice take place. In any event, it may be doubted whether the beneficiaries can permit a trustee to retire without the consent of his co-trustee or co-trustees[1]. However, all collectively entitled beneficiaries if of full age and capacity may be able, instead, to rely on s 19 of the Trusts of Land and Appointment of Trustees Act 1996, discussed below.

1   Cf *Re Brockbank* [1948] Ch 206, [1948] 1 All ER 287; discussed at para 69.24 above.

Retirement by order of the court

72.15 Retirement by order of the court is now a comparatively rare method of retirement from a trust. It might arise where the trustee wishes to retire and either cannot procure a person to take his place, or, being himself the appointing party, has a dispute with his beneficiaries in relation to the person to be appointed, or where the persons with power to appoint are out of the country, or cannot be found[1]. In such cases the trustee would be justified in issuing a Part 8 claim under RSC Order 5, rule 3, for the appointment of a new trustee in his place and it is conceived that ordinarily he would not only be exempt from bearing the costs of the application, but would also be entitled to his own costs[2].

1   See *Re Humphry's Estate* (1855) 1 Jur NS 921; and *Re Somerset* [1887] WN 122.
2   See *Re Chetwynd's Settlement* [1902] 1 Ch 692; *Re Merry* [2003] WTLR 424.

72.16 The court also has jurisdiction in an administration action or on a claim inter partes asking for administration or execution of the trusts (but not on a claim under the Trustee Act 1925[1]) to discharge one of two or more trustees without appointing another person to succeed him[2]. It will not do so unless there remain at least two trustees or a trust corporation to perform the trust.

1   *Re Chetwynd's Settlement* [1902] 1 Ch 692. The device of re-appointing the continuing trustees in place of themselves and the retiring trustee (as in *Re Stokes' Trusts* (1872) LR 13 Eq 333; and *Re Harford's Trusts* (1879) 13 Ch D 135) was disapproved in *Re Aston* (1883) 23 Ch D 217; following a decision of Cotton LJ in *Re Colyer* (1880) 50 LJ Ch 79, and is not now followed.
2   See *Re Chetwynd's Settlement* [1902] 1 Ch 692, and *Re Stretton* [1942] WN 95.

Retiring trustees not released from liability

72.17 Where a trustee hands over to another trustee he is not entitled to a formal release from the trusteeship, since the only persons who can give, or are called on to give, a formal release to trustees are the beneficiaries when the trust is wound up[1].

1   *Tiger v Barclays Bank Ltd* [1951] 2 KB 556, [1951] 2 All ER 262; affd [1952] 1 All ER 85, CA, where this point was not in issue.

72.18 Setting aside deed of retirement for undue influence

72.19 Where a trustee (or a protector) executes a deed of retirement due to another's undue influence, the deed can be set aside[1]

1   *Daniel v Drew* [2005] WTLR 807,CA.

Paragraph 2(a)

Illustration of express power to remove a trustee

72.20 An instance of a trustee being removable under an express power is afforded by the form of bankers' mortgage, namely, containing a declaration by a mortgagor who has deposited his title deeds that he will hold the legal estate in trust for the mortgagees, with power for the mortgagees, during the continuance of the security, to remove him or any other trustee from the trusteeship, and to appoint themselves or any other person in his place. In such cases the mortgagees can, by a deed removing the trustee and appointing another person, without even the necessity for an express vesting declaration[1], take the legal estate out of the mortgagor, or even of an assign to whom he has conveyed it with notice[2]. Sometimes, the settlor will reserve to himself or confer on a protector the right to remove a trustee at any time and replace him with a new trustee. This will almost always be a fiduciary power[3] to be exercised in the best interests of the beneficiaries as discussed under Article 73(1)(a) below.

1   See para 75.3 above.
2   *London and County Banking Co v Goddard* [1897] 1 Ch 642.
3   Eg *Re Osiris Trustees Ltd* [2000] WTLR 933.

Problem where remove without replacing

72.21 If A, B and C are trustees and C is removed pursuant to an express power of removal that permits removal other than by replacement, legal title remains in A, B and C because s 39 does not apply to vest title in A and B alone (C not having executed a deed retiring from the trusteeship). It will thus be necessary to appoint a replacement trustee, D, who can then execute a deed of retirement benefiting from ss 39 and 40(2) of the Trustee Act so as to vest legal title in A and B alone.

72.22 On the other hand, it is clear that removing a trustee without replacement under an express power of removal does not engage the statutory prohibition on the number of trustees falling below two[1], as that only applies on the appointment of a trustee[2].

1   Trustee Act 1925, s 37(1)(c); see para 72.3 above.
2   *Chamberlain v IRC* [1945] 2 All ER 351, at 355D, CA.

Paragraph 2(b)

Qualifying Requirements

72.23 Where there is at the time in question no person nominated for the purpose of appointing new trustees by the trust instrument[1] and the beneficiaries under the trust are all of full age and capacity and between them are collectively entitled to the trust property[2], then they may collectively give a written direction requiring the trustee(s) to retire and if they wish, also requiring the retiring trustee(s) to appoint the person(s) specified in the direction[3]. This right can be excluded by a provision in a post-1996 trust[4], while in the case of pre-1997 trusts it can be excluded by a provision in a post-1996 deed only if such a deed is executed by the settlor(s)[5]. The beneficiaries' collective right is personal to them so they can appoint one or more of themselves to be new trustees if they wish. The retiring trustees should do as they are told unless aware of facts indicating that the participation of one beneficiary thereby placed in a vulnerable position has been obtained by fraud or undue influence.

1   For example, if by then the person nominated in the trust instrument has died.
2   TLATA 1996, s 19(1).
3   TLATA 1996, s 19(2).
4   TLATA 1996, s 21(5).
5   TLATA 1996, s 21(6). The deed is irrevocable: s 21(7).

72.24 The purpose of the provision is to save those beneficiaries who have collective *Saunders v Vautier* rights from having to terminate the trust (with disadvantageous tax consequences) and create a new trust on the same terms where they simply want to replace the trustees. Thus, beneficiaries under a discretionary trust with collective *Saunders v Vautier* rights should be able to force the trustees to retire in favour of new trustees nominated by the beneficiaries when 'beneficiary' is defined[1] as 'any person who under the trust has an interest in property subject to the trust (including a person who has such an interest as trustee or as a trustee or a personal representative)'.

1   TLATA 1996, s 22(1): it includes an annuitant (whose interest in the trust property is only excluded from being an interest in possession by s 22(3)).

72.25 However, it is a question whether 'beneficiary' for this purpose extends to an object of a power of appointment who only has a hope of obtaining 'an interest in property subject to the trust' if the trustees happen to exercise their discretion in his favour, the trustees not being obliged to exercise any discretion at all[1]. In the estate duty context the House of Lords held that 'interest' did not extend to an interest as beneficiary under a discretionary trust, and *a fortiori* not to the hope of an object of a power of appointment[2], but "interest" in other contexts can extend to discretionary trust beneficiaries[3]. The Privy Council has said obiter that even the object of a power is necessary to join in a *Saunders v Vautier* application to the trustees to terminate the trust[4], and the House of Lords refused to distinguish the two classes (objects of discretionary trust and objects of fiduciary power) in the context of certainty of objects[5].

72.25 *The death, retirement, or removal of trustees*

1   See paras 1.67–1.69.
2   In *Gartside v IRC* [1968] AC 553, at 607.
3   *Knocker v Youle* [1986] 2 All ER 914 at 916–917.
4   *Rosewood Trust Ltd v Schmidt* [2003] UKPC 26, [2003] 2 AC 709, para 41.
5   *McPhail v Doulton* [1971] AC 424.

72.26 Where the interest of a beneficiary has passed by operation of law to his personal representative or to his trustee in bankruptcy or has been assigned to B beneficially or to T on various trusts ,then it will be the personal representative or trustee in bankruptcy or B or T who will need to join with the other beneficiaries to require the trustees to retire.

Beneficiaries' Directions

72.27 The beneficiaries' directions may require the retirement of a trustee or trustees without any new trustee being appointed (provided there will be either a trust corporation or at least two trustees left to perform the trust) or require both the retirement of a trustee or trustees and the appointment of a new trustee or trustees (provided as above) or require the appointment of an additional trustee or trustees (subject to the usual restrictions on the number of trustees)[1]. A single direction may be given by all the beneficiaries jointly or by each of them (whether solely or jointly with one or more of the others) specifying the same person or persons for retirement and appointment[2]. A written withdrawal by any one beneficiary before compliance with the direction(s) makes the direction(s) ineffective[3]. Retirement directions need to be served on the retiring trustee(s), while appointment directions must be served on all the trustees.

1   TLATA 1996, s 19(2) and (3)(c). A direction may be given to the personal representative of
     the last trustee.
2   TLATA 1996, s 21(1).
3   TLATA 1996, s 21(1).

Implementation of Directions

72.28 A trustee shall make a deed declaring his retirement and be deemed to have retired and be discharged from his trust where (a) he has been given a direction, (b) 'reasonable arrangements have been made for the protection of any rights of his in connection with the trust', (c) there will be a trust corporation or at least two trustees after he has retired and (d) either another person is to be appointed to be a new trustee on his retirement or the continuing trustees by deed consent to his retirement[1]. Where a trustee retires, he and the continuing trustees (together with any new trustee) must (subject to any arrangements for the protection of his rights)[2] do anything necessary to vest the trust property in the continuing trustees (or the continuing and new trustees). It thus seems that, as in the case of voluntary retirements, it is envisaged that, rather than require the retired trustee to rely solely on his equitable non-possessory lien, he and the other trustees will come to reasonable arrangements, eg including an indemnity given by them to him against contingent and future liabilities.

1   TLATA 1996, s 19(3).
2   TLATA 1996, s 19(4).

72.29 If the trustee fails to execute the requisite deed e.g. because not satisfied with the arrangements for his protection, then the beneficiaries may seek a mandatory order from the court, with the trustee being at risk as to the costs if he loses the case, and the court ultimately having power to nominate a person to execute the deed on his behalf[1].

1   Supreme Court Act 1981, s 39.

72.30 A retirement by deed under the statutory power without the appointment of any new trustee operates under s 40(2) of the Trustee Act 1925 to vest the trust property in the remaining trustees (other than property excepted by s 40(3)). While an appointment of new trustees must, at the least, be in writing[1], it will be better for it to be by deed so as to obtain the benefit of s 40 for much trust property, although specific steps will be necessary for other trust property (eg stocks and shares) to be vested in the new trustees together with any continuing trustees.

1   TLATA 1996, s 19(2)(b).

Where trustee is mentally disordered

72.31 If there is another trustee who is of sound mind he will normally exercise his powers under s 36(1) of the TA 1925 (but see s 36(9). If a trustee lacks capacity to exercise his functions as trustee and there is no person entitled to appoint a replacement trustee under s 36(1) of the Trustee Act 1925, then the collectively absolutely entitled beneficiaries of full age and capacity can arrange for a replacement trustee[1]. They need to give a written direction to a receiver of the trustee or an attorney acting for him under a registered enduring or lasting power of attorney or a person authorised for the purpose by the authority (the Court of Protection) having jurisdiction under the Mental Health Act 1983, Pt VII, requiring the recipient to appoint by writing the person or persons specified in the direction to be a trustee or trustees in place of the incapable trustee[2].

1   TLATA 1996, s 20(1) subject to s 21 in the same way as s 19.
2   TLATA 1996, s 20(2). Section 20 will normally be used to appoint two or more trustees, implicitly subject to the maximum of four for land.

Paragraph 2(c) and (d)

72.32 Where the relationship between trustees and beneficiaries breaks down, it may be sensible to terminate it[1]. The court has an inherent power to remove a trustee for cause[2], or can by statute appoint a new trustee in substitution for another. The removal of a trustee under the statutory power of appointing new trustees, or by the court, is so mixed up with the appointment of new trustees, that reference should be made to the next Article for further information on the subject[3]. In Jersey it has been held that by analogy with the court's inherent jurisdiction to remove a trustee for cause, it has the like power to remove a protector for cause[4].

1   *Eiro v Lombardo* [2005] JRC 172, R Ct Jersey.
2   See para 73.42 ff.
3   An executor who is incapable of performing his duties can, in effect, be removed by revocation of the grant of probate. See *Re Galbraith* [1951] P 422, [1951] 2 All ER 470n; but see *Re Cope's Estate* [1954] 1 All ER 698, [1954] 1 WLR 608. But the Family Division has no jurisdiction to order the removal of a trustee: *Compton (Marquess of Northampton) v Compton (Marchioness of Northampton) and Hussey* [1960] P 201, [1960] 2 All ER 70. The High Court now has jurisdiction to remove a personal representative: Administration of Justice Act 1985, s 50.
4   *Re Freiburg Trust* [2004] JRC 056, R Ct Jersey. Also Isle of Man High Court dicta in *Re Papadimitriou* [2004] WTLR 1141.

ARTICLE 73
APPOINTMENT OF NEW TRUSTEES[1]

73.1

(1)   New trustees of a settlement may be appointed:
   (a)   under an express or a necessarily implied[2] power;
   (b)   under the statutory power conferred by section 36 of the Trustee Act 1925;
   (c)   by the High Court (or where the trust fund does not exceed £30,000 in value, the county court[3]) on the application of any trustee or beneficiary[4], whenever it is expedient to appoint a new trustee or new trustees, and it is found inexpedient, difficult or impracticable to do so without the court's assistance; and particularly where it is desirable to appoint a new trustee in substitution for a trustee who is incapable, by reason of mental disorder within the meaning of the Mental Health Act 1983[5], of exercising his functions as trustee, or is a bankrupt, or is a corporation which is in liquidation or has been dissolved[6]. Where, however, there is a donee of a power of appointing new trustees able and willing to exercise it, the court has no power to appoint new trustees contrary to his wishes[7]; or
   (d)   by the authority having jurisdiction under Part VII of the Mental Health Act 1983, in cases where such authority has concurrent jurisdiction with the High Court by virtue of section 54 of the Trustee Act 1925, as amended by the Mental Health Act 1983, section 148(1) and Schedule 4[8];
   (e)   if a trustee of a pension trust scheme has been removed by the Pensions Regulator or has ceased to be a trustee by reason of his disqualification the Regulator may appoint another trustee in his place[9].
(2)   In the case of pension trust schemes an independent trustee must be appointed, where the employer is insolvent, by the insolvency

practitioner in relation to such employer or the official receiver if satisfied that there is no independent trustee[10].

(3) Every new trustee, appointed pursuant to the statutory power or by the court, both before and after the trust property is vested in him, has the same powers, authorities, and discretions (incident to the office of trustee)[11], and may in all respects act as if he had been an original trustee[12], while the newly appointed independent trustee of a pension trust scheme will have all the trustees' discretionary powers vested in him alone[13].

(4) Any person, including a corporation[14], who can hold property, is capable of being appointed to be a trustee except, in the case of pension trust schemes, a person disqualified by reason of dishonesty, insolvency and other prejudicial matters within section 29 of the Pensions Act 1995; but an infant cannot be appointed, and serious consideration should be given before appointing a person who resides out of the jurisdiction of the court, or one who is a beneficiary, or husband of a beneficiary.

(5) Where there are more than four trustees of a trust of land no new trustee can be appointed (except where on the appointment the number is reduced to four or less) until the number is reduced to less than four, and thereafter the number cannot be increased beyond four[15].

(6) Where an attempted appointment is invalid the old trustee remains liable, and the invalidly appointed new trustee also becomes liable as a trustee de son tort if he intermeddles with the trust property[16].

1   The appointment of a judicial trustee is treated separately in Article 76 below.
2   *Davis v Richards and Wallington Industries Ltd* [1991] 2 All ER 563 at 581.
3   County Courts Act 1959, s 52, as amended.
4   TA 1925, s 58. The court can charge the costs of such appointment, and of vesting orders, on the trust estate (TA 1925, s 60).
5   See s 1(2) of the 1983 Act.
6   TA 1925, s 41, as amended by Mental Health Act 1983, s 148(1) and Sch 4, and by Criminal Law Act 1967, s 10(2) and Sch 3, Pt III.
7   *Re Higginbottom* [1892] 3 Ch 132. But this does not relate to applications for this appointment of a judicial trustee under the Judicial Trustees Act 1896, as to which see Article 76, below, and *Douglas v Bolam* [1900] 2 Ch 749; nor, it is apprehended, to cases in which a judgment for general administration has been given, as to which see Article 68.
8   For the relevant powers under the 1983 Act, see s 96 thereof. See also paras 73.44 and 75.73 below.
9   Pensions Act 1995, s 7. The Pensions Regulator has taken over the powers of the abolished Occupational Pensions Regulatory Authority: Pensions Act 2004 s 7.
10 Pensions Act 1995, s 23.
11 As to the difference between powers incident to the office and powers confided to persons who are also trustees, see per Farwell J in *Re Smith* [1904] 1 Ch 139 at 144; and Art 74, above.
12 Trustee Act 1925, ss 36(7), 43.
13 Pensions Act 1995, s 25.
14 *Re Thompson's Settlement Trusts* [1905] 1 Ch 229. A corporation could not be a joint tenant prior to the Bodies Corporate (Joint Tenants) Act 1899.
15 TA 1925, s 34 as amended by the TLATA 1996, Sch 3, para 3(9). The restrictions do not apply in the case of land for charitable, ecclesiastical or public trusts, or to the trustees of portions terms etc. See TA 1925, s 34(3).

[16] *Pearce v Pearce* (1856) 22 Beav 248; *Adam & Co International Trustees Ltd v Theodore Goddard* [2000] WTLR 349.

Paragraph 1(a)

Appointment of new trustees under express power

73.2–73.5 Express powers to appoint new trustees are construed somewhat strictly. Thus, where an express power to appoint new trustees is vested in:

'the surviving or continuing trustees or trustee, or executors or administrators of the last surviving and continuing trustee,'

73.6 All the trustees are desirous of retiring, they cannot do so by appointing new trustees in their place by a single deed. Instead, a new trustee must be appointed in the place of the first retiring trustee by one deed, and then the new trustee must join in a second deed appointing another new trustee in the place of the second retiring trustee, and so on[1].

[1] *Lord Camoys v Best* (1854) 19 Beav 414; *Re Coates to Parsons* (1886) 34 Ch D 370; *Re Norris* (1884) 27 Ch D 333. This notion was strongly disapproved by Bacon V-C in *Re Glenny and Hartley* (1884) 25 Ch D 611; but the Vice-Chancellor's dicta were equally strongly disapproved by Pearson J in *Re Norris*, above, and by North J in *Re Coates to Parsons*, above.

73.7 This singular instance of verbal subtlety all turns upon the idea that trustees who are *about to retire cannot be said to be continuing*[1], but that if one retired first, the other would be a continuing trustee, although he might intend to retire the next day. If, in addition to the words 'surviving and continuing', the words 'or other trustee or trustees' had been added, the retiring trustees might have appointed new ones by the same deed[2].

[1] With regard to appointments made under the statutory power this is not so, as the statute enacts that a continuing trustee shall include a refusing or retiring trustee, *if willing to act*, as donee of the power (TA 1925, s 36(8)); but he is not a necessary party if unwilling to act (see *Re Norris* (1884) 27 Ch D 333).

[2] With regard to appointments made under the statutory power this is not so, as the statute enacts that a continuing trustee shall include a refusing or retiring trustee, *if willing to act*, as donee of the power (TA 1925, s 36(8)); but he is not a necessary party if unwilling to act (see *Re Norris* (1884) 27 Ch D 333).

73.8 So, again, the words 'unfit and incapable' are very strictly construed. Thus, where a new trustee was to be appointed if a trustee became 'incapable of acting', it was held that the bankruptcy of one of the trustees did not fulfil the condition, as it only rendered him *unfit* but not *incapable*[1]. Similarly, where the words were 'unable to act', it was held that absence in China or Australia did not *disable*[2], although it clearly unfitted[3], a trustee for the office. But where the power was to arise in case a trustee should 'be abroad', the fact of his having taken a five years' lease of a residence in Normandy was held to be sufficient to enable the donee of the power to displace him[4]. It has been held that unsoundness of mind *disables* a trustee so as to bring a power into operation[5].

1   *Turner v Maule* (1850) 15 Jur 761; see *Re Watts' Settlement* (1851) 9 Hare 106.
2   *Withington v Withington* (1848) 16 Sim 104; *Re Harrison's Trusts* (1852) 22 LJ Ch 69; *Re May's Will Trusts* [1941] Ch 109 (trustee resident in enemy-occupied territory not incapable of acting); but see *Re Bignold's Settlement Trusts* (1872) 7 Ch App 223.
3   *Mesnard v Welford* (1853) 1 Sm & G 426; and *Re Harrison's Trusts* (1852) 22 LJ Ch 69. A mere temporary absence abroad will not unfit a trustee for the office (*Re Moravian Society* (1858) 26 Beav 101), especially with the ease of communication in the 21st Century.
4   *Re Earl of Stamford* [1896] 1 Ch 288.
5   *Re East* (1873) 8 Ch App 735.

73.9 With regard to a trustee becoming *unfit* to act, bankruptcy (at all events where the trust property consists of money or other property capable of being misappropriated, and where the beneficiaries desire his removal[1]) an arrangement or composition with creditors[2], or conviction of a dishonesty crime[3], are grounds for removal *by the court*, under s 41 of the Trustee Act 1925[4]. It thus seems likely that they would enable a donee of a power of appointing new trustees to displace the trustee in hostile proceedings on the ground of *unfitness*. Under the old law it was held that infancy was not *unfitness*, although an infant would be removed by the court[5]; but by s 20 of the Law of Property Act 1925 it is provided that 'the appointment of an infant to be a trustee in relation to any settlement or trust shall be void, but without prejudice to the power to appoint a new trustee to fill the vacancy'[6]. Lastly, with regard to *incapacity*, the word is strictly limited to incapacity of the trustee arising from some personal defect[7], as illness, physical or mental[8], or infancy.

1   See *Re Barker's Trusts* (1875) 1 Ch D 43; *Re Adams' Trust* (1879) 12 Ch D 634.
2   See *Re Barker's Trusts* (1875) 1 Ch D 43; *Re Adams' Trust* (1879) 12 Ch D 634.
3   *Turner v Maule* (1850) 15 Jur 761.
4   Replacing s 25 of the Trustee Act 1893. The Criminal Law Act 1967, s 1, has abolished the distinction between felonies and misdemeanours and s 10 and Sch 3, P III, therefore repeal the words in s 41 of the TA 1925 which refer specifically to a trustee being convicted of felony. It is clear none the less that the trustee's conviction for a serious crime would make it expedient to replace him.
5   *Re Tallatire* [1885] WN 191. Minors, as infants are now known, attain majority at the age of 18 years under the Family Law Reform Act 1969.
6   See *Re Vinogradoff* [1935] WN 68.
7   See *Re Watts' Settlement* (1851) 9 Hare 106; *Turner v Maule* (1850) 15 Jur 761; *Re Bignold's Settlement Trusts* (1872) 7 Ch App 223.
8   *Re East* (1873) 8 Ch App 735; *Re Blake* [1887] WN 173.

Power personal and not incident to donee's interest

73.10 Where the power is vested in a beneficiary he may exercise it even after alienating his interest by way of a mortgage assignment[1]. On the other hand, where a decree for administration by the court has been made, the donee of a power (whether express or statutory) can only appoint a new trustee under the supervision of the court. But the court will accept his nominee, unless there be strong grounds for rejecting him[2].

1   *Hardaker v Moorhouse* (1884) 26 Ch D 417.
2   *Re Gadd* (1883) 23 Ch D 134; *Re Hall* (1885) 33 WR 508; *Re Sales* [1911] WN 194, followed, *Re Cotter* [1915] 1 Ch 307.

73.11 *The death, retirement, or removal of trustees*

Power normally fiduciary

73.11 Where a power to remove trustees by replacing them with new trustees is vested in a beneficiary who is the primary object of the settlor's bounty and whose power is not restricted to a few specified eventualities, the obvious inference is that the power has been conferred on the beneficiary to look after his own personal interests and not those of the beneficiaries as a whole. However, if it is someone who is not a beneficiary (such as the settlor or, a *fortiori*, a designated protector) who has such power, there is a strong presumption that this kind of power is a fiduciary one[1] to be exercised only in the best interests of the beneficiaries as a whole[2]. This is because the subject-matter of the power is the office of the trustee at the very core of the trust, also obliged to act in the best interests of the beneficiaries as a whole. Thus the function of a protector who is not himself a beneficiary is naturally presumed to be to protect the same interests. On the other hand, the initial protector may be a beneficiary with a significant interest to protect[3] (eg the settlor's widow life-tenant or a son being managing director of the company which is a major trust asset) or may be the settlor's foreign lawyer, whom the settlor expects to protect a significant interest of the settlor not as beneficiary under the trust but as managing director (at a good salary with good perquisites) of a company controlled by the trustees or in which the trustees have a significant shareholding[4].

---

[1]   *Steele v Paz* [1993–95] Manx LR 426, CA; *IRC v Schroder* [1983] STC 480; *Re Osiris Trustees* (2000) 2 ITELR 404. See para 1.76–1.78 above.
[2]   It should be noted that the fact that the duties are light in proportion to the fees chargeable has been held not to be a good ground for refusing to allow retiring trustees to appoint the Public Trustee: *Re Drake's Settlement* [1926] WN 132.
[3]   *Rawson Trust v Perlman* Butts OCM, Vol 11, pp 35–54 (Bahamas Sup Ct); and see *Re Z Trust* [1997] Cayman ILR 248; *Re Papadimetriou* [2004] WTLR 1141 (IOM High Ct), and *Virani v Guernsey International Trustees Ltd*, (4 December 2002, unreported), R Ct Guernsey.
[4]   As in *Von Knierem v Bermuda Trust Co* Butts OCM, Vol 1, p 116.

73.12 To avoid the operational problems that will arise if the purportedly replaced trustees argue that their replacement was in breach of the equitable and fiduciary duties placed upon the donor of the power of appointment so that they remain the trustees, it will help if the trust instrument spells out the limited nature of the donee's duties rather than having to fall back upon necessary implications. It also helps if the trust assets are held by a custodian trustee so the replaced old trustees need not be told who are the new trustees to whom assets need to be transferred (no trust assets needing to be transferred), and so that the trust continues to operate smoothly with the custodian trustee taking its instructions from the new trustees. This custodian trusteeship structure is also essential to the effectiveness of automatic 'flee' (or should it be 'flea') clauses where, in certain specified events, T Co Ltd in Suntopia is to cease to be a trustee and E Trust Co Ltd in Erewhon is to become trustee, for otherwise Suntopian assets can be frozen and the Suntopian trustees enjoined from any activities.

Exercise of express power by a minor

73.13 It would seem that a minor can validly exercise an express power of appointment[1], but a minor is not bound by an act which is either imprudent or prejudicial to his interests or which, where he is executing an authority with which he is entrusted, touches his interest. Where therefore a minor, having an express power to appoint new trustees and being himself beneficially entitled to the property on attaining twenty-five, appointed his mother, to whom the income was payable for his benefit until he attained twenty-five, as sole trustee, the court held the appointment to be invalid[2].

[1]   *Re D'Angibeau* (1880) 15 Ch D 228; *Pouey v Horden* [1900] 1 Ch 492 at 494.
[2]   *Re Parsons* [1940] Ch 973, [1940] 4 All ER 65.

Exercise of express power on behalf of person who is mentally ill

73.14 Where a power of appointment is vested in a person who lacks capacity to manage and administeri his property and affairs[1], the judge[2] may exercise the power[3] and may also make consequential vesting orders[4].

[1]   See the Mental Health Act 1983, s 94.
[2]   'The judge' in this context is defined in s 94 of the 1983 Act.
[3]   Mental Health Act 1983, s 96(1). See also, as cases decided under ss 128, 129 of the Lunacy Act 1890 (which was replaced by the 1959 Act); *Re Shortridge* [1895] 1 Ch 278; *Re Fuller* [1900] 2 Ch 551; *Re Blake* [1887] WN 173, CA. These provisions apply whether or not the patient is a trustee, but if he is and a vesting order is required the better practice on grounds of expense may be to proceed under the TA 1925, s 54; see para 75.23 below.
[4]   Mental Health Act 1983, s 96(2). See also the preceding footnote.

Attack on exercise of express power

73.15 The exercise of the power to appoint new trustees cannot be attacked under the rule in *Hastings-Bass*[1].

[1]   *Re Duxbury's Settlement Trust* [1995] 3 All ER 145. See para 61.24 above.

Paragraph 1(b)

Appointment of new trustees under the statutory power

73.16 If there be no express power, or even if there is one but the statutory power is not expressly negatived or modified[1], and the express power is for some reason inapplicable to the state of circumstances that has arisen, new trustees may be appointed under the provisions of s 36 of the Trustee Act 1925. That section and ss 37 and 38 of the Act are in the following words:

> 36.—(1)
> Where a trustee, either original or substituted, and whether appointed by a court or otherwise, is dead, or remains out of the United Kingdom for more than twelve months, or desires to be discharged from all or any of the trusts or powers reposed in or conferred on him, or refuses or is unfit to act therein, or is

incapable of acting therein, or is an infant, then, subject to the restrictions imposed by this Act on the number of trustees—

    (a)   the person or persons nominated for the purpose of appointing new trustees by the instrument, if any, creating the trust[2]; or

    (b)   if there is no such person, or no such person able and willing to act, then the surviving or continuing trustees or trustee for the time being, or the personal representatives of the last surviving or continuing trustee[3]:

may, by writing[4], appoint one or more other persons (whether or not being the persons exercising the power) to be a trustee or trustees in the place of the trustee so deceased remaining out of the United Kingdom, desiring to be discharged, refusing, or being unfit or being incapable, or being an infant, as aforesaid.

    (2)   Where a trustee has been removed under a power contained in the instrument creating the trust, a new trustee or new trustees may be appointed in the place of the trustee who is removed, as if he were dead, or, in the case of a corporation, as if the corporation desired to be discharged from the trust, and the provisions of this section shall apply accordingly, but subject to the restrictions imposed by this Act on the number of trustees.

    (3)   Where a corporation being a trustee is or has been dissolved, either before or after the commencement of this Act, then, for the purposes of this section and of any enactment replaced thereby, the corporation shall be deemed to be and to have been from the date of the dissolution incapable of acting in the trusts or powers reposed in or conferred on the corporation.

    (4)   The power of appointment given by subsection (1) of this section or any similar previous enactment to the personal representatives of a last surviving or continuing trustee shall be and shall be deemed always to have been exercisable by the executors for the time being (whether original or by representation) of such surviving or continuing trustee who have proved the will of their testator or by the administrators for the time being of such trustee without the concurrence of any executor who has renounced or has not proved.

    (5)   But a sole or last surviving executor intending to renounce, or all the executors where they all intend to renounce, shall have and shall be deemed always to have had power, at any time before renouncing probate, to exercise the power of appointment given by this section, or by any similar previous enactment, if willing to act for that purpose and without thereby accepting the office of executor.

    (6)   Where in the case of any trust, there are not more than three trustees[5]–

        (a)   the person or persons nominated for the purpose of appointing new trustees by the instrument, if any, creating the trust; or

        (b)   if there is no such person, or no such person able and willing to act, then the trustee or trustees for the time being;

may, by writing, appoint another person or other persons[6] to be an additional trustee or additional trustees, but it shall not be obligatory to appoint any additional trustee, unless the instrument, if any, creating the trust, or any statutory enactment provides to the contrary, nor shall the number of trustees be increased beyond four by virtue of any such appointment.

(6A)   A person who is either—

    (a)   both a trustee and attorney for the other trustee (if one other), or for both of the other trustees (if two others), under a registered power; or

    (b)   attorney under a registered power for the trustee (if one) or for both or each of the trustees (if two or three),

may, if subsection (6B) of this section is satisfied in relation to him, make an appointment under subsection (6)(b) of this section on behalf of the trustee or trustees[7].

(6B)   This subsection is satisfied in relation to an attorney under a registered power for one or more trustees if (as attorney under the power)—

    (a)   he intends to exercise any function of the trustee or trustees by virtue of section 1(1) of the Trustee Delegation Act 1999; or

    (b)   he intends to exercise any function of the trustee or trustees in relation to any land, capital proceeds of a conveyance of land or income from land by virtue of its delegation to him under section 25 of this Act or the instrument (if any) creating the trust.

(6C)   In subsections (6A) and (6B) of this section "registered power" means an enduring power of attorney or a lasting power of attorney registered under the Mental Capacity Act 2005.

(6D)   Subsection (6A) of this section—

    (a)   applies only if and so far as a contrary intention is not expressed in the instrument creating the power of attorney (or, where more than one, any of them) or the instrument (if any) creating the trust; and

    (b)   has effect subject to the terms of those instruments.

(7)   Every new trustee appointed under this section as well before as after all the trust property becomes by law, or by assurance, or otherwise, vested in him, shall have the same powers, authorities, and discretions, and may in all respects act as if he had been originally appointed a trustee by the instrument, if any, creating the trust.

(8)   The provisions of this section relating to a trustee who is dead include the case of a person nominated trustee in a will but dying before the testator, and those relative to a continuing trustee include a refusing or retiring trustee[8] if willing to act in the execution of the provisions of this section.

(9)   Where a trustee lacks capacity to exercisie his functions as trustee and is also entitled in possession to some beneficial interest in the trust property, no appointment of a new trustee in his place shall be made by virtue of paragraph (b) of subsection (1) of this section unless leave to make the appointment has been given by the Court of Protection.

37.—(1)

On the appointment of a trustee for the whole or any part of trust property–

    (a)   the number of trustees may, subject to the restrictions imposed by this Act on the number of trustees, be increased; and

    (b)   a separate set of trustees, not exceeding four, may be appointed for any part of the trust property held on trusts distinct from those relating to any other part or parts of the trust property, notwithstanding that no new trustees or trustee are or is to be appointed for other parts of the trust property, and any existing trustee may be appointed or remain one of such separate set of trustees, or, if only one trustee was originally appointed, then, save as hereinafter provided, one separate trustee may be so appointed; and

      (c)   it shall not be obligatory, save as hereinafter provided, to appoint more than one new trustee where only one trustee was originally appointed[9], or to fill up the original number of trustees where more than two trustees were originally appointed, but, except where only one trustee was originally appointed, and a sole trustee when appointed will be able to give receipts for all capital money, a trustee shall not be discharged from his trust unless there will be either a trust corporation or at least two persons[10] to act as trustees to perform the trust; and

      (d)   any assurance or thing requisite for vesting the trust property, or any part thereof, in a sole trustee, or jointly in the persons who are the trustees, shall be executed or done.

(2)   Nothing in this Act shall authorise the appointment of a sole trustee, not being a trust corporation, where the trustee, when appointed, would not be able to give valid receipts for all capital money arising under the trust.

38.—(1)

A statement, contained in any instrument coming into operation after the commencement of this Act by which a new trustee is appointed for any purpose connected with land, to the effect that a trustee has remained out of the United Kingdom for more than twelve months or refuses or is unfit to act, or is incapable of acting, or that he is not entitled to a beneficial interest in the trust property in possession, shall, in favour of a purchaser of a legal estate, be conclusive evidence of the matter stated.

(2)   In favour of such purchaser any appointment of a new trustee depending on the statement, and any vesting declaration, express or implied, consequent on the appointment, shall be valid.

---

[1] *Cecil v Langdon* (1884) 28 Ch D 1; and *Re Wheeler and de Rochow* [1896] 1 Ch 315, followed in *Re Sichel* [1916] 1 Ch 358. If the events contemplated by a limited express power of appointment have not occurred then the statutory power applies.

[2] In *Re Wheeler and de Rochow* [1896] 1 Ch 315, Kekewich J held that if there is a limited express power of appointment in certain events and no such event occurs so that reliance is placed on the statutory power then the nominee with the limited power is not the 'person nominated for the purpose of appointing new trustees' within s 36(1)(a) so that the proper nominating person is to be found in s 36(1)(b). Neville J reluctantly followed this in *Re Sichel* [1916] 1 Ch 358. Section 36 in substance merely re-enacts Trustee Act 1893, s 10(1), so the position seems the same.

[3] See *Re Shafto's Trusts* (1885) 29 Ch D 247; *Nicholson v Field* [1893] 2 Ch 511; *Re Coates to Parsons* (1886) 34 Ch D 370.

[4] Query whether those who have actually proved can exercise the power without the joinder of those who have not renounced; cf *Re Boucherett* [1908] 1 Ch 180. An executor who has not proved his trustee-testator's will can exercise this power, but the trustee appointed in such circumstances can only prove his title by reference to a proper grant of representation establishing that the appointor was executor under the testator's last will, so that a grant of probate or of letters of administration with the will annexed is vital in practice: *Re Crowhurst Park* [1974] 1 All ER 991, [1974] 1 WLR 583.

[5] Nevertheless the power cannot be exercised by will; see *Re Parker's Trusts* [1894] 1 Ch 707. A deed will attract the benefit of s 40 of the TA 1925.

[6] As amended by TLATA 1996, Sch 3, para 3(11).

[7] The appointor cannot appoint himself to be an additional trustee, though he could under sub-s (1) appoint himself to fill a vacancy (*Re Power's Settlement Trusts* [1951] Ch 1074, [1951] 2 All ER 513, CA; and see *Re Sampson* [1906] 1 Ch 435).

[8] This has effect only where the power, or (where more than one) each of them, was created after commencement of the Trustee Delegation Act 1999 (on 1 March 2000) which by s 8 inserted subs (6A)–(6D). The purpose is to deal with the situation where one co-owner of land has, before losing capacity, delegated his trustee functions to the other co-owner by enduring power of attorney, and two trustees are needed to give a good receipt for the proceeds of sale of the land.

9   A trustee who is compulsorily removed (eg on account of absence abroad) is not a 'refusing or retiring trustee' within this provision (*Re Stoneham's Settlement Trusts* [1953] Ch 59, [1952] 2 All ER 694).

10   Mere disclaimer by one of two trustees does not enable the other to retire and appoint one only in his place: *Earl of Lonsdale v Beckett* (1850) 4 De G & Sm 73; and see *Re Birchall* (1889) 40 Ch D 436.

Inviolability of the statutory power

73.17 The statutory power deserves the greatest respect, and is one with which the court will not interfere[1]. It would not aid the beneficiaries, even when all concurred, to control the exercise of the power[2] but now the beneficiaries collectively absolutely beneficially entitled and of full age and capacity can retire and replace the trustees under s 19 of the Trusts of Land and Appointment of Trustees Act 1996[3].

1   'Persons' substituted for 'individuals' by TLATA 1996, Sch 3, para 3(12).
2   *Re Gadd* (1883) 23 Ch D 134; *Re Higginbottom* [1892] 3 Ch 132.
3   *Re Brockbank* [1948] Ch 206, [1948] 1 All ER 287.

When the statutory power is exercisable

73.18 It will be observed that the statutory power is exercisable in seven cases, namely:

(1)   where a trustee is dead;
(2)   where he remains out of the United Kingdom for more than twelve months;
(3)   where he desired to be discharged;
(4)   where he refuses to act;
(5)   where he is unfit to act;
(6)   where he is incapable of acting; and
(7)   where he is an infant[1].

1   This is now a minor under 18 years of age.

Deceased trustee

73.19 This head includes the case of a person nominated trustee in a will but dying before the testator. However, it should be noted that if a will creates trusts but all the intended trustees predecease the testator, so that no one has ever been a trustee, then no trustee can be appointed under this head[1] because there can then be no surviving or continuing trustees. In such a case the personal representative of the testator has title to the property[2] until the court appoints trustees[3], equity not allowing a trust to fail for want of a trustee.

1   *Nicholson v Field* [1893] 2 Ch 511.
2   Administration of Estates Act 1925, ss 1, 2.
3   *Re Williams* (1887) 36 Ch D 231.

73.20 *The death, retirement, or removal of trustees*

Trustee residing abroad

73.20 The second ground enables a new trustee to be appointed in the place of a trustee who has been resident abroad for 12 months even against his will[1], '12 months' for this purpose meaning residence for an unbroken period of 12 months[2]. To facilitate matters whilst abroad a trustee may by power of attorney[3] delegate his duties and discretions for a period not exceeding 12 months.

1   *Re Stoneham's Settlement Trusts* [1953] Ch 59, [1952] 2 All ER 694.
2   *Re Walker* [1901] 1 Ch 259.
3   TA 1925, s 25, 55.34.

Trustee desiring to be discharged

73.21 The third ground is clearly applicable to the case of an executor who, having paid debts, and funeral and testamentary expenses, has assented to a settled legacy where the testator has not appointed trustees to administer it. In such cases, where the executor has assented to the legacy, he becomes functus officio qua executor, and thenceforth holds the legacy as trustee[1], and can, like any other trustee, retire, and appoint a new one in his place under the section now under consideration[2]. Further, it is now clear that the section is equally applicable where the legacy is not settled (eg a legacy to an infant for which the executor cannot get a receipt), or where an administrator holds a share of residue. This appears from the judgment of Danckwerts J in *Re Cockburn's Will Trusts*[3], where he said:

> 'Whether persons are executors or administrators, once they have completed the administration in due course, they become trustees holding for the benefici-aries, either on an intestacy or under the terms of the will, and are bound to carry out the duties of the trustees, though in the case of personal representa-tives, they cannot be compelled to go on indefinitely acting as trustees and are entitled to appoint new trustees in their place and thus clear themselves from duties which were not expressly conferred on them under the terms of the testator's will and which, for that purpose, they are not bound to accept. It seems to me that if they do not appoint new trustees to proceed to execute the trusts of the will they will become trustees in the full sense. Further, it seems to me that they have the power, under the trusts (*sic*) conferred by section 36 of the Trustee Act 1925 to appoint new trustees of the will to act in their place.'

1   See *Re Smith* (1889) 42 Ch D 302; *Re Earl of Stamford* [1896] 1 Ch 288; *Re Willey* [1890] WN 1; *Re Timmis* [1902] 1 Ch 176; and *Re De Sommery* [1912] 2 Ch 622.
2   *Re Smith* (1889) 42 Ch D 302; *Re Earl of Stamford* [1896] 1 Ch 288; *Re Willey* [1890] WN 1; *Re Timmis* [1902] 1 Ch 176; and *Re De Sommery* [1912] 2 Ch 622 and *Re Pitt* (1928) 44 TLR 371; *Re Yerburgh* [1928] WN 208; and see also *Re Moore* (1882) 21 Ch D 778; and comments thereon of Kekewich J in *Eaton v Daines* [1894] WN 32; Administra-tion of Estates Act 1925, s 42 may be available to enable a personal representative to obtain a discharge: see para 66.7.
3   [1957] Ch 438, [1957] 2 All ER 522. See also *Re Ponder* [1921] 2 Ch 59; *Re Pitt* (1928) 44 TLR 371. So far as the observations of the CA in *Harvell v Foster* [1954] 2 QB 367, [1954] 2 All ER 736, CA, cast any doubt on these cases they were obiter and in the view of Danckwerts J in *Re Cockburn's Will Trusts*, above, were probably unjustified.

73.22 The judge went on to say that it had been recognised for a great number of years, and he felt no doubt that a personal representative who had 'completed his duties in a proper manner' can appoint new trustees[1].

1   In the case of land, personal representatives should execute a written assent in their own favour as trustees before they appoint new trustees; since, although the new trustees are no doubt validly appointed as such even if there has been no assent, the legal estate in the land will not vest in them under s 40 of the TA 1925 (para 75.3) unless it was vested in the appointors as trustees and this will not be so if the appointors have not made a written assent: *Re King's Will Trusts* [1964] Ch 542, [1964] 1 All ER 833. See also paras 40.4 and 75.8.

Filling up place of trustee who has already retired

73.23 Where one of three or more trustees has retired under s 39 of the Act of 1925[1], without a new trustee having been appointed in his place, his place can be subsequently filled up before another vacancy occurs, by virtue of s 36(6)[2], which gives power to appoint additional trustees even where there is no vacancy, where there are not more than three trustees and that the result of the appointment will not be to make the trustees more than four in number.

1   See para 72.11 above.
2   See para 73.16 above.

Refusal to act as trustee

73.24 It is apprehended that the fourth case, namely, refusal to act, clearly extends to the case of a disclaimer—ie to a case where the person nominated as trustee has never accepted the office[1].

1   See *Re Hadley* (1851) 5 De G & Sm 67; *Re Birchall* (1889) 40 Ch D 436.

Unfitness or incapacity

73.25 The case of a trustee becoming unfit to act (eg by virtue of his bankruptcy) or incapable of acting (eg by virtue of mental disorder) has already been dealt with[1].

1   See para 73.8 above.

73.26 Where a trustee, who lacks capacity to exercise the functions of a trustee, is also entitled in possession to some beneficial interest, no appointment of a new trustee in his place under s 36(1)(b) may be made without leave of the Court of Protection[1]. Thus a co-trustee cannot replace him, but the person (if any) having express power in the trust instrument may replace him under s 36(1)(a). Similarly, if his co-owner of land is his attorney under a registered lasting or enduring power of attorney, that co-owner[2] may appoint an additional trustee under s 36(6)(b), so that there are two trustees to give a valid capital receipt for the proceeds of sale of the land under an overreaching sale.

73.26 *The death, retirement, or removal of trustees*

1   Section 36(9) of the TA 1925, as amended by the Mental Health Act 1983; see para 73.16 above.
2   Section 36(6A) of the TA 1925 as amended by the Trustee Delegation Act 1999, s 8: see para 73.16 above.

The appointor(s)

73.27 In the above statutory cases, the appointment of new trustees must be made in writing (normally a deed to take advantage of the vesting provisions in s 40 of the Trustee Act 1925[1]). The appointment must be made by the person(s) nominated for the purpose of appointing new trustees by the trust instrument, or if there be no such person (or no such person able and willing to act), then by the surviving or continuing trustee(s) or the personal representatives of the last surviving or continuing trustee. A 'continuing' trustee includes a refusing or a retiring trustee if willing to act in making the new appointment[2]: the practice is for them to participate in the appointment if possible. A sole surviving trustee cannot appoint new trustees by his will[3] so that in that case it will fall to his personal representatives to appoint new trustees.

1   See para 75.3 below.
2   TA 1925, s 36(8).
3   *Re Parker's Trusts* [1894] 1 Ch 707.

Increase or reduction in number of trustees

73.28 By s 37 of the Trustee Act 1925[1], on an appointment under the statutory power, the number of the trustees may be increased (but not to more than four in the case of trusts of land) or diminished so long as there will then be either a trust corporation (as defined[2]) or at least two persons to perform the trust[3], unless only one trustee was originally appointed and a sole trustee will be able to give valid receipts for all capital money. Thus a sole surviving trustee will not be discharged by the appointment of one only in his place, unless the new trustee is a trust corporation. The question whether the number could be increased or diminished under a special power, depended on the interpretation of the power itself[4], but, as the statutory power is exercisable by the same persons as would exercise the express power, the point appears to be merely academic. The court is generally indisposed to reduce the number unless an administration action is pending, or the fund is about to be paid into court or is immediately divisible[5]. By s 36(6) of the Act of 1925[6] the number of trustees can be increased by the appointment of an additional trustee when no vacancy exists if there are not more than three trustees (none of them being a trust corporation).

1   See para 73.16 above.
2   See paras 79.5–79.6 below.
3   But the trust instrument may authorise trustees to replace themselves and be discharged even if they appoint a corporate trustee not incorporated in a European Union State, so long as no land in England and Wales is part of the trust property: see para 37.3.
4   *Meinertzhagen v Davis* (1844) 1 Coll 335 at 341; *Miller v Priddon* (1852) 1 De GM & G 335; *Re Bathurst's Estate* (1854) 2 Sm & G 169; See *Earl of Lonsdale v Beckett* (1850) 4 De G & Sm 73; but cf *Re Cunningham and Bradley to Wilson* [1877] WN 258; and *West of England and South Wales District Bank v Murch* (1883) 23 Ch D 138.

5   *Re Skeats' Settlement* (1889) 42 Ch D 522; *Re Newen* [1894] 2 Ch 297; *Re Gardiner's Trusts* (1886) 33 Ch D 590.
6   See para 73.16 above.

Severance of trusts

73.29   The provision in s 37(1)(b) of the Trustee Act 1925[1], authorising the severance of trusts by donees of the power of appointing new trustees applies notwithstanding that the trusts, although separate for a time when there are two life tenants, may ultimately again unite in favour of one individual[2].

1   See para 73.16 above.
2   *Re Hetherington's Trusts* (1886) 34 Ch D 211; *Re Moss's Trusts* (1888) 37 Ch D 513.

73.30   It is conceived that four existing trustees of a will could not split themselves into two sets, two of the trustees taking over fund A and the other two trustees taking over fund B, for there would be no appointment of a *new* trustee for the whole *or any part* of the trust property. Whether, after a total extinguishment of all the trustees, new trustees can be appointed of part of the trust property, leaving the residue in the hands of the executors of the last surviving trustee, seems doubtful, and the question has been answered in the negative by the Irish Courts[1].

1   *Re Nesbitt* (1887) 19 LR Ir 509.

Where donees of express power differ, or one incapable, the statutory power is available

73.31   Where there are joint donees of a power of appointment named in the settlement, and they differ as to the person to be appointed, they will be deemed to be 'unable or unwilling', to appoint, so as to vest the statutory power in the surviving or continuing trustees[1]. It may be observed that the statutory power is not imperative, and imposes no obligation on the donee of the power to appoint new trustees[2]. Moreover, it is exercisable by an express donee notwithstanding that the personal representatives of the last surviving trustee have acted as trustees[3].

1   *Re Sheppard's Settlement Trusts* [1888] WN 234.
2   *Peacock v Colling* (1885) 33 WR 528; *Re Knight's Will* (1884) 26 Ch D 82.
3   *Re Routledge* [1909] 1 Ch 280.

Paragraph 1(c)

Appointment of new trustees by the court

73.32   The court has an inherent jurisdiction to appoint trustees in proceedings where an order has been made for administration or execution of the trusts[1]. But the jurisdiction of the court to appoint new trustees most frequently exercised is that conferred and governed by the following section of the Trustee Act 1925:

41.—(1)

The court[2] may, whenever it is expedient to appoint a new trustee or new trustees, and it is found inexpedient difficult or impracticable so to do without the assistance of the court, make an order appointing a new trustee or new trustees, either in substitution for or in addition to any existing trustee or trustees, or although there is no existing trustee.

In particular and without prejudice to the generality of the foregoing provision, the court may make an order appointing a new trustee in substitution for a trustee who lacks capacity to exercise his functions as trustee, or is a bankrupt, or is a corporation which is in liquidation or has been dissolved[3].

(2)   The power conferred by this section may, in the case of a deed of arrangement within the meaning of the Deeds of Arrangement Act 1914, be exercised either by the High Court or by the court having jurisdiction in bankruptcy in the district in which the debtor resided or carried on business at the date of the execution of the deed.

(3)   An order under this section, and any consequential vesting order or conveyance, shall not operate further or otherwise as a discharge to any former or continuing trustee than an appointment of new trustees under any power for that purpose contained in any instrument would have operated.

(4)   Nothing in this section gives power to appoint an executor or administrator.

42.—Where the court appoints a corporation, other than the Public Trustee, to be a trustee either solely or jointly with another person, the court may authorise the corporation to charge such remuneration for its services as trustee as the court may think fit.

43.—Every trustee appointed by a court of competent jurisdiction shall, as well before as after the trust property becomes by law, or by assurance, or otherwise, vested in him, have the same powers, authorities, and discretions, and may in all respects act as if he had been originally appointed a trustee by the instrument, if any, creating the trust.

1   See Article 88.
2   Ie the High Court, or where the trust state does not exceed £30,000 in value, the county court. See County Courts Act 1984, s 23.
3   This provision has been amended by the Mental Capacity Act 2005, the Mental Health Act 1983 and by the Criminal Law Act 1967.

73.33 It should be noted that a corporation appointed by the court in any particular case to be a trustee ranks as a trust corporation[1] and so is able on its own to give a valid receipt for capital moneys derived from land.

1   TA 1925, s 68(18).

Examples of cases in which application to court is proper

73.34 Application should only be made to the court to appoint new trustees in cases where, for some reason or other, it is difficult, inexpedient, or impracticable to appoint them otherwise. Thus, where the donee of a power was anxious to exercise it corruptly, the court could not *under the statutory* *power* appoint over his head; although, of course, in an *action* to restrain him and to administer the trust it would have been a different matter[1].

[1] See *Re Hodson's Settlement* (1851) 9 Hare 118. And cf *Middleton v Reay* (1849) 7 Hare 106. But sometimes where the donee neglects to appoint (*Finlay v Howard* (1842) 2 Dr & War 490).

No donee of the power, or none capable of acting

73.35 However, situations still arise in which it is inexpedient or impracticable to appoint new trustees out of court. Thus, if a last surviving or a sole trustee dies intestate, and leaves no estate, so that no one will take out letters of administration to him, and no one is named in the settlement to appoint new trustees, it may be necessary to apply to the court.

73.36 Under similar powers conferred by earlier Acts the court has replaced a trustee who has, through old age and infirmity, become incapable of acting in the trust[1].

[1] *Re Lemann's Trusts* (1883) 22 Ch D 633; *Re Phelps' Settlement Trusts* (1885) 31 Ch D 351.

Appointment by court where no original trustees of will

73.37 Where, by inadvertence, or by reason of predeceasing the testator, or otherwise, there never were any original trustees of a will trust, and no express power of appointing any, the court will appoint some[1].

[1] *Dodkin v Brunt* (1868) LR 6 Eq 580; *Re Smirthwaite's Trusts* (1871) LR 11 Eq 251; *Re Davis' Trusts* (1871) LR 12 Eq 214; *Re Moore* (1882) 21 Ch D 778; *Re Williams' Trusts* (1887) 36 Ch D 231.

Appointment by court where a minor is trustee or donee of an express power

73.38 Where a minor is appointed to be a trustee, and the statutory power is not available[1], the court will appoint another in his place, for the appointment of a minor to be a trustee in relation to any settlement or trust is void[2]. Where the donee of an express power of appointing new trustees is a minor it will almost always be desirable to seek the aid of the court. Though it appears that a minor can exercise such a power after he has reached years of some discretion, yet any appointment he may make will be liable to be set aside, and cannot therefore safely be acted upon[3].

[1] Infancy or minority of a trustee is one of the events in which the statutory power is exercisable; see TA 1925, s 36(1), para 73.16.
[2] LPA 1925, s 20.
[3] *Re Parsons* [1940] Ch 973, [1940] 4 All ER 65.

Appointment by court in cases of doubt

73.39 If there be a doubt whether the statutory (or an express) power applies, the court will solve it by appointing new trustees itself[1].

1   *Re Woodgate's Settlement* (1856) 5 WR 448.

Appointment by court where the donees of power cannot agree

73.40 In an old case it was held that, where the power of appointing new trustees was given to a husband and wife jointly, and they were judicially separated, the husband being resident in Australia, it was inexpedient or difficult to appoint new trustees without the assistance of the court which, therefore, made the appointment on the petition of the wife and her children who were the sole beneficiaries[1]. The position is the same where the donees of the power cannot agree upon the choice of the new trustees[2].

1   *Re Somerset* [1887] WN 122.
2   See as to this, para 73.31 above.

73.41 Where there are not more than three trustees, the current trustees in the absence of someone with an express power of appointing new trustees can appoint an additional trustee without waiting for a vacancy so long as the total number is not increased beyond four[1]. If there is disagreement between co-trustees then the court may appoint an additional trustee. But it will not normally appoint an additional trustee against the wishes of a sole trustee appointed by the settlor, even at the unanimous request of the existing beneficiaries[2], in the absence of allegations against his honesty. But it is otherwise where there is a trust of land, when, unless the sole trustee is a trust corporation, a valid receipt cannot be given by fewer than two trustees[3]. However, in an exceptional case the court could appoint an additional trustee to ensure that repeated deficiencies in the administration of the trust ceased[4].

1   TA 1925, s 36(6); para 73.16.
2   *Re Badger* [1915] WN 166; see *Re Rendell's Trusts* (1915) 139 LT Jo 249.
3   LPA 1925, s 27(2); and see Article 74, below.
4   See *Titterton v Oates* [2001] WTLR 319.

Appointment by the court in cases of friction

73.42 The court will not in exercise of its statutory jurisdiction remove a trustee against his will and appoint another in his place where there is a dispute as to fact; but where there is no such dispute the court may resolve friction between trustees by making an order for the substitution of a new trustee for one of the existing trustees[1]. Where there is a dispute as to any relevant fact, the proper course is to invoke the inherent jurisdiction of the court over trustees in a claim for administration or execution of the trusts, brought under CPR Part 7[2].

1   *Re Henderson* [1940] Ch 764, [1940] 3 All ER 295.
2   See Article 87.

73.43 It is not necessary that the trustee to be removed should have been guilty of any dishonesty or other misconduct. It is sufficient that his continuance as trustee would impede the effectual execution of the trusts. Indeed, the court will remove a trustee and appoint a new one in his stead where the only complaint against him is that, from faults of temper, it has become impossible to transact the trust business with him. This sometimes appears to be a slur upon a perfectly honest but impracticable trustee; but, as Lord Blackburn said in *Letterstedt v Broers*[1]:

> 'In exercising so delicate a jurisdiction as that of removing trustees, their lordships do not venture to lay down any general rule beyond the very broad principle ... that their main guide must be the welfare of the beneficiaries. Probably it is not possible to lay down any more definite rule in a matter so essentially dependent on details often of great nicety ... It is quite true that friction or hostility between trustees and the immediate possessor of the trust estate, is not of itself a reason for the removal of trustees. But where the hostility is grounded on the mode in which the trust has been administered, ... it is certainly not to be disregarded ... If it appears clear that the continuance of the trustee would be detrimental to the execution of the trusts, even if for no other reason than that human infirmity would prevent those beneficially interested, or those who act for them, from working in harmony with the trustee, and if there is no reason to the contrary from the intentions of the framer of the trust to give this trustee a benefit or otherwise, the trustee is always advised by his own counsel to resign, and does so. If, without any reasonable ground he refuses to do so, it seems to their lordships that the court might think it proper to remove him.'

[1] (1884) 9 App Cas 371 at 386, 387; and see *Earl of Portsmouth v Fellows* (1820) 5 Madd 450.

Appointment by court where trustee is a criminal or bankrupt

73.44 Where a trustee has been convicted of a serious crime[1] or is a bankrupt[2], and refuses to join in the appointment of a new trustee in his place, the court can and will remove him, and appoint another person if the beneficiaries desire it[3]. So also where a trustee lacks capacity to exercise his functions as trustee[4], or has gone to reside permanently abroad[5], or has absconded.

[1] See note 4, at para 73.43.
[2] As to the procedure for appointing new trustees of a bankrupt solicitor's client account, see *Re A Solicitor* [1952] Ch 328, [1951] 1 All ER 133.
[3] TA 1925, s 41, as amended: see para 73.32 above. And see *Coombes v Brookes* (1871) LR 12 Eq 61; *Re Adams' Trust* (1879) 12 Ch D 634; *Re Foster's Trusts* (1886) 55 LT 479; *Re Danson* (1899) 48 WR 73; *Re Henderson* [1940] Ch 764, [1940] 3 All ER 295.
[4] TA 1925, s 41, as amended: see para 73.32 above.
[5] *Re Bignold's Settlement Trusts* (1872) 7 Ch App 223. As to the length of absence abroad, see *Hutchinson v Stephens* (1834) 5 Sim 498. For a case in which the court held it proper to displace a trustee resident in enemy-occupied territory in time of war, see *Re May's Will Trusts* [1941] Ch 109.

Removal and appointment where breach of trust

73.45 It does not necessarily follow that new trustees will be appointed to replace trustees who have been guilty of a breach of trust, even if such trustees have defended their conduct till judgment has been given against them. It is still necessary to find 'something which induces the court to think either that the trust property will not be safe, or that the trust will not properly be executed in the interests of the beneficiaries'[1]. Thus, where trustees were held liable for a breach of trust, no order removing them and appointing new trustees was made where the trust fund had become distributable between beneficiaries of full age and capacity, some of whom did not want the trustees removed, taking into account the extra costs thereby involved which it seemed unnecessary to incur[2].

1   *Re Wrightson* [1908] 1 Ch 789 at 803. See also *Nissen v Grunden* (1912) 14 CLR 297; *Princess Anne of Hesse v Field* [1963] NSWR 998.
2   *Re Wrightson* [1908] 1 Ch 789 at 803. See also *Nissen v Grunden* (1912) 14 CLR 297; *Princess Anne of Hesse v Field* [1963] NSWR 998.

73.46 The general rule for removal of a trustee is that his 'acts or omissions must be such as to endanger the trust property or to show a want of honesty or a want of proper capacity to execute the duties or a want of reasonable fidelity'[1]. As Dixon CJ said in *Miller v Cameron*[2]:

> 'The jurisdiction to remove a trustee is exercised with a view to the interest of the beneficiaries, to the security of the trust property and to an efficient and satisfactory execution of the trusts and a faithful and sound exercise of the powers conferred upon the trustee.'

1   *Letterstedt v Broers* (1884) 9 App Cas 371 at 386.
2   (1936) 54 CLR 572 at 580 followed in *Re Roberts* (1983) 70 FLR 158; *Titterton v Oates* [2001] WTLR 319 and *Monty v Delmo* [1996] 1 VR 65.

73.47 If hostility between the trustees prevents them from acting unanimously (as they must unless otherwise authorised) then one or all should be removed and replaced[1].

1   *Re Consigli's Trusts* (1973) 36 DLR (3d) 658.

73.48 Section 41 does not confer the power simply to remove a trustee without appointing a new trustee in his place. However, the court has *inherent* power to do so if sufficient trustees remain or a receiver is appointed to safeguard the assets[1]. Indeed, in an emergency trustees may be removed on an interim application without notifying the defendants, and a receiver appointed of the trust assets until appointment of new trustees after hearing the defendants[2].

1   *Re Harrison's Settlement Trusts* [1965] 3 All ER 795 at 799; *Re Chetwynd's Settlement* [1902] 1 Ch 692; *Re Henderson* [1940] Ch 764; *Clarke v Heathfield (No 2)* [1985] ICR 606.
2   *Clarke v Heathfield* [1985] ICR 203.

Appointment defeating trustee's rights

73.49 In *Re Pauling's Settlement Trusts*[1] the plaintiff had previously brought a successful action against the defendant bank as trustee for breach of trust, and it had been ordered that two or more persons should be appointed new trustees of the settlement under s 41. On the reference pursuant to that order, the trustee bank objected to the appointment of new trustees at a time when an appeal and a cross-appeal were pending in the main action. One ground of objection was that such an appointment would defeat the bank's right to impound the interest of the life tenant (who was said to have instigated the breaches of trust). However, Wilberforce J held that a trustee's equitable right to impound is not defeated by the appointment of new trustees, because it does not depend upon the trustee being in actual possession of the trust fund, and that the right of indemnity by way of impounding under s 62 of the Trustee Act 1925[2] extends in favour of a former trustee. Nevertheless, he held that the order for appointment of new trustees should not be implemented for the time being because (inter alia) it would deprive the bank of its security for costs and also of the funds from which to pay the estate duty for which it might (depending on the result of the appeal) be liable and remain liable even if replaced by new trustees.

[1] [1963] Ch 576, [1963] 1 All ER 857.
[2] See Article 99, below.

Trustee charged with breach of trust appointing a new trustee against claimant's wishes

73.50 Where a trustee, charged with breach of trust, appointed a new trustee against the claimant's wishes, both were removed[1]. A similar course was followed where the donee of a power appointed a new trustee because the old one would not commit a breach of trust[2].

[1] *Peatfield v Benn* (1853) 17 Beav 522.
[2] *Pepper v Tuckey* (1844) 2 Jo & Lat 95.

Summary procedure only applicable where trust is clear

73.51 The regular procedure for the appointment of new trustees by the court under the statutory jurisdiction is by claim form under Part 8 of the Civil Procedure Rules[1]. However, it would seem that where the trust is not clear on the face of written documents (eg where a conveyance is taken in the name of some other person than the real purchaser[2]), the court first requires the trust to be established to its satisfaction by a claim under Pt 7 of the Rules so as to resolve a substantial dispute of fact, as where the inherent jurisdiction to remove a trustee is invoked.

[1] Even where the trustee whom it is desired to displace opposes (*Re Danson* (1899) 48 WR 73).
[2] *Re Martin's Trusts Lands etc Improvement Co v Martin* (1887) 34 Ch D 618; and see also *Re Carpenter* (1854) Kay 418; and *Re Weeding's Estate* (1858) 4 Jur NS 707.

Appointing person to perform the duties incident to office of executor

73.52 Although s 41(4) of the Trustee Act 1925[1] expressly prohibits the court from appointing an executor or administrator, yet where a testator has not appointed a trustee of trust legacies (and, consequently, the trusteeship is incident to the office of executor), the court has jurisdiction, when the estate has been cleared, to appoint some one to perform those fiduciary duties in his place[2].

1   See para 73.32 above.
2   *Re Moore* (1882) 21 Ch D 778; *Eaton v Daines* [1894] WN 32; and *Re Willey* [1890] WN 1; *Re Earl of Stamford* [1896] 1 Ch 288; and see TA 1925, s 68(17); (interpretation of 'trust' and 'trustee'); and see also *Re Ponder* [1921] 2 Ch 59; *Re Cockburn's Will Trusts* [1957] Ch 438, [1957] 2 All ER 522.

73.53 Section 50 of the Administration of Justice Act 1985 now confers power on the High Court to appoint a substitute for, or to remove, a personal representative where application in this behalf is made by a beneficiary interested in the deceased's estate or by a personal representative[1].

1   See para 1.48.

Practice on applications to the court

73.54 With regard to the practice on applications for the appointment of new trustees, ss 58, 59, and 60 of the Trustee Act 1925 provide as follows:

Persons entitled to apply for orders

73.55 58—(1) An order under this Act for the appointment of a new trustee or concerning any interest in land, stock, or thing in action subject to a trust, may be made on the application of any person beneficially interested[1] in the land, stock or thing in action, whether under disability or not, or on the application of any person duly appointed trustee thereof.

(2) An order under this Act concerning any interest in land, stock, or thing in action subject to a mortgage may be made on the application of any person beneficially interested in the equity of redemption, whether under disability or not, or of any person interested in the money secured by the mortgage[2].

1   Held to include a contingent beneficiary (*Re Sheppard's Trusts* (1863) 4 De GF & J 423) and a purchaser of trust property (*Ayles v Cox* (1853) 17 Beav 584).
2   See *Re Peacock* (1880) 14 Ch D 212.

Power to give judgment in absence of a trustee

73.56 59.—Where in any action the court is satisfied that diligent search has been made for any person who, in the character of trustee, is made a defendant in any action, to serve him with a process of the court, and that he cannot be found, the court may hear and determine the action and give judgment therein against that person in his character of a trustee as if he had been duly served, or had entered an appearance in the action, and had also appeared by his counsel and solicitor at the hearing, but without prejudice to any interest he may have in the matters in question in the action in any other character.

Power to charge costs on trust estate

73.57 60.—The court may order the costs and expenses of and incident to any application for an order appointing a new trustee, or for a vesting order, or of and incident to any such order or any conveyance or transfer in pursuance thereof, to be raised and paid out of the property in respect whereof the same is made, or out of the income thereof, or to be borne and paid in such manner and by such persons as to the court may seem just.

Procedure under the Act was originally by originating summons, and now by Part 8 claim form, even where the existing trustee resists[1], as long as there is no dispute of fact. Where there is a dispute of fact, the court may decline to exercise the statutory jurisdiction, and leave the parties to invoke the inherent jurisdiction of the court over trustees in an action[2].

[1] *Re Danson* (1899) 48 WR 73.
[2] See per Bennett J in *Re Henderson* [1940] Ch 764 at 767, [1940] 3 All ER 295 at 298.

Paragraph 1(d)

Concurrent mental health jurisdiction

73.58 Section 54 of the Trustee Act 1925, as amended by the Mental Health Act 1983[1], provides for the concurrent jurisdiction of the High Court and the Court of Protection in the four cases therein mentioned, namely in relation to (a) mortgaged property of which the person lacking capacity has become a trustee merely because the mortgage has been paid off, (b) matters consequent on the making of provision by such authority for the exercise of a power of appointing trustees or retiring from a trust, (c) matters consequent on the making of provision by such authority for the carrying out of any contract entered into by the person lacking capacity, and (d) property to some interest in which the patient is beneficially entitled but which, or some interest in which, is held by that person under an express, implied or constructive trust.

[1] And the Mental Capacity Act 2005.

73.59 In these cases application may still be made to the Court of Protection and this procedure will often be advantageous upon the score of convenience and economy as compared with an application in the Chancery Division. But if there is any substantial part of the trust property in which the patient has no beneficial interest, the application should be made in the Chancery Division[1].

[1] *Jackson v Nerman* (1933) unreported. For the practice on applications see Heywood & Massey *Court of Protection Practice*, Ch 15.

Paragraph 2

Only such powers pass to new trustees as are incident to the office

73.60   As above stated, every new trustee appointed pursuant to the statutory power or by the court has the same powers, authorities, and discretions as if he had been an original trustee[1]. This, however, only applies to powers, authorities, and discretions which, on the true construction of the trust instrument, are incident to the office, and not to mere naked or personal powers given to the original trustees personally. The same principles are applicable to this as those already discussed under Article 71, above, in relation to the survivorship of powers on the death of one of several trustees. Prima facie such powers are so incident[2].

1   Trustee Act 1925, ss 36(7), 43.
2   *Re de Sommery* [1912] 2 Ch 622; and see *Innes (Inspector of Taxes) v Harrison* [1954] 1 All ER 884, [1954] 1 WLR 668.

Paragraph 3

Persons proper to be appointed new trustees

73.61   In selecting persons to be new trustees, the court acts upon the following principles, and it is apprehended that donees of powers *ought* to be guided by the same considerations. However, trustees have plenty of leeway in the exercise of their discretion. So long as their exercise of their power of appointment does not amount to a fraud on the power which in the eyes of equity[1] would make the exercise void, they only commit a breach of trust if the appointment is one that no properly informed trustee could make[2].

1   *Cloutte v Storey* [1911] 1 Ch 18 at 31, so at common law a purchaser could acquire a legal title from the trustees having the legal title and be protected as a purchaser thereof without notice' see paras 101.2 and 101.12.
2   *Richard v Mackay* (1997) Trust LI 23, Millett J (as he then was) pointing out that proposed appointment would be unchallengeable if 'not so inappropriate that no reasonable trustee could entertain it'. If it were so inappropriate then it would be liable to be set aside at the instance of a beneficiary who had not consented to it: *Re Whitehead's Will Trusts* [1971] 1 WLR 833 at 837.

73.62   First, regard will be paid to the wishes of the settlor as expressed in, or plainly deduced from, the settlement.

73.63   Second, a person will not be appointed with a view to promoting the interest of some of the beneficiaries in opposition to the interest of others. It is said to be not proper to appoint new trustees without communicating with the beneficiaries and hearing their objections; at all events where it is likely that they would object[1]. The reason for this is that the attitude of the beneficiaries towards the new trustee could create bad relationships and impair the efficiency with which trusteeship duties are performed.

1   *Marshall v Sladden* (1849) 7 Hare 428, and *O'Reilly v Alderson* (1849) 8 Hare 101.

73.64 Third, regard will be had to the question whether the appointment will promote or impede the execution of the trust. However, the mere fact of a continuing trustee refusing to act with the proposed new trustee will not be sufficient to induce the court to refrain from appointing him[1], because that would give the continuing trustee a power of veto. On the other hand, it may well be necessary to remove the continuing trustee if the trust is to be operated smoothly and efficiently.

1   *Re Tempest* (1866) 1 Ch App 485.

73.65 Fourth, a person will not normally be appointed if to do so would place him in a position in which his interest and his duty would be apt to conflict, unless of course the settlement contemplates the possibility of such conflict, eg where the trustee of a pension fund may well also be a beneficiary[1].

1   *Re Parsons* [1940] Ch 973, [1940] 4 All ER 65.

Appointment by the donee of the power of himself

73.66 It was not clear before the Trustee Act 1925 to what extent the donee of a power of appointing new trustees could appoint himself[1]. However, the point is now settled by s 36(1) of the Trustee Act 1925[2] which expressly authorises the appointment of:

> 'one or more other persons (*whether or not being the persons exercising the power*)',

but this does not enable donees to appoint themselves to be additional trustees where no vacancy exists[3].

1   See *Re Sampson* [1906] 1 Ch 435; *Montefiore v Guedalla* [1903] 2 Ch 723; *Tempest v Lord Camoys* (1888) 58 LT 221; *Re Skeats' Settlement* (1889) 42 Ch D 522; and *Re Newen* [1894] 2 Ch 297; *Re Shortridge* [1895] 1 Ch 278.
2   See para 73.16 above.
3   *Re Power's Settlement Trusts* [1951] Ch 1074, [1951] 2 All ER 513, CA.

Appointment of person entitled to life interest

73.67 The appointment of a person entitled for life has been held to be not improper[1]. But such an appointment is certainly not advisable, for one of the main objects of a trustee is to protect the reversioner interested in capital against the person entitled to income.

1   *Forster v Abraham* (1874) LR 17 Eq 351; and see *Briggs v Parsloe* [1937] 3 All ER 831.

Appointment of remainderman

73.68 It has been held[1] that a reversioner is not a person whom *the court* will appoint, at all events where there is an infant entitled for life. For the interest of a person entitled in remainder is somewhat opposed to that of a tenant for life; and it would be for his advantage to lay out trust income in making improvements on the property, instead of making accumulations for the benefit of the tenant for life. Of course, however, such an objection would be inapplicable where a tenant for life is of full age and capacity and consents to the appointment, and in special circumstances the court will appoint a beneficiary[2].

1   *Re Paine's Trusts* (1885) 28 Ch D 725.
2   *Ex p Conybeare's Settlement* (1853) 1 WR 458.

Appointment of solicitor to the trust

73.69 The solicitor to the trust is normally not a proper person to be appointed a new trustee. Thus, the court will seldom make, or sanction, such an appointment unless a very special case is made out[1]. But such an appointment out of court would not, however, be bad, so as to invalidate the acts of the trustee so appointed. When such an appointment is made the appointee is generally required to undertake, should he become sole trustee, forthwith to appoint another to act with him.

1   *Re Norris* (1884) 27 Ch D 333; and *Re Earl of Stamford* [1896] 1 Ch 288. The same rule is equally applicable to appointments of trustees for purposes of the Settled Land Act: *Re Kemp's Settled Estates* (1883) 24 Ch D 485; *Re Spencer's Settled Estates* [1903] 1 Ch 75. For acceptance of the appointor's own solicitor see *Re Cotter* [1915] 1 Ch 307.

Appointment of beneficiaries' bankers

73.70 In *Re Northcliffe's Settlements*[1] it was held by the Court of Appeal that there is no principle which would prevent a bank being appointed trustee merely because the beneficiaries are customers of the bank and, in fact, have overdrawn accounts.

1   [1937] 3 All ER 804, CA.

Near relations

73.71 It used to be said that the court would never appoint a near relation of a beneficiary, except in case of necessity[1]. But this seems to be a counsel of perfection, and is not now followed in practice.

1   *Wilding v Bolder* (1855) 21 Beav 222.

Persons out of jurisdiction appointed trustee

73.72 The provision in s 36(1) of the Trustee Act 1925 which enables a trustee who remains out of the UK for more than twelve months to be replaced does not make persons resident abroad ineligible to be appointed trustees. In *Re Whitehead's Will Trusts* Pennycuick V-C in 1971 summarised the traditional position as follows[1]:

'The law has been quite well established for upwards of a century that there is no absolute bar to the appointment of persons resident abroad as trustees of an

English trust. I say "no absolute bar" in the sense that such an appointment would be prohibited by law and would consequently be invalid. On the other hand, apart from exceptional circumstances, it is not proper to make such an appointment, that is to say, the court would not, apart from exceptional circumstances, make such an appointment; nor would it be right for the donees of such a power to make an appointment out of court. If they did, presumably the court would be likely to interfere at the instance of the beneficiaries. There do, however, exist exceptional circumstances in which such an appointment can properly be made. The most obvious are those in which the beneficiaries have settled permanently in some country outside the UK and what is proposed to be done is to appoint new trustees in that country.'

1   [1971] 1 WLR 833 at 837. See also *Re Windeatt's Will Trusts* [1969] 1 WLR 692.

73.73 Clearly, it will be proper to appoint as new trustees persons resident in another jurisdiction if the beneficiaries are resident in that jurisdiction, the trust assets are in, or will be transferred to, that jurisdiction, and the jurisdiction has its own trust law[1] or recognises and gives effect to foreign trusts[2]. In these circumstances the English court itself will be prepared to appoint non-resident trustees or approve an arrangement under the Variation of Trusts Act 1958 by which non-resident trustees are appointed and the trust fund is exported. Indeed, in *Re Chamberlain*[3] an arrangement was approved for the export of a trust to Guernsey with Guernsey trustees where the primary beneficiaries were domiciled in France and the remaindermen were domiciled in Indonesia.

1   *Re Freeman's Settlement Trusts* (1887) 37 Ch D 148; *Re Liddiard* (1880) 14 Ch D 310; *Re Cunard's Trusts* (1878) 27 WR 52; *Re Austen's Settlement* (1878) 38 LT 601; *Re Hill's Trusts* [1874] WN 228; *Re Seale's Marriage Settlement* [1961] Ch 574, [1961] 3 All ER 136; *Meinertzhagen v Davis* (1844) 1 Coll 335.
2   *Re Windeatt's Will Trusts* [1969] 2 All ER 324, [1969] 1 WLR 692; *Re Whitehead's Will Trusts* [1971] 2 All ER 1334, [1971] 1 WLR 833. In *Re Weston's Settlements* [1969] 1 Ch 223, [1968] 3 All ER 338, CA, para 47.67, an arrangement to export to Jersey was held not for the benefit of beneficiaries who had just settled in Jersey (perhaps temporarily). Jersey now has a trust law of its own: Trusts (Jersey) Law 1983. Implementation of The Hague 1984 Convention on The Law Applicable to Trusts and on their Recognition will assist: see Article 105, below.
3   Discussed in (1976) 126 NLJ 1034.

73.74 Nowadays, when it is the trustees who are proposing to exercise their discretion so as to appoint foreign trustees and who are considering seeking the declaratory authorisation of the court that this is within the leeway afforded to them, it seems that so long as there are some grounds for the trustees to believe that the proposed appointment is for the benefit of the beneficiaries there is no need to seek the protection of the court. As Millett J stated back in 1987[1]:

'The appropriateness is for the trustees to decide, and different minds may have different views on what is appropriate in particular circumstances. Certainly, in the conditions of today when one can have an international family with international interests and where they are as likely to make their home in one country as in another and as likely to choose one jurisdiction as another for the investment of their capital, I doubt that the language of Sir John Pennycuick is really in tune with the times. In my judgment, where the trustees retain their discretion, as they do in the present case, the court should need to be satisfied only that the proposed transaction is not so inappropriate that no reasonable trustee could entertain it.'

1   *Richard v Mackay* (1997) 11 Trust LI 23 reporting 4 March 1987 judgment followed by Vinelott J in *Re Beatty's Will Trusts (No 2)* (28 February 1991, reported in (1997) 11 Trust LI 77.

73.75 Thus, he held that the trustees could properly transfer part of the trust fund to the trustees of an ad hoc trust to be established in Bermuda with Bermudan resident trustees even though the beneficiaries had no connection with Bermuda. Although this did not involve the appointment of new trustees of an existing trust nothing turns on this distinction as recognised in *Re Whitehead's Will Trusts[1]*. However, Millett J did contrast cases where the court is asked to exercise a discretion of its own (eg under the Variation of Trusts Act 1958 or s 41 of the Trustee Act 1925) because in these cases the applicants have to make out a positive case for the court to exercise its discretion 'and the court is unlikely to assist them where the scheme is nothing more than a device to avoid tax and has no other advantages of any kind'.

1   [1971] 1 WLR 833 at 838.

73.76 It is crucial to ensure that the English trustees are duly discharged under s 37(1)(c) of the Trustee Act 1925[1], noting that the reference there to a trust corporation only covers European Union companies carrying on trust business[2].

1   See para 73.32 above.
2   See paras 79.5–79.6 below.

Settlements subject to a foreign trust law

73.77 Even in the case of a foreign settlement the English court has held itself to have inherent jurisdiction to make *in personam* orders removing and replacing foreign trustees so long as the trustees are subject to the jurisdiction of the English court[1]. Trustees are so subject when either they are within the territory of England and Wales, or they have submitted to the jurisdiction of the court. However, due to the Recognition of Trusts Act 1987, incorporating Article 8(2)(a) of the Hague Trusts Convention, it would seem that removal and replacement should be made according to the governing law of the trust in question.

1   *Chellaram v Chellaram* [1985] Ch 409.

73.78 In drafting a settlement, if the possibility of appointing foreign trustees is considered a clause should expressly authorise the appointment of foreign trustees wherever resident and exempt the appointors from any liability so long only as they act in good faith. Indeed, in modern settlements express power is commonly conferred on the trustees (perhaps with the consent of a 'protector') to replace the law governing validity of the trust, as well as the law governing matters of administration, with another law[1].

1   See para 102.162.

Appointment of an alien

73.79 The court usually refuses to appoint an alien as trustee of an English law trust unless he be permanently resident in England, or special circumstances are present justifying appointment of a non-resident trustee (such as the migration abroad of an English resident trust[1], where this is for the benefit of those entitled).

1   See paras 47.75–47.77.

Appointment of a trust company

73.80 Subject to the fact that a corporation could not hold real property in trust which it could not hold for its own benefit without licence in mortmain[1] an incorporated company could always be appointed an original sole trustee; but owing to the impossibility of making it a joint tenant with a natural person, it was impracticable to appoint such a company to be one of two or more trustees. This difficulty was, however, obviated by the Bodies Corporate (Joint Tenancy) Act 1899 by which a body corporate was rendered capable of being a joint tenant. In *Re Thompson's Settlement Trusts*[2] Swinfen-Eady J held that a company could be appointed one of several trustees under a power the words of which authorised the appointment 'of a new trustee or new trustees'. It is apparent that the statutory power contained in s 36 of the Trustee Act 1925[3] equally authorises the appointment of a company, for although that section empowers the appointment of 'another person or other persons', yet by the Interpretation Act 1978 the word 'person' in an Act of Parliament includes a corporation. It seems the same result should follow under a special power in similar terms since a company is a legal person, so that one would expect the word 'individual' to be used if human persons alone are to be trustees.

1   *Sonley v Clock-makers Co* (1780) 1 Bro CC 81. The Mortmain Acts are now repealed: Charities Act 1960, ss 38 and 48, and Sch 7, Pt II.
2   [1905] 1 Ch 229. As to the effect on the legal estate of a corporation trustee being wound up see *Hastings Corpn v Letton* [1908] 1 KB 378; *Re No 9 Bomore Road* [1906] 1 Ch 359; and *Re Nos 56 and 58 Albert Road, Norwood* [1916] 1 Ch 289. But distinguish *Re Queenstown Dry Docks Shipbuilding and Engineering Co* [1918] 1 IR 356; after 1925 the court has express statutory jurisdiction to create a corresponding estate and vest it in the person entitled (LPA 1925, s 181).
3   See para 73.16 above.

Corporation sole

73.81 A corporation sole may be a trustee: there is no principle that a conveyance to a corporation sole cannot take effect when a trust is imposed[1].

1   *Bankes v Salisbury Diocesan Council of Education Inc* [1960] Ch 631, [1960] 2 All ER 372.

Paragraph 5

Effect of invalid appointment of new trustee

73.82 An illustration of this paragraph of the present article is afforded by the case of *Pearce v Pearce*[1]. There A and B were trustees when a deed was prepared appointing C a new trustee in place of B. This was executed by C but by inadvertence it was not executed by the donees of the power to appoint trustees. It was therefore invalid. The trust fund was nevertheless transferred from the names of A and B into those of A and C. Afterwards A and C authorised the husband of the life tenant to receive the fund, and it was lost.

1   (1856) 22 Beav 248. Also *Adam & Co International Trustees Ltd v Theodore Goddard* [2000] WTLR 349.

73.83 It was held that both B and C were liable—B because he had never ceased to be a trustee, and had yet denuded himself of the trust property, and C because she had intermeddled with trust property, and therefore became a constructive trustee. Whether B would now get full or partial relief under such circumstances under s 61 of the Trustee Act 1925[1] is, of course, another matter, depending on his honesty and the reasonableness of his conduct and on whether it appears to the court that he 'ought fairly to be excused'.

1   See Article 95.

ARTICLE 74
APPOINTMENT OF TRUSTEES FOR SALE OF LAND

74.1

(1)   Appointments of new trustees of land and of new trustees of any trust of the proceeds of sale of the land shall, subject to any order of the court be effected by separate instruments, but in such manner as to secure that the same persons become the trustees of land and trustees of the trust.

(2)   Where new trustees of land are appointed, a memorandum of the persons who are for the time being the trustees of the land shall be endorsed on or annexed to the conveyance by which the land was vested in trustees of land; and that conveyance shall be produced to the persons who are for the time being the trustees of the land by the person in possession of it in order for that to be done when the trustees require its production.

74.2 This article states the effect of s 35(1), (3), (4), of the Trustee Act 1925 as amended by the Trusts of Land and Appointment of Trustees Act 1996, Sch 3, para 3(10).

74.3 In view of the fact that unless a trust corporation[1] is a sole trustee there must be at least two trustees to give a receipt for proceeds of sale arising on the exercise of a trust for sale of English or Welsh land[2], it should be seen that appointment of individuals as new trustees of such trusts always results in there being at least two trustees.

1   See paras 79.5–79.6.
2   See Article 63 above.

ARTICLE 75
VESTING OF TRUST PROPERTY IN NEW TRUSTEES

75.1

(1)   On a change in the trusteeship out of court, the trust property should be vested jointly in the persons who as a result of such change become the trustees[1]. This may be done:
   (a)   by the ordinary modes of transferring property of the type concerned;
   (b)   except in relation to the classes of property set out in section 40(4) of the Trustee Act 1925[2], by a vesting declaration, express or implied by statute, contained in a deed of appointment of a new trustee or in a deed of discharge of a retiring trustee;
   (c)   where neither of the foregoing means is available, by a vesting order made by a competent court[3].
(2)   On the appointment of a new trustee by the court, a vesting order will be made vesting the trust property in the new trustee or trustees, either alone, or jointly with the continuing trustee or trustees, as the case may require.

1   TA 1925, s 37(1)(d).
2   See para 75.4 below.
3   Normally the application will be to the Chancery Division of the High Court, but in certain cases of small trust estates the county court has jurisdiction; TA 1925, s 63A inserted by County Courts Act 1984, Sch 2, para 1.

Paragraph 1(a)

Need to vest trust property in new or continuing trustees

75.2 Trust property is vested in the original trustees of a trust by virtue of the complete constitution of the trust at the outset[1]. When a trustee retires from the trust, or a new trustee is appointed, some means must be found to divest the retiring trustee of, or invest the new trustee with, the trust assets. The mere fact of a valid retirement or appointment having taken place will confer a right on the new or continuing trustee to call for the trust assets to be vested in him[2]. But it does not, in the absence of statutory sanction, go further than that, and the trustee obtains neither equitable[3] nor legal[4] interest in the property merely by virtue of appointment. Thus steps must be taken to achieve it separately.

1   As to which see Article 9.
2   *East Anglia Roman Catholic Diocese Trustee v Milthorn Enginerring Co Ltd* (1983) 18 Tru LI 160.
3   *East Anglia Roman Catholic Diocese Trustee v Milthorn Enginerring Co Ltd* (1983) 18 Tru LI 160.
4   *Bankes v Salisbury Diocesan Council of Education Inc* [1960] Ch 631, [1960] 2 All ER 372.

Paragraph 1(b)

Vesting declarations on appointments out of court

75.3   However, section 40 of the Trustee Act 1925[1] provides a statutory basis for automatic vesting in some cases. The section has two beneficial effects. First, it provides that a vesting declaration in a *deed*[2] of appointment of new trustees will operate to transfer most trust assets (though not registered land, company assets or certain leases) automatically to the new and any continuing trustees. Secondly, if the deed is made after 1925 and does not contain such a vesting declaration, then, subject to any express provision in the deed to the contrary, one is implied into it. Similar effects apply to any deed of retirement and discharge under s 39 of the Act, where of course there are no new trustees, but the retiring trustee needs to be divested.

1   Re-enacting the Trustee Act 1893, s 12, which in its turn re-enacted the Conveyancing Act 1881, s 34.
2   A deed is not generally needed for the appointment, but the benefit of the statute attaches only if one is used.

75.4   Section 40 of the Trustee Act 1925 is in the following terms:

(1)   Where by a deed a new trustee is appointed to perform any trust, then—
    (a)   if the deed contains a declaration by the appointor to the effect that any estate or interest in any land subject to the trust, or in any chattel so subject, or the right to recover or receive any debt or other thing in action so subject, shall vest in the persons who by virtue of the deed become or are the trustees for performing the trust, the deed shall operate, without any conveyance or assignment, to vest in those persons as joint tenants and for the purposes of the trust the estate interest or right to which the declaration relates[1], and
    (b)   if the deed is made after the commencement of this Act and does not contain such a declaration, the deed shall, subject to any express provision to the contrary therein contained, operate as if it had contained such a declaration by the appointor extending to all the estates interests and rights with respect to which a declaration could have been made.
(2)   Where by a deed a retiring trustee is discharged under section 39 of this Act or section 19 of the Trusts of Land and Appointment of Trustees Act 1996[2] without a new trustee being appointed, then—

(a)   if the deed contains such a declaration as aforesaid by the retiring and continuing trustees, and by the other person, if any, empowered to appoint trustees, the deed shall, without any conveyance or assignment, operate to vest in the continuing trustees alone, as joint tenants, and for the purposes the trust, the estate, interest or right to which the declaration relates; and

(b)   if the deed is made after the commencement of this Act and does not contain such a declaration, the deed shall, subject to any express provision to the contrary therein contained, operate as if it had contained such a declaration by such persons as aforesaid extending to all the estates, interests and rights with respect to which a declaration could have been made.

(3)   An express vesting declaration, whether made before or after the commencement of this Act, shall, notwithstanding that the estate, interest, or right to be vested is not expressly referred to, and provided that the other statutory requirements were or are complied with, operate and be deemed always to have operated (but without prejudice to any express provision to the contrary contained in the deed of appointment or discharge) to vest in the persons respectively referred to in subsections (1) and (2) of this section, as the case may require, such estates, interests and rights as are capable of being and ought to be vested in those persons.

(4)   This section does not extend—

(a)   to land conveyed by way of mortgage for securing money subject to the trust, except land conveyed on trust for securing debentures or debenture stock;

(b)   to land held under a lease which contains any covenant, condition or agreement against assignment or disposing of the land without licence or consent, unless, prior to the execution of the deed containing expressly or impliedly the vesting declaration, the requisite licence or consent has been obtained, or unless, by virtue of any statute or rule of law, the vesting declaration, express or implied, would not operate as a breach of covenant or give rise to a forfeiture;

(c)   to any share, stock, annuity or property which is only transferable in books kept by a company or other body, or in manner directed by or under an Act of Parliament.

In this subsection 'lease' includes an underlease and an agreement for a lease or underlease.

(5)   For purposes of registration of the deed in any registry, the person or persons making the declaration expressly or impliedly, shall be deemed the conveying party or parties, and the conveyance shall be deemed to be made by him or them under a power conferred by this Act.

[1]   See also, as to legal estates, s 9(1) of the LPA 1925 so that the estate if not vested is the appointor may vest in the appointees but not so as to obviate the difficulties apparent in *Re King's Will Trusts* [1964] Ch 542.

[2]   Inserted by the TLATA 1996, Sch 3, para 3(14). Note that s 40(1) is unrestricted, so applying to appointments by deed under express powers, while s 40(2) does not cover retirements under express powers or the removal of a trustee under an express power.

75.5 Assets which do not pass by a vesting declaration (set out in sub-s (4)) are of three main kinds. First are mortgages. They are invariably transferred without disclosing the trust, so as to keep it off the face of the mortgagor's title. Second are leases the transfer of which would breach a covenant or work a forfeiture. Thus a lease that does not contain a covenant against assignment or a forfeiture clause is not within this class. Nor is a lease that *does* contain such a covenant or clause, but in respect of which the appropriate licence or consent has already been obtained, or for some other reason the vesting declaration would not cause a breach or a forfeiture.

75.6 The third class is property which is transferable in the books of a company or under statutory procedures. There are two main categories. First, company stocks, shares, etc, are transferred via the CREST system or by transfer form, duly registered with the company. It is not settled whether equitable interests requiring to be transferred by signed writing[1] pass by a vesting declaration. One view is that such a declaration extends only to *legal* debts or other choses in action. On the other hand, if the section is intended to extend to legal choses in action it should be *a fortiori* extend to lesser interests like equitable choses in action. This is the preferable view. Where nominees hold assets on trust for the trustees, as often is the case, it makes sense for the new and continuing trustees to ensure that the nominees' register or electronic records duly acknowledge their entitlement. If no transfer by the retiring trustee is possible then an application to the court[2] is necessary.

[1] See s 53(1)(c) of the Law of Property Act 1925, para 12.14 ff .
[2] Under s 44 of the Trustee Act; see para 75.16.

75.7 The second category in the third class is registered land, transferable under statute. Whereas in unregistered land the vesting declaration *itself* transfers the legal estate to the new or continuing trustees, in registered land this is not enough, and the declaration must first be registered[1]. The vesting declaration is a registrable disposition, which must be submitted to the Land Registry, together with a certificate from the conveyancer or other evidence that the persons making the declaration were entitled to do so[2]. To obviate the need for the Registry to check on the validity of the deed of appointment, it is more convenient for the retiring current registered proprietors to execute a transfer to the new trustees as new proprietors, to be registered in the usual way[3].

[1] Land Registration Act 2002, s 58.
[2] Land Registration Act 2002, s 27(5); Land Registration Rules 2003, r 161(3).
[3] See Land Registration Act 2002, s 27.

Declaration operative only on property vested in trustees as trustees

75.8 In *Re King's Will Trusts*[1] several points on the interpretation of s 40 were considered. In that case a will which imposed certain trusts upon freehold land was proved by two of the persons named as executors and trustees. Later, when the administration was complete and one of the proving executors had died, the surviving executor appointed another person to act jointly with him as trustee of the will. No assent had been executed in respect of the land. The question arose as to whether, by virtue of s 40, the legal estate was currently vested in these two persons as *trustees* of the will. Since the

Deed of Appointment contained no express declaration vesting the land in them, their ownership of the legal estate depended upon the operation of the vesting declaration implied by s 40(1)(b).

¹   [1964] Ch 542, [1964] 1 All ER 833. It has not been followed in Ireland: *Mohan v Roche* [1991] 1 IR 560.

75.9 Two main arguments were put forward to show that the legal estate was vested in the two persons concerned. First, it was said that no written assent was necessary to transfer a legal estate in land from a person in his capacity as executor to the same person in his capacity as trustee; that since administration of the estate had been completed the surviving executor therefore held the legal estate as trustee when he made the Deed of Appointment; and that s 40 therefore operated in the usual, straightforward way.

75.10 This argument was rejected. A written assent was necessary to transfer the legal estate from an executor to a trustee, even when the executor and the trustee were one and the same person¹. Since no written assent had been made, the legal estate was therefore vested in the appointor as *executor* when he made the appointment.

¹   Administration of Estates Act 1925, s 36; see para 40.3.

75.11 Secondly, it was argued that the Deed of Appointment was, under s 40(1)(b), deemed to include a declaration by the appointor which operated to vest in himself and the new trustee 'any estate or interest in any land subject to the trust'; and that since the appointor was in this case also the executor the implied declaration must extend to land which he held in his capacity as executor, so that the Deed of Appointment amounted also to an assent or conveyance by which the surviving executor vested the land in himself and the new trustee as trustees of the will.

75.12 This argument was supported by a reference to s 9(1) of the Law of Property Act 1925 which, so far as material, provides that:

> '... every vesting declaration (express or implied) under any statutory power ... which is made for the purpose of vesting, conveying, or creating a legal estate, shall operate to convey or create the legal estate disposed of in like manner as if the same had been a conveyance executed by the estate owner of the legal estate ...'.

75.13 This was said to make it clear that the Deed of Appointment must be read as containing a conveyance by the surviving executor in that capacity (he being 'the estate owner') to the two persons who were to become the trustees. But this argument was also rejected. The implied vesting declaration operates only upon 'land subject to the trust', and this meant land which was already trust property and could not include land which was still vested in the executor as such.

75.14 *The death, retirement, or removal of trustees*

Paragraphs 1(c) and 2

Vesting orders made by the Chancery Division

75.14 The jurisdiction of the Chancery Division of the High Court to make orders vesting trust property in the trustees for the time being of a settlement is codified in ss 44, 45, 49, 50–56 and 58 of the Trustee Act 1925, which are set out below. For the sake of clarity comments on the sections are relegated to the footnotes.

75.15 The jurisdiction extends to trust property in any part of Her Majesty's dominions except Scotland.[1] The width of this jurisdiction[2] is unlikely to be invoked nowadays[3] when the relevant overseas jurisdiction where the land or other assets are situate would seem more appropriate. But in principle it would cover, for example, Bermuda, BVI, Cayman Islands, the Channel Islands and Gibraltar as British Overseas Territories or Dependencies. As an enactment of the Imperial Parliament, these provisions[4] extend directly as part of the local law. But they would not extend to an independent Commonwealth country of which The Queen was merely head of state (eg The Bahamas) because it is no longer a dominion of the Crown in right of the United Kingdom.

1 TA 1925, s 56. As to procedure where there are both English and Scottish assets, see *Practice Direction* [1945] WN 80, and *Practice Direction* [1987] 1 WLR 93 at 101.
2 See *Halsbury's Laws of England* (4th edn) Vol 6, para 803.
3 For instances of the use of the predecessor jurisdiction under the Trustee Act 1850 in relation to land abroad, see *Re Groom's Trusts* (1864) 11 LT 336 (Canada), and *Re Taitt's Trusts* [1870] WN 257 (Ireland).
4 Section 56 being express on the face of Trustee Act 1925, s 71(3)(which otherwise confines the operation of the Act to England and Wales).

Vesting orders of land

75.16 44.—In any of the following cases, namely—

  (i) Where the court appoints or has appointed a trustee or where a trustee has been appointed out of court under any statutory or express power;

  (ii) Where a trustee entitled to or possessed of any land[1] or interest therein, whether by way of mortgage or otherwise, or entitled to a contingent right therein, either solely or jointly with any other person—
    (a) is under disability[2], or
    (b) is out of the jurisdiction of the High Court[3]; or
    (c) cannot be found, or, being a corporation, has been dissolved[4];

  (iii) Where it is uncertain who was the survivor of two or more trustees jointly entitled to or possessed of any interest in land[5];

  (iv) Where it is uncertain whether the last trustee known to have been entitled to or possessed of any interest in land is living or dead[6];

  (v) Where there is no personal representative of a deceased trustee who was entitled to or possessed of any interest in land, or where it is uncertain who is the personal representative of a deceased trustee who was entitled to or possessed of any interest in land[7];

  (vi) Where a trustee jointly or solely entitled to or possessed of any interest in land, or entitled to a contingent right therein, has been required, by or on behalf of a person entitled to require a conveyance of the land or interest or a release of the right, to convey the land or interest or to release the right, and has wilfully refused or neglected to convey[8] the land or interest or release the right for twenty-eight days after the date of the requirement;

(vii) Where land or any interest therein is vested in a trustee whether by way of mortgage or otherwise, and it appears to the court to be expedient;

the court may make an order (in this Act called a vesting order) vesting the land or interest therein in any such person in any such manner and for any such estate or interest as the court may direct, or releasing or disposing of the contingent right to such person as the court may direct:

Provided that—

(a) Where the order is consequential on the appointment of a trustee the land or interest therein shall be vested for such estate as the court may direct in the persons who on the appointment are trustees; and

(b) Where the order relates to a trustee entitled or formerly entitled jointly with another person, and such trustee is under disability or out of the jurisdiction of the High Court or cannot be found, or being a corporation has been dissolved, the land interest or right shall be vested in such other person who remains entitled, either alone or with any other person the court may appoint[9].

[1] This includes leaseholds; see definition of 'land', TA 1925, s 68. Since 1997 it also includes and undivided share in land: TLATA 1886, s 25(2) and Sch 4.

[2] This includes mental illness: see s 54.

[3] A mere temporary absence (eg that a sailor) is not sufficient: *Hutchinson v Stephens* (1834) 5 Sim 498.

[4] This is intended to put an end to such question as arose in *Re Nos 56 and 58 Albert Road, Norwood* [1916] 1 Ch 289; and *Re Queenstown Dry Docks Shipbuilding and Engineering Co* [1918] 1 IR 356.

[5] Cf s 55.

[6] Cf s 55.

[7] Cf s 55, and see *Re William's Trusts* (1887) 36 Ch D 231; *Re Rackstraw's Trusts* (1885) 52 LT 612; and *Re Pilling's Trusts* (1884) 26 Ch D 432.

[8] A trustee's conduct in not conveying cannot be considered wilful, if the title of the applicant to call for a conveyance is subject to a dispute which leads the trustee to entertain a bona fide doubt as to his title (*Re Mills' Trusts* (1888) 40 Ch D 14). But if he has acted unreasonably he may have to pay the costs (*Re Knox's Trust* [1895] 1 Ch 538; affd [1895] 2 Ch 483, CA). The summons must not even be issued until the twenty-eight days have elapsed (*Re Knox's Trust*, above). The Law Reform Committee 23rd Report (Cmnd 8733) para 5.8 recommends removal of 'wilfully' from s 44(vi) in line with s 51(1)(ii). Where one or more beneficiaries are absolutely beneficially entitled to the land so as having rights to replace the trustees under s 19 of the TLATA 1996 it seems the court will vest the land directly in such person or persons preferring the approach in *Re Godfrey's Trusts* (1883) 23 Ch D 205 to that in *Re Holland* (1881) 16 Ch D 672 and *Re Currie* (1878) 10 Ch D 93. Saving expense and circuity of action fits in with the philosophy reflected in the Civil Procedure Rules.

[9] *Re Watson* (1881) 19 Ch D 384 (vesting order made in remaining trustees to facilitate immediate distribution to beneficiaries); *Re Harrison's Settlement Trusts* [1965] 1 WLR 1492 (court has jurisdiction to make vesting order in favour of remaining trustees even though trustee concerned not yet discharged).

Orders as to contingent rights of unborn persons

75.17 45.—Where any interest in land is subject to a contingent right in an unborn person or class of unborn persons[1] who, on coming into existence would, in respect thereof, become entitled to or possessed of that interest on any trust, the court may make an order releasing the land or interest therein from the contingent right, or may make an order vesting in any person the estate or interest to or of which the unborn person or class of unborn persons would, on coming into existence, be entitled or possessed in the land.

1   See *Basnett v Moxon* (1875) LR 20 Eq 182.

Effect of vesting order

75.18 49.—A vesting order under any of the foregoing provisions shall in the case of a vesting order consequential on the appointment of a trustee, have the same effect

    (a)   as if the persons who before the appointment were the trustees, if any, had duly executed all proper conveyances of the land for such estate or interest as the court directs; or

    (b)   if there is no such person, or no such person of full capacity, as if such person had existed and been of full capacity and had duly executed all proper conveyances of the land for such estate or interest as the court directs;

and shall in every other case have the same effect as if the trustee or other person or description or class of persons to whose rights or supposed rights the said provisions respectively relate had been an ascertained and existing person of full capacity, and had executed a conveyance or release to the effect intended by the order.

Power to appoint person to convey

75.19 50.—In all cases where a vesting order can be made under any of the foregoing provisions, the court may, if it is more convenient[1], appoint a person to convey the land or any interest therein or release the contingent right, and a conveyance or release by that person in conformity with the order shall have the same effect as an order under the appropriate provision.

1   On the question of convenience, compare *Hancox v Spittle* (1857) 3 Sm & G 478 (numerous parties under disability: person appointed to convey) and *Shepherd v Churchill* (1857) 25 Beav 21 (vesting order made to avoid expense). See also *Hipkin v Hipkin* [1962] 1 WLR 491 (sale out of court to as yet unknown purchaser: person appointed to convey).

Vesting orders as to stock and things in action

75.20 51.—(1) In any of the following cases, namely:—

    (i)   Where the court appoints or has appointed a trustee, or where a trustee has been appointed out of court under any statutory or express power,

    (ii)   Where a trustee entitled, whether by way of mortgage or otherwise, alone or jointly with another person to stock[1] or to a thing in action[2]—

    (a)   is under disability[3], or

    (b)   is out of the jurisdiction of the High Court[4]; or

(c)   cannot be found, or, being a corporation, has been dissolved[5]; or

(d)   neglects or refuses to transfer stock or receive the dividends or income thereof, or to sue for or recover a thing in action, according to the direction of the person absolutely entitled[6] thereto for twenty-eight days next after a request in writing has been made to him by the person so entitled[7]; or

(e)   neglects or refuses to transfer stock or receive the dividends or income thereof, or to sue for or recover a thing in action for twenty-eight days next after an order of the court for that purpose has been served on him;

        (iii)   Where it is uncertain whether a trustee entitled alone or jointly with another person to stock or to a thing in action is alive or dead;

        (iv)   Where stock is standing in the name of a deceased person whose personal representative is under disability;

        (v)   Where stock or a thing in action is vested in a trustee[8] whether by way of mortgage or otherwise and it appears to the court to be expedient;

the court may make an order vesting the right to transfer or call for a transfer of stock, or to receive the dividends or income thereof, or to sue for or recover the thing in action, in any such person[9] as the court may appoint[10]:

Provided that—

        (a)   Where the order is consequential on the appointment of a trustee, the right shall be vested in the persons who, on the appointment, are the trustees; and

        (b)   Where the person whose right is dealt with by the order was entitled jointly with another person, the right shall be vested in the last-mentioned person either alone or jointly with any other person whom the court may appoint.

(2)   In all cases where a vesting order can be made under this section, the court may, if it is more convenient, appoint some proper person to make or join in making the transfer:

Provided that the person appointed to make or join in making a transfer of stock shall be some proper officer of the bank, or the company or society whose stock is to be transferred[11].

(3)   The person in whom the right to transfer or call for the transfer of any stock is vested by an order of the court under this Act, may transfer the stock to himself or any other person, according to the order, and the Bank of England and all other companies shall obey every order under this section according to its tenor.

(4)   After notice in writing of an order under this section it shall not be lawful for the Bank of England or any other company to transfer any stock to which the order relates or to pay any dividends thereon except in accordance with the order.

(5)   The court may make declarations and give directions concerning the manner in which the right to transfer any stock or thing in action vested under the provisions of this Act is to be exercised[12].

(6)   The provisions of this Act as to vesting orders shall apply to shares in ships registered under the Acts relating to merchant shipping as if they were stock.

[1]   As to meaning of stock, see s 68(14).
[2]   *Re Defense Supplies Corpn's Application* (1948) 65 RPC 172 (patent application).
[3]   *Re Dehaynin (Infants)* [1910] 1 Ch 223.
[4]   *Re Trubee's Trusts* [1892] 3 Ch 55.

5   *Re General Accident Assurance Corpn* [1904] 1 Ch 147; cf *Re Straithblaine Estates Ltd* [1948] Ch 228.
6   *Re Ellis's Settlement* (1857) 24 Beav 426; *Re Cane's Trusts* [1895] 1 IR 172 (new trustees held absolutely entitled).
7   *Re Knox's Trusts* [1895] 2 Ch 483; *Re Struve's Trust* (1912) 56 Sol Jo 551.
8   Where stock is vested in the Public Trustee by virtue of the Administration of Estates Act 1925, s 9 as amended by Law of Property (Miscellaneous Provisions) Act 1994, s 14 he seems not a trustee within the meaning of this para because such vesting 'does not impose on him any duty, obligation or liability in respect of the property' so that a grant of representation will need to be taken out: *Re Deans* [1954] 1 All ER 496.
9   Nowadays to save expense and circuitry of action, if there is a beneficiary who is absolutely entitled, it is believed that the court will normally vest the property directly in such beneficiary rather than in trustees for him as was the old practice (*Re Holland* (1881) 16 Ch D 672, CA): and see *Orwin v A-G* [1998] 2 BCLC 693, CA.
10 In *Re Harrison's Settlement Trusts* [1965] 3 All ER 795, [1965] 1 WLR 1492, Cross J considered the situation where one of the trustees has become disabled through mental illness and the court is asked to vest the trust property in the other trustees alone (under ss 44 and 51 of the TA 1925, above), without removing the disabled trustee from the trusteeship. He said that the court would very seldom take this course if the trust was a continuing one, because it was preferable to replace the disabled trustee entirely. Accordingly, following *Re Nash* (1881) 16 Ch D 503, he refused to accede to the application in the present case, which did involve a continuing trust. He referred to the cases of *Re Watson* (1881) 19 Ch D 384, and *Re Martyn* (1884) 26 Ch D 745, in which the court had acceded to such an application, but pointed out that in these cases the trusts were not continuing, the trust property being in fact due for distribution, so that the situation was different and the decisions in those cases were justified for that reason. He considered that the two reported cases in which the court had acceded to such an application in the case of a continuing trust, *Re Leon* [1892] 1 Ch 348, and *Re Lees' Settlement Trusts* [1896] 2 Ch 508, must be treated as exceptional and pointed out that the applications in those cases were unopposed.
11 *Re Price's Settlement* [1883] WN 202.
12 *Re Gregson* [1893] 3 Ch 233, CA; see also *Re CMG* [1898] 2 Ch 324, CA.

Vesting orders of charity property

75.21 52.—The powers conferred by this Act as to vesting orders may be exercised for vesting any interest in land, stock, or thing in action in any trustee of a charity or society over which the court would have jurisdiction upon action duly instituted, whether the appointment of the trustee was made by instrument under a power or by the court under its general or statutory jurisdiction.

Vesting orders in relation to infant's beneficial interests

75.22 53.—Where an infant is beneficially entitled to any property the court may, with a view to the application of the capital or income thereof for the maintenance, education, or benefit[1] of the infant, make an order—

(a)   appointing a person to convey such property[2]; or
(b)   in the case of stock, or a thing in action, vesting in any person the right to transfer or call for a transfer of such stock or to receive the dividends or income thereof, or to sue for and recover such thing in action, upon such terms as the court may think fit.

1   These words are of the widest import (*Re Heyworth's Contingent Reversionary Interest* [1956] Ch 364, [1956] 2 All ER 21). They cover not merely expenditure but capital investment such as the purchase of a house to live in or a share in a partnership or even, in

some cases, placing of money on deposit for an infant (*Re Baron Vestey's Settlement* [1951] Ch 209, [1950] 2 All ER 891, CA). However, to bring the jurisdiction into play there must be 'a view to the application' of the capital or income for the maintenance, education or benefit of the infant. In *Re Heyworth's Contingent Reversionary Interest*, above, what was proposed was the sale of an infant's contingent reversionary interest to the life tenant for cash, thus putting an end to the settlement. There was no suggestion that the transaction was necessary to enable the infant to be maintained till attaining full age and Upjohn J held that he had no jurisdiction under the section to sanction it. This case was distinguished in *Re Meux* ([1958] Ch 154, [1957] 2 All ER 630), where it was proposed to convey the entailed interest of an infant tenant in tail to his father the tenant for life and protector of the settlement for a proper price to be paid to trustees and settle it on virtually the same trusts as those under which the entailed interest arose except that the father would have no beneficial interest and the infant would have a contingent, as opposed to a vested interest. It was held that the settlement of the proceeds of sale, which on the authority of *Re Ropner's Settlement Trusts* [1956] 3 All ER 332n, [1956] 1 WLR 902, was an 'application', was an absolutely essential part of the transaction looked at as a whole, for no court would consider it fair merely to bar the entail and sell the property without making provision for interests subsequent to that of the infant. That led Wynn Parry J to the conclusion that he was dealing with one single transaction which was overwhelmingly in favour of the infant and that he had jurisdiction to approve it. For further cases in which the court appointed a person under s 53 to execute a disentailing deed, see *Re Bristol's Settled Estates* [1964] 3 All ER 939, [1965] 1 WLR 569, and *Re Lansdowne's Will Trusts* [1967] Ch 603, [1967] 1 All ER 888 (in which *Re Meux*, above, was applied).

2   See *Re Gower's Settlement* [1934] Ch 365, where the court authorised a mortgage of an infant's estate tail in remainder.

Jurisdiction of the High Court in regard to mental patients

75.23 54.—(1) Subject to subsection (2), the Court of Protection may not make an order, or give a direction or authority, in relation to a person who lacks capacity to exercise his functions as trustee, if the High Court may make an order to that effect under this Act.

(2)   Where a person lacks capacity to exercise his functions as a trustee and a deputy is appointed for him by the Court of Protection or an application for the appointment of a deputy has been made but not determined, then, except as respects a trust which is subject to an order for administration made by the High Court, the Court of Protection shall have concurrent jurisdiction with the High Court in relation to—

(a)   mortgaged property of which the person concerned has become a trustee merely by reason of the mortgage having been paid off;

(b)   matters consequent on the making of provision by the Court of Protection for the exercise of a power of appointing trustees or retiring from a trust;

(c)   matters consequent on the making of a provision by the Court of Protection for the carrying out of any contract entered into by the person concerned;

(d)   property to some interest in which the person concerned is beneficially entitled but which, or some interest in which, is held by the person concerned under an express, implied or constructive trust.

(2A)   Rules may be made in accordance with Part 1 of Schedule 1 to the Constitutional Reform Act 2005 with respect to the exercise of the jurisdiction referred to in subsection (2).

Orders made upon certain allegations to be conclusive evidence

75.24 55.—Where a vesting order is made as to any land under this Act or under sections 15 to 20 of the Mental Capacity Act 2005 or any corresponding provisions having effect in Northern Ireland, founded on an allegation of any of the following matters namely—

(a)   the personal incapacity of a trustee or mortgagee; or

(b)   that a trustee or mortgagee or the personal representative of or other person deriving title under a trustee or mortgagee is out of the jurisdiction of the High Court or cannot be found, or being a corporation has been dissolved; or

(c)   that it is uncertain which of two or more trustees, or which of two or more persons interested in a mortgage, was the survivor; or

(d)   that it is uncertain whether the last trustee or the personal representative of or other person deriving title under a trustee or mortgagee, or the last surviving person interested in a mortgage is living or dead; or

(e)   that any trustee or mortgagee has died intestate without leaving a person beneficially interested under the intestacy or has died and it is not known who is his personal representative or the person interested;

the fact that the order has been so made shall be conclusive evidence of the matter so alleged in any court upon any question as to the validity of the order; but this section does not prevent the court from directing a reconveyance or surrender or the payment of costs occasioned by any such order if improperly obtained.

Application of vesting order to property out of England

75.25 56.—The powers of the court to make vesting orders under this Act shall extend to all property in any part of His Majesty's dominions except Scotland[1].

[1]   Where there are investments or property situate in Scotland the court will give leave to the trustees to make application to the appropriate court in Scotland for a vesting order: See *Practice Direction* [1945] WN 80 and [1987] 1 All ER 884.

Persons entitled to apply for orders

75.26 58.—(1) An order under this Act for the appointment of a new trustee or concerning any interest in land, stock, or thing in action subject to a trust, may be made on the application of any person beneficially interested[1] in the land, stock, or thing in action, whether under disability or not, or on the application of any person duly appointed trustee thereof.

(2)   An order under this Act concerning any interest in land, stock or thing in action subject to a mortgage may be made on the application of any person beneficially interested in the equity of redemption, whether under disability or not, or of any person interested in the money secured by the mortgage[2].

[1]   This includes a person contingently interested (*Re Sheppard's Trusts* (1862) 4 De GF & J 423), and also a purchaser of trust property (*Ayles v Cox, ex p Attwood* (1853) 17 Beav 584).

2   Where the trust funds are invested in unauthorised stocks, the order will give the new trustees, *or purchasers from them*, the right to call for a transfer etc (*Re Peacock* (1880) 14 Ch D 212).

Chapter 17

APPOINTMENT OF A JUDICIAL TRUSTEE

ARTICLE 76
STATUTORY POWER OF THE COURT TO APPOINT A
JUDICIAL TRUSTEE

76.1

(1) Where application is made to the court[1] by or on behalf of the person creating or intending to create a trust[2], or by or on behalf of a trustee or beneficiary, the court may in its discretion appoint a person (called a judicial trustee) to be a trustee for that trust, either jointly with any other person, or as sole trustee, and, if sufficient cause is shown, in place of all or any existing trustees[3]. An injunction may be granted to preserve the position until the hearing of the summons for the appointment of a judicial trustee. Where the application relates to the estate of a deceased person the court may if it thinks fit proceed as if the application were, or included, an application under section 50 of the Administration of Justice Act 1985 conferring power to appoint a substitute for, or to remove, a personal representative.

(2) Any fit and proper person nominated in the application may be appointed, including, a beneficiary, or the husband, wife, or relation of a beneficiary, or a solicitor to any of such parties or to the trust[4], or a person who is already a trustee[5]. In the absence of such nomination, or if the court disapproves it[6], the official solicitor of the court, or some other person approved by the judge, may be appointed[7]. An unofficial judicial trustee must give security by way of guarantee unless the court otherwise directs[8].

(3) Remuneration may be assigned by the court to the judicial trustee[9].

(4) The evidence in support of an application must include an affidavit containing the following particulars so far as obtainable:

(a) a short description of the trust instrument;

(b) short particulars of the trust property with an approximate estimate of its income, and capital value;

(c) short particulars of any incumbrances affecting the property;

(d) particulars as to persons possessing trust documents;

(e) names and addresses of beneficiaries and short particulars of their interests;

(f) name, address and description of the proposed judicial trustee together with remuneration proposals[10].

(5) Once in every year the accounts of a judicial trustee have to be audited by an officer of the court, or a professional accountant appointed by the court or, in the case of a corporate judicial trustee, submitted to such persons as the court may direct, whereupon only if such person or a beneficiary objects will accounts have to be lodged with the court for examination by or on behalf of the court[11].

(6) The accounts, with a note of any corrections made on the audit, must be filed as the court directs, and the judicial trustee must send a copy of the accounts, or if the court thinks fit, a summary of the accounts to such beneficiaries or other persons as the court thinks proper[12].

(7) Where a judicial trustee has failed to comply with the 1896 Act or the 1983 Rules or any direction of the court or has otherwise misconducted himself in relation to the trust the court may subsequently disallow any remuneration; if he failed to pay any sum into the trust account within a reasonable period of time the court may charge him with interest currently payable in respect of judgment debts[13].

(8) The court may direct an inquiry into the administration of the trust by the judicial trustee[14], and may, either with or without any request, give any special or general directions in regard to the trust or its administration[15].

(9) In all cases a judicial trustee is to be subject to the control and supervision of the court as an officer thereof[16], and may at any time request the court to give him directions[17].

(10) Where a judicial trustee fails to submit his account or do any other thing which he is required to do he may be required to attend in chambers to show cause for the failure and the court may give such directions as it thinks proper including directions for the discharge of the trustee and the appointment of another and the payment of costs[18].

(11) The appointment of an official of the court as a judicial trustee is an ex officio appointment so that no further order or appointment is necessary by reason only of the person appointed dying or ceasing to hold office: any property vested in such person on

his dying or ceasing to hold office vests in the person appointed
to succeed him without any conveyance assignment or transfer[19].

(12) An official of the court cannot be appointed as judicial trustee;

    (a) for any persons in their capacity as members or debenture
holders of, or being in any other relation to, any corporation or unincorporated body; or

    (b) of a trust which involves the carrying on of any trade or
business unless the court, with or without special conditions, specifically directs[20].

---

1   The High Court or any county court judge to whom jurisdiction may be assigned under the
Act by rules made thereunder (Judicial Trustees Act 1896, s 2). The appointment may be
made by a master or district judge of the High Court: CPR, r 2.4, Practice Direction B to
Part 2, para 5.

2   The administration of the estate of a deceased testator or intestate is a trust, and his
personal representative a trustee for the purposes of the Act (Judicial Trustees Act 1896,
s 1(2)). The Act, however, contains no complete definition of the word 'trust', which must
therefore be given its ordinary meaning, with the result that Settled Land Act trustees are
trustees of a trust for the purposes of the Act. See *Re Marshall's Will Trusts* [1945] Ch 217,
[1945] 1 All ER 550.

3   Judicial Trustees Act 1896, s 1(1); Judicial Trustee Rules 1983, r 3. For an instance of
appointment of two banks, each as sole judicial trustee of part of the trust estate, see *Re
Cohen* [1918] WN 252. But this case related to trusteeship and was distinguished in *Re
Wells* [1967] 3 All ER 908, [1968] 1 WLR 44, which was concerned with executorship: it
was held that the court had no power to appoint a judicial trustee to deal with part only of
an estate since the executorship was indivisible and the administration of this part of the
estate was not a separate trust; and in the circumstances it would not be right to appoint a
judicial trustee of the whole estate.

4   Recognised originally by Judicial Trustee Rules 1897, r 5(1) which Rules were revoked and
replaced by Judicial Trustee Rules (SI 1972/1096) which were revoked and replaced by
Judicial Trustee Rules 1983 (SI 1983/370).

5   Recognised originally by Judicial Trustee Rules 1897, r 5(1) which Rules were revoked and
replaced by Judicial Trustee Rules (SI 1972/1096) which were revoked and replaced by
Judicial Trustee Rules 1983 (SI 1983/370).

6   Judicial Trustees Act 1896, s 1(3).

7   *Douglas v Bolam* [1900] 2 Ch 749; *Marcus v Marcus* [1997] EWCA Civ 796; *Davies v
Sweeney*, (14 April 1999, unreported) CA.

8   Judicial Trustees Act 1896, s 4(1), and Judicial Trustee Rules 1983, r 6.

9   Judicial Trustees Act 1896, s 1(5).

10   Judicial Trustee Rules, r 3.

11   Judicial Trustees Act 1896, s 1(6), and Judicial Trustee Rules, rr 9, 12, 13. See *Marcus v
Marcus* [1997] EWCA Civ 796.

12   Judicial Trustee Rules, rr 12, 13. The beneficiaries should be sent copies of any corrections
or comments made on the audit in order that they may be in a position to take such
proceedings as they may be advised in respect of any matters which are open to question.
See *Re Ridsdel* [1947] Ch 597, [1947] 2 All ER 312, and *Marcus v Marcus* [1997] EWCA
Civ 796.

13   Judicial Trustee Rules, r 14.

14   Judicial Trustees Act 1896, s 1(6).

15   Judicial Trustees Act 1896, s 1(4).

16   Judicial Trustees Act 1896, s 1(3).

17   Judicial Trustee Rules, r 8. This may be done quite informally by a simple letter addressed
to the officer of the court. This right to apply for directions does not exclude the ordinary
power of a trustee to compromise claims under the Trustee Act 1925, s 15(f). See *Re
Ridsdel* [1947] Ch 597, [1947] 2 All ER 312.

18   Judicial Trustee Rules, r 14.

19   Judicial Trustee Rules, r 16.

20   Judicial Trustee Rules, r 15.

76.2 *Appointment of a judicial trustee*

Purpose of the Act

76.2 The object of the Judicial Trustees Act 1896 was to provide a middle course in cases where the administration of the estate by the ordinary trustees had broken down and it was not desired to put the estate to the expense of a full administration[1]. A high degree of protection for the property is secured—

(1)   by the appointment of an official, or
(2)   in the alternative, of a person who gives security for his honesty, and
(3)   by having his accounts audited once a year, and
(4)   generally requiring him to act in concert with the court and under conditions which enable the court to supervise his transactions.

[1]   *Re Ridsdel* [1947] Ch 597, [1947] 2 All ER 312.

76.3 Having regard to the fact that judicial trustees are almost always appointed in chambers, it is difficult to judge as to the extent to which this Act has been utilised, but it is believed not to have found great favour. There have, however, been cases where the appointment of a judicial trustee has been of the greatest benefit to the beneficiaries; in one unreported case, which came to the knowledge of the late Sir Arthur Underhill, such an appointment was the means of extricating a fund and its beneficiaries from a morass of cost and complexity such that, but for the appointment of a judicial trustee, the parties would have felt constrained, having regard to their limited means, to abandon their attempt to secure the fund. For similar reasons it may be helpful and cost-efficient for members of a pension scheme trust to have a judicial trustee appointed to help unscramble the muddled affairs of the trust[1]. Again, in the well-known and complicated *Diplock* litigation[2] the appointment of a judicial trustee was clearly an advantage as was recognised by the fact that he was allowed a separate set of costs in the actions by the next of kin to recover moneys paid away by the executors under an invalid residuary bequest. In a more recent case a judicial trustee was appointed to replace a trustee who had an acute conflict of interest, had failed to provide information to the beneficiaries, was dishonest, and was evading service on him.[3]

[1]   *McDonald v Horn* (1993) Times, 12 October, Vinelott J (on appeal see [1995] 1 All ER 961, CA).
[2]   *Chichester Diocesan Fund and Board of Finance Inc v Simpson* [1944] AC 341, [1944] 2 All ER 60, HL; *Re Diplock* [1948] Ch 465, [1948] 2 All ER 318, CA; affd sub nom *Ministry of Health v Simpson* [1951] AC 251, [1950] 2 All ER 1137, HL. Also see *Bowen-Jones v Bowen-Jones* [1986] 3 All ER 163 where both sides agreed to the court appointing a chartered accountant to be judicial trustee to resolve the accounts and distribute property between the absolutely entitled beneficiaries.
[3]   *Davies v Sweeney*, (14 April 1999, unreported) CA.

76.4 When there was no machinery for the retirement of a personal representative the machinery for the appointment of a judicial trustee in his place could be invoked, but a replacement can now more conveniently be achieved by appointment of a replacement under s 50 of the Administration of Justice Act 1985[1]. In an application under the Judicial Trustees Act 1896 the court may now proceed as if the application were under the 1985 Act and vice versa[2].

¹ See eg *Green v Gaul* [2006] EWCA Civ 1124.
² Administration of Justice Act 1985, s 50(4), Judicial Trustees Act 1896, s 1(7) added by the 1985 Act.

Discretion of the court

76.5 The power of the court to appoint a judicial trustee is purely discretionary, and will not be exercised where no charge of improper conduct is made against an existing trustee who opposes the application, even where he or she is a sole trustee[1]; nor where the donee of the power of appointing trustees has appointed persons able and willing to act[2]; nor will the court as a rule appoint a judicial trustee to act with a private one[3].

¹ *Re Ratcliff* [1898] 2 Ch 352 (an ordinary trustee was appointed instead, nominated by the sole executrix).
² *Re Chisholm* (1898) 43 Sol Jo 43.
³ See also *Re Martin* [1900] WN 129.

Rules

76.6 In compliance with s 4 of the Act, a code of thirty-five rules was made in 1897, but the position is now governed by the Judicial Trustee Rules 1983. Remuneration has to be authorised by the court under rule 11.The draft order for the appointment of a judicial trustee should normally provide for the remuneration to be in such amount as may be approved by the court upon application for payment on examination of the accounts; for application for payment to be by letter (copied to the beneficiaries) setting out the basis for the claim, the scales or rates of any professional charges, the work done and time spent, any information concerning the complexity of the trusteeship and any other matters the judicial trustee invites the court to take into account, with the judicial trustee certifying that he considers the claim reasonable and proportionate[1]. The court may require further information and can refer the mater to a costs judge. Remuneration any year of account cannot exceed 15% of the capital value of the property, which must be certified in the accounts.

¹ Practice Direction, Chancery Division, Judicial Trustees: Remuneration [2003] 3 All ER 974 [2003] 1 WLR 1653.

Chapter 18

THE PUBLIC TRUSTEE

ARTICLE 77
THE NATURE AND FUNCTIONS OF THE PUBLIC TRUSTEE, AND
THE GUARANTEE OF THE STATE TO BE ANSWERABLE FOR HIS
BREACHES OF TRUST

77.1

(1)   The Public Trustee is a corporation sole established by statute[1]. He is a salaried official, prohibited from acting for personal reward[2] and empowered to act where appointed[3]:
    (a)   as an ordinary trustee either alone or jointly with others[4];
    (b)   as a mere 'custodian trustee', or treasurer, the administration being confided to ordinary trustees called 'managing trustees';
    (c)   as a judicial trustee[5]; and
    (d)   in certain other capacities not falling within the law of private trusts[6].
(2)   The Public Trustee is, on the other hand, forbidden to accept:
    (a)   any trust exclusively for religious or charitable purposes[7];
    (b)   any trust made solely by way of security for money[8];
    (c)   any trust for the benefit of creditors[9];
    (d)   any trust involving the management or carrying on of a business[10]; save only—

975

        (i)   where he is merely custodian trustee without power of management, and either holds no property which exposes him to risk, or the circumstances are exceptional, and he is fully indemnified; or

        (ii)   where, being an ordinary trustee, the circumstances are exceptional, and he either obtains the consent of the Treasury, or accepts the trusteeship for a time not exceeding 18 months with a view only to winding up the business, and is satisfied that it can be carried on without risk or loss.

(3)   The Public Trustee is only offered by the State as an alternative to ordinary private persons, and therefore can only act where appointed as mentioned in Article 78, below. Moreover, he may decline to act, or may prescribe conditions on which alone he will accept the appointment; save only that he is forbidden to decline merely on the ground that the estate is of small value[11].

(4)   The Public Trustee has the same powers, duties, and liabilities, and is entitled to the same rights and immunities and is subject to the same control and jurisdiction of the court, as a private person acting in the same capacity[12].

(5)   For the services of the Public Trustee and the State guarantee, the State charges an acceptance fee, an administration fee and a withdrawal fee in respect of all trusts together with additional fees for special services[13].

(6)   Where a person dies intestate his estate vest in the Public Trustee until the grant of administration to such estate as also is the position where a testator dies and at the time of his death there is no executor with power to obtain probate of the will or at any time before probate of the will is granted there ceases to be any executor with power to obtain probate: the vesting of the estate in the Public Trustee does not confer on him any beneficial interest in, or impose on him any duty, obligation or liability in respect of, the property[14].

---

1   Public Trustee Act 1906. The statute only applies to English trusts, and the Public Trustee has no power to accept the trusts of a foreign instrument, eg a Scottish trust disposition and settlement (*Re Hewitt's Settlement* [1915] 1 Ch 228; but cf *Re Ardagh's Estate* [1914] 1 IR 5). One appointee is both Public Trustee and Official Solicitor to the Supreme Court.

2   Public Trustee Act 1906, s 11(1).

3   Public Trustee Act 1906, s 2(1).

4   Public Trustee Act 1906, s 5(1).

5   As to judicial trustees, see Article 76, above.

6   Such as the office of executor or administrator, the administration of small estates under £1,000 (which means estates of deceased persons not trust estates) (*Re Devereux* [1911] 2 Ch 545).

7   Public Trustee Act 1906, s 2(5). This includes trusts under which the trustee has to select charitable objects (*Re Hampton* (1918) 88 LJ Ch 103).

8   Public Trustee Rules 1912, r 6.

9   Public Trustee Act 1906, s 2(4).

10   Public Trustee Act 1906, s 2(4).

11   Public Trustee Act 1906, s 2(3).

12   Public Trustee Act 1906, s 2(2).

13 Public Trustee Act 1906, s 9; Public Trustee (Fees) Act 1957; and Public Trustee (Fees) Orders 1999, SI 1999/855.
14 Administration of Estate, Act 1925, s 9 as substituted by Law of Property (Miscellaneous Provisions) Act 1994, s 14.

Paragraph 1

Establishment of a Public Trustee

77.2 The Public Trustee Act 1906 was passed not only with the object of meeting the increasing difficulty of finding suitable persons to act as trustees, but also to safeguard beneficiaries against those fraudulent misappropriations by trustees which had previously been unpleasantly frequent. The Act also contains provisions for the appointment of what are in the Act called custodian trustees (as distinguished from those trustees who actively manage the trust), and for the auditing of trust accounts. The Act further provides for the administration of small estates not exceeding £1,000 in value by the Public Trustee in place of the court, and enables the Public Trustee to accept the offices of executor or administrator. As, however, those are matters outside the law of trusts, it is proposed in this work to confine the consideration of the Act to matters affecting the appointment of the Public Trustee (and certain corporate bodies) to trusteeships, custodian and ordinary. The provisions relating to the auditing of ordinary trust accounts by the Public Trustee will be considered later on in Article 86, below.

Paragraph 2

Trusts the Public Trustee may not accept

77.3 It is considered that the exception of trusts *exclusively* for religious or charitable purposes does not include the trusts of a will some of which are private and others charitable; e g where residue is given to the testator's widow for life, and after her death to divers charities[1].

1   The Public Trustee accepted the trusts of the will of George Bernard Shaw containing gifts in aid of the reform of the alphabet, which were, however, held by Harman J not to be charitable; *Re Shaw* [1957] 1 All ER 745, [1957] 1 WLR 729; compromised on appeal [1958] 1 All ER 245n.

77.4 The exception of trusts by way of security for money rules out trust deeds for securing debentures or debenture stock, and those rare mortgages which are drafted in the form of trusts. Deeds of arrangement for the benefit of creditors do not, it is conceived, include those trust deeds which are made for the convenience of the debtor rather than for the benefit of the creditors, which have been discussed at para 8.252 ff.

77.5 The exception of trusts which involve the management of a business was obviously necessary, as no public official could be expected to carry on commercial undertakings.

Paragraph 3

Not compulsory

77.6   The Public Trustee is merely offered as a convenience and safeguard to those who care to avail themselves of his services, and not to all of those, as he is given a discretion as to whether or not he will accept a trust, the only restriction being that he must not refuse solely on the ground that the property is small. No appointment of the Public Trustee as a trustee should be made without his formal consent to act[1], which is usually incorporated in the deed of appointment. A testamentary appointment will only become effective if and when the formal consent is given[2].

1   Public Trustee Rules 1912, r 8, though a subsequent formal consent will be effective if given: *Re Shaw* [1914] WN 141.
2   Public Trustee Rules 1912, r 8.

Paragraph 4

Liability: State guarantee

77.7   The Public Trustee is in exactly the same position as a private trustee with regard to the beneficiaries[1]. Formerly there was provision that the State guaranteed that it would make good *any losses which an ordinary trustee would be liable to make good*, taking into account the terms of the trust instrument as in the case of a private trustee. At one time there seems to have been an impression among the general public that the State not only gave this guarantee, but went further, and guaranteed the beneficiaries against all loss, whether arising from breach of trust or depreciation of securities. Needless to say that was a popular error. The State guarantee itself has been abolished[2].

1   Public Trustee Act 1906, s 2(2).
2   Public Trustee (Liability and Fees) Act 2002, s 1(1).

Paragraph 5

Fees payable to the Public Trustee

77.8   The Lord Chancellor has power to fix fees chargeable in respect of the duties of the Public Trustee[1]. The power is exercised by order made by statutory instrument, which must prescribe whether each fee is to be paid out of capital or income. Power is conferred on the Public Trustee, where a fee is payable out of capital, to direct, with the consent of the beneficiary entitled to the income, if he is of full age, that it shall be paid out of income[2].

1   Public Trustee Act 1906, s 9(1), as amended by Public Trustee (Liability and Fees) Act 2002.
2   Public Trustee (Fees) Act 1957, s 1, as amended by the Public Trustee (Liability and Fees) Act 2002, s 2(3).

77.9   The Public Trustee (Fees) Order 1999[1] prescribes the fees payable. Since these fees change quite often the current figures are not set out here, but the fees are an acceptance fee, an administration fee and a withdrawal fee, whilst additional fees are prescribed for certain particular services.

¹   SI 1999/855, as amended by SI 2002/2232, SI 2003/690, SI 2004/799, and 2005/351.

77.10 All these fees are to be paid out of capital, except the following which are to be paid out of income[1]:

(a)   Fees which under s 1(3) of the Act of 1957 the Public Trustee directs to be paid out of income.

(b)   The administration fee payable in respect of annuities and similar terminable payments.

(c)   The insurance fee.

(d)   The income-collection fee.

(e)   The management fees where the Public Trustee acts as a trustee of a superannuation scheme or on behalf of the trustees of a friendly society or runs a common investment scheme.

(f)   VAT where the fee in respect of which VAT is payable is itself payable out of income.

¹   Section 1(2) of the Public Trustee (Fees) Act 1957 provides that 'Every fees order made after the passing of this Act shall indicate, with respect to every fee fixed by the order, whether it is to be paid out of capital or out of income'. See also Public Trustee Act 1906, s 9(5).

77.11 Fees to the Public Trustee which are payable out of income have to be borne rateably by the several persons entitled to the trust income[1], and not exclusively by persons entitled to the income of residue.

¹   *Re Roberts' Will Trusts* [1937] Ch 274, [1937] 1 All ER 518.

77.12 The position of annuitants, however, can cause difficulty. In one case it was held that annuitants must bear their share of an income fee payable under an earlier fee order[1]. But in *Re Riddell*[2], Farwell J (it is respectfully submitted, rightly) dissented from this on the ground that the provision of these payments is a part of the expenses of administration and must be paid out of the estate but not out of the portions thereof given before the residue is disposed of. So where the direction was to set aside such a fund as would provide an annuity of a stated amount, the income fee was held to be payable out of the income of the fund; but the fund set aside had to be sufficient to discharge by the income thereof both the stated annuity in full and the income fee[3]. Where the Public Trustee was appointed a trustee after the appropriation of annuity funds but there was power to resort to capital if the income of any fund should be insufficient to answer the annuity, Vaisey J directed that out of the income of each fund the annuity and the Public Trustee's income fee should be paid and that in case of a deficiency of income to meet these two payments recourse should be had to the capital of the particular fund[4].

¹   *Re Bentley* [1914] 2 Ch 456.
²   [1936] Ch 747, [1936] 2 All ER 1600. Cf *Re Hulton* [1936] Ch 536, [1936] 2 All ER 207, and *Re Godwin* [1938] Ch 341, [1938] 1 All ER 287.
³   *Re Godwin* [1938] Ch 341, [1938] 1 All ER 287.
⁴   *Re Evans' Will Trusts* [1948] Ch 185, [1948] 1 All ER 381.

77.13 The fact that the duties are light in proportion to the fees chargeable has been held not to be a good ground for refusing to allow retiring trustees to appoint the Public Trustee[1].

1   *Re Drake's Settlement* [1926] WN 132.

ARTICLE 78
THE APPOINTMENT OF THE PUBLIC TRUSTEE AS AN
ORDINARY TRUSTEE

78.1

(1)   The Public Trustee may be appointed an ordinary trustee of any trust (other than those which he is forbidden to accept[1]), whether the trust was created before or since the Act, unless the instrument creating the trust contains a direction to the contrary; and even then he may be appointed if the court so orders[2].

(2)   The appointment must be made either[3]:
   (a)   by the creator of the trust;
   (b)   by the person having power to appoint new trustees; or
   (c)   by the court.

(3)   Unless appointed by the will of a settlor the consent of the Public Trustee under his official seal must be obtained before he is appointed. Where appointed by such a will the appointment does not take effect until he so consents[4].

(4)   Where he is appointed to be a new trustee he may (unlike an ordinary individual) be appointed sole trustee (even where the trust instrument or a statute forbids the appointment of a sole trustee)[5], and correspondingly all his co-trustees may retire under section 39 of the Trustee Act 1925 leaving him sole trustee, and without any of the consents required by that section[6].

(5)   Where, however, it is proposed to appoint the Public Trustee to be a new trustee or additional trustee, notice of the proposed appointment must, where practicable, be given to all the beneficiaries in the United Kingdom whose addresses are known or to the guardians of such of them as are infants, and any person to whom such notice has been given may within 21 days apply to the court to prohibit the appointment, which the court may do if it considers it expedient. Nevertheless, failure to give the notice does not invalidate the appointment[7].

1   Article 77(2) above; and Public Trustee Act 1906, s 2(4), and Public Trustee Rules 1912, r 6.
2   Public Trustee Act 1906, s 5(1) and (3).
3   Public Trustee Act 1906, s 5(1).
4   Public Trustee Rules 1912, r 8(2); and see *Re Shaw* [1914] WN 141; and Public Trustee Rules 1916, r 3.
5   *Re Leslie's Hassop Estates* [1911] 1 Ch 611.
6   Public Trustees Act 1906, s 5(1) and (2).
7   Public Trustee Act 1906, s 5(4). See *Re Drake's Settlement* [1926] WN 132.

Paragraphs 1, 2, and 3

How the Public Trustee is appointed

78.2 The Public Trustee can be appointed by will or codicil without any previous communication to him, but he does not become a trustee until he has accepted the appointment[1]. In the case of trusts created inter vivos he cannot be appointed without his previous consent given under his corporate seal, which is usually given by his execution of the instrument appointing him[2]. The effect of this would seem to be to make such purported appointments mere offers, although when he does subsequently consent the appointment becomes ipso facto effective[3].

[1]   Public Trustee Rules 1912, r 8(2).
[2]   Public Trustee Rules 1912, r 8 and Public Trustee Rules 1916, r 3.
[3]   *Re Shaw* [1914] WN 141.

78.3 Where a person is appointed by a testator to act jointly with the Public Trustee and does not disclaim, it is his duty to communicate the Public Trustee's appointment to him as soon as practicable[1].

[1]   Public Trustee Rules 1912, r 8(3).

Appointment by the court

78.4 The tendency of the court is not to appoint the Public Trustee against the wishes of any considerable proportion of the beneficiaries[1], or against the wishes of a continuing trustee, where nothing is alleged against him[2], unless for some special reason it is 'expedient'[3].

[1]   *Re Drake's Settlement* [1926] WN 132.
[2]   See per Neville J *Re Kensit* [1908] WN 235.
[3]   *Re Henderson* [1940] Ch 764, [1940] 3 All ER 295.

78.5 Where it is proposed to appoint the Public Trustee in place of a retiring judicial trustee, the court ought to make an order that there shall cease to be a judicial trustee[1].

[1]   *Re Johnston* [1911] WN 234.

Paragraph 4

Appointment as sole trustee

78.6 The Act provides that the Public Trustee may be appointed a sole trustee in cases where no other sole trustee could be appointed without breach of trust[1]. This applies not only to cases where the appointment of a sole trustee is forbidden by law, but also to cases where it is expressly directed by the settlement that (a) the trustees shall be kept up to a prescribed number[2], or (b) that discretions and powers cannot be exercised if there are fewer than two trustees, so that despite such directions the Public Trustee can effectively act on his own[3].

1 Public Trustee Act 1906, ss 2(2), 5.
2 *Re Leslie's Hassop Estates* [1911] 1 Ch 611; *Re Moxon* [1916] 2 Ch 595.
3 *Re Duxbury's Settlement Trusts* [1995] 1 WLR 425, CA.

78.7 Since the Public Trustee is a trust corporation[1], he can, even though sole trustee, give a good receipt for proceeds of sale arising under a trust for sale of land[2].

1 Trustee Act 1925, s 68(18); Law of Property Act 1925, s 205(1)(xxviii). As to trust corporations, see paras 79.5–79.6.
2 Trustee Act 1925, s 14(2); Law of Property Act 1925, s 27(2).

Paragraph 5

Effect of not giving beneficiaries notice of intention to appoint Public Trustee as a new trustee

78.8 The sole effect of failure to give notice of the proposed appointment of the Public Trustee appears to be that it is a ground on which any beneficiary may *at any time* (and not merely within 21 days) apply to the court to remove the Public Trustee. This provision as to notice is however confined to cases where the Public Trustee is appointed an ordinary trustee, and has no application in the case of his appointment as a custodian trustee.

ARTICLE 79
THE APPOINTMENT AND REMOVAL OF THE PUBLIC TRUSTEE OR CERTAIN CORPORATE BODIES AS MERE 'CUSTODIAN TRUSTEE'

79.1

(1) The Public Trustee (with regard to trusts which he is not forbidden to accept[1]), if he consents to act as such, and also any banking or insurance company, or other body corporate entitled by rules under the Public Trustee Act 1906 to act as such, may be appointed custodian trustee of any trust[2].
(2) The appointment may be made[3]:
  (a) by the creator of the trust;
  (b) by the court on the application of anyone who could apply for the appointment of a new trustee;
  (c) by the person having power to appoint new trustees, even (semble) where the trust instrument forbids it[4].
(3) The court may terminate the custodian trusteeship on the application of the custodian trustee or the managing trustee or of any beneficiary, if:
  (a) it is the general wish of the beneficiaries; or

(b)   it is expedient on any other grounds[5], and thereupon the court may give general directions and make the requisite vesting orders[6].

[1]   See Article 77(2), above; and Public Trustee Act, 1906, s 2(4) and Public Trustee Rules 1912, r 7.
[2]   Public Trustee Act 1906, s 4(1) and (3), and Public Trustee Rules 1912, r 6(d); and with regard to other corporate trustees, r 30, as amended by the Public Trustee (Custodian Trustee) Rules 1975, SI 1975/1189 (amended by SI 1976/836; SI 1981/318; SI 1984/109; SI 1985/132; SI 1987/1891).
[3]   Public Trustee Act 1906, s 4(1).
[4]   *Re Cherry's Trusts* [1914] 1 Ch 83.
[5]   Eg if it is desired to appoint the custodian trustee to be managing trustee, in which case the custodian trusteeship must first be terminated: *Re Squire's Settlement* (1946) 115 LJ Ch 90.
[6]   Public Trustee Act 1906, s 4(2)(i).

Advantages of custodian trusteeship

79.2 The appointment of a custodian trustee has practical advantages, for

(1)   it safeguards the capital against loss from obvious breaches of trust, whether fraudulent or not, and
(2)   it saves the periodic expense caused by the necessity of transferring the trust property on every appointment of new trustees, and
(3)   it makes it more likely that the trust will continue to be run effectively if the managing trustee is removed and replaced by another of whose identity it is ignorant, yet is aggrieved by its removal.

79.3 On the other hand, it leaves the management in the hands of ordinary active trustees. Custodian trusteeship has not however greatly commended itself to the public, despite the fact that it has become common to appoint either the Public Trustee or one of the great banks or insurance societies to be a corporate trustee in the full sense of a managing trustee.

Certain corporate bodies may be appointed custodian trustees

79.4 The Public Trustee Act 1906 authorises the appointment as custodian trustee not only of the Public Trustee but also of any banking or insurance company or other body corporate which is entitled by rules made under the Act to act as custodian trustee; and any such body so appointed may charge fees not exceeding those charged by the Public Trustee[1].

[1]   But see *Forster v Williams Deacon's Bank Ltd* [1935] Ch 359, CA; where it was held that a bank which has been appointed to be (a) managing trustee, and (b) custodian trustee, was not entitled to charge fees under the Public Trustee Act 1906, s 4(3). Followed in *Arning v James* [1936] Ch 158.

79.5 Rule 30 of the Public Trustee Rules 1912, as substituted in 1975[1], and as subsequently amended[2], provides:

'The following corporations shall be entitled to act as custodian trustees:
(a)   the Treasury Solicitor;

(b)   any corporation which:

    (i)   is constituted under the law of the United Kingdom or of any part thereof, or under the law of any other Member State of the European Union or of any part thereof;

    (ii)   is empowered by its constitution to undertake trust business (which for the purpose of this rule means the business of acting as trustee under wills and settlements and as executor and administrator) in England and Wales[3]:

    (iii)   has one or more places of business in the United Kingdom; and

    (iv)   is a company incorporated by special Act of Parliament or Royal Charter, or

a company registered (with or without limited liability) in the United Kingdom under the Companies Act 1948 or 1985 or under the Companies Act (Northern Ireland) 1960 or in another Member State of the European Union and having a capital (in stock or shares) for the time being issued of not less than £250,000 (or its equivalent in the currency of the State where the company is registered), of which not less than £100,000 (or its equivalent) has been paid up in cash, or

a company which is registered without limited liability in the United Kingdom under the Companies Act 1948 [or 1985] or the Companies Act (Northern Ireland) 1960 or in another Member State of the European Union and of which one of the members is a company within any of the classes defined in this sub-paragraph;

(c)   any corporation which is incorporated by the special Act or Royal Charter or under the Charitable Trustees Incorporation Act 1872[4] which is empowered by its constitution to act as a trustee for any charitable purposes, but only in relation to trusts in which its constitution empowers it to act;

(d)   any corporation which is constituted under the law of the United Kingdom or of any part thereof and having its place of business there, and which is either:

    (i)   established for the purpose of undertaking trust business for the benefit of Her Majesty's Navy, Army, Air Force or Civil Service or of any unit, department, member or association of members thereof, and having among its directors or members any persons appointed or nominated by the Defence Council or any Department of State or any one or more of those Departments, or

    (ii)   authorised by the Lord Chancellor to act in relation to any charitable, ecclesiastical or public trusts as a trust corporation, but only in connection with any such trust as is so authorised;

(e)(i)   any Strategic Health Authority, Health Authority or special health authority, but only in relation to any trust which the authority is authorised to accept or hold by virtue of section 90 of the National Health Service Act 1977;

    (ii)   any preserved Board as defined by section 15(6) of [The National Health Reorganisation Act 1973], but only in relation to any trust which the Board is authorised to accept or hold by virtue of an order made under that section;

(f)   the British Gas Corporation[5], or any subsidiary of the British Gas Corporation but only in relation to a pension scheme or pension fund established or maintained by the Corporation by virtue of section 36 of the Gas Act 1972;

(g)   the London Transport Executive[6], but only in relation to a pension scheme or pension fund—

    (i)   which is established or administered by the Executive by virtue of section 6 of the Transport (London) Act 1969, or

(ii) in relation to which rights, liabilities and functions have been transferred to the Executive by an order under section 74 of the Transport Act 1962 as applied by section 18 of the Transport (London) Act 1969;

(h) any of the following, namely:—
  (i) the Greater London Council[7],
  (ii) the corporation of any London borough (acting by the council),
  (iii) a county council, district council, parish council or community council,
  (iv) the Council of the Isles of Scilly,
  (v) the Common Council of the City of London,

but only in relation to charitable or public trusts (and not trusts for an ecclesiastical charity or for a charity for the relief of poverty) for the benefit of the inhabitants of the area of the local authority concerned and its neighbourhood, or any part of that area.

(i) any of the following, namely:—
  (i) a metropolitan district council[8] or a non-metropolitan county council,
  (ii) the corporation of any London borough (acting by the council),
  (iii) the Common Council of the City of London,
  (iv) the Council of the Isles of Scilly,

but only in relation to any trust under which property devolves for the sole benefit of a person who occupies residential accommodation provided under section 21(1)(a) of the National Assistance Act 1948 by the local authority concerned or is in the care of that authority; and a corporation acting as a custodian trustee by virtue of this paragraph in relation to any trust shall be entitled to continue so to act in relation to that trust until a new custodian trustee is appointed, notwithstanding that the person concerned ceases to occupy such accommodation or to be in the care of that authority, as the case may be.

(j) the National Coal Board[9] or any subsidiary of the National Coal Board, but only in relation to a scheme or arrangements established under regulations made under section 37 of the Coal Industry Nationalisation Act 1946.'

[1] Public Trustee (Custodian Trustee) Rules 1975, SI 1975/1189, r 2.
[2] SI 1976/836, r 2; SI 1981/358, r 2; SI 1984/109, r 2; SI 1985/132, r 2; SI 1987/1891, r 2; SI 1994/2519, r 2; SI 2002/2469, reg 4, Sch 1, Pt 2, para 32.
[3] See *Re Bigger* [1977] 2 All ER 644 (Bank of Ireland effectively empowered by its constitution, because Ireland had joined the European Economic Community, to undertake trust business in England and Wales).
[4] Repealed by Charities Act 1993: see Pt VII of that Act.
[5] Dissolved by British Gas Corporation Dissolution Order 1990 SI 1990/147 under Gas Act 1986: for property vesting in British Gas plc see 1986 Gas Act, Pt II, 1986 SI 1986/1317.
[6] Under London Regional Transport Act 1984 London Regional Transport takes over London transport functions.
[7] Abolished along with metropolitan councils by Local Government Act 1985. As to the transfer of functions, see Pt II of that Act.
[8] Abolished along with metropolitan councils by Local Government Act 1985. As to the transfer of functions, see Pt II of that Act.
[9] The British Coal Corporation has replaced the National Coal Board. The 1946 Act has been repealed but regulations under Coal Industry Act 1994, Sch 5, para 2, continue such pension schemes so that they remain trust corporations: Public Trustee (Custodian Trustee) Rules 1994, SI 1994/2519.

79.6 To this list has been added:

(k)   any corporation in relation to it, acting as trustee of a pension scheme established or maintained by the British Broadcasting Corporation[1];

(l)   any corporation appointed by the Secretary of State as a trustee of any scheme having effect by virtue of regulations made under section 37 of the Coal Industry Nationalisation Act 1946[2]for purposes relating to pensions, gratuities or other like benefits and in relation to which provision is, or has been, made by regulations made under paragraph 2(1) of Schedule 5 to the Coal Industry Act 1994[4]for the scheme to continue in force notwithstanding the repeal by the Coal Industry Act 1994 of section 37 of the Coal Industry Nationalisation Act 1946 and of the enactments modifying that section, but only in relation to such a scheme[2].

[1]   SI 1987/1891.
[2]   SI 1994/2519.

Custodian trustee making profit from trust

79.7   The rule that a trustee must not profit from his trust applies to custodian trustees, and a corporate custodian trustee has been held to be unable (without the authority of the court) lawfully to contract for its own benefit with the managing trustee[1].

[1]   *Re Brooke Bond & Co Ltd's Trust Deed* [1963] Ch 357, [1963] 1 All ER 454.

ARTICLE 80
THE RESPECTIVE DUTIES, RIGHTS AND LIABILITIES OF THE
CUSTODIAN TRUSTEE AND MANAGING TRUSTEES

80.1

The respective functions and rights of a custodian trustee and the managing trustees are as follows[1]:

(a)   the trust property must be transferred to the custodian trustee as if he were sole trustee, and for that purpose vesting orders may, where necessary, be made under the Trustee Act 1925[2]. And, subject and without prejudice to the rights of any other persons, the custodian trustee is to have the custody of all securities and documents of title relating to the trust property; but the managing trustees are to have free access thereto, and to be entitled to take copies thereof or extracts therefrom[3];

(b)   the management of the trust property, and the exercise of any power or discretion exercisable by the trustees under the trust, remain vested in the managing trustee[4];

(c)   the custodian trustee must concur in and perform all acts necessary to enable the managing trustees to exercise their powers of management, or any other power or discretion vested in them (including the power to pay money or securities into court), unless the matter in which he is requested to concur is a breach of trust, or involves a personal liability upon him in respect of calls or otherwise. But, unless he so concurs, the custodian trustee is not liable for any act or default on the part of the managing trustees or any of them[5];

(d) all sums payable to, or out of, the income or capital of the trust property, must be paid to or by the custodian trustee: provided that the custodian trustee may allow the dividends and other income derived from the trust property to be paid to the managing trustees, or to such person as they direct, or into such bank to the credit of such person as they may direct, and in such case is exonerated from seeing to the application thereof, and is not answerable for any loss or misapplication thereof[6];

(e) the custodian trustee, if he acts in good faith, is not liable for accepting as correct, and acting upon the faith of, any written statement by the managing trustees as to any birth, death, marriage, or other matter of pedigree or relationship, or other matter of fact, upon which the title to the trust property or any part thereof may depend, nor for acting upon any legal advice obtained by the managing trustees independently of the custodian trustee[7];

(f) the power of appointing new trustees, when exercisable by the trustees, is to be exercised by the managing trustees alone, and in determining the number of trustees the custodian trustee is not to be counted, but the custodian trustee has the same right of applying to the court to appoint a new trustee as any other trustee has[8];

(g) a custodian trustee holding land is not a necessary party to proceedings by the managing trustees for possession as against a trespasser[9].

[1]   Public Trustee Act 1906, s 4(2).
[2]   Public Trustee Act 1906, s 4(2)(a). As to such vesting orders, see para 75.14 ff.
[3]   Public Trustee Act 1906, s 4(2)(c).
[4]   Public Trustee Act 1906, s 4(2)(b).
[5]   Public Trustee Act 1906, s 4(2)(d).
[6]   Public Trustee Act 1906, s 4(2)(e).
[7]   Public Trustee Act 1906, s 4(2)(h).
[8]   Public Trustee Act 1906, s 4(2)(f) and (g).
[9]   *Muman v Nagasena* [1999] 4 All ER 178.

Management of the trust where custodian trustee appointed

80.2 The distinction between a custodian trustee and a bare trustee is a fine one, but it is a real one. A bare trustee has to do what he is told. A custodian trustee, while generally having to do or he is told, does not have to do what he is told and must not do it if it would involve him knowingly participating in a breach of trust[1]. He will so participate not only where he has actual knowledge but also, it seems, where he turns a Nelsonian blind-eye to what would otherwise appear a breach of trust or where he deliberately or recklessly fails to make the inquiries an honest and reasonable man would make despite having his suspicions aroused over the propriety of his instructions: his want of probity will justify the imposition of personal liability[2].

1   See *IRC v Silverts Ltd* [1951] Ch 521, [1951] 1 All ER 703, CA; *Unidare plc v Cohen* [2005] EWHC 1410 (Ch), [2006] Ch 489, para 51.
2   See Article 100; *Royal Brunei Airlines v Tan* [1995] 2 AC 378, [1995] 3 All ER 97.

ARTICLE 81
SPECIAL RULES RELATING TO THE PUBLIC TRUSTEE

81.1

(1)   Any person aggrieved by any act or omission or decision of the Public Trustee in relation to the trust may apply to the court, which may make such order as it thinks fit[1]. The application is made to a judge of the Chancery Division by summons in Chambers[2].

(2)   The Public Trustee may employ, for the purposes of the trust, such solicitors, bankers, accountants, and brokers, or other persons as he may deem necessary, having regard to the interests of the trust; and in doing so must, where practicable, take into consideration the wishes of:
(a)   the creator of the trust;
(b)   the other trustees (if any); and
(c)   the beneficiaries;
either expressed or implied from the previous practice of the creator or trustees[3]. He may also take and use professional advice and assistance in regard to legal and other matters, and act on credible information (though less than legal evidence) of facts[4].

(3)   The Public Trustee may make advances out of public money for the purposes of any trust estate of which he is trustee[5].

(4)   The entry of the name of the Public Trustee in the books of a company does not constitute notice of the trust, nor is any one affected with notice of a trust by the mere fact of dealing with the Public Trustee[6].

(5)   The Public Trustee is bound to keep a register setting out the date of acceptance, particulars of the trust property, particulars of the person entitled to the income, particulars of any notices received as to dealings with any beneficial interest or of any exercise or release of any power, and entries of any decision or opinion of the court in respect of the trust estate and of decisions of his own relating thereto of every trust of which he is trustee[7].

1   Public Trustee Act 1906, s 10.
2   RSC Ord 93, r 2. For form of originating summons, see 41 Atkin's Court Forms (1991) p 186.
3   Public Trustee Act 1906, s 11(2).
4   Public Trustee Rules 1912, r 26.

⁵ Public Trustee Act 1906, r 25.
⁶ Public Trustee Act 1906, s 11(5).
⁷ Public Trustee Rules 1912, r 16.

Procedure by way of appeal from decisions of Public Trustee

81.2 The procedure for appealing from a decision of the Public Trustee to a judge is by Part 8 claim to a judge of the Chancery Division, the summons being entitled in the matter of the will, settlement, or other trust, and in the matter of the Public Trustee Act 1906 and s 10 of that Act being specified in the body of the claim as the section under which relief is sought. If the parties desire to be heard the Public Trustee ought to hear them, before deciding a point judicially against them[1]. Section 10 applies to all decisions of the Public Trustee in discharge of his judicial functions under the Act[2].

¹ Per Parker J *Re Oddy* [1911] 1 Ch 532.
² *Re Oddy* [1911] 1 Ch 532 approved in *Re Utley* [1912] WN 147.

81.3 In one case[1], a beneficiary had disappeared and the Public Trustee refused under the Public Trustee Rules 1912, r 27 (which enables him to refuse payment until evidence is produced that the beneficiary is alive) to make the income payments otherwise due to him. The beneficiary's wife, who had obtained a sequestration order, applied to the court under s 10, above. It was held that the Public Trustee had a discretion under r 27 to refuse payment and since the wife (on whom the onus lay) had not produced the necessary evidence the court would not interfere with the exercise of that discretion; nor would the court interfere with the Public Trustee's decision not to apply under r 28 for the court's directions.

¹ *Re Wilson* [1964] 1 All ER 196, [1964] 1 WLR 214.

81.4 It should be noted that the simple procedure for taking the opinion of the court on any question arising in the course of *any administration* without judicial proceedings under s 3(4) of the Act has no application to cases where the Public Trustee is *acting as trustee*, but is confined to 'the administration of small estates'[1] ie of deceased persons[2]. All applications in relation to trusts must either be by beneficiaries in the nature of appeals from the Public Trustee under s 10 of the Public Trustee Act 1906 or by the Public Trustee or a beneficiary under the general law of trusts as made applicable to the Public Trustee by s 2(2).

¹ *Re Oddy* [1911] 1 Ch 532.
² *Re Oddy* [1911] 1 Ch 532, and *Re Oddy* (1910) 104 LT 338.

Chapter 19

ADMINISTRATION OF NEW TRUSTS CREATED UNDER LIMITED POWERS IN THE ORIGINAL SETTLEMENT

ARTICLE 82
BY WHOM NEW TRUSTS CREATED UNDER POWERS OF APPOINTMENT ARE TO BE CARRIED OUT

82.1

(1) Where the donee of a general power creates new trusts:
   (a) if the appointment is made by an instrument inter vivos he can nominate new trustees for carrying them out, to whom the old trustees must transfer the property;
   (b) if the appointment is made by a testamentary instrument the old trustees must transfer the property to the personal representatives of the appointor to be dealt with by them as part of his assets in due course of administration[1].

(2) Where the donee of a special power creates new trusts, it seems that he cannot create separate trusts under the administration of new trustees unless the power is in a wider than usual form which either expressly or impliedly authorises him to do so[2]. In contrast the usual form of a power of advancement is of such width that it can, but need not necessarily, be exercised so as to create separate trusts under the administration of new trustees[3].

(3) A resettlement on separate trusts pursuant to a special power will incorporate the statutory power of advancement[4], but will not be able to contain discretionary or protective trusts or powers of appointment[5] unless the special power for the benefit of objects thereof is construed as wide enough to permit delegation of such discretions to the trustees of the settlement.

---

[1] *Re Hoskin's Trusts* (1877) 5 Ch D 229; on appeal (1877) 6 Ch D 281; *Hayes v Oatley* (1872) LR 14 Eq 1; *Re Philbrick* (1865) 13 WR 570; *Re Peacock's Settlement* [1902] 1 Ch 552 (administration with will annexed).

[2] *Bond (Inspector of Taxes) v Pickford* [1983] STC 517, CA; *Roome v Edwards (Inspector of Taxes)* [1982] AC 279, [1981] 1 All ER 736, HL; *Busk v Aldam* (1874) LR 19 Eq 16; *Von Brockdorff v Malcolm* (1885) 30 Ch D 172; *Re Tyssen* [1894] 1 Ch 56; and per Cotton LJ in *Scotney v Lomer* (1886) 31 Ch D 380.

991

3   *Pilkington v IRC* [1964] AC 612, [1962] 3 All ER 622, HL; *Bond v Pickford*, supra; *Roome v Edwards*, supra. See para 67.7 above.
4   *Re Mewburn* [1934] Ch 112; *Re Morris* [1951] 2 All ER 528 at 533, CA.
5   *Re Morris* [1951] 2 All ER 528, CA; *Re Hunter's Will Trusts* [1963] Ch 372; *Re Hay's Settlement Trusts* [1981] 3 All ER 786.

Paragraph 1(a)

Donee of general power may appoint by deed to new trustees

82.2 A general power, being a power to appoint to anyone in the world, is tantamount to ownership and the donee can exercise it in whatever way he pleases[1]. It follows that the donee may, by instrument inter vivos, appoint not merely in favour of persons to take beneficially, but in favour of persons who are to hold upon new special trusts. In either case the trusts of the old settlement are spent, and the trustees' sole remaining duty is to transfer the property to the appointees, whether they be beneficial or fiduciary.

1   *Re Triffitt's Settlement* [1958] Ch 852, [1958] 2 All ER 299.

82.3 Exceptionally, if the general power is vested in trustees ex officio so that the power is fiduciary and not a personal beneficial power then the trustees can only exercise the power in ways contemplated by the settlor[1].

1   *Re Beatty's Will Trusts* [1990] 3 All ER 844 at 846–847.

Paragraph 1(b)

Where general power exercised by will, property must in first instance be transferred to personal representative

82.4 Where the appointment is made by a testamentary instrument the matter is somewhat different. In that case the appointor, by exercising the power, makes the property assets for the payment of his debts in due order of administration[1]. By the mere fact of the appointment, therefore, he gives an interest to his personal representative, who may require the fund for debts or death duties. Consequently, the trustees of the settlement must transfer the fund to the personal representative or according to his direction[2]. If the appointor has declared new trusts, and appointed new trustees for carrying them out, then, of course, it will be the duty of the personal representative to transfer or direct the transfer to such new trustees of so much as he may not require for debts or duties. In either case, however, the functions of the old trustees cease on the death of the appointor.

1   *Lassells v Cornwallis* (1704) 2 Vern 465; *Holmes v Coghill* (1802) 7 Ves 499; affd (1806) 12 Ves 206; *Pardo v Bingham* (1868) LR 6 Eq 485. This is the case even where the consent of the trustees is necessary to the exercise of the power: *Re Phillips* [1931] 1 Ch 347.
2   See cases cited, note 1, para 82.1.

Paragraph 2

Whether donee of special power can appoint to new trustees is a question of construction

82.5 Appointments creating new trusts under special or limited powers give rise to more difficulty. As is stated in *Farwell on Powers*[1]:

'If other indications of intention be lacking, at all events in the case of personalty, a settlor or testator who vests funds in trustees, and provides machinery for filling up vacancies in their number, may well be taken to have intended that the fund shall remain in the custody of the persons to whom he has entrusted it, until some beneficiary absolutely entitled is ready to receive it; although he has given power to another to say who the beneficiary shall be. He may well trust (say) his daughter, to select which of her children shall take the fund, and yet not desire her to nominate the trustees who are to hold it.'

[1] Farwell on Powers (3rd edn) p 374.

Mere power of selection

82.6 In *Re Tyssen*[1] under a special power in favour of children, the donees appointed in favour of one daughter upon certain trusts in favour of another daughter; but it was held that the fund ought not to be transferred to the first daughter as trustee under the appointment, but instead should be retained by the trustees of the settlement. The same view had been previously taken in *Busk v Aldam*[2].

[1] [1894] 1 Ch 56.
[2] (1874) LR 19 Eq 16; and see per Cotton LJ in *Scotney v Lomer* (1886) 31 Ch D 380.

Power to appoint in such manner and form as donee may think fit

82.7 On the other hand, in the subsequent case of *Re Redgate*[1] Buckley J held that, under a power to appoint to children 'for such estate or estates manner and form' as the donee of the power should direct, the power was well exercised by an appointment to new trustees upon trust for sale and distribution of the proceeds among the children. This seems to have ben based upon the presence of the words 'manner and form', which, by contrast with the words 'estate or estates', seemed to the judge to imply a power to do something else than to give an estate to children.

[1] [1903] 1 Ch 356; distinguished by Astbury J in *Re Mackenzie* [1916] 1 Ch 125.

82.8 In the later case of *Re Adams' Trustees and Frost's Contract*[1], Warrington J came to the same conclusion even where the words 'manner and form' were absent and the settlement merely directed the trustees to transfer 'or pay'.

[1] [1907] 1 Ch 695; and see *Re Falconer's Trusts* [1908] 1 Ch 410, as to the power of a donee of a special power of appointment to enlarge the range of investments; and see also *Re Taylor*, not reported, but decided on 28 February 1912, where Parker J went a step further,

and held that a donee of a power to appoint the proceeds of sale of real and *personal estate, directed to be sold* can stop the direction for sale and appoint a house to A (an object of the power) so long as she remains a spinster and inhabits it.

82.9 In *Re Rank's Settlement Trusts[1]* Slade J held that a special power of appointment on trusts 'with such provisions for maintenance education and advancement and otherwise *at the discretion of* any person and with such gifts over and *generally in such manner* for the benefit of' certain issue conferred upon the donee of the power the authority to give new trustees all such administrative powers as were reasonably ancillary to the appointed beneficial interests, including wider powers of investment than were contained in the trust instrument conferring the power of appointment.

[1]   [1979] 1 WLR 1242.

Special powers in the wider form

82.10 In *Bond v Pickford[1]* Slade LJ characterised as powers in the wider form 'powers to alter the presently operative trusts of a settlement which expressly or by necessary implication authorise the trustees to remove assets altogether from the original settlement (without rendering any person absolutely beneficially entitled to them)'. Powers of this nature which do not confer on the trustees such authority are regarded as 'powers in the narrower form'.

[1]   [1983] STC 517 at 523, CA.

82.11 This distinction is of great importance for capital gains tax purposes. It has developed as a more precise and workable distinction than that between special powers of appointment and powers of advancement[1], especially when the latter distinction became blurred in the case of certain wide express powers, eg of appropriation or allocation of trust assets.

[1]   'Advancement' has the connotation of receiving part of the capital earlier than one would expect, taking into account one's vested or contingent interest in capital.

82.12 If there is a separate settlement created under a power in the wider form there will be a deemed disposal for capital gains tax purposes, the trustees of the separate settlement having become absolutely entitled to the subject matter thereof as against the trustees of the original settlement[1]. If there is no separate settlement, then the trustees of the sub-settlement and the trustees of the head settlement will be treated as a single and continuing body of trustees[2]. This means there will be no deemed disposal, but if there are two UK head trustees and the two non-resident sub-trustees realise their gains on their sub-trust assets abroad the UK trustees will be liable for CGT thereon[3].

[1]   Taxation of Chargeable Gains Act 1992, s 71. Further see Whiteman, *Capital Gains Tax* (4th edn) paras 26–29 to 26–41.
[2]   Taxation of Chargeable Gains Act 1992, s 69.
[3]   *Roome v Edwards* [1982] AC 279, [1981] 1 All ER 736, HL.

82.13 A power in the narrower form is ex hypothesi incapable of being exercised so as to create a separate settlement. An appointment under a special power to appoint to beneficiaries in the classical form (which is frequently found as the primary provision of a discretionary settlement—the discretionary trusts being expressed to apply only until and in default of appointment) cannot create a separate settlement in the absence of further terms in the trust instrument expressly or by necessary implication authorising such creation[1]. This reflects two basic principles of English trust law. The office of a trustee being one of personal confidence, it is well settled that a trustee may not delegate the exercise of his trusts, powers and discretions to other persons except where so authorised by the trust instrument or by statute. Secondly, when a special power of appointment is exercised the limitations created under it are treated as written into the original instrument which created the power[2].

1   *Bond v Pickford* [1983] STC 517 at 522–533, 529, CA.
2   *Muir (or Williams) v Muir* [1943] AC 468, HL; *Roome v Edwards* [1982] AC 279, [1981] 1 All ER 736, HL; *Clarkson v Clarkson* [1994] BCC 921, CA.

82.14 A power in the wider form is ex hypothesi capable of being exercised so as to create a separate settlement but it is also capable of being exercised in narrow fashion so as not to create a separate settlement. Such a power will include a power to appoint to anyone except certain named persons[1] or to appoint to anyone living at a specified date[2], whether or not such power is vested in joint appointors[3] or is subject to the consent of some named person[4]. It includes a power to 'pay or apply the whole or any part or parts of the Capital to or for the benefit of all or any one or more of the specified class [freed and released from the trusts concerning the same][5] or [in such manner as the Trustees shall in their absolute discretion think fit]'[6]. However, a power in the narrower form was held to exist where it was a power to 'apply capital for the benefit of any one or more of the Beneficiaries by allocating or appropriating to such Beneficiary such sum out of or investments forming part of the Capital as the Trustees think fit either absolutely or contingently upon the attainment by him or her of a specified age and so that the provisions of s 31 of the Trustee Act 1925 and the powers of the Trustees to invest and vary investments shall apply to any moneys or investments so allocated or appropriated[7].

1   *Re Triffitt's Settlement* [1958] Ch 852, [1958] 2 All ER 299.
2   *Re Jones* [1945] Ch 105.
3   *Re Earl of Coventry's Indentures* [1974] Ch 77, [1973] 3 All ER 1.
4   *Re Triffitt's Settlement* [1958] Ch 852, [1958] 2 All ER 299.
5   *Hart (Inspector of Taxes) v Briscoe* [1979] Ch 1, [1978] 1 All ER 791; *Swires v Renton* [1991] STC 490 (wide power exercised not so as to re-settle on separate trusts but to sub-settle by grafting new trusts on to old trusts).
6   *Bond v Pickford* [1983] STC 517, CA. This is similar to the power of advancement in Trustee Act 1925, s 32. Also see *Ewart v Taylor (Inspector of Taxes)* [1983] STC 721.
7   *Bond v Pickford* [1983] STC 517, CA.

Whether separate settlement created under wider form of power

82.15 In *Roome v Edwards*[1] Lord Wilberforce provided the following guidelines as to whether a power had been exercised so as to create a separate settlement.

'I think that the question whether a particular set of facts amounts to a settlement should be approached by asking what a person, with knowledge of the legal context of the word under established doctrine and applying this knowledge in a practical and commonsense manner to the facts under examination, would conclude. To take two fairly typical cases. Many settlements contain powers to appoint a part or a proportion of the trust property to beneficiaries; some may also confer power to appoint separate trustees of the property so appointed or such power may be conferred by the Trustee Act 1925, s 37. It is established doctrine that the trusts declared by a document exercising a special power of appointment are to be read into the original settlement. If such a power is exercised, whether or not separate trustees are appointed, I do not think that it would be natural for such a person as I have presupposed to say that a separate settlement had been created; still less so if it were found that provisions of the original settlement continued to apply to the appointed fund, or that the appointed fund were liable, in certain events, to fall back into the rest of the settled property. On the other hand, there may be a power to appoint and appropriate a part of the trust property to beneficiaries and to settle it for their benefit. If such a power is exercised, the natural conclusion might be that a separate settlement was created, all the more so if a complete new set of trusts were declared as to the appropriated property, and if it could be said that the trusts of the original settlement ceased to apply to it. There can be many variations on these cases each of which will have to be judged on its facts.[2]'

1 [1982] AC 279, [1981] 1 All ER 736, HL.
2 See also *Swires v Renton* [1991] STC 490.

82.16 The Board of Inland Revenue in a Statement of Practice has stated[1]:

'It is now clear that a deemed disposal under s 71 [TGCA 1992] cannot arise unless the power exercised by the trustees, or the instrument conferring the power, expressly or by necessary implication, confers on the trustees authority to remove assets from the original settlement by subjecting them to the trusts of a different settlement. Such powers (which may be powers of advancement or appointment) are referred to by the Court of Appeal [in *Bond v Pickford*] as "powers in the wider form." However, the Board considers that a deemed disposal will not arise when such a power is exercised and trusts are declared in circumstances such that—
(a)   the appointment is revocable; or
(b)   the trusts declared of the advanced or appointed funds are not exhaustive so that there exists a possibility at the time when the advancement or appointment is made that the funds covered by it will on the occasion of some event cease to be held upon such trusts and once again come to be held upon the original trusts of the settlement.

Further, when such a power is exercised the Board considers it unlikely that a deemed disposal will arise when trusts are declared if duties in regard to the appointed assets still fall to the trustees of the original settlement in their capacity as trustees of that settlement, bearing in mind the provision in s 69(1), TCGA 1992, that the trustees of a settlement form a single and continuing body (distinct from the persons who may from time to time be the trustees).

Finally, the Board accept that a Power of Appointment or Advancement can be exercised over only part of the settled property and that the above consequences would apply to that part.'

1 SP 7/84, [1983] STC 517 at 699, reissued IR 131 (Supp)(1997).

Paragraph 3

Delegation of discretions to new trustees

82.17 Since *Pilkington v IRC*[1] the statutory power of advancement 'for the benefit of' a beneficiary, B, has been construed broadly so as to enable advancements to be made by way of resettlement on separate new trusts, freed and discharged from the old trusts. These new trusts may confer discretions on the new trustees if this is 'for the benefit of' B, so that the power authorises the delegation by the old trustees to the new trustees being an authorised one. If a special power of appointment is in the 'wider' form already discussed, then it may be exercised to resettle all or part of the trust property on new separate trusts which will automatically incorporate the statutory power of advancement in favour of beneficiaries interested in capital[2].

[1] [1964] AC 612; see para 67.7 ff.
[2] *Re Mewburn* [1934] Ch 112; *Re Morris* [1951] 2 All ER 528 at 533. Logically this would also be the case if the statutory power were extended to cover not just half, but all the capital, as pointed out in J Kessler *Drafting Trusts and Will Trusts* (7th edn) para 10–5, footnote 22 and *Lewin on Trusts* (17th edn) para 29–46 footnote 27.

82.18 It is then a question of construing the terms of the special power to see if they are broad enough to enable the resettlement to confer discretions on the new trustees by way of creating a protective trust (which may become a discretionary trust on bankruptcy of the life tenant) or an immediate discretionary trust and whether or not containing discretionary powers of appointment. In the past, case law gave a restrictive Victorian approach to construction of special powers[1], whereas the modern trend is to give words like 'for the benefit of' a wide unrestricted meaning[2]. However, in modern practice it is usual to draft special powers of appointment in the wider form which do expressly confer the widest possible power to confer discretions on the new trustees of the resettled trust property, thereby avoiding problems.

[1] *Re Morris* [1951] 2 All ER 528, CA; *Re Hunter's Will Trust* [1963] Ch 372; *Re Hay's Settlement Trust* [1981] 3 All ER 786.
[2] *Pilkington v IRC* [1964] AC 612, HL; *Re Hampden's Settlement Trusts* [1977] TR 177, [2001] WTLR 195 (a special power); plus *Re Pocock's Policy* (1871) 6 Ch App 445. Further see G Thomas *Powers* (Sweet & Maxwell 1998), paras 7–58 to 7–83.

Chapter 20

THE RIGHTS OF THE TRUSTEE

ARTICLE 83
RIGHT TO REIMBURSEMENT AND INDEMNITY

83.1

(1)   A trustee is entitled to be reimbursed out of the trust funds or
       may pay out of the trust funds[1] all expenses which he has
       properly incurred when acting on behalf of the trust[2], having
       regard to the circumstances of each particular case[3], but without
       interest[4], unless he has paid an interest-bearing claim, in which
       case he stands in the shoes of the creditor by subrogation[5].
       Exceptionally, where expenses were incurred without authorisa-
       tion but the trustee in good faith conferred a benefit on the trust
       property he will have a right of indemnity to the value of the
       benefit conferred[6].

(2)   The trustee's lien covers present and future liabilities[7] and
       extends over both capital and income[8] so as to confer upon him
       a beneficial interest in the nature of a non-possessory equitable
       lien with priority over the claims of the beneficiaries[9]. After
       retirement or removal of a trustee his lien automatically binds the
       trust fund in the hands of the successor trustees[10]. When trustees
       exercise discretionary powers to distribute trust funds to a
       beneficiary they may be regarded as releasing any equitable lien
       of themselves or any predecessors unless such lien is expressly
       preserved[11]. When trustees are obliged to distribute trust funds to
       persons absolutely entitled under the terms of the trust they have
       a right to retain assets to cover future liabilities[12] and a right to

preserve their lien (though they may rely on personal covenants of indemnity): if they do not expressly exercise such rights, it seems they will lose them[13].

(3)   Where the only beneficiary is a person of full age and capacity, who himself created the trust or accepted the beneficial owner-ship with knowledge that the legal ownership of the trust property was vested in the trustee, the right of the trustee to indemnity against liabilities incident to the legal ownership is not limited to the trust property, but is enforceable in equity against the beneficiary personally, unless he is in a position to disclaim the property[14]. The principle is equally applicable where all the beneficiaries between them absolutely entitled are each of full age and capacity[15].

(4)   Where a trustee has committed a breach of trust, his right of indemnity is limited to the extent to which the liabilities properly incurred exceed the compensation due from him to the trust estate[16].

(5)   A person against whose claims the trustee is, by the settlement, entitled to be indemnified, is allowed to stand in the trustee's place, by way of subrogation, against the fund which the settlor has authorised the trustee to use in the enterprise in question[17]. Such person will therefore need to show that the debt was properly incurred and that the state of accounts between the trustee and the beneficiaries (taking into account any losses flowing from any breach of trust) is such that there is some balance in the trustee's favour to which the right of indemnity may attach[18].

---

1   *Re Earl of Winchilsea's Policy Trusts* (1888) 39 Ch D 168.
2   Trustee Act 2000, s 31(1); *Worrall v Harford* (1802) 8 Ves 4; *Re German Mining Co* (1853) 4 De GM & G 19; *Re Grimthorpe* [1958] Ch 615, [1958] 1 All ER 765; *Holding and Management Ltd v Property Holding and Investment Trust plc* [1990] 1 All ER 938, [1989] 1 WLR 1313, CA.
3   *Leedham v Chawner* (1858) 4 K & J 458.
4   *Gordon v Trail* (1820) 8 Price 416; *Foster v Spencer* [1996] 2 All ER 672 at 678.
5   *Re Beulah Park Estate* (1872) LR 15 Eq 43; *Finch v Pescott* (1874) LR 17 Eq 554.
6   *Vyse v Foster* (1872) 8 Ch App 309 at 336–337; *Re Smith's Estate* [1937] Ch 636, [1937] 3 All ER 472; *Conway v Fenton* (1888) 40 Ch D 512 at 518: an independent restitutionary right to prevent unjust enrichment.
7   *X v A* [2000] 1 All ER 490.
8   *Stott v Milne* (1884) 25 Ch D 710; *Re Davis* (1832) 1 Deac & Ch 272; *Re German Mining Co* (1853) 4 De GM & G 19; and see *Walters v Woodbridge* (1878) 7 Ch D 504, CA (considered and explained in *Re Spurling's Will Trusts* [1966] 1 All ER 745, [1966] 1 WLR 920.
9   *Dodds v Tuke* (1884) 25 Ch D 617; *Mathias v Mathias* (1858) 3 Sm & G 552; *Re Griffith* [1904] 1 Ch 807; *Octavo Investments Pty Ltd v Knight* (1979) 144 CLR 360.
10 *Dimos v Dikeakos Nominees Ltd* (1996) 68 FCR 39, (1997) 149 ALR 113; *Rothmore Farms Pty Ltd v Belgravia Pty Ltd* [1999] FCA 745, (1999) 2 ITELR 159.
11 See para 83.34 below.
12 *X v A* [2000] 1 All ER 490.
13 See para 83.34 below.

14   *Hardoon v Belilios* [1901] AC 118; *J W Broomhead (Vic) Pty Ltd (in liquidation) v J W Broomhead Pty Ltd* [1985] VR 891. The previous cases at law, such as *Hosegood v Pedler* (1896) 66 LJQB 18, are inapplicable, the right being peculiarly an equitable one; cf *Jervis v Wolferstan* (1874) LR 18 Eq 18 at 24; *Fraser v Murdoch* (1881) 6 App Cas 855 at 872; *Re German Mining Co* (1853) 4 De GM & G 19 at 54; *Hobbs v Wayet* (1887) 36 Ch D 256.
15   *Balkin v Peck* (1997) 43 NSWLR 706.
16   *Re Knott* (1887) 56 LJ Ch 318; *Re Kidd* (1894) 70 LT 648 at 649. *Re Evans* (1887) 34 Ch D 597 at 601, CA; *RWG Management Ltd v Corporate Affairs Comr* [1985] VR 385.
17   *Ex p, Garland* (1804) 10 Ves 110; *Fraser v Murdoch* (1881) 6 App Cas 855, HL.
18   See cases cited in note 2 and paras 83.46–83.50 below.

Paragraph 1

Right to indemnity

83.2 As was said by Danckwerts J in *Re Grimthorpe[1]*:

> 'It is a commonplace that persons who take the onerous and sometimes dangerous duty of being trustees are not expected to do any of the work on their own expense; they are entitled to be indemnified against the costs and expenses which they incur in the course of their office; of course, that necessarily means that such costs and expenses are properly incurred and not improperly incurred. The general rule is quite plain; they are entitled to be paid back all that they have had to pay out.'

1   [1958] Ch 615 at 623, [1958] 1 All ER 765 at 769; *Alhamrani v Russa Management Ltd* (2006) JRC 081, R Ct Jersey. As to when costs are properly and reasonably incurred see *Bonham v Blake Lapthorn Linell* [2006] EWHC 2513 (Ch).

83.3 Indeed, the right of indemnity is inseparable from the office of the trustee[1]. This rule, however, applies only to costs incurred for the purpose of benefiting the trust estate. Obviously trustees are not entitled to their costs on an indemnity basis in respect of hostile litigation with the beneficiaries designed to define and secure their personal rights as individuals[2].

1   *Worrall v Harford* (1802) 8 Ves 4 at 8; *Re Exhall Coal Co Ltd* (1866) 35 Beav 449 at 453.
2   *Re Dargie* [1954] Ch 16, [1953] 2 All ER 577. They are so entitled where they successfully defend themselves against an action for breach of trust, but they may be deprived of part of such costs where they put forward unsuccessful arguments that prolonged the case: *Armitage v Nurse* [1998] Ch 241 at 262–263.

83.4 Section 31(1) of the Trustee Act 2000[1], reflecting the position in equity given statutory force since 1859, provides 'A trustee (a) is entitled to be reimbursed from the trust funds[2] or (b) may pay out of the trust funds, expenses properly incurred by him when acting on behalf of the trust'. Unlike its predecessors[3], this provision[4] cannot be ousted by the contrary provision in the trust. It was earlier thought that if the trustee were willing to accept office where the trust instrument ousted his indemnity right then there was no reason why he should not be free to do so[5]. However, where exclusion of the statutory right to claim an indemnity would have frustrated a subrogation claim it is possible that equity could have intervened where a fraud would

otherwise have been perpetrated by a settlor-beneficiary or volunteer beneficiaries, all of full capacity and claiming to take benefits without any burdens[6].

1   Section 31(2) extends s 31(1) to a trustee exercising functions as agent, nominee or
     custodian.
2   Defined in Trustee Act 2000 s 339 to mean 'income and capital funds of the trust' thereby
     affording greater discretion as to the ultimate incidence of expenses than before: see paras
     51.2–51.4 above.
3   Eg Trustee Act 1925 s 69(2).
4   Effective for expenses incurred after commencement of the Trustee Act 2000: s 33(1).
5   *Re German Mining Co* (1854) 4 De GM & G 19 at 52; *RWG Management Ltd v
     Corporate Affairs Comr* [1985] VR 385 at 395. There may be a liberal charging clause.
6   *Re Johnson* (1880) 15 Ch D 548 at 550.

83.5 The right to an indemnity is normally of crucial importance to a trustee.
Since a trust is not a legal entity that can enter into contracts, sue or be sued,
it is the trustees who are personally liable to third parties unless as a matter of
contract law[1] the trustees can persuade a third party to agree that the trustees'
liability should be limited or excluded, or that the trustees should only pay the
debt out of the trust property under the statutory right to indemnity in s 31(1)
of the Trustee Act 2000. Trustees can never plead their contract was ultra vires
and void (as companies could plead at common law) because the trustees
contract as individuals who have no restriction on their capacity as individuals[2].

1   *Muir v City of Glasgow Bank* (1879) 4 App Cas 337 at 355, 362, HL; *Perring v Draper*
     [1997] EGCS 109; *Marston Thompson & Evershed plc v Benn* [1998] CLY No 4875;
     Watling v Lewis [1911] 1 Ch 414 at 424; *Re Robinson's Settlement* [1912] 1 Ch 717 at
     729. Further see Trust Law Committee Consultation Paper and the Report on 'Rights of
     Creditors against Trustees and Trust Funds'.
2   See Lord Upjohn in *De Vigier v IRC* [1964] 2 All ER 907 at 914, HL; *Hammersmith and
     Fulham London Borough Council v Monk* [1992] 1 AC 478 at 493, per Lord Browne
     Wilkinson; *Rolled Steel Products (Holdings) Ltd v British Steel Corpn* [1986] Ch 246 at
     303, per Browne-Wilkinson LJ.

Damages recovered by third parties

83.6 In *Benett v Wyndham*[1] a trustee, in the due execution of his trust,
directed a bailiff, employed on the trust property, to have certain trees felled.
The bailiff ordered the wood-cutters usually employed on the property to fell
the trees. In doing so they negligently allowed a bough to fall on to a
passer-by, who, being injured, recovered heavy damages from the trustee in a
court of law. These damages were, however, allowed to the trustee out of the
trust property.

1   (1862) 4 De GF & J 259; and see *Re Raybould* [1900] 1 Ch 199.

Calls on shares

83.7 Where a trustee of shares has been obliged to pay calls upon them, he is
entitled to be reimbursed[1]; and the right to be indemnified accrues directly the
liability is proved to exist[2]. However, there must be some proof that the
liability is not merely hypothetical, for a person entitled to be indemnified
cannot claim a declaration of his right to indemnity before the contingency

which creates the damage has arisen[3]. Therefore, although a trustee may, as such, be a member of a company which is being wound up, he cannot bring an action to establish his right to an indemnity, unless he can establish the fact that calls *must* be made[4]. And where the court makes an order for the distribution of a trust fund it will not set aside any part of the fund to indemnify the testator's executors against possible liabilities which may arise in respect of leases formerly held by him, unless there is privity of estate between the executors and the lessors[5] and no assent has been executed[6].

1   *James v May* (1873) LR 6 HL 328; *Re National Financial Co* (1868) 3 Ch App 791; *Fraser v Murdoch* (1881) 6 App Cas 855. See also, as to right of executor to recover calls from a residuary legatee, *Whittaker v Kershaw* (1890) 45 Ch D 320.
2   *Hobbs v Wayet* (1887) 36 Ch D 256.
3   *Hughes-Hallett v Indian Mammoth Gold Mines Co* (1882) 22 Ch D 561.
4   However, contrast *X v A* [2000] 1 All ER 490 where the court upheld a lien in respect of potential future liability under an Act not in force and Mason P in *Comr of Stamp Duties v ISPT* (1999) 2 ITELR 1 at 18, 'A trustee's right of indemnity arises at the time when a liability is incurred, and, it is at this stage that the lien over trust assets arises: *Custom Credit Corpn Ltd v Ravi Nominees Pty Ltd* (1982) 8 WAR 42 at 53–53'.
5   *Re Nixon* [1904] 1 Ch 638; *Re Owers* [1941] Ch 389, [1941] 2 All ER 589. A sum paid into court as a protection to executors will be paid out when all claims against them are barred by lapse of time (*Re Lewis* [1939] Ch 232, [1939] 3 All ER 269).
6   *Re Bennett* [1943] 1 All ER 467.

Liability from holding title to trust property

83.8 Unless protected by statute (as in the case of inheritance tax[1]) a trustee is personally liable to the extent of his own wealth for liabilities imposed upon him as owner of trust property, but he has a right of indemnity out of the trust property where the property was properly acquired. Liability under Pt IIA of the Environmental Protection Act 1990 for the costs of cleaning up contaminated land is of particular concern to trustees and, to this end, they may retain and manage trust assets even after beneficiaries have otherwise become absolutely entitled to the trust property[2]. Perhaps the courts may develop a principle as in the USA that the trustee's liability should be limited to the extent it is sufficient to indemnify him where he is without fault for the liability and the insufficiency of the fund to be able to satisfy the liability[3].

1   Inheritance Tax Act 1984, s 204(2).
2   *X v A* [2000] 1 All ER 490.
3   Scott on Trusts (4th edn), para 265.4; Restatement (Second) of Trusts, para 265; section 1010(b) Uniform Trust Code.

Indemnity for liabilities incurred in carrying on trust business

83.9 So where trustees or executors have *rightly* carried on a business in accordance with the provisions of a will or settlement, they are entitled to be indemnified out of the trust estate against any liabilities which they have properly incurred[1]. This right will not, however prevail against creditors *of the testator* himself unless they have assented to the business being carried on in the interest as well of themselves as of the beneficiaries under the will, and their assent will not be assumed because they have not actively interfered with the continuance of the business[2]. But where the settlement has directed a trustee to employ a specific portion only of the estate for the purpose of carrying on the business, the rule is that, although the trustee is personally liable to creditors for debts incurred by him in carrying on the trade pursuant to the settlement, his right to indemnity is limited to the specific assets so directed to be employed[3].

1   *Re Oxley* [1914] 1 Ch 604, explaining *Dowse v Gorton* [1891] AC 190; *Re Evans* (1887) 34 Ch D 597, dissenting from *Re Brooke* [1894] 2 Ch 600, and *Re Hodges* [1899] 1 IR 480. For the clearest exposition of the law see *Vacuum Oil Co Pty Ltd v Wiltshire* (1945) 72 CLR 319.
2   *Re Oxley* [1914] 1 Ch 604, explaining *Dowse v Gorton* [1891] AC 190; *Re Evans* (1887) 34 Ch D 597, dissenting from *Re Brooke* [1894] 2 Ch 600, and *Re Hodges* [1899] 1 IR 480. For the clearest exposition of the law see *Vacuum Oil Co Pty Ltd v Wiltshire* (1945) 72 CLR 319.
3   *Re Johnson* (1880) 15 Ch D 548; *Re Webb* (1890) 63 LT 545. As to the right of creditors of the business to be placed in the shoes of the trustee by way of subrogation, see para 83.47 ff.

Solicitor's costs

83.10 A trustee or executor will be allowed the amount of a solicitor's bill of costs which he has paid for services rendered in the matter of the trust[1], even, it would seem, where the necessity for the services arose through want of caution on the part of the trustee, eg where proceedings had to be taken by an administrator against an agent to whom he had entrusted money to make payments[2]. However, under the Solicitors Act 1974, s 71(3), beneficiaries may, at the discretion of the court, obtain an order to tax the costs of the trustee's solicitor[3].

1   *Macnamara v Jones* (1784) 2 Dick 587.
2   *Re Davis* [1887] WN 186.
3   See *Re Miles* [1903] 2 Ch 518; *McIlwraith v McIlwraith* [2002] EWHC 9028 (Costs).

Basis on which costs of litigation are assessed

83.11 In cases to which trustees are parties in their capacity as such, the general rule is that they should be indemnified as to their proper costs and expenses of the proceedings out of the trust fund, to the extent that they are not recovered from any other person[1]. Accordingly, the order as to the costs of the trustees should direct assessment (formerly known as taxation) on the indemnity basis out of the trust fund[2].

1   CPR, r 48.4(2); see eg *Turner v Kleinwort Benson* [2005] EWHC 2442 (Ch); *Alhamrani v Russa Management Ltd* (2006) JRC 081, R Ct Jersey.
2   CPR, r 48.4(3), replacing (after a hiatus) RSC, Ord 62 r 6(2); *McDonald v Horn* [1995] 1 All ER 961, CA.

83.12 On an assessment on the indemnity basis all costs shall be allowed except insofar as they are of an unreasonable amount or have been unreasonably incurred and any doubts as to whether the costs were reasonably incurred or were reasonable in amount should be resolved in favour of the recieving party[1]. Unlike the standard basis of assessment[2], there is no requirement that the costs be proportionate to the matters in issue.

¹ CPR, r 44.4(3). See *Bowen-Jones v Bowen-Jones* [1986] 3 All ER 163 at 164 where it is pointed out that the previous five main bases of taxation set out in *EMI Records Ltd v Ian Cameron Wallace Ltd* [1983] Ch 59, [1982] 2 All ER 980 now appear to have been reduced to two. See also *Re Basham* [1986] 1 WLR 1498 at 1511, and para 87.37 below.
² CPR, r 44.4(2)(a).

83.13 If the trust fund is likely to prove insufficient to indemnify the trustees, they may decline to become involved in the litigation unless given suitable security from elsewhere.¹

¹ *Concord Trust v Law Debenture Trust Corpn* [2005] UKHL 27, [2005] 1 WLR 1591, CA.

Other instances of costs, charges, and expenses allowed trustees

83.14 It has been held that a trustee is entitled to be reimbursed costs of former trustees, paid by him to their personal representatives before the latter transfer the trust estate¹. He is also entitled to be reimbursed costs incurred by him prior to his appointment in obtaining a statement of the trust property and ascertaining that the power of appointing new trustees is being properly exercised²; and also costs incurred by the donee of the power of appointment in relation to the trustee's appointment³.

¹ *Harvey v Olliver* [1887] WN 149.
² *Re Pumfrey* (1882) 22 Ch D 255. This case was considered in *De Vigier v IRC* [1964] 2 All ER 907, HL, where it was considered relevant as showing that a trustee who had made payments for trust purposes was entitled in equity to a charge on the trust property and his bank was subrogated to his rights having provided the relevant money by way of loan.
³ See penultimate note.

Expenses incurred in litigation with third parties

83.15 Where a trustee takes upon himself the responsibility of defending an action in relation to the trust estate without procuring the sanction of the court, then if the action succeeds the onus lies upon him of proving that he had reasonable grounds for defending it. If he cannot prove such grounds, he is not entitled to retain out of the trust property the costs of the action beyond the amount which he would have incurred if he had applied for leave to defend¹. The position is similar where the trustee commences an action on behalf of the trust if such action fails. In attempting to ascertain whether the costs were properly incurred the court puts itself 'in the position in which the court would have been had an application been made to the court, as it ought to have been made if it was intended to throw the costs of the proceedings on the estate before commencing the action which has been brought and tried'².

¹ *Leedham v Chawner* (1858) 4 K & J 458; *Re Beddoe* [1893] 1 Ch 547; followed, *Re England's Settlement Trusts* [1918] 1 Ch 24. For successful recovery of costs out of the trust fund see *Bonham v Blake Lapthorn Linell* [2006] EWHC 2513 (Ch).
² *Re Yorke* [1911] 1 Ch 370; *Singh v Bhasin* [2000] WTLR 101.

83.16 The rights of the trustee

A protective Beddoe application

83.16 The moral is always to apply to the court for its sanction. As Lightman J pointed out in *Alsop Wilkinson v Neary*[1]:

'Trustees have a duty to protect and preserve the trust estate for the benefit of the beneficiaries and accordingly to represent the trust in a third party dispute … trustees are well advised to seek court authorisation before they sue or defend. The right to an indemnity and a lien will ordinarily extend to the costs of such an application. The form of application is a separate action to which all the beneficiaries are parties (either in person or by a representative defendant). With the benefit of their views the judge thereupon exercising his discretion determines what course the interests of justice require to be taken in the proceedings (see *Evans v Evans*[2] considered in *McDonald v Horn*)[3]. So long as the trustees make full disclosure of the strength, and weaknesses of their case, if the trustees act as authorised by the court their entitlement to an indemnity and lien is secure.'

1 [1995] 1 All ER 431; *Smith v Croft* [1986] 2 All ER 551 at 558. Further see para 87.48 below.
2 [1985] 3 All ER 289 [1986] 1 WLR 101, CA.
3 [1995] 1 All ER 961.

83.17 Where the opposing party in the litigation is himself a beneficiary he is either not present at the application[1] or (if present) not supplied with the privileged legal advice available to the trustees[2].

1 *Re Moritz* [1960] Ch 251, [1959] 3 All ER 767.
2 *Re Eaton* [1964] 3 All ER 229n, [1964] 1 WLR 1269.

A protective clause ousting need for a Beddoe Application

83.18 The costs and delay occasioned by a need for a *Beddoe* application make it desirable to insert a clause in the original trust instrument permitting trustees to recover their expenses out of the trust fund on an indemnity basis if they act on the advice of experienced counsel (as the judge on a *Beddoe* application does to a great extent). To this end the following clause has been suggested[1]:

'A Trustee shall not be liable for acting in accordance with the advice of Counsel, of at least ten years standing, with respect to the settlement. The Trustees may in particular conduct legal proceedings in accordance with such advice without obtaining a Court Order. A Trustee may recover from the Trust Fund any expenses where he acted in accordance with such advice'.

1 J Kessler, *Drafting Trusts and Will Trusts* (6th edn), para 5.28.

83.19 But this provision

'does not apply if the trustee knows or has reasonable cause to suspect that the advice was given in ignorance of material facts; if proceedings were pending to obtain the decision of the court in the matter; in relation to a Trustee who has a personal interest in the subject matter of the advice; or in relation to a Trustee who has committed a breach of trust relating to the subject matter of the advice'.

83.20 Alternatively, it would be open for a trusting settlor to go much further. The trust instrument could even authorise the trustee to indemnify himself in respect of all costs and expenses incurred as trustee in acting as claimant or defendant as concerns third parties unless the beneficiaries prove that he did not act in good faith.

Unreasonable expenses disallowed

83.21 The general rule is that trustees will not be allowed to reimburse themselves *every* out-of-pocket expense, but only such as are reasonable and proper under the circumstances. Thus in one case the expenses of a trustee's journey to Paris, in order that he might be present at the hearing of a suit brought in the French courts (the sole question being one of French law, and not of fact), were disallowed[1].

[1]   *Malcolm v O'Callaghan* (1837) 3 My & Cr 52; see also *Virani v Guernsey International Trustees Ltd* [2004] WTLR 1035, paras 48–52.

Voluntary subscriptions

83.22 As a general rule, the payment by trustees of voluntary subscriptions for public or charitable objects is not allowed. But nevertheless they may be in exceptional cases—for instance, where the subscriptions are reasonable in amount and made in the honest belief that the payment will benefit the estate[1]. As to charitable subscriptions made under the power of advancement, see para 67.5 above.

[1]   *How v Earl of Winterton* (1902) 51 WR 262 (subscriptions to a church school allowed, as otherwise a school board would have been necessary and the estate would have been liable for an increase in rates exceeding the amount of the subscriptions). See also *Re Walker* [1901] 1 Ch 879, where the court sanctioned the payment of charitable subscriptions.

Unnecessary law costs

83.23 A trustee, although entitled to obtain legal advice in relation to the execution of the trust, is not entitled, out of an excess of caution, to charge the estate with unnecessary legal costs. For instance, on retirement he is not entitled to have an attested copy of the settlement, or of the appointment of new trustees, made at the expense of the estate[1]. And on an appeal between beneficiaries it has been said that trustees ought not, as a rule, to brief counsel[2]. However, the practice is that trustees served with notice of appeal upon the construction of a will should have their costs of appearing by counsel[3]. If trustees appeal from an order of the court they will have to pay the costs if they are unsuccessful[4]. Indeed, where trustees have sought guidance from the court so as to be protected by the court's order then it is not for them to appeal: that should be done by a beneficiary[5].

[1]   *Warter v Anderson* (1853) 11 Hare 301; and see Article 84 below.
[2]   *Carroll v Graham* [1905] 1 Ch 478; see per contra *Catterson v Clark* (1906) 95 LT 42; and cf *Re Barry's Trusts* [1906] 2 Ch 358.
[3]   See old RSC Ord 59 r 10.

4   *Re Earl of Radnor's Will Trusts* (1890) 45 Ch D 402.
5   *Re Londonderry's Settlement* [1965] Ch 918 at 930, [1964] 3 All ER 855 at 858 per
     Harman LJ (with whom, it seems, Danckwerts LJ agreed) though the non-Chancery lawyer
     Salmon LJ disagreed at 936 and 862 because the trustees believed an appeal was essential
     for the protection of the general body of the beneficiaries; the trustee's appeal was
     successful so they were allowed their costs out of the trust fund.

83.24 Where the dispute is essentially between claimants of the trust property
on the one hand and the beneficiaries under the trust on the other hand, the
trustees will obtain their costs of adopting a neutral stance and making
disclosure but will not recover their costs to the extent that they side with the
losing party[1].

1   *Alsop Wilkinson v Neary* [1995] 1 All ER 431, para 87.37 below.

Interest

83.25 Although a trustee is entitled to be reimbursed his out-of-pocket costs
and expenses, he is not, as a rule, entitled to interest on them—a rule not
altogether in accordance with justice[1]. And although by s 66(a) of the
Solicitors Act 1974, a solicitor may be allowed on taxation with respect to
contentious business, interest on disbursements made for his client, this does
not seem to apply to disbursements made by a solicitor trustee. There is,
however, an exception to the rule, namely, that where a trustee has paid out of
his own moneys an interest-bearing claim against the estate, he stands by way
of subrogation in the shoes of the creditor, and is entitled to interest[2].

1   *Gordon v Trail* (1820) 8 Price 416.
2   *Re Beulah Park Estate, Sargood's Claim* (1872) LR 15 Eq 43; *Finch v Pescott* (1874) LR
     17 Eq 554.

Expenses paid out of taxed income

83.26 The income expenses of the trustees are borne out of the net income of
the trust after payment of income tax[1].

1   *Aiken v Macdonald's Trustees* (1894) 3 TC 306; *Murrary v IRC* 1926 SLT 714;
     Macfarlane v IRC 1929 SC 453. Income & Corporation Taxes Act 1988, s 686; J Tiley
     Revenue Law (4th edn) pp 559 and 563.

Paragraph 2

Trustees' paramount lien on trust property for expenses

83.27 If, in an administration action, it appears probable that the trust fund
will be insufficient for the payment of the whole of the costs in full, the
trustees are entitled to have inserted in the order a direction that their costs,
charges, and expenses shall be paid in priority to those of the beneficiaries[1]. In
short, the trustees' lien takes precedence over all beneficial interests, and this
not only as against original beneficiaries but also against all purchasers or
mortgagees claiming through or under them[2].

1 *Dodds v Tuke* (1884) 25 Ch D 617. But even without this direction the trustees would be
   entitled to be paid in priority to the other parties (*Re Griffith* [1904] 1 Ch 807; *Re Turner*
   [1907] 2 Ch 126).
2 *Re Knapman* (1881) 18 Ch D 300, CA; cf *Re Andrews* (1885) 30 Ch D 159.

83.28 A trustee who successfully defends proceedings brought against him as
trustee by a beneficiary and arising out of the execution of the trust is entitled
to his costs out of the trust fund and to a lien for their payment[1].

1 *Re Spurling's Will Trusts* [1966] 1 All ER 745, [1966] 1 WLR 920, in which *Turner v
   Hancock* (1882) 20 Ch D 303, and *Re Grimthorpe's* [1958] Ch 615, [1958] 1 All ER 765,
   were applied, *Re Dunn* [1904] 1 Ch 648, was distinguished, and *Walters v Woodbridge*
   (1878) 7 Ch D 504, CA, was considered and explained.

Trustees' lien for legal costs where settlement void or avoided

83.29 In *Re Holden*[1] Holden executed a post-nuptial voluntary settlement.
He subsequently commenced an action to set it aside for undue influence, but
failed in his contention, the action being dismissed with costs against him,
which he did not pay. He then became bankrupt within two years of the date
of the settlement, which accordingly became void under the Bankruptcy Act
then in force. It was held that, although the settlement was void, yet, as it had
originally been valid, but voidable, and as the trustees had incurred costs in
the execution of their duty which they could not recover from the bankrupt,
they were entitled to be fully indemnified out of the trust funds.

1 (1887) 20 QBD 43.

83.30 Where there is a dispute between rival claimants to the beneficial
interest in the trust property the trustee's normal duty is to remain neutral and
offer to submit to the court's directions, leaving it to the rivals to fight their
battles[1]. If this stance be adopted the trustee will be entitled to an indemnity
and lien in respect of costs necessarily and properly incurred, eg in serving a
defence agreeing to submit to the court's directions and in making discovery. If
the rival claimant's cannot agree how the trust fund should be invested and
managed until the claims are resolved, appropriate directions can be obtained
from the court under CPR Part 64[2]. If the trustee actively defends the trust but
fails then, unless the circumstances are exceptional[3], he will not be entitled to
his costs out of the trust fund, although he will be if he succeeds in his
defence[4].

1 *Alsop Wilkinson v Neary* [1995] 1 All ER 431 at 435; see para 87.37 below.
2 As to which see Article 87.
3 *Bullock v Lloyds Bank Ltd* [1955] Ch 317, [1954] 3 All ER 726 as explained in *Alsop
   Wilkinson v Neary* [1995] 1 All ER 431 at 436.
4 See paras 87.38 and 87.49.

No paramount lien where trustee has mixed his money with trust fund

83.31 Where a trustee for purchase advanced money of his own to enable a
particular property to be purchased and the price of the property exceeded the

83.31 *The rights of the trustee*

whole trust fund, it was held that he had not a *first* charge on the property for reimbursing himself his advance, but that the beneficiaries had a first charge on the estate for the amount of the trust fund, and that he only had a second charge for the amount of his advance[1]. The ratio decidendi in this case would seem to have been that it was not so much a question of indemnity for *costs and expenses incurred in the performance of his duty* as of a gratuitous mixing of his own moneys with the trust moneys; and that this (as will be seen later on)[2] gave the trust estate a first and paramount charge. So where a trustee paid premiums on a settled policy out of his own pocket, instead of applying a fund provided for that purpose by the settlement, he was disallowed the payments[3].

¹ *Re Pumfrey* (1882) 22 Ch D 255, approved in *De Vigier v IRC* [1964] 2 All ER 907, HL.
² Article 92, below.
³ *Clack v Holland* (1854) 19 Beav 262.

Trustee can refuse to transfer property to new trustees or absolutely entitled beneficiaries until his lien is satisfied

83.32 By virtue of his lien a trustee has the right to retain sufficient trust assets to cover actual and contingent liabilities and also possible potential liabilities that can be identified[1]. This can lead to the trustee continuing to manage the trust property after all the beneficiaries have otherwise become entitled to it, exercising its powers under the trust instrument for the benefit of itself and those beneficiaries, fairly considering the interests of itself and of them[2].

¹ *X v A* [2000] 1 All ER 490; Trusts of Land and Appointment of Trustee Act 1996, s 19(3)(b).
² *X v A* [2000] 1 All ER 490 at 494–495.

Trustee's lien continues to bind trust property in hands of successor trustees

83.33 A trustee may choose not to exercise his right of retention if satisfied that his interests are adequately protected. He may overlook some possible liability, wrongly assuming that liabilities of trustees attach to the holders of the office from time to time. Where he is replaced by new trustees his beneficial interest in the nature of a non-possessory lien[1] continues to bind the trust assets just like the interests of the beneficiaries[2], and affords him an independent right of recourse to the trust assets that is not dependent in any way upon either possession of the trust fund or the successor trustees' right of indemnity against the trust assets.

¹ *Dimos v Dikeakos Nominees Ltd* (1996) 68 FCR 39 (1997) 149 ALR 113; *Rothmore Farms Pty Ltd v Belgravia Pty Ltd* (1999) 2 ITELR 159.
² There are two classes of beneficiaries: (1) the trustee with a beneficial interest commensurate with his right of indemnity, (2) the persons designated as beneficiaries in the trust instrument: see *Octavo Investments Pty Ltd v Knight* (1979) 144 CLR 360; *Kemtron Industries Pty Ltd v Comr of Stamp Duties* [1984] 1 Qd R 576 at 590.

Assets distributed to beneficiaries no longer subject to lien unless it is expressly preserved

83.34 Where a trustee exercises discretionary powers of appointment or discretionary trusts and appoints an asset in favour of an object it seems that the asset will be released not only from the equitable interests of (default) beneficiaries designated in the trust instrument but also from the equitable interest commensurate with any right of indemnity of a trustee[1]. In such a case it is implicit – if not made explicit – that the distribution is of assets freed and discharged from the trusts affecting them[2], unless otherwise stipulated.

[1] *Octavo Investments Pty Ltd v Knight* (1979) 144 CLR 360; *Kemtron Industries Pty Ltd v Comr of Stamp Duties* [1984] 1 Qd R 576; and an authorised overreaching (explaining *Vandervell v IRC* [1967] 2 AC 291) see RC Nolan [2002] Camb LJ 169 and C Harpum [1990] Camb LJ 277.

[2] In *Rothmore Farms Pty Ltd v Belgravia Pty Ltd* [1999] FCA 745 (1999) 2 ITELR 159 at para 116 counsel for the sole distributee, who was party to a scheme to evade a right of indemnity and defraud creditors, did not seek to argue that the distributee took free from an original trustee's right of indemnity that survived the appointment of the distributor as new trustee. If the trustee-distributor is guilty of a fraud on a power in exercising his discretion so as to defraud an earlier trustee the exercise of the power will be void: *Cloutte v Storey* [1911] 1 Ch 18, CA.

83.35 When the trust terminates, so that whatever trust assets remain must be transferred to the beneficiaries absolutely entitled to them, the trustee who knows he has a beneficial interest in the assets may be treated as releasing or giving away that beneficial interest in assets he transfers to the beneficiaries freed and discharged from the trusts affecting them. But it is more difficult to see how the non-possessory interest of a former trustee can be given up in this way, unless the present trustee has the authority of the former to give it up.

Transfer subject to indemnity from new trustees

83.36 Often, to guard against known or potential liabilities, retiring trustees will refuse to transfer trust property to new trustees until the new trustees provide an indemnity for the old trustees by virtue of the powers conferred by s 15 of the Trustee Act 1925 or by the trust instrument. To protect themselves, the new trustees will want their liability under the indemnity to be restricted to the value of the trust fund in their hands, but to protect the old trustees, it is common to provide that in calculating that value distributions of assets out of the trust fund are only to be excluded from calculation of that value if and to the extent that the beneficiaries receiving such distributions enter into direct covenants with the old trustees to indemnify them. Because procuring such covenants is necessary for the new trustees to protect themselves they can be relied upon to do so[1].

[1] Further see Trust Law Committee Consultation Paper, 'The Proper Protection by Liens, Indemnities or Otherwise of those who cease to be Trustees': www.kcl.ac.uk/schools/law/research/tlc/consult.html

Paragraph 3

Personal indemnity by beneficiary under a simple trust

83.37 In one case shares in a company were placed in the plaintiff's name as bare trustee for his employers, and later for the defendant, as successor in title of the employers. When a call was made on the shares which the plaintiff was obliged to pay, the defendant was held liable to indemnify him personally. Lord Lindley said[1]:

> 'The plainest principles of justice require that the cestui que trust who gets all the benefit of the property should bear its burdens unless he can show some good reason why his trustee should bear them himself. The obligation is equitable and not legal, and the legal decisions negativing it unless there is some contract or custom imposing the obligation, are wholly irrelevant and beside the mark. Even where trust property is settled on tenants for life and children, the right of the trustee to be indemnified *out of the whole trust estate* against any liabilities arising out of any part of it is clear and indisputable; although, if that which was once one large trust estate has been converted by the trustees into several smaller distinct trust estates, the liabilities incidental to one of them cannot be thrown on the beneficial owners of the others ... But where the only cestui que trust is a person sui juris, the right of the trustee to indemnity by him against liabilities incurred by the trustee by his retention of the trust property has never been limited to the trust property; it extends further, and imposes upon the cestui que trust a personal obligation enforceable in equity to indemnify his trustee. This is no new principle, but as old as trusts themselves ... Although the defendant did not create the trust, he accepted a transfer of the beneficial ownership in the shares ... with full knowledge of the fact that they were registered in the plaintiff's name as trustee for their original purchasers and their assigns, whoever they might be.'

[1]   *Hardoon v Belilios* [1901] AC 118 at 123; also see *Jervis v Wolferstan*(1874) LR 18 Eq 18 at 24 and *Fraser v Murdoch* (1881) 6 App Cas 855.

83.38 In another case two partners had taken a lease, as trustees, for the firm, and ultimately the executors of one of the trustees were compelled to pay large arrears of rent. It was held that they could insist upon contribution from all the co-partners, and that the fact of the lease having been assigned to a limited company which made default in paying the rent, did not free the co-partners from the trustees' right to contribution[1].

[1]   *Matthews v Ruggles-Brise* [1911] 1 Ch 194.

83.39 In an Australian case, the defendants formed a company to carry on a trade as corporate trustee and to pay or apply the net income to the defendants in accordance with the number of units they had under the trust (100 units had been divided into 42, 10, 24 and 24). It was held that the defendants had personally to indemnify the corporate trustee, though each defendant's share of the liability was not to exceed his proportion of the beneficial interest[1]. It was irrelevant that some of the beneficiaries had declared sub-trusts of their units for infant children. In principle, it would seem that persons who purchase units of a unit trust can thus be called on to indemnify the trustee, unless the trust instrument excludes the trustee's right to be indemnified personally by the beneficiaries[2].

1 *J W Broomhead (Vic) Pty Ltd (in liquidation) v J W Broomhead Pty Ltd* [1985] VR 891.
2 The right can be excluded: *Gillan v Morrison* (1847) 1 De G & Sm 421; *Hardoon v Belilios* [1901] AC 118, PC; *RWG Management Ltd v Corporate Affairs Comr* [1985] VR 385.

83.40 Just as a right of subrogation may subsist in respect of the right of indemnity out of the trust property[1] so it should subsist in respect of the right of indemnity against the beneficiaries personally[2]. In principle there should be no distinction between the two rights of indemnity[3].

1 See para 83.48 ff.
2 Unless personal liability of beneficiaries has been excluded by the trust instrument: *McLean v Burns Philp Trustee Co Pty Ltd* (1985) 2 NSWLR 623 at 641.
3 See Scott on Trusts (4th edn), para 478; *Poland v Beal* 192 Mass 559 (1906); *Countryside (No 3) Pty Ltd v Bayside Brunswick Pty Ltd* (20 April 1994, unreported) NSW Sup Ct, Brownie J.

Limits upon right to personal indemnity

83.41 The above decisions, however, only relate to the case of simple trusts in favour of a person or persons absolutely entitled who created the trust themselves or who accepted a transfer of the beneficial ownership in the trust property with full knowledge of the facts. As Lord Lindley observed[1]:

> 'it is quite unnecessary to consider in this case the difficulties which would arise if these shares were held by the plaintiff on trust for tenants for life, or for infants, or upon special trusts limiting the right to indemnity. In those cases there is no beneficiary who can be justly expected or required personally to indemnify the trustee against the ... burdens incident to his legal ownership; and the trustee accepts the trust *knowing that under such circumstances and in the absence of special contract his right to indemnity cannot extend beyond the trust estate* i e beyond the respective interests of his cestuis que trust. In this case their lordships have only to deal with a person sui juris beneficially entitled to shares which he cannot disclaim.'

1 *Hardoon v Belilios* [1901] AC 118 at 127.

83.42 The justification for making A, B, C, and D personally liable to indemnify the trustees (and creditors subrogated to the trustees) where the property is held in trust for A, B, C and D absolutely seems to rest on the principle that A, B, C and D can terminate the trust at any time as the beneficiaries of full age and capacity between them absolutely entitled to the trust property[1]. One can thus infer a continuing request by them to the trustees to incur liabilities in duly administering the trust property. Thus A, B, C and D should also be personally liable to indemnify the trustees if of full age and capacity and between them entitled to the trust property by virtue of successive rather than concurrent interests. In one case[2] the New South Wales Court of Appeal held that where property was held on trust for A for life, remainder to B, C and D equally and English trustees had to pay overlooked inheritance tax on the death of A, (resident in England) then the trustees had a

83.42 *The rights of the trustee*

personal right of indemnity against B, C and D in Australia to whom the trustees had transferred the trust assets. In another case the principle was slightly extended, where the sole member of a company pension scheme (whose wife had a contingent interest) brought in an independent trustee who incurred liability, and the member was held liable to indemnify the trustee personally.[3]

1   *Saunders v Vautier* (1841) 4 Beav 115 principle discussed in Article 69, above.
2   *Balkin v Peck* (1997) 43 NSWLR 706, (1998) 1 ITELR 717.
3   *Independent Trustee Services Ltd v Rowe* [1998] OPLR 77.

83.43 In any event if any beneficiary of full age and capacity, whether with a life interest or only interested under a discretionary trust, requests the trustee to incur a liability the beneficiary becomes personally liable to indemnify the trustee[1]. The settlor who requests the trustee to assume the office of a trustee (from which liabilities will inevitably flow) does not thereby make himself personally liable to indemnify the trustee unless he retains such wide powers to direct the trustee that the relationship of principal and agent is established between them[2].

1   *Balsh v Hyham* (1728) 2 P Wms 453; *Hobbs v Wayet* (1887) 36 Ch D 256; *J W Broomhead (Vic) Pty Ltd v JW Broomhead Pty Ltd* [1985] VR 891.
2   *Fraser v Murdoch* (1881) 6 App Cas 855; *Trident Holdings Ltd v Danand Investments Ltd* (1988) 49 DLR (4th) 1.

Trustees of clubs have no right to personal indemnity

83.44 As an illustration of the remarks in the last paragraph the case of trustees of a members' club may be cited. It is a usual condition of club membership that members are not legally liable to any one beyond the amount of their subscriptions. There is, therefore, in the nature of the transaction no implied bargain, unless the rules of the club provide to the contrary (as they certainly ought to do), that the members shall as beneficiaries be liable to indemnify the trustees[1], and the trustees are taken to accept the office with knowledge of this condition.

1   *Wise v Perpetual Trustee Co Ltd* [1903] AC 139, PC; Marston, *Thompson & Evershed plc v Benn* [1998] CLY 4875, Ch D.

83.45 However, if the members authorise the trustees to enter into a contract (eg of insurance of club property) expressly on behalf of all the members, then those members will be able to sue or be sued in respect of such contract[1].

1   *Howells v Dominion Insurance Co Ltd* [2005] EWHC 552 (QB) where when H & J took out representative orders for the other members, Cox J held those other members could not be liable for costs.

Paragraph 4

Trustee can only receive indemnity where he has discharged his own indebtedness to the estate

83.46 If the state of accounts between the trustee and the beneficiaries taking account of any losses caused by any breach of trust by the trustee is such that the trustee is in deficit then he has no right to any indemnity till that deficit has been made good[1]. This will prejudice the derivative right of any creditor seeking to be subrogated to the trustee's right of indemnity[2]. However, where there are two trustees and one is indebted to the trust but the other is not, the creditors can take advantage of the latter's right to an indemnity[3]. It sometimes happens that, in the course of an administration action or summons, a trustee is ordered to refund to the estate moneys lost by reason of some breach of trust for which he is responsible, but that he is nevertheless allowed his costs of the litigation, either in the whole[4], or limited to costs incurred after the judgment. In all such cases, however, he will not be permitted to receive the costs in fact allowed to him (or his costs, charges, and expenses properly incurred outside the litigation) until he has made good the loss to the estate caused by his breach[5]. In practice the costs are set off against the liability, the trustee either receiving or paying the balance only. The principle sometimes causes hardship to the solicitor of an insolvent trustee, as he loses the security of the estate for the costs of what may have been a costly litigation, and cannot recover them from his own insolvent client[6].

[1] *Re Johnson* (1880) 15 Ch D 548 at 552; *Re Frith* [1902] 1 Ch 342 at 345; *Re Evans* (1887) 34 Ch D 597 at 601.
[2] *Ex p Edmonds* (1862) 4 De G F & J 488 at 498.
[3] *Re Firth* [1902] 1 Ch 342 at 346.
[4] On which see para 87.27 ff.
[5] *Re Knott* (1887) 56 LJ Ch 318.
[6] *Lewis v Trask* (1882) 21 Ch D 862; *Re Basham* (1883) 23 Ch D 195; *McEwan v Crombie* (1883) 25 Ch D 175. But cf *Clare v Clare* (1882) 21 Ch D 865.

Paragraph 5

Persons employed by, or who supply goods to, the trustee have no direct claim on estate but may have a subrogation claim

83.47 Persons to whom a trustee has incurred liability have no original or direct right to claim payment out of the trust estate. This question usually arises in relation to the business of a testator carried on, rightly or wrongly, by his trustees. If a testator's will is silent on the question, his business ought to be sold as a going concern, or wound up with reasonable despatch. If (as sometimes happens) trustees carry it on for the benefit of the family, they do so at their own risk. If losses ensue, they have no right to reimbursement out of the trust property, though they may have personal claims against members of the family of full age and capacity.

83.48 On the other hand, a testator not infrequently directs his business to be carried on, and authorises the employment in it of all, or a specific portion, of his assets. In that case, of course, the trustees are entitled to reimbursement of losses out of the assets so appropriated. Now in such cases the creditors of the business have no original right to claim payment of their debts out of the *trust estate*[1], their remedy being against the trustee whom they trusted; but nevertheless, they have also a right to be *put in his place* against the trust estate by subrogation.

1   *Re Johnson* (1880) 15 Ch D 548; *Re Webb* (1890) 63 LT 545; *Strickland v Symons* (1884) 26 Ch D 245; and see also *Redman v Rymer* (1889) 60 LT 385; *Baroness Wenlock v River Dee Co* (1887) 19 QBD 155; *Moore v M'Glynn* [1904] 1 IR 334; and as to torts, *Re Raybould* [1900] 1 Ch 199.

83.49 The right, however, is strictly limited to the right of the trustee himself. Therefore, if he is (by reason of breach of trust or otherwise) himself indebted to the trust estate to an extent exceeding his claim to indemnity, then, inasmuch as he cannot be entitled to an indemnity except upon the terms of making good his own indebtedness to the trust, the creditors are in no better position, and can have no claim against the estate[1].

1   *Re Johnson* (1880) 15 Ch D 548; *Ex p Garland* (1804) 10 Ves 110; recognised in *Re Blundell* (1890) 44 Ch D 1 at 11; *Re Frith* [1902] 1 Ch 342; *Re British Power Traction and Lighting Co* [1910] 2 Ch 470. A defaulting trustee cannot claim any beneficial interest before making good his default (*Doering v Doering* (1889) 42 Ch D 203; *Re Dacre* [1916] 1 Ch 344 at 347) is the underlying principle. Further see Trust Law Committee Consultation Paper and their Report on 'Rights of Creditors against Trustees and Trust Funds'.

83.50 A creditor has four hurdles to surmount. He needs to show that the contractual liability incurred by the trustee was not improperly incurred (1) by lack of capacity due to limits imposed by the trust instrument; (2) by lack of due authorisation where there is power to enter into the transaction but only in accordance with some requisite internal procedure which was not observed, eg the holding of a meeting before taking the decision or a unanimous (not a majority) decision, or the consent of X to a decision; (3) by breach of some equitable duty, eg to diversify investments, to exercise the duty of care in appointing and supervising agents and in making investment or managerial decisions. He must also show that the trustee (4) is not indebted to the trust by reason of conduct totally unconnected with the creditor's transaction but by virtue of some unrelated breach of trust occurring before or after such transaction.

83.51 There is very little a potential creditor can do about the fourth hurdle. The best may be an argument that the trustee's power under the trust to enter into the transaction with the creditor itself authorises the insertion of a term in the contract which confers on the creditor a direct unsecured right of recourse to the trust fund irrespective of any indebtedness of the trustee to the trust which is unrelated to the transaction and such a term is inserted in the contract[1]. Clearly, no term in the contract can protect the creditor where the liability incurred by the trustee was improperly incurred because this would enable the trustee to commit breaches of trust wholly undermining the effectiveness of the settlor's trust. The problem for a creditor in negotiating a deal with the trustees is that the better the deal is for the creditor, the more likely it is to be in breach of the trustee's duty of care, so ousting any subrogation rights of the creditor if the trustees do not discharge their liability to the creditor.

1   See JG Merralls QC (1993) Australian Bar Review 248; Scott on Trusts (4th edn) Vol IIIA, pp 499–500.

83.52 Recourse can only be made to the right of subrogation where the personally liable trustee is insolvent or the circumstances are such as to lead to the reasonable conclusion that a judgment against the trustee would be pointless[1].

1   *Owen v Delamere* (1872) LR 15 Eq 134; *Re Morris* (1889) 23 LR Ir 333; *Fairland v Percy* (1875) LR 3 P & D 217.

83.53 Where a testator authorises trustees to carry on a business but directs that a limited part of his estate is to be used for that purpose, then the trustees' right of indemnity and, thus, the claims of creditors subsequent to the testator's death are limited to that part[1]. Similarly, if executors exercise a power of appropriation to sever the estate so that they hold half including a business for X and her family and the other half for Y and her family there is no right of recourse against Y's half for business debts arising after the severance[2]. Old case law[3] (which may require reconsideration in modern conditions) indicates that for the right of subrogation to subsist there must have been a positive express dedication or appropriation of the property to be used for the purposes of trade. This view may be confined to cases where the trustees have not been expressly authorised to carry on the business but have had to carry it on for a period by way of salvage to enable it to be sold for a reasonable price. Even here though, the court will as between the trustees and the beneficiaries allow the trustees an indemnity out of the estate so it is difficult to see why a right of subrogation should not subsist to that extent.

1   *Ex p Garland* (1804) 10 Ves 110.
2   *Fraser v Murdoch* (1881) 6 App Cas 855, HL.
3   *Strickland v Symons* (1853) 26 Ch D 245; and see *Re German Mining Co* (1853) 4 De GM & G 19; and *Labouchere v Tupper* (1857) 11 Moo PCC 198. But contrast *Re Raybould* [1900] 1 Ch 199.

Protection of third parties via direct claims on estate

83.54 Trustees may and often do have power to create an immediate fixed charge over specific assets comprised in the trust estate. However, whether they may be given express power to create a floating charge over the trust estate generally, in the sense of the assets from time to time comprised within the estate, is a more difficult question. The traditional view was that because the basis of a floating charge is contract law[1] and the burden of a contract with T1 cannot without a novation be imposed on his successor T2, a charge of future property created by T1 will not operate upon property acquired after the appointment of T2. However, the Law Reform Committee's Twenty-Third Report (1982)[2] saw 'no reason to doubt that a trust instrument could be so worded' to confer just that sort of power[3], with the instrument spelling out the events in which such charge will crystallise.

83.54 *The rights of the trustee*

1   *Holroyd v Marshall* (1862) 10 HL Cas 191; *Tailby v Official Receiver* (1888) 13 App Cas 523; *Akrom Tyre Co Pty Ltd v Kittson* (1951) 82 CLR 477.
2   Para 2.21.
3   It seems that a power for value to make a creditor an equitable beneficiary in the trust fund in its state from time to time until payment of the debt would in substance be held to be a security interest by way of floating charge.

83.55 However, to accord with the traditional contract basis of floating charges, the deed creating the floating charge should ensure that there will be no change of trustee without the chargee's consent, so as to enable a new contractual arrangement to be entered into with the new trustee, and that the charge will automatically crystallise if a change of trustees does occur without consent. The deed should also restrict the trustee's exercise of powers that could detrimentally affect the chargee (eg distributive powers over capital); it could indeed provide for the trustee's personal liability to extend to the value of assets distributed to the beneficiaries except to the extent that such beneficiaries entered into direct covenants to indemnify the chargee. Whether the trustees should properly exercise their powers to create such a floating charge must of course depend on the circumstances.

83.56 Taking account of an analogy with the trustee's lien conferring upon him a beneficial interest in the trust *fund*[1] (although superior to the beneficial interests of the designated beneficiaries) it has been argued that a power to create a floating charge over the assets from time to time comprised in the trust fund, when exercised, creates an equitable interest binding the trust fund, not just in the hands of the trustee-chargors but also their successors as trustees. But this ignores the contractual nexus needed to bring the equitable interest into existence and for Equity to look on as done that which ought to be done. The successor trustee made no contract binding the assets subsequently acquired by him. Without that, there is no basis for subjecting those assets to any charge on the occurrence of the prescribed events. The analogy with the trustee's lien is not a good one, T1, on being replaced by T2, being incapable of incurring further liabilities and having incurred liabilities in respect of which he has a fixed overreachable interest.

1   *Kemtron Industries Pty Ltd v Commissioner of Stamp Duties* [1984] 1 QdR 576 at 590; *Octavo Investments Pty Ltd v Knight* (1979) 144 CLR 360; *Dimos v Dikeakos Nominees Ltd* (1996) 68 FCR 39, (1997) 149 ALR 113.

Where trustee is insolvent

83.57 On insolvency the right of indemnity vests in the trustee in bankruptcy or remains with the insolvent trustee[1]. The benefit of the right of indemnity out of the trust fund is available only for payment of creditors of the trust and not the general creditors of the insolvent trustee[2].

1   *St Thomas' Hospital Governors v Richardson* [1910] 1 KB 271, CA; *Re Richardson* [1911] 2 KB 705 at 717, CA.
2   *Re Richardson* [1911] 2 KB 705; *Re Byrne Australia Pty Ltd* [1981] 1 NSWLR 394; *Re Byrne Australia Pty Ltd (No 2)* [1981] 2 NSWLR 364; *Collie v Merlaw Nominees Pty Ltd* [2001] VSC 39.

ARTICLE 84
RIGHT TO DISCHARGE ON COMPLETION OF TRUSTEESHIP

84.1

Upon the completion of his trusteeship, a trustee is entitled to have his accounts examined and settled by the beneficiaries; and either to have a formal discharge given to him or to have the accounts taken in court. He cannot, however, as a rule, demand a release by deed[1], nor to have deeds relating to the trust, or to the title of an assign of one of the original beneficiaries, handed over to him; but it seems that he is entitled to an examined copy and to an acknowledgment for production and an undertaking for safe custody.

[1] *Chadwick v Heatley* (1845) 2 Coll 137; *Re Wright's Trusts* (1857) 3 K & J 419; *King v Mullins* (1852) 1 Drew 308; *Tiger v Barclay's Bank Ltd* [1951] 2 KB 556, [1951] 2 All ER 262; affd [1952] 1 All ER 85, CA, where this point was not in issue; and see *Re Earl of Stamford* [1896] 1 Ch 288 at 301; Law of Property (Miscellaneous Provisions) Act 1989, s 1 (now contains the formal requirements for a deed).

Release by deed cannot usually be required

84.2 A trustee, on finally transferring trust assets to a beneficiary absolutely entitled is not entitled to a deed of release[1].

[1] *Chadwick v Heatley* (1845) 2 Coll 137; *King v Mullins* (1852) 1 Drew 308 at 311.

Right to settlement of account restricted to the actual trust fund

84.3 Although a trustee is entitled to have his accounts settled before handing over the trust fund, this right is confined to the accounts of that particular trust. Where, therefore, a person is trustee of two distinct trusts for the same beneficiaries, he cannot mix up the two, and refuse to pay over the first fund until all questions as to the second have been settled[1].

[1] *Price v Loaden* (1856) 21 Beav 508.

Release may be required in exceptional cases

84.4 Where trust monies have been resettled, the trustees or executors of the original settlement or will are entitled to a release by deed from their beneficiaries, though they are entitled only to a mere receipt from the trustees to whom they pay the moneys[1]. On the other hand, where a person having a *general* power of appointment by will appoints the fund in pursuance of the power, and then appoints executors, the trustees of the fund can safely hand it over to the executors on their receipt, and cannot demand a release by deed from the beneficiaries[2]; for, by appointing, the donee of the power makes the property assets of his own[3].

[1] *Re Cater's Trusts (No 2)* (1858) 25 Beav 366.

84.4 *The rights of the trustee*

2   *Re Hoskin's Trusts* (1877) 5 Ch D 229; on appeal 6 Ch D 281.
3   See para 82.2 above.

Trustee cannot demand custody of assignments of shares of the original beneficiaries

84.5 It is well settled that, on the distribution of a trust fund, a share in which has been previously assigned, the trustee has no right to require the delivery to him of the assignment and other documents of title before payment of his share to the assignee[1]; and of course it follows that a trustee cannot require a power of attorney to be handed to him[2]. However, he is entitled to retain custody of the trust instrument and of appointments of new trustees.

1   *Re Palmer* [1907] 1 Ch 486.
2   *Re Palmer* [1907] 1 Ch 486.

How far a trustee is entitled to copies of deeds, etc

84.6 This, however, does not dispose of the question whether a trustee can demand *copies* of those documents which justify his doing what he has in fact done. This certainly does not seem unreasonable in principle, especially where he is paying money to a person who claims as attorney or assignee of one of the original beneficiaries. It seems that he can demand plain examined copies, but not attested copies or, a fortiori, duplicates, except perhaps at his own expense. Thus in one case[1] the representative of a deceased trustee was held not to be entitled, upon transferring the property to new trustees, to be furnished at the expense of the trust with a duplicate of the appointment of the new trustees, nor even to an attested copy thereof, although the court considered that he had a right to have an examined copy and possibly at his own expense an attested copy or even a duplicate.

1   *Warter v Anderson* (1853) 11 Hare 301; and see *Clayton v Clayton* [1930] 2 Ch 12.

84.7 Further, it would seem that a trustee may be entitled to insist upon an acknowledgment for production and an undertaking for safe custody as well as to a copy[1].

1   *Re Palmer* [1907] 1 Ch 486.

ARTICLE 85
RIGHT TO PAY TRUST FUNDS INTO COURT IN
CERTAIN CIRCUMSTANCES

85.1

(1)   Trustees, or the majority of trustees, having in their hands or under their control money or securities belonging to a trust, may pay them into court[1].

(2)   Payment into court is not, however, justifiable merely in order to raise some question which can be determined more cheaply by

way of a claim under CPR Part 8 (formerly by originating summons)[2]; nor where the equities are perfectly clear[3], and, if trustees pay into court in such circumstances, they may have to pay the costs of obtaining payment out[4].

[1]   Ie the High Court, or where the funds paid in are of less than £30,000 in value the county court; see the Trustee Act 1925, s 63, and the County Courts Act, 1984, s 23.
[2]   *Re Giles* (1886) 34 WR 712. As to Part 8 claims, see para 87.1.
[3]   *Re Cull's Trusts* (1875) LR 20 Eq 561; *Re Elliot's Trusts* (1873) LR 15 Eq 194.
[4]   *Re Cull's Trusts* (1875) LR 20 Eq 561; *Re Elliot's Trusts* (1873) LR 15 Eq 194; *Re Leake's Trusts* (1863) 32 Beav 135; *Re Heming's Trust* (1856) 3 K & J 40.

Payment into court where beneficiaries are under disability

85.2 A trustee is justified in paying money into court where he cannot get a valid discharge; as, for instance, where beneficiaries who are absolutely entitled are infants[1] or of unsound mind[2].

[1]   *Re Cawthorne* (1848) 12 Beav 56; *Re Beauclerk* (1862) 11 WR 203; *Re Coulson's Trust* (1857) 4 Jur NS 6. It was unsafe to keep and invest an infant's legacy as if the investment depreciated the executor was liable (*Re Salomons* [1920] 1 Ch 290). After 1925 instead of paying it into court the better course is for the personal representatives to appoint trustees of the legacy under the power given by the Administration of Estates Act 1925, s 42; or to make an appropriation under s 41 thereof.
[2]   *Re Upfull's Trust* (1851) 3 Mac & G 281; *Re Irby* (1853) 17 Beav 334; and see *Re Carr's Trusts* [1904] 1 Ch 792.

Where money claimed by a representative

85.3 It has been said that a trustee may properly pay money into court where it is claimed by the representative of a beneficiary because the beneficiary may have disposed of it[1], but a Part 8 claim would seem to be the more appropriate course[2].

[1]   *Re Lane's Trust* (1854) 24 LTOS 181; *King v King* (1857) 1 De G & J 663.
[2]   See para 87.1.

Payment to one who claims in default of appointment

85.4 A trustee ought not to hesitate to pay the money to a beneficiary who claims in default of appointment, if he has no notice of any appointment by the donee of the power, and no ground for believing that any appointment has been made. For in that case he could not be made liable if he paid over the fund, even if an appointment were subsequently discovered[1]. Anyhow, now, a trustee in such a case would only be allowed the costs of a summons.

[1]   Per Jessel MR in *Re Cull's Trusts* (1875) LR 20 Eq 561, distinguishing *Re Wylly's Trusts* (1860) 28 Beav 458; but see also *Re Swan* (1864) 2 Hem & M 34; *Re Roberts' Trust* (1869) 17 WR 639; *Re Bendyshe* (1857) 5 WR 816; *Re Williams' Settlement* (1858) 4 K & J 87.

85.5 The rights of the trustee

Reasonable doubt or claim

85.5 Again, where the trustee is uncertain as to the persons entitled[1], as when he has a bona fide doubt as to the law[2], or has received a bona fide claim sanctioned by respectable solicitors[3], he may properly pay the fund into court, unless the question can be settled by a Part 8 claim[4] or the trustee will be protected by taking advantage of s 27 of the Trustee Act 1925[5] or s 48 of the Administration of Justice Act 1985[6]. For instance, where a necessary party to a claim is out of the jurisdiction, and for some reason service out of the jurisdiction is not possible, so that the proceedings could not be served, payment into court would be justifiable.

[1]   *Re Headington Trust* (1857) 6 WR 7.
[2]   *King v King* (1857) 1 De G & J 663; *Re Metcalfe* (1864) 2 De GJ & Sm 122; *Gunnell v Whitear* (1870) LR 10 Eq 664.
[3]   *Re Maclean's Trusts* (1874) LR 19 Eq 274.
[4]   See para 87.1.
[5]   See para 54.16.
[6]   See Article 87(2).

Undue caution

85.6 Where, however, a beneficiary in reversion who had gone to Australia, and had not been heard of for some years, suddenly reappeared, and there was no reasonable doubt as to his identity, it was held that the trustee was not entitled to pay the trust fund into court, and he was ordered to *pay* the costs of all parties[1].

[1]   *Re Elliot's Trusts* (1873) LR 15 Eq 194; *Re Foligno's Mortgage* (1863) 32 Beav 131; *Re Knight's Trusts* (1859) 27 Beav 45; *Re Woodburn's Will* (1857) 1 De G & J 333; *Re Culis Trusts* (1875) LR 20 Eq 561 and see AJ Hawkins (1968) 84 LQR 64 at 65–67. As to when payment into court is justifiable, see *Re Davies' Trusts* (1914) 59 Sol Jo 234.

General warning

85.7 Lastly, now that most questions of doubt or difficulty can be decided on a Part 8 claim, the right of paying money into court can only be exercised with safety in somewhat rare cases as a last resort. The apparently unconditional invitation extended to trustees by the words of s 63(1) of the Trustee Act 1925 is one which can only be accepted at the risk of having to pay costs.

Chapter 21

THE RIGHT OF TRUSTEES AND BENEFICIARIES TO SEEK THE ASSISTANCE OF THE PUBLIC TRUSTEE OR THE COURT IN AUDITING OR IN ADMINISTERING THE TRUST

Article

ARTICLE 86
RIGHT OF TRUSTEE OR BENEFICIARY TO OFFICIAL AUDIT OF THE TRUST THROUGH THE PUBLIC TRUSTEE

86.1

On an application being made to the Public Trustee[1] and notice thereof given by any trustee or beneficiary[2], the condition and accounts of any trust must, unless the court orders otherwise, be investigated and audited by such solicitor or public accountant as may be agreed on by the applicant and the trustees or, in default of agreement[3], by the Public Trustee or some person appointed by him[4]. A trustee or beneficiary cannot be appointed to make the investigation or audit[5]. The Public Trustee may require a deposit from the applicant for payment of any expenses of the investigation or audit ordered by the Public Trustee to be paid by the applicant personally[6].

[1]   Public Trustee Rules 1912, r 31.
[2]   The notice must, unless the Public Trustee directs otherwise, be given to every other trustee or beneficiary (Public Trustee Rules 1912, r 12).
[3]   If no solicitor or public accountant has been appointed within one month from the date of the application, there is deemed to be a default of agreement and the applicant may apply to the Public Trustee accordingly (Public Trustee Rules 1912, r 34).
[4]   Public Trustee Act 1906, s 13(1).
[5]   See Public Trustee Act 1906, s 13(1).
[6]   Public Trustee Rules 1912, r 32.

86.2 Except with the permission of the court, the investigation and audit must not be required within twelve months of any previous investigation and audit[1]. On the other hand, s 22(4) of the Trustee Act, which gives power to the trustees to cause the accounts to be audited, provides that, except in special circumstances, an audit shall not be made more than once in every three years[2]. When trustees require a more frequent audit than a triennial one it will usually be because 'special circumstances' such as are contemplated by s 22(4) of the 1925 Act exist. The Public Trustee may restrict the investigation and audit, eg to a specified period or particular trust property[3].

1   See the proviso to Public Trustee Act 1906, s 13(1).
2   See para 51.37 above.
3   Public Trustee Rules 1912, r 33.

86.3 The costs of the investigation and audit, including the auditor's remuneration[1] will normally be paid out of the trust fund, but the Public Trustee may order the applicant or trustee to pay such costs personally or partly by one and partly by the other[2]. Before making any such order, the Public Trustee should hear the parties[3]. Where an application is unreasonable and vexatious the Public Trustee would be right to make the applicant pay the costs[4]. A person aggrieved by any act or omission or decision of the Public Trustee may apply to the court. The application should be made, under CPR Part 8[5], to a judge of the Chancery Division of the High Court sitting in private[6].

1   For fees see Public Trustees (Fees) Order 1999, SI 1999/855, as amended.
2   Public Trustee Act 1906, s 13(5).
3   *Re Oddy* [1911] 1 Ch 532.
4   *Re Oddy* [1911] 1 Ch 532; *Utley* [1912] WN 147.
5   See para 87.1.
6   Public Trustee Act 1906, s 10; see CPR Sch 1 RSC Ord 93 r 2.

86.4 The Law Reform Committee has recommended the repeal of s 13: it has been invoked only occasionally and its operation has not been found to be particularly effective since there are no powers to enforce the Public Trustee's findings[1].

1   Cmnd 8733 para 4.48

ARTICLE 87
RIGHT OF TRUSTEE OR BENEFICIARY TO TAKE THE DIRECTIONS OF THE COURT IN RELATION TO SPECIFIC QUESTIONS

87.1

(1)   A claim may be brought for the determination of any question arising in the execution of a trust[1]. The following are examples of the types of claims which may be brought[2]:

(a)   A claim for the determination of any of the following questions[3]:

(i)   any question as to the composition of any class of persons having a beneficial interest in any property subject to a trust;

     (ii)   any question as to the rights or interests of a person claiming to be beneficially entitled under a trust.

(b)   A claim for any of the following remedies[4]:

    (i)   an order requiring a trustee to furnish and, if necessary, verify accounts;

    (ii)   an order requiring a trustee to pay money which he holds in that capacity[5];

    (iii)   an order directing a trustee to do or not to do a particular act[6];

    (iv)   an order approving any sale, purchase, compromise or other transaction by a trustee[7];

    (v)   an order directing any act to be done in the execution of a trust which the court could order to be done if the trust were being executed under the direction of the court.

It is also common practice to add a claim for the execution of the trusts under the court's direction 'if and so far as may be necessary'. This may not be wanted, but it avoids a multitude of objections if it does prove necessary[8]. The court will only make an administration order if it considers that the issues between the parties between the parties cannot be resolved in any other way[9].

A claim brought to determine specific questions in the execution of a trust is normally made brought under CPR Part 8[10]. If, however, the claim involves an allegation of fraud or wilful default or other breach of trust against the trustees and is likely to involve some substantial dispute of fact, this procedure should not be used[11], and it should be brought under CPR Part 7. Neither should third party disputes[12] be decided this way[13]. Contingent or future questions cannot normally be decided[14]. The court will also not accept a general surrender of a discretion which is exercisable from time to time in changing circumstances[15].

(2) If a question of construction of a will or a trust has arisen and the opinion in writing of a person with a ten year High Court qualification[16] has been obtained, then the court on the application of the personal representatives or trustees without hearing any argument, may make an order authorising them to take such steps in reliance on the opinion as are specified in the order[17]. The court will not make such an order if it appears that a dispute exists which makes it inappropriate to make the order without hearing argument[18].

(3) Where the trustees or by analogy other parties bring a claim to have the trust instrument construed for their guidance or to have determined some question arising in the administration, the costs of all parties will normally be ordered to be paid out of the trust fund, and generally those costs will be ordered to be assessed on the indemnity basis[19]. Where the claim concerns rival claims to the trust fund or it is, in

substance, hostile litigation, the court will normally order the unsuccessful party to pay the costs of the successful party[20]. A trustee, beneficiary or other persons concerned in relation to the administration of a trust may apply to the court at any stage of proceedings for an order that his costs be paid out of the trust fund[21]. An application can be made to the court (a *Beddoe* application) for directions whether or not the trustee should bring or defend proceedings in his capacity as trustee[22].

(4) No claim for the determination of specific questions can be brought after the trust has been completely administered and the property handed over by the trustees; any relief claimed by beneficiaries after that must be the subject of a claim brought by standard claim form under Part 7 of CPR[23].

1   This paragraph sets out the effect of CPR, r 64.2(a)(ii) and Practice Direction to Part 64, para 1.
2   Practice Direction to Part 64, para 1.
3   Practice Direction to Part 64, para 1(1).
4   Practice Direction to Part 64, para 1(2).
5   *Nutter v Holland* [1894] 3 Ch 408.
6   This procedure is not appropriate to compel trustees to concur in a sale of property in a partition action: *Suffolk v Lawrence* (1884) 32 WR 899. See also *Re Leask* (1891) 65 LT 199. The court does not generally interfere with the exercise of trustees' powers, see para 61.14 above.
7   See *Re Robinson* (1885) 31 Ch D 247.
8   *Re Berens* [1888] WN 95; and see also *Re Freme's Contract* [1895] 2 Ch 256; affd [1895] 2 Ch 778.
9   Practice Direction to Part 64, para 3(1).
10 For the necessary contents of a Part 8 claim form see CPR Pt 8, r 8.2. In particular, the claim form must contain a statement showing the representative role of the trustee in the proceedings (CPR, r 8.2(d) and (e)).
11 *Re Weall* (1889) 42 Ch D 674; *Dowse v Gorton* [1891] AC 190 at 202; *Re Thorpe* [1891] 2 Ch 360; *Nutter v Holland* [1894] 3 Ch 408; *Broere v Mourant & Co* [2003] JCA 091, Jersey CA; *Federal Trust Co Ltd v Macdonald-Smith* (2001) 4 ITELR 21, R Ct Guernsey.
12 Ie disputes with persons, otherwise than in the capacity of beneficiaries, in respect of rights and liabilities assumed by the trustees as such in the administration of the trust (see *Alsop Wilkinson v Neary* [1995] 1 All ER 431 at 434).
13 See *Marley v Mutual Security Merchant Bank* [1991] 3 All ER 198 at 201; *Federal Trust Co Ltd v Macdonald-Smith* (2001) 4 ITELR 21, R Ct Guernsey.
14 *Re Berens* [1888] WN 95; see para 87.25 below.
15 *Re Allen-Meyrick's Will Trusts* [1966] 1 WLR 499; see para 87.10 below.
16 As to which see Courts and Legal Services Act 1990, s 71(2), Sch 10 para 63.
17 Under Administration of Justice Act 1985, s 48(1). The claim is brought by Part 8 procedure in the Chancery Division (Practice Direction to CPR Pt 8, Section A, Table 1; CPR, r 64.3). No defendant should be named under CPR Pt 8, r 8.2A. No separate application for permission under r 8.2A need be made (see Practice Direction B to Part 64, para 5). For the procedure generally see para 26.36 of the Chancery Guide.
18 Administration of Justice Act 1985, s 48(2). This procedure will not be inappropriate where the dispute is between two rival constructions of which one is obviously wrong.
19 *Re Buckton* [1907] 2 Ch 406; see CPR Pt 48, r 48.4(2). The general principles set out in *Re Buckton* have not been superseded by CPR (*see D'Abo v Paget (No 2)* [2000] WTLR 863, Ch D).
20 *Re Buckton* [1907] 2 Ch 406.
21 Practice Direction to CPR Part 64 para 6.3. Where trustees have power to agree to pay the costs of a party, and exercise properly such a power, CPR, r 48.3 applies. In such a case, an order is not required and the trustees are entitled to recover out of the trust fund any costs which they pay pursuant to the agreement made in exercise of the power (Practice Direction at para 6.2).

22 *Re Beddoe* [1893] 1 Ch 547; see paras 83.16 and 87.48 below.
23 *Wightman v Cousins* [1932] NI 61, CA.

Paragraph 1

JURISDICTION

87.2–87.4 Trustees are entitled to seek the assistance of the court in determining how the trust instrument should be construed or as to the proper administration of the trust so as to enable them to execute their duties properly. They can then act in accordance with that guidance without fear that they are in breach of trust. It is clear that a beneficiary is also entitled to seek the court's guidance[1], as is a protector[2]. In Jersey it has been held that the guardian ad litem (in England, litigation friend) of a beneficiary may do so[3].

1 See, eg, the nature of the remedies set out in CPR, r 2(3).
2 *Von Knierem v Bermuda Trust Co Ltd,* Butts OCM Vol 1, 116; *Re Omar Family Trust* [2000] WTLR 713 at 714; *Re Hare Trust* (2001) 4 ITELR 288. The court has inherent power to appoint a protector where otherwise the office would not be filled and, presumably, to replace a wrongdoing protector: *Steele v Paz Ltd* [1993–95] Manx LR 102 and, on appeal, 426; *Re Papadimitriou* [2004] WTLR 1141, para 71.
3 *P v P and W Trustees,* (16 December 2002, unreported) R Ct Jersey.

87.5 Any attempt to exclude this right to apply to the court on questions of law (eg by a provision in a will that the determination by the trustees of any questions and matters arising in the execution of the trusts shall be conclusive and binding on all parties) is void[1]. Questions of fact, however, may be left to be determined by trustees[2].

1 *Phillips v Bury* (1696) Skin 447 at 469; *Re Raven* [1915] 1 Ch 673; *Re Wynn* [1952] Ch 271, [1952] 1 All ER 341; see P Matthews, Trustees as Judges, (1983) 133 New LJ 915.
2 *Dundee General Hospitals Board of Management v Walker* [1952] 1 All ER 896, HL; *Re Coxen* [1948] Ch 747, [1948] 2 All ER 492; *Re Tuck's Settlement* [1978] Ch 49, [1978] 1 All ER 1047, CA. See para 8.56 ff.

87.6 Where the court is asked to make a decision on a course of action proposed or actually taken by trustees, the court may be exercising its own discretion or simply protecting the trustees in an exercise of their own. The act of seeking the court's guidance does not however necessarily involve the trustees in a surrender of discretion[1]. The four-fold analysis of Robert Walker J in an unnamed and unreported decision, set out in large part in the later case of *Public Trustee v Cooper*[2], provides guidance.

1 *Public Trustee v Cooper* [2001] WTLR 901.
2 *Public Trustee v Cooper* [2001] WTLR 901 at 922–924.

87.7 First, there are proceedings for guidance as to whether some proposed action is within the trustees' powers. That is ultimately a question of construction of the trust instrument or statute or both[1].

1 Eg *Philean Trust Co Ltd v Taylor* [2003] JRC 038, R Ct Jersey; *Re The Double Happiness Trust* [2003] WTLR 367, R Ct Jersey; *Re Pinto's Settlement* [2004] WTLR 878, R Ct Jersey; *A-G v Trustees of the British Museum* [2005] EWHC 1089 (Ch), [2005] Ch 397.

87.8 Second, there are cases in which the question is whether the proposed course of action is a proper exercise of the trustees' power but no real doubt exists as to the nature and extent of the power and the trustees have decided how they want to exercise it. The trustees wish to obtain the blessing of the court because the decision is particularly momentous[1].

[1]   *Re the Estate of Dawes*, (7 December 2000, unreported), R Ct Guernsey; *Re Representation of I* (2002) 4 ITELR 446, R Ct Jersey; *Concord Trust v Law Debenture Trust Corpn* [2003] 1 WLR 1591, HL; *Rathbone Trustee Co (Jersey) Ltd v Kane* [2004] JRC 041, R Ct Jersey; *Re Representation Securitas Services Ltd* [2004] JRC 122, R Ct Jersey; *Rysaffe Trustee Co Ltd v Hexagon Trust Co (CI) Ltd*, (2 November 2004, unreported), R Ct Guernsey; *Re Representation of the Trustees of the H Settlement* [2005] JRC 077, R Ct Jersey; *X Trust Co Ltd v RW* [2006] JRC 057, R Ct Jersey.

87.9 Merely applying to the court for directions does not automatically involve a surrender of discretion[1]. In this second class of case, there is no question of surrender of discretion. Indeed it is most unlikely that the court will be persuaded in the absence of special circumstances to accept a surrender of discretion on questions of that sort, since the trustees are prima facie in a much better position than the court to know what is in the best interests of the beneficiaries. The task of the court here is not to say how it would itself exercise the discretion, but merely to ensure (via an inquisitorial process[2]) that the proposed exercise is lawful in the sense that the trustees can properly form the view which they have[3]. The consequence of the court being so satisfied is that the beneficiaries will be deprived of the opportunity to allege that it constitutes a breach of trust, and thus the court will act with caution[4].

[1]   Per Robert Walker J in the unnamed case referred to in *Public Trustee v Cooper* [2001] WTLR 901 at 922–924, explaining that that the case of *Marley v Mutual Security Merchant Bank and Trust Co Ltd* [1991] 3 All ER 198 was not authority for the contrary proposition; see also *Re Fletcher Challenge Energy Employees Educational Fund* [2004] WTLR 199, H Ct of NZ.
[2]   *Marley v Mutual Security Merchant Bank and Trust Co* [1991] 3 All ER 198.
[3]   *Richard v McKay* (1987) 11 Tru LI 23, 24; *X v A* [2005] EWHC 2706 (Ch), [2006] 1 All ER 952 at paras 27–30.
[4]   *Richard v McKay* (1987) 11 Tru LI 23, 24; *X v A* [2005] EWHC 2706 (Ch), [2006] 1 All ER 952 at paras 27–30.

87.10 Third, there are cases of surrender of discretion properly so called[1]. There the court will only accept a surrender of discretion for a good reason, the most obvious being either that the trustees are deadlocked (but honestly deadlocked, so that the question cannot be resolved by removing one trustee rather than another) or because the trustees are disabled as a result of a conflict of interest. But there is not always a clear distinction between the second and third classes of case on the facts[2], even though the distinction is clear in principle[3].

[1]   *Re M and L Trusts* [2003] WTLR 491, R Ct Jersey.
[2]   *Public Trustee v Cooper* [2001] WTLR 901.
[3]   *Re Drexel Burnham Lambert UK Pension Plan* [1995] 1 WLR 32; *Public Trustee v Cooper* [2001] WTLR 901.

87.11 Fourth, there are cases where trustees have actually taken action, and that action is attacked as being either outside their powers or an improper exercise of their powers.

PROCEDURE

HOW TO START PROCEEDINGS

87.12 All claims under the Civil Procedure Rules ('CPR') are begun by standard claim form under Part 7 of the CPR unless the claimant is entitled to use the Part 8 procedure[1]. The procedure under CPR Part 8 can be used when the claimant seeks the court's decision on a question which is unlikely to involve a substantial dispute of fact or a rule or practice direction requires the Part 8 procedure to be used[2]. The rules in fact require that a claim for the court to determine any question arising in the execution of a trust must be brought under CPR Part 8[3]. However, the court has power at any stage to order the claim to continue as a standard claim under CPR Part 7[4], and, if it involves an allegation of fraud, wilful default or other breach of trust, and there is likely to be a substantial dispute of fact, it is likely to do so[5].

[1]   CPR, r 8.1(2) and Practice Direction to Part 8 Section A paras 1.1 and 1.2.
[2]   CPR, r 8.1(2) and (6).
[3]   CPR, r 64.3.
[4]   CPR, r 8.13.
[5]   See *Re Sir Lindsay Parkinson & Co Ltd Settlement Trusts* [1965] 1 All ER 309, [1965] 1 WLR 372, decided under the previously applicable Rules of the Supreme Court.

PARTIES

87.13 All the trustees must be parties[1]. If the claim is brought by some of the trustees any other trustee who does not consent to being joined as a claimant must be made a defendant[2]. A person with more than one capacity should not appear twice on the record, whether on the same side[3] or (a fortiori) on opposite sides of the record[4].

[1]   CPR, r 64.4(1)(a).
[2]   CPR, r 64.4(1)(b).
[3]   *Hardie and Lane Ltd v Chiltern* [1928] 1 KB 663.
[4]   Eg *Neale v Turton* (1827) 4 Bing 149; *Allnutt v Wilding* [2006] EWHC 1905 (Ch) 150 Sol Jo LB 1057.

87.14 All the beneficiaries need not be made parties, but the claimant may make such of them parties as is appropriate having regard to the nature of the order sought[1]. If there are only two views as to the appropriate course, and one is advocated by one beneficiary who will be joined, it may not be necessary for other beneficiaries to be joined since the trustees may be able to present the other argument[2]. If the trustees are unsure as to which beneficiaries need to be joined, they may issue the claim form without naming any defendants[3] and apply for directions[4] as to which ones should be joined in or notified of the proceedings[5].

[1]   CPR, r 64.4(1)(c).
[2]   Practice Direction B to CPR Part 64, para 4.1.
[3]   Under CPR, r 8.2A.
[4]   Practice Direction B to CPR Part 64, para 4.3.
[5]   Under CPR, r 19.8A(2).

87.15 The rules permit a claim to be brought by or against trustees without adding as parties any beneficiaries[1]. Any judgment or order given or made in such a claim will be binding on the beneficiaries unless the court orders otherwise[2]. Hence it is not the normal practice to make representation orders[3] on an application for directions[4]. The trustees will have all the authority they need without having to join every beneficiary.

1   CPR, r 19.7A(1).
2   CPR, r 19.7A(2).
3   Under CPR, r 19.7.
4   Practice Direction to CPR Sch 1 RSC Ord 85 para 8.

87.16 However, where a beneficiary of the trust is a party to the litigation about which directions are sought, with an interest opposed to that of the trustees, that beneficiary should be a defendant to the trustees' application[1]. Indeed, where separately from particular litigation the trustees make a *Beddoe* application in relation to recovery of the costs thereof out of the trust fund, the beneficiaries must be parties even though not parties to the litigation against the trustee[2].

1   Practice Direction B to CPR Part 64, para 7.6.
2   *Alsop Wilkinson v Neary* [1995] 1 All ER 431; [1996] 1 WLR 1220, *STG Valmet Trustees Ltd v Brennan* [2002] WTLR 273 (Gibraltar CA, comprising three retired English L.JJ.). Further see *Breadner v Granville Grossman* [2001] WTLR 377 at 390.

EVIDENCE

87.17 The trustees' evidence should be given by witness statement. In order to ensure that, if directions are given, the trustees are properly protected by the order, they must ensure full disclosure of relevant matters, even if the case is to proceed with the participation of beneficiaries as defendants[1]. All applications for directions should be supported by evidence showing the value of the trust assets, the significance of any proposed litigation or other courses of action for the trust and why directions are needed[2]. In the case of a pension trust the evidence should include the latest actuarial valuation and describe the membership profile and, if a deficit on winding up is likely, the priority provisions and their likely effect[3].

1   *Marley v Mutual Security Merchant Bank* [1991] 3 All ER 198 at 201; *Alhamrani v Russa Management Ltd* [2003] JRC 229, R Ct Jersey; see also Practice Direction B to CPR Part 64, para 7.1, and Practice Direction to CPR Part 64, para 6.7 (in relation to prospective costs orders).
2   Practice Direction B to CPR Part 64, para 7.4.
3   Practice Direction B to CPR Part 64, para 7.4.

87.18 One type of application which is of considerable importance in practice is for the court's guidance as to whether the trustees should or should not bring or defend litigation (a *Beddoe* application)[1]. Such applications should be supported by evidence including the advice of an appropriately qualified lawyer[2] as to the prospects of success and other matters relevant to be taken into account, including a cost estimate for the proceedings and any known facts concerning the means of the opposite party to the proceedings and a draft of any proposed statement of case[3]. In such a case the evidence should also state whether, in relation to the proposed litigation, (i) any relevant Pre-Action Protocol has been followed, and (ii) the trustees have proposed or undertaken, or intend to propose, mediation by ADR, and (in each case) if not why not[4].

1 [1893] 1 Ch 547; see para 87.48 below.
2 As to which see Practice Direction B to CPR Part 64, para 7.3.
3 Practice Direction B to CPR Part 64, para 7.2.
4 Practice Direction B to CPR Part 64, para 7.5.

87.19 If a beneficiary is party to the proposed litigation, he should be a party to the claim for directions but any material which would be privileged as regards that beneficiary should be put in evidence as exhibits to the trustees' witness statement and should not be served on the beneficiary[1]. The beneficiary defendant may be excluded from part of the hearing, including that which relates to the material withheld[2]. The evidence should also explain what consultation, if any, there has been with beneficiaries[3]. The trustees will be expected to have canvassed the proposed course of action with all the adult beneficiaries of a private trust or, if there are numerous beneficiaries, with the principal adult beneficiaries.

1 Practice Direction B to CPR Part 64, para 7.6. See also *Re Moritz decd* [1960] Ch 251, [1959] 3 All ER 767; *Re Eaton* [1964] 3 All ER 299n, [1964], 1 WLR 1269.
2 Practice Direction B to CPR Part 64, para 7.6. See also *Re Moritz decd* [1960] Ch 251, [1959] 3 All ER 767; *Re Eaton* [1964] 3 All ER 299n, [1964], 1 WLR 1269.
3 Practice Direction B to CPR Part 64, para 7.7.

87.20 If a child beneficiary is a defendant, the court will expect to have put before it the instructions to and advice of an appropriately qualified lawyer as to the benefits and disadvantages of the proposed, and any other relevant, course of action from the point of view of the child[1].

1 Practice Direction B to CPR Part 64, para 7.10.

CASE MANAGEMENT, HEARINGS AND LEVEL OF JUDGE

87.21 The claim will be referred to the master or district judge to consider directions for the management of the case[1]. This will happen when either a defendant has acknowledged service or the period for doing so has expired or, if no defendant is named, as soon as the claimants' evidence has been filed[2]. Such directions may be given without a hearing in some cases including directions as to parties or as to notice of proceedings.

1 Practice Direction B to CPR Part 64, para 5.1.
2 Practice Direction B to CPR Part 64, para 5.1.

87.22 The court will always consider whether it is possible to deal with the application on paper without a hearing[1]. The trustees must always consider whether a hearing is needed for any reason[2]. If a party considers that a hearing is needed, this should be stated and the reasons explained in his evidence or otherwise in a letter to the court[3]. If the court is minded to refuse to give directions asked for on a consideration of the papers alone, the parties will be notified and given the opportunity to ask for a hearing[4].

1   Practice Direction B to CPR Part 64, para 6.1; see also Practice Direction to CPR Part 64, para 6.5 (in relation to prospective costs orders).
2   Practice Direction B to CPR Part 64, para 6.1; see also Practice Direction to CPR Part 64, para 6.5 (in relation to prospective costs orders).
3   Practice Direction B to CPR Part 64, para 6.1; see also Practice Direction to CPR Part 64, para 6.5 (in relation to prospective costs orders).
4   Practice Direction B to CPR Part 64, para 6.2; see also Practice Direction to CPR Part 64, para 6.6 (in relation to prospective costs orders).

87.23   The claim will usually be listed and heard in private[1]. Accordingly, the order made and the other documents among the court records (apart from the claim form itself) will not be open to inspection by third parties without the court's permission[2]. If the matter is disposed of without a hearing, the order made will be expressed to have been made in private[3]. If confidentiality of the directions sought is important (eg directions relating to actual or proposed litigation with a third party who could find out what directions the claimants are seeking through access to the claim form[4]) the statement of the remedy[5] in the claim form may be expressed in general terms. The trustees must, in that case, state specifically in the evidence what directions they seek.

1   See CPR Pt 39, r 39.2(3)(f); see also Practice Direction to CPR Part 39 para. 1.5 (in relation to *Beddoe's* applications).
2   CPR, r 5.4(2), (5).
3   Practice Direction B to CPR Part 64, para 3.
4   Under CPR Pt 5, r 5.4(2), (5).
5   For the purposes of CPR, r 8.2(b).

87.24   A master or district judge may give the directions sought though, if the directions relate to actual or proposed litigation, only if it is a plain case, and therefore usually without a hearing[1]. A master or district judge may not deal with questions of law or the construction of a document[2].

1   Practice Direction to Pt 2 para 5.1(e); see also Practice Direction B to CPR Part 64, para. 7.11.
2   Practice Direction to Pt 2 para 5.1(d).

CONTINGENT OR FUTURE QUESTIONS NOT USUALLY DECIDED

87.25   The court is very reluctant to decide academic[1] or hypothetical[2] issues, or questions which have not yet arisen or may never arise, particularly where the decision affects the rights, or possible rights, of unborn persons. But exceptions are made where a beneficiary's rights under the trust depend on an event which is presently contemplated, so that until the question is decided he is practically unable to shape his conduct. Thus a daughter could raise a claim as to the validity of the trusts of her father's will forbidding marriage with a person of different faith[3]. And a life tenant could raise the question as to exactly when the class of remaindermen (his own children) closed, as he wished to surrender his life interest for their benefit[4]. On the other hand, in a case where Sir Arthur Underhill appeared for the trustees, the court refused to consider the question whether a tenant for life (who had been married some years and had no issue) would, if he died without issue, be absolutely entitled to the trust fund, or whether there would be a gift over to his brother's issue. His evidence was that if it was decided that he would be absolutely entitled he need not save so much of his income as would otherwise be necessary, but this was held to be insufficient.

¹ *Ainsbury v Milligan* [1987] 1 All ER 929.
² *Mercury Communications Ltd v Director General of Telecommunications* [1994] 36 LSG Rep 36, CA.
³ See *Re Berens* [1888] WN 95; and see also *Curtis v Sheffield* (1882) 21 Ch D 1; *Re Staples* [1916] 1 Ch 322; *Re Freme's Contract* [1895] 2 Ch 256; affd [1895] 2 Ch 778.
⁴ *Bassett v Bassett* [2003] NSWSC 691. [2005] WTLR 51.

87.26 The moral seems to be that contingent questions will not be decided unless the contingent event depends on the applicant's volition, and he convinces the court that he intends to exercise that volition forthwith if the result of doing so would not deprive him of his rights under the trust. For example, if a will gave income of a trust fund to a testator's son until he quits the kingdom and then over to another, it is probable that if the son contemplated accepted an official appointment abroad the court would say whether the effect of doing so would cause a forfeiture, but it would probably not decide the question if the son had no present intention of quitting the kingdom unless the son was arguing that the contingent event was void for uncertainty¹.

¹ Cf *Sifton v Sifton* [1938] AC 656, [1938] 3 All ER 435. But in this case, and in such English cases as *Re Gape* [1952] Ch 418, [1952] 1 All ER 827; affd [1952] Ch 743, [1952] 2 All ER 579; the question decided was whether the gift over was void for uncertainty or not. On academic issues see *Ainsbury v Millington* [1987] 1 All ER 929, and on the need for a current dispute rather than a hypothetical or future question see *Mercury Communications Ltd v Director General of Telecommunications* [1994] 36 LS Gaz R 36, CA.

Paragraph 3

COSTS

COURT'S JURISDICTION

87.27 The court's jurisdiction to deal with litigation¹ costs is based upon s 51 of the Supreme Court Act 1981. The court has a wide discretion to determine by whom and to what extent the costs are to be paid². This includes payment by a non-party³. This discretion is however by no means untrammelled and must be exercised in accordance with the rules of the court and established principles⁴.

¹ Including administration of trusts (see Supreme Court Act 1981, s 51(4)).
² Supreme Court Act 1981, s 51(3).
³ *Aiden Shipping Ltd v Interbulk Ltd (No 2)* [1986] 1 AC 965, HL.
⁴ *McDonald v Horn* [1995] 1 All ER 961 at 969.

RULES OF THE COURT

87.28 In their original form, the CPR only provided for the assessment of costs. Unlike the old RSC[1], they failed to deal with entitlement to costs out of the trust fund. The gap was soon exposed[2], however, and dealt with[3]. Now the position is largely returned to that under the RSC. Where a person is party to proceedings in the capacity of trustee, the normal rule is that he is entitled to costs, in so far as not recovered from or paid by any other person, out of the trust fund[4].

1   Ord 62, r 6(2).
2   *Breadner v Granville-Grossman* (2000) [2006] WTLR 411, 417–419.
3   By SI 2001/4015.
4   CPR, r 48.4(2).

87.29 The relevant practice direction provides that a trustee will be entitled to an indemnity out of the fund for costs 'properly incurred', which may include costs awarded against the trustee in favour of another party[1]. Whether costs were properly incurred depends on all the circumstances of the case, but factors include (1) whether the trustee obtained the directions of the court; (2) whether the trustee was acting in the interests of the fund or in another interest; and (3) whether the trustee acted unreasonably[2].

1   Practice Direction to Part 48, para 50A.1.
2   Practice Direction to Part 48, para 50A.2. See *Holding and Management Ltd v Property Holding and Investment Trust plc* [1988] 2 All ER 702, [1988] 1 WLR 644; affd [1990] 1 All ER 938, [1989] 1 WLR 1313, CA. Defending a claim in which relief is sought against a trustee personally does not by itself mean that the trustee is not acting in the interests of the fund: para 50A.3.

87.30 Where the trustees are entitled to costs out of the trust fund, CPR, r 44.4 provides that such costs will normally be assessed on the indemnity basis[1]. The court will not allow costs which have been unreasonably incurred[2] or are unreasonable in amount[3]. In assessing costs on the indemnity basis, the court must have regard to all the circumstances of the case in deciding whether costs were unreasonably incurred or unreasonable in amount[4]. The court will however resolve any doubt in favour of the receiving party[5].

1   Similarly, the costs of a claim properly brought or defended by a beneficiary will be assessed in the indemnity basis: *Re Buckton* [1907] 2 Ch 406 at 414 ff. The general principles in *Buckton* have not been superseded by the CPR: *D'Abo v Paget (No 2)* [2000] WTLR 863.
2   On acting unreasonably see *Re Spurling's Will Trusts* [1966] 1 All ER 745, [1966] 1 WLR 920. See also *Re Knox's Trust* [1895] 2 Ch 483 and *Re Ruddock* (1910) 102 LT 89.
3   See CPR, r 44.4(1).
4   CPR, r 44.5(1)(b).
5   CPR, r 44.4(3).

ESTABLISHED PRINCIPLES

87.31 The principles underlying the trustees' entitlement to costs out of the trust fund and the extension of these principles to other parties are set out in the case of *Re Buckton*[1] (summarised by Hoffmann LJ in *McDonald v Horn*[2]). A three-fold classification was adopted by Kekewich J in *Re Buckton*[3].

[1]   *Re Buckton* [1907] 2 Ch 406.
[2]   *McDonald v Horn* [1995] 1 All ER 961 at 970. For recent discussion, see *Machin v National Power plc* [1998] Pen LR 295, [2001] WTLR 741 and *Chessels v British Telecommunications plc* [2002] WTLR 719.
[3]   *Re Buckton* [1907] 2 Ch 406 at 413 ff. Applied in *D'Abo v Paget (No 2)* [2000] WTLR 863 where a beneficiary raised a point against another beneficiary that would have justified a construction claim brought by the trustees.

87.32 The first category was proceedings brought by trustees to have the guidance of the court as to the construction of the trust instrument or some other question arising in the course of administration. In such cases, the costs of all parties were normally treated as incurred for the benefit of the trust and ordered to be paid out of the trust fund.

87.33 Second, there were cases in which the application was made by someone other than the trustees, but raising the same kind of point as in category (1) and would have justified a claim being brought by the trustees. That is treated in the same way as category (1)[1].

[1]   Eg *D'Abo v Paget (No 2)* [2000] WTLR 863.

87.34 Third, there are cases in which a beneficiary is making a hostile claim against the trustees or another beneficiary. In such cases the unsuccessful party will usually be ordered to pay the costs of the successful party, as in ordinary litigation[1].

[1]   CPR, r 44.3(2). See also *Alsop Wilkinson v Neary* [1996] 1 WLR 1220 at 1225. For a recent decision see *Breadner v Granville-Grossman* [2001] WTLR 377.

87.35 Categories (1) and (2) are usually concerned with friendly litigation, seeking the necessary guidance of the court on issues of difficulty in relation to the construction or management of a trust. Exceptionally such cases may, in substance, be hostile litigation in which costs should follow the event[1]. Hoffmann LJ in *McDonald v Horn* also referred[2] to *Beddoe's* applications, following the case of that name[3], in which the trustees can seek advance approval from the court for incurring litigation costs on behalf of the trust[4].

[1]   See *Breadner v Granville-Grossman* [2001] WTLR 377 at 389.
[2]   At p 970.
[3]   [1893] 1 Ch 547.
[4]   See para 83.16 above.

HOSTILE LITIGATION

87.36 In a case where the dispute is, in substance, between rival claimants to the trust fund (category (3) in *Re Buckton*), the trustees must normally take a neutral and passive role – filing a defence that the trustees submit to the court's directions and disclosing relevant documents, in which event they will be entitled to an indemnity for their (comparatively modest) costs out of the trust fund[1]. If they choose actively to favour one side or another, or defend the trust against claims of invalidity, and their contention is successful (eg in rejecting the settlor's claim to set aside for undue influence) they should be entitled to their costs out of the trust fund for preserving the interests of the beneficiaries under the trust[2]. However, if they fail, they will normally not be entitled to any indemnity because they will have incurred costs in an unsuccessful attempt to prefer one class of beneficiaries (eg the specified beneficiaries) over another (eg the trustee in bankruptcy or the creditors) and so have acted unreasonably and otherwise than for the benefit of the trust estate[3]. There may be exceptional cases where it the trustee should perform an active role, eg if the claim only relates to part of the fund, the beneficiaries are unborn, unascertained or minors, or cannot obtain legal aid, or the claim may be a 'try-on' susceptible to a strike out application[4].

[1]   *Alsop Wilkinson v Neary* [1996] 1 WLR 1220 at 1225.
[2]   See *Re Holden* (1887) 20 QBD 43.
[3]   *Alsop Wilkinson v Neary* [1995] 1 All ER 431 at 436.
[4]   See *Re Hall* [1994–95] Cayman ILR 456; *Re Representation Bank America Trust Co (Jersey) Ltd* [1995] JLR N-29; *Showlag v Bank America Trust Co (Jersey) Ltd* [1995] JLR N-30; *STG Valmet Trustees Ltd v Brennan* [2002] WTLR 273.

TRUST DISPUTES, BENEFICIARIES' DISPUTES AND THIRD PARTY DISPUTES

87.37 A different threefold classification was adopted by Lightman J in *Alsop Wilkinson v Neary*[1], although overlapping with that in *Re Buckton*. Trustees may be involved in three types of cases[2]. The first are disputes ('trust disputes') as to the trusts on which trustees hold the subject matter of the trusts. It may be friendly litigation[3], involving the true construction of the trust instrument or some other question arising in the course of administration of the trust. It may be hostile, involving a challenge in whole or in part to the validity of the settlement by the settlor on grounds of undue influence or by a trustee in bankruptcy or a defrauded creditor of the settlor so that the trustees hold as trustees for the settlor, the trustee in bankruptcy or creditor in place of or in addition to the beneficiaries. This first category covers the ground of categories (1) and (2) in *Re Buckton*.

[1]   [1996] 1 WLR 1220.
[2]   *Alsop Wilkinson v Neary* [1996] 1 WLR 1220 at 1223–1224.
[3]   The line between friendly and hostile litigation which is relevant to costs is not always easy to draw (see *Re Buckton* [1907] 2 Ch 406 at 415; *Alsop Wilkinson v Neary* [1996] 1 WLR 1220 at 1224; and *D'Abo v Paget (No 2)* [2000] WTLR 863 at 868–869).

87.38 As already stated above, in hostile litigation the trustees should normally remain neutral, leaving it to the rival claimants to fight their own battles and offering to submit to the court's directions. If they adopt this stance, they will be entitled to be reimbursed their costs out of the trust fund[1].

[1]   *Alsop Wilkinson v Neary* [1996] 1 WLR 1220 at 1225.

87.39 Second, there are disputes ('beneficiaries' disputes') with one or more of the beneficiaries as to the propriety of any action which the trustees have taken or omitted to take or may or may not take in the future[1], eg an action for breach of trust and removal of trustees. Such a dispute is regarded as ordinary hostile litigation in which costs follow the event and do not come out of the trust estate[2].This category covers the cases in category (2) of *Re Buckton*.

1   *Alsop Wilkinson v Neary* [1995] 1 All ER 431 at 434.
2   *McDonald v Horn* [1995] 1 All ER 961; *Holding and Management Ltd v Property Holding & Investment Trust plc* [1990] 1 All ER 938, [1989] 1 WLR 1313 (trustee of maintenance fund for block of flats not entitled to costs out of fund where tenant-beneficiaries successfully claimed proposed works were not repairs but improvements); cf *Brown v Orion Trust Ltd*, (10 May 2004, unreported) R Ct Guernsey.

87.40 Third, there are disputes ('third party disputes') with third parties, otherwise than in the capacity of beneficiary, in respect of rights and liabilities assumed by the trustees as such in the administration of the trust. The trustees have a duty to protect and preserve the trust estate and accordingly represent the trust in third party disputes. Before doing so however, they are well advised to make an application (a *Beddoe* application) to the court for permission to bring or defend proceedings at the expense of the trust fund[1].

1   See para 87.48 below.

COSTS ON APPEAL

87.41 Trustees and beneficiaries are able in appropriate cases to seek authoritative guidance of the High Court at the expense of the trust fund. However, once such guidance has been obtained, then in the absence of some special circumstances (eg difficulties arising from that decision itself) the parties have the authoritative guidance they need[1]. The fact that they do not like it will not justify the costs of appeal. If the trustees appeal, they do so at their own risk as to costs and will usually be ordered to pay costs if the appeal is unsuccessful. If the beneficiary appeals unsuccessfully, he will usually be ordered to pay the trustee's costs on the standard basis. In the latter case, the respondent trustees will usually be entitled to the difference between their costs on the standard and indemnity basis out of the trust fund[2]. The court will only order payment of the costs of an unsuccessful appeal out of the trust fund in exceptional circumstances, as where large interests, and particularly those of unborn persons, are at stake[3]. In the House of Lords, trustees passively interested are not required to lodge a separate case, but should ensure their position is explained in one of the cases lodged[4].

1   *Re Earl of Radnor's Will Trusts* (1890) 45 Ch D 402 and *Re Londonderry's Settlement* [1965] Ch 918 at 930–931 per Harman LJ, at 936 per Salmon LJ and costs out of trust fund at 940, the appeal being successful. For recent decisions see *Machin v National Power plc* [2001 WTLR 746 and *Chessels v British Telecommunications plc* [2002] WTLR 735.
2   *Re Stuart* [1940] 4 All ER 80. See now CPR, r 48.4(2).
3   *Re Stuart* [1940] 4 All ER 80.
4   HL Practice and Standing Orders, 16.11.

ONE SET OF COSTS ONLY ALLOWED UNLESS SEVERANCE NECESSARY

87.42 Except under special circumstances discussed below, trustees should bring and defend claims jointly. They will only be allowed one set of costs between them[1], to be apportioned by the costs judge[2]. If a trustee improperly refuses to join with his co-trustee as claimant, and consequently has to be made a defendant, he may be deprived of costs altogether. On the other hand, where, owing to one trustee being also a beneficiary, it is necessary that one should be claimant, and the other defendant, they will each be allowed separate sets of costs on an indemnity basis[3].

1   *Hughes v Key* (1885) 20 Beav 395; *Gompertz v Kensit* (1872) LR 13 Eq 369. But on an appeal, the appellant beneficiary should give notice to the respondents that he will ask the court to make only one order for costs against him on the basis there only needs be one ad idem representation against him: *Re Stuart* [1940] 4 All ER 80.
2   *Re Isaac* [1897] 1 Ch 251.
3   *Re Love* (1885) 29 Ch D 348; *Re Morgan* [1927] WN 180.

87.43 There are other cases where trustees may properly sever their statements of case and if successful recover separate sets of costs where there are reasonable grounds for doing so. These include: (1) where one trustee has a personal interest which conflicts with his duty as a trustee; (2) where one trustee is able to admit facts which the others do not believe to be true; and (3) where allegations of fraud or improper conduct are made against one trustee[1]. To this may be added (4) where hostile litigation is brought against one of the trustees, in which case he may employ two counsel[2].

1   *Re Spurling's Will Trusts* [1966] 1 All ER 745, [1966] 1 WLR 920.
2   *Re Maddock* [1899] 2 Ch 588.

PROSPECTIVE COSTS ORDERS

87.44 A trustee, beneficiary, or any other person concerned in relation to the administration of a trust, including questions of construction, questions relating to the exercise of powers conferred by the trust, or questions as to the validity of the trust, may apply to the court at any stage of proceedings for an order (a 'prospective costs order') that his costs be paid out of the trust fund[1]. In the case of the trustees' costs, the court may authorise the trustees to raise and meet such costs out of the trust fund[2]. In the case of the costs of any other party, the court may authorise or direct the trustees to pay such costs (or any part of them, or the costs incurred up to a particular time) out of the trust fund to be assessed, if not agreed by the trustees, on the indemnity basis or, if the court directs, on the standard basis, and to make payments from time to time on account of such costs[3].

1   Practice Direction to Part 64, para 6.3. Where trustees have power to agree to pay the costs of a party, and exercise properly such a power, CPR, r 48.3 applies. In such a case, an order is not required and the trustees are entitled to recover out of the trust fund any costs which they pay pursuant to the agreement made in exercise of the power (Practice Direction to Part 64, para 6.2).
2   Practice Direction to Part 64, para 6.4(a).
3   Practice Direction to Part 64, para 6.4(b).

87.45 In deciding whether to make a prospective costs order, the court will have regard to (1) the applicant's prospects of success of the claim or defence sought to be made or resisted (2) the general reluctance of the court to deal with costs before, rather than after, trial unless satisfied that it is clear that the judge at trial would be bound to make an order in favour of the applicant[1] (3) the degree of risk that such an order might work injustice and (4) the existence of any special circumstances[2].

1 It is not necessary however for the applicant to show that no reasonable trial judge would have ordered otherwise (*Re British Airways Pension Schemes* [2000] Pen LR 311, 315.
2 See *National Anti-Vivisection Society v Duddington* (1989) 12 Tru LI 113, Mummery J; *Re Westdock Realisations Ltd* [1988] BCLC 354; see also *Evans v Evans* [1985] 3 All ER 289, [1986] 1 WLR 101; *Re Biddencare Ltd* [1994] 2 BCLC 160; *McDonald v Horn* [1995] 1 All ER 961; *Re British Airways Pension Schemes* [2000] Pen LR 311; *Weth v A-G* [2001] WTLR 155; *Machin v National Power plc* [2001] WTLR 741; *STG Valmet Trustees Ltd v Brennan* [2002] WTLR 273; and *Chessels v British Telecommunications plc* [2002] WTLR 719.

87.46 It will often be unjust for the successful claimant to property in dispute being placed in a position where, even if he wins, property held to be his is burdened with payment of the unsuccessful parties' costs. That is a powerful consideration where the persons who would benefit from the prospective costs order are all adult and of full age and capacity[1]. In a case which depends on the determination of the question whether property is held in trust by the defendants for the claimant, the very existence of the trustee/beneficiary relationship is in issue. Since that involves hostile litigation between two rival claimants it is normally wrong for the court to fetter the discretion of the trial judge by making a prospective costs order in favour of the defendants to be paid out of the property in dispute which might operate unjustly against the claimant[2].

1 *Evans v Evans* [1985] 3 All ER 289, [1986] 1 WLR 101 CA.
2 *National Anti-Vivisection Society Ltd v Duddington* (1989) 12 Tru LI 113, Mummery J; *STG Valmet Trustees Ltd v Brennan* [2002] WTLR 273 (Gibraltar CA). In *Re Omar Family Trust* [2000] WTLR 713 the trustee obtained a prospective order for its costs to be paid out of the trust fund where the protector had brought an action to replace the trustee which was opposed by the principal beneficiary but not the trustee, since no impropriety was alleged against it, although it intended to present its concerns about the purported exercise of removal without compromising its neutrality.

87.47 In one case[1], the representative members of a pension scheme obtained a prospective costs order in an action against their employers and the trustees. The representative employees did not have the resources to pursue major litigation but their claims were so strong that it was inconceivable that an independent trustee, if appointed, would not have applied for and obtained such an order. In another case[2], the court decided that it was reasonable to make a prospective costs order in favour of a representative beneficiary joined as a defendant, where he represented a significant class of members in respect of a pension scheme. There were two classes of beneficiary and, although there was no obvious conflict between them, separate legal representation was requested. The court was entitled to take into account the suspicions which existed between the two classes and the desirability of having the ultimate decision (as to whether to merge two pension schemes) accepted with good grace.

1 *McDonald v Horn* [1995] 1 All ER 961.
2 *Re British Airways Pensions Schemes* [2000] Pens LR 311.

87.48 *The right of the trustees and beneficiaries*

BEDDOE APPLICATIONS[1]

87.48 Trustees may need to bring claims against, or defend claims brought by, third parties which could affect the trust estate. They have a duty to protect and preserve the trust estate and accordingly represent the trust in third party disputes[2]. If the trustees bring or defend the claim properly for the benefit of the trust, they will be entitled to be reimbursed for their costs from the trust fund, even if they lose the litigation[3]. However, it is open to them, and prudent, to make an application (a *Beddoe* application) to the court for permission to bring or defend proceedings at the expense of the trust fund[4]. If they are given permission, they will be entitled to their costs out of the trust fund, win or lose, together with any costs which they may be ordered to pay to the third party. If however they fail to obtain permission, they do so at their own risk as to costs. If they lose the litigation, they will not receive their costs unless they establish that the costs were properly incurred. Even if they have been advised by counsel, they will not receive their costs unless the court is satisfied that it would have authorised the claim or defence had an application been made[5].

[1] See also para 83.16 above.
[2] See *Alsop Wilkinson v Neary* [1995] 1 All ER 431 at 434, [1996] 1 WLR 1220 at 1224.
[3] CPR, r 48.4(2), Practice Direction, paras 50A.1, 50A.2.
[4] The application is made under CPR Part 64: see Practice Direction B. For the procedure see paras 87.16–87.18 above. In a case of urgency, such as where a limitation period or period for service of proceedings is about to expire, the court may be able to give directions on a summary consideration of the evidence to cover the steps which need to be taken urgently, but limiting those directions so that the application needs to be renewed on fuller consideration at an early stage (see old Practice Direction to Ord 85 para 7.9).
[5] *Singh v Bhasin* [2000] WTLR 275.

87.49 In a case where the dispute in substance is between rival claimants to the entire fund the court will normally direct the trustees to take a passive role. The beneficiaries will be ordered to be joined as defendants and left to fight the claim, if they so wish, at their own expense rather than at the expense of the trust fund[1]. Where there are reasonable doubts as to whether the case is an exceptional one for the trustee to take active defensive steps against a rival claimant to all or part of the trust fund as where, otherwise, there is no viable defendant, a *Beddoe* application should be made, though such application is quite different from the ordinary *Beddoe* application, having a close affinity to a prospective costs order. In the case of a trustee who is defending personal charges of misconduct or maladministration the trustee will almost always have to defend the claim, which is a personal one, at his own risk as to costs[2].

[1] *Evans v Evans* [1986] 1 WLR 101; *Alsop Wilkinson v Neary* [1996] 1 WLR 1220; *Breadner v Granville-Grossman* [2001] WTLR 377.
[2] The ordinary rules as to costs of hostile litigation apply to breach of trust claims: *McDonald v Horn* [1995] 1 All ER 961 at 972; *Alsop Wilkinson v Neary* [1996] 1 WLR 1220 at 1224; but see *Brown v Orion Trust Ltd*, (10 May 2004, unreported), R Ct Guernsey.

ARTICLE 88
RIGHT UNDER CERTAIN CIRCUMSTANCES TO HAVE THE TRUST
ADMINISTERED UNDER THE DIRECTION OF THE COURT

88.1

(1)   Where the trustee reasonably wishes to be discharged from the *office of trustee*, or where difficulties arise which cannot be determined summarily under CPR, rule 64.2, or where it is dangerous to administer the trust except under the direction of the court, any trustee or any beneficiary may bring a claim for the administration of the trust under the court's direction[1], and this can normally now be done by claim form under CPR Part 8. But it is not obligatory on the court to make an order for administration, if the questions between the parties can be properly determined without it[2].

(2)   Where the equities are perfectly clear and unambiguous[3]; or a trustee-claimant merely craves to be released from caprice or laziness, or there is no real difficulty in administering the trust, and no reasonable allegation of dishonesty or incompetence against the trustees[4], the claimant will have to pay all the costs. Even where he acts bona fide but without any real cause, he will not be allowed his own costs[5]; and where he brings an action when the same object might have been obtained by payment into court or by a claim made under CPR, rule 64.2[6], he will not be allowed the extra costs[7] occasioned thereby. He will always appeal from an order of the court at his own risk[8].

[1]   *Talbot v Earl of Radnor* (1834) 3 My & K 252; *Goodson v Ellisson* (1827) 3 Russ 583; and for precedents, see 41 Atkin's Court Forms, Forms (2000 issue) forms 17, 201 ff.
[2]   RSC Ord 85, r 5; *Re Blake* (1885) 29 Ch D 913; *Re De Quetteville* (1903) 19 TLR 383.
[3]   *Re Knight's Trusts* (1859) 27 Beav 45; *Lowson v Copeland* (1787) 2 Bro CC 156; *Re Elliot's Trusts* (1873) LR 15 Eq 194; *Re Foligno's Mortgage* (1863) 32 Beav 131; *Re Woodburn's Will* (1857) 1 De G & J 333; *Beaty v Curson* (1868) LR 7 Eq 194; *Re Hoskin's Trusts* (1877) 5 Ch D 229.
[4]   *Forshaw v Higginson* (1855) 20 Beav 485; *Re Stokes' Trusts* (1872) LR 13 Eq 333; *Re Cabburn* (1882) 46 LT 848.
[5]   *Re Leake's Trusts* (1863) 32 Beav 135; *Re Heming's Trust* (1856) 3 K & J 40; *Re Hodgkinson* [1895] 2 Ch 190; and see CPR, Pt 44, r 44.4(1).
[6]   *Re Giles* (1886) 34 WR 712.
[7]   *Wells v Malbon* (1862) 31 Beav 48; but see *Smallwood v Rutter* (1851) 9 Hare 24.
[8]   *Rowland v Morgan* (1848) 13 Jur 23; *Tucker v Hernaman* (1853) 4 De GM & G 395; *Re Earl of Radnor's Will Trusts* (1890) 45 Ch D 402 at 423.

When general administration will be ordered

88.2 Before provision was made in the rules for seeking the directions of the court, the only way for a trustee in difficulty to know what to do was to seek to transfer the whole administration to the court. Before the making of RSC Ord 55, r 10 (later Ord 85, r 5, and now Practice Direction to CPR Part 64, para 3), a decree for general administration was granted to a trustee or beneficiary as of course. As a result of the rule change, actions for the actual administration of a trust by the court are now very rare, although it is quite common to add a claim for general administration, if and so far as may be necessary, to a claim under CPR, r 64.2, so as to give the court jurisdiction to go further than that order would otherwise authorise. In such cases, although an order pro forma is made, all further proceedings are stayed. The Practice Direction to Part 64, para 3.1, provides, however, that the court will only make an administration order if it considers that the issues between the parties cannot properly be resolved in any other way, as mentioned in Article 87.

88.3 The principles on which the court will, under Practice Direction para 3, grant or refuse general administration, were discussed, in relation to the corresponding provision (Order 55, rule 10) of the earlier Rules, in two cases; one before Pearson J[1] and the other before the Court of Appeal[2], in which the learned Lords Justices were more inclined to restrict the right to a decree than was Pearson J. Cotton LJ in the latter case said:

> 'Where there are questions which cannot properly be determined without some accounts and inquiries or directions which would form part of an ordinary administration decree, then the right of the party to have the decree or order is not taken away, but the court may restrict the order simply to those points which will enable the question which requires to be adjudicated upon to be settled. That is the result of Order, 55, rule 10 [now CPR Sch 1, Order 85, rule 5]. Then we have Order 65, rule 1 [now revoked but see Supreme Court Act 1981 s 51 and CPR, Partt 44], which says: 'Subject to the provisons of the Acts and these Rules, the costs of and incident to all proceedings in the Supreme Court, including the administration of estate and trusts, shall be in the discretion of the court of judge'. These two rules must be read together, and we then find this: that if a party comes and insists that there is a question to be determined, and, for the purposes of determining that question, asks for an administration judgment, the court cannot refuse the judgment, unless it sees that there is no question which requires its decision; but rule 1 of Order 65 puts the party who applies for the judgment and insists upon it in this position—that if it turns out that what has been represented as the substantial question requiring adjudication is one which was not a substantial question, or that the applicant was entirely wrong in his contention as to that particular question, the court can, and, in my opinion, ought ordinarily to make the person who gets the judgment pay the costs of all the proceedings consequent upon his unnecessary or possibly vexatious application to the court'[3].

[1] *Re Wilson* (1885) 28 Ch D 457.
[2] *Re Blake* (1885) 29 Ch D 913; and see also *Re Gyhon* (1885) 29 Ch D 834.
[3] A trustee may first seek protection under *Re Beddoe* [1893] 1 Ch 547; see para 83.16 above.

Deduction from Lord Justice Cotton's judgment

88.4 It will be seen from the above judgment that, since almost all isolated questions of construction or administrative difficulty can be dealt with singly, cases necessitating general administration can seldom arise; except:

(1)   where the trustees cannot pull together, or

(2)   the circumstances of the estate give rise to ever-recurring difficulties requiring the frequent direction of the court, or

(3)   where a prima facie doubt is thrown on the bona fides or the discretion of one or more of the trustees.

88.5 Possibly, also, a trustee would be held entitled to a judgment for general administration to relieve him of trouble and annoyance. where there were divers disputes as to the proper beneficiaries, out of which disputes several actions had sprung, to all of which the trustee was a necessary defendant[1]. For if he brings the money into court under the Act, he still remains a trustee; and though he would be under no liability quoad the fund brought in, he would not be discharged from liability quoad the past income. Moreover, he must be served with notice of all proceedings in relation to the fund, and this of necessity would compel him to incur some expense in employing a solicitor.

1   *Barker v Peile* (1865) 2 Drew & Sm 340.

88.6 It has also been held that the court will not necessarily order general administration because a testator has directed his trustees to commence an action for it[1]; for the court is for the benefit of the living and not the dead.

1   *Wells v Malbon* (1862) 31 Beav 48.

88.7 In *McLean v Burns Philp Trustee Co Pty Ltd*[1] Young J, in a thorough judgment, accepted that a general administration order would be made only in the three summarised cases deduced from Cotton LJ's judgment, but pointed out that in the second and third categories the court takes a relatively benign view and might act on relatively weak evidence because if the claimant puts forward a case which seems to require the court's investigation, and it turns out not to be a proper case, the court will visit on the plaintiff the costs of the proceedings. This heavy potential burden of costs seems to have been a prime weapon for keeping administration actions within proper bounds[2]. He empha-sised that the court does not make an administrative decree if the only possible result would be that the whole trust fund would be spent in costs or where there would not be likely to be any benefit to the beneficiaries[3]. Secondly, where the trustee has been given a discretion by the trust instrument, the court does not enforce the exercise of the power against the wish of the trustees, but it does prevent them exercising it improperly[4].

1   [1985] 2 NSWLR 623.
2   *Fane v Fane* (1879) 13 Ch D 228.
3   *Re Customs and Excise Officers' Mutual Guarantee Fund* [1917] 2 Ch 18 at 26–27.
4   *Tempest v Lord Camoys* (1882) 21 Ch D 571 at 578, CA; but see *Mettoy Pension Trustees Ltd v Evans* [1991] 2 All ER 513 and paras 8.46 and 8.86 above.

Division Five

THE CONSEQUENCES OF A BREACH OF TRUST

Chapter 22

THE LIABILITY OF THE TRUSTEES

ARTICLE 89
THE MEASURE OF THE TRUSTEE'S LIABILITY FOR BREACH
OF TRUST

89.1

(1)   Where a trustee loses or misapplies trust property in an unau-
       thorised transaction entered into in breach of his core duty to
       hold and disburse the trust fund solely in accordance with the
       trust terms, he can be ordered to restore the trust property in
       specie, or to pay a money substitute. In the latter case, the
       trustee's liability is a 'primary' liability to render substitutive
       performance of his core duty, rather than a wrong-based 'second-
       ary' liability to repair the harm caused by his breach of duty, and
       so there is no need for the beneficiaries to plead or prove that he
       has breached his duty[1], nor do they need to establish a causal
       link between his breach of duty and any loss which they may
       have suffered[2]. The measure of the trustee's liability is, instead,
       the objective value of the property which he should have had in
       his possession when the beneficiaries called on him to account
       for his stewardship of the trust fund[3]. Equity regards the trustee
       as inducing the settlor to transfer ownership of the trust assets to

the trustee on the trustee's undertaking of fidelity to the trust's terms, and he is not allowed to deny that he observed this undertaking by subsequently asserting that he actually did something which he was not allowed to do[4]. The trustee's accounts are therefore 'falsified' to delete unauthorised outgoings from the record[5], and he must then make up any shortfall out of his own pocket.

(2) Where a trustee's conduct is authorised by the trust deed, but he fails to comply with the duties imposed upon him, he can be ordered to pay reparation to make good the harm caused by his breach of duty. In this case, the measure of his liability is the loss which the beneficiaries have actually suffered[6], using a 'but-for' causation test in all cases, regardless of whether the trustee's breach of duty was innocent, negligent, or fraudulent[7]. In the case of a reparation claim, the trustee's accounts are 'surcharged' with the amount of the beneficiaries' loss as if the trustee has received this amount for the beneficiaries, and the trustee must then pay this sum into the trust funds in order to make the accounts balance[8].

(3) Where a trustee makes an unauthorised gain, title to the property or its traceable product must be transferred as an accretion to the trust fund (subject in appropriate cases to the trustee's lien for reimbursing his acquisition expenses)[9] unless the beneficiaries are content for the trustee simply to pay over the amount of his gain[10]. In that case, the beneficiaries may surcharge the accounts with the amount of the trustee's unauthorised gain, so that he becomes personally liable to pay over the relevant sum[11]. Hence, where the trustee acquires an asset, the value of which depreciates, the beneficiaries may choose not to adopt the transaction, so that the trustee becomes personally liable to pay over the amount paid to acquire the asset, and the beneficiaries may then exploit their lien over the property to have title to the property transferred as an accretion to the trust fund in part satisfaction of the trustee's personal liability to account[12].

(4) Where a trustee's failure properly to perform his functions causes a beneficiary to suffer an individual loss over and above any loss remediable through falsifying or surcharging the trust accounts and such special loss would not have occurred but for such failure, then equitable compensation in the amount of that loss will be payable by the trustee to that beneficiary. By the same token, a trustee might also be ordered to pay exemplary damages directly to a beneficiary in cases of outrageous misconduct, were the courts to decide that awards of this kind should be made in appropriate circumstances.

(5) Apart from the above personal or proprietary liability of a trustee who has committed a breach of trust, such trustee may be

liable to a direction[13] or declaration[14] of the court or may be enjoined from pursuing a particular course of conduct[15] or removed or replaced by another trustee[16].

[1] *Bacon v Clarke* (1837) 3 My & Cr 294; *Re Anglo-French Co-operative Society* (1882) 21 Ch D 492 at 506; *Re Stevens* [1898] 1 Ch 162; *Ahmed Angullia bin Hadjee Mohamed Salleh Angullia v Estate and Trustees Agencies* (1927) Ltd [1938] AC 624 at 637, PC.

[2] *Cocker v Quayle* (1830) 1 Russ & M 535; *Magnus v Queensland National Bank* (1888) 37 Ch D 466 at 471–2 per Lord Halsbury LC, CA; *British American Elevator Co v Bank of Bank of North America* [1919] AC 658 at 663–4 per Viscount Haldane; *Youyang Pty Ltd v Minter Ellison Morris Fletcher* (2003) 212 CLR 484 at [63] and [69].

[3] *New Cap Reinsurance Corpn Ltd v General Cologne Re Australia Ltd* (2004) 7 ITELR 295 at [55] per Young CJ in Eq, NSW Sup Ct.

[4] *Re Smith* [1896] 1 Ch 71 at 77; *Re Biss (deceased)* [1903] 2 Ch 40.

[5] *Knott v Cottee* (1852) 16 Beav 77 at 79–80; *Re Bennion* (1889) 60 LT 859; *Re Salmon* (1889) 42 Ch D 351 at 357.

[6] *Elder's Trustee and Executor Co Ltd v Higgins* (1963) 113 CLR 426 at 453; *Fales v Canada Permanent Trust Co* [1977] 2 SCR 302 at 320.

[7] *Target Holdings Ltd v Redferns (a firm)* [1996] AC 421 at 436; *Collins v Brebner* [2000] Lloyd's Rep PN 587; *Hulbert v Avens* [2003] EWHC 76 (Ch), [2003] WTLR 387 at [56]; *Gwembe Valley Developments Ltd v Koshy (No 3)* [2003] EWCA Civ 1048, [2004] 1 BCLC 131 at [147].

[8] *Meehan v Glazier Holdings Pty Ltd* (2002) 54 NSWLR 146 at 149–150, NSWCA; *Re Ambrazevicius Estate* (2002) 164 Man R (2d) 5, Manitoba QB; *Man Fong Hang v Man Ping Nam* [2003] HKCFI 967.

[9] See Article 83.

[10] *Boardman v Phipps* [1967] 2 AC 46, HL.

[11] *Re Blake* [1977] 1 ACWS 524, Ontario CA.

[12] *Re Lake* [1903] 1 KB 439.

[13] For example, Trustee Act 1925, s 61, RSC Ord 85.

[14] *Cowan v Scargill* [1985] Ch 270 at 286, 296, 299 per Megarry VC; *Public Trustee v Cooper* [2001] WTLR 903.

[15] For example, Article 93 below.

[16] *Letterstedt v Broers* (1884) 9 App Cas 371, PC.

Paragraphs 1 and 2

Personal liability via the taking of accounts

89.2 At the core of the trust is the duty of trustees to produce accounts that are available for the beneficiaries to examine. The beneficiaries are entitled to accounts and supporting documents and information without any court order[1]. However, they can also obtain an order for an account as a means of enforcing their right to performance of the trustee's core duties or reparation for losses flowing from the trustee's breaches of duty, by 'falsifying' or 'surcharging' the accounts, as explained by Lewison J in *Ultraframe (UK) Ltd v Fielding*[2]:

'The taking of an account is the means by which a beneficiary requires a trustee to justify his stewardship of trust property. The trustee must show what he has done with that property. If the beneficiary is dissatisfied with the way that a trustee has dealt with trust assets, he may surcharge or falsify the account. He surcharges the account when he alleges that the trustee has not obtained for the benefit of the trust all that he might have done, if he had exercised due care and diligence. If the allegation is proved, then the account is taken as if the trustee had received, for the benefit of the trust, what he would have received if he had exercised due care and diligence. The beneficiary falsifies the account when he alleges that the trustee has applied trust property in a way that he should not have done (e.g. by making an unauthorised investment). If the allegation is proved, then the account will be taken as if the expenditure had not been made; and as if the unauthorised investment had not formed part of the assets of the trust. Of course, if the unauthorised investment has appreciated in value, the beneficiary may choose not to falsify the account: in which case the asset will remain a trust asset and the expenditure on it will be allowed in taking the account.'

1   See Article 60 above.
2   [2005] EWHC 1638 (Ch) at [1513].

89.3 As explained by Austin J in an Australian case, *Glazier Holdings Pty Ltd v Australian Men's Health Pty Ltd (No 2)*[1] there are two forms of account, with an order to pay any sum found to be due to the trust estate when the accounting process is complete: the common account and the account on the footing of wilful default. Where the trustees have acted beyond their powers by doing something they are not authorised to do (eg distributing trust money by way of gift to themselves or to someone else who is not a beneficiary or purchasing an unauthorised asset) the accounts will be falsified, deleting unauthorised entries of disbursements or transfers or acquisitions of assets, so that the appropriate sums or assets are deemed to remain in the trust fund and the trustees must reconstitute the trust fund as it would have been but for the unauthorised transactions, it being 'well recognised that the basis on which a trustee is liable to make good a misapplication of trust moneys is strict and harsh, especially where there has been a huge depreciation in the value of the asset acquired', as where there is a dramatic fall in the property market or the stock market[2]. Where the trustees have not exceeded their powers, but have failed to act as they should have acted to comply with their equitable or statutory duties, their accounts will be surcharged to add the value that the trust fund would have had but for such failure[3].

1   [2001] NSWSC 6. Austin J's decision was overturned on appeal, but nothing was said by the NSWCA that contradicted his analysis of the forms of equitable accounting: (2002) 54 NSWLR 146. For additional discussion, see R Chambers 'Liability' in P Birks and A Pretto (eds) *Breach of Trust* (2002) 1 at pp. 16–20.
2   *Re Duckwari plc* [1999] Ch 253 at 265 per Nourse LJ; *Pitt v Cholmondeley* (1754) 2 Ves Sen 565, 28 ER 360; *Knott v Cottee* (1852) 16 Beav 77 at 79. Where unauthorised investments have been made 'the case must either be treated as if these investments had not been made, or had been made for his own benefit out of his own moneys and that he had at the same time retained moneys of the [trust] in his Lands'; *Wallersteiner v Moir* [1975] QB 373 at 397 per Buckley LJ.
3   *Re Tebbs* [1976] 2 All ER 858; *Bartlett v Barclays Bank Trust Co Ltd* (No 2) [1980] Ch 515 at 543; *Glazier Holdings Pty Ltd v Australian Men's Health Pty Ltd (No 2)* [2001] NSWSC 6.

89.4 While the taking of such accounts will reveal instances where a trustee acted beyond his powers by diverting to himself proceeds of sale of trust assets or dividends on trust shares, it may be that a trustee profited from his trust in a less direct manner from personal activities that conflicted with his obligation of undivided loyalty. Here the beneficiaries need to obtain an order for an account of profits springing from a particular breach[1]: this provides a remedy for specific wrongdoing and nothing more[2].

1   For example, *Boardman v Phipps* [1967] 2 AC 46.
2   *Glazier Holdings Pty Ltd v Australian Men's Health Pty Ltd (No 2)* [2001] NSWSC 6.
    Where an asset is received by way of a bribe or in breach of the fiduciary duty of undivided
    loyalty the fiduciary will be personally liable for the highest value of the asset while he
    owns it: *Nant-y-glo and Blaina Ironworks Co v Grave* (1878) 12 Ch D 738 accepted in
    Target Holdings Ltd v Redferns [1996] AC 421 at 440, HL.

89.5 The order for an account of administration in common form is available
without any allegation of wrongdoing[1], and requires the defendant to account
only for what has actually been received, what has been disbursed in
management expenses[2] and what has been distributed[3]. In contrast, an order
for an account on the basis of wilful default is grounded on the trustee's
misconduct, and requires him to account not only for what he has received,
but for what he should have received if he had not committed a breach of
duty[4]. The term 'wilful default' is a misleading one in this context since it
extends to all breaches of duty, running from negligence through to deliberate
fraud[5].

1   *Partington v Reynolds* (1858) 4 Drew 253 at 256. See too *Templeton Insurance Ltd v
    Penningtons Solicitors LLP* [2005] EWHC 2885 (Ch).
2   Note the Trustee Act 2000 s 31, which empowers trustees to take properly incurred
    expenses out of the trust funds. For discussion of the question whether trustees can recover
    an indemnity for expenses incurred in the course of unauthorised conduct, see *Fitzwood
    Pty Ltd v Unique Goal Pty Ltd (in liquidation)* (2001) 188 ALR 566, Fed Ct of Aus.
3   *Glazier Holdings Pty Ltd v Australian Men's Health Pty Ltd (No 2)* [2001] NSWSC 6.
4   *Gordon v Gonda* [1955] 2 All ER 762 at 768, CA; *Armitage v Nurse* [1998] Ch 241 at
    252; *Coulthard v Disco Mix Club Ltd* [1999] 2 All ER 457 at 481; *Glazier Holdings
    Pty Ltd v Australian Men's Health Pty Ltd (No 2)* [2001] NSWSC 6; *Iliffe v Trafford*
    [2001] EWHC 469 (Ch) at [9]; *Garcia v Delfino* [2003] NSWSC 1001 at [31]–[33]. See
    too *Re Tebbs* [1976] 2 All ER 858 and *Northey v Juul* [2005] NSWSC 933, in both of
    which the order was limited to an account only of part of the administration.
5   *Walker v Symonds* (1818) 3 Swan 1 at 69; *Re Chapman* [1896] 2 Ch 763 at 776 and
    779–780. See too J H Stannard 'Wilful Default' [1979] Conv 345 esp at p. 348.

89.6 In all cases, the onus lies on the trustee to prove and justify his records,
and evidential presumptions are made against him if he fails to do so[1]. Where
the trustee can show that he paid trust funds away in an authorised
transaction which entailed no breach of duty he will be discharged from his
duty to hold the relevant funds for the beneficiaries[2]. However, where the
court decides, following its scrutiny of the trust accounts, that he owes the
beneficiaries a personal liability, different forms of order can be made,
according to the nature of the trust. Where the trust is absolute and there is no
need to reconstitute the fund, the court can simply order the trustee to transfer
trust assets or pay money directly to the beneficiaries[3]. In the more common
case where the trust is still on foot, the trustee will be ordered to reconstitute
the fund in a proper state, or where he has been replaced by new trustees, to
transfer assets or pay money to the new trustees, to be held by them under the
terms of the trust[4].

1   *Maintemp Heating & Air Conditioning Inc v Monat Developments Inc* (2002) 59 OR (3d)
    270, esp at [40]–[44]; *Wong v Wong* [2002] BCSC 779 at [25].
2   *Soar v Ashwell* [1893] 2 QB 390 at 394, CA.
3   *Target Holdings Ltd v Redferns* [1996] AC 421 at 435; *Roxborough v Rothmans of Pall
    Mall Australia Ltd* (2002) 185 ALR 335 at 353.

4   *Partridge v Equity Trustees Executors and Agency Co Ltd* (1947) 75 CLR 149; *Hillsdown plc v Pensions Ombudsman* [1997] 1 All ER 862 at 897; *Chellaram v Chellaram (No 2)* [2002] EWHC 632 (Ch), [2002] 3 All ER 17 at [159]; *Patel v London Borough of Brent (No 2)* [2003] EWHC 3081, [2004] WTLR 577 at [32].

Compensation claims against trustees

89.7 Equity recognises two different types of compensation claim against trustees, which will be termed substitutive performance claims and reparation claims[1]. Substitutive performance claims are claims for a money payment as a substitute for performance of the trustees' obligation to account for and deliver trust assets *in specie*. Claims of this sort are apposite when trust property has been lost or misapplied in an unauthorised transaction, and the amount claimed is the objective value of the property for which the trustees should have been able to account. Reparation claims are claims for a money payment to make good the damage caused by a breach of trust, and the amount claimed is measured by reference to the actual loss sustained by the beneficiaries. Claims of this sort are often brought where trustees have carelessly mismanaged trust property, but they lie more generally wherever a trustee has harmed his beneficiaries by committing a breach of duty.

1   Adopting Dr Steven Elliott's terminology in Compensation Claims against Trustees (Oxford DPhil thesis, 2002). Parts of this are published as: SB Elliott, 'Remoteness Criteria in Equity' (2002) 65 MLR 588; SB Elliott and C Mitchell 'Remedies for Dishonest Assistance' (2004) 67 MLR 16, pp.23–34; SB Elliott and J Edelman 'Money Remedies against Trustees' (2004) 18 Tru LI 116. For additional discussion, see R Chambers 'Liability' in P Birks and A Pretto (eds) Breach of Trust (2002) 1; DJ Hayton 'Unique Rules for the Unique Institution, the Trust' in S Degeling and J Edelman (eds) Equity in Commercial Law (2005) 279.

Substitutive performance claims

89.8 A trustee's 'paramount obligation' is 'recovering, securing and duly applying the trust fund'[1]: he must get in the trust assets where the trust deed requires him to do so[2], 'properly ... preserve the trust fund', and 'pay the income and the corpus to those who are entitled to them respectively'[3]. The beneficiaries have corresponding primary rights to have the trust assets collected, maintained, and disbursed in accordance with the trust deed[4], and the courts can give direct effect to these rights, without proof that the trustee has committed a breach of duty, in various ways: eg by making a declaration setting out the nature of a beneficiary's interest[5], or a trustee's duty[6]; by directing the trustee to exercise an obligatory discretionary power of appointment;[7] by directing the trustee to transfer trust assets to an absolutely entitled beneficiary;[8] or by issuing a prohibitory injunction, restraining the trustee from acting inconsistently with his primary obligations[9].

1   *Re Brogden* (1888) 38 Ch D 546 at 571 per Fry LJ.
2   *Maitland v Bateman* (1843) 13 LJ Ch 273; *Coppard v Allen* (1864) 4 Giff 497; *M'Donnel v White* (1865) 9 HL Cas 570 at 585, per Lord Westbury LC.
3   *Low v Bouverie* [1891] 3 Ch 82 at 99 per Lindley LJ.
4   *Target Holdings Ltd v Redferns* [1996] AC 421 at 434, per Lord Browne-Wilkinson.

5   *Smith v Acton* (1858) 26 Beav 210. The proper form of a declaration of equitable interest
    under CPR Rule 40.20 is discussed in *Powell v Wilshire [2004] EWCA Civ 534*, [2005]
    QB 117 at [39]–[45] per Arden LJ. The Trusts of Land and Appointment of Trustees
    Act 1996 s 14(2)(b) enables a person with an interest in property that is subject to a trust
    of land to obtain an order declaring the nature or extent of his interest, as in eg *Oxley v
    Hiscock* [2004] EWCA Civ 546, [2004] 2 FLR 295, [2005] Fam 211.
6   *Cowan v Scargill* [1985] Ch. 270. The court should not make declarations merely to enable
    a party to argue that there were a greater number of issues decided in his favour for the
    purposes of the determination of costs, and in any case 'the degree to which parties
    relevantly succeeded or lost will be assessed for the purposes of the costs determination
    independently of the form of the orders and will not depend mechanically on what is or is
    not spelt out into orders': *Lewis v Nortex Pty Ltd (in liquidation)* [2006] NSWSC 480
    at [6].
7   *Re Locker's Settlement Trusts* [1977] 1 WLR 1323.
8   *Re Knox's Trusts* [1895] 2 Ch 483; *Re Sandeman's Will Trust* [1937] 1 All ER 368. See too
    the Trustee Act 1925, ss 44(vi) and 51(1)(d).
9   *Fox v Fox* (1870) LR 11 Eq 142 (improper distribution of assets); *Buttle v Saunders* [1950]
    2 All ER 193 (sale of assets at an undervalue); *George v Macdonald NSW Sup Ct (Eq Div)*
    6 February 1992 (sale of assets at an undervalue). It is no bar to the issue of an injunction
    restraining the unauthorised disposal of trust assets that the trustees have entered a binding
    contract with a third party: *Fouche v Superannuation Fund Board* (1952) 88 CLR 609;
    and see too *Ord v Noel* (1820) 5 Madd 438; *Dance v Goldingham* (1873) 8 Ch App 902.

89.9 In just the same way, the court can also give direct effect to the
beneficiaries' primary rights without proof of wrongdoing where a trustee
cannot perform his core obligation to deliver trust assets *in specie* because he
has lost or misapplied them in an unauthorised transaction. In such cases, the
court can order the trustee to pay money as a substitute for performance of his
core duty. The amount due is calculated by requiring the trustee to produce a
set of accounts which omits no relevant incomings and records only authorised outgoings, by inspecting these accounts to determine what assets make up
the trust fund, and then, where the trustee cannot produce these assets in
specie, by ordering him to pay over a money substitute – either directly to the
beneficiaries, or more usually, into the trust fund so that the trust can remain
on foot. Thus, as Kekewich J stated in *Head v Gould*[1]:

> 'As against a trustee who, on the accounts being taken, is shewn to have
> improperly applied part of the trust estate, the right of a cestui que trust is to
> have those accounts set straight – that is, to compel the trustee to pay such a
> sum as will make them balance.'

1   [1898] 2 Ch 250 at 266. See too *Wiglesworth v Wiglesworth* (1852) 16 Beav 269 at 272
    per Romilly MR; *Chaplin v Young* (1864) 33 Beav 330 at 343 per Romilly MR. Also Sir P
    Millett 'Equity's Place in the Law of Commerce' (1998) 114 LQR 214 at p. 225.

89.10 The courts have often said that claims of this sort resemble claims for
'an equitable debt' and that the trustees' liability is a 'liability in the nature of
a debt'[1]. The point of this comparison is that the beneficiaries' claim is not
comparable to a common law claim for damages because it is not founded on
an assertion that the trustees have committed a wrong[2]. Hence it makes no
difference whether the beneficiaries have been caused a loss by the trustees'
actions or omissions[3], for the amount payable 'looks not so much to the loss
suffered as to what is required to restore the trust fund'[4]. Nor does it matter
whether the trustees have behaved negligently or dishonestly[5]. Nor do the
concepts of remoteness[6] and contributory negligence[7] have any bearing on the
beneficiaries' claim.

89.10 *The liability of the trustees*

1   Ex p Adamson (1878) 8 Ch D 807 at 819 per James LJ; Ex p Kelly & Co (1879) 11 Ch D 306 at 311 per James LJ; *Wickstead v Brown* (1992) 30 NSWLR 1 at 14–5; *Armstrong v East West Airlines (Operations) Ltd* NSW Sup Ct (Eq Div) 3 February 1994; *Turner v TR Nominees Pty Ltd* NSW Sup Ct (Eq Div) 3 November 1995.
2   Cf *Jervis v Harris* [1996] Ch 195 at 202–3: 'The plaintiff who claims payment of a debt need not prove anything beyond the occurrence of the event or condition on the occurrence of which the debt becomes due. He need prove no loss; the rules as to remoteness of damage and mitigation of loss are irrelevant.'
3   *Cocker v Quayle* (1830) 1 Russ & M 535; *Salway v Salway* (1831) 2 Russ & M 215; *Magnus v Queensland National Bank* (1888) 37 Ch D 466 at 471–2 per Lord Halsbury LC, CA; British *American Elevator Co v Bank of Bank of North America* [1919] AC 658 at 663–4 per Viscount Haldane; *Island Realty Investments Ltd v Douglas* (1985) 19 ETR 56 at 64; *Youyang Pty Ltd v Minter Ellison Morris Fletcher* (2003) 212 CLR 484 at [63] and [69].
4   *New Cap Reinsurance Corpn Ltd v General Cologne Re Australia Ltd* (2004) 7 ITELR 295 at [55] per Young CJ in Eq, NSW Sup Ct. See too *Re Anglo-French Co-operative Society* (1882) 21 Ch D 492 at 506; *Re Windsor Steam Coal Co* (1901) Ltd [1929] 1 Ch 151 at 166–7.
5   *Caffrey v Darby* (1801) 6 Ves 488; *Clough v Bond* (1838) 3 My & Cr 490 at 496–7 per Lord Cottenham LC, endorsed in *Target Holdings Ltd v Redferns* [1996] AC 421 at 434.
6   *Clough v Bond* (1838) 3 My & Cr 490; *Magnus v Queensland* National Bank (1888) 37 Ch D 466; *Re Duckwari plc (No 2)* [1999] Ch 268 at 272; *McCann v Switzerland Insurance Australia Ltd* (2000) 203 CLR 579 at 621–2.
7   *Nationwide Building Society v Bulmer Radmore (a firm)* [1999] PNLR 606 per Blackburne J: 'contributory negligence has never been a defence open to a trustee sued by his beneficiary for breach of trust in wrongfully paying away the trust fund'.

89.11   The nature of the trustee's liability is well brought out in the judgment of Street J (as he then was) in *Re Dawson*[1] in the following passage, although the language of 'restitution' is now best avoided in this context as it is frequently used in other contexts to describe gain-based liabilities:

'The obligation of a defaulting trustee is essentially one of effecting a restitution to the estate. The obligation is of a personal character and its extent is not to be limited by common law principles governing remoteness of damages. In *Caffrey v Darby*[2], trustees were charged with neglect in failing to recover possession of part of the trust assets. The assets were lost and it was argued by the trustees that the loss was not attributable to their neglect. The Master of the Rolls, in stating his reasons, asked "will they be relieved from that by the circumstance that the loss has ultimately happened by something that is not a direct and immediate consequence of their negligence?" His answer to this question was that, even supposing that "they could not look to the possibility" of the actual event which occasioned the loss, "yet, if they have already been guilty of negligence they must be responsible for any loss in any way to that property; for whatever may be the immediate cause the property would not have been in a situation to sustain that loss if it had not been for their negligence. If they had taken possession of the property it would not have been in his possession. If the loss had happened by fire, lightning, or any other accident, that would not be an excuse for them, if guilty of previous negligence. That was their fault." *Caffrey v Darby* is consistent with the proposition that if a breach has been committed then the trustee is liable to place the trust estate in the same position as it would have been in if no breach had been committed. Considerations of causation, foreseeability and remoteness do not readily enter into the matter. To the same effect is the case of *Clough v Bond*[3]. It was argued before Lord Cottenham LC that "the principle of the court is to charge persons in the situation of trustees as parties to a breach of trust, wherever they have acted irregularly, and the irregularity, however well intended, has in the result enabled their co-trustees to commit a breach of trust, or has been, however remotely, the origin of the loss." ... The principles embodied in this approach do not appear to involve any inquiry as to whether the loss was caused by or flowed from the breach. Rather the inquiry in each instance would appear to be whether the loss would have happened if there had been no breach ... The cases to which I have referred demonstrate that the obligation to make restitution, which courts of equity have from very early times imposed on defaulting trustees and other fiduciaries, is of a more absolute nature than the common-law obligation to pay damages for tort or breach of contract. Moreover the distinction between common law damages and relief against a defaulting trustee is strikingly demonstrated by reference to the actual form of relief granted in equity in respect of breaches of trust. The form of relief is couched in terms appropriate to require the defaulting trustee to restore to the estate the assets of which he deprived it. Increases in market values between the date of breach and the date of recoupment are for the trustee's account: the effect of such increases would, at common law, be excluded from the computation of damages but in equity a defaulting trustee must make good the loss by restoring to the estate the assets of which he deprived it notwithstanding that market values may have increased in the meantime. The obligation to restore to the estate the assets of which he deprived it necessarily connotes that, where a monetary compensation is to be paid in lieu of restoring assets, that compensation is to be assessed by reference to the value of the assets at the date of restoration and not at the date of deprivation. In this sense the obligation is a continuing one and ordinarily, if the assets are for some reason not restored in specie, it will fall for quantification at the date when recoupment is to be effected, and not before.'

1   [1966] 2 NSWR 211. This passage was endorsed by Brightman LJ in *Bartlett v Barclays Bank Trust Co Ltd* [1980] Ch 515 and by *Lord Browne-Wilkinson in Target Holdings Ltd v Redferns* [1996] AC 421, HL.
2   (1801) 6 Ves 488.
3   (1838) 3 My & Cr 490.

89.12 Further authorities supporting this analysis include *Bacon v Clark*[1], where a trustee received assets out of which he was bound to pay money to the beneficiaries, but the beneficiaries never received the money, and where Lord Cottenham LC held that[2]:

'whether a breach of trust was committed or not ... [the trustee's] estate must remain liable to pay what is due in respect of that sum, unless payment or a sufficient excuse for non-payment can be shewn.'

1   (1837) 2 My & Cr 294.
2   (1837) 2 My & Cr 298–9.

89.13 A century later, in a Privy Council appeal from Singapore, *Ahmed Angullia bin Hadjee Mohamed Salleh Angullia v Estate and Trust Agencies (1927) Ltd*[1], the defendant trustee contended that he should be chargeable with money spent for an unauthorised purpose only if the beneficiaries pleaded that this money had been spent in breach of trust. Lord Romer rejected this, ruling that the trustee owed the beneficiaries a duty to account for the trust assets, that 'it was incumbent upon [the trustee] to justify his payments, and those that he could not justify would necessarily have to be disallowed' from the account, leaving him under a primary duty to pay over the outstanding balance[2].

89.13 *The liability of the trustees*

1   [1938] AC 624. See too *Green v Weatherill* [1929] 2 Ch 213 at 222–3.
2   *Green v Weatherill* [1929] 2 Ch 213 at 627, citing *Re Stevens* [1898] 1 Ch 162 at 172 per
     Cotton LJ: 'on taking the common account of their receipts, executors can properly be, and
     are often, charged with a devastavit arising on the accounts themselves ... they stand
     charged with their receipts; and if they seek to discharge themselves by unlawful payments,
     their discharge is disallowed.' See also Lindley MR's comment in *Re Stevens* at 170 that 'A
     wrongful payment is one thing, and can be set right by disallowing it when the executor
     brings in his account. But if it is sought to charge him with loss attributable to some other
     breach of duty, call it wilful default or by any other name, such breach of duty must be
     proved'.

89.14 When deciding whether a trustee's payments are justified and should
therefore be allowed to stand on the taking of the account, the court will
generally disallow unauthorised disbursements, but there are exceptional cases
where these will be allowed, and the trustee exonerated from performance of
his duty to hold the relevant property for the beneficiaries. One such is where
the beneficiaries elect to adopt the trustee's actions and ask the court to treat
these as though they had been authorised all along. Beneficiaries would wish
to do this where the trustee has bought an unauthorised investment which has
increased in value[1], or where the trustee has wrongfully sold trust assets
whose current value is less than the value of the sale proceeds in the trustees'
hands[2].

1   *Re Patten* (1883) 52 LJ Ch 787; *Re Jenkins* [1903] 2 Ch 362; *Wright v Morgan* [1926] AC
     788 at 799. If the beneficiaries choose to adopt the investment, they cannot also demand
     that the trustees pay in the difference between the current value of the investment and the
     (higher) current value of an authorised asset that was sold to make the purchase: *Thornton
     v Stokill* (1855) 1 Jur NS 751; sed contra *Re Lake* [1903] 1 KB 439.
2   *Watts v Girdlestone* (1843) 6 Beav 188; *Shepherd v Mouls* (1845) 4 Hare 500 at 504.

89.15 The courts may also relieve a trustee from the performance of his duty
where they consider that requiring him to perform the duty would be
inequitable. For example, in *Jones v Lewis*, Lord Hardwicke LC held that[1]:

> 'if a trustee is robbed, that robbery properly proved shall be a discharge [in an
> action of account], provided he keeps [the trust assets] so as he would keep his
> own.'

1   (1750) 2 Ves Sen 240 at 241. See too *Morley v Morley* (1678) 2 Cas in Ch 2; *Jobson v
     Palmer* [1893] 1 Ch 71. And cf *Ex p Belchier* (1754) Amb 218 at 219 per Lord Hard-
     wicke LC (trustee not answerable for funds lost on banker's bankruptcy); *Job v Job* (1877)
     6 Ch D 562 at 563–4 per Jessel MR (laying down a similar rule for executors).

89.16 It is tempting, but wrong, to conclude from the fact that trustees need
not account for stolen trust property which they have kept with reasonable
care that the courts will never require trustees to reach into their own pockets
unless they have committed a breach of duty[1]. Various cases have already been
cited for the proposition that proof of wrongdoing is unnecessary in substitutive performance claims. Another is *Eaves v Hickson*[2], where Romilly MR
declined to relieve a trustee who made unauthorised distributions on presentation of a forged document. No finding was made that the trustee had failed
to examine this document carefully, and although counsel cited *Jones* and
other robbery cases[3], his Lordship concluded that the trustee was still 'bound
to pay the trust fund to the right person'[4].

1   As argued in R Chambers 'Liability' in P Birks and A Pretto (eds) *Breach of Trust* (2002) 1, at p.9.
2   (1861) 30 Beav 136 (whilesee also *Ashby v Blackwell* (1765) 2 Eden 299; *Bostock v Floyer* (1865) LR 1 Eq 26; *Sutton v Wilders* (1871) LR 12 Eq 373).
3   (1861) 30 Beav 139.
4   (1861) 30 Beav 141.

89.17 To give some examples of substitutive performance claims in practice, let it be supposed that a trustee T makes an unauthorised distribution of £x to A, who is now bankrupt; that T makes an unauthorised investment of £y in a villa in South Africa, which has now halved in value; and that T makes an unauthorised transfer of assets worth £z to an agent, B, who has now absconded with the money. Because T had no power under the trust to distribute the £x to A or to spend the £y on the villa, he will be treated as though he carried out these transactions with his own money, and he will be required to pay £x and £y back into the trust fund[1], with compound interest at 1% above the clearing banks' base rate[2]. So far as the assets worth £z are concerned, T will now have to pay their replacement value back into the trust fund, even if this has risen to £2z in the interim[3], and it makes no difference whether the assets were lost through an innocent accident or through B's negligence or dishonesty[4].

1   *Knott v Cottee* (1852) 16 Beav 77; *Re Duckwari plc (No 2)* [1999] Ch 268 at 272; *Royal Trust Corpn of Canada v Barter* [2000] BCSC 1842 at [46]–[50]; *Wong v Burt* (2004) 7 ITELR 263 at [59], NZCA.
2   *Wallersteiner v Moir (No 2)* [1975] QB 373 at 397.
3   *Shepherd v Mouls* (1845) 4 Hare 500 at 504; *Re Massingberd* (1890) 63 LT 296.
4   *Clough v Bond* (1838) 3 My & Cr 490 at 496–7 per Lord Cottenham LC, endorsed in *Target Holdings Ltd v Redferns* [1996] AC 421 at 434 per Lord Browne-Wilkinson; *Caffrey v Derby* (1801) 6 Ves 488.

TARGET HOLDINGS LTD V REDFERNS

89.18 In *Target Holdings Ltd v Redferns*[1], the claimant agreed to lend money to a borrower to purchase property. Repayment of the loan was to be secured by a charge on the property. The money was placed with the defendant solicitors on trust for payment to the borrower's order, once a duly executed charge over the property and with supporting documents of title were delivered. The solicitors paid the money over to the borrower's order without first obtaining the charge or other documents, although these were later delivered. The borrower defaulted on the loan and it then transpired that the property had been fraudulently over-valued, so that the claimant was left substantially out of pocket after it had exercised its power of sale. The Court of Appeal held that the solicitors had committed a breach of trust by releasing the money before receiving the documents, and that at this moment there had been 'an immediate loss placing the trustee under an immediate duty to restore the moneys to the trust fund'[2]. They concluded that the solicitors were liable for the full amount of the money, but to prevent double recovery they required the claimant to give credit for the amount realised by the sale of the property.

1   [1996] AC 421.
2   [1994] 1 WLR 1089 at 1103 per Peter Gibson LJ.

89.19 The House of Lords agreed that there had been a breach of trust, but disagreed that the clock should be stopped at the date of breach for the purpose of quantifying the solicitors' liability. Their Lordships held that the relevant date was the date of judgment, ie after the transaction had been completed, and that the solicitors would therefore be liable only if the claimant could prove that its loss would not have occurred but for the early payment of the money without taking any security. Hence the case was sent back to the High Court for determination of this point.

89.20 In his leading speech, Lord Browne-Wilkinson clearly thought that the claimant should have to prove a causal link between its loss and the solicitor's breach of duty. However, as Lord Millett has observed in later extra-judicial writings[1], the claim was for substitutive performance of the solicitor's duty to hold and disburse the trust money in accordance with the trust terms, and so the question whether the claimant had suffered a loss as a result of the solicitor's breach of duty was beside the point[2]. In Lord Millett's view, the case should therefore have been decided on the different basis that the solicitor's release of the money without a contemporaneous receipt of the title documents was a breach of trust, but that where a trustee has misapplied trust assets, his 'obligation to restore the trust property is not an obligation to restore it in the very same form in which he disbursed it, but an obligation to restore it in any form authorised by the trust[3]'. Hence, when the solicitor later acquired the title documents and delivered them to the claimant, it performed its obligation to restore the trust property, not *in specie*, but in the form of an authorised substitute. Hence the solicitor should not have been liable to a substitutive performance claim, having obtained the title documents as he was supposed to do, albeit later than he was supposed to do. He should only have been liable to a reparation claim, which, of course, does require proof of a causal link between the loss and the breach of duty, so this matter had to be remitted to the High Court by the House of Lords.

[1] Sir P Millett 'Equity's Place in the Law of Commerce' (1998) 114 LQR 214, at pp. 225–7. See too Lord Millett 'Proprietary Restitution' in S Degeling and J Edelman (eds) Equity in Commercial Law (2005) 309, at p. 311.
[2] In essence, it seems that Lord Browne-Wilkinson introduced the causation rule for reparation claims into a case concerned with a substitutive performance claim. The ultimate source of this confusion was the Supreme Court of Canada's decision in *Canson Enterprises Ltd v Boughton & Co* [1991] 3 SCR 534, as explained in J Edelman and SB Elliott 'Money Remedies against Trustees' (2004) 18 Tru LI 116, at pp.122–5.
[3] (1998) 114 LQR 214 at p. 227.

89.21 This rationalisation of the case leaves intact Lord Browne-Wilkinson's finding that the quantum of the liability owed by a trustee who misapplies trust property is not determined at the date of breach, even though he comes under an immediate liability to restore the property[1]. However, this does not mean that the court can look at events occurring after the breach to see whether the beneficiaries would ultimately have suffered the same loss anyway[2]. Instead, its significance lies in the fact that the court can look to see whether the trustee has rectified matters in an authorised fashion since the date of breach. Also, if the trustee has not done this, then the value of his obligation to hand over the property will vary according to its current market value, or, where the property is money, according to the amount of (compound) interest accrued on the money between the date of breach and the date of judgment.

1   See too *Youyang Pty Ltd v Minter Ellison Morris Fletcher* (2003) 212 CLR 484 at [35].
2   *Cocker v Quayle* (1830) 1 Russ & M 535.

No deduction for fiscal liabilities

89.22 In *Re Bell's Indenture*[1] Vinelott J held that no deduction will be made when calculating the replacement value of trust property for the purposes of a substitutive performance claim, to reflect the fact that fiscal liabilities would have been incurred on the property if the trustee had performed his duty and kept the trust fund property intact. However, the Estate Duty Office accepted that the misapplied property could not be reconstituted or recovered by tracing, so that duty would not be exacted on any money that was replaced.

1   [1980] 3 All ER 425, [1980] 1 WLR 1217.

89.23 In *Bartlett v Barclays Bank Trust Co Ltd (No 2)*[1] Brightman LJ rejected the defendant trustee's contention that if the money to be accounted for to the beneficiaries were to escape taxation, which otherwise would have been payable had the breach of trust never been committed, the Bank should not have to pay over more than the requisite net sum:

> 'My reasoning is this: the obligation of a trustee who is held liable for breach of trust is fundamentally different from the obligation of a contractual or tortious wrongdoer. The trustee's obligation is to restore to the trust estate the assets of which he has deprived it. The tax liability of individual beneficiaries, who have claims qua beneficiaries to the capital and income of the trust estate, do not enter into the picture because they arise not at the point of restitution to the trust estate but at the point of distribution of capital or income out of the trust estate. These are different stages despite the fact they coalesce in the draft minutes.'

1   [1980] Ch 515 at 543, [1980] 2 All ER 92 at 96.

89.24 Unfortunately, the above cases were not cited in *O'Sullivan v Management Agency and Music Ltd*[1]. The plaintiff sought an account of profits flowing from the defendant's breach of fiduciary duty and procurement of a contract by undue influence. The Court of Appeal held that no deductions should be made in respect of the six most recent years when the defendant had paid tax on the improperly obtained profits since the defendant would be able to re-open the tax assessments to exclude such improper profits. However, irrecoverable tax paid by the defendant on improperly obtained profits in earlier years was deductible. *O'Sullivan* was thus concerned not with the plaintiff's position but with calculating compensation so as to put the defendant in the same net of tax position he would have achieved but for breach of his fiduciary duty. This is the obverse of the common law rule laid down in *Gourley*[2] requiring such damages to be calculated so as to put the plaintiff in the same net of tax position.

89.24 *The liability of the trustees*

1 [1985] QB 428, [1985] 3 All ER 351, CA. The defendant was not allowed to deduct tax in
   Guardian Ocean Cargoes v Banco da Brasil [1992] 2 Lloyd's Rep 193.
2 *British Transport Commission v Gourley* [1956] AC 185, [1955] 3 All ER 796, HL.

89.25 In *John v James*[1] a similar problem arose where the defendants had
retained excessive fees in breach of a fiduciary duty owed to the plaintiff. The
defendants first sought to reduce the profit for which they had to account by
tax that they had paid on those profits in the past. Nicholls LJ said this would
mean that 'the plaintiffs would be penalised because of the defendants' breach
of fiduciary duty. In principle that cannot be right'. Moreover, *Gourley* applies
if non-taxable damages compensate for taxable losses, so that a mirror-image
Gourley for defendants would seem to arise only if the profits are taxable in
the defendant's hands but compensation payable by him is not deductible for
tax purposes, and Nicholls LJ strongly suspected that the defendants' payments would be treated as allowable deductions. This issue was not dealt with
in *O'Sullivan*.

1 [1986] STC 352.

89.26 The defendants further sought to reduce the amount of their liability
by a standard *Gourley* deduction to take account of the plaintiff's exemption
from tax on moneys payable in respect of loss of income that would have been
taxable in his hands had it been paid at the proper time. It seemed likely that
the moneys recoverable by the plaintiff and his associates should be treated as
recovery of an old debt referable to a period behind the relevant six year
period and so exempt from tax. Nicholls LJ did not rule on this but rejected
the defendants' submission on the grounds of the complexity of the outcome
and 'the impracticality of the course involved' since it would be necessary to
investigate the tax position of several persons in several countries over many
years. Is it really a justifiable outcome that plaintiffs suffer the *Gourley*
deductions if their tax affairs are straightforward but not if they are 'impracticably complicated'?

89.27 Nicholls LJ further rejected the defendants' claim that compound
interest (at the agreed rate of 1% above minimum lending rate or its
equivalent) should be paid less the tax which would have been paid by the
defendants (following the approach taken in *O'Sullivan*[1]) since this exercise
'also would be an impracticably complicated one'. He further stated[2], 'unlike
the position where the court orders an account to be taken of the defendant's
profits, a compound interest calculation is not intended or expected to
correspond precisely with the amount of a defendant's profits. It is a
convenient yardstick.'

1 [1985] QB 428 at 460, [1985] 3 All ER 351 at 368, CA.
2 [1986] STC 352 at 363–364.

89.28 To cover himself, Nicholls LJ made it clear that his case was a special
one decided on its own particular facts. He refused to say whether the
O'Sullivan decision was reached per incuriam. He distinguished it, since there
the court was fixing the terms on which agreements were to be set aside in

equity and thought it just that the defendant's liability should be limited to accounting for their actual profit which did not include tax paid and irrecoverable: since the court's purpose was to remove from the defendants the profits to which they were not entitled it was necessary in calculating compound interest to deduct the tax which would have been paid by the defendants thereon. It seems *O'Sullivan* was a decision turning on its own particular facts.

89.29 It is submitted that the proper approach will normally be that appearing from *Re Bell's Indenture* and *Bartlett* except where there are very special particular facts to justify equity not looking after its own as scrupulously as possible and deterring wrongdoers as much as possible.

Reparation claims

89.30 Reparation claims are claims that trustees should make good the harm which the beneficiaries have suffered as a consequence of the trustees' breach of duty. They depend on the assertion that the trustees have committed a wrong[1], and the award made is calculated by reference to the loss suffered by the beneficiaries[2], including the loss of a chance to avoid a detriment or make a gain[3]. The beneficiaries must prove that their loss has been factually caused by the trustees' breach of duty, using a 'but-for' causation test in all cases, regardless of whether the breach was innocent, negligent, or fraudulent[4]. Canadian authorities also indicate that their claims are subject to the principle of *novus actus interveniens*[5], and that where the beneficiaries have become aware that their trustees are not to be trusted, losses flowing from clearly unreasonable behaviour by the beneficiaries thereafter will be judged to have been caused by this behaviour and not by the breach[6].

[1]   *Partington v Reynolds* (1858) 4 Drew 253 at 255–6; *Dowse v Gorton* [1891] AC 190 at 202; *Re Stevens* [1898] 1 Ch 162 at 170.

[2]   *Elder's Trustee and Executor Co Ltd v Higgins* (1963) 113 CLR 426 at 453; *Fales v Canada Permanent Trust Co* [1977] 2 SCR 302 at 320.

[3]   *Sanders v Parry* [1967] 1 WLR 753 at 767; *Nestle v National Westminster Bank plc* [1993] 1 WLR 1260 at 1269; *Colour Control Centre Pty Ltd v Ty* (24 July 1995, unreported) NSW Sup Ct (Eq Div); *Bank of New Zealand v New Zealand Guardian Trust Co Ltd* [1999] 1 NZLR. 664 at 685–6. In the NZCA *Chirnside v Fay (No 2)* [2005] 3 NZLR 689 compensation was also assessed on a loss of a chance bais, but on appeal the NZSC considered an account of profits to be a more appropriate remedy: [2006] NZSC 68.

[4]   *Target Holdings Ltd v Redferns* [1996] AC 421 at 436; *Collins v Brebner* [2000] Lloyds Rep PN 587; *Hulbert v Avens* [2003] EWHC 76 (Ch), [2003] WTLR 387 at [56]; *Gwembe Valley Development Co Ltd v Koshy (No 3)* [2004] 1 BCLC 131 at [147]. But cf *Bairstow v Queen's Moat Houses plc* [2001] EWCA Civ 712, [2001] 2 BCLC 531 at [53]–[54]. On the question whether reparation claims are subject to a remoteness cap, see SB Elliott 'Remoteness Criteria in Equity' (2002) 65 MLR 588; and also *Olszanecki v Hillocks* [2003] EWHC 1997 (Ch), [2004] WTLR 975 and para 89.33.

[5]   *Hodgkinson v Simms* [1994] 3 SCR 377 at 443; *Waxman v Waxman* (2004) 7 ITELR 162 at [663], Ontario CA.

[6]   *Canson Enterprises Ltd v Boughton & Co* [1991] 3 SCR 534 at 554, endorsed in *Corporaçion del Cobre de Chile v Sogemin Metals Ltd* [1997] 1 WLR 1396 at 1403–4. See too *Lipkin Gorman v Karpnale Ltd* [1992] 4 All ER 331 at 361.

89.31 A reparation claim might be brought, for example, where a trustee T fails to exhibit the requisite duty of care in negligently making an authorised investment which subsequently declines in value, or fails to strike a fair balance between the interests of a life tenant and a remainderman when investing the trust assets[1], or fails to diversify the trust investments[2], or to sell particular assets[3], or to monitor the activities of a 99 per cent owned company[4]. In cases where the trustee's breach of duty consists of a negligent omission, it must be shown that the beneficiaries' loss could not have occurred, but for T's failure to do what no reasonable trustee (*viz* a properly informed trustee exhibiting the due standard of care) could have failed to do. Proving this can be difficult[5], but it seems that a claim would lie where trustees take a positive decision to take specific action, eg to sell particular shares as soon as practicable, and then fail to implement their decision without any conscious reason. Another way of analysing this situation, however, would be to draw an analogy with the case where a trust instrument requires a particular original investment to be sold as soon as practicable. If the trustees fail to perform this duty, then a substitutive performance claim will lie against them for the amount that would have been realised if they had sold investment within a reasonable time[6].

1   *Re Mulligan* [1998] 1 NZLR 481.
2   *Nestle v National Westminster Bank plc* [1993] 1 WLR 1260 at 1281.
3   *Wight v Olswang (No 2)* [2000] WTLR 783; revsd [2001] WTLR 291; *Re Ambrazevicius Estate* (2002) 164 Man R (2d) 5.
4   *Bartlett v Barclays Bank Trust Co Ltd* [1980] Ch 515.
5   Consider *Nestle v National Westminster Bank* [1993] 1 WLR 1260.
6   *Fry v Fry* (1859) 27 Beav 144; *Fales v Canada Permanent Trust Co* (1976) 70 DLR (3d) 257 at 274. What if the trustees decide to appoint capital to O by executing the requisite deed before the date when the power expires, and then fail to execute the deed in time, so that the deed is void and the default beneficiaries get the capital, as in *Breadner v Granville-Grossman* [2001] Ch 523? Should the trustees compensate O for his loss? Falsification of accounts would be impossible but equitable compensation should be payable as happened out of court in Breadner. Further, see DJ Hayton 'Unique Rules for the Unique Institution, the Trust' in S Degeling and J Edelman (eds) *Equity in Commercial Law* (2005) 279.

89.32 In *Bartlett v Barclays Bank Trust Co Ltd (No 2)*, Brightman LJ thought that in cases where trustees are ordered to pay money to make good the harm caused to the beneficiaries by the trustees' negligence, the award made is 'not readily distinguishable from damages except with the aid of a powerful legal microscope'[1]. This comment was later echoed by Millett LJ in *Bristol and West Building Society v Mothew*, where he held in a case involving a solicitor but not a trustee that[2]:

> 'Equitable compensation for breach of the duty of skill and care [owed by a fiduciary] resembles common law damages in that it is awarded by way of compensation to the plaintiff for his loss. There is no reason in principle why the common law rules of causation, remoteness of damage and measure of damages should not be applied by analogy in such a case. It should not be confused with equitable compensation for breach of fiduciary duty, which may be awarded in lieu of rescission or specific restitution.'

1   [1980] Ch 515 at 545.

2   [1998] Ch 1 at 18, adopting *Permanent Building Society v Wheeler* (1994) 11 WAR 187 at 237. See too *Bank of New Zealand v New Zealand Guardian Trust Co Ltd* [1999] 1 NZLR 664 at 687; *Hilton v Barker Booth and Eastwood (a firm)* [2005] 1 WLR 567 at [29] per Lord Walker, HL.

89.33 Others consider it a controversial question whether trustees and other fiduciaries who harm their principals by their negligent acts or omissions should be treated in the same way as tortfeasors at common law, or whether the fact that they are fiduciaries justifies treating them more stringently, especially if they are trustees who could, perhaps, be treated as if positively undertaking not to act negligently, so that negligent acts are unauthorised acts leading to a substitutive performance claim and not a reparation claim[1]. Proponents of the stringent view emphasise that a fiduciary and his principal are not 'independent and equal actors, concerned primarily with their own self-interest' but parties in a special relationship under which one 'pledges itself to act in the best interest of the other', so that 'when breach occurs, the balance favours the person wronged'[2]. Proponents of the opposite view deny that there is a valid reason to treat a trustee or other fiduciary differently from anyone else who injures another person by his negligence, and that 'regardless of the doctrinal underpinning, plaintiffs should not be able to recover higher damage awards merely because their claim is characterised as a breach of fiduciary duty, as opposed to breach of contract or tort'[3]. In modern times there seems much to be said for not even imposing on trustees the same stringent liability for negligent conduct as for unauthorised conduct.

1   Thus, if trustees sold Microwhizzo Ltd shares negligently because not obtaining any appropriate advice they would have to restore such shares to the fund even if appreciated one hundred times in value, it being immaterial that if they had taken appropriate advice they would have been advised to sell.
2   *Canson Enterprises Ltd v Boughton & Co* [1991] 3 SCR 534 at 543 per McLachlin J, quoted with approval in *Youyang Pty Ltd v Minter Ellison Morris Fletcher* (2003) 212 CLR 484 at [40]. See too *Norberg v Wynrib* [1992] 2 SCR 226 at 272 per McLachlin J, quoted with approval in *Pilmer v Duke Group Ltd (in liquidation)* (2001) 207 CLR 165 at [71]; *Maguire v Makaronis* (1997) 188 CLR 449 at 473. For the argument that equity should exert prophylactic pressure on fiduciaries by stringent treatment of their breaches of skill and care as well as their breaches of fiduciary duty, see too Justice Heydon 'Are the Duties of Company Directors to Exercise care and Skill Fiduciary?' and J Getzler 'Am I My Beneficiary's Keeper? Fusion and Loss-Based Fiduciary Remedies' in S Degeling and J Edelman (eds), *Equity in Commercial Law* (2005) 185 and 239.
3   *Martin v Goldfarb* (1998) 41 OR (3d) 161 at 173 per Finlayson JA. See too *Day v Mead* [1987] 2 NZLR 443 at 451 per Cooke P; *Canson Enterprises Ltd v Boughton & Co* [1991] 3 SCR 534 at 585–9 per La Forest J; *Waxman v Waxman* (2004) 7 ITELR 162 at [660]–[662]; J Edelman and SB Elliott 'Money Remedies against Trustees' (2004) 18 Tru LI 116, at pp. 119–122; AS *Burrows Remedies for Torts and Breach of Contract* 3rd edn (2004) at pp. 600–606.

89.34 However, this debate need not be conducted in all-or-nothing terms: it is better to acknowledge that it can be appropriate to treat different kinds of fiduciary in different ways[1]. In the case of commercial contracts involving an incidental temporary trust for one contracting party (eg a solicitor holding property purchase money for the purchaser) or modern commercial trusts for absolutely entitled sophisticate investors where huge sums are involved and the management role of the trustee is extensive and complex there is surely no justification for imposing the same stringent liability for negligent conduct as for unauthorised conduct.

1   See further CEF Rickett 'Compensating for Loss in Equity: Choosing the Right Horse for Each Course' in P Birks and FD Rose (eds) Restitution and Equity (2000) 178; DJ Hayton 'Unique Rules for the Unique Institution, the Trust' in S Degeling and J Edelman (eds) Equity in Commercial Law (2005) 279.

Unauthorised investments

89.35 Where trustees make an unauthorised investment they are liable for the amount of the money improperly invested, but they are entitled to claim a credit for the sale proceeds of the property when it is sold, as held in *Knott v Cottee*[1]. There Romilly MR held that unless a trustee invests in authorised securities the case is either treated:

> 'as if the investments had not been made, or had been made for his own benefit out of his own moneys, and that he had at the same time retained moneys of the testator in his hands ... I cannot concur in the argument that the court must charge him as if the money had been invested in consols. If that were so, the court must charge him the other way where the funds have fallen, which it never does ... The persons interested were entitled to earmark them [the unauthorised investments], as being bought with the testator's assets, in the same manner as if the executor had bought a house with the trust funds; and, though they do not recognise the investment, they had a right to make it available for what was due.'

1   (1852) 16 Beav 77; and see *Re Whiteley* (1886) 33 Ch D 347 at 354.

89.36 Thus, where the unauthorised investments were ordered into court and sold at a loss the trustees were liable to make up the difference between the sale proceeds and the amount for which the investments had been purchased even though at the date of the subsequent court decree there would have been no loss if these investments had been retained[1]. As Buckley LJ subsequently stated, the trustee's liability in cases of this kind rests[2]:

> 'on the notional ground that the money so applied was in fact the trustee's own money and that he has retained the misapplied trust money in his own hands and used it for his own purposes.'

1   Where trustees still have unauthorised investments that have proved profitable such investment may be adopted (and retained or be sold) on behalf of the trust so that the trust profits. If they proved unprofitable the beneficiaries can reprobate the transaction and claim compensation and take over the investment in part satisfaction of such claim; but they should make it clear that they are not approbating the transaction and are not taking over the investments as approbated authorised investments, for then the loss claim would itself be lost: cf *Thornton v Stokill* (1855) 1 Jur NS 751; *Re Lake* [1903] 1 KB 439.
2   *Wallersteiner v Moir (No 2)* [1975] QB 373 at 397, [1975] 1 All ER 849 at 863.

89.37 Thus, it can be said that equity presumes the trustee to have acted honestly and not in breach of his duty, not letting him take advantage of his own wrong. If £10,000 is spent on an unauthorised asset which falls to a value below £10,000 then the trustee must replace the £10,000 with interest. If an authorised investment was sold for £10,000 in order to enable purchase of an unauthorised investment then the trustee must replace the authorised investment if the unauthorised investment is worth less than it, though if the authorised investment and the unauthorised investment are both worth less than £10,000, then the trustee must replace £10,000 with interest. Note, though, that if the unauthorised investment soared in value, say doubling its value, in the period between the breach and the court order, before falling below £10,000, this does not enable the measure of liability to be calculated by reference to the highest value of that asset in that period[1].

> [1] See the overruling of *Jaffrey v Marshall* [1994] 1 All ER 143 in *Target Holdings Ltd v Redferns* [1996] AC 421. Such calculation is possible, however, for an asset received as a secret commission or bribe: *Nant-y-glo and Blaina Ironworks v Grave* (1878) 12 Ch D 738.

89.38 In *Target Holdings Ltd v Redferns*[1] the court endorsed Lord Cottenham's views in *Clough v Bond*[2] that if a trustee or personal representative invests funds in unauthorised securities or puts them within the control of persons who are not authorised to be entrusted with them and a loss be sustained, then such trustee or personal representative will be liable to make it good, however unexpected the result, however little likely to arise from the course adopted and however free such conduct may have been from any improper motive. On this basis if trustees delegated management of their investment portfolio to a discretionary manager where not authorised to do so, then the trustees would be automatically liable even if the loss in value of the portfolio was caused by an unforeseeable market crash. The beneficiaries could therefore derive a significant advantage from framing their claim as a substitutive performance claim rather than as a reparation claim, in a case where the trustee's decision to delegate management of the trust portfolio is negligent as well as unauthorised. In such a case, their reparation claim for breach of the trustee's equitable duty of care would be subject to principles relating to causation, foreseeability and remoteness that would not apply to their substitutive performance claim.

> [1] [1994] AC 421, HL.
> [2] (1838) 3 My & Cr 490 at 496–497.

Negligent investments

89.39 In *Nestle v National Westminster Bank plc*[1] the plaintiff proved that the Bank was in breach of trust in failing to obtain legal advice as to the scope of the investment clause, in failing to understand its broad investment powers, and in failing to conduct regular periodic reviews of the portfolio. However, she had to go on to prove that a prudent trustee knowing of the broad scope of the investment clause and conducting regular reviews would so have invested the trust fund as to make it worth more than it was worth when she became entitled to it. Until she proved any loss there was no cause of action and no recourse could be had to any presumptions against a wrongdoing trustee[2] where the trustee was merely doing badly what it was authorised to do[3].

> [1] [1994] 1 All ER 118.
> [2] [1994] 1 All ER 118 at 141.
> [3] If the trustee acted recklessly, so as not to be acting in good faith then it seems it would be a wrongdoer so the onus would lie on the trustee to prove the loss did not flow from his breach: see Millett LJ on recklessness and lack of good faith in *Armitage v Nurse* [1998] Ch 241, CA and *Bristol and West Building Society v Mothew* [1998] Ch 1, CA.

89.40 *The liability of the trustees*

89.40 As Dillon LJ stated[1]:

'The onus is on her to prove that she has suffered loss because from 1922 to 1960 the equities in the fund were not diversified. In some cases it is sufficient to prove loss of a chance because in such cases the outcome, if the plaintiff had not lost the chance, can never be proved. But in the present case, if the annuity fund had been invested wholly in fixed interest securities, it would have been relatively easy to prove, even though the event never happened, that the fund would have been worth much more if a substantial part had been invested in equities. Consequently, fair compensation could have been assessed. Equally, it would have been possible, if it be the fact, that the equities in the fund would have performed even better if diversified than they did as concentrated in bank and insurance shares. But Miss Nestle has not provided any such proof. She has not even provided any material which would enable the court to assess the strength of, or value, the chance which she claims she has lost. Therefore her claim must fail.'

1   [1994] 1 All ER 118 at 127.

89.41 Dillon and Staughton LJJ directly and Leggatt LJ indirectly indicated that nineteenth-century authority to the effect that compensation should be limited to the difference between the actual performance of the fund and the very least that a trustee acting properly might have achieved was flawed. As Dillon LJ emphasised[1], investment conditions were very different 50 years ago, let alone 150 years ago, so that too much weight should not be accorded to the actual decisions of the courts in those days. It seems that credence should no longer be given to decisions[2] indicating that where trustees have a choice of investments (eg real securities or Government securities) but invest in unauthorised securities the beneficiaries can only claim to have the trust fund made good with interest. It seems clear that the beneficiaries cannot choose a particular authorised security which has appreciated dramatically to claim that the trustees should have invested in that particular security[3]. Instead, they can claim 'fair compensation' based, it seems, on the average performance of investments within the authorised class of investments[4].

1   [1994] 1 All ER 118 at 126.
2   *Robinson v Robinson* (1851) 1 De GM & G 247, *Shepherd v Mouls* (1845) 4 Hare 500.
3   *Robinson v Robinson* (1851) 1 De G M & G 247, *Shepherd v Mouls* (1845) 4 Hare 500, but if the investment to be made is directed by the trust instrument and not left to the discretion of the trustees then so much of the investment as would have been obtained by a purchase at the proper time can be obtained less any outgoings (ie calls on shares) which would necessarily have been payable if the investment had been made: *Byrchall v Bradford* (1822) 6 Madd 235; *Pride v Fooks* (1840) 2 Beav 430; *Briggs v Massey* (1882) 30 WR 325 (and see also *Re Hulkes* (1886) 33 Ch D 552 and *Elder's Trustee & Executor Co Ltd v Higgens* (1963) 113 CLR 426).
4   *Nestlé v National Westminster Bank plc* [1994] 1 All ER 118, CA.

89.42 Indeed this was the approach in *Re Mulligan*[1] where the trustees favoured the life tenant by not investing in equities so as to provide capital growth and protection against inflation. The New Zealand High Court held the trustees should have diversified in 1972 to the extent of investing 40% of the capital in equities which should then be treated as appreciating at 75% of an appropriate index of equities. The 25% discount took account of dealing costs that would need to have been incurred and the fact that the fund was not large enough to be expected to rival a broad-based index. Nowadays, however, one needs to bear in mind the possibility of investing small funds in 'tracker funds' which track and reflect the index, so obviating the need for a discount based on the size of the fund in question.

¹ [1998] 1 NZLR 481.

89.43 Similarly if trustees do invest in authorised fashion but do not diversify sufficiently though having a broad spread of equities as well as gilts then again fair compensation should be payable, eg if trustees left five million pounds on deposit for nine months in a year like 1986 when one would have expected a 20% gain in the average price of ordinary shares in such period¹.

¹ See *Midland Bank Trustee (Jersey) Ltd v Federated Pension Services Ltd* [1995] JLR 352, PLR, [1996] 179, CA Jersey.

89.44 No problems arise over beneficiaries suing for diminution in the value of a trust shareholding caused by the trustees' failure to keep themselves fully informed of the activities of a company controlled by them or in which they have a substantial shareholding where the shares have been sold. Where the shares remain part of the trust property there is the *Prudential Assurance¹* principle to consider, that a shareholder cannot sue for damages in respect of the diminution in value of his shares caused by a wrong to the company where the company itself has a cause of action entitling it to recover for the wrong to it. However, the Court of Appeal² has held that this principle does not operate where a beneficiary is suing a trustee where the breach of trust has caused loss to the trust fund or the beneficiary that is separate from any loss that may have been occasioned to the company in which the beneficiary is financially interested: the mere fact that the defendant's conduct may also have given rise to a cause of action at the suit of the company in which the beneficiary is interested will not deprive the claimant beneficiary of his right of action.

¹ *Prudential Assurance Co Ltd v Newman Industries Ltd (No 2)* [1982] Ch 204, CA. See too *Johnson v Gore Wood & Co* [2002] 2 AC 1 and other cases discussed in C Mitchell 'Shareholders' Claims for Reflective Loss' (2004) 120 LQR 457.
² *Walker v Stones* [2001] QB 902, CA.

Loss of interest

89.45 A trustee who is guilty of unreasonable delay in investing trust funds will be answerable to the beneficiaries for simple interest during the relevant period¹; for if he had done his duty, interest would in fact have been received. On the same ground, where an executrix allowed trust money to remain uninvested in her solicitor's hands for nine years during the infancy of the beneficiary, she was charged with compound interest, with half-yearly rests, as it was her duty to have accumulated the income, by investing it from time to time in consols². A fortiori is this the case where there is an express trust for accumulation³.

¹ *Stafford v Fiddon* (1857) 23 Beav 386; *Jones v Foxall* (1852) 15 Beav 388 at 392. In the light of *Nestlé v National Westminster Bank plc* [1994] 1 All ER 118 JLR CA and *Midland Bank Trustee (Jersey) Ltd v Federated Pension Services Ltd* [1995] JLR 352, [1996] PLR

179, CA, there may be an alternative claim for loss of the profit that would have been made if the trustee had exercised his power to invest in a broad range of shares.

2   *Gilroy v Stephens* (1882) 30 WR 745 (Fry J); and see also *Re Emmet's Estate* (1881) 17 Ch D 142.
3   *Re Barclay* [1899] 1 Ch 674; *Raphael v Boehm* (1805) 11 Ves 92.

Rate of interest in ordinary circumstances

89.46 Where income has been lost due to the trustees' default in respect of the capital Brightman LJ has stated (at a time when inflation had led to high interest rates)[1]:

'In former days a trustee was as a rule charged only with interest at 4% unless there were special circumstances ... In these days I think it would be unrealistic for a court of equity to abide by the modest rate of interest which was current in the stable times of our forefathers. ... In my judgment a proper rate of interest to be awarded, in the absence of special circumstances, to compensate beneficiaries and trusts for non-receipt from a trustee of money that ought to have been received is that allowed from time to time on the courts' short-term investment account, established under section 6(1) of the Administration of Justice Act 1965. To some extent the high interest rates payable reflect and compensate for the continued erosion in the value of money by reason of galloping inflation. It seems to me arguable, therefore, that if a high rate of interest is payable in such circumstances, a proportion of that interest should be added to capital in order to help maintain the value of the corpus of the trust estate. It may be, therefore, that there will have to be some adjustment as between life tenant and remainderman.'

1   *Bartlett v Barclays Bank Trust Ltd (No 2)* [1980] Ch 515 at 547, [1980] 2 All ER 92 at 97–99.

89.47 This approach was adopted in *Jaffray v Marshall*[1] where the interest was apportioned equally between income and capital. The rate on the short-term investment account, now the special investment account under the Court Fund Rules 1987, is generally in line with that offered by National Savings. Changes are made in the rate much less frequently than those made to the clearing banks' base rate.

1   [1994] 1 All ER 143, but note that the decision on liability for lost capital was overruled by *Target Holdings Ltd v Redferns* [1996] AC 421, HL.

Higher rate in special circumstances

89.48 *Bartlett* and *Jaffray* both concerned money lost by the neglect of the trustees rather than by the positive misapplication of trust funds. As Buckley LJ has pointed out[1], in the latter event liability to replace the lost capital with interest arises 'on the notional ground that the money so applied was in fact the trustee's own money and that he has retained the misapplied trust moneys in his own hands and used it for his own purposes' so that the appropriate rate is the commercial rate of 1% above the London and Scottish clearing banks' base lending rates, and interest will be compounded with yearly units where such represents what the trust can be presumed to have lost or what the trustee can be presumed to have obtained[2].

1   *Wallersteiner v Moir (No 2)* [1975] QB 373 at 397.
2   See para 89.52 ff below.

89.49 Nevertheless the court has a discretion which it may exercise so as to favour the defendant in special circumstances. Thus, in *Re Evans[1]* the defendant administrator of her intestate father's estate believed her brother was dead, not having heard from him for over 30 years. Acting on legal advice she purchased a missing beneficiary policy to cover half the estate (as better than incurring the expense of a *Benjamin[2]* order). Four years later the claimant brother appeared, claiming interest, the policy not extending to interest. The judge rejected the claim to interest at 1% above base lending rate from time to time and the defendant's claim that 6% was appropriate as the rate payable on unpaid legacies. The rate payable on the special investment court account had fluctuated between 8 and 14.5%. The judge awarded 8% interest throughout the period, taking account of the fact the defendant was a lay person and not a professional administrator.

1   [1999] 2 All ER 777 at 788.
2   [1902] 1 Ch 723: see para 47.49 above.

89.50 However, a trustee who, without proper authority, calls in trust property properly invested at a higher rate than the ordinarily appropriate current rate of interest will be liable for that higher rate of interest; for although he may not actually have received that rate, he would have done so[1] but for his unauthorised act. Similarly, where the trustee actually received a higher rate he will be accountable therefor[2].

1   See judgment in *Jones v Foxall* (1852) 15 Beav 388; and see principles stated in *Re Massingberd's Settlement* (1890) 63 LT 296; and *Mosley v Ward* (1805) 11 Ves 581.
2   *Re Emmet's Estate* (1881) 17 Ch D 142. This should include the case where the trustee has used the trust money to reduce his overdraft and so save paying an actual interest rate: *Farnell v Cox* (1898) 19 LR NSW Eq 142.

89.51 Where a trustee makes unauthorised use of trust money for his own purposes and the profits made are unascertainable or less than the amount produced by applying a commercial rate of interest of one per cent above the London clearing banks' base rate, then such commercial rate will be payable, perhaps at compound interest with yearly rests[1].

1   *O'Sullivan v Management Agency & Music Ltd* [1985] QB 428, [1985] 3 All ER 351, CA, see para 89.57 below.

Mixing trust funds with trustee's own moneys

89.52 Liability for interest relating to innocent breaches of trust is supposed to be based on the actual amount of loss, but if a trustee keeps the money in his hands, meaning to appropriate it, or even to use it temporarily only (and indeed even where he does so in order that the beneficiaries may have a larger income[1]), the actual loss ceases to be the measure of his responsibility. As Lord Cranworth said in the leading case of *A-G v Alford*[2] (when 4% was the norm):

> 'in such a case I think the court would be justified in dealing in point of interest very hardly with an executor, *because it might fairly infer that he used the money in speculation, by which he either did make 5%, or ought to be estopped from saying that he did not:* the court would not there inquire what had been the actual proceeds, but in application of the principle, in odium spoliatoris omnia praesumuntur, would assume that he did make the higher rate, *that is, if that were a reasonable conclusion.*'

1   *Re Davis* [1902] 2 Ch 314.
2   (1855) 4 De GM & G 843 at 852; *Stafford v Fiddon* (1857) 23 Beav 386; *Jones v Foxall* (1852) 15 Beav 388; *Re Jones* (1883) 49 LT 91; *Re Emmet's Estate* (1881) 17 Ch D 142; and *Re Davis* [1902] 2 Ch 314.

Solicitor-trustee using trust funds in his business[1]

89.53 In *Burdick v Garrick*[2] a solicitor, as the agent of the plaintiff, held a power of attorney from him, under the authority of which he received divers sums of money, and paid them into the bank to the credit of his (the solicitor's) firm. On a bill being filed by the client for an account, the Vice-Chancellor made a decree for payment of the principal with *compound interest*.

1   The Solicitors' Account Rules are designed to prevent trust moneys from being so used. As to the enforcement of such rules, see the Solicitors Act 1974 s 32.
2   (1870) 5 Ch App 233. See also *Hale v Sheldrake* (1889) 60 LT 292; where a husband of the tenant for life was ordered to replace a trust fund, but without interest, as the wife had allowed him to receive the income.

89.54 The Court of Appeal, however, reversed this decision, Lord Hatherley saying:

> 'The Vice-Chancellor has directed interest to be charged at the rate of 5%, which appears to me to be perfectly right, and for this reason that the money was retained in the defendants' own hands, and was made use of by them[1]. That being so, the court presumes the rate of interest made upon the money to be 5%. I cannot, however, think the decree correct in directing half-yearly rests, because the principle laid down in the case of *Attorney-General v Alford* appears to be the sound principle, namely, that the court does not proceed against an accounting party by way of punishing him for making use of the plaintiff's money by directing rests, or payment of compound interest, but proceeds upon this principle, either that he has made, or has put himself into such a position as that he is to be presumed to have made, 5%, or compound interest, as the case may be.'

1   See to same effect *Bate v Scales* (1806) 12 Ves 402; *Re Pilling, ex p Ogle* (1873) 8 Ch App 711; *Jones v Foxall* (1852) 15 Beav 388; *Heathcote v Hulme* (1819) 1 Jac & W 122; *Docker v Somes* (1834) 2 My & K 655; *Berwick-upon-Tweed Corpn v Murray* (1857) 7 De GM & G 497; and *Gordon v Gonda* [1955] 2 All ER 762, [1955] 1 WLR 885, CA.

89.55 His Lordship then pointed out that no doubt where a trustee employs money in ordinary trade he may be made liable for compound interest, where trade capital is presumed to yield it; but that that reason had no application to capital employed in a solicitor's business, upon which a solicitor is frequently receiving no interest at all.

Trustee allowing trust fund to remain in his business

89.56 In order to charge a trustee with compound interest, or with actual profits for employing the trust funds in trade, there must be an active calling in of the trust moneys for the purpose of embarking them in the trade or speculation; a mere neglect to withdraw funds *already embarked by the settlor in the trustee's trade* is not sufficient[1].

1   *Vyse v Foster* (1872) 8 Ch App 309; affd (1874) LR 7 HL 318; *Smith v Nelson* (1905) 92 LT 313; *Brown v Sansome* (1825) M'Cle & Yo 427; but cf *Townend v Townend* (1859) 1 Giff 201.

Rate of interest to be charged against trustee using money

89.57 It will be perceived that in the old cases the rate was 5% interest[1]. However, in *Wallersteiner v Moir (No 2)*[2] the Court of Appeal, applying principles applicable to trustees to a director of a company who is in a fiduciary position similar to a trustee, held that where a fiduciary used his beneficiaries' money in his own commercial transactions he should be debited with compound interest at the commercial rate of 1% above minimum lending rate (or official bank rate) with yearly rests. This commercial rate is now 1% above the London and Scottish clearing banks' base rate[3] as held by the Court of Appeal in *O'Sullivan v Management Agency and Music Ltd*[4], though awarding simple interest only since the money was used in a joint venture benefiting the plaintiff as well as the defendant.

1   See also *Bate v Scales* (1806) 12 Ves 402; *Re Davis* [1902] 2 Ch 314 and *Gordon v Gonda* [1955] 2 All ER 762, [1955] 1 WLR 885, CA.
2   [1975] QB 373, [1975] 1 All ER 849, CA. See further *Westdeutsche Landesbank Girozentrale v Islington Borough Council* [1994] 4 All ER 890, CA and, on appeal, [1996] AC 669, HL and *Mather v TM Sutton Ltd* [1994] 4 All ER 793 (fiduciary relationship between pawnbroker and pawnor liable to pay interest in equity on surplus proceeds of sale: interest rate to be fixed after inquiry as to actual high interest-bearing use of money in trade).
3   *Buckingham v Francis* [1986] 2 All ER 738 at 743–744; *Shearson Lehman Hutton Inc v Maclaine Watson & Co Ltd (No 2)* [1990] 3 All ER 723 at 732–733, though a party may prove special circumstances justifying instead LIBOR (London Inter-Bank Offer Rate) plus one-eighth, or 1% above New York prime rate: *Guardian Ocean Cargoes Ltd v Banco da Brasil (No 3)* [1992] 2 Lloyd's Rep 193.
4   [1985] QB 428, [1985] 3 All ER 351, CA.

89.58 Compound interest is awarded not as a punishment but as fairly representing what the defendant is presumed to have received in the commercial context[1], though the presumption is often more readily made where stress has been laid on fraud or gross misconduct on the defendant's part[2]. In *Re Duckwari plc (No 2)*[3] the Court of Appeal held that interest should be given at a commercial rate where money has been withheld from a commercial concern, and viewed *Bartlett v Barclays Bank Co Ltd*[4] as authority for the view that interest need only be paid at the lower trustee rate where money is taken from a private trust. However, this distinction implicitly rests on the doubtful proposition that the use of money is more valuable to a commercial entity than a private person[5]

1   *Wallersteiner v Moir* (No 2) [1975] QB 373, [1975] 1 All ER 849, CA; *Guardian Ocean Cargoes Ltd v Banco da Brasil* (No 3) [1992] 2 Lloyd's Rep 193.
2   *Jones v Foxall* (1852) 15 Beav 388; *Gordon v Gonda* [1955] 2 All ER 762, CA.
3   [1999] Ch 268 at 273, CA.
4   [1980] Ch 515 at 547, CA.
5   S B Elliott 'Rethinking Interest on Withheld and Misapplied Trust Money' [2001] Conv 313 at p. 331, arguing that interest on trust money withheld from a beneficiary should be payable at a commercial rate irrespective of whether the beneficiary is a commercial entity.

89.59 The cost and difficulty of ascertaining actual profits, and thus whether or not they represent a return exceeding the commercial rate, is such that it is often best to elect for charging interest at the presumed commercial rate, with compound interest at yearly rates where the money was used by the defendant in his own business. An election must be made since the plaintiff cannot both approbate and reprobate: of course, it would also be inequitable to allow the plaintiff to claim actual profits for profitable periods and a commercial rate of interest for unprofitable periods[1].

1   *Heathcote v Hulme* (1819) 1 Jac & W 122; *Vyse v Foster* (1872) 8 Ch App 309 at 334; *Tang Man Sit v Capacious Investments Ltd* [1996] AC 514, [1996] 1 All ER 193, PC.

Retention of unauthorised investment or improper retention of authorised investment

89.60 A trustee who retains an unauthorised investment is liable for the difference between the price obtainable by sale at the proper time and the actual proceeds of sale. Thus in *Fry v Fry*[1] trustees were liable for the difference between the price offered for an inn in 1837 and the price to be received on sale in 1859, which would be very low due to the diversion of road traffic by the opening of a railway in 1843.

1   (1859) 27 Beav 144.

89.61 Where the trustees have a duty to sell but a power to postpone sale and in breach of trust they postpone sale for too long, difficulties arise where during the period over which the trustees should have sold the asset its value has fluctuated considerably. In *Fales v Canada Permanent Trust Co*[1] the Supreme Court of Canada held the proper measure of compensation was the average of the highest and lowest prices of the asset in the period from when it could first have been sold to advantage till the date by which it should reasonably have been sold. No authority was cited for this, though it is supported by American cases[2] and is consistent with *Re Bell's Indenture*[3]. Subsequently, in *Jaffray v Marshall*[4] it was held that a defaulting trustee under a continuous obligation to restore property or its value must pay compensation on the footing of the highest price obtainable during the relevant period, everything being presumed against the wrongdoer. However, while this very strict approach seems appropriate for a trustee who has personally benefited by taking trust assets for himself[5], it is too harsh for a trustee who has merely caused a loss to the beneficiaries by negligently doing what he is authorised to do, and for this reason the House of Lords overruled *Jaffray in Target Holdings Ltd v Redferns*[6].

1   (1976) 70 DLR (3d) 257.
2   See Scott on Trusts (4th edn) para 209.
3   [1980] 3 All ER 425 (property sold in breach of trust in 1947 resold in 1949, and the 1949 sale price was accepted as the measure of the trustee's liability when 1949 was a time at which the trustees could properly have sold).
4   [1994] 1 All ER 143 at 153. See too *Michael v Hart & Co* [1901] 2 KB 867 at 869–870 and on appeal the observation of Collins MR at [1902] 1 KB 482 at 488.
5   See *Nant-y-glo and Blaina Ironworks Co v Grave* (1878) 12 Ch D 738 (in an account of profits, fiduciary-director liable for highest value of shares given to him as a secret commission between date of receipt and the trial).
6   [1996] AC 421 at 440.

Improper sale of authorised investment

89.62 It is a breach of trust if trustees sell an authorised investment for the purpose of investing in an unauthorised investment or of paying the proceeds to the life tenant in breach of trust[1]. The trustees are liable to replace the authorised investment or the proceeds of sale thereof, whichever is the greater burden[2]. Replacement of the authorised investment will be at its value at the date it is actually replaced, so remedying the breach, or at the subsequent date of the court judgment[3]. Exceptionally, where the authorised investment would in any event have been sold, the date when such sale should have occurred will be the relevant date for valuing the loss[4].

1   *Re Bell's Indenture* [1980] 3 All ER 425, [1980] 1 WLR 1217.
2   *Shepherd v Mouls* (1845) 4 Hare 500 at 504.
3   *Re Bell's Indenture* [1980] 3 All ER 425, where it was pointed out that in *Re Massingberd's Settlement* (1890) 63 LT 296 the reference to the date of the writ rather than the date of judgment was per incuriam.
4   *Re Bell's Indenture* [1980] 3 All ER 425, [1980] 1 WLR 1217 followed by Megarry V-C in *Re Montagu's Settlements* (1985) 131 Sol Jo 411.

89.63 A strict deterrent policy underlies the decisions. Thus, where an authorised investment is sold but with a view to investing in an unauthorised investment the liability is to replace the authorised investment and not merely to make good the proceeds misapplied[1], though some argue that the latter measure of liability should suffice: although the *motive* for the sale of the authorised investment was to reinvest in an unauthorised security, the sale itself was authorised, so that liability should extend no further than making up the proceeds of such sale if the unauthorised investment has depreciated in value.

1   *Re Massingberd's Settlement* (1890) 63 LT 296; and see also *Re Bennison* (1889) 60 LT 859; and *Stokes v Prance* [1898] 1 Ch 212. In *Re Bell's Indenture* (supra) it was pointed out that the date of the judgment should replace date of the writ in *Re Massingberd's Settlement*; counsel expressly reserved the right to challenge the correctness of Massingberd in a higher court.

Liability of executors of deceased trustee who was party to a breach for loss incurred after his death

89.64 In *Lander v Weston*[1] two trustees, in breach of trust, sold consols and advanced the proceeds to the husband of the life tenant. He subsequently repaid the advance to the surviving trustee, who reinvested it in unauthorised stock for a few days, and then sold such stock and again lent the proceeds to the husband, with the result that the fund was lost.

---

[1] *Lander v Weston* (1855) 3 Drew 389; and see also *Bacon v Clark* (1836) 3 My & Cr 294; and *Clough v Bond* (1838) 3 My & Cr 490.

89.65 It was held that not only was the surviving trustee liable for the loss (which was obvious), but so also were the executors of the deceased trustee because, but for the original sale of the stock to make the advance to the husband, that stock would have remained intact. The mere repayment by the husband to the surviving trustee and the investment in unauthorised stock did not set matters right and so condone the original breach because the original consols were not replaced, quite apart from the fact that the repayment for a few days was a sham. Consequently the executors of the deceased trustee were liable for all loss which happened (even after his death) before the fund was ultimately replaced.

Paragraph 3

Unauthorised gains

89.66 The rule that a trustee may not make an unauthorised gain has already been considered in Article 33. It takes in situations where the trustee uses trust funds to acquire an asset for himself which rises in value, or receives a bribe to influence his behaviour as a trustee, or diverts to himself a business opportunity offered to the trust, or uses trust funds for his own business or professional purposes. Alternatively, the trustee may use trust funds to purchase an unauthorised investment for the beneficiaries which rises in value, or leave the trust funds invested in unauthorised investments which rise in value. In all such cases the trustee is personally accountable in respect of the trust property and profits made therefrom, and a proprietary remedy may also be possible if the property or its traceable equivalent still subsists in the trustee's hands[1]. In the case where the trustee uses trust funds for his own business or professional purposes, instead of seeking an account of profits, the beneficiaries may seek compensation with interest at the mercantile rate[2], eg if there are difficulties assessing how much profit was made or if it seems that not much profit was made. As already seen, an election must be made between these two inconsistent remedies[3].

---

[1] See Art 104. See further *Warman International Ltd v Dwyer* (1995) 69 ALJR 362.
[2] See para 89.51 above.
[3] *Heathcote v Hulme* (1819) 1 Jac & W 122, para 89.59 above.

Election between accounting for profits or compensation for loss

89.67 In respect of a particular breach of duty, it is not possible to approbate and to reprobate, to adopt and to disavow, to blow hot and to blow cold. Suing for profits adopts the trustee's conduct whilst claiming compensation rejects such conduct. Thus, if T holds 16 houses on trust to transfer them to C, but without C's knowledge, leases them, C must elect[1] whether to sue for the actual profit made by T from renting out the houses or for the loss caused to C in not being able to rent out the houses.

1   *Tang Man Sit v Capacious Investments Ltd* [1996] AC 514, PC.

89.68 If a trustee breaks the self-dealing rule the beneficiary has to elect between (1) claiming the purchased property or its traceable equivalent (with whatever income it produced or should have produced) or its value before it was dissipated or given away (with interest thereafter) or (2) claiming compensation equal to the difference between actual market value at the date of the trustee's purchase and the lower price paid by the trustee, with interest on such lost capital since such date[1].

1   Cf *McKenzie v McDonald* [1927] VLR 134.

89.69 If trustees sell £10,000 of authorised shares to purchase £10,000 of unauthorised shares then which election should be made depends on the current values of these shares. If the unauthorised shares are valued at more than the authorised shares and more than £10,000, then the trustees' actions should be adopted and the shares taken over as proper trust shares, making the trustees personally liable to account for these profitable shares (and the dividends thereon)[1]. If the unauthorised shares are worth less than the authorised shares which are worth more than £10,000, then the trustees' actions should be disavowed and the trustees made to replace the authorised shares that they improperly sold or pay compensation of a sum equal to such replacement cost[2]. It will be possible, if acceptable to the beneficiaries, to take over the unauthorised shares in part satisfaction of the trustees' personal liability to compensate the trust[3]. If both the authorised and unauthorised shares are worth less than £10,000, then the trustees must compensate the trust by repaying the £10,000 with interest thereon from the date of the improper sale of the authorised securities[4].

1   Cf *Boardman v Phipps* [1967] 2 AC 46, [1966] 3 All ER 721, HL; *Docker v Somes* (1834) 2 My & K 655; *Scott v Scott* (1963) 109 CLR 649.
2   *Re Bell's Indenture* [1980] 3 All ER 425, [1980] 1 WLR 1217. Interest will be payable thereon: *Re Dawson* [1966] 2 NSWR 211 (semble on the original £4,700 rather than the replacement cost of £5,829).
3   It should be made clear that this is what is being done as opposed to adopting or ratifying the investment as if it had originally been authorised: see *Thornton v Stockill* (1855) 1 Jur NS 751 and *Re Lake* [1903] 1 KB 439.
4   *Shepherd v Mouls* (1845) 4 Hare 500 at 504.

89.70 If the beneficiaries lack capacity to elect which remedy to pursue it seems that the court should enforce the most advantageous remedy available to the beneficiaries in the circumstances[1]. After all, if the unborn or minor beneficiaries were relegated to their compensation remedy, because they could not positively adopt the transaction and claim the profits, the trustees would be allowed to profit from their trust in breach of their fundamental duty[2]. However, where the profitable investment is an unauthorised investment, then it will need to be sold[3] and converted into an authorised investment, unless all the beneficiaries between them absolutely entitled to the trust property and of full age and capacity elect to adopt the investment as authorised, despite the trust restrictions on a limited class of authorised investments[4].

1   Scott on Trusts (4th edn) para 208.5.
2   See Article 59.
3   This sale, pursuant to the trustees' duty to sell unauthorised investments will overreach the beneficiaries interests: *Re Jenkins and HE Randall & Co's Contract* [1903] 2 Ch 362.
4   *Wright v Morgan* [1926] AC 788, PC; *Re Patten and Edmonton Union* (1883) 52 LJ Ch 787; *Re Jenkins and H E Randall & Co's Contract* [1903] 2 Ch 362.

Paragraph 4

Loss sustained by particular beneficiary

89.71 A trustee may negligently perform his functions so as to cause no loss to the trust fund but to cause loss to a particular beneficiary. Take the case of T who, in accordance with the purposes of the settlor in creating an accumulation and maintenance trust with flexible powers, decides to make an appointment of half the trust capital to O before he attains 25 years of age on 2 August when the power of appointment will cease to be exercisable. The deed of appointment is duly prepared but is not executed by T *before* 2 August but *on* 2 August, so the deed is ineffective[1] and the beneficiaries entitled in default of any appointment are entitled to all and not just half of the trust capital – and T must duly account to them for the whole capital. O will surely be entitled to equitable compensation in the amount of half the capital. This could be on the basis that T had negligently broken his equitable duty of care to O. Alternatively, while T actually has to account to the default beneficiaries for the whole capital, T is estopped from denying that he is personally liable to render an account to O for half the capital (and income subsequently arising therefrom) that T put himself under a duty to transfer to O, Equity looking on as done (as between T and O) that which ought to have been done before T's neglectful mistake put it out of his power to do what he ought to have done.

1   See the facts in *Breadner v Granville-Grossman [2001] Ch 523, [2000] 4 All ER 705*.

89.72 Another scenario is where B tells T that she is £100,000 in debt at a crippling 18% interest, so that she is desperately looking forward to receiving from T £100,000 to which she becomes entitled under the trust in two months time on attaining 35 years of age. Despite this, T does not get round to paying her the £100,000 till three months after her birthday because he and his wife were taking a four month round-the-world trip of a lifetime. While T must account for three months interest on the £100,000 at the mercantile higher than ordinary rate as if he had used the money for his own purposes, it seems clear that he will be forced by way of equitable compensation to make up the difference between that rate and the 18% paid by B.

89.73 In *Bank of New Zealand v New Zealand Guardian Trust Co Ltd*[1] a beneficiary claimed for an individual loss extraneous to the trust estate. The Bank claimed that the trustee of a secured debenture trust had failed in its duty to monitor the conduct of the company which had borrowed money from the Bank and other lenders and which had itself made unsecured advances to its subsidiaries in breach of its obligations under the debenture deed. The Bank claimed that because it was not notified of the breach it had lost the opportunity to withdraw from the loan facility at a time when it would have recovered the full amount due.

1   [1999] 1 NZLR 664, CA.

89.74 The New Zealand Court of Appeal held that the strict 'but for' test of causation did not apply because there had been no breach of the duty of fidelity and loyalty, only a breach of the duty to exercise reasonable care. There was no reason to approach the trustee's breach of its duty to act diligently in any different manner as regards causation and remoteness than would be the case if the cause of action were in contract or tort rather than in equity. On this basis the scope of the trustee's duty was to maintain (and not permit diminution of) the value of the secured debenture by monitoring the company's compliance and, if necessary, threatening to enforce or enforcing the charge over the company's property. The Bank's loss flowed not from any diminution in the value of the trust property but from the loss of opportunity to exit the loan syndicate. The scope and purpose of the trustee's duty did not extend to protecting the Bank from the loss it suffered from the company's insolvency through causes unconnected with the unsecured advances to its subsidiaries which the trustee failed to detect and report. Thus, the Bank's claim failed.

Exemplary damages

89.75 In *Re Brogden*[1], North J said that 'the court will not punish a trustee pecuniarily for his breach of trust except so far as loss has resulted therefrom to the trust estate', and historically no English court has ever awarded exemplary damages against a defaulting trustee[2]. Until recently, it was thought that the English courts had no power to award exemplary damages in respect of equitable wrongdoing because there was no case pre-dating 1964 where this had been done[3]. However, they may wish to reconsider their position, now that the restrictive cause of action test for the award of exemplary damages has been discredited in *Kuddus v Chief Constable of Leicestershire*[4]. Elsewhere, the appellate courts of Canada and New Zealand have held that an award of exemplary damages can be made in relation to a breach of fiduciary duty[5]. In Australia, the leading case is now *Harris v Digital Pulse Pty Ltd*[6], where Heydon JA vehemently opposed the award of exemplary damages for equitable wrongdoing, but Mason P strongly favoured their award in suitable cases. The third judge, Spiegleman CJ, considered it unnecessary and undesirable to decide the case on the basis that a punitive monetary award can never be awarded in equity because remedial flexibility is a characteristic of equity jurisprudence. In principle there is much to be said for the view that Equity, like the common law, should be able to award exemplary damages in cases of outrageous misconduct by trustees and other fiduciaries[7].

1   (1886) 38 Ch D 546 at 557. See too *A-G v Alford* (1855) 4 De G M & G 843; *Vyse v Foster* (1872) 8 Ch App 309 at 333, affirmed (1874) LR 7 HL 318.
2   The Pensions Act 1995, s 10 authorises the imposition of 'civil penalties' for maladministration of occupational pension schemes, but to date no such penalty has been levied in a reported case.
3   *AB v South West Water Services Ltd* [1993] QB 507. See too Law Commission Aggravated, Exemplary, and Restitutionary Damages (Law Com No 247, 1997) paras [5.54]–[5.56], recommending legislation to give the courts a power to award exemplary damages in relation to breaches of equitable duty. This recommendation has not been acted upon by Parliament.
4   [2001] UKHL 29, [2002] 2 AC 122.
5   *Norberg v Wynrib* [1992] 2 SCR 226; *KM v HM* [1992] 3 SCR 6; *Whiten v Pilot Insurance Co* [2002] 1 SCR 595; *Aquaculture Corp v New Zealand Green Mussel Co Ltd* [1990] 3 NZLR 299; *Cook v Evatt (No 2)* [1992] 1 NZLR 676.
6   (2003) 56 NSWLR 298.
7   For further discussion see A Burrows 'Remedial Coherence and Punitive Damages in Equity' and D Hayton "Unique Rules for the Unique Institution,the Trust" in S Degeling and J Edelman (eds) Equity in Commercial Law (2005) 381 and 300–303; A Duggan 'Exemplary Damages in Equity: A Law and Economics Perspective' (2006) 26 OJLS 303.

ARTICLE 90
JOINT AND SEVERAL LIABILITY OF TRUSTEES

90.1

(1)   Each trustee is, in general, liable for the whole loss when caused by the joint[1] default of all the trustees, even although all may not have been equally blameworthy[2]; and a decree against all may be enforced against one or more only[3].

(2)   But although the liability is several as well as joint, all the actual trustees or the personal representatives of the last surviving trustee are necessary parties to the action[4].

1   See Article 98 as to when a trustee is not answerable for the default of a co-trustee.
2   *Wilson v Moore* (1833) 1 My & K 126; *Lyse v Kingdon* (1844) 1 Coll 184; *Re Biddulph* (1869) 4 Ch App 280. This applies not only to express trustees, but to all persons who meddle with the trust property with notice of the trust. See *Cowper v Stoneham* (1893) 68 LT 18.
3   *A-G v Wilson* (1840) Cr & Ph 1 at 28; *Fletcher v Green* (1864) 33 Beav 426.
4   *Re Jordan* [1904] 1 Ch 260.

90.2 Trustees are liable only for their *own* breaches of duty, and they are not vicariously liable for breaches committed by their co-trustees. However, it often happens the joint actions or omissions of several trustees entail a joint breach of trust. Note, too, that it constitutes a breach of duty for a trustee to leave the trust affairs in the hands of a co-trustee to be dealt with as he sees fit[1], or to leave trust property in his sole control[2], or to stand by with knowledge that he is committing a breach of duty[3], or to take no steps to obtain redress on becoming aware that he has committed a breach of trust[4], or to retire from being a trustee with the object of facilitating a breach of trust which the remaining, or new, trustees then commit[5]. Trustees who cause the same damage to their beneficiaries by their respective breaches of duty are jointly and severally liable, with the result that the beneficiaries can require two or more of them jointly, or one of them individually, to discharge their common liability[6]. If a trustee is obliged to pay more than his fair share, then he can recover a contribution from the others, or even require them to reimburse him in full, as discussed below in Article 99.

1   *Wynne v Tempest* (1897) 13 TLR 360; *Re Lucking's Will Trusts* [1968] 1 WLR 866. This assumes that there has been no proper delegation, eg under the Trustee Act 2000 ss 11 and 12. Exceptionally a settlor may provide that a trustee must act as his co-trustee directs, in which case he will not be liable unless he dishonestly assists his co-trustee to commit a breach: *Re Arnott* [1899] 1 IR 201.
2   *Lewis v Nobbs* (1878) 8 Ch D 591. This assumes that the co-trustee is not an authorised nominee or custodian under the Trustee Act 2000, s 19.
3   *Booth v Booth* (1838) 1 Beav 125; *Gough v Smith* [1872] WN 18.
4   *Wilkins v Hogg* (1861) 8 Jur NS 25 at 26.
5   *Head v Gould* [1898] 2 Ch 250 at 273–274; *Kingdom v Castleman* (1877) 36 LT 141.
6   *Charitable Corpn v Sutton* (1742) 2 Atk 400 at 406; *Walker v Symonds* (1818) 3 Swan 1 at 75; *Ashurst v Mason* (1875) LR 20 Eq 225 at 233; *Re Duckwari plc* [1999] Ch 253 at 262.

ARTICLE 91
SET-OFF OF GAIN ON ONE BREACH AGAINST LOSS ON ANOTHER NOT ALLOWED

91.1

A trustee is liable only for the actual loss in each distinct and complete transaction which amounts to a breach of trust, and not for the loss in each particular item thereof[1]. A loss in one transaction or fund is not, however, compensated by a gain in another and distinct one[2].

1   *Vyse v Foster* (1872) 8 Ch App 309; affd (1874) LR 7 HL 318.
2   *Wiles v Gresham* (1854) 2 Drew 258; affd 5 De GM & G 770; *Dimes v Scott* (1828) 4 Russ 195; *Re Leonard, ex p Lewis* (1819) 1 Gl & J 69.

91.2 In *Bartlett v Barclays Bank Trust Co Ltd (No 2)*[1], Brightman J stated:

'The general rule is that where a trustee is liable in respect of distinct breaches of trust, one of which resulted in a loss and the other in a gain, he is not entitled to set off the gain against the loss, unless they arise in the same transaction.'

1   [1980] Ch 515 at 538.

91.3 The principle is illustrated by *Wiles v Gresham*[1] where the trustees of a marriage settlement negligently failed to get in a bond debt for £2,000 due from the husband, and the money was totally lost. Certain other of the trust funds were without proper authority invested in the purchase of land upon the trusts of the settlement. The husband, out of his own money, greatly added to the value of this land, and upon a claim being made against the trustees for the

£2,000 they sought to set off against that loss the gain which had accrued to the trust by the increased value of the land. However, their contention was disallowed, the two transactions being separate and distinct.

1   (1854) 2 Drew 258; *Re Barker* (1898) 77 LT 712.

91.4 Again, in *Dimes v Scott*[1] trustees had kept invested on unauthorised security at 10% a sum of money which they ought to have invested in consols, at a far lower rate of interest. The whole interest was wrongfully paid to the life tenant instead of just 3% then applicable under the rule in *Howe v Dartmouth*. Later the money was invested in consols when they were at a low price so that more consols were purchased than would have been the case if they had earlier been purchased at the proper time. The trustees claimed to set off the gain against the loss, but were not allowed to do so, because 'at whatever period the unauthorised security was realised, the estate was entitled to the whole of the consols that were then bought, and if it was sold at a later period than it ought to have been the executor was not entitled to any accidental advantage thence accruing'.

1   (1828) 4 Russ 195. For investment portfolio theory see para 53.9 above.

91.5 There is scope, however, for trustees to escape the consequences of the 'no set-off' rule by arguing that their actions have all formed part of a single transaction. Thus in *Vyse v Foster*[1] a testator devised his real and personal estates upon common trusts for sale, making them a mixed fund. His trustees were advised that a few acres of freehold land which belonged to him might be advantageously sold in lots for building purposes, and that, to develop their value, it was desirable to build a villa upon part of them. They accordingly built one at a cost of £1,600 out of the testator's personal estate. The evidence showed that the outlay had benefited the estate, but Vice-Chancellor Bacon disallowed the £1,600 to the trustees in passing their accounts. The Court of Appeal (and subsequently the House of Lords), however, reversed this, James LJ saying:

> 'As the real and personal estate constituted one fund, we think it neither reasonable nor just to fix the trustees with a sum, part of the estate, bona fide laid out on other part of the estate in the exercise of their judgment as the best means of increasing the value of the whole.'

1   (1872) 8 Ch App 309.

91.6 Further examples include *Fletcher v Green*[1], where trustees committed a breach of trust in lending trust moneys on mortgage, and upon a suit by them the mortgaged property was sold, and the money paid into court, and invested in consols pending the suit, and the consols rose in value, the trustees were allowed to set off the gain in the value of the consols against the loss under the mortgage, for the gain and loss arose out of one transaction. Again, in *Bartlett* the defendant trustees negligently invested trust funds in separate property development projects but Brightman LJ concluded that these transactions all formed part of a single breach of trust so that gains on one project could be set off against losses on another:

'The Guildford development stemmed from exactly the same policy and exemplified the same folly as the Old Bailey project. Part of the profit was used to finance the Old Bailey disaster. By sheer luck the gamble paid off handsomely on capital account. I think it would be unjust to deprive the bank of this element of salvage. My order will therefore reflect the bank's right to an appropriate set-off.'

1   (1864) 33 Beav 426.

91.7 Finally, in *Hulbert v Avens*[1], trustees failed to pay sums properly due as capital gains tax and thereby incurred liabilities to pay interest and penalties. The trustees successfully argued that they were entitled to pay these liabilities with money which had been earned as interest on trust money in a deposit account which would not have been earned had the trust money been paid as tax to the Revenue.

1   [2003] EWHC 76 (Ch), [2003] WTLR 287.

ARTICLE 92
PROPERTY ACQUIRED BY TRUSTEE OR FIDUCIARY CAN BE
TRACED AND CLAIMED BY THE BENEFICIARIES OR PRINCIPAL

92.1

(1)   If a trustee or other fiduciary has, in breach of trust or other fiduciary obligation, converted trust or fiduciary property into some other form, the property into which it has been so converted becomes subject to the trust or other fiduciary obligation. If *all* the beneficiaries are of full age and capacity, they can collectively elect to adopt the transaction, and take the property as it then stands; but failing such election, the property must be reconverted if it is not an authorised investment. In that case any gain accrues for the benefit of the beneficiaries and any loss falls on the trustee or other fiduciary[1]. Where a trustee or other fiduciary has made an unauthorised use of the trust or fiduciary property or has otherwise exploited his position in breach of his duty[2] so as purportedly to obtain a personal profit for himself, then such profit into whatever form it may be converted is also trust property and must be invested in authorised investments and held for the trust beneficiaries unless they are all of full age and capacity and elect to take the property as it then stands.

(2)   If a trustee has mixed trust moneys with his own, or has, partly with his own and partly with trust moneys, purchased other property, then the beneficiaries cannot elect to take the whole of the mixed fund or the entire property so purchased. However, the beneficiaries can trace into the mixed fund or property so purchased and either assert a proprietary claim to a proportionate share, or alternatively take a first charge on the traced assets to secure restoration of the trust fund[2]. Moreover, if there is an

increase in the value of the property paid for partly with trust money, in substance, the trustee and the beneficiaries are treated as co-owners of the appreciated property in proportions corresponding to their respective contributions to the purchase price[3].

(3)   Where assets of two trusts have been mixed (other than in a current banking account) any losses or gains in the value of the mixed fund are shared rateably according to the values of the mixed assets of each trust[4]. Where mixing occurs in a current banking account the rule in *Clayton's Case* has traditionally been applied to attribute the first drawings out to the first payments in[5] unless this produces an inequitable result[6]. However the courts are now so quick to find that application of the rule in *Clayton's Case* would be inequitable that it is effectively a dead letter.

(4)   Traditionally, the equitable right to trace required a continuing right of property recognised in equity or its concomitant, a fiduciary or quasi-fiduciary relationship. The right to trace thus extended well beyond the pure trustee-beneficiary relationship since the concept of fiduciary or quasi-fiduciary relationship was stretched to the limit in the interests of protecting quasi-beneficiaries so that equity in its auxiliary jurisdiction might assist a plaintiff who was sole legal beneficial owner of a stolen asset where legal remedies were inadequate in the circumstances. The tracing cases to this effect should now be regarded as superseded by the House of Lords' judgment in *Foskett v McKeown*[7] where Lord Steyn and Lord Millett both explained that there is no need to show a trust or fiduciary relationship in order to bring the 'equitable' tracing rules into play, because there is only one set of tracing rules which can be invoked by common law and equitable claimants alike.

(5)   The right to trace is lost when no traceable product of trust or other fiduciary property can be identified or the traceable product is found (as Article 101 reveals) in the hands of a third party who is a bona fide purchaser of a legal interest for value without notice or who makes out the defence of change of position.

---

1   See per Pearson J in *Re Patten and Edmonton Union* (1883) 52 LJ Ch 787; *Re Hallett's Estate* (1880) 13 Ch D 696; *Taylor v Plumer* (1815) 3 M & S 562; *Frith v Cartland* (1865) 2 Hem & M 417; *Hopper v Conyers* (1866) LR 2 Eq 549; *Lane v Dighton* (1762) Amb 409; *Scales v Baker* (1859) 28 Beav 91; *Cook v Addison* (1869) LR 7 Eq 466; *Ernest v Croysdill* (1860) 2 De GF & J 175; *Re Anslow* (1880) 28 WR 522; *Wright v Morgan* [1926] AC 788.
2   *A-G for Hong Kong v Reid* [1994] 1 AC 324, [1994] 1 All ER 1, PC.
3   *Foskett v McKeown* [2001] 1 AC 102 at 131, per Lord Millett. See too *Re Hallett's Estate* (1880) 13 Ch D 696; *Re Oatway* [1903] 2 Ch 356; *Lupton v White* (1808) 15 Ves 432; *Pennell v Deffell* (1853) 4 De GM & G 372; and *Re Diplock* [1948] Ch 465, [1948] 2 All ER 318, CA; affd sub nom *Ministry of Health v Simpson* [1951] AC 251, [1950] 2 All ER 1137, HL; *El Ajou v Dollar Land Holdings plc* [1993] 3 All ER 717 at 735–736, [1994] 2 All ER 685 at 701.
4   *Sinclair v Brougham* [1914] AC 398 at 442; *Re Diplock* [1948] Ch 465 at 533, 534, 539; *Foskett v McKeown* [2001] 1 AC 102 at 132, per Lord Millett.

5   *Re Hallett's Estate* (1879) 13 Ch D 696 (Fry J); *Hancock v Smith* (1889) 41 Ch D 456 at 461; *Re Stenning* [1895] 2 Ch 433; *Re Diplock* [1948] Ch 465 at 553–554.
6   *Barlow Clowes International Ltd v Vaughan* [1992] 4 All ER 22 at 39 and 44; *Re Ontario Securities Commission* (1987) 30 DLR (4th) 1, *Re Registered Securities* [1991] 1 NZLR 545.
7   [2001] 1 AC 102 at 113 and 128.

Paragraph 1

Tracing, following, and claiming

92.2 In *Foskett v McKeown*[1], Lord Millett distinguished 'tracing', 'following', and 'claiming' in these terms:

> '[Tracing and following] are both exercises in locating assets which are or may be taken to represent an asset belonging to the plaintiffs and to which they assert ownership. The processes of following and tracing are, however, distinct. Following is the process of following the same asset as it moves from hand to hand. Tracing is the process of identifying a new asset as the substitute for the old. Where one asset is exchanged for another, a claimant can elect whether to follow the original asset into the hands of the new owner or to trace its value into the new asset in the hands of the same owner ... Tracing is also distinct from claiming. It identifies the traceable proceeds of the claimant's property. It enables the claimant to substitute the traceable proceeds for the original asset as the subject matter of his claim. But it does not affect or establish his claim. That will depend on a number of factors including the nature of his interest in the original asset. He will normally be able to maintain the same claim to the substituted asset as he could have maintained to the original asset ... But his claim may also be exposed to potential defences as a result of intervening transactions.'

1   [2001] 1 AC 102 at 129–130, adopting the terminology suggested in L D Smith The Law of Tracing (1997). See too *Boscawen v Bajwa* [1996] 1 WLR 328 at 334, CA; *Waxman v Waxman* (2004) 7 ITELR 162 at [582], Ontario CA.

92.3 In Lord Millett's view, therefore, 'the rules of following and tracing ... are essentially evidential in nature', and they are essentially distinct from 'rules which determine substantive rights': the former are concerned with identifying property in other hands or in another form; the latter with the rights that a claimant can assert against the property in its present form'[1].

1   *Glencore International AG v Metro Trading Inc* [2001] 1 Lloyd's Rep 284 at 329.

92.4 Where trust property has been wrongfully converted into a different form by the trustee, either by exchanging the trust property for another asset, or by mixing the trust property with other property, or by a combination of the two, and the substitute asset or mixture remains in the trustee's hands, there is no need for the beneficiaries to 'follow' their property or its traceable product into the hands of a third party, before they can assert a proprietary claim to the new asset or mixture[1]. However, it will be necessary for the beneficiaries to 'trace' the value inherent in the trust property through the trustee's substitutions or mixtures into the value inherent in the substitute asset or mixture, as they can only assert a proprietary claim to the new asset or mixture once they have established that this is the traceable product of trust property.[1]

1 The process of following trust property or its traceable proceeds into the hands of third parties is discussed in Article 101, below.

Proprietary claims to trust assets and their traceable proceeds

92.5 In *Foskett v McKeown*[1] the majority of the House of Lords held that the beneficiaries are given a proprietary claim to the whole or part of a traced asset in order to vindicate their proprietary rights in the trust fund. To understand what this means we must first distinguish proprietary claims to trust assets in their original form from proprietary claims to the traceable proceeds of trust assets. Suppose that a trustee misappropriates a trust asset for himself. In this case, nothing happens to interrupt the beneficiaries' continuing equitable ownership of the asset, and they can enforce their continuing rights by obtaining a declaration of ownership and an order for reconveyance if necessary.

1 [2001] 1 AC 102.

92.6 Now contrast the case where a trustee uses trust assets to buy an unauthorised investment for the beneficiaries, or a new asset for himself. Here the beneficiaries can trace into the new asset and assert a proprietary claim to the new asset. But, strictly speaking, their proprietary right to the new asset cannot be exactly the same right as their proprietary right to the original trust property. The reason is that a property right is a right to a specific thing which cannot be detached from the thing to which it relates and reattached to some new thing[1]. For example, an ownership right in land relates to the land, and so it cannot be the same right as the right to the sale proceeds of the land, even if one right is exchanged for the other.

1 P Birks 'Tracing, Property, and Unjust Enrichment' (2002) 54 CLP 231 at pp. 244–5; R Chambers 'Tracing and Unjust Enrichment' in JW Neyers et al (eds) Understanding Unjust Enrichment (2004) 263 at pp. 273–4.

92.7 In *Foskett* their Lordships averted their eyes from this, focussing their attention on the beneficiaries' interests as interests in the trust fund established by the settlor. Thus Lord Browne-Wilkinson held that[1]:

'The only trusts at issue are the express trusts of the purchasers' trust deed. Under those express trusts the purchasers were entitled to equitable proprietary interests in the original moneys [which they paid over to the trustee]. Like any other equitable proprietary interest, those equitable proprietary interests under the purchasers' trust deed which originally existed in the moneys paid to [the trustee] now exist in any other property which, in law, now represents the original trust assets.'

1 *Foskett v McKeown* [2001] 1 AC 102 at 110. Cf *Taylor v Plumer* (1815) 3 M & S 562 at 575.

92.8 Similarly, Lord Millett held that the beneficiaries have 'a continuing beneficial interest not merely in the trust property but in its traceable proceeds also'[1], and he has since written extra-judicially that '"the fiction of persistence" is not a fiction [because the] beneficiaries' interests in the new investment are exactly the same as their interest in the old'[2]. However, this cannot be literally true: the new asset is not the old asset, and prior to the acquisition of the new asset with trust funds, no one owed any obligation to the beneficiaries in respect of the new asset. It follows that the beneficiaries' right in the new asset after it has been acquired must be a new right whose existence calls for explanation.

1   *Foskett v McKeown* [2001] 1 A.C. 102 at 127.
2   Lord Millett 'Proprietary Restitution' in S Degeling and J Edelman (eds) Equity in Commercial Law (2005) pp 315–316, adding that 'wrongfully substituted assets are [not] held on a constructive trust … [but] continue to be held on the same trusts throughout. If the claimant was the beneficiary under an express trust, the substituted assets are held on the same express trusts.'

92.9 To the extent that they recognised this, the majority of the House of Lords in *Foskett* explained the beneficiaries' new right as a right which arose in order to 'vindicate their property rights' in the trust fund[1]. However, the mere fact of the beneficiaries' ownership of the original trust property is not enough in itself to explain their acquisition of a new proprietary right in a traceable substitute[2]. To explain the beneficiaries' new right, one must look instead to the substitution by means of which the new asset was acquired with the trust property. Take the case where a trustee uses trust funds to purchase an authorised investment. Here, by virtue of an agreement between the settlor and the trustee, the trustee holds the original trust property, subsequently added property, and property substituted for such property as a trust fund for the beneficiaries. When the trustee buys an authorised investment with trust money, the beneficiaries' interest in the money is overreached, and they acquire a new interest in the new investment by a process which the beneficiaries cannot subsequently dispute. In this case, the source of the beneficiaries' new rights is the settlor's intention, agreed to by the trustee, to give the beneficiaries' proprietary rights in the original trust assets and the proceeds thereof, mediated through the trustee's authorised exercise of his powers of sale and investment to acquire new assets for the beneficiaries, to be held by him on the same terms as those on which he held the original trust assets. The same analysis can also be used to explain the case where the trustees purport to acquire new assets for the beneficiaries, but act beyond the scope of their powers. As noted above, the beneficiaries can retrospectively adopt the unauthorised investment, which looks like an *ad* hoc variation of the trust, retrospectively giving the beneficiaries rights whose source, again, is the settlor's intention, agreed to by the trustee, to create such rights in their favour, the trustee being under an obligation always to act in the beneficiaries' best interests.

1   [2001] 1 AC 102 at 129 per Lord Millett. See too Lord Browne-Wilkinson's comments at 110 and Lord Hoffmann's comments at 115.
2   As argued in R Grantham and C Rickett 'Property and Unjust Enrichment' [1997] NZL Rev 668,at pp. 675–684; G Virgo 'Tracing and Property Rights: The Categorical Truth' (2000) 63 MLR 905.

92.10 The case where a trustee misappropriates trust funds and uses them to acquire new assets for himself resembles the case where a trustee makes an unauthorised profit from his position. As previously discussed in Article 33, the constructive trust imposed on the trustee's gain in the latter situation responds to the fact that a trustee binds himself by agreement at the moment when he assumes office to act exclusively in the beneficiaries' best interests (not his own) and so hold all the profits of his office for the beneficiaries as and when he receives them. *A fortiori*, one can also say that a trustee binds himself to hold whatever traceable proceeds of trust funds come into his hands for the beneficiaries.

Stock bought with trust or fiduciary money

92.11 Where money is handed to a broker for the purpose of purchasing stock, and he invests it in unauthorised stock, and absconds, the stock which he has purchased will belong to the principal, and not to the broker's trustee in bankruptcy, for a broker is a fiduciary or constructive trustee for his principal; and, as was said by Lord Ellenborough[1]:

'the property of a principal entrusted by him to his factor for any special purpose belongs to the principal, notwithstanding any change which that property may have undergone in point of form, so long as such property is capable of being identified, and distinguished from all other property.'

[1]   *Taylor v Plumer* (1815) 3 M & S 562 clarified by L Smith (1995) LMCLQ 240 and Millett LJ in *Trustee of Property of FC Jones & Sons v Jones* [1997] Ch 159 at 169; see also *Re Strachan* (1876) 4 Ch D 123 at 128, CA; *Re Hallett's Estate* (1880) 13 Ch D 696 at 717.

92.12 Nor does a personal judgment against the trustee to make good the loss release the lien of the beneficiaries on an unauthorised investment[1].

[1]   *Francis v Francis* (1854) 5 De GM & G 108.

Money produced by trust or fiduciary chattels

92.13 If goods consigned to a factor be sold by him and reduced into money, yet if the money can be traced – as, for instance, where it has been kept separate and apart from the factor's own moneys, or kept in bags, or the like[1], or has been changed into bills or notes[2], or into any other form[3], or has been paid into the factor's account at the bank[4] – the employer, and not the creditors of the factor, will, upon his bankruptcy, be entitled to the property into which it has been converted. For the creditors of a defaulting trustee can have no better right to the trust property than the trustee himself[5]. However, where a person whose business it is to act as an agent in turning to account the property of his principal, ceases to carry on this business actively, there is no general rule that he cannot keep the proceeds of the principal's property for himself, and even if the agency relationship comes to an end because the agent is forced into administrative receivership, this cannot alter the agent's right to seek outstanding sums from customers, nor can it alter the right of the agent's bank to enforce a charge against these book debts, unless this would be wholly unconscionable[6].

1   *Tooke v Hollingworth* (1793) 5 Term Rep 215.
2   *Re Jullian, ex p Dumas* (1754) 2 Ves Sen 582; *Scott v Surman* (1742) Willes 400.
3   *Frith v Cartland* (1865) 2 Hem & M 417; *Birt v Burt* (1877) 11 Ch D 773n.
4   *Re Hallett's Estate* (1880) 13 Ch D 696.
5   *Taylor v Plumer* (1815) 3 M & S 562.
6   *Triffit Nurseries v Salads Etcetera Ltd* [2000] 1 BCLC 761.

Money produced by misuse of fiduciary position

92.14 If in breach of fiduciary duty a fiduciary receives a bribe which he then invests in property, such bribe and then such property is held on trust for the person injured, Equity considering as done that which ought to be done[1], the fiduciary having agreed to act exclusively in such person's best interests (and not his own) and so hold any profits, like bribes, for that person.

1   *A-G for Hong Kong v Reid* [1994] 1 AC 324, [1994] 1 All ER 1, PC.

Wrongful sale by vendor

92.15 A vendor who, after entering into a contract for sale of land[1], sells it to another person will hold the proceeds of sale (and anything purchased therewith) on constructive trust for the original contracting purchaser subject to that purchaser paying over the agreed purchase price[2].

1   See Article 36.
2   *Lake v Bayliss* [1974] 2 All ER 1114, [1974] 1 WLR 1073.

Sale by trustees of property wrongfully acquired out of trust moneys

92.16 Where the trustees of a will invested trust moneys in an unauthorised purchase of land, and afterwards contracted to sell it for a largely increased price, it was held that they were acting properly in so doing, and that the concurrence of one beneficiary was sufficient to make a good overreaching title[1]. For, as Pearson J put it:

> 'I see no reason why the trustees should not now do what it was all along their duty to do, and what the court would have ordered them to do. At the same time, I agree that it would be proper to take the concurrence of one of the cestuis que trust; because, if all of them elected to take their shares of the land after it had been purchased, they would have been entitled to do so.'

1   *Re Patten and Edmonton Union* (1883) 52 LJ Ch 787. See Birks and Prett (ed) *Breach of Trust* (Hart Publishing, 2002) Chapter 4 'Overreaching' by D Fox.

92.17 The report states that the learned judge said that a good title could be made on the purchasers seeing that the purchase-money was invested in the names of the trustees as trustees; but no such requirement has been suggested in subsequent cases and it seems to be quite inconsistent with s 14 of the

Trustee Act 1925, s 27 of the Law of Property Act 1925 and the language of Cozens-Hardy J in *Power v Banks*[1] where he said:

> 'by means of the sales ... the purchase-money got into ... the proper hands, and I cannot see what harm was done by this. To affect the purchasers ... with the consequences of any subsequent misappropriation ... would be unjust unless the sale itself was a wrongful act'.

[1] *Re Jenkins and H E Randall & Co's Contract* [1903] 2 Ch 362; and see *Power v Banks* [1901] 2 Ch 487 at 496. A purchaser would only have problems if not acting in good faith by purchasing knowingly at an undervalue: *Cowan de Groot Properties v Eagle Trust plc* [1992] 4 All ER 700.

92.18 On the same principle, where the beneficiaries or any of them are infants, the trustees can sell the wrongfully acquired unauthorised investment without anyone's consent; because in that case the beneficiaries collectively are not in a position to adopt the breach[1].

[1] *Re Jenkins and H E Randall & Co's Contract* [1903] 2 Ch 362.

Paragraph 2

Trust or fiduciary property mixed with other property so as to lose its discrete identity

92.19 The case is comparatively simple where (as in the foregoing illustrations) the trustee has spent or converted the trust property, and nothing but the trust property. It becomes more difficult when the trustee has mixed the trust moneys with his own so that uncertainty of subject-matter of the trust arises, and either kept the mixed fund or spent it in the purchase of other property. The case then turns entirely upon the question whether the mixed fund, so formed, can still be identified; or, if it has been spent, whether it can be traced into the property which has been purchased with it. As Lord Greene[1] has stated:

> 'The equitable remedies pre-suppose the continued existence of the money either as a separate fund or as part of a mixed fund or as latent in property acquired by means of such a fund'.

[1] In *Re Diplock* [1948] Ch 465 at 521, [1948] 2 All ER 318 at 347, CA; affd sub nom *Ministry of Health v Simpson* [1951] AC 251, [1950] 2 All ER 1137, HL.

92.20 However, as Lord Millett brings out[1]:

> 'In principle it should not matter ... whether the trustee mixes the trust money with his own and buys the new asset with the mixed fund or makes separate payments of the purchase price (whether simultaneously or sequentially) out of the different funds. In every case the value formerly inherent in the trust property has become located within the value inherent in the new asset'.

[1] *Foskett v McKeown* [2001] 1 AC 102 at 130.

92.21 If the trust property has ceased to have any continued existence, because it has been dissipated[1], then, as the actual property is gone, and nothing can be identified as standing in its place, the beneficiary can only proceed against the trustee personally for the breach of trust, or, if the latter be bankrupt, can prove only as a creditor[2]. For the right of the beneficiary is only to have the actual trust property or that which stands in its place, or to have a charge on it[3].

[1] Although the payment of a debt was traditionally regarded as a dissipation, in this context (*Re Diplock* [1948] Ch 465 at 549), it now seems that the beneficiaries may 'backwards trace' through such payments into an asset, or trace into an extinguished charge which they may then acquire, by a legal fiction via subrogation. See para 92.62 below.

[2] *Re Jullian, ex p Dumas* (1754) 2 Ves Sen 582; *Scott v Surman* (1742) Willes 400; *Re Hallett & Co* [1894] 2 QB 237; *Foskett v McKeown* [2001] 1 AC 102 at 130.

[3] See *Re Diplock* [1948] Ch 465, [1948] 2 All ER 318, CA; affd sub nom *Ministry of Health v Simpson* [1951] AC 251, [1950] 2 All ER 1137, HL.

92.22 It has been suggested[1] that, even though a plaintiff's £x has been dissipated, the plaintiff should have an equitable lien or charge for £x over all the defendant fiduciary's remaining unencumbered assets which had earlier been swollen by the plaintiff's £x. This suggestion has been rejected by the Court of Appeal in *Re Hallett & Co*[2] and *Bishopsgate Investment Management Ltd v Homan*[3]: it would so dramatically affect the rights of the unsecured creditors of the defendant on his insolvency that only legislation should alter the position if a full consideration of the problems justifies such legislation or some limited legislation covering special types of defendants in specified circumstances.

[1] *Space Investments Ltd v Canadian Imperial Bank of Commerce Trust Co (Bahamas) Ltd* [1986] 3 All ER 75 at 77, [1986] 1 WLR 1072 at 1074.

[2] [1894] 2 QB 237 at 245.

[3] [1995] Ch 211, [1995] 1 All ER 347.

Trust property mixed with trustee's property

92.23 If a trustee mixes assets with his own the onus of proof is on the trustee to distinguish the separate assets and, to the extent that he fails to do so, they belong to the trust[1]. Moreover as Staughton J stated[2], 'If the wrongdoer has destroyed or impaired the evidence by which the innocent party could show how much he has lost the wrongdoer must suffer from the resulting uncertainty.' The tracing rules which apply in this situation thus dovetail with the more general rule of evidence that where evidential uncertainty is created by wrongdoing, evidential presumptions will be made against the wrongdoer[3].

[1] *Lupton v White* (1808) 15 Ves 432, *Westdeutsche Landesbank Girozentrale v Islington Borough Council* [1996] AC 669.

[2] *Indian Oil Corpn Ltd v Greenstone Shipping SA* [1987] 3 All ER 893 at 906.

[3] *Armory v Delamirie* (1722) 1 Stra 505; *Infabrics Ltd v Jaytex Ltd* [1985] FSR 75.

92.24 The starting point is that the beneficiaries will have a first charge for their money on the mixed fund and any property purchased thereout[1]. In Lord Millett's words[2], 'As against the wrongdoer and his successors, the beneficiary is entitled to locate his contribution in any part of the mixture and to subordinate their claims to share in the mixture until his own contribution has been satisfied'. Thus, if trust money is mixed with the trustee's own money in account No. 1 and the trustee then transfers money therefrom into account No 2 and account No 3 (thereby acquiring choses in action) and purchases with money in account No 1 a painting and a flat the beneficiaries will have an equitable charge for their moneys over whatever money remains in the No 1, No 2 and No 3 accounts and over the painting and the flat. Equity imposes such charges over the new assets because they are derived from a fund which is treated as if subject to a charge in favour of the beneficiaries[3]. If the defendant does not personally satisfy their claim they can assert their charge over any of the traced assets to satisfy their claim. Only if they seek more than a charge by seeking a proportionate share of an appreciated asset will they need to consider relying upon artificial presumptions against a wrongdoer, whether the presumption[4] that he acted honestly in first using his own money or the presumption[5] that he used trust money because he cannot allege he used his own money until he reinstated the trust money in a trust account.

[1]   *Re Hallett's Estate* (1880) 13 Ch D 696; *Re Oatway* [1903] 2 Ch 356; *Re Diplock* [1948] Ch 465 at 539, CA, *El Ajou v Dollar Land Holdings plc* [1993] 3 All ER 717 at 735; revsd, [1994] 2 All ER 685 at 699, 701.
[2]   *Foskett v McKeown* [2001] 1 AC 102 at 132.
[3]   *El Ajou v Dollar Land Holdings plc* [1993] 3 All ER 717 at 736.
[4]   *Re Hallett's Estate* (1880) 13 Ch D 696 at 727–728; *Halley v Law Society* [2002] EWHC 139 (Ch) at [160] (not challenged on appeal [2003] EWCA Civ 97, [2003] WTLR 845).
[5]   *Re Oatway* [1903] 2 Ch 356.

92.25   Where mixing takes place in a current account of a bank the trustee is presumed to draw out his own moneys[1] first and not to draw on the trust moneys until his own moneys have been exhausted[2]. However, once trust moneys have been drawn upon a beneficiary cannot claim that subsequent payments in to the trustee's own account are meant to be trust moneys unless such payments represent the proceeds of sale of traceable trust property[3]. This rule, established in *James Roscoe (Bolton) Ltd v Winder*[4], is known as the 'lowest intermediate balance rule'. It has been summarised as follows: 'absent any payment in of money with the intention of making good earlier depredations, tracing cannot occur through a mixed account for any larger sum than is the lowest balance in the account between the time the beneficiary's money goes in, and the time the remedy is sought'[5] .

[1]   *Re Tilley's Will Trusts* [1967] Ch 1179, [1967] 2 All ER 303; *Scott v Scott* (1963) 109 CLR 649; *Paul A Davies (Australia) Pty Ltd (in liquidation) v Davies* [1983] 1 NSWLR 440.
[2]   *Re Hallett's Estate* (1880) 13 Ch D 696 followed in *Grabowski v Grangemore Investments* [2002] EWHC 851 (Ch).
[3]   *Westdeutsche Landesbank Girozentrale v Islington London Borough Council* [1994] 4 All ER 890 at 939.
[4]   [1915] 1 Ch 62, endorsed in *Re Goldcorp Exchange Ltd* [1995] 1 AC 74 and *Bishopsgate Investment Management Ltd v Homan* [1995] Ch 211, CA.
[5]   *Re French Caledonia Travel Service Pty Ltd* (2003) 59 NSWLR 361 at [175] per Campbell J. For application of the principle where goods are successively withdrawn and deposited in an unascertained bulk, see *Glencore International AG v Metro Trading Inc* [2001] 1 Lloyd's Rep 284 at [201]–[202], revisited in *Glencore International AG v Alpina Insurance Co Ltd [2004] EWHC 66 (Comm)*, [2004] 1 All ER (Comm) 858 at [14]–[20]. The 'lowest intermediate balance' role was unfortunately abrogated by the Ontario Court of Appeal without appreciating that the role does not resolve evidential uncertainties, but rather, helps to identify what is evidentially certain about the trustees' actions: *Law Society of Upper Canada v Toronto Dominion Bank* (1998) 169 DLR (4th) 353, noted LD Smith (2000) 33 Can Bar LJ 75; significantly, however, this case was distinguished by the same court in *Re Graphicshoppe Ltd* (2005) 78 OR (3d) 401.

92.26 Where moneys are withdrawn to purchase what turns out to be a profitable investment the beneficiaries can claim such investment even if at the time of the purchase the trustee's own moneys (mixed with the trust moneys) could have sufficed to effect the purchase[1]. The presumption that the trustee is presumed to draw out his own moneys first and the 'first in first out' principle enshrined in *Clayton's Case* cannot be invoked by the wrongdoing trustee to his own advantage to control the book-keeping and allocate profitable investments to himself. His conduct prevented proper accounts from being kept so it is up to the beneficiaries to resolve the book-keeping as they wish, and it is the trustee's own fault that his mixing of moneys prevents him from disputing such book-keeping. The beneficiaries can choose to treat withdrawals that are dissipated as representing the trustee's money and profitable withdrawals as representing the trust moneys. The trustee cannot take advantage of his own wrongdoing to put himself in the position of 'Heads I win, tails you lose'; 'everything is presumed against him'[2], and the beneficiaries are free to 'cherry pick' from the presumptions raised to resolve the evidential difficulties created by the trustee's wrongdoing in order to reach the best results for themselves[3].

---

[1] *Re Oatway* [1903] 2 Ch 356. There seems no justification for restricting this claim to the situation where insufficient moneys are left in the account to cover the trust moneys, though such restriction may (accidentally?) be implicit in the final sentence of the penultimate paragraph of the judgment of Ungoed-Thomas J in *Re Tilley's Will Trusts* [1967] Ch 1179, [1967] 2 All ER 303. A subsequent fortuitous dissipation or not of the balance in the account by the trustee should be immaterial.

[2] *Gray v Haig* (1855) 20 Beav 219 at 226 per Romilly MR; *Jaffray v Marshall* [1994] 1 All ER 143 at 151.

[3] *Shalson v Russo* [2003] EWHC 1637 (Ch), [2005] Ch 281 at [144] per Rimer J. In *Turner v Jacob* [2006] EWHC 1317 (Ch) at [102] Patten J held to the contrary that 'in a case … where the trustee maintains in the account an amount equal to the remaining trust fund, the beneficiary's right to trace is limited to that fund.' However Shalson does not appear to have been cited to his Lordship and in principle Rimer J's cherry-picking rule is to be preferred.

92.27 Where a trustee mixes, say, £10,000 of trust money with £10,000 of his own, so as to purchase Whizzo Ltd shares for £20,000, then the trust beneficiaries can choose either to take a 50% ownership interest in the shares, or to take charge over the shares to the value of £10,000, depending on which of these is most advantageous to them[1]. Exceptionally, if the trustee would not have been able to purchase the shares but for being the trustee, as where the offer was made to him qua trustee, the shares should belong exclusively to the trust, subject to him being reimbursed his own expenditure[2]. Similarly, if investments had, for example, to be in minimum £100,000 blocks which the trust, but not the trustee personally, could provide, the trustee only having £10,000 spare which he invested with £90,000 of trust moneys, then it seems that the investment should belong to the trust beneficiaries, subject to reimbursement of the £10,000 with interest. A trustee must not profit from his trust (unless authorised by the trust instrument): Equity should regard him as having done what he was duty-bound to do, namely to acquire the investments for the benefit of the trust beneficiaries and not himself.

---

[1] *Foskett v McKeown* [2001] 1 AC 102; *Mitchell v O'Brien* [2002] All ER (D) 125 (Feb), Ch D. See too *Re Tilley's Will Trusts* [1967] Ch 1179; *Wedderburn v Wedderburn* (1838) 4 My & CR 41.

[2] Eg *Keech v Sandford* (1726) 2 Eq Cas Abr 741.

92.28 A trustee of course may reinstate the trust fund and so right the wrong[1] and thereafter, having distinguished his own private property from the trust property, he may invest his private property profitably or unprofitably. Until he has done that he cannot prove that it was not trust moneys that were used to purchase the profitable investment[2].

[1]   *Re Oatway* [1903] 2 Ch 356 at 361. If T mixed £10,000 of trust money with his own £5,000 to purchase shares worth £15,000, which he later sells for £30,000, he can only reinstate the trust fund by paying £20,000 and not £10,000 into a designated trust account.

[2]   Thus if T mixes £20,000 trust money with £10,000 of his own money and spends £18,000 on a profitable investment which doubles in value the trust beneficiaries should be able to claim a £2,000 charge on the moneys remaining in the mixed account as well as the £36,000 investment representing the £18,000 balance of the £20,000 trust money. The wrongdoing trustee can hardly be heard to claim that it would be fairer to allow him to make a profit either by claiming 10 eighteenths of the investment for himself or 10 thirtieths thereof.

Causation problems and the alternative remedies

92.29 Equity's minimum remedy is the imposition of a lien or charge over the identifiable product of the claimant's property to satisfy his claim in respect of such property. However, in some circumstances Equity will impose a constructive trust over such identifiable product to the extent of such share therein as reflects the value of the claimant's traceable interest, thereby enabling the claimant to recover more than would be achieved by the imposition of a lien.

92.30 To achieve this favourable result it is submitted that a claimant needs to prove not just the transactional proprietary links. It is fundamental that he should also establish as a matter of causation that the defendant was unjustly enriched at the claimant's expense because, but for the value input from the claimant's property, the defendant probably would not have acquired the asset in which the claimant asserts a whole or partial share. This is the crucial justification for the imposition of the constructive trust which captures the profit for the claimant and makes it unavailable to the defendant and his creditors on his insolvency.

92.31 A helpful and illuminating case is *Re Tilley's Will Trusts*[1] where Ungoed-Thomas J was prepared to find that there were transactional proprietary links to justify the imposition of a lien but held that no constructive trust of a profitable proportionate share would be imposed. The plaintiff argued that £179 of trust money had been used by the trustee in purchasing a £1,000 house and £83 in purchasing a £2,050 house because the trust moneys had been paid into the trustee's bank account whence the purchase moneys had been paid, leaving her account overdrawn, so that logically there were clear transactional links. She was a woman of substantial wealth having (in 1939) overdraft facilities of £22,000. In the 1950s her account was substantially in credit when she paid in three trust sums totalling £1,975 and later purchased houses in her name when her account, if including the overdraft facility, contained more than enough, without regard to the trust moneys, to pay for such purchases.

1   [1967] Ch 1179.

92.32 Ungoed-Thomas J took the view[1] that if the trustee had been dishonest, deliberately using trust money in the purchases, then the beneficiaries would be entitled to proportionate shares in the property purchased. One can see that here there would be clear transactional and causative links because she would not be in a position (due to her intentions, quite apart from her mixing of the funds) to prove the moneys invested in the houses were not trust moneys. However, he held that the trustee, an elderly widow who was also life tenant under her spouse's will, had innocently but misguidedly intermingled trust money with her own. He then held that her wealthy financial circumstances meant that she would have bought the properties anyhow, so that the beneficiaries were not entitled to proportionate shares in the properties.

> 'The trustee's breach halted at the mixing of funds in her bank account. Although properties bought out of those funds would, like the bank account itself, ... be charged with repayment of the trust moneys ... yet the trust moneys were not invested in properties at all but merely went in reduction of the trustee's overdraft which was in reality the source of the purchase moneys.'

1   [1967] Ch 1179 at 1193.

92.33 One can thus see that it was not a case where the defendant would not have bought the houses but for the trust money. Therefore she had not obtained the houses and thereby enriched herself at the expense of the trust beneficiaries, though she had obtained a benefit of £2,237, making her personally liable to account for the £2,237 but without interest since she was the life tenant.

92.34 Because the £2,237 was readily available out of the deceased trustee's estate the question of any lien to secure payment did not arise. However, the judge indicated[1] that he would have been prepared to impose a lien 'on the properties purchased by the widow out of the bank account as security for repayment of the £2,237 trust moneys paid into her bank account in accordance with the principle in *Re Oatway*'[2] if 'the moneys in the bank account were inadequate' to satisfy a lien on such account.

1   [1967] Ch 1179 at 1193.
2   [1903] 2 Ch 356.

92.35 The defendant was fortunate in having as the judge Ungoed-Thomas J, renowned for severely distinguishing between honesty and dishonesty and for his concentration upon the merits of individuals rather than upon lofty legal principles. The deterrent philosophy underpinning the integrity of trusteeship as reflected in *Boardman v Phipps*[1], *A-G for Hong Kong v Reid*[2] and *Foskett v McKeown*[3] indicates that, as a trustee wrongfully mixing trust funds with her own, the defendant (or rather her personal representative) should not have been allowed to argue that the profitable investments belonged to her and not to the trust beneficiaries and that she had done for herself what she could have done for the beneficiaries. After all, throughout her trusteeship she had acted recklessly, cavalierly and in clear breach of trust by not taking easy elementary steps to keep the trust money separate from her own, so that she could not prove that trust money had not actually been used towards the purchase of houses: she could not really disprove the causative link with the houses, as recognised by the preparedness of Ungoed-Thomas to impose a lien on the houses if her estate had not easily been able to pay the £2,237.

¹   [1967] 2 AC 46.
²   [1994] 1 AC 324, PC.
³   [2001] 1 AC 102 at 134, HL.

92.36 It is submitted that an express trustee who wrongly mixes trust money with her or his own, so that it cannot be established whose money was used to purchase particular assets, cannot be allowed to escape liability by arguing that he would have bought the assets anyway, having more than enough capacity to buy them without the assistance of the trust money, so that he is entitled to these profitable assets. Moreover, there ought not to be different approaches for lay trustees as opposed to professional trustees, or, within the category of lay trustees, for elderly housewives as opposed to entrepreneurial businessmen. Moreover, innocent volunteers who take from wrongdoing trustees cannot be placed in a better position than the trustees themselves, as the majority of the House of Lords made clear in *Foskett v McKeown*¹.

¹   [2001] 1 AC 102 at 127 and 131, per Lord Millett.

92.37 However, if the defendant does not know that he is a trustee but is a constructive trustee, like the defendants in *Boardman v Phipps*¹, then he should be able to argue that he would have bought the relevant assets anyway so that he has not been unjustly enriched at the expense of the trust and no constructive trust should therefore attach to those assets. Thus, if the millionaire, Tom Boardman, had sold the shares subject to the constructive trust for £50,000 and, believing the proceeds to be his, had then used them with another £50,000 of his to purchase Great Co shares which doubled in value, he should not hold half such shares on a constructive trust. Instead, he should simply hold the shares subject to a lien for £50,000 and interest.

¹   [1967] 2 AC 46.

92.38 A fortiori this should be the position for an innocent donee, D, having no actual, Nelsonian or naughty knowledge¹ that he had received trust property.

¹   'Nelsonian' and 'naughty' knowledge represent the knowledge that D is deemed to have from wilfully shutting his eyes to the obvious, or from wilfully or recklessly failing to make the enquiries an honest and reasonable man would make in the suspicious circumstances, ie categories (ii) and (iii) in *Baden Delvaux v Société Generale* [1992] 4 All ER 161 at 235. See paras 100.72–100.73 below. Strictly, an innocent volunteer means one without actual constructive or imputed notice (as assumed in *Re Diplock* [1948] Ch 465) but in line with the liberal approaches in *Re Tilley's Will Trusts* [1967] Ch 1179 and *Re Montagu's Settlements* [1987] Ch 264 it is submitted that there should be scope for D not to be in as

strict a position as an express trustee, so that he can be allowed to prove that he has not actually enriched himself at the expense of beneficiaries because he would have bought the relevant asset anyway: see para 101.37 below.

Tracing trust funds into property insurance proceeds

92.39 Problems arise over the proceeds of insurance in respect of property that is the traceable product of property of a claimant, C, where the premiums were paid by a defendant, D, out of his own money. Robert Goff J[1] considered that the 'insurance money is the product, not of the property involved, but of the premiums'. However, but for D acquiring the property he would not have had an insurable interest entitling him to pay the premiums and receive the proceeds of the policy in the event of the loss or destruction of the property. Thus, D should be personally liable for the insurance proceeds subject to a credit for the premiums paid by him. It would further seem that D should be liable to the proprietary remedy if he be an errant fiduciary under an express or implied duty[2] to insure the trust property (or even with a power to insure trust property) so that equity will look on as done that which ought to be done[3] (or estop D from denying the presumption[4] that he used his fiduciary insurance power): the insurance policy and its proceeds will then be held upon the same trusts as the insured property, subject to D having a lien for the cost of the premiums he paid himself. However, if D were an innocent donee he would be under no duty to insure the property and have no fiduciary powers that he could be presumed to have used, so that C should have no proprietary right to insurance proceeds, capable of prejudicing D's unsecured creditors upon the insolvency of D.

1.   *Ellerman Lines Ltd v Lancaster Maritime Co Ltd* [1980] 2 Lloyd's Rep 497 at 502 applying *Rayner v Preston* (1881) 18 Ch D 1. The House of Lords showed no inclination to reach a similar conclusion by way of analogy in the recent life insurance proceeds case of *Foskett v McKeown* [2001] 1 AC 102.
2.   Nowadays, standards of care should require a trustee (under s 19 Trustee Act 1925 substituted by s 34 Trustee Act 2000) to insure trust property to the full value where a reasonable businessman would do so.
3.   Eg *A-G for Hong Kong v Reid [1994] 1 AC 324*, [1994] 1 All ER 1.
4.   Omnia praesumuntur rite esse acta ('all acts are presumed to have been duly performed') and 'every presumption must be made against him as a wrongdoer' as appears from *Foskett v McKeown* [2001] 1 AC 102 at 132, HL.

Purchase of property with mortgage loan

92.40 *Paul A Davies Pty (Australia) Ltd (in liquidation) v Davies*[1] illustrates tracing possibilities arising from loans. Take two brothers who innocently but erroneously believe they can borrow £20,000 from their private company to use as a deposit on a private venture involving purchase of a restaurant for £200,000. They go into occupation for a monthly fee and defer completion for three years on a further payment of £20,000, similarly borrowed from the company, and on agreeing to raise the purchase price from £200,000 to £250,000. After two years they complete the purchase early, taking out a mortgage on the restaurant to secure the necessary £210,000 bank loan and personally covenanting to repay the loan. A year later they sell out to a

92.40 *The liability of the trustees*

purchaser for £320,000, paying off the £210,000 loan out of the proceeds. The company is not just entitled to four twenty-fifths of the profits. After all, the company's £40,000 gave it an equitable interest in the restaurant, which the brothers then used as security for the £210,000 loan, which was repaid out of the proceeds of sale and not out of the brothers' money. Thus the company is entitled to all the profit.

¹ [1983] 1 NSWLR 440; *Re Marriage of Wagstaff* (1990) 14 Fam LR 78, 99 FLR 390; *Australian Postal Corpn v Lutak* (1991) 21 NSWLR 584. In the last case the plaintiff's $20,000 had been used with an equitable mortgagee's $70,000 to buy a $90,000 house sold for $110,000 when $103,000 capital and interest were due to the mortgagee. Bryson J held the plaintiffs were entitled to $40,000, representing their $20,000 charge and the $20,000 profit, so the equitable mortgagee received only $70,000. Because the house could not have been purchased but for the mortgage it is difficult to see why the mortgagee did not have priority over the plaintiff for the $103,000: c f *Abbey National Building Society v Cann* [1991] 1 AC 56; *Equity and Law Home Loans Ltd v Prestidge* [1992] 1 WLR 137.

Paragraph 3

Trust assets mixed with assets of another trust

92.41 If the assets of Trust 'A' and the assets of Trust 'B' are mixed (other than in a current bank account) then any loss is borne rateably according to the values of the mixed assets of the two trusts, eg if £20,000 from Trust 'A' and £10,000 from Trust 'B' were used to purchase a £30,000 car now depreciated to £10,000 in value then the car would be subject to a charge in favour of 'A' and 'B' in the proportions 2 to 1¹. Any gains should similarly be rateably shared².

¹ *Sinclair v Brougham* [1914] AC 398: *Re Diplock* [1948] Ch 465 at 533, 534, 539, CA.
² *Edinburgh Corpn v Lord Advocate* (1879) 4 App Cas 823.

92.42 Until recently, there was generally considered to be an exception to this principle, deriving from *Clayton's* case¹. This case concerned a dispute centring on the appropriation of payments as between a bank and its customer, but it came to be seen as authority for the rule that if a trustee places money belonging to two different sets of beneficiaries into the same unbroken running account², any withdrawals that he makes from the account are deemed to be made in the same order as the payments in, on a 'first in, first out' basis³. Thus, for example, if he puts £10,000 from Trust A into a current bank account, and then puts in £10,000 from Trust B, and then withdraws £10,000 and loses it (or uses it to buy an asset which triples in value), then the loss (or gain) will be attributed solely to the beneficiaries of Trust A.

¹ (1816) 1 Mer 529. For the history of the case see L D Smith The Law of Tracing (1997) pp. 183–194; *Re French Caledonia Travel Service Pty Ltd* (2003) 59 NSWLR 361 at [20]–[172].
² Eg a current bank account, a solicitor's trust account, or a moneylender's account. The rule does not apply where there are distinct and separate debts: *The Mecca* [1897] AC 286; *Re Sherry* (1884) 25 Ch D 692 at 702. Nor does the rule apply to entries on the same day: it is the end-of-day balance which counts: The Mecca at 291.
³ *Pennell v Deffell* (1853) 4 De GM & G 372; *Hancock v Smith* (1889) 41 Ch D 456 at 461; *Re Stenning* [1895] 2 Ch 433; *Re Diplock* [1948] Ch 465 at 553–4.

92.43 As between the beneficiaries of Trust A and Trust B this is an arbitrary and unfair result, and for this reason the 'first in, first out' rule has been discarded in many Commonwealth jurisdictions, in favour of a *pro rata* approach[1]. In *Barlow Clowes International Ltd v Vaughan*[2], the Court of Appeal reaffirmed the general application of *Clayton's* case in English law, except where its application would be impracticable or would result in injustice between the parties. However, a series of more recent English cases suggests that the rule will not often be applied, for the courts are now swift to find that the rule is an impracticable or unjust method of resolving disputes between the victims of shared misfortune, particularly in cases of large-scale fraud[3]. Thus, it now appears that 'in terms of its actual application between beneficiaries who have in any sense met a shared misfortune, it might be more accurate to refer to the exception that is, rather than the rule in, *Clayton's* case'[4].

[1] *Re Ontario Securities Commission* (1985) 30 DLR (4th) 1, affirmed [1988] 2 SCR 172; *Re Registered Securities Ltd* [1991] 1 NZLR 545; *Keefe v Law Society of New South Wales* (1998) 44 NSWLR 451; *Re Esteem Settlement* [2002] JLR 53; *Re French Caledonia Travel Service Pty Ltd* (2003) 59 NSWLR 361; *Re International Investment Unit Trust* [2005] 1 NZLR 270.
[2] [1992] 4 All ER 22.
[3] *El Ajou v Dollar Land Holdings plc (No 2)* [1995] 2 All ER 213 at 222; *Russell-Cooke Trust Co v Prentis [2002] EWHC 2227 (Ch)*, [2003] 2 All ER 478 at [54]–[58]; *Commerzbank Aktiengesellschaft v IMB Morgan plc [2004] EWHC 2771 (Ch)*, [2005] 1 Lloyd's Rep 298 at [43]–[49]; *Re Ahmed & Co (a firm)* [2006] EWHC 480 (Ch) 150 Sol Jo LB 402 at [131]–[138].
[4] *Russell-Cooke Trust Co v Prentis [2002] EWHC 2227 (Ch)*, [2003] 2 All ER 478 at [55].

92.44 *Barlow Clowes* concerned the liquidation of an investment company whose fraudulent managers had stolen most of the company's assets, leaving thousands of investors out of pocket. The question arose as to how the surviving assets should be distributed between the investors. The court held that the rule in *Clayton's* case should not be used to resolve this question because the investors had all intended that their money should be pooled in a single fund for investment purposes, so that it would conform with their original intentions if they all shared rateably in what remained in the pool. However, Woolf and Leggatt LJJ[1] also indicated that a 'rolling charge' solution might be fairer than rateable sharing so that claimants should share losses and gains to the fund in proportion to their interest in the fund immediately prior to each withdrawal.

[1] [1992] 4 All ER 22 at 35 and 44.

92.45 This would work as follows. Suppose that a trustee pays £2,000 from Trust A and then £4,000 from Trust B into an empty current bank account. He then withdraws £3,000 and loses it. He then pays in £3,000 from Trust C before withdrawing another £3,000 to buy shares whose value increases tenfold. He then withdraws the remaining £3,000 and loses it. Applying the "rolling charge" rule, the first loss must be borne by A and B in the ratio 1:2, and C need not bear this loss at all. Immediately after the first withdrawal the remaining £3,000 would be attributed to A and B in the ratio 1:2, and after the next deposit, the £6,000 in the account would be attributable to A, B, and C in the ratio 1:2:3. Hence, the shares should be attributed to them in the same proportion, leaving A with shares worth £5,000, B with shares worth £10,000 and C with shares worth £15,000. In contrast, the *pro rata* rule would attribute all gains and losses in proportion to the total contributions made by each Trust, giving a ratio of 2:4:3, and leaving A with shares worth £6,667, B with shares worth £13,333, and C with shares worth £10,000. The 'first in, first out' rule, meanwhile, would produce the result that all of A's money is lost, that £1000 of B's money is lost, that all the shares belong to B, and that all of C's money is lost.

92.46 In *Shalson v Russo*[1], Rimer J suggested that the rolling charge rule should always be used to resolve cases of this kind, because the *pro rata* rule ignores evidence of what has actually happened to the claimants' money: thus, in the example, we know that no part of Trust C's £3,000 can have gone into the trustee's first withdrawal, suggesting that Trust C should not have to share this loss with Trust A and Trust B. Rimer J's position can certainly be supported by reference to *Roscoe v Winder*[2], but in a case involving thousands of investors and hundreds of thousands of deposits and withdrawals, the expense and practical difficulties of calculation using the rolling charge rule may be prohibitive, leaving the claimants with a choice between the rough justice of the *pro rata* rule, and the even rougher justice of 'first in, first out'.

[1]   [2005] EWHC 1637 (Ch), [2005] Ch 281 at [150].
[2]   [1915] 1 Ch 62.

Trust assets mixed with trustee's assets and assets of another trust

92.47 If the mixed fund contains not just the moneys of trust funds but also the trustee's own money, one must first apply the principles applicable to a trustee's own money mixed with trust money of an amount corresponding to the aggregate value of all the mixed trust funds. Once the total entitlement of those mixed funds has been determined then one applies the principles above discussed in apportioning such mixed funds between different trusts.

Paragraph 4

Common law and equitable tracing rules

92.48 The traditional view for many years has been that there are different tracing rules in equity and at common law, and that the equitable tracing rules are more favourable to claimants than the common law tracing rules, most noticeably because it is impossible to trace through mixtures of money in bank accounts at common law, something which the equitable tracing rules allow[1]. It has also been said by the courts for many years that claimants must show that their property was held on trust or that it was subject to some other fiduciary relationship before they can take advantage of the equitable tracing rules with a view to tracing through mixtures in bank accounts[2].

[1]   *Sinclair v Brougham* [1914] AC 398 at 419–420 per Viscount Haldane LC; *Banque Belge pour l'Étranger v Hambrouck* [1921] 1 KB 321 at 328 per Bankes LJ and at 330 per Scrutton LJ; *Re Diplock* [1948] Ch 465 at 518 per curiam; *Agip (Africa) Ltd v Jackson*

[1991] Ch 547 at 566 per Fox LJ. See too *Taylor v Plumer* (1815) 3 M & S 562 at 575 per Lord Ellenborough, which has often been said to stand for the proposition that tracing through mixtures in bank accounts is not possible at common law, but which in fact lays down a rule about claiming – moreover, the case was ultimately decided on equitable principles, as confirmed in *Trustee of FC Jones & Son (a firm) v Jones* [1997] Ch 159 at 169 per Millett LJ.

2   *Sinclair v Brougham* [1914] AC 398 at 421 per Viscount Haldane LC; *Re Diplock* [1948] Ch 465 at 536–537 per curiam; *Agip (Africa) Ltd v Jackson* [1991] Ch 547 at 566 per Fox LJ; *Boscawen v Bajwa* [1995] 4 All ER 769 at 777 per Millett LJ.

92.49 These findings were always suspect as a matter of authority[1]. They were inconsistent with a long line of cases in which the courts did not require claimants to establish a fiduciary relationship before invoking the equitable tracing rules with a view to showing that their money had been used to pay off securities to which they sought to be subrogated[2]. They were also inconsistent with *Marsh v Keating*[3], in which the House of Lords advised by 12 common law judges was willing to accept that the common law could trace through a mixed bank account. Finally, Viscount Haldane LC's finding in *Sinclair v Brougham*[4] that there can be no tracing at common law where money has been lent and placed in a bank account was founded on a misunderstanding of Thesiger LJ's previous, undoubtedly correct statement in *Re Hallett's Estate*[5] that a claimant who makes an unsecured loan to a defendant cannot as a general rule make a proprietary claim to the defendant's assets to secure repayment of the loan.

1   L D Smith The Law of Tracing (1997) at pp 123–130 and 168–174.
2   For example, *Marlow v Pitfeild* (1719) 1 P Wms 558; *Baroness Wenlock v River Dee Co* (1887) 19 QBD 155; *Orakpo v Manson Investments Ltd* [1978] AC 95.
3   (1834) 2 Cl & Fin 250, discussed in J Edelman 'Marsh v Keating' in C Mitchell and P Mitchell (eds) Landmark Cases in the Law of Restitution (2006) 97.
4   [1914] AC 398 at 419–421.
5   (1880) 13 Ch D 696 at 723–724. Also *Halifax Building Society v Thomas [1996] Ch 217*,[1995] 4 All ER 673,CA (secured loan)

92.50 These objections to the traditional view are now of subsidiary importance, however, following the House of Lords' landmark speeches in *Foskett v McKeown*[1]. Lord Steyn and Lord Millett both explained that there is now only one set of tracing rules in English law, applicable to common law and equitable claimants alike, and although their observations on this point were obiter, it seems most unlikely that they will not be followed in future cases[2]. Hence, it is now clear that English law does not distinguish between two sets of tracing rules, and does not restrict the availability of a more claimant-friendly set of 'equitable' rules to claimants who can show that their property was held subject to a fiduciary relationship.

1   [2001] 1 AC 102.
2   For dicta following Foskett on this point, see *Bracken Partners Ltd v Gutteridge [2003] EWHC 1064 (Ch),* [2003] 2 BCLC 84 at [121] (not relevant on appeal: [2003] EWCA Civ 1875, [2004] 1 BCLC 377 though at [29] Mantell LJ cited Lord Millett's dicta that the tracing rules are the same at common law and in equity); *Dick v Harper* [2006] BPIR 20 at [43]. But compare *Shalson v Russo [2003] EWHC 1637 (Ch)* [2005] Ch 281 at [103]-[104]; *Compagnie Noga D'importation et D'Exportation SA v Australia and New Zealand Banking Group Ltd* [2005] EWHC 225 (Comm) at [16].

92.51 In the relevant part of Lord Steyn's speech, he observed that[1]:

'counsel for the purchasers from time to time invoked "the rules of tracing". By that expression he was placing reliance on a corpus of supposed rules of law, divided into common law and equitable rules. In truth tracing is a process of identifying assets: it belongs to the realm of evidence. It tells us nothing about legal or equitable rights to the assets traced. In a crystalline analysis Professor Birks ("The Necessity of a Unitary Law of Tracing", essay in *Making Commercial Law, Essays in Honour of Roy Goode* (1997), pp 239–258) explained, at p 257, that there is a unified regime for tracing and that "it allows tracing to be cleanly separated from the business of asserting rights in or in relation to assets successfully traced". Applying this reasoning Professor Birks concludes, at p 258:

"that the modern law is equipped with various means of coping with the evidential difficulties which a tracing exercise is bound to encounter. The process of identification thus ceases to be either legal or equitable and becomes, as is fitting, genuinely neutral as to the rights exigible in respect of the assets into which the value in question is traced. The tracing exercise once successfully completed, it can then be asked what rights, if any, the plaintiff can, on his particular facts, assert. It is at that point that it becomes relevant to recall that on some facts those rights will be personal, on others proprietary, on some legal, and on others equitable."

I regard this explanation as correct. It is consistent with orthodox principle. It clarifies the correct approach to so-called tracing claims. It explains what tracing is about without providing answers to controversies about legal or equitable rights to assets so traced.'

1   [2001] 1 AC 102 at 113.

92.52   Lord Millett agreed[1]:

'Given its nature, there is nothing inherently legal or equitable about the tracing exercise. There is thus no sense in maintaining different rules for tracing at law and in equity. One set of tracing rules is enough. The existence of two has never formed part of the law in the United States: see *Scott on Trusts*, 4th ed (1989), section 515, at pp 605–609. There is certainly no logical justification for allowing any distinction between them to produce capricious results in cases of mixed substitutions by insisting on the existence of a fiduciary relationship as a precondition for applying equity's tracing rules. The existence of such a relationship may be relevant to the nature of the claim which the plaintiff can maintain, whether personal or proprietary, but that is a different matter.'

1   [2001] 1 AC 102 at 129–130.

92.53 In the past, the courts have been tempted to discover fiduciary relationships between the parties to litigation not because the parties' relationship has been of the sort that would normally attract the imposition of fiduciary duties, but because the courts have wished to enable the claimant to take advantage of the equitable tracing rules. So, for example, it has been held that a thief owes a fiduciary duty to his victim, with the result that the victim can invoke the equitable tracing rules in order to trace through the thief's sale of the stolen property and mixing of the proceeds in a bank account, so as to make a proprietary claim to the traceable proceeds of the victim's property[1]. Findings of this sort debase the currency of the fiduciary concept, and run counter to Sopinka J's warning in the Supreme Court of Canada, in *Norberg v*

Wynrib[2], that 'equitable doctrines cannot be imported simply in order to improve the nature and extent of the remedy'. One effect of the findings in *Foskett* will be to relieve the courts from the need to do this in order to give claimants access to the equitable tracing rules.

[1] *Black v Freedman* (1910) 12 CLR 105 at 110, endorsed by Lord Templeman in *Lipkin Gorman v Karpnale Ltd* [1991] 2 AC 548 at 565–6; *Bishopsgate Investment Management Ltd v Maxwell* [1993] Ch 1 at 70; *Westdeutsche Landesbank Girozentrale v Islington London Borough Council* [1996] AC 669 at 716, distinguished in *Box v Barclays Bank plc* [1998] Lloyd's Rep Bank 185, on the basis that the rule does not extend to fraudulently induced transfers.

[2] (1992) 92 DLR (4th) 449 at 481.

Paragraph 5

Need for identified traced product of trust or fiduciary property

92.54 The equitable remedies of an equitable charge or of a constructive trust of a proportionate share can only be imposed in respect of an identified traced product of property subject to a trust or other fiduciary relationship[1]. The claimant has to identify his original proprietary right in respect of a particular asset and then show that there are transactional links between such original asset and a new asset in the defendant's hands so that the value of the original asset is represented in the new asset.

[1] *Napier and Ettrick v Kershaw* [1993] AC 713, [1993] 1 All ER 385, HL; *Bishopsgate Investment Management Ltd v Homan* [1995] Ch 211, [1995] 1 All ER 347, CA and paras 92.21–92.22 above.

92.55 A wrongdoing trustee who, deliberately or fortuitously, has transactional links occurring in foreign jurisdictions having no concept of equitable proprietary ownership cannot thereby thwart the tracing process of the English forum to determine the amount for which he is personally liable[1] nor should he thereby thwart a proprietary claim to the traced assets that establish the amount of that personal liability. Factually, nothing will be traceable if the original asset is sold and the proceeds spent on a holiday or on a horse which dies or on a painting which is destroyed in circumstances where no insurance compensation[2] is available. As a matter of law if the claimant authorises his proprietary interest to be displaced by a transaction creating only a debtor-creditor relationship he will only have a personal claim against that debtor, ie if the trustee or fiduciary is authorised to lend the claimant's money to himself[3] or to mix the claimant's resin with his own materials so as to produce chipboard[4] (there being no agreement as to the claimant then becoming a proportionate owner of the chipboard[5]).

[1] *El Ajou v Dollar Land Holdings Ltd plc* [1993] 3 All ER 717 at 736–737 accepted on appeal, [1994] 2 All ER 685. The case involved personal liability, but the principle is broad enough to compel a defendant in the jurisdiction to treat assets within the jurisdiction as trust assets, if having regard to their history and his state of knowledge, it would be unconscionable for him to treat them as his own: see Millet LJ at 737h. The defendant could be compelled by an in personam order to bring foreign assets within the jurisdiction or transfer title to foreign immovables: cf *Webb v Webb* [1992] 1 All ER 17; affd [1994] QB 696; *Cook Industries Inc v Galliher* [1979] Ch 439; *Derby & Co Ltd v Weldon* (No 6)

92.55 *The liability of the trustees*

[1990] 1 WLR 1139. However if the defendant is an innocent donee who acquired a good clean title in a foreign lex situs the English court should recognise the effect of the lex situs.
2   See para 92.39 above.
3   *Space Investments Ltd v Canadian Imperial Bank of Commerce Trust Co* [1986] 3 All ER 75, [1986] 1 WLR 1072, HL; *Re Goldcorp Exchange Ltd [1995] 1 AC 74,* [1994] 2 All ER 806; *Customs and Excise Comrs v Richmond Theatre Management Ltd* [1995] STC 257.
4   *Borden (UK) Ltd v Scottish Timber Products Ltd* [1981] Ch 25.
5   *Coleman v Harvey* [1989] 1 NZLR 723.

Money and bank accounts

92.56 Once a wrongdoing fiduciary has mixed trust funds with his own in a bank account an equitable lien or charge will automatically attach to that account and therefore to moneys paid out of that account, whether into other accounts (so purchasing a chose in action) or to purchase a painting or Whizzo shares, until the fiduciary discharges the burden of showing that he has reinstated the trust fund and remedied the breach of trust[1]. Once it has been established with the help, if need be, of any presumptions against wrongdoers that a bank account or some shares or some land is subject to an equitable charge then such charge will automatically bind a transferee of such property other than a bona fide purchaser of a legal interest without notice[2].

1   *El Ajou v Dollar Land Holdings plc* [1993] 3 All ER 717 at 735–736; *Foskett v McKeown* [2001] 1 AC 102 at 130.
2   *El Ajou v Dollar Land Holdings plc* [1993] 3 All ER 717 at 735–736 and [1994] 2 All ER 685 at 701 per Hoffmann LJ.

92.57 Money passing through a clearing system raises difficulties because of the netting off that occurs between banks that are members of such systems. The courts look at 'the substance of the matter'[1] to see if there is a sufficient nexus between the debit to X's account and the credit to Y's account to enable the latter to be treated as representing the former. In *Agip (Africa) Ltd v Jackson*[2] it was accepted that equity can trace money through a clearing system and even identify a credit with a debit where the credit entry was the first in time while in *El Ajou v Dollar Land Holdings plc*[3] money was traced through back to back credit facilities.

1   *Agip (Africa) Ltd v Jackson* [1991] Ch 547 at 561, [1992] 4 All ER 451 at 462.
2   [1990] Ch 265; affd [1991] Ch 547, the plaintiff's banker buying on credit from Lloyds Bank a payment to Baker Oil and then debiting the plaintiff's account with the payment.
3   [1993] 3 All ER 717 accepted by CA [1994] 2 All ER 685.

92.58 The tracing process is used to identify what is trust property[1] so that one can then tell whether or not a breach of trust has occurred in respect of that property. In clearing systems, through which pass the proceeds of sale of trust property or dividends on trust shares, it seems that there will be an equitable charge over a very valuable chose in action.

1   In *Re Hallett's Estate* (1889) 13 Ch D 696 at 708–709 Jessel MR emphasised 'there is no distinction between what is a rightful and wrongful disposition of the property so far as regards the right of the beneficial owner to follow the proceeds.'

92.59 Take the C Bank with a £100 million credit with the Bank of England operating the clearing system and the D Bank with a £90 million credit with the Bank of England. During the day transactions occur such that C Bank owes D Bank £15 million while D Bank owes C Bank £20 million necessitating C Bank being credited with £5 million so that its credit stands at £105 million while D Bank's credit stands at £85 million. If a purchaser of trust property paid the £50,000 price out of his account with C Bank in favour of the trust account with D Bank, the £50,000 will be regarded as within the £15 million treated as passing[1] (despite the 'netting off') to the D Bank, so that there will be an equitable charge for £50,000 arising by operation of law over the £85 million credit balance with the Bank of England. The chose in action with the Bank of England charged with payment of the trust's £50,000 will cease to be so upon D Bank crediting the trust account with the £50,000 under an authorisation to deposit the money with itself by way of loan (enabling money to be loaned to the Bank of England). The trust will then own a chose in action against the D Bank[2] so that if the trustee then uses it by withdrawing £50,000 to buy a painting the beneficiaries will be able to trace and claim the painting.

[1]   *Re Harmony and Montague Tin Mining Co Ltd Spargo's Case* (1873) 8 Ch App 407.
[2]   *Space Investments Ltd v Canadian Imperial Bank of Commerce Trust Co (Bahamas) Ltd* [1986] 3 All ER 75; *Customs and Excise Comrs v Richmond Theatre Management Ltd* [1995] STC 257. For further discussions of the issues explored here, see L D Smith 'Tracing and Electronic Funds Transfers' in F D Rose (ed) Restitution and Banking Law (Mansfield Press 1998) p. 120.

Payment of debts with trust money

92.60 In *Re Diplock*[1], the Court of Appeal considered that a tracing process would come to an end, and that a claimant would be left with nothing into which he might trace the value inherent in his property, where the property or its traceable proceeds are used to pay off a debt. The better view, however, is that where a trustee misappropriates trust money and uses it to pay off a debt which he owes to a creditor, there are two ways in which the beneficiaries might trace into an asset to which they can then assert a proprietary claim.

[1]   [1948] Ch 465 at 549; followed in *Euroactividade AG v Mason Investments Ltd* [1994] NPC 55.

92.61 First, if the trustee's debt to the creditor was secured by a charge over the trustee's property, the beneficiaries can ask the court to treat them, by a legal fiction, as though the creditor's charge had not been extinguished after all, but had instead been assigned by the creditor to the beneficiaries, in order that the beneficiaries might enforce the charge against the trustee's property to secure restoration of the trust fund[1]. This remedy is known as subrogation. In *Boscawen v Bajwa*[2], Millett LJ (as he then was) observed that, contrary to the Court of Appeal's finding in *Re Diplock*, 'the discharge of the creditor's security is certainly not a bar to subrogation in equity; it is rather a precondition'. In *Banque Financière de la Cité v Parc (Battersea) Ltd*[3], Lord Hoffmann stressed the fictional nature of the subrogation remedy, and held that it lies in the court's discretion to tailor the remedy to fit the circumstances of a case, by varying the extent to which a claimant is entitled to be treated as though he has acquired the creditor's rights, to ensure that his fictional acquisition of these rights does not unfairly prejudice the position of third parties[4].

1   *M'Mahon v Fetherstonehaugh* [1895] 1 IR 83; *McCullough v Marsden* (1919) 45 DLR 645; *Scotlife Homes Ltd (No 2) v Melinek* [1999] NSWSC 898; *Primlake Ltd (in liquidation) v Matthews Associates* [2006] EWHC 1227 (Ch).
2   [1996] 1 WLR 328 at 340.
3   [1999] 1 AC 221 at 236.
4   For further judicial consideration of this point, see *Halifax Mortgage Services Ltd v Muirhead* (1997) 76 P & CR 418, CA, and for general discussion, see C Mitchell 'Subrogation: Persistent Misunderstandings' in A Burrows and Lord Rodger (eds) Mapping the Law: Essays in Honour of Peter Birks (2006).

92.62 Secondly, if the trustee borrows £10,000 from a creditor, and uses this money to purchase an asset, and then uses money which he has misappropriated from the trust to pay off his debt, then the beneficiaries should be able to 'trace backwards' through the payment of the debt into the asset which was purchased with the borrowed money, and identify the value inherent in the asset as the traceable proceeds of the value inherent in the trust property. In other words, the wrongdoing trustee should not be able to deny the beneficiaries' claims to be treated as if they had been original co-purchasers. This analysis, suggested by Professor Smith[1], has support in England at Court of Appeal level[2]: from Dillon LJ *in Bishopsgate Investment Management v Homan*[3] (although in the same case it was disapproved by Leggatt LJ[4]), and from Scott V-C in *Foskett v McKeown*[5]. However, in the latter case, Scott V-C considered that it should only be possible to 'trace backwards' through a wrongdoing trustee's payment of a debt into the asset purchased with the borrowed money if it can be shown that it was the trustee's intention at the time of borrowing the money that he would later wrongfully use the trust money to repay his creditor. With respect, however, this proposed restriction, in favouring the trustee, seems likely to cause evidential difficulties in practice, and, in principle, there is no compelling reason why the beneficiaries' right to 'backwards tracing' should be made contingent on the trustee's state of mind at the time of the original loan transaction.

1   L D Smith 'Tracing into the Payment of a Debt' [1995] CLJ 290, esp pp 292–295, expanded in L D Smith The Law of Tracing (1997), pp 146–152.
2   Cf *Re Agricultural Credit Corpn of Saskatchewan v Pettyjohn* [1991] 3 WWR 689 (Sask CA).
3   [1995] Ch 211 at 216–217.
4   [1995] Ch 211 at 221–212. One could argue that if the trustee's personal creditworthiness enables him to become legal beneficial owner of an asset, then his full ownership should not be affected by subsequent events (other than the owner's voluntary disposition of all or part of his title).
5   [1998] Ch 265 at 283–284, not considered on appeal to HL: [2001] 1 AC 102.

ARTICLE 93
APPLICATION BY INTERIM CLAIM TO SAFEGUARD THE TRUST PROPERTY IF ENDANGERED

93.1

(1)   Where the court is satisfied that trust property[1] is in danger:

(a) by reason of the active[2] or passive[3] misconduct of the trustees; or

(b) by reason of the trustees residing out of the jurisdiction of the court[4];

an injunction will be granted on an interim claim[5] at the instance of any person with a right to make the trustees account[6] for the trust property (including a co-trustee[7], even if he himself breached his trust[8]) either compelling the trustees to do their duty[9], or restraining them from interfering with the trust property[10], as the case may require; and, if expedient, a receiver will be appointed[11].

(2) Where a trustee has admitted that he has trust moneys in his hands, and the court considers the trust property is endangered, an interim order may be made for payment of the amount into court; but there must be an admission direct or implied, written or verbal, and no dispute as to the defendant's liability, as the court cannot try the question on an interim claim[12].

[1] As to what amounts to trust property, see *A-G for Hong Kong v Reid* [1994] 1 AC 324, [1994] 1 All ER 1, PC, discussed at paras 33.3–33.5 above; *Eldan Services Ltd v Chandag Motors Ltd* [1990] 3 All ER 459; *A v C* [1981] QB 956n.

[2] *Earl Talbot v Hope-Scott* (1858) 4 K & J 139; *Middleton v Dodswell* (1806) 13 Ves 266; *Dance v Goldingham* (1873) 8 Ch App 902.

[3] *Foley v Burnell* (1783) 1 Bro CC 274; *Fletcher v Fletcher* (1844) 4 Hare 67.

[4] *Noad v Backhouse* (1843) 2 Y & C Ch Cas 529; *Dickins v Harris* (1866) 14 LT 98.

[5] See CPR Pt 25, r 25 for an order for the detention, custody or preservation of trust property by way of interim remedy.

[6] See Article 60. In Australia an injunction was granted to preserve the interest of a child en vetre sa mere at the instance of the child's father who was appointed by the court to represent the child: *Yunghams v Candoora No 19 Pty Ltd* (2000)2 ITELR 589; CPR Pt 19, r 19.7 for English representation orders.

[7] *Young v Murphy* [1996] 1 VR 279 (a thorough survey); *Re Forest of Dean Coal Mining Co* (1878) 10 Ch D 450; *Space Investments Ltd v Canadian Imperial Bank of Commerce Trust Co (Bahamas) Ltd* [1986] 1 WLR 1072 at 1074, PC.

[8] *Baynard v Woolley* (1855) 20 Beav 583.

[9] See note 3 above.

[10] See note 2 above.

[11] See cases in note 325, above, and *Bennett v Colley* (1832) 5 Sim 182; Supreme Court Act 1981, s 37.

[12] *London Syndicate v Lord* (1878) 8 Ch D 84 at 90; *Freeman v Cox* (1878) 8 Ch D 148; *Hampden v Wallis* (1884) 27 Ch D 251; *Dunn v Campbell* (1879) 27 Ch D 254n; *Porrett v White* (1885) 31 Ch D 52, CA; *Wanklyn v Wilson* (1887) 35 Ch D 180; *Re Beeny* [1894] 1 Ch 499; *Neville v Matthewman* [1894] 3 Ch 345, CA; *Re Benson* [1899] 1 Ch 39.

Paragraph 1

Interim injunction principles

93.2 The approach prescribed by *American Cynamid Co v Ethicon Ltd[1]* needs to be followed. First, the plaintiff must show an arguable case. If an arguable case is shown then the balance of convenience should be applied. If the scale appears very evenly balanced it is then legitimate to take into account the strength or weakness of the claimant's case. However, even if the claimant's case is weak the court may grant him protection falling short of a full preservation order. Thus in one case[2] the Court of Appeal ordered the defendant, Central Bank of Cyprus, to earmark the £8 million, representing the plaintiff's claimed traceable money, in a separate account and to refrain from dealing with it otherwise than in the normal course of its banking business and only to the extent that no other funds were available in England for that purpose. The Bank was also required to inform the plaintiff's solicitors in advance of any proposed use to be made of the £8 million and, at the same time, to give details of all foreign currency reserves for the time being held in England. It may be that such flexibility might enable a court to preserve a proportion of the disputed assets relative to the strength of a claimant's case.

1   [1975] AC 396 [1975] 1 All ER 504, HL.
2   *Polly Peck International plc v Nadir (No 2)* [1992] 4 All ER 769 at 784 and 787, CA.

Loss of a portion of the trust property

93.3 The loss of a portion of the trust property affords prima facie ground for appointing a receiver on an interim claim[1]; and so does reasonable anticipation of a loss.

1   *Evans v Coventry* (1854) 5 De GM & G 911.

Trust property in danger

93.4 In support of an interim injunction where the trust property is in danger, there may be claimed an interim order directing information to be provided about the location of trust property or property claimed to be trust property or the traceable product of trust property[1]. Such order can be made in respect of foreign proceedings where no claim is made over which the English court has jurisdiction[2].

1   CPR Pt 25, r 25.1(1); *Norwich Pharmacal Co v Customs and Excise Comrs* [1974] AC 133, HL. Equity does not want to act in vain and wants its orders to be effective: *Banker's Trust Co v Shapira* [1980] 1 WLR 1274 at 1280, CA.
2   CPR Pt 25, r 25.4.

93.5 If trust property is in a jurisdiction that neither recognises trusts nor would recognise an order of the English court, the court may order the property to be brought within the jurisdiction[1].

1   *Derby & Co Ltd v Weldon (No 6)* [1990] 1 WLR 1139, CA.

93.6 The court will appoint a receiver and grant an injunction where, from the character or condition of the trustee, he is not a fit person to have the control of the trust property; as, for instance, where he is insolvent[1], or about to become bankrupt[2], or is a person of dissolute habits, or dishonest[3] or in contempt of court orders[4].

1   *Mansfield v Shaw* (1818) 3 Madd 100; *Gladdon v Stoneman* (1808) 1 Madd 143n, followed in *Bowen v Phillips* [1897] 1 Ch 174.
2   *Re H's Estate* (1875) 1 Ch D 276.

3   See *Everett v Prythergch* (1841) 12 Sim 363.
4   *Clarke v Heathfield* [1985] ICR 203, CA.

93.7 So where, there being some disagreement between three trustees, the majority acted alone and took securities in their own names, omitting the name of the dissentient trustee, it was held that the plaintiff (a beneficiary) was entitled to a receiver[1].

1   *Swale v Swale* (1856) 22 Beav 584.

93.8 Now that trustees can be removed and replaced on a wide variety of grounds it will rarely be necessary to appoint a receiver except as an interim measure where the affairs of the trust are in special disorder requiring a troubleshooter to resolve matters that most trustees could not reasonably be expected to do. One such special case involved the National Union of Mineworkers during the lengthy miners' strike where the union trustees were salting money away in devious ways in various countries and were in contempt of court orders: the Court of Appeal[1] even upheld an ex parte (without notice) order for the removal of the trustees and the appointment of a receiver.

1   *Clarke v Heathfield* [1985] ICR 203, CA.

93.9 The appointment of a receiver does not necessarily involve removing the trustees since it may be a temporary expedient in the interests of continuing the management of the trust where it is needed pending resolution of a problem. As Megarry V-C said in *A-G v Schonfield*[1], 'The remedy is one to be moulded to the needs of the situation: within proper limits a receiver may be given such powers as the court considers to be appropriate to the particular case.' Thus, a receiver may even be appointed of assets worldwide[2].

1   [1980] 1 WLR 1182 at 1187.
2   *Derby & Co Ltd v Weldon (Nos 3 & 4)* [1990] Ch 65, CA.

Where same persons trustees under conflicting settlements

93.10 In *Earl Talbot v Hope-Scott*[1] lands were vested in trustees by Act of Parliament upon trust for sale, and, subject thereto, upon trusts inalienably annexing the rents to the earldom of Shrewsbury. The Earl of Shrewsbury attempted to disentail (which of course he could not do effectually), and demised the lands to the same trustees, upon trust for a particular claimant of the title. The trustees accepted this trust, and claimed to receive the rents in that character, pending proceedings by the plaintiff to establish his claim to the earldom. A receiver of the rents was, however, appointed on his application, upon the ground that the trusts of the will were in conflict with the prior trusts upon which the trustees held the estate.

1   (1858) 4 K & J 139; and see to same effect *Price v Loaden* (1856) 21 Beav 508.

93.11 *The liability of the trustees*

Injunction granted to restrain improper sale

93.11 Again, the court will grant an injunction to restrain a sale by trustees at an undervalue[1] or a sale of land held on trust for sale without appointing a second trustee and without consulting the beneficiaries[2].

1   *Anon* (1821) 6 Madd 10; and see *Webb v Earl of Shaftesbury* (1802) 7 Ves 480; *Milligan v Mitchell* (1833) 1 My & K 446; *Dance v Goldingham* (1873) 8 Ch App 902; *Wheelwright v Walker* (1883) 31 WR 912; *Buttle v Saunders* [1950] 2 All ER 193.
2   *Waller v Waller* [1967] 1 All ER 305, [1967] 1 WLR 451.

Where new trustees or co-trustees sue for redress of breach of trust

93.12 When new trustees or continuing co-trustees sue for restoration of lost assets or value to the trust fund they need not make the beneficiaries parties, because they sufficiently represent the beneficiaries interests[1] unless it seems[2], all the beneficiaries are ascertained and of full age and capacity and might wish an unauthorised investment to be retained and not sold.

1   CPR Pt 50, r 50.1 and Sch1, RSC Ord 15 r 14; see *Re Cross* (1881) 20 Ch D 109; *Williams v Barton* [1927] 2 Ch 9; *Young v Murphy* [1996] 1 VR 279.
2   *Butler v Butler* (1877) 7 Ch D 116 at 120, CA.

Paragraph 2

Payment into court ordered on motion

93.13 It is obviously a severe measure to order a trustee to pay money into court pending the trial of an action. It will, therefore, only be done where the trustee has admitted that he has the money *in his hands*, or possibly where he has admitted that he has had it and has either misappropriated it or not accounted for it[1], or not invested it[2], or has invested or paid it away improperly[3], and it is clear that he has no real defence.

1   *Freeman v Cox* (1878) 8 Ch D 148.
2   *Wiglesworth v Wiglesworth* (1852) 16 Beav 269.
3   *Bourne v Mole* (1845) 8 Beav 177; *Re Whiteley* (1886) 33 Ch D 347; affd sub nom *Learoyd v Whiteley* (1887) 12 App Cas 727; *Scott v Becher* (1817) 4 PR 346; *Meyer v Montriou* (1841) 4 Beav 343; but cf *Crompton and Evans' Union Bank v Burton* [1895] 2 Ch 711.

Practice no longer favoured

93.14 The court does not, however, favour these interim applications as readily as it once did; and the Court of Appeal laid it down in *Neville v Matthewman*[1] that:

'unless care is taken in making such orders a very dangerous precedent may be established. Such orders may easily become very oppressive. Under the old practice of the Court of Chancery such an order could only have been made upon an admission contained in the defendant's answer. We all know with what

1108

care answers were framed; and if by his answer the defendant admitted that he had in his hands money belonging to the plaintiff, there could be no danger in ordering him to pay it into court.'

1   *Neville v Matthewman* [1894] 3 Ch 345 at 353, CA, per Lindley LJ. The subsequent case of *Nutter v Holland* [1894] 3 Ch 408, was an application by originating summons under Ord 55, r 3 (now Ord 85, r 2). See also *Crompton and Evans' Union Bank v Burton* [1895] 2 Ch 711.

93.15 Lord Justice Davey added that an extension of the doctrine was made by Jessel MR in *Freeman v Cox*[1], and that he (the Lord Justice) was not disposed to carry the practice any further. In his opinion such orders ought to be made only when it is made out to the satisfaction of the court that the defendant has the sum claimed *in his hands and that he has no real defence*. In *Re Benson*[2], however, North J ordered payment into court, although the trustee deposed that he had spent it.

1   (1878) 8 Ch D 148.
2   [1899] 1 Ch 39 but cf *Re Clinton's Will* (1910) 10 SRNSW 465.

ARTICLE 94
DISHONEST BREACH OF TRUST MAY BE A CRIME

94.1

A trustee will be guilty of theft under the Theft Act 1968 if he dishonestly appropriates property belonging to another with the intention of permanently depriving the other of it[1].

1   Theft Act 1968, s 1. For general commentary, see Sir J Smith The Law of Theft 8th edn (1997); E Griew The Theft Acts 7th edn (1995).

Actus reus

'APPROPRIATES'

94.2 Any assumption of the rights of an owner amounts to an appropriation, including, after acquisition without stealing, a later assumption of a right to it by keeping or dealing with it as owner[1]. A disposal for his own purposes of goods held in trust by a trustee will constitute theft[2].

1   Theft Act 1968, s 3(1). A transferee for value acting in good faith is protected by s 3(2) from the consequences that might otherwise arise from a defect in the transferor's title.
2   *International Factors Ltd v Rodriguez* [1979] QB 351 at 358, [1979] 1 All ER 17 at 21, CA.

'PROPERTY'

94.3 Property includes money and all other property, real or personal, including things in action and other intangible property[1]. A trustee, unlike other persons, may steal land or anything forming part of the land where he deals with it in breach of the confidence[2] reposed in him[3].

1   Theft Act 1968, s 4(1). Thus in *R v Hilton* [1997] 2 Cr App Rep 445, where the defendant
     was a designated signatory of a bank account belonging to a charity, and he instructed the
     bank to transfer the charity's funds to settle his personal debts, it was held that he stole the
     charity's chose in action against the bank.
2   'Confidence' was intended as a word of general meaning, replacing 'trust' in the Criminal
     Law Revision Committee's draft Bill; see 291 HL Official Report (6th series) col 22.
3   Theft Act 1968, s 4(2)(a).

'BELONGING TO ANOTHER'

94.4 Property is regarded as belonging to any person having possession or
control of it, or having in it any proprietary right or interest (not being an
equitable interest arising solely from an agreement to grant or transfer an
interest)[1]. Where property is subject to a trust, the persons to whom it belongs
include any person having a right to enforce the trust[2]. In the case of
charitable trusts, such person is the Attorney General[3]. In the case of a non-
charitable purpose trust recognised as valid under the Recognition of Trusts
Act 1987 it will be the person nominated as enforcer under the trust
instrument.

1   Theft Act 1968, s 5(1).
2   Theft Act 1968, s 5(2).
3   *National Anti-Vivisection Society v IRC* [1948] AC 31 at 62, HL, [2001] EWCA Crim
     2184, per Lord Simonds. Cf *R v Dyke and Munro* [2002] 1 Cr App Rep 404 where the CA
     held that money stolen from collecting boxes belonged to the charity on whose behalf the
     money was given, which cannot have been correct if the legal form through which the
     charitable purposes were pursued was a trust: only the trustees (and not the trust) have the
     capacity to own property.

94.5 Where a person receives property from or on account of another, and is
under an obligation to the other to retain and deal with that property or its
proceeds in a particular way, the property or proceeds are regarded (as against
him) as belonging to the other[1]. In *R v Mainwaring*[2] in a passage endorsed by
R v Dubar[3] Lawton LJ stated:

   'Whether or not an obligation arises is a matter of law, because an obligation
   must be a legal obligation. But a legal obligation arises only in certain
   circumstances, and in many cases the circumstances cannot be known until the
   facts have been established. It is for the jury, not the judge, to establish the facts
   if they are in dispute. What, in our judgment, a judge ought to do is this: if the
   facts relied upon by the prosecution are in dispute he should direct the jury to
   make their findings on the facts and then say to them: if you find the facts to be
   such and such then I direct you as a matter of law that a legal obligation arose
   to which section 5(3) applies.'

1   Theft Act 1968, s 5(3). See *R v Wills* (1990) 92 Cr App Rep 297; *R v Wain* [1995] 2 Cr
     App Rep 660; *R v Preddy* [1996] AC 815; *R v Klineberg* [1999] 1 Cr App R 427.
     Section 5(3) should cover Quistclose trusts as explained by Lord Millett in *Twinsectra v
     Yardley* [2002] UKHL 12, [2002] 2 AC 164.
2   (1981) 74 Cr App Rep 99 at 107.
3   [1995] 1 All ER 781 at 787 and 789.

CONSTRUCTIVE TRUSTS

94.6 As ever, one must clearly distinguish the constructive trust of specific property from the constructive trustee*ship* imposed upon a defendant so that he may be made personally liable to account as if he had been an express trustee[1]. In the case of personal liability as a constructive trustee where there is simply a debtor—creditor relationship, there being no specific trust property or its traceable equivalent, there can be no question of theft of property belonging to another[2].

[1]   See Article 100 below.
[2]   *A-G's Reference (No 1 of 1985)* [1986] QB 491, [1986] 2 All ER 219, CA, though see paras 94.8–94.10 below.

94.7 Section 5(2) treats property 'as belonging to any person having in it any proprietary right or interest not being an equitable interest arising only' from a specifically enforceable contract. This must surely cover equitable interests under trusts—whether express, resulting or constructive[1]. Thus if an express trustee uses trust property to make a profit for himself and spends the profit on a holiday for his wife and himself the actus reus of theft should be satisfied. The position should be similar if a trustee privately in his own name renewed the trust lease or purchased the freehold reversion to the trust lease[2], then sold his interest at a profit and dissipated the profit in paying off his debts.

[1]   In *R v Clowes* (No 2) [1994] 2 All ER 316 at 335–336 the Court of Appeal held that even equitable interests in bank accounts, to which trust moneys can be traced and over which an equitable charge is imposed, suffice. See too *Re Holmes [2004] EWHC 2020 (Admin),* [2005] 1 Cr App Rep 229 at [21]–[22], where Stanley Burnton J held that money mistakenly paid to a fraudster would be held on constructive trust for the payor following *Westdeutsche Landesbank Girozentrale v Islington London Borough Council* [1996] AC 669 at 716 per Lord Browne-Wilkinson, and that 'the beneficial interest on property held on constructive trust is "property" within the meaning of the 1968 Act, and is regarded as belonging to the person entitled to that beneficial interest.'
[2]   See Article 33, above.

94.8 The legal position has been obscured somewhat by the Court of Appeal in *A-G's Reference (No 1 of 1985)*[1] where a public house manager, with his barman's assistance, bought beer from a wholesaler intending to make a secret profit from the unauthorised sale of the beer to customers in the pub. They were charged with going equipped for theft when found secretly bringing their own beer into the pub, and they were acquitted.

[1]   [1986] QB 491, [1986] 2 All ER 219, CA.

94.9 The referred questions were 'On a charge of theft, where an employee has used his employer's premises and facilities to make a secret profit, will that secret profit be subject to a constructive trust in favour of the employer? And, if so, does that constructive trust give the employer a proprietary right or interest in the secret profit within section 5(1) of the Theft Act?' The two answers were 'If, which we do not believe, it is properly described as a trust, it is not such a trust as falls within the ambit of section 5(1)' and 'No'.

94.10 Unfortunately, the court did not appreciate that property derived from use of property entrusted to a fiduciary should be regarded as held on a proprietary constructive trust or did not appreciate that the manager's use of his employer's beer pumps, beer glasses, cellars, bar, heating and lighting invoked the application of proprietary constructive trust principles. The court thus overlooked *Reid-Newfoundland Co v Anglo-American Telegraph Co Ltd*[1] where the appellants were entitled to use a special telegraphic wire but not to transmit any commercial messages except for the benefit of the respondents. The appellants made a profit from using the wire for their own business purposes. The Privy Council held[2] 'an obligation in the nature of a trust arose on their part to keep an account of the profits accruing from such use of the wire and to set their profits aside as money belonging to the respondents'. As Page-Wood V-C has stated[3], 'where a chattel is entrusted to an agent to be used for the owner's benefit, all the profits which the agent may make by using that chattel belong to the owner'.

[1]   [1912] AC 555, PC.
[2]   [1912] AC 555 at 559.
[3]   *Shallcross v Oldhan* (1862) 2 John & H 609 at 616.

94.11 On inadequate consideration of the position the court concluded that no constructive trust of the secret profit existed, basing itself on *Lister & Co v Stubbs*[1] which held that where a fiduciary does not use trust property but only uses his fiduciary position (eg to take a bribe) then he is only personally liable to account for the money obtained by use of such position. Since then, a strong Privy Council in *A-G for Hong Kong v Reid*[2] has rejected the difficult distinction between use of fiduciary property and use of fiduciary position, has pointed out case law overlooked in *Lister & Co v Stubbs*, and has refused to apply *Lister v Stubbs*, which can therefore now be regarded as wholly discredited[3]. Moneys like bribes and secret profits, obtained by virtue of a fiduciary position are now held on constructive trust, equity regarding as done that which ought to be done.

[1]   (1890) 45 Ch D 1, CA.
[2]   [1994] 1 AC 324, [1994] 1 All ER 1, discussed at para 33.65 above.
[3]   The Court of Appeal is free to follow the Privy Council decision: *Worcester Works Finance Ltd v Gooden Engineering Ltd* [1972] 1 QB 210. In *Daraydan Holdings Ltd v Solland International Ltd [2005] EWHC 622 (Ch),* [2005] Ch 119 at [75]–[85], Lawrence Collins J considered that the rules of precedent also allowed him to follow Reid in preference to Lister (but see further *National Westminster Bank plc v Spectrum Plus Ltd [2005] UKHL 41,* [2005] 2 AC 680 at [93], [155] and [163]).

94.12 Surprisingly, the court then stated[1]:

'assuming that, contrary to our views, s 5(1) does import the constructive trust into the 1968 Act, on the facts of the case the employers still obtain no proprietary interest. A trustee is not permitted to make a profit from his trust. Therefore, if he uses trust property to make a profit from the trust he is accountable for that profit. If and when such property is identified as a separate piece of property, he may be a constructive trustee of it. However, until the profit is identifiable as a separate piece of property it is not trust property and his obligation is to account only.'

[1]   [1986] 2 All ER 219 at 225, CA.

94.13 With the greatest of respect, these dicta are wholly misconceived since they were uttered without any consideration of the equitable rules which give the claimant an equitable proprietary interest in the traceable product or profit of trust property, even though such may not be a separate piece of property but part of a mixed fund or a property amalgam. The claimant will either have a charge on such fund or amalgam or, if more beneficial, he will be a co-owner thereof according to the proportion of traceable trust property therein[1]. Appreciating this, the Court of Appeal[2] has since held that beneficiaries' equitable interests in bank accounts and withdrawals from them arising from the application of equity's tracing rules are proprietary rights or interests within s 5(1) of the Theft Act 1968.

1 See Article 92, above.
2 *R v Clowes (No 2)* [1994] 2 All ER 316 at 335–336.

94.14 Where two or more persons are involved in fraudulent schemes to sell their own beer or sandwiches and not their employer's on his premises it is now safe[1] to charge them with common law conspiracy to defraud in addition to a statutory conspiracy involving the commission of a specific offence if appropriate. If a defendant is charged under s 25 of the 1968 Act there are problems since it may well be that passengers or customers would not have refused to purchase refreshments from the defendant if they had known he was operating a fraud on his employer so the defendant cannot be said to have been going equipped to cheat the passengers or customers[2]. If charged under s 17 there is the difficulty that since the defendant will not have used his employer's supplies but private supplies, which will not show up in the employer's accounts, there will be no false accounting[3].

1 *R v Cooke* [1986] AC 909, [1986] 2 All ER 985, HL.
2 *R v Cooke* [1986] AC 909, [1986] 2 All ER 985, HL.
3 *R v Cooke* [1986] AC 909, [1986] 2 All ER 985, HL.

Mens rea

'DISHONESTY'

94.15 The issue of dishonesty is a question of fact for the jury[1]. Dishonesty does not necessarily depend upon a correct understanding by an accused of all the legal implications of his conduct: The test is that laid down in *R v Ghosh*[2], namely, whether the accused was acting dishonestly by the standards of ordinary and decent people and, if so, whether he himself must have realised that what he was doing was, by those standards, dishonest[3].

1 *R v Feely* [1973] QB 530, [1973] 1 All ER 341, CA.
2 [1982] QB 1053.
3 *R v Clowes (No 2)* [1994] 2 All ER 316 at 330–331, CA.

94.16 A person's appropriation of property belonging to another is not dishonest if he appropriates it believing (1) he has in law the right to deprive the other of it, (2) he would have the other's consent if the other knew of the circumstances, (3) (except where the property came to him as trustee or personal representative) that the person to whom the property belongs cannot be discovered by taking reasonable steps[1]. Before the Theft Act 1968 a fiduciary who abstracted money from a fund intending to repay shortly without causing any loss was guilty of larceny[2]. Now it is up to the jury to decide whether the fiduciary was acting dishonestly[3]. It has been suggested[4] that the Act might usefully be amended so that 'A person is not guilty of theft by reason only of the fact that, being in lawful control of money or a monetary fund, he appropriates the whole or part of it, intending to repay promptly, in the sure belief that he has resources presently available for virtually immediate repayment, and being certain that he will be able to repay it so as to cause no loss or inconvenience to the owner' since in such circumstances it is hardly likely that a jury would find such person was acting dishonestly.

1   Theft Act 1968, s 2(1). The trustee cannot assert that his inability to discover the beneficiary leads to his own absolute entitlement.
2   *R v Williams* [1953] 1 QB 660.
3   *R v Feely* [1973] QB 530.
4   G Williams (1985) 5 Legal Studies 183 at 189.

'INTENTION OF PERMANENTLY DEPRIVING'[1]

94.17   Where the property is subject to a trust, an intention to defeat the trust is regarded as an intention to deprive of the property any person having the right to enforce the trust[2]. Borrowings do not involve permanent deprivation unless moneys or fungible goods (like bottles of claret) are involved, when the very same notes or bottles are not returned.

1   Theft Act 1968, s 6.
2   Theft Act 1968, s 5(2); and see note 2 at para 94.4 above.

Other offences

94.18   There are six further offences under the Theft Act 1968 which may be committed by a dishonest trustee. These are:

(1)   Obtaining property by deception[1].
(2)   Obtaining a money transfer by deception[2]
(2)   Obtaining a pecuniary advantage by deception[3].
(3)   False accounting[4].
(4)   Publication of false, deceptive or misleading statements by officers of a body corporate or unincorporated association[5].
(5)   Suppression of documents[6].

1   Theft Act 1968, s 15.
2   Theft Act 1968, s 15A. This section was inserted by the Theft (Amendment) Act 1996 in response to *R v Preddy* [1996] AC 815 where the HL held that a defendant cannot be guilty of obtaining property belonging to another where his account is credited following a transfer from another party's bank account, the reason being that the defendant's chose in action against his own bank is a new piece of property that cannot previously have belonged to anyone else.
3   Theft Act 1968, s 16.
4   Theft Act 1968, s 17.

94.19 Where two or more co-trustees agree to do an unlawful act, or to do a lawful act by unlawful means, they will be guilty of conspiracy[1].

1   The Criminal Law Act 1977, ss 1–5, abolishes the common law offence of conspiracy and creates a statutory offence. The 1977 Act does not apply to conspiracy to defraud, on which, see *Scott v Metropolitan Police Comr* [1975] AC 819, [1974] 3 All ER 1032, HL. For the relationship between common law conspiracy to defraud and statutory conspiracy under Criminal Law Act 1977, s 1 see *R v Cooke* [1986] AC 909, [1986] 2 All ER 985, HL. Now see Criminal Justice Act 1987, s 12, intended to allow common law conspiracy to defraud to have the same meaning and width as it had before the 1977 Act.

Chapter 23

PROTECTION ACCORDED TO TRUSTEES IN CASE OF BREACH OF TRUST

ARTICLE 95
GENERAL PROTECTION OF TRUSTEES WHO HAVE ACTED
REASONABLY AND HONESTLY

95.1

If it appears to the court that a trustee (or personal representative) is or may be personally liable for any breach of trust, but that he:
(a)   has acted honestly;
(b)   has acted reasonably; and
(c)   ought fairly to be excused for the breach *and* for omitting to obtain the directions of the court in the matter in which he committed such breach,
then the court may relieve him, either wholly or partly, from personal liability for breach[1]. The onus of proving honesty and reasonableness and that he ought fairly to be excused is cast upon the trustee[2], and whether a trustee acted reasonably and honestly is a question of fact depending on the circumstances of each case, no general principle or rule being possible[3].

---

[1]   Trustee Act 1925, s 61; and see *National Trustees Co of Australasia v General Finance Co of Australasia* [1905] AC 373. The relief could be given without the Act being pleaded: *Singlehurst v Tapscott Steamship Co Ltd* [1899] WN 133; *Re Pawson's Settlement* [1917]

    1 Ch 541; but, in view of CPR Pt 16, r 16.5(2)(a), a trustee or personal representative whose defence did not raise the issue of s 61 and the requisite financial basis could have problems.
2   *Re Stuart* [1897] 2 Ch 583; *Marsden v Regan* [1954] 1 WLR 423.
3   *Re Turner* [1897] 1 Ch 536; *Re Barker* (1898) 77 LT 712; *Re Stuart* [1897] 2 Ch 583; and see *Re Windsor Steam Coal Co (1901) Ltd* [1929] 1 Ch 151.

Reasonableness required as well as honesty

95.2 This statutory rule, now contained in s 61 of the Trustee Act 1925[1] was designed to protect honest trustees, and ought not to be construed in a narrow sense[2]. However all three circumstances must co-exist to entitle a trustee to the benefit of the section, namely,

(1)   he must have acted honestly, and
(2)   he must also have acted reasonably (honest folly is not excused[3]), and
(3)   he ought fairly (that is to say in fairness to himself and other persons who may be detrimentally affected[4]) to be excused not just for the breach but also for omitting to obtain the directions of the court in the matter in which he committed the breach[5].

1   The rule was originally introduced by s 3 of the Judicial Trustees Act 1896. For useful surveys see L A Sheridan 'Excusable Breaches of Trust' (1955) 19 Conv 420; C Stebbings *The Private Trustee in Victorian England* (2002) Chap 6; and J Lowry and R Edmunds 'Excuses' in P Birks & A Pretto (eds) *Breach of Trust* (2002) Chap 9. Similar protection is afforded to company directors by the Companies Act 1985, s 727.
2   *Re Allsop* [1914] 1 Ch 1 at 11 per Cozens-Hardy MR and *Re Grindey* [1898] 2 Ch 593 at 601 per Chitty LJ, CA. As discussed in Article 100, below, those who dishonestly assist in breaches of trust or who knowingly receive misapplied trust property can incur personal liability to the beneficiaries which has traditionally been described as 'personal liability as a constructive trustee'. However defendants who incur such liability may not hold any property on constructive trust, and even if they do, they lie outside the merits of s 61, as would innocent recipients of misapplied trust property who incurred a strict restitutionary liability to the beneficiaries.
3   *Re Turner* [1897] 1 Ch 536; *Re Barker* (1898) 77 LT 712; *Re Stuart* [1897] 2 Ch 583; *Mitchell v Halliwell* [2005] EWHC 937 (Ch) at [49] (no relief for honest trustee who unreasonably failed to ensure that beneficiaries took independent advice); *Barraclough v Mell* [2006] WTLR 203 at [98] (no relief for honest trustee who negligently paid trust assets to wrong people).
4   *Marsden v Regan* [1954] 1 All ER 475, [1954] 1 WLR 423, CA.
5   *National Trustees Co of Australasia v General Finance Co of Australasia* [1905] AC 373.

95.3 The section in its concern for the case where a trustee 'is or *may* be personally liable' extends to actual or possible past liability but not so as to authorise future liability. A trustee can thus invoke the section where he 'may' be liable for breach of trust in respect of past actions, whether or not a breach of trust has actually been committed, but he cannot use the section to obtain immunity in respect of contemplated future actions.

95.4 In *Re Rosenthal*[1] the defendants, who had been acting in the administration of a deceased's estate, transferred a house to the specific devisee without making any provision for payment of the estate duty which should have been borne by the house. The devisee sold the house and the proceeds were remitted to her in Israel where she lived. The defendant paid £270 of the estate duty on the house out of the residuary estate, leaving about £1,500 of estate duty still to be found. The residuary legatee obtained a declaration that the defendants were not entitled to pay the £1,500 out of the residuary estate. Plowman J held that no breach of trust had yet occurred in respect of the outstanding £1,500 to enable the defendants to invoke s 61. The £270 had been paid out of the residuary estate in breach of trust but the defendants were professional trustees and although they had acted honestly they had neither acted reasonably nor ought they fairly to be excused for such a breach of trust.

¹   [1972] 1 WLR 1273.

95.5 The section is not only broad enough to enable the court to excuse surchargeable breaches of trust in the management of trust property[1]; falsifiable payments to the wrong persons[2] and unauthorised acquisitions or dispositions[3] can also be excused.

¹   *Re Smith* (1902) 86 LT 401.
²   *Re Allsop* [1914] 1 Ch 1. Where a trustee or personal representative pays the wrong persons because he does not have notice of illegitimate or legitimated or adopted persons he may have protection under Trustee Act 1925, s 27 (where advertisements placed), Legitimacy Act 1976, s 7 and Adoption Act 1976, s 45.
³   *Perrins v Bellamy* [1898] 2 Ch 521; affd [1899] 1 Ch 797, CA.

What conduct is reasonable

95.6 The requirement of honesty, that is, that the trustee should have acted in good faith for the welfare of the trust, needs no elaboration. As to reasonableness each case must depend upon its own facts.

95.7 A trustee cannot be considered to have acted reasonably, if he has neglected to obtain skilled advice where this is called for[1]. Trustees vested with a discretion are not protected by the section if they refer to counsel for advice as to how they should exercise the discretion, although they may be protected if they act on legal advice as to whether they are entitled to exercise their discretion in particular ways[2]. When considering what level of advice is required, regard must be had to the estate of which he is a trustee. In a large estate it may be only reasonable that he should consult counsel of the first rank or apply for the directions of the court, whereas it would not be reasonable to insist upon this where the estate is small[3]. In such a case it may be reasonable to act upon the advice of a solicitor, without going to counsel[4]. However, merely taking advice, without more, is not necessarily a passport to relief[5]. Counsel must be adequately instructed and allowed sufficient time to give properly considered advice[6]. But even this may not be enough to save the trustees in some cases: for example, where they resolve to implement a scheme, having been told that it could come under critical legal scrutiny, as being an allegedly unlawful device, their reasonable course would be to ask the court for directions[7].

¹   *Bergliter v Cohen* [2006] EWHC 123 (Ch) at [39]–[42] per Morritt C. Cf *Arakella Pty Ltd v Paton (No 2)* (2004) 49 ACSR 706 at [38] per Austin J, NSW Sup Ct.

2   *Perpetual Trustee Co v Watson (No 2)* (1927) 28 SR (NSW) 43 at 47 per Harvey CJ in Eq (considering analogous legislation), followed in *Re Investa Properties Ltd* (2001) 40 ACSR 124, NSW Sup Ct.
3   *Re Allsop* [1914] 1 Ch 1 at 13. Where a barrister of at least ten years' standing has given a written opinion on a question of construction the High Court, without hearing argument, can authorise trustees or personal representatives safely to take steps in reliance on the opinion: Administration of Justice Act 1985, s 48.
4   *Re Evans* [1999] 2 All ER 777.
5   *Marsden v Regan* [1954] 1 All ER 475 at 482 per Evershed MR; and see *National Trustees Co of Australasia v General Finance Co of Australasia* [1905] AC 373, PC.
6   *Baden v Societe General* [1992] 4 All ER 161 at 272.
7   *Wong v Burt* [2005] 1 NZLR 91, NZCA.

95.8 It appears that high standards are expected of trustees. In *Roome v Edwards*[1] a UK set of trustees was charged to capital gains tax in respect of the transactions of a Cayman Islands set of trustees appointed by the UK trustees but over which they had no control, since both sets of trustees were regarded as a single and continuing body of trustees[2] of the settlement comprising the UK and the foreign assets. Lord Roskill stated[3]:

'Your Lordships were strongly pressed with the submission that this conclusion would or might jeopardise trustees such as the taxpayers who have no legal control over the assets which were the subject of the deemed disposal. Your Lordships were assured that in the present case the taxpayers were properly and adequately protected by the beneficiaries in relation to any liability which might fall on them. My Lords, the short answer to this powerfully urged plea is surely this. Persons, whether professional men or not, who accept appointment as trustees of settlements such as these are clearly at risk under [what is now the Taxation of Chargeable Gains Act 1992] and have only themselves to blame if they accept the obligations of trustees in these circumstances without ensuring that they are sufficiently and effectively protected whether by their beneficiaries or otherwise for fiscal or other liabilities which may fall on them personally or as a result of the obligations which they had felt able to assume.'

1   [1982] AC 279, [1981] 1 All ER 736, HL.
2   Taxation of Chargeable Gains Act 1992, s 69(3).
3   [1982] AC 279 at 299, [1981] 1 All ER 736 at 744.

95.9 Of course, it was not necessary to consider the application of s 61 of the Trustee Act as it would have been if the UK trustees had created a sub-trust with Cayman Islands trustees, whose activities led to a tax charge, in respect of the Cayman property, which the UK trustees had had to pay out of the UK property to the prejudice of UK beneficiaries. The strong implication is that in such circumstances the court would be most reluctant to relieve the UK trustees under s 61 of the Trustee Act.

95.10 While this may be justifiable in the case of professional trustees there may well be a case for excusing a non-professional co-trustee like Mrs Wohlleben (a married woman with four children) in *Wohlleben v Canada Permanent Trust Co*[1] where Dickson CJ stated:

'She tried to the best of her ability to keep herself informed but Canada Permanent failed to make known to her the contents of papers which were essential to informed opinion. She made all decisions which she had to make within the limits of her experience and knowledge, and I cannot find that she failed to listen to reason or that she responded irrationally or obdurately ... this is the very sort of case for which the section was intended. Mrs Wohlleben ought fairly to be excused from her breach of trust.'

1   (1976) 70 DLR (3d) 257 at 275 (Can SC); contrast *Re Mulligan* [1998] 1 NZLR 481.

95.11 This had the effect of throwing all the liability on the professional trustee, so having the same effect as the indemnity given to a lay trustee against a co-trustee who is a solicitor, whose advice and control caused the lay trustee's participation in the breach of trust[1].

1   *Re Partington* (1887) 57 LT 654 and paras 99.16–99.18.

95.12 In *Re Evans*[1] the defendant administrator of her intestate father's estate wound up his estate and distributed the property to herself, assuming that her brother was dead, not having heard from him for over 30 years. On her solicitor's advice, she took out a missing beneficiary policy to cover half the estate as less expensive and more effective than procuring a *Benjamin* order[2]. Four years later her brother turned up, took the proceeds of the policy covering his capital entitlement but sued for interest. She was held liable to account for interest but was granted partial relief under s 61 being relieved to the extent that the interest claim could not be satisfied out of the proceeds of sale of a property derived from the deceased's estate which was still at the defendant's disposal. The judge took account of the relatively small size of the estate, the unwarranted expense of applying to the court, the defendant being a lay person unaccustomed to problems of this nature who was at all times willing to abide by the advice of solicitors.

1   [1999] 2 All ER 777, but cf P Kenny in [1999] Conv 375 at 376.
2   [1902] 1 Ch 723; para 47.49.

95.13 In *Segbedzi v Segbedzi*[1] the defendant army officer was one of four administrators of a Ghanaian who died intestate in Ghana, leaving Ghanaian and English estate. Because he took up a new job in Swaziland he decided to resign as administrator and this was accepted at a family meeting by the head of the family who received his letter of resignation and then wrote to him telling him that 'the Solicitor for the Estate [of the deceased] has been informed and you will be instructed as to what legal procedures to follow'. Nothing further happened, but the defendant (in breach of duty) left it to the other three administrators to deal with the estate. This led to substantial losses occurring. The judge however, granted relief under s 61 to the defendant in respect of claims by those beneficially interested in the estate despite the defendant's knowledge that further formalities were required to effect his removal. As a condition of resealing the Ghanaian letters of administration, the English court had required a guarantee against losses up to £104,000 from two guarantors, who provided, this at the request of the administrators, and so had an implied contractual right of indemnity from them jointly and severally. Relief under s 61 from the beneficiaries' claims could have no effect on the guarantors' right to recover their £104,000 from the defendant alone, who would then need to seek contribution from the other three administrators. The defendant's appeal was dismissed.

95.13 *Protection accorded to trustees in case of breach of trust*

1   [2002] WTLR 83. The guarantors had not been notified of the defendant's intention to resign and not act further.

95.14 Note that a person found liable for a breach of trust which involves lack of reasonable care can nonetheless satisfy a court that he acted reasonably for the purposes of s 61[1].

1   Compare the discussions of the Companies Act 1985, s 727, in *Re D'Jan of London Ltd* [1994] 1 BCLC 561 at 564 per Hoffmann LJ, and *Barings plc (in liquidation) v Coopers & Lybrand (a firm)* [2003] EWHC 1319 (Ch), [2003] Lloyd's Rep IR 566 at [1125]–[1148] per Evans-Lombe J.

Examples of unreasonable conduct

95.15 Where the breach of trust consisted in investing the trust funds upon insufficient mortgage security, prima facie the statutory requirements in the now repealed s 8 of the Trustee Act 1925 as to the employment of an independent surveyor constitute a standard by which reasonableness of conduct should be judged; although non-compliance with those requirements was not necessarily a fatal obstacle to an application for relief. It was also a matter of consideration whether the trustee would have acted in the same way if he had been a prudent person lending money of his own[1]. Where, therefore, the trustee acted on the valuation of a valuer employed by the solicitor *who acted for the mortgagors also*, and the valuation in one case merely stated the amount for which the property was a good security, without stating the value of the property itself, and in another, although the value was stated, the sum advanced exceeded two-thirds of that value, it was held that no relief could be given to the trustee[2].

1   *Re Turner* [1897] 1 Ch 536 at 542; *Re Lord de Clifford's Estate* [1900] 2 Ch 707 at 716.
2   *Re Stuart* [1897] 2 Ch 583; and see *Khoo Tek Keong v Ch'ng Joo Tuan Neoh* [1934] AC 529, PC where, although the power of investment was extremely wide, it was held that it was unreasonable to lend trust money merely on a personal promise to repay it with interest, although the testator had been accustomed to make such loans during his lifetime.

95.16 So, again, where the trustee invested the trust fund on the security of a second mortgage in Ireland he was not excused where he took no advice on the matter, employing the mortgagor's solicitor and not really considering the risks[1].

1   *Chapman v Browne* [1902] 1 Ch 785.

95.17 So, also, it has been held that a trustee does not act reasonably (however honest he may have been) in allowing his co-trustee to receive trust money without inquiry as to its application[1], or in allowing his co-trustee to act without check or inquiry[2], even where he is a solicitor who transacts the trust business[3]. The section is not meant to be used as a sort of general indemnity clause for honest men who neglect their own duties as trustee[4]. Thus, a bank trustee that acted honestly obtained no relief when it acted unreasonably in failing to keep in touch with the activities of a company in which it had a 99.8% shareholding so that a large loss flowed from the company's disastrous property speculation[5]. However, the above cases, and those which follow, must only be taken as examples of the general trend of judicial opinion; for, in the words of Byrne J, it is 'impossible to lay down any general rules or principles to be acted on in carrying out the provisions of the section, and each case must depend upon its own circumstances'[6].

1 *Wynne v Tempest* (1897) 13 TLR 360.
2 *Re Second East Dulwich etc Building Society* (1899) 68 LJ Ch 196. See note 9, below.
3 *Re Turner* [1897] 1 Ch 536; *Williams v Byron* (1901) 18 TLR 172. If the solicitor is a co-trustee then he may be obliged to indemnify the lay trustee against loss suffered by the lay trustee liable for breach of trust: *Re Partington* (1887) 57 LT 654; *Head v Gould* [1898] 2 Ch 250.
4 *Williams v Byron* (1901) 18 TLR 172 at 176.
5 *Bartlett v Barclays Bank Trust Co Ltd* [1980] Ch 515, [1980] 1 All ER 139.
6 Per Byrne J in *Re Turner* [1897] 1 Ch 536, and per Romer J in *Re Kay* [1897] 2 Ch 518 at 524.

Examples of reasonable conduct

95.18 Trustees who acted throughout bona fide and in accordance with what was the generally held view of the law, supported by judicial authority until that authority was overruled by the House of Lords, were held to have acted honestly and reasonably and to be fairly entitled to be excused[1]. But no relief was given in a case in which a solicitor-trustee had formed a wrong view of the effect of a statute by failing to notice one of its provisions: 'A prudent man whose affairs were affected by a statute would either satisfy himself that he fully understood its effect or would seek legal advice. A solicitor-trustee could not be heard to say that it was reasonable to apply a lower standard to him'[2].

1 *Re Wightwick's Will Trusts* [1950] Ch 260, [1950] 1 All ER 689.
2 *Ward-Smith v Jebb* (1964) 108 Sol Jo 919. The co-trustee was not a lawyer but, in the absence of evidence that he was given specific advice on the point in question by the solicitor-trustee or some other legal adviser, he was not granted relief. He might have had a right of indemnity against the solicitor-trustee, but that matter was not before the court.

95.19 The sale of leaseholds under a mistake of law, where there was no power of sale, has been held to be reasonable and excusable[1], and so has the payment by executors to their solicitor of money for the specific purpose of paying debts and administration expenses, which the solicitor misappropriated[2]. Wilful default in not suing a debtor to the estate has been excused, where the trustee had reasonable grounds for believing the proceedings would have been ineffectual[3]; and also where the debt was small, and he reasonably believed that the debtor was a man of good credit, and that, having regard to the testator's will, he was not bound to take proceedings[4].

1 *Perrins v Bellamy* [1898] 2 Ch 521; affd [1899] 1 Ch 797, and so also has a mistaken interpretation of the trust instrument (*Re Allsop* [1914] 1 Ch 1, CA).
2 *Re Lord De Clifford's Estate* [1900] 2 Ch 707.
3 *Re Roberts* (1897) 76 LT 479; and see Art 68.
4 *Re Grindey* [1898] 2 Ch 593.

95.20 So where a testator left an estate of £22,000, and it appeared that his debts only amounted to £100 or so, it was held that the executor acted reasonably in paying the widow an immediate legacy of £300, and in permitting her (under the trusts of the will) to receive so much of the income of the estate as was necessary for the maintenance of herself and family, before advertising for claims, although it subsequently turned out that there was a large claim for fraudulent misappropriation of rents received and not accounted for by the testator, which caused his estate to be insolvent[1]. But the executor was not excused for allowing the widow to take the income after the claimant had issued his writ; and, apparently, Romer J felt considerable doubts as to whether he ought to have excused payment of income after the executor had notice of the claim.

1   *Re Kay* [1897] 2 Ch 518. Also see *Guardian Trust Co of New Zealand v Public Trustee of New Zealand* [1942] AC 115, PC.

95.21 Again where a testator authorised his trustees to employ agents to act for them under his will and declared that they should be indemnified for the acts and omissions of such agents, it was held that, even if such words did not authorise them to pay money to their solicitor for the discharge of death duties (which was doubtful), yet their conduct was honest and reasonable, and that they ought to be excused[1].

1   *Re Mackay* [1911] 1 Ch 300.

Honesty and reasonableness do not always suffice if the court thinks that the trustees nevertheless ought not to be excused

95.22 It must not be assumed, however, that where a trustee has acted both honestly and reasonably he ought to be excused as a matter of course; for relief is always within the discretion of the court and an appellate court will be reluctant to interfere with the exercise of its discretion by a lower court[1]. Unless honesty and reasonableness are proved:

> 'the court cannot help the trustees; but if both are made out, there is then a case *for the court to consider* whether the trustee ought fairly to be excused for the breach, looking at all the circumstances'[2].

1   *Marsden v Regan* [1954] 1 All ER 475, [1954] 1 WLR 423, CA.
2   *National Trustees Co of Australasia v General Finance Co of Australasia* [1905] AC 373, PC.

95.23 One factor which can affect the courts' exercise of its discretion is 'whether the trustee is unpaid for services rendered'[1]. The court will be more loath to excuse a paid professional trustee who is now[2] expected to exhibit such care and skill as is reasonable having regard to any knowledge or experience that it is objectively reasonable to expect of a professional trustee as well as to any special knowledge or experience that he subjectively has or holds himself out as having, previously having been expected to exercise a higher standard of diligence and knowledge than a gratuitous trustee[3]. Thus in *Re Windsor Steam Coal Company (1901) Ltd*[4] PO Lawrence LJ speaking of the claim of a liquidator of a company, who had neglected to apply to the court for directions before making a large payment from the company's fund, said:

'Even if the appellant had himself taken the best possible advice and had made the payment acting on such advice, I am of opinion that that would not be sufficient to excuse him having regard to the fact that he was a paid trustee, and paid for his skill and services in performing his duties.'

[1] *Pateman v Heyen* (1993) 35 NSWLR 188 at 199 per Cohen J (considering analogous legislation and declining to relieve an unpaid trustee from liability who had failed to insure trust property which burned down).
[2] Trustee Act 2000, s 1; para 52.2 ff.
[3] *Re Waterman's Will Trusts* [1952] 2 All ER 1054; *Bartlett v Barclays Bank Trust Co Ltd* [1980] Ch 515, [1980] 1 All ER 139; see paras 52.3–52.4. Further see *Re Cooper (No 2)* (1978) 90 DLR (3d) 715.
[4] [1929] 1 Ch 151.

95.24 And in *Re Pauling's Settlement Trusts*[1], where a bank had not only accepted the office of professional trustee but had done so under a settlement created by one of its customers, the Court of Appeal said that since it had thus deliberately placed itself in a position where its duty as trustee conflicted with its interest as banker, the court should be very slow to relieve it under the provisions of s 61.

[1] [1964] Ch 303, [1963] 3 All ER 1, CA. See especially pp 339 and 11 (letter F), respectively.

95.25 Where a non-professional trustee has honestly and reasonably acted on the ill-advice obtained on behalf of the trust from a solicitor, the court will not excuse him if he abstains from recovering the loss from the solicitor where the latter is responsible for negligence because such abstention will not be reasonable[1].

[1] *National Trustees Co of Australasia v General Finance Co of Australasia* [1905] AC 373, PC.

Breaches of trust creating profit for trustees

95.26 All the above cases concerned trustees or personal representatives seeking relief from personal liability for losses arising from a breach of trust. In theory it could extend to relief from personal liability for profits, but this would be of little assistance if proprietary liability still remained in respect of the property (and its traceable product) acquired by the trustee. Thus, in practice, relief is accorded to honest hard-working trustees by awarding them an allowance for their endeavours[1].

[1] See para 58.13 ff.

ARTICLE 96
LIMITATION OF ACTIONS BY BENEFICIARIES AGAINST TRUSTEES

96.1

(1) No statutory period of limitation applies to an action by a beneficiary under a trust[1], being an action:
  (a) in respect of any fraud or fraudulent breach of trust to which the trustee was party or privy; or

(b)   to recover from the trustee trust property or the proceeds thereof in the trustee's possession, or previously received by him and converted to his use[2].

(2)   Where a trustee who is also a beneficiary under the trust receives or retains trust property or its proceeds as his share on a distribution of trust property made honestly and reasonably, his liability under (b) above is limited to the excess over his proper share, if an action is brought to recover the trust property more than six years after the distribution[3].

(3)   Subject as aforesaid, an action by a beneficiary to recover trust property or in respect of any breach of trust, not being an action for which a period of limitation is prescribed by some specific provision of the Limitation Act 1980, will be barred if brought after the expiration of six years from the date on which the right of action accrued; but a right of action is not deemed to have accrued to any beneficiary entitled to a future interest in the trust property, until the interest falls into possession[4].

(4)   No beneficiary as against whom there would be a good defence under the Limitation Act 1980, can derive any greater or other benefit from a judgment or order obtained by any other beneficiary than he could have obtained if he had brought the action and the Act had been pleaded in defence[5].

(5)   Subject to the provisions of paragraphs 1 and 2, above, no action in respect of any claim to the personal estate of a deceased person or to any share or interest therein, whether under a will or on intestacy, can be brought after the expiration of twelve years from the date when the right to receive such share or interest accrued[6] nor can any action to recover arrears of interest in respect of any legacy, or damages in respect of such arrears, be brought after the expiration of six years from the date on which the interest became due[7].

(6)   An action for an account cannot be brought after the expiration of any time limit under the Act which is applicable to the claim which is the basis of the duty to account[8].

(7)   All statutory limitation periods are extended where any necessary party to the action is or has been an enemy or prisoner of war, so as not to expire before the end of twelve months from his ceasing to be an enemy or to be detained as a prisoner[9].

(8)   Where periods of limitation are expressly provided by statute, the doctrine of laches (as distinct from acquiescence: see para 97.7 below) has no application[10] but if no statutory period of limitation is laid down then laches may bar a claim.

(9)   The general provisions in the Limitation Act 1980, sections 28 and 32, which extend limitation periods in cases of disability, fraud, deliberate concealment or mistake apply to actions against trustees.

1　This includes constructive and resulting trusts, as well as express trusts. See the Limitation Act 1980, s 38, which gives to the terms 'trust' and 'trustee' the same meaning as is given to them by s 68 of the Trustee Act 1925. However, in historical context, only one category of true constructive trust is covered: *Paragon Finance plc v DB Thakerar & Co* [1999] 1 All ER 400, CA; see para 96.8 below. Actions by the Attorney General to enforce charitable trusts are not 'actions by a beneficiary under a trust': *A-G v Cocke* [1988] Ch 414.

2　Limitation Act 1980, s 21(1).

3　Limitation Act 1980, s 21(2).

4　Limitation Act 1980, s 21(3). As to when the statute begins to run in cases where the claimant has always been in possession, but acquires a new title, see *Mara v Browne* [1895] 2 Ch 69 (reversed on another point) where a person with an interest in possession and a reversionary interest was not barred as to the latter though barred as to the former. If trustees make a valid advance to a remainderman with a future interest, it seems that his interest falls (pro tanto) into possession; but this is not so if the advance is invalid: *Re Pauling's Settlement Trusts* [1964] Ch 303, [1963] 3 All ER 1, CA, in which the Court of Appeal confirmed on this point the judgment of Wilberforce J at first instance ([1961] 3 All ER 713 at 735).

5　Limitation Act 1980, s 21(4).

6　Limitation Act 1980, s 22(a).

7　Limitation Act 1980, s 22(b).

8　Limitation Act 1980, s 23.

9　Limitation (Enemies and War Prisoners) Act 1945.

10　*Re Pauling's Settlement Trusts* [1962] 1 WLR 86 at 115, per Wilberforce J; [1964] Ch 303 at 353, per Willmer LJ.

The Limitation Act 1980

96.2 These paragraphs state the effect of ss 21, 22 and 23 of the Limitation Act 1980 which to a large extent restate ss 19 and 20 of the Limitation Act 1939. Express, resulting and constructive trustees of property are dealt with on the same footing[1]. However there is a major distinction between (i) trustees who have been guilty of fraud or who have retained trust property (or its product) or converted it to their use, and (ii) trustees who have committed an 'innocent' or 'negligent' breach of trust. In the former case no limitation period applies[2] although the trustees may plead laches or acquiescence. In the latter case a six year limitation period is prescribed as for proprietary claims against innocent strangers[3], unless, it seems, such innocent strangers derive their title from a fraudulent breach of trust[4].

1　Limitation Act 1980, s 38(1) referring to Trustee Act 1925, s 68(17). However, the pre-1939 Limitation Act distinction between express trustees and one category of constructive trustees expounded in *Taylor v Davies* [1920] AC 636 continues to subsist: *Paragon Finance plc v DB Thakerar & Co* [1999] 1 All ER 400, CA; *Halton International Inc v Guernroy Ltd* [2006] EWCA Civ 801; para 96.8 ff.

2　Limitation Act 1980, s 21(1).

3　Limitation Act 1980, s 21(3).

4　Limitation Act 1980, s 21(1)(a); *GL Baker Ltd v Medway Building and Supplies Ltd* [1958] 1 WLR 1216 at 1221–1222; Law Com CP No 151 Limitation of Actions, 1998, para 4.16.

96.3 Exceptionally, a 12 year period is prescribed for 'any claim to the personal estate of a deceased person' so that an underpaid or unpaid creditor, legatee or next of kin has 12 years in which to sue the personal representatives (even if they hold such estate as trustees upon completing their administration) or other persons who received such estate[1].

¹ Limitation Act 1980, s 22(a) replacing Limitation Act 1939, s 20: *Re Diplock* [1948] Ch 465 at 511–513 approved seemingly on appeal in *Ministry of Health v Simpson* [1951] AC 251 at 276, HL, and followed in *Davies v Sharples* [2006] EWHC 362 (Ch), [2006] WTLR 839 at [26]–[33] per Patten J (explaining at [42] –[47] that once the personal representatives have administered the estate and become trustees of settled property, then if a beneficiary later sues for a breach of trust committed by the trustees qua trustees the relevant section is not s 22 but s 21). Protection against s 21 or s 22 claims may be available under Trustee Act 1925, s 27, para 54.16.

96.4 Oddly, ss 21(1) and (3) only apply at face value to actions by a beneficiary under a trust, so that an action by a trustee on behalf of his beneficiaries (who may be unborn or unascertained) against a co-trustee or former trustees or a third party (owning trust property or its traceable product or personally liable in respect of dishonest assistance in breach of trust or dishonest dealings with the trust property) is neither helped nor hindered, so the result of an action against such a defendant depends on whether it be brought by a beneficiary or a trustee. This cannot be justified: the courts will surely apply the six year period by analogy with the statutory period for actions by beneficiaries so that the position is as it was under the Trustee Act 1888¹. However, it has been held that an action by the Attorney-General to enforce a charitable trust is subject to no statutory time-bombs².

¹ *Re Bowden* (1890) 45 Ch D 444. On applying the six year period by analogy see *Companhia de Seguros Imperio v Heath (REBX) Ltd* [2001] 1 WLR 112, CA.
² *A-G v Cocke* [1988] Ch 414.

Paragraph 1

Perpetual liability (subject to laches)

96.5 No period of limitation applies for actions in respect of any fraud or fraudulent breach of trust to which the trustee was a party or privy nor to recover from the trustee trust property or the proceeds thereof in the possession of the trustee or previously received by the trustee and converted to his use¹ eg to pay off his private debts.

¹ Limitation Act 1980, s 21(1). WJ Swadling in 'Limitation' in P Birks and A Pretto (eds) *Breach of Trust* (2002) reveals there should be a different starting point for resolving the current messy situation if one examines the historical context, but the modern starting point has to be *Paragon Finance plc v DB Thakerar & Co* [1999] 1 All ER 400, CA.

96.6 The trustee needs to be a party or privy to actual dishonesty¹ viz pursuit of a course of action knowing it to be contrary to the beneficiaries' interests or being recklessly indifferent whether it is so contrary². An innocent trustee is not liable for the fraud of his co-trustee³ or of his solicitor or other agent⁴.

¹ *Armitage v Nurse* [1998] Ch 241 at 260 (though not supported by the reference to *Beaman v ARTS Ltd* [1949] 1 KB 550 at 558 which did not concern the predecessor to s 21 which was Limitation Act 1939 s 19, but concerned s 26 of the latter Act which was the predecessor to s 32 of the 1980 Act); *Thorne v Heard* [1895] AC 495, HL.
² *Armitage v Nurse* [1998] Ch 241 at 251 and 260.
³ *Re Tufnell* (1902) 18 TLR 705.

4   *Re Fountaine* [1909] 2 Ch 382, CA; *Thorne v Heard* [1895] AC 495 (but no longer
     authoritative on the effect of fraud or concealment of a trustee's agent in view of
     Limitation Act 1980, s 32(1)(a)and (b)).

96.7 Because s 21(1) is not restricted on its face to actions against the trustee
it seems that an action against an innocent donee from the trustee may be
regarded[1] as one 'in respect of any fraud or fraudulent breach of trust to
which the trustee was a party or privy'. The fact that the innocent donee takes
title forthwith subject to the beneficiaries' interests of which he may be
ignorant for many years till being informed of their claims, does not require
him to be treated as a trustee for the purposes of s 21[2]. However, since there is
no justification for treating an *innocent* recipient differently depending upon
whether the trustee was or was not acting dishonestly when transferring title
to him, it may be that the courts might restrict s 21(1) to actions against
trustees, leaving s 21(3) for actions against third parties.

1   *GL Baker Ltd v Medway Building Supplies Ltd* [1958] 1 WLR 1216 at 1221–1222.
2   *Paragon Finance plc v DB Thakerar & Co* [1999] 1 All ER 400, CA.

Two classes of constructive trustee

96.8 It then becomes crucial that the Court of Appeal has restricted perpetual
liability (subject only to laches) to only one category of constructive trustee.
The Court of Appeal[1] has distinguished two classes of constructive trustee: (1)
where the defendant acquired the property or control over the property as a
trustee or other fiduciary in an unimpeached arrangement before the conduct
complained of when he abused the trust and confidence reposed in him; and
(2) where the wrongful conduct of the defendant in asserting his selfish
interests leads to an equitable obligation being placed upon him. Before the
Trustee Act 1888 intervened, Courts of Equity treated the former category as
being express trustees against whom time did not run, while, when the 1888
Act expressly made clear that the express trustee position covered constructive
trustees, it was held that the second category of constructive trustees could
still plead limitation as a defence[2]. The Court of Appeal has held that this
distinction was preserved in the 1939 and 1980 Limitation Acts, so that
constructive trustees within the second category can raise a limitation defence
even in cases of fraud and retention or conversion of trust property, as for
equivalent situations at common law (subject to limitation periods not
running till the fraud was discovered or could with reasonable diligence have
been discovered).

1   *Paragon Finance plc v DB Thakerar & Co* [1999] 1 All ER 400 at 408–414; reaffirmed by
     CA in: *Cia De Seguros Imperio v Heath (REBX) Ltd* [2001] 1 WLR 112 at 122; *JJ
     Harrison (Properties) Ltd v Harrison* [2001] EWCA Civ 1467, [2002] 1 BCLC 162
     at [27]–[29]; *Gwembe Valley Development Co Ltd v Koshy (No 3)* [2003] EWCA Civ
     1048, [2004] 1 BCLC 131 at [86]–[91]; *Halton International Inc v Guernroy* [2006]
     EWCA Civ 801 at [10]–[11].
2   *Taylor v Davies* [1920] AC 636, PC; *Clarkson v Davies* [1923] AC 100 at 110–111, PC.

96.9 Persons within the first category of constructive trustee include trustees
de son tort[1], executors de son tort[2] voluntarily undertaking executorship
functions, secret trustees[3], and agents such as a solicitor receiving trust

property agreeing to treat it as such but subsequently dealing with it inconsistently with the trusts affecting it[4]. Within the second category entitled to a limitation defence are included persons who knowingly receive trust property in breach of trust[5], persons who innocently receive trust property for their own benefit but then retain and deal with it as if it were their own property after becoming aware that it was trust property, and persons who dishonestly assist in a breach of trust or other fiduciary duty[6].

1   *Paragon Finance plc v DB Thakerar & Co* [1999] 1 All ER 400 at 408.
2   *Jones v Williams* [2000] Ch 1, CA in ignorance of *Paragon Finance* held no limitation period applied to an executor de son tort due to Limitation Act 1980, s 21(1)(b) but it would seem that the executor de son tort intermeddled on purely selfish (not altruistic) grounds so that he should have fallen outside s 21(1) and within s 21(3).
3   *Paragon Finance plc v DB Thakerar & Co* [1999] 1 All ER 400 at 409 where Millett LJ also instanced *Rochefoucauld v Banstead* [1897] 1 Ch 196 (where the defendant agreed to buy property for the claimant but the trust was imperfectly recorded) and *Pallant v Morgan* [1952] 2 All ER 951 (where the defendant sought to keep for himself property which the claimant had trusted him to buy for both parties).
4   *Lee v Sankey* (1873) LR 15 Eq 204; *Soar v Ashwell* [1893] 2 QB 390.
5   *Taylor v Davies* [1920] AC 636, PC.
6   *Schulman v Hewson* [2002] EWHC 855 (Ch). Cf *Akai Holdings Ltd (in compulsory liquidation) v Ko Cheong Wing* [2006] HKCFI 494 at [41] per Stone J (Hong Kong CFI); but the contrary view was taken in *Peconic Industrial Development Ltd v Chio Ho Cheong* [2006] HKCFI 447 at [625]–[673] per Cheung J (Hong Kong CFI). For further discussion see C Mitchell 'Assistance' in P Birks and A Pretto *Breach of Trust* (2002) at pp 209–211.

96.10 Some recent cases on company directors nicely illustrate the considerations which might lead a court to place a defendant into one category or the other. In *JJ Harrison (Properties) Ltd v Harrison*[1], a director bought property from the claimant company without disclosing that a valuer had told him that it had development potential. He sold the property at a profit and the company sued for an account of the proceeds of sale. His limitation defence failed because the court found him to be a constructive trustee within the first category. In *Gwembe Valley Development Co Ltd v Koshy (No 3)*[2] a director caused the claimant company to borrow foreign currency from a second company in which he owned shares. The loans were valued at the official exchange rate although the currency advanced had actually been obtained by the second company at a much more favourable rate. The claimant company sued on the basis that the director did not disclose his interest in the loan transactions to the board, and the court held that in the absence of fraud the claim would have been time-barred, because the director was liable to account for the secret profit as a constructive trustee within the second category (the claim ultimately succeeded on the basis that the director had fraudulently concealed his interest in the second company and the true cost of the foreign currency). The difference between these two cases, as Carnwath LJ subsequently observed in *Halton International Inc v Guernroy Ltd*, was that[3]:

> 'in the former the director had a pre-existing "trustee-like responsibility" in relation to the particular property which was the subject of the action, [but] in the latter he did not.'

1   [2003] EWCA Civ 1467, [2001] WTLR 1327,
2   [2003] EWCA Civ 1048, [2004] 1 BCLC 131.
3   [2006] EWCA Civ 801 at [16]. See also Mummery LJ's comments in *Gwembe* at [118]–[119].

96.11 Where an action is brought under s 21(1)(b) a trustee who remains in actual physical occupation of trust property for his own purposes cannot be heard to say that he has not received any rents or profits in respect of the property. He will be charged a notional occupation rent, and, unless he can discharge himself by showing that he has paid moneys away[1]:

> 'he must be considered as still having it in his pocket at the material date, and, therefore, cannot escape under the provisions of the Limitation Act.'

1   *Re Howlett* [1949] Ch 767 at 778, [1949] 2 All ER 490 at 495, per Danckwerts J.

Paragraph 2

Overpayment to trustees as beneficiaries

96.12 Where trustees paid themselves as beneficiaries annuities without deducting tax it was held they could not plead any limitation period in respect of these overpayments to themselves but that they could in respect of over-payments to other beneficiaries.

96.13 Under a novel provision in the Limitation Act 1980, s 21(2), if a trustee, who is also a beneficiary, receives or retains trust property or its proceeds as his beneficial share on a distribution of the trust property made by him honestly and reasonably, then his liability will be limited to the excess over his proper share, if an action is brought to recover the trust property more than six years after the distribution. Thus, if T distributed one-third of the trust property to himself, honestly and reasonably believing that only three beneficiaries exist, he will be liable to a fourth beneficiary after six years not for a quarter share but only for the one-twelfth difference between the one-third share he took and the one-quarter share which was truly his.

Paragraphs 3 and 4

Six Year Period

96.14 Assuming that s 21(1) does not apply (with the result that the claim is not subject to any limitation period), s 21(3) provides that an action by a beneficiary to recover trust property or in respect of any breach of trust cannot be brought after six years from the date on which the right of action accrued (unless the action is to recover land[1], or the twelve year period in s 22 applies in the case of personal representatives who have been appointed trustees under the will[2]). Because recovering trust property from the trustee (including the first but not the second category of constructive trustee) falls within s 21(1)(b), s 21(3) only covers claims to recover trust property (including its traceable product) from a third party. Prima facie, s 21(3) will therefore protect an innocent third party receiving title to property for his own benefit from a trustee six years after receipt of such property: because he falls within the second category of constructive trustee he is not regarded as a trustee within s 21(1). However, the rule laid down in s 21(3) is stated to be 'subject to the preceding provisions of this section', suggesting that in cases where an innocent recipient has received property from a fraudulent trustee, s 21(1)(a) will apply so as to make the recipient liable, irrespective of time[3]. This is unsatisfactory because it creates different limitation regimes for claims against innocent recipients, according to whether or not the trustee from whom they received trust property acted fraudulently. The only way of avoiding this unsatisfactory outcome would be for the courts to restrict s 21(1) to actions against trustees and not against third parties. Support for this reading of the sub-section can be derived from Carnwath LJ's judgment in *Halton International Inc v Guernroy Ltd* where he explained the rationale behind s 21(1) in terms which are consistent with the view that the sub-section applies to actions against trustees only[4]:

> 'Section 21(1) provides an exception to the ordinary limitation rule that civil actions are barred after six years. Such an exception needs to be clearly justified by reference to the statutory language and the policy behind it. It is important therefore to keep in mind the reasoning behind the exception. It is not about culpability as such; fraud may not be sufficient to avoid the ordinary rule[5]. It is about deemed possession: the fiction that the possession of a property by a trustee is treated from the outset as that of the beneficiary. In the words of Millett LJ, the possession of the trustee is "taken from the first for and on behalf of the beneficiaries" and is "consequently treated as the possession of the beneficiaries". An action by the beneficiary to recover that property is not time-barred, because in legal theory it has been in his possession throughout.'

1   Twelve years is normally available to recover unregistered land (Limitation Act 1980, s 15) while Land Registration Act 2002, Sch 6 contains special rules enabling an adverse possessor to apply to become registered proprietor after ten years but the current registered proprietor who must be notified can prevent this except in very limited circumstances.
2   *Re Diplock* [1948] Ch 465 at 511–513; *Ministry of Health v Simpson* [1951] AC 251 at 276–277. See note 1 at para 96.3 and see para 96.28.
3   *GL Baker Ltd v Medway Building & Supplies Ltd* [1958] 1 WLR 1216 at 1221–1222.
4   [2006] EWCA Civ 801 at [22].
5   Citing *Paragon Finance plc v DB Thakerar & Co* [1999] 1 All ER 400 at 411; *Clarkson v Davies* [1923] AC 100. His Lordship added that 'although the judgment in *Gwembe* (to which I was a party) proceeded on the premise that fraud was sufficient to bring the case within section 21(1)(a)) (para [120]), the ultimate decision may be better explained by reference to the alternative ground of fraudulent concealment: s 32.'

96.15 Personal actions against trustees not perpetually vulnerable under s 21(1) and personal actions against third parties involved in a breach of trust are barred six years after the right of action accrued, not from the date on which loss was first suffered eg six years from the date an unauthorised or improper investment was made[1]. The payment of the full amount of income due to the life tenant is not an acknowledgment that capital is intact so as to prevent time running against the beneficiary[2].

1   *Re Somerset* [1894] 1 Ch 231, CA.
2   *Re Fountaine* [1909] 2 Ch 282, CA. On acknowledgments see Limitation Act 1980, ss 29, 30, 31.

96.16 Although a life tenant may be barred at the expiration of six years from the date of a breach of trust (eg the date of an improper mortgage) the remainderman will not be barred until six years after his interest falls into possession. If he compels the trustees to replace the loss during the life tenancy after the life tenant has become barred, the trustees are entitled to receive for themselves the income of the sum replaced by them, but until they have replaced the whole loss the income must be accumulated towards such replacement[1].

¹   *Re Somerset* [1894] 1 Ch 231, CA.

96.17 A beneficiary who has both an interest in possession and a future interest may sue in reliance on his future interest after his interest in possession claim has become barred[1] (but not so as to receive any income which the trustees may retain for themselves) except in the case of land, where s 15(5) applies to bar the future interest once the interest in possession has been barred.

¹   *Mara v Browne* [1895] 2 Ch 69 at 96–97 (reversed on another point [1896] 1 Ch 199, CA).

Trustees of discretionary trusts

96.18 Where a beneficiary is merely interested under a discretionary trust until obtaining a life interest upon attaining 25 years the Court of Appeal[1] has held that time does not run until the beneficiary obtains an interest in possession on his 25th birthday, applying section 22(3) 'the right of action shall not be treated as having accrued to any beneficiary entitled to a future interest in the trust property until the interest fell into possession'. It matters not that at 18 a beneficiary, whether or not having an interest in possession, is entitled to see the trust accounts with supporting information so as to be able to discover whether there has been a breach of trust.

¹   *Armitage v Nurse* [1998] Ch 241.

96.19 Millett LJ has stated[1] that the rationale for time not running till an interest in possession has been acquired 'is not that a beneficiary with a future interest has not the means of discovery [because he has], but that the beneficiary should not be compelled to litigate (at considerable personal expense) in respect of an injury to an interest which he may never live to enjoy. Similar reasoning would apply to exclude a person who is merely the object of a discretionary trust or power which may never be exercised in his favour'.

¹   *Armitage v Nurse* [1998] Ch 241 at 261.

96.20 At face value this indicates that a right of action of any such object to have property restored to the trust fund should not accrue until such object has received some trust property so as to have obtained an interest in possession therein. This means that the liability of trustees of a discretionary trust is open-ended because towards the end of the trust period there will almost always be some beneficiary under a discretionary trust or some object of a power of appointment who will not have received any trust income or capital and who will therefore be able to claim that losses from breaches of trust over the last 70 or 80 years should be restored to the trust fund (or it may be that the person ultimately absolutely receiving what remains of the trust property could sue on his own behalf alleging there would have been much more passing to him but for breaches of trust in the preceding 70 or 80 years). It thus makes sense to exclude objects of powers from having any right to make the trustees account and to appoint a small amount to each beneficiary on attaining 18 years of age but this still leaves trustees exposed, although if they arrange for an independent annual audit this will make it most unlikely that actions will be brought years later, especially if a clause in the trust instrument provides that accounts approved by independent auditors shall be regarded as conclusively correct unless any trustee, knowing there had been a breach of trust, deliberately concealed it from the auditors.

96.21 The mandatory statutory limitation rules cannot be directly ousted because this would be contrary to public policy. However, just as determinable interests enduring only until bankruptcy are valid, perhaps one could validly provide that the interests of anyone interested under the settlement in whatever should be restored to the trust fund as a result of any breaches of duty by the trustees shall endure only until six years have elapsed since the relevant breach of trust or, in the case where the trustee, knowing he had committed a breach, deliberately concealed it, until six years have elapsed since discovery of such concealed breach or the time when such concealment could with reasonable diligence have been discovered.

96.22 Alternatively, a clause in the trust instrument could provide that if anyone interested under the trust brings an action in respect of a breach of trust that occurred more than six years previously or, in the case where the trustee knowing he had committed a breach deliberately concealed it, more than six years after discovery of it or the time when it could with reasonable diligence have been discovered, then anything recovered in such action shall be held on trust for the trustee held liable for the breach. To prevent the circuity of a beneficiary exercising his right of action against the trustee, who would then be entitled to the fruits of the action, the trustee is entitled to prevent the beneficiary's action from being pursued[1].

[1]   *Ingram v IRC* [1997] 4 All ER 395 at 424 per Millett LJ.

96.23 However, in light of the unanimous view of the New Zealand Court of Appeal in *Johns v Johns*[1] after examining the *dicta* of Millett LJ, there should be no need to rely on the above devices. Section 21(3) and its exact New Zealand counterpart is restricted to rights of action not accruing to 'any beneficiary *entitled to a future interest in* the trust property until the interest fell into possession".The object of a discretionary trust or power is not *entitled* to any future interest in the trust property, merely having a hope of benefiting. Thus, the normal limitation rules apply to such objects.

[1]   [2004] 3 NZLR 202 at [40].

Breach of self-dealing and fair-dealing rules

96.24 In *Tito v Waddell (No 2)*[1] Megarry V-C held that the self-dealing rule (enabling beneficiaries as of right to set aside purchases of trust property) and the fair-dealing rule (enabling a beneficiary to have the purchase of his equitable interest set aside unless the trustee shows the purchase was scrupulously fair) amount to disabilities of the trustee so that infractions of such rules are not breaches of trust with the result that s 21(3) of the Limitation Act 1980 is inapplicable, leaving laches as the only time-based defence. All fiduciaries are subject to these rules, not just trustees, and Megarry V-C considered that breach of trust within s 21 concerns only breaches by trustees of duties confined to trustees as such.

¹   [1977] Ch 106.

96.25 These findings were reviewed, and rejected as a 'needless complication', by the Court of Appeal in *Gwembe Valley Development Co Ltd v Koshy (No 3)*¹, which considered it unjustifiable to apply different limitation rules to claims founded on breaches of the self- and fair-dealing rules, and claims founded on other breaches of fiduciary duty. The court held that such a distinction²:

> 'is inconsistent with Millett LJ's exposition of the nature of fiduciary duties [in *Paragon Finance*]. Whether viewed as duties or disabilities, all such incidents are aspects of the fiduciary's primary obligation of loyalty. Contrary to the Vice-Chancellor's concern, this does not lead to any anomalous distinction between trustees and others subject to the fair-dealing rule. They are all subject, directly or by analogy, to section 21. On the contrary, the *Tito v Waddell* distinction would itself lead to anomaly. Across the wide spectrum of conduct which may give rise to fiduciary liability, the six year limitation would apply except at the two extremes. At one end, fraud would be excepted by section 21(1)(a); at the other, innocent breach of the no-profit rule would be excepted because it relates to a disability rather than a duty. The former exception is defensible in legal policy terms; the latter is not.'

¹   [2003] EWCA Civ 1048, [2004] 1 BCLC 131 at [104]–[109].
²   [2004] 1 BCLC 13 at [108].

Paragraph 5

Legacies

96.26 By s 22 of the Limitation Act 1980 it is provided that the period of limitation for all actions in respect of any claim to the personal estate of a deceased person shall be 12 years, but this has no application to an action to remove a personal representative¹.

¹   *Green v Gaul* [2006] EWCA Civ 1124.

96.27 The wording of the section, which refers to 'actions in respect of' personal estate and not to 'actions to recover' personal estate, is important, since it has been held by the Court of Appeal¹ to be wide enough to apply not only to an action by an unpaid beneficiary against a personal representative but also to an action by an unpaid beneficiary direct against one overpaid or wrongly paid. After expressing his complete agreement with the reasoning and conclusion of the Court of Appeal in this case, when appealed to the House of Lords, Lord Simonds (with whom their other Lordships concurred) said:

> 'there is nothing in the ancestry of this section which justifies, much less requires, a narrower meaning being given to its words than they ordinarily bear'[2].

1   *Re Diplock* [1948] Ch 465, CA; affd sub nom *Ministry of Health v Simpson* [1951] AC 251; followed in *Davies v Sharples* [2006] EWHC 362 (Ch), [2006] WTLR 839, at [26]–[32] per Patten J.
2   *Ministry of Health v Simpson* [1951] AC 251 at 276–277, HL.

96.28 Note, however, that s 22(a) has no application to cases of trusts created by will once the administration of an estate is complete and the personal representatives have ceased to act as such, and continue in office only as trustees. In this case, it seems that any claims arising out of breaches of trust committed by the trustees will fall exclusively within the scope of s 21(3)[1].

1   *Davies v Sharples* [2006] EWHC 362 (Ch), [2006] WTLR 839 at [43]–[47] per Patten J, relying on *Re Timmis* [1902] 1 Ch 176 and *Re Oliver* [1927] 2 Ch 323. However, land is covered by Limitation Act 1980 s 15 and Sched 1, Part 1.

96.29 Lord Simonds also held that time started to run for the purposes of the statutory precursor to s 22(a) from the date when the next of kin or legatee could obtain an order for the due administration of the estate against the personal representative, which would be no later than the end of the year allowed to personal representatives to complete administration of an estate under the Administration of Estates Act 1925 s 44[1] Subsequently, in *Re Loftus, deceased*[2], Lawrence Collins J held without referring to Lord Simonds' dictum that time starts to run 'from the later of the end of the executor's year and the date when the relevant interest falls into possession'[3], deriving support for this proposition from *Re Johnson*[4]. There Chitty J held that the limitation period in respect of claims arising out of the administration of a deceased estate, where the next of kin are entitled to a reversionary asset belonging to the intestate, do not start to run:

> 'before [the asset] falls into possession and is possessed by [the administrator], nor where he is compelled to take proceedings to recover an outstanding asset, before he recovers it or obtains possession of it.'

1   *Ministry of Health v Simpson* [1951] AC 251 at 277.
2   [2005] EWHC 406 (Ch), [2005] 1 WLR 1890 at [156].
3   [2005] 1 WLR 1890 at [156].
4   (1885) 29 Ch D 964 at 970–1.

96.30 However in *Davies v Sharples*[1] Patten J stressed the exceptional nature of the rule established by *Re Johnson*, which he took to apply only where administrators have difficulty getting in the estate, and where the beneficiaries' interest has yet to fall into possession. The more general rule laid down by Lord Simonds he took to be[2]:

> 'simply the consequence ... of merging the limitation period for restitutionary claims by beneficiaries and next of kin with that applicable to claims against the personal representatives for the due administration of the estate. A failure to distribute legacies and the residuary estate to those immediately entitled to it is

easily catered for by a limitation period of 12 years commencing with the death of the testator or intestate, particularly when one bears in mind the application of the exceptions for cases of fraud or the continuing possession by the personal representative of trust property contained in s 21 (1) and (2) of the 1980 Act which are incorporated by the opening words of s 22 (a). ... The application of [ss 21 and 22] to ... restitutionary claims by beneficiaries against third parties where the third party is not also one of the personal representatives can cause ... difficulties ... [but] I am bound by the weight of authority to regard time as running in such cases from the same starting point.'

Inconsistently, Patten J had earlier[3] correctly referred to Lord Simonds[4] as considering a claimant to have 12 years after the expiration of the executor's year. Subsequently, when *Re Loftus* was appealed under the name of *Green v Gaul* [5], the Court of Appeal made no reference to Patten J's decision, but shared his view that *Re Johnson* is of limited assistance in this context. Moreover, Chadwick LJ could not see how time could run before the grant of letters of administration to an intestate's estate: indeed, he took the view that time could not run till the administrator had concluded administration of the estate by paying debts, funeral and testamentary expenses etc so as to ascertain the net residuary estate that he then became under a duty to distribute under the intestacy rules[6].

[1]   [2006] EWHC 632 (Ch), [2006] WTLR 839 at [39].
[2]   [2006] EWHC 632 (Ch) at [40].
[3]   [2006] EWHC 632 (Ch) at [37].
[4]   *Ministry of Health v Simpson* [1951] AC 251 at 277.
[5]   [2006] EWCA Civ 1124; (2006) 9 ITELR 107.
[6]   [2006] EWCA Civ 1124 at [30] which happens to coincide with the views of the deputy judge in *Evans v Westcombe* [1999] 2 All ER 777.

Paragraph 6

Action for account

96.31 An action for an account must not be brought after the expiration of any time limit under the Limitation Act 1980 which is applicable to the claim which is the basis of the account. It would seem[1] that this provision in s 23 of the 1980 Act should, in historical context, be restricted to claims within Equity's concurrent or auxiliary jurisdiction and not claims like those of beneficiaries under trusts within Equity's exclusive jurisdiction so their claims to accounts should fall outside s 23, as held in *A-G v Cocke*[2], though for other reasons. However, merely because a beneficiary seeks an account *simpliciter* a trustee cannot be deprived of a limitation defence otherwise available to him, so he can restrict the period for which he has to account if he makes out such a defence[3].

[1]   See W J Swadling 'Limitation' in P Birks & A Pretto (eds) *Breach of Trust* (2002) at pp 336–7. There may be no limit as in *Green v Gaul* [2006] EWCA Civ 1124 where under s 21(1)(b) there was no limitation period applicable.
[2]   [1988] Ch 414, where no limitation period applied to the A-G's action.
[3]   *Paragon Finance plc v DB Thakerar & Co* [1999] 1 All ER 400 at 415–416, CA, criticising *Nelson v Rye* [1996] 1 WLR 1378 at 1390; *Gwembe Valley Development Co Ltd v Koshy (No 3)* [2004] 1 BCLC 131 at [110], CA, criticising *Gwembe Valley Development Co Ltd v Koshy* [1998] 2 BCLC 613 at 621–623.

Paragraph 7

War-time extensions

96.32 The limitation periods prescribed by ss 21 and 22 of the Limitation Act 1980 are extended in cases where any necessary party to the action is or has been an enemy or a prisoner of war by s 1 of the Limitation (Enemies and War Prisoners) Act 1945 which, though passed to meet conditions arising in the last war, is permanent legislation, and is in the following terms:

(1)   If at any time before the expiration of the period prescribed by any statute of limitation for the bringing of any action any person who would have been a necessary party to that action if it had then been brought was an enemy or was detained in enemy territory, the said period shall be deemed not to have run while the said person was an enemy or was so detained, and shall in no case expire before the end of twelve months from the date when he ceased to be an enemy or to be so detained, or from the date of the passing of this Act, whichever is the later:

Provided that, where any person was only an enemy as respects a business carried on in enemy territory, this section shall only apply, so far as that person is concerned, to actions arising in the course of that business.

(2)   If it is proved that any person was resident or carried on business or was detained in enemy territory at any time, he shall for the purposes of this Act be presumed to have continued to be resident or to carry on business or to be detained, as the case may be, in that territory until it is proved that he ceased to be resident or to carry on business or to be detained in that territory at an earlier date.

(3)   If two or more periods have occurred in which any person who would have been such a necessary party as aforesaid was an enemy or was detained in enemy territory, those periods shall be treated for the purposes of this Act as one continuous such period beginning with the beginning of the first period and ending with the end of the last period.

96.33 By s 2(1), 'enemy' is defined as meaning any person who is or is deemed to be an enemy for any purposes of the Trading with the Enemy Act 1939 and may therefore include British subjects resident in enemy territory; 'enemy territory' is given a very wide meaning and includes territory under the sovereignty of or occupied by an enemy Power or which the Department of Trade and Industry has directed to be treated as enemy territory, and in respect whereof no cessation order has been made; and 'statute of limitation' includes the Limitation Act 1939 and 1980.

96.34 References to the period during which any person was detained in enemy territory are by s 2(3) to be construed as including references to any immediately succeeding period during which that person remained in enemy territory.

Paragraph 8

Whether doctrine of laches available

96.35 It is clear that if statute specifically provides for an express period of limitation then there is no room for the equitable doctrine of laches, though there may still be scope for a defence of acquiescence to arise[1]. Equally clearly if statute altogether omits mention of any limitation period for certain circumstances then the doctrine of laches must apply. However, the question arises whether there is room for the doctrine of laches to operate where statute specifically states as in s 21(1) of the 1980 Act that 'no period of limitation prescribed by this Act shall apply' to claims of the relevant kind. In principle this should be insufficient to oust the doctrine of laches especially since s 36(2) of the 1980 Act states that 'nothing in the Act shall affect any equitable jurisdiction to refuse relief on the grounds of acquiescence or otherwise'. Moreover Blackburne J expressly held in *Schulman v Hewson*[2] that the defence of laches was available to a dishonest assistant falling within the scope of s 21(1)(a). However in obiter dicta in *Gwembe Valley Development Co Ltd v Koshy (No 3)*[3] the Court of Appeal held that in the case of a fraudulent breach of trust falling within s 21(1)(a), 'the defence of laches is not available'; and in *Patel v Shah*[4] the Court of Appeal accepted that where a claim is brought to recover trust property falling under s 21(1)(b), the defence of laches is not available in the 'general run of claims' arising in connection with donative trusts 'in which a beneficiary is not expected by anyone to do anything other than to receive the gift' – although it may be available where the trust has arisen in a commercial context as the result of arms'-length dealings between the parties[5].

[1] *Re Pauling's Settlement Trusts* [1964] Ch 303 at 353, [1962] 1 WLR 86 at 115.
[2] [2002] EWHC 855 (Ch) at [44].
[3] [2004] 1 BCLC 131 at [140], critiqued in G Scanlan (2006) 27 Co Law 186. The court's statement was obiter because it also held at [141] that there were no grounds for applying the doctrine of laches on the facts of the case.
[4] [2005] EWCA Civ 157, [2005] WTLR 359.
[5] [2005] EWCA Civ 157 at [30].

96.36 Laches consists of a substantial lapse of time coupled with circumstances 'where it would be practically unjust to give a remedy either because the party has by his conduct done that which might fairly be regarded as equivalent to a waiver of it, or where by his conduct and neglect he has, though perhaps not waiving that remedy, yet put the other party in a situation in which it would not be reasonable to place him if the remedy were afterwards asserted'[1].In *Patel v Shah*[2] the Court of Appeal, in rejecting claims by beneficiaries involved under a commercial resulting trust venture to assert their rights against the trustee, endorsed a more modern approach of Aldous LJ in *Frawley v Neill* [3]

> 'the more modern approach should not require an inquiry as to whether the circumstances can be fitted within the confines of a pre-conceived formula derived from old cases. The inquiry should require a broad approach directed to ascertaining whether it would in all the circumstances be unconscionable for a party to be permitted to assert his beneficial right. No doubt the circumstances which gave rise to a particular result in decided cases are relevant to the

question whether or not it would be conscionable or unconscionable for the relief to be asserted, but each case has to be decided on its facts applying the broad approach.'

1   *Lindsay Petroleum Co v Hurd* (1874) LR 5 PC 221 at 239–240, per Lord Selborne LC. Also see *Fysh v Page* (1956) 96 CLR 233 (Aust HC) (12-year delay barred claim to set aside purchase by fiduciary). Further, see G Watt 'Laches, Estoppel and Election' in P Birks & A Pretto (eds) *Breach of Trust* (2002) 353.
2   [2005] EWCA Civ 157. [2005] WTLR 359 at [32].
3   [2000] CP Rep 20.

96.37 A bare trustee cannot plead laches against his beneficiary with an undisputed equitable title[1] nor can express trustees of a charitable trust for the public make out a case of laches against the public[2].

1   *Joyce v Joyce* [1978] 1 WLR 1170; *Frawley v Neill* (1999) Times, 5 April; *Mills v Drewitt* (1855) 20 Beav 632 at 638, 52 ER 748 at 750. Laches can bar a personal as opposed to a proprietary claim: *Bright v Legerton* (1861) 2 De G F & J 606.
2   *Brisbane City Council v A-G for Queensland* [1979] AC 411, PC.

Paragraph 9

Extension of limitation period

96.38 Where in the case of an action for which a limitation period is prescribed by the 1980 Act (a) an action is based upon the fraud of the defendant[1] or his agent or of any person through whom he claims[2] or his agent or (b) any fact relevant to the claimant's right of action has been deliberately concealed from him by any such person aforesaid or (c) the action is for relief from the consequences of a mistake[3], then the limitation period does not begin to run until the claimant has discovered the fraud, concealment or mistake or could with reasonable diligence have discovered it[4]. Section 32(3) and (4) provide protection for purchasers for value without notice of the fraud, concealment or mistake. The burden of proof is on the claimant 'to establish that he could not have discovered the fraud (or concealment) earlier than he did (whenever that was) without exceptional measures which he could not reasonably have been expected to take'[5].

1   This requires fraud to be an ingredient essential to the cause of action: *Beaman v ARTS Ltd* [1949] 1 KB 550 at 558, CA. It seems that fraud will be regarded as unambiguously referring to dishonesty: *Armitage v Nurse* [1998] Ch 241 at 260. Historically, such extension was not needed for claims within Equity's exclusive jurisdiction: W J Swadling 'Limitation' in P Birks & A Pretto (eds) *Breach of Trust* (2002) at pp 325, 330 and 334.
2   See *Eddis v Chichester Constable* [1969] 2 Ch 345, [1969] 2 All ER 912.
3   See *Phillips-Higgins v Harper* [1954] 1 QB 411.
4   Limitation Act 1980, s 32. On reasonable diligence see *Peco Arts Inc v Hazlitt Gallery Ltd* [1983] 3 All ER 193, [1983] 1 WLR 1315 and *Davies v Sharples* [2006] EWHC 362 (Ch), [2006] WTLR 839 at [57] to [59]. What must be discovered or known are all the facts which together constitute the cause of action: *Official Assignee of Collier v Creighton* [1993] 2 NZLR 534 at 538–540.
5   *Schulman v Hewson* [2002] EWHC 855 (Ch) at [42] per Blackburne J, following *Paragon Finance v DB Thakerar & Co* [1999] 1 All ER 400 at 418.

96.39 No limitation period is prescribed for any fraud or fraudulent breach of trust involving the trustee, but facts concerning an innocent or negligent breach of trust could be deliberately concealed by acts or omissions of the trustee once he became aware that he had committed such breach[1].

1   Limitation Act 1980, s 32(2) as interpreted in *Cave v Robinson Jarvis and Rolf [2002] UKHL 18, [2003] 1 AC 384*.

96.40 Section 32(1)(b) operates to postpone the running of time wherever there is a deliberate concealment, whether such concealment was contemporaneous with or subsequent to the accrual of the cause of action[1].

1   *Sheldon v RHM Outhwaite (Underwriting Agencies) Ltd* [1996] AC 102, [1995] 2 All ER 558, HL. If a life tenant wrongfully sells an heirloom and says nothing about this, this amounts to deliberate concealment: *Eddis v Chichester Constable* [1969] 2 Ch 345 at 356, CA.

ARTICLE 97
CONCURRENCE OF OR WAIVER OR RELEASE BY
THE BENEFICIARIES

97.1

(1)   A beneficiary who has assented to, or concurred in, a breach of trust[1], or who has subsequently released or confirmed it[2], or even acquiesced in it[3], cannot afterwards charge the trustees with it. Provided:
    (a)   that the beneficiary was of full age and capacity at the date of such assent or release[4];
    (b)   that he had full knowledge of the facts, and knew what he was doing[5] and the legal effect thereof[6], though, if in all the circumstances it is not fair and equitable that, having given his concurrence or acquiescence, he should subsequently turn round and sue the trustees, it is not necessary that he should know that what he is concurring or acquiescing in is a breach of trust (provided he fully understands what he is concurring or acquiescing in) and it is not necessary (though it is significant[7]) that he should himself have directly benefited by the breach of trust[8];
    (c)   that no undue influence was brought to bear upon him to extort the assent or release[9].

(2)   Where a beneficiary has obtained judgment in an action for breach of trust, or merely for general administration, it is not competent for him afterwards in that action to charge the trustees with breaches of trut committed before action and not alleged in the pleadings and proved at the trial, or even to ask for their removal on that ground[10]; nor, it seems, can a fresh action be brought for that purpose without the leave of the court[11].

97.1 Protection accorded to trustees in case of breach of trust

1. Brice v Stokes (1805) 11 Ves 319; 2 White & Tud LC 631; Wilkinson v Parry (1828) 4 Russ 272; Nail v Punter (1832) 5 Sim 555; Life Association of Scotland v Siddal (1861) 3 De GF & J 58; Walker v Symonds (1818) 3 Swan 1; Evans v Benyon (1887) 37 Ch D 329; Re Pauling's Settlement Trusts [1964] Ch 303, [1963] 3 All ER 1, CA).

2. French v Hobson (1803) 9 Ves 103; Wilkinson v Parry (1828) 4 Russ 272; Cresswell v Dewell (1863) 4 Giff 460.

3. See Broadhurst v Balguy (1841) 1 Y & C Ch Cas 16; Brewer v Swirles (1854) 2 Sm & G 219; Stafford v Stafford (1857) 1 De G & J 193; Re Jarvis [1958] 2 All ER 336, [1958] 1 WLR 815; Re Pauling's Settlement Trusts [1964] Ch 303, [1963] 3 All ER 1, CA.

4. Lord Montford v Lord Cadogan (1816) 19 Ves 635; Overton v Banister (1844) 3 Hare 503 at 506.

5. Re Garnett (1885) 31 Ch D 1; Buckeridge v Glasse (1841) Cr & Ph 126; Hughes v Wells (1852) 9 Hare 749; Cockerell v Cholmeley (1830) 1 Russ & M 418; Strange v Fooks (1863) 4 Giff 408; March v Russell (1837) 3 My & Cr 31; Aveline v Melhuish (1864) 2 De GJ & Sm 288; Walker v Symonds (1818) 3 Swan 1. Paragraph 1 of this Article, as it stood in the 1960 edition was referred to by Wilberforce J in Re Pauling's Settlement Trusts [1961] 3 All ER 713, [1962] 1 WLR 86; (on appeal [1964] Ch 303, [1963] 3 All ER 1, CA).

6. Re Garnett (1885) 31 Ch D 1; Cockerell v Cholmeley (1830) 1 Russ & M 418; Marker v Marker (1851) 9 Hare 1; Burrows v Walls (1855) 5 De GM & G 233; Stafford v Stafford (1857) 1 De G & J 193; Strange v Fooks (1863) 4 Giff 408; Re Howlett [1949] Ch 767 at 775, [1949] 2 All ER 490 at 492.

7. Stafford v Stafford (1857) 1 De G & J 193 (benefits from breach of trust accepted for 15 years); Roeder v Blues (2004) 248 DLR (4th) 210 at [33], BCCA.

8. Holder v Holder [1968] Ch 353 at 369, 394, 399 (CA) approving Re Pauling's Settlement Trusts [1962] 1 WLR 86 at 108. Also Re Freeston's Charity [1979] 1 All ER 51 at 62, CA.

9. Bowles v Stewart (1803) 1 Sch & Lef 209; Earl Chesterfield v Janssen (1751) 2 Ves Sen 125; Stevens v Robertson (1868) 18 LT 427; White & Tud LC 630. In Re Pauling's Settlement Trusts [1964] Ch 303, [1963] 3 All ER 1, CA, the Court of Appeal expressed the view that a trustee who carried out a transaction with the beneficiary's apparent consent might still be liable if the trustee knew or ought to have known that the beneficiary was acting under the undue influence of another, or might be presumed to have so acted, but that the trustee would not be liable if it could not be established that he knew or ought to have known. The Court added that the trustee's liability might still exist even if he had received no benefit from the breach of trust.

10. Re Wrightson [1908] 1 Ch 789.

11. Re Wrightson [1908] 1 Ch 789 at 800.

Paragraph 1

Distinction between right to plead concurrence and the right to indemnity

97.2 One must carefully distinguish between the rules stated in the present article and those stated in Article 99, below. The present article is concerned only with the circumstances in which a trustee may plead concurrence or assent by way of defence to an action by the concurring or assenting beneficiary. Article 99, on the other hand, deals with the question as to the circumstances in which a trustee, who may possibly have no defence to an action for breach of trust, may yet call upon his co-trustee, or a concurring or assenting beneficiary, to indemnify him against the consequences of the breach.

Claimant party to breach of trust

97.3 The principle that a party concurring in a breach of trust cannot afterwards complain of it is well illustrated in an old case where stock was settled on a married woman for her separate use for life, with a power of appointment by will. The trustees, at the instance of the husband, sold out the stock, and paid the proceeds to him. The wife filed a bill to compel the trustees to replace the stock, and obtained a decree, under which the trustees transferred part of the stock into court, and were allowed time to re-transfer the remainder. The wife then died, having by her will appointed the stock to the husband. He then filed a bill against the trustees, claiming the stock under the appointment, and praying for the same relief as his wife might have had. It is needless to say that his claim was promptly rejected[1].

1   *Nail v Punter* (1832) 5 Sim 555.

Release need not be under seal

97.4 A formal release in a deed, or an express confirmation, will, of course, estop a beneficiary from instituting subsequent proceedings[1] except that a release which relates to a transaction that is void in equity, being beyond the trustees' power like a fraud on the power, is not binding on the beneficiary executing it[2]. It would seem that any positive act or expression indicative of a clear intention to waive a breach of trust will, if supported by valuable consideration (however slight), be equivalent to a release[3]. Thus, in *Ghost v Waller*[4] a marriage being in contemplation, the lady executed a settlement of real estate under which, in default of issue and in the event of her surviving the husband, she became once more absolutely entitled to the settled property. Between the date of the settlement and the marriage a breach of trust took place through the fraud of the trustees' agent; but in consideration of the trustees undertaking to assist in getting back part of the loss from the agent's estate she through her solicitor agreed (merely by letter) 'to give up all claims if she has any against her trustees for negligence'. Years afterwards, after the death of the husband without issue, she sought to sue the trustees, but it was held that she had effectually released them.

1   See *Re Montagu's Settlements* [1987] 2 WLR 1192 at 1212.
2   *Thomson v Eastwood* (1877) 2 App Cas 215 at 234 and 247, HL.
3   See *Stackhouse v Barnston* (1805) 10 Ves 453, per Sir W. Grant, and *Farrant v Blanchford* (1863) 1 De GJ & Sm 107 at 119–120 per Lord Westbury LC.
4   (1846) 9 Beav 497.

97.5 Section 10 of the Unfair Contract Terms Act 1977 does not affect releases or compromises relating to events that had already occurred so as to make such not binding because unreasonable: the Act is concerned only with prospective liabilities[1].

1   *Tudor Grange Holdings Ltd v Citibank NA* [1992] Ch 53, [1991] 4 All ER 1.

Release may be inferred from conduct

97.6 A release may be inferred from conduct. Thus, where a mother bequeathed property to her son and 'prohibited him from setting up any claim on account of any error, irregularity, or impropriety in the execution of the trusts' of her father's will, it was held that having accepted the bequest the son could not sue the executor of his grandfather's will for employing part of the estate in his own business[1].

1   *Egg v Devey* (1847) 10 Beav 444.

Acquiescence

97.7 Even before the limitation periods now contained in s 21 of the Limitation Act 1980[1] were introduced[2], a beneficiary under a declared trust would disentitle himself to relief by acquiescence over a period. Thus, where a trustee with the knowledge, but without the consent, of the beneficiary, accepted a reduced rent from a lessee of the trust property, and the beneficiary complained of the abatement, but took no steps to put an end to it for some years, it was held that, after the expiration of the lease, the trustee could not be called upon to make up the deficiency[3]. Generally speaking, the same result follows where, with full knowledge of a breach of trust, the beneficiaries take no steps for many years[4], but where the delay can be reasonably explained, and the trustees have not been damnified by it, it is otherwise[5].

1   See para 96.14 ff.
2   By the Trustee Act 1888.
3   *McDonnel v White* (1865) 11 HL Cas 570; and see to same effect *Fletcher v Collis* [1905] 2 Ch 24.
4   *Sleeman v Wilson* (1871) LR 13 Eq 36; and see also *Life Association of Scotland v Siddal* (1861) 3 De GF & J 58 at 72, 74 per Turner LJ; *Jones v Higgins* (1866) LR 2 Eq 538; *Broadhurst v Balguy* (1841) 1 Y & C Ch Cas 16; *Newham v Newham* (1822) 1 LJOS 23; *Griffiths v Porter* (1858) 25 Beav 236; *Davies v Hodgson* (1858) 25 Beav 177; *Hourigan v Trustees Executors and Agency Co Ltd* (1934) 51 CLR 619. See also *Nocton v Lord Ashburton* [1914] AC 932 at 944 and 958 in respect of the claim relating to a 1904 mortgage being barred by acquiescence.
5   See *Story v Gape* (1856) 2 Jur NS 706. See also *Re Pauling's Settlement Trusts* [1964] Ch 303, [1963] 3 All ER 1, CA, where the Court of Appeal held that a delay of four years was explicable on the ground that the case was a complicated one demanding exploration before proceedings could be instituted; *Reader v Fried* [2001] Victoria SC 495 and *Orr v Ford* (1989) 167 CLR 316.

Acquiescence by reversioner

97.8 It must not, however, be assumed that where a person entitled in reversion knows of a breach of trust, and protests, but takes no steps until he becomes entitled in possession, he thereby loses his remedy. In such cases it is apprehended that much must depend on the surrounding circumstances. For instance, where the reversioner was a young lady living with her mother, and the breach consisted in a loan by the trustees at the mother's request to her son (which the daughter objected to), it was held that seven years' delay was no evidence of acquiescence, having regard to her relationship to the mother and brother and the difficulty of taking proceedings without a family quarrel[1]. But where there were no similar circumstances a reversioner was held to be barred after fourteen years' acquiescence[2].

1   *Phillipson v Gatty* (1848) 7 Hare 516. See also *Life Association of Scotland v Siddal* (1861) 3 De GF & J 58.

² *Farrar v Barraclough* (1854) 2 Sm & G 231; and see also *Bate v Hooper* (1855) 5 De GM & G 338; *Browne v Cross* (1851) 14 Beav 105; *Farrant v Blanchford* (1863) 1 De GJ & Sm 107.

97.9 Acquiescence in a past breach does not constitute a licence for the trustee to commit future breaches[1].

¹ *Swain v Law Society* [1982] 1 WLR 17, CA, reversed on the other issues [1983] 1 AC 598, HL.

When acquiescence is a bar

97.10 Although long acquiescence is a bar to relief, the reason for so holding is that the fact of lying by for a considerable period is evidence of an intention or election on the part of the beneficiary not to exercise his strict rights. Consequently, where the circumstances are such as to afford no ground for any such presumption, acquiescence, however long, will be no bar to relief:

(1)   unless the Limitation Act 1980 is applicable[1], or
(2)   unless in the circumstances it appears to be for the general convenience that a suit in respect of a long dormant grievance should be disallowed.

¹ Consider *Re Cross* (1882) 20 Ch D 109.

97.11 In the latter case the court will refuse relief on the ground that 'expedit reipublicae ut sit finis litium'. For instance, where a claimant seeks to set aside a purchase obtained from him by his solicitor, a delay of less than twenty years *may* bar the right to relief, if it would be inconvenient to grant it[1]. So where, in an action for an account, the claimant, by lying by, has rendered it impossible or very inconvenient for the defendant to render the account, he will get no relief[2].

¹ *Gresley v Mousley* (1859) 4 De G & J 78; *Gregory v Gregory* (1815) Coop G 201. See also *Official Assignee of Collier v Creighton* [1993] 2 NZLR 534.
² See per *Lord Alvanley* in *Pickering v Earl Stamford* (1793) 2 Ves 272; and see also *Tatam v Williams* (1844) 3 Hare 347 and *Nelson v Rye* [1996] 2 All ER 186.

97.12 Where the claim is against a constructive trustee on account of the profits of a business the remedy must in all cases be sought with reasonable celerity. As Knight Bruce LJ said in *Clegg v Edmondson*[1]:

'In such cases a man having an adverse claim in equity on the ground of constructive trust should pursue it promptly, and not by empty words only. He should show himself in good time willing to participate in possible loss as well as profit, not play a game in which he alone risks nothing.'

¹ (1857) 8 De GM & G 787. See *Re Jarvis* [1958] 2 All ER 336, [1958] 1 WLR 815.

97.13 *Protection accorded to trustees in case of breach of trust*

Paragraph 1(a)

Minors incapable of release or acquiescence

97.13 A minor cannot lose his right to relief, either by concurrence or release, for the law presumes that he has not the requisite discretion to judge. Nor would this be in any way affected (at least it is so submitted) by the fact that he falsely represented himself to be of age, unless he thereby fraudulently caused the breach of trust of which he complains[1].

[1] See *Cory v Gertcken* (1816) 2 Madd 40; *Overton v Banister* (1844) 3 Hare 503; *Wright v Snowe* (1848) 2 De G & Sm 321.

Paragraph 1(b)

Full knowledge of beneficiary essential

97.14 According to Lawrence Collins J in *Challaram v Chellaram (No 2)*[1]:

'the court can consider all the circumstances with a view to seeing whether it is fair and equitable that a beneficiary who has acquiesced in, or given his concurrence to, a breach of trust should be able to turn round and sue the trustees ... [but] that inquiry is concerned with the requisite degree of knowledge. There is no principle of the law of ... trusts which makes a release ineffective simply because it is unfair.'

[1] [2002] EWHC 632 (Ch), [2002] 3 All ER 17 at [187].

97.15 Even where the beneficiary has executed a deed of release, however, and a fortiori where he has merely concurred or subsequently acquiesced in the breach of trust, the beneficiary must have had full knowledge for the release to be effective. Thus a release to a trustee has been set aside after the lapse of more than twenty years, after the death of the trustee, on evidence of the claimant (corroborated by the tenor of the release) that it was executed in error, although no fraud was imputed[1].

[1] *Re Garnett* (1885) 31 Ch D 1; and see also *Sawyer v Sawyer* (1885) 28 Ch D 595; and *Burrows v Walls* (1855) 5 De GM & G 233.

97.16 So where, on the footing of a supposed illegitimacy, the title of a beneficiary to a trust legacy was disputed and denied by the trustee, and the former was thereby induced to accept from the trustee a smaller sum than that to which he was entitled under the will, and, by deed, to release the trustee from the payment of the legacy, the court would not permit the release to stand even after the lapse of more than 25 years[1].

[1] *Thomson v Eastwood* (1877) 2 App Cas 215, HL; and see *McDonnel v White* (1865) 11 HL Cas 570; *Dougan v Macpherson* [1902] AC 197, HL; and *National Trustees Co of Australasia v General Finance Co of Australasia* [1905] AC 373.

97.17 Although there was some authority[1] for the view that a man is not bound by his concurrence or acquiescence unless and until he knows his legal rights this is not a hard and fast rule. In *Re Pauling's Settlement Trusts*[2] Wilberforce J after considering older cases[3], said:

'The result of these authorities appears to me to be that the court has to consider all the circumstances in which the concurrence of the cestui que trust was given with a view to seeing whether it is fair and equitable that, having given his concurrence, he should afterwards turn round and sue the trustees: that, subject to this, it is not necessary that he should know that what he is concurring in is a breach of trust, provided that he fully understands what he is concurring in, and that it is not necessary that he should himself have directly benefited by the breach of trust.'

[1] *Cockerell v Cholmeley* (1830) 1 Russ & M 418 at 425; *Willmott v Barber* (1880) 15 Ch D 96 at 105; *Farrant v Blanchford* (1863) 1 De GJ & Sm 107 at 119–120.
[2] [1962] 1 WLR 86 at 108.
[3] *Walker v Symonds* (1818) 3 Swan 1; *Evans v Benyon* (1887) 37 Ch D 329; *Re Garnett* (1884) 50 LT 172; on appeal (1885) 31 Ch D 1, CA; *Re Somerset* [1894] 1 Ch 231; *Chillingworth v Chambers* [1896] 1 Ch 685, CA.

97.18 In the later case of *Holder v Holder*[1], these dicta were followed by Cross J at first instance, and expressly approved and applied by the Court of Appeal, Harman LJ stating[2]:

'There is, therefore, no hard and fast rule that ignorance of a legal right is a bar [to the trustee's defence] but the whole circumstances must be looked at to see whether it is just that the complaining beneficiary should succeed against the trustee'.

[1] [1968] Ch 353, [1966] 2 All ER 116, on appeal [1968] Ch 353, [1968]1 All ER 665, CA.
[2] [1968] Ch 353 at 394, CA. Also *Goldsworthy v Brickell* [1987] 1 All ER 853 at 873, CA

97.19 The dicta of Cross J and Harman LJ's statement were endorsed by the Court of Appeal in *Re Freeston's Charity*[1]. Another approach that the Court of Appeal[2] has adopted is that a claimant's right will be lost if 'it would be dishonest or unconscionable for the claimant to seek to enforce it'.

[1] [1979] 1 All ER 51 at 62, [1978] 1 WLR 741 at 754–755, CA.
[2] *Shaw v Applegate* [1978] 1 All ER 123 at 131, [1977] 1 WLR 970 at 978, CA; *Swain v Law Society* [1981] 3 All ER 797 at 810, CA (where the defence of acquiescence succeeded for the solicitors' indemnity insurance commission paid to the Law Society prior to 1979 but not thereafter, but in the Lords [1983] 1 AC 598, [1982] 2 All ER 827, para 33.34, the point did not arise). Further see *Knight v Frost* [1999] 1 BCLC 364 where acquiescence in a breach of fiduciary duty by a director was not established in respect of a £300,000 loan but was established in respect of a subsequent £75,000 loan though disputed by J Payne 'Consent' in P Birks & A Pretto *Breach of Trust* (2002) 297 at pp. 304–8.

97.20 Where trustees wish to obtain the consent of beneficiaries of full age and capacity to activities that will profit the trustees particular care must be taken to ensure that the fully informed consent of the beneficiaries is obtained[1]. Where the trustees know that a breach of trust is involved they must so inform the beneficiaries.

[1] *Phipps v Boardman* [1964] 2 All ER 187 at 204–205, 207. The point was not pressed in the appeals. See too *Mitchell v Halliwell* [2005] EWHC 937 (Ch) esp at [41]–[52].

Necessity of reciting actual breaches of trust in a deed of release

97.21 For these reasons a release, where intended to cover known breaches of trust, must contain recitals showing fully and precisely the circumstances under which the breach took place, including the amount of the loss (if any) and that such circumstances did in fact amount to a breach of trust. If this be not done, the general words will be controlled and restricted in their operation by the recitals to the matters actually stated[1]. Indeed, it is the duty of the trustees to see that the beneficiary, who is about to execute a release, is properly advised as to his rights[2]. Where the trustees rely on the beneficiary having been separately advised, so as to oust a finding of undue influence, they must *prove* that he did in point of fact employ a separate solicitor, and not merely someone nominated by the trustees or their solicitor[3].

1 *Lindo v Lindo* (1839) 8 LJ Ch 284; *Ramsden v Hylton* (1751) 2 Ves Sen 304; *Pritt v Clay* (1843) 6 Beav 503.
2 This point, and the extent of the solicitor's duty to advise, were considered in *Re Pauling's Settlement Trusts* [1964] Ch 303, [1963] 3 All ER 1, CA.
3 *Lloyd v Attwood* (1859) 3 De G & J 614.

Ignorance of beneficiary where he has had the advantage of the breach

97.22 It seems that where a beneficiary has, for valuable consideration (eg marriage), had the advantage of a breach of trust, but without any knowledge of the breach, he can sue the trustee without replacing the amount which he himself has received by reason of the breach. Thus, where part of the proceeds of trust funds misappropriated by a father were made subject to the marriage settlement of his son (a beneficiary in remainder who was ignorant of the source whence the property proceeded, and thought it was a gift from his father), it was held that the son's representatives were entitled to have his share of the trust funds replaced without deducting the value of the proceeds settled[1].

1 *Crichton v Crichton* [1896] 1 Ch 870, reversing decision of North J [1895] 2 Ch 853; *Re Pauling's Settlement Trusts* [1964] Ch 303 at 354, 357–358 (Anthony, an innocent volunteer, did not have to account for benefits indirectly received through his mother, but Ann conceded that £300 spent directly for her benefit on furniture had to be brought into account).

Paragraph 1(c)

97.23 A release made by a beneficiary who has just attained his majority will be subject to considerable scrutiny in case it was obtained by undue influence. Thus in *Wade v Cox*[1] a release executed by a twenty-three year old man in favour of his trustee was set aside eighteen years afterwards.

1 (1835) 4 LJ Ch 105. However, times have changed so that 18 years is now the age of majority and persons normally become independent minded by the time they reach 23 years.

97.24 Similarly, where beneficiaries aged between twenty-one and twenty-seven years consented to breaches of trust for the benefit of their parents the

Court of Appeal held that 'a trustee carrying out a transaction in breach of trust may be liable if he knew, or ought to have known, that the beneficiary was acting under the undue influence of another, or may be presumed to have done so, but will not be liable if it cannot be established that he knew or ought to have known'[1]. When a young adult may be presumed to be fully emancipated from parental influence is a question of fact in all the circumstances of a particular case[2].

1   *Re Pauling's Settlement Trusts* [1964] Ch 303 at 338.
2   See *Bullock v Lloyds Bank Ltd* [1955] Ch 317 where a settlement created one month after attaining majority was set aside for undue influence, despite some lengthy but explicable delay.

ARTICLE 98
PROTECTION AGAINST THE ACTS OF CO-TRUSTEE

98.1

(1)   A trustee is not vicariously answerable for the receipts, acts, or defaults of his co-trustee[1], but only for his *own* acts or defaults such as:
       (a)   where he *hands* the trust property to his co-trustee without seeing to its proper application[2];
       (b)   where he allows his co-trustee to *receive* the trust property without making due inquiry as to his dealing with it[3];
       (c)   where he becomes aware of a breach of trust, either committed or meditated, and abstains from taking the needful steps to obtain restitution and redress, or to prevent the meditated wrong[4].

(2)   Even in the above three cases the trustee may be relieved from responsibility by express declaration in the trust deed.

1   Trustee Act 1925, s 30 before its repeal by the Trustee Act 2000; *Dawson v Clarke* (1811) 18 Ves 247; and see *Welch v Bank of England* [1955] Ch 508, [1955] 1 All ER 811.
2   *Walker v Symonds* (1818) 3 Swan 1; and *Bone v Cooke* (1824) 13 Price 332. The case of *Re Fryer* (1857) 3 K & J 317, merely turned upon a question of procedure, wilful default not having been pleaded.
3   See *Wynne v Tempest* (1897) 13 TLR 360; *Bradwell v Catchpole* (1700) 3 Swan 78n; *Marriott v Kinnersley* (1830) Taml 470.
4   *Millar's Trustees v Polson* (1897) 34 SLR 798.

Position apart from statute

98.2 In the leading case of *Wilkins v Hogg*[1] a testatrix, after appointing three trustees, declared that each of them should be answerable only for losses arising from his own default, and not for involuntary acts or for the acts or defaults of his co-trustees; and, particularly, that any trustee who should pay over to his co-trustees, or should do or concur in any act enabling his co-trustees to receive any moneys for the general purposes of her will, should not be obliged to see to the due application thereof, nor should such trustee be subsequently rendered liable by any express notice or intimation of the actual misapplication of the same moneys. The three trustees joined in signing and giving receipts to insurance companies for sums of money paid by them, but two of the trustees permitted their co-trustee to obtain the money without ascertaining whether he had invested it. This trustee having misapplied it, it was sought to make his co-trustees responsible, but Lord Westbury held that they were not, saying:

> 'There are three modes in which a trustee would become liable *according to the ordinary rules of law*—first, where, being the recipient, he hands over the money without securing its due application; secondly, where he allows a co-trustee to receive money without making due inquiry as to his dealing with it; and thirdly, where he becomes aware of a breach of trust, either committed or meditated, and abstains from taking the needful steps to obtain restitution or redress. The framer of the clause under examination knew these three rules, and used words sufficient to meet all these cases. There remained, therefore, only personal misconduct, in respect of which a trustee acting under this will would be responsible. He would still be answerable for collusion if he handed over trust money to his co-trustee with reasonable ground for believing or suspecting that that trustee would commit a breach of trust; but no such case as this was made by the bill.'

¹ (1861) 31 LJ Ch 41; and see *Pass v Dundas* (1880) 43 LT 665; *Dix v Burford* (1854) 19 Beav 409; *Mucklow v Fuller* (1821) Jac 198; *Brumridge v Brumridge* (1858) 27 Beav 5.

98.3 However, an exculpatory clause cannot protect a trustee who commits a breach of trust dishonestly (which includes reckless indifference to the beneficiaries' interests) or honestly if no reasonable trustee in his shoes could have honestly done what he did¹.

¹ *Armitage v Nurse* [1998] Ch 241, CA; *Walker v Stones* [2001] QB 902, CA.

98.4 Commonly, a trustee is liable for the acts of a co-trustee where he is a passive trustee who allows his co-trustee to exercise alone discretions which it is their duty to exercise jointly so that he himself is at fault. However, where trustees who are majority shareholders in a company have one trustee representing them on the board of the company then:

> 'one ought not to regard him as performing a duty to the trust which it was incumbent on the trustees to perform personally so that [the trustees] become automatically responsible for any deficiencies in [him], as does a passive trustee who allows his co-trustee to exercise alone discretions which it is their duty to exercise jointly. If these trustees had decided as they might have done, to be represented on the board by a nominee they would have been entitled to rely upon the information given to them by that nominee as to the way in which the company's affairs were being managed even though such information was inaccurate or inadequate, *unless they* had some reason to suspect that it was inaccurate or inadequate'¹.

¹ *Re Lucking's Will Trusts* [1967] 3 All ER 726 at 733.

Statutory indemnity 1859 to 2000

98.5 By s 30(1) of the Trustee Act 1925¹ it was provided as follows:

A trustee shall be chargeable only for moneys and securities actually received by him notwithstanding his signing any receipt for the sake of conformity, and shall be answerable and accountable only for his own acts, receipts, neglects, or defaults, and not for those of any other trustee, nor for any banker, broker, or other person with whom any trust money or securities may be deposited, nor for the insufficiency or deficiency of any securities, nor for any other loss[2], unless the same happens through his own wilful default.

1   See *Re Munton* [1927] 1 Ch 262, CA, and *Re Windsor Steam Coal Co (1901) Ltd* [1929] 1 Ch 151; per Maugham J in *Re Vickery* [1931] 1 Ch 572 at 580.
2   Of a similar sort: *Re Vickery* [1931] 1 Ch 572 at 582.

98.6 This section replaced s 24(1) of the Trustee Act 1893 which replaced s 31 of the Law of Property Amendment Act 1859 which 'incorporated, into instruments creating trusts the common indemnity clause which was usually inserted in such instruments. It does not substantially alter the law as it was administered by courts of equity'[1] which construed such express indemnity clauses very strictly against trustees attempting to rely upon them. Thus 'wilful default' was construed as including 'want of ordinary prudence'[2] though in *Re Vickery*[3] Maugham J, somewhat surprisingly relying on company law cases, treated 'wilful default' as meaning only a consciousness of committing a breach of duty or a recklessness as to whether or not a breach was being committed.

1   *Re Brier* (1884) 26 Ch D 238 at 243, per Lord Selborne.
2   *Re Chapman* [1896] 2 Ch 763 at 776, per Lindley LJ; *Underwood v Stevens* (1816) 1 Mer 712.
3   [1931] 1 Ch 572.

98.7 Then, in *Armitage v Nurse*[1] the Court of Appeal endorsed this, before the Trustee Act 2000 repealed s 30, having made express provision concerning trustee's liabilities for agents, nominees or custodians that they employ, but leaving the question of the liability for the conduct of a co-trustee to the general law treating trusteeship as a joint office[2] and the provisions of particular trust instruments.

1   [1998] Ch 241, CA, but no detailed consideration was given to substantial criticisms of *Re Vickery's* interpretation of 'wilful default' eg by G H Jones (1959) 22 MLR 381; J E Stannard [1979] Conv 345 and 15th edn hereof pp 623–624.
2   See Article 56 above.

Post Trustee Act 2000

98.8 Repeal of the earlier statutory provision has had two significant consequences. In cases formerly within s 30 a trustee is no longer protected unless guilty of 'wilful default', so that the presence or absence of an exemption clause in the trust instrument becomes crucial, while he also loses the protection of the onus of proof falling upon the beneficiary-claimants[1].

1   *Re Brier* (1882) 26 Ch D 238, CA.

98.9 The burden of proving that he acted properly in fulfilling the functions of his joint office falls back upon him[1]. Otherwise, it is not believed that the repeal has made much difference, the earlier statutory provisions having been declaratory of the position in equity. Joining in receipts for the sake of conformity and permitting a co-trustee to receive money in the first instance will be safe behaviour, but money must not be allowed to be retained by the co-trustee for longer than reasonably necessary[2], while if the co-trustee says that the money has been duly invested this needs to be checked[3]. The safest course is for money to be paid into a joint bank account of the trustees.

[1]   *Brice v Stokes* (1805) 11 Ves 319.
[2]   *Brice v Stokes* (1805) 11 Ves 319; *Lewis v Nobbs* (1878) 8 Ch D 591; *Wynne v Tempest* (1897) 13 TLR 360.
[3]   *Mendes v Guedalla* (1861) 2 John & H 259; *Thompson v Finch* (1856) 22 Beav 316.

ARTICLE 99
TRUSTEES' CLAIMS FOR CONTRIBUTION OR INDEMNITY AGAINST CO-TRUSTEES, BENEFICIARIES WHO INSTIGATED BREACH, OR THIRD PARTIES IMPLICATED IN BREACH

99.1

(1)   Where several trustees have been held jointly and severally liable in respect of the same 'damage' caused by their respective breaches of duty[1], and one pays more than his fair share of their common liability, he can recover a contribution or even a complete indemnity from one or more of the others, according to the court's assessment of the proportions in which the burden of paying for the 'damage' should properly be borne[2].

(2)   When apportioning liability between the trustees for the purposes of a contribution claim, the court will apply the following general principles:

   (a)   trustees are presumed to share equal responsibility to the beneficiaries, and so must bear an equal share of the burden of paying for the damage unless there is a reason why an unequal apportionment should be made[3];

   (b)   an unequal apportionment will be made against a trustee who derives a personal benefit from his breach of trust, either by wrongfully misapplying trust funds to his personal use[4], or by taking a benefit from the breach in his capacity as beneficiary[5];

   (c)   an unequal apportionment will be made against a trustee who has acted dishonestly where the others have acted in good faith[6];

   (d)   an unequal apportionment may also be made against a professional trustee upon whose guidance a lay trustee has reasonably relied[7].

(3)   Where a trustee commits a breach of trust at the instigation or request[8], or with the consent in writing, of a beneficiary, the court may make such order as it deems just, for impounding all

or any part of the beneficiary's interest in the trust property by way of indemnity to the trustee or persons claiming through him[9].

(4)   Third parties who are implicated in a breach of trust and who are liable for the same damage as the trustees are jointly and severally liable, both with one another, and with the trustees, with the result that any one of them may have to pay for the whole damage[10], in which case he may be entitled to recover a contribution or even a complete indemnity from the others[213], according to the court's assessment of the equities.

1   *Charitable Corpn v Sutton* (1742) 2 Atk 400 at 406; *Walker v Symonds* (1818) 3 Swan 1 at 75; *Ashurst v Mason* (1875) LR 20 Eq 225 at 233; *Re Duckwari plc* [1999] Ch 253 at 262.
2   Civil Liability (Contribution) Act 1978, ss 1, 2, 6.
3   *Lingard v Bromley* (1812) 1 V & B 114; *Jesse v Bennett* (1856) 6 De GM & G 609; *Robinson v Harkin* [1896] 2 Ch 415 at 426.
4   *Lincoln v Wright* (1841) 4 Beav 427; *Thompson v Finch* (1856) 22 Beav 316 at 327; *Wynne v Tempest* [1897] 1 Ch 110.
5   *Chillingworth v Chambers* [1896] 1 Ch 685.
6   *Baynard v Woolley* (1855) 20 Beav 583 at 585–6; *Re Smith* [1896] 1 Ch 71.
7   *Lockhart v Reilly* (1856) 25 LJ Ch 697, aff'd (1857) LJ Ch 54; *Thompson v Finch* (1856) 22 Beav 316; *Re Linsley* [1904] 2 Ch 785.
8   The request need not be in writing, although a mere consent must be: per Kekewich J in *Griffith v Hughes* [1892] 3 Ch 105 at 109; and per Lindley LJ in *Re Somerset* [1894] 1 Ch 231 at 266.
9   Trustee Act 1925, s 62. In *Re Pauling's Settlement Trusts (No 2)* [1963] Ch 576, [1963] 1 All ER 857, Wilberforce J said that a trustee's rights to impound, under s62 and in equity, did not depend upon his being still a trustee at the date of the impounding order.
10   *Rowland v Witherden* (1851) 21 LJ Ch 480 at 482; *Pearce v Pearce* (1856) 22 Beav 248; *Blyth v Fladgate* [1891] 1 Ch 337 at 353; *Cowper v Stoneham* (1893) 68 LT 18; *Young v Murphy* [1996] 1 VR 279 at 300.
11   Civil Liability (Contribution) Act 1978, ss 1, 2, 6; *Dubai Aluminium Co Ltd v Salaam* [2002] UKHL 48, [2003] 2 AC 366.

Paragraph 1

Joint and several liability

99.2 Trustees are liable only for their own breaches of duty, and are not vicariously liable for breaches of trust committed by their co-trustees. However, it often happens that the beneficiaries suffer the same damage as a result of various breaches of trust committed by several trustees, either because the trustees have collectively done an act which entails a breach of duty by each trustee, or because one 'active trustee' has committed a breach of trust while another 'passive trustee' has committed a distinct breach of duty, eg by standing by with knowledge that the other is committing a breach of duty[1], or by failing to take steps to obtain redress after becoming aware that a breach has been committed[2]. In the event that several trustees are liable for the same damage, their liability is joint and several, with the result that the whole amount of the damage can be recovered from any or all of them[3]. In these circumstances, it can happen that one may be forced to pay more than his fair share of their common liability, in which case he may be entitled to recover a contribution or indemnity may lie against one or more of the others. Note, though, that no such claim will lie against a co-trustee who is not liable to the beneficiaries, eg because he has been excused from liability under the Trustee Act 1925, s 61[4]; nor will a claim lie against a co-trustee who is liable only in respect of some other damage than the damage for which the claimant trustee was liable to pay[5].

1   *Booth v Booth* (1838) 1 Beav 125; *Gough v Smith* [1872] WN 18.
2   *Wilkins v Hogg* (1861) 8 Jur NS 25 at 26.
3   *Vandebende v Levingston* (1674) 3 Swan 625; *Charitable Corpn v Sutton* (1742) 2 Atk 400 at 406; *Walker v Symonds* (1818) 3 Swan 1 at 75; *A-G v Daugars* (1864) 33 Beav 621 at 624; *Ashurst v Mason* (1875) LR 20 Eq 225 at 233; *Jackson v Dickinson* [1903] 1 Ch 947 at 952; *Re Mulligan* [1998] 1 NZLR 481 at 511, NZ High Ct; *Re Duckwari plc* [1999] Ch 253 at 262, CA.
4   Cf *Wohlleben v Canada Permanent Trust Co* (1976) 70 DLR (3d) 257.
5   *Alexander v Perpetual Trustee (WA) Ltd* (2003) 216 CLR 109.

The Civil Liability (Contribution) Act 1978

99.3 Equitable claims for contribution and indemnity between trustees were allowed by the Chancery courts for many years, but such claims must now be brought under the Civil Liability (Contribution) Act 1978. Section 1(1) entitles 'any person liable in respect of any damage suffered by any other person' to claim contribution from 'any other person liable in respect of the same damage', and s 6(1) expressly states that a person is relevantly liable for 'damage' if the legal basis for his liability is 'breach of trust'[1]. Section 2(2) empowers the court 'to direct that the contribution to be recovered from any person shall amount to a complete indemnity'; thus indemnity claims fall within the scope of the statute as well as contribution claims to recover a smaller proportion of a shared liability. Section 7(3) then stipulates that the right to recover contribution under the Act 'supersedes any right, other than an express contractual right, to recover contribution (as distinct from indemnity) otherwise than under [the] Act in corresponding circumstances'. It is suggested that the parenthesised words in s 7(3) should be read to mean 'as distinct from a *contractual* indemnity', as otherwise one arrives at the absurd conclusion that claims by trustees for a contribution of up to 99.99% from co-trustees are covered by the statute, but that claims for a 100% indemnity are not[2].

1   In this context the word 'damage' is not synonymous with 'damages' but rather means 'harm' or 'loss': *Royal Brompton NHS Trust v Hammond* [2002] UKHL 12, [2002] 1 WLR 1397 at 1401, HL.
2   Loose usage of the term 'indemnity' can lead to several different sorts of misunderstanding and ideally the term should be used solely in connection with contractual claims, leaving the term 'reimbursement' to describe non-contractual 100% contribution claims: C Mitchell *The Law of Contribution and Reimbursement* (2003) paras 1.15–1.17.

99.4 The 1978 Act came into force on 1 January 1979[1]. It does not apply where the damage in question occurred before 1979[2] and a person is not to be entitled to recover contribution or be liable to make contribution 'by reference to any liability based on breach of any obligation assumed by him' before 1979[3]. These words are entirely apt to describe the consensual acceptance of obligations as an express trustee[4]. Thus persons appointed trustees before 1979 should not be affected by the statute.

[1] Section 10(2). Once B and C are each persons against whom liability had been, or could be, established in an action brought against them by A in an English court (applying the appropriate law in accordance with English private international law rules) then the Act confers on B a right of contribution against C: *Arab Monetary Fund v Hashim (No 9)* (1994) Times, 11 October; *RA Lister & Co Ltd v EG Thomson Shipping Ltd* [1987] 3 All ER 1032 at 1038, citing Donaldson MR in *Logan v Uttlesford District Council* [1984] CA Transcript 263, interpreting s 1(6).
[2] Section 7(1).
[3] Section 7(2).
[4] *Lampitt v Poole Borough Council* [1990] 2 All ER 887 at 892, CA.

99.5 It seems probable that the courts will generally be guided by the pre-1978 equitable jurisprudence when deciding claims by trustees for a contribution or indemnity from their co-trustees. In one respect, however, it seems that they have departed from the earlier authorities. It was formerly the case that the 'clean hands' rule debarred a fraudulent trustee from recovering a contribution from another fraudulent trustee in the Chancery court[1]. However the 1978 Act (and its precursor the Law Reform (Married Women and Tortfeasors) Act 1935, s 6) was enacted with the express purpose of allowing claimants to rely on their own wrongdoing when seeking contribution from other wrongdoers, and the statute makes no stipulation that claimants should be debarred from claiming by the fact that they acted illegally or immorally. In *K v P* these considerations led Ferris J to conclude that 'the ex turpi causa defence is not available as an answer to a claim for contribution under the Act of 1978'[2]. However, he went on to say that[3]:

'section 2(1) and (2) give the court ample power to fix the amount of the contribution at a level, including a zero level, which takes account of all the factors which, in relation to common law claims, are relevant to the ex turpi causa defence.'

[1] *A-G v Wilson* (1840) Cr & Ph 1 at 28 per Lord Cottenham LC.
[2] [1993] Ch 140 at 148–9.
[3] [1993] Ch 140 at 149.

99.6 No action to recover contribution under the 1978 Act can be brought after the expiration of two years from the date of judgment or award of damages against the person seeking contribution or, otherwise, the date such person agreed to make a payment in satisfaction of his liability[1].

[1] Limitation Act 1980, s 10. For discussion of the interplay between s 10(3) and (4), which lay down different rules for cases where a third party has won judgment against a contribution claimant, and cases where his action has been settled, see *Knight v Rochdale Healthcare NHS Trust* (QB) [2004] 1 WLR 371, reviewed in *Aer Lingus plc v Gildacroft Ltd* [2006] EWCA Civ 4, [2006] 2 All ER 290.

Paragraph 2

Principles of apportionment

99.7 In any proceedings for contribution made under s 1 the amount of the contribution recoverable from any person is to be 'such as may be found by the court to be just and equitable having regard to the extent of that person's responsibility for the damage in question'[1]. It is likely that the courts will look to the cases decided prior to the enactment of the legislation for guidance when apportioning liability between trustees.

[1]   Civil Liability (Contribution) Act 1978, s 2(1).

Paragraph 2(a)

Equal responsibility is the default rule

99.8 Trustees are presumed to share equal responsibility for trust losses[1]. The sanction of equal liability serves a useful salutary function for breach of what is a joint obligation par excellence. Moreover, trustees undertake an active joint obligation: this should not be undermined by encouraging hopes that passivity might help a trustee reduce the extent of his liability[2]. By sitting back and leaving everything to a co-trustee, a trustee fundamentally breaks his duty of fidelity and loyalty and cannot be heard to deny that the breach would not have occurred but for him doing the opposite of what he had undertaken to do.

[1]   *Lingard v Bromley* (1812) 1 Ves & B 114; *Jesse v Bennett* (1856) 6 De GM & G 609; *Robinson v Harkin* [1896] 2 Ch 415 at 426; *Gilchrist v Dean* [1960] VR 266 at 271–2, Victoria Sup Ct.
[2]   See *Bahin v Hughes* (1886) 31 Ch D 390, CA for emphasis on culpability of inactive trustee. Where the trustees are authorised to act by a majority then the dissenting minority if not protected, as usual, by a clause in the trust instrument, will need to seek the directions of the court (at the expense of the trust fund) if they believe the majority may be committing a breach of trust.

Paragraph 2(b)

Trustee-beneficiary generally bound to indemnify co-trustee to extent of his beneficial interest

99.9 This rule is established by *Chillingworth v Chambers*[1], where the whole of the authorities were elaborately discussed by the Court of Appeal. The claimant and defendant, the trustees of a will, had committed breaches of trust by investing on insufficient securities, bearing a high rate of interest, and were declared to be jointly and severally liable to make good the loss to the trust estate. The claimant trustee, after some and before others of the investments in question had been made, became also beneficially entitled to a share in the trust estate, as the successor in title of his deceased wife. He claimed to be entitled to contribution from the defendant trustee on the ground that they were both in pari delicto (equally to blame).

[1]   [1896] 1 Ch 685. See also *Moxham v Grant* [1900] 1 QB 88 (where directors of a company were held entitled to indemnity from shareholders who had been paid capital ultra vires); *Palmer v Permanent Trustee Co* (1915) 16 SR (NSW) 162; *MacDonald v Hauer* (1976) 72 DLR (3d) 110. The loss caused by the breach must have occurred in connection with the same trust as that under which the trustee is a beneficiary: *Re Towndrow* [1911] 1 Ch 662; *Harris v Harris* (1919) 20 SR(NSW) 61; *Macphillamy v Fox* (1932) 32 SR (NSW) 427.

99.10 The court, however, rejected this claim, on the ground that the rule as to the right of a trustee to contribution from his co-trustee for loss occasioned to the estate by a breach of trust for which both are equally to blame, does not apply where one of them is also a beneficiary, until he has made good any loss sustained to the extent of his own beneficial share in the property. In that case, the rule to be applied is that under which the *share or interest* of a trustee-beneficiary who has assented to a breach of trust has to bear the whole loss; and the trustee who is a beneficiary must therefore indemnify his co-trustee to the extent of his share or interest in the trust estate, and not merely to the extent of the benefit he has received. Lindley MR, in giving judgment, made the following important observations:

> 'The plaintiff and the defendant being *in pari delicto*, the plaintiff's right as trustee to contribution from the defendant as co-trustee to the extent of one-half the loss is established by a long series of authorities, of which it is only necessary to mention *Lingard v Bromley*[1] and *Bahin v Hughes*[2]. On the other hand, the right of the defendant as trustee to be indemnified out of the share of the plaintiff as cestui que trust against the consequences of a breach of trust committed at his request and for his benefit is equally indisputable. It was treated by Lord Eldon as clear law in his day that a cestui que trust who concurs in a breach of trust is not entitled to relief against his co-trustees in respect of it: see *Walker v Symonds*[3]. ... Lord Eldon's statement of the law was distinctly approved and followed in *Farrant v Blanchford*[4]. Moreover ... it was decided, in *Evans v Benyon*[5], that this doctrine applies to a person who becomes a cestui que trust after his concurrence. Further, in *Butler v Carter*[6], Lord Romilly stated distinctly that where one of two trustees was himself a cestui que trust he could not call upon his co-trustee to replace stock which they had both permitted to be misapplied. These cases are all based on obvious good sense; for if I request a person to deal with my property in a particular way, and loss ensues, I cannot justly throw that loss on him. Whatever our liabilities may be to other people, still, as between him and me, the loss clearly ought to fall on me. Whether I am solely entitled to the property, or have only a share or a limited interest, still the loss which I sustain in respect of my share or interest must clearly be borne by me, not by him ... The plaintiff contended, on the authority of *Raby v Ridehalgh*[7], that the plaintiff's liability as cestui que trust to indemnify the defendant, and the extent of the plaintiff's inability to obtain relief against the defendant, was limited, not by the amount of the plaintiff's share in the trust estate, *but by the benefit derived by the plaintiff from the breach of trust.*'

[1] (1812) 1 Ves & B 114.
[2] (1886) 31 Ch D 390.
[3] (1818) 3 Swan 1 at 64.
[4] (1863) 1 De GJ & Sm 107.
[5] (1887) 37 Ch D 329.
[6] (1868) LR 5 Eq 276 at 281.
[7] (1855) 7 De GM & G 104.

99.11 His Lordship then showed that that case was no authority for such a proposition, and continued:

> 'Suppose a cestui que trust in remainder to induce his trustees to commit a breach of trust for the benefit of the tenant for life—perhaps his own father or mother—can such a remainderman compel the trustees to make good the loss or resist their claim to have it made good out of his interest when it falls in, if some other cestui que trust compels them to make the loss good? *I apprehend*

> not; and yet, in the case supposed, the cestui que trust in remainder might not himself have derived any benefit at all from the breach.'

99.12 Kay LJ in the same case does not seem to have been willing to commit himself to the extent of the words above italicised[1]; but decided that, as in that case, the claimant *had* received some benefit from the breach, he was primarily liable not merely to the extent of that benefit, but to the extent of his whole share.

1   *Chillingworth v Chambers* [1896] 1 Ch 685 at 707.

Trustee benefiting incidentally by breach not always liable to indemnify co-trustee

99.13 Although, as stated by Cotton LJ in *Bahin v Hughes*[1], a trustee who has got the trust money into his own hands and made use of it, will in general be liable to indemnify his co-trustee, yet he will not have to do so where his breach of trust is only remotely connected with the loss; unless, of course, he was guilty of actual fraud. Thus the fact of a borrower of trust funds on insufficient security repaying out of the money so borrowed a debt due from him to one of the trustees is not, of itself, sufficient to render the trustee accepting repayment liable, since the borrower is under no restriction as to its application[2].

1   (1886) 31 Ch D 390.
2   *Chillingworth v Chambers* [1896] 1 Ch 685; *Butler v Butler* (1877) 7 Ch D 116; and see also *Whitney v Smith* (1869) 4 Ch App 513.

Liability of trustee-beneficiary confined to breaches of trust to which he was privy

99.14 The primary liability of a trustee-beneficiary for a breach of trust is confined to breaches committed with his privity, and does not extend to the case where his only breach consists in failing to take steps to put the original breach right when he subsequently becomes a trustee, even although, if he had done so, it is probable that no loss would have been suffered. In such a case the trustee who committed the original breach and the beneficiary subsequently appointed to be a trustee who merely failed in his duty of not insisting on the breach being set right are not *in pari delicto*. Both may be liable to the other beneficiaries, but the original breach is the *fons et origo mali*, and the original trustee who alone committed it is primarily responsible as between himself and the trustee subsequently appointed. This was decided by Warrington J in *Re Fountaine*[1] (in which the late Sir Arthur Underhill was counsel), but the case is reported only on other points which were appealed.

1   [1909] 2 Ch 382.

Paragraph 2(c)

Relative moral blameworthiness

99.15 Notwithstanding the importance of keeping trustees up to the mark by refusing to make apportionments in their favour where they have passively stood by while other trustees have actively committed breaches of trust, the courts have sometimes allowed trustees who have acted in good faith to shift the burden of making good the trust losses onto other trustees who have acted dishonestly[1].

[1] *Baynard v Woolley* (1855) 20 Beav 583 at 585–6; *Elwes v Barnard* (1865) 13 LT 426; *Bellemore v Watson* (1885) 1 TLR 241 at 242, CA ; *Re Smith* [1896] 1 Ch 71; *Deloitte Haskins & Sells v Coopers and Lybrand Ltd* (Alberta QB, 29 November 1996) at para 92.

Paragraph 2(d)

Professional and lay trustees

99.16 In *Bahin v Hughes[1]*, Cotton LJ said:

'On going into the authorities, there are very few cases in which one trustee, who has been guilty with a co-trustee of breach of trust and held answerable, has successfully sought indemnity as against his co-trustee. *Lockhart v Reilly[2]* and *Thompson v Finch[3]* are the only cases which appear to be reported. Now in *Lockhart v Reilly* it appears from the report of the case in the Law Journal that the trustee by whom the loss was sustained had been not only trustee, but had been and was a solicitor, and acting as solicitor for himself and his co-trustee, and it was on his advice that Lockhart had relied in making the investment which gave rise to the action of the cestui que trust[4]... Of course where one trustee has got the money into his own hands, and made use of it, he will be liable to his co-trustee to give him an indemnity[5]. Now I think it wrong to lay down any limitation of the circumstances under which one trustee would be held liable to the other for indemnity, both having been held liable to the cestui que trust; but so far as cases have gone at present, relief has only been granted against a trustee *who has himself got the benefit of the breach of trust, or between whom and his co-trustees there has existed a relation, which will justify the court in treating him as solely liable for the breach of trust.*'

[1] (1886) 31 Ch D 390 at 394; and see also *Robinson v Harkin* [1896] 2 Ch 415. For an interesting historical account of the nineteenth century Chancery courts' reluctance to accept that a lay trustee might rely on a professional trustee, see C Stebbings *The Private Trustee in Victorian England* (2002) chap 4.
[2] (1856) 25 LJ Ch 697.
[3] (1856) 22 Beav 316; but see also *Warwick v Richardson* (1842) 10 M & W 284.
[4] See also to same effect *Re Turner* [1897] 1 Ch 536; and *Re Linsley* [1904] 2 Ch 785, where Warrington J made a solicitor-trustee indemnify his co-trustee against costs, merely because he was negligent in furnishing accounts to the beneficiaries.
[5] See *Fetherstone v West* (1871) IR 6 Eq 86.

99.17 These italicised dicta may be invoked not just against a trustee who is a solicitor but also against a trustee who is a Chancery barrister or a bank manager or a professional trustee. An 'innocent' non-professional trustee misled by the advice of such a co-trustee might alternatively be able to claim relief under s 61 of the Trustee Act 1925.

99.18 It must not, however, be assumed from the above citation that a solicitor-trustee who advises the commission of a breach of trust is necessarily bound to indemnify his co-trustees; for where the co-trustee has himself been an active participator in the breach of trust, and has not participated in it merely in consequence of the advice and control of the solicitor, he will have no right to be indemnified. Thus, where a female trustee joined in the importunities of her brother, and thus induced her co-trustee (a solicitor) to commit a breach of trust for the brother's benefit, it was held that she was not entitled to call upon the solicitor-trustee for an indemnity[1].

1   *Head v Gould* [1898] 2 Ch 250. See also *Ward-Smith v Jebb* (1964) 108 Sol Jo 919;para 95.18, where the question of indemnity by a solicitor-trustee who had wrongly interpreted a statute was raised but not decided.

99.19 Again, in *Re Mulligan*[1] the lay trustee who was life tenant, and the trust corporation co-trustee were held jointly and severally liable to beneficiaries on the death of the life tenant, the beneficiaries having suffered losses from the trust money on sale of a farm being invested solely in fixed interest securities for many years. The life tenant's personal representatives claimed an indemnity from the trust corporation, which itself claimed an indemnity from them on the basis the life tenant had alone benefited from the breach of trust designed to favour her over the remaindermen interested in capital growth investments protecting against inflation. Surprisingly, the judge found that her subjective intent to benefit herself at the expense of the remaindermen was not of itself sufficient when it so happened that, objectively, her strategy had been mistaken, because a mix of fixed-interest and share investments would have enabled her to enjoy a higher income than the one actually received. On the other hand, despite her vociferousness the trust corporation as such should not have meekly acquiesced in her selfish policy[2], so one can appreciate a reluctance to permit it to be indemnified out of her estate. Her estate's claim to be indemnified by the trust corporation was rejected because she herself was a person of some business acumen whose overriding of the advice of her co-trustee was not the product of her ignorance or vulnerability. A draw was thus a fair result.

1   [1998] 1 NZLR 481 (at 511 in particular).
2   It should have applied to the court for directions which the life tenant-trustee would have to comply with or be replaced as trustee.

Justifications for treating lay trustees differently from professional trustees

99.20 One justification for the rule that professional trustees should bear a greater proportion of responsibility for trust losses than lay trustees is that they are paid, and so might be characterised as having derived a benefit from their breaches of trust in the form of remuneration for work done badly[1]. Another is that professional trustees by reason of their greater knowledge and experience owe a duty to explain the ins-and-outs of trust administration to less well-informed lay trustees, so as to give them the opportunity to raise objections; hence a professional trustee's failure to do this constitutes a more potent cause of the trust losses than the failure of the lay trustees to keep themselves informed about such matters[2]. A third is that the beneficiaries are entitled to expect more of professional trustees who have held themselves out as possessing special skill and knowledge[3], and that their breaches of trust are therefore more morally reprehensible than those of lay trustees who have made no such false promises[4]. It is consistent with both the second and third of these explanations that a lay trustee who is actually as well-informed as a professional co-trustee in respect of a particular transaction undertaken bythe trustees in breach of trust should not be able to escape all liability for resulting trust losses[5].

[1]   There is a hint of this in *Re Waterman's Will Trusts* [1952] 2 All ER 1054.
[2]   *MacDonald v Eastern Trust Co* (1957) 12 DLR (2d) 92 at 123, New Brunswick Sup Ct; *Fales v Canada Permanent Trust Co* [1977] 2 SCR 304 at 317.
[3]   *Australian Securities Commission v AS Nominees Ltd* (1995) 18 ACSR 459 at 470, Fed Ct of Aus, citing *National Trustee Co of Australasia Ltd v General Finance Co of Australasia Ltd* [1905] AC 373, PC; *Bartlett v Barclays Trust Co Ltd* [1980] Ch 515 at 534; *Gill v Eagle Star Nominees Ltd* (NSW Sup Ct 22 September 1993).
[4]   H Arthur *Pensions and Trusteeship* (1998) at p. 249.
[5]   *Head v Gould* [1898] 2 Ch 250; *Re Mulligan* [1998] 1 NZLR 481, NZ High Ct; and c f *Ward-Smith v Jebb* (1964) 108 Sol Jo 919.

Paragraph 3

Breaches of trust committed at the instigation, or request, or with consent of beneficiaries

99.21 Paragraph 3 of the present Article is based on s 62 of the Trustee Act 1925[1]. As Wilberforce J (as he then was) said in *Re Pauling's Settlement Trusts (No 2)*[2] 'the statutory right is extending the equitable right and not limiting it'. To invoke the equitable jurisdiction to impound it had previously been necessary in the cases of instigation or request to prove a motive of personal benefit on the part of the beneficiary[3] and in the case of consent or concurrence to prove personal benefit actually obtained by the beneficiary[4]. This is no longer the case although the factors of motive and benefit will no doubt influence the court in exercising its discretion. Both under s 62 and in equity a trustee's right to impound does not depend upon him still being a trustee at the date of the impounding order[5]. Note, though, that relief under s 62 can only be given after a finding of breach of trust has been made[6], and so the trustee cannot ask for relief under the section in respect of contemplated future acts.

[1]   It replaces the Trustee Act 1893, s 45, which replaced Trustee Act 1888, s 6. With regard to the procedure where the claimant is an innocent beneficiary and the trustee desires to claim indemnity against another beneficiary, see *Re Holt* [1897] 2 Ch 525; *Molyneux v Fletcher* [1898] 1 QB 648 at 656.
[2]   [1963] Ch 576 at 584.
[3]   *Raby v Ridehalgh* (1855) 7 De GM & G 104; *Hanchett v Briscoe* (1856) 22 Beav 496.
[4]   *Cocker v Quayle* (1830) 1 Russ & M 535 at 538; *Booth v Booth* (1838) 1 Beav 125; *Williams v Allen (No 2)* (1863) 32 Beav 650; *Blyth v Fladgate* [1891] 1 Ch 337 at 363.
[5]   *Re Pauling's Settlement Trusts (No 2)* [1963] Ch 576.
[6]   *Mitchell v Halliwell* [2005] EWHC 937 (Ch) at [64].

99.22 *Protection accorded to trustees in case of breach of trust*

To render beneficiary liable to indemnify trustee, he must have known all the facts amounting to a breach of trust

99.22 To make a beneficiary liable under s 62 of the Act of 1925, he or she must not only have instigated or requested or consented in writing to the breach, but must also have known all the facts which would render what was done a breach of trust, without necessarily appreciating that these facts amounted in law to a breach of trust. Thus, where a tenant for life undeniably requested trustees to invest the trust fund on a certain security, but it did not appear that he intended to be a party to a breach of trust, and in effect he left it to the trustees to determine whether the security was a proper one for the sum to be advanced, it was held that the trustees could not impound his life interest to make good the breach[1], but if the tenant for life had been proved to have *knowingly requested a breach of trust*, the decision would have been otherwise[2]. Subsequently, it has been held that, quite apart from the statute, a tenant for life who consents to the trustee handing over the capital to his (the life tenant's) wife, cannot, and neither can his trustee in bankruptcy, deny the right of the trustee who has had to replace the capital, to impound the income by way of indemnity during the life of the life tenant; and this notwithstanding that the consent was not in writing[3]. The justification for this is that the life tenant is debarred from suing for breach of trust since he consented to it[4].

1   *Re Somerset* [1894] 1 Ch 231; *Mara v Browne* [1895] 2 Ch 69. Also see impounding of life tenant's interest in *Jaffrey v Marshall* [1994] 1 All ER 143 at 154 (though the decision was overruled on liability by *Target Holdings Ltd v Redferns* [1996] AC 421, HL.)
2   *Raby v Ridehalgh* (1855) 7 De GM & G 104; *Bolton v Curre* [1895] 1 Ch 544.
3   *Fletcher v Collis* [1905] 2 Ch 24; and see for other instances of income being impounded to make good mistakes, *Re Ainsworth* [1915] 2 Ch 96; *Re Robinson* [1911] 1 Ch 502; *Re Reading* [1916] WN 262 (in which the judgment of Warrington J in *Re Horne* [1905] 1 Ch 76, was said not to be of general application); *Re Musgrave* [1916] 2 Ch 417 (income-tax, omitted to be deducted under testamentary trust to pay annuity 'without deduction', where such words do not cover income tax, recoverable out of future annuity payments, and *Re Horne* (supra) restrictively interpreted) and see *Re Gordon's Settlement* [1924] 1 Ch 146.
4   See Article 97, above.

No right to impound in order to make good the trustee's beneficial interest

99.23 The right of a trustee to impound the interest of beneficiaries who have instigated a breach is, however, only applicable for the purpose of indemnifying him against the claims of other beneficiaries. It does not enable him to obtain an indemnity against other losses. Thus, where a trustee subsequently became entitled to share in the trust fund as one of the next of kin of a beneficiary, it was held that he could not call on a beneficiary at whose instigation the breach was committed to indemnify him against loss as such next of kin, even although the beneficiary had given him an express covenant of indemnity[1]. It is submitted that the same principle would apply a fortiori to the statutory right, which is not so strong in favour of the trustee as an express covenant.

1   *Evans v Benyon* (1887) 37 Ch D 329; cf *Orrett v Corser* (1855) 21 Beav 52.

1162

*Where trustees have wrongfully parted with trust fund to trustees of
subsidiary settlement*

99.24 Where trustees, at the request of a beneficiary, advance the trust fund
to her, with notice that she has settled it by another settlement, they cannot
impound her income under such other settlement, because that income is not
the interest of a beneficiary in the trust estate *of which they are the trustees*[1].

1   *Ricketts v Ricketts* (1891) 64 LT 263.

Paragraph 4

*Joint and several liability of trustees and third parties liable in respect of
same damage*

99.25 As discussed in Article 100, third parties who are implicated in a
breach of trust may incur personal liability to the beneficiaries, as trustees de
son tort, dishonest assistants, or knowing recipients of misdirected trust funds;
conceivably they may also be strictly liable in unjust enrichment to repay the
value of misdirected trust funds which they have received. All such third
parties are jointly and severally liable with the trustees, and with one another,
for the harm suffered by the beneficiaries[1]. Hence any one may have to make
good the loss in full, opening up the possibility that he might be entitled to
recover a contribution or indemnity from the others, as accepted by *Morritt V-C in Charter plc v City Index Ltd*[2].

1   *Rowland v Witherden* (1851) 21 LJ Ch 480 at 482; *Pearce v Pearce* (1856) 22 Beav 248;
     Blyth v Fladgate [1891] 1 Ch 337 at 353; *Cowper v Stoneham* (1893) 68 LT 18; *Efstratiou
     v Glantschnig* [1972] NZLR 594 at 599, NZCA; *Macdonald v Hauer* (1976) 72 DLR (3d)
     110 at 130, Saskatchewan CA; *United States Surgical Corp v Hospital Products Inter-
     national Pty Ltd* [1982] 2 NSWLR 766 at 817, NSW Sup Ct (Eq Div); *Winslow v Richter*
     (1989) 61 DLR (4th) 549 at 563, British Columbia Sup Ct; *Young v Murphy* [1996] 1 VR
     279 at 300, Victoria CA.
2   Times LR [2006] 27 October.

The Civil Liability (Contribution) Act 1978

99.26 Most claims of this kind must be brought under the 1978 Act as they
are relevantly claims against defendants who are liable 'in respect of the same
damage', as specified under s 1. In this context, the word 'damage' does not
mean 'damages', but 'loss' or 'harm'[1], and so parties can be covered by the
statute even though their liability is not a liability to pay damages, but eg a
liability to reconstitute the trust fund. However it is clear that when enacting
the statute Parliament intended that it should apply only to contribution
claims between wrongdoers, and that it should not apply to parties whose
liability is not wrong-based[2]. Acting as a trustee de son tort is a wrong; so too
is dishonest assistance in a breach of trust; so too, probably, is knowing
receipt of trust property[3]. It follows that contribution claims between trustees
and parties liable under any of these heads fall within the scope of the 1978
Act. However, in the event that the courts recognise strict liability in unjust
enrichment to repay the value of misapplied trust assets, a party liable on this

basis would not fall within the scope of the legislation, as liability for unjust enrichment is not a wrong-based liability[4]. A contribution or indemnity claim by or against a third party liable on this basis would therefore have to be brought in equity, and although there is no authority directly in point confirming that such a claim would lie, strong support for this can be derived from *Niru Battery Manufacturing Co Ltd v Milestone Trading Ltd (No 2)*[5] where the Court of Appeal allowed a common law claim for reimbursement by a party liable for the tort of negligence against a party liable in unjust enrichment to make restitution of a mistaken payment.

[1] *Royal Brompton NHS Trust v Hammond* [2002] UKHL 14, [2002] 1 WLR 1397 at 1401.
[2] See references cited in C Mitchell *The Law of Contribution and Reimbursement* (2003) paras 4.35–4.38.
[3] *Dubai Aluminium Co Ltd v Salaam* [2002] UKHL 48, [2003] 2 AC 366 at [87] per Lord Millett, citing *John v Dodwell & Co Ltd* [1918] AC 563.
[4] *Royal Brompton NHS Trust v Hammond* [2002] UKHL 14, [2002] 1 WLR 1397 at 1412–3 per Lord Steyn, disagreeing obiter with *Friends' Provident Life Office v Hiller Parker May & Rowden (a firm)* [1997] QB 85 at 102 per Auld LJ (so Morritt V-C in *Charter plc v City Index Ltd*, Times LR [2006] 27 October felt bound to regard *Friends' Provident* as still good law.
[5] [2004] 2 Lloyd's Rep 219.

Principles of apportionment

99.27 When deciding how to apportion liability between trustees and third parties implicated in a breach of trust the courts can be expected to start from their usual default position that the parties are all equally liable[1], and then to ask whether there are any reasons to make one party bear a larger share of the burden of paying for the loss than the others. The fact that one party has personally benefited as a result of the breach of trust, whereas the others have not is likely to be seen as a strong reason for making that party bear the burden of making good the trust losses; so too is the fact that one party has acted dishonesty while the others have acted in good faith.

[1] As in e g *Cowper v Stoneham* (1893) 68 LT 18, a case concerning apportionment between trustees and a trustee de son tort.

99.28 Thus, for example, in *Eaves v Hickson*[1] trustees were fraudulently induced to pay trust property to the wrong persons, in reliance on a forged marriage certificate that was presented to them by the recipients' father. The trustees, the recipients, and the recipients' father were all joined as defendants to an action by the beneficiaries, and Romilly MR ordered that the recipients should repay the sums they had received, that their father should then be liable for so much of the trust fund as could not be recovered from the recipients, and that the trustees should finally have to pay so much as still had not been recovered. More recently, in *Dubai Aluminium Co Ltd v Salaam*[2] various defendants were assumed to have incurred liability to a company for breach of fiduciary duty and dishonest assistance in connection with a scheme to defraud the company of around US$50 million. The House of Lords upheld Rix J's decision at first instance to make an apportionment of liability between the parties that was heavily weighted against those defendants who still retained the misappropriated funds, reasoning that it would be unacceptable to leave them in possession of their spoils at the expense of their co-conspirators[3].

1   (1861) 30 Beav 136.
2   [2002] UKHL 48, [2003] 2 AC 366.
3   Cf *Burke v LFOT Pty Ltd* (2002) 209 CLR 282, where the High Court of Australia drew a similar conclusion.

Chapter 24

LIABILITY OF THIRD PARTIES AND BENEFICIARIES

ARTICLE 100
PERSONAL LIABILITY OF THIRD PARTIES OR BENEFICIARIES WHO ARE INVOLVED IN A BREACH OF TRUST

100.1

(1) A person who is neither a trustee, nor authorised by the trustees, but who takes it on himself to intermeddle with trust matters or do acts characteristic of the office of trustee makes himself a trustee de son tort, becoming personally liable to account to the beneficiaries, in addition to holding the trust property or its traceable product as constructive trustee for the beneficiaries[1];

(2) a person who is not a trustee, but who lawfully receives trust property from the trustees in his capacity as the trustees' agent, and who subsequently deals with the property in a way that he knows to be inconsistent with the trust, will be personally liable to compensate the beneficiaries for the loss which they sustain as a result of his dishonest dealing with the trust property, or to disgorge the profits of his wrongdoing to them[2];

(3) a person who dishonestly assists in a breach of trust or other fiduciary duty will be personally liable to compensate the beneficiaries for their loss to the same extent as the trustee or fiduciary whose breach he has assisted, or to disgorge the profits of his wrongdoing to them[3];

(4) a person who dishonestly receives property for his own benefit with knowledge of the fact that it is misapplied trust property, or

1167

who receives such property innocently but subsequently acquires knowledge of its improper provenance and then dishonestly deals with the property for his own benefit, will be personally liable to compensate the beneficiaries for their loss or to disgorge the profits of his wrongdoing to them[4]; moreover, it seems likely that even if he does not know of the property's improper provenance at the time of receipt, and does not subsequently acquire such knowledge by the time when he innocently deals with it for his own benefit, he will still be personally liable to make restitution of the value of the property to the beneficiaries on the ground that he has been unjustly enriched at their expense, subject to his ability to establish a change of position defence to their claim[5];

(5)   where a person is indebted to the trust estate[6] (whether by reason of his involvement in a breach of trust or in respect of a simple contract debt), and he has an equitable interest in the trust property (whether original or derivative[7]), his interest may be impounded to make good his liability, and this remedy will not only affect him personally[8], but will also affect all persons claiming under him, including purchasers for value without notice.

1   *Mara v Browne* [1896] 1 Ch 199; *Kennedy v Lyell* (1889) 14 App Cas 437.
2   *Lee v Sankey* (1873) LR 15 Eq 204; *Soar v Ashwell* [1893] 2 QB 390.
3   *Royal Brunei Airline Sdn Bhd v Tan* [1995] 2 AC 378; *Twinsectra Ltd v Yardley* [2002] UKHL 12, [2002] 2 AC 164; *Ultraframe (UK) Ltd v Fielding* [2005] EWHC 1638 (Ch); *Barlow Clowes International Ltd (in liquidation) v Eurotrust International Ltd* [2005] UKPC 37, [2006] 1 All ER 333.
4   *Belmont Finance Corp v Williams Furniture Ltd (No 2)* [1980] 1 All ER 393; *Re Montagu's Settlement Trusts* [1987] Ch 264; *BCCI v Akindele* [2001] Ch 437.
5   *Grupo Torras SA v Al-Sabah (No 5)* [2001] Lloyd's Rep Bank 36 at 62; *Twinsectra Ltd v Yardley* [2002] UKHL 12, [2002] 2 AC 164 at 194; *Dubai Aluminium Co Ltd v Salaam* [2002] UKHL 48, [2003] 2 AC 366 at [87]. See too Lord Nicholls, 'Knowing Receipt: The Need for a New Landmark', in W R Cornish et al (eds) *Restitution: Past, Present and Future* (1998) 231; Lord Walker, 'Dishonesty and Unconscionable Conduct in Commercial Life – Some Reflections on Accessory Liability and Knowing Receipt' (2005) 27 Sydney LR 187 at p. 202.
6   *Re Taylor* [1894] 1 Ch 671.
7   *Jacubs v Rylance* (1874) LR 17 Eq 341; *Doering v Doering* (1889) 42 Ch D 203; *Chillingworth v Chambers* [1896] 1 Ch 685.
8   *Woodyatt v Gresley* (1836) 8 Sim 180; *Fuller v Knight* (1843) 6 Beav 205; *M'Gachen v Dew* (1851) 15 Beav 84; *Vaughan v Noble* (1861) 30 Beav 34; *Jacubs v Rylance* (1874) LR 17 Eq 341; *Re Taylor* [1894] 1 Ch 671; *Re Weston* [1900] 2 Ch 164.

Paragraph 1

Trustees de son tort – strangers purporting to act as trustees

100.2 As A L Smith LJ stated in *Mara v Browne*[1]:

'If one, not being a trustee and not having authority from a trustee, takes upon himself to intermeddle with trust matters or to do acts characteristic of the office of trustee he may thereby make himself what is called in law a trustee of his own wrong, ie a trustee de son tort, or as it is also termed, a constructive trustee.'

¹ [1896] 1 Ch 199 at 209. See too *Carl Zeiss Stiftung v Herbert Smith & Co (No 2)* [1969] 2 Ch 276 at 289.

100.3 A trustee de son tort does not claim to act in his own right, but to act for the beneficiaries. Nevertheless, intermeddling with their equitable property rights in this way is a civil wrong, and so the traditional language of 'trusteeship de son tort' says something about the nature of liability under this head that is not captured by the language of 'de facto trusteeship' for which Lord Millett expressed a preference in *Dubai Aluminium Co Ltd v Salaam*¹. However, Lord Millett was certainly right to stress in that case that liability as a trustee de son tort differs in certain fundamental respects from the liabilities of those who intermeddle in other ways, by dishonestly assisting in breaches of trust or dishonestly receiving and dealing with misdirected trust property.

¹[2002] UKHL 48, [2003] 2 AC 366 at [138].

100.4 As his Lordship observed, a trustee de son tort is treated 'in every respect as if [he] had been duly appointed', with the result that he is 'fully subject to fiduciary obligations'¹. Hence the court will treat him as having assumed a duty to account for his management of the trust property, a breach of which duty will render him personally liable to compensate the beneficiaries for their loss². Like an express trustee he must familiarise himself with the extent of his powers and duties on taking office, and thereafter he may be liable for a breach of these duties³. The liability of a trustee de son tort is not a secondary liability, in the way that the liability of those who dishonestly assist in a breach of trust is a secondary liability because it is predicated on the commission of a primary breach of trust by the trustees⁴. It is rather a primary liability which is incurred when the trustee de son tort himself breaches the trust duties which he previously constructively assumed when he intermeddled with the trust property. Thus in *Blyth v Fladgate*⁵ where a sole trustee had solicitors invest trust funds in Exchequer Bills and, after his death and before the appointment of any new trustees, the bills were sold by the solicitors and the proceeds invested in a loan on mortgage, the solicitors were personally accountable for the loss arising when the security proved insufficient.

¹ [2002] UKHL 48, [2003] 2 AC 366 at [138]–[139], following *Taylor v Davies* [1920] AC 636 at 651 per Viscount Cave. See too *Life Association of Scotland v Siddal* (1861) 3 De GF & J 58 at 72; *Selangor United Rubber Estates Ltd v Cradock (No 3)* [1968] 1 WLR 1555 at 1579; *Paragon Finance plc v D B Thackerar & Co (a firm)* [1999] 1 All ER 400 at 408–409 per Millett LJ. In contrast, executors de son tort are not generally constructive trustees of the estate which they take it upon themselves to administer, but cf *Jones v Williams* [2000] Ch 1 (decided in ignorance of Millett LJ's twofold classification of constructive trusteeship in *Paragon Finance*), where an executor de son tort knew that he was not solely entitled to inherited property, and so was unusually held by the Court of Appeal to hold a proportionate share of the property on constructive trust for the others entitled to share in the estate.
² *Montreal Trust Co of Canada v Hickman* [2001] NFCA 42 at para 44.
³ *Pearce v Pearce* (1856) 22 Beav 248 at 252.
⁴ See para 100.19 below.
⁵ [1891] 1 Ch 337. See too *Goddard v DFC New Zealand Ltd* [1991] 3 NZLR 580.

100.5 *Liability of third parties and beneficiaries*

100.5 There is no need to show that an intermeddler has acted dishonestly in order to fix him with liability as a trustee de son tort – he may have been honest and well intentioned, a busybody of excessive probity[1]. To show that a defendant has relevantly 'intermeddled' with the trust affairs, it is not enough to show that he has attended meetings of the trustees without participating in the trustees' decision making – he must take it on himself to assume a more active role in the management of the trust affairs than this[2].

1   *Kennedy v Lyell* (1889) 14 App Cas 437 at 459; *Mara v Browne* [1896] 1 Ch 199 at 209; *Life Association of Scotland v Siddal* (1861) 3 De G F & J 58; *Baden, Delvaux v Société Générale pour Favoriser le Développement du Commerce et de l'Industrie en France SA* [1993] 1 WLR 509n at 577.
2   *Clay v Clay* [1999] WASCA 8 at para 16.

100.6 One should be alert to the fact that some authors and judges have formerly used the expression 'trustee de son tort' to cover not the primary liability described here, but the secondary or accessory liability that is incurred by a person who dishonestly assists in a breach of trust.

Paragraph 2

Elements of liability for dishonest dealing by trustees' lawful agents

100.7 To make the lawful agent of trustees personally liable for dishonest dealing it is necessary to establish that there was:

(1)   a trust or other fiduciary relationship;
(2)   a lawful receipt of trust property or other fiduciary property by the agent of the trustees or fiduciary, in his ministerial capacity;
(3)   a subsequent dealing with the property by the agent that is inconsistent with the rights of the beneficiaries or the principal;
(4)   a dishonest state of mind on the part of the agent at the time of this dealing.

100.8 If an agent lawfully receives trust property, but then dishonestly takes it on himself to treat the property as his own, and misapplies it for his own benefit, then he will be liable for dishonest dealing in line with Article 100(4), but it should be noted that agents can also incur liability for dishonest dealing where they have misapplied trust property while purporting to act in their agency role, and without benefiting themselves. If a defendant does not purport to act as an agent, but instead takes it on himself to do acts characteristic of the office of trustee, then there is no need to prove dishonesty against him with a view to fixing him with liability as a dishonest dealer, as he will be liable as a trustee de son tort[1]. If a defendant receives misapplied trust property from the trustees in his capacity as the trustees' agent, and then applies it in accordance with their instructions, knowing that the trustees are acting in breach of trust, then he will not incur the primary liability of a dishonest dealer, but he will incur the secondary, accessory liability of a dishonest assistant in a breach of trust[2].

¹   *Blyth v Fladgate* [1891] 1 Ch 337; *Williams-Ashman v Price and Williams* [1942] Ch 219
at 228. See paras 100.3–100.5.
²   See para 100.17 below.

Agents who lawfully receive trust property

100.9 In relation to the liability of agents who cause a loss to the beneficiaries
by dealing with trust property that they have lawfully received from the
trustees one must bear in mind Lord Selborne LC's warning in *Barnes v Addy*
against extending the scope of their liability too far¹:

> 'Those who create a trust clothe the trustee with a legal power and control over
> the trust property, imposing on him a corresponding responsibility. That
> responsibility may no doubt be extended in equity to others who are not
> properly trustees if they are found either making themselves trustees de son tort
> or actually participating in any fraudulent conduct of the trustee to the injury of
> the cestui que trust. But on the other hand strangers are not to be made
> constructive trustees merely because they act as the agents of trustees in
> transactions within their legal powers, transactions, perhaps, of which a Court
> of Equity may disapprove, unless those agents receive and become chargeable
> with some part of the trust property, or unless they assist with knowledge in a
> dishonest and fraudulent design on the part of the trustees²... If those principles
> were disregarded I know not how anyone could in transactions admitting of
> doubt as to the view which a Court of Equity might take of them, safely
> discharge the office of solicitor, of banker or of agent of any sort to the trustees.
> But, on the other hand, if persons dealing honestly as agents are at liberty to
> rely on the legal power of the trustees, are not to have the character of trustees
> constructively thrust upon them, then the transactions of mankind can safely be
> carried through; and I apprehend those who create trusts do expressly intend, in
> the absence of fraud and dishonesty, to exonerate such agents of all classes from
> the responsibilities which are expressly incumbent by reason of the fiduciary
> relation upon the trustees.'

¹   (1874) 9 Ch App 244 at 251–252. See too *Williams v Williams* (1881) 17 Ch D 437 at
442; *Carl Zeiss Stiftung v Herbert Smith & Co (a firm)* [1969] 2 Ch 276 at 299 and 304;
Competitive Insurance Co v Davies Investments Ltd [1975] 3 All ER 254 at 264.
²   NB the rule that liability for dishonest assistance can be incurred only by those who assist
in a dishonest breach of trust was abrogated by *Royal Brunei Airlines Sdn Bhd v Tan*
[1995] 2 AC 378, approved in *Twinsectra Ltd v Yardley* [2002] UKHL 12, [2002] 2 AC
164.

Dishonest dealing by agents

100.10 In line with Lord Selborne LC's observations, and in line with the
Privy Council's decision in *Royal Brunei Airlines Sdn Bhd v Tan*¹, with regard
to the state of mind which must be established against defendants to fix them
with (secondary) liability for dishonestly assisting in a breach of trust, a
defendant must have acted dishonestly before he can be fixed with (primary)
liability for the equitable wrong of dealing with trust property that he has
lawfully received in his capacity as the trustees' agent, in a manner that is
inconsistent with the terms of the trust². Support for this view may be derived
from various sources. In *Williams-Ashman v Price and Williams*, Bennett J
considered that³:

'An agent in possession of money which he knows to be trust money, *so long as he acts honestly*, is not accountable to the beneficiaries interested in the trust money unless he intermeddles in the trust by doing acts characteristic of a trustee and outside the duties of an agent.'

1   [1995] 2 AC 378. See too *Twinsectra Ltd v Yardley* [2002] UKHL 12, [2002] 2 AC 164 and *Barlow Clowes International Ltd (in liq) v Eurotrust International Ltd [2005] UKHL 37,* [2006] 1 All ER 333.
2   In Canada, the cases on this subject are grouped under the heading 'knowing dealing': *Citadel General Assurance Co v Lloyds Bank Canada* [1997] 3 SCR 805 at 821.
3   [1942] Ch 219 at 228. Emphasis added.

100.11 In *Carl Zeiss Stiftung v Herbert Smith & Co (a firm)*, Sachs LJ stated that[1]:

'professional men and agents who have received moneys as such and acted bona fide are accountable only to their principals unless dishonesty as well as cognisance of trusts is established against them.'

1   [1969] 2 Ch 276 at 299, approving the statement which appeared in the 11th edn of *Underhill* at p 599: 'Where the agent of the trustees acts honestly and confines himself to the duties of an agent then, though he will not be accountable to the beneficiaries, they will have their remedy against the persons who are the real trustees.'

100.12 Finally, in *Cukurooa Celik Enduustrisi AS v Hill Taylor Dickinson (a firm)*[1], Morison J followed Sachs LJ's dictum in the *Carl Zeiss* case, and held that solicitors who had lawfully received money from a client that was allegedly subject to a trust in the claimant's favour, and had placed the money in their client account, owed duties to the client 'to pay the monies out in accordance with their instructions and to give proper advice to their clients', but could not be liable to the alleged beneficiary for dealing with the property in a manner inconsistent with the alleged trust 'unless something akin to impropriety or dishonesty is alleged.'

1   (1 June 1996, unreported), QBD (Comm Ct).

100.13 In *Williams-Ashman,* solicitors who followed the instructions of the sole trustee in making an unauthorised loan to the trustee's son and in making other unauthorised investments were held not to be liable to compensate the beneficiaries even though they could have checked the terms of the trust instrument, which they had drawn up themselves, placed in their safe, and forgotten. They had not acted dishonestly, and had followed the trustee's instructions in good faith. Likewise, in *Williams v Williams*[1] a settlor suppressed the existence of a settlement on his wife and children and the defendant solicitor carried out the sale of various lands which were in fact subject to the settlement and disposed of the proceeds in accordance with the instructions of the settlor's widow and executrix. The solicitor honestly believed that there was no settlement, and although the circumstances were such that it was negligent of the solicitor to hold this belief, Kay J considered that he was not liable to compensate the beneficiaries. In *Lee v Sankey*[2], on the other hand, solicitors were found liable where they were employed by two trustees to receive the proceeds of sold trust properties, and with knowledge of the terms of the trust paid the proceeds over to only one of the trustees, who dissipated the money and died insolvent. These cases are all consistent with the view that the defendant must have acted with the objective dishonesty identified by the Privy Council in *Royal Brunei Airlines Sdn Bhd v Tan*[3] and *Barlow Clowes International Ltd (in liquidation) v Eurotrust International Ltd*[4] as the requisite state of mind for liability as a dishonest assistant in a breach of trust[5].

[1]   (1881) 17 Ch D 437, treated in this category by Brightman J in *Karak Rubber Co Ltd v Burden (No 2)* [1972] 1 All ER 1210 at 1242.
[2]   (1873) LR 15 Eq 204.
[3]   [1995] 2 AC 378.
[4]   [2005] UKPC 37, [2006] 1 All ER 333.
[5]   See para 100.27 ff.

Pleading dishonesty

100.14 The courts have issued various guidelines with regard to the pleading of claims in which dishonesty is alleged against a defendant. These guidelines should be followed whether the claim is for dishonest dealing with trust property, dishonest assistance in a breach of trust, or dishonest receipt and dealing with trust property for one's own benefit.

100.15 Defendants are entitled to have their conduct judged against distinct allegations of dishonesty as pleaded[1], and 'in order to allege fraud it is not sufficient to sprinkle a pleading with words like "wilfully" or "recklessly" (but not "fraudulently" or "dishonestly") … [as this] may still leave it in doubt whether the words are being used in a technical sense or merely to give colour by way of pejorative emphasis to the complaint'[2]. 'Where fraud has not been sufficiently pleaded, it is … no answer to say that if it had been sufficiently pleaded no further evidence would be called for the defence', for 'the presence or absence of a charge of fraud may … affect the whole manner in which a defence is conducted'[3]. Hence, it is 'generally no answer to a demand for particulars … that the defendant already knows the information … [as] the defendant is entitled to pin the [claimant] down by his or her pleading so that the case to be met will be known'[4].

[1]   *Three Rivers District Council v Bank of England DC (No 3)* [2003] 2 AC 1 at [183]–[189], following *Jonesco v Beard* [1930] AC 298 at 300. See too *Armitage v Nurse* [1998] Ch 241 at 251, following *Davy v Garrett* (1878) 7 Ch D 473 at 489; also *Practice Direction*, Part 16, rule 16.2(5). Under the Bar Code of Conduct, para 606(c), counsel must have reasonably credible material to enable fraud properly to be pleaded, but the Code does not require full disclosure of this material to the defendant: *Rigby v Den Decorating Systems Ltd* (15 March 1999, unreported), CA. In the event that a defendant defeats allegations of dishonesty, claimant's counsel will not be liable to a wasted costs order, provided that a reasonable lawyer might have decided to plead dishonesty on the available material: *Brown v Bennett (No 2)* [2002] 1 WLR 713.
[2]   *Armitage v Nurse* [1998] Ch 241 at 257.
[3]   *Belmont Finance Corpn Ltd v Williams Furniture Ltd* [1979] Ch 250 at 270.
[4]   *Montreal Trust Co v Hickman* [2001] NFCA 42 at para 60.

100.16 'It is not necessary to use the word "fraud" or "dishonesty" [in the pleadings] if the facts which make the conduct complained of fraudulent are pleaded, but if the facts pleaded are consistent with innocence, then it is not open to the court to find fraud'[1]. Nor is it necessary to provide particulars of knowledge in a fraud claim, provided that actual knowledge is pleaded, but it is open to the defendant to seek further particulars of such a pleading of actual knowledge, and 'if there is a pleading that a person "knew or ought to have known" particular matters, then that rolled-up plea should be particularised'[2]. It is usually harder to prove an allegation of dishonesty than an allegation of negligence, as 'the more serious the allegation the less likely it is that the event occurred and, hence, the stronger should be the evidence before the court concludes that the allegation is established on the balance of probability'[3]. Before a court is likely to reach such a conclusion in an application for summary judgment, the pleaded facts must therefore be particularly clear[4].

1   *Armitage v Nurse* [1998] Ch 241 at 251, following *Belmont Finance Corpn Ltd v Williams Furniture Ltd* [1979] Ch 250 at 268.
2   *Rigby v Decorating Den Systems Ltd* (15 March 1999, unreported), CA.
3   *Re H* [1996] AC 563 at 586 per Lord Nicholls, followed in *Grupo Torras v Al-Sabah (No 5)* [2001] Lloyd's Bank Rep 36 at 45, CA.
4   *Houghton v Fayers* [2000] Lloyd's Rep Bank 145 at 149; *Gencor ACP Ltd v Dalby* [2000] 2 BCLC 734 at 758.

Paragraph 3

Elements of liability as a dishonest assistant

100.17 To make a defendant personally liable for dishonest assistance in a breach of trust or other fiduciary duty it is necessary to establish[1]:

(1)   a trust or other fiduciary relationship;
(2)   a breach of trust or other fiduciary duty on the part of the trustee or other fiduciary;
(3)   a causal link between the breach and a loss to the beneficiaries, or between the breach and a gain to the defendant, depending on the remedy which is sought;
(4)   assistance by the defendant in the breach;
(5)   a dishonest state of mind on the part of the assistant.

1   *Royal Brunei Airline Sdn Bhd v Tan* [1995] 2 AC 378; *Twinsectra Ltd v Yardley* [2002] UKHL 12, [2002] 2 AC 164.

100.18 Each of these requirements will be discussed in turn. It should also be noted that liability for dishonest assistance in a breach of trust or other fiduciary duty 'is not dependent upon receipt of trust property' and 'arises even though no trust property has reached the hands of the accessory'[1]. Where a defendant has in fact received trust property, however, there is nothing to stop the beneficiaries from suing him for dishonest assistance if they wish to do so[2]. In practice, they will generally prefer to make a proprietary claim, or alternatively to make a claim in knowing receipt, for which the mental element may be easier to prove, but they may be unable to pursue the first option if the property has been dissipated, and the second if the defendant has received the property ministerially and not beneficially[3].

1   *Royal Brunei Airline Sdn Bhd v Tan* [1995] 2 AC 378 at 382; *Houghton v Fayers* [2000] Lloyd's Rep Bank 145 at 149.

2   *Baden, Delvaux v Société Générale pour Favoriser le Développement du Commerce et de l'Industrie en France SA* [1993] 1 WLR 509n at 572–573; *Equiticorp Industries Group Ltd (in stat man) v R (No 47)* [1998] 2 NZLR 481 at 539; *Primlake Ltd (in liquidation) v Matthews Associates* [2006] EWHC 1227 (Ch) at [334].
3   *Twinsectra Ltd v Yardley* [2002] UKHL 12, [2002] 2 AC 164 at 194. See para 100.32 below.

100.19 The courts often use the language of constructive trusteeship to describe liability for dishonest assistance. However it follows from the fact that liability can arise whether or not the defendant has received property that the courts do not mean that the defendant is a trustee of property for which he must account to the claimant: 'there is no real trust and usually no chance of a proprietary remedy' against him[1], and 'he is in fact not a trustee at all'[2]. Instead, the courts mean that he should be treated, by a legal fiction, as though he were the trustee or fiduciary in whose breach of duty he has participated: his liability derives from and duplicates theirs[3]. Another way of putting this is to say that liability for dishonest assistance is a civil secondary liability, analogous to the criminal secondary liability of those who procure, aid, or abet a criminal offence[4]. As discussed below, this has consequences for the causation rules which govern liability under this head, and also for the remedies which are awarded to successful claimants[5].

1   *Coulthard v Disco Mix Club Ltd* [2000] 1 WLR 707 at 731.
2   *Dubai Aluminium Co Ltd v Salaam* [2002] UKHL 48, [2003] 2 AC 366 at [141] per Lord Millett. See too *Belmont Finance Corp Ltd v Williams Furniture Ltd* [1979] Ch 250 at 272.
3   *Rolfe v Gregory* (1865) 4 De GJ & Sm 576 at 579, *per* Lord Westbury LC; *US Surgical Corp v Hospital Products International Pty Ltd* [1982] 2 NSWLR 766 at 817 (not considered on appeal); *Arab Monetary Fund v Hashim* QBD 29 July 1994, *per* Chadwick J; *Royal Brunei Airlines Sdn Bhd v Tan* [1995] 2 AC 378 at 385; *Australian Securities Commission v AS Nominees Ltd* (1995) 62 FCR 504 at 523; *Equiticorp Industries Ltd v R (No 47)* [1998] 2 NZLR 481 at 658; *Bankgesellschaft Berlin AG v Makris* (22 January 1999, *unreported*) QBD (Comm Ct) *per* Cresswell J; *Grupo Torras v Al-Sabah (No 5)* [2001] Lloyd's Rep Bank 36 at 61–2.
4   *Ultraframe (UK) Ltd v Fielding* [2005] EWHC 1638 (Ch) at [1506], *per* Lewison J.
5   See para 100.23 and 100.43 below.

Existence of trust or other fiduciary relationship

100.20 Claims for dishonest assistance are not limited to the situation where an express trustee has misappropriated trust property. They can also lie against defendants who have assisted in the misappropriation of property by other fiduciaries who have voluntarily assumed responsibility for managing the property – for example, partners[1], joint venturers[2], company directors[3], and other agents and/or employees[4]. Claims can also clearly lie where a defendant has helped a constructive or resulting trustee to misapply the trust property[5]. However, it is currently unclear on the authorities whether liability as a dishonest assistant can be incurred by a defendant who has assisted in a breach of trust or other fiduciary duty that does not entail the misapplication of property[6]. It is submitted that in principle a claim should lie in such a case, consistently with the courts' general desire to preserve the integrity of fiduciary relations.

1   *Alers-Hankey v Teixeira* (2002) 5 ITELR 171, British Columbia CA.

2   *Abou-Rahmah v Abacha* [2005] EWHC 2662 (QB), [2006] 1 All ER (Comm) 247
     at [34]–[37], not challenged on appeal: [2006] EWCA Civ 1492 [62].
3   *Selangor United Rubber Estates Ltd v Cradock (No 3)* [1968] 1 WLR 1555; *Belmont
     Finance Corpn Ltd v Williams Furniture Ltd (No 2)* [1980] 1 All ER 393; *Heinl v Jyske
     Bank (Gibraltar) Ltd* [1999] Lloyd's Rep Bank 511.
4   *Norwich Union Fire Insurance Soc Ltd v Central Auto Salvage (London) Ltd* (30 July
     1993, unreported), CA; *Brinks Ltd v Abu-Saleh (No 3)* (1995) Times, 23 October; *Comax
     Secure Business Services Ltd v Wilson* [2001] All ER (D) 222 (Jun), QBD.
5   *Bank Tejerat v Hong King and Shanghai Banking Corpn (CI) Ltd* [1995] 1 Lloyd's Rep
     239; *Bankgesellschaft Berlin AG v Makris* (22 January 1999, unreported), QBD (Comm
     Ct); *Heinl v Jyske Bank (Gibraltar) Ltd* [1999] Lloyd's Rep Bank 511.
6   Yes: *Waxman v Waxman* (2004) 7 ITELR 162 at [546] (Ontario CA). Maybe: *Brown v
     Bennett* [1999] 1 BCLC 649 at 657–659; *Fyffes Group Ltd v Templeman* [2000] 2 Lloyd's
     Rep 643; *Goose v Wilson Sandford & Co (No 2)* [2001] Lloyd's Rep PN 189, CA at
     para 88; *Gencor ACP Ltd v Dalby* [2000] 2 BCLC 734 at 757. No: *Cowan de Groot
     Properties Ltd v Eagle Trust plc* [1991] BCLC 1045 at 1103; *Bankgesellschaft Berlin AG v
     Makris* (22 January 1999, unreported), QBD (Comm Ct); *Satnam Investments Ltd v
     Dunlop Heywood & Co Ltd* [1999] 1 BCLC 385 at 404; *Petrotrade Inc v Smith* [2000]
     1 Lloyd's Rep 486 at 491–492.

Breach of trust or fiduciary duty

100.21   There was originally no requirement that the breach of trust in which
a defendant has assisted should itself have been a dishonest breach[1], but then,
in an unreserved judgment not discussing the earlier cases, Lord Selborne LC
held that assistants in a breach of trust could not be liable unless (inter alia)[2]:

   'they assist with knowledge in a dishonest and fraudulent design on the part of
   the trustees.'

1   *Fyler v Fyler* (1841) 3 Beav 550; *A-G v Corpn of Leicester* (1844) 7 Beav 176.
2   *Barnes v Addy* (1874) 9 Ch App 244 at 252.

100.22   The requirement that a defendant must have assisted in a dishonest
breach of trust was confirmed by the Court of Appeal in *Belmont Finance
Corp Ltd v Williams*[1], but subsequently, in his speech for the Privy Council in
Royal Brunei Airlines Sdn Bhd v Tan[2], Lord Nicholls refused to follow the
Court of Appeal's decision on this point, holding that there is no need to show
that the breach of trust assisted by a defendant was itself a dishonest breach.
His finding in this regard was subsequently approved by the House of Lords,
in *Twinsectra Ltd v Yardley*[3].

1   [1979] Ch 250 at 257.
2   [1995] 2 AC 378.
3   [2002] UKHL 12, [2002] 2 AC 164 at 171 and 195.

*Causal link between the breach of trust and loss to the beneficiaries or gain
to the defendant*

100.23   Generally speaking, the law of civil wrongs, like the criminal law, is
'moulded on the philosophy of autonomy'[1], with the result that it does not
generally regard loss flowing from the actions of a primary wrongdoer as
having been caused by the actions of a participant who has induced or assisted
in the commission of the wrong[2]. However, civil secondary liability for

dishonest assistance is an exception to this general rule: a defendant fixed with liability of this sort is liable for loss flowing from the primary wrong even where there is no direct causal link between his actions and the loss. Thus, as Mance LJ held in *Grupo Torras SA v Al-Sabah (No 5)*[3]:

> 'The starting point ... is that the requirement of dishonest assistance relates not to any loss or damage which may be suffered, but to the breach of trust or fiduciary duty. The relevant enquiry is ... what loss or damage resulted from the breach of trust or fiduciary duty which has been dishonestly assisted.'

[1]   G Williams, 'Complicity, Purpose and the Draft Code' [1990] Crim LR 4 at p. 6.
[2]   HLA Hart and AM Honoré, *Causation in the Law* 2nd edn (1985) at p. 385.
[3]   [1999] CLC 1469.

100.24 This was affirmed on appeal[1], and then reaffirmed by a differently constituted Court of Appeal, in *Casio Computer Ltd v Sayo*, where Tuckey LJ stated that[2]:

> '*Grupo Torras* ... establishes that in a claim for dishonest assistance it is not necessary to show a precise causal link between the assistance and the loss ... [and that loss] caused by the breach of fiduciary duty is recoverable from the accessory.'

[1]   [2001] Lloyd's Rep Bank 36 at 61.
[2]   [2001] EWCA Civ 661, [2001] 06 LS Gaz R 45 at [15].

100.25 Of course, where a defendant's actions have made no difference at all to the implementation of a breach of trust or fiduciary duty, 'there is no causative effect and therefore no assistance ... [and so] the requirements of conscience [do not] require any remedy'[1]. Hence a claimant must at least show that the defendant's actions have made the fiduciary's breach of duty easier than it would otherwise have been. But the causation requirement for dishonest assistance is no stronger than this, and it is no answer to a claim, for example, that the claimant's loss would have occurred anyway, because the wrongdoing fiduciary would have committed the breach even if the defendant had not assisted him.

[1]   *Brown v Bennett* [1999] 1 BCLC 649 at 659, *per* Morritt LJ.

Assistance

100.26 The requirement that a defendant must have assisted the breach of duty reflects the foregoing principle that the defendant's actions must have had *some* causative impact, in the sense that he cannot relevantly have assisted in a breach if his actions or omissions have either hampered the trustee or fiduciary or have been of 'minimal importance' to him[1]. There is no need for the claimant to show that the dishonest assistant's action 'inevitably [had] the consequence that a loss [was suffered]'[2], nor is it an answer to a claim that a dishonest assistant 'only participated in a part of a chain of events all of which led to [the breach], or to assert that the [breach] would probably have occurred without his assistance'[3]. A defendant might well incur liability for actions or omissions which precede the commission of the breach[4], but he cannot be liable if his actions or omissions only occurred after the breach was fully implemented[5]. However, where the breach has entailed the misapplication of funds, the courts are likely to hold that the breach was not fully implemented until the funds were hidden away where the beneficiaries could not find them, with the consequence that those who assist in money-laundering activities after trust funds have been removed from a trust account can be fixed with liability for dishonest assistance[6]. If a trustee or other fiduciary has committed a series of breaches, a defendant can only be liable for dishonest assistance in respect of those breaches to the commission of which his own actions or omissions have made a difference[7].

1   *Baden, Delvaux v Société Générale pour Favoriser le Développement du Commerce et de l'Industrie en France SA* [1993] 1 WLR 509n at 574.
2   *Baden, Delvaux v Société Générale pour Favoriser le Développement du Commerce et de l'Industrie en France SA* [1993] 1 WLR 509n at 575.
3   *Balfron Trustees Ltd v Peterson* [2001] IRLR 758 at 761.
4   R P Austin, 'Constructive Trusts' in P D Finn (ed), *Essays in Equity* (1985) 196, 236–7, discussing *Adams v Bank of New South Wales* [1984] 1 NSWLR 285. See too *Aequitas Ltd v Sparad No 100 Ltd* [2001] NSWSC 14.
5   *Brown v Bennett* [1998] 2 BCLC 97 at 105.
6   *Heinl v Jyske Bank (Gibraltar) Ltd* [1999] Lloyd's Rep Bank 511 at 523, approving *Agip (Africa) Ltd v Jackson* [1990] Ch 265 at 293. See too *Casio Computer Co Ltd v Sayo* [2001] EWCA Civ 661, [2001] 06 LS GAZ R 45 at para 22.
7   *Grupo Torras SA v Al-Sabah (No 5)* [1999] CLC 1469, QBD (Comm Ct).

Dishonest state of mind

100.27 The mental state required for liability as a dishonest assistant has been reviewed in three important cases of recent vintage: *Royal Brunei Airlines Sdn Bhd v Tan*[1], *Twinsectra Ltd v Yardley*[2], and *Barlow Clowes International Ltd (in liquidation) v Eurotrust International Ltd*[3]. These will be discussed after the background to *Royal Brunei* has been described.

1   [1995] 2 AC 378.
2   [2002] UKHL 12, [2002] 2 AC 164.
3   [2005] UKPC 37, [2006] 1 All ER 333.

100.28 Prior to *Royal Brunei*, in *Baden, Delvaux v Société Générale pour Favoriser le Développement du Commerce et de l'Industrie en France SA*[1], Peter Gibson J held that a defendant might be liable for assisting in a breach of trust even if his behaviour fell short of dishonesty[2], and he accepted that any of five types of knowledge would serve to render a defendant liable as an assistant in a breach of trust: (i) actual knowledge; (ii) wilfully shutting one's eyes to the obvious; (iii) wilfully and recklessly failing to make such inquiries as an honest and reasonable man would make; (iv) knowledge of circumstances which would indicate the facts to an honest and reasonable man; (v) knowledge of circumstances which would put an honest and reasonable man on inquiry[3]. He also held that types (ii)–(v) could all be distinguished from type (i), as constituting various types of 'imputed' or 'constructive knowledge'[4]. The *Baden, Delvaux* classification of knowledge subsequently formed the starting point for discussion in a series of English cases on liability for assisting in a breach of trust. The points were made in these cases, that categories (ii) and (iii) should more properly be understood as types of actual, rather than constructive knowledge[5]; that constructive knowledge is not the same thing as constructive notice[6]; that in commercial transactions, men of business do not normally make inquiries unless the facts are such as to raise suspicion, suggesting that constructive notice, as that term is generally understood in relation to dealings with land, has only a limited role to play in the context of commercial transactions[7]; that categories (i), (ii), and (iii) certainly suffice for liability as an assistant[8]; and that categories (iv) and (v) are phrased in a way that might take in dishonest as well as negligent states of mind[9]. A consensus also emerged that, contrary to Peter Gibson J's finding on the point in *Baden, Delvaux*, a defendant must have been dishonest to incur liability[10].

[1]   [1993] 1 WLR 509n. Although the case was finally decided in 1983, it was not reported for another ten years.
[2]   [1993] 1 WLR 509n at 577.
[3]   [1993] 1 WLR 509n at 575–587.
[4]   [1993] 1 WLR 509n at 576.
[5]   *Agip (Africa) Ltd v Jackson* [1990] Ch 265 at 293; *Cowan de Groot Properties Ltd v Eagle Trust plc* [1991] BCLC 1045 at 1103.
[6]   *Re Montagu's Settlement Trusts* [1987] Ch 264 at 277–9.
[7]   *Cowan de Groot Properties Ltd v Eagle Trust plc* [1991] BCLC 1045 at 1112; *Eagle Trust plc v SBC Securities Ltd* [1993] 1 WLR 484 at 492–493; *El Ajou v Dollar Land Holdings plc* [1993] BCLC 735 at 758.
[8]   *Re Montagu's Settlement Trusts* [1987] Ch 264 at 272; *Lipkin Gorman v Karpnale Ltd* [1987] 1 WLR 987 at 1005–1006, affirmed [1989] 1 WLR 1340 at 1355, not considered on appeal to HL [1991] 2 AC 548.
[9]   *Agip (Africa) Ltd v Jackson* [1990] Ch 265 at 293; *Cowan de Groot Properties Ltd v Eagle Trust plc* [1991] BCLC 1045 at 1112.
[10] *Re Montagu's Settlement Trusts* [1987] Ch 264 at 285; *Agip (Africa) Ltd v Jackson* [1990] Ch 265 at 292–293, on appeal: [1991] Ch 547 at 569; *Eagle Trust plc v SBC Securities Ltd* [1993] 1 WLR 484 at 495; *Lipkin Gorman v Karpnale Ltd* [1989] 1 WLR 1340 at 1354–1355, not considered on appeal to HL; *Cowan de Groot Properties Ltd v Eagle Trust plc* [1991] BCLC 1045 at 1101; *Polly Peck International v Nadir (No2)* [1993] BCLC 187 at 203–204; *Bank Tejerat v Hong Kong and Shanghai Banking Corpn (CI) Ltd* [1995] 1 Lloyd's Rep 239 at 248.

100.29 The view that dishonesty is a pre-requisite for liability was not beyond doubt, however, as a line of cases pre-dating *Baden, Delvaux* and holding that a defendant can be liable if he has honestly but negligently failed to investigate the circumstances of an impugned transaction, was never overruled[1]. The body of law founded on the *Baden, Delvaux* classification also suffered from the more general problem that it had become over-theorised: as Lord Nicholls subsequently put it in *Royal Brunei*, the courts had been led into 'tortuous convolutions' in their efforts to investigate the 'sort' of knowledge possessed by defendants, 'when the truth is that "knowingly" is inapt as a criterion when applied to the gradually darkening spectrum where the differences are of degree and not kind'[2].

[1]   *Selangor United Rubber Estates Ltd v Cradock (No 3)* [1968] 1 WLR 1555; *Karak Rubber Co Ltd v Burden (No 2)* [1972] 1 WLR 602; *Rowlandson v National Westminster Bank Ltd* [1978] 1 WLR 798
[2]   [1995] 2 AC 378 at 391.

100.30 In *Royal Brunei*, Lord Nicholls was therefore determined to start afresh. He held that knowledge is best avoided as a defining ingredient of liability, and that the *Baden, Delvaux* scale is best forgotten in this context[1].

100.30 *Liability of third parties and beneficiaries*

He rejected the idea that unconscionability should be the touchstone for liability, unless it is made clear 'what, *in this context*, unconscionable *means*'[2], and he held instead that to fix a defendant with liability, it must be shown that he has acted dishonestly. In line with this decision, the English courts, along with the courts of most other Commonwealth jurisdictions other than Canada[3], no longer refer to this head of liability as liability for 'knowing assistance', and have come instead to refer to it as liability for 'dishonest assistance'[4].

[1] [1995] 2 AC 378 at 392.
[2] [1995] 2 AC 378 at 392 (his emphasis).
[3] The leading Canadian case remains *Air Canada v M & L Travel Ltd* [1993] 3 SCR 787, in which Iacobucci J held at 811 that 'the knowledge requirement for this type of liability is actual knowledge ... recklessness or wilful blindness', and at 826 that 'it is unnecessary ... to find that the [assistant] himself acted in bad faith or dishonestly'. In line with this decision, the Canadian courts have persisted with the language of 'knowing assistance': *Gold v Rosenberg* [1997] 3 SCR 767 at 780; *Citadel General Assurance Co v Lloyd's Bank Canada* [1997] 3 SCR 805 at 819; *Glenko Enterprises Ltd v Keller* [2001] 1 WWR 229 at 248.
[4] England: *Walker v Stones* [2001] 2 WLR 623 at 665; *Twinsectra Ltd v Yardley* [2002] 2 AC 164 at 168 and 171; *Barlow Clowes International Ltd v Eurotrust International Ltd* [2005] UKPC 37, [2006] 1 All ER 333 at [18]. Australia: *Burger King Corp v Hungry Jack's Pty Ltd* (21 June 2001, unreported), NSWCA; *Pilmer v Duke Group Ltd (in liquidation)* (2001) 207 CLR 165 at para 3. Hong Kong: *Bardissy v D'Souza* [1999] HKCFI 85. Malaysia: *Industrial Concrete Products Bhd v Concrete Engineering Products Ltd* [2001] 2 MLJ 332 at 363. New Zealand: *Equiticorp Industries Group Ltd (in stat man) v R (No 47)* [1998] 2 NZLR 481 at 540. Singapore: *Banque Nationale de Paris v Hew* [2001] 1 SLR 300.

100.31 In the *Royal Brunei* case, Lord Nicholls made it clear that the test for dishonesty in this context is not purely subjective, in the sense that individuals are not 'free to set their own standards of honesty in particular circumstances'[1], and must instead be judged by reference to the objective standards of right-thinking members of society. So, as the courts have put it in subsequent cases, there is no 'Robin Hood' defence to an action for dishonest assistance[2]. Lord Nicholls also clearly stated that[3]:

'honesty ... does have a strong subjective element in that it is a description of a type of conduct assessed in the light of what a person actually knew at the time, as distinct from what a reasonable person would have known or appreciated.'

[1] [1995] 2 AC 378 at 389.
[2] *Grupo Torras SA v Al-Sabah (No 5)* [2001] Lloyd's Rep Bank 36 at 60; *Walker v Stones* [2001] QB 902 at 939; *Twinsectra Ltd v Yardley* [2002] UKHL 12, [2002] 2 AC 164 at 172. Cf *Consul Developments Pty Ltd v DPC Estates Pty Ltd* (1975) 132 CLR 373 at 398.
[3] [1995] 2 AC 378 at 389.

100.32 Rather surprisingly, however, the House of Lords subsequently divided in *Twinsectra Ltd v Yardley*[1], over the question whether Lord Nicholls meant to lay down a test for dishonesty which incorporated any further subjective element than this. More specifically, the question which divided their Lordships was whether he meant to lay down a test which requires it to be shown not merely that a defendant's behaviour has been dishonest by the standards of right-thinking people, but also that the defendant was conscious of this fact at the time when he acted. In the language of criminal lawyers, the question was therefore whether Lord Nicholls meant to lay down a test for dishonesty that was analogous to the test for dishonesty laid down in the context of criminal proceedings by Lord Lane CJ in *R v Ghosh*[2]?

1   [2002] 2 AC 164, [2002] 2 AC 164.
2   [1982] QB 1053.

100.33 There were powerful reasons for thinking that this was not Lord Nicholls' intention. One was the fact that Lord Nicholls found the defendant liable for dishonest assistance on the facts of the *Royal Brunei* case, even though the claimant never argued, and Lord Nicholls did not hold, that the defendant knew that right-thinking people would have thought his behaviour dishonest. Another was the fact that Lord Nicholls expressly stated that[1]:

'Whatever may be the position in some criminal or other contexts (see, for instance, *R v Ghosh* [1982] QB 1053), in the context of the accessory liability principle acting dishonestly, or with a lack of probity, which is synonymous, means simply not acting as an honest person would in the circumstances. This is an objective standard.'

1   [1995] 2 AC 378 at 389.

100.34 Nonetheless, and notwithstanding some powerful dissenting remarks on the subject by Lord Millett[1], the majority of the House of Lords in *Twinsectra* held that Lord Nicholls had meant to introduce a test of self-conscious dishonesty. Thus, Lord Hutton stated that[2]:

'dishonesty requires knowledge by the defendant that what he was doing would be regarded as dishonest by honest people, although he should not escape a finding of dishonesty because he sets his own standards of honesty and does not regard as dishonest what he knows would offend the normally accepted standards of honest conduct.'

1   [2002] UKHL 12, [2002] 2 AC 164 at 194–202.
2   [2002] UKHL 12, [2002] 2 AC 164 at [36].

100.35 Likewise, Lord Hoffmann held that 'more than knowledge of the facts which make the conduct wrongful [is required]' and that there must be 'a dishonest state of mind, that is to say, consciousness that one is transgressing ordinary standards of honest behaviour' [1]. Applying this test to the facts of the case, the majority concluded that a solicitor who had enabled a client to commit a breach of trust by releasing trust money to the client absolutely had not acted dishonestly, although he was aware from the terms of an undertaking given by another solicitor that the client had been meant to take the money as trustee and not as absolute owner.

1   [2002] UKHL 12, [2002] 2 AC 164 at [20].

100.36 The majority judgments in *Twinsectra* depended on a very strained reading of Lord Nicholls' words in *Royal Brunei*. However matters did not end there as the point was then revisited by the Privy Council, in *Barlow Clowes International Ltd v Eurotrust International Ltd*[1]. Judgment was delivered by Lord Hoffmann, and the panel presided over by Lord Nicholls[2]. The relevant facts were as follows. A fraudster laundered several million pounds stolen from the claimant company through bank accounts held in the names of various Isle of Man companies administered by Eurotrust, another company in the Isle of Man which provided offshore financial services. One of the Eurotrust directors was found by the trial judge to have strongly suspected that the money passing through his hands had been misappropriated, but to have consciously decided not to make inquiries lest he discover the truth. The judge also held that he might have seen nothing wrong with this behaviour, because he had had an[3]:

> 'exaggerated notion of dutiful service to clients, which produced a warped moral approach that it was not improper to treat carrying out clients' instructions as being all important.'

1   [2005] UKPC 37, [2006] 1 All ER 333.
2   The panel also included Lord Walker, who had extra-judicially doubted 'whether the law as stated in *Royal Brunei* [was] clearer after *Twinsectra*': Lord Walker, "Dishonesty and Unconscionable Conduct in Commercial Life" (2005) 27 Sydney LR 187, at p 197.
3   [2004] WTLR 1365 at [133].

100.37 On appeal from the finding that the director was liable for dishonest assistance, counsel argued that on these facts as found by the trial judge he could not have been relevantly dishonest because he had not been aware that his actions were dishonest by ordinary standards, as required by the majority in *Twinsectra*. Lord Hoffmann rejected this. Conceding that there had been 'an element of ambiguity' in Lord Hutton's remarks in *Twinsectra*, he held that neither he nor Lord Hutton had meant to say there that a defendant must have considered what normally acceptable standards of honest conduct might be: they had merely meant to say that a defendant must have known about those aspects of the relevant transaction which made his participation transgress those standards[1]. Applying this test to the facts of *Eurotrust*, the defendant was therefore liable.

1   [2005] UKPC 37, [2006] 1 All ER 333 at [15]–[16].

100.38 Lord Hoffmann saw no inconsistency between the Privy Council's judgment in *Eurotrust* and the majority judgments in *Twinsectra*, and he rationalised the decision in *Twinsectra* on the basis that the defendant solicitor had not been objectively dishonest because[1]:

> 'he honestly believed that the undertaking [given by the other solicitor that his client would use the money solely for trust purposes] did not, so to speak, run with the money and that, as between him and his client, he held it for his client unconditionally.'

1   [2005] UKPC 37, [2006] 1 All ER 333 at [17].

100.39 This rationalisation of the result in *Twinsectra* is plausible if there is truly room for doubt whether professional ethics permit a solicitor to disregard another solicitor's undertaking affecting property when he receives the property with notice of this undertaking. Lord Hoffmann's account of the reasoning in *Twinsectra* is less convincing, but the courts have taken him at his word and followed *Eurotrust* in subsequent cases[1]. Hence it may now be said that the mental element for dishonest assistance is not self-conscious dishonesty of the kind described by Lord Lane CJ in *Ghosh* but objective dishonesty of the kind described by Lord Nicholls in *Royal Brunei* and Lord Hoffmann in *Eurotrust*.

[1] *Fresh 'N' Clean Wales Ltd v Miah* [2006] EWHC 903 (Ch) at [18]; *Abouh-Rahmah v Abacha* [2006] 1 All ER (Comm) 247 at [43], approved [2006] EWCA Civ 1492 [66]–[69] (Arden LJ).

Dishonesty and knowledge

100.40 Although he held that knowledge is not the defining ingredient of accessory liability in *Royal Brunei*, Lord Nicholls acknowledged there that the honesty of a defendant's conduct can only be assessed in the light of what he knew when he acted. Obviously, the facts which a defendant must have known before he can be said to have acted dishonestly will vary from case to case, but it seems that at the very least the defendant must have known 'that the person he is assisting is not entitled to do what he is doing'[1]. He need not have understood the legal characterisation of the primary wrongdoer's actions, so that 'a person may dishonestly assist in the commission of a breach of trust without any idea of what a trust means,' as Lord Hoffmann said in *Twinsectra*[2]. Nor need he have known all the details of the primary wrongdoer's whole design, according to Lewison J in *Ultraframe (UK) Ltd v Fielding*, although by analogy with criminal accessory liability, he must have known in broad terms what the design was, and his liability should not extend to unforeseen and uncontemplated actions by the primary wrongdoer which lay outside the scope of the joint enterprise in which he participated[3].

[1] *Ultraframe (UK) Ltd v Fielding* [2005] EWHC 1638 (Ch) at [1504], *per* Lewison J.
[2] [2002] UKHL 12, [2002] 2 AC 164 at [19]. Lord Hoffmann made the same point in *Barlow Clowes International Ltd v Eurotrust International Ltd [2005] UKPC 37*, [2006] 1 All ER 333 at [28]. See too *Abou-Rahmah v Abacha* [2006] 1 All ER (Comm) 247 at [43]; [2006] EWCA Civ 1492 [23].
[3] [2005] EWHC 1638 (Ch) at [1506].

100.41 The question has arisen whether a defendant is relevantly dishonest if he thinks that he is participating in some wrongful transaction other than the breach of trust in which he has actually participated? The cases are divided on this point[1], but in principle, defendants should not be allowed to make the disreputable argument that they did not think they were helping to steal from the claimant because they thought they were helping to steal from someone else. As Fox LJ held in *Agip (Africa) Ltd v Jackson*[2]:

'persons who [need] to demonstrate that they [have] acted honestly [cannot] shelter behind transactions or objects which [are] themselves disreputable.'

[1] Yes: *Agip (Africa) Ltd v Jackson* [1990] Ch 265 at 295, affirmed [1991] Ch 547 at 569; *Ultraframe (UK) Ltd v Fielding* [2005] EWHC 1638 (Ch) at [1500], *Abou-Rahmah v Abacha* [2006] EWCA Civ 1492 [39]. No: *Brink's Ltd v Abu-Saleh* [1999] CLC 133; *Grupo Torras SA v Al-Sabah (No 5)* [1999] CLC 1469 at 1665–6, affirmed [2001] Lloyd's Rep Bank 36 at 59.
[2] [1991] Ch 547 at 569.

100.42 The different question has also arisen in the context of accessory liability cases, whether a corporate defendant can ever be said to possess a dishonest 'state of mind' because it 'knows' relevant facts. Pursuant to the principles governing the corporate identification doctrine which were laid down by Lord Hoffmann in his speech for the Privy Council in *Meridian Global Funds Management Asia Ltd v Securities Commission*[1] *it is possible to fix a c*ompany with liability on this basis provided that an employee with whom the company can be 'identified' has assisted in a breach of trust with the requisite degree of fault. In practice, though, it is far easier to succeed with arguments of this kind against 'one-man companies'[2] than against larger organisations where responsibilities and relevant knowledge are fragmented and dispersed among many people. In some Australian and New Zealand cases on accessory liability, the courts have been willing to aggregate the knowledge of several corporate employees, with a view to fixing the company with knowledge of particular facts[3]. However, this process has not recommended itself to the English courts when it has been urged upon them in criminal cases, and they are particularly unhappy with the notion that a consciously dishonest corporate 'mind' can be conjured up by aggregating the knowledge of several employees, none of whom, individually, is consciously dishonest[4]. Representative of this attitude is Harman J's statement in *Galmerrow Securities Ltd v National Westminster Bank plc* that[5]:

> 'knowledge held by a corporation depends on the knowledge of all its employees ... [but] one cannot put the knowledge of one employee, who acts honestly in the course of his duties, together with the knowledge of another employee in a separate department, who acts honestly in the course of his duties, and conclude that the corporation has acted dishonestly because had the two employees pooled their information it would have become apparent that an act was dishonest.'

1   [1995] 2 AC 500 at 507. See too *London Underground Ltd v NURMTW* [2001] ICR 647 at 662, where Robert Walker LJ considered the 'essential point' of *Meridian* to be that: 'in determining the mental state of an artificial person (when some ... rule requires that rather fictional exercise to be carried out) it may be necessary to look, not only at the body's formal constitution, but also at the way it actually organises its activities, and at the scope and purpose of the ... rule'.
2   As in eg *Fresh 'N' Clean (Wales) Ltd v Miah* [2006] EWHC 903 (Ch).
3   *Macquarie Bank Ltd v Sixty-Fourth Throne Pty Ltd* [1998] 3 VR 133 at 161; *Equiticorp Industries Group Ltd (in stat man) v R (No 47)* [1998] 2 NZLR 481 at 627–9.
4   *R v HM Coroner for East Kent, ex p Spooner* (1987) 88 Cr App Rep 10 at 15–17; *A-G's Ref (No 2 of 1999)* [2000] 3 WLR 195 at 211–212.
5   [2002] WTLR 125 at 151–152.

Remedies

100.43 Because liability for dishonest assistance is a civil secondary liability which derives from and duplicates the liability of the trustee or fiduciary whose breach has been assisted, the compensatory remedies available against the dishonest assistant are identical with the remedies available against the trustee or fiduciary. Thus, dishonest assistants can be ordered to account for the value of misapplied trust property as a form of substitutive performance of the trustees' obligation to apply the property in accordance with the trust[1], and compound interest will be payable on top of the capital sum found to be due[2]. They can also be ordered to pay the same measure of compensation as the trustee or fiduciary would have to pay if the principal sued him for reparation[3].

[1] For discussion of this method of quantifying the trustee's liability see para 89.7 ff. Awards of this sort were made against dishonest assistants in *Macdonald v Hauer* (1976) 72 DLR (3d) 110 at 129; *Re Bell's Indenture* [1980] 1 WLR 1217 at 1231–1233; *Commercial Union Life Assurance Co of Canada v John Ingle Insurance Group Inc* (2002) 22 CCLI 221, affirmed (2002) 217 DLR (4th) 178; *NCR Australia v Credit Connection Pty Ltd (in liquidation)* [2004] NSWSC 1 at [150]; *Lewis v Nortex Pty Ltd (in liquidation)* [2005] NSWSC 480.

[2] As in eg *Orix Australia Corpn Ltd v Moody Kiddell & Partners Pty Ltd* [2005] NSWSC 1209 at [161].

[3] Awards of this sort were made against dishonest assistants in eg *Colour Control Centre Pty Ltd v Ty* NSW Sup Ct (Eq Div) 24 July 1995; *Equiticorp Industries Group Ltd v R. (No 47)* [1998] 2 NZLR 481 at 658; *Fyffes Group Ltd v Templeman* [2000] 2 Lloyd's Rep 643.

100.44 Consistently with the view that liability for dishonest assistance derives from and duplicates the liability of the primary wrongdoer, one would also expect the courts to hold that a dishonest assistant must pay over the amount of unauthorised profits made by the wrongdoing trustee or fiduciary, even though these do not correspond to a loss in the claimant's hands, and even though the dishonest assistant has not shared in them. There are a series of Canadian cases to this effect[1], and several English decisions at first instance[2]. However, in *Ultraframe (UK) Ltd v Fielding*[3], Lewison J declined to hold that a dishonest assistant should incur liability of this kind because he thought that this would amount to a punitive measure.

[1] Running from *Canada Safeway Ltd v Thompson* [1951] 3 DLR 295 through to *Glenko Enterprises Ltd v Keller* [2001] 1 WWR 229 at 257–258.

[2] *Ostrich Farming Corpn Ltd v Wallstreet* LLC Ch D, Lawtel Report 8 October 1998; *Comax Secure Business Services Ltd v Wilson* [2001] All ER (D) 222 (Jun) QBD 21 June 2001; *CMS Dolphin Ltd v Simonet* [2001] 2 BCLC 704, followed in *Quarter Master UK Ltd v Pyke* [2004] EWHC 1815 (Ch), [2005] 1 BCLC 245.

[3] [2005] EWHC 1638 (Ch) at [1589]–[1601].

100.45 It sometimes happens that a dishonest assistant makes a profit for himself by assisting in a breach of trust or fiduciary duty which does not correspond to a loss suffered by the claimant. In these circumstances, the trustee or fiduciary owes no primary liability for the dishonest assistant's gain, and so the dishonest assistant cannot be made liable to pay over the amount of his profit on the basis that he is secondarily liable to do so. To avoid the conclusion that he is therefore not liable to disgorge his profit, the courts have dealt with cases of this sort by abandoning the theory that liability for dishonest assistance is a civil secondary liability, and ordering an account of profits against the dishonest assistant[1].

[1] *Consul Development Pty Ltd v DFC Estates Pty Ltd* (1972) 132 CLR 373 at 397, followed in *United States Surgical Corp v Hospital Products International Pty Ltd* [1982] 2 NSWLR 766 at 817, and quoted with approval in *Fyffes Group Ltd v Templeman* [2000] 2 Lloyd's Rep 643 at 672. See too *Crown Dilmun v Sutton* [2004] EWHC 52 (Ch), [2004] 1 BCLC 468 at [204]; *Ultraframe (UK) Ltd v Fielding* [2005] EWHC 1638 (Ch) at [1595]. And cf *Nanus Asia Co Inc v Standard Chartered Bank* [1990] 1 HKLR 396 at 417–9 where the judge went one step further and held that a dishonest assistant's profits

were held on constructive trust.See also *Alers-Hankey v Teixera* [2006] BCCA 224, where a dishonest assistant was ordered to disgorge his profits but was permitted an equitable allowance for his time and efforts.

100.46 In a case in the New South Wales Court of Appeal, *Yeshiva Properties No 1 Pty Ltd v Marshall*[1], Bryson JA expressed the obiter view that a claimant should not be awarded a remedy against a dishonest assistant if he has released the wrongdoing trustee or fiduciary from liability, or decided not to sue him. In his Honour's view[2]:

'A plaintiff who seeks an equitable remedy commits himself to a suit in which all equities in the controversy will be resolved together, and the court should not allow the plaintiff to decide which party to sue and which party to ignore or give a release, perhaps for forensic advantages related to assessed readiness to contest the claim.'

1   (2005) 7 ITELR 577.
2   (2005) 7 ITELR 577 at [80].

100.47 For an English court to follow these dicta would require a departure from long-established authorities which hold that claimants are free to sue all or any of those who are jointly and severally liable with the wrongdoing trustees for their participation in a breach of trust[1].

1   *Rowland v Witherden* (1851) 3 Mac & G 568, esp at 573; *Pearce v Pearce* (1856) 22 Beav 248; *Blyth v Fladgate* [1891] 1 Ch 337 at 353.

Vicarious liability of a defendant's partners

100.48 In *Dubai Aluminium Co Ltd v Salaam*[1], the House of Lords held that where a partner incurs liability for dishonest assistance, his fellow partners may be vicariously liable for his wrongdoing under the Partnership Act 1890, s 10. This statute was enacted before certain of the core principles of English agency law as they are now understood were fully developed, and significantly the statute predates Diplock LJ's account of actual and apparent authority in *Freeman and Lockyer v Buckhurst Park Properties (Mangal) Ltd*[2] by some 70 years. Hence Parliament did not have as sharply focused an idea of apparent authority as that articulated by Diplock LJ when it enacted section 10, which ambiguously provides that:

'Where, by any wrongful act or omission of any partner acting in the ordinary course of the business of the firm, or with the authority of his co-partners, loss or injury is caused to any person not being a partner in the firm, or any penalty is incurred, the firm is liable therefor to the same extent as the partner so acting or omitting to act.'

1   [2002] UKHL 48, [2003] 2 AC 366.
2   [1964] 2 QB 480.

100.49 Does this mean that a partner will be vicariously liable for the apparently or actually authorised acts of a fellow partner, and for nothing else? Or does it mean that he will be vicariously liable for a wider class of acts which may or may not have been actually or apparently authorised, but which the partner has in any case enabled his fellow partner to perform by placing him in a position to perform them? In *Dubai Aluminium* the Court of Appeal gave the first answer, Evans and Aldous LJJ taking the view that the question whether an agent's actions are actually or apparently authorised is essentially identical to the question whether an employee has acted in the course of his employment[1]. However, the House of Lords took a different approach, holding that a partner can be vicariously liable under section 10 for the acts of a fellow partner, even if these have not been actually or apparently authorised, because the words 'in the ordinary course of business of the firm' take in a wider class of acts. These include both actually and apparently authorised acts, and also acts that are 'so closely connected with acts that [the partner] ... was authorised to do that ... the wrongful conduct [can] fairly and properly be regarded as done ... while acting in the course of the firm's business'[2] .This 'close connection' test was taken by their Lordships from the Supreme Court of Canada's decision in *Bazley v Curry*[3]. To determine whether or not it is satisfied a court must look to the underlying policy imperatives discussed there, and also in the House of Lords' decision in *Lister v Hesley Hall Ltd*[4]. Taken in conjunction with *Dubai Aluminium*, these cases make it clear that a dishonest assistant's partners may be vicariously liable for his acts even though he acted without his partners' knowledge or authority, and even though they expressly prohibited him from doing what he did, if by their decision to carry on the business of the firm they increased the risk that third parties would be harmed by his actions.

1 [2001] QB 113 at 133, *per* Evans LJ, and 141–2, *per* Aldous LJ.
2 [2002] UKHL 48, [2003] 2 AC 366 at [23] *per* Lord Nicholls.
3 (1999) 174 DLR (4th) 45.
4 [2001] UKHL 22, [2002] 1 AC 215. See too *Majrowksi v Guy's and St Thomas' NHS Trust* [2006] UKHL 34 [2006] 4 All ER 395 at [9]–[10] per Lord Nicholls. The reasons given by the courts for imposing vicarious liability in these cases are critiqued in J W Neyers 'A Theory of Vicarious Liability' (2005) 43 Alberta LR 287.

Protection for suspicious agents or advisers

100.50 Banks, building societies, and other financial institutions, as well as lawyers and accountants, are now required to take many more precautions than hitherto against the possibility that their clients are engaged in laundering the proceeds of criminal activity or terrorism. Several statutes now make it a criminal offence to assist in money laundering, to fail to report information relating to the activities of money launderers, and to tip off money launderers that they are under criminal investigation. The mens rea requirements for these offences range from actual knowledge or suspicion of relevant facts, as in the Criminal Justice Act 1988, s 93A, and the Drug Trafficking Act 1994, s 50, for example, to the more draconian requirements of the Criminal Justice Act 1988, s 39C(2), of the Terrorism Act 2000, s 21A, and of the Proceeds of Crime Act 2002, s 330, which also catch defendants who have had 'reasonable grounds for knowing or suspecting' the relevant facts[1]. Even standing alone, these provisions would obviously give financial and other professional intermediaries a considerable incentive to create internal checking and monitoring procedures, with a view to protecting themselves against liability. But these institutions must additionally take due heed of the Money Laundering

100.50 *Liability of third parties and beneficiaries*

Regulations 1993, the Money Laundering Guidance Notes issued by the Joint Money Laundering Steering Group, and the Money Laundering Rules issued by the Financial Services Authority under powers conferred by the Financial Services and Markets Act 2000. These variously require financial institutions to establish internal procedures, eg to check the identity of customers, keep records, appoint compliance officers, train staff, or describe how to achieve best practice in these areas. Taken collectively, they represent an extensive and detailed description of how professional intermediaries ought to behave, and failure to live up to the standards which they demand seems certain to be construed by the courts as a relevant matter when considering the honesty of an intermediary's conduct in the context of civil proceedings for dishonest assistance.

[1] Section 21A(6) of the Terrorism Act 2000, and s 330(8) of the Proceeds of Crime Act 2002, both also provide that in deciding whether a person has committed an offence under the section, 'the court must consider whether he followed any relevant guidance' approved by the Treasury or other supervisory body.On the meaning of 'suspicion' in this context note *R v Da Silva* [2006] 2 Cr App R 35, followed in *K Ltd v National Westminster Bank plc* [2006] EWCA Civ 1039.

100.51 The question arises as to how agents and advisers might protect themselves in the event that they receive money from a client and become suspicious about its provenance, given that they owe contractual and fiduciary duties to their clients, and might face civil suits by their clients for breach of these duties in the event that they fail to follow their client's instructions, but given too that they may incur criminal sanctions or civil liability for dishonest assistance in the event that they comply with them[1]. Depending on the circumstances, intermediaries in this position are advised to apply to the Serious Fraud Office for directions, as recommended by the Court of Appeal in *Bank of Scotland v A Ltd*[2], or alternatively to the court, as in *Finers v Miro*[3].

[1] For cases exploring the tensions created for financial institutions wishing to avoid civil liability from these two possible directions, see *TTS International v Cantrade Private Bank* (Royal Court of Jersey, 1995), noted D Banks (1995) 4 JITCP 60; *Wavefront Trading Ltd v Po Sang Bank Ltd* [1999] HKFCI 5; *US International Marketing Ltd v National Bank of New Zealand Ltd* [2004] 1 NZLR 589, NZCA.
[2] [2001] 1 WLR 751.
[3] [1991] 1 WLR 35. See too *C v S* [1999] 1 WLR 1551.

Paragraph 4

Elements of liability where misapplied trust property has been received and dealt with by a defendant for his own benefit

100.52 To make a defendant personally liable where he has received misapplied trust property and dealt with the property for his own benefit it is currently necessary to establish that there was:

(1)   property held on trust or subject to some other fiduciary duty;
(2)   misapplication of the property by the trustees or fiduciary in breach of trust or fiduciary duty;
(3)   receipt of the property or its traceable proceeds by the defendant;

(4)   a causal link between the defendant's receipt and the breach of trust or fiduciary duty;

(5)   a dealing with the property by the defendant for his own benefit, and not in his character as agent for another party;

(6)   knowledge by the defendant that the property has been transferred in breach of trust or breach of fiduciary duty, either at the time of receipt or at any other time prior to his dealing with the property for his own benefit.

100.53 Although the courts have discussed this final requirement in many cases, it still cannot be said that it has been definitively settled what states of mind will suffice to incur liability. However, some recent judicial observations on the nature of liability under this head suggest that the time is now ripe for the courts to take a more radical approach to this question[1], by recognising not only that it is a fault-based equitable wrong to receive and deal with misapplied trust property for one's own benefit with a dishonest state of mind, but also that a strict liability claim in unjust enrichment will alternatively lie against the recipients of misapplied trust property, subject to the recipients' ability to raise the defence of change of position. In the following account, each of the current requirements for liability will be considered, and the future direction of the law will then be discussed.

[1]   Of particular importance are Lord Nicholls' extra-judicial observations in his article 'Knowing Receipt: The Need for a New Landmark' in W R Cornish et al (eds) *Restitution: Past, Present and Future* (1998) 231, and Lord Walker's supportive extra-judicial comments in his article 'Dishonesty and Unconscionable Conduct in Commercial Life – Some Reflections on Accessory Liability and Knowing Receipt' (2005) 27 Sydney LR 187 at p. 202. See too *Grupo Torras SA v Al-Sabah (No 5)* [2001] Lloyd's Rep Bank 36 at 62, CA; *Twinsectra Ltd v Yardley* [2002] UKHL 12, [2002] 2 AC 164 at 194; *Dubai Aluminium Co Ltd v Salaam* [2003] 2 AC 366 at [87].

Property held on trust or subject to fiduciary duty

100.54 Liability is not confined to cases where the misapplied property has been held on trust, but may also be incurred where a defendant has received property that has been controlled by a person, such as a company director or employee, who owed fiduciary duties to a principal in respect of his handling of the property[1]. In the absence of a trust or fiduciary duty, however, liability will not arise[2].

[1]   *Competitive Insurance Co v Davies Investments Ltd* [1975] 3 All ER 254; *Belmont Finance CorpN Ltd v Williams Furniture Ltd (No 2)* [1980] 1 All ER 393; *Baden, Delvaux v Société Générale pour Favoriser le Développement du Commerce et de l'Industrie en France SA* [1993] 1 WLR 509n; *Rolled Steel Products (Holdings) Ltd v British Steel Corpn* [1986] Ch 246; *Precision Dippings Ltd v Precision Dippings Marketing Ltd* [1986] Ch 447; *Agip (Africa) Ltd v Jackson* [1991] Ch 547; *Heinl v Jyske Bank (Gibraltar) Ltd* [1999] Lloyd's Rep Bank 511; *CMS Dolphin Ltd v Simonet* [2001] 2 BCLC 704; *Primlake Ltd (in liquidation) v Matthews Associates* [2006] EWHC 1227 (Ch).

[2]   *Walker v Standard Chartered Bank* [1998] NPC 29, Ch D; *Box v Barclays Bank plc* [1998] Lloyd's Rep Bank 185.

100.55 *Liability of third parties and beneficiaries*

Misapplication of property in breach of trust or fiduciary duty

100.55 It must be shown that the trustee or fiduciary who controlled the property misapplied it in breach of trust or breach of fiduciary duty, but there is no need to show that he committed this breach with a dishonest state of mind[1].

1   *Polly Peck International plc v Nadir (No 2)* [1992] 4 All ER 769 at 777; *El Ajou v Dollar Land Holdings plc* [1994] 2 All ER 685 at 700; *Brown v Bennett* [1999] 1 BCLC 649.

Receipt of the property or its traceable proceeds by the defendant

100.56 The defendant must have received legal title to the property; for if he has not, then he is strictly liable at common law to repay the amount of the property, and there is no need for equity's intervention[1] .The defendant's receipt of the property or its traceable proceeds must not be protected by the overreaching provisions of the 1925 property legislation, nor by the exceptions to the *nemo dat quod non habet* principle such as those embodied in the Factors Act 1889, the Sale of Goods Act 1979, and the Consumer Credit Act 1974. Nor must the defendant be in a position to raise the defence of bona fide purchase for value of the legal estate without notice of the beneficiaries' interest[2]. However, if the defendant knowingly colludes with the trustee to purchase trust property at an undervalue, then the sale can be impeached under the Trustee Act 1925 s 13(2), and the trustee and the defendant will both be liable to make good the difference between the sale price and the fair market value of the property[3].

1   *Criterion Properties plc v Stratford, [2004] UKHL 28, [2004] 1 WLR 1846; cf Trustee of the Property of FC Jones & Sons (a firm) v Jones* [1997] Ch 159. Trustees generally have the power to transfer legal title to trust property even where they act in breach of trust: *Rolled Steel Products (Holdings) Ltd v British Steel Corpn* [1986] Ch 246 at 304; *Hammersmith and Fulham London Borough Council v Monk* [1992] 1 AC 478 at 493.
2   *Re Diplock* [1948] Ch 465 at 535 and 544, CA; *Carl Zeiss Stiftung v Herbert Smith & Co (a firm) (No 2)* [1969] 2 Ch 276 at 289 per Danckwerts LJ; *Cowan de Groot Properties Ltd v Eagle Trust plc* [1992] 4 All ER 700 at 767.
3   *Myatt v Browne* [2005] All ER (D) 276 (Nov).

100.57 In the absence of fraud, a company's receipt of property will not be treated as receipt by its shareholders for the purposes of fixing the shareholders with liability, even if the company is wholly owned[1]. In the case of fraud, however, 'the court is entitled to "pierce the corporate veil" and recognise the receipt of the company as that of the individual(s) in control of it if the company was used as a device or facade to conceal the true facts thereby avoiding or concealing any liability of those individual(s)'[2].

1   *Trustor AB v Smallbone (No 2)* [2001] 3 All ER 987 at 994, per Morritt V-C following *Cowan de Groot Properties Ltd v Eagle Trust plc* [1992] 4 All ER 700 at 762, and *El Ajou v Dollar Land Holdings plc* [1993] 3 All ER 717 at 738.
2   *Trustor AB v Smallbone (No 2)* [2001] 3 All ER 987 at 995. See too *Gencor ACP Ltd v Dalby* [2000] 2 BCLC 734 at 744. It is a controversial issue whether the same effect can be achieved by fixing the company's director/shareholders with secondary liability as dishonest assistants for the company's profits: see cases cited at note 1, para 100.44 above.

100.58 Receipt of trust property by a defendant clearly includes receipt of the traceable proceeds of the trust property, as identified in accordance with the relevant tracing rules. Thus, in *El Ajou v Dollar Land Holdings plc*, Hoffmann LJ considered that a claimant must show[1]:

> 'first, a disposal of his assets in breach of fiduciary duty; secondly, the beneficial receipt by the defendant of assets which are traceable as representing the assets of the [claimant]; and thirdly, knowledge on the part of the defendant that the assets he received are traceable to a breach of fiduciary duty.'

1   [1994] 2 All ER 685 at 700. See too *Agip (Africa) Ltd v Jackson* [1990] Ch 265 at 289–292; *Boscawen v Bajwa* [1996] 1 WLR 328 at 334; *Foskett v McKeown* [2001] 1 AC 102 at 128; *Trustor AB v Smallbone (No 2)* [2001] 3 All ER 987 at 994.

100.59 The question arises whether the courts are tied to a strict transactional approach to identifying the traceable proceeds of trust property, or whether they might instead use a causative ('but for') approach to determining whether a defendant has received the traceable proceeds of trust property. Take the case where a trustee wrongfully gives a cheque for £10,000 drawn on a trust account to D1, and D1 pays the cheque into his own current account. The following day D1 receives a cheque from X for £10,000 for work done which he endorses in favour of his son, D2, believing that he can afford to make such a gift to D2 in the circumstances, although he would not otherwise have made such a gift. The beneficiaries have no proprietary remedy against D2 because they cannot trace *their* £10,000 into D2's hands. However, the substance of the matter is that D2 would not have received D1's endorsed cheque but for D1 having previously received the trustee's payment, and in these circumstances it is submitted that D2 should be liable to a personal claim by the beneficiaries, assuming that the knowledge requirement is satisfied[1]. This result could have been reached if D1 had paid X's cheque into his current account, and had then paid D2 out of this account, and to deny the beneficiaries a claim for knowing receipt in the situation described, on the ground that they cannot prove transactional proprietary links between the money withdrawn from the trust account and the money received by D2, is surely 'to adopt an unnecessary "proprietary analysis" in what is otherwise a personal claim'[2], there being no question of the beneficiaries obtaining any priority prejudicial to D2's creditors in the event of D2's insolvency[3].

1   The same analysis could also be adopted in the event that the courts were to recognise that D2 was strictly liable to the beneficiaries in an action for unjust enrichment, and indeed, might also be adopted in the context of claims for dishonest assistance, as suggested by the facts of *Agip (Africa) Ltd v Jackson* [1991] Ch 547 esp at 561.
2   S Fennell, 'Misdirected Funds: Problems of Uncertainty and Inconsistency', (1994) 57 MLR 38 at 45.
3   The underlying issue here is whether the applicable tracing rules should reflect an abstract or property-specific conception of wealth transfers. Causal tracing rules are consistent only with the former conception, but the HL insisted on the latter in *Foskett v McKeown* [2001] 1 AC 102. For discussion, see L Smith 'Tracing' in A Burrows and A Rodger (eds) *Mapping the Law* (2006) at pp.135–7, considering P Birks *Unjust Enrichment* (2005) at p.70. See too C Rotherham 'The Metaphysics of Tracing: Substituted Title and Property Rhetoric' (1996) 34 Osgoode Hall LJ 321; S Evans 'Rethinking Tracing and the law of Restitution' (1999) 115 LQR 469.

Causal link between the breach of trust or fiduciary duty and the defendant's receipt

100.60 In *Brown v Bennett*[1] Morritt LJ held that the defendant's receipt of misapplied trust property 'must be the direct consequence of the alleged breach of trust or fiduciary duty of which the recipient is said to have notice', and he amplified this finding as follows[2]:

> 'The matter, I think, can be tested in this way. Let us assume a mansion house vested in trustees. The trustees fail to perform their fiduciary duties and allow it to fall into appalling disrepair. They are then replaced by other trustees who decide that the matter has gone too far and decide to sell the property. They sell the property to a next-door neighbour, who for the previous 40 years has watched the mansion house falling into disrepair. The sale by the new trustees to the neighbour is entirely proper, at a proper price. The neighbour unquestionably has notice of the previous breaches of duty, because he watched them happen, but the breaches of duty did not give rise to any receipt by the neighbour; the neighbour was not in any way responsible for them and he paid the full value for what he received from the new trustees when he bought. I can see no reason why in those circumstances there should be any [knowing receipt] liability imposed upon the neighbour merely because he watched the house fall into disrepair before he was enabled to buy it.'

1   [1999] 1 BCLC 649 at 655.
2   [1999] 1 BCLC 649 at 655. This principle does not apply in the case where a defendant receives and deals with an unlawful dividend for his own benefit, where the case is not pleaded on the basis that the defendant has dishonestly received and dealt with the property with knowledge that the directors breached their fiduciary duty to the company when they authorised the dividend, but is pleaded on the different basis that the defendant owes the company a restitutionary obligation in the law of unjust enrichment, based on the fact that the company lacked the capacity to pay him the unlawful dividend: *Allied Carpets Group plc v Nethercott* (QBD 28 January 2000).

100.61 Applying this principle to the facts of *Brown v Bennett*, Morritt LJ concluded that even if the defendant had purchased the assets of an insolvent company in the knowledge that the company had been forced into insolvency as a consequence of the directors' breaches of fiduciary duty, it could not be said that there was a direct causal link between the defendant's acquisition of the corporate assets and the directors' breaches of duty, and it followed from this that the defendant could not be liable[1].

1   [1999] 1 BCLC 649 at 654–657, affirming the trial judge's analysis to the same effect, reported at [1998] 2 BCLC 97 at 104.

Beneficial receipt

100.62 Under the present law, a defendant cannot be liable for receiving and dealing with misapplied trust property for his own benefit, if he has acted in a ministerial capacity – ie if he has received property as agent for a principal to whom he owes an immediate duty to account for the property (or an equivalent sum), and who is himself immediately liable to the claimant on the defendant's receipt from the claimant[1]. In these circumstances, however, the defendant can be liable for dishonest assistance if he has dealt with the property in accordance with his principal's instructions, knowing that he is thereby facilitating a breach of trust, and knowing that his actions would be regarded as dishonest by right-thinking people[2]. The reason for this is that liability for dishonest assistance is a wrong-based liability that does not turn on the question whether the defendant has derived a benefit from his actions.

[1] *Barnes v Addy* (1874) 9 Ch App 244 at 254–255; *Adams v Bank of New South Wales* [1984] 1 NSWLR 285 at 290–292; *Westpac Banking Corp v Savin* [1985] 2 NZLR 41 at 69; *Agip (Africa) Ltd v Jackson* [1990] Ch 265 at 291–292; *Cukurooa Celik Enduustrisi AS v Hill Taylor Dickinson (a firm)* (QBD (Comm Ct) 1 June 1996); *Trustor AB v Smallbone (No 2)* [2001] 3 All ER 987 at 994; *Twinsectra Ltd v Yardley* [2002] UKHL 12, [2002] 2 AC 164 at 194.

[2] See eg *British North American Elevator Co v Bank of British North America* [1919] AC 658, but note that this case predates the discussion of the mental element required for liability as a dishonest assistant in *Royal Brunei Airline Sdn Bhd v Tan* [1995] 2 AC 378 and *Twinsectra Ltd v Yardley* [2002] UKHL 12, [2002] 2 AC 164.

100.63 If the courts were to hold that dishonestly receiving and dealing with misapplied trust property for one's own benefit is an equitable wrong analogous to the wrong of dishonest dealing by agents described in Article 100(2), then consistently with what has been said about dishonest assistants, it would not be open to a defendant to rely on the fact that he has acted in a ministerial capacity in his defence to an action based on this wrong. However, if the courts also hold that those who receive misapplied trust property and deal with it for their own benefit are strictly liable to make restitution to the beneficiaries on the ground of unjust enrichment, then defendants could rely on the defence of ministerial receipt in reply to an action of this sort, just as they can currently rely on the defence in reply to other claims in unjust enrichment[1].

[1] *National Westminster Bank Ltd v Barclays Bank International Ltd* [1975] QB 654; *Chase Manhattan Bank NA v Israel-British Bank (London) Ltd* [1981] Ch 105; *Australia and New Zealand Banking Group Ltd v Westpac Banking Corpn* (1988) 164 CLR 662; *Portman Building Society v Hamlyn Taylor Neck (a firm)* [1998] 4 All ER 202 at 207.

100.64 The question has arisen in a series of cases concerned with the liability of banks who have received and dealt with misapplied trust property, whether they should properly be sued on the basis that they have received and dealt with the property for their own benefit, or on the basis that they have acted ministerially, with the result that they can only be sued for dishonest assistance in a breach of trust[1]. To answer this question it is necessary to distinguish the situation where the misapplied trust property has been deposited with the bank by the account-holder from the situation where the property has been deposited with the bank by a third party.

[1] The following discussion draws on the arguments contained in J P Moore, 'Restitution from Banks', unpublished DPhil dissertation, University of Oxford, 2000.

100.65 In the first situation, the bank always receives the money beneficially, and never receives it ministerially: there is simply a loan of money from the account-holder to the bank, or if the account is overdrawn, a repayment of the debt owed to the bank by the account-holder. Hence, the bank is potentially liable to claims that are predicated on the basis that it has received and dealt with misapplied trust property for its own benefit, where a trustee or fiduciary himself deposits trust money into his personal account[1]. It is submitted that cases to the contrary, which suggest that in this situation a bank can only be liable as a dishonest assistant, are incorrect in principle[2].

[1]   As in eg *Director, Real Estate and Business Brokers v NRS Mississauga Inc* (2001) 194 DLR (4th) 527.
[2]   For example, *Polly Peck International plc v Nadir (No 2)* [1993] BCLC 187.

100.66 In the second situation, where cash is deposited with a bank by a person other than the account holder, or the bank's own account with a central clearing bank is credited as result of instructions from such a person, the bank will almost always take the proceeds of the transaction ministerially as agent for the account-holder[1] – and it follows that the bank cannot be sued on the basis that it has received and dealt with the property for its own benefit, although it can be liable for dishonest assistance. It has been hard for the courts and academic commentators to accept this proposition, although cases can be marshalled in its support. One reason for their reluctance may be that they have not always clearly understood that a bank which receives a third-party deposit on its customer's behalf does not receive 'beneficially' simply because it takes good title to the money and thereafter uses the money as its own[2]: 'beneficial receipt' as distinguished from 'ministerial receipt' of money entails not merely that a defendant takes good title to the money, but also that the defendant should not have to account for an equivalent sum to a principal who is himself legally liable to the claimant from the moment of the defendant's receipt. A second, related reason may be that it is not immediately obvious what happens when a bank receives a third-party deposit on a customer's behalf, particularly where the account is overdrawn. Properly understood, though, such transactions always work in the same way, regardless of the state of the account between the bank and the customer: first, the bank receives the deposit ministerially, as agent for its customer; then, in a separate transaction, the bank either borrows the money from its customer and credits the amount in its books as a debt which it owes to the customer, or where his account is overdrawn, applies the amount on his behalf in reduction of the debt which he owes to the bank.

[1]   The only exception to this rule arises where the bank has some prior right of its own to be paid by the third party, pursuant to an arrangement previously entered by the third party and the bank: *Continental Caoutchouc and Gutta Percha Co v Kleinwort Sons & Co* (1904) 90 LT 474 at 476 per Collins MR. In *Standard Bank London Ltd v Canara Bank* [2002] EWHC 1032 (Comm) at para 99, Moore-Bick J considered that Collins MR's observations on this point were irreconcilable with *Barclays Bank Ltd v W J Simms, Son & Cooke (Southern) Ltd* [1980] QB 677 at 695, and *Lloyds Bank plc v Independent Insurance Co Ltd* [2000] QB 110. With respect, though, these two lines of authority are not irreconcilable because they are not concerned with the same issue.
[2]   Cf R Cranston, *Principles of Banking Law* (1997) 207–8; M Bryan, 'Recovering Misdirected Money from Banks: Ministerial Receipt at Law and in Equity' in F D Rose (ed) *Restitution and Banking Law* (1998) 161, 181–187; L D Smith 'Unjust Enrichment, Property, and the Structure of Trusts' (2000) 116 LQR 412 at 433; E P Ellinger, E Lomnicka, and R J A Hooley, *Modern Banking Law* (3rd edn, 2002) 239–242.

100.67 Authority for this analysis, at least where the customer's account is in credit, can be found in *Agip (Africa) Ltd v Jackson*[1], where Millett J (as he then was) stated that:

'The essential feature of [claims in knowing receipt] ... is that the recipient must have received the property for his own use and benefit. This is why neither the paying nor the collecting bank can normally be brought within it.'

¹ [1990] Ch 265, 291; affd [1991] Ch 547.

100.68 It can also be found in a recent Scottish case, *Compagnie Commerciale Andre SA v Artibell Shipping Co Ltd* where Lord Macfadyen held that¹:

'There is, no doubt, a sense in which money paid to a bank to the credit of the account of one of its customers becomes, on receipt, the bank's money – as Lord Mackay said in *Royal Bank of Scotland v Skinner*² it is "simply consumed by the banker." But in that simple situation, the bank is not thereby enriched, because it grants an immediate obligation of corresponding amount to its customer. Receipt by the bank in that way would not ... afford the necessary foundation for an argument that in the event of the money becoming repayable by the customer to the payer, the bank had been unjustly enriched.'

¹ 2001 SC 653 at 661–662.
² 1931 SLT 382 at 384.

100.69 There are also earlier cases which support the proposition that the same analysis applies where misdirected money is credited to an overdrawn account by a third party. In *Continental Caoutchouc and Gutta Percha Co v Kleinwort Sons & Co*¹, Collins MR considered that a bank can rely on the defence of ministerial receipt where it has not received money in its own right pursuant to some prior agreement between the bank and the third party, but has instead received the money purely in its capacity as the customer's agent, and has then credited the money to the customer's overdrawn account, as in these circumstances the bank will have 'constructively sent [the money on] and received it back, and [will have] done nothing incompatible with [its] position as a conduit-pipe or intermediary'. In *British North American Elevator Co v Bank of British North America*², the Privy Council held a bank liable as an accessory to a breach of trust, but not as a beneficial recipient of trust property, where the bank had 'knowingly [become a party] to a misapplication of what were trust funds'³ paid into an overdrawn account by a person other than the bank's customer. Finally, in *Bank of New South Wales v Vale Corpn (Management) Ltd*⁴, the corporate manager of a unit trust wrongfully deposited money it had received as subscriptions for units into the overdrawn account of companies belonging to the same corporate group, and the New South Wales Court of Appeal considered that 'it was not the [defendant] bank, but rather it was the [corporate group] which was the recipient of almost the entirety of the moneys paid out of [the manager's] account.'

¹ (1904) 90 LT 474 at 476.
² [1919] AC 658.
³ [1919] AC 658 at 663.
⁴ (21 October 1981, unreported), NSWCA.

100.70 Against this line of authority are a number of decisions and dicta, which include Millett J's further statement in the *Agip* case that¹:

'if the collecting bank uses the money to reduce or discharge the company's overdraft ... it receives the money for its own benefit.'

1   [1990] Ch 265 at 292; affd [1991] Ch 547. See too *Foxton v Manchester and Liverpool District Banking Co* (1881) 44 LT 406; *Coleman v Bucks and Oxon Union Bank* [1897] 2 Ch 243; *Citadel General Assurance Co v Lloyds Bank Canada* [1997] 3 SCR 805; *Peppiatt v Nichol* (21 August 1998, unreported), Ontario Ct (Gen Div) at paras 316–346.

100.71 Lord Millett (as he has since become) shifted his position after the *Agip* case, writing extra-judicially that a bank can only be said to have received third-party deposits beneficially where there has been 'some conscious appropriation of the sum paid into the account in reduction of the overdraft'[1]. Against this, however, it must be said that when a bank receives a payment from a third party who designates the relevant account at the time of his payment, the bank has no choice which account to credit with the money, and so is not in a position to make a 'conscious appropriation' of the third party's deposit.

1   Sir P Millett (now Lord Millett) 'Tracing the Proceeds of Fraud' (1991) 107 LQR 70, 83, n 46, noted without deciding the issue by the NZCA in *Westpac Banking Corpn v M M Kembla New Zealand Ltd* [2001] 2 NZLR 298 at 316–317.

Knowledge of the breach of trust

100.72 In common with the cases on liability for assisting in a breach of trust which were decided prior to *Royal Brunei Airlines Sdn Bhd v Tan*[1], the cases on personal liability where misapplied trust property has been received and dealt with by a defendant for his own benefit have often adopted the classification of knowledge approved by Peter Gibson J in *Baden, Delvaux v Société Générale pour Favoriser le Développement du Commerce et de l'Industrie en France SA*[2], namely: (i) actual knowledge; (ii) wilfully shutting one's eyes to the obvious; (iii) wilfully and recklessly failing to make such inquiries as an honest and reasonable man would make; (iv) knowledge of circumstances which would indicate the facts to an honest and reasonable man; (v) knowledge of circumstances which would put an honest and reasonable man on inquiry. There is no clear alignment between actual knowledge, *Baden, Delvaux* categories (i)–(iii), and dishonesty on the one hand, and between constructive knowledge, *Baden, Delvaux* categories (iv)–(v), and negligence on the other. Hence it is difficult to translate decisions which are expressed in the language of *Baden, Delvaux* into the language of dishonesty and negligence. However, while some cases suggest that carelessness of the kind which is typically exhibited by defendants falling into categories (iv)–(v) will not suffice for liability[3], the weight of authority indicates that something less than dishonesty of the sort displayed by defendants falling into categories (i)–(iii) will be enough[4].

1   [1995] 2 AC 378.
2   [1993] 1 WLR 509n at 577.
3   *Re Montagu's Settlement Trusts* [1987] Ch 264; *Lipkin Gorman v Karpnale Ltd* [1987] 1 WLR 987 at 1005; *Barclays Bank plc v Quincecare Ltd* [1992] 4 All ER 363 at 375; *Eagle Trust plc v SBC Securities Ltd* [1992] 4 All ER 488 at 509; *Cowan de Groot Properties Ltd v Eagle Trust plc* [1992] 4 All ER 700 at 759; *Polly Peck International plc v Nadir (No 2)* [1992] 4 All ER 769 at 777; *Jonathan v Tilley* (1988) 12 Tru LI 36. Authorities expressly requiring dishonesty are: *Dubai Aluminium Co Ltd v Salaam* [1999] 1 Lloyd's Rep 415 at 453 (not considered by CA on appeal); *Bank of America v Arnell* [1999] Lloyd's Rep Bank 399 at 406–407 per Aikens J, citing *Twinsectra Ltd v Yardley*

[1999] Lloyds Rep Bank 438 at 463–466, where however Potter LJ seems to have been concerned solely with the question whether the defendant had been dishonest for the purposes of a claim in dishonest assistance; *Bank of Credit and Commerce International (Overseas) Ltd v Akindele* [1999] BCC 669, Ch D, overruled on this point in the CA: [2001] Ch 437 at 448.

4   *Selangor United Rubber Estates Ltd v Cradock (No 3)* [1968] 1 WLR 1555; *Belmont Finance Corp v Williams Furniture Ltd (No 2)* [1980] 1 All ER 393 at 405, CA; *International Sales and Agencies Ltd v Marcus* [1982] 3 All ER 551 at 558; *Baden, Delvaux v Société Générale pour Favoriser le Développement du Commerce et de l'Industrie en France SA* [1993] 1 WLR 509n at 582; *Houghton v Fayers* [2000] 1 BCLC 511, CA.

100.73 Clearly, though, a person who receives trust or fiduciary property for his own benefit in circumstances where he has actual, 'Nelsonian' or 'naughty' knowledge of a misapplication will be liable. 'Nelsonian' knowledge (after Admiral Nelson putting his telescope to his blind eye to avoid knowledge of flag signals ordering him to withdraw at the Battle of Copenhagen) covers the deliberate shutting of eyes to what would otherwise be obvious[1]. A defendant has 'naughty' knowledge where he deliberately or recklessly fails to make the inquiries that an honest, reasonable man would make in circumstances where the defendant's suspicions were aroused[2]. Moreover, if the circumstances were such that the suspicions of an honest, reasonable man would have been aroused then the court will be slow to accept the defendant's protestations that his suspicions were not aroused, and so will be ready to infer that his suspicions were aroused[3]. Essentially it is a matter of fact – a jury question[4] – whether the defendant exhibited a sufficient degree of fault by virtue of having actual, Nelsonian, or naughty knowledge of the misapplication, bearing in mind that where he 'knows of circumstances which may on the one hand make the payment a misapplication but which may on the other hand be consistent with perfect propriety ... such a case might be determined on its particular facts by the principle that a party to a commercial agreement should not be fixed with notice simply because in a loose sense he has been put on inquiry'[5].

1   *Baden, Delvaux* [1993] 1 WLR 509n at 576. See too *The Star Sea* [2003] 1 AC 469 at [112], *per* Lord Scott: 'an imputation of blind-eye knowledge requires an amalgam of suspicion that certain facts may exist and a decision to refrain from taking any step to confirm their existence'.
2   As pointed out in *Assets Co Ltd v Mere Roihi* [1905] AC 176 at 201: 'If it can be shown that his suspicions were aroused and that he abstained from making inquiries for fear of learning the truth ... fraud may be ascribed to him.' Also see *White v White* [2001] UKHL 9 {2001] 1 WLR 481 at [16] and [53] per Lord Nicholls and Lord Scott.
3   *Eagle Trust plc v SBC Securities Ltd* [1992] 4 All ER 488 at 509; *El Ajou v Dollar Land Holdings plc* [1993] 3 All ER 717 at 739.
4   *Agip (Africa) Ltd v Jackson* [1990] Ch 265 at 293.
5   *Criterion Properties plc v Stratford UK Properties LLC* [2002] 2 BCLC 151 at 173; not doubted on appeal [2002] EWCA Civ 1783, [2003] 2 BCLC 129; affd [2004] UKHL 28, [2004] 1 WLR 1846.

100.74 A defendant will not be liable if he knows that it would constitute a breach of trust if he were to receive trust property from the trustees, but he genuinely forgets this before he receives and deals with the property for his own benefit[1].If a defendant knows at the time of receiving the property that it is misapplied trust property, then his conscience will be affected and he will hold the property on constructive trust for the beneficiaries from that time onwards, with the result that he will be liable by way of surcharging and falsifying his accounts to restore the trust fund, to compensate the beneficiaries, or to disgorge his gains to them, in the event that he deals with the property for his own benefit[2]. If a defendant receives misapplied trust property innocently, however, and only subsequently acquires knowledge of its improper provenance, then he will only be personally liable to the beneficiaries in respect of those dealings with the property that have taken place after he acquired knowledge[3]. On the basis that the defendant holds the property on constructive trust for the beneficiaries from the time that his conscience is affected with knowledge that the property is theirs, he will be strictly liable to restore the trust fund by way of falsification of his accounts even in the exceptional case where the property is stolen or destroyed by an act of God after he knows that it should be returned to the beneficiaries.

1   *Re Montagu's Settlement Trusts* [1987] Ch 264.
2   *Rolled Steel Products (Holdings) Ltd v British Steel Corpn* [1986] 1 Ch 246 at 303–4; *Westdeutsche Landesbank Girozentrale v Islington London Borough Council* [1996] AC 669 at 707.
3   *Re Diplock* [1948] Ch 465 at 477; *Allan v Rea Brothers Trustees Ltd [2002] EWCA Civ 85,* (2002) 4 ITELR 627 at 642–3 and 645–6.

Future development of the law

100.75 An attempt was recently made to cut through the terminological problems engendered by the *Baden, Delvaux* classification of knowledge by Nourse LJ in *BCCI (Overseas) Ltd v Akindele*[1], where he held that dishonesty will suffice, but is not required, to make a defendant liable where he has received and dealt with misapplied trust property for his own benefit[2], and that as a general rule a defendant will be liable whenever his 'state of knowledge [is] ... such as to make it unconscionable for him to retain the benefit of the receipt'[3]. With respect to Nourse LJ, however, unconscionability is an uncertain concept, reference to which seems unlikely to bring clarity to this area of the law[4]. Indeed, unconscionability was expressly rejected by Lord Nicholls in the *Royal Brunei* case as the test for assistance liability for precisely this reason[5].

1   [2001] Ch 437.
2   [2002] EWHC 496 (Ch), [2001] Ch 437 at 448, followed in *Criterion Properties plc v Stratford UK Properties LLC* [2002] EWCA 496 (Ch), [2002] 2 BCLC 151 at 171.
3   [2001] Ch 437 at 455.
4   Consider the different readings of *Akindele* in *Papamichael v National Westminster Bank plc [2003] EWHC 164 (Comm)* [2003] 1 Lloyd's Rep 341 at [246]–[247] and *Criterion Properties plc v Stratford UK Properties LLC* [2002] EWCA Civ 1783, [2003] 2 BCLC 129 at [20]–[39], not reviewed on appeal [2004] UKHL 28, [2004] 1 WLR 1846.
5   [1995] 2 AC 378 at 392.

100.76 It is submitted that the courts would do better to develop the law in this area by holding that dishonestly receiving and dealing with misapplied trust property for one's own benefit is a fault-based equitable wrong analogous to the wrong of dishonest dealing with trust property by agents described in Article 100(2). This could be achieved by reinterpreting the cases requiring fault for liability in this area as having been concerned with equitable wrongdoing. At the same time, the courts should also recognise that a strict liability claim in unjust enrichment will also lie against the recipients of misapplied trust property. These twin developments have been advocated extra-judicially by Lord Nicholls[1] and Lord Walker[2].

[1] In his article 'Knowing Receipt: The Need for a New Landmark', in W R Cornish et al (eds) *Restitution: Past, Present and Future* (1998) at p 231. See too P Birks, 'Receipt', in P Birks and A Pretto (eds), *Breach of Trust* (2002) at p 213; but for a different view, see L D Smith, 'Unjust Enrichment, Property, and the Structure of Trusts' (2000) 116 LQR 412, reviewed in M. Bryan, 'The Liability of the Recipient: Restitution at Common Law or Wrongdoing in Equity?' in S Degelman and J Edelman (eds), *Equity in Commercial Law* (2005).

[2] In his article 'Dishonesty and Unconscionable Conduct in Commercial Life – Some Reflections on Accessory Liability and Knowing Receipt' (2005) 27 Sydney LR 187 at p. 202.

100.77 Judicial observations suggesting that the courts are poised to develop the law relating to beneficial receipt and dealing with misapplied trust property in this way include[1]: Lord Nicholls' statement in *Royal Brunei Airlines Sdn Bhd v Tan* that 'recipient liability is restitution-based'[2]; the Court of Appeal's statement in *Grupo Torras SA v Al-Sabah (No 5)* that liability for knowing receipt is 'a receipt-based liability which may on examination prove to be either a vindication of persistent property rights or a personal restitutionary claim based on unjust enrichment by subtraction'[3]; and Lord Millett's statement in *Twinsectra Ltd v Yardley* that[4]:

'Liability for 'knowing receipt' is receipt-based. It does not depend on fault. The cause of action is restitutionary and is available only where the defendant received or applied the money in breach of trust for his own use and benefit ... There is no basis for requiring actual knowledge of the breach of trust, let alone dishonesty, as a condition of liability. Constructive notice is sufficient, and may not even be necessary. There is powerful academic support for the proposition that the liability of the recipient is the same as in other cases of restitution, that is to say strict but subject to a change of position defence.'

[1] See too *Powell v Thompson* [1991] 1 NZLR 597 at 607; *Equiticorp Industries Group Ltd v R* [1996] 3 NZLR 586 at 604 (Smellie J); *Kooratang Nominees Pty Ltd v Australia and New Zealand Banking Group Ltd* [1998] 3 VR 16 at 99 ff; *Say-Dee Pty Ltd v Farah Constructions Pty Ltd* [2005] NSWCA 309 at [217] ff. A different model has been pursued in Canada, where knowing receipt has been held to be a fault-based claim in unjust enrichment, contrary to the general position that liability in unjust enrichment is strict: see *Gold v Rosenberg* [1997] 3 SCR 767 and *Citadel General Assurance Co v Lloyds Bank Canada* [1997] 3 SCR 805, criticised in P Birks, 'The Role of Fault in the Law of Unjust Enrichment', in W Swadling and G Jones (eds), The Search for Principle (1999) 235, at 235–238 and 268–271; M Bryan, 'The Receipt-Based Constructive Trust: A Case Study of Personal and Proprietary Restitution in the Supreme Court' (1999) 37 Alberta LR 73, at 90–93.
[2] [1995] 2 AC 378 at 382.
[3] [2001] Lloyd's Rep Bank 36 at 62.
[4] [2002] UKHL 12, [2002] 2 AC 164 at 194.

100.78 Again, in *Dubai Aluminium Co Ltd v Salaam*, Lord Millett held that[1]:

'Dishonest receipt gives rise to concurrent liability, since the claim can be based on the defendant's dishonesty, treating the receipt itself as incidental, being merely the particular form taken by the defendant's participation in the breach of fiduciary duty; but it can also be based simply on the receipt, treating it as a restitutionary claim independent of any wrongdoing.'

1   [2002] UKHL 48, [2003] 2 AC 366 at [87], citing *John v Dodwell & Co Ltd* [1918] AC 563.

100.79 A dissenting note was struck by Nourse LJ in *Bank of Credit and Commerce International (Overseas) Ltd v Akindele*[1], who remarked of claims against those who receive and deal with misapplied trust property for their own benefit that 'it may be possible to sympathise with a tendency to subsume a further part of our law of restitution under the principles of unjust enrichment', but who begged 'leave to doubt whether strict liability coupled with a change of position defence would be preferable to fault-based liability in many commercial transactions.' In the same case, Nourse LJ also considered that to develop the law in the manner advocated here, it would be necessary for a claimant to take his case to the House of Lords[2]. However, if the existing authorities requiring fault for liability were construed to mean that fault is required for a wrong-based liability, then arguably they would not contradict the proposition that a separate, strict liability claim in unjust enrichment can also lie.

1   [2001] Ch 437 at 456.
2   [2001] Ch 437 at 456.

100.80 In addition to the dicta which have already been cited, there are three further sources of authority upon which a claimant might draw to support the introduction of a strict liability claim in unjust enrichment against the recipients of misapplied trust property. First, it was held by the House of Lords in *Ministry of Health v Simpson*[1] that the recipients of funds improperly distributed in the administration of a deceased person's estate are strictly liable to repay the persons properly entitled to the estate, and it is submitted that there is no compelling reason of principle why this situation should be treated differently from the situation where trust assets are misdirected[2]. Secondly, it was held by the House of Lords in *Lipkin Gorman v Karpnale Ltd*[3] that a common law action for money had and received would lie where a claimant's property was wrongfully taken from him by a third party and transferred without his knowledge to the defendant, and again it is submitted that there is no compelling reason of principle why this situation should be treated differently from the situation where trust assets are misdirected. Thirdly, it has been held that where assets are misappropriated by a trustee or fiduciary and used to pay off a security charged on property belonging to an innocent third party, the beneficiaries are entitled to be subrogated to the extinguished rights which were formerly possessed by the charge-holder, and to be treated, by a legal fiction, as though these rights were not extinguished, but were instead assigned to the beneficiaries in order that they might enforce them against the innocent third party for their own benefit[4]. The English courts have now recognised that in this kind of case subrogation is a remedy awarded to reverse unjust enrichment[5], and it clearly follows from the fact that the beneficiaries can acquire proprietary rights against innocent third parties via subrogation on the ground of unjust enrichment, that they are also entitled to a direct personal claim[6] in unjust enrichment against innocent third parties who are enriched at their expense.

1   [1951] AC 251, affirming the CA's decision to this effect, sub nom *Re Diplock* [1948] Ch 465.
2   Note, though, that the two types of claim are currently governed by different limitation rules, as they respectively fall within the scope of s 21(3) and s 22(a) of the Limitation Act 1980: *Davies v Sharples* [2006] EWHC 362 (Ch) [2006] WTLR 839, following *Re Diplock* [1948] Ch 465.
3   [1991] 2 AC 548.
4   *Primlake Ltd (in liquidation) v Matthews Associates* [2006] EWHC 1227 (Ch) at [337]–[340]. See too *McCullough v Marsden* (1919) 45 DLR 645 at 646–647, Alberta CA; subsequent proceedings: *McCullough v Elliott* (1922) 62 DLR 257. *Boscawen v Bajwa* [1996] 1 WLR 328 might also be viewed as a relevant authority, if it is correct to say that the claimant's entitlement to subrogation in the case derived from the fact that the money used to pay off the charge to which it was subrogated had been impressed with a *Quistclose* trust in its favour.
5   *Banque Financière de la Cité v Parc (Battersea) Ltd* [1999] 1 AC 221 at 228 per Lord Steyn and at 234 per Lord Hoffmann (also emphasising at 236 the fictional nature of treating the claimant as though the creditor's extinguished rights have been 'kept alive' and transferred to him); *Birmingham Midshires Mortgage Services Ltd v Sabherwal* (1999) 80 P & CR 256 at 264; *Cheltenham & Gloucester plc v Appleyard* [2004] EWCA Civ 291 148 Sol Jo LB 356 at [33]; *Niru Battery Manufacturing Co v Milestone Trading Ltd (No 2)* [2004] EWCA Civ 487, [2004] 2 All ER (Comm) 289 at [27]–[28]; *Filby v Mortgage Express (No 2) Ltd* [2004] EWCA Civ 759 at [62].
6   *Cheltenham & Gloucester plc v Appleyard* [2004] EWCA Civ 291 148 Sol Jo LB 356 at [36]; *Filby v Mortgage Express (No 2) Ltd* [2004] EWCA Civ 759 [2004] 29 LS Gaz R 30 at [59] and [64].

100.81 In the event that the recipients of misapplied trust property were made strictly liable to make restitution to the beneficiaries on the ground of unjust enrichment, the question arises whether any room would then be left in practice for a wrong-based knowing receipt action, where proof of fault was required: ie would circumstances ever arise in which a claimant might wish to bring a wrong-based claim? One answer to this question is that a defendant who received trust property ministerially would have a good defence to the unjust enrichment claim, but would not have a defence against the wrong-based claim[1]. Another is that a claimant might suffer a loss that is greater than the benefit received by the defendant, with the result that the claimant would be better off seeking a compensatory rather than a restitutionary remedy. Extra-judicially, Lord Nicholls has argued that in such a case, the claimant should be entitled to recover compensation from the defendant, provided that the defendant has acted dishonestly[2]. One example of a situation where such an award might be appropriate would be where a defendant receives half of a claimant's 60% company shareholding, where the shares received by the defendant are worth less to him (as a minority holding) than they are to the claimant (as the difference between a minority and a majority holding). Another example is provided by the facts of a recent Canadian case, *Treaty Group Inc v Simpson*[3], where the claimant company successfully pursued an action for 'knowing receipt' and was awarded 'aggravated damages' over and above the amount of money which the defendant had received at its expense, to compensate the claimant for the loss of profits which it had sustained when its employees' time and energy had been diverted from their usual duties into the task of unravelling the wrongdoing fiduciary's fraud.

1   See para 100.62 above.
2   Lord Nicholls, 'Knowing Receipt: The Need for a New Landmark', in W R Cornish et al (eds) *Restitution: Past, Present and Future* (1998) 231 at 244: 'in the case of dishonest recipients, liability is not confined to the value of the property received'.
3   (2001) 103 ACWS (3d) 1072 at paras 29–31.

Change of position defence

100.82 If the courts do hold that a claim in unjust enrichment lies against the recipients of misapplied trust property, it seems likely that recipients who are sued on this basis will often attempt to raise a change of position defence. It therefore seems apposite to give a brief account of the circumstances in which this defence is available.

100.83 In practice, the defence of change of position is most often relied upon by defendants who have incurred extraordinary expenditure in reliance on their receipt of the benefit which forms the subject-matter of the claim: ie because they have received the benefit, they have been led to spend their money on something which they would not otherwise have bought. However, the defence is available to a wider class of defendants than this, and there is no need to show that the change in a defendant's position came about because he consciously incurred expenditure in reliance on his receipt of the benefit, although there must be a causal link 'at least on a "but-for" test' between the receipt of the benefit and the change in the defendant's position[1]. Thus, a defendant who is paid £5000 and then immediately loses it when his wallet is stolen can raise the defence even though it cannot be said that he changed his position in reliance on his receipt. A defendant who changes his position in anticipation of a benefit which is subsequently paid to him can also raise the defence[2]. In the event that a defendant changes his position by purchasing an asset which remains in his possession at the time when the claim is made, he cannot rely on the defence to the extent that he remains enriched by his possession of the asset[3].

1   For *obiter dicta* to this effect, see *Scottish Equitable plc v Derby [2001] EWCA Civ 369*, [2001] 3 All ER 818 at 827; *Rose v AIB Group (UK) plc [2003] EWHC 1737 (Ch)*, [2003] 2 BCLC 374 at [49]; *Cressman v Coys of Kensington [2004] EWCA Civ 47 [2004] 1 WLR 2775 at [49]*. In principle these *dicta* are preferable to the contrary findings in *Streiner v Bank Leumi (UK) plc* QBD 31 October 1985; *Credit Suisse (Monaco) SA v Attar [2004] EWHC 374 (Comm)*.
2   *Dextra Bank & Trust Co Ltd v Bank of Jamaica [2001] UKPC 50, [2002] 1 All ER (Comm) 193.*
3   *Lipkin Gorman v Karpnale Ltd [1991] 2 AC 548 at 560.*

100.84 In *Lipkin Gorman v Karpnale Ltd*[1], Lord Goff held that the defence is not available to those who act in bad faith and wrongdoers. This good faith requirement clearly excludes defendants who have been self-consciously dishonest, but it can also exclude those who have failed 'to act in a commercially acceptable way' and those who have engaged in 'sharp practice of a kind that falls short of outright dishonesty'[2]. On the other hand, 'mere negligence on the part of the recipient is not sufficient to deprive him of the defence of change of position'[3]. In *Abou-Rahmah v Abacha*[4] the question arose whether a bank acts in good faith where it suspects in a general way that its customers are involved in money-laundering, but has no transaction-specific suspicion that there is anything wrong with the payments on which it later rests its defence. Rix LJ strongly felt that the bank should not be entitled to the defence in these circumstances, as it is not 'commercially acceptable' for a bank to operate an account for customers whom it suspects of money-laundering. However Arden and Pill LJ thought that transaction-specific suspicions are needed for bad faith, and Rix LJ did not press his disagreement to the point of dissent.

1   [1991] 2 AC 548 at 580.
2   *Niru Battery Manufacturing Co v Milestone Trading Ltd* [2002] EWHC 1425 (Comm), [2002] 2 All ER (Comm) 705 at [125], *per* Moore-Bick J, affirmed [2003] EWCA Civ 1446, [2004] 1 Lloyd's Rep 344.
3   *Niru Battery Manufacturing Co v Milestone Trading Ltd* [2002] EWHC 1425 (Comm), [2002] 2 All ER (Comm) 705 at [125], *per* Moore-Bick J., relying on *Dextra Bank & Trust Co Ltd v Bank of Jamaica [2001] UKPC 50*, [2002] 1 All ER (Comm) 193, where at [42]–[45] the Privy Council declined to hold that the relative fault of the claimant and the defendant can affect the availability of the defence.
4   [2006] EWCA Civ 1492, esp [49]–[58] (Rix LJ), [81]–[84] (Arden LJ) and [101] Pill LJ.

100.85 In *Barros Mattos Junior v MacDaniels Ltd*[1], the question arose whether a defendant is relevantly a 'wrongdoer' debarred from relying on the defence if he does something illegal. Relying on the House of Lords' decision in *Tinsley v Milligan*[2], Laddie J held that the answer to this question is always in the affirmative, and he denied that the courts have any discretion in the matter[3] subject to a *de minimis* threshold, they must always disallow the change of position defence in line with the maxim *ex dolo malo non oritur actio*, even if this effectively means imposing an arbitrarily heavy penalty on a defendant. This led him to conclude that the defendants could not raise the defence, even though they had acted in good faith when they had received stolen money and paid it on to third parties, because they had converted the money from US dollars into Nigerian naira before paying it away, contrary to a Nigerian law which requires foreign exchange dealings in Nigeria to be conducted through authorised intermediaries. In the result, the defendants were liable to repay US $8 million.

1   [2004] EWHC 1188 (Ch), [2005] 1 WLR 247.
2   [1994] 1 AC 340.
3   [2004] EWHC 1188 (Ch), [2005] 1 WLR 247 at [22]–[30] and [42]–[43].

100.86 On Laddie J's reasoning, the defendants would have escaped liability if they had paid the money away without converting it into naira first. But why should so much have turned on a breach of the Nigerian foreign exchange laws that was unconnected with the circumstances in which the claimant's money had been stolen and placed in the defendants' hands? The courts would do better to take a more nuanced approach to assessing the gravity of the illegal acts committed by defendants, along with all the other circumstances of a case, before jumping to the conclusion that the change of position defence should be disallowed. It is by no means obvious that the rule in *Tinsley* debarring *claims* founded on evidence of illegality should necessarily be extended to knock out *defences*, even assuming that the rule for claims works well, something which may be doubted[1].

1   See paras 30.20–30.21.

Paragraph 5

Where one of the beneficiaries has joined in the breach his beneficial interest is liable to make good the loss

100.87 As stated in the fifth paragraph of the present Article, the equitable interest of one of several beneficiaries, who has made himself liable by joining in a breach of trust, may be stopped at the instance of his co-beneficiaries, until the whole loss to the estate has been made good. This right *of the beneficiaries* must not, however, be confused with the limited right *of the trustee* (treated of in Article 99, above) to impound the interest of a beneficiary who has requested, instigated, or consented in writing to a breach of trust, by way of indemnifying the trustee himself. The two rights are essentially different, and it is apprehended that beneficiaries might have the right referred to in paragraph 5 of the present Article in cases where the trustee (who as particeps criminis) might not be allowed to impound the interest of the instigating beneficiary. It must also be understood that the rule laid down in paragraph 5 of the present Article applies a fortiori to the case of a beneficiary who is also a trustee.

100.88 It should be noted that a trustee will not be ordered to pay a debt to the trust fund if (or to the extent that) it can be recouped simply by withholding from him the property to which he would otherwise be entitled as beneficiary[1].

[1]   *Re VGM Holdings Ltd* [1942] Ch 235, [1942] 1 All ER 224; *Selangor United Rubber Estates Ltd v Cradock (No 4)* [1969] 3 All ER 965, [1969] 1 WLR 1773.

Retainer of income to make good breach instigated by tenant for life

100.89 A trustee, in breach of trust, lent the trust fund to AB, the tenant for life. The trustee afterwards concurred in a creditor's deed, by which AB's life interest was to be applied in payment of his debts, and the trustee received thereunder a debt due to him from AB. Before the other creditors had been paid, the trustee retained the life income to make good the breach of trust. It was held that the court would not restrain the trustee from making good the breach of trust out of the life income; for although the trustee, being a creditor and party to the deed, had, qua himself, no right to retain the life interest, yet, as representing the beneficiaries, he was justified in so doing[1].

[1]   *Fuller v Knight* (1843) 6 Beav 205; and see also *Carson v Sloane* (1884) 13 LR Ir 139; *Bolton v Curre* [1895] 1 Ch 544.

Rule applies to derivative as well as to original shares

100.90 The rule applies not only to shares taken directly under the settlement creating the trust, but also to shares purchased from or otherwise derived through or under immediate beneficiaries. Thus, where a Mrs D, who was trustee and life tenant under a will, took assignments from two of the beneficiaries entitled in remainder, and committed divers breaches of trust which only came to light on her death, it was held that the two shares which she had purchased were liable to make good the loss to the estate. Moreover, this right of the beneficiaries was held to take priority over the rights of persons to whom Mrs D had mortgaged the shares in question[1]. The fact that the mortgagees were bona fide mortgagees for value without notice was immaterial, for the equitable interest in question was a chose in action, and purchasers of choses in action take subject to all equities. Indeed, so far has this been carried, that such purchasers have been held to take subject to breaches of trust committed *after* the purchase[2].

1 *Doering v Doering* (1889) 42 Ch D 203 and cases there cited; and see also *Re Akerman* [1891] 3 Ch 212; *Re Dacre* [1915] 2 Ch 480; on appeal [1916] 1 Ch 344; *Re Melton* [1918] 1 Ch 37; and *Re Jewell's Settlement* [1919] 2 Ch 161.
2 Per Hall V-C in *Hooper v Smart* (1875) 1 Ch D 90 at 98; and see also *Morris v Livie* (1842) 1 Y & C Ch Cas 380; *Irby v Irby (No 3)* (1858) 25 Beav 632; *Barnett v Sheffield* (1852) 1 De GM & G 371; *Cole v Muddle* (1852) 10 Hare 186; and *Re Pain* [1919] 1 Ch 38; *Re Knapman* (1881) 18 Ch D 300 at 307, CA.

But not to independent trust created by same instrument

100.91 The rule, however, has no application to beneficial interests under independent trusts even although created by the same settlor and by the same instrument. Thus where a person is beneficially interested in (or even a trustee of) settled residuary estate and is liable for a breach of trust committed in relation thereto, his beneficial interest under a trust of specific property created by the same will cannot be impounded[1].

1 *Re Towndrow* [1911] 1 Ch 662.

Retainer of beneficiary's interest to make good a debt due from him to the trust estate, even where statute barred

100.92 The rule now under consideration is not confined to cases of breach of trust, but is equally applicable where a beneficiary is indebted to the trust estate. By a separation deed, after reciting that the husband and wife had agreed to live apart, the husband assigned certain leaseholds to trustees in trust to pay the rents to the wife for life[1], and then to sell and hold the proceeds (in the events which happened) in trust for himself; and he covenanted to make up the wife's income to £300 a year. The husband paid nothing under the covenant, and he was subsequently adjudicated a bankrupt. The trustees proved for arrears due down to the date of the bankruptcy, but there were further arrears due to them since that date. On the death of the wife, the husband's assignee in bankruptcy claimed the leaseholds. It was held, however, that the trustees were entitled to retain them until the arrears were satisfied, and it seems that the right of trustees to retain trust property as against a beneficiary who owes money to them as trustees under the instrument creating the trust, exists in favour of trustees of a voluntary settlement which has been so completed as to be enforceable by the court[2]. The rule applies even where the debt is statute barred[3], provided that it was a debt for which, but for the statute[4], the debtor could have been sued[5]. Trustees cannot, however, retain the share of a beneficiary as against *future instalments* of a debt repayable by instalments[6].

1   Since this was long before the Settled Land Act 1925 the leaseholds did not become settled land.
2   *Re Weston* [1900] 2 Ch 164; *Re Akerman* [1891] 3 Ch 212; and see and consider analogous right of executors, *Re Taylor* [1894] 1 Ch 671.
3   *Re Akerman* [1891] 3 Ch 212; *Re Wheeler* [1904] 2 Ch 66.
4   Now the Limitation Act 1980.
5   See *Re Wheeler* [1904] 2 Ch 66.
6   *Re Abrahams* [1908] 2 Ch 69.

Acceptance of a composition from defaulting trustee-beneficiary

100.93 Where a defaulting trustee who is also a beneficiary in remainder makes a composition which is accepted by the new trustees they cannot afterwards claim to retain his beneficial interest to make good the balance of the loss[1].

1   *Re Sewell* [1909] 1 Ch 806.

Where claimant is also the residuary legatee of person who has benefited by breach

100.94 A somewhat curious complication arises where money has, in breach of trust, been paid to a person whose estate subsequently devolves on or is bequeathed to the claimant. Thus, where a trustee had wrongfully paid part of the capital of the trust fund to the claimant's father under whose intestacy the claimant was entitled to and received two-thirds of his estate, it was held that the father's assets in the hands of the claimant were primarily liable to make good two-thirds of the trust fund in exoneration of the trustee[1].

1   *Orrett v Corser* (1855) 21 Beav 52.

How far beneficiary who has been innocently overpaid is liable to refund

100.95 Where a trustee has made any over-payment to a beneficiary in error, whether of fact or law[1], he can, on behalf of the other beneficiaries, and where the trust property is still in his hands on behalf of himself if he is also a beneficiary[2], recoup the trust out of the overpaid beneficiary's interest or capital or income which subsequently becomes due to such beneficiary[3]: this is part of the equitable accounting process in the administration of the trust, the trustee's set-off being a defence for him[4]. On the other hand, the court will not, as a rule, order the over-paid beneficiary personally to refund to the trustee who has been disallowed the item in his accounts[5]. However, it may be that a *co-beneficiary* could compel repayment of the excess or so much thereof as could not be recovered from the trustee as the party responsible for the over-payment[6], but the onus would lie upon him of proving that what the other beneficiary has received was an over-payment, having regard to the value of the estate at the date of the payment, and did not arise merely by reason of *subsequent* depreciation[7]. This, of course, presupposes that payment at all, at the date in question, was proper, for otherwise, if the date for payment to the knowledge of the payee had not arisen, the payment would itself have been a breach of trust to which the payee would have been privy.

[1]   *Re Musgrave* [1916] 2 Ch 417; *Re Wooldridge* [1920] WN 78.

[2]   *Re Reading* [1916] WN 262, in which the contrary decision of Warrington J in *Re Horne* [1905] 1 Ch 76 (criticised by Goff & Jones, *Law of Restitution* (6th edn, 2002) at para 5–011) was said not to be of general application.

[3]   *Livesey v Livesey* (1827) 3 Russ 287; *Dibbs v Goren* (1849) 11 Beav 483; *IVS Enterprises Ltd v Chelsea Cloisters Management Ltd* (1999) 13 Tru LR 111, and discussed by P Matthews [1994] Rest LR 44. *Re Musgrave* [1916] 2 Ch 417 (but there is no such right where the income arises under a covenant, and not a trust: *Re Hatch* [1919] 1 Ch 351).

[4]   He has a lien for this purpose: *Dibbs v Goren* (1849) 11 Beav 483, *Williams v Allen (No 2)* (1863) 32 Beav 650.

[5]   *Downes v Bullock* (1858) 25 Beav 54; *Bate v Hooper* (1855) 5 De GM & G 338; but cf *Hood v Clapham* (1854) 19 Beav 90, where it was allowed; and consider *Allcard v Walker* [1896] 2 Ch 369 at 384, as to the converse case, where funds have been erroneously paid to the trustees.

[6]   *Harris v Harris (No 2)* (1861) 29 Beav 110; *Baynard v Woolley* (1855) 20 Beav 583, *Re Robinson* [1911] 1 Ch 502 at 508; *Ministry of Health v Simpson* [1951] AC 251 at 274.

[7]   *Re Winslow* (1890) 45 Ch D 249; *Fenwick v Clarke* (1862) 4 De GF & J 240; *Peterson v Peterson* (1866) LR 3 Eq 111; and *Hilliard v Fulford* (1876) 4 Ch D 389.

100.96 Where personal representatives have acted upon a wrong view of the effect of a will, and have distributed the estate amongst persons who have no title at all but are mere strangers to the estate, the recipients are personally liable, at the suit of the true beneficiaries or of creditors, to refund the sums paid to them, so far as such sums cannot be recovered from the personal representatives[1]. Such strict liability, subject to the defence of change of position, should extend to wrongful recipients of trust property, whether a mistake of fact or law is involved[2], so as to reverse the unjust enrichment of such recipients[3].

[1]   *Ministry of Health v Simpson* [1951] AC 251; *Barraclough v Mell* [2005] EWHC B17 (Ch) at [76].

[2]   The rule that an action in unjust enrichment will not lie to recover money paid under a mistake of law was abolished in *Kleinwort Benson Ltd v Lincoln City Council* [1999] 2 AC 349.

[3]   See para 100.76 ff.

No recouping of excess income derived from improper investment

100.97 It appears to be settled that, where a beneficiary for life has received a high rate of interest from a security on which the trustees ought not to have invested, and which subsequently turns out to be insufficient, he will not be liable to account for any part of the income received[1] unless he was either one of the trustees[2], or with full knowledge, a consenting party to the investment[3]. On the other hand, he will not get any arrears of income on realisation of the security without bringing into hotchpot all income received by him during its continuance[4]; but this will not be so where the investment was not improperly made (eg where it was made by the testator himself)[5].

1   See *Re Bird* [1901] 1 Ch 916, and comments thereon of Warrington KC arguendo in *Re Alston* [1901] 2 Ch 584 at 587; *Re Horne* [1905] 1 Ch 76.
2   See *Re Sharp* [1906] 1 Ch 793 at 796.
3   See *Griffiths v Porter* (1858) 25 Beav 236.
4   *Griffiths v Porter* (1858) 25 Beav 236.
5   *Re Coaks* [1911] 1 Ch 171; and see Article 53, above.

ARTICLE 101
TRACING AND FOLLOWING TRUST PROPERTY AND ITS PROCEEDS
INTO THE HANDS OF THIRD PARTIES

101.1

(1)   If trust property or its traceable product is found in the hands of any person in circumstances inconsistent with the trust, he will hold it as constructive trustee[1] subject to the interests of beneficiaries under the trust except to the extent that he proves[2] that the defence of change of position is available to him, or that he or some person through whom he claims[3] has bona fide acquired the property for valuable consideration and without receiving notice, before the transaction was completed[4], that the acquisition was a breach of trust, and:

(a)   has acquired the legal (as distinguished from a mere equitable) title[5]; or

(b)   having acquired a mere equitable title has been induced to acquire it for value by the fraud or negligence of the persons having the legal title[6]; or

(c)   the property, being a chose in action[7], consists of a negotiable instrument[8], or an instrument which was intended by the parties thereto to be transferable free from all equities attaching to it[9].

(2)   A person who purchases property with notice of an equitable interest affecting that property will hold such property subject thereto unless it has been validly discharged[10].

1   *Peffer v Rigg* [1977] 1 WLR 285 at 294; *Baden v Société Générale* [1992] 4 All ER 161 at 231; *Re Montagu's Settlement Trusts* [1987] Ch 264 at 270, 276, 285 [1992] 4 All ER 308 at 318, 322, 329; *Polly Peck International plc v Nadir (No 2)* [1992] 4 All ER 769 at 781 per Scott LJ; *Boscawen v Bajwa* [1996] 1 WLR 328 at 335, per Millett LJ; *Bankgesellschaft Berlin AG v Makris* (22 January 1999, unreported), QBD (Comm Ct).
2   The defendant prima facie, cannot claim a better title than the trustee-transferor to him, so to defend wholly or pro tanto the prior equitable interest which burdens his title it is up to him to establish a defence: *Re Nisbett & Pott's Contract* [1905] 1 Ch 391 at 398; *Barclays Bank plc v Boulter* [1999] 4 All ER 513 at 518, per Lord Hoffmann.
3   *Harrison v Forth* (1695) Prec Ch 51; *Mertins v Joliffe* (1756) Amb 311; *M'Queen v Farquhar* (1885) 11 Ves 467.
4   *Bassett v Nosworthy* (1673) Cas temp Finch 102, 2 White & Tud LC 163; *Boursot v Savage* (1866) LR 2 Eq 134; *Mackreth v Symmons* (1808) 15 Ves 329, 2 White & Tud LC 946; *Pilcher v Rawlins* (1872) 7 Ch App 259; *London and Canadian Loan and Agency Co v Duggan* [1893] AC 506; and as to the time at which the notice is effectual, *Lady Bodmin v Vandenbendy* (1683) 1 Vern 179; *Jones v Thomas* (1734) 3 P Wms 243; *A-G v Gower* (1736) 2 Eq Cas Abr 685, pl 11; *More v Mayhow* (1663) 1 Cas in Ch 34. Registered land requires separate consideration: see para 101.68.

5   See per Lord Westbury in *Phillips v Phillips* (1861) 4 De GF & J 208; *Rimmer v Webster* [1902] 2 Ch 163.
6   See *Walker v Linom* [1907] 2 Ch 104.
7   *Turton v Benson* (1718) 1 P Wms 496; *Ord v White* (1840) 3 Beav 357; *Mangles v Dixon* (1852) 3 HL Cas 702; *Doering v Doering* (1889) 42 Ch D 203.
8   *Anon* (1697) 1 Com 43.
9   *Re Blakely Ordnance Co* (1867) 3 Ch App 154; *Re General Estates Co* (1868) 3 Ch App 758; *Crouch v Credit Foncier of England* (1873) LR 8 QB 374.
10 *Jared v Clements* [1903] 1 Ch 428 (vendor, who had failed to disclose an equitable mortgage, subsequently produced a forged discharge which the purchaser relied upon in completing the purchase, having discovered and raised requisitions on the equitable mortgage, but the purchaser was bound by the mortgage); *Boursot v Savage* (1866) LR 2 Eq 134.

Paragraph 1

Relative rights of legal and equitable claimants

101.2 The rule enunciated in this paragraph is derived from well-known property principles namely:

(1)   where the equities are equal the law prevails so a bona fide purchaser for value of a legal interest without notice of an equitable interest prevails over the holder of the equitable interest; and

(2)   as between mere equitable claimants qui prior in tempore, potior in jure est – he who is first in time has the strongest claim in law.

101.3 In fact, where one of two innocent parties must suffer, then as equity is not called upon to interfere on behalf of either of them, the common law must take its course; and the one who has the legal estate, or its equivalent, will take priority over the one who has a mere equitable claim, notwithstanding that the title of the legal claimant may have accrued after that of the equitable one. The rule is very strikingly and completely illustrated by the case of *Cave v Cave*[1] where a trustee, who was a solicitor, fraudulently misappropriated the trust fund, and with it bought an estate which was conveyed to his brother. The brother then mortgaged the property, by legal, and afterwards by equitable, mortgages, the solicitor-trustee acting on all such occasions as the solicitor both for mortgagor *and mortgagees*. The parties beneficially entitled under the trust claimed to follow their trust money into the property which had been bought with it, on the ground that, as the solicitor of the mortgagees had notice of the breach of trust, that notice must be imputed to the mortgagees themselves.

1   (1880) 15 Ch D 639; and see also *Powell v London and Provincial Bank* [1893] 2 Ch 555, CA; and *Capell v Winter* [1907] 2 Ch 376.

101.4 It was held, however, that, as the solicitor was a party to the fraud, notice of the equity of the beneficiaries could not be imputed constructively to the clients, the mortgagees, for the conduct of the agent raised a conclusive presumption that he would not communicate to the client the facts in controversy. Consequently their equities and the equity of the beneficiaries were equal, whence it followed, on the maxim 'where the equities are equal the law prevails', that the legal mortgagee, having the legal estate, took priority over the beneficiaries, but that the latter took priority over the equitable mortgagees because their equity was first in point of date[1].

1   See also *Pilcher v Rawlins* (1872) 7 Ch App 259.

101.5 Another instructive case is *Kleinwort Benson v Vaughan*[1] where V stole £248,000 from his employer to buy a house in the name of himself and his wife with the further assistance of a £70,000 mortgage loan from the employer, which sold the mortgage to N. Ultimately, the employer, B, discovered what had happened and traced its money into the house, and so the court charged the house with repayment of the money and B was enabled to sell the house but only after paying N off so as to be able to confer an unincumbered title on the purchaser. Having paid off N, the employer claimed to recoup from Mr and Mrs V the money paid to discharge their mortgage. This claim was rejected. After all, N was a bona fide purchaser of a legal mortgage without notice of the employer's equitable interest, so that qua mortgagee N could have sold the house and taken the moneys due to it, thereby preventing from arising any question of the employer having any claim against Mr and Mrs V in respect of such moneys by subrogation or otherwise. The fact that it was the employer chargee, rather than N, which exercised the power of sale could not change matters: the employer's right extended only to the equity of redemption subject to N's charge and it could not enlarge such rights by voluntarily paying off N's charge to enable it to sell a title unencumbered by such charge rather than encumbered thereby.

1   [1994] NPC 31.

Notice of doubtful equity

101.6 To deprive a person who has acquired a legal right to property for valuable consideration, the notice of a superior equity must be notice of facts which would clearly show the existence of such equity, at all events, to a lawyer. Thus, a bona fide purchaser for value is not bound by notice of a very doubtful equity, as where the construction of a trust is ambiguous or equivocal[1].

1   *Hardy v Reeves* (1800) 5 Ves 426; *Cordwell v Mackrill* (1766) Amb 515; *Warrick v Warrick and Kniveton* (1745) 3 Atk 291; but see and consider per Lord St Leonards in *Thompson v Simpson* (1841) 1 Dr & War 459.

101.7 Thus, in *Carl Zeiss Stiftung v Herbert Smith & Co (No 2)*[1] a firm of solicitors received money in payment of their costs from a company for which they acted. These costs were incurred in an action in which another organisation or foundation claimed all the assets of their client company and alleged that their client company held all its assets upon trust for the other foundation; but these claims were unresolved when the payment was received and they involved complicated questions of fact and of law, both English and German. The other foundation then brought a subsidiary action against the solicitors to recover the money paid to them on the ground that they had received it with knowledge of the facts averred in the main action and thus with notice that the money belonged to the foundation.

1   [1969] 2 Ch 276, [1969] 2 All ER 367, CA.

101.8 The Court of Appeal held, however, that such notice was merely notice of a doubtful equity. When they received the money, the solicitors did not know whether the claim was well founded or not and the mere knowledge of its existence was not enough to make them constructive trustees for the foundation.

Purchasing from two sets of trustees who are mortgagees under a contributory mortgage

101.9 It has been held that where two sets of trustees have joined in advancing money on a contributory mortgage (on the face of which their fiduciary characters appeared), and they sell under their power of sale, the purchaser is not bound to see that each set of trustees gets their due proportion of the purchase-money on the ground, apparently, that the purchase-money is not the debt, but only a security therefore[1].

1   *Re Parker and Beech's Contract* (1887) 56 LJ Ch 358, sed quaere. Now see ss 107, 111, 113 of the Law of Property Act 1925 so that a purchaser may assume the mortgagees are entitled on a joint account and may jointly give a valid receipt.

Trust money paid in to trustee's private overdrawn account

101.10 Where a trustee has overdrawn his banking account, his bankers have a first and paramount legal lien on all moneys paid in by him, unless they have notice, not only that they are trust moneys[1], but also that payment to them constitutes a breach of trust[2].

1   *Thomson v Clydesdale Bank* [1893] AC 282, HL (considered in *Selangor United Rubber Estates Ltd v Cradock* [1968] 2 All ER 1073, [1968] 1 WLR 1555). As to notice, see *Texas Co v Bombay Banking Co* (1919) LR 46 Ind App 250.
2   *Coleman v Bucks and Oxon Union Bank* [1897] 2 Ch 243; *Union Bank of Australia Ltd v Murray-Aynsley* [1898] AC 693, PC; *Re Spencer* (1881) 51 LJ Ch 271; but cf *Mutton v Peat* [1900] 2 Ch 79.

Costs paid by defaulting trustee to his solicitor

101.11 On similar grounds it has been held that the solicitor of a trustee is not debarred from accepting payments out of the estate in respect of costs properly incurred, unless he had knowledge that, at the time when he accepted them, the trustee had been guilty of such a breach of trust as would preclude him from resorting to the trust estate for payment of costs[1]. Where, however, a solicitor receives money with knowledge of a breach of trust, a summary order may be made upon him to pay into court, without the necessity of an action[2].

1   *Re Blundell* (1888) 40 Ch D 370.
2   *Re Carroll* [1902] 2 Ch 175.

What constitutes notice

101.12 The subject of notice is now governed by s 199 of the Law of Property Act 1925 which is in the following words:

(1)   A purchaser shall not be prejudicially affected by notice of—
  (i)   any instrument or matter capable of registration under the provisions of the Land Charges Act 1925, or any enactment which it replaces, which is void or not enforceable as against him under that Act or enactment, by reason of the non-registration thereof[1];
  (ii)   any other instrument or matter or any fact or thing unless—

(a) it is within his own knowledge, or would have come to his knowledge if such inquiries and inspections had been made as ought reasonably to have been made by him[2], or

(b) in the same transaction with respect to which a question of notice to the purchaser arises, it has come to the knowledge of his counsel, as such, or of his solicitor or other agent, as such, or would have come to the knowledge of his solicitor or other agent, as such, if such inquiries and inspections had been made as ought reasonably to have been made by the solicitor or other agent.

(2)   Paragraph (ii) of the last subsection shall not exempt a purchaser from any liability under, or any obligation to perform or observe, any covenant, condition, provision, or restriction contained in any instrument under which his title is derived, mediately or immediately; and such liability or obligation may be enforced in the same manner and to the same extent as if that paragraph had not been enacted.
(3)   A purchaser shall not by reason of anything in this section be affected by notice in any case where he would not have been so affected if this section had not been enacted.

1   In connection with the sale of land, it is necessary to consider also the provisions of ss 24 and 25 of the Law of Property Act 1969, which came into force on 1 January 1970. Briefly, s 24 provides that where under a contract for the sale of unregistered land, any question arises as to whether the purchaser had notice, at the time of entering into it, of a registered land charge, that question is to be determined by reference to his actual knowledge and without regard to the provisions of s 198 of the Law of Property Act 1925 (whereby registration is deemed to constitute actual notice). Section 25 is concerned with cases in which the purchaser completes his purchase in ignorance of a registered land charge which he has failed to discover because it is registered against the name of someone who does not figure in the title to the property (ie, generally because the title commences too late to include him), and provides for compensation to be paid to such a purchaser.
2   Nowadays, a purchaser is under a duty to inquire of a wife in occupation whether or not she claims any equitable interest: *Kingsnorth Trust Ltd v Tizard* [1986] 2 All ER 54, [1986] 1 WLR 783.

101.13 It will be perceived that sub-s (1)(ii)(a) relates to actual or constructive notice of the party affected personally, and that sub-s (1)(ii)(b) relates to actual or constructive notice of his agents which is imputed to him.

101.14 The protection afforded by the legal estate to a purchaser of land is further extended by statute, so that in many cases he is able to purchase free from equitable interests even though he has notice of them. The provisions having this effect are contained in s 2 of the Law of Property Act 1925 which, as amended by the Law of Property (Amendment) Act 1926 and the Trusts of Land and Appointment of Trustees Act 1996 is in the following words:

   (1)   A conveyance to a purchaser of a legal estate in land shall overreach[1] any equitable interest or power affecting that estate, whether or not he has notice thereof, if—

        (i)   the conveyance is made under the powers conferred by the Settled Land Act, 1925, or any additional powers conferred by a settlement, and the equitable interest or power is capable of being overreached thereby, and the statutory requirements respecting the payment of capital money arising under the settlement are complied with;

        (ii)   the conveyance is made by trustees of land and the equitable interest or power is at the date of the conveyance capable of being overreached by such trustees under for provisions of subsection (2) of this section or independently of that subsection, and the requirements of section 27 of this Act respecting the payment of capital money arising on such a conveyance;

        (iii) the conveyance is made by a mortgagee or personal representative in the exercise of his paramount powers, and the equitable interest or power is capable of being overreached by such conveyance, and any capital money arising from the transaction is paid to the mortgagee or personal representative;

        (iv) the conveyance is made under an order of the court and the equitable interest or power is bound by such order, and any capital money arising from the transaction is paid into, or in, accordance with the order of, the court.

   (2)   [Where the legal estate affected is subject to a trust of land, then if at the date of a conveyance made after the commencement of this Act by the trustees, trustees (whether original or substituted) are either—

        (a)   two or more individuals approved or appointed by the court or the successors in office of the individuals so approved or appointed; or

        (b)   a trust corporation;

[any equitable interest or power having priority to the trust] shall, notwithstanding any stipulation to the contrary, be overreached by the conveyance, and shall, according to its priority, take effect as if created or arising by means of a primary trust affecting the proceeds of sale and the income of the land until sale.

   (3)   The following equitable interests and powers are excepted from the operation of subsection (2) of this section, namely—

        (i)   Any equitable interest protected by a deposit of documents relating to the legal estate affected;

        (ii)   The benefit of any covenant or agreement restrictive of the user of land;

        (iii) Any easement, liberty, or privilege over or affecting land and being merely an equitable interest (in this Act referred to as an 'equitable easement');

      (iv)   The benefit of any contract (in this Act referred to as an 'estate contract') to convey or create a legal estate, including a contract conferring either expressly or by statutory implication a valid option to purchase, a right of pre-emption, or any other like right;

      (v)   Any equitable interest protected by registration under the Land Charges Act 1925 or 1972 other than—

(a) an annuity within the meaning of Part II of that Act;

(b) a limited owner's charge or a general equitable charge within the meaning of that Act.

    (4)   Subject to the protection afforded by this section to the purchaser of a legal estate, nothing contained in this section shall deprive a person entitled to an equitable charge of any of his rights or remedies for enforcing the same.

    (5)   So far as regards the following interests, created before the commencement of this Act (which accordingly are not within the provisions of the Land Charges Act 1925 or 1972), namely—

      (a)   the benefit of any covenant or agreement restrictive of the user of the land;

      (b)   any equitable easement;

      (c)   the interest under a puisne mortgage within the meaning of the Land Charges Act 1925 or 1972, unless and until acquired under a transfer made after the commencement of this Act;

      (d)   the benefit of an estate contract, unless and until the same is acquired under a conveyance made after the commencement of this Act;

a purchaser of a legal estate shall only take subject thereto if he has notice thereof, and the same are not overreached under the provisions contained or in the manner referred to in this section.

[1]   Overreaching occurs whether or not the mortgagor receives any capital money from the mortgagee at the time of the mortgage: *State Bank of India v Soud* [1997] Ch 276, CA.

101.15 By s 3, however, although a purchaser is free from liability, the person having the power of sale has to give effect to all equitable interests and powers which have been overreached by the sale. Save as above, the old rules as to notice (whether actual or constructive) still remain in force.

Actual notice

101.16 With regard to actual notice, knowledge is absolutely necessary except where registration under the Land Charges Act 1925 or 1972 is deemed to give persons actual notice[1]. Mere gossip or report is not sufficient. It does not seem that the notice must be given by a party interested or his agent.

[1]   Law of Property Act 1925, s 198.

101.17 The statutory definition of actual notice (therein differing from the definition of imputed notice) does not state that the instrument, fact, or thing must have come to the party's knowledge in the *same* transaction, nor have been notified by a party interested. Indeed, it would seem that actual notice is entirely a matter of evidence; and if the court comes to the conclusion that a party had in fact, at the date of the transaction, such knowledge as would operate on the mind of any rational man, or man of business, and make him act with reference to the knowledge he has so acquired, then he will be taken to have had actual notice. Whether he acquired his knowledge before or at the time of the transaction, and whether he acquired it from a party interested or not, appears to be immaterial[1].

---

1   *Lloyd v Banks* (1868) 3 Ch App 488; and see also *London and Canadian Loan and Agency Co Ltd v Duggan* [1893] AC 506, PC; and *Redman v Rymer* (1889) 60 LT 385; and see also on the subject of actual (and forgotten) knowledge *Re Montagu's Settlements* [1987] Ch 264 discussed at para 100.74.

Constructive notice

101.18 A purchaser has constructive notice of matters that would have come to his knowledge if such inquiries and inspections had been made as *ought*[1] reasonably to have been made by him. Where the purchase of land is concerned there are elaborate inquiries and inspections that have to be made but a wise purchaser employs a solicitor or licensed conveyancer to make these, with the result that any actual or constructive notice obtained by such person will be imputed to the purchaser[2]. In the purchase of property other than land, the purchaser usually acts for himself since matters are normally straightforward, there being no duty to make investigations as to title in the absence of suspicious circumstances, since the courts are most reluctant to import a duty of inquiry as to title which would restrict the flow of commerce[3].

---

1   What *ought* to have been done in all the circumstances and thus the nature and extent of the *duty* to make reasonable inquiries will vary according to the circumstances: *Carl Zeiss Stiftung v Herbert Smith & Co (a firm) (No 2)* [1969] 2 Ch 276 at 297; *Polly Peck International plc v Nadir (No 2)* [1992] 4 All ER 769 at 782; *Eagle Trust Securities plc v SBC Securities Ltd* [1992] 4 All ER 488 at 497–498; *Criterion Properties plc v Stratford UK Properties LLC* [2002] EWHC 496 (Ch) [2002] 2 BCLC 151 at 173. A donee does not have to look a gift horse in the mouth and is under no duty of inquiry unless the circumstances are very suspicious: *Re Diplock* [1948] Ch 465 at 478–479, *Re Montagu's Settlements* [1987] Ch 264. A volunteer must return trust property or its product in his possession irrespective of notice.
2   Constructive notice is thus considered when discussing agents at para 101.22 ff.
3   *Baden Delvaux and Lecuit v Société Generale* [1992] 4 All ER 161; *Joseph v Lyons* (1884) 15 QBD 280 CA; *Manchester Trust v Furness* [1895] 2 QB 539, CA; *Feuer Leather Corpn v Frank Johnstone & Sons* [1981] Com LR 251, *Eagle Trust plc v SBC Securities Ltd* [1992] 4 All ER 488 at 507–508.

101.19 While Megarry V-C has emphasised[1] the differences between the artificialities of the cold calculus of constructive *notice* and the realities of *knowledge*, it now seems that in the commercial context (not involving conveyancing procedures) a purchaser will not have 'constructive notice' unless suspicious circumstances existed but he deliberately or recklessly failed to make the inquiries an honest reasonable man would have made so as to have 'naughty knowledge' of the relevant matter[2].

1   *Re Montagu's Settlement Trusts* [1987] Ch 264.
2   *Polly Peck International plc v Nadir (No 2)* [1992] 4 All ER 769, CA.

Imputed notice

101.20 With regard to imputed notice, on the other hand, it is quite clear that a man is not liable for notice acquired by his counsel, solicitor, or agent, unless it has come to the latter's knowledge in the very transaction with respect to which the question of notice arises. The fact that a solicitor has been in the habit of acting for a particular person cannot reasonably constitute that solicitor the agent of the client to bind him by receiving notices or information; for apart from the burden which it would impose on the memory of a solicitor, it may well be that the client has ceased to regard him as his solicitor[1]. On similar grounds Parliament has enacted that:

> 'A trustee or personal representative acting for the purposes of more than one trust or estate shall not, in the absence of fraud, be affected by notice of any instrument, matter, fact or thing in relation to any particular trust or estate if he has obtained notice thereof merely by reason of his acting or having acted for the purposes of another trust or estate'[2].

1   *Saffron Walden Second Benefit Building Society v Rayner* (1880) 14 Ch D 406, CA.
2   Trustee Act 1925, s 28.

101.21 It has also been held in *Cave v Cave*[1] that constructive notice of an equity through counsel, solicitor, or agent is not imputed to the client, where the counsel, solicitor, or agent is party to a fraud which would be exposed if he had communicated the notice to his client. This case must, however, be carefully distinguished from the earlier cases of *Boursot v Savage*[2] and *Bradley v Riches*[3], which seem at first sight in direct conflict with it. The point in *Boursot v Savage* was that where a client has *notice of the existence of a trust* and intends to get the equitable interests of beneficiaries *from them*, the fact that he gets the legal estate from a trustee who happens to be his solicitor does not protect him if the solicitor forges the signatures of the beneficiaries; for he had notice of the equitable interests, and the fact that he was the innocent victim of a forgery does not give him an equal equity with the beneficiaries. In *Bradley v Riches* the point decided was that the presumption that a solicitor has communicated to his client facts which he ought to have made known is not rebutted by proof that it was to the solicitor's *interest* to conceal the facts. There the fact omitted to be communicated was the existence of a valid mortgage, whereas in *Cave v Cave* the fact omitted to be communicated was the prior commission of a fraud by the solicitor himself[4].

1   (1880) 15 Ch D 639, discussed at para 101.3 above, also see *Selangor United Rubber Estates Ltd v Cradock (No 3)* [1968] 2 All ER 1073, [1968] 1 WLR 1555.
2   (1866) LR 2 Eq 134.
3   (1878) 9 Ch D 189.
4   And see also and distinguish *Lloyds Bank v Bullock* [1896] 2 Ch 192; *Halifax Mortgage Services Ltd v Stepsky* [1996] Ch 207.

Constructive notice of agent imputed to principal

101.22 The imputed notice mentioned in s 199(1) of the Law of Property Act 1925[1] extends to notice of:

> an instrument, fact, or thing which has come to the party's knowledge, or to the knowledge of his counsel, solicitor or agent as such, or would have come to the knowledge of his solicitor or other agent (not his counsel) as such, if such inquiries or inspections had been made as ought reasonably to have been made by them.

[1]   See para 101.12 above. And see *Newman v Real Estate Debenture Corpn Ltd and Flower Decorations Ltd* [1940] 1 All ER 131.

101.23 Thus in *Patman v Harland*[1] it was held that a lessee had imputed constructive notice of those matters he would have discovered if he had stipulated for full investigation of title even though under an open contract he was deprived by statute of his right to investigate the superior title: he could have contracted out of the statute and by not doing so he was in the same position as if he had agreed to accept a short title not going back for the full period over which title should be investigated. This has been reversed by Law of Property Act 1925, s 44(5), though a lessee may still find himself bound by a land charge registered against the name of a superior owner whom he could not have discovered[2].

[1]   (1881) 17 Ch D 353.
[2]   *White v Bijou Mansions Ltd* [1937] Ch 610, [1937] 3 All ER 269, CA, revealing that Law of Property Act 1925, s 198, prevails over s 44(5). No compensation under Law of Property Act 1969, s 25 is available: see s 25(9), (10).

101.24 It must also be borne in mind that notice of the existence of a deed affecting the title, or which *necessarily* affects it, is notice of its contents if the deed can be viewed:

> 'Of course there may be cases where the deed cannot be got at, or for some other reason, where, with the exercise of all the prudence in the world, you cannot see it, and then there may be no constructive notice affecting the title ... There is a class of cases, of which I think *Jones v Smith*[1] is the most notorious, where the purchaser was told of a deed which might or might not affect the title, and was told at the same time that it did not affect the title [and in such cases there is no constructive notice[2]]. Supposing you are buying land of a married man as in *Jones v Smith*, and you are told at the same time that there is a marriage settlement, but the deed does not affect the land in question, you have no constructive notice of its contents, because although you know there is a settlement you are told it does not affect the land. If every marriage settlement necessarily affected all a man's land then you would have constructive notice, but as a settlement may not relate to his land at all, or only to some other portions of it, the mere fact of you having heard of a settlement does not give you constructive notice of its contents, if you are told at the same time that it does not affect the land'[3].

[1]   (1841) 1 Hare 43.
[2]   A fortiori where he has no notice of the existence of any settlement.
[3]   Per Jessel MR in *Patman v Harland* (1881) 17 Ch D 353.

101.25 In addition to documents, constructive notice may be imputed to a purchaser from the state, appearance or occupation[1] of property. Thus the existence of a sea-wall bounding property has been held to give constructive notice of a liability to keep it in repair[2]. So notice of a tenancy is notice of its terms though there is no duty to inquire of the tenant whether the terms of his tenancy accurately reflect his agreement with his landlord, so that there is no constructive notice of any right of the tenant to rectify the tenancy for mistake[3]. Generally, where a person purchases property where a visible state of things exists, which could not legally exist, or is very unlikely to exist without the property being subject to some burden, he is taken to have notice of the nature and extent of the burden[4].

[1] See *Hunt v Luck* [1902] 1 Ch 428; *Kingsnorth Trust Ltd v Tizard* [1986] 2 All ER 54, [1986] 1 WLR 783.
[2] *Morland v Cook* (1868) LR 6 Eq 252.
[3] *Smith v Jones* [1954] 2 All ER 823, [1954] 1 WLR 1089 though such mere equity of an actual occupier of registered land will be an overriding interest within Land Registration Act 1925, s 70(1)(g): *Blacklocks v JB Developments (Godalming) Ltd* [1982] Ch 183, [1981] 3 All ER 392; *Collings v Lee* [2001] 2 All ER 332; all doubts now being resolved by the Land Registration Act 2002, s 116.
[4] *Allen v Seckham* (1879) 11 Ch D 790, and note 1, above.

Imputing knowledge to a company

101.26 In *El Ajou v Dollar Land Holdings plc*[1] the Court of Appeal emphasised that an individual's knowledge can be imputed to a company either if the individual was its directing mind and will in relation to the act or omission in point or was its agent in the relevant transaction. These are separate alternatives though it is easy to confuse them.

[1][1994] 2 All ER 685.

101.27 For the first ground it suffices that the individual had de facto control and management of the relevant arrangements even if he had ceased to have such when some of the arrangements put in train by him were actually carried into effect. Different persons may for different purposes be 'identified' with the company for the purpose of imputing knowledge or a particular state of mind to the company, a point which was subsequently elaborated by Lord Hoffmann in the Privy Council decision, *Meridian Global Funds Management Asia Ltd v Securities Commission*[1]. In *London Underground Ltd v NURMTW*[2], Robert Walker LJ considered the 'essential point' of *Meridian* to be that:

> 'in determining the mental state of an artificial person (when some ... rule requires that rather fictional exercise to be carried out) it may be necessary to look, not only at the body's formal constitution, but also at the way it actually organises its activities, and at the scope and purpose of the ... rule'.

[1] [1995] 2 AC 500.
[2] [2001] ICR 647 at 662.

101.28 For the second ground the knowledge of its agent will be imputed to a company where the company is under a duty to investigate or to make disclosure and employs the agent to discharge such duty (so long as the agent is not committing a fraud against his principal) or where the agent has actual or ostensible authority to receive communications on behalf of the principal. It does not suffice that the agent had private knowledge of facts into which his principal had no duty to inquire, even if he was under a duty to inform his principal of such facts, so long as he did not actually so inform his principal.

101.29 In the particular circumstances the Court of Appeal applying the above principles of law held that F's knowledge could be imputed to the defendant company on the first ground but not the second.

Absence of notice will not protect a volunteer

101.30 If a transferee of trust property is a volunteer, then the estate will remain burdened with the trust, whether or not he had notice of the trust[1], because a volunteer has no equity against a true owner. Where, therefore, the trust property can be followed into the hands of a volunteer, and no question of mixing arises, an order for restoration will be made against him. Indeed, a volunteer will be personally liable to repay the beneficiaries if after acquiring knowledge of the trust he dissipated the trust property so that no proprietary tracing claim lies against him, as should also be the case even if he had no knowledge of the trust at the time of dissipation[2], though then the defence of change of position may be available to such innocent volunteer.

1 *Mansell v Mansell* (1732) 2 P Wms 678; *Re Strachan* (1876) 4 Ch D 123, CA; *Spurgeon v Collier* (1758) 1 Eden 55; *Banque Belge Pour l'Etranger v Hambrouck* [1921] 1 KB 321.
2 See para 100.76 ff.

Tracing, following, and claiming

101.31 In *Foskett v McKeown*[1], Lord Millett distinguished 'tracing', 'following', and 'claiming':

> '[Tracing and following] are both exercises in locating assets which are or may be taken to represent an asset belonging to the plaintiffs and to which they assert ownership. The processes of following and tracing are, however, distinct. Following is the process of following the same asset as it moves from hand to hand. Tracing is the process of identifying a new asset as the substitute for the old. Where one asset is exchanged for another, a claimant can elect whether to follow the original asset into the hands of the new owner or to trace its value into the new asset in the hands of the same owner ... Tracing is also distinct from claiming. It identifies the traceable proceeds of the claimant's property. It enables the claimant to substitute the traceable proceeds for the original asset as the subject matter of his claim. But it does not affect or establish his claim. That will depend on a number of factors including the nature of his interest in the original asset. He will normally be able to maintain the same claim to the substituted asset as he could have maintained to the original asset ... But his claim may also be exposed to potential defences as a result of intervening transactions.'

1 [2001] 1 AC 102 at 129–130, adopting the terminology suggested in L D Smith *The Law of Tracing* (1997). See too *Boscawen v Bajwa* [1996] 1 WLR 328 at 334.

101.32 Thus, 'the rules of following and tracing ... [are] evidential in nature', and they are distinct from 'rules which determine substantive rights': 'the former are concerned with identifying property in other hands or in another form; the latter with the rights that a claimant can assert against the property in its present form'[1].

1   *Glencore International AG v Metro Trading International Inc* [2001] 1 Lloyd's Rep 284 at [180], *per* Moore-Bick J. See too *Boscawen v Bajwa* [1996] 1 WLR 328 at 334, *per* Millett LJ; *Waxman v Waxman* (2004) 7 ITELR 162 at [582].

101.33 It follows that where a trustee has misdirected trust assets to a third party who still has them in the form in which he received them it will be unnecessary for the beneficiaries to 'trace' the value inherent in their property into some other asset, and they need merely 'follow' their property into the third party's hands, before asserting a proprietary claim to the property. However, it will be necessary for the beneficiaries to 'trace' and 'follow', before they can assert a claim to assets in the hands of a third party, in the event that the trustee has mixed trust assets with other property, or substituted trust assets for other property, before transferring the traceable proceeds of the trust property to the third party; and the same can also be said of the situation where the third party mixes the trust assets or their traceable proceeds with other property, or substitutes trust assets or their traceable proceeds after receiving them.

Trust funds mixed with volunteer's own moneys: Re Diplock approach

101.34 Where trust funds are wrongfully mixed with the moneys of an innocent volunteer then, provided means of identification or disentanglement exist, the volunteer and the beneficiary will each be entitled to a pari passu charge on the mixed fund for his own money, and this is so whether the mixing was done by the trustee[1] or by the volunteer himself[2]. If the mixing has occurred through trust moneys being paid into the volunteer's current account at the bank then the rule in *Clayton's Case*[3] has traditionally been applied, the money first paid in being deemed to be that first drawn out. However, the rule will not be applied where stocks are bought out of a mixed fund consisting of trust moneys and the volunteer's own moneys and then sold piecemeal, as in such case each sum of stock sold will be treated as containing an aliquot proportion of that bought with the trust money[4]. Furthermore, for reasons which have already been discussed, it is submitted that the courts should now hold that the rule in *Clayton's* case is no longer applicable in this situation, and that the *Re Diplock* rateable proportion approach should be used instead[5]. Recent cases suggest that the English courts have now effectively moved to this position, as they are swift to find that the facts satisfy the requirement laid down in *Barlow Clowes International Ltd v Vaughan*[6], that departures from the rule in Clayton's Case are permissible where its application would result in injustice between the parties[7].

1   *Sinclair v Brougham* [1914] AC 398, HL.
2   *Re Diplock* [1948] Ch 465, [1948] 2 All ER 318, CA; affd sub nom *Ministry of Health v Simpson* [1951] AC 251, [1950] 2 All ER 1137, where only the in personam claim was considered.

3   *Devaynes v Noble, Clayton's Case* (1816) 1 Mer 529 at 572, applied in *Re Diplock* [1948] Ch 465.
4   *Re Diplock* [1948] Ch 465, [1948] 2 All ER 318, CA.
5   See para 92.42 ff.
6   [1992] 4 All ER 22.
7   *Russell-Cooke Trust Co v Prentis* [2002] *EWHC* 2227 *(Ch)*, [2003] 2 All ER 478 at 495; *Commerzbank Aktiengesellschaft v IMB Morgan plc* [2004] *EWHC* 2771 *(Ch)*, [2004] *EWHC* 2771 *(Ch)*, [2005] 1 Lloyd's Rep 298 at [43]–[49]; *Re Ahmed & Co* [2006] EWHC 480 (Ch) 150 Sol Jo LB 402 at [131]–[138].

101.35 Where, however, trust moneys are spent by an innocent volunteer on the improvement or alteration of some asset of its own, such as land and buildings, the Court of Appeal has held the moneys 'cannot be traced in any true sense,' so, the volunteer will hold the resulting 'mixed asset' free from any trust and the beneficiaries will be confined to their personal remedy[1]. This finding was recently reaffirmed by Lord Browne-Wilkinson in *Foskett v McKeown*[2], on the basis that:

> 'cases where the money of one person has been expended on improving or maintaining the physical property of another raise special problems [because the] property left at the end of the day is incapable of being physically divided into its separate constituent assets, ie the land and the money spent on it'.

1   *Re Diplock* [1948] Ch 465, CA; followed in *Re Esteem Settlement* 2002 JLR 53 at 106. A volunteer who knowingly so spent trust moneys will not as a constructive trustee be able to complain if the trust claims a charge or a proportionate share in respect of the improved property. See para 92.27 above.
2   [2001] 1 AC 102 at 109.

101.36 However, his Lordship went on to say that such expenditure might still give rise to a proprietary lien, which is difficult to square with his view that it leaves no traceable residue in the hands of the recipient.

Modern approach for innocent volunteers

101.37 Where trust property is wrongly transferred gratuitously to D, D must take the property subject to the trust. If such property be money, or if he sells such property so converting it into money, and he then mixes the money with his own money in a deposit account which he draws upon to purchase assets various questions arise. If D had actual, Nelsonian or naughty knowledge[1] that he had received trust property then any asset so purchased must belong to the trust until D has reinstated the trust fund, D (like a wrongdoing trustee[2]) not being able until then to prove that he used his own money[3]. Otherwise, at most the asset will belong to the trust and D pro rata according to the proportion that the trust money in the mixed account bore to D's own money when the asset was purchased[4]. However, if D can prove that he could have bought the asset without the assistance of the trust money and would have done so if he had known that the trust money was trust money, then he has not unjustly enriched himself at the expense of the trust, so that the asset should not be held on a constructive trust for D and the trust beneficiaries in proportionate shares. Instead, the asset should belong to D subject only to a lien for the trust money[5], as Ungoed-Thomas J would have held in *Re Tilley's*

Will Trusts[6] if he had been dealing with an innocent donee, whose position is a fortiori that of the innocent trustee, Mrs Tilley. However, as the majority of the House of Lords recently made clear in *Foskett v McKeown*[7], this argument is not open to the innocent donee of an asset purchased with trust money by a fraudulent trustee who could have used his own money to buy the asset, since the argument would not be open to the trustee himself and the donee can be in no better position than the fraudster from whom he received the gift.

1   'Nelsonian' and 'naughty' knowledge represent the knowledge that D is deemed to have from wilfully shutting his eyes to the obvious, or from wilfully or recklessly failing to make the enquiries an honest and reasonable man would make when aware of suspicious circumstances: he does not ask because he does not want to receive a likely unfavourable answer: see para 100.73 above. Strictly, an innocent volunteer means one without actual constructive or imputed notice (as assumed in *Re Diplock* [1948] Ch 465) but in line with the liberal approaches in *Re Tilley's Will Trusts* [1967] Ch 1179 and *Re Montagu's Settlements* [1987] Ch 264 it is submitted that, nowadays, the state of *knowledge* of D's conscience has more relevance and, in any event, a donee is almost inevitably only going to have constructive notice of matters of which he has naughty knowledge, a donee not normally having any duty to make inquiries.
2   See para 92.28 above.
3   *Boscawen v Bajwa* [1996] 1 WLR 328 at 336–8; *Banton v CIBC Trust Corp* (2001) 197 DLR (4th) 212.
4   *Re Diplock* [1948] Ch 465 at 524, 539, 546, 554 but in the context of the claimant only claiming a charge which was held not to rank in priority over the volunteer without notice but pari passu with such innocent volunteer's claim, each being regarded as having proprietary interests of the same priority.
5   See *Scott on Trusts* (4th edn) Vol V, pp 588–589; DJ Hayton (1990) 106 LQR 87 at 100 and in 'Equity's Identification Rules', Chapter 1 in P Birks (ed) *Laundering and Tracing*, Clarendon, Oxford 1995.
6   [1967] Ch 1179, discussed at para 92.31 ff.
7   See especially [2001] 1 AC 102 at 127 and 131, per Lord Millett; for the minority's finding to the contrary, see Lord Steyn's speech at 112–113.

101.38 The position ought not to be different where no mixing has occurred because D has innocently received X Ltd shares which he sold and replaced with Y Ltd shares which he sold and replaced with Z Ltd shares. Instead of a 'money input' of his there has been an 'expertise input'. If D can prove that he could have bought the Y Ltd and Z Ltd shares without the assistance of the proceeds of sale of the X Ltd shares and would have done so if he had known that the X Ltd shares were trust property, then he has not unjustly enriched himself at the expense of the trust, so that the Z Ltd shares should not be held on constructive trust for the trust beneficiaries. D should own the shares subject to a lien for the value of the X Ltd shares at the time he received them[1].

1   See *Scott on Trusts* (4th edn) Vol V, pp 588–589.

101.39 What, however, if D's investments produced a loss, the Z Ltd shares being worth less than the value of the X Ltd shares when received by D? Clearly the trust must be able to fall back upon a lien over the Z Ltd shares to secure the value of the X Ltd shares[1]. Will the position be any different if the loss flowed from a mixing of assets[2] as where D innocently spent his £10,000 and the trust's £10,000 on a £20,000 car which has halved in value? Can the trust claim a lien over the car, so entitling it to the car to the exclusion of D, who thereby loses all his £10,000?

¹ *Scott on Trusts* (4th edn) Vol V, pp 588–589; *Re Diplock* [1948] Ch 465.
² It is here assumed that the mixing and withdrawals do not relate to a current account
   where *Re Diplock* [1948] Ch 465 applied *Clayton's* case: on the justifiability of this see
   para 101.34 above.

New potential in defence of change of position

101.40 D can argue that he changed his position in reliance upon the belief
that he had £20,000 available to purchase a car: if he had known that only
half of the £20,000 was available then he would only have bought a £10,000
car so as only to lose half its value, namely £5,000. This change of position
makes it inequitable for the trust to have a lien over the car¹ for more than
£5,000, so that the trust and D should rateably bear the loss.

¹ See car example of Lord Templeman in *Lipkin Gorman v Karpnale* [1991] 2 AC 548 at
   559–560.

101.41 This result is already achieved by *Re Diplock* treating the trust and D
as each having equitable proprietary interests of the same priority, so that
assets purchased out of their mixed moneys are owned equally (or technically
subject to two equal priority liens for £10,000 each) when it comes to
allocation of losses. This approach will probably continue where it achieves a
rough and ready measure of justice so avoiding complications. However,
strictly speaking there ought to be scope for D to argue that the depreciation
on a £10,000 car is less than that on the £20,000 car, so that if he had
purchased a £10,000 car it would now be worth £6,000, so that his change of
position defence should entitle him to have a lien for £6,000 on the car and
the trust only to a lien for £4,000.

101.42 The availability of the defence of change of position¹ enables one to
see that in *Re Diplock* the Court of Appeal should have found that the
claimant's moneys could have been traced into altered or improved real
property to enable a charge to have been imposed thereon, but that the
defence of change of position should have been available at least to the extent
that the defendant charities in the case should have been given time to go back
to the charge-holders whose securities they had paid off with the claimants'
money, and take out new loans from the lenders on terms as favourable as
those which the defendants had originally enjoyed².

¹ For existing case law see para 100.82 ff and for possible ramifications see P Birks (ed)
   Laundering and Tracing (Clarendon,Oxford, 1995).
² As Millett LJ held in *Boscawen v Bajwa* [1996] 1 WLR 328.

101.43 In *Lipkin Gorman v Karpnale Ltd¹*, Lord Goff stated that the defence
of change of position is:

> 'available to a person whose position has so changed that it would be
> inequitable in all the circumstances to require him to make restitution, or to
> make restitution in full'.

¹ [1991] 2 AC 548 at 580.

101.44 Lord Goff also recognised that change of position would help the development of 'a more consistent approach to tracing claims', and there seems scope for change of position to replace the peculiar tracing rules applicable to innocent volunteers, as appears from the example discussed four paragraphs above. Rather than a pro rata rule for the trust's money mixed with D's money or, in the case of a current account, a first in first out *Clayton's Case* approach, should the court not consider simply whether the position of the innocent volunteer, D, has so changed that it would be inequitable in all the circumstances to require him to make restitution or restitution in full, especially when the justification for both the change of position defence and the tracing rules is a combination of the prevention of unjust enrichment and the avoidance of hardship to innocent persons?

101.45 Take the case where D is wrongly paid £1,200 from a trust fund of which P is a beneficiary and pays this into his deposit account containing £600. Then, D takes a holiday costing £1,200 which he would not have taken but for receiving £1,200. According to traditional case law the £600 remaining in D's account should be charged pro rata in favour of P and D and so be shared £400 for P and £200 for D; while if the account had been a current account D would have been taken to have spent all his £600 first so that the £600 remaining would belong to P though if P's £1,200 had been paid in before D's £600 then the £600 remaining would belong to D. The impact of the change of position defence is that the remaining £600 should belong to D because D has a complete defence to the claim for £1,200.

101.46 Essentially, the position is that P's claim is a restitutionary power to vest himself with a proprietary interest in traced assets by way of a lien or charge over such assets as security for the value of his claim which abates to the extent that the defence of change of position is established. He only has power to claim a lien or charge to the value of such abated claim. Thus, in the above example P can establish no lien, so there is no need to consider tracing a fund over which a lien could be imposed. However, if D's holiday only cost £1,100 then there should be a lien for £100 over anything remaining in the account or purchased with money from the account.

101.47 Where change of position is not directed at proving that the defendant is not in fact enriched but is directed at proving that the enduring enrichment of the defendant is just, D must surely have a defence to P's claim for a proportionate share of an appreciated asset if D can prove that he would anyhow have bought the asset with his own money alone if he had known that the money derived from P was such and therefore should not be taken to have detrimentally changed his position, having accidentally and unknowingly used P's money, for this would be unjustly to enrich P at D's expense. It thus suffices to allow P a lien over D's asset for P's money (and interest) until D reimburses P for the use of P's money.

No need to sue trustee personally before making proprietary claim

101.48 The strict personal claim available to unpaid creditors, legatees or next of kin against recipients of a deceased's estate can only be made after the personal claim against the blundering personal representatives has been exhausted. Thus, in *Re Diplock*[1] where such a personal claim was brought as well as a proprietary claim and £15,000 was recovered from the personal representatives, it followed that the money had to be credited rateably to all the defendant innocent volunteers 'prima facie and subject to discussion.' However, where beneficiaries are bringing a proprietary tracing claim to recover their property or its traceable product there can be no possible ground for restricting exercise of such proprietary right until personal claims against the trustee have been exhausted. Significantly, Oliver J in *Re J Leslie Engineers Co Ltd*[2] having mentioned the need to exhaust personal claims against the wrongdoing fiduciary before proceeding with a personal claim against third parties did not mention such prior need when going on to deal with a proprietary tracing claim. Thus one can assert one's proprietary rights without first taking advantage of any personal claims as was held in *Hagan v Waterhouse*[3].

[1] [1948] Ch 465 at 556. Writing extra-judicially, Lord Nicholls considered that this was an unfair rule and that in the event that a strict liability personal claim in *Re Diplock* was extended to all recipients of misapplied trust funds, 'the opportunity should be taken to decided that this form of relief is no longer subject to the pre-condition that a claimant must first exhaust his remedies against the trustees': 'Knowing Receipt: The Need for a New Landmark' in WR Cornish et al (eds) *Restitution: Past, Present and Future* (1998) at pp 231 and 241.
[2] [1976] 2 All ER 85 at 91–92.
[3] (1994) 34 NSWLR 308 at 369–370.

Can defendant plead equitable jus tertii?

101.49 In *El Ajou v Dollar Land Holdings plc*[1] the defendant was found to have been in knowing receipt of £2.325 million, representing the traceable proceeds of fraud, so as not to be a bona fide purchaser without notice. The claimant was the most significant of the 1,986 victims and had brought a personal money claim for the whole £2.325 million, while the defendant argued that the claimant could only claim 24% or 40% or 70%.

[1] [1993] 3 All ER 717 reversed by CA imputing knowledge of its director to the defendant company [1994] 2 All ER 685 and remitted the case to the High Court for assessment of compensation.

101.50 Millett J and the Court of Appeal found that 6.673 million dollars of the claimant were within 9.547 million dollars of victims traceable via Panama into assets whose proceeds of sale amounted to £2.325 million. The fraudulent boiler-room operation was run from Amsterdam via Dutch companies and a Mr Apeldoorn had been appointed by the Dutch courts to look after the interests of the victims without the need for any powers of attorney from them (though to assist with Swiss proceedings 1,590 victims had given powers of attorney to Mr Apeldoorn). Apeldoorn and the claimant entered into a sharing agreement in 1988 providing for the claimant's compensation in the English action and his costs to be divided in shares of 70:30 between the claimant and Apeldoorn.

101.51 Walker J pointed out[1] that the tracing of the claimant's money had not been on a pro rata basis with that of the other victims as in *Barlow Clowes International v Vaughan*[2] but on a more stringent basis, which would entitle the claimant to an equitable charge over the £2.325 million to cover his net losses in excess of 5 million dollars. He concluded that there was nothing inequitable in permitting the claimant to claim the whole £2.325 million when no other claimant was seeking to assert a charge ranking rateably with the claimant's charge and there was no realistic possibility of such a claim being made in the future. He stated:

> 'There is not any rigid rule to be applied as to whether a defendant can ever plead a sort of equitable jus tertii in this type of case. It must depend on the circumstances.'

1   *El Ajou v Dollar Land Holdings plc (No 2)* [1995] 2 All ER 213.
2   [1992] 4 All ER 22, CA.

101.52 He indicated that the court would not be inclined to look with favour upon a defendant 'who has no claim to retain the traceable money subject to the equitable charges'. This finding has recently been followed in *Campden Hill Ltd v Chakrani*[1].

1   [2005] EWHC 911 (Ch) at [76]–[77].

Tracing through non-trust jurisdictions

101.53 A wrongdoer cannot exploit transactions occurring in foreign non-trust jurisdictions to thwart the tracing processes of the English forum to determine the amount for which he is personally liable[1], nor should he thereby thwart a proprietary claim to the traced English assets that establish the amount of that personal liability. However, it would seem that an innocent defendant (an innocent volunteer) who acquired title under a foreign lex situs should have a good defence if subsequently sued in England over the relevant asset brought into England when he had acquired an unimpeachable title under the lex situs[2].

1   *El Ajou v Dollar Land Holdings plc* [1993] 3 All ER 717 at 736–737, accepted on appeal [1994] 2 All ER 685.
2   Cf *Winkworth v Christie Manson & Woods Ltd* [1980] Ch 496.

Transfer of fund into court equivalent to alienation for value

101.54 Some transfers, apparently voluntary, have been held to be equivalent to alienations for value. Thus, in *Thorndike v Hunt*[1] a trustee of two different settlements having applied to his own use funds subject to one of the settlements, replaced them by funds which, under a power of attorney from his co-trustee under the other, he transferred into the names of himself and his co-trustee in the former. In a suit in respect of breaches of trust of the former settlement, the trustees of it transferred the fund thus replaced into court.

1   (1859) 3 De GF & J 563; and see *Case v James* (1861) 3 De GF & J 256; *Re Bankhead's Trust* (1856) 2 K & J 560; and *Dawson v Prince* (1857) 2 De G & J 41; but c f *Cloutte v Storey* [1911] 1 Ch 18.

101.55 It was held by the Court of Appeal that the transfer into court was equivalent to an alienation for value without notice, and that the beneficiaries under the other settlement could not follow the trust fund. The transfer was to satisfy an existing debt and so was for value and the legal title was in the Accountant General on trust for beneficiaries under the former settlement.

101.56 So incumbrancers on a fund in court which has been transferred to a separate account before the incumbrances were created, are not postponed to prior equitable claims of other beneficiaries under the same settlement, subsequently discovered[1]. This is because, when a fund is carried over to a separate account in an action for administering the trust, it is released from the general questions in the action, and becomes ear-marked as subject only to the questions arising upon the particular matter referred to in the heading of the account[2]. All other questions are in fact treated as res judicata. The fund has been awarded by the court to the parties falling under the heading of the separate account, and it is too late for others to try to upset the court's award. It is, in fact, equivalent to a transfer of the legal estate or interest.

1   *Re Eyton* (1890) 45 Ch D 458.
2   Per Lord Langdale MR in *Re Jervoise* (1849) 12 Beav 209.

Purchaser with notice from purchaser without

101.57 A purchaser with notice (or a donee) from a purchaser without notice is safe. If he were not, an innocent purchaser for value would be prejudiced, being incapable of ever alienating the property which he had acquired without breach of duty and without loss, and such a restraint on alienation would necessarily create that stagnation against which the law has always set its face[1]. However, if a trustee wrongfully disposes of trust property to a purchaser without notice and later re-acquires the property he will again hold it subject to the trusts if the beneficiaries prefer this to claiming the traceable product of the wrongful sale[2].

1   See *Brandlyn v Ord* (1738) 1 Atk 571; *Lowther v Carlton* (1741) 2 Atk 242; *Peacock v Burt* (1834) 4 LJ Ch 33; but the doctrine is not to be extended (*West London Commercial Bank v Reliance Permanent Building Society* (1885) 29 Ch D 954, CA).
2   *Re Stapleford Colliery Co* (1880) 14 Ch D 432 at 445; *Gordon v Holland* (1913) 82 LJPC 81.

Where purchaser has only acquired equitable interest

101.58 The preceding examples all refer to cases in which the third party has acquired the legal title to property the subject of a trust, in which case the validity of his title depends entirely on the absence of notice. Where, however, the third party has only acquired an equitable interest, the question of notice is, as a rule, immaterial, for he does not have the legal estate, and therefore his equity, being no stronger than that of the beneficiaries, the maxim 'qui prior in tempore, potior in jure est' applies (he who is first in time has the strongest claim in law)[1].

1   But the beneficiaries will be postponed where their title is based on a document misleading in form and the third parties acted wholly innocently and were misled by the settlor through whom the beneficiaries claim (*Re King's Settlement* [1931] 2 Ch 294). As between competing equitable interests the first in time prevails unless the person having the first equitable interest (or someone claiming under him) is estopped from claiming such priority through having misled the second person by his fraud or negligent conduct: *Abigail v Lapin* [1934] AC 491, PC; *Freeguard v Royal Bank of Scotland* (1998) 79 P & CR 81.

Where equities are equal and no legal estate in either claimant

101.59 Thus, where a trustee, holding a mortgage[1] or a lease[2], deposits the deed with another to secure an advance to himself, the lender as equitable mortgagee will have no equity against the beneficiaries however bona fide he may have acted, and however free he may have been of notice of the trustee's fraud.

1   *Newton v Newton* (1868) 4 Ch App 143; and *Joyce v De Moleyns* (1845) 2 Jo & Lat 374.
2   *Re Morgan* (1881) 18 Ch D 93. After the Law of Property (Miscellaneous Provisions) Act 1989 the equitable mortgage needs to be in signed writing: *United Bank of Kuwait plc v Sahib* [1997] Ch 107, CA.

101.60 On the same principle, where a trustee has wrongfully spent trust funds in the purchase of property, which he has afterwards contracted to sell to a third party without notice, then, if the legal estate has not been conveyed to the third party, the beneficiaries will have priority over him[1]. For they have a right to trace the trust fund into the property into which it has been converted, and to take it or to have a charge upon it, at their election; and as their right was prior in time to that of the third party, and as he does not have the legal estate, the maxim above referred to applies[2].

1   *Frith v Cartland* (1865) 2 Hem & M 417.
2   And see, as to deposit of share certificates with blank transfers forming part of a trust estate, *Powell v London and Provincial Bank* [1893] 2 Ch 555, CA.

When protection of legal estate may be lost against later equitable interest

101.61 One line of authorities lays down the principle that either direct fraud, or negligence so gross as to amount to evidence of fraud, must be proved against a legal owner, to estop him from claiming the protection afforded by the legal estate[1]. Another line of authorities supplements this by asserting that where the relation between the legal owner and custodian of the deeds and other persons claiming beneficially is that of trustee and beneficiary or solicitor and client, then the beneficiary or client does not lose priority by reason of the improper or negligent acts of the trustee or solicitor, unless of course the beneficiary or client has notice of, and is privy to, the impropriety or negligence[2]. Thus, the equitable interests of a beneficiary under a trust where the legal estate is vested in trustees will prevail over subsequent equitable interests, whether or not involving fraud or negligence on the trustees' part, unless the beneficiary's involvement precludes the beneficiary from asserting priority in time or the overreaching provisions of the 1925 legislation protect the subsequent equitable owner. Exceptionally, in *Walker v Linom*[3], Parker J, after elaborately reviewing all the authorities, came to the conclusion that where trustees of a marriage settlement (to whom the legal fee simple in lands had been conveyed) negligently failed to obtain from the settlor-husband the deed by which he had purchased the property, and thus enabled him to pose as the owner and mortgage it, their negligence was such that their legal estate must be postponed to the subsequent equitable estate of the mortgagee and a purchaser from him, *and that the beneficiaries were in no better position than the trustees.* The position would have been different if the trustees had obtained all the relevant title deeds, but the trustees and the beneficiaries had to take the unprotected title conferred upon them by the settlor subject to any risks inherent in such title.

[1]   *Evans v Bicknell* (1801) 6 Ves 174; *Hewitt v Loosemore* (1851) 9 Hare 449; *Ratcliffe v Barnard* (1871) 6 Ch App 652, CA; *Northern Counties of England Fire Insurance Co v Whipp* (1884) 26 Ch D 482, CA; *Re Greer* [1907] 1 IR 57; and see doubt expressed by HL in *Taylor v Russell* [1892] AC 244 at 262; *Re Castell & Brown Ltd* [1898] 1 Ch 315; *Re Valletort Sanitary Steam Laundry Co Ltd* [1903] 2 Ch 654.

[2]   Per Stirling LJ in *Taylor v London and County Banking Co* [1901] 2 Ch 231 at 261; and see *Oliver v Hinton* [1899] 2 Ch 264; *Capell v Winter* [1907] 2 Ch 376; *Cave v Cave* (1880) 15 Ch D 639, *Newton v Newton* (1868) 4 Ch App 143.

[3]   [1907] 2 Ch 104. No point was taken over the preparedness of the mortgagee to lend money on the strength of only one recent title deed.

101.62 Things (or 'choses') in action are generally taken subject to all equities affecting them, because at law they were originally not transferable; and although by statute they are now transferable, it is directed that they should be transferred subject to all equities. Thus, in *Turton v Benson*[1] a mother agreed to give her son, on his marriage, as a portion a sum equal to that with which his intended father-in-law should endow the intended wife. The son, in order to induce the mother to give him a larger portion, entered into a collusive arrangement with the father-in-law, whereby, in consideration of the latter nominally endowing his daughter with £3,000, the son gave him a bond to repay him £1,000, part of it. This bond, being made upon a fraudulent consideration, was void in the hands of the father-in-law, and it was held that, being a chose in action, he could not confer a better title upon his assignee.

[1]   (1718) 1 P Wms 496.

Negotiable instruments

101.63 Negotiable instruments are, however, an exception to the rule as to choses in action passing subject to all prior equities, for the *common law*, with regard to them, adopted the custom of merchants, and recognised that such instruments were transferable. Consequently, the transferee of a negotiable instrument has a legal, as well as an equitable, interest; and where the equities are equal he is protected against prior equities by his legal title[1]. Of course, however, the transferee will be postponed where he has notice[2] of prior equities.

1   *London Joint Stock Bank v Simmons* [1892] AC 201, HL.
2   See *Earl of Sheffield v London Joint Stock Bank* (1888) 13 App Cas 333, HL.

Bona fide purchasers from trustees cannot get legal estate from them after notice

101.64 The bona fide purchaser of an equitable interest, without notice of an express trust, cannot defend his position by subsequently, and after notice, getting in an outstanding legal estate *from the trustee*; for by so doing he would be guilty of taking part in a new breach of trust[1]. If, however, he can perfect his legal title without being a party to a new breach of trust (as, for instance, by registering a transfer of shares which have been actually transferred before notice, or by getting in the legal estate from a third party), he may legitimately do so[2].

1   *Saunders v Dehew* (1692) 2 Vern 271; *Collier v M'Bean* (1865) 34 Beav 426; affd 1 Ch App 81; *Sharples v Adams* (1863) 32 Beav 213; *Carter v Carter* (1857) 3 K & J 617; *McCarthy & Stone Ltd v Julian Hodge & Co Ltd* [1971] 1 WLR 1547 at 1556.
2   *Dodds v Hills* (1865) 2 Hem & M 424.

Dealings with equitable interests under trusts

101.65 Priority depends upon the order in which notice in writing of the mortgage or other dealing is received by the trustees for sale of land or the Settled Land Act trustees or, otherwise, by the estate owner of land or legal owner of other property, unless the trust instrument or the trustees have nominated a trust corporation to receive notices instead, when notice should be given to such corporation[1]. If for any reason a valid notice cannot be served (eg because there are no trustees) a purchaser (eg a mortgagee) can protect himself by having a memorandum indorsed on the trust instrument[2]. On the application of any person interested in the equitable interest the trustees or legal title holder must produce any notices served on them or their predecessors[3].

1   Law of Property Act 1925, ss 137, 138; *Dearle v Hall* (1828) 3 Russ 1, *Re Dallas* [1904] 2 Ch 385; Ward.
2   Law of Property Act 1925, s 137(4), (5), (6).
3   Law of Property Act 1925, s 137(8), (9) emasculating *Law v Bouverie* [1891] 3 Ch 82.

101.66 Exceptionally, a mortgagee who had actual or constructive notice of a prior mortgage when he lent his money cannot gain priority by giving notice first[1]. However, if he had no notice of a prior mortgage when he lent his money he will not be prevented from claiming priority under a notice given by him to the trustees after learning of the prior mortgage[2].

1   *Re Holmes* (1885) 29 Ch D 786.

² *Mutual Life Assurance Society v Langley* (1886) 32 Ch D 460. If the second assignee be a volunteer he cannot gain priority over the earlier assignee by giving notice: he can take no more than the assignor could give: *Justice v Wynne* (1860) 12 I Ch R 289, *Fraser v Imperial Bank* (1912) 10 DLR 232.

101.67 It is advisable to give notice to all trustees¹ so that it remains effective indefinitely even though they all die or retire without communicating the notice to their successors. Of course, the written notices should be preserved with the trust documents but if they are not and new trustees, without notice of the incumbrance, distribute the trust fund to other incumbrancers or the beneficiaries they will not be personally liable².

¹ Notice to one of several trustees was not effective against incumbrancers who lent money after the death or retirement of that trustee unless he had communicated the notice to one or more of the continuing trustees: *Timson v Ramsbottom* (1837) 2 Heen 35.
² *Hallows v Lloyd* (1888) 39 Ch D 686.

Registered land

101.68 Where trust property is registered land and it is transferred to a purchaser such purchaser will take the property subject only to minor interests protected by entry on the register and to overriding interests¹, though if the purchaser is party to some fraud then an equitable in personam remedy may lie against him². The doctrine of notice has no application to overriding interests³ such as the proprietary rights of persons in actual occupation save where inquiry is made of such persons and the rights are not disclosed. A purchaser will thus be absolutely bound by the proprietary rights of such persons irrespective of questions of notice. A wife will be treated as herself in actual occupation if the husband appears as sole registered proprietor though her presence is explicable qua wife of the actual occupier⁴. An interest under a Settled Land Act settlement can only be a minor interest⁵ though it has been held⁶ that rights under a trust of land can be overriding interests if supported by actual occupation and not duly overreached by payment of purchase moneys to two trustees or a trust corporation⁷.

¹ Land Registration Act 1925, ss 20(1), 23(1) and Land Registration Act 2002, ss 29 and 30, minor interests being those interests that are not registered and do not rank as overriding interests. Payment of capital moneys to trustees in accordance with the entry of a restriction will overreach the beneficiaries' interests: *City of London Building Society v Flegg* [1988] AC 54, [1987] 3 All ER 435, HL.
² *Lyus v Prowsa Developments Ltd* [1982] 2 All ER 953; *Ashburn Anstalt v Arnold* [1989] Ch 1, and Article 100.
³ *Williams and Glyn's Bank v Boland* [1981] AC 487, [1980] 2 All ER 408, HL; *Blacklocks v JB Developments (Godalming) Ltd* [1982] Ch 183, [1981] 3 All ER 392; *Kling v Keston Properties Ltd* (1983) 49 P & CR 212.
⁴ *Williams and Glyn's Bank v Boland* [1981] AC 487, [1980] 2 All ER 408, HL. Minors are not capable of being in actual occupation in their own right unless aged 16 years and co-habiting in emancipated fashion: *Hypo-Mortgage Services Ltd v Robinson* [1997] 2 FLR 71, CA.
⁵ Land Registration Act 1925, s 86(2). Under the Land Registration Act 2002, s 33(a) it can only be protected by a restriction and not a notice.
⁶ *Williams and Glyn's Bank v Boland* [1981] AC 487, [1980] 2 All ER 408, HL.
⁷ *City of London Building Society v Flegg* [1988] AC 54, [1987] 2 WLR 1266.

Division Six

THE HAGUE
TRUSTS CONVENTION

Chapter 25

CONFLICT OF LAWS AND THE HAGUE TRUSTS CONVENTION

102.1 The choice of law rules for England and Wales, Northern Ireland and Scotland are set out in the Hague Convention on the Law Applicable to Trusts and on their Recognition, as implemented and extended by the Recognition of Trusts Act 1987, except that preliminary issues concerning the creation or launching of a trust are outside the scope of such Convention and Act which are now set out.

ARTICLE 102

THE HAGUE CONVENTION ON THE LAW APPLICABLE TO TRUSTS AND ON THEIR RECOGNITION, IMPLEMENTED BY THE RECOGNITION OF TRUSTS ACT 1987

The Hague Convention

CHAPTER ONE—SCOPE

Article 1

102.2 This Convention specifies the law applicable to trusts and governs their recognition.

Article 2

102.3 For the purposes of this Convention, the term 'trust' refers to the legal relationships created—inter vivos or on death—by a person, the settlor, when assets have been placed under the control of a trustee for the benefit of a beneficiary or for a specified purpose.

102.4 A trust has the following characteristics—

(a)   the assets constitute a separate fund and are not a part of the trustee's own estate;
(b)   title to the trust assets stands in the name of the trustee or in the name of another person on behalf of the trustee;
(c)   the trustee has the power and the duty, in respect of which he is accountable, to manage, employ or dispose of the assets in accordance with the terms of the trust and the special duties imposed upon him by law.

102.5–102.6 The reservation by the settlor of certain rights and powers and the fact that the trustee may himself have rights as a beneficiary, are not necessarily inconsistent with the existence of a trust.

Article 3

102.7 The Convention applies only to trusts created voluntarily and evidenced in writing.

Article 4

102.8 The Convention does not apply to preliminary issues relating to the validity of wills or of other acts by virtue of which assets are transferred to the trustee.

Article 5

102.9 The Convention does not apply to the extent that the law specified by Chapter II does not provide for trusts or the category of trusts involved.

Chapter II—Applicable Law

Article 6

102.10 A trust shall be governed by the law chosen by the settlor. The choice must be express or be implied in the terms of the instrument creating or the writing evidencing the trust, interpreted, if necessary, in the light of the circumstances of the case.

102.11 Where the law chosen under the previous paragraph does not provide for trusts or the category of trust involved, the choice shall not be effective and the law specified in Article 7 shall apply.

Article 7

102.12 Where no applicable law has been chosen, a trust shall be governed by the law with which it is most closely connected.

102.13 In ascertaining the law with which a trust is most closely connected reference shall be made in particular to—

(a)   the place of administration of the trust designated by the settlor;
(b)   the situs of the assets of the trust;
(c)   the place of residence or business of the trustee;
(d)   the objects of the trust and the places where they are to be fulfilled.

Article 8

102.14 The law specified by Article 6 or 7 shall govern the validity of the trust, its construction, its effects, and the administration of the trust.

102.15 In particular that law shall govern—

(a)   the appointment, resignation and removal of trustees; the capacity to act as a trustee, and the devolution of the office of trustee;
(b)   the rights and duties of trustees among themselves;
(c)   the right of trustees to delegate in whole or in part the discharge of their duties or the exercise of their powers;
(d)   the power of trustees to administer or to dispose of trust assets, to create security interests in the trust assets, or to acquire new assets;
(e)   the powers of investment of trustees;
(f)   restrictions upon the duration of the trust, and upon the power to accumulate the income of the trust.
(g)   the relationships between the trustees and the beneficiaries including the personal liability of the trustees to the beneficiaries;
(h)   the variation or termination of the trust;
(i)   the distribution of the trust assets;
(j)   the duty of trustees to account for their administration.

Article 9

102.16 In applying this Chapter a severable aspect of the trust, particularly matters of administration, may be governed by a different law.

Article 10

102.17 The law applicable to the validity of the trust shall determine whether that law or the law governing a severable aspect of the trust may be replaced by another law.

CHAPTER III—RECOGNITION

Article 11

102.18 A trust created in accordance with the law specified by the preceding Chapter shall be recognised as a trust. Such recognition shall imply, as a minimum, that the trust property constitutes a separate fund, that the trustee may sue and be sued in his capacity as trustee, and that he may appear or act in this capacity before a notary or any person acting in an official capacity.

102.19 In so far as the law applicable to a trust requires or provides, such recognition shall imply, in particular—

(a)   that personal creditors of the trustee shall have no recourse against the trust assets;

(b)   that the trust assets shall not form part of the trustee's estate upon his insolvency or bankruptcy;

(c)   that the trust assets shall not form part of the matrimonial property of the trustee or his spouse nor part of the trustee's estate upon his death;

(d)   that the trust assets may be recovered when the trustee, in breach of trust, has mingled trust assets with his own property or has alienated trust assets. However, the rights and obligations of any third party holder of the assets shall remain subject to the law determined by the choice of law rules of the forum.

Article 12

102.20 Where the trustee desires to register assets, movable or immovable, or documents of title to them, he shall be entitled, in so far as this is not prohibited by or inconsistent with the law of the State where registration is sought, to do so in his capacity as trustee or in such other way that the existence of the trust is disclosed.

Article 13

102.21 No State shall be bound to recognise a trust the significant elements of which, except for the choice of the applicable law, the place of administration and the habitual residence of the trustee, are more closely connected with States which do not have the institution of the trust or the category of trust involved.

Article 14

102.22 The Convention shall not prevent the application of rules of law more favourable to the recognition of trusts.

Chapter IV—General Clauses

Article 15

102.23 The Convention does not prevent the application of provisions of the law designated by the conflicts rules of the forum, in so far as those provisions cannot be derogated from by voluntary act, relating in particular to the following matters—

(a)   the protection of minors and incapable parties;

(b)   the personal and proprietary effects of marriage;
(c)   succession rights, testate and intestate, especially the indefeasible shares of spouses and relatives;
(d)   the transfer of title to property and security interests in property;
(e)   the protection of creditors in matters of insolvency;
(f)   the protection, in other respects, of third parties acting in good faith.

102.24 If recognition of a trust is prevented by application of the preceding paragraph, the court shall try to give effect to the objects of the trust by other means.

Article 16

102.25 The Convention does not prevent the application of those provisions of the laws of the forum which must be applied even to international situations, irrespective of rules of conflict of laws.

102.26 If another State has a sufficiently close connection with a case then, in exceptional circumstances, effect may also be given to rules of that State which have the same character as mentioned in the preceding paragraph.

102.27 Any Contracting State may, by way of reservation, declare that it will not apply the second paragraph of this article.

Article 17

102.28 In the Convention the word 'law' means the rules of law in force in a State other than its rules of conflict of laws.

Article 18

102.29 The provisions of the Convention may be disregarded when their application would be manifestly incompatible with public policy (*ordre public*).

Article 19

102.30 Nothing in the Convention shall prejudice the powers of States in fiscal matters.

Article 20

102.31 Any Contracting State may, at any time, declare that the provisions of the Convention will be extended to trusts declared by judicial decisions.

102.32 This declaration shall be notified to the Ministry of Foreign Affairs of the Kingdom of the Netherlands and will come into effect on the day when this notification is received.

102.33 Article 31 is applicable to the withdrawal of this declaration in the same way as it applies to a denunciation of the Convention.

Article 21

102.34 Any Contracting State may reserve the right to apply the provisions of Chapter III only to trusts the validity of which is governed by the law of a Contracting State.

Article 22

102.35 The Convention applies to trusts regardless of the date on which they were created.

102.36 However, a Contracting State may reserve the right not to apply the Convention to trusts created before the date on which, in relation to that State, the Convention enters into force.

Article 23

102.37 For the purpose of identifying the law applicable under the Convention, where a State comprises several territorial units each of which has its own rules of law in respect of trusts, any reference to the law of that State is to be construed as referring to the law in force in the territorial unit in question.

Article 24

102.38 A State within which different territorial units have their own rules of law in respect of trusts is not bound to apply the Convention to conflicts solely between the laws of such units.

RECOGNITION OF TRUSTS ACT 1987

102.39

(1)   The provisions of the Convention set out in the Schedule hereto [Articles 1–12, 14–18 and 22 above set out] shall have the force of law[1] in the United Kingdom.
(2)   Those provisions shall, so far as practicable, have effect not only in relation to the trusts described in Articles 2 and 3 of the Convention but also in relation to any other trusts of property arising under the law of any part of the United Kingdom or by virtue of a judicial decision whether in the United Kingdom or elsewhere.

(3)   In accordance with Articles 15 and 16 such provisions of the law as are there mentioned shall, to the extent there specified, apply to the exclusion of the other provisions of the Convention.

(4)   In Article 17 the reference to a State includes a reference to any country or territory (whether or not a party to the Convention and whether or not forming part of the United Kingdom) which has its own system of law.

(5)   Article 22 shall not be construed as affecting the law to be applied in relation to anything done or omitted before the coming into force of this Act.

¹   As from 1 August 1987 by SI 1987/1177.

The Conflict of Laws

102.40 The conflict of laws is concerned with situations where a matter has connections with the legal systems of more than one State (with some States like the UK and the USA having many legal systems within them). Such a conflict might arise if eg a settlor domiciled in England and Wales creates a trust of property located in Scotland and Ontario, to be held on trust by Ontarian trustees for New York and Saskatchewan beneficiaries. It might also arise if a settlor domiciled in England and Wales wishes to create a trust which is in all respects purely domestic to England and Wales, save that he chooses the law of another legal system, eg New South Wales, to govern the trust.

102.41 Essentially, three key questions arise: in what circumstances will an English court be prepared to hear and decide transnational litigation (being the technical question whether it will exercise jurisdiction over the case); which legal system will it apply to resolve the dispute on the merits (the choice of law question); and in which circumstances will an English court recognise and enforce a judgment delivered overseas?

102.42 Discussion in this chapter will focus on the choice of law rules applicable to international trusts. These rules are mostly contained in the Hague Convention on the Law Applicable to Trusts and on their Recognition. Brief discussion will follow on the law concerning the English courts' jurisdiction relating to transnational trusts litigation¹ and the recognition and enforcement of foreign judgments.

¹   Most of the rules of jurisdiction are not trusts specific and it is accordingly not intended to cover them in detail here. Discussion will be confined to the trusts specific bases of jurisdiction.

The Hague Trusts Convention – Basic Concepts

Background

102.43 The Hague Trusts Convention was adopted at the Fifteenth Session of the Hague Conference on Private International Law in 1984¹. It has now been ratified by[2], and has entered into force in, Australia[3], Canada[4], Hong Kong[5], Italy[6], Liechtenstein[7], Luxembourg[8], Malta[9], the Netherlands,[10] San Marino[11] and the United Kingdom[12]. It has also been signed, though not ratified by Cyprus[13], France[14], and the United States[15]. Legislation has been tabled in Switzerland which is expected to lead to the ratification of the Convention in early 2007[16].

[1] See the Proceedings of the Fifteenth Session of the Hague Conference on Private International Law (1984), Book II – Trusts – Applicable Law and Recognition (hereafter 'The Proceedings'). For detailed discussion of the Convention, see J Harris *The Hague Trusts Convention* (2002) Hart Publishing, Oxford. See also F Albisinni and R Gambino (1993) 2 J Int P 73; L Collins (gen ed) Dicey, Morris and Collins, *The Conflict of Laws* (14th edn 2006) Sweet and Maxwell, London, Chapter 29; A Dyer (1999) 32 Van J Trans Law; E Gaillard and D Trautman (1987) 35 Am J Comp Law 307; D Hayton (1987) 36 ICLQ 260; D Hayton (1994) 1 J Int P 23; D Hayton in J Glasson (ed) *International Trust Laws*, Jordans, looseleaf, Bristol, Chapter C3; H Kötz in D Hayton (ed) *Modern International Developments in Trust Law* (1999) Kluwer, The Hague, Chapter 3; D Hayton and C Mitchell, *Commentary and Cases on the Law of Trusts and Equitable Remedies*, (12th edn, 2005) Sweet and Maxwell, London, Chapter 13; M Lupoi (1995) 1(3) Trusts and Trustees 15; M Lupoi *Trusts: a Comparative Study* (1997) Giuffrè, Milan, translated by S Dix, (2001) Cambridge University Press, Cambridge, Chapter 6; J Mowbray, L Tucker, N Le Poidevin and E Simpson *Lewin on Trusts* (17th edn, 2000) Sweet and Maxwell, London, Chapter 11; P North and J Fawcett Cheshire and North's *Private International Law* (13th edn, 1999) Butterworths, London, Chapter 35; A Oakley Parker and Mellows, *The Modern Law of Trusts* (8th edn, 2003), Chapter 23; J Schoenblum, (1994) 3 J Int Corp P 5; G Thomas and A Hudson, *The Law of Trusts* (2004) Oxford University Press, Oxford, Chapter 41; D Waters in M Graziadei, U Mattei and L Smith (eds) *Commercial Trusts in European Private Law* (2005) , Cambridge University Press, Cambridge, Part I, Chapter 3. A bibliography to the Hague Trusts Convention is provided by the Hague Conference on Private International Law and is updated regularly. It can be found at http://hcch.e-vision.nl/index_en.php

[2] For a list of States which have signed and/or ratified the Convention and the date of entry into force of the Convention into those countries, see http://hcch.e-vision.nl/index_en.php?act=conventions.status&cid=59.

[3] See the Trusts (Hague Convention) Act 1991. It entered into force on 1 January 1992.

[4] It entered into force on 1 January 1993 in Alberta, British Columbia, New Brunswick, Newfoundland and Prince Edward Island. The Convention currently applies to the States of Alberta, British Columbia, Manitoba (entry into force in Manitoba: 1 July 1994), New Brunswick, Newfoundland and Prince Edward Island and Saskatchewan (entry into force in Saskatchewan: 1 September 1994).

[5] The United Kingdom had extended the application of the Convention to Hong Kong with effect from 1 January 1992. The Government of the People's Republic of China determined that the Convention would continue to apply to the Hong Kong Special Administrative Region with effect from 1 July 1997 .

[6] It entered into force on 1 January 1992. The Italian ratification instrument (Law 364 of 16 October 1989) can be found in M Lupoi *Trust Laws of the World* (1996), ETI, Rome, 26.

[7] Liechtenstein is a non-Member State of the Hague Conference. The Convention entered into force in Liechtenstein on 1 April 2006.

[8] It entered into force on 1 January 2004.

[9] It entered into force on 1 March 1996.

[10] It entered into force on 1 February 1996.

[11] San Marino is a non-Member State of the Hague Conference. The Convention entered into force in Liechtenstein on 1 August 2006.

[12] This includes Bermuda, British Antarctic Territories, the British Virgin Islands, the Falkland Islands, Gibraltar, Guernsey (the UK extended the operation of the Convention to Guernsey on 28 April 1993), the Isle of Man, Jersey (the UK Recognition of Trusts Act 1987 was not extended to Jersey, but Jersey became a party to the Convention on 1 March 1992, having brought its Trusts (Jersey) Law 1984 into line with the Convention by the Trusts (Amendment No 2) (Jersey) Law 1991), Montserrat, St Helena and Dependencies, South Georgia, the South Sandwich Islands and the Turks and Caicos

Islands (entry into force in Turks and Caicos: 1 July 1993). See also Recognition of Trusts Act 1987, s 2. The United Kingdom signed the Convention on 10 January 1986 and ratified it on 17 November 1989. It entered into force in the United Kingdom and in the territories to which it was initially extended on 1 January 1992.

13 Signed on 11 March 1998.
14 Signed on 26 November 1991. There is a distinct possibility that France will enact a bill for the creation of La Fiducie, a ring-fenced fund for companies to create, and then ratify the Convention : D Hayton in J Glasson (ed) *International Trust Laws*, Chapter C3, p 4.
15 Signed on 13 June 1988.
16 For discussion, see F Noseda, (2005) 19(1) Tru LI 37; F Noseda, (2005) 20(1) Tru LI 3; P Gutzwiller (2006) PCB 19; S Pallister (2006) PCB 147.

102.44 In the United Kingdom, the Recognition of Trusts Act 1987 gives effect to the Convention. It appears as a Schedule to s 1 of the 1987 Act[1]. Section 1(1) of the Act states that 'the provisions of the Convention set out in the Schedule hereto shall have the force of law in the United Kingdom'. In the initial ratifying States of the United Kingdom, Australia and Italy, the Convention came into force on 1 January 1992.

1 Not all provisions of the Convention eg Article 13, are scheduled to the Act.

102.45 It is beyond doubt that the Convention is the dominant source of choice of law rules in England for trusts. The United Kingdom extended the ambit of the Convention, so that now only a small minority of international trusts fall outside its scope. For those trusts which do fall outside the Convention's scope, the common law choice of law rules will apply. However, these differ little from the Convention in any event. Accordingly, discussion will focus on the Convention. The common law rules will be referred to only in those few areas where they are significantly different from the Convention position.

102.46 The Explanatory Report on the Convention by Professor von Overbeck[1] details the evolution of the Convention and provides detailed commentary on each Article of the Convention. The courts of Contracting States may, of course, refer to this and may find it persuasive in resolving ambiguities[2].

1 The Official Report by Professor A von Overbeck, (hereafter 'the von Overbeck Report'), starts at p 370 of The Proceedings, note 2 above.
2 See also *Tod v Barton* [2002] EWHC 264 (Ch), (2002) 4 ITELR 715 , para 30 of Lawrence Collins J.

The effect of the Convention in non-trust States

102.47 The Convention does not introduce the trust nor equitable proprietary interests of trust beneficiaries into the domestic law of States which do not have the trust concept. It requires those States to recognise trusts falling within the Convention's scope for private international law purposes only[1]. Of course, it is quite possible that this will act as a catalyst for such States to develop their own domestic trust concept of a segregated ring-fenced fund immune from the claims of the owner creditors and heirs[2]; but there is absolutely no obligation on them to do so.

1 But they must recognise it *qua* trust, rather than translating it into an analogous institution in their domestic legal systems, so the domestic law must recognise that the trustee's trust property is immune from claims of the trustee's own creditors and heirs: von Overbeck Report, para 108.

2 See L Thevenoz *Trusts in Switzerland (Ratification of The Hague Convention on Trusts and Codification of Fiduciary Transfers)* (2001) Schulthess, Zurich (but see R Pease (2004) 11(1) Trusts and Trustees 17). The ratification of the Convention in Luxembourg was accompanied by a reform of its law on the *fiducia* in the Law of 27 July 2003: see *Trust & Fiducie- la Convention de la Haye et la nouvelle legislation luxembourgeoise*; (Montchrestien, Paris 2005); P Matthews (2003) 17(4) Tru LI 188; R Niland (2004) 19(1) JIBLR 6. Art. 6(1) of the Law states that fiduciary assets constitute a separate fund from the fiduciary's own wealth in his private patrimony. Belgium, which has not ratified the Hague Convention, has nonetheless introduced trusts provisions in its new Code of Private International Law: see P Matthews (2005) 19(4) Tru LI 191.

The open-ended nature of the Convention

102.48 The Convention is not reciprocal in nature. For matters within its scope there is no territorial limit and it applies even if the law applicable to the trust is that of a non-Contracting State. However, a Contracting State may enter a reservation[1] so that it only applies the Convention to trusts governed by the law of a Contracting State. The United Kingdom has made no such reservation[2].

1 Pursuant to Article 21.
2 Article 21 is omitted from the schedule to the Recognition of Trusts Act 1987.

The time factor

102.49 Article 22 provides that, 'the Convention applies to trusts regardless of the date on which they were created' but permits Contracting States to reserve the right not to apply the Convention to trusts created before the date on which the Convention enters into force in that Contracting State[1]. By the Recognition of Trusts Act 1987, s 1(5), out of an abundance of caution in case of the slightest possibility that the Convention rules differed from the common law rules on which there was a paucity of authority (much of which dated from a bygone era), the United Kingdom provided that, 'Article 22 shall not be construed as affecting the law to be applied in relation to anything done or omitted before the coming into force of this Act', so that breaches of trust committed before such date (but not after) are to be judged according to the common law rules applicable before that date (1 August 1987)[2].

1 See also the decision of the Supreme Court of New South Wales in *Saliba v Falzon* [1998] NSWSC 302.
2 See SI 1987/1177. Lawrence Collins J applied a number of provisions of the Hague Trusts Convention to a trust created in 1975 in *Chellaram v Chellaram (No 2)* [2002] EWHC 632 (Ch), [2002] 3 All ER 17, esp paras 164 and 166 However, the alleged breaches of trust occurred before 1987, so that the common law rules would apply and prevail if leading to a different result as he indicated at para 164, but he doubted there was any significant difference between them: para 166. See also *Re Carapiet's Trusts, Manoogian (Armenian Patriarch of Jerusalem) v Sonsino* [2002] EWHC 1304 (Ch),[2002] WTLR 989 paras 147, 160–162, 166–167.

The two main functions of the Convention: choice of law rules and the recognition of trusts

102.50 The Convention serves two key functions: it harmonises the choice of law rules applicable in Contracting States and then expressly provides for the recognition of trusts falling within its scope. The former function helps bring clarity to an area previously governed by common law rules which were never highly developed or clear. As to the recognition of trusts, it is important to understand what we mean. The word 'recognition' does not have anything to do with recognition of foreign trust judgments. The Hague Convention does not affect the rules on recognition of foreign judgments. Recognition and enforcement of foreign judgments must be and is still governed by the 'general' rules on recognition of foreign judgments of the State addressed[1]. The Hague Convention's 'recognition' rules are to be understood as simply giving guidance to Contracting non-trust States faced with a trust governed by the law of Trustopia as to what effect they must give that trust in their legal system, rather than leave it to their judges and notaries to work out for themselves the logical implications flowing from application of the Trustopian applicable law ascertained by applying the Convention's choice of law rules.

¹ See para 102.222 ff.

Exclusion of fiscal matters

102.51 Article 19 states that 'nothing in the Convention shall prejudice the powers of States in fiscal matters'. Although this is not scheduled to the Recognition of Trusts Act 1987, it goes without saying that a Convention on the private international law of trusts will not affect the taxation of trusts in the United Kingdom. Non-trust States will need to develop rules for the taxation of trusts[1].

¹ See F Sonneveldt in F Sonneveldt and H van Mens (eds) *The Trust-Bridge or Abyss between Common and Civil Law Jurisdictions?* (1992) Kluwer, Deventer, Chapter 1, p 17. On the position in Switzerland, see C Kälin, (2005) 11(10) Trusts and Trustees 19; F Noseda (2006) 20(1) Tru LI 8.

Types of Trusts falling within the Convention

What is a 'trust' for Convention purposes?

102.52 The Convention seeks to lay down the key characteristics of a trust. This is not intended as an exhaustive statement of its characteristics, still less a definition. The Convention is not limited to the common law trust and is also intended to cover civil law institutions which exhibit certain core characteristics of the trust as a special entity but not a juristic person[1]. Structurally similar institutions to the common law trust, such as exist in States such as Argentina, Egypt, Ethiopia, Israel, Japan, Liechtenstein[2], Louisiana, Panama, Peru, Quebec and Venezuela may very well be 'trusts' for the purposes of the Convention[3].

¹ So the institution must not have legal personality enabling it to own property.

²   See J Niegel (2004) 10(6) Trusts and Trustees 19.
³   See further M Graziadei, U Mattei and L Smith (eds) *Commercial Trusts in European Private Law* (2005); Waters (2004) 11(4) J Int Pl 199, 223.

102.53 The first paragraph of Article 2 explains that a trust is a relationship created inter vivos or on death by which a settlor places assets under the control of a trustee for a beneficiary. However, it also makes clear that purpose trusts shall be included within the Convention's scheme. Whilst some provision for purpose trusts was necessary to cover Scots purpose trusts, which may be valid even if non-charitable, and a limited number of anomalous testamentary purpose trusts permitted by English and many American States' laws, the unrestricted scope of this provision means that the Convention can apply to non-charitable purpose trusts, even though such trusts are usually invalid in English domestic law¹.

¹   See para 8.144 ff; also the discussion of public policy and of the recognition of trusts at para 102.204 ff below.

102.54 Article 2 does not refer to the fiduciary nature of trusteeship since civil law lawyers argued the word 'fiduciary' as adjective or noun could not meaningfully be translated into their legal language. Although, to an English or other trust lawyer, fiduciary duties inevitably are implicit in the fact that the trustee holds assets of another person for the benefit of another, this is not expressed as an essential characteristic of a Convention 'trust'.

102.55 Where a settlor declares himself as trustee, so switching particular assets from his private property to fiduciary property, it is doubtful whether it can be said that 'assets have been placed under the control of a trustee' within the meaning of Article 2. This might suggest that declarations of trust are excluded from the Convention¹. However, there seems to be no reason why a declaration by the settlor of himself as trustee should be excluded; provided that the trust is validly created², its applicable law and its entitlement to recognition should be identical to that of a trust created by transfer of assets to a trustee. Accordingly, it is suggested that trusts created by the declarations of the settlor of himself as trustee do fall within the Convention, at least once they have been 'launched'³.

¹   See the United Kingdom delegate's remarks: *Actes et Documents* 237), and M Lupoi *Trusts: a Comparative Study*, 335. See also M Lupoi in *The Reform of Property Law* (1997) Ashgate, Aldershot, 222, 228.
²   Which is a preliminary matter falling outside the scope of the Convention, discussed below.
³   M Lupoi also argues that, 'On balance, the arguments in favour of extending the Convention to include self-declared trusts seem to me to be convincing': *Trusts: a Comparative Study*, 335.

102.56 Article 2(2)(a) emphasises that trust assets constitute a separate fund which is not part of the trustee's own private estate or patrimony. It is not necessary that the concept of equitable ownership be known in a legal system for it to have a 'trust' within the meaning of the Convention¹. Accordingly, the trusts of India, Scotland, South Africa, Liechtenstein, Quebec² and Japan fall within the Convention.

¹ For example, ring-fenced funds immune from the claims of the owner's creditors and heirs. See D Hayton (ed) *Modern International Developments in Trust Law*, Chapter 2, p 23 and D Hayton (ed) *Extending the Boundaries of Trusts and Similar Ring-Fenced Funds* (2002) Kluwer Law International, pp. 1–133.
² Title to the assets has to be vested in the trustee, the trust not being a legal person.

102.57 Sub-paragraph (b) of Article 2(2) is designed to make clear that title to the trust assets need not necessarily be held by the trustee, provided that it is held 'in the name of another person to hold on behalf of the trustee', as where legal title to shares is vested in a custodian (although the equitable title therein is vested in the trustee). The danger is that the sub-paragraph appears at first sight to be broad enough to cover some forms of agency or mandate (although there is no provision in the Convention dealing with its relationship to the earlier Hague Convention on Agency) eg the transfer by an owner to an agent of control (but not ownership) of assets for the benefit of the owner and others¹. This risk is exacerbated by Article 2(1) referring only to assets being placed under the 'control' of the trustee. The word 'ownership' is not used. Indeed, it has been suggested that if this makes Article 2 cover agency-management as well as ownership-management, then 'non-trust' States within the meaning of the Convention are extremely rare, or even non-existent², in which case there is no scope for the application of Article 13 applicable only where significant elements are more closely connected with non-trust States. Thus, the Convention should be construed as concerned with ownership management and not agency management, so covering situations where the trustee owns what laymen regard as trust assets directly or indirectly via a nominee (eg in the case of shares), so that the assets do not form part of his own private estate³. Accordingly, agency and mandate should fall outside the scope of the Convention.

¹ See also D Hayton, S Kortmann & R Verhagen *Principles of European Trusts Law* (1999) Kluwer Law International, pp. 39–40 and D Hayton (2000) 8 J Int Corp P 159, 167.
² M Lupoi (1995) 1(3) Trusts and Trustees 15. He describes Italy as a trust State under the terms of Article 2 and argues that the shapeless trust can be found 'from Ecuador to Russia to the Philippines.'
³ D Hayton (2000) 11 KCLJ 48, 53.

102.58 Indeed, it is noteworthy that by sub-paragraph (a) 'the assets constitute a separate fund and are not a part of the trustee's own estate', which is not needed at all if the assets remain owned by the owner and have not become owned by the trustee. Furthermore, by sub-paragraph (b) 'title to the trust assets stands in the name of the trustee *or* in another person *on behalf of the trustee*'. However, where assets are owned by O, so that he has title to them, but he places them under the control of an agent, A, this is surely not a case where title is in the name of O '*on behalf of*' A: title is vested in O on behalf of O, while control is vested in A on behalf of O.

102.59 Sub-paragraph (c) of Article 2(2) of the Convention makes clear that a trustee is subject to any obligations specified in the trust instrument, and also to duties imposed on him by law. It does not say to whom he is accountable, although under orthodox English trust law there is accountability to the beneficiaries (or the Attorney-General or the Charity Commission for charitable purpose trusts) and not the settlor once he has dropped out of the picture, having completed his gift to the trustee. There seems no good reason, however, why a foreign trust, like an American charitable trust or a Chinese or Liechtenstein trust, should not be covered by the Convention merely because the trustee was accountable to the settlor[1]. This, though, runs the serious risk that the trust will be viewed as nothing but a sham unless, in addition, the trustee is also accountable to the beneficiaries. A non-charitable purpose trust which specifies an 'enforcer' to uphold the terms of the trust, such as is permitted in a number of offshore States, should fall within Article 2.

1   M Lupoi asks 'How could an "institution" be "analogous" to the Anglo-Saxon trust if the trustee were to be accountable to the "settlor"?' (1995) 1(3) Trusts and Trustees 15, 16, but so long as there is also accountability to other enforcers there are sufficient obligations to persons other than the settlor for there to be a proper trust within Article 2.

102.60 The final paragraph of Article 2 indicates that a trustee may himself be a beneficiary, although not the sole beneficiary. Equally, the settlor may be a beneficiary of the trust. The 'reservation by the settlor of certain rights and powers'[1] is also permitted. The Convention does not say which rights they are. To the extent that the assets remain effectively under the control of the settlor, the trust should be treated as a sham trust, not for the designated beneficiaries but for the settlor alone.

1   See the extensive powers permitted by some offshore jurisdictions discussed by D W M Waters in D Hayton *Extending the Boundaries of Trusts and Similar Ring-Fenced Funds*, pp. 243–290.

What types of trust are governed by the Hague Convention?

EVIDENCED IN WRITING

102.61 Article 3 states that the Convention applies only to 'trusts created voluntarily and evidenced in writing'. A trust created orally may fall within the Convention, if it is subsequently evidenced in writing as, indeed, is required for trusts of land under s 53(1)(b) of the Law of Property Act 1925 and as envisaged by Article 5(6) of the Brussels Convention on Jurisdiction and Enforcement of Judgments which was the inspiration for Article 3 of the Trusts Convention[1] .It appears that a trust can be sufficiently 'evidenced in writing' even if it has not been signed by the settlor. Indeed, it seems that the trustee could put the terms of an orally declared trust in writing and that this would suffice to bring it within the Convention's ambit. That said, 'evidenced in writing' must mean sufficiently evidenced to represent the will of the settlor. Whilst it cannot be said that the written evidence of the trust *must* be signed by any particular party, there must be sufficient evidence that the settlor intended to create the trust. This should require more than the mere existence of a written document eg signed only by the claimant, stating that fact. In practice, it is best for the written instrument to be signed by the settlor or, failing him, by the trustee.

1   As von Overbeck points out in paragraph 52 of his Report. See now Art. 5(6) of Regulation (EC) No 44/2001 of 22 December 2000 ('the Brussels I Regulation') which is needed where it is sought to sue a trustee domiciled in one Member State in another Member State, not where a person is being sued in the Member State where he is domiciled under the basic jurisdictional rule in Art 2.1.

102.62 A trust which satisfies the formality requirements continues to fall within the Convention, even if affected by a later court decision replacing a trustee or varying the trust[1].

1   Von Overbeck, para 50, p 380.

102.63 Where a party transfers additional assets to be held on the terms of a pre-existing trust which was created and evidenced in writing, it is not certain whether this has also to be evidenced in writing at some stage eg in the trust accounts. To err on the side of caution, it is wise for the fact that the transferee of these additional assets is intended to hold them on trust also to be evidenced in writing eg provided by the settlor or the trustee at the time of the transfer.

VOLUNTARY TRUSTS

102.64 The trust must reflect the will of the settlor (even if he did not expressly declare and constitute that trust). Trusts voluntarily created as a means of discharging an obligation imposed by law, eg to discharge a maintenance obligation, are not, however, excluded[1]. Moreover, once there is an expressly created voluntary trust evidenced in writing, subsequent actions of the court will not lead to the trust's exclusion, eg where the court intervenes to appoint a trustee[2] or to vary trusts pursuant to powers under the Matrimonial Causes Act 1973 or the Variation of Trusts Act 1958, or to use the cy-près doctrine in the case of charitable purpose trusts.

1   Von Overbeck, para 49, p 380.
2   Von Overbeck, para 50, p 380.

102.65 The terms 'trusts created voluntarily' or 'voluntary trusts' are new open-textured terms that are not terms of art known to trust lawyers, so creating difficulties in ascertaining the position of 'resulting trusts' and 'constructive trusts'. These types of trusts in English trust law (the basis for Commonwealth trust laws) do not have to satisfy the formalities required of 'express trusts'. Resulting and constructive trusts arise in well-known circumstances taken for granted by pragmatic trust lawyers whose language has been contradictory in referring to these trusts variously as arising by law or by operation of law or arising from presumed intention or implied intention or an express, but inadequately evidenced, intention or operating as an incident of an express trust or in order to remedy some wrongdoing 'in equity' as opposed to 'at law'. Part of this confusion flowed from differences within the categories. The main problem, however, was the lack of analysis of the events to which different types of resulting trusts and of constructive trusts are a response, such analysis now being found in Division 3 hereof, but non-existent when the Trusts Convention was prepared in 1982–84 and when there were fears about judicial trusts imposed by courts (based on North American developments concerning 'remedial'– as opposed to traditional or institutional – trusts[1]).

[1]   See para 28.15 above.

102.66   It seems the intention of the drafting committee was to use language that provided leeway for extending the scope of the Convention as persons became more comfortable with the concept of trusts, but which prima facie excluded constructive trusts[1]. Little thought was given to resulting trusts except for considering that resulting trusts arising from failure of express trusts should be covered by the Convention[2]. Nowadays, greater familiarity with the trust concept and more detailed analysis of the events giving rise to different types of resulting and constructive trusts may lead courts to expand the scope of the 'accordion' language used in Article 3, particularly when most resulting or constructive trusts can be a response to voluntary acts of free will of the settlor and the trustee.

[1]   Von Overbeck para 49.
[2]   Von Overbeck, para 51.

RESULTING TRUSTS

102.67   Once there has been an express declaration of trust created or evidenced in writing so as to fall within the Convention, the Convention must also extend to the resulting trusts that arise when express trusts fail to deal completely with the beneficial interest in the trust fund[1]. It makes sense that the law governing an express trust and any failure thereof should determine the effect of such failure as giving rise to a resulting trust[2].

[1]   Von Overbeck, para 51, pp. 380–381.
[2]   R Stevens, 'Resulting Trusts in the Conflict of Laws' in P Birks and F Rose (eds) *Restitution and Equity, Volume 1: Resulting Trusts and Equitable Compensation* (2000) Mansfield Press, London, pp. 147, 157.

102.68   The position with regard to purchase money resulting trusts[1], such as arise where a jointly purchased property is registered in the name of one party only, is less clear. Suppose S and T jointly purchase a house in England, which is conveyed into T's sole name. T then sells the house and reinvests the proceeds of sale in a villa situated in Civilopia (a Contracting State to The Hague Convention and an EU Member State). If T remains domiciled in England S can have an English court hold that T is trustee of an English resulting trust of half the English house for S, then half the proceeds of sale and then half the villa. T then flees England, leaving no English assets and having only Civilopian assets If a Civilopian court was faced with a claim by S to be recognised as a beneficiary under this resulting trust, should Civilopia recognise the trust under the Convention? It can be argued that the trust was created 'voluntarily', in the sense that it is presumed to reflect the settlor's intention in contributing to the purchase price as purchaser of half the house bought in T's name. The difficulty is that the resulting trust does not appear itself to be 'evidenced in writing'[2], but if an English court has already declared the terms of the resulting trust, it could be said that the English court's declaration is *itself* the necessary written element that conclusively evidences a voluntarily created trust, so that its recognition in Civilopia should fall within the Convention[3]. It is a straightforward matter and why should the open-textured language of the Convention not be used to further a proper and just solution against a wrongdoer? In any event, the judgment that T holds half the villa for S should be recognised and enforced under the Brussels 1 Regulation.

[1]   The questions whether the Recognition of Trusts Act 1987 extends to these resulting trusts was left open by Peter Gibson LJ in *Lightning v Lightning Electrical Contractors Ltd [1998] NPC 71*. See para 31.1 ff on these trusts.
[2]   And Article 3 states that the trust in issue must be both created voluntarily and evidenced in writing.
[3]   D Hayton (1987) 36 ICLQ 260 at 264;cf Case C–294/92 *Webb v Webb* [1994] ECR I–1717, [1994] QB 696.

102.69 However, if T had bought the Civilopian villa as a residence and so become domiciled there for the purposes of the Brussels 1 Regulation, then S has problems because the English court has no jurisdiction unless Article 5(6) thereof applies. This allows a defendant domiciled in Civilopia to be sued as settlor or trustee 'of a trust created by the operation of a statute, or by a written instrument, or created orally and evidenced in writing, in the courts of the Member State in which the trust is domiciled'. The first hurdle relates to the domicile of the trust which the Regulation leaves to each Member State to determine. By UK law the trust is domiciled in a part of the UK only if the system of law of that part is the system of law with which the trust has its closest and most real connection[1]. The governing birth law was English as was the land, while Civilopia has no municipal trust law[2], so this hurdle can be overcome. By operation of law all beneficially co-owned land is held on trust for the beneficial co-owners[3], though the critical identity of such co-owners in the S-T purchase money relationship cannot be ascertained by written evidence until the English court, having heard oral evidence, declares that T holds the house on the statutory trusts for S and T equally. Thus, it appears that the English court cannot take jurisdiction to hear the matter.

[1]   SI 2001/3929, Sch 1, para 12.
[2]   As Article 5 of the Trusts Convention recognises,a law of a non-trust State could be that of closest connection , but English law seems more apt.
[3]   Law of Property Act 1925 ss 34,36 as amended by Trusts of Land and Appointment of Trustees Act 1996; *Bull v Bull* [1955] 1 QB 234, para 31.2 above.

102.70 If S therefore decides to sue T in Civilopia where T is domiciled (and which has implemented the Trusts Convention) in order to establish the existence of the trust, his claim will fail as outside Article 3,not being evidenced in any writing save his own, which self-serving evidence is not adequate. Query whether the Civilopian court would be prepared to prevent the unjust enrichment of T by using rules of its own that are more favourable than those under the Convention (as encouraged by Article 14 of the Convention).

CONSTRUCTIVE TRUSTS

102.71 It is clear that the personal remedy imposed upon a third party involved in a breach of an express trust making him liable to account as a 'constructive trustee' and so pay compensation for losses or gains made as if he were an express trustee[1] cannot be within Article 3, since the Convention is concerned only with trusts of specific property as a ring-fenced fund and with the trustee-beneficiary relationship and the office and powers of trustees under article 8[2].

[1] See para 100.1 above.
[2] D Hayton (1987) 36 ICLQ 260 at 264.

102.72 In the case of the normal expressly declared trust which has been 'created voluntarily and evidenced in writing', then the trustee in accepting the office of trustee has voluntarily agreed to act exclusively in the best interests of his beneficiaries (and not himself) and to hold the trust fund (comprising the original trust assets, subsequently added assets and substituted assets[1]) for the beneficiaries. Assets substituted in authorised fashion for trust assets are held on the terms of the express trusts, as are substituted assets acquired for the trust in unauthorised fashion[2], and as are substituted assets that the trustee tried to acquire for himself so as to profit his private patrimony at the expense of the beneficiaries interested in the trust fund[3]. This is absolutely fundamental to the ring-fenced nature of trust assets from time to time comprised in the trust fund[4]. The crucial ring-fenced protection would be wholly illusory if the trustee-guardian of the fence could easily take trust assets outside the ring-fence and make them part of his private patrimony available for his private creditors eg by simply taking the proceeds of sale of trust assets into his private patrimony and buying assets for himself with such proceeds[5].

[1] See paras 1.1 and 33.3–33.5 above.
[2] Where the beneficiaries either retrospectively ratify the trustee's unauthorised conduct or claim the unauthorised assets as security for the personal liability of the trustee to pay compensation for the loss caused by his unauthorised conduct. See para 92.24 and Article 92(2).
[3] *Foskett v McKeown* [2001] 1 AC 102
[4] Note the use of 'fund' in Article 2(2)(a) and Article 11(2).
[5] Theoretically, as recognised in Article 11 para 3, by the introductory words 'In so far as the law applicable to a trust requires or provides' a very inefficient ,weak form of trust law could provide protection only for assets acquired by the trustee on behalf of the trust and not on behalf of himself: however, there would then be no protection against dishonest trustees, only against honest trustees who had the misfortune to become insolvent. One could justify this if under regulatory laws only licensed corporate financial bodies could act as trustees.

102.73 Analytically, such substituted assets acquired by the express trustee for his private patrimony are forthwith held on the terms of the express trusts[1], though, traditionally judges have reached this conclusion by speaking of the trustee holding such assets on constructive trust for the beneficiaries under the express trust. Nevertheless, for the crucial vindication of the expressly created ring-fenced trust fund such trusts of substituted assets must fall within the Convention, whether regarded strictly as express trusts or loosely as constructive trusts.

1   *Foskett v McKeown* [2001] 1 AC 102 at 110 and 127, emphasising the continuing
    equitable interest of the beneficiaries in the assets from time to time comprising the trust
    fund (a life policy bought privately for the trustee with premiums paid with trust money,
    and the substantial policy moneys paid out on the trustee's death, when matters came to
    light); Lord Millett in 'Proprietary Restitution' in S Degeling & J Edelman (eds) *Equity in
    Commercial Law* (2005) pp. 315–316 stating that wrongfully substituted assets are not
    held on constructive trust but "continue to be held on the same trusts throughout. If the
    claimant was the beneficiary under an express trust, the substituted assets are held on the
    same express trusts."

102.74 Indeed, sub-paragraph (d) of paragraph 2 in Article 11 requires it to
be possible to recover trust assets *from the trustee* if he has mingled them with
his own assets (eg bought a painting for himself, the purchase price being
provided half with trust money and half his own money) or if he has alienated
trust assets (eg sold them for 1million Euros in order to buy a flat purportedly
for himself with the 1 million, but actually as a traced substituted asset
comprised in the trust fund).

102.75 It is noteworthy, however, that when the trustee wrongfully transfers
trust assets *to a third party* (without receiving anything in return to be treated
as a substituted trust asset) the effect of such transfer of title to property (and
of the receipt of the proceeds of sale of such property) is determined according
to the choice of law rules of the forum[1], which will normally designate the lex
situs as the governing law. While a common law lex situs[2] will find the third
party to be bound by the equitable proprietary interests of the beneficiaries,
and so to be a constructive trustee of the property for those beneficiaries
unless the third party is a bona fide purchaser for value (or protected by
special statutory provisions), it seems likely that other jurisdictions not
knowing equitable proprietary interests will not find there to be a constructive
trust[3]. Where a common law lex situs recognises equitable interests and finds
a third party to be bound by those interests, then it will make the necessary
order for the protection of those prior interests eg an order that the third
party transfer the property to a new trustee who has replaced the wrongdoing
trustee.

1   See Articles 11(3) (d) and 15(d); paras 102.198 and 102.215 below.
2   Or a mixed jurisdiction having trusts and constructive trusts like Jersey or Guernsey: *Nabb
    Brothers Ltd v Lloyd's Bank International (Guernsey) Ltd* [2005] EWHC 405 (Ch), [2005]
    IL Pr 506.
3   See F Noseda (2005) 20 (1) Tru LI 3 at 5. However, the third party may be liable to pay
    compensation to prevent his unjust enrichment or, if knowingly involved in a scheme to
    defraud the beneficiaries, may have to return the property. Further see para 102.217 below.

102.76 Moving on from the core characteristics of an express trust of a fund
in the hands of a trustee, to specific types of constructive trust, a type of
constructive trust within the scope of Article 3 arises where duly executed
written mutual wills are made[1]. There will be written documentation which
reflects the voluntary intention of the parties to be contractually bound by the
mutual wills and, if necessary, to have them enforced by a constructive trust[2].

1   M Lupoi Trusts: a Comparative Study, 342–343.
2   Generally see para 33.53 ff.

102.77   Also, in the case of a specifically enforceable written contract for the purchase of English land which gives rise to a constructive trust of the land (and the proceeds of a wrongful sale[1]), there can probably be said to be a voluntarily created trust evidenced in writing[2]. The parties are taken to intend the inevitable legal consequences of their voluntary actions, just as a person can speak prose without knowing it or create a trust without knowing it.

1   *Lake v Bayliss* [1974] 2 All ER 1114 and para 36.1 ff.
2   J Harris, The Hague Trusts Convention, p 128.

102.78   Indeed, a secret testamentary trust (especially if half-secret) should also fall within the Convention where a testator leaves property by will to T, but only because T had agreed with him to hold the property after his death for X, and there is sufficient written evidence provided by him or T to X or, perhaps, a written court decision[1], to establish that T holds the property on constructive trust for X[2].

1   See paras 102.68–102.69 above and para 102.29 below.
2   Generally see para 12.78 ff.

102.79   Where the sole owner of a house, T, voluntarily intends there to be a trust of the family home for himself and his cohabitant, C, which cannot take effect as an express trust because of a failure to comply with the requisite statutory formalities (under s 53(1)(b) of the Law of Property Act 1925), the court intervenes to vindicate the unenforceable but valid express trust by imposing a common intention constructive trust[1], so as to prevent T from fraudulently retaining the property wholly for himself after C's detrimental reliance[2]. This constructive trust clearly reflects T's intentions (whether subjective or as objectively reasonably perceived by the misled C), and the court order, that declares that T has held on trust for T and C since C's detrimental reliance on T's intention to hold on trust for C, can be regarded as evidence of the pre-existing trust. The fact that T changes his mind does not alter the fact that originally he voluntarily intended to become a trustee of his house. What if T sells the house and buys a villa in Civilopia or shares in a Civilopian company?

1   Generally see para 35.9 ff.
2   D Hayton (1987) 36 ICLQ 260, 264; see also P Matthews (1995) 1 Trusts and Trustees 7.

102.80   C can bring an action in the English court against T domiciled in England and obtain the court decree that can be regarded as conclusive evidence of the trust that T voluntarily created before changing his mind. C can then have her rights under the trust recognised and enforced under the Brussels 1 Regulation.However, if T had become domiciled in Civilopia or another EU State, then C could make no claim in England against him and would therefore have great difficulty in trying to bring a successful claim in Civilopia or another EU State when the trust would be outside the Convention[1].

1   See paras 102.69–102.70 above.

102.81 Leaving aside the EU Regulation and focusing only on the Trusts Convention it can be argued that the common intention constructive trust should not be regarded as 'created voluntarily' because it effectively acts as a *substitute* for an express trust and this constructive trust is not a trust *itself* created voluntarily[1], but one imposed by law, the defendant fighting against the trust all the way until final judgment against him.

1   See J Harris The Hague Trusts Convention, 128–134.

102.82 At this stage, an important point of principle arises. If evidence that a trust was created voluntarily can be supplied by a court decree that the trust exists, the scope of Article 3 is very wide, so only trusts imposed regardless of the intention of the parties should be excluded from Article 3 eg constructive trusts arising out of a person killing another to obtain a benefit that could not otherwise have been obtained[1].Thus the constructive trust imposed in the case of oral testamentary secret trusts and family home constructive trusts are both within the Convention. On the other hand, it can be argued that Article 3 requires the instant trust *itself* to have been both created voluntarily and evidenced in writing. The constructive trusts considered here are imposed to reflect the ascertained intentions of the parties, but they are not themselves created voluntarily by the objecting settlor. They are imposed by the court, albeit as a result of the settlor's conduct which is the *causa sine qua non* for the retrospective declaration of the court.

1   See para 35.79 above. The constructive trust imposed on a bribe taken by the Head of the Anti-Corruption Crime Squad can be said to arise voluntarily, because if asked by an officious bystander 'Can the officer take bribes not to prosecute corrupt people?'the officer and his employer would forthwith reply 'Of course not!'.

102.83 Clearly, the courts have much leeway in interpreting Article 3. On balance, in order to make persons, who have voluntarily agreed to hold property for the benefit of others, honour their agreement, and to provide justifiable protection to vulnerable persons, a trust should fall within the Convention so long as the trust in some sense reflects a voluntary undertaking and is sufficiently evidenced in some writing (and what better evidence for a court than a court decree of a court very much experienced in trust matters)[1].

1   But see J Harris *The Hague Trusts Convention*, 128–34, preferring a more literal and narrower construction of the Convention's scope. Because of fear of a narrow interpretation of the ambit of the Recognition of Trusts Act 1987, s 1(2) paras 102.39 and 102.86 is broad.

102.84 In EU countries – and Lugano Convention countries – an English resulting or constructive trust decree against a defendant 'domiciled' in England will, in any event, be recognised and enforced in those countries. However, it will not be possible for there to be any such decree of an English court against a person as a settlor or trustee domiciled elsewhere in the EU – or EFTA – in relation to an English domiciled trust, because no jurisdiction exists unless the trust was 'created by the operation of a statute, or by a written instrument, or created orally and evidenced in writing'[1]. It is odd that it is so easy in the 21st century for a defendant dramatically to improve his position by moving from one EU country to another unless EU countries are going to develop their own laws to cover such situations.

[1] Regulation Art 5(6).

STATUTORY TRUSTS

102.85 Statutory trusts, such as those which arise upon a person's intestacy or the co-purchase of land[1], and which are automatically triggered by certain scenarios, appear to be excluded from the Convention because not 'voluntarily' created. Although the settlor has voluntarily chosen not to make a will or to be a co-purchaser, the statutory trust is imposed without his consent: he may very well be ignorant that a trust would arise.

[1]   Administration of Estates Act 1925, s 33; Law of Property Act 1925 ss 34–36; Trusts of Land and Appointment of Trustees Act 1996. A purchase money resulting trust could, however, fall within the Convention: see para 102.68 above.

EXTENDED SCOPE OF THE CONVENTION IN THE UNITED KINGDOM

102.86 Article 20(1) allows a State to extend the ambit of the Convention. Those States which are comfortable with applying the Convention's rules to trusts declared[1] by judicial decision are free to do so[2]; indeed, a sovereign State is free to extend the Convention within its own boundaries as it wishes, eg to cover any trusts arising under its own or a foreign law that would not otherwise fall within the Convention. In the United Kingdom[3], s 1(2) of the Recognition of Trusts Act 1987 states that:

> 'Those provisions [of the Convention] shall, so far as applicable, have effect not only in relation to the trusts described in Articles 2 and 3 of the Convention but also in relation to any other trusts of property arising under the law of any part of the United Kingdom or by virtue of a judicial decision whether in the United Kingdom or elsewhere.'

[1]   Contrast the French 'créés'. The English version suggests that Convention may be extended to trust whose existence is affirmed by the court; the French version tends to suggest that the trust must be *imposed* by the court.
[2]   Luxembourg extended the scope of the Convention upon its ratification.
[3]   In Canada, '... all the ... provinces that have implemented the Convention have exercised the option in the Convention to extend its application to trusts created by virtue of judicial decision, including constructive trusts and resulting trusts.' J Walker, *Castel & Walker, Canadian Conflict of Laws*, 6th ed (2005) (Markham, Ontario, LexisNexis Canada Inc.) , pp. 28–8.

102.87 For the UK this makes academic much of the above debate about which trusts should fall within Article 3 of the Convention. In so far as the Convention has been extended to cover resulting and constructive trusts, one would normally focus upon 'the law with which it is most closely connected'[1], so it is very curious that the Hague Convention's choice of law rules receive almost no discussion in the few English cases where the existence of a constructive trust in a transnational context has been at issue[2]. However, where the constructive trust inevitably applies to the property from time to time representing the original trust property held under an express trust, the law governing the latter must govern the former, just as the law governing property held on a resulting trust upon failure of all or part of an express trust must be the same as the law governing the express trust. In the case of purchase resulting trusts of property the lex situs should be the key factor.

1   J Walker, *Castel & Walker, Canadian Conflict of Laws*, 6th ed, pp. 28–14; save, of course, in the rare case where an express or implied choice of law can be found (an example might be a purported express trust which contained a choice of law clause for English law, where the trust failed for want of formalities, but where equity stepped in to impose a trust to prevent a statute being used as a cloak for fraud).

2   For example, *El Ajou v Dollar Land Holdings plc* [1993] 3 All ER 717 (reversed on different grounds: [1994] 2 All E.R. 685); *Arab Monetary Fund v Hashim (No 9)*, Times, 11 October, 1994; *Trustor AB v Smallbone*, (9 May 2000, unreported), CA; *Kuwait Oil Tanker v Al Bader* [2000] 2 All ER (Comm) 271; *Grupo Torras SA v Al Sabah* [2001] CLC. 221 (CA); *Barros Mattos Jnr v Macdaniels Ltd* [2005] EWHC 1323, [2005] I.L. Pr. 630. In *Arab Monetary Fund v Hashim (No 9)*, Chadwick J remarked that '[I]n cases involving a foreign element in which an English court is asked to treat a defendant as a constructive trustee of assets which he has acquired through misuses of his powers, the relevant questions are: (i) what is the proper law which governs the relationship between the defendant and the person for whose benefit those powers have been conferred; (ii) what, under that law, are the duties to which the defendant is subject in relation to those powers; (iii) is the nature of those duties such that they would be regarded by an English court as fiduciary duties; and (iv) if so, is it unconscionable for the defendant to retain those assets.' See further *Dicey, Morris and Collins*, pp. 1327–8.

TRUSTS ARISING UNDER THE LAW OF A PART OF THE UNITED KINGDOM

102.88 The Convention applies to 'any other trusts of property arising under the law of any part of the United Kingdom'[1]. This creates something of a paradox since until one knows what choice of law rules to apply to the trust, one cannot know if it is governed by the law of a part of the United Kingdom; but one cannot know which choice of law rules to apply until one knows whether the Convention applies or not. Accordingly, the extension must apply if it *appears* that the law of a part of the United Kingdom is *putatively* applicable.

1   This also means that the Convention rules will apply to disputes solely between the application of English and Scottish law.

102.89–102.99 Statutory trusts such as those arising on intestacy or the co-purchase of land clearly are 'trusts arising under the law of any part of the UK'.

102.100 As Lord Browne-Wilkinson points out in *Westdeutsche Landesbank v Islington Borough Council*[1], 'Under an institutional constructive trust the trust arises by operation of law as from the date of the circumstances which give rise to it: the function of the court is merely to declare that such trust has arisen in the past'. Thus institutional constructive trusts of property – and resulting trusts – which are declared to have arisen under the law of any part of the UK are covered by s 1(2) of the 1987 Act to the extent not already covered by Article 3 of the Convention.

1   [1996] AC 669 at 716.

TRUSTS 'ARISING' BY JUDICIAL DECISION IN ANY LEGAL SYSTEM

102.101 It is easy to see that 'statutory jurisdiction trusts'[1] are covered by this provision. Hence, if an English or foreign court were to create a new trust of property pursuant to a divorce jurisdiction or a Mental Health Act jurisdiction or a statutory jurisdiction for damages for personal injuries of infants, such a trust would fall within the Act.

1   These are 'trusts created pursuant to a court order made under a statutory jurisdiction and dealing with unique factual circumstances ...': D Hayton (1987) 36 ICLQ 260, 266.

102.102 The question then needing to be answered is whether constructive or resulting trusts of property not arising under the law of a part of the UK but under some foreign law are trusts 'arising by virtue of a judicial decision' within s 1(2) (assuming they fall outside Article 3 as earlier discussed[1]). It has already been seen that, traditionally, in England resulting trusts and most constructive trusts of property are retrospectively confirmed or declared by the court as old trusts that arose earlier as a result of the law's view of the voluntary actions of relevant parties, rather than being new trusts arising by virtue of a judicial decision. Thus, if the foreign law responsible for the existence of a constructive or resulting trust of property operates on the same basis as English law, then s 1(2) and the Convention will be inapplicable[2]. It will then only be in respect of remedial constructive trusts (not yet part of English law)[3] that are first created and imposed by a court order that the Convention will apply.

1   See para 102.68 ff.
2   See R Stevens in F Rose (ed) *Restitution and The Conflict of Laws* (1995) Mansfield Press, Oxford, Chapter 5, pp. 216–218.
3   *Re Polly Peck International (No 5)* [1998] 3 All ER 812, CA; *Westdeutsche Landesbank v Islington London Borough Council* [1996] AC 669 at 716.

102.103 This strict literal approach[1] has the curious effect that trusts arising by virtue of a discretionary judicial decision are included within the Act, while the well-known institutional constructive and resulting trusts arising other than under the law of a part of the UK are excluded. Because it is odd so to discriminate against foreign constructive or resulting trusts and because Article 20, that underlies the enactment of s 1(2), refers to trusts 'declared' by judicial decision, it may well be that a broad purposive approach should then be taken to treat s 1(2) as a broad sweeping-up provision, so as to treat 'arising ... by virtue of a judicial decision' as covering 'declared or created': then foreign (as well as UK) constructive and resulting trusts will be covered.

1   Favoured by J Harris *The Hague Trust Convention*, pp. 145–147. See also A Chong (2005) 54 ICLQ 855.

Preliminary Matters Excluded from the Convention

The 'rocket' and the 'rocket launcher'

102.104 The Convention is applicable only to matters which concern the validity of the trust itself. However, for a trust to be brought into existence, it must be validly declared and constituted. When contained in a written instrument, that written instrument must itself be valid, both as to form and substance. When involving the transfer of property into the hands of the trustee, the property must have been validly transferred. When the type of trust in question can be created only by certain types of person, then the settlor must have the capacity to create the trust. Article 4 states that these preliminary matters are outside the scope of the Convention. 'The image employed was that of the launcher and the rocket; it will always be necessary to have a "launcher", for example a will, a gift or another act with legal effects, which then launches the "rocket", the trust. The preliminary act with legal effects, the "launcher", does not fall under the Convention's coverage.'[1]

1   Von Overbeck Report, para 53 at p 381. Professor Hayton introduced this analogy: see D McClean, 'Common Lawyers and The Hague Conference' in A Borras, A Bucher, T Struycken & M Verwilghen (eds) *E Pluribus Unum: Liber Amicorum Georges Droz* p 217.

102.105 The choice of law rules applicable to many of these 'rocket launching' matters are themselves highly uncertain. Moreover, it is difficult in some cases to determine precisely where the distinction between 'rocket-launcher' and 'rocket' should be drawn.

102.106 It is contended that the essential distinction to be drawn is between those rules which are applicable to *any* disposition of property and those which specifically affect the ability to create a trust of property. The former should be seen as 'rocket launching' preliminary matters outside the scope of the Convention; the latter as 'rocket' matters within the Convention's scope[1].

1   This view appears to be supported by the decision in *Tod v Barton* [2002] EWHC 264 (Ch), (2002) 4 ITELR 715), judgment of Lawrence Collins J.

102.107 It is possible to say that certain issues are clearly part of the rocket-launching process and outside the Convention. These include the transfer of property to trustees, the validity of a will as to form and substance and the capacity of the settlor to create the trust. But it is not possible to say that other, more specific legal rules, such as rules on forced heirship or rules against perpetuities, are or are not outside the Convention. In so far as they relate to the right to transfer property at all, they are outside; in so far as they relate to the creation of the trust structure, they are inside.

102.108 It is now necessary to look at some of the most important preliminary issues that might arise[1].

1   For more detailed coverage, see J Harris, 'Launching the Rocket: Capacity and the Creation of Inter Vivos Transnational Trusts', in J Glasson (ed) *International Trust Laws*, Chapter C2; J Harris *The Hague Trusts Convention*, Part 1; P Matthews (2002) 6(2) Edin. L.R. 2002, 176. See also *Dicey, Morris and Collins*, pp 1308–9. Sophisticated "rocket-launching" choice of law rules have been adopted in the British Virgin Islands: see the Trustee Ordinance 1961 (as amended; see in particular, the B.V.I. Trustee (Amendment) Act 2003), s. 83A; J Harris in J Glasson (ed) *International Trust Laws*, Chapter C2, pp 24–;31; A Lynton (2004) 10(4) Trusts and Trustees 18.

Capacity to create a trust

102.109 Capacity rules define a particular class of persons who by a given law cannot enter into a transaction into which other people generally may enter.

THE SETTLOR

102.110 The capacity of a settlor to transfer assets to the trustee is an issue which appears to fall outside the Hague Convention[1]. There is very little cogent authority on the choice of law rule governing the settlor's capacity to create a trust[2]. There is some support for application of the law of the settlor's domicile[3]. However, these cases are from a completely different era over 100 years ago and almost all are largely concerned with matrimonial capacity or marriage settlements.

1   'In the end the Commission did not expressly exclude general capacity, although a consensus emerged that this was not to be governed by the Convention, while the specific capacity to become a trustee was to be so governed': von Overbeck Report, para 59 at p 382.
2   At least outside the context of marriage settlements.
3   See *Sottomayor v De Barros* (1877) 3 PD 1, 5; *Re Cooke's Trusts* (1877) 56 LJ Ch 637, 639; *Cooper v Cooper* (1888) 13 App Cas 88, 99–100. See also *Viditz v O'Hagan* [1900] 2 Ch 87 (a case relied upon by the authors of *Lewin on Trusts* (17th edn), p 303). See also *Re Bankes* [1902] 2 Ch 333.

102.111 It is important to appreciate that there are in fact two distinct aspects to the capacity to create a trust: the capacity of the settlor to alienate property *at all* and the capacity of the settlor to create the trust structure with that property[1]. The first question arises because a settlor who seeks to transfer property to a trustee is disposing of his property no less than an owner who simply gives away or sells his property to another person absolutely. Since the alienation by the settlor ultimately affects title to property and since it is important that any decision on capacity be enforceable in the courts of the place where the property is located, it is suggested that the law of the place where the property is situated (lex situs) should apply to this first question[2], at least where the trust is to be created inter vivos[3].

1   This two staged approach has now been adopted in the British Virgin Islands: see the Trustee Ordinance 1961 (as amended; see in particular, the B.V.I. Trustee (Amendment) Act 2003), s. 83A.
2   But see *Black v Black's Trustees* 1950 SLT (Notes) 32, where the lex situs was applied only in respect of immovable trust property and not in respect of movable property.
3   In the case of testamentary trusts of movable property, it is suggested that the lex successionis, the law of the deceased's domicile at death should be applied, as this is consistent with the law applied to the essential validity of testamentary transfers of movables.

102.112 There is then a second question as to whether the settlor, who has capacity to alienate property according to the lex situs, has capacity to create the trust structure with that property. Here, it is suggested that there is a much stronger case for settlor autonomy. The restrictions upon a settlor seem legitimately targeted at the question whether he may dispose of property at all, not whether he may dispose thereof on trust[1]. Moreover, use of any other law on this second question might lead to a trust failing because the law in question does not know the trust concept at all.

[1]   A view supported by P Nygh and M Davies *Conflict of Laws in Australia* (7th edn, 2002) Butterworths, Australia, p 627.

102.113 How should this test apply if the settlor simply declares himself trustee of his property? Arguably, he has not alienated his legal title, so the first question above does not apply[1].The settlor has merely created the trust structure with the property, which, on the view advocated here, would be a second question issue, to be resolved by the chosen law. However, if the first step of asking whether the settlor has capacity to alienate his property is not taken where declarations of trust are concerned, the effect might be the equitable alienation of property of which the settlor may not dispose *at all* according to the lex situs. Rather, it is suggested that, in the case of the declaration of trust, one should ask (i) does the settlor have power to alienate *any* interest in his property by the lex situs; (ii) if so, does he have power to create a trust according to the proper law of the trust?

[1]   This is the approach that has been adopted in the British Virgin Islands for declarations of trusts, so that the law applicable to the trust alone applies: see the Trustee Ordinance 1961 (as amended), 83A(10).

102.114 In summary, the following choice of law is suggested as appropriate to determine the capacity of a settlor to create an inter vivos trust:

(1)   The capacity of a settlor to dispose of any property right inter vivos is governed by the lex situs at the time of the purported transfer[1].

(2)   The capacity of any settlor to create a trust of any property of which he may, according to rule (1), dispose is governed by the proper law of the trust[2].

[1]   For testamentary trusts of movables, the law of the deceased's last domicile should apply.
[2]   Which will normally be the law chosen by the settlor to govern the trust.

THE CAPACITY OF THE TRUSTEE

102.115 Article 8(2)(a) of the Convention states that the capacity of the intended trustee is governed by the law applicable to the trust[1]. However, it is suggested that this deals only with the specific issue of his capacity to act as trustee. The intended trustee must also have 'general' capacity to receive property at all[2].

[1]   See also von Overbeck, para 59, p 382.
[2]   An example of a 'general' property rule regulating capacity in England is the Trusts of Land and Appointment of Trustees Act 1996, s 1(1), Sch 1, which provides that a purported transfer of land to a minor is ineffective to pass legal title, but operates as a declaration that the land is to be held in trust for the minor.

102.116 Accordingly, the following choice of law rule is suggested:

(1)   The capacity of a 'trustee'[1] to receive any property right inter vivos[2] is governed by the lex situs at the time of the purported transfer.

(2)   The capacity of a 'trustee' to act as trustee of any property which he may, according to rule (1), receive is governed by the proper law of the trust.

[1]   Ie a putative trustee.
[2]   In the case of a testamentary disposition of movables, the law of the deceased's last domicile would apply.

THE CAPACITY OF THE BENEFICIARY

102.117 A putative beneficiary likewise requires capacity to receive property at all[1], and specifically to receive a benefit under a trust. Where a beneficiary lacks capacity in English domestic law, he will not normally be able to give a good receipt for trust capital and/or income and alternative arrangements will need to be made.

[1]   We are concerned here with restrictions which the law imposes on the receipt of a benefit by a person or class of persons, not with further restrictions which the trust instrument might expressly impose on a person as to when he may become entitled to an interest in possession.

102.118 It might appear that a beneficiary's capacity is a trusts specific issue, and should be subjected to the law governing the trust. However, since the governing law of the trust might allow the beneficiary to terminate the trust and claim the property absolutely, the lex situs is likely also to have a legitimate interest in the matter. It is submitted that the 'general' capacity of a beneficiary to receive any form of benefit under the trust should be determined by the lex situs. It is then suggested that the 'specific' question whether a person in principle entitled to take a benefit may do so in the capacity of a beneficiary under a trust (including the question of whether he is presently entitled to take a beneficial interest in possession under the trust) should be seen as a trusts specific matter for the law applicable to the trust.

102.119 Accordingly, the following choice of law rule is suggested:

(1)   The capacity of a person to receive property at all inter vivos[1] is determined by the lex situs at the time of the purported transfer of property to the trustee.

(2)   The capacity of a person who may, according to rule (1), receive property, to assert a beneficial interest under a trust, including the question of whether he is presently entitled to that benefit, is governed by the proper law of the trust.

[1]   In the case of a testamentary disposition of movables, the law of the deceased's last domicile would be applicable to this matter.

The vesting of property in the trustee

102.120 'Article 4 is intended to exclude from the Convention's scope of application both the substantive validity and the formal validity of the transfers which are preliminary to the creation of the trust.'[1] The question whether property has successfully been vested in the trustees is thus excluded from the Convention. This must be governed by the general choice of laws rules for the transfer of property, which will be set out below.

[1] Von Overbeck Report, para 55, p 382.

102.121 Technically, one could argue that two questions arise as to the passing of property: (i) the transfer of legal title to the trustee; (ii) the transfer of equitable title to the beneficiary. However, civil law systems know nothing of equitable title and, once legal title has validly been transferred to B, the 'rocket-launching' process is concluded. It follows that the sole question with which the lex situs should concern itself is whether legal title to an interest may be alienated. It should not be a reason to invalidate the rocket-launching process that the situs does not know the trust concept. The particular interest which the beneficiary acquires under the trust should be seen as an aspect of the relationship between trustee and beneficiary[1], and governed by the applicable law of the trust, as determined by the rules of The Hague Trusts Convention.

[1] Which Article 8(2)(g) states to be within the Convention's scope: para 102.175 below.

102.122 Where the settlor declares himself trustee of property, matters are less certain. Although there will be no transfer of legal title, there will still be the passing of a property right or of a ring-fenced right from the would-be settlor. It is suggested the question whether *any* property right capable of binding third parties has passed from the settlor should be governed by the lex situs, so as not to evade the application of that law to property matters[1]; but the question of the beneficial rights of the beneficiaries against the trustee should be determined by the proper law of the trust[2].

[1] But note that the authors of *Lewin on Trusts* (17th edn), p 288 disagree and take the view that as there is no transfer of legal title, there is no preliminary issue to be decided about any transfer. This is also the approach taken by in the British Virgin Islands: see the Trustee Ordinance 1961 (as amended), 83A(10).
[2] The lex situs should not apply to this question. If it did, a trust could fail simply because the lex situs does not know the concept of a trust. However, an equitable interest e g under an English trust may not be given full effect if a foreign lex situs of a transfer does not recognise beneficiaries as having a property right capable of binding third party recipients from a wrongdoing trustee.

CLASSIFICATION OF PROPERTY

102.123 For conflict of laws purposes, the distinction drawn in English domestic law between real and personal property is not used. Rather, a distinction is made between movable and immovable property. Within the former category, the law distinguishes between tangible and intangible property. It is the law of the situs of the property which decides whether that property is movable or immovable[1]. Where the situs is England, English law treats mortgages[2] and leases of land[3] as immovable property. The same is true for land subject to a trust for sale[4], at least prior to sale[5].

[1] *Re Berchtold* [1923] 1 Ch 192; *Philipson-Stow v IRC* [1961] AC 727.

2   *Re Hoyles* [1911] 1 Ch 179.
3   *Freke v Carbery* (1873) LR 16 Eq 461; *Pepin v Bruyère* [1902] 1 Ch 24.
4   *Re Berchtold* [1923] 1 Ch 192.
5   Interests in the proceeds of sale of land are not treated as immovable: *Re Piercy* [1895] 1 Ch 83.

102.124   In order to understand what we mean when we say that the transfer of legal title to the trustee should be governed by the lex situs, it is necessary to look at the various types of property in turn[1].

1   For more detailed discussion, see J Carruthers, *The Transfer of Property in the Conflict of Laws* (2005) Oxford University Press, Oxford.

IMMOVABLE PROPERTY

102.125   The lex situs applies to the essential validity[1] and formalities[2] necessary for a transfer of immovable property[3]. This is justified by the fact that the courts of the situs have exclusive control over land located within the jurisdiction. This makes it futile to decide a dispute other than the way that a judge in the courts of the situs would decide it, since any English order would otherwise probably be ineffective.

1   *Nelson v Bridport* (1846) 8 Beav 547.
2   *Adams v Clutterbuck* (1883) 10 QBD 403.
3   However, a contract to transfer an interest in land need not satisfy the formal requirements of the lex situs – *Re Smith, Lawrence v Kitson* [1916] 2 Ch 206. Article 9(2) of the Rome Convention states that a contract is formally valid if it satisfies the formal requirements of either the applicable law of the contract or the law of the place where either party was at the time of conclusion of the contract. Article 9(6) states that in the case of contracts for the sale of land, these formality rules still apply but are subject to 'the mandatory requirements of form of the law of the country where the property is situated if by that law those requirements are imposed irrespective of the country where the contract is concluded and irrespective of the law governing the contract.'

102.126   The doctrine of *renvoi* will also be applied here[1]. *Renvoi* essentially entails the English court seeking to decide a case using the substantive law that a judge in the courts of the situs would use. In other words, the whole of the law of the situs will apply, including its rules of private international law. If the law of the situs has its own choice of law rules which leads to the application of a different law, then an English court must apply the choice of law rule of the situs.

1   On which, see Dicey, Morris and Collins, Chapter 4; Cheshire and North, Chapter 5.

102.127   The doctrine of *renvoi* can lead to something of a logical paradox. Suppose that an English court has to determine title to land located in Utopia purportedly transferred by one English domiciliary to another. English choice of law rules point to the law of the situs, Utopian law. Suppose that on the facts a Utopian judge would apply the law of England to resolve the dispute[1]. Application of *renvoi* leads back to English law. But we know already that English choice of law rules refer to *Utopian* law. So which law should an English court apply? The answer is that it depends if Utopia *itself* has a doctrine of *renvoi*. If not, an English court should apply English law, since when Utopian law stated that English law should apply, it meant simply the *domestic* law of England, ignoring its choice of law rules. This is known as single *renvoi*[2]. However, if Utopia *itself* has a doctrine of *renvoi* (or, to put it another way, when Utopian law stated that English law should apply, it meant all of English law, including its choice of law rules), the matter is sent back to Utopian law and it is that law which an English court should apply. This is known as double *renvoi*[3].

[1]   This might be because it applies the law of the domicile, where buyer and seller are domiciled in the same State.
[2]   See *Re Duke of Wellington* [1947] Ch 506.
[3]   See *Re Annesley* [1926] Ch 692.

102.128   Succession to immovables is also governed by the lex situs[1]. The doctrine of *renvoi* is also applicable to succession to immovables[2].

[1]   *Nelson v Bridport* (1846) 8 Beav 547; *Freke v Carbery* (1873) LR 16 Eq 461; *Duncan v Lawson* (1889) 41 Ch D 394; *Re Ross* [1930] 1 Ch 377. On the question of reform, see the *Green Paper on Succession and Wills* COM/2005/0065 Final; see also D Hayton (2005) 66 T.E.L. & T.J. 11; H Dörner and P Lagarde, *Conflicts of Law of Succession in the European Union: Perspectives for Harmonisation*, available at http://www.dnoti.de/arbeitshilfen.htm#Familienrecht.
[2]   *Re Ross* [1930] 1 Ch 377; *Re Duke of Wellington* [1947] Ch 506. The exception is formal validity, where the application of *renvoi* is excluded by Wills Act 1963, s 6(1).

TANGIBLE MOVABLE PROPERTY

102.129   Individual[1] transfers of tangible movable property inter vivos are governed by the lex situs. This means the law of the place where the property was located at the time of the last purported transfer of that property[2]. There are a few exceptions to this rule, such as (a) where goods are in transit, with a casual or unknown presence[3]; (b) where the application of the lex situs is contrary to English public policy; (c) where an English statute prescribes the mandatory application of English law.

[1]   Special rules apply to general assignments on bankruptcy, which are normally governed by the law of the domicile of the bankrupt: *Dicey, Morris and Collins*, Chapter 31.
[2]   *Cammell v Sewell* (1858) 3 H & N 617; *Winkworth v Christie* [1980] Ch 496.
[3]   *Winkworth v Christie* [1980] Ch 496 at 501. For the applicable law in such a case, see *Cheshire and North*, 951–2. It is likely that the law with which the transaction is objectively most closely connected will apply.

102.130   There is some support for the application of this doctrine in relation to inter vivos transfers of tangible movable property in *Winkworth v Christie*, where Slade J stated that he 'supposes' it would be open to a claimant to plead *renvoi*[1]. Application of the doctrine is also supported by *Dicey, Morris and Collins*[2]. The main reason for application of the lex situs is to decide a dispute as it would be decided by a judge in the courts of the situs for reasons of enforceability. For this reason, application of the doctrine of *renvoi* should be supported, since it means that an English court will apply the same law as a judge would in the courts of that State.

[1]   *Winkworth v Christie* [1980] Ch 496 at 514.
[2]   Dicey, Morris and Collins at 1167.

102.131 By contrast, transfers of tangible movable property on death are governed by the law of the deceased's domicile at the time of death[1]. It appears that the doctrine of *renvoi* is applicable[2]. Some writers argue that *renvoi* should not be applied to testamentary transfers of movables[3]. There is something to be said for this view, since a testator might expect that, in so far as the law of his domicile at death determines succession to his property, the domestic law of that State would apply. However, even here, *renvoi* has much to commend it, as it promotes unity of outcome. Without it, an English court might apply a different law from that which the courts of the testator's domicile would apply. This might mean that English courts take a different view as to who succeeds to property from the courts of the State of the deceased's domicile. It also provides an incentive for a claimant to forum-shop[4]. On balance, it is suggested that the doctrine of *renvoi* should be preserved in this area.

1   *Re Groos* [1915] 1 Ch 572; *Re Annesley* [1926] Ch 692; *Re Ross* [1930] 1 Ch 377. For a recent example of the determination of domicile in a succession context, see *Cyganik v Agulian* [2006] EWCA Civ 129; [2006] 1 FCR 406. On the question of reform, see footnote 1 at para 102.128.
2   *Re Annesley* [1926] Ch 692; *Re Ross* [1930] 1 Ch 377; *Re O'Keefe* [1940] Ch 124. The exception is formal validity, where the application of *renvoi* is excluded by Wills Act 1963, s 6(1).
3   *Lewin on Trusts* (17th edn) at p 284. The authors contend that, since the relevant authorities are at first instance, the Court of Appeal should restrict the application of *renvoi* to immovables.
4   Ie to choose a State to sue in where he thinks he will get the most favourable outcome on the merits.

INTANGIBLE MOVABLE PROPERTY

102.132 Although it might seem curious to ascribe a situs to intangible property, the law does exactly that[1]. Shares have their situs in the country where they may be dealt with between shareholder and company. So, if shares are only transferable by entry on the register, they are situated in the country where the register is kept[2]. If the company has a register in two countries, and the transfer may be registered in either, the situs is the place where in the ordinary course of business the transfer would be registered[3].

1   See also the more detailed rules in the British Virgin Islands' Trustee Ordinance 1961 (as amended), Schedule 1.
2   See eg *Brassard v Smith* [1925] AC 371; *Eric Beach Co v A-G for Ontario* [1930] AC 161; *R v Williams* [1942] AC 541; *Macmillan Inc v Bishopsgate Trust plc (No 3)* [1996] 1 WLR 387.
3   *Treasurer of Ontario v Blonde* [1947] AC 24; *Standard Chartered Bank Ltd v IRC* [1978] 3 All ER 644.

102.133 A beneficial interest under a trust is located where the trustees of the original trust might be sued to enforce the terms of the trust. This will apply if the claimant has at present only a right to enforce the trust[1]. An interest in an as yet unadministered estate is located in the place where the estate ought naturally to be administered[2]. However, if the claimant asserts equitable ownership of property held subject to a trust, that equitable title is located where the property which is subject to the trust is itself located[3].

1 *Re Smyth* [1898] 1 Ch 89; *A-G v Johnson* [1907] 2 KB; *Favorke v Steinkopff* [1922]
   1 Ch 174; *Re Cigala's Settlement Trusts* (1878) 7 Ch D 351. See Dicey, Morris and Collins,
   p 1127; Harris, The Hague Trusts Convention, pp 34–9.
2 *Lord Sudeley v A-G* [1897] AC 11; *Barnado's Homes v Comrs Special Purposes Income
   Tax Acts* [1921] 2 AC 1; *Commissioner of Stamp Duties Comr (Queensland) v Livingstone*
   [1965] AC 694.
3 *Re Berchtold* [1923] 1 Ch 192; *Philipson-Stow v IRC* [1961] AC 727.

102.134 Transfers of a debt due under a contract[1] give rise to certain
problems. A debt is generally regarded as having its situs where the debtor
resides[2], because that is where it generally needs to be enforced. If he has more
than one residence, it is where the creditor stipulates for the debt to be paid[3]
and in the absence of such a stipulation, where it is payable in the normal
course of business[4].

1 Or any contractual right.
2 *New York Life Insurance Co v Public Trustee* [1924] 2 Ch 101.
3 *Kwok Chi Leung Karl v Estate Duty Comrs* [1988] 1 WLR 1035.
4 *Power Curber International Ltd v National Bank of Kuwait SAK* [1981] 3 All ER 607.

102.135 Where a purported assignment of a debt[1] occurs, questions relating
to the assignability of the debt and to the relationship between that debtor and
assignee are to be governed by the law governing the right which is to be
assigned[2]. Whether a debt which *can* be assigned actually *has* been assigned is
a matter for the law applicable to the contract of assignment[3].

1 Or a contractual right.
2 Ie the law applicable to the contract which created the debt. For matters within the scope
   of the Rome Convention, this is stated in Article 12(2). Article 1(2)(g), Rome Convention
   excludes from the scope of the Convention the constitution of trusts. However, it appears
   that the same approach is taken at common law: *Trendtex v Crédit Suisse* [1980] QB 629.
3 See Article 12(1), Rome Convention; *Trendtex v Crédit Suisse* [1980] QB 629.

CONCLUSION ON TRANSFERS OF PROPERTY

102.136 The following choice of law rule is suggested to determine the
essential validity of purported transfers of property on trust:

(1)   The question whether any proprietary interest has been transferred
      inter vivos[1] from a would-be settlor to a would-be trustee is determined
      by the lex situs at the time of transfer[2].
(2)   Whether such disposition is effective to transfer an equitable title or
      other protected beneficial rights to the would-be beneficiary[3] is deter-
      mined by the proper law of the trust.

1 For testamentary transfers of movables, the law of the deceased's domicile at death should
   apply.
2 However, in the case of debts, the assignability of the debt will be determined by the law
   under which the debt arose; and the question whether the debt has been assigned to the
   trustee will be determined by the law governing the assignment itself.
3 The Convention does not introduce into municipal law the concept of trusts and equitable
   proprietary interests. States not knowing such concepts will use their own municipal law to
   determine whether a beneficiary's rights against a third party are non-existent or a personal
   claim to compensation or an *in personam ad rem* claim – or perhaps even an *in rem* claim.
   Further see para 102.217 below, notes 327 & 328.

Perpetuity

102.137 It is suggested that the English rules both against perpetuities and accumulations should be treated as 'rocket' matters and applicable when (but only when) English law is the law governing the trust[1]. This is because, in practice, they are predominantly focused upon the validity of trusts, trusts being necessary where property is to be tied up for a period of time. After all, '... the problems of future interests, apart from questions of construction and of tax liability, essentially resolve themselves into the question of the application of the perpetuity rule to equitable interests under trusts'[2]. Moreover, the fact that the trust contravenes the rule against accumulations or the rule against remoteness of vesting does not prevent the trust from being launched: it only means the accumulations cannot continue beyond the applicable accumulation period and the trust itself cannot continue beyond the statutory 'wait and see' period of statutory lives in being plus twenty-one years[3].

1   This view is supported by the decision of the Supreme Court of New South Wales in *Saliba v Falzon* [1998] NSWSC 302, where a testamentary disposition infringed the rule against accumulations of English law, but not New South Wales law and where the court felt bound to consider the law applicable to the trust to determine whether the accumulation period was infringed.
2   E Burn *Cheshire and Burn's Real Property* (16th edn, 2000) Butterworths, London, p 309. See also *Re Fitzgerald* [1904] 1 Ch 573.
3   See further D Hayton, (2006) 13(2) J Int Trust & Corp Pl 55.

Forced heirship

102.138 The classification of forced heirship claims is complex where, say, the deceased's three children are entitled to three quarters of his estate, extending to include property given away to individuals or to a trustee in an unlimited or prescribed period before death. The key question is whether a claim affects the trust structure itself or the transfer of title to the trustee. In so far as it affects only the ability to create the trust structure (because it does not impeach the alienation of legal title to the trustee) it falls within the Trusts Convention, and the mandatory rules of the law applicable to succession may be applied pursuant to Article 15(1)(c)[1]. Only if the alleged forced heirship rule impugns the transfer of title to the trustee, as in the case of a testamentary gift to a trustee where the lex successionis has forced heirship rules, should it be regarded as affecting the initial transfer and thus fall outside the Convention (but the general rule for inter vivos gifts is that the deceased is free while alive to transfer his property[2], so the transferee is only liable to pay compensation to the heirs to the extent necessary to make up the value of three quarters of the aggregate of the deceased's actual estate at death plus the value of the earlier valid gifts).

1   See the discussion of mandatory rules and Article 15(1)(c) of the Convention below.
2   See D Hayton (ed) *European Succession Laws* (2nd edn, 2002) Jordan Publishing.

102.139 In the case of a vitiated transfer, since forced heirship rules are most naturally to be classified as rules of succession[1], the law governing succession to the deceased's estate[2] should determine whether, and to what extent, a

testamentary disposition should be restricted by forced heirship rules[3]. However, it should be noted that where assets have already validly been disposed of
on inter vivos trust, then in the English (or a similar common law) forum there
is no question of that trust being affected by forced heirship rules of the law
applicable to succession. This is because that law should only be applied to
assets which the law of the forum regards as forming part of the deceased's
estate at death, rather than having been taken out of such estate by an earlier
transfer, unimpeachable according to the applicable lex situs[4].

[1]   See A Duckworth in J Glasson (ed) *International Trust Laws*, Chapter B1, p 32, who
     considers other possible classifications, but concludes that the succession classification is
     the most likely.
[2]   And not just the mandatory rules of the law of succession.
[3]   A view supported by *Re Annesley* [1926] Ch 692. For discussion of the position in the
     United States, see E Scoles, P Hay, P Borchers and S Symeonides *The Conflict of Laws* (4th
     edn, 2004), pp 1133–1136; *Bullen v Wisconsin* 240 US 625, 36 Sup Ct 473; *In Re Estate
     of Clark* 21 NY 2d 478, 288 NYS 2d 993; contrast *Re Estate of Renard* 56 NY 2d 973,
     453 NYS 3d 625 (considered by M Lupoi *Trusts: a Comparative Study*, 152).
[4]   See further the discussion of mandatory rules and Article 15(1)(c) below, para 102.193.

Determining the Governing Law of a Trust under The Hague Convention

Express choice of law

102.140 Article 6 provides that the settlor may choose the law to govern a
trust. This reflects the common law approach to express trusts[1]. However, it
does not matter under the Convention that the chosen law has no objective
connection with the trust. This appears to be a departure from the common
law position, where it was thought that the settlor must choose a law with
some objective connection to the trust[2]. However, Article 13[3] affords a State
or its judicial officers the option to refuse to recognise a trust which has (save
for its chosen law, the place of administration and the habitual residence of
the trustee) its other significant connections with a non-trust State. Nor is
there a requirement that a trust be objectively connected to more than one
State; it is possible to choose the law of trusts State A to govern a trust
objectively connected entirely to State B.

[1]   See eg *Re Hernando* (1884) 27 Ch D 284; *Re Fitzgerald* [1904] 1 Ch 573; *Iveagh v IRC*
     [1954] Ch 364; *Trustees Executors and Agency Co. Ltd v Margottini* [1960] VR 417. M
     Lupoi *Trusts: a Comparative Study*, 349 points out that even the Cour d'appel of Paris,
     (10 January 1970, [1971] Revue Critique de Droit International Privé 518) accepted the
     freedom to choose the applicable law of a trust created by a Frenchman over securities
     situated in the United States.
[2]   In the Australian case of *Augustus v Permanent Trustee Company (Canberra) Ltd* (1971)
     124 CLR 245 Walsh J expressed the view that the general choice of law principles
     applicable to contracts at common law should extend to trusts. In contract, it was required
     at common law that a choice be '*bona fide* and legal': per Lord Wright in *Vita Foods
     Products Inc v Unus Shipping Co Ltd* [1939] AC 277 at 290.
[3]   This Article was deliberately omitted from the Recognition of Trusts Act 1987: see para
     102.220 below.

102.141 It should be noted that the settlor is free to choose the governing
law, even in respect of trusts of land located overseas. This is something of a
departure from the English common law, where it was necessary for a trust of

land retained overseas to be valid by the law of the situs of the land[1]. Such an approach was justified by the fact that the courts of the situs of land have exclusive control thereof, so that there was little point in an English court deciding a dispute differently from the way that a judge in the courts of the situs would, as any English order might prove unenforceable overseas. The Hague Convention, however, places a higher currency on settlor autonomy than on the risk of unenforceability overseas.

1   *Re Piercy* [1895] 1 Ch 83. But once the land was sold, the law of the situs of the land no longer applied and the law chosen by the settlor to govern the trust alone applied. See also *Re Berchtold* [1923] 1 Ch 192. See further *Webb v Webb* [1994] ECR I–1717, where the ECJ held that a claim to assert a beneficial interest in land did not have as its object 'right *in rem* in immovable property' for the purposes of [what was then] Article 16(1) of the Brussels Convention (now Article 22(1) of the Brussels I Regulation, considered in the discussion of jurisdiction below).

102.142 The choice must be that of an individual legal system. Article 23 provides that 'where a State comprises several territorial units each of which has its own rules of law in respect of trusts, any reference to the law of that State is to be construed as referring to the law in force in the territorial unit.'[1] The intent of this infelicitously drafted Article is that, whilst it would be possible to choose the law of Ontario to govern a trust, a choice of Canadian law to govern a trust would be treated as meaningless and ignored[2]. Thus, in the absence of a choice of a valid law, the governing law will be determined under Article 7.

1   This Article is not scheduled to the Recognition of Trusts Act 1987.
2   See von Overbeck Report para 176 and also D Hayton (1987) 36 ICLQ 260, 269.

102.143 The settlor must choose the law of a trust State to govern a trust. Article 6(2) states that where a law has been chosen to govern a trust and that law, 'does not provide for trusts or the category of trust involved[1], the choice shall not be effective and the law ... [applicable in the absence of choice] ... shall apply.' If application of Article 7 points to the law of closest connection being that of a non-trust State, the Convention's rules[2] shall not be applicable. However, von Overbeck comments that, in searching for the law of closest connection in this context, 'one would think that ... the judge will have a tendency to conclude that a trust is most closely connected with a State which has this institution.'[3]

1   So that a choice of English law to govern a non-charitable purpose trust would probably fail, as such trusts are normally invalid in English law (subject to certain limited exceptions): see para 8.144 ff.
2   Including, paradoxically, Article 7.
3   Von Overbeck Report, para 61, p 383. See also Report of the Special Commission, Preliminary Document No. 9 of 9 March 1984, No 50.

102.144 A difficult question might arise if a settlor creates a trust by vesting assets in the trustee and then subsequently another person transfers assets to the trustee to be held under the same settlement[1]. What if the original settlor chooses the law of Utopia to govern the trust but the subsequent transferor-settlor of assets to the trust chooses the law of Ruritania? It is suggested that the latter choice would be ineffective[2]. Where a person transfers assets to be held on the terms of a pre-existing trust, he has no choice but to submit to the law already governing that trust. Of course, the subsequent disposition must still be 'launched' by the rules which determine the transfer of assets to a trustee[3].

1   D Hayton (1987) 36 ICLQ 260 at 270 gives the examples of a unit trust and of the establishment of a pension fund, friendly society or unincorporated association.
2   See *Galmerrow Securities Ltd v National Westminster Bank plc [2002] WTLR 125*, Harman J.
3   On which, see para 102.120 above.

Implied choice of law

102.145 If the settlor has not made a valid express choice of law, one should then look to see if he impliedly made a choice. The factors to which regard should be had in ascertaining whether the settlor impliedly made a choice of law are ones which reveal something of the settlor's subjective intentions; accordingly, those factual matters showing where the centre of gravity of the trust lies are not relevant at this stage.

102.146 An implied choice must be determined from the 'terms of the instrument creating the trust or the writing evidencing the trust, interpreted, if necessary, in the light of the circumstances of the case'. The court should begin by confining itself to the trust instrument as the first point of reference in the search for an implied choice[1], but if the position is then ambiguous it will become necessary to look at the circumstances of the case to reveal the settlor's intentions. Thus, in the trust instrument the use of terms resonant of a particular legal system, or the reference to powers contained in a specified Statute of a particular system or to purposes charitable under the law of a specified system, or the specification of a place of administration or a choice of court clause for resolution of disputes, should normally determine the issue without the need to refer to extrinsic circumstances which, in any event, will not be relevant if not indicative of the settlor's intentions.

1   Von Overbeck Report, para 69, p 385.

102.147 If helpful, common law case law can still be referred to by English courts in deciding whether a choice can be implied, but an implied intention may not be inferred only from the circumstances of the case in the absence of assistance from the trust instrument or other written evidence thereof[1]. The common law cases reveal a number of interesting points[2]. In the case of testamentary trusts, it appears that the deceased's last domicile is normally a most influential circumstance in ascertaining the settlor's intentions. However, it is far from determinative[3]. In the case of inter vivos trusts, the insertion of a jurisdiction clause will be a powerful indicator of the settlor's intention[4]. Furthermore, if the trust is created by virtue of, or pursuant to, a judicial settlement[5], the inference that the law of the forum was intended to govern will be strong[6]. Use of terminology resonant of a particular legal system, or of a form known in only one system, will be a strong indicator of the settlor's intentions, although it has not proved to be anything like determinative[7]. The place of administration will frequently be given great prominence[8]. However, since under The Hague Convention the principal focus is on the trust instrument itself, this factor should be treated as especially important only where the place of administration is expressly specified therein. Little inference can normally be drawn from the domicile or residence of the original trustees[9]. However, there are two obvious exceptions to this principle. First, where all the original trustees are domiciled or resident in one State, and their identity was stipulated in the trust instrument, this may itself lead to an irresistible inference as to where the settlor intended the trust to be administered[10]. That place of administration itself becomes a key factor in the search for an implied intention. Secondly, where the trustee is a company established specifically to hold the trust assets, the inference is that the law of the place of incorporation of the trust company will govern[11].

[1] Von Overbeck Report, para 69, p 385.
[2] See further J Harris *The Hague Trusts Convention*, pp 198–211. However, most of the common law cases do not distinguish between an implied choice of law and the applicable law in the absence of choice.
[3] See, in particular, *A-G v Campbell* (1872) LR 5 HL 524; *Saliba v Falzon* [1998] NSWSC 302; *Tod v Barton* [2002] EWHC 264 (Ch), (2002) 4 ITELR 715, Lawrence Collins J.
[4] As in *A-G v Jewish Colonization Association* [1901] 1 KB 123.
[5] Since, in the United Kingdom, the Hague Convention has been extended to apply to such trusts by s 1(2) of the Recognition of Trusts Act 1987.
[6] As in *Revenue Comrs v Pelly* [1940] IR 122.
[7] *Peillon v Brooking* (1858) 25 Beav 218; *Re Lord Cable* [1977] 1 WLR 7; *Lindsay v Miller* [1949] VR 13; *Revenue Comrs v Pelly* [1940] IR 122; *Iveagh v IRC* [1954] Ch 364.
[8] As in *Chellaram v Chellaram* [1985] Ch 409, *Lindsay v Miller* [1949] VR 13. However, it was accorded far less prominence in *Chellaram v Chellaram (No 2)* [2002] EWHC 632 (Ch), [2002] 3 All ER 17.
[9] *Revenue Comrs v Pelly* [1940] IR 122; *Iveagh v IRC* [1954] Ch 364.
[10] *Chellaram v Chellaram* [1985] Ch 409; *Re Carapiet's Trusts, Manoogian (Armenian Patriarch of Jerusalem) v Sonsino* [2002] EWHC 1304 (Ch), [2002] WTLR 989.
[11] As in *A-G v Jewish Colonization Association* [1901] 1 KB 123.

102.148 The situs of the assets may prove to be an important factor where the bulk of the trust property is immovable. However, where movable property is concerned, the situs appears to be a relevant, but not especially important factor and may tell a court little about the settlor's intentions[1]. Personal connecting factors relating to the settlor[2] or a primary beneficiary are unlikely to be given much weight in the case of inter vivos trusts, save in the case of a family settlement where all parties to the trust are domiciled or resident in one State[3]. The place where a deed was prepared and executed does not normally reveal very much about the settlor's intentions[4], but it may[5]. The policy underlying the trust might tell the court something of the settlor's intentions but should only prove relevant where that policy is readily apparent[6].

[1] *A-G v Campbell* (1872) LR 5 HL 524; *Lindsay v Miller* [1949] VR 13; *Iveagh v IRC* [1954] 1 Ch 364.
[2] But see *Re Carapiet's Trusts, Manoogian (Armenian Patriarch of Jerusalem) v Sonsino* [2002] EWHC 1304 (Ch), [2002] WTLR 989.
[3] As in *Iveagh v IRC* [1954] Ch 364.
[4] *Duke of Marlborough v AG* [1945] Ch 78; *Harris Investment Ltd v Smith* [1934] 1 DLR 748; *Lindsay v Miller* [1949] VR 13; *Iveagh v IRC* [1954] 1 Ch 364.

5   *Chellaram v Chellaram (No 2)* [2002] EWHC 632 (Ch), [2002] 3 All ER 17, Lawrence Collins J at para 167, re Art 7.
6   This is suggested by the comments of von Overbeck, para 67, p 384.

102.149 It is not clear if a court may assume that the settlor intended to choose a law by which the trust is valid. Presumably, the settlor's purpose can be considered as one of the 'circumstances of the case' relevant to shedding light on the construction of the written trust document. However, such a purpose cannot itself be conclusive as to the intended applicable law, since Article 6 requires that the choice derives from the written instrument itself (or the written evidence thereof), interpreted, if necessary, by reference to the surrounding factors[1].

1   *Augustus v Permanent Trustee Co (Canberra) Ltd* (1971) 124 CLR 24. This appears to accord with the policy of the Convention, whereby a choice of a non-trust State is disregarded altogether and the law of closest connection is used (Article 6(2)).

102.150 It appears that the settlor's intention should be ascertained as of the time of creation of the trust. Subsequent factors should only prove relevant in so far as they shed light on the settlor's intentions at the time of creation of the trust[1].

1   As for sham trusts see para 4.6 and *Midland Bank v Wyatt* [1995] 1 FLR 697.See also *Dicey, Morris and Collins*, 1560 and P Nygh *Autonomy in International Contracts* (1999) Clarendon Press, Oxford, p 112, for a similar view in relation to contracts.

Applicable law in the absence of choice

102.151 If the settlor has neither expressly nor impliedly chosen a law or has made an invalid choice of a non-trust State, the governing law of a trust must be objectively determined under Article 7. In trust-States the courts take into account a bewildering array of different factors with different weights attached to those factors in the circumstances of particular cases, where the nature of the trust is of much significance eg inter vivos or testamentary or a charitable trust or a marriage settlement or a fixed interest trust or a very broad discretionary trust. However non-trust States required simple guidance, preferably with a hierarchy or cascade of only the four most significant factors. The Convention therefore specifies 'in particular' (and so without prejudice to taking account of other factors) four factors which are to be regarded as of especial importance in ascertaining the law of closest connection for all trusts, albeit being of significance primarily for inter vivos trusts: the place of administration of the trust designated by the settlor; the situs of the trust assets; the residence or place of business of the trustees; and the place of performance of the purposes of the trust. As the von Overbeck Report states, this enables non-trust judges and notaries to regard these factors as 'an implicit hierarchy which would satisfy the needs of practice. But the text will also allow the judges of the common law countries to take into account, as they have the habit of doing, all factors at the same time.'[1]

1   Von Overbeck Report, para 77 at p 387.In *Chellaram v Chellaram (No 2)* [2002] EWHC 632 (Ch), [2002] 3 All ER 17, Lawrence Collins J stated at para 166,'I doubt if there is any significant difference between Article 7 and the likely approach at common law'. See also P Beaumont [2006] Jur Rev 2.

102.152 In practice, the potential for a Civilopian judge to reach a different result from a Trustopian judge, eg in the case of a testamentary trust (where the testator's Trustopian domicile is a most significant factor, though not determinative) is very limited[1]. Normally, it will be left to the Trustopian courts to determine matters affecting the trustee-beneficiary obligation and the Civilopian court will accept such determination, it normally being concerned only with the rights of third parties dealing in Civilopia with the trust property. In the exceptionally rare case where the Civilopian court has to work out for itself the governing law of the trust, then the Trustopian expert will be able to produce clear evidence as to which one or two factors (not limited to the four specified) are the key ones for determining the governing law – and which the court is free to take into account under the flexible wording of Article 7.

1 Fear of a different result from a Civilopoian judge led Ontario to refuse to implement the Convention, though note how in *Tod v Barton* [2002] WTLR 469, (2002) 4 ITELR 715 a Texan domiciled testator subject to the Texan *lex successionis* created a testamentary trust governed by English law of English assets for B for life remainder to X charity company and B and X, resident in England, were able to split the capital between them under *Saunders v Vautier*, though this was not possible under Texan law.

102.153 It should be noted that where the place of administration is designated by the settlor, this will be a very strong indicator of an implied choice of law pursuant to Article 6; in which case, the cases where Article 7(2)(a) may be relied upon to establish the law of closest connection will indeed be rare. As to the situs of the assets, since the character of the Convention is to treat the trust rather more as a matter of the law of obligations than the law of property, its role may not be especially significant. That said, one might expect the role of the situs to be stronger where the trust property consists wholly or principally of immovables. The difficulties which might arise in enforcing an order relating to the trust property itself in the State where the property is located mean that an English court should be slow to decide a dispute differently from the way that a judge in the court of the situs would decide it, unless the court can exercise *in personam* jurisdiction over the defendant landowner to compel him to do as it orders[1]. The third factor mentioned, namely the place of residence or business of the trustee, is one whose importance in the common law cases varied from almost irrelevance[2] to near decisiveness. Where the original trustees are domiciled or habitually resident in different States, this factor is likely to be of very little relevance; on the other hand, if the trustees are domiciled or habitually resident in the same State, or the settlor sets up a trust company in a certain State, the factor may well be of considerable importance[3]. The final factor mentioned in Article 7 is the objects of the trust and their place of fulfilment. It is submitted that, under Article 7, a great deal of importance should not ordinarily be attached to a trust's 'objects' or purposes. Article 7 is about determining the law of closest connection objectively. The objects of the trust do not tell the court much about this, unless it is possible to infer from them something objective about the trust, such as where the assets should be invested, or the trust administered[4].

1 Case C–294/92 *Webb v Webb* [1994] ECR I–1717, [1994] QB 696.; *Chellaram v Chellaram* [1985] Ch 409.

2   The trustees' residence was discounted in *Harris Investments Ltd v Smith* [1934] 1 DLR 748 and *Jewish National Fund Inc v Royal Trust Co* (1965) 53 DLR (2d) 577. Little importance was attached to it in *Chellaram v Chellaram (No 2)* [2002] EWHC 632 (Ch), [2002] 3 All E.R. 17.

3   *A-G v Jewish Colonization Association* [1901] 1 KB 123; But see *Re Carapiet's Trusts, Manoogian (Armenian Patriarch of Jerusalem) v Sonsino* [2002] EWHC 1304 (Ch), [2002] WTLR 989.

4   In *Chellaram v Chellaram* [1985] Ch 409, Scott J took the view that the trust before him was created, in part, to escape Indian tax and exchange control regulation and that the trust was to be administered in England. However, in *Chellaram v Chellaram (No 2)* [2002] EWHC 632 (Ch), [2002] 3 All ER 17, at para 167, Lawrence Collins J still found that the law of closest connection to the trust at the time of its creation was Indian law.

102.154 It should be noted that the domicile of a testator-settlor and the residence of the beneficiaries and the settlor are omitted from the list of factors mentioned in Article 7. However, as explained above, the list of Article 7 factors is not closed[1], so these factors can still be considered, though in *Tod v Barton*[2] Lawrence Collins J, in taking account of the law of Texas, the law of the testator's domicile, for Article 7 purposes, did not find it to be the governing law of the testamentary trust.

1   In *Chellaram v Chellaram (No 2)* [2002] EWHC 632 (Ch), [2002] 3 All ER 17, Collins J found that the four factors listed in Article 7 did not clearly reveal a law of closest connection. Rather, he determined the law of closest connection by reference to factors not mentioned in Article 7, such as the place of drafting and the origin of the family for whose benefit the trust was created.

2   *Tod v Barton* [2002] EWHC 264 (Ch), (2002) 4 ITELR 715, at para 36.

102.155 A court is likely to be reluctant to find that a trust is most closely connected with the law of a non-trust State, since this will take the trust outside the Convention altogether. However, in principle at least, the law of closest connection is to be determined entirely objectively and such a consideration ought not to be relevant.

102.156 A related question is whether, in ascertaining the law of closest connection, any relevance should be attached to the fact that by X law the trust is valid, whereas by Y law, it is not[1]. Although not mentioned in the non-exhaustive list in Article 7, some commentators appear to suggest validity is a relevant matter[2]. Moreover, it could be said that one of the 'objects of the trust' is to create a valid trust in the first place. However, the better view is that no such presumption of validity exists. It is true that a settlor would probably not have chosen a law by which the trust was invalid. However, where there is no choice of law, the law of closest connection is a purely objective concept. A law of closest connection remains the law of closest connection regardless of whether it leads to the validity or invalidity of the trust.

1   Compare *National Shawmut Bank v Cumming* 325 Mass 457.

2   A von Overbeck at http://isdc.ch/en/default.asp . See also P Nygh and M Davies *Conflict of Laws in Australia* (7th edn), p 624, considering *Augustus v Permanent Trustee Company (Canberra) Ltd* (1971) 124 CLR 245. The same view is expressed by A Oakley *Parker and Mellows, The Modern Law of Trusts* (8th edn), pp 858–9.

102.157 Article 7 does not say at what time the law of closest connection should be ascertained. Nevertheless, it is submitted that, in principle, the law of closest connection to an inter vivos trust should be determined as of the time when the trust was created[1], since if a trust is to be validly created, it must be subject to a particular legal system from the moment of commencement[2]. This accords with the common law approach[3].

[1]   In the case of testamentary trusts, this rule would be unsatisfactory, however, since the trust will not come into existence until the testator's death, and not at the time of creation of the will. In the intervening period, the testator's domicile may change, as may that of the trustees or beneficiaries. Accordingly, it is suggested that the Article 7 factors should, in the case of testamentary trusts, be determined as of the date of creation of a will. This view is supported by the decision in *Jewish National Fund Inc v Royal Trust Co* (1965) 53 DLR (2d) 577, where the Supreme Court of Canada refused to consider supervening changes in the determining the law of closest connection. But cf M O'Sullivan (1993) 2 J Int Corp P 65 at 69.

[2]   This is also the view of *Cheshire and North*, 1037 and of P Nygh and M Davies *Conflict of Laws in Australia* (7th edn), p 625. *Dicey, Morris and Collins* state (at 1313), that it is 'clear' that the law should be ascertained as at the point of creation 'at least in the case of inter vivos trusts'.

[3]   At common law, subsequent changes clearly did not affect the law of closest connection (at least where it was not alleged that the applicable law had been changed): see *Duke of Marlborough v A-G* [1945] Ch 78; *Iveagh v IRC* [1954] Ch 364; *Devos v Devos* (1970) 10 DLR (3d) 603; *Chellaram v Chellaram* [1985] Ch 409. A similar position prevailed at common law in contract (see *Amin Rasheed Corp v Kuwait Insurance Co* [1984] AC 50, discussed in *Dicey, Morris and Collins*, pp 1559–1560), but it now appears that, under the Rome Convention, supervening factors may be considered: Giuliano and Lagarde Report, OJ 1980 C282/4, p 20.

Exclusion of renvoi

102.158 Article 17 excludes the application of the doctrine of *renvoi*[1]. In other words, once the governing law of the trust has been determined, its domestic law is applied, without regard to any choice of law rules of the State identified. Suppose that a settlor chooses Utopian law to govern a trust. As a matter of Utopian private international law, the settlor may not choose the applicable law and a trust is governed by the law with which it has its closest connection. It may be that a Utopian judge would actually apply Ruritanian domestic law to the trust. Under the Convention, this fact is ignored and Utopian domestic law applied.

[1]   On which see the discussion of the preliminary issue of the vesting of property in the trustee above.

Splitting the applicable law; the distinction between validity and administration of trusts

102.159 The Convention permits the use of *dépeçage*, so that separate aspects of the trust may be subjected to different laws. This separation may be especially appropriate in relation to matters of administration[1]. Hence the settlor might provide, for example, that the validity of the trust be governed by English law, whereas its administration be governed by New South Wales law. However, the scope of Article 9 is wider than this and any severable[2] aspect of the trust might be subjected to a different law from that which governed the rest of the trust. Furthermore, although the splitting of the trust will usually be effected by express choice of the settlor, it may in an appropriate case be achieved under Article 7 in the absence of choice, if a particular aspect of the trust (eg Manitoban land where no perpetuity rules are applicable under Manitoban law, though they are under the law of the jurisdiction objectively applicable to the rest of the trust) is objectively more closely connected with a law other than that which governs the rest of the trust[3].

1   The settlor may choose the law of any trust State to govern administration, but it is envisaged that the place of administration may provide the most appropriate law: von Overbeck Report, para 91, pp 389–90. For the common law position, see A Wallace, (1987) 36 ICLQ 454 at 473–482.

2   The meaning of the word 'severable' is not wholly clear. P Matthews *Trusts: Migration and Change of Proper Law* (1997) Key Haven, London, p 60 argues that '…"severable" must mean *either* a qualitative difference in the type of exercise being done, eg construction of the substantive provisions as opposed to matters of administration, or a physical division of the trust into two or more parts, each having separate assets and being governed by separate substantive provisions, for example like separate appointments constituting separate trusts for capital gains tax purposes.'

3   Von Overbeck Report, paras 93–94, pp 390–391.

102.160 Of course, distinguishing matters of validity from matters of administration can be very difficult in practice[1]. It might be said that the difference between validity and administration is essentially one between matters which affect the substantive rights and interests of the beneficiaries and matters which simply go to the obligations of the trustees to take due care of the trust property and manage and invest it properly[2]. Certain issues will on any view be treated as matters of administration. These would include the trustees' powers of investment, right to remuneration, the appointment and removal of trustees, the power of the courts to confer additional powers on the trustees, the trustees' powers of delegation, of acquisition and disposal of trust assets and of paying debts and expenses and settling claims. The distinction between what constitutes capital and income is also most naturally to be seen as a matter of administration[3]. Powers of maintenance and advancement, on the other hand, have such a potentially significant impact on the nature and extent of the beneficiaries' interests that they may better be seen as matters affecting validity[4].

1   *Chellaram v Chellaram* [1985] Ch 409; (compare *Re Hewitt's Settlement* [1915] 1 Ch 228). See also the Ontarian decision in *Branco v Veira* (1995) 8 ETR (2d) 49.

2   But see the critical views of Scott J in *Chellaram v Chellaram* [1985] Ch 409 at 432: 'The rights and duties of trustees, for example, may be regarded as matters of administration but they also concern the effect of the settlement. The rights of the trustees are enjoyed as against the beneficiaries; the duties of the trustees are owed to the beneficiaries'; Scott J's words were approved by the South Australian Full Court in *Re Estate of Webb (dec'd)* (1992) 57 SASR 193. In *Chellaram v Chellaram (No 2)* [2002] EWHC 632 (Ch), [2002] 3 All ER 17, Lawrence Collins J was happier with the distinction

3   But, of course, the *nature and extent* of the interests of the beneficiaries in the capital and income is a matter of validity.

4   So that the powers contained in ss 31 and 32 of the Trustee Act 1925 would apply when English law governed the validity of a trust, even if the administration of the trust was governed by a different law but would not apply in the converse scenario.

102.161 However, it is important to appreciate that the words 'administration' and 'validity' are not terms of art and do not have an autonomous meaning. Essentially the issue in question is one of construction. If a settlor states eg that he wishes New South Wales law to govern the administration of the trust, a court should determine what *he* meant by the word 'administration': ideally, the settlor should define the term in his trust instrument so as to exclude any ambiguity. Whichever law governs the construction of the trust should determine what is meant respectively by 'validity' and 'administration'[1]. Where the settlor does not specify a law to govern construction and only subjects the administration of the trust to a separate law, it may be assumed that construction is to be subjected to the same law as that which governs validity.

1   Compare *Lindsay v Miller* [1949] VR 13.

Changing the governing law

102.162 Article 10 states that the law applicable to the validity of a trust shall decide if that law or the law governing a severable aspect thereof (eg administration) may be replaced by another law[1]. So, if it is purported to change from the law of England to the law of Ontario, English law will decide if the change is permissible. A right to replace the governing law with another can be expressly contained in the trust instrument[2], but it is doubtful whether it can be implied into the trust instrument, even though judges normally allow what could be expressly contained in an instrument to be capable of being necessarily implied therein[3]. An example of where such implication might be drawn is where the trust instrument authorises the trustees to retire in favour of foreign trustees in another trust State and to transfer the assets to those new trustees: can one not necessarily infer that at least the law governing administration was then intended by the settlor to change to the law of the new State of administration?

1   Where property is transferred from an initial settlement to another settlement, the original settlements' perpetuity period is applicable: *West v Trennery* [2005] UKHL 5, [2005] 1 All ER 827, para 41, *per* Lord Walker.
2   In English domestic law, the right to change the governing law may be expressly contained in the trust instrument or an application may be made to change the governing law under the Variation of Trusts Act 1958. See *Richard v Mackay* (4 March 1987, unreported), Ch D, (transcript in (1997) 11 Trust Law International 22); *Chellaram v Chellaram (No 2)* [2002] EWHC 632 (Ch), [2002] 3 All ER 17, at para 146.
3   In *Duke of Marlborough v A-G* [1945] Ch 78, the Court of Appeal took the view that, in the absence of an express provision in the trust instrument, the applicable law could be changed only with the concurrence of all the beneficiaries, and that this would result in a new settlement being created. However, it is difficult to see why an implied power to change the governing law of an existing settlement should not be permitted, providing it is clear that the settlor did intend this. That is a question of degree of evidence, not of substance. See also P Nygh and M Davies *Conflict of Laws in Australia* (7th edn), p 625 who tentatively supports implied change, citing the case of *Duyvewaardt v Barber* (1992) 43 RFL (Can) (3rd) 139 in support. J Walker, *Castel & Walker, Canadian Conflict of Laws*, 6th ed , pp 28–3 suggests that 'Once the trust has been created, the law governing its validity cannot be changed unless it is done by a power reserved to the settlor to that effect, or by an agreement by the beneficiaries to change it, or by the court sanctioning such a change under the relevant law.'. See also *Chellaram v Chellaram (No 2)* [2002] EWHC 632 (Ch), [2002] 3 All ER 17, at para 146.

102.163 Where there was no initial choice of law, what happens if it is argued that the law of closest connection has changed[1]? If, for example, the trust assets are vested in the hands of new trustees who are resident in a different State, it may be that the law of closest connection changes. It seems then that the relevant question is whether, according to the law of closest connection at the time of the trust's creation, the applicable law may be changed in this manner.

¹   Such 'objective' change of law is also covered by Article 10: von Overbeck Report, para 99, p 392.

102.164 Where the governing law has been purportedly replaced by another governing law pursuant to an express power in that behalf, does this amount to the creation of a new trust altogether, like a re-settlement¹? The Supreme Court of Delaware believed so in *Wilmington Trust Co v Wilmington Trust Co*². On the other hand, it might be said that such a power is like a power of appointment that permits the creation of a sub-trust within the umbrella of the original or head trust, so that a change from English to Suntopian law is only permitted because the English 'birth' law so decrees and the English trust should be treated as a continuing subsisting head trust when the applicable law is changed to Suntopian law, so that any provisions of Suntopian law (eg as to perpetuities and accumulations or to trusts always being revocable or being revocable in limited circumstances) which go beyond provisions of English law are inoperative – which, if overlooked, would invalidate the exercise of the power on *Re Hastings-Bass* principles³. If a replacement of the applicable law involves the creation of a new trust, there may be very unattractive capital gains tax implications for the trust⁴, as well as very unattractive income tax implications eg if such change could possibly enable the settlor or his spouse to benefit in any way⁵. The safest advice is to insert powers to change the governing law only when considered essential, perhaps restricting the power to one to change the law governing administration only. When used, such clauses need very careful drafting and consideration of the possible taxation implications, eg such powers being expressed to be exercisable only to the extent no possible benefit is conferred on the settlor or his spouse⁶.

¹   P Matthews Trusts: Migration and Change of Proper Law, 67.
²   26 Del Ch 397; P Matthews Trusts: Migration and Change of Proper Law, 68.
³   Discussed at para 61.18 above.
⁴   Taxation of Chargeable Gains Act 1992, s 71; *Hart v Briscoe* [1979] Ch 1; *Bond v Pickford* [1983] STC 517.
⁵   Income and Corporation Taxes Act 1988, s 660A(2), *IRC v Botnar* [1999] STC 711, CA.
⁶   P Matthews *Trusts: Migration and Change of Proper Law*, pp 80–81. As he points out (at 73–74) a preferable strategy may be to appoint assets of an English trust to an existing foreign trust having the same beneficiaries: indeed, the trust instrument might specify a particular foreign trust to which assets may be appointed, allowing the assets to be moved from their existing location in times of economic or political difficulty (a 'pilot' trust).

Scope of the Governing Law of the Trust

General matters

102.165 The list of factors to be determined by the applicable law is not intended to be exhaustive¹. Indeed, it is meant in part to assist non-trust States to understand the nature of the issues involved in dealing with trusts.

¹   Von Overbeck Report, para 81, pp 387–388.

102.166 Under Article 8(1) the applicable law not only governs the validity[1] and effects of a trust, as one might expect, but also governs the construction and the administration of the trust. At common law[2] the law governing validity normally governs construction; indeed, validity often hinges on a question of construction. However, it is possible under Article 9 for a settlor expressly to choose another law to govern construction eg under a trust governed by English law the settlor could provide that a specified clause defining the terms used, like 'Beneficiaries', in the Trust Deed, shall be determined under Bahamian law at the date of the Trust Deed (thereby excluding non-marital issue). The law applicable to the administration of a trust may be less straightforward. It may be that the settlor will have selected a law to govern the administration of the trust which differs from that which governs the trust as a whole[3]. The 'effects' of the trust are also governed by the applicable law. This rather general term does not reveal much[4]. Presumably, the effects are primarily those stated in Article 8 (and also in Article 11).

[1]   *Tod v Barton* [2002] WTLR 469, (2002) 4 ITELR 715; but see *Minwalla v Minwalla* [2004] EWHC 2823 (Fam), [2005] 1 FLR. 771.
[2]   *Re Pilkington's Will Trusts* [1937] Ch 574; *Trustees Executors and Agency Co Ltd v Margottini* [1960] VR 417; *Philipson-Stow v IRC* [1961] AC 727; *Re Levick's Will Trusts* [1963] 1 WLR 311; *Perpetual Executors and Trustees Association of Australia Ltd v Roberts* [1970] VR 732.
[3]   Pursuant to Article 9.
[4]   If anything.

Specific matters subject to the governing law of the trust

102.167 Article 8(2) lays down a list of matters which are to be subjected to the governing law of the trust.

102.168 Article 8(2)(a) covers 'the appointment, resignation and removal of trustees'. This is an important departure from the English common law position under which the English court may make *in personam* orders according to English law where trustees of a trust governed by a foreign law are properly brought before the court. Provided that the relevant court has jurisdiction to remove and replace trustees of a foreign settlement, it should now use the applicable law to determine whether to do so[1]. The other important matter covered by Article 8(2)(a) is the capacity to act as a trustee. It was argued above that it is only the trustee's capacity to act *qua* trustee which is covered by Article 8(2)(a). The questions whether he has 'general' capacity to receive a property interest *at all* (as opposed to whether he can act as trustee of that interest) is not a trusts specific matter and ought to be governed by general property principles, which would tend to point to the lex situs[2].

[1]   Where English law governs the trust, it appears that a *court* will not appoint a trustee resident overseas to an existing trust (of which the trustees are presently English residents) unless the trust has subsequently acquired a very strong connection with an overseas State, such as where the beneficiaries have become resident there: *Re Liddiard* (1880) 14 Ch D 310; *Re Whitehead's Trusts* [1971] 1 WLR 833; see also *In the Estate of Ardagh* [1914] 1 IR 5. However, English courts now take a more relaxed view when a *trustee* with an express power of appointment chooses to appoint foreign trustees and will not intervene unless no reasonable trustee could have made such a choice: *Richard v Mackay* (4 March

1987, unreported), Ch D (transcript included in (1997) 11 Trust Law International 22) and
Re Beatty's Will Trust (No 2) (28 February 1991, unreported), Ch D (transcript included in
(1997) Trust Law International 77).

2   In the case of inter vivos transfers. In the case of testamentary transfers of movables, it
would point to the law of the deceased's last domicile. See the discussion of the capacity of
the trustee above.

102.169 Article 8(2)(b) subjects the rights and duties of the trustees among
themselves to the applicable law. Despite this, it should be noted that where a
trustee has been sued for breach of trust and then brings a contribution claim
against the others, the Civil Liability (Contribution) Act 1978 applies in an
English court regardless of the applicable law of the trust and to the exclusion
of that applicable law[1].

1   *Arab Monetary Fund v Hashim (No 9)* (1994) Times, 11 October; A Briggs, [1995]
LMCLQ 437. See also *The Kapetan Georgis* [1988] 1 Lloyd's Rep 352 at 357–359;
Petroleo Brasiliero SA v Mellitus Shipping Inc [2001] 2 Lloyd's Rep 203.

102.170 Article 8(2)(c) provides that the trustee's right to delegate is determined by the applicable law. However, whilst this provision deals with the
right to delegate, it does not deal with the consequences of such delegation. It
is suggested that whilst the applicable law of the trust should determine if and
when a trustee might be liable for the acts of a properly appointed delegate,
the nature and terms of the relationship formed between the trustee and the
delegate is a matter for whatever law governs the relationship between them[1].

1   Of course, there may very well be a contract between the trustee and the delegate; in which
case, the governing law of the contract will determine the relationship between them. See
also *Dicey, Morris and Collins*, p 1914.

102.171 Article 8(2)(d) deals with the administration of the trust and the
trustee's power to deal with and acquire trust property. In the absence of
dépeçage, it is important to note that the vast body of law that is administration of trusts is subjected to the law applicable to the trust. Whilst this might
seem not in the least surprising, there is English common law authority which
applies certain English statutory provisions concerning trustees' powers to
trusts governed by a foreign law, where the trustee is appointed in an English
court[1]. It has been held that where a grant of administration is made in
England, s 33(1) of the Administration of Estates Act 1925 (which grants
statutory powers to the trustee to postpone sale) applies irrespective of the law
applicable to the trust[2]. The same is true of the maintenance and advancement
powers contained in ss 31 and 32, Trustee Act 1925[3]. *Dicey, Morris and
Collins* state that 'It is not certain how these common law authorities are
affected by Art. 8(2)(d).'[4] It might be argued that these provisions are
overriding mandatory rules of English law, or that they relate to the administration of estates, rather than to the law of trusts. However, this view should
be rejected. These are powers which arise pursuant to a valid trust and there is
no pressing reason to insist upon the application of these statutory provisions
to trusts governed by foreign law. It follows that their application should be
governed by the Hague Convention and it is suggested that such statutory
provisions should not be applied to a trust governed by a foreign law.

1 Or, more precisely, where the trustee is appointed according to English law in an English court. See *Re Wilks* [1935] Ch 645; *Re Kehr* [1952] Ch 26; *Re Ker's Settlement Trusts* [1963] Ch 553; *Chellaram v Chellaram* [1985] Ch 409.
2 *Re Wilks* [1935] Ch 645.
3 *Re Kehr* [1952] Ch 26. See also *Dicey, Morris and Collins*, p 1315.
4 *Dicey, Morris and Collins*, p 1315. See also pp 1330–1331, Illustration 10.

102.172 The other matter mentioned in Article 8(2)(d) is the trustees' power to create security interests in trust property. Although the governing law of the trust decides whether a security interest in trust property can be created, or trust property disposed of, the title acquired by the transferee is a property law question and is a matter for the lex situs as recognised by Article 15(1)(d).

102.173 Article 8(2)(e) deals with the investment powers of the trustees. The power of investment is one of the key aspects of the proper administration of the trust. It follows that English legislative provisions on investment should only be applied if English law governs the trust. Such rules should not be treated as mandatory rules of English law, since even in a domestic context they can be derogated from if the settlor lays down different investment rules in the trust instrument.

102.174 Restrictions upon the duration of the trust, and upon the power to accumulate the income of the trust are covered by Article 8(2)(f). In England, s 164 of the Law of Property Act 1925, the Perpetuities and Accumulations Act 1964 and the rule against inalienability (also known as the rule against purpose trusts of excessive duration) should, accordingly, be applied only where English law is the governing law of the trust[1].

1 Even if the property is located overseas. See also the discussion of perpetuities when considering preliminary issues, paras 102.107 and 102.137 above.

102.175 Article 8(2)(g) states that the 'relationships between the trustees and the beneficiaries, including the personal liability of the trustees to the beneficiaries', are subject to the governing law of the trust. It seems this law will also determine the fiduciary duties owed by the trustee to the beneficiary under the Convention. The question of whether a fiduciary relationship arises in a transnational context appears not to be the subject of an orthodox choice of law rule at all, at least where there is no other 'specific relationship' between claimant and defendant[1], so that the Federal Court of Australia in *Paramasivam v Flynn*[2], treated the law of the forum as the governing law for 'general' breaches of fiduciary duty. However, in the context of the trustee/beneficiary relationship, it is submitted that the law governing the trust should determine the trustee's fiduciary duties. Article 8(2)(g) is not expressly confined to the personal liability of the trustee to the beneficiary *qua trustee*. Furthermore, that provision only 'includes' personal liability as one aspect of 'the relationships between the trustees and the beneficiaries'. Moreover, the court in *Paramasivam v Flynn* expressly excluded from its ruling fiduciary duties arising from agreement, suggesting that they might better be governed by the law applicable to the specific relationship from which they arise. Although the fiduciary relationship is not trusts specific, in so far as the rights and obligations arise because of the existence of a valid trust, it only makes sense for the law governing the trust also to regulate that relationship.

1 *Paramasivam v Flynn* (1998–99) 160 ALR 203. See also *El Ajou v Dollar Land Holdings plc* [1993] 3 All ER 717 (reversed on different grounds: [1994] 2 All ER 685); *Arab Monetary Fund v Hashim* [1993] 1 Lloyd's Rep 543, reversed on other grounds [1996] 1 Lloyd's Rep. 589 (CA); *Kuwait Oil Tanker SAK v Al Bader* [2000] 2 All ER (Comm) 271 (CA); *Grupo Torras SA v Al Sabah* [2001] CLC. 221 (CA); *Barros Mattos Jnr v Macdaniels Ltd* [2005] EWHC 1323 (Ch.), [2005] IL.Pr 630. See also *Base Metal Trading Ltd v Shamurin* [2004] EWCA Civ 1316, [2005] 1 WLR 1157.
2 (1998–99) 160 ALR 203.See also Dicey, Morris and Collins, pp 1884–5; T Yeo, Choice of Law for Equitable Doctrines, pp 293–4.

102.176 Article 8(2)(g) does not deal with the liability of the trustees to third parties. Von Overbeck makes clear that this is quite deliberate[1]. If a trustee harms a third party's interest eg by breaking a contract with him or wrongfully misappropriating his property and mixing it with the trust fund, there is no reason why the third party's personal or proprietary right of recovery should in any way be affected by a trust to which he was not party. Of course, the Convention also does not deal with the personal liability of a third party who receives trust property and then dishonestly or innocently deals with it inconsistently with the trust, or who dishonestly assists in a breach of trust[2].

1 Von Overbeck Report, para 87, p 389.
2 Claims for dishonest assistance in a breach of fiduciary duty have been treated for the purposes of Article 5(3) of the Brussels Convention as matters relating to tort: see *Casio Computer Co Ltd v Sayo* [2001] EWCA Civ 661,[2001] IL Pr 694 ; *Dexter v Harley* (2001) Times, 2 April, Ch D (both cases are discussed by T Yeo (2001) 117 LQR 560). The same cases also assumed that claims based on dishonest dealings with fiduciary property received for one's own benefit could be classified for Brussels Convention purposes as matters relating to tort. For choice of law purposes, however, *Dicey, Morris and Collins*, Chapter 34, p 1882, suggest that '... equitable claims to disgorge the value of the enrichment of the defendant fall within the scope of [the choice of law rules for restitution].' However, 'equitable claims for compensation fall outside the scope of [this rule].', relying, in particular, on *Grupo Torras SA v Al-Sabah* [2001] CLC. 221 (CA); and *Base Metal Trading Ltd v Shamurin* [2004] EWCA Civ. 1316, [2005] 1 WLR. 1157. They conclude that '... an equitable claim which is founded on an allegation of unlawful or knowing receipt, or any other equitable claim to disgorge an unjust enrichment, will fall within the scope of the present Rule [on restitution]. But a claim which is founded on an allegation of wrongdoing for which compensation is sought does not do so, even if English domestic law would regard the liability as equitable.' For detailed discussion, see T Yeo, *Choice of Law for Equitable Doctrines* (2004), Oxford University Press, Oxford, esp. Chapters 7–9.

102.177 Article 8(2)(h) deals with the variation and termination of trusts. The variation of trusts raises particularly complex questions in England[1]. The matter is complicated by statutory provisions of English law which purport to confer 'jurisdiction' on an English court to vary a settlement[2]. It is not clear what happens where that 'jurisdiction' is lacking. Furthermore, pre-Convention case-law suggests that the English statutory variation provisions[3] may be applied to trusts governed by foreign law.

1 The subject is examined in detail in J Harris *The Hague Trusts Convention*, 256–270. See also *Dicey, Morris and Collins*, pp 1323–4; K Byrne, (2004) 11(2) J Int Corp 93.

² This is not a reference to *in personam* jurisdiction of the court over the defendant, which must, of course, still be established (and is considered below). The 'jurisdiction' here is rather the conferral of competence to vary a trust on an English court which already has *in personam* jurisdiction.

³ On the Variation of Trusts Act 1958, see *Re Ker's Settlement Trusts* [1963] Ch 553; *Re Paget's Settlement* [1965] 1 WLR 1046. On the Matrimonial Causes Act 1973, see *Nunneley v Nunneley and Marrian* (1890) 15 PD 186.

102.178 It is clear from s 24(1)(c) of the Matrimonial Causes Act 1973[1] that an English court has the power to vary a trust governed by English law when it has jurisdiction over divorce, nullity or legal separation proceedings involving the same parties[2]. Section 17 of the Matrimonial and Family Proceedings Act 1984 confers a similar power on the court in respect of foreign decrees. In both cases, the decision to vary is at the court's discretion. Section 24 further provides a basis of competence to vary a trust governed by foreign law. However, whether a court with competence should actually vary a foreign trust raises a choice of law question. Article 8(2)(h) of the Trusts Convention makes clear that if a foreign law governs the trust, then it is that foreign law's substantive provisions on variation of trusts which should be applied, not those of English law[3]. It must follow that it is to the applicable law of the trust that an English court should first look when deciding whether to vary the trust.

¹ Family Law Act 1996, s 15, was intended to introduce certain changes in this area, including allowing ancillary orders to be made prior to a divorce or legal separation. However, it has not entered into force. See also Sch 2 to the 1996 Act.

² It may also adjust the interests of the parties, or extinguish the interest of one party: s 24(1)(d). See also *Cammell v Cammell* [1965] P 467; *Tallack v Tallack* [1927] P 211.

³ Subject to the application of mandatory rules and public policy (on which, see Articles 15(1)(b), 16 and 18, below).

102.179 Notwithstanding Article 8(2)(h), the Court of Appeal in *Charalambous v. Charalambous*[1] held that the power in section 24(1)(c) of the 1973 Act should be exercised in accordance with English law as part of the whole range of powers exercisable in the context of such proceedings and that the Recognition of Trusts Act 1987 does not affect the position. This is on the basis that although Article 8(2)(h) of the Convention refers the question of variation to the law applicable to the trust, this is subject to the mandatory rules identified in Article 15[2]. Section 24 of the 1973 Act was treated as a mandatory rule of the English law relating to matrimonial causes, applicable irrespective of the law applicable to the trust.

¹ [2004] EWCA Civ 1030, [2005] Fam 250.

² On which, see below. Although Art. 15 does not expressly refer to matrimonial causes (referring only to the 'personal and proprietary effects of marriage', the Court of Appeal in *Charalambous* noted that the list in Art. 15 is not intended to be exhaustive and that this area falls within the scope of the Article. See also *Minwalla v Minwalla* [2004] EWHC 2823 (Fam.), [2005] 1 FLR 771.

102.180 However, this can be criticised[1]. Prior to the entry into force of the Convention, English courts simply applied the lex fori as the choice of law rule applicable to variation of trusts. Article 8(2)(h) makes it clear that the law applicable to the trust now applies to the question of variation; and it is to this law that the court should turn first and foremost. Nor is there any pressing reason to treat section 24 of the 1973 Act as a mandatory rule. Rather, it is suggested that the rules of variation of the law applicable to the trust should be applied, subject to their disapplication if, but only if, they are manifestly incompatible with English public policy under Article 18.

¹   See J Harris (2005) 120 LQR. 16, 18–22. See also on the position in the Isle of Man: J Rimmer, (2004) 10(10) Trusts and Trustees 16; J Rimmer [2005] PCB 88.

102.181 A similar approach should be taken to the Variation of Trusts Act 1958, s 1. In *Re Paget's Settlement¹*, Cross J suggested that an English court would be empowered to vary a foreign settlement. However, it might choose in its discretion not to do so. 'Obviously, however, where there are substantial foreign elements in the case, the court must consider carefully whether it is proper for it to exercise the jurisdiction.'² However, there was no suggestion in *Re Paget's Settlement* that the power to vary should be exercised in accordance with the applicable law of the trust. Instead, an English statute was applied to a foreign settlement. Such an approach would now appear incompatible with Article 8(2)(h)³.

¹   [1965] 1 WLR 1046.
²   [1965] 1 WLR 1046 at 1050.
³   Unless it could be said to be a mandatory statutory rule of English law applicable under Article 16. However, there seems no principled reason why an English court should insist on applying English rules on variation to a foreign trust. See further J Harris *The Hague Trusts Convention*, pp 264–9.

102.182 There must also be limits to the English court's willingness to exercise its *jurisdiction* to vary a trust governed by a foreign law¹. In particular, if an English court were to vary a trust governed by foreign law and with no objective connection to England, this would risk incurring the displeasure of foreign courts and might render any variation order unenforceable overseas². It is submitted that the test which the English court should apply is to ask whether, (assuming that it has *in personam* jurisdiction over the defendant) it is a natural forum in which to grant the particular variation order sought. In deciding this, it should attach considerable weight to the law governing the trust and to the strength of objective connection of the trust to England. However, against this, it must weigh three main factors: (i) that the philosophy of Article 8(2)(h) makes clear that the mere fact that a foreign law governs the trust is nothing like a conclusive reason for the forum not to exercise the jurisdiction to vary in accordance with such law; (ii) that England may well be the natural forum on the basis that it is more appropriate eg for divorce proceedings and a variation order of what in English law rank as ante-nuptial or post-nuptial settlements, to be dealt with by the same court; and (iii) an English court should be reluctant to refuse to vary a trust if it appears that no other court overseas would be competent, or willing, to vary the trust.

¹   Especially if there is a concern as to whether the variation order will be recognised overseas.
²   See *Goff v Goff* [1934] P 107 at 114 and *Re Rabaiotti 1989 Settlement* [2000] WTLR 953, [2000] 3 ITELR 763 commented upon in (2000) 4 Jersey Law Review 317; D Benest (2000) 6 Trusts and Trustees 6; D Benest (2001) 7 Trusts and Trustees 16; C Davies (2000) 6 Trusts and Trustees 33. But see *Charalambous v Charalambous* [2004] EWCA Civ 1030, [2005] Fam 250, at para 54; *Compass Trustees v McBarnett* [2002] JLR 321 (Royal Court

of Jersey). See also *Otobo v Otobo* [2002] EWCA Civ 949, [2003] 1 FLR 192. See further M Hanson and T Renouf (2005) 35 Fam. L.J. 794 and [2006] PCB 310 on Jersey case law and the new Article 9 of Jersey Trust Law in the Trusts (Amendment No 4) (Jersey) Law 2006.

102.183 In divorce proceedings, where final resolution of matters is a fundamental goal and where the court in *Charalambous* has shown itself inclined to invoke Articles 15(1) (and, if necessary, Articles 16 and 18) to buttress the Matrimonial Causes Act, the English court should be prepared to exercise its MCA jurisdiction, but probably subject to acceptance by the court in the jurisdiction of the applicable law before final resolution of the divorce issues. However, this will be pointless if the policy of the foreign applicable law eg The Bahamas[1] is specifically to protect the settled property from rights conferred by foreign law upon any person by reason of a personal relationship to the settlor, such as marriage. Otherwise, even if the State whose law governs the trust happens to have no legislation conferring equivalent powers on its own courts, it may well be that such courts will not object to the impact of the overriding powers of the English court, treating interests under such trust as from the outset subject to such foreign overriding process where key persons involved as settlor or trustee or beneficiaries thereunder have legitimately been subjected to the jurisdiction of the English court.

[1] Trusts (Choice of Governing Law) Act 1989, s 8(b).

102.184 As to the termination of a trust, Article 8(2)(h) will cover the rights of both trustee (under an express power) and beneficiary (under the English *Saunders v Vautier*[1] principle, which only applies in one USA State) to terminate the trust. Where the right to terminate is exercised, the vesting of the property in the beneficiary ought to be determined by the applicable law of the trust[2].

[1] (1841) 4 Beav 115.
[2] Only when it comes to a transfer of the legal title to the beneficiary will the lex situs be applied.

102.185 Article 8(2)(i) deals with the distribution of trust assets. This provision will cover the decision of a trustee of a discretionary trust as to whom should benefit from the trust and in what proportions. Presumably, it also covers the interpretation of the trust deed, in order to determine who are the permissible beneficiaries under the trust.

102.186 Finally, the core duty of the trustee to produce accounts for falsification or surcharge in respect of breaches of trust is subject to the trust's governing law under Article 8(2)(j). This will extend to the duties to inform adult beneficiaries they be such, to keep and produce accounts for inspection and verification and to produce trust documents for inspection which may, perhaps, extend to letters of wishes.

Limits on the Scope of the Governing Law of the Trust

102.187 For matters within the scope of the Convention, the role of the law applicable to the trust or a severable aspect is not unlimited. The provisions of Articles 15, 16 and 18 respectively preserve the application of domestic mandatory rules in areas related to the law of trusts, the international mandatory rules of the forum and the public policy of the forum.

Mandatory rules and public policy distinguished

102.188 Mandatory rules are *positive* rules of law of a legal system which a State insists upon applying, even where a different law is applicable to the cause of action. They are superimposed onto the governing law. Mandatory rules are ones from which the settlor is not free to derogate. They contrast with use of public policy, which is a negative process. A court invokes its public policy where giving effect to the governing law would be unacceptable on the facts. It is a *negative* process leading to the disapplication of the governing law in whole or in part.

Mandatory rules of the law applicable to related areas of law

102.189 Article 15 preserves the application of domestic mandatory rules in areas related to trusts law. In case of conflict, the law applicable to the trust must[1] give way, but only in so far as the rules in a related area are mandatory. Article 15 is concerned not with the mandatory rules of the forum in related areas, but with the mandatory rules of the State whose law is designated by the forum's choice of law rules as applicable to those areas.

[1]   Although Article 15 (based on a French text then translated into English) states that it 'shall not prevent' the application of mandatory rules, s 1(3) of the Recognition of Trusts Act 1987 makes it clear that the provisions of Articles 15 and 16 positively '*shall* to the extent there specified, apply to the exclusion of other provisions of the Convention' (emphasis added).

102.190 Article 15 provides a non-exhaustive list of areas of law related to the trust.

102.191 Article 15(1)(a) deals with rules for the protection of minors and incapable parties. This will often manifest itself in rules on capacity. Its scope of application may be rather narrow, since the capacity of a settlor to create a trust is in any event a preliminary issue excluded from the Convention[1]; and it appears that the capacity of a beneficiary to receive a benefit is also excluded[2]. The capacity to act as a trustee is, however, within the Convention[3]. A State might eg designate a personal connecting factor, or the lex situs, to determine the capacity of a party to hold and manage property. The mandatory rules of that State will be superimposed over the trust[4].

[1]   See the discussion of the settlor's capacity in relation to the preliminary issues considered above.
[2]   See Article 8(2)(a), above.

3   Article 8(2)(a). More accurately, the specific capacity to act as a trustee is included; the 'general' capacity to receive property at all is excluded.

4   But a State should be slow to reach this conclusion. It is the contention of this author that 'general' rules of property law should be applied only to the 'rocket-launching' matter of vesting legal title in the trustee and not to the 'rocket' matter of the creation of the trust structure with that property. Accordingly, mandatory rules should be applied under Article 15(1)(a) only where the restriction on the trustee's capacity relates specifically to his competence to hold and manage *trust* property.

102.192 Article 15(1)(b) concerns the effects of marriage[1] on the trust[2], especially marital regimes having a form of community of property and the effects to be given to an ante-nuptial contract. Community of property is a common phenomenon in a number of States[3]. Where there is no contract, an English court will apply the law of the matrimonial domicile[4] to determine the effects of marriage on title to movable property[5]. Where there is a marriage contract, its effect is to be governed by the proper law of the contract[6]. The parties may expressly or impliedly agree on this law[7]; in the absence of choice, the law of the matrimonial domicile will govern[8].

1   On the effects of divorce, see *Charalambous v Charalambous* [2004] EWCA Civ. 1030, [2005] Fam 250.

2   See generally Dicey, Morris and Collins, Chapter 28; Cheshire and North, Chapter 34.

3   See the brief survey in *Dicey, Morris and Collins*, p 1282. They divide the various systems of community of property into three categories: full community (giving the examples of the Netherlands and South Africa), community of gains (Spain) and community of chattels and gains.

4   *Dicey, Morris and Collins*, Rule 156 at p 1280. The rule is expressly limited to movable property. On immovables, see *Re De Nicols (No 2)* [1900] 2 Ch 410.

5   Where the spouses have different domiciles at the time of marriage, historically the husband's domicile prevails. However, such a rule has very little to commend it today and *Dicey, Morris and Collins* (at 1283) prefer to apply the 'law of the country with which the parties and the marriage have the closest connection …'.

6   Dicey, Morris and Collins, Rule 157 at p 1288.

7   For example, *Re Hernando* (1884) 27 Ch D 284; *Re Hewitt's Settlement* [1915] 1 Ch 228.

8   *Duke of Marlborough v AG* [1945] Ch 78; Dicey, Morris and Collins, Rule 157 at p 1288. On the reform of the rules relating to matrimonial property, see the Green Paper on Conflict of Laws in Matters Concerning Matrimonial Property Regimes, including the question of Jurisdiction and Mutual Recognition COM/2006/0400 Final.

102.193 Article 15(1)(c) applies to succession rights, testate and intestate, especially the indefeasible shares of spouses and relatives. It may apply, in particular, to preserve forced heirship rights under the law applicable to succession. However, the scope of Article 15(1)(c) is much narrower than might first appear because Article 4 will operate to prevent a testamentary trust from getting off the ground to the extent it purports to cover that part of the deceased's estate reserved for the heirs[1].

1   A Duckworth, in J Glasson (ed) *International Trust Laws*, Chapter B1, p 24.

102.194 The most serious concern regarding forced heirship from an English or common lawyer's viewpoint (but not that of a civil law lawyer) is the fear that even an inter vivos trust might fall prey to 'claw-back' claims of the law applicable to succession, although it is more appropriate to regard these as 'add-back' claims.

102.195 Take S, who transfers English assets worth £24 million to English resident trustees of a trust governed by English law and then dies a few years later with a £12 million estate. Under his Civilopian lex situs S had power to make valid gifts of his property, but the value of them has to be added back to the value of his estate at death in order to calculate his three children's reserved three quarter shares of the notional £36million estate. To obtain their £27 million the three children take the whole £12 million in S's actual estate and have a personal claim to recover £15 million from the donee-trustees of the £24 million gift (or, perhaps, from beneficiaries who had actually received part thereof).

102.196 However, it is almost certain that an English court will not permit a validly created inter vivos trust subsequently to be impugned by foreign forced heirship rules[1], just as it would not permit the operation of S's inter vivos joint account of money or other investments to be frustrated by any heir's claim against the surviving joint tenant even if S's lex successionis considered the joint account arrangement to be a testamentary one[2]. Characterisation of an issue as testamentary or inter vivos is a matter for the English forum. The English court will surely characterise a transfer by a live settlor to trustees (or into a joint account) as the case of an inter vivos transfer which is a preliminary issue outside the Trusts Convention, although, if within it, its paramount effect would be recognised under Article 15(1)(d). The only relevant question then is whether, at the time when the settlor purported to create an inter vivos trust, he could, and did, validly alienate his property to the trustee according to the lex situs. If the transfer is valid by the lex situs (and the trust itself is valid by its applicable law), it has validly come into effect and cannot later be impugned on the testator's death by forced heirship rules under the law happening to be the law applicable to succession because it so happened that the settlor died many years later domiciled in a forced heirship jurisdiction and left an actual estate inadequate to cover the amount of the reserved shares. It can also be argued that it would hardly be consistent with English public policy (protected by Article 18) to require trustees to have to wait upon such uncertainties for many years (adding back rules in States like France and Italy being without limit of time) and so not exercise their distributive powers beyond the value of the property received from the settlor, not having any protection such as that provided by s 13 of the Inheritance (Provision for Family and Dependants) Act 1975.

[1] *Lewin on Trusts* (17th edn, 2000), para 11–59; P Matthews (2001) 5 Chase Journal 15; D Hayton (ed) *European Succession Laws* (2nd edn, 2002), paras 1–67 to 1–69.
[2] *Sanchez v Sanchez* 547 So 2d 945 (1989); *Hutchinson v Ross* 211 Ne 2d 637.

102.197 An English court should only apply the law applicable to succession to assets which are part of the deceased's estate at death. Thus, in *Pouey v Hordern*[1] property, appointed by will by a French-domiciled testatrix pursuant to a special power of appointment in her 1880 inter vivos settlement, was not subject to her children's forced heirship claims because there was 'no disposition of property belonging to the testatrix'. Assets which have been validly disposed of on inter vivos trusts are not part of the deceased's estate and so the law applicable to succession should not be applied to them.

However, a judge in a civil law jurisdiction, faced with an English trust of some assets located in his jurisdiction or with some beneficiaries resident therein, is likely to consider that these issues are succession issues from his forum's viewpoint, and so enforce forced heirs' rights against such assets or beneficiaries[2].

1   [1900] 1 Ch 492 at 494.
2   D Hayton in J Glasson (ed) *International Trust Laws*, Chapter C3, p 15. See *Holzberg v Sasson* (1986) 75 Revue Critique de Droit International Privé 685 and *Caron v Odell* (1986) 75 Revue Critique de Droit International Privé 66.

102.198 Article 15(1)(d) preserves the application of mandatory rules concerning transfer of title to property and security interests in property. The term 'transfer of title to property' is intended to emphasise that not every property issue falls within the sub-paragraph[1]. Article 15(1)(d) cannot be concerned, as one might first think, with the transfer of property to the trustee, since this is a 'rocket-launching' matter within Article 4 and so is outside the scope of the Convention. For common law trusts, it might be applied to questions of transfer of equitable title to the beneficiary[2]. Questions such as whether equitable title has vested in the beneficiary and at what stage, whether the beneficiary's interest in the property transferred is in possession, vested, contingent or determinable and whether a beneficiary absolutely entitled can terminate the trust and call for the trust property to be transferred to him might be covered by this provision. It can also apply to the circumstances in which a good title to trust property might be passed to a third party.

1   Compare the German proposal in Working Document No 44 (discussed by von Overbeck, para 143, p 402) to refer simply to 'property'; see also A von Overbeck at http://isdc.ch/en/default.asp.
2   D Hayton (1996) 5 J Int Trust & Corp P 127 at 128. If a settlor declares himself trustee of his property, in order to defraud his personal creditors, in common law jurisdictions and civilian systems with their actions based on the Roman actio Pauliana , the creditors will be able to claim the trust assets.

102.199 Article 15(1)(e) covers the protection of creditors in matters of insolvency. It is not necessary that a creditor should have acted in good faith[1]. Article 15(1)(e) should be taken to concern the protection of creditors upon the beneficiary's insolvency, not the trustee's insolvency, for otherwise there would be no ring-fenced fund, which 'is an essential element of a trust, without which its recognition would have no meaning'[2]. The protective trust might be viewed as a means of frustrating the claims of a creditor and may be vulnerable to the mandatory rules of the designated foreign law[3].

1   Von Overbeck, para 145 at p 403; Working Document No 58.
2   Von Overbeck Report para 108.
3   Or, indeed, be seen under Article 18 as contrary to the public policy of a State asked to recognise a protective trust governed by English law.

102.200 Article 15(1)(f) preserves the application of mandatory rules for the protection of third parties acting bona fide. It is not limited to purchasers and might extend to other third party recipients of trust property[1].

1   A third party who has dissipated the trust property may be personally liable as discussed at para 100.52 ff: but this personal claim is not covered by the Convention in any event and it may be that it is subject to the choice of law rules governing claims in unjust enrichment. See *Dicey, Morris and Collins*, p 1882. See also eg *Chase Manhattan Bank NA v Israel-British Bank (London) Ltd* [1981] Ch 105; *Re Jogia (A Bankrupt)* [1988] 1 WLR 484; *El Ajou v Dollar Land Holdings plc* [1993] 3 All ER 717 (reversed on different grounds: [1994] 2 All ER 685); *Arab Monetary Fund v Hashim (No 9)* (1994) Times, 11 October; *Trustor AB v Smallbone* (9 May 2000, unreported), CA; *Kuwait Oil Tanker v Al Bader* [2000] 2 All ER (Comm) 271; *Grupo Torras v Al-Sabah* [2001] CLC 221; *Douglas v Hello! Ltd (No.3)* [2005] EWCA Civ 595, [2005] 3 WLR 881; *Barros Mattos Jnr v Macdaniels Ltd* [2005] EWHC 1323 (Ch), [2005] IL Pr 630 But contrast the views of Yeo, *Choice of Law for Equitable Doctrines* (2004), Chapter 8.

102.201 Article 15(2) states that where a mandatory rule is applied under Article 15(1), 'the court shall try to give effect to the objects of the trust by other means'. There is no obligation to do so. However, it might allow a non-trust State which cannot recognise the trust *qua* trust to give some effect to it by 'translating' it into the nearest domestic law analogue[1].

1   On which, see D Hayton in J Glasson (ed) *International Trust Laws*, Chapter C3 at pp 19–26.

International mandatory rules of the forum

102.202 Article 16 preserves the application of the forum's international mandatory rules (a nebulous flexible concept for common law States) and not the domestic mandatory rules of the jurisdiction designated by application of the forum's choice of law rules. These are those rules which the settlor may not derogate from and which are intended to be applied *irrespective* of the law governing the trust[1]. This will allow a State to apply its own international mandatory rules in any areas that might affect particular trusts so as to override such trust's terms so far as necessary eg so as to prevent export of heritage objects to a beneficiary or, perhaps, requiring exercise of its statutory variation of trust rules to produce a final resolution of a divorce of spouses whose affairs involve international ante-nuptial or post-nuptial trusts[2].

1   The wording used to describe these mandatory rules is much more emphatic than in Article 15. Article 16 speaks of rules which must be applied 'even to international situations, irrespective of rules of conflict of laws'. See also von Overbeck, para 149 at pp 404–405.
2   'Among the laws which fall in this category, mention may be made of those which are intended to protect the cultural heritage of a country, public health, certain vital economic interests, the protection of employees or of the weaker party to another contract. The French delegation asked that in the Report currency exchange regulations be mentioned in this connection.': von Overbeck, para 149 at pp 403–404.

102.203 Article 16(2) permits the application 'in exceptional circumstances' of the international mandatory rules of a State of close connection with the case, whose law is neither the law of the forum nor the applicable law. However, for some States the extraordinary uncertainties engendered by this provision represented a step too far. Article 16(3) thus offers Contracting States the option to enter a reservation as to the application of Article 16(2)[1]. The Recognition of Trusts Act 1987 simply omits Article 16(2)[2], so that only the international mandatory rules of the forum may be applied[3]. Despite that, an English court is hardly likely to require a trustee to act in a manner which is illegal in the place where it is to be effected[4].

1   The procedural mechanism for making a reservation is dealt with in Article 26. Luxembourg has entered this reservation upon its ratification of the Convention.
2   Nor does the provision apply in Alberta: s 1(4) of the International Convention Implementation Act 1990.
3   The United Kingdom has done exactly the same in the contract sphere. Article 7(1), Rome Convention allows a State to apply the international mandatory rules of 'another country with which the situation has a close connection'. Article 22(1)(a) allowed Contracting States to enter a reservation on the application of this provision. The United Kingdom did so in s 2(2) of the Contracts (Applicable Law) Act 1990, which states that Article 7(1) 'shall not have the force of law in the United Kingdom.' However, it should be noted that Australia has not entered this reservation, even though Australian courts appear to give very little effect to the mandatory rules of third States at common law: see P Nygh and M Davies *Conflict of Laws in Australia* (7th edn), at pp 376–9, 628.
4   'Since a Court of Equity will do nothing in vain and will not require a person to do an act that is illegal where it is to be done, so that sufficient defined protection exists, there seems no need for a common law country to adopt this paragraph [ie Article 16(2)] of worryingly indefinite ambit'. (D Hayton, in J Glasson (ed) *International Trust Laws*, Chapter C3 at p 16).

Public policy

102.204 Article 18 states that 'the provisions of the Convention may be disregarded when their application would be manifestly contrary to public policy'. The provision encompasses the choice of law rules and the recognition of trusts. It may be applied to any[1] or all provisions of the Convention.

1   Although Article 18 strictly refers to disapplication of 'the provisions of the Convention' and not to 'any one or more of the Convention provisions', it would be extraordinary if the public policy provision could only be applied to the Convention on an all or nothing basis.

102.205 However, it is likely that Article 18 will be interpreted restrictively[1], in order not to undermine the other provisions of the Convention. The word 'manifestly' indicates a strong threshold. In particular, the fact that a technique necessitated by the trust is unfamiliar in a given State is not in itself grounds to invoke public policy[2]. Thus one would expect Article 18 to be confined to rules which are discriminatory, oppressive, infringe human rights or are impossible to give effect to[3] or contravene the irreducible core content of ownership rights, but, otherwise, it is better to utilise Articles 15 or 16 or rules that apply to preliminary issues which fall outside the Convention by virtue of Article 4 thereof[4]. However, if particular English property is held on valid foreign trusts preventing that very property from being alienated in any way for a period exceeding that permitted by the Perpetuities and Accumulations Act 1964, then it would seem that English public policy would not permit such infringement of a very fundamental English property right attached to ownership[5]. On the other hand, if the trust property is freely alienable, but the interests of the beneficiaries in the changing investments representing the trust fund from time to time may arise outside the English perpetuity period laid down in the Perpetuities and Accumulations Act, then there seems no adequate reason to allow Article 18 to be invoked to trump Article 8(2)(f)[6].

1   M Koppenol-Laforce *Het Haagse Trustverdrag*, 270 remarks of Articles 16 and 18: 'From experiences with similar articles it follows that such articles are hardly ever applied. I see no reason why this should be different in trust-cases. Article 15 is the real danger to recognition of the trust.' However, the unique problems created by the recognition of the trust in States which do not know the institution in their domestic law provides a real prospect that Article 18 may be used more widely than corresponding provisions of other Convention as a route of last resort to prevent recognition of a trust.

2   Thus in *Re Fitzgerald* [1904] 1 Ch 573, CA the non-assignability of a life interest under a Scots trust (which would have been assignable if the trust had been English) was recognised, so that a mortgage of it by the English domiciled life tenant to his English creditors was invalid. See also See further D Hayton, (2006) 13(2) J Int Corp Pl 55, 59.

3   *Oppenheim v Cattermole* [1976] AC 249; see also *Kuwait Airways Corpn v Iraqi Airways Co* [2002] UKHL 19, [2002] 2 AC 883: On the use of public policy in the conflict of laws, see *Dicey, Morris and Collins*, Chapter 5; *Cheshire and North* at pp 123–132.Typical cases where public policy is invoked (largely taken from contract law) include where the applicable law is fundamentally contrary to basic principles of human liberty (eg *Forbes v Cochrane* (1824) 2 B & C 448), English standards of justice (eg *Royal Boskalis Westminster NV v Mountain* [1999] QB 674) or English morality (eg *Lemenda Trading Co Ltd v African Middle East Petroleum Ltd* [1988] QB 448; though it may also be necessary in this 'weaker' category that the place of performance take the same view as to the morality of the agreement). Public policy may also be invoked where the United Kingdom's interests are adversely affected by the applicable law (eg *Dynamit Actein-Gesellschaft v Rio Tinto Co Ltd* [1918] AC 260) or where good relations with a friendly foreign State may be adversely affected (eg *Foster v Driscoll* [1929] 1 KB 4709).

4   However, D Hayton and C Mitchell, *Commentary and Cases on the Law of Trusts and Equitable Remedies,* (12th edn, 2005), p 850, n 50 suggest that English courts would be likely to invoke public policy where a settlor chooses Belize or Cook Islands law to settle his property on protective trust for himself for life (relying on *Re Lawrence* (2003) 5 ITELR 1); or creates an asset protection trust intending to defraud a creditor who can only challenge the trust's validity within a short limitation period, or by discharging an unusually onerous burden of proof.

5   (1917) 33 LQR 11 (E Jenks); Megarry & Wade *The Law of Real Property* (6th edn) at para 3–071.

6   See *Lewin on Trusts* (17th edn) at para 11–34. It may be tempting to invoke Art 18 where an English settlor transfers English assets, particularly land, to English trustees for descendants of his grandfather, John Bull, for ever under a trust governed by a law (like Manitoban law) validating such trust, so as not to allow settlors to undermine and 'cock a snook' at English trust law. However, once Manitoban or other foreign settlors under a favourable foreign trust law can do this for English investments that are comprised in their trust funds the pass is sold, even dramatically different treatment under a foreign trust law not being a reason to refuse to recognise it: *Re Fitzgerald* [1904] 1 Ch 573, CA. No line should be drawn between trust laws that permit 80 years or 125 years or 150 years or unlimited periods, so for Article 13 purposes, trusts with unlimited lives should not be regarded as a separate 'category of trust' from trusts with limited lives. In any event English law permits an extensive 'wait & see' period which could last for 100–125 years before the English court would need to consider the issue, by which time it will surely have a very relaxed attitude to perpetual trusts.

102.206 Article 18 says only that the applicable law *may* be disregarded. It imposes no obligation. However, it is difficult to imagine a State whose own public policy is manifestly infringed not invoking its public policy.

102.207 Article 18 does not state that only the forum's public policy may be applied. However, it is extremely unlikely that an English court would anything other than its own public policy. It would indeed be very curious if a third State's public policy were applied by an English court, when the international mandatory rules of such a State may not be[1].

1   But see J Schoenblum in E McKendrick (ed) *Commercial Aspects of Trusts and Fiduciary Obligations*, Chapter 11 at pp 238–239, who points out that *Dicey and Morris* at one stage asserted that the strong public policy of the law with which the trust had its closest connection would also be applied at common law.

102.208 One question of particular practical importance is the effect to be given to non-charitable purpose trusts in England and whether their recognition should be refused on public policy grounds. In particular, should STAR trusts be enforced in England[1]? These trusts, originating from the Cayman Islands, allow a settlor to create a trust for beneficiaries or for purposes, or for both. Such purposes may be charitable or non-charitable. The beneficiaries do not have any rights in the trust property itself unless and until it is transferred to them. The trusts are enforced by appointed enforcers. The beneficiary has no right to enforce the trust unless also appointed as an enforcer of the trust. Although the matter is far from clear, it is submitted that, in general, such trusts should be recognised in England. Provided that the trust has an appointed enforcer, there is someone who can compel the trustee to fulfil his duties; and though an English court might dislike the tying up of capital for non-charitable purposes, it is by no means impossible to give effect to the trust[2]. English courts should be very slow to use public policy simply because a trust governed by a foreign law shows different characteristics from the English domestic trust[3], when the Convention asks contracting non-trust States to go much further and to recognise an institution not known in their legal system[4].

1   See the Special Trusts (Alternative Regime) Law 1997, now incorporated into the Trusts Law (2001) Revision, Pt VIII. See A Duckworth, *STAR Trusts*; A Duckworth, in J Glasson (ed) *International Trust Laws*, Chapter A7 at pp 29–36; G Thomas in J Glasson (ed) *International Trust Laws*, Chapter B4, pp 63–73; G Thomas and A Hudson, *The Law of Trusts* (2004), Chapter 40. See also D Hayton (1998) 4 Amicus Curiae 13; D Hayton (1998) 8 Offshore Taxation Review 43; P Matthews (1997) 11 Trust Law International 67; A Duckworth (1998) 12 Trust Law International 16; P Matthews (1998) 12 Trust Law International 98; A Duckworth (1999) 13 Trust Law International 158.
2   D Hayton (2001) 117 LQR 96, 100.
3   For example, *Re Fitzgerald* [1904] 1 Ch 573, CA.
4   A point made by A Duckworth (1999) 13 Trust Law International 158, 162.

102.209 Exceptionally, if the STAR trust is for beneficiaries (eg a discretionary trust for the descendants of X for ever), the irreducible core content of the trust obligation[1] requires that a beneficiary (as opposed to an object of a power of appointment) must have rights to make the trustee account for its trusteeship. If some beneficiaries are not expressly appointed as enforcers there is the problem that, as stated by Millett LJ in *Armitage v Nurse*[2], 'There is an irreducible core of obligations owed by the trustees to the beneficiaries and enforceable by them which is fundamental to the concept of a trust. If the beneficiaries have no rights enforceable against the trustees there are no trusts' for the beneficiaries, only a resulting trust for the settlor, with the 'beneficiaries' being characterised by the English forum as mere objects of a personal (non-fiduciary) power of appointment to whom the trustee is authorised to distribute trust assets till the settlor (beneficially entitled under a resulting trust) countermands his gratuitous mandate[3].

¹   See D Hayton 'The Irreducible Core Content of Trusteeship', Chapter 3 in AJ Oakley (ed) *Trends in Contemporary Trust Law* (1996) Oxford and D Hayton 'The Obligation Characteristic of The Trust' (2001) 117 LQR 97.
²   [1998] Ch 241 at 253.
³   As he can: *Vandervell v IRC* [1967] 2 AC 291 at 317 per Lord Upjohn.

102.210 Where there is a true trust for non-charitable purposes so that the beneficial interest is exhausted (the income actually being spent an achieving some purpose eg the furthering of the purposes of the Jersey Conservative Party or of the Manx legal profession) the trust should be upheld by the English court, as where it is alleged that there is a resulting trust of English assets so that they are available to creditors or heirs of the settlor. However, if the purpose of the trust is the inward or self-serving purpose to hold a particular shareholding or a collection of paintings or a ship¹ or to develop the value of the trust fund, so that the terms of the trust do not dispose of the settlor's underlying beneficial interest then there should simply be a resulting trust for the settlor or if the trust is simply to hold the shares in X Co Ltd so as to promote the business of the X Co Ltd then the trust is treated as one for the benefit of the shareholders in that company. Use of a legal person, such as a foundation, to carry out such purposes is safer.

¹   If the specific asset was to be wholly inalienable for longer than the permitted English perpetuity period, then this should contravene English public policy.

Recognition of Trusts

The requirements of recognition

102.211 A trust demonstrating the characteristics described in Article 2, meeting the requirement of Article 3¹ and governed by the law of a trust State is entitled to recognition under Article 11. The word 'recognition' has nothing to do with the effects to be given to foreign judgments in trust matters. A Contracting State to the Hague Convention will not be compelled to recognise an English trust judgment unless the English court is jurisdictionally competent in the eyes of the State of recognition. Likewise, a non-contracting, non-trust State will be compelled to recognise an English judgment if its criteria for the recognition of foreign judgments are met.

¹   Unless the Contracting State has extended the operation of the Convention pursuant to Article 20 beyond such trusts, as the United Kingdom has done in s 1(2) of the Recognition of Trusts Act 1987.

102.212 Article 11 simply explains certain key consequences of giving effect to a trust under its applicable law determined by the earlier Articles, primarily for the benefit of non-trust States. It is intended to lay down minimum requirement of recognition. A State which wishes to apply more favourable rules for the recognition of trusts is free to do so¹. Article 11(2) lays down a uniform rule and states that the trust assets are separate from the personal assets of the trustee. The trustee's capacity to sue and be sued is also covered by Article 11(2). It makes clear that this extends beyond lawsuits and covers any relevant appearances before an authority or public notary².

1 Article 14. Of course, Contracting States might choose to extend the operation of the Convention's rules, so that recognition of a broader range of trusts would automatically follow. This is what the United Kingdom has done in s 1(2) of the Recognition of Trusts Act 1987.

2 See also K Lipstein in K Lipstein (ed) *International Encyclopaedia of Comparative Law*, Chapter 23 at p 27.

102.213 Article 11(3) spells out more detailed consequence of recognition. However, these consequences are not required as a matter of uniform law and only apply in so far as the law governing the trust so provides. The trust assets are not available to satisfy claims brought against the trustee by his personal creditors, or upon the trustee's bankruptcy or insolvency, nor do they form part of his matrimonial property or estate[1]. Whilst these seem uncontroversial, it should be noted that Article 11 is subject to the mandatory rule provisions of Articles 15 and 16[2], which throws some doubt on the question whether the trust assets *must* be treated as a separate fund from the trustee's personal wealth. What happens if the requirement in Article 11 that the trust property constitutes a separate fund from the trustee's personal assets itself infringes the mandatory rules of property law of the forum, or the law designated by the forum to apply to property matters[3]? Could a trust still function without the separate fund element, or would it be stripped of any meaning or function[4]? As pointed out in the von Overbeck Report at paragraph 108, the separate fund requirement 'is an essential element of a trust, without which its recognition would have no meaning'.

1 On these provisions, see von Overbeck, para 112 at pp 394–395.

2 Von Overbeck, para 105 at pp 393–394.

3 Article 15(1)(d) preserves the mandatory rules of the law applicable to transfers of title to property and security interests in property; Article 16 preserves the mandatory rules of the law of the forum.

4 D Hayton (1996) 5 J Int Corp P 127 at 128.

102.214 It should therefore be the case that Article 15 preserves the application of mandatory rules in relation to matters of transfer of property and security interests in property in so far as they affect the beneficiary's interest under the trust. They should not normally be applied to affect the nature of the trustee's interest[1]. It follows that Article 15 does not detract from the separate status of the trust assets from the trustee's personal wealth and that this separation of the trust assets is required by the Convention[2]. This view is also supported by the Dutch ratification of the Convention. Although Dutch law did not permit separation of personal and fiduciary patrimony[3], the legislation implementing the Hague Convention[4] provides that Dutch laws on transfer of property, security interests and creditor protection shall not prevent the recognition of a trust otherwise satisfying the Hague Convention's requirements[5].

1 Unless, of course, the trustee is also a beneficiary of the fund.

2 For the likely interpretation of Article 15(1)(d) and (e) if and when Switzerland ratifies the Convention, see A von Overbeck (1996) 4 Trusts and Trustees 6, 9.

3 Article 84, s (3) of Book 3, Dutch Civil Code.

4 Article 4, Wet Conflichtenrecht Trusts 1995.

5 See also M Koppenol-Laforce *Het Haagse Trustverdrag*, 271. See also D Hayton (1996) 5 J Int Corp P 127.

Following and tracing trust assets

102.215 Article 11(3)(d) deals with the tracing of assets or their value and the recovery of them in providing 'that the trust assets may be recovered when the trustee, in breach of trust, has mingled trust assets with his own property or has alienated trust assets'. The provision covers recovery of the trust assets, which should clearly cover assets from time to time representing the trust fund itself in the trustee's hands, whether assets acquired for himself wholly by alienating trust assets (by selling or exchanging them) or assets acquired for himself by mixing trust money half and half with his own money so as to become half owner of the purchased property. However, Article 11(3)(d) does not expressly deal with the case where a third party, to whom the trustee wrongfully gifted trust assets, sells them and uses them wholly to buy an asset for himself or mixes the proceeds of sale with his own money half and half. Although the lex situs may not have equitable tracing rules, it may have less-refined proprietary subrogation principles dealing with, for example, property substituted for marital regime property or commercial partnership property or property in a deceased's estate before being accepted with benefit of inventory.

102.216 More fundamentally, although para (d) provides for trust assets to be recovered where the trustee has alienated assets to a third party eg by way of gift (so that no proceeds of sale have become substituted assets comprised in the trust fund) or to hold as a custodian, the final sentence of Article 11(3)(d) provides that the third party's 'rights and obligations shall remain subject to the law determined by the choice of law rules of the forum', while Article 15(d) preserves the effect on the transfer of title to property of the mandatory rules of the law determined by the choice of law rules of the forum. This is of crucial significance where that law is the lex situs of a civil law[1] or Muslim jurisdiction not knowing of equitable proprietary interests or tracing processes.

[1]   An Explanatory Report published in December 2005 by the Swiss Government considers any claim against a third party to fall outside the Convention. For criticism, see F Noseda (2005) 20(1) Tru LI 3, 5.

102.217 However, it is suggested that the above Convention provisions should only be invoked in England where the issue concerns acquisition by the third party and whether under the lex situs he takes an unimpeachable title[1]. It would not be relevant to the question whether the trust assets or their value could be traced into the third party's hands, which is determined under the first sentence of Article 11(3)(d) by the law applicable to the trust[2].

[1]   Which should be a matter for the lex situs: see *Macmillan Inc v Bishopsgate Investment Trust Plc (No 3)* [1996] 1 WLR 387. Most *leges situs* confer unimpeachable title upon donees as well as purchasers (unless an intent to defraud creditors is involved) though compensation may be payable to prevent unjust enrichment or an *in personam ad rem* remedy may be available in special circumstances, while Scots law even protects purchasers in bad faith from trustees. Further see F Noseda (2005) 20 (1) Trs L I 3 at 5.

[2]   There seems no good reason for the rules on *identification* of property to be subject to different laws, depending upon whether a third party is involved. However, the question whether identifiable property may be *claimed* from a third party depends on whether that third party took good title to it; and that is a property law question: see preceding note.

102.218 Accordingly, there should be a two-stage process to determine the ability to recover trust assets or their value from the hands of a third party under the Convention:

(1)   The law governing the trust determines whether the assets or their value can be followed or traced into the hands of the third party. If they may not be, then they cannot be recovered from the third party;

(2)   If they can, the lex situs shall determine whether a third party recipient has taken free of the claims of the beneficiaries under the trust. If he has, the assets or their value cannot be recovered from him; if he has not, then their value can be recovered or even the assets themselves, depending on whether the lex situs recognises the beneficiaries as not merely having a personal claim but an *in personam ad rem* claim or, even an *in rem* proprietary claim where the donee actually knew the trustee had wrongfully transferred the assets to her without authority[1].

[1]   For detailed discussion of the choice of law rules applicable to tracing, see Harris (2002) 73 BYIL 65. See also *Dicey, Morris and Collins*, pp 1885–8; G Panagopoulos, (2005) 1 J. Priv. Int L 69.

Right to refuse recognition to trusts objectively connected to non-trust States

102.219 Article 13 is concerned with cases where the settlor has selected the law of a trust State to govern the trust, or has designated that the trust be administered in such a State, or has chosen trustees who are habitually resident in that State, but where the other significant elements point objectively to the law of one or more non-trust States[1]. This provision allows a court to refuse to recognise a trust otherwise qualifying for recognition under Article 11[2]. It reinforces the fact that the trust is not introduced by the Convention into non-trust States' domestic legal systems. It also applies if the State of closest connection knows the concept of the trust in its domestic legal system, but does not provide for the category of trust in question.

[1]   Article 13 refers only to 'States' in the plural, but it would be extraordinary if it did not apply when all objective elements pointed to a single non-trust State: see von Overbeck, para 122 at p 397.

[2]   Rather than relying on wholesale use of mandatory rules and pubic policy to prevent recognition, Article 13 was adopted in Italy (see A Paton and R Grosso (1994) 43 ICLQ, 654 at 655), but not Malta and is not recommended for Switzerland in L Thevenoz *Trusts in Switzerland*, Schulthess, Zurich. The Cayman Isles have not implemented the Convention, fearing that this will encourage the invocation of Art 13 against its trusts, but Civilopian judges under existing Civilopian laws have plenty of power to refuse to recognise Cayman trusts that are Civilopian except for choosing Cayman law, and, perhaps a Cayman trustee, too.

102.220 Article 13 was considered to have no useful application in the United Kingdom and is omitted from the schedule to the Recognition of Trusts Act 1987. However, the non-enactment of Article 13 may have considerable ramifications. The broad scope of Article 2 of the Convention means that an English court might be faced with a number of institutions qualifying for recognition under Article 11 and that it will be compelled to recognise them. Such institutions would include non-charitable purpose trusts, so that '… pure purpose trusts, variant types of trusts, and so on, can now be formed by

Englishmen under the law of, say, Belize or Cyprus, even if all the elements of the trust are connected with England.'[1] The Recognition of Trusts Act 1987 appears to have the effect of authorising an English settlor in an otherwise wholly domestic context to create a trust[2] unknown or unauthorised in English domestic trust law, by the simple expedient of choosing a foreign law to govern it. Moreover, it was argued above that non-charitable trusts should not be denied recognition on public policy grounds[3]. If a person is identified by the settlor as responsible for enforcing a non-charitable purpose trust[4], to whom the trustee owes obligations, it is not obvious why recognition of the trust should not be permitted in English law: after all, the core accounting obligation of the trustee to someone able to enforce it is present[5].

[1] M Lupoi in P Jackson and D Wilde (eds) *The Reform of Property Law*, 222 at 225; see also M Lupoi *Trusts: a Comparative Study*, 362.
[2] Ie a 'trust' as that term is understood in Article 2.
[3] See the discussion of public policy in considering limits on the scope of the governing law of the trust above.
[4] The concept of an 'enforcer' of the trust is well known in offshore jurisdictions.
[5] Although it was suggested above that public policy might be invoked in respect of trust assets located in England if those specific assets were intended to be wholly inalienable for longer than the permitted English perpetuity period. See further D Hayton, (2006) 13(2) J TCP 55.

Registration of Trusts

102.221 Article 12 is primarily concerned with the need to reflect on the public registers of non-trust States the existence of a trust if the trust property is to be protected against the insolvency of the otherwise apparent beneficial owner. It also applies to private registers having a public function, such as a shareholders' register[1]. Where a trust is entitled to recognition, the trustee may ask for the trust to appear on the register, or, if this cannot be done, for it otherwise to be reflected on it[2]. He will need to produce any relevant documentation and comply with the requisite formalities of the place of purported registration[3]. In Italy it had been held that the Land Registrar, if requested, must register the existence of the trust, even where it is the registered proprietor who is declaring foreign trusts over his property[4]. Article 2645-ter of the Italian Civil Code now provides a mechanism for the registration of trusts[5]. Article 12 of the Hague Convention states that registration may be refused to the extent that it is prohibited by or inconsistent within the law of the State addressed. Clearly, registration will be prohibited if the trust is not entitled to recognition under Article 11[6]. Since in England the crucially important doctrine of overreaching is available, details of a trust of English land or of shares in English companies are not inserted on the registers of land or shares[7].

[1] Von Overbeck Report, para 121 at p 396.
[2] Von Overbeck Report, para 119 at p 396.
[3] Von Overbeck Report, para 119 at p 396.
[4] *Daniele Muritano v Agencia del Territorio, Ufficio Provinciale di Pisa* Tribunale di Pisa (22 December 2001), reported in Trusts e attivita fiduciarie (April 2002) at p 241.
[5] Although it does not expressly mention the word 'trust' in the legislation: see F Mazzocchi, (2006) 12(6) Trusts and Trustees 21. For the position in Luxembourg, see R Niland (2004) 19(1) JIBLR 6, 8.

6   On the problems which might be experienced in civil law States from registration of the
     trust, see A Dyer and H van Loon *Report on Trusts and Analogous Institutions*, para 177
     at p 91.
7   See s 360 of the Companies Act 1985, which precludes registration of a trust on the share
     register of an English company.

**Jurisdiction and the enforcement of foreign judgments in transnational
trusts litigation**

Synopsis

102.222 The law which determines the jurisdiction of English courts[1] in
transnational litigation is a complex and detailed subject. A brief consideration of the most important rules in this area is given here[2].

1   On the use of alternative dispute resolution in trusts litigation, see further L Cohen and M
     Staff, (1999) 7 J Int Corp 203; D Hayton, (2006) 13(2) J Int Corp 55, 71.
2   For more detail, see J Harris 'Jurisdiction and the Enforcement of Foreign Judgments' in J
     Glasson (ed) *International Trusts Laws*, Chapter C1. See also G Thomas and A Hudson,
     The Law of Trusts (2004) Oxford University Press, Oxford, Chapter 42. See also A Briggs
     and P Rees *Civil Jurisdiction and Judgments* (LLP, 4th edn, 2005).

102.223 In England, two[1] principal sets of jurisdictional rules exist: the
harmonised rules contained in the relevant European Regulation (and Conventions) and the common law. The European harmonised rules are now the
first point of reference. The application of the common law rules is residual.
Moreover, the European harmonised rules do not apply only to disputes
between domiciliaries of Member States. In civil and commercial matters[2], the
European rules will apply if the defendant is domiciled in a Member State and
even, in some cases, when neither party is domiciled in Europe.

1   The Hague Conference on Private International Law concluded a Convention on Choice of
     Court Agreements on 30 June 2005. For discussion of the position of the Convention with
     respect to trusts, see J Harris in J Glasson (ed) *International Trust Laws,* Chapter C1, pp
     52–6.
2   Falling within Article 1 of the Regulation on Jurisdiction and the Recognition and
     Enforcement of Judgments in Civil and Commercial Matters (the Brussels I Regulation),
     the Brussels Convention or the Lugano Convention on Jurisdiction and the Enforcement of
     Judgments in Civil and Commercial Matters 1988 (the Lugano Convention), as amended.

Jurisdiction under the European regime

102.224 The Regulation on Jurisdiction and the Recognition and Enforcement of Judgments in Civil and Commercial Matters ('the Brussels I Regulation')[1] provides a set of uniform jurisdictional rules for European Member
States. It entered into force on 1 March 2002[2].

1   Regulation (EC) No 44/2001 of 22 December 2000: OJ 2001 L 12/1.
2   Save in the case of jurisdictional disputes between Denmark and one or more other
     European Member States. As the Brussels I Regulation does not apply to Denmark, an
     English court must continue to apply the Brussels Convention to such jurisdictional
     disputes. However, see the Agreement between the European Community and the Kingdom
     of Denmark on Jurisdiction and the Recognition and Enforcement of Judgments in Civil
     and Commercial Matters [2005] O.J. L 299/62, which will apply the provisions of the

Brussels I Regulation to the relations between the Community and Denmark, subject to certain modifications. There exists also a parallel Convention to the Brussels Convention, concluded at Lugano on 16 April 1988 (the Lugano Convention) (see Sch 3C of the Civil Jurisdiction and Judgments Act 1982 (CJJA), inserted by Sch 1 of the CJJA 1991. The Lugano Convention applies between European Union Member States and certain European Union non-Member States. Today, the Lugano Convention must still be applied in an English court to jurisdictional disputes between Member States and Iceland, Norway and Switzerland. There are also separate provisions, closely modelled on the European regime, for Anglo-Scottish conflicts contained in the CJJA 1982 and in Sch 4 to the Act (as substituted by the Civil Jurisdiction and Judgments (Amendment) Order 2001, SI 2001/3929).

102.225 The Regulation applies to civil and commercial matters[1]. It excludes such matters as the status or legal capacity of natural persons, matrimonial property rights, wills and succession, bankruptcy and insolvency and arbitration. While not absolutely free from doubt, once the law concerning wills and succession has fully applied (so becoming *functus officio*) so that the relevant property has become vested in the trustee on trusts which give rise to litigation, say 20 years later, the Regulation should apply to this 20 year old trust in the same way it would apply to a 20 years old inter vivos trust or to a contractual or delictual claim relating to a Ming vase that twenty years earlier had been the subject of a legacy. Where applicable, the Regulation lays down a general rule in Article 2, to the effect that the defendant is entitled to be sued in the courts of his domicile[2]. Exceptions to this rule are to be construed narrowly[3].

[1]   Article 1.
[2]   There is a European autonomous definition of domicile for corporate defendants, contained in Article 60(1), Brussels I Regulation. There is no such definition of domicile for individual defendants. In order to determine whether an individual defendant is domiciled in the United Kingdom (and, if so, in which part of the United Kingdom), a court should apply the rules contained in Sch 1, para 9 of the Civil Jurisdiction and Judgments Order 2001 SI 2001/3929.
[3]   See, eg, *Reichert v Dresdner Bank* [1990] ECR I-27; *Kalfelis v Schroeder* [1988] ECR 5565; *Marinari v Lloyds Bank plc* [1995] ECR I-2719.

102.226 The most powerful exception to the defendant domicile principle is contained in Article 22(1), which provides that jurisdiction shall vest in the following courts regardless of the domicile of the defendant: 'in proceedings which have as their object rights *in rem* in immovable property or tenancies of immovable property, the court of the Member State in which the property is situated.' However, the ECJ held in *Webb v Webb*[1] that where a party asserts a beneficial interest under a trust of land, the right asserted is to be treated for Regulation purposes as *in personam*, so that this provision does not apply.

[1]   [1994] ECR I–1717. The instant claim was to be declared beneficial owner under a resulting trust. For recent discussion of the *Webb* case, see *Ashurst v Pollard* [2001] Ch 595; *Prazic v Prazic* [2006] EWCA Civ 497.

102.227 The other key exception to the defendant domicile rule in the trusts context is where a valid choice of court clause is inserted in a trust instrument[1]. A choice of court clause contained in a trust deed for a Member State will be binding and confer exclusive[2] jurisdiction on the chosen State 'in any proceedings brought against a settlor, trustee or beneficiary, if relations between these persons or their rights or obligations under the trust are involved'³. However, it is not absolutely clear whether Article 23(4) applies to litigation between trustee and beneficiary, since neither party will ordinarily have executed the trust instrument. Although it has been suggested that an exclusive jurisdiction clause for another Member State would not prevent a beneficiary of a trust governed by English law from suing in England⁴, it is submitted that this view is incorrect. The interest received by a beneficiary will be subject to any terms or conditions of the trust instrument, which includes the jurisdiction clause. Put differently, with the 'benefit' of the interest under the trust goes the 'burden' of the jurisdiction clause. Moreover, Article 23(4) is a trusts specific provision. As such, it is intended to extend the effect of jurisdiction clauses in the trust context beyond the scope of expressly consenting parties⁵. Accordingly, a jurisdiction clause must also bind the beneficiaries of a trust⁶.

1   Special rules apply if the clause is caught by the rules protecting consumers, employees or insured parties under the Regulation.
2   Unless the clause states to the contrary.
3   Article 23(4) of the Brussels I Regulation.
4   A Oakley Parker and Mellows: Modern Law of Trusts (8th edn) at pp 847–8.
5   Explanatory Report on the Brussels Convention, as amended by the United Kingdom, Irish and Danish Accession Convention, by Prof Dr P Schlosser ('Schlosser Report') [1979] OJ C 59 p 71 at para 178.
6   On the interpretation of jurisdiction clauses in trust instruments, see *Green v Jernigan* (2003–4) 6 ITELR 330, Sup Ct (British Columbia); *Koonmen v Bender* [2002] JCA 218. (Jersey); P Matthews, (2003) 7 Jersey LR 232.

102.228 Where neither of the above exceptions applies and jurisdiction is available against the defendant on the basis of his domicile¹, there are also rules contained in Article 5 and 6 which provide the claimant with further fora in which he can sue. However, although the claimant has a choice, he may only commence proceedings in one State of jurisdictional competence².

1   Note that Articles 5 and 6 do not apply if one of the exceptions to the defendant domicile rule discussed above is applicable.
2   See Articles 27 and 28. The court 'first seised' of a dispute alone has jurisdiction (see Article 30). See further *Prazic v Prazic* [2006] EWCA Civ 497.

102.229 The most important of these additional bases of competence in the trusts context is Article 5(6), which allows a defendant domiciled in a Member State also to be sued 'as settlor, trustee or beneficiary¹ of a trust² created by the operation of a statute, or by a written instrument, or created orally and evidenced in writing, in the courts of the Member State in which the trust is domiciled'³. This provision applies to the internal relationship between the parties: 'as between the trustees themselves, between persons claiming the status of trustees and, above all, between trustees on the one hand and the beneficiaries of a trust on the other'⁴.

1   The defendant must be a trustee or beneficiary at the time at which proceedings are instituted: *Chellaram v Chellaram (No 2)* [2002] EWHC 632 (Ch), [2002] 3 All ER 17.
2   Note that the scope of this provision is broader than Art 3 of the Hague Trusts Convention, which applies to trusts created voluntarily and evidenced in writing: see above.

3   It appears that constructive trusts fall outside the scope of this provision: *Chellaram v Chellaram (No 2)* [2002] EWHC 632 (Ch), [2002] 3 All ER 17, esp. para 138.
4   Schlosser Report, para 111.

102.230 The place where a trust is domiciled is left to Member States to determine[1]. In the United Kingdom, the relevant rules are to be found in the Civil Jurisdiction and Judgments Order 2001[2] ,which provides that 'A trust is domiciled in a part of the United Kingdom if and only if the system of law of that part[3] is the system of law with which the trust has its closest and most real connection'[4].

1   Article 60(3) states that 'in order to determine whether a trust is domiciled in the Member State whose courts are seised of the matter, the court shall apply its rules of private international law'.
2   SI 2001/3929, Sch.1, para.12. The proceedings should be brought in the particular part of the UK in which the trust is domiciled: para.7(2). See also Civil Jurisdiction and Judgments Act 1982, s.45.
3   If different laws are applicable under the trust to questions of validity and administration, the relevant law for these purposes is the law governing validity: *Chellaram v Chellaram (No 2)* [2002] EWHC 632 (Ch), [2002] 3 All ER 17.
4   Lawrence Collins J stated in *Chellaram v Chellaram (No 2)* that if the settlor had chosen law X to govern a trust, this fact could be used to negate a claim that law Y was the law of closest connection. This must be on the basis that while SI 2001/3929, Sch.1, para.12 lays down an apparently objective test to determine the domicile of a trust, the law giving birth to the trust is the expressly chosen law and as the *sine qua non* of the trust is the closest and most real connection. This will make it simple and certain to determine where most trusts are domiciled, but it does not appear that the point was fully argued.

Jurisdiction at common law

102.231 At common law, an English court has jurisdiction as of right over a defendant who can be served with a claim form whilst he is within the jurisdiction[1]. A company registered in England may be served at its registered office[2]. If the company is incorporated abroad but has a branch in England, it must file with the registrar of companies the name and address of those persons resident in Britain who are authorised to accept service on its behalf[3]. The position for service of process has ostensibly been liberalised by CPR Part 6, since the requirement in the Companies Act 1985 for there to be a sufficient connection between the claim and the activities of a branch in England does not exist[4] .The court will also have jurisdiction as of right if a defendant submits to proceedings in England (though not if he merely contests the court's jurisdiction)[5].

1   *Maharanee of Baroda v Wildenstein* [1972] 2 QB 283. But note that even if an English court has *in personam* jurisdiction, it will not hear a case which is solely concerned with legal title to land situated overseas: *British South Africa Co v Companhia de Moçambique* [1893] AC 602.
2   Companies Act 1985, s 725.
3   Companies Act 1985, s 690A(2).
4   See *Saab v Saudi Arabian Bank* [1999] 1 WLR 1861; *Sea Assets v Garuda Indonesia* [2000] 4 All ER 371. However, it might be argued that CPR Part 6 should not be seen as creating any additional basis of jurisdiction and simply provides for alternative means of service on a company over whom the court has jurisdiction: *Harrods v Dow Jones*, [2003] EWHC 1162 (QB), para 33, Eady J and *Lakah Group v Al Jazeera Satellite Channel* [2003] EWHC 1231 (QBD), (2003) Times, 18 April.
5   *Williams and Glyn's Bank plc v Astro Dinamico Cia Naviera SA* [1984] 1 All ER 760.

102.232 If the court has jurisdiction as of right, the defendant may seek a stay of proceedings. He must show that, objectively, the natural forum for the litigation is in an overseas State. Even then, he will denied a stay if the claimant can show that it would be (subjectively) unjust for him to be denied the right to sue in England[1]. However, special rules apply if the proceedings were brought in England in breach of a foreign exclusive jurisdiction clause. Then, the defendant would have to show strong reasons why the stay should not be granted[2].

1   These principles were laid down by the House of Lords in *Spiliada Maritime Corpn v Cansulex Ltd* [1987] AC 460.
2   See eg *The Elefthria* [1970] P 94; *The El Amria* [1981] 2 Lloyd's Rep 119; *The Pioneer Container* [1994] 2 AC 324; *Bouygues Offshore SA v Caspian Shipping Co* [1998] 2 Lloyd's Rep 461. For an example of a stay case concerning an exclusive jurisdiction clause contained in a trust instrument, see the Royal Court of Jersey's decision in *EMM Capricorn Trustees Ltd v Compass Trustees Ltd* (2002) 4 ITELR 34. See further A Briggs and P Rees, *Civil Jurisdiction and Judgments*, 4th ed, pp 328–345.

102.233 If the defendant is outside the jurisdiction and does not submit to proceedings in England, the claimant must ask the court for permission to serve the defendant with a claim form outside the jurisdiction. In order to do so, he must show, *inter alia*, a good arguable case that his claim falls within one of the provisions of the Civil Procedure Rules (CPR), r 6.20[1]. He must also show that the natural forum for the litigation is England[2] and must assert in his application that he believes that he has a reasonable prospect of success on the merits[3].

1   *Seaconsar (Far East) Ltd v Bank Markazi Jomhouri Iran* [1994] 1 AC 438. However, the good arguable case test applies only to factual matters. Where satisfaction of a head of CPR, r 6.20 depends on a matter of law or construction, the court must authoritatively decide that issue, rather than applying the good arguable case test. So, in the case of CPR, r 6.20(11), the court must decide at the jurisdiction stage whether the trust is governed by English law. See *Chellaram v Chellaram (No 2)*) [2002] EWHC 632 (Ch), [2002] 3 All ER 17.
2   CPR, r 6.21(2)(a). *Spiliada Maritime Corp v Cansulex Ltd* [1987] AC 460; *Seaconsar (Far East) Ltd v Bank Markazi Jomhouri Iran* [1994] 1 AC 438. For a recent example of the application of the natural forum test to trusts litigation, see *Chellaram v Chellaram (No 2)* [2002] EWHC 632 (Ch), [2002] 3 All ER 17.
3   CPR, r 6.21(1)(b).

102.234 Several of the provisions of CPR, r 6.20 are specifically concerned with trusts[1]. They are as follows[2]:

(11)   a claim is made for any remedy which might be obtained in proceedings to execute the trusts of a written instrument where–
    (a)   the trusts ought to be executed according to English law[3]; and
    (b)   the person on whom the claim form is to be served is a trustee of the trusts;

(12)   a claim is made for any remedy which might be obtained in proceedings for the administration of the estate of a person who died domiciled within the jurisdiction;

(13)   a claim is made in probate proceedings which includes a claim for the rectification of a will;

(14)   a claim is made for a remedy against the defendant as constructive trustee where the defendant's alleged liability arises out of acts committed within the jurisdiction[4];

(15)   a claim is made for restitution where the defendant's alleged liability arises out of acts committed within the jurisdiction[5].

1   Specifically, CPR, r 6.20(11)–(15).
2   Note also that CPR, r 6.20(10) might be used in respect of trusts of land. It applies where 'the whole subject-matter of a claim relates to property located within the jurisdiction.'
3   If different laws govern the validity and the administration of a trust, it would suffice that either is governed by English law: *Chellaram v Chellaram (No 2)* [2002] EWHC 632 (Ch), [2002] 3 All ER 17. It should be noted that the applicable law should be ascertained at the time at which permission to serve out is sought, not at the time when the cause of action allegedly accrued.
4   In *ISC Technologies v Guerin* [1992] 2 Lloyd's Rep 430, Hoffmann J remarked *obiter* that it would suffice that some of the acts inducing liability occurred in England, even if other acts occurred overseas.
5   For recent discussion, see *Nabb Brothers Ltd v Lloyd's Bank International (Guernsey) Ltd* [2005] EWHC 405 (Ch), [2005] IL Pr 506.

Recognition and enforcement of foreign judgments under the European regime

102.235 A judgment given in a Member State of the European Union in a civil and commercial matter[1] will normally be enforced in other Member States without any special procedure being required[2]. The defendant might apply to have registration set aside if: recognition is manifestly contrary to the State of recognition's public policy; the judgment was a default one and the defendant was not duly served in sufficient time and in such a way as to enable him to arrange his defence; the judgment is irreconcilable with a judgment of the courts of the State of recognition; or the judgment is irreconcilable with an earlier judgment delivered in another Member State, or in a non-Member State, if that earlier judgment also meets the conditions for recognition in the State addressed[3].

1   Ie a judgment falling within the subject matter of Article 1 of the Brussels I Regulation, Brussels Convention or Lugano Convention.
2   Article 41 of the Brussels I Regulation. However, Article 35(1) states that a judgment should not be recognised if the foreign State which gave judgment did so in violation of the exclusive jurisdiction provisions of Article 22 or the insurance or consumer contract provisions.
3   These defences are contained in Article 34.

Enforcement of foreign judgments under the statutory schemes and at common law

102.236 Where a judgment was not given in a Member State of the European Union[1], its recognition will be governed by the Administration of Justice Act 1920, the Foreign Judgments (Reciprocal Enforcement) Act 1933 or the common law. The statutory schemes apply on a reciprocal basis to money judgments delivered in superior courts of certain States[2]; if there is no such arrangement, the common law applies[3].

1   Or falls outside the scope of Article 1 of the Brussels or Lugano scheme.

2   In countries to which an Order in Council has been made extending its provisions. See
     Briggs and Rees, p 576, note 575 and p 578, notes 602–604.
3   But note that there are different and much more liberal rules for the enforcement of a
     judgment from one part of the United Kingdom in another part: The CJJA 1982 provides
     for the free recognition and enforcement of a judgment of the courts of one part of the
     United Kingdom in any other part: see, in particular, ss 18 and 19; Schs 6 and 7 (as
     amended).

102.237 Whichever of these three scheme applies, the substantive[1] rules on
recognition are very similar. The judgment will be recognised if and only if the
defendant was resident (or, in the case of the common law, it seems, present)[2]
in the foreign State at the time that proceedings were instituted[3], or the
defendant submitted to proceedings there[4]. Even then, the defendant may
resist recognition if he can show that the judgment was procured by the
judgment creditor's fraud, was in breach of natural justice, infringed English
public policy, violated a choice of court clause[5] or was inconsistent with
another judgment[6]. A judgment will not be enforced[7] unless final, conclusive
and for a fixed sum of money, and it must not order the payment of penal
damages to the State[8], or the payment of multiple damages[9].

1   The procedure differs. A scheme of registration is used under the statutes. At common law,
     the claimant must commence proceedings to have the judgment enforced.
2   *Adams v Cape Industries* [1990] Ch 433.
3   For a corporate defendant, it was decided in *Adams v Cape Industries* [1990] Ch 433 that
     there must be a fixed place of business maintained at the company's own expense from
     which it has carried out its own business in the overseas jurisdiction. It will suffice that its
     business is transacted at that place through representatives of the company carrying out the
     corporation's business (*Littauer Glove Corp v FW Millington* (1928) 44 TLR 746).
4   Appearance by the defendant solely to contest the court's jurisdiction, or to seek a stay,
     does not constitute submission: s 33 of the CJJA 1982.
5   CJJA 1982, s 32(1).
6   Under the statutory schemes, recognition may also be resisted pending an appeal in the
     State of origin.
7   A judgment needs to be recognised and enforced where a person asks the English court to
     give effect to a remedy granted in a foreign court eg an award of damages. Recognition
     alone will suffice where no remedy is sought eg where the judgment relates to status, or is
     used as a defence to further proceedings against a defendant in England.
8   If it does and it is possible to identify which part of the damages is compensatory and
     which penal, the judgment may be enforced solely in respect of the compensatory part:
     Raulin v Fisher [1991] KB 93.
9   Protection of Trading Interests Act 1980, s 5.

Index

Index

Index

Index

Index

Index

Index

Index

Index

Index

Index